GRADE 9 | TEACHER'S EDITION

myPerspectives™

ENGLISH LANGUAGE ARTS

Pearson

NEW YORK, NEW YORK • BOSTON, MASSACHUSETTS
CHANDLER, ARIZONA • GLENVIEW, ILLINOIS

Photo locators denoted as follows: Top (T), Center (C), Bottom (B), Left (L), Right (R), Background (Bkgd)

Cover image “Birds on Wire” is a combination of illustrations from various artists, and credited to; Rodica Bruma/123RF, Laschi Adrian/123RF, and Peony/Fotolia. T3: londoneye/Getty Images; T20: karandaev/fotolia; T23: Jojje/Shutterstock; T25: Nikada/Getty Images; T26B: Creativa Images/Shutterstock; T32: Monkey Business Images/Shutterstock; T34: artagent/Fotolia; T33: Hocus Focus Studio/Getty Images;

Acknowledgments of third-party content appear on page R81, which constitutes an extension of this copyright page.

ISBN-13: 978-0-133-33868-3
ISBN-10: 0-133-33868-1
7 17

Pearson

Welcome!

*my*Perspectives™ *English Language Arts* is a student-centered learning environment where you will analyze text, cite evidence, and respond critically about your learning. You will take ownership of your learning through goal-setting, reflection, independent text selection, and activities that allow you to collaborate with your peers.

Each unit of study includes selections of different genres—including multimedia—all related to a relevant and meaningful Essential Question. As you read, you will engage in activities that inspire thoughtful discussion and debate with your peers allowing you to formulate, and defend, your own perspectives.

*my*Perspectives *ELA* offers a variety of ways to interact directly with the text. You can annotate by writing in your print consumable, or you can annotate in your digital Student Edition. In addition, exciting technology allows you to access multimedia directly from your mobile device and communicate using an online discussion board!

We hope you enjoy using *my*Perspectives *ELA* as you develop the skills required to be successful throughout college and career.

Authors' Perspectives

*my*Perspectives is informed by a team of respected experts whose experiences working with students and study of instructional best practices have positively impacted education. From the evolving role of the teacher to how students learn in a digital age, our authors bring new ideas, innovations, and strategies that transform teaching and learning in today's competitive and interconnected world.

"The teaching of English needs to focus on engaging a new generation of learners. How do we get them excited about reading and writing? How do we help them to envision themselves as readers and writers? And, how can we make the teaching of English more culturally, socially, and technologically relevant? Throughout the curriculum, we've created spaces that enhance youth voice and participation and that connect the teaching of literature and writing to technological transformations of the digital age."

Ernest Morrell, Ph.D.

is the Macy professor of English Education at Teachers College, Columbia University, a class of 2014 Fellow of the American Educational Research Association, and the Past-President of the National Council of Teachers of English (NCTE). He is also the Director of Teachers College's Institute for Urban and Minority Education (IUME). He is an award-winning author and in his spare time he coaches youth sports and writes poems and plays. Dr. Morrell has influenced the development of *my*Perspectives in Assessment, Writing & Research, Student Engagement, and Collaborative Learning.

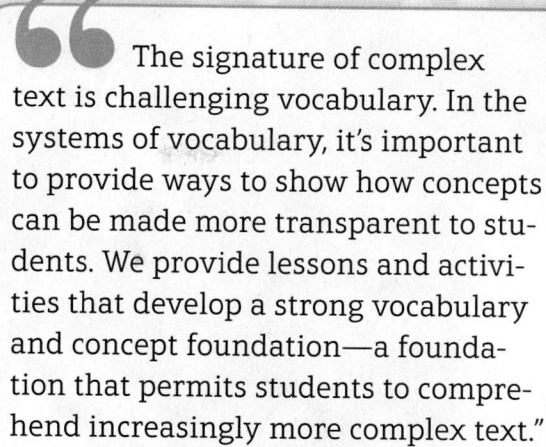

"The signature of complex text is challenging vocabulary. In the systems of vocabulary, it's important to provide ways to show how concepts can be made more transparent to students. We provide lessons and activities that develop a strong vocabulary and concept foundation—a foundation that permits students to comprehend increasingly more complex text."

Elfrieda Hiebert, Ph.D.

is President and CEO of TextProject, a nonprofit that provides resources to support higher reading levels. She is also a research associate at the University of California, Santa Cruz. Dr. Hiebert has worked in the field of early reading acquisition for 45 years, first as a teacher's aide and teacher of primary-level students in California and, subsequently, as a teacher and researcher. Her research addresses how fluency, vocabulary, and knowledge can be fostered through appropriate texts. Dr. Hiebert has influenced the development of *my*Perspectives in Vocabulary, Text Complexity, and Assessment.

"The *my*Perspectives classroom is dynamic. The teacher inspires, models, instructs, facilitates, and advises students as they evolve and grow. When teachers guide students through meaningful learning tasks and then pass them ownership of their own learning, students become engaged and work harder. This is how we make a difference in student achievement—by putting students at the center of their learning and giving them the opportunities to choose, explore, collaborate, and work independently."

Kelly Gallagher, M.Ed.

teaches at Magnolia High School in Anaheim, California, where he is in his thirty-first year. He is the former co-director of the South Basin Writing Project at California State University, Long Beach. Mr. Gallagher has influenced the development of *my*Perspectives in Writing, Close Reading, and the Role of Teachers.

"It's critical to give students the opportunity to read a wide range of highly engaging texts and to immerse themselves in exploring powerful ideas and how these ideas are expressed. In *my*Perspectives, we focus on building up students' awareness of how academic language works, which is especially important for English language

Jim Cummins, Ph.D.

is a Professor Emeritus in the Department of Curriculum, Teaching and Learning of the University of Toronto. His research focuses on literacy development in multilingual school contexts as well as on the potential roles of technology in promoting language and literacy development. In recent years, he has been working actively with teachers to identify ways of increasing the literacy engagement of learners in multilingual school contexts. Dr. Cummins has influenced the development of *my*Perspectives in English Language Learner and English Language Development support.

Each unit focuses on an engaging topic related to the Essential Question.

VOLUME ONE

UNIT 1 American Voices

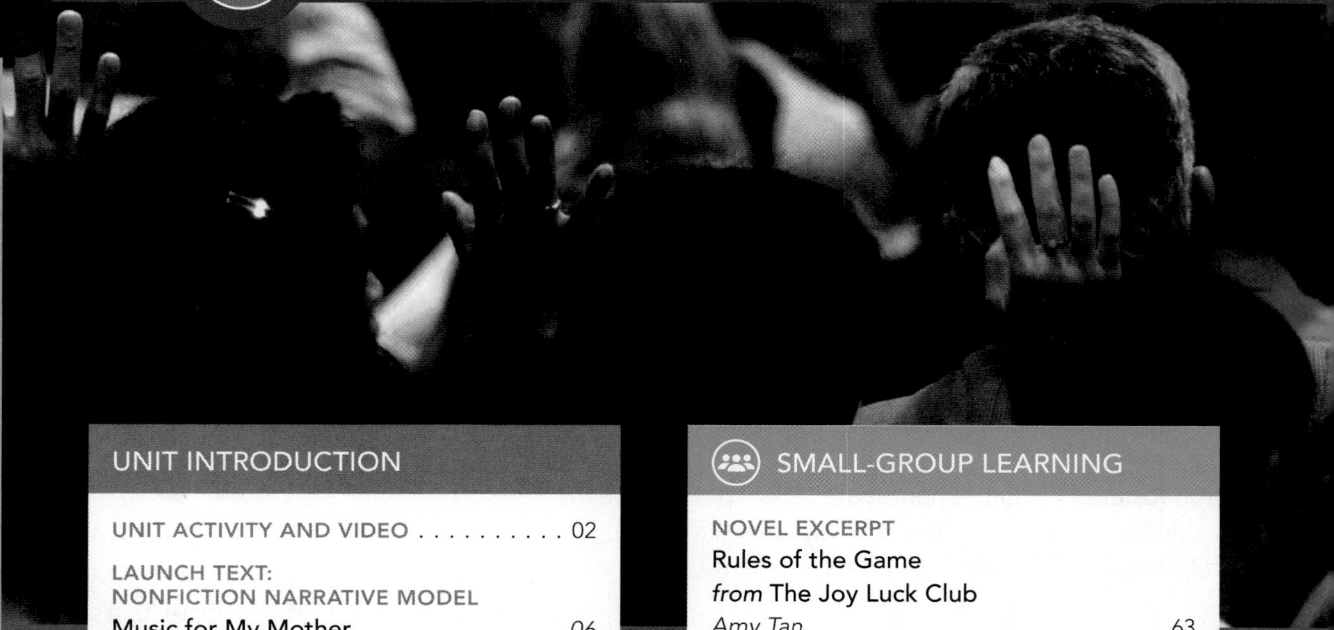

UNIT INTRODUCTION

WHOLE-CLASS LEARNING

SMALL-GROUP LEARNING

An Essential Question frames all unit activities and discussions.

ESSENTIAL QUESTION: What does it mean to be "American"?

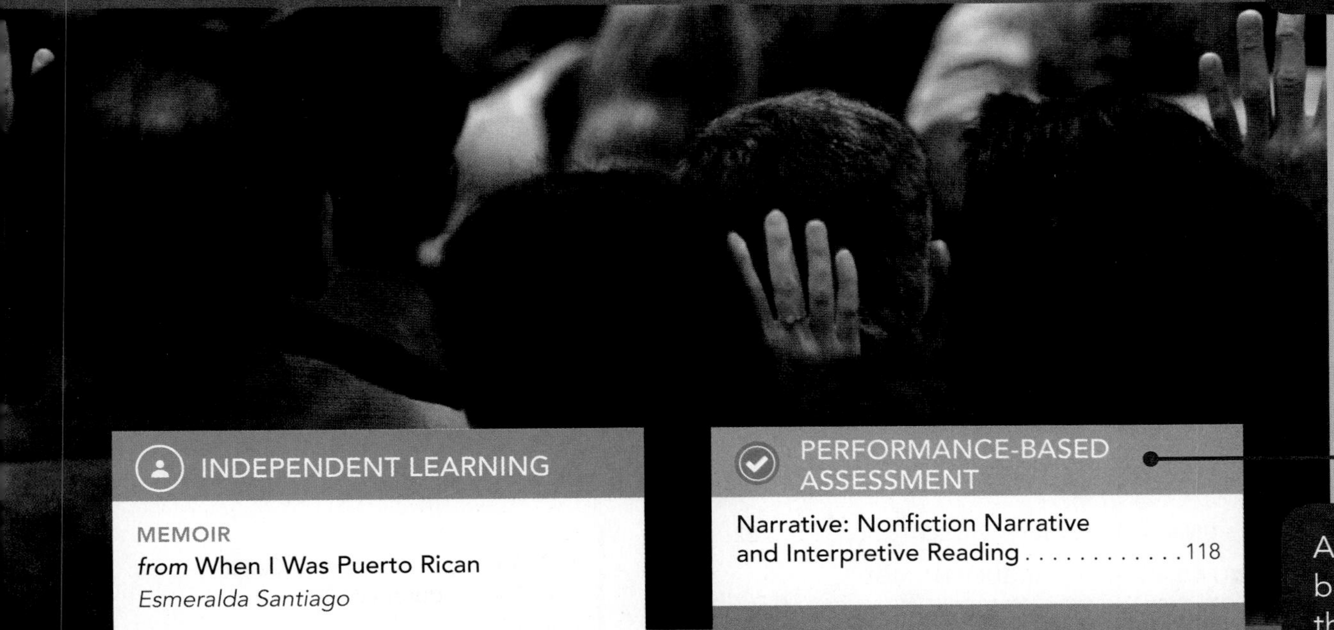

INDEPENDENT LEARNING

These selections can be accessed via the Interactive Student Edition.

PERFORMANCE-BASED ASSESSMENT

UNIT REFLECTION

All unit activities are backwards-designed to the Performance-Based Assessment.

DIGITAL PERSPECTIVES

SCAN FOR MULTIMEDIA

Use the BouncePage app whenever you see "Scan for Multimedia" to access:

- Unit Introduction Videos
- Media Selections
- Modeling Videos
- Selection Audio Recordings

Additional digital resources can be found in:

- Interactive Student Edition
- *my*Perspectives+

VOLUME ONE

UNIT 2 Survival

The Launch Text introduces a perspective on the unit topic.

Teachers lead the shared reading experience, providing modeling and support, as students begin exploring perspectives on the unit topic.

Students encounter diverse perspectives on the unit topic, working in collaborative teams.

UNIT INTRODUCTION

WHOLE-CLASS LEARNING

SMALL-GROUP LEARNING

Students self-select a text to explore an aspect of the unit topic and share their learning with the class.

INDEPENDENT LEARNING

These selections can be accessed via the Interactive Student Edition.

PERFORMANCE-BASED ASSESSMENT

UNIT REFLECTION

DIGITAL PERSPECTIVES

SCAN FOR MULTIMEDIA

Use the BouncePage app whenever you see "Scan for Multimedia" to access:

- Unit Introduction Videos
- Media Selections
- Modeling Videos
- Selection Audio Recordings

Additional digital resources can be found in:

- Interactive Student Edition
- *my*Perspectives+

The Launch Text models the mode of writing that will be at the core of the Performance-Based Assessment.

Performance Tasks build toward and prepare students for the Unit Performance-Based Assessment.

VOLUME ONE

UNIT 3 The Literature of Civil Rights

UNIT INTRODUCTION

WHOLE-CLASS LEARNING

SMALL-GROUP LEARNING

INDEPENDENT LEARNING

These selections can be accessed via the Interactive Student Edition.

PERFORMANCE-BASED ASSESSMENT

UNIT REFLECTION

DIGITAL PERSPECTIVES

SCAN FOR MULTIMEDIA

Use the BouncePage app whenever you see "Scan for Multimedia" to access:

- Unit Introduction Videos
- Media Selections
- Modeling Videos
- Selection Audio Recordings

Additional digital resources can be found in:

- Interactive Student Edition
- *my*Perspectives+

Students pull together their notes, evidence, completed activities, and Performance Tasks to prepare for the Performance-Based Assessment.

VOLUME TWO

UNIT 4 Star-Crossed Romances

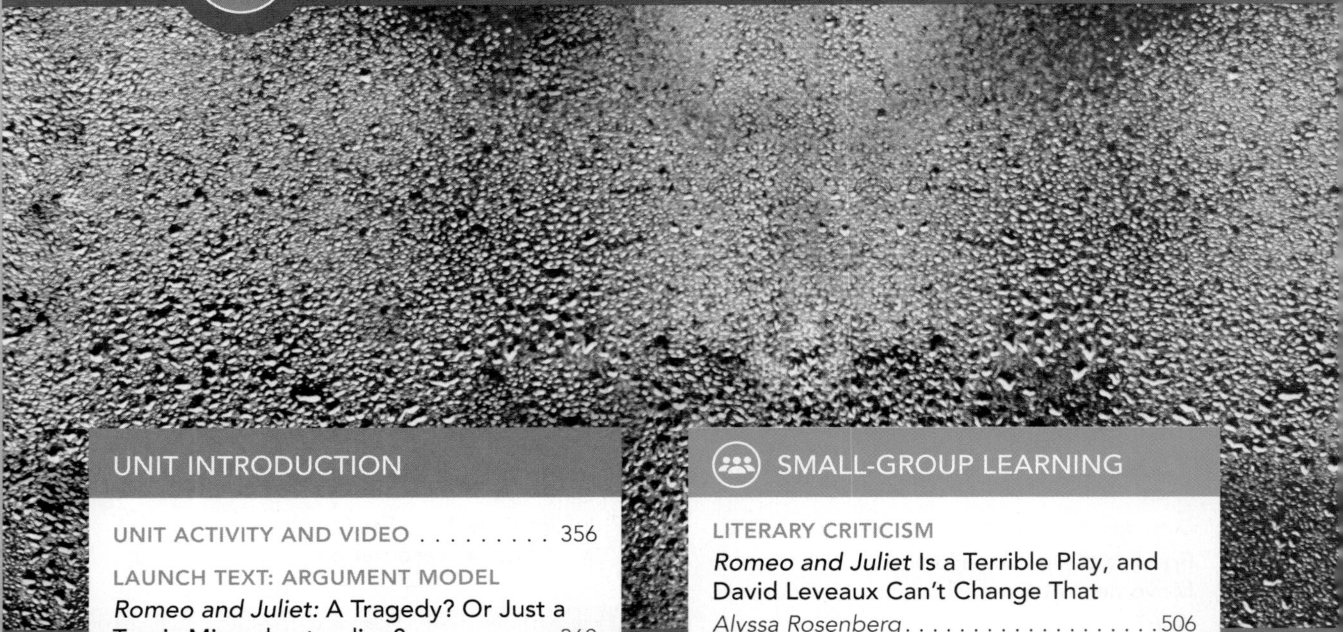

UNIT INTRODUCTION

WHOLE-CLASS LEARNING

Comparing a text and media version of classic literature deepens the learning experience and develops critical skills.

A rich array of media selections engage students in multi-modal learning.

SMALL-GROUP LEARNING

ESSENTIAL QUESTION: Do we determine our own destinies?

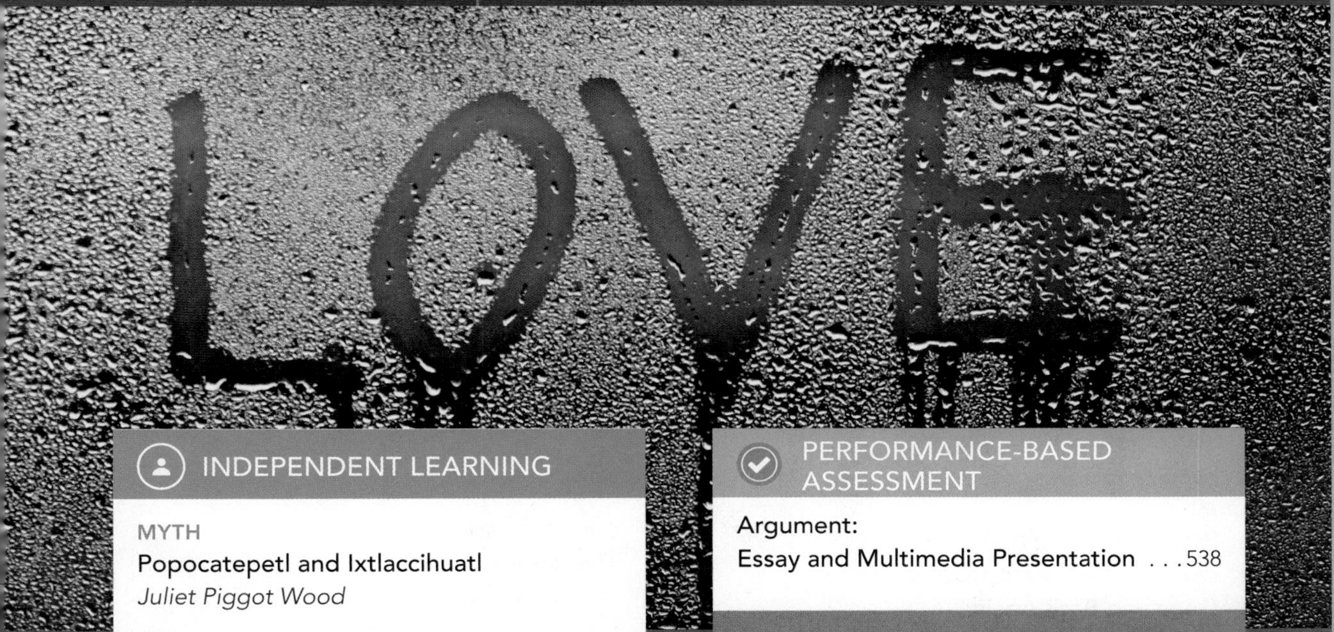

INDEPENDENT LEARNING

These selections can be accessed via the Interactive Student Edition.

PERFORMANCE-BASED ASSESSMENT

UNIT REFLECTION

DIGITAL PERSPECTIVES

SCAN FOR MULTIMEDIA

Use the BouncePage app whenever you see "Scan for Multimedia" to access:

- Unit Introduction Videos
- Media Selections
- Modeling Videos
- Selection Audio Recordings

Additional digital resources can be found in:

- Interactive Student Edition
- *my*Perspectives+

Access multimedia resources directly from print by using your mobile or tablet device.

Digital resources, including editable worksheets, can be found in *my*Perspectives+.

VOLUME TWO

UNIT 5 Journeys of Transformation

UNIT INTRODUCTION

WHOLE-CLASS LEARNING

Comparing classic literature to graphic novels brings relevance and engagement to the classroom.

SMALL-GROUP LEARNING

ESSENTIAL QUESTION: What can we learn from a journey?

INDEPENDENT LEARNING

These selections can be accessed via the Interactive Student Edition.

PERFORMANCE-BASED ASSESSMENT

UNIT REFLECTION

Unit Reflection allows students to revisit learning goals and review skills and content learned.

DIGITAL PERSPECTIVES

SCAN FOR MULTIMEDIA

Use the BouncePage app whenever you see "Scan for Multimedia" to access:

- Unit Introduction Videos
- Media Selections
- Modeling Videos
- Selection Audio Recordings

Additional digital resources can be found in:

- Interactive Student Edition
- *my*Perspectives+

UNIT 6 World's End

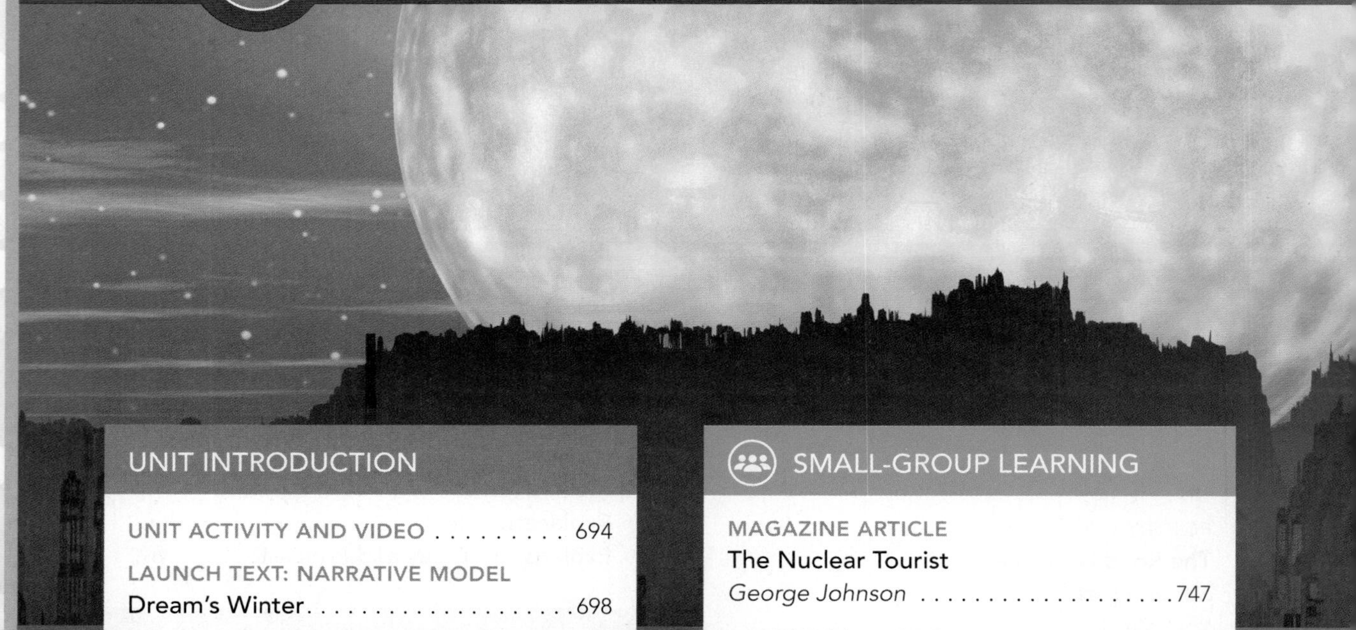

UNIT INTRODUCTION

WHOLE-CLASS LEARNING

SMALL-GROUP LEARNING

ESSENTIAL QUESTION: Why do we try to imagine the future?

INDEPENDENT LEARNING

These selections can be accessed via the Interactive Student Edition.

PERFORMANCE-BASED ASSESSMENT

UNIT REFLECTION

DIGITAL PERSPECTIVES

SCAN FOR MULTIMEDIA

Use the BouncePage app whenever you see "Scan for Multimedia" to access:

- Unit Introduction Videos
- Media Selections
- Modeling Videos
- Selection Audio Recordings

Additional digital resources can be found in:

- Interactive Student Edition
- *my*Perspectives+

Student-Centered Learning

*my*Perspectives promotes student-centered learning through a unit organization that:

- gives students increasing responsibility for the learning process as they understand expectations, set goals, use self-assessment measures, and monitor and reflect on their learning.
- supports active learning in which students annotate texts, answer questions, pose questions of their own, and construct knowledge as they search for meaning.
- promotes social collaboration and interaction among learners in ways that strengthen positive interdependence and individual accountability.
- engages students in making choices in their learning and work they are producing.
- provides flexibility for teachers to manage resources to match learner needs.

UNIT INTRODUCTION

- An open-ended Essential Question is posed to stimulate thoughtful student inquiry into the richness of a topic.
- The Launch Text, unit opener video, and discussion board engage students by provoking and generating interest in the unit topic.
- Unit goals link directly to the demands of the Performance-Based Assessment.

WHOLE-CLASS LEARNING

- Teachers model, instruct, and support with anchor texts as the class broadens its perspective of the unit topic.
- Activities focus on making meaning, language development, and effective expression.
- Students develop and share their perspectives on the unit topic through writing in a targeted mode.

SMALL-GROUP LEARNING

- Students work collaboratively to broaden their perspectives on the unit topic.
- Teachers facilitate and encourage collaboration as students work in groups.
- Students develop presentations, participate in group discussions and debates, and share their learning with the class in an array of speaking and listening activities.

INDEPENDENT LEARNING

- Students select one online text to read independently.
- Teachers advise and encourage students as they implement close-reading strategies.

PERFORMANCE-BASED ASSESSMENT

Students are required to demonstrate their learning by pulling together the content knowledge, process skills, and learning habits they acquired, practiced, and engaged in throughout the unit.

Interactive Student Edition

Whether your students use the print or digital version, the Student Edition is interactive!

Provides easy access to background, author, and standards information.

Integrated notebook captures student responses to activities and allows for easy submission to the teacher.

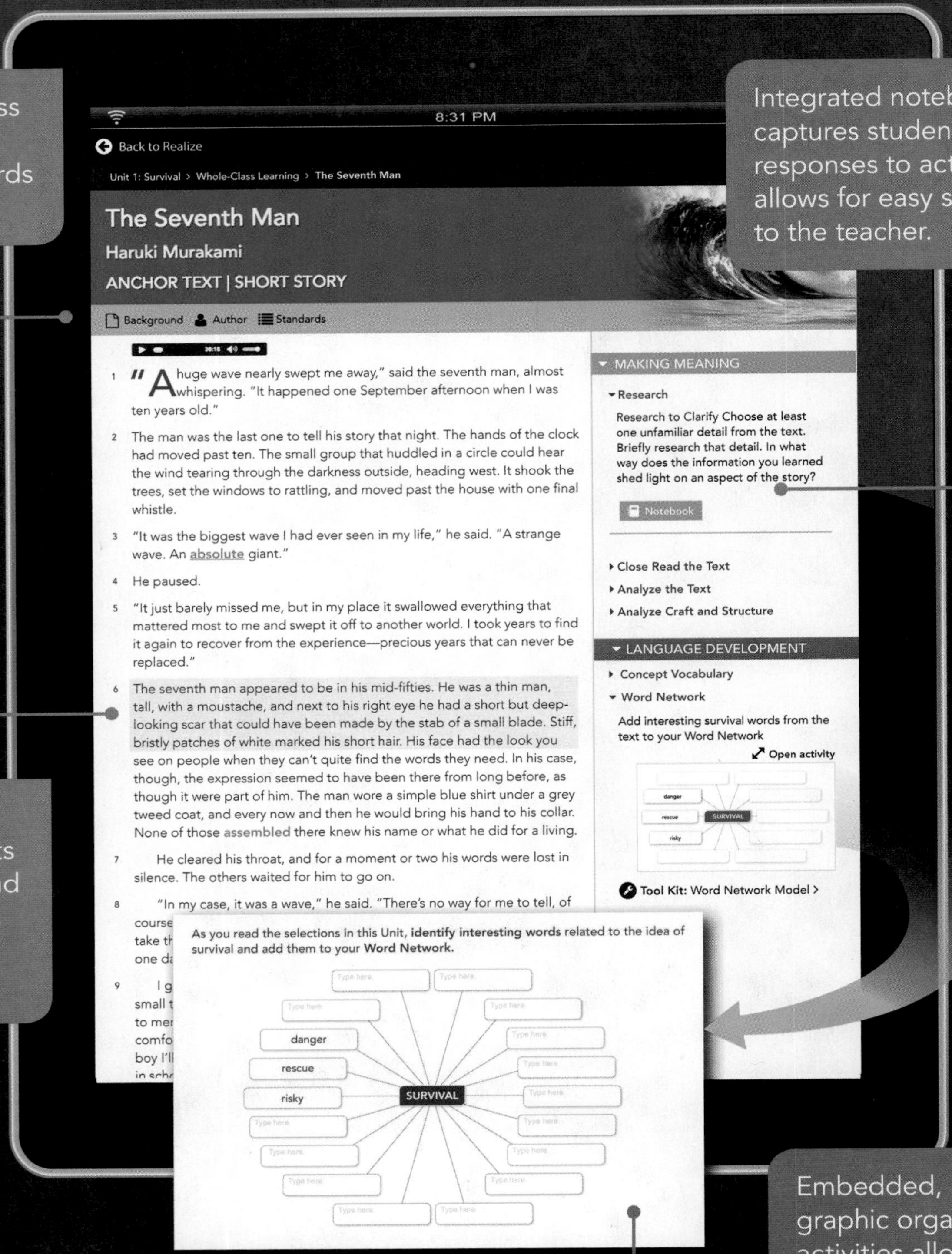

Inline annotation tools allow students to highlight text and write comments as they apply close-reading strategies.

Embedded, interactive graphic organizers and activities allow for interaction at point-of-use.

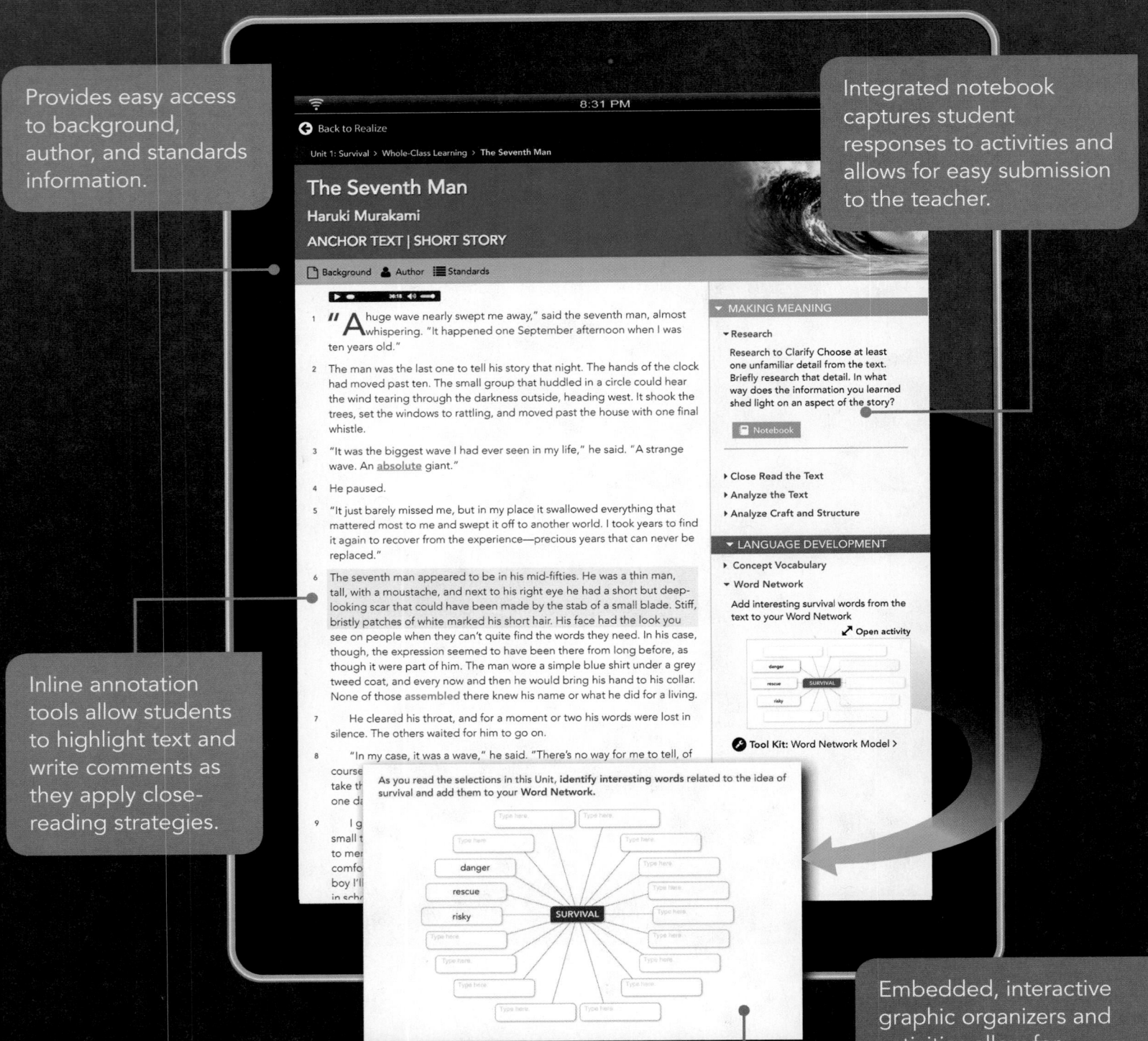

Download the Pearson BouncePages App to access audio, video, and multimedia selections through your mobile device!

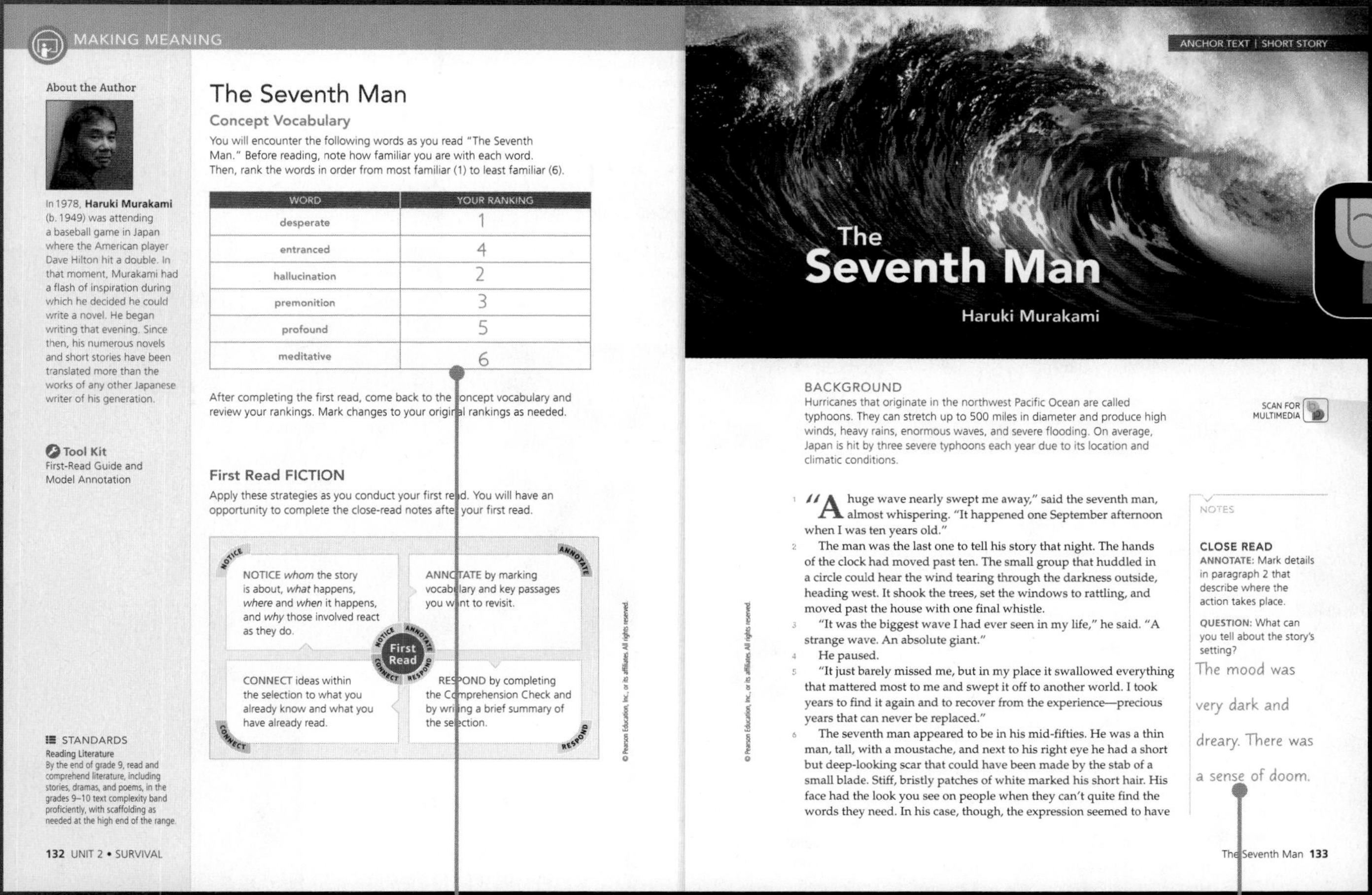

MAKING MEANING

About the Author

In 1978, **Haruki Murakami** (b. 1949) was attending a baseball game in Japan where the American player Dave Hilton hit a double. In that moment, Murakami had a flash of inspiration during which he decided he could write a novel. He began writing that evening. Since then, his numerous novels and short stories have been translated more than the works of any other Japanese writer of his generation.

Tool Kit
First-Read Guide and Model Annotation

STANDARDS
Reading Literature
By the end of grade 9, read and comprehend literature, including stories, dramas, and poems, in the grades 9–10 text complexity band proficiently, with scaffolding as needed at the high end of the range.

The Seventh Man

Concept Vocabulary

You will encounter the following words as you read "The Seventh Man." Before reading, note how familiar you are with each word. Then, rank the words in order from most familiar (1) to least familiar (6).

WORD	YOUR RANKING
desperate	1
entranced	4
hallucination	2
premonition	3
profound	5
meditative	6

After completing the first read, come back to the concept vocabulary and review your rankings. Mark changes to your original rankings as needed.

First Read FICTION

Apply these strategies as you conduct your first read. You will have an opportunity to complete the close-read notes after your first read.

NOTICE *whom* the story is about, *what* happens, *where* and *when* it happens, and *why* those involved react as they do.

ANNOTATE by marking vocabulary and key passages you want to revisit.

CONNECT ideas within the selection to what you already know and what you have already read.

RESPOND by completing the Comprehension Check and by writing a brief summary of the selection.

First Read: NOTICE, ANNOTATE, CONNECT, RESPOND

© Pearson Education, Inc., or its affiliates. All rights reserved.

132 UNIT 2 • SURVIVAL

ANCHOR TEXT | SHORT STORY

The Seventh Man

Haruki Murakami

BACKGROUND
Hurricanes that originate in the northwest Pacific Ocean are called typhoons. They can stretch up to 500 miles in diameter and produce high winds, heavy rains, enormous waves, and severe flooding. On average, Japan is hit by three severe typhoons each year due to its location and climatic conditions.

SCAN FOR MULTIMEDIA

1 "A huge wave nearly swept me away," said the seventh man, almost whispering. "It happened one September afternoon when I was ten years old."

2 The man was the last one to tell his story that night. The hands of the clock had moved past ten. The small group that huddled in a circle could hear the wind tearing through the darkness outside, heading west. It shook the trees, set the windows to rattling, and moved past the house with one final whistle.

3 "It was the biggest wave I had ever seen in my life," he said. "A strange wave. An absolute giant."

4 He paused.

5 "It just barely missed me, but in my place it swallowed everything that mattered most to me and swept it off to another world. I took years to find it again and to recover from the experience—precious years that can never be replaced."

6 The seventh man appeared to be in his mid-fifties. He was a thin man, tall, with a moustache, and next to his right eye he had a short but deep-looking scar that could have been made by the stab of a small blade. Stiff, bristly patches of white marked his short hair. His face had the look you see on people when they can't quite find the words they need. In his case, though, the expression seemed to have

NOTES

CLOSE READ
ANNOTATE: Mark details in paragraph 2 that describe where the action takes place.

QUESTION: What can you tell about the story's setting?

The mood was very dark and dreary. There was a sense of doom.

© Pearson Education, Inc., or its affiliates. All rights reserved.

The Seventh Man 133

A write-in Student Edition allows students to annotate the text and respond to questions.

Close-Reading Routine

myPerspectives motivates students to read a text thoughtfully, apply strategies as they read, and critically examine the text.

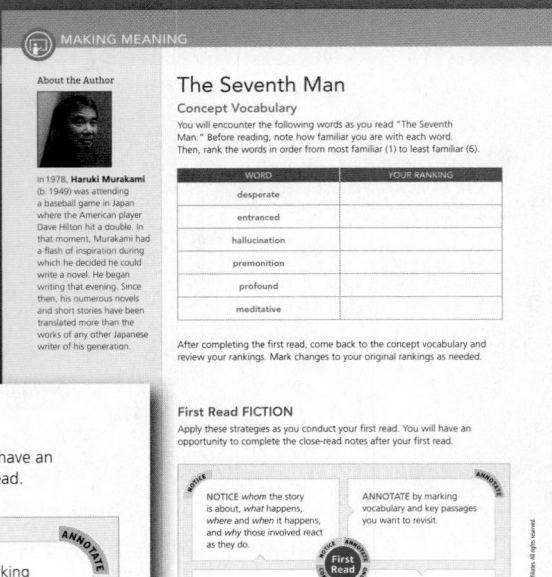

MAKING MEANING

About the Author

In 1978, **Haruki Murakami** (b. 1949) was attending a baseball game in Japan where the American player Dave Hilton hit a double. In that moment, Murakami had a flash of inspiration during which he decided he could write a novel. He began writing that evening. Since then, his numerous novels and short stories have been translated more than the works of any other Japanese writer of his generation.

The Seventh Man

Concept Vocabulary

You will encounter the following words as you read "The Seventh Man." Before reading, note how familiar you are with each word. Then, rank the words in order from most familiar (1) to least familiar (6).

WORD	YOUR RANKING
desperate	
entranced	
hallucination	
premonition	
profound	
meditative	

After completing the first read, come back to the concept vocabulary and review your rankings. Mark changes to your original rankings as needed.

First Read FICTION

Apply these strategies as you conduct your first read. You will have an opportunity to complete the close-read notes after your first read.

NOTICE *whom* the story is about, *what* happens, *where* and *when* it happens, and *why* those involved react as they do.

ANNOTATE by marking vocabulary and key passages you want to revisit.

CONNECT ideas within the selection to what you already know and what you have already read.

RESPOND by completing the Comprehension Check and by writing a brief summary of the selection.

First Read: NOTICE, ANNOTATE, CONNECT, RESPOND

Students apply first-read routines as they independently read and annotate texts.

First Read FICTION

Apply these strategies as you conduct your first read. You will have an opportunity to complete the close-read notes after your first read.

NOTICE *whom* the story is about, *what* happens, *where* and *when* it happens, and *why* those involved react as they do.

ANNOTATE by marking vocabulary and key passages you want to revisit.

CONNECT ideas within the selection to what you already know and what you have already read.

RESPOND by completing the Comprehension Check and by writing a brief summary of the selection.

MAKING MEANING

THE SEVENTH MAN

Close Read the Text

1. The model, from paragraph 5 of the story, shows two sample annotations, along with questions and conclusions. Close read the passage, and find another detail to annotate. Then, write a question and your conclusion.

Close Read: ANNOTATE, QUESTION, CONCLUDE

ANNOTATE: This phrase describes the wave in almost human terms.

QUESTION: What effect does this word choice create?

CONCLUDE: This description makes the wave seem alive and evil.

"It just barely missed me, but in my place it swallowed everything that mattered most to me and swept it off to another world. I took years to find it again and to recover from the experience—precious years that can never be replaced."

ANNOTATE: This word is repeated.

QUESTION: Why does the author repeat the word *years*?

CONCLUDE: The repetition emphasizes how long it takes the man to recover from the experience.

Models show students how to close read the text.

Students close read complex and rich text passages, studying structures, diction, and other elements of author's craft.

... not seem to have reached him. He might have been so absorbed in whatever it was he had found that my call made no impression on him. K. was like that. He would get involved with things to the point of forgetting everything else. Or possibly I had not yelled as loudly as I had thought. I do recall that my voice sounded strange to me, as though it belonged to someone else.

29 Then I heard a deep rumbling sound. It seemed to shake the earth.

NOTES

CLOSE READ

ANNOTATE: In paragraph 27, mark the details the author uses to describe the waves.

QUESTION: Why does the author include so many contrasting descriptions?

CONCLUDE: In what ways is the author preparing you for what comes next?

Closer Look notes, found only in the Teacher's Edition, provide additional close-reading opportunities.

Digital Annotation Highlights focus on passages in the Interactive Teacher's Edition.

TEACHING

CLOSER LOOK

Analyze Character

Students may have marked paragraph 10 during their first read. Use this paragraph to help students understand the seventh man's friendship with K.

ANNOTATE: Have students mark details in the paragraph that describe K.'s appearance and personality.

QUESTION: What overall impression does the author create of K.? How does the author characterize the relationship between K. and the seventh man?

Possible response: K. is an artistic, sensitive boy who is often picked on because he is physically different from most boys his age. His speech impediment and difficulty with academics lead most people to think something is wrong with him. K. and the seventh man are best friends. The seventh man feels protective of K., and often stands up for him when he is picked on by others.

CONCLUDE: How does the author's characterization of K. and his friendship with the seventh man help you understand the impact of K.'s death?

Possible response: The seventh man viewed himself as K.'s protector. When K. was lost to the wave the seventh man lost his best friend, and he blamed himself for failing to protect K., carrying that guilt with him for most of his life.

Remind students that there are two types of characterization. In **direct characterization**, ... a character's traits. ...**tion**, an author ...aracter by describing ..., does, and says, as ...ers react to him or ...o draw conclusions ...

NOTES

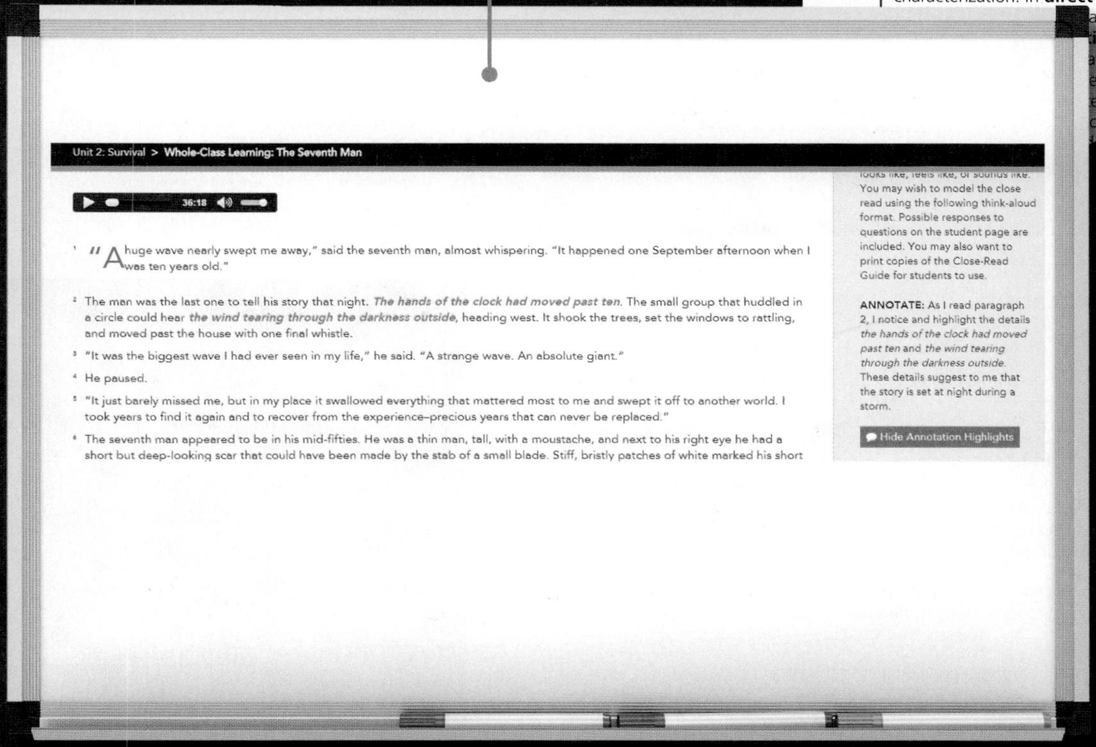

Unit 2: Survival > Whole-Class Learning: The Seventh Man
36:18
1 "A huge wave nearly swept me away," said the seventh man, almost whispering. "It happened one September afternoon when I was ten years old."
2 The man was the last one to tell his story that night. The hands of the clock had moved past ten. The small group that huddled in a circle could hear the wind tearing through the darkness outside, heading west. It shook the trees, set the windows to rattling, and moved past the house with one final whistle.
3 "It was the biggest wave I had ever seen in my life," he said. "A strange wave. An absolute giant."
4 He paused.
5 "It just barely missed me, but in my place it swallowed everything that mattered most to me and swept it off to another world. I took years to find it again and to recover from the experience–precious years that can never be replaced."
6 The seventh man appeared to be in his mid-fifties. He was a thin man, tall, with a moustache, and next to his right eye he had a short but deep-looking scar that could have been made by the stab of a small blade. Stiff, bristly patches of white marked his short
You may wish to model the close read using the following think-aloud format. Possible responses to questions on the student page are included. You may also want to print copies of the Close-Read Guide for students to use.
ANNOTATE: As I read paragraph 2, I notice and highlight the details the hands of the clock had moved past ten and the wind tearing through the darkness outside. These details suggest to me that the story is set at night during a storm.
Hide Annotation Highlights

Building Literacy

For each selection, students **Make Meaning** through first- and close-read routines and by analyzing author's craft and structure. Students also complete **Language Development** activities with concept vocabulary and conventions practice tasks. **Effective Expression** activities provide students with opportunities to share their learning through written and oral projects.

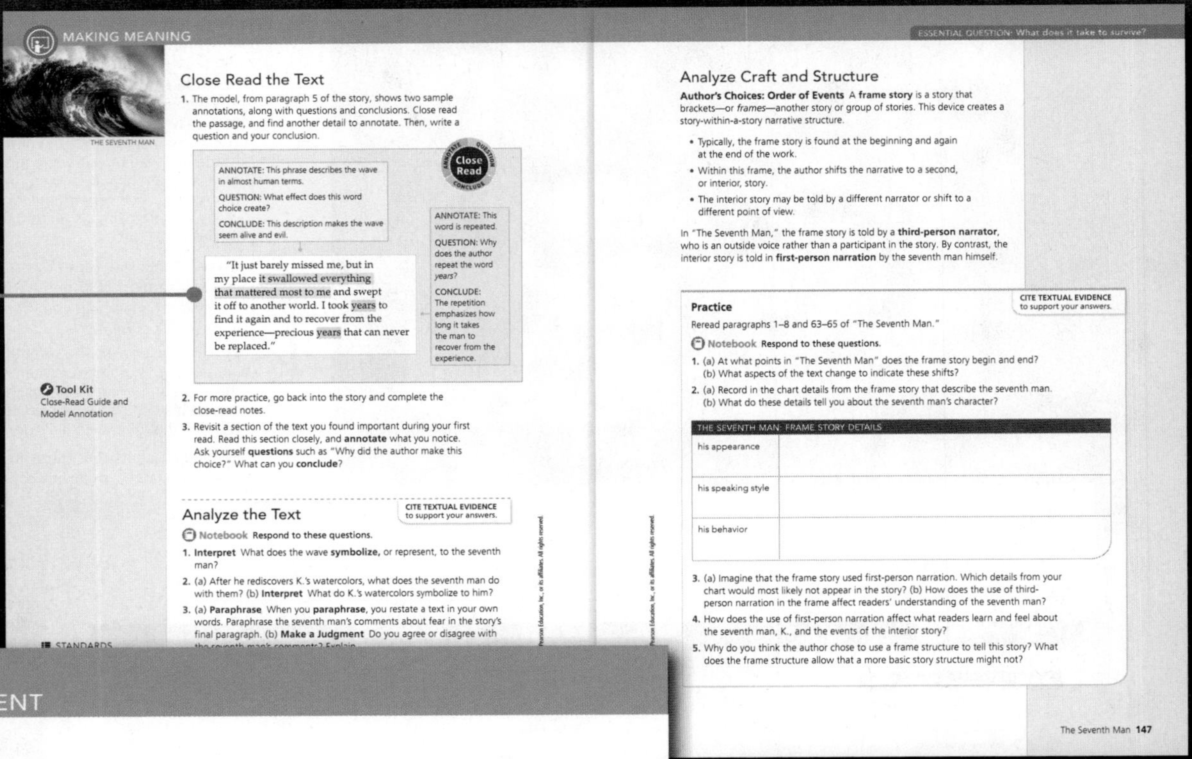
MAKING MEANING

THE SEVENTH MAN

Close Read the Text

1. The model, from paragraph 5 of the story, shows two sample annotations, along with questions and conclusions. Close read the passage, and find another detail to annotate. Then, write a question and your conclusion.

ANNOTATE: This phrase describes the wave in almost human terms.
QUESTION: What effect does this word choice create?
CONCLUDE: This description makes the wave seem alive and evil.

"It just barely missed me, but in my place it swallowed everything that mattered most to me and swept it off to another world. I took years to find it again and to recover from the experience—precious years that can never be replaced."

ANNOTATE: This word is repeated.
QUESTION: Why does the author repeat the word *years*?
CONCLUDE: The repetition emphasizes how long it takes the man to recover from the experience.

Tool Kit
Close-Read Guide and Model Annotation

2. For more practice, go back into the story and complete the close-read notes.
3. Revisit a section of the text you found important during your first read. Read this section closely, and **annotate** what you notice. Ask yourself **questions** such as "Why did the author make this choice?" What can you **conclude**?

Analyze the Text

CITE TEXTUAL EVIDENCE to support your answers.

Notebook Respond to these questions.

1. **Interpret** What does the wave **symbolize**, or represent, to the seventh man?
2. (a) After he rediscovers K.'s watercolors, what does the seventh man do with them? (b) **Interpret** What do K.'s watercolors symbolize to him?
3. (a) **Paraphrase** When you **paraphrase**, you restate a text in your own words. Paraphrase the seventh man's comments about fear in the story's final paragraph. (b) **Make a Judgment** Do you agree or disagree with

STANDARDS

ESSENTIAL QUESTION: What does it take to survive?

Analyze Craft and Structure

Author's Choices: Order of Events A **frame story** is a story that brackets—or *frames*—another story or group of stories. This device creates a story-within-a-story narrative structure.

- Typically, the frame story is found at the beginning and again at the end of the work.
- Within this frame, the author shifts the narrative to a second, or interior, story.
- The interior story may be told by a different narrator or shift to a different point of view.

In "The Seventh Man," the frame story is told by a **third-person narrator**, who is an outside voice rather than a participant in the story. By contrast, the interior story is told in **first-person narration** by the seventh man himself.

Practice

CITE TEXTUAL EVIDENCE to support your answers.

Reread paragraphs 1–8 and 63–65 of "The Seventh Man."

Notebook Respond to these questions.

1. (a) At what points in "The Seventh Man" does the frame story begin and end? (b) What aspects of the text change to indicate these shifts?
2. (a) Record in the chart details from the frame story that describe the seventh man. (b) What do these details tell you about the seventh man's character?

THE SEVENTH MAN: FRAME STORY DETAILS	
his appearance	
his speaking style	
his behavior	

3. (a) Imagine that the frame story used first-person narration. Which details from your chart would most likely not appear in the story? (b) How does the use of third-person narration in the frame affect readers' understanding of the seventh man?
4. How does the use of first-person narration affect what readers learn and feel about the seventh man, K., and the events of the interior story?
5. Why do you think the author chose to use a frame structure to tell this story? What does the frame structure allow that a more basic story structure might not?

The Seventh Man 147

MAKING MEANING

Students make meaning of the text through close reading and analysis.

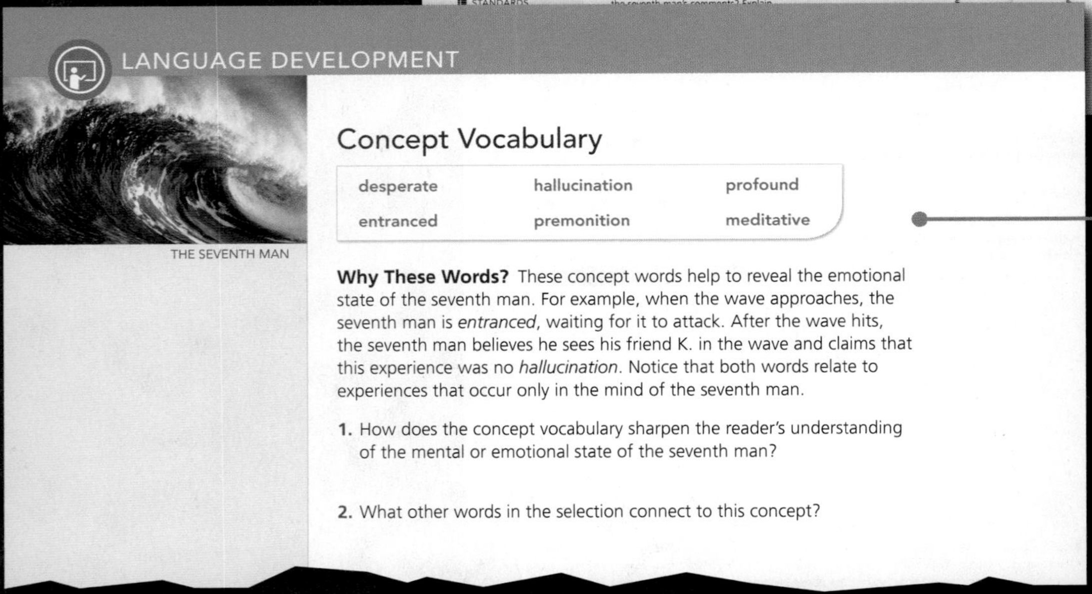
LANGUAGE DEVELOPMENT

THE SEVENTH MAN

Concept Vocabulary

desperate	hallucination	profound
entranced	premonition	meditative

Why These Words? These concept words help to reveal the emotional state of the seventh man. For example, when the wave approaches, the seventh man is *entranced*, waiting for it to attack. After the wave hits, the seventh man believes he sees his friend K. in the wave and claims that this experience was no *hallucination*. Notice that both words relate to experiences that occur only in the mind of the seventh man.

1. How does the concept vocabulary sharpen the reader's understanding of the mental or emotional state of the seventh man?
2. What other words in the selection connect to this concept?

LANGUAGE DEVELOPMENT

Concept Vocabulary words are taught in conjunction with each text. The selected words enable students to study words within meaningful clusters.

EFFECTIVE EXPRESSION

Students are provided with frequent opportunities to practice writing within the unit's focus mode.

Throughout the unit, students participate in speaking and listening, writing, and research activities that enable them to share learning.

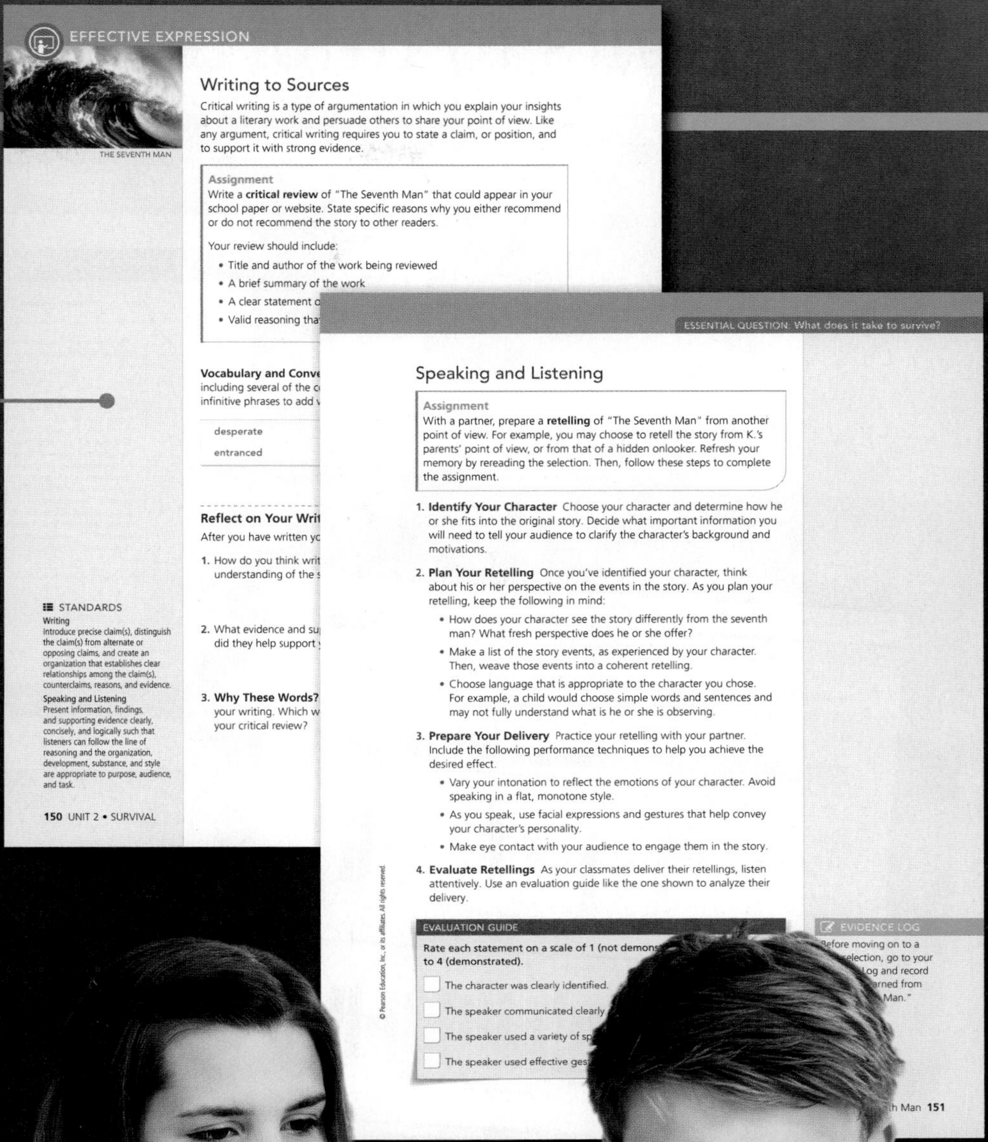

EFFECTIVE EXPRESSION

THE SEVENTH MAN

Writing to Sources

Critical writing is a type of argumentation in which you explain your insights about a literary work and persuade others to share your point of view. Like any argument, critical writing requires you to state a claim, or position, and to support it with strong evidence.

Assignment

Write a **critical review** of "The Seventh Man" that could appear in your school paper or website. State specific reasons why you either recommend or do not recommend the story to other readers.

Your review should include:

- Title and author of the work being reviewed
- A brief summary of the work
- A clear statement o
- Valid reasoning tha

Vocabulary and Conve including several of the c infinitive phrases to add v

desperate

entranced

Reflect on Your Writ

After you have written yo

1. How do you think writ understanding of the s

2. What evidence and su did they help support y

3. **Why These Words?** your writing. Which w your critical review?

STANDARDS

Writing

Introduce precise claim(s), distinguish the claim(s) from alternate or opposing claims, and create an organization that establishes clear relationships among the claim(s), counterclaims, reasons, and evidence.

Speaking and Listening

Present information, findings, and supporting evidence clearly, concisely, and logically such that listeners can follow the line of reasoning and the organization, development, substance, and style are appropriate to purpose, audience, and task.

150 UNIT 2 • SURVIVAL

ESSENTIAL QUESTION: What does it take to survive?

Speaking and Listening

Assignment

With a partner, prepare a **retelling** of "The Seventh Man" from another point of view. For example, you may choose to retell the story from K.'s parents' point of view, or from that of a hidden onlooker. Refresh your memory by rereading the selection. Then, follow these steps to complete the assignment.

1. **Identify Your Character** Choose your character and determine how he or she fits into the original story. Decide what important information you will need to tell your audience to clarify the character's background and motivations.

2. **Plan Your Retelling** Once you've identified your character, think about his or her perspective on the events in the story. As you plan your retelling, keep the following in mind:
   - How does your character see the story differently from the seventh man? What fresh perspective does he or she offer?
   - Make a list of the story events, as experienced by your character. Then, weave those events into a coherent retelling.
   - Choose language that is appropriate to the character you chose. For example, a child would choose simple words and sentences and may not fully understand what is he or she is observing.

3. **Prepare Your Delivery** Practice your retelling with your partner. Include the following performance techniques to help you achieve the desired effect.
   - Vary your intonation to reflect the emotions of your character. Avoid speaking in a flat, monotone style.
   - As you speak, use facial expressions and gestures that help convey your character's personality.
   - Make eye contact with your audience to engage them in the story.

4. **Evaluate Retellings** As your classmates deliver their retellings, listen attentively. Use an evaluation guide like the one shown to analyze their delivery.

EVALUATION GUIDE

Rate each statement on a scale of 1 (not demons to 4 (demonstrated).

- The character was clearly identified.
- The speaker communicated clearly
- The speaker used a variety of sp
- The speaker used effective ges

EVIDENCE LOG

Before moving on to a selection, go to your Log and record arned from Man."

© Pearson Education, Inc., or its affiliates. All rights reserved.

h Man 151

Assessments to Inform Instruction

Assessments can be administered in print and/or online.

Pearson Realize™ provides powerful data reporting.

YEAR-LONG ASSESSMENT

Beginning-of-Year Test

- Tests all standards that will be taught in the school year.
- Allows you to use test data to plan which standards need focus.

Mid-Year Test

- Tests mastery of standards taught in the first half of the year.
- Provides an opportunity to remediate; if administered online, remediation is assigned automatically.

End-of-Year Test

- Allows you to use results to determine mastery of standards, place students in classes for the following school year, and to capture final assessment data.

UNIT-LEVEL ASSESSMENT

Selection Activities

- Instructional activities can be used to assess students' grasp of critical concepts.

Formative Assessments

- Selection activities can be used as formative checks.
- Notes in the Teacher's Edition offer suggestions for reteaching.

Selection Tests

- Test items track student progress toward mastering standards taught with the selection.

Performance Tasks

- Each unit includes both a writing and a speaking and listening performance task.
- Performance Tasks prepare students for success on the end-of-unit Performance-Based Assessment.

Unit Tests

- Students apply standards taught in the unit with new texts.
- These tests provide an opportunity to remediate; if administered online, remediation is assigned automatically.

Performance-Based Assessments

- All unit activities are backwards-mapped to the end-of-unit Performance-Based Assessment.
- Students use their notes, knowledge, and skills learned to complete a project.

Technology-enhanced items allow students to experience next-generation assessment formats.

Personalize for Learning

The Teacher's Edition provides support before, during, and after each selection to help you personalize learning for your students.

A continuous improvement loop is built in to help teachers perform formative assessment and remediation.

A full range of reading supports is provided for each text, based on text complexity rubrics.

PERSONALIZE FOR LEARNING WHOL

Reading Support

Text Complexity Rubric: The Seventh Man	
Quantitative Measures	
Lexile: 910 **Text Length:** 5,860 words	
Qualitative Measures	
Knowledge Demands ①—❷—③—④—⑤	Life experience demands: The situations may be unfamiliar to some readers (experiencing a typhoon, tragedy of losing someone in a natural disaster), but the situations and emotions are clearly explained.
Structure ①—❷—③—④—⑤	Use of flash-back, flash-forward (transitions from narration in third person and the seventh man's story told in first person)
Language Conventionality and Clarity ①—②—❸—④—⑤	Figurative language; complex descriptions
Levels of Meaning/Purpose ①—②—❸—④—⑤	Multiple levels of meaning (events are described that also signify emotions of guilt or of self-forgiveness); concepts and meanings are mostly explained and easy to grasp.

DECIDE AND PLAN

English Language Support

Provide English Learners with support for context and vocabulary as they read the selection. **PI.8; PI.12**

Knowledge Demands Tell students that this short story is about an event that occurred during a typhoon. They should expect to see language that describes weather and the sea. (high tide, low tide,...)

Language Conventiality and Clarity Students may find the use of sensory language difficult to grasp. Explain that the author often uses words in a figurative way to create feelings or sensations. Figurative language is language that is used imaginatively rather than literally. Such expressions can be difficult for second-language learners.

Strategic Support

Provide students with strategic support to ensure that they can successfully read the text.

Knowledge Demands Use the background information to discuss typhoons. Determine students' prior knowledge and experience with natural disasters. Provide additional background if needed.

Structure Discuss what it means to flash-back or flash-forward in a text. Point out that a story might switch back and forth to different time periods. If students continue to have difficulty with the time sequence, point out clues to transitions between past and present; for example, sentences that say that the man is telling a story, or use of first and third person. When students reread, have them note each transition from past to present.

Challenge

Provide students who need to be challenged with ideas for how they can go beyond a simple interpretation of the text.

Text Analysis For students that grasp the time transitions, have them identify the use of first person when the seventh man is speaking, and descriptions in third person when the story moves to the present.

Written Response Ask students to speculate on what might have happened if the seventh man had made different choices in his life. Have them analyze each choice he made and determine how his life might have differed if he had chosen differently. Have them rewrite the story with reflection the choices.

TEACH

Read and Respond

Have the class do their first read of the selection. Then have them complete their close read. Finally, work with them on the Making Meaning, Language Development, and Effective Expression activities.

98C

Standards Support Throug

IDENTIFY NEEDS

Analyze results of the Beginning-of-Year Assessment, focusing on the items relating to Unit 2. Also take into consideration student performance to this point and your observations of where particular students struggle.

ANALYZE AND REVISE

- Analyze student work for evidence of student learning.
- Identify whether or not students have met the expectations in the standards.
- Identify implications for future instruction.

TEACH

Implement the planned lesson, and gather evidence of student learning.

- If students hav scaffolds befor
- If students hav keep progressi
- Use the Selecti students contir

Instructional S

	Cat
Reading	Revi stud unde have diffe You the to he the narr
Writing	You the Ane stud anec an a
Speaking and Listening	You the work help to p exce
Language	You the help func Revi stud unde have diffe

Text complexity rubrics provide targeted suggestions for learner levels, including English Language supports that are based on the demands of the text.

PERSONALIZE FOR LEARNING

Challenge
Encourage interested students to expand the Research to Explore activity by learning about the motto of other branches of the U.S. military, including the Air Force, Army, Coa[...] in addition to the Marines. Students can also [...] branch and present their results in a poster [...]

PERSONALIZE FOR LEARNING

English Language Support
Idioms Explain to students that *eye of the storm* in paragraph 15 is an idiomatic expression—the words used are not meant literally. If students struggle to understand idioms, encourage them to look for context clues. Instruct students to keep reading to get clues about the meaning of this expression (*No such "eye" existed, of course: we were just in that momentary quiet spot at the center of the pool of whirling air*). Make sure students understand that eye of the storm means "a calm in the middle of a turbulent situation. **ALL LEVELS**

English Language Support notes provide support for skills and concepts such as idioms, figurative language, and multiple-meaning words.

Practical and easy-to-implement supports ensure that all students' needs are met as they practice and apply standards with each text.

d Learning Cycle

ND PLAN

tching these standards, then provide selection sson provided in the Student Edition.

-Year Assessment, then challenge them to opportunities to practice the skills in depth.

ing Pages for The Seventh Man to help ster the standards.

	Looking Forward
4 Determine the of words and phrases e used in the text.	Have students analyze the subtleties and nuances of various word choices.
5 Analyze how an choices concerning ructure a text, nts within it, and te time create such mystery, tension, or	Have students recast the beginning of the story without the frame and analyze the impact on the story as a whole.
.a-e Write narratives p real or imagined es or events using technique, well- etails, and well- d event sequences.	Encourage students to incorporate both real and fictional anecdotes in their writing.
4.b Plan, memorize ent a recitation veys the meaning ection and includes te performance es (e.g., tone, rate, dulation) to achieve ed aesthetic effect.	You may wish to challenge students to memorize and recite increasingly longer or more complex selections.
Use various types s to convey specific s and add variety est to writing or tions.	You may wish to challenge students to use increasingly complex phrases and clauses in their writing.
a Use context as a e meaning of a word .	Have students analyze the subtleties and nuances of various word choices in different contexts.

Customize and Enrich

DIGITAL PERSPECTIVES

Enriching the Text In 2013, the environmental scientist Tim Jarvis re-created Shackleton's voyage from Elephant Island to South Georgia in a replica of the *James Caird*. Jarvis and his crew used the same clothing, food, and navigational equipment that Shackleton had. The documentary *Shackleton: Death or Glory* chronicles the journey. Find a clip from the documentary online and show students (after previewing it yourself). Then, have students write a paragraph explaining how the clip enhances their understanding of the selection "The Voyage of the *James Caird*." For example, students might gain a better understanding of the size of the boat and the harsh conditions Shackleton and his men endured.

Digital Perspectives offers suggestions for using digital resources to strengthen concepts being taught.

AUTHOR'S PERSPECTIVE **Jim Cummins**

Importance of Background Knowledge It is important for all students, and especially English Language Learners, to tap into background knowledge when they read a text. It is incumbent on teachers to help students access this knowledge and integrate it with new textual information. One way to do this is to encourage groups to share what they know about the topic of the text before they begin reading. For example, on a superficial level, some students may have prior knowledge about sailing, which can help to scaffold understanding of "The Voyage of the *James Caird*." On a deeper level, more students may be able to relate to the idea of forcing oneself to go to extremes or taking risks in order to help others. After students have completed their first read, have them discuss how their background knowledge helped them understand the text.

Author's Perspective notes offer expert insights on topics, including incorporating first-language knowledge, building background knowledge, and academic and conversational vocabulary.

FORMATIVE ASSESSMENT
Analyze Craft and Structure

- **If** students fail to identify the frame, **then** have them look for clues that indicate the point of view. For example, the person narrating the frame may not be involved in the interior story.

A formative assessment opportunity with recommended prescriptive activities is provided with

English Language Support

myPerspectives provides supports for English Language Learners at the Emerging, Expanding, and Bridging levels. Various resources can be used flexibly in print and online to meet your students' individual needs.

Selection audio can be found in the Interactive Student Edition and via BouncePages in the print Student Edition.

The Moral Logic of Survivor Guilt

Nancy Sherman

ANCHOR TEXT | OPINION PIECE

Background Author Standards

11:44

1 If there is one thing we have learned from returning war veterans—especially those of the last decade—it's that the emotional reality of the soldier at home is often at odds with that of the civilian public they left behind. And while friends and families of returning service members may be experiencing gratefulness or relief this holiday,[1] many of those they've welcomed home are likely struggling with other emotions.

Is the sense of responsibility soldiers feel toward each other irrational?

2 High on that list of emotions is guilt. Soldiers often carry this burden home—survivor guilt being perhaps the kind most familiar to us. In war, standing here rather than there can save your life but cost a buddy his. It's flukish luck, but you feel responsible. The guilt begins an endless loop of counterfactuals—thoughts that you could have or should have done otherwise, though in fact you did nothing wrong. The feelings are, of course, not restricted to the battlefield. But given the magnitude[2] of loss in war, they hang

Glossary terms are defined at point of use and include English and Spanish audio.

BACKGROUND

Traumatic events take a toll on the physical and mental well-being of the individuals who must endure them. Survivors of the Holocaust, rescue workers, and war veterans, for example, might wonder how they were able to make it out alive when others did not. The term "survivor guilt" is used to describe these feelings.

SCAN FOR MULTIMEDIA

1 If there is one thing we have learned from returning war veterans—especially those of the last decade—it's that the emotional reality of the soldier at home is often at odds with that of the civilian public they left behind. And while friends and families of returning service members may be experiencing gratefulness or relief this holiday,[1] many of those they've welcomed home are likely struggling with other emotions.

Is the sense of responsibility soldiers feel toward each other irrational?

2 High on that list of emotions is guilt. Soldiers often carry this burden home—survivor guilt being perhaps the kind most familiar to us. In war, standing here rather than there can save your life but cost a buddy his. It's flukish luck, but you feel responsible. The guilt begins an endless loop of counterfactuals—thoughts that you could have or should have done otherwise, though in fact you did nothing wrong. The feelings are, of course, not restricted to the battlefield. But given the magnitude[2] of loss in war, they hang heavy there and are pervasive. And they raise the question of just how irrational those feelings are, and if they aren't, of what is the basis of their reasonableness.

NOTES

burden (BURD n) *n.* something that is carried with difficulty or obligation

CLOSE READ

ANNOTATE: Mark words in paragraph 1 that show opposites.

QUESTION: What groups of people are being contrasted by using these opposites?

CONCLUDE: What does this contrast suggest about the two groups?

1. **this holiday** This essay was originally published the day before the 4th of July (Independence Day).
2. **magnitude** *n.* great size or extent.

GLOSARIO: VOCABULARIO ACADÉMICO

VOCABULARIO ACADÉMICOS/ VOCABULARIO DE CONCEPTOS

El vocabulario académico está en letra azul.

Pronunciation Key

Symbol	Sample Words	Symbol	Sample Words
a	*at, catapult, Alabama*	ihr	
a	*father, charms, argue*	o	
ahr	*far, archaic, argument*	oh	
ar	*marry, various, arrogant*	o͝o [lig]	
aw	*law, maraud, caution*	o͞o	*boot, soup, crucial*
awr	*pour, organism, forewarn*	ow	*now, stout, flounder*
ay	*ape, sails, implication*	oy	*boy, toil, oyster*
ayr	*Mary, compare, hair*	u	*us, disrupt, understand*
ee	*even, teeth, really*	uh	*ago, focus, contemplation*
eer	*sneer, veneer, sincere*	uhr	*under, guttural, discolor*
eh	*ten, repel, elephant*	ur	*bird, urgent. perforation*
ehr	*merry, verify, terribly*	y	*by, delight, identify*
ih	*is, continue, fugitive*		

Concept and Academic Vocabulary words are defined in Spanish.

A

abash / avergonzar *v.* apenar

ambiguity / ambigüedad *s.* estado o cualidad de ser indefinido; vago

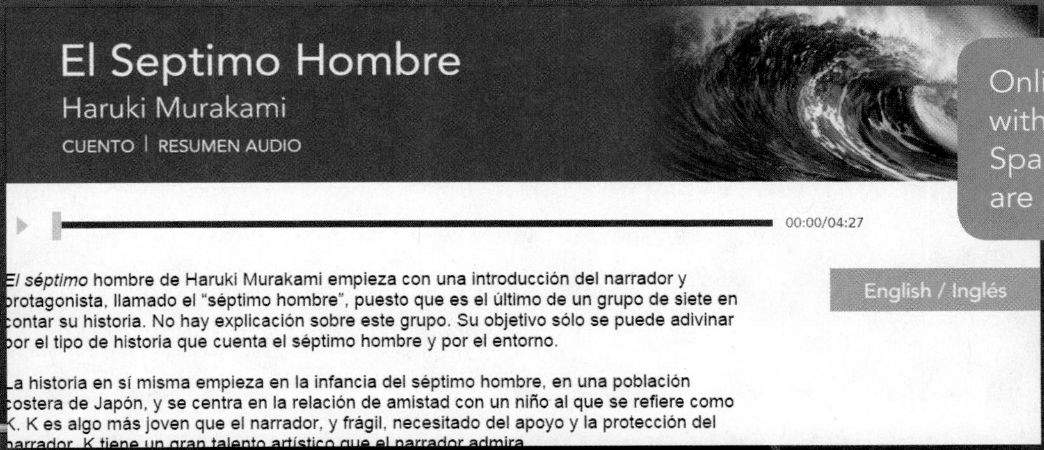
El Septimo Hombre
Haruki Murakami
CUENTO | RESUMEN AUDIO
00:00/04:27
English / Inglés
El séptimo hombre de Haruki Murakami empieza con una introducción del narrador y protagonista, llamado el "séptimo hombre", puesto que es el último de un grupo de siete en contar su historia. No hay explicación sobre este grupo. Su objetivo sólo se puede adivinar por el tipo de historia que cuenta el séptimo hombre y por el entorno.
La historia en sí misma empieza en la infancia del séptimo hombre, en una población costera de Japón, y se centra en la relación de amistad con un niño al que se refiere como K. K es algo más joven que el narrador, y frágil, necesitado del apoyo y la protección del narrador. K tiene un gran talento artístico que el narrador admira.

Online selection summaries with both English and Spanish audio and text are assignable.

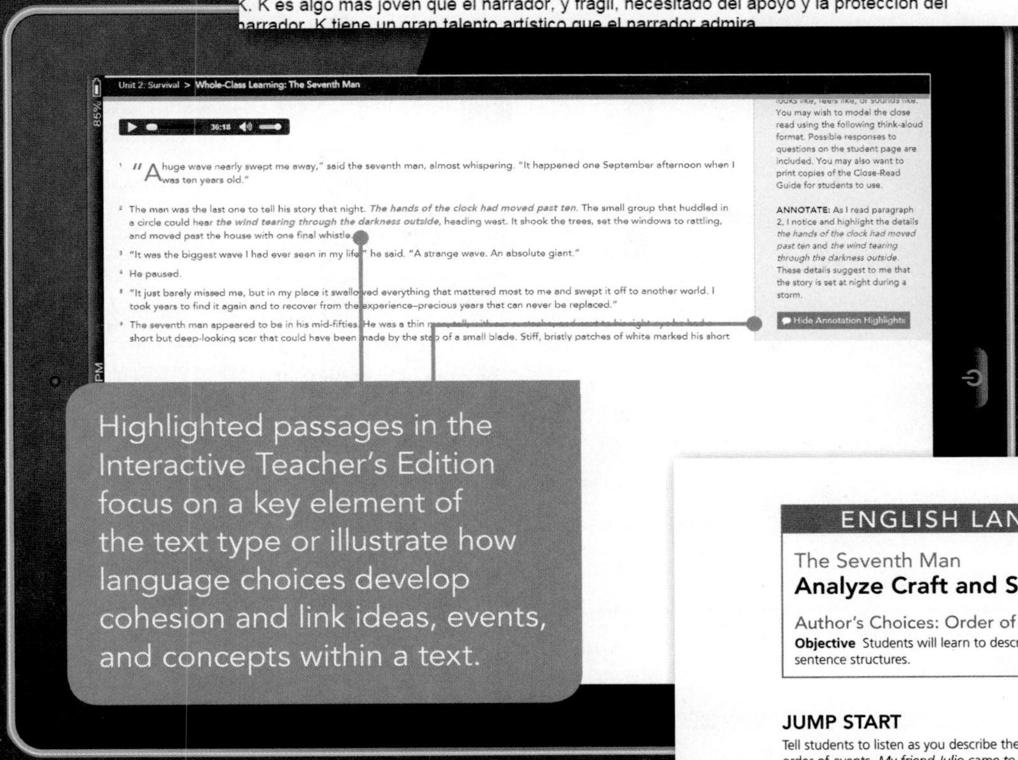
Unit 2: Survival > Whole-Class Learning: The Seventh Man
36:18
1 "A huge wave nearly swept me away," said the seventh man, almost whispering. "It happened one September afternoon when I was ten years old."
2 The man was the last one to tell his story that night. The hands of the clock had moved past ten. The small group that huddled in a circle could hear the wind tearing through the darkness outside, heading west. It shook the trees, set the windows to rattling, and moved past the house with one final whistle.
3 "It was the biggest wave I had ever seen in my life," he said. "A strange wave. An absolute giant."
4 He paused.
5 "It just barely missed me, but in my place it swallowed everything that mattered most to me and swept it off to another world. I took years to find it again and to recover from the experience–precious years that can never be replaced."
6 The seventh man appeared to be in his mid-fifties. He was a thin
short but deep-looking scar that could have been made by the st of a small blade. Stiff, bristly patches of white marked his short
You may wish to model the close read using the following think-aloud format. Possible responses to questions on the student page are included. You may also want to print copies of the Close-Read Guide for students to use.
ANNOTATE: As I read paragraph 2, I notice and highlight the details the hands of the clock had moved past ten and the wind tearing through the darkness outside. These details suggest to me that the story is set at night during a storm.
Hide Annotation Highlights

Highlighted passages in the Interactive Teacher's Edition focus on a key element of the text type or illustrate how language choices develop cohesion and link ideas, events, and concepts within a text.

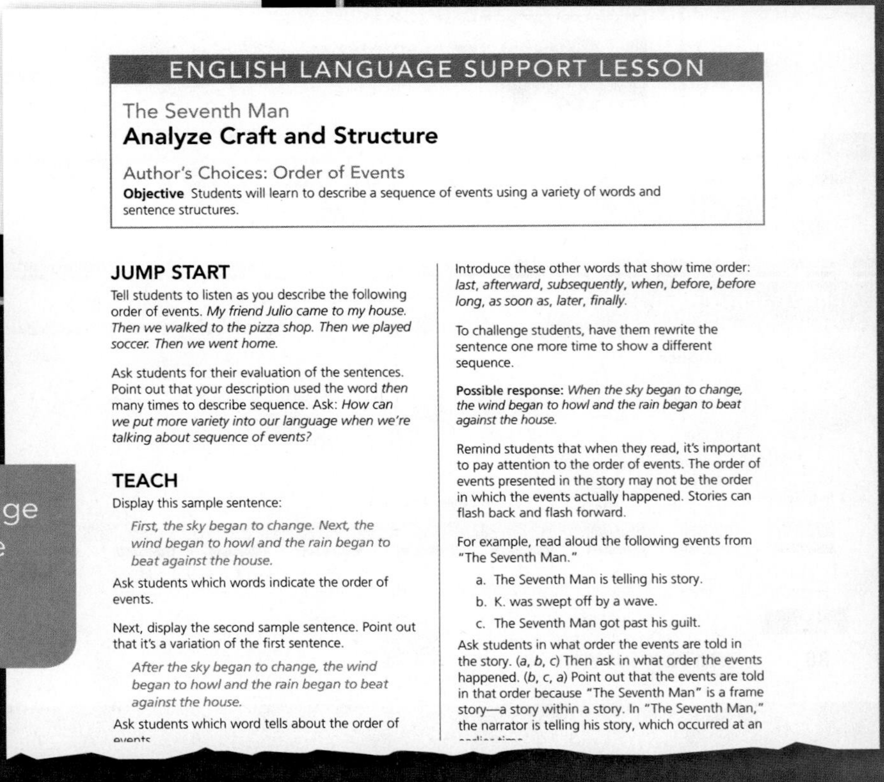

ENGLISH LANGUAGE SUPPORT LESSON

The Seventh Man

Analyze Craft and Structure

Author's Choices: Order of Events

Objective Students will learn to describe a sequence of events using a variety of words and sentence structures.

JUMP START

Tell students to listen as you describe the following order of events. *My friend Julio came to my house. Then we walked to the pizza shop. Then we played soccer. Then we went home.*

Ask students for their evaluation of the sentences. Point out that your description used the word *then* many times to describe sequence. Ask: *How can we put more variety into our language when we're talking about sequence of events?*

TEACH

Display this sample sentence:

First, the sky began to change. Next, the wind began to howl and the rain began to beat against the house.

Ask students which words indicate the order of events.

Next, display the second sample sentence. Point out that it's a variation of the first sentence.

After the sky began to change, the wind began to howl and the rain began to beat against the house.

Ask students which word tells about the order of events.

Introduce these other words that show time order: *last, afterward, subsequently, when, before, before long, as soon as, later, finally.*

To challenge students, have them rewrite the sentence one more time to show a different sequence.

Possible response: *When the sky began to change, the wind began to howl and the rain began to beat against the house.*

Remind students that when they read, it's important to pay attention to the order of events. The order of events presented in the story may not be the order in which the events actually happened. Stories can flash back and flash forward.

For example, read aloud the following events from "The Seventh Man."

a. The Seventh Man is telling his story.

b. K. was swept off by a wave.

c. The Seventh Man got past his guilt.

Ask students in what order the events are told in the story. (*a*, *b*, *c*) Then ask in what order the events happened. (*b*, *c*, *a*) Point out that the events are told in that order because "The Seventh Man" is a frame story—a story within a story. In "The Seventh Man," the narrator is telling his story, which occurred at an earlier time.

Printable English Language Support Lessons provide additional instructional opportunities.

Personalize for Teaching

Lesson planning is easy and efficient with clearly labeled support at point of use in the Teacher's Edition.

A trade book alignment with suggestions for integrating longer works within the unit is provided. Lesson plans for recommended titles are available online.

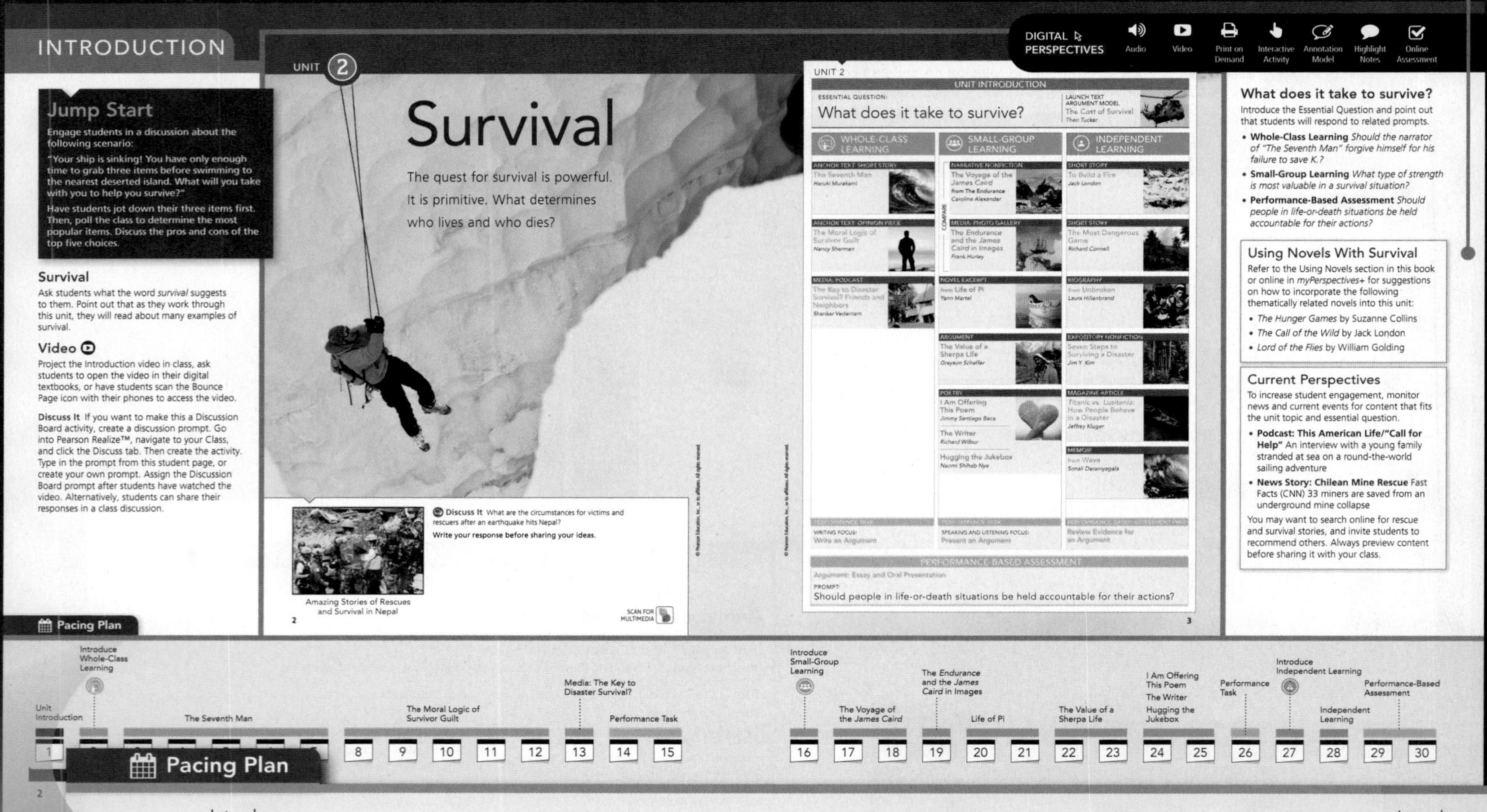

INTRODUCTION

DIGITAL PERSPECTIVES
Audio | Video | Print on Demand | Interactive Activity | Annotation Model | Highlight Notes | Online Assessment

Jump Start

Engage students in a discussion about the following scenario:

"Your ship is sinking! You have only enough time to grab three items before swimming to the nearest deserted island. What will you take with you to help you survive?"

Have students jot down their three items first. Then, poll the class to determine the most popular items. Discuss the pros and cons of the top five choices.

Survival

Ask students what the word *survival* suggests to them. Point out that as they work through this unit, they will read about many examples of survival.

Video

Project the Introduction video in class, ask students to open the video in their digital textbooks, or have students scan the Bounce Page icon with their phones to access the video.

Discuss It If you want to make this a Discussion Board activity, create a discussion prompt. Go into Pearson Realize™, navigate to your Class, and click the Discuss tab. Then create the activity. Type in the prompt from this student page, or create your own prompt. Assign the Discussion Board prompt after students have watched the video. Alternatively, students can share their responses in a class discussion.

UNIT 2

Survival

The quest for survival is powerful. It is primitive. What determines who lives and who dies?

Discuss It What are the circumstances for victims and rescuers after an earthquake hits Nepal?

Write your response before sharing your ideas.

Amazing Stories of Rescues and Survival in Nepal

SCAN FOR MULTIMEDIA

2

UNIT 2

UNIT INTRODUCTION

ESSENTIAL QUESTION: What does it take to survive?

LAUNCH TEXT ARGUMENT MODEL The Cost of Survival *Theo Tucker*

WHOLE-CLASS LEARNING	SMALL-GROUP LEARNING	INDEPENDENT LEARNING
ANCHOR TEXT: SHORT STORY The Seventh Man *Haruki Murakami*	NARRATIVE NONFICTION The Voyage of the James Caird from The Endurance *Caroline Alexander*	SHORT STORY To Build a Fire *Jack London*
ANCHOR TEXT: OPINION PIECE The Moral Logic of Survivor Guilt *Nancy Sherman*	MEDIA: PHOTO GALLERY The Endurance and the James Caird in Images *Frank Hurley*	SHORT STORY The Most Dangerous Game *Richard Connell*
MEDIA: PODCAST The Key to Disaster Survival? Friends and Neighbors *Shankar Vedantam*	NOVEL EXCERPT from Life of Pi *Yann Martel*	BIOGRAPHY from Unbroken *Laura Hillenbrand*
	ARGUMENT The Value of a Sherpa Life *Grayson Schaffer*	EXPOSITORY NONFICTION Seven Steps to Surviving a Disaster *Jim Y. Kim*
	POETRY I Am Offering This Poem *Jimmy Santiago Baca* / The Writer *Richard Wilbur* / Hugging the Jukebox *Naomi Shihab Nye*	MAGAZINE ARTICLE Titanic vs. Lusitania: How People Behave in a Disaster *Jeffrey Kluger*
		MEMOIR from Wave *Sonali Deraniyagala*
PERFORMANCE TASK WRITING FOCUS: Write an Argument	PERFORMANCE TASK SPEAKING AND LISTENING FOCUS: Present an Argument	PERFORMANCE-BASED ASSESSMENT PREP Review Evidence for an Argument

PERFORMANCE-BASED ASSESSMENT

Argument: Essay and Oral Presentation

PROMPT: Should people in life-or-death situations be held accountable for their actions?

3

What does it take to survive?

Introduce the Essential Question and point out that students will respond to related prompts.

- **Whole-Class Learning** *Should the narrator of "The Seventh Man" forgive himself for his failure to save K.?*
- **Small-Group Learning** *What type of strength is most valuable in a survival situation?*
- **Performance-Based Assessment** *Should people in life-or-death situations be held accountable for their actions?*

Using Novels With Survival

Refer to the Using Novels section in this book or online in *myPerspectives+* for suggestions on how to incorporate the following thematically related novels into this unit:

- *The Hunger Games* by Suzanne Collins
- *The Call of the Wild* by Jack London
- *Lord of the Flies* by William Golding

Current Perspectives

To increase student engagement, monitor news and current events for content that fits the unit topic and essential question.

- **Podcast: This American Life/"Call for Help"** An interview with a young family stranded at sea on a round-the-world sailing adventure
- **News Story: Chilean Mine Rescue** Fast Facts (CNN) 33 miners are saved from an underground mine collapse

You may want to search online for rescue and survival stories, and invite students to recommend others. Always preview content before sharing it with your class.

Pacing Plan

Unit Introduction 1 | Introduce Whole-Class Learning 2 | The Seventh Man 3–7 | The Moral Logic of Survivor Guilt 8–12 | Media: The Key to Disaster Survival? 13 | Performance Task 14–15 | Introduce Small-Group Learning 16 | The Voyage of the James Caird 17–18 | The *Endurance* and the *James Caird* in Images 19 | Life of Pi 20–21 | The Value of a Sherpa Life 22–23 | I Am Offering This Poem, The Writer, Hugging the Jukebox 24–25 | Performance Task 26 | Introduce Independent Learning 27 | Independent Learning 28 | Performance-Based Assessment 29–30

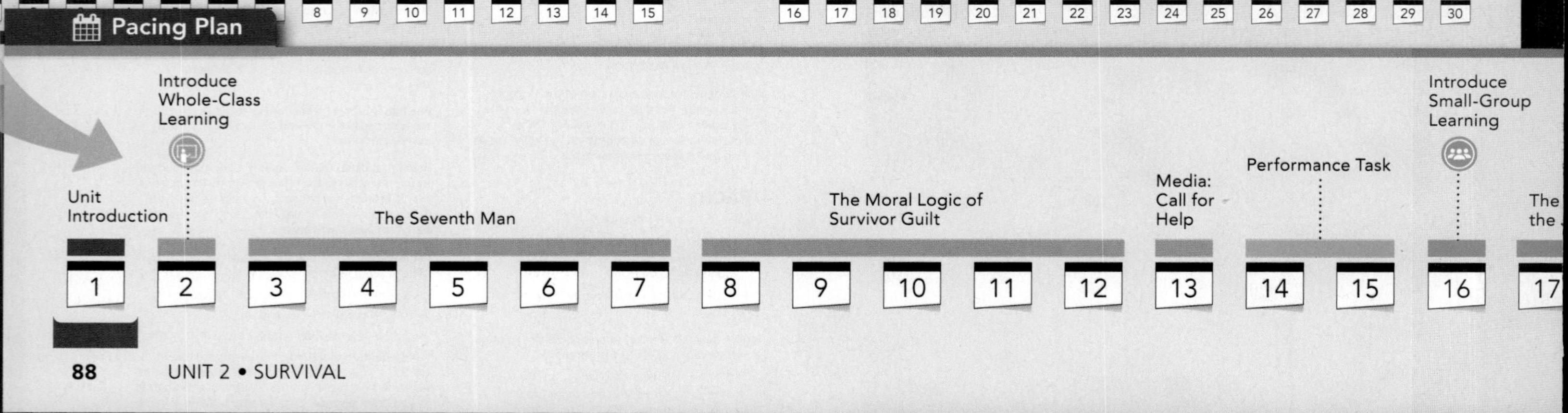

PLANNING WHOLE-CLASS LEARNING • THE SEVENTH MAN

The Seventh Man

AUDIO SUMMARIES
Audio summaries of "The Seventh Man" are available in both English and Spanish and can be assigned to students in Pearson Realize™. Assigning these summaries prior to reading the selection may help students build additional background knowledge and set a context for their first read.

Summary

"The Seventh Man" begins on a stormy night in a house where a group of people is sharing stories. The unnamed seventh man tells his story last and describes a huge wave that changed his life forever. He explains that he grew up in a seaside town in Japan, where he and his best friend, described only as K., were as close as brothers. A typhoon strikes and when the eye of the storm passes over, the seventh man's father allows the boys to go outside. They go down to the beach to play. When the a tsunami strikes, the seventh man runs for his life, leaving K. behind. He struggles with guilt for into his adult life. Forty years later, the seventh man makes an important realization.

Insight

The choices survivors make are not always easy or clear. Reading "The Seventh Man" will help students begin their reflections on how complicated survival can be. Although a survivor may have escaped with his or her life, that life may never be the same.

Some students may find "The Seventh Man" disturbing. The realization that a childhood decision might color someone's whole life is sobering and may require support.

Planning pages provide essential information, including selection summaries, insights, and links to the Essential Question.

Digital Perspectives identifies online resources.

DIGITAL PERSPECTIVES — Audio | Video | Print on Demand | Interactive Activity | Annotation Model | Highlight Notes | Online Assessment

Lesson Resources provides at-a-glance listings of standards, student-facing resources, on-level and reteaching support, and even a place for you to write in your own resources!

LESSON RESOURCES

	Making Meaning	Language Development	Effective Expression
Lesson	**First Read** **Close Read** **Analyze the Text** **Analyze Craft and Structure**	**Concept Vocabulary** **Word Study** **Conventions**	**Writing to Sources** **Speaking and Listening**
Instructional Standards	RL.9–10.4 RL.9–10.5 PI.5 PI.6a	L.9–10.1b L.9–10.4a PII.3, PII.4, PII.5	W.9–10.3.a–e SL.9–10.4.b PI.1, PI.5, PI.11
STUDENT RESOURCES	Search for these resources in myPerspectives Digital Student Edition or myPerspectives+		
Selection Resources	Audio Selection Student Modeling Video Close-Read Guide First-Read Guide	Word Network	Evidence Log
TEACHER RESOURCES	Search for these resources in myPerspectives Digital Teacher's Edition or myPerspectives+		
Selection Resources	Annotation Model Audio Summaries Additional English Language Support Analyze Text Frame Story Graphic Organizer Order of Events	Dependent Clause Tree Concept Vocabulary Suffixes Clauses	Anecdotes Recitations
Reteach and Practice	Analyze the Text Frame Story	Concept Vocabulary Suffixes Clauses	Anecdotes Recitations
Assessment			Selection Test
My Resources*	• Map of Japan • _____ • _____ • _____	• Sentence Strips • Tree diagram for dependent clauses • _____ • _____	• _____ • _____ • _____

* These resources are suggested at point of use in this lesson.

Whole-Class Learning 98B

e Endurance d the James ird in Images	*from* Life of Pi		The Value of a Sherpa Life		I Am Offering This Poem The Writer Hugging the Jukebox		Performance Task	Introduce Independent Learning	Independent Learning	Performance-Based Assessment	
9	20	21	22	23	24	25	26	27	28	29	30

A Pacing Plan provides recommended pacing.

Resources for Flexibility

myPerspectives+ includes hundreds of additional teacher resources you can use to customize your lessons. Interactive lessons, grammar tutorials, digital novels, and more are student-facing to allow students to work independently.

- Digital novels, including classics such as *Great Expectations, Pride and Prejudice, The Adventures of Tom Sawyer, Alice in Wonderland, The Scarlet Letter,* and *Romeo and Juliet*
- Novel lesson plans for over 100 titles, including those aligned to each unit
- Interactive lessons to help students develop critical writing, speaking, and listening skills
- High-interest readings and resources for struggling students
- Engaging grammar and academic vocabulary tutorials
- Writing Whiteboard Activities for an interactive and engaging classroom experience
- Editable grammar worksheets for extra practice with this crucial skill
- Generic graphic organizers and rubrics that can be used with any lesson

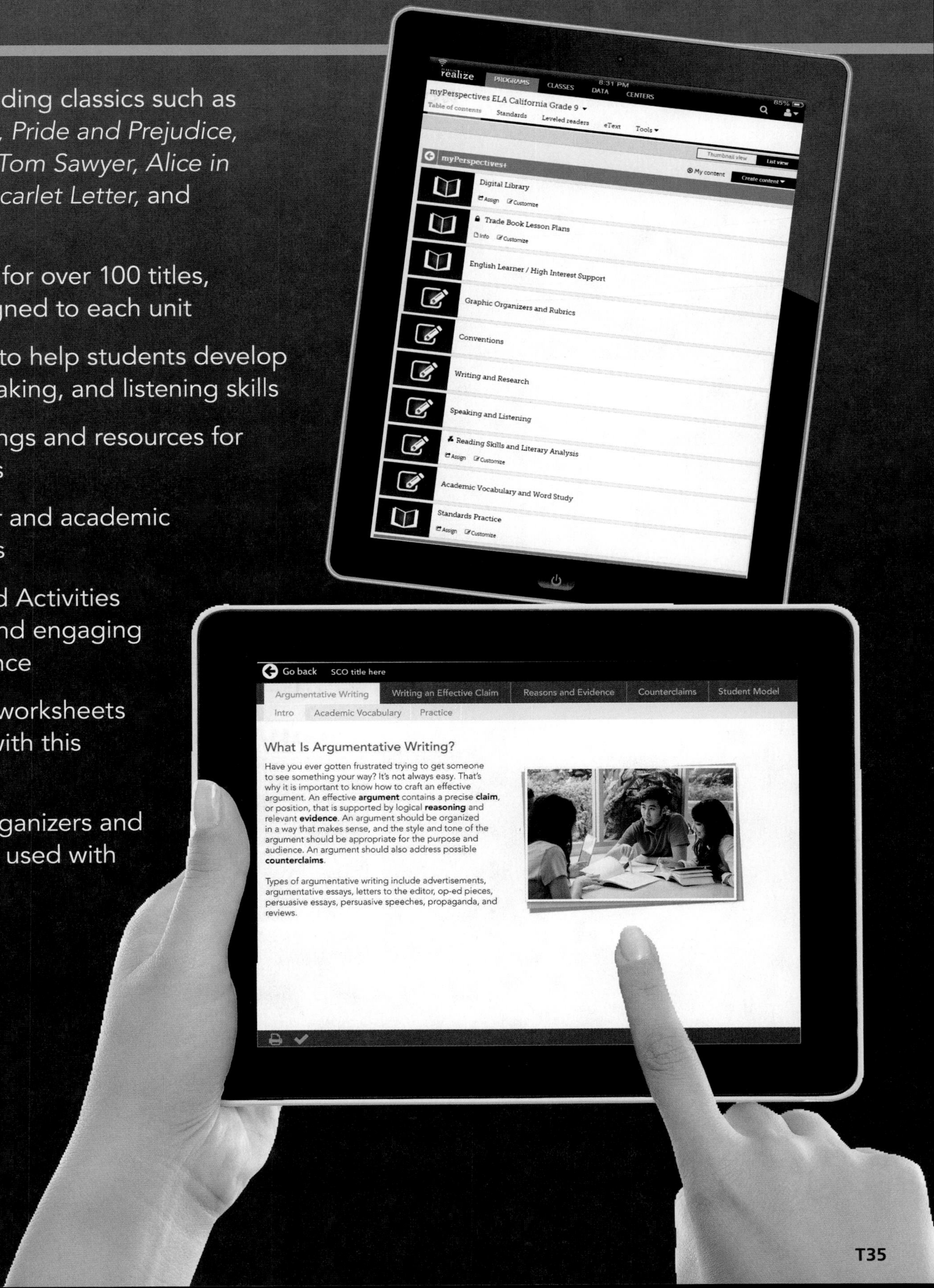

PEARSON realize™

Pearson Realize™ is your online destination for digital resources, assessments, and data. Flexible classroom management tools give you an amazing amount of freedom and control.

Easily manage your classes and data.

YOU HAVE THE POWER

Customize the program to make it your own.

- Rearrange content
- Upload your own content
- Add links to online media
- Edit resources and assessment

All program-specific resources, flexible agnostic resources, and assessments are available in one location for easy lesson planning and presentation.

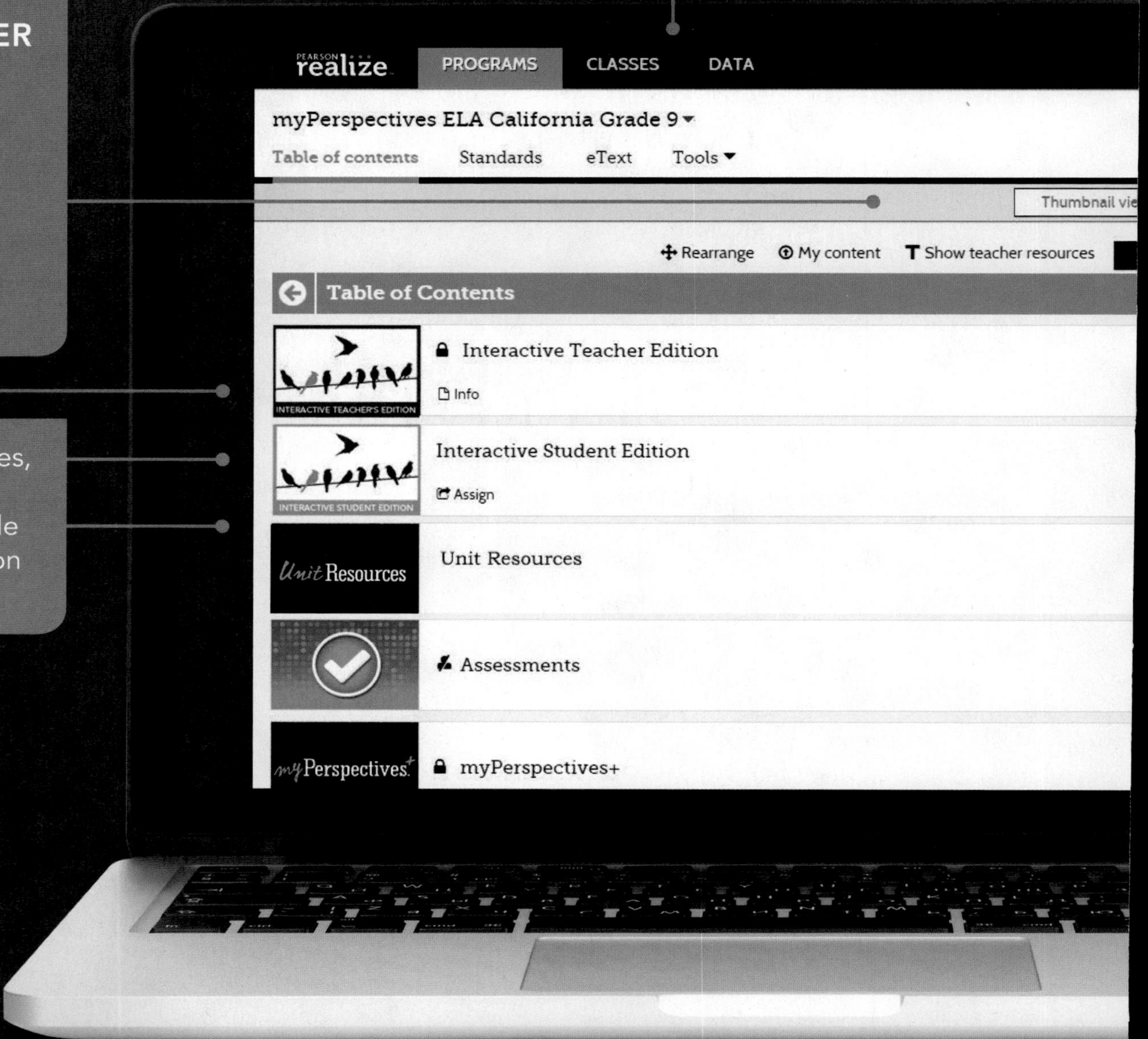

Selection resources are available at point of use!

DIGITAL PERSPECTIVES

Audio | Video | Document | Annotation Highlights | EL Highlights | Online Assessment

Digital Perspectives in the Teacher's Edition identifies digital resources available for each lesson.

UNIT 1: American Voices

Integrating Trade Books with *my*Perspectives

These titles provide students with another perspective on the topic of what it means to be an American, touching upon many of the ideas found within the unit selections.

Depending on your objectives for the unit, as well as your students' needs, you may choose to integrate the trade book into the unit in several ways, including:

- **Supplement the unit** Form literature circles and have the students read one of the trade books throughout the course of the unit as a supplement to the selections and activities.
- **Substitute for unit selections** If you replace unit selections with a trade book, review the standards taught with those selections. Teacher Resources that provide practice with all standards are available.
- **Extend Independent Learning** Extend the unit by replacing independent reading selections with one of these trade books.
- **Pacing** However you choose to integrate trade books, the Pacing Guide below offers suggestions for aligning the trade books with this unit.

Trade Book Lesson Plans

Trade book lesson plans for *The Joy Luck Club, My Antonia,* and *Stargirl* are available online in *my*Perspectives+.

Pacing Guide: Unit Supplement

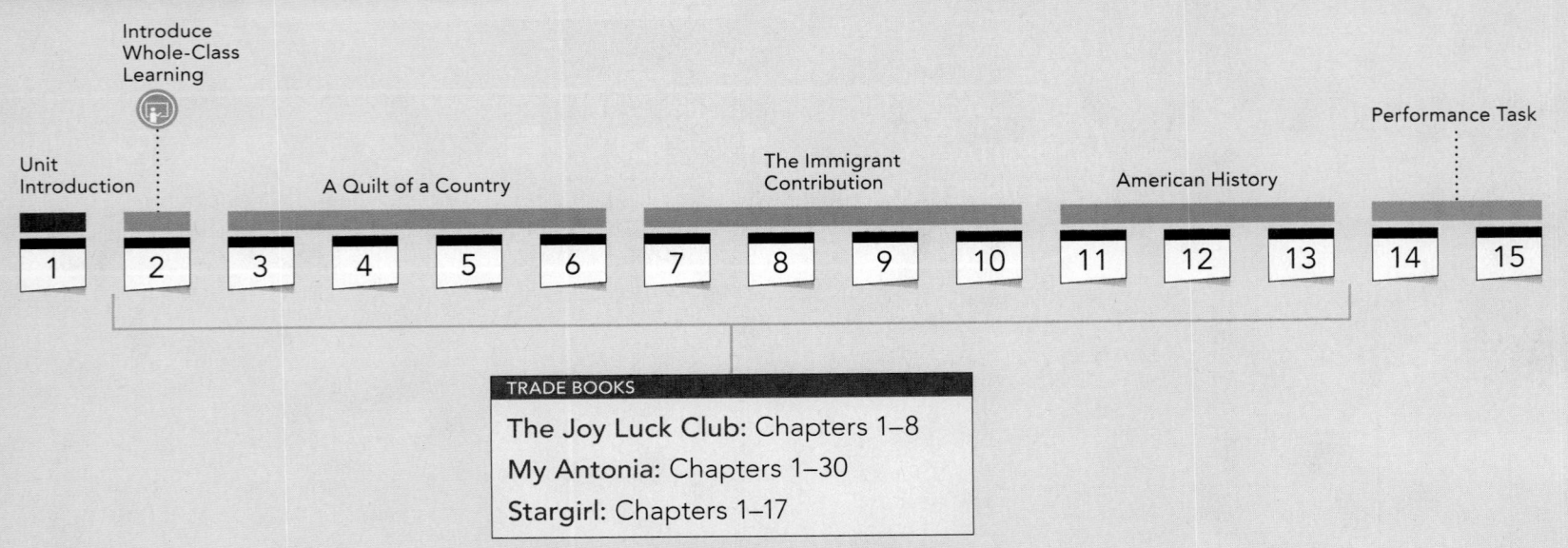

Unit Introduction: 1
Introduce Whole-Class Learning: 2
A Quilt of a Country: 3, 4, 5, 6
The Immigrant Contribution: 7, 8, 9, 10
American History: 11, 12, 13
Performance Task: 14, 15

TRADE BOOKS (2–13)

The Joy Luck Club: Chapters 1–8
My Antonia: Chapters 1–30
Stargirl: Chapters 1–17

Suggested Trade Books

The Joy Luck Club

Amy Tang

Lexile: 930

Four families of Chinese immigrants in San Fransisco learn to live in America and come to terms with their pasts.

Connection to Essential Question

A classic presentation of how immigrants become "American," this novel shows the challenges and triumphs of four women and their daughters as they navigate life in San Francisco. Their experiences reveal multiple answers to the Essential Question: *What does it mean to be "American"?*

My Antonia

Willa Cather

Lexile: 990

Jim Burden is an orphan and Antonia Shimerda is an immigrant. They meet as pioneers in rural Nebraska, making a bond that helps both of them manage their new lives.

Connection to Essential Question

The pioneer experience is a classic feature of American literature. Jim and Antonia face the demands of the landscape and the problems it brings. Both these young characters join their families in a new environment and their lives help provide a 19th century response to the Essential Question: *What does it mean to be "American"?*

Stargirl

Jerry Spinelli

Lexile: 590

A quirky new student expresses happiness and optimism and challenges the attitudes at her high school, pushing others to question themselves in the process.

Connection to Essential Question

This contemporary novel describes the consequences of Stargirl's unique ways of expressing her personality. Her nonconformist ways upset some of the other students, and even Stargirl begins to question her own behaviors. Stargirl's core message of creativity and independence is very much at the center of the Essential Question *What does it mean to be "American"?*

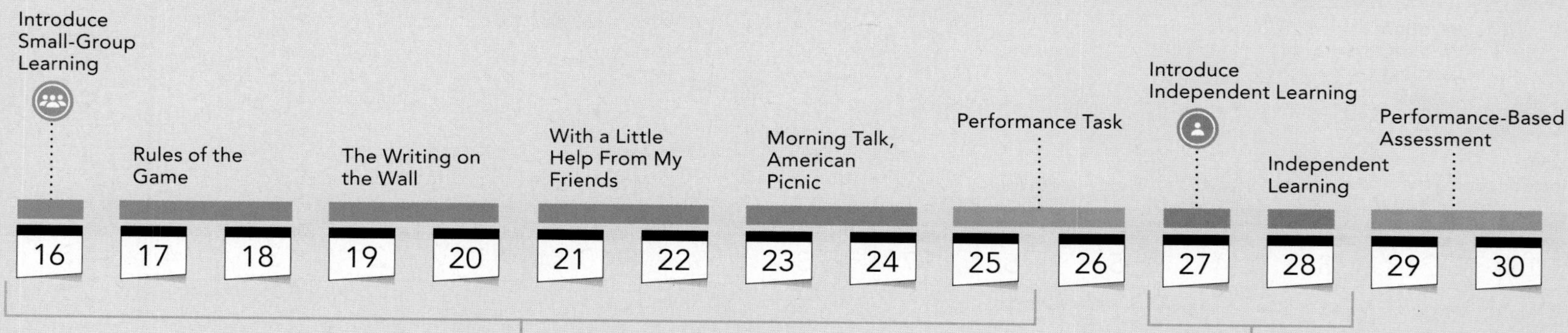

TRADE BOOKS

The Joy Luck Club: Chapters 9–14

My Antonia: Chapters 31–48

Stargirl: Chapters 18–29

TRADE BOOKS

The Joy Luck Club: Chapters 15–16

My Antonia: Chapters 49–55

Stargirl: Chapters 30–33

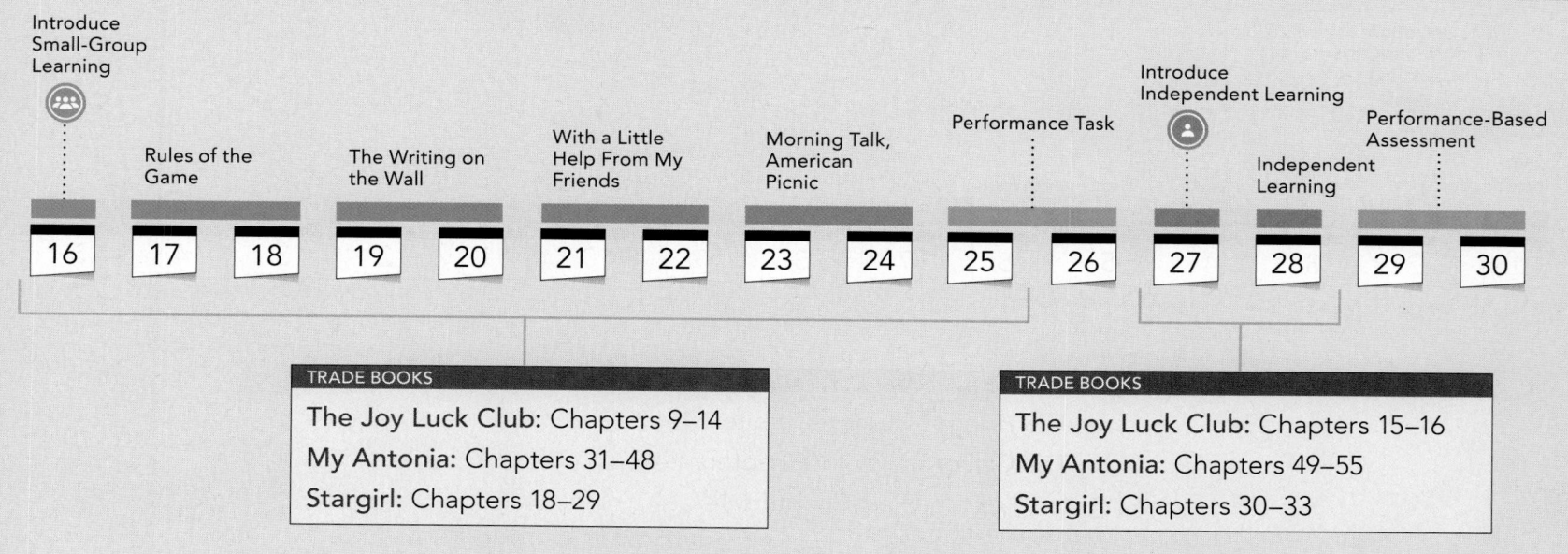

UNIT 2: Survival

Integrating Trade Books with *my*Perspectives

These titles provide students with another perspective on the topic of survival, touching upon many of the ideas found within the unit selections.

Depending on your objectives for the unit, as well as your students' needs, you may choose to integrate the trade book into the unit in several ways, including:

- **Supplement the unit** Form literature circles and have the students read one of the trade books throughout the course of the unit as a supplement to the selections and activities.
- **Substitute for unit selections** If you replace unit selections with a trade book, review the standards taught with those selections. Teacher Resources that provide practice with all standards are available.
- **Extend Independent Learning** Extend the unit by replacing independent reading selections with one of these trade books.
- **Pacing** However you choose to integrate trade books, the Pacing Guide below offers suggestions for aligning the trade books with this unit.

Trade Book Lesson Plans

Trade book lesson plans for *The Hunger Games, The Call of the Wild,* and *Lord of the Flies* are available online in *my*Perspectives+.

Pacing Guide: Unit Supplement

- Unit Introduction: 1
- Introduce Whole-Class Learning: 2
- The Seventh Man: 3, 4, 5, 6, 7, 8
- Moral Logic: 9, 10, 11
- Call for Help: 12, 13
- Performance Task: 14, 15

TRADE BOOKS (days 2–13)

The Hunger Games: Chapters 1–15
The Call of the Wild: Chapters 1–4
Lord of the Flies: Chapters 1–7

Suggested Trade Books

The Hunger Games

Suzanne Collins

Lexile: 810

In a televised battle of life and death, a young woman faces long odds playing a game in which the only rules are kill or be killed.

Connection to Essential Question

The moral dilemma at the heart of *The Hunger Games* challenges students to consider the choices one faces when confronting life-or-death situations, and the decisions that must be taken, no matter how difficult or unwanted they are. Driven by necessity, these choices and their impact provide insight into the Essential Question: *What does it take to survive?*

The Call of the Wild

Jack London

Lexile: 1120

When a pet dog is sold into service pulling a sled during the Yukon gold rush of the 1890s, he sheds his domesticated tendencies and must rely on his instincts in order to survive.

Connection to Essential Question

What if surviving means shedding all vestiges of civilization and returning to the unrestrained but savage call of the wild? *The Call of the Wild* provides an interesting perspective on the Essential Question: *What does it take to survive?*, as Buck ultimately chooses to bet on his own destiny rather than depend on the humans who have failed him time and again.

Lord of the Flies

William Golding

Lexile: 770

After a group of students is marooned on an island, what initially looked like paradise without adult supervision soon turns into a harrowing experience in this brutal portrait of human nature.

Connection to Essential Question

Lord of the Flies offers a unique perspective into the Essential Question: *What does it take to survive?* by connecting students with the timeless theme of society versus the individual, and the savagery possible in human nature when faced with survival situations.

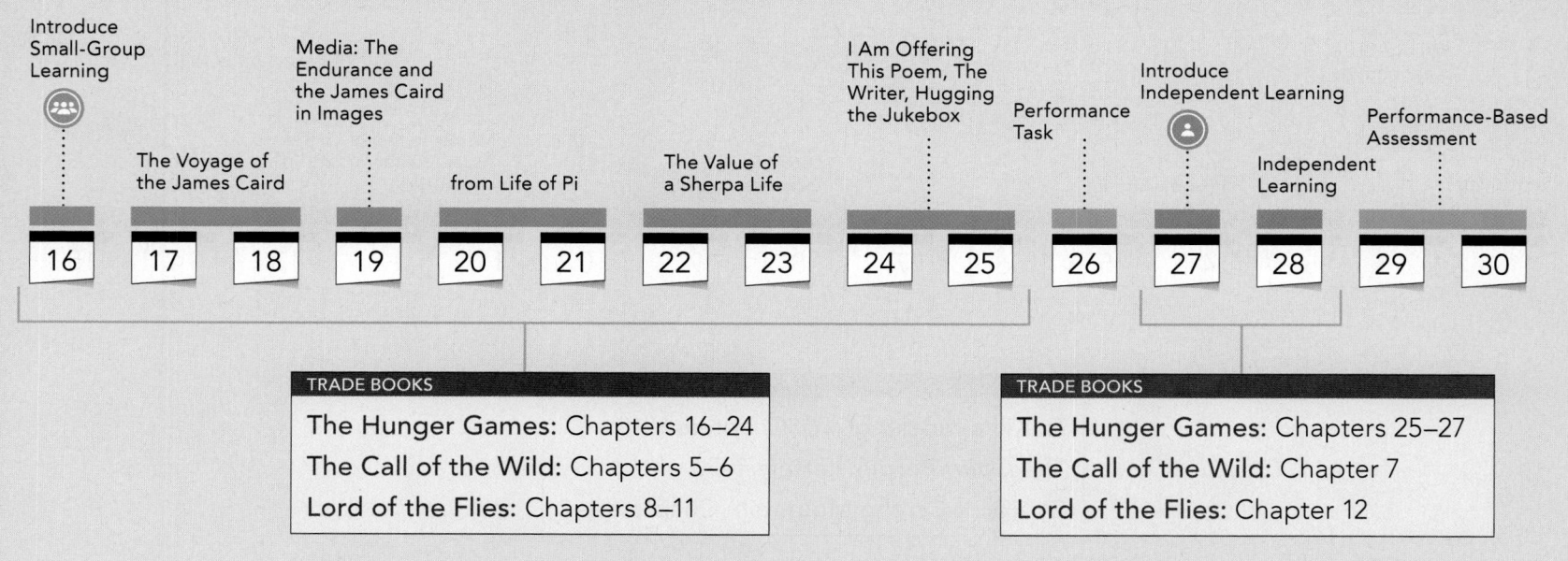

Day	Activity
16	Introduce Small-Group Learning
17–18	The Voyage of the James Caird
19	Media: The Endurance and the James Caird in Images
20–21	from Life of Pi
22–23	The Value of a Sherpa Life
24–25	I Am Offering This Poem, The Writer, Hugging the Jukebox
26	Performance Task
27	Introduce Independent Learning
28	Independent Learning
29–30	Performance-Based Assessment

TRADE BOOKS (Days 16–25)

The Hunger Games: Chapters 16–24

The Call of the Wild: Chapters 5–6

Lord of the Flies: Chapters 8–11

TRADE BOOKS (Days 27–28)

The Hunger Games: Chapters 25–27

The Call of the Wild: Chapter 7

Lord of the Flies: Chapter 12

UNIT 3: The Literature of Civil Rights

Integrating Trade Books with *my*Perspectives

These titles provide students with another perspective on the topic of the literature of civil rights, touching upon many of the ideas found within the unit selections.

Depending on your objectives for the unit, as well as your students' needs, you may choose to integrate the trade book into the unit in several ways, including:

- **Supplement the unit** Form literature circles and have the students read one of the trade books throughout the course of the unit as a supplement to the selections and activities.
- **Substitute for unit selections** If you replace unit selections with a trade book, review the standards taught with those selections. Teacher Resources that provide practice with all standards are available.
- **Extend Independent Learning** Extend the unit by replacing independent reading selections with one of these trade books.
- **Pacing** However you choose to integrate trade books, the Pacing Guide below offers suggestions for aligning the trade books with this unit.

Trade Book Lesson Plans

Trade book lesson plans for *To Kill a Mockingbird, The Color Purple,* and *Go Tell It On the Mountain* are available online in *my*Perspectives+.

Pacing Guide: Unit Supplement

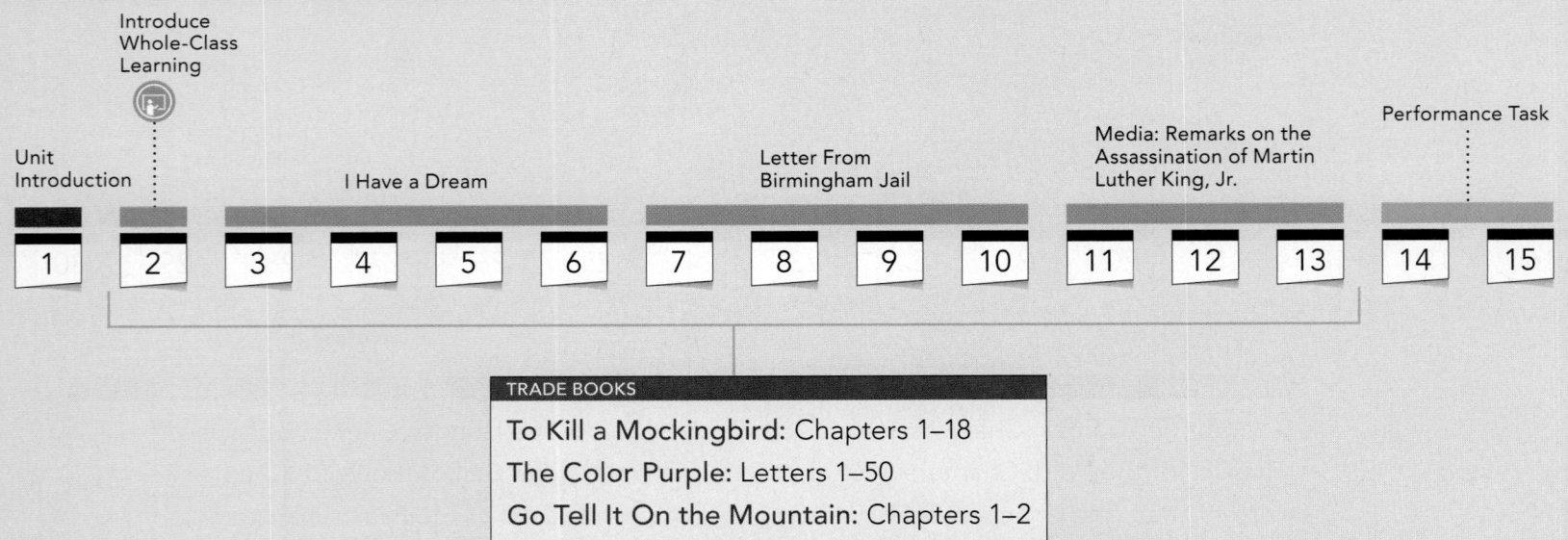

- Day 1: Unit Introduction
- Day 2: Introduce Whole-Class Learning
- Days 3–6: I Have a Dream
- Days 7–10: Letter From Birmingham Jail
- Days 11–13: Media: Remarks on the Assassination of Martin Luther King, Jr.
- Days 14–15: Performance Task

TRADE BOOKS (Days 2–13)

To Kill a Mockingbird: Chapters 1–18
The Color Purple: Letters 1–50
Go Tell It On the Mountain: Chapters 1–2

Suggested Trade Books

To Kill a Mockingbird

Harper Lee

Lexile: 870

A black man in rural Alabama is accused of a crime, and the protagonist's father is the only lawyer willing to defend him in this classic coming-of-age novel.

Connection to Essential Question

The court case at the heart of *To Kill a Mockingbird* centers on the use of truth and rhetoric to inspire change. Yet Harper Lee's perspective is pessimistic; here, even the best use of language fails to overcome engrained prejudice. This leaves open the Essential Question: *How can words inspire change?* and suggests there may be no perfect answer.

The Color Purple

Alice Walker

Lexile: 670

The Color Purple follows the lives of two African-American sisters growing up in the 1930s, showing how they resist sexism and racism.

Connection to Essential Question

Central to *The Color Purple* are the relationships it portrays. The characters are dynamic, and their conversations change each other both for better and for worse—offering insight into the Essential Question: *How can words inspire change?*

Go Tell It On The Mountain

James Baldwin

Lexile: 1030

In this coming-of-age novel, a young boy in Harlem struggles with his father's dislike for him. He develops renewed hope for his future through community and religion.

Connection to Essential Question

The protagonist's father is a preacher, and characters regularly weave allusions to Biblical language into their speech. The power of language is key to the story, as is the Essential Question: *How can words inspire change?*

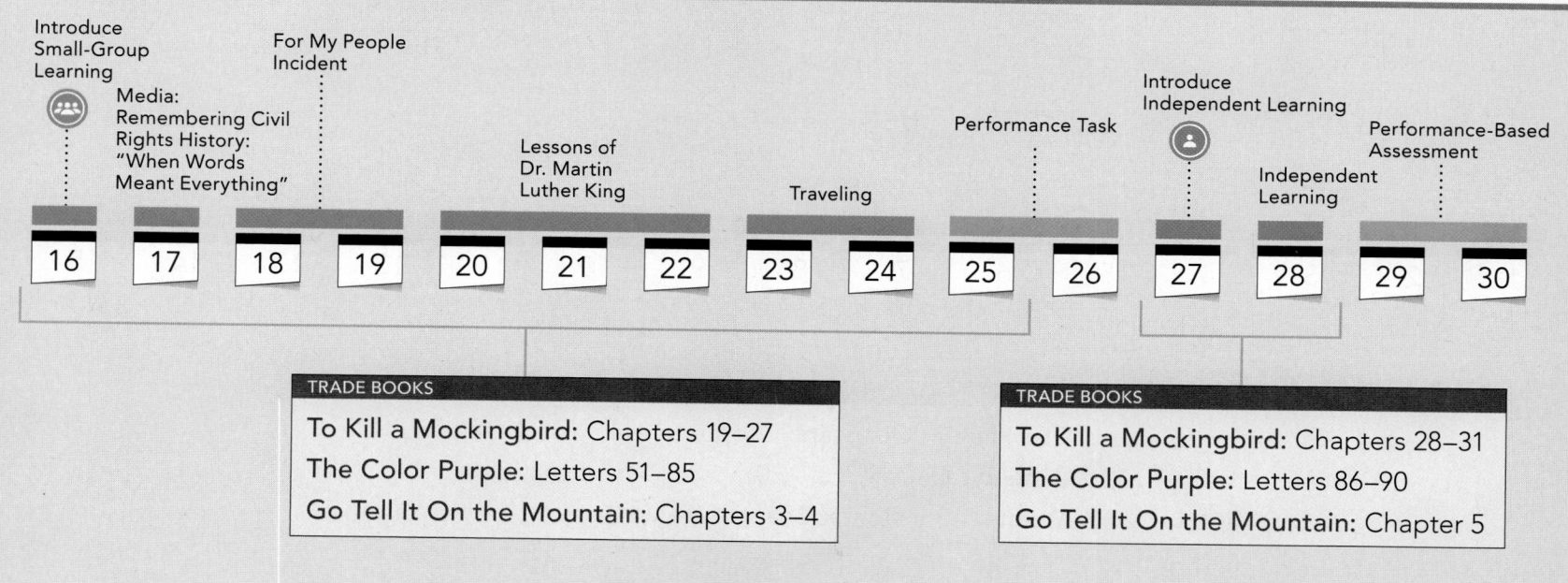

- 16 — Introduce Small-Group Learning
- 17 — Media: Remembering Civil Rights History: "When Words Meant Everything"
- 18 — For My People / Incident
- 19
- 20 — Lessons of Dr. Martin Luther King
- 21
- 22
- 23 — Traveling
- 24
- 25 — Performance Task
- 26
- 27 — Introduce Independent Learning
- 28 — Independent Learning
- 29 — Performance-Based Assessment
- 30

TRADE BOOKS (16–25)

To Kill a Mockingbird: Chapters 19–27

The Color Purple: Letters 51–85

Go Tell It On the Mountain: Chapters 3–4

TRADE BOOKS (27–28)

To Kill a Mockingbird: Chapters 28–31

The Color Purple: Letters 86–90

Go Tell It On the Mountain: Chapter 5

UNIT 4: Star-Crossed Romances

Integrating Trade Books with *my*Perspectives

These titles provide students with another perspective on the topic of star-crossed romances, touching upon many of the ideas found within the unit selections.

Depending on your objectives for the unit, as well as your students' needs, you may choose to integrate the trade book into the unit in several ways, including:

- **Supplement the unit** Form literature circles and have the students read one of the trade books throughout the course of the unit as a supplement to the selections and activities.
- **Substitute for unit selections** If you replace unit selections with a trade book, review the standards taught with those selections. Teacher Resources that provide practice with all standards are available.
- **Extend Independent Learning** Extend the unit by replacing independent reading selections with one of these trade books.
- **Pacing** However you choose to integrate trade books, the Pacing Guide below offers suggestions for aligning the trade books with this unit.

Trade Book Lesson Plans

Trade book lesson plans for *The Fault in Our Stars, Jane Eyre,* and *Wuthering Heights* are available online in *my*Perspectives+.

Pacing Guide: Unit Supplement

- Day 1: Unit Introduction
- Day 2: Introduce Whole-Class Learning
- Day 3: Literature and Culture
- Days 4–12: *The Tragedy of Romeo and Juliet, Acts I-V*
- Day 13: Pyramus and Thisbe
- Days 14–15: Performance Task

Days 2–13:

TRADE BOOKS

The Fault in Our Stars: Chapters 1–14

Jane Eyre: Chapters 1–20

Wuthering Heights: Chapters 1–17

Suggested Trade Books

The Fault in Our Stars

John Green

Lexile: 850

A romance between two high school-aged cancer patients is at the center of this touching bestseller.

Connection to Essential Question

The protagonists' health is outside their control, yet they find great meaning and adventure despite the constraints they face. While they cannot change their chances of survival, the book reveals an optimistic approach to the Essential Question: *Do we determine our own destinies?*

Jane Eyre

Charlotte Brontë

Lexile: 890

The witty, individualistic protagonist of this proto-feminist novel grows up in painful circumstances. Still, she finds her way to happiness and family.

Connection to Essential Question

19th-century women had little freedom, and Jane's life is frequently steered by events outside her control. Her choices, most famously her answers to two marriage proposals, are pivotal —providing insight into the Essential Question: *Do we determine our own destinies?*

Wuthering Heights

Emily Brontë

Lexile: 880

A blistering critique of Victorian society and ideals, *Wuthering Heights* tells the complicated story of a relationship and its legacy for generations that followed.

Connection to Essential Question

Birth and social standards terribly warp the characters' lives and keep them from happiness, providing a compelling answer to the Essential Question: *Do we determine our own destinies?*

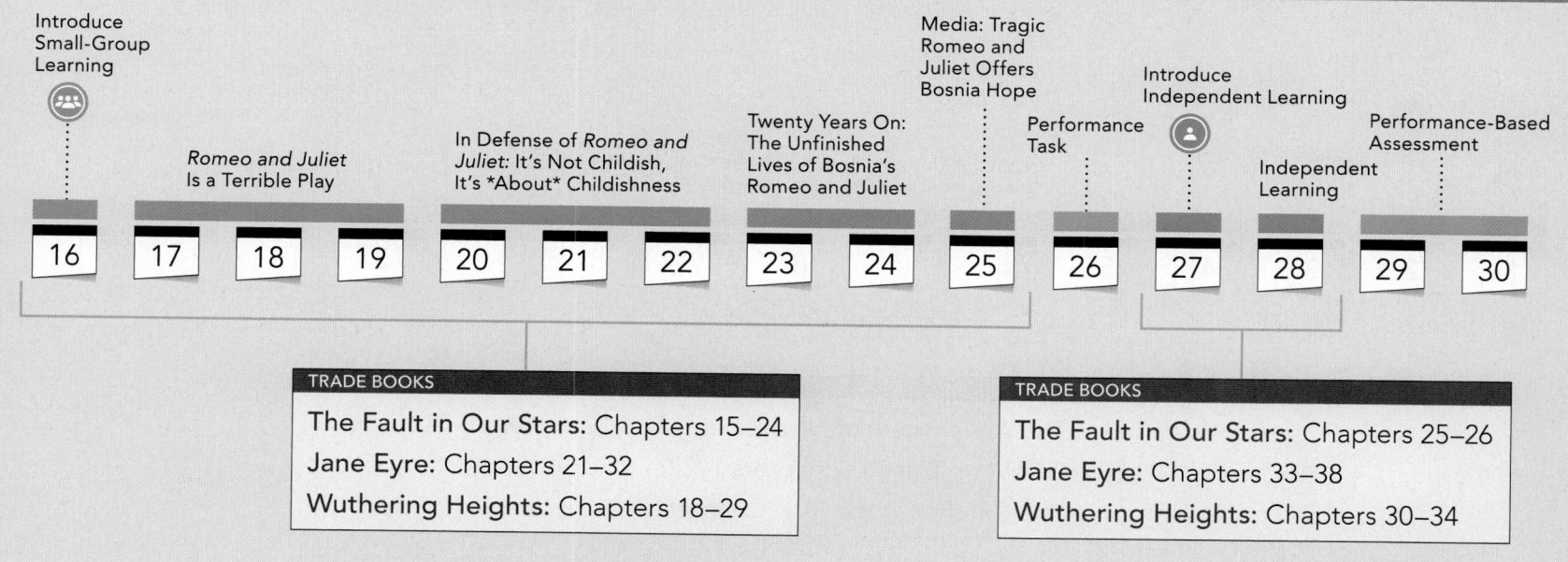

16 — Introduce Small-Group Learning

17–19 — *Romeo and Juliet* Is a Terrible Play

20–22 — In Defense of *Romeo and Juliet:* It's Not Childish, It's *About* Childishness

23–24 — Twenty Years On: The Unfinished Lives of Bosnia's Romeo and Juliet

25 — Media: Tragic Romeo and Juliet Offers Bosnia Hope

26 — Performance Task

27 — Introduce Independent Learning

28 — Independent Learning

29–30 — Performance-Based Assessment

TRADE BOOKS (Days 16–25)

The Fault in Our Stars: Chapters 15–24

Jane Eyre: Chapters 21–32

Wuthering Heights: Chapters 18–29

TRADE BOOKS (Days 27–28)

The Fault in Our Stars: Chapters 25–26

Jane Eyre: Chapters 33–38

Wuthering Heights: Chapters 30–34

UNIT 5: Journeys of Transformation

Integrating Trade Books with *my*Perspectives

These titles provide students with another perspective on the topic of journeys of transformation, touching upon many of the ideas found within the unit selections.

Depending on your objectives for the unit, as well as your students' needs, you may choose to integrate the trade book into the unit in several ways, including:

- **Supplement the unit** Form literature circles and have the students read one of the trade books throughout the course of the unit as a supplement to the selections and activities.
- **Substitute for unit selections** If you replace unit selections with a trade book, review the standards taught with those selections. Teacher Resources that provide practice with all standards are available.
- **Extend Independent Learning** Extend the unit by replacing independent reading selections with one of these trade books.
- **Pacing** However you choose to integrate trade books, the Pacing Guide below offers suggestions for aligning the trade books with this unit.

Trade Book Lesson Plans

Trade book lesson plans for *The Adventures of Huckleberry Finn, Gulliver's Travels,* and *The Catcher in the Rye* available online in *my*Perspectives+.

Pacing Guide: Unit Supplement

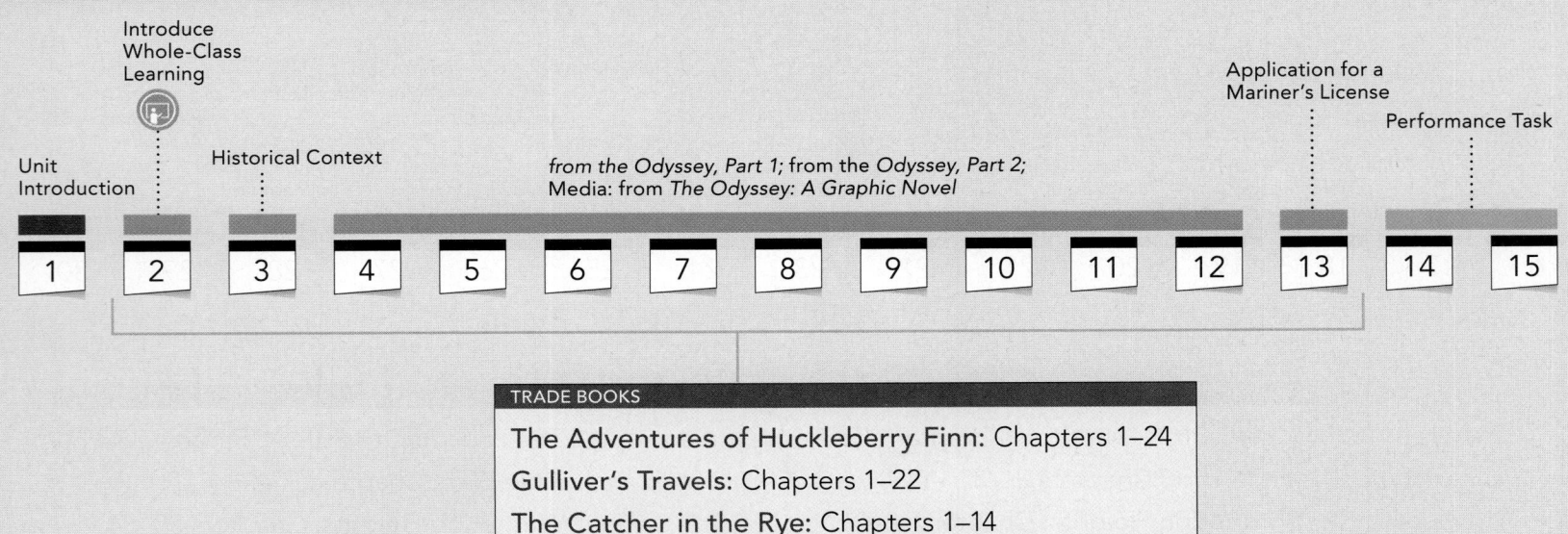

- 1: Unit Introduction
- 2: Introduce Whole-Class Learning
- 3: Historical Context
- 4–12: *from the Odyssey, Part 1; from the Odyssey, Part 2;* Media: *from The Odyssey: A Graphic Novel*
- 13: Application for a Mariner's License
- 14–15: Performance Task

TRADE BOOKS (Days 2–13)

The Adventures of Huckleberry Finn: Chapters 1–24

Gulliver's Travels: Chapters 1–22

The Catcher in the Rye: Chapters 1–14

Suggested Trade Books

The Adventures of Huckleberry Finn

Mark Twain

Lexile: 990

A young boy runs away from home and details his adventures along the Mississippi with Jim, an escaped slave.

Connection to Essential Question

Huck and Jim's journey is crucially important; while Huck ends the story in the same place he set out, he has learned greatly from his journey. As a result, he doesn't intend to stay back at home for long. All in all, this classic takes a strong stance on the Essential Question: *Which matters more, the journey or the destination?*

Gulliver's Travels

Jonathan Swift

Lexile: 1330

This satire follows a traveler across four lands of exaggerated societies. Swift uses these adventures to critique institutions of his time and to make incisive points about human nature.

Connection to Essential Question

Gulliver meets people who seem very different from him, yet they force him to re-consider life as he knows it. Readers who take the adventures with him will have a new approach to the Essential Question: *Which matters more, the journey or the destination?*

The Catcher in the Rye

Lexile: 790

The definitive story of adolescent angst and alienation follows a few days in the life of Holden Caulfield, a teenager in New York City.

Connection to Essential Question

Among the most interesting questions about *The Catcher in the Rye* is whether Holden is actually any different at the end than he was at the beginning. He has certainly been through a journey, but has he gone back on the revelations he's had? In many ways, it asks the Essential Question: *Which matters more, the journey or the destination?*

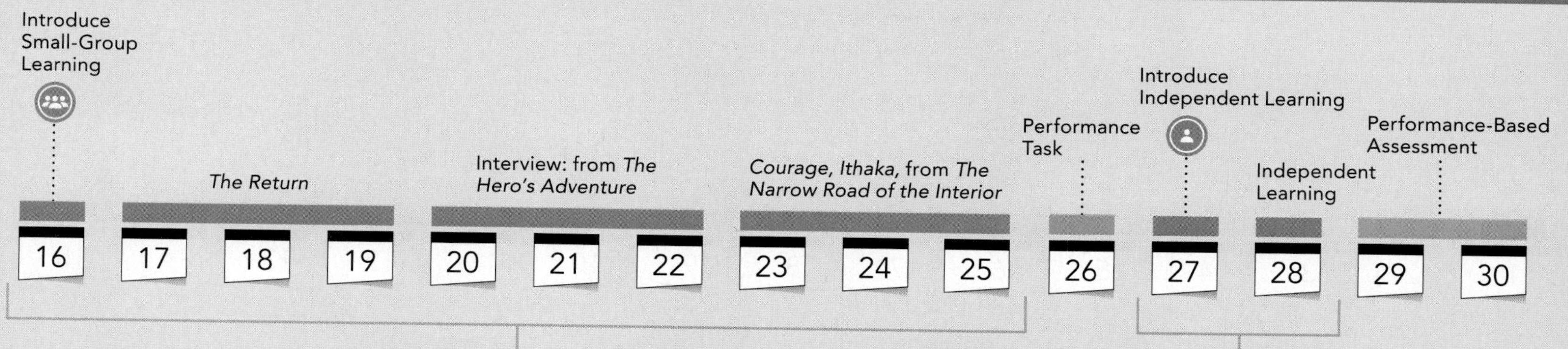

TRADE BOOKS

The Adventures of Huckleberry Finn: Chapters 25–38

Gulliver's Travels: Chapters 23–35

The Catcher in the Rye: Chapters 15–24

TRADE BOOKS

The Adventures of Huckleberry Finn: Chapters 39–43

Gulliver's Travels: Chapters 36–39

The Catcher in the Rye: Chapters 25–26

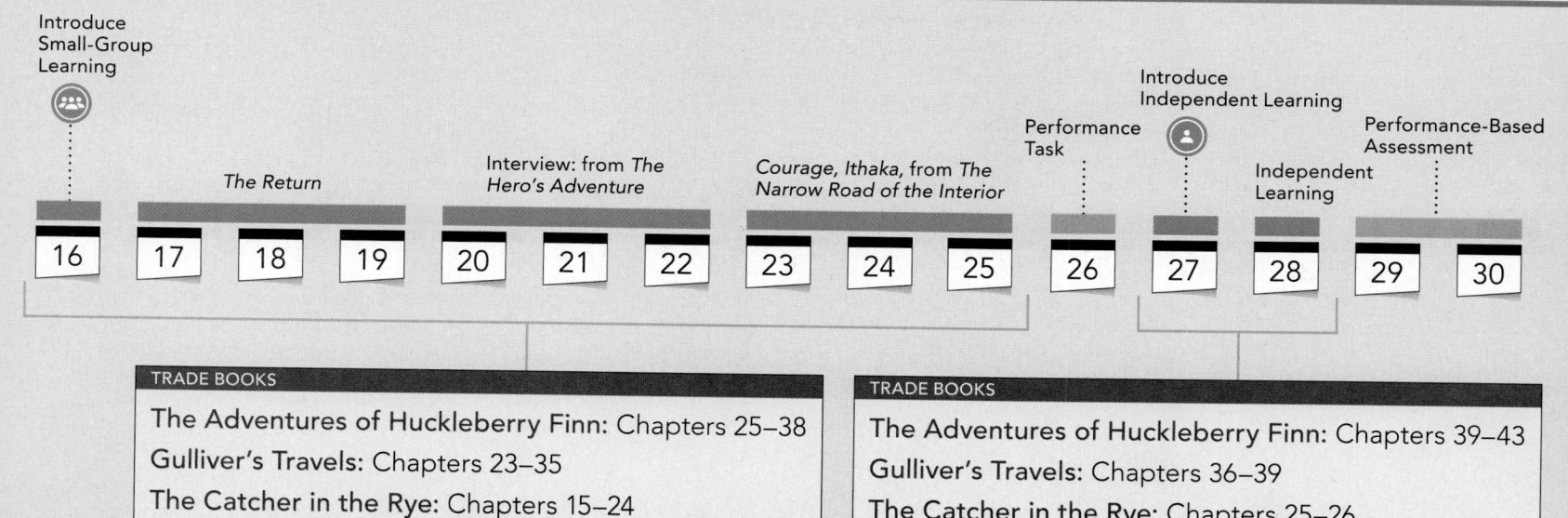

UNIT 6: World's End

Integrating Trade Books with *my*Perspectives

These titles provide students with another perspective on the topic of the end of the world, touching upon many of the ideas found within the unit selections.

Depending on your objectives for the unit, as well as your students' needs, you may choose to integrate the trade book into the unit in several ways, including:

- **Supplement the unit** Form literature circles and have the students read one of the trade books throughout the course of the unit as a supplement to the selections and activities.
- **Substitute for unit selections** If you replace unit selections with a trade book, review the standards taught with those selections. Teacher Resources that provide practice with all standards are available.
- **Extend Independent Learning** Extend the unit by replacing independent reading selections with one of these trade books.
- **Pacing** However you choose to integrate trade books, the Pacing Guide below offers suggestions for aligning the trade books with this unit.

Trade Book Lesson Plans

Trade book lesson plans for *The Road, Fahrenheit 451,* and *Paradise Lost* & *Paradise Regained* are available online in *my*Perspectives+.

Pacing Guide: Unit Supplement

Unit Introduction: 1

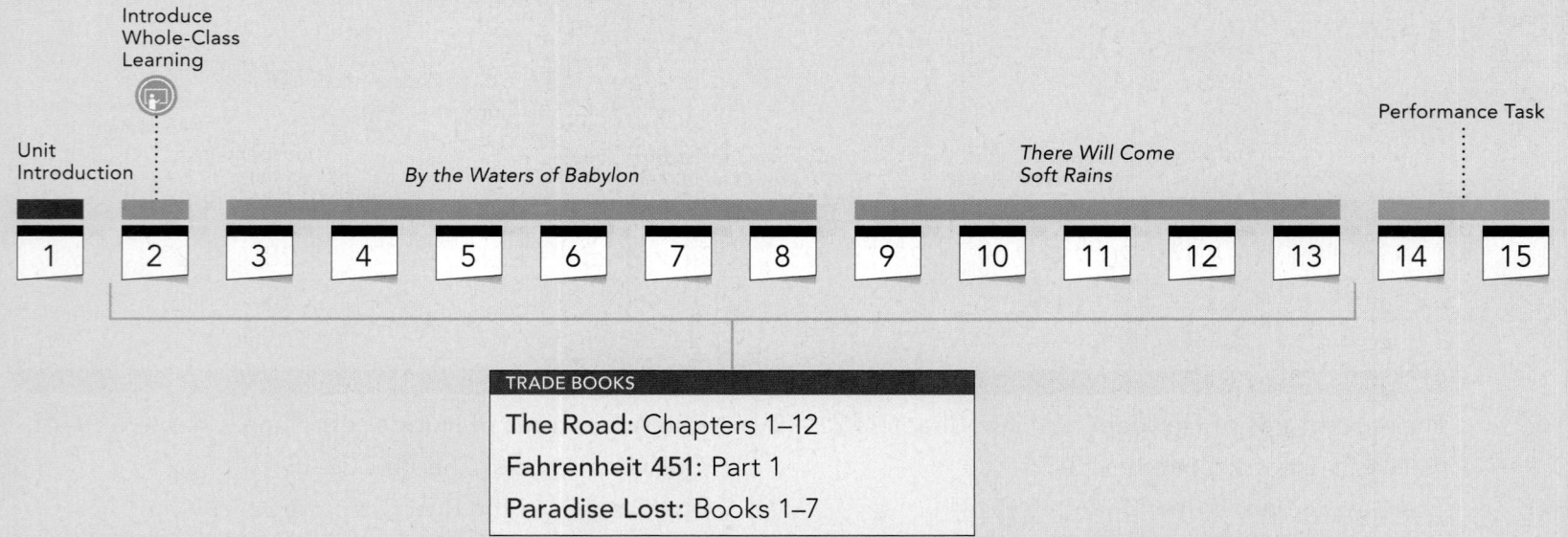

Introduce Whole-Class Learning: 2

By the Waters of Babylon: 3 4 5 6 7 8

There Will Come Soft Rains: 9 10 11 12 13

Performance Task: 14 15

TRADE BOOKS (2–13)

The Road: Chapters 1–12

Fahrenheit 451: Part 1

Paradise Lost: Books 1–7

Suggested Trade Books

The Road

Cormac McCarthy

Lexile: 670

Journeying across a relentlessly bleak landscape, a man and his son struggle for life in the wake of apocalypse.

Connection to Essential Question

The Road centers on questions of morality. In the face of horror and despair beyond anything that exists today, what do good people do? What right do we have to help ourselves at others' expense? In order to consider these central questions, one must ask the Essential Question: *What do stories about the future say about the present?*

Fahrenheit 451

Ray Bradbury

Lexile: 890

In an America where books are outlawed and burned, one of the "firemen" who burn them breaks the rules and begins to read.

Connection to Essential Question

Fahrenheit 451 is most famous as an allegory for censorship, but Bradbury himself said his message was a critique of television and an endorsement of literature. How do changes in the media we consume affect society? Given those changes, how can we answer the Essential Question: *What do stories about the future say about the present?*

Paradise Lost & Paradise Regained

John Milton

Lexile: 1460

This highly influential epic poem focuses on religious themes, telling the story of a war in heaven and how humans first learn of good and evil.

Connection to Essential Question

Paradise Lost mainly concerns the past, but its characters are often swayed by prophecies of the future. It also serves as an allegory for the English Civil War, and reflects Milton's dread of another. In *Paradise Regained*, Milton describes the future return to a state of grace, speaking to his understanding of the world as the result of sin and rebellion. Both classic texts reveal interesting perspectives on the Essential Question: *What do stories about the future say about the present?*

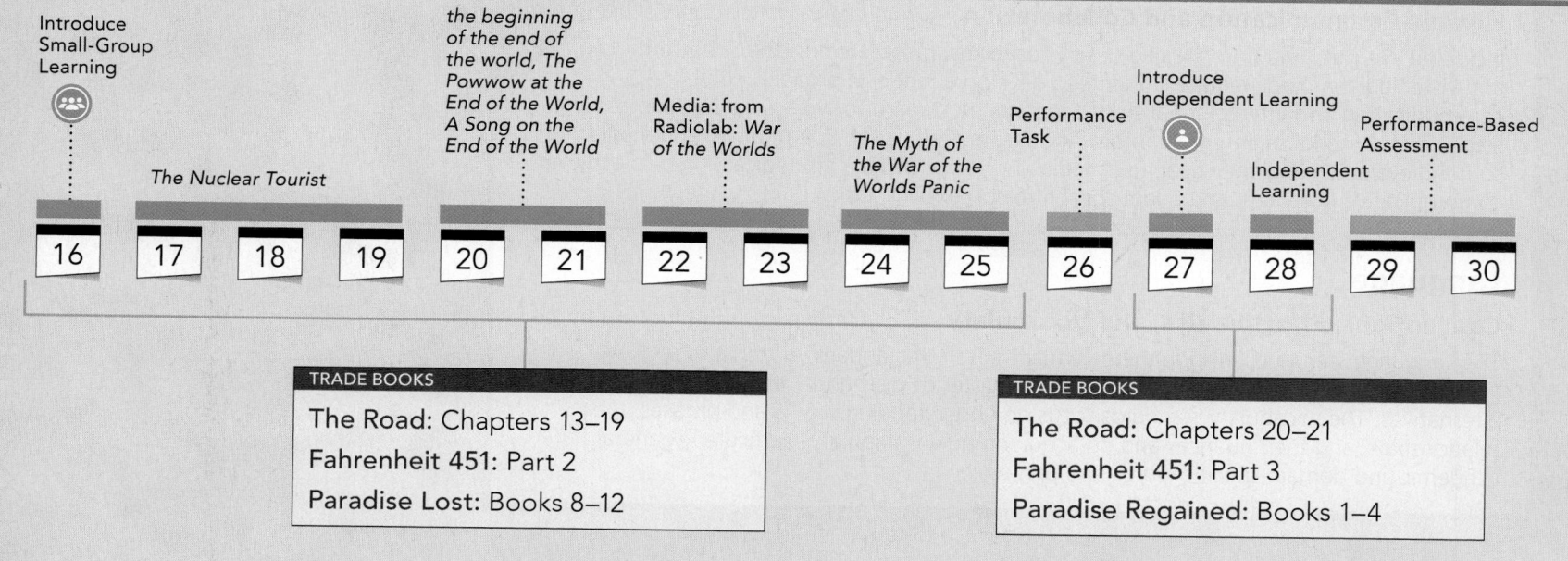

- 16 — Introduce Small-Group Learning
- 17–19 — *The Nuclear Tourist*
- 20–21 — *the beginning of the end of the world, The Powwow at the End of the World, A Song on the End of the World*
- 22–23 — Media: from Radiolab: *War of the Worlds*
- 24–25 — *The Myth of the War of the Worlds Panic*
- 26 — Performance Task
- 27 — Introduce Independent Learning
- 28 — Independent Learning
- 29–30 — Performance-Based Assessment

TRADE BOOKS (16–25)

The Road: Chapters 13–19

Fahrenheit 451: Part 2

Paradise Lost: Books 8–12

TRADE BOOKS (27–28)

The Road: Chapters 20–21

Fahrenheit 451: Part 3

Paradise Regained: Books 1–4

Standards Correlation

Key Features of the Standards

The following summary of key features is from the Introduction to the Common Core State Standards for English Language Arts © 2010, National Governors Association for Best Practices and Council of Chief State School Officers. All rights reserved.

Reading

Text Complexity and the Growth of Comprehension

The Reading standards place equal emphasis on the sophistication of what students read and the skill with which they read. Standard 10 defines a grade-by-grade "staircase" of increasing text complexity that rises from beginning reading to the college and career readiness level. Whatever they are reading, students must also show a steadily growing ability to discern more from and make fuller use of text. This process should include making an increasing number of connections among ideas and between texts, considering a wider range of textual evidence, and becoming more sensitive to inconsistencies, ambiguities, and poor reasoning in texts.

Writing

Text Types, Responding to Reading, and Research

The Standards acknowledge the fact that whereas some writing skills, such as the ability to plan, revise, edit, and publish, are applicable to many types of writing, other skills are more properly defined in terms of specific writing types: arguments, informative/explanatory texts, and narratives. Standard 9 stresses the importance of the writing-reading connection by requiring students to draw upon and write about evidence from literary and informational texts. Because of the centrality of writing to most forms of inquiry, research standards are prominently included in this strand, though skills important to research are infused throughout the document.

Speaking and Listening

Flexible Communication and Collaboration

Including but not limited to skills necessary for formal presentations, the Speaking and Listening standards require students to develop a range of broadly useful oral communication and interpersonal skills. Students must learn to work together, express and listen carefully to ideas, integrate information from oral, visual, quantitative, and media sources, evaluate what they hear, use media and visual displays strategically to help achieve communicative purposes, and adapt speech to context and task.

Language

Conventions, Effective Use, and Vocabulary

The Language standards include the essential "rules" of standard written and spoken English, but they also approach language as a matter of craft and informed choice among alternatives. The vocabulary standards focus on understanding words and phrases, their relationships, and their nuances and on acquiring new vocabulary, particularly general academic and domain-specific words and phrases.

Correlation to *myPerspectives*™ *English Language Arts*

The following correlation shows points at which focused standards instruction is provided in the Student Edition. The Teacher's Edition provides further opportunity to address standards through Personalize for Learning notes and additional resources available only in the Interactive Teacher's Edition.

Grade 9 Standards for Literature	
Standard	**Print and Interactive Editions**
Key Ideas and Details	
RL.9.1 Cite strong and thorough textual evidence to support analysis of what the text says explicitly as well as inferences drawn from the text.	**SE/TE:** *The Immigrant Contribution:* 30, *The Moral Logic of Survivor Guilt:* 158, *The Endurance and the James Caird in Images:* 199, *"I Have a Dream":* 266, *Letter from Birmingham Jail:* 288, *Whole Class Performance Task*: Unit 4: 496, *Application for a Mariner's License:* 638, *By the Waters of Babylon:* 704, *The Nuclear Tourist:* 754, Students will address this standard in *Analyze the Text* features which appear with every literature selection.
RL.9.2 Determine a theme or central idea of a text and analyze in detail its development over the course of the text, including how it emerges and is shaped and refined by specific details; provide an objective summary of the text.	**SE/TE:** *I Am Offering This Poem; The Writer; Hugging the Jukebox*: 234, *the beginning of the end of the world; The Powwow at the End of the World; A Song on the End of the World*: 766
RL.9.3 Analyze how complex characters develop over the course of a text, interact with other characters, and advance the plot or develop the theme.	**SE/TE:** *American History:* 46, *Rules of the Game*: 74, *Life of Pi*: 212, *Romeo and Juliet:* 398, 480, *The Odyssey, Part 1*: 592, *By the Waters of Babylon*: 718
Craft and Structure	
RL.9.4 Determine the meaning of words and phrases as they are used in the text, including figurative and connotative meanings; analyze the cumulative impact of specific word choices on meaning and tone.	**SE/TE:** *I Am Offering This Poem; The Writer; Hugging the Jukebox*: 236, *Courage; Ithaka; The Narrow Road of the Interior:* 680, *There Will Come Soft Rains*: 730
RL.9.5 Analyze how an author's choices concerning how to structure a text, order events within it (e.g., parallel plots), and manipulate time (e.g., pacing, flashbacks) create such effects as mystery, tension, or surprise.	**SE/TE:** *Morning Talk; Immigrant Picnic:* 106, *The Seventh Man*: 146, *For My People; Incident*: 318, *Romeo and Juliet:* 398, 448, 464, 480, *The Odyssey, Part 1:* 592, *The Return*: 656, *By the Waters of Babylon*: 716, *There Will Come Soft Rains*: 730, *the beginning of the end of the world; The Powwow at the End of the World; A Song on the End of the World*: 768
RL.9.6 Analyze a particular point of view or cultural experience reflected in a work of literature from outside the United States, drawing on a wide reading of world literature.	**SE/TE:** *The Life of Pi:* 212, *The Odyssey, Part 1*: 592, *The Odyssey, Part 2*: 618, *The Return*: 656

Standards Correlation

Grade 9 Standards for Literature (continued)	
Standard	**Print and Interactive Editions**
Integration of Knowledge and Ideas	
RL.9.7 Analyze the representation of a subject or a key scene in two different artistic mediums, including what is emphasized or absent in each treatment.	**SE/TE:** *Romeo and Juliet*: 485, *The Odyssey; The Odyssey: A Graphic Novel*: 632
RL.9.8 (Not applicable to literature)	
RL.9.9 Analyze how an author draws on and transforms source material in a specific work (e.g., how Shakespeare treats a theme or topic from Ovid or the Bible or how a later author draws on a play by Shakespeare).	**SE/TE:** *Pyramus and Thisbe*: 492, *The Odyssey; The Odyssey: A Graphic Novel*: 632
Range of Reading and Text Complexity	
RL.9.10 By the end of grade 9, read and comprehend literature, including stories, dramas, and poems, in the grades 9–10 text complexity band proficiently, with scaffolding as needed at the high end of the range.	**SE/TE:** *American History*: 36, *Morning Talk; Immigrant Picnic*: 98, *First Read Guide*: 114, 242, 348, 534, 686, 786, *Close Read Guide*: 115, 243, 349, 535, 687, 787, *The Seventh Man*: 132, *Life of Pi*: 202, *I Am Offering This Poem; The Writer; Hugging the Jukebox*: 224, *For My People; Incident*: 312, *Romeo and Juliet*: 374, 400, 424, 450, 466, *Pyramus and Thisbe*: 486, *The Odyssey, Part 1*: 558, *The Odyssey, Part 2*: 594, *The Odyssey: A Graphic Novel*: 624, *The Return*: 650, *Courage; Ithaka; The Narrow Road of the Interior*: 668, *By the Waters of Babylon*: 704, *There Will Come Soft Rains*: 722, *the beginning of the end of the world; The Powwow at the End of the World; A Song on the End of the World*: 758

Grade 9 Standards for Informational Text	
Standard	**Print and Interactive Editions**
Key Ideas and Details	
RI.9.1 Cite strong and thorough textual evidence to support analysis of what the text says explicitly as well as inferences drawn from the text.	**SE/TE:** *The Immigrant Contribution:* 30, *The Moral Logic of Survivor Guilt:* 158, *The Endurance and the James Caird in Images*: 199, *I Have a Dream*: 266, *Letter From Birmingham Jail:* 288, *Application for a Mariner's License:* 638, *Radiolab: War of the Worlds:* 773, Students will address this standard in *Analyze the Text* features which appear with every informational text selection.
RI.9.2 Determine a central idea of a text and analyze its development over the course of the text, including how it emerges and is shaped and refined by specific details; provide an objective summary of the text.	**SE/TE:** *The Writing on the Wall*: 84, *The Moral Logic of Survivor Guilt*: 158, *Radiolab: War of the Worlds:* 773
RI.9.3 Analyze how the author unfolds an analysis or series of ideas or events, including the order in which the points are made, how they are introduced and developed, and the connections that are drawn between them.	**SE/TE:** *With a Little Help From My Friends*: 94, *The Voyage of the James Caird*: 192, *Letter From Birmingham Jail*: 288, *Lessons of MLK, Jr.*: 330, *Traveling*: 340, *Romeo and Juliet Is a Terrible Play; In Defense of Romeo and Juliet*: 514, *The Hero's Adventure*: 664, *Radiolab: War of the Worlds:* 773
Craft and Structure	
RI.9.4 Determine the meaning of words and phrases as they are used in a text, including figurative, connotative, and technical meanings; analyze the cumulative impact of specific word choices on meaning and tone.	**SE/TE:** *A Quilt of a Country:* 20, *A Quilt of a Country; The Immigrant Contribution:* 34, *The Writing on the Wall*: 86, *The Voyage of the James Caird*: 192
RI.9.5 Analyze in detail how an author's ideas or claims are developed and refined by particular sentences, paragraphs, or larger portions of a text.	**SE/TE:** *A Quilt of a Country*: 18, *The Immigrant Contribution*: 30, *The Value of a Sherpa Life*: 220, *Traveling*: 340, *Twenty Years On:* 522, *Application for a Mariner's License:* 638
RI.9.6 Determine an author's point of view or purpose in a text and analyze how an author uses rhetoric to advance that point of view or purpose.	**SE/TE:** *A Quilt of a Country*: 18, *The Immigrant Contribution*: 30, *The Value of a Sherpa Life*: 222, *I Have a Dream*: 266
Integration of Knowledge and Ideas	
RI.9.7 Analyze various accounts of a subject told in different mediums, determining which details are emphasized in each account.	**SE/TE:** *The Endurance and the James Caird in Images*: 194, *The Voyage of the James Caird; The Endurance and the James Caird in Images:* 201, *Tragic Romeo and Juliet Offers Bosnia Hope*: 524, 528, *Radiolab: War of the Worlds; The Myth of the War of the Worlds Panic:* 780
RI.9.8 Delineate and evaluate the argument and specific claims in a text, assessing whether the reasoning is valid and the evidence is relevant and sufficient; identify false statements and fallacious reasoning.	**SE/TE:** *The Moral Logic of Survivor Guilt*: 158, *"I Have a Dream"; Letter From Birmingham Jail:* 292–293, *Romeo and Juliet Is a Terrible Play; In Defense of Romeo and Juliet*: 512, 515
RI.9.9 Analyze seminal U.S. documents of historical and literary significance, including how they address related themes and concepts.	**SE/TE:** *I Have a Dream*: 266, *Letter From Birmingham Jail*: 288
Range of Reading and Level of Text Complexity	
RI.9.10 By the end of grade 9, read and comprehend literary nonfiction in the grades 9–10 text complexity band proficiently, with scaffolding as needed at the high end of the range.	**SE/TE:** *A Quilt of a Country*: 12, *The Writing on the Wall*: 78, *With a Little Help From My Friends*: 88, *First Read Guide*: 114, 242, 348, 534, 686, 786, *Close Read Guide*: 115, 243, 349, 535, 687, 787, *The Moral Logic of Survivor Guilt*: 152, *The Voyage of the James Caird*: 178, *The Value of a Sherpa Life*: 216, *I Have a Dream*: 260, *Letter From Birmingham Jail*: 270, *Remarks on the Assassination of Martin Luther King, Jr.*: 294, *Remembering Civil Rights History, When "Words Meant Everything"*: 308, *Lessons of MLK, Jr.*: 322, *Traveling:* 334, *Romeo and Juliet Is a Terrible Play; In Defense of Romeo and Juliet*: 504, *Twenty Years On*: 516, *The Hero's Adventure*: 660, *The Nuclear Tourist*: 746, *The Myth of the War of the Worlds Panic:* 774

Standards Correlation

Grade 9 Writing Standards	
Standard	**Print and Interactive Editions**
Text Types and Purpose	
W.9.1 Write arguments to support claims in an analysis of substantive topics or texts, using valid reasoning and relevant and sufficient evidence.	**SE/TE:** *Whole Class Performance Task*: Unit 2: 168, Unit 4: 494, *Life of Pi:* 214, *Performance-Based Assessment:* Unit 2: 246, *Romeo and Juliet*: 465, 484, *Tragic Romeo and Juliet Offers Bosnia Hope*: 528, *Radiolab: War of the Worlds; The Myth of the War of the Worlds Panic:* 781
W.9.1.a Introduce precise claim(s), distinguish the claim(s) from alternate or opposing claims, and create an organization that establishes clear relationships among claim(s), counterclaims, reasons, and evidence.	**SE/TE:** *The Seventh Man*: 150, *Whole Class Performance Task*: Unit 2: 168–169, Unit 4: 494–495, *Life of Pi*: 214, *Performance-Based Assessment*: Unit 2: 245, Unit 4: 537–538, *Romeo and Juliet Is a Terrible Play; In Defense of Romeo and Juliet*: 515, *The Odyssey; The Odyssey: A Graphic Novel:* 632
W.9.1.b Develop claim(s) and counterclaims fairly, supplying evidence for each while pointing out the strengths and limitations of both in a manner that anticipates the audience's knowledge level and concerns.	**SE/TE:** *Whole Class Performance Task*: Unit 2: 169, Unit 4: 496, 497, *Performance-Based Assessment:* Unit 2: 246, Unit 4: 538
W.9.1.c Use words, phrases, and clauses to link the major sections of the text, create cohesion, and clarify the relationships between claim(s) and reasons, between reasons and evidence, and between claim(s) and counterclaims.	**SE/TE:** *Whole Class Performance Task*: Unit 2: 171, Unit 4: 497, *Performance-Based Assessment:* Unit 2: 246
W.9.1.d Establish and maintain a formal style and objective tone while attending to the norms and conventions of the discipline in which they are writing.	**SE/TE:** *Whole Class Performance Task*: Unit 2: 172, Unit 3: 303, Unit 4: 498, Unit 5: 644, *Performance-Based Assessment:* Unit 2: 246, *Remarks on the Assassination of Martin Luther King, Jr.*: 297, *Performance-Based Assessment:* 246
W.9.1.e Provide a concluding statement or section that follows from and supports the argument presented.	**SE/TE:** *Whole Class Performance Task:* Unit 2: 170, Unit 4: 494, 498, *Performance-Based Assessment:* 246
W.9.2 Write informative/explanatory texts to examine and convey complex ideas, concepts, and information clearly and accurately through the effective selection, organization, and analysis of content.	**SE/TE:** *A Quilt of a Country; The Immigrant Contribution:* 34, *With a Little Help From My Friends*: 97, *I Have a Dream; Letter From Birmingham Jail*: 292, *Performance-Based Assessment*: Unit 3: 351, *Romeo and Juliet:* 449, *Pyramus and Thisbe*: 492, 689, 690, *Whole Class Performance Task*: Unit 3: 298, Unit 5: 640, *The Return*: 658
W.9.2.a Introduce a topic; organize complex ideas, concepts, and information to make important connections and distinctions; include formatting (e.g., headings), graphics (e.g., figures, tables), and multimedia when useful to aiding comprehension.	**SE/TE:** *The Moral Logic of Survivor Guilt*: 162, *Letter From a Birmingham Jail*: 292, *Whole Class Performance Task*: Unit 3: 300, Unit 5: 641, 642, *Performance-Based Assessment*: Unit 3: 352
W.9.2.b Develop the topic with well-chosen, relevant, and sufficient facts, extended definitions, concrete details, quotations, or other information and examples appropriate to the audience's knowledge of the topic.	**SE/TE:** *With a Little Help From My Friends*: 97, *Remarks on the Assassination of Martin Luther King, Jr.*: 297, *Whole Class Performance Task*: Unit 3: 300, Unit 5: 641, *Performance-Based Assessment*: Unit 3: 352
W.9.2.c Use appropriate and varied transitions to link the major sections of the text, create cohesion, and clarify the relationships among complex ideas and concepts.	**SE/TE:** *Whole Class Performance Task*: Unit 3: 302, Unit 5: 644, *Lessons of MLK, Jr.*: 332, *Romeo and Juliet Is a Terrible Play; In Defense of Romeo and Juliet*: 514
W.9.2.d Use precise language and domain-specific vocabulary to manage the complexity of the topic.	**SE/TE:** *Whole Class Performance Task*: Unit 3: 300, 302, Unit 5: 643
W.9.2.e Establish and maintain a formal style and objective tone while attending to the norms and conventions of the discipline in which they are writing.	**SE/TE:** *Remarks on the Assassination of Martin Luther King, Jr.*: 297, *Whole Class Performance Task*: Unit 2: 172, Unit 3: 302, Unit 4: 498, Unit 5: 644
W.9.2.f Provide a concluding statement or section that follows from and supports the information or explanation presented.	**SE/TE:** *Whole Class Performance Task*: Unit 3: 302, Unit 5: 640–645, *Performance-Based Assessment:* Unit 3: 353, Unit 5: 691

Grade 9 Writing Standards (continued)	
Standard	**Print and Interactive Editions**
Text Types and Purpose (continued)	
W.9.3 Write narratives to develop real or imagined experiences or events using effective technique, well-chosen details, and well-structured event sequences.	**SE/TE:** *American History*: 50, *Whole Class Performance Task:* Unit 1: 52, Unit 6: 736, *Performance-Based Assessment*: Unit 1: 118, Unit 6: 790, *By the Waters of Babylon*: 720, *There Will Come Soft Rains*: 734, *the beginning of the end of the world; The Powwow on the End of the World; A Song on the End of the World*: 769
W.9.3.a Engage and orient the reader by setting out a problem, situation, or observation, establishing one or multiple point(s) of view, and introducing a narrator and/or characters; create a smooth progression of experiences or events.	**SE/TE:** *Whole Class Performance Task:* Unit 1: 52–57, Unit 6: 736–741, *Performance-Based Assessment:* 790–791
W.9.3.b Use narrative techniques, such as dialogue, pacing, description, reflection, and multiple plot lines, to develop experiences, events, and/or characters.	**SE/TE:** *Whole Class Performance Task:* Unit 1: 53–55, Unit 6: 738, *By the Waters of Babylon*: 720
W.9.3.c Use a variety of techniques to sequence events so that they build on one another to create a coherent whole.	**SE/TE:** *Whole Class Performance Task:* Unit 1: 52–57, Unit 6: 736–741, *Performance-Based Assessment:* 790–791
W.9.3.d Use precise words and phrases, telling details, and sensory language to convey a vivid picture of the experiences, events, setting, and/or characters.	**SE/TE:** *Whole Class Performance Task:* Unit 1: 56, Unit 6: 739, *There Will Come Soft Rains*: 734
W.9.3.e Provide a conclusion that follows from and reflects on what is experienced, observed, or resolved over the course of the narrative.	**SE/TE:** *American History*: 50, *Whole Class Performance Task:* Unit 1: 56
Production and Distribution of Writing	
W.9.4 Produce clear and coherent writing in which the development, organization, and style are appropriate to task, purpose, and audience.	**SE/TE:** *Whole Class Performance Task:* Unit 1, Unit 2, Unit 3, Unit 4, Unit 5, Unit 6, *I Have a Dream; Letter From Birmingham Jail*: 292, *The Odyssey, Part 2*: 622
W.9.5 Develop and strengthen writing as needed by planning, revising, editing, rewriting, or trying a new approach, focusing on addressing what is most significant for a specific purpose and audience.	**SE/TE:** *Whole Class Performance Task*: Unit 1, Unit 2, Unit 3, Unit 4, Unit 5, Unit 6
W.9.6 Use technology, including the Internet, to produce, publish, and update individual or shared writing products, taking advantage of technology's capacity to link to other information and to display information flexibly and dynamically.	**SE/TE:** *The Writing on the Wall:* 87, *Small Group Performance Task*: Unit 1: 110, Unit 3: 334–345, Unit 5: 682–683, Unit 6: 782–783, *The Voyage of the James Caird, The Endurance and the James Caird in Images:* 200–201, *The Hero's Adventure:* 667, *By the Waters of Babylon:* 721, *Radiolab: War of the Worlds; The Myth of the War of the Worlds Panic:* 780–781, *Performance-Based Assessment:* Unit 3: 354, Unit 4: 540, Unit 6: 792
Research to Build and Present Knowledge	
W.9.7 Conduct short as well as more sustained research projects to answer a question (including a self-generated question) or solve a problem; narrow or broaden the inquiry when appropriate; synthesize multiple sources on the subject, demonstrating understanding of the subject under investigation.	**SE/TE:** *The Writing on the Wall*: 86, *Whole Class Performance Task*: Unit 3: 298, *Remembering Civil Rights History, When "Words Meant Everything"*: 311, *Lessons of MLK, Jr.*: 332, *Performance-Based Assessment*: Unit 3: 352, *The Hero's Adventure*: 666, *The Nuclear Tourist*: 757
W.9.8 Gather relevant information from multiple authoritative print and digital sources, using advanced searches effectively; assess the usefulness of each source in answering the research question; integrate information into the text selectively to maintain the flow of ideas, avoiding plagiarism and following a standard format for citation.	**SE/TE:** *Whole Group Performance Task*: Unit 3: 299, 301, *Performance-Based Assessment*: Unit 3: 352, *The Nuclear Tourist:* 757

Standards Correlation

Grade 9 Writing Standards (continued)	
Standard	**Print and Interactive Editions**
Research to Build and Present Knowledge (continued)	
W.9.9 Draw evidence from literary or informational texts to support analysis, reflection, and research.	**SE/TE:** *Performance-Based Assessment*: Unit 1: 118, Unit 2: 246, Unit 3: 352, Unit 4: 538, *The Hero's Adventure*: 666, *The Nuclear Tourist*: 757, *Radiolab: War of the Worlds; The Myth of the War of the Worlds Panic:* 781
W.9.9.a Apply grades 9–10 Reading standards to literature.	**SE/TE:** *Pyramus and Thisbe*: 492, *The Odyssey; The Odyssey: A Graphic Novel:* 632
W.9.9.b Apply grades 9–10 Reading standards to literary nonfiction.	**SE/TE:** *A Quilt of a Country; The Immigrant Contribution:* 34, *I Have a Dream; Letter From Birmingham Jail:* 292, *Radiolab: War of the Worlds; The Myth of the War of the Worlds Panic:* 780
Range of Writing	
W.9.10 Write routinely over extended time frames (time for research, reflection, and revision) and shorter time frames (a single sitting or a day or two) for a range of tasks, purposes, and audiences.	**SE/TE:** *Whole Class Performance Task*: Unit 1: 52, Unit 2: 168, Unit 4: 494, Unit 5: 640, Unit 6: 736, *Performance-Based Assessment:* Unit 2: 246, Unit 3: 298, Unit 3: 352, Unit 4: 538, Unit 5: 690

Grade 9 Speaking and Listening Standards	
Standard	**Print and Interactive Editions**
Comprehension and Collaboration	
SL.9.1 Initiate and participate effectively in a range of collaborative discussions with diverse partners on grades 9–10 topics, texts, and issues, building on others' ideas and expressing their own clearly and persuasively.	**SE/TE:** *Share Your Independent Learning*: 116, 244, 350, 688, 788, *The Odyssey, Part 1*: 593, *The Odyssey, Part 2*: 622, *Courage; Ithaka; The Narrow Road of the Interior*: 681
SL.9.1.a Come to discussions prepared, having read and researched material under study; explicitly draw on that preparation by referring to evidence from texts and other research on the topic or issue to stimulate a thoughtful, well-reasoned exchange of ideas.	**SE/TE:** *Small Group Performance Task:* Unit 1: 110–111, *I Am Offering This Poem; The Writer; Hugging the Jukebox*: 237, *The Odyssey, Part 1*: 593
SL.9.1.b Work with peers to set rules for collegial discussions and decision-making (e.g., informal consensus, taking votes on key issues, presentation of alternate views), clear goals and deadlines, and individual roles as needed.	**SE/TE:** *I Am Offering This Poem; The Writer; Hugging the Jukebox:* 237, *The Odyssey, Part 1*: 593, Students will address this standard in *Working as a Team* features which appear in the Small Group Learning Overview lessons.
SL.9.1.c Propel conversations by posing and responding to questions that relate the current discussion to broader themes or larger ideas; actively incorporate others into the discussion; and clarify, verify, or challenge ideas and conclusions.	**SE/TE:** *Morning Talk; Immigrant Picnic:* 109, *Traveling*: 343, Students will address this standard in *Launch Activity* features which appear in the Unit Introduction and in *Working as a Team* features which appear in the Small Group Learning Overview lessons.
SL.9.1.d Respond thoughtfully to diverse perspectives, summarize points of agreement and disagreement, and, when warranted, qualify or justify their own views and understanding and make new connections in light of the evidence and reasoning presented.	**SE/TE:** *Morning Talk; Immigrant Picnic:* 109, Students will address this standard in *Launch Activity* features which appear in the Unit Introduction, in *Working as a Team* features which appear in the Small Group Learning Overview lessons, and *Group Discussion Tips* which appear throughout the program.
SL.9.2 Integrate multiple sources of information presented in diverse media or formats (e.g., visually, quantitatively, orally) evaluating the credibility and accuracy of each source.	**SE/TE:** *Remembering Civil Rights History, When "Words Meant Everything"*: 310, *By the Waters of Babylon*: 720, *the beginning of the end of the world; The Powwow at the End of the World; A Song on the End of the World*: 769
SL.9.3 Evaluate a speaker's point of view, reasoning, and use of evidence and rhetoric, identifying any fallacious reasoning or exaggerated or distorted evidence.	**SE/TE:** *The Key to Disaster Survival? Friends and Neighbors*: 166, *Remarks on the Assassination of Martin Luther King, Jr.*: 296, *The Odyssey, Part 2*: 622
Presentation of Knowledge and Ideas	
SL.9.4 Present information, findings, and supporting evidence clearly, concisely, and logically such that listeners can follow the line of reasoning and the organization, development, substance, and style are appropriate to purpose, audience, and task.	**SE/TE:** *Rules of the Game:* 77, *Small Group Performance Task*: Unit 1: 110, Unit 2: 238, Unit 3: 344, Unit 4: 530, Unit 5: 682, Unit 6: 782, *Performance-Based Assessment*: Unit 1: 120, Unit 2: 248, Unit 3: 354, Unit 4: 540, Unit 5: 692, 693, *The Seventh Man:* 150, *The Moral Logic of Survivor Guilt:* 162, *Remarks on the Assassination of Martin Luther King, Jr.*: 297, *For My People; Incident*: 321, *Romeo and Juliet*: 423, 465, 484, *By the Waters of Babylon*: 720, *There Will Come Soft Rains:* 734, *the beginning of the end of the world; The Powwow at the End of the World; A Song on the End of the World*: 769, *Radiolab: War of the Worlds; The Myth of the War of the Worlds Panic:* 781
SL.9.5 Make strategic use of digital media (e.g., textual, graphical, audio, visual, and interactive elements) in presentations to enhance understanding of findings, reasoning, and evidence and to add interest.	**SE/TE:** *The Writing on the Wall*: 86, *Small Group Performance Task*: Unit 1: 110, Unit 2: 239, Unit 3: 345, Unit 4: 531, Unit 5: 683, Unit 6: 783, *The Voyage of the James Caird & The Endurance and the James Caird in Images*: 201, *The Value of a Sherpa Life*: 222, *Performance-Based Assessment*: Unit 3: 354, Unit 4: 540, Unit 6: 792, *By the Waters of Babylon*: 720, *Radiolab: War of the Worlds; The Myth of the War of the Worlds Panic:* 780, 781
SL.9.6 Adapt speech to a variety of contexts and tasks, demonstrating command of formal English when indicated or appropriate.	**SE/TE:** *Small Group Performance Task*: Unit 1: 110, Unit 3: 345, Unit 5: 683, Unit 6: 783, *I Am Offering This Poem; The Writer; Hugging the Jukebox*: 237, *Performance-Based Assessment*: Unit 3: 352, Unit 4: 540, *Romeo and Juliet:* 423

Standards Correlation

Grade 9 Language Standards	
Standard	**Print and Interactive Editions**
Conventions of Standard English	
L.9.1 Demonstrate command of the conventions of standard English grammar and usage when writing or speaking.	**SE/TE:** *Rules of the Game:* 76, *Life of Pi:* 214, *I Have a Dream:* 268, *Romeo and Juliet:* 482, *The Odyssey, Part 2:* 620, *The Return:* 658, *The Hero's Adventure*: 666, *Courage; Ithaka; The Narrow Road of the Interior*: 680, *Whole Class Performance Task*: Unit 6: 740
L.9.1.a Use parallel structure.	**SE/TE:** *I Have a Dream*: 268, *Romeo and Juliet:* 482, *There Will Come Soft Rains*: 732
L.9.1.b Use various types of phrases and clauses to convey specific meanings and add variety and interest to writing or presentations.	**SE/TE:** *The Immigrant Contribution:* 32, *American History*: 48, *Rules of the Game:* 76, *The Seventh Man:* 148, *Whole Class Performance Task*: Unit 6: 739, *The Voyage of the James Caird*: 192, *The Life of Pi*: 214, *Letter From Birmingham Jail:* 290, *Twenty Years On*: 523, *The Hero's Adventure:* 666
L.9.2 Demonstrate command of the conventions of standard English capitalization, punctuation, and spelling when writing.	**SE/TE:** *The Moral Logic of Survivor Guilt*: 160, *For My People; Incident:* 320, *Traveling*: 342, *By the Waters of Babylon*: 718, *There Will Come Soft Rains:* 732
L.9.2.a Use a semicolon (and perhaps a conjunctive adverb) to link two or more closely related independent clauses.	**SE/TE:** *The Moral Logic of Survivor Guilt*: 160, *For My People; Incident*: 320, *Lessons of MLK, Jr.:* 332
L.9.2.b Use a colon to introduce a list or quotation.	**SE/TE:** *The Moral Logic of Survivor Guilt*: 160, *Whole Class Performance Task:* Unit 4: 497
L.9.2.c Spell correctly.	**SE/TE:** *I Have a Dream:* 268, *Whole Class Performance Task*: Unit 5: 643, 645, Unit 6: 740
Knowledge of Language	
L.9.3 Apply knowledge of language to understand how language functions in different contexts, to make effective choices for meaning or style, and to comprehend more fully when reading or listening.	**SE/TE:** *A Quilt of a Country; The Immigrant Contribution:* 34, *Morning Talk; Immigrant Picnic:* 108, *Whole Class Performance Task*: Unit 2: 168, 172, *The Odyssey, Part 2:* 620, *The Nuclear Tourist*: 756
L.9.3.a Write and edit work so that it conforms to the guidelines in a style manual (e.g., *MLA Handbook,* Turabian's *Manual for Writers)* appropriate for the discipline and writing type.	**SE/TE:** *Research*: R30–33
Vocabulary Acquisition and Use	
L.9.4 Determine or clarify the meaning of unknown and multiple-meaning words and phrases based on grades 9–10 reading and content, choosing flexibly from a range of strategies	**SE/TE:** *Morning Talk; Immigrant Picnic:* 98, 106, *The Voyage of the James Caird*: 191, *Life of Pi*: 202, *I Am Offering This Poem; The Writer; Hugging the Jukebox*: 224, *The Return:* 650
L.9.4.a Use context as a clue to the meaning of a word or phrase.	**SE/TE:** *Rules of the Game*: 62, *The Writing on the Wall*: 78, *With a Little Help From My Friends*: 88, *The Voyage of the James Caird*: 178, *The Value of a Sherpa Life*: 216, *For My People; Incident:* 312, *Lessons of MLK, Jr.:* 322, *Traveling:* 334, *Romeo and Juliet Is a Terrible Play; In Defense of Romeo and Juliet*: 504, *The Hero's Adventure*: 660, *Courage; Ithaka; The Narrow Road of the Interior*: 668, *The Nuclear Tourist:* 746, *The Myth of the War of the Worlds Panic:* 774
L.9.4.b Identify and correctly use patterns of word changes that indicate different meanings or parts of speech.	**SE/TE:** *A Quilt of a Country*: 20, *The Immigrant Contribution*: 32, *The Writing on the Wall*: 84, *With a Little Help From My Friends*: 94, *The Seventh Man*: 148, *The Moral Logic of Survivor Guilt*: 160, *Life of Pi*: 212, *The Value of a Sherpa Life:* 220, *I Am Offering This Poem; The Writer; Hugging the Jukebox*: 224, 234, *I Have a Dream*: 268, *Letter From Birmingham Jail*: 290, *For My People; Incident*: 318, *Lessons of MLK, Jr.*: 330, *Traveling*: 340, *Romeo and Juliet:* 397, 421, 447, 463, *Romeo and Juliet Is a Terrible Play; In Defense of Romeo and Juliet*: 512, *Twenty Years On*: 516, 521, *The Odyssey, Part 1:* 591, *The Odyssey, Part 2*: 620, *The Return*: 650, 656, *Courage; Ithaka; The Narrow Road of the Interior*: 678, *By the Waters of Babylon*: 718, *There Will Come Soft Rains*: 732, *The Nuclear Tourist:* 754, *the beginning of the end of the world; The Powwow on the End of the World; A Song on the End of the World*: 758, 766

Grade 9 Language Standards (continued)	
Standard	**Print and Interactive Editions**
Vocabulary Acquisition and Use (continued)	
L.9.4.c Consult general and specialized reference materials, both print and digital, to find the pronunciation of a word or determine or clarify its precise meaning, its part of speech, or its etymology.	**SE/TE:** *American History: 48, The Moral Logic of Survivor Guilt:* 160, *For My People; Incident:* 318, *The Hero's Adventure:* 664, *Whole Class Performance Task*: Unit 5: 643, 645, *The Nuclear Tourist:* 754, *the beginning of the end of the world; The Powwow at the End of the World; A Song on the End of the World:* 766
L.9.4.d Verify the preliminary determination of the meaning of a word or phrase.	**SE/TE:** *The Immigrant Contribution:* 22, *Rules of the Game:* 74, *Traveling*: 334, *Twenty Years On*: 521, *Courage; Ithaka; The Narrow Road of the Interior:* 668, *There Will Come Soft Rains:* 732
L.9.5 Demonstrate understanding of figurative language, word relationships, and nuances in word meanings.	**SE/TE:** *American History*: 48, *I Am Offering This Poem; The Writer; Hugging the Jukebox*: 236, *Letter From Birmingham Jail*: 290, *Romeo and Juliet:* 463, 482, *Pyramus and Thisbe*: 491, *The Odyssey, Part 1:* 591, *The Return*: 656, *The Hero's Adventure*: 664, *Courage; Ithaka; The Narrow Road of the Interior*: 678, *By the Waters of Babylon*: 718, *There Will Come Soft Rains*: 730
L.9.5.a Interpret figures of speech in context and analyze their role in the text.	**SE/TE:** *With a Little Help From My Friends:* 96, *Morning Talk; Immigrant Picnic:* 108, *I Am Offering This Poem; The Writer; Hugging the Jukebox:* 237, *Romeo and Juliet*: 399, 464
L.9.5.b Analyze nuances in the meaning of words with similar denotations.	**SE/TE:** *Rules of the Game*: 74, *The Seventh Man*: 148, *Letter From Birmingham Jail:* 290, *Romeo and Juliet:* 482
L.9.6 Acquire and use accurately general academic and domain-specific words and phrases, sufficient for reading, writing, speaking, and listening at the college and career readiness level; demonstrate independence in gathering vocabulary knowledge when considering a word or phrase important to comprehension or expression.	**SE/TE:** *Unit Goals*: Unit 1: 4, Unit 2: 124, Unit 3: 252, Unit 4: 358, Unit 5: 544, Unit 6: 696, *The Key to Disaster Survival? Friends and Neighbors*: 164, *The Endurance and the James Caird in Images*: 194, *Tragic Romeo and Juliet Offers Bosnia Hope*: 524, 527, *The Odyssey: A Graphic Novel*: 624, 631, *Application for a Mariner's License*: 634, *By the Waters of Babylon*: 716, *The Nuclear Tourist*: 756, *Radiolab: War of the Worlds:* 770, 772

UNIT 1

American Voices

INTRODUCTION

Jump Start

Give students a few minutes to write as many words as they can about what it means to them to be American. Engage the class by letting them vote for their favorite words/phrases, and choose the three most popular results. Ask students if they think that the list of words about what it means to be American might be different twenty years from now. Fifty years from now? Fifty years ago?

American Voices

Ask students what the phrase *American voices* suggests to them. Point out that as they work through this unit, they will read many examples about how the diversity of American voices reflects the diversity of the American people.

Video

Project the introduction video in class, ask students to open the video in their digital textbooks, or have students scan the Bounce Page icon with their phones to access the video.

Discuss It If you want to make this a digital activity, go online and navigate to the Discussion Board. Alternatively, students can share their responses in a class discussion.

Block Scheduling

Each day in this pacing calendar represents a 40–50 minute class period. Teachers using block scheduling may combine days to reflect their class schedule. In addition, teachers may revise pacing to differentiate and support core instruction by integrating components and resources as students require.

UNIT 1

American Voices

The people who call the United States home are diverse in their histories and experiences. Is there such a thing as a "correct" way to be "American"?

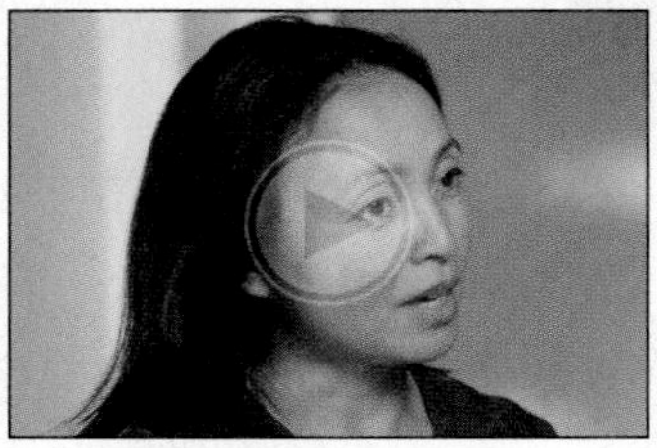

Define American: Hiep Le

Discuss It Is being "American" a matter of geography or choice?

Write your response before sharing your ideas.

2

SCAN FOR MULTIMEDIA

Pacing Plan

- Unit Introduction: 1
- Introduce Whole-Class Learning: 2
- A Quilt of a Country: 3, 4, 5, 6
- The Immigrant Contribution: 7, 8, 9, 10
- American History: 11, 12, 13
- Performance Task: 14, 15

DIGITAL PERSPECTIVES — Audio | Video | Document | Annotation Highlights | EL Highlights | Online Assessment

UNIT 1

UNIT INTRODUCTION

ESSENTIAL QUESTION:

What does it mean to be "American"?

LAUNCH TEXT
NONFICTION
NARRATIVE MODEL
Music for My Mother

WHOLE-CLASS LEARNING

COMPARE

ANCHOR TEXT: ESSAY
A Quilt of a Country
Anna Quindlen

ANCHOR TEXT: ESSAY
The Immigrant Contribution
from A Nation of Immigrants
John F. Kennedy

ANCHOR TEXT: SHORT STORY
American History
Judith Ortiz Cofer

PERFORMANCE TASK
WRITING FOCUS:
Write a Nonfiction Narrative

SMALL-GROUP LEARNING

NOVEL EXCERPT
Rules of the Game
from The Joy Luck Club
Amy Tan

MEDIA: BLOG POST
The Writing on the Wall
Camille Dungy

MEMOIR
With a Little Help From My Friends
from Funny in Farsi
Firoozeh Dumas

POETRY COLLECTION
Morning Talk
Roberta Hill Whiteman

Immigrant Picnic
Gregory Djanikian

PERFORMANCE TASK
SPEAKING AND LISTENING FOCUS:
Present a Nonfiction Narrative

INDEPENDENT LEARNING

MEMOIR
from When I Was Puerto Rican
Esmeralda Santiago

AUTOBIOGRAPHICAL ESSAY
Finding a Voice: A Taiwanese Family Adapts to America
Diane Tsai

POETRY
The New Colossus
Emma Lazarus

POETRY
Legal Alien
Pat Mora

MEDIA: VIDEO
Grace Abbott and the Fight for Immigrant Rights in America
BBC

PERFORMANCE-BASED ASSESSMENT PREP
Review Evidence for a Nonfiction Narrative

PERFORMANCE-BASED ASSESSMENT

Narrative: Nonfiction Narrative and Interpretive Reading

PROMPT:
How is an American identity created?

3

What does it mean to be "American"?

Introduce the Essential Question and point out that students will respond to related prompts.

- **Whole-Class Learning** *How does your generation define what it means to be an American today?*
- **Small-Group Learning** *How do the realities of immigrants' experiences reflect or fail to reflect American ideals?*
- **Performance-Based Assessment** *How is an American identity created?*

Using Trade Books

Refer to the Teaching with Trade Books section in this book or online in *my*Perspectives+ for suggestions on how to incorporate the following thematically-related novels into this unit.

- *The Joy Luck Club* by Amy Tan
- *My Antonia* by Willa Cather
- *Stargirl* by Jerry Spinelli

Current Perspectives

To increase student engagement, search online for stories about what being an American means to different people, and invite your students to recommend stories they find. Always preview content before sharing it with your class.

- **News Story: "We All Belong to the Sea Between Us," (NPR)** A profile of Cuban-American poet Richard Blanco, who spoke at President Obama's second inauguration.
- **Video: *I Am an Undocumented Immigrant* (The Atlantic)** Interview with filmmaker Pang Tubhirun about her short documentary of the same name.

Day	Activity
16	Introduce Small-Group Learning
17–18	Rules of the Game
19–20	The Writing on the Wall
21–22	With a Little Help From My Friends
23–24	• Morning Talk, • Immigrant Picnic
25–26	Performance Task
27	Introduce Independent Learning
28	Independent Learning
29–30	Performance-Based Assessment

About the Unit Goals

These unit goals were backward designed from the Performance-Based Assessment at the end of the unit and the Whole-Class and Small-Group Performance Tasks. Students will practice and become proficient in many more standards over the course of this unit.

Unit Goals

Review the goals with students and explain that as they read and discuss the selections in this unit, they will improve their skills in reading, writing, research, language, and speaking and listening.

- Have students watch the video on Goal Setting.
- A video on this topic is available online in the Professional Development Center.

Reading Goals Tell students they will read and evaluate various nonfiction narratives.

Writing and Research Goals Tell students that they will learn the elements of nonfiction narrative writing. They will also write their own nonfiction narratives. They will conduct research to clarify and explore ideas.

Language Goal Tell students that they will develop a deeper understanding of exposition and dialogue to convey meaning and add variety to their writing.

Speaking and Listening Explain to students that they will work together to build on one another's ideas, develop consensus, and communicate with one another. They will also learn to incorporate audio, visuals, and text in presentations.

HOME Connection

A Home Connection letter to students' parents or guardians is available in myPerspectives+. The letter explains what students will be learning in this unit and how they will be assessed.

Unit Goals

Throughout this unit, you will deepen your understanding of what it means to be "American" by reading, writing, speaking, presenting, and listening. These goals will help you succeed on the Unit Performance-Based Assessment.

Rate how well you meet these goals right now. You will revisit your ratings later when you reflect on your growth during this unit.

SCALE	1	2	3	4	5
	NOT AT ALL WELL	NOT VERY WELL	SOMEWHAT WELL	VERY WELL	EXTREMELY WELL

READING GOALS	1	2	3	4	5
• Evaluate written narratives by analyzing how authors sequence and describe experiences and events.	○	○	○	○	○
• Expand your knowledge and use of academic and concept vocabulary.	○	○	○	○	○

WRITING AND RESEARCH GOALS	1	2	3	4	5
• Write a nonfiction narrative in which you develop characters and events using specific details and descriptions.	○	○	○	○	○
• Conduct research projects of various lengths to explore a topic and clarify meaning.	○	○	○	○	○

LANGUAGE GOAL	1	2	3	4	5
• Correctly use exposition and dialogue to convey meaning and add variety and interest to your writing and presentations.	○	○	○	○	○

SPEAKING AND LISTENING GOALS	1	2	3	4	5
• Collaborate with your team to build on the ideas of others, develop consensus, and communicate.	○	○	○	○	○
• Integrate audio, visuals, and text in presentations.	○	○	○	○	○

STANDARDS

Language

Acquire and use accurately grade-appropriate general academic and domain-specific words and phrases, sufficient for reading, writing, speaking, and listening at the college and career readiness level; demonstrate independence in gathering vocabulary knowledge when considering a word or phrase important to comprehension or expression.

SCAN FOR MULTIMEDIA

AUTHOR'S PERSPECTIVE Ernest Morrell, Ph.D.

Why Goal Setting Matters Establishing goals helps students take responsibility for their own learning and become independent scholars and thinkers. One way to encourage students to set, follow, and achieve goals is to have them write down their goals. Students can use the following process for crafting well-defined and measurable goals:

- *Decide What You Want:* Have students skim the Unit Table of Contents and decide what they most want to learn. Guide students to set specific, realistic goals, such as "learn and use five new concept words from the unit."
- *Write Down Goals:* Have students draft the goals in clear, precise language. Students should include a way to measure results so they can assess progress.
- *Set a Time Frame:* Have students include a realistic schedule for completion. Have students break down large goals into smaller ones to make the goal more likely to be completed.

When students take responsibility, they may rely more on themselves and take interest in their success.

Academic Vocabulary: Narrative Writing

Academic terms appear in all subjects and can help you read, write, and discuss with more precision. Here are five academic words that will be useful to you in this unit as you analyze and write narratives.

Complete the chart.

1. Review each word, its root, and the mentor sentences.
2. Use the information and your own knowledge to predict the meaning of each word.
3. For each word, list at least two related words.
4. Refer to a dictionary or other resources if needed.

TIP

FOLLOW THROUGH
Study the words in this chart, and highlight them or their forms wherever they appear in the unit.

WORD	MENTOR SENTENCES	PREDICT MEANING	RELATED WORDS
conflict ROOT: ***-flict-*** "strike"; "hit"	1. Alice and Nora resolved their *conflict* by sharing the toy they both wanted. 2. In the story I'm writing, I want the *conflict* to resolve happily.		inflict, afflict
description ROOT: ***-scrip-*** "writing"	1. Pat Mora's skill with *description* is one reason her poems are so good. 2. Your comedy routine will be funnier if you include detailed *description* of the scene.		
dialogue ROOT: ***-log-*** "word"	1. Milton has memorized every word of *dialogue* in the film and will gladly recite it. 2. Greta enjoys writing fiction but has a hard time making *dialogue* sound realistic.		
exposition ROOT: ***-posit-*** "sit"; "place"; "put"	1. The story contains very little *exposition*, so it took me awhile to figure out the characters' relationships. 2. Kennedy's essay about American identity is a well-organized *exposition* of important ideas.		
sequence ROOT: ***-sequ-*** "follow"	1. A movie director may plan a scene by breaking it into a *sequence* of separate shots. 2. After Anika finished the experiment, she explained the *sequence* of steps she had followed.		

DIGITAL PERSPECTIVES

Academic Vocabulary: Narrative Writing

Introduce the blue academic vocabulary words in the chart on the student page. Point out that the root of each word provides a clue to its meaning. Discuss the mentor sentences to ensure students understand each word's usage. Students should also use the mentor sentences as context to help them predict the meaning of each word. Check that students are able to fill the chart in correctly. Complete pronunciations, parts of speech, and definitions are provided for you. Students are only expected to provide the definition.

Possible responses:

conflict *n.* (KON flickt)
Meaning: a struggle, problem, or fight
Related words: conflicted; conflicting
Additional words related to the root *-flict-*: inflict, afflict, affliction

description *n.* (di SKRIP shuhn)
Meaning: writing or speech that tells about something
Related words: describe; describing
Additional words related to the root *-scrip-*: scripture, post-script, prescription, inscription

dialogue *n.* (DAHY uh log)
Meaning: conversation between characters in writing, film, or drama
Related words: dialogic
Additional words related to the root *-log-*: logistics, monologue, logo, prologue

exposition *n.* (ek spuh ZIH shuhn)
Meaning: writing that explains or shows
Related words: expose; exposure
Additional words related to the root *-posit-*: position; deposition; imposition; posit; reposition

sequence *n.* (SEE kwuh ns)
Related words: sequential
Meaning: order, as a linear order of steps or events
Additional words related to the root *-sequ-*: consequential, consequence, inconsequential

PERSONALIZE FOR LEARNING

English Language Support

Cognates Many of the academic words have Spanish cognates. Use these cognates with students whose home language is Spanish.

ALL LEVELS

conflict – conflicto   description – descripción
dialogue – diálogo   sequence – secuencia

Purpose of the Launch Text

The Launch Text provides students with a common starting point to address the unit topic. After reading the Launch Text, all students will be able to participate in discussions about American voices.

Lexile: 770 The easier reading level of this selection makes it perfect to assign for homework. Students will need little or no support to understand it.

Additionally, "Music for My Mother" provides a writing model for the Performance-Based Assessment students complete at the end of the unit.

Launch Text: Narrative Model

Ask students to think about the story the author is telling and how she uses details to weave a vivid and meaningful narrative.

Have students pay attention to the way the author uses the opening paragraph to establish how her mother was homesick, and the way the subsequent paragraphs describe her parents' difficulty in adapting to their new country. They should notice that the story concludes by drawing a connection to its opening.

Encourage students to read this text on their own and annotate unfamiliar words and sections of text they think are particularly important.

AUDIO SUMMARIES

Audio summaries of "Music for My Mother" are available in both English and Spanish in the Interactive Teacher's Edition or Unit Resources. Assigning these summaries before students read the Launch Text may help them build additional background knowledge and set a context for their reading.

LAUNCH TEXT | NARRATIVE MODEL

This selection is an example of a **nonfiction narrative,** a type of writing in which an author tells a true story. This is the type of writing you will develop in the Performance-Based Assessment at the end of the unit.

As you read, look at the way the writer builds the story. Mark the text to help you answer this question: What details make this narrative vivid and meaningful?

Music for My Mother

NOTES

1 After dinner my older brother liked to play the guitar. He preferred the music he heard on the radio, but he played the traditional songs for Mama. She enjoyed things that reminded her of home.

2 Her eyes hurt and her fingers would get sore from long hours of work as a seamstress. I remember washing dishes while Pedrito sang: "And seeing myself so lonely and sad like a leaf in the wind, I want to cry . . . from this feeling."

3 He sang in Spanish, which is how the lyrics were written. That song is more than 100 years old now. Mama learned it when she was a girl.

4 Papa tried to nudge Mama out of her nostalgia sometimes. He would answer her in English when she spoke to him in Spanish. His English was not very good at first, but he worked at it until it got better.

5 Mama usually answered him in Spanish. They would go back and forth in either language, talking about work or homesickness or family. Pedrito or I would occasionally correct them or help them finish their sentences in English. Papa would thank us. Mama would just smile and shake her head. But she always repeated the words we

SCAN FOR MULTIMEDIA

CROSS-CURRICULAR PERSPECTIVES

Social Studies Have students conduct research to learn about children of immigrants who went on to make significant contributions to the culture, economy, or government of the United States. Possible examples include Steve Jobs, Nikki Haley, Marco Rubio, and Maria Elena Salinas.

Have students write a brief essay about how those individuals had to overcome the challenge of being the child of an immigrant in order to become successful.

had helped her with. In time her English got better too, but she was far more at ease in her native tongue.

6 I was seven years old when we came to the United States. Pedrito was 11. Papa was a carpenter who also knew a little about plumbing and electricity. From an early age, my brother and I learned how to take care of ourselves in our new home. Our parents worked long hours, and they counted on us to be independent.

7 At first we were almost like guides for Mama and Papa. In big busy places, like the mall or the registry of motor vehicles, they felt uncomfortable, if not overwhelmed. It was easier for us to adjust to environments that were fast-paced and not always friendly. I felt protective of my parents and also proud of how quickly I learned my way around.

8 It would hurt my feelings to see the way some people looked at us. For a while, on Sundays and holidays we would wear our best clothes from home. Before long, we learned to wear casual clothes almost all the time, like most people in this country do. And after a while, our parents became more at ease in stores or government offices. They relaxed a little, I suppose, and we attracted less attention.

9 Mama and Papa live with Pedrito now, in a two-family home outside of Houston. Pedrito is now known as Peter. He runs a construction business that employs 14 men and women.

10 Papa is in his seventies now. Pedrito would like for him to slow down a little and enjoy retirement, but Papa says that Mama wouldn't want him sitting around the house getting in her way. He rises at dawn almost every day and goes to work with Pedrito, building houses.

11 I am a teacher. This summer I will be taking my son, Michael, to visit his grandparents. He is twelve. He wants to learn to play the guitar. I want Mama and his Uncle Peter to teach him a few of the good old songs.

NOTES

WORD NETWORK FOR AMERICAN VOICES

Vocabulary A Word Network is a collection of words related to a topic. As you read the selections in this unit, identify interesting words related to the idea of American identity and add them to your Word Network. For example, you might begin by adding words from the Launch Text, such as *traditional*, *native*, and *environment*. Continue to add words as you complete the unit.

Tool Kit
Word Network Model

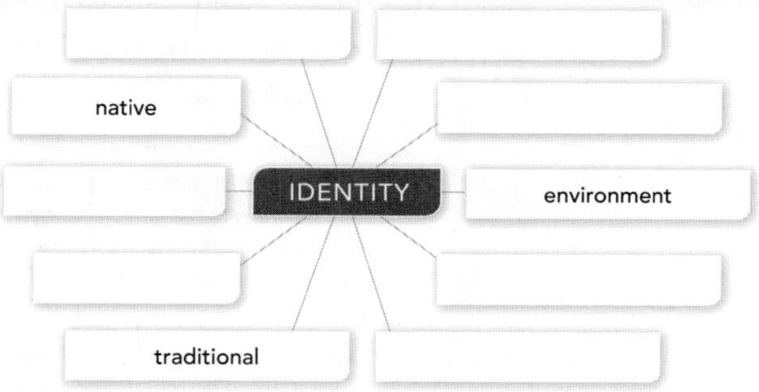

Word Network for American Voices

Tell students that they can fill in the Word Network as they read texts in the unit, or they can record the words elsewhere and add them later. Point out to students that people may have personal associations with some words. A word that one student thinks is related to the topic of American identity might not be a word another student would pick. However, students should feel free to add any word they personally think is relevant to their Word Network. Each person's Word Network will be unique. If you choose to print the Word Network, distribute it to students at this point so they can use it throughout the rest of the unit.

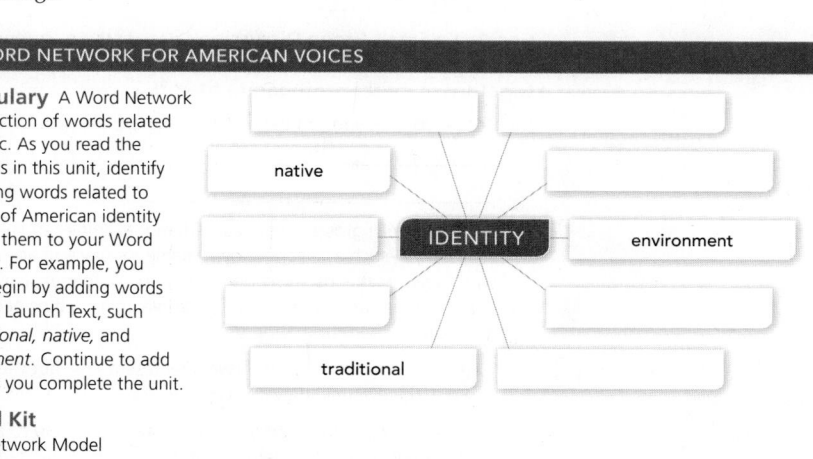

AUTHOR'S PERSPECTIVE Elfrieda Hiebert, Ph.D.

Word Networks Vocabulary word networks enable students to learn, use, and retain a large number of useful words related to a particular concept. In addition, generating vocabulary in this way can help students appreciate the subtleties of an author's word choice and evaluate the effectiveness of an author's style. Using vocabulary word networks also helps students choose more precise words when they write and edit. Finally, forging connections among related words, as opposed to teaching the words individually, allows students to approach new words with confidence and knowledge.

When students discuss the unit's theme, they can choose from a wide variety of related words, each with its own connotation, to create a word network. While students may not know more complex words at first, they do know common conversation words and words that get at the big idea. These words can serve as a gateway to the more complex words they will encounter in these selections.

INTRODUCTION

Summary

Have students read the introductory paragraph. Provide them with tips for writing a summary:

- Write in the present tense.
- Make sure to include the title of the work.
- Be concise: a summary should not be equal in length to the original text.
- If you need to quote the words of the author, use quotation marks.
- Don't put your own opinions, ideas, or interpretations into the summary. The purpose of writing a summary is to accurately represent what the author says, not to provide a critique.

If necessary, students can refer to the Tool Kit for help in understanding the elements of a good summary.

See possible summary on Student page.

Launch Activity

Explain to students that as they work on this unit they will have many opportunities to discuss the topic of American identity. Remind them that there are many possible ways that creative expression can either bring people together or divide them, but their examples should be personal to one of the members of the group. Students should listen to the different examples and think about how theirs are similar and different.

Summary

Write a summary of "Music for My Mother." A **summary** is a concise, complete, and accurate overview of a text. It should not include a statement of your opinion or an analysis.

Possible response: In this narrative text, the narrator speaks about music and her family's early days in the United States. The family sang and played old songs while doing chores. The narrator's mother was often homesick, and never entirely comfortable with English rather than with Spanish. From an early age, the children learned to take care of themselves and be independent, because their parents worked long hours. They often acted like guides for their parents, helping them find their way around busy and fast-paced places. Over time, everyone got more used to living in the US and fit in better. The narrator now works as a teacher, and intends to come back home to pass the family tradition of music on to the next generation.

Launch Activity

Conduct a Small-Group Discussion Consider this question: **In what ways can music or other creative expression bring people together or, perhaps, separate them?**

- Record your feelings on the question and explain your thinking.

  ____

  ____

- Gather in small groups to discuss different examples of creative expression—such as a song, poem, game, or piece of art—you learned with family or friends, at school, or during another experience. As a group, choose an example that you agree either brings people together or separates them from others.
- Gather the small groups and have a representative from each one describe the example they have chosen.
- As a class, discuss the examples. Would each one help to bring people of different backgrounds together or to keep them separated?

VOCABULARY DEVELOPMENT

Academic Vocabulary Reinforcement Students will benefit from additional examples and practice with the academic vocabulary. Reinforce their comprehension with "show-you-know" sentences. The first part of the sentence uses the vocabulary word in an appropriate context. The second part of the sentence—the "show-you-know" part—clarifies the first. Model the strategy with this example.

The brothers were in constant *conflict,* always *arguing* about everything.

Then give students these sentence prompts and coach them to create the clarification parts.

1. By improving the script's *dialogue* in the second draft, the screenwriter _____.
2. The author used vivid *descriptions* to _____.
3. Bogged down by too much *exposition*, the story _____.
4. The *sequence* of exciting events _____.

QuickWrite

Consider class discussions, presentations, the video, and the Launch Text as you think about the prompt. Record your first thoughts here.

PROMPT: **How is an "American" identity created?**

Possible response: I think being yourself and using your talents as you learn to navigate and adapt to your environment creates an American identity. Your identity is who you are and who people see when they encounter you. Would you want to come off as unmemorable or—even worse—as a phony? Of course not!

The author explains in "Music for My Mother," that the family often attracted looks that were hurtful. They stood out because the parents were overwhelmed, and they dressed up more than other people. They adapted by dressing more casually. The author's brother learned to play and sing songs in Spanish and became a carpenter. This is his identity. He created it by being himself and using his talents to become the person others see.

EVIDENCE LOG FOR AMERICAN VOICES

Review your QuickWrite. Summarize your thoughts in one sentence to record in your Evidence Log. Then, record textual details or evidence from "Music for My Mother" that support your thinking.

Prepare for the Performance-Based Assessment at the end of the unit by completing the Evidence Log after each selection.

Tool Kit
Evidence Log Model

Title of Text: ______ Date: ______

CONNECTION TO PROMPT	TEXT EVIDENCE/DETAILS	ADDITIONAL NOTES/IDEAS

How does this text change or add to my thinking? Date: ______

SCAN FOR MULTIMEDIA

DIGITAL PERSPECTIVES

QuickWrite

In this QuickWrite, students should present their own response to the prompt based on the material they have read and viewed in the Unit Overview and Introduction. This initial response will help inform their work when they complete the Performance-Based Assessment at the end of the unit. Students should present their thoughts clearly and support their ideas with well-reasoned thinking and examples.

See possible QuickWrite on Student page.

Evidence Log for American Voices

Students should record their initial thinking in their Evidence Logs along with evidence from "Music for My Mother" that supports this thinking.

If you choose to print the Evidence Log, distribute it to students at this point so they can use it throughout the rest of the unit.

Performance-Based Assessment: Refining Your Thinking

- Have students watch the video on Refining Your Thinking.
- A video on this topic is available online in the Professional Development Center.

WriteNow Express and Reflect

Description The author describes the challenges that her parents and family faced as outsiders in the United States. Have students write a two-paragraph essay about a time in their lives when they felt like outsiders, and what made that time so challenging. Remind students to provide details that will illustrate how difficult the situation was. Point out to students that the author used vivid details to show the reader that adapting to America was difficult for her family.

OVERVIEW

WHOLE-CLASS LEARNING

What does it mean to be "American"?

The concept of being "American" can mean a wide variety of things to a wide variety of people. America is a nation that was founded and built by immigrants, and American culture reflects our unique mixture of people and traditions from around the world. Everyone has different experiences and stories to share. During Whole-Class Learning, students will read selections about what it truly means to be American, and how the diversity of our culture continues to define us.

Whole-Class Learning Strategies

Review the Learning Strategies with students and explain that as they work through Whole-Class Learning they will develop strategies to work in large-group environments.

- Have students watch the video on Whole-Class Learning Strategies.
- A video on this topic is available online in the Professional Development Center.

You may wish to discuss some action items to add to the chart as a class before students complete it on their own. For example, for "Listen actively," you might solicit the following from students:

- If you think you might have misunderstood someone's point, ask her to make sure.
- Take notes so that you can remember important details.

Block Scheduling

Each day in this Pacing Plan represents a 40–50 minute class period. Teachers using block scheduling may combine days to reflect their class schedule. In addition, teachers may revise pacing to differentiate and support core instruction by integrating components and resources as students require.

OVERVIEW: WHOLE-CLASS LEARNING

ESSENTIAL QUESTION:

What does it mean to be "American"?

America has been described as a "melting pot" of people from different places and cultures—but is that description accurate? Does American identity represent a "melting" or merging of cultures? Or is it more like a salad in which the separate ingredients are still visible? You will work with your whole class to explore the concept of American identity. The selections you are going to read present different perspectives on what it means to be "American."

Whole-Class Learning Strategies

Throughout your life, in school, in your community, and in your career, you will continue to learn and work in large-group environments.

Review these strategies and the actions you can take to practice them as you work with your whole class. Add ideas of your own for each step. Get ready to use these strategies during Whole-Class Learning.

STRATEGY	ACTION PLAN
Listen actively	• Eliminate distractions. For example, put your cell phone away. • Keep your eyes on the speaker. •
Clarify by asking questions	• If you're confused, other people probably are, too. Ask a question to help your whole class. • If you see that you are guessing, ask a question instead. •
Monitor understanding	• Notice what information you already know and be ready to build on it. • Ask for help if you are struggling. •
Interact and share ideas	• Share your ideas and answer questions, even if you are unsure. • Build on the ideas of others by adding details or making a connection. •

SCAN FOR MULTIMEDIA

Pacing Plan

Unit Introduction: 1

Introduce Whole-Class Learning: 2

A Quilt of a Country: 3, 4, 5, 6

The Immigrant Contribution: 7, 8, 9, 10

American History: 11, 12, 13

Performance Task: 14, 15

WHOLE-CLASS LEARNING

CONTENTS

COMPARE

ANCHOR TEXT: ESSAY

A Quilt of a Country

Anna Quindlen

In the aftermath of the terror attacks of September 11, 2001, a journalist emphasizes the importance of diversity.

ANCHOR TEXT: ESSAY

The Immigrant Contribution

from A Nation of Immigrants

John F. Kennedy

Before he was president of the United States, John F. Kennedy described how the American way of life has been created by the efforts of immigrants.

ANCHOR TEXT: SHORT STORY

American History

Judith Ortiz Cofer

A girl faces challenges at school and at home on the day that President Kennedy is assassinated.

PERFORMANCE TASK

WRITING FOCUS

Write a Nonfiction Narrative

All three Whole-Class readings deal with issues of cultural diversity and citizenship in the United States. After reading, you will write your own nonfiction narrative about the topic of American identity.

Overview: Whole-Class Learning 11

Contents

Anchor Texts Preview the anchor texts and media with students to generate interest. Encourage students to discuss other texts they may have read or movies or television shows they may have seen that discuss or explore how Americans from different time periods define American identity.

You may wish to conduct a poll to determine which selection students think looks more interesting, and discuss the reasons for their preferences. Students can return to this poll after they have read the selections to see if their preferences changed.

Performance Task

Write a Nonfiction Narrative Explain to students that after they have finished reading the selections, they will write a nonfiction narrative about Americans from different time periods and whether those individuals see American identity differently. To help them prepare, encourage students to think about the topic as they progress through the selections and as they participate in the Whole-Class Learning experience.

Introduce Small-Group Learning

16

Rules of the Game

17 18

The Writing on the Wall

19 20

With a Little Help From My Friends

21 22

- Morning Talk
- Immigrant Picnic

23 24

Performance Task

25 26

Introduce Independent Learning

27

Independent Learning

28

Performance-Based Assessment

29 30

A Quilt of a Country

AUDIO SUMMARIES
Audio summaries of "A Quilt of a Country" are available in both English and Spanish in the Interactive Teacher's Edition or Unit Resources. Assigning these summaries prior to reading the selection may help students build additional background knowledge and set a context for their first read.

Summary

In her essay "A Quilt of a Country," Anna Quindlen compares America to a patchwork quilt made up many bits and pieces, just as America is made up of many different groups of people. She says that we can all live together as one nation, united by the principle that we are all created equal. The reality she describes, however, is that there is a lot of hostility and violence between the different groups. These different groups unite when America faces the threat of war. However, as soon as those threats go away, the divisions return. Even so, most Americans think of America as great because of its great diversity. They see that recent immigrant groups are like their own families, who worked hard to make it in America. Those who died in the World Trade Center attacks of September 11, 2001, reflected America's diversity. Americans feel patriotic towards the country that defines itself by the diversity of those who died.

Insight

Reading "A Quilt of a Country" will help students begin to reflect on the complicated nature of a nation made up of people from so many other nations, some of whom have fought wars over their cultural and religious differences. The author delivers criticism and praise in almost equal measure as she analyzes the paradox of America as a great nation.

ESSENTIAL QUESTION:
What does it mean to be "American"?

Connection to Essential Question

"A Quilt of a Country" provides a paradoxical perspective on the Essential Question. According to Quindlen, being American means dividing along lines of ethnicity, while simultaneously embracing the idea of "Out of many, one." The response of American people to the terrorism that brought down the World Trade Center and killed so many Americans of different ethnicities encapsulates a different and contradictory idea about America. It unified the American people in mourning for the loss of their fellow Americans.

WHOLE-CLASS LEARNING PERFORMANCE TASK
How does your generation define what it means to be an American today?

UNIT PERFORMANCE-BASED ASSESSMENT
How is an American identity created?

Connection to Performance Tasks

Whole-Class Learning Performance Task In this Performance Task, students will consider the concept of American identity as defined by people in different eras. "A Quilt of a Country" provides a contemporary perspective that refuses to whitewash the reality of life in America for so many, while at the same time embracing the diversity of America's population as integral to its identity.

Unit Performance-Based Assessment This selection suggests an American identity created through diversity and conflict and an American sense of national unity only when faced with enormous tragedy. However, the selection also acknowledges an American identity created through diversity and acceptance. Most patriotic Americans are proud to attribute America's unique greatness to its unique cultural diversity, and to identify themselves as contributors to that diversity.

DIGITAL PERSPECTIVES — Audio | Video | Document | Annotation Highlights | EL Highlights | Online Assessment

LESSON RESOURCES

	Making Meaning	Language Development
Lesson	**First Read** **Close Read** **Analyze the Text** **Analyze Craft and Structure**	**Concept Vocabulary** **Word Study** **Conventions**
Instructional Standards	**RI.10** By the end of grade 9, read and comprehend . . . **RI.5** Analyze in detail how an author's ideas . . . **RI.6** Determine an author's point of view . . .	**RI.4** Determine the meaning of words and phrases . . . **L.4.b** Identify and correctly use patterns of word changes . . .
STUDENT RESOURCES		
Available online in the Interactive Student Edition or Unit Resources	Selection Audio First-Read Guide: Nonfiction Close-Read Guide: Nonfiction	Word Network Evidence Log
TEACHER RESOURCES		
Selection Resources Available online in the Interactive Teacher's Edition or Unit Resources	Audio Summaries Annotation Highlights EL Highlights Analyze Craft and Structure: Purpose and Rhetoric English Language Support Lesson: Rhetoric	Concept Vocabulary and Word Study Author's Style: Word Choice
Reteach/Practice (RP) Available online in the Interactive Teacher's Edition or Unit Resources	Analyze Craft and Structure: Purpose and Rhetoric (RP)	Word Study: Latin Prefix *dis-* (RP) Author's Style: Word Choice (RP)
Assessment Available online in Assessments	Selection Test	
My Resources	A Unit 1 Answer Key is available online and in the Interactive Teacher's Edition.	

Reading Support

Text Complexity Rubric: A Quilt of a Country	
Quantitative Measures	
Lexile: 1310 **Text Length:** 1,082 words	
Qualitative Measures	
Knowledge Demands ①—②—③—❹—⑤	Numerous historical and literary references may be unfamiliar (names of historians, writers, theorists); many challenging abstract concepts; historical context necessary for selection written just after Sept 11, 2001.
Structure ①—②—③—❹—⑤	Complex structure and organization with multiple pathways that are not sequential or predictable; shifts between statements of political opinion and historical examples.
Language Conventionality and Clarity ①—②—③—❹—⑤	Long and complex sentences with multiple clauses and challenging vocabulary; abstract descriptions and metaphorical language.
Levels of Meaning/Purpose ①—②—③—❹—⑤	Multiple levels of meaning not always explicit; subtle concepts; abstract and theoretical elements.

DECIDE AND PLAN

English Language Support

Provide English Learners with support for context and vocabulary as they read the selection.

Knowledge Demands Ask students to listen actively as you share this background information. Tell students that the article was written just after September 11, 2001. They should expect to see language that describes architecture, politics, community, and terrorist tactics. Review the meaning of the word *quilt*.

Language Write the following words and phrases: *mongrel nation, calico, disparate parts, bits and pieces, splintered whole, one spirit*. Involve students in a discussion of the meaning of each word and phrase and relate it to the idea of America as a nation made up of many kinds of people.

Strategic Support

Provide students with strategic support to ensure that they can successfully read the text.

Knowledge Demands Use the background information to discuss America as a nation made up of many kinds of people. Determine students' prior knowledge and experience, historical and personal, of the advantages and disadvantages of American cultural diversity. Provide additional background if needed.

Meaning / Purpose Ask students to analyze the first two sentences and the last two sentences. Discuss reasons for the repetition of two key phrases: *improbable idea* and *mongrel nation*. Point out the word *spirit*, which appears only in the penultimate sentence. Discuss what it means to have one spirit in the context of the essay, as well as beyond the context of the essay.

Challenge

Provide students who need to be challenged with ideas for how they can go beyond a simple interpretation of the text.

Text Analysis Ask students to comment on how the author seeks to balance positive and negative elements in her discussion of America as a nation made up of many different kinds of people. Ask them to cite examples from the text of both positive and negative attitudes to similar aspects of being American.

Written Response Ask students to write an essay giving their own ideas about the advantages and disadvantages of being in a country made up of many different cultures. Encourage them to be specific, using examples from current events or from personal experience about people of different origins and cultures living in the same country.

TEACH

Read and Respond

Have the class do their first read of the selection. Then have them complete their close read. Finally, work with them on the Making Meaning and Language Development activities.

Standards Support Through Teaching and Learning Cycle

IDENTIFY NEEDS

Analyze results of the Beginning-of-Year Assessment, focusing on the items relating to Unit 1. Also take into consideration student performance to this point and your observations of where particular students struggle.

DECIDE AND PLAN

- If students have performed poorly on items matching these standards, then provide selection scaffolds before assigning them the on-level lesson provided in the Student Edition.
- If students have done well on the Beginning-of-Year Assessment, then challenge them to keep progressing and learning by giving them opportunities to practice the skills in depth.
- Use the Selection Resources listed on the Planning pages for "A Quilt of a Country" to help students continually improve their ability to master the standards.

Instructional Standards: A Quilt of a Country

	Catching Up	This Year	Looking Forward
Reading	You may wish to administer the **Analyze Craft and Structure: Purpose and Rhetoric (RP)** worksheet to help students distinguish among different purposes authors have for writing an informational selection. You may wish to administer the **Author's Style: Word Choice (RP)** worksheet to help students understand how vivid language and precise adjectives make informational writing more interesting and convincing.	**RI.6** Determine an author's point of view or purpose in a text and analyze how an author uses rhetoric to advance that point of view or purpose. **RI.4** Determine the meaning of words and phrases as they are used in a text, including figurative language, connotative and technical meanings; analyze the cumulative impact of specific word choices or meaning and tone.	Have students analyze the selection through the author's writing style and rhetorical choices—including choice of words, phrases, and figurative language. Ask students to explain how the author's rhetoric supports her purpose, as well as the power and beauty of the text.
Language	You may wish to administer the **Word Study: Latin Prefix *dis-* (RP)** worksheet to help students understand that the meaning of the prefix contributes to the overall meaning of a word, as in the words *disparate* and *discordant*.	**L.4.b** Identify and correctly use patterns of word changes that indicate different meanings or parts of speech.	Have students locate sentences in the selection in which words appear that contain the prefix *dis-*. Challenge them to determine the part of speech for each of those words, based on how they are used in the sentences.

TEACH

Implement the planned lesson, and gather evidence of student learning.

ANALYZE AND REVISE

- Analyze student work for evidence of student learning.
- Identify whether or not students have met the expectations in the standards.
- Identify implications for future instruction.

Jump Start

FIRST READ What is a patchwork quilt? Ask students to identify the single essential characteristic of a patchwork quilt that makes it different from other quilts. Engage students in a discussion about why patchwork quilts are so valued. Are the components valuable, or just the quilt as a whole?

A Quilt of a Country

Who is the author? How do you think her experience of working and living in New York City affects her view of the impact immigrant populations have had on the United States? Modeling the questions readers might ask as they read "A Quilt of a Country" for the first time brings the text alive for students and connects it to the Whole-Class Performance Task assignment. Selection audio and print capability for the selection are available in the Interactive Teacher's Edition.

Concept Vocabulary

Support students as they rank their words. Ask if they've ever heard, read or used the words. Reassure them that the definitions for these words are listed in the selection.

FIRST READ

As they read, students should perform the steps of the first read:

NOTICE: You may want to encourage students to notice details that present and support important ideas.

ANNOTATE: Remind students to mark passages that support the author's central ideas.

CONNECT: Encourage students to go beyond the text to make connections—When have they encountered times when differences and diversity were celebrated?

RESPOND: Students will answer questions and write a summary to demonstrate understanding.

Point out to students that while they will always complete the Respond step at the end of the first read, the other steps will probably happen somewhat concurrently. You may wish to print copies of the **First-Read Guide: Nonfiction** for students to use.

Remind students that during their first read, they should not answer the close-read questions that appear in the selection.

MAKING MEANING

A QUILT OF A COUNTRY

Comparing Texts

In this lesson, you will read and compare the essay "A Quilt of a Country" and the essay "The Immigrant Contribution." First, complete the first-read and close-read activities for "A Quilt of a Country." The work you do on this selection will help prepare you for the comparing task.

THE IMMIGRANT CONTRIBUTION

About the Author

Anna Quindlen (b. 1953) started working in the newspaper business at the age of 18 as an assistant. After graduating from Barnard College in 1974, she wrote for the *New York Post* and then for the *New York Times,* where her career in journalism began to flourish. She was only the third woman to have a column in the *Times's* Opinion Pages, for which she won a Pulitzer Prize in 1992. Three years later, Quindlen decided to leave the newspaper and pursue her passion for writing fiction. She has written several best-selling novels, as well as nonfiction and children's books.

Tool Kit
First-Read Guide and Model Annotation

STANDARDS
Reading Informational Text
By the end of grade 9, read and comprehend literary nonfiction in the grades 9–10 text complexity band proficiently, with scaffolding as needed at the high end of the range.

A Quilt of a Country

Concept Vocabulary

You will encounter the following words as you read "A Quilt of a Country." Before reading, note how familiar you are with each word. Then, rank them each on a scale of 1 (most familiar) to 6 (least familiar).

WORD	YOUR RANKING
disparate	
discordant	
pluralistic	
interwoven	
diversity	
coalescing	

After completing the first read, return to the concept vocabulary and review your rankings. Mark changes to your original rankings as needed.

First Read NONFICTION

Apply these strategies as you conduct your first read. You will have an opportunity to complete the close-read notes after your first read.

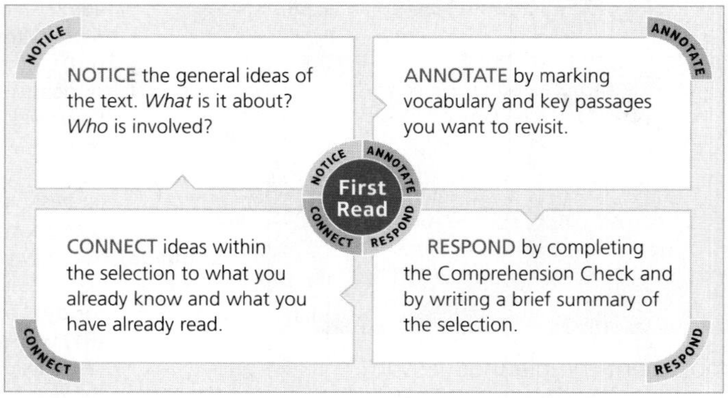

NOTICE
NOTICE the general ideas of the text. *What* is it about? *Who* is involved?
ANNOTATE
ANNOTATE by marking vocabulary and key passages you want to revisit.
First Read
NOTICE ANNOTATE CONNECT RESPOND
CONNECT ideas within the selection to what you already know and what you have already read.
RESPOND by completing the Comprehension Check and by writing a brief summary of the selection.
CONNECT
RESPOND

AUTHOR'S PERSPECTIVE **Kelly Gallagher, M.Ed.**

Teacher as the Best Reader in the Class Rather than being the wizard behind the curtain, use modeling to do the work of reading in front of students. When students see that even good readers wrestle with difficult text, they gain confidence. Use these methods:

- **Using think-alouds.** Choose a passage from this unit and model read alouds/think alouds to show students what effective readers do when they are confused. The *Annotate Question Conclude* feature and the teacher edition support the importance of this work. Additional suggestions include marking the texts in different colors for what is understood and what is not.

ANCHOR TEXT | ESSAY

A Quilt of a Country

Anna Quindlen

DIGITAL PERSPECTIVES

BACKGROUND

This essay was published in *Newsweek* magazine about two weeks after the terrorist attacks of September 11, 2001. In New York City, almost 3,000 people were killed when hijackers crashed two airliners into the World Trade Center. In Washington, D.C., 224 people were killed when a hijacked jet crashed into the Pentagon. On hijacked United Airlines Flight 93, passengers tried to regain control of the plane. All 44 people on board died when the aircraft crashed in a field near Shanksville, Pennsylvania.

SCAN FOR MULTIMEDIA

1 America is an improbable idea. A mongrel nation built of ever-changing **disparate** parts, it is held together by a notion, the notion that all men are created equal, though everyone knows that most men consider themselves better than someone. "Of all the

NOTES

disparate (DIHS puhr iht) *adj.* essentially different in kind

- **Marking the text.** If students say they don't understand, have them use a yellow highlighter (or sticky notes) for parts they understand and a pink highlighter for those they don't.
- **Using sentence starters.** To identify where students are having comprehension problems, have them complete this sentence starter: *I don't understand…* Then, as a class, work to resolve the issues. Use these additional sentence starters: *I noticed…; I wonder…; I think…; I'm surprised that…; I realized…; I'm not sure…*
- It is also important for students to know that applying tools like these doesn't always work: sometimes, readers decide to live with ambiguity.

TEACHING

CLOSE READ

Remind students to focus on the author's word choices as they read paragraph 2, and how word choice sets a mood for the text. You may wish to model the Close Read using the following think-aloud format. Possible responses to questions on the Student page are included. You may also want to print copies of the **Close-Read Guide: Nonfiction** for students to use.

ANNOTATE: As I read paragraph 2, I notice and mark the repeated adjective that I see here.

QUESTION: I wonder why the author chose to use the adjective *enormous* to describe two very different things. It seems like the author is trying to create a parallel between the tragedies and the blessings.

CONCLUDE: These details suggest that both tragedies and blessings can have a significant impact on people.

Additional **English Language Support** is available in the Digital Teacher's Edition.

NOTES

discordant (dihs KAWR duhnt) *adj.* unrelated; out of place

pluralistic (plur uh LIHS tihk) *adj.* having multiple parts or aspects

CLOSE READ

ANNOTATE: Reread the final sentence in paragraph 2. Mark the repeated adjective in this statement.

QUESTION: Why has the author chosen to use the same adjective to describe two very different things?

CONCLUDE: What effect does this deliberate use of repetition create?

nations in the world, the United States was built in nobody's image," the historian Daniel Boorstin wrote. That's because it was built of bits and pieces that seem **discordant**, like the crazy quilts that have been one of its great folk-art forms, velvet and calico[1] and checks and brocades.[2] Out of many, one. That is the ideal.

2 The reality is often quite different, a great national striving consisting frequently of failure. Many of the oft-told stories of the most **pluralistic** nation on earth are stories not of tolerance, but of bigotry. Slavery and sweatshops, the burning of crosses and the ostracism of the other. Children learn in social-studies class and in the news of the lynching of blacks, the denial of rights to women, the murders of gay men. It is difficult to know how to convince them that this amounts to "crown thy good with brotherhood," that amid all the failures is something spectacularly successful. Perhaps they understand it at this moment, when enormous tragedy, as it so often does, demands a time of reflection on enormous blessings.

3 This is a nation founded on a conundrum, what Mario Cuomo[3] has characterized as "community added to individualism." These two are our defining ideals; they are also in constant conflict. Historians today bemoan the ascendancy of a kind of prideful apartheid[4] in America, saying that the clinging to ethnicity, in background and custom, has undermined the concept of unity. These historians must have forgotten the past, or have gilded it. The New York of my children is no more Balkanized,[5] probably less so, than the Philadelphia of my father, in which Jewish boys would walk several blocks out of their way to avoid the Irish divide of Chester Avenue. (I was the product of a mixed marriage, across barely bridgeable lines: an Italian girl, an Irish boy. How quaint it seems now, how incendiary then.) The Brooklyn of Francie Nolan's famous tree,[6] the Newark of which Portnoy complained,[7] even the uninflected WASP[8] suburbs of Cheever's[9] characters: they are ghettos, pure and simple. Do the Cambodians and the Mexicans in California coexist less easily today than did the Irish and Italians of Massachusetts a century ago? You know the answer.

4 What is the point of this splintered whole? What is the point of a nation in which Arab cabbies chauffeur Jewish passengers through the streets of New York—and in which Jewish cabbies chauffeur Arab passengers, too, and yet speak in theory of hatred, one for the other? What is the point of a nation in which one part seems to be

1. **calico** *n.* printed cotton cloth
2. **brocades** *n.* fabrics with raised patterns in gold or silver.
3. **Mario Cuomo** politician and former New York governor.
4. **apartheid** (uh PAHR tyd) *n.* system of racial segregation and discrimination.
5. **Balkanized** *adj.* broken up into smaller, often hostile groups.
6. **Nolan's famous tree . . .** reference to Betty Smith's novel *A Tree Grows in Brooklyn.*
7. **the Newark of which Portnoy complained . . .** reference to Philip Roth's novel *Portnoy's Complaint.*
8. **WASP** short for white Anglo-Saxon Protestant; typically refers to a member of the dominant and most privileged class of people in the United States.
9. **Cheever's** reference to John Cheever, an American novelist and short story writer.

PERSONALIZE FOR LEARNING

English Language Support

Figurative Language Have students reread this sentence in paragraph 5: *Once these disparate parts were held together by a common enemy, by the fault lines of world wars and the electrified fence of communism.* Explain to students that this sentence contains an example of **metaphor**, a type of figurative language in which an expression describes a person or object by referring to something that is considered to possess similar characteristics.

Ask students why they think the author chose to use the metaphor to describe the common enemy. **ALL LEVELS**

always on the verge of fisticuffs with another, blacks and whites, gays and straights, left and right, Pole and Chinese and Puerto Rican and Slovenian? Other countries with such divisions have in fact divided into new nations with new names, but not this one, impossibly **interwoven** even in its hostilities.

5 Once these disparate parts were held together by a common enemy, by the fault lines of world wars and the electrified fence of communism. With the end of the cold war there was the creeping concern that without a focus for hatred and distrust, a sense of national identity would evaporate, that the left side of the hyphen—African-American, Mexican-American, Irish-American—would overwhelm the right. And slow-growing domestic traumas like economic unrest and increasing crime seemed more likely to emphasize division than community. Today the citizens of the United States have come together once more because of armed conflict and enemy attack. Terrorism has led to devastation—and unity.

6 Yet even in 1994, the overwhelming majority of those surveyed by the National Opinion Research Center agreed with this statement: "The U.S. is a unique country that stands for something special in the world." One of the things that it stands for is this vexing notion that a great nation can consist entirely of refugees from other nations, that people of different, even warring religions and cultures can live, if not side by side, then on either side of the country's Chester Avenues. Faced with this **diversity** there is little point in trying to isolate anything remotely resembling a national character, but there are two strains of behavior that, however tenuously, abet the concept of unity.

7 There is that Calvinist[10] undercurrent in the American psyche that loves the difficult, the demanding, that sees mastering the impossible, whether it be prairie or subway, as a test of character, and so glories in the struggle of this fractured **coalescing**. And there is a grudging fairness among the citizens of the United States that eventually leads most to admit that, no matter what the English-only advocates try to suggest, the new immigrants are not so different from our own parents or grandparents. Leonel Castillo, former director of the Immigration and Naturalization Service and himself the grandson of Mexican immigrants, once told the writer Studs Terkel proudly, "The old neighborhood Ma-Pa stores are still around. They are not Italian or Jewish or Eastern European any more. Ma and Pa are now Korean, Vietnamese, Iraqi, Jordanian, Latin American. They live in the store. They work seven days a week. Their kids are doing well in school. They're making it. Sound familiar?"

8 Tolerance is the word used most often when this kind of coexistence succeeds, but tolerance is a vanilla-pudding word, standing for little more than the allowance of letting others live

NOTES

interwoven (ihn tuhr WOH vuhn) *adj.* intermingled; combined

diversity (duh VUR suh tee) *n.* variety of different ethnic or cultural groups

coalescing (koh uh LEHS ihng) *n.* coming together in one body or place

10. **Calvinist** *adj.* related to Calvinism, a set of Christian beliefs based on the teachings of John Calvin that stresses God's power, the moral weakness of humans, the idea that one's destiny is set and unchangeable.

DIGITAL PERSPECTIVES

Enriching the Text To help students understand how "Ma and Pa" stores look, have them research photos of small shops in a variety of cities and neighborhoods over a period of time in U.S. history, particularly those in which the owners also live in or above the shops. Guide students to notice and evaluate the conditions of the stores and the types of people who own them. What conclusions can they draw about how modern day Ma and Pa store owners differ from the old neighborhood Ma and Pa store owners as discussed in paragraph 7?

CLOSER LOOK

Figurative Language

Students may have marked paragraph 8 during their first read. Use this paragraph to help students understand how the author uses figurative language to describe her feelings about ethnic diversity in America. Encourage them to talk about the annotations that they marked. You may want to model a close read with the class based on the highlights shown in the text.

ANNOTATE: Have students mark details in paragraph 8 that describe the author's feelings about the ethnic diversity found in America.

QUESTION: Guide students to consider what these details might tell them. Ask what a reader can infer from what was marked, and accept student responses.

Possible response: The author does not like the word *tolerance*, and compares it to vanilla pudding, which is symbolic of something that is bland.

CONCLUDE: Help students to formulate conclusions about the importance of these details in the text. Ask students why the author might have included these details.

Possible response: The details reveal that the author values ethnic diversity, but believes that people of varying backgrounds should not simply tolerate one another; rather, there should be more of a connection among those who inhabit this country.

Remind students that a **metaphor** is a figure of speech that compares two apparently unlike things without using the words *like, as, than,* or *resembles.* An **extended metaphor** is a metaphor that is sustained and developed over several lines or an entire literary work.

NOTES

unremarked and unmolested. Pride seems excessive, given the American willingness to endlessly complain about them, them being whoever is new, different, unknown or currently under suspicion. But patriotism is partly taking pride in this unlikely ability to throw all of us together in a country that across its length and breadth is as different as a dozen countries, and still be able to call it by one name. When photographs of the faces of all those who died in the World Trade Center destruction are assembled in one place, it will be possible to trace in the skin color, the shape of the eyes and the noses, the texture of the hair, a map of the world. These are the representatives of a mongrel nation that somehow, at times like this, has one spirit. Like many improbable ideas, when it actually works, it's a wonder. ❧

PERSONALIZE FOR LEARNING

English Language Support

Domain-Specific Vocabulary The domain-specific vocabulary that appears in "A Quilt of a Country" may present challenges to English Learners. Support them in understanding the text by reviewing the following terms:

Pride: an emotion that refers to an inflated sense of status

Patriotism: the devotion and dedication to one's country

Have students locate these terms in paragraph 8, and read the sentence containing each term. Then, have students rewrite the sentences, replacing the domain-specific term with its definition. **ALL LEVELS**

DIGITAL PERSPECTIVES

Comprehension Check

Complete the following items after you finish your first read.

1. According to Quindlen, what familiar object serves as an ideal representation of America?

2. According to Quindlen, how have people's attitudes about her being a product of a mixed marriage changed over time?

3. What does Quindlen think unified America's diverse ethnic groups before the end of the cold war?

4. According to Quindlen, how have other countries often handled deep ethnic divisions?

5. According to the former head of the Immigration and Naturalization Service, how are today's neighborhood stores similar to and different from the old neighborhood stores?

6. **Notebook** Write a summary of "A Quilt of a Country" to confirm your understanding of the essay.

RESEARCH

Research to Clarify Choose at least one unfamiliar detail from the text. Briefly research that detail. In what way does the information you learned shed light on an idea expressed in the essay?

Research to Explore Choose something that interests you from the text, and formulate a research question.

PERSONALIZE FOR LEARNING

Challenge

Conclusions Ask students about the impact of the last paragraph of the essay. Point out that the last paragraph of an essay often includes a conclusion, or take-away. Reread the last paragraph of the selection, asking students whether they think this final paragraph concludes the essay. Ask students to consider other final paragraphs that have had meaning for them. Then, have students write a short essay that compares and contrasts the final paragraphs of several articles, stories, or books they have read. What do these final paragraphs have in common? How are they different?

Comprehension Check

Possible Responses

1. A crazy quilt, since it is a single garment made from a number of distinct fabrics joined together.
2. The ethnic division that was previously unthinkable and full of strife is now barely noticeable and quaint; it would no longer even be considered a mixed marriage.
3. A common enemy and a division between America as a whole and an external threat, such as the Axis Powers in World War II or the Soviet Union in the cold war.
4. Other countries have often divided or partitioned, creating multiple countries without internal divisions of such scale; the United States has remained whole and coherent to the end.
5. They are alike in still having the same basic social role and success. They differ in that, rather than being run by Eastern European, Italian, or other immigrant populations from the early 1900s, the new Ma-Pa stores belong to a new wave of immigrants from Korea, Latin America, Vietnam, Iraq, and more.
6. The United States of America is a unique nation in that its national image is fluid and always changing. Like a crazy quilt, it is made of many different people. This has not always been a successful experience; history shows that great tragedy has come out of the fusion of many peoples from many places, but much good has come out of it as well. Distrust of "others" cannot be the only glue that holds a nation together. It takes a national consciousness that rises to challenges and is generally fair in its outlook. When this happens, it is a wonderful thing to behold and take pride in.

Research

Research to Clarify If students struggle to come up with a detail to research further, you may want to suggest that they choose a detail from the text that is evidence of a "splintered whole."

Research to Explore If students struggle to come up with a research topic, you may want to suggest that they focus on one of the following topics: national identity; historic events that have brought Americans together; patchwork quilts.

Jump Start

CLOSE READ Ask students what they know about quilts. Dig deeper into the title, creating an analogy between America's diverse population and quilts. Explain that quilts come together through a series of patches. The patches are sewn together to create one big piece of fabric. The stitches must be sewn tight to prevent the patches from falling apart. Ask students if they think that America could fall apart if the seams were not strong enough.

Close Read the Text

Walk students through the annotation model on the Student page. Encourage them to complete items 2 and 3 on their own. Review and discuss the sections students have marked. If needed, continue to model close reading by using the Annotation Highlights in the Interactive Teacher's Edition.

Analyze the Text

Possible responses:

1. (a) Mario Cuomo's conundrum is that America thrives on individualism, yet Americans must accept the idea that we are all bound together as a community in order to survive as a nation. (paragraph 3) **DOK 2** (b) This detail supports Quindlen's key metaphor: we are multicultural nation of diverse ethnicity, but we are unified as one people under one government. (paragraph 1) **DOK 2**
2. (a) The idea that the United States is "a mongrel nation," the result of many different ethnic groups that become unified as one, makes it pointless to try and isolate any one group as uniquely American. (paragraph 1) **DOK 1** (b) One quality she proposes as essentially American is the belief in rewarding, difficult work that allows one to "get ahead." **DOK 2**
3. (a) The ethnic groups of today interact in the same ways that the ethnic groups of earlier time periods did. (b) Quindlen likely wants readers to come to this conclusion on their own.
4. **Responses will vary.**

FORMATIVE ASSESSMENT

Analyze the Text

- **If** students fail to cite evidence, **then** remind them to support their ideas with specific information.
- **If** students fail to understand the ways in which immigrants view American beliefs, **then** remind them to find examples of ethnic tensions in the text.

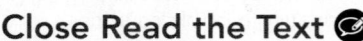

A QUILT OF A COUNTRY

Close Read the Text

1. The model, from paragraph 5 of the essay, shows two sample annotations, along with questions and conclusions. Close read the passage and find another detail to annotate. Then, write a question and your conclusion.

Close Read — ANNOTATE · QUESTION · CONCLUDE

ANNOTATE: These phrases make comparisons between people's emotions and physical barriers placed by warring nations.

QUESTION: Why does the author use these comparisons?

CONCLUDE: The comparisons create a sense of danger and clarify the idea of a "common enemy."

Once these disparate parts were held together by a common enemy, by the fault lines of world wars and the electrified fence of communism. With the end of the cold war there was the creeping concern that without a focus for hatred and distrust, a sense of national identity would evaporate, that the left side of the hyphen—African-American, Mexican-American, Irish-American—would overwhelm the right.

ANNOTATE: These words characterize a new concern that arose at the end of the cold war.

QUESTION: What do these words suggest about the nature of the problem?

CONCLUDE: "Creeping" suggests that the problem grew slowly and secretly. "Evaporate" adds that it was hidden and not immediately noticed.

Tool Kit
Close-Read Guide and Model Annotation

2. For more practice, go back into the text, and complete the close-read notes.
3. Revisit a section of the text you found important during your first read. Read this section closely, and **annotate** what you notice. Ask yourself **questions** such as "Why did the author choose these words?" What can you **conclude**?

Analyze the Text

CITE TEXTUAL EVIDENCE to support your answers.

Notebook Respond to these questions.

1. (a) **Analyze** Explain Mario Cuomo's conundrum. (b) How does this detail contribute to the development of Quindlen's ideas?
2. (a) **Generalize** Why is Quindlen reluctant to define "anything remotely resembling a national character"? (b) **Connect** What qualities does she propose are essentially American? Explain.
3. (a) **Deduce** At the end of paragraph 3, Quindlen says, "You know the answer." Explain what that answer is. (b) **Interpret** Why do you think she leaves that answer open-ended?
4. **Essential Question:** ***What does it mean to be "American"?*** What have you learned about American identity from reading this essay?

STANDARDS
Reading Informational Text
• Analyze in detail how an author's ideas or claims are developed and refined by particular sentences, paragraphs, or larger portions of a text.
• Determine an author's point of view or purpose in a text and analyze how an author uses rhetoric to advance that point of view or purpose.

WriteNow Analyze and Interpret

Reflection Have students write a short reflection about how immigrants may experience America. How might immigrants feel about this country's values? Do they think people in America are really equal? Encourage students to draw upon the text for examples of ethnic diversity. Is this country strong enough to support its diverse population? Why or why not?

Analyze Craft and Structure

Purpose and Rhetoric An **author's purpose** is his or her reason for writing. The four general purposes for writing are to inform, to persuade, to entertain, and to reflect. Writers also have specific purposes for writing that vary with the topic and occasion. A writer may want to explain a particular event or reach a special audience. Those intentions shape the choices the writer makes, including those of structure and **rhetoric**, or language devices.

Anna Quindlen organizes this essay around a central **analogy**—a comparison of two unlike things that works to clarify an idea. Quindlen was moved to write this essay shortly after the terrorist attacks of September 11, 2001. Consider how her purpose and use of analogy reflect the concerns of that moment in history.

Practice

CITE TEXTUAL EVIDENCE to support your answers.

Notebook **Respond to these questions.**

1. **(a)** Identify three details in the first paragraph that support Quindlen's idea that America is a mash-up of different cultures. **(b)** According to Quindlen, what "notion" unites American culture into a single whole?
2. For Quindlen, why does the idea of a crazy quilt capture a tension at the heart of American culture?
3. **(a)** Use the chart to explain how each passage adds to Quindlen's analogy of the crazy quilt. **(b)** Select a fourth passage from the essay that you think belongs on the chart. Explain your choice.

PARAGRAPH	PASSAGE	HOW IT DEVELOPS THE ANALOGY
2	*Many of the oft-told stories . . . ostracism of the other.*	This presents a contrasting image of America, one of disharmony, which is shown to be no more representative than one of unity.
4	*Other countries with such . . . even in its hostilities.*	The uniqueness of the American situation is stressed, as well as the combination of distinct parts, which is what the quilt best represents.
8	*When photographs of the faces . . . a map of the world.*	This makes for a direct comparison between the visual appearance of a quilt and the mosaic of different American faces that will be seen.
8	(b) "this unlikely ability ... by one name."	(b) By stressing the combination of many elements into a single whole, and the singular nature of that whole, this supports the analogy of a quilt.

4. Why might the analogy of a quilt have seemed fitting at a time that the nation was suffering from a great trauma? Explain.

DIGITAL PERSPECTIVES

Analyze Craft and Structure

Discuss with students why an author might choose to use rhetoric or language devices, such as analogy or imagery, in a text. Have them think about the advantages and disadvantages of doing so. How does rhetoric shape the text? How does it establish the author's purpose? Students should recognize that the author uses the quilt analogy to develop her central ideas. For more support, see **Analyze Craft and Structure: Purpose and Rhetoric.**

Practice

Possible responses:

1. (a) "Built in nobody's image"; "built of bits and pieces"; "out of many, one"; (b) The notion that unites American culture is that a great nation can consist entirely of refugees from other nations and be woven together of different and even opposing cultures.
2. The crazy quilt is a coherent whole with a particular artistic quality that only arises from the combination of many very different elements.
3. **See possible responses in chart on student page.**
4. A quilt is a familiar, comforting item, and at the time Americans felt in need of comfort and togetherness.

FORMATIVE ASSESSMENT

Analyze Craft and Structure

- **If** students fail to identify the author's purpose, **then** direct them back to the main ideas the author develops in the text.
- **If** students are unable to cite evidence of rhetoric used in the text, **then** have students locate instances in which the author uses analogies to make comparisons.

For Reteach and Practice, see **Analyze Craft and Structure: Purpose and Rhetoric (RP).**

PERSONALIZE FOR LEARNING

English Language Support

Rhetoric Have English learners discuss how rhetoric is used to get a point across and to achieve the intended effect on readers.

Ask pairs of students to work together to write a mock political speech. Tell them to use an analogy in their speech, and suggest that the analogy refer to the economy. For example, a comparison could be made between a struggling economy and a sputtering car. **EMERGING**

Ask students to independently write a mock political speech. Tell them to use an analogy in their speech, and suggest that the analogy refer to the tensions among ethnic groups. For example, a comparison could be made between ethnic tensions and a tug-of-war competition. **EXPANDING**

Ask students to write a mock political speech independently. Tell them to use an analogy in their speech, and suggest that the analogy refer to e-commerce. **BRIDGING**

An expanded **English Language Support Lesson** on Rhetoric is available in the Interactive Teacher's Edition.

Concept Vocabulary

Why These Words

Possible responses:

1. Words that emphasize *unity* include: *interwoven* and *coalescing*. Words that emphasize *fragmentation* include: *disparate*, *discordant*, and *diversity*. The word *pluralistic* emphasizes both fragmentation and unity.
2. *bits and pieces, tolerance, conundrum, unity, Balkanized, coexist, splintered, common, fault lines, distrust, national identity,* and *fractured.*

Practice

Possible responses:

1. pluralistic, disparate, discordant, diversity, coalescing, interwoven
2. Responses will vary. Students should identify context clues within each sentence that help them identify the missing word's part of speech and meaning.

Word Network

Possible words: *community, folk-art, tolerance, brotherhood, custom*

Word Study

For more support, see **Concept Vocabulary and Word Study**

Possible responses:

1. disbelieve, "not believe"; disappear, "go away"; discomfort, "lack of comfort"
2. distrust, "lack of trust"

FORMATIVE ASSESSMENT

Concept Vocabulary

If students fail to see the connection between the words, **then** have them use each word in a sentence and think about what is similar about the sentences.

Word Study

If students fail to use prefixes correctly, **then** have them create a list of five common prefixes and write one word using each one, using each word in a sentence. For Reteach and Practice, see **Word Study: Latin Prefix: *dis-* (RP).**

LANGUAGE DEVELOPMENT

A QUILT OF A COUNTRY

Concept Vocabulary

disparate	pluralistic	diversity
discordant	interwoven	coalescing

Why These Words? These concept words convey unity and fragmentation. For example, at the beginning of the first paragraph, the author describes America as "a mongrel nation built of ever-changing disparate parts." The word *mongrel*, a mixed-breed dog, reinforces the idea of disparate elements that come together to form a unique whole.

1. Which concept vocabulary words contribute to the idea of unity, and which contribute to the idea of fragmentation?
2. What other words in the selection connect to the concepts of unity and fragmentation?

WORD NETWORK

Add interesting words related to American identity from the text to your Word Network.

Practice

Notebook The concept vocabulary words appear in "A Quilt of a Country."

1. Use the concept vocabulary words to complete the paragraph.

   America is a _____ society, a nation in which groups of people from many _____ backgrounds come together to live. The members of these groups often raise their voices in disagreement, but their _____ opinions are essential to our democracy. Despite the great _____ of America's population, Americans find ways to bridge their differences, usually by _____ around important social, economic, or political principles. Indeed, the strength of our nation seems to originate from the _____ strands that create its fabric.
2. Write the context clues that help you determine the correct words.

Word Study

Latin prefix: *dis-* The prefix *dis-* shows negation or expresses the idea of being apart or away. In the word *discordant, dis-* combines with the Latin root *-cord-,* meaning "heart." Over time, the word became associated with music that was harsh or out of tune. Today, *discordant* is often used to describe anything that is out of place.

1. Write another word you know that begins with the prefix *dis-*. Explain how the prefix helps you understand the meaning of the word.
2. Reread paragraph 5 of "A Quilt of a Country." Mark a word (other than *disparate*) that begins with the prefix *dis-*. Write a definition for the word.

STANDARDS

Reading Informational Text
Determine the meaning of words and phrases as they are used in a text, including figurative, connotative, and technical meanings; analyze the cumulative impact of specific word choices on meaning and tone.

Language
Identify and correctly use patterns of word changes that indicate different meanings or parts of speech.

AUTHOR'S PERSPECTIVE Elfrieda Hiebert, Ph.D.

Author's Word Choice Teachers can show the power of vocabulary to convey theme by selecting a text from the unit and guiding students to find words and phrases that are part of a network. The words should be related because of their denotations, connotations, or imagery. Model for students how to choose words that belong in a network. For example, if the passage describes cooking, students can select words from the passage such as *warm, clean, fragrant,* and *sweetness*. Be sure the list is narrowly focused and students can explain the relationship among the words and why they chose each word. Then have students explore the effect of the words and explain how they convey the author's ideas and make the text richer.

Author's Style

Word Choice Fiction writers and poets are not the only ones who choose words carefully. Nonfiction writers like Anna Quindlen also use **vivid language**, or strong, precise words, to bring ideas to life and to communicate them forcefully. Strong verbs and precise adjectives make informational writing more interesting and convincing.

Ordinary adjective: We sailed through the *rough* water.
Precise adjective: We sailed though the *churning* water.

Ordinary verb: I *fell* into the hole.
Strong verb: I *tumbled* into the hole.

Read It

Read the passages from "A Quilt of a Country" and identify the precise adjectives and strong verbs in each one. Then, rewrite each passage, changing the vivid word choices to ordinary ones. Explain how Quindlen's original word choices contribute to the accuracy and liveliness of her writing. Use the chart to record your answers.

PASSAGE	PRECISE ADJECTIVE OR STRONG VERB	REWRITE	EFFECT
What is the point of this splintered whole? (paragraph 4)	splintered	What is the point of this broken whole?	makes the kind of break – into many small parts – clear.
Historians today bemoan . . . (paragraph 3)	bemoan	Historians today complain…	makes the historians seem less petty and more somber
. . . but tolerance is a vanilla-pudding word . . . (paragraph 8)	vanilla-pudding	…but tolerance is a bland word…	emphasizes how weak and unimpressive the word is
And there is a grudging fairness among the citizens of the United States . . . (paragraph 7)	grudging	And there is a reluctant fairness among the citizens of the United States	expresses the scope and emotional tenor of the reluctance

Write It

Notebook **Revise each sentence by replacing verbs or adjectives with stronger, more vivid word choices.**

1. The crowd yelled at the player after the game.
2. Eloise was happy when she got her driver's license.
3. The campers carried their gear through the tall grass.
4. The garbage smelled bad after it was in the sun.

CROSS-CURRICULAR PERSPECTIVE

Art Have students find images on the Internet that depict immigrants or immigration. Ask them to write down what they see and how the pictures make them feel. What do the images mean? What kinds of stories do these images tell? Ask students to share their images and ideas in small groups.

DIGITAL PERSPECTIVES

Author's Style

Discuss word choice with students. Explain that words are powerful tools for persuasion and that they can be used to influence how the reader feels. Making deliberate word choices is a strategy for authors to increase their ability to encourage others to agree with their beliefs. Some words are more powerful than others. Have students come up with a list of strong words and a list of weak words related to the topic of conflict. For more support, see **Author's Style: Word Choice.**

MAKE IT INTERACTIVE

Have students write a sentence in which they must argue for something they want at school, such as longer lunchtime. Then, have the students rewrite their sentence using "stronger" words. Ask students to talk about whether their stronger sentences are more convincing than the original sentences.

Read It

See possible responses in chart on Student page.

Write It

Possible responses:

1. The crowd *screeched* at the player after the game.
2. Eloise was *ecstatic* when she got her driver's license.
3. The campers *lugged* their gear through the tall grass.
4. The garbage *reeked* horribly after it was in the sun.

Evidence Log Support students in completing their Evidence Log. This paced activity will help prepare them for the Performance-Based Assessment at the end of the unit.

FORMATIVE ASSESSMENT

Author's Style

- **If** students cannot identify the author's strategic word choice, **then** have them pinpoint sentences that evoke a strong feeling.

For Reteach and Practice, see **Author's Style: Word Choice (RP).**

Selection Test

Administer the "A Quilt of a Country" Selection Test, which is available in both print and digital formats online in Assessments.

The Immigrant Contribution

AUDIO SUMMARIES
Audio summaries of "The Immigrant Contribution" are available in both English and Spanish in the Interactive Teacher's Edition or Unit Resources. Assigning these summaries prior to reading the selection may help students build additional background knowledge and set a context for their first read.

Summary

In his essay, "The Immigrant Contribution," John F. Kennedy celebrates America as a country of immigrants. Immigrants were among the signers of the Declaration of Independence. Since 1776, every immigrant seeking freedom from injustice has strengthened America's dedication to liberty. Immigrants have contributed to the economy. He recognizes the contribution of immigrants whose labor made America's industrial greatness possible. Immigrants figure among our greatest writers, artists, architects, and musicians. The cultural influence of immigrants is apparent in the way we talk, the food we eat, and the ways we worship. Life for immigrants as strangers in a new country can be hard, and communities can be unwelcoming. Coming to America, however, is an act of hope for a better life – and keeping that hope alive is the greatest contribution an immigrant can make to America.

Insight

Reading "The Immigrant Contribution" will help students understand the crucial part that immigrants have played historically in the creation, development, and success of America and understand why this country's future wealth and vitality depend on continuing immigration. The essay will also help students begin to understand why Kennedy was so popular in his time and why he continues to be admired. Kennedy interprets American history as progress, each generation building on the achievements of the last. His view of his own times is always optimistic – he regards the hardships of new immigrants as useful and necessary for the future citizens, and although his terminology reflects a different time period, his ideas about expanding the rights and opportunities of "the Negro" quickly became part of a progressive policy.

ESSENTIAL QUESTION:
What does it mean to be "American"?

Connection to Essential Question

"The Immigrant Contribution" addresses the Essential Question by honoring the diversity of America. Kennedy suggests that to be American means that we recognize and appreciate the various immigrant groups who have settled here at various times in our history, along with the contributions they have made to the nation.

WHOLE-CLASS LEARNING PERFORMANCE TASK
How does your generation define what it means to be an American today?

UNIT PERFORMANCE-BASED ASSESSMENT
How is an American identity created?

Connection to Performance Tasks

Whole-Class Learning Performance Task In this Performance Task, students will consider the idea of American identity as defined by their own generation. "The Immigrant Contribution" takes an optimistic view. Students will have the option of referring to this perspective, as well as the perspectives provided in the other selections in this module, when they write their narratives.

Unit Performance-Based Assessment This selection proposes that an American identity is created through the active pursuit of the American dream. As immigrants embrace American ideals, seek to create better lives, and contribute to the culture and success of America as a nation, the very core of what it means to be American is reinforced.

DIGITAL PERSPECTIVES — Audio | Video | Document | Annotation Highlights | EL Highlights | Online Assessment

LESSON RESOURCES

	Making Meaning	Language Development	Effective Expression
Lesson	**First Read** **Close Read** **Analyze the Text** **Analyze Craft and Structure**	**Concept Vocabulary** **Word Study** **Conventions**	**Writing to Compare**
Instructional Standards	**RI.10** By the end of grade 9, read and comprehend . . . **RI.5** Analyze in detail how an author's ideas . . . **RI.6** Determine an author's point of view . . .	**L.4.b** Identify and correctly use patterns . . . **L.1.b** Use various types of phrases and clauses . . .	**RI.4** Determine the meaning of words and phrases . . . **W.2** Write informative/explanatory texts . . . **W.9.b** Apply grades 9–10 Reading standards . . .
STUDENT RESOURCES			
Available online in the Interactive Student Edition or Unit Resources	Selection Audio First-Read Guide: Nonfiction Close-Read Guide: Nonfiction	Word Network	Evidence Log
TEACHER RESOURCES			
Selection Resources Available online in the Interactive Teacher's Edition or Unit Resources	Audio Summaries Annotation Highlights EL Highlights Analyze Craft and Structure: Purpose and Persuasion	Concept Vocabulary and Word Study Conventions: Sentence Types English Language Support Lesson: Independent and Dependent Clauses	Writing to Compare: Essay
Reteach/Practice (RP) Available online in the Interactive Teacher's Edition or Unit Resources	Analyze Craft and Structure: Purpose and Persuasion (RP)	Word Study: Latin Root *-nat-* (RP) Conventions: Sentence Types (RP)	
Assessment Available online in Assessments	Selection Test		
My Resources	A Unit 1 Answer Key is available online and in the Interactive Teacher's Edition.		

Reading Support

Text Complexity Rubric: The Immigrant Contribution	
Quantitative Measures	
Lexile: 1320 **Text Length:** 1,702 words	
Qualitative Measures	
Knowledge Demands (1–2–**3**–4–5)	Text explores themes of varying levels of complexity that may be unfamiliar (contribution and influence of immigrants on the US in areas of culture, religion, science and industry).
Structure (1–2–**3**–4–5)	Text is dense and covers a variety of points. Paragraph structure helps, as each paragraph covers a different aspect of immigrant contribution, supported by examples.
Language Conventionality and Clarity (1–2–3–**4**–5)	Many long sentences with multiple clauses, conditional phrases *(If we were to restrict….we would have to … our society would have… if they had..)*, and difficult vocabulary
Levels of Meaning/Purpose (1–2–**3**–4–5)	Purpose of text is clear and explicit (exploring the contribution of immigrants). However, some of the concepts and details throughout the text are intricate or theoretical.

DECIDE AND PLAN

English Language Support

Provide English Learners with support for structure and language as they read the selection.

Structure Help students to use the paragraph structure to outline the main ideas of the text. As students read, guide them to highlight sentences, phrases, or words in each paragraph that give information about the main idea of that paragraph - for example, (paragraph 2) *two great hopes, personal freedom, economic opportunity*.

Language Students may need help understanding complex sentences and difficult vocabulary. Encourage them to highlight and prepare long or complex sentences for analysis. Help to define key phrases that suggest the main ideas of each paragraph -for example, (paragraph 14) *adjustment and assimilation*.

Strategic Support

Provide students with strategic support to ensure that they can successfully read the text.

Knowledge Demands Discuss the meaning of the two words in the title, *immigrant* and *contribution*. Point out that the selection will cover many kinds of contributions. List areas of interest for them to look for as they read - for example, professions and arts, religion, industrialists, scientists, vocabulary, foods.

Meaning/Purpose Stop to discuss the main point of each paragraph - for example, (paragraph 14) *This paragraph talks about some of the difficulties of being an immigrant*. Then ask students to find and discuss an example of that point in that paragraph – what it means, why it was chosen, etc. *(racketeers, unscrupulous businessmen)*.

Challenge

Provide students who need to be challenged with ideas for how they can go beyond a simple interpretation of the text.

Text Analysis Have students reread paragraph 14 on adjustment and assimilation. Discuss this line: *The ideal of the "melting pot" symbolized the process of blending many strains into a single nationality, and we have come to realize in modern times that the "melting pot" need not mean the end of particular ethnic identities or traditions.* Ask students to explain the difference between blending cultures and maintaining cultural identity, and to give their opinion on which is preferable.

Read and Research Have students research information about JFK, the background of the book *A Nation of Immigrants*, and why he wrote it. Have them read additional excerpts from the book.

TEACH

Read and Respond

Have the class do their first read of the selection. Then, have them complete their close read. Finally, work with them on the Making Meaning, Language Development, and Effective Expression activities.

Standards Support Through Teaching and Learning Cycle

IDENTIFY NEEDS

Analyze results of the Beginning-of-Year Assessment, focusing on the items relating to Unit 1. Also take into consideration student performance to this point and your observations of where particular students struggle.

DECIDE AND PLAN

- If students have performed poorly on items matching these standards, then provide selection scaffolds before assigning them the on-level lesson provided in the Student Edition.
- If students have done well on the Beginning-of-Year Assessment, then challenge them to keep progressing and learning by giving them opportunities to practice the skills in depth.
- Use the Selection Resources listed on the Planning pages for "The Immigrant Contribution" to help students continually improve their ability to master the standards.

Instructional Standards: The Immigrant Contribution

Reading	You may wish to administer the **Conventions: Sentence Types (RP)** worksheet to help students understand the differences between independent and dependent clauses. You may wish to administer the **Analyze Craft and Structure: Purpose and Persuasion (RP)** worksheet to help students identify and distinguish among different ways in which authors successfully appeal to and persuade readers.	**L.1.b** Use various types of phrases and clauses to convey specific meanings and add variety and interest to writing or presentations. **RI.5** Analyze in detail how an author's ideas or claims are developed and refined by particular sentences, paragraphs, or larger portions of a text. **RI.6** Determine an author's point of view or purpose in a text and analyze how an author uses rhetoric to advance that point of view or purpose.	Have students examine a specific portion of the text, identifying the independent and dependent clauses and their impact on the meaning of the text. Ask students to identify sections of the text where the author is attempting to persuade the reader, and the type of persuasive appeal being used.
Language	You may wish to administer the **Word Study: The Latin Root *-nat-* (RP)** worksheet to help students understand that the meaning of a Latin root contributes to the overall meaning of a word, as in the word *national*.	**L.4.b** Identify and correctly use patterns of word changes that indicate different meanings or parts of speech.	Have students locate sentences in the selection in which words that contain the Latin root *-nat-* appear. Then challenge them to determine the part of speech for each of those words, based on how they are used in the sentences.

TEACH

Implement the planned lesson, and gather evidence of student learning.

ANALYZE AND REVISE

- Analyze student work for evidence of student learning.
- Identify whether or not students have met the expectations in the standards.
- Identify implications for future instruction.

TEACHING

Jump Start

FIRST READ Prior to students' first read, discuss examples of immigrant contributions that have become part of American culture. Which foods do they enjoy from other ethnic groups? What are some local street or city names that come from languages other than English? What are some inventions from immigrants?

The Immigrant Contribution

Who is the author? How might JFK's family history have shaped his opinions of immigrants and their contributions to America? What might his purpose be for writing? Modeling questions such as these will help students connect to "The Immigrant Contribution" and to the performance task assignment. Selection audio and print capability for the selection are available in the Interactive Teacher's Edition.

Concept Vocabulary

Support students as they rank their words. Ask if they've ever heard, read, or used them. Reassure them that the definitions for these words are listed in the selection.

FIRST READ

As they read, students should perform these steps:

NOTICE: Encourage students to notice the author's definition and description of immigrants.

ANNOTATE: Remind students to mark key passages, such as the ones that illuminate the author's depiction of immigrants. Students may want to revisit these passages in their close read.

CONNECT: Encourage students to make connections to their own family histories. Did their families come to the United States a very long time ago or very recently? Ask them how they might have felt coming to a new country.

RESPOND: Students will answer questions and write a summary to demonstrate understanding.

You may wish to print copies of the **First-Read Guide: Nonfiction** for students to use.

Remind students that during their first read, they should not answer the close-read questions that appear in the selection.

MAKING MEANING

Comparing Texts

You will now read "The Immigrant Contribution," which is a chapter from *A Nation of Immigrants*. First, complete the first-read and close-read activities. Then, compare the author's purpose and use of persuasive techniques in "A Quilt of a Country" with those of "The Immigrant Contribution."

About the Author

Born into a family of politicians, **John F. Kennedy** (1917–1963) did not take schooling seriously and was known as a trickster in the classroom. In his junior year at Harvard University, he developed an interest in political philosophy and became more studious. After school, he served in the U.S. Navy during World War II. In 1961, he became the thirty-fifth president of the United States. Tragically, Kennedy was assassinated on November 22, 1963, in Dallas, Texas.

Tool Kit
First-Read Guide and Model Annotation

STANDARDS
Reading Informational Text
By the end of grade 9, read and comprehend literary nonfiction in the grades 9–10 text complexity band proficiently, with scaffolding as needed at the high end of the range.

The Immigrant Contribution

Concept Vocabulary

You will encounter the following words as you read "The Immigrant Contribution." Before reading, note how familiar you are with each word. Then, rank the words in order from most familiar (1) to least familiar (6).

WORD	YOUR RANKING
descendants	
stock	
minority	
naturalization	
factions	
assimilation	

After completing the first read, come back to the concept vocabulary and review your rankings. Mark any changes to your original rankings.

First Read NONFICTION

Apply these strategies as you conduct your first read. You will have an opportunity to complete the close-read notes after your first read.

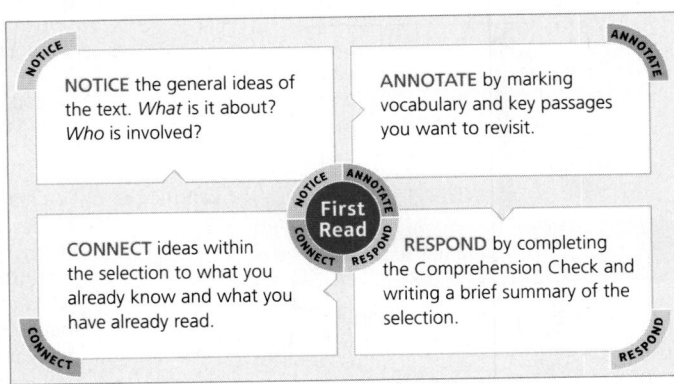

NOTICE the general ideas of the text. *What* is it about? *Who* is involved?

ANNOTATE by marking vocabulary and key passages you want to revisit.

CONNECT ideas within the selection to what you already know and what you have already read.

RESPOND by completing the Comprehension Check and writing a brief summary of the selection.

22 UNIT 1 • AMERICAN VOICES

VOCABULARY DEVELOPMENT

Word Map Have students fill out a word map for the word *descendant*. **Possible responses** are shown here.

descendant

Definition in your own words
The children or the lineage of children from a person.

Synonyms
heir, offspring, kin

Antonyms
ascendant, parent, origin, predecessor

Use it in a sentence
Although I was born in the United States, I am the ***descendant*** of people from Spain.

DIGITAL PERSPECTIVES

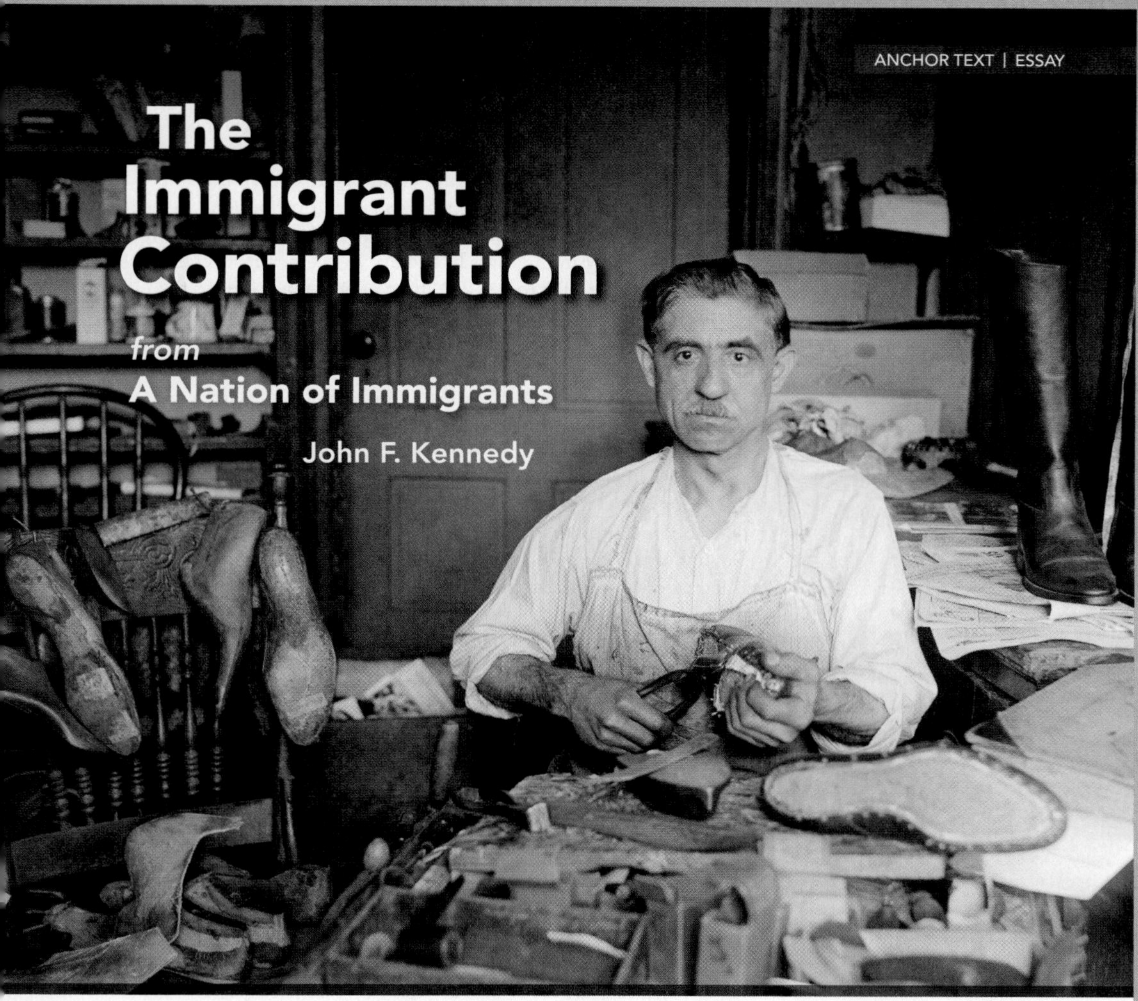

ANCHOR TEXT | ESSAY

The Immigrant Contribution

from **A Nation of Immigrants**

John F. Kennedy

BACKGROUND

John F. Kennedy wrote the book from which this excerpt was taken when he was a United States senator. He was a prominent supporter of immigrant rights, and ran for president on a platform that included the extension of those rights. He opposed legal distinctions between native-born and naturalized citizens, stating, "There is no place for second-class citizenship in America." He greatly influenced and inspired the immigration reforms of the late twentieth century.

SCAN FOR MULTIMEDIA

1 Oscar Handlin has said, "Once I thought to write a history of the immigrants in America. Then I discovered that the immigrants *were* American history." In the same sense, we cannot really speak of a particular "immigrant contribution" to America because all Americans have been immigrants or the **descendants** of immigrants;

NOTES

descendants (dih SEHN duhnts) *n.* people who are the offspring of an ancestor

DIGITAL PERSPECTIVES

Illuminating the Text To help students understand how the country viewed immigrants, invite them to watch clips from John F. Kennedy's Anti-Defamation League address, "We Are a Nation of Immigrants." Then, have students evaluate the purpose of Kennedy's speech and how the video provided insight into the text. Encourage students to discuss whether they believe the speech was, or was not, effective, and explain why.

TEACHING

CLOSE READE

Remind students to focus on the author's purpose. You may wish to model the Close Read using the following think-aloud format. Possible responses to questions on the Student page are included. You may also want to print copies of the **Close-Read Guide: Nonfiction** for students to use.

ANNOTATE: As I read paragraph 1, I notice and highlight the sentence containing the pronouns that Kennedy uses.

QUESTION: I wonder why JFK uses these pronouns. It seems as though he is trying to include everyone when he describes immigrants.

CONCLUDE: The pronouns create a sense of inclusiveness, which helps aid in persuasion. If I am a member of *we*, then I am more likely to arrive on the same side of the argument.

NOTES

CLOSE READ

ANNOTATE: In paragraph 1, mark the pronouns Kennedy uses.

QUESTION: How do these pronouns show that Kennedy is trying to connect with the reader?

CONCLUDE: What is the effect of using this approach in an essay about a social issue?

stock (stok) *n.* descendants of a particular individual or ethnic group; family or lineage

minority (muh NAWR uh tee) *n.* group of people that differs in some way from the larger population

naturalization (NACH uhr uh luh ZAY shuhn) *n.* process of becoming a citizen

even the Indians, as mentioned before, migrated to the American continent. We can only speak of people whose roots in America are older or newer. Yet each wave of immigration left its own imprint on American society; each made its distinctive "contribution" to the building of the nation and the evolution of American life. Indeed, if, as some of the older immigrants like to do, we were to restrict the definition of immigrants to the 42 million people who came to the United States *after* the Declaration of Independence, we would have to conclude that our history and our society would have been vastly different if they all had stayed at home.

2 As we have seen, people migrated to the United States for a variety of reasons. But nearly all shared two great hopes: the hope for personal freedom and the hope for economic opportunity. In consequence, the impact of immigration has been broadly to confirm the impulses in American life demanding more political liberty and more economic growth.

3 So, of the fifty-six signers of the Declaration of Independence, eighteen were of non-English **stock** and eight were first-generation immigrants. Two immigrants—the West Indian Alexander Hamilton, who was Washington's Secretary of the Treasury, and the Swiss Albert Gallatin, who held the same office under Jefferson—established the financial policies of the young republic. A German farmer wrote home from Missouri in 1834,

> If you wish to see our whole family living in . . . a country where freedom of speech obtains, where no spies are eavesdropping, where no simpletons criticize your every word and seek to detect therein a venom that might endanger the life of the state, the church and the home, in short, if you wish to be really happy and independent, then come here.

4 Every ethnic **minority**, in seeking its own freedom, helped strengthen the fabric of liberty in American life.

5 Similarly, every aspect of the American economy has profited from the contributions of immigrants. We all know, of course, about the spectacular immigrant successes: the men who came from foreign lands, sought their fortunes in the United States and made striking contributions, industrial and scientific, not only to their chosen country but to the entire world. In 1953 the President's Commission on Immigration and **Naturalization** mentioned the following:

6 Industrialists: Andrew Carnegie (Scot), in the steel industry; John Jacob Astor (German), in the fur trade; Michael Cudahy (Irish), of the meat-packing industry; the Du Ponts (French), of the munitions and chemical industry; Charles L. Fleischmann (Hungarian), of the yeast business; David Sarnoff (Russian), of the radio industry; and William S. Knudsen (Danish), of the automobile industry.

7 Scientists and inventors: Among those whose genius has benefited the United States are Albert Einstein (German), in physics; Michael

HOW LANGUAGE WORKS

Word Choice As students perform their Close Read, explain that the author chose his words very carefully in order to convey meaning and tone with elegance and style. Word choice, called **diction**, also creates clarity and evokes emotion, which are effective tools for persuasion. Instruct students to find words and word phrases related to immigrants on this page and analyze the persuasive effect of the author's word choice on the reader's perception.

Words and Word Phrases	Effects of Words (possible responses)
distinctive "contribution"	Immigrants giving (rather than taking) from our society
evolution of American life	Gives the impression that our country would be "less" if not for the contribution of immigrants
strengthen the fabric of liberty	Gives a sense that immigrants have made the U.S. stronger
spectacular immigrant successes	Makes readers feel fortunate that they benefit from the successes of immigrants. Using "spectacular" gives those successes more weight.

^ This photo shows the first Chinese telephone operator in San Francisco in the early part of the twentieth century.

NOTES

Pupin (Serbian), in electricity; Enrico Fermi (Italian) in atomic research; John Ericsson (Swedish), who invented the ironclad ship and the screw propeller; Giuseppe Bellanca (Italian) and Igor Sikorsky (Russian), who made outstanding contributions to airplane development; John A. Udden (Swedish), who was responsible for opening the Texas oil fields; Lucas P. Kyrides (Greek), industrial chemistry; David Thomas (Welsh), who invented the hot blast furnace; Alexander Graham Bell (Scot), who invented the telephone; Conrad Hubert (Russian), who invented the flashlight; and Ottmar Mergenthaler (German), who invented the linotype machine[1].

8 But the anonymous immigrant played his indispensable role too. Between 1880 and 1920 America became the industrial and agricultural giant of the world as well as the world's leading creditor nation.[2] This could not have been done without the hard labor, the technical skills and the entrepreneurial[3] ability of the 23.5 million people who came to America in this period.

1. **linotype machine** printing machine that sets type in whole lines, instead of letter by letter, in order to print faster.
2. **creditor nation** country that owes less money to other countries than other countries owe to it.
3. **entrepreneurial** (on truh pruh NUR ee uhl) *adj.* related to being an entrepreneur, or someone who starts a business and is willing to risk loss in order to make money.

Additional **English Language Support** is available in the Interactive Teacher's Edition.

PERSONALIZE FOR LEARNING

English Language Support

Figurative Language Figurative language can be confusing to English learners. Explain that the term *giant* in paragraph 8 is used to express that the United States was a leader in the world in industrial and agricultural progress. It compares the country to a very large figure or person that is much bigger than others. The narrator could have expressed this fact with literal wording, but chose to use the word *giant*.

Ask students why they think the author chose to use figurative language to describe the United States.

Possible response: The use of figurative language creates an emotion that literal language would not evoke. It makes readers believe that the United States was (and still is) mighty.

ALL LEVELS

NOTES

9 Significant as the immigrant role was in politics and in the economy, the immigrant contribution to the professions and the arts was perhaps even greater. Charles O. Paullin's analysis of the *Dictionary of American Biography* shows that, of the eighteenth- and nineteenth-century figures, 20 percent of the businessmen, 20 percent of the scholars and scientists, 23 percent of the painters, 24 percent of the engineers, 28 percent of the architects, 29 percent of the clergymen, 46 percent of the musicians and 61 percent of the actors were of foreign birth—a remarkable measure of the impact of immigration on American culture. And not only have many American writers and artists themselves been immigrants or the children of immigrants, but immigration has provided American literature with one of its major themes.

10 Perhaps the most pervasive influence of immigration is to be found in the innumerable details of life and the customs and habits brought by millions of people who never became famous. This impact was felt from the bottom up, and these contributions to American institutions may be the ones which most intimately affect the lives of all Americans.

11 In the area of religion, all the major American faiths were brought to this country from abroad. The multiplicity of sects established the American tradition of religious pluralism and assured to all the freedom of worship and separation of church and state pledged in the Bill of Rights.

12 So, too, in the very way we speak, immigration has altered American life. In greatly enriching the American vocabulary, it has been a major force in establishing "the American language," which, as H. L. Mencken demonstrated thirty years ago, had diverged materially from the mother tongue as spoken in Britain. Even the American dinner table has felt the impact. One writer has suggested that "typical American menus" might include some of the following dishes: "Irish stew, chop suey, goulash, chile con carne, ravioli, knackwurst mit sauerkraut, Yorkshire pudding, Welsh rarebit, borscht, gefilte fish, Spanish omelet, caviar, mayonnaise, antipasto, baumkuchen, English muffins, Gruyère cheese, Danish pastry, Canadian bacon, hot tamales, wiener schnitzel, petits fours, spumone, bouillabaisse, maté, scones, Turkish coffee, minestrone, filet mignon."

13 Immigration plainly was not always a happy experience. It was hard on the newcomers, and hard as well on the communities to which they came. When poor, ill-educated and frightened people disembarked in a strange land, they often fell prey to native racketeers, unscrupulous businessmen and cynical politicians. Boss Tweed said, characteristically, in defense of his own depredations[4] in New York in the 1870's, "This population is too hopelessly split into races and **factions** to govern it under universal suffrage,[5] except by bribery of patronage, or corruption."

factions (FAK shuhnz) *n.* groups of people inside a political party, club, government, etc., working against another group

4. **depredations** (dehp ruh DAY shuhnz) *n.* acts of plundering or robbery.
5. **universal suffrage** right to vote for all adults

PERSONALIZE FOR LEARNING

Strategic Support

Background Knowledge Students may need help in understanding the following sentence in paragraph 14, *Today we are belatedly, but resolutely, engaged in ending this condition of national exclusion and shame and abolishing forever the concept of second-class citizenship in the United States.*

Explain to students that the meaning of this sentence cannot be fully understood without some background information. Provide students with additional information about segregation, the U.S. Supreme Court's decision on Brown v. Board of Education in 1954, Jim Crow laws that relegated African-Americans to second-class citizens, and the Civil Rights movement. When this excerpt was written, the Civil Rights movement was underway.

14 But the very problems of adjustment and **assimilation** presented a challenge to the American idea—a challenge which subjected that idea to stern testing and eventually brought out the best qualities in American society. Thus the public school became a powerful means of preparing the newcomers for American life. The ideal of the "melting pot" symbolized the process of blending many strains into a single nationality, and we have come to realize in modern times that the "melting pot" need not mean the end of particular ethnic identities or traditions. Only in the case of the Negro has the melting pot failed to bring a minority into the full stream of American life. Today we are belatedly, but resolutely, engaged in ending this condition of national exclusion and shame and abolishing forever the concept of second-class citizenship in the United States.

15 Sociologists call the process of the melting pot "social mobility." One of America's characteristics has always been the lack of a rigid class structure. It has traditionally been possible for people to move up the social and economic scale. Even if one did not succeed in moving up oneself, there was always the hope that one's children would. Immigration is by definition a gesture of faith in social mobility. It is the expression in action of a positive belief in the possibility of a better life. It has thus contributed greatly to developing the spirit of personal betterment in American society and to strengthening the national confidence in change and the future. Such confidence, when widely shared, sets the national tone. The opportunities that America offered made the dream real, at least for a good many; but the dream itself was in large part the product of millions of plain people beginning a new life in the conviction that life could indeed be better, and each new wave of immigration rekindled the dream.

Immigration is by definition a gesture of faith in social mobility.

16 This is the spirit which so impressed Alexis de Tocqueville,[6] and which he called the spirit of equality. Equality in America has never meant literal equality of condition or capacity; there will always be inequalities in character and ability in any society. Equality has meant rather that, in the words of the Declaration of Independence, "all men are created equal . . . [and] are endowed by their Creator with certain unalienable rights"; it has meant that in a democratic society there should be no inequalities in opportunities or in freedoms. The American philosophy of equality has released the energy of the people, built the economy, subdued the continent, shaped and reshaped the structure of government, and animated the American attitude toward the world outside.

NOTES

assimilation (uh sihm uh LAY shuhn) *n.* process of adapting to the culture of an adopted country

CLOSE READ

ANNOTATE: Mark nouns and verbs that have positive connotations, or emotional associations, in paragraphs 15 and 16.

QUESTION: What common thread of meaning connects these words?

CONCLUDE: How do these words add to the author's argument?

6. **Alexis de Tocqueville** (uh LEHK sihs duh TOHK vihl) (1805–1859) French political thinker who traveled through America in 1831. Afterward, he wrote about his experiences in a book called *Democracy in America.*

DIGITAL PERSPECTIVES

CLOSE READ

Remind students to focus on nouns and verbs that have positive connotations or add to the persuasive nature of the text. You may wish to model the Close Read using the following think-aloud format. Possible responses to questions on the Student page are included.

ANNOTATE: As I read paragraphs 15 and 16, I notice some nouns and verbs are positive and uplifting.

QUESTION: I wonder if these words are symbolic of the changed views people in the country had toward immigrants. The common thread connecting these words is one of hope and achievement. They seem to describe immigrants in a positive light.

CONCLUDE: By using these words, I can infer that the author is trying to invoke feelings of pride, hope, and brotherhood in his discussion of immigrants.

WriteNow Express and Reflect

Reflection Direct students' attention to the description of equality in paragraph 16. Have students write a paragraph in which they discuss the author's use of the word *equality* in comparison to the literal definition of the word. Have students write a reflection about the types of equality discussed in the text, and whether or not people are ever truly equal.

NOTES

17 The *continuous* immigration of the nineteenth and early twentieth centuries was thus central to the whole American faith. It gave every old American a standard by which to judge how far he had come and every new American a realization of how far he might go. It reminded every American, old and new, that change is the essence of life, and that American society is a process, not a conclusion. The abundant resources of this land provided the foundation for a great nation. But only people could make the opportunity a reality. Immigration provided the human resources. More than that, it infused the nation with a commitment to far horizons and new frontiers, and thereby kept the pioneer spirit of American life, the spirit of equality and of hope, always alive and strong. "We are the heirs of all time," wrote Herman Melville," and with all nations we divide our inheritance." ❧

PERSONALIZE FOR LEARNING

English Language Support

Difficult Concepts Direct students' attention to the middle of paragraph 17: *American society is a process, not a conclusion*. Explore the meaning of this statement with students. Discuss what it would mean if American society *were* a conclusion. If it were, would there be space for growth from immigrants coming to America? Lead a discussion about how describing American society as *a process* is different and how this description allows for the changes and progress with new groups of immigrants in the United States. **ALL LEVELS**

Comprehension Check

Complete the following items after you finish your first read.

1. According to Kennedy, why is it impossible to speak about a particular "immigrant contribution" to the United States?

2. What does Kennedy state are the two main reasons immigrants come to the United States?

3. List five areas in which Kennedy says immigrants have made important contributions to American society.

4. In the case of which minority does Kennedy say the "melting pot" has failed?

5. According to Kennedy, what qualities in American culture impressed Alexis de Tocqueville?

6. **Notebook** Write a brief summary of "The Immigrant Contribution."

RESEARCH

Research to Clarify Choose at least one unfamiliar detail from the text. Briefly research that detail. In what way does the information you learned shed light on an aspect of the essay?

Research to Explore Choose one of the immigrant industrialists, scientists, or inventors that Kennedy mentions. Conduct research to learn more about this figure.

DIGITAL PERSPECTIVES

Comprehension Check

1. It's impossible because everyone in America is an immigrant or a descendant of one.
2. The two main reasons immigrants came to America were their hopes for personal freedom and economic opportunity.
3. Kennedy offers examples of immigrant contributions in politics, economics, inventions, writing, and cuisine.
4. Kennedy points out that the melting pot has failed for African Americans ("Negros").
5. deTocqueville was impressed by the widely held American belief that "things could get better."
6. **Responses will vary.** Summaries should include the idea that Kennedy believed all immigrant groups made a significant contribution to the development of America and that he argues that even "ordinary" immigrants contributed by passing along their dreams for a better life to their descendants.

Research

Research to Clarify If students struggle to come up with a detail to clarify, you might want to suggest that they focus on one of the following topics: John F. Kennedy, Anti-Defamation League, or the President's Commission on Immigration and Naturalization.

Research to Explore If students struggle to choose an immigrant figure to research, suggest that they review paragraphs 6–7 and choose a person, contribution, or invention with which they are unfamiliar.

PERSONALIZE FOR LEARNING

Challenge

Research Have students research contributions to the United States from historical figures who share their ethnic backgrounds or an ethnic group of their choosing. Keep in mind that many students will have more than one culture of origin. These contributions can vary from popular foods like pizza to historical inventions like the telephone. Have students share their findings with the class, creating a master list of contributions from various ethnic groups.

TEACHING

Jump Start

CLOSE READ Have students close read the title, "The Immigrant Contribution." Whom does Kennedy say are immigrants? What does Kennedy mean when he says "contribution?"

Close Read the Text

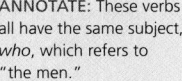

Walk students through the annotation model on the student page. Encourage them to complete items 2 and 3 on their own. Review and discuss the sections students have marked. If needed, continue to model close reading by using the Annotation Highlights in the Interactive Teacher's Edition.

Analyze the Text

Possible responses:

1. Handlin believes that there would be no history of America without the various immigrant groups that came here. Handlin's statement supports and parallels Kennedy's belief that "all Americans are immigrants or the descendants of immigrants." **DOK 2**
2. (a) Kennedy notes that eighteen of the signers were of non-English stock, eight were first-generation immigrants, and two—Alexander Hamilton and Albert Gallatin—were of West Indian and Swiss origins respectively. (paragraph 3) **DOK 1** (b) This confirms Kennedy's point that all Americans are immigrants. **DOK 2**
3. (a) The melting pot described "the process of blending many strains into a single nationality" to create the American identity. (paragraph 14) **DOK 1** (b) Kennedy states that the modern understanding of the melting pot is that it does not need to completely blend strains of culture but rather just allow them to coexist. **DOK 3**
4. Responses will vary. **DOK 3**

FORMATIVE ASSESSMENT

Analyze the Text

- **If** students fail to cite evidence, **then** remind them to support their ideas with specific information.
- **If** students struggle with the symbolism of "The Melting Pot," **then** discuss the term *symbolize* and explore the original and modern meanings of the term "melting pot."

MAKING MEANING

THE IMMIGRANT CONTRIBUTION

Close Read the Text

1. The model, from paragraph 5 of the essay, shows two sample annotations, along with questions and conclusions. Close read the passage and find another detail to annotate. Then, write a question and your conclusion.

ANNOTATE QUESTION Close Read CONCLUDE

ANNOTATE: These words refer to knowledge that "we all" have in common.

QUESTION: Why does the writer make this reference?

CONCLUDE: The reference adds to a sense that the writer and the reader are part of one community.

We all know, of course, about the spectacular immigrant successes: the men who came from foreign lands, sought their fortunes in the United States and made striking contributions, industrial and scientific, not only to their chosen country but to the entire world.

ANNOTATE: These verbs all have the same subject, *who*, which refers to "the men."

QUESTION: What is the effect of this string of related verbs and objects?

CONCLUDE: This construction creates a strong sense of forward progress, emphasizing how each action leads to the next.

2. For more practice, go back into the selection, and complete the close-read notes.
3. Revisit a section of the selection you found important during your first read. Read this section closely, and **annotate** what you notice. Ask yourself **questions** such as "Why did the author choose these words?" What can you **conclude**?

Analyze the Text

CITE TEXTUAL EVIDENCE to support your answers.

Notebook Respond to these questions.

1. **Analyze** Does Oscar Hanlin's statement support or refute Kennedy's main idea as it is expressed in the first paragraph of this selection? Explain.
2. (a) What information does Kennedy provide about the immigrant status of some of the signers of the Declaration of Independence?
(b) **Analyze** How does this information connect to his earlier point about all Americans?
3. (a) According to Kennedy, what did the idea of the "melting pot" once mean? (b) **Infer** For Kennedy, how has that ideal changed in modern times? Explain.
4. **Essential Question:** *What does it mean to be "American"?* What have you learned about the nature of American identity from reading this essay?

STANDARDS

Reading Informational Text

- Cite strong and thorough textual evidence to support analysis of what the text says explicitly as well as inferences drawn from the text.
- Analyze in detail how an author's ideas or claims are developed and refined by particular sentences, paragraphs, or larger portions of a text.
- Determine an author's point of view or purpose in a text and analyze how an author uses rhetoric to advance that point or view or purpose.

PERSONALIZE FOR LEARNING

Strategic Support

Analyzing Text Some students may struggle to find and analyze evidence to help them address the essential question. Pair them with other students and have pairs look for points in the text that answer the essential question. Have pairs examine one example of textual evidence at a time, taking the time to discuss the meaning of each example. Pairs should decide on a brief summary for each example of evidence from the text.

Students can then use these notes to help them answer the essential question using textual evidence.

Analyze Craft and Structure

Purpose and Persuasion An **author's purpose** is his or her reason for writing. A writer may want to inform or explain, to persuade, to entertain, or to reflect. Writers may also have more than one purpose for creating a particular text. For example, a writer may want to inform readers about a topic while also persuading them to see something in a new way. Those purposes direct the writer's choices, including the types of **persuasive appeals,** or methods of informing and convincing readers, to use. There are three main types of persuasive appeals:

- **Appeals to Authority:** the statements of experts on the topic.
- **Appeals to Reason:** logical arguments based on verifiable evidence, such as facts or data.
- **Appeals to Emotion:** statements intended to affect readers' feelings about a subject. These statements may include **charged language**—words with strong positive or negative associations.

In this essay, John F. Kennedy uses all three types of appeal to great effect. As you read, think about Kennedy's purpose for writing. Ask yourself, "Why does the writer include this information?"

Practice

CITE TEXTUAL EVIDENCE to support your answers.

Notebook **Respond to these questions.**

1. Use the chart to record at least two examples of each of the persuasive techniques Kennedy uses in this essay. Explain in what ways each example makes Kennedy's ideas more or less convincing.

PERSUASIVE TECHNIQUE	EXAMPLES FROM THE TEXT	EFFECTIVE OR INEFFECTIVE?
Appeal to Authority	Oscar Handlin has said . . .	Effective; sets the premise for defining immigrants to include all Americans.
Appeal to Emotion, including charged language	when poor, ill-educated, and frightened people . . . fell prey to native racketeers, unscrupulous businessmen and cynical politicians	Effective; shows how Kennedy could create sympathy for immigrants
Appeal to Reason	Between 1880 and 1920 … 23.5 million people who came to America.	Effective; cites useful information, supporting his argument

2. **(a)** Which technique does Kennedy use the most? Explain. **(b)** Why do you think he emphasizes this technique over the others? Explain.

3. Which type of persuasive technique do you find most effective in this essay? Why?

DIGITAL PERSPECTIVES

Illuminating the Standard To help students further understand the three persuasive techniques, find examples online of ethos, logos, and pathos. Connect the new terms with the three strategies discussed and read several examples of each. Then, ask students to find two more examples of each in political speeches or commercials. Finally, have students construct two new examples for each technique.

DIGITAL PERSPECTIVES

Analyze Craft and Structure

Discuss with students why an author might choose to use all three types of persuasive appeals. Have them think about the advantages of using more than one type of persuasion. Direct their attention to all the parts of the text, including the title, quotes and images, as well as the main content. Remind students that some readers may respond more strongly to some types of persuasion over others. For more support, see **Analyze Craft and Structure: Purpose and Persuasion.**

MAKE IT INTERACTIVE

After students have their Practice, ask them to rate the effectiveness of each of the techniques on a scale of 1-5 (with 5 ranked the highest), then tally scores for each persuasive technique. Poll students to see which technique they ranked the highest.

Practice

1. **See possible responses in chart on Student page**.
2. **Possible responses:** (a) Kennedy leans most on the Appeal to Emotion, as most of his discussion comprises anecdotes and strong moral appeals, liberally sprinkled with charged language. (b) His speech is primarily meant to sway the populace towards a positive emotional connection with immigrants; the purpose is to win hearts, and the appeal to emotion is ideal for that.
3. Responses will vary. Accept responses students can defend.

FORMATIVE ASSESSMENT

Analyze Craft and Structure

- **If** students struggle to find two examples of each persuasive technique, **then** review the definitions of each and give examples from popular media like a television show in order to clarify concepts.
- **If** students find the concept of charged language in appeals to emotion challenging to understand, **then** provide them with easy-to-understand examples and non-examples.

For Reteach and Practice, see **Analyze Craft and Structure: Purpose and Persuasion. (RP)**

TEACHING

Concept Vocabulary

Why These Words?

Possible responses:

1. Responses will vary. *Naturalization* and *assimilation* are both words that refer to processes related to immigrant populations.
2. Other words in the selection related to these concepts include: *society, nation, professions, sects, pluralism,* and *communities.*

Practice

Possible responses:

1. Makes sense; sentence implies that a faction is less than the whole society.
2. Does not make sense; naturalization is the process by which immigrants become citizens.
3. Makes sense; the U.S. Constitution and Bill of Rights apply to everyone who is a citizen.
4. Does not make sense; assimilation involves immigrants adapting their behavior to the social norms of American culture.
5. Makes sense; the word *stock* in this case refers to the origins of a minority group.
6. Makes sense; descendants include the later generations of immigrants who often marry members of other groups.

Word Network

Possible words: *national, nationality, freedom, opportunity, liberty*

Word Study

For more support, see **Concept Vocabulary and Word Study.**

Possible responses:

1. "the act of obtaining the rights or status of someone who was born in a place"
2. native, "born in a place"; nationality, "status of belonging to a particular nation by birth"; national, "relating to those born in a particular country or nation"
3. **Nationality** (nation + ality), identification with a certain nation. **National** (nation + al), belonging to or applying to a certain nation.

LANGUAGE DEVELOPMENT

THE IMMIGRANT CONTRIBUTION

Concept Vocabulary

descendants	minority	factions
stock	naturalization	assimilation

Why These Words? These concept words are related to populations and group identities. For example, in the first paragraph of the selection, John F. Kennedy asserts that "all Americans have been immigrants or descendants of immigrants." The word *descendants* refers to the offspring of immigrants.

1. Select two concept vocabulary words other than *descendants*. How does each word relate to ideas about populations and group identities? Explain.

2. What other words in the selection connect to the concepts of populations and group identities?

Practice

Notebook The concept vocabulary words appear in "The Immigrant Contribution." Tell whether each sentence does or does not make sense. Explain your reasoning.

1. Over time, the opinions of certain *factions* may become more popular.
2. American citizens returning from Europe must go through a process of *naturalization*.
3. The U.S. Constitution and Bill of Rights were intended to protect the rights of all American citizens, including those from a *minority* background.
4. Some immigrants may prefer *assimilation* as a way of preserving their cultures of origin.
5. Some historians believe that Native Americans were originally of Asian *stock*.
6. Many third-generation Americans are *descendants* of several different ethnic groups.

WORD NETWORK

Add interesting words related to American identity from the text to your Word Network.

Word Study

Latin root: *-nat-* The Latin root *-nat-* means "birth" or "to be born." The root appears in many common words related to populations and group identities.

1. Write a definition of the word *naturalization* that demonstrates your understanding of how the Latin root *-nat-* contributes to its meaning.

2. Reread paragraphs 13 and 14 of "The Immigrant Contribution." Mark two other words that contain the Latin root *-nat-*. Write a definition for each word.

STANDARDS

Language

- Use various types of phrases and clauses to convey specific meanings and add variety and interest to writing or presentations.
- Identify and correctly use patterns of word changes that indicate different meanings or parts of speech.

32 UNIT 1 • AMERICAN VOICES

FORMATIVE ASSESSMENT

Word Study

If students find words that are not related to the root *-nat-*, **then** explain that word parts should be combined with context clues in order to determine if they affect meaning. For Reteach and Practice, see **Word Study: Latin Root *-nat-* (RP).**

Conventions

Sentence Structure Sentences can be classified by the number of independent and dependent clauses they contain. An **independent clause** has a subject and verb and can stand alone as a complete thought. A **dependent,** or **subordinate, clause** also has a subject and verb, but it cannot stand alone as a complete thought. A dependent clause begins either with a subordinating conjunction, such as *when, although, because*, or *while*, or with a relative pronoun, such as *who, whose, which*, or *that*.

TIP

CLARIFICATION

Refer to the Grammar Handbook to learn more about these terms.

This chart shows the four basic sentence structures. Independent clauses are underlined once, and dependent clauses are underlined twice.

SENTENCE STRUCTURE	ELEMENTS	EXAMPLE
simple	a single independent clause	Anand saw the audience for the first time.
compound	two or more independent clauses, joined either by a comma and a coordinating conjunction or by a semicolon	The lights came on, and Anand saw the audience for the first time.
complex	one independent clause and one or more dependent clauses	When the lights came on, Anand saw the audience for the first time.
compound-complex	two or more independent clauses and one or more dependent clauses	When the lights came on, Anand saw the audience for the first time, and he waved to his parents, who were sitting in the front row.

Read It

Label each of these sentences from "The Immigrant Contribution" *simple, compound, complex,* or *compound-complex.*

1. This impact was felt from the bottom up, and these contributions to American institutions may be the ones which most intimately affect the lives of all Americans.

2. Immigration provided the human resources.

3. Equality in America has never meant literal equality of condition or capacity; there will always be inequalities in character and ability in any society.

4. We can only speak of people whose roots in America are older or newer.

Write It

Notebook Write a paragraph containing a simple sentence, a compound sentence, a complex sentence, and a compound-complex sentence.

DIGITAL PERSPECTIVES

Conventions

Sentence Structure Discuss the definition of dependent and independent clauses and create several examples of each as a class. Read both independent and dependent clauses aloud to aid students' understanding of the distinction between them. You may want to consider reviewing the parts of speech used in the lesson with students. For more support, see **Conventions: Sentence Structure.**

MAKE IT INTERACTIVE

Have students write three examples of dependent and independent clauses in random order on a piece of paper. Then, have students exchange these papers with classmates in order to identify each example. Review incorrect classifications as a class in order to further clarify the distinctions.

Read It

1. compound-complex
2. simple
3. compound
4. complex

Write It

Possible responses:

Answers will vary. Confirm that students' writing reflects sentence structure as directed.

FORMATIVE ASSESSMENT

Conventions

- **If** students struggle to identify dependent and independent clauses, **then** instruct them to read them out loud to determine if the clause makes sense by itself.
- **If** students struggle with identifying the structure of the sample sentences, **then** guide them in identifying the dependent and independent clauses first, then compare those identifications with the sentence type chart in order to categorize each.

For Reteach and Practice, see **Conventions: Sentence Structure. (RP).**

PERSONALIZE FOR LEARNING

English Language Support

Sentences Ask students to write three complete sentences to summarize "The Immigrant Contribution." **EMERGING**

Ask students to write their opinion on "The Immigrant Contribution." Encourage students to use both nouns and pronouns as their subjects and to use action words as well as forms of *to be* for their verbs. **EXPANDING**

Ask students to write a paragraph identifying the central idea and three supporting details from "The Immigrant Contribution."

Remind students that they can use simple sentences, or they can connect two clauses. Point out that at least one of the clauses has to be an independent clause. **BRIDGING**

An expanded **English Language Support Lesson** on Independent and Dependent Clauses is available in the Digital Teacher's Edition.

Writing to Compare

As students analyze the diction in these two texts, they will see that each author achieves a specific tone through the vocabulary that he or she chooses. Help students see that words have power to make a writer's work seem formal, informal, friendly, or academic.

Prewriting

1. Responses will vary, but students should be able to defend their analysis.
2. Responses will vary. Quindlen wrote in a magazine following a terrorist attack. She is writing to allay fear and to persuade her readers. Kennedy's more formal tone reflects his purpose of informing his audience about the multiple contributions immigrants made to the country.

A QUILT OF A COUNTRY

THE IMMIGRANT CONTRIBUTION

Writing to Compare

You have read two essays that discuss American cultural diversity. Deepen your understanding of both texts by comparing each writer's diction. **Diction** is a writer's way of using language to create a unique voice.

Assignment

Diction is a writer's choice and arrangement of words and phrases.

- Diction may be formal, informal, ordinary, technical, sophisticated, down-to-earth, old-fashioned, modern, or even slangy.
- The types of diction an author uses reflect the readers, or **audience,** for whom he or she is writing. A writer's diction also reveals his or her **tone,** or attitude.

The essays by Quindlen and Kennedy share a topic, but are very different in diction and tone. Write an **essay** in which you consider how diction and tone reflect each author's purpose, audience, and message.

Prewriting

Analyze the Texts Scan the two texts, and choose two passages from each one that you think use especially interesting language. Describe the type of diction each passage displays. You may use the following categories or add categories of your own. Note that writers may use more than one type of diction in a single passage.

Informal / Formal / Poetic / Ordinary / Sophisticated / Slangy
Technical / Scientific / Concrete / Abstract

Gather your observations in the chart.

PASSAGES	TYPE(S) OF DICTION
A Quilt of a Country	
1.	1.
2.	2.
The Immigrant Contribution	
1.	1.
2.	2.

Notebook Respond to these questions.

1. For each passage in your chart, explain the tone the diction creates.
2. How does each author's diction and tone reflect his or her purpose for writing and the audience he or she is trying to reach?

STANDARDS

Reading Informational Text
Determine the meaning of words and phrases as they are used in a text, including figurative, connotative, and technical meanings; analyze the cumulative impact of specific word choices on meaning and tone.

Writing
- Write informative/explanatory texts to examine and convey complex ideas, concepts, and information clearly and accurately through the effective selection, organization, and analysis of content.
- Apply *grades 9–10 Reading standards* to literary nonfiction.

PERSONALIZE FOR LEARNING

English Language Support

Nuances of Language English learners may struggle with the nuances of the English language that require understanding in order to evaluate diction choices. Pair them with an English-speaking student for this assignment to help them explore language nuances or phrases that confuse them. Encourage them to discuss similar phrases they may use and compare them with the authors' language choices. **ALL LEVELS**

Drafting

Identify Passages and Ideas Use your Prewriting notes to identify passages to use as examples in your essay. Make sure each passage clearly displays an aspect of Quindlen's or Kennedy's diction that you think offers a clear difference or a clear similarity. Identify the passages, and note the idea you will use each one to support.

Example Passage: ______________________________
Point It Will Support:

Example Passage: ______________________________
Point It Will Support:

Example Passage: ______________________________
Point It Will Support:

Example Passage: ______________________________
Point It Will Support:

Write a Thesis In one sentence, state the central idea you will explore in your essay. As you write, feel free to modify this statement to reflect changes to your ideas.

Central Idea/Thesis: ______________________________
____

Organize Ideas Make some organizational decisions before you begin to write. Consider using one of these two structures:

- **Grouping Ideas:** discuss all the similarities in the diction and tone of the two essays and then all of the differences
- **Grouping Texts:** discuss the diction and tone of one essay and then the diction and tone of the other essay

Elaborate With Examples Start with a statement, and then add examples.

Statement: Some writers use concrete diction to clarify abstract ideas.

With Example: Some writers use concrete diction to clarify abstract ideas. For example, when discussing conflicts in American culture, Quindlen uses concrete terms such as "slavery and sweatshops."

Review, Revise, and Edit

Once you are done drafting, review your essay. Because your essay is about multiple subjects—the diction and tone of two different texts—clarity and balance are critical. If you see an imbalance or unclear statements, add more analysis, detail, or examples.

DIGITAL PERSPECTIVES

Drafting

Identify Passages and Ideas As students find the evidence they will use in their essays, encourage them to use the strongest examples to convey their ideas.

Write a Thesis Students' working thesis statements should be supported by the examples they have chosen and should make a statement that compares or contrasts the two selections.

Organize Ideas Students may choose to use the organization of grouping ideas, or point-by-point organization, if they feel the comparison and contrasts align well. They may decided to use the organization of grouping texts, or block organization, if they have a stronger overall comparison to make.

Review, Revise and Edit You may want students to work in pairs to review their essays. For more support, see **Writing to Compare: Essay.**

FORMATIVE ASSESSMENT

Writing to Compare

- **If** students struggle with their comparisons, **then** suggest that they find at least two similar elements of each quilt to compare and contrast.
- **If** students are unsure of how to organize their paragraphs, **then** suggest that they devote one paragraph to each of the two elements they've chosen to compare and contrast.

Selection Test

Administer the "The Immigrant Contribution" Selection Test, which is available in both print and digital formats online in **Assessments.**

American History

AUDIO SUMMARIES
Audio summaries of "American History" are available in both English and Spanish in the Interactive Teacher's Edition or Unit Resources. Assigning these summaries prior to reading the selection may help students build additional background knowledge and set a context for their first read.

Summary

In Judith Ortiz Cofer's short story, "American History," ninth-grader Elena is miserable during recess. Elena is freezing and tormented by the bigger, stronger black girls. The only thing that Elena is happy about these days is her new neighbor, Eugene. After spying into his house for weeks, Elena finally gets the nerve to talk to him. To her joy, and her mother's disapproval, they become friends.

On this cold day, a teacher tells the students to go home early because the president has been shot. Elena wants to feel sad, but she's too happy. She's going to Eugene's house for the first time, despite her mother's warning. After Elena meets Eugene's mother, she is able to cry with the rest of the country, but not for the same reason.

Insight

Reading "American History" will help students begin to understand the opportunities and limitations for American immigrants. Elena is smart enough for advanced courses, but she's not allowed to take them because English isn't her first language. She's included in the recess games of the African-American girls but teased mercilessly for being Puerto Rican. She's accepted by Eugene, but Eugene's mother and her own mother see only the differences between them and discourage the friendship.

ESSENTIAL QUESTION:
What does it mean to be "American"?

Connection to Essential Question

"American History" provides an historical and a personal perspective on the Essential Question. From the historical perspective, the characters in the story are bonded as Americans while they grieve over the death of President Kennedy. Even Eugene's mother, with her superior attitude, feels the same way as Elena's mother about Kennedy's death. From the more personal perspective, both women also harbor dreams of a better life for their families—the classic American dream. More poignantly, Elena's personal experience shows us that being American for immigrants is a back-and-forth struggle between belonging and being seen as an outsider.

WHOLE-CLASS LEARNING PERFORMANCE TASK
How does your generation define what it means to be an American today?

UNIT PERFORMANCE-BASED ASSESSMENT
How is an American identity created?

Connection to Performance Tasks

Whole-Class Learning Performance Task In this Performance Task, students will consider the concept of American identity as defined by people in their generation. The characters in "American History" live during the Kennedy years, and it is his death that helps to define them as Americans, in that they join together to mourn.

Unit Performance-Based Assessment This selection connects to the question of the creation of an American identity by showing how one event can erase the differences between diverse groups and bond them together as a nation. The text also shows, in the depictions of Elena's parents and Eugene's mother, that an American identity is created when people have faith that their sacrifices and hard work will lead to a better life.

DIGITAL PERSPECTIVES — Audio | Video | Document | Annotation Highlights | EL Highlights | Online Assessment

LESSON RESOURCES

	Making Meaning	Language Development	Effective Expression
Lesson	**First Read** **Close Read** **Analyze the Text** **Analyze Craft and Structure**	**Concept Vocabulary** **Word Study** **Conventions**	**Writing to Sources** **Speaking and Listening**
Instructional Standards	**RL.10** By the end of grade 9, read and comprehend . . . **RL.3** Analyze how complex characters develop . . .	**L.4.c** Consult general and specialized reference materials . . . **L.5** Demonstrate understanding of figurative language . . . **L.1.b** Use various types of phrases and clauses . . .	**W.3** Write narratives . . . **W.3.e** Provide a conclusion . . .
STUDENT RESOURCES			
Available online in the Interactive Student Edition or Unit Resources	Selection Audio First-Read Guide: Fiction Close-Read Guide: Fiction	Word Network	Evidence Log
TEACHER RESOURCES			
Selection Resources Available online in the Interactive Teacher's Edition or Unit Resources	Audio Summaries Annotation Highlights EL Highlights Analyze Craft and Structure: Narrative Structure English Language Support Lesson: Conflict	Concept Vocabulary and Word Study Conventions: Types of Phrases	Writing to Sources: Alternative Endings Speaking and Listening: Monologue
Reteach/Practice (RP) Available online in the Interactive Teacher's Edition or Unit Resources	Analyze Craft and Structure: Narrative Structure (RP)	Word Study: Cognates (RP) Conventions: Types of Phrases (RP)	Writing to Sources: Alternative Endings (RP) Speaking and Listening: Monologue (RP)
Assessment Available online in Assessments	Selection Test		
My Resources	A Unit 1 Answer Key is available online and in the Interactive Teacher's Edition.		

Reading Support

Text Complexity Rubric: American History	
Quantitative Measures	
Lexile: 1000 **Text Length:** 3,490 words	
Qualitative Measures	
Knowledge Demands 1 — 2 — 3 — **4** — 5	Themes explored are uncommon to many readers: the immigrant experience, Puerto Rican culture, the lives of Puerto Ricans in a barrio in New Jersey, President Kennedy's assassination.
Structure 1 — **2** — 3 — 4 — 5	Plot elements are told chronologically, but selection also has some background stories of other characters (the father, the neighbors); story is narrated by one person and includes some dialogue.
Language Conventionality and Clarity 1 — 2 — **3** — 4 — 5	Language is contemporary, familiar and conversational; mostly simple and compound sentences with some more complex constructions; some Spanish words are included.
Levels of Meaning/Purpose 1 — 2 — **3** — 4 — 5	Theme is mostly clear but contains some subtlety; readers must infer some meanings from character's speech (for example, attitudes of neighbor toward main character.)

DECIDE AND PLAN

English Language Support

Provide English Learners with support for knowledge demands and language as they read the selection.

Knowledge Demands Invite students to listen actively as you list before students the characters, setting, and other important information, for example:

Characters: a girl in 9th grade, mother, teacher, friend, a neighbor

Setting: New Jersey, Puerto Rican neighborhood, 1963, the day of presidential assassination.

Language Pair students. As students read, ask each partner to write a list of unfamiliar words. Have them compare lists to help each other with any of the words. Then have them look up words in a dictionary. Ask Spanish speakers to explain the Spanish words.

Strategic Support

Provide students with strategic support to ensure that they can successfully read the text.

Knowledge Demands Using the background information, discuss that the narrator is one of many immigrants from Puerto Rico. Point out that the story takes place in 1963 on the day that President Kennedy was assassinated.

Meaning Guide students to look for meanings that may not be explicit. For example, discuss the unspoken attitude in the conversation between the main character and her neighbor. Point out the contradictions the narrator describes: for example, she has a "sweet-sounding" or "honey-drenched" voice, but her tone is unfriendly or angry. Have two students read the dialogue aloud, trying to imitate the voice and tone.

Challenge

Provide students who need to be challenged with ideas for how they can go beyond a simple interpretation of the text.

Text Analysis Ask students to discuss the scene between the main character and her neighbor. Have them give their interpretation of why the neighbor tells the girl to leave.

Written Response Have students look up other short stories, poems, or essays from Judith Ortiz Cofer's collection, *The Latin Deli*. Ask them to write a response to what they've read. In their responses, ask them to include a comparison to this selection, commenting on the common themes in the selections.

TEACH

Read and Respond

Have the class do their first read of the selection. Then, have them complete their close read. Finally, work with them on the Making Meaning, Language Development, and Effective Expression activities.

Standards Support Through Teaching and Learning Cycle

IDENTIFY NEEDS

Analyze results of the Beginning-of-Year Assessment, focusing on the items relating to Unit 1. Also take into consideration student performance to this point and your observations of where particular students struggle.

DECIDE AND PLAN

- If students have performed poorly on items matching these standards, then provide selection scaffolds before assigning them the on-level lesson provided in the Student Edition.
- If students have done well on the Beginning-of-Year Assessment, then challenge them to keep progressing and learning by giving them opportunities to practice the skills in depth.
- Use the Selection Resources listed on the Planning pages for "American History" to help students continually improve their ability to master the standards.

Instructional Standards: American History

	Catching Up	This Year	Looking Forward
Reading	You may wish to administer the **Analyze Craft and Structure: Narrative Structure (RP)** worksheet to help students understand how conflict drives narrative.	**RL.3** Analyze how complex characters develop over the course of a text, interact with other characters, and advance the plot or develop the theme.	Have students summarize Elena's overall conflict in the story and then identify where in the text the author introduces a part of Elena's conflict that is external and a part of Elena's conflict that is internal to show the complexity.
Writing	You may wish to administer the **Writing to Sources: Alternative Endings (RP)** worksheet to help students understand how resolutions to conflict may suggest authentic solutions.	**W.3.e** Provide a conclusion that follows from and reflects on what is experienced, observed, or resolved over the course of the narrative.	Challenge students to revisit a previous selection and
Speaking and Listening	You may wish to use the **Speaking and Listening: Monologue (RP)** worksheet to help students understand the purpose and point of view to use in a monologue.	**SL.4** Present information, findings, and supporting evidence clearly, concisely, and logically such that listeners can follow the line of reasoning and the organization, development, substance, and style are appropriate to purpose, audience, and task.	Encourage students to plan and organize a monologue that one of the people described in "American History" may have given on the topic of Americans with immigrant roots.
Language	Review the **Word Study: Cognates (RP)** worksheet to help students identify words in different languages that have similar spelling, meaning, and pronunciation.	**L.4.c** Consult general and specialized reference materials, both print and digital, to find the pronunciation of a word or determine or clarify its precise meaning, its part of speech, or its etymology.	Ask students to identify English words with Spanish cognates in the selection.

TEACH

Implement the planned lesson, and gather evidence of student learning.

ANALYZE AND REVISE

- Analyze student work for evidence of student learning.
- Identify whether or not students have met the expectations in the standards.
- Identify implications for future instruction.

Jump Start

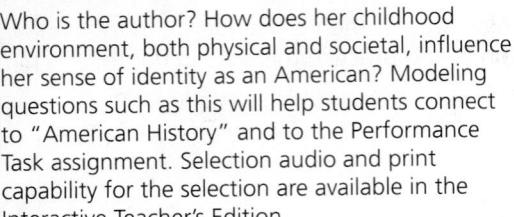

FIRST READ Ask students to name the most important historical event they can remember. Do they remember the day it happened? Do they remember what they were doing when they heard the news?

American History

Who is the author? How does her childhood environment, both physical and societal, influence her sense of identity as an American? Modeling questions such as this will help students connect to "American History" and to the Performance Task assignment. Selection audio and print capability for the selection are available in the Interactive Teacher's Edition.

Concept Vocabulary

Support students as they rank the words. Ask if they've ever heard, read, or used them. Reassure them that the definitions for these words are listed in the selection.

FIRST READ

As they read, students should perform the steps of the first read:

NOTICE: Encourage students to notice details about where the narrator lives, about her family and neighbors—and why they react so powerfully to the death of President Kennedy.

ANNOTATE: Remind students to mark passages they feel are particulary evocative or worthy of analysis in their close read. For example, students may want to focus on passages that describe the setting or the importance of the day.

CONNECT: Encourage students to think about how the text connects with their own experiences. Have they ever developed an important friendship with someone from a different culture or background?

RESPOND: Students will answer questions and write a summary to demonstrate understanding.

Point out to students that while they will always complete the Respond step at the end of the first read, the other steps will probably happen somewhat concurrently. You may wish to print copies of the **First Read Guide: Fiction** for students to use.

Remind students that, during their first read, they should not answer the close read questions that appear in the selection.

About the Author

Judith Ortiz Cofer (1952–2016) spent her childhood in two different cultures. Born in Puerto Rico, she moved with her parents to Paterson, New Jersey, when she was very young. She grew up mostly in Paterson, but she also spent time in Puerto Rico with her *abuela* (grandmother). It was from her grandmother that Ortiz Cofer learned the art of storytelling. In her own work, Ortiz Cofer teaches readers about the richness and difficulty of coming of age in two cultures at once.

American History

Concept Vocabulary

You will encounter the following words as you read "American History." Before reading, note how familiar you are with each word. Then, rank the words in order from most familiar (1) to least familiar (6).

WORD	YOUR RANKING
anticipated	
infatuated	
enthralled	
devoted	
elation	
impulse	

After completing the first read, return to the concept vocabulary and review your rankings. Make changes to your original rankings as needed.

First Read FICTION

Apply these strategies as you conduct your first read. You will have an opportunity to complete the close-read notes after your first read.

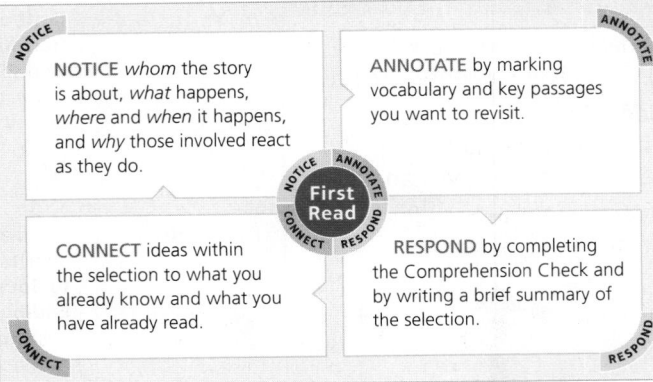

NOTICE *whom* the story is about, *what* happens, *where* and *when* it happens, and *why* those involved react as they do.

ANNOTATE by marking vocabulary and key passages you want to revisit.

CONNECT ideas within the selection to what you already know and what you have already read.

RESPOND by completing the Comprehension Check and by writing a brief summary of the selection.

Tool Kit
First-Read Guide and Model Annotation

STANDARDS
Reading Literature
By the end of grade 9, read and comprehend literature, including stories, dramas, and poems, in the grades 9–10 text complexity band proficiently, with scaffolding as needed at the high end of the range.

DIGITAL PERSPECTIVES

Illuminating the Text

President Kennedy Find and preview an excerpt of the film *PT-109*, the story of Lieutenant John F. Kennedy's courage and leadership during an encounter with a Japanese destroyer in World War II. Share the clip with your students. Though two of his crewmen were killed in the attack, Lt. Kennedy was instrumental in saving the remaining 10 crew members. This will help students understand the grief that blanketed the nation when this war hero turned President of the United States was assassinated. Have students name other influential figures or celebrities whose deaths have had a similar effect.

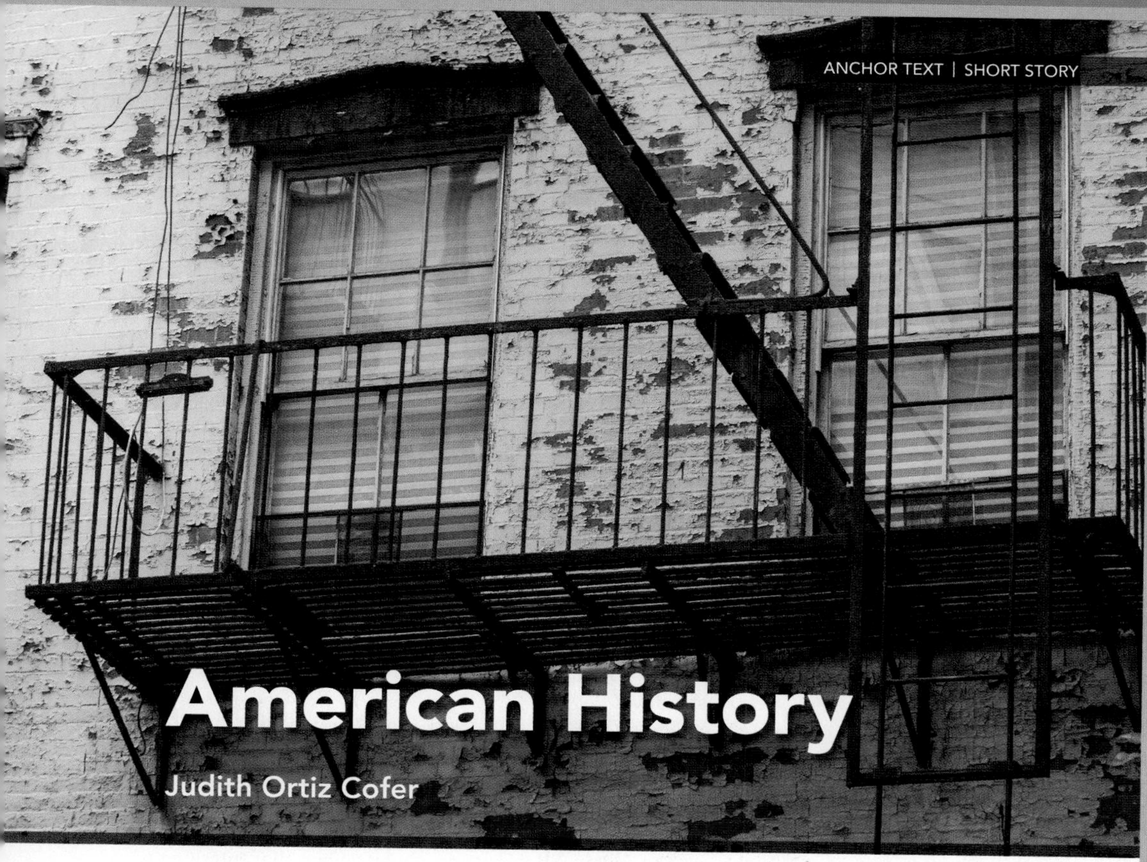

American History

Judith Ortiz Cofer

BACKGROUND

On November 22, 1963, President John F. Kennedy was shot and killed in Dallas, Texas, and the United States was plunged into mourning. Most people who lived through that time can still remember where they were when they heard the news. Kennedy's assassination and the nation's grief defined a generation. Key events in this story take place on that fateful day.

SCAN FOR MULTIMEDIA

1 I once read in a "Ripley's Believe It or Not" column that Paterson, New Jersey, is the place where the Straight and Narrow (streets) intersect. The Puerto Rican tenement known as *El Building* was one block up from Straight. It was, in fact, the corner of Straight and Market; not "at" the corner, but *the* corner. At almost any hour of the day, El Building was like a monstrous jukebox, blasting out *salsas*[1] from open windows as the residents, mostly new immigrants just up from the island, tried to drown out whatever they were currently enduring with loud music. But the day President Kennedy was shot there was a profound silence in El Building; even the abusive tongues of viragoes,[2] the cursing of the unemployed, and the screeching of

NOTES

1. **salsas** (SAHL suhz) songs written in a particular Latin American musical style.
2. **viragoes** (vih RAH gohz) fierce, irritable women with loud voices.

DIGITAL PERSPECTIVES

CLOSER LOOK

Analyze Character

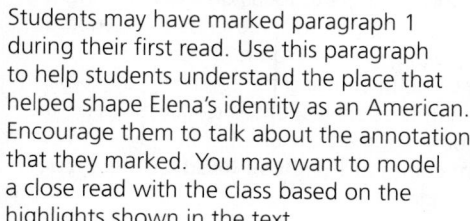

Students may have marked paragraph 1 during their first read. Use this paragraph to help students understand the place that helped shape Elena's identity as an American. Encourage them to talk about the annotations that they marked. You may want to model a close read with the class based on the highlights shown in the text.

ANNOTATE: Have students mark details in paragraph 1 that show the characteristics of *El Building,* or have students participate while you highlight them.

QUESTION: Guide students to consider what these details might tell them. Ask what a reader can infer about *El Building*, and accept student responses.

Possible response: *El Building* was an imposing figure, home to segregated, mostly low-income, Spanish speaking immigrants. The silence in the building demonstrates that those who lived there viewed the American president with much love and respect.

CONCLUDE: Help students to formulate conclusions about the importance of these details in the text. Ask students why the author might have included these details.

Possible responses: The residents of *El Building* are, essentially, relegated to a sub-culture in a Puerto Rican ghetto, even though they are U.S. citizens and hold the U.S. president in high esteem. *El Building* could be viewed as an antagonistic character, limiting the ability to fully identify as "American."

Remind students that a **character** plays a role in the action of a literary work. Sometimes a character can be an inanimate object or thing, rather than a person or animal. Have students watch for character traits that can be ascribed to *El Building* in passages to come.

Additional **English Language Support** is available in the Interactive Teacher's Edition.

PERSONALIZE FOR LEARNING

English Language Support

Figurative Language In paragraph 1, the author states: *El Building was like a monstrous jukebox, blasting out salsas from open windows at the residents...* Explain to students that this is an example of a **simile**, a type of figurative language that shows similarities between two different things by making a direct comparison using the words *like* or *as*.

Explain to students that a jukebox is a machine that automatically plays a selected musical recording when a coin is inserted. Jukeboxes were commonly found in many public places, such as casual restaurants, in the 1960s.

Ask students what this comparison does to add to their understanding of *El Building*. Help students to see that the silence of a building that was normally as loud as a jukebox made a strong impact. **ALL LEVELS**

TEACHING

CLOSE READ

Remind students to focus on the vivid language in paragraph 5 used to describe the temperature on the playground. You may want to model the Close Read using the following think-aloud format. Possible responses to questions on the Student page are included. You may also want to print copies of the **Close-Read Guide: Fiction** for students to use.

ANNOTATE: In paragraph 5, I mark the following words related to temperature. I see words that describe how warm or cold it is, and words that describe what happens when it is warm or cold.

QUESTION: I think the author's focus on heat and cold shows that Elena is preoccupied with her physical misery, which seems to her to be something only she suffers.

CONCLUDE: Not everyone has experienced the sense of displacement that Elena describes, but every reader knows what it is to be miserably cold. Every reader can empathize with her suffering—and that opens the way to a greater emotional empathy for the character.

NOTES

small children had been somehow muted. President Kennedy was a saint to these people. In fact, soon his photograph would be hung alongside the Sacred Heart and over the spiritist altars that many women kept in their apartments. He would become part of the hierarchy of martyrs they prayed to for favors that only one who had died for a cause would understand.

2 On the day that President Kennedy was shot, my ninth grade class had been out in the fenced playground of Public School Number 13. We had been given "free" exercise time and had been ordered by our P.E. teacher, Mr. DePalma, to "keep moving." That meant that the girls should jump rope and the boys toss basketballs through a hoop at the far end of the yard. He in the meantime would "keep an eye" on us from just inside the building.

3 It was a cold gray day in Paterson. The kind that warns of early snow. I was miserable, since I had forgotten my gloves, and my knuckles were turning red and raw from the jump rope. I was also taking a lot of abuse from the black girls for not turning the rope hard and fast enough for them.

4 "Hey, Skinny Bones, pump it, girl. Ain't you got no energy today?" Gail, the biggest of the black girls had the other end of the rope, yelled, "Didn't you eat your rice and beans and pork chops for breakfast today?"

5 The other girls picked up the "pork chops" and made it into a refrain: "pork chop, pork chop, did you eat your pork chop?" They entered the double ropes in pairs and exited without tripping or missing a beat. I felt a burning on my cheeks and then my glasses fogged up so that I could not manage to coordinate the jump rope with Gail. The chill was doing to me what it always did; entering my bones, making me cry, humiliating me. I hated the city, especially in winter. I hated Public School Number 13. I hated my skinny flat-chested body, and I envied the black girls who could jump rope so fast that their legs became a blur. They always seemed to be warm while I froze.

6 There was only one source of beauty and light for me that school year. The only thing I had **anticipated** at the start of the semester. That was seeing Eugene. In August, Eugene and his family had moved into the only house on the block that had a yard and trees. I could see his place from my window in El Building. In fact, if I sat on the fire escape I was literally suspended above Eugene's backyard. It was my favorite spot to read my library books in the summer. Until that August the house had been occupied by an old Jewish couple. Over the years I had become part of their family, without their knowing it, of course. I had a view of their kitchen and their backyard, and though I could not hear what they said, I knew when they were arguing, when one of them was sick, and many other things. I knew all this by watching them at mealtimes. I could see their kitchen table, the sink, and the stove. During good times, he

CLOSE READ

ANNOTATE: In paragraph 5, mark words and phrases related to temperature.

QUESTION: Why is the narrator so focused on feelings of hot and cold?

CONCLUDE: How do these details help readers understand Elena's feelings of isolation?

anticipated (an TIHS uh payt ihd) *v.* eagerly expected

VOCABULARY DEVELOPMENT

Word Forms Model other forms of the word *anticipated* in sentences. Have students fill in a chart similar to the one below, identify the part of speech for each form, and note the meaning.

We don't anticipate any objections to our proposal.
Just the anticipation of riding the roller coaster made her knees weak!
He took the anticipatory step of buying a flashlight before the camping trip.

Word	Part of Speech	Meaning
anticipate	verb	To think of something that might happen in the future
anticipation	noun	A feeling of excitement about something upcoming
anticipatory	adjective	In anticipation, or expectation

sat at the table and read his newspapers while she fixed the meals. If they argued, he would leave and the old woman would sit and stare at nothing for a long time. When one of them was sick, the other would come and get things from the kitchen and carry them out on a tray. The old man had died in June. The last week of school I had not seen him at the table at all. Then one day I saw that there was a crowd in the kitchen. The old woman had finally emerged from the house on the arm of a stocky, middle-aged woman, whom I had seen there a few times before, maybe her daughter. Then a man had carried out suitcases. The house had stood empty for weeks. I had had to resist the temptation to climb down into the yard and water the flowers the old lady had taken such good care of.

NOTES

7 By the time Eugene's family moved in, the yard was a tangled mass of weeds. The father had spent several days mowing, and when he finished, from where I sat, I didn't see the red, yellow, and purple clusters that meant flowers to me. I didn't see this family sit down at the kitchen table together. It was just the mother, a red-headed tall woman who wore a white uniform—a nurse's, I guessed it was; the father was gone before I got up in the morning and was never there at dinner time. I only saw him on weekends when they sometimes sat on lawn chairs under the oak tree, each hidden behind a section of the newspaper; and there was Eugene. He was tall and blond, and he wore glasses. I liked him right away because he sat at the kitchen table and read books for hours. That summer, before we had even spoken one word to each other, I kept him company on my fire escape.

I saw then that he was blushing deeply. Eugene liked me, but he was shy.

8 Once school started I looked for him in all my classes, but P.S. 13 was a huge, overpopulated place and it took me days and many discreet questions to discover that Eugene was in honors classes for all his subjects; classes that were not open to me because English was not my first language, though I was a straight A student. After much maneuvering, I managed "to run into him" in the hallway where his locker was—on the other side of the building from mine—and in study hall at the library where he first seemed to notice me, but did not speak; and finally, on the way home after school one day when I decided to approach him directly, though my stomach was doing somersaults.

9 I was ready for rejection, snobbery, the worst. But when I came up to him, practically panting in my nervousness, and blurted out: "You're Eugene. Right?" he smiled, pushed his glasses up on his nose, and nodded. I saw then that he was blushing deeply. Eugene liked me, but he was shy. I did most of the talking that day. He nodded and smiled a lot. In the weeks that followed, we walked home together. He would linger at the corner of El Building for a few minutes then walk down to his two-story house. It was not until

PERSONALIZE FOR LEARNING

English Language Support

Idioms Idioms may confuse many English Language learners, because the meaning of the phrase cannot be deduced from the individual words that make up the phrase.

Explain that the phrase to *run into him* in paragraph 8 is an idiom, since Elena did not literally run into Eugene. The idiom means to meet someone by chance. Ask students why they think the author used quotation marks around the idiom "to run into him," in view of its meaning. Then ask students to evaluate the author's choice to do this. **ALL LEVELS**

CLOSER LOOK

Analyze Characterization

Students may have marked paragraph 12 during their first read. Use this paragraph to help students understand Elena's infatuation with Eugene. Encourage them to talk about the annotations that they marked. You may want to model a close read with the class based on the highlights shown in the text.

ANNOTATE: Have students mark details in paragraph 12 where Elena describes her feelings for Eugene, or have students participate while you highlight them.

QUESTION: Guide students to consider what these details might tell them. Ask what a reader can infer about Elena, and accept student responses.

Possible response: Elena secretly fantasizes about sharing her life with Eugene.

CONCLUDE: Help students to formulate conclusions about the importance of these details in the text. Ask students why the author might have included these details.

Possible response: These details show that the author is lonely and naïve, looking for a place where she fits in.

Remind students that **characterization** is the way a writer develops and reveals a character's personality and temperament. Authors may simply tell the reader what a character is like; this is direct characterization. Sometimes the author will give the reader enough information to infer what the character is like; this is indirect characterization.

NOTES

infatuated (ihn FACH oo ayt ihd) *adj.* briefly but intensely in love

enthralled (ehn THRAWLD) *v.* captivated

devoted (dih VOHT ihd) *adj.* loving, loyal, and concerned with another's well-being

Eugene moved into that house that I noticed that El Building blocked most of the sun, and that the only spot that got a little sunlight during the day was the tiny square of earth the old woman had planted with flowers.

10 I did not tell Eugene that I could see inside his kitchen from my bedroom. I felt dishonest, but I liked my secret sharing of his evenings, especially now that I knew what he was reading since we chose our books together at the school library.

11 One day my mother came into my room as I was sitting on the window-sill staring out. In her abrupt way she said: "Elena, you are acting 'moony.'" *Enamorada*[3] was what she really said, that is—like a girl stupidly **infatuated**. Since I had turned fourteen my mother had been more vigilant than ever. She acted as if I was going to go crazy or explode or something if she didn't watch me and nag me all the time about being a *señorita*[4] now. She kept talking about virtue, morality, and other subjects that did not interest me in the least. My mother was unhappy in Paterson, but my father had a good job at the bluejeans factory in Passaic and soon, he kept assuring us, we would be moving to our own house there. Every Sunday we drove out to the suburbs of Paterson, Clifton, and Passaic, out to where people mowed grass on Sundays in the summer, and where children made snowmen in the winter from pure white snow, not like the gray slush of Paterson which seemed to fall from the sky in that hue. I had learned to listen to my parents' dreams, which were spoken in Spanish, as fairy tales, like the stories about life in the island paradise of Puerto Rico before I was born. I had been to the island once as a little girl, to grandmother's funeral, and all I remembered was wailing women in black, my mother becoming hysterical and being given a pill that made her sleep two days, and me feeling lost in a crowd of strangers all claiming to be my aunts, uncles, and cousins. I had actually been glad to return to the city. We had not been back there since then, though my parents talked constantly about buying a house on the beach someday, retiring on the island—that was a common topic among the residents of El Building. As for me, I was going to go to college and become a teacher.

12 But after meeting Eugene I began to think of the present more than of the future. What I wanted now was to enter that house I had watched for so many years. I wanted to see the other rooms where the old people had lived, and where the boy spent his time. Most of all, I wanted to sit at the kitchen table with Eugene like two adults, like the old man and his wife had done, maybe drink some coffee and talk about books. I had started reading *Gone with the Wind*. I was **enthralled** by it, with the daring and the passion of the beautiful girl living in a mansion, and with her **devoted** parents and the slaves who did everything for them. I didn't believe such a world had ever really existed, and I wanted to ask Eugene some questions since he and his

3. ***Enamorada*** (ay nah moh RAH dah) Spanish for "enamored; lovesick."
4. ***señorita*** (seh nyoh REE tah) Spanish for "young lady."

PERSONALIZE FOR LEARNING

Strategic Support

Background Knowledge To enhance the students' understanding of this passage in paragraph 12, they may want to get more information about the novel *Gone with the Wind*. Have students research the storyline of the novel, which is set during a pivotal period in American history. Emphasizing connections between already known information and that acquired during their research, lead a class discussion about Elena's enthrallment with the book and her disbelief that *"such a world had ever really existed."* Have students draw conclusions about why Elena may not be familiar with the cultural context of *Gone with the Wind*.

NOTES

parents, he had told me, had come up from Georgia, the same place where the novel was set. His father worked for a company that had transferred him to Paterson. His mother was very unhappy, Eugene said, in his beautiful voice that rose and fell over words in a strange, lilting way. The kids at school called him "the hick" and made fun of the way he talked. I knew I was his only friend so far, and I liked that, though I felt sad for him sometimes. "Skinny Bones" and the "Hick" was what they called us at school when we were seen together.

13 The day Mr. DePalma came out into the cold and asked us to line up in front of him was the day that President Kennedy was shot. Mr. DePalma, a short, muscular man with slicked-down black hair, was the science teacher, P.E. coach, and disciplinarian at P.S. 13. He was the teacher to whose homeroom you got assigned if you were a troublemaker, and the man called out to break up playground fights, and to escort violently angry teenagers to the office. And Mr. DePalma was the man who called your parents in for "a conference."

14 That day, he stood in front of two rows of mostly black and Puerto Rican kids, brittle from their efforts to "keep moving" on a November day that was turning bitter cold. Mr. DePalma, to our complete shock, was crying. Not just silent adult tears, but really sobbing. There were a few titters from the back of the line where I stood shivering.

15 "Listen," Mr. DePalma raised his arms over his head as if he were about to conduct an orchestra. His voice broke, and he covered his face with his hands. His barrel chest was heaving. Someone giggled behind me.

16 "Listen," he repeated, "something awful has happened." A strange gurgling came from his throat, and he turned around and spat on the cement behind him.

17 "Gross," someone said, and there was a lot of laughter.

PERSONALIZE FOR LEARNING

English Language Support

Abbreviations Abbreviations can be confusing to English Language Learners. In paragraph 13, the author uses the abbreviations P.E. and P.S. 13. Explain to students that often they can use context clues to help determine the meaning of unfamiliar abbreviations. In this story, the context helps us understand both abbreviations in this paragraph. In fact, P.E. is an abbreviation for Physical Education and P.S. 13 is an abbreviation for Public School #13. Ask students where else they can access the meanings of abbreviations. If students are unsure, suggest that online resources may help. **ALL LEVELS**

NOTES

18 "The President is dead, you idiots. I should have known that wouldn't mean anything to a bunch of losers like you kids. Go home." He was shrieking now. No one moved for a minute or two, but then a big girl let out a "Yeah!" and ran to get her books piled up with the others against the brick wall of the school building. The others followed in a mad scramble to get to their things before somebody caught on. It was still an hour to the dismissal bell.

19 A little scared, I headed for El Building. There was an eerie feeling on the streets. I looked into Mario's drugstore, a favorite hangout for the high school crowd, but there were only a couple of old Jewish men at the soda-bar talking with the short order cook in tones that sounded almost angry, but they were keeping their voices low. Even the traffic on one of the busiest intersections in Paterson—Straight Street and Park Avenue—seemed to be moving slower. There were no horns blasting that day. At El Building, the usual little group of unemployed men were not hanging out on the front stoop making it difficult for women to enter the front door. No music spilled out from open doors in the hallway. When I walked into our apartment, I found my mother sitting in front of the grainy picture of the television set.

"You are going out *today*?" The way she said "today" sounded as if a storm warning had been issued.

20 She looked up at me with a tear-streaked face and just said: *"Dios mio,"*[5] turning back to the set as if it were pulling at her eyes. I went into my room.

elation (ee LAY shuhn) *n.* great happiness and excitement

21 Though I wanted to feel the right thing about President Kennedy's death, I could not fight the feeling of **elation** that stirred in my chest. Today was the day I was to visit Eugene in his house. He had asked me to come over after school to study for an American history test with him. We had also planned to walk to the public library together. I looked down into his yard. The oak tree was bare of leaves and the ground looked gray with ice. The light through the large kitchen window of his house told me that El Building blocked the sun to such an extent that they had to turn lights on in the middle of the day. I felt ashamed about it. But the white kitchen table with the lamp hanging just above it looked cozy and inviting. I would soon sit there, across from Eugene, and I would tell him about my perch just above his house. Maybe I should.

22 In the next thirty minutes I changed clothes, put on a little pink lipstick, and got my books together. Then I went in to tell my mother that I was going to a friend's house to study. I did not expect her reaction.

23 "You are going out *today*?" The way she said "today" sounded as if a storm warning had been issued. It was said in utter disbelief.

5. ***Dios mío*** (DEE ohs MEE oh) Spanish for "My God!"

PERSONALIZE FOR LEARNING

Strategic Support

Choral Reading Employ choral reading to help students develop good pacing, fluency, and appropriate expression. Ask students to follow along as you model a fluent reading of paragraph 21. Though lengthy, this selection does not contain any difficult words. As you read, point out and discuss important details in the text, such as the meaning of the vocabulary word *elation*, which is contained in the paragraph. Next, the entire class should read aloud in unison. Pay attention to the pacing, fluency, and expression. Lead a class discussion about the content of the paragraph to make sure the students comprehend what they have read.

DIGITAL PERSPECTIVES

Before I could answer, she came toward me and held my elbows as I clutched my books.

24 "*Hija*,[6] the President has been killed. We must show respect. He was a great man. Come to church with me tonight."

25 She tried to embrace me, but my books were in the way. My first **impulse** was to comfort her, she seemed so distraught, but I had to meet Eugene in fifteen minutes.

26 "I have a test to study for, Mama. I will be home by eight."

27 "You are forgetting who you are, *Niña*[7]. I have seen you staring down at that boy's house. You are heading for humiliation and pain." My mother said this in Spanish and in a resigned tone that surprised me, as if she had no intention of stopping me from "heading for humiliation and pain." I started for the door. She sat in front of the TV holding a white handkerchief to her face.

28 I walked out to the street and around the chainlink fence that separated El Building from Eugene's house. The yard was neatly edged around the little walk that led to the door. It always amazed me how Paterson, the inner core of the city, had no apparent logic to its architecture. Small, neat, single residences like this one could be found right next to huge, dilapidated apartment buildings like El Building. My guess was that the little houses had been there first, then the immigrants had come in droves, and the monstrosities had been raised for them—the Italians, the Irish, the Jews, and now us, the Puerto Ricans and the blacks. The door was painted a deep green: *verde*, the color of hope, I had heard my mother say it: *Verde-Esperanza*.[8]

29 I knocked softly. A few suspenseful moments later the door opened just a crack. The red, swollen face of a woman appeared. She had a halo of red hair floating over a delicate ivory face—the face of a doll—with freckles on the nose. Her smudged eye make-up made her look unreal to me, like a mannequin seen through a warped store window.

30 "What do you want?" Her voice was tiny and sweet-sounding, like a little girl's, but her tone was not friendly.

31 "I'm Eugene's friend. He asked me over. To study." I thrust out my books, a silly gesture that embarrassed me almost immediately.

32 "You live there?" She pointed up to El Building, which looked particularly ugly, like a gray prison with its many dirty windows and rusty fire escapes. The woman had stepped halfway out and I could see that she wore a white nurse's uniform with St. Joseph's Hospital on the name tag.

33 "Yes. I do."

34 She looked intently at me for a couple of heartbeats, then said as if to herself, "I don't know how you people do it." Then directly to me: "Listen. Honey. Eugene doesn't want to study with you. He is a smart

6. **Hija** (EE hah) Spanish for "daughter."
7. **Niña** (NEE nyah) Spanish for "child," used here as an endearment.
8. **Verde-Esperanza** (vehr day ehs pay RAHN sah) Spanish for "green-hope."

NOTES

impulse (IHM puls) *n.* sudden urge to act or do something

CLOSE READ

ANNOTATE: In paragraphs 29 and 30, mark details that describe Eugene's mother's appearance and behavior.

QUESTION: Which details suggest softness or sweetness, and which suggest hardness or harshness?

CONCLUDE: What is the effect of these contrasting details?

CLOSE READ

Remind students to focus on the author's choice of words, in particular the words she uses to paint a vivid picture of Eugene's mother. You may wish to model the Close Read using the think-aloud format. Possible responses to questions on the Student page are included.

ANNOTATE: In paragraphs 29 and 30, I mark the words and phrases that describe the appearance and behavior of Eugene's mother.

QUESTION: I see that words like *delicate* and *sweet-sounding* suggest softness, and *mannequin* and *not-friendly* suggest harshness.

CONCLUDE: I think the effect of these contrasting details shows the difference between appearance and reality. They show that Eugene's mother is strongly characterized as someone who presents herself as friendly and welcoming while actually holding strong prejudices and acting cruelly. Elena has learned an important lesson in the dangers of confusing fantasy and reality.

CROSS-CURRICULAR PERSPECTIVES

Social Studies In paragraph 28, the author describes El Building as a huge, dilapidated apartment building that housed immigrants who had come in droves. Have students search the Internet for information about New York's Tenement Museum. Explore the site and read about modern-day efforts to preserve a slice of American immigrant history—apartments that housed over 7,000 immigrants from 1863 until 1935.

CLOSER LOOK

Infer Motivation

Students may have marked parts of paragraph 38 during their first read. Use this paragraph to help students understand Elena's emotional response to her encounter with Eugene's mother, and to the other distressing events of the day. Encourage them to talk about the annotations that they marked. You may want to model a read with the class based on the highlights shown in the text.

ANNOTATE: Have students mark details in paragraph 38 where Elena reveals her motivation for her actions involving Eugene, or have students participate while you highlight them.

QUESTION: Guide students to consider what these details might tell them. Ask what a reader can infer from these details, and accept student responses.

Possible response: Elation over a personal experience stood in the way before, and now her sense of bereavement for a lost dream allows her tears to flow.

CONCLUDE: Help students to formulate conclusions about the importance of these details in the text. Ask students why the author might have included these details.

Possible response: Elena is determined to be truthful in her efforts to make sense of her emotional confusion. The author included these details because she, too, wanted to be truthful—to the complexity and agony of an adolescent girl's emotional life.

Remind students that **motivation** is the reason for a character's actions. It may come from internal causes like loneliness or jealousy, or from external causes like danger or poverty. Most characters' motivations are a combination of internal and external factors.

NOTES

boy. Doesn't need help. You understand me. I am truly sorry if he told you you could come over. He cannot study with you. It's nothing personal. You understand? We won't be in this place much longer, no need for him to get close to people—it'll just make it harder for him later. Run back home now."

35 I couldn't move. I just stood there in shock at hearing these things said to me in such a honey-drenched voice. I had never heard an accent like hers, except for Eugene's softer version. It was as if she were singing me a little song.

36 "What's wrong? Didn't you hear what I said?" She seemed very angry, and I finally snapped out of my trance. I turned away from the green door, and heard her close it gently.

37 Our apartment was empty when I got home. My mother was in someone else's kitchen, seeking the solace she needed. Father would come in from his late shift at midnight. I would hear them talking softly in the kitchen for hours that night. They would not discuss their dreams for the future, or life in Puerto Rico, as they often did; that night they would talk sadly about the young widow and her two children, as if they were family. For the next few days, we would observe *luto*[9] in our apartment; that is, we would practice restraint and silence—no loud music or laughter. Some of the women of El Building would wear black for weeks.

38 That night, I lay in my bed trying to feel the right thing for our dead President. But the tears that came up from a deep source inside me were strictly for me. When my mother came to the door, I pretended to be sleeping. Sometime during the night, I saw from my bed the streetlight come on. It had a pink halo around it. I went to my window and pressed my face to the cool glass. Looking up at the light I could see the white snow falling like a lace veil over its face. I did not look down to see it turning gray as it touched the ground below. ❧

9. ***luto*** (LOO toh) Spanish for "mourning."

WriteNow Evaluate and Judge

Conclusion In paragraph 37, Elena's parents mourn and talk about the First Lady and her children rather than their own affairs. Have students write a short statement that draws a conclusion about why Elena does not do the same.

Comprehension Check

Complete the following items after you finish your first read.

1. On what memorable day in history does this story take place?

2. How does the narrator first become aware of Eugene?

3. Why does the narrator like Eugene even before she meets him?

4. According to her mother, how does Elena seem to feel about Eugene?

5. How does Eugene's mother react to Elena's visit?

6. **Notebook** Write a summary of "American History."

RESEARCH

Research to Clarify Choose at least one unfamiliar detail from the text. Briefly research that detail. In what way does the information you learned shed light on an aspect of the story?

Research to Explore Choose something from the text that interested you, and formulate a research question.

DIGITAL PERSPECTIVES

Comprehension Check

Possible responses:

1. November 22, 1963, the day President Kennedy was assassinated.
2. She sees him from her fire escape, where she likes to go to read.
3. She can see that he spends a lot of time reading, like her; she feels as though they are sharing that experience when she sees him from the fire escape.
4. She is being unrealistic, forgetting that they live in different parts of society, and she is only setting herself up for humiliation and pain.
5. Eugene's mother is cruel and disrespectful. She thinks Elena is nothing but trouble for Eugene. She tells Elena to go away.
6. **Notebook:** Write a summary of "American History."

Possible response: Elena lives in Paterson, where she is an outcast because she is poor and Puerto Rican. Over time, Elena develops hope because of her relationship with Eugene, a boy whose house she can see from her apartment window. On the day Kennedy is killed, Elena has plans to go to Eugene's house for the first time. Elena's mother discourages her, telling her she is being disrespectful to the president. Elena arrives at Eugene's house only to be turned away by Eugene's mother. Eugene's mother doesn't want a girl like Elena anywhere near her son. Elena goes home feeling rejected and despondent.

Research

Research to Clarify If students struggle to come up with a detail to research, suggest that they focus on one of the following topics: Ambassador Caroline Kennedy; El Yunque National Forest, Puerto Rico; prominent figures who have died and are considered by some to be martyrs.

Research to Explore If students have difficulty formulating a research question, suggest that they use their findings from Research to Clarify as a starting point.

PERSONALIZE FOR LEARNING

Challenge

Research Have students research the history of U.S. jurisdiction over the islands of Puerto Rico. Write a brief report that includes information on five influential Puerto Ricans, past or present.

As an alternative, have students learn more about the day that President Kennedy was shot and about how the nation expressed its grief in the days that followed.

Jump Start

CLOSE READ Ask students to tell which period of America's history they find most interesting. American Revolution? Civil rights era? The new millennium? Ask students how they think the present period of time will be described in history books of the future.

Close Read the Text

Walk students through the annotation model on the Student page. Encourage them to complete items 2 and 3 on their own. Review and discuss the sections students have marked. If needed, continue to model close reading by using the Annotation Highlights in the Interactive Teacher's Edition.

Analyze the Text

Possible responses:

1. Elena feels disappointed in her home, but she feels a very strong affection toward Eugene's house and sees it as a better way to live. She explicitly compares it favorably to her own apartment, with descriptive details like, "Small, neat, single residences like this one could be found next to huge, dilapidated apartment buildings like El Building." (Paragraph 28) **DOK 3**
2. Elena's family are Puerto Rican immigrants, trying to achieve a middle-class life. Elena herself is facing outright discrimination from Eugene's mother. **DOK 4**
3. (a) American History. **DOK 1** (b) The events of the story are also shaped by the assassination of President Kennedy. More than that, the conditions of growing up in America, the influx of immigrants, and shifting class lines all reflect the history of that period of time. **DOK 2**
4. **Possible Response** I've learned that to truly feel American, a person must feel that he or she *belongs*. At the end of this story, Elena still didn't feel like she belonged, so she did not feel like a part of America. **DOK 2**

FORMATIVE ASSESSMENT

Analyze the Text

- **If** students fail to cite evidence, **then** remind them to support their ideas with specific information.
- **If** students struggle to find a connection between Elena's environment and the reaction of Eugene's mother, **then** discuss the term "social issues" (Conditions that influence society that some believe should be corrected; often called "social problems").

MAKING MEANING

AMERICAN HISTORY

Close Read the Text

1. The model, from paragraph 1 of the story, shows two sample annotations, along with questions and conclusions. Close read the passage and find another detail to annotate. Then, write a question and your conclusion.

ANNOTATE: This clause includes strong, emotionally charged language.

QUESTION: What do these words suggest about the nature of life in El Building?

CONCLUDE: *Whatever* and *currently* suggest that the people had many different problems, while the word *enduring* suggests that they faced long-term struggles with no easy solutions.

At almost any hour of the day, El Building was like a monstrous jukebox, blasting out *salsas* from open windows as the residents, mostly new immigrants just up from the island, tried to drown out whatever they were currently enduring with loud music.

ANNOTATE: These two words are especially colorful.

QUESTION: What picture of El Building is the narrator painting with these word choices?

CONCLUDE: *Monstrous* suggests El Building is large, strange, and dangerous. *Blasting* suggests loudness and aggression. It is a big, fierce place.

2. For more practice, go back into the selection, and complete the close-read notes.
3. Revisit a section of the text you found important during your first read. Read this section closely, and **annotate** what you notice. Ask yourself **questions** such as "Why did the author make this choice?" What can you **conclude**?

Tool Kit
Close-Read Guide and Model Annotation

Analyze the Text

CITE TEXTUAL EVIDENCE to support your answers.

Notebook Respond to these questions.

1. **Compare and Contrast** Explain the contrast in Elena's feelings toward her own home and Eugene's house. Cite descriptive details that reflect these feelings.
2. **Analyze** In what ways does this story reflect social issues facing America in the 1960s? Consider descriptions of Elena's school and neighborhood, as well as Eugene's mother's reaction to Elena.
3. **(a)** What subject is Elena planning to study with Eugene?
   (b) Interpret What other reasons might Ortiz Cofer have for calling this story "American History"?
4. **Essential Question:** *What does it mean to be "American"?* What have you learned about American identity from reading this selection?

STANDARDS
Reading Literature
Analyze how complex characters develop over the course of a text, interact with other characters, and advance the plot or develop the theme.

CROSS-CURRICULAR PERSPECTIVES

Math Provide students with these figures that represent the number of Puerto Ricans who left the island to relocate to mainland United States from 1970 through 2013. Have students chart these figures as a graph. Students can use the graph style of their choice, such as bar graph, time plot, scatter graph, and so on. Have students project the years 2014 through 2020 before graphing. Ask students to write a summary about the changes in migration from Puerto Rico over time.

Measuring Migration from Puerto Rico to the Mainland U.S. 1970 to 1980 – 27,000; 1980 to 1990 – 126,400; 1990 to 2000 – 111,300; 2000 to 2010 – 192,000; 2010 to 2013 – 144,000

Analyze Craft and Structure

Narrative Structure Every story is driven by a **conflict**, or struggle between opposing forces. Characters in stories may face two different types of conflict—internal and external.

- In an **internal conflict**, a character grapples with his or her own beliefs, values, needs, or desires. For example, a character may know something is wrong but still be pulled to do it.
- In an **external conflict**, a character struggles against an outside force. This force may be another character, nature, or society. For example, a character trying to survive a hurricane at sea is experiencing an external conflict.

A character's efforts to resolve, or fix, a conflict form the basis for the plot of a story. In "American History," the main character, Elena, experiences both internal and external conflicts.

Practice

CITE TEXTUAL EVIDENCE to support your answers.

Notebook Respond to these questions.

1. (a) What is the main conflict in this story? (b) Is that main conflict primarily external or internal? Explain.
2. Use the chart to identify conflicts Elena faces in addition to the main conflict. For each conflict you note, identify at least one story detail that supports your answer.

ELENA VS. AN OUTSIDE FORCE	ELENA VS. HERSELF
Elena vs. her schoolmates, who mock her in the schoolyard	Elena has to overcome her reluctance to make friends with Eugene
Elena vs. Eugene's mother, who intentionally interferes with her relationship with Eugene	Elena's relationship with her mother suffers when her own preoccupations make her unable to understand her mother

3. (a) In the last scene of the story, why does Elena say that her tears are just for herself? (b) In what ways does the assassination of the president both add to and minimize the importance of Elena's suffering? Explain.

PERSONALIZE FOR LEARNING

English Language Support

Describing Story Elements Some students may need support to understand how the conflict in a story relates to the rest of the story.

Ask pairs of students to work together to identify the rising action, conflict, and climax of "American History." **EMERGING**

Ask students to identify the story elements of "American History," including exposition, rising action, conflict, climax, falling action, and resolution. **EXPANDING**

Ask students to write a paragraph that describes the story elements of "American History," including exposition, rising action, conflict, climax, falling action, and resolution. **BRIDGING**

An expanded **English Language Support Lesson** on Conflict is available in the Interactive Teacher's Edition.

DIGITAL PERSPECTIVES

Analyze Craft and Structure

Narrative Structure Discuss with students why the author might feel that the use of internal and external conflict is an effective way to tell Elena's "American" story. Have them think about others in the story who also may be struggling with their own values or societal pressures. Remind students that, if there is no conflict, there is no story. For more support, see **Analyze Craft and Structure: Narrative Structure.**

MAKE IT INTERACTIVE

Elena is not the only character in "American History" who is conflicted. Have students write a short paragraph (three or four sentences) from Eugene's point of view. What does he say about his relationship with Elena, since that is not explored in the story? Invite a few students to read their selections aloud.

Practice

Possible responses:

1. (a) Elena does not fit in with anyone around her. The only person she feels close to is unavailable. (b) It is primarily external, as Elena is at odds with her environment and the people she knows.
2. See possible responses on Student page.
3. (a) She can't feel strongly emotional about the assassination of Kennedy, but she is strongly emotional about her own misfortune. (b) It both shows that the nation is dealing with a far more universal and painful tragedy, making hers look personal and relatively unimportant; on the other hand, her pain being more immediate and personal means that the sadness the people of *El Building* feel for the death of a distant politician is less easily relatable than her social problems.

FORMATIVE ASSESSMENT

Analyze Craft and Structure

- **If** students have difficulty identifying an example of internal conflict, **then** have them re-read paragraph 10, where such an example is apparent.
- **If** students have difficulty identifying an example of external conflict, **then** have them re-read paragraph 23, where such an example is apparent. For Reteach and Practice, see **Analyze Craft and Structure: Narrative Structure (RP).**

Concept Vocabulary

Why These Words?

Possible responses:

1. Each vocabulary word helps to describe how characters are excited about the different interests in their lives.
2. Passion, miserable, violently, shock, distraught

Practice

Possible responses:

1. I *anticipated* my reward. Magda was *infatuated* with a handsome movie star. The kids were *enthralled* by the movie. She was *devoted* to President Kennedy's memory. I felt *elation* when the Mets won. My first *impulse* was to laugh when I saw my brother's costume.
2. I *expected* my reward. Magda was *fascinated* by a handsome movie star. The kids were *excited* by the movie. She was *loyal* to President Kennedy's memory. I felt *delight* when the Mets won. My first *urge* was to laugh when I saw my brother's costume.

Students may say that some synonyms change the intensity of the sentences.

Word Network

Possible words: *residents, immigrants, suburbs, mealtimes*

Word Study

For more support, see **Concept Vocabulary and Word Study**

1. See possible responses in chart on Student page.
2. enamored, "in love" or "captivated"

FORMATIVE ASSESSMENT

Concept Vocabulary

If students have trouble finding synonyms to vocabulary words, **then** introduce them to a thesaurus, if they are not already familiar with it.

Word Study

If students struggle with the concept of cognates, **then** demonstrate an online English to Spanish translator, showing the difference between what constitutes a cognate and what does not. For Reteach and Practice, see **Word Study: Cognates (RP).**

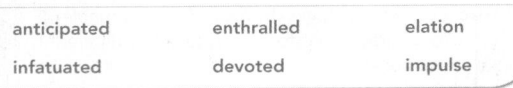

LANGUAGE DEVELOPMENT

AMERICAN HISTORY

Concept Vocabulary

anticipated	enthralled	elation
infatuated	devoted	impulse

Why These Words? The six concept vocabulary words from the text all involve having a fascination with or an attraction to something. For example, Elena is *enthralled* by the book *Gone With the Wind*. She is captivated by the story, which is set in a romantic and tragic place.

1. How do the vocabulary words help the writer describe characters' emotions?

2. Find two other words in the selection that describe a strong emotion.

Practice

Notebook The concept vocabulary words appear in "American History."

1. Use each concept vocabulary word in a sentence that demonstrates its meaning.
2. Rewrite each sentence using a synonym for the concept vocabulary word. How does the replacement change the meaning of the sentence?

WORD NETWORK

Add interesting words related to American identity from the text to your Word Network.

Word Study

Cognates When two words in different languages share a common origin, they are called **cognates**. Often, they are spelled and pronounced similarly in the two languages and still share a common meaning. Recognizing when two words are cognates can help you determine an unfamiliar word's meaning. If you know Spanish, for example, you can quickly guess the meanings of the English words *bicycle* and *paradise* from knowing their Spanish cognates: *bicicleta* and *paraíso*.

1. For each Spanish word in the chart, write its English cognate. Then, write the meaning the pair of cognates shares.

SPANISH WORD	ENGLISH COGNATE	MEANING
anticipación	anticipation	expecting or preparing for something
pasión	passion	a strong feeling for something

2. Look back at paragraph 11 of "American History." What English word is a cognate of the Spanish word *enamorada*? Write the word and its definition. Consult a bilingual dictionary if necessary.

STANDARDS

Language

- Use various types of phrases and clauses to convey specific meanings and add variety and interest to writing or presentations.
- Consult general and specialized reference materials, both print and digital, to find the pronunciation of a word or determine or clarify its precise meaning, its part of speech, or its etymology.
- Demonstrate understanding of figurative language, word relationships, and nuances in word meanings.

AUTHOR'S PERSPECTIVE **Elfrieda Hiebert, Ph.D.**

Word Networks Vocabulary word networks enable students to learn, use, and retain a large number of useful words related to a particular concept. In addition, generating vocabulary in this way can help students appreciate the subtleties of an author's word choice and evaluate the effectiveness of an author's style. Using vocabulary word networks also helps students choose more precise words when they write and edit. Finally, forging connections among related words, as opposed to teaching the words individually, allows students to approach new words with confidence and knowledge.

When students discuss the unit's theme, they can choose from a wide variety of related words, each with its own connotation, to create a word

Conventions

Types of Phrases A **preposition** is a word such as *of, in, to, for* or *with* that relates a noun or a pronoun to another word in the sentence. A **prepositional phrase** is a group of words that begins with a preposition and ends with a noun or pronoun, called the **object of the preposition**.

When a prepositional phrase modifies a noun or a pronoun, by telling *what kind* or *which one*, it is an **adjective phrase.** When it modifies a verb, an adjective, or an adverb, by pointing out *where, why, when, in what way,* or *to what extent,* it is an **adverb phrase.** In the chart, the prepositional phrases are italicized, and the words they modify are underlined.

TIP

CLARIFICATION
Refer to the Grammar Handbook to learn more about these terms.

SENTENCE	TYPE OF PHRASE	HOW PHRASE FUNCTIONS
Let's take a picture *of the Eiffel Tower*.	adjective phrase	tells *what kind*
The snowball *on the table* melted.	adjective phrase	tells *which one*
I left my wallet *in the car*.	adverb phrase	tells *where*
The other team played *with more skill*.	adverb phrase	tells *in what way*

Read It

1. Mark every prepositional phrase in each of these sentences. Then, indicate whether each phrase is an adjective phrase or an adverb phrase.
   - **a.** Elena's mother was unhappy in Paterson.
   - **b.** When Elena sat on the fire escape, she was above Eugene's backyard.
   - **c.** The boys tossed basketballs through a hoop in the yard.
2. Reread paragraph 29 of "American History." Mark one adjective phrase and one adverb phrase. Then, note which word each phrase modifies.

Write It

Notebook Add either an adjective phrase or an adverb phrase to each sentence. Label each phrase you add.

Example
We drove.
We drove *to the suburbs.* (adverb phrase)
We drove to the suburbs *of Paterson and Clifton.* (adjective phrase)

1. Elena observed Eugene.
2. I could see the snow falling like a lace veil.

DIGITAL PERSPECTIVES

Conventions

Types of Phrases

Discuss with students the definition of a prepositional phrase, an adjective phrase, and an adverb phrase. As you review the examples with students, explain that a prepositional phrase functions as either an adverb or an adjective, depending on what it modifies. Consider defining the following term:

modifier: a word, phrase, or clause that functions to describe a word or make its meaning more specific

For more support, see **Conventions: Types of Phrases.**

MAKE IT INTERACTIVE
Have students write each sentence on a sentence strip using one color marker for adverb phrases and another color marker for adjective phrases.

Read It

Possible responses:

1. a. *in Paterson* (adverb phrase); b. *above Eugene's backyard* (adverb phrase); c. *through a hoop* (adverb phrase); *in the yard* (adverb phrase)
2. But the white kitchen table *with the lamp hanging just above it* looked cozy and inviting. (adjective phrase - paragraph 21)

   I would hear them talking softly *in the kitchen* for hours that night. (adverb phrase - paragraph 37)

Write It

Possible responses:

1. Elena observed Eugene *at his locker.* (adverb phrase)
2. I could see the snow falling like a lace veil *around my shoulders.* (adjective phrase)

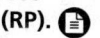

network. While students may not know more complex words at first, they do know common conversation words and words that get at the big idea. These words can serve as a gateway to the more complex words they will encounter in these selections.

PERSONALIZE FOR LEARNING

Strategic Support

Roles and Power Ask students this question: How would you define your role in society? Ask them to consider their age, cultural background, economic status and any other demographic factors they feel are appropriate. How do these social factors affect their own efforts at advancement in society? Finally, ask students to list those institutions in society that they consider most powerful.

FORMATIVE ASSESSMENT

Conventions

- **If** students struggle to isolate an adverb phrase, **then** remind them that an adverb phrase answers the questions "how, where, when, why?".
- **If** students struggle to isolate an adjective phrase, **then** remind them that an adjective phrase answers the question "which?".

Types of For Reteach and Practice, see **Conventions: Types of Phrases (RP).**

Writing to Sources

Explain to students that a story's ending is what leaves a lasting impression on the reader. The author can guide the reader to a specific conclusion, or cause the reader to have certain thoughts and feelings that last long after the book is closed. If you want your story to stay on the reader's mind, write it with a powerful ending. For more support, see **Writing to Sources: Alternative Endings.**

Reflect on Your Writing

Possible responses:

1. Responses will vary. Make sure students include their explanation of how the characters in the alternative ending remain consistent with the earlier part of the story even though they have addressed the conflict in a different way.
2. Responses will vary. Adjective phrases and adverb phrases can be used to help the alternative ending flow logically from the story's earlier events.
3. **Why These Words?** Responses will vary, with students listing words that convey feeling and emotion, such as the vocabulary words.
4. **Essential Question:** Answers will vary; students may answer that Elena does not feel especially "American" because she does not grieve after the death of President Kennedy as the adults do. Or, they may answer that events of national importance cause many Americans to experience similar emotions.

FORMATIVE ASSESSMENT

Writing to Sources

- **If** students have difficulty formulating an alternative ending, **then** ask them to think about what they did not like about the ending of the original story and what they would like to see happen instead. For Reteach and Practice, see **Writing to Sources: Alternative Endings (RP).**

EFFECTIVE EXPRESSION

AMERICAN HISTORY

Writing to Sources

A story can be a way of exploring and even of explaining a topic. The conflicts a writer chooses to address in a work of fiction often reflect issues people encounter in real life. The resolutions to those conflicts may suggest authentic solutions.

Assignment

Consider the conflicts Elena faces in "American History" and the choices she makes as she faces them. Ask yourself whether she could have made different choices and whether those other options might have had a better or, perhaps, a worse result. Then, write an **alternative ending** to the story. Start your ending after Elena knocks on Eugene's door. Consider how you will either resolve or leave open the main conflicts Elena faces in the story.

- Your new ending should flow logically from the story's earlier events.
- Your new ending should be consistent with your understanding of the characters.
- Your new ending should either provide a resolution to the conflict or demonstrate a realization Elena experiences.

Vocabulary and Conventions Connection Consider including several concept vocabulary words in your alternative ending. Also, consider using prepositional phrases to make your writing more precise.

anticipated	enthralled	elation
infatuated	devoted	impulse

Reflect on Your Writing

After you have written your alternative ending, answer these questions.

1. How did you make your portrayal of the characters consistent with the earlier part of the story? Explain.
2. Did you include any prepositional phrases in your writing? If so, how did they help you be more descriptive or precise?
3. **Why These Words?** Which words in your writing do you feel are especially effective in portraying characters' thoughts or feelings? List a few of these words.
4. **Essential Question:** *What does it mean to be "American"?* What have you learned about American identity from reading this selection?

STANDARDS

Writing

- Write narratives to develop real or imagined experiences or events using effective technique, well-chosen details, and well-structured event sequences.
- Provide a conclusion that follows from and reflects on what is experienced, observed, or resolved over the course of the narrative.

Speaking and Listening

Assignment

Write and present a **monologue** from the point of view of a character in "American History" other than Elena. A monologue is an uninterrupted speech often used in drama. It is delivered by one character to an audience of silent listeners and allows the character to present his or her version of events. For example, your monologue may present Eugene's thoughts and feelings after his mother sends Elena away.

1. **Choose a Character** Other than Elena, which character in the story would have something interesting and important to say? When choosing your character, consider the following elements:
   - the character's knowledge, attitude, and feelings about the story's events
   - the character's relationship to Elena and connection to the main events of the story
2. **Plan and Write** Brainstorm for ideas, perceptions, experiences, and thoughts your chosen character would have and might want to explain to others. Then, write your monologue.
   - Adopt the character's point of view and write using first-person pronouns—*I, me, us,* and *we.*
   - Create an authentic voice by working to "hear" the character's voice in your head as you write. Include details that show how he or she sees the setting, events, and other characters.
   - Remember that your character's knowledge is limited. Include only what he or she actually knows about the events of the story.
3. **Prepare and Deliver** Practice your delivery before you present to the class.
   - Speak clearly without rushing.
   - Employ body language and gestures to add drama or create emphasis. Try to be true to the type of movements or speech patterns your character would use.
   - Vary your speech cadence and emphasis to express your character's ideas.
4. **Evaluate** Use the evaluation guide to evaluate your classmates' monologues.

MONOLOGUE EVALUATION GUIDE

Rate each item on a scale of 1 (not demonstrated) to 5 (demonstrated) for each speaker.

- ☐ The speaker spoke clearly and effectively.
- ☐ The monologue sounded authentic and accurately reflected the story's setting and events.
- ☐ The speaker varied tone and cadence to enhance meaning.
- ☐ The speaker's body language helped express ideas.

EVIDENCE LOG

Before moving on to a new selection, go to your Evidence Log and record what you learned from "American History."

DIGITAL PERSPECTIVES

Illuminating the Standard To help students understand the elements of an effective monologue, show videos of presentations that include examples of effective and ineffective techniques. Lead a discussion with students analyzing reasons why some monologues moved the audience and others did not. Make a master list of techniques deemed to be effective and distribute to the students.

DIGITAL PERSPECTIVES

Speaking and Listening

1. **Choose a Character** You may want to guide students in choosing a character by asking them to consider whose perspective they most understand.
2. **Plan and Write** Tell students that their monologue should have an arresting opening and a clear closing—one that does not leave the audience wondering if they are done.
3. **Prepare and Deliver** Direct students to record their practice sessions (perhaps on a cell phone) and review them using the Monologue Evaluation Guide.
4. **Evaluate** Encourage students to make at least one supportive comment about each monologue.

For more support, see **Speaking and Listening: Monologue.**

Evidence Log Support students in completing their Evidence Log. This paced activity will help prepare them for the Performance-Based Assessment at the end of the unit.

FORMATIVE ASSESSMENT

Speaking and Listening

- **If** students struggle to identify a character, **then** have them list all the possible characters and choose the one they find most interesting.
- **If** students struggle to put their thoughts on paper, **then** remind them to think about what thoughts their character may want to tell others and to write them using first-person pronouns.

For Reteach and Practice, see **Speaking and Listening: Monologue (RP).**

Selection Test

Administer the "American History" Selection Test, which is available in both print and digital formats online in Assessments.

TEACHING

Jump Start

What does it mean to be an American?

Ask students to write examples of the different ways Americans are connected to one another after reading "A Quilt of a Country," "The Immigrant Contribution," and "American History." You might guide them with the question: "What do Americans have in common with each other?"

As students share, ask them to cite specific examples from the texts to support their ideas.

Write a Nonfiction Narrative

Ensure students understand what they are being asked to do in the Assignment. Explain that the question is related to the topic of American identity because the writer of each piece has a unique perspective on what makes a country's identity.

Students should complete the assignment using word processing software to take advantage of editing tools and features.

Elements of a Nonfiction Narrative

Remind students that an effective nonfiction narrative such as "American History" includes the listed required elements, flows well, and uses word choice and tone to create a mood and a feeling.

MAKE IT INTERACTIVE

Project "Music for My Mother" from the Interactive Teacher's Edition and have students identify the elements of a nonfiction narrative, such as situation or problem, a well-structured, logical sequence of events, and a reflective conclusion.

Academic Vocabulary

Ask students to explain which academic vocabulary word is most applicable to each of the selections.

PERFORMANCE TASK: WRITING FOCUS

WRITING TO SOURCES

- A QUILT OF A COUNTRY
- THE IMMIGRANT CONTRIBUTION
- AMERICAN HISTORY

Write a Nonfiction Narrative

You've read an essay, an excerpt from a nonfiction book, and a short story that deal with issues of American identity. In "A Quilt of a Country," written shortly after September 11, 2001, author Anna Quindlen explores how well the United States holds "the many" together as one. In the "The Immigrant Contribution," published in 1958, then-Senator John F. Kennedy explains how immigrants have contributed to the country. Finally, in "American History," the narrator describes how a personal experience of discrimination overshadowed her grief on the day in 1963, when President Kennedy was assassinated.

Tool Kit
Student Model of a Narrative

Assignment

Think about how the authors of "A Quilt of a Country," "The Immigrant Contribution," and "American History" explore American identity. Consider how the idea of American identity has changed over time. Then, use your own experience, or that of someone you know or have studied, to write a brief narrative that explores this question:

How does your generation define what it means to be an American today?

Elements of a Nonfiction Narrative

A **nonfiction narrative** is a true story, a series of events that occurred in real life rather than in an author's imagination. A nonfiction narrative describes real experiences or events along with reflections on those experiences. An effective nonfiction narrative includes these elements:

- a clearly described situation or problem
- a well-structured, logical sequence of events
- details that show time and place
- effective story elements such as dialogue, description, and reflection
- a reflective conclusion
- your thoughts, feelings, or views about the significance of events
- correct grammar

ACADEMIC VOCABULARY

As you craft your narrative, consider using some of the academic vocabulary you learned in the beginning of the unit.

conflict
description
dialogue
exposition
sequence

Model Narrative For a model of a well-crafted narrative, see the Launch Text, "Music for My Mother."

LAUNCH TEXT

Challenge yourself to find all of the elements of an effective narrative in the text. You will have the opportunity to review these elements as you start to write your own narrative.

As you consider how to capture an aspect of today's American identity in a story, it can help to imagine your narrative being included in a time capsule. Ask yourself: What would you want a future American to know about Americans today?

STANDARDS

Writing

- Write narratives to develop real or imagined experiences or events using effective technique, well-chosen details, and well-structured event sequences.
- Write routinely over extended time frames and shorter time frames for a range of tasks, purposes, and audiences.

AUTHOR'S PERSPECTIVE **Kelly Gallagher, M.Ed.**

Pump up the Volume of Writing Spend some time talking to kids about why they should write--not just how. Students should write more than the teacher can grade. To help students get the most from their writing, teachers can use techniques such as these:

- **Confer** Teachers can achieve more in a two-minute conference than they can by spending five-to-seven minutes writing comments on a paper. Developing writers need face time with the most experienced writer in the class—the teacher.
- **Model** Teachers can model how they write by frequently writing in front of students. Show students that effective writing extends far past correctness. Teachers can do this in short bursts, and model authentic writing,

Prewriting / Planning

Choose an Event to Explore Now that you have read the selections and thought about American identity, think of a true story that captures something unique about American identity today. It could have happened to you or someone you know—or to someone you have only heard or read about. Write a sentence describing the experience.

Experience: ____

____.

Structure the Sequence Create a detailed record of the **sequence of events**, or the events in the order that they happened, by filling out the chart below. Each event should be a part of an overall narrative that captures what it means to be an American today.

Event 1: ____.

Event 2: ____.

Event 3: ____.

Event 4: ____.

Gather Details Before you draft, gather details about people, places, and actions that will bring them to life for readers. Include the following:

- **descriptive words and phrases** that show how different people look and speak
- **precise language** about how people behave
- **sensory details**—words that appeal to the senses of sight, smell, taste, touch, and hearing—about key places

Using strong details adds interest and depth to your writing. For example, in the Launch Text, the writer uses lyrics of a specific song her brother sang for their mother. This detail helps readers understand the characters' feelings better.

I remember washing dishes while Pedrito sang: "And seeing myself so lonely and sad like a leaf in the wind, I want to cry . . . from this feeling."

—"Music for My Mother"

Develop Situation and Point of View Use remaining time to figure out how to describe the central situation or problem memorably. Sharpen your description by emphasizing key conflicts or describing how an important moment felt. Your narrative will be even more memorable if it conveys strong points of view. For added depth, you can take a step back and consider how other people might have perceived the same events as well.

EVIDENCE LOG

Review your Evidence Log and identify key details you may want to cite in your narrative.

STANDARDS

Writing

- Engage and orient the reader by setting out a problem, situation, or observation, establishing multiple point(s) of view, and introducing a narrator and/or characters; create a smooth progression of experiences or events.
- Use narrative techniques, such as dialogue, pacing, description, reflection, and multiple plot lines, to develop experiences, events, and/or characters.

DIGITAL PERSPECTIVES

Prewriting/Planning

Choose an Event to Explore Explain to students that the key to writing a compelling nonfiction narrative is to select an event or experience that is meaningful to the writer. Remind them that they will write a stronger narrative if they have a personal connection to the event or experience.

Structure the Sequence Point out to students that they when they begin to write, it will help to have already listed the important events that show what it means to be an American today. Tell them that if at this stage they have difficulty noting the significance of an event, it might not be worth including in the narrative.

Gather Details Explain that an essential component of a compelling narrative is the creation of strong characters. Provide examples of strong characters from classic movies or books to illustrate how descriptive words and precise language help readers understand their lives and the challenges or struggles they face. Recommend that they take a moment to brainstorm and write down all the details that come to mind about the characters and settings.

Develop Situation and Point of View Encourage students to plan the ways they will make their narratives convey feeling. Suggest that students write a single sentence to identify the emotion they want their readers to understand. Students should keep this idea in mind as they begin to draft.

whether brainstorming a topic, working to add details, or revising to find the right word. Note: other times the teacher can bring a model to class that has already been written for the students to study.

- **Share models of excellent writing** Show students models from a professional writer and from other students. As they study mentor texts, students begin to see the moves a writer has made, and they can work to emulate those moves.
- **Use a Rubric** Experiment with changing the rubric. Encourage students to help you build it. This creates buy-in when the students see that each rubric is personalized to some degree to their needs.

Drafting

Organize Your Narrative Review the plot diagram with students. Explain to students that without strong exposition, in which the story's characters and their situation are presented in a compelling way, a reader will be uninterested in learning about the conflict or problem that needs to be addressed. Have students think about some of their favorite stories and draw lessons from them.

Use Narrative Techniques Some narrative techniques make changes to a completely linear chronological order. Help students see that these time-order changes can increase interest. Remind students that they should include language in their narratives that helps readers follow the events of the story, especially if those events are presented out of order.

Write a First Draft Remind students that the main goal of the first draft is to get their ideas on paper, incorporating all the elements of writing a nonfiction narrative. Instruct them to include details that will interest readers and make them want to read the whole story. Encourage students to grab the reader's attention by beginning the narrative with an especially interesting detail.

PERFORMANCE TASK: WRITING FOCUS

Drafting

Organize Your Narrative Most narratives describe events in *chronological* order, or the sequence in which they occurred. They also center on a *conflict,* or problem, that is somehow resolved. As the conflict develops, the tension should increase until it reaches its *climax,* or point of greatest intensity. After that, the tension should decrease as you move toward the ending, or *resolution.* Use a basic narrative structure like the one shown here.

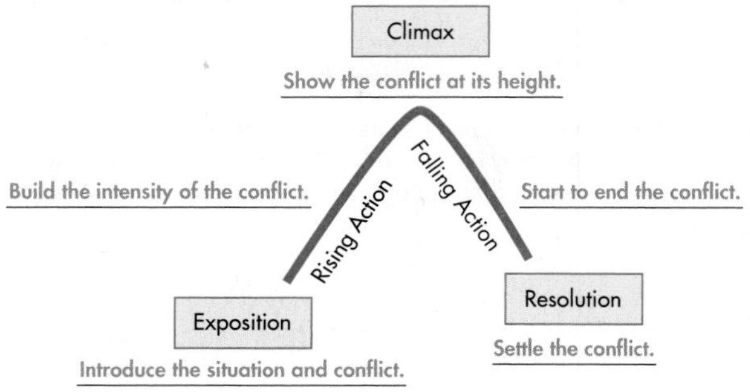

Use Narrative Techniques Once you have established the basic narrative structure, you can consider using narrative techniques to add interest. For example, you might jump back in time with a *flashback* to add a memory that will give readers insight into a person's thinking. Alternatively, you could jump forward in time and add a *flash-forward*. Finally, you could add a subplot, a minor narrative that sheds light on the main story.

Whatever you choose to do, make sure that the events you describe are true and tie together into a story that makes sense as whole, so readers will be able to follow along. Notice that the Launch Text actually starts *in medias res*—in the middle of the story, chronologically—and then goes backward then forward in time. Readers are still able to follow the sequence of events.

First event described ("middle" of story): The author's brother Pedrito is singing a traditional Spanish song because his mother misses life in her native country.

Second event described ("beginning" of story): The family arrives in the United States, and the parents have a more difficult time adjusting than the children have.

Third event described ("end" of story): Everyone has fully adjusted to life in the United States. Both children have successful careers, and the parents live with Pedrito.

Write a First Draft Consider the narrative techniques you plan to include in your story, and write a first draft. Remember to introduce a clear situation in the exposition and use descriptive details as you write about characters and places. Also be sure to include your own thoughts and feelings as you describe events and what they show about this generation of Americans.

STANDARDS

Writing

- Use narrative techniques, such as dialogue, pacing, description, reflection, and multiple plot lines, to develop experiences, events, and/or characters.
- Use a variety of techniques to sequence events so that they build on one another to create a coherent whole.

AUTHOR'S PERSPECTIVE **Jim Cummins, Ph.D.**

Writing Enhances Student Identity Writing is an expression of oneself, and writing projects that self into new social spheres. However, students learning English are often defined by what they are missing rather than by what they possess. While teaching writing through the Performance Tasks in *myPerspectives*, you may want to supplement the writing instruction and practice for English learners by using *identity texts.* These texts allow students to invest their identities into their writing. The results hold up a mirror to students and reflect their identities in a positive light. Teachers can use this process:

1. Encourage students to have a hand in picking the topic to ensure they are writing about something that reflects themselves or their

LANGUAGE DEVELOPMENT: AUTHOR'S STYLE

Exposition and Dialogue

Exposition In every narrative, certain elements need to be established, including the setting, the characters, and the situation. As you begin your narrative, think about showing the reader your story, instead of just telling it. Give clues instead of always stating information. When readers have to figure small things out, they become more involved in the story.

TELL IT
I was in the desert and it was morning. My brother and sister were with me. We had our bikes and we were going to ride. We were being careful because riding in the desert can be dangerous.

SHOW IT
The sun was just rising, throwing golden light over the miles of sand in front of us. My brother Gio checked our bikes one last time for any problems. My sister Lisa was on her cell phone, giving our parents our exact location. Just in case.

Dialogue It's not always necessary to include dialogue in a narrative, but it can often bring a story to life. What happens if we add dialogue to the exposition above?

The sun was rising, throwing golden light over the miles of sand in front of us.
"Bikes are ready," said my brother Gio. "I checked everything. Twice."
"Cool," I said. "Don't want a breakdown."
"Mom and Dad have our coordinates," said my sister Lisa, putting her cell phone back into her pack.

If you want your dialogue to sound real, you need to write the way people actually talk. Try listening to people talking in the lunchroom or after school. These are some of the things you may notice:

- short, incomplete sentences
- slang and other informal word choices
- repetition

Pacing Both description and dialogue can dramatically affect the *pacing*, or speed, of a story. For example, a large amount of description can slow down the pace, while short bursts of clipped dialogue can speed it up. Good writers read over their narratives, deciding when they want a reader to slow down and enjoy a description or deciding when to speed up and allow readers to get caught up in an exciting event.

Write It As you write your narrative, use these techniques: tell instead of show, use realistic dialogue, and vary your pacing.

TIP

STYLE

Make sure to use precise language in your narrative as you describe events.

- Use a dictionary if you are not sure you are using a word correctly.
- Use a thesaurus to find synonyms for words you know.

STANDARDS

Writing
Use narrative techniques, such as dialogue, pacing, description, reflection, and multiple plot lines, to develop experiences, events, and/or characters.

DIGITAL PERSPECTIVES

Exposition and Dialogue

Exposition Emphasize how important it is for a writer to show readers what is happening and that simply telling them flat details might cause readers to lose interest in the narrative. Have students skim "American History," making note of the places where the writer shows, rather than tells, the reader what is going on.

Dialogue Remind students that dialogue can help establish each character's personality. Through the use of distinct word choices, a writer can establish that each person in the story has his or her own voice.

identities. Have students write their drafts in English, illustrate them, and work with various sources, such as parents and older students fluent in their home language, to translate the drafts into their home language.

2. Publish these texts. Help students share identity texts with multiple audiences including peers, teachers, parents, grandparents, sister classes, and the media.

It is critical that students share their writing with broad audiences to build this positive experience. Students are likely to receive positive feedback and affirmation of self by providing true audiences with which to share their work. Writing and publishing identity texts helps ELL students take active control and ownership of the learning process and invest their identities in their drafts.

PERSONALIZE FOR LEARNING

English Language Support

Predict Meaning Provide students with the key terms used in the unit: *conflict, dialogue, description, exposition,* and *sequence.* Discuss aspects of the words that will help them understand their meanings; for example, the root of *description* is *describe*, or that *exposition* helps *expose* information about a character. After discussing the key terms, students can work as a group to use the terms in sentences. **ALL LEVELS**

Revising

Evaluating Your Draft Before students begin revising their writing, they should first evaluate their draft to determine that it contains all the required elements, is organized well, and adheres to the norms and conventions of nonfiction narratives.

Conclusion Remind students that in a nonfiction narrative, the purpose of the conclusion is the same as it is in other forms of writing. It should wrap up the narrative in a meaningful way and help the reader understand its message.

Exposition Have students review their narratives to find areas where they failed to show the reader what's occurring and instead simply told them. You might suggest that they share their narratives with a partner who can review key details with an unbiased eye.

Dialogue Remind students that dialogue is an opportunity to illustrate how each person is unique. Have them review all instances of dialogue to find areas where the people do not come across as real or where their words don't sound distinctive.

PERFORMANCE TASK: WRITING FOCUS

Revising

Evaluating Your Draft

Use the following checklist to evaluate the effectiveness of your first draft. Then, use your evaluation and the instruction on this page to guide your revision.

FOCUS AND ORGANIZATION	EVIDENCE AND ELABORATION	CONVENTIONS
☐ Provides an introduction to a real situation and develops a narrative. ☐ Introduces the key people involved in the narrative. ☐ Relates a problem or conflict. ☐ Provides a smooth progression of events. ☐ Concludes with a reflection on the significance of events.	☐ Includes interesting exposition that shows as well as tells the reader. ☐ Uses various techniques to create natural-sounding dialogue.	☐ Follows the norms and conventions of a nonfiction narrative, especially in structure and in the punctuation of dialogue.

WORD NETWORK

Include interesting words from your Word Network in your narrative.

Revising for Focus and Organization

Conclusion Reread your narrative, paying attention to how the conclusion works with the rest of the piece. Do you include reflections on the significance of events? Do you consider whether Americans from different time periods see American identity differently? When you are finished considering these questions, revise your conclusion to make it more meaningful to readers. End your narrative with a reflection, an observation, or an insight that ties the story to the theme of American identity today.

Revising for Evidence and Elaboration

Exposition Go to the beginning of your narrative, where you establish the setting, key people, and situation. Have you done all you can to make the exposition interesting to the reader by showing these elements and leaving details for the reader to infer? Put a star next to passages that feel insubstantial or do not give readers enough of a feel for what an experience was like. Then, go back into these passages, and find precise words or phrases that describe thoughts or physical sensations.

Dialogue Look over the dialogue you have included in your narrative. Does it sound like real people talking? Can you improve it by shortening sentences or using more casual language? Look for other places in your narrative where dialogue might bring your story to life.

STANDARDS

Writing

- Use precise words and phrases, telling details, and sensory language to convey a vivid picture of the experiences, events, setting, and/or characters.
- Provide a conclusion that follows from and reflects on what is experienced, observed, or resolved over the course of the narrative.

HOW LANGUAGE WORKS

Dialogue As students revise their narratives, remind them to ensure they used quotation marks whenever dialogue appears. Explain that quotation marks alert the reader that the character, rather than the narrator, is "speaking." Also explain that the speaker of a line of dialogue doesn't necessarily have to be identified if the context makes it clear who is talking, thereby streamlining the dialogue.

PEER REVIEW

Exchange narratives with a classmate. Use the checklist to evaluate your classmate's narrative and provide supportive feedback.

1. Is the exposition clear?
☐ yes ☐ no If no, explain what confused you.
2. Are the events sequenced logically?
☐ yes ☐ no If no, what about the sequence did not work?
3. Does the author include thoughts, feelings, and reflections?
☐ yes ☐ no If no, write a brief note explaining what you thought was missing.
4. What is the strongest part of your classmate's narrative? Why?

Editing and Proofreading

Edit for Conventions Reread your draft for accuracy and consistency. Correct errors in grammar and word usage. Check your narrative to make sure you have used commas correctly in compound and complex sentences.

Proofread for Accuracy Read your draft carefully, looking for errors in spelling and punctuation. Double-check the capitalization of names and places. Common nouns name general categories and are lowercase. Proper nouns name specific people, places, or things and are capitalized.

Publishing and Presenting

Create a final version of your narrative. Share it with a small group so that your classmates can read it and make comments. In turn, review and comment on your classmates' work. Together, determine what your different narratives convey about Americans today. Listen and respond respectfully to comments about your work.

Reflecting

Think about what you learned while writing your narrative. What techniques did you learn that you could use when writing another nonfiction narrative? How might you make your main point clearer? For example, you might write more reflections on why the events of the narrative were important.

DIGITAL PERSPECTIVES

Peer Review

Before they begin their peer review, remind students that they are reviewing their classmate's narrative for its success in telling the story, not whether the writer should have chosen to tell that story. However, they might point out places where the writer could use more detail to add interest to the narrative.

Editing and Proofreading

As students proofread, they should check for grammar, spelling, and punctuation errors. Remind them that they should not rely on word processing programs to find all mistakes, because these programs can, for example, sometimes fail to recognize an incorrect form of a homonym or a grammatical error. They should also be aware that it's easy to misspell names of people and places.

Publishing and Presenting

Before students review their classmates' nonfiction narratives, remind them to:

- Keep comments positive.
- Use formal rather than informal language—this includes grammar and punctuation.
- Avoid using all capital letters—it reads as if you're yelling.
- Provide examples of both positive facets of the narrative and areas in need of improvement.
- Disagree respectfully. Give your opinion, but be sure to support your position with evidence.
- Be brief. It's not the number of words, but the clarity of the message that's important.

Reflecting

Explain that by reflecting on their narrative and the comments from their peers, students can gain a new appreciation for the significance of the story they told. Tell them that by hearing the perspectives of others, they may think of something that had never occurred to them.

PERSONALIZE FOR LEARNING

Challenge

Write a Play Invite students to adapt their narrative into a play. Explain to them that since a play doesn't have a narrator, the story must be told solely through dialogue and acting. They can feel free to fictionalize parts of the narrative, creating new dialogue, as long as the play still conveys the larger truth that is being told. Remind them to include stage directions so that the actors understand what emotions to convey.

OVERVIEW

SMALL-GROUP LEARNING

What does it mean to be American?

The United States is a fusion of cultures from all over the world. As a result, being "American" can have a different meaning to different people. Discuss with the class how the way in which immigrants are treated affects their understanding of what it means to be American. During Small-Group Learning, students will read selections that highlight experiences of Americans who emigrated from other countries.

Small-Group Learning Strategies

Review the Learning Strategies with students and explain that as they work through Small-Group Learning they will develop strategies to work in small-group environments.

- Have students watch the video on Small-Group Learning Strategies.
- A video on this topic is available online in the Professional Development Center.

You may wish to discuss some action items to add to the chart as a class before students complete it on their own. For example, for "Support others" you might solicit the following from students:

- Give positive feedback when others share their ideas.
- Take turns so that all group members get a chance to be heard.

Block Scheduling

Each day in this Pacing Plan represents a 40-50 minute class period. Teachers using block scheduling may combine days to reflect their class schedule. In addition, teachers may revise pacing to differentiate and support core instruction by integrating components and resources as students require.

OVERVIEW: SMALL-GROUP LEARNING

ESSENTIAL QUESTION:

What does it mean to be "American"?

What is it like to build a new life in America? And what happens when newcomers are greeted with confusion or suspicion rather than welcome? The selections you will read present different perspectives on the experience of becoming American. You will work in a group to continue your exploration of American identity.

Small-Group Learning Strategies

Throughout your life, in school, in your community, and in your career, you will continue to learn and work with others.

Review these strategies and the actions you can take to practice them as you work in teams. Add ideas of your own for each step. Use these strategies during Small-Group Learning.

STRATEGY	ACTION PLAN
Prepare	• Complete your assignments so that you are prepared for group work. • Organize your thinking so that you can contribute to your group's discussion. •
Participate fully	• Make eye contact to signal that you are listening and taking in what is being said. • Use text evidence when making a point. •
Support others	• Build off ideas from others in your group. • Invite others who have not yet spoken to join the discussion. •
Clarify	• Paraphrase the ideas of others to ensure that your understanding is correct. • Ask follow-up questions. •

SCAN FOR MULTIMEDIA

Pacing Plan

Introduce Whole-Class Learning

Unit Introduction: 1

2

A Quilt of a Country: 3, 4, 5, 6

The Immigrant Contribution: 7, 8, 9, 10

American History: 11, 12, 13

Performance Task: 14, 15

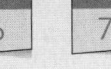

DIGITAL PERSPECTIVES

CONTENTS

Contents

Selections Circulate among groups as they preview the selections. You might encourage groups to discuss any knowledge they already have about any of the selections or the situations and settings shown in the photographs. Students may wish to take a poll within their group to determine which selections look most interesting.

Remind students that communicating and collaborating in groups are important skills that they will use throughout their lives—in school, in their careers, and in their community.

Performance Task

Present a Nonfiction Narrative Give groups time to read about and briefly discuss the nonfiction narrative about American identity they will create after reading. Encourage students to do some preliminary thinking about the types of media they may want to use. This may help focus their subsequent reading and group discussion.

Introduce Small-Group Learning — 16
Rules of the Game — 17, 18
The Writing on the Wall — 19, 20
With a Little Help From My Friends — 21, 22
• Morning Talk
• Immigrant Picnic — 23, 24
Performance Task — 25, 26
Introduce Independent Learning — 27
Independent Learning — 28
Performance-Based Assessment — 29, 30

SMALL-GROUP LEARNING

OVERVIEW

SMALL-GROUP LEARNING

Working as a Team

1. **Take a Position** Remind groups to let all members share their responses. You may wish to set a time limit for this discussion.
2. **List Your Rules** You may want to have groups share their lists of rules and consolidate them into a master list to be displayed and followed by all groups.
3. **Apply the Rules** As you circulate among the groups, ensure that students are staying on task. Consider a short time limit for this step.
4. **Name Your Group** This task can be creative and fun. If students have trouble coming up with a name, suggest that they think of something related to the unit topic. Encourage groups to share their names with the class.
5. **Create a Communication Plan** Encourage groups to plan for times during the day to share ideas. They should also devise a method for recording and saving their communications.

Accountable Talk

Remind students that groups should communicate politely. You can post these Accountable Talk suggestions and encourage students to add their own. Students should:

Remember to . . .
Ask clarifying questions.

Which sounds like . . .
I think you said _____. Did I hear you correctly?
I'm not sure I understand what you're saying about _____. Can you elaborate?

Remember to . . .
Explain your thinking.

Which sounds like . . .
My reason for thinking _____ is _____.
I came to my conclusion after _____.

OVERVIEW: SMALL-GROUP LEARNING

Working as a Team

1. **Take a Position** In your group, discuss the following question:

   Which do you think would be easier, immigrating to America from another country, or emigrating from America to another country?

   As you take turns sharing your positions, be sure to provide reasons for your choice. After all group members have shared, discuss some of the political and social realities that could make such transitions challenging.

2. **List Your Rules** As a group, decide on the rules that you will follow as you work together. Samples are provided; add two more of your own. As you work together, you may add or revise rules based on your experience together.
   - Everyone should participate in group discussions.
   - Build upon each other's ideas.
   - ____________________
   - ____________________

3. **Apply the Rules** Share what you have learned about American identity. Make sure each person in the group contributes. Take notes and be prepared to share with the class one thing that you heard from another member of your group.

4. **Name Your Group** Choose a name that reflects the unit topic.

   Our group's name: ____________________

5. **Create a Communication Plan** Decide how you want to communicate with one another. For example, you might use online collaboration tools, email, or instant messaging.

   Our group's decision: ____________________

   ____

FACILITATING SMALL-GROUP LEARNING

Forming Groups

You may wish to form groups for Small-Group Learning so that each consists of students with different learning abilities. Some students may be adept at organizing information, whereas others may have strengths related to generating or synthesizing information. A good mix of abilities can make the experience of Small-Group Learning dynamic and productive.

Making a Schedule

First, find out the due dates for the Small-Group activities. Then, preview the texts and activities with your group and make a schedule for completing the tasks.

SELECTION	ACTIVITIES	DUE DATE
Rules of the Game		
The Writing on the Wall		
With a Little Help From My Friends		
Morning Talk Immigrant Picnic		

Working on Group Projects

As your group works together, you'll find it more effective if each person has a specific role. Different projects require different roles. Before beginning a project, discuss the necessary roles, and choose one for each group member. Some possible roles are listed here. Add your own ideas to the list.

Project Manager: monitors the schedule and keeps everyone on task
Researcher: organizes information-gathering activities
Recorder: takes notes during group meetings

SCAN FOR MULTIMEDIA

DIGITAL PERSPECTIVES

Making a Schedule

Encourage groups to preview the reading selections and to consider how long it will take them to complete the activities accompanying each selection. Point out that they can adjust the due dates for particular selections as needed as they work on their small-group projects; however, they must complete all assigned tasks before the group Performance Task is due. Encourage groups to review their schedules upon completing the activities for each selection to make sure they are on track to meet the final due date.

Working on Group Projects

Point out to groups that the roles they assign can also be changed later. Students might have to make changes based on who is best at each task. Try to make sure that there is no favoritism, cliquishness, or stereotyping by gender or other means in the assignment of roles.

Also, you should review the roles each group assigns to its members. Based on your understanding of students' individual strengths, you might find it necessary to suggest some changes.

AUTHOR'S PERSPECTIVE **Kelly Gallagher, M.Ed.**

Meaningful Talk Instead of asking teacher-directed questions that lead students to see specific elements, give the power back to the students. Help them find their own big ideas and support them by building in talk opportunities. Use these two strategies to help students achieve deeper comprehension.

- *See the Relevance in Reading:* Teachers can have students read great works of literature to give students an opportunity to think deeply about issues that will affect their lives. Asking students "What is worth talking about here?" helps them find themes and interpretations.
- *One Question; One Comment Strategy:* To generate an in-depth discussion of the text, teachers can ask students to come to class with one question and one comment generated from their reading. Have the first student share one comment or question. The next student can answer, respond, or build on the discussion. Continue the process until everyone in class has participated.
- *Silent Talk*: Students write their thoughts quietly for four minutes and then rotate their papers. The next student then continues the "conversation."

These strategies will lessen student dependence on the teacher and help to build independence.

Rules of the Game

AUDIO SUMMARIES
Audio Summaries of "Rules of the Game" are available online in both English and Spanish in the Interactive Teacher's Edition or Unit Resources. Assigning these summaries prior to reading the selection may help students build additional background knowledge and set a context for their first read.

Summary

Amy Tan's short story "Rules of the Game" focuses on the relationship between a mother and her nine-year-old daughter, Waverly. The mother is an immigrant from China. Waverly was born in the United States. Her life changes after her older brother is given a chess set as a Christmas present. Previously happy playing in the streets of San Francisco's Chinatown, Waverly now devotes all of her energy to learning the secrets of chess. With hard work, she improves her game until she is winning chess championships against older, more experienced players. Her success brings her into conflict with her mother. To her mother, Waverly's success belongs to the family, but for Waverly it is hers alone. An argument erupts between them and Waverly runs off. When she returns, it is clear the test of wills with her mother is not over.

Insight

Reading "Rules of the Game" will help students consider the difficulties that come from trying to comply with the customs, beliefs, and laws of two completely different cultures. As the daughter of immigrants and a U.S. citizen by birth, Waverly tries to navigate two worlds. She uses her deftness with all things American against her mother, essentially rejecting the Chinese culture of which her mother is a symbol. She also uses Chinese forms of knowledge and power to become unbeatable at chess, and to arm herself for the ongoing psychological battle against her mother. In the end, her mother uses her Chinese wisdom against Waverly, but she's taught Waverly well. By combining the power she's gained as the "Great American Hope" and the invisible strength she learned from her mother, Waverly is going to be a formidable match for her mother.

ESSENTIAL QUESTION:
What does it mean to be "American"?

Connection to Essential Question

"Rules of the Game" provides a complex perspective on the Essential Question. Waverly and her brothers are American by birth, unlike their immigrant parents. Waverly is also American by virtue of her embrace of American attitudes in direct opposition to her mother, who remains fiercely loyal to her Chinese heritage. As Waverly grows more successful at chess, she embraces the idea that she really is the "Great American Hope," and she creates more and more distance between her American self and her Chinese self.

SMALL-GROUP READING PERFORMANCE TASK
How do the realities of immigrants' experiences reflect or fail to reflect American ideals?

UNIT PERFORMANCE-BASED ASSESSMENT
How is an American identity created?

Connection to Performance Tasks

Small-Group Reading Performance Task In this Performance Task, students will consider how the lives of immigrants in America reflect or fail to reflect American ideals. This selection provides students with depictions of both. Waverly is given opportunities she would not have had in China. The way she works hard to turn those opportunities into great personal achievement reflects American ideals. Her mother's claim that Waverly's achievement belongs not to her but to her family reflects Chinese values rather than American ideals.

Unit Performance-Based Assessment This selection will contribute to students' understanding of how an American identity is created, by illustrating the difficulties an American-born child of immigrant parents might face in creating an American identity when one or both parents refuse to accept the American way of life.

DIGITAL PERSPECTIVES: Audio | Video | Document | Annotation Highlights | EL Highlights | Online Assessment

LESSON RESOURCES

	Making Meaning	Language Development	Effective Expression
Lesson	**First Read** **Close Read** **Analyze the Text** **Analyze Craft and Structure**	**Concept Vocabulary** **Word Study** **Conventions**	**Speaking and Listening**
Instructional Standards	**RL.10** By the end of grade 9, read and comprehend . . . **RL.3** Analyze how complex characters develop . . .	**L.4.a** Use context as a clue . . . **L.4.d** Verify the preliminary determination . . . **L.5.b** Analyze nuances in the meaning of words . . . **L.2** Demonstrate command of the conventions . . . **L.1.b** Use various types of phrases and clauses . . .	**SL.4** Present information, findings, and supporting evidence . . .
STUDENT RESOURCES			
Available online in the Interactive Student Edition or Unit Resources	Selection Audio First-Read Guide: Fiction Close-Read Guide: Fiction	Word Network	Evidence Log
TEACHER RESOURCES			
Selection Resources Available online in the Interactive Teacher's Edition or Unit Resources	Audio Summaries Annotation Highlights EL Highlights Rules of the Game: Text Questions Analyze Craft and Structure: Complex Characters English Language Support Lesson: Character Traits	Conventions: Participles and Participial Phrases Concept Vocabulary and Word Study	Speaking and Listening: Act Out a Scene
Reteach/Practice (RP) Available online in the Interactive Teacher's Edition or Unit Resources	Analyze Craft and Structure: Complex Characters (RP)	Conventions: Participles and Participial Phrases (RP) Word Study: Connotation and Denotation (RP)	Speaking and Listening: Act Out a Scene (RP)
Assessment Available online in Assessments			Selection Test
My Resources	A Unit 1 Answer Key is available online and in the Interactive Teacher's Edition.		

Reading Support

Text Complexity Rubric: Rules of the Game	
Quantitative Measures	
Lexile: 1000 **Text Length:** 4,486 words	
Qualitative Measures	
Knowledge Demands ①—②—❸—④—⑤	Some themes and situations may be unfamiliar (Chinese immigrant experience, growing up in urban Chinese neighborhood), but they are explained in the narrative.
Structure ①—②—❸—④—⑤	Story is told chronologically, with some shifts in time to span several years in character's life; dialogue breaks up text and makes it easier to read.
Language Conventionality and Clarity ①—②—③—❹—⑤	Story contains rich descriptive language and metaphorical phrases; intentional grammatical errors are used for mother's speech (as a Chinese immigrant).
Levels of Meaning/Purpose ①—②—③—❹—⑤	Multiple levels of meaning (*rules of the game, next move* refer to chess, to adjustment of immigrant to American life, or to character's family life and relationship with mother).

DECIDE AND PLAN

English Language Support

Provide English Learners with support for language and meaning as they read the selection.

Language Point out that the author intentionally employs grammatical errors for the mother's speech because she is a Chinese immigrant with a contempt for learning anything beyond the most basic English. Ask students to work in pairs to find errors in specific sentences and to suggest ways to correct them—for example *What you say? What did you say?*

Meaning/Purpose Discuss the meanings of metaphorical phrases—for example, *I pondered my next move*. Tell students that to *ponder* means to think about, and the phrase *next move* comes from chess and other strategic board-games in which the opponents take turns to "make a move." Here it means the strategy the girl will use to get along with her mother.

Strategic Support

Provide students with strategic support to ensure that they can successfully read the text.

Knowledge Demands Discuss the situation in the story—an American-born girl growing up with a mother who is a Chinese immigrant who refuses to adopt American culture. Ask students to look for references to Chinese culture—for example, in descriptions of Chinatown, Chinese names and foods, and a Chinese proverb.

Meaning/Purpose Guide students to understand metaphorical phrases—for example: *I closed my eyes and pondered my next move.* Ask questions to help with the meaning: *If you ponder your next move in a chess game, what do you do?* (think about where to move the piece). *The girl is imagining a chess game. What is she also pondering?* (how to resolve the fight with her mother)

Challenge

Provide students who need to be challenged with ideas for how they can go beyond a simple interpretation of the text.

Text Analysis Ask students to describe the emotions that the girl and the mother are feeling at various points in the story—for example, after their conflict at the end. Encourage them to give specific examples of how the emotions are expressed or repressed by the characters.

Written Response Have students look up the website of the author Amy Tan: https://www.amytan.net/

Ask them to read the bio and to write a paragraph describing the most interesting thing they have learned about the author.

TEACH

Read and Respond

Have the groups read the selection and complete the Making Meaning, Language Development, and Effective Expression activities.

Standards Support Through Teaching and Learning Cycle

IDENTIFY NEEDS

Analyze results of the Beginning-of-Year Assessment, focusing on the items relating to Unit 1. Also take into consideration student performance to this point and your observations of where particular students struggle.

DECIDE AND PLAN

- If students have performed poorly on items matching these standards, then provide selection scaffolds before assigning them the on-level lesson provided in the Student Edition.
- If students have done well on the Beginning-of-Year Assessment, then challenge them to keep progressing and learning by giving them opportunities to practice the skills in depth.
- Use the Selection Resources listed on the Planning pages for "Rules of the Game" to help students continually improve their ability to master the standards.

Instructional Standards: Rules of the Game

	Catching Up	This Year	Looking Forward
Reading	You may wish to administer the **Analyze Craft and Structure: Complex Characters (RP)** worksheet to help students understand and distinguish ways in which authors present the traits of a character directly and indirectly.	**RL.3** Analyze how complex characters develop over the course of a text, interact with other characters, and advance the plot or develop the theme.	Ask students to work in small groups to identify how the relationship between mother and daughter is introduced. Then challenge groups to trace how the author conveys the feelings of these two characters toward one another, as the events of the story unfold.
Speaking and Listening	You may wish to administer the **Speaking and Listening: Act Out a Scene (RP)** worksheet to help students understand that characterization is reflected in how a character speaks and what a character says in a given situation.	**SL.4** Present information, findings, and supporting evidence clearly, concisely, and logically such that listeners can follow the line of reasoning and the organization, development, substance, and style are appropriate to purpose, audience, and task.	Challenge students to choose a character from the selection and present an oral narrative based on a diary entry that character could have written about an event in the story. Record the narratives. Then encourage students to listen to, revise, and then re-record their presentations. Suggest they share the final recordings with the class.
Language	You may wish to administer the **Conventions: Participles and Participial Phrases (RP)** worksheet to help students understand the function of participial phrases and their impact on meaning.	**L.1.b** Use various types of phrases and clauses to convey specific meanings and add variety and interest to writing or presentations.	Have students identify examples of participial phrases used in the selection and determine what the participial phrases modify.

TEACH

Implement the planned lesson, and gather evidence of student learning.

ANALYZE AND REVISE

- Analyze student work for evidence of student learning.
- Identify whether or not students have met the expectations in the standards.
- Identify implications for future instruction.

FACILITATING

Jump Start

FIRST READ Have students discuss what games (other than chess) they have played that involve using strategies to win. Have they ever applied these strategies to real-life situations? Were these strategies useful?

Rules of the Game

How important is it to play by the rules? Should rules given by parents or adults in authority always be followed? When does it make sense to challenge these rules? Modeling the questions a reader might ask as they read "Rules of the Game" for the first time brings the text alive for students and connects it to the Small-Group Performance Task assignment. Selection audio and print capability for the selection are available in the Interactive Teacher's Edition.

Concept Vocabulary

Encourage groups to discuss the four concept vocabulary words and share their familiarity or knowledge of each one. Ask students to study the modeling of context clues. Have groups discuss how words surrounding an unknown word help them narrow down possibilities of meaning, especially when the unknown word has multiple meanings.

FIRST READ

Have students perform the steps of the first read independently:

NOTICE: Encourage students to notice main characters and to pay attention to ways in which they follow (or break) rules and use strategies when interacting with one another or with other people.

ANNOTATE: Remind students to mark passages that include vivid details, figurative language, and dialogue.

CONNECT: Encourage students to go beyond the text to make connections with other stories they know, movies, TV shows, or their own personal experiences.

RESPOND: Students will answer questions and write a summary to demonstrate understanding.

Point out to students that while they will always complete the Respond step at the end of the first read, the other steps will probably happen somewhat concurrently. You may wish to print copies of the **First-Read Guide: Fiction** for students to use.

MAKING MEANING

About the Author

Amy Tan (b. 1952) grew up in Oakland, California, across the bay from where "Rules of the Game" takes place. Tan first published "Rules of the Game" in a magazine and then expanded the story into the novel *The Joy Luck Club. The Joy Luck Club* was praised for how it depicted the complicated relationships between Chinese mothers and their Chinese American daughters. It was hugely successful, receiving critical acclaim, and was a *New York Times* bestseller. Tan has received numerous awards, and her books have been translated into 25 languages.

Rules of the Game

Concept Vocabulary

As you perform your first read of "Rules of the Game," you will encounter these words.

deftly	relented	plotted	concessions

Context Clues To infer the meaning of an unfamiliar word, look to its context—the words and sentences that surround it.

Example: The emergency exit doors were clearly marked to allow for rapid and safe **evacuation** from the building.

Explanation: The underlined context clues provide hints that an *evacuation* is a fast exit from a dangerous situation.

Example: The **simulation** of the crash seemed so life-like, it was a relief to discover that it was not real.

Explanation: The underlined context clues help you infer that the word *simulation* refers to something that is not real, but is an enactment of events.

Apply your knowledge of context clues and other vocabulary strategies to determine the meanings of unfamiliar words you encounter during your first read. Confirm your definitions using a print or online dictionary.

First Read FICTION

Apply these strategies as you conduct your first read. You will have an opportunity to complete a close read after your first read.

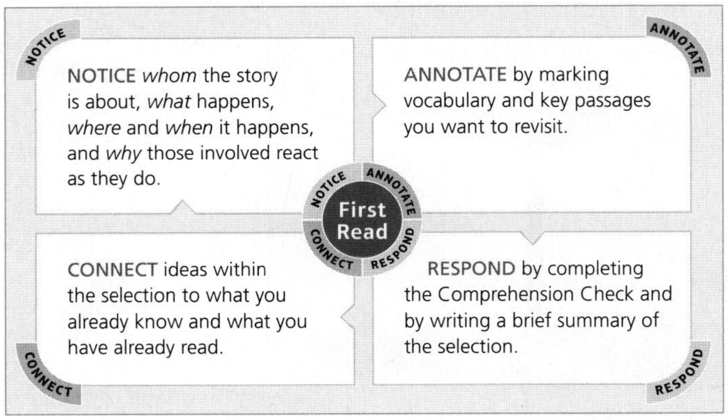

NOTICE
NOTICE *whom* the story is about, *what* happens, *where* and *when* it happens, and *why* those involved react as they do.
ANNOTATE
ANNOTATE by marking vocabulary and key passages you want to revisit.
First Read
NOTICE ANNOTATE CONNECT RESPOND
CONNECT
CONNECT ideas within the selection to what you already know and what you have already read.
RESPOND
RESPOND by completing the Comprehension Check and by writing a brief summary of the selection.

STANDARDS

Reading Literature
By the end of grade 9, read and comprehend literature, including stories, dramas, and poems, in the grades 9–10 text complexity band proficiently, with scaffolding as needed at the high end of the range.

Language
Use context as a clue to the meaning of a word or phrase.

PERSONALIZE FOR LEARNING

English Language Support

Proverbs Throughout their 4,000 year history, the Chinese have produced more proverbs than any other culture. Sayings that offer wisdom in the form of homespun advice are called proverbs. Often these sayings are written in figurative descriptive language, language used imaginatively rather than literally. In paragraph 2, Waverly learns *the art of invisible strength* through a proverb when her mother tells her, "Wise guy, he not go against wind. In Chinese we say, Come from South, blow with wind—poom!—North will follow. Strongest wind cannot be seen." Have students discuss the image created by the proverb and ask what they think the proverb means, or might have meant in its native Chinese. Then, have students share proverbs from their own cultural heritage. **ALL LEVELS**

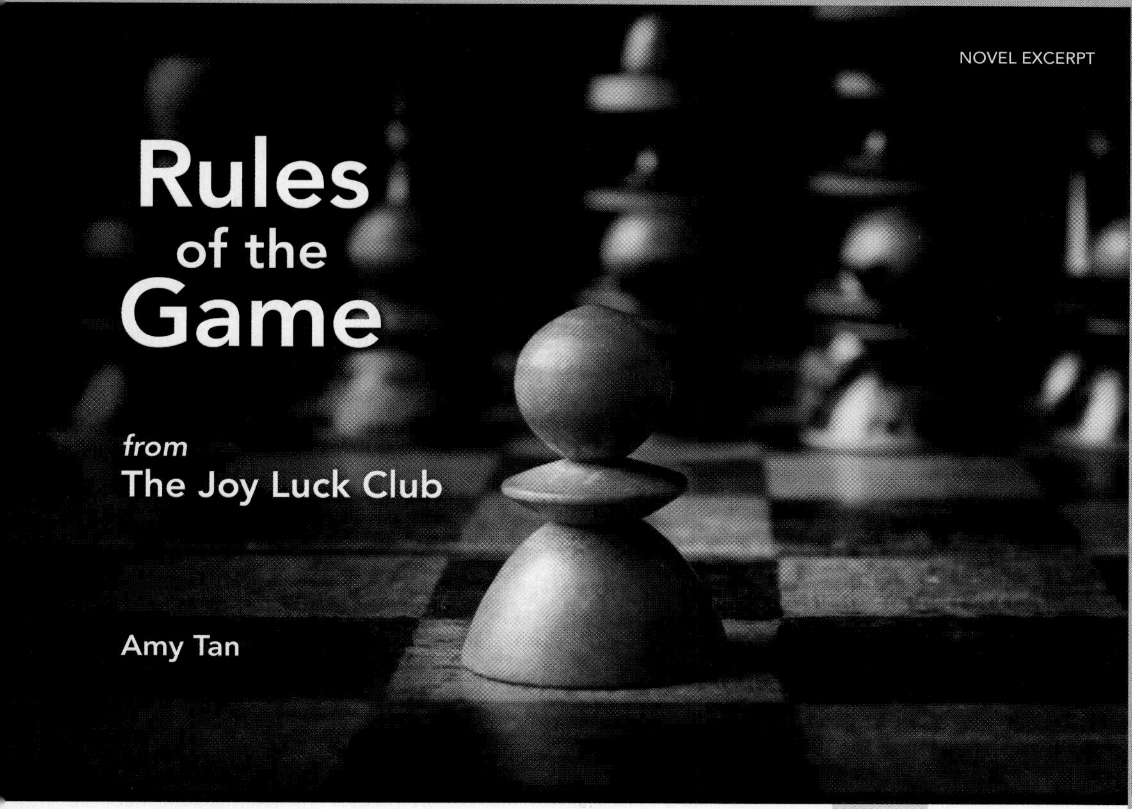

NOVEL EXCERPT

Rules of the Game

from
The Joy Luck Club

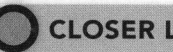

Amy Tan

BACKGROUND

Chess is a game of strategy that has gained world-wide popularity. Winning a game of chess requires capturing the opposing king piece, using your own pieces. Chess organizations record the rankings of players. The most successful players are called *grand masters.*

SCAN FOR MULTIMEDIA

NOTES

1 I was six when my mother taught me the art of invisible strength. It was a strategy for winning arguments, respect from others, and eventually, though neither of us knew it at the time, chess games.

2 "Bite back your tongue," scolded my mother when I cried loudly, yanking her hand toward the store that sold bags of salted plums. At home, she said, "Wise guy, he not go against wind. In Chinese we say, Come from South, blow with wind—poom!—North will follow. Strongest wind cannot be seen."

3 The next week I bit back my tongue as we entered the store with the forbidden candies. When my mother finished her shopping, she quietly plucked a small bag of plums from the rack and put it on the counter with the rest of the items.

* * *

DIGITAL PERSPECTIVES

CLOSER LOOK

Analyze Idioms

Circulate among groups as students conduct their close read. Suggest that groups close read paragraph 2. If needed, provide the following support.

ANNOTATE: Have students mark details in paragraph 2 that demonstrate the use of an idiom, or work with small groups to have students participate as you highlight them together.

QUESTION: Guide students to consider what these details might tell them. Ask what a reader can infer from these details, and accept student responses.

Possible response: The mother is telling Waverly to be quiet and control her impulse to ask for things. In her attempt to be emphatic she shows her incomplete grasp of the English idiom; the correct expression is "bite your tongue."

CONCLUDE: Help students to formulate conclusions about the importance of these details in the text. Ask students why the author might have included these details.

Possible response: Tan wishes to illuminate essential aspects of the mother through the way she speaks. The confidence with which the mother alters an English idiom demonstrates her determination to express herself forcibly in the language of her adopted country.

Remind students than an **idiom** is an expression that is peculiar to a given language, region, community, or class of people. It cannot be understood literally. Idioms often arise from a figure of speech (for example, *show your hand, follow suit, poker face,* or *take the wrong tack*).

AUTHOR'S PERSPECTIVE **Jim Cummins, Ph.D.**

Literacy Engagements. The more students are engaged with print texts, the more they can develop their academic language proficiency. Conversational fluency is faster to achieve than academic proficiency, so students working in small groups can build language. To support academic language growth and help enhance student engagement with literacy, use these methods:

- **Increase access to print:** To build academic vocabulary, reading is key. Encourage students to read the texts in *myPerspectives* as well as other selections of their choice.
- **Scaffold Meaning:** Teachers can support students' understanding by using visuals such as illustrations and graphic organizers in the text. Next, teachers can use students' first language to help them understand content in their second language by using electronic translators and bilingual dictionaries.
- **Connect to Students' Lives:** Students' background knowledge is activated by the instruction. This may or may not occur through a student's first language. Help students build from what they already know.
- **Extend Language:** Use instructional strategies across the curriculum to expand students' language base. For example, make an effort to call out new words, unusual syntax, or other language challenges when the opportunities arise.

Concept Vocabulary

DEFTLY If groups are struggling to define the word *deftly* in paragraph 7, point out that one of the meanings of the base word *deft* is "skillful and clever." Remind students that the suffix *–ly* can mean "in a manner specified by the adjective." Point out that it is used with reference to the gutting of fish. Then ask students to define the word.

Possible response: *Deftly* must mean "appearing to be skillful; skilfully."

NOTES

4 My mother imparted her daily truths so she could help my older brothers and me rise above our circumstances. We lived in San Francisco's Chinatown. Like most of the other Chinese children who played in the back alleys of restaurants and curio shops, I didn't think we were poor. My bowl was always full, three five-course meals every day, beginning with a soup full of mysterious things I didn't want to know the names of.

5 We lived on Waverly Place, in a warm, clean, two-bedroom flat that sat above a small Chinese bakery specializing in steamed pastries and dim sum.[1] In the early morning, when the alley was still quiet, I could smell fragrant red beans as they were cooked down to a pasty sweetness. By daybreak, our flat was heavy with the odor of fried sesame balls and sweet curried chicken crescents. From my bed, I would listen as my father got ready for work, then locked the door behind him, one-two-three clicks.

6 At the end of our two-block alley was a small sandlot playground with swings and slides well-shined down the middle with use. The play area was bordered by wood-slat benches where old-country people sat cracking roasted watermelon seeds with their golden teeth and scattering the husks to an impatient gathering of gurgling pigeons. The best playground, however, was the dark alley itself. It was crammed with daily mysteries and adventures. My brothers and I would peer into the medicinal herb shop, watching old Li dole out onto a stiff sheet of white paper the right amount of insect shells, saffron-colored seeds, and pungent leaves for his ailing customers. It was said that he once cured a woman dying of an ancestral curse that had eluded the best of American doctors. Next to the pharmacy was a printer who specialized in gold-embossed wedding invitations and festive red banners.

7 Farther down the street was Ping Yuen Fish Market. The front window displayed a tank crowded with doomed fish and turtles struggling to gain footing on the slimy green-tiled sides. A hand-written sign informed tourists, "Within this store, is all for food, not for pet." Inside, the butchers with their bloodstained white smocks **deftly** gutted the fish while customers cried out their orders and shouted, "Give me your freshest," to which the butchers always protested, "All are freshest." On less crowded market days, we would inspect the crates of live frogs and crabs which we were warned not to poke, boxes of dried cuttlefish, and row upon row of iced prawns, squid, and slippery fish. The sanddabs made me shiver each time; their eyes lay on one flattened side and reminded me of my mother's story of a careless girl who ran into a crowded street and was crushed by a cab. "Was smash flat," reported my mother.

Mark context clues or indicate another strategy you used that helped you determine meaning.

deftly (DEHFT lee) *adv.*

MEANING:

8 At the corner of the alley was Hong Sing's, a four-table café with a recessed stairwell in front that led to a door marked "Tradesmen." My brothers and I believed the bad people emerged from this door

1. **dim sum** small dishes of traditional Chinese foods meant to be shared.

FACILITATING SMALL-GROUP CLOSE READING

CLOSE READ: Narrative Fiction As groups perform their close read, circulate and offer support as needed.

- Remind groups that when they read fiction, they should be sure to identify the leading characters, distinguish the main events, and follow the plot.
- If a group struggles to work out why particular events are important, remind them that in narrative fiction, events are created through the interaction—usually conflict—between characters, and guide them toward points of conflict and resolution involving Waverly and her mother.
- Challenge groups to determine the theme of the text and the specific details that support their determination.

at night. Tourists never went to Hong Sing's, since the menu was printed only in Chinese. A Caucasian man with a big camera once posed me and my playmates in front of the restaurant. He had us move to the side of the picture window so the photo would capture the roasted duck with its head dangling from a juice-covered rope. After he took the picture, I told him he should go into Hong Sing's and eat dinner. When he smiled and asked me what they served, I shouted, "Guts and duck's feet and octopus gizzards!" Then I ran off with my friends, shrieking with laughter as we scampered across the alley and hid in the entryway grotto of the China Gem Company, my heart pounding with hope that he would chase us.

9 My mother named me after the street that we lived on: Waverly Place Jong, my official name for important American documents. But my family called me Meimei, "Little Sister." I was the youngest, the only daughter. Each morning before school, my mother would twist and yank on my thick black hair until she had formed two tightly wound pigtails. One day, as she struggled to weave a hard-toothed comb through my disobedient hair, I had a sly thought.

10 I asked her, "Ma, what is Chinese torture?" My mother shook her head. A bobby pin was wedged between her lips. She wetted her palm and smoothed the hair above my ear, then pushed the pin in so that it nicked sharply against my scalp.

11 "Who say this word?" she asked without a trace of knowing how wicked I was being. I shrugged my shoulders and said, "Some boy in my class said Chinese people do Chinese torture."

12 "Chinese people do many things," she said simply. "Chinese people do business, do medicine, do painting. Not lazy like American people. We do torture. Best torture."

* * *

13 My older brother Vincent was the one who actually got the chess set. We had gone to the annual Christmas party held at the First Chinese Baptist Church at the end of the alley. The missionary ladies had put together a Santa bag of gifts donated by members of another church. None of the gifts had names on them. There were separate sacks for boys and girls of different ages.

14 One of the Chinese parishioners had donned a Santa Claus costume and a stiff paper beard with cotton balls glued to it. I think the only children who thought he was the real thing were too young to know that Santa Claus was not Chinese. When my turn came up, the Santa man asked me how old I was. I thought it was a trick question; I was seven according to the American formula and eight by the Chinese calendar. I said I was born on March 17, 1951. That seemed to satisfy him. He then solemnly asked if I had been a very, very good girl this year and did I believe in Jesus Christ and obey my parents. I knew the only answer to that. I nodded back with equal solemnity.

NOTES

DIGITAL PERSPECTIVES

CLOSER LOOK

Analyze First Person Point of View

Circulate among groups as students conduct their close read. Suggest that groups close read paragraph 14. Encourage them to talk about the annotations that they mark. If needed, provide the following support.

ANNOTATE: Have students mark details in paragraph 14 that indicate the narrator's memories and views regarding the Chinese Santa Claus, or work with small groups to have students participate while you highlight them together.

QUESTION: Guide students to consider what these details might tell them. Ask what a reader can infer from what was annotated, and accept student responses.

Possible response: Waverly knows that Santa Claus is not Chinese, so she is not fooled by the costume. She is, however, confused by his question because the two cultures she embodies have two different calendars, according to which she can give two different answers.

CONCLUDE: Help students to formulate conclusions about the importance of these details in the text. Ask students why the author might have included these details.

Possible response: The author shows how astute and intelligent Waverly is, especially with regard to any conflict between her two cultural influences. The author uses first-person narrative—she remembers and comments on her memories. However, she can still see and hear things as she saw and heard them as a child. This dual point of view often infuses the narrative with humor and irony.

Remind students that in a fictional work, a first-person narrator is a character who tells the story and speaks "I." With a first-person narrator, the reader sees, hears, and understands only what this character sees, hears, and understands—and only what this character chooses to reveal. Stories told by a first-person narrator are told from the **first-person point of view**.

VOCABULARY DEVELOPMENT

Multiple Meanings Tell students the word *capture* in paragraph 8 has multiple meanings. Discuss the following sentences with students.

1. The army wanted to *capture* the city that day. (to gain control by force)
2. She decided to *capture* the knight on her third move. (to take possession of something belonging to your opponent)
3. The hotel management *captures* credit card information during registration. (to read electronically and retain)
4. The artist hoped to *capture* the brilliant colors of the sunset. (to reproduce precisely as a record)

Have students reread the following sentence in paragraph 8, *He had us move . . . so the photo would capture the roasted duck with its head dangling from a juice-covered rope*. Guide them to identify which meaning is used in the sentence. Remind students to look for context clues to help define words with multiple meanings.

CLOSER LOOK

Analyze Hyperbole

Circulate among groups as students conduct their close read. Suggest that groups close read paragraph 19. Encourage them to talk about the annotations that they mark. If needed, provide the following support.

ANNOTATE: Have students mark details in paragraph 19 that use hyperbole to convey the power of the chessboard over Waverly's brothers, or work with small groups to have students participate while you highlight them together.

QUESTION: Guide students to consider what these details might tell them. Ask what a reader can infer from what was annotated, and accept student responses.

Possible response: The narrator uses hyperbole to describe Waverly's perception of the chessboard's transformative powers over her brothers. She uses exaggeration as a very effective way to convey the amazing change in the two boys, and to describe how seriously they took the game.

CONCLUDE: Help students to formulate conclusions about the importance of these details in the text. Ask students why the author might have included these details.

Possible response: Tan wants the reader to understand the impact that chess has on Waverly, who sees the game as being more powerful than anything she has ever witnessed before. The author is hinting strongly that this will lead to a very significant development in Waverly's life.

Remind students that **hyperbole** is a figure of speech that uses deliberate overstatement, or exaggeration—either for comic effect or to express heightened emotion. Sometimes overstatement is used as a synonym for hyperbole, but overstatement is really the means by which hyperbole creates its figurative (nonliteral) effect.

NOTES

15 Having watched the other children opening their gifts, I already knew that the big gifts were not necessarily the nicest ones. One girl my age got a large coloring book of biblical characters, while a less greedy girl who selected a smaller box received a glass vial of lavender toilet water. The sound of the box was also important. A ten-year-old boy had chosen a box that jangled when he shook it. It was a tin globe of the world with a slit for inserting money. He must have thought it was full of dimes and nickels, because when he saw that it had just ten pennies, his face fell with such undisguised disappointment that his mother slapped the side of his head and led him out of the church hall, apologizing to the crowd for her son who had such bad manners he couldn't appreciate such a fine gift.

16 As I peered into the sack, I quickly fingered the remaining presents, testing their weight, imagining what they contained. I chose a heavy, compact one that was wrapped in shiny silver foil and a red satin ribbon. It was a twelve-pack of Life Savers and I spent the rest of the party arranging and rearranging the candy tubes in the order of my favorites. My brother Winston chose wisely as well. His present turned out to be a box of intricate plastic parts; the instructions on the box proclaimed that when they were properly assembled he would have an authentic miniature replica of a World War II submarine.

As I peered into the sack, I quickly fingered the remaining presents, testing their weight, imagining what they contained.

Vincent got the chess set, which would have been a very decent present to get at a church Christmas party, except it was obviously used and, as we discovered later, it was missing a black pawn and a white knight. My mother graciously thanked the unknown benefactor, saying, "Too good. Cost too much." At which point, an old lady with fine white, wispy hair nodded toward our family and said with a whistling whisper, "Merry, merry Christmas."

18 When we got home, my mother told Vincent to throw the chess set away. "She not want it. We not want it," she said, tossing her head stiffly to the side with a tight, proud smile. My brothers had deaf ears. They were already lining up the chess pieces and reading from the dog-eared instruction book.

* * *

19 I watched Vincent and Winston play during Christmas week. The chess board seemed to hold elaborate secrets waiting to be untangled. The chessmen were more powerful than Old Li's magic herbs that cured ancestral curses. And my brothers wore such serious faces that I was sure something was at stake that was greater than avoiding the tradesmen's door to Hong Sing's.

20 "Let me! Let me!" I begged between games when one brother or the other would sit back with a deep sigh of relief and victory,

PERSONALIZE FOR LEARNING

Strategic Support

Description Guide students as they review paragraphs 15 and 16 As a class, reread the descriptions of children choosing their presents and Waverly as she chooses her own present. Discuss how these differences give the reader important details about how Waverly approaches a problem or challenge. Have students compare and contrast the two approaches to picking gifts, and ask what it might convey to them about Waverly's character and about her method of solving a problem or meeting a challenge.

the other annoyed, unable to let go of the outcome. Vincent at first refused to let me play, but when I offered my Life Savers as replacements for the buttons that filled in for the missing pieces, he **relented**. He chose the flavors: wild cherry for the black pawn and peppermint for the white knight. Winner could eat both.

21 As our mother sprinkled flour and rolled out small doughy circles for the steamed dumplings that would be our dinner that night, Vincent explained the rules, pointing to each piece. "You have sixteen pieces and so do I. One king and queen, two bishops, two knights, two castles, and eight pawns. The pawns can only move forward one step, except on the first move. Then they can move two. But they can only take men by moving crossways like this, except in the beginning, when you can move ahead and take another pawn."

22 "Why?" I asked as I moved my pawn. "Why can't they move more steps?"

23 "Because they're pawns," he said.

24 "But why do they go crossways to take other men. Why aren't there any women and children?"

25 "Why is the sky blue? Why must you always ask stupid questions?" asked Vincent. "This is a game. These are the rules. I didn't make them up. See. Here. In the book." He jabbed a page with a pawn in his hand. "Pawn. P-A-W-N. Pawn. Read it yourself."

26 My mother patted the flour off her hands. "Let me see book," she said quietly. She scanned the pages quickly, not reading the foreign English symbols, seeming to search deliberately for nothing in particular.

27 "This American rules," she concluded at last. "Every time people come out from foreign country, must know rules. You not know, judge say, Too bad, go back. They not telling you why so you can use their way go forward. They say, Don't know why, you find out yourself. But they knowing all the time. Better you take it, find out why yourself." She tossed her head back with a satisfied smile.

28 I found out about all the whys later. I read the rules and looked up all the big words in a dictionary. I borrowed books from the Chinatown library. I studied each chess piece, trying to absorb the power each contained.

29 I learned about opening moves and why it's important to control the center early on; the shortest distance between two points is straight down the middle. I learned about the middle game and why tactics between two adversaries are like clashing ideas; the one who plays better has the clearest plans for both attacking and getting out of traps. I learned why it is essential in the endgame[2] to have foresight, a mathematical understanding of all possible moves, and patience; all weaknesses and advantages become evident to a strong adversary and are obscured to a tiring opponent. I discovered that

2. **endgame** final stage of a chess game, when few pieces remain.

NOTES

Mark context clues or indicate another strategy you used that helped you determine meaning.

relented (rih LEHNT ihd) *v.*

MEANING:

DIGITAL PERSPECTIVES

Concept Vocabulary

RELENTED If groups are struggling to define the word *relented* in paragraph 20, point out that the surrounding words and phrases refer to Vincent's attitude toward Waverly playing chess and her response. These include "at first refused" and "when I offered my Life Savers." These details should lead the students to infer that initially Vincent will not let Waverly play, but then he changes his mind because her Life Savers are attractive replacements for the missing pieces.

Possible response: *Relented* means "agree to do something after resisting it before."

Additional **English Language Support** is available in the Interactive Teacher's Edition.

PERSONALIZE FOR LEARNING

English Language Support

Cohesion If students struggle with "long sentences," explain that the author is presenting thoughts as a single unit. Have students read the sentence from paragraph 20: "He chose the flavors: wild cherry for the black pawn and peppermint for the white knight." For this type of sentence, have students look "backward" to find the "wild cherry" and "peppermint" references.

Have students read the sentence from paragraph 21: "As our mother sprinkled flour and rolled out small doughy circles for the steamed dumplings that would be our dinner that night, Vincent explained the rules, pointing to each piece." Have students discuss the two main actions in the sentence. Then assist students in determining to what "that" refers. **ALL LEVELS**

FACILITATING

CLOSER LOOK

Analyzing Situational Irony

Circulate among groups as students conduct their close read. Suggest that groups close read paragraph 33. Encourage them to talk about the annotations that they mark. If needed, provide the following support.

ANNOTATE: Have students mark details in paragraph 33 that set the reader up to expect something the characters may not expect.

QUESTION: Guide students to consider what these details might tell them. Ask what a reader can infer from Lau Po's reaction to Waverly's question, and accept student responses.

Possible response: Lau Po makes the assumption that the box under Waverly's arm is full of dolls. In so doing he dismisses Waverly as a little girl who would not be able to understand chess. His words carry the clear connotation that since Waverly is just a *little* girl, he has absolutely no intention of playing chess with her.

CONCLUDE: Help students to formulate conclusions about the importance of these details in the text. Ask students why the author might have included these details.

Possible response: Tan interjects humor through Lau Po's response to Waverly's request. Unlike the reader, who has been following her amazing progress, Lau Po has no idea that he's addressing a gifted chess player. The reader can take pleasure in Lao Po's ignorant scorn, and look forward to seeing him taken down by this brilliant child.

Remind students that **situational irony** is a form of irony that exists when something happens that directly contradicts the expectations of the characters, the readers, or the audience. In situational irony, or irony of situation, what happens is often the opposite of what we expect to happen, or what seems appropriate. Stories with surprise endings are ironic in this way—but situational irony encompasses more than just a plot twist.

NOTES

for the whole game one must gather invisible strengths and see the endgame before the game begins.

30 I also found out why I should never reveal "why" to others. A little knowledge withheld is a great advantage one should store for future use. That is the power of chess. It is a game of secrets in which one must show and never tell.

31 I loved the secrets I found within the sixty-four black and white squares. I carefully drew a handmade chessboard and pinned it to the wall next to my bed, where at night I would stare for hours at imaginary battles. Soon I no longer lost any games or Life Savers, but I lost my adversaries. Winston and Vincent decided they were more interested in roaming the streets after school in their Hopalong Cassidy cowboy hats.

32 On a cold spring afternoon, while walking home from school, I detoured through the playground at the end of our alley. I saw a group of old men, two seated across a folding table playing a game of chess, others smoking pipes, eating peanuts, and watching. I ran home and grabbed Vincent's chess set, which was bound in a cardboard box with rubber bands. I also carefully selected two prized rolls of Life Savers. I came back to the park and approached a man who was observing the game.

33 "Want to play?" I asked him. His face widened with surprise and he grinned as he looked at the box under my arm. "Little sister, been a long time since I play with dolls," he said, smiling benevolently. I quickly put the box down next to him on the bench and displayed my retort.

34 Lau Po, as he allowed me to call him, turned out to be a much better player than my brothers. I lost many games and many Life Savers. But over the weeks, with each diminishing roll of candies, I added new secrets. Lau Po gave me the names. The Double Attack from the East and West Shores. Throwing Stones on the Drowning Man. The Sudden Meeting of the Clan. The Surprise from the Sleeping Guard. The Humble Servant Who Kills the King. Sand in the Eyes of Advancing Forces. A Double Killing Without Blood.

35 There were also the fine points of chess etiquette. Keep captured men in neat rows, as well-tended prisoners. Never announce "Check" with vanity, lest someone with an unseen sword slit your throat. Never hurl pieces into the sandbox after you have lost a game, because then you must find them again, by yourself, after apologizing to all around you. By the end of the summer, Lau Po had taught me all he knew, and I had become a better chess player.

36 A small weekend crowd of Chinese people and tourists would gather as I played and defeated my opponents one by one. My mother would join the crowds during these outdoor exhibition games. She sat proudly on the bench, telling my admirers with proper Chinese humility, "Is luck."

WriteNow Inform and Explain

Exposition In paragraph 34, Lau Po teaches Waverly a number of chess plays, all of which are given special names. Have students write briefly on a game they have played (athletic or board) in which certain moves or strategies have been named after the players who created them or made them their own by executing them with unique brilliance. Students should describe these moves and strategies and explain why their names are appropriate and well-deserved.

NOTES

37 A man who watched me play in the park suggested that my mother allow me to play in local chess tournaments. My mother smiled graciously, an answer that meant nothing. I desperately wanted to go, but I bit back my tongue. I knew she would not let me play among strangers. So as we walked home I said in a small voice that I didn't want to play in the local tournament. They would have American rules. If I lost, I would bring shame on my family.

38 "Is shame you fall down nobody push you," said my mother.

39 During my first tournament, my mother sat with me in the front row as I waited for my turn. I frequently bounced my legs to unstick them from the cold metal seat of the folding chair. When my name was called, I leapt up. My mother unwrapped something in her lap. It was her *chang,* a small tablet of red jade which held the sun's fire. "Is luck," she whispered, and tucked it into my dress pocket. I turned to my opponent, a fifteen-year-old boy from Oakland. He looked at me, wrinkling his nose.

40 As I began to play, the boy disappeared, the color ran out of the room, and I saw only my white pieces and his black ones waiting on the other side. A light wind began blowing past my ears. It whispered secrets only I could hear.

41 "Blow from the South," it murmured. "The wind leaves no trail." I saw a clear path, the traps to avoid. The crowd rustled. "Shhh! Shhh!" said the corners of the room. The wind blew stronger. "Throw sand from the East to distract him." The knight came forward ready for the sacrifice. The wind hissed, louder and louder. "Blow, blow, blow. He cannot see. He is blind now. Make him lean away from the wind so he is easier to knock down."

PERSONALIZE FOR LEARNING

English Language Support

Personification Note the last two sentences of paragraph 40: "A light wind began blowing past my ears. It whispered secrets only I could hear." Explain to students that these sentences contain an example of personification, a type of figurative language in which a nonhuman subject is given human characteristics. The author is attributing human qualities to the wind. Have students look for more examples of personification, and encourage them to invent some examples of their own. Have them discuss why they think the author chose to use personification to describe the wind. **ALL LEVELS**

CLOSER LOOK

Analyze Dialect

Circulate among groups as students conduct their close read. Suggest that groups close read paragraphs 43, 45, and 47. Encourage them to talk about the annotations that they mark. If needed, provide the following support.

ANNOTATE: Have students mark details in these paragraphs that reveal unusual language patterns, or work with small groups to have students participate while you highlight them together.

QUESTION: Guide students to consider what these details might tell them. Ask what a reader can infer from what was annotated, and accept student responses.

Possible response: Waverly's mother speaks quickly and emphatically, but she has never fully learned English and speaks in a hybrid form of English that is unique to herself. Her manner of speech indicates either an unwillingness or an inability to absorb or be absorbed into the culture of the country to which she came as an immigrant.

CONCLUDE: Help students to formulate conclusions about the importance of these details in the text. Ask students why the author might have included these details.

Possible response: Tan reveals important aspects of character by having Waverly's mother speak in this curious form of Chinese English. The confidence and fluency with which she incorrectly uses the English language indicates a powerful and intelligent character who expects to be understood and obeyed, whatever comes out of her mouth.

Remind students that **dialect** is the form of a language spoken by people in a particular region or group. Dialects differ from one another in grammar, syntax, vocabulary, and pronunciation. Writers often use dialect to make a character sound more realistic and to create local color in a literary work.

NOTES

42 "Check,"[3] I said, as the wind roared with laughter. The wind died down to little puffs, my own breath.

* * *

43 My mother placed my first trophy next to a new plastic chess set that the neighborhood Tao society had given to me. As she wiped each piece with a soft cloth, she said, "Next time win more, lose less."

44 "Ma, it's not how many pieces you lose," I said. "Sometimes you need to lose pieces to get ahead."

45 "Better to lose less, see if you really need."

46 At the next tournament, I won again, but it was my mother who wore the triumphant grin.

47 "Lost eight piece this time. Last time was eleven. What I tell you? Better off lose less!" I was annoyed, but I couldn't say anything.

48 I attended more tournaments, each one farther away from home. I won all games, in all divisions. The Chinese bakery downstairs from our flat displayed my growing collection of trophies in its window, amidst the dust-covered cakes that were never picked up. The day after I won an important regional tournament, the window encased a fresh sheet cake with whipped-cream frosting and red script saying, "Congratulations, Waverly Jong, Chinatown Chess Champion." Soon after that, a flower shop, headstone engraver, and funeral parlor offered to sponsor me in national tournaments. That's when my mother decided I no longer had to do the dishes. Winston and Vincent had to do my chores.

49 "Why does she get to play and we do all the work," complained Vincent.

50 "Is new American rules," said my mother. "Meimei play, squeeze all her brains out for win chess. You play, worth squeeze towel."

51 By my ninth birthday, I was a national chess champion. I was still some 429 points away from grand-master status, but I was touted as the Great American Hope, a child prodigy and a girl to boot. They ran a photo of me in *Life* magazine next to a quote in which Bobby Fischer[4] said, "There will never be a woman grand master." "Your move, Bobby," said the caption.

52 The day they took the magazine picture I wore neatly plaited braids clipped with plastic barrettes trimmed with rhinestones. I was playing in a large high school auditorium that echoed with phlegmy coughs and the squeaky rubber knobs of chair legs sliding across freshly waxed wooden floors. Seated across from me was an American man, about the same age as Lau Po, maybe fifty. I remember that his sweaty brow seemed to weep at my every move. He wore a dark, malodorous suit. One of his pockets was stuffed with

3. **Check** term in chess meaning a player's king is in danger.
4. **Bobby Fischer** (1943–2008) American chess prodigy who attained the top rank of grand master in 1958.

PERSONALIZE FOR LEARNING

Strategic Support

Research The story is set in the 1950s. During that time, Bobby Fischer, the most famous chess player in American history, stated that there would never be a woman who would reach grandmaster status in chess. This is no longer true.

Have students research the first woman grandmaster in chess. If the students are doing their research on the Internet, discuss the importance of search terms. For example, searching "chess" will result in many interesting links, but will not help them immediately find information on the first female grandmaster. Have students try more than one term in their search and evaluate the result.

a great white kerchief on which he wiped his palm before sweeping his hand over the chosen chess piece with great flourish.

53 In my crisp pink-and-white dress with scratchy lace at the neck, one of two my mother had sewn for these special occasions, I would clasp my hands under my chin, the delicate points of my elbows poised lightly on the table in the manner my mother had shown me for posing for the press. I would swing my patent leather shoes back and forth like an impatient child riding on a school bus. Then I would pause, suck in my lips, twirl my chosen piece in midair as if undecided, and then firmly plant it in its new threatening place, with a triumphant smile thrown back at my opponent for good measure.

* * *

54 I no longer played in the alley of Waverly Place. I never visited the playground where the pigeons and old men gathered. I went to school, then directly home to learn new chess secrets, cleverly concealed advantages, more escape routes.

55 But I found it difficult to concentrate at home. My mother had a habit of standing over me while I **plotted** out my games. I think she thought of herself as my protective ally. Her lips would be sealed tight, and after each move I made, a soft "Hmmmmph" would escape from her nose.

56 "Ma, I can't practice when you stand there like that," I said one day. She retreated to the kitchen and made loud noises with the pots and pans. When the crashing stopped, I could see out of the corner of my eye that she was standing in the doorway. "Hmmmph!" Only this one came out of her tight throat.

57 My parents made many **concessions** to allow me to practice. One time I complained that the bedroom I shared was so noisy that I couldn't think. Thereafter, my brothers slept in a bed in the living room facing the street. I said I couldn't finish my rice; my head didn't work right when my stomach was too full. I left the table with half-finished bowls and nobody complained. But there was one duty I couldn't avoid. I had to accompany my mother on Saturday market days when I had no tournament to play. My mother would proudly walk with me, visiting many shops, buying very little. "This my daughter Wave-ly Jong," she said to whoever looked her way.

My mother had a habit of standing over me while I plotted out my games. I think she thought of herself as my protective ally.

58 One day, after we left a shop I said under my breath, "I wish you wouldn't do that, telling everybody I'm your daughter." My mother stopped walking. Crowds of people with heavy bags pushed past us on the sidewalk, bumping into first one shoulder, then another.

NOTES

Mark context clues or indicate another strategy you used that helped you determine meaning.

plotted (PLOT ihd) *v.*

MEANING:

concessions (kuhn SEHSH uhnz) *n.*

MEANING:

DIGITAL PERSPECTIVES

Concept Vocabulary

PLOTTED If groups are struggling to define the word *plotted* in paragraph 56, point out to students that the words that follow it in paragraph 55, *out my games,* clearly refer to chess, and to whatever plans Waverly is putting together. Have them think of other examples of the word *plot,* either as a noun or a verb. Guide them toward its popular use as a term in films and novels for storyline. These details of context and alternative applications should lead the students to infer that Waverly needs to create plans to become a serious winner in tournament chess.

Possible response: Plotted means "planned a series of actions."

CONCESSIONS If students are struggling to define the word *concessions* in paragraph 57, point out that its context in the story is rich in clues: "One time I complained that the bedroom I shared was so noisy that I couldn't think. Thereafter, my brothers slept in a bed in the living room facing the street." "I said I couldn't finish my rice; my head didn't work right when my stomach was too full. I left the table with half-finished bowls and nobody complained." These details should lead students to infer that concessions are not ideal solutions: people are making allowances for her, accommodating her particular needs. Explain that the verb form is "to concede," which can mean "to allow as a right or privilege," and "to yield to pressure or circumstances."

Possible response: *Concessions* are "allowances that are made for the benefit of another person."

VOCABULARY DEVELOPMENT

How Language Works

Present Participles and Gerunds Help students to understand the difference between a present participle and a gerund. Explain that both end in *-ing*, but a present participle may act as an adjective, while a gerund is always a noun. Assist students with an example of a present participle in paragraph 57:

"My mother would proudly walk with me, visiting many shops, buying very little." Have students discuss the function of "visiting many shops" and "buying very little" in the sentence. Have students read an example of a gerund from paragraph 56: "When the crashing stopped . . ." Have students discuss the function of "the crashing" in the subordinate clause. Have students identify the underlined word in each sentence as a gerund or a present participle.

1. Waverly's brothers slept in the room facing the street. (present participle, functioning as an adjective, describing the room)
2. Shopping at the market with her mother was a weekly obligation for Waverly. (gerund, functioning as a noun and the subject of the sentence)

CLOSER LOOK

Analyze Conflict

Circulate among groups as students conduct their close read. Suggest that groups close read paragraphs 59–65. Encourage them to talk about the annotations that they mark. If needed, provide the following support.

ANNOTATE: Have students mark details in these paragraphs that indicate conflict between Waverly and her mother, or work with small groups to have students participate while you highlight them together.

QUESTION: Guide students to consider what these details might tell them. Ask what a reader can infer from what was annotated, and accept student responses.

Possible response: Waverly is struggling to establish and protect her own identity. Her mother is infuriated by her daughter's disrespect for her and ingratitude for all her efforts to improve Waverly's life.

CONCLUDE: Help students to formulate conclusions about the importance of these details in the text. Ask students why the author might have included these details.

Possible response: Tan presents the core conflict between Waverly and her mother, which parallels the theme of chess in the story. In their ongoing power struggle, Waverly knows she is making a mistake when she tells her mother to learn to play chess, but she is too frustrated with her mother's overbearing behavior to remain submissive any longer.

Remind students that a **conflict** is a struggle between opposing forces. There are two kinds of conflicts: external and internal. In an **external conflict**, a character struggles against an outside force: another character, an element of nature, or some aspect of society. In an **internal conflict**, the conflict is within a single character who is struggling with opposing feelings, beliefs, needs, or desires. Characters in conflict form the basis of narrative literature because most plots develop from conflicts. If there is no conflict, there is no story.

NOTES

59 "Aiii-ya. So shame be with mother?" She grasped my hand even tighter as she glared at me.

60 I looked down. "It's not that, it's just so obvious. It's just so embarrassing."

61 "Embarrass you be my daughter?" Her voice was cracking with anger.

62 "That's not what I meant. That's not what I said."

63 "What you say?"

64 I knew it was a mistake to say anything more, but I heard my voice speaking. "Why do you have to use me to show off? If you want to show off, then why don't you learn to play chess."

65 My mother's eyes turned into dangerous black slits. She had no words for me, just sharp silence.

66 I felt the wind rushing around my hot ears. I jerked my hand out of my mother's tight grasp and spun around, knocking into an old woman. Her bag of groceries spilled to the ground.

67 "Aii-ya! Stupid girl!" my mother and the woman cried. Oranges and tin cans careened down the sidewalk. As my mother stooped to help the old woman pick up the escaping food, I took off.

68 I raced down the street, dashing between people, not looking back as my mother screamed shrilly, "Meimei! Meimei!" I fled down an alley, past dark curtained shops and merchants washing the grime off their windows. I sped into the sunlight, into a large street crowded with tourists examining trinkets and souvenirs. I ducked into another dark alley, down another street, up another alley. I ran until it hurt and I realized I had nowhere to go, that I was not running from anything. The alleys contained no escape routes.

69 My breath came out like angry smoke. It was cold. I sat down on an upturned plastic pail next to a stack of empty boxes, cupping my chin with my hands, thinking hard. I imagined my mother, first walking briskly down one street or another looking for me, then giving up and returning home to await my arrival. After two hours, I stood up on creaking legs and slowly walked home.

70 The alley was quiet and I could see the yellow lights shining from our flat like two tiger's eyes in the night. I climbed the sixteen steps to the door, advancing quietly up each so as not to make any warning sounds. I turned the knob; the door was locked. I heard a chair moving, quick steps, the locks turning—click! click! click!—and then the door opened.

71 "About time you got home," said Vincent. "Boy, are you in trouble."

72 He slid back to the dinner table. On a platter were the remains of a large fish, its fleshy head still connected to bones swimming upstream in vain escape. Standing there waiting for my punishment, I heard my mother speak in a dry voice.

73 "We not concerning this girl. This girl not have concerning for us."

74 Nobody looked at me. Bone chopsticks clinked against the insides of bowls being emptied into hungry mouths.

DIGITAL PERSPECTIVES

Enriching the Text The 1993 feature film *The Joy Luck Club* contains scenes based on this excerpt from the novel. After the students complete their close read, show these clips from the movie–particularly the scene where Waverly argues with her mother. Have students compare them with the written text. Ask them how the movie scenes contribute to their understanding of the narrative. Preview all videos before showing them in class.

75 I walked into my room, closed the door, and lay down on my bed. The room was dark, the ceiling filled with shadows from the dinnertime lights of neighboring flats.

76 In my head, I saw a chessboard with sixty-four black and white squares. Opposite me was my opponent, two angry black slits. She wore a triumphant smile. "Strongest wind cannot be seen," she said.

77 Her black men advanced across the plane, slowly marching to each successive level as a single unit. My white pieces screamed as they scurried and fell off the board one by one. As her men drew closer to my edge, I felt myself growing light. I rose up into the air and flew out the window. Higher and higher, above the alley, over the tops of tiled roofs, where I was gathered up by the wind and pushed up toward the night sky until everything below me disappeared and I was alone.

78 I closed my eyes and pondered my next move. ❧

NOTES

Comprehension Check

Complete the following items after you finish your first read. Review and clarify details with your group.

1. How does Waverly first obtain a chess set?

2. What advice does Waverly's mother give her about finding out "why" important things are done?

3. Why does Waverly become angry with her mother at the market?

4. **Notebook** Write a summary of the story to check your understanding.

RESEARCH

Research to Explore Choose an aspect of the story to research. For example, you may want to learn more about chess or San Francisco's Chinatown.

DIGITAL PERSPECTIVES

Comprehension Check

Possible responses:

1. The chess set originally belonged to her brother Vincent, but when he lost interest in it, Waverly appropriated the game.
2. Waverly's mother tells her that it's better if she finds out "why" herself rather rely on someone to tell her.
3. Waverly becomes angry with her mother at the grocery store because she feels like her mother is using her to "show off."
4. Waverly, a young first-generation Chinese-American girl, becomes fascinated with the game of chess, studies its strategies seriously, and works her way up to championship status. While her mother is supportive of Waverly's talent, she is also overbearing and controlling. Frustrated from her mother's constant showing her off to others, Waverly gets into an ugly argument in the street and runs away. When she returns home several hours later, she is dismissed by her family during dinner time. The story ends with Waverly plotting her next move against her mother, just as she plots her next move in a game of chess.

Research

Research to Explore If groups struggle to come up with a research topic, you may choose to suggest that they focus on one of these topics: the history of Chinatown in San Francisco; the history of Chinese immigration to America in the nineteenth and twentieth centuries; reasons for surges and declines in the popularity of chess tournaments in the United States.

PERSONALIZE FOR LEARNING

Challenge Have students learn the rules of chess and play the game. Ask them to share the experience of playing the game, commenting on what skills are necessary for success. Would they like to continue to play the game? Why, or why not?

Jump Start

CLOSE READ Ask students to consider the following prompt: *What is the figurative meaning of the title?* As students discuss the prompt in their group, have them describe a situation where they or someone they knew had to follow the rules of someone in authority to get what they wanted.

Close Read the Text

If needed, model close reading by using the Annotation Highlights in the Interactive Teacher's Edition. Remind students to use Accountable Talk in their discussions and to support one another as they complete the close read.

Analyze the Text

1. **Possible response:** The message of Waverly's mother at the beginning of the story is that the most powerful forces in your life are the ones you do not recognize. Tan returns to the image at the end of the story because Waverly finally understands what her mother was saying.
2. **Passages will vary by group.** Remind students to explain why they chose the passage they presented to the group members.
3. **Responses will vary by group.**

Concept Vocabulary

Why These Words? Possible response: The words are all associated with strategy and competition. Much of Waverly's life revolves around competing against others in chess. Another word that fits this category would be *deceive*.

Practice

Sample responses: Waverly's mother **deftly** rolled out dough to make dumplings for dinner that night; Lau Po at first resisted playing chess with Waverly, but he later **relented** and became her mentor; When playing a game in a tournament, Waverly **plotted** her chess moves very carefully; The **concessions** Waverly's parents provided to encourage her chess-playing were often not fair to her brothers.

Word Network

Possible words: *ancestral, neighborhood, regional*

Word Study

For more support, see **Concept Vocabulary and Word Study**

Possible responses:
scurried - connotes fear, weakness, smallness;
hurl - connotes savagery, strength, suddenness

MAKING MEANING

RULES OF THE GAME

TIP

GROUP DISCUSSION
Be sure to identify specific events or passages so your classmates can follow your thinking. Use precise words and specific details to express your thoughts.

Close Read the Text

With your group, revisit sections of the text you marked during your first read. **Annotate** details that you notice. What **questions** do you have? What can you **conclude**?

ANNOTATE QUESTION Close Read CONCLUDE

Analyze the Text

CITE TEXTUAL EVIDENCE to support your answers.

Notebook Complete the activities.

1. **Review and Clarify** With your group, reread paragraphs 1–3 and 76–77 of "Rules of the Game." What does the image of the "strongest wind" represent to you? Why does Tan return to the "strongest wind" image at the end of the story? Explain.
2. **Present and Discuss** Now, work with your group to share other key passages from the story. Discuss parts of the text that you found to be most meaningful, as well as questions you asked and the conclusions you reached as a result of reading those passages.
3. **Essential Question:** ***What does it mean to be "American"?*** What has this selection taught you about American identity? Discuss this idea with your group.

WORD NETWORK
Add interesting words about American identity from the text to your Word Network.

LANGUAGE DEVELOPMENT

Concept Vocabulary

deftly	relented	plotted	concessions

Why These Words? The four concept vocabulary words are related. With your group, determine what the words have in common. Write your ideas, and add another word that fits the category.

Practice

Notebook Use a dictionary to confirm the definitions for the concept vocabulary words. Then, write a sentence using each of the words. How did the concept vocabulary words make your sentences more vivid?

STANDARDS
Reading Literature
Analyze how comple characters develop over the course of a text, interact with other characters and advance the plot or develop the theme.
Language
• Verify the preliminary determination of the meaning of a word or phrase.
• Analyze nuances in the meaning of words with similar denotations.

Word Study

Connotation and Denotation The **denotation** of a word is its literal dictionary definition. The same word may also have a **connotation**, a suggested meaning that evokes either positive or negative feelings. In "Rules of the Game," for example, Waverly is described as *plotting* out her games. The word *plotting* has overtones of a dark conspiracy. Its connotation is more negative than the neutral word *planning*. Find two other words in the text, and describe their connotative meanings.

74 UNIT 1 • AMERICAN VOICES

FORMATIVE ASSESSMENT

Analyze the Text

If students struggle to close read the text, **then** provide the **Rules of the Game: Text Questions** available online in the Interactive Teacher's Edition or Unit Resources. Answers and DOK levels are also available.

Concept Vocabulary

If students struggle to identify the concept, **then** have them search the text for other words with similar meanings that can be read denotatively and connotatively.

Word Study

If students fail to identify other words, **then** have them search for verbs that evoke a vivid image. From there, they may be able to discern these words denotatively and connotatively. For Reteach and Practice, see **Word Study: Connotation and Denotation (RP).**

Analyze Craft and Structure

Complex Characters In the best stories, the main characters are interesting and **complex**, or well-rounded. You can identify complex characters in the following ways:

- They show multiple or even contradictory **traits**, or qualities.
- They struggle with conflicting **motivations**, or reasons for acting as they do.
- They change or learn something important by the end of the story.

Characters Advance Plot As characters interact with one another and struggle to overcome problems, their choices move the story along. A character's action—or decision *not* to take action—can lead to new plot developments and may intensify the conflict, heightening tension or suspense in the story.

Characters Develop Theme A character's struggles with a conflict can teach a general lesson. In this way, characters help develop a story's **theme**—the central insight that it conveys. As you read a short story, pay close attention to the ways that characters change and to the lessons that they learn. These details will point you toward the story's theme.

Find your own examples in "Rules of the Game" where the author builds characters. Identify each character's traits, motivations, and actions, and interpret how these details help to establish theme.

Practice

CITE TEXTUAL EVIDENCE to support your answers.

Notebook Work with your group to complete the following activities.

1. Use the chart to identify at least two conflicts Waverly and her mother face. For each conflict, explain how the character responds and the reasons for her responses.

CHARACTER	CONFLICTS	CHARACTER'S RESPONSE	CHARACTER'S MOTIVATIONS
Waverly	a. See answers in Teacher's Edition.	b.	c.
Mrs. Jong	c.	d.	e.

2. **(a)** Cite at least two ways in which Waverly's actions or reactions change the situation and move the plot forward. **(b)** Do the same for Mrs. Jong.
3. Do Waverly and Mrs. Jong change or grow as a result of their experiences? If so, in what ways? If not, why?
4. **(a)** What central ideas do Waverly and her mother's conflict emphasize? **(b)** What insights about life or the human condition does the story express?

DIGITAL PERSPECTIVES

Analyze Craft and Structure

Complex Characters Discuss with students how main characters in fictional narratives often have conflicting traits and motivations which heighten the tension of a story. Have students discuss stories they have read where main characters are parent and child. Ask which type of conflicts these characters would have. For more support, see **Analyze Craft and Structure: Complex Characters.**

Possible responses:

1. a. Her brothers won't let her play chess.
   b. She offers candy to the winner.
   c. She wants to play.
   d. She worries that Waverly is not getting enough sleep.
   e. She moves the boys out of the shared bedroom. She wants Waverly to be successful.
2. (a) She reads to learn more about chess. This prepares her for competitions. Later, she decides not to play in the alley, which lets her focus on studying chess. (b) Mrs. Jong reacts to Waverly's tournament by giving her a charm. This shows she supports her daughter. She reacts to Waverly's success by freeing her from her chores.
3. The characters grow. Waverly gets better at chess but must learn how to deal with her mother.
4. (a) Their conflict emphasizes the struggle between parent and child over who is in control. (b) The story shows that the relationship is complicated. Parents want the best but may seem controlling.

FORMATIVE ASSESSMENT

Analyze Craft and Structure

If students struggle to understand how a actions character's advance the plot of a story, **then** discuss which specific events of the story result from a character's personality and movements. For Reteach and Practice, see **Analyze Craft and Structure: Complex Characters (RP).**

PERSONALIZE FOR LEARNING

English Language Support

Character Traits Have students create a fictional character and describe him or her with specific traits.

Ask students to think of a character that they have read about recently. Have them write three traits that apply to the character. Ask each student to explain how their created character exhibits the three traits. **EMERGING**

Ask students to write a few sentences that compare and contrast two characters that they have read about recently. Remind students to describe the characters using specific traits. **EXPANDING**

Ask students to write a paragraph that indirectly describes two characters that they have read about recently.

Ask students to describe the characters indirectly. Have them try to avoid using specific adjectives to describe the characters. **BRIDGING**

An expanded **English Language Support Lesson** on Character Traits is available in the Digital Teacher's Edition.

FACILITATING

Conventions

Participles and Participial Phrases

Participial phrases are often used to add extra detail, a purpose, or a reason to a sentence or thought.

As you review the examples of both types of participial phrases (present and past), consider providing additional examples.

Present Participial Phrase
Helping her mother with yard work, Cassandra felt tired.

Past Participial Phrase
Exhausted from a long's day work, she was happy to watch a movie that night.

For more support, see **Conventions: Participles and Participial Phrases.**

MAKE IT INTERACTIVE

Read It

1. specializing in steamed pastries and dim sum; modifies "bakery"
2. smiling benevolently; modifies "he"
3. rushing around my hot ears; modifies "wind"
4. slowly marching to each successive level as a single unit; modifies "men"

Write It

Possible response:

Our school talent show was tonight. The winner was my best friend, Rita. Dressed in a simple gown, she stepped onto the stage quietly. Hitting every note perfectly, she was a star.

FORMATIVE ASSESSMENT

Conventions

If students are unable to identify the difference between present and past participial phrases, **then** have them look for words ending in *–ing* and *–ed*. For Reteach and Practice, see **Conventions: Participles and Participial Phrases (RP).**

LANGUAGE DEVELOPMENT

RULES OF THE GAME

Conventions

Participles and Participial Phrases A **participle** is a verb form that acts as an adjective. The **present participle** of a verb ends in *-ing (frightening, entertaining).* The **past participle** of a regular verb ends in *-ed (frightened, entertained).* The past participle of an irregular verb may have any of a variety of endings, such as *-t (burnt)* or *-en (written).*

A **participial phrase** consists of a participle and its objects, complements, or modifiers, all acting together as an adjective. A participial phrase may either precede or follow the word it modifies.

In the chart, participles are italicized, participial phrases are highlighted, and the nouns or pronouns they modify are underlined.

SENTENCE	HOW PHRASE FUNCTIONS
Exhausted by the arduous climb, we rested by the side of the trail.	modifies the subject
The movers carefully unloaded the van *packed* with antiques.	modifies the direct object
Rosa handed the woman *wearing* the gray suit her application.	modifies the indirect object
The hallways were clogged with students *going* to class.	modifies the object of the preposition
Ann Pace is a scientist *known* for her work in aeronautics.	modifies the subject complement

Read It

Work individually. Mark the participial phrase in each of these sentences from "Rules of the Game," and write the word it modifies. When you have finished, compare your responses with those of your team.

1. We lived on Waverly Place, in a warm, clean, two-bedroom flat that sat above a small Chinese bakery specializing in steamed pastries and dim sum.
2. "Little sister, been a long time since I play with dolls," he said, smiling benevolently.
3. I felt the wind rushing around my hot ears.
4. Her black men advanced across the plane, slowly marching to each successive level as a single unit.

Write It

Notebook Work individually. Write a short paragraph about "Rules of the Game," using two participial phrases. Mark the participial phrases, and identify the words they are modifying.

STANDARDS

Language

- Demonstrate command of the conventions of standard English grammar and usage when writing or speaking.
- Use various types of phrases and clauses to convey specific meanings and add variety and interest to writing or presentations.

PERSONALIZE FOR LEARNING

English Language Support

Past Participles and Past Tense Words If students struggle to understand whether a word ending in *–ed* is functioning as a past tense verb or a past participle, have students read sentences that have words that end in *–ed*. Discuss which of these words are showing the action of a noun or pronoun and which are describing a noun or pronoun.

Then have students identify the underlined words in each sentence as a past tense verb or a past participle.

Maxwell carried three boxes of books up three flights of steps. (past tense verb)

Drenched from the rain, Rosario was happy to change into dry clothes. (past participle)

ALL LEVELS

EFFECTIVE EXPRESSION

Speaking and Listening

Assignment

With your group, present a **scene** that further develops characters and events Amy Tan describes in "Rules of the Game." Assign roles to members of your group, rehearse, and then perform your scene in front of the class. You may develop one of the following options or pick an alternative your group prefers.

- ☐ Waverly confronts her mother about what happened on the street.
- ☐ Waverly meets Bobby Fischer after he says there will never be a female grand master.
- ☐ Waverly and Lau Po have a phone conversation in which she thanks him for influencing her and tells him about an achievement that he inspired.

Project Plan Make a list of tasks that your group will need to carry out. Write a script for your scene, and obtain any props you may need.

Practice Practice your scene before you present it to your class. Include the following performance techniques to achieve the desired effect.

- Speak clearly and comfortably without rushing.
- Use your voice in a way that reflects your character's emotions and situation. Vary your tone and pitch and avoid speaking in a flat, monotonous style.
- Make sure your body language is appropriate for the character and is neither too limited nor too exaggerated.

Evaluate Scenes Use a presentation evaluation guide like the one shown to analyze your classmates' scenes.

PRESENTATION EVALUATION GUIDE

Rate each statement on a scale of 1 (not demonstrated) to 5 (demonstrated).

- ☐ The speakers communicated events that fit well with the story.
- ☐ The speakers included details from the story to demonstrate shifts in feeling.
- ☐ The speakers used their voices effectively to reflect the characters and situations.
- ☐ The speakers used gestures and other body language effectively.
- ☐ The dialogue was clear and easy to follow.

EVIDENCE LOG

Before moving on to a new selection, go to your Evidence Log and record what you learned from "Rules of the Game."

STANDARDS

Speaking and Listening
Present information, findings, and supporting evidence clearly, concisely, and logically such that listeners can follow the line of reasoning and the organization, development, substance, and style are appropriate to purpose, audience, and task.

DIGITAL PERSPECTIVES

Speaking and Listening

Remind students that before they choose a scene to perform, they can close read the selection again to help them analyze how each character thinks or behaves. Discuss with students the importance of understanding a character before writing and acting out a scene.

Project Plan Encourage students to discuss each scene option carefully before the group decides which one to perform. Have the students make a list of what they need to do to create the scene, including writing and approving dialogue, auditioning roles, and choosing a group member to direct the scene.

Practice As students practice their scenes, they should check to make sure they are acting in a manner that mirrors the way the character behaves in the narrative.

Evaluate Scene After each group presents their scene, discuss how each scene provides a better understanding of each character. Encourage students to discuss whether they felt the scenes would have fit naturally into the narrative. For more support, see **Speaking and Listening: Act Out a Scene.**

Evidence Log Support students in completing their Evidence Log. This paced activity will help prepare them for the Performance-Based Assessment at the end of the unit.

FORMATIVE ASSESSMENT

Speaking and Listening

If students are struggling with how to act like their character, **then** ask them if their character reminds them of someone they know or a character they have seen in a movie. Encourage students to demonstrate the behavior or attitude of that person or character, if appropriate. For Reteach and Practice, see **Speaking and Listening: Act Out a Scene (RP).**

Selection Test

Administer the "The Rules of the Game" Selection Test, which is available in both print and digital formats online in Assessments.

The Writing on the Wall

AUDIO SUMMARIES
Audio summaries of "The Writing on the Wall" are available in both English and Spanish in the Interactive Teacher's Edition or Unit Resources. Assigning these summaries prior to reading the selection may help students build additional background knowledge and set a context for their first read.

Summary

In her blog post "The Writing on the Wall," Camille Dungy describes the poems and messages written on the walls of the Angel Island Detention Center. There are hundreds of poems and messages etched into the walls of the old immigrant station on Angel Island in San Francisco Bay. Their creators were among the 175,000 Chinese immigrants detained there between 1910 and 1940 because of problems with health or documentation. Some poems were ancient writings, and others were new ideas written by the men who were held as prisoners. Many of the men may have written to give hope to others after them. Dungy tells the story of how the poems were nearly lost under layers of paint, and how the buildings fell into disrepair and were scheduled for demolition. The story of their survival is as extraordinary as the hope that they affirm.

Insight

American voices are often the voices of those who suffered to become American. Reading "The Writing on the Wall" will help students begin to reflect on the human need to speak to and be heard by not only one's fellow inhabitants of the world, but also by people of the future—people like us—especially when the subject is injustice and unnecessary suffering. The value of those communications then becomes a part of the moral history of America. The importance of the poems is recognized in the effort to reveal and preserve them, and in the moral necessity to ensure that the buildings on Angel Island are preserved.

Some students may find it upsetting to face the reality of the way America treated its immigrants by holding them in detention centers.

ESSENTIAL QUESTION:
What does it mean to be "American"?

Connection to Essential Question

"The Writing on the Wall" provides a very unusual and disturbing perspective on the Essential Question. While the immigrants detained on Angel Island had their American citizenship denied or delayed, there were those who believed that testimony contained in the poetry they wrote and left behind would one day be an important part of the fabric of American history. Is acknowledging the wrongs done to immigrants part of what it means to be American?

SMALL-GROUP LEARNING PERFORMANCE TASK
How do the realities of immigrants' experiences reflect or fail to reflect American ideals?

UNIT PERFORMANCE-BASED ASSESSMENT
How is an American identity created?

Connection to Performance Tasks

Small-Group Learning Performance Task In this Performance Task, students will consider the connection between the immigrant experience and America's values. This selection describes a harsh reality for many immigrants in America, focusing especially on the mistreatment of Chinese immigrants.

Unit Performance-Based Assessment This selection does not speak of the American identities that the detained immigrants might have created once they lived in America. However, the experience of being detained would have contributed to their sense of themselves as Americans, as the process of becoming American had involved unreasonable pain and suffering.

DIGITAL PERSPECTIVES — Audio | Video | Document | Annotation Highlights | EL Highlights | Online Assessment

LESSON RESOURCES

	Making Meaning	Language Development	Effective Expression
Lesson	**First Read** **Close Read** **Analyze the Text** **Analyze Craft and Structure**	**Concept Vocabulary** **Word Study** **Author's Style**	**Research**
Instructional Standards	**RL.10** By the end of grade 9, read and comprehend . . . **RI.2** Determine a central idea of a text . . .	**L.4.a** Use context as a clue . . . **L.4.b** Identify and correctly use patterns of word changes . . . **RI.4** Determine the meaning of words and phrases . . .	**W.7** Conduct short as well as more sustained research projects . . . **SL.5** Make strategic use of digital media . . .
STUDENT RESOURCES			
Available online in the Interactive Student Edition or Unit Resources	Selection Audio First-Read Guide: Nonfiction Close-Read Guide: Nonfiction	Word Network	Evidence Log
TEACHER RESOURCES			
Selection Resources Available online in the Interactive Teacher's Edition or Unit Resources	Audio Summaries Annotation Highlights EL Highlights The Writing on the Wall: Text Questions Analyze Craft and Structure: Informative Text	Author's Style: Alliteration, Assonance, and Consonance Concept Vocabulary and Word Study	Research: Digital Presentation English Language Support Lesson: Digital Presentation
Reteach/Practice (RP) Available online in the Interactive Teacher's Edition or Unit Resources	Analyze Craft and Structure: Informative Text (RP)	Author's Style: Alliteration, Assonance, and Consonance (RP) Word Study: Latin Root *-mem-* (RP)	Research: Digital Presentation (RP)
Assessment Available online in Assessments			Selection Test
My Resources	A Unit 1 Answer Key is available online and in the Interactive Teacher's Edition.		

Reading Support

Text Complexity Rubric: The Writing on the Wall	
Quantitative Measures	
Lexile 1,160 **Text Length** 1355 words	
Qualitative Measures	
Knowledge Demands ① ② ③ ❹ ⑤	Main theme in selection (experiences of immigrants in early 1900s) will be unfamiliar to most readers.
Structure ① ② ③ ❹ ⑤	Structure is not predictable, as descriptions (of Angel Island) are interspersed with examples of poetry and commentary about the immigrant experience.
Language Conventionality and Clarity ① ② ③ ❹ ⑤	Many sentences are long and complex, with multiple clauses; selection contains a lot of above-level vocabulary. Poetry examples contain figurative language.
Levels of Meaning/Purpose ① ② ❸ ④ ⑤	Concepts are explicitly explained, but full explanation of the topic (Chinese immigrants entering the US) does not appear until halfway through the text and is not easily located. Pictures and examples help to support concepts.

DECIDE AND PLAN

English Language Support

Provide English Learners with support for structure and language as they read the selection.

Structure Guide students to navigate the structure of the text. Before they begin reading, preview what the structure contains: information about the immigrant experience, descriptions of the Angel Island Detention Center, historical information, and examples of the poetry on the walls. Encourage students to mark or color code which section gives which type of information.

Language Help students break down long sentences into comprehensible chunks of language. Have them highlight or copy lengthy sentences. Then guide them to create shorter sentences out of each piece of information given in the sentence.

Strategic Support

Provide students with strategic support to ensure that they can successfully read the text.

Structure Point out to students that the selection switches between information about immigrants' experiences, historical information, descriptive information, and examples of the writing on the wall. As students read, have them make notes of which sections convey each kind of content.

Meaning/Purpose Ask students to take notes as they read about the main concept in each paragraph—for example, the first full paragraph describes what it was like to travel by sea from China to America between 1910 and 1940.

Challenge

Provide students who need to be challenged with ideas for how they can go beyond a simple interpretation of the text.

Text Analysis Pair students and ask them both to write journal entries as though they were the Chinese immigrants described in the first paragraph. Encourage them to draw from the details they have read and to include the emotions they might be feeling.

Written Response Have students find the author's site on the Internet. Ask them to read other poems or essays on that site. Have them pick one selection and write a summary. Have them read their summaries to the class.

TEACH

Read and Respond

Have the groups read the selection and complete the Making Meaning, Language Development, and Effective Expression activities.

Standards Support Through Teaching and Learning Cycle

IDENTIFY NEEDS

Analyze results of the Beginning-of-Year Assessment, focusing on the items relating to Unit 1. Also take into consideration student performance to this point and your observations of where particular students struggle.

DECIDE AND PLAN

- If students have performed poorly on items matching these standards, then provide selection scaffolds before assigning them the on-level lesson provided in the Student Edition.
- If students have done well on the Beginning-of-Year Assessment, then challenge them to keep progressing and learning by giving them opportunities to practice the skills in depth.
- Use the Selection Resources listed on the Planning pages for "The Writing on the Wall" to help students continually improve their ability to master the standards.

Instructional Standards: The Writing on the Wall

	Catching Up	This Year	Looking Forward
Reading	You may wish to administer the **Analyze Craft and Structure: Informative Text (RP)** worksheet to help students understand how to introduce, develop, and refine central ideas.	**RL.2** Determine a theme or central idea of a text and analyze in detail its development over the course of the text, including how it emerges and is shaped and refined by specific details; provide an objective summary of the text.	Challenge students to identify the central idea from a previous selection. Working in small groups, ask students to identify the central idea(s) and cite text in the selection that supports their responses. Encourage listeners to ask questions for clarification.
Research	You may wish to administer the **Research: Digital Presentation (RP)** worksheet to help students select research findings and present them through digital modes that engage the senses and the mind.	**W.7** Conduct short as well as more sustained research projects to answer a question or solve a problem; narrow or broaden inquiry when appropriate; synthesize multiple sources on the subject, demonstrating understanding of the subject under investigation.	Encourage students to write a description of a short research project that could be conducted about another selection in this unit. The description should include a question or problem that the research would answer, along with various print and digital sources.
Language	You may wish to administer the **Word Study: Latin Root *-mem-* (RP)** worksheet to help students understand that the meaning of a Latin root contributes to the overall meaning of a word, as in the word *memento*. You may wish to administer the **Author's Style: Alliteration, Assonance, and Consonance (RP)** worksheet to help students understand the use of sound devices.	**L.4.b** Identify and correctly use patterns of word changes that indicate different meanings or parts of speech. **RI.4** Determine the meaning of words and phrases as they are used in a text, including figurative, connotative, and technical meanings; analyze the cumulative impact of specific word choices on meaning and tone.	Have students list other words from this and other selections in the unit that contain the Latin root *mem*. Challenge students to determine the part of speech for each of those words. Have students write a descriptive paragraph with at least one example each of alliteration, assonance, and consonance.

ANALYZE AND REVISE

- Analyze student work for evidence of student learning.
- Identify whether or not students have met the expectations in the standards.
- Identify implications for future instruction.

TEACH

Implement the planned lesson and gather evidence of student learning.

Jump Start

FIRST REVIEW Encourage students to think about characters in literature, movies, or songs who felt sad or lonely. How did those characters deal with their emotions? Ask students to consider the ways people can express their emotions and discuss specific factors that impact people's means of expression.

The Writing on the Wall

Where is the wall mentioned in the title of this blog post, and what was written on it? How do people feel about the writing? Who has been affected by it? Modeling the questions a reader might ask as they read "The Writing on the Wall" for the first time brings the text alive for students and connects it to the Small-Group Performance Task assignment. Selection audio and print capability for the selection are available in the Interactive Teacher's Edition.

Concept Vocabulary

Ask groups to look closely at the three types of context clues—synonyms, restatement of an idea, and contrast of ideas and topics—and discuss how these types of clues can help clarify meaning. Encourage groups to think of one other type of context clue that they might encounter in a text. Possibilities include examples, antonyms, and definitions.

FIRST REVIEW

Have students perform the steps of the first review independently.

NOTICE: Encourage students to notice new information about the wall and why people interacted with it.

ANNOTATE: Remind students to mark passages they feel evoke an emotion in readers or are worthy of analysis in their close read.

CONNECT: Encourage students to go beyond the text to make connections. Have them consider how a person might react to spending time in a jail or a prison.

RESPOND: Students will answer questions and write a summary to demonstrate understanding. Point out to students that while they will always complete the Respond step at the end of the first review, the other steps will probably happen somewhat concurrently. You may wish to print copies of the **First-Read Guide: Nonfiction** for students to use.

About the Author

Camille Dungy (b. 1972) often moved during her childhood because her father taught medicine at different schools around the country. Dungy studied English at Stanford University and became a poet and professor. Her poems have been published widely and have won several awards. Her interest in social issues and nature led her to edit a collection of African American poets and their writings on nature.

The Writing on the Wall

Concept Vocabulary

As you perform your first read of "The Writing on the Wall," you will encounter these words.

memento composed inscribed

Context Clues If these words are unfamiliar to you, try using context clues. There are various types of context clues that you may encounter.

Similarity of Ideas: The ineffective laws revealed the **futility** of the fight against oppression.

Restatement of Ideas: Once the rations were **apportioned**, the men had to live on their share of the food.

Contrast of Ideas: Once the refugees **emigrated** from their war-torn country, they settled in a new home in a peaceful land.

Apply your knowledge of context clues and other vocabulary strategies to determine the meanings of unfamiliar words you encounter during your first read.

First Review NONFICTION

Apply these strategies as you conduct your first read. You will have an opportunity to complete a close read after your first read.

NOTICE the general ideas of the text. *What* is it about? *Who* is involved?

ANNOTATE by marking vocabulary and key passages you want to revisit.

First Read

CONNECT ideas within the selection to what you already know and what you have already read.

RESPOND by completing the Comprehension Check and by writing a brief summary of the selection.

STANDARDS

Reading Informational Text
By the end of grade 9, read and comprehend literary nonfiction in the grades 9–10 text complexity band proficiently, with scaffolding as needed at the high end of the range.

Language
Use context as a clue to the meaning of a word or a phrase.

DIGITAL PERSPECTIVES

Illuminating the Text Find and show a video about Angel Island, and provide a brief description of this former immigration station. This will help students understand the experiences described in "The Writing on the Wall." After you show the footage, create a Main Idea and Details chart. Students should write a phrase or sentence to describe the main idea of the video and include several key details that support it. Be sure to preview any video before showing it to the class.

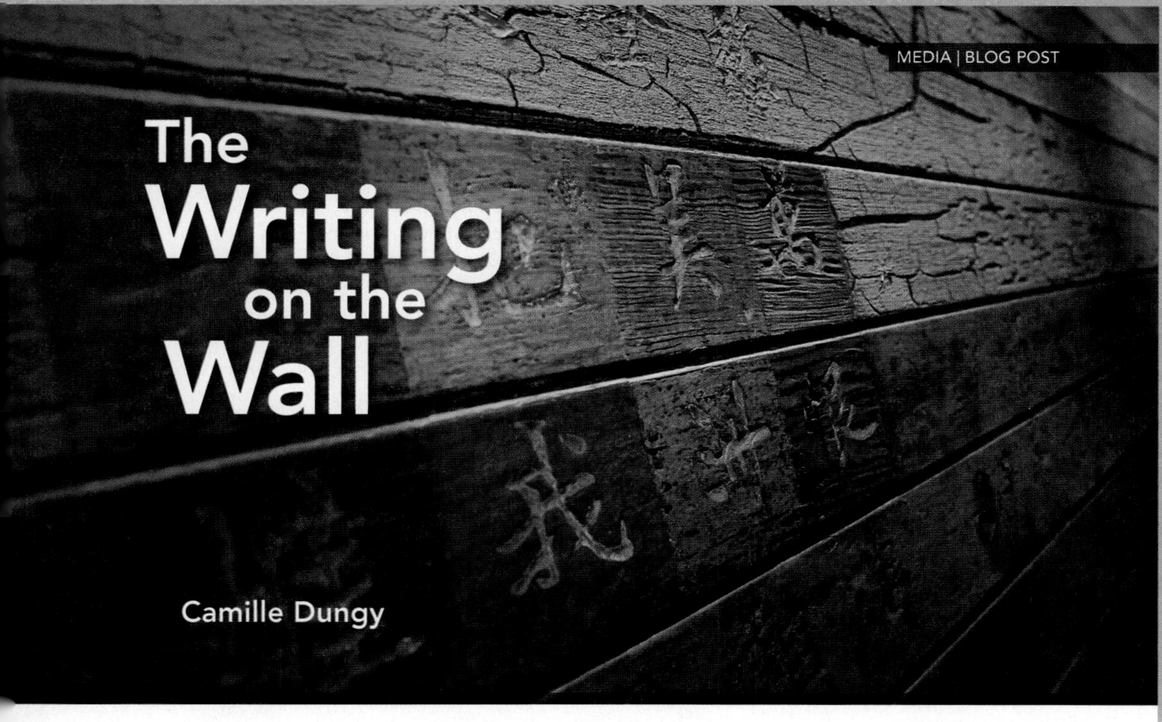

MEDIA | BLOG POST

The Writing on the Wall

Camille Dungy

DIGITAL PERSPECTIVES

BACKGROUND

Between 1882 and 1943, the United States severely restricted the number of immigrants from Asia who were allowed to enter the country. Many people wanted to move from Asia to America, and many whose families had come to the United States before 1882 wanted to visit China and then return to the United States. As a result of the restrictions, many travelers between Asia and the United States encountered delays and difficulties.

SCAN FOR MULTIMEDIA

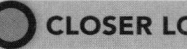

1 "Over a hundred poems are on the walls.
Looking at them, they are all pining[1] at the delayed progress.
What can one sad person say to another?
Unfortunate travelers everywhere wish to commiserate . . ."

(Island: Poetry and History of Chinese Immigrants on Angel Island, 1910–1940, Eds *Him Mark Lai, Genny Lim, and Judy Yung)*

2 Imagine you have traveled on a ship from China to America. Imagine it is sometime between 1910 and 1940, and you may or may not know the man who you will call your father when you arrive in the new country whose language you likely do not know. Imagine that when you arrive you are not admitted to the country you've traveled so far and paid so dearly to reach, but instead you are taken to an island in the middle of one of the world's 10 largest bays. It's called Angel Island, but you may not know that. All you might know is that you have been ushered into a room filled with perhaps

NOTES

1. **pining** *v.* wasting away, as if in ill health.

CLOSER LOOK

Determine the Mode of Discourse

Circulate among groups as students conduct their close read. Suggest that groups close read paragraph 2. Encourage them to talk about the annotations that they mark. If needed, provide the following support.

ANNOTATE: Have students mark details in paragraph 2 that help the reader determine the mode of discourse the author uses, or work with small groups to have students participate while you highlight them together.

QUESTION: Guide students to consider what these details might tell them. Ask what a reader can infer from the mode of discourse, and accept student responses.

Possible response: Throughout the first paragraph the narrator adopts a persuasive, repetitive style to tell a story at the beginning of an expository text. This is an ideal mode to introduce the reader to a world where nothing is explained and nothing makes sense.

CONCLUDE: Help students to formulate conclusions about the importance of these details in the text. Ask students why the author might have included these details.

Possible response: The author includes these details to provide background for the reader. The insistent repetition of the word "imagine" is the author's attempt to build empathy for the men on the island.

Remind students that the phrase **mode of discourse** can refer to narration, description, exposition and argumentation, and in particular the way the writer chooses to present any of those categories. The mode of discourse has a strong impact on the author's ability to convey a message to the reader.

Additional **English Language Support** is available in the Interactive Teacher's Edition.

PERSONALIZE FOR LEARNING

English Language Support

Syntax Help students analyze the sentence structure of the poem excerpt in paragraph 1 in order to better understand conventional English syntax. Have students rewrite the poem in prose form, removing the line breaks within poetry. Ask them to read the rewritten sentences and make observations. Have students consider how reading the text as a paragraph instead of as a poem affects their understanding of the text. **ALL LEVELS**

Concept Vocabulary

MEMENTO If groups are struggling to define *memento* in paragraph 3, point out that surrounding words and phrases can help students determine the meaning of the word. Phrases and words such as *an expression*, *leave*, and *to encourage fellow souls* should suggest that a memento is a tangible thing that is left behind and can evoke a response in people. In this case, the memento is a poem written on a wall. It describes one immigrant's experience at Angel Island, and it may encourage other immigrants who read it in the future.

Possible response: A memento is something that reminds people of an event or an experience and can affect their emotions.

NOTES

Mark context clues or indicate another strategy you used that helped you determine meaning.

memento (muh MEHN toh) *n.*

MEANING:

250 other men. You will not know that men from as many as 80 other countries have suffered the same fate as you, but you will know that the women and small children are kept in another building, that the Asian men are separated from the European men, that the European men received comparably better treatment than the Asian men, and that though you can see Oakland through the window of the wooden building you do not know if you will ever walk its streets. The air on the island is by turns foggy and cool and salty and warm. There are moss roses and fragrant stands of eucalyptus. You might call it beautiful, but you are a detainee, not a vacationer, and you are very far from any place that you could call home. Imagine if, in these circumstances, lying in bunks stacked three high and 6 deep, you glanced at the wooden walls around you and saw poems.

3 "On a long voyage I traveled across the sea.
Feeding on wind and sleeping on dew, I tasted hardships.
Even though Su Wu was detained among the barbarians,
he would one day return home.
When he encountered a snow storm, Wengong sighed,
thinking of bygone years.
In days of old, heroes underwent many ordeals.
I am, in the end, a man whose goal is unfulfilled.
Let this be an expression of the torment which fills my belly.
Leave this as a **memento** to encourage fellow souls."

4 Imagine you saw not just one poem written on or etched into the walls, but hundreds. Imagine nearly every inch of available wall space was taken up by a poem, and there was only a little space left. Imagine you were one of the most educated men in your village, the man on whom several families had penned their hopes. Imagine you had little but a knife or a pen and your calligraphy was beautiful. Would you take the opportunity to add a new poem to that wall?

5 ". . . Do not treat these words as idle words.
Why not let them deport you back to China?
You will find some work and endure to earn a couple of meals."

6 What I am describing is not fantasy. What I am describing was the reality for hundreds of Chinese immigrants who sought entry into America through the immigration station in the San Francisco Bay. If an immigrant's papers were in order, they could go straight away into their new lives in America. But if there were health concerns or irregularities with papers, if the would-be immigrant suffered the fate of so many as a result of the Chinese Exclusion Act of 1882, they were sent to a detention center on Angel Island, in the middle of the Bay. Held there for 2 days, 2 weeks, 2 months, and in one case as long as 2 years, many of these would-be immigrants took to writing on the walls.

FACILITATING SMALL-GROUP LEARNING

CLOSE READ: Nonfiction As groups perform their close read, you should circulate and offer assistance as required.

Remind groups that with informative and explanatory texts there should be a sentence that clearly identifies the topic. Readers should locate the topic and notice the ways the author develops it through the text.

If any group members struggle to identify the topic sentence, remind them that it does not always appear at the beginning of an article. Use tips and hints to point them toward the end of paragraph 6.

Have groups discuss and identify techniques employed to support and develop the topic.

7 These were not just idle scribbles. The Chinese immigrants, in particular, raised with a tradition of public poetry, **composed** carefully crafted verses that drew on Classical traditions, forms, and allusions. There is often little way to know whether a poem was written in 1910 or 1935, the poems these men wrote would stand the test of time.

8 "The insects chirp outside the four walls.
The inmates often sigh.
Thinking of affairs back home,
Unconscious tears wet my lapel."[2]

9 The poem above may well reference a poem written in the 6th century AD. The first poem I copied references a poet who wrote in the 8th century AD. The poets held at the Angel Island Immigration Station were partaking of a centuries-old tradition, creating a camaraderie[3] far beyond the confines of the walls they found themselves isolated inside. Likely separated from friends and family by thousands of miles and piles of bureaucracy,[4] these writers turned to the ancient tradition of public poetry to reconstruct their sense of self.

10 "The west wind ruffles my thin gauze clothing.
On the hill sits a tall building with a room of wooden planks.
I wish I could travel on a cloud far away, reunite my wife and son.
When the moonlight shines on me alone, the night seems even longer.
At the head of the bed there is wine and my heart is constantly drunk.
There is no flower beneath my pillow and my dreams are not sweet.
To whom can I confide my innermost feelings?
I rely solely on close friends to relieve my loneliness."

11 Here is a picture of San Francisco State University Professor Charles Egan pointing at the poem quoted above. Here we are, at least 60 years after this poem was penned, with a man from a different country, reading this lonely man's words and sharing them with people who have come to read them.

12 In the early 1940s the administration building of the Angel Island Immigration burned, and the facilities were turned over to the Army for the war

San Francisco State University Professor Charles Egan

NOTES

Mark context clues or indicate another strategy you used that helped you determine meaning.

composed (kuhm POHZD) *v.*

MEANING:

2. **lapel** (luh PEHL) *n.* fold of the front of a coat underneath the collar.
3. **camaraderie** (kom uh ROD uh ree) *n.* friendship or fellowship
4. **bureaucracy** (byu ROK ruh see) *n.* inflexible routines related to government.

DIGITAL PERSPECTIVES

CLOSER LOOK

Understand Imagery

Circulate among groups as students conduct their close read. Suggest that groups close read paragraph 10. Encourage them to talk about the annotations that they mark. If needed, provide the following support.

ANNOTATE: Have students mark details in paragraph 10 that are examples of imagery, or work with small groups to have students participate while you highlight them together.

QUESTION: Guide students to consider what these details might tell them. Ask what a reader can infer from what was marked, and accept student responses.

Possible response: The author uses imagery in the poem to convey a sense of loss and loneliness. The text helps the reader imagine someone who is completely alone with only the elements of nature surrounding him or her. It suggests a place that is isolated and empty of warmth.

CONCLUDE: Help students to formulate conclusions about the importance of these details in the text. Ask students why the author might have included these details.

Possible response: The poet employs personification, and suggests that nature is focusing special attention on him—not to comfort him, but to intensify his sorrows. These details help readers imagine how lonely and isolating it must have felt to be detained at Angel Island during the early 1900s.

Remind students that **imagery** in poetry refers to visual effects created from descriptive or figurative language, often with symbolic, emotionally evocative, or associative significance.

Concept Vocabulary

Composed If groups are struggling to define *composed* in paragraph 7, point out that surrounding words and phrases can help students determine the meaning of the word. Phrases and words such as *idle scribbles, public poetry,* and *carefully crafted verses* all relate to writing. These details should suggest that something that is composed has been written down or drafted.

Possible response: Something that is composed has been drafted, written, or put together.

PERSONALIZE FOR LEARNING

Strategic Support

Background If students struggle to understand the concept of public poetry, provide them with additional sources on this topic. You may wish to have students in each group create poems, either individually or working collaboratively. After they complete their poems, they can read them aloud among their groups or post them in one section of the classroom. Have students consider how experiencing poetry this way differs from reading a poem on your own in a magazine or a book.

FACILITATING

CLOSER LOOK

Infer the Author's Attitude

Circulate among groups as students conduct their close read. Suggest that groups close read paragraph 16. Encourage them to talk about the annotations that they mark. If needed, provide the following support.

ANNOTATE: Have students mark details in the paragraph about the work to preserve the poems on the walls at the detention center on Angel Island.

QUESTION: Guide students to consider what these details might tell them. Ask students to identify the author's attitude or opinion on efforts to preserve the poetry on the walls of the detention center, and accept student responses.

Possible response: The author believes that the poems written on the walls of the detention center have value. As a result, preserving them is important work. She also states that one result of this work is that now the Angel Island Detention Center has a place of honor in the new State Park. The preservation efforts also allow scholars to study the poems and allow other people to become inspired by them.

CONCLUDE: Help students to formulate conclusions about the importance of these details in the text. Ask students why the author might have included these details.

Possible response: The author is pleased with the efforts to preserve the poetry written on the walls. She thinks it is useful and important work that will help many people.

Remind students that the **author's attitude** toward his or her audience is expressed as the **tone** of a text. It can often be described with a single adjective, such as formal or informal.

Concept Vocabulary

INSCRIBED If groups are struggling to define *inscribed* in paragraph 16, point out that surrounding words and phrases can help students determine the meaning of the word. The phrase *poems on the wall* relates to something that has been written and carved into walls. These details should suggest that something that is written has been carved into something else.

Possible response: Something that is inscribed is writing that is carved or engraved into something.

NOTES

effort. The buildings were painted again, and after the war the barracks were deserted for years. Eventually derelict, there was talk of selling the whole island off as Army surplus. There was talk of letting local fire departments use all the island's buildings for practice. (This was the fate of several of the Julia Morgan designed employee cottages), but for the male detainee's barracks, poetry once again came to save the day.

13 Look at this picture and notice how difficult it might be to spot the poetry.

Park superintendent Roy McNamee shines a light on a poem written on a wall of the barracks.

14 If you didn't know what you were looking for, you might miss it entirely. I'm reminded of a Lucille Clifton poem, "mulberry fields," in which she talks about a similar problem.

> "they say that the rocks were shaped
> some of them scratched with triangles and other forms they
> must have been trying to invent some new language they say"

15 In the case of the Angel Island Detention Center, as in the case of the Clifton poem, the language, actually "marked an old tongue." But it was years before many people recognized what was being said and why it mattered.

16 Or, I should say in the case of the detention center that it was years before anyone who was not being directly addressed recognized the language and understood why it mattered. Because so many of the poets actually spoke to each other in their "posts," we know that the poems mattered to the people to whom they were addressed at the time. Eventually someone else saw the value as well. Someone walked through the detention center and recognized the language, recognized the poems on the wall, the hundreds of poems that documented the lives of nearly 175,000 people. Once the need inscribed on those walls was translated, efforts began to preserve the detention center and to give the Angel Island Detention Center a place of honor in a newly created State Park. Now this world

Mark context clues or indicate another strategy you used that helped you determine meaning.

inscribed (ihn SKRYBD) *adj.*

MEANING:

PERSONALIZE FOR LEARNING

English Language Support

Idioms Idioms can be confusing to English Language learners. Explain that the phrase *marked an old tongue* in paragraph 15 is an idiom. To help them understand the usage in the paragraph, explain that the word *tongue* can be used to mean "language." Since this text is about poetry written in Chinese long ago, the phrase refers to the fact that the poetry was written in a style that is out of date or no longer in use. **ALL LEVELS**

history record is preserved and available for viewing. Scholars are researching the poems, and people and poets like me, who need to believe in the power of poetry to speak beyond the here and now, can stand in front of those walls and understand the power of poetry: to calm, to communicate, to commiserate, and to conserve. ❧

NOTES

Comprehension Check

Complete the following items after you finish your first read. Review and clarify details with your group.

1. Who was sent to Angel Island and under what circumstances?

2. Why were the poems inscribed on the walls at Angel Island so hard to see?

3. According to the writer, how will preservation of the Angel Island Detention Center poetry benefit her as a poet?

4. **Notebook** Write a summary of the text to confirm your understanding.

RESEARCH

Research to Clarify Choose at least one unfamiliar detail from the text. Briefly research that detail. In what way does the information you learned shed light on an aspect of the blog post?

Research to Explore Further explore an aspect of the text that you find interesting. For example, you might want to learn more about the Chinese Exclusion Act of 1882.

DIGITAL PERSPECTIVES

Comprehension Check

Possible responses:

1. Any immigrant whose papers were not in order because of health concerns or any other irregularities was sent to Angel Island. Chinese people were especially likely to be sent there because of the Chinese Exclusion Act of 1882.
2. The poems were hard to see for several reasons: the carvings and inscriptions were painted over; they were written a long time ago and the walls were in bad condition; and the writers used all the space they could find, so some poems may have overlapped others.
3. Poets like her can become inspired to create their own works on similar themes. Other people can learn about the experiences and concerns of immigrants from that time period.
4. This article describes the poetry that has been inscribed on the walls of a building at the Angel Island Detention Center that once served as the barracks for male detainees. The detainees wrote or carved poetry on the walls to share their experiences with other men like them. Recently, the poems have been preserved as part of the newly-created State Park on Angel Island.

Research

Research to Clarify If groups struggle to come up with a research topic, you may want to suggest that they focus on one of the following topics: How were immigrants processed at Angel Island? What happened to the detainees after they left Angel Island?

Research to Explore If groups struggle to come up with a research topic, you may want to suggest that they focus on one of the following topics: The Chinese Exclusion Act of 1882; events that led up the passage of the Act; the effects of the passage of this law.

PERSONALIZE FOR LEARNING

Challenge

Research Have students research Asian immigration to the United States during this period in history to learn more about other kinds of experiences that many immigrants had. Possible subjects include the employment of Chinese immigrants to build railroads or the creation of Chinatowns in several cities along the Pacific Coast. After all of the students have completed their work, have each group hold a roundtable discussion to talk about what the students have learned about Asian immigration in the late 1800s and early 1900s.

Jump Start

CLOSE READ Ask students to identify examples of writing that appears on walls, such as graffiti. Discuss the fact that some may consider it vandalism, while others may consider it art. Ask students to consider how the poetry written on the walls of Angel Island relates to these ideas.

Close Read the Text

If needed, model close reading by using the Annotation Highlights in the Interactive Teacher's Edition.

Remind students to use Accountable Talk in their discussions and to support one another as they complete the close read.

Analyze the Text

1. **Possible response:** In some ways, the speaker feels similar to heroes Su Wu and Wengong. Like them, he has suffered hardships, is being detained among "barbarians," and longs to return home. But unlike the heroes of the past, he sees his goal as "unfulfilled."
2. **Passages will vary by group.** Remind students to explain why they chose the passages they presented to the group members.
3. **Responses will vary by group.**

Concept Vocabulary

Why These Words? Possible response: The words relate to something that might be written or contain writing. Another word that fits this category is *etched*.

Practice

We stopped by the souvenir shop to get a **memento** that would remind us of our trip.
She **composed** the lyrics for her new song one afternoon in the studio.
He had the bracelet **inscribed** with the words "I love you."

Word Network

Possible responses: *fellow, tradition, camaraderie*

Word Study

For more support, see **Concept Vocabulary and Word Study**

Possible responses:
memorial: a structure built to remember someone; **memoir:** book that recalls the past; **memorandum:** note that should be remembered

MAKING MEANING

THE WRITING ON THE WALL

Close Read the Text

Close Read: Annotate, Question, Conclude

With your group, revisit sections of the text you marked during your first read. **Annotate** details that you notice. What **questions** do you have? What can you **conclude**?

TIP

GROUP DISCUSSION
Take notes on your group members' comments so that you can refer to them later or ask for clarification.

Analyze the Text

CITE TEXTUAL EVIDENCE to support your answers.

Notebook Complete the activities.

1. **Review and Clarify** With your group, reread the poem in paragraph 3 of the selection. How do you interpret this poem? How does the speaker compare with the heroes of the past?
2. **Present and Discuss** Now, work with your group to share the passages from the text that you found especially important. Take turns presenting your passages. Discuss what you notice in the text, the questions you asked, and the conclusions you reached.
3. **Essential Question:** ***What does it mean to be "American"?*** What have you learned about American identity from reading this text? Discuss with your group.

WORD NETWORK
Add interesting words related to American identity from the text to your Word Network.

LANGUAGE DEVELOPMENT

Concept Vocabulary

memento	composed	inscribed

Why These Words? The three concept vocabulary words are related. With your group, determine what the words have in common. Write your ideas, and add another word that fits the category.

Practice

Notebook Use a print or online dictionary to confirm the definitions of the three concept vocabulary words. Write a sentence using each of the words. How did the concept vocabulary words make your sentences more vivid? Discuss.

Word Study

Latin Root: *-mem-* The word *memento* comes from Latin and contains the root *-mem-*, which means "to remember." In fact, the word *remember* itself was also formed from this root. Identify two other words that were formed from the root *-mem-*. Write the words and their definitions.

STANDARDS
Reading Informational Text
Determine a central idea of a text and analyze its development over the course of the text, including how it emerges and is shaped and refined by specific details; provide an objective summary of the text.
Language
Identify and correctly use patterns of word changes that indicate different meanings or parts of speech.

FORMATIVE ASSESSMENT

Analyze the Text

- **If** students struggle to close read the text, **then** provide the **The Writing on the Wall: Text Questions** available online in the Interactive Teacher's Edition or Unit Resources. Answers and DOK levels are also available.

Concept Vocabulary

If students struggle to explain how the vocabulary words make their sentences more vivid, **then** have them restate the sentences using more generic terms and consider the difference.

Word Study

If students struggle to identify other words with the Latin root *-mem-*, **then** ask them to name things that provide a way to recall someone or something.

For Reteach and Practice, see **Word Study: Latin Root *-mem-* (RP).**

Analyze Craft and Structure

Informative Text Many blog posts, including "The Writing on the Wall," are essentially essays that are posted online. Like all effective essays, this blog post expresses a **central idea**, the main idea the author wants readers to understand. The author **develops and refines** the central idea by explaining it and making connections to other, related ideas. Pieces of information that illustrate, expand on, or prove an author's ideas are called **supporting details.** These are some types of supporting details:

- **Facts:** information that can be proved true
- **Statistics:** numbers used to compare groups of people or things
- **Examples:** specific cases of a general concept
- **Descriptions:** details that tell what something looks like, feels like, and so on
- **Reasons:** logical claims that justify a belief
- **Expert opinions:** comments of people with special knowledge

An essay may not include every type of supporting detail, but most writers try to include a variety. Doing so makes a text more interesting and convincing.

Practice

CITE TEXTUAL EVIDENCE to support your answers.

Work individually to complete the activities. Then, discuss your responses with your group.

1. (a) At what point in "The Writing on the Wall" does Dungy state her central idea?

(b) In your own words, restate that idea.

2. Use the chart to identify one or more examples from the text of each type of detail listed. Explain how the detail develops or refines the central idea.

SUPPORTING DETAIL	HOW IT DEVELOPS OR REFINES CENTRAL IDEA
Description	Description in paragraph 1 helps readers imagine the writing and the experiences the men had to endure.
Example	Excerpts of poetry in paragraphs 5 and 8 help readers see what kinds of poems the men wrote. They show the emotion the men were conveying.
Fact	Details such as the fire in paragraph 12 help readers understand the history of the building. Readers may appreciate the poetry more.
Reasons	In paragraph 16, the writer talks about why these poems remain important and valuable.

DIGITAL PERSPECTIVES

Analyze Craft and Structure

Informative Text Discuss with students different examples of informative texts, such as magazine articles, encyclopedia entries, or blog posts. Discuss the various types of supporting details that writers use to develop a supporting idea. Point out to students that the support for a central idea is critical because it helps readers understand and accept the author's premise. Explain that it is often useful to include a variety of support types. Explain that each type of text focuses on one central idea. This is the main point authors want readers to know and understand after completing the text.

For more support, see **Analyze Craft and Structure: Informative Text.**

Practice

1. Dungy states her central idea in paragraph 6 and 7.
2. In the late 1800s and early 1900s, male Chinese detainees at Angel Island wrote poetry on the wall of the detention center to share their struggles and experiences.
3. See possible responses in chart on student page.

FORMATIVE ASSESSMENT

Analyze Craft and Structure

If students fail to identify the central idea, **then** have them point to different details in the blog post and explain what they have in common and what they help support. For Reteach and Practice, see **Analyze Craft and Structure: Informative Text (RP).**

FACILITATING

Author's Style

Word Choice Discuss with students how sound devices contribute to the tone of a text. Identifying and understanding them can help readers determine the tone, which is the author's attitude or opinion about the central idea. As you review the examples of sound devices with students, consider providing additional examples:

alliteration:
The bouquet of *pink* and *purple peonies* looks very *pretty*.

assonance:
In a *deep sleep*, I *dream* of *meeting* you.

consonance:
We had a *chuckle* when she dropped the *pickle* and *kicked* it.

For more support, see **Author's Style: Word Choice**.

Read It

MAKE IT INTERACTIVE
Have students write each sentence on a sentence strip, using a different color for each type of sound device, and circling which words are examples of alliteration, assonance, or consonance.

See possible responses in chart on Student page.

Write It

Responses will vary. Be sure that students include at least one example of alliteration, one example of assonance, and one example of consonance. As you evaluate student writing, look for attention to details. Common errors may include a misunderstanding of each type of sound device.

FORMATIVE ASSESSMENT

Author's Style

If students fail to use sound devices correctly, **then** have them read their sentences aloud to listen for the different sounds and consider ways to improve their writing. For Reteach and Practice, see **Author's Style: Word Choice (RP).**

LANGUAGE DEVELOPMENT

THE WRITING ON THE WALL

TIP

GROUP DISCUSSION
If you feel confused during the discussion, don't be afraid to ask questions. Other members of the group may be thankful that you asked for clarification.

Author's Style

Word Choice Both poems and prose are enhanced by the use of sound devices, such as **alliteration, assonance,** and **consonance**. The use of sound devices may emphasize meaning, create a particular mood, or express **tone**—the author's attitude toward the subject or audience.

SOUND DEVICES IN POETRY AND PROSE

SOUND DEVICE	DEFINITION	EXAMPLE
alliteration	repetition of first consonant sound in stressed syllables of consecutive or nearby words	• *The snake sneaked past the snail.*
assonance	repetition of vowel sounds within consecutive or nearby words	• *The green leaves fluttered in the breeze.*
consonance	repetition of internal or ending consonant sounds within consecutive or nearby words	• *The king sang a rousing song.*

Read It

Work individually. Find examples of alliteration, assonance, and consonance in "The Writing on the Wall." You may consider both Dungy's prose and the poetry examples she cites. Then, discuss with your group how each example emphasizes meaning or helps to convey a specific tone.

SOUND DEVICE	EXAMPLE FROM "THE WRITING ON THE WALL"
alliteration	• to calm, to communicate, to commiserate, and to conserve • west wind • moonlight shines on me alone • composed carefully crafted
assonance	• dreams are not sweet • reunite my wife • China to America • solely on close friends to relieve my loneliness
consonance	• women and small children • Island Immigration

Write It

Notebook Write a paragraph in which you use one example each of alliteration, assonance, and consonance.

STANDARDS

Reading Informational Text
Determine the meaning of words and phrases as they are used in a text, including figurative, connotative, and technical meanings; analyze the cumulative impact of specific word choices on meaning and tone.

Writing
Conduct short as well as more sustained research projects to answer a question or solve a problem; narrow or broaden the inquiry when appropriate; synthesize multiple sources on the subject, demonstrating understanding of the subject under investigation.

Speaking and Listening
Make strategic use of digital media in presentations to enhance understanding of findings, reasoning, and evidence and to add interest.

PERSONALIZE FOR LEARNING

Challenge
Invite students to think of a situation where a person might feel sad or lonely, and ask them to write poems expressing those feelings. Encourage students to use a variety of sound devices (alliteration, assonance, and consonance) in their poems. Have students display their poems on a wall in the classroom.

Research

Assignment

With your group, conduct research using a variety of sources and prepare a **digital presentation**. Gather relevant visual evidence to strengthen your presentation. Choose from the following topics:

- ☐ **Angel Island** Research the Angel Island Immigration Station. Find maps, photos, records, blueprints, and other items to give your audience an understanding of exactly where the station was and what it was like. Make sure your presentation addresses questions such as: Who exactly was brought to Angel Island? Were all inmates immigrants? Where were the groups (Europeans, women and children, Asians) each housed and under what conditions did they live?
- ☐ **Poetry** The poems of Angel Island are said to follow the classic style of well-known Chinese poets. Research one or two of these poets and compare their work with that of one of the poets on Angel Island. Classic poets to investigate include Li Bai, Tu Fu, and Wang Wei.
- ☐ **Chinese Immigration** Research Chinese immigration to the United States from 1910 to 1940. How many Chinese immigrants arrived? What were the common reasons that most of these immigrants came to San Francisco? How did their motivations and expectations influence the poetry at Angel Island?

Finding Materials Your presentation may include photos, video, and audio as well as text. Use the Internet and other sources to obtain these materials.

Presentation Plan Work with your group to plan your presentation. Try out different approaches and ideas. Take notes to mark down which ideas work best. Use the chart to plan your presentation.

VISUALS	NOTES
VISUAL 1:	
VISUAL 2:	
VISUAL 3:	
VISUAL 4:	

EVIDENCE LOG

Before moving on to a new selection, go to your Evidence Log and record what you learned from "The Writing on the Wall."

DIGITAL PERSPECTIVES

Research

Explain to students that a digital presentation should achieve the same goals as a written, informative text. It should focus on a central idea and include evidence to support it. All of the visual evidence that is included should be relevant, which means it should relate to the central idea. There should be no extra material that strays from the topic because it will confuse the audience.

After each group completes its research, guide students to work together to decide on a central idea for their digital presentation. Have them write it out and refer to it as they choose supporting visual evidence to include. For more support, see **Research: Digital Presentation.**

Finding Materials As they research their digital presentations, guide students to use credible sources to find photographs, maps, or other materials.

Presentation Plan Have students in each group work together to complete the plan for their digital presentation. Each presentation should include at least four pieces of visual evidence. Encourage students to use different kinds of materials. Some examples include photographs, maps, diagrams, charts, or lists.

Evidence Log Support students in completing their Evidence Log. This paced activity will help prepare them for the Performance-Based Assessment at the end of the unit.

FORMATIVE ASSESSMENT

Research

If students have difficulty finding visual evidence, **then** have them brainstorm a list of different key words to use to help aid their research. For Reteach and Practice, see **Research: Digital Presentation (RP).**

Selection Test

Administer the "The Writing on the Wall" Selection Test, which is available in both print and digital formats online in Assessments.

PERSONALIZE FOR LEARNING

English Language Support

Planning a Digital Presentation Support English learners in creating an effective digital presentation.

Ask pairs of students to plan a digital presentation that compares and contrasts the immigration experience at Angel Island with that of Ellis Island. Encourage students to make a list of the kinds of tools they will use, including the information that will be addressed by each one. **EMERGING**

Ask pairs of students to plan a digital presentation that compares and contrasts the immigration experience at Angel Island with that of Ellis Island. Encourage students to create a storyboard that illustrates the kinds of media they will use and the information that will be addressed by the media. **EXPANDING**

Ask pairs of students to plan a digital presentation that compares and contrasts the immigration experience at Angel Island with that of Ellis Island. Encourage students to create a storyboard that illustrates the kinds of media they will use and the information that will be addressed by the media. Students should also write an introduction for their presentation. **BRIDGING**

An expanded **English Language Support Lesson** on Digital Presentation is available in the Interactive Teacher's Edition.

With a Little Help From My Friends

AUDIO SUMMARIES
Audio summaries of "With a Little Help From My Friends" are available in both English and Spanish in the Interactive Teacher's Edition or Unit Resources. Assigning these summaries prior to reading the selection may help students build additional background knowledge and set a context for their first read.

Summary

Firoozeh Dumas's memoir "With a Little Help From My Friends" begins in 1972, when she and her family moved to the United States from Iran. She is seven years old. Dumas is surprised that Americans know so little about Iran—many of them don't even know where it is. Many of her neighbors and classmates ask questions that show that they have no knowledge of Iran at all. However, Dumas receives much more from Americans than silly questions and crazy ideas about Iran. She receives genuine hospitality and true kindness. After two years in California, she and her family find it very hard to leave the country and go back to Iran. Dumas considers herself lucky to have come to America when she did. The silly questions and crazy ideas were harmless, and the hospitality and kindness were real. Not many years later, Iranians coming to this country may not have felt quite so welcome.

Insight

Reading "With a Little Help From My Friends" will help students consider how Americans are perceived by their friends and enemies—and also by those about whom they know nothing.

ESSENTIAL QUESTION:
What does it mean to be "American"?

Connection to Essential Question

"With a Little Help From My Friends" provides an autobiographical perspective on the Essential Question. Dumas's memoir covers only two years as a guest resident in America, but during that time of her childhood, she fully embraced American life. For Dumas, being American meant offering hospitality and kindness to a foreigner from a country that many Americans couldn't locate on a map. Students may also look at Dumas's experiences with American ignorance, and determine whether being American necessarily involves a practice of neglecting to learn about other countries.

SMALL-GROUP READING PERFORMANCE TASK
How do the realities of immigrants' experiences reflect or fail to reflect American ideals?

UNIT PERFORMANCE-BASED ASSESSMENT
How is an American identity created?

Connection to Performance Tasks

Small-Group Reading Performance Task In this Performance Task, students will consider how the lives of particular immigrants might benefit by reflecting American ideals. This selection shows that with the right political mood, the American ideals of tolerance and acceptance might surprise immigrants and contrast with their expectations, just as the ease and adaptability of immigrants might surprise Americans and contrast with their expectations. If the time isn't right, however, such ideals and expectations may not apply.

Unit Performance-Based Assessment Although Dumas returned to Iran during the period covered by this selection, she creates her notion of an American identity out of her gratitude to the American people for the care and protection they extended to her and her family while they were here.

DIGITAL PERSPECTIVES — Audio | Video | Document | Annotation Highlights | EL Highlights | Online Assessment

LESSON RESOURCES

	Making Meaning	Language Development	Effective Expression
Lesson	**First Read** **Close Read** **Analyze the Text** **Analyze Craft and Structure**	**Concept Vocabulary** **Word Study** **Author's Style**	**Writing to Sources**
Instructional Standards	**RL.10** By the end of grade 9, read and comprehend . . . **RI.3** Analyze how the author unfolds an analysis or series of ideas or events . . .	**L.4.a** Use context as a clue . . . **L.4.b** Identify and correctly use patterns of word changes . . . **L.5.a** Interpret figures of speech . . .	**W.2** Write informative/explanatory texts . . . **W.2.b** Develop the topic . . .
STUDENT RESOURCES			
Available online in the Interactive Student Edition or Unit Resources	Selection Audio First-Read Guide: Nonfiction Close-Read Guide: Nonfiction	Evidence Log Word Network	
TEACHER RESOURCES			
Selection Resources Available online in the Interactive Teacher's Edition or Unit Resources	Audio Summaries Annotation Highlights EL Highlights With a Little Help from My Friends: Text Questions Analyze Craft and Structure: Literary Nonfiction	Author's Style: Humor English Language Support Lesson: Hyperbole Concept Vocabulary and Word Study	Writing to Sources: Essay
Reteach/Practice (RP) Available online in the Interactive Teacher's Edition or Unit Resources	Analyze Craft and Structure: Literary Nonfiction (RP)	Author's Style: Humor (RP) Word Study: The Latin Prefix *inter-* (RP)	Writing to Sources: Essay (RP)
Assessment Available online in Assessments	Selection Test		
My Resources	A Unit 1 Answer Key is available online and in the Interactive Teacher's Edition.		

Reading Support

Text Complexity Rubric: With a Little Help From My Friends	
Quantitative Measures	
Lexile: 920 Text Length: 1,715 words	
Qualitative Measures	
Knowledge Demands ①—②—③—**4**—⑤	Explores themes of varying levels of complexity that are uncommon to most readers (Iranian immigrant experience, people's misconceptions about other cultures).
Structure ①—②—**3**—④—⑤	Organization of individual ideas is clear, but ideas flow from one to another without a predictable organization.
Language Conventionality and Clarity ①—②—**3**—④—⑤	Language is mostly contemporary, conversational, and familiar; language is explicit and literal; vocabulary is mostly familiar, with occasional unfamiliar vocabulary (e.g., *tabulae rasae*)
Levels of Meaning/Purpose ①—②—**3**—④—⑤	Main ideas and meaning are clearly expressed most of the time, but in some sections meaning has to be inferred from dialogue.

DECIDE AND PLAN

English Language Support

Provide English Learners with support for knowledge demands and meaning as they read the selection.

Knowledge Demands Collect and record information about the writer and setting to review with students. Invite students to listen actively as you share this background. Writer: *an immigrant from Iran* Setting: *a city outside* Los Angeles, *in 1972 when the writer is seven years old.* The memoir is written many years later.

Discuss the fact that the author is talking about people with no understanding of Iranian culture. Define the term *tabulae rasae* (blank slate).

Meaning List words and phrases pertaining to stereotypes or misunderstandings about Iranian culture - for example, *camels, Lawrence of Arabia, Persian cats*. Make sure students understand the words. Then discuss the incorrect beliefs described in the reading - for example, that all Iranians have camels.

Strategic Support

Provide students with strategic support to ensure that they can successfully read the text.

Knowledge Demands Explain that students will be reading about the experiences of an immigrant from Iran, and that the writer describes many stereotypes about Iran. Discuss the possibility that sometimes stereotypes come to exist because of lack of real information about a culture.

Meaning Ask students to list as many of the stereotypes the writer shares about Iran as possible, and then correct them by setting them beside the reality—for example, *One boy thought everyone had camels and not cars. The writer had never seen a camel. Her family had a car.*

Challenge

Provide students who need to be challenged with ideas for how they can go beyond a simple interpretation of the text.

Text Analysis Ask students to comment on how the author felt when she was confronted with a wide variety of stereotypes, representing a wide variety of misunderstandings and absences of fact. Then ask them to give ideas on the various ways a person might respond to stereotypes, to describe what in their opinion represents the best possible response, and to explain why.

Written Response Suggest that students read other chapters of the book *Funny in Farsi*, from which this selection is taken. They may also search for information on the author, Firoozeh Dumas. Ask students to explain in writing what they enjoyed most about the selections, or the most interesting thing they learned about the author, and to give reasons for their picks.

TEACH

Read and Respond

Have groups read the selection and complete the Making Meaning, Language Development, and Effective Expression activities.

Standards Support Through Teaching and Learning Cycle

IDENTIFY NEEDS

Analyze results of the Beginning-of-Year Assessment, focusing on the items relating to Unit 1. Also take into consideration student performance to this point and your observations of where particular students struggle.

DECIDE AND PLAN

- If students have performed poorly on items matching these standards, then provide selection scaffolds before assigning them the on-level lesson provided in the Student Edition.
- If students have done well on the Beginning-of-Year Assessment, then challenge them to keep progressing and learning by giving them opportunities to practice the skills in depth.
- Use the Selection Resources listed on the Planning pages for "With a Little Help From My Friends" to help students continually improve their ability to master the standards.

Instructional Standards: With a Little Help from My Friends

	Catching Up	This Year	Looking Forward
Reading	You may wish to administer the **Analyze Craft and Structure: Literary Nonfiction (RP)** worksheet to help students understand features of a memoir that are similar and/or different from other forms of literary nonfiction.	**RI.3** Analyze how the author unfolds an analysis or series of ideas or events, including the order in which the points are made, how they are introduced and developed, and the connections that are drawn between them.	Have students identify a theme about the United States from before the Iranian Revolution of 1973 and a theme from after the Revolution. In small groups, have students share the themes they identified and cite text that supports the theme from each time period.
Writing	You may wish to administer the **Writing to Sources: Essay (RP)** worksheet to help students focus on details and quotations from literary nonfiction as a source and focal point for a interpretive narrative essay.	**W.2** Write informative/explanatory texts to examine and convey complex ideas, concepts, and information clearly and accurately through the effective selection, organization, and analysis of content.	Encourage students to work with partners to revise their narrative interpretation essays and make them more vivid by discussing precise words, telling details, or sensory language that could be included.
Language	You may wish to administer the **Word Study: Latin Prefix *inter-* (RP)** worksheet to help students understand that related words are used differently, according to the part of speech they represent, such as *interpreter* (noun) and *interpret* (verb). You may wish to administer the **Author's Style: Humor (RP)** worksheet to help students understand how metaphors, similes, and hyperbole can add zest and humor to writing.	**L.4.b** Identify and correctly use patterns of word changes that indicate different meanings or parts of speech. **L.5.a** Interpret figures of speech in context and analyze their role in the text.	Have students list words from this selection along with other, related words that have a same word part, such as *interpreter* (from the selection) and *interpretation, interpret, and interpretive* (related words that share a word part). Then ask students to write the meaning and part of speech for each word. Have students identify examples of metaphors, similes, and hyperbole from the selection and analyze their impact on meaning.

TEACH

Implement the planned lesson, and gather evidence of student learning.

ANALYZE AND REVISE

- Analyze student work for evidence of student learning.
- Identify whether or not students have met the expectations in the standards.
- Identify implications for future instruction.

Jump Start

FIRST READ What would it be like to settle in a foreign country where the language, the food, and the climate are totally new? Engage students in the meaning and usefulness of the word "foreign." Ask them if they would try to learn the local language and customs and become part of the community, or whether they would be happy to remain a foreigner.

With a Little Help From My Friends

What are the biggest concerns about moving somewhere new? What makes people feel that they belong to their community? Model these questions for students before they read "With a Little Help From My Friends" to help bring the text alive and also connect it to the Small-Group Performance Task. Selection audio and print capability for the selection are available in the Interactive Teacher's Edition.

Concept Vocabulary

Encourage groups to discuss the three concept vocabulary words and share their familiarity or knowledge of each one. Then, ask groups to study the modeling of familiar word parts. Encourage students to look for roots along with context to help them determine the meaning of an unknown word.

FIRST READ

Have students perform the steps of the first read independently:

NOTICE: You may want to encourage students to notice the opening image of the selection and the mood it conveys. Also, point out the importance of footnotes in this selection.

ANNOTATE: Remind students to focus on passages of key importance or of particular interest.

CONNECT: Encourage students to go beyond the text to make connections with their own personal experiences or the experiences of someone they know or have heard of through movies or television.

RESPOND: Students will answer questions and write a summary to demonstrate understanding.

Point out to students that while they will always complete the Respond step at the end of the first read, the other steps will probably happen somewhat concurrently. You may wish to print copies of the **First-Read Guide: Non-Fiction** for students to use.

About the Author

Firoozeh Dumas (b. 1966) split her childhood between Iran, the country of her birth, and California. Her father loved to tell stories of his life, and she decided to tell stories, too. She originally wrote her first book, *Funny in Farsi*, for her children. It was published in 2003 and became a bestseller. Today, Dumas travels throughout the world spreading a message of humor and shared humanity.

With a Little Help From My Friends

Concept Vocabulary

As you perform your first read of "With a Little Help From My Friends," you will encounter these words.

proximity correspondents interpreter

Base Words If these words are unfamilar to you, see whether they contain a base word you know. Use your knowledge of the "inside" word, along with context, to determine the meaning. Here is an example of how to apply the strategy.

Unfamiliar Word: *translation*

Familiar "Inside" Word: *translate*, with meanings including "convert words from one language to another language"

Context: The *translation* of the German author's novel sold very well throughout the United States.

Conclusion: *Translation* is being used as a noun. It must mean "a work which has been translated, or converted from one language to another."

Apply your knowledge of base words and other vocabulary strategies to determine the meanings of unfamiliar words you encounter during your first read.

First Read NONFICTION

Apply these strategies as you conduct your first read. You will have an opportunity to complete a close read after your first read.

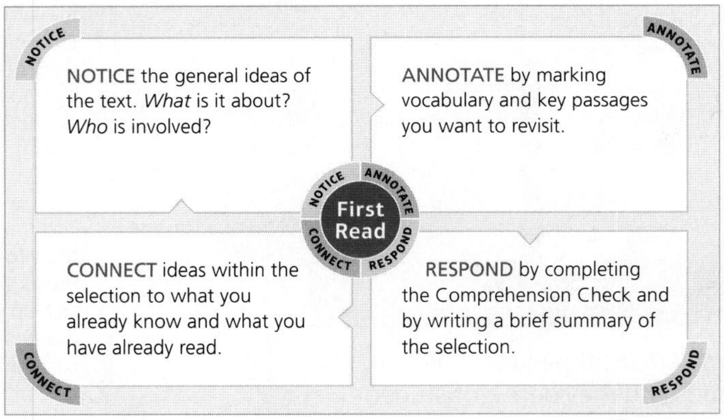
NOTICE
NOTICE the general ideas of the text. *What* is it about? *Who* is involved?
ANNOTATE
ANNOTATE by marking vocabulary and key passages you want to revisit.
First Read
CONNECT ideas within the selection to what you already know and what you have already read.
CONNECT
RESPOND by completing the Comprehension Check and by writing a brief summary of the selection.
RESPOND

STANDARDS

Reading Informational Text
By the end of grade 9, read and comprehend literary nonfiction in the grades 9–10 text complexity band proficiently, with scaffolding as needed at the high end of the range.

Language
Use context as a clue to the meaning of a word or phrase.

MEMOIR

With a Little Help From My Friends

from Funny in Farsi

Firoozeh Dumas

DIGITAL PERSPECTIVES

CLOSER LOOK

Infer Tone

Circulate among groups as students conduct their close read. Suggest that groups close read paragraphs 1 and 2 and think about the author's tone. Encourage them to talk about the annotations they mark. If needed, provide the following support.

ANNOTATE: Have students mark details in paragraphs 1 and 2 that show the author's opinion of Americans, or work with small groups as you highlight them together.

QUESTION: Guide students to consider what these details might tell them. Ask what a reader can infer from the author's initial impressions of Americans, and accept student responses.

Possible response: These initial details tell us that even though most Americans didn't know much about the author and the country she came from, they were kind to her.

CONCLUDE: Help students to formulate conclusions about the importance of these details in the text. Ask students why the author might have included these details.

Possible response: These first impressions clearly occupy an important place in her memories. They formed the foundation of a long and happy relationship with America, and they set a tone for her writing.

Remind students that **tone** reveals the author's attitude towards her subject and toward her audience. Tone is established by word choice, and shows the character of the writer.

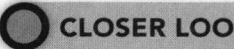

Additional **English Language Support** is available in the Interactive Teacher's Edition.

BACKGROUND

Once known as Persia, Iran is an oil-rich country in the Middle East. In 1953, the United States had helped to remove Iran's government and to place a Shah, or king, in power. In 1972, when this excerpt begins, the Iranian government was still a monarchy led by the Shah. However, seven years later, during the Iranian Revolution of 1979, the country would undergo the political upheaval the author refers to in her first sentence. The Shah would be overthrown and replaced with a government that was unfriendly to the United States. Many Americans returned the hostility.

SCAN FOR MULTIMEDIA

NOTES

1 I was lucky to have come to America years before the political upheaval in Iran. The Americans we encountered were kind and curious, unafraid to ask questions and willing to listen. As soon as I spoke enough English to communicate, I found myself being interviewed nonstop by children and adults alike. My life became one long-running *Oprah* show, minus the free luxury accommodations in Chicago, and Oprah.

2 On the topic of Iran, American minds were tabulae rasae.[1] Judging from the questions asked, it was clear that most Americans in 1972 had never heard of Iran. We did our best to educate. "You know Asia? Well, you go south at the Soviet Union and there we are." Or we'd try

1. **tabulae rasae** (TAB yuh lee RAY see) *n.* blank slates, or minds free from preconceived ideas.

PERSONALIZE FOR LEARNING

Strategic Support

Context In order to give students a clearer understanding of this author and her family, use online maps that show the country of Iran and its location on the Asian continent. Images of the larger cities such as Tehran, its architecture, and common foods of the region will help provide students with a feel for this writer's country.

FACILITATING

Concept Vocabulary

PROXIMITY If groups are struggling to define the word *proximity* in paragraph 2, point out that the meaning of the root word *proxim* is "nearest." Context clues will also help students understand the word. If the mentions of Iraq and Afghanistan are of no immediate help to students, an online map of Iran will show that it shares borders with both those nations. Students should then be able to infer that proximity means, "being close to or near."
Possible response: Proximity must mean "being near or close to."

NOTES

Mark base words or indicate another strategy you used that helped you determine meaning.

proximity (prok SIHM uh tee) *n.*

MEANING:

to be more bucolic, mentioning being south of the beautiful Caspian Sea, "where the famous caviar comes from." Most people in Whittier did not know about the famous caviar and once we explained what it was, they'd scrunch up their faces. "Fish eggs?" they would say. "Gross." We tried mentioning our **proximity** to Afghanistan or Iraq, but it was no use. Having exhausted our geographical clues, we would say, "You've heard of India, Japan, or China? We're on the same continent."

3 We had always known that ours is a small country and that America is very big. But even as a seven-year-old, I was surprised that so many Americans had never noticed us on the map. Perhaps it's like driving a Yugo[2] and realizing that the eighteen-wheeler can't see you.

4 In Iran, geography is a requirement in every grade. Since the government issues textbooks, every student studies the same material in the same grade. In first-grade geography, I had to learn the shape of Iran and the location of its capital, Tehran. I had to memorize that we shared borders with Turkey, Afghanistan, Pakistan, Iraq, and the USSR.[3] I also knew that I lived on the continent of Asia.

5 None of the kids in Whittier, a city an hour outside of Los Angeles, ever asked me about geography. They wanted to know about more important things, such as camels. How many did we own back home? What did we feed them? Was it a bumpy ride? I always disappointed them by admitting that I had never seen a camel in my entire life. And as far as a ride goes, our Chevrolet was rather smooth. They reacted as if I had told them that there really was a person in the Mickey Mouse costume.

6 We were also asked about electricity, tents, and the Sahara. Once again, we disappointed, admitting that we had electricity, that we did not own a tent, and that the Sahara was on another continent. Intent to remedy the image of our homeland as backward, my father took it upon himself to enlighten Americans whenever possible. Any unsuspecting American who asked my father a question received, as a bonus, a lecture on the successful history of the petroleum industry in Iran. As my father droned on, I watched the faces of these kind Americans, who were undoubtedly making mental notes never to talk to a foreigner again.

7 My family and I wondered why Americans had such a mistaken image of Iran. We were offered a clue one day by a neighbor, who told us that he knew about Iran because he had seen *Lawrence of Arabia*.[4] Whoever Lawrence was, we had never heard of him, we said. My father then explained that Iranians are an Indo-European people; we are not Arabs. We do, however, have two things in common with Saudi Arabia, he continued: "Islam and petroleum." "Now, I

2. **Yugo** (YOO goh) small car manufactured in Yugoslavia.
3. **USSR** Union of Soviet Socialist Republics, name for a former country composed of 15 states, including Russia, that disbanded in 1991.
4. ***Lawrence of Arabia*** movie made in 1962 about a military officer in the Arabian Peninsula during World War I.

FACILITATING SMALL-GROUP CLOSE READ

CLOSE READING: Memoir As groups perform the close read, circulate and offer support as needed.

- Remind groups that when they read a memoir, they should be sure to identify the narrator.
- If a group is confused about why particular events are important, remind them to think about how they relate to the narrator's experience and why the narrator felt it was important to mention.
- Challenge groups to determine the main idea of the text and the specific details that refine the main idea.

won't bore you with religion," he said, "but let me tell you about the petroleum industry."

8 Another neighbor, a kindly old lady who taught me how to take care of indoor plants, asked whether we had many cats back home. My father, with his uncanny ability to forge friendships, said, "We don't keep pets in our homes. They are dirty." "But your cats are so beautiful!" our neighbor said. We had no idea what she was talking about. Seeing our puzzled expressions, she showed us a picture of a beautiful, longhaired cat. "It's a Persian cat," she said. That was news to us; the only cats we had ever seen back home were the mangy strays that ate scraps behind people's houses. From that day, when I told people I was from Iran, I added "where Persian cats come from." That impressed them.

9 I tried my best to be a worthy representative of my homeland, but, like a Hollywood celebrity relentlessly pursued by paparazzi, I sometimes got tired of the questions. I, however, never punched anybody with my fists; I used words. One boy at school had a habit of asking me particularly stupid questions. One day he inquired about camels, again. This time, perhaps foreshadowing a vocation in storytelling, I told him that, yes, we had camels, a one-hump and a two-hump. The one-hump belonged to my parents and the two-hump was our family station wagon. His eyes widened.

10 "Where do you keep them?" he asked.

11 "In the garage, of course," I told him.

12 Having heard what he wanted to hear, he ran off to share his knowledge with the rest of the kids on the playground. He was very angry once he realized that I had fooled him, but at least he never asked me another question.

13 Often kids tried to be funny by chanting, "I ran to I-ran, I ran to I-ran." The correct pronunciation, I always informed them, is "Ee-rahn." "I ran" is a sentence, I told them, as in "I ran away from my geography lesson."

14 Older boys often asked me to teach them "some bad words in your language." At first, I politely refused. My refusal merely increased their determination, so I solved the problem by teaching them phrases like *man kharam*, which means "I'm an idiot." I told them that what I was teaching them was so nasty that they would have to promise never to repeat it to anyone. They would then spend all of recess running around yelling, "I'm an idiot! I'm an idiot!" I never told them the truth. I figured that someday, somebody would.

15 But almost every person who asked us a question asked with kindness. Questions were often followed by suggestions of places to visit in California. At school, the same children who inquired about camels also shared their food with me. "I bet you've never tried an Oreo! Have one," or "My mom just baked these peanut butter cookies and she sent you one." Kids invited me to their houses to show me what their rooms looked like. On Halloween, one family brought over a costume, knowing that I would surely be the only

NOTES

DIGITAL PERSPECTIVES

CLOSER LOOK

Understanding Memoir

Circulate among groups as students conduct their close read. Suggest that groups close read paragraphs 14–15. Encourage them to talk about the annotations they mark. If needed, provide the following support.

ANNOTATE: Have students mark details in paragraphs 14–15 that the author uses to describe the questions she is asked, or work with small groups as you highlight them together.

QUESTION: Guide students to consider what these details might tell them. Ask what a reader can infer from these questions, and accept student responses.

Possible response: The narrator was asked many questions and a few, especially from the boys in her class, were irritating. However, mostly they showed that both adults and children were interested in her and where she came from.

CONCLUDE: Help students to formulate conclusions about the importance of these details in the text. Ask students why the author might have included these details.

Possible response: This is a memoir and the questions she is asked by people give the reader a more complete view of her experience.

Remind students that a **memoir** is a type of nonfiction autobiographical writing that tells about a person's own life, usually focusing on the writer's involvement in historically or culturally significant events.

DIGITAL PERSPECTIVES

Illuminating the Text Dumas was asked about camels and Persian cats, even though she had never actually seen either one. Show students images or brief video clips of each of these animals. Be sure to preview all material before you show it in class. These animals had become symbols of Iran that the author did not experience. Ask students if there are animals or activities in American culture that are unfamiliar to them.

Concept Vocabulary

CORRESPONDENTS If groups are struggling to define the word *correspondents*, in paragraph 15, point out that the meaning of the root-word *correspond* is "to communicate with letters." Context clues will also help students understand the word. Point out these phrases in the same sentence. Ask students to think about who writes letters or communicates in a war as part of his or her job.

Possible response: *Correspondent* must mean "a person who writes letters or files reports for a news organization."

INTERPRETER If groups are struggling to define the word *interpreter,* in paragraph 18, explain to students that this word has both a prefix and a suffix. The prefix is *inter-* meaning "between" and the suffix *-er*, means "one who." So this is someone who is between two experiences or activities. Context clues will also help students understand the word.

Possible response: *Interpreter* must mean, "a person who translates speech."

NOTES

Mark base words or indicate another strategy you used that helped you determine meaning.

correspondents (kawr uh SPON duhnts) *n.*

MEANING:

Mark base words or indicate another strategy you used that helped you determine meaning.

interpreter (ihn TUR pruh tuhr) *n.*

MEANING:

kid in the Halloween parade without one. If someone had been able to encapsulate the kindness of these second-graders in pill form, the pills would undoubtedly put many war **correspondents** out of business.

16 After almost two years in Whittier, my father's assignment was completed and we had to return home. The last month of our stay, I attended one slumber party after another, all thrown in my honor. This avalanche of kindness did not make our impending departure any easier. Everyone wanted to know when we would come back to America. We had no answer, but we invited them all to visit us in Iran. I knew no one would ever take us up on our offer, because Iran was off the radar screen for most people. My friends considered visiting their grandmothers in Oregon to be a long trip, so visiting me in Iran was like taking a left turn at the next moon. It wasn't going to happen. I didn't know then that I would indeed be returning to America about two years later.

17 Between frenzied shopping trips to Sears to buy presents for our relatives back home, my mother spent her last few weeks giving gifts to our American friends. I had wondered why my mother had brought so many Persian handicrafts with her; now I knew. Everyone, from my teachers to the crossing guard to the Brownie leader to the neighbors, received something. "Dees eez from my countay-ree. Es-pay-shay-ley for you," she would explain. These handicrafts, which probably turned up in garage sales the following year, were received with tears and promises to write.

18 My mother was particularly sad to return to Iran. I had always assumed that she would be relieved to return to her family and to a land where she spoke the language and didn't need me to act as her **interpreter.** But I realized later that even though my mother could not understand anything the crossing guard, Mrs. Popkin, said, she understood that this woman looked out for me. And she understood her smiles. Even though my mother never attended a Brownie meeting, she knew that the leader, Carrie's mom, opened up her home to us every week and led us through all kinds of projects. No one paid her for this. And my mother knew that when it had been my turn to bring snacks for the class, one of the moms had stepped in and baked cupcakes. My best friend Connie's older sister, Michele, had tried to teach me to ride a bike, and Heather's mom, although single with two daughters, had hosted me overnight more times than I can remember. Even though I had been the beneficiary of all the attention, my mother, watching silently from a distance, had also felt the warmth of generosity and kindness. It was hard to leave.

19 When my parents and I get together today, we often talk about our first year in America. Even though thirty years have passed, our memories have not faded. We remember the kindness more than ever, knowing that our relatives who immigrated to this country after the Iranian Revolution did not encounter the same America. They saw

PERSONALIZE FOR LEARNING

English Language Support

Figurative Language Note the sentence in paragraph 16: *This avalanche of kindness did not make our impending departure any easier.* Explain to the students that this sentence contains an example of **hyperbole**, a figure of speech that uses deliberate overstatement, or exaggeration—either for comic effect or to express heightened emotion. The author is emphasizing the kindness she and her family experience by calling it an avalanche. (Make certain students understand the word *avalanche).* Ask students why they think the author chose to use hyperbole to describe kindness. **ALL LEVELS**

Americans who had bumper stickers on their cars that read "Iranians: Go Home" or "We Play Cowboys and Iranians." The Americans they met rarely invited them to their houses. These Americans felt that they knew all about Iran and its people, and they had no questions, just opinions. My relatives did not think Americans were very kind. ❧

NOTES

Comprehension Check

Complete the following items after you finish your first read. Review and clarify details with your group.

1. How did most Americans treat Dumas and her family during their first year in the United States?

2. What surprised the young Dumas about Americans' knowledge of geography?

3. What joke did Dumas play on boys who pestered her to teach them bad words in her native language?

4. According to Dumas, how did things change for Iranian immigrants to the United States after the Iranian Revolution?

5. **Notebook** Write a summary of the selection.

RESEARCH

Research to Clarify Choose at least one unfamiliar detail from the text. Briefly research that detail. In what way does the information you learned shed light on an aspect of the memoir?

Research to Explore Choose something from the text that interested you, and formulate a research question.

DIGITAL PERSPECTIVES

Comprehension Check

Possible responses:

1. They treated her and her family with acute curiosity and well-meaning but ignorant friendliness.
2. The Americans did not know where Iran was, to the point of not being able to find the country on a map.
3. Dumas taught the older boys to say, *"man kharam" or* "I'm an idiot" in Farsi.
4. After the Iranian Revolution they were no longer welcomed with friendliness and confusion.
5. Firoozeh's family came to Whittier, California, when she was seven. In the beginning, Firoozeh had problems explaining where she had come from. As Firoozeh spent time in America, she learned American ways. When it was time to return to Iran, Firoozeh and her family began to recognize how kind her American friends had been to the family. Members of her family who immigrated later received a different reception due to the Iranian Revolution.

Research

Research to Clarify If groups struggle to come up with a detail to clarify, you may want to suggest that they review their annotations for details that are unfamiliar to them.

Research to Explore If groups struggle to come up with a research topic, you may want to suggest that they focus on one of the following topics: the Iranian Revolution; caviar and the Caspian Sea; geography in American schools.

PERSONALIZE FOR LEARNING

Challenge

Personal Memoir Have the students write their own personal memoirs. Students should recount a childhood experience that shaped the goals they have today. Student memoirs should be about an experience that is still relevant to their ideals now. What shaped them and assisted their growth? Emphasize that this writing needs rich details and vivid language to draw in the reader.

Jump Start

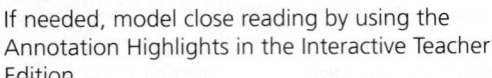

CLOSE READ Ask students to imagine how this selection would be different if Firoozeh had only known America after the Iranian Revolution. Would she have been treated with kindness? What view would she have of America?

Close Read the Text

If needed, model close reading by using the Annotation Highlights in the Interactive Teacher's Edition.

Remind students to use Accountable Talk in their discussions and to support one another as they complete the close read.

Analyze the Text

1. **Possible response:** Firoozeh saw that the attitude of kindness and good will of Americans toward Iran turn to scorn, mistrust, and hostility. The cause of change was the Iranian Revolution in which Iranian militants took Americans as hostages. Though the actions of militants in Iran were brutal, Firoozeh implies that they were not representative of the Iranian people themselves.
2. **Passages will vary by group.** Remind students to explain why they chose the passages they presented to the group members.
3. **Responses will vary by group.**

Concept Vocabulary

Possible responses:

Why These Words? All of these words emphasize travel and communication between people from different places and cultures. Another word that fits the concept is *translation*.

Practice

Do not smoke in close *proximity* to gas pumps; The *correspondents* for the sports section take every game seriously; We still have not found an *interpreter* for our Japanese investors.

In discussion, students may address how these words make their sentences seem detailed and professional.

Word Network

Possible words: *borders, homeland, foreigner*

Word Study

For more support, see **Concept Vocabulary and Word Study.**

Possible Response: *interviewed*, When one person interviews another, there is a series of questions and answers *between* them.

MAKING MEANING

WITH A LITTLE HELP FROM MY FRIENDS

Close Read the Text

With your group, revisit sections of the text you marked during your first read. **Annotate** details that you notice. What **questions** do you have? What can you **conclude**?

ANNOTATE QUESTION Close Read CONCLUDE

Analyze the Text

CITE TEXTUAL EVIDENCE to support your answers.

Notebook Complete the activities.

1. **Review and Clarify** With your group, reread paragraphs 18–19 of "With a Little Help From My Friends." What change in the attitude of Americans toward Iran did Dumas see in a few short years? How did Dumas feel about the change, and were her feelings justified?
2. **Present and Discuss** Now, work with your group to share the passages from the text that you found especially important. Take turns presenting your passages. Discuss what you notice in the text, the questions you asked, and the conclusions you reached.
3. **Essential Question:** ***What does it mean to be "American"?*** What has this selection taught you about American identity? Discuss with your group.

TIP

GROUP DISCUSSION
If you do not fully understand a classmate's comment, don't hesitate to ask for clarification. Use a friendly and respectful tone when you ask.

LANGUAGE DEVELOPMENT

Concept Vocabulary

proximity	correspondents	interpreter

Why These Words? The three concept vocabulary words are related. With your group, determine what the words have in common. Write your ideas, and add another word that fits the category.

WORD NETWORK
Add interesting words related to American identity from the text to your Word Network.

Practice

Notebook Use a print or online dictionary to confirm the definitions of the three concept vocabulary words. Write a sentence using each of the words. How did they make your sentences more vivid? Discuss.

Word Study

Latin Prefix: *inter-* The Latin prefix *inter-*, which begins the word *interpreter*, means "between" or "among." For instance, an *international* agreement is an agreement between or among different nations.

Reread paragraph 1 of "With a Little Help From My Friends." Mark the word that begins with the prefix *inter-*. Write the word here, and explain how the prefix *inter-* contributes to its meaning.

STANDARDS

Reading Informational Text
Analyze how the author unfolds an analysis or series of ideas or events, including the order in which the points are made, how they are introduced and developed, and the connections that are drawn between them.

Language
Identify and correctly use patterns of word changes that indicate different meanings or parts of speech.

FORMATIVE ASSESSMENT

Analyze the Text

If students struggle to close read the text, **then** provide **With a Little Help From My Friends: Text Questions** available online in the Interactive Teacher's Edition or Unit Resources. Answers and DOK levels are also available.

Concept Vocabulary

If students struggle to identify the concept **then** have them revisit the context in which the words were used in the story.

Word Study

If students fail to identify one other word that uses the *inter-* prefix, **then** remind them that the prefix *inter* refers to activity that occurs between or among people and things that come together. For Reteach and Practice, see **Word Study: Latin Prefix *inter-* (RP).**

Analyze Craft and Structure

Literary Nonfiction Autobiographical writing is any type of nonfiction in which an author tells his or her own story. A full autobiography usually covers the author's entire life or a large span of time. A **memoir**, by contrast, is a limited kind of autobiographical writing that focuses on one period or aspect of the writer's life. Memoirs share these elements:

- written in first person, using the pronouns *I*, *me*, *we*, and *us*
- written in story form; may read like a work of fiction
- expresses the writer's attitude and insights

Memoirs often show how the writer's personal life intersects the **social and historical context**, or the circumstances of the time and place in which the story occurs. Aspects of the context include politics, language, values, beliefs, foods, customs, and traditions. In this memoir, Dumas expresses insights about the social and historical context of her childhood.

CITE TEXTUAL EVIDENCE to support your answers.

Practice

Work independently. Use the chart to identify details from the memoir that show each aspect of the social and historical context. Add a fifth category of your own. Then, discuss with your group how Dumas uses each detail to support an insight.

ASPECT OF THE CONTEXT	TEXTUAL DETAIL(S)	DUMAS'S INSIGHT
Politics		
Traditions	a.	b.
Foods	c.	d.
Values or Beliefs	e.	f.
Other	g.	h.

DIGITAL PERSPECTIVES

Analyze Craft and Structure

Literary Nonfiction It is important to discuss with students that autobiographical writing may be biased. Taking note of the perspective in which a person's story is told is important. In "With a Little Help From My Friends," the author is talking about the political climate at the time of her childhood. In terms of accuracy, the reader must note that Dumas is remembering things and writing them down through a child's lens.

However, this also shows that social and historical context memoirs can be similar to primary source documents of a time period. They lend personal and emotional layers to history that might otherwise be lost. For more support, see **Analyze Craft and Structure: Literary Nonfiction**

a. "We remember the kindness . . . knowing that our relatives who immigrated . . . after the Iranian Revolution did not encounter the same America" (paragraph 19)

b. America changed after the Iranian Revolution, turning against Iranians.

c. "On Halloween, one family brought over a costume" (paragraph 15)

d. While the Americans were confused about Iranian culture, they realized that Dumas wouldn't know American traditions.

e. "I bet you've never tried an Oreo! Have one" (paragraph 15)

f. People were eager to share their culture as an aspect of multicultural friendship.

g. "I won't bore you with religion," he said, "but let me tell you about the petroleum industry." (paragraph 7)

h. It's made clear that the cultural differences between were less important to Dumas' father than their similarities.

FORMATIVE ASSESSMENT

Analyze Craft and Structure

If students struggle to identify details that show aspects of social and historical context, **then** revisit key passages to discuss what Dumas is conveying to the reader about the habits and beliefs of herself, her family, and her neighbors. For Reteach and Practice, see **Analyze Craft and Structure: Literary Nonfiction (RP).**

FACILITATING

Author's Style

Humor Discuss with students that a variety of jokes that they know are actually examples of figurative language. Writers have been using figurative language to amuse their readers since well before Shakespeare, and Dumas is following in this tradition.

As you review the examples of metaphor, simile, and hyperbole, consider providing additional examples:

> The sound of the cash register *is music to my ears.* (metaphor)
>
> He is *like a balloon*, just full of hot air. (simile)
>
> She is so rich *she wipes her tears away with dollar bills*. (hyperbole)

For more support, see **Author's Style: Humor.**

Read It

See possible responses in chart on Student page.

Write It

Possible responses

Paragraphs will vary, but make sure that students include at least one metaphor, simile, and hyperbole. Suggest that students underline and label their figurative language to assist in evaluating any confusion among the different kinds of figurative language devices.

FORMATIVE ASSESSMENT

Author's Style

If students fail to identity figurative language devices, **then** have students look for exaggeration and comparisons between unlike objects that bring humor to the text. For Reteach and Practice, see **Author's Style: Humor (RP).**

LANGUAGE DEVELOPMENT

WITH A LITTLE HELP FROM MY FRIENDS

Author's Style

Humor Language that is used imaginatively rather than literally is called **figurative language**. Writers often use figurative language to make their ideas more vivid and rich. As figurative language involves surprising contrasts, writers also use it to make their writing funny. In this memoir, Dumas uses three types of figurative language—metaphor, simile, and hyperbole—to add zest and humor to her story.

A **metaphor** compares by describing one thing as if it were another.
Example: My chores were a mountain waiting to be climbed.

A **simile** uses the word *like* or *as* to compare two unlike items.
Example: Gerald is like a pesky housefly that keeps coming around again and again.

Hyperbole is a deliberate, extreme exaggeration.
Example: The cake was ten stories tall.

Read It

On your own, identify each type of figurative language from "With a Little Help From My Friends." Then, share your work with your group.

EXAMPLE FROM THE TEXT	TYPE OF FIGURATIVE LANGUAGE	EFFECT
My life became one long-running Oprah show, minus the free luxury accommodations in Chicago, and Oprah. (paragraph 1)	metaphor	The exaggerated metaphor is established, then slowly admitted to be false and absurd by pointing out what about it doesn't make sense.
I tried my best to be a worthy representative of my homeland, but, like a Hollywood celebrity relentlessly pursued by paparazzi, I sometimes got tired of the questions. (paragraph 9)	simile	It humorously compares her experiences with childhood friends to a far more adult situation.
This avalanche of kindness did not make our impending departure any easier. (paragraph 16)	metaphor	The kindness is characterized as something normally dangerous or destructive.
If someone had been able to encapsulate the kindness of these second-graders in pill form, the pills would undoubtedly put many war correspondents out of business. (paragraph 15)	hyperbole	The idea that one could use make a pill out of kindness is inherently humorous, as is the absurd hopefulness of using that to fix major world problems.

Write It

Notebook Write a paragraph describing daily events in your school. Use at least one metaphor, simile, and hyperbole.

STANDARDS
Language
Interpret figures of speech in context and analyze their role in the text.

96 UNIT 1 • AMERICAN VOICES

PERSONALIZE FOR LEARNING

English Language Support

Hyperbole Have pairs of students work together to write a few sentences about a fictitious Paul Bunyan-like character.

Tell students to describe what the character can do using hyperbole. For example, Paul Bunyan grew so fast that he had to start wearing his father's clothes as a baby. **EMERGING**

Have students write a paragraph about a fictitious Paul Bunyan-like character. Tell students to describe what the character can do using hyperbole. For example, Paul Bunyan could eat 50 pancakes in one minute. **EXPANDING**

Have students write two paragraphs about a fictitious Paul Bunyan-like character. Tell students to write the first paragraph describing the character and what he or she does in plain language. Tell them to write the second paragraph using hyperbole. **BRIDGING**

An expanded **English Language Support Lesson** on Hyperbole is available in the Digital Teacher's Edition.

EFFECTIVE EXPRESSION

Writing to Sources

Assignment

Write an **essay** in which you interpret an important detail or quotation from the selection. Explain what the quote you chose means and how it adds to the portrait Dumas paints of herself as a child, her family, and their relationship to their community in California.

With your group, choose one of the following quotations:

- ☐ "After almost two years in Whittier, my father's assignment was completed and we had to return home. The last month of our stay, I attended one slumber party after another, all thrown in my honor."
- ☐ "They wanted to know about more important things, such as camels. How many did we own back home? What did we feed them? Was it a bumpy ride?"
- ☐ "We remember the kindness more than ever, knowing that our relatives who immigrated to this country after the Iranian Revolution did not encounter the same America."

Writing Plan Consider the steps of the writing process—planning/prewriting, drafting, revising, and editing. Discuss options for organizing the work of group writing. For example, you may plan and prewrite as a group, but then have one person draft the essay, another revise it, and another edit. Alternatively, you may choose to have all group members write first drafts and then organize the various versions into a single, finished piece. Find the best way to make sure that all group members contribute equally and that you create a polished essay.

As a group, choose the quote you will write about. Then, brainstorm for ideas you will include in your essay. Use the chart to record your notes.

Brainstorming and Discussion Notes

Chosen Quote: ________________________________

WHAT THE QUOTE SHOWS ABOUT...	EXPLANATION
Dumas as a child:	
Dumas's parents:	
The relationship of Dumas and her family to their community in California:	

EVIDENCE LOG

Before moving on to a new selection, go to your Evidence Log and record what you learned from "With a Little Help From My Friends."

STANDARDS

Writing
- Write informative/explanatory texts to examine and convey ideas, concepts, and information clearly and accurately through the effective selection, organization, and analysis of content.
- Develop a topic with well-chosen, relevant, and sufficient facts, extended definitions, concrete details, quotations, or other information and examples appropriate to the audience's knowledge of the topic.

DIGITAL PERSPECTIVES

Writing to Sources

Explain to students that they should organize to build a structurally sound and logical essay. The introduction, body, and concluding paragraphs should be clearly distinguishable from one another.

Then, explain that the students can organize their essay in the following ways:

- The introduction should introduce the chosen quotation and how it is important to the memoir as a whole in a general way.
- The body paragraphs should correspond to the graphic organizer on the bottom of this page. Students may draw other details from the memoir that supports their interpretation, but should not add details that distract from their interpretation.
- The conclusion should summarize all the main points of the body paragraphs and express an idea or conclusion about the text as a whole.

For more support, see **Writing to Sources: Essay.**

Evidence Log Support students in completing their Evidence Log. This paced activity will help prepare them for the Performance-Based Assessment at the end of the unit.

FORMATIVE ASSESSMENT

Writing to Sources

If students are not able to interpret important details or quotations, **then** have students choose the listed quote that seems most important in the memoir and explain why. For Reteach and Practice, see **Writing to Sources: Essay. (RP).**

Selection Test

Administer the "With A Little Help From My Friends" Selection Test, which is available in both print and digital formats online in Assessments.

PERSONALIZE FOR LEARNING

Strategic Support

Interpreting Text Deconstruct the writing process for students struggling with interpreting important textual details. Have each student write their own rough draft, then, partner students and have them read through each other's essays with two colored pens. Using one pen, they should highlight the details from the text or important quotations. Then, in another color, they should highlight the explanations of these details. This will allow visual learners to map their writing process.

Morning Talk • Immigrant Picnic

AUDIO SUMMARIES
Audio Summaries of "Morning Talk" and "Immigrant Picnic" are available in both English in the Interactive Teacher's Edition or Unit Resources. Assigning these summaries prior to reading the selections may help students build additional background knowledge and set a context for their first read.

Summary

In "Morning Talk," a poem by Roberta Hill Whiteman, the speaker starts a conversation with a bird in her garden. She tells him he is not really a robin because robins live in England. Instead, she says, he is a red-breasted thrush. The robin responds with the name that the native people gave him. In the end, the bird questions the speaker's roots, too.

Gregory Djanikian's poem "Immigrant Picnic" is set at a holiday cookout on the Fourth of July. The speaker has classic American foods prepared. His father is confused by the names of the foods. He doesn't know how to order a hot dog, and can't tell a hot dog from a hamburger—and he doesn't care. As the speaker tries to cook the food, his family sets about mangling American figures of speech. When the speaker tries to correct them, his explanations only lead to more confusion.

Insight

Reading these two poems will give students a deeper understanding of the power of language to create an American identity.

ESSENTIAL QUESTION:
What does it mean to be "American"?

Connection to Essential Question

"Morning Talk" and "Immigrant Picnic" both provide a humorous perspective on the Essential Question.

In "Morning Talk," being American means acknowledging one's roots, and understanding that the process of naming an object, a living thing, or a natural feature conveys more about the namer than it does about the named.

The speaker of "Immigrant Picnic" thinks being American means having a classic American Fourth of July cookout. His family, however, ruins his American moment because they don't have his mastery of American language.

SMALL-GROUP READING PERFORMANCE TASK
How do the realities of immigrants' experiences reflect or fail to reflect American ideals?

UNIT PERFORMANCE-BASED ASSESSMENT
How is an American identity created?

Connection to Performance Tasks

Small-Group Reading Performance Task In this Performance Task, students will consider how the lives of immigrants in America succeed or fail to reflect American ideals. "Morning Talk" illustrates that the identification of Native Americans as immigrants denies their claims to be indigenous Americans. "Immigrant Picnic" shows that the adoption of American traditions can cause conflicts of identity among immigrants.

Unit Performance-Based Assessment In "Morning Talk, the speaker's assertions of indigenous American identity are challenged by the robin, who regards himself as the true American of the pair. The speaker of "Immigrant Picnic" tries desperately to create an American identity appropriate to the Fourth of July.

DIGITAL PERSPECTIVES — Audio | Video | Document | Annotation Highlights | EL Highlights | Online Assessment

LESSON RESOURCES

	Making Meaning	Language Development	Effective Expression
Lesson	**First Read** **Close Read** **Analyze the Text** **Analyze Craft and Structure**	**Concept Vocabulary** **Word Study** **Author's Style**	**Speaking and Listening**
Instructional Standards	**RL.10** By the end of grade 9, read and comprehend . . . **RL.5** Analyze how an author's choices . . .	**L.4** Determine or clarify the meaning . . . **L.5.a** Interpret figures of speech . . .	**SL.1.c** Propel conversations . . . **SL.1.d** Respond thoughtfully . . .
STUDENT RESOURCES			
Available online in the Interactive Student Edition or Unit Resources	Selection Audio First-Read Guide: Poetry Close-Read Guide: Poetry	Word Network	Evidence Log
TEACHER RESOURCES			
Selection Resources Available online in the Interactive Teacher's Edition or Unit Resources	Audio Summaries Annotation Highlights EL Highlights Poetry Collection: Text Questions Analyze Craft and Structure: Poetic Structures	Author's Style: Word Choice Concept Vocabulary and Word Study	Speaking and Listening: Panel Discussion English Language Support Lesson: Panel Discussion
Reteach/Practice (RP) Available online in the Interactive Teacher's Edition or Unit Resources	Analyze Craft and Structure: Poetic Structures (RP)	Author's Style: Word Choice (RP) Word Study: Multiple-Meaning Words (RP)	Speaking and Listening: Panel Discussion (RP)
Assessment Available online in Assessments	Selection Test		
My Resources	A Unit 1 Answer Key is available online and in the Interactive Teacher's Edition.		

Reading Support

Text Complexity Rubric: Morning Talk • Immigrant Picnic	
Quantitative Measures	
Lexile NP Text Length 32 lines; 52 lines	
Qualitative Measures	
Knowledge Demands ①—②—③—❹—⑤	"Morning Talk'': themes of indigenous pride, Native American folklore; "Immigrant Picnic'' requires understanding these expressions: a *chicken with its head cut off, on a roll, go nuts, roll out the barrels.*
Structure ①—②—❸—④—⑤	Both "Morning Talk'' and "Immigrant Picnic'' have a free verse structure (non rhyming) and both contain dialogue.
Language Conventionality and Clarity ①—②—③—❹—⑤	"Morning Talk'' has rich nature imagery, mix of formal and informal language; "Immigrant Picnic" has figurative language, similes, idioms, and multiple meaning words.
Levels of Meaning/Purpose ①—②—③—❹—⑤	"Morning Talk" has multiple levels of meaning. While it seems to be about a conversation, the topic of naming may be difficult to grasp. "Immigrant Picnic" is a light-hearted approach to the challenges of learning a new culture and language.

DECIDE AND PLAN

English Language Support

Provide English Learners with support for knowledge demands and meaning as they read the selection.

Knowledge Demands Write key words and phrases to define and discuss with students. For "Morning Talk," make sure students understand the meaning of the word *indigenous*. For "Immigrant Picnic," write these expressions: *a chicken with its head cut off, on a roll, go nuts, roll out the barrels*. For each one, find out if students have heard the expression. Explain the meanings if needed.

Meaning After discussing the meaning of key words and phrases, have students reread the lines or stanzas where the words and phrases appear. Discuss the meanings of these stanzas, and of the way the words and phrases function in the stanzas – for instance, in terms of rhyme and meter. In "Immigrant Picnic," locate and discuss the sources of the misunderstandings that occur.

Strategic Support

Provide students with strategic support to ensure that they can successfully read the text.

Knowledge Demands Discuss key words and phrases that are central to the poems. For "Morning Talk," discuss the word *indigenous*. Point out that one theme in the poem is pride about a person's roots. For "Immigrant Picnic," discuss with students the significance of the fact that the characters are misunderstanding each other's use of a language that is not their own.

Meaning For "Morning Talk," discuss the phrases that refer to the robin's identity and authenticity (*not the real robin, call you a red-breasted thrush, you are indigenous, Jis ko ko*). For "Immigrant Picnic," ask students to identify the humorous technique that's responsible for all the comedy in the poem.

Challenge

Provide students who need to be challenged with ideas for how they can go beyond a simple interpretation of the text.

Text Analysis For "Morning Talk," have students read about the author and discuss an analysis of the poem. Ask them to write the two most interesting things they have discovered in the bio and the analysis. For "Immigrant Picnic," pair students and ask them to adopt, if possible, contrasting interpretations of the poem.

Written Response Ask students to write an essay about cultural pride. Encourage them to spread their net wide. They might offer reasons why they think it's important to feel and convey pride in one's culture, or maybe share an experience that has made them feel proud of their cultural identity.

TEACH

Read and Respond

Have the groups read the selection and complete the Making Meaning and Language Development activities.

Standards Support Through Teaching and Learning Cycle

IDENTIFY NEEDS

Analyze results of the Beginning-of-Year Assessment, focusing on the items relating to Unit 1. Also take into consideration student performance to this point and your observations of where particular students struggle.

DECIDE AND PLAN

- If students have performed poorly on items matching these standards, then provide selection scaffolds before assigning them the on-level lesson provided in the Student Edition.
- If students have done well on the Beginning-of-Year Assessment, then challenge them to keep progressing and learning by giving them opportunities to practice the skills in depth.
- Use the Selection Resources listed on the Planning pages for "Morning Talk" and "Immigrant Picnic" to help students continually improve their ability to master the standards.

Instructional Standards: Poetry: "Morning Talk," "Immigrant Picnic"

	Catching Up	This Year	Looking Forward
Reading	You may wish to administer the **Analyze Craft and Structure: Poetic Structures (RP)** worksheet to help students understand different ways in which poems convey ideas.	**RL.5** Analyze how an author's choices concerning how to structure a text, order events within it, and manipulate time create such effects as mystery, tension, or surprise.	Have students work with partners to identify the structure of each poem with respect to time and place, as well as other times or places that each poem references. Working together, have students cite text that supports the theme from each time or place, and have them report their findings to the class.
Speaking and Listening	You may wish to administer the **Speaking and Listening: Panel Discussion (RP)** worksheet to help students organize and conduct such a discussion successfully.	**SL.1.c** Propel conversations by posing and responding to questions that relate the current discussion to broader themes or larger ideas; actively incorporate others into the discussion; and clarify, verify, or challenge ideas and conclusions.	Encourage student groups to organize and conduct a panel discussion around a question that probes the meaning, purpose, and quality of another selection from this unit.
Language	You may wish to administer the **Word Study: Multiple-Meaning Words (RP)** worksheet to help students understand that many English words have more than one meaning, as in the word *pipes*. You may wish to administer the **Author's Style: Word Choice (RP)** worksheet to help students understand that idioms are informal expressions in which the literal meaning is not the same as the actual meaning.	**L.4** Determine or clarify the meaning of unknown and multiple-meaning words and phrases based on grades 9-10 reading and content, choosing flexibly from a range of strategies. **L.5.a** Interpret figures of speech in context and analyze their role in the text.	Have students work in groups to list multiple-meaning words from "Immigrant Picnic," and identify the meaning as well as the part of speech for each, such as for the word *pipes* (present-tense verb, singular form, meaning "starts to speak."). Have students review other selections in this unit, and identify idioms used in those texts.

TEACH

Implement the planned lesson, and gather evidence of student learning.

ANALYZE AND REVISE

- Analyze student work for evidence of student learning.
- Identify whether or not students have met the expectations in the standards.
- Identify implications for future instruction.

FACILITATING

Jump Start

FIRST READ America has been called a "melting pot" because people from all over the world have come here to live. What does it mean to be an immigrant? Do you know any people or families who have immigrated? What challenges did they face? Engage students in a discussion about what it means to immigrate to help set the context for reading "Morning Talk" and "Immigrant Picnic."

Morning Talk
Immigrant Picnic

How might someone feel if his or her name and identity was changed or challenged based on place of birth? How might an Independence Day celebration be different for an immigrant? Modeling questions such as these will help students connect "Morning Talk" and "Immigrant Picnic" to the Small-Group Performance Task assignment. Selection audio and print capability for the selection are available in the Interactive Teacher's Edition.

MAKING MEANING

POETRY COLLECTION

Morning Talk
Immigrant Picnic

Concept Vocabulary

As you perform your first read, you will encounter these words.

chirruped	teased	pipes

Context Clues To find the meaning of unfamiliar words, look for **context clues**, or other words and phrases in nearby text. There are several different types of context clues.

Definition: The word is clearly defined in the text.

Example: Rick was surprised that he liked **ornithology** so much. He did not expect the study of birds to be so interesting.

Contrast: A word or phrase signaling a contrast appears near the word.

Example: Simone's room is **pristine**, but Olivia's room is disorganized and messy.

Synonym: A word with a similar meaning appears nearby.

Example: It is a pleasure to teach these students because they are so insightful and **perceptive**.

Apply your knowledge of context clues and other vocabulary strategies to determine the meanings of unfamiliar words you encounter during your first read.

First Read POETRY

Apply these strategies as you conduct your first read. You will have an opportunity to complete a close read after your first read.

NOTICE *who* or *what* is "speaking" the poem and whether the poem tells a story or describes a single moment.

ANNOTATE by marking vocabulary and key passages you want to revisit.

CONNECT ideas within the selection to what you already know and what you have already read.

RESPOND by completing the Comprehension Check.

First Read

STANDARDS

Reading Literature
By the end of grade 9, read and comprehend literature, including stories, dramas, and poems, in the grades 9–10 text complexity band proficiently, with scaffolding as needed at the high end of the range.

Language
Determine or clarify the meaning of unknown and multiple-meaning words and phrases based on *grades 9–10 reading and content*, choosing flexibly from a range of strategies.

98 UNIT 1 • AMERICAN VOICES

About the Poets

Roberta Hill Whiteman (b. 1947) is a nationally recognized poet, scholar, and member of the Oneida Nation of Wisconsin. Born in Baraboo, Wisconsin, Hill holds an MFA in Creative Writing and a PhD in American Studies. Her doctoral dissertation centered on her grandmother, and inspiration, Dr. Lillie Rose Minoka, one of the first Native American physicians. Hill's work draws on her experience as a Native American woman and on Oneida history. In addition to two critically acclaimed poetry collections, she has written a biography of her grandmother.

Gregory Djanikian (b. 1949) moved from his birthplace of Alexandria, Egypt, to Williamsport, Pennsylvania, when he was eight years old. He became interested in writing poetry while studying English at the University of Pennsylvania, and is now Director of Creative Writing at his alma mater. He has published six volumes of poetry, which often deal with family, culture, and the ways immigrants to America enrich the English language. He believes that "poetry is a communication between people on the most intense level, even if it's only between two people—writer and reader."

Backgrounds

Morning Talk

The songbird commonly referred to as the North American "robin" is actually a thrush. It was named "robin" by the Europeans who settled the Americas because it looks like the European robin. The two birds are not actually related. These facts play a key role in this poem.

Immigrant Picnic

This poem is full of wordplay, including puns and malapropisms, that is both funny and pointed. *Puns* are jokes that play on differences in the meanings of words with similar sounds. *Malapropisms* involve the mistaken use of a wrong word that shares similar pronunciation with the right word—for example, "a hypodermic question," rather than "a hypothetical question."

DIGITAL PERSPECTIVES

Concept Vocabulary

Encourage groups to discuss the three concept vocabulary words. Have they seen the words in texts before? Do they use any of the words in their speech or writing? Do they recognize any word parts, such as a base word, a prefix, or a suffix?

Have students look closely at the words and punctuation that surround the unknown words in the example sentences. Discuss how these types of context clues can help determine meaning. Encourage groups to think of one other type of context clue they might encounter in a text, such as synonyms, antonyms, and restatements of an idea.

FIRST READ

Have students perform the steps of the first read independently.

NOTICE: Encourage students to focus on the basic elements of each poem to ensure that they understand the message the author is conveying.

ANNOTATE: Remind students to mark lines or stanzas they would like to revisit in order to enhance comprehension or to increase their aesthetic appreciation.

CONNECT: Encourage students to compare the thoughts and feelings expressed in the poems with what it means to immigrate.

RESPOND: Students will answer questions and write a summary to demonstrate understanding.

Point out to students that while they will always complete the Respond step at the end of the first read, the other steps will probably happen somewhat concurrently. You may wish to print copies of the **First-Read Guide: Poetry** for students to use.

PERSONALIZE FOR LEARNING

English Language Support

Syntax Help students analyze the unusual sentence structure of free verse poetry in order to develop an understanding of conventional English syntax. Ask students to rewrite the poem in prose format, removing line breaks from within the poetry. Have them read aloud the rewritten sentences and make observations, paying particular attention to sound devices, such as alliteration and assonance. Remind students that alliteration is the repetition of initial consonant sounds, as in *Lately, Lucy was lazy*. Assonance is the repetition of vowel sounds, as in *The sweet and easy taste of cheesecake.* **ALL LEVELS**

POETRY

Morning Talk

Roberta Hill Whiteman

FACILITATING SMALL-GROUP CLOSE READING

CLOSE READ: Poetry As groups perform the close read, circulate and offer support as needed.

- Remind groups that when they read poetry, they should identify the speaker and pay attention to the figurative language.
- If a group is confused about a poem's meaning, suggest that they examine each stanza, and discuss what is taking place in each one.
- Challenge group members to discuss the poem's overall meaning to develop an understanding of the theme or message.

SCAN FOR MULTIMEDIA

for Melissa L Whiteman

"Hi, guy," said I to a robin
perched on a pole in the middle
of the garden. Pink and yellow
firecracker zinnias, rough green
leaves of broccoli,
and deep red tomatoes on dying stems
frame his still presence.

"I've heard you're not
THE REAL ROBIN. Bird watchers have
agreed," I said. "THE REAL ROBIN
lives in England. They claim
you are misnamed and that we ought
to call you 'a red-breasted thrush'
because you are
indigenous."

He fluffed up. "Am I not
*Jis ko ko?"** he cried, "that persistent
warrior who carries warmth
northward every spring?"
He seemed so young, his red belly
a bit light and his wings, still
faded brown. He watched me
untangling the hose to water squash.

"Look who's talking!" he **chirruped**.
"Your people didn't come
from Europe or even India.
The turtles say you're a relative
to red clay on this great island."
Drops of crystal water
sparkled on the squash.

"Indigenous!" he **teased**
as he flew by.

* ***Jis ko ko*** (jihs koh koh) Iroquoian name for "robin."

NOTES

Mark context clues or indicate another strategy you used that helped you determine meaning.

chirruped (CHIHR uhpt) *v.*

MEANING:

Mark context clues or indicate another strategy you used that helped you determine meaning.

teased (TEEZD) *v.*

MEANING:

DIGITAL PERSPECTIVES

Concept Vocabulary

CHIRRUPED If groups are struggling to define the word *chirruped* in line 24, point out that the base word is *chirrup*. Ask students to think about how the word sounds when spoken, and who speaks the word in the poem. Then have them define the word.

Possible response: *Chirruped* means uttered a series of chirps or high-pitched sounds.

TEASED If groups are struggling to define the word *teased* in line 31, point out that the base word is *tease*. Ask students to use context clues from lines 24 to 32 to determine the attitude of the robin as he speaks. The clues in these lines should prompt them to recognize the bird is kidding or joking in order to make a point. Then have them define the word.

Possible response: *Teased* means to have laughed at, criticized, or annoyed someone in a way that is either playful or unkind.

Additional **English Language Support** is available in the Interactive Teacher's Edition.

PERSONALIZE FOR LEARNING

Strategic Support

Theme Students may require support to identify the theme of a poem because it is typically implied rather than directly stated. Remind students that the theme is not the subject of the poem, but rather the message or insight about life that the poet conveys. To figure out the poem's message, direct students to examine stanzas 2 through 4, paying specific attention to the dialogue between the speaker and the bird. Ask them to think about how the details of this conversation relate to one another and contribute to the overall meaning.

CLOSER LOOK

Analyze Dialogue

Circulate among groups as students conduct their close read. Suggest that groups close read lines 18 to 22. Encourage them to talk about the annotations that they mark. If needed, provide the following support.

ANNOTATE: Have students mark details in these lines that show the speaker's reaction to his family's use of English phrases, or work with small groups to have students participate while you highlight them together.

QUESTION: Guide students to consider what these details might tell them. Ask what the reader can infer from the dialogue in the poem. Accept student responses.

Possible response: The speaker seemed frustrated by his family's mistakes in using English phrases.

CONCLUDE: Help students to formulate conclusions about the importance of these details in the text. Ask students why the author might have included these details.

Possible response: The author is illustrating that there are differences between the speaker, who was born in America, and his parents, who are immigrants. The author might have included these details to show that sometimes younger family members are able to learn more easily than older family members.

Remind students that **dialogue** is a conversation between or among characters. Writers use dialogue to reveal character and relationships and to add variety and naturalness to poetry.

POETRY

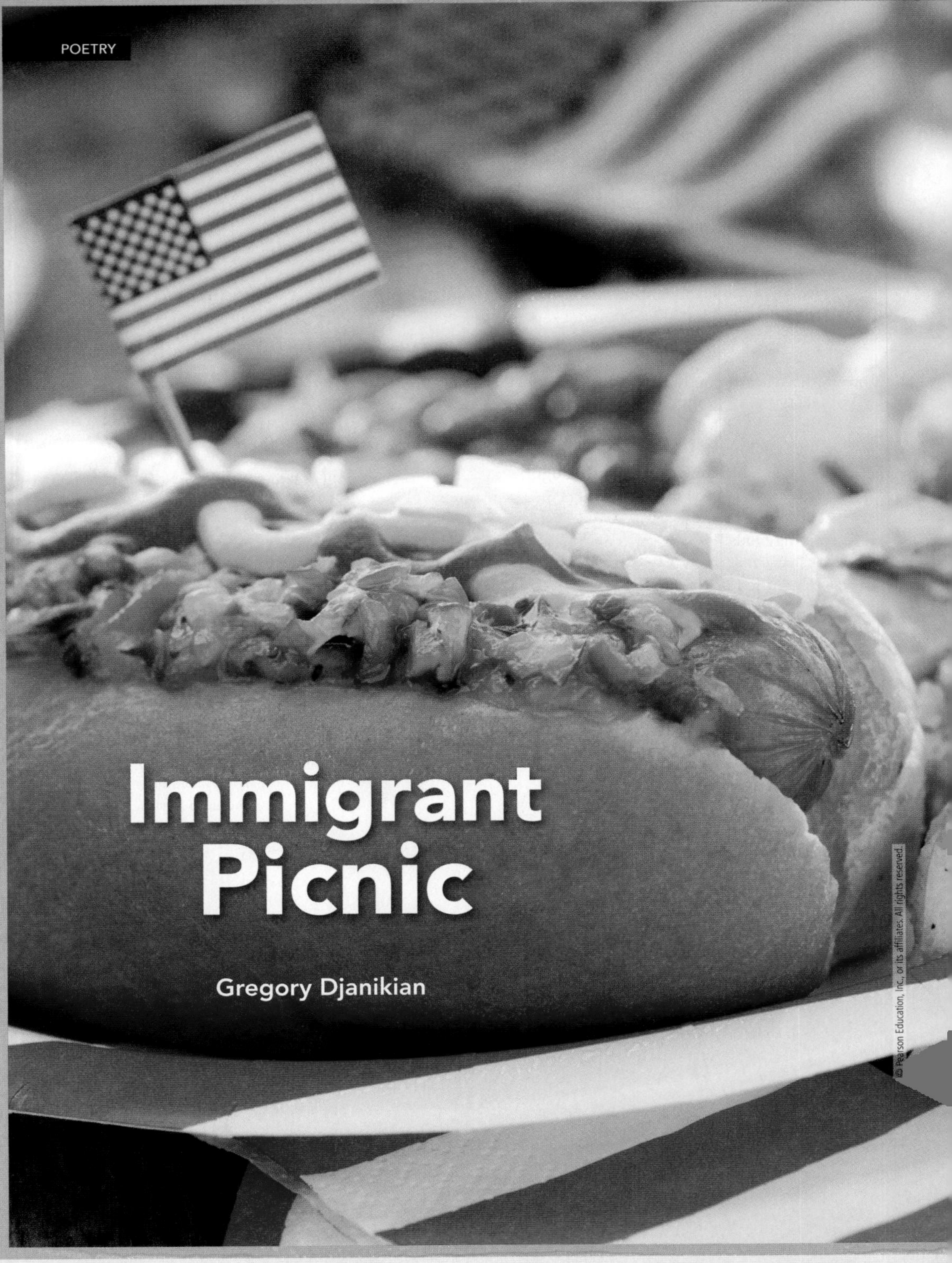

Immigrant Picnic

Gregory Djanikian

VOCABULARY DEVELOPMENT

Word Map Have students complete a word map for the word *immigrant*.

Definition in your own words | Synonyms

immigrant

Antonyms | Use it in a sentence

SCAN FOR MULTIMEDIA

It's the Fourth of July, the flags
are painting the town,
the plastic forks and knives
are laid out like a parade.

And I'm grilling, I've got my apron,
I've got potato salad, macaroni, relish,
I've got a hat shaped
like the state of Pennsylvania.

I ask my father what's his pleasure
and he says, "Hot dog, medium rare,"
and then, "Hamburger, sure,
what's the big difference,"
as if he's really asking.

I put on hamburgers and hot dogs,
slice up the sour pickles and Bermudas,[1]
uncap the condiments. The paper napkins
are fluttering away like lost messages.

"You're running around," my mother says,
"like a chicken with its head loose."

"Ma," I say, "you mean cut off,
loose and cut off being as far apart
as, say, son and daughter."

She gives me a quizzical look as though
I've been caught in some impropriety.
"I love you and your sister just the same," she says,
"Sure," my grandmother **pipes** in,
"you're both our children, so why worry?"

That's not the point I begin telling them,
and I'm comparing words to fish now,
like the ones in the sea at Port Said,[2]
or like birds among the date palms by the Nile,[3]
unrepentantly elusive, wild

1. **Bermudas** sweet onions grown on the island of Bermuda.
2. **Port Said** (sah EED) city in northeast Egypt.
3. **Nile** river in northeast Africa, considered the longest in the world.

NOTES

Mark context clues or indicate another strategy you used that helped you determine meaning.

pipes (pyps) *v.*

MEANING:

DIGITAL PERSPECTIVES

Concept Vocabulary

PIPES If groups are struggling to define the word *pipes* in line 26, remind them that the word has multiple meanings depending on whether the word is used as a noun or a verb. Point out the most common definitions as well as the idiomatic, informal meanings.

1. long, hollow tubes that carry fluids or gases (noun)
2. musical instruments in the shape of a tube like a flute (noun)
3. to carry or move substances through a pipe (verb)
4. to play a tune on a pipe or the bagpipes (verb)
5. a singer's voice (noun - idiomatic/informal)
6. to start talking (verb - idiomatic/informal)

Have students examine the context clues to determine the appropriate meaning of the word *pipes* in the poem.

Possible response: ***Pipes*** means "to start talking." It is being used in an informal way.

PERSONALIZE FOR LEARNING

Challenge

Personification Poets use figurative language to make their writing more interesting. Personification is a figure of speech in which a nonhuman subject is given human characteristics ("the wind howled," "the house groaned"). Effective personification lends vivid imagery and life to writing. Have students identify a few instances of personification in the poem, such as *the flags are painting the town* in the first stanza, and then invite them to write their own poems about a celebration in which they utilize personification to give human characteristics to a few nonhuman objects, ideas, or animals.

CLOSER LOOK

Analyze Characters

Circulate among groups as students conduct their close read. Suggest that groups close read lines 36–43. Encourage them to talk about the annotations that they mark. If needed, provide the following support.

ANNOTATE: Have students mark details in these lines that show the actions of various family members, or work with small groups to have students participate while you highlight them together.

QUESTION: Guide students to consider what these details tell them. Ask what a reader can infer about the characters, and accept student responses.

Possible response: The speaker throws up his hands because he's frustrated. In response, the father claps his hands, and the mother and father dance. These details show that the parents are good-natured, happy people, and take the mistakes that they make in stride. The uncle's reaction to the situation reinforces that, despite their differences, they are all one family.

CONCLUDE: Help students formulate conclusions about the importance of these details in the text. Ask students why the author might have included these details.

Possible response: The author might have included these details to show that even though different generations in an immigrant family may not understand American ideas and expressions the same way, those differences are not as important as being together and enjoying a celebration. These details provide insight into the different members of the family.

Remind students that **characterization** is the way a writer develops and reveals a character's personality and temperament. With **direct characterization**, a writer simply tells us what a character is like. With **indirect characterization**, the writer shows us a character's traits, by showing a character's actions and behavior or presenting a character's words and thoughts.

NOTES

"Sonia," my father says to my mother,
"what the hell is he talking about?"
"He's on a ball," my mother says.

"That's roll!" I say, throwing up my hands,
"as in hot dog, hamburger, dinner roll. . . ."

"And what about roll out the barrels?" my mother asks,
and my father claps his hands, "Why sure," he says,
"let's have some fun," and launches
into a polka, twirling my mother
around and around like the happiest top,

and my uncle is shaking his head, saying
"You could grow nuts listening to us,"

and I'm thinking of pistachios in the Sinai[4]
burgeoning without end,
pecans in the South, the jumbled
flavor of them suddenly in my mouth,
wordless, confusing,
crowding out everything else.

4. **Sinai** (SY ny) triangular peninsula in Egypt.

PERSONALIZE FOR LEARNING

English Language Support

Idioms Idioms can be confusing to English Language learners. Explain that in lines 35 and 36 the terms *on the ball* and *on a roll* are both idioms. To help them understand the usage in the poem, explain that *on the ball* means knowledgeable and alert and that *on a roll* means experiencing a series of successes or ongoing good fortune. Explain that the parents in the poem are accidentally mixing up idiomatic phrases and that the speaker is trying to explain their mistake to them. **ALL LEVELS**

Comprehension Check

Complete the following items after you finish your first read. Review and clarify details with your group.

MORNING TALK

1. According to the speaker, what have bird watchers agreed?

2. According to the robin, where did the speaker's people come from?

IMMIGRANT PICNIC

1. On what day does the picnic take place?

2. What type of food is the speaker thinking of at the end of the poem?

RESEARCH

Research to Clarify Choose at least one unfamiliar detail from one of the poems. Briefly research that detail. In what way does the information you found shed light on an aspect of the poem?

Research to Explore These poems may spark your curiosity to learn more. Briefly research a topic that interests you. You may want to share what you discover with your group.

DIGITAL PERSPECTIVES

Comprehension Check

Morning Talk

Possible responses:

1. Bird watchers have agreed that real robins live in England and that the birds that live in the United States should be named red-breasted thrushes.
2. The robin is saying that the speaker's people are Native American with "red" skin.

Immigrant Picnic

Possible responses:

1. The picnic takes place on the Fourth of July.
2. The speaker is thinking about pistachios, a type of nut that is common in Egypt.

Research

Research to Clarify If students struggle to come up with an unfamiliar detail, have them reread the poems and notice an idea or concept that might be new to them, such as the background of the argument over the naming of robins in the United States or where various nuts are popular.

Research to Explore If students are having difficulty selecting a research topic, suggest that they consider researching other poems by Gregory Djanikian, such as "Alexandria, 1953," "So Much of the World," "Absences," or "When I First Saw Snow."

PERSONALIZE FOR LEARNING

Challenge

Research Have students research Gregory Djanikian. Ask them to write a brief biography of the man, outlining his professional career, including what inspired him to write poetry. How is his life reflected in the themes of his poetry? Have students read some of his other works and, if possible, play recordings of these for the class.

Jump Start

CLOSE READ Ask students to consider the following prompt: Imagine you are an immigrant to a new country. How would you go about learning the language? How would you learn about the culture of your new home? As students discuss the prompt in their groups, have them consider what kinds of support someone would need to successfully immigrate to a new country.

Close Read the Text

If needed, model close reading by using the Annotation Highlights in the Interactive Teacher's Edition.

Remind students to use Accountable Talk in their discussions and to support one another as they complete the close read.

Analyze the Text

1. **Possible response:** The poet is once again demonstrating how just a slight alteration of a word can create an image that is wildly different than what the speaker intended.
2. **Passages will vary by group.** Remind students to explain why they chose the passages they presented to the group members.
3. **Responses will vary by group.**

Concept Vocabulary

Possible response:

Why These Words? The words all describe ways of speaking or making sounds. Other words that fit the category include *yelled, whispered,* or *cheered*.

Practice

The bird *chirruped* outside my window; its constant, high-pitched twittering woke me up early.

My cousin often *teased* me, and even his good-natured taunting annoyed me.

Sandy's brother often *pipes* up and interrupts our conversation with his chatter.

Word Network

Possible response: indigenous, relative

Word Study

For more support, see **Concept Vocabulary and Word Study**

Possible responses:

Pipes: "speaks up cheerily and loudly" and "tubes used to transfer liquids or gasses"
Relish: "enjoy" and "pickle spread"
State: "government of a region" and "say"

MAKING MEANING

POETRY COLLECTION

Close Read the Text

With your group, revisit sections of the text you marked during your first read. **Annotate** details that you notice. What **questions** do you have? What can you **conclude**?

Analyze the Text

CITE TEXTUAL EVIDENCE to support your answers.

Notebook Complete the activities.

1. **Review and Clarify** With your group, reread lines 45–50 of "Immigrant Picnic." What recognition is the poet making when he compares words to nuts? Explain.
2. **Present and Discuss** Share with your group the passages from the texts that you found important. Take turns presenting your passages. Discuss what you noticed in the text, the questions you asked, and the conclusions you reached.
3. **Essential Question:** ***What does it mean to be "American"?*** What have these poems taught you about American identity? Discuss this question with your group.

TIP

GROUP DISCUSSION
Try having group members read each poem aloud. Discuss how the oral reading changes the poem's impact.

WORD NETWORK
Add interesting words related to American identity from the text to your Word Network.

STANDARDS

Reading Literature
Analyze how an author's choices concerning how to structure a text, order events within it, and manipulate time create such effects as mystery, tension, or surprise.

Language
Determine or clarify the meaning of unknown and multiple-meaning words and phrases based on *grades 9–10 reading and content*, choosing flexibly from a range of strategies.

LANGUAGE DEVELOPMENT

Concept Vocabulary

chirruped teased pipes

Why These Words? The three concept vocabulary words are related. With your group, determine what the words have in common. Write your ideas, and add another word that fits the category.

Practice

Notebook Use a dictionary to confirm the definitions of the three concept vocabulary words. Write a sentence using each of the words. Be sure to use context clues that hint at each word's meaning.

Word Study

Multiple-Meaning Words Some words in English have multiple meanings, or more than one distinct definition. For example, the word *pipes*, which appears in "Immigrant Picnic," has several different meanings. Write the meaning of *pipes* as the poet uses it. Then, write another definition of the word. Finally, find two other multiple-meaning words. Write down the words and two of their definitions.

FORMATIVE ASSESSMENT

Analyze the Text

If students struggle to close read the text, **then** provide the **Poetry Collection: Text Questions** available online in the Interactive Teacher's Edition or Unit Resources. Answers and DOK levels are also available.

Concept Vocabulary

If students struggle to identify the unifying concept, **then** have them revisit the context in which the words were used in the poems.

Word Study

If students fail to identify more words with multiple meanings, **then** have them scan the poems looking for words that can be used as both nouns and verbs. For Reteach and Practice, see **Word Study: Multiple-Meaning Words (RP).**

Analyze Craft and Structure

Poetic Structures The basic structures of poetry are lines and stanzas. A **line** is a group of words arranged in a row. A line of poetry may break, or end, in different ways.

- An **end-stopped line** is one in which both the grammatical structure and sense are complete at the end of the line. It may include punctuation, such as a comma or period. Example: *How do I love thee?/ Let me count the ways.*
- A **run-on, or enjambed, line** is one in which both the grammatical structure and sense continue past the end of the line. Example: *I love thee to the depth and breadth and height / My soul can reach, when feeling out of sight / For the ends of Being and ideal Grace.*

A **stanza** is a group of lines, usually separated from other stanzas by space. Like a paragraph in prose, a stanza often expresses a single idea. The ways in which a poet organizes a poem into lines and stanzas affects how a poem looks and sounds and even what it means. See possible responses in Teacher's Edition.

Practice

CITE TEXTUAL EVIDENCE to support your answers.

Working on your own, use the chart to analyze the stanzas and line breaks in these poems. Record and share your observations.

MORNING TALK	IMMIGRANT PICNIC
Summarize the action of each stanza. a	Which stanzas set the scene? Explain. d
What type of line breaks appear in stanzas 1, 2, 3, and 5? Explain. b	In which stanza does the first incorrect use of an English expression appear? How does the stanza length change? Why? e
How do the line breaks in stanza 4 differ from those in the rest of the poem? Why? c	How do the last lines of stanzas 11 and 12 break? How do the line breaks reinforce the actions and feelings that are expressed? f

DIGITAL PERSPECTIVES

Analyze Craft and Structure

Poetic Structures Explain to students that while there is no one correct way to write a poem, there is a correct way to read one. For more support, see **Analyze Craft and Structure: Poetic Structures.**

Practice

Possible responses:

"Morning Talk"

a. Stanza 1: The poet greets a robin in their garden.
Stanza 2: The poet accuses the robin of not being "THE REAL ROBIN."
Stanza 3: The robin replies with indignation.
Stanza 4: The robin accuses the poet of being hypocritical in calling an American robin not "real."
Stanza 5: The robin teases the poet by calling her "indigenous."

b. Almost all the line breaks are enjambed. Only a few lines end with periods or commas.

c. Every other line is end-stopped in order to create a regular structure.

"Immigrant Picnic"

d. Stanzas 1 and 2.

e. Stanza 5. The line cuts off when the mother uses the wrong words, which should be "cut off" rather than "loose."

f. The ellipses create a feeling of confusion in the language of the poem.

FORMATIVE ASSESSMENT

Analyze Craft and Structure

If students are unable to differentiate between end-stopped lines and enjambed lines, **then** remind them to look at the starting point of the sentence or line and the end punctuation mark. For Reteach and Practice, see **Analyze Craft and Structure: Poetic Structures (RP).**

PERSONALIZE FOR LEARNING

English Language Support

Have students use the words *stanza, end-stopped line*, and *enjambed line* in a paragraph in which they analyze what is taking place in a portion of one of the poems. Remind students to quote lines or words from the poem in their analysis. Encourage them to use any new vocabulary they discovered while reading the poems in their writing. **ALL LEVELS**

Author's Style

Word Choice Discuss with students that idioms exist in every language and are common in everyday speech. Idioms are words or phrases that cannot be taken literally. The difficulty with idioms is that the meaning cannot be deduced through analyzing the meaning of the words in the idioms themselves. Idioms are lively phrases that are unique to each culture, and learning them is like unlocking a secret code in language.

As you review the examples of idioms from the poems with students, consider providing additional examples:

Turn over a new leaf – means to begin anew, start over

When pigs fly –means that something is highly unlikely

A chip on your shoulder - means you have a bad attitude or are holding a grudge

To sit on the fence – means to remain neutral or undecided

For more support see **Author's Style: Word Choice.**

Read It

Possible Responses:

a. Correct

b. You have the same problem that you are complaining about.

c. The flags are painting the town red.

d. The flags make the day festive.

e. You are running around like a chicken with its head cut off.

f. You are running around in a panic with no clear direction.

g. Correct.

h. He's having a series of successes.

Write It

Responses will vary, but make sure that students list at least three idioms and that their explanations are not literal interpretations.

FORMATIVE ASSESSMENT

Author's Style

If students are unable to identify the idioms, **then** have students look for images in the poems that do not seem to make literal sense.

For Reteach and Practice, see **Author's Style: Word Choice (RP).**

LANGUAGE DEVELOPMENT

POETRY COLLECTION

Author's Style

Word Choice Poets may draw on informal types of language to make scenes, settings, and characters come alive. **Idioms** are informal expressions in which the literal meanings of the words do not add up to the actual meaning. For example, the idiom "raining cats and dogs" does not mean cats and dogs are falling from the sky. It means it is raining very hard. In "Immigrant Picnic," the speaker's family members attempt to use idioms in their new language. Their mistakes create humor and are an important part of the poem.

Examples of Common English Idioms

SENTENCE	MEANING OF THE IDIOM
Grilling hot dogs and hamburgers is not **rocket science**.	Grilling is not very difficult.
First they told him he wasn't born here; then to **add insult to injury**, they told him he wasn't really a robin.	They made the situation worse.
When it comes to understanding what *indigenous* means, they completely **missed the boat**.	They failed to understand.

Read It

Work individually. Use this chart to define idioms that are either used or referred to in the poems. If the idiom is not used correctly, correct it. Then, rewrite the idiom in formal language that means the same thing.

See possible responses in Teacher's Edition.

IDIOM	CORRECTION IF NEEDED	REWRITE IN FORMAL LANGUAGE
Look who's talking! (from "Morning Talk')	a.	b.
the flags / are painting the town (from "Immigrant Picnic")	c.	d.
like a chicken with its head loose (from "Immigrant Picnic")	e.	f.
He's on a ball. (from "Immigrant Picnic")	g.	h.

STANDARDS

Language

Interpret figures of speech in context and analyze their role in the text.

Write It

Notebook Write at least three idioms with which you are familiar. Explain what each one means. Then, use each idiom in a sentence.

PERSONALIZE FOR LEARNING

English Language Support

Idioms Idioms and colloquial expressions can be confusing to English language learners. Review the definition of idioms. Ask students to think of idioms from their native languages and to share them with the group.

Assist students with identifying an example or two from the poems and have them use the idiomatic expressions in their own sentences. Ensure that they have correctly interpreted the meanings of the idioms instead of interpreting them literally. Support students in completing as many of these steps as they can. **EMERGING/EXPANDING**

Speaking and Listening

Assignment

With your group, organize a **panel discussion** to discuss the poems. Panel members should ask and answer questions to clarify and politely challenge one another's ideas. Choose one of the following topics:

- [ ] **Poetry Comparison** Compare and contrast the two poems. Discuss the attitudes of the speakers, each poet's use of language, and the message or insight each poem conveys. Which poem is more positive in its message?
- [ ] **Poetry Ranking** Rate the two poems on a scale of 1 to 5, with 1 being ineffective and 5 being extremely effective. Then, share your ratings, and discuss your reasons for making them.
- [ ] **Poetry Definition** What is a poem? Is it simply a string of words set up in lines and stanzas, or is there more to it? Propose and discuss various definitions of poetry, using the two poems as examples.

Discussion Plan Once the group has chosen the focus for the panel discussion, work individually to gather ideas about the topic and the poems that you would like to work into the conversation. Jot down your ideas in the chart.

POEM	INSIGHTS TO SHARE	SPECIFIC PASSAGES TO CITE
Morning Talk		
Immigrant Picnic		

Participation Plan As you participate in the panel discussion, do not read your notes aloud, but use them to remind yourself of insights you had earlier. Speak clearly, using language that is appropriate for an academic setting. Make sure you understand one another's points by summarizing them before contributing your own ideas. Ask follow-up questions respectfully.

EVIDENCE LOG

Before moving on to a new selection, go to your Evidence Log and record what you learned from "Morning Talk" and "Immigrant Picnic."

STANDARDS

Speaking and Listening

- Propel conversations by posing and responding to questions that relate the current discussion to broader themes or larger ideas; actively incorporate others into the discussion; and clarify, verify, or challenge ideas and conclusions.
- Respond thoughtfully to diverse perspectives, summarize points of agreement and disagreement, and, when warranted, qualify or justify their own views and understanding and make new connections in light of the evidence and reasoning presented.

DIGITAL PERSPECTIVES

Speaking and Listening

You may wish to explain to students that panel discussions are presentations in which several people (a panel) engage in a conversation about a specific topic, usually in front of an audience. At the very end of a panel discussion, the audience participates by asking questions. You may choose to help students create groups for the panel discussion based on the topic in which they have shown interest.

Discussion Plan Tell students that when they analyze their topics or interpret their poems, they should focus on specific stanzas or lines in the poems to illustrate the points they are making.

Participation Plan Remind students that each panel member should know the points he or she wants to raise ahead of time. Having students summarize their points verbally to each other before the actual panel discussion may ensure that each student is familiar with the material. For more support, see **Speaking and Listening: Panel Discussion.**

Evidence Log Support students in completing their Evidence Log. This paced activity will help prepare them for the Performance-Based Assessment at the end of the unit.

FORMATIVE ASSESSMENT

Speaking and Listening

If students have difficulty comparing and contrasting poems, **then** have them fill out a Venn diagram to visually illustrate the similarities and differences between the two. For Reteach and Practice, see **Speaking and Listening: Panel Discussion (RP).**

Selection Test

Administer the "Poetry Collection" Selection Test, which is available in both print and digital formats online in Assessments.

PERSONALIZE FOR LEARNING

English Language Support

Panel Discussion Ask small groups of students to choose a topic for a panel discussion, and write a list of sample questions that could be asked during the discussion. **EMERGING**

Ask small groups of students to choose a topic for a panel discussion, write a list of questions that could be asked, and have a mock panel discussion. One member of the group should act as the moderator, and each panelist should answer one question, justifying opinions and persuading others. **EXPANDING**

Ask small groups of students to choose a topic for a panel discussion, write a list of questions that could be asked, and have a mock panel discussion. One member of the group should act as the moderator, and each panelist should have an opening statement prepared and answer at least one question. Students should be prepared to justify opinions and persuade others. **BRIDGING**

An expanded **English Language Support Lesson** on Panel Discussion is available in the Digital Teacher's Edition.

Produce a Podcast

Assignment Before groups begin work on their projects, have them clearly differentiate the role each group member will play. Remind groups to consults the schedule for Small-Group Learning to guide their work during the Performance Task.

Students should complete the assignment using presentation software to take advantage of text, graphics, and sound features.

Plan With Your Group

Analyze the Text Instruct students to be thorough as they list the different experiences included in the reading selections, and the way those experiences reflect American ideals. Each author has a unique perspective, and taken together, all the readings present a broad representation of the immigrant experience.

Remind students that they can include stories about the immigration experience from other sources. Perhaps they have read books or articles about famous immigrants or have a personal experience to share.

Gather Evidence and Media Examples Remind students that they need to provide evidence to support any conclusions they draw about the immigrant experience and how it reflects American ideals. Encourage students to consider community members to include in their interviews.

PERFORMANCE TASK: SPEAKING AND LISTENING FOCUS

SOURCES

- THE RULES OF THE GAME
- THE WRITING ON THE WALL
- WITH A LITTLE HELP FROM MY FRIENDS
- MORNING TALK
- IMMIGRANT PICNIC

Produce a Podcast

Assignment

You have read about immigrants' experiences as they strove to adjust to the United States. Work with your group to develop a podcast that addresses this question:

How do the realities of immigrants' experiences reflect or fail to reflect American ideals?

Plan With Your Group

Analyze the Text With your group, discuss the types of experiences that new immigrants to the United States have. Consider new immigrants' social interactions, their efforts to acquire a new language, and the economic challenges they face. Use the chart to list your ideas. First, discuss how you would define American ideals. Then, for each selection, identify key immigrant experiences and whether or not they reflect American ideals, such as fairness and equality of opportunity.

TITLE	KEY EXPERIENCES / AMERICAN IDEALS
The Rules of the Game	
The Writing on the Wall	
With a Little Help From My Friends	
Morning Talk	
Immigrant Picnic	

Gather Evidence and Media Examples Identify specific examples from the selections to support your group's claims. Then, brainstorm ideas for types of media you can use to illustrate or elaborate on each example. Consider having group members research various aspects of the immigrant experience and integrate their findings into the podcast. Group members could also conduct interviews with former or current immigrants about American ideals and their experiences, then select clips to include in the podcast.

STANDARDS

Speaking and Listening

- Present information, findings, and supporting evidence clearly, concisely and logically such that listeners can follow the line of reasoning and the organization, development, substance, and style are appropriate to purpose, audience, and task.
- Make strategic use of digital media in presentations to enhance understanding of findings, reasoning, and evidence and to add interest.
- Adapt speech to a variety of contexts and tasks, demonstrating a command of formal English when indicated or appropriate.
- Use technology, including the Internet, to produce, publish, and update individual or shared writing products, taking advantage of technology's capacity to link to other information and to display information flexibly and dynamically.

AUTHOR'S PERSPECTIVE **Ernest Morrell, Ph.D.**

How to Prepare for a Speech/Oral Presentation The small-group speaking and listening activity will help students learn how to engage an audience during a presentation. This is important for students as they prepare for college, careers, or public service. Help students learn to become better speakers by reminding them to ask themselves these questions as they practice and rehearse their speeches and oral presentations:

- *Posture*: Does my posture convey authority and ease? Do I look relaxed and comfortable as I'm presenting?
- *Body language*: How do I connect with my audience? For instance, do I make eye contact, lean forward at key points to show emphasis, and use appropriate gestures?
- *Voice*: Am I changing my voice by varying my pitch and volume to show emotion and convey meaning? Does my voice project to the back rows?
- *Humor*: How do I add humor when it suits my audience and purpose? Do I tell jokes or anecdotes, for instance?
- *Tone*: Do I speak with passion to engage my audience?

Organize Your Ideas Use the **Podcast Script** chart to organize the script for your podcast presentation. Assign roles for each part of the podcast that you plan to present. Note when each segment will begin, and record what the speaker will say. Plan where audio clips and music will be used.

PODCAST SCRIPT		
	Audio	Script
Speaker 1		
Speaker 2		
Speaker 3		

Rehearse With Your Group

Practice With Your Group As you run through rehearsals, use this checklist to evaluate the effectiveness of your podcast.

CONTENT	USE OF MEDIA	PRESENTATION TECHNIQUES
☐ The podcast has a clear introduction, explaining the focus of the story. ☐ The podcast presents a clear story and point of view. ☐ Main ideas are supported with evidence from the texts.	☐ The media support the main points. ☐ The media communicate key ideas. ☐ Media are used evenly throughout the podcast. ☐ Equipment functions properly.	☐ Media are audible. ☐ Transitions between speakers' segments and other audio clips are smooth. ☐ Each speaker speaks clearly.

Fine-Tune the Content To make your podcast stronger, review each speaker's segment to make sure it supports the group's response to the question about American ideals and the immigrant experience. Be sure that group members touch on aspects of the immigrant experience they encountered in the literature they read in this unit, as well as in their research and interviews. Check with your group to identify key points that are not clear. Find another way to word these ideas.

Improve Your Use of Media Review all audio clips and sound effects to make sure they communicate key ideas and help create a cohesive story. Ensure that the equipment is working properly.

Present and Evaluate

When you present as a group, be sure that each member has taken into account each of the checklist items. As you listen to other groups, evaluate how well they meet the checklist.

DIGITAL PERSPECTIVES

Organize Your Ideas Let students know that a strong podcast uses a conversational tone that helps the listener connect to the podcast hosts.

Rehearse With Your Group

Practice With Your Group Remind students that practicing their parts ahead of time will reduce the likelihood that they'll make a mistake when they "record" their podcast. Rehearsal will also allow them to detect areas where the script copy is awkward and doesn't flow.

Improve Your Use of Media Groups might find that the media they've chosen does little to enhance the presentation. Remind them that this is an opportunity to explore other options.

Present and Evaluate

Before beginning the presentations, set the expectations for the audience. You may wish to have students consider these questions as groups present.

- Which American ideals did the groups discuss?
- How did the immigrant experiences reflect these ideals?
- Did the multimedia enhance the presentations?
- What presentation skills did the groups excel at?

Remind students that positive feedback is as valuable as constructive criticism.

PERSONALIZE FOR LEARNING

Strategic Support

Comparison Group members might have difficulty seeing how the different sources present different perspectives on the immigrant experience. To help students better understand, have them skim "With a Little Help From My Friends," "The Writing on the Wall," and "Rules of the Game." As they are skimming, have them place sticky notes in the text whenever a challenging situation is discussed.

OVERVIEW

INDEPENDENT LEARNING

What does it mean to be "American"?

Encourage students to think carefully about what they have already learned and what more they want to know about the unit topic of American voices. This is a key first step to previewing and selecting the text or media they will read or review in Independent Learning.

Independent Learning Strategies

Review the Learning Strategies with students and explain that as they work through Independent Learning they will develop strategies to work on their own.

- Have students watch the video on Independent Learning Strategies.
- A video on this topic is available online in the Professional Development Center.

Students should include any favorite strategies that they might have devised on their own during Whole-Class and Small-Group Learning. For example, for the strategy "Take notes," students might include:

- Compare notes with a classmate.
- Identify ideas that seem especially important, and write them down.

Block Scheduling

Each day in this Pacing Plan represents a 40-50 minute class period. Teachers using block scheduling may combine days to reflect their class schedule. In addition, teachers may revise pacing to differentiate and support core instruction by integrating components and resources as students require.

OVERVIEW: INDEPENDENT LEARNING

ESSENTIAL QUESTION:

What does it mean to be "American"?

Being an American is different for everyone. In this section, you will complete your study of American identity by exploring an additional selection related to the topic. You'll then share what you learn with classmates. To choose a text, follow these steps.

Look Back Think about the selections you have already studied. What more do you want to know about the topic of American identity?

Look Ahead Preview the selections by reading the descriptions. Which one seems most interesting and appealing to you?

Look Inside Take a few minutes to scan the text you chose. Choose a different one if this text doesn't meet your needs.

Independent Learning Strategies

Throughout your life, in school, in your community, and in your career, you will need to rely on yourself to learn and work on your own. Review these strategies and the actions you can take to practice them during Independent Learning. Add ideas of your own for each category.

STRATEGY	ACTION PLAN
Create a schedule	• Understand your goals and deadlines. • Make a plan for what to do each day. •
Practice what you have learned	• Use first-read and close-read strategies to deepen your understanding. • Evaluate the usefulness of the evidence to help you understand the topic. • Consider the quality and reliability of the source. •
Take notes	• Record important ideas and information. • Review your notes before preparing to share with a group. •

SCAN FOR MULTIMEDIA

Pacing Plan

Unit Introduction: 1
Introduce Whole-Class Learning: 2
A Quilt of a Country: 3, 4, 5, 6
The Immigrant Contribution: 7, 8, 9, 10
American History: 11, 12, 13
Performance Task: 14, 15

Choose one selection. Selections are available online only.

CONTENTS

MEMOIR

from When I Was Puerto Rican
Esmeralda Santiago

When a young Puerto Rican girl moves to New York and achieves her dreams, does she become a different person?

AUTOBIOGRAPHICAL ESSAY

Finding a Voice: A Taiwanese Family Adapts to America
Diane Tsai

How long, and how much commitment, does it take before a new immigrant can feel American?

POETRY

The New Colossus
Emma Lazarus

What does the Statue of Liberty really stand for?

POETRY

Legal Alien
Pat Mora

How does someone move through the world with dual identities?

MEDIA: VIDEO

Grace Abbott and the Fight for Immigrant Rights in America
BBC

This video asks the question: What does it mean to be a citizen? Is it simply that you live in a particular place?

PERFORMANCE-BASED ASSESSMENT PREP

Review Evidence for a Nonfiction Narrative
Complete your Evidence Log for the unit by evaluating what you've learned and synthesizing the information you've recorded.

SCAN FOR MULTIMEDIA

DIGITAL PERSPECTIVES

Contents

Selections Encourage students to scan and preview the selections before choosing the one they would like to read or review. Suggest that they consider the genre and subject matter of each one before making their decision. You can use the information on the following Planning pages to advise students in making their choice.

Remind students that the selections for Independent Learning are only available in the Interactive Student Edition of ***myPerspectives.*** Allow students who do not have digital access at home to preview the selections or review the media selection(s) using classroom or computer lab technology. Then either have students print the selection they choose or provide a printout for them.

Performance Based-Assessment Prep

Review Evidence for a Nonfiction Narrative Point out to students that collecting evidence during Independent Learning is the last step in completing their Evidence Log. After they finish their independent reading, they will synthesize all the evidence they have compiled in the unit.

The evidence students collect will serve as the primary source of information they will use to complete the writing and oral presentation for the Performance-Based Assessment at the end of the unit.

Introduce Small-Group Learning — 16
Rules of the Game — 17, 18
The Writing on the Wall — 19, 20
With a Little Help From My Friends — 21, 22
• Morning Talk, • Immigrant Picnic — 23, 24
Performance Task — 25, 26
Introduce Independent Learning — 27
Independent Learning — 28
Performance-Based Assessment — 29, 30

INDEPENDENT LEARNING

from When I Was Puerto Rican

Summary

In her memoir "When I Was Puerto Rican" Esmeralda Santiago says she never wanted to be a nurse or a teacher – those things her guidance counselor dreamed up. Esmeralda wanted to be an actress. The High School of Performing Arts in Manhattan would be the first big step, and it would get her out of crowded, dangerous Brooklyn. She worked hard to get ready for her audition, but on the day it was scheduled, she took one look at the panel of teachers waiting to judge her and froze. The audition was a disaster. The teachers, however, gave her another chance, and this time something magical happened. Many years later, Esmeralda revisits her old high school. She thinks about how much she learned, how far she's come, and how far she still plans to go.

Insight

This excerpt from "When I Was Puerto Rican" will help students understand how the children of immigrants, as American citizens from birth, can feel confined in immigrant communities. Their need to escape and lead independent, American lives can take the form of intense ambition, especially in the performing arts, where self-expression is central. Santiago's immature dissatisfaction develops into high-sighted ambitions and provides the energy to achieve them.

Connection to Essential Question

This excerpt from "When I Was Puerto Rican" provides a very personal perspective on the Essential Question. At first, Esmeralda Santiago rejects her identity as an American, abandoning the dreams she once had. However, the taste of success gives her an appetite for more. She eventually comes to realize that only America provides opportunities capable of fulfilling ambitions as large as hers.

Connection to Performance-Based Assessment

In this task, students will consider how an American identity is created. Esmeralda Santiago creates her identity by dreaming of a better future and overcoming obstacles.

SELECTION RESOURCES

- First Read-Guide: Nonfiction
- Close-Read Guide: Nonfiction
- *from* When I Was Puerto Rican: Text Questions
- Audio Summaries
- Selection Audio
- Selection Test

Text Complexity Rubric: *from* When I Was Puerto Rican	
Quantitative Measures	
Lexile: 900 **Text Length:** 3,771 words	
Qualitative Measures	
Knowledge Demands ①—②—❸—④—⑤	Explores several themes (a teen struggling with identity; trying to succeed and auditioning; growing up as a bilingual immigrant). Experiences portrayed are common to many readers.
Structure ①—②—❸—④—⑤	Mostly clear chronological structure, but story spans many years and includes a sudden time shift; narrative structure and abundant dialogue improve readability.
Language Conventionality and Clarity ①—②—❸—④—⑤	Language is mostly clear and explicit; contains some long sentences with complex constructions, and a lot of descriptive language.
Levels of Meaning/Purpose ①—②—❸—④—⑤	Theme is clear but conveyed with some subtlety. At times, reader must infer meaning from character's actions or dialogue.

DIGITAL PERSPECTIVES

Audio | Video | Document | Annotation Highlights | EL Highlights | Online Assessment

SELECTION RESOURCES

- First Read-Guide: Nonfiction
- Close-Read Guide: Nonfiction
- Finding a Voice: A Taiwanese Family Adapts to America: Text Questions
- Audio Summaries
- Selection Audio
- Selection Test

Finding a Voice: A Taiwanese Family Adapts to America

Summary

Diane Tsai's autobiographical essay "Finding a Voice: A Taiwanese Family Adapts to America" starts with an account of the first day of school in America for Diane and her younger sister, Linda. The two girls have lived in Taiwan their whole lives, and can barely speak English. When Linda discovers she doesn't have enough money to buy lunch, she can't explain what's wrong and bursts into tears. Diane's first day isn't much better. She has no one to play with because she and the other kids can't understand each other. Today, the sisters are American. They speak English fluently and are fully integrated with their fellow citizens. The story of how Diane and Linda became American is a story they share with many children of immigrants.

Insight

Reading "Finding a Voice: A Taiwanese Family Adapts to America" will help students consider the power of a common language. For Diane and Linda, that means learning to speak English without a trace of an accent. It also means learning that the language of humans trying to connect with each other is universal. This is what Diane's mother means when she explains to Diane that she doesn't need to ask to play with her classmates – she just needs to join in and start playing with them.

Connection to Essential Question

"Finding a Voice: A Taiwanese Family Adapts to America" provides an autobiographical perspective on the Essential Question: What does it mean to be "American"? For Diane and her sister, being American means taking the initiative, and learning the language and customs of America through their daily life as students at an American school. It means honoring their parents' hard work through their own commitment to learn what it means to be American.

Connection to Performance-Based Assessment

In this task, students will consider how an American identity is created. The author's American identity is created not just by learning to speak English flawlessly. Nor is it the rejection of her Taiwanese heritage that makes her American. It is her ability to have both "Taiwanese" and "American" exist side by side within her. Diane owes her American identity not only to the sacrifices of her parents, but also to her acknowledgment of the cultural influence of her Taiwanese roots on her American life.

Text Complexity Rubric: Finding a Voice	
Quantitative Measures	
Lexile: 1180 **Text Length:** 648 words	
Qualitative Measures	
Knowledge Demands ①—②—❸—④—⑤	Explores a single theme. Experiences portrayed (adjustment as immigrants) may not be common to all readers, but experiences and feelings are fully explained.
Structure ①—②—❸—④—⑤	Narrative is told chronologically, starting with the past. It jumps to present-day experience, and then concludes with a reflection on the past.
Language Conventionality and Clarity ①—❷—③—④—⑤	Narrative is written in contemporary, conversational language; mostly explicit and easy to understand; some long sentences with multiple clauses.
Levels of Meaning/Purpose ①—❷—③—④—⑤	Theme is clear (difficulties of transitioning as immigrants), but situation is not explained right away. Meaning is revealed over the entirety of the text.

SELECTION RESOURCES

- First Read-Guide: Poetry
- Close-Read Guide: Poetry
- The New Colossus: Text Questions
- Audio Summaries
- Selection Audio
- Selection Test

The New Colossus

Summary

"The New Colossus" is a poem written by Emma Lazarus in 1883, three years before the Statue of Liberty in New York Harbor was completed. Lazarus wrote it as a celebration of America's promise of a better life to the poor and oppressed people of the world. The poem compares a new statue to the Colossus of Rhodes, a terrifying figure. Instead, this new statue welcomes the tired and poor of the world. She will raise a lamp to guide the way for these new immigrants.

Insight

Reading "The New Colossus" will help students see that America's hospitality to all immigrants, however desperate their need, is a defining principle of America. Recognizing that principle is necessary to understanding what it means to be American.

Connection to Essential Question

"The New Colossus" provides an idealized perspective on the Essential Question: What does it mean to be "American"? The speaker of the last six lines of this sonnet is the Mother of Exiles herself, and she reminds the nation that immigration is the lifeblood of America. The poem contrasts the desire of other nations to create great empires and keep the masses down with America's compassion for all.

Connection to Performance-Based Assessment

In this task, students will consider how an American identity is created. The American identity—the spirit that identifies the nation and her people as depicted in this poem—comes from the differences between America and other countries. America welcomes the people who have been oppressed by those other countries and offers them a better life.

Text Complexity Rubric: The New Colossus

Quantitative Measures	
Lexile: NP **Text Length:** 14 lines	
Qualitative Measures	
Knowledge Demands ① — ② — ③ — ❹ — ⑤	Background is needed about the Statue of Liberty (name is never stated). Many references need explanation (*brazen giant of Greek fame* is the Colossus of Rhodes, *Mother of Exiles* the Statue of Liberty).
Structure ① — ② — ③ — ❹ — ⑤	Poem is a sonnet of 14 lines; includes two different rhyme schemes; point of view shifts (second stanza is meant to be the statue's words).
Language Conventionality and Clarity ① — ② — ③ — ④ — ❺	Very complex language, multiple instances of archaic and above-level vocabulary, unfamiliar syntax, figurative language, including metaphors and oxymorons (*imprisoned lightning, speak with silent lips*).
Levels of Meaning/Purpose ① — ② — ③ — ❹ — ⑤	Multiple levels of meaning; subject of poem is not directly stated and much background knowledge is needed in order to understand meaning of individual lines and theme of poem.

DIGITAL PERSPECTIVES

Audio | Video | Document | Annotation Highlights | EL Highlights | Online Assessment

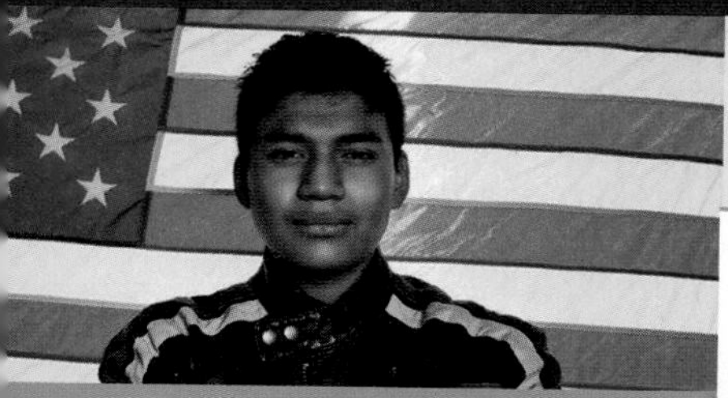

SELECTION RESOURCES

- First Read-Guide: Poetry
- Close-Read Guide: Poetry
- Legal Alien: Text Questions
- Audio Summaries
- Selection Audio
- Selection Test

Legal Alien

Summary

The speaker of Pat Mora's poem, "Legal Alien," describes a woman who has two languages and two cultures. As she talks, she slides naturally from colloquial English into colloquial Spanish. She can write memos in formal English and order Mexican food in Spanish. She's not just American, but Mexican-American. To Mexicans she's American, and to Americans she's Mexican. She doesn't belong wholly to either world, but moves between the fringes of both with a smile. With that smile she pretends that she doesn't mind being judged by both sides.

Insight

Reading "Legal Alien" will help students reflect on the complicated cultural conflict within some American voices. Is it necessary for Americans of mixed ethnicities to deny one part of their hyphenated label in order to find their American voice, or is that dance back and forth over the hyphen the essential characteristic that can make some voices authentically American?

Connection to Essential Question

"Legal Alien" approaches the Essential Question: What does it mean to be "American"? from the point of view of one who straddles two nationalities. The woman described in the poem cannot be entirely American. The hyphen in her label as Mexican-American reminds her that she is not quite American. She may feel distanced from both nationalities. On the other hand, perhaps for her, being American means containing both parts.

Connection to Performance-Based Assessment

In this task, students will consider how an American identity is created. The woman in this poem experiences a conflict of identities: she identifies herself as both American and Mexican, but believes that neither Americans nor Mexicans can accept her as both.

Text Complexity Rubric: Legal Alien

Quantitative Measures	
Lexile: NP **Text Length:** 22 lines	
Qualitative Measures	
Knowledge Demands 1 — 2 — **3** — 4 — 5	Experiences portrayed may be common to some readers who are bilingual or bicultural, but other readers will find the themes unfamiliar (cultural tensions in the lives of Mexican-American).
Structure 1 — 2 — **3** — 4 — 5	Poem is written in free verse; no rhyme scheme, varying meter; some repetition is used within groups of phrases *(able to sit, able to order; perhaps exotic, perhaps inferior).*
Language Conventionality and Clarity 1 — 2 — **3** — 4 — 5	Language is contemporary and familiar; some repetitive language; mostly literal language with some figurative phrases; Spanish answer is given to an English question (not translated).
Levels of Meaning/Purpose 1 — 2 — **3** — 4 — 5	Theme is clear, but meaning of specific phrases may be difficult to identify for some readers.

Grace Abbott and the Fight for Immigrant Rights in America

SELECTION RESOURCES

- First-Review Guide: Media—Video
- Close-Review Guide: Media—Video
- Grace Abbott and the Fight for Immigrant Rights: Media Questions
- Audio Summaries
- Selection Video

Summary

This video discusses immigrant rights in the early twentieth century. Grace Abbott was a teacher who campaigned for immigrant rights. Abbott worked as a social worker in Chicago. She was particularly worried about girls who fell into forced labor. She set up an Immigrant Protective League, staffed by women who could speak the same languages as new arrivals and offer them protection and advice. Abbott felt that honoring where you come from strengthened your loyalty to America. When asked "What is an American?" she answered, "We are many nationalities, scattered over a continent."

Insight

This video shows that the idea that immigrants are equally American is not new. Some Americans whose families have been here for a long time have always worked to protect people whose families have been here a short time.

Connection to Essential Question

The video connects the meaning of the Essential Question: What does it mean to be "American"? to the relationship between people who have lived in America for awhile and those who are newly arrived.

Connection to Performance-Based Assessment

The prompt is "How is an American identity created?" In her final words of the video, Abbott says that Americans come from many places and can "meet the American opportunity" by living together and respecting differences.

Media Complexity Rubric: Grace Abbott and the Fight for Immigrant Rights in America	
Quantitative Measures	
Format and Length Video of 3 minutes, 37 seconds	
Qualitative Measures	
Knowledge Demands ① ② ③ **❹** ⑤	Subject of video (immigration rights and issues in early 20th century) and references (sweat shops, saloons), will be unfamiliar to viewers. Content is explained, but background is necessary.
Structure ① ② **❸** ④ ⑤	Explanations are logically and sequentially organized. Much of audio is supported by visuals with one-to-one correspondence (e.g., picture of Grace Abbott while introducing name and role).
Language Conventionality and Clarity ① ② **❸** ④ ⑤	Narration of video contains language that is mostly contemporary and sometimes formal. It has some complex sentences with multiple clauses. Speech is clear and well enunciated.
Levels of Meaning/Purpose ① ② **❸** ④ ⑤	Purpose of video is explicit and concrete. Subject covered is narrowly focused, but requires understanding; purpose requires understanding of background information.

MY NOTES

ADVISING

You may wish to direct students to use the generic **First-Read** and **Close-Read Guides** in the Print Student Edition. Alternatively, you may wish to print copies of the genre-specific **First-Read** and **Close-Read Guides** for students. These are available online in the Interactive Student Edition or Unit Resources.

FIRST READ

Students should perform the steps of the first read independently:

NOTICE: Students should focus on the basic elements of the text to ensure they understand.

ANNOTATE: Students should mark any passages they wish to revisit during their close read.

CONNECT: Students should increase their understanding by connecting what they've read to other texts or personal experiences.

RESPOND: Students will write a summary to demonstrate their understanding.

Point out to students that while they will always complete the Respond step at the end of the first read, the other steps will probably happen somewhat concurrently. Students will revisit their first-read annotations during the close read.

After students have completed the First-Read Guide, you may wish to assign the Text Questions for the selection that are available in the Interactive Teacher's Edition.

Anchor Standards

In the first two sections of the unit, students worked with the whole class and in small groups to gain topical knowledge and greater understanding of the skills required by the anchor standards. In this section, they are asked to work independently, applying what they have learned and demonstrating increased readiness for college and career.

INDEPENDENT LEARNING

First-Read Guide

Tool Kit
First-Read Guide and Model Annotation

Use this page to record your first-read ideas.

Selection Title: ______________________________

NOTICE new information or ideas you learn about the unit topic as you first read this text.

ANNOTATE by marking vocabulary and key passages you want to revisit.

CONNECT ideas within the selection to other knowledge and the selections you have read.

RESPOND by writing a brief summary of the selection.

STANDARD
Reading Read and comprehend complex literary and informational texts independently and proficiently.

PERSONALIZE FOR LEARNING

English Language Support

Skim, Predict, and Use a KWL Chart Use the Text Complexity Rubrics to help individual students select a text appropriate for their English proficiency level. Help students identify the genre of the selection they chose: poem, short story, or opinion piece. Then have them skim the selection to notice text features, such as headings or visuals. They can also look for quotation marks and words that stand out to them. Explain to students that when they skim, they should focus on understanding the general idea and should not stop to figure out unfamiliar words.

Next, have students work with a partner to predict what their selection will be about. Instruct them to ask and answer *Wh-* questions. Provide sample question frames such as *What ______? Who______? How ______?*

Finally, help partners complete a KWL chart to note what they already know about the topic and what they want to learn, and then finally, what they learned: **ALL LEVELS,**

Know	Want to Know	Learned

DIGITAL PERSPECTIVES

Close-Read Guide

Tool Kit
Close-Read Guide and Model Annotation

Use this page to record your close-read ideas.

Selection Title: ____________________

Close Read the Text

Revisit sections of the text you marked during your first read. Read these sections closely and **annotate** what you notice. Ask yourself **questions** about the text. What can you **conclude?** Write down your ideas.

ANNOTATE · QUESTION · CONCLUDE — Close Read

Analyze the Text

Think about the author's choices of patterns, structure, techniques, and ideas included in the text. Select one, and record your thoughts about what this choice conveys.

QuickWrite

Pick a paragraph from the text that grabbed your interest. Explain the power of this passage.

STANDARD
Reading Read and comprehend complex literary and informational texts independently and proficiently.

CLOSE READ

Students should begin their close read by revisiting the annotations they made during their first read. Then, students should analyze one of the author's choices regarding the following elements:

- a clearly described situation or problem
- a well-structured, logical sequence of events
- details that show time and place
- effective story elements such as dialogue, description, and reflection
- a reflective conclusion

MAKE IT INTERACTIVE
Group students according to the selection they have chosen. Then, have students meet to discuss the selection in depth. Their discussions should be guided by their insights and questions.

PERSONALIZE FOR LEARNING

English Language Support

Read Aloud, Confirm Predictions, and Complete a KWL Chart Pair students or put them in groups so they can take turns reading aloud to one another. Each student can read one paragraph, or you can split up the text in any other way that makes sense. For example, for a short story, you may wish to assign different characters and the role of the narrator to individual students to take turns reading aloud. Have students make predictions as they listen, then have partners or groups discuss, compare, and confirm the predictions they made. Ask: *Did anything surprise you? Were any predictions correct? Which ones?* Finally, have partners or groups work together to add more details about what they learned to the Close Read the Text box on their Close-Read Guide. **ALL LEVELS**

ADVISING

Share Your Independent Learning

Prepare to Share

Explain to students that sharing what they learned from their Independent Learning selection provides classmates who read a different selection with an opportunity to consider the text as a source of evidence during the Performance-Based Assessment. As students prepare to share, remind them to highlight how their selection contributed to their knowledge of the concept of survival as well as how the selection connects to the question *What does it mean to be "American"?*

Learn From Your Classmates

As students discuss the Independent Learning selections, direct them to take particular note of how their classmates' chosen selections align with their current position on the Performance-Based Assessment question.

Reflect

Students may want to add their reflection to their Evidence Log, particularly if their insight relates to a specific selection from the unit.

MAKE IT INTERACTIVE

Have students sketch a character from one of the unit's selections. Have them mark the sketch with five identity words that best describe the character. After students have completed their sketches, post them on the wall and conduct a gallery walk. As students circulate, have them choose the sketch that best represents the selected character and take note of the identity words used to describe the character. Then, lead students in a discussion about their choices and what makes a good character in a narrative.

Evidence Log Support students in completing their Evidence Log. This paced activity will help prepare them for the Performance-Based Assessment at the end of the unit.

INDEPENDENT LEARNING

EVIDENCE LOG

Go to your Evidence Log and record what you learned from the text you read.

Share Your Independent Learning

Prepare to Share

What does it mean to be "American"?

Even when you read something independently, your understanding continues to grow when you share what you have learned with others. Reflect on the text you explored independently, and write notes about its connection to the unit. In your notes, consider why this text belongs in this unit.

Learn From Your Classmates

Discuss It Share your ideas about the text you explored on your own. As you talk with your classmates, jot down ideas that you learn from them.

Reflect

Review your notes, and mark the most important insight you gained from these writing and discussion activities. Explain how this idea adds to your understanding of American identity.

STANDARDS

Speaking and Listening
Initiate and participate effectively in a range of collaborative discussions with diverse partners on *grades 9–10 topics, texts, and issues*, building on others' ideas and expressing their own clearly and persuasively.

AUTHOR'S PERSPECTIVE **Ernest Morrell, Ph.D.**

Learning From Others Independent Learning helps students build vocabulary, background knowledge, and fluency. Teach students how to learn from each other by modeling how to ask clarifying questions when other students are sharing their experiences. Questions like these can guide the discussion:

- Why did you choose this text? For example, did the topic interest you? Have you heard of the author or read anything else by the author?
- For narrative text: What is the problem in the story? When and where does the story take place? Why?
- For nonfiction text: How is the information organized? What is the most interesting thing you've learned so far?
- What parts of the text do you think were most important? Why?
- Did the text meet your expectations? Why or why not? Would you recommend this text to a classmate? Explain your answer.
- How does the text relate to other texts you have read on this subject? How does it relate to your life?

Review Evidence for a Nonfiction Narrative

At the beginning of the unit, you expressed a point of view about the following question:

How is an "American" identity created?

EVIDENCE LOG

Review your Evidence Log and your QuickWrite from the beginning of the unit. What have you learned?

NOTES	NOTES
Identify at least three pieces of evidence that interested you about the experiences of immigrants, both past and present.	Identify at least three pieces of evidence that reinforced your initial point of view.
1.	1.
2.	2.
3.	3.

Identify a real-life experience that illustrates one of your revised ideas about American identity: ______________________________

____

____

Develop your thoughts into a topic sentence for a nonfiction narrative. Complete this sentence starter:

I learned a great deal about the experience of immigrant life in America when ______________________________

____

____

Evaluate the Strength of Your Evidence Consider your point of view. How did the texts you read impact your point of view?

DIGITAL PERSPECTIVES

Review Evidence for Nonfiction Narrative

Evidence Log Students should understand that their thinking could evolve as they learn more about the subject and are exposed to additional points of view. Point out that just because they took an initial point of view on the question *How is an American identity created?* doesn't mean that their thinking can't change after careful consideration of their learning and evidence.

Evaluate the Strength of Your Evidence

Remind students to think about the evidence they gathered from the texts that can support their initial point of view, including:

- experiences of immigrants both past and present
- negative or positive descriptions of life as an immigrant
- examples of immigrants' American identity
- facts and opinions about life in America

In addition to ensuring that they have sufficient evidence to reinforce their initial point of view, students should consider what they learned from the texts and think about what, if anything, made them change their point of view.

ASSESSING

Writing to Sources: Nonfiction Narrative

Students should complete the Performance-Based Assessment independently, with little to no input or feedback during the process. Students should use word processing software to take advantage of editing tools and features.

Prior to beginning the Assessment, ask students to think about how immigrants and native-born Americans might have different perspectives about American identity.

Review the Elements of Nonfiction Narrative Students can review the work they did earlier in the unit as they complete the Performance-Based Assessment. They may also consult other resources such as:

- the elements of nonfiction narrative, including sequence, exposition, and dialogue available in Whole-Class Learning
- their Evidence Log
- their Word Network

Although students will use information from unit selections for their nonfiction narrative, they may need to collect additional information, including facts, meaningful events, quotations, or examples.

PERFORMANCE-BASED ASSESSMENT

SOURCES

- WHOLE-CLASS SELECTIONS
- SMALL-GROUP SELECTIONS
- INDEPENDENT LEARNING

PART 1

Writing to Sources: Nonfiction Narrative

In this unit, you read about various characters, both real and fictional, who moved from other countries and had to work to build an American identity. It was easier for some than for others.

Assignment

Write a **nonfiction narrative** on the following topic:

How is an "American" identity created?

Use your own experience or the experience of someone you know to write a narrative answering this question. Consider geographical, social, legal, and emotional aspects of this question. What is the connection between a sense of one's personal identity and one's national identity? Do those aspects of identity ever come into conflict? As you write your narrative, draw comparisons to the real or imagined experiences described in the selections in this unit. Ensure that the ideas you want to express are fully developed by meaningful details, and that you establish a clear sequence of events.

Reread the Assignment Review the assignment to be sure you fully understand it. The assignment may reference some of the academic words presented at the beginning of the unit. Be sure you understand each of the words in order to complete the assignment correctly.

Academic Vocabulary

conflict	dialogue	sequence
description	exposition	

Review the Elements of Effective Nonfiction Narrative Before you begin writing, read the Nonfiction Narrative Rubric. Once you have completed your first draft, check it against the rubric. If one or more of the elements is missing or is not as strong as it could be, revise your narrative to add or strengthen that component.

WORD NETWORK

As you write and revise your narrative, use your Word Network to help vary your word choices.

STANDARDS

Writing

- Write narratives to develop real or imagined experiences or events using effective technique, well-chosen details, and well-structured event sequences.
- Draw evidence from literary or informational texts to support analysis, reflection, and research.

AUTHOR'S PERSPECTIVE Kelly Gallagher, M. Ed.

Building a Writing Portfolio With Students Teachers can create a portfolio that enables students to demonstrate the variety of writing they complete over the year. There are three elements of keeping a portfolio—collection of all the writing a student has done, selection of the best pieces, and reflection to evaluate growth.

Teachers can set the criteria using such categories as *Best Argument, Best Narrative Piece, Best Informative Piece, Best On-Demand Writing, Best Poetry, Best Blended Genre, Best Writing From Another Class, Best Model of Revision,* and *Best Single Line You Wrote This Year*. Students should also include a reflective letter at the end of the year.

- Where does your writing still need improvement? How will you improve it?
- Reflect on a struggle you faced during this unit. How did you overcome it?
- Discuss a specific writing strategy you used and how it worked for you.
- What strengths have you developed as a writer? Where are those strengths found in this portfolio?

At the end of the year, students can review these pieces to see their growth as writers.

Nonfiction Narrative Rubric

	Focus and Organization	Evidence and Elaboration	Language Conventions
4	The narrative engages and orients the reader by setting out a clear problem, situation, or observation. The narrative includes a variety of narrative techniques. The narrative includes a smooth sequence of events or ideas. The conclusion follows from the events in the narrative and provides insightful reflection on the experiences related in the narrative.	The specific details and descriptions create a vivid picture of events and characters. The narrative includes story elements such as dialogue, pacing, and reflection. The language in the narrative is always precise and appropriate for the audience and purpose. The tone of the narrative is always engaging.	The narrative intentionally follows standard English conventions of usage and mechanics.
3	The narrative orients the reader by setting out a problem, situation, or observation. The narrative includes narrative techniques. The narrative includes a sequence of events or ideas. The conclusion follows from the events in the narrative and restates important ideas.	The details and descriptions create a picture of events and characters. The narrative includes some story elements, such as dialogue, pacing, and reflection. The language in the narrative is precise and appropriate for the audience and purpose. The tone of the narrative is mostly narrative engaging.	The narrative demonstrates accuracy in standard English conventions of usage and mechanics.
2	The narrative sets out a problem, situation, or observation. The narrative includes at least one narrative technique. The narrative includes a somewhat logical sequence of events or ideas. The conclusion follows from the events in the narrative.	Some details and descriptions are included to create a picture of events and characters. The narrative includes at least one story element. The language in the narrative is sometimes precise and appropriate for the audience and purpose. The tone of the narrative is occasionally engaging.	The narrative demonstrates some accuracy in standard English conventions of usage and mechanics.
1	The narrative does not clearly set out a problem, situation, or observation. The narrative does not include narrative techniques. The sequence of events or ideas is not presented smoothly or logically. The conclusion does not follow from the events in the narrative, or the narrative has no conclusion.	Details and descriptions are not included to create a picture of events and characters. The narrative does not include story elements. The language in the narrative is not precise or appropriate for the audience and purpose. The tone of the narrative is not engaging.	The narrative contains mistakes in standard English conventions of usage and mechanics.

DIGITAL PERSPECTIVES

Nonfiction Narrative Rubric

As you review the Nonfiction Narrative Rubric with students, remind them that the rubric is a resource that can guide their revisions. Students should pay particular attention to the differences between a narrative that contains all the required elements (a score of 3) and a narrative that is comprehensive, engaging, and progresses in a logical and thoughtful manner (a score of 4).

Speaking and Listening: Interpretive Reading

Students should annotate their written nonfiction narrative in preparation for the interpretive reading, marking the important elements (dialogue, exposition, and sequence) as well as meaningful events.

Remind students that the effectiveness of an interpretive reading relies on how the speaker establishes credibility with his or her audience. If a speaker comes across as confident, it will be easier to engage the audience and sustain their interest.

Review the Interpretive Reading Rubric As you review the Interpretive Reading Rubric with students, remind them that it is a valuable tool that can help them plan their presentation. They should strive to include all of the criteria required to achieve a score of 3. Draw their attention to some of the subtle differences between scores of 2 and 3.

PERFORMANCE-BASED ASSESSMENT

PART 2

Speaking and Listening: Interpretive Reading

Assignment
After completing the final draft of your nonfiction narrative, plan and present a brief **interpretive reading.**

Do not simply read your narrative aloud. Take the following steps to make your presentation lively and engaging.

- Go back to your narrative, and annotate the ideas that provide reflection on your experiences and events.
- Refer to your annotations to guide your presentation.
- Use appropriate eye contact, adequate volume, and clear pronunciation.

STANDARDS

Speaking and Listening
Present information, findings, and supporting evidence clearly, concisely, and logically such that listeners can follow the line of reasoning and the organization, development, substance, and style are appropriate to purpose, audience, and task.

Review the Rubric The criteria by which your narrative will be evaluated appear in the rubric below. Review these criteria before presenting to ensure that you are prepared.

	Content	Organization	Presentation Technique
3	The narrative engages and orients listeners by setting out a clear problem, situation, or observation. The presentation includes a variety of story elements and narrative techniques. The conclusion follows from and reflects on what is in the rest of the presentation.	The speaker uses time very effectively by spending the right amount of time on each part. The narrative includes a smooth sequence of events or ideas. Listeners can always follow the presentation.	The speaker makes occasional eye contact and speaks clearly with adequate volume. The speaker varies tone and emphasis to create an engaging presentation.
2	The narrative sets out a problem, situation, or observation. The presentation includes some story elements and narrative techniques. The conclusion follows from what is in the rest of the presentation.	The speaker uses time effectively by spending the right amount of time on each part. The narrative includes a sequence of events or ideas. Listeners can mostly follow the presentation.	The speaker makes minimal eye contact and speaks clearly with adequate volume. The speaker sometimes varies tone and emphasis to create an engaging presentation.
1	The narrative does not set out a problem, situation, or observation. The presentation does not include story elements or narrative techniques. The conclusion does not follow from what is in the rest of the presentation.	The speaker does not use time effectively by spending the right amount of time on each part. The narrative does not include a sequence of events or ideas. Listeners cannot follow the presentation.	The speaker does not maintain effective eye contact or speak clearly with adequate volume. The speaker does not vary tone and emphasis to create an engaging presentation.

DIGITAL PERSPECTIVES

Preparing for the Assignment You can help students understand what makes a nonfiction narrative compelling by showing them short video clips from the Internet. You can also play them a clip from a podcast, noting how the narrator grabs the listener's attention. While projecting the video or playing the podcast, have students note the ways exposition and dialogue are used. Be sure to preview the video clips or podcast before sharing with the class.

Reflect on the Unit

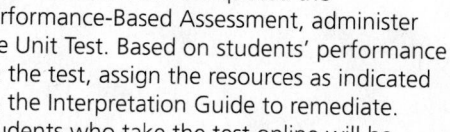

Now that you've completed the unit, take a few moments to reflect on your learning.

Reflect on the Unit Goals

Look back at the goals at the beginning of the unit. Use a different-colored pen to rate yourself again. Think about readings and activities that contributed the most to the growth of your understanding. Record your thoughts.

Reflect on the Learning Strategies

Discuss It Write a reflection on whether you were able to improve your learning based on your Action Plans. Think about what worked, what didn't, and what you might do to keep working on these strategies. Record your ideas before a class discussion.

Reflect on the Text

Choose a selection that you found challenging and explain what made it difficult.

Explain something that surprised you about a text in the unit.

Which activity taught you the most about what it means to be "American"? What did you learn?

SCAN FOR MULTIMEDIA

Reflect on the Unit

- Have students watch the video on Reflecting on Your Learning
- A video on this topic is available online in the Professional Development Center

Reflect on the Unit Goals

Students should re-evaluate how well they met the unit goals now that they have completed the unit. You might ask them to provide a written commentary on the goal they made the most progress with as well as the goal they feel warrants continued focus.

Reflect on the Learning Strategies

Discuss It If you want to make this a digital activity, go online and navigate to the Discussion Board. Alternatively, students can share their learning strategies reflections in a class discussion.

Reflect on the Text

Consider having students share their text reflections with one another.

MAKE IT INTERACTIVE

Have students prepare one slide using presentation software that summaries their reflection.

Collate student slides into a presentation that can be viewed by the class. Students should be prepared to give a 30-second oral summary for their slide.

Unit Test and Remediation

After students have completed the Performance-Based Assessment, administer the Unit Test. Based on students' performance on the test, assign the resources as indicated on the Interpretation Guide to remediate. Students who take the test online will be automatically assigned remediation, as warranted by test results.

UNIT 2

Survival

INTRODUCTION

Jump Start

Engage students in a discussion about the following scenario:

"Your ship is sinking! You have only enough time to grab three items before swimming to the nearest deserted island. What will you take with you to help you survive?"

Have students jot down their three items first. Then, poll the class to determine the most popular items. Discuss the pros and cons of the top five choices.

Survival

Ask students what the word *survival* suggests to them. Point out that as they work through this unit, they will read about many examples of survival.

Video

Project the Introduction video in class, ask students to open the video in their interactive textbooks, or have students scan the Bounce Page icon with their phones to access the video.

Discuss It If you want to make this a digital activity, go online and navigate to the Discussion Board. Alternatively, students can share their responses in a class discussion.

Block Scheduling

Each day in this Pacing Plan represents a 40–50 minute class period. Teachers using block scheduling may combine days to reflect their class schedule. In addition, teachers may revise pacing to differentiate and support core instruction by integrating components and resources as students require.

UNIT 2

Survival

The quest for survival is a powerful human instinct. What determines who lives and who dies?

Amazing Stories of Rescues and Survival in Nepal

Discuss It What are the circumstances for victims and rescuers after an earthquake hits Nepal?

Write your response before sharing your ideas.

SCAN FOR MULTIMEDIA

Pacing Plan

Day	Activity
1	Unit Introduction
2	Introduce Whole-Class Learning
3–7	The Seventh Man
8–12	The Moral Logic of Survivor Guilt
13	Media: The Key to Disaster Survival?
14–15	Performance Task

DIGITAL PERSPECTIVES: Audio | Video | Document | Annotation Highlights | EL Highlights | Online Assessment

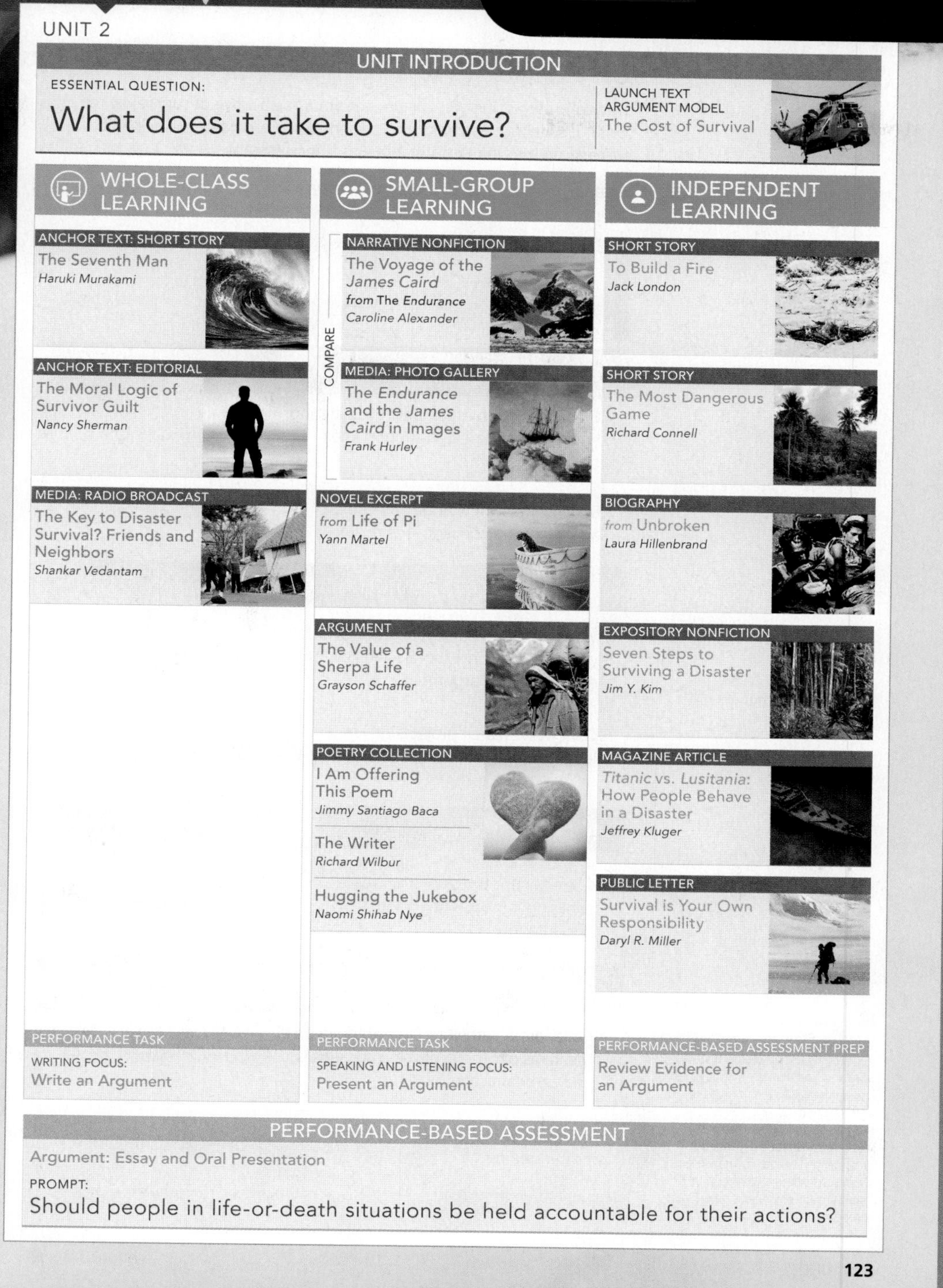

UNIT 2

UNIT INTRODUCTION

ESSENTIAL QUESTION:

What does it take to survive?

LAUNCH TEXT
ARGUMENT MODEL
The Cost of Survival

WHOLE-CLASS LEARNING	SMALL-GROUP LEARNING	INDEPENDENT LEARNING
ANCHOR TEXT: SHORT STORY The Seventh Man *Haruki Murakami*	NARRATIVE NONFICTION The Voyage of the *James Caird* from *The Endurance* *Caroline Alexander*	SHORT STORY To Build a Fire *Jack London*
ANCHOR TEXT: EDITORIAL The Moral Logic of Survivor Guilt *Nancy Sherman*	MEDIA: PHOTO GALLERY The *Endurance* and the *James Caird* in Images *Frank Hurley* (COMPARE)	SHORT STORY The Most Dangerous Game *Richard Connell*
MEDIA: RADIO BROADCAST The Key to Disaster Survival? Friends and Neighbors *Shankar Vedantam*	NOVEL EXCERPT from Life of Pi *Yann Martel*	BIOGRAPHY from Unbroken *Laura Hillenbrand*
	ARGUMENT The Value of a Sherpa Life *Grayson Schaffer*	EXPOSITORY NONFICTION Seven Steps to Surviving a Disaster *Jim Y. Kim*
	POETRY COLLECTION I Am Offering This Poem *Jimmy Santiago Baca* The Writer *Richard Wilbur* Hugging the Jukebox *Naomi Shihab Nye*	MAGAZINE ARTICLE *Titanic* vs. *Lusitania*: How People Behave in a Disaster *Jeffrey Kluger*
		PUBLIC LETTER Survival is Your Own Responsibility *Daryl R. Miller*
PERFORMANCE TASK WRITING FOCUS: Write an Argument	PERFORMANCE TASK SPEAKING AND LISTENING FOCUS: Present an Argument	PERFORMANCE-BASED ASSESSMENT PREP Review Evidence for an Argument

PERFORMANCE-BASED ASSESSMENT

Argument: Essay and Oral Presentation

PROMPT:

Should people in life-or-death situations be held accountable for their actions?

123

What does it take to survive?

Introduce the Essential Question and point out that students will respond to related prompts.

- **Whole-Class Learning** *Should the narrator of "The Seventh Man" forgive himself for his failure to save K.?*
- **Small-Group Learning** *What type of strength is most valuable in a survival situation?*
- **Performance-Based Assessment** *Should people in life-or-death situations be held accountable for their actions?*

Using Trade Books

Refer to the Teaching With Trade Books section for suggestions on how to incorporate the following thematically-related titles into this unit:

- *The Hunger Games* by Suzanne Collins
- *The Call of the Wild* by Jack London
- *Lord of the Flies* by William Golding

Current Perspectives

To increase student engagement, search online for rescue and survival stories, and invite your students to recommend stories they find. Always preview content before sharing it with your class.

- **Podcast: This American Life / 525: "Call for Help"** (NPR) An interview with a young family stranded at sea on a round-the-world sailing adventure
- **News Story: Chilean Mine Rescue Fast Facts** (CNN) 33 miners are saved from an underground mine collapse

Day	Lesson
16	Introduce Small-Group Learning
17–18	The Voyage of the *James Caird*
19	Media: The *Endurance* and the *James Caird* in Images
20–21	*from* Life of Pi
22–23	The Value of a Sherpa Life
24–25	I Am Offering This Poem; The Writer; Hugging the Jukebox
26	Performance Task
27	Introduce Independent Learning
28	Independent Learning
29–30	Performance-Based Assessment

About the Unit Goals

These unit goals were backward designed from the Performance-Based Assessment at the end of the unit and the Whole-Class and Small-Group Performance Tasks. Students will practice and become proficient in many more standards over the course of this unit.

Unit Goals

Review the goals with students and explain that as they read and discuss the selections in this unit, they will improve their skills in reading, writing, research, language, and speaking and listening.

- Have students watch the video on Goal Setting.
- A video on this topic is available online in the Professional Development Center.

Reading Goals Tell students they will read and evaluate arguments. They will also read fiction, essays, and articles to better understand the ways writers express ideas.

Writing and Research Goals Tell students that they will learn the elements of argumentative writing. They will write their own argument, and they will also write for a variety of other reasons, including organizing and sharing ideas, reflecting on experiences, and gathering evidence. They will conduct research to clarify and explore ideas.

Language Goal Tell students that they will develop a deeper understanding of how authors use phrases and clauses. They will then practice using phrases and clauses in their own writing.

Speaking and Listening Goals Explain to students that they will work together to build on one another's ideas, develop consensus, and communicate with one another. They will also learn to incorporate audio, visuals, and text in presentations.

HOME Connection

A Home Connection letter to students' parents or guardians is available in myPerspectives+. The letter explains what students will be learning in this unit and how they will be assessed.

Unit Goals

Throughout this unit you will deepen your perspective of survival by reading, writing, speaking, listening, and presenting. These goals will help you succeed on the Unit Performance-Based Assessment.

Rate how well you meet these goals right now. You will revisit your ratings later when you reflect on your growth during this unit.

SCALE	1	2	3	4	5
	NOT AT ALL WELL	NOT VERY WELL	SOMEWHAT WELL	VERY WELL	EXTREMELY WELL

READING GOALS	1	2	3	4	5
• Evaluate written arguments by analyzing how authors state and support their claims.	○	○	○	○	○
• Expand your knowledge and use of academic and concept vocabulary.	○	○	○	○	○

WRITING AND RESEARCH GOALS	1	2	3	4	5
• Write an argumentative essay in which you effectively incorporate the key elements of an argument.	○	○	○	○	○
• Conduct research projects of various lengths to explore a topic and clarify meaning.	○	○	○	○	○

LANGUAGE GOAL	1	2	3	4	5
• Correctly use transitions to create cohesion in your writing and presentations.	○	○	○	○	○

SPEAKING AND LISTENING GOALS	1	2	3	4	5
• Collaborate with your team to build on the ideas of others, develop consensus, and communicate.	○	○	○	○	○
• Integrate audio, visuals, and text in presentations.	○	○	○	○	○

STANDARDS

Language

Acquire and use accurately general academic and domain-specific words and phrases, sufficient for reading, writing, speaking, and listening at the college and career readiness level; demonstrate independence in gathering vocabulary knowledge when considering a word or phrase important to comprehension or expression.

SCAN FOR MULTIMEDIA

AUTHOR'S PERSPECTIVE Ernest Morrell, Ph.D.

Self-Assessing Progress The Unit Goals will help students share responsibility for their learning. This is an important ownership for students as they prepare for life in higher education, in their professional career, and as leaders in their families and communities. One way to encourage students to practice monitoring their own learning is to give them guiding questions like these to help them assess their progress as they work through the unit. Remind students to ask themselves such questions as they complete each selection or activity in the unit so they can track their progress.

- Do I have a better understanding of the parts of an argument and how to recognize them when reading and use them when writing?
- Do I have a better understanding of the difference between academic and thematic vocabulary?
- Am I recognizing different types of phrases and clauses?
- Am I effective when I collaborate with others?

Academic Vocabulary: Argument

Academic terms appear in all subjects and can help you read, write, and discuss with more precision. Here are five academic words that will be useful to you in this unit as you analyze and write arguments.

Complete the chart.

1. Review each word, its root, and the mentor sentences.
2. Use the information and your own knowledge to predict the meaning of each word.
3. For each word, list at least two related words.
4. Refer to a dictionary or other resources if needed.

WORD	MENTOR SENTENCES	PREDICT MEANING	RELATED WORDS
evidence ROOT: ***-vid-*** "to see"	1. The receipt from the cashier was *evidence* that she had paid the bill. 2. The students' outstanding short film is *evidence* of their creativity.		evident; evidently
credible ROOT: ***-cred-*** "to believe"	1. Marco is a *credible* witness because he pays attention and tells the truth. 2. Even if a story seems *credible*, confirm the details before you accept it as fact.		
valid ROOT: ***-val-*** "worth"	1. An answer is *valid* if it can be proved true. 2. Jon's license is *valid* for another three years, and then he will renew it.		
formulate ROOT: ***-form-*** "shape"	1. A researcher has to carefully *formulate* a topic that will be worth studying. 2. It took time for Erika to *formulate* a response to the complex question.		
logical ROOT: ***-log-*** "word"; "reason"	1. If your reasoning is *logical*, you will be able to show the connections between your ideas. 2. Mathematics is *logical* because it is based on rules and patterns.		

TIP

FOLLOW THROUGH
Study the words in this chart, and highlight them or their forms wherever they appear in the unit.

DIGITAL PERSPECTIVES

Academic Vocabulary: Argument

Introduce the blue academic vocabulary words in the chart on the student page. Point out that the root of each word provides a clue to its meaning. Discuss the mentor sentences to ensure students understand each word's usage. Students should also use the mentor sentences as context to help them predict the meaning of each word. Check that students are able to fill the chart in correctly. Complete pronunciations, parts of speech, and definitions are provided for you. Students are expected to provide only the definition.

Possible responses:

evidence *n.* (EHV uh dehns)
Meaning: facts or details that support a position or claim; proof
Related words: evident; evidently
Additional words related to the root *-vid-*: evidentiary, inevitable

credible *adj.* (KREHD uh buhl)
Meaning: believable; convincing
Related words: credit; credibly
Additional words related to the root *-cred-*: credibility, incredible, incredulous, credulity

valid *adj.* (VAL ihd)
Meaning: well-founded; sound; effective
Related words: validate; validity
Additional words related to the root *-val-*: value, validation, invalid

formulate *v.* (FOHR myoo layt)
Meaning: build; state definitely; develop
Related words: formula; formulaic
Additional words related to the root *-form-*: inform, formation

logical *adj.*(LOJ ih kuhl)
Meaning: based on reason or sound judgment
Related words: logic; logically
Additional words related to the root *-log-*: illogical, logician

PERSONALIZE FOR LEARNING

English Language Support

Cognates Many of the academic vocabulary words have Spanish cognates:

evidence – evidencia   valid – válido
formulate – formular   logical – lógico

Not all English learners will recognize and use these cognates automatically. Help students build their cognate awareness by pointing out that these cognates share the same root in both English and Spanish. **ALL LEVELS**

Purpose of the Launch Text

The Launch Text provides students with a common starting point to address the unit topic. After reading the Launch Text, all students will be able to participate in discussions about survival.

Lexile: 1070 The easier reading level of this selection makes it perfect to assign for homework. Students will need little or no support to understand it.

Additionally, "The Cost of Survival" provides a writing model for the Performance-Based Assessment students will complete at the end of the unit.

Launch Text: Argument Model

Remind students to determine the main point of the argument and how the author supports that point.

Have students pay attention to the structure of the text. They should note that the author's position is clearly stated in the opening paragraph—"The adventurer should be the one to foot the bill"—and that the following paragraphs provide details supporting that position. The concluding paragraph restates the author's position.

Encourage students to read this text on their own and annotate unfamiliar words and sections of text they think are particularly important.

AUDIO SUMMARIES

Audio summaries of "The Cost of Survival" are available online in both English and Spanish in the Interactive Teacher's Edition or Unit Resources. Assigning these summaries before students read the Launch Text may help them build additional background knowledge and set a context for their reading.

LAUNCH TEXT | ARGUMENT MODEL

This selection is an example of an **argumentative text,** a type of writing in which an author states and defends a position on a topic. This is the type of writing you will develop in the Performance-Based Assessment at the end of the unit.

As you read, look at the way the writer builds a case. Mark the text to help you answer this question: What is the writer's position and what evidence supports it?

The Cost of Survival

NOTES

1 Some people willingly put themselves in life-and-death situations. Mountain climbers and base jumpers knowingly face danger, and they usually walk away safely. However, when things don't turn out well, a lost climber or an injured base jumper may need help. The police, fire department, rescue workers, and medical teams do their best to save an adventurer's life. These efforts can cost a lot of money. The adventurer should be the one to foot the bill.

2 Two big news stories of 2014 involved rescue missions. In one, a family of four called for help when their child became ill. They were on a sailboat 900 miles off the coast of Mexico. Their rescue involved the U.S. Navy, the Coast Guard, and the California Air National Guard. In another news story, a caver in Germany was nearly 4,000 feet underground when he was hit by a falling rock. It took rescue teams 11 days to get him safely back to the surface.

SCAN FOR MULTIMEDIA

CROSS-CURRICULAR PERSPECTIVES

Math Challenge students to write math questions based on the numerical information in "The Cost of Survival." Possible questions might include:

What percentage of the national park rescues in 2012 were caused by risky decisions?

What was the average cost per mile for the rescue of the family in the sailboat?

Tell students that they must know how to answer any questions they write. Once students have vetted their own questions, have them exchange questions with a partner and challenge their partner to answer the questions correctly.

3 It is easy to argue that people should be stopped from putting themselves in danger. However, this would be impossible to enforce. Usually, when people need to be rescued, it is because something unexpected happened. In 2012, millions of people hiked, climbed, and boated in national parks, but only 2,876 needed help. More than 1,600 of those emergencies may have been caused by risky decisions. Someone has to pay for those rescues. The rescue of the family stranded at sea cost $663,000. That figure does not include pay for the rescue workers. Getting the caver safely to the surface involved 728 people.

4 Some people wind up in trouble because of bad luck, but others make dangerous choices. We need to treat these two groups differently. People who take extreme risks should pay for their rescue operation. Some states have passed laws to reflect this belief. In New Hampshire, for example, hikers who get lost or injured because of reckless behavior can be billed for rescue services.

5 Not everyone agrees that people should be responsible for the costs of their rescue. Howard Paul, a spokesman for the National Association for Search and Rescue, says, "We know that when people believe that they are going to receive a large bill for an SAR mission, they delay a call for help or they refuse to call for help." He can list many examples of people making their problems worse by not calling for help because they are worried about the cost. And a second lieutenant in the California Air National Guard who helped rescue the family at sea put it this way: "We're out there to save lives. You can't put a price on that."

6 However, arguments against charging for rescue miss an important point. Many rescue workers have lost their own lives saving others. In addition, the idea of holding people responsible is not to stop rescuing them. It's to discourage them from behaving in foolish and dangerous ways. That can only be a good thing!

7 In the end, taxpayers cover the cost of rescue for those who put themselves at risk. Maybe there are better uses for our money. ❧

NOTES

WORD NETWORK FOR SURVIVAL

Vocabulary A Word Network is a collection of words related to a topic. As you read the selections in this unit, identify interesting words related to the idea of survival and add them to your Word Network. For example, you might begin by adding words from the Launch Text, such as *danger, rescue,* and *risky*. Continue to add words as you complete this unit.

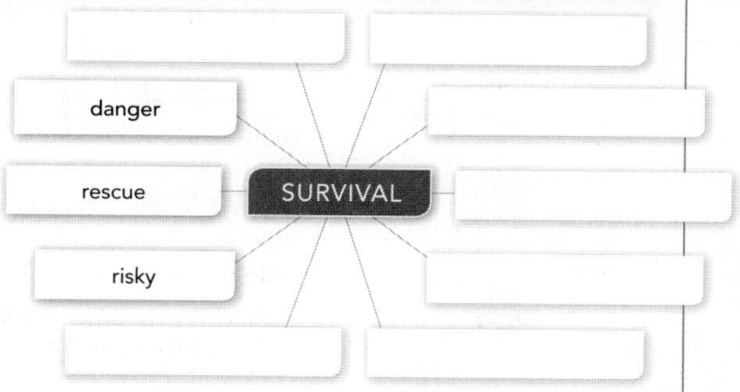

Tool Kit
Word Network Model

DIGITAL PERSPECTIVES

Word Network for Survival

Tell students that they can fill in the Word Network as they read the texts in the unit, or they can record the words elsewhere and add them later. Point out to students that people may have personal associations with some words. A word that one student thinks is related to the concept of survival might not be a word another student would pick. However, students should feel free to add any word they personally think is relevant to their Word Network. Each person's Word Network will be unique. If you choose to print the Word Network, distribute it to students at this point so they can use it throughout the rest of the unit.

AUTHOR'S PERSPECTIVE Elfrieda Hiebert, Ph.D.

Word Networks Vocabulary word networks enable students to learn a large number of words related to a particular concept. Using a word network helps to draw students' attention to words and helps students understand the essential attributes, qualities, or characteristics of a word's meaning. Generating vocabulary in this way can support reading, writing, and conversational skills. In reading and listening, word networks build students' appreciation of the subtleties of an author's word choice. In writing and speaking, they help students choose more precise words when they communicate. Making connections among the words (as opposed to teaching the words individually) allows students to approach new words with confidence and knowledge.

Word networks are different depending on the type of word they help capture. Maps for concepts that describe people and social situations are different from those that describe physical phenomena. In networks about social phenomena, students will find synonyms that help express the concept. For example, *sluggish* is related to *sulky*, *inert*, *soggy*, *torpid*, *slow*, and *dull*. However, these words have subtle differences and cannot necessarily be substituted for one another.

When exploring survival in this unit, students can identify and track a wide variety of words, each with its own connotation. For example, using the word *peril* instead of *danger* communicates a much more extreme situation. Engaging students in this generative approach to vocabulary will help them gain knowledge of a deep and varied body of words related to the topic.

INTRODUCTION

Summary

Have students read the introductory paragraph. Provide them with tips for writing a summary:

- Write in the present tense.
- Make sure to include the title of the work.
- Be concise: a summary should not be equal in length to the original text.
- If you need to quote the words of the author, use quotation marks.
- Don't put your own opinions, ideas, or interpretations into the summary. The purpose of writing a summary is to accurately represent what the author says, not to provide a critique.

If necessary, students can refer to the Tool Kit for help in understanding the elements of a good summary.

See a possible summary on the Student page.

Launch Activity

Explain to students that as they work on this unit, they will have many opportunities to discuss the topic of survival. Remind them that there is no right or wrong position, but they should be able to support their positions with evidence from the material they've viewed, read, and analyzed so far in the unit as well as their prior knowledge.

Encourage students to keep an open mind and listen to their classmates.

Summary

Write a summary of "The Cost of Survival." A **summary** is a concise, complete, and accurate overview of a text. It should not include a statement of your opinion or an analysis.

Possible response: In "The Cost of Survival," the author proposes that adventurers who willingly put themselves in danger should be responsible for the costs of being rescued.

Two well-known rescue missions that took place in 2014 each cost a great deal of money and required the use of multiple resources—all paid for by taxpayers.

Rescue missions fall into two groups. Some rescues occur because of misfortune. Others result from adventurers choosing to participate in dangerous activities or acting recklessly. People in the second group should be treated differently because they willingly put themselves at risk. Still, some rescuers do not agree, though many have lost their own lives rescuing adventurers.

Taxpayers pay for rescues, but this money could be spent more wisely.

Launch Activity

Conduct a Four-Corner Debate Consider this statement: **Adventurers should be held responsible for their rescue.**

- Record your position on the statement and explain your thinking.

  ☐ Strongly Agree ☐ Agree ☐ Disagree ☐ Strongly Disagree

  ____

  ____

- Form a group with like-minded students in one corner of the classroom. Discuss questions such as "What examples from the text or your own prior knowledge led you to take this position?"
- After your discussion, have a representative from each group present a two- to three-minute summary of the group's position.
- After all the groups have presented their views, move into the four corners again. If you change your corner, be ready to explain why.

VOCABULARY DEVELOPMENT

Academic Vocabulary Reinforcement Students will benefit from additional examples and practice with the academic vocabulary. Reinforce their comprehension with "show-you-know" sentences. The first part of the sentence uses the vocabulary word in an appropriate context. The second part of the sentence—the "show-you-know" part—clarifies the first. Model the strategy with this example for *evidence*:

The *evidence* presented in the trial was irrefutable; it proved that Samuel was out of town when the crime took place.

Then give students these sentence prompts and coach them in creating the clarification part:

1. Kawan's story was not *credible*; ____________

   Possible response: his version of what happened was not logical.
2. To rent a car you need a *valid* driver's license; ____________

   Possible response: you must prove that you can legally drive.
3. Brianna took some time to *formulate* her answer; ____________

   Possible response: she methodically included everything she knew on the topic.
4. His argument wasn't *logical*; ____________

   Possible response: his facts were contradictory.

QuickWrite

Consider class discussions, presentations, the video, and the Launch Text as you think about the prompt. Record your initial position here.

PROMPT: **Should people in life-or-death situations be held accountable for their actions?**

Possible response: I think that people who put themselves willingly in life-or-death situations should be held accountable for their actions. If you choose to swim with sharks, is it really their fault if they attack you? That's what sharks do.

As the author points out in "The Cost of Survival," when rescuers need to help those who have intentionally exposed themselves to danger, it is not only expensive, but these rescuers are placing themselves in harm's way. And, if rescuers are busy helping those who needlessly put themselves at risk, they might not be available to help those who are in danger through no fault of their own.

EVIDENCE LOG FOR SURVIVAL

Review your QuickWrite. Summarize your thoughts in one sentence to record in your Evidence Log. Then, record textual details or evidence from "The Cost of Survival" that support your thinking.

Prepare for the Performance-Based Assessment at the end of the unit by completing the Evidence Log after each selection.

Tool Kit
Evidence Log Model

Title of Text: ____________ Date: ______

CONNECTION TO PROMPT	TEXT EVIDENCE/DETAILS	ADDITIONAL NOTES/IDEAS

How does this text change or add to my thinking? Date: ______

DIGITAL PERSPECTIVES

QuickWrite

In this QuickWrite, students should present their own response to the prompt based on the material they have read and viewed in the Unit Overview and Introduction. This initial response will help inform their work when they complete the Performance-Based Assessment at the end of the unit. Students should make sure they present their position clearly and support it with well-reasoned evidence and accurate details.

See a possible QuickWrite on the Student page.

Evidence Log for Survival

Students should record their initial position in their Evidence Logs along with evidence from "The Cost of Survival" that supports this position.

If you choose to print the Evidence Log, distribute it to students at this point so they can use it throughout the rest of the unit.

Performance-Based Assessment: Refining Your Thinking

- Have students watch the video on Refining Your Thinking.
- A video on this topic is available online in the Professional Development Center.

OVERVIEW

WHOLE-CLASS LEARNING

What does it take to survive?

Engage students in a conversation about the universality of guilt. Point out that everyone feels guilty about something at one time or another. It could be canceling a date with a friend at the last minute or not doing well on a test. During Whole-Class Learning, students will read two selections about the guilt survivors sometimes feel and how it affects their lives.

Whole-Class Learning Strategies

Review the Learning Strategies with students and explain that as they work through Whole-Class Learning, they will develop strategies to work in large-group environments.

- Have students watch the video on Whole-Class Learning Strategies.
- A video on this topic is available online in the Professional Development Center.

You may wish to discuss some action items to add to the chart as a class before students complete it on their own. For example, for "Listen actively," you might solicit the following actions from students:

- If you don't understand someone's point, ask for clarification.
- Take notes to help retain information.

Block Scheduling

Each day in this Pacing Plan represents a 40–50 minute class period. Teachers using block scheduling may combine days to reflect their class schedule. In addition, teachers may revise pacing to differentiate and support core instruction by integrating components and resources as students require.

OVERVIEW: WHOLE-CLASS LEARNING

ESSENTIAL QUESTION:

What does it take to survive?

Everyone knows what it feels like to be ashamed to have done something—but why do people sometimes feel guilty for things they *didn't* do? Survivors' feelings can be complicated. You will work with your whole class to explore the concept of survival. The selections you are going to read present insights into some less-examined costs of survival.

Whole-Class Learning Strategies

Throughout your life, in school, in your community, and in your career, you will continue to learn and work in large-group environments.

Review these strategies and the actions you can take to practice them as you work with your whole class. Add ideas of your own for each step. Get ready to use these strategies during Whole-Class Learning.

STRATEGY	ACTION PLAN
Listen actively	• Eliminate distractions. For example, put your cell phone away. • Keep your eyes on the speaker. •
Clarify by asking questions	• If you're confused, other people probably are, too. Ask a question to help your whole class. • If you see that you are guessing, ask a question instead. •
Monitor understanding	• Notice what information you already know and be ready to build on it. • Ask for help if you are struggling. •
Interact and share ideas	• Share your ideas and answer questions, even if you are unsure. • Build on the ideas of others by adding details or making a connection. •

SCAN FOR MULTIMEDIA

Pacing Plan

Unit Introduction: 1

Introduce Whole-Class Learning: 2

The Seventh Man: 3, 4, 5, 6, 7

The Moral Logic of Survivor Guilt: 8, 9, 10, 11, 12

Media: The Key to Disaster Survival?: 13

Performance Task: 14, 15

WHOLE-CLASS LEARNING

DIGITAL PERSPECTIVES

CONTENTS

ANCHOR TEXT: SHORT STORY

The Seventh Man

Haruki Murakami

A man recalls a childhood tragedy that changed his life forever.

ANCHOR TEXT: EDITORIAL

The Moral Logic of Survivor Guilt

Nancy Sherman

Does it make sense to feel guilty that you survived when others didn't?

MEDIA: RADIO BROADCAST

The Key to Disaster Survival? Friends and Neighbors

Shankar Vedantam

Who is more helpful during and after a disaster: friends and family or emergency services?

PERFORMANCE TASK

WRITING FOCUS

Write an Argument

Both Whole-Class readings deal with the guilt that haunts people who have survived when others have died. The radio broadcast deals with finding help to survive a disaster. After reading and listening, you will write an argument on the topic of survivor guilt.

Contents

Anchor Texts Preview the anchor texts with students to generate interest. Encourage students to discuss other texts they have read or movies or television shows they have seen that deal with the issues of survival and survivor guilt.

You might wish to conduct a poll to determine which selection students think looks more interesting and discuss the reasons for their preference. Students can return to this poll after they have read both selections to see if their preference changed.

Performance Task

Write an Argument Explain to students that after they have finished reading the selections, they will write an argument about survivor guilt. To help them prepare, encourage students to think about the topic as they progress through both selections and as they participate in the Whole-Class Learning experience.

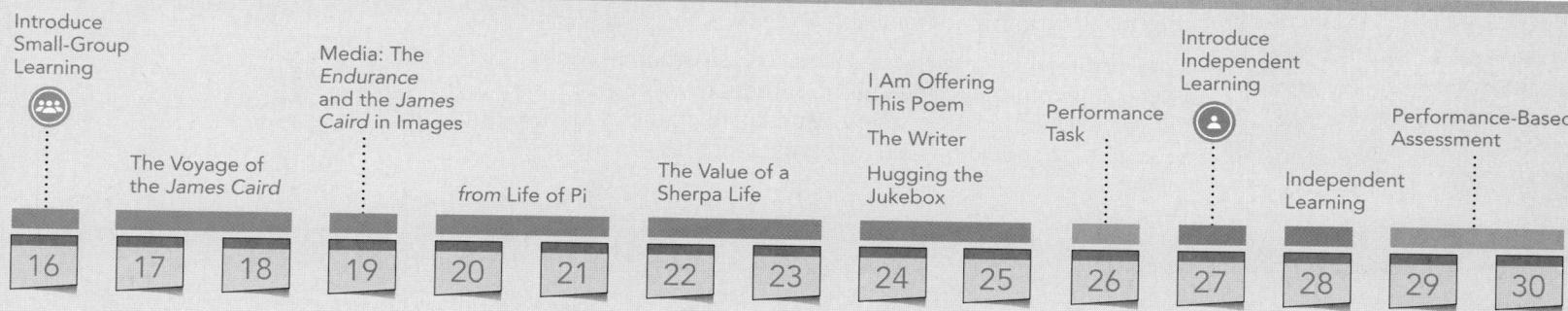

16 Introduce Small-Group Learning
17–18 The Voyage of the *James Caird*
19 Media: The *Endurance* and the *James Caird* in Images
20–21 *from* Life of Pi
22–23 The Value of a Sherpa Life
24–25 I Am Offering This Poem; The Writer; Hugging the Jukebox
26 Performance Task
27 Introduce Independent Learning
28 Independent Learning
29–30 Performance-Based Assessment

The Seventh Man

AUDIO SUMMARIES
Audio summaries of "The Seventh Man" are available online in both English and Spanish in the Interactive Teacher's Edition or Unit Resources. Assigning these summaries prior to reading the selection may help students build additional background knowledge and set a context for their first read.

Summary

In Haruki Murakami's "The Seventh Man," seven people tell stories on a stormy night. The seventh man tells the story of a great wave that devastated his life. He explains that as a child, he lived by the ocean in Japan. When he was ten years old, a typhoon hit his town. People stayed safely inside, but during the calm at the center of the storm, he and his best friend K. walked to the beach. As they looked around, he saw a great wave approaching. He called to K., but K. didn't hear. The seventh man ran for safety; K. was drowned. He could have reached K.—but could he have saved him, or would they both have died? For forty years, the seventh man is haunted by guilt and uncertainty—but then something makes him reconsider what he did, or failed to do, that day.

Insight

The choices survivors make are not always easy or clear. Reading "The Seventh Man" will help students begin their reflections on how complicated survival can be. Although a survivor may have escaped with his or her life, that life may never be the same.

Some students may find "The Seventh Man" disturbing. The realization that a childhood decision might color someone's whole life is sobering and may require support.

ESSENTIAL QUESTION:
What does it take to survive?

Connection to Essential Question

"The Seventh Man" provides an unusual perspective on the Essential Question, "What does it take to survive?" The main character physically survives a giant wave by reacting almost instinctively: Fear causes him to run away from the beach. However, the guilt that he feels about having left his best friend behind persists for years. The seventh man only truly begins to survive emotionally when he faces and overcomes his guilt.

WHOLE-CLASS LEARNING PERFORMANCE TASK
Should the seventh man forgive himself for his failure to save K.?

UNIT PERFORMANCE-BASED ASSESSMENT
Should people in life-or-death situations be held accountable for their actions?

Connection to Performance Tasks

Whole-Class Learning Performance Task In this Performance Task, students will consider the concept of survivor's guilt. "The Seventh Man" provides a literary perspective on the price survivors pay. Students will be combining this perspective with facts about survivor's guilt that they glean from further reading.

Unit Performance-Based Assessment This selection provides an interesting insight into the question students will respond to on the Performance-Based Assessment. Students should consider whether the seventh man should be held accountable for his actions.

DIGITAL PERSPECTIVES: Audio | Video | Document | Annotation Highlights | EL Highlights | Online Assessment

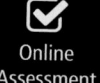

LESSON RESOURCES

	Making Meaning	Language Development	Effective Expression
Lesson	**First Read** **Close Read** **Analyze the Text** **Analyze Craft and Structure**	**Concept Vocabulary** **Word Study** **Conventions**	**Writing to Sources** **Speaking and Listening**
Instructional Standards	**RL.10** By the end of grade 9, read and comprehend literature . . . **RL.5** Analyze how an author's choices . . .	**L.1.b** Use various types of phrases and clauses . . . **L.4.b** Identify and correctly use patterns of word changes . . . **L.5.b** Analyze nuances in the meaning of words . . .	**W.1.a** Introduce precise claim(s) . . . **SL.4** Present information, findings, and supporting evidence . . .
STUDENT RESOURCES			
Available online in the Interactive Student Edition or Unit Resources	Selection Audio First-Read Guide: Fiction Close-Read Guide: Fiction	Word Network	Evidence Log
TEACHER RESOURCES			
Selection Resources Available online in the Interactive Teacher's Edition or Unit Resources	Audio Summaries Annotation Highlights EL Highlights Analyze Craft and Structure: Order of Events English Language Support Lesson: Order of Events	Concept Vocabulary and Word Study Conventions: Infinitives and Infinitive Phrases	Writing to Sources: Critical Review Speaking and Listening: Retelling
Reteach/Practice (RP) Available online in the Interactive Teacher's Edition or Unit Resources	Analyze Craft and Structure: Order of Events (RP)	Word Study: Latin Suffix *–tion* (RP) Conventions: Infinitives and Infinitive Phrases (RP)	Writing to Sources: Critical Review (RP) Speaking and Listening: Retelling (RP)
Assessment Available online in Assessments	Selection Test		
My Resources	A Unit 2 Answer Key is available online and in the Interactive Teacher's Edition		

Reading Support

Text Complexity Rubric: The Seventh Man	
Quantitative Measures	
Lexile: 910 Text Length: 5,860 words	
Qualitative Measures	
Knowledge Demands ① ❷ ③ ④ ⑤	The situations may be unfamiliar to some readers (experiencing a typhoon, tragedy of losing someone in a natural disaster), but the situations and emotions are clearly expressed.
Structure ① ❷ ③ ④ ⑤	Use of flashback, flash-forward (transitions from narration in third person and first person)
Language Conventionality and Clarity ① ② ❸ ④ ⑤	Figurative language; complex descriptions
Levels of Meaning/Purpose ① ② ❸ ④ ⑤	Multiple levels of meaning (events are described that also signify emotions of guilt or self-forgiveness); concepts and meanings are mostly explained and easy to grasp.

DECIDE AND PLAN

English Language Support

Provide English Learners with support for structure and language as they read the selection.

Structure If students have difficulty following the narration, draw their attention to the use of first person when the seventh man is speaking. This would be a good opportunity to review pronouns in first person *(I, me, my, mine)* and third person *(he/she, him/her, his/her, his/hers)*.

Language If students have difficulty with some of the complex or figurative language, have them break down the sentences into smaller chunks. Then have them highlight any words that are confusing because they are used figuratively; for example, *the wave swallowed everything . . . it swept it to another world.*

Strategic Support

Provide students with strategic support to ensure that they can successfully read the text.

Knowledge Demands Use the background information to discuss typhoons. Determine students' prior knowledge and experience with natural disasters. Provide additional background if needed.

Structure Discuss what it means to flash-back or flash-forward in a text. Point out that a story might switch back and forth to different time periods. If students continue to have difficulty with the time sequence, point out clues to transitions between past and present; for example, sentences that say that the man is telling a story, or use of first and third person. When students reread, have them note each transition from past to present.

Challenge

Provide students who need to be challenged with ideas for how they can go beyond a simple interpretation of the text.

Text Analysis Ask students to identify the use of first person when the seventh man is speaking, and descriptions in third person when the story moves to the present. Ask students to consider how the story would change if the author had told the man's story as a narrative in the third person. Would it be as effective? How does using first person give it more impact?

Written Response Ask students to speculate on what might have happened if the seventh man had made different choices in his life. Have them analyze each choice he made and determine how his life might have changed if he had chosen differently. Have them rewrite the story with these choices in mind.

TEACH

Read and Respond

Have the class do their first read of the selection. Then, have them complete their close read. Finally, work with them on the Making Meaning, Language Development, and Effective Expression activities.

Standards Support Through Teaching and Learning Cycle

IDENTIFY NEEDS

Analyze results of the Beginning-of-Year Assessment, focusing on the items relating to Unit 2. Also take into consideration student performance to this point and your observations of where particular students struggle.

DECIDE AND PLAN

- If students have performed poorly on items matching these standards, then provide selection scaffolds before assigning them the on-level lesson provided in the Student Edition.
- If students have done well on the Beginning-of-Year Assessment, then challenge them to keep progressing and learning by giving them opportunities to practice the skills in depth.
- Use the Selection Resources listed on the Planning pages for "The Seventh Man" to help students continually improve their ability to master the standards.

Instructional Standards: The Seventh Man

	Catching Up	This Year	Looking Forward
Reading	You may wish to administer the **Analyze Craft and Structure: Order of Events (RP)** worksheet to help students understand the basic sequence of a narrative.	**RL.5** Analyze how an author's choices concerning how to structure a text, order events within it, and manipulate time create such effects as mystery, tension, or surprise.	Have students recast the beginning of the story without the frame and analyze the impact on the story as a whole.
Writing	You may wish to administer the **Writing to Sources: Critical Review (RP)** worksheet to help students understand how to evaluate or critique a literary work.	**W.1.a** Introduce precise claim(s), distinguish the claim(s) from alternate or opposing claims, and create an organization that establishes clear relationships among claim(s), counterclaims, reasons, and evidence.	You may wish to challenge students to write a critical review of a text of their own choosing.
Speaking and Listening	You may wish to administer the **Speaking and Listening: Retelling (RP)** worksheet to help students understand how to plan and deliver a retelling.	**SL.4** Present information, findings, and supporting evidence clearly, concisely, and logically such that listeners can follow the line of reasoning and the organization, development, substance, and style are appropriate to purpose, audience, and task.	You may wish to challenge students to retell increasingly longer or more complex selections.
Language	You may wish to administer the **Conventions: Infinitives and Infinitive Phrases (RP)** worksheet to help students understand the function of infinitives and infinitive phrases.	**L.1.b** Use various types of phrases and clauses to convey specific meanings and add variety and interest to writing or presentations.	You may wish to challenge students to use increasingly complex phrases and clauses in their writing.
	Review context clues with students to ensure they understand that words can have different meanings in different contexts.	**L.4.b** Identify and correctly use patterns of word changes that indicate different meanings or parts of speech.	Have students analyze the subtleties and nuances of various word choices in different contexts.

ANALYZE AND REVISE

- Analyze student work for evidence of student learning.
- Identify whether or not students have met the expectations in the standards.
- Identify implications for future instruction.

TEACH

Implement the planned lesson, and gather evidence of student learning.

TEACHING

Jump Start

FIRST READ Prior to students' first read, engage them in a discussion about severe storms to help them make connections between the text and their own experiences.

The Seventh Man

Who is the seventh man? How does his story connect to the concept of survival? Should he forgive himself for his failure to save K.? Modeling the questions a reader might ask as they read "The Seventh Man" brings the text alive for students and connects it to the Performance Task question. Selection audio and print capability for the selection are available in the Interactive Teacher's Edition.

Concept Vocabulary

Support students as they rank their words. Ask if they've ever heard, read, or used them. Reassure them that the definitions for these words are listed in the selection.

FIRST READ

As they read, students should perform the steps of the first read:

NOTICE: You may want to encourage students to notice who the seventh man and K. are.

ANNOTATE: Remind students to mark passages they feel are particularly evocative or worthy of analysis in their close read. For example, students may want to focus on passages that have vivid figurative language or description.

CONNECT: Encourage students to make connections beyond the text. If they cannot make connections to their own lives or other texts, have them consider movies and TV shows as well.

RESPOND: Students will answer questions and write a summary to demonstrate understanding.

Point out to students that while they will always complete the Respond step at the end of the first read, the others steps will probably happen somewhat concurrently. You may wish to print copies of the **First-Read Guide: Fiction** for students to use.

Remind students that during their first read, they should not answer the close-read questions that appear in the selection.

MAKING MEANING

About the Author

In 1978, **Haruki Murakami** (b. 1949) was attending a baseball game in Japan where the American player Dave Hilton hit a double. In that moment, Murakami had a flash of inspiration during which he decided he could write a novel. He began writing that evening. Since then, his numerous novels and short stories have been translated more than the works of any other Japanese writer of his generation.

The Seventh Man

Concept Vocabulary

You will encounter the following words as you read "The Seventh Man." Before reading, note how familiar you are with each word. Then, rank the words in order from most familiar (1) to least familiar (6).

WORD	YOUR RANKING
desperate	
entranced	
hallucination	
premonition	
profound	
meditative	

After completing the first read, come back to the concept vocabulary and review your rankings. Mark changes to your original rankings as needed.

Tool Kit
First-Read Guide and Model Annotation

First Read FICTION

Apply these strategies as you conduct your first read. You will have an opportunity to complete the close-read notes after your first read.

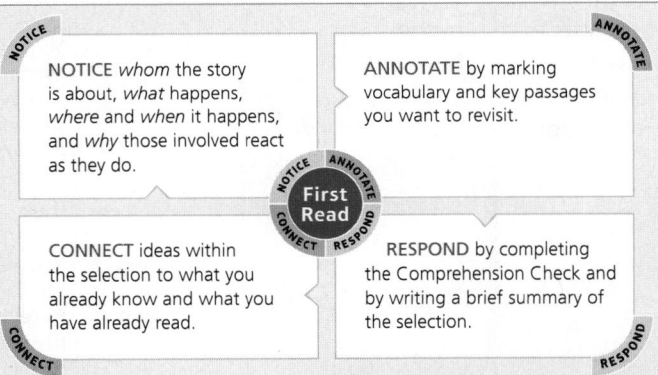

NOTICE *whom* the story is about, *what* happens, *where* and *when* it happens, and *why* those involved react as they do.

ANNOTATE by marking vocabulary and key passages you want to revisit.

CONNECT ideas within the selection to what you already know and what you have already read.

RESPOND by completing the Comprehension Check and by writing a brief summary of the selection.

First Read: NOTICE, ANNOTATE, CONNECT, RESPOND

STANDARDS
Reading Literature
By the end of grade 9, read and comprehend literature, including stories, dramas, and poems, in the grades 9–10 text complexity band proficiently, with scaffolding as needed at the high end of the range.

AUTHOR'S PERSPECTIVE **Kelly Gallagher, M.Ed.**

First Read Strategies As students encounter unfamiliar and challenging text for the first time, some may hit a frustration point early. Students often think that if they don't understand something on the first try, they'll never understand it. Comprehension when reading is not an all-or-nothing situation. Share these strategies for getting through the gray areas:

- ***Read on with Uncertainty*** Students who are "a little bit lost" may be able to read a little further to resolve confusion. Model this mindset with the opening paragraphs of a novel or long work. Read the text, and show students what questions you already have. Demonstrate that many questions arise at the beginning as readers place themselves in the world the writer has created. Good readers can live with this confusion because within a few paragraphs or pages, key ideas often become more clear.
- ***Monitor Comprehension*** To make their comprehension more concrete, have students use

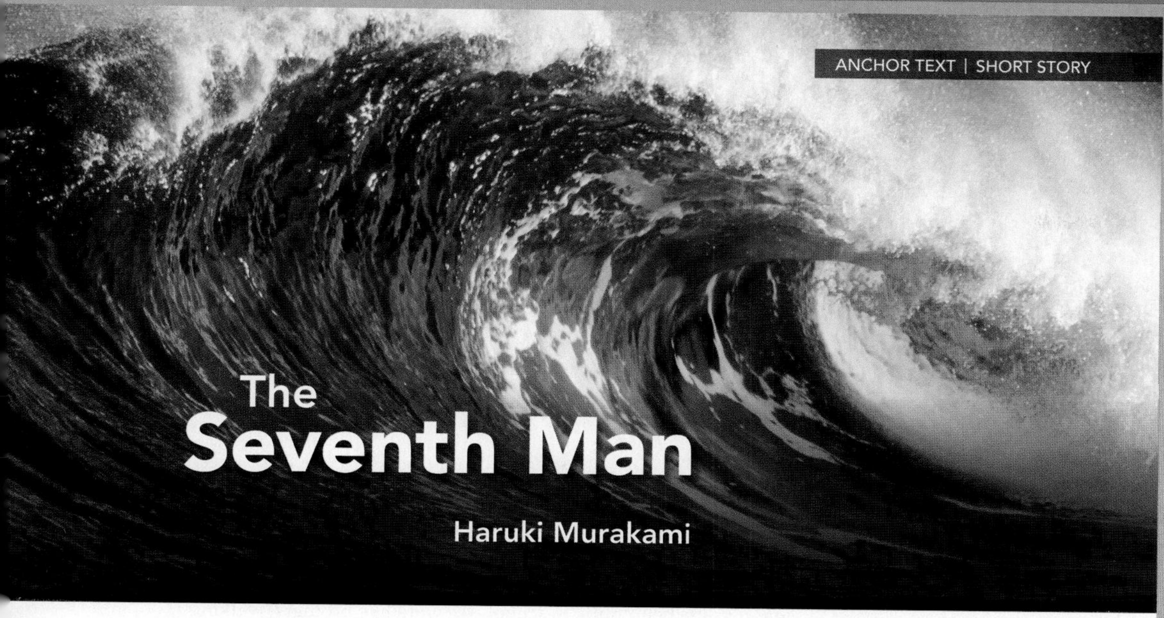

ANCHOR TEXT | SHORT STORY

The Seventh Man

Haruki Murakami

DIGITAL PERSPECTIVES

CLOSE READE

As students look for descriptive details, remind them to find the words that tell what something looks like, feels like, or sounds like. You may wish to model the close read using the following think-aloud format. Possible responses to questions on the Student page are included. You may also want to print copies of the **Close-Read Guide: Fiction** for students to use.

ANNOTATE: As I read paragraph 2, I notice and highlight the details that suggest to me that the story is set at night during a storm.

QUESTION: I know that the story is set during a storm late at night, sometime past ten o'clock, but none of the details tell me the actual place where the story is set. I also don't know the year in which the story takes place. Maybe I will learn these details later in the story.

CONCLUDE: These details make me feel frightened. After all, the trees are shaking, and the windows are rattling. I would describe the mood as ominous, gloomy, and scary.

BACKGROUND

Hurricanes that originate in the northwest Pacific Ocean are called typhoons. They can stretch up to 500 miles in diameter and produce high winds, heavy rains, enormous waves, and severe flooding. On average, Japan is hit by three severe typhoons each year due to its location and climatic conditions.

SCAN FOR MULTIMEDIA

1 "A huge wave nearly swept me away," said the seventh man, almost whispering. "It happened one September afternoon when I was ten years old."

2 The man was the last one to tell his story that night. The hands of the clock had moved past ten. The small group that huddled in a circle could hear the wind tearing through the darkness outside, heading west. It shook the trees, set the windows to rattling, and moved past the house with one final whistle.

3 "It was the biggest wave I had ever seen in my life," he said. "A strange wave. An absolute giant."

4 He paused.

5 "It just barely missed me, but in my place it swallowed everything that mattered most to me and swept it off to another world. I took years to find it again and to recover from the experience—precious years that can never be replaced."

6 The seventh man appeared to be in his mid-fifties. He was a thin man, tall, with a moustache, and next to his right eye he had a short but deep-looking scar that could have been made by the stab of a small blade. Stiff, bristly patches of white marked his short hair. His face had the look you see on people when they can't quite find the words they need. In his case, though, the expression seemed to have

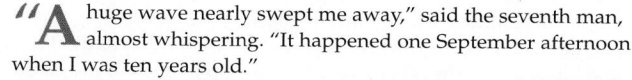

NOTES

CLOSE READ

ANNOTATE: Mark details in paragraph 2 that describe where the action takes place.

QUESTION: What can you tell about the story's setting?

What details about the setting are left unclear?

CONCLUDE: Describe the **mood**, or feeling, that the annotated details create.

two different colors to mark the text: one color for text they understand, and another color to highlight the text that is challenging to them. This will help pinpoint areas of confusion and show how much of the text they understand.

- ***Apply Fix-It Strategies*** Students who are struggling with comprehension may use fix-it strategies to start by rereading at the word level and decoding words they don't know. They can then move to the sentence level to make sure that they are following the text. When students have the tools to monitor their comprehension, they may feel more empowered to get through their first read. Once they can get past the literal interpretation of text, they can then move toward uncovering deeper meaning.

CLOSER LOOK

Analyze Character

Students may have marked paragraph 10 during their first read. Use this paragraph to help students understand the seventh man's relationship with K. Encourage them to talk about the annotations that they marked. You may want to model a close read with the class based on the highlights shown in the text.

ANNOTATE: Have students mark details in paragraph 10 that describe K.'s appearance and personality, or have students participate while you highlight them.

QUESTION: Guide students to consider what these details might tell them. Ask what a reader can infer from these descriptions about K.'s character, and accept student responses.

Possible response: K. is an artistic, sensitive boy who is often bullied because he is weak and has a speech impediment. Most people think that there is something wrong with him.

CONCLUDE: Help students to formulate conclusions about the importance of these details in the text. Ask students why the author might have included these details.

Possible responses: The descriptions explain why K. might need protection. They also explain why the seventh man likes and admires K. By adding these details, the author gives reasons why the seventh man makes himself responsible for K.'s safety.

Remind students that there are two types of characterization. In **direct characterization,** the author directly states a character's traits. In **indirect characterization,** an author provides clues about a character by describing the character's appearance, actions, and feelings, as well as how other characters react to him or her. With indirect characterization, the reader has to add up the details to draw conclusions about the character's personality.

Additional **English Language Support** is available in the Interactive Teacher's Edition.

NOTES

been there from long before, as though it were part of him. The man wore a simple blue shirt under a gray tweed coat, and every now and then he would bring his hand to his collar. None of those assembled there knew his name or what he did for a living.

7 He cleared his throat, and for a moment or two his words were lost in silence. The others waited for him to go on.

8 "In my case, it was a wave," he said. "There's no way for me to tell, of course, what it will be for each of you. But in my case it just happened to take the form of a gigantic wave. It presented itself to me all of a sudden one day, without warning. And it was devastating."

* * *

9 I grew up in a seaside town in the Province of S. It was such a small town, I doubt that any of you would recognize the name if I were to mention it. My father was the local doctor, and so I led a rather comfortable childhood. Ever since I could remember, my best friend was a boy I'll call K. His house was close to ours, and he was a grade behind me in school. We were like brothers, walking to and from school together, and always playing together when we got home. We never once fought during our long friendship. I did have a brother, six years older, but what with the age difference and differences in our personalities, we were never very close. My real brotherly affection went to my friend K.

10 K. was a frail, skinny little thing, with a pale complexion and a face almost pretty enough to be a girl's. He had some kind of speech impediment,[1] though, which might have made him seem retarded to anyone who didn't know him. And because he was so frail, I always played his protector, whether at school or at home. I was kind of big and athletic, and the other kids all looked up to me. But the main reason I enjoyed spending time with K. was that he was such a sweet, pure-hearted boy. He was not the least bit retarded, but because of his impediment, he didn't do too well at school. In most subjects, he could barely keep up. In art class, though, he was great. Just give him a pencil or paints and he would make pictures that were so full of life that even the teacher was amazed. He won prizes in one contest after another, and I'm sure he would have become a famous painter if he had continued with his art into adulthood. He liked to do seascapes. He'd go out to the shore for hours, painting. I would often sit beside him, watching the swift, precise movements of his brush, wondering how, in a few seconds, he could possibly create such lively shapes and colors where, until then, there had been only blank white paper. I realize now that it was a matter of pure talent.

11 One year, in September, a huge typhoon hit our area. The radio said it was going to be the worst in ten years. The schools were closed, and all

1. **speech impediment** (ihm PEHD uh muhnt) obstacle to speaking clearly, such as a lisp or stammer.

WriteNow Express and Reflect

Description The narrator's description of K. in paragraph 10 brings their friendship alive. Have students write a one-page description of someone close to them, reflecting on what that person means to them. Remind students to include details that reveal the person's personality, not just his or her appearance. Point out that the seventh man draws attention to K.'s physical attributes as well as his personality. Some of these details are positive, while others are somewhat negative. As a whole, they create a more complete picture of what K. was like.

Draw students' attention to the fact that the narrator describes his relationship with K. both overtly ("I played his protector") and implicitly (descriptions of K.'s art reveal the narrator's admiration). Students should convey their feelings for the person they are writing about in a similar manner.

DIGITAL PERSPECTIVES

the shops in town lowered their shutters in preparation for the storm. Starting early in the morning, my father and brother went around the house nailing shut all the storm-doors, while my mother spent the day in the kitchen cooking emergency provisions. We filled bottles and canteens with water, and packed our most important possessions in rucksacks[2] for possible evacuation. To the adults, typhoons were an annoyance and a threat they had to face almost annually, but to the kids, removed as we were from such practical concerns, it was just a great big circus, a wonderful source of excitement.

12 Just after noon the color of the sky began to change all of a sudden. There was something strange and unreal about it. I stayed outside on the porch, watching the sky, until the wind began to howl and the rain began to beat against the house with a weird dry sound, like handfuls of sand. Then we closed the last storm-door and gathered together in one room of the darkened house, listening to the radio. This particular storm did not have a great deal of rain, it said, but the winds were doing a lot of damage, blowing roofs off houses and capsizing ships. Many people had been killed or injured by flying debris. Over and over again, they warned people against leaving their homes. Every once in a while, the house would creak and shudder as if a huge hand were shaking it, and sometimes there would be a great crash of some heavy-sounding object against a storm-door. My father guessed that these were tiles blowing off the neighbors' houses. For lunch we ate the rice and omelettes my mother had cooked, waiting for the typhoon to blow past.

13 But the typhoon gave no sign of blowing past. The radio said it had lost momentum[3] almost as soon as it came ashore at S. Province, and now it was moving north-east at the pace of a slow runner. The wind kept up its savage howling as it tried to uproot everything that stood on land.

14 Perhaps an hour had gone by with the wind at its worst like this when a hush fell over everything. All of a sudden it was so quiet, we could hear a bird crying in the distance. My father opened the storm-door a crack and looked outside. The wind had stopped, and the rain had ceased to fall. Thick, gray clouds edged across the sky, and patches of blue showed here and there. The trees in the yard were still dripping their heavy burden of rainwater.

15 "We're in the eye of the storm," my father told me. "It'll stay quiet like this for a while, maybe fifteen, twenty minutes, kind of like an intermission. Then the wind'll come back the way it was before."

16 I asked him if I could go outside. He said I could walk around a little if I didn't go far. "But I want you to come right back here at the first sign of wind."

17 I went out and started to explore. It was hard to believe that a wild storm had been blowing there until a few minutes before. I looked

2. **rucksacks** *n.* knapsacks.
3. **momentum** *n.* force or speed of movement.

NOTES

CLOSE READ

ANNOTATE: In paragraph 12, annotate at least four vivid details about the storm. Underline those that compare one thing to another.

QUESTION: What is being compared? What picture does each detail create in the reader's mind?

CONCLUDE: How do these descriptions help you visualize the typhoon?

CLOSE READ

Remind students that vivid details tap into some or all of the five senses: sound, sight, touch, taste, and smell. As a result, vivid details make the setting, characters, and action come alive. You may wish to model the close read using the following think-aloud format. Possible responses to questions on the Student page are included.

ANNOTATE: As I read paragraph 12, I notice and highlight phrases that describe the storm and appeal to the sense of sound. Then I find details that appeal to the sense of sight.

QUESTION: I see that the sound of rain beating against the house is compared to handfuls of sand, and that the creak and shudder of the house are compared with the motion of a huge hand. Based on these details, I imagine a monster trying to get into the house.

CONCLUDE: I can infer from these descriptions that the typhoon is extremely dangerous. I think that this fierce storm foreshadows—or hints—that something bad is going to happen in the story.

PERSONALIZE FOR LEARNING

English Language Support

Idioms Explain to students that *eye of the storm* in paragraph 15 is an idiomatic expression—the words used are not meant literally. If students struggle to understand idioms, encourage them to look for context clues. Instruct students to keep reading to get clues about the meaning of this expression (*No such "eye" existed, of course: we were just in that momentary quiet spot at the center of the pool of whirling air*). Make sure students understand that *eye of the storm* means "a calm in the middle of a turbulent situation." **ALL LEVELS**

NOTES

up at the sky. The storm's great "eye" seemed to be up there, fixing its cold stare on all of us below. No such "eye" existed, of course: we were just in that momentary quiet spot at the center of the pool of whirling air.

18 While the grown-ups checked for damage to the house, I went down to the beach. The road was littered with broken tree branches, some of them thick pine boughs that would have been too heavy for an adult to lift alone. There were shattered roof tiles everywhere, cars with cracked windshields, and even a doghouse that had tumbled into the middle of the street. A big hand might have swung down from the sky and flattened everything in its path.

19 K. saw me walking down the road and came outside.

20 "Where are you going?" he asked.

21 "Just down to look at the beach," I said.

22 Without a word, he came along with me. He had a little white dog that followed after us.

23 "The minute we get any wind, though, we're going straight back home," I said, and K. gave me a silent nod.

24 The shore was a 200-yard walk from my house. It was lined with a concrete breakwater—a big dyke[4] that stood as high as I was tall in those days. We had to climb a short flight of steps to reach the water's edge. This was where we came to play almost every day, so there was no part of it we didn't know well. In the eye of the typhoon, though, it all looked different: the color of the sky and of the sea, the sound of the waves, the smell of the tide, the whole expanse of the shore. We sat atop the breakwater for a time, taking in the view without a word to each other. We were supposedly in the middle of a great typhoon, and yet the waves were strangely hushed. And the point where they washed against the beach was much farther away than usual, even at low tide. The white sand stretched out before us as far as we could see. The whole, huge space felt like a room without furniture, except for the band of flotsam[5] that lined the beach.

25 We stepped down to the other side of the breakwater and walked along the broad beach, examining the things that had come to rest there. Plastic toys, sandals, chunks of wood that had probably once been parts of furniture, pieces of clothing, unusual bottles, broken crates with foreign writing on them, and other, less recognizable items: it was like a big candy store. The storm must have carried these things from very far away. Whenever something unusual caught our attention, we would pick it up and look at it every which way, and when we were done, K.'s dog would come over and give it a good sniff.

26 We couldn't have been doing this more than five minutes when I realized that the waves had come up right next to me. Without any sound or other warning, the sea had suddenly stretched its long,

4. **dyke** (dyk) *n.* barrier built along the edge of a body of water to prevent flooding.
5. **flotsam** (FLOT suhm) *n.* refuse or debris from a ship.

DIGITAL PERSPECTIVES

Illuminating the Text Some students may not be familiar with the words *breakwater* or *flotsam* used in paragraph 24. To help them visualize these key parts of the scene, find images of concrete breakwaters and flotsam online, and project them for students. Remind them that breakwaters are barriers that help protect land from waves, but they can be breached by a powerful storm like a typhoon that generates damaging winds and waves. Flotsam is debris that can include a wide variety of items. After students have examined the images, have them discuss how their ability to visualize the scene has changed. Additionally, have students consider what the images and descriptions in the story suggest about the force of a typhoon. **(Research to Clarify)**

NOTES

smooth tongue out to where I stood on the beach. I had never seen anything like it before. Child though I was, I had grown up on the shore and knew how frightening the ocean could be—the savagery with which it could strike unannounced.

27 And so I had taken care to keep well back from the waterline. In spite of that, the waves had slid up to within inches of where I stood. And then, just as soundlessly, the water drew back—and stayed back. The waves that had approached me were as unthreatening as waves can be—a gentle washing of the sandy beach. But something ominous about them—something like the touch of a reptile's skin—had sent a chill down my spine. My fear was totally groundless—and totally real. I knew instinctively that they were alive. The waves were alive. They knew I was here and they were planning to grab me. I felt as if some huge, man-eating beast were lying somewhere on a grassy plain, dreaming of the moment it would pounce and tear me to pieces with its sharp teeth. I had to run away.

28 "I'm getting out of here!" I yelled to K. He was maybe ten yards down the beach, squatting with his back to me, and looking at something. I was sure I had yelled loud enough, but my voice did not seem to have reached him. He might have been so absorbed in whatever it was he had found that my call made no impression on him. K. was like that. He would get involved with things to the point of forgetting everything else. Or possibly I had not yelled as loudly as I had thought. I do recall that my voice sounded strange to me, as though it belonged to someone else.

29 Then I heard a deep rumbling sound. It seemed to shake the earth. Actually, before I heard the rumble I heard another sound, a weird gurgling as though a lot of water was surging up through a hole

CLOSE READ

ANNOTATE: In paragraph 27, mark how the author divides sentences 3, 4, 5, and 6 into parts.

QUESTION: Why do you think the author uses dashes? What patterns does this punctuation create?

CONCLUDE: What is the effect of dividing these sentences in this way?

CLOSE READ

Remind students to focus on the punctuation marks that appear within several of the sentences in paragraph 27. Explain that these punctuation marks divide the sentences into parts, and have students think about why the author chose to include them. You may wish to model the Close Read using the following think-aloud format. Possible responses to questions on the Student page are included.

ANNOTATE: As I read paragraph 27, I notice and mark the dashes that the author uses in sentences 3, 4, 5, and 6. These dashes divide the sentences into parts.

QUESTION: The dashes allow the author to highlight a part of a sentence, to add important descriptive details, and to help create a mood. The use of dashes in consecutive sentences creates a stop-and-start pattern that reflects the tense mood: There is hesitation, uncertainty, and fear as the tension builds.

CONCLUDE: From his use of dashes, I can conclude that the author is trying to build the drama and tension in this important scene. The breaks in the sentences are meant to reflect the author's scattered, confused, and fearful thinking.

PERSONALIZE FOR LEARNING

English Language Support

Figurative Language Note this sentence in paragraph 26: *Without any sound or other warning, the sea had suddenly stretched its long, smooth tongue out to where I stood on the beach.* Explain to students that this sentence contains an example of **personification**, a type of figurative language in which a nonhuman subject is given human characteristics. The author is giving the sea human qualities (stretching out a tongue). Make sure students understand that the *tongue* refers to the wave and that the author is comparing the wave to a huge animal that has a long tongue.

Ask students why they think the author chose to use personification to describe the wave. (Possible response: *The use of personification creates a mental image that expresses a feeling of danger and terror.*) **ALL LEVELS**

CLOSE READ

Analyze Motivation

Remind students to focus on the author's word choice. This will help students to tell the difference between what the narrator thinks he should do and what he actually does. You may wish to model the Close Read using the following think-aloud format. Possible responses to questions on the Student page are included.

ANNOTATE: As I read paragraph 30, I notice and mark what the narrator thought and what he actually did. The phrase "I told myself" indicates that the narrator is thinking something. The phrase "I found myself running" tells what the narrator is actually doing.

QUESTION: I notice that the narrator's thoughts and actions don't match. He knows that he should run over and save his friend, but fear and the desire to stay alive motivate him to run away.

CONCLUDE: From the details that the author provides, I can conclude that the narrator is conflicted. He thinks one thing, but he does something else.

NOTES

CLOSE READ

ANNOTATE: In paragraph 30, mark thoughts the narrator had. Then, mark actions the narrator actually took.

QUESTION: What do you notice about the thoughts and the actions?

CONCLUSION: What do these details reveal about the narrator's character?

desperate (DEHS puhr iht) *adj.* involving extreme danger or disaster

in the ground. It continued for a while, then stopped, after which I heard the strange rumbling. Even that was not enough to make K. look up. He was still squatting, looking down at something at his feet, in deep concentration. He probably did not hear the rumbling. How he could have missed such an earth-shaking sound, I don't know. This may seem odd, but it might have been a sound that only I could hear—some special kind of sound. Not even K.'s dog seemed to notice it, and you know how sensitive dogs are to sound.

30 I told myself to run over to K., grab hold of him, and get out of there. It was the only thing to do. I *knew* that the wave was coming, and K. didn't know. As clearly as I knew what I ought to be doing, I found myself running the other way—running full speed towards the dyke, alone. What made me do this, I'm sure, was fear, a fear so overpowering it took my voice away and set my legs to running on their own. I ran stumbling along the soft sand beach to the breakwater, where I turned and shouted to K.

31 "Hurry, K.! Get out of there! The wave is coming!" This time my voice worked fine. The rumbling had stopped, I realized, and now, finally, K. heard my shouting and looked up. But it was too late. A wave like a huge snake with its head held high, poised to strike, was racing towards the shore. I had never seen anything like it in my life. It had to be as tall as a three-story building. Soundlessly (in my memory, at least, the image is soundless), it rose up behind K. to block out the sky. K. looked at me for a few seconds, uncomprehending. Then, as if sensing something, he turned towards the wave. He tried to run, but now there was no time to run. In the next instant, the wave had swallowed him.

32 The wave crashed on to the beach, shattering into a million leaping waves that flew through the air and plunged over the dyke where I stood. I was able to dodge its impact by ducking behind the breakwater. The spray wet my clothes, nothing more. I scrambled back up on to the wall and scanned the shore. By then the wave had turned and, with a wild cry, it was rushing back out to sea. It looked like part of a gigantic rug that had been yanked by someone at the other end of the earth. Nowhere on the shore could I find any trace of K., or of his dog. There was only the empty beach. The receding wave had now pulled so much water out from the shore that it seemed to expose the entire ocean bottom. I stood alone on the breakwater, frozen in place.

33 The silence came over everything again—a **desperate** silence, as though sound itself had been ripped from the earth. The wave had swallowed K. and disappeared into the far distance. I stood there, wondering what to do. Should I go down to the beach? K. might be down there somewhere, buried in the sand . . . But I decided not to leave the dyke. I knew from experience that big waves often came in twos and threes.

34 I'm not sure how much time went by–maybe ten or twenty seconds of eerie emptiness–when, just as I had guessed, the next wave came. Another gigantic roar shook the beach, and again, after

DIGITAL PERSPECTIVES

Illuminating the Text To help students grasp the power and violence of waves like the ones described in paragraph 32, use the search term "typhoon waves" to find video footage online showing the roar of giant waves crashing. Have students discuss how seeing and hearing these waves help illuminate the author's use of figurative language.

Then, have students write a paragraph explaining how the video footage helps clarify one example of the figurative language in the story, such as the following:

- *It looked like part of a gigantic rug that had been yanked by someone at the other end of the earth.*
- *Another gigantic roar shook the beach, and...another huge wave raised its head to strike. It towered before me, blocking out the sky, like a deadly cliff.* **(Research to Clarify)**

the sound had faded, another huge wave raised its head to strike. It towered before me, blocking out the sky, like a deadly cliff. This time, though, I didn't run. I stood rooted to the sea wall, **entranced**, waiting for it to attack. What good would it do to run, I thought, now that K. had been taken? Or perhaps I simply froze, overcome with fear. I can't be sure what it was that kept me standing there.

35 The second wave was just as big as the first—maybe even bigger. From far above my head it began to fall, losing its shape, like a brick wall slowly crumbling. It was so huge that it no longer looked like a real wave. It was like something from another, far-off world, that just happened to assume the shape of a wave. I readied myself for the moment the darkness would take me. I didn't even close my eyes. I remember hearing my heart pound with incredible clarity.

36 The moment the wave came before me, however, it stopped. All at once it seemed to run out of energy, to lose its forward motion and simply hover there, in space, crumbling in stillness. And in its crest,[6] inside its cruel, transparent tongue, what I saw was K.

37 Some of you may find this impossible to believe, and if so, I don't blame you. I myself have trouble accepting it even now. I can't explain what I saw any better than you can, but I know it was no illusion, no **hallucination**. I am telling you as honestly as I can what happened at that moment—what really happened. In the tip of the wave, as if enclosed in some kind of transparent capsule, floated K.'s body, reclining on its side. But that is not all. K. was looking straight at me, smiling. There, right in front of me, so close that I could have reached out and touched him, was my friend, my friend K. who, only moments before, had been swallowed by the wave. And he was smiling at me. Not with an ordinary smile—it was a big, wide-open grin that literally stretched from ear to ear. His cold, frozen eyes were locked on mine. He was no longer the K. I knew. And his right arm was stretched out in my direction, as if he were trying to grab my hand and pull me into that other world where he was now. A little closer, and his hand would have caught mine. But, having missed, K. then smiled at me one more time, his grin wider than ever.

38 I seem to have lost consciousness at that point. The next thing I knew, I was in bed in my father's clinic. As soon as I awoke the nurse went to call my father, who came running. He took my pulse, studied my pupils, and put his hand on my forehead. I tried to move my arm, but I couldn't lift it. I was burning with fever, and my mind was clouded. I had been wrestling with a high fever for some time, apparently. "You've been asleep for three days," my father said to me. A neighbor who had seen the whole thing had picked me up and carried me home. They had not been able to find K. I wanted to say something to my father. I *had* to say something to him. But my numb and swollen tongue could not form words. I felt as if some kind of creature had taken up residence in my mouth. My father asked me

6. **crest** *n.* top of a wave.

NOTES

entranced (ehn TRANST) *adj.* in a state of wonder or amazement

hallucination (huh loo suh NAY shuhn) *n.* something perceived that has no reality

DIGITAL PERSPECTIVES

CLOSER LOOK

Analyze First-Person Narrative

Students may have marked paragraph 37 during their first. Encourage them to talk about the annotations that they marked. You may want to model a close read with the class based on the highlights shown in the text.

ANNOTATE: Have students mark details in the paragraph that demonstrate that events are being described as they were perceived by the narrator, or have students participate while you highlight them.

QUESTION: Guide students to consider what these details might tell them. Ask what a reader can infer from these details of the seventh man's first-person narrative, and accept student responses.

Possible responses: The seventh man realizes that parts of his story might seem unbelievable, but he is telling the truth as he remembers it.

CONCLUDE: Help students to formulate conclusions about the importance of these details in the text. Ask students why the author might have included these details.

Possible responses: These details of the seventh man's narrative demonstrate his determination to be believed, even though he admits he can hardly believe what he saw. By adding these details, the author demonstrates that the seventh man is not necessarily a reliable narrator.

Explain that first-person narrators are characters in their own stories. Authors often use the first person to create a version of events that is only as reliable as the narrator's memory—or as questionable as his or her grasp of what was happening at the time. A first-person narrative might not convey an accurate account of events, but it can reveal important truths about the narrator.

PERSONALIZE FOR LEARNING

Strategic Support

Plot Was K. really in the wave as described in paragraph 37? Are the seventh man's memories reliable? To help students probe this issue, form small groups, and have them create a chart in which they list the evidence on each side and then evaluate the results:

Evidence that K. was in the wave	Evidence that K. was not in the wave	Conclusion
• "K. was looking straight at me...." • "His cold, frozen eyes were locked on mine." • "His right arm was stretched out in my direction...."	• "And he was smiling at me." • "I myself have trouble accepting it even now."	It is not likely that a body would be visible in the water at all, especially given the magnitude of the wave.

CLOSER LOOK

Infer Characters' Attitudes

Students may have marked paragraph 41 during their first read. Use this paragraph to show that other characters don't hold the seventh man responsible for K.'s death. Encourage them to talk about the annotations that they marked. You may want to model a close read with the class based on the highlights shown in the text.

ANNOTATE: Have students mark details in the paragraph that demonstrate contradictory attitudes about who is responsible for K.'s death, or have students participate while you highlight them.

QUESTION: Guide students to consider what these details might tell them. Ask what a reader can infer from these characters' attitudes, and accept student responses.

Possible responses: K.'s parents don't blame the seventh man because they know he loved and protected their son and must therefore believe he would have done everything possible to save him. The seventh man's parents don't hold him responsible because they love him and therefore believe the best of him. Everyone else is silent on the subject because they don't know what happened. The seventh man blames himself because he believes that he alone knows the truth.

CONCLUDE: Help students to formulate conclusions about the importance of these details in the text. Ask students why the author might have included these details.

Possible responses: Other characters' attitudes are important because they create a context within which readers may judge for themselves. By adding these details, the author shows how other characters' attitudes have no effect on the seventh man's sense of guilt. They may, however, have an effect on readers' attitudes.

Remind students that authors often compare and contrast characters' attitudes in their narratives to create a sense of moral debate. In first-person narratives, other characters' attitudes are vital because they provide alternatives to the narrator's own attitudes, which otherwise dominate this form of storytelling.

NOTES

to tell him my name, but before I could remember what it was, I lost consciousness again, sinking into darkness.

39 Altogether, I stayed in bed for a week on a liquid diet. I vomited several times, and had bouts of delirium. My father told me afterwards that I was so bad that he had been afraid I might suffer permanent neurological[7] damage from the shock and high fever. One way or another, though, I managed to recover—physically, at least. But my life would never be the same again.

40 They never found K.'s body. They never found his dog, either. Usually when someone drowned in that area, the body would wash up a few days later on the shore of a small inlet to the east. K.'s body never did. The big waves probably carried it far out to sea—too far for it to reach the shore. It must have sunk to the ocean bottom to be eaten by the fish. The search went on for a very long time, thanks to the cooperation of the local fishermen, but eventually it petered out.[8] Without a body, there was never any funeral. Half crazed, K.'s parents would wander up and down the beach every day, or they would shut themselves up at home, chanting sutras.[9]

41 As great a blow as this had been for them, though, K.'s parents never chided me for having taken their son down to the shore in the midst of a typhoon. They knew how I had always loved and protected K. as if he had been my own little brother. My parents, too, made a point of never mentioning the incident in my presence. But I knew the truth. I knew that I could have saved K. if I had tried. I probably could have run over and dragged him out of the reach of the wave. It would have been close, but as I went over the timing of the events in memory, it always seemed to me that I could have made it. As I said before, though, overcome with fear, I abandoned him there and saved only myself. It pained me all the more that K.'s parents failed to blame me and that everyone else was so careful never to say anything to me about what had happened. It took me a long time to recover from the emotional shock. I stayed away from school for weeks. I hardly ate a thing, and spent each day in bed, staring at the ceiling.

42 K. was always there, lying in the wave tip, grinning at me, his hand outstretched, beckoning. I couldn't get that picture out of my mind. And when I managed to sleep, it was there in my dreams—except that, in my dreams, K. would hop out of his capsule in the wave and grab my wrist to drag me back inside with him.

43 And then there was another dream I had. I'm swimming in the ocean. It's a beautiful summer afternoon, and I'm doing an easy breaststroke far from shore. The sun is beating down on my back, and the water feels good. Then, all of a sudden, someone grabs my right leg. I feel an ice-cold grip on my ankle. It's strong, too strong to shake off. I'm being dragged down under the surface. I see K.'s face there.

7. **neurological** (nur uh LOJ uh kuhl) *adj.* relating to the nervous system.
8. **petered out** came to an end.
9. **sutras** (SOO truhz) *n.* short religious texts meant to be chanted.

CROSS-CURRICULAR PERSPECTIVES

Science The seventh man mentions in paragraphs 42 and 43 that after K. was swept away by the wave, he had recurring nightmares about the event that involved K. dragging him into the wave or pulling him underwater. Nightmares can be common after an event that causes anxiety and trauma. Have students conduct research about recurring nightmares and create a bulleted list addressing the following questions:

- What is the difference between nightmares and recurring nightmares?
- What causes recurring nightmares?
- What treatment exists for recurring nightmares?
- What might the seventh man have been able to do to resolve his nightmares?

Have volunteers share their responses with the class.

He has the same huge grin, split from ear to ear, his eyes locked on mine. I try to scream, but my voice will not come. I swallow water, and my lungs start to fill.

44 I wake up in the darkness, screaming, breathless, drenched in sweat.

45 At the end of the year I pleaded with my parents to let me move to another town. I couldn't go on living in sight of the beach where K. had been swept away, and my nightmares wouldn't stop. If I didn't get out of there, I'd go crazy. My parents understood and made arrangements for me to live elsewhere. I moved to Nagano Province in January to live with my father's family in a mountain village near Komoro.[10] I finished elementary school in Nagano and stayed on through junior and senior high school there. I never went home, even for holidays. My parents came to visit me now and then.

46 I live in Nagano to this day. I graduated from a college of engineering in the City of Nagano and went to work for a precision toolmaker in the area. I still work for them. I live like anybody else. As you can see, there's nothing unusual about me. I'm not very sociable, but I have a few friends I go mountain climbing with. Once I got away from my home town, I stopped having nightmares all the time. They remained a part of my life, though. They would come to me now and then, like debt collectors at the door. It happened whenever I was on the verge of forgetting. And it was always the same dream, down to the smallest detail. I would wake up screaming, my sheets soaked with sweat.

47 That is probably why I never married. I didn't want to wake someone sleeping next to me with my screams in the middle of the night. I've been in love with several women over the years, but I never spent a night with any of them. The terror was in my bones. It was something I could never share with another person.

48 I stayed away from my home town for over forty years. I never went near that seashore—or any other. I was afraid that if I did, my dream might happen in reality. I had always enjoyed swimming, but after that day I never even went to swim in a pool. I wouldn't go near deep rivers or lakes. I avoided boats and wouldn't take a plane to go abroad. Despite all these precautions, I couldn't get rid of the image of myself drowning. Like K.'s cold hand, this dark **premonition** caught hold of my mind and refused to let go.

49 Then, last spring, I finally revisited the beach where K. had been taken by the wave.

50 My father had died of cancer the year before, and my brother had sold the old house. In going through the storage shed, he had found a cardboard carton crammed with childhood things of mine, which he sent to me in Nagano. Most of it was useless junk, but there was one bundle of pictures that K. had painted and given to me. My parents had probably put them away for me as a keepsake of K., but

10. **Nagano Province . . . village near Komoro** northwestern area of Japan and a town in that area.

NOTES

CLOSE READ
ANNOTATE: In paragraphs 45 and 46, mark verbs that reveal the time frame.

QUESTION: Why has the writer switched from past tense verbs in paragraph 45 to present tense verbs in paragraph 46?

CONCLUDE: What shift in the story's time frame is revealed through the use of verbs?

premonition (prehm uh NIHSH uhn) *n.* feeling that something bad will happen

DIGITAL PERSPECTIVES

CLOSE READ

Remind students to focus on past-tense verbs and present-tense verbs and how the author uses them to reveal the time frame. You may wish to model the Close Read using the following think-aloud format. Possible responses to questions on the student page are included.

ANNOTATE: As I read paragraphs 45 and 46, I notice and mark the verbs that reveal the time frame. One clue to identifying past-tense verbs is that many of them end in *-ed.*

QUESTION: The author has switched from past-tense verbs in paragraph 45 to present-tense verbs in paragraph 46 to show that the time period has changed.

CONCLUDE: The shift in the story's time frame is from childhood to adulthood. In paragraph 45, the narrator is describing the past—a period in his childhood. In paragraph 46, the narrator is speaking in the present—he is an adult at this point.

PERSONALIZE FOR LEARNING

Strategic Support

Plot Explain to students that the turning point in the story occurs in paragraph 49 when the seventh man says, "Then, last spring, I finally revisited the beach where K. had been taken by the wave." If students have difficulty understanding why the seventh man made this decision, have them find the details that lead up to it. These details include the fact that his father had died, and his brother had sold the house and sent him a box that contained some pictures that K. had painted. Invite students to debate whether or not they think the seventh man made the right decision to revisit the beach.

CLOSER LOOK

Analyze Ephiphany

Students may have marked paragraph 51 during their first read. Use this paragraph to help students understand the sudden insight the seventh man has. Encourage them to talk about the annotations that they marked. You may want to model a close read with the class based on the highlights shown in the text.

ANNOTATE: Have students mark details in paragraph 51 that contribute to the narrator's epiphany, or have students participate while you highlight them.

QUESTION: Guide students to consider what these details might tell them. Ask what a reader can infer from these details about the narrator's response to the pictures, and accept student responses.

Possible responses: The author is reminded of landscapes and scenes from childhood and of how skilled K. was at portraying them. He remembers so vividly the times they shared that he realizes that he is seeing everything through K.'s eyes.

CONCLUDE: Help students to formulate conclusions about the importance of these details in the text. Ask students why the author might have included these details.

Possible response: This insight might free the seventh man from the guilt that has constrained him his entire life. Perhaps he will be able to lead a normal life, interact with people more fully, and finally be happy. Explain to students that narratives often contain an **epiphany**, a sudden flash of insight into a conflict or situation. These insights are usually sudden and dramatic and often affect the plot arc.

NOTES

the pictures did nothing but reawaken the old terror. They made me feel as if K.'s spirit would spring back to life from them, and so I quickly returned them to their paper wrapping, intending to throw them away. I couldn't make myself do it, though. After several days of indecision, I opened the bundle again and forced myself to take a long, hard look at K.'s watercolors.

51 Most of them were landscapes, pictures of the familiar stretch of ocean and sand beach and pine woods and the town, and all done with that special clarity and coloration I knew so well from K.'s hand. They were still amazingly vivid despite the years, and had been executed with even greater skill than I recalled. As I leafed through the bundle, I found myself steeped in warm memories. The deep feelings of the boy K. were there in his pictures—the way his eyes were opened on the world. The things we did together, the places we went together began to come back to me with great intensity. And I realized that his eyes were my eyes, that I myself had looked upon the world back then with the same lively, unclouded vision as the boy who had walked by my side.

52 I made a habit after that of studying one of K.'s pictures at my desk each day when I got home from work. I could sit there for hours with one painting. In each I found another of those soft landscapes of childhood that I had shut out of my memory for so long. I had a

HOW LANGUAGE WORKS

Word Choice As students perform their close read, explain that authors choose their words very carefully to enable them to convey their precise meaning and tone with elegance and style. Word choice, called **diction**, also creates clarity. As the famous American writer Mark Twain said, "The difference between the right word and the almost right word is the difference between lightning and a lightning bug." Have students complete this chart to analyze the effect of the author's word choice in paragraphs 50 and 51.

Words	Effect of the Words
terror	evokes a feeling of uncontrollable fear
clarity and coloration	the alliteration creates smoothness and beauty
unclouded	evokes a feeling of serenity and wide vistas
soft landscapes	conveys the softness of K's character

sense, whenever I looked at one of K.'s works, that something was permeating my very flesh.

53 Perhaps a week had gone by like this when the thought suddenly struck me one evening: I might have been making a terrible mistake all those years. As he lay there in the tip of the wave, surely K. had not been looking at me with hatred or resentment; he had not been trying to take me away with him. And that terrible grin he had fixed me with: that, too, could have been an accident of angle or light and shadow, not a conscious act on K.'s part. He had probably already lost consciousness, or perhaps he had been giving me a gentle smile of eternal parting. The intense look of hatred I thought I saw on his face had been nothing but a reflection of the **profound** terror that had taken control of me for the moment.

54 The more I studied K.'s watercolor that evening, the greater the conviction with which I began to believe these new thoughts of mine. For no matter how long I continued to look at the picture, I could find nothing in it but a boy's gentle, innocent spirit.

55 I went on sitting at my desk for a very long time. There was nothing else I could do. The sun went down, and the pale darkness of evening began to envelop the room. Then came the deep silence of night, which seemed to go on for ever. At last, the scales tipped, and dark gave way to dawn. The new day's sun tinged the sky with pink.

56 It was then I knew I must go back.

57 I threw a few things in a bag, called the company to say I would not be in, and boarded a train for my old home town.

58 I did not find the same quiet, little seaside town that I remembered. An industrial city had sprung up nearby during the rapid development of the Sixties, bringing great changes to the landscape. The one little gift shop by the station had grown into a mall, and the town's only movie theatre had been turned into a supermarket. My house was no longer there. It had been demolished some months before, leaving only a scrape on the earth. The trees in the yard had all been cut down, and patches of weeds dotted the black stretch of ground. K.'s old house had disappeared as well, having been replaced by a concrete parking lot full of commuters' cars and vans. Not that I was overcome by sentiment. The town had ceased to be mine long before.

59 I walked down to the shore and climbed the steps of the breakwater. On the other side, as always, the ocean stretched off into the distance, unobstructed, huge, the horizon a single straight line. The shoreline, too, looked the same as it had before: the long beach, the lapping waves, people strolling at the water's edge. The time was after four o'clock, and the soft sun of late afternoon embraced everything below as it began its long, almost **meditative**, descent to the west. I lowered my bag to the sand and sat down next to it in silent appreciation of the gentle seascape. Looking at this scene, it was impossible to imagine that a great typhoon had once raged here, that a massive wave had swallowed my best friend in all the world. There was almost no one left now, surely, who remembered those

NOTES

profound (pruh FOWND) *adj.* intense; deep

CLOSE READ

ANNOTATE: In paragraph 58, mark details that suggest harshness or hardness. Then, mark details in paragraph 59 that suggest softness and calm.

QUESTION: Why does the author use these particular details in this way?

CONCLUDE: What change in the narrator's perspective is revealed by the author's word choice?

meditative (MEHD uh tay tihv) *adj.* given to extended thought

DIGITAL PERSPECTIVES

CLOSE READ

Remind students to focus on the author's word choice and how word choice helps to set a scene. You may wish to model the Close Read using the following think-aloud format. Possible responses to questions on the student page are included.

ANNOTATE: As I read paragraph 58, I notice and mark words that suggest harshness or hardness. To do this, I look for descriptive words that tell me about the town in which the narrator lived as a child. As I read paragraph 59, I notice and mark words that suggest softness and calm.

QUESTION: The author uses details that suggest harshness or hardness when describing the narrator's childhood hometown and details that suggest softness and calm when describing the seascape to set up a contrast between what the narrator expected to find in each place and what the reality was.

CONCLUDE: The town in which the narrator grew up has changed—it is no longer small and quiet. And the seascape, which the narrator thought might be a source of anxiety, is calming. The contrasts cause the narrator to question things: If his perspective of the places could change, then perhaps his perspective of K.'s death could change, too. And that might allow him to overcome his guilt and get on with his life.

CLOSE READ

Remind students to focus on the author's word choices and to consider how word choice can help to convey ideas that go beyond the surface level of meaning. You may wish to model the Close Read using the following think-aloud format. Possible responses to questions on the student page are included.

ANNOTATE: As I read paragraph 62, I notice and mark words or phrases that suggest things that are in dramatic motion and words or phrases that suggest stillness. These words or phrases will describe forceful, powerful movement or no movement at all.

QUESTION: These words and phrases provide an analogy to help the reader better understand what is happening to the narrator physically.

CONCLUDE: The narrator physically collapses into the water just as the fears and guilt that have built up inside him collapse "like a dilapidated house." The narrator has undergone a change and is confronting fear. He is no longer afraid, and I can infer that he is no longer going to live a life ruled by fear and guilt.

NOTES

CLOSE READ

ANNOTATE: In paragraph 62, mark words or phrases that suggest dramatic motion and stillness.

QUESTION: How do these words and phrases show what is happening to the narrator physically?

CONCLUDE: What deeper idea is the author conveying through this word choice?

terrible events. It began to seem as if the whole thing were an illusion that I had dreamed up in vivid detail.

60 And then I realized that the deep darkness inside me had vanished. Suddenly. As suddenly as it had come. I raised myself from the sand and, without bothering to take off my shoes or roll up my cuffs, walked into the surf to let the waves lap at my ankles.

61 Almost in reconciliation, it seemed, the same waves that had washed up on the beach when I was a boy were now fondly washing my feet, soaking black my shoes and pant cuffs. There would be one slow-moving wave, then a long pause, and then another wave would come and go. The people passing by gave me odd looks, but I didn't care.

62 I looked up at the sky. A few gray cotton chunks of cloud hung there, motionless. They seemed to be there for me, though I'm not sure why I felt that way. I remembered having looked up at the sky like this in search of the "eye" of the typhoon. And then, inside me, the axis of time gave one great heave. Forty long years collapsed like a dilapidated house, mixing old time and new time together in a single swirling mass. All sounds faded, and the light around me shuddered. I lost my balance and fell into the waves. My heart throbbed at the back of my throat, and my arms and legs lost all sensation. I lay that way for a long time, face in the water, unable to stand. But I was not afraid. No, not at all. There was no longer anything for me to fear. Those days were gone.

63 I stopped having my terrible nightmares. I no longer wake up screaming in the middle of the night. And I am trying now to start life over again. No, I know it's probably too late to start again. I may not have much time left to live. But even if it comes too late, I am grateful that, in the end, I was able to attain a kind of salvation, to effect some sort of recovery. Yes, grateful: I could have come to the end of my life unsaved, still screaming in the dark, afraid.

* * *

64 The seventh man fell silent and turned his gaze upon each of the others. No one spoke or moved or even seemed to breathe. All were waiting for the rest of his story. Outside, the wind had fallen, and nothing stirred. The seventh man brought his hand to his collar once again, as if in search of words.

65 "They tell us that the only thing we have to fear is fear itself; but I don't believe that," he said. Then, a moment later, he added: "Oh, the fear is there, all right. It comes to us in many different forms, at different times, and overwhelms us. But the most frightening thing we can do at such times is to turn our backs on it, to close our eyes. For then we take the most precious thing inside us and surrender it to something else. In my case, that something was the wave." ❧

VOCABULARY DEVELOPMENT

Dictionary Use Help students choose the correct dictionary entry for the word *reconciliation*. Read aloud the following text from paragraph 61: "Almost in reconciliation, it seemed, the same waves that had washed up on the beach when I was a boy were now fondly washing my feet, soaking black my shoes and pant cuffs." Tell students that dictionaries sometimes include example sentences or phrases within their definitions to show the different ways a word might be used. Then, read aloud the following dictionary entry for *reconciliation*:

1. the restoration of friendly relations; *his reconciliation with his aunt.* 2. the action of making one view compatible with another; *a reconciliation between art and technology.* 3. the action of making financial accounts consistent; *the bank reconciliation process updated the accounts.*

Guide students to see that the example in the first definition parallels the author's usage in the story. Help students list synonyms for the word *reconciliation*, such as *accord* or *harmony*. Then, ask students to use the word *reconciliation* in a sentence to share with the class.

Comprehension Check

Complete the following items after you finish your first read.

1. What traumatic event changes the seventh man's life?

2. Why does the seventh man's father allow him to go outside during the storm?

3. At the beach, why doesn't K. respond when his friend calls out to him?

4. What does the seventh man see inside the second wave?

5. What does the seventh man do when he returns to his hometown that shows he has finally recovered from his traumatic experience?

6. **Notebook** To confirm your understanding, write a summary of "The Seventh Man."

RESEARCH

Research to Clarify Choose at least one unfamiliar detail from the text. Briefly research that detail. In what way does the information you learned shed light on an aspect of the story?

Research to Explore Choose something from the text that interested you and formulate a research question.

DIGITAL PERSPECTIVES

Comprehension Check

Possible responses:

1. The seventh man's life is changed when he does not try to rescue his best friend K. from a giant wave. As a result, K. drowns.
2. The seventh man's father allows him to go outside during the storm because it is during the eye of the storm and everything is calm.
3. K. doesn't respond when the seventh man calls out to him because K. was likely absorbed in something that interested him, or the seventh man's voice did not reach him.
4. Inside the second wave, the seventh man sees K. grinning and reaching out to him.
5. When he returns to his hometown, the seventh man goes into the ocean, an act that shows he has finally recovered from his traumatic experience.
6. Summaries will vary; however, students should include a description of the storm, K.'s death, the narrator's years of guilt, and the narrator's recovery in the end.

Research to Clarify If students struggle to come up with a detail to research, you may want to suggest that they focus on one of the following topics: typhoons, Nagano Province, watercolors.

Research to Explore If students aren't sure how to go about formulating a research question, suggest that they use their findings from Research to Clarify as a starting point. For example, if students researched what watercolor painting is, they might formulate a question such as *What is the history of watercolor painting?*

PERSONALIZE FOR LEARNING

Challenge

Typhoon Research Encourage interested students to research typhoons. What causes them to form? How are they ranked? What damage do they cause? Students should also include information about how typhoon-prone regions are trying to safeguard people and property. Students can present their results as a pamphlet on typhoon safety.

Jump Start

CLOSE READ Have students close read the title "The Seventh Man." Ask students what they know about the number seven. Explain that the number seven is considered a lucky number in Japanese culture. Knowing this, one might wonder if the author intended the reader to infer that the seventh man is really "The Lucky Man." Ask students if they think the seventh man is truly lucky.

Close Read the Text

Walk students through the annotation model on the student page. Encourage them to complete items 2 and 3 on their own. Review and discuss the sections students have marked. If needed, continue to model close reading by using the Annotation Highlights in the Interactive Teacher's Edition.

Analyze the Text

Possible responses:

1. To the seventh man, the wave symbolizes the loss of his childhood innocence and joy. Paragraph 65 **DOK 2**
2. (a) After he rediscovers K.'s watercolors, the seventh man looks at one for hours every day when he gets home from work. **DOK 1** (b) To the seventh man, K.'s paintings symbolize the rediscovery of who he was before K. was killed. Paragraph 52 **DOK 2**
3. (a) Ignoring your fear will destroy your life. You must face your fear in order to overcome it. **DOK 2** (b) I agree, because if the seventh man hadn't ignored his fear, he could have forgiven himself much earlier and lived a happier life. **DOK 3**
4. Most students will observe that the seventh man suffered terribly after the wave took K.'s life. Paragraph 53 **DOK 3**
5. Students may conclude that a person can survive a life-threatening event physically, but be hurt in other ways. **DOK 3**

FORMATIVE ASSESSMENT

Analyze the Text

- **If** students fail to cite evidence, **then** remind them to support their ideas with specific information.
- **If** students struggle to identify what the wave or K.'s watercolors symbolize, **then** discuss the term *symbolize*, and illustrate with examples.

THE SEVENTH MAN

Close Read the Text

1. The model, from paragraph 5 of the story, shows two sample annotations, along with questions and conclusions. Close read the passage, and find another detail to annotate. Then, write a question and your conclusion.

ANNOTATE · QUESTION · CONCLUDE — Close Read

ANNOTATE: This phrase describes the wave in almost human terms.

QUESTION: What effect does this word choice create?

CONCLUDE: This description makes the wave seem alive and evil.

"It just barely missed me, but in my place it swallowed everything that mattered most to me and swept it off to another world. I took years to find it again and to recover from the experience—precious years that can never be replaced."

ANNOTATE: This word is repeated.

QUESTION: Why does the author repeat the word *years*?

CONCLUDE: The repetition emphasizes how long it takes the man to recover from the experience.

Tool Kit
Close-Read Guide and Model Annotation

2. For more practice, go back into the story and complete the close-read notes.
3. Revisit a section of the text you found important during your first read. Read this section closely, and **annotate** what you notice. Ask yourself **questions** such as "Why did the author make this choice?" What can you **conclude**?

Analyze the Text

CITE TEXTUAL EVIDENCE to support your answers.

Notebook Respond to these questions.

1. **Interpret** What does the wave **symbolize,** or represent, to the seventh man?
2. (a) After he rediscovers K.'s watercolors, what does the seventh man do with them? (b) **Interpret** What do K.'s watercolors symbolize to him?
3. (a) **Paraphrase** When you **paraphrase**, you restate a text in your own words. Paraphrase the seventh man's comments about fear in the story's final paragraph. (b) **Make a Judgment** Do you agree or disagree with the seventh man's comments? Explain.
4. **Evaluate** Although the seventh man did not die, did he truly escape the wave? Explain your position, citing story details.
5. **Essential Question:** *What does it take to survive?* What have you learned about the nature of survival by reading this story?

STANDARDS
Reading Literature
Analyze how an author's choices concerning how to structure a text, order events within it, and manipulate time create such effects as mystery, tension, or surprise.

Analyze Craft and Structure

Author's Choices: Order of Events A **frame story** is a story that brackets—or *frames*—another story or group of stories. This device creates a story-within-a-story narrative structure.

- Typically, the frame story is found at the beginning and again at the end of the work.
- Within this frame, the author shifts the narrative to a second, or interior, story.
- The interior story may be told by a different narrator or shift to a different point of view.

In "The Seventh Man," the frame story is told by a **third-person narrator**, who is an outside voice rather than a participant in the story. By contrast, the interior story is told in **first-person narration** by the seventh man himself.

Practice

CITE TEXTUAL EVIDENCE to support your answers.

Reread paragraphs 1–8 and 63–65 of "The Seventh Man."

Notebook Respond to these questions.

1. (a) At what points in "The Seventh Man" does the frame story begin and end? (b) What aspects of the text change to indicate these shifts?
2. (a) Record in the chart details from the frame story that describe the seventh man. (b) What do these details tell you about the seventh man's character?

THE SEVENTH MAN: FRAME STORY DETAILS	
his appearance	mid-fifties; thin; tall; moustache; scar near his right eye; stiff, bristly patches of white in his short hair; looks slightly confused; blue shirt; gray tweed coat
his speaking style	almost whispering; words lost in silence
his behavior	touches his hand to collar; clears throat

3. (a) Imagine that the frame story used first-person narration. Which details from your chart would most likely not appear in the story? (b) How does the use of third-person narration in the frame affect readers' understanding of the seventh man?
4. How does the use of first-person narration affect what readers learn and feel about the seventh man, K., and the events of the interior story?
5. Why do you think the author chose to use a frame structure to tell this story? What does the frame structure allow that a more basic story structure might not?

PERSONALIZE FOR LEARNING

English Language Support

Order of Events Have English Learners describe a sequence of events using a variety of words and sentence structures. Display words and phrases that tell about order of events: *first, next, after, last, afterward, subsequently, before, before long, as soon as, later,* and *finally.*

Present three events from "The Seventh Man" and have students use time-order words to explain the sequence in which they occur in the story. **EMERGING**

Have students practice using the time-order words and phrases to describe the order of events in a section of "The Seventh Man." **EXPANDING**

As students become more comfortable describing order of events, have them combine sentences and create more complex sentences to describe events in the story. **BRIDGING**

An expanded **English Language Support Lesson** on Order of Events is available in the Interactive Teacher's Edition.

DIGITAL PERSPECTIVES

Analyze Craft and Structure

Discuss with students why an author might choose to use a frame story as a narrative technique. Have them think about the advantages of telling parts of a story from two different points of view. Students should recognize that the frame in "The Seventh Man" allows the author to create a sense of mystery. For more support, see **Analyze Craft and Structure: Order of Events.**

MAKE IT INTERACTIVE

Have students sketch an image of the seventh man using the descriptions from the text. Conduct a gallery walk of student work, asking students to observe the differences and similarities among the sketches. What details were best captured by the sketches?

Practice

Possible responses:

1. (a) The interior story begins with paragraph 9 and ends with paragraph 63. (b) After paragraph 8, the narration changes from third-person to first-person. The quotation marks around the words spoken by the seventh man are dropped. The "he" of the first eight paragraphs becomes the "I."
2. (a) **See possible responses in chart on Student page.** (b) These details inform the reader that the seventh man is a quiet, reserved individual.
3. (a) Readers may not learn what the seventh man looks like or how he behaves. (b) Third-person narration affects readers' understanding of the seventh man by revealing his appearance and behavior as other people might see him.
4. First person allows readers to feel sympathy for the seventh man, his experience of losing K., and his sadness during his lonely life. Readers learn how he feels as his life falls apart and as he rediscovers himself.
5. The author chose the frame structure because he needed a reason to allow for the seventh man to tell his story. The frame structure allows the author to transition from the seventh man as an adult to his experiences as a child.

FORMATIVE ASSESSMENT

Analyze Craft and Structure

- **If** students fail to identify the frame, **then** have them look for clues that indicate the point of view. For example, the person narrating the frame may not be involved in the interior story.
- **If** students are unable to identify the point of view, **then** remind them to pay close attention to pronoun usage. For Reteach and Practice, see **Analyze Craft and Structure: Order of Events (RP).**

Concept Vocabulary

Why These Words?

Possible responses:

1. The concept vocabulary allows the reader to more clearly understand what the seventh man is thinking and feeling.
2. *delirium* (paragraph 39), *crazed* (paragraph 40)

Practice

Possible responses:

1. Her *desperate*, last-minute shot scored the winning points. Ramal was *entranced* as he watched the ants carry the crumbs away. He had a *hallucination* that he saw K. smiling at him in the wave. Before Brianna took the test, she had a *premonition* she would pass. K.'s death had a *profound* impact on the seventh man. Doing yoga puts me in a *meditative* state.
2. Her *frantic*, last-minute shot scored the winning points. Ramal was *mesmerized* as he watched the ants carry the crumbs away. He had a *vision* that he saw K. smiling at him in the wave. Before Brianna took the test, she had a *hunch* she would pass. K.'s death had a *deep* impact on the seventh man. Doing yoga puts me in a *calm* state. *Answers will vary regarding the effect, strength, and meaning when substituting with synonyms.*

Word Network

Possible words: *evacuation, terror, threat, fear, accident*

Word Study

For more support, see **Concept Vocabulary and Word Study.**

Possible responses:

1. A *hallucination* is a false perception.
2. *Direction* (paragraph 37): a line or course along which something is moving or aimed. Root word: *direct*
   Cooperation (paragraph 40): the process of moving together toward the same end. Root word: *cooperate*

FORMATIVE ASSESSMENT

Concept Vocabulary

If students fail to see the connection among the words, **then** have them use each word in a sentence and think about what is similar about the sentences.

Word Study

If students misspell the root words, **then** point out that there are no hard and fast rules about spelling changes when adding the suffix *-tion*, and have them check spellings in a dictionary. For Reteach and Practice, see **Word Study: Latin Suffix *-tion* (RP).**

LANGUAGE DEVELOPMENT

THE SEVENTH MAN

Concept Vocabulary

desperate	hallucination	profound
entranced	premonition	meditative

Why These Words? These concept words help to reveal the emotional state of the seventh man. For example, when the wave approaches, the seventh man is *entranced*, waiting for it to attack. After the wave hits, the seventh man believes he sees his friend K. in the wave and claims that this experience was no *hallucination*. Notice that both words relate to experiences that occur only in the mind of the seventh man.

1. How does the concept vocabulary sharpen the reader's understanding of the mental or emotional state of the seventh man?
2. What other words in the selection connect to this concept?

Practice

Notebook The concept vocabulary words appear in "The Seventh Man."

1. Use each concept word in a sentence that demonstrates your understanding of the word's meaning.
2. Challenge yourself to replace the concept word with one or two synonyms. How does the word change affect the meaning of your sentence? For example, which sentence is stronger? Which has a more positive meaning?

WORD NETWORK

Add interesting words related to survival from the text to your Word Network.

Word Study

Latin Suffix: *-tion* The Latin suffix *-tion* often indicates that a word is a noun. Sometimes this suffix is spelled *-ion* or *-ation*. In any of its forms, it means "act, state, or condition of." In "The Seventh Man," the word *premonition* means "the state of being forewarned."

1. Record a definition of *hallucination* based on your understanding of its root word and the meaning of the suffix *-tion*.
2. Look back at paragraphs 37–40 and find two other words that end with the suffix *-tion*. In each case, identify the root word that has been combined with the suffix. Record a definition for each word.

STANDARDS

Language

- Use various types of phrases and clauses to convey specific meanings and add variety and interest to writing or presentations.
- Identify and correctly use patterns of word changes that indicate different meanings or parts of speech.
- Analyze nuances in the meaning of words with similar denotations.

AUTHOR'S PERSPECTIVE Elfrieda Hiebert, Ph.D.

Collecting Sentences To help students become more adept with words, give them the experience of working with them. By studying sentences that use new vocabulary well, students can build their vocabulary strength. Encourage students to collect model sentences using two strategies:

- **Find sentences in the text.** Help students locate sentences that use new vocabulary, or have students identify sentences where word choice truly packs power into the text. Discuss how the words are used, and have students emulate the writer by writing similar sentences.
- **Find sentences in online vocabulary resources.** When students are learning new words, it is useful to see the word used correctly in a variety of contexts. Many online dictionaries provide contemporary and cross-curricular examples to help learners see the words in action.

There are several benefits to this approach. First, a study of words and the way they are used can help students appreciate and understand writers. Second, looking closely at vocabulary and the spectrum of related words can help students improve their own writing.

Conventions

Infinitives and Infinitive Phrases An **infinitive** is a verb form that generally appears with the word *to* in front of it and acts as a noun, an adjective, or an adverb. An **infinitive phrase** consists of an infinitive and its objects, complements, or modifiers, all acting together as a single part of speech. Like an infinitive, an infinitive phrase acts as a noun, an adjective, or an adverb.

The examples in the chart show uses of infinitives and infinitive phrases.

TIP

CLARIFICATION

Don't confuse infinitives with prepositional phrases. A prepositional phrase always ends with a noun or a pronoun. An infinitive always ends with a verb.

INFINITIVE	INFINITIVE PHRASE
Used as a Noun To succeed requires dedication. (functions as the subject of the sentence)	Used as a Noun We chose to take the old foot path. (functions as the direct object of the verb *chose*)
Used as an Adjective I wish I had the ability to fly. (tells *what kind* of ability)	Used as an Adjective Dana's desire to do well made Mama proud. (tells *which* desire)
Used as an Adverb When Derrick sat down to study, he concentrated. (tells *why* Derrick sat down)	Used as an Adverb She called the editor to voice her opinion. (tells *why* she called)

Read It

1. Mark the infinitive in each sentence from "The Seventh Man." Then, label each infinitive phrase as a noun, an adjective, or an adverb.
   a. I didn't want to wake someone sleeping next to me with my screams in the middle of the night.
   b. It took me a long time to recover from the emotional shock.
   c. This was where we came to play almost every day, so there was no part of it we didn't know well.
2. Reread paragraph 31 of "The Seventh Man." Mark each infinitive, and label each infinitive phrase as a noun, an adjective, or an adverb.

Write It

Notebook For each of these sentences, write a new sentence that expresses a similar idea but includes an infinitive or infinitive phrase. Mark each infinitive, and note whether each infinitive or infinitive phrase is a noun, an adjective, or an adverb.

1. K. was an unimaginably gifted artist for his age.
2. The seventh man was so filled with grief he never married.

PERSONALIZE FOR LEARNING

English Language Support

Parts of Speech Review the definitions of the parts of speech referenced in this lesson (noun, verb, adjective, adverb). Have students identify an example of each and use their examples in sentences. Support students in completing as many of these steps as they can. **EMERGING / EXPANDING**

Conventions

Infinitives and Infinitive Phrases Discuss the definition of an *infinitive* and an *infinitive phrase* with students. As you review the examples of infinitive phrases with students, explain that in order to figure out the infinitive phrase in a sentence, they must determine what it is modifying. Consider defining the following terms:

modifier: a word, phrase, or clause that functions as an adjective or an adverb to describe a word or make its meaning more specific

complement: a word (or words) that's needed to complete the meaning of an expression

For more support, see **Conventions: Infinitives and Infinitive Phrases.**

MAKE IT INTERACTIVE

Have students write each sentence on a sentence strip using a different colored marker for the infinitive.

Read It

1. a. to wake, noun (direct object)
   b. to recover, adjective (modifies *time*)
   c. to play, adverb (modifies *came*)
2. to strike, adverb (modifies *poised*); to block out, adverb (modifies *rose up*); to run, noun (direct object); to run, adjective (modifies *time*)

Write It

Possible responses:

1. To be such a gifted artist at K.'s age was unimaginable. (To be, noun)
2. The seventh man was filled with too much grief to marry. (to marry, adverb)

FORMATIVE ASSESSMENT

Conventions

- **If** students can't locate the infinitive or infinitive phrase, **then** remind them to look for the word *to*.
- **If** students can't identify the type of infinitive or infinitive phrase, **then** have them think about the role it plays in the sentence. For Reteach and Practice, see **Conventions: Infinitives and Infinitive Phrases (RP).**

TEACHING

Writing to Sources

Explain to students that when they write a critical review of a narrative, they should focus on the aspects of the text that allow them to say something meaningful. For example, they might want to focus on theme, structure, and the author's use of language.

One way that a writer can strengthen his or her critical review is to provide specific examples of how other readers may view the text differently. Then, the writer can illustrate why his or her position is more persuasive. For more support, see **Writing to Sources: Critical Review.**

Reflect on Your Writing

1. Responses will vary. If students need support, ask them to consider the insights they gained in writing their critical review.
2. Responses will vary. Be sure that students make connections between their claim and the evidence they cite.
3. **Why These Words?** Responses will vary. Have students list specific examples of words they have chosen that add power to their review.

FORMATIVE ASSESSMENT

Writing to Sources

If students struggle to identify their position, **then** ask them to consider what they liked (or did not like) about the story or what they learned about survival from reading the story. For Reteach and Practice, see **Writing to Sources: Critical Review (RP).**

EFFECTIVE EXPRESSION

THE SEVENTH MAN

Writing to Sources

Critical writing is a type of argumentation in which you explain your insights about a literary work and persuade others to share your point of view. Like any argument, critical writing requires you to state a claim, or position, and to support it with strong evidence.

Assignment

Write a **critical review** of "The Seventh Man" that could appear in your school paper or website. State specific reasons why you either recommend or do not recommend the story to other readers.

Your review should include:

- Title and author of the work being reviewed
- A brief summary of the work
- A clear statement of your claim, or position
- Valid reasoning that is supported by text evidence

Vocabulary and Conventions Connection In your review, consider including several of the concept vocabulary words. Also, consider using infinitive phrases to add variety to your sentences.

desperate	hallucination	profound
entranced	premonition	meditative

Reflect on Your Writing

After you have written your critical review, answer the following questions.

1. How do you think writing your critical review strengthened your understanding of the story?
2. What evidence and supporting details did you use in your writing? How did they help support your claim?
3. **Why These Words?** The words you choose make a difference in your writing. Which words did you specifically choose to add power to your critical review?

STANDARDS

Writing
Introduce precise claim(s), distinguish the claim(s) from alternate or opposing claims, and create an organization that establishes clear relationships among the claim(s), counterclaims, reasons, and evidence.

Speaking and Listening
Present information, findings, and supporting evidence clearly, concisely, and logically such that listeners can follow the line of reasoning and the organization, development, substance, and style are appropriate to purpose, audience, and task.

PERSONALIZE FOR LEARNING

English Language Support

Condensing Ideas As students write the critical reviews, take this opportunity to support them in applying the sentence strategies of condensing ideas. Introduce these methods for writing more concisely and creating more powerful sentences.

1. *Use Compound Verbs* Tell students that they can avoid a choppy writing style by using compound verbs instead of writing two separate sentences. Share these example sentences:

   K. felt afraid after the storm.

   K. did not seek help for many years to come.

   K. felt afraid but did not seek help after the storm and for many years to come.

2. *Embed clauses* Show students how to embed clauses. Share these example sentences:

   K. vividly remembers the storm.

   K. was only a young boy.

   K. who was only a young boy, remembered the storm vividly.

ALL LEVELS

Speaking and Listening

Assignment

With a partner, prepare a **retelling** of "The Seventh Man" from another point of view. For example, you may choose to retell the story from K.'s parents' point of view, or from that of a hidden onlooker. Refresh your memory by rereading the selection. Then, follow these steps to complete the assignment.

1. **Identify Your Character** Choose your character and determine how he or she fits into the original story. Decide what important information you will need to tell your audience to clarify the character's background and motivations.
2. **Plan Your Retelling** Once you've identified your character, think about his or her perspective on the events in the story. As you plan your retelling, keep the following in mind:
   - How does your character see the story differently from the seventh man? What fresh perspective does he or she offer?
   - Make a list of the story events, as experienced by your character. Then, weave those events into a coherent retelling.
   - Choose language that is appropriate to the character you chose. For example, a child would choose simple words and sentences and may not fully understand what is he or she is observing.
3. **Prepare Your Delivery** Practice your retelling with your partner. Include the following performance techniques to help you achieve the desired effect.
   - Vary your intonation to reflect the emotions of your character. Avoid speaking in a flat, monotone style.
   - As you speak, use facial expressions and gestures that help convey your character's personality.
   - Make eye contact with your audience to engage them in the story.
4. **Evaluate Retellings** As your classmates deliver their retellings, listen attentively. Use an evaluation guide like the one shown to analyze their delivery.

EVALUATION GUIDE

Rate each statement on a scale of 1 (not demonstrated) to 4 (demonstrated).

☐ The character was clearly identified.

☐ The speaker communicated clearly and expressively.

☐ The speaker used a variety of speaking tones and pitches.

☐ The speaker used effective gestures and other body language.

EVIDENCE LOG

Before moving on to a new selection, go to your Evidence Log and record what you learned from "The Seventh Man."

DIGITAL PERSPECTIVES

Illuminating the Standard To help students understand the elements of an effective oral presentation, find videos online of presentations that include examples of effective and ineffective techniques. Show the videos to students, and ask them to consider whether the example shown increases the effectiveness of the presentation or distracts from it. Then, ask students to locate additional examples of the dos and don'ts of effective and ineffective presentations, and create one slide that embeds an eight-second video of each. Finally, review the slide show with the class, giving enough time after each slide for students to discuss their reactions to the videos. **(Research to Clarify)**

DIGITAL PERSPECTIVES

Speaking and Listening

1. **Identify Your Character** You may wish to guide students in choosing a character by asking them to consider whose perspective most interests them.
2. **Plan Your Retelling** Tell students that when they retell the story from their chosen character's point of view, they should remember to include only those details that the character would have knowledge of.
3. **Prepare Your Delivery** Have pairs video record each other's presentations. Then have them use the Evaluation Guide to provide feedback to their partner prior to presenting to the class.
4. **Evaluate Retelling** Encourage students to make one supportive comment about each presentation. For more support, see **Speaking and Listening: Retelling.**

Evidence Log Support students in completing their Evidence Log. This paced activity will help prepare them for the Performance-Based Assessment at the end of the unit.

FORMATIVE ASSESSMENT

Speaking and Listening

- **If** students struggle to identify a character, **then** have them list all of the possible characters and choose the one that most interests them.
- **If** students struggle with their character's perspective, **then** have them think about how the character might have reacted to the events in the story. For Reteach and Practice, see **Speaking and Listening: Retelling (RP).**

Selection Test

Administer "The Seventh Man" Selection Test, which is available in both print and digital formats online in Assessments.

The Moral Logic of Survivor Guilt

AUDIO SUMMARIES
Audio summaries of "The Moral Logic of Survivor Guilt" are available online in both English and Spanish in the Interactive Teacher's Edition or Unit Resources. Assigning these summaries prior to reading the selection may help students build additional background knowledge and set a context for their first read.

Summary

In her opinion piece "The Moral Logic of Survivor Guilt," Nancy Sherman consults war veterans and philosophers to explore survivor guilt. She first explains the difference between objective guilt, which one feels as a result of wrongdoing, and subjective guilt, which is not caused by wrongdoing and is thought to be irrational. She then examines whether subjective guilt, such as the survivor guilt soldiers often feel, is truly irrational after all. Although this type of guilt does not reflect any fault on the part of the survivor, it does reflect one's values and morality. Survivor guilt also helps soldiers humanize the horrors of war.

Insight

Survival may hurt. Reading "The Moral Logic of Survivor Guilt" will help students see that, rather than being unreasonable, survivor guilt serves the purpose of reaffirming one's humanity and character, while making it possible to fix the moral ruin that can result when one feels responsible for someone's death.

Some students may have difficulty grasping the crushing weight of responsibility that soldiers deal with and may require support.

ESSENTIAL QUESTION:
What does it take to survive?

Connection to Essential Question

"The Moral Logic of Survivor Guilt" has a two-part connection to the Essential Question, "What does it take to survive?" Firstly, soldiers who survive often do so because they aren't in the wrong place at the wrong time, so survival becomes a question of luck. Secondly, those people who survive death must then try to live with the guilt they feel; for them, survival becomes a question of allowing those feelings to exist in order to arrive at a sense of redemption.

WHOLE-CLASS LEARNING PERFORMANCE TASK
Should the seventh man forgive himself for his failure to save K.?

UNIT PERFORMANCE-BASED ASSESSMENT
Should people in life-or-death situations be held accountable for their actions?

Connection to Performance Tasks

Whole-Class Learning Performance Task In this Performance Task, students will consider the concept of survivor guilt. "The Moral Logic of Survivor Guilt" provides an informative and analytical perspective on the reasons survivors experience guilt. Students will be combining this perspective with the literary perspective they gleaned from reading "The Seventh Man."

Unit Performance-Based Assessment In terms of the question of whether or not people in life-or-death situations should be held accountable for their actions, this selection provides a real-life perspective. "The Moral Logic of Survivor Guilt" applies the question to soldiers, people who face life-or-death situations as part of the normal course of their lives.

DIGITAL PERSPECTIVES: Audio | Video | Document | Annotation Highlights | EL Highlights | Online Assessment

LESSON RESOURCES

	Making Meaning	Language Development	Effective Expression
Lesson	**First Read** **Close Read** **Analyze the Text** **Analyze Craft and Structure**	**Concept Vocabulary** **Word Study** **Conventions**	**Writing to Sources** **Speaking and Listening**
Instructional Standards	**RI.10** By the end of grade 9, read and comprehend literary nonfiction . . . **RI.1** Cite strong and thorough textual evidence . . . **RI.2** Determine a central idea of a text . . . **RI.8** Delineate and evaluate the argument and specific claims in a text . . .	**L.4.b** Identify and correctly use patterns of word changes . . . **L.4.c** Consult general and specialized reference materials . . . **L.1** Demonstrate command of the conventions . . . **L.2.a** Use a semicolon . . . **L.2.b** Use a colon . . .	**W.2.a** Introduce a topic . . . **SL.4** Present information, findings, and supporting evidence . . .
STUDENT RESOURCES			
Available online in the Interactive Student Edition or Unit Resources	Selection Audio First-Read Guide: Nonfiction Close-Read Guide: Nonfiction	Word Network	Evidence Log
TEACHER RESOURCES			
Selection Resources Available online in the Interactive Teacher's Edition or Unit Resources	Audio Summaries Annotation Highlights EL Highlights Analyze Craft and Structure: Development of Ideas English Language Support Lesson: Central Idea and Specific Details	Concept Vocabulary and Word Study Conventions: Punctuation	Writing to Sources: Encyclopedia Entry Speaking and Listening: Pep Talk
Reteach/Practice (RP) Available online in the Interactive Teacher's Edition or Unit Resources	Analyze Craft and Structure: Development of Ideas (RP)	Word Study: Greek Root *-path-* (RP) Conventions: Punctuation (RP)	Writing to Sources: Encyclopedia Entry (RP) Speaking and Listening: Pep Talk (RP)
Assessment Available online in Assessments	Selection Test		
My Resources	A Unit 2 Answer Key is available online and in the Interactive Teacher's Edition.		

Reading Support

Text Complexity Rubric: The Moral Logic of Survivor Guilt	
Quantitative Measures	
Lexile: 1100 **Text Length:** Word Count: 1,746	
Qualitative Measures	
Content/ Knowledge Demands (rating: 4 of 5)	Explores complex themes that will be unfamiliar (survivor guilt of war veterans); explanation is provided for only some of the complex ideas.
Structure (rating: 3 of 5)	Organization is evident and sequential, but paragraphs contain a lot of information that is not broken up with any headings or graphics to organize it.
Language Conventionality and Clarity (rating: 4 of 5)	The syntax includes many complex sentences that have several subordinate clauses or phrases, or sentences with unclear pronoun antecedents; selection has a lot of above-level vocabulary.
Levels of Meaning/Purpose/Concept Level (rating: 3 of 5)	The main idea is revealed early, but the concept may be hard for some to grasp because of sophisticated language and complex supporting concepts.

DECIDE AND PLAN

English Language Support

Provide English Learners with support for Language and Meaning as they read the selection.

Language Help students reword long and complex sentences. Using the language from the selection, suggest simpler sentences that convey the same meaning. For example, paragraph 1: *Friends and families experience gratefulness or relief. Returning war veterans are struggling with other emotions.* Ask students to read the new sentences and discuss.

Meaning Make sure students understand the meaning of the words *survivor* and *guilt.* It may be helpful to Spanish speakers to see the word *sobrevivir.* Point out that the word *survivor* contains *-viv-,* from the Latin word *vivar,* which means "to live."

Strategic Support

Provide students with strategic support to ensure that they can successfully read the text.

Knowledge Demands Make sure students understand the term *survivor guilt*—guilt that survivors feel for living while others die. Relate this to students' possible experiences of feeling guilty if they are healthy or happy when someone else is ill or sad.

Language If students have difficulty with complex sentences, work together to break down sentences into smaller chunks. Ask students to highlight words or phrases that they don't understand. Have the whole group help to define difficult terms.

Challenge

Provide students who need to be challenged with ideas for how they can go beyond a simple interpretation of the text.

Text Analysis Ask students to read aloud the paragraph about the sacred bond among soldiers (paragraph 7). Ask students to explain why they think having a strong bond increases the feeling of survivor guilt.

Written Response Ask students to write a description of a fictional character who feels survivor guilt. Ask them to explain the situation, the reason for the guilt, and the feelings of the character. Encourage them to explain why the character feels guilt. Ask students to read their work to a partner and discuss the descriptions they wrote.

TEACH

Read and Respond

Have the class do their first read of the selection. Then have them complete their close read. Finally, work with them on the Making Meaning, Language Development, and Effective Expression activities.

Standards Support Through Teaching and Learning Cycle

IDENTIFY NEEDS

Analyze results of the Beginning-of-Year Assessment, focusing on the items relating to Unit 2. Also take into consideration student performance to this point and your observations of where particular students struggle.

DECIDE AND PLAN

Instructional Standards: The Moral Logic of Survivor Guilt

	Catching Up	This Year	Looking Forward
Reading	You may want to use the **Analyze Craft and Structure: Development of Ideas (RP)** worksheet to help students understand how an author unfolds an argument through careful reasoning.	**RI.8** Delineate and evaluate the argument and specific claims in a text, assessing whether the reasoning is valid and the evidence is relevant and sufficient; identify false statements and fallacious reasoning.	Have students develop the author's argument further by providing specific suggestions about why guilt is appropriate or fitting for soldiers to feel.
Writing	You may wish to administer the **Writing to Sources: Encyclopedia Entry (RP)** worksheet to help students understand how to define key concepts.	**W.2.a** Introduce a topic, organize complex ideas, concepts, and information to make important connections and distinctions; include formatting, graphics, and multimedia when useful to aiding comprehension.	Have students choose a key concept from another text in the unit and write an encyclopedia entry.
Speaking and Listening	You may wish to administer the **Speaking and Listening: Pep Talk (RP)** worksheet to help students develop an outline to communicate ideas.	**SL.4** Present information, findings, and supporting evidence clearly, concisely, and logically such that listeners can follow the line of reasoning and the organization, development, substance, and style are appropriate to purpose, audience, and task.	Ask students to write and present a speech that taps a historical experience of survivor guilt. Ask them to include an explanation of what the guilty survivor or survivors did or might do to overcome their guilt and feel whole.
Language	You may wish to administer the **Conventions: Punctuation (RP)** worksheet to help students understand how punctuation can connect ideas. You may wish to administer the **Word Study: Greek Root -*path*- (RP)** worksheet to help students understand how to increase their vocabulary using their knowledge of Greek roots.	**L.1** Demonstrate command of the conventions of standard English grammar and usage when writing or speaking. **L.4.b** Identify and correctly use patterns of word changes that indicate different meanings or parts of speech.	Ask students to evaluate whether the author has overused dashes in this piece of writing and to provide a few examples of how different punctuation in some sentences might yield similarly effective or more effective results. Have students identify other words that have the Greek root -*path*-.

ANALYZE AND REVISE

- Analyze student work for evidence of student learning.
- Identify whether or not students have met the expectations in the standards.
- Identify implications for future instruction.

TEACH

Implement the planned lesson, and gather evidence of student learning.

Jump Start

FIRST READ We all know the famous question: "Am I my brother's keeper?" What responsibility do we have for others, especially those we consider "brothers" through kinship, friendship, or duty? Engage students in a discussion about the aftermath of death or tragedy for the people who survive. This can set the context for reading "The Moral Logic of Survivor Guilt."

The Moral Logic of Survival Guilt

Why do some people survive a catastrophic event and others don't? What emotions might a survivor have? How do the survivors cope with these emotions? Modeling the questions a reader might ask as they read "The Moral Logic of Survival Guilt" brings the text alive for students and connects it to the Whole-Class Performance Task question. Selection audio and print capability for the selection are available in the Interactive Teacher's Edition.

Concept Vocabulary

Support students as they rank the words. Ask if they've ever heard, read, or used them. Reassure them that the definitions for these words are listed in the selection.

FIRST READ

As they read, students should perform the steps of the first read.

NOTICE: Have students notice who Bonenberger and Prior are.

ANNOTATE: Remind students to mark passages that explain why the profiled men feel guilty and how the author tries to explain or understand their guilt.

CONNECT: Encourage students to think about veterans they know or have met. Have these people experienced survivor guilt?

RESPOND: Students will answer questions and write a summary to demonstrate understanding.

Point out to students that while they will always complete the Respond step at the end of the first read, the other steps will probably happen somewhat concurrently. You may wish to print copies of the **First-Read Guide: Nonfiction** for students to use.

Remind students that during their first read, they should not answer the close-read questions that appear in the selection.

About the Author

Nancy Sherman (b. 1951) always wanted to understand more about what her father went through as a soldier during World War II. Her opportunity came when she served as the first Distinguished Chair in Ethics at the U.S. Naval Academy from 1997–99. Sherman is now a University Professor of Philosophy at Georgetown University, and her research includes military ethics, the history of moral philosophy, and moral psychology.

Tool Kit
First-Read Guide and Model Annotation

STANDARDS
Reading Informational Text
By the end of grade 9, read and comprehend literary nonfiction in the grades 9–10 text complexity band proficiently, with scaffolding as needed at the high end of the range.

The Moral Logic of Survivor Guilt

Concept Vocabulary

You will encounter the following words as you read "The Moral Logic of Survivor Guilt." Before reading, note how familiar you are with each word. Then, rank the words in order from most familiar (1) to least familiar (6).

WORD	YOUR RANKING
burden	
culpability	
conscience	
remorse	
entrusted	
empathic	

After completing your first read, review your original rankings. Make any changes to your rankings as needed.

First Read NONFICTION

Apply these strategies as you conduct your first read. You will have an opportunity to complete the close-read notes after your first read.

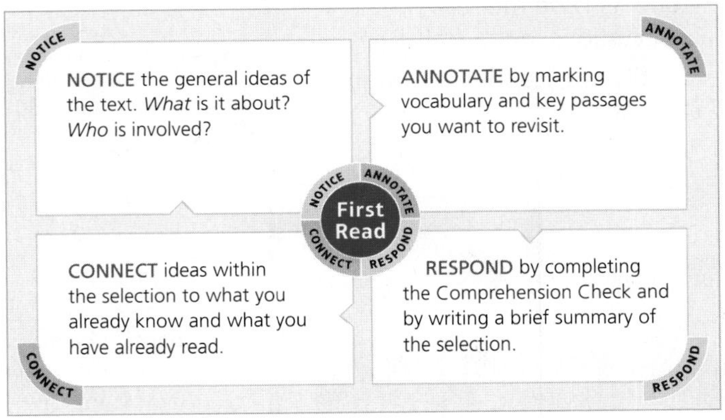
NOTICE the general ideas of the text. *What* is it about? *Who* is involved?
ANNOTATE by marking vocabulary and key passages you want to revisit.
CONNECT ideas within the selection to what you already know and what you have already read.
RESPOND by completing the Comprehension Check and by writing a brief summary of the selection.
First Read
NOTICE
ANNOTATE
CONNECT
RESPOND

ANCHOR TEXT | EDITORIAL

The Moral Logic of Survivor Guilt

Nancy Sherman

BACKGROUND

Traumatic events take a toll on the physical and mental well-being of the individuals who must endure them. Survivors of the Holocaust, rescue workers, and war veterans, for example, might wonder how they were able to make it out alive when others did not. The term "survivor guilt" is used to describe these feelings.

SCAN FOR MULTIMEDIA

1 If there is one thing we have learned from returning war veterans—especially those of the last decade—it's that the emotional reality of the soldier at home is often at odds with that of the civilian public they left behind. And while friends and families of returning service members may be experiencing gratefulness or relief this holiday,[1] many of those they've welcomed home are likely struggling with other emotions.

Is the sense of responsibility soldiers feel toward each other irrational?

2 High on that list of emotions is guilt. Soldiers often carry this **burden** home—survivor guilt being perhaps the kind most familiar to us. In war, standing here rather than there can save your life but cost a buddy his. It's flukish luck, but you feel responsible. The guilt begins an endless loop of counterfactuals—thoughts that you could have or should have done otherwise, though in fact you did nothing wrong. The feelings are, of course, not restricted to the battlefield. But given the magnitude[2] of loss in war, they hang heavy there and are pervasive. And they raise the question of just how irrational those feelings are, and if they aren't, of what is the basis of their reasonableness.

1. **this holiday** This essay was originally published the day before the Fourth of July (Independence Day).
2. **magnitude** *n.* great size or extent.

NOTES

CLOSE READ

ANNOTATE: Mark words in paragraph 1 that show opposites.

QUESTION: What groups of people are being contrasted by using these opposites?

CONCLUDE: What does this contrast suggest about the two groups?

burden (BURD uhn) *n.* something that is carried with difficulty or obligation

DIGITAL PERSPECTIVES

CLOSE READ

Remind students to focus on the two groups of citizens. You may wish to model the close read using the following think-aloud format. Possible responses to questions on the student page are included. You may also want to print copies of the **Close-Read Guide: Nonfiction** for students to use.

ANNOTATE: As I read the first paragraph, I notice phrases that show how the author emphasizes the opposed realities and emotions of two groups.

QUESTION: I can see that the reality and emotions of returning veterans are contrasted with those of their friends and family—members of the civilian public.

CONCLUDE: I think that the contrast shows that the two groups are experiencing very different realities, suggesting that they might have a hard time understanding each other.

Additional **English Language Support** is available in the Interactive Teacher's Edition.

PERSONALIZE FOR LEARNING

English Language Support

Idioms Idioms can be confusing to English Language learners. Explain that the term *hang heavy* in paragraph 2 is an idiom. To help them understand its usage in the paragraph, explain that feelings that *hang heavy* may be feelings that are hard to move past. Ask students to think of a time that they felt sad and to remember what that emotion is like. Since the author is referring to a soldier's feelings of guilt in the phrase "they hang heavy there," explain that the author is saying that survivor guilt is a feeling that doesn't go away quickly. **ALL LEVELS**

TEACHING

CLOSE READ

Remind students to focus on what it means to be a good person. You may wish to model the Close Read using the following think-aloud format. Possible responses to questions on the student page are included.

ANNOTATE: As I read paragraph 6, I notice that the author discusses what it means to be a good person. She talks about virtue and its relationship to emotions and actions.

QUESTION: The author focuses on defining what it means to be good because soldiers who return home from combat can be good people, yet they may experience a sense of guilt—despite having no reason to feel guilty.

CONCLUDE: The definitions and examples serve to point out a conflict: A person may feel guilty—not virtuous—precisely because he or she is a good person.

NOTES

culpability (kuhl puh BIHL uh tee) *n.* guilt or blame that is deserved; blameworthiness

conscience (KON shuhns) *n.* inner sense of what is morally right or wrong in one's actions

remorse (rih MAWRS) *n.* deep sense of regret for having done wrong

CLOSE READ

ANNOTATE: In paragraph 6, mark the words or passages that describe what it means to be a good person.

QUESTION: Why does the writer focus on defining what it is to be "good"?

CONCLUDE: What purpose do these definitions and examples serve?

3 Capt. Adrian Bonenberger, head of a unit in Afghanistan, pondered those questions recently as he thought about Specialist Jeremiah Pulaski, who was killed by police in the wake of a deadly bar fight shortly after he returned home. Back in Afghanistan, Pulaski had saved Bonenberger's life twice on one day, but when Pulaski needed help, Bonenberger couldn't be there for him: "When he was in trouble, he was alone," Captain Bonenberger said. "When we were in trouble, he was there for us. I know it's not rational or reasonable. There's nothing logical about it. But I feel responsible."

4 But how unreasonable is that feeling? Subjective guilt, associated with this sense of responsibility, is thought to be irrational because one feels guilty despite the fact that he knows he has done nothing wrong. Objective or rational guilt, by contrast—guilt that is "fitting" to one's actions—accurately tracks real wrongdoing or **culpability**: guilt is appropriate because one acted to deliberately harm someone, or could have prevented harm and did not. Blameworthiness, here, depends on the idea that a person could have done something other than he did. And so he is held responsible or accountable, by himself or others.

5 But as Bonenberger's remarks make clear, we often *take* responsibility in a way that goes beyond what we can reasonably be *held* responsible for. And we feel the guilt that comes with that sense of responsibility. Nietzsche is the modern philosopher who well understood this phenomenon: "Das schlechte Gewissen," (literally, "bad **conscience**")—his term for the consciousness of guilt where one has done no wrong, doesn't grow in the soil where we would most expect it, he argued, such as in prisons where there are actually "guilty" parties who should feel **remorse** for wrongdoing. In "The Genealogy of Morals," he appeals to an earlier philosopher, Spinoza, for support: "The bite of conscience," writes Spinoza in the "Ethics," has to do with an "offense" where "something has gone unexpectedly wrong." As Nietzsche adds, it is not really a case of "I ought not to have done that."

6 But what then is it a case of? Part of the reasonableness of survivor guilt (and in a sense, its "fittingness") is that it tracks a moral significance that is broader than moral *action*. Who I am, in terms of my character and relationships, and not just what I do, matters morally. Of course, character is expressed in action, and when we don't "walk the walk," we are lacking; but it is also expressed in emotions and attitudes. Aristotle[3] in his "Nicomachean Ethics" insists on the point: "virtue is concerned with emotions and actions;" to have good character is to "hit the mean"[4] with respect to both. Moreover, many of the feelings that express character are not about what one has done or should have done, but rather about what one cares deeply about. Though Aristotle doesn't himself talk about guilt, it is the emotion that best expresses that conflict—the desire or obligation to help frustrated by the inability, through no fault of one's

3. **Aristotle** (AR ihs tot uhl) (384–322 B.C.) ancient Greek philosopher and scientist.
4. **mean** *n.* middle point between two things.

PERSONALIZE FOR LEARNING

Strategic Support

First-Read Support If students struggle to comprehend the text during the first read, have a partner conduct a think-aloud to explain the thought process as he or she works through the NOTICE, ANNOTATE, CONNECT, and RESPOND steps. For example, the student can isolate the key details and explain what they reveal.

own, to do so. To not feel the guilt is to be numb to those pulls. It is that vulnerability, those pulls, that Bonenberger feels when he says he wasn't there for Pulaski when he needed him.

The sacred bond among soldiers originates not just in duty, but in love.

7 In many of the interviews I've conducted with soldiers over the years, feelings of guilt and responsibility tangle with feelings of having betrayed fellow soldiers. At stake is the duty to those soldiers, the imperative[5] to hold intact the bond that enables them to fight for and with each other in the kind of "sacred band" that the ancients memorialized and that the Marine motto *semper fidelis*[6] captures so well. But it is not just duty at work. It is love.

8 Service members, especially those higher in rank, routinely talk about unit members as "*my* soldiers," "*my* Marines," "*my* sailors." They are family members, their own children, of sorts, who have been **entrusted** to them. To fall short of unconditional care is experienced as a kind of perfidy, a failure to be faithful. Survivor guilt piles on the unconscious thought that luck is part of a zero-sum game. To have good luck is to deprive another of it. The anguish of guilt, its sheer pain, is a way of sharing some of the ill fate. It is a form of **empathic** distress.

9 Many philosophers have looked to other terms to define the feeling. What they have come up with is "agent-regret" (a term coined by the British philosopher Bernard Williams, but used by many others). The classic scenario is not so much one of good luck (as in survivor guilt), but of bad luck, typically having to do with accidents where again, there is little or no culpability for the harms caused. In these cases, people may be *causally* responsible for harm—they bring about the harm through their agency—but they are not morally responsible for what happened.

10 But to my ear, agent-regret is simply tone-deaf to how subjective guilt feels. Despite the insertion of "agent," it sounds as passive and flat as "regretting that the weather is bad." Or more tellingly, as removed from empathic distress as the message sent to the next of kin, after an official knock on the door: "The Secretary of Defense regrets to inform you that . . . ."[7]

11 Indeed, the soldiers I've talked to, involved in friendly fire accidents that took their comrades' lives, didn't feel regret for what happened, but raw, deep, unabashed guilt. And the guilt persisted long after they were formally investigated and ultimately exonerated. In one wrenching case in April 2003 in Iraq, the gun on a Bradley

NOTES

entrusted (ehn TRUHST ihd) *v.* given the responsibility of doing something or caring for someone or something

empathic (ehm PATH ihk) *adj.* characterized by empathy, the ability to identify with the feelings or thoughts of others

5. **imperative** *n.* act or duty that is very important or required.
6. ***semper fidelis*** (SEHM puhr fih DAY lihs) Latin phrase that means "always faithful." It is the motto of the United States Marine Corps, a branch of the military.
7. **"The Secretary of Defense regrets to inform you that. . . ."** first sentence of a scripted message spoken by United States military officers when they report the death of a soldier to that soldier's closest living relative.

DIGITAL PERSPECTIVES

CLOSER LOOK

Analyze Terminology

Students may have marked paragraph 7 during their first read. Use this paragraph to help students understand what the author means by the "sacred band." Encourage them to talk about the annotations that they marked. You may want to model a close read with the class based on the highlights shown in the text.

ANNOTATE: Have students mark details in paragraph 7 that suggest chivalric codes of honor and dishonor rather than military duty and the failure to do one's duty, or have students participate while you highlight them.

QUESTION: Guide students to consider what these details might tell them. Ask what a reader can infer from the use of this kind of elevated language, and accept student responses.

Possible responses: Readers can infer that armies are held together by something more mysterious and much more powerful than military discipline and obedience to orders.

CONCLUDE: Help students to formulate conclusions about the importance of these details in the text. Ask students why the author might have included these details.

Possible responses: Terms that suggest chivalric codes of honor and dishonor convey the idea that soldiers are and always have been bound together by a sacred trust. By adding these details, the author shows that this dedication originates not in duty or obedience to orders, but in love.

Remind students that since ancient times, authors have been both idealistic and truthful in describing armies as "sacred bands" of warriors bound together ultimately by love.

HOW LANGUAGE WORKS

Italics Italics are often used to emphasize a word or a phrase in a sentence, as is the case in paragraph 8: "*my* soldiers," "*my* Marines," "*my* sailors." Explain that the author is emphasizing the word *my* to demonstrate the closeness of the relationship between soldiers and *their* unit members. Use the following sentences to model how italics can alter the meaning of a word or phrase:

I *really* don't care what you think.

I really don't care what *you* think.

Have students read each sentence aloud, emphasizing the italicized word. Ask students if the change in emphasis affects the meaning of the sentence. Guide students to understand that changing the emphasis affects the meaning of the author's words. Ask students to write their own examples of sentence pairs with alternate emphases and note how the change in emphasis influences the meaning of the sentence.

CLOSE READ

Remind students to focus on looking for the author's observations. You may wish to model the Close Read using the following think-aloud format. Possible responses to questions on the student page are included.

ANNOTATE: As I read paragraph 14, I notice and mark the author's observations. These are sentences in which the author adds her own opinion rather than simply relating facts.

QUESTION: The quotation from Prior supports the author's observations. For example, the author describes Prior's connection with Mayek's mother as "painful." Prior calls it "terrible." And the author uses the word *fratricide* or the "killing of a brother or sister." Prior describes the letters from Mayek's mother to him being "like a mother writing to her son."

CONCLUDE: The author's choice to quote Prior adds weight to her argument that soldiers can be burdened with guilt and feel a sense of responsibility even though they have done nothing wrong.

NOTES

fighting vehicle misfired, blowing off most of the face of Private Joseph Mayek who was standing guard near the vehicle. The accident was ultimately traced to a faulty replacement battery that the commander in charge had authorized. When the Bradley's ignition was turned on, the replacement battery in the turret (a Marine battery rather than an Army one) failed to shut off current to the gun. Mayek, who was 20, died.

12 The Army officer in charge, then Capt. John Prior, reconstructed the ghastly scene for me, and the failed attempts in the medic tent to save Mayek's life. He then turned to his feelings of responsibility: "I'm the one who placed the vehicles; I'm the one who set the security. As with most accidents, I'm not in jail right now. Clearly I wasn't egregiously responsible. But it is a comedy of errors. Any one of a dozen decisions made over the course of a two-month period and none of them really occurs to you at the time. Any one of those made differently may have saved his life. So I dealt with and still deal with the guilt of having cost him his life essentially. . . . There's probably not a day that doesn't go by that I don't think about it, at least fleetingly."

13 What Prior feels are feelings of guilt, and not simply regret that things didn't work out differently. He feels the awful weight of self-indictment,[8] the empathy with the victim and survivors, and the need to make moral repair. If he didn't feel that, we would probably think less of him as a commander.

CLOSE READ

ANNOTATE: In paragraph 14, mark sentences in which the author states her own observations.

QUESTION: How does the quotation from Prior add to or support the author's observations?

CONCLUDE: What is the effect of the author's choice to quote Prior?

14 In his case, moral repair came through an empathic, painful connection with Mayek's mother. After the fratricide, Prior and his first sergeant wrote a letter to Mayek's mother. And for some time after, she replied with care packages to the company and with letters. "Oh it was terrible," said Prior. "The letters weren't just very matter of fact—here's what we did today; it was more like a mother writing to her son." Prior had become the son who was no longer. "It was her way of dealing with the grief," said Prior. "And so I had a responsibility to try to give back."

15 In all this we might say guilt, subjective guilt, has a redemptive side. It is a way that soldiers impose moral order on the chaos and awful randomness of war's violence. It is a way they humanize war for themselves, for their buddies, and for us as civilians, too.

16 But if that's all that is involved, it sounds too moralistic. It makes guilt appropriate or fitting because it's good for society. It is the way we all can deal with war. Maybe, instead, we want to say it is fitting because it is evolutionarily adaptive in the way that fear is. But again, this doesn't do justice to the phenomenon. The guilt that soldiers feel isn't just morally expedient[9] or species-adaptive. It is fitting because it gets right certain moral (or evaluative) features of a soldier's world—that good soldiers depend on each other, come to

8. **self-indictment** (sehlf ihn DYT muhnt) *n.* expression of strong disapproval toward oneself; self-blame.
9. **expedient** (ehk SPEE dee uhnt) *adj.* providing an easy way to do something; quick.

VOCABULARY DEVELOPMENT

Word Forms Expand students' vocabulary by helping them learn related forms of the concept vocabulary words. Four of the words have related forms. Give students a blank **Word Forms Chart (myPerspectives+)** with *burden, culpability, conscience,* and *empathic* in the correct columns. Work with the class to determine the related forms. The final chart should look like this:

Noun	Verb	Adjective	Adverb
burden	burden	burdensome	burdensomely
culpability		culpable	culpably
conscience		conscientious	conscientiously
empathy	empathize	**empathic**	empathically

love each other, and have duties to care and bring each other safely home. Philosophers, at least since the time of Kant,[10] have called these "imperfect duties": even in the best circumstances, we can't perfectly fulfill them. And so, what duties to others need to make room for, even in a soldier's life of service and sacrifice, are duties to self, of self-forgiveness and self-empathy. These are a part of full moral repair. ❧

NOTES

10. **Kant** (1724–1804) Immanuel Kant, German philosopher who was a foremost thinker of the European Enlightenment.

Comprehension Check

Complete the following items after you finish your first read.

1. What is survivor guilt?

2. According to the writer, what other emotions do soldiers describe when they talk about feeling guilt?

3. What happened to Private Joseph Mayek, and why does Captain John Prior feel responsible?

4. **Notebook** Write a summary of "The Moral Logic of Survivor Guilt" to confirm your understanding of the text.

RESEARCH

Research to Clarify Choose at least one unfamiliar detail from the text. Briefly research that detail. In what way does the information you learned shed light on an aspect of the editorial?

Research to Explore Conduct research to learn about the history of the official Marine code, *semper fidelis*, and what it signifies.

DIGITAL PERSPECTIVES

Comprehension Check

Possible responses:

1. "Survivor guilt" is the feeling of guilt about being alive when someone close to you has died.
2. The soldiers talk about feelings of responsibility and feeling that they have betrayed fellow soldiers.
3. In April 2003, the gun on a Bradley fighting vehicle misfired, blowing off most of Mayek's face. Captain Prior feels responsible because he placed the vehicles and set the security.
4. Survivors of traumatic events, especially soldiers, may feel guilty for being alive, a phenomenon called "survivor' guilt." When people take responsibility for events that are out of their control, they may feel guilty because of the conflict between the desire to help and the inability to do so. Soldiers develop a sacred bond out of love as well as duty.

Research to Clarify If students struggle to come up with a detail to research further, you may want to suggest that they focus on one of the following details: the beliefs of Aristotle, Bernard Williams, or Kant; the meaning of "species-adaptive."

Research to Explore Students should discover that *Semper Fidelis* has long been used as a motto by various military branches around the world, including the Irish Brigade of France, who helped Americans fight during the Revolutionary War. Their involvement most likely later inspired the Marines to adopt the motto.

PERSONALIZE FOR LEARNING

Challenge

Military Research Encourage interested students to expand the Research to Explore activity by learning about the motto of other branches of the U.S. military, including the Air Force, Army, Coast Guard, and Navy, in addition to the Marines. Students can also draw the crests for each branch and present their results in a poster or an online presentation.

Jump Start

CLOSE READ Ask students to consider the following prompt: *How would you help someone who is experiencing "survivor guilt"? What do you think you might say or do to help the person cope with his or her feelings?* As students discuss in their groups, ask them to consider the author's discussion of this phenomenon among the military.

Close Read the Text

Walk students through the annotation model on the student page. Encourage them to complete items 2 and 3 on their own. Review and discuss the sections students have marked. If needed, continue to model close reading by using the Annotation Highlights in the Interactive Teacher's Edition.

Analyze the Text

Possible responses:

1. (a) Some people find "survivor guilt" unreasonable because the person feeling the guilt was not responsible for the other's death. **DOK 1**
(b) Sherman responds to this opinion by saying that we often take responsibility to a degree that goes beyond what we can reasonably be held responsible for. **DOK 2**
2. Sherman means that the logic is based on our feelings (morals) rather than on objective facts (logic). This is an oxymoron, a seeming contradiction. **DOK 2**
3. (a) The two men's experiences are similar because both men feel responsible for another man's death. Captain Bonenberger was not in any way involved in the death of his friend, as the death occurred after the friend had returned home. Captain Prior, in contrast, gave orders that indirectly contributed to his friend's death, which occurred while the men were on active duty. **DOK 2**
(b) Both their stories support the idea of "survivor guilt." **DOK 3**
4. Responses will vary; however, students should note that survival entails dealing with the emotional aftermath of life-or-death situations. **DOK 3**

MAKING MEANING

THE MORAL LOGIC OF SURVIVOR GUILT

Close Read the Text

1. This model, from paragraph 4 of the text, shows two sample annotations, along with questions and conclusions. Close read the passage, and find another detail to annotate. Then, write a question and your conclusion.

ANNOTATE: This phrase signals that the writer is contrasting two ideas.

QUESTION: What two ideas are being contrasted here?

CONCLUDE: The writer contrasts subjective and objective guilt.

Subjective guilt, associated with this sense of responsibility, is thought to be irrational because one feels guilty despite the fact that he knows he has done nothing wrong. Objective or rational guilt, by contrast—guilt that is "fitting" to one's actions—accurately tracks real wrongdoing or culpability: guilt is appropriate because one acted to deliberately harm someone, or could have prevented harm and did not.

ANNOTATE: These details define subjective and objective guilt.

QUESTION: Why does the author add these details?

CONCLUDE: The writer is making sure to define key concepts so that readers are not confused and can follow her logic.

2. For more practice, go back into the text and complete the close-read notes.
3. Revisit a section of the text you found important during your first read. Read this section closely, and **annotate** what you notice. Ask yourself **questions** such as "Why did the author make this choice?" What can you **conclude**?

Tool Kit
Close-Read Guide and Model Annotation

STANDARDS

Reading Informational Text
- Cite strong and thorough textual evidence to support analysis of what the text says explicitly as well as inferences drawn from the text.
- Determine a central idea of a text and analyze its development over the course of the text, including how it emerges and is shaped and refined by specific details; provide an objective summary of the text.
- Delineate and evaluate the argument and specific claims in a text, assessing whether the reasoning is valid and the evidence is relevant and sufficient; identify false statements and fallacious reasoning.

Analyze the Text

CITE TEXTUAL EVIDENCE to support your answers.

Notebook **Respond to these questions.**

1. (a) **Make Inferences** Why do many people consider survivor guilt to be irrational, or unreasonable? (b) **Draw Conclusions** How does Sherman respond to this opinion? Explain.
2. **Interpret** What does Sherman mean when she refers to "moral logic" in the title of her essay?
3. (a) **Compare and Contrast** How are Captain Bonenberger's and Captain Prior's experiences similar and different? (b) **Connect** What idea do both of their stories support? Explain.
4. **Essential Question**: *What does it take to survive?* What have you learned about the nature of survival by reading this text?

158 UNIT 2 • SURVIVAL

FORMATIVE ASSESSMENT

Analyze the Text

- **If** students fail to cite evidence, **then** remind them to support their ideas with specific information.
- **If** students struggle to identify the rationale for feelings of survivor guilt, **then** discuss the different types of guilt, and illustrate them with examples.
- **If** students are unable to draw conclusions, **then** explain that drawing conclusions involves "reading between the lines" of the information in the text by adding what students already know to the facts stated.

Analyze Craft and Structure

Development of Ideas "The Moral Logic of Survivor Guilt" is an editorial, a form of argumentative writing. As with all types of arguments, an effective editorial must include a clear claim, or central idea, and specific supporting details.

- The **claim** or **central idea** of a text is more than the topic—it is the key message that the writer wants to communicate about the topic.
- **Specific details** are the evidence a writer uses to support and develop the central idea. Facts, examples, numerical data, personal observations, and expert opinions are different types of supporting details.

In "The Moral Logic of Survivor Guilt," the writer unfolds an argument through careful reasoning. She supports her argument with examples, quotations from or references to the ideas of famous philosophers, and her own observations as a professional in her field.

Practice

CITE TEXTUAL EVIDENCE to support your answers.

Notebook Respond to these questions.

1. (a) What key question does Sherman ask early in this editorial? (b) In your own words, briefly state her answer, which is her central idea.
2. Use the chart to record examples of each type of supporting detail Sherman uses to develop her claim, or central idea.

EXAMPLES FROM REAL LIFE	FAMOUS PHILOSOPHERS' IDEAS	AUTHOR'S IDEAS
Soldiers carry home feelings of guilt.	Nietzsche's work with a "bad conscience."	Subjective versus objective or rational guilt: blameworthiness depends on the idea that a person could have done something other than what he did.
Captain Adrian Bonenberg's guilt over the death of Specialist Jeremiah Pulaski	Spinoza's writing in *Ethics*	We often *take* responsibility in a way that goes beyond what we can reasonably be *held* responsible for.
Soldiers feel guilt, responsibility, and having betrayed fellow soldiers.	Aristotle's *Nicomachean Ethics*	Sharing guilt is a form of empathic distress.

3. Choose one of the supporting details you identified in the chart. Explain how Sherman's use of that detail adds to the development of her central idea.
4. (a) In paragraph 8, Sherman compares survivor guilt to "a zero-sum game." Define *zero-sum game.* (b) How does Sherman's use of this mathematical term support her argument?
5. Is Sherman's claim and support well-reasoned and convincing? Explain, citing specific details to support your position.

PERSONALIZE FOR LEARNING

English Language Support

Development of Ideas Have English Learners analyze an essay's central ideas and supporting details.

Display: *In all this we might say that . . ., Indeed . . . As his/her remarks make clear . . ., In here/his/this case . . .*

Ask students to write a summary of the essay, stating the central idea and three specific details using the connection word *because.* **EMERGING**

Ask students to write a summary of the essay, stating the central idea and three specific details using the phrases displayed, such as *In all this we might say that* or *In her case.* **EXPANDING**

Ask students to write a summary of the essay, stating the central idea and presenting two other people's views mentioned in the essay using the phrases that emphasize agreement, such as *Indeed,* or *As his remarks make clear.* **BRIDGING**

An expanded **English Language Support Lesson** on Central Idea and Specific Details is available in the Interactive Teacher's Edition.

DIGITAL PERSPECTIVES

Analyze Craft and Structure

Explain that effective writers use specific details (as opposed to vague generalities) to bolster their points and add to their credibility. For example, in this essay the author cites specific examples from the works of famous philosophers in order to add more weight to her argument. For more support, see **Analyze Craft and Structure: Development of Ideas.**

MAKE IT INTERACTIVE

Project the digital version of "The Moral Logic of Survivor Guilt," and read aloud paragraph 3. Model how to locate an example from real life (Captain Bonenberger's story) to help students understand what they have to do to complete the chart correctly.

Practice

Possible responses:

1. (a) *Is the sense of responsibility soldiers feel toward each other irrational?* (b) Even though it might be irrational, survivor guilt has a redemptive side. It creates empathy and helps impose moral order on the chaos and violence of war.
2. **See possible responses in chart on Student page.**
3. By including the reference to Aristotle's *Nicomachean Ethics*, the author further develops her idea that "the feelings that express character are . . . about what one cares deeply about."
4. (a) In a zero-sum game, each participant's loss (or gain) is exactly balanced by the losses (or gains) of the other participants. (b) Sherman's use of the term provides an analogy to her point that even though survivors feel guilty about something over which they have no control, this guilt is balanced by the positive effects of the underlying emotions, such as imposing a moral order on the chaos and violence of war.
5. Responses will vary but should be supported with specific details from the text.

FORMATIVE ASSESSMENT

Analyze Craft and Structure

If students are unable to identify the specific details in "The Moral Logic of Survivor Guilt," **then** have them start by filling in the third column of the chart (author's ideas), and work back to columns 1 and 2. For Reteach and Practice, see **Analyze Craft and Structure: Development of Ideas (RP).**

Concept Vocabulary

Why These Words? Discuss with students the difference between saying the *burden* of guilt and the *issue* of guilt. How is the connotation, the emotional overtone, of the word *issue* different from that of the word *burden*?

Possible responses:

1. The concept vocabulary helps readers feel the emotional aspect of guilt.
2. *responsibility* (paragraph 2), *accountable* (paragraph 4), *help* (paragraph 6)

Practice

Possible responses:

1. Her backpack weighed 20 pounds and so was a significant *burden* to carry.
   The child's *conscience* bothered him when he told a lie, and he found the guilt difficult to endure.
   The criminal showed *remorse* when he appeared before the judge.
   Marcia *entrusted* her sister to keep her secret.
   The child's downcast eyes were a tacit admission of *culpability* in the issue of the cookie theft.
   The psychologist was a close listener and had *empathic* ability.
2. Students are likely to find the sentences with the shorter words easier to complete.

Word Network

Possible words: medic, redemptive, adaptive, exonerated

Word Study

For more support, see **Concept Vocabulary and Word Study.**

Possible responses:

1. *Empathic* means "identifying with the feelings of others."
2. *Empathize* means "to identify with the feelings of others."
   Sympathy means "sharing the feelings of others, especially in times of sorrow or grief."

FORMATIVE ASSESSMENT

Concept Vocabulary

If students are unable to see how these words express the experience and necessity of survivor guilt, **then** have them use these words in sentences to discuss what they learned about survivor guilt from the reading.

Word Study

If students are unable to define the words, **then** have students focus on the meaning of the root, *-path-*. For Reteach and Practice, see **Word Study: Greek Root *-path-* (RP).**

LANGUAGE DEVELOPMENT

THE MORAL LOGIC OF SURVIVOR GUILT

Concept Vocabulary

burden	conscience	entrusted
culpability	remorse	empathic

Why These Words? These concept words help us describe how people take care of others—or fail to do so. For example, Sherman explains that soldiers often carry the burden of guilt home with them. The word *burden* emphasizes that this guilt is both difficult to carry and an obligation. She later discusses *conscience* in order to emphasize the moral dimension of soldiers' emotional responses.

1. How does the concept vocabulary help readers understand the complex experience of survivor guilt?
2. What other words in the selection connect to the idea of taking care of others?

WORD NETWORK

Add interesting words related to survival from the text to your Word Network.

Practice

Notebook The concept vocabulary words appear in "The Moral Logic of Survivor Guilt."

1. Use each concept word in a sentence that demonstrates your understanding of the word's meaning. Then, create fill-in puzzles by taking turns reading a sentence aloud, but leaving out the concept word. Invite listeners to guess the missing word.
2. Discuss each fill-in puzzle. Which sentences were easy for listeners to complete, and which were difficult? Why?

Word Study

Greek Root: *-path-* The Greek root *-path-*, which appears in the concept vocabulary word *empathic*, means "feeling." It comes from the Greek word *pathos*, meaning "feeling" or "suffering."

1. Write a definition of *empathic* based on your understanding of its root.
2. Define these words that include the same root: *pathetic*, *empathize*, *sympathy*. Consult a college-level dictionary if necessary.

STANDARDS

Language

- Demonstrate command of the conventions of standard English capitalization, punctuation, and spelling when writing.
- Use a semicolon to link two or more closely related independent clauses.
- Use a colon to introduce a list or quotation.
- Identify and correctly use patterns of word changes that indicate different meanings or parts of speech.
- Consult general and specialized reference materials, both print and digital, to find the pronunciation of a word or determine or clarify its precise meaning, its part of speech, or its etymology.

160 UNIT 2 • SURVIVAL

CROSS-CURRICULAR PERSPECTIVES

Science Discuss with students some possible functions of guilt. For example, guilt helps people try to make amends to resolve something they've done wrong. Guilt might also teach a lesson, so it helps prevent the same negative actions that brought about the bad feeling. Finally, guilt helps uphold the moral guidelines of social groups, so everyone behaves better and society functions with less stress. Have students debate whether or not they believe that guilt fulfills these functions in society.

Conventions

Punctuation Writers use punctuation to clarify the relationships among ideas, establish rhythm, and add sentence variety. This chart shows uses for three punctuation marks: **colons (:)**, **semicolons (;)**, and **dashes (—)**.

USE COLONS TO . . .	EXAMPLES
• introduce a list	We bought the following: milk, eggs, and cheese.
• introduce a quotation, when it is formal or lengthy or when there is no introductory expression	Holmes wrote this about freedom: "It is only through free debate and free exchange of ideas that government remains responsive to the will of the people."
• introduce a sentence that summarizes or explains the sentence before it	His explanation for being late was believable: He had had a flat tire on the way.
USE SEMICOLONS TO . . .	**EXAMPLES**
• join closely related complete sentences, without a coordinating conjunction	We explored the attic together; we were amazed at all the useless junk we found there.
• join closely related complete sentences, with a transitional word or phrase	They visited shops in eight counties in only two days; consequently, they had no time to relax.
• avoid confusion when items in a list or series already contain commas	I sent letters to Alex, my friend from camp; Alana, my pen pal; and Hassan, my cousin.
USE DASHES TO . . .	**EXAMPLES**
• indicate an abrupt change of thought or a dramatic interrupting idea	The pagoda was built—you may find this hard to believe—in a single month.
• set off a summary statement at the end of a sentence	To see her jersey hanging from the rafters—this was Cherie's greatest dream.
• set off a nonessential appositive that is long or already punctuated	The cause of the damage—a rare South American termite—went undiscovered for years.

Read It

In these sentences from "The Moral Logic of Survivor Guilt," mark each colon, semicolon, or dash. Then, explain its function in the sentence.

1. The guilt begins an endless loop of counterfactuals—thoughts that you could have or should have done otherwise. . . .
2. Objective or rational guilt . . . tracks real wrongdoing or culpability: Guilt is appropriate because one acted to deliberately harm. . . .
3. "The letters weren't just very matter of fact—here's what we did today; it was more like a mother writing to her son."

Write It

Notebook Write three sentences about the editorial. Use at least one colon, one semicolon, and one dash.

PERSONALIZE FOR LEARNING

Strategic Support

Semicolons Students will often incorrectly combine an independent and dependent clause with a semicolon. Explain to students that a semicolon functions like the coordinating conjunction *and* to connect two complete sentences (independent clauses). Remind students that a sentence must have a subject (noun or pronoun) and a verb, and it must express a complete thought. Have students write complete sentences based on "The Moral Logic of Survivor Guilt." Then, have them combine related sentences with semicolons.

For example:

Prior wrote a letter to Mayek's mother. He explained the circumstances of her son's death.

Prior wrote a letter to Mayek's mother; he explained the circumstances of her son's death.

DIGITAL PERSPECTIVES

Conventions

Punctuation Provide the following model to explore the different effects each mark of punctuation creates.

The general public likely doesn't understand how returning soldiers feel; the soldiers often carry a heavy load of guilt.

Point out how this example uses a semicolon to link two related independent clauses (complete sentences).

The general public likely doesn't understand how returning soldiers feel—the soldiers often carry a heavy load of guilt.

Point out how this example uses a dash to link the two related independent clauses but emphasizes the information in the second clause. For more support, see **Conventions: Punctuation.**

Read It

Possible responses:

1. dash, sets off an appositive
2. colon, introduces an explanation
3. dash, indicates an interrupting idea; semicolon, joins closely related complete sentences

Write It

Possible response:

Soldiers struggle with many emotions when they return home: guilt, disorientation, and loneliness. Soldiers must develop strategies for handling wartime violence; they must also adjust to the peace of civilian life. Their feelings of guilt—regardless of responsibility—can be overwhelming.

FORMATIVE ASSESSMENT

Conventions

- **If** students cannot use a colon to introduce a list or example, **then** have them write the independent clause on the left of their paper and the list on the right to see the relationship.
- **If** students cannot use a semicolon to link two closely related clauses, **then** have them find the subject and verb in each independent clause.
- **If** students cannot use a dash to set off material for emphasis, **then** have them read the sentences aloud to hear the emphasis. For Reteach and Practice, see **Conventions: Punctuation (RP).**

TEACHING

Writing to Sources

Explain to students that a definition can take different forms. A brief *dictionary entry*, for instance, is usually no more than a phrase or two. An encyclopedia entry, in contrast, is more detailed and far longer—often several paragraphs in length. Point out that the form is related to the function of each: A brief dictionary definition deals with a simple idea, while an encyclopedia entry definition addresses a far more complex idea.

Writers make their extended definitions clear and precise by using different kinds of support, especially **details** and **anecdotes**. Point out to students that anecdotes, as with all narratives, can be fiction or nonfiction. Be sure students understand that they can make up anecdotes that best illustrate their point. For more support, see **Writing to Sources: Encyclopedia Entry.**

Vocabulary and Conventions Connection As students write their encyclopedia entries, they should include several of the concept vocabulary words as well as colons, semicolons, and em dashes to make their points clearly and succinctly.

Reflect on Your Writing

Possible responses:

1. The anecdote provided an interesting and specific example.
2. Students might advise classmates to create a plan, such as an outline, before they write.
3. **Why These Words?** Have students list specific examples of words they chose that added power to their encyclopedia entry.

FORMATIVE ASSESSMENT

Writing

If students are unable to create an anecdote to use in their writing, **then** have them work in pairs to tell each other brief stories that illustrate the point they are making in their writing. For Reteach and Practice, see **Writing to Sources: Encyclopedia Entry (RP).**

EFFECTIVE EXPRESSION

THE MORAL LOGIC OF SURVIVOR GUILT

Writing to Sources

The ability to define concepts can be key to a successful argument. When you introduce an unfamiliar or academic idea, it is important to give your readers a clear and accurate definition so that they understand the concept. For example, if you are writing an essay about survivor guilt, you need to explain what is meant by this term before you continue your analysis.

Assignment

Write an **encyclopedia entry** in which you define the idea of imperfect duty, discussed in paragraph 16 of "The Moral Logic of Survivor Guilt." Present a clear definition of the concept, and then clarify your definition with two types of information:

- key details from Sherman's essay that help you understand this concept (see paragraph 16).
- an anecdote, or brief story, that illustrates the concept. Use your own anecdote, not one provided by Sherman in her essay.

Vocabulary and Conventions Connection You might consider using some of the concept vocabulary in your definition, explanation, and anecdote. Use colons, semicolons, and dashes to clarify connections between ideas and add emphasis.

burden	conscience	entrusted
culpability	remorse	empathic

Reflect on Your Writing

After you have written your encyclopedia entry, answer the following questions:

1. How did providing an anecdote help you clarify the concept of an imperfect duty?
2. What advice would you give to another student writing an encyclopedia entry?
3. **Why These Words?** The words you choose make a difference in your writing. Which words did you specifically choose to add power or clarity to your entry?

STANDARDS

Writing
Introduce a topic; organize complex ideas, concepts, and information to make important connections and distinctions; include formatting, graphics, and multimedia when useful to aiding comprehension.

Speaking and Listening
Present information, findings, and supporting evidence clearly, concisely, and logically such that listeners can follow the line of reasoning and the organization, development, substance, and style are appropriate to purpose, audience, and task.

PERSONALIZE FOR LEARNING

Challenge

Letters Have students write letters to active service members. Their letters should be creative and positive and should include an uplifting message to the service member. More information about writing letters to service members can be found at the following websites:

- **Operation Gratitude**
- **A Million Thanks**

Speaking and Listening

Assignment

Write and deliver a **pep talk** you might give to a group of firefighters, a Scout troop, or members of another service organization who have experienced a failure. Explain why it is important that they strive to fulfill their vows, but also forgive themselves when they fail. Include ideas from Sherman's essay, explaining or simplifying them as needed.

1. **Organize Your Talk** Use an outline to gather ideas for your pep talk. Once you have gathered details, organize them logically and delete unneeded information.

Introduction	Describe the reasons for your speech, including your knowledge of the recent failure. State your central idea clearly and in inspiring language.
Body	Provide details that explain your ideas. Arrange the details logically, in an order that makes sense. Note the ideas from Sherman's essay that you will include. For example, you might point out that your listeners' vows are "imperfect duties."
Conclusion	Summarize your main points.

2. **Prepare Your Delivery** Using the notes in your outline, practice giving your pep talk. Record yourself rehearsing, or ask a partner to listen and respond. While rehearsing, keep these techniques in mind:
   - Maintain eye contact with your audience.
   - Use body language to emphasize important ideas.
   - Speak clearly without rushing, taking care to pronounce unfamiliar terms slowly.
3. **Evaluate Presentations** As your classmates deliver their pep talks, listen attentively. Use a presentation evaluation guide like the one shown to analyze their presentations.

PRESENTATION EVALUATION GUIDE

Rate each statement on a scale of 1 (not demonstrated) to 6 (demonstrated).

- [ ] The speaker communicated a positive message clearly and effectively.
- [ ] The speaker used examples from Sherman's essay effectively.
- [ ] The speaker maintained eye contact with the audience.
- [ ] The speaker used effective gestures and other body language.
- [ ] The information was presented logically and effectively.
- [ ] The pep talk concluded with a restatement of the speaker's main points.

EVIDENCE LOG

Before moving on to a new selection, go to your Evidence Log and record what you learned from "The Moral Logic of Survivor Guilt."

DIGITAL PERSPECTIVES

Speaking and Listening

1. **Organize Your Talk** You may wish to help students create their outline by having them note any ideas that will make their pep talk more interesting and effective. For instance, next to "State your central idea clearly and in inspiring language," have students jot down an inspirational quotation to use as a model for their choice of language.
2. **Prepare Your Delivery** Guide students to mark their script to help them know where to raise the pitch of their voice for effect and where to slow down and pause for emphasis. Also remind students to pronounce all words fully, such as "going" instead of "gonna." Finally, have students monitor themselves to avoid using interrupters such as "um" and "like." Suggest that they pause and make eye contact instead.
3. **Evaluate Presentations** Encourage students to make supportive comments about each speaker's words, ideas, and delivery.

For more support, see **Speaking and Listening: Pep Talk.**

Evidence Log Support students in completing their Evidence Log. This paced activity will help prepare them for the Performance-Based Assessment at the end of the unit.

DIGITAL PERSPECTIVES

Illuminating the Standard Watching others give uplifting speeches and presentations can often illuminate the subtle ways in which speakers vary the tone and style of their presentations to match their purpose. Find videos of motivational speakers to help guide students' pep talks. Possible examples include:

- Les Brown's "It's Not Over" speech
- Tony Robbins's "Raise Your Standards and Change Your Rituals" presentation

As students watch the videos, have them note examples of inspiring language and summarize the main points. Preview all videos before showing them to your class.

FORMATIVE ASSESSMENT

Speaking and Listening

If students are unable to speak in front of the class without significant distress, **then** have them deliver their speech to a small group of students instead of the entire class. For Reteach and Practice, see **Speaking and Listening: Pep Talk (RP).**

Selection Test

Administer "The Moral Logic of Survivor Guilt" Selection Test, which is available in both print and digital formats online in Assessments.

The Key to Disaster Survival? Friends and Neighbors

AUDIO SUMMARIES of "The Key to Disaster Survival? Friends and Neighbors" are available in both English and Spanish in the Interactive Teacher's Edition or Unit Resources. Assigning these summaries prior to reviewing the selection may help students build additional background knowledge and set a context for their first review.

Summary

In his podcast, "The Key to Disaster Survival? Friends and Neighbors," NPR Science Correspondent Shankar Vedantam talks to political scientist Daniel Aldrich.

In late August, 2005, Aldrich was a newcomer to New Orleans. He had heard the storm warnings, but he didn't plan to leave town until a neighbor advised him to take his family someplace safe without delay. It was nearly midnight on Saturday, but he and his wife bundled the children into the car and left the city. Hurricane Katrina struck New Orleans early Monday morning.

Since that night, Aldrich has researched disaster sites all over the world. He finds that while emergency services and government aid can rescue, restore, and rebuild, it is good neighbors that are the key to the survival of neighborhoods, communities, and cities.

Insight

Survival may come down to whom you know. Reviewing "The Key to Disaster Survival? Friends and Neighbors" will help students begin to reflect on the social aspect of survival. The relationships people foster in their communities may make the difference between life and death.

ESSENTIAL QUESTION:
What does it take to survive?

Connection to Essential Question

"The Key to Disaster Survival? Friends and Neighbors" provides a sociological perspective on the Essential Question—*What does it take to survive?* Daniel Aldrich's research shows that people with close ties to their community and those who know their neighbors have a better chance of surviving a disaster. Even after the disaster has passed, and the professionals step in to fix the damage, the survival of the community depends on the relationships among its members.

WHOLE-CLASS LEARNING PERFORMANCE TASK
Should the seventh man forgive himself for his failure to save K.?

UNIT PERFORMANCE-BASED ASSESSMENT
Should people in life-or-death situations be held accountable for their actions?

Connection to Performance Tasks

Whole-Class Learning Performance Task In this Performance Task, students will consider the concept of survivor guilt. "The Key to Disaster Survival? Friends and Neighbors" provides students with examples of ways in which people may feel guilty by not helping their neighbors during times of natural disasters.

Unit Performance-Based Assessment The podcast offers an interesting perspective on the question of accountability in life-or-death situations in that it addresses the life, or the potential death, of entire communities as a result of the actions of neighbors.

DIGITAL PERSPECTIVES — Audio | Video | Document | Annotation Highlights | EL Highlights | Online Assessment

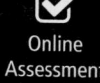

LESSON RESOURCES

	Making Meaning	Effective Expression
Lesson	**Media Vocabulary** **First Review** **Close Review** **Analyze the Media**	**Writing to Sources** **Speaking and Listening**
Instructional Standards	**L.6** Acquire and use accurately general academic and domain-specific words and phrases . . .	**SL.3** Evaluate a speaker's point of view . . . **SL.4** Present information, findings, and supporting evidence . . .
STUDENT RESOURCES		
Available online in the Interactive Student Edition or Unit Resources	Selection Audio First-Review Guide: Media-Audio Close-Review Guide: Media-Audio Word Network	Evidence Log
TEACHER RESOURCES		
Selection Resources Available online in the Interactive Teacher's Edition or Unit Resources	Audio Summaries Media Vocabulary	Writing to Sources: Listener Comment Speaking and Listening: Oral Presentation

Media Complexity Rubric: The Key to Disaster Survival? Friends and Neighbors

Quantitative Measures	
Format and Length: audio of 5 minutes, 37 seconds	
Qualitative Measures	
Knowledge Demands ① ② **❸** ④ ⑤	The central situation (needing rescue from a disaster) may not be familiar to all students, but the concepts of neighbors helping is familiar and is explained clearly.
Structure ① **❷** ③ ④ ⑤	For both reading and listening, the story is told in a straightforward, linear way; conversational language and alternating voices make it easy to follow.
Language Conventionality and Clarity ① ② **❸** ④ ⑤	Some sentences in the explanation are complex, with multiple clauses and difficult vocabulary, but the selection also has many quotations that include conversational language.
Levels of Meaning/Purpose ① ② **❸** ④ ⑤	Selection has only one level of meaning. The main concept and supporting ideas are clearly stated when reading or listening.

Jump Start

FIRST REVIEW Ask students to consider the following prompt: *How many people do you know in your neighborhood?* As students discuss in groups, ask them to consider why knowing your neighbors might be important and how the question might relate to the concept of survival.

The Key to Disaster Survival? Friends and Neighbors

How can friends and neighbors be the key to surviving a disaster? Does that mean you can expect your neighbor to row his boat to your door the next time it floods? Modeling the questions readers might ask as they review "The Key to Disaster Survival? Friends and Neighbors" brings the radio broadcast alive for students and connects it to the Whole-Class Performance Task question. Selection audio is available in the Interactive Teacher's Edition.

Media Vocabulary

Encourage students to discuss the media vocabulary. Have they seen or used these words or concepts before? Have students brainstorm three examples of Expert Commentary and share with the class. For more support, see **Media Vocabulary**.

FIRST REVIEW

As they listen, students should perform the steps of the first review:

LISTEN: Remind students to listen to the different speakers in the radio broadcast and note who is speaking when.

NOTE: Encourage students to listen to the reporter to note key ideas.

CONNECT: Encourage students to make connections beyond the radio broadcast. If they cannot make connections to their own lives, have them consider other news reports they may have heard or read.

RESPOND: Students will answer questions to demonstrate understanding.

Point out to students that while they will always complete the Respond step at the end of the first review, the other steps will probably happen concurrently. You may wish to print copies of the **First-Review Guide: Media-Audio** for students to use.

About the Narrator

Shankar Vedantam
(b. 1969) worked as a reporter for the *Washington Post* for ten years before joining National Public Radio as a science correspondent in 2011. Inspired by a story he had done about hidden biases, Vedantam wrote *The Hidden Brain*, a book that examines the complexities of the unconscious. His reporting ties together his interests in both human behavior and the social sciences, giving readers and listeners unique insight into daily news.

The Key to Disaster Survival? Friends and Neighbors

Media Vocabulary

The following words or concepts will be useful to you as you analyze, discuss, and write about media.

Introduction: context and background information about the topic of a radio broadcast, provided at its beginning	• The introduction is meant to grab listeners' attention so they'll want to keep listening and learn more about the story. • The introduction is usually brief and functions to "set the stage" for the full story.
Expert Commentary: information delivered by a person who has special knowledge of the subject	• Expert commentary is often used to support a specific point of view. • Although expert commentary may be used to validate a story, it is still up to listeners to decide whether it is credible.
Interpreter: person who changes the words of one language into another for the benefit of listeners	• Listeners will often hear a response in the speaker's language before the interpreter restates the words in the listeners' language.

First Review MEDIA: AUDIO

Apply these strategies as you listen to the radio broadcast.

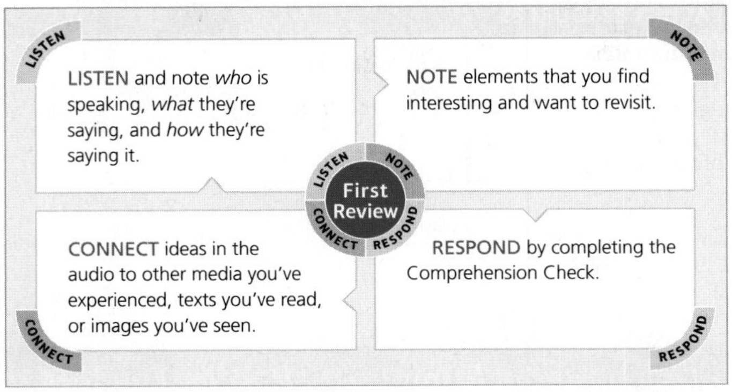

LISTEN
NOTE
LISTEN and note *who* is speaking, *what* they're saying, and *how* they're saying it.
NOTE elements that you find interesting and want to revisit.
First Review
CONNECT ideas in the audio to other media you've experienced, texts you've read, or images you've seen.
RESPOND by completing the Comprehension Check.
CONNECT
RESPOND

Listening Strategy: Take Notes

Notebook As you listen, write down your observations and questions, making sure to note time codes so you can easily revisit sections later.

STANDARDS
Language
Acquire and use accurately general academic and domain-specific words and phrases, sufficient for reading, writing, speaking, and listening at the college and career readiness level; demonstrate independence in gathering vocabulary knowledge when considering a word or phrase important to comprehension or expression.

MEDIA | RADIO BROADCAST

The Key to Disaster Survival? Friends and Neighbors

Shankar Vedantam

BACKGROUND

Since the beginning of the twenty-first century, there have been numerous large-scale natural disasters. The earthquake and tsunami that hit the east coast of Japan in 2011 killed more than 15,000 people and caused an estimated 300 billion dollars' worth of damage. The tragic, catastrophic 2004 Indian Ocean tsunami killed more than 230,000 people. In the wake of natural disaster, governments and NGOs—nongovernment organizations—try to rebuild the affected regions. In areas at risk of disaster, people are encouraged to make preparations such as drafting a survival plan, stockpiling resources, and designating a storm shelter in their home.

SCAN FOR MULTIMEDIA

NOTES

CLOSER REVIEW

Analyze Evidence

Students may have noted the section of the broadcast from 5:36 to 6:38 during their first review. Use this segment to help students understand how evidence is used to support a claim. Encourage them to talk about what they noted. You may want to model a close review with the class based on the notes below.

NOTE: Have students note the details in the broadcast that describe the narrator's claim and the evidence used to support it, or have students participate while you note them.

Possible response: NGOs can hurt those they are trying to help. Prior to the tsunami in Southeast Asia in 2004, some villagers owned boats, but others comprised a support network for the fishing industry. Once everyone was made an owner by the NGOs, this support network disappeared as new boat owners competed for fish and the human resources necessary for fishing.

QUESTION: Guide students to consider what these details might tell them. Ask what a listener can infer from these details, and accept student responses.

Possible response: Sometimes NGOs take actions that they think are helpful, but unless they consider the underlying dynamics of a community, their actions might harm those they are trying to help.

CONCLUDE: Help students to formulate conclusions about the importance of these details in the radio broadcast. Ask students why the narrator might have included these details.

Possible response: Providing real-life examples of the effects of an NGO's actions provides evidence to support the narrator's claim and helps the listener better understand.

Remind students that even when claims are made orally, they should be supported by **evidence**.

PERSONALIZE FOR LEARNING

English Language Support

Taking Notes Support students as they listen to the podcast. Form groups and have them listen to the podcast in 30 second increments. Students should take notes on the key ideas and details spoken during each segment. After listening for 30 seconds, have group members compare their notes. Repeat the process until students have listened to the entirety of the podcast. **ALL LEVELS**

TEACHING

Comprehension Check

Possible responses:

1. The narrator begins by listing recent disasters and reporting that we've heard a lot about the emergency personnel who responded to those disasters.
2. Daniel Aldridge's neighbor knocked on his door because Hurricane Katrina was approaching and the neighbor knew Aldridge was unfamiliar with this type of weather.
3. Aldridge studied the Indian villages hit by the 2004 tsunami and the aftereffects of the earthquake in 1995 in Kobe, Japan.
4. Watanabe's neighbors provided a generator which allowed his father to continue to use his breathing machine.

Close Review

Model how to listen closely by using the Closer Look note for the podcast. Remind students to clarify anything they did not understand during their first review. You may wish to print the **Close-Review Guide: Media-Audio** for students to use.

Analyze the Media

Possible responses:

1. (a) Watanabe's story provides a personal anecdote that supports the reporter's position. **DOK 1**
(b) Responses will vary, but students will most likely respond that Watanabe's account allows an English-speaking audience to see how this phenomenon happens across different societies. **DOK 2**
2. (a) One of the most successful groups at rebuilding in New Orleans was one that ignored officials who told them not to return and rebuild. **DOK 1** (b) Including the views of economists provides support for the claim made in the podcast that friends and neighbors can be critically important in disaster situations. **DOK 2**
3. The story of the fishing villages provides evidence to support the narrator's claim that NGOs can actually hurt people recovering from a disaster. **DOK 3**
4. Students may conclude that survival depends most on those around you. **DOK 3**

Word Network

Possible words: victim, decisive, forces, infrastructure

FORMATIVE ASSESSMENT

Analyze the Media

If students struggle to determine the importance of Watanabe's first-hand account, **then** remind them how anecdotes can strengthen a claim.

MAKING MEANING

Comprehension Check

Complete the following items after you finish your first review.

1. What information does the show's host give the listener during the introduction of the broadcast?
2. What event causes Daniel Aldridge's neighbor to knock on Aldridge's door late at night?
3. What event does Aldridge use to study the effect of neighbors' helping one another in Japan?
4. Who helped Michinori Watanabe save his father?

MEDIA VOCABULARY

Use these words as you discuss and write about the broadcast.

introduction
expert commentary
interpreter

WORD NETWORK

Add interesting survival words from the broadcast to your Word Network.

STANDARDS

Speaking and Listening

- Evaluate a speaker's point of view, reasoning, and use of evidence and rhetoric, identifying any fallacious reasoning or exaggerated or distorted evidence.
- Present information, findings, and supporting evidence clearly, concisely, and logically such that listeners can follow the line of reasoning and the organization, development, substance, and style are appropriate to purpose, audience, and task.

Close Review

Listen to the broadcast again. Write down any new observations that seem important. What **questions** do you have? What can you **conclude**?

REVIEW QUESTION Close Review CONCLUDE

Analyze the Media

CITE TEXTUAL EVIDENCE to support your answers.

Notebook Respond to these questions.

1. **(a)** What does Michinori Watanabe's story add to the broadcast? **(b) Evaluate** Is it important to hear Watanabe's firsthand account translated for an English audience? Explain.
2. **(a)** What information does Emily Chamlee-Wright provide? **(b) Draw a Conclusion** Why do you think Shankar Vedantam includes the economist's thoughts after the stories of people in disaster situations?
3. The central idea is reiterated at the end of the broadcast. How does the story of the fishing villages contribute to the central idea?
4. **Essential Question:** ***What does it take to survive?*** What have you learned about the nature of survival by listening to this broadcast?

Writing to Sources

Many radio-show websites include a comments section and invite listeners to share their thoughts about the shows.

Assignment

Write a **listener comment** about this radio broadcast. In one to three paragraphs, explain how the show affected you and evaluate the points of view of the people documented in the broadcast, their reasoning, and their explanations.

- Use a friendly but formal tone.
- Develop your ideas by jotting down answers to these questions:
  - Does the broadcast convince you that neighbors can be more effective at helping than authorities? Explain your thinking.
  - Are there other questions you think Shankar Vedantam should have asked? If so, what are they?
  - How do you think professional rescue workers might respond to this broadcast? What do you think a government official would say?

THE KEY TO DISASTER SURVIVAL? FRIENDS AND NEIGHBORS

Speaking and Listening

This broadcast summarizes the circumstances of a few individuals who faced disaster scenarios.

Assignment

Consider this question: *Does the radio broadcast present the full picture?* With a partner, research disaster relief efforts. Consult primary and secondary sources: newspapers, broadcast media, and accounts written by disaster survivors. Plan, write, and present your findings in an informal **oral presentation**.

- Organize your information into talking points—a list of brief statements you can refer to while sharing your findings.
- Include a statement that answers the research question.
- Using your talking points, present your findings to the class.

EVIDENCE LOG

Before moving on to a new selection, go to your Evidence Log and record what you learned from "The Key to Disaster Survival? Friends and Neighbors."

DIGITAL PERSPECTIVES

Writing to Sources

Explain to students that when evaluating media sources, they should consider not only the claims made, but also the reasons and evidence presented to support the claim.

MAKE IT INTERACTIVE

Have students record and share their listener comments. Explain to students that often, listeners can comment not only on the radio broadcast but on the comments of other listeners. Give students several minutes to formulate responses to the shared listener comments. Have students share their responses with the class. Ask students to evaluate the effectiveness of the responses by identifying any claims, reasons, and evidence to support the reasons found in the responses. For more support, see **Writing to Sources: Listener Comment**.

Speaking and Listening

Remind students that there are many different types of evidence they can use to support their talking points, including facts, statistics, anecdotes, quotations from authorities, and examples.

In addition to ensuring they have sufficient evidence to support their talking points, students should evaluate the reliability of their evidence. Discuss the characteristics that make evidence reliable:

- reliable sources, including government, educational, and professional organizations
- degree to which experts have reviewed the evidence for accuracy
- credibility of references and confirmation provided by the source of the evidence

For more support, see **Speaking and Listening: Oral Presentation**.

Evidence Log Support students in completing their Evidence Log. This paced activity will help prepare them for the Performance-Based Assessment at the end of the unit.

DIGITAL PERSPECTIVES

Enriching the Media Locate and project one or more Internet resources related to disaster-preparedness planning. For example:

- City of Los Angeles' 5 Steps to Neighborhood Preparedness
- Neighbors Helping Neighbors
- Federal Emergency Management Agency

As you review these sites with your students, engage them in a discussion about how they might interact with these resources to help protect themselves and their family. Consider having students create a family or neighborhood disaster-preparedness plan and share it with the class.

FORMATIVE ASSESSMENT

Writing to Sources

If students struggle with identifying the point of view of the speakers in the podcast, **then** have them listen to the podcast again, taking notes on what each speaker says.

Speaking and Listening

If students struggle to identify resources to support their talking points, **then** have them refine the search terms they are using to locate resources.

TEACHING

Jump Start

What is survivor guilt?

Ask students to write down two things they have learned about survivor guilt after reading "The Seventh Man" and "The Moral Logic of Survivor Guilt" and reviewing "The Key to Disaster Survival? Friends and Neighbors." You might guide them with the question "How does survivor guilt affect the survivors?"

As students share, ask them to cite specific examples from the texts or radio broadcast to support their ideas.

Write an Argument

Make sure students understand what they are being asked to do in the Assignment. Explain that the question on which they will take a position is related to the topic of survivor guilt because the seventh man suffers from this problem.

Students should complete the assignment using word processing software to take advantage of editing tools and features.

Elements of an Argument

Remind students that an effective argument, such as "The Cost of Survival," contains all of the listed required elements, is organized in a logical manner, and uses word choice and tone to create a sense of seriousness and authority.

MAKE IT INTERACTIVE

Project "The Cost of Survival" from the Interactive Teacher's Edition, and have students identify the elements of an argument, such as the claim, counterclaims, reasons, evidence, and concluding statement.

Academic Vocabulary

Consider polling students for examples of sentences they might use in their arguments that incorporate the academic vocabulary.

PERFORMANCE TASK: WRITING FOCUS

WRITING TO SOURCES

- THE SEVENTH MAN
- THE MORAL LOGIC OF SURVIVOR GUILT
- THE KEY TO DISASTER SURVIVAL? FRIENDS AND NEIGHBORS

Write an Argument

You've read a short story and a newspaper opinion piece that deal with the issue of survivor guilt. You've also listened to a radio broadcast about the ways in which friends can help one another in survival situations. In "The Seventh Man," the narrator describes the loss of his closest friend. In "The Moral Logic of Survivor Guilt," the author makes an argument about the guilt that surviving soldiers often feel for their fallen comrades. In the radio broadcast, neighbors and friends come to one another's aid.

Assignment

Use your knowledge of "The Seventh Man," "The Moral Logic of Survivor Guilt," and "The Key to Disaster Survival…" to take and defend a position on the topic. Write a brief **argument** in which you state and support your position on this question:

> **Should the narrator of "The Seventh Man" forgive himself for his failure to save K.?**

Elements of an Argument

An **argument** is a logical way of presenting a viewpoint, belief, or stand on an issue. A well-written argument may convince the reader, change the reader's mind, or motivate the reader to take a certain action.

An effective argument contains these elements:

- a precise claim
- consideration of counterclaims, or opposing positions, and a discussion of their strengths and weaknesses
- logical organization that makes clear connections among claim, counterclaim, reasons, and evidence
- valid reasoning and relevant and sufficient evidence
- a concluding statement or section that logically completes the argument
- formal and objective language and tone
- error-free grammar, including accurate use of transitions

ACADEMIC VOCABULARY

As you craft your argument, consider using some of the academic vocabulary you learned in the beginning of the unit.

evidence
credible
valid
formulate
logical

Model Argument For a model of a well-crafted argument, see the Launch Text, "The Cost of Survival."

Challenge yourself to find all of the elements of an effective argument in the text. You will have an opportunity to review these elements as you prepare to write your own argument.

STANDARDS

Writing

Write arguments to support claims in an analysis of substantive topics or texts, using valid reasoning and relevant and sufficient evidence.

- Write routinely over extended time frames and shorter time frames for a range of tasks, purposes, and audiences.

AUTHOR'S PERSPECTIVE **Kelly Gallagher, M.Ed.**

The Best Writer in the Room Intensive modeling is one of the most effective ways to improve writing instruction. When you model at every stage of the writing process, you stop *assigning* writing and start *teaching* it. While you are teaching writing through this Performance Task, show your students how you attack these parts of the assignment:

Prewriting Brainstorm counterclaims and ask students to add their own ideas to your list. List types of evidence you could use.

Drafting Outline the argument, and draft alongside students.

Revising Use your model or a student model as an example.

Do this work in front of students each time. While it may seem more efficient to follow the same steps with each class or show a perfectly polished essay, don't take this path. If you authentically model the work of writing, students may be more open to the work of writing. It is important for the students to see the teacher struggle a bit with the work.

Prewriting / Planning

Write a Claim Now that you have thought about how the authors of the selections in this unit make their arguments, write a sentence in which you state your **claim**, or position on the question posed in this assignment. As you continue to write, you may revise your claim or even change it entirely. For now, it will help you choose reasons and supporting evidence.

Claim: ____

____.

Consider Possible Counterclaims Remember that part of your job is to address **counterclaims**, or opposing positions. Complete these sentences to address a counterclaim.

Another reader might say that ______________________________.

The reason he or she might think this is because ______________________.

The evidence that supports this is ______________________________.

However, my position is stronger because ______________________________.

Gather Evidence From Sources There are many different types of evidence you can use to support your argument:

- **facts:** statements that can be proved true
- **statistics:** facts presented in the form of numbers
- **anecdotes:** brief stories that illustrate a point
- **quotations from authorities:** statements from experts
- **examples:** facts, ideas, or events that support a general idea

The use of varied evidence can make your argument stronger. For example, you could use the following quotation from the Launch Text to support the point that even professionals sometimes fail in rescue attempts.

However, arguments against charging for rescue miss an important point. Many rescue workers have lost their own lives saving others.

—"The Cost of Survival"

Connect Across Texts As you write your argument, you will be using evidence from one text to support your analysis of another. Incorporate that evidence in different ways. If the precise words are important, use **exact quotations**. To clarify a complex idea, **paraphrase**, or restate it in your own words. Make sure that your paraphrases accurately reflect the original text.

EVIDENCE LOG

Review your Evidence Log and identify key details you may want to cite in your argument.

STANDARDS

Writing

- Introduce precise claim(s), distinguish the claim(s) from alternate or opposing claims, and create an organization that establishes clear relationships among claim(s), counterclaims, reasons, and evidence.
- Develop claim(s) and counterclaims fairly, supplying evidence for each while pointing out the strengths and limitations of both in a manner that anticipates the audience's knowledge level and concerns.

DIGITAL PERSPECTIVES

Prewriting/Planning

Write a Claim Remind students that the first step in writing an argument is to take a position on the question. Explain that for this assignment, their claim will stem from whether they think the seventh man should forgive himself.

Consider Possible Counterclaims Explain that by considering counterclaims, students can make their argument stronger, demonstrating that they are well informed about both sides of the question by providing evidence to refute these possible counterclaims.

Gather Evidence From Sources Have students review their Evidence Log to find possible support for their claim. Remind them that if they have sufficient evidence in their Evidence Log, they may want to go back and review the selections to identify additional or stronger evidence for their argument. Students should also consider using other sources to support their claim and should make a plan for identifying and citing evidence from these sources.

Connect Across Texts Make sure students understand that paraphrasing is restating in their own words what an author has written. A paraphrase retains the meaning of the original text but is usually expressed in a simpler way. Remind students that it's very important to use different words when they paraphrase in order to avoid plagiarizing.

PERSONALIZE FOR LEARNING

English Language Support

Writing a Claim Support students as they write a claim for their argument.

Have students review the definition of argument. Encourage them to write their claim in a short, complete sentence. **EMERGING**

Have students review the definition of argument. Encourage them to write their claim in a complete sentence, paying attention to how their statement is organized. **EXPANDING**

Ask students to keep in mind that they are writing an argument. Encourage them to write their claim and offer supporting reasons. **BRIDGING**

TEACHING

Drafting

Organize Your Argument Explain to students the difference between the *elements* of an argument (claim, counterclaims, valid reasoning and evidence, and concluding statement) and the *organization* of an argument (introduction, body, and conclusion). Students should use their working claim, possible counterclaims, and evidence to complete an Argument Outline of their own.

Write a First Draft As students write their first draft, they should focus on getting their ideas on paper, incorporating all of the elements of an argument. Students should remember to include sufficient details to ensure that a reader with no knowledge of the subject can understand their claim and reasoning.

Encourage students to grab the reader's attention in the introduction by including a pertinent quotation from one of the selections or a compelling statistic that relates to their claim.

PERFORMANCE TASK: WRITING FOCUS

Drafting

Organize Your Argument Most arguments are composed of three parts:

- the **introduction**, in which you state your claim
- the **body**, in which you provide analysis, supporting reasons, and evidence
- the **conclusion**, in which you summarize or restate your claim

Each part of your argument should build on the part that came before, and every point should connect directly to your main claim. This outline shows the key sections of the Launch Text. Notice that each paragraph fulfills a specific purpose.

LAUNCH TEXT

Model: "The Cost of Survival" Outline

INTRODUCTION
Paragraph 1 states claim: *The adventurer should be the one to foot the bill.*

BODY
Paragraph 2 establishes importance: *Two big news stories of 2014 involved rescue missions.*

Paragraph 3 presents/refutes counterclaim: *It is easy to argue that people should be stopped from putting themselves in danger. However, this would be impossible to enforce.*

Paragraph 4 presents support for main claim: *People who take extreme risks should pay for their rescue operation.*

Paragraph 5 presents counterclaim: *Not everyone agrees that people should be responsible for the costs of their rescue.*

Paragraph 6 refutes counterclaim: *However, arguments against charging for rescue miss an important point. Many rescue workers have lost their own lives saving others.*

CONCLUSION
Paragraph 7 restates claim: *In the end, taxpayers cover the cost of rescue for those who put themselves at risk. Maybe there are better places for our money.*

Argument Outline

INTRODUCTION

BODY

CONCLUSION

Write a First Draft Use your outline to write your first draft. Remember to include a precise claim and to address possible counterclaims. Use a variety of evidence and make clear connections to your claim and counterclaims. Keep your audience in mind as you craft your argument. Begin with an interesting point to engage them, and conclude by logically completing your argument. Keep in mind what your audience might already know and what might be unfamiliar to them.

STANDARDS
Writing
Provide a concluding statement or section that follows from and supports the argument presented.

170 UNIT 2 • SURVIVAL

AUTHOR'S PERSPECTIVE **Jim Cummins, Ph.D.**

Sentence Frames Students learning English may be challenged by a blank page. Support them with scaffolding to help them organize their arguments and flesh out their outlines. They may benefit from using sentence frames like the following to help them map out their writing.

Introduction: I believe the seventh man should/should not forgive himself for not saving K. because ______________ ________.

Evidence from the text: My point of view is supported by the fact that ________.

Counterclaim: Others may say that he should/should not forgive himself because ________, but this view is problematic because ____________.

Conclusion: Although it may seem like the seventh man should/should not forgive himself because ________, ultimately, he should/should not because ________.

Remind students that the writing process is recursive and they will be able to refine their outlines and sentence frames as they draft. These are simply tools to help them organize their thoughts before they begin writing.

LANGUAGE DEVELOPMENT: AUTHOR'S STYLE

Create Cohesion: Transitions

Transitions are words and phrases that connect and show relationships between ideas. Transitional words and phrases perform an essential function in an argument. They help the writer guide the reader through a line of reasoning.

Read It

These sentences from the Launch Text use transitions to show specific connections between ideas.

- However, *when things don't turn out well, a lost climber or an injured base jumper may need help.* (shows contrast)
- Even so, *someone has to pay for those rescues.* (shows emphasis)
- *In New Hampshire,* for example, *hikers who get lost or injured because of reckless behavior can be billed for rescue services.* (illustrates or shows)
- In addition, *the idea of holding people responsible is not to stop rescuing them.* (adds idea)

Write It

As you draft your argument, choose transitions that accurately show specific relationships between your ideas. Transitions are especially important when connecting one paragraph to the next.

If you want to . . .	consider using one of these transitions
list or add ideas	*first of all, secondly, next, lastly, in addition*
compare	*also, equally, likewise*
contrast	*although, however, on the other hand*
emphasize	*most of all, immediately, in fact*
show effect	*therefore, as a result, so, consequently*
illustrate or show	*for example, for instance, specifically*

TIP

PUNCTUATION

Make sure to punctuate transitional expressions correctly.

- Use a comma after a transitional expression at the beginning of a sentence.
- Use a comma before and after a transitional expression in the middle of a clause or sentence unless the transition follows a semicolon. In that case, add a comma only *after* the transition.

STANDARDS

Writing

Use words, phrases, and clauses to link the major sections of the text, create cohesion, and clarify the relationships between claim(s) and reasons, between reasons and evidence, and between claim(s) and counterclaims.

DIGITAL PERSPECTIVES

Create Cohesion: Transitions

Read It

Emphasize that transitions are essential to developing a strong argument because they add clarity and cohesion.

MAKE IT INTERACTIVE

Project "The Cost of Survival" from the Interactive Teacher's Edition and ask students to identify additional examples of transitions.

- list: **In one,** *a family of four called for help when their child became ill.* (paragraph 2)
- add ideas: **In addition***, the idea of holding people responsible is not to stop rescuing them.* (paragraph 6)

Write It

As students revise their draft, they should think about the relationships between their ideas and use the suggested transitions to improve the clarity of their argument.

Consider reviewing additional examples of comma use with transitional expressions. For example:

- The seventh man believes he could have saved K., **but** there is nothing he could have done.
- **In fact,** had the seventh man tried to save K., he may have been swept away as well.
- **On the other hand,** perhaps the seventh man could have made more of an effort to warn K.

PERSONALIZE FOR LEARNING

Strategic Support

Transitions Some students may require additional support in using transitions when revising their argument. Pair students with a partner and have them identify places in each other's argument where transition words might clarify what the writer is trying to say or help the flow of the argument. Have them consider the specific relationships among the ideas. Finally, have students review the suggested transitions for the appropriate type of relationship and revise their argument.

TEACHING

Revising

Evaluating Your Draft

Before students begin revising their writing, they should first evaluate their draft to make sure it contains all of the required elements, is organized in a logical manner, and adheres to the norms and conventions of argumentative writing.

Internal Logic Students should also ensure that their argument flows smoothly and that they used transitions to link ideas together and create cohesion.

You might suggest that students read their arguments aloud to a partner or record themselves reading as a strategy for identifying necessary revisions.

Word Choice and Tone Remind students as they revise their argument that using precise language and maintaining a formal tone is an important part of argumentative writing. Explain that the purpose of an argument is to convince readers of a claim, so the word choices and tone they use should match that of a conversation with a teacher and not an informal conversation with a friend.

PERFORMANCE TASK: WRITING FOCUS

Revising

Evaluating Your Draft

Use the following checklist to evaluate the effectiveness of your first draft. Then, use your evaluation and the instruction on this page to guide your revision.

FOCUS AND ORGANIZATION	EVIDENCE AND ELABORATION	CONVENTIONS
☐ Provides an introduction that leads to the argument.	☐ Develops the claim and opposing claims fairly, supplying evidence for each, while pointing out the strengths and limitations of both.	☐ Attends to the norms and conventions of the discipline, especially the correct use and punctuation of transitions.
☐ Introduces a precise claim.	☐ Provides adequate examples for each major idea.	
☐ Distinguishes the claim from opposing claims.	☐ Uses vocabulary and word choice that are appropriate for the audience and purpose.	
☐ Provides a conclusion that follows from the argument.	☐ Establishes and maintains a formal style and an objective tone.	
☐ Establishes a logical organization and develops a progression throughout the argument.		
☐ Uses words, phrases, and clauses to clarify the relationships between and among ideas.		

WORD NETWORK

Include interesting words from your Word Network in your argument.

STANDARDS

Writing

• Write arguments to support claims in an analysis of substantive topics or texts, using valid reasoning and relevant and sufficient evidence.

b. Establish and maintain a formal style and objective tone while attending to the norms and conventions of the discipline in which they are writing.

• Produce clear and coherent writing in which the development, organization, and style are appropriate to task, purpose, and audience.

• Develop and strengthen writing as needed by planning, revising, editing, rewriting, or trying a new approach, focusing on addressing what is most significant for a specific purpose and audience.

Revising for Focus and Organization

Internal Logic Reread your argument, paying attention to the flow of ideas. Are they presented in a logical order? Have you made the connections between your ideas clear?

Revising for Evidence and Elaboration

Word Choice Review your draft. Identify and replace words that are vague, or imprecise. Then, look for words that are repeated throughout your draft. Consider replacing overused words with synonyms. Refer to your Word Network for help varying your word choice.

Tone A writer's **tone** is his or her attitude toward the audience or subject. Because the purpose of an argument is to convince readers of the accuracy of your claim, the tone you use should convey a sense of seriousness and authority.

Apply the following steps to create and maintain a formal tone:

- Avoid slang and abbreviations, and limit the use of contractions.
- Make use of academic vocabulary whenever possible.
- Generally, avoid the use of idioms, which tend to be less formal in tone.
- Refer to places, people, or formal concepts by their proper names.
- A pure argument does not generally use "I" statements. For example, instead of writing, "I think that survivors owe a debt to society," shorten and strengthen the thought: "Survivors owe a debt to society."

HOW LANGUAGE WORKS

Transitions As students revise their arguments, remind them to use transitional words and phrases to connect and show relationships among ideas and create cohesion in their writing. Explain that using transitions is a key element in a logically organized argument. You may want to suggest students consider the following types of transitions as they revise their argument:

When . . .	Transition Type
Considering possible counterclaims	Contrast
Providing reasons to support your claim	List or add ideas; illustrate or show
Using evidence to support your reasons	Show effect; compare
Concluding your argument	Emphasize

PEER REVIEW

Exchange papers with a classmate. Use the checklist to evaluate your classmate's argument and provide supportive feedback.

1. Is the claim clear?
   ☐ yes ☐ no If no, explain what confused you.
2. Is the counterclaim clearly stated? Is there sufficient evidence to counter it?
   ☐ yes ☐ no If no, point out what is missing.
3. Did you find the argument convincing?
   ☐ yes ☐ no If no, write a brief note explaining what you thought was missing.
4. What is the strongest part of your classmate's paper? Why?

Editing and Proofreading

Edit for Conventions Reread your draft for accuracy and consistency. Correct errors in grammar and word usage. Consult a grammar handbook or use online tools if you need help.

Proofread for Accuracy Read your draft carefully, correcting for errors in spelling and punctuation. Check the spelling of plurals. You can make most words plural by simply adding *-s*, but there are some words, such as *libraries*, *arches*, and *echoes*, that don't follow this rule. If you are unsure, use a resource to help you.

Publishing and Presenting

Create a final version of your essay. Share it with your class so that your classmates can read it and make comments. In turn, review and comment on your classmates' work. Consider the ways in which other students' arguments are both similar to and different from your own. Always maintain a polite and respectful tone when commenting.

Reflecting

Think about what you learned by writing your argument. What could you do differently the next time you need to write an argument to make the writing experience easier and to make your argument stronger?

DIGITAL PERSPECTIVES

Peer Review

Remind students before they begin their peer review that they are reviewing for clarity and completeness, not whether they agree with the author's position. However, they might raise a point of disagreement that could be incorporated as a counterclaim to strengthen the argument.

Editing and Proofreading

As students proofread, they should check for grammar, spelling, and punctuation errors. Remind them that although many word processing programs catch grammar and spelling mistakes, they are not foolproof. Students should still manually review their work.

Publishing and Presenting

Before students review their classmates' arguments, remind them of the folowing:

- Keep comments positive.
- Use formal rather than informal language—this includes grammar and punctuation.
- Avoid using all capitals—it reads as if you're yelling.
- Don't just agree; move the discussion forward by building on the ideas of others.
- Disagree respectfully. Give your opinion, but be sure to support your position with evidence.
- Be brief. It's not the number of words, but the clarity of the message that's important.

Reflecting

Students should reflect not only on their argument and the process of writing it, but also on the comments received from their peers.

PERSONALIZE FOR LEARNING

English Language Support

Subject-Verb Agreement English Learners often struggle with subject-verb agreement when writing. Remind students that the subject and the verb in a sentence need to agree. For example, singular subjects need a singular verb (The boy runs), and plural subjects need a plural verb (The girls run). Suggest that students review their argument for subject-verb agreement as part of their editing process. **ALL LEVELS**

OVERVIEW

SMALL-GROUP LEARNING

What does it take to survive?

Explain that survival involves more than just escaping immediate danger. The effects of survival can have life-long repercussions. During Small-Group Learning, students will read selections that examine the strengths needed to survive both immediate danger and the aftermath of an ordeal.

Small-Group Learning Strategies

Review the Learning Strategies with students, and explain that as they work through Small-Group Learning, they will develop strategies to work in small-group environments.

- Have students watch the video on Small-Group Learning Strategies.
- A video on this topic is available online in the Professional Development Center.

You may wish to discuss some action items to add to the chart as a class before students complete it on their own. For example, for "Participate fully," you might solicit the following actions from students:

- Offer an opinion when it differs from the group's ideas.
- Take on an equal share of the work.

Block Scheduling

Each day in this Pacing Plan represents a 40–50 minute class period. Teachers using block scheduling may combine days to reflect their class schedule. In addition, teachers may revise pacing to differentiate and support core instruction by integrating components and resources as students require.

OVERVIEW: SMALL-GROUP LEARNING

ESSENTIAL QUESTION:

What does it take to survive?

Survival is not always straightforward. What is required for survival in one situation may be a detriment in another. You will read selections that examine characteristics that helped people survive life-and-death situations. You will work in a group to continue your exploration of the concept of survival.

Small-Group Learning Strategies

Throughout your life, in school, in your community, in college, and in your career, you will continue to learn and work with others.

Look at these strategies and the actions you can take to practice them as you work in teams. Add ideas of your own for each step. Use these strategies during Small-Group Learning.

STRATEGY	ACTION PLAN
Prepare	• Complete your assignments so that you are prepared for group work. • Organize your thinking so you can contribute to your group's discussions. •
Participate fully	• Make eye contact to signal that you are listening and taking in what is being said. • Use text evidence when making a point. •
Support others	• Build off ideas from others in your group. • Invite others who have not yet spoken to do so. •
Clarify	• Paraphrase the ideas of others to ensure that your understanding is correct. • Ask follow-up questions. •

SCAN FOR MULTIMEDIA

Pacing Plan

Day	Activity
1	Unit Introduction
2	Introduce Whole-Class Learning
3–7	The Seventh Man
8–12	The Moral Logic of Survivor Guilt
13	Media: The Key to Disaster Survival?
14–15	Performance Task

DIGITAL PERSPECTIVES

CONTENTS

COMPARE

NARRATIVE NONFICTION

The Voyage of the *James Caird*

from The Endurance

Caroline Alexander

Can six men sail a small boat into fierce, icy seas to find help for their stranded Antarctic expedition?

MEDIA: PHOTO GALLERY

The *Endurance* and the *James Caird* in Images

Frank Hurley

How incredible is it that a photographer was able to bring back pictures from a harrowing 22-month trip to the Antarctic?

NOVEL EXCERPT

from **Life of Pi**

Yann Martel

Can a young man survive a devastating shipwreck followed by months in a lifeboat with a surprising traveling companion?

ARGUMENT

The Value of a Sherpa Life

Grayson Schaffer

What are the risks to the Sherpas who guide climbers up the tallest mountain in the world?

POETRY COLLECTION

I Am Offering This Poem *Jimmy Santiago Baca*

The Writer *Richard Wilbur*

Hugging the Jukebox *Naomi Shihab Nye*

Does love help us survive? Do stories, poems, and music help keep us alive?

PERFORMANCE TASK

SPEAKING AND LISTENING FOCUS

Present an Argument

The Small-Group readings feature people who exhibit different types of strength as they face life-or-death situations. After reading, your group will create a multimedia presentation about strength and survival.

Contents

Selections Circulate among the groups as they preview the selections. You might encourage groups to discuss any knowledge they already have about any of the selections or the situations and settings shown in the photographs. Students may wish to take a poll within their group to determine which selections look most interesting.

Remind students that communicating and collaborating in groups is an important skill that they will use throughout their lives—in school, in their careers, and in their community.

Performance Task

Present an Argument Give groups time to read about and briefly discuss the multimedia presentation they will create after reading. Encourage students to do some preliminary thinking about the types of media they might want to use. This may help focus their subsequent reading and group discussion.

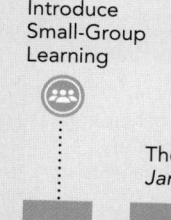

Introduce Small-Group Learning — 16

The Voyage of the *James Caird* — 17, 18

Media: The *Endurance* and the *James Caird* in Images — 19

from Life of Pi — 20, 21

The Value of a Sherpa Life — 22, 23

I Am Offering This Poem / The Writer / Hugging the Jukebox — 24, 25

Performance Task — 26

SMALL-GROUP LEARNING

Introduce Independent Learning — 27

Independent Learning — 28

Performance-Based Assessment — 29, 30

OVERVIEW

SMALL-GROUP LEARNING

Working as a Team

1. **Take a Position** Remind groups to let all members share their responses. You may wish to set a time limit for this discussion.
2. **List Your Rules** You may want to have groups share their lists of rules and consolidate them into a master list to be displayed and followed by all the groups.
3. **Apply the Rules** As you circulate among the groups, ensure that students are staying on task. Consider a short time limit for this step.
4. **Name Your Group** This task can be creative and fun. If students have trouble coming up with a name, suggest that they think of something related to the unit topic. Encourage groups to share their names with the class.
5. **Create a Communication Plan** Encourage groups to include in their plans agreed-upon times during the day to share ideas. They should also devise a method for recording and saving their communications.

Accountable Talk

Remind students that groups should communicate politely. You can post these Accountable Talk suggestions and encourage students to add their own. Students should:

Remember to . . .
Ask clarifying questions.

Which sound like . . .
Can you say that again?
Would you give me an example?
I think you said _____. Did I understand you correctly?

Remember to . . .
Explain your thinking.

Which sounds like . . .
I believe this is true because _____.

Remember to . . .
Build on the ideas of others.

Which sounds like . . .
When _____ said _____, it made me think of _____.

OVERVIEW: SMALL-GROUP LEARNING

Working as a Team

1. **Take a Position** In your group, discuss the following question:

   Would you rather be stranded at the top of a mountain, on a deserted island, or in the middle of the ocean?

   As you take turns sharing your positions, be sure to provide reasons for your choice. After all group members have shared, discuss some of the personal attributes that might be required to survive each of these situations.

2. **List Your Rules** As a group, decide on the rules that you will follow as you work together. Samples are provided; add two more of your own. You may add or revise rules based on your experience together.
   - Everyone should participate in group discussions.
   - People should not interrupt.
   - ______________________________
   - ______________________________

3. **Apply the Rules** Share what you have learned about survival. Make sure each person in the group contributes. Take notes and be prepared to share with the class one thing that you heard from another member of your group.

4. **Name Your Group** Choose a name that reflects the unit topic.

   Our group's name: ______________________________

5. **Create a Communication Plan** Decide how you want to communicate with one another. For example, you might use online collaboration tools, email, or instant messaging.

   Our group's decision: ______________________________

FACILITATING SMALL-GROUP LEARNING

Forming Groups
You may wish to form the groups for Small-Group Learning so that each consists of students with different abilities. Some students may be adept at organizing information whereas others may have strengths related to generating or synthesizing information. A good mix of abilities can make the experience of Small-Group Learning dynamic and productive.

Making a Schedule

First, find out the due date for the Small-Group activities. Then, preview the texts and activities with your group, and make a schedule for completing the tasks.

SELECTION	ACTIVITIES	DUE DATE
The Voyage of the *James Caird* The *Endurance* and the *James Caird* in Images		
from Life of Pi		
The Value of a Sherpa Life		
I Am Offering This Poem The Writer Hugging the Jukebox		

Working on Group Projects

As your group works together, you'll find it more effective if each person has a specific role. Different projects require different roles. Before beginning a project, discuss the necessary roles and choose one for each group member. Here are some possible roles; add your own ideas.

Project Manager: monitors the schedule and keeps everyone on task
Researcher: organizes research activities
Recorder: takes notes during group meetings

____

____

____

____

____

SCAN FOR MULTIMEDIA

DIGITAL PERSPECTIVES

Making a Schedule

Encourage groups to preview the reading selections and to consider how long it will take them to complete the activities accompanying each selection. Point out that they can adjust the due dates for particular selections as needed as they work on their small-group projects; however, they must complete all assigned tasks before the group Performance Task is due. Encourage groups to review their schedules upon completing the activities for each selection to make sure they are on track to meet the final due date.

Working on Group Projects

Point out to groups that the roles they assign can be changed later. Students might have to make changes based on who is best at doing what.

Also, you should review the roles each group assigns to its members. Based on your understanding of students' individual strengths, you might find it necessary to suggest some changes.

AUTHOR'S PERSPECTIVE **Ernest Morrell, Ph.D.**

Supporting Small-Group Learning Because the dominant mode of discourse in classrooms has historically been teacher-led, many students may not be immediately comfortable discussing and collaborating in groups. The first few times students meet in their groups, you may need to provide additional support by setting expectations for collaborative behavior and discussions.

Remind students that it's important for all group members to contribute to discussions, but that no one member of the group should monopolize discussion. Whether students are speaking or listening, they should be active participants. Visit groups to explain that even when students aren't speaking, they should be listening to other group members and noting important points that they would like to build upon when it's their turn to speak.

The Voyage of the *James Caird* from *The Endurance*

AUDIO SUMMARIES
Audio summaries of "The Voyage of the *James Caird*" are available online in both English and Spanish in the Interactive Teacher's Edition or Unit Resources. Assigning these summaries prior to reading the selection may help students build additional background knowledge and set a context for their first read.

Summary

"The Voyage of the *James Caird*" is Caroline Alexander's narrative account of how Ernest Shackleton and his five-man crew made an epic 16-day voyage aboard the lifeboat *James Caird*. On April 24, 1916, six exhausted, half-starved men climbed into the small boat in a desperate bid to escape the harsh Antarctic conditions of Elephant Island. They then sailed 800 miles across one of the most treacherous bodies of water on Earth to reach South Georgia Island, where they could summon help.

Prior to the journey, Shackleton had failed to cross Antarctica (his original mission) and had witnessed his ship, *Endurance*, sink. However, his leadership aboard the *James Caird* earned him a place of honor among the world's heroes.

Insight

Reading "The Voyage of the *James Caird*" will help students begin to understand the struggle to survive in desperate situations. The firsthand descriptions and the way the author plunges readers into the punishing conditions will show students what it means to face death again and again.

ESSENTIAL QUESTION:
What does it take to survive?

Connection to Essential Question

"The Voyage of the *James Caird*" provides a clear-cut connection to the Essential Question, "What does it take to survive?" Leadership and teamwork are key to survival for Shackleton and his men. Shackleton's wise decisions, the men's unflagging commitment to their duties, and the sheer determination they all share not to give in to pain, exhaustion, thirst, and cold keep them on course and alive.

SMALL-GROUP LEARNING PERFORMANCE TASK
What type of strength is most valuable in a survival situation?

UNIT PERFORMANCE-BASED ASSESSMENT
Should people in life-or-death situations be held accountable for their actions?

Connection to Performance Tasks

Small-Group Learning Performance Task In this Performance Task, students will present an argument about the most valuable strength in a survival situation. This selection provides students with examples of several strengths, including physical endurance, faith, and perseverance.

Unit Performance-Based Assessment The fact that Shackleton and his men survived their arduous journey and were able to secure rescue for the other men in the expedition might seem to make the question of their accountability moot. However, students should consider the choices that were made during the trip, such as anchoring the boat instead of running with the wind and heading for the uninhabited coast of the island and having to maneuver a treacherous reef. Did the benefits of those choices outweigh the risks the men faced because of them?

DIGITAL PERSPECTIVES — Audio | Video | Document | Annotation Highlights | EL Highlights | Online Assessment

LESSON RESOURCES

	Making Meaning	Language Development
Lesson	**First Read** **Close Read** **Analyze the Text** **Analyze Craft and Structure**	**Concept Vocabulary** **Word Study** **Author's Style**
Instructional Standards	**RL.10** By the end of grade 9, read and comprehend literary nonfiction . . . **RI.3** Analyze how the author unfolds an analysis . . . **L.4.a** Use context as a clue . . .	**L.4** Determine or clarify the meaning . . . **RI.4** Determine the meaning of words and phrases . . . **L.1.b** Use various types of phrases and clauses . . .
STUDENT RESOURCES		
Available online in the Interactive Student Edition or Unit Resources	Selection Audio First-Read Guide: Nonfiction Close-Read Guide: Nonfiction	Evidence Log Word Network
TEACHER RESOURCES		
Selection Resources Available online in the Interactive Teacher's Edition or Unit Resources	Audio Summaries Annotation Highlights EL Highlights The Voyage of *James Caird*: Text Questions Analyze Craft and Structure: Series of Events	Concept Vocabulary and Word Study Author's Style: Word Choice English Language Support: Participles and Participial Phrases
Research and Practice Available online in the Interactive Teacher's Edition or Unit Resources	Analyze Craft and Structure: Series of Events (RP)	Word Study: Multiple-Meaning Words (RP) Author's Style: Word Choice (RP)
Assessment Available online in Assessments	Selection Test	
My Resources	A Unit 2 Answer Key is available online and in the Interactive Teacher's Edition.	

Reading Support

Text Complexity Rubric: The Voyage of the *James Caird*	
Quantitative Measures	
Lexile: 1160 **Text Length:** 4,722 words	
Qualitative Measures	
Knowledge Demands ①—②—③—❹—⑤	It's very unlikely that students will be familiar with the situation that is central to the selection. Clear explanations are made of many, but not all, of the elements in the selection.
Structure ①—❷—③—④—⑤	Organization of narrative is mostly sequential; paragraphs contain a lot of information, but quotes break up the text somewhat; graphic with list of dates and events helps reader to understand the content.
Language Conventionality and Clarity ①—②—③—❹—⑤	Sentences are long with embedded clauses, above-level vocabulary, and frequent use of passive voice. Selection includes quotes written long ago by men on the ship, so language style changes and some styles or expressions may be unfamiliar.
Levels of Meaning/Purpose ①—❷—③—④—⑤	Meaning and concepts are straightforward. The main purpose of the selection is to convey the details of an amazing and harrowing voyage.

DECIDE AND PLAN

English Language Support

Provide English Learners with support for knowledge demands and language as they read the selection.

Knowledge Demands Before reading the text, have students summarize the background information. For example, *British explorer failed to cross Antarctic in 1914. Ship* Endurance *got stuck in ice and sank. Men marched across ice. They sailed lifeboats to an island. Six of them sailed one lifeboat, the* James Caird, *800 miles.* Making notes of what they know so far will help them as they read the text.

Language Students will likely have difficulty with the numerous complex sentences and above-level vocabulary. Instead of trying to understand every word, encourage students to scan each paragraph to find events that they understand. Ask them to write sentences restating the information they understood.

Strategic Support

Provide students with strategic support to ensure that they can successfully read the text.

Knowledge Demands After students read the background information, make sure they understand the situation that is the focus of the selection—an 800-mile journey in a lifeboat with six men. Ask students to name some of the hardships that could come with a journey of this kind, such as storms, cold, risks of capsizing, or lack of sleep.

Language/Clarity Encourage students who may have difficulty with complex sentences to break the sentences down into smaller chunks or to identify the meaning of unfamiliar words or phrases. Then, have them reread the whole sentences.

Challenge

Provide students who need to be challenged with ideas for how they can go beyond a simple interpretation of the text.

Text Analysis Pair students and have them each retell a paragraph to their partner, using their own words. Encourage them to include details and descriptive language. They may refer to the text as needed to remember details.

Written Response Ask students to identify expressions in quotations that are not ones we hear in modern speech. Have them write how we might say the same thing today. For example, from paragraph 44: "Our need of water and rest was well nigh desperate." (We were extremely thirsty, and we were desperate for sleep.) Ask partners to read their sentences aloud to compare the different ways they said the same thing.

TEACH

Read and Respond

Have the groups read the selection and complete the Making Meaning and Language Development activities.

Standards Support Through Teaching and Learning Cycle

IDENTIFY NEEDS

Analyze results of the Beginning-of-Year Assessment, focusing on the items relating to Unit 2. Also take into consideration student performance to this point and your observations of where particular students struggle.

DECIDE AND PLAN

- If students have performed poorly on items matching these standards, then provide selection scaffolds before assigning them the on-level lesson provided in the Student Edition.
- If students have done well on the Beginning-of-Year Assessment, then challenge them to keep progressing and learning by giving them opportunities to practice the skills in depth.
- Use the Selection Resources listed on the Planning Pages for "The Voyage of the *James Caird*" to help students continually improve their ability to master the standards.

Instructional Standards: The Voyage of the *James Caird*

	Catching Up	This Year	Looking Forward
Reading	You may want to administer the **Analyze Craft and Structure: Series of Events (RP)** worksheet to help students understand how an author's interpretation of events can shape a story.	**RI.3** Analyze how the author unfolds an analysis or series of ideas or events, including the order in which the points are made, how they are introduced and developed, and the connections that are drawn between them.	Ask students to draw a timeline reflecting the various points in the selection where the author says that the boat moved a certain number of miles.
Language	You may wish to administer the **Author's Style: Word Choice (RP)** worksheet to help students understand what a participle is and the effect it has on meaning. Review context clues with students to ensure they understand that words can have multiple meanings in different contexts. You may wish to administer the **Word Study: Multiple-Meaning Words (RP)** worksheet to help students understand that some words have several meanings and can be used in several different ways.	**L.1.b** Use various types of phrases and clauses to convey specific meanings and add variety and interest to writing or presentations. **L.4.a** Use context as a clue to the meaning of a word or phrase. **RI.4** Determine the meaning of words and phrases as they are used in a text, including figurative, connotative, and technical meanings; analyze the cumulative impact of specific word choices on meaning and tone.	Have students choose a section of the text and rewrite several sentences using participles. Have students analyze the subtleties and nuances of various word choices in different contexts. Have students identify the multiple uses of one or more nautical terms in the selection and explain how the term(s) are used in slightly different ways in different contexts.

ANALYZE AND REVISE

- Analyze student work for evidence of student learning.
- Identify whether or not students have met the expectations in the standards.
- Identify implications for future instruction.

TEACH

Implement the planned lesson, and gather evidence of student learning.

FACILITATING

Jump Start

FIRST READ How much suffering can people take before they break? Why do some people endure no matter how much hardship they undergo—while others fall apart? Engage students in a discussion about suffering that sets the context for reading "The Voyage of the *James Caird*." As students share their thoughts, guide them to identify specific factors that affected their decisions.

The Voyage of the *James Caird*

How much of survival depends on strength, skill, teamwork, and planning—and how much on luck? Modeling the questions readers might ask as they read "The Voyage of the *James Caird*" brings the text alive for students and connects it to the Small-Group Performance Task question. Selection audio and print capability for the selection are available in the Interactive Teacher's Edition.

Concept Vocabulary

Ask groups to look closely at the three types of context clues—synonym, elaborating details, and contrast of ideas and topics—and discuss how these types of clues can help clarify meaning. Encourage groups to think of one other type of context clue that they might encounter in a text. Possibilities include examples, antonyms, and definitions.

FIRST READ

Have students perform the steps of the first read independently.

NOTICE: Encourage students to notice the six sailors and differences in their responses to challenges.

ANNOTATE: Remind students to mark any passages that describe how the men reacted to moments of great danger and hardship.

CONNECT: Have students compare the performance of Shackleton's men with that of other men and women who have faced extreme hardship and danger.

RESPOND: Students will answer questions and write a summary to demonstrate understanding.

Point out to students that while they will always complete the Respond step at the end of the first read, the other steps will probably happen somewhat concurrently. You may wish to print out the **First-Read Guide: Nonfiction** for students to use.

MAKING MEANING

Comparing Texts

THE VOYAGE OF THE *JAMES CAIRD*

In this lesson, you will read and compare the narrative nonfiction "The Voyage of the *James Caird*" and review the photo gallery "The *Endurance* and the *James Caird* in Images." First, you will complete the first-read and close-read activities for "The Voyage of the *James Caird*." The work you do with your group on this title will help prepare you for the comparing task.

THE *ENDURANCE* AND THE *JAMES CAIRD* IN IMAGES

About the Author

Caroline Alexander (b. 1956) was born in Florida and has lived in Europe, Africa, and the Caribbean. In her writing, Alexander often combines literary detective work with travel writing. She is also drawn to the reinterpretation of legendary figures, including Achilles, the hero of Homer's *Iliad*, and Ernest Shackleton, the true-life adventurer whose spectacular failed expedition serves as the subject of Alexander's critically acclaimed book, *The Endurance*.

The Voyage of the *James Caird*

Concept Vocabulary

As you perform your first read of "The Voyage of the *James Caird*," you will encounter these words.

pitched | reeling | upheaval

Context Clues If these words are unfamiliar to you, try using context clues to help you determine their meanings. There are various types of context clues that you may encounter as you read.

Restatement, or Synonyms: The recent **dearth** of milk has resulted in a shortage of other dairy products.

Elaborating details: Singing protest songs and waving placards, the demonstrators were clearly **ardent** about their cause.

Contrast of ideas: After the coach **derided** the team during the whole game, it was strange that she praised them afterward.

Apply your knowledge of context clues and other vocabulary strategies to determine the meanings of unfamiliar words you encounter during your first read.

First Read NONFICTION

Apply these strategies as you conduct your first read. You will have an opportunity to complete a close read after your first read.

First Read

NOTICE the general ideas of the text. What is it about? Who is involved?

ANNOTATE by marking vocabulary and key passages you want to revisit.

CONNECT ideas within the selection to what you already know and what you have already read.

RESPOND by completing the Comprehension Check and by writing a brief summary of the selection.

STANDARDS

Reading Informational Text
By the end of grade 9, read and comprehend literary nonfiction in the grades 9–10 text complexity band proficiently, with scaffolding as needed at the high end of the range.

Language
Use context as a clue to the meaning of a word or phrase.

AUTHOR'S PERSPECTIVE Jim Cummins, Ph.D.

Importance of Background Knowledge It is important for all students, and especially English Learners, to tap into their background knowledge when they read a text. Teachers can help students access this knowledge and integrate it with new textual information. One way to do this is to encourage groups to share what they know about the topic of the text before they begin reading. For example, some students may have prior knowledge about sailing, which can help scaffold understanding of "The Voyage of the *James Caird*." On a deeper level, students may be able to relate to the idea of forcing oneself to go to extremes or taking risks in order to help others. After students have completed their first read, have them discuss how their background knowledge helped them understand the text.

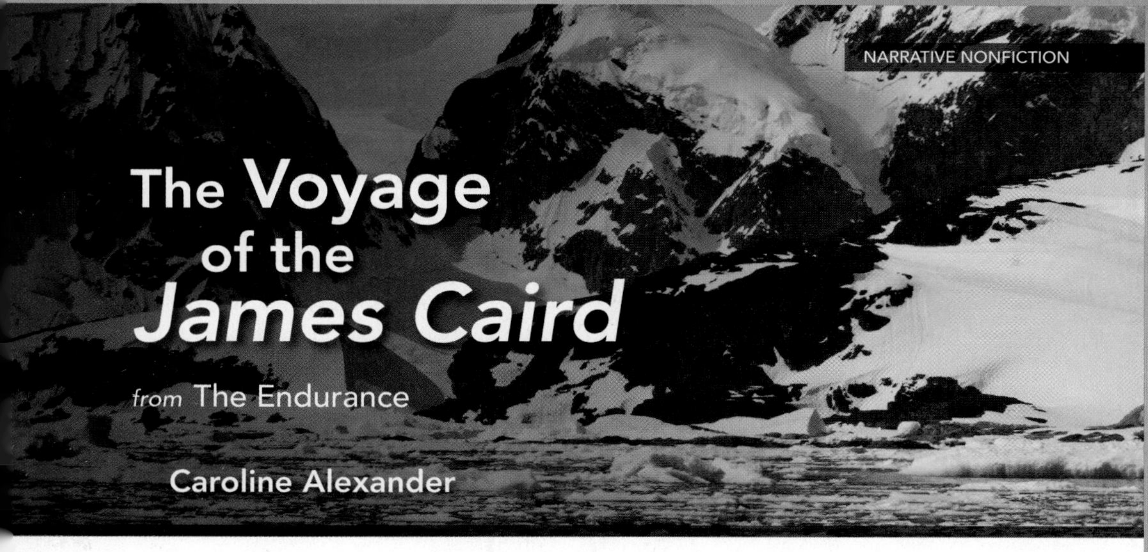

NARRATIVE NONFICTION

The Voyage of the *James Caird*

from The Endurance

Caroline Alexander

BACKGROUND

Ernest Shackleton was a British explorer famous for his failed attempt to cross Antarctica. His ship, *Endurance*, sailed from London in August of 1914 and crossed the Antarctic Circle in December. Icebound, the ship drifted for months and finally sank. Encamped on Elephant Island, Shackleton decided that he and five others would sail in one of the lifeboats—the *James Caird*—800 miles to South Georgia Island, where there was a whaling station.

SCAN FOR MULTIMEDIA

> Tues 25th Fine WSW breeze running all day sky overcast.
> Wed 26th W.SW gale squally & cloudy run 105 mile
> Thurs 27th Northerly gale overcast & heavy squalls hove too.
> Friday 28th Light N.W to W winds misty high NW swell
> Sat 29th Fresh W to SW breeze sqaly running high seas
> Sunday 30th hove too at 8 AM & put out sea anchor at 3 PM heavy sprays breaking over the boat & freezing solid.
> Mon May 1st SSW gale laying to sea anchor & mizzen
> Tues May 2nd —
>
> —Henry McNish, *diary*

NOTES

1 "The tale of the next sixteen days is one of supreme strife amid heaving waters," wrote Shackleton. The crew of the *Caird* had departed on a day of rare sunshine that made the water sparkle and dance, and the peaks and glacial slopes of Elephant Island glittered with deceptive beauty as they slowly fell away behind the boat. An hour and a half after taking leave of the line of dark figures on the lonely beach, the *Caird*'s crew ran into their old enemy, the pack. Once again, they entered the eerie landscape of fantastically shaped ancient, wrecked bergs. A channel they had spotted before departure

DIGITAL PERSPECTIVES

CLOSER LOOK

Analyze Description

Circulate among groups as students conduct their close read. Suggest that groups close read paragraph 1. Encourage them to talk about the annotations that they mark. If needed, provide the following support.

ANNOTATE: Have students mark details in paragraph 1 that describe the opening scene, or work with small groups to have students participate while you highlight them together.

QUESTION: Guide students to consider what these details might tell them. Ask them what impression the author creates with this description, and accept student responses.

Possible response: The author uses intense, vivid language to describe how sunshine transforms Elephant Island and the surrounding waters into a vision of glittering beauty—but sunshine is rare, and it creates a beauty that she describes as "deceptive." By adding these details, the author warns the reader that despite its fantastic splendor, the Antarctic is dangerous and unpredictable.

CONCLUDE: Help students to formulate conclusions about the importance of these details in the text. Ask students why the author might have included these details.

Possible response: This sparkling beauty lies and conceals the cruelty and weirdness of the place. The pack-ice is "eerie," "ancient," "fantastically shaped," and "strangely-rustling." The day seems calm and mild, but out in open sea, the spray soaks the men to the skin, and the boat takes on water.

Remind students that writers often use rich language and vivid imagery to describe the beauty of a natural landscape. If the beauty astonishes the viewer, the writer's description should aim to astonish the reader.

PERSONALIZE FOR LEARNING

English Language Support

Abbreviations Abbreviations can be confusing to English Language Learners. For example, in his diary entry, Henry McNish uses WSW, NW, SW, W, and SSW to indicate the wind and current directions. Explain to students that when they encounter abbreviations that they do not recognize, they can use context clues to help determine their meaning. Have students highlight the abbreviations used by McNish in his diary, including the word following each abbreviation (breeze, gale, winds). Ask students what information the author might be trying to convey about breezes or gales or winds. Guide students through questioning to understand that the abbreviations represent the direction of the air currents: north (N), south (S), east (E), and west (W). Consider projecting or displaying a map to help students understand the direction represented by WSW, NW, or SW. **ALL LEVELS**

CLOSER LOOK

Examine Character

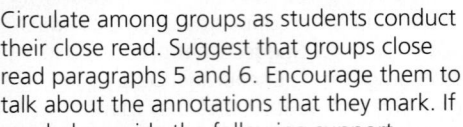

Circulate among groups as students conduct their close read. Suggest that groups close read paragraphs 5 and 6. Encourage them to talk about the annotations that they mark. If needed, provide the following support.

ANNOTATE: In paragraphs 5 and 6, have students mark the details that reveal something about Shackleton's character, or work with small groups to have students participate while you highlight them together.

QUESTION: Guide students to consider what these details might tell them. Ask them to note the difference between Shackleton's own comment about his sailing ability and the author's account of his sailing ability. Accept student responses.

Possible response: Shackleton downplays his knowledge of sailing and claims he knows nothing about it. The author notes that Shackleton had 20 years' experience in the Merchant Service, so Shackleton's claim seems dubious.

CONCLUDE: Help students to formulate conclusions about the importance of these details in the text. Ask students why the author might have included these details.

Possible response: Shackleton could have been telling the truth. Despite his 20 years in the Merchant Navy, he really might never have been aboard a sailboat. He is clearly encouraging Worsley to be confident in his own abilities and not to depend on him. By adding this detail, the author demonstrates Shackleton's concern with the morale of his crew.

Additional **English Language Support** is available in the Interactive Teacher's Edition.

NOTES

from the beach led them through the heaving, strangely rustling pack to open water by nightfall. Even on this first, relatively easy day the *Caird* shipped water, soaked by spray and soused by breaking waves. The crew wore woolen underwear under ordinary cloth trousers, Jaeger sweaters, woolen socks, mitts, and balaclavas.[1] Over these, each man had his Burberry overalls and helmet.

2 "These, although windproof, were unfortunately not waterproof," Worsley observed.

3 Shackleton hoped to run north for a few days, away from the ice and towards warmer weather, before bearing east and setting a course for South Georgia Island. This was not the nearest landfall—Cape Horn was closer—but the prevailing westerly gales made it the only one feasible.

4 The men took their first meal under the low canvas deck in a heavy swell, fighting to steady the little Primus stove on which hot food depended. Unable to sit upright, they ate with great difficulty, their chests almost pressed against their stomachs. The staple of their diet was "hoosh," a brick of beef protein, lard, oatmeal, sugar, and salt originally intended as sledging rations[2] for the transcontinental trek that now lay on the fringe of memory. Mixed with water, hoosh made a thick stew over which the coveted Nut Food could be crumbled. All but Worsley and McCarthy were seasick. After the meal, McNish, Crean, McCarthy, and Vincent crawled into their wet bags and lay down on the hard, shifting ballast of stones, while Worsley and Shackleton shared the first watch. With the Southern Cross shining from the clear, cold sky overhead, they sailed north by the stars.

5 "Do you know I know nothing about boat-sailing?" Worsley reports Shackleton as saying with a laugh, on this first night watch. He continues: "'Alright, Boss,' I replied, 'I do, this is my third boat-journey.'"

6 Worsley's report of the conversation was intended as a tribute to Shackleton's courage in undertaking such a dangerous voyage as a land explorer whose seafaring days were behind him. But in fact, it is striking how many of the British polar explorers were experienced sailors. Not only had Shackleton served twenty years in the Merchant Service, but each member of the *James Caird*'s small crew had so many years of experience at sea that expertise was taken for granted. Each man had the assurance that when he went "below deck" to crawl into his bag, his companions above who worked the sails and tiller knew, even under the unprecedented conditions, exactly what they were doing.

7 By dawn, when Crean emerged to light the Primus, the *Caird* had made forty-five miles from Elephant Island. Breakfast was prepared below deck, with the sea breaking over the canvas covering and running down the men's necks. In the afternoon, the wind rose to

1. **balaclavas** (bol uh KLOV uhz) *n.* hats that cover all but part of the head and face, usually leaving the eyes, mouth, and nose open.
2. **sledging rations** food to be eaten while sledging, or sledding.

CROSS-CURRICULAR PERSPECTIVES

Social Studies Other British polar explorers include Robert Falcon Scott, Brian Blessed, Ann Daniels, Martin Frobisher, Jonas Poole, Hugh Willoughby, and Edward Adrian Wilson. Have students select one of these explorers and learn more about his or her life and exploits. As a class, have students debate how the achievements of the explorer they researched compare to those of Shackleton. **(Research to Clarify)**

a gale from the west-southwest, with a dangerous high cross sea that racked the heavily ballasted boat with a hard, jerky motion. Shackleton divided the crew into two watches, with himself, Crean, and McNish taking one, and Worsley, McCarthy, and Vincent the other, rotating four-hour shifts.

8 "The routine," wrote Worsley, "was, three men in bags deluding themselves that they were sleeping, and three men 'on deck'; that is one man steering for an hour, while the other two when not pumping, baling or handling sails were sitting in our 'saloon' (the biggest part of the boat, where we generally had grub)." Going "below" was a dreaded ordeal: The space amid the increasingly waterlogged ballast was only five by seven feet. The men had to line up one behind the other and crawl, in heavy, wet clothes, over the stones and under a low thwart to reach their bags. With the boat rolling and shipping water, entrapment in this narrow space held all the horror of being buried alive, and many times men who had nodded off awoke to the sickening sensation that they were drowning.

9 "Real rest we had none," wrote Shackleton. The worn-out reindeer-skin bags were shedding badly, and their bristly hairs appeared everywhere—in the men's clothes, in their food, in their mouths. There was nothing to relieve the long hours of darkness, from six at night until seven in the morning; the boat carried only a makeshift oil lamp and two candles, which provided meager, carefully hoarded light. On the first night out, the cries of penguins coming from the dark sea reminded the men of lost souls.

10 On the third day, despite snowy, stormy weather, Worsley snatched the journey's first observation of the sun between patches of racing cloud. Kneeling on a thwart while Vincent and McCarthy strained to brace him in the pitching boat, Worsley managed to fix his sextant[3] and take his "snap." The precious almanac and logarithm charts, against which the observations were calculated, had become dangerously pulpy, the pages sticking together and the numbers blurred. Nonetheless, Worsley's calculations revealed that they had come 128 miles from Elephant Island.

11 They were, however, widely off the position he had previously reckoned. Worsley wrote,

12 Navigation is an art, but words fail to give my efforts a correct name. Dead reckoning or DR—the seaman's calculation of courses and distance—had become a merry jest of guesswork. . . . The procedure was: I peered out from our burrow—precious sextant cuddled under my chest to prevent seas falling on it. Sir Ernest stood by under the canvas with chronometer pencil and book. I shouted "Stand by," and knelt on the thwart—two men holding me up on either side. I brought the sun down to where the horizon ought to be and as the boat

NOTES

3. **sextant** *n.* instrument used by navigators to measure the position of the stars and the sun to determine location.

DIGITAL PERSPECTIVES

CLOSER LOOK

Analyze Conflict

Circulate among groups as students conduct their close read. Suggest that groups close read paragraph 8. Encourage them to talk about the annotations that they mark. If needed, provide the following support.

ANNOTATE: Have students mark details in paragraph 8 that describe the setting, or work with small groups to have students participate while you highlight them together.

QUESTION: Guide students to consider what these details might tell them. Ask which images they find the most terrifying, and accept student responses.

Possible response: The most terrifying images are of tired men in completely waterlogged clothes trying to sleep in a tiny space below deck and feeling as though they are drowning.

CONCLUDE: Help students to formulate conclusions about the importance of these details in the text. Ask students why the author might have included these details.

Possible response: The description shows the increasingly desperate struggle of the men against the weather and the ocean. By adding these details, the author conveys the extreme discomfort and sheer horror of their living conditions.

Remind students that conflicts can be internal or external. An **internal conflict** is a struggle between opposing desires or forces in one's mind. An **external conflict** is a struggle against an outside force. Students should be able to recognize that the conflict in this selection is external.

PERSONALIZE FOR LEARNING

Strategic Support

Technical Vocabulary If group members struggle to comprehend the technical vocabulary, have each group find a domain-specific word and define it. Words include *sextant, logarithm,* and *almanac.* Have groups share their words with the class. Keep track of the words from each group, and compile them in a class dictionary that all class members can consult as they read.

Concept Vocabulary

PITCHED If groups are struggling to define the word *pitched* in paragraph 16, point out that because the word has multiple meanings, they need to use context clues to determine the correct meaning here. Draw students' attention to the context clues *and rolled* and *high lumpy sea,* and have them use these context clues to define the word.

Possible response: In this context, *pitched* means "moved up and down."

NOTES

leaped frantically upward on the crest of a wave, snapped a good guess at the altitude and yelled, "Stop," Sir Ernest took the time, and I worked out the result. . . . My navigation books had to be half opened page by page till the right one was reached, then opened carefully to prevent utter destruction.

13 Steering at night was especially difficult. Under dense skies that allowed no light from moon or stars, the boat charged headlong into the darkness, the men steering by the "feel" of the wind, or the direction of a small pennant attached to the mast. Once or twice each night, the wind direction was verified by compass, lit by a single precious match. And yet navigation was every bit as critical as keeping the boat upright; the men knew that even a mile off course could result in a missed landfall, and the *Caird* would be swept into 3,000 miles of ocean.

14 In the afternoon of the third day, the gale backed to the north, and then blew continuously the next twenty-four hours. The heaving waves were gray, the sky and lowering clouds were gray, and all was obscured with mist. Heavy seas poured over the *Caird*'s port quarter. The canvas decking, sagging under the weight of so much water, threatened to pull loose the short nails McNish had extracted from packing cases. As if to underscore their own vulnerability, a flotsam of ship wreckage drove past them.

15 "We were getting soaked on an average every three or four minutes," wrote Worsley. "This went on day and night. The cold was intense." Particularly hateful was the task of working the pump, which one man had to hold hard against the bottom of the boat with bare hands—a position that could not be endured beyond five or six minutes at a time.

16 In the afternoon of April 28, the fifth day, the wind died and the seas settled into the towering swells characteristic of the latitude; "The highest, broadest and longest swells in the world," as Worsley wrote. So high were the waves that the *Caird*'s sails slackened in the artificial calm between wave crests; then the little craft was lifted onto the next hill of water, and hurled down an ever-steepening slope. On the following day, a west-southwest gale **pitched** and rolled the *Caird* in a high lumpy sea, but gave an excellent run of ninety-two miles on the desired northeast course. They had now come 238 miles from Elephant Island, "but not in a straight line," as Worsley observed ruefully.

Mark context clues or indicate another strategy you used that helped you determine meaning.

pitched (PIHCHT) *v.*

MEANING:

17 On April 30, the gale strengthened and shifted from the south, blowing off the ice fields behind them, as they knew by the increasing cold. Shackleton wanted to run before the wind, but realizing that the *Caird* was in danger of being swung broadside to the surging waves, or driven headlong into the sea, he reluctantly gave the order to head into the wind and stand by.

18 "We put out a sea anchor to keep the *James Caird*'s head up into the sea," Shackleton wrote. "This anchor consisted of a triangular canvas

VOCABULARY DEVELOPMENT

Concept Vocabulary Reinforcement Students will benefit from additional examples and practice with the concept vocabulary. Reinforce their comprehension with "show-you-know" sentences. The first part of the sentence uses the vocabulary word in an appropriate context. The second part of the sentence—the show-you-know part—clarifies the first. Model the strategy with this example for *pitched*:

The ship *pitched* in the rough waters; the bow and stern of the boat moved up and down as it rose over the crests of each wave.

Then, give students these sentence prompts, and coach them in creating the clarification part:

1. The sudden rock of the ship sent him *reeling* across the deck; ________.

   Possible response: he lost his balance and staggered to find something to hold on to

2. Mountains are often caused by an *upheaval* in the earth's crust; ________.

   Possible response: when two tectonic plates collide, the crust is displaced upward

bag fastened to the end of the painter[4] and allowed to stream out from the bows." The drag of the sea anchor counteracted the boat's drift to the lee, and held her head into the wind so that she met the sea head-on. Up until now, however much the *Caird* was battered, however much icy water she shipped, she had moved forward, slowly, perceptibly closing the distance that lay between them and South Georgia. Now, soaked by bitter spray, the men waited anxiously in the pitching darkness and knew their suffering brought little progress.

19 "Looking out abeam," wrote Shackleton, "we would see a hollow like a tunnel formed as the crest of a big wave toppled over on to the swelling body of water." The spray that broke upon the **reeling** boat froze almost on impact, and towards the end of the eighth day, the *Caird's* motion had changed alarmingly. No longer rising with the swell of the sea, she hung leaden in the water. Every soaking inch of wood, canvas, and line had frozen solid. Encased in icy armor fifteen inches thick, she was sinking like a dead weight.

20 Immediate action had to be taken. While the wind howled and the sea shattered over them, the men took turns crawling across the precariously glassy deck to chip away the ice. Worsley tried to evoke the unimaginable "difficulty and the peril of that climb in the darkness up that fragile slippery bit of decking. . . . Once, as the boat gave a tremendous lurch, I saw Vincent slide right across the

4. **painter** *n.* rope used for towing or tying a boat.

NOTES

Mark context clues or indicate another strategy you used that helped you determine meaning.

reeling (REEL ihng) *adj.*

MEANING:

DIGITAL PERSPECTIVES

Concept Vocabulary

REELING If groups are struggling to define the word *reeling* in paragraph 19, remind them to use context clues. Point out the context clue *no longer rising with the swell of the sea.* Have students use this context clue to define the word.

Possible response: In this context, *reeling* means "rocking; lurching; swaying."

CLOSER LOOK

Examine Suspense

Circulate among groups as students conduct their close read. Suggest that groups close read paragraph 19. Encourage them to talk about the annotations that they mark. If needed, provide the following support.

ANNOTATE: Have students mark details in paragraph 19 that the author uses to create suspense, or work with small groups to have students participate while you highlight them together.

QUESTION: Guide students to consider what these details might tell them. Ask them why ice poses such a threat, and accept student responses.

Possible response: Ice is heavy, so it prevents the boat from moving forward and, even worse, may cause the boat to sink.

CONCLUDE: Help students to formulate conclusions about the importance of these details in the text. Ask students why the author might have included these details.

Possible response: The boat is in a state of suspension; lead sinks in water. By adding these details, the author tells us that the boat is ready to plummet like lead into the ocean, but for now it hangs in the water. The crew waits for the inevitable, and so do we.

Remind students that **suspense** is a feeling of anxious uncertainty about the outcome of events. Authors create suspense by raising questions about what will happen and delaying the answers.

PERSONALIZE FOR LEARNING

English Language Support

Domain-specific Vocabulary The domain-specific vocabulary that appears in "The Voyage of the *James Caird*" may present challenges to English Learners. Support them in understanding the text by reviewing the following nautical terms:

port the left side of the ship when facing forward

quarter the stern (back) sides of a ship; **craft** a boat or ship

broadside the side of the ship

abeam at a right angle to the ship's length

Have students locate these terms in paragraphs 13–20 and read each sentence containing a term. Then, have them paraphrase the sentences by replacing the nautical term with its definition. For example:

- Heavy seas poured over the *port quarter* of the ship.
- Heavy seas poured over the *left back* side of the ship.

You may wish to have students create an illustrated glossary of these terms by sketching an outline of a ship and placing each term in the appropriate place on the diagram. **ALL LEVELS**

FACILITATING

CLOSER LOOK

Understand Figurative Language

Circulate among groups as students conduct their close read. Suggest that groups close read paragraph 25. Encourage them to talk about the annotations that they mark. If needed, provide the following support.

ANNOTATE: Have students mark the phrases in paragraph 25 that Worsley uses to describe Shackleton's actions. Or, work with small groups to have students participate while you highlight the words together. Help students find the phrase Worsley uses in a figurative rather than a literal sense.

QUESTION: Guide students to consider what these details might tell them. Ask how they think Shackleton treats his crew, and accept student responses.

Possible response: Shackleton treats his men with great care, making sure that any man who is colder than normal gets a hot drink. The author includes these details to show that he does this in a way that protects the man's self-esteem.

CONCLUDE: Help students to formulate conclusions about the importance of these details in the text. Ask students why the author might have included these details.

Possible response: By writing that Shackleton *keeps a finger on each man's pulse,* Worsley shows that Shackleton is closely and very discreetly following his men's physical and mental well-being. Worsley uses figurative language to convey that Shackleton is concerned, but he has an admirably light touch.

Remind students that authors may use **figurative language,** words and expressions whose meaning is different from a literal interpretation, to help characterize someone indirectly.

NOTES

icy sheathing of the canvas. . . . Fortunately he managed to grasp the mast just as he was going overboard."

21 Three times the boat had to be chipped clear. Whether using an axe or a knife, the task required strength, but also delicacy as the canvas decking had to be protected from damage at all cost. Flimsy though it was, it was their only shelter, and without it they could not survive. Two of the hated sleeping bags were now discarded; they had frozen solid in the night and had previously begun to putrefy—Shackleton estimated that they weighed as much as forty pounds apiece. By these painstaking efforts, the *Caird* rose incrementally in the water and began to rise and fall again with the movement of the swell.

22 The next morning, the *Caird* gave a sudden, sickening roll leeward; the painter carrying the sea anchor had been severed by a block of ice that had formed on it, out of reach. Beating the ice off the canvas, the men scrambled to unfurl the frozen sails, and once they succeeded in raising them, headed the *Caird* into the wind. It was on this day, May 2, that McNish abruptly gave up any attempt to keep a diary.

23 "We held the boat up to the gale during that day, enduring as best we could discomforts that amounted to pain," wrote Shackleton, in an uncharacteristically direct reference to their physical suffering. The men were soaked to the bone and frostbitten. They were badly chafed by wet clothes that had not been removed for seven months, and afflicted with saltwater boils. Their wet feet and legs were a sickly white color and swollen. Their hands were black—with grime, blubber, burns from the Primus and frostbite. The least movement was excruciating.

24 "We sat as still as possible," wrote Worsley. "[I]f we moved a quarter of an inch one way or the other we felt cold, wet garments on our flanks and sides. Sitting very still for a while, life was worth living." Hot meals afforded the only relief. Shackleton ensured that the men had hot food every four hours during the day and scalding powdered milk every four hours of the long night watches.

25 "Two of the party at least were very close to death," Worsley wrote. "Indeed, it might be said that [Shackleton] kept a finger on each man's pulse. Whenever he noticed that a man seemed extra cold and shivered, he would immediately order another hot drink of milk to be prepared and served to all. He never let the man know that it was on his account, lest he became nervous about himself." To stave off cold, they also drank the blubber oil that had been intended to calm the troubled seas. As Worsley noted, the oil would have sufficed for only one gale; there were ten days of gales on the journey.

26 Their ordeal had already taken a heavy toll on Vincent, who from late April, to use Shackleton's enigmatic words, had "ceased to be an active member of the crew." Worsley attributed the trouble to rheumatism,[5] but the collapse appears to have been mental as much

5. **rheumatism** (ROO muh tihz uhm) *n.* disease characterized by pain in the joints.

PERSONALIZE FOR LEARNING

Strategic Support

Brackets Review paragraph 25. Explain to students that brackets are used to include explanatory words or phrases within a direct quote. These brackets show that the information was not part of the speaker's words. Remind students that a direct quote is a speaker's exact words and is set off with quotation marks. Have students examine the use of Shackleton's name in brackets in the direct quote in paragraph 25. Explain that writers will use brackets to clarify the subject of the sentence—the person who is doing the action.

as physical, for later in the journey he does not appear to have been entirely incapacitated. Physically, he had been the strongest member of the entire *Endurance* company.

27 McCarthy shamed them all.

28 "[He] is the most irrepressable optimist I've ever met," Worsley wrote in his navigating book. "When I relieve him at the helm, boat iced & seas pourg: down yr neck, he informs me with a happy grin 'It's a grand day, sir.'"

29 Between Shackleton and Crean was a special rapport. As Worsley wrote,

30 Tom Crean had been so long and done so much with Sir E that he had become a priviledged retainer. As they turned in, a kind of wordless rumbling, muttering, growling noise could be heard issuing from the dark & gloomy lair in the bows sometimes directed at one another, sometimes at things in general, & sometimes at nothing at all. At times they were so full of quaint conceits & Crean's remarks were so Irish that I ran risk of explosion by suppressed laughter. "Go to sleep Crean & don't be clucking like an old hen." "Boss I can't eat those reindeer hairs. I'll have an inside on me like a billygoats neck. Let's give 'em to the Skipper & McCarthy. They never know what they're eating" & so on.

31 Worsley, despite the rank discomfort, was in his element. He was conscious of being in the midst of a great adventure—which had been his life's ambition. The fact that he was able to continue taking bemused stock of his shipmates is proof that he retained his sense of humor. Of McNish, there is little record. Shackleton stated only, "The carpenter was suffering particularly, but he showed grit and spirit." McNish appears to have endured each day's developments with his customary dour, matter-of-fact forbearance; he had not been born to a life that had promised things to be easy. Shackleton himself was in extreme discomfort; on top of everything else, his sciatica[6] had returned.

32 At midnight on May 2, Shackleton relieved Worsley at the helm just as he was being struck full in the face by a torrent of water. The gale had been gaining strength for eight hours, and a heavy cross sea was running under snow squalls. Alone at the helm, Shackleton noticed a line of clear sky behind them, and called out to the men below that it was at last clearing.

33 "Then a moment later I realized that what I had seen was not a rift in the clouds but the white crest of an enormous wave," wrote Shackleton. "During twenty-six years' experience of the ocean in all its moods I had not encountered a wave so gigantic. It was a mighty **upheaval** of the ocean, a thing quite apart from the big white-capped

NOTES

Mark context clues or indicate another strategy you used that helped you determine meaning.

upheaval (uhp HEE vuhl) *n.*

MEANING:

6. **sciatica** (sy AT uh kuh) *n.* pain in the lower back, hip, or leg caused by damage to the sciatic nerve.

DIGITAL PERSPECTIVES

Concept Vocabulary

UPHEAVAL If groups are struggling to define the word *upheaval* in paragraph 23, point out that they can use context clues to infer the meaning. Draw their attention to the context clue *a wave so gigantic*. Point out that this is a context clue that restates an idea. Have students use this context clue to define the word.

Possible response: In this context, *upheaval* means "a lifting up." You may wish to point out that the word has another meaning as well: "strong or violent change or disturbance, as in a society."

DIGITAL PERSPECTIVES

Illuminating the Text To illustrate the dramatic action in paragraphs 32 and 33, play videos of ships traveling in sea storms. Point out that the *James Caird* was 22.5 feet long; the average cruise ship today, in contrast, is around 1,000 feet long. Encourage students to discuss what the waves must have felt like on a boat as small as the *James Caird.* Then, discuss the danger the men on the *James Caird* faced in such waves. **(Research to Clarify)**

CLOSER LOOK

Analyze Diction

Circulate among groups as students conduct their close read. Suggest that groups close read paragraph 34. Encourage them to talk about the annotations that they mark. If needed, provide the following support.

ANNOTATE: Have students mark phrases in paragraph 34 that contain vividly expressive diction, or work with small groups to have students participate while you highlight them together.

QUESTION: Guide students to consider what these details might tell them. Ask them how the author's word choice affects the reader, and accept student responses.

Possible response: By choosing vividly expressive diction rather than purely descriptive or technically accurate words, the author aims to convey the intense drama of the scene.

CONCLUDE: Help students to formulate conclusions about the importance of these details in the text. Ask students why the author might have included these details.

Possible response: The author uses vividly expressive diction in order to make the events on board the *James Caird* as terrifying and dramatic for the reader as they were for Shackleton's crew. By adding these stylistic details, the author re-creates the human drama of the scene.

Remind students that **diction**—the author's choice of words—is a crucial element of an author's style. It gives us a sense of who the author is. It should also tell us what's happening, who the characters are, and what they are experiencing, thinking, and feeling. Appropriate diction allows the reader access to the world on the page and to the characters who inhabit it.

NOTES

seas that had been our tireless enemies for so many days. I shouted, 'For God's sake, hold on! It's got us!'"

34 After an unnatural lull, a torrent of thundering foam broke over them. Staggering under the flood, the boat nonetheless rose, emerging, to use Shackleton's words, "half-full of water, sagging to the dead weight and shuddering under the blow." The men bailed with all their energy until they felt the *Caird* float true beneath them. Then it took a full hour of bailing to clear her.

35 On the morning of May 3, after blowing for forty-eight hours at its height, this fierce, bitter gale at last subsided, and the sun appeared amid great, clean cumulus clouds. The sails were unreefed, and the wet sleeping bags and clothing were hung from the mast and the deck, as they set course for South Georgia Island. It was still clear and bright at noon, enabling Worsley to take a sighting for their latitude; they had been six days without taking an observation. His calculations revealed that despite the monstrous difficulties, they had covered 444 miles since leaving Elephant Island—more than half the required distance. Suddenly, success seemed possible.

36 The good weather held, affording them "a day's grace," as Worsley said. On May 5, the twelfth day at sea, the *Caird* made an excellent run of ninety-six miles—the best of the journey—in lumpy swell that raked the boat. Willis Island, off the western tip of South Georgia, was 155 miles away. On May 6, a return of heavy seas and a northwest gale caused them to lay to again, with a reefed jib sail. The next day, the gale moderated, and they set course once more.

37 Worsley was now increasingly worried about getting his observational sights for their position. Since leaving Elephant Island fourteen days earlier, he had been able to sight the sun only four times. "Two of these," he noted, were "mere snaps or guesses through slight rifts in the clouds." He continued:

> 38 It was misty, the boat was jumping like a flea, shipping seas fore and aft and there was no "limb" to the sun so I had to observe the center by guesswork. Astronomically, the limb is the edge of sun or moon. If blurred by cloud or fog it cannot be accurately "brought down" to the horizon. The center is the spot required, so when the limb is too blurred you bring the center of the bright spot behind the clouds down to the horizon. By practice and taking a series of "sights" you can obtain an average that has no bigger error than one minute of arc.

39 When Worsley informed Shackleton that he "could not be sure of our position to ten miles," it was decided that they would aim for the west coast of South Georgia, which was uninhabited, rather than the east coast where the whaling stations—and rescue—lay. This ensured that if they missed their landfall, the prevailing westerlies would carry them towards the other side of the island. Were they to fail to make an eastern landfall directly, the westerlies would carry them out

WriteNow Inform and Explain

Diary Entry In paragraph 28, the author uses primary sources, the diaries of Shackleton and Worsley, to add vivid details and description. Explain to students that **primary sources** (such as diaries, letters, and the ship's logs) are first-hand accounts by participants, while **secondary sources** (such as encyclopedia entries) are accounts based on first-hand sources. Have students write a diary entry about a journey they took. The journey can be as familiar as a bus ride to school or as unfamiliar as a trip to a foreign land. Guide them to include description and specific details, modeled on Worsley's diary entry.

Draw students' attention to the fact that Worsley uses figurative language ("the boat was jumping like a flea" is a simile), technical words ("limb," "brought down"), and sensory words and phrases ("misty," "shipping seas fore and aft"). Students should describe their journey in a similar style.

NOTES

to sea. If Worsley's calculations were correct, the *James Caird* was now a little more than eighty miles from South Georgia Island.

40 Before darkness fell on May 7, a piece of kelp floated by. With mounting excitement the crew sailed east-northeast through the night, and at dawn on the fifteenth day, they spotted seaweed. The thrill of anticipation made them momentarily forget the most recent setback: One of the kegs of water was discovered to have become brackish from seawater that evidently had got in when the *Caird* had almost capsized shortly before leaving Elephant Island. They were now plagued with mounting thirst.

41 Cape pigeons such as they had admired so many months before at Grytviken made frequent appearances, along with mollyhawks and other birds whose presence hinted at land. Worsley continued anxiously to monitor the sky, but heavy fog obscured the sun, and all else that might lie ahead. Two cormorants were spotted, birds known not to venture much beyond fifteen miles from land. There were heavy, lumpy cross swells, and when the fog cleared around noon low, hard-driving clouds bore in from the west-northwest, with misty squalls. Then at half past noon, McCarthy cried out that he saw land.

42 "There, right ahead through a rift in the flying scud our glad but salt-rimmed eyes saw a towering black crag with a lacework of snow around its flank," wrote Worsley. "One glimpse, and it was hidden again. We looked at each other with cheerful foolish grins. The thoughts uppermost were 'We've done it.'" The land, Cape Demidov, was only ten miles distant, and it was on course with Worsley's calculations.

DIGITAL PERSPECTIVES

CLOSER LOOK

Infer Key Ideas

Circulate among groups as students conduct their close read. Suggest that groups close read paragraph 40. Encourage them to talk about the annotations that they mark. If needed, provide the following support.

ANNOTATE: Have students mark details in paragraph 40 that explain why the men were growing excited, or work with small groups to have students participate while you highlight them together.

QUESTION: Guide students to consider what these details might tell them. Ask them what the crew—and the reader—infers from the presence of kelp and seaweed, and accept student responses.

Possible response: Both the kelp and the seaweed suggest that land is close by.

CONCLUDE: Help students to formulate conclusions about the importance of these details in the text. Ask students why the author might have included these details.

Possible response: The author does not directly state that the men are approaching land because she wants readers to see events through the men's eyes, so as to increase suspense and allow readers to share the process of inference and realization with the crew.

Remind students that authors often make readers **infer key ideas**, or fill in the gaps that the text leaves out. When authors do not state important information outright, readers get more deeply involved in the narrative, thereby increasing interest.

FACILITATING SMALL-GROUP CLOSE READING

CLOSE READ: Nonfiction As groups perform the close read, circulate and offer support as needed.

- Remind groups that when they read a narrative, they should be sure to identify the main characters and the plot.
- If a group is confused about why particular events are important, remind group members to think about how the events are related to the narrative's full plot.
- Challenge groups to determine the main idea of the text and the specific details that refine the main idea.

FACILITATING

CLOSER LOOK

Analyze Imagery

Circulate among groups as students conduct their close read. Suggest that groups close read paragraph 43. Encourage them to talk about the annotations that they mark. If needed, provide the following support.

ANNOTATE: Have students mark the details in paragraph 43 that show where the men want to be and why they can't get there, or work with small groups to have students participate while you highlight them together.

QUESTION: Guide students to consider what these details might tell them. Ask why Cape Demidov was so appealing, and accept student responses.

Possible response: The "green tussock grass" is the first living vegetation they've seen in 17 months. They've had no fresh water in 48 hours. The alternatives are distant and impossible, and this is tantalizingly close.

CONCLUDE: Help students to formulate conclusions about the importance of these details in the text. Ask students why the author might have included these details.

Possible response: These images, situated at the beginning and end of the paragraph, show how close together hope and despair can be. By adding these details, the author shows how the goal can be so near and so far away.

Remind students that imagery can act like illustrations or photographs in a text. Just as a picture can be worth a thousand words, a well-placed verbal image can be more expressive and dramatic than a long description.

NOTES

43 By three in the afternoon, the men were staring at patches of green tussock grass that showed through the snow on the land ahead—the first living vegetation they had beheld since December 5, 1914, seventeen months before. It was impossible to make for the whaling stations: The nearest lay 150 miles away—a formidable distance given the conditions and changing winds. Also, they had been without fresh water for forty-eight hours. Two alternative landing sites were considered: Wilson Harbor, which lay north, but to windward, and was thus impossible to reach; and King Haakon Sound, which opened to the West, and where a westerly swell shattered on jagged reefs, spouting surf up to forty feet in the air.

44 "Our need of water and rest was wellnigh desperate," wrote Shackleton, "but to have attempted a landing at that time would have been suicidal. There was nothing for it but to haul off till the following morning." As he well knew, making landfall could be the most dangerous part of sailing.

45 A stormy sunset closed the day, and the men prepared to wait out the hours of darkness. Although they were weak in the extreme, their swollen mouths and burning thirst made eating almost impossible. The small crew tacked through the darkness until midnight, when they stood to, eighteen miles offshore. Then, in the bleak, early hours of the morning, the wind strengthened and, as the *Caird* rose and fell, increased to a gale that showered sleet and hail upon the men. Although they hove to with only a reefed jib, they were shipping water and forced to bail continuously. By break of day, the *Caird* was trapped in a perilously heavy cross sea and enormous swell that was driving them towards the coast.

46 Rain, hail, sleet, and snow hammered down, and by noon the gale had become a full-fledged hurricane whipping a mountainous sea into foam and obscuring every trace of land.

47 "None of us had ever seen anything like it before," wrote Worsley. The storm, he continued, "Was driving us, harder than ever, straight for that ironbound coast. We thought but did not say those words, so fateful to the seaman, 'a lee shore.'"

48 At one in the afternoon, the clouds rent, suddenly exposing a precipitous front to their lee. The roar of breakers told them they were heading dead for unseen cliffs. In desperation, Shackleton ordered the double-reefed sails set for an attempt to beat into wind and pull away from the deadly course.

49 "The mainsail, reefed to a rag, was already set," wrote Worsley, "and in spite of the smallness of the reefed jib and mizzen it was the devil's own job to set them. Usually such work is completed inside of ten minutes. It took us an hour."

50 As the *James Caird* clawed her way against the wind, she struck each heaving swell with a brutal thud. With each blow, her bow planks opened, and water squirted in; caulked with oil paints and seal blood, the *Caird* was straining every joint. Five men pumped and

CROSS-CURRICULAR PERSPECTIVES

Science As paragraph 46 shows, one of the perils that Ernest Shackleton and the crew of the *James Caird* faced was constant exposure to the cold, which can lead to hypothermia. Have interested students conduct research about hypothermia and prepare a brief presentation for the class. Ask them to describe situations that may lead to hypothermia and actions that can be taken to either prevent or overcome the condition.

bailed, while the sixth held her on her fearful course. She was not so much inching forward as being squeezed sideways.

51 "At intervals we lied, saying 'I think she'll clear it,'" Worsley wrote. After three hours of this battle, the land had safely receded, when suddenly the snow-covered mountains of Annenkov Island loomed out of the dusk to their lee. They had fought their way past one danger only to be blown into the path of another.

52 "I remember my thoughts clearly," wrote Worsley. "Regret for having brought my diary and annoyance that no one would ever know we had got so far."

53 "I think most of us had a feeling that the end was very near," wrote Shackleton. It was growing dark as the *Caird* floundered into the backwash of waves breaking against the island's precipitous coastline. Suddenly the wind veered round to the southwest. Coming about in the foaming, confused current, the *Caird* sheered away from the cliffs, and from destruction. Darkness fell, and the hurricane they had fought for nine hours abated.

54 "We stood offshore again, tired almost to the point of apathy," wrote Shackleton. "The night wore on. We were very tired. We longed for day."

55 When the morning of May 10 dawned, there was virtually no wind at all, but a heavy cross sea. After breakfast, chewed with great difficulty through parched lips, the men steered the *Caird* towards King Haakon Bay. The few charts at their disposal had been discovered to be incomplete or faulty, and they were guided in part by Worsley's instinct for the lay of the land.

56 Setting course for the bay, they approached a jagged reef line, which, in Shackleton's words, seemed "like blackened teeth" to bar entrance to the inlet. As they steered towards what appeared to be a propitious gap, the wind shifted once again, blowing right out of the bay, against them. Unable to approach directly, they backed off and tried to tack in, angling for entry. Five times they bore up and tacked, and on the last attempt the *Caird* sailed through the gap and into the mouth of the bay.

57 It was nearly dusk. A small cove guarded by a reef appeared to the south. Standing in the bows, Shackleton directed the boat through a narrow entrance in the reef.

58 "In a minute or two we were inside," wrote Shackleton, "and in the gathering darkness the *James Caird* ran in on a swell and touched the beach."

59 Jumping out, he held the frayed painter and pulled against the backward surge; and when the boat rolled in again with the surf, the other men stumbled ashore and loosely secured her. The sound of running water drew them to a small stream nearly at their feet. They fell upon their knees and drank their fill.

60 "It was," wrote Shackleton, "a splendid moment."

61 McNish's handiwork had stood up to all that the elements had flung at it. Throughout their seventeen-day ordeal, Worsley had

NOTES

DIGITAL PERSPECTIVES

CLOSER LOOK

Connect to Essential Question

Circulate among groups as students conduct their close read. Suggest that groups close read paragraph 56. Encourage them to talk about the annotations that they mark. If needed, provide the following support.

ANNOTATE: Have students mark phrases in paragraph 56 that connect to the Essential Question, *What does it take to survive?* Or work with small groups to have students participate while you highlight them together.

QUESTION: Guide students to consider what these details might tell them. Ask students what the men do to fight for their survival, and accept student responses.

Possible response: They headed for a dangerous reef and, despite their exhaustion, made five attempts to sail through a gap in the reef to the bay beyond. The author makes it clear that reaching the bay represents their only hope of survival.

CONCLUDE: Help students to formulate conclusions about the importance of these details in the text. Ask students why the author might have included these details.

Possible response: The bay is protected by a jagged line of reef. When the men first approach, the wind shifts, blowing them away from the bay they must reach to survive. Despite the manifest threat of death, the crew makes the approach five times. By adding these details, the author shows the desperation of their situation.

Remind students that in order to survive, it is sometimes necessary to risk one's life.

PERSONALIZE FOR LEARNING

Challenge

Interview Encourage interested students to create a brief video in which they imagine that they are a news crew interviewing Shackleton and his men right after they have landed on South Georgia Island. The men have traveled 920 miles in seventeen days. What questions should students ask? What would the men say? Students can write scripts upon which to base their interviews and then use mobile devices to film the interviews. **(Research to Clarify)**

Comprehension Check

Possible responses:

1. Readers get the points of view of Shackleton and Worsley from their diary entries as well as the point of view of the author.
2. The purpose of the voyage of the *James Caird* is to get to others who can then rescue the men stranded on Elephant Island after the loss of their ship, the *Endurance*.
3. The author reconstructed what happened during the voyage of the *James Caird* from the diaries the men kept.
4. The obstacles included hunger, thirst, injuries, frostbite and other effects of extreme cold; the psychological effects of fear and despair. The crew overcame these obstacles through perseverance and teamwork.

Research

Research to Clarify If groups struggle to narrow their research topic, you may want to suggest that they focus on one of the following aspects of Antarctic exploration: Roald Amundsen's journey to the South Pole as it compares to Robert Falcon Scott's journey, additional expeditions by Shackleton, the provisions needed to venture on such a trip, or weather conditions and their repercussions.

NOTES

never allowed his mind to relax and cease its calculations. Together, the six men had maintained a ship routine, a structure of command, a schedule of watches. They had been mindful of their seamanship under the most severe circumstances a sailor would ever face. They had not merely endured; they had exhibited the grace of expertise under ungodly pressure.

62 Undoubtedly they were conscious of having achieved a great journey. They would later learn that a 500-ton steamer had foundered with all hands in the same hurricane they had just weathered. But at the moment they could hardly have known—or cared—that in the carefully weighed judgment of authorities yet to come, the voyage of the *James Caird* would be ranked as one of the greatest boat journeys ever accomplished. ❧

Comprehension Check

Complete the following items after you finish your first read. Review and clarify details with your group.

1. Whose points of view are represented in this piece?

2. What is the purpose of the voyage of the *James Caird*?

3. How does the author know what happened during the voyage of the *James Caird*?

4. **Notebook** Confirm your understanding of the text by listing the obstacles the crew of the *James Caird* faced during their voyage and explaining how they overcame those obstacles.

RESEARCH

Research to Clarify Choose at least one unfamiliar detail from the text. Briefly research that detail. In what way does the information you learned shed light on an aspect of the story?

DIGITAL PERSPECTIVES

Enriching the Text In 2013, the environmental scientist Tim Jarvis re-created Shackleton's voyage from Elephant Island to South Georgia in a replica of the *James Caird*. Jarvis and his crew used the same clothing, food, and navigational equipment that Shackleton had. The documentary *Shackleton: Death or Glory* chronicles the journey. Find and preview a clip from the documentary online and show it to students. Then, have students write a paragraph explaining how the clip enhances their understanding of the selection "The Voyage of the *James Caird.*" For example, students might gain a better understanding of the size of the boat and the harsh conditions Shackleton and his men endured. **(Research to Clarify)**

Close Read the Text

With your group, revisit sections of the text you marked during your first read. **Annotate** details that you notice. What **questions** do you have? What can you **conclude**?

ANNOTATE · QUESTION · Close Read · CONCLUDE

THE VOYAGE OF THE *JAMES CAIRD*

Analyze the Text

CITE TEXTUAL EVIDENCE to support your answers.

Notebook Complete the activities.

1. **Review and Clarify** With your group, reread paragraph 29 of the selection. Why do you think the author describes Worsley's character at this point in the selection? What is the author trying to say about Worsley?
2. **Present and Discuss** Now work with your group to share passages from the selection that you found especially important. Take turns presenting your passages. Discuss what you notice in the selection, the questions you asked, and the conclusions you reached.
3. **Essential Question:** ***What does it take to survive?*** What has this narrative taught you about survival? Discuss with your group.

LANGUAGE DEVELOPMENT

Concept Vocabulary

pitched reeling upheaval

Why These Words? The three concept vocabulary words from the text are related. With your group, determine what the words have in common. How do these word choices enhance the impact of the text?

Practice

Notebook Confirm your understanding of these words from the text by using them in a paragraph. Be sure to use context clues that hint at each word's meaning.

Word Study

Notebook **Multiple-Meaning Words** Many words in English have multiple meanings, or more than one distinct definition. For example, the word *pitched*, which appears in "The Voyage of the *James Caird,*" has several different meanings. Write the meaning of *pitched* as Caroline Alexander uses it. Then, write two more definitions of the word. Finally, find two other multiple-meaning words in the text. Record the words, and list two definitions for each.

WORD NETWORK

Add interesting words related to survival from the text to your Word Network.

STANDARDS

Language

Determine or clarify the meaning of unknown and multiple-meaning words and phrases based on *grades 9–10 reading and content*, choosing flexibly from a range of strategies.

Jump Start

CLOSE READ Ask groups to consider the following prompt: *Why do you think the men on the* James Caird *survived? Was it their training, their temperament, their integrity, good fortune, something else—or a combination of factors?* As students discuss in their groups, ask them to consider the dangers the men faced and how they reacted to each of them.

Close Read the Text

If needed, model close reading by using the Annotation Highlights in the Interactive Teacher's Edition.

Remind students to use Accountable Talk in their discussions and to support one another as they complete the close read.

Analyze the Text

1. **Possible response:** The author is describing Worsley at this moment because she has just quoted Worsley's diary and wants to give the reader some insight into Worsley's mood at the time of his writing. The author is saying that despite the difficulties the men were facing, Worsley was able to maintain his sense of humor.
2. **Passages will vary by group.** Remind students to explain why they chose the passage they presented to group members.
3. **Responses will vary by group.**

Concept Vocabulary

Why These Words? Possible response: The words all describe violent motion, which helps readers visualize the dramatic movements of the boat in the ocean.

Practice

Sample response: The tiny boat **pitched** in the pounding surf—it was tossed back and forth like a toy. The **upheaval** sent anything not tied down flying into the air and the men **reeling** up and down.

Word Network

Possible responses: blubber, frostbite, excruciating

Word Study

For more support, see **Concept Vocabulary and Word Study.**

Possible responses:

pitched – moved up and down in a rocking motion; threw a baseball for a batter to hit; set up a tent **rare** – coming or occurring far apart in time; unusual; uncommon; not dense; admirable, fine; undercooked **pack** – a bundle; a definite quantity or standard measure of something wrapped up or otherwise assembled for sale; a group of people or things; a form of sea ice **rest** – the absence of motion; sleep; relief or freedom

FORMATIVE ASSESSMENT

Analyze the Text

If students struggle to close read the text, **then** provide the **The Voyage of the *James Caird*: Text Questions** available online in the Interactive Teacher's Edition or Unit Resources. Answers and DOK levels are also available.

Concept Vocabulary

If students fail to see the connection among the words, **then** have them use each word in a sentence and think about what is similar about the sentences.

Word Study

If students are unable to locate multiple-meaning words, **then** have them reread a section of the text, highlighting words that have more than one meaning. For Reteach and Practice, see **Word Study: Multiple-Meaning Words (RP).**

FACILITATING

Analyze Craft and Structure

Series of Events Discuss with students the difference between *primary sources* (first-hand accounts such as diaries, photographs, eyewitness reports, ship's logs) and *secondary sources* (accounts such as encyclopedia entries magazine articles constructed from primary sources). Discuss with students how primary sources offer immediacy and a distinctive voice to a narrative. For more support, see **Analyze Craft and Structure: Series of Events.**

MAKE IT INTERACTIVE

Project the Interactive Teacher's Edition for "The Voyage of the *James Caird,*" and model locating a primary source. Point out that brief quotations from primary sources are set off with quotation marks, while those that are longer than five lines are inset in the text.

Possible responses:

- **a.** courageous, able to use humor to defuse a tense situation; stoic; takes good care of his men; a fine commander with deep knowledge and wisdom
- **b.** selected text from paragraphs 5–6, 23, 25, and 44
- **c.** detail-oriented, precise, knowledgeable about the sea; resourceful
- **d.** The diary that prefaces the selection; selected text from paragraph 14
- **e.** recognizes Shackleton's skill; possesses a good sense of humor; a skilled navigator; courageous; loves adventure
- **f.** selected text from paragraphs 5–6, 8, 10, 12, 20, and 21
- **g.** strong
- **h.** selected text from paragraph 12
- **i.** Shackleton's favorite; has a good sense of humor
- **j.** selected text from paragraph 30
- **k.** strongest member of the crew; courageous and hard-working, but succumbs to depression
- **l.** selected text from paragraphs 12, 20, and 26

1. Responses will vary. Encourage students to support their answers.
2. Responses will vary. Some students may suggest that the story is exciting and compelling.

FORMATIVE ASSESSMENT

Analyze Craft and Structure

If students are unable to identify the specific textual examples, **then** have them skim the selection and summarize each paragraph. For Reteach and Practice, see **Analyze Craft and Structure: Series of Events (RP).**

MAKING MEANING

THE VOYAGE OF THE *JAMES CAIRD*

Analyze Craft and Structure

Series of Events Writing that tells a real-life story is called **narrative nonfiction**. Even though the events of a nonfiction narrative are true, the story is still shaped by the **author's perspective**—his or her interpretations of the events and the people involved. To be believable, that interpretation needs to be supported with evidence. In this account, the author uses **primary sources** in the form of sailors' journals as evidence that supports her interpretation. Her use of the journals also allows her to incorporate the sailors' voices to make their personalities and experiences more vivid.

TIP

GROUP DISCUSSION
Keep in mind that members of your group might have different impressions of Shackleton and the other sailors than you do. There's no right impression or conclusion, but talking out differing opinions and the reasons for them will help you clarify your thoughts and learn from one another.

CITE TEXTUAL EVIDENCE to support your answers.

Practice

In your own words, describe the people who appear in this narrative. Cite details from the text that support your descriptions. Work on your own to gather your ideas in the chart. Then, share with your group.

PERSON	DESCRIPTION	TEXTUAL EVIDENCE
Shackleton	a. See possible responses in Teacher's Edition	b.
McNish	c.	d.
Worsley	e.	f.
McCarthy	g.	h.
Crean	i.	j.
Vincent	k.	l.

Notebook Respond to these questions.

1. Which member of the expedition do you think Alexander admires most? Why?
2. The story of the *Endurance* was famous even before Alexander wrote her book. Why do you think she felt the story was worth retelling? Explain, citing evidence from this excerpt.

STANDARDS

Reading Informational Text
- Analyze how the author unfolds an analysis or series of ideas or events, including the order in which the points are made, how they are introduced and developed, and the connections that are drawn between them.
- Determine the meaning of words and phrases as they are used in a text, including figurative, connotative, and technical meanings; analyze the cumulative impact of specific word choices on meaning and tone.

Language
Use various types of phrases and clauses to convey specific meanings and add variety and interest to writing or presentations.

CROSS-CURRICULAR PERSPECTIVES

Art Ernest Shackleton brought a photographer with him on the Trans-Antarctic Expedition, an Australian named Frank Hurley, who took motion pictures as well as still photographs. As a result, almost every part of the epic journey was recorded on film. Have students do research to locate these films and photographs, download them onto presentation software, and share their findings with the class. (You may want to have them look ahead to the next selection for inspiration.) Discuss how the motion pictures and photos compare with students' visualizations of the subject matter from this text.

LANGUAGE DEVELOPMENT

Author's Style

Word Choice A **description** is a portrait in words of a person, place, or thing. Descriptions include details that appeal to the senses: sight, hearing, taste, smell, and touch. The effectiveness of a description depends upon **vivid word choice**, or the language a writer uses to create a specific impression.

In "The Voyage of the *James Caird*," the author makes extensive use of participles and participial phrases. A **participle** is a verb form that acts as an adjective. A **participial phrase** consists of a participle and its objects, complements, or modifiers, all acting together as an adjective. Because they are formed from verbs, participles and participial phrases often add energy to sentences by conveying to the reader a vivid sense of motion or action.

Example / Participle: On the third day, despite snowy, stormy weather, Worsley snatched the journey's first observation of the sun between patches of **racing** cloud.
Example / Participial Phrase: The canvas decking, **sagging under the weight of so much water**, threatened to pull loose the short nails McNish had extracted from packing cases.

Read It

Working individually, use this chart to identify each participle in these sentences from "The Voyage of the *James Caird*." Then, discuss with your group how each participial affects what you picture as you read the sentence.

PASSAGE	PARTICIPLE(S)	EFFECT
"The tale of the next sixteen days is one of supreme strife amid heaving waters," wrote Shackleton. (paragraph 1)	a. See possible responses in Teacher's Edition	b.
. . . in the foaming, confused current, the Caird sheered away from the cliffs, and from destruction. (paragraph 53)	c.	d.
After the meal, McNish, Crean, McCarthy, and Vincent crawled into their wet bags and lay down on the hard, shifting ballast of stones. . . . (paragraph 4)	e.	f.

Write It

Notebook Write a paragraph in which you explain what you learned about navigating uncharted waters from "The Voyage of the *James Caird*." Use participles and participial phrases to make your language more vivid and precise or to create a sense of motion.

DIGITAL PERSPECTIVES

Author's Style

Word Choice As you review the participles in the selection with students, consider providing additional examples to reinforce the difference between a verb and a participle.

- The whining sound came from the mast straining against the boards.
- The cracking ice looked like shards of glass.
- The howling wind unsettled the men.

For more support, see **Author's Style: Word Choice.**

Read It

Possible responses:

a. heaving

b. makes the water seem fierce and alive

c. foaming; confused

d. helps readers visualize the waves, and creates a sense of turbulent motion

e. shifting

f. helps readers feel how uncomfortable the men must have been

Write It

Paragraphs will vary, but make sure that students use participial phrases to make their writing vivid and to help readers visualize the action.

FORMATIVE ASSESSMENT

Author's Style

If students are unable to identify participles, **then** have students look for words that end in *–ing* and come before a noun.

For Reteach and Practice, see **Author's Style: Word Choice (RP).**

Selection Test

Administer "The Voyage of the *James Caird*" Selection Test, which is available in both print and digital formats online in Assessments.

PERSONALIZE FOR LEARNING

English Language Support

Participles and Participial Phrases Have English Learners identify and use participles and participial phrases in order to add variety to speaking and writing.

Ask student pairs to work together to summarize the events in "The Voyage of the *James Caird*," using participles and participial phrases. **EMERGING**

Ask students to use participles and participial phrases to describe a moment in the text when a member of the crew thought he might not survive.

Ask students to then use participles to compare how he or she might react to a moment such as this. **EXPANDING**

Ask students to consider which of the crew members of the *James Caird* disagreed with Shackleton's point of view the most. Then, ask students to write a critique of Shackleton from this crew member's point of view, using participles and participial phrases. **BRIDGING**

An expanded **English Language Support Lesson** on Participles and Participial Phrases is available in the Interactive Teacher's Edition.

The *Endurance* and the *James Caird* in Images

AUDIO SUMMARIES
Audio summaries of "The *Endurance* and the *James Caird* in Images" are available online in both English and Spanish in the Interactive Teacher's Edition or Unit Resources. Assigning these summaries prior to reviewing the images may help students build additional background knowledge and set a context for their first review.

Summary

"The Voyage of the *James Caird*" is Caroline Alexander's narrative account of how Ernest Shackleton and his five-man crew made an epic 16-day voyage aboard the lifeboat *James Caird*. On April 24, 1916, six exhausted, half-starved men climbed into the small boat in a desperate bid to escape the harsh Antarctic conditions of Elephant Island. They then sailed 800 miles across one of the most treacherous bodies of water on Earth to reach South Georgia Island, where they could summon help.

Prior to the journey, Shackleton had failed to cross Antarctica (his original mission) and had witnessed his ship, *Endurance,* sink. However, his leadership aboard the *James Caird* earned him a place of honor among the world's heroes.

Insight

Reviewing "The *Endurance* and the *James Caird* in Images" will help students realize what a threat to survival looks like. The bright white landscape in the photos contains a certain beauty, but the men and the ships are contrasted sharply against the white, suggesting that they don't belong in that landscape. The contrast highlights the danger the men are in and their need to escape.

ESSENTIAL QUESTION:
What does it take to survive?

Connection to Essential Question

"The *Endurance* and the *James Caird* in Images" provides a visual perspective on the Essential Question—*What does it take to survive?* The photographs clearly depict the bleak and deadly landscape in which the crew of the *Endurance* was trapped, and students can see the attempts the men made to save the *Endurance* before they were forced to take drastic steps to survive. The image of the crew of the *James Caird* launching the uncomfortably small boat into the icy water is especially powerful. In conjunction with "The Voyage of the *James Caird*," that image should help students understand that bravery plays a large part in survival.

SMALL-GROUP LEARNING PERFORMANCE TASK
What type of strength is most valuable in a survival situation?

UNIT PERFORMANCE-BASED ASSESSMENT
Should people in life-or-death situations be held accountable for their actions?

Connection to Performance Tasks

Small-Group Learning Performance Task In this Performance Task, students will present an argument about the most valuable type of strength in a survival situation. This selection provides students with visual examples of Shackleton facing the reality of his situation, as well as the bravery and perseverance he and his men needed to survive.

Unit Performance-Based Assessment The media selection does not speak directly to the concept of accountability in life-or-death situations, but students may consider the choices that Shackleton made (as represented in the photos) as evidence.

DIGITAL PERSPECTIVES — Audio | Video | Document | Annotation Highlights | EL Highlights | Online Assessment

LESSON RESOURCES

	Making Meaning	Effective Expression
Lesson	**First Review** **Close Review** **Analyze the Media** **Media Vocabulary**	**Writing to Compare**
Instructional Standards	**RI.7** Analyze various accounts of a subject . . . **L.6** Acquire and use accurately general academic and domain-specific words and phrases . . . **RL.1** Cite strong and thorough textual evidence . . .	**RI.7** Analyze various accounts of a subject . . . **SL.5** Make strategic use of digital media . . .
STUDENT RESOURCES		
Available online in the Interactive Student Edition or Unit Resources	Selection Audio First-Review Guide: Media Art/Photography Close-Review Guide: Media Art/Photography	Evidence Log
TEACHER RESOURCES		
Selection Resources Available online in the Interactive Teacher's Edition or Unit Resources	Audio Summaries The *Endurance* and the *James Caird* in Images: Media Questions Media Vocabulary	Writing to Compare: Compare the Text and Photographs

Media Complexity Rubric: The *Endurance* and the *James Caird* in Images

Quantitative Measures

Lexile: NP **Text Length:** Photo essay: six photos

Qualitative Measures

Knowledge Demands ① ❷ ③ ④ ⑤	The photographs in this media selection directly relate to the selection students have just read: "The Voyage of the *James Caird*." Students will therefore be familiar with the subject matter, but some review to help in recalling specific details may be necessary.
Structure ① ❷ ③ ④ ⑤	The structure is straightforward, with numbered photos accompanied by descriptive captions.
Language Conventionality and Clarity ① ② ❸ ④ ⑤	The language used in the photo captions is informative, direct, and clear. Some technical terms are used, such as "pack ice," "port side," and "sled dogs."
Levels of Meaning/Purpose ① ② ❸ ④ ⑤	Concepts will be familiar to students. The purpose is to inform and provide visual support for a selection students have just read.

FACILITATING

Jump Start

FIRST READ We all know the phrase, "A picture is worth a thousand words." Engage students in a discussion about how photographs, like words, tell a story. How might a story told through photographs be different from the same one told through words?

The *Endurance* and the *James Caird* in Images

What special challenges to survival might a photographer face—especially a photographer in Antarctica? Modeling the questions readers might ask as they review "The *Endurance* and the *James Caird* in Images" brings the photographs alive for students and connects them to the Small-Group Performance Task question. Selection audio and print capability for the selection are available in the Interactive Teacher's Edition.

Media Vocabulary

Encourage groups to discuss the media vocabulary. Have they seen the terms in texts before? Do they use any of them in their speech and writing?

Ask groups to look closely at the three terms to see what they have in common. Students will notice that each of the terms has a very specific meaning when used in the context of media. For example, when used in an English class, "composition" refers to an essay, but when used to refer to media, the word means "arrangement of the parts of a picture."

FIRST REVIEW

Have students perform the steps of the first review independently.

NOTICE: Students should focus on the basic elements of the photos and captions to ensure they understand what the photos show.

ANNOTATE: Students should mark any photos they wish to revisit during their close review.

CONNECT: Students should increase their understanding by connecting the photos here to other photographs or media they have seen.

RESPOND: Students will answer questions and write a description to demonstrate understanding.

Point out to students that while they will always complete the Respond step at the end of the first review, the other steps will probably happen somewhat concurrently. You may wish to print copies of the **First-Review Guide: Media Art/Photography** for students to use.

MAKING MEANING

THE VOYAGE OF THE
JAMES CAIRD

Comparing Text to Media

The photographs on the following pages were taken by the *Endurance* expedition photographer Frank Hurley. While looking at this selection, you will compare the differences between how written text and photographs can tell a story.

THE ENDURANCE AND THE
JAMES CAIRD IN IMAGES

About the Photographer

Frank Hurley (1885–1962) was an Australian photographer known for the stunning photos he took during Shackleton's *Endurance* expedition. In the words of one of the crew members, "Hurley [was] a warrior with his camera and would go anywhere or do anything to get a picture." Remarkably, Hurley was able to save many plate glass negatives from the *Endurance* as well as an album of photos he had already printed. After the ship sank, Hurley had to leave his photographic equipment behind. From that point on, he used a small hand-held camera to take an additional 38 photos, all of which survived.

STANDARDS

Reading Informational Text
Analyze various accounts of a subject told in different mediums, determining which details are emphasized in each account.

Language
Acquire and use accurately grade-appropriate general academic and domain-specific words and phrases, sufficient for reading, writing, speaking, and listening at the college and career readiness level; demonstrate independence in gathering vocabulary knowledge when considering a word or phrase important to comprehension or expression.

The *Endurance* and the *James Caird* in Images

Media Vocabulary

These words will be useful to you as you analyze, discuss, and write about photographs.

Composition: arrangement of the parts of a picture; the *foreground* is closest to the camera lens, while the *background* is farther away	• The composition may stress one part of an image more than another. • The composition may show what the photographer thinks is important in the subject.
Perspective or Angle: vantage point from which a photo is taken	• The camera may be looking down, looking up, or looking head on at the subject. • The subject may seem very far away, at a middle distance, or very close.
Lighting and Color: use of light, shadow, and color in a picture	• Some images are full color, while others are black and white. There are countless variations of color options. • Some parts of an image are brighter or darker than others.

First Review MEDIA: ART AND PHOTOGRAPHY

Study each photograph and its caption using these strategies.

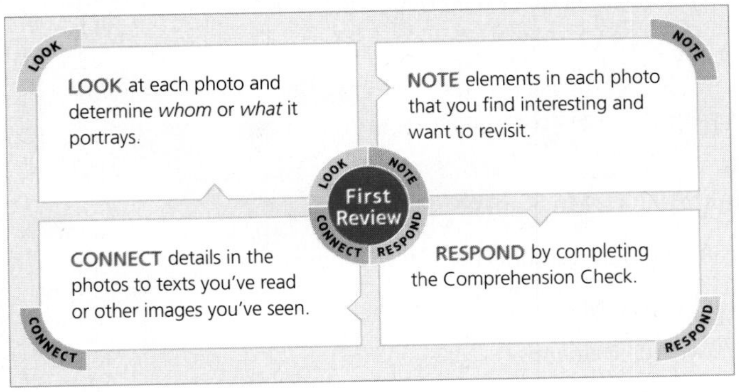
LOOK
LOOK at each photo and determine *whom* or *what* it portrays.
NOTE
NOTE elements in each photo that you find interesting and want to revisit.
First Review
CONNECT
CONNECT details in the photos to texts you've read or other images you've seen.
RESPOND
RESPOND by completing the Comprehension Check.

PERSONALIZE FOR LEARNING

Strategic Support
Zoom In To help students who are visually impaired, project the photographs on a screen to enlarge the images. As necessary, zoom in on specific parts of each photograph to help students appreciate the detail in the images, especially the shadows in the pack ice that make it look like waves in the ocean.

MEDIA | PHOTO GALLERY

The *Endurance* and the *James Caird* in Images

Frank Hurley

BACKGROUND

Sir Ernest Shackleton's trans-Antarctica expedition of 1914–1917 was a true-life adventure that rivals any work of fiction for drama, bravery, and daring. Shackleton's goal was to cross the Antarctic continent from one coast to the other. The expedition never made it. Instead, Shackleton and his men were forced to abandon their ship, the *Endurance*, when it became stuck in Antarctic pack ice in 1915. The crew set up camp on an ice floe and eventually reached Elephant Island in April 1916. From there, Shackleton and five crewmen sailed the *James Caird*—a small lifeboat—800 miles to South Georgia Island to seek help at a whaling station. That August, using a boat on loan from Chile, Shackleton finally rescued the rest of the crew from Elephant Island.

SCAN FOR MULTIMEDIA

PHOTO 1: *Endurance* in the ice To photographer Frank Hurley, the pack ice often looked like ocean waves.

NOTES

FACILITATING SMALL-GROUP CLOSE REVIEWING

CLOSE REVIEW: Photography As groups perform the close review, circulate and offer support as needed.

- Remind groups that when they view photographs, they should be sure to identify the subject and setting.
- If a group is confused about why particular photographs are important, remind group members to think about the significant events in "The Voyage of the *James Caird*."
- Challenge groups to rewrite the captions that accompany the photographs.

DIGITAL PERSPECTIVES

CLOSER REVIEW

Analyze Perspective and Angle

Circulate among groups as students conduct their close review. Suggest that groups close review Photo 1. Encourage them to talk about the notes that they make. If needed, provide the following support.

ANNOTATE: Explain to students that **perspective** refers to the relative size of objects in a photograph, as determined by the distance of each object from the camera lens; the **angle** refers to the photographer's point of view. Have students note aspects of the photograph that demonstrate **perspective** and **angle,** or work with small groups to have students participate while you note them together.

QUESTION: Guide students to consider what these details might tell them. Ask how perspective and angle affect this photograph of the *Endurance*, and accept student responses.

Possible response: The *Endurance* looks like a tiny ship on a mountainous ocean—almost engulfed by foam and spray. Hurley shoots the ship from a long distance and with pack ice in the close foreground. He angles the shot for a broadside view of the ship to dramatize its apparent movement from right to left.

CONCLUDE: Help students to formulate conclusions about the importance of perspective and angle in the photograph. Ask students why Hurley might have used perspective and angle as he does here. What overall impression of the voyage does the photographer convey with his choice of perspective and angle?

Possible response: The image is playful and inventive rather than realistic, but by using perspective and angle, the photographer comments on the real danger the ship is in.

Explain to students that the **perspective** and **angle** of a photograph often reveal the photographer's attitude and emotional response to the subject. They often express the photographer's style.

CLOSER REVIEW

Analyze Lighting

Circulate among groups as students conduct their close review. Suggest that groups close review Photo 3. Encourage them to talk about the notes that they make. If needed, provide the following support.

ANNOTATE: Have students note details in the photograph that demonstrate its **lighting** (the use of light and shadow), or work with small groups to have students participate while you note them together.

QUESTION: Guide students to consider what the lighting might tell them. Ask what they can infer from the contrast between the dark ship and the brilliant white snow, and accept student responses.

Possible response: The contrast between the ship and the ice suggests that the ice is swallowing up the ship—as a fierce predator might consume its prey.

CONCLUDE: Help students to formulate conclusions about the importance of these details of light and shade. Ask students why the photographer might have included these details.

Possible response: What remains of the ship is a dark, ragged skeleton against the white glow of the sky. It casts no shadow. The image is like an illustration from a ghost story. By his use of lighting, the photographer suggests an atmosphere of eerie unreality.

Remind groups that **lighting** can transform and sometimes undermine the reality of a scene. It often reveals clues about the kind of story the photographer aims to tell.

PHOTO 2: The port side of the ship, October 19, 1915 Shackleton is the man leaning over the side of the ship in the foreground. He called this photo "The Beginning of the End."

NOTES

PHOTO 3: The end The expedition's sled dogs are shown in the foreground looking at the trapped and ruined ship.

NOTES

VOCABULARY DEVELOPMENT

Media Vocabulary If groups are struggling with the concept of *composition* as they review Photo 3, remind them that the word has multiple meanings. Point out four of the most common definitions:

1. manner of being composed; structure
2. the act of combining parts or elements to form a whole
3. the resulting state or product
4. a short writing assignment; essay

Explain to groups that when used to refer to photographs or any work of art, *composition* has the first meaning: "manner of being composed; structure." Have groups brainstorm possible parts of the composition of a photograph.

Possible responses: pattern, symmetry, texture, depth of field, lines, perspective, shape, framing

PHOTO 4: Hauling the *James Caird* After the *Endurance* sank, the men dragged the *James Caird* three quarters of a mile to a new camp. The boat weighed approximately 2,000 pounds.

NOTES

PHOTO 5: Launching the *Caird* As they attempted to launch the boat in heavy surf, two of the men were thrown overboard.

NOTES

DIGITAL PERSPECTIVES

CLOSER REVIEW

Analyze Composition

Circulate among groups as students conduct their close review. Suggest that groups close review Photo 4. Encourage them to talk about the notes that they make. If needed, provide the following support.

ANNOTATE: Guide groups to note characteristics of the **composition** (the arrangement of the elements in the image), or work with small groups to have students participate while you note them together.

QUESTION: Guide students to consider what these details might tell them. Ask them why the photographer composes the two main elements of the image in this way, and accept student responses.

Possible response: The two main elements are the men and the boat. The photographer gives equal weight to both: the men are on the left; the boat is on the right. This arrangement balances the composition. The two elements are equally crucial to survival.

CONCLUDE: Help students to formulate conclusions about the importance of these details in the photograph. Ask students why the photographer might have included these details of composition.

Possible response: The binary arrangement of elements in the composition—men on one side, boat on the other—suggests the men and boat have equal weight in the battle for survival. The men will use the boat to reach the help they need.

Remind students that good **composition** in photography is the arrangement of elements to suit the idea, the attitude, or the meaning of the whole image.

PERSONALIZE FOR LEARNING

Challenge

Color Photographs Review Photo 5 with students. Point out to students that a number of classic black-and-white photographs have been "colorized," so the photographs are now in color. Locate several of these photographs by using the Internet, and display both the before and after images. Have students discuss which version they prefer and why, using the media vocabulary (*composition, lighting and color, perspective or angle*) in their analysis. Then have students use a software coloring program to color one of Hurley's photographs and analyze the results in the same way. How does the color affect the impact of the photograph?

CLOSER REVIEW

Analyze Composition

Circulate among groups as students conduct their close review. Suggest that groups close review Photo 6. Encourage them to talk about the notes that they make. If needed, provide the following support.

ANNOTATE: Have students note the elements of the photograph's **composition** (arrangement of the parts), or work with small groups to have students participate while you note them together.

QUESTION: Guide students to consider what these details might tell them. Ask which of the two main elements is in the foreground and which is in the background, and accept student responses.
Possible response: The men are in the foreground; the rescue boat is barely visible in the background.

CONCLUDE: Help students to formulate conclusions about the importance of these details in the text. Ask students why the photographer might have included these details.
Possible response: The composition demonstrates the photographer's judgment of what is really important in this scene. In formal terms, the rescue ship is the subject. The men's eyes are all focused on it, so the viewer's eyes are too. The ship, however, is in the far distance. It's tiny. The men dominate the close foreground, and their jubilation dominates the entire composition.

Remind students that **composition** enables the viewer to see where every element stands in order of importance.

Comprehension Check

Possible responses:

1. Details include the ship not only trapped in the ice but also clearly listing to one side and in imminent danger of capsizing and sinking further into the icy water.
2. In Photo 3, the *Endurance* is trapped and ruined, rendered immobile by the ice.
3. The frothy waves, snow-capped rocks, and frozen chunks of ice show the surf is rough and frigid.
4. Descriptions will vary; however, students should include elements of the setting, people, and events the images show.

PHOTO 6: The rescue The crew members who were left on Elephant Island welcome the rescue ship.

NOTES

Comprehension Check

Complete the following items after you finish your first review.

1. Which details help explain why Shackleton would call Photo 2 "The Beginning of the End"?

2. What is happening to the *Endurance* in Photo 3?

3. In Photo 5, which details show the conditions of the surf when the *James Caird* was launched?

4. **Notebook** Confirm your understanding of the *Endurance* and the *James Caird* photo gallery by writing a description of the setting, people, and events the images portray.

Close Review

With your group, revisit the photographs and your first-review notes. Record any new observations that seem important. What **questions** do you have? What can you **conclude**?

Close Review (REVIEW · QUESTION · CONCLUDE)

THE *ENDURANCE* AND THE *JAMES CAIRD* IN IMAGES

Analyze the Media

Notebook **Complete the activities.**

1. **Present and Discuss** Choose the photo you find most interesting or powerful. Share your choice with the group and discuss why you chose it. Explain what you notice in the photo, the questions it raises for you, and the conclusions you reach about it.
2. **Review and Synthesize** With your group, review all the photos. Do they do more than simply document the expedition? Are they examples of journalism, of art, or of both? Explain.
3. Notebook **Essential Question:** ***What does it take to survive?*** What challenges did the men face when they lost the *Endurance*? What qualities do you think their survival required? Support your response with evidence from the photographs.

LANGUAGE DEVELOPMENT

Media Vocabulary

composition	perspective or angle	lighting and color

Use the vocabulary words in your responses to the questions.

1. **(a)** In Photo 1, what is the position of the ship in relation to the ice around it? **(b)** What might Hurley have wanted to convey in this photograph?
2. In Photo 2, which aspects help to emphasize the condition of the *Endurance*?
3. In Photo 4, what effect does the contrast between the background and the subjects create?

STANDARDS

Reading

Cite strong and thorough textual evidence to support analysis of what the text says explicitly as well as inferences drawn from the text.

DIGITAL PERSPECTIVES

Jump Start

CLOSE REVIEW Ask students to consider the following prompt: *Would you rather be the photographer or a regular sailor on the Endurance?* As students discuss the prompt in their groups, have them consider the importance of each position to history and to the crew's survival.

Close Review

If needed, model close reviewing by using the Closer Review notes in the Interactive Teacher's Edition.

Remind students to use Accountable Talk in their discussions and to support one another as they complete the close review.

Analyze the Media

You may wish to review the following definitions with groups before they complete the activities:

- Art – the expression of human creative skill and imagination
- Journalism – the activity of gathering, assessing, creating, and presenting news and information

1. **Responses will vary by group.** Remind students to review their notes from the first review to get details that support their assertions before discussing with the group.
2. **Responses will vary by group.** Groups should support their explanations with evidence from the photographs.
3. **Possible response:** When the *Endurance* was lost, the crew of the ship were faced with surviving in the harsh conditions of Antarctica with little to no access to shelter, food, or water. This situation required the men to be resourceful and steadfast in their efforts to find help.

Media Vocabulary

For more support, see **Media Vocabulary.**

Possible responses:

1. (a) The ship is centered in the ice, so the *perspective* is head on. (b) This *composition* enables Hurley to convey that the ship is surrounded by ice, that the voyage is perilous, and that survival is unsure.
2. Aspects that emphasize the terrible condition of the *Endurance* include its *angle* in the ocean, the broken boards, and the snow and ice packed into the tools on the side.
3. The contrast between the background and the subjects creates a feeling of desolation that reinforces the enormous struggle for survival the men face. The stark *lighting and color* differences reinforce this contrast.

FORMATIVE ASSESSMENT

Analyze the Media

If students struggle to close review the photographs, **then** provide **The *Endurance* and the *James Caird* in Images: Media Questions** available online in the Interactive Teacher's Edition or Unit Resources. Answers and DOK levels are also available.

Media Vocabulary

If students struggle to identify the effect contrast creates in the photographs, **then** have them review the definition of *contrast* and look for examples of contrasts in photographs.

FACILITATING

Writing to Compare

As students prepare to compare information they've gathered about the *James Caird*, they will create a multimedia presentation to synthesize what they have learned.

Compare the Text and Photographs Discuss with students what factors to consider as they locate similarities and differences between the photographs and the text. For example, in studying the photos, students should consider each caption, image, composition, perspective or angle, use of lighting and color, contrast, pattern, symmetry, perspective, and shape. In the text, students should consider the topic or subject, main idea, word choice, tone, details, dialogue, primary sources, characterization, plot, and suspense. For more support, see **Writing to Compare: Compare the Text and Photographs.**

MAKE IT INTERACTIVE

Project the Interactive Teacher's Edition of photo 1 of "The *Endurance* and the *James Caird* in Images" and paragraph 1 of "The Voyage of the *James Caird,*" and model comparing them.

Both examples describe the difficulty the men faced: the photo shows the *Endurance* surrounded by ice, while the paragraph from "The Voyage of the *James Caird*" quotes Shackleton's description of "the supreme strife amid heaving waters" that the men faced. The two works are primarily different because of their topics. "The Voyage of the *James Caird*" describes the trip the lifeboat undertook, while photo 1 of "The *Endurance* and the *James Caird* in Images" shows the *Endurance*.

Analyze the Text

See **possible responses** in chart on Student page.

Possible responses:

1. The photographs give readers a sense of what the ship and landscape looked like—and how difficult the conditions were.
2. The text communicates specific details and offers personal insights. It gives readers a fuller picture of events than the photographs.

EFFECTIVE EXPRESSION

THE VOYAGE OF THE *JAMES CAIRD*

THE *ENDURANCE* AND THE *JAMES CAIRD* IN IMAGES

Writing to Compare

Both "The Voyage of the *James Caird*" by Caroline Alexander and the photographs taken by Frank Hurley provide information about the legendary Antarctic expedition led by Sir Ernest Shackleton. Now, analyze the texts and consider how the medium in which information is provided—visual or verbal—affects what you learn about the subject.

Assignment

Create a **multimedia presentation** about the Shackleton expedition in which you weave together Alexander's text, Hurley's photographs, and your own commentary. In your presentation, explain how verbal accounts and photographs provide information that is valuable in different ways. Choose from these options:

- ☐ a **museum exhibit guide** for a show about the Shackleton expedition
- ☐ a page plan and content for a **website** about the Shackleton expedition
- ☐ the script for a **slide show** about the Shackleton expedition

Analyze the Texts

Compare the Text and Photographs With your group, identify ways in which the verbal text and the photographs convey information. Use the chart to capture your observations.

INFORMATION ABOUT THE EXPEDITION	WHAT I LEARNED FROM "THE VOYAGE OF THE *JAMES CAIRD*"	WHAT I LEARNED FROM THE EXPEDITION PHOTOGRAPHS	HOW TEXT COMPARES TO PHOTOGRAPHS
hardships the crew faced	Possible responses: Extreme cold, hunger, and thirst; fear; overcrowding; physical danger, pain from injuries; psychological terror; great physical exertion	Possible responses: Physical danger; loss of boat (loss of shelter, food, clothing, transportation); psychological terror; extreme cold; great physical exertion	Possible responses: The text is more descriptive, especially the primary sources, the journals of Shackleton and Worsley
actions they took to survive	Tried to calculate their position; bailed the water out of the boat; drank hot liquids; took shifts to allow for some rest; tried to stay upbeat and positive; chipped ice from the mast	Men dragged the *James Caird*, which was very heavy, across the ice to a new camp; they launched the *James Caird* into the ocean to find help; they saved the sled dogs	The text is more descriptive, especially the primary sources, the journals of Shackleton and Worsley
details about the crew	Personalities of crew members; anecdotes about the crew and the hardships and challenges they faced	Some of the actions that the crew took, such as hauling and launching the *James Caird*.	The text provides more specific and detailed information.

Notebook Respond to these questions.

1. Do the photographs reveal aspects of the story that the text does not? Explain.
2. Does the text communicate aspects of the men's experience that the photographs do not? Explain.

PERSONALIZE FOR LEARNING

Strategic Support

Comparison Group members may have difficulty seeing how both sources work together to convey more information about the expedition. To help them learn more about the challenges the crew faced, have students skim "The Voyage of the *James Caird.*" Ask them to suggest where the photos could be placed in the text to clarify, reinforce, and illustrate the text. Have students discuss their choices.

Planning and Prewriting

Organize Tasks Make a list of tasks you will have to accomplish in order to get your presentation done. Assign the tasks to individual group members. You may add to or modify this list as needed.

TASK LIST

Research and Choose Photographs: Decide whether you need additional photos of the expedition or its members. If you do, research and choose those images.

Assigned To: ______________________

Research and Choose Texts: Decide whether you need additional writings about the expedition or by its members. If you do, research and choose those texts.

Assigned To: ______________________

Locate Other Media: Find additional media—audio, video, or other visuals—to add interest and information. For example, you may want to include maps that show the routes Shackleton had planned and the ones the expedition actually took.

Assigned To: ______________________

Make a Rough Outline: Set a sequence for your content as well as any special sections of information you may want to include. You may always revise the sequence later as your project takes shape.

Assigned To: ______________________

Drafting

Provide Thorough Information As you organize photos and texts and write content, work to answer five basic questions:

- What happened?
- Who was involved?
- Where did the events happen?
- Why did the events happen?
- What were the results or consequences of the events?

Include Comparisons of Texts to Photographs Use your notes from the analysis you did earlier to explain how images and texts contribute to readers' and viewers' understanding of the Shackleton expedition in similar and different ways.

Revising

Make sure all the images or other media you have chosen add value to the presentation. If necessary, cut content to make your presentation more focused and effective.

EVIDENCE LOG

Before moving on to a new selection, go to your Evidence Log and record what you've learned from "The Voyage of the *James Caird*" and "The *Endurance* and the *James Caird* in Images."

STANDARDS

Reading Informational Text
Analyze various accounts of a subject told in different mediums, determining which details are emphasized in each account.

Speaking and Listening
Make strategic use of digital media in presentations to enhance understanding of findings, reasoning, and evidence and to add interest.

PERSONALIZE FOR LEARNING

Challenge

Museum Exhibition When everyone is finished writing, challenge students to arrange all the projects to create a museum exhibition about Shackleton, his crew, and their remarkable story of survival. Students can add additional visuals, including three-dimensional models, shadowboxes, and audio-visual features. Invite other classes to tour the exhibition.

DIGITAL PERSPECTIVES

Planning and Prewriting

Organize Tasks Remind students to make a list of tasks for the project and assign tasks to individual group members. Although group members will work individually for a time, the overall effort is collaborative, and group members should check in with one another during the process, asking for and offering opinions and feedback in a respectful way. You may wish to monitor groups to ensure that all members are participating equally.

Review and Revise Groups should be mindful of which photos, texts, and media they choose to include in their presentations. Each part of the presentation should contribute to the overall effect, and extraneous materials should be omitted. **For more support, see Writing to Compare: Multimedia Presentation.**

Evidence Log Support students in completing their Evidence Log. This paced activity will help prepare them for the Performance-Based Assessment at the end of the unit.

FORMATIVE ASSESSMENT

Writing to Compare

If students are unable to provide specific examples and details, **then** have them skim "The Voyage of the *James Caird*" and look back at the photos in "The *Endurance* and the *James Caird* in Images" for ideas.

from Life of Pi

AUDIO SUMMARIES
Audio summaries of this excerpt from *Life of Pi* are available online in both English and Spanish in the Interactive Teacher's Edition or Unit Resources. Assigning these summaries prior to reading the selection may help students build additional background knowledge and set a context for their first read.

Summary

In this excerpt from *Life of Pi* by Yann Martel, Pi tries to come to terms with a disturbing fact about his continuing survival adrift at sea. He shares a boat with Richard Parker, a tiger, and unless Pi provides him with fresh meat the tiger will eat him. Pi decides to take up fishing, but he has no bait and the fish don't bite. Suddenly the air is full of flying fish fleeing from a school of dorado. Some of them land in the bottom of the boat, providing Pi with bait. As a lifelong vegetarian, he can hardly bring himself to kill a fellow creature, but when he baits his hook with a flying fish's head he quickly finds himself battling with an enormous dorado. Now Pi is not just fighting for his survival. He has become a predator—like the tiger he must feed.

Insight

Reading this excerpt from *Life of Pi* will help students begin to think about how the need for survival can challenge one's humanity. When people are pitted against nature, they may be surprised by the measures they are willing to take to survive external forces of nature.

ESSENTIAL QUESTION:
What does it take to survive?

Connection to Essential Question

This excerpt from *Life of Pi* provides a strong connection to the Essential Question, "What does it take to survive?" Pi's struggle to survive forces him to act against his fundamental beliefs, and he becomes a killer of animals. Yet, he maintains a hold on his identity and the distinction between him and Richard Parker, whom he works hard to tame, so he survives with his humanity intact.

SMALL-GROUP LEARNING PERFORMANCE TASK
What type of strength is most valuable in a survival situation?

UNIT PERFORMANCE-BASED ASSESSMENT
Should people in life-or-death situations be held accountable for their actions?

Connection to Performance Tasks

Small-Group Learning Performance Task In this Performance Task, students will present an argument about the most valuable strength in a survival situation. This selection provides students with examples of Pi's adaptability, cunning, and barbarism.

Unit Performance-Based Assessment This selection should contribute to students' ideas about the accountability of people in life-or-death situations in that Pi betrays his beliefs and essentially tortures Richard Parker in order to survive.

DIGITAL PERSPECTIVES: Audio | Video | Document | Annotation Highlights | EL Highlights | Online Assessment

LESSON RESOURCES

	Making Meaning	Language Development	Effective Expression
Lesson	**First Read** **Close Read** **Analyze the Text** **Analyze Craft and Structure**	**Concept Vocabulary** **Word Study** **Conventions**	**Writing to Sources**
Instructional Standards	**RL.10** By the end of grade 9, read and comprehend literature . . . **RL.3** Analyze how complex characters develop . . . **L.4** Determine or clarify the meaning . . .	**L.4.b** Identify and correctly use patterns of word changes . . . **L.2** Demonstrate command of the conventions . . . **L.1.b** Use various types of phrases and clauses . . .	**W.1** Write arguments to support claims . . . **W.1.a** Introduce precise claim(s) . . .
STUDENT RESOURCES			
Available online in the Interactive Student Edition or Unit Resources	Selection Audio First-Read Guide: Fiction Close-Read Guide: Fiction	Word Network	Evidence Log
TEACHER RESOURCES			
Selection Resources Available online in the Interactive Teacher's Edition or Unit Resources	Audio Summaries Annotation Highlights EL Highlights Life of Pi: Text Questions Analyze Craft and Structure: Complex Characters English Language Support Lesson: Character	Concept Vocabulary and Word Study Conventions: Participial Versus Absolute Phrases	Writing to Sources: Argument, Claims, and Counterclaims
Reteach/Practice (RP) Available online in the Interactive Teacher's Edition or Unit Resources	Analyze Craft and Structure: Complex Characters (RP)	Word Study: Latin Suffixes *-ory* and *-ary* (RP) Conventions: Participial Versus Absolute Phrases (RP)	Writing to Sources: Argument, Claims, and Counterclaims (RP)
Assessment Available online in Assessments	Selection Test		
My Resources	A Unit 2 Answer Key is available online and in the Interactive Teacher's Edition		

Reading Support

Text Complexity Rubric: Life of Pi	
Quantitative Measures	
Lexile: 870 **Text Length:** 4,924 words	
Qualitative Measures	
Knowledge Demands ①—②—❸—④—⑤	Unfamiliar and fantastical situation (being stranded at sea with wild animals); though students will not be able to relate to the experiences, the situation and feelings are explained.
Structure ①—②—❸—④—⑤	Linear story, but plot elements are mixed with internal commentary; the only dialogue is the character's conversations with himself.
Language Conventionality and Clarity ①—②—❸—④—⑤	Selection has complex sentences with embedded clauses, figurative language, and some idiomatic phrases; contains some ironic or sarcastic statements; many descriptive passages.
Levels of Meaning/Purpose ①—②—③—❹—⑤	Multiple levels of meaning; description of events is interspersed with introspective comments by the main character and with observations and generalizations about human and animal nature; some sophisticated concepts.

DECIDE AND PLAN

English Language Support

Provide English Learners with support for language and meaning as they read the selection.

Language Students may get confused reading passages with figurative language, such as, *It was an investment that would bring him an excellent return* (paragraph 2); *His tail jumped to life* (paragraph 3). Ask questions to guide students to understand that these are figurative rather than literal phrases.

Levels of Meaning/Purpose To help students sort out the events and ideas in the story, suggest that they keep a log of the main events, stating them in their own words. For example, (paragraph 2) *He tried to go fishing. He had a problem with bait. He wanted to use the fish, but he was afraid to steal it from the tiger.*

Strategic Support

Provide students with strategic support to ensure they can successfully read the text.

Knowledge Demands Using the background information in the selection, discuss the situation depicted in the story, asking what aspects of it are most based in reality. Discuss that the selection has fantastical as well as realistic elements. Point out that students will read to find out the actions of Pi and the tiger, and also the main character's feelings and observations about animals and people.

Levels of Meaning/Purpose If students have difficulty understanding the multiple levels of meaning, focus on individual paragraphs. Ask students to first state the events that happen. Then, ask them to reread the paragraph to determine what feelings or ideas are conveyed by the man or the tiger.

Challenge

Provide students who need to be challenged with ideas for how they can go beyond a simple interpretation of the text.

Text Analysis Ask students to describe the conflict the boy feels about the first time he kills a fish. What are some of the factors that contribute to his difficulty? Ask them to comment on how the boy's ability to imagine the feelings of the fish contributes to his conflict. What makes him want to stop? What makes him continue?

Written Response After discussing the boy's ability to have empathy for the fish, ask students to write a paragraph about how this ability helps him to tame the tiger. How does thinking like an animal help the boy to survive?

TEACH

Read and Respond

Have groups read the selection and complete the Making Meaning, Language Development, and Effective Expression activities.

Standards Support Through Teaching and Learning Cycle

IDENTIFY NEEDS

Analyze results of the Beginning-of-Year Assessment, focusing on the items relating to Unit 2. Also take into consideration student performance to this point and your observations of where particular students struggle.

DECIDE AND PLAN

- If students have performed poorly on items matching these standards, then provide selection scaffolds before assigning them the on-level lesson provided in the Student Edition.
- If students have done well on the Beginning-of-Year Assessment, then challenge them to keep progressing and learning by giving them opportunities to practice the skills in depth.
- Use the Selection Resources listed on the Planning pages for *Life of Pi* to help students continually improve their ability to master the standards.

Instructional Standards: Life of Pi

	Catching Up	This Year	Looking Forward
Reading	You may wish to administer the **Analyze Craft and Structure: Complex Characters (RP)** worksheet to help students understand the relationships between complex characters and a text.	**RL.3** Analyze how complex characters develop over the course of a text, interact with other characters, and advance the plot or develop the theme.	Have students introduce a new character to Pi's lifeboat and write one paragraph in which the character and Pi interact.
Writing	You may wish to administer the **Writing to Sources: Argument, Claims, and Counterclaims (RP)** worksheet to help students understand how to develop a claim, identify opposing claims, and support their reasons with evidence.	**W.1** Write arguments to support claims in an analysis of substantive topics or texts, using valid reasoning and relevant and sufficent evidence.	Have students develop an argument that uses as its claim one of the counterclaims from their original argument.
Language	You may wish to administer the **Conventions: Types of Phrases (RP)** worksheet to help students understand participial and absolute phrases.	**L.1.b** Use various types of phrases and clauses to convey specific meanings and add variety and interest to writing or presentations.	You may wish to challenge students to use increasingly complex participial and absolute phrases in their speaking and writing.

ANALYZE AND REVISE

- Analyze student work for evidence of student learning.
- Identify whether or not students have met the expectations in the standards.
- Identify implications for future instruction.

TEACH

Implement the planned lesson, and gather evidence of student learning.

FACILITATING

Jump Start

FIRST READ Which do you think would be more dangerous: being marooned on a lifeboat in the middle of an ocean or being confined in a small space with a hungry tiger? Engage students in a discussion about survival that sets the context for reading this excerpt from *Life of Pi*.

Life of Pi

How do people change when confronted with life-and-death decisions? Modeling the questions readers might ask as they read the excerpt from *Life of Pi* brings the text alive for students and connects it to the Small-Group Performance Task question. Selection audio and print capability for the selection are available in the Interactive Teacher's Edition.

Concept Vocabulary

Encourage groups to discuss the concept vocabulary words. Have they seen the words in any text before? Do they use any of the words in their speech or writing? Do they recognize any word parts, such as a base word, a prefix, or a suffix?

Ask groups to look closely at the three words to see what they have in common. Students will notice that each of the unfamiliar words contains most or all of a smaller, familiar word. Groups of words that share a common root or base are called *word families*. Encourage groups to think of one other word family. For example, the word family for *word* includes *wordy, wordsmith, reword,* and *wordless*.

FIRST READ

Have students perform the steps of the first read independently.

NOTICE: Encourage students to notice the interactions of Pi and Richard Parker with the flying fish.

ANNOTATE: Remind students to mark any passages that describe how Pi's character changes as he fishes for food.

CONNECT: Have students compare Pi's actions when fishing with his beliefs as a vegetarian.

RESPOND: Students will answer questions and write a summary to demonstrate understanding.

Point out to students that while they will always complete the Respond step at the end of the first read, the other steps will probably happen somewhat concurrently. You may wish to print copies of the **First-Read Guide: Fiction** for students to use.

MAKING MEANING

About the Author

Yann Martel (b. 1963) was born in Spain to Canadian parents and lived in many different places, including Costa Rica, Mexico, Alaska, and Canada. After graduating from college, he worked various jobs, such as dishwasher and security guard. Unsure about what he wanted to pursue as a career, he started to write. Though he found critical success, sales of his stories did not follow. Eventually, Martel traveled to India, where he found the inspiration for his most successful work, *Life of Pi*.

from Life of Pi

Concept Vocabulary

As you perform your first read of the excerpt from *Life of Pi*, you will encounter the following words.

irresolvable   predatory   adversary

Base Words If these words are unfamiliar to you, analyze each one to see whether it contains a base word you know. Then, use your knowledge of the "inside" word, along with context, to determine the meaning of the concept word. Here is an example of how to apply the strategy.

Unfamiliar Word: *willful*

Familiar "Inside" Word: *will*, with meanings including "choose," "intention," "determination"

Context: A lifetime of peaceful vegetarianism stood between me and the **willful** beheading of a fish.

Conclusion: The narrator is a vegetarian, and would not want to behead a fish, at least not on purpose. *Willful* might mean "with will," or "intentionally."

Apply your knowledge of base words and other vocabulary strategies to determine the meanings of unfamiliar words you encounter during your first read.

First Read FICTION

Apply these strategies as you conduct your first read. You will have an opportunity to complete a close read after your first read.

NOTICE *whom* the story is about, *what* happens, *where* and *when* it happens, and *why* the main characters react as they do.

ANNOTATE by marking vocabulary and key passages you want to revisit.

CONNECT ideas within the selection to what you already know and what you have already read.

RESPOND by completing the Comprehension Check and by writing a brief summary of the selection.

First Read: NOTICE, ANNOTATE, CONNECT, RESPOND

STANDARDS

Reading Literature

By the end of grade 9, read and comprehend literature, including stories, dramas, and poems, in the grades 9–10 text complexity band proficiently, with scaffolding as needed at the high end of the range.

Language

Determine or clarify the meaning of unknown and multiple-meaning words and phrases based on *grades 9–10 reading and content*, choosing flexibly from a range of strategies.

NOVEL EXCERPT

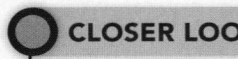

from
Life of Pi

Yann Martel

BACKGROUND

In the novel *Life of Pi* by Yann Martel, the main character is a teenager whose family owns a zoo in India. The family decides to leave India with their animals and sail to Canada, but while traveling, their ship is struck by a violent storm and sinks. Pi escapes on a lifeboat with four of the family's animals: a hyena, a zebra, an orangutan—and a Bengal tiger named Richard Parker. The hyena kills the zebra and the orangutan but is in turn killed by the tiger. Pi constructs a raft for himself, where he can retreat to safety from the tiger, and sets about taming Richard Parker.

SCAN FOR MULTIMEDIA

Chapter 61

NOTES

1 The next morning I was not too wet and I was feeling strong. I thought this was remarkable considering the strain I was under and how little I had eaten in the last several days.

2 It was a fine day. I decided to try my hand at fishing, for the first time in my life. After a breakfast of three biscuits and one can of water, I read what the survival manual had to say on the subject. The first problem arose: bait. I thought about it. There were the

DIGITAL PERSPECTIVES

CLOSER LOOK

Analyze Tone

Circulate among groups as students conduct their close read. Suggest that groups close read paragraph 1. Encourage them to talk about the annotations that they mark. If needed, provide the following support.

ANNOTATE: Have students mark details in paragraph 1 that reveal **tone**—the author's attitude toward his subject and his audience. Point out that the tone of a literary work such as a story may be serious, eerie, or ironic.

QUESTION: Guide students to consider what these details might tell them. Ask them to describe the tone of Pi's remarks and to say what impression it conveys of Pi. Accept student responses.

Possible response: Pi's account of his morning is delivered in a calm, matter-of-fact tone. This conveys the impression that Pi is a practical young man who is dealing with his situation without fear or distaste.

CONCLUDE: Help students to formulate conclusions about the importance of these details in the text. Ask students why the author might have included these details.

Possible response: Pi's calm tone suggests that he will cope with what comes his way and that he will do whatever is necessary to feed himself and (crucially) the tiger.

Remind students that authors often use **tone** to help establish character. By adding these details, the author makes it clear that Pi is capable of seeing the funny side of his terrible situation. For example, Pi's humorous remark that he "was not too wet" suggests that he realizes that while his situation is dire, it could always be worse—and likely will be, if he can't keep the tiger well fed.

PERSONALIZE FOR LEARNING

English Language Support

Idioms Tell students that the expression *to try my hand* in paragraph 2 is an idiom. Remind students that an idiom is a commonly used expression that is not meant literally.

Explain that *to try your hand* at something means "to try to do something, or to make an attempt at." Have students look at the second part of the sentence, ". . . for the first time in my life." Point out that this statement supports the meaning of the idiom. When you do something for the first time, you have no idea how you'll do. All you can do is to try. You may wish to introduce students to other idioms that include the word *hand*.

- To be *at hand* means to be within reach.
- Something that *changes hands* passes from one person or owner to another.
- When you are in *good hands* you are safe and protected.
- *To be on hand* is to be available in case you are needed.

Remind students that when they come across an idiom in their reading, they may be able to find context clues to help them figure out the idiom's meaning. **ALL LEVELS**

FACILITATING

CLOSER LOOK

Analyze Conflict

Circulate among groups as students conduct their close read. Suggest that groups close read paragraph 5. Encourage them to talk about the annotations that they mark. If needed, provide the following support.

ANNOTATE: Have students mark details in paragraph 5 that refer to Pi's involvement in a **conflict.**

QUESTION: Guide students to consider what these details might tell them. Ask them which details show how Pi's fight for survival becomes an exasperating conflict with a slippery opponent, and accept student responses.

Possible response: By dragging out the details of Pi's attempt—fish by fish, hook by hook—Martel makes the reader more and more eager to find out if Pi is ever going to outmaneuver these happy freeloading fish.

CONCLUDE: Help students to formulate conclusions about the importance of these details in the text. Ask students why the author might have included these details. What type of conflict does the author show here to create suspense?

Possible answer: The conflict here is between Pi and the fish he is relying on for his survival. The tone is humorous. It is unlikely that the "happy freeloading fish" would have acknowledged any conflict. By adding these details, the author shows that Pi's battle for survival will be fought on many fronts—there are enemies and potential enemies everywhere.

Remind students that authors often use **conflict** to dramatize a hero's precarious relationship with a hostile world. In Pi's world, survival is a well-fed tiger—but if the fish refuse to bite, Pi's only hope of survival will disappear down Richard Parker's throat.

NOTES

dead animals, but stealing food from under a tiger's nose was a proposition I was not up to. He would not realize that it was an investment that would bring him an excellent return. I decided to use my leather shoe. I had only one left. The other I had lost when the ship sank.

3 I crept up to the lifeboat and I gathered from the locker one of the fishing kits, the knife and a bucket for my catch. Richard Parker was lying on his side. His tail jumped to life when I was at the bow[1] but his head did not lift. I let the raft out.

4 I attached a hook to a wire leader, which I tied to a line. I added some lead weights. I picked three that had an intriguing torpedo shape. I removed my shoe and cut it into pieces. It was hard work; the leather was tough. I carefully worked the hook into a flat piece of hide, not through it but into it, so that the point of the hook was hidden. I let the line down deep. There had been so many fish the previous evening that I expected easy success.

5 I had none. The whole shoe disappeared bit by bit, slight tug on the line by slight tug on the line, happy freeloading fish by happy freeloading fish, bare hook by bare hook, until I was left with only the rubber sole and the shoelace. When the shoelace proved an unconvincing earthworm, out of sheer exasperation I tried the sole, all of it. It was not a good idea. I felt a slight, promising tug and then the line was unexpectedly light. All I pulled in was line. I had lost the whole tackle.

6 This loss did not strike me as a terrible blow. There were other hooks, leader wires and weights in the kit, besides a whole other kit. And I wasn't even fishing for myself. I had plenty of food in store.

7 Still, a part of my mind—the one that says what we don't want to hear—rebuked me. "Stupidity has a price. You should show more care and wisdom next time."

8 Later that morning a second turtle appeared. It came right up to the raft. It could have reached up and bit my bottom if it had wanted to. When it turned I reached for its hind flipper, but as soon as I touched it I recoiled in horror. The turtle swam away.

9 The same part of my mind that had rebuked me over my fishing fiasco scolded me again. "What exactly do you intend to feed that tiger of yours? How much longer do you think he'll last on three dead animals? Do I need to remind you that tigers are not carrion eaters?[2] Granted, when he's on his last legs he probably won't lift his nose at much. But don't you think that before he submits to eating puffy, putrefied zebra he'll try the fresh, juicy Indian boy just a short dip away? And how are we doing with the water situation? You know how tigers get impatient with thirst. Have you smelled his breath recently? It's pretty awful. That's a bad sign. Perhaps you're hoping that he'll lap up the Pacific and in quenching his thirst

1. **bow (bow)** *n.* forward part of the ship.
2. **carrion eaters** animals that eat the flesh of other, dead animals.

FACILITATING SMALL-GROUP CLOSE READING

CLOSE READ: Fiction As groups perform the close read, circulate and offer support as needed.

- Remind groups that when they read a narrative, they should be sure to identify the main characters and the plot.
- If a group is confused about why particular events are important, remind them to think about the cultural experiences reflected in the selection.
- Challenge groups to determine the theme of the text and the specific details that refine the theme.

allow you to walk to America? Quite amazing, this limited capacity to excrete salt that Sundarbans tigers have developed. Comes from living in a tidal mangrove forest, I suppose. But it *is* a limited capacity. Don't they say that drinking too much saline water makes a man-eater of a tiger? Oh, look. Speak of the devil. There he is. He's yawning. My, my, what an enormous pink cave. Look at those long yellow stalactites[3] and stalagmites.[4] Maybe today you'll get a chance to visit."

10 Richard Parker's tongue, the size and color of a rubber hot-water bottle, retreated and his mouth closed. He swallowed.

11 I spent the rest of the day worrying myself sick. I stayed away from the lifeboat. Despite my own dire predictions, Richard Parker passed the time calmly enough. He still had water from the rainfall and he didn't seem too concerned with hunger. But he did make various tiger noises—growls and moans and the like—that did nothing to put me at ease. The riddle seemed **irresolvable**: to fish I needed bait, but I would have bait only once I had fish. What was I supposed to do? Use one of my toes? Cut off one of my ears?

12 A solution appeared in the late afternoon in a most unexpected way. I had pulled myself up to the lifeboat. More than that: I had climbed aboard and was rummaging through the locker, feverishly looking for an idea that would save my life. I had tied the raft so that it was about six feet from the boat. I fancied that with a jump and a pull at a loose knot I could save myself from Richard Parker. Desperation had pushed me to take such a risk.

13 Finding nothing, no bait and no new idea, I sat up—only to discover that I was dead center in the focus of his stare. He was at the other end of the lifeboat, where the zebra used to be, turned my way and sitting up, looking as if he'd been patiently waiting for me to notice him. How was it that I hadn't heard him stir? What delusion was I under that I thought I could outwit him? Suddenly I was hit hard across the face. I cried out and closed my eyes. With feline speed he had leapt across the lifeboat and struck me. I was to have my face clawed off—this was the gruesome way I was to die. The pain was so severe I felt nothing. Blessed be shock. Blessed be that part of us that protects us from too much pain and sorrow. At the heart of life is a fuse box. I whimpered, "Go ahead, Richard Parker, finish me off. But please, what you must do, do it quickly. A blown fuse should not be over-tested."

14 He was taking his time. He was at my feet, making noises. No doubt he had discovered the locker and its riches. I fearfully opened an eye.

15 It was a fish. There was a fish in the locker. It was flopping about like a fish out of water. It was about fifteen inches long and it had wings. A flying fish. Slim and dark gray-blue, with dry, featherless wings and round, unblinking, yellowish eyes. It was this flying fish

3. **stalactites** (stuh LAK tyts) *n.* pointed pieces of rock that hang from a cave ceiling.
4. **stalagmites** (stuh LAG myts) *n.* pointed pieces of rock formed on the floor of a cave.

NOTES

Mark base words or indicate another strategy you used to help you determine meaning.

irresolvable (ihr ih ZOL vuh buhl) *adj.*

MEANING:

DIGITAL PERSPECTIVES

Concept Vocabulary

IRRESOLVABLE If groups are struggling to define the word *irresolvable* in paragraph 11, remind them to think about the base of the word, *resolve,* which means "to settle or find a solution for." Point out that the suffix *-able* means "capable of." Taken together, these word parts mean "something that is not capable of being solved."

Possible response: *Irresolvable* means "impossible to resolve or settle."

Additional **English Language Support** is available in the Interactive Teacher's edition.

PERSONALIZE FOR LEARNING

Strategic Support

First-Read Support If group members struggle to comprehend the text during the first read, have another group member conduct a think-aloud to explain the thought process as he or she works through the NOTICE, ANNOTATE, CONNECT, and RESPOND steps. For example, in paragraph 13, the student might notice that Pi has reached a turning point in his quest for food to feed Richard Parker. The student might annotate "What delusion was I under that I thought I could outwit him?" to return to in the close read to see what it reveals about Pi's perspective.

CLOSER LOOK

Analyze Figurative Language

Circulate among groups as students conduct their close read. Suggest that groups close read paragraph 17. Encourage them to talk about the annotations that they mark. If needed, provide the following support.

ANNOTATE: Have students mark details of **figurative language** that the author uses in paragraph 17 to describe the fish, or work with small groups to have students participate while you highlight them together.

QUESTION: Guide students to consider what these details might tell them. Ask what the author's use of figurative language conveys to the reader about the effect of the flying fish on Pi, and accept student responses.

Possible response: The four highlighted instances of figurative language in turn convey intense confusion, disgust, alarm, and severe physical pain.

CONCLUDE: Help students to formulate conclusions about the importance of these details in the text. Ask students why the author might have included these details.

Possible response: Through figurative language the reader gets a vivid impression of the experience of being overwhelmed by flying fish. By adding these details, the author gives the reader a clear sense of how Pi feels about this infestation.

Remind students that authors may use **figurative language**—words and expressions whose meanings are not literal—to emphasize something, to place a certain interpretation on events, or to intensify an impression, a feeling, or an experience.

NOTES

that had struck me across the face, not Richard Parker. He was still fifteen feet away, no doubt wondering what I was going on about. But he had seen the fish. I could read a keen curiosity on his face. He seemed about ready to investigate.

16 I bent down, picked up the fish and threw it towards him. This was the way to tame him! Where a rat had gone, a flying fish would follow. Unfortunately, the flying fish flew. In mid-air, just ahead of Richard Parker's open mouth, the fish swerved and dropped into the water. It happened with lightning speed. Richard Parker turned his head and snapped his mouth, jowls flapping, but the fish was too quick for him. He looked astonished and displeased. He turned to me again. "Where's my treat?" his face seemed to inquire. Fear and sadness gripped me. I turned with the half-hearted, half-abandoned hope that I could jump onto the raft before he could jump onto me.

17 At that precise instant there was a vibration in the air and we were struck by a school of flying fish. They came like a swarm of locusts. It was not only their numbers; there was also something insect-like about the clicking, whirring sound of their wings. They burst out of the water, dozens of them at a time, some of them flick-flacking over a hundred yards through the air. Many dived into the water just before the boat. A number sailed clear over it. Some crashed into its side, sounding like firecrackers going off. Several lucky ones returned to the water after a bounce on the tarpaulin. Others, less fortunate, fell directly into the boat, where they started a racket of flapping and flailing and splashing. And still others flew right into us. Standing unprotected as I was, I felt I was living the martyrdom of Saint Sebastian. Every fish that hit me was like an arrow entering my flesh. I clutched at a blanket to protect myself while also trying to catch some of the fish. I received cuts and bruises all over my body.

18 The reason for this onslaught became evident immediately: dorados were leaping out of the water in hot pursuit of them. The much larger dorados couldn't match their flying, but they were faster swimmers and their short lunges were very powerful. They could overtake flying fish if they were just behind them and lunging from the water at the same time and in the same direction. There were sharks too; they also leapt out of the water, not so cleanly but with devastating consequence for some dorados. This aquatic mayhem didn't last long, but while it did, the sea bubbled and boiled, fish jumped and jaws worked hard.

19 Richard Parker was tougher than I was in the face of these fish, and far more efficient. He raised himself and went about blocking, swiping and biting all the fish he could. Many were eaten live and whole, struggling wings beating in his mouth. It was a dazzling display of might and speed. Actually, it was not so much the speed that was impressive as the pure animal confidence, the total absorption in the moment. Such a mix of ease and concentration, such a being-in-the-present, would be the envy of the highest yogis.

PERSONALIZE FOR LEARNING

Strategic Support

Background Students may need help in understanding the sentence "Where a rat had gone a flying fish would follow" in paragraph 16.

Explain to students that the meaning of this sentence cannot be fully understood without some background information. Tell them that previously in the story—before the starting point of the selection—a rat suddenly appears and runs up onto Pi's head. Pi grabs the rat and throws it at the tiger, who eats it. This gives Pi time to escape to his raft.

NOTES

20 When it was over, the result, besides a very sore body for me, was six flying fish in the locker and a much greater number in the lifeboat. I hurriedly wrapped a fish in a blanket, gathered a hatchet and made for the raft.

21 I proceeded with great deliberation. The loss of my tackle that morning had had a sobering effect on me. I couldn't allow myself another mistake. I unwrapped the fish carefully, keeping a hand pressed down on it, fully aware that it would try to jump away to save itself. The closer the fish was to appearing, the more afraid and disgusted I became. Its head came into sight. The way I was holding it, it looked like a scoop of loathsome fish ice cream sticking out of a wool blanket cone. The thing was gasping for water, its mouth and gills opening and closing slowly. I could feel it pushing with its wings against my hand. I turned the bucket over and brought its head against the bottom. I took hold of the hatchet. I raised it in the air.

22 Several times I started bringing the hatchet down, but I couldn't complete the action. Such sentimentalism may seem ridiculous considering what I had witnessed in the last days, but those were the deeds of others, of **predatory** animals. I suppose I was partly responsible for the rat's death, but I'd only thrown it; it was Richard Parker who had killed it. A lifetime of peaceful vegetarianism stood between me and the willful beheading of a fish.

Mark base words or indicate another strategy you used to help you determine meaning.

predatory (PREHD uh tawr ee) *adj.*

MEANING:

Concept Vocabulary

PREDATORY If groups are struggling to define the word *predatory* in paragraph 22, remind them to look for a smaller word within the larger one. Point out the word *predator* in *predatory*. Have students use this technique to define the word.

Possible response: *Predatory* means "prone to attack or exploit other creatures."

CROSS-CURRICULAR PERSPECTIVES

Science Paragraph 18 describes an attack of flying fish. Do fish really fly? Not really, but flying fish often make stupendous leaps into the air, which makes it appear as though they are flying. Once out of the water, the fish use their wing-like fins to glide through the air, a skill useful for avoiding predators below. Flying fish are eaten around the world, but are especially significant in the Caribbean island of Barbados, a country whose nickname is "land of the flying fish." Have groups research more about these fascinating creatures, including how they are trapped and cooked. Then have each group briefly share their findings with the class.

FACILITATING

CLOSER LOOK

Analyze Character Development

Circulate among groups as students conduct their close read. Suggest that groups close read paragraph 26. Encourage them to talk about the annotations that they mark. If needed, provide the following support.

ANNOTATE: Have students mark details in paragraph 26 that describe Pi's reassessments of his own character in the light of what he has just done, or work with small groups to have students participate while you highlight them together.

QUESTION: Guide students to consider what these details might tell them. Ask them what a reader might infer about Pi's character from his own self-assessments, and accept student responses.

Possible response: They reveal that he has strong religious convictions that forbid the taking of any life. However, his recognition that he's now a killer suggests that he knows he'll go on killing. He'll pray for the fish, but he's not prepared either to starve to death or be eaten by a tiger.

CONCLUDE: Help students to formulate conclusions about the importance of these details in the text. Ask students why the author might have included these details.

Possible response: Pi's words of self-recrimination show his bitter regret that he will never again be a harmless, bookish, religious boy: he has lost his innocence. By adding these details, the author shows that it takes courage and self-awareness for Pi to admit this—and maybe even more courage to admit that he means to go on taking life to save his own.

Remind students that characters develop out of conflict and learn from experience. Authors use **character development** to show how characters respond to events and to open up new possibilities for a story.

NOTES

23 I covered the fish's head with the blanket and turned the hatchet around. Again my hand wavered in the air. The idea of beating a soft, living head with a hammer was simply too much.

24 I put the hatchet down. I would break its neck, sight unseen, I decided. I wrapped the fish tightly in the blanket. With both hands I started bending it. The more I pressed, the more the fish struggled. I imagined what it would feel like if I were wrapped in a blanket and someone were trying to break my neck. I was appalled. I gave up a number of times. Yet I knew it had to be done, and the longer I waited, the longer the fish's suffering would go on.

25 Tears flowing down my cheeks, I egged myself on until I heard a cracking sound and I no longer felt any life fighting in my hands. I pulled back the folds of the blanket. The flying fish was dead. It was split open and bloody on one side of its head, at the level of the gills.

26 I wept heartily over this poor little deceased soul. It was the first sentient[5] being I had ever killed. I was now a killer. I was now as guilty as Cain. I was sixteen years old, a harmless boy, bookish and religious, and now I had blood on my hands. It's a terrible burden to carry. All sentient life is sacred. I never forget to include this fish in my prayers.

27 After that it was easier. Now that it was dead, the flying fish looked like fish I had seen in the markets of Pondicherry. It was something else, something outside the essential scheme of creation. I chopped it up into pieces with the hatchet and put it in the bucket.

28 In the dying hours of the day I tried fishing again. At first I had no better luck than I'd had in the morning. But success seemed less elusive. The fish nibbled at the hook with fervor. Their interest was evident. I realized that these were small fish, too small for the hook. So I cast my line further out and let it sink deeper, beyond the reach of the small fish that concentrated around the raft and lifeboat.

29 It was when I used the flying fish's head as bait, and with only one sinker, casting my line out and pulling it in quickly, making the head skim over the surface of the water, that I finally had my first strike. A dorado surged forth and lunged for the fish head. I let out a little slack, to make sure it had properly swallowed the bait, before giving the line a good yank. The dorado exploded out of the water, tugging on the line so hard I thought it was going to pull me off the raft. I braced myself. The line became very taut. It was good line; it would not break. I started bringing the dorado in. It struggled with all its might, jumping and diving and splashing. The line cut into my hands. I wrapped my hands in the blanket. My heart was pounding. The fish was as strong as an ox. I was not sure I would be able to pull it in.

30 I noticed all the other fish had vanished from around the raft and boat. No doubt they had sensed the dorado's distress. I hurried. Its struggling would attract sharks. But it fought like a devil. My arms

5. **sentient** (SEHN shuhnt) *adj.* living and capable of feeling.

WriteNow Take a Stand

Argument Paragraph 26 describes Pi's reaction to killing a fish. Pi is likely Hindu, and as such, a vegetarian—someone who does not eat any animal flesh. For Hindus, vegetarianism arises from the principle of nonviolence, as slaughtering animals for food, cooking their meat, and serving it are all considered to have a negative effect on the person who does so. Most Hindu vegetarians avoid eggs but eat dairy products. Non-Hindus may be vegetarians because they believe that it is a more healthful diet and better for the planet. Have students write a one-page argument, taking a position on the claim "Everyone should be a vegetarian." Have students include a counterclaim and evidence, and share their argument with their group.

were aching. Every time I got it close to the raft, it beat about with such frenzy that I was cowed into letting out some line.

31 At last I managed to haul it aboard. It was over three feet long. The bucket was useless. It would fit the dorado like a hat. I held the fish down by kneeling on it and using my hands. It was a writhing mass of pure muscle, so big its tail stuck out from beneath me, pounding hard against the raft. It was giving me a ride like I imagine a bucking bronco would give a cowboy. I was in a wild and triumphant mood. A dorado is a magnificent-looking fish, large, fleshy and sleek, with a bulging forehead that speaks of a forceful personality, a very long dorsal fin as proud as a rooster's comb, and a coat of scales that is smooth and bright. I felt I was dealing fate a serious blow by engaging such a handsome **adversary**. With this fish I was retaliating against the sea, against the wind, against the sinking of ships, against all circumstances that were working against me. "Thank you, Lord Vishnu, thank you!" I shouted. "Once you saved the world by taking the form of a fish. Now you have saved *me* by taking the form of a fish. Thank you, thank you!"

32 Killing it was no problem. I would have spared myself the trouble—after all, it was for Richard Parker and he would have dispatched it with expert ease—but for the hook that was embedded in its mouth. I exulted at having a dorado at the end of my line—I would be less keen if it were a tiger. I went about the job in a direct way. I took the hatchet in both my hands and vigorously beat the fish on the head with the hammerhead (I still didn't have the stomach to use the sharp edge). The dorado did a most extraordinary thing as it died: it began to flash all kinds of colors in rapid succession. Blue, green, red, gold and violet flickered and shimmered neon-like on its surface as it struggled. I felt I was beating a rainbow to death. (I found out later that the dorado is famed for its death-knell iridescence.) At last it lay still and dull-colored, and I could remove the hook. I even managed to retrieve a part of my bait.

33 You may be astonished that in such a short period of time I could go from weeping over the muffled killing of a flying fish to gleefully bludgeoning to death a dorado. I could explain it by arguing that profiting from a pitiful flying fish's navigational mistake made me shy and sorrowful, while the excitement of actively capturing a great dorado made me sanguinary and self-assured. But in point of fact the explanation lies elsewhere. It is simple and brutal: a person can get used to anything, even to killing.

34 It was with a hunter's pride that I pulled the raft up to the lifeboat. I brought it along the side, keeping very low. I swung my arm and dropped the dorado into the boat. It landed with a heavy thud and provoked a gruff expression of surprise from Richard Parker. After a sniff or two, I heard the wet mashing sound of a mouth at work. I pushed myself off, not forgetting to blow the whistle hard several times, to remind Richard Parker of who had so graciously provided him with fresh food. I stopped to pick up some biscuits and a can of

NOTES

Mark base words or indicate another strategy you used to help you determine meaning.

adversary (AD vuhr sehr ee) *n.*

MEANING:

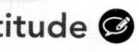

Concept Vocabulary

ADVERSARY If groups are struggling to define the word *adversary* in paragraph 31, remind them to look for a smaller word within the larger one. Point out the word *advers*[e] in *adversary*. Have students use this technique to define the word.

Possible response: *Adversary* means "a person or group that opposes or attacks; a foe."

CLOSER LOOK

Analyze Attitude

Circulate among groups as students conduct their close read. Suggest that groups close read paragraph 33. Encourage them to talk about the annotations that they mark. If needed, provide the following support.

ANNOTATE: Have students mark details in paragraph 33 that show Pi's feeling about killing, or work with small groups to have students participate while you highlight them together.

QUESTION: Guide students to consider what these details might tell them. Ask them how Pi's attitude about killing has changed in the last 24 hours, and accept student responses.

Possible response: Twenty-four hours earlier, killing a fish caused him great grief, but now he's bloodthirsty and confident; he feels excitement and glee. He's gotten over his problem with killing.

CONCLUDE: Help students to formulate conclusions about the importance of these details in the text. Ask students why the author might have included these details.

Possible response: As Pi gets used to doing what he must in order to survive, his attitude toward "sacred sentient life" changes: it becomes prey. By adding these details, the author shows how Pi's attitude of religious respect transforms into the attitude of a hunter.

Remind students that an author often uses a character's changing **attitudes** to indicate success or failure in adapting to changing circumstances.

PERSONALIZE FOR LEARNING

English Language Support

British vs. American English Direct students' attention to the word *biscuits* near the end of paragraph 34. Ask if anyone knows what a biscuit is. Responses will probably involve the American meaning of the word: a thick, flaky type of bread or roll.

Remind students that Pi was born and raised in India. Explain that he would have learned the British form of English rather than the American form. The grammar is mostly the same, but many things have different names in the two countries. When Pi says he is getting some biscuits, he is referring to what an American would call a cookie.

You may wish to provide other examples of differing words. Ask students if they have heard either the American or the British terms before.

American	British
elevator	lift
truck	lorry
wrench	spanner
vacation	holiday
sweater	jumper
sneakers	trainers

ALL LEVELS

CLOSER LOOK

Analyze Character

Circulate among groups as students conduct their close read. Suggest that groups close read paragraph 35. Encourage them to talk about the annotations that they mark. If needed, provide the following support.

ANNOTATE: Have students mark details in paragraph 35 that describe what Pi does at the end of the day, or work with small groups to have students participate while you highlight them together.

QUESTION: Guide students to consider what these details might tell them. Ask what Pi's actions at the end of the day tell them about his state of mind, and accept student responses.

Possible response: He washes himself and cleans up his equipment like any good hunter. Removing another creature's blood from his hands doesn't spoil his appetite.

CONCLUDE: Help students to formulate conclusions about the importance of these details in the text. Ask students why the author might have included these details.

Possible response: Pi is calm, tidy, and methodical, and he never mentions the tiger. By adding these details, the author shows that Pi's state of mind is untroubled by fear or religious principles. He has learned that he can survive with courage and ingenuity.

Remind students that authors often describe a character's **state of mind**, especially at the end of a dramatic day, to show how the character is coping emotionally and practically with the day's events.

NOTES

water. The five remaining flying fish in the locker were dead. I pulled their wings off, throwing them away and wrapped the fish in the now-consecrated fish blanket.

35 By the time I had rinsed myself of blood, cleaned up my fishing gear, put things away and had my supper, night had come on. A thin layer of clouds masked the stars and the moon, and it was very dark. I was tired, but still excited by the events of the last hours. The feeling of busyness was profoundly satisfying; I hadn't thought at all about my plight or myself. Fishing was surely a better way of passing the time than yarn-spinning or playing I Spy. I determined to start again the next day as soon as there was light.

36 I fell asleep, my mind lit up by the chameleon-like flickering of the dying dorado. ❧

DIGITAL PERSPECTIVES

Enriching the Text Show students a section of the movie version of *Life of Pi* that corresponds with one of the excerpts from the novel here. Be sure to preview the clip in advance to make sure the content is appropriate for your class.

After students have viewed the clip, have them compare and contrast the movie version with the novel. You might wish to capture the similarities and differences in a Venn diagram or a chart. Encourage students to consider the following elements: missing or added details, depictions of the characters, and details about the setting. Finally, engage students in a discussion about how or if the movie version enhances their understanding of the text. **(Research to Clarify)**

DIGITAL PERSPECTIVES

Comprehension Check

Complete these items after you finish your first read. Review and clarify details with your group.

1. Briefly describe the problem that Pi faces.

2. At the beginning of the selection, what does Pi plan to do to solve his problem?

3. (a) What main problem does Pi face in executing his plan? (b) What event provides him with a solution?

4. What fact about Pi explains why he has such difficulty in killing his first flying fish?

5. (a) Compare and contrast Pi's attitude toward killing the flying fish with his attitude toward killing the dorado. (b) What does Pi believe explains the difference?

6. **Notebook** Write a summary of the excerpt from *Life of Pi*.

RESEARCH

Research to Clarify Choose at least one unfamiliar detail from the text. Briefly research that detail. In what way does the information that you found shed light on an aspect of the story?

Comprehension Check

Possible responses:

1. The narrator is adrift in the ocean with an untamed, hungry tiger.
2. The narrator plans to learn how to fish so he can feed the tiger.
3. (a) The narrator's main problem is that he has no bait. (b) His problem is solved when a school of flying fish land on the boat. Pi now has enough fish to use as bait and the tiger has filled his stomach.
4. The narrator believes that all life is sacred.
5. (a) The narrator is very upset about killing the flying fish, but very cool and matter-of-fact about killing the dorado. (b) The narrator explains the difference by saying: "It is simple and brutal: a person can get used to anything, even to killing."
6. Summaries will vary; however, students should include the narrator's predicament, the main events in the plot, and a brief description of how the narrator changes.

Research to Clarify Students will likely be unfamiliar with many details in the story. If they have trouble figuring out what to focus on, you may want to suggest the following details: the significance of the name Richard Parker, facts about flying fish and dorado, behavior of tigers.

PERSONALIZE FOR LEARNING

Challenge

Text-to-World Connection While *Life of Pi* is a work of fiction, author Yann Martel was inspired by the real-life experiences of Poon Lim, a steward aboard the British ship *Ben Lomond*. Lim was stranded at sea for 133 days after a German U-boat torpedoed his ship in 1942. Have students research the historical account of Lim's journey. Encourage them to draw comparisons between the journeys of Pi and Lim. Which aspects of Pi's journey are drawn from Lim's experience, and which are drawn from the imagination of the author? Ask students to draw conclusions about why Martel might have added these fictional aspects, and how they contribute to the overall meaning and message of the story.

Jump Start

Close Review Ask students to consider the following prompt: *How would you go about training a man-eating tiger? Training the tiger is essential to your survival.* As students discuss the prompt in their groups, have them consider what character traits someone would need to accomplish this task.

Close Read the Text

If needed, model close reading by using the Annotation Highlights in the Interactive Teacher's Edition.

Remind students to use Accountable Talk in their discussions and to support one another as they complete the close read.

Analyze the Text

1. Responses will vary by group. Suggest to groups that they close read the text to resolve any confusion or disagreement.
2. Passages will vary by group. Remind students to explain why they chose the passages they presented to the group members.
3. Responses will vary by group.
4. Responses will vary by group.

Concept Vocabulary

Why These Words? Possible response:
The words can all be used to describe hostile relationships. The words highlight conflict that Pi faces.

Practice

Possible responses:

- Pi's challenges with Richard Parker seem ***irresolvable*** because there is no way he can get the tiger out of the boat.
- Tigers are ***predatory*** animals, attacking and eating other creatures to survive.
- Richard Parker is Pi's ***adversary,*** because the tiger is the boy's natural enemy.

Word Network

Possible words: *fishing, thirst, dire*

Word Study

For more support, see **Concept Vocabulary and Word Study**.

Possible responses:
complimentary – having to do with a compliment, praise; **advisory** – tending to advise, give advice; **dietary** – having to do with diet, eating; **temporary** – having to do with time, not lasting

MAKING MEANING

from LIFE OF PI

Close Read the Text

With your group, revisit sections of the text you marked during your first read. **Annotate** details that you notice. What **questions** do you have? What can you **conclude**?

ANNOTATE • QUESTION • CONCLUDE — Close Read

TIP

GROUP DISCUSSION
If you do not fully understand a classmate's contribution to the discussion, don't hesitate to ask for clarification. To ensure an effective exchange, use a respectful and friendly tone. State exactly what it is you don't understand. In some cases, it might be helpful to pose alternatives: "When you said . . . , did you mean . . . or . . . ?"

Analyze the Text

CITE TEXTUAL EVIDENCE to support your answers.

Notebook Complete the activities.

1. **Review and Clarify** Work with your group to review your responses to the Comprehension Check questions. If there is any confusion or disagreement, review the text as a group to clarify and gain consensus.
2. **Present and Discuss** Share with your group the passages from the text that you found especially significant, taking turns with others. Discuss what you notice in the text, what questions you asked, and what conclusions you reached.
3. **Vote and Post** Vote on the passage your group would like to share with the whole class. Invite comments from the class.
4. **Essential Question:** ***What does it take to survive?*** What has this text taught you about survival? Discuss with your group.

WORD NETWORK
Identify words related to the idea of survival in *LIfe of Pi.* Add these words to your Word Network.

LANGUAGE DEVELOPMENT

Concept Vocabulary

irresolvable predatory adversary

Why These Words? The three concept vocabulary words from the excerpt are related. With your group, discuss the words and identify a concept they have in common. How do these word choices enhance the text?

Practice

Notebook Confirm your understanding of these words from the text by using them in sentences. In each sentence, provide context clues that hint at the word's meaning.

Word Study

Notebook **Latin suffixes: *-ory* and *-ary*** In *LIfe of Pi,* the narrator uses the words *predatory,* which ends with the Latin suffix *-ory*, and *sanguinary*, which ends with the Latin suffix *-ary*. These two suffixes are related and often mean "having to do with," "characterized by," or "tending to." Find four other words that feature either of these suffixes. Record the words and their meanings. Explain how the meaning of the suffix contributes to the meaning of each word.

STANDARDS
Reading Literature
Analyze how complex characters develop over the course of a text, interact with other characters, and advance the plot or develop the theme.
Language
Identify and correctly use patterns of word changes that indicate different meanings or parts of speech.

FORMATIVE ASSESSMENT

Analyze the Text

If students struggle to close read the text, **then** provide the **Life of Pi: Text Questions** available online in the Interactive Teacher's Edition or Unit Resources. Answers and DOK levels are also available.

Concept Vocabulary

If students struggle to identify the concept, **then** have them revisit the context in which the words were used in the story.

Word Study

If students fail to identify other words, **then** have them search the text for the letter combinations *-ory* and *-ary*. For Reteach and Practice, see **Word Study: Latin Suffixes *-ory* and *-ary* (RP)**.

Analyze Craft and Structure

Characters In the best fiction, the main characters are interesting and well-rounded, or complex. **Complex characters** are those that show both strengths and weaknesses and experience a mix of emotions. They have a variety of reasons, or multiple motivations, for behaving and reacting as they do. As the story progresses, they change. They are **dynamic**, rather than **static**, or unchanging.

Characterization is the way a writer develops a character's traits and personality. Writers may include the following elements as clues to a character's nature:

- descriptions of the character's appearance and actions
- descriptions of the character's emotions
- the character's spoken words, or **dialogue,** and thoughts

Life of Pi is narrated by the title character himself. To show Pi's thoughts with more dimension, the author uses **internal monologue**, a kind of "conversation" or dialogue Pi has with himself.

To better understand how Yann Martel develops Pi as a complex character, consider both *what* you learn about Pi and *how* you learn that information.

Practice

CITE TEXTUAL EVIDENCE to support your answers.

Working independently, use the chart to identify details from the excerpt that reveal Pi's character. Note that each set of paragraphs may not include every type of detail. Then, gather your notes and share them with your group.

PARAGRAPHS	PI'S ACTIONS	PI'S FEELINGS	PI'S WORDS OR THOUGHTS	WHAT IS PI LIKE?
paragraphs 4–5	a. See possible responses in Teacher's Edition.	b.	c.	d.
paragraphs 7–9	e.	f.	g.	h.
paragraphs 23–27	i.	j.	k.	l.
paragraphs 28–35	m.	n.	o.	p.

PERSONALIZE FOR LEARNING

English Language Support

Complex Characters Have English Learners describe what makes a character static or dynamic in speech and writing.

Have students use the words *static* and *dynamic* to summarize the events that show Pi is a dynamic character. **EMERGING**

Have students use the words *static* and *dynamic* to compare Pi's initial and later reactions to killing a fish and the tiger's reactions to killing fish. Have students incorporate any new adjectives they discovered while reading the text. **EXPANDING**

Have students write a paragraph discussing the degree to which Pi is a dynamic character. Remind them to include text evidence such as quotations and paraphrases. Ensure that they use the words *static* and *dynamic* along with any new vocabulary they discovered while reading the text. **BRIDGING**

An expanded **English Language Support Lesson** on Character is available in the Interactive Teacher's Edition.

DIGITAL PERSPECTIVES

Analyze Craft and Structure

Complex Characters Discuss with students how the main characters in a literary work are often complex characters because they are the focus of the story and help develop the theme. As a result, authors show how they change and develop over the course of the story.

Characterization Remind students that authors often use both **direct characterization** and **indirect characterization**. In the former, the author directly states the character's traits; in the latter, the author provides clues about a character through describing the character's actions, appearance, and the reactions of others to the character. In *Life of Pi*, the author uses both direct and indirect characterization to make Pi come alive on the page. For more support, see **Analyze Craft and Structure: Complex Characters**.

Possible responses:

a. He is methodical and careful at first, but then acts without thought.
b. sheer exasperation
c. his need to feed the tiger
d. He wants to be calm and collected, but is prone to impulsiveness.
e. He tries to psyche himself up.
f. regret, shame
g. his failure to catch fish to feed the tiger
h. He is determined to survive, and therefore is hard on himself for his failures.
i. He is able to kill the fish, but feels enormous guilt and sorrow for taking a life.
j. guilt and sorrow
k. his need to get bait so he can fish
l. He is willing to do whatever it takes to survive, but is also mindful of the personal toll it is taking on his morals.
m. He successfully catches a huge fish and gets used to killing.
n. gratitude to Vishnu, pride in his hunting ability
o. his need to survive
p. He is adaptable.

FORMATIVE ASSESSMENT

Analyze Craft and Structure

If students struggle to determine character traits of the narrator, **then** revisit key passages to discuss what specific actions or experiences imply about strengths, weaknesses, or character traits. For Reteach and Practice, see **Analyze Craft and Structure: Complex Characters (RP).**

FACILITATING

Conventions

Participial versus Absolute Phrases Discuss with students that sentences using these types of phrases are common in our everyday speech patterns. Participial and absolute phrases are often used to add extra detail, a purpose, or a reason.

As you review the examples of participial and absolute phrases with students, consider providing additional examples:

participial phrase:

Having borrowed the book, he rushed home from the library.

absolute phrase:

Roxanne's teacher being out sick, the substitute teacher taught the class. For more support, see **Conventions: Participial Versus Absolute Phrases**.

Read It

MAKE IT INTERACTIVE

Have students write each sentence on a sentence strip using a different colored marker for the participle, and underlying the participal or absolute phrase.

Possible responses:

1. Tears flowing down my cheeks; absolute
2. keeping very low; participial (modifies *I*)
3. tugging on the line; absolute
4. rolling; participial (modifies *boat*)

Write It

Paragraphs will vary, but make sure that students include at least two participial phrases and one absolute phrase. Suggest that students use participial phrases to elaborate on the setting, action, or character details. As you evaluate student writing, look for attention to details. Common errors may include run-on sentences.

FORMATIVE ASSESSMENT

Conventions

If students are unable to identify the participial or absolute phrases, **then** have students look for words ending in *-ing* or *-ed*. For Reteach and Practice, see **Conventions: Participial Versus Absolute Phrases (RP).**

LANGUAGE DEVELOPMENT

from LIFE OF PI

TIP

COLLABORATION TIP

Discuss the definitions and examples of these phrases as a group. If you have a good grasp of the concepts, explain them to others. If your group is still having difficulty, consult with your teacher.

Conventions

Participial versus Absolute Phrases A **participle** is a form of a verb used as an adjective. Participles often end with *-ed* or *-ing*. A **participial phrase** is a participle and its modifiers, objects, or complements.

catching	the ball	quickly
PARTICIPLE	OBJECT	MODIFIER

having seemed	obvious
PARTICIPLE	COMPLEMENT

The entire participial phrase functions as an adjective. It modifies a noun or pronoun in the sentence.

Catching the ball quickly, Sam helped make a double play.

An **absolute phrase** features a noun or pronoun and its modifiers. Often, the modifiers include a participle or participial phrase. Sometimes, the participle *being* or *having been* is omitted as understood.

everyone's	**pencils**	[having been] sharpened
MODIFIER	NOUN	PARTICIPLE

Rather than modifying an individual word, an absolute phrase modifies an entire clause or sentence. It may comment upon the clause or sentence, or it may place it in context.

Everyone's pencils sharpened, we were ready to take our test.

Read It

Work individually. Mark the participle in each of these sentences from *LIfe of Pi*. Then, identify each phrase as a participial phrase or an absolute phrase. When you have finished, compare your responses with those of your team. Resolve any differences you see in your responses.

1. Tears flowing down my cheeks, I egged myself on. . . .
2. I brought it along the side, keeping very low.
3. Finding nothing, no bait and no new idea, I sat up—only to discover that I was dead center in the focus of his stare.
4. Richard Parker turned his head and snapped his mouth, jowls flapping, but the fish was too quick for him.

Write It

Notebook Write a paragraph summarizing a scene from the excerpt from *Life of Pi*. In your paragraph, use at least two participial phrases and one absolute phrase.

STANDARDS

Writing

- Write arguments to support claims in an analysis of substantive topics or texts, using valid reasoning and relevant and sufficient evidence.
- Introduce precise claim(s), distinguish the claim(s) from alternate or opposing claims, and create organization that establishes clear relationships among claim(s), counterclaims, reasons, and evidence.

Language

- Demonstrate command of the conventions of standard English grammar and usage when writing or speaking.
- Use various types of phrases and clauses to convey specific meanings and add variety and interest to writing or presentations.

Writing to Sources

Assignment

Write an **argument** that includes **claims**, or statements that express a position, and evidence that supports these claims. In your argument, also address and refute opposing opinions, called **counterclaims.** Once you have completed the writing, present your work to the class. Choose from the following topics:

- ☐ Take a position about the following statement: *Pi becomes a different person after he kills the flying fish.* Write a brief **essay** in which you state and support your position. Include a paragraph in which you discuss an opposing position.
- ☐ A **pitch** is a concise description of an idea for a movie. Write a pitch to persuade studio executives to make a movie version of *Life of Pi*. Anticipate and address objections executives might have to the project. Be sure to include passages from the text in your pitch.
- ☐ Pi is a vegetarian who abandons his principles by fishing. Is he right to do so? Take a position and write either a **defense** or a **criticism** of Pi. Include a paragraph in which you consider the opposing view.

Project Plan Before you begin, make a list of the tasks you will need to complete to fulfill the assignment. Decide how you will organize the work. Then, appoint individual group members to each task.

Clarifying Ideas and Evidence Write a sentence in which you clearly state your claim. Then, brainstorm for at least two reasons that support it. Identify evidence from *Life of Pi* that supports each reason. Use the chart to organize your reasons and supporting textual evidence.

Claim: ______________________________

____

REASONS	TEXT EVIDENCE

Present After you have completed your argument, present the finished work to the class. Make sure all group members have a role to play in the presentation.

EVIDENCE LOG

Before moving on to a new selection, go to your Evidence Log and record what you learned from *Life of Pi*.

PERSONALIZE FOR LEARNING

Strategic Support

Finding Evidence If students who choose the third topic have difficulty finding persuasive outside sources concerning vegetarianism, suggest they refine their search terms and use respected databases such as those that index respected newspapers, magazines, and journals.

Writing to Sources

Explain to students that building an argument is like building a house, as both depend on strong support. A house rests on a strong foundation; an argument rests on strong evidence.

Then, explain that students can address counterclaims in three ways:

- Present evidence to show that the counterclaim is wrong;
- Present evidence to show that the counterclaim is valid, but that their position is as strong;
- Present evidence to show that the counterclaim is valid, but that their position is much stronger.

Project Plan Encourage students to include different kinds of evidence, such as facts, examples, anecdotes, and statistics. As students research evidence, have them carefully note their sources, including paragraph numbers from the selection. Remind groups to consult the schedule for Small-Group Activities as they create their Project Plan. Check to make sure each group has made assignments, and that the work is divided evenly among group members.

Finding Evidence As students write their claims, counterclaims, and supporting evidence, they should check to make sure they have quoted all textual citations correctly. Remind students to document any outside sources carefully—including visuals—to avoid plagiarism. For more support, see **Writing to Sources: Argument, Claims, and Counterclaims.**

Evidence Log Support students in completing their Evidence Log. This paced activity will help prepare them for the Performance-Based Assessment at the end of the unit.

FORMATIVE ASSESSMENT

Writing to Sources

If students are unable to form counterclaims, **then** have students insert the word *not* in their claims to see the other side of the issue. For Reteach and Practice, see **Writing to Sources: Argument, Claims, and Counterclaims (RP).**

Selection Test

Administer the *Life of Pi* Selection Test, which is available in both print and digital formats online in Assessments.

The Value of a Sherpa Life

AUDIO SUMMARIES
Audio summaries of "The Value of a Sherpa Life" are available in both English and Spanish online in the Interactive Teacher's Edition or Unit Resources. Assigning these summaries prior to reading the selection may help students build additional background knowledge and set a context for their first read.

Summary

On the morning of April 18, 2014, an avalanche swept down the west shoulder of Mount Everest and claimed the lives of sixteen Sherpas. In his magazine article, "The Value of a Sherpa Life," Grayson Schaffer writes that the high casualty rate among Nepal's Sherpa community is accepted as a matter of routine. He argues that the unsafe conditions responsible for such fatalities will improve only when the tourist climbers realize that Sherpa lives are as valuable as their own. These "adventure tourists," he says, prefer not to carry their own equipment and supplies and expect Sherpas to perform dangerous ascents while burdened by heavy loads.

Insight

Are social position and survival connected? Reading "The Value of a Sherpa Life" will help students consider the relationship between social status and survival. When an entire group of people is undervalued, such as the Sherpa guides of Nepal, their deaths occur more frequently than do the deaths of people who are more greatly valued by society.

Some students may have trouble with the injustices described in this selection and may require support.

ESSENTIAL QUESTION:
What does it take to survive?

Connection to Essential Question

"The Value of a Sherpa Life" will help students answer the Essential Question—"What does it take to survive?"—by demonstrating to them that survival sometimes depends on external forces. The survival of Sherpa guides is threatened because their lower status places them in greater danger than the people who hire them. The selection suggests that survival is directly tied to a shift in the pervasive attitude about Sherpa guides. Students may also look at the question from the other side and determine that the survival of Western climbers is less threatened as a result of their having money and social status.

SMALL-GROUP LEARNING PERFORMANCE TASK
What type of strength is most valuable in a survival situation?

UNIT PERFORMANCE-BASED ASSESSMENT
Should people in life-or-death situations be held accountable for their actions?

Connection to Performance Tasks

Small-Group Learning Performance Task In this Performance Task, students will present an argument about the most valuable asset in a survival situation. Since Westerners don't die as frequently as Sherpa guides, students may determine that money and status are valuable strengths.

Unit Performance-Based Assessment The evidence in this selection that will help students with their arguments about the accountability of people in life-or-death situations lies in the relationship between employer and employee. The Westerners who hire Sherpa guides place Sherpas in a more dangerous position in order to make their own lives easier, which often results in the death of Sherpas.

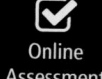

LESSON RESOURCES

	Making Meaning	Language Development	Effective Expression
Lesson	**First Read** **Close Read** **Analyze the Text** **Analyze Craft and Structure**	**Concept Vocabulary** **Word Study** **Author's Style**	**Speaking and Listening**
Instructional Standards	**RL.10** By the end of grade 9, read and comprehend literary nonfiction . . . **RI.5** Analyze in detail how an author's ideas . . . **L.4.a** Use context as a clue . . .	**L.4.b** Identify and correctly use patterns of word changes . . . **RI.6** Determine an author's point of view . .	**SL.5** Make strategic use of digital media . . .
STUDENT RESOURCES			
Available online in the Interactive Student Edition or Unit Resources	Selection Audio First-Read Guide: Nonfiction Close-Read Guide: Nonfiction English Language Support: Parallelism	Word Network	Evidence Log
TEACHER RESOURCES			
Selection Resources Available online in the Interactive Teacher's Edition or Unit Resources	Audio Summaries Annotation Model EL Highlights The Value of a Sherpa Life: Text Questions Analyze Craft and Structure: Author's Claims and Ideas	English Language Support: Parallelism Concept Vocabulary and Word Study Author's Style: Use of Rhetoric	Speaking and Listening: Group Presentation
Reteach/Practice (RP) Available online in the Interactive Teacher's Edition or Unit Resources	Analyze Craft and Structure: Author's Claims and Ideas (RP)	Word Study: Latin Root *-mort-* (RP) Author's Style: Use of Rhetoric (RP)	Speaking and Listening: Group Presentation (RP)
Assessment Available online in Assessments	Selection Test		
My Resources	A Unit 2 Answer Key is available online and in the Interactive Teacher's Edition.		

Reading Support

Text Complexity Rubric: The Value of a Sherpa Life	
Quantitative Measures	
Lexile: 1230 **Text Length:** 885 words	
Qualitative Measures	
Knowledge Demands ①—②—❸—④—⑤	Contains references to Mount Everest, the porter workforce, the tourism industry, and insurance standards, not all of which are explained. Students may need more background about these terms.
Structure ①—②—❸—④—⑤	Information in the selection is logically organized, but connections between ideas are not always completely explicit or in a predictable sequence.
Language Conventionality and Clarity ①—②—③—❹—⑤	Many difficult words; many complex sentences; language is used for figurative power (*. . . the solution is increasing the value of a Sherpa life; . . . what a Sherpa life is worth)* without explanation.
Levels of Meaning/Purpose ①—②—❸—④—⑤	Concepts have multiple meanings (*worth* and *value* used in reference to importance and also monetary value); meaning is not always explicit; the main idea is clear, but some of the supporting concepts are complicated.

DECIDE AND PLAN

English Language Support

Provide English Learners with support for context and vocabulary as they read the selection.

Knowledge Demands Before students read, make a list of some of the terms and phrases they will need to understand: *Mount Everest, Sherpas, porter workforce, tourism industry*. Discuss and define each term as needed.

Language Discuss the meaning and use of the words *value* and *worth*. Ask students to read sentences in paragraphs 4 and 5 with these words. Point out the use of the words as different parts of speech:

(adjective) . . . *what a Sherpa life is worth?*

(noun) . . . *the value of a Sherpa life.*

(verb) . . . *the industry clearly values life . . .*

Help students use the words in other sentences.

Strategic Support

Provide students with strategic support to ensure that they can successfully read the text.

Knowledge Demands Using the background information for the selection, discuss who *Sherpas* are and what it means to be a *porter*. Discuss the meanings of *value:* how much money a possession is worth or how important something is. Ask students to be on the lookout for the different meanings of the words *value* and *worth* used in the selection.

Levels of Meaning/Purpose If students have difficulty with multiple meanings, have them identify all sentences using the word *worth* or *value*. Then have them reread each sentence to try to determine the meaning.

Challenge

Provide students who need to be challenged with ideas for how they can go beyond a simple interpretation of the text.

Text Analysis Have students take the numerical data presented in paragraphs 4 and 7 and make charts or tables to compare the different sets of information given.

Written Response Ask students to read more about the Sherpa people. Have them write a page explaining aspects of their culture that students find most interesting.

TEACH

Read and Respond

Have the groups read the selection and complete the Making Meaning, Language Development, and Effective Expression activities.

Standards Support Through Teaching and Learning Cycle

IDENTIFY NEEDS

Analyze results of the Beginning-of-Year Assessment, focusing on the items relating to Unit 2. Also take into consideration student performance to this point and your observations of where particular students struggle.

DECIDE AND PLAN

- If students have performed poorly on items matching these standards, then provide selection scaffolds before assigning them the on-level lesson provided in the Student Edition.
- If students have done well on the Beginning-of-Year Assessment, then challenge them to keep progressing and learning by giving them opportunities to practice the skills in depth.
- Use the Selection Resources listed on the Planning pages for "The Value of a Sherpa Life" to help students continually improve their ability to master the standards.

Instructional Standards: The Value of a Sherpa Life

	Catching Up	This Year	Looking Forward
Reading	You may wish to administer the **Analyze Craft and Struture: Author's Claims and Ideas (RP)** worksheet to help students understand how an author introduces, develops, and refines an argument.	**RI.5** Analyze in detail how an author's ideas or claims are developed and refined by particular sentences, paragraphs, or larger portions of a text.	Have students develop the author's argument further by providing specific suggestions for how to change the climbing industry to benefit Sherpas.
Speaking and Listening	You may wish to administer the **Speaking and Listening: Group Presentation (RP)** worksheet to help students understand how to plan and present a digital presentation.	**SL.5** Make strategic use of digital media in presentations to enhance understanding of findings, reasonings, and evidence and to add interest.	You may wish to challenge students to create their own artwork to accompany their presentation.
Language	You may wish to administer the **Author's Style: Use of Rhetoric (RP)** worksheet to help students understand the function of parallelism and other rhetorical devices as language techniques.	**RI.6** Determine an author's point of view or purpose in a text and analyze how an author uses rhetoric to advance that point of view or purpose.	You may wish to challenge students to use increasingly complex examples of parallelism and other rhetorical devices in their speaking and writing.

TEACH

Implement the planned lesson, and gather evidence of student learning.

ANALYZE AND REVISE

- Analyze student work for evidence of student learning.
- Identify whether or not students have met the expectations in the standards.
- Identify implications for future instruction.

Jump Start

FIRST READ Should all lives be valued equally?

Engaging students in a discussion about the value of a life sets the context for reading "The Value of a Sherpa Life." As students share their thoughts, have them explain the factors that influence their opinion.

The Value of a Sherpa Life

We've all heard the phrase "only the strong survive." What happens when they don't? Who is responsible for those they leave behind? Modeling the questions readers might ask as they read "The Value of a Sherpa Life" brings the text alive for students and connects it to the Small-Group Performance Task question. Selection audio and print capability for the selection are available in the Interactive Teacher's Edition.

Concept Vocabulary

Ask groups to study the three types of context clues and discuss how they can help clarify meaning. Encourage groups to think of one other type that they might encounter in a text. Possibilities include antonyms, examples, and definitions.

FIRST READ

Have students perform the steps of the first read independently:

NOTICE: Encourage students to note the problems the author calls out and what his main point is.

ANNOTATE: Suggest that students mark key passages that support the author's argument.

CONNECT: If students cannot make connections to their own lives or other texts, have them consider current news events that might relate.

RESPOND: Students will answer questions and write a summary to demonstrate understanding.

Point out to students that while they will always complete the Respond step at the end of the first read, the other steps will probably happen somewhat concurrently. You may wish to print copies of the **First-Read Guide: Nonfiction** for students to use.

About the Author

Grayson Schaffer is a senior editor and writer at *Outside* magazine. As a climber himself, he became disturbed by the media attention that was paid to Westerners who died while climbing Mount Everest, while the deaths of Sherpas were largely ignored. He has written extensively about the working conditions of Sherpas on Everest.

The Value of a Sherpa Life

Concept Vocabulary

As you perform your first read of "The Value of a Sherpa Life" you will encounter these words.

physiology	mortality	reincarnation

Context Clues If these words are unfamiliar to you, try using **context clues**—other words and phrases that appear in a text—to help you determine their meanings. There are various types of context clues that you may encounter as you read.

Restatement: The major wreck on the highway was a **calamity**, or terrible misfortune.

Definition: There are millions of **illiterate** people in the world—those who cannot read or write.

Contrast of ideas and topics: Abandoning his usual **veracity**, Greg decided to lie about why he missed practice.

Apply your knowledge of context clues or other vocabulary strategies to determine the meanings of unfamiliar words you encounter during your first read of "The Value of a Sherpa Life." For example, you may look for familiar word parts or use a dictionary to unlock meaning.

First Read NONFICTION

Apply these strategies as you conduct your first read. You will have an opportunity to complete a close read after your first read.

NOTICE the general ideas of the text. *What* is it about? *Who* is involved?

ANNOTATE by marking vocabulary and key passages you want to revisit.

CONNECT ideas within the selection to what you already know and what you have already read.

RESPOND by completing the Comprehension Check and by writing a summary of the selection.

First Read: NOTICE, ANNOTATE, CONNECT, RESPOND

STANDARDS

Reading Informational Text
By the end of grade 9, read and comprehend literary nonfiction in the grades 9–10 text complexity band proficiently, with scaffolding as needed at the high end of the range.

Language
Use context as a clue to the meaning of a word or phrase.

ARGUMENT

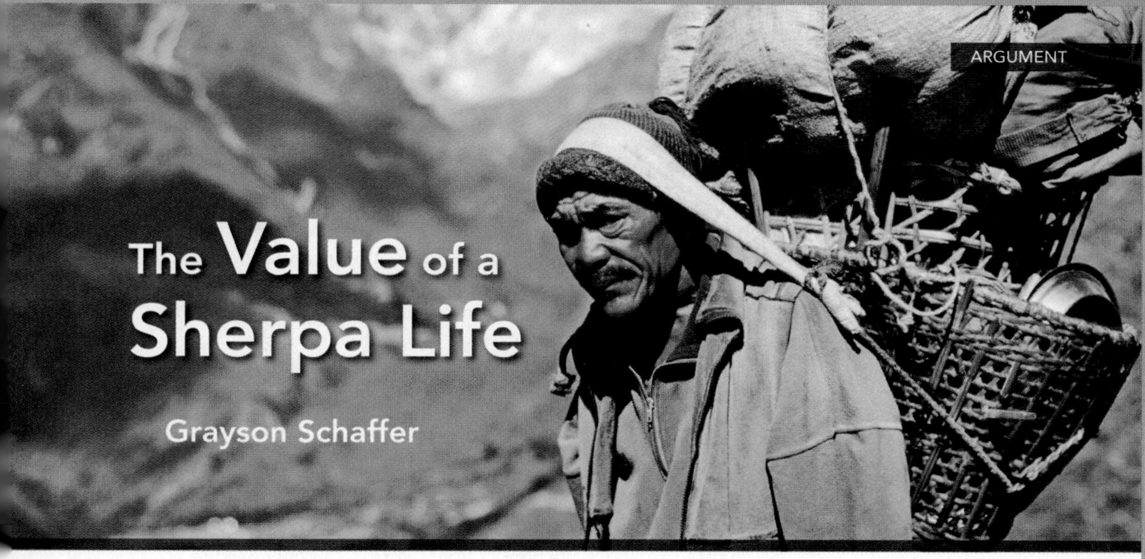

The Value of a Sherpa Life

Grayson Schaffer

DIGITAL PERSPECTIVES

Concept Vocabulary

PHYSIOLOGY If groups are struggling to define the word *physiology* in paragraph 1, point out that many of the surrounding words and phrases refer to the physical abilities of the Sherpa porters. These include *backbone, carrying 80-pound loads,* and *hard work*. These details should lead students to understand that the Sherpa porters are able to carry heavy loads thousands of feet up Mount Everest. Students should then be able to infer that these men and women must be very strong and adapted to the altitudes of the mountain. So Sherpas, unlike the American and European climbers, have a far-above-average physiology for the mountain environment and the tasks necessary to climbing expeditions. Now have students write their definition.

Possible response: *Physiology* must mean "the way a person's body functions."

BACKGROUND

Located between Tibet and Nepal in southern Asia, Mount Everest is the tallest mountain in the world and one of the most dangerous to climb. More than 200 people have died attempting to reach the summit, including 17 Sherpa porters in 2014. Sherpas are a Nepalese ethnic group famous for their superior mountaineering skills. Companies that run expeditions up the mountain often employ Sherpas to guide climbers.

SCAN FOR MULTIMEDIA

1 On April 18, at about 6:30 a.m. local time, an avalanche swept down off the west shoulder of Everest and killed 16 climbers. To anybody who's familiar with Everest climbing, it should come as no surprise that all of the men were Sherpa porters. Sherpas are Everest's workforce—the literal backbone of the climbing industry there. The men who were struck were either carrying 80-pound loads to Camps I and II,[1] or they were on their way back to Base Camp.[2] Without the hard work of the Sherpa porters, it would be largely impossible for Americans and Europeans with slightly above-average **physiology**, and well above-average disposable income, to scale the world's tallest mountain.

2 Increasingly, the pinnacle of adventure tourism—the summit of Everest—comes at too steep a cost. In the August 2013 issue, I wrote a story titled "Disposable Man," about the routinization of Sherpa deaths on Everest. Today's avalanche was the worst accident in the history of the mountain. Add to this the April 2 death of Sherpa Mingma Tenzing, who was working for the Peak Freaks expedition, as well as at least a dozen serious injuries from the avalanche, and 2014 stands out as the bloodiest year in Everest history—all before most teams have even set foot on the mountain.

1. **Camps I and II** campsites located at 19,500 feet and 21,000 feet, respectively.
2. **Base Camp** campsite located at 17,500 feet, on the south side of Everest, in Nepal; where the true climb up the mountain begins.

NOTES

Mark context clues or indicate another strategy you used that helped you determine meaning.

physiology (fihz ee OL uh jee) *n.*

MEANING:

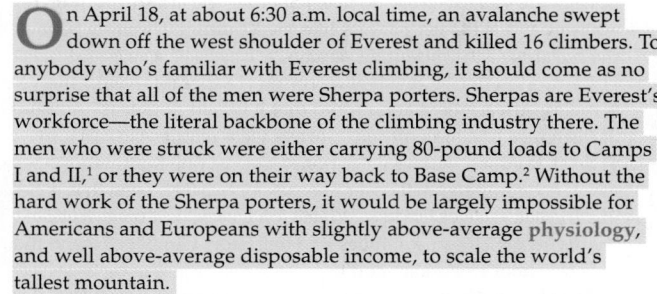

Additional **English Language Support** is available in the Digital Teacher's Edition.

PERSONALIZE FOR LEARNING

Strategic Support

First-Read Support If group members struggle to comprehend the text during the first read, have another group member conduct a think-aloud to explain the thought process as he or she works through the NOTICE, ANNOTATE, CONNECT, and RESPOND steps. For example, in paragraph 1, the student might notice that an avalanche that killed 16 Sherpas is the impetus for the author to write. The student might annotate powerful language ("literal backbone," the whole last sentence) to return to in the close read to see what it reveals about the author's perspective.

FACILITATING

Concept Vocabulary

MORTALITY If groups are struggling to define the word *mortality*in paragraph 4, point out the sentence in paragraph 4 with the phrases *1 percent* and *were dying on the job* as well as the phrase *extremely dangerous* in the following sentence. Have students use these context clues to define the word.

Possible response: "death rate"

CLOSER LOOK

Infer Tone

Circulate among groups as students conduct their close read. Suggest groups close read paragraph 4. If needed, provide the following support.

ANNOTATE: Have students mark details in paragraph 4 that reveal **tone**, or work with small groups to have students participate while you highlight them together.

QUESTION: Guide students to consider what these details might tell them. Ask about the difference in tone between the author's descriptions of early travelers to Everest and his description of today's climbers, and accept student responses.

Possible response: The author is respectful toward the Himalayan climbers who honor the romantic roots of their activities, but has contempt for "recreational" tourists.

CONCLUDE: Help students to formulate conclusions about the importance of these details in the text. Ask students why the author might have included these details.

Possible response: Putting Sherpa lives at risk for nothing more than someone's vacation raises important ethical questions.

Remind students that **tone** reveals the author's attitude toward his or her subject and toward his or her audience. Tone is established by word choice and shows the character of the writer.

NOTES

Mark context clues or indicate another strategy you used that helped you determine meaning.

mortality (mawr TAL uh tee) *n.*

MEANING:

3 Yes, something needs to be done.

4 There's no question that guiding on Everest is ethically fraught. But shutting the industry down would anger the outfitters, clients, and, most of all, the Sherpas. That last group would lose jobs that pay between $2,000 and $6,000 per season, in a country where the median income is $540 per year. If, say, 1 percent of American college-aged raft guides or ski instructors were dying on the job—the **mortality** rate of Everest Sherpas—the guiding industry would vanish. But Himalayan climbing is understood to be extremely dangerous, and people who play the game still cling to its romantic roots in exploration rather than its current status as recreational tourism.

5 The answer isn't decreasing, or ending, the climbing business on Everest; the solution is increasing the value of a Sherpa life. Because right now—despite what anybody may feel in their heart—the industry clearly values life on a two-tiered basis: Westerners at the top, Sherpas at the bottom.

6 Want to know what a Sherpa life is worth? You only need to review the numbers that I reported last year: lower pay, lower standards for rescue insurance, lower payouts on accidental-death coverage in general. And, perhaps most significantly, the amount of time that Sherpas spend making laps through the deadly Khumbu Icefall[3] and up the Lhotse Face,[4] ferrying loads for predominantly Western expeditions so that clients can arrive fresh and minimize their exposure to the hazards of the mountain. Several organizations, including the Juniper Fund and Alex Lowe Charitable Foundation, have made valiant efforts to teach Sherpas the latest climbing, rescue, and first-aid skills via projects like the Khumbu Climbing School, but the hazards of the mountain remain.

7 Last June, after I'd finished reporting "Disposable Man," the Nepalese government announced that it would double the amount of insurance that high-altitude porters were required to carry, to $11,000. But for about $200 per policy, at least one Kathmandu[5]-based insurance company will cover Sherpas for $23,000. Even that is clearly insufficient to cover the loss. What's left instead is a patchwork of charity, in which some families find help from climbers to send their kids to school and others don't.

8 The change I'd most like to see would start at the very beginning of the tragedy, when outfitters describe what has happened to these men, in words that, at this point, sound rote. A typical blog post on an expedition website follows a predictable pattern, like this one from earlier this month: "Our team is overwhelmed with sadness. Our prayers go out to his family at this extremely difficult time. Tea lights have been lit, we hang our heads in sorrow." But after sorrow should come an acknowledgement of the deep sense of responsibility that is

3. **Khumbu** (KUHM boo) **Icefall** dangerous area between Base Camp and Camp I where ice often shifts and snaps off over the heads of climbers.
4. **Lhotse** (loht SEE) **Face** 3,700-foot wall of glacial ice on the southern face of Lhotse, the fourth-highest mountain in the world; connected to Everest and in the path of climbers.
5. **Kathmandu** (kot mon DOO) capital of Nepal.

FACILITATING SMALL-GROUP CLOSE READING

CLOSE READ: Nonfiction As groups perform the close read, circulate and offer support as needed.

- Remind groups that when they read an argument, they should be sure to identify the claim and how the claim is supported.
- If a group is confused about the author's claim, point out that the claim is not always in the first paragraph of a text. Challenge them to find the claim. (In this case, it appears in paragraph 3.)
- Challenge groups to find all the types of evidence the author uses (facts, statistics, anecdotes, quotations from authorities, or examples).

tied in to hiring somebody to do such a dangerous job—for an end result that's ultimately meaningless.

9 In the press, largely as a result of a faulty translation to English, the deceased are always referred to as Sherpa "guides." It's generally a misleading job title for the men—and one or two women—who, each day, lean into their pack straps and haul supplies up the mountain for paying clientele.

10 As guides and Sherpas begin to wake up today in Nepal, they'll commit themselves to finding the remaining bodies. They'll loiter for hours, shovels in hand, under the same serac[6] that killed their friends. The Buddhist tradition is strict about needing a body to cremate if the deceased is to find a speedy **reincarnation**.

11 In the days to come, there will be 16 different puja[7] funeral ceremonies, most of them in the small villages of the Khumbu Valley.[8] In every village, there are already houses with missing men. Their photos, usually faded, smiling, and standing on the summit of the world, are still hung for visitors to see. Now there are 16 more. ❧

6. **serac** (suh RAK) *n.* pinnacle, sharp ridge, or block of ice among the large cracks in glaciers.
7. **puja** (POO jah) *n.* (in Buddhism) expressions of honor, worship, and devotion.
8. **Khumbu Valley** valley below Everest on the Nepalese side.

NOTES

Mark context clues or indicate another strategy you used that helped you determine meaning.

reincarnation (ree ihn kahr NAY shuhn) *n.*

MEANING:

Comprehension Check

Complete the following items after you finish your first read. Review and clarify details with your group.

1. What event prompted the author to write this argumentative essay?
2. According to the author, why would Sherpa porters likely object to scaling back or shutting down the climbing business on Everest?
3. What is the author saying about the value of a Sherpa life?
4. **Notebook** Confirm your understanding of the text by writing a summary.

RESEARCH

Research to Explore This essay may spark your curiosity to learn more. Briefly research a topic that interests you. You may want to share what you discover with your group.

DIGITAL PERSPECTIVES

Concept Vocabulary

REINCARNATION If groups are struggling to define the word *reincarnation* in paragraph 10, point out that the last sentence in the paragraph contains the phrases *The Buddhist tradition, a body to cremate,* and *if the deceased is to find.* Have students use these context clues to define the word.

Possible response: *Reincarnation* means "the rebirth of a soul in a new body."

Comprehension Check

Possible responses:

1. The deaths of sixteen Sherpa porters prompted the author to write the essay.
2. Sherpas earn above-average incomes. If climbing were cut back, they would not be able to earn as good a living.
3. The value of a Sherpa life is less than the value of a western climber's life.
4. Summaries will vary; however, students should include the following points in their summary:
   - the author's claim
   - the reasons that support the author's claim

Research

If groups struggle to come up with a research topic, you may want to suggest that they focus on one of the following topics: a specific climbing expedition on Everest, mountain climbing fatalities, the physical challenges of mountain climbing, or Sherpa culture.

DIGITAL PERSPECTIVES

Illuminating the Text To help students understand the work Sherpas do and the risks they take, find photos online of Sherpas carrying heavy loads as well as photos or video footage of avalanches. Display the photos and videos for students after they have finished reading, and have groups discuss how the images enhance their understanding of "The Value of a Sherpa Life." Then, have groups share how the photos and videos provided insight to the text. Encourage them to consider how or if their view of Sherpas' working conditions changed in reaction to the photos and videos.

Jump Start

CLOSE READ Ask students to brainstorm about other sports and activities, such as skydiving, in which participants run the risk of losing their lives. As students discuss in their groups, ask them to consider whether it's fair for people to partake in such activities knowing that others may be forced to put their own lives at risk to rescue them.

Close Read the Text

If needed, model close reading by using the Annotation Highlights in the Interactive Teacher's Edition.

Remind groups to use Accountable Talk in their discussions and to support one another as they complete the close read.

Analyze the Text

1. **Possible response:** Although the author discusses shutting down the Everest industry, in paragraph 5 he explicitly states that "the answer isn't decreasing, or ending, the climbing business." Instead the author is taking the position that the solution is "increasing the value of a Sherpa life."
2. Passages will vary by group. Remind students to explain why they chose the passage they present to the group members.
3. Responses will vary by group.

Concept Vocabulary

Why These Words?

Possible response:

These three words are related to life, death, and the human body. They enhance the impact of the text by emphasizing the life-and-death nature of the climbing industry.

Practice

Possible responses:

- Kenton studied ***physiology*** in college so that he could become a doctor.
- A funeral reminds me of my own ***mortality***.
- ***Reincarnation*** is a central belief in the Hindu religion.

Word Network

Possible words: *deadly, injuries, sorrow*

Word Study

For more support, see **Concept Vocabulary and Word Study.**

MAKING MEANING

THE VALUE OF A SHERPA LIFE

Close Read the Text

With your group, revisit sections of the text you marked during your first read. **Annotate** details that you notice. What **questions** do you have? What can you **conclude**?

Analyze the Text

CITE TEXTUAL EVIDENCE to support your answers.

Notebook Complete the activities.

1. **Review and Clarify** With your group, reread paragraph 4 of the selection. Discuss the author's counterargument to shutting down the Everest industry. Do you think that he would prefer the climbing industry to stop, or is there another alternative?
2. **Present and Discuss** Now, work with your group to share the passages from the selection that you found especially important. Take turns presenting your passages. Discuss what you notice in the selection, what questions you asked, and what conclusions you reached.
3. **Essential Question:** ***What does it take to survive?*** What has this essay taught you about survival? Discuss with your group.

TIP

GROUP DISCUSSION
Keep in mind that group members will have different interpretations of the text. These different perspectives enable group members to learn from one another and to clarify their own thoughts. Very often there is no single interpretation or conclusion.

LANGUAGE DEVELOPMENT

Concept Vocabulary

physiology	mortality	reincarnation

Why These Words? The concept vocabulary words from the text are related. With your group, determine what the words have in common. How do these word choices enhance the impact of the text?

Practice

Notebook Confirm your understanding of these words from the text by using them in sentences. Be sure to use context clues that hint at each word's meaning.

WORD NETWORK

Add interesting words related to survival from the text to your Word Network.

Word Study

Latin root: *-mort-* In "The Value of a Sherpa Life," the author draws attention to the *mortality* rate of Everest Sherpas. The word *mortality* was formed from the Latin root *-mort-*, which means "death." Find several other words that contain this root. Record the words and their meanings.

STANDARDS

Reading Informational Text
Analyze in detail how an author's ideas or claims are developed and refined by particular sentences, paragraphs, or larger portions of a text.

Language
Identify and correctly use patterns of word changes that indicate different meanings or parts of speech.

FORMATIVE ASSESSMENT

Analyze the Text

If students struggle to close read the text, **then** provide the **The Value of a Sherpa Life: Text Questions** available online in the Interactive Teacher's Edition or Unit Resources. Answers and DOK levels are also available.

Concept Vocabulary

If students struggle to identify the concept, **then** have them use each word in a sentence and think about what is similar about the sentences.

Word Study

If students fail to identify other words, **then** suggest they use a dictionary to browse words that begin with *-mort-*. For Reteach and Practice, see **Word Study: Latin Root *-mort-* (RP).**

Analyze Craft and Structure

Author's Claims and Ideas An **argumentative essay** is a brief nonfiction work in which an author attempts to persuade readers to accept his or her point of view. The writer presents a position, or **claim**, and develops it through a sequence of logically linked ideas and evidence. Most essays follow a standard structure:

- **Introduction:** The writer introduces the topic, engages the reader, and states the main claim.
- **Body:** The writer develops the main claim with explanations, evidence, and reasons. The author may introduce additional claims that relate to the main claim. The author may also refine the main claim by making it narrower or more specific.
- **Conclusion:** The writer ends the essay in a memorable way. He or she may restate or summarize the main claim.

TIP

CLARIFICATION

An introduction or a conclusion may consist of multiple paragraphs, not just one.

Practice

CITE TEXTUAL EVIDENCE to support your answers.

Working with your group, analyze how the author of "The Value of a Sherpa Life" introduces, develops, and refines his argument.

1. Identify the paragraphs that make up the separate sections of the essay. (Use paragraph numbers or ranges, such as "paragraph 1," or "paragraphs 7-9.")

   Introduction: *paragraph(s)* 1–3

   Body: *paragraph(s)* 4–8

   Conclusion: *paragraph(s)* 9–11

Notebook

2. Create a "reverse" outline of the essay. Using outline format, state the topic or main idea of each paragraph. Then, for each paragraph, list the evidence or reasons the author uses to support or develop that idea.
3. (a) What is the main claim of the essay? (b) Cite two pieces of evidence or reasons that develop or support that idea.
4. (a) At what point in the essay does the author refine the main claim by making it more specific? Cite the paragraph or sentence. (b) What specifically does the author want readers to think or to do?
5. (a) What is noteworthy or memorable about the essay's conclusion? (b) Is this conclusion persuasive? Explain.

DIGITAL PERSPECTIVES

Analyze Craft and Structure

Author's Claims and Ideas Remind students that an effective argument supports a claim with reasons, as well as evidence to support those reasons. For more support, see **Analyze Craft and Structure: Author's Claims and Ideas.**

Practice

Possible responses:

1. See responses in the chart on the Student page.
2. Students should state the topic or main idea of each paragraph of the selection and note the support that the author uses.
3. (a) The main claim of the essay is that media attention has been given to the dangers faced by Westerners who climb Mount Everest, but not enough attention has been paid to the risks taken by Sherpas, who perform very difficult, dangerous work for little money. (b) Sixteen Sherpas were killed on April 18th; Sherpas carry 80-pound loads; Sherpas earn between $2,000 and $6,000 per season.
4. (a) In the first sentence of paragraph 5, the author says that "the solution is increasing the value of a Sherpa life," and he further refines his claim by stating in paragraph 8 that the Westerners who benefit from the Sherpas' labor should feel a greater sense of responsibility for their deaths. (b) The author wants readers to understand the problem he's describing—Sherpas perform dangerous work for relatively low pay, and their deaths aren't being given the same weight in the media as the Western climbers who hire them.
5. (a) In the conclusion, the author reiterates the number sixteen, which is the number of Sherpa deaths that he mentions in the first paragraph. The author also uses powerful imagery—photos of those who were killed and the phrase "houses with missing men." (b) The conclusion is persuasive because the author uses repetition and emotional appeals to underscore his point.

FORMATIVE ASSESSMENT

Analyze Craft and Structure

If students are unable to identify elements of the argument, **then** have them reread each paragraph and ask which element is addressed in the paragraph. For Reteach and Practice, see **Analyze Craft and Structure: Author's Claims and Ideas (RP).**

PERSONALIZE FOR LEARNING

Strategic Support

Clarifying Elements of an Argument If students struggle to comprehend the elements of an argument in "The Value of a Sherpa Life," suggest that they identify a passage or detail that is confusing or overwhelming and have a group member summarize the text in his or her own words.

FACILITATING

Author's Style

Use of Rhetoric As you review the examples of rhetoric with students, consider providing additional examples to reinforce the definitions of the different rhetorical devices.

"I have a dream that my four little children will one day live in a nation where they will not be judged by the color of their skin but by the content of their character."
—Martin Luther King, Jr. (parallelism)

Is the sky blue? (rhetorical question)

Class warfare (charged language)

For more support, see **Author's Style: Use of Rhetoric.**

Read It

Possible responses:

a. parallelism

b. compares the characteristics of Sherpas to the characteristics of Westerners

c. charged language

d. emphasizes the differences between Westerners and Sherpas

e. rhetorical question

f. emphasizes the point that there is no way to quantify the value of a person's life

Write It

Paragraphs will vary but make sure students include at least one example of parallelism, a rhetorical question, and charged language.

FORMATIVE ASSESSMENT

Author's Style

If students struggle to identify examples of rhetorical devices, **then** review the definitions of each type of rhetorical device, providing additional examples as needed. For Reteach and Practice, see **Author's Style: Use of Rhetoric (RP).**

LANGUAGE DEVELOPMENT

THE VALUE OF A SHERPA LIFE

Author's Style

Use of Rhetoric **Rhetorical devices** are patterns of words that an author uses to support and emphasize ideas, create rhythm, and make a work memorable. Review the common rhetorical devices described here. Then, discuss the examples of each device with your group.

Parallelism: the use of similar grammatical structures to express related ideas
Example: We shall pay any price, bear any burden, oppose any foe . . .

Rhetorical Question: a question to which no response is expected because the answer is obvious or is the point the writer intends to prove
Example: If winter comes, can spring be far behind?

Charged Language: strong words that appeal to the emotions and create a powerful impression on readers
Example: Only a fool or a cheat would oppose these new rules.

STANDARDS

Reading Informational Text
Determine an author's point of view or purpose in a text and analyze how an author uses rhetoric to advance that point of view or purpose.

Speaking and Listening
Make strategic use of digital media in presentations to enhance understanding of findings, reasoning, and evidence and to add interest.

Read It

Work individually. Use this chart to identify each passage from "The Value of a Sherpa Life" as an example of parallelism, rhetorical question, or charged language. Then, explain how each example helps to convey the author's point of view. When you finish, reconvene as a group to discuss your responses.

SELECTION PASSAGE	RHETORICAL DEVICE	HOW IT CONVEYS POINT OF VIEW
slightly above-average physiology, and well above-average disposable income (paragraph 1)	a.	b.
people who play the game still cling to its romantic roots (paragraph 4)	c.	d.
Want to know what a Sherpa life is worth? (paragraph 6)	e.	f.

Write It

Notebook Write a paragraph in which you explain what you learned about Everest expeditions from this essay. Use an example of parallelism, a rhetorical question, or charged language.

PERSONALIZE FOR LEARNING

English Language Support

Parallelism Support English Learners in understanding how parallelism in texts makes an impact on the reader and establishes relationships between ideas.

Ask students to write about a routine at school using parallelism for effect. **EMERGING**

Ask students to write a paragraph analyzing another moment of parallelism in the text and discuss its effect on the reader. **EXPANDING**

Ask students to write about the tourists who climb Everest, using parallelism for effect, to express their support or criticism for the tourism industry on Mt. Everest. **BRIDGING**

An expanded **English Language Support Lesson** on Parallelism is available in the Interactive Teacher's Edition.

EFFECTIVE EXPRESSION

Speaking and Listening

Assignment

Create a **digital presentation** in which you incorporate text and images to explain a subject. Choose from the following topics:

- ☐ a set of **illustrated maps** showing the route taken by most Everest expeditions conducted for tourists, including base camp locations and key topographical points
- ☐ a **profile** of the Sherpa people, including information about Sherpa history and culture
- ☐ a **report** about a historic expedition to the summit of Everest, including information about Westerners and Sherpas who participated and descriptions of key events

Project Plan Before you begin, make a list of the tasks you will need to accomplish in order to complete your digital presentation. Then, assign individual group members to each task. Finally, determine how you will make decisions about choices of images, text, and the overall design of your project.

Finding Visuals Make sure the visuals you choose accurately illustrate and enhance the text. Use this chart to collect your ideas. Consult a variety of research sources to gather information and images you will need. Remember to include appropriate citations.

TEXT IMAGE ILLUSTRATES	DESCRIPTION OF IMAGE	SOURCE INFORMATION FOR CITATION

EVIDENCE LOG

Before moving on to a new selection, go to your Evidence Log and record what you learned from "The Value of a Sherpa Life."

PERSONALIZE FOR LEARNING

English Language Support

Figurative Language English Learners may struggle with the figurative language often present in rhetoric. Suggest that they identify any words or phrases that are confusing, and have another group member paraphrase in simpler language. For example, some students may struggle to understand that calling the Sherpas "the literal backbone of the climbing industry" (Paragraph 1) is a figurative expression that means the Sherpas are the foundation of the climbing industry. **ALL LEVELS**

DIGITAL PERSPECTIVES

Speaking and Listening

Assignment If groups have trouble deciding which type of presentation to choose, encourage them to consider which option plays to their group's strengths the most. For example, if the group is artistically inclined, the illustrated maps might be the best option. If they excel at straightforward research reports, the report on the historic expedition might be best. Remind them, however, that all of the options will require them to conduct research and find visuals.

Project Plan Remind groups to consult the schedule for Small-Group Activities as they create their Project Plan. Check to make sure each group has made assignments and that the work is divided evenly among group members.

Finding Visuals The chart on the student page will help groups organize their presentation and keep track of their sources. Point out to groups that they will have a stronger presentation if they think about why they're including each image. They can then fill in the first column of the chart with the idea they want to convey with the image. Groups can then brainstorm possible images. Once they have chosen, they should record the description in the second column and the citation in the third column. For more support see **Speaking and Listening: Group Presentation**.

MAKE IT INTERACTIVE

Using the Interactive Teacher's Edition, project the image from the first page of "The Value of a Sherpa Life." Ask students to consider the different messages a viewer might receive if the photo had the following captions:

- Sherpa porters provide the heavy lifting for those scaling Mount Everest.
- How come I have to carry the heavy stuff?
- Sherpas are unfairly exploited by the climbing community.

Evidence Log Support students in completing their Evidence Log. This paced activity will help prepare them for the Performance-Based Assessment at the end of the unit.

FORMATIVE ASSESSMENT

Speaking and Listening

If students struggle with locating images, **then** have them refine their search terms to more accurately describe the text an image illustrates.

For Reteach and Practice, see **Speaking and Listening: Group Presentation (RP).**

Selection Test

Administer "The Value of a Sherpa Life" Selection Test, which is available in both print and digital formats online in Assessments.

I Am Offering This Poem • The Writer • Hugging the Jukebox

AUDIO SUMMARIES
Audio summaries of "I Am Offering This Poem," "The Writer," and "Hugging the Jukebox" are available online in both English and Spanish in the Interactive Teacher's Edition or Unit Resources. Assigning these summaries prior to reading the selections may help students build additional background knowledge and set a context for their first read.

Summary

The speaker in Jimmy Santiago Baca's "I Am Offering This Poem" compares his poem with a variety of useful things: a warm coat, a pair of socks, a pot of yellow corn, and a set of directions that the woman he loves can use if ever she gets lost. The poem offers all that is really necessary to survive: love.

In Richard Wilbur's "The Writer," the speaker pauses on the stairs as he hears his daughter typing a story. He employs maritime imagery as he develops his line of thought. The house has a "prow"; the typewriter sounds "like a chain hauled over a gunwale"; her young life carries "a great cargo"; he wishes her "a lucky passage." Then the speaker remembers something with no apparent connection to the clatter of the keys or to the ships that shape and give mystery to his thoughts.

Naomi Shihab Nye's "Hugging the Jukebox" is set on a Caribbean island, where six-year-old Alfred has learned every song on the jukebox in his grandparents' cafe. His parents have put Alfred into their care, and now he hugs the jukebox and sings in a voice that holds the customers spellbound, carries to the harbor, and travels like a wave across the sea.

Insight

Reading these three poems will help students begin to think about the aspects of survival that go beyond whether one lives or dies. Each poem addresses the struggle to live through difficult times—difficulties that don't necessarily threaten one's life, but that need to be overcome with the help of others.

ESSENTIAL QUESTION:
What does it take to survive?

Connection to Essential Question

These three poems will help students answer the Essential Question by illustrating that survival can involve emotional support from others. In "I Am Offering This Poem," the speaker offers his love—so that the recipient will survive. In "The Writer," the speaker gives his daughter the freedom she needs to make her own mistakes, to recover from them, and to live an independent life. In "Hugging the Jukebox," Alfred survives because of music and his grandparents' acceptance, and he, in turn, gives his grandmother hope for the future.

SMALL-GROUP LEARNING PERFORMANCE TASK
What type of strength is most valuable in a survival situation?

UNIT PERFORMANCE-BASED ASSESSMENT
Should people in life-or-death situations be held accountable for their actions?

Connection to Performance Tasks

Small-Group Learning Performance Task In these poems, the strengths that lead to survival are gifts that come from someone else, such as the love and guidance offered in "I Am Offering This Poem," the independence offered in "The Writer," or the hope offered in "Hugging the Jukebox." The overall strength is the ability to forge relationships that offer protection from the harshness of life.

Unit Performance-Based Assessment Students may wish to use the poems in this collection as a source for anecdotes when writing their argument in the Performance-Based Assessment.

DIGITAL PERSPECTIVES — Audio | Video | Document | Annotation Highlights | EL Highlights | Online Assessment

LESSON RESOURCES

	Making Meaning	Language Development	Effective Expression
Lesson	**First Read** **Close Read** **Analyze the Text** **Analyze Craft and Structure**	**Author's Style** **Concept Vocabulary** **Word Study**	**Speaking and Listening**
Instructional Standards	**RL.10** By the end of grade 9, read and comprehend literature . . . **L.4** Determine or clarify the meaning . . . **RL.2** Determine a theme or central idea of a text . . . **L.4.b** Identify and correctly use patterns of word changes . . .	**L.4.b** Identify and correctly use patterns of word changes . . . **RL.4** Determine the meaning of words and phrases . . . **L.5** Demonstrate understanding of figurative language . . .	**L.5.a** Interpret figures of speech . . . **SL.1.a** Come to discussions prepared . . . **SL.6** Adapt speech to a variety of contexts . . . **SL.1.b** Work with peers to set rules for collegial discussions . . .
STUDENT RESOURCES			
Available online in the Interactive Student Edition or Unit Resources	Selection Audio First-Read Guide: Poetry Close-Read Guide: Poetry	Word Network	Evidence Log
TEACHER RESOURCES			
Selection Resources Available online in the Interactive Teacher's Edition or Unit Resources	Audio Summaries Annotation Highlights EL Highlights Poetry Collection: Text Questions Analyze Craft and Structure: Development of Theme	Author's Style: Figurative Language English Language Support Lesson: Figurative Language Concept Vocabulary and Word Study	Speaking and Listening: Oral Presentation
Reteach and Practice Available online in the Interactive Teacher's Edition or Unit Resources	Analyze Craft and Structure: Development of Theme (RP)	Author's Style: Figurative Language (RP) Word Study: Latin Root *-lum-* (RP)	Speaking and Listening: Oral Presentation (RP)
Assessment Available online in Assessments	Selection Test		
My Resources	A Unit 2 Answer Key is available online and in the Interactive Teacher's Edition		

Reading Support

Text Complexity Rubric: I Am Offering This Poem • The Writer • Hugging the Jukebox	
Quantitative Measures	
Lexile: NP Text Length: 30 lines; 33 lines; 51 lines	
Qualitative Measures	
Knowledge Demands ① ❷ ③ ④ ⑤	Mostly familiar situations, but written from point of view of parents and grandparents rather than children or teens. Some references may not be familiar to students (the sound of typewriter keys; records and needle in a jukebox).
Structure ① ❷ ③ ④ ⑤	All three poems have conventional poetic structure.
Language Conventionality and Clarity ① ② ❸ ④ ⑤	"The Writer" and "Hugging the Jukebox" contain metaphors, similes, and more difficult vocabulary.
Levels of Meaning/Purpose ① ② ❸ ④ ⑤	Multiple levels of meaning: poems describe observations or communication between parents/grandparents and children. They also touch on growth and change and parents' experience of watching children get older.

DECIDE AND PLAN

English Language Support

Provide English Learners with support for language and meaning as they read the selection.

Language Students may need help not only with the metaphors and similes but also with the structure of the language and the vocabulary. For example, in "I Am Offering This Poem" point out that the word *it* in all the verses is the pronoun replacing *the poem*. Ask students to reread some of the phrases making this replacement to make sure they understand. For example, *The poem is all I have to give.* Then have them reread the poem's original language.

Meaning Work with students to help them understand the meaning of metaphors by first understanding the literal meaning. For example, explain that in "Hugging the Jukebox," the "giant whale in a small pool" means a very big voice in a small body.

Strategic Support

Provide students with strategic support to ensure that they can successfully read the text.

Language Remind students that the poems they are about to read contain metaphors and similes. Discuss the difference—similes use the word *like* to compare, whereas metaphors do not. Give an example, such as *like a chain* or *born with a trumpet in my throat.* Ask students to be on the lookout for other such similes or metaphors.

Meaning For students who have difficulty understanding metaphors and similes, have them underline or list the phrases that they don't understand. Then have them read those phrases again and work with a partner to try to figure out the comparison the poet is making.

Challenge

Provide students who need to be challenged with ideas for how they can go beyond a simple interpretation of the text.

Text Analysis Ask students to make a list of all the metaphors and similes they find in the poems. Pair students and have one say a simile or metaphor (for example, *a poem like a warm coat*). Have the other describe the image conveyed by these words and give an analysis of what the poet is trying to describe (for example, *The poem is like a warm coat because it is comforting and protective.*)

Written Response Ask students to use the similes and metaphors in the poems to write their own images. For example, ask them what other images they could use to convey a loving and comforting poem.

TEACH

Read and Respond

Have the groups read the selection and complete the Making Meaning, Language Development, and Effective Expression activities.

Standards Support Through Teaching and Learning Cycle

IDENTIFY NEEDS

Analyze results of the Beginning-of-Year Assessment, focusing on the items relating to Unit 2. Also take into consideration student performance to this point and your observations of where particular students struggle.

DECIDE AND PLAN

- If students have performed poorly on items matching these standards, then provide selection scaffolds before assigning them the on-level lesson provided in the Student Edition.
- If students have done well on the Beginning-of-Year Assessment, then challenge them to keep progressing and learning by giving them opportunities to practice the skills in depth.
- Use the Selection Resources listed on the Planning pages for this Poetry Collection to help students continually improve their ability to master the standards.

Instructional Standards: I Am Offering This Poem • The Writer • Hugging the Jukebox

	Catching Up	This Year	Looking Forward
Reading	You may wish to administer the **Analyze Craft and Structure: Development of Theme (RP)** worksheet to help students understand how to identify the theme of a text.	**RL.2** Determine a theme or central idea of a text and analyze its development over the course of the text, including how it emerges and is shaped and refined by specific details; provide an objective summary of the text.	Have students select a theme from one of the poems and write their own poem around that theme.
Speaking and Listening	You may wish to administer the **Speaking and Listening: Oral Presentation (RP)** worksheet to help students understand what makes an effective presentation.	**SL.6** Adapt speech to a variety of contexts and tasks, demonstrating command of formal English when indicated or appropriate.	You may wish to challenge students to perform their Reader's Theater or show their video presentation to a community-based organization.
Language	You may wish to administer the **Word Study: Latin Root *-lum-*** worksheet to help students understand that knowing the meaning of roots helps them unlock the meaning of many words. You may wish to administer the **Speaking and Listening: Oral Presentation (RP)** worksheet to help students understand the effectiveness of figures of speech.	**L.4.b** Identify and correctly use patterns of word changes that indicate different meanings or parts of speech. **L.5** Demonstrate understanding of figurative language, word relationships, and nuances in word meaning.	Have students identify other Latin roots that mean "light" and find several words that have this root. You may wish to challenge students to rewrite one of the poems, selecting words and phrases and replacing them with other figurative language.

ANALYZE AND REVISE

- Analyze student work for evidence of student learning.
- Identify whether or not students have met the expectations in the standards.
- Identify implications for future instruction.

TEACH

Implement the planned lesson, and gather evidence of student learning.

Jump Start

FIRST READ How can poetry help people survive? Engage students in a discussion about how writing and reading poetry can help people process difficulties. Suggest that contemporary music is a form of poetry, and ask students to discuss how songs can help people survive challenging circumstances.

I Am Offering This Poem
The Writer
Hugging the Jukebox

What tools do people use to help themselves survive emotionally? Modeling the questions readers might ask as they read "I Am Offering This Poem," "The Writer," and "Hugging the Jukebox" brings the text alive for students and connects it to the Small-Group Performance Task question. Selection audio and print capability for the selections are available in the Interactive Teacher's Edition.

POETRY COLLECTION

I Am Offering This Poem
The Writer
Hugging the Jukebox

Concept Vocabulary

As you perform your first read of these three poems, you will encounter the following words.

treasure	iridescent	luminous

Familiar Word Parts When determining the meaning of an unfamiliar word, look for word parts, such as roots or suffixes, that you know. Doing so may help you unlock word meanings.

Root: The words *thermos* and *thermometer* are built on the same root, *-therm-*, which refers to heat. If you know the root *-therm-*, you could guess that the word *thermal* has something to do with heat.

Suffix: The suffix *-ence* appears at the ends of words such as *dependence* and *residence*. It means "state or quality of being." If you know the suffix *-ence*, you can conclude that the word *emergence* means "state or quality of emerging"—arising or coming to be.

Apply your knowledge of familiar word parts and other vocabulary strategies to determine the meanings of unfamiliar words you encounter during your first read.

First Read POETRY

Apply these strategies as you conduct your first read. You will have an opportunity to complete a close read after your first read.

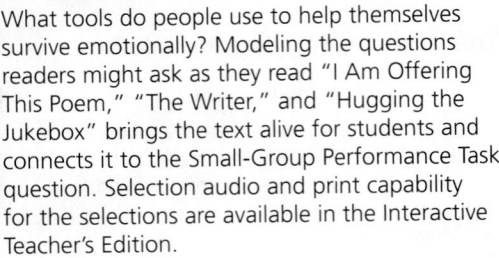

NOTICE who or what is "speaking" the poem and whether the poem tells a story or describes a single moment.

ANNOTATE by marking vocabulary and key passages you want to revisit.

CONNECT ideas within the selection to what you already know and what you have already read.

RESPOND by completing the Comprehension Check.

STANDARDS

Reading Literature
By the end of grade 9, read and comprehend literature, including stories, dramas, and poems, in the grades 9–10 text complexity band proficiently, with scaffolding as needed at the high end of the range.

Language
- Determine or clarify the meaning of unknown and multiple-meaning words and phrases based on *grades 9–10 reading and content*, choosing flexibly from a range of strategies.
- Identify and correctly use patterns of word changes that indicate different meanings or parts of speech.

About the Poets

Jimmy Santiago Baca (b. 1952) was born in New Mexico. He initially lived with his grandmother but was later sent to an orphanage. Baca ran away at age 13, and circumstances led him to illegal activities and prison. During his time in prison, he learned to read and write. Some of his poems were sent to a publisher, who included them in a book published the year Baca left prison. He continues to write and teach those who are experiencing hardship.

Richard Wilbur (b. 1921) earned his first dollar as a poet when he was eight years old. At the time, he did not think that he would pursue a literary career because he was more interested in painting and journalism. As a soldier during World War II, he wrote poems to calm his nerves. After the war, a college friend read the poems and asked Wilbur to write for his literary magazine. Wilbur went on to win two Pulitzer Prizes for Poetry and to serve as the second Poet Laureate of the United States.

Naomi Shihab Nye's (b. 1952) experiences as a woman of mixed Palestinian and American heritage give her a unique perspective. Before attending college in Texas, she lived in Palestine and Jerusalem. In her writing, she often celebrates the extraordinary nature of everyday, ordinary life. After the terrorist attacks on the World Trade Center, Nye became an activist for Arab Americans, advocating for peace and tolerance.

Backgrounds

I Am Offering This Poem

Jimmy Santiago Baca's work draws on features of the American Southwest, including the imagery of the natural landscape and the indigenous ways of life. For example, in this poem, the speaker mentions the comforts of home by referencing the Navajo hogan, a traditional dwelling built out of logs and covered with mud. The entrance of a hogan typically faces east, toward the rising sun.

The Writer

Before computers becam household items, anyone who did not want to write out a manuscript by hand used a typewriter. Typewriters could be noisy because the typists had to strike each key with enough force to push a typebar against an ink ribbon. In turn, the typebar made the impression on the ribbon to create each letter. In this poem, the speaker listens as a young writer uses a typewriter to work on a story.

Hugging the Jukebox

A jukebox is a device that contains a number of vinyl records and a record player. The user typically inserts money and then selects which record to play. Jukeboxes were often found in dance halls and restaurants, and people could select the music for the crowd to hear. Jukeboxes were a major method of playing popular music for much of the twentieth century.

DIGITAL PERSPECTIVES

Concept Vocabulary

Encourage groups to discuss the three concept vocabulary words. Have they seen the words in texts before? Do they use any of the words in their speech and writing? Do they recognize any word parts, such as a root word or a suffix?

Ask students to look closely at word parts and discuss how these types of clues can help clarify meaning. Encourage groups to think of one other type of word part that they might encounter in a word (prefixes).

FIRST READ

Have students perform the steps of the first read independently.

NOTICE: Students should focus on the basic elements of the text to ensure they understand the message the author is conveying.

ANNOTATE: Students should mark any passages they wish to revisit during their close read.

CONNECT: Students should increase their understanding by connecting what they've read to other texts or personal experiences.

RESPOND: Students will answer questions and write a summary to demonstrate understanding.

Point out to students that while they will always complete the Respond step at the end of the first read, the other steps will probably happen somewhat concurrently. You may wish to print copies of the **First-Read Guide: Poetry** for students to use.

PERSONALIZE FOR LEARNING

English Language Support

Syntax Help students analyze the unusual sentence structure of poetry in order to develop a better understanding of conventional English syntax. Have students rewrite the poem in prose format, removing the line breaks from within the poetry. Ask them to read the rewritten sentences and make observations. Help students understand that the rewritten poem is composed of many run-on sentences. In prose, these sentences wouldn't be acceptable, but with poetry, an author can write outside the conventional rules of English.

ALL LEVELS

CLOSER LOOK

Interpret Images

Circulate among groups as students conduct their close read. Suggest that groups examine the photograph, and have them note details of imagery in the photograph. Encourage them to talk about the notes that they make. If needed, provide the following support.

ANNOTATE: Have students note the details in the photograph that relate directly or indirectly to the poem, or work with small groups to have students participate while you highlight them together.

QUESTION: Guide students to consider what these details might tell them. Ask how the photograph might help readers to understand the poem better, and accept student responses.

Possible response: The poem says "I love you" and affirms that love is all we need to survive and endure. Rock is a symbol of solidity and permanence; the heart-shaped rock in the photo symbolizes the survival and endurance of love. Like the poem, it is offered as a gift. The heart-shaped stone in the photograph held by a hand represents love that is being offered from one to another.

CONCLUDE: Help students to formulate conclusions about the importance of these details in the photograph. Ask students why the photographer might have included these details. How does the photograph help you predict the meaning of the poem?

Possible response: The photograph tells me that the poem is about someone offering love to another.

Remind students that illustrating poetry can be a way of interpreting poetry. Poets often make use of imagery. A drawing, painting, or photograph can sometimes help to **interpret images** in a poem.

POETRY

I Am Offering This Poem

Jimmy Santiago Baca

VOCABULARY DEVELOPMENT

Concept Vocabulary Reinforcement
Students will benefit from additional examples and practice with the concept vocabulary. Reinforce their comprehension with "show-you-know" sentences.
The first part of the sentence uses the vocabulary word in an appropriate context. The second part of the sentence—the "show-you-know" part—clarifies the first.

Model the strategy with this example for *treasure:*

Richard will *treasure* the time he spends with his Papa; their relationship is very important to him.

Then give students these sentence prompts and coach them in creating the clarification part:

1. The oil floating in the water was *iridescent;* ____________.

   Possible response: It gave off bright colors that seemed to change when seen from different angles

2. He checked the time on the *luminous* dial of his watch; ____________.

   Possible response: It was easy to read, as it glowed in the dark

SCAN FOR MULTIMEDIA

I am offering this poem to you,
since I have nothing else to give.
Keep it like a warm coat
when winter comes to cover you,
or like a pair of thick socks
the cold cannot bite through,

I love you,

I have nothing else to give you,
so it is a pot full of yellow corn
to warm your belly in winter,
it is a scarf for your head, to wear
over your hair, to tie up around your face,

I love you,

Keep it, **treasure** this as you would
if you were lost, needing direction,
in the wilderness life becomes when mature;
and in the corner of your drawer,
tucked away like a cabin or hogan*
in dense trees, come knocking,
and I will answer, give you directions,
and let you warm yourself by this fire,
rest by this fire, and make you feel safe,

I love you,

It's all I have to give,
and all anyone needs to live,
and to go on living inside,
when the world outside
no longer cares if you live or die;
remember,

I love you.

NOTES

Mark familiar word parts or indicate another strategy you used that helped you determine meaning.

treasure (TREHZH uhr) *v.*

MEANING:

* **hogan** *n.* Navajo Indian dwelling made of logs and mud.

DIGITAL PERSPECTIVES

Enriching the Text Show students a video of writer Jimmy Santiago Baca reading his poem, "I Am Offering This Poem," available by searching on the Internet.

After students have viewed the video, have them compare and contrast the video version with the text. In poetry, breaking a sentence into lines is one way to create emphasis. How does the emphasis created by the written lines compare with Baca's reading? Does the difference between the two alter the poem's meaning or the listener's emotional response to the poem?

Reading poetry involves our eyes and our mind. Hearing poetry requires our ears, mind, and sometimes our eyes as we watch the speaker. Ask students to consider how adding the sensory input of sound affects our interpretation and response to poetry. **(Research to Clarify)**

DIGITAL PERSPECTIVES

Concept Vocabulary

TREASURE If groups are struggling to define the word *treasure* in line 14, remind them to look for context clues. Have them annotate the clauses *as you would if you were lost, needing direction* and *come knocking, and I will answer, give you directions.* Point out that these two clauses together compare a treasure with directions for someone who is lost, which you would hold dear.

Possible response: In this context, *treasure* means "to retain carefully, to cherish." It is being used as a verb, not a noun.

CLOSER LOOK

Analyze Figurative Language

Circulate among groups as students conduct their close read. Suggest that groups examine the photograph. Encourage them to talk about the annotations that they mark on the poem. If needed, provide the following support.

ANNOTATE: Have students mark details in the first stanza that refer to the comforts that the poem can provide in winter, or work with small groups to have students participate while you highlight them together.

QUESTION: Guide students to consider what these details might tell them. Ask what a reader can infer from the speaker's advice to wear the poem as winter clothing in cold weather, and accept student responses.

Possible response: The speaker seems to believe that the poem will take the place of a number of items of winter clothing.

CONCLUDE: Help students to formulate conclusions about the importance of these details in the text. Ask students why the author might have included these details.

Possible response: The first stanza introduces the poem's connection to survival. The poet uses figurative language to great comic effect as he introduces the theme—the notion of wearing the poem like a pair of winter socks is clearly absurd. By adding these details so early in the poem, the writer gives himself time to develop his idea of survival and love to a level of urgent necessity.

Additional **English Language Support** is available in the Interactive Teacher's Edition.

CLOSER LOOK

Examine Symbols

Circulate among groups as students conduct their close read. Suggest that groups close read the third stanza. Encourage them to talk about the annotations that they mark. If needed, provide the following support.

ANNOTATE: As students work through the poem, have them mark details with nautical or maritime associations, or work with small groups to have students participate while you highlight them together.

QUESTION: Guide students to consider what these details might tell them. Ask if these details might derive from the speaker's feelings about his daughter, and accept student responses.

Possible response: Wilbur's use of figurative language of nautical origin applies to his daughter's imminent voyage through life. She is young and ready to set sail. The speaker wishes her a "lucky passage."

CONCLUDE: Help students to formulate conclusions about the importance of these details in the text. Ask students why the author might have included these details. What do the "cargo" and the "passage" symbolize, or represent, in the poem? Why does the author use symbols rather than stating the meaning outright?

Possible response: Many of the nautical symbols apply to the daughter's journey, and Wilbur talks of her room "at the prow of the house," her typewriter sounding "like a chain hauled over a gunwale," and he recalls the starling "beating a smooth course" (a sailing term for heading into the wind). By adding these details, the author intends to show how the world is transformed by the prospect of the voyage.

Remind students that **symbols** stand both for themselves and for something beyond themselves. Authors often use them to evoke intense emotion and to convey subtle shades of meaning. Point out that symbols are especially useful in poetry, as the words are all subtly interrelated and depend on one another for precision and dramatic impact.

POETRY

The Writer

Richard Wilbur

SCAN FOR MULTIMEDIA

NOTES

In her room at the prow[1] of the house
Where light breaks, and the windows are tossed with linden,[2]
My daughter is writing a story.

I pause in the stairwell, hearing
From her shut door a commotion of typewriter-keys
Like a chain hauled over a gunwale.[3]

Young as she is, the stuff
Of her life is a great cargo, and some of it heavy:
I wish her a lucky passage.

1. **prow** *n.* front of a ship.
2. **linden** *n.* type of tree with yellowish-white flowers and heart-shaped leaves.
3. **gunwale** (GUH nuhl) *n.* upper edge of a ship's side.

FACILITATING SMALL-GROUP CLOSE READING

CLOSE READ: Poetry As groups perform the close read, circulate and offer support as needed.

- Remind groups that when they read poetry, they should pay particular attention to the figurative language.
- If a group is confused about the poem's meaning, suggest that they consider each word the poet uses and think about every possible meaning the word may have.
- Challenge group members to debate the poem's meaning with one another to develop a deeper understanding about the message.

But now it is she who pauses,
As if to reject my thought and its easy figure.
A stillness greatens, in which

The whole house seems to be thinking,
And then she is at it again with a bunched clamor[4]
Of strokes, and again is silent.

I remember the dazed starling[5]
Which was trapped in that very room, two years ago;
How we stole in, lifted a sash

And retreated, not to affright it;
And how for a helpless hour, through the crack of the door,
We watched the sleek, wild, dark

And **iridescent** creature
Batter against the brilliance, drop like a glove
To the hard floor, or the desk-top,

And wait then, humped and bloody,
For the wits to try it again; and how our spirits
Rose when, suddenly sure,

It lifted off from a chair-back,
Beating a smooth course for the right window
And clearing the sill of the world.

It is always a matter, my darling,
Of life or death, as I had forgotten. I wish
What I wished you before, but harder.

NOTES

Mark familiar word parts or indicate another strategy you used that helped you determine meaning.

iridescent (ihr uh DEHS uhnt) *adj.*

MEANING:

4. **clamor** (KLAM uhr) *n.* loud, continuous noise.
5. **starling** *n.* dark brown or black bird that is common in Europe and the United States.

CROSS-CURRICULAR CONNECTION

Art This poem describes the creative process, as suggested by lines 13–15. Have students interpret the poem through artistic expression. Students can create drawings, collages, or graphic designs that represent the messages Wilbur is trying to convey in "The Writer." As students conduct a gallery walk of the artwork, have them note which pieces they feel best represent the meaning of the poem.

Concept Vocabulary

IRIDESCENT If groups are struggling to define the word *iridescent* in line 22, point out that the word is based on the Latin root *iris,* which means "rainbow." Have students use this root to define the word.

Possible response: *Iridescent* means "rainbow colored, displaying a play of lustrous colors like those of the rainbow."

CLOSER LOOK

Analyze Theme

Circulate among groups as students conduct their close read. Suggest that groups close read the last stanza. Encourage them to talk about the annotations that they mark. If needed, provide the following support.

ANNOTATE: Have students mark details and description in the last stanza that convey the speaker's desolation at the prospect of his daughter leaving home, or work with small groups to have students participate while you highlight them together.

QUESTION: Guide students to consider what these details might tell them. Ask them to look at the last stanza, which identifies the real theme of the poem and sums up the speaker's feelings about it. Ask what "it" refers to in line 31 and accept student responses.

Possible response: The speaker himself says that "it" has always been "a matter of life or death." He therefore intensifies the wish he made for her before. Acknowledging the peril of the enterprise—he has experienced it himself—he wishes her "a lucky passage" once more: "but harder." "It" is therefore the voyage.

CONCLUDE: Help students to formulate conclusions about the importance of these details in the text. Ask students why the author might have included these details.

Possible response: "It" is the voyage: a matter of life or death. By adding these details, the author reveals his underlying theme. The voyage is life, and, to paraphrase the first half of the last stanza, "Life is a battle for survival."

Remind students that the **theme** is what a poem or narrative is really "about." It's the idea that gives depth, structure and meaning to every form of creative writing. In Richard Wilbur's poem, it is "it."

POETRY

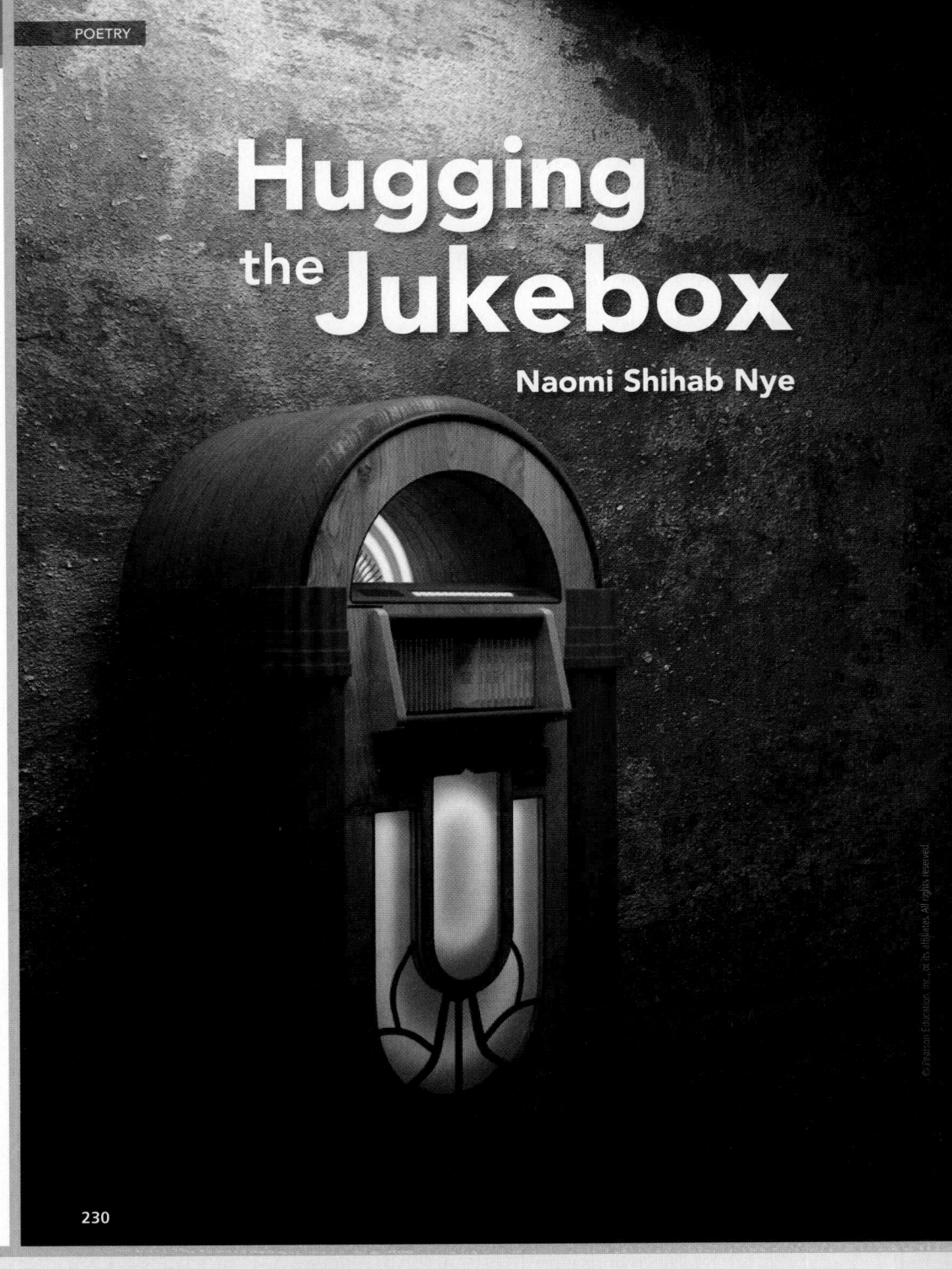

Hugging the Jukebox

Naomi Shihab Nye

PERSONALIZE FOR LEARNING

Challenge

Poetry Readings Poetry readings bring poetry alive, and, through the reader's voice, tempo, and tone, can reveal nuances that might otherwise be overlooked.

Have students select one of the poems in this collection and prepare a reading. Explain to them that in their readings, they should not simply read the words on the page, but think about the relationship among meaning, sound, and rhythm. As students give their readings, ask those who are listening to think about how the different approaches to reading the same poem change the perspective the listener has on the meaning of the poem.

SCAN FOR MULTIMEDIA

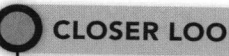

On an island the soft hue of memory,
moss green, kerosene[1] yellow, drifting, mingling
in the Caribbean Sea,
a six-year-old named Alfred
learns all the words to all the songs
on his grandparents' jukebox, and sings them.
To learn the words is not so hard.
Many barmaids and teenagers have done as well.
But to sing as Alfred sings—
how can a giant whale live in the small pool of his chest?
How can there be breakers[2] this high, notes crashing
at the beach of the throat,
and a reef of coral so enormous only the fishes know its size?

The grandparents watch. They can't sing.
They don't know who this voice is, trapped in their grandson's body.
The boy whose parents sent him back to the island
to chatter mango-talk and scrap with chickens—
three years ago he didn't know the word "sad"!
Now he strings a hundred passionate sentences on a single line.
He bangs his fist so they will raise the volume.

What will they do together in their old age?
It is hard enough keeping yourself alive.
And this wild boy, loving nothing but music—
he'll sing all night, hugging the jukebox.
When a record pauses, that live second before dropping down,
Alfred hugs tighter, arms stretched wide
head pressed on the **luminous** belly. "Now!" he yells.
A half-smile when the needle breathes again.

They've tried putting him to bed, but he sings in bed.
Even in Spanish—and he doesn't speak Spanish!
Sings and screams, wants to go back to the jukebox.
O mama I was born with a trumpet in my throat
spent all these years tryin' to cough it up . . .

He can't even read yet. He can't *tell time.*
But he sings, and the chairs in this old dance hall jerk to attention.
The grandparents lean on the counter, shaking their heads.
The customers stop talking and stare, goosey bumps[3] surfacing on
their arms.

NOTES

Mark familiar word parts or indicate another strategy you used that helped you determine meaning.

luminous (LOO muh nuhs) *adj.*

MEANING:

1. **kerosene** (KEHR uh seen) *n.* type of oil that is burned as fuel.
2. **breakers** *n.* waves that break into foam when they hit the shore.
3. **goosey bumps** variation of *goose bumps*, small bumps on the skin caused by cold, fear, or sudden excitement.

DIGITAL PERSPECTIVES

Concept Vocabulary

LUMINOUS If groups are struggling to define the word *luminous* in line 27, point out that they can use the root *–lum–,* which means "light." Have students use this root to define the word.

Possible response: *Luminous* means "shining, radiating light."

CLOSER LOOK

Analyze Figurative Language

Circulate among groups as students conduct their close read. Suggest that groups close read the fifth stanza. Encourage them to talk about the annotations that they mark. If needed, provide the following support.

ANNOTATE: Have students mark an example of figurative language in lines 34–38, or work with small groups to have students participate while you highlight it together.

QUESTION: Guide students to consider what these details might tell them. Ask what two images are linked in the example. Ask how the figure of speech works, and accept student responses.

Possible response: *Chairs in this old dance hall jerk to attention* links the chairs to their occupants. Clearly, it's not the chairs but the people who jerk to attention: "The people sitting around this old dance hall jerk to attention." That doesn't work. It needs the chairs—but does the original figure of speech work because we visualize empty chairs jerking to attention? Obviously we don't. It works as we hear it, and not as we see it.

CONCLUDE: Help students to formulate conclusions about the importance of these details in the text. Ask students why the author might have included these details.

Possible response: The example appears to report fact: Alfred's voice casts a spell—which is interrupted by chairs scraping as their occupants jerk to attention. The chairs *sound* empty because their occupants *are* stunned into silence. It's only a short step to say they *are* empty—and a figure of speech gives Alfred the power to move objects with his mind.

Remind students that **figurative language** is language that is not meant to be read literally. Instead, it helps poets make comparisons that ask readers to think of people, actions, objects, or ideas in fresh ways.

FACILITATING

Comprehension Check

I Am Offering This Poem

Possible responses:

1. The speaker has "nothing else to give."
2. The author feels the poem will protect the subject of the poem from the cold, warm the subject's belly in winter, tie up the subject's hair, summon the poet, and offer love.
3. The speaker repeats the phrase "I love you."

NOTES

His voice carries out to the water where boats are tied
and sings for all of them, *a wave.*
For the hens, now roosting in trees,
for the mute boy next door, his second-best friend.
And for the hurricane, now brewing near Barbados[4]—
a week forward neighbors will be hammering boards over their
windows,
rounding up dogs and fishing lines,
the generators will quit with solemn clicks in every yard.

But Alfred, hugging a sleeping jukebox, the names of the tunes gone
dark,
will still be singing, doubly loud now, teasing his grandmother,
"Put a coin in my mouth!" and believing what she wants to believe;
this is not the end of the island, or the tablets this life has been
scribbled on, or the song.

Utila,[5] Honduras

4. **Barbados** (bahr BAY dohs) island nation in the southeastern Caribbean Sea.
5. **Utila** (OO tee lah) smallest of the Bay Islands of Honduras.

Comprehension Check

Complete the following items after you finish your first read. Review and clarify details with your group.

I AM OFFERING THIS POEM

1. Why does the speaker offer the poem to the reader rather than some other gift?

2. What are some of the benefits that the speaker hopes the poem will have for the reader?

3. What phrase does the speaker repeat at the end of every stanza?

THE WRITER

1. Early in the poem, what sound does the speaker hear?

2. What memory of a starling does the speaker describe?

3. What wish for the daughter does the speaker express twice?

HUGGING THE JUKEBOX

1. What three things does the speaker say Alfred cannot do? What remarkable thing can Alfred do?

2. According to the speaker, what will Alfred continue to do during the upcoming hurricane?

RESEARCH

Research to Clarify Choose at least one unfamiliar detail from one of the poems. Briefly research that detail. In what way does the information you learned shed light on an aspect of the poem?

DIGITAL PERSPECTIVES

Comprehension Check

The Writer

1. The speaker hears the sound of his daughter typing on a typewriter.
2. The speaker describes a time when a starling was trapped in the room in which his daughter is now typing.
3. The speaker wishes that his daughter might have a "lucky passage."

Hugging the Jukebox

1. Alfred cannot read, tell time, or stop singing. He knows all the words to all the songs on his grandparents' jukebox.
2. Alfred will continue to sing during the hurricane.

Research

Research to Clarify If students struggle to come up with an unfamiliar detail, have them reread the poems and notice an idea or concept that might be new to them, such as hogans or jukeboxes.

PERSONALIZE FOR LEARNING

Challenge

Writing a Poem Invite students to write their own poem, based on one of these three. Students can change the point of view; for instance, they might write as the recipient of the poem in "I Am Offering This Poem," or as the daughter in "The Writer." Or, they can take the situation in "Hugging the Jukebox" and extend it into the future, showing what Alfred's life will be like when he is an adult. Encourage students to use symbols and figures of speech, as the poets do. As students share their poems, guide listeners to identify the themes and poetic techniques.

Jump Start

CLOSE READ Engage students in a discussion about what makes poetry a unique way of addressing the concept of survival. What is different about the way poetry affects the reader? How is the type of survival that these authors address different from that of other selections in the unit?

Close Read the Text

If needed, model close reading by using the Annotation Highlights in the Interactive Teacher's Edition.

Remind groups to use Accountable Talk in their discussions and to support one another as they complete the close read.

Analyze the Text

1. **Possible response:** A person carries his or her cargo in his or her memory, but also in his or her heart. "Heavy" cargo can be experiences that have a deep impact on the person directly, such as loss, love, heartbreak, betrayal, or disappointment.
2. **Possible response:** Passages will vary by group. Remind students to explain why they chose the passage they shared with the group members.
3. Responses will vary by group.

Concept Vocabulary

Why These Words? Possible response: The words are related by their ability to catch the light or shine. Both *iridescent* and *luminous* may be related to a bright spot or hope in an otherwise difficult situation. Another word that fits the category is *brilliant.*

Practice

Possible responses:

- MacKenzie will always *treasure* her prized sea glass collection.
- Opals are *iridescent* gemstones.
- His watch had a *luminous* dial.
- Things that are *iridescent* or *luminous* are shiny or bright and emit or reflect light.

Word Network

Possible words: lost, bloody, trapped

Word Study

For more support, see **Concept Vocabulary and Word Study.**

Possible words: *illuminate* (light up); *luminary* (an inspirational or influential person); *luminescence* (the emission of light from sources other than heat)

MAKING MEANING

POETRY COLLECTION

Close Read the Text

With your group, revisit sections of the text you marked during your first read. **Annotate** details that you notice. What **questions** do you have? What can you **conclude**?

ANNOTATE · QUESTION · Close Read · CONCLUDE

TIP

GROUP DISCUSSION

Keep in mind that personal experience can affect how a reader perceives a poem. Be aware and supportive of the impressions of others as your group discusses the poetry.

Analyze the Text

CITE TEXTUAL EVIDENCE to support your answers.

Notebook Complete the activities.

1. **Review and Clarify** With your group, reread stanza 3 (lines 7–9) of "The Writer." Discuss the idea of the "cargo" of life. Where does a person carry his or her cargo? What does the speaker mean when saying some of the cargo can be heavy?
2. **Present and Discuss** Now work with your group to share key passages from "Hugging the Jukebox" and "I Am Offering This Poem." Why did you choose these passages? Take turns presenting your passages. Discuss what you notice in the text, what questions you asked, and what conclusions you reached.
3. **Essential Question:** ***What does it take to survive?*** What do these poems reveal about the idea of survival? Discuss with your group.

LANGUAGE DEVELOPMENT

Concept Vocabulary

treasure	iridescent	luminous

Why These Words? The concept vocabulary words from the poems are related. With your group, determine what the words have in common. Write your ideas and add another word that fits the category.

WORD NETWORK

Add interesting words related to survival from the text to your Word Network.

Practice

Notebook Confirm your understanding of each vocabulary word by answering this question: What are the qualities of something that is *iridescent* or *luminous*?

STANDARDS

Reading Literature

Determine a theme or central idea of a text and analyze in detail its development over the course of the text, including how it emerges and is shaped and refined by specific details; provide an objective summary of the text.

Language

Identify and correctly use patterns of word changes that indicate different meanings or parts of speech.

Word Study

Latin Root: *-lum-* In "Hugging the Jukebox," the author refers to the jukebox as having a *luminous* belly. The word *luminous* was formed from the Latin root *-lum-*, which means "light." Find several other words that contain this root. Record the words and their meanings.

FORMATIVE ASSESSMENT

Analyze the Text

If students struggle to close read the text, **then** provide the **Poetry Collection: Text Questions** available online in the Interactive Teacher's Edition or Unit Resources. Answers and DOK levels are also available.

Concept Vocabulary

If students struggle to identify the concept, **then** discuss the words in more detail, emphasizing the qualities of things that can be described by the words.

Word Study

If students fail to identify other words, **then** suggest they use a dictionary to browse words that begin with *-lum-*.

Word Study: Latin Root *-lum-* (RP).

Analyze Craft and Structure

Development of Theme The **theme** of a poem is the central idea, message, or insight it expresses. In most poems, the theme is not stated directly. Instead, it is suggested through details and poetic elements. In some poems, the poet uses a central symbol to help develop a theme. A **symbol** is anything—an object, a person, an animal, a place, or an image—that has its own meaning, but also stands for something larger than itself, usually an abstract idea.

Practice

CITE TEXTUAL EVIDENCE to support your answers.

Working independently, use the chart to analyze how the poets use symbols to develop the themes of these poems. Gather your notes and then share with your group.

SYMBOL: The poem in "I Am Offering This Poem"
What details does the speaker use to describe the poem? a. See possible responses in Teacher's Edition.
What does the poem represent to the speaker? b.
What is the poem's theme? How does the symbol help develop that theme? c.
SYMBOL: The starling in "The Writer"
What details describe the starling? d.
What does the starling represent to the speaker? e.
What is the poem's theme? How does the use of the symbol help develop the theme? f.
SYMBOL: Alfred's voice in "Hugging the Jukebox"
What details describe Alfred's voice? g.
What does Alfred's voice represent to the speaker? h.
What is the poem's theme? How does the symbol help develop the theme? i.

PERSONALIZE FOR LEARNING

Strategic Support

Theme Students may require support to identify the theme of a poem because it is typically implied rather than explicitly stated. Remind students that a poem's theme is not the topic of the poem, but rather the "big idea" about life that the author is trying to convey. Have students create T-charts, with one side for identifying the theme, and the other for recording details that prove the theme. If students continue to need support, have them identify important details from the poem and ask them to think about how these details relate to one another.

DIGITAL PERSPECTIVES

Analyze Craft and Structure

Development of Theme Engage students in a discussion about symbolism in their lives. Discuss how symbols can convey very deep sentiments quickly, without using a lot of words. What makes symbolism so important in poetry? How is it different from the use of symbolism in prose? For more support, see **Analyze Craft and Structure: Development of Theme**.

MAKE IT INTERACTIVE

Choose an image that is easily recognizable as a symbol of something of importance to your students and project it to the class. Ask students to take a minute to write down what the symbol means to them. Then, ask students to discuss in their groups similarities or differences in their interpretation of the symbol.

Possible responses:

a. warm coat, pair of thick socks, pot full of yellow corn, scarf, directions for someone lost

b. The poem represents a treasure.

c. The poem is shown to be needed for survival. One possible theme is that feeling secure and loved is just as important as being warm, well-fed, and protected.

d. dazed, frightened, helpless, sleek, wild, dark, iridescent

e. The starling represents the daughter's struggle to break free and express herself.

f. The theme of the poem is the need to express oneself. Although the starling flails away, it eventually finds the window and breaks free.

g. a giant whale living in a small pool, high breakers crashing at the beach, a reef of coral so big only fishes know its size

h. Alfred's voice represents the joy of life.

i. The theme of the poem is joy. Alfred's singing shows that life is a joyful experience if you allow it to be.

FORMATIVE ASSESSMENT

Analyze Craft and Structure

If students are unable to identify what the symbols represent, **then** have them think about the people, places, or things that the symbols are identified with. For Reteach and Practice, see **Analyze Craft and Structure: Development of Theme (RP).**

FACILITATING

Author's Style

Figurative Language Ask students to describe figurative language in their own words. Remind them that sometimes we use figures of speech to illustrate a point. For more support, see **Author's Style: Figurative Language.**

Read It

Possible responses:

a. simile

b. a poem to socks

c. It suggests that the "truth" in a poem will keep you "warm."

d. metaphor

e. a house to a ship

f. It suggests that life is a journey.

g. metaphor

h. Alfred's voice to a whale

i. It tells you that Alfred's voice is powerful.

Write It

Possible responses:

1. To Alfred, the jukebox is as colorful as a holiday festival. (simile)
2. In "The Writer," the sound of typewriter keys is a crackling fire. (metaphor)
3. In "I Am Offering This Poem," the individual words of a poem are as important as the ingredients in a cake. (simile)

FORMATIVE ASSESSMENT

Author's Style

If students struggle to create metaphors and similes, **then** ask them to consider what the examples could be compared to. For Reteach and Practice, see **Author's Style: Figurative Language. (RP)**

LANGUAGE DEVELOPMENT

Author's Style

Figurative Language Poets often use figurative language, or language that is not meant to be taken literally. Most figurative language points out a striking similarity between dissimilar things. Through these unexpected comparisons, poets help readers see familiar experiences or objects in a fresh new light. Metaphors and similes are two types of figurative language.

Metaphor: A figure of speech in which one thing is spoken of as though it were something else.
Examples: "The clouds are a thick blanket" or "My couch is a rock."

Simile: A figure of speech in which the words *like* or *as* are used to compare two seemingly dissimilar things.
Examples: "The clouds are as comforting as a thick blanket" or "My couch is like a rock."

Read It

Work individually. Use this chart to identify and analyze metaphors and similes from the poems. Then gather as a group to discuss your responses.

PASSAGE	METAPHOR OR SIMILE	WHAT IT COMPARES	HOW IT ADDS MEANING
Keep it . . . / . . . like a pair of thick socks / the cold cannot bite through. (I Am Offering This Poem, line 5)	**a.** See possible responses in Teacher's Edition.	**b.**	**c.**
In her room at the prow of the house . . . (The Writer, line 1)	**d.**	**e.**	**f.**
. . . how can a giant whale live in the small pool of his chest? (Hugging the Jukebox, line 10)	**g.**	**h.**	**i.**

Write It

Complete each sentence. Write in words and phrases to create a metaphor or a simile. Be as imaginative as possible in your writing. Identify each comparison you write as a metaphor or a simile.

1. To Alfred, the jukebox is ______________________________.
2. In "The Writer," the sound of typewriter keys ______________________________.
3. In "I Am Offering This Poem," the individual words of a poem are ______________________________.

STANDARDS

Reading Literature
Determine the meaning of words and phrases as they are used in the text, including figurative and connotative meanings; analyze the cumulative impact of specific word choices on meaning and tone.

Language
Demonstrate understanding of figurative language, word relationships, and nuances in word meanings.

PERSONALIZE FOR LEARNING

English Language Support

Figurative Language Support English Learners in analyzing how an author uses figurative language to achieve different effects. Have students write a paragraph explaining the metaphor of a whale in the boy's chest in "Hugging the Jukebox" (line 10). Ensure that they describe the effect or added meaning of the line. **EMERGING**

Have students write a paragraph comparing the metaphor of a whale in the boy's chest (line 10) with a more mundane version of the line, such as "How can such a powerful voice come from such a small boy?" Make sure students explain how the metaphor creates interest and adds meaning. **EXPANDING**

Have students write a few paragraphs about the cumulative impact of several metaphors regarding the boy's voice. **BRIDGING**

An expanded **English Language Support Lesson** on Figurative Language is available in the Interactive Teacher's Edition.

Speaking and Listening

Assignment

Create an **oral presentation** of the poem of your choice. When delivering your presentation, pay close attention to your eye contact, body language, pronunciation, tone, speaking rate, and voice modulation. Choose from the following options.

- ☐ **Theater Production** Perform one of the poems as a theater production that might include music, sound effects, costumes, stage props, and images. Dramatize the poem, using techniques such as alternating speakers and acting out the images in the poem. Aim to make your production convey the true meaning of the poem to the audience.
- ☐ **Video Presentation** Choose your favorite poem and create a brief, entertaining video in which your group performs the poem.
- ☐ **Discussion and Presentation** In "The Writer," the author says, "It is always a matter of life and death." With your group, discuss the following questions:
  - What is the "it" to which the speaker of Wilbur's poem refers—what is "always a matter of life and death"?
  - What might always be a matter of life and death for the speakers of the other two poems?
  - Organize notes from the discussion into a brief presentation to share with the class.

Discussion Plan If you choose the discussion, make decisions about who the participants will be and which question each student will discuss. Write out a list of at least five discussion questions, including the ones provided.

Presentation Plan Before you begin the theater production or video presentation, make decisions about things such as the order of speakers, the music, props, images, costumes, and other items that might be needed. Create a written outline that provides that information for all members of the group. Then, gather the items and materials that you will need. Use this chart to organize your ideas.

POEM STANZA	READER(S)	MUSIC/SOUND	PROPS, COSTUMES, IMAGES	PLAN
1–2				
3				
4				

EVIDENCE LOG

Before moving on to a new selection, go to your Evidence Log and record what you learned from "I Am Offering This Poem," "The Writer," and "Hugging the Jukebox."

STANDARDS

Speaking and Listening
- Come to discussions prepared, having read and researched material under study; explicitly draw on that preparation by referring to evidence from texts and other research on the topic or issue to stimulate a thoughtful, well-reasoned exchange of ideas.
- Work with peers to set rules for collegial discussions and decision-making, clear goals and deadlines, and individual roles as needed.
- Adapt speech to a variety of contexts and tasks, demonstrating command of formal English when indicated or appropriate.

Language
Interpret figures of speech in context and analyze their role in the text.

DIGITAL PERSPECTIVES

Speaking and Listening

Assignment If groups have trouble deciding which type of presentation to do, encourage them to consider which option plays to their group's strengths the most. For example, if the group is tech savvy, the video presentation might be the best option. Remind them that no matter which option they choose, all group members should participate in the oral presentation.

Discussion Plan Ensure that all group members have a role during the group's discussion. Suggest that group members not directly discussing a question take a supporting role, such as discussion moderator.

Presentation Plan Remind groups to consult the schedule for Small-Group activities as they create their Project Plan. Check to make sure each group has made assignments and that the work is divided evenly among group members. For more support, see **Speaking and Listening: Oral Presentation.**

Evidence Log Support students in completing their Evidence Log. This paced activity will help prepare them for the Performance-Based Assessment at the end of the unit.

FORMATIVE ASSESSMENT

Speaking and Listening

If groups struggle to create meaningful presentations, **then** review one stanza of each poem, asking students to think about the best option for sharing their insights with the class. For Reteach and Practice, see **Speaking and Listening: Oral Presentation (RP).**

Selection Test

Administer the "Poetry Collection" Selection Test, which is available in both print and digital formats online in Assessments.

FACILITATING

Present an Argument

Assignment Before groups begin work on their projects, have them clearly differentiate the role each group member will play. Remind groups to consult the schedule for Small-Group Learning to guide their work during the Performance Task.

Students should complete the assignment using presentation software to take advantage of text, graphics, and sound features.

Plan With Your Group

Analyze the Text Students should understand that even though one text may provide the majority of the evidence to support the type of strength they choose, it is likely that all of the texts contain some evidence to support their position. Students can potentially use this evidence as a basis for addressing counterclaims.

Remind groups that in addition to evidence from the readings, they might also include facts, statistics, anecdotes, quotations from authorities, or examples to support their argument. Groups should provide citations for any evidence they use, including media. They may also choose to paraphrase complex ideas from sources in order to clarify their evidence.

Gather Evidence and Media Examples Suggest that groups brainstorm about what to look for as they search for media to represent different types of strength: athletes, warriors, superheroes (physical), world leaders, well-known local political figures, historical figures who display wealth (economic), social-change leaders, spiritual leaders (emotional). Explain that while students may find many media examples, they'll want to use the ones that will be most strategic for their presentation.

PERFORMANCE TASK: SPEAKING AND LISTENING FOCUS

SOURCES

- THE VOYAGE OF THE *JAMES CAIRD*
- THE *ENDURANCE* AND THE *JAMES CAIRD* IN IMAGES
- *from* LIFE OF PI
- THE VALUE OF A SHERPA LIFE
- I AM OFFERING THIS POEM
- THE WRITER
- HUGGING THE JUKEBOX

Present an Argument

Assignment

You have read about people who showed different types of strength as they struggled to survive in life-or-death situations. Work with your group to develop and refine a multimedia presentation about emergency situations to present to a school or civic group. Your presentation should present an argument that addresses the following question:

What type of strength is most valuable in a survival situation?

Plan With Your Group

Analyze the Text With your group, discuss the various types of strength—such as physical and emotional strength—that factor into the survival stories you have read. Use the chart to list your ideas. For each selection, identify the type of strength that plays the most vital role. Then, come to a consensus about which type of strength your group believes is most valuable.

TITLE	TYPES OF STRENGTH
The Voyage of the *James Caird*	
The *Endurance* and the *James Caird* in Images	
from Life of Pi	
The Value of a Sherpa Life	
I Am Offering This Poem The Writer Hugging the Jukebox	
Most Valuable Type of Strength:	

Gather Evidence and Media Examples Scan the selections to record specific examples that support your group's claim. Then, brainstorm for types of media you can use to illustrate or elaborate on each example. Consider photographs, illustrations, music, charts, graphs, and video clips. Allow each group member to make suggestions. Keep your purpose and audience directly in mind while choosing media.

STANDARDS

Speaking and Listening
Present information, findings, and supporting evidence clearly, concisely, and logically such that listeners can follow the line of reasoning and the organization, development, substance, and style are appropriate to purpose, audience, and task.

AUTHOR'S PERSPECTIVE **Ernest Morrell, Ph.D.**

Strategic Use of Media Media is becoming more important as a communication tool, but teachers need to guide students to understand media's value. As groups plan their presentation, remind them that it is important to use media and visuals strategically so that they support the presentation but don't dominate it. Share these suggestions:

- Students should ensure that each piece of media has a specific purpose and is not mere "filler."
- Encourage students to let the content of their argument drive their decisions about which media support to include, rather than finding appealing media and trying to force it into a presentation where it might not work.
- Remind groups that although media and visuals can enhance a presentation, the content of what students say during the presentation is what is most important.

Ultimately, the presentation should be able to stand alone without media support and still make sense.

Organize Your Ideas Use a chart like this one to organize your script. Assign roles for each part of the presentation, note when each part begins, and record what the presenter will say.

MULTIMEDIA PRESENTATION SCRIPT		
	Media Cues	Script
Presenter 1		
Presenter 2		
Presenter 3		

Rehearse With Your Group

Practice With Your Group Use this checklist to evaluate the effectiveness of your group's first run-through. Then, use your evaluation and the instructions here to guide your revision.

CONTENT	USE OF MEDIA	PRESENTATION TECHNIQUES
☐ The presentation presents a clear thesis. ☐ Main ideas are supported with evidence from the texts in Small-Group Learning.	☐ The media support the thesis. ☐ The media communicate key ideas. ☐ Media are used evenly throughout the presentation. ☐ Equipment functions properly.	☐ Media are visible and audible. ☐ Transitions between media segments are smooth. ☐ The speaker uses eye contact and speaks clearly.

Fine-Tune the Content To make your presentation stronger, you may need to go back into the texts to find more support for your ideas. Check with your group to identify key points that are not clear to listeners. Find another way to word these ideas. Remember to always keep your purpose and audience in mind.

- **Purpose:** Because your purpose is to inform your audience about how to behave in an emergency, make sure you address both mental and physical strength.
- **Audience:** If your audience is young children, keep your language and ideas simple and use plenty of visuals. If adults are your audience, don't "talk down" to them.

Improve Your Use of Media If media are not evenly distributed throughout the presentation, work to change the pacing.

Present and Evaluate

When you present as a group, be sure that each member has taken into account each of the checklist items. As you watch other groups, evaluate how well they meet the criteria in the checklist.

STANDARDS
Speaking and Listening
Make strategic use of digital media in presentations to enhance understanding of findings, reasoning, and evidence and to add interest.

DIGITAL PERSPECTIVES

Organize Your Ideas Remind groups that all group members should have an opportunity to speak and that no one member should dominate the presentation.

Rehearse With Your Group

Practice With Your Group Remind students that each group member should practice his or her part ahead of time. Other group members should provide constructive feedback. Rehearsing can help with the timing and flow of the presentation, and can expose any equipment issues that may need to be resolved.

You may wish to pair groups so that they can rehearse their presentations with each other.

Fine-Tune the Content Groups may also use additional media examples to support their main ideas.

Improve Your Use of Media Groups may want to time themselves as they rehearse their presentation to ensure it doesn't run too long or isn't too brief.

MAKE IT INTERACTIVE
Suggest that groups video record their rehearsal and watch together as a strategy for refining their presentation.

Present and Evaluate

Before beginning the presentations, set the expectations for the audience. You may wish to have students consider these questions as groups present.

- What was the presenting group's claim?
- What were some of their supporting ideas?
- Which multimedia best illustrated their claim?
- What presentation skills did this group excel at?

As students provide feedback to the presenting group, remind them that compliments are just as valuable as constructive criticism.

PERSONALIZE FOR LEARNING

Strategic Support

Understanding Evidence Some groups may require more time to complete the planning process. Be prepared to assist these students in understanding why their evidence represents a specific type of strength. Use key words such as *because* and *therefore* as you model for students.

- *I think physical strength plays the most vital role for Sherpas* **because** *they have to carry heavy 80-pound loads as they climb Mount Everest.*
- *Being stranded at sea involves enduring long periods of solitude;* **therefore**, *I think emotional strength is most vital to survive.*

OVERVIEW

INDEPENDENT LEARNING

What does it take to survive?

Encourage students to think carefully about what they have already learned and what more they want to know about the unit topic of survival. This is a key first step to previewing and selecting the text they will read in Independent Learning.

Independent Learning Strategies

Review the Learning Strategies with students and explain that as they work through Independent Learning they will develop strategies to work on their own.

- Have students watch the video on Independent Learning Strategies.
- A video on this topic is available online in the Professional Development Center.

Students should include any favorite strategies that they might have devised on their own during the Whole-Class and Small-Group Learning. For example, for the strategy "Create a schedule," students might include:

- Review my plan at the end of each day.
- Remain flexible and make adjustments as needed.

Block Scheduling

Each day in this Pacing Plan represents a 40–50 minute class period. Teachers using block scheduling may combine days to reflect their class schedule. In addition, teachers may revise pacing to differentiate and support core instruction by integrating components and resources as students require.

OVERVIEW: INDEPENDENT LEARNING

ESSENTIAL QUESTION:

What does it take to survive?

The ways in which people survive life-or-death situations can be inspiring. In this section, you will complete your study of survival by exploring an additional selection related to the topic. You'll then share what you learn with classmates. To choose a text, follow these steps.

Look Back Think about the selections you have already studied. What more do you want to know about the topic of survival?

Look Ahead Preview the texts by reading the descriptions. Which one seems most interesting and appealing to you?

Look Inside Take a few minutes to scan the text you chose. Choose a different one if this text doesn't meet your needs.

Independent Learning Strategies

Throughout your life, in school, in your community, and in your career, you will need to rely on yourself to learn and work on your own. Review these strategies and the actions you can take to practice them during Independent Learning. Add ideas of your own for each category.

STRATEGY	ACTION PLAN
Create a schedule	• Understand your goals and deadlines. • Make a plan for what to do each day. •
Practice what you have learned	• Use first-read and close-read strategies to deepen your understanding. • Evaluate the usefulness of the evidence to help you understand the topic. • Consider the quality and reliability of the source. •
Take notes	• Record important ideas and information. • Review your notes before preparing to share with a group. •

SCAN FOR MULTIMEDIA

Pacing Plan

Day	Activity
1	Unit Introduction
2	Introduce Whole-Class Learning
3–7	The Seventh Man
8–12	The Moral Logic of Survivor Guilt
13	Media: The Key to Disaster Survival?
14–15	Performance Task

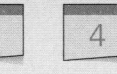

CONTENTS

Choose one selection. Selections are available online only.

SCAN FOR MULTIMEDIA

Contents

Selections Encourage students to scan and preview the selections before choosing the one they would like to read. Suggest that they consider the genre and subject matter of each one before making their decision. You can use the information on the following planning pages to advise students in making their choice.

Remind students that the selections for Independent Learning are available only in the interactive edition of *myPerspectives*™. Allow students who do not have digital access at home to preview the digital selections using classroom or computer lab technology. Then either have students print the selection they choose or provide a printout for them.

Performance-Based Assessment Prep

Review Evidence for an Argument Point out to students that collecting evidence during Independent Learning is the last step in completing their Evidence Log. After they finish their independent reading they will synthesize all the evidence they have compiled in the unit.

The evidence students collect will serve as their primary source of information they will use to complete the writing and oral presentation for the Performance-Based Assessment at the end of the unit.

To Build a Fire

Summary

Jack London's short story, "To Build a Fire," is a tale of survival set in the Yukon region of Canada during the depth of winter. A man is on the long trail back to camp in the frigid cold. He's a newcomer to the Yukon. He has no experience of having to fight for survival in a hostile environment, and doesn't seem to understand the need to learn. His dog, however, knows all about survival. He is a husky, with the instincts of a wolf-dog. Survival is bred into him.

There are springs under the snow that never freeze. When the man sinks up to his knees in water, he lights a big fire to dry out—right under a spruce tree, its branches heavy with snow. As he's getting comfortable, he and his fire are buried under an avalanche of wet snow. His dog knows his way to the camp from here, and trots off to find another fire.

Insight

Reading "To Build a Fire" will help students reflect on the relationship between humans and nature. People, in all their arrogance, think they can outsmart the natural world. But nature is a powerful force, not to be taken lightly. Only those who respect that force will survive it.

SELECTION RESOURCES

- First-Read Guide: Fiction
- Close-Read Guide: Fiction
- To Build a Fire: Text Questions
- Audio Summaries
- Selection Audio
- Selection Test

Connection to Essential Question

"To Build a Fire" will help students answer the Essential Question—*What does it take to survive?*—by showing them that it takes more than strength and knowledge to survive. It takes instinct. The man in the story does not survive, because his overconfidence in his ability to survive the harsh conditions in the Yukon doom him, whereas the dog survives because his natural instincts protect him.

Connection to Performance-Based Assessment

This selection has an interesting take on the question of people's accountability in life-or-death situations. The man tries but fails to kill his dog in order to survive. If he had been successful, would his actions have been justified?

Text Complexity Rubric: To Build a Fire

Quantitative Measures	
Lexile: 970 **Text Length:** 7,099 words	
Qualitative Measures	
Knowledge Demands ①—❷—③—④—⑤	Students will lack prior knowledge of the situation (a man freezing to death in wilderness), but the experience is explained graphically.
Structure ①—②—❸—④—⑤	Plot follows a straightforward, linear structure. Events are described in sequence. Paragraphs are long and not broken up with any dialogue.
Language Conventionality and Clarity ①—②—③—❹—⑤	The story has multiple instances of above-level vocabulary, unconventional descriptions, and a lot of figurative language. Sentence structure can be difficult to understand.
Levels of Meaning/Purpose ①—②—③—❹—⑤	The main events are clear, but there are sophisticated themes and levels of meaning. The man's actions can be seen through the dog's eyes, which allows for generalizations about people, nature, behavior, instinct, and the wisdom needed for survival.

DIGITAL PERSPECTIVES

Audio | Video | Document | Annotation Highlights | EL Highlights | Online Assessment

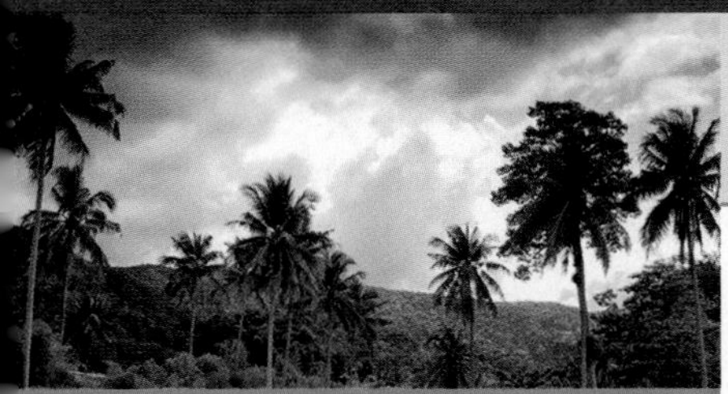

SELECTION RESOURCES

- First-Read Guide: Fiction
- Close-Read Guide: Fiction
- The Most Dangerous Game: Text Questions
- Audio Summaries
- Selection Audio
- Selection Test

The Most Dangerous Game

Summary

In "The Most Dangerous Game" by Richard Connell, Sanger Rainsford, a famous big-game hunter, falls overboard from a yacht while cruising in the Caribbean. He is a strong swimmer and takes refuge on a nearby island. The island is the private domain of General Zaroff, a sinister European aristocrat. Zaroff, too, is a fanatical hunter, and he is familiar with Rainsford's reputation. He invites Rainsford to be his guest in his grand house up in the hills. Zaroff tells Rainsford that he has become bored with hunting animals because they present no real opposition. Zaroff can't lose because humans have cunning, courage, and reason, while animals have only instinct. He has come to this island to hunt the only prey that can match his own abilities.

Insight

The survival instinct is extremely powerful. Reading "The Most Dangerous Game" will help students see that humans are capable of almost anything when their survival is threatened. When people are pushed to the brink, their animal side emerges and the strictures of civilization become meaningless.

Some students may require support when faced with the idea of humans hunting humans. They may also be disturbed by the question of which side of Rainsford impels him to kill Zaroff—his instinctive animal side or his reasoning human side.

Connection to Essential Question

"The Most Dangerous Game" will help students answer the Essential Question—*What does it take to survive?*—by demonstrating that in certain circumstances survival requires the melding of human reasoning and animal instinct. Sanger Rainsford, who values his human primacy over animals, is forced to accept his primeval animal nature before he can beat the truly animalistic General Zaroff.

Connection to Performance-Based Assessment

The selection provides a surprising perspective on the question of people's accountability in life-or-death situations. This is the first selection in the unit in which the life-or-death situation results in the murder of a human being. Are Rainsford's actions justified? Does he have any other choice?

Text Complexity Rubric: The Most Dangerous Game

Quantitative Measures	
Lexile: 740 **Text Length:** 8,001 words	
Qualitative Measures	
Knowledge Demands 1 — **2** — 3 — 4 — 5	Some situations (falling off yacht, swimming to island, being hunted) will be unfamiliar, but they are clearly explained.
Structure 1 — **2** — 3 — 4 — 5	Straightforward, linear story. Frequent use of dialogue makes the story sequences mostly easy to understand.
Language Conventionality and Clarity 1 — **2** — 3 — 4 — 5	Syntax includes some complex sentences; there is some above-level vocabulary; conversational language is used throughout because there is a lot of dialogue.
Levels of Meaning/Purpose 1 — 2 — **3** — 4 — 5	Meaning is not always explicit. In many parts of the story, the reader must infer meaning and plot elements from clues.

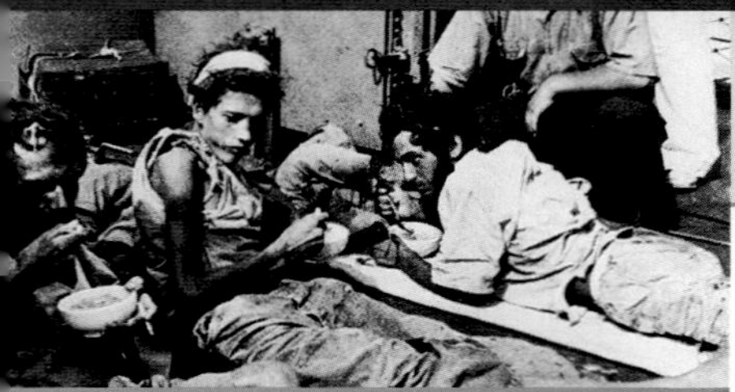

SELECTION RESOURCES

- First-Read Guide: Nonfiction
- Close-Read Guide: Nonfiction
- Unbroken: Text Questions
- Audio Summaries
- Selection Audio
- Selection Test

from Unbroken

Summary

This excerpt from *Unbroken* by Laura Hillenbrand chronicles nineteen days in the lives of three crew members of an American bomber plane, shot down over the southeast Pacific in World War II. When we first encounter them, Louie, Mac, and Phil have been adrift for twenty-seven days in two small inflatable rafts that they have tied together. Attacked repeatedly by gunfire from an enemy aircraft and sharks and deprived of food and fresh water, their survival is made possible by courage, cooperation, incredible luck, and extraordinary self-sacrifice.

Insight

Survivors never give up. Reading this excerpt from *Unbroken* will help students reflect on the astounding tenacity that people throughout history have been forced to find within themselves so that they could survive life-or-death situations.

Connection to Essential Question

This excerpt from *Unbroken* will help students answer the Essential Question—*What does it take to survive?*—by illustrating that when the survival of more than one person is at stake, perseverance and teamwork are essential. There's no question that Louie's ingenuity and his refusal to give up help to keep him and Phil alive, but the text also makes it clear that without the combined efforts of the three men they all would have died.

Connection to Performance-Based Assessment

The selection raises a difficult question about whether people in life-or-death situations should be held accountable for their actions. Phil refuses to give a dying Mac a sip of his precious water. It is clear that Mac understands Phil's choice, but the question remains for students to consider.

Text Complexity Rubric: *from* Unbroken	
Quantitative Measures	
Lexile: 910 **Text Length:** 6,204 words	
Qualitative Measures	
Knowledge Demands ① ② ❸ ④ ⑤	Story assumes knowledge of aspects of war (World War II) such as bombers, gunners, and means of survival (flares, rafts); main situation (survival from sharks) is unfamiliar to most, but clear explanations and context clues are provided.
Structure ① ❷ ③ ④ ⑤	Straightforward, linear story; plot events are told sequentially; no dialogue is included.
Language Conventionality and Clarity ① ② ❸ ④ ⑤	Vocabulary and syntax are generally simple, with some difficult words or sentences (vocabulary related to war, survival gear); some figurative language is used (metaphors, similes).
Levels of Meaning/Purpose ① ❷ ③ ④ ⑤	Straightforward purpose (to describe survival experience); theme is clear but with some subtlety at times (emotions of men are inferred rather than explicit).

DIGITAL PERSPECTIVES
Audio | Video | Document | Annotation Highlights | EL Highlights | Online Assessment

Seven Steps to Surviving a Disaster

Summary

In his "Seven Steps to Surviving a Disaster," President of the World Bank Group Jim Yong Kim proposes a series of policies that he believes would alleviate the human suffering and calamitous damage caused by natural disasters. Kim believes the potential for full-scale catastrophe is intensified by climate change and booming urbanization, but intends his seven steps to be simple, practical, and easy to put into effect on a personal, local, and national level. Kim stresses that these steps are not designed to prevent natural disasters, but to prevent some of the catastrophic but avoidable destruction that is so often the consequence of natural disasters.

Insight

Entire nations face the possibility that they might not survive a disaster intact. Reading "Seven Steps to Surviving a Disaster" will help students reflect on the issue of global survival and on what it means to rely on policies and politicians to stay safe.

SELECTION RESOURCES

- First-Read Guide: Nonfiction
- Close-Read Guide: Nonfiction
- Seven Steps to Surviving a Disaster: Text Questions
- Audio Summaries
- Selection Audio
- Selection Test

Connection to Essential Question

"Seven Steps to Surviving a Disaster" will help students answer the Essential Question—*What does it take to survive?*—by showing them that surviving large-scale disasters requires large-scale planning and action. The steps make it clear that governments need to become resilient so they can anticipate and prepare for the risks of natural disasters in order to ensure the greatest number of survivors.

Connection to Performance-Based Assessment

The selection provides a twist on the question of *Should people in life-or-death situations be held accountable for their actions?* by presenting preventative steps that can be taken before disaster strikes. Students should consider whether government officials should be held accountable for the actions they take in the face of life-or-death situations.

Text Complexity Rubric: Seven Steps to Surviving a Disaster

Quantitative Measures

Lexile: 1340 **Text Length:** 732 words

Qualitative Measures	
Knowledge Demands: 1 — 2 — **3** — 4 — 5	Students may not have experience with the concepts—natural disasters and survival policies of cities (building codes, political champions, risk assessment). However, clear explanations are given about most information.
Structure: 1 — **2** — 3 — 4 — 5	The selection is very straightforward and information is well organized in a numerical list, making it easy to find information.
Language Conventionality and Clarity: 1 — 2 — **3** — 4 — 5	Includes some above-level vocabulary and long sentences that have multiple clauses.
Levels of Meaning/Purpose: 1 — **2** — 3 — 4 — 5	Concepts in the selection are very straightforward, with only one level of meaning. Main ideas are easy to grasp, though some concepts that support the main idea are complex.

SELECTION RESOURCES

- First-Read Guide: Nonfiction
- Close-Read Guide: Nonfiction
- *Titanic* vs. *Lusitania:* How People Behave in a Disaster: Text Questions
- Audio Summaries
- Selection Audio
- Selection Test

Titanic vs. *Lusitania:* How People Behave in a Disaster

Summary

In his magazine article "*Titanic vs. Lusitania*: How People Behave in a Disaster," Jeffrey Kluger looks into the two greatest maritime disasters of the early twentieth century: the *Titanic* and the *Lusitania*. He asks, Who died, and why? The two ships were alike in many ways: the Titanic was carrying 2,207 passengers and crew; the *Lusitania* held 1,949. 68.7 percent of crew and passengers died on the *Titanic*; the death rate on the Lusitania was 67.3 percent. There the similarities end. The differences between the ways people behaved and treated one another aboard the two stricken ships provide some disturbing insights into the darker side of our nature and the fragility of our codes of civilized conduct.

Insight

Reading "*Titanic* vs. *Lusitania*: How People Behave in a Disaster" will help students consider the behavioral and scientific factors of survival. Although two disasters may seem almost identical, their results may be quite different.

Connection to Essential Question

"*Titanic* vs. *Lusitania*: How People Behave in a Disaster" will help students answer the Essential Question—*What does it take to survive?*—by proving to them that many complex factors affect the possibility of surviving a disaster, including the speed with which the disaster takes hold, social considerations such as class, and the science of biology. Such factors help explain why certain people were survivors or victims when these two famous ships went down.

Connection to Performance-Based Assessment

This selection provides a scientific perspective on the question of whether people in life-or-death situations should be held accountable for their actions. Students have the opportunity to compare the different, scientifically based actions of people who faced similar fates—in one case, actions that amounted to self-sacrifice, and in the other case, actions that contributed to the deaths of others.

Text Complexity Rubric: *Titanic* vs. *Lusitania*: How People Behave in a Disaster

Quantitative Measures	
Lexile: 1240 **Text Length:** 1,048 words	
Qualitative Measures	
Knowledge Demands ①—❷—③—④—⑤	Some knowledge of the *Titanic* and *Lusitania* is helpful, but necessary details of the events are explained sufficiently to understand the selection.
Structure ①—②—❸—④—⑤	Information is presented with clear, straightforward organization, but the amount of information presented without headings, subheadings, or summaries makes it challenging.
Language Conventionality and Clarity ①—②—❸—④—⑤	Selection contains some long, complex sentences with embedded clauses and some above-level vocabulary.
Levels of Meaning/Purpose ①—②—❸—④—⑤	The details explaining the concepts are clearly explained, but the main idea is stated in complex sentences with phrases and metaphors that could be unclear to students.

DIGITAL PERSPECTIVES

Audio | Video | Document | Annotation Highlights | EL Highlights | Online Assessment

SELECTION RESOURCES

- First-Read Guide: Nonfiction
- Close-Read Guide: Nonfiction
- Survival Is Your Own Responsibility: Text Questions
- Audio Summaries
- Selection Audio
- Selection Test

Survival is Your Own Responsibility

Summary

The remote and rugged mountains of Alaska's backcountry draw thousands of climbers every year. In his article "Survival is Your Own Responsibility," retired mountaineering ranger Daryl R. Miller explains that wilderness survival skills used to be a way of life in the backcountry. These days, most travelers to the backcountry have no experience with the hostility of wild nature. Climbers often rely on hi-tech equipment they can't use. Cell-phones give climbers a false impression that rescue is only a call away, which encourages unnecessary risk. Miller proposes a program for climbers designed to prepare them to take responsibility for their own decisions, their own risks, and their own survival.

Insight

Expecting to survive without doing any of the work is foolish. Reading "Survival is Your Own Responsibility" will help students think about survival not as the result of luck or even just brute strength, but as a personal responsibility. Miller is angry at the current trend of irresponsible adventurers. He bemoans the nonchalant attitude that many people have toward hiking in Alaska's backcountry.

Connection to Essential Question

"Survival is Your Own Responsibility" provides an expert's perspective on the Essential Question, "What does it take to survive?" Daryl Miller, a retired mountaineering ranger, is very clear about what he thinks it takes to survive in the backcountry of Alaska, and he holds nothing back as he lays most of the blame for not surviving on the shoulders of the people seeking adventure. For him, survival depends on the knowledge, common sense, preparation, and perseverance of the adventurer.

Connection to Performance Task

Unit Performance-Based Assessment This selection almost directly answers the question students will address in this Unit Performance-Based Assessment: *Should people in life-or-death situations be held accountable for their actions?* Miller thinks the answer is a resounding "Yes." In this selection, a life-or-death situation is something that people should be completely prepared to face. They should anticipate the possibility of danger, know what actions to take and not to take to get out of danger, and use their best judgment to survive. These responsibilities are the ultimate accountability.

Text Complexity Rubric: Survival Is Your Own Responsibility

Quantitative Measures	
Lexile: 1120 **Text Length:** 1119 words	
Qualitative Measures	
Knowledge Demands (1)—(2)—(3)—**(4)**—(5)	Selection explores ideas that may be unfamiliar to many readers (survival in the wilderness), though the ideas are concrete and fully explained.
Structure (1)—**(2)**—(3)—(4)—(5)	Organization is clear and straightforward. Connections among ideas are logical and explicit. Bulleted points at end of piece summarize ideas, making it easier to understand the text.
Language Conventionality and Clarity (1)—(2)—(3)—**(4)**—(5)	Language is dense and complex; style is journalistic and formal, but mixed with personal accounts; many sentences are complex, with multiple clauses, conditional phrases, and difficult vocabulary.
Levels of Meaning/Purpose (1)—**(2)**—(3)—(4)—(5)	Purpose is explicit, clear, concrete, and narrowly focused (exploring factors that affect survival).

ADVISING

You may wish to direct students to use the generic **First-Read** and **Close-Read Guides** in the Print Student Edition. Alternatively, you may wish to print copies of the genre-specific **First-Read** and **Close-Read Guides** for students. These are available online in the Interactive Student Edition or Unit Resources.

FIRST READ

Students should perform the steps of the first read independently:

NOTICE: Students should focus on the basic elements of the text to ensure they understand what is happening.

ANNOTATE: Students should mark any passages they wish to revisit during their close read.

CONNECT: Students should increase their understanding by connecting what they've read to other texts or personal experiences.

RESPOND: Students will write a summary to demonstrate their understanding.

Point out to students that while they will always complete the Respond step at the end of the first read, the other steps will probably happen somewhat concurrently. Remind students that they will revisit their first-read annotations during the close read.

After students have completed the First-Read Guide, you may wish to assign the Text Questions for the selection that are available in the Interactive Teacher's Edition.

Anchor Standards

In the first two sections of the unit, students worked with the whole class and in small groups to gain topical knowledge and greater understanding of the skills required by the anchor standards. In this section, they are asked to work independently, applying what they have learned and demonstrating increased readiness for college and career.

INDEPENDENT LEARNING

First-Read Guide

Tool Kit
First-Read Guide and Model Annotation

Use this page to record your first-read ideas.

Selection Title: ______________________________

NOTICE

NOTICE new information or ideas you learn about the unit topic as you first read this text.

ANNOTATE

ANNOTATE by marking vocabulary and key passages you want to revisit.

NOTICE ANNOTATE First Read CONNECT RESPOND

CONNECT ideas within the selection to other knowledge and the selections you have read.

RESPOND by writing a brief summary of the selection.

CONNECT

RESPOND

STANDARD
Reading Read and comprehend complex literary and informational texts independently and proficiently.

PERSONALIZE FOR LEARNING

Strategic Support
Text Preview To help students who struggle to notice words, passages, and other features that might unlock the meaning of a text, have them first conduct a text preview. Ask them to notice the text title, visuals, captions, headings, or other text features (including text enclosed in quotation marks, words shown in all capital letters, or the use of different type treatments such as italic or bold). Based on their observations, remind students to speculate on the topic or genre of the text and the author's purpose for writing. Have students meet in small groups to share their preview observations and speculations about the text they will read. After their first read, encourage groups to meet again to discuss how their speculations actually fit the content of the text.

Close-Read Guide

Tool Kit
Close-Read Guide and Model Annotation

Use this page to record your close-read ideas.

Selection Title: ______________________________

Close Read the Text

Revisit sections of the text you marked during your first read. Read these sections closely and **annotate** what you notice. Ask yourself **questions** about the text. What can you **conclude?** Write down your ideas.

ANNOTATE · QUESTION · CONCLUDE · Close Read

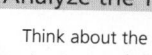

Analyze the Text

Think about the author's choices of patterns, structure, techniques, and ideas included in the text. Select one, and record your thoughts about what this choice conveys.

QuickWrite

Pick a paragraph from the text that grabbed your interest. Explain the power of this passage.

STANDARD
Reading Read and comprehend complex literary and informational texts independently band proficiently.

DIGITAL PERSPECTIVES

CLOSE READ

Students should begin their close read by revisiting the annotations they made during their first read. Then, students should analyze one of the author's choices regarding the following:

- **patterns,** such as repetition or parallelism
- **structure,** such as cause-and-effect or problem-solution
- **techniques,** such as description or dialogue
- **ideas,** such as the author's main idea or claim

MAKE IT INTERACTIVE
Group students according to the selection they have chosen. Then, have students meet to discuss the selection in-depth. Their discussions should be guided by their insights and questions.

PERSONALIZE FOR LEARNING

Strategic Support
Annotations Reinforce the strategies of close reading for students who struggle with its benefits. After they complete the Close-Read Guide, review the experience. Have students choose a first-read annotation that helped them understand the text more deeply during the close read. Discuss the following questions with students:

- How did a revisit of the first-read annotation help you better understand the text during your close read?
- What did you learn about that passage during the close read? What strategies did you use to study the passage you marked?
- What can you conclude about the text, based on the passage you selected?

Ask for student volunteers to discuss how using the First-Read and Close-Read Guides helped them understand the text better.

Share Your Independent Learning

Prepare to Share

Explain to students that sharing what they learned from their Independent Learning selection provides classmates who read a different selection with an opportunity to consider the text as a source of evidence during the Performance-Based Assessment. As students prepare to share, remind them to highlight how their selection contributed to their knowledge of the concept of survival as well as how the selection connects to the question *Should people in life-or-death situations be held accountable for their actions?*

Learn From Your Classmates

As students discuss the Independent Learning selections, direct them to take particular note of how their classmates' chosen selections align with their current position on the Performance-Based Assessment question.

Reflect

Students may want to add their reflection to their Evidence Log, particularly if their insight relates to a specific selection from the unit.

MAKE IT INTERACTIVE

Create a gallery walk of student reflections. Have students write their insight on a blank sheet of paper and arrange the reflections around the room. As students circulate, have them respond to three of the reflections using one of the following sentence starters:

- I agree with your insight and . . .
- I understand your insight, but have you considered . . .?
- I am confused by your insight. Did you mean . . .?

Evidence Log Support students in completing their Evidence Log. This paced activity will help prepare them for the Performance-Based Assessment at the end of the unit.

INDEPENDENT LEARNING

EVIDENCE LOG

Go to your Evidence Log and record what you learned from the text you read.

Share Your Independent Learning

Prepare to Share

What does it take to survive?

Even when you read something independently, your understanding continues to grow when you share what you have learned with others. Reflect on the text you explored independently and write notes about its connection to the unit. In your notes, consider why this text belongs in this unit.

Learn From Your Classmates

Discuss It Share your ideas about the text you explored on your own. As you talk with your classmates, jot down ideas that you learn from them.

Reflect

Review your notes, and underline the most important insight you gained from these writing and discussion activities. Explain how this idea adds to your understanding of the topic of survival.

STANDARDS

Speaking and Listening

Initiate and participate effectively in a range of collaborative discussions with diverse partners on grades 9–10 topics, texts, and issues, building on others' ideas and expressing their own clearly and persuasively.

244 UNIT 2 • SURVIVAL

AUTHOR'S PERSPECTIVE Ernest Morrell, Ph.D.

Active Listening and Learning It's important to support students as they learn and develop the skills of participating in small-group discussions. As students discuss their Independent Learning selection with classmates, remind them that it is important to be an active, but not dominant, participant. Explain that an active participant is one who speaks confidently but also listens carefully to others, while a dominant participant is one who takes over and does not allow others to contribute. Remind students that being an active listener involves these strategies:

- Taking notes (capturing the speaker's main points; noting ideas to contribute once the speaker is done talking)
- Restating others' ideas to show understanding ("This is what I heard you saying. . ."; "I think this is what you meant when you said . . .")
- Asking clarifying questions ("Could you explain what you meant when you said . . .?")

Review Evidence for an Argument

At the beginning of this unit, you took a position on the following question:

Should people in life-or-death situations be held accountable for their actions?

EVIDENCE LOG

Review your Evidence Log and your QuickWrite from the beginning of the unit. Has your position changed?

☐ YES	☐ NO
Identify at least three pieces of evidence that convinced you to change your mind.	Identify at least three pieces of evidence that reinforced your initial position.
1.	1.
2.	2.
3.	3.

State your position now: ____________________

Identify a possible counterclaim: ____________________

Evaluate the Strength of Your Evidence Consider your argument. Do you have enough evidence to support your claim? Do you have enough evidence to refute a counterclaim? If not, make a plan.

- ☐ Do more research
- ☐ Talk with my classmates
- ☐ Reread a selection
- ☐ Ask an expert
- ☐ Other: ____________________

STANDARDS

Writing

Introduce precise claim(s), distinguish the claim(s) from alternate or opposing claims, and create an organization that establishes clear relationships among claim(s), counterclaims, reasons, and evidence.

DIGITAL PERSPECTIVES

Review Evidence for Argument

Evidence Log Students should understand that their position on an issue can evolve as they learn more about the subject and are exposed to additional points of view. Point out that just because they took an initial position on the question *Should people in life-or-death situations be held accountable for their actions?*, doesn't mean that their position can't change after careful consideration of their learning and evidence.

Evaluate the Strength of Your Evidence

Remind students that there are many different types of evidence they can use to support their argument, including:

- facts
- statistics
- anecdotes
- quotations from authorities
- examples

In addition to ensuring they have sufficient evidence to support their claim and address counterclaims, students should evaluate the reliability of their evidence. Discuss the characteristics that make evidence credible:

- reliable sources, including government, educational, and professional organizations
- degree to which experts have reviewed the evidence for accuracy
- credibility of references and confirmation provided by the source of the evidence

ASSESSING

Writing to Sources: Argument

Students should complete the Performance-Based Assessment independently, with little to no input or feedback during the process. Students should use word processing software to take advantage of editing tools and features.

Prior to beginning the Assessment, ask students to think about actions that people in survival situations might need to take that would be considered inappropriate in everyday situations.

Review the Elements of Effective Argument
Students can review the work they did earlier in the unit as they complete the Performance-Based Assessment. They may also consult other resources such as:

- the elements of an effective argument, including language, tone, and grammar, as well as how to organize an argument, available in Whole-Class Learning
- their Evidence Log
- their Word Network

Although students will use evidence from the unit selections for their argument, they may need to collect additional evidence, including facts, statistics, anecdotes, quotations from authorities, or examples that support their position.

PERFORMANCE-BASED ASSESSMENT

SOURCES
- WHOLE-CLASS SELECTIONS
- SMALL-GROUP SELECTIONS
- INDEPENDENT LEARNING

PART 1

Writing to Sources: Argument

In this unit, you read about various characters, both real and fictional, who found themselves in life-or-death situations. Some made choices of which they were most likely proud, while others did not.

Assignment

Write an **argument** in which you state and defend a claim responding to the following question:

Should people in life-or-death situations be held accountable for their actions?

Use credible evidence from at least three of the selections you read and researched in this unit to support your claim. Ensure that your claim is fully supported, that you use a formal tone, and that your organization is logical and easy to follow.

Reread the Assignment Review the assignment to be sure you fully understand it. The task may reference some of the academic words presented at the beginning of the unit. Be sure you understand each of the words given below in order to complete the assignment correctly.

Academic Vocabulary

evidence	valid	logical
credible	formulate	

Review the Elements of Effective Argument Before you begin writing, read the Argument Rubric. Once you have completed your first draft, check it against the rubric. If one or more of the elements is missing or not as strong as it could be, revise your essay to add or strengthen that component.

WORD NETWORK

As you write and revise your argument, use your Word Network to help vary your word choices.

STANDARDS

Writing
- Write arguments to support claims in an analysis of substantive topics or texts, using valid reasoning and relevant and sufficient evidence.
- Draw evidence from literary or informational texts to support analysis, reflection, and research.
- Write routinely over extended time frames and shorter time frames for a range of tasks, purposes, and audiences.

AUTHOR'S PERSPECTIVE **Kelly Gallagher, M.Ed.**

Building a Writing Portfolio with Students You can create a portfolio to show the variety of writing students complete over the year. You can set the criteria using such categories as *Best Argument, Best Narrative Piece, Best Informative Piece, Best On-Demand Writing, Best Poetry, Best Writing from Another Class, Best Model of Revision,* and *Best Single Line You Wrote this Year.* You might also ask students to include a reflective letter at the end of the year. To help them learn to reflect, use questions like this throughout the year.

- Where does your writing still need improvement? How will you improve?
- Reflect on a struggle you faced during this unit. How did you overcome it?
- Discuss a specific writing strategy you used and how it worked for you.

At the end of the year, students can review these pieces to see their growth as writers.

Argument Rubric

	Focus and Organization	Evidence and Elaboration	Language Conventions
4	The introduction is engaging and establishes the claim in a compelling way. Includes valid reasons and evidence that address and support the claim while acknowledging counterclaims. Ideas progress logically, and include a variety of sentence transitions. The conclusion offers fresh insights into claim.	Sources of evidence are comprehensive and specific and contain relevant information. The tone of the argument is formal and objective. Uses vocabulary strategically and appropriately for the audience and purpose.	The argument intentionally uses standard English conventions of usage and mechanics. Uses transitions to create cohesion.
3	The introduction is engaging and establishes the claim in a way that grabs readers' attention. Includes reasons and evidence that address and support the claim while acknowledging counterclaims. The ideas progress logically, and include sentence transitions that connect readers to the argument. The conclusion restates information.	Sources of evidence contain relevant information. The tone of the argument is mostly formal and objective. Uses vocabulary that is generally appropriate for the audience and purpose.	The argument demonstrates accuracy in standard English conventions of usage and mechanics. Sometime uses transitions to create cohesion.
2	The introduction establishes a claim. Includes some reasons and evidence that address and support the claim while briefly acknowledging counterclaims. Ideas progress somewhat logically. Includes a few sentence transitions that connect readers to the argument. The conclusion offers some insight into the claim and restates information.	Sources of evidence contain some relevant information. The tone of the argument is occasionally formal and objective. Uses vocabulary that is somewhat appropriate for the audience and purpose.	The argument demonstrates some accuracy in standard English conventions of usage and mechanics. Uses few transitions to create cohesion.
1	The claim is not clearly stated. Does not include reasons or evidence to support the claim. Does not acknowledge counterclaims. Ideas do not progress logically. The sentences are often short and choppy and do not connect readers to the argument. The conclusion does not restate any information that is important.	Does not include reliable or relevant evidence. The tone of the argument is informal. The vocabulary is limited or ineffective.	The argument contains mistakes in standard English conventions of usage and mechanics. Fails to use transitions to create cohesion.

Argument Rubric

As you review the Argument Rubric with students, remind them that the rubric is a resource that can guide their revisions. Students should pay particular attention to the differences between an argument that contains all of the required elements (a score of 3) and one that is comprehensive, engaging, and progresses in a logical and thoughtful manner (a score of 4).

Speaking and Listening: Oral Presentation

Students should annotate their written argument in preparation for the oral presentation, marking the important elements (claim, reasons, evidence, and counterclaims) as well as critical anecdotes or facts.

Remind students that the effectiveness of an oral argument relies on how the speaker establishes credibility with his or her audience. If a speaker comes across as confident and authoritative, it will be easier for the audience to give credence to the speaker's claim.

Review the Oral Presentation Rubric As you review the Oral Presentation Rubric with students, remind them that it is a valuable tool that can help them plan their presentation. They should strive to include all of the criteria required to achieve a score of 3. Draw their attention to some of the subtle differences between scores of 2 and 3.

PERFORMANCE-BASED ASSESSMENT

PART 2

Speaking and Listening: Oral Presentation

Assignment

After completing the final draft of your argument, use it as the foundation for a three- to five-minute oral presentation.

Instead of simply reading your essay aloud, take the following steps to make your oral presentation lively and engaging.

- Go back to your essay and annotate the most important claims and supporting details from your introduction, body paragraphs, and conclusion.
- Refer to your annotated text to guide your presentation and keep it focused.
- Deliver your argument with conviction. Look up from your annotated text frequently, and make eye contact with listeners.

STANDARDS

Speaking and Listening
Present information, findings, and supporting evidence clearly, concisely, and logically such that listeners can follow the line of reasoning and the organization, development, substance, and style are appropriate to purpose, audience, and task.

Review the Oral Presentation Rubric Before you deliver your presentation, check your plans against this rubric. If one or more of the elements is missing or not as strong as it could be, revise your presentation.

	Content	Organization	Presentation Technique
3	Introduction is engaging and establishes a claim in a compelling way. Presentation has strong valid reasons and evidence that support the claim while clearly acknowledging counterclaims. Conclusion offers fresh insight into the claim.	The speaker uses time very effectively by spending the right amount of time on each part. Ideas progress logically, supported by a variety of sentence transitions. Listeners can follow the presentation.	The speaker maintains effective eye contact. The speaker presents with strong conviction and energy.
2	Introduction establishes a claim. Presentation has valid reasons and evidence that support the claim while acknowledging counterclaims.	The speaker uses time effectively by spending the right amount of time on most parts. Ideas progress logically, supported by some sentence transitions. Listeners mostly follow the presentation.	The speaker mostly maintains effective eye contact. The speaker presents with some level of conviction and energy.
1	Introduction does not clearly state a claim. Presentation does not have reasons or evidence to support a claim or acknowledge counterclaims. Conclusion does not restate important information about a claim.	The speaker does not use time effectively; some parts of the presentation are too long or too short. Ideas do not progress logically. Listeners have difficulty following the presentation.	The speaker does not establish eye contact. The speaker presents without conviction or energy.

DIGITAL PERSPECTIVES

Preparing for the Assignment To help students understand what an effective oral argument looks and sounds like, find examples on the Internet of students or adults presenting arguments. Project the examples for the class, and have students note the techniques that make each speaker successful (that is, gestures, pacing, tone, and so on). Suggest that students record themselves presenting their arguments prior to presenting to the class so that they can practice incorporating some of the elements in the examples you showed them.

Reflect on the Unit

Now that you've completed the unit, take a few moments to reflect on your learning.

Reflect on the Unit Goals

Look back at the goals at the beginning of the unit. Use a different colored pen to rate yourself again. Then, think about readings and activities that contributed the most to the growth of your understanding. Record your thoughts.

Reflect on the Learning Strategies

Discuss It Write a reflection on whether you were able to improve your learning based on your Action Plans. Think about what worked, what didn't, and what you might do to keep working on these strategies. Record your ideas before joining a class discussion.

Reflect on the Text

Choose a selection that you found challenging, and explain what made it difficult.

Describe something that surprised you about a text in the unit.

Which activity taught you the most about survival? What did you learn?

SCAN FOR MULTIMEDIA

DIGITAL PERSPECTIVES

Reflect on the Unit

- Have students watch the video on Reflecting on Your Learning.
- A video on this topic is available online in the Professional Development Center.

Reflect on the Unit Goals

Students should re-evaluate how well they met the unit goals now that they have completed the unit. You might ask them to provide a written commentary on the goal they made the most progress with as well as the goal they feel warrants continued focus.

Reflect on the Learning Strategies

Discuss It If you want to make this a digital activity, go online and navigate to the Discussion Board. Alternatively, students can share their learning strategies reflections in a class discussion.

Reflect on the Text

Consider having students share their text reflections with one another.

MAKE IT INTERACTIVE

Have students prepare one slide using presentation software that summarizes their reflection.

Collate student slides into a presentation that can be viewed by the class. Students should be prepared to give a 30-second oral summary of their slide.

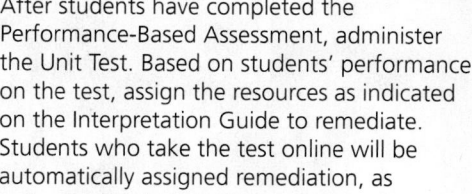

Unit Test and Remediation

After students have completed the Performance-Based Assessment, administer the Unit Test. Based on students' performance on the test, assign the resources as indicated on the Interpretation Guide to remediate. Students who take the test online will be automatically assigned remediation, as warranted by test results.

los Pesticidas
COACH COMPANY
45

The Literature of Civil Rights

UNIT 3

Jump Start

Engage students in a discussion about changes they would like to see happen in school, their communities, and their extracurricular activities. Ask students how would they go about convincing the proper authorities to implement the changes they want. Have students consider what they do, and do not, have the right to do.

The Literature of Civil Rights

Ask students what the unit theme, *The Literature of Civil Rights,* suggests to them. Point out that as they work through this unit, they will read many examples about the literature that arose from the civil rights movement, which led to widespread social reforms.

Video

Project the introduction video in class, ask students to open the video in their digital textbooks, or have students scan the Bounce Page icon with their phones to access the video.

Discuss It If you want to make this a digital activity, go online and navigate to the Discussion Board. Alternatively, students can share their responses in a class discussion.

Block Scheduling

Each day in this pacing calendar represents a 40–50 minute class period. Teachers using block scheduling may combine days to reflect their class schedule. In addition, teachers may revise pacing to differentiate and support core instruction by integrating components and resources as students require.

UNIT 3

The Literature of Civil Rights

During the Civil Rights movement, writings and speeches inspired sweeping social change. What gave those words the power to change a nation?

Civil Rights Movement and Martin Luther King

Discuss It How was Dr. Martin Luther King, Jr., important to the Civil Rights movement?

Write your response before sharing your ideas.

SCAN FOR MULTIMEDIA

250

Pacing Plan

- Unit Introduction: 1
- Introduce Whole-Class Learning: 2
- I Have a Dream: 3, 4, 5, 6
- Letter From Birmingham Jail: 7, 8, 9, 10
- Media: Remarks on the Assassination of Martin Luther King, Jr.: 11, 12, 13
- Performance Task: 14, 15

DIGITAL PERSPECTIVES

Audio | Video | Document | Annotation Highlights | EL Highlights | Online Assessment

UNIT 3

UNIT INTRODUCTION

ESSENTIAL QUESTION:

How can words inspire change?

LAUNCH TEXT
INFORMATIVE MODEL
1963: The Year That Changed Everything

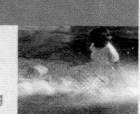

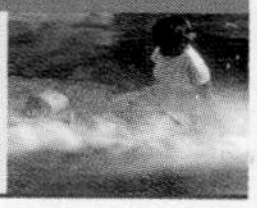

WHOLE-CLASS LEARNING

COMPARE

ANCHOR TEXT: SPEECH
"I Have a Dream"
Dr. Martin Luther King, Jr.
MEDIA CONNECTION: "I Have a Dream"

ANCHOR TEXT: LETTER
Letter From Birmingham Jail
Dr. Martin Luther King, Jr.

MEDIA: VIDEO
Remarks on the Assassination of Martin Luther King, Jr.
Robert F. Kennedy

PERFORMANCE TASK
WRITING FOCUS:
Write an Informative Essay

SMALL-GROUP LEARNING

MEDIA: NEWSCAST
Remembering Civil Rights History, When "Words Meant Everything"
PBS NewsHour

POETRY COLLECTION
For My People
Margaret Walker
Incident
Natasha Trethewey

SPEECH
Lessons of Dr. Martin Luther King, Jr.
Cesar Chavez

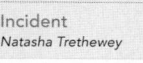

MEMOIR
Traveling
Grace Paley

PERFORMANCE TASK
SPEAKING AND LISTENING FOCUS:
Multimedia Presentation

INDEPENDENT LEARNING

MEDIA: NEWSCAST
Frank McCain Dies—Helped Start Sit-In Movement at Greensboro Lunch Counter
Jeff Tiberii

NEWS ARTICLE
How the Children of Birmingham Changed the Civil-Rights Movement
Lottie L. Joiner

NARRATIVE NONFICTION
Sheyann Webb
from Selma, Lord, Selma
as told to Frank Sikora

MAGAZINE ARTICLE
The Many Lives of Hazel Bryan
David Margolick

MEDIA: VIDEO
Fannie Lou Hamer
BBC

PERFORMANCE-BASED ASSESSMENT PREP
Review Evidence for an Informative Essay

PERFORMANCE-BASED ASSESSMENT PREP

Informative Text: Essay and Multimedia Presentation

PROMPT:
Explain how words have the power to provoke, calm, or inspire.

251

How can words inspire change?

Introduce the Essential Question and point out that students will respond to related prompts.

- **Whole-Class Learning** *How did the selections in this section affect those who first heard them or read them?*
- **Small-Group Learning** *Why do words and actions in some time periods produce meaningful change—and in others do not?*
- **Performance-Based Assessment** *Explain how words have the power to provoke, calm, or inspire.*

Using Trade Books

Refer to the Teaching with Trade Books section in this book or the Interactive Teacher's Edition for suggestions on how to incorporate the following thematically-related novels into this unit.

- *To Kill a Mockingbird* by Harper Lee
- *The Color Purple* by Alice Walker
- *Go Tell It On The Mountain* by James Baldwin

Current Perspectives

To increase student engagement, search online for stories about the literature of the civil rights movement, and how it continues to shape our world half a century later, and invite your students to recommend stories they find. Always preview content before sharing it with your class.

- **Article: Obama pays tribute to Civil Rights Act at 50 (PBS)** An article about President Obama's tribute on the 50th anniversary of the Civil Rights Act of 1964.
- **Podcast: This Fight Begins in the Heart (NPR)** A podcast that relates the works of James Baldwin to the civil unrest in Ferguson, Missouri.

Day	Activity
16	Introduce Small-Group Learning
17	Media: Remembering Civil Rights History: "When Words Meant Everything"
18–19	• For My People • Incident
20–22	Lessons of Dr. Martin Luther King, Jr.
23–24	Traveling
25–26	Performance Task
27	Introduce Independent Learning
28	Independent Learning
29–30	Performance-Based Assessment

About the Unit Goals

These unit goals were backward designed from the Performance-Based Assessment at the end of the unit and the Whole-Class and Small-Group Performance Tasks. Students will practice and become proficient in many more standards over the course of this unit.

Unit Goals

Review the goals with students and explain that as they read and discuss the selections in this unit, they will improve their reading, writing, research, language, and speaking and listening skills.

- Have students watch the video on Goal Setting.
- A video on this topic is available online in the Professional Development Center.

Reading Goals Tell students they will read and evaluate informative essays. They will also read literary criticisms, nonfiction narratives, and arguments to understand the ways writers express ideas.

Writing and Research Goals Tell students that they will learn the elements of writing an informative essay. They will also write their own informative essays. Students will write to organize and share ideas, reflect on experiences, and gather evidence. They will conduct research to clarify and explore ideas.

Language Goal Tell students that they will develop a deeper understanding of how to learn to use clauses and parallelism in writing and presentations and smoothly integrate information from varied sources to create cohesion. They will then conduct research projects.

Speaking and Listening Explain to students that they will work together to build on one another's ideas, develop consensus, and communicate with one another. They will also learn to incorporate audio, visuals, and text in presentations.

HOME Connection

A Home Connection letter to students' parents or guardians is available in the Interactive Teacher's Edition. The letter explains what students will be learning in this unit and how they will be assessed.

Unit Goals

Throughout the unit, you will deepen your perspective of the literature of civil rights by reading, writing, speaking, presenting, and listening. These goals will help you succeed on the Unit Performance-Based Assessment.

Rate how well you meet these goals right now. You will revisit your ratings later when you reflect on your growth during this unit.

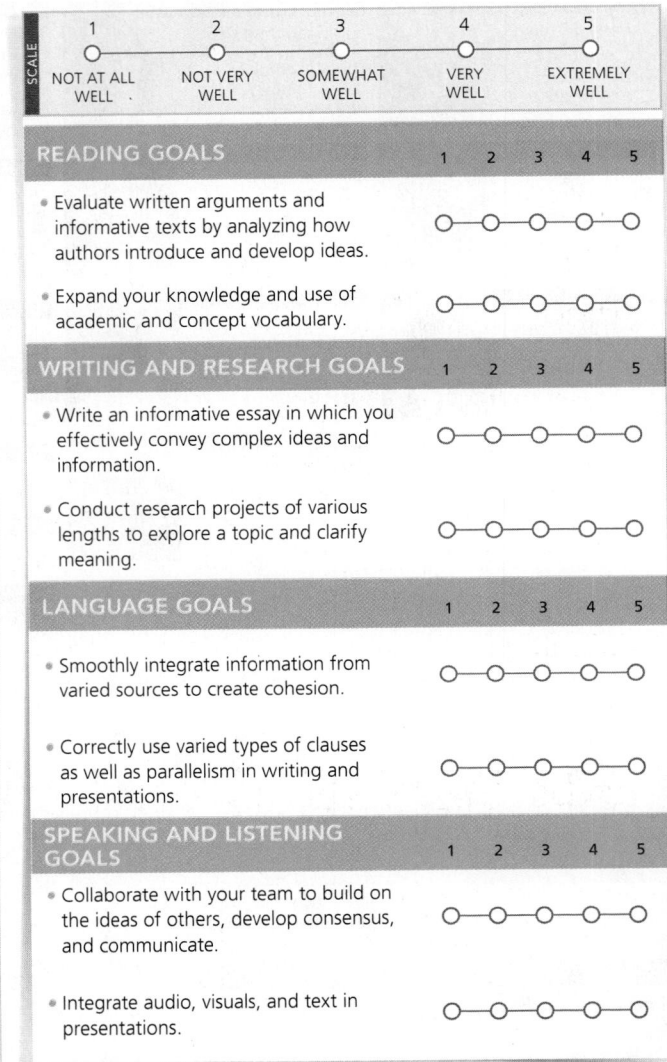

SCALE	1	2	3	4	5
	NOT AT ALL WELL	NOT VERY WELL	SOMEWHAT WELL	VERY WELL	EXTREMELY WELL

READING GOALS	1	2	3	4	5
• Evaluate written arguments and informative texts by analyzing how authors introduce and develop ideas.	○	○	○	○	○
• Expand your knowledge and use of academic and concept vocabulary.	○	○	○	○	○

WRITING AND RESEARCH GOALS	1	2	3	4	5
• Write an informative essay in which you effectively convey complex ideas and information.	○	○	○	○	○
• Conduct research projects of various lengths to explore a topic and clarify meaning.	○	○	○	○	○

LANGUAGE GOALS	1	2	3	4	5
• Smoothly integrate information from varied sources to create cohesion.	○	○	○	○	○
• Correctly use varied types of clauses as well as parallelism in writing and presentations.	○	○	○	○	○

SPEAKING AND LISTENING GOALS	1	2	3	4	5
• Collaborate with your team to build on the ideas of others, develop consensus, and communicate.	○	○	○	○	○
• Integrate audio, visuals, and text in presentations.	○	○	○	○	○

STANDARDS

Language

Acquire and use accurately general academic and domain-specific words and phrases, sufficient for reading, writing, speaking, and listening at the college and career readiness level; demonstrate independence in gathering vocabulary knowledge when considering a word or phrase important to comprehension or expression.

SCAN FOR MULTIMEDIA

AUTHOR'S PERSPECTIVE Ernest Morrell, Ph.D.

Goals and Identity Setting and meeting goals is closely linked to our sense of self, so it is important to help students learn to think of themselves as powerful readers, writers, and speakers. Introduce the importance of goal setting by comparing it to the actions of outstanding high school athletes. How do these athletes excel and make it to the college or professional level? They continue to improve by establishing and working to reach challenging new goals.

Then ask students: "What goals do you need to set in order to continue to develop as a powerful reader? As a skilled writer? As an effective speaker?" Have students decide on their own goals and write them down. As they work through this unit, direct students to refer back to their goals to assess how successfully they have

DIGITAL PERSPECTIVES

Academic Vocabulary: Informative Texts

Academic terms appear in all subjects and can help you read, write, and discuss with more precision. Here are five academic words that will be useful to you in this unit as you analyze and write informative texts.

Complete the chart.

1. Review each word, its root, and the mentor sentences.
2. Use the information and your own knowledge to predict the meaning of each word.
3. For each word, list at least two related words.
4. Refer to a dictionary or other resources if needed.

TIP

FOLLOW THROUGH
Study the words in this chart, and highlight them or related word forms wherever they appear in the unit.

WORD	MENTOR SENTENCES	PREDICT MEANING	RELATED WORDS
disrupt ROOT: ***-rupt-*** "break"; "burst"	1. We were worried a storm would *disrupt* the drive-in movie. 2. Golf fans are very quiet, so they do not *disrupt* the match.		disruptive; disrupting
coherent ROOT: ***-her-*** "stick"; "cling"	1. It is important to organize academic writing in a logical and *coherent* manner. 2. Although the philosopher spoke well, his argument was not *coherent*.		
notation ROOT: ***-not-*** "mark"; "sign"	1. The *notation* in the margin told more about the play. 2. The recipe contained a *notation* to substitute oil for butter.		
aggregate ROOT: ***-greg-*** "herd"; "flock"	1. The pavers are an *aggregate* of three types of stone. 2. The collage was an *aggregate* of the artist's photographs.		
express ROOT: ***-press-*** "push"; "press down"	1. *Express* your thoughts logically and clearly so that others can understand them. 2. We gave a gift because words alone could not fully *express* our gratitude.		

Academic Vocabulary: Informative Texts

Introduce the blue academic vocabulary words in the chart on the student page. Point out that the root of each word provides a clue to its meaning. Discuss the mentor sentences to ensure students understand each word's usage. Students should also use the mentor sentences as context to help them predict the meaning of each word. Check that students are able to fill the chart in correctly. Complete pronunciations, parts of speech, and definitions are provided for you. Students are only expected to provide the definition.

Possible responses:

disrupt *v.* (dihs RUHPT)
Meaning: to break up; upset
Additional words related to root *-rupt-*: disruptive, interrupt

coherent adj. (koh HIHR int)
Meaning: sticking together, holding together
Related words: coherent; incoherent; cohesive
Additional words related to root *-her-*: adhere; adhesive; inherent

notation *n.* (noh TAY shuhn)
Meaning: information put in writing
Related words: note, annotate, annotation,
Additional words related to root *-not:* *denote, denotation, connote, connotation, footnote, endnote, keynote*

aggregate *n.* (AG rih git)
Meaning: a collection, a sum of many parts
Related words: aggregation, disaggregate, disaggregation
Additional words related to root *-greg-:* *congregate, congregation, segregate, segregation*

express *v.* (eks PREHS)
Meaning: to say, to convey, to reveal
Related words: expression, expressive
Additional words related to root *-press-:* *pressure, impress, impression, depress, suppress, repress*

achieved them. Guide students to develop reasonable benchmarks for assessment. Possibilities include increased reading fluency, greater comprehension, improved grades on essays, and more comfort speaking up in groups, for instance. Then have students set goals for developing these skills as they finish high school and prepare to enter college and the workplace.

PERSONALIZE FOR LEARNING

English Language Support

Cognates Many of the academic words have Spanish cognates. Use these cognates with students whose home language is Spanish. **ALL LEVELS**

aggregate – agregar   social – social

Not all English learners will recognize and use these cognates automatically. Help students build their cognate awareness by pointing out that these cognates share the same root in both English and Spanish. **ALL LEVELS**

Purpose of the Launch Text

The Launch Text provides students with a common starting point to address the unit topic. After reading the Launch Text, all students will be able to participate in discussions about the literature of civil rights.

Lexile: 1030 The easier reading level of this selection makes it perfect to assign for homework. Students will need little or no support to understand it.

Additionally, "1963: The Year That Changed Everything" provides a writing model for the Performance-Based Assessment students complete at the end of the unit.

Launch Text: Informative Model

Ask students to think about the main idea and how the author supports it by presenting a sequence of events that happened in 1963.

Have students note that after briefly providing historical context, the author clearly states the main idea in the first paragraph: "A number of major events in the dramatic battle took place in 1963." The following paragraphs provide a series of examples to support this position. The concluding paragraph sums up everything that happened that year in the struggle for civil rights.

Encourage students to read this text on their own and annotate unfamiliar words and sections of text they think are particularly important.

AUDIO SUMMARIES

Audio summaries of "1963: The Year That Changed Everything" are available in both English and Spanish in the Interactive Teacher's Edition or Unit Resources. Assigning these summaries before students read the Launch Text may help them build additional background knowledge and set a context for their reading.

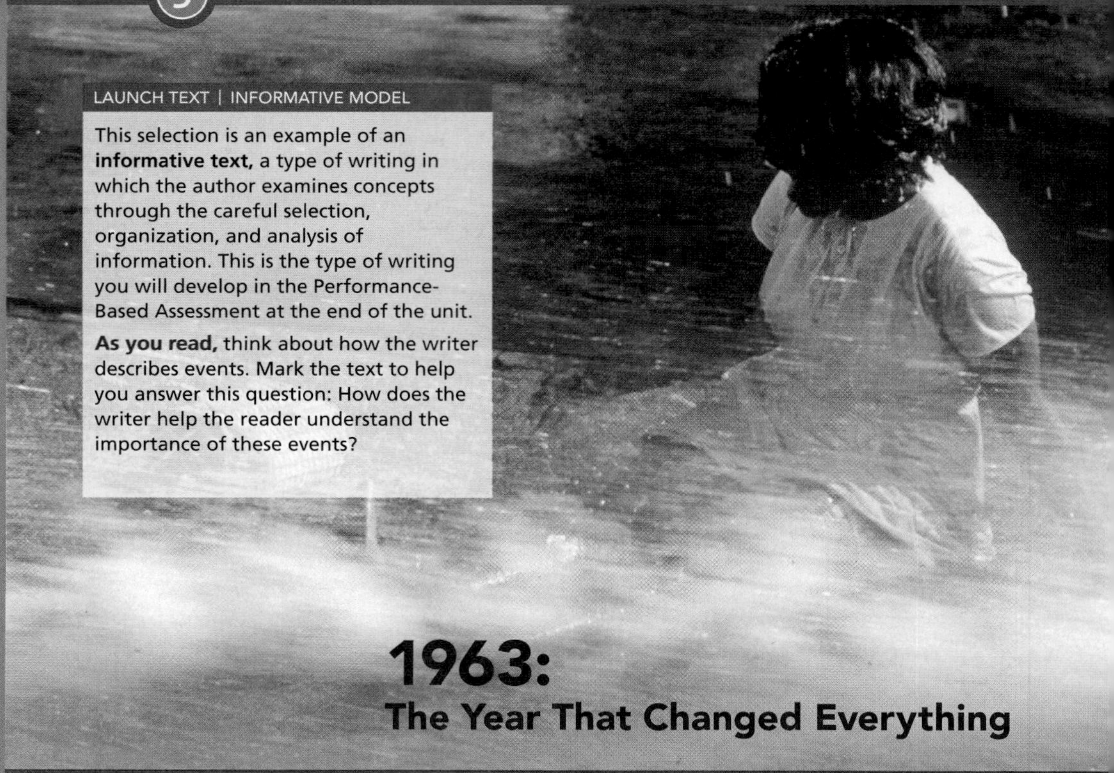

LAUNCH TEXT | INFORMATIVE MODEL

This selection is an example of an **informative text,** a type of writing in which the author examines concepts through the careful selection, organization, and analysis of information. This is the type of writing you will develop in the Performance-Based Assessment at the end of the unit.

As you read, think about how the writer describes events. Mark the text to help you answer this question: How does the writer help the reader understand the importance of these events?

1963:
The Year That Changed Everything

During the Children's Crusade of May 1963, police turned fire hoses on young civil rights protesters, including this girl who was knocked to the ground by the force of the water.

NOTES

1 In 1865, the Thirteenth Amendment to the United States Constitution ended slavery. Nearly a century later, African Americans continued to struggle for equality under the law. A number of major events in this dramatic battle took place in 1963.

2 In April of that year—from behind the bars of a jail cell in Birmingham, Alabama—Dr. Martin Luther King, Jr., wrote a message that would inspire countless others. King had been arrested for breaking a law banning public protest. His message, the famous "Letter From Birmingham Jail," defends nonviolent resistance to injustice. "Injustice anywhere is a threat to justice everywhere," King wrote. He added, "Whatever affects one directly, affects all indirectly."

3 In early May, the young people of Birmingham took King's message to heart. Disobeying a court order, more than 1,000 African American students marched from the 16th Street Baptist Church. The next day, the students marched through Kelly Ingram Park. They were met by an angry white mob as well as police who blasted

SCAN FOR MULTIMEDIA

CROSS CURRICULAR PERSPECTIVES

Social Studies Instruct students to conduct research to learn about the actions Congress took to respond to the events of 1963. You might want to encourage them to learn more about the Civil Rights Act of 1964 and the Voting Rights Act of 1965.

Have students write an essay about how these pieces of legislation protected civil rights and how they made a difference in people's lives.

AUTHOR'S PERSPECTIVE Elfrieda Hiebert, Ph.D.

Word Networks Vary by Word Type Concept maps or nets—the graphic organizers that help students understand the essential attributes, qualities, or characteristics of a word's meaning—vary depending on the type of word they help capture. For example, maps for concepts that explain phenomena in the physical world and those that describe features of people and social situations can be different.

- In concept maps related to physical phenomena, the words are typically not synonyms; rather, they are connected by topic. For example, for

them with water from fire hoses and terrified them with dogs. The teenagers were jailed in temporary cells at the county fairgrounds. On the seventh day of the Children's Crusade, city officials agreed to negotiate with the African American community. A few days later, the two sides reached an agreement to end local segregation.

4 News of the Children's Crusade spread in the media, helping to transform the way Americans saw the civil rights movement. The *New York Times* ran more stories about civil rights in the two weeks after the Children's Crusade than it had in the previous two years combined. Scenes of children under attack were filmed and broadcast all over the world, setting off a global outcry. Polls showed that Americans across the land believed racial justice was the nation's biggest problem.

5 The struggle for civil rights continued to be marked by violence. On May 28, 1963, four African American college students in Jackson, Mississippi, were assaulted for sitting at a segregated lunch counter. Two weeks later, on June 12, an assassin killed civil rights activist Medgar Evers outside his home in Jackson.

6 That summer brought a landmark event in civil rights history. This was the March for Jobs and Freedom that took place in Washington, D.C., on August 28. Under the shadow of the Lincoln Memorial, Dr. King delivered his famous "I Have a Dream" speech to a crowd of 200,000 people from all walks of life. The peace and hope of that event did not last long. On September 15, a bomb exploded inside Birmingham's 16th Street Baptist Church. The attack killed four little African American girls and injured twenty-two other people.

7 The struggle continued throughout 1963. The Southern Regional Council has records of protests that took place in more than 100 southern towns. Approximately 20,000 demonstrators were arrested. With words and actions, they delivered a demand for justice that could not be ignored.

NOTES

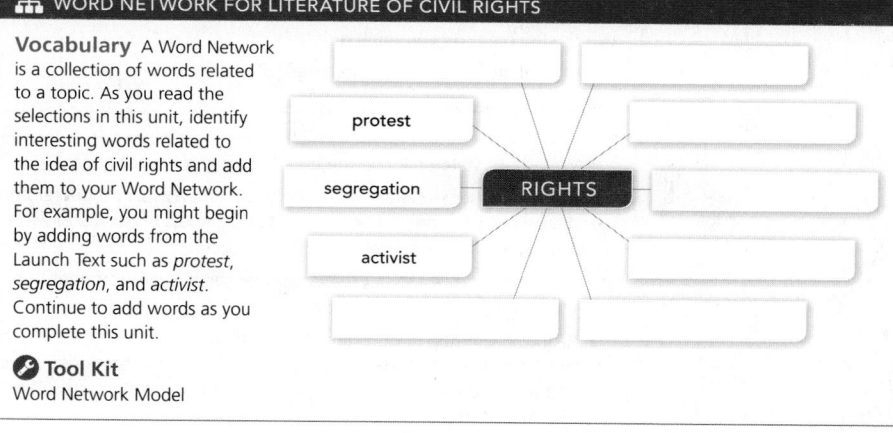

WORD NETWORK FOR LITERATURE OF CIVIL RIGHTS

Vocabulary A Word Network is a collection of words related to a topic. As you read the selections in this unit, identify interesting words related to the idea of civil rights and add them to your Word Network. For example, you might begin by adding words from the Launch Text such as *protest*, *segregation*, and *activist*. Continue to add words as you complete this unit.

Tool Kit
Word Network Model

Word Network for The Literature of Civil Rights

Tell students that they can fill in the Word Network as they read texts in the unit, or they can record the words elsewhere and add them later. Point out to students that people may have personal associations with some words. A word that one student thinks is related to the topic of civil rights might not be a word another student would pick. However, students should feel free to add any word they personally think is relevant to their Word Network. Each person's Word Network will be unique. If you choose to print the Word Network, distribute it to students at this point so they can use it throughout the rest of the unit.

the topic *the outdoors,* the words *mountains, trees, rivers, and parks* all have different meanings, but each could be used in a word network.

- Concept maps about people and social situations contain words that have subtle differences in meaning and cannot necessarily be substituted for one another. For example, for the network built around the word *leader,* the words *director, manager,* and *ruler* carry similar meanings but are not interchangeable.

To help students build their word knowledge, help them understand the power of word networks. Often, especially in narratives, the concepts represented by rare words are known by common words that most students understand. In part, that's because in describing traits of characters or features of a problem or context, an author will use a number of different words to describe the same concept rather than repeating the same word over and over. For example, *battle, struggle,* and *clash* are all more complex words for *fight*.

1963: The Year That Changed Everything 255

INTRODUCTION

Summary

Have students read the introductory paragraph. Provide them with tips for writing a summary:

- Write in the present tense.
- Make sure to include the title of the work.
- Be concise: a summary should not be equal in length to the original text.
- If you need to quote the words of the author, use quotation marks.
- Don't put your own opinions, ideas, or interpretations into the summary. The purpose of writing a summary is to accurately represent what the author says, not to provide a critique.

If necessary, students can refer to the Tool Kit for help in understanding the elements of a good summary.

See possible Summary on Student page.

Launch Activity

Explain to students that as they work on this unit they will have many opportunities to discuss the topic of civil rights. Remind them that social progress is challenging to implement. As students listen to their classmates' opinions, encourage them to evaluate each idea to determine if they agree or disagree.

Summary

Write a summary of "1963: The Year That Changed Everything." A **summary** is a concise, complete, and accurate overview of a text. It should not include a statement of your opinion or an analysis.

Possible response: In "1963: The Year That Changed Everything," the author discusses the many events that took place in 1963 that paved the way for the recognition of African American civil rights.

The first event that the author mentioned was Martin Luther King, Jr.'s "Letter From a Birmingham Jail," in which he defended nonviolent resistance. The next month, African American students marched in the Children's Crusade. In May, African American college students were assaulted for sitting at a segregated lunch counter. King's "I Have a Dream" speech was delivered in August, and the next month a bomb exploded at the 16th Street Baptist Church in Birmingham. Other events took place as the struggle continued.

Launch Activity

Group Discussion Consider these statements:

1. **Social progress is only possible if you have a powerful leader.**
2. **Social progress is only possible if it comes from the people.**

Which statement do you think is right?

☐ statement 1 ☐ statement 2

Explain your reasons: ______

- Write both statements on the board, leaving room for notes.
- Find two other students who share your response. Get together and discuss your reasons. Choose the three strongest reasons and write each one on a self-sticking note.
- Place the notes with your reasons under the relevant statement on the board.
- Read through the reasons and identify the ones that are similar. Group them together on the board. As a class, discuss the categories of reasons and evaluate their validity. Has your position changed as a result of the class discussion?

VOCABULARY DEVELOPMENT

Parts of Speech Point out that the word *aggregate* can be a verb, a noun, and an adjective. Model different forms of the word *aggregate* in sentences.

NOUN: The *aggregate* of his debt was becoming difficult to manage.

ADJECTIVE: The *aggregate* total of her investment earnings has been increasing at an impressive rate.

VERB: The editor's job is to *aggregate* content from different websites.

Word (pronunciation)	Part of Speech	Meaning
aggregate (AG ri git)	noun	the total or whole
aggregate (AG ri git)	adjective	formed by the combination of particulars
aggregate (AG ri gayt)	verb	to combine into a whole

QuickWrite

Consider class discussions, presentations, the video, and the Launch Text as you think about the prompt. Record your first thoughts here.

PROMPT: **Explain how words have the power to provoke, calm, or inspire.**

Possible response: Words have the power to provoke, calm, or inspire because words often carry a lot of meaning. Words that are uplifting and hopeful can encourage people to try to fight for positive change, whereas negative and discouraging words can provoke people to commit harmful acts.

Martin Luther King, Jr. used positive, uplifting words to inspire people to fight for the recognition of African American civil rights. Other people throughout history have also used uplifting rhetoric, such as John F. Kennedy and Barack Obama. Some people, like Adolf Hitler, used negative, hateful rhetoric.

EVIDENCE LOG FOR THE LITERATURE OF CIVIL RIGHTS

Review your QuickWrite. Summarize your thoughts in one sentence and record it in your Evidence Log. Then, record textual details or evidence from "1963: The Year That Changed Everything" that support your thinking.

Prepare for the Performance-Based Assessment at the end of the unit by completing the Evidence Log after each selection.

Tool Kit
Evidence Log Model

Title of Text: ______ Date: ______

CONNECTION TO PROMPT	TEXT EVIDENCE/DETAILS	ADDITIONAL NOTES/IDEAS

How does this text change or add to my thinking? Date: ______

SCAN FOR MULTIMEDIA

DIGITAL PERSPECTIVES

QuickWrite

In this QuickWrite, students should present their own response to the prompt based on the material they have read and viewed in the Unit Overview and Introduction. This initial response will help inform their work when they complete the Performance-Based Assessment at the end of the unit. Students should think about the power of words and the ways that supportive, loving, or harmful words can have an impact on people.

See possible QuickWrite on Student page.

Evidence Log for The Literature of Civil Rights

Students should record their initial thinking in their Evidence Logs along with evidence from "1963: The Year That Changed Everything" that support this thinking.

If you choose to print the Evidence Log, distribute it to students at this point so they can use it throughout the rest of the unit.

Performance-Based Assessment: Refining Your Thinking

- Have students watch the video on Refining Your Thinking.
- A video on this topic is available online in the Professional Development Center.

OVERVIEW

WHOLE-CLASS LEARNING

How can words inspire change?

Engage students in conversation about the phrase "I have a dream." Ask students: Where have they heard it before? Why do they remember it? What other famous phrases do they remember from history? During Whole-Class Learning, students will read selections by and about Martin Luther King, Jr. and how his words became a part of the Civil Rights movement.

Whole-Class Learning Strategies

Review the Learning Strategies with students and explain that as they work through Whole-Class Learning they will develop strategies to work in large-group environments.

- Have students watch the video on Whole-Class Learning Strategies.
- A video on this topic is available online in the Professional Development Center.

You may wish to discuss some action items to add to the chart as a class before students complete it on their own. For example, for "Monitor understanding," you might solicit the following from students:

- Take detailed notes.
- If you are unsure that you understand something, ask about it afterwards for clarification.

Block Scheduling

Each day in this Pacing Plan represents a 40–50 minute class period. Teachers using block scheduling may combine days to reflect their class schedule. In addition, teachers may revise pacing to differentiate and support core instruction by integrating components and resources as students require.

OVERVIEW: WHOLE-CLASS LEARNING

ESSENTIAL QUESTION:

How can words inspire change?

During the 1960s, the fight for racial equality in the United States gave rise to powerful literary statements. In speeches, essays, poetry, and fiction, writers rose to the challenge of documenting injustice and inspiring change. You will work with your whole class to explore the literature of the Civil Rights movement. The selections you are going to read capture the struggles and hopes of an important era in American history.

Whole-Class Learning Strategies

Throughout your life, in school, in your community, and in your career, you will continue to learn and work in large-group environments.

Review these strategies and the actions you can take to practice them as you work with your whole class. Add ideas of your own for each step. Get ready to use these strategies during Whole-Class Learning.

STRATEGY	ACTION PLAN
Listen actively	• Eliminate distractions. For example, put your cell phone away. • Keep your eyes on the speaker. •
Clarify by asking questions	• If you're confused, other people probably are, too. Ask a question to help your whole class. • If you see that you are guessing, ask a question instead. •
Monitor understanding	• Notice what information you already know and be ready to build on it. • Ask for help if you are struggling. •
Interact and share ideas	• Share your ideas and answer questions, even if you are unsure. • Build on the ideas of others by adding details or making a connection. •

SCAN FOR MULTIMEDIA

Pacing Plan

- 1: Unit Introduction
- 2: Introduce Whole-Class Learning
- 3–6: I Have a Dream
- 7–10: Letter From Birmingham Jail
- 11–13: Media: Remarks on the Assassination of Martin Luther King, Jr.
- 14–15: Performance Task

WHOLE-CLASS LEARNING (days 2–15)

CONTENTS

COMPARE

ANCHOR TEXT: SPEECH

"I Have a Dream"
Dr. Martin Luther King, Jr.

The speech that inspired millions to support the Civil Rights movement continues to inspire to this day.

▸ MEDIA CONNECTION: "I Have a Dream"

ANCHOR TEXT: LETTER

Letter From Birmingham Jail
Dr. Martin Luther King, Jr.

Read the letter that Dr. King wrote after he was jailed for staging a public protest.

MEDIA: VIDEO

Remarks on the Assassination of Martin Luther King, Jr.
Robert F. Kennedy

In one of the great speeches of the era, Senator Robert F. Kennedy both delivers terrible news and honors Dr. King.

PERFORMANCE TASK

WRITING FOCUS

Write an Informative Essay
Both Whole-Class readings and the two videos deal with the struggle for civil rights in the United States. After reading the selections and viewing the videos, you will conduct research and write your own informative essay about the power of the written and spoken word in the American Civil Rights movement.

DIGITAL PERSPECTIVES

Contents

Anchor Texts Preview the anchor texts and media with students to generate interest. Encourage students to discuss other texts they may have read or movies or television shows they may have seen that deal with the issues of the role that Martin Luther King, Jr. played in the Civil Rights movement.

You may wish to conduct a poll to determine which selection students think looks more interesting, and discuss the reasons for their preference. Students can return to this poll after they have read the selections to see if their preference changed.

Performance Task

Write an Informative Essay Explain to students that after they have finished reading the selections, they will write an informative essay about how the texts in this section affected those who first heard or read them. To help them prepare, encourage students to think about the topic as they progress through the selections and as they participate in the Whole-Class Learning experience.

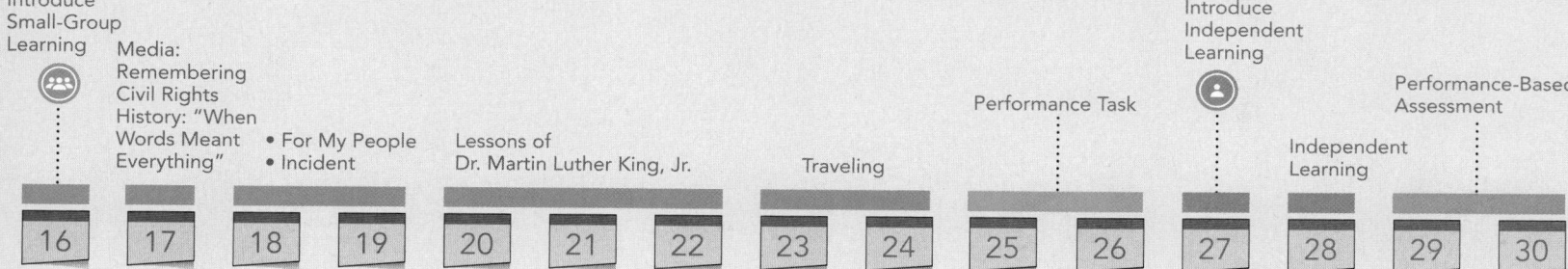

- 16: Introduce Small-Group Learning
- 17: Media: Remembering Civil Rights History: "When Words Meant Everything"
- 18–19: • For My People • Incident
- 20–22: Lessons of Dr. Martin Luther King, Jr.
- 23–24: Traveling
- 25–26: Performance Task
- 27: Introduce Independent Learning
- 28: Independent Learning
- 29–30: Performance-Based Assessment

"I Have a Dream"

AUDIO SUMMARIES
Audio summaries of "I Have a Dream" are available online in both English and Spanish in the Interactive Teacher's Edition or Unit Resources. Assigning these summaries prior to reading the selection may help students build additional background knowledge and set a context for their first read.

Summary

In this speech, perhaps the most famous in American history, Dr. Martin Luther King, Jr. lays out his vision of a renewed America. He emphasizes the failure of the government to establish equal rights, and the persistence of discrimination that attacks both people's bodies and their dignity. After an unflinching look at the suffering of the past and the present, King turns to the future. He describes his dream that, one day, justice and equality will prevail even in the most challenging places; that regardless of race people will treat each other fairly, work together, and establish freedom across the land.

Insight

This speech was one of the most important moments of the 1960s Civil Rights Movement; all students should be familiar with it. In addition to its historical importance, the unreached vision it calls for is still very resonant today.

ESSENTIAL QUESTION:
How can words inspire change?

Connection to Essential Question

When Americans think of words that have inspired generation after generation, Martin Luther King's "I Have a Dream" speech is probably one of the most often cited texts.

WHOLE-CLASS LEARNING PERFORMANCE TASK
How did the selections in this section affect those who first heard them or read them?

UNIT PERFORMANCE-BASED ASSESSMENT
Explain how words have the power to provoke, calm, or inspire.

Connection to Performance Tasks

Whole-Class Learning Performance Task "I Have a Dream" galvanized a generation of Americans the moment the speech was delivered by King. Students will have little difficulty identifying the many ways in which King's speech affected those who first heard or read it.

Unit Performance-Based Assessment Students can dissect what gives this speech its emotional power, ranging from the language itself to the references.

DIGITAL PERSPECTIVES — Audio | Video | Document | Annotation Highlights | EL Highlights | Online Assessment

LESSON RESOURCES

	Making Meaning	Language Development
Lesson	**First Read** **Close Read** **Analyze the Text** **Analyze Craft and Structure**	**Concept Vocabulary** **Word Study** **Conventions**
Instructional Standards	**RI.10** By the end of grade 9, read and comprehend literary nonfiction . . . **RI.1** Cite strong and thorough textual evidence . . . **RI.6** Determine an author's point of view . . . **RI.9** Analyze seminal U.S. documents . . .	**L.2** Demonstrate command of the conventions of standard English grammar and usage . . . **L.1.a** Use parallel structure. **L.2.c** Spell correctly. **L.4.b** Identify and correctly use patterns of word changes . . .
STUDENT RESOURCES		
Available online in the Interactive Student Edition or Unit Resources	Selection Audio First-Read Guide: Nonfiction Close-Read Guide: Nonfiction	Word Network Evidence Log
TEACHER RESOURCES		
Selection Resources Available online in the Interactive Teacher's Edition or Unit Resources	Audio Summaries Annotation Highlights EL Highlights Analyze Craft and Structure: Argument	Concept Vocabulary and Word Study Conventions: Parallel Structure English Language Support Lesson: Parallelism
Reteach/Practice (RP) Available online in the Interactive Teacher's Edition or Unit Resources	Analyze Craft and Structure: Argument (RP)	Word Study: Word Changes (RP) Conventions: Parallel Structure (RP)
Assessment Available online in Assessments	Selection Test	
My Resources	A Unit 3 Answer Key is available online and in the Interactive Teacher's Edition.	

Reading Support

Text Complexity Rubric: "I Have a Dream"	
Quantitative Measures	
Lexile: 1140 **Text Length:** 1,597 words	
Qualitative Measures	
Knowledge Demands ① ② ❸ ④ ⑤	Understanding the speech requires some prior knowledge of the identity of Martin Luther King, Jr. and civil rights inequalities in the 1960s and before.
Structure ① ② ❸ ④ ⑤	Selection has a logical progression of ideas, starting with historical perspective, followed by the situation at time of speech, and ending with hopes and dreams for the future.
Language Conventionality and Clarity ① ② ③ ❹ ⑤	Speech contains extensive use of metaphors embedded within complex, long sentences. To understand language, reader must be able to distinguish literal from metaphorical language.
Levels of Meaning/Purpose ① ② ③ ❹ ⑤	To understand the meaning of concepts within the speech, the reader must be able to interpret meaning of multiple and contrasting metaphors.

DECIDE AND PLAN

English Language Support

Provide English Learners with support for language and meaning as they read the selection.

Language Write phrases that may be unfamiliar, for example, *five score years ago*. Explain words as necessary (for example a *score* is 20 years) and ask them to figure out the meaning of the phrase. As students read, have them highlight or list words that they need to find out about.

Meaning Point out that the speech contains many *metaphors*. Help students decipher the metaphorical meaning by first making sure they understand the literal meanings. For example, write (from paragraph 5) *insufficient funds in the great vaults of opportunity*. Define the meaning of the individual words. Then talk about the metaphorical meaning of the phrase.

Strategic Support

Provide students with strategic support to ensure that they can successfully read the text.

Language Point out the use of metaphors that show a contrast. Give an example: (paragraph 6) *dark and desolate valley of segregation/sunlit path of racial justice*. Ask students to find a second set of contrasting metaphors in that same paragraph *(quicksand of racial injustice/solid rock of brotherhood)*.

Meaning Guide students to understand the meaning of each section. For example, in the second paragraph, ask about the "great American" and "five score years ago." Confirm that they understand that it is about the freeing of the slaves by Lincoln, about 100 years before the speech. As students listen or read, stop periodically to discuss the meaning.

Challenge

Provide students who need to be challenged with ideas for how they can go beyond a simple interpretation of the text.

Text Analysis Ask students to highlight or list all of the metaphors they can find in the text (for example, in paragraph 2: *a joyous daybreak to end the long night of captivity)*. For more complex metaphors (for example in paragraph 5: *insufficient funds in the great vaults of opportunity)*, ask students to explain what they think each of the metaphors means. Discuss as a group.

Written Response Pair students and ask them to write alternate metaphors to express some of the same ideas in the speech (for example, *freedom from slavery was a ray of sunshine in dark cave of captivity*.)

TEACH

Read and Respond

Have the class do their first read of the selection. Then have them complete their close read. Finally, work with them on the Making Meaning and Language Development.

Standards Support Through Teaching and Learning Cycle

IDENTIFY NEEDS

Analyze results of the Beginning-of-Year Assessment, focusing on the items relating to Unit 3. Also take into consideration student performance to this point and your observations of where particular students struggle.

DECIDE AND PLAN

- If students have performed poorly on items matching these standards, then provide selection scaffolds before assigning them the on-level lesson provided in the Student Edition.
- If students have done well on the Beginning-of-Year Assessment, then challenge them to keep progressing and learning by giving them opportunities to practice the skills in depth.
- Use the Selection Resources listed on the Planning pages for "I Have a Dream" to help students continually improve their ability to master the standards.

Instructional Standards: I Have a Dream

	Catching Up	This Year	Looking Forward
Reading	You may wish to administer the **Analyze Craft and Structure: Argument (RP)** worksheet to help students understand that rhetorical devices create emphasis and emotion.	**RI.6** Determine an author's point of view or purpose in a text and analyze how an author uses rhetoric to advance that point of view or purpose.	Challenge students to rewrite a portion of King's speech in which his rhetoric is removed. Compare the rewritten speech's effectiveness in communicating Kings' message to the original speech.
Language	You may wish to administer the **Conventions: Parallel Structure (RP)** worksheet to help students understand that parallelism is both a rhetorical device and a grammatical rule. You may wish to administer the **Word Study: Word Changes (RP)** worksheet to understand that when added to a base word, the suffix *-tion* changes verbs to nouns.	**L.1.a** Use parallel structure. **L.4.b** Identify and correctly use patterns of word changes that indicate different meanings or parts of speech.	Have students find sections of text that demonstrate parallelism and rewrite them without parallel structure to point out the effectiveness of the technique. Have students identify other words in the selection that can be changed to nouns by adding the suffix *-tion*. Have students use each in a sentence.

TEACH

Implement the planned lesson, and gather evidence of student learning.

ANALYZE AND REVISE

- Analyze student work for evidence of student learning.
- Identify whether or not students have met the expectations in the standards.
- Identify implications for future instruction.

Jump Start

FIRST READ Prior to students' first read, ask them to talk about their perception of fairness and justice in the world. Do we live in a just and fair world? If not, what would this kind of society look like? What steps can we take to ensure that we can leave a better world for future generations?

"I Have a Dream"

Who is the speaker? What was going on in the U.S. when the speaker gave his speech? How does the speaker suggest we move forward as a country? Modeling the questions a reader might ask as they read, "I Have a Dream" for the first time brings the text alive for students and connects it to the Whole-Class Performance Task assignment. Selection audio and print capability for the selection are available in the Interactive Teacher's Edition.

Concept Vocabulary

Support students as they rank their words. Ask if they've ever heard, read, or used them. Reassure them that the definitions for these words are listed in the selection.

FIRST READ

Have students perform the steps of the first read independently:

NOTICE: Encourage students to notice when, as well as where, and to whom Dr. King gave this speech, and any other background information to help explain its context and historical significance.

ANNOTATE: Remind students to mark passages that illustrate Dr. King's use of figurative language.

CONNECT: Encourage students to consider the speech in the context of its time and then in the context of their own time and their own lives. Are Dr. King's words relevant today?

RESPOND: Students will answer questions and write a summary to demonstrate understanding.

Point out to students that while they will always complete the Respond step at the end of the first read, the other steps will probably happen somewhat concurrently. You may wish to print copies of the **First-Read Guide: Nonfiction** for students to use.

Remind students that, during their first read, they should not answer the close read questions that appear in the selection.

MAKING MEANING

"I HAVE A DREAM"

Comparing Texts

In this lesson, you will read and compare two of Dr. Martin Luther King, Jr.'s most famous works. First, you will complete the first-read and close-read activities for the "I Have a Dream" speech. Then, you will compare the speech to the letter King wrote while a prisoner in a jail cell in Birmingham, Alabama.

LETTER FROM BIRMINGHAM JAIL

About the Author

Dr. Martin Luther King, Jr. (1929–1968) was a prominent leader of the African American civil rights movement from 1955 until his assassination in 1968. His dedication to nonviolent resistance made him both a moral and a political leader. As a Baptist minister, he was a religious leader as well. Dr. King organized many of the largest and most effective civil rights protests of the era.

"I Have a Dream"

Concept Vocabulary

You will encounter the following words as you read King's speech. Before reading, note how familiar you are with each word. Then, rank the words in order from most familiar (1) to least familiar (6).

WORD	YOUR RANKING
prosperity	
hallowed	
tribulations	
redemptive	
oppression	
exalted	

After completing the first read, come back to the concept vocabulary and review your rankings. Mark any changes to your original rankings as needed.

Tool Kit
First-Read Guide and Model Annotation

First Read NONFICTION

Apply these strategies as you conduct your first read. You will have an opportunity to complete the close-read notes after your first read.

NOTICE the general ideas of the text. *What* is it about? *Who* is involved?

ANNOTATE by marking vocabulary and key passages you want to revisit.

First Read

CONNECT ideas within the selection to what you already know and what you have already read.

RESPOND by completing the Comprehension Check and by writing a brief summary of the selection.

STANDARDS
Reading Informational Text
By the end of grade 9, read and comprehend literary nonfiction in the grades 9–10 text complexity band proficiently, with scaffolding as needed at the high end of the range.

AUTHOR'S PERSPECTIVE **Kelly Gallagher, M.Ed.**

The Value of Rereading To get the most out of a text, it is important for students to move beyond surface-level comprehension into deeper, inferential meaning. Give students rereading strategies that allow them to break free from the habit of complaining, "I read it, but I don't get it" by having them ask themselves the following four questions, in order, as they read:

1. What does it say?
2. What does it mean?
3. How is it said?
4. Why does it matter?

Question 1 taps literal comprehension, necessary before students can move on to uncovering

ANCHOR TEXT | SPEECH

"I Have a Dream"

Dr. Martin Luther King, Jr.

BACKGROUND

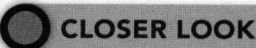

Because speeches are written to be spoken aloud, they are a more fluid form of literature than most other nonfiction. A strong speaker will react to unspoken signals from his or her listeners and adjust a speech accordingly. He or she might change words or add whole phrases. This is the case with Dr. Martin Luther King, Jr., one of the great speakers of the modern age. The text that appears here represents the speech exactly as it was delivered by Dr. King on the steps of the Lincoln Memorial.

SCAN FOR MULTIMEDIA

1 I am happy to join with you today in what will go down in history as the greatest demonstration for freedom in the history of our nation.

2 Five score[1] years ago, a great American, in whose symbolic shadow we stand today, signed the Emancipation Proclamation. This momentous decree came as a great beacon light of hope to millions of Negro slaves who had been seared in the flames of withering injustice. It came as a joyous daybreak to end the long night of their captivity.

3 But one hundred years later, the Negro still is not free. One hundred years later, the life of the Negro is still sadly crippled by the manacles of segregation and the chains of discrimination. One hundred years later, the Negro lives on a lonely island of poverty in the midst of a vast ocean of material prosperity. One hundred years later, the Negro is still languished in the corners of American society and finds himself an exile in his own land. And so we've come here today to dramatize a shameful condition.

4 In a sense we've come to our nation's capital to cash a check. When the architects of our republic wrote the magnificent words of the Constitution and the Declaration of Independence, they were signing a promissory note[2] to which every American was to fall heir.

NOTES

prosperity (pros PEHR uh tee) *n.* good fortune; success

1. **score** *n.* twenty. "Five score" is one hundred years.
2. **promissory note** (PROM ih sawr ee) *n.* written promise to pay a specific amount.

DIGITAL PERSPECTIVES

CLOSER LOOK

Analyze Metaphor

Students may have marked paragraph 3 during their first read. Use this paragraph to help students understand Dr. King's use of metaphor. Encourage them to talk about the annotations that they marked. You may want to model a close read with the class based on the highlights shown in the text.

ANNOTATE: Have students mark details in paragraph 3 that demonstrate Dr. King's use of metaphor, or have students participate while you highlight them.

QUESTION: Guide students to consider what these details might tell them. Ask what a reader can infer from these metaphors, and accept student responses.

Possible response: A "lonely island" is a simple and effective metaphor for the social isolation imposed by poverty. "Manacles" and "chains" show the powerlessness and confinement suffered by African Americans as a result of segregation and discrimination. Manacles and chains also connect to slavery.

CONCLUDE: Help students to formulate conclusions about the importance of these details in the text. Ask students why the author might have included these details.

Possible response: Metaphors enable Dr. King's audience to visualize his ideas and the ideas of his opponents as participants in a drama, or as warriors in the epic battle for equality. His metaphors often revealed the uncomfortable truth in words that had developed an undeserved respectability.

Remind students that a **metaphor** is a figure of speech in which a word or phrase for one thing is used to refer to another thing in order to show or suggest they are similar.

Additional **English Language Support** is available in the Interactive Teacher's Edition.

deeper meaning. Question 2 requires students to provide evidence for their interpretation by citing specific details and passages. Question 3 asks students to think about the author's technique. Question 4 asks them to think deeply about the issues that will affect their lives, as recognizing the universals in great literature enables students to consider their place in society. After all, asking "Why does it matter?" is the reason why we read and teach great literature.

TEACHING

CLOSE READ

Remind students to focus on sentences that present two highly contrasting or opposing images or ideas. You may wish to model the Close Read using the following think-aloud format. Possible responses to questions on the Student page are included. You may also want to print copies of the **Close-Read Guide: Nonfiction** for students to use.

ANNOTATE: As I read paragraphs 6 and 7, I notice and highlight metaphorical imagery that illustrates a series of contrasts between opposing ideas of racial injustice and racial justice.

QUESTION: Each pair of contrasting images represents a journey from a bad place to a better place. In each journey the bad place is the present, and the better place is a vision of the future. The speaker clearly regards the present as a time of racial injustice and discontent, but believes that the future will see the establishment of freedom, justice, and equality.

CONCLUDE: The speaker adds urgency to his message by using stark, uncomfortable, and dangerous imagery to dramatize the injustice and suffering of the present, and contrasts it with bright, strong, and uplifting imagery to dramatize the promise of the future.

NOTES

hallowed *adj.* (HAL ohd) holy; sacred

CLOSE READ

ANNOTATE: In paragraphs 6 and 7, mark sentences that present two highly contrasting or opposing images or ideas.

QUESTION: What do these images suggest about the speaker's view of both the present and the future?

CONCLUDE: How do these images add urgency to the speaker's message?

This note was a promise that all men, yes, black men as well as white men, would be guaranteed the "unalienable Rights" of "Life, Liberty, and the pursuit of Happiness." It is obvious today that America has defaulted on this promissory note, insofar as her citizens of color are concerned. Instead of honoring this sacred obligation, America has given the Negro people a bad check, a check which has come back marked "insufficient funds."

5 But we refuse to believe that the bank of justice is bankrupt. We refuse to believe that there are insufficient funds in the great vaults of opportunity of this nation. And so, we've come to cash this check, a check that will give us upon demand the riches of freedom and the security of justice.

6 We have also come to this **hallowed** spot to remind America of the fierce urgency of Now. This is no time to engage in the luxury of cooling off or to take the tranquilizing drug of gradualism. Now is the time to make real the promises of democracy. Now is the time to rise from the dark and desolate valley of segregation to the sunlit path of racial justice. Now is the time to lift our nation from the quicksands of racial injustice to the solid rock of brotherhood. Now is the time to make justice a reality for all of God's children.

7 It would be fatal for the nation to overlook the urgency of the moment. This sweltering summer of the Negro's legitimate discontent will not pass until there is an invigorating autumn of freedom and equality. Nineteen sixty-three is not an end, but a beginning. And those who hope that the Negro needed to blow off steam and will now be content will have a rude awakening if the nation returns to business as usual. And there will be neither rest nor tranquility in America until the Negro is granted his citizenship rights. The whirlwinds of revolt will continue to shake the foundations of our nation until the bright day of justice emerges.

8 But there is something that I must say to my people, who stand on the warm threshold which leads into the palace of justice. In the process of gaining our rightful place, we must not be guilty of wrongful deeds. Let us not seek to satisfy our thirst for freedom by drinking from the cup of bitterness and hatred. We must forever conduct our struggle on the high plane of dignity and discipline. We must not allow our creative protest to degenerate into physical violence. Again and again, we must rise to the majestic heights of meeting physical force with soul force.

9 The marvelous new militancy which has engulfed the Negro community must not lead us to a distrust of all white people, for many of our white brothers, as evidenced by their presence here today, have come to realize that their destiny is tied up with our destiny. And they have come to realize that their freedom is inextricably bound to our freedom.

10 We cannot walk alone.

11 And as we walk, we must make the pledge that we shall always march ahead.

PERSONALIZE FOR LEARNING

Strategic Support

Roles and Power As students read paragraph 7 of this speech, pose this question to students: How would you define the roles of different people in society? Guide students to consider age, race, ethnicity, education status, socioeconomic background, and other demographic factors of interest. Then, ask them to consider how these demographics affect the way people might perceive and treat others. How do these identifiers affect the roles and power of various groups, as well as their ability to progress?

12 We cannot turn back.

13 There are those who are asking the devotees of civil rights, "When will you be satisfied?" We can never be satisfied as long as the Negro is the victim of the unspeakable horrors of police brutality. We can never be satisfied as long as our bodies, heavy with the fatigue of travel, cannot gain lodging in the motels of the highways and the hotels of the cities. We cannot be satisfied as long as the Negro's basic mobility is from a smaller ghetto to a larger one. We can never be satisfied as long as our children are stripped of their self-hood and robbed of their dignity by signs stating: "For Whites Only." We cannot be satisfied as long as a Negro in Mississippi cannot vote and a Negro in New York believes he has nothing for which to vote. No, no, we are not satisfied, and we will not be satisfied until "justice rolls down like waters, and righteousness like a mighty stream."

14 I am not unmindful that some of you have come here out of great trials and **tribulations**. Some of you have come fresh from narrow jail cells. And some of you have come from areas where your quest—quest for freedom left you battered by the storms of persecution and staggered by the winds of police brutality. You have been the veterans of creative suffering. Continue to work with the faith that unearned suffering is **redemptive**. Go back to Mississippi, go back to Alabama, go back to South Carolina, go back to Georgia, go back to Louisiana, go back to the slums and ghettos of our northern cities, knowing that somehow this situation can and will be changed.

15 Let us not wallow in the valley of despair, I say to you today, my friends.

16 And so even though we face the difficulties of today and tomorrow, I still have a dream. It is a dream deeply rooted in the American dream.

17 I have a dream that one day this nation will rise up and live out the true meaning of its creed: "We hold these truths to be self-evident, that all men are created equal."

18 I have a dream that one day on the red hills of Georgia, the sons of former slaves and the sons of former slave owners will be able to sit down together at the table of brotherhood.

19 I have a dream that one day even the state of Mississippi, a state sweltering with the heat of injustice, sweltering with the heat of **oppression**, will be transformed into an oasis of freedom and justice.

20 I have a dream that my four little children will one day live in a nation where they will not be judged by the color of their skin but by the content of their character.

21 I have a *dream* today!

22 I have a dream that one day, down in Alabama, with its vicious racists, with its governor having his lips dripping with the words of "interposition" and "nullification"[3]—one day right there in Alabama

NOTES

tribulations (trihb yuh LAY shuhnz) *n.* great trouble or misery

redemptive (rih DEHMP tihv) *adj.* serving to deliver from sorrow; make amends or pay back

oppression (uh PREHSH uhn) *n.* cruel or unjust treatment

3. **"interposition"** (ihn tuhr puh ZIHSH uhn) **and "nullification"** (nuhl uh fih KAY shuhn) disputed doctrine that a state can reject federal laws considered to be violations of its rights. Governor George C. Wallace of Alabama used this doctrine to reject federal civil rights legislation.

DIGITAL PERSPECTIVES

Enriching the Text To give students a better understanding of the "I Have a Dream" speech and to contextualize the Civil Rights movement show students a documentary or film highlighting some of the events of the Jim Crow era and events leading up to Martin Luther King, Jr.'s famous speech at the Lincoln Memorial. Be sure to preview the documentary or film before sharing it with the class.

Then, have students write a page about how the documentary or film enhances their understanding of the speech and why it was critical for Dr. King to have delivered it when he did. **(Research to Clarify)**

CLOSE READ

Remind students to focus on phrases that refer to music or which come from songs. You may wish to model the Close Read using the following think-aloud format. Possible responses to questions on the Student page are included.

ANNOTATE: As I read paragraphs 26–27, I notice and highlight the details that refer to sounds or music.

QUESTION: Dr. King has a vision of America as a great orchestra and chorus who should be able to create beautiful, harmonious music, but who instead produce jangling discord.

CONCLUDE: The emotional impact is powerful. Dr. King is saying that the fulfillment of his dream will restore harmony and cause all people to join together in this great anthem of patriotism and shared conviction.

NOTES

exalted (ehg ZAWL tihd) *adj.* elevated

CLOSE READ

ANNOTATE: Mark words and phrases in paragraphs 26–27 that refer to sounds or music.

QUESTION: How do these references help define the transformation in society King is seeking?

CONCLUDE: What effect do these references have on both the meaning and the emotional impact of the speech?

little black boys and black girls will be able to join hands with little white boys and white girls as sisters and brothers.

23 I have a *dream* today!

24 I have a dream that one day every valley shall be **exalted**, and every hill and mountain shall be made low, the rough places will be made plain, and the crooked places will be made straight; "and the glory of the Lord shall be revealed and all flesh shall see it together."[4]

25 This is our hope, and this is the faith that I go back to the South with.

26 With this faith, we will be able to hew out of the mountain of despair a stone of hope. With this faith, we will be able to transform the jangling discords of our nation into a beautiful symphony of brotherhood. With this faith, we will be able to work together, to pray together, to struggle together, to go to jail together, to stand up for freedom together, knowing that we will be free one day.

27 And this will be the day—this will be the day when all of God's children will be able to sing with new meaning:

My country 'tis of thee, sweet land of liberty, of thee I sing.
Land where my fathers died, land of the Pilgrim's pride,
From every mountainside, let freedom ring!

28 And if America is to be a great nation, this must become true.

29 And so let freedom ring from the prodigious hilltops of New Hampshire.

30 Let freedom ring from the mighty mountains of New York.

31 Let freedom ring from the heightening Alleghenies[5] of Pennsylvania.

32 Let freedom ring from the snow-capped Rockies of Colorado.

33 Let freedom ring from the curvaceous slopes of California.

34 But not only that:

35 Let freedom ring from Stone Mountain of Georgia.

36 Let freedom ring from Lookout Mountain of Tennessee.

37 Let freedom ring from every hill and molehill of Mississippi.

38 From every mountainside, let freedom ring.

39 And when this happens, when we allow freedom to ring, when we let it ring from every village and every hamlet, from every state and every city, we will be able to speed up that day when all of God's children, black men and white men, Jews and Gentiles,[6] Protestants and Catholics, will be able to join hands and sing in the words of the old Negro spiritual:

40 Free at last! Free at last!

41 Thank God Almighty, we are free at last! ❧

4. **every valley . . . all flesh shall see it together** reference to a biblical passage (Isaiah 40:4–5). King is likening the struggle of African Americans to the struggle of the Israelites.
5. **Alleghenies** (al uh GAY neez) mountain range that runs through Pennsylvania, Maryland, West Virginia, and Virginia.
6. **Gentiles** (JEHN tylz) people who are not Jewish; often refers to Christians.

PERSONALIZE FOR LEARNING

English Language Support

Taking Notes Support students as they listen to a recording of the "I Have a Dream" speech. Form groups and have them listen to the podcast in 30-second increments. Students should take notes on the key ideas and details spoken during each segment. After listening for 30 seconds, have group members compare their notes. Repeat the process until students have listened to the entirety of the recording.
ALL LEVELS

MEDIA CONNECTION

"I Have a Dream"

Discuss It How does Dr. King's delivery contribute to the power and impact of the speech?

Write your response before sharing your ideas.

SCAN FOR MULTIMEDIA

Comprehension Check

Complete the following items after you finish your first read.

1. About how much time has passed between the signing of the Emancipation Proclamation and Dr. King's speech?

2. When his audience returns home after his speech, what does Dr. King want them to know about the situation African Americans face?

3. What dream does Dr. King have for his four children?

4. **Notebook** Write a summary of Dr. King's "I Have a Dream" speech.

RESEARCH

Research to Clarify Choose at least one unfamiliar detail from the text. Briefly research that detail. In what way does the information you learned shed light on an aspect of the speech?

DIGITAL PERSPECTIVES

Comprehension Check

1. Almost 100 years have passed between the signing of the Emancipation Proclamation and Dr. King's speech.
2. King wants his audience to return home knowing that the situation can and will be changed.
3. King dreams that his children will one day live in a nation where they will not be judged by their skin color but by the content of their character.
4. King's key message was that African Americans were not still treated equally as many faced poverty, discrimination, and lack of opportunities. Dr. King urged his audience that "now" was the time for America to heal the injustices that African Americans still faced. He says that African Americans had been waiting too long, almost 100 years after the signing of the Emancipation Proclamation. He urged Americans to recognize that individual freedoms were tied to everyone's freedoms. He discouraged the breeding of hatred and the use of violence to achieve outcomes. In the end, King shared his dream of a future in America where racial harmony and integration is the standard.

Research

Research to Clarify If students struggle to come up with a detail to research, suggest that they focus on the following topics: "My Country 'Tis of Thee," Emancipation Proclamation, segregation, or Governor George C. Wallace of Alabama and his role in civil rights.

PERSONALIZE FOR LEARNING

Challenge

Conclusions Ask students about the impact that the conclusion of the speech has on Dr. King's message and the audience. Point out that speeches typically end with a "take-away" or a call to action. Reread paragraphs 26–44. Ask students to consider Dr. King's call to action at the end of the speech. Have them write a short essay about the lasting impact of Dr. King's speech, reflecting on his concluding statements. How have things changed since Dr. King gave his speech? What aspects of our society have stayed the same? Has Dr. King's dream materialized?

Jump Start

CLOSE READ Have students close read the selection, "I Have a Dream." Ask students what they know about this famous speech and who delivered it. Ask students if they think Dr. King's "dream" has come to fruition.

Close Read the Text

Walk students through the annotation model on the Student page. Encourage them to complete items 2 and 3 on their own. Review and discuss the sections students have marked. If needed, continue to model close reading by using the Annotation Highlights in the Interactive Teacher's Edition.

Analyze the Text

Possible responses:

1. An "exile"is a person who has been barred from his/her native country. King uses "exile" to show how African Americans exist in a state of punitive exclusion. (Paragraph 3) **DOK 2**
2. In King's comparison, the check is a debt owed to African Americans. They were promised equality but America didn't come through. King's speech is a demand for America to fulfill its "payment" or promise. (Paragraph 5) **DOK 2**
3. (a) King says that "Now" is the only time to act. He says it is not the time to let ideas cool off or get sleepy with the idea of "some day." (Paragraph 6) **DOK 2** (b) King is likely directing this part of his argument to white leaders or other potential supporters who have refrained from engaging in the movement, possibly in hopes that the issue might resolve itself. **DOK 3**
4. King is saying that people who have suffered unjustly will eventually be rewarded. **DOK 3**
5. **Responses will vary.** Students may conclude that words can appeal to an audience's emotions, causing them to act immediately in support of an idea or a cause. **DOK 3**

FORMATIVE ASSESSMENT

Analyze the Text

- **If** students fail to cite evidence, **then** remind them to support their ideas with specific information.
- **If** students struggle with the concept of African Americans in exile in the United States, **then** reframe the concept of exile and offer examples of groups that have been in exile.

MAKING MEANING

"I HAVE A DREAM"

Close Read the Text

1. This model, from paragraph 8 of the text, shows two sample annotations, along with questions and conclusions. Close read the passage, and find another detail to annotate. Then, write a question and your conclusion.

ANNOTATE: The use of the word "thirst" relates to a physical need, something people must have in order to live.

QUESTION: How does this choice of words add intensity to King's argument?

CONCLUDE: The powerful choice of words shows that freedom isn't simply something King and his followers want; it is a basic human need.

Let us not seek to satisfy our thirst for freedom by drinking from the cup of bitterness and hatred.

ANNOTATE: This phrase develops the idea of thirst.

QUESTION: What does this phrase suggest about King's view of the struggle for freedom?

CONCLUDE: The phrase implies that thirst can be quenched in various ways. King warns his listeners against taking a dark path.

Tool Kit
Close-Read Guide and Model Annotation

2. For more practice, go back into the text, and complete the close-read notes.
3. Revisit a section of the text you found important during your first read. Read this section closely, and **annotate** what you notice. Ask yourself **questions** such as "Why did the author make this choice?" What can you **conclude**?

Analyze the Text

CITE TEXTUAL EVIDENCE to support your answers.

Notebook Respond to these questions.

1. **Interpret** What does King mean when he refers to the African American as an "exile in his own land"?
2. **Summarize** Explain the comparison King makes between the African American struggle for equality and the cashing of a check.
3. **Paraphrase** (a) When you **paraphrase**, you restate a text in your own words. Paraphrase King's comments on the urgency of "Now." (b) **Speculate** To which group of people might King have been directing that part of his argument? Explain.
4. **Evaluate** What idea is King trying to convey when he says that "unearned suffering is redemptive"?
5. **Essential Question:** *How can words inspire change?* What have you learned about the power of words by reading this speech?

STANDARDS

Reading Informational Text

- Cite strong and thorough textual evidence to support analysis of what the text says explicitly as well as inferences drawn from the text.
- Determine an author's point of view or purpose in a text and analyze how an author uses rhetoric to advance that point of view or purpose.
- Analyze seminal U.S. documents of historical and literary significance, including how they address related themes and concepts.

WriteNow Express and Reflect

Argument Some historians may argue that Dr. King's "I Have a Dream" speech single-handedly shaped the outcomes of the Civil Rights Movement. Have students write a one-page essay taking a position on this claim. Encourage students to use other texts or conduct research online to support their claims. Remind students to include a counterclaim and evidence, and give students an opportunity to share their arguments with their classmates.

Analyze Craft and Structure

Argument In a **persuasive speech**, the speaker tries to convince listeners to think or act in a certain way. Strong persuasive speakers present information and supporting evidence clearly and logically so listeners can follow the reasoning. Persuasive speakers may charged language—language that appeals to emotions. In addition, they often use **rhetorical devices**—patterns of words and ideas that create emphasis and emotion. These devices include the following forms:

- **Parallelism:** repeating a grammatical structure or an arrangement of words to create rhythm and momentum
- **Repetition:** using the same words frequently to reinforce concepts and unify the speech
- **Analogy:** drawing a comparison that shows a similarity between two unlike things

Practice

CITE TEXTUAL EVIDENCE to support your answers.

Notebook **Reread the speech. Then, respond to the questions.**

1. In this speech, what is King attempting to persuade his listeners to think or do? Explain.
2. Use the chart to record at least one example of each type of rhetorical device used in this speech. Explain why each choice is a good example of that device.

RHETORICAL DEVICE	EXAMPLE FROM THE SPEECH	EXPLANATION
charged language	*lonely island of poverty* **(Paragraph 3)**	a. This phrase strongly describes the state of isolation brought on by poverty.
parallelism	*But one hundred years later, . . . a vast ocean of material prosperity.* (Paragraph 3)	b. Shows that since the Emancipation Proclamation, African Americans have made little progress toward freedom.
repetition	*I have a dream...* Paragraphs 17–24	c. Shows a glimpse of what King hopes the nation will achieve.
analogy	American civil rights are compared to a bad check. Paragraph 5	d. The freedoms accorded African Americans are not worth the paper they are printed on.

3. For each example from your chart, state whether the rhetorical device serves to clarify an idea, stir listeners' emotions, or both. For each determination, explain your reasoning.
4. This speech has become an iconic part of American history. Do you think it deserves this standing? Support your answer with text evidence and your analysis of King's use of rhetoric.

PERSONALIZE FOR LEARNING

English Language Support

Idioms English Language learners may find Idioms confusing. Explain that the phrase *cooling off* in paragraph 6 is an idiom. To help them understand the usage in the paragraph, explain that asking someone to cool off means you're asking him or her to calm down. Ask students to think of a book or movie where a character was upset about something important. How did the character react to being told to "cool off"? What did Dr. King mean when he said, "this is no time to engage in the luxury of cooling off"? **ALL LEVELS**

DIGITAL PERSPECTIVES

Analyze Craft and Structure

Discuss with students why an author might choose to use emotionally charged language in a persuasive speech or argument. Have them think about the advantages and disadvantages of appealing to the audience's emotions. Students should recognize that this technique helps the author connect with the audience. In this case, using emotionally charged language helps listeners recognize that social injustices impact all Americans. For more support, see **Analyze Craft and Structure: Argument.**

MAKE IT INTERACTIVE

Have students break up into pairs. Assign the pairs opposite sides of the same argument and ask each student to write a short persuasive speech using rhetorical devices such as emotionally charged language, parallelism, repetition, and/or analogy. Each student should have a chance to present the speech to his or her partner.

Practice

1. In the speech, Dr. King is attempting to persuade listeners to help fight for the rights of African Americans in the United States so they can experience the liberties outlined in the Constitution.
2. Possible responses:

   See possible responses in pink on student page.
3. **Charged language:** These examples stir listener's emotions. These phrases are powerful and persuasive ways of describing the effect of poverty and hatred. **Parallelism:** King uses this example to stir listener's emotions and to clarify an idea. **Repetition:** This example stirs listener's emotions. Its repetition heightens its impact. **Analogy:** This analogy is used to clarify an idea.
4. **Responses will vary.** Students should be able to support their answer with evidence from the text and their own analysis.

FORMATIVE ASSESSMENT

Analyze Craft and Structure

If students struggle with rhetorical devices, **then** have them practice writing their own examples. For Reteach and Practice, see **Analyze Craft and Structure: Argument (RP).**

Concept Vocabulary

Why These Words

Possible responses:

1. *Tribulations* (paragraph 14), *oppression* (paragraph 19) express how African Americans suffered. King says that suffering will be *redemptive* (paragraph 14), or rewarded. *Hallowed* (paragraph 6) indicates the sacred nature of the U.S. capitol, where King stood and recalled the nation's promise of equality. African Americans had not shared in the nation's prosperity. King says they will be *exalted* (paragraph 24), or rise from their suffering.
2. Other words that relate to the concept vocabulary: *persecution* (paragraph 14), *injustice* (paragraph 2), *crippled* (paragraph 3), *discrimination* (paragraph 3), *sacred* (paragraph 4), *lift* (paragraph 6), *justice* (paragraph 5)

Practice

Possible responses:

1. The rise in the sale of new products brought an era of *prosperity* to the nation. The *redemptive* power of music was evident in people's faces. They understood the importance of standing on such *hallowed* ground. We must end *oppression* for all people to live freely. The explorers turned back after the *tribulations* caused by the storm. We were honored to be in such *exalted* company.
2. The rise in the sale of new products brought an era of *economic success* to the nation. The *rewarding* power of music was evident in people's faces. They understood the importance of standing on such *revered* ground. We must end *injustice* for all people to live freely. The explorers turned back after the *problems* caused by the storm. We were honored to be in such *illustrious* company.

Word Network

Possible words: *justice, discrimination, dignity*

Word Study

For more support, see **Concept Vocabulary and Word Study.**

1. (a) assumption, (b) reception, (c) prescription
2. For once, his *assumption* was correct. The band received a warm *reception*. The doctor refilled Dad's *prescription*.

FORMATIVE ASSESSMENT

Concept Vocabulary

If students fail to see the connections between the words, **then** have them use each one in a sentence.

Word Study

If students misspell words, **then** point out that adding the suffix *-tion* can be challenging and have them use a dictionary to check spellings. For Reteach and Practice, see **Word Study: Word Changes (RP).**

"I HAVE A DREAM"

Concept Vocabulary

prosperity	tribulations	oppression
hallowed	redemptive	exalted

Why These Words? The six concept vocabulary words are all related to overcoming a challenge. For example, Dr. Martin Luther King, Jr., speaks of overcoming the *tribulations* that African Americans face.

1. How does the concept vocabulary help express both the difficulties and the possible rewards of the struggle for equality?
2. What other words in the selection connect to this concept?

Practice

Notebook Complete the activities.

1. Use each concept vocabulary word in a sentence that demonstrates its meaning.
2. Rewrite each of your sentences, replacing the concept vocabulary word with a synonym. How do your replacements change the meaning of each sentence?

WORD NETWORK

Add interesting words related to civil rights from the text to your Word Network.

Word Study

Patterns of Word Changes When added to a base word, the suffix *-tion* changes a verb to a noun. In some words, that change requires other adjustments to spelling. For example, in the word *describe*, the letters *be* are deleted and replaced with a *p* plus *-tion* to get *description*.

1. Form nouns by adding the suffix *-tion* to each of the following verbs. Make any adjustments to spelling that might be required.
   a. **assume** ____________________
   b. **receive** ____________________
   c. **prescribe** ____________________
2. Now that you have changed the verbs into nouns, use them in your own sentences.

STANDARDS

Language

- Demonstrate command of the conventions of standard English grammar and usage when writing or speaking.
- Use parallel structure.
- Spell correctly.
- Identify and correctly use patterns of word changes that indicate different meanings or parts of speech.

AUTHOR'S PERSPECTIVE Elfrieda Hiebert, Ph.D.

Frequency of Concepts in Narrative Texts In describing character traits or problems, skilled authors rarely repeat the same word, other than to achieve unity through repetition. Instead, authors use different words to create an interesting style. For instance, authors use a variety of words to describe setting, such as *lagoon, swales, bog*. Specifically, in *The Wizard of Oz*, L. Frank Baum describes what Dorothy and her companions see on arriving in the Emerald City with these words: *brilliance, dazzled, glittering*. Word variety also helps authors build characterization in jobs (*actor, lawyer, expert*) and roles *(adult/relative, female, male*). Especially in stories, the concepts represented by rare words are often known by common words that most students understand, such as *down* and *blah* for the rare words *lethargic*, *listless*, *slothful*, and

Conventions

Parallel Structure Parallelism, or **parallel structure**, is the use of similar grammatical forms or patterns to express similar ideas. Effective use of parallelism adds rhythm and balance to your writing and strengthens connections among your ideas.

When writing lacks parallelism, it presents equal ideas in an unnecessary mix of grammatical forms. This inconsistency can be awkward, confusing, or distracting for readers. By contrast, parallel constructions place equal ideas in words, phrases, or clauses of similar types.

This chart shows examples of nonparallel and parallel structure.

TIP

CLARIFICATION
Always check for parallelism when your writing contains items in a series, draws a comparison between two or more things, or includes a correlative conjunction, such as *both . . . and* or *not only . . . but also.*

ELEMENTS	NONPARALLEL STRUCTURE	PARALLEL STRUCTURE
words	Planning, drafting, and **revision** are three steps in the writing process.	Planning, drafting, and **revising** are three steps in the writing process.
phrases	I could not wait to try my new surfboard, to catch some waves, and **for a visit to the beach**.	I could not wait to try my new surfboard, to catch some waves, and **to visit the beach**.
clauses	Olivia likes her school: The teachers are good, the students are nice, and **she likes the new building.**	Olivia likes her school: The teachers are good, the students are nice, and **the building is new.**

Read It

1. Read each sentence from Dr. King's "I Have a Dream" speech. Mark the elements that are parallel. Then, note what type of parallel structure is being used—words, phrases, or clauses.

a. One hundred years later, the life of the Negro is still sadly crippled by the manacles of segregation and the chains of discrimination.

b. This is no time to engage in the luxury of cooling off or to take the tranquilizing drug of gradualism.

c. With this faith, we will be able to work together, to pray together, to struggle together, to go to jail together, to stand up for freedom together, knowing that we will be free one day.

Write It

Notebook Add a parallel phrase or clause to each of the following sentences.

1. But we refuse to believe that the bank of justice is bankrupt.

2. And so, we've come to cash this check.

3. And so, even though we face the difficulties of today and tomorrow, I still have a dream.

DIGITAL PERSPECTIVES

Conventions

Parallel Structure Discuss the definition of parallelism with students. For more support, see **Conventions: Parallel Structure.**

Read It

Possible responses:

1. (a) the manacles of segregation / the chains of discrimination; phrase (b) to engage in the luxury of cooling off / to take the tranquilizing drug of gradualism; phrase (c) to work together / to pray together / to struggle together / to go to jail together / to stand up for freedom together; phrase

Write It

Possible responses:

1. But we refuse to believe that the bank of justice, the repository of equality, and the store of goodness are bankrupt. (phrase)
2. And so, we've come to cash this check and to get our share. (verb)
3. And so, even though we face the difficulties of today and we face the difficulties of tomorrow, I still have a dream. (clause)

FORMATIVE ASSESSMENT

Conventions

If students struggle with parallel structure, **then** remind them to look for repetitive clauses or phrases. For Reteach and Practice, see **Conventions: Parallel Structure (RP).**

Selection Test

Administer the "I Have a Dream" Selection Test, which is available in both print and digital formats online in Assessments.

sluggish. However, the more complex the text, the rarer the words that describe a particular concept will be. For instance, in a complex text, rather than describing a character as *calm*, the author might use *phlegmatic*. However, be sure that students understand that words such as these in a concept network have subtle differences in meaning and cannot necessarily be substituted for one another.

PERSONALIZE FOR LEARNING

English Language Support

Justifying an Opinion about Parallelism Have students read a short excerpt of a fiction or nonfiction work that features parallelism. For example, see the first sentence of *A Tale of Two Cities.*

Ask pairs of students to form an opinion about the effect the parallelism has on the reader and the understanding of the text. **EMERGING ELD**

Ask students to form an opinion about the effect the parallelism has on the reader's understanding of the text and then write a few sentences stating the opinion and using text evidence to support it. **EMERGING ELD**

Ask students to form an opinion about the effect the parallelism has on the reader's understanding of the text and then write a paragraph stating the opinion and using text evidence to support it. **EMERGING ELD**

An expanded **English Language Support Lesson** on Parallelism is available in the Digital Teacher's Edition.

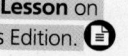

Letter From Birmingham Jail

AUDIO SUMMARIES
Audio summaries of "Letter From Birmingham Jail" are available online in both English and Spanish in the Interactive Teacher's Edition or Unit Resources. Assigning these summaries prior to reading the selection may help students build additional background knowledge and set a context for their first read.

Summary

In his "Letter From Birmingham Jail," Martin Luther King responds to his critics in the church who urged him against nonviolent protest. He begins by explaining why he is in Birmingham. The city's laws call for deep segregation. He says that injustice anywhere challenges injustice everywhere. Although his critics don't support the demonstrations, King says he has taken every step to avoid these protests. His teams have studied the situation and they have worked to negotiate to change the laws. King says that freedom is not given, but must be demanded. Next, King describes two forces within the African-American community. There is one of complacency or acceptance, and there is one of hatred. King calls for action that falls between these two extremes. He calls for the church to be braver and to act on the injustices that exist. Finally, he says that one day the South will recognize the heroes of the movement who were brave enough to stand up to the injustice of segregation.

Insight

This letter thoroughly and rigorously lays down the case for civil disobedience. But on top of the letter's logic, King gives compelling, relatable, vivid examples to show the reader the importance of the cause.

ESSENTIAL QUESTION:
How can words inspire change?

Connection to Essential Question

As students consider the Essential Question, this text will be critical. This letter was widely republished, and became a key text in the civil rights movement.

WHOLE-CLASS LEARNING PERFORMANCE TASK
How did the selections in this section affect those who first heard them or read them?

UNIT PERFORMANCE-BASED ASSESSMENT
Explain how words have the power to provoke, calm, or inspire.

Connection to Performance Tasks

Whole-Class Learning Performance Task King's letter was important to his efforts. This task calls for outside research into how this letter was received at the time.

Unit Performance-Based Assessment The letter uses careful reasoning, citations of authorities its target audience respected, and evocative explanations. Both its logic and its rhetoric are sound, and King had a deliberate goal in mind. He wanted to get more people to participate in nonviolent protest.

DIGITAL PERSPECTIVES — Audio | Video | Document | Annotation Highlights | EL Highlights | Online Assessment

LESSON RESOURCES

	Making Meaning	Language Development	Effective Expression
Lesson	**First Read** **Close Read** **Analyze the Text** **Analyze Craft and Structure**	**Concept Vocabulary** **Word Study** **Conventions**	**Writing to Compare**
Instructional Standards	**RI.1** Cite strong and thorough textual evidence... **RI.10** By the end of grade 9, read and comprehend literary nonfiction . . . **RI.3** Analyze how the author unfolds an analysis . . . **RI.9** Analyze seminal U.S. documents . . .	**L.1.b** Use various types of phrases and clauses . . . **L.4.b** Identify and correctly use patterns of word changes . . . **L.5** Demonstrate understanding of figurative language . . .	**W.2** Write informative/explanatory texts . . . **W.4** Produce clear and coherent writing . . . **W.9.b** Apply grades 9–10 Reading standards . . .
STUDENT RESOURCES			
Available online in the Interactive Student Edition or Unit Resources	Selection Audio First-Read Guide: Nonfiction Close-Read Guide: Nonfiction	Word Network	Evidence Log
TEACHER RESOURCES			
Selection Resources Available online in the Interactive Teacher's Edition or Unit Resources	Audio Summaries Annotation Highlights EL Highlights English Language Support Lesson: Allusion Analyze Craft and Structure: Argument	Concept Vocabulary and Word Study Conventions: Relative Clauses	Writing to Compare: Compare-and-Contrast Essay
Reteach/Practice (RP) Available online in the Interactive Teacher's Edition or Unit Resources	Analyze Craft and Structure: Argument (RP)	Word Study: Latin Root *-plac-* (RP) Conventions: Relative Clauses (RP)	
Assessment Available online in Assessments	Selection Test		
My Resources	A Unit 3 Answer Key is available online and in the Interactive Teacher's Edition.		

Reading Support

Text Complexity Rubric: Letter From Birmingham Jail

Quantitative Measures	
Lexile: 1190 **Text Length:** 6,936 words	
Qualitative Measures	
Knowledge Demands ①—②—❸—④—⑤	To understand text, reader needs context of the reason for the letter and the non-violent resistance in Birmingham leading to the arrest. Some, but not all, of the context is explained.
Structure ①—②—③—❹—⑤	The structure of a formal letter has organization that is logical and sequential, but includes multiple pathways and a large range of ideas. Connections between ideas is not always explicit.
Language Conventionality and Clarity ①—②—③—❹—⑤	Langauge is dense and complex, with a lot of formal language patterns; use of metaphorical phrases with contrasting concepts; many complex sentences with multiple clauses.
Levels of Meaning/Purpose ①—②—❸—④—⑤	Overall purpose of text is easily identified, but concepts that back up the main ideas are intricate, with a lot of figurative language used to express meaning.

DECIDE AND PLAN

English Language Support

Provide English Learners with support for structure and language as they read the selection.

Structure Help students to navigate the structure by providing clues to the overall organization. For example, first King makes an introduction and states that he is responding to a recent statement by the clergy. In the next paragraph, he explains his affiliations in Birmingham. In the third, he talks about the injustice he sees there, and in the fourth, he writes about how all communities are affected by injustice.

Language The text contains difficult language. Encourage students to work to get the gist of each paragraph without trying to understand every word. Write some of the difficult phrases or metaphors to discuss with students.

Strategic Support

Provide students with strategic support to ensure that they can successfully read the text.

Language Point out words that make the language sound formal. For example, (paragraph 2) King says *I think I should indicate why I am here*. If the style were conversational style he might say *I'll tell you why I'm here*.

Discuss the metaphors that are used to make contrasts, for example: (paragraph 9) dark depths of prejudice/majestic heights of understanding and brotherhood.

Structure Point out that when there is a long selection like this one, students can break down the text to look at the purpose of each section. Ask them to read paragraph by paragraph and help them identify the main ideas. Then have them reread the text with these concepts in mind.

Challenge

Provide students who need to be challenged with ideas for how they can go beyond a simple interpretation of the text.

Text Analysis Ask students to analyze the language style that King uses in his writing. First have them highlight sentences that make the letter sound very formal and to say how the sentences might sound if the language were informal. Then have them identify examples of metaphorical language, for example (paragraph 12) *Asia and Africa are moving at jetlike speed/ we still move at a horse and buggy pace.*

Written Response Have students imagine they are writing a letter about injustice they see in their communities or in the world. Ask them to write a paragraph in a formal style. Ask them to include metaphorical language.

TEACH

Read and Respond

Have the class do their first read of the selection. Then have them complete their close read. Finally, work with them on the Making Meaning, Language Development, and Effective Expression activities.

Standards Support Through Teaching and Learning Cycle

IDENTIFY NEEDS

Analyze results of the Beginning-of-Year Assessment, focusing on the items relating to Unit 3. Also take into consideration student performance to this point and your observations of where particular students struggle.

DECIDE AND PLAN

- If students have performed poorly on items matching these standards, then provide selection scaffolds before assigning them the on-level lesson provided in the Student Edition.
- If students have done well on the Beginning-of-Year Assessment, then challenge them to keep progressing and learning by giving them opportunities to practice the skills in depth.
- Use the Selection Resources listed on the Planning pages for "Letter From Birmingham Jail" to help students continually improve their ability to master the standards.

Instructional Standards: Letter From Birmingham Jail

	Catching Up	This Year	Looking Forward
Reading	You may wish to administer the **Analyze Craft and Structure: Argument (RP)** worksheet to help students understand the basic elements of persuasion.	**RI.3** Analyze how the author unfolds an analysis or series of ideas or events, including the order in which the points are made, how they are introduced and developed, and the connections that are drawn between them.	Challenge students to think of other rhetorical devices that may aid an argument.
Language	You may wish to administer the **Conventions: Relative Clauses (RP)** worksheet to help students understand the function of relative clauses and relative pronouns. Review the **Word Study: Latin Root *-plac-* (RP)** worksheet with students to ensure they understand the meaning of the root word.	**L.1.b** Use various types of phrases and clauses to convey specific meanings and add variety and interest to writing or presentations. **L.4.b** Identify and correctly use patterns of word changes that indicate different meanings or parts of speech.	Have students find sentences within the selection that use relative clauses, then rewrite them without the relative clauses to point out the effectiveness of the technique. Have students identify other words in the selection that use Latin or Greek roots they may recognize.

ANALYZE AND REVISE

- Analyze student work for evidence of student learning.
- Identify whether or not students have met the expectations in the standards.
- Identify implications for future instruction.

TEACH

Implement the planned lesson, and gather evidence of student learning.

Jump Start

FIRST READ Prior to students' first read, ask them to talk about the Civil Rights movement and some of its prominent leaders, including Martin Luther King, Jr. What do they know about Dr. King's role? What kind of impact did he have on the movement?

Letter From Birmingham Jail

What is the purpose of the letter, and does the writer achieve his or her intended goal? Is nonviolence an effective method for addressing injustice? Modeling the questions a reader might ask as they read "Letter from Birmingham Jail" for the first time brings the text alive for students and connects it to the Whole-Class Performance Task assignment. Selection audio and print capability for the selection are available in the Interactive Teacher's Edition.

Concept Vocabulary

Support students as they rank their words. Ask if they've ever heard, read, or used them. Reassure them that the definitions for these words are listed in the selection.

FIRST READ

As they read, students should perform the steps of the first read:

NOTICE: Have students notice that the letter was written while Dr. King was in jail in Birmingham, Alabama, to eight white ministers who published a letter criticizing him.

ANNOTATE: Remind students to mark passages they find particularly memorable and may wish to return to. These may include passages that demonstrate Dr. King's effective use of figurative language and historical allusions.

CONNECT: Encourage students to go beyond the text to think about how Dr. King's "I Have a Dream" speech compares to "Letter From Birmingham Jail." Are Dr. King's messages similar or different in the two selections?

RESPOND: Students will answer questions and write a summary to demonstrate understanding.

Point out to students that while they will always complete the Respond step at the end of the first read, the other steps will probably happen somewhat concurrently. You may wish to print copies of the **First-Read Guide: Nonfiction** for students to use.

MAKING MEANING

"I HAVE A DREAM"

Comparing Texts

In this part of the lesson, you will read Dr. King's "Letter From Birmingham Jail." First, complete the first read and close read activities. Then, compare the ways in which Dr. King uses language to appeal to different audiences.

LETTER FROM BIRMINGHAM JAIL

About the Author

Dr. Martin Luther King, Jr. (1929–1968) was one of the most charismatic leaders of the civil rights movement. King first came to national attention in Montgomery, Alabama in 1956 when he organized a boycott by African-Americans of the city's segregated buses. He went on to lead other protests and to speak out against poverty and social injustice. He was assassinated on April 4, 1968.

Tool Kit
First-Read Guide and Model Annotation

STANDARDS
Reading Informational Text
By the end of grade 9, read and comprehend literary nonfiction in the grades 9–10 text complexity band proficiently, with scaffolding as needed at the high end of the range.

Letter From Birmingham Jail

Concept Vocabulary

You will encounter the following words as you read "Letter From Birmingham Jail." Before reading, note how familiar you are with each word. Then, rank the words in order from most familiar (1) to least familiar (6).

WORD	YOUR RANKING
idly	
postpone	
stagnation	
complacency	
yearning	
languished	

After completing the first read, come back to the concept vocabulary and review your rankings. Mark changes to your original rankings as needed.

First Read NONFICTION

Apply these strategies as you conduct your first read. You will have an opportunity to complete a close read after your first read.

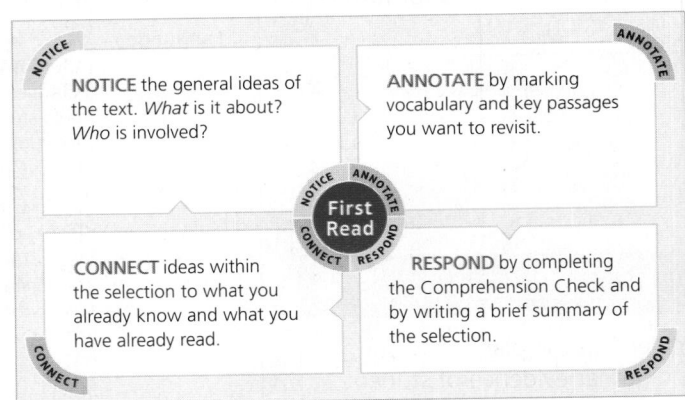

NOTICE the general ideas of the text. *What* is it about? *Who* is involved?

ANNOTATE by marking vocabulary and key passages you want to revisit.

CONNECT ideas within the selection to what you already know and what you have already read.

RESPOND by completing the Comprehension Check and by writing a brief summary of the selection.

Letter From Birmingham Jail

Dr. Martin Luther King, Jr.

BACKGROUND

By the late 1950s, Dr. Martin Luther King, Jr. had emerged as a key figure of the Civil Rights movement. During the Kennedy administration, Dr. King was arrested in April, 1963, for protesting racial segregation in Birmingham, Alabama. As he sat in jail, he read a newspaper article in which eight white clergymen criticized him for "unwise and untimely" demonstrations. Without proper writing paper, Dr. King drafted a response—this letter—in the cramped margins of that newspaper.

SCAN FOR MULTIMEDIA

16 April 1963

My Dear Fellow Clergymen:

1 While confined here in the Birmingham city jail, I came across your recent statement calling my present activities "unwise and untimely." Seldom do I pause to answer criticism of my work and ideas. If I sought to answer all the criticisms that cross my desk, my secretaries would have little time for anything other than such correspondence in the course of the day, and I would have no time for constructive work. But since I feel that you are men of genuine good will and that

NOTES

DIGITAL PERSPECTIVES

CLOSER LOOK

Analyze Diction

Students may have marked paragraph 1 during their first read. Use this paragraph to help students understand Dr. King's choice to show respect and civility as he addresses the eight white clergymen who criticized him for organizing peaceful demonstrations. Encourage them to talk about the annotations that they marked. You may want to model a close read with the class based on the highlights shown in the text.

ANNOTATE: Have students mark details in paragraph 1 that demonstrate Dr. King's non-confrontational approach, or have students participate while you highlight them.

QUESTION: What can we infer about Dr. King's attitude and mindset based on the language he uses?

Possible response: Dr. King chose to behave respectfully toward his fellow clergymen while he answered their criticisms of his actions.

CONCLUDE: Help students to formulate conclusions about the importance of these details in the text. Ask students why the author might have included these details.

Possible response: Dr. King was not only addressing these clergymen. He was writing a public letter which would be read by millions of people, who would judge it not only on its merits as an answer to the criticisms expressed by those clergymen, but by Dr. King's tone as he framed his answer.

Remind students that an author's **diction**—the words the author chooses to convey his message—reveals his attitude toward his subject.

WriteNow Express and Reflect

Write a Speech Ask students to reflect on an issue or a cause that means a lot to them; for example, cancer, animal rights, or equal pay for women. As a class, review how Dr. King opens his letter in paragraph 1 of "Letter From Birmingham Jail." Note the details, the language, the tone, and the style. Instruct students to write the introduction of a letter about the issue or cause they chose to someone who might not feel as strongly about that issue or cause. Remind students that they want to demonstrate sincerity in order to win their opponents over. Encourage them to use Dr. King's opening as inspiration.

CLOSE READ

Remind students to focus on Dr. King's firm but respectful attitude to the clergymen as he begins to reply to their criticisms. You may wish to model the Close Read using the following think-aloud format. Possible responses to questions on the Student page are included. You may also want to print copies of the **Close-Read Guide: Nonfiction** for students to use.

ANNOTATE: As I read paragraph 5, I notice that Dr. King expresses regret that there must be demonstrations in Birmingham and for the underlying causes of those demonstrations.

QUESTION: Dr. King uses the respectful tone of an apology as a way of respectfully correcting the clergymen for overlooking the root causes of the demonstrations.

CONCLUDE: Dr. King's approach changes the focus from the demonstrations themselves to the underlying causes of the demonstrations, which are the problems he feels need to be addressed.

Additional **English Language Support** is available in the Digital Teacher's Edition.

NOTES

your criticisms are sincerely set forth, I want to try to answer your statement in what I hope will be patient and reasonable terms.

2 I think I should indicate why I am here in Birmingham, since you have been influenced by the view which argues against "outsiders coming in." I have the honor of serving as president of the Southern Christian Leadership Conference, an organization operating in every southern state, with headquarters in Atlanta, Georgia. We have some eighty five affiliated organizations across the South, and one of them is the Alabama Christian Movement for Human Rights. Frequently we share staff, educational, and financial resources with our affiliates. Several months ago the affiliate here in Birmingham asked us to be on call to engage in a nonviolent direct action program if such were deemed necessary. We readily consented, and when the hour came we lived up to our promise. So I, along with several members of my staff, am here because I was invited here. I am here because I have organizational ties here.

3 But more basically, I am in Birmingham because injustice is here. Just as the prophets of the eighth century B.C. left their villages and carried their "thus saith the Lord" far beyond the boundaries of their home towns, and just as the Apostle Paul left his village of Tarsus and carried the gospel of Jesus Christ to the far corners of the Greco-Roman world, so am I compelled to carry the gospel of freedom beyond my own home town. Like Paul, I must constantly respond to the Macedonian call for aid.

idly (YD lee) *adv.* lazily; without taking action

4 Moreover, I am cognizant of the interrelatedness of all communities and states. I cannot sit **idly** by in Atlanta and not be concerned about what happens in Birmingham. Injustice anywhere is a threat to justice everywhere. We are caught in an inescapable network of mutuality, tied in a single garment of destiny. Whatever affects one directly, affects all indirectly. Never again can we afford to live with the narrow, provincial "outside agitator" idea. Anyone who lives inside the United States can never be considered an outsider anywhere within its bounds.

CLOSE READ

ANNOTATE: In paragraph 5, mark details that reveal what King is apologizing for.

QUESTION: Why would King express his apology in this way?

CONCLUDE: How does this approach emphasize what King believes is the real problem to address?

5 You deplore the demonstrations taking place in Birmingham. But your statement, I am sorry to say, fails to express a similar concern for the conditions that brought about the demonstrations. I am sure that none of you would want to rest content with the superficial kind of social analysis that deals merely with effects and does not grapple with underlying causes. It is unfortunate that demonstrations are taking place in Birmingham, but it is even more unfortunate that the city's white power structure left the Negro community with no alternative.

6 In any nonviolent campaign there are four basic steps: collection of the facts to determine whether injustices exist; negotiation; self purification; and direct action. We have gone through all these steps in Birmingham. There can be no gainsaying[1] the fact that racial

1. **gainsaying** *v.* denying or disproving.

PERSONALIZE FOR LEARNING

Strategic Support

Research In paragraph 2, Dr. King begins to explain why he has come to Birmingham. Throughout "Letter From Birmingham Jail," Dr. King references various injustices happening in Birmingham. Ask students to use the Internet to research some of the events that transpired between 1960 and 1963 in Birmingham and how those events might have angered the African-American community. If students are having a difficult time, suggest search terms they can use; for example, *civil rights in Birmingham* or *Dr. King's arrest in Birmingham*.

injustice engulfs this community. Birmingham is probably the most thoroughly segregated city in the United States. Its ugly record of brutality is widely known. Negroes have experienced grossly unjust treatment in the courts. There have been more unsolved bombings of Negro homes and churches in Birmingham than in any other city in the nation. These are the hard, brutal facts of the case. On the basis of these conditions, Negro leaders sought to negotiate with the city fathers. But the latter consistently refused to engage in good faith negotiation.

7 Then, last September, came the opportunity to talk with leaders of Birmingham's economic community. In the course of the negotiations, certain promises were made by the merchants—for example, to remove the stores' humiliating racial signs. On the basis of these promises, the Reverend Fred Shuttlesworth and the leaders of the Alabama Christian Movement for Human Rights agreed to a moratorium[2] on all demonstrations. As the weeks and months went by, we realized that we were the victims of a broken promise. A few signs, briefly removed, returned; the others remained.

8 As in so many past experiences, our hopes had been blasted, and the shadow of deep disappointment settled upon us. We had no alternative except to prepare for direct action, whereby we would present our very bodies as a means of laying our case before the conscience of the local and the national community. Mindful of the difficulties involved, we decided to undertake a process of self purification. We began a series of workshops on nonviolence, and we repeatedly asked ourselves: "Are you able to accept blows without retaliating?" "Are you able to endure the ordeal of jail?" We decided to schedule our direct action program for the Easter season, realizing that except for Christmas, this is the main shopping period of the year. Knowing that a strong economic-withdrawal program would be the by-product of direct action, we felt that this would be the best time to bring pressure to bear on the merchants for the needed change.

9 Then it occurred to us that Birmingham's mayoral election was coming up in March, and we speedily decided to **postpone** action until after election day. When we discovered that the Commissioner of Public Safety, Eugene "Bull" Connor, had piled up enough votes to be in the run off, we decided again to postpone action until the day after the run off so that the demonstrations could not be used to cloud the issues. Like many others, we waited to see Mr. Connor defeated, and to this end we endured postponement after postponement. Having aided in this community need, we felt that our direct action program could be delayed no longer.

10 You may well ask: "Why direct action? Why sit-ins, marches, and so forth? Isn't negotiation a better path?" You are quite right in calling for negotiation. Indeed, this is the very purpose of direct action.

NOTES

postpone (pohst POHN) *v.* delay

2. **moratorium** (mawr uh TAWR ee uhm) *n.* time when a particular activity is not allowed.

CLOSE READD

Remind students to focus on any repeated words or phrases as they read. You may wish to model the Close Read using the following think-aloud format. Possible responses to questions on the Student page are included.

ANNOTATE: As I read paragraph 10, I notice that Dr. King uses the word *tension* six times.

QUESTION: Dr. King is demonstrating that the word *tension* can have positive and negative meanings, and making a distinction between "violent tension" and "creative tension."

CONCLUDE: The effect is one of "tension" itself. Its repetition builds in the mind and makes it more memorable.

NOTES

CLOSE READ

ANNOTATE: In paragraph 10, mark the word that King repeats.

QUESTION: Why does King revisit this word? What is he trying to show or explain?

CONCLUDE: What is the effect of King's effort to clarify what he means in using this word?

Nonviolent direct action seeks to create such a crisis and foster such a tension that a community which has constantly refused to negotiate is forced to confront the issue. It seeks so to dramatize the issue that it can no longer be ignored. My citing the creation of tension as part of the work of the nonviolent resister may sound rather shocking. But I must confess that I am not afraid of the word "tension." I have earnestly opposed violent tension, but there is a type of constructive, nonviolent tension which is necessary for growth. Just as Socrates felt that it was necessary to create a tension in the mind so that individuals could rise from the bondage of myths and half truths to the unfettered realm of creative analysis and objective appraisal, so must we see the need for nonviolent gadflies[3] to create the kind of tension in society that will help men rise from the dark depths of prejudice and racism to the majestic heights of understanding and brotherhood.

11 The purpose of our direct action program is to create a situation so crisis-packed that it will inevitably open the door to negotiation. I therefore concur with you in your call for negotiation. Too long has our beloved Southland been bogged down in a tragic effort to live in monologue rather than dialogue.

12 One of the basic points in your statement is that the action that I and my associates have taken in Birmingham is untimely. Some have asked: "Why didn't you give the new city administration time to act?" The only answer that I can give to this query is that the new Birmingham administration must be prodded about as much as the outgoing one, before it will act. We are sadly mistaken if we feel that the election of Albert Boutwell as mayor will bring the millennium[4] to Birmingham. While Mr. Boutwell is a much more gentle person than Mr. Connor, they are both segregationists, dedicated to maintenance of the status quo. I have hope that Mr. Boutwell will be reasonable enough to see the futility of massive resistance to desegregation. But he will not see this without pressure from devotees of civil rights. My friends, I must say to you that we have not made a single gain in civil rights without determined legal and nonviolent pressure. Lamentably, it is an historical fact that privileged groups seldom give up their privileges voluntarily. Individuals may see the moral light and voluntarily give up their unjust posture; but, as Reinhold Niebuhr[5] has reminded us, groups tend to be more immoral than individuals.

13 We know through painful experience that freedom is never voluntarily given by the oppressor; it must be demanded by the oppressed. Frankly, I have yet to engage in a direct action campaign that was "well timed" in the view of those who have not suffered unduly from the disease of segregation. For years now I have heard

3. **gadflies** *n.* people who annoy others by being very critical.
4. **bring the millennium** In some forms of Christianity, the world is believed to enter a thousand-year period of peace and happiness before the end of time.
5. **Reinhold Niebuhr** (NEE bur) (1892–1971) American professor of theology who advocated nonviolence and social reform.

^ Police officers arrest Dr. King on September 3, 1958, in Montgomery, Alabama. Dr. King was charged with loitering outside the courtroom in which his colleague was testifying.

NOTES

the word "Wait!" It rings in the ear of every Negro with piercing familiarity. This "Wait" has almost always meant "Never." We must come to see, with one of our distinguished jurists, that "justice too long delayed is justice denied."

14 We have waited for more than 340 years for our constitutional and God given rights. The nations of Asia and Africa are moving with jetlike speed toward gaining political independence, but we still creep at horse and buggy pace toward gaining a cup of coffee at a lunch counter. Perhaps it is easy for those who have never felt the stinging darts of segregation to say, "Wait." But when you have seen vicious mobs lynch your mothers and fathers at will and drown your sisters and brothers at whim; when you have seen hate filled policemen curse, kick and even kill your black brothers and sisters; when you see the vast majority of your twenty million Negro brothers smothering in an airtight cage of poverty in the midst of an affluent society; when you suddenly find your tongue twisted and your speech stammering as you seek to explain to your six year old daughter why she can't go to the public amusement park that has just been advertised on television, and see tears welling up in her eyes when she is told that Funtown is closed to colored children, and see ominous clouds of inferiority beginning to form in her little mental sky, and see her beginning to distort her personality by developing an unconscious bitterness toward white people; when you have to concoct an answer for a five year old son who is asking: "Daddy,

PERSONALIZE FOR LEARNING

English Language Support

Metaphors Note this sentence in paragraph 14: *The nations of Asia and Africa are moving with jetlike speed toward gaining political independence, but we still creep at horse and buggy pace toward gaining a cup of coffee at a lunch counter.*

Explain to students that this sentence contains **metaphors**, a type of figurative language that compares two different objects, but unlike similes, does not use *like* or *as*. The author is comparing the move toward political independence in Asia and Africa to the pace of a jet, whereas he compares America's move toward desegregation to that of a horse and buggy.

Ask students why they think Dr. King chose to use these metaphors. **Possible response:** The metaphors are used to create a visual image to demonstrate the difference between the speed of political change in Africa and Asia and that of America.
ALL LEVELS

NOTES

why do white people treat colored people so mean?"; when you take a cross-county drive and find it necessary to sleep night after night in the uncomfortable corners of your automobile because no motel will accept you; when you are humiliated day in and day out by nagging signs reading "white" and "colored"; when your first name becomes "nigger," your middle name becomes "boy" (however old you are) and your last name becomes "John," and your wife and mother are never given the respected title "Mrs."; when you are harried by day and haunted by night by the fact that you are a Negro, living constantly at tiptoe stance, never quite knowing what to expect next, and are plagued with inner fears and outer resentments; when you are forever fighting a degenerating sense of "nobodiness"—then you will understand why we find it difficult to wait. There comes a time when the cup of endurance runs over, and men are no longer willing to be plunged into the abyss of despair. I hope, sirs, you can understand our legitimate and unavoidable impatience.

> I would agree with St. Augustine that "an unjust law is no law at all."

15 You express a great deal of anxiety over our willingness to break laws. This is certainly a legitimate concern. Since we so diligently urge people to obey the Supreme Court's decision of 1954 outlawing segregation in the public schools, at first glance it may seem rather paradoxical for us consciously to break laws. One may well ask: "How can you advocate[6] breaking some laws and obeying others?" The answer lies in the fact that there are two types of laws: just and unjust. I would be the first to advocate obeying just laws. One has not only a legal but a moral responsibility to obey just laws. Conversely, one has a moral responsibility to disobey unjust laws. I would agree with St. Augustine that "an unjust law is no law at all."

16 Now, what is the difference between the two? How does one determine whether a law is just or unjust? A just law is a man made code that squares with the moral law or the law of God. An unjust law is a code that is out of harmony with the moral law. To put it in the terms of St. Thomas Aquinas:[7] An unjust law is a human law that is not rooted in eternal law and natural law. Any law that uplifts human personality is just. Any law that degrades human personality is unjust. All segregation statutes are unjust because segregation distorts the soul and damages the personality. It gives the segregator a false sense of superiority and the segregated a false sense of inferiority. Segregation, to use the terminology of the Jewish philosopher Martin Buber, substitutes an "I it" relationship for an "I thou" relationship and ends up relegating persons to the status of things. Hence segregation is not only politically, economically

6. **advocate** *v.* argue for or support a cause or policy.
7. **St. Thomas Aquinas** (uh KWY nuhs) (1225–1274) influential Christian philosopher who made lasting contributions to Western philosophy.

WriteNow Inform and Explain

Use of First Person In "Letter from Birmingham Jail," Dr. King's use of first person point-of-view makes his letter more authentic, as his audience quickly realizes that he's writing, not only about the experiences of other African Americans, but also about his own experiences with injustice across southern states. Point out Dr. King's use of the first person throughout this letter, but focus on paragraphs 18 and 19. Ask students to think about a social or political problem happening in the world today and write about its effects on people, using the first person point-of-view. Have them explain how writing about this event from the first person point-of-view makes their account more powerful.

and sociologically unsound, it is morally wrong and sinful. Paul Tillich[8] has said that sin is separation. Is not segregation an existential expression of man's tragic separation, his awful estrangement, his terrible sinfulness? Thus it is that I can urge men to obey the 1954 decision of the Supreme Court, for it is morally right; and I can urge them to disobey segregation ordinances,[9] for they are morally wrong.

17 Let us consider a more concrete example of just and unjust laws. An unjust law is a code that a numerical or power majority group compels a minority group to obey but does not make binding on itself. This is difference made legal. By the same token, a just law is a code that a majority compels a minority to follow and that it is willing to follow itself. This is sameness made legal.

18 Let me give another explanation. A law is unjust if it is inflicted on a minority that, as a result of being denied the right to vote, had no part in enacting or devising the law. Who can say that the legislature of Alabama which set up that state's segregation laws was democratically elected? Throughout Alabama all sorts of devious methods are used to prevent Negroes from becoming registered voters, and there are some counties in which, even though Negroes constitute a majority of the population, not a single Negro is registered. Can any law enacted under such circumstances be considered democratically structured?

19 Sometimes a law is just on its face and unjust in its application. For instance, I have been arrested on a charge of parading without a permit. Now, there is nothing wrong in having an ordinance which requires a permit for a parade. But such an ordinance becomes unjust when it is used to maintain segregation and to deny citizens the First-Amendment privilege of peaceful assembly and protest.

20 I hope you are able to see the distinction I am trying to point out. In no sense do I advocate evading or defying the law, as would the rabid segregationist. That would lead to anarchy. One who breaks an unjust law must do so openly, lovingly, and with a willingness to accept the penalty. I submit that an individual who breaks a law that conscience tells him is unjust, and who willingly accepts the penalty of imprisonment in order to arouse the conscience of the community over its injustice, is in reality expressing the highest respect for law.

21 Of course, there is nothing new about this kind of civil disobedience. It was evidenced sublimely in the refusal of Shadrach, Meshach and Abednego to obey the laws of Nebuchadnezzar,[10] on the ground that a higher moral law was at stake. It was practiced superbly by the early Christians, who were willing to face hungry lions and the excruciating pain of chopping blocks rather than submit to certain unjust laws of the Roman Empire. To a degree, academic freedom is a reality today because Socrates practiced civil

8. **Paul Tillich** (1886–1965) German American, Christian philosopher.
9. **ordinances** *n.* laws or regulations made by a city or town government.
10. **refusal . . . Nebuchadnezzar** story from the Bible about three Jews who refused to worship a golden statue; Nebuchadnezzar sentenced them to death by burning, but God protected them from harm.

NOTES

CLOSE READ

ANNOTATE: In paragraphs 17 and 18, mark words and phrases that sound as though King is actually speaking to his readers.

QUESTION: Why does King seem to be walking his readers through his reasoning?

CONCLUDE: How might this approach affect how King's readers understand and respond to his argument?

CLOSE READ

Remind students to focus on phrases or words that indicate that Dr. King is speaking to his readers. You may wish to model the Close Read using the following think-aloud format. Possible responses to questions on the Student page are included.

ANNOTATE: As I read paragraph 17, I notice and highlight the details that show Dr. King is having a conversation with his readers and walking them through his line of reasoning.

QUESTION: King is trying to make the information more accessible and personal to the reader.

CONCLUDE: Readers may respond more favorably to King's argument because he includes his readers in the struggle by using the pronoun *us*.

CLOSER LOOK

Analyze Word Meanings

Remind students to focus on Dr. King's concern with the meanings of words as they read. You may wish to model the Close Read using the following think-aloud format. Possible responses to questions on the Student page are included.

ANNOTATE: As I read paragraphs 22–23, I notice and highlight the words and phrases Dr. King puts in quotation marks.

QUESTION: Dr. King puts these words, phrases, and sentences in quotation marks because he wishes to draw them to the attention of his readers so that they might examine them.

CONCLUDE: Dr. King points out the difference between "legal" and "right," and states that it is right to break unjust laws. He notes the difference between the "order" created by obedience to unjust laws and the "positive peace" created by justice. He asserts that justice is never "convenient."

Remind students that the words they choose as writers can have a strong impact on their audience. If they are trying to persuade their audience, they will want to choose words that have the power to influence their audience to think in a new way.

NOTES

disobedience. In our own nation, the Boston Tea Party represented a massive act of civil disobedience.

22 We should never forget that everything Adolf Hitler did in Germany was "legal" and everything the Hungarian freedom fighters did in Hungary was "illegal." It was "illegal" to aid and comfort a Jew in Hitler's Germany. Even so, I am sure that, had I lived in Germany at the time, I would have aided and comforted my Jewish brothers. If today I lived in a Communist country where certain principles dear to the Christian faith are suppressed, I would openly advocate disobeying that country's antireligious laws.

23 I must make two honest confessions to you, my Christian and Jewish brothers. First, I must confess that over the past few years I have been gravely disappointed with the white moderate. I have almost reached the regrettable conclusion that the Negro's great stumbling block in his stride toward freedom is not the White Citizen's Counciler or the Ku Klux Klanner, but the white moderate, who is more devoted to "order" than to justice; who prefers a negative peace which is the absence of tension to a positive peace which is the presence of justice; who constantly says: "I agree with you in the goal you seek, but I cannot agree with your methods of direct action"; who paternalistically believes he can set the timetable for another man's freedom; who lives by a mythical concept of time and who constantly advises the Negro to wait for a "more convenient season." Shallow understanding from people of good will is more frustrating than absolute misunderstanding from people of ill will. Lukewarm acceptance is much more bewildering than outright rejection.

24 I had hoped that the white moderate would understand that law and order exist for the purpose of establishing justice and that when they fail in this purpose they become the dangerously structured dams that block the flow of social progress. I had hoped that the white moderate would understand that the present tension in the South is a necessary phase of the transition from an obnoxious negative peace, in which the Negro passively accepted his unjust plight, to a substantive and positive peace, in which all men will respect the dignity and worth of human personality. Actually, we who engage in nonviolent direct action are not the creators of tension. We merely bring to the surface the hidden tension that is already alive. We bring it out in the open, where it can be seen and dealt with. Like a boil that can never be cured so long as it is covered up but must be opened with all its ugliness to the natural medicines of air and light, injustice must be exposed, with all the tension its exposure creates, to the light of human conscience and the air of national opinion before it can be cured.

25 In your statement you assert that our actions, even though peaceful, must be condemned because they precipitate violence. But is this a logical assertion? Isn't this like condemning a robbed man because his possession of money precipitated the evil act of

robbery? Isn't this like condemning Socrates because his unswerving commitment to truth and his philosophical inquiries precipitated the act by the misguided populace in which they made him drink hemlock?[11] Isn't this like condemning Jesus because his unique God consciousness and never-ceasing devotion to God's will precipitated the evil act of crucifixion? We must come to see that, as the federal courts have consistently affirmed, it is wrong to urge an individual to cease his efforts to gain his basic constitutional rights because the quest may precipitate violence. Society must protect the robbed and punish the robber.

26 I had also hoped that the white moderate would reject the myth concerning time in relation to the struggle for freedom. I have just received a letter from a white brother in Texas. He writes: "All Christians know that the colored people will receive equal rights eventually, but it is possible that you are in too great a religious hurry. It has taken Christianity almost two thousand years to accomplish what it has. The teachings of Christ take time to come to earth." Such an attitude stems from a tragic misconception of time, from the strangely irrational notion that there is something in the very flow of time that will inevitably cure all ills. Actually, time itself is neutral; it can be used either destructively or constructively. More and more I feel that the people of ill will have used time much more effectively than have the people of good will. We will have to repent in this generation not merely for the hateful words and actions of the bad people but for the appalling silence of the good people. Human progress never rolls in on wheels of inevitability; it comes through the tireless efforts of men willing to be coworkers with God, and without this hard work, time itself becomes an ally of the forces of social **stagnation**. We must use time creatively, in the knowledge that the time is always ripe to do right. Now is the time to make real the promise of democracy and transform our pending national elegy[12] into a creative psalm[13] of brotherhood. Now is the time to lift our national policy from the quicksand of racial injustice to the solid rock of human dignity.

27 You speak of our activity in Birmingham as extreme. At first I was rather disappointed that fellow clergymen would see my nonviolent efforts as those of an extremist. I began thinking about the fact that I stand in the middle of two opposing forces in the Negro community. One is a force of **complacency**, made up in part of Negroes who, as a result of long years of oppression, are so drained of self respect and a sense of "somebodiness" that they have adjusted to segregation; and in part of a few middle-class Negroes who, because of a degree of academic and economic security and because in some ways they profit by segregation, have become insensitive to the problems of the masses. The other force is one of bitterness and hatred, and it

NOTES

stagnation (stag NAY shuhn) *n.* state of being inactive and not moving or changing

complacency (kuhm PLAY suhn see) *n.* state of unthinking or satisfied acceptance

11. **hemlock** *n.* highly poisonous plant.
12. **elegy** (EHL uh jee) *n.* song expressing sorrow or grief.
13. **psalm** (sahm) *n.* biblical song that praises God.

VOCABULARY DEVELOPMENT

Concept Vocabulary Reinforcement Reinforce students' grasp of concept vocabulary with "show-you-know" sentences. The first part of the sentence uses the vocabulary word in an appropriate context. The second part of the sentence – the "show-you-know" part – clarifies the first. Model the strategy with this example for *stagnation* (paragraph 26):

The *stagnation* of water in a birdbath is a health risk; sitting water is a breeding ground for mosquitoes.

Then give students these sentence prompts and coach them in creating the clarification part:

1. Her *complacency* over the issue was frustrating; _____.
   Possible response: she just didn't care.
2. John was *yearning* for a change; _____.
   Possible response: he had an intense desire to switch careers.
3. Brooke can't sit *idly* for very long; _____.
   Possible response: her limitless energy drives her toward physical activity.

CLOSER LOOK

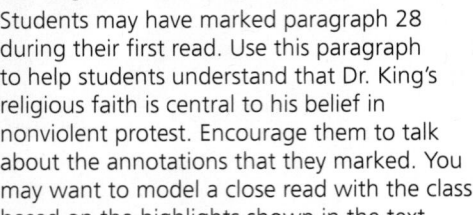

Analyze Motivation

Students may have marked paragraph 28 during their first read. Use this paragraph to help students understand that Dr. King's religious faith is central to his belief in nonviolent protest. Encourage them to talk about the annotations that they marked. You may want to model a close read with the class based on the highlights shown in the text.

ANNOTATE: Have students mark details in paragraph 28 that demonstrate how Dr. King differentiates himself from black nationalists, or have students participate while you highlight them.

QUESTION: Guide students to consider what these details might tell them. Ask what a reader can infer from what was marked, and accept student responses.

Possible response: Dr. King regards the black nationalist as being in opposition to Christianity, and created by despair. Dr. King, in contrast, thanks God and his church for helping him to recognize nonviolent protest as the best way for the Civil Rights movement to achieve its ends.

CONCLUDE: Help students to formulate conclusions about the importance of these details in the text. Ask students why the author might have included these details.

Possible response: Dr. King wanted people to know that he regarded his role in the Civil Rights movement as an essential part of his duty as a minister of the church. Unrest and discontentment in the African-American community took many forms in the 1960s, and Dr. King wanted people to understand that, unlike other action groups, the Civil Rights movement was dedicated to nonviolence and looked to the Bible and the church to authorize its just demands.

Remind students that **motivation** is the reason or reasons for a speaker's actions. This motivation may come from internal causes such as loneliness or jealousy, or from external causes such as danger or poverty. Most motives are a combination of internal and external factors.

^ A crowd gathers on the steps of the Sixteenth Street Baptist Church in Birmingham, Alabama, during protests led by Dr. King in an effort to end racial segregation in the city.

NOTES

comes perilously close to advocating violence. It is expressed in the various black nationalist groups that are springing up across the nation, the largest and best known being Elijah Muhammad's[14] Muslim movement. Nourished by the Negro's frustration over the continued existence of racial discrimination, this movement is made up of people who have lost faith in America, who have absolutely repudiated Christianity, and who have concluded that the white man is an incorrigible "devil."

28 I have tried to stand between these two forces, saying that we need emulate neither the "do-nothingism" of the complacent nor the hatred and despair of the black nationalist. For there is the more excellent way of love and nonviolent protest. I am grateful to God that, through the influence of the Negro church, the way of nonviolence became an integral part of our struggle.

29 If this philosophy had not emerged, by now many streets of the South would, I am convinced, be flowing with blood. And I am further convinced that if our white brothers dismiss as "rabble rousers" and "outside agitators" those of us who employ nonviolent direct action, and if they refuse to support our nonviolent efforts, millions of Negroes will, out of frustration and despair, seek solace

14. **Elijah Muhammad** (1897–1975) African American leader of the Nation of Islam and a mentor to Malcolm X.

and security in black nationalist ideologies—a development that would inevitably lead to a frightening racial nightmare.

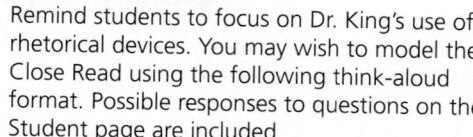

30 Oppressed people cannot remain oppressed forever. The **yearning** for freedom eventually manifests itself, and that is what has happened to the American Negro. Something within has reminded him of his birthright of freedom, and something without has reminded him that it can be gained. Consciously or unconsciously, he has been caught up by the Zeitgeist,[15] and with his black brothers of Africa and his brown and yellow brothers of Asia, South America and the Caribbean, the United States Negro is moving with a sense of great urgency toward the promised land of racial justice. If one recognizes this vital urge that has engulfed the Negro community, one should readily understand why public demonstrations are taking place. The Negro has many pent up resentments and latent frustrations, and he must release them. So let him march; let him make prayer pilgrimages to the city hall; let him go on freedom rides—and try to understand why he must do so. If his repressed emotions are not released in nonviolent ways, they will seek expression through violence; this is not a threat but a fact of history. So I have not said to my people: "Get rid of your discontent." Rather, I have tried to say that this normal and healthy discontent can be channeled into the creative outlet of nonviolent direct action. And now this approach is being termed extremist.

31 But though I was initially disappointed at being categorized as an extremist, as I continued to think about the matter I gradually gained a measure of satisfaction from the label. Was not Jesus an extremist for love: "Love your enemies, bless them that curse you, do good to them that hate you, and pray for them which despitefully use you, and persecute you." Was not Amos an extremist for justice: "Let justice roll down like waters and righteousness like an ever flowing stream." Was not Paul an extremist for the Christian gospel: "I bear on my body the marks of the Lord Jesus." Was not Martin Luther[16] an extremist: "Here I stand; I cannot do otherwise, so help me God." And John Bunyan:[17] "I will stay in jail to the end of my days before I make a butchery of my conscience." And Abraham Lincoln: "This nation cannot survive half slave and half free." And Thomas Jefferson: "We hold these truths to be self evident, that all men are created equal." So the question is not whether we will be extremists, but what kind of extremists we will be. Will we be extremists for hate or for love? Will we be extremists for the preservation of injustice or for the extension of justice? In that dramatic scene on Calvary's hill three men were crucified. We must never forget that all three were crucified for the same crime—the crime of extremism. Two were

15. **Zeitgeist** (ZYT gyst) *n.* general intellectual, moral, and cultural spirit of an era.
16. **Martin Luther** (1483–1546) German priest and professor of theology who was an important figure in the Protestant Reformation.
17. **John Bunyan** (1628–1688) English writer and preacher who wrote *The Pilgrim's Progress*.

NOTES

yearning (YUR nihng) *n.* strong desire; longing

CLOSE READ

ANNOTATE: In paragraph 31, mark references to historic figures.

QUESTION: What qualities do these historic figures have in common?

CONCLUDE: How is King attempting to redefine what the word "extremist" means?

CLOSE READ

Remind students to focus on Dr. King's use of rhetorical devices. You may wish to model the Close Read using the following think-aloud format. Possible responses to questions on the Student page are included.

ANNOTATE: As I read paragraph 31, I notice Dr. King's references to famous people who were called extremists who were fighting for change.

QUESTION: These were some of the greatest people in history, including many biblical figures and great statesmen. Each was working to change the world in an important way.

CONCLUDE: The word was intended to damage Dr. King's reputation, but the effect of his close examination is to make it not only harmless, but honorable.

DIGITAL PERSPECTIVES

Enriching the Text Look for an audio clip of "Letter From Birmingham Jail," making sure to listen to the entire clip before sharing with students. Play the entire clip for students, or choose important excerpts from the selection and have students listen to these sections. Then, ask them to write a paragraph explaining how the audio clip enhances their understanding of Dr. King's words. Why was it necessary for him to write this letter?

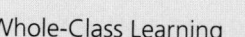

CLOSE READ

Remind students to focus on Dr. King's belief that the church should be actively involved with the Civil Rights movement. You may wish to model the Close Read using the following think-aloud format. Possible responses to questions on the Student page are included.

ANNOTATE: As I read paragraph 34, I notice that Dr. King points out his love and loyalty for the church.

QUESTION: I think that Dr. King adds these details to show his history with the church. He is not attacking the church as an outsider, but questioning its actions as a person who loves the church. By noting only two small examples of any white church's support for civil rights, Dr. King emphasizes how little the white clergy has done to address injustice and inequality.

CONCLUDE: Dr. King wants his readers to understand that he wants to stay with the church. He is demonstrating his disappointment with the inaction of church leaders regarding the issue of civil rights.

NOTES

languished (LANG gwihsht) *v.* grown weak; lived under distressing conditions

CLOSE READ

ANNOTATE: In paragraph 34, mark sentences in which King mentions his affection for and loyalty to the church.

QUESTION: Why does King present his religious credentials and emotions so emphatically?

CONCLUDE: What does King want his readers to understand about the target or point of his criticism?

extremists for immorality, and thus fell below their environment. The other, Jesus Christ, was an extremist for love, truth and goodness, and thereby rose above his environment. Perhaps the South, the nation, and the world are in dire need of creative extremists.

32 I had hoped that the white moderate would see this need. Perhaps I was too optimistic; perhaps I expected too much. I suppose I should have realized that few members of the oppressor race can understand the deep groans and passionate yearnings of the oppressed race, and still fewer have the vision to see that injustice must be rooted out by strong, persistent and determined action. I am thankful, however, that some of our white brothers in the South have grasped the meaning of this social revolution and committed themselves to it. They are still all too few in quantity, but they are big in quality. Some—such as Ralph McGill, Lillian Smith, Harry Golden, James McBride Dabbs, Ann Braden and Sarah Patton Boyle—have written about our struggle in eloquent and prophetic terms. Others have marched with us down nameless streets of the South. They have **languished** in filthy, roach infested jails, suffering the abuse and brutality of policemen who view them as "dirty nigger-lovers." Unlike so many of their moderate brothers and sisters, they have recognized the urgency of the moment and sensed the need for powerful "action" antidotes to combat the disease of segregation.

33 Let me take note of my other major disappointment. I have been so greatly disappointed with the white church and its leadership. Of course, there are some notable exceptions. I am not unmindful of the fact that each of you has taken some significant stands on this issue. I commend you, Reverend Stallings, for your Christian stand on this past Sunday, in welcoming Negroes to your worship service on a nonsegregated basis. I commend the Catholic leaders of this state for integrating Spring Hill College several years ago.

34 But despite these notable exceptions, I must honestly reiterate that I have been disappointed with the church. I do not say this as one of those negative critics who can always find something wrong with the church. I say this as a minister of the gospel, who loves the church; who was nurtured in its bosom; who has been sustained by its spiritual blessings and who will remain true to it as long as the cord of life shall lengthen.

35 When I was suddenly catapulted into the leadership of the bus protest in Montgomery, Alabama, a few years ago, I felt we would be supported by the white church. I felt that the white ministers, priests and rabbis of the South would be among our strongest allies. Instead, some have been outright opponents, refusing to understand the freedom movement and misrepresenting its leaders; all too many others have been more cautious than courageous and have remained silent behind the anesthetizing security of stained glass windows.

36 In spite of my shattered dreams, I came to Birmingham with the hope that the white religious leadership of this community would see the justice of our cause and, with deep moral concern, would serve as

the channel through which our just grievances could reach the power structure. I had hoped that each of you would understand. But again I have been disappointed.

37 I have heard numerous southern religious leaders admonish their worshipers to comply with a desegregation decision because it is the law, but I have longed to hear white ministers declare: "Follow this decree because integration is morally right and because the Negro is your brother." In the midst of blatant injustices inflicted upon the Negro, I have watched white churchmen stand on the sideline and mouth pious irrelevancies and sanctimonious trivialities. In the midst of a mighty struggle to rid our nation of racial and economic injustice, I have heard many ministers say: "Those are social issues, with which the gospel has no real concern." And I have watched many churches commit themselves to a completely other-worldly religion which makes a strange, un-Biblical distinction between body and soul, between the sacred and the secular.

38 I have traveled the length and breadth of Alabama, Mississippi, and all the other southern states. On sweltering summer days and crisp autumn mornings I have looked at the South's beautiful churches with their lofty spires pointing heavenward. I have beheld the impressive outlines of her massive religious education buildings. Over and over I have found myself asking: "What kind of people worship here? Who is their God? Where were their voices when the lips of Governor Barnett dripped with words of interposition and nullification? Where were they when Governor Wallace gave a clarion call for defiance and hatred? Where were their voices of support when bruised and weary Negro men and women decided to rise from the dark dungeons of complacency to the bright hills of creative protest?"

39 Yes, these questions are still in my mind. In deep disappointment I have wept over the laxity of the church. But be assured that my tears have been tears of love. There can be no deep disappointment where there is not deep love. Yes, I love the church. How could I do otherwise? I am in the rather unique position of being the son, the grandson and the great grandson of preachers. Yes, I see the church as the body of Christ. But, oh! How we have blemished and scarred that body through social neglect and through fear of being nonconformists.

40 There was a time when the church was very powerful—in the time when the early Christians rejoiced at being deemed worthy to suffer for what they believed. In those days the church was not merely a thermometer that recorded the ideas and principles of popular opinion; it was a thermostat that transformed the mores of society. Whenever the early Christians entered a town, the people in power became disturbed and immediately sought to convict the Christians for being "disturbers of the peace" and "outside agitators." But the Christians pressed on, in the conviction that they were "a colony of heaven," called to obey God rather than man. Small in number,

NOTES

HOW LANGUAGE WORKS

Prepositional Phrases Call students' attention to the language at work in paragraph 38. If students struggle to comprehend the difference between an adverb phrase and an adjective phrase, assist them by giving examples of both kinds of prepositional phrase. Have students complete sentences like these with prepositional phrases, and identify them as adverb phrases or adjective phrases:

- . . . I have looked at the South's beautiful churches *with their lofty spires pointing heavenward.* Paragraph 38 (adjective phrase that modifies the noun *churches*)
- There was a time when the church was very powerful – *in the time when the early Christians rejoiced at being deemed worthy to suffer for what they believed.* Paragraph 40 (adverb phrase that modifies the adjective *powerful*)

TEACHING

CLOSE READ

Remind students to focus on Dr. King's use of rhetorical devices. You may wish to model the Close Read using the following think-aloud format. Possible responses to questions on the Student page are included.

ANNOTATE: As I read paragraph 42, I notice that Dr. King asks if the church has sacrificed its spiritual authority by allowing itself to accept the current situation.

QUESTION: Dr. King perceives that the church is in a state of crisis, and his question indicates that he wants to involve his readers in the search for a solution.

CONCLUDE: Dr. King believes that the future of the church depends on those ministers of the church who have dared to defy their leaders and risked dismissal by joining the Civil Rights movement. Dr. King believes that their actions have preserved the true meaning of the gospel, and will in time be crucial to the survival and renewal of the church.

NOTES

they were big in commitment. They were too God-intoxicated to be "astronomically intimidated." By their effort and example they brought an end to such ancient evils as infanticide and gladiatorial contests. Things are different now. So often the contemporary church is a weak, ineffectual voice with an uncertain sound. So often it is an arch defender of the status quo. Far from being disturbed by the presence of the church, the power structure of the average community is consoled by the church's silent—and often even vocal—sanction of things as they are.

41 But the judgment of God is upon the church as never before. If today's church does not recapture the sacrificial spirit of the early church, it will lose its authenticity, forfeit the loyalty of millions, and be dismissed as an irrelevant social club with no meaning for the twentieth century. Every day I meet young people whose disappointment with the church has turned into outright disgust.

42 Perhaps I have once again been too optimistic. Is organized religion too inextricably bound to the status quo to save our nation and the world? Perhaps I must turn my faith to the inner spiritual church, the church within the church, as the true ekklesia[18] and the hope of the world. But again I am thankful to God that some noble souls from the ranks of organized religion have broken loose from the paralyzing chains of conformity and joined us as active partners in the struggle for freedom. They have left their secure congregations and walked the streets of Albany, Georgia, with us. They have gone down the highways of the South on tortuous rides for freedom. Yes, they have gone to jail with us. Some have been dismissed from their churches, have lost the support of their bishops and fellow ministers. But they have acted in the faith that right defeated is stronger than evil triumphant. Their witness has been the spiritual salt that has preserved[19] the true meaning of the gospel in these troubled times. They have carved a tunnel of hope through the dark mountain of disappointment.

CLOSE READ

ANNOTATE: In paragraph 42, mark King's use of a question.

QUESTION: Why do you think King begins the paragraph with a question?

CONCLUDE: Does the rest of the paragraph help us find an answer to the question? If so, what would that answer be?

43 I hope the church as a whole will meet the challenge of this decisive hour. But even if the church does not come to the aid of justice, I have no despair about the future. I have no fear about the outcome of our struggle in Birmingham, even if our motives are at present misunderstood. We will reach the goal of freedom in Birmingham and all over the nation, because the goal of America is freedom. Abused and scorned though we may be, our destiny is tied up with America's destiny. Before the pilgrims landed at Plymouth, we were here. Before the pen of Jefferson etched the majestic words of the Declaration of Independence across the pages of history, we were here. For more than two centuries our forebears labored in this country without wages; they made cotton king; they built the homes of their masters while suffering gross injustice and shameful

18. **ekklesia** (ih KLEE zhee uh) *n.* Greek word for a group of believers.
19. **spiritual salt that has preserved** Salt has traditionally been used to preserve food so that it remains edible.

humiliation—and yet out of a bottomless vitality they continued to thrive and develop. If the inexpressible cruelties of slavery could not stop us, the opposition we now face will surely fail. We will win our freedom because the sacred heritage of our nation and the eternal will of God are embodied in our echoing demands.

NOTES

44 Before closing I feel impelled to mention one other point in your statement that has troubled me profoundly. You warmly commended the Birmingham police force for keeping "order" and "preventing violence." I doubt that you would have so warmly commended the police force if you had seen its dogs sinking their teeth into unarmed, nonviolent Negroes. I doubt that you would so quickly commend the policemen if you were to observe their ugly and inhumane treatment of Negroes here in the city jail; if you were to watch them push and curse old Negro women and young Negro girls; if you were to see them slap and kick old Negro men and young boys; if you were to observe them, as they did on two occasions, refuse to give us food because we wanted to sing our grace together. I cannot join you in your praise of the Birmingham police department.

If the inexpressible cruelties of slavery could not stop us, the opposition we now face will surely fail.

45 It is true that the police have exercised a degree of discipline in handling the demonstrators. In this sense they have conducted themselves rather "nonviolently" in public. But for what purpose? To preserve the evil system of segregation. Over the past few years I have consistently preached that nonviolence demands that the means we use must be as pure as the ends we seek. I have tried to make clear that it is wrong to use immoral means to attain moral ends. But now I must affirm that it is just as wrong, or perhaps even more so, to use moral means to preserve immoral ends. Perhaps Mr. Connor and his policemen have been rather nonviolent in public, as was Chief Pritchett in Albany, Georgia, but they have used the moral means of nonviolence to maintain the immoral end of racial injustice. As T. S. Eliot has said: "The last temptation is the greatest treason: To do the right deed for the wrong reason."

46 I wish you had commended the Negro sit inners and demonstrators of Birmingham for their sublime courage, their willingness to suffer and their amazing discipline in the midst of great provocation. One day the South will recognize its real heroes. They will be the James Merediths,[20] with the noble sense of purpose that enables them to face jeering and hostile mobs, and with the agonizing loneliness that characterizes the life of the pioneer. They will be old, oppressed, battered Negro women, symbolized in a seventy two year old woman in Montgomery, Alabama, who rose up with a sense of dignity and with her people decided not to

20. **James Meredith** (b. 1933) civil rights activist who, in 1962, became the first African American student admitted to the segregated University of Mississippi.

PERSONALIZE FOR LEARNING

English Language Support

Domain-specific Vocabulary The domain-specific vocabulary that appears in "Letter From Birmingham Jail" may present challenges to English Learners. Support them in understanding the text by reviewing the following vocabulary:

inhumane – cruel
treason – betraying something or someone
immoral – wicked and unprincipled

Have students locate these terms in paragraphs 44–45 and read the sentence containing each term. Then, have them rephrase the sentences, replacing the vocabulary word with its definition. For example:

Those bullies were *inhumane* toward the elementary school students.

Those bullies were *cruel* toward the elementary school students.

You may wish to have students create a glossary of these terms and update with new words and phrases over time.
ALL LEVELS

CLOSE READ

Remind students to focus on the fact that Dr. King is writing not only for the eight white clergymen, but for all the other people who will read this letter when it is published. You may wish to model the Close Read using the following think-aloud format. Possible responses to questions on the Student page are included.

ANNOTATE: As I read paragraph 47, I notice that Dr. King talks about himself and his immediate circumstances as he composes this letter in a jail cell.

QUESTION: Dr. King reminds the clergymen and the other readers of the letter that he is sitting in a jail cell in enforced solitude and idleness. He is clearly aware of the larger audience and the effect this description of his circumstances will have on them.

CONCLUDE: Dr. King recognizes that the letter is long. His circumstances make it so that he cannot join the peaceful demonstrations he calls for in the letter.

NOTES

CLOSE READ

ANNOTATE: In paragraph 47, mark King's descriptions of himself.

QUESTION: What part of his character is King emphasizing in this paragraph?

CONCLUDE: What is the effect of King's describing himself like this at the very end of his letter?

ride segregated buses, and who responded with ungrammatical profundity[21] to one who inquired about her weariness: "My feets is tired, but my soul is at rest." They will be the young high school and college students, the young ministers of the gospel and a host of their elders, courageously and nonviolently sitting in at lunch counters and willingly going to jail for conscience' sake. One day the South will know that when these disinherited children of God sat down at lunch counters, they were in reality standing up for what is best in the American dream and for the most sacred values in our Judeo-Christian heritage, thereby bringing our nation back to those great wells of democracy which were dug deep by the founding fathers in their formulation of the Constitution and the Declaration of Independence.

47 Never before have I written so long a letter. I'm afraid it is much too long to take your precious time. I can assure you that it would have been much shorter if I had been writing from a comfortable desk, but what else can one do when he is alone in a narrow jail cell, other than write long letters, think long thoughts and pray long prayers?

48 If I have said anything in this letter that overstates the truth and indicates an unreasonable impatience, I beg you to forgive me. If I have said anything that understates the truth and indicates my having a patience that allows me to settle for anything less than brotherhood, I beg God to forgive me.

49 I hope this letter finds you strong in the faith. I also hope that circumstances will soon make it possible for me to meet each of you, not as an integrationist or a civil-rights leader but as a fellow clergyman and a Christian brother. Let us all hope that the dark clouds of racial prejudice will soon pass away and the deep fog of misunderstanding will be lifted from our fear-drenched communities, and in some not too distant tomorrow the radiant stars of love and brotherhood will shine over our great nation with all their scintillating beauty.

Yours for the cause of Peace and Brotherhood,

Martin Luther King, Jr. ❧

21. **profundity** (pruh FUHN duh tee) *n.* quality of having intellectual depth.

Comprehension Check

Complete the following items after you finish your first read.

1. What circumstance or event is Dr. Martin Luther King, Jr., responding to in this letter?

2. According to Dr. King, what are the four basic steps that a nonviolent campaign must follow?

3. According to Dr. King, what are the two types of laws?

4. According to Dr. King, who are the South's real heroes?

Notebook Write a summary of "Letter From Birmingham Jail."

RESEARCH

Research to Clarify Choose at least one unfamiliar detail from the text. Briefly research that detail. In what way does the information you learned shed light on an aspect of the letter?

Research to Explore Choose something that interested you from the text, and formulate a research question.

DIGITAL PERSPECTIVES

Comprehension Check

Possible responses:

1. In this letter, Dr. King is responding to white clergy members who criticized him for protesting racial segregation in Birmingham, Alabama.
2. The four basic steps that a nonviolent campaign must face are 1) collection of the facts to determine whether injustices actually exist; 2) negotiation; 3) self purification; and 4) direct action.
3. According to Dr. King, there are two types of laws: just and unjust laws. Just laws are those that people have a moral responsibility to obey. Unjust laws are codes that do not align with moral laws and degrade human beings or the human condition.
4. According to Dr. King, the real heroes of the South are those civil rights activists who have endured violence when doing what was right.

Summary: After being criticized by members of the clergy, Dr. King writes from a prison cell to defend his actions. He calls for more actions in the name of civil peace and justice.

Research

Research to Clarify If students struggle to come up with a detail to research, suggest that they focus on one of the following topics: Alabama Bus Boycotts, Eugene Bull Connor, or Elijah Muhammad.

Research to Explore If students have a difficult time formulating a research question, suggest that they research the four steps of nonviolent campaign, or focus on one specific step.

PERSONALIZE FOR LEARNING

Challenge

Research Have students research another important figure of the Civil Rights movement who helped fight against social injustices and violence against minorities. Possible subjects include Malcolm X, Rosa Parks, Ella Baker, John Lewis,and President John F. Kennedy. Who was this individual? What was his or her involvement in the Civil Rights movement? What was his or her legacy? Have students report their findings to the class.

Jump Start

CLOSE READ Have students close read the title, "Letter From Birmingham Jail." What might motivate someone to write a letter from jail?

Close Read the Text

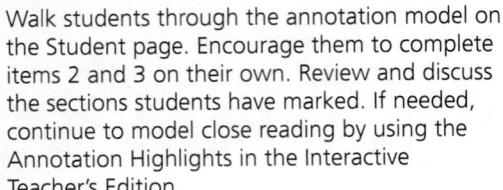

Walk students through the annotation model on the Student page. Encourage them to complete items 2 and 3 on their own. Review and discuss the sections students have marked. If needed, continue to model close reading by using the Annotation Highlights in the Interactive Teacher's Edition.

Analyze the Text

Possible responses:

1. (a) King believes that his fellow clergy are "men of good will" and will do the right thing. (paragraph 1) **DOK 2** (b) He emphasizes his attitude about that outcome because it puts pressure on the clergy to join him in this fight. **DOK 3**
2. While Dr. King urges people to obey the Supreme Court's desegregation laws, he justifies the breaking of laws that are "unjust." He describes unjust laws as ones that do not meet with moral law and are degrading to "human personality." (paragraphs 15–16) **DOK 2**
3. King is more concerned with the "white moderate" clergy because they are not doing anything with their good intentions. He considers these people much more frustrating than those who misunderstand the cause and reject its principles. (paragraph 23) **DOK 2**
4. **Responses will vary.** Students may say, for example, that words have the power to invoke certain emotions, thus swaying listeners or readers or moving them to a desired action. **DOK 3**

FORMATIVE ASSESSMENT

Analyze the Text

- **If** students fail to cite evidence, **then** remind them to support their ideas with specific information from the text.
- **If** students fail to make the correct inferences about Dr. King's attitude about the clergy **then** have them reread key paragraphs in the selection.

MAKING MEANING

LETTER FROM BIRMINGHAM JAIL

Close Read the Text

1. This model, from paragraph 10 of the text, shows two sample annotations, along with questions and conclusions. Close read the passage, and find another detail to annotate. Then, write a question and your conclusion.

Close Read (ANNOTATE · QUESTION · CONCLUDE)

ANNOTATE: The author directly addresses the reader using the pronoun *you*.

QUESTION: What relationship with the reader is King trying to establish?

CONCLUDE: His use of "you" establishes a sense of connection; it suggests Dr. King is open to his critic's ideas.

You may well ask: "Why direct action? Why sit-ins, marches, and so forth? Isn't negotiation a better path?" You are quite right in calling for negotiation. Indeed, this is the very purpose of direct action.

ANNOTATE: The author asks a series of questions readers might ask.

QUESTION: What purpose do these questions serve?

CONCLUDE: The questions show that King is taking his readers' concerns into account. This makes his argument stronger.

2. For more practice, go back into the selection and complete the close-read notes.
3. Revisit a section of the text you found important during your first read. Read this section closely, and **annotate** what you notice. Ask yourself **questions** such as "Why did the author make this choice?" What can you **conclude**?

Tool Kit
Close-Read Guide and Model Annotation

Analyze the Text

CITE TEXTUAL EVIDENCE to support your answers.

Notebook **Respond to these questions.**

1. (a) In the first paragraph, what reasons does King give for his confidence in the outcome of the struggle? (b) **Infer** Why do you think he emphasizes his attitude about that outcome? Explain.
2. Reread paragraphs 13–18. How does Dr. King explain his decision to break the law?
3. Why is Dr. King more concerned with the attitudes of "white moderates" than he is with those of outright enemies of integration? Explain.
4. **Essential Question:** *How can words inspire change?* What have you learned about the power of words from reading this text?

STANDARDS

Reading Informational Text

- Cite strong and thorough textual evidence to support analysis of what the text says explicitly as well as inferences drawn from the text.
- Analyze how the author unfolds an analysis or series of ideas or events, including the order in which the points are made, how they are introduced and developed, and the connections that are drawn between them.
- Analyze seminal U.S. documents of historical and literary significance, including how they address related themes and concepts.

PERSONALIZE FOR LEARNING

Strategic Support

Clarifying Elements of an Argument If students struggle to comprehend the elements of the argument presented in paragraphs 13–18 in "Letter From Birmingham Jail," suggest that they identify a detail that is confusing or overwhelming and have a group member summarize the text in their own words.

Analyze Craft and Structure

Argument "Letter from Birmingham Jail" can be considered a persuasive essay in the form of a letter. A **persuasive essay** is a short nonfiction work in which a writer seeks to convince the reader to think or act in a certain way. Persuasive writers often use **rhetorical devices,** or special patterns of language that help to clarify ideas and evoke emotions. A persuasive essay may include the following types of rhetorical devices:

- **Antithesis:** a form of parallelism that emphasizes strong contrasts
  Example: It was the best of times; it was the worst of times.
- **Allusion:** a brief, unexplained reference to a well-known person, historical event, organization, literary work, or place
  Example: We all got the feeling that we were not in Kansas anymore. (reference to *The Wizard of Oz*)
- **Rhetorical Question:** a question asked to make a point rather than to invite an answer
  Example: If you poison us, do we not die?

Practice

CITE TEXTUAL EVIDENCE to support your answers.

Go back and reread paragraph 27 in "Letter From Birmingham Jail."

Notebook Respond to these questions.

1. In this letter, what is King attempting to persuade his listeners to think or do? Explain.
2. Use the chart to record at least one example of each type of rhetorical device used in King's letter.
3. For each example, explain whether the rhetorical device serves to clarify an idea, stir listeners' emotions, or both. For each determination, explain your reasoning.

RHETORICAL DEVICE	EXAMPLE FROM THE LETTER	EXPLANATION
antithesis	*Whatever affects one directly, affects all indirectly.* (paragraph 40)	King contrasts the individual against the whole.
allusion	*...to use the terminology of the Jewish philosopher Martin Buber...* (paragraph 16)	King alludes to this philosopher to explain how segregation affects the status of a person.
rhetorical question	*How could I do otherwise?* (paragraph 39)	King asks this question to show the inevitability of his love for the church.

4. This letter is widely regarded as a powerful defense of nonviolent protest. Do you think it deserves this recognition? Support your answer with text evidence and your analysis of King's use of rhetoric.

DIGITAL PERSPECTIVES

Analyze Craft and Structure

Explain to students that, in addition to presenting a solid case with good evidence, a writer may use rhetorical devices to strengthen a persuasive essay, including antithesis, allusions, and rhetorical questioning. In "Letter From Birmingham Jail," Dr. King uses these strategies to invoke a sense of urgency in his fellow clergymen and other readers. For more support, see **Analyze Craft and Structure: Argument.**

MAKE IT INTERACTIVE

Have students select one of the following rhetorical devices: antithesis, allusion, or rhetorical question. Ask each student to identify a topic around which they will construct three examples of the rhetorical device they have chosen. As students share their responses with the class, discuss the effectiveness of the rhetorical device in clarifying ideas and evoking emotions.

Practice

1. In his essay, King is trying to convince readers of the need for direct action in the Civil Rights movement.
2. See possible response in chart on Student page.
3. **Responses will vary.** Be sure students explain their reasoning.
4. **Responses will vary.** Remind students to support their responses with evidence from the text.

FORMATIVE ASSESSMENT

Analyze Craft and Structure

- **If** students fail to identify the elements of an argument or persuasive essay, **then** review the elements with them.
- **If** students fail to understand how rhetorical devices are used, **then** review additional examples with them.

For Reteach and Practice, see **Analyze Craft and Structure: Argument (RP).**

PERSONALIZE FOR LEARNING

English Language Support

Making Allusions Ask pairs of students to collaborate on a brief description of a person, place, or thing that includes an allusion. Remind them that allusions can be a literary, historical, or cultural reference. **EMERGING**

Ask students to write a brief description of a person, place, or thing that includes an allusion. Remind them that allusions can be a literary, historical, or cultural reference. **EXPANDING**

Ask students to write two brief descriptions of a person, place, or thing – one that includes a historical allusion and one that includes a literary allusion. **BRIDGING**

An expanded **English Language Support lesson** on Allusion is available in the Digital Teacher's Edition.

TEACHING

Concept Vocabulary

Why These Words

Possible responses:

1. *Stagnation* (paragraph 26) is the physical state of inaction. It means standing still or not moving. *Idly* (paragraph 4) is an adverb used to show how a person can act in an inactive or lazy way.
2. *laxity* (paragraph 39), *lukewarm* (paragraph 23), *wait* (paragraphs 13, 14, 23), *never* (paragraphs 3, 14, 23, etc.)

Practice

Possible responses:

1. I can no longer wait *idly* as graffiti takes over the neighborhood. The board of education *postponed* plans for building a new school. When I saw the *stagnation* at the intersection, I knew it would take twice as long to drive home. The *complacency* of the voters was sure to guarantee the incumbent another four years. The group's *yearning* for freedom was evident in their impassioned pleas before the crowd. Without any books or proper teaching, the students *languished* in their studies.
2. **Responses will vary.**

Word Network

Possible words: *nonviolent, demonstrations, prejudice, tension, negotiating, suppressed*

Word Study

For more support, see **Concept Vocabulary and Word Study.**

Possible responses:

placate: to soothe or make less angry

placid: calm, not easily excited

placebo: a medicine that has no medical benefit, but is perceived to have a benefit by the user

implacable: impossible to please, satisfy, or change

FORMATIVE ASSESSMENT

Concept Vocabulary

If students do not see the connection between the words, **then** have them write additional sentences using the words.

Word Study

If students fail to understand how to use the root word, **then** use words that have the root in sentences and have students figure out their definitions. For Reteach and Practice, see **Word Study: Latin Root *–plac-* (RP).**

LANGUAGE DEVELOPMENT

LETTER FROM BIRMINGHAM JAIL

Concept Vocabulary

idly	stagnation	yearning
postpone	complacency	languished

Why These Words? These concept words are related to inaction. For example, in paragraph 27 of the selection, Dr. King claims that he stands in the middle of two forces at work in the African American community. One of those forces is *complacency*. Those who are complacent are satisfied and passive. That is, they will not work for change.

1. Select two concept vocabulary words other than *complacency*. How does each word contribute to the idea of inaction? Explain.
2. What other words in the selection connect to the concept of inaction?

Practice

Notebook The concept vocabulary words appear in "Letter From Birmingham Jail."

1. Use each concept word in a sentence that demonstrates your understanding of the word's meaning.
2. Challenge yourself to replace the concept word with one or two synonyms. How does each word affect the meaning of your sentence? For example, which sentence is stronger? Which has a more positive meaning?

WORD NETWORK

Add interesting words related to civil rights from the selection to your Word Network.

Word Study

Latin Root: *-plac-* The Latin root *-plac-* means "calm," "peaceful," or "pleasing." The word *complacency* suggests a sense of relaxed or satisfied pleasure in a situation. Using your understanding of the root *-plac-*, define each of the words listed here. Consult a dictionary if necessary.

placate ______________________________

placid ______________________________

placebo ______________________________

implacable ______________________________

STANDARDS

Language

- Use various types of phrases and clauses to convey specific meanings and add variety and interest to writing or presentations.
- Identify and correctly use patterns of word changes that indicate different meanings or parts of speech.
- Demonstrate understanding of figurative language, word relationships, and nuances in word meanings.

CROSS-CURRICULAR PERSPECTIVES

Art

Civil Rights Posters The Civil Rights era is an important time in American history. Ask students to identify and research one important moment in Civil Rights history and create a poster that communicates their understanding of that moment in time.

Conventions

Relative Clauses A **clause** is a group of words that contains a subject and a verb. A **relative clause** is a type of clause that modifies a noun or pronoun in another clause by telling what kind or which one. It usually begins with a **relative pronoun**, such as that, which, who, whom, or whose.

This chart shows examples of sentences containing relative clauses. The relative pronouns are italicized, and the relative clauses are highlighted.

SENTENCE	FUNCTION OF RELATIVE CLAUSE
The month *that* has 28 days is February.	modifies *month, telling which one*
The dinner, *which* includes dessert, is not expensive.	modifies *dinner,* telling *what kind*
This is the player *who* broke the record.	modifies *player,* telling *which one*
The next-door neighbor *whom* my sister has known since college is named Mario.	modifies *neighbor,* telling *which one*
The senator *whose* opinion was in question spoke to the press.	modifies *senator,* telling *which one*

Read It

1. Mark the relative pronoun and the relative clause in each of these sentences from "Letter From Birmingham Jail." Then, indicate the noun or pronoun each clause modifies.
   a. One who breaks an unjust law must do so openly, lovingly, and with a willingness to accept the penalty.
   b. Every day I meet young people whose disappointment with the church has turned into outright disgust.
   c. Now, there is nothing wrong in having an ordinance which requires a permit for a parade.
2. Reread paragraph 23 of "Letter From Birmingham Jail." Mark the relative clauses and relative pronouns, and tell what each clause modifies.

Write It

Notebook Add a relative clause to each sentence. Mark the relative clause and relative pronoun, and tell what word the clause modifies.

1. Segregation is an injustice.
2. Some church leaders stood up against discrimination.

DIGITAL PERSPECTIVES

Conventions

Explain to students that relative clauses can be either essential or nonessential. An essential clause is one that is needed to identify the person or thing that it modifies. The relative clause in the first sentence in the chart on the student page is essential because it identifies the month. The second sentence in the chart is nonessential because it adds information that is not critical to the reader's understanding. Nonessential clauses are set apart with commas. For more support, see **Conventions: Relative Clauses.**

Read It

Possible responses:

1. a. One who breaks an unjust law must do so openly. Used as an adjective to modify *one*.
   b. Every day I meet young people whose disappointment with the church has turned into outright disgust. Used as an adjective to modify people.
   c. Now, there is nothing wrong in having an ordinance which requires a permit for a parade. Used as an adjective to modify ordinance.
2. The relative clauses are: *who is more devoted to "order" than to justice; who prefers a negative peace which is the absence of tension to a positive peace which is the presence of justice; who constantly says ...; who paternalistically believes he can set the timetable for another man's freedom; who lives by a mythical concept of time and who constantly advises the Negro to wait for a "more convenient season."* Each clause modifies "the white moderate."

Write It

Possible responses:

1. Segregation is an injustice that has its origins in complacency. The clause modifies injustice.
2. Some church leaders, who were far ahead of their time, stood up against discrimination. The clause modifies the church leaders.

FORMATIVE ASSESSMENT

Conventions

If students cannot locate relative clauses, **then** review additional examples with them. For Reteach and Practice, see **Conventions: Relative Clauses (RP).**

TEACHING

Writing Compare

As students prepare to complete this assignment, review the multiple approaches to persuasion that Dr. King uses in his writing. He uses both logical and emotional appeals in his famous speech, "I Have a Dream" and in his "Letter From Birmingham Jail."

Logos, or logical appeal, is possibly the most important element of any argument, as claims must be supported with evidence and by reasoning.

Pathos, or emotional appeal, is also important because it can help readers and listeners connect the argument to their own lives and feelings.

Prewriting

Clarify audience and occasion. Help students see that Dr. King's purpose for writing each of these works is very different. The speech was written to motivate a huge crowd. It was given on the day of a momentous march. In contrast, the letter was written in a time of reflection when Dr. King, writing from a jail cell, wanted to express his frustration with the church.

Possible responses:

1. Students may expect that Dr. King's speech at the march would include more pathos and that a letter written from jail might include more logos. Most students may say their expectations were met.
2. The speech includes some logical reasoning but focuses on the rhetoric and charged language of motivation. The letter is far more scholarly, providing Dr. King's argument for his actions and beliefs.

EFFECTIVE EXPRESSION

"I HAVE A DREAM"

LETTER FROM BIRMINGHAM JAIL

Writing to Compare

You have studied two famous works by Dr. Martin Luther King, Jr.—his "I Have a Dream" speech and his "Letter From Birmingham Jail." Now, deepen your analysis and formalize your observations in writing.

Assignment

Both works by Dr. King are arguments, or persuasive texts, and use two main types of persuasive appeals.

- **Logical appeal,** or ***logos*:** using a clear line of reasoning supported by evidence, such as facts, data, or expert testimony
- **Emotional appeal,** or ***pathos*:** using loaded or charged language and other devices to arouse emotions

Write a **comparison-and-contrast essay** in which you analyze Dr. King's use of persuasive appeals in these two texts. Explain how the appeals he chooses fit the occasions and audiences for each text.

Prewriting

Clarify Audience and Occasion Dr. King's use of the two main types of appeals reflects both the **occasion,** or circumstances of the writing, and the **audience,** or listeners and readers, he seeks to reach. Make sure you are clear about the audiences and occasions that prompted the writing of each text. If necessary, reread the Background notes to clarify that information.

"I Have a Dream" speech audience and occasion: ______________

____

"Letter From Birmingham Jail" audience and occasion: ______________

____

STANDARDS

Writing

- Write informative/explanatory texts to examine and convey ideas, concepts, and information clearly and accurately through the effective selection, organization, and analysis of content.
- Produce clear and coherent writing in which the development, organization, and style are appropriate to task, purpose, and audience.
- Apply *grades 9–10 Reading standards* to literary nonfiction.

Gather Evidence Reread the two texts, and identify passages from each one that you feel are especially persuasive. Categorize each passage as an example of either logos or pathos. Explain why it fits that category.

PASSAGE	LOGOS OR PATHOS	EXPLANATION

Notebook Respond to these questions.

1. What types of appeals would you expect Dr. King to use to persuade the audience for each of these texts? Were your expectations met? Explain.
2. Does one text use more pathos or more logos than the other? Explain.

Drafting

Determine Your Central Idea In one sentence state the central idea or thesis you will develop:

Central Idea/Thesis: ______________________________

____

As you write, your ideas may come into clearer focus. If necessary, refine your thesis so that it expresses your position more precisely.

Choose a Structure Decide how best to organize your essay. Point-by-point organization and block organization are two commonly used structures for essays of comparison.

Point-by-Point Organization

I. Main Topic: Dr. King's Use of Logos in Two Texts
   A. Appeals to Logic in "I Have a Dream" Speech
   B. Appeals to Logic in "Letter from Birmingham Jail"
II. Main Topic: Dr. King's Use of Pathos in Two Texts
   A. Appeals to Emotion in "I Have a Dream" Speech
   B. Appeals to Emotion in "Letter from Birmingham Jail"

Block Organization

I. Main Topic: Types of Appeals in Dr. King's "I Have a Dream" Speech
   A. Appeals to Logic
   B. Appeals to Emotion
II. Main Topic: Types of Appeals in Dr. King's "Letter from Birmingham Jail"
   A. Appeals to Logic
   B. Appeals to Emotion

No matter the organizational structure you choose, weave in quotations from the two texts to support your analysis.

Review, Revise and Edit

Once you are done drafting, review and revise your essay. Make sure you have given specific examples of Dr. King's use of logos and pathos. In addition, make sure you have explained how those appeals fit the occasion and audience of each text. If necessary, add support for your ideas by incorporating additional examples from the texts.

EVIDENCE LOG

Before moving on to a new selection, go to your Evidence Log and record what you have learned from Dr. King's "I Have a Dream" speech and "Letter From Birmingham Jail."

DIGITAL PERSPECTIVES

Drafting

- Remind students that a thesis statement should be specific and address only what they will discuss in the essay. The thesis should be supported with evidence from both selections. Usually, the thesis appears at the end of the first paragraph.
- Explain to students that if their topic changes as they write, they may need to revise the thesis statement to reflect those changes.
- Remind students that brainstorming or creating a web is a useful way to structure an essay. Encourage students to use the point-by-point or block organization as guides for structuring the essay.

Review, Revise, and Edit

Encourage students to use two colors to evaluate the balance in their writing. Students may use one color for the speech and one color for the letter. This technique will allow students to see if they have written more about one text than the other.

For more support, see **Writing to Compare: Compare-and-Contrast Essay.**

Evidence Log Support students in completing their Evidence Log. This paced activity will help prepare them for the Performance-Based Assessment at the end of the unit.

FORMATIVE ASSESSMENT

Writing to Compare

- **If** students struggle with writing a thesis, **then** have them read examples and practice writing their own.
- **If** students struggle with structuring their essays, **then** ask them to brainstorm a series of potential topic statements before they start.

Selection Test

Administer the "Letter From Birmingham Jail" Selection Test, which is available in both print and digital formats online in Assessments.

PERSONALIZE FOR LEARNING

Strategic Support

Thesis Statements Students may struggle with constructing a thesis statement for their essays. Remind students that a thesis should capture the main idea of the entire paper. Have students create graphic organizers with sections for the thesis, each of the topic sentences, and evidence that supports each of the topic sentences. If students continue to struggle, ask them to think about how each of their topic sentences relates to the others and to the thesis statement.

Remarks on the Assassination of Martin Luther King, Jr.

AUDIO SUMMARIES
Audio summaries of "Remarks on the Assassination of Martin Luther King, Jr." are available online in both English and Spanish in the Interactive Teacher's Edition or Unit Resources. Assigning these summaries prior to reviewing the video may help students build additional background knowledge and set a context for listening to the speech.

Summary

On April 4, 1968, Robert F. Kennedy was expected to give a campaign speech. Instead, in "Remarks on the Assassination of Martin Luther King, Jr.," he puts aside his plans and shares the news that Martin Luther King, Jr. has been killed in Memphis. Kennedy urges the audience to dedicate their lives and energy to love and justice. He takes the opportunity to ask the crowd to think about the type of nation the United States should become. He suggests that one option is to act on bitterness, hatred, and revenge, which might lead to greater polarization. He says that he has felt these emotions and he reminds the crowd that his own brother was killed by an assassin. Kennedy asks the crowd to try to pursue the other option—to understand and to move beyond. He calls for love, wisdom, and compassion, and he says that the majority of Americans want the same thing.

Insight

This speech addresses the anticipated, widespread hopelessness and rage that followed King's death, and counters it with calls to carry on.

Several months later Kennedy, like King and like his brother John F. Kennedy, was assassinated.

ESSENTIAL QUESTION:
How can words inspire change?

Connection to Essential Question

This speech provides a connection to the Essential Question. At a critical moment in history, Kennedy's words helped calm people who were upset, afraid, and angry. This may have helped them stay on track and avoid harming their own cause.

WHOLE-CLASS LEARNING PERFORMANCE TASK
How did the selections in this section affect those who first heard them or read them?

UNIT PERFORMANCE-BASED ASSESSMENT
Explain how words have the power to provoke, calm, or inspire.

Connection to Performance Tasks

Whole-Class Learning Performance Task Kennedy's speech was delivered to a largely African-American crowd on the night Dr. King was killed. This task calls for outside research into how this speech was received at the time.

Unit Performance-Based Assessment In this speech, Kennedy tries to calm and inspire people in a terrible time. His references to his own experiences and to the ideas of Aeschylus were meant to help the crowd who struggled with the news of the assassination.

DIGITAL PERSPECTIVES — Audio | Video | Document | Annotation Highlights | EL Highlights | Online Assessment

LESSON RESOURCES

	Making Meaning		Effective Expression
Lesson	**First Review** **Analyze the Media**	**Close Review** **Media Vocabulary**	**Writing to Sources** **Speaking and Listening**
Instructional Standards	**RI.10** By the end of grade 9, read and comprehend literary nonfiction . . . **SL.3** Evaluate a speaker's point of view . . .		**W.2.b** Develop a topic . . . **W.1.d** Establish and maintain a formal style . . . **SL.4** Present information, findings, and supporting evidence . . .
STUDENT RESOURCES			
Available online in the Interactive Student Edition or Unit Resources	Selection Audio First-Review Guide: Media Video Close- Review Guide: Media Video		Evidence Log
TEACHER RESOURCES			
Selection Resources Available online in the Interactive Teacher's Edition or Unit Resources	Audio Summaries Media Vocabulary		Writing to Sources: Newspaper Report Speaking and Listening: Newscast
Assessment Available online in Assessments	Selection Test		
My Resources	A Unit 3 Answer Key is available online and in the Interactive Teacher's Edition.		

Media Complexity Rubric: Remarks on the Assassination of Martin Luther King, Jr.

Quantitative Measures	
Format and Length:	Video; 6 minutes 28 seconds
Qualitative Measures	
Knowledge Demands ① ② ❸ ④ ⑤	Prior knowledge is required of the assassination of Martin Luther King, Jr., and the tension between African Americans and whites at that time.
Structure ① ❷ ③ ④ ⑤	Video shows Robert F. Kennedy delivering the speech. No other images or graphics are included, but they are not necessary in order to understand the excerpt.
Language Conventionality and Clarity ① ❷ ③ ④ ⑤	Language is mostly easy to understand, but some sentences are complex with multiple clauses; diction is clear and easy to understand, and pace of delivery is slow.
Levels of Meaning/Purpose ① ② ❸ ④ ⑤	Purpose of speech is clear, explicit, and narrowly focused (honoring King after his death); listener also needs to infer the other purpose of speech—encouraging a non-violent reaction to the assassination.

Jump Start

FIRST READ Ask the following prompt: *Does seeking revenge promote peace and justice?* As students discuss the prompt, ask them to think of the kind of actions Martin Luther King, Jr. was known for, and what he might have wanted people to say in response to his assassination.

Remarks on the Assassination of Martin Luther King, Jr.

Is peace the cowardly option? How did Dr. King and Senator Kennedy contribute to Civil Rights movement in a peaceful way? Have their methods proven effective over time? Modeling the questions a viewer might ask as they review "Remarks on the Assassination of Martin Luther King, Jr." brings the speech alive for students and connects it to the Whole-Class Performance Task assignment. Selection audio is available in the Interactive Teacher's Edition.

Media Vocabulary

Encourage students to discuss the media vocabulary. Have they seen the terms before? Do they use any of them in their speech and writing? For more support, see **Media Vocabulary.**

FIRST REVIEW

As they listen, students should perform the steps of the first review:

WATCH: Remind students to listen to Kennedy's tone of voice and observe how the audience reacts to him.

NOTE: Encourage students to take note of key ideas and themes in Kennedy's speech.

CONNECT: Encourage students to make connections beyond the speech with what they know of other assassinations in American history—Abraham Lincoln, or John F. Kennedy, for instance. If possible, have them make connections to their reactions to other acts of political violence.

RESPOND: Students will answer questions to demonstrate understanding.

Point out to students that while they will always complete the Respond step at the end of the first read, the other steps will probably happen somewhat concurrently. You may wish to print copies of the **First-Read Guide: Media Video** for students to use.

About the Author

Robert F. Kennedy (1925–1968) was named United States Attorney General beginning when his brother President John F. Kennedy took office in 1961. Robert Kennedy was known for fighting organized crime and championing civil rights. As Attorney General, Kennedy fought for racial equality and provided critical help in passing the landmark Civil Rights Act of 1964. Kennedy was a leading presidential candidate when he was killed in Los Angeles, a few months after the assassination of Dr. Martin Luther King, Jr.

Remarks on the Assassination of Martin Luther King, Jr.

Media Vocabulary

The following words or concepts will be useful to you as you analyze, discuss, and write about recordings of speeches.

oratory: formal public speaking	• Speeches given on formal, serious, or ceremonial occasions are often examples of oratory. • Oratory is typically more dramatic and passionate than everyday speech.
delivery: manner in which a speaker gives a speech	• Delivery involves all aspects of a speaker's presentation: his or her voice, tone, emotional expressiveness, use of gestures, and overall personality.
gesture: movement of the hands or body that conveys meaning	• Gestures play an important role in oratory, helping to emphasize the speaker's ideas or emotions. • Gestures may help create a visual sense of a speaker's ideas.
cadence: rhythm and flow of language	• Cadence may have many different rhythms, from slow and steady to smooth and flowing. • Effective speakers often vary cadence to emphasize ideas and add drama.

First Review MEDIA: VIDEO

Apply these strategies as you conduct your first review.

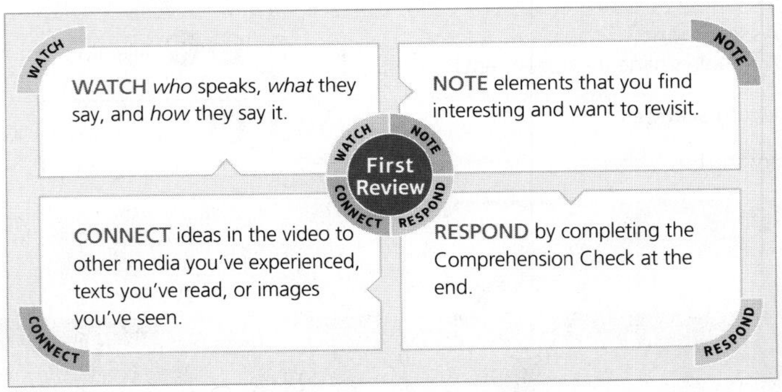
WATCH
WATCH *who* speaks, *what* they say, and *how* they say it.
NOTE
NOTE elements that you find interesting and want to revisit.
First Review
CONNECT ideas in the video to other media you've experienced, texts you've read, or images you've seen.
RESPOND by completing the Comprehension Check at the end.
CONNECT
RESPOND

STANDARDS

Reading Informational Text

By the end of grade 9, read and comprehend literary nonfiction in the grades 9–10 text complexity band proficiently, with scaffolding as needed at the high end of the range.

Media Strategy: Tone and Context

Notebook Start your review of the speech by focusing on Kennedy's tone, or emotional attitude, and how it relates to the occasion. What makes the situation so difficult? What kind of assumptions must Kennedy have made about his audience? Why is his tone important in this situation?

VOCABULARY DEVELOPMENT

Media Vocabulary If students are struggling with the concept of *cadence,* remind them that the word has multiple meanings. Point out a few of the most common definitions:

1. A rhythmic sequence or flow of sounds in language.
2. The beat, time, or measure of rhythmical motion or activity.
3. The modulated and rhythmic recurrence of a sound, especially in nature.

Explain to students that the *cadence* of a speech refers to the first meaning: its rhythmic sequence, or flow of sounds. Have students consider why the rhythm and flow of our normal speech patterns change. Why, at times, do we speak faster or slower, quieter or louder?

DIGITAL PERSPECTIVES

MEDIA | VIDEO

Remarks on the Assassination of Martin Luther King, Jr.

Robert F. Kennedy

BACKGROUND

Martin Luther King, Jr., was assassinated on April 4, 1968, in Memphis, Tennessee. On that day, Senator Robert F. Kennedy, who was then running for president, was in Indianapolis to give a campaign speech. After hearing news of King's murder, Kennedy chose not to give his planned speech. Instead, he announced that King had been killed and made the following impromptu remarks.

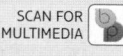

SCAN FOR MULTIMEDIA

NOTES

PERSONALIZE FOR LEARNING

Challenge

Research Have students research the assassination of president John F. Kennedy. Students should report back with a brief account of what happened, what JFK stood for as a civil rights leader, and the public response to this event in history. Discuss the significance of John F. Kennedy's death and how this experience made his brother Robert Kennedy qualified in many ways to address the sensitive subjects of this speech.

CLOSER LOOK

Analyze Diction

Students may have noted the cry of anguish that follows Robert Kennedy's announcement that Martin Luther King had just died that evening by an assassin's bullet. Use the potential danger of this moment to help students understand how Robert Kennedy's choice of words in the speech affects the audience. Encourage them to talk about what they noted. You may want to model a close review with the class based on the notes below.

NOTE: Have students note the details in the video that demonstrate how Robert Kennedy's choice of words calms, comforts, or inspires the audience.

QUESTION: Guide students to consider what these details might tell them. Ask what a listener can infer from Robert Kennedy's choice of words, and accept student responses.

Possible response: Robert Kennedy draws on his own loss of a brother by assassination to share his profound sympathy with his audience, and talks about "our" feelings, and how "we" should react to this act of violence. He uses Dr. King's own words as he appeals to his audience to reject "bitterness" and "hatred," and to respond to violence with "compassion," "love" and "wisdom." The audience is audibly moved and inspired by Kennedy's call for "justice."

CONCLUDE: Help students to formulate conclusions about the importance of these details in the speech. Ask students why the speaker might have included these details.

Possible response: Robert Kennedy sought to offer his audience solace for their loss, and to keep them from responding with violence. He achieved these aims by using words—many drawn from Dr. King himself—that expressed compassion, understanding, love, unity, and hope.

Remind students that **diction,** an author's word choice, is crucial to the way an audience responds to a speaker. A speaker who wishes to gain the attention and support of the people in an audience should address them in their own words, in words that have important associations and special meaning to them, and in words that carry particular emotional appeal and power to encourage, unify, and inspire.

Comprehension Check

Possible responses:

1. Kennedy shares the news that Dr. Martin Luther King, Jr. had been assassinated in Memphis, TN.
2. Kennedy fears that his African American listeners might be hateful, mistrustful, or seek revenge. He also fears that African Americans and white Americans will form opposing groups in hatred of each other.
3. He wants America to make an effort to understand and go beyond difficult times to choose compassion and love.
4. Kennedy quotes the ancient Greek dramatist Aeschylus.
5. Kennedy was in Indianapolis, Indiana.

Close Review

Model how to listen closely by using the Close Review note for the speech. Remind students to clarify anything they did not understand during their first review. You may wish to print the **Close-Review Guide: Media Video** for students to use.

Analyze the Media Speech

Possible responses:

1. The audience's astonished screams showed that people were not expecting the news. **DOK 2**
2. (a) Kennedy references the temptation to be filled with hatred. He asks his audience for compassion and understanding. **DOK 1** (b) Responses will vary. His approach seems effective because people are cheering at the end of the speech. **DOK 3**
3. Responses will vary. It seems from hearing this speech that words can have a soothing and reassuring effect during difficult times. **DOK 3**

Word Network

Possible words: *polarization, justice, bitterness, hatred, revenge, compassion, distrust, injustice, division, lawlessness*

FORMATIVE ASSESSMENT

Analyze the Speech

If students struggle to determine the impact and key points of Kennedy's speech on the audience, **then** remind them of past outraged responses to crimes committed in this country and how quickly the situation has turned to violence.

MAKING MEANING

Comprehension Check

Complete the following items after you finish your first review.

1. What news does Kennedy communicate to his audience?
2. What fear does Kennedy have with respect to the African American members of his audience?
3. What response to the news does Kennedy urge his listeners to choose?
4. What poet does Kennedy quote at the end?
5. Where was Kennedy when he gave these remarks?

MEDIA VOCABULARY

Use these words as you discuss and write about the speech.

oratory
delivery
gesture
cadence

WORD NETWORK

Add interesting words related to civil rights from the video to your Word Network.

STANDARDS

Speaking and Listening
Evaluate a speaker's point of view, reasoning, and use of evidence and rhetoric, identifying any fallacious reasoning or exaggerated or distorted evidence.

Close Review

Watch the video again. Write down any new observations that seem important. What **questions** do you have? What can you **conclude?**

Review · Close Review · Question · Conclude

Analyze the Media

CITE TEXTUAL EVIDENCE to support your answers.

Notebook Respond to these questions.

1. **Infer** What does the response of the audience at the beginning of the speech tell you about the occasion and listeners' expectations? Explain.
2. **(a)** In what specific ways does Kennedy address his fear that the nation might erupt in violence? **(b) Evaluate** Do you think his approach is effective? Explain.
3. **Essential Question:** *How can words inspire change?* What have you learned about the power of words from reading this selection?

296 UNIT 3 • THE LITERATURE OF CIVIL RIGHTS

PERSONALIZE FOR LEARNING

Strategic Support

Allusions Students might not see the relevance of Kennedy's chosen Aeschylus quote. It might seem to pause the speech unnecessarily as opposed to building it up. However, making an allusion to this particular Greek dramatist is a mark of the time and Kennedy's education at Harvard. Ask students for a few examples of what allusions they might make, or what songs or texts they might find appropriate to quote at such a serious moment.

EFFECTIVE EXPRESSION

Writing to Sources

Robert Kennedy was seeking election as president when Martin Luther King, Jr., was assassinated. He delivered this speech at an event that was supposed to be an ordinary campaign stop.

Assignment

Imagine that you are a newspaper reporter assigned to Senator Kennedy's presidential campaign. You have been traveling with the Senator and are on the spot when he delivers this speech. Write the **newspaper report** that you post later that day.

- Answer the five journalistic questions about the event. These are as follows: *Who is involved? What happened? Where did it happen? When did it happen?* and *Why did it happen?*
- Use precise, descriptive language that accurately captures the circumstances of the events and provides readers with a sense of how people reacted and seemed to feel.
- A news report is not a personal, first-person account. Use third-person pronouns, such as "he," and "they," as well as an appropriately serious tone. Focus attention on the events you observed, not on personal feelings or experiences.

Speaking and Listening

TV journalism follows many of the same rules as print journalism but requires strong speaking skills.

Assignment

Adapt your newspaper report as a **newscast** that might have aired on national television. You may deliver your newscast live to the class. Alternatively, you may work with a partner to record it and present or post it.

- TV journalists do not usually read their reports. Work to memorize your article so that you can deliver it smoothly. You may need to shorten it or make other changes so that it works as a spoken text.
- As you deliver your report, pay attention to your cadence and do not rush. Use an appropriately serious, somber tone.
- Add realism by using an actual microphone or a prop.
- If you are recording your report, look into the camera. In addition, keep gestures to a minimum.

REMARKS ON THE ASSASSINATION OF MARTIN LUTHER KING, JR.

EVIDENCE LOG

Before moving on to a new selection, go to your Evidence Log and record what you learned from "Remarks on the Assassination of Martin Luther King, Jr."

STANDARDS

Writing

- Develop a topic with well-chosen, relevant, and sufficient facts, extended definitions, concrete details, quotations, or other information and examples appropriate to the audience's knowledge of the topic.
- Establish and maintain a formal style and objective tone while attending to the norms and conventions of the of the discipline in which they are writing.

Speaking and Listening

- Present information, findings, and supporting evidence clearly, concisely, and logically such that listeners can follow the line of reasoning and the organization, development, substance, and style are appropriate to purpose, audience and task.

DIGITAL PERSPECTIVES

Enriching the Text To assist students in writing a detailed newspaper report, show the seven-minute documentary *Awful Grace,* directed and edited by Zachary Shields. This video will show them images of the location of the speech and interviews with people who were in the crowd that night. Use these questions to prompt discussion:

- How does this information add dimensions to students' understanding of the speech?
- What is this documentary telling us about how Kennedy's peaceful example influenced civil rights today?

Preview all videos before showing them in class.

DIGITAL PERSPECTIVES

Writing to Sources

Explain to students that when writing a news report they have a complex task. They need to set the scene for the rest of the world and make the experience resonate with communities everywhere. However, a reporter must also stay objective. A news report is not a place to voice personal emotions or opinions. For more support, see **Writing to Sources: Newspaper Report.**

Speaking and Listening

Remind the students that their spoken reports will need to be concise and have a defined beginning, middle, and end. Adding relevant background information about Kennedy or King would help the *why* and *what* of their reporting and strengthen their spoken report.

As students are practicing or recording their report, remind them to pay attention to speech patterns and pausing. Encourage them to check if they are using phrases like "um," "you know," or "like" to fill the gaps in their report. These behaviors will take away from the professional tone of the report and should be avoided. For more support see, **Speaking and Listening: Newscast.**

Evidence Log Support students in completing their Evidence Log. This paced activity will help prepare them for the Performance-Based Assessment at the end of the unit.

FORMATIVE ASSESSMENT

Writing to Sources

If students struggle with writing a news report about Kennedy's speech, **then** have them watch the video again while answering the five journalistic questions: *who, what, when, where* and *why*.

Speaking and Listening

If students struggle to adapt their newspaper report to a newscast, **then** have them watch a local or international newscaster in order to imitate cadence, eye contact, and tone of delivery.

TEACHING

Jump Start

What are civil rights? After students have read "I Have a Dream" and "Letter From Birmingham Jail" and watched "Remarks on the Assassination of Martin Luther King, Jr.," lead a discussion about the different ways that the civil rights of African Americans were violated. You might ask, "What are rights that many people take for granted that have been denied to African Americans?"

Write an Informative Essay

Make sure students understand what they are being asked to do in the assignment. Suggest that their research should seek answers to these questions: How did people present respond to King and Kennedy? How were government officials affected? What did contemporary news reports say?

Students should complete the assignment using word processing software to take advantage of editing tools and features.

Elements of an Informative Text

Reminds students that an effective piece of informative text is organized, such as "1963: The Year That Changed Everything," contains all the listed required elements. It is sequenced and informs the reader by providing plenty of facts and evidence.

MAKE IT INTERACTIVE

Project "1963: The Year That Changed Everything" from the interactive Teacher's Edition and have students identify the elements of a piece of informative text, such as a clear thesis statement; facts and evidence from reliable sources; and a clear introduction, body, and conclusion.

Academic Vocabulary

Ask students how the word *coherent* applies to the way informative text should be organized.

PERFORMANCE TASK: WRITING FOCUS

WRITING TO SOURCES

- "I HAVE A DREAM"
- LETTER FROM BIRMINGHAM JAIL
- REMARKS ON THE ASSASSINATION OF MARTIN LUTHER KING, JR.

Write an Informative Essay

You've read an essay, a speech, and a letter and viewed two videos of speeches, all of which have to do with the struggle for civil rights in the United States. In his "I Have a Dream" speech, Dr. Martin Luther King, Jr., speaks of the long struggle of the movement and of the need to persevere. In "Letter From Birmingham Jail," Dr. King writes to the white moderate religious leaders who would have him move more slowly to end segregation. Finally, in "Remarks on the Assassination of Martin Luther King, Jr.," Robert Kennedy announces to a crowd that Dr. King has been shot, and strives to give solace while appealing for peace and prayer. Now you will use your knowledge of the topic to write an informative text about the literature of civil rights.

Tool Kit
Student Model of an Informative Text

Assignment

Think about how Dr. Martin Luther King, Jr., and Robert Kennedy choose to address the question of civil rights in the United States, and how their listeners would have responded at the time. Conduct research to write an **informative essay** on this question:

How did the selections in this section affect those who first heard them or read them?

ACADEMIC VOCABULARY

As you craft your informative essay, consider using some of the academic vocabulary you learned in the beginning of the unit.

coherent
aggregate
disrupt
notation
express

Elements of an Informative Text

A **informative text** presents and interprets information gathered through the extensive study of a subject.

An effective informative text includes these elements:

- a clear thesis statement
- facts and evidence from a variety of reliable, credited sources
- a clear organization that seamlessly integrates quotations, paraphrases, and analysis from various sources
- smooth transitions that show the relationships between ideas
- correct grammar, formal style, and an objective tone

STANDARDS

Writing

- Write informative/explanatory texts to examine and convey complex ideas, concepts, and information clearly and accurately through the effective selection, organization, and analysis of content.
- Conduct short as well as more sustained research projects to answer a question or solve a problem; narrow or broaden the inquiry when appropriate; synthesize multiple sources on the subject, demonstrating understanding of the subject under investigation.
- Write routinely over extended time frames and shorter time frames for a range of tasks, purposes, and audiences.

Model Informative Text For a model of a well-crafted informative text, see the Launch Text, "1963: The Year That Changed Everything."

Challenge yourself to find all of the elements of effective informative writing in the text. You will have the opportunity to review these elements as you start to write your own informative text.

AUTHOR'S PERSPECTIVE **Kelly Gallagher, M.Ed.**

Revision E.B. Write once said, "The best writing is rewriting." Unfortunately, many students come to us with the "I wrote it once; I'm done" philosophy. Demonstrate the importance of *revision* – making writing better by looking at it again-- through teacher modeling. First, write with the class for fifteen minutes on a specific topic Then,. Complete the activity with the class.

1. Display your first draft on the screen. Use think alouds as you use RADAR strategies for revision: REPLACE; ADD; DELETE; REORDER. For each change you implement, mark the type of change you made.
2. Have students use the same process on their first drafts. Remind students that they will work on making their papers *correct* later; for now, they are to revise with the goal of being able to point out places where their second draft is better than their first.
3. Last, have students hold their two drafts side-by-side as you modeled, and indicate which RADAR strategies they used to revise their first drafts.

Prewriting / Planning

Focus Your Research Now that you have read the selections and thought about how words can inspire change, use the research question to focus your research. Plan to use a variety of sources. Consider:

- **primary sources**, which are firsthand or original accounts, such as newspaper articles
- **secondary sources**, such as encyclopedia entries
- **digital sources**, or material accessed on the Internet
- **print sources**, such as books or journal articles, which may be edited more carefully than digital material
- **original research**, such as eyewitness interviews or survey results

Create a list of sources to consult, and add new sources to your list as you find them.

Source List: ____

____.

Search Terms Write down terms you plan to research online. Deciding on terms before going online may help you to stay focused on your topic. Use your search engine's advanced search function to narrow your results and find more relevant hits.

Search Terms: ____

____.

Evaluate Sources To ensure that the sources you use are reliable, evaluate them carefully by asking yourself the following types of questions:

- Is the writer an authority on the subject?
- Is the information current, and does the publisher have a good reputation?
- Do other sources confirm the information in this source?

You can find out the answers to the first two questions by examining the author's and publisher's credentials. Do a quick Internet search to find out about the author's background, previous publications, and reputation. Consider the author's bias, or leanings, before accepting a conclusion. Check publication dates to make sure information is current. If you find conflicts in information between two sources, check the facts in a third source.

Take notes as you find relevant information, and keep a reference list of every source you use. Note each source's author, title, publisher, city, and date of publication. For Internet sources, record the name and Web address of the site, and the date you accessed the information. For print sources, note the page numbers on which you found useful information.

EVIDENCE LOG

Review your Evidence Log and identify key details you may want to cite in your informative essay.

STANDARDS

Writing
Gather relevant information from multiple authoritative print and digital sources, using advanced searches effectively; assess the usefulness of each source in answering the research question; integrate information into the text selectively to maintain the flow of ideas, avoiding plagiarism and following a standard format for citation.

DIGITAL PERSPECTIVES

Prewriting/Planning

Focus Your Research Tell students that there is a wealth of sources that could supply the information they're seeking. Encourage them to be strategic when choosing sources for their research and to think about specific facts or details they would like to find.

Search Terms Explain that using general search terms for research will usually bring back too many results. Encourage students to think about narrowing the information they are looking for to one or two specific terms.

Evaluate Sources Remind students that their online sources should be credible and reliable. Help students see that all web addresses are not equally valid, and encourage students to review each site critically. The student edition provides recommendations about how to document each resource. Encourage students to build this habit, as research will be an important part of their high school and college careers.

PERSONALIZE FOR LEARNING

Strategic Support

Gathering Information Students might have difficulty organizing all the information they discover during their research. Suggest they take notes on notecards while reading books and other print sources. For online research, encourage students to list the URLs of the helpful websites in a document, and to copy and paste relevant passages into the document.

TEACHING

Drafting

Organize Your Informative Text Explain to students that the structure they choose will depend upon what the purpose of their essay is. Point out that they are writing about King's speech and Kennedy's remarks and that they will want to show how the words affect people.

Adequate Support Remind students that there are a variety of ways to support their ideas. They might add primary sources including direct quotations or paraphrases from the text, or they might include secondary sources such as information from those who have read and analyzed the texts.

Remember Your Audience As students draft their essays, encourage them to think of their readers and to place them on a spectrum to rate their knowledge level of the topic. Those on the low-end may need support with basic ideas, but those who are more familiar with the subject may not need deep background. It is the writer's responsibility to help readers learn more about the subject without spending too much time summarizing ideas they may already know.

PERFORMANCE TASK: WRITING FOCUS

Drafting

Organize Your Informative Text Start by writing a **thesis statement**—a sentence that states your position. Your thesis for this essay will be a concise statement that summarizes the impact of the words of Dr. Martin Luther King, Jr., and Robert F. Kennedy on their audiences. This thesis can help shape the way you choose to organize your essay beyond the introduction.

- If your thesis emphasizes the connections between the impact of the words of the two men, you might consider a *point-by-point organization*. Each section of the essay would examine a new aspect of the men's influence and show their similarities.
- If your thesis emphasizes distinctions, you might consider a *block organization*. First you would describe multiple aspects of one man's words on his audience. Then, you would examine those same aspects with the words of the second man as the focus.

Adequate Support One of the main ingredients of a strong informative essay is the evidence you assemble to support your ideas. For example, you might be making a point about how Kennedy's speech affected the mood of the crowd. You could support that point with an exact quotation from an eyewitness or with details about the emotions that people in the crowd experienced, based on your sources. If you use an exact quotation, be sure to cite the source.

- **Exact Quotation:** Vechel Rhodes, who was there that night, later described the Kennedy event for CBS News: "A white man coming in this neighborhood, especially seeking for [the office of] president, it was a big deal for the blacks [for Kennedy] to be in this area."
- **Details:** The Indianapolis police chief was afraid Kennedy would be attacked by the crowd if he told them that King had been shot… The crowd's mood seemed to shift during the course of the speech.

Remember Your Audience While selecting facts, details, and quotations, keep your audience and their knowledge level firmly in mind. For instance, if your audience has with very limited knowledge, you might have to supply an extended definition of *segregation*—explaining how the system of inequality came about and how it affected communities. Use this space to record some notes about who your audience is and what they might already know.

STANDARDS

Writing

- Introduce a topic; organize complex ideas, concepts, and information to make important connections and distinctions; include formatting, graphics, and multimedia when useful to aiding comprehension.
- Develop the topic with well-chosen, relevant, and sufficient facts, extended definitions, concrete details, quotations, or other information and examples appropriate to the audience's knowledge of the topic.
- Use precise language and domain-specific vocabulary to manage the complexity of the topic.

AUTHOR'S PERSPECTIVE **Jim Cummins, Ph.D.**

The Importance of Frequent Writing Writing develops a different awareness from reading. Second-language learners need abundant opportunities to write for varied audiences and purposes to determine what they do and do not know. Frequent writing can be accomplished through a combination of low-stakes (informal, ungraded) and high stakes (formal, revised, graded) writing. Using this approach allows the teacher to nurture writing without needing to grade everything. Here are some suggestions for fostering regular writing:

- Do QuickWrites daily to review lessons and learning.
- Assign public writing, aimed at real audiences.
- Include personal writing, such as journals and diaries.
- Have students write reactions in response to their readings. Students can upload their reviews to class or school webpages.
- Have students write across genres. Try each one, having students pay attention to the conventions of each genre, such as stage directions in drama and dialogue in fiction. All genres have value; for example, poetry is powerful and likely easier for ESL students because of its condensed vocabulary. These assignments can be linked to word networks, too.

LANGUAGE DEVELOPMENT: AUTHOR'S STYLE

Create Cohesion: Integrate Different Types of Information

As you write your draft, use the following methods to incorporate the facts, examples, and quotations you have found:

- **Direct Quotations:** Place a writer's exact words in quotation marks. Any omitted words or sentences should not alter the intent of the passage. Indicate omitted material with **ellipses,** or dots.
- **Paraphrase:** Restate a writer's specific ideas in your own words, accurately reflecting the writer's meaning.
- **Summary:** Condense an extended idea into a brief statement in your own words to introduce background information or review key ideas.

When paraphrasing or quoting text, provide proper credit for all sources. There are several citation formats that are widely accepted. Those offered by the Modern Language Association (MLA) and the American Psychological Association (APA) are two of the most common. Each has different rules about the source information to include, as well as how to order and punctuate it. The style guides treat quotations and in-text citations differently, as well. Follow the citation format your teacher specifies.

Read It

These sentences from the Launch Text show the different methods of incorporating information.

- *"Injustice anywhere is a threat to justice everywhere," King wrote. He added, "Whatever affects one directly, affects all indirectly."* (uses direct quotation from "Letter From Birmingham Jail")
- *His message, the famous "Letter From Birmingham Jail," defends nonviolent resistance to injustice.* (paraphrases Dr. King's ideas)
- *In 1865, the Thirteenth Amendment to the United States Constitution ended slavery.* (summarizes the text of the Amendment)

STANDARDS

Writing
Gather relevant information from multiple authoritative print and digital sources, using advanced searches effectively; assess the usefulness of each source in answering the research question; integrate information into the text selectively to maintain the flow of ideas, avoiding plagiarism and following a standard format for citation.

Language
Write and edit work so that it conforms to the guidelines in a style manual appropriate for the discipline and writing type.

Write It

Use this chart to begin collecting source material and to plan your use of it.

SOURCE MATERIAL	QUOTATION	PARAPHRASE	SUMMARY

DIGITAL PERSPECTIVES

Create Cohesion: Integrate Different Types of Information

Read It

Explain that good writers vary the types of information they use in order to bolster their point and to make their communication more interesting to readers.

MAKE IT INTERACTIVE

Project "1963: The Year That Changed Everything" from the Interactive Teacher's Edition and ask students to identify additional examples of information types.

- **Paraphrase:** The peace and hope of that event did not last long. (paragraph 6)
- **Summary:** The struggle continued throughout 1963. The Southern Regional Council has records of protests that took place in more than 100 southern towns. Approximately 20,000 demonstrators were arrested. In words and actions, they delivered a demand for justice that could not be ignored. (paragraph 7)

Write It

As students organize the information they've gathered through their research, have them present each piece in a chart as a direct quote, a paraphrased sentence or paragraph, and a summary. Explain to students that this exercise will add interest as they sit down to write. Remind them that they shouldn't present information in only one way and that their informational essay will benefit from variety.

PERSONALIZE FOR LEARNING

English Language Support

Metaphors Read aloud this sentence from paragraph 15 of "I Have a Dream": *Let us not wallow in the valley of despair, I say to you today, my friends.* Explain to students that the phrase "valley of despair" is a metaphor that King used to describe the plight of African Americans. Let them know that King chose the words because the imagery of a lowly valley helps portray the difficult conditions that African Americans were enduring. You might also want to point out that the word "valley" appears again in paragraph 24, in a reference to a biblical passage. **ALL LEVELS**

Revising

Evaluating Your Draft

Point out to students that it's especially important in an informative essay that the facts and evidence support the thesis statement. Remind them that "1963: The Year That Changed Everything" effectively accomplished this goal. Encourage them to review the facts and evidence they've included to ensure that they are relevant to the thesis statement and support it.

Revising for Purpose and Organization

Review Your Conclusion Encourage students to compare their introductions to their conclusions to ensure that these important paragraphs align. These functional paragraphs should match so that readers see a clear connection and understand the goal of the essay.

Use Transitions As students highlight their drafts to find gaps in transitions, encourage them to add these directional words. Transitions help readers see the connections writers intended.

Revising for Evidence and Elaboration

Use Precise Language Encourage students to review their drafts for such vague words as *many, a lot, people, society,* and *justice.* When they locate words like this, ask them to consider choosing more specific words that convey their thoughts more accurately.

Revising

Evaluating Your Draft

Use the following checklist to evaluate the effectiveness of your first draft. Then, use your evaluation and the instruction on this page to guide your revision.

FOCUS AND ORGANIZATION	EVIDENCE AND ELABORATION	CONVENTIONS
☐ Provides a clear thesis statement.	☐ Includes specific reasons, details, facts, and quotations to support the thesis.	☐ Attends to the norms and conventions of the discipline especially regarding crediting sources properly.
☐ Includes a clear introduction, body, and conclusion.	☐ Provides adequate support for each major idea.	
☐ Uses facts and evidence from a variety of reliable, credited sources.	☐ Uses precise language that is appropriate for the audience and purpose.	
☐ Provides a logical text structure.	☐ Establishes a formal, objective tone.	
☐ Concludes with a summary of the thesis and supporting evidence.		

Revising for Focus and Organization

Review Your Conclusion Reread your conclusion. Make sure that it fully addresses the prompt and summarizes information you presented in your essay.

Use Transitions Make sure the flow of your ideas is clear to your readers. Reread your draft, highlighting places where the addition of a transition word or phrase would clarify your thinking. Words or phrases such as *in contrast, finally, additionally,* and *similarly* serve as signposts for the next idea.

WORD NETWORK

Include interesting words from your Word Network in your informative text.

Revising for Evidence and Elaboration

Use Precise Language Choose words that say exactly what you mean. The author of the Launch Text uses precise language to describe the effects of the Children's Crusade. Words such as *transform, under attack,* and *global outcry* help capture the dramatic impact of the events described.

As you choose precise words, make sure you avoid overgeneralizations. Look through your draft for clue words, such as *all, none,* or *never* that suggest an overgeneralization. Circle these words in your draft and—if you can't back them up with support—consider qualifying, or limiting, your statements.

> **Overgeneralization:** *Everyone who heard King's words was inspired to change American society.*
> **Qualified statement:** *Many who heard King's words were inspired to change American society.*

STANDARDS

Writing

- Use appropriate and varied transitions to link the major sections of the text, create cohesion, and clarify the relationships among complex ideas and concepts.
- Use precise language and domain-specific vocabulary to manage the complexity of the topic.
- Provide a concluding statement or section that follows from and supports the information or explanation presented.

HOW LANGUAGE WORKS

Precision and Clarity Explain to students that in an informative text, precision is essential, whereas in certain forms of fictional writing, like poetry, establishing a feeling is more important than precisely conveying information. Refer to "1963: The Year That Changed Everything" and note the different ways in which the author used precise language (e.g., the use of dates). Point out that without precision and clarity, the reader might have difficulty understanding the essay.

PEER REVIEW

Exchange papers with a classmate. Use the checklist to evaluate your classmate's informative essay and provide supportive feedback.

1. Is the thesis clear?
   ☐ yes ☐ no If no, explain what confused you.
2. Is the essay organized logically?
   ☐ yes ☐ no If no, what about the organization does not work?
3. Does the essay fully address the writing prompt?
   ☐ yes ☐ no If no, write a brief note explaining what you thought was missing.
4. What is the strongest part of your classmate's essay? Why?

____

____

____

____

Editing and Proofreading

Edit for Formal Language Reread your draft to make sure that you did not use any slang or informal language. Also, keep in mind that informative writing requires an objective tone, so avoid adding personal opinions when presenting facts and information about the time period.

Proofread for Accuracy Read your draft carefully, looking for errors in spelling and punctuation. Double-check that you have used quotation marks correctly, and that there is an ending quotation mark for every beginning quotation mark.

Publishing and Presenting

Create a final version of your draft. Share it with a small group so that your classmates can read it and make comments. In turn, review and comment on your classmate's work. Together, determine what your different reports convey about the initial impact of Dr. King's and Senator Kennedy's words. Listen and respond respectfully to comments about your work.

Reflecting

Think about what you learned while writing your essay. What techniques did you learn that you could use when writing another informative text? How could you improve the process? For example, you might take more notes as you read over reliable sources of information.

STANDARDS

Writing
Establish and maintain a formal style and objective tone while attending to the norms and conventions of the discipline in which they are writing.

DIGITAL PERSPECTIVES

Peer Review

Explain to students that the main purpose of their peer review is to provide helpful feedback to the author. Encourage them to take close look at the strength of the thesis and the relevance of the facts and evidence. Remind them that when they provide feedback to the author, it should be done in a constructive, not critical, way.

Editing and Proofreading

Remind students that while the overall purpose of the essay, its organization, strength of thesis, and relevant evidence are what matters most, a piece of writing can be undermined by poor grammar and spelling errors. Encourage students to proofread carefully.

Reflecting

Ask students what they learned from the process of writing their informative essays. Ask them to reflect on both what they learned about writing and what they learned about the Civil Rights era.

PERSONALIZE FOR LEARNING

Challenge

Interview Instruct students to create a podcast in which they interview both Martin Luther King, Jr. and Robert F. Kennedy after their speeches. Tell students to think about the questions they'd ask the men, asking them to keep in mind that they both have just experienced something very emotional. Remind students that neither King nor Kennedy knew how their speeches would be received.

OVERVIEW

SMALL-GROUP LEARNING

How can words inspire change?

Words have the tremendous power to inspire meaningful and widespread change. Many authors who wrote during the Civil Rights movement used their words to draw global attention to the racial inequality in the United States. During Small-Group Learning, students will read selections that show how powerful words can be.

Small-Group Learning Strategies

Review the Learning Strategies with students and explain that as they work through Small-Group Learning they will develop strategies to work in small-group environments.

- Have students watch the video on Small-Group Learning Strategies.
- A video on this topic is available online in the Professional Development Center.

You may wish to discuss some action items to add to the chart as a class before students complete it on their own. For example, for "Participate fully," you might solicit the following from students:

- Offer suggestions to help the group.
- Ask questions to make sure that you and others in your group understand the topic.

Block Scheduling

Each day in this Pacing Plan represents a 40-50 minute class period. Teachers using block scheduling may combine days to reflect their class schedule. In addition, teachers may revise pacing to differentiate and support core instruction by integrating components and resources as students require.

OVERVIEW: SMALL-GROUP LEARNING

ESSENTIAL QUESTION:

How can words inspire change?

The 1960s marked a time of great change in American history. However, we should never forget the hardships of those who lived under segregation. The selections you will read present insights into different accounts of what took place during this important period. You will work in a group to continue your exploration of the civil rights movement.

Small-Group Learning Strategies

Throughout your life, in school, in your community, in college, and in your career, you will continue to learn and work with others.

Look at these strategies and the actions you can take to practice them as you work in teams. Add ideas of your own for each step. Use these strategies during Small-Group Learning.

STRATEGY	ACTION PLAN
Prepare	• Complete your assignments so that you are prepared for group work. • Organize your thinking so you can contribute to your group's discussion. •
Participate fully	• Make eye contact to signal that you are listening and taking in what is being said. • Use text evidence when making a point. •
Support others	• Build off ideas from others in your group. • Invite others who have not yet spoken to join the discussion. •
Clarify	• Paraphrase the ideas of others to ensure that your understanding is correct. • Ask follow-up questions. •

SCAN FOR MULTIMEDIA

Pacing Plan

- Unit Introduction: 1
- Introduce Whole-Class Learning: 2
- I Have a Dream: 3, 4, 5, 6
- Letter From Birmingham Jail: 7, 8, 9, 10
- Media: Remarks on the Assassination of Martin Luther King, Jr.: 11, 12, 13
- Performance Task: 14, 15

CONTENTS

MEDIA: NEWSCAST

Remembering Civil Rights History, When "Words Meant Everything"

PBS Newshour

Guided by poet Natasha Trethewey, take a journey through some of the dramatic events of the civil rights era.

POETRY

For My People *Margaret Walker*

This poem celebrates the resilience and strength of the African American people.

Incident *Natasha Trethewey*

An autobiographical poem presents frightening images from a painful time in American life.

SPEECH

Lessons of Dr. Martin Luther King, Jr.

Cesar Chavez

One political activist connects his purpose to the words and actions of a leader who came before him.

MEMOIR

Traveling

Grace Paley

In stories from different decades, members of one family confront the ugliness of segregation.

PERFORMANCE TASK

SPEAKING AND LISTENING FOCUS

Multimedia Presentation

The Small-Group readings present the experiences of people who were eyewitnesses to civil rights history. After reading, your group will develop a research presentation about civil rights in the United States.

Contents

Selections Circulate among groups as they preview the selections. You might encourage groups to discuss any knowledge they already have about any of the selections or the situations and settings shown in the photographs. Students may wish to take a poll within their group to determine which selections look the most interesting.

Remind students that communicating and collaborating in groups is an important skill that they will use throughout their lives—in school, in their careers, and in their community.

Performance Task

Present an Informative Essay Give groups time to read about and briefly discuss the podcast they will create after reading. Encourage students to do some preliminary thinking about the types of media they may want to use. This may help focus their subsequent reading and group discussion.

Introduce Small-Group Learning — 16

Media: Remembering Civil Rights History: "When Words Meant Everything" — 17

• For My People • Incident — 18, 19

Lessons of Dr. Martin Luther King, Jr. — 20, 21, 22

Traveling — 23, 24

Performance Task — 25, 26

SMALL-GROUP LEARNING

Introduce Independent Learning — 27

Independent Learning — 28

Performance-Based Assessment — 29, 30

OVERVIEW

SMALL-GROUP LEARNING

Working as a Team

1. **Take a Position** Remind groups to let all members share their responses. You may wish to set a time limit for this discussion.
2. **List Your Rules** You may want to have groups share their lists of rules and consolidate them into a master list to be displayed and followed by all groups.
3. **Apply the Rules** As you circulate among the groups, ensure that students are staying on task. Consider a short time limit for this step.
4. **Name Your Group** This task can be creative and fun. If students have trouble coming up with a name, suggest that they think of something related to the unit topic. Encourage groups to share their names with the class.
5. **Create a Communication Plan** Encourage groups to include in their plans agreed-upon times during the day to share ideas. They should also devise a method for recording and saving their communications.

Accountable Talk

Remind students to communicate politely. Post these Accountable Talk ideas and ask students to add more. They should:

Remember to . . . Ask clarifying questions.

Which sounds like . . .
Can you please repeat what you said?
Would you give me an example?
I think you said _____. Did I understand you correctly?

Remember to . . . Explain your thinking.

Which sounds like . . .
I believe _____ is true because _____.
I feel _____ because _____.

Remember to . . . Build on the ideas of others.

Which sounds like . . .
When _____ said _____, it made me think of _____.

OVERVIEW: SMALL-GROUP LEARNING

Working as a Team

1. **Take a Position** In your group, discuss the following question:

   If you saw an injustice in your community, how might you start to change it?

   As you take turns sharing your ideas, be sure to provide reasons. After all group members have shared, discuss the strengths and weaknesses of different types of approaches to social change.

2. **List Your Rules** As a group, decide on the rules that you will follow as you work together. Two samples are provided. Add two more of your own. As you work together, you may add or revise rules based on your experience together.
   - Everyone should read all of the texts.
   - People should stay focused during discussions.
   - ____
   - ____

3. **Apply the Rules** Share what you have learned about the Civil Rights movement. Make sure each person in the group contributes. Take notes and be prepared to share with the class one thing that you have heard from another member of your group.

4. **Name Your Group** Choose a name that reflects the unit topic.

   Our group's decision: ________________________________

5. **Create a Communication Plan** Decide how you want to communicate with one another. For example, you might use online collaboration tools, email, or instant messaging.

   Our group's decision: ________________________________

FACILITATING SMALL-GROUP LEARNING

Forming Groups You may wish to form groups for Small-Group Learning so that each consists of students with different learning abilities. Some students may be adept at organizing information whereas other may have strengths related to generating or synthesizing information. A good mix of abilities can make the experience of Small-Group Learning dynamic and productive.

Making a Schedule

First, find out the due dates for the Small-Group activities. Then, preview the texts and activities with your group, and make a schedule for completing the tasks.

SELECTION	ACTIVITIES	DUE DATE
Remembering Civil Rights History, When "Words Meant Everything"		
For My People Incident		
Lessons of Dr. Martin Luther King, Jr.		
Traveling		

Working on Group Projects

As your group works together, you'll find it more effective if each person has a specific role. Different projects require different roles. Before beginning a project, discuss the necessary roles, and choose one for each group member. Some possible roles are listed here. Add your own ideas to the list.

Project Manager: monitors the schedule and keeps everyone on task
Researcher: organizes information-gathering activities
Recorder: takes notes during group meetings
Role: ______________________________
Role: ______________________________
____
____

SCAN FOR MULTIMEDIA

DIGITAL PERSPECTIVES

Making a Schedule

Encourage groups to preview the reading selections and to consider how long it will take them to complete the activities accompanying each selection. Point out that they can adjust the due dates for particular selections as needed as they work on their small-group projects. However, they must complete all assigned tasks before the group Performance Task is due. Encourage groups to review their schedules upon completing the activities for each selection to make sure they are on track to meet the final due date.

Working on Group Projects

Point out to groups that the roles they assign can also be changed later. Students might have to make changes based on who is best at a given task. Try to make sure that there is no favoritism, cliquishness, or stereotyping by gender or other means in the assignment of roles.

Also, you should review the roles each group assigns to its members. Based on your understanding of students' individual strengths, you might find it necessary to suggest some changes.

AUTHOR'S PERSPECTIVE **Kelly Gallagher, M.Ed.**

The Teacher's Role After the ability to read and write with fluency, the skill that employers value most is the ability to collaborate successfully. Talking with other people can help us all learn more, change our opinions, and make us more intelligent because we hear ideas that we may not have previously considered. Student collaboration also serves as a useful formative assessment tool. An effective strategy for identifying students' opinions about what they read and for pinpointing the information they're missing about a text is to ask, "What is worth talking about?" Hearing what they get and what they've missed informs further instruction. Here are some additional strategies for encouraging effective collaboration:

- *Flow in and out of groups* as students work. Circulate from group to group, modeling and encouraging meaningful talk, a lifelong literacy skill.
- *Take notes* on what is being said outright and what is being implied. See what prior knowledge and background individuals contribute.

Plan pathways for subsequent lessons from what you've heard and observed.

Remembering Civil Rights History, When "Words Meant Everything"

AUDIO SUMMARIES
Audio summaries of "Remembering Civil Rights History, When 'Words Meant Everything'" are available online in both English and Spanish in the Interactive Teacher's Edition or Unit Resources. Assigning these summaries prior to reading the selection may help students build additional background knowledge and set a context for their first read.

Summary

In this newscast, journalist Jeffrey Brown follows Poet Laureate Natasha Trethewey. They join in on a journey, the Congressional Civil Rights Pilgrimage, to commemorate key events from the era. As part of this event, politicians from both major political parties discuss the events and their relevance today. Trethewey and such luminaries as John Lewis discuss the role poetry played during the Civil Rights movement. Poetry and music helped propel the movement, allowing protestors to express thoughts that are difficult to convey otherwise.

Insight

Too often, the Civil Rights Movement is taught as if no one but Dr. King was involved in it. This video helps show the range of people whose language contributed to the movement, and reflects on their legacy today.

ESSENTIAL QUESTION:
How can words inspire change?

Connection to Essential Question

This selection investigates the role of language in the Civil Rights movement. Well-used words can have great power to affect social change.

SMALL-GROUP LEARNING PERFORMANCE TASK
Why do words and actions in some time periods produce meaningful change—and in others do not?

UNIT PERFORMANCE-BASED ASSESSMENT
Explain how words have the power to provoke, calm, or inspire.

Connection to Performance Tasks

Small-Group Learning Task Words are important not only for swaying the unpersuaded, but also for convincing people on your side to keep up through difficult work.

Unit Performance-Based Assessment This video shows the way that words can positively provoke change, stirring up people's passion to make a difference.

DIGITAL PERSPECTIVES

Audio | Video | Document | Annotation Highlights | EL Highlights | Online Assessment

LESSON RESOURCES

	Making Meaning	Effective Expression
Lesson	**Media Vocabulary** **First Review** **Close Review** **Analyze the Media**	**Research** **Writing to Sources**
Instructional Standards	**RL.10** By the end of grade 9, read and comprehend literary nonfiction . . . **SL.2** Integrate multiple sources of information presented in diverse media . . .	**W.7** Conduct short as well as more sustained research projects . . .
STUDENT RESOURCES		
Available online in the Interactive Student Edition or Unit Resources	Selection Audio First-Review Guide: Media-Video Close-Review Guide: Media-Video Word Network	
TEACHER RESOURCES		
Selection Resources Available online in the Interactive Teacher's Edition or Unit Resources	Audio Summaries Media Vocabulary Remembering Civil Rights History: Media Questions	Research: Report Writing to Sources: Short Essay
My Resources	A Unit 3 Answer Key is available online and in the Interactive Teacher's Edition.	

Media Complexity Rubric: Remembering Civil Rights History, When "Words Meant Everything"

Quantitative Measures	
Format and Length: video of 7 minutes, 38 seconds	
Qualitative Measures	
Knowledge Demands ① ② ❸ ④ ⑤	Some background information is helpful about the Civil Rights movement, though all is explained fully. Multiple references are given to people and locations important in the movement.
Structure ① ② ❸ ④ ⑤	Video follows documentary style, including narration and interviews; footage is shown and interspersed with interviews; images correspond to narration, telling the story sequentially.
Language Conventionality and Clarity ① ② ❸ ④ ⑤	Language is contemporary and conversational; some figurative language is used (reading of poem "Incident"); multiple speakers are interviewed, so students hear speech of different styles and speed.
Levels of Meaning/Purpose ① ❷ ③ ④ ⑤	Purpose of video (explaining the Civil Rights Pilgrimage) is explicitly stated at beginning of video and explained. Details about the pilgrimage (locations, reasons) are also explained.

FACILITATING

Jump Start

FIRST READ Ask groups to discuss the following prompt: *Do people learn from their mistakes?* Remind students to support their discussion with specific examples from their reading or connections to the lives of important figures in human history.

Remembering Civil Rights History, When "Words Meant Everything"

Are words more important than actions? Or do the two need to go hand in hand? Modeling the questions a reader might ask as they review "Words Meant Everything" brings the video alive for students and connects it to the Small-Group Performance Task assignment. Selection audio is available in the Interactive Teacher's Edition.

Media Vocabulary

Encourage students to discuss the media vocabulary. Ask groups to give examples for each term from school or their community. For example, the *secondary sources* we use in class are textbooks and videos that analyze and study events in the past. An *eyewitness* could write or make something that would be a *primary source*. For more support, see **Media Vocabulary.**

FIRST REVIEW

As they listen, students should perform the steps of the first review:

WATCH: Remind students to notice the different historical locations visited on this journey through civil rights history.

NOTE: Encourage students to note the people, locations, and events in this video that they are naturally intrigued by or drawn to.

CONNECT: Encourage students to make connections beyond this video from other memoirs, movies, and songs about social and political change that they have heard or read.

RESPOND: Students will answer questions and write a summary to demonstrate understanding.

Point out to students that while they will always complete the Respond step at the end of the first read, the other steps will probably happen somewhat concurrently. You may wish to print copies of the **First-Read Guide: Media-Video** for students to use.

MAKING MEANING

About the Newscast

The poet featured in this newscast, **Natasha Trethewey** (b. 1966), was born in Gulfport, Mississippi, the daughter of a biracial couple. Trethewey has won numerous awards and honors for her poetry. In 2007, her book *Native Guard* was awarded the Pulitzer Prize. In 2012, Trethewey was named the Poet Laureate of the United States, 2012–2014.

Jeffrey Brown (b. 1956) is the Chief Correspondent for Arts, Culture, and Society at *PBS NewsHour.* His work as both a correspondent and a news producer has been recognized with numerous honors, including an Emmy.

Remembering Civil Rights History, When "Words Meant Everything"

Media Vocabulary

The following words or concepts will be useful to you as you analyze, discuss, and write about media.

Point of View: perspective from which the creators of a media piece approach a topic	• A media creator's perspective includes his or her attitudes and assumptions as well as his or her knowledge of a topic.
Primary Source: document, recording, image, or other source that was created at the same time as the events it describes or shows	• In journalism, someone with information to share or experience of an event may be referred to as a "source." • Newspaper articles are one type of written primary source.
Eyewitness: someone who has firsthand experience of an event	• Information from eyewitnesses is often used in newscasts. • Information from eyewitnesses is often seen as more credible than content from other sources.
Secondary Source: document, recording, image, or other source that is written or created after an event by someone who did not witness it firsthand	• Secondary sources include history books, documentary films, and other works. • Secondary sources often include references to or interpretations of primary sources.

First Review MEDIA: VIDEO

Apply these strategies as you conduct your first review.

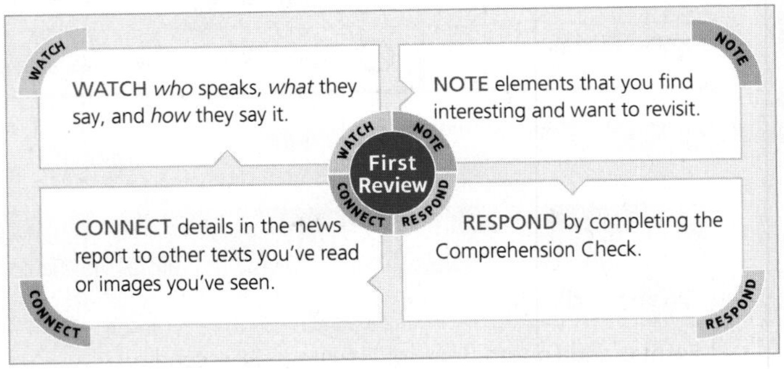
WATCH
NOTE
WATCH *who* speaks, *what* they say, and *how* they say it.
NOTE elements that you find interesting and want to revisit.
First Review
CONNECT details in the news report to other texts you've read or images you've seen.
RESPOND by completing the Comprehension Check.
CONNECT
RESPOND

STANDARDS

Reading Informational Text
By the end of grade 9, read and comprehend literary nonfiction in the grades 9–10 text complexity band proficiently, with scaffolding as needed at the high end of the range.

AUTHOR'S PERSPECTIVE **Jim Cummins, Ph.D.**

Critical Literacies Recent research shows that even early-stage English learners can use higher-order thinking skills and engage with complex social issues with the appropriate instructional support. The following questions illustrate how teachers can support the development of critical thinking:

Step 1: Textual Dimension In order to help students read deeply to understand how the language and multimodal dimensions of the text construct meaning, ask, "When, where, and how did it happen?" and "Who did it? Why?"

Step 2: Personal Dimension Encourage students to reflect critically on the text in relation to their experiences and emotions. Ask, "Have

MEDIA | NEWSCAST

Remembering Civil Rights History, When "Words Meant Everything"

Jeffrey Brown

BACKGROUND

This video describes key people, places, and events of the civil rights era, including the murder of activist Medgar Evers. Evers was an African American civil rights leader in Mississippi who helped desegregate the University of Mississippi in 1962. One year later, he was shot by a member of the Ku Klux Klan, a racist hate group, in his own driveway. His home, where this video begins, is now a museum.

SCAN FOR MULTIMEDIA

NOTES

DIGITAL PERSPECTIVES

CLOSE REVIEW

Analyze Sources

Circulate among groups as students conduct their first review. Suggest that groups review the section of the video from 4:08 to 5:56. Encourage them to talk about what they notice. If needed, provide the following support.

NOTE: Have students note the speakers in the video who describe how civil rights history is connected to the present, or work with small groups to have students participate while you note them together.

QUESTION: Guide students to consider what these details might tell them. Ask them what a viewer can infer about the inclusion of the variety of different sources, and accept student responses.

Possible response: Many politicians contribute to this video—white and African American, Republican and Democrat. The different perspectives give the video validity as a thoroughly researched, objective secondary source that includes and shows respect to multiple points of view.

CONCLUDE: Help students formulate conclusions about the importance of these details in the video. Ask students why the editors might have included these details.

Possible response: Those creating and editing this video used a multitude of people from different backgrounds to convey the impact of civil rights history on present-day students and citizens. It's significant that multiple voices express the same opinion: They want to see the history of the Civil Rights movement kept alive so that America may continue to progress toward the fulfillment of Martin Luther King's dream.

Remind students that this segment is a news report, so it needs to give its audience the *who, what, when, where,* and *why* that make its contents relevant. Eyewitness interviews and interviews from a wide variety of beliefs and backgrounds give this segment appeal to many different viewing audiences.

you ever seen, felt, or experienced something like this?" or "Have you ever wanted something similar?"

Step 3: Critical Dimension Engage students in critical analysis of issues in the text, by asking questions such as, "Is what this person said valid? Always? Under what conditions? Are there any alternatives to this situation?"

Step 4: Creative/Transformative Dimension Engage students in creative, constructive actions that address the social realities discussed. Ask, "How can the problem or issues be resolved?" and "What role can we play in helping resolve the problem?" Projects can involve drama, role play, art, poetry, stories, and newsletter publication.

FACILITATING

Comprehension Check

Possible responses:

1. Jeffrey Brown and Natasha Tretheway attended a march to Selma, Alabama, that commemorated key events of the Civil Rights era.
2. The pilgrimage lasted three days. More than 100 people attended, traveling through the Mississippi Delta to Selma.
3. Natasha Trethaway read a poem about the burning of a cross on her childhood lawn.
4. Rep. John Lewis was one of the original marchers to return to the bridge, where he was beaten for his participation.
5. Terri Sewell is the first African American valedictorian of Selma High School and the first African American congresswoman of Alabama. Her current status shows how people can rise to greater positions after being given equal opportunities.

Close Review

Ask students to think about who was involved in the Civil Rights movement. What types of people have they learned about? While you discuss this with the class, have students consider why these people were so influential and what they have in common.

Model how to listen closely by using the Close Review note for the video. Remind students to clarify anything they did not understand during their first review. You may wish to print the **Close-Review Guide: Media-Video** for students to use.

Analyze the Media

Possible responses:

1. Responses will vary.
2. Responses will vary.
3. Tretheway's poem could make a person more aware of the importance of the Civil Rights era. Her poem gives a personal look at why things needed to change.

Word Network

Possible words: *activists, organizers, intersections, memorialize*

FORMATIVE ASSESSMENT

Analyze the Media

If students struggle to close review the video, **then** provide the **Remembering Civil Rights History: Media Questions** available online in the Interactive Teacher's Edition or Unit Resources. Answers and DOK levels are also available.

MAKING MEANING

Comprehension Check

Complete the following items after you finish your first review. Review and clarify details with your group..

1. What event did Jeffrey Brown and Natasha Trethewey attend?
2. How long did the pilgrimage last, where did it go, and how many people participated?
3. What is the topic of the poem that Natasha Trethewey reads during the newscast?
4. What special status does Representative John Lewis have among the marchers?
5. Who is Terri Sewell and how does her current status demonstrate the ways life in Selma has changed?

MEDIA VOCABULARY

Use these words as you discuss and write about the newscast.

point of view
primary source
eyewitness
secondary source

WORD NETWORK

Add interesting words arelated to civil rights from the newscast to your Word Network.

STANDARDS

Speaking and Listening
Integrate multiple sources of information presented in diverse media or formats evaluating the credibility and accuracy of each source.

Close Review

With your group, revisit the newscast and your first-review notes. Share your observations and brainstorm new ones that might seem important. What **questions** do you have? What can you **conclude?**

Review Question Conclude — Close Review

Analyze the Media

1. **Present and Discuss** Choose the part of the newscast that you find most interesting or powerful. Share your choice with the group and discuss why you chose it. Explain what you notice in that portion, the questions it raises for you, and the conclusions you reached about it.
2. **Review and Synthesize** With your group, review all of the scenes included in the newscast. How do they work together? How does the newscast add to your understanding of the topic of civil rights? Explain.
3. Notebook **Essential Question:** *How can words inspire change?* Do you think the poem included in the newscast might help change someone's opinion about the Civil Rights era? Explain why or why not.

Research

Assignment

The newscast refers to a number of important events from the Civil Rights era. Choose one of those events to research. Then, write a **research report** of your findings. Consider these topics or choose another one that was mentioned in the newscast:

- ☐ the killing of Medgar Evers
- ☐ the murders of civil rights workers James Chaney, Andrew Goodman, and Michael Schwerner
- ☐ "Bloody Sunday" in Selma, Alabama

As you research, identify at least three reliable sources to cite. Then, note unique information from each source that you will synthesize, or weave together, to create a complete picture of events. As you write, include the following elements:

- background information that will help readers understand the context, or bigger social and historical issues, of the event.
- clear presentation of basic information, such as who was involved, what happened, and where it happened.
- explanation of the impact the event had on people both at the time and in years to follow.

REMEMBERING CIVIL RIGHTS HISTORY, WHEN "WORDS MEANT EVERYTHING"

Writing to Sources

Assignment

Starting at about the 3:50 point in the newscast, listen to Natasha Trethewey's description of "sacred language." Then, write a short **essay** in which you consider how various types of "sacred language"—such as songs, poetry, or stories—can affect what people understand, know, and feel about social problems. Use these questions to guide your thinking:

- What does Natasha Trethewey mean by the term "sacred language"?
- What role does Trethewey believe "sacred language" played in the Civil Rights movement?
- Does "sacred language" like Trethewey describes exist today? If you think it does, provide examples. If you think it does not, explain your thinking.

STANDARDS

Writing

Conduct short as well as more sustained research projects to answer a question, or solve a problem; narrow or broaden the inquiry when appropriate; synthesize multiple sources on the subject, demonstrating understanding of the subject under investigation.

DIGITAL PERSPECTIVES

Research

Remind the students to use multiple sources for their research. A report that is rich in detail and still relevant to civil rights issues today requires more than a casual perusal of Wikipedia. Primary source documents and academic studies should be included whenever possible. If additional databases and research tools are available at your school library, consider signing the class up for a tutorial with the staff librarian. For more support, see **Research: Report.**

Writing to Sources

Remind students to have one main thesis in their "sacred languages" essay. Whatever stance they take on the importance of these "sacred languages" in the Civil Rights movement, it must be supported in the short essay's introduction, body, and conclusion. Every example of "sacred languages" that they draw in from the past or present day should clearly support this thesis. For more support, see **Writing to Sources: Short Essay.**

FORMATIVE ASSESSMENT

Research

If students struggle with finding research questions, **then** have them review their notes, and look for what they found engaging or powerful.

Writing to Sources

If students have trouble writing their essays, **then** help them identify the main points in their argument.

PERSONALIZE FOR LEARNING

Strategic Support

Music and Lyrics If students struggle to give examples of music and poetry that demonstrate the idea of equality, make certain that you have a few examples of current songs on hand. Two examples are "A Change is Gonna Come," written by Sam Cooke, and "One Woman," written for the United Nations Entity for Gender Equality and the Empowerment of Women. Preview these songs before playing them for the class. Ask what the artists are trying to communicate. Ask them whose music they listen to that represents the values of equality.

For My People • Incident

AUDIO SUMMARIES
Audio summaries of "For My People" and "Incident" are available online in both English and Spanish in the Interactive Teacher's Edition or Unit Resources. Assigning these summaries prior to reading the selection may help students build additional background knowledge and set a context for their first read.

Summary

Margaret Walker's "For My People" addresses the humble and hardworking. It describes trials and joys of life, from childhood to old age. The tone flies between spiritual and mundane, between everyday life and the struggle between right and wrong that is inevitably entwined into our lives. Walker calls for rebirth, a new and better world.

Natasha Trethewey's "Incident" is smaller in scale. It tells of how her family one night saw the KKK burning a cross on their lawn. The story is tense and frightening, but anticlimactic. Nothing happened that year—but her family tells the story every year.

Insight

These poems capture the fear and hope that comes with living in a marginalized position. Both of these poems have relatively happy conclusions, but in neither do the characters seem safe. Great travails are clearly ahead, even in Walker's optimistic vision of rising up to remake the world.

ESSENTIAL QUESTION:
How can words inspire change?

Connection to Essential Question

The theme of words inspiring change is expressed very vividly in "For My People." In "Incident," words—the family telling the story every year—seem more there for caution than for change.

SMALL-GROUP LEARNING PERFORMANCE TASK
Why do words and actions in some time periods produce meaningful change—and in others do not?

UNIT PERFORMANCE-BASED ASSESSMENT
Explain how words have the power to provoke, calm, or inspire.

Connection to Performance Tasks

Small-Group Learning Task Walker envisions creating the new world through language and action, with the seemingly paradoxical line: "Let a bloody peace be written in the sky." Trethewey's family retells the story every year, lest their vigilance lapse.

Unit Performance-Based Assessment Walker's poem invokes language in scenes of kindness and happiness, as well as prayer. It is also worth noting that in "Incident," the KKK threatens the family with a symbol and *not* with words.

DIGITAL PERSPECTIVES — Audio | Video | Document | Annotation Highlights | EL Highlights | Online Assessment

LESSON RESOURCES

	Making Meaning	Language Development	Effective Expression
Lesson	**First Read** **Close Read** **Analyze the Text** **Analyze Craft and Structure**	**Concept Vocabulary** **Word Study** **Author's Style**	**Speaking and Listening**
Instructional Standards	**RL.10** By the end of grade 9, read and comprehend literature . . . **RL.5** Analyze how an author's choices . . .	**L.4.a** Use context as a clue . . . **L.4.b** Identify and correctly use patterns of word changes . . . **L.4.c** Consult general and specialized reference materials . . . **L.2** Demonstrate command of the conventions . . . **L.2.a** Use a semicolon . . .	**SL.4** Present information, findings, and supporting evidence . . . **SL.5** Make strategic use of digital media . . . **SL.6** Adapt speech to a variety of contexts . . .
STUDENT RESOURCES			
Available online in the Interactive Student Edition or Unit Resources	Selection Audio First-Read Guide: Poetry Close-Read Guide: Poetry	Word Network	Evidence Log
TEACHER RESOURCES			
Selection Resources Available online in the Interactive Teacher's Edition or Unit Resources	Audio Summaries Annotation Highlights EL Highlights English Language Support Lesson: Multimedia Presentation Poetry Collection: Text Questions Analyze Craft and Structure: Poetic Structures	Concept Vocabulary and Word Study Author's Style: Punctuation	Speaking and Listening: Multimedia Presentation
Reteach/Practice (RP) Available online in the Interactive Teacher's Edition or Unit Resources	Analyze Craft and Structure: Poetic Structures (RP)	Word Study: Latin Root *-trem-* (RP) Author's Style: Punctuation (RP)	Speaking and Listening: Multimedia Presentation (RP)
Assessment Available online in Assessments	Selection Test		
My Resources	A Unit 3 Answer Key is available online and in the Interactive Teacher's Edition.		

Reading Support

Text Complexity Rubric: For My People • Incident	
Quantitative Measures	
Lexile: NP **Text Length:** 58 lines; 20 lines	
Qualitative Measures	
Knowledge Demands ① ② ③ ❹ ⑤	"For My People," about slavery, is fairly accessible without background. "Incident" requires specific knowledge of the Klu Klux Klan. References will be unfamiliar without background.
Structure ① ② ③ ❹ ⑤	Both poems are in free verse. "For My People" has many repetitive patterns, (many verses start *For my people*; in last verse, all sentences start with *Let a . . .*) "Incident" has a few repeated lines.
Language Conventionality and Clarity ① ② ③ ❹ ⑤	Both poems have descriptive language and metaphorical phrases. "For My People" has abstract concepts, many repetitive structures (phrases with multiple verbs, repeated phrases to begin lines), and difficult vocabulary.
Levels of Meaning/Purpose ① ② ③ ❹ ⑤	Understanding the meaning of the poems requires prior background information, and an understanding of metaphors and descriptive phrases. Some abstract concepts in "For My People" may be hard to understand.

DECIDE AND PLAN

English Language Support

Provide English Learners with support for language and structure as they read the selection.

Language Ask students to list the verbs that they find in "For My People." Pair students and have them check the list to see which ones they understand and which ones they need to look up. Discuss the author's choice of verbs that have similar meanings (for example *blundering, groping, floundering*). For both poems, have students highlight phrases they don't understand. Discuss as a group.

Structure Discuss "For My People" by asking students to highlight the repetitive phrases that begin each stanza (*for my people, for my playmates*, etc). In "Incident," ask them to find lines used more than once (first and last lines, line repeated in last two stanzas).

Strategic Support

Provide students with strategic support to ensure that they can successfully read the text.

Knowledge Demands When reading "For My People," discuss aspects of slavery that are mentioned in the poem, for example, types of work that slaves had to do, or the organizing that had to happen to create change. For "Incident," make sure students understand the background information about the Klu Klux Klan.

Meaning Encourage students to read the poems multiple times. Ask them to highlight or list phrases that they don't understand. Discuss the meaning of metaphors, and encourage students to look up words they don't understand.

Challenge

Provide students who need to be challenged with ideas for how they can go beyond a simple interpretation of the text.

Text Analysis Have students look up information about the two poems on the Internet, such as interviews with the authors, or analyses or information that have been written about the poems. Ask students to report to the class about what they read. Then, discuss the poems. Encourage students to be specific when reporting what they read or giving their own analysis.

Written Response Ask students to write responses to each of the poems. Ask them to include the feelings that the poems evoke, their interpretations of the poems, or questions they may have about their meaning.

TEACH

Read and Respond

Have the class do their first read of the selection. Then have them complete their close read. Finally, work with them on the Making Meaning, Language Development, and Effective Expression activities.

Standards Support Through Teaching and Learning Cycle

IDENTIFY NEEDS

Analyze results of the Beginning-of-Year Assessment, focusing on the items relating to Unit 3. Also take into consideration student performance to this point and your observations of where particular students struggle.

DECIDE AND PLAN

- If students have performed poorly on items matching these standards, then provide selection scaffolds before assigning them the on-level lesson provided in the Student Edition.
- If students have done well on the Beginning-of-Year Assessment, then challenge them to keep progressing and learning by giving them opportunities to practice the skills in depth.
- Use the Selection Resources listed on the Planning pages for "For My People" and "Incident" to help students continually improve their ability to master the standards.

Instructional Standards: For My People, Incident

	Catching Up	This Year	Looking Forward
Reading	You may wish to administer the **Analyze Craft and Structure: Poetic Structures (RP)** worksheet to help students understand how lyric poems describe an emotion or mood through images and vivid word choice.	**RL.5** Analyze how an author's choices concerning how to structure a text, order events within it, and manipulate time create such effects as mystery, tension, or surprise.	Challenge students to rewrite one of the poems using a more straightforward structure to point out the effect of lyrical language.
Speaking and Listening	You may wish to administer the **Speaking and Listening: Multimedia Presentation (RP)** worksheet to help students understand how to effectively combine text with audio, graphics, or both.	**SL.5** Make strategic use of digital media in presentations to enhance understanding of findings, reasonings, and evidence and to add interest.	Have students ponder the practical applications of this lesson. How will learning to prepare and perform multimedia presentation now help them later in their careers?
Language	You may wish to administer the **Author's Style: Punctuation (RP)** worksheet to help students understand how poets respect the rules of grammar, but punctuate with purpose. Review the **Word Study: Latin Root *-trem-* (RP)** worksheet with students to ensure they understand the meaning of the root word.	**L.2.a** Use a semicolon to link two or more closely related independent clauses. **L.4.b** Identify and correctly use patterns of word changes that indicate different meanings or parts of speech.	Have students rewrite a section of one of the poems without the colons or semicolons to point out the effectiveness of these punctuations. Have students identify other words in the selection that use Latin or Greek roots they may recognize.

ANALYZE AND REVISE

- Analyze student work for evidence of student learning.
- Identify whether or not students have met the expectations in the standards.
- Identify implications for future instruction.

TEACH

Implement the planned lesson, and gather evidence of student learning.

FACILITATING

Jump Start

FIRST READ Imagine you grew up in a period when the United States was in turmoil that caused suffering for various groups of people. How might someone feel growing up knowing that his or her opportunities were limited? How might people feel if they were ostracized for being different? Engage students in a discussion about inequality to help set the context for reading "For My People" and "Incident."

Concept Vocabulary

Encourage groups to discuss the three concept vocabulary words. Have they seen the words in texts before? Do they use any of the words in their speech or writing? Encourage students to study the types of context clues modeled. Have students look closely at the words, punctuation, and images that surround the unknown word and discuss how these types of context clues can help determine meaning. Encourage groups to think of one other type of context clue they might encounter in a text, such as synonyms, antonyms, and restatements of an idea.

FIRST READ

As they read, students should perform the steps of the first read:

NOTICE: You may want to encourage students to notice the basic elements of each poem, including point of view, to ensure that they understand the message and feelings the author is conveying.

ANNOTATE: Remind students to mark lines or stanzas they would like to revisit in order to enhance comprehension or to increase their aesthetic appreciation.

CONNECT: Encourage students to compare the thoughts and feelings expressed in the poems and how it might have felt to be part of a minority group prior to Civil Rights legislation.

RESPOND: Students will answer questions and write a summary to demonstrate understanding.

Point out to students that while they will always complete the Respond step at the end of the first read, the other steps will probably happen somewhat concurrently. You may wish to print copies of the **First-Read Guide: Poetry** for students to use.

MAKING MEANING

POETRY COLLECTION

For My People

Incident

Concept Vocabulary

As you perform your first read of "For My People" and "Incident," you will encounter these words.

bewildered	blundering	trembling

Context Clues If these words are unfamiliar to you, try using context clues. **Context clues** are other words and phrases that appear in a text and may provide hints about the meanings of unfamiliar words. There are various types of context clues that you may encounter as you read.

Definition: Tonight there will be a **lunar** eclipse—an eclipse of the moon!

Synonym: Oscar was known for his **acerbic,** or sharp, wit.

Elaborating Details: Curtis angered his father and was **disinherited,** which left his siblings with a much larger portion of the family fortune.

Apply your knowledge of context clues and other vocabulary strategies to determine the meanings of unfamiliar words you encounter during your first read.

First Read POETRY

Apply these strategies as you conduct your first read. You will have an opportunity to complete a close read after your first read.

NOTICE who or *what* is "speaking" the poem and whether the poem tells a story or describes a single moment.

ANNOTATE by marking vocabulary and key passages you want to revisit.

CONNECT ideas within the selection to what you already know and what you have already read.

RESPOND by completing the Comprehension Check.

First Read: NOTICE, ANNOTATE, CONNECT, RESPOND

STANDARDS

Reading Literature
By the end of grade 9, read and comprehend literature, including stories, dramas, and poems, in the grades 9–10 text complexity band proficiently, with scaffolding as needed at the high end of the range.

Language
Use context as a clue to the meaning of a word or phrase.

About the Poets

A writer, a teacher, and an activist, **Margaret Walker** (1915–1998) was 22 years old when she published her first volume of poetry, *For My People*. In 1942, she became the first African American to win the Yale Younger Poets Prize. She is also known for her epic novel *Jubilee*, which was based on the life of her great-grandmother and took 30 years to write, and for establishing one of the first African American–studies centers in the nation.

Natasha Trethewey (b. 1966) was Poet Laureate, or official poet, of the United States from 2012 to 2014. Born in Mississippi to an African American mother and a white father, Trethewey grew up in the South at a time when laws enforcing segregation had just been overturned, but stark divisions between African Americans and whites were still common. Much of her poetry addresses her biracial heritage, as well as the forgotten histories of African American men and women in the deep South.

Backgrounds

For My People

Margaret Walker wrote this poem as part of a book of poetry, also titled *For My People*. True to its name, Walker's collection of sonnets, ballads, and free verse was intended to honor and celebrate the joys, struggles, and ordinary lives of African Americans—in her words, to "write the songs of my people—to frame their dreams into words, their souls into notes."

Incident

During the 1960s, the Ku Klux Klan, a white supremacist hate group that had been active in the late nineteenth and early twentieth centuries, reemerged in response to the growing Civil Rights movement. One of their typical acts of terrorism was a cross-burning, during which a wooden cross would be set on fire in front of an African American home or church.

DIGITAL PERSPECTIVES

For My People
Incident

What was it like living in pre-Civil Rights America? Do you know anyone or have you spoken with anyone who lived through those experiences? Modeling the questions a reader might ask as they read "For My People" and "Incident" for the first time brings the text alive for students and connects it to the Small-Group Performance Task assignment. Selection audio and print capability for the selection are available in the Interactive Teacher's Edition.

FACILITATING SMALL-GROUP LEARNING

CLOSE READ: Poetry

- Remind groups that when they read poetry, they should identify the speaker and pay attention to the figurative language.
- If a group is confused about a poem's meaning, suggest that they examine each stanza and discuss what is taking place or being described.
- Challenge group members to discuss the poem's overall meaning to develop an understanding of the theme or message.

CLOSER LOOK

Analyze Language

Circulate among groups as students conduct their close read. Suggest that groups close read stanzas 1, 2, and 3. Encourage them to talk about the annotations they mark. If needed, provide the following support.

ANNOTATE: Have students mark details in stanzas 1, 2, and 3 that seem similar, or work with small groups as you highlight them together.

QUESTION: Guide students to consider what these details might tell them. Ask what a reader can infer from the repetition in each stanza, and accept student responses.

Possible response: It seems as though the author uses repetition at the start of each stanza to emphasize a feeling or idea.

CONCLUDE: Help students to formulate conclusions about the importance of repetition in the poem. Ask students why the author might have included these details.

Possible response: The author may have chosen to use repetition to emphasize the intended audience of the poem, to develop a sense of unity, to show a sense of urgency, and to create a rhythm.

Remind students that **repetition** is the repeated use of any element of language (a sound, a word, a phrase, a clause, or a sentence) and that a **refrain** is a type of repetition in which a line or group of lines is repeated.

Concept Vocabulary

BEWILDERED If groups are struggling to define the word *bewildered* in line 17, point out lines 17–22. Explain to students that these lines describe children going to school to learn about the world and finding that none of the information taught pertained to them or their history, and it confused them.

Possible response: In this context, *bewildered* is being used as an adjective meaning "perplexed and confused."

Additional **English Language Support** is available in the Interactive Teacher's Edition.

POETRY

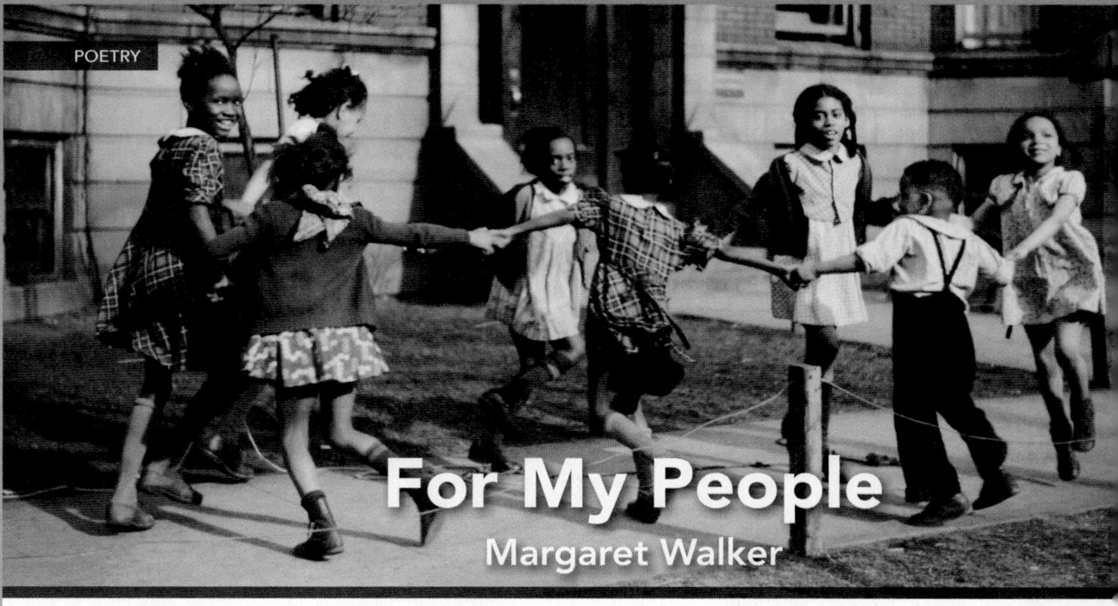

For My People

Margaret Walker

SCAN FOR MULTIMEDIA

NOTES

For my people everywhere singing their slave songs
repeatedly: their dirges[1] and their ditties and their blues
and jubilees, praying their prayers nightly to an
unknown god, bending their knees humbly to an
unseen power;

For my people lending their strength to the years, to the
gone years and the now years and the maybe years,
washing ironing cooking scrubbing sewing mending
hoeing plowing digging planting pruning patching
dragging along never gaining never reaping never
knowing and never understanding;

For my playmates in the clay and dust and sand of Alabama
backyards playing baptizing and preaching and doctor
and jail and soldier and school and mama and cooking
and playhouse and concert and store and hair and
Miss Choomby and company;[2]

For the cramped **bewildered** years we went to school to learn
to know the reasons why and the answers to and the
people who and the places where and the days when, in
memory of the bitter hours when we discovered we
were black and poor and small and different and nobody
cared and nobody wondered and nobody understood;

Mark context clues or indicate another strategy you used that helped you determine meaning.

bewildered (bih WIHL duhrd) *adj.*

MEANING:

1. **dirges** (DURJ uhz) *n.* slow songs expressing sorrow.
2. **Miss Choomby and company** Margaret Walker and her sister would play house, which they referred to as playing "Miss Choomby," because her father had said that Miss Choomby was a name for a black lady.

PERSONALIZE FOR LEARNING

Strategic Support

Parallelism Lead students in reviewing the lists the poet uses in lines 6 through 16. Remind them that parallelism is the repetition of words, phrases, clauses, or sentences that have the same grammatical structure. Have them reread these listings and discuss the effect of the use of parallel structure in the poem.

For the boys and girls who grew in spite of these things to
be man and woman, to laugh and dance and sing and
play and drink their wine and religion and success, to
marry their playmates and bear children and then die
of consumption[3] and anemia[4] and lynching;

For my people thronging 47th Street in Chicago and Lenox
Avenue in New York and Rampart Street in New
Orleans,[5] lost disinherited dispossessed[6] and happy
people filling the cabarets and taverns and other
people's pockets and needing bread and shoes and milk and
land and money and something—something all our own;

For my people walking blindly spreading joy, losing time
being lazy, sleeping when hungry, shouting when
burdened, drinking when hopeless, tied, and shackled
and tangled among ourselves by the unseen creatures
who tower over us omnisciently[7] and laugh;

For my people **blundering** and groping and floundering in
the dark of churches and schools and clubs
and societies, associations and councils and committees and
conventions, distressed and disturbed and deceived and
devoured by money-hungry glory-craving leeches,
preyed on by facile force of state and fad and novelty, by
false prophet and holy believer;

For my people standing staring trying to fashion a better way
from confusion, from hypocrisy and misunderstanding,
trying to fashion a world that will hold all the people,
all the faces, all the adams and eves and their countless
generations;

Let a new earth rise. Let another world be born. Let a
bloody peace be written in the sky. Let a second
generation full of courage issue forth; let a people
loving freedom come to growth. Let a beauty full of
healing and a strength of final clenching be the pulsing
in our spirits and our blood. Let the martial songs
be written, let the dirges disappear. Let a race of men now
rise and take control.

3. **consumption** (kuhn SUHMP shuhn) *n.* tuberculosis, a lung disease that was widespread in poor communities.
4. **anemia** (uh NEE mee uh) *n.* blood disease caused by a lack of iron, often due to a lack of good nutrition suffered by the poor.
5. **47th Street . . . New Orleans** African American communities which were thriving but poor.
6. **dispossessed** *adj.* deprived of the possession of something, especially land or a house.
7. **omnisciently** (om NIHSH uhnt lee) *adv.* acting with complete knowledge of the world.

NOTES

Mark context clues or indicate another strategy you used that helped you determine meaning.

blundering (BLUHN duhr ihng) *adj.*

MEANING:

DIGITAL PERSPECTIVES

Illuminating the Text The poet makes several specific geographic references in lines 28 and 29. Students may not be familiar with 47th Street in Chicago, Lenox Avenue in New York, or Rampart Street in New Orleans. To help them visualize these references in the poem, find images of each area in the 1940s, the time in which the poem was written, when each place was a thriving, but poor, African-American community. Have students consider how viewing these images helps them understand the sentiments expressed in the poem.

DIGITAL PERSPECTIVES

CLOSER LOOK

Analyze Alliteration

Circulate among groups as students conduct their close read. Suggest that groups read stanza 8 (lines 39–45). Encourage them to talk about the annotations they mark. If needed, provide the following support.

ANNOTATE: Have students mark details in stanza 8 (lines 39–45) that stand out to them because of a noticeable pattern, or work with small groups as you highlight them together.

QUESTION: Guide students to consider what these details might tell them. Ask what a reader can infer from the repeated pattern in some of the words, and accept student responses.

Possible response: The speaker seems to be listing items that all begin with the same consonant sounds.

CONCLUDE: Help students to formulate conclusions about the effect of repeated sound in the text. Ask students why the author uses repetition.

Possible response: The author may have included these details to emphasize these words, link these words, and create a sense of monotony, persecution, and hopelessness.

Remind students that **alliteration** is the repetition of initial consonant sounds in nearby syllables (as in "slippery slope" or "weak and weary"). Writers, especially poets, use alliteration to emphasize and link words, to imitate sounds, and to create musical and rhythmic effects.

Concept Vocabulary

BLUNDERING If groups are struggling to define the word *blundering* in line 39, explain point out line 39, which reads *For my people blundering and groping and floundering in*. Explain that the synonym floundering means "to struggle" mentally or show or feel great confusion.

Possible response: In this context, *blundering* means "making unforeseen mistakes."

FACILITATING

CLOSER LOOK

Analyze Imagery

Circulate among groups as students conduct their close read. Suggest that groups read stanza 3. Encourage them to talk about the annotations they mark. If needed, provide the following support.

ANNOTATE: Have students mark details in stanza 3 that are typically connected with religion, or work with small groups as you highlight them together.

QUESTION: Guide students to consider what these details might tell them. Ask what a reader can infer from the details describing religion, and accept student responses.
Possible response: The details and images used seem to depict a quiet religious ceremony.

CONCLUDE: Help students formulate conclusions about the importance of these details in the text. Ask students why the author might have included these details.
Possible response: The author may have included these details to create the imagery of a religious ceremony and to highlight the juxtaposition between a true religious ceremony and what was actually taking place outside the speaker's window.

Remind students that the term **imagery** refers to the use of language that appeals to the senses to create a picture in the mind of the reader. Poets use imagery to help readers experience a poem more fully.

Concept Vocabulary

TREMBLING If groups are struggling to define the word *trembling* in line 12, explain that in order to understand the meaning of the word, students need to comprehend the action taking place in the poem. They should consider the fright the speaker and her family feel and how it might compare to a flame and how it flickers.

Possible response: In this context, *trembling* means "to shake involuntarily from excitement, anger, or fear; to quake."

POETRY

Incident

Natasha Trethewey

SCAN FOR MULTIMEDIA

NOTES

Mark context clues or indicate another strategy you used that helped you determine meaning.

trembling (TREHM blihng) *v.*

MEANING:

We tell the story every year—
how we peered from the windows, shades drawn—
though nothing really happened,
the charred grass now green again.

We peered from the windows, shades drawn,
at the cross trussed[1] like a Christmas tree,
the charred grass still green. Then
we darkened our rooms, lit the hurricane lamps.

At the cross trussed like a Christmas tree,
a few men gathered, white as angels in their gowns.
We darkened our rooms and lit hurricane lamps,
the wicks[2] **trembling** in their fonts of oil.

It seemed the angels had gathered, white men in their gowns.
When they were done, they left quietly. No one came.
The wicks trembled all night in their fonts of oil;
by morning the flames had all dimmed.

When they were done, the men left quietly. No one came.
Nothing really happened.
By morning all the flames had dimmed.
We tell the story every year.

1. **trussed** *v.* tied up tightly.
2. **wicks** *n.* strings in lamps or candles that are lit to burn off oil or wax.

PERSONALIZE FOR LEARNING

English Language Support

Background Knowledge Line 10 of "Incident" presents an image that may be unfamiliar to some students. Some students may struggle with the images presented in the poem as they represent an aspect of American culture with which they may not be familiar. Lead a class discussion about the Ku Klux Klan and show them images of the typical outfits worn by members of this organization and the crosses they burned to help clarify the descriptions in the poem. **ALL LEVELS**

316 UNIT 3 • THE LITERATURE OF CIVIL RIGHTS

Comprehension Check

Complete the following items after you finish your first read. Review and clarify details with your group.

FOR MY PEOPLE

1. Who are the "people" that the speaker refers to in the title and text of the poem "For My People"?

2. In stanza four, what discovery does the speaker say "we" made?

3. What wish does the speaker express in the final stanza of the poem?

INCIDENT

1. What story does the speaker's family tell every year?

2. To the speaker, what do the gathered men look like?

3. At the end of the poem, what has happened by morning?

RESEARCH

Research to Clarify Choose at least one unfamiliar detail from one of the poems. Briefly research that detail. In what way does the information you learned shed light on an aspect of the poem?

DIGITAL PERSPECTIVES

Comprehension Check

Possible responses:

For My People

1. The speaker refers to fellow African Americans living throughout the nation.
2. They discovered that they were black, poor, small, and different. They discovered that nobody cared or understood.
3. The speaker hopes for a new world where her people have freedom and courage. The speaker wishes for a world where her people rise and take control.

Incident

1. They retell the story of the burning of a cross by the Ku Klux Klan.
2. The speaker says they look like angels.
3. By morning, the flames had dimmed, and it seems as if it never really happened.

Research

Research to Clarify If groups struggle to narrow their research topic, you may want to suggest that they focus on one of the following aspects: civil rights issues, local and state governments' roles in ending harassment of citizens.

PERSONALIZE FOR LEARNING

Challenge

Research Have students research Natasha Trethewey and consider her biography, professional career, and inspiration for writing poetry. Have students read some of her other works, such as "Enlightenment" and "Flounder." Then, have students write a brief essay that examines how Trethewey's life is reflected in the themes of her poetry.

FACILITATING

Jump Start

CLOSE READ Have groups close read the title of the poem "For My People." Ask them to discuss who they consider "their people" to be.

Close Read the Text

If needed, model close reading by using the Annotation Highlights in the Interactive Teacher's Edition.

Remind students to use Accountable Talk in their discussions and to support one another as they complete the close read.

Analyze the Text

Possible responses:

1. The speaker doesn't provide specifics because the children learned about a history that didn't include them. Because of this idea, actual details were unknown to them.
2. The speaker begins and ends the poem with "We tell this story every year." This line contradicts the idea that "nothing really happened." The speaker might have done this to show the family's attempts to cope with, or society's denial of, the magnitude of the event.
3. **Responses will vary.**

Concept Vocabulary

Why These Words? Possible response: These words can all be used to describe people who make mistakes and are confused and frightened.

Practice

Sample response:

As she stood at the podium, her *trembling* fingers shook the papers she held. She was *bewildered* by the hand-drawn map, which provided unclear information. We went *blundering* through the woods until we found the trail. A person would most likely feel nervous, confused, and unsteady if he or she were *trembling, bewildered*, and *blundering*.

Word Network

Possible words: *thronging, hypocrisy, misunderstanding, disinherited, dispossessed*

Word Study

For more support, see **Concept Vocabulary and Word Study.**

Possible responses:

tremor: shake, shiver
tremendous: towering, enormous, huge
tremulous: shaky, wobbly

MAKING MEANING

POETRY COLLECTION

TIP

GROUP DISCUSSION

Remember that personal experiences can affect how a reader perceives a poem. Some readers will be familiar with the imagery and context of a poem, whereas other readers may not relate to these poetic elements. Keep these differences in mind as your group discusses the poems.

Close Read the Text

With your group, revisit sections of the text you marked during your first read. **Annotate** details that you notice. What **questions** do you have? What can you **conclude**?

Close Read (ANNOTATE, QUESTION, CONCLUDE)

Analyze the Text

CITE TEXTUAL EVIDENCE to support your answers.

Notebook Complete the activities.

1. **Review and Clarify** With your group, reread stanza 4 (lines 17–22) of "For My People." Discuss what the speaker claims African American children learned in school. Why does the speaker refer to "the reasons why and the answers to and the / people who and the places where and the days when," rather than provide specific examples of people, places, and events?
2. **Analyze** How does the speaker begin and end "Incident"? Does this line support or contradict the speaker's statement in the final stanza, "Nothing really happened"? Discuss why you think the poet made these choices.
3. **Essential Question:** ***How can words inspire change?*** What have you learned about the literature of civil rights from reading these poems?

LANGUAGE DEVELOPMENT

Concept Vocabulary

bewildered   blundering   trembling

Why These Words? The three concept vocabulary words are related. With your group, determine what the words have in common. Write your ideas, and add at least one other word that fits the category.

WORD NETWORK

Add interesting words related to civil rights from the text to your Word Network.

Practice

Notebook Use a print or online dictionary to confirm your understanding of each concept vocabulary word. Then, use each word in an original sentence. What emotions might a person be feeling if he or she were *trembling, bewildered*, or *blundering*?

STANDARDS

Reading Literature
Analyze how an author's choices concerning how to structure a text, order events within and manipulate time create such effects as mystery, tension, or surprise.

Language
- Identify and correctly use patterns of word changes that indicate different meanings or parts of speech.
- Consult general and specialized reference materials, both print and digital, to find the pronunciation of a word or determine or clarify its precise meaning, its part of speech, or its etymology.

Word Study

Latin Root: *-trem-* The word *trembling* contains the Latin root *-trem-*, meaning "to shake" or "to shiver." Use an online thesaurus to look up these words that also contain the root *-trem-*: *tremor, tremendous, tremulous.* Write a synonym for each word.

FORMATIVE ASSESSMENT

Analyze the Text

If students struggle to close read the text, then provide the, **Poetry Collection: Text Questions** available online in the Interactive Teacher's Edition or Unit Resources. Answers and DOK levels are also available.

Concept Vocabulary

If students fail to identify the relationship between the words, **then** have them revisit the context in which the words were used in the poem.

Word Study

If students fail to find an online thesaurus on their own, **then** give them the Web address of one you trust. For Reteach and Practice, see **Word Study: Latin Root *-trem-* (RP).**

Analyze Craft and Structure

Poetic Structure A **lyric poem** expresses the thoughts and feelings of a single speaker, often in vivid, musical language. Although it may describe characters and events, a lyric poem does not tell a complete story. Instead, it captures an emotion or a moment in time. Lyric poems may follow a particular **poetic form**, or structure. This may involve a pattern of lines, stanzas, rhyme, meter, or a combination of all of those elements. Stanzas are named for the number of lines they contain:

Couplet: two-line stanza
Tercet: three-line stanza
Quatrain: four-line stanza
Sextet: six-line stanza
Septet: seven-line stanza
Octet: eight-line stanza

The form of a poem may contribute to its effect in different ways. The form may emphasize words or sounds, create rhythm or flow, or build a sense of order or sequence.

Natasha Trethewey's poem "Incident" is an example of an ancient form called a **pantoum**. Margaret Walker's "For My People" is **free verse**, or a poem that does not follow a set pattern. Nevertheless, Walker includes elements that add structure and help organize the poem.

TIP

CLARIFICATION

Repeating lines in a poem may not be identical. Look for similar lines that share many—but perhaps not all—of the same words.

Practice

CITE TEXTUAL EVIDENCE to support your answers.

Notebook Work independently to answer the questions and complete the activities. Then, share your responses with your group.

1. (a) What basic type of stanza appears in "Incident"? Explain. (b) Use the chart to identify by number which lines from stanza 1 repeat in stanza 2, which lines from stanza 2 repeat in stanza 3, and so on.

STANZA	LINES REPEATED FROM PREVIOUS STANZAS
2	a. See possible responses in Teacher's Edition.
3	b.
4	c.
5	d.

2. (a) At what point does the first line of "Incident" repeat? (b) Does the meaning of the first line change when it is repeated? Explain.
3. Using "Incident" as a model, outline the structure of a pantoum.
4. (a) Which elements of "For My People" repeat, either exactly or very closely? (b) What qualities connect the separate images in each stanza? (c) In what ways does the final stanza differ from the preceding stanzas?

PERSONALIZE FOR LEARNING

Strategic Support

Pantoums If students have difficulty identifying the pantoum format of the poem "Incident," suggest that they closely examine the lines of the poem to see if they notice a pattern of repetition. Specifically, have them examine how lines 2 and 4 in the first stanza are repeated as lines 1 and 3 in the second stanza. Also, have them note how the first line of the poem is repeated as the last line of the poem. Have them consider the effect of this repetition.

DIGITAL PERSPECTIVES

Analyze Craft and Structure

Poetic Structures We hear lyric poetry every single day in the form of songs on the radio or TV. In fact, the Greek word *lyrikos*, from which the word *lyric* derives, means "singing to the lyre." Most lyric poems are written in the first-person point of view and express intense personal feelings or other strong emotions. Lyric poems usually have an obvious musical rhythm. Poems written as **pantoums**, the form that "Incident" follows, have also been set to music, although not nearly as often. Review the poetic structures outlined on the student page. For more support, see **Analyze Craft and Structure: Poetic Structures.**

Practice

Possible responses:

1. "Incident" is built from quatrains or 4-line stanzas. It does not have a rhyme scheme.
   (a) First stanza's Lines 2 and 4 repeat in second stanza's line 1 and 3
   (b) Second stanza's Lines 2 and 4 repeat in third stanza's line 1 and 3
   (c) Third stanza's Lines 2 and 4 repeat in fourth stanza's line 1 and 3
   (d) Fourth stanza's Lines 2 and 4 repeat in fifth stanza's line 1 and 3
2. (a) The first line is also the last line.
   (b) Responses may vary.
3. A pantoum is a poem whose stanzas follow a formula for repeated lines. Each stanza's second and fourth line repeat as the first and third line in the following stanza.
4. (a) The first line of each stanza follows a pattern.
   (b) People are working in most of the stanzas.
   (c) The final stanza expresses hope for a more powerful future.

FORMATIVE ASSESSMENT

Analyze Craft and Structure

If students struggle to identify the musical qualities of lyric poetry, **then** have them consider the elements of a popular song, such as rhyming, repetition, and refrains. For Reteach and Practice, see **Analyze Craft and Structure: Poetic Structures (RP).**

Author's Style

Punctuation

Discuss with students that correct punctuation makes the meaning of writing easier to comprehend. Remind students that when listing items, a comma should be placed after the last item listed and before the conjunction. This is commonly called the Oxford comma because it is used by the Oxford University Press. It is also often called the serial comma because it describes items in a series. Also, remind students that a sentence that introduces a list must be a complete sentence, followed by a colon. As you review the examples of commas with items in a series and colons that introduce lists, consider providing additional examples:

Commas with items in a series:

- The Irish flag is green, white, and orange.
- The puppies played in the yard, chased the ball, and wagged their tails.

Colons that introduce lists:

- The lesson covered many topics: poetic verse, alliteration, and imagery.
- I enjoy all sorts of sporting events: hockey, baseball, basketball, and football.

For more support, see **Author's Style: Punctuation.**

Read It

MAKE IT INTERACTIVE

Have students write their own sentences which contain complex listings or items that already contain commas. Have them use a separate color of marker or pen for the commas and the semicolons. Have them consider how difficult it would be to read and understand the sentences if the semicolons were incorrectly replaced with commas.

Write It

Responses will vary, but make sure students include commas, colons, and semicolons to enhance the meanings of their poems. Suggest that students use listings in their poems to add description and to make inclusion of punctuation a bit easier.

FORMATIVE ASSESSMENT

Conventions

If students struggle to identify how the em dash sets off explanatory phrases from the rest of a sentence, **then** have them practice with sentences in which they can replace the comma and conjunction with an em dash, or replace the colon or semicolon with an em dash. For Reteach and Practice, see **Author's Style: Punctuation (RP).**

POETRY COLLECTION

Author's Style

Punctuation Poets respect the rules of grammar and punctuation, but they may break them to add emphasis or to create a particular effect. Before examining how poets use interior punctuation (punctuation *within* a sentence), review the functions of commas, semicolons, and dashes.

Commas separate independent clauses linked by a coordinating conjunction (*and, but, or, nor, so, yet,* or *for*). Commas also separate words, phrases, or clauses in a series.

Semicolons separate independent clauses without a conjunction or items in a series, especially when one or more of the items already includes a comma.

Dashes set off a word, phrase, or clause from the rest of a sentence.

COMMAS	SEMICOLONS	DASHES
I caught my bus, yet was still late to practice.	I just missed my bus; Coach Carlos was pretty upset.	The bus—ten feet away—belched fumes in my face.
Our grocery list started with beef, onions, and peas.	We needed beef, peas, and onions; sugar for cookies; and fruit.	Start with beef, peas, and onions—for stew.

In "For My People," Margaret Walker breaks some of the traditional rules of punctuation. In "Incident," Natasha Trethewey uses conventional punctuation—commas, semicolons, and dashes—throughout. Complete this organizer with your group. The first and last items are done.

POEM	PUNCTUATION	HOW IT IS USED	EFFECT
"For My People"	comma	separates phrases in a series (lines 23–27)	creates a simple style that reinforces the humble images
	semicolon		
	dash		
"Incident"	comma		
	semicolon		
	dash	sets off explanatory material	creates suspense

Read It

Notebook Work individually to identify and record examples of conventional and unconventional punctuation from the second stanza of "For My People." Think about the effect of the punctuation on the poem's meaning, and jot down your ideas. Then, discuss your findings with your group.

Write It

Notebook Write a poem that describes an "incident" from your life. You may want to write it in complete sentences. You could then delete parts of sentences to leave meaningful phrases, and then make line breaks to create stanzas of free verse. Use commas, semicolons, and dashes for effect.

STANDARDS

Language

- Demonstrate command of the conventions of standard English capitalization, punctuation, and spelling when writing.
- Use a semicolon to link two or more closely related independent clauses.

Speaking and Listening

Assignment

Create a **multimedia presentation** using the poem of your choice. In your presentation, combine text with audio, graphics, or both. When delivering your presentation, pay special attention to your pronunciation, tone, speaking rate, and voice modulation. Be sure to make eye contact with your audience and to use body language to add emphasis or reflect your meaning. Choose from among the following options.

- ☐ **Soundtrack or Playlist** Record a soundtrack or playlist to accompany an oral reading of one of the poems. Decide what type of music you will include to enhance or support your oral reading. Practice your oral presentation of the poem using your finished soundtrack or playlist in the background. Prepare brief explanations of why you selected the music or songs you used.
- ☐ **Historical Context Report** Prepare an oral report that explains the circumstances of the era one of the poems reflects. In your report, be sure to include factual details and events of the period and explain how these elements relate to images and language used in the poem.
- ☐ **Annotated Illustration** Select images from period photographs and art that show a vision of the "new earth" the speaker imagines at the end of "For My People." Prepare comments and excerpts from the poem to accompany and explain how each image is related to the speaker's vision.

Use this chart or one like it to help gather and record the text excerpts, images, musical selections, and notes/comments you will use in your multimedia presentation.

Poem: ____________________

TEXT EXCERPT	IMAGE	MUSIC/SONG	NOTES/COMMENTS

EVIDENCE LOG

Before moving on to a new selection, go to your Evidence Log and record what you learned from "For My People" and "Incident."

STANDARDS

Speaking and Listening
- Present information, findings, and supporting evidence clearly, concisely, and logically such that listeners can follow the line of reasoning and the organization, development, substance, and style are appropriate to purpose, audience, and task.
- Make strategic use of digital media in presentations to enhance understanding of findings, reasoning, and evidence and to add interest.
- Adapt speech to a variety of contexts and tasks, demonstrating command of formal English when indicated or appropriate.

DIGITAL PERSPECTIVES

Speaking and Listening

The term *multimedia* means "multiple forms of media and content." A multimedia presentation usually contains one of the following elements: a video or movie clip, audio, animation, still images, and so on. For your multimedia presentation, you might choose to use a combination of music and photographic images, hand-outs and film, or a technological application. The important factor is that the individual presenting a multimedia presentation delivers the content to the intended audience via the use of a variety of formats. For more support, see **Speaking and Listening: Multimedia Presentation.**

Evidence Log Support students in completing their Evidence Log. This paced activity will help prepare them for the Performance-Based Assessment at the end of the unit.

FORMATIVE ASSESSMENT

Speaking and Listening

If students are unable to choose a poem upon which to base their presentations, **then** have them consider which poem evoked more feelings or images for them upon the first read.

If students struggle to locate historical images to include in their presentations, **then** guide them in choosing more accurate search terms.

For Reteach and Practice, see **Speaking and Listening: Multimedia Presentation (RP).**

Selection Test

Administer the "Poetry Collection" Selection Test, which is available in both print and digital formats online in Assessments.

PERSONALIZE FOR LEARNING

English Language Support

Planning a Multimedia Presentation

Students will plan a multimedia presentation based on one of the places that Margaret Walker mentions in her poem such as 47th Street in Chicago, Lenox Avenue in New York, or Rampart Street in New Orleans.

Ask students to work in pairs. Encourage students to make a list of the kinds of media they will use, including the information that will be addressed by the media. **EMERGING**

Encourage students to create a storyboard that illustrates the kinds of media they will use and the information that will be addressed by the media. **EXPANDING**

Encourage students to create a storyboard that illustrates the kinds of media they will use and the information that will be addressed by the media. Students should write an introduction for the presentation. **BRIDGING**

An expanded **English Language Support Lesson** on Multimedia Presentations is available in the Interactive Teacher's Edition.

Lessons of Dr. Martin Luther King, Jr.

AUDIO SUMMARIES
Audio summaries of "Lessons of Dr. Martin Luther King, Jr." are available online in both English and Spanish in the Interactive Teacher's Edition or Unit Resources. Assigning these summaries prior to reading the selection may help students build additional background knowledge and set a context for their first read.

Summary

In this speech, Cesar Chavez discusses what he has learned from Dr. King's methods. He emphasizes the power of nonviolent direct action as a way to obtain peace and justice. Chavez then addresses social ills that remain, noting that Dr. King died while working to support workers' rights. Chavez, who was most famous for his support of agricultural workers, goes through a number of problems of the day, including misuse of 1970s pesticides. He calls for the audience to fight for social change, and to keep in mind the way their work echoes Dr. King's.

Insight

This speech reminds us that Dr. King's advocacy was not only for civil rights. His method can also be applied to many other kinds of social change. There are still plenty of social challenges that need advocacy.

ESSENTIAL QUESTION:
How can words inspire change?

Connection to Essential Question

Chavez invokes Dr. King's successful inspiration of change, and tries to inspire people in turn.

SMALL-GROUP LEARNING PERFORMANCE TASK
Why do words and actions in some time periods produce meaningful change—and in others do not?

UNIT PERFORMANCE-BASED ASSESSMENT
Explain how words have the power to provoke, calm, or inspire

Connection to Performance Tasks

Small-Group Learning Task Chavez discusses both speeches and demonstrations that helped create progress. He calls for nonviolent resistance; he doesn't call for *calling for* nonviolent resistance. Speech with no action has less power than speech coupled with action.

Unit Performance-Based Assessment This speech is an inspiring example of activism.

DIGITAL PERSPECTIVES — Audio | Video | Document | Annotation Highlights | EL Highlights | Online Assessment

LESSON RESOURCES

	Making Meaning	Language Development	Effective Expression
Lesson	**First Read** **Close Read** **Analyze the Text** **Analyze Craft and Structure**	**Concept Vocabulary** **Word Study** **Author's Style**	**Writing to Sources**
Instructional Standards	**RI.10** By the end of grade 9, read and comprehend literary nonfiction . . . **RI.3** Analyze how the author unfolds . . .	**L.4.a** Use context as a clue . . . **L.4.b** Identify and correctly use patterns of word changes . . . **W.2.c** Use appropriate and varied transitions . . . **L.2.a** Use a semicolon . .	**W.7** Conduct short as well as more sustained research projects . . .
STUDENT RESOURCES			
Available online in the Interactive Student Edition or Unit Resources	Selection Audio First-Read Guide: Nonfiction Close-Read Guide: Nonfiction	Word Network	Evidence Log
TEACHER RESOURCES			
Selection Resources Available online in the Interactive Teacher's Edition or Unit Resources	Audio Summaries Annotation Highlights EL Highlights Lessons of Dr. Martin Luther King, Jr.: Text Questions Analyze Craft and Structure: Development of Ideas	Concept Vocabulary and Word Study Author's Style: Transitions English Language Support Lesson: Cause and Effect	Research: Team Report
Reteach/Practice (RP) Available online in the Interactive Teacher's Edition or Unit Resources	Analyze Craft and Structure: Development of Ideas (RP)	Word Study: Latin Root *-voc-* (RP) Author's Style: Transitions (RP)	Research: Team Report (RP)
Assessment Available online in Assessments	Selection Test		
My Resources	A Unit 3 Answer Key is available online and in the Interactive Teacher's Edition.		

Reading Support

Text Complexity Rubric: Lessons of Dr. Martin Luther King, Jr.	
Quantitative Measures	
Lexile: 1060 **Text Length:** 2,021 words	
Qualitative Measures	
Knowledge Demands ①—❷—③—④—⑤	Selection is about Martin Luther King Jr., who is very familiar to students at this age level; information and details about his actions and beliefs are also clearly explained.
Structure ①—❷—③—④—⑤	Text has clear and logical organization, from background of Dr. King to persuasive argument about United Farm Workers; main ideas of paragraphs are clear; examples and quotations break up text.
Language Conventionality and Clarity ①—②—❸—④—⑤	Selection contains some complex sentences with embedded clauses; metaphors used occasionally *(sound the trumpets of change; trampled by…iron feet of oppression).*
Levels of Meaning/Purpose ①—❷—③—④—⑤	Persuasive purpose of text is explicitly stated. Main concepts of each paragraph are explained and their connection to purpose of text is explicit and clear.

DECIDE AND PLAN

English Language Support

Provide English Learners with support for language and meaning as they read the selection.

Language Write complex sentences and help students with sentence construction that may be difficult or confusing. Rephrase or explain meanings as needed. For example, (paragraph 33): *The children live in communities surrounded by the grape fields that employ their parents.* Explain that *surrounded by the grape fields* means that there are grape fields all around the community, and that *fields that employ their parents* means that the parents work in the grape fields.

Meaning After explaining individual words and phrases, make sure students understand the whole meaning. Ask them to tell you the main idea of the sentence or paragraph.

Strategic Support

Provide students with strategic support to ensure that they can successfully read the text.

Language Ask students to highlight long and complex sentences. Then guide them to unpack the sentences, listing each piece of information they find. For example, *The children live in communities surrounded by the grape fields that employ their parents.* (unpacked:) *Grape fields surround the community. Children and their parents live in the community. The parents work in the grape fields.*

Language After unpacking complex sentences, have students reread the sentences. Then ask them to explain in their own words what it is about.

Challenge

Provide students who need to be challenged with ideas for how they can go beyond a simple interpretation of the text.

Text Analysis Pair students. Ask partners to work together to write a list of all of the arguments Chavez makes for why people should boycott table grapes, (for example use of pesticides, bad conditions for workers in the hot sun, the pressure to meet quotas, or harassment and assault of women) and how a boycott would help.

Written Response Ask students to read more about Cesar Chavez, the United Farm workers, or the grape boycott discussed in the selection. Have them prepare a written report giving information on what they have learned.

TEACH

Read and Respond

Have the class do their first read of the selection. Then have them complete their close read. Finally, work with them on the Making Meaning, Language Development, and Effective Expression activities.

Standards Support Through Teaching and Learning Cycle

IDENTIFY NEEDS

Analyze results of the Beginning-of-Year Assessment, focusing on the items relating to Unit 3. Also take into consideration student performance to this point and your observations of where particular students struggle.

DECIDE AND PLAN

- If students have performed poorly on items matching these standards, then provide selection scaffolds before assigning them the on-level lesson provided in the Student Edition.
- If students have done well on the Beginning-of-Year Assessment, then challenge them to keep progressing and learning by giving them opportunities to practice the skills in depth.
- Use the Selection Resources listed on the Planning pages for "Lessons of Dr. Martin Luther KIng, Jr." to help students continually improve their ability to master the standards.

Instructional Standards: Lessons of Dr. Martin Luther King, Jr.

	Catching Up	This Year	Looking Forward
Reading	You may wish to administer the **Analyze Craft and Structure: Development of Ideas (RP)** worksheet to help students develop ideas by identifying cause-and-effect relationships.	**RI.3** Analyze how the author unfolds an analysis or series of ideas or events, including the order in which the points are made, how they are introduced and developed, and the connections that are drawn between them.	Challenge students to think of how a lack of cause-and-effect development would weaken Chavez's argument.
Writing	You may wish to administer the **Author's Style: Transitions (RP)** worksheet to help students understand how transitions bridge the gaps between sections in a text. You may wish to administer the **Research: Team Report (RP)** worksheet to help students understand how to effectively conduct research within a group setting.	**W.2.c** Use appropriate and varied transitions to link the major sections of the text, create cohesion, and clarify the relationships among the complex ideas and topics. **W.7** Conduct short as well as more sustained research projects to answer a question (including a self-generated question) or solve a problem; narrow or broaden the inquiry when appropriate; synthesize multiple sources on the subject, demonstrating understanding of the subject under investigation.	Have students find transitions within Chavez's speech and omit them to point out how the tool is effective. After the team report is finished, challenge students to consider how the work on their reports would have been different if they hadn't worked in a team.
Language	Review the Word Study: **Latin Root *-voc-* (RP)** worksheet with students to ensure they understand the meaning of the root word.	**L.4.b** Identify and correctly use patterns of word changes that indicate different meanings or parts of speech.	Have students identify other words in the selection that use Latin or Greek roots they may recognize.

ANALYZE AND REVISE

- Analyze student work for evidence of student learning.
- Identify whether or not students have met the expectations in the standards.
- Identify implications for future instruction.

TEACH

Implement the planned lesson, and gather evidence of student learning.

FACILITATING

Jump Start

FIRST READ What does bravery feel like? Recall when someone you knew or heard about did something brave for someone else. What were the possible consequences? Were the risks worth the possible benefits? Exploring these ideas of bravery, empathy and righteousness, and weighing risks and benefits will help students.

Lessons of Dr. Martin Luther King, Jr.

What qualities make great leaders? How do the values and goals of activist leaders and other leaders sometimes conflict? Modeling the questions a reader might ask as they read "Lessons of Dr. Martin Luther King, Jr." for the first time brings the text alive for students and connects it to the Small-Group Performance Task assignment. Selection audio and print capability for the selection are available in the Interactive Teacher's Edition.

Concept Vocabulary

Ask groups to study the two types of context clues and discuss how they can help clarify meaning. Encourage groups to think of other kinds of context clues that they might encounter. Possibilities include antonyms and examples.

FIRST READ

Have students perform the steps of the first read independently:

NOTICE: Encourage students to notice not only what leadership and activist qualities Chavez wants us to learn from Dr. King but also what qualities and methods we can learn from Chavez himself in this speech.

ANNOTATE: Remind students to mark passages that relay Chavez's primary argument, what he is persuading listeners to do, the evidence he presents, and the values and tactics that he and Dr. King believe in.

CONNECT: Urge students to make connections between Chavez, Dr. King, and their own leaders and role models.

RESPOND: Students will answer questions and write a summary to demonstrate understanding.

Point out to students that while they will always complete the Respond step at the end of the first read, the other steps will probably happen somewhat concurrently. You may wish to print copies of the **First-Read Guide: Nonfiction** for students to use.

MAKING MEANING

About the Speaker

Cesar Chavez (1927–1993) was the founder of the United Farm Workers Union (UFW). In the 1960s, Chavez recognized that the predominantly Latino field workers who picked grapes, lettuce, and other crops were being poorly treated. Chavez tried to put an end to this mistreatment by organizing the workers into the UFW, a union that fought for higher wages and better treatment.

Lessons of Dr. Martin Luther King, Jr.

Concept Vocabulary

As you perform your first read, you will encounter these words.

activist radical advocating

Context Clues To infer the meaning of an unfamiliar word, look to the context, the text that surrounds the word. Consider these lines from "Lessons of Dr. Martin Luther King, Jr."

Context Clues: Word Position

Our nation continues to ***wage*** *war upon its neighbors, and upon itself.*

You can gather clues about a word's meaning based on its role in a sentence. Here, *wage* is a verb; it is something that a nation is doing to another nation in the context of warfare. That helps you understand that the correct meaning of *wage* here is to "carry on a war."

Context Clue: Series

When our workers complain, or try to organize, they are fired, ***assaulted****, and even murdered.*

The sequence of *fired, assaulted,* and *murdered* is arranged so that each term names a more serious offense than the previous term. Since *assaulted* is the middle term, it must refer to something more serious than *fired* but less serious than *murdered.* So, assaulted may mean "attacked."

Apply your knowledge of context clues and other vocabulary strategies to help you determine the meanings of unfamiliar words you encounter during your first read.

First Read NONFICTION

Apply these strategies as you conduct your first read. You will have an opportunity to complete a close read after your first read.

First Read

NOTICE the general ideas of the text. *What* is it about? *Who* is involved?

ANNOTATE by marking vocabulary and key passages you want to revisit.

CONNECT ideas within the selection to what you already know and what you have already read.

RESPOND by completing the Comprehension Check and by writing a brief summary of the selection.

STANDARDS

Reading Informational Text
By the end of grade 9, read and comprehend literary nonfiction in the grades 9–10 text complexity band proficiently, with scaffolding as needed at the high end of the range.

Language
Use context as a clue to the meaning of a word or phrase.

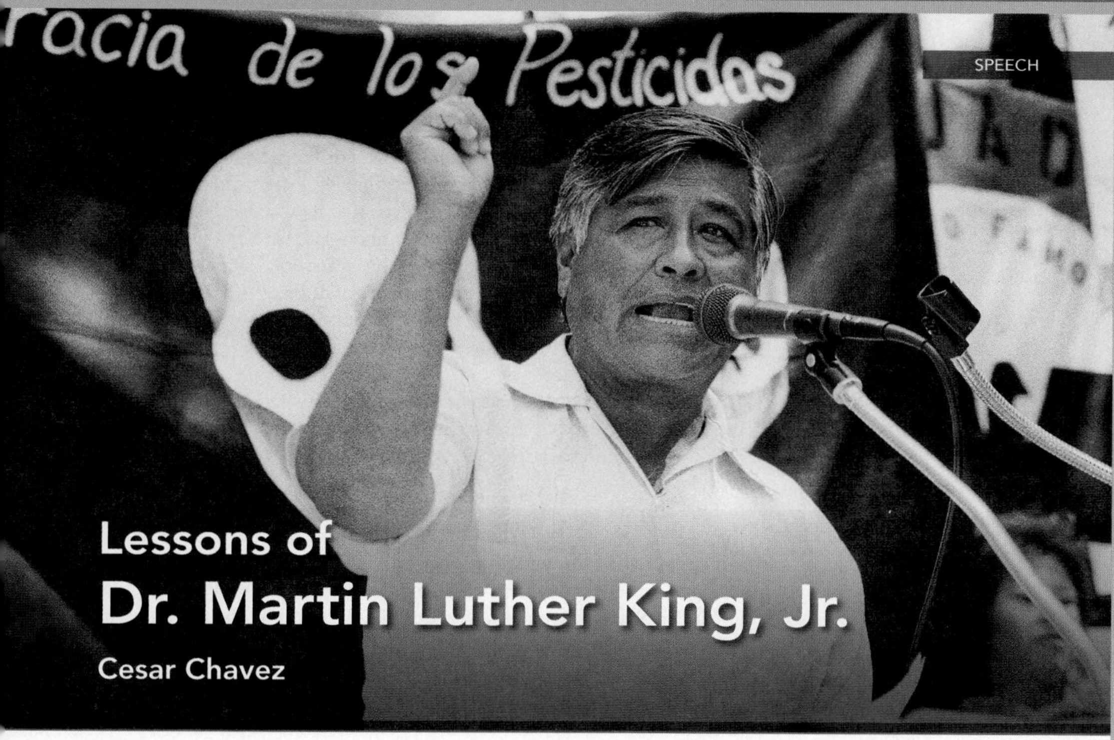

SPEECH

Lessons of Dr. Martin Luther King, Jr.

Cesar Chavez

BACKGROUND

Starting with the 1962 publication of *Silent Spring,* by Rachel Carson, an American anti-pesticide movement worked to reduce the amount and variety of toxic chemicals used to kill insects that feed on crops or spread disease. Cesar Chavez, shown here at an anti-pesticide rally in 1985, was one such activist. Chavez gave many speeches, including the following, against the use of pesticides on California grapes. One major success of the anti-pesticide movement was the banning of DDT, a powerful pesticide, in cases other than disease control.

SCAN FOR MULTIMEDIA

1 January 12, 1990

2 My friends, today we honor a giant among men: today we honor the reverend Martin Luther King, Jr.

3 Dr. King was a powerful figure of destiny, of courage, of sacrifice, and of vision. Few people in the long history of this nation can rival his accomplishment, his reason, or his selfless dedication to the cause of peace and social justice.

4 Today we honor a wise teacher, an inspiring leader, and a true visionary, but to truly honor Dr. King we must do more than say words of praise.

5 We must learn his lessons and put his views into practice, so that we may truly be free at last.

6 Who was Dr. King?

7 Many people will tell you of his wonderful qualities and his many accomplishments, but what makes him special to me, the truth many

NOTES

DIGITAL PERSPECTIVES

CLOSER LOOK

Analyze Parallelism

Circulate among groups as students conduct their close read. Suggest that groups read paragraphs 2–4. Encourage them to talk about the annotations they mark. If needed, provide the following support.

ANNOTATE: Have students mark details in paragraphs 2–4 that show the speaker's use of repetition of words as parallelism, or work with small groups to have students participate as you highlight them together.

QUESTION: Guide students to consider what these details might tell them. Ask what a reader can infer from Chavez's use of parallelism, and accept student responses.

Possible response: Chavez uses parallelism to emphasize the importance of why people have gathered together—to honor Dr. King. to emphasize the importance of why people have gathered together—to honor Dr. King.

CONCLUDE: Help students formulate conclusions about the importance of these details in the text. Ask students why the author might have included these details.

Possible response: By using parallelism, Chavez emphasizes that if we learn from King and carry on with putting his lessons into action, we become part of that history.

Remind students that **parallelism** is the repetition of words, phrases, clauses, or sentences that have the same structure or meaning, and that it is used to emphasize, link, and balance related ideas or to contrast ideas.

PERSONALIZE FOR LEARNING

English Language Support

Hyperbole Help students analyze Chavez's language. Tell students that the expression *a giant among men* in paragraph 2 is hyperbole. Remind students that hyperbole is a figure of speech in which exaggeration is used for emphasis, such as *a giant among men*.

Explain that *a giant among men* means a person who accomplishes huge feats and who is an exceptionally effective leader.

Have students analyze the words in paragraph 3, "a powerful figure of destiny, of courage, of sacrifice, and of vision. Few people in the long history of this nation can rival his accomplishment, his reason, or his selfless dedication." Point out that these words help define the meaning of hyperbole.

Remind students that when they come across hyperbole, they may be able to find context clues to help them figure out the hyperbole's meaning.

ALL LEVELS

Concept Vocabulary

ACTIVIST If groups are struggling to define the word *activist* (paragraph 7), point out that *activist* is followed by Chavez's definition of what kind of activist he considers Dr. King to be.

Possible response: *Activist* must mean "a person who fights for radical social change with radical methods."

RADICAL If groups are struggling to define the word *radical* (paragraph 7), point out that the sentence, *While other people talked about change, Dr. King used direct action to challenge the system*. Have students use these context clues to define the word.

Possible response: *Radical* must mean "extremely different from the usual."

ADVOCATING If groups are struggling to define the word *advocating* (paragraph 11), point out that the sentence *We are not advocating violence* is followed by goals that are the opposite of violence, *We want to love our enemies. I want you to love our enemies. Be good to them. This is what we live by. We must meet hate with love*. Remind students that *advocating* is a verb. Have students use context clues to define the word.

Possible response: *Advocating* must mean "arguing or acting in favor of an ideal."

NOTES

Mark context clues or indicate another strategy you used that helped you determine meaning.

activist (AK tuh vihst) *n.*
MEANING:

radical (RAD uh kuhl) *adj.*
MEANING:

advocating (AD vuh kayt ihng) *v.*
MEANING:

people don't want you to remember, is that Dr. King was a great **activist**, fighting for **radical** social change with radical methods.

8 While other people talked about change, Dr. King used direct action to challenge the system. He welcomed it, and used it wisely.

9 In his famous letter from the Birmingham jail, Dr. King wrote that "The purpose of direct action is to create a situation so crisis-packed that it will inevitably open the door to negotiation."

10 Dr. King was also radical in his beliefs about violence. He learned how to successfully fight hatred and violence with the unstoppable power of nonviolence.

11 He once stopped an armed mob, saying: "We are not **advocating** violence. We want to love our enemies. I want you to love our enemies. Be good to them. This is what we live by. We must meet hate with love."

12 Dr. King knew that he very probably wouldn't survive the struggle that he led so well. But he said "If I am stopped, the movement will not stop. If I am stopped, our work will not stop. For what we are doing is right. What we are doing is just, and God is with us."

13 My friends, as we enter a new decade, it should be clear to all of us that there is an unfinished agenda,[1] that we have miles to go before we reach the promised land.

14 The men who rule this country today never learned the lessons of Dr. King, they never learned that non-violence is the only way to peace and justice.

15 Our nation continues to wage war upon its neighbors, and upon itself.

16 The powers that be rule over a racist society, filled with hatred and ignorance.

17 Our nation continues to be segregated along racial and economic lines.

18 The powers that be make themselves richer by exploiting the poor. Our nation continues to allow children to go hungry, and will not even house its own people. The time is now for people, of all races and backgrounds, to sound the trumpets of change. As Dr. King proclaimed "There comes a time when people get tired of being trampled over by the iron feet of oppression."

19 My friends, the time for action is upon us. The enemies of justice want you to think of Dr. King as only a civil rights leader, but he had a much broader agent. He was a tireless crusader for the rights of the poor, for an end to the war in Vietnam long before it was popular to take that stand, and for the rights of workers everywhere.

20 Many people find it convenient to forget that Martin was murdered while supporting a desperate strike on that tragic day in Memphis, Tennessee. He died while fighting for the rights of sanitation workers.

1. **agenda** (uh JEHN duh) *n.* plan or goal that guides someone's behavior.

FACILITATING SMALL-GROUP LEARNING

Close Read As groups perform the close read, circulate and offer support as needed.

- Remind groups that when they read an argument, they should be sure to identify the author's opinions/claims and purpose.
- Challenge groups to identify all the opinions on the page and find all the types of evidence the author uses (facts, quotations, examples).
- Have groups focus in on two places where Chavez states his purpose (paragraphs 13 and 19, both marked by the phrase "my friends.")

21 Dr. King's dedication to the rights of the workers who are so often exploited by the forces of greed has profoundly touched my life and guided my struggle.

22 During my first fast in 1968, Dr. King reminded me that our struggle was his struggle too. He sent me a telegram which said "Our separate struggles are really one. A struggle for freedom, for dignity, and for humanity."

23 I was profoundly moved that someone facing such a tremendous struggle himself would take the time to worry about a struggle taking place on the other side of the continent.

24 Just as Dr. King was a disciple of Ghandi[2] and Christ, we must now be Dr. King's disciples.

25 Dr. King challenged us to work for a greater humanity. I only hope that we are worthy of his challenge.

26 The United Farm Workers are dedicated to carrying on the dream of reverend Martin Luther King, Jr. My friends, I would like to tell you about the struggle of the farm workers who are waging a desperate struggle for our rights, for our children's rights and for our very lives.

27 Many decades ago the chemical industry promised the growers that pesticides would bring great wealth and bountiful harvests to the fields.

28 Just recently, the experts are learning what farm workers, and the truly organized farmers have known for years.

29 The prestigious National Academy of Sciences recently concluded an exhaustive five-year study which determined that pesticides do not improve profits and do not produce more crops.

30 What, then, is the effect of pesticides? Pesticides have created a legacy of pain, and misery, and death for farm workers and consumers alike.

31 The crop which poses the greatest danger, and the focus of our struggle, is the table grape crop. These pesticides soak the fields, drift with the wind, pollute the water, and are eaten by unwitting consumers.

32 These poisons are designed to kill, and pose a very real threat to consumers and farm workers alike. The fields are sprayed with pesticides: like Captan, Parathion, Phosdrin, and Methyl Bromide. These poisons cause cancer, DNA mutation, and horrible birth defects.

33 The Central Valley of California is one of the wealthiest agricultural regions in the world. In its midst are clusters of children dying from cancer.

34 The children live in communities surrounded by the grape fields that employ their parents. The children come into contact with the poisons when they play outside, when they drink the water, and when they hug their parents returning from the fields.

2. **Gandhi** Mohandas Karamchand Gandhi (1869–1948), an Indian leader who used nonviolent resistance to fight for Indian independence from Britain. He is considered to have been a major influence on Dr. Martin Luther King, Jr.

NOTES

DIGITAL PERSPECTIVES

CLOSER LOOK

Identify Purpose

Circulate among groups as students conduct their close read. Suggest that groups read paragraphs 21–26. Encourage them to talk about the annotations they mark. If needed, provide the following support.

ANNOTATE: Have students mark details in paragraphs 21–26 that reveal the author's purpose in this speech, or work with small groups as you highlight them together.

QUESTION: Guide students to consider what these details might tell them. Ask what a reader can infer from these details about Chavez's purpose.

Possible response: The reader can infer that one of Chavez's purposes in speaking was to encourage others to follow the example of Dr. King in his struggle for workers' rights, children's rights, and for their right to live free of the poison of pesticides.

CONCLUDE: Help students formulate conclusions about the importance of these details in the text. Ask students why the author might have included these details.

Possible response: The details in paragraphs 21–26 indicate that the author gave this speech on Martin Luther King, Jr. Day not only to honor Dr. King, but also to call civil rights activists and other listeners to join the struggle for the rights of farm workers.

Remind students that an **author's purpose** is his or her reason for writing. An author may want to entertain, inform, or persuade the reader. Sometimes an author's main purpose is to convey a moral lesson or to draw and communicate meaning from an experience, an event, or a series of events by seeing them in a larger historical context.

PERSONALIZE FOR LEARNING

Strategic Support

Roles and Power Pose this question to students: *How would you define your role in society?* Guide them to consider age, cultural background, economic status, and any other demographic factors that students note. Then ask them to consider how these social roles affect their power to advance their own agendas. Finally, ask students what they consider the main institutions of power in today's world.

Additional **English Language Support** is available in the Interactive Teacher's Edition.

CLOSER LOOK

Analyze Analogy

Circulate among groups as students conduct their close read. Suggest that groups read paragraph 51. Encourage them to talk about the annotations they mark. If needed, provide the following support.

ANNOTATE: Have students mark details in paragraph 51 that demonstrate Chavez's use of analogy, or work with small groups to have students participate as you highlight them together.

QUESTION: Guide students to consider what these details might tell them. Ask what a reader can infer from Chavez's choice of analogy.

Possible response: Bull Connor was the notorious Commissioner of Public Safety for the City of Birmingham who used fire hoses and released dogs on civil rights activists. By likening the growers to Connor, Chavez is making a direct connection between the fruit workers' struggle for rights and the civil rights movement of the 1960s.

CONCLUDE: Help students formulate conclusions about the importance of these details in the text. Ask students why the author might have included these details.

Possible response: This is a very powerful analogy to draw on Martin Luther King Day. Chavez uses it to inspire the workers by comparing their suffering with the heroic suffering of the civil rights activists of the 1960s, and by the nonviolent, loving example of Dr. King.

Discuss with students that an **analogy** is a comparison that points out the similarities between two things, often explaining something unfamiliar by likening it to something familiar. Analogies are usually extended comparisons.

NOTES

35 And the children are dying.

36 They are dying slow, painful, cruel deaths in towns called cancer clusters, in cancer clusters like McFarland, where the children cancer rate is 800 percent above normal. A few months ago, the parents of a brave little girl in the agricultural community of Earlimart came to the United Farm Workers to ask for help.

37 The Ramirez family knew about our protests in nearby McFarland and thought there might be a similar problem in Earlimart. Our union members went door to door in Earlimart, and found that the Ramirez family's worst fears were true:

38 There are at least four other children suffering from cancer in the little town of Earlimart, a rate 1200 percent above normal.

39 In Earlimart, little Jimmy Caudillo died recently from leukemia at the age of three.

40 Three other young children in Earlimart, in addition to Jimmy and Natalie, are suffering from similar fatal diseases that the experts believe are caused by pesticides.

41 These same pesticides can be found on the grapes you buy in the stores.

42 My friends, the suffering must end. So many children are dying, so many babies are born without limbs and vital organs, so many workers are dying in the fields.

43 We have no choice, we must stop the plague of pesticides.

44 The growers responsible for this outrage are blinded by greed, by racism, and by power.

45 The same inhumanity displayed at Selma, in Birmingham, in so many of Dr. King's battlegrounds, is displayed every day in the vineyards of California.

46 The farm labor system in place today is a system of economic slavery.

47 My friends, even those farm workers who do not have to bury their young children are suffering from abuse, neglect, and poverty.

48 Our workers labor for many hours every day under the hot sun, often without safe drinking water or toilet facilities.

49 Our workers are constantly subjected to incredible pressures and intimidation to meet excessive quotas.[3]

50 When our workers complain, or try to organize, they are fired, assaulted, and even murdered.

51 Just as Bull Connor turned the dogs loose on non-violent marchers in Alabama, the growers turn armed foremen on innocent farm workers in California.

52 The stench of injustice in California should offend every American. Some people, especially those who just don't care, or don't understand, like to think that the government can take care of these problems. The government should, but won't.

3. **quotas** (KWOHT uhz) *n.* specific amounts that are expected to be achieved.

326 UNIT 3 • THE LITERATURE OF CIVIL RIGHTS

Viramontes, Xavier (1947) © Copyright Smithsonian American Art Museum, Washington, DC/Art Resource, NY

Posters like the one pictured here were used to gain support for Chavez's cause.

NOTES

understand, like to think that the government can take care of these problems. The government should, but won't.

53 The growers used their wealth to buy good friends like Governor George Deukmajian, Ronald Reagan, and George Bush.

54 My friends, if we are going to end the suffering, we must use the same people power that vanquished injustice in Montgomery, Selma and Birmingham.

55 I have seen many boycotts succeed. Dr. King showed us the way with the bus boycott, and with our first boycott we were able to get DDT, Aldrin, and Dieldrin banned in our first contracts with grape growers. Now, even more urgently, we are trying to get deadly pesticides banned.

56 The growers and their allies have tried to stop us for years with intimidation, with character assassination,[4] with public relations campaigns, with outright lies, and with murder.

57 But those same tactics did not stop Dr. King, and they will not stop us.

58 Once social change begins, it cannot be reversed.

59 You cannot uneducate the person who has learned to read. You cannot humiliate the person who feels pride. And you cannot oppress the people who are not afraid anymore.

4. **character assassination** *n.* saying false things about a person in order to make the public stop liking or trusting that person.

VOCABULARY DEVELOPMENT

Graphic Organizer

Word Map Have students fill out a word map for the word *vanquish,* which appears in paragraph 54.

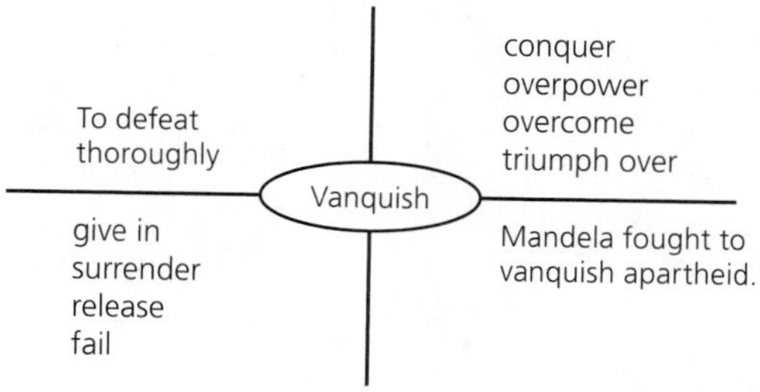

CLOSER LOOK

Analyze Intention

Circulate among groups as students conduct their close read. Suggest that groups read paragraphs 62–75. Encourage them to talk about the annotations they mark. If needed, provide the following support.

ANNOTATE: Have students mark details in paragraphs 62–75 that demonstrate the speaker's intentions, or work with small groups to have students participate as you highlight them together.

QUESTION: Guide students to consider what these details might tell them. Ask what a reader can infer from this conclusion, and accept student responses.

Possible response: Chavez intends to gain support for the boycott of table grapes, for the campaign against harmful pesticides, and for the United Farm Workers in their struggle for peaceful change.

CONCLUDE: Help students formulate conclusions about the importance of these details in the text. Ask students why the author might have included these details.

Possible response: Chavez intends to commemorate Martin Luther King on his memorial day by using his message as a call to action in the campaign against the use of poisonous pesticides.

Remind students that a **speaker's intention** can be expressed in a number of ways: by direct statement; by suggestion; and by presenting his or her case in such a way that the listeners' intentions and the speakers' intentions are united.

NOTES

60 In our life and death struggle for justice we have turned to the court of last resort: the American people. And the people are ruling in our favor.

61 As a result, grape sales keep falling. We have witnessed truckloads of grapes being dumped because no one would stop to buy them. As demand drops, so do prices and profits. The growers are under tremendous economic pressure.

62 We are winning, but there is still much hard work ahead of us. I hope that you will join our struggle.

63 The simple act of refusing to buy table grapes laced with pesticides is a powerful statement that the growers understand.

64 Economic pressure is the only language the growers speak, and they are beginning to listen.

65 Please, boycott table grapes. For your safety, for the workers, and for the children, we must act together.

66 My friends, Dr. King realized that the only real wealth comes from helping others.

67 I challenge each and every one of you to be a true disciple of Dr. King, to be truly wealthy.

68 I challenge you to carry on his work by volunteering to work for a just cause you believe in.

69 Consider joining our movement because the farm workers, and so many other oppressed peoples, depend upon the unselfish dedication of its volunteers, people just like you.

70 Thousands of people have worked for our cause and have gone on to achieve success in many different fields.

71 Our non-violent cause will give you skills that will last a lifetime. When Dr. King sounded the call for justice, the freedom riders answered the call in droves. I am giving you the same opportunity to join the same cause, to free your fellow human beings from the yoke[5] of oppression.

72 I have faith that in this audience there are men and women with the same courage and the same idealism, that put young Martin Luther King, Jr. on the path to social change.

73 I challenge you to join the struggle of the United Farm Workers. And if you don't join our cause, then seek out the many organizations seeking peaceful social change.

74 Seek out the many outstanding leaders who will speak to you this week, and make a difference.

75 If we fail to learn that each and every person can make a difference, then we will have betrayed Dr. King's life's work. The reverend Martin Luther King, Jr. had more than just a dream, he had the love and the faith to act.

76 God Bless You. ❧

5. **yoke** (yohk) *n.* type of collar used on working animals to pull wagons or plows; here, used figuratively to indicate something that causes people to be treated cruelly and unfairly.

Comprehension Check

Complete the following items after you finish your first read. Review and clarify details with your group.

1. According to Chavez, what must people do to truly honor Dr. Martin Luther King, Jr.?

2. What was the primary message that Dr. Martin Luther King, Jr., wanted to communicate in the telegram he sent to Chavez?

3. What evidence does Chavez offer to make the case for banning pesticides?

4. What was Chavez doing to fight back against what he saw as oppression of the farm workers in California's central valley?

5. **Notebook** Write a summary of "Lessons of Dr. Martin Luther King, Jr." to confirm your understanding of the text.

RESEARCH

Research to Clarify Choose at least one unfamiliar detail from the text. Briefly research that detail. In what way does the information you learned shed light on an aspect of the speech?

Research to Explore Choose something that interested you from the text, and formulate a research question.

DIGITAL PERSPECTIVES

Comprehension Check

1. According to Chavez, in order to truly honor Dr. Martin Luther King, Jr., people must learn his lessons of peace and social justice and then put them into practice.
2. King wanted to communicate that all people share the same struggle: a struggle for freedom, dignity, and humanity.
3. Chazez cites evidence about how pesticides cause cancer, DNA mutation, and birth defects.
4. Chavez was organizing boycotts of California's table grapes.
5. **Responses will vary.** Cesar Chavez is commemorating the legacy of Dr. Martin Luther King, Jr. Chavez asks his audience to emulate Dr. King's practice of nonviolent protest. He wants listeners to participate in his own campaign for safer conditions for California's farm workers. In particular, listeners could help by joining his boycott.

RESEARCH

Research to Clarify If students struggle to find a topic, suggest that they learn more about Gandhi, Dr. King's position on Vietnam, Dr. King's relationship to the sanitation workers in Memphis, Chavez's 1968 fast, or details related to pesticides or children working on farms.

Research to Explore If students struggle to find a topic for a research question, suggest that they write a question about Dr. King's assassination or a question about Chavez's concerns about pesticides.

PERSONALIZE FOR LEARNING

Challenge

Research To help students understand what a "giant amongst men" Cesar Chavez himself was, have students conduct research and write a brief biography, focusing on how "roles and power" determined the course of Chavez's life, agenda, sacrifices, and accomplishments.

FACILITATING

Jump Start

CLOSE READ Have students close read the title "Lessons of Dr. Martin Luther King, Jr." Ask them to discuss in their groups whether or not they think America has learned Dr. King's lessons.

Close Read the Text

If needed, model close reading by using the Annotation Highlights in the Interactive Teacher's Edition.

Remind students to use Accountable Talk in their discussions and to support one another as they complete the close read.

Analyze the Text

1. Possible response: Chavez uses the term "economic slavery" to compare the farm workers' terrible working conditions to what slaves faced. Even though the workers are paid, they are oppressed as slaves were. Chavez's use of the term is justified because like slaves, California farm workers are not able to get better conditions on their own.
2. Passages will vary.
3. Responses will vary.

Concept Vocabulary

Why These Words? Possible response: These words might be used in stories about people trying to change government or protest laws.

Practice

Possible responses:

Activist: The *activist* for prison reform spent the day lobbying for sentencing legislation at the nation's capitol. *Radical*: The conventional leaders rejected the *radical* ideas of the fringe group. *Advocating*: If we spend our time *advocating* for change rather than talking about change, our group might get results.

Word Network

Possible words: *injustice, boycott, oppressed*

Word Study

For more support, see **Concept Vocabulary and Word Study.**

Possible responses

vocal: spoken, verbal
vociferous: loud, boisterous
invoke, invocate: to call forth

MAKING MEANING

LESSONS OF DR. MARTIN LUTHER KING, JR.

Close Read the Text

Close Read: ANNOTATE · QUESTION · CONCLUDE

With your group, revisit sections of the text you marked during your first read. **Annotate** details that you notice. What **questions** do you have? What can you **conclude**?

Analyze the Text

CITE TEXTUAL EVIDENCE to support your answers.

Notebook Complete the activities.

1. **Review and Clarify** With your group, reread paragraphs 45–50 of "Lessons of Dr. Martin Luther King, Jr." What does Chavez mean when he refers to "economic slavery"? Do you think Chavez's use of this term is justified based on the evidence he presents? Explain.
2. **Present and Discuss** Now, work with your group to share other key passages from "Lessons of Dr. Martin Luther King, Jr." What made you choose these particular sections? Take turns presenting your choices. Discuss parts of the text that you found to be most meaningful, the questions you asked, and the conclusions you reached as a result of reading those passages.
3. **Essential Question:** ***How can words inspire change?*** What have your learned about the power of words from reading this speech?

TIP

GROUP DISCUSSION

Keep in mind that the struggle for fair pay and good working conditions is ongoing in today's world. Different people have different ideas for how to solve these problems in the best possible way.

LANGUAGE DEVELOPMENT

Concept Vocabulary

activist radical advocating

Why These Words? Use a print or online dictionary to confirm your definitions of the three vocabulary words. Write a sentence using each vocabulary word. In what news stories would you hear these words commonly used? Discuss.

Practice

Notebook Confirm your understanding of these words from the text by using them in sentences. Be sure to use context clues that hint at each word's meaning.

WORD NETWORK

Add interesting words related to civil rights from the selection to your Word Network.

Word Study

Latin root: *-voc-* In this speech, Cesar Chavez discusses Dr. King's assertion that he was not advocating violence. The word *advocating* contains the Latin root *-voc-* or *-vok-*, meaning "to call," "to name," or "voice." Find several other words that were formed from this same root. Record the words and their meanings.

STANDARDS

Reading Informational Text
Analyze how the author unfolds an analysis or series of ideas or events, including the order in which the points are made, how they are introduced and developed, and the connections that are drawn between them.

Language
Identify and correctly use patterns of word changes that indicate different meanings or parts of speech.

FORMATIVE ASSESSMENT

Analyze the Text

If students struggle to close read the text, then provide the **Lessons of Dr. Martin Luther King, Jr.: Text Questions** available online in the Interactive Teacher's Edition or Unit Resources. Answers and DOK levels are also available.

Concept Vocabulary

If students struggle to identify the type of stories these words might appear in, **then** have them revisit the context in which the words were used in the passage.

Word Study

If students fail to identify other words, **then** have them search the text for the letter combination *voc-*. For Reteach and Practice, see **Word Study: Latin Root *-voc-* (RP).**

Analyze Craft and Structure

Development of Ideas One way in which an author can build a persuasive argument is by identifying **cause-and-effect relationships,** showing how one event or situation leads to another. Many complex issues, such as those Cesar Chavez discusses in this speech, have multiple causes or multiple, different effects.

To show the true seriousness of a problem, an author may present related aspects of an issue in a **cause-and-effect chain**. This means that the author demonstrates how a single cause results in an effect, which leads to a second effect, which causes a third effect, and so on. Cause-and-effect organization allows an author to show how one issue is part of a series or network of connected issues.

TIP

CLARIFICATION

Keep in mind the difference between a cause-and-effect chain and a single cause with multiple effects. Imagine the chain as having a linear shape, and a cause with multiple effects having a fanlike shape.

Practice

CITE TEXTUAL EVIDENCE to support your answers.

1. Work with your group to complete the chart. (a) Identify three effects resulting from each of the causes noted. (b) Identify another cause from the speech and at least two of its effects.

TRACING CAUSE AND EFFECT
CAUSE: *The men who rule this country today never learned the lessons of Dr. King, they never learned that non-violence is the only way to peace and justice. (par. 14)* **EFFECT:** The society is still racist. **EFFECT:** The nation still has segregation in the economy. **EFFECT:** Children are still hungry.
CAUSE: *Many decades ago the chemical industry promised the growers that pesticides would bring great wealth and bountiful harvests to the fields. (par. 27)* **EFFECT:** The country continued to use pesticides. **EFFECT:** Pesticides have proven dangerous for farm workers and consumers. **EFFECT:** There are clusters with increased childhood cancers.
CAUSE: Answers will vary. **EFFECT:** **EFFECT:**

Notebook Answer the following questions.

2. What connections does Chavez make between Dr. King's approach to social change and the work of the UFW?
3. What effects does Chavez say those who volunteer to work for a just cause will experience?

DIGITAL PERSPECTIVES

Analyze Craft and Structure

Development of Ideas

Discuss with students how cause-and-effect events can be analyzed and organized in a timeline format. One event causes another event, the effect, to occur. When identifying which event is the cause and which is the effect, ask students to think about the order in which they occur. The effect cannot occur without the cause.

Demonstrate how one cause can have many effects. Discuss with students the many effects that a hurricane can have on a community, point out that all of the mentioned effects are derived from one cause, the hurricane. For more support, see **Analyze Craft and Structure: Development of Ideas.**

1. See answers in chart on student page.
2. Chavez says that both the UFW and Dr. King struggled to gain freedom, dignity, and human rights.
3. Chavez says they will gain new skills and go on to success in their lives.

FORMATIVE ASSESSMENT

Analyze Craft and Structure

If students struggle to identify cause-and-effect relationships, **then** revisit paragraph 55 to determine what effect boycotting had on the production of grapes. For Reteach and Practice, see **Analyze Craft and Structure: Development of Ideas (RP).**

WriteNow Take a Stand

Social Issues Cesar Chavez and Martin Luther King, Jr. both promoted societal change through non-violence. They were both successful activists, and their actions caused great change in the world we live in. Have students write a one-page argument, taking a position about a social issue of their choice. Provide a few relevant examples for students who have a hard time developing a topic. Have students include a counterclaim and evidence, and share their argument with their group.

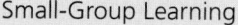

FACILITATING

Author's Style

Cohesion and Clarity Discuss with students that sentences using these types of transitional words or phrases are common in our everyday language. Transitions are often used to join sentences or phrases. Using transitions between ideas allows writing to flow more smoothly. They can help an author provide additional information about a topic or signal changes. Transition words have different functions.

As you review the examples of transitions with students, consider providing additional examples:

Contrasting Transition: The rain continued, *despite* the weather forecaster's prediction of sunny skies.

Time Transition: The score was tied, *before* he scored the winning touchdown. For more support, see **Author's Style: Transitions.**

MAKE IT INTERACTIVE

Have students write individual phrases (without the transition word/phrase) on sentence strips. Write the transitional words or phrases on additional strips. Try to fit the phrases together using different transitional words to see how they change the meaning of the sentence based on their function.

Read It

See possible responses in chart on Student page.

Write It

Possible responses:

As a result of the spraying of pesticides, some California towns are developing cancer clusters. (cause and effect) For example, the child cancer rate in the town of McFarland is 800 percent above normal. (example) The pesticides are found on the grapes sold across the nation, but many people don't realize how their purchases affect these children. (contrast)

FORMATIVE ASSESSMENT

Author's Style

If students are unable to identify the transitional word/phrase within a sentence, **then** have students look for the word or phrase in the sentence that provides a signal or bridges the phrases. For Reteach and Practice, see **Author's Style: Transitions (RP).**

LANGUAGE DEVELOPMENT

LESSONS OF DR. MARTIN LUTHER KING, JR.

STANDARDS

Writing

- Use appropriate and varied transitions to link the major sections of the text, create cohesion, and clarify the relationships among complex ideas and concepts.
- Conduct short as well as more sustained research projects to answer a question, or solve a problem; narrow or broaden the inquiry when appropriate; synthesize multiple sources on the subject, demonstrating understanding of the subject under investigation.

Language

Use a semicolon to link two or more closely related independent clauses.

Author's Style

Cohesion and Clarity **Transitions** are the words and phrases that link sections of a text. Writers and speakers use transitions to create cohesion and to clarify the relationships among the ideas they are presenting.

When a transitional word or phrase begins a sentence, or when it joins two closely related independent clauses connected with a semicolon, follow it with a comma. When it appears in the middle of a word or phrase, set it off with two commas.

Here are examples of transitions and the types of relationships they indicate.

Similarity: *also, likewise, similarly, in the same way*
Example: Dr. King advocated for nonviolent resistance. *Similarly*, Chavez encourages the community to seek peaceful social change.

Contrast: *although, however, nevertheless, on the other hand*
Example: The workers protested; *however*, the growers refused to change.

Addition of Ideas: *also, in addition, moreover, even more so*
Example: Workers were underpaid. *Moreover*, they were treated poorly.

Cause-and-effect: *so, thus, therefore, consequently, as a result*
Example: Buyers boycotted. *As a result*, growers changed their practices.

Example: *for example, for instance, specifically, in particular*
Example: Growers were paying to receive favorable treatment. One grower, *for example*, gave over a million dollars to the governor.

Read It

Work individually. Read these pairs of sentences based on the "Lessons of Dr. Martin Luther King, Jr." For each pair, indicate a transitional word or phrase that could be used to effectively link the sentences. Then, write the type of relationship the transition is conveying.

PASSAGE	TRANSITION	RELATIONSHIP
Dr. King knew that he probably would not survive the struggle. He believed that if he were stopped, the movement would not stop.	however	contrast
The children live in communities surrounded by grape fields. They come into contact with poisons whenever they play outside.	as a result	cause-and-effect
Our workers labor for man hours every day under the hot sun. They are subjected to incredible pressures to meet excessive quotas.	moreover	addition of ideas

Write It

Notebook Write a short description of the issues the farm workers faced. In your description, use at least three different transitional words or phrases. Identify the relationship each transition conveys.

332 UNIT 3 • THE LITERATURE OF CIVIL RIGHTS

PERSONALIZE FOR LEARNING

English Language Support

Using Cause and Effect Ask pairs of students to write down one cause and effect of that cause from the selection, "Lessons from Dr. Martin Luther King, Jr." **EMERGING**

Ask students to write down two causes and the effects of those causes from the selection, "Lessons from Dr. Martin Luther King, Jr." **EXPANDING**

Have students write a brief argumentative essay in which they take a position on the information presented in the selection. Tell students to include causes and effects when making their argument. **BRIDGING**

An expanded **English Language Support lesson** on Cause and Effect is available in the Digital Teacher's Edition.

EFFECTIVE EXPRESSION

Research

Assignment

Write a **team report** on one of the following topics:

- ☐ A **strategy analysis** that addresses the following questions: *Was Chavez's strategy of asking consumers to boycott grapes morally responsible? Were Chavez and the UFW able to make the plight of farm workers clear and compelling? How likely was it that some consumers feel manipulated or resentful at being told what they could and could not buy? Given what happened in other boycotts, was Chavez's strategy likely to be successful?*
- ☐ A **public opinion report** that addresses the following questions: *How did the general public view Chavez's work during the era of the grape boycott? Did workers in general support Chavez and the UFW? How does the public view Chavez's legacy today?*
- ☐ A **status report** that addresses the following questions: *How are farm workers in California and other places treated today? Do they have full rights? Are their wages comparable to workers in other industries? Have working conditions improved since Chavez's time? Have the problems presented by pesticides been solved?*

EVIDENCE LOG

Before moving on to a new selection, go to your Evidence Log and record what you learned from "Lessons of Dr. Martin Luther King, Jr."

Research Plan Before you write, work together to identify a variety of sources, including the following types:

- **Primary Sources:** firsthand or original accounts
- **Secondary Sources:** texts that analyze, retell, or report on events
- **Specialized Sources:** almanacs, government publications, and other texts that provide specific information or data

List the sources you consult and consider their usefulness. Make sure the authors have the knowledge to speak with authority on the topic. In addition, determine whether any show bias or make unfair judgments. You can then decide whether to use the information or to discard it.

EVALUATING USEFULNESS OF SOURCES

Primary Source(s)	authoritative? fair and unbiased?
Secondary Source(s)	authoritative? fair and unbiased?
Specialized Source(s)	authoritative? fair and unbiased?

DIGITAL PERSPECTIVES

Research

When writing a team report, it is important that the report include the work of the entire team. Remind groups to consult the schedule for Small-Group Activities as they create their Report Plan. Check to make sure each group member has been given a topic, and that the work is divided evenly among group members.

Explain that students should first identify the questions they are asking. Then they can begin looking for answers to their questions. Encourage students to include different kinds of evidence, such as facts, examples, anecdotes, and statistics, in their work. As students research evidence, have them carefully note their sources, including paragraph numbers from the selection. For more support, see **Research: Team Report.**

Evidence Log Support students in completing the Evidence Log. This paced activity will help prepare them for the Performance-Based Assessment at the end of the unit.

FORMATIVE ASSESSMENT

Writing to Sources

If students are unable to develop enough topics for their report, **then** have them identify additional related information to include. For Reteach and Practice, see **Research: Team Report (RP).**

Selection Test

Administer the "Lessons of Dr. Martin Luther King, Jr." Selection Test, which is available in both print and digital formats online in Assessments.

PERSONALIZE FOR LEARNING

Strategic Support

Research If students are doing their research on the Internet, discuss the importance of search terms. Identify the key words in the information they are trying to find. What is the specific information they need to answer the question? For example, searching *Cesar Chavez* will result in many possible resources, but may not provide the specific details they are looking for. Have students use narrower search terms to guide their online research and evaluate the results.

Traveling

AUDIO SUMMARIES
Audio summaries of "Traveling" are available online in both English and Spanish in the Interactive Teacher's Edition or Unit Resources. Assigning these summaries prior to reading the selection may help students build additional background knowledge and set a context for their first read.

Summary

In "Traveling," a memoir by Grace Paley, the author describes her family's experiences traveling to the South during the Jim Crow era. Paley's family is white and Jewish, but they were sympathetic to the African Americans who endured the segregation laws. When Paley was a child, her mother and sister traveled to visit her brother who was at medical school in Virginia. They were sitting toward the back of the bus and the driver directed them to move forward, but her mother refused. Later, in a bus trip of her own, Paley challenged the Jim Crow laws when she helped a tired mother who was carrying her baby on a crowded bus.

Insight

In retrospect, Paley's family realizes that these moments had a strong influence on their lives. This memoir is a story of empathy. It shows how it feels to look back on a terrible time and be glad you did the right thing.

ESSENTIAL QUESTION:
How can words inspire change?

Connection to Essential Question

This memoir may help students see how words and actions can be powerful agents of change—even for one person at a time. Paley's mother's quiet refusal to go along with a discriminatory law and her experience decades later reinforces this idea.

SMALL-GROUP LEARNING PERFORMANCE TASK
Why do words and actions in some time periods produce meaningful change—and in others do not?

UNIT PERFORMANCE-BASED ASSESSMENT
Explain how words have the power to provoke, calm, or inspire.

Connection to Performance Tasks

Small-Group Learning Performance Task The text makes a strong connection to the performance task. Paley's mother fights against the Jim Crow laws of the same time period.

Unit Performance-Based Assessment As students prepare for the Unit Performance-Based Assessment, they can access several points of evidence in this memoir. It is important to note the references to Paley's family's experiences with anti-Semitism and to consider how those might have impacted their ability to empathize with others. The most vivid example in this selection is how the man's casual cruelty provokes and enrages Paley.

DIGITAL PERSPECTIVES — Audio · Video · Document · Annotation Highlights · EL Highlights · Online Assessment

LESSON RESOURCES

	Making Meaning	Language Development	Effective Expression
Lesson	**First Read** **Close Read** **Word Study** **Analyze Craft and Structure**	**Analyze the Text** **Concept Vocabulary** **Author's Style**	**Speaking and Listening**
Instructional Standards	**RI.10** By the end of grade 9, read and comprehend literary nonfiction . . . **RI.3** Analyze how the author unfolds . . . **RI.5** Analyze in detail how an author's ideas or claims . . .	**L.4.a** Use context as a clue . . . **L.4.d** Verify the preliminary determination . . . **L.4.b** Identify and correctly use patterns of word changes . . . **L.1** Demonstrate command of the conventions . . .	**SL.1.c** Propel conversations . . .
STUDENT RESOURCES			
Available online in the Interactive Student Edition or Unit Resources	Selection Audio First-Read Guide: Nonfiction Close-Read Guide: Nonfiction	Word Network	Evidence Log
TEACHER RESOURCES			
Selection Resources Available online in the Interactive Teacher's Edition or Unit Resources	Audio Summaries Annotation Highlights EL Highlights English Language Support Lesson: Punctuation Traveling: Text Questions Analyze Craft and Structure: Structure	Concept Vocabulary and Word Study Author's Style: Punctuation	Speaking and Listening: Debate
Reteach/Practice (RP) Available online in the Interactive Teacher's Edition or Unit Resources	Analyze Craft and Structure: Structure (RP)	Word Study: Etymology (RP) Author's Style: Punctuation (RP)	Speaking and Listening: Debate (RP)
Assessment Available online in Assessments	Selection Test		
My Resources	A Unit 3 Answer Key is available online and in the Interactive Teacher's Edition.		

Reading Support

Text Complexity Rubric: Traveling	
Quantitative Measures	
Lexile: 820 **Text Length:** 1,418 words	
Qualitative Measures	
Knowledge Demands ①—②—❸—④—⑤	Single theme is explored; it is helpful for reader to have knowledge of racial segregation and attitudes at the time the experience took place—the 1920s and 1940s, before segregation was outlawed.
Structure ①—②—③—❹—⑤	Selection includes time shifts to three periods, from events in 1927, events of 1943, and reflections from 1990s intertwined with memory of earlier events; some times shifts may be unclear.
Language Conventionality and Clarity ①—②—❸—④—⑤	Language is explicit and easy to understand; contemporary, familiar vocabulary is used; sentences are mostly simple, but some are more complex with multiple clauses.
Levels of Meaning/Purpose ①—②—❸—④—⑤	Theme is revealed early in text. Meaning is not always explicit; reader needs to infer people's feelings based on ability to empathize with their situations; ending has multiple meanings.

DECIDE AND PLAN

English Language Support

Provide English Learners with support for structure and meaning as they read the selection.

Structure To help students understand the text, make sure they realize that the structure includes an account of three different time periods – 1927, 1943, and 1993 when the author is reflecting on long ago. At times, the author switches back and forth between those time periods. As students read, have them mark where the time periods change.

Knowledge Demands Engage students in a discussion about segregation. Write *racial segregation* and ask students if they know the meaning. Help define it if necessary. Write *1964* and remind students that racial segregation was outlawed at this time. Then write the dates of the time periods in the memoir. Point out that segregation existed in the first two.

Strategic Support

Provide students with strategic support to ensure that they can successfully read the text.

Knowledge Demands Before reading, review some background information about racial segregation. Ask students to describe what segregation means and to recall when it was outlawed (1964). Ask students to find the time periods the memoir is about (1927, 1943, 1993) by reading. Then ask them if racial segregation still existed in those times.

Meaning Discuss the final paragraph of the memoir, in which Paley draws a parallel between the stranger's child she held in 1943 and the grandson she now knows and who reminds her of that child from 1943. If necessary, clarify that she is speaking metaphorically when she says *first knew my grandson*.

Challenge

Provide students who need to be challenged with ideas for how they can go beyond a simple interpretation of the text.

Text Analysis Ask students to explain the last paragraph. What does Paley mean when she says that she *first knew my grandson* back on that bus? Ask them to comment on what they think she is saying about the difference between being able to protect a black child in 1943 or fifty years later.

Written Response Have students research Grace Paley on the internet and read about her life. Ask them to write a paragraph about something they learned about her life that they think might relate to the memoir they have just read.

TEACH

Read and Respond

Have the class do their first read of the selection. Then have them complete their close read. Finally, work with them on the Making Meaning, Language Development, and Effective Expression activities.

Standards Support Through Teaching and Learning Cycle

IDENTIFY NEEDS

Analyze results of the Beginning-of-Year Assessment, focusing on the items relating to Unit 3. Also take into consideration student performance to this point and your observations of where particular students struggle.

DECIDE AND PLAN

- If students have performed poorly on items matching these standards, then provide selection scaffolds before assigning them the on-level lesson provided in the Student Edition.
- If students have done well on the Beginning-of-Year Assessment, then challenge them to keep progressing and learning by giving them opportunities to practice the skills in depth.
- Use the Selection Resources listed on the Planning pages for "Traveling" to help students continually improve their ability to master the standards.

Instructional Standards: Traveling

	Catching Up	This Year	Looking Forward
Reading	You may wish to administer the **Analyze Craft and Structure: Structure (RP)** worksheet to help students understand the significance of the overall shape of a literary work.	**RI.5** Analyze in detail how an author's ideas or claims are developed and refined by particular sentences, paragraphs, or larger portions of a text.	To help them understand the effect structure has on a literary work's meanings, challenge students to identify with other ways Paley could have structured her memoir.
Speaking and Listening	You may wish to administer the **Speaking and Listening: Debate (RP)** worksheet to help students understand how to effectively stage a debate.	**SL.1.c** Propel conversations by posing and responding to questions that relate the current discussion to broader themes or larger ideas; actively incorporate others into the discussion; and clarify, verify, or challenge ideas and conclusions.	Have students find videos or transcripts online of examples of strong and/or poor debates to help them better appreciate the form.
Language	You may wish to administer the **Author's Style: Punctuation (RP)** worksheet to help students understand how authors may alter the standards of punctuation to add more impact to dialogue. Review the **Word Study: Etymology (RP)** worksheet with students to further their understanding of the origins of language.	**L.1** Demonstrate command of the conventions of standard English grammar and usage when writing or speaking. **L.4.b** Identify and correctly use patterns of word changes that indicate different meanings or parts of speech.	Have students rewrite some of the dialogue using standard punctuation to help them see how the author's choices affected the piece. Challenge students to compose a list of words whose origins they would like to know. Then have them research these origins using online or library resources.

TEACH

Implement the planned lesson, and gather evidence of student learning.

ANALYZE AND REVISE

- Analyze student work for evidence of student learning.
- Identify whether or not students have met the expectations in the standards.
- Identify implications for future instruction.

FACILITATING

Jump Start

FIRST READ Can a person of one racial or ethnic group ever truly experience what it feels like to be a person of another group? What role does personal perspective play in public discourse? As groups discuss, have students support their opinions with examples, anecdotes, and facts.

Traveling

How much courage does it take to stand up for what you believe in? When is it better to just "fit in?" Modeling the questions a reader might ask as they read "Traveling" for the first time brings the text alive for students and connects it to the Small-Group Performance Task assignment. Selection audio and print capability for the selection are available in the Interactive Teacher's Edition.

Concept Vocabulary

Ask groups to study the three types of context clues and discuss how they can help clarify meaning of a text. Encourage students to think of another type of context clue that they might encounter during their reading of "Traveling," such as antonyms and restatements.

FIRST READ

Have students perform the steps of the first read independently:

NOTICE: Encourage students to notice details in the text that help explain the author's experiences and reflection.

ANNOTATE: Remind students to focus on passages that feel powerful. These may be paragraphs that are key to meaning.

CONNECT: Encourage students to make connections to the text, either through their own experience or through reading, TV, movies or other sources.

RESPOND: Students will answer questions and write a summary to demonstrate understanding.

Point out to students that while they will always complete the Respond step at the end of the first read, the other steps will probably happen somewhat concurrently. You may wish to print copies of the **First-Read Guide: Nonfiction** for students to use.

MAKING MEANING

About the Author

Grace Paley (1922–2007) grew up in New York, the daughter of Russian Jewish immigrants. Before writing as a career, she spent many hours in parks with her children, getting to know the women who would eventually become the focus of her literary output. In addition to writing, Paley also participated in many activist causes, such as the feminist and peace movements.

Traveling

Concept Vocabulary

As you perform your first read of "Traveling," you will encounter these words.

absolute   sheer   adamant

Context Clues If these words are unfamiliar to you, try using **context clues**—other words and phrases that appear in a text—to help you determine their meanings. There are various types of context clues that you may encounter as you read.

Definition: Her mood yesterday seemed **pensive,** or deeply thoughtful.

Elaborating Details: Many of their comments were **unintelligible**—because they mumbled or spoke too quietly to be heard.

Contrast of Ideas and Topics: Failing to display his usual **tenacity,** Patrick decided to abandon his science project.

Apply your knowledge of context clues and other vocabulary strategies to determine the meanings of unfamiliar words you encounter during your first read. Use a resource such as a dictionary or a thesaurus to verify the meanings you identify.

First Read NONFICTION

Apply these strategies as you conduct your first read. You will have an opportunity to complete a close read after your first read.

NOTICE the general ideas of the text. *What* is it about? *Who* is involved?

ANNOTATE by marking vocabulary and key passages you want to revisit.

First Read

CONNECT ideas within the selection to what you already know and what you have already read.

RESPOND by completing the Comprehension Check and by writing a brief summary of the selection.

STANDARDS

Reading Informational Text
By the end of grade 9, read and comprehend literary nonfiction in the grades 9–10 text complexity band proficiently, with scaffolding as needed at the high end of the range.

Language
- Use context as a clue to the meaning of a word or phrase.
- Verify the preliminary determination of the meaning of a word or phrase.

MEMOIR

Traveling

from Just as I Thought

Grace Paley

DIGITAL PERSPECTIVES

BACKGROUND

Some of the most visible Jim Crow laws (state laws establishing segregation between African American and white citizens) were those affecting public transportation. During the Civil Rights era, laws requiring African American travelers to sit in the back of buses became the focus of organized protest.

SCAN FOR MULTIMEDIA

1 My mother and sister were traveling south. The year was 1927. They had begun their journey in New York. They were going to visit my brother, who was studying in the South Medical College of Virginia. Their bus was an express and had stopped only in Philadelphia, Wilmington, and now Washington. Here, the darker people who had gotten on in Philadelphia or New York rose from their seats, put their bags and boxes together, and moved to the back of the bus. People who boarded in Washington knew where to seat themselves. My mother had heard that something like this would happen. My sister had heard of it, too. They had not lived in it. This reorganization of passengers by color happened in silence. My mother and sister remained in their seats, which were about three-quarters of the way back.

2 When everyone was settled, the bus driver began to collect tickets. My sister saw him coming. She pinched my mother: Ma! Look! Of

NOTES

CLOSER LOOK

Analyze Memoir

Circulate among groups as students conduct their close read. Suggest that groups close read paragraph 1. Encourage them to talk about the annotations they mark. If needed, provide the following support.

ANNOTATE: Have students mark details in paragraph 1 that demonstrate the author's concern for accuracy, or work with small groups to have students participate as you highlight them together.

QUESTION: Guide students to consider what these details might tell them. Ask what a reader can infer from the author's recollections, and accept student responses.

Possible response: The author reports precisely what she observed on the bus as a kind of natural and orderly human reorganization carried out in silence.

CONCLUDE: Help students to formulate conclusions about the importance of these observations in the text. Ask students why the author might have chosen to write about these particular details.

Possible response: The importance of this event in the author's young life, and the impression it made at the time, is apparent in the care and precision with which she recalls and reports it.

Remind students that a **memoir** is a type of nonfiction autobiographical writing that tells about a person's own life, usually focusing on the writer's involvement in historically or culturally significant events—either as a participant or an eyewitness.

Additional **English Language Support** is available in the Interactive Teacher's Edition.

PERSONALIZE FOR LEARNING

English Language Support

Syntax Students may struggle with complex sentence structures that contain subordinate or embedded clauses. Encourage them to rewrite a few of these sentences from paragraph 1, removing the embedded clauses that are set off by commas. *They were going to visit my brother, who was studying in the South Medical College of Virginia. My mother and sister remained in their seats, which were about* three-quarters *of the way back.* Ask them to read the rewritten sentences and make observations about whether the text is easier to understand. **ALL LEVELS**

CLOSER LOOK

Analyze Point of View

Circulate among groups as students conduct their close read. Suggest that groups close read paragraphs 4–7. Encourage them to talk about the annotations they mark. If needed, provide the following support.

ANNOTATE: Have students mark details in paragraphs 4–7 that reveal the author's point of view, or work with small groups to have students participate as you highlight them together.

QUESTION: Guide students to consider what these details might tell them. Ask what a reader can infer from the details about the author's point of view, and accept student responses.

Possible response: The author's point of view is that of a detached but intense observer of events. The conversation is recalled without comment. Later, in discussing this event with her mother, the writer learns that her mother was rebellious, not polite.

CONCLUDE: Help students to formulate conclusions about the importance of these details in the text. Ask students why the author might have included these details.

Possible response: The author states that her mother and sister were aware that segregation would take place on the bus as it traveled south.

They had a specific reaction, and the author is sharing that experience without commentary. She is giving the reader a window into the events. By jumping forward to the time when the writer discusses the event with her mother, the author provides readers with perspective about the event.

Remind students that **point of view** is the perspective, or vantage point, from which a narrative is related. In autobiographical writing it is crucial to the reader to know whether events are being narrated from the point of view of the author looking back through time or the point of view of someone observing them as they occurred.

NOTES

course, my mother saw him, too. What frightened my sister was the quietness. The white people in front, the black people in back—silent.

3 The driver sighed, said, You can't sit here, ma'am. It's for them, waving over his shoulder at the Negroes, among whom they were now sitting. Move, please.

4 My mother said, No.

5 He said, You don't understand, ma'am. It's against the law. You have to move to the front.

6 My mother said, No.

7 When I first tried to write this scene, I imagined my mother saying, That's all right, mister, we're comfortable. I can't change my seat every minute. I read this invention to my sister. She said it was nothing like that. My mother did not try to be friendly or pretend innocence. While my sister trembled in the silence, my mother said, for the third time, quietly, No.

8 Somehow finally, they were in Richmond. There was my brother in school among so many American boys. After hugs and my mother's anxious looks at her young son, my sister said, Vic, you know what Mama did?

9 My brother remembers thinking, What? Oh! She wouldn't move? He had a classmate, a Jewish boy like himself, but from Virginia, who had had a public confrontation with a Negro man. He had punched that man hard, knocked him down. My brother couldn't believe it. He was stunned. He couldn't imagine a Jewish boy wanting to knock anyone down. He had never wanted to. But he thought, looking back, that he had been set down to work and study in a nearly foreign place and had to get used to it. Then he told me about the Second World War, when the disgrace of black soldiers being forced to sit behind white German POWs[1] shook him. Shamed him.

10 About fifteen years later, in 1943, in early summer, I rode the bus for about three days from New York to Miami Beach, where my husband in sweaty fatigues,[2] along with hundreds of other boys, was trudging up and down the streets and beaches to prepare themselves for war.

11 By late afternoon of the second long day, we were well into the South, beyond Richmond, maybe South Carolina or Georgia. My excitement about travel in the wide world was damaged a little by a sudden fear that I might not recognize Jess or he, me. We hadn't seen each other for two months. I took a photograph out of my pocket; yes, I would know him.

12 I had been sleeping waking reading writing dozing waking. So many hours, the movement of the passengers was something like a tide that sometimes ebbed[3] and now seemed to be noisily rising. I opened my eyes to the sound of new people brushing past my aisle seat. And looked up to see a colored woman holding a large sleeping

1. **POWs** abbreviation for "prisoners of war."
2. **fatigues** (fuh TEEGZ) *n.* uniforms soldiers wear while doing physical work.
3. **ebbed** *v.* flowed outward from the land, lowering the level of the water.

FACILITATING SMALL-GROUP LEARNING

Close Read As groups perform the close read, circulate and offer support as needed.

- Remind groups that when they read a memoir, they should be sure to identify the author's purpose. They should also be aware that a memoir is told from the perspective of the author, which is important to consider when analyzing a text.
- If a group is confused about the author's purpose, point out that the purpose is not always obvious or clearly stated. Challenge students to find evidence throughout the text that support why the author wrote this memoir.
- Ask groups to find evidence of the author's personal perspective versus facts from that time in history.

This photograph depicts how segregation looked on public buses in the Jim Crow South.

baby, who, with the heaviness of sleep, his arms so tight around her neck, seemed to be pulling her head down. I looked around and noticed that I was in the last white row. The press of travelers had made it impossible for her to move farther back. She seemed so tired and I had been sitting and sitting for a day and a half at least. Not thinking, or maybe refusing to think, I offered her my seat.

13 She looked to the right and left as well as she could. Softly she said, Oh no. I became fully awake. A white man was standing right beside her, but on the other side of the invisible **absolute** racial border. Of course, she couldn't accept my seat. Her sleeping child hung mercilessly from her neck. She shifted a little to balance the burden. She whispered to herself, Oh, I just don't know. So I said, Well, at least give me the baby. First, she turned, barely looking at the man beside her. He made no move. So, to my surprise, but obviously out of **sheer** exhaustion, she disengaged the child from her body and placed him on my lap. He was deep in child-sleep. He stirred, but not enough to bother himself or me. I liked holding him, aligning him along my twenty-year-old young woman's shape. I thought ahead to that holding, that breathing together that would happen in my life if this war would ever end.

14 I was so comfortable under his nice weight. I closed my eyes for a couple of minutes, but suddenly opened them to look up into the face of a white man talking. In a loud voice he addressed me: Lady, I wouldn't of touched that thing with a meat hook.

15 I thought, Oh, this world will end in ice. I could do nothing but look straight into his eyes. I did not look away from him. Then I held that boy a little tighter, kissed his curly head, pressed him even closer so that he began to squirm. So sleepy, he reshaped himself

NOTES

Mark context clues or indicate another strategy you used that helped you determine meaning.

absolute (AB suh loot) *adj.*

MEANING:

sheer (sheer) *adj.*

MEANING:

Concept Vocabulary

ABSOLUTE If groups are struggling to define the word *absolute*, point out the sentence in which it is used in paragraph 13. Have students look for context clues from the surrounding words and phrases. For example, the use of the word *border* in the sentence suggests that there is some kind of distinguishable line being drawn. Ask students what they can infer from this to determine the meaning of the word.

Possible response: *Absolute* means "complete."

SHEER If groups are struggling to define the word *sheer*, point out that some of the surrounding words can provide context clues. This is especially helpful because the word *sheer* can have multiple meanings. For instance, in paragraph 13, *sheer* is being used as an adjective to describe a feeling of exhaustion. This detail should allow students to infer the meaning as they come up with other words that can relate to exhaustion.

Possible response: *Sheer* means "true, deep, or complete."

DIGITAL PERSPECTIVES

Enriching the Text This text describes the author's experiences with Jim Crow, beginning with paragraph 10. To help students understand segregation in the South during the time of Jim Crow laws, find photos online that depict what segregation was like. This might include photos of all African-American schools, segregated buses, or diners. Display the photos for students after they have finished reading, and have groups discuss how the images enhance their understanding of "Traveling." Then, have groups share how the photos provided insight to the text. Encourage them to consider whether these issues are still present today, or how things have changed.

FACILITATING

CLOSER LOOK

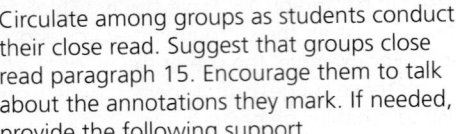

Analyze Author's Purpose

Circulate among groups as students conduct their close read. Suggest that groups close read paragraph 15. Encourage them to talk about the annotations they mark. If needed, provide the following support.

ANNOTATE: Have students mark details in paragraph 15 that provide descriptive clues about the author's purpose in writing about the woman and her baby, or work with small groups as you highlight them together.

QUESTION: Guide students to consider what these details might tell them. Ask what a reader can infer from what was marked, and accept student responses.

Possible response: A reader can infer that when the child is put in her lap the writer experiences the natural instincts of a mother, regardless of the color of the child. The child is beautiful to her, and her body adapts naturally to its shape. Meanwhile the child's actual mother shows her maternal instincts by registering fear for the consequences.

CONCLUDE: Help students to formulate conclusions about the importance of these details in the text. Ask students why the author might have included these details.

Possible response: The author included these details to indicate that the mother, the author, and the baby were acting in obedience to nature, rather than to the law. The mother was too tired to carry the child, the author had a vacant lap, and the child was sleeping.

Remind students that an **author's purpose** is his or her main reason for writing. For example, an author may want to entertain, inform, or persuade the reader. Sometimes an author is trying to teach a moral lesson or reflect on an experience. An author may also have more than one purpose.

Concept Vocabulary

ADAMANT If groups are struggling to define the word *adamant* in paragraph 21, point out that many of the surrounding words and phrases refer to the mother's characteristics. These include *principled* and *shy*. Have students draw upon what they have already learned about the mother from the text. Students should be able to infer that the mother is a woman who does what she believes in, even if others frown upon it.

Possible response: *Adamant* must mean "hard" or "stubborn."

NOTES

inside my arms. His mother tried to narrow herself away from that dangerous border, too frightened at first to move at all. After a couple of minutes, she leaned forward a little, placed her hand on the baby's head, and held it there until the next stop. I couldn't look up into her mother face.

16 I write this remembrance more than fifty years later. I look back at that mother and child. How young she is. Her hand on his head is quite small, though she tries by spreading her fingers wide to hide him from the white man. But the child I'm holding, his little face as he turns toward me, is the brown face of my own grandson, my daughter's boy, the open mouth of the sleeper, the full lips, the thick little body of a child who runs wildly from one end of the yard to the other, leaps from dangerous heights with certain experienced caution, muscling his body, his mind, for coming realities.

17 Of course, when my mother and sister returned from Richmond, the family at home wanted to know: How was Vic doing in school among all those gentiles?[4] Was the long bus ride hard, was the anti-Semitism really bad or just normal? What happened on the bus? I was probably present at that supper, the attentive listener and total forgetter of information that immediately started to form me.

18 Then last year, my sister, casting the net of old age (through which recent experience easily slips), brought up that old story. First I was angry. How come you never told me about your bus ride with Mama? I mean, really, so many years ago.

19 I don't know, she said, anyway you were only about four years old, and besides, maybe I did.

20 I asked my brother why we'd never talked about that day. He said he thought now that it had had a great effect on him; he had tried unraveling its meaning for years—then life family work happened. So I imagined him, a youngster really, a kid from the Bronx in Virginia in 1927; why, he was a stranger there himself.

21 In the next couple of weeks, we continued to talk about our mother, the way she was principled, **adamant**, and at the same time so shy. What else could we remember . . . Well, I said, I have a story about those buses, too. Then I told it to them: How it happened on just such a journey, when I was still quite young, that I first knew my grandson, first held him close, but could protect him for only about twenty minutes fifty years ago. — 1997

Mark context clues or indicate another strategy you used that helped you determine meaning.

adamant (AD uh muhnt) *adj.*

MEANING:

4. **gentiles** (JEHN tylz) *n.* people who are not Jewish.

Comprehension Check

Complete the following items after you finish your first read. Review and clarify details with your group.

1. Why does the bus driver ask the author's mother and sister to change their seats?

2. On her way by bus to Miami, how does the author attempt to help one of her fellow passengers?

3. How does the author react when a white man addresses her in a loud voice?

4. About how much time separates the third part of the memoir from the second part?

5. In the last part of the memoir, what does the author come to realize about her mother?

6. **Notebook** Confirm your understanding of "Traveling" by writing a timeline of events.

RESEARCH

Research to Clarify Choose at least one unfamiliar detail from the text. Briefly research that detail. In what way does the information you learned shed light on an aspect of the memoir?

Research to Explore Choose something that interested you from the text, and formulate a research question.

DIGITAL PERSPECTIVES

Comprehension Check

Possible responses:

1. The bus driver asked the writer's mother and sister to change seats because they were sitting in seats designated for African Americans.
2. The writer attempted to give up her seat to another passenger.
3. The writer stared into the eyes of the man who addressed her loudly.
4. About 50 years separate the second and third parts of the memoir.
5. In the last part of the memoir, the writer learns about how stubborn and principled her mother is.
6. 1927—The writer's mother and sister take a bus trip down south during which they sat in the back and refused to move.
   1943—The narrator travels via bus from New York to Miami Beach and offers her seat to an African-American woman who was standing and holding a child. The woman refuses out of custom and, perhaps, fear. Ultimately the writer holds the woman's child in her lap and endures the disrespect of another white passenger.
   Somewhere around 1993, the writer hears the story of her mother's bus ride. A year later, she writes the memoir.

Research

Research to Clarify If groups struggle to choose an unfamiliar detail from the text, suggest they research segregation laws during the 1920s and discuss ways the information sheds light on aspects of the memoir.

Research to Explore If groups struggle to find something interesting about which to formulate a research question suggest they research the similarities and differences between society's treatment of Jewish Americans and African Americans during the 1920s.

PERSONALIZE FOR LEARNING

Challenge

Relating to Personal Experience Have students think about what they would have done if they were in the author's position. Would they have offered to hold the child? Why or why not? Ask them to think of a similar situation that might arise today. Ask them to write a paragraph describing the situation, what they would do, and the risks that would involved.

Jump Start

CLOSE READ Ask students to consider the following prompt: *Would you do something or make choices that other people might object to or might not do themselves?*

Close Read the Text

If needed, model close reading by using the Annotation Highlights in the Interactive Teacher's Edition.

Remind students to use Accountable Talk in their discussions and to support one another as they complete the close read.

Analyze the Text

1. Possible response: The writer's mother was coming from the North where there weren't any Jim Crow laws and people sat wherever they wanted on public transportation.
2. **Responses will vary.**
3. **Responses will vary.**

Concept Vocabulary

Why These Words? Possible response: The words are all adjectives that indicate extremeness or completeness.

Practice

Possible Responses:

Absolute: The leader's power was so *absolute* that it took years to usher in change.

Sheer: He accomplished the feat by *sheer* strength and will.

Adamant: I was *adamant* that Jim Crow laws were wrong and therefore refused to give up my seat.

Word Network

Possible words: *racial, anti-Semitism, reorganization, confrontation*

Word Study

For more support, see **Concept Vocabulary and Word Study.**

Possible responses:

invention: in–, "on"; *venire,* "to come"; something that is come upon, a discovery

disengage: dis–, "do the opposite of"; *gage,* "pledge"; release, detach

attentive: ad–, "to"; *tendere,* "stretch"; stretching one's mind to, paying attention to

remembrance: re–, "again"; *memori,* "be mindful of"; *–ance,* "state of"; the state of being mindful again

MAKING MEANING

TRAVELING

Close Read the Text

With your group, revisit sections of the text you marked during your first read. **Annotate** details that you notice. What **questions** do you have? What can you **conclude**?

Close Read — ANNOTATE · QUESTION · CONCLUDE

TIP

GROUP DISCUSSION
Keep in mind that group members will have different interpretations of the text. These different perspectives will help you to learn from one another and clarify your own thoughts. Very often there is no single interpretation or conclusion.

Analyze the Text

CITE TEXTUAL EVIDENCE to support your answers.

Notebook Complete the activities.

1. **Review and Clarify** Reread paragraphs 1–4 of the selection. Discuss why you think that the author's mother refused to change her seat.
2. **Present and Discuss** Now work with your group to share the passages from the selection that you found especially important. Take turns presenting your passages. Discuss what you notice in the selection, the questions you asked, and the conclusions you reached.
3. **Essential Question:** *How can words inspire change?* What has this text taught you about the power of words to effect change?

LANGUAGE DEVELOPMENT

Concept Vocabulary

absolute · sheer · adamant

Why These Words? The three concept vocabulary words are related. With your group, discuss the words, and determine what they have in common. How do these word choices enhance the impact of the text?

WORD NETWORK
Add interesting words related to civil rights from the text to your Word Network.

Practice

Notebook Confirm your understanding of these words by using them in sentences. Include context clues that hint at each word's meaning.

STANDARDS

Reading Informational Text
- Analyze how the author unfolds an analysis or series of ideas or events, including the order in which the points are made, how they are introduced and developed, and the connections that are drawn between them.
- Analyze in detail how an author's ideas or claims are developed and refined by particular sentences, paragraphs, or larger portions of a text.

Language
Identify and correctly use patterns of word changes that indicate different meanings or parts of speech.

Word Study

Notebook **Etymology** A word's origins are called its **etymology**. You will find every word's etymology in its dictionary entry. For example, if you look up the word *adamant* in a dictionary, you will see that it comes from the Greek word *adamas*, which was formed in Greek from the prefix *a-*, meaning "not," and the root *-daman-*, meaning "to subdue" or "to tame." Thus, the original meaning of *adamant* was "untameable" or "unbreakable."

Use a good dictionary to research the etymology of the following words: *invention, disengaged, attentive,* and *remembrance*. Write each word's etymology, and then write its meaning.

340 UNIT 3 • THE LITERATURE OF CIVIL RIGHTS

FORMATIVE ASSESSMENT

Analyze the Text

If students struggle to close read the text, **then** provide the **Traveling: Text Questions** available online in the Interactive Teacher's Edition or Unit Resources. Answers and DOK levels are also available.

Concept Vocabulary

If students fail to describe the tone, **then** have them revisit the context of the words as they were used in the text.

Word Study

If students fail to identify a word's etymology, **then** have them look up the words in a dictionary and apply the words' origins to the connotation of the text. For Reteach and Practice, see **Word Study: Etymology (RP).**

Analyze Craft and Structure

Author's Choices: Point of View and Structure The **author's point of view** is the perspective from which events are related. In a memoir like "Traveling," the author's point of view can be compared to a physical position. For example, an author may look at events from a distance, reflecting on them from the perspective of an older, wiser self. Alternatively, a writer may choose a much closer perspective, perhaps attempting to recreate the feeling of a long ago moment.

The **structure** of a work is its overall shape, including the relationship of its different parts or sections to one another. In this memoir, Grace Paley employs a different point of view in each of the work's three sections. The point of view and the structure she uses are fully intertwined.

TIP

GROUP DISCUSSION
Members of your group may have responded in various ways to these questions. As you discuss your responses, be sure to allow group members to explain their thinking.

Practice

CITE TEXTUAL EVIDENCE to support your answers.

Notebook **Work independently to answer these questions. Then, share your responses with the group.**

1. Reread paragraphs 1–6. Did Paley herself live through the experience she describes in those paragraphs? Explain.
2. (a) What shift in author's perspective happens in paragraph 7? (b) How does this shift allow the author to clarify the memoir's opening scene? Explain.
3. (a) What is the author's perspective in the memoir's second section, paragraphs 1 through 15? (b) Explain the shift in perspective that happens at paragraph 16. (c) How does the perspective shift again in the final section, paragraphs 17–21?
4. Explain how the changes in perspective in each section of the memoir follow the chronology of the author's life.
5. Why do you think the author chose to structure the memoir as she did? What does the shifting chronology and point of view allow that a more basic story structure might not?
6. (a) "Traveling" is a work of nonfiction. Identify at least two sections in which Paley uses techniques commonly found in works of fiction. **(b)** How does her use of fictional elements add to or detract from the power of the story? Explain.
7. Does the fact that this is a true story make it more powerful or less powerful than a fictionalized version might be? Explain.

PERSONALIZE FOR LEARNING

English Language Support

Subject-Verb Agreement English Learners often struggle with subject-verb agreement when writing. Remind students that the subject and the verb in a sentence need to agree. For example, singular subjects need singular verbs (The boy runs.), and plural subjects need plural verbs (The girls run.). Suggest that students review their subject-verb agreement as part of their editing process. **ALL LEVELS**

DIGITAL PERSPECTIVES

Analyze Craft and Structure

Point of View and Structure

Discuss with students that authors often use structure as a way to create a purpose or tone for their stories. Structure has to do with the shape of the text. In "Traveling," the author starts out describing events from her youth, and then jumps to a later point in her life. This structure allows the reader to catch glimpses of the author's experiences, as well as make connections between the author's childhood and how it shaped her adult beliefs. For more support, see **Analyze Craft and Structure: Structure.**

Possible responses:

1. She did not have the experience. She is writing about it.
2. (a) The author's perspective moves from describing a scene to a recent interaction. (b) It allows her to tell her readers she wasn't on the bus with her family.
3. (a) The author is describing an event from her past, but she writes from the perspective of what it felt like to live it. (b) Paragraph 16 jumps in time to revisit the event 50 years later. (c) Paragraph 17 returns to the original perspective—describing an event as though she were living it. Paragraphs 18–21 reflect on the events from the author's life.
4. The first section describes events she was too young to experience. The second section describes her own experiences. The third is a reflection on these experiences.
5. This structure allows the reader to understand what happened and then appreciate the reflection.
6. (a) Responses will vary. (b) Students may suggest it makes the text more engaging.
7. Responses will vary. As a piece of nonfiction, the text carries the weight of actual events.

FORMATIVE ASSESSMENT

Analyze Craft and Structure

If students fail to understand the structure of the text, **then** revisit the story and point out where the story divides into three sections. For Reteach and Practice, see **Analyze Craft and Structure: Structure (RP).**

FACILITATING

Author's Style

Punctuation

Discuss with students that the author uses an unusual, nonstandard punctuation style, in which her direct quotes are not enclosed by punctuation marks. This can make it tricky to fully understand when the text represents dialogue.

As you review the text with students, look for any other types of nonstandard punctuation that the author uses. Encourage students to think about the author's purpose for not using traditional punctuation. For more support, see **Author's Style: Punctuation.**

Read It

MAKE IT INTERACTIVE

Have students write down a conversation between three or more characters that they make up. Instruct students to avoid using proper punctuation, such as quotation marks. Then, have students write the same conversation using proper punctuation. Ask students what happens to the characters' conversation with the proper punctuation compared to the improper punctuation. Does it change the tone of the text? Does it make it harder or easier to follow the conversations? Why or why not?

Responses will vary. Be sure students include their thoughts in the chart on the Student page about the effect of leaving the marks out on how they read each item of dialogue.

Write It

Responses will vary. Be sure that students include some direct speech without the use of quotation marks.

FORMATIVE ASSESSMENT

Author's Style

If students are unable to identify the missing punctuation, **then** have them look for lines of dialogue throughout the text. For Reteach and Practice, see **Author's Style: Punctuation (RP).**

LANGUAGE DEVELOPMENT

TRAVELING

Author's Style

Punctuation In her memoir, Paley uses a nonstandard format for punctuating **dialogue.** In standard English, a speaker's exact words are enclosed by punctuation marks in a direct quotation. When Paley quotes the words spoken by her mother, her sister, her brother, and the bus driver in paragraphs 1–9 of "Traveling," however, she does not use quotation marks.

In addition, Paley occasionally omits punctuation marks, such as commas, that are standard for lists or series. For example, in paragraph 12, she writes this way about her bus ride to Miami: "I had been sleeping waking reading writing dozing waking."

Read It

Work individually. For each quotation from dialogue in the left column of the chart, examine the context. Then, write a note in the right column that comments on Paley's use of direct speech without standard quotation marks. Include your thoughts about the effect of Paley's punctuation choices.

QUOTATION	NOTES ON DIALOGUE
The driver sighed, said, You can't sit here, ma'am. . . . (paragraph 3)	
My mother said, No. (paragraph 6)	
Softly she said, Oh no. (paragraph 13)	
In a loud voice, he addressed me: Lady, I wouldn't of touched that thing with a meat hook. (paragraph 14)	
I don't know, she said, anyway you were only about four years old, and besides, maybe I did. (paragraph 19)	
Well, I said, I have a story about those buses, too. (paragraph 21)	

STANDARDS

Language
Demonstrate command of the conventions of standard English capitalization, punctuation, and spelling when writing.

Write It

Notebook Write a brief anecdote about something that happened recently to you and someone you know, such as a friend or classmate. Include some direct speech without the use of quotation marks.

PERSONALIZE FOR LEARNING

English Language Support

Punctuating Dialogue Ask pairs of students to each write a line of dialogue with a dialogue tag and then trade with their partner and punctuate their sentence. **EMERGING**

Ask pairs of students to take turns writing down lines of dialogue instead of having a verbal conversation. After each student writes a line, he or she should give it to his or her partner to punctuate. **EXPANDING**

Ask pairs of students to take turns writing down lines of dialogue instead of having a verbal conversation. Have students focus their dialogue on the use of different points of view in the selection. After each student writes a line, he or she should give it to his or her partner to punctuate. **BRIDGING**

An expanded **English Language Support Lesson** on Punctuation in Dialogue is available in the Digital Teacher's Edition.

EFFECTIVE EXPRESSION

Speaking and Listening

Assignment

In the memoir "Traveling," two generations of women make difficult choices in the segregated South. Each decision has the potential to produce both positive and negative results for all of those involved. With a group, plan a **debate** about a question raised by Paley's memoir. Choose from among these options for your debate.

- ☐ Was Paley's mother right to refuse to move to the front of the bus? Was her attitude helpful?
- ☐ Was Paley right to hold the baby on the bus to Miami? Was she standing up for her principles, or was she endangering the child?
- ☐ Which story—Paley's experience on a segregated bus or her mother's—best reflects the tensions caused by the belief in "separate but equal" treatment?

Support Your Position Working individually, identify at least three specific supporting reasons for your position as well as passages from Paley's memoir that you could use to support your position. Collect your ideas in the chart.

SUPPORTING REASONS	SUPPORTING PASSAGES OR OTHER EVIDENCE
1	
2	
3	

Come to a Consensus Invite each member of your group to share their positions on the debate questions. Discuss one another's positions, asking questions and clarifying your responses. Work together to reach a conclusion that identifies the strongest argument. This conclusion may draw on points from several group members.

EVIDENCE LOG

Before moving on to a new selection, go to your Evidence Log and record what you learned from "Traveling."

STANDARDS

Speaking and Listening
Propel conversations by posing and responding to questions that relate the current discussion to broader themes or larger ideas; actively incorporate others into the discussion; and clarify, verify, or challenge ideas and conclusions.

DIGITAL PERSPECTIVES

Speaking and Listening

Remind students that the memoir "Traveling" depicts a sensitive and controversial topic regarding segregation in the South. The memoir is told from the perspective of the author and main character, but her mother is also an important figure in the text.

Explain to students that controversial issues are often debated because people have differing ideas about whether the issues are right, wrong, correct, or incorrect. Prepare students for a debate. Remind them that a debate involves using good speaking and listening skills.

- Good speaking skills are necessary for presenting your side of the argument. They allow students to clearly and correctly make their points and expand on their evidence.
- Good listening skills are needed for making sure to hear your opponent and being able to respond appropriately.

For more support, see **Speaking and Listening: Debate.**

Evidence Log Support students in completing their Evidence Log. This paced activity will help prepare them for the Performance-Based Assessment at the end of the unit.

FORMATIVE ASSESSMENT

Speaking and Listening

If students are unable to articulate their claims clearly, **then** have them practice writing down what they want to say and reading their sentences aloud. For Reteach and Practice, see **Speaking and Listening: Debate (RP).**

Selection Test

Administer the "Traveling" Selection Test, which is available in both print and digital formats online in Assessments.

DIGITAL PERSPECTIVES

Enriching the Text Show students clips of movies that depict segregation, desegregation, or other Civil Rights issues. Be sure to preview the clips in advance to make sure the content is appropriate for your class, especially due to the sensitive nature of the material.

After students have viewed the clips, have them discuss how they relate to "Traveling." Encourage students to consider if, after watching the clips, they agree with the decisions of the author and her mother. Why, or why not?

Multimedia Presentation

Assignment Before groups begin work on their projects, have them clearly differentiate the role each group member will play. Remind groups to consult the schedule for Small-Group Learning to guide their work during the Performance Task.

Students should complete the assignment using presentation software to take advantage of text, graphics, and sound features.

Plan With Your Group

Analyze the Text Point out to students that they have read and watched a variety of selections. One is a personal memoir ("Traveling"), another is a speech ("Lessons of Dr. Martin Luther King, Jr."), two are poems ("For My People" and "Incident"), and one is a news report about a poet ("Remembering Civil Rights History: When 'Words Meant Everything'").

Explain that different forms of writing can use language in different ways to effect change. You might want to mention how the style of writing that Cesar Chavez used differs significantly from the styles used by Margaret Walker and Natasha Trethewey.

Gather Evidence and Media Examples Suggest that students examine words and actions from specific time periods that produced—or did not produce—meaningful change. Remind students of famous historic speeches that were given to effect change, such as Abraham Lincoln's Gettysburg Address, John F. Kennedy's inaugural speech, and Ronald Reagan's "tear down this wall" speech.

You might also want to discuss protest music, such as "We Shall Overcome," "The Times They Are a Changin'," and "We Shall Not Be Moved." Point out that music has an ability to inspire.

Encourage students to find recordings of these songs and video clips of the speeches.

PERFORMANCE TASK: SPEAKING AND LISTENING FOCUS

SOURCES

- REMEMBERING CIVIL RIGHTS HISTORY, WHEN "WORDS MEANT EVERYTHING"
- FOR MY PEOPLE
- INCIDENT
- LESSONS OF DR. MARTIN LUTHER KING, JR.
- TRAVELING

Multimedia Presentation

Assignment

You have read stories, poems, and a speech that deal with the struggle for civil rights in the United States. Work with your group to develop a **multimedia presentation** that addresses this question:

Why do words and actions in some time periods produce meaningful change—and in others do not?

Plan With Your Group

Analyze the Text With your group, analyze each selection and consider what it suggests about the ways in which words and actions either did or could lead to change. Use the chart to record your notes.

TITLE	WHAT ACTIONS OR WORDS LEAD TO CHANGE?
Remembering Civil Rights History, When "Words Meant Everything"	
For My People	
Incident	
Lessons of Dr. Martin Luther King, Jr.	
Traveling	

STANDARDS

Speaking and Listening

- Present information, findings, and supporting evidence clearly, concisely and logically such that listeners can follow the line of reasoning and the organization, development, substance, and style are appropriate to purpose, audience, and task.

Gather Evidence and Media Examples After your group has finished filling in the chart, list ways in which the words of civil rights leaders and political activists produced change in the 1960s. This will help you draw comparisons and contrasts with other eras, such as today. Consider using audio clips from speeches or news programs to emphasize points in your presentation. You may also include music and other sound effects. Allow each group member to make suggestions for how to integrate media that is appropriate for your audience and task.

AUTHOR'S PERSPECTIVE **Ernest Morrell, Ph.D.**

Mastering Classroom Talk Complex texts can be intimidating and alien to some students, especially those who have had limited exposure to such texts. However, these same students often show deep critical and analytical skills when considering popular culture. Teachers can use their students' background knowledge of popular culture and their enthusiasm for it to increase motivation and classroom talk, especially debate skills, small-group work, and formal public presentations. Start by incorporating elements of popular culture such as rap and hip-hop, movies, or sports into a traditional unit of study. Place popular culture alongside the other historical/literacy periods covered in the unit so students can use their knowledge of the familiar works as a lens through which to evaluate the new ones. Second, have students evaluate one literary work in the program, such as a poem, alongside a contemporary reference of their choice. This approach helps students gain the understanding and confidence they need to discuss classroom texts and enhance their critical perspectives.

Organize Your Ideas As a group, organize the script for your presentation. Decide who will do what job in each part of the presentation. Then, take note of when each section begins, and record what the speaker will say. Also, note when you will use excerpts from texts in this section, other sources, sound effects, and music.

MULTIMEDIA PRESENTATION SCRIPT		
	Media Cues	Script
Speaker 1		
Speaker 2		
Speaker 3		

Rehearse With Your Group

Practice With Your Group As you work through the script for your presentation, use this checklist to evaluate the effectiveness of your group's first run-through. Then, use your evaluation and the instruction here to guide your revision.

CONTENT	USE OF MEDIA	PRESENTATION TECHNIQUES
☐ The presentation has a clear purpose and focus. ☐ Main ideas are supported with evidence from the texts and from research.	☐ The media support and enhance understanding of the topic. ☐ Media are used evenly throughout the report. ☐ Equipment functions properly.	☐ Media are audible. ☐ Transitions are smooth. ☐ Each speaker speaks clearly and with conviction.

Fine-Tune the Content Work with your group to identify key points that are not clear to listeners. Add material to support your points or find another way to word these ideas. Make sure that you address the main prompt by offering an analysis of why some eras produce meaningful change, while others do not.

Improve Your Use of Media Review all audio clips, music, and sound effects to make sure they add interest and help create a cohesive presentation. If a sound cue is not clearly related to the presentation, replace it with a more relevant item.

Present and Evaluate

When you present, be sure that each member has taken into account each of the checklist items. As you listen to other groups' presentations, evaluate how well they meet the items on checklist.

STANDARDS

Speaking and Listening

- Make strategic use of digital media (e.g., textual, graphical, audio, visual, and interactive elements) in presentations to enhance understanding of findings, reasoning, and evidence and to add interest.
- Adapt speech to a variety of contexts and tasks, demonstrating a command of formal English when indicated or appropriate.

DIGITAL PERSPECTIVES

Organize Your Ideas Remind students that it's important to set up each piece of media (e.g., video of a speech, recording of a song) with an introduction so that the audience will understand why they are being played or shown.

Rehearse With Your Group

Practice With Your Group Remind students that each group member should practice his or her part ahead of time. Explain that rehearsing will be especially helpful in ensuring that the transitions between speaking and playing media go smoothly, pointing out that equipment malfunctions are a common problem for presenters.

Improve Your Use of Media Explain to students that during rehearsal, other members of the group might think of better choices of audio or video. Encourage them not to hesitate to make changes to their presentation if it's clear it could be stronger.

PERSONALIZE FOR LEARNING

Strategic Support

The Power of Words Ask students to think about times in their lives when they've used words with friends or family to make a convincing case for something they wanted. Encourage them to consider the effectiveness of their approach, how they might do it differently if given another opportunity, and how they could use that strategy in other arenas. Discuss current social justice issues with students and how their strategic use of words could make a difference.

OVERVIEW

INDEPENDENT LEARNING

How can words inspire change?

Encourage students to think carefully about what they have already learned and what more they want to know about the unit topic of The Literature of Civil Rights. This is a key first step to previewing and selecting the text or media they will read or review in Independent Learning.

Independent Learning Strategies

Review the Learning Strategies with students and explain that as they work through Independent Learning they will develop strategies to work on their own.

- Have students watch the video on Independent Learning Strategies.
- A video on this topic is available online in the Professional Development Center.

Students should include any favorite strategies that they might have devised on their own during Whole-Class and Small-Group Learning. For example, for the strategy "Create a schedule," students might include:

- Make an outline of the topics that you want to discuss.
- Allot an amount of time to each point you'd like to make, to avoid running out of time.

Block Scheduling

Each day in this Pacing Plan represents a 40–50 minute class period. Teachers using block scheduling may combine days to reflect their class schedule. In addition, teachers may revise pacing to differentiate and support core instruction by integrating components and resources as students require.

OVERVIEW: INDEPENDENT LEARNING

ESSENTIAL QUESTION:

How can words inspire change?

Words, as well as actions, were crucial to the fight for civil rights. In this section, you will complete your study of the literature of civil rights by exploring an additional selection related to the topic. You'll then share what you learn with classmates. To choose a text, follow these steps.

Look Back Think about the selections you have already studied. What more do you want to know about the topic of civil rights?

Look Ahead Preview the texts by reading the descriptions. Which one seems most interesting and appealing to you?

Look Inside Take a few minutes to scan the text you chose. Choose a different one if this text doesn't meet your needs.

Independent Learning Strategies

Throughout your life, in school, in your community, and in your career, you will need to rely on yourself to learn and work on your own. Review these strategies and the actions you can take to practice them during Independent Learning. Add ideas of your own for each category.

STRATEGY	ACTION PLAN
Create a schedule	• Understand your goals and deadlines. • Make a plan for what to do each day. •
Practice what you've learned	• Use first-read and close-read strategies to deepen your understanding. • After you read, evaluate the usefulness of the evidence to help you understand the topic. • Consider the quality and reliability of the source. •
Take notes	• Record important ideas and information. • Review your notes before preparing to share with a group. •

SCAN FOR MULTIMEDIA

Pacing Plan

Day	Activity
1	Unit Introduction
2	Introduce Whole-Class Learning
3–6	I Have a Dream
7–10	Letter From Birmingham Jail
11–13	Media: Remarks on the Assassination of Martin Luther King, Jr.
14–15	Performance Task

DIGITAL PERSPECTIVES

Choose one selection. Selections are available online only.

CONTENTS

MEDIA: NEWSCAST

Frank McCain Dies—Helped Start Sit-In Movement at Greensboro Lunch Counter

Jeff Tiberii

How far-reaching can one small act of bravery be?

NEWS ARTICLE

How the Children of Birmingham Changed the Civil-Rights Movement

Lottie L. Joiner

They were beaten, jailed, and scared, but the young people of the Children's Crusade did not give up.

NARRATIVE NONFICTION

Sheyann Webb

from Selma, Lord, Selma *as told to* Frank Sikora

Sheyann Webb recounts her experience as a young girl during a dramatic and terrifying episode of the civil rights era.

MAGAZINE ARTICLE

The Many Lives of Hazel Bryan

David Margolick

An iconic photograph from the civil rights era shapes the lives of two women in surprising ways.

MEDIA: VIDEO

Fannie Lou Hamer

BBC

From sharecropper to civil rights activist to congresswoman, Fannie Lou Hamer faced life with courage and dignity.

PERFORMANCE-BASED ASSESSMENT PREP

Review Evidence for an Informative Essay

Complete your Evidence Log for the unit by evaluating what you've learned and synthesizing the information you have recorded.

SCAN FOR MULTIMEDIA

Contents

Selections Encourage students to scan and preview the selections before choosing the one they would like to read or review. Suggest that they consider the genre and subject matter of each one before making their decision. You can use the information on the following Planning pages to advise students in making their choice.

Remind students that the selections for Independent Learning are only available in the Interactive Student Edition. Allow students who do not have digital access at home to preview the selections or review the media selections using classroom or computer lab technology. Then either have students print the selection they choose or provide a printout for them.

Performance-Based Assessment Prep

Review Evidence for an Informative Essay Point out to students that collecting evidence during Independent Learning is the last step in completing their Evidence Log. After they finish their independent reading, they will synthesize all the evidence they have compiled in the unit.

The evidence students collect will serve as the primary source of information they will use to complete the writing and oral presentation for the Performance-Based Assessment at the end of the unit.

Introduce Small-Group Learning — 16
Media: Remembering Civil Rights History, When "Words Meant Everything" — 17
• For My People • Incident — 18, 19
Lessons of Dr. Martin Luther King, Jr. — 20, 21, 22
Traveling — 23, 24
Performance Task — 25, 26
Introduce Independent Learning — 27
Independent Learning — 28
Performance-Based Assessment — 29, 30

INDEPENDENT LEARNING

Frank McCain Dies—Helped Start Sit-In Movement at Greensboro Lunch Counter

Summary

In this newscast, Jeff Tiberii explains how Frank McCain inspired a movement that used sit-in protests to great success. As a young man, he and three fellow university students sat at the whites-only section of a segregated lunch counter and refused to leave. The store closed early to avoid serving them. The next day, they did the same thing—and twenty more students joined them. The movement spread, and within months, the chain of stores they targeted agreed to desegregate. McCain went on to study chemistry and biology, spent three decades working as a chemist, and is survived by three sons. His college built a statue that commemorates the students who engaged in that first sit-in.

Insight

Frank McCain's story shows the power of using activism to create change. It also shows that activism can easily fit into a full life.

SELECTION RESOURCES

- First-Review Guide: Media—Audio
- Close-Review Guide: Media—Audio
- Frank McCain Dies: Media Questions
- Audio Summaries
- Selection Audio

Connection to Essential Question

An older, white woman helped cement McCain's resolve that what he was doing was right, along with his faith in kindness and support from unexpected places. This may help students answer "How can words inspire change?"

Connection to Performance-Based Assessment

The prompt here is "Explain how words have the power to provoke, calm, or inspire." Students may note that McCain's explanation of how the protest made him feel is inspiring; the words of unexpected support he received helped calm his fears about the chances of success.

Media Complexity Rubric: Franklin McCain Dies—Helped Start Sit-In Movement at Greensboro Lunch Counter	
Quantitative Measures	
Format and Length: Audio, 5 min, 13 seconds	
Qualitative Measures	
Knowledge Demands 1—2—**3**—4—5	To understand the audio, prior knowledge is helpful about "sit-ins" and their role in protest movements, particularly in the Civil Rights movement.
Structure 1—2—**3**—4—5	Audio features narrator plus voices of people who were interviewed. Changes of voice make audio easier to listen to, but organization makes the audio a bit difficult to follow because basic information about McCain is not provided right away—students may need to listen more than once.
Language Conventionality and Clarity 1—2—**3**—4—5	Language is contemporary, in the style of documentary. Some sentences are complex and long. Narration is spoken at quick pace which may make language in those sections a little harder to follow.
Levels of Meaning/Purpose 1—2—**3**—4—5	Main concept (importance of sit-ins to the Civil Rights movement) is revealed in the course of the video, but not immediately presented.

DIGITAL PERSPECTIVES

Audio | Video | Document | Annotation Highlights | EL Highlights | Online Assessment

How the Children of Birmingham Changed the Civil-Rights Movement

Summary

This newspaper article by Lottie L. Joiner is about a high school student protest in 1963. Thousands of students marched to Birmingham, an infamously pro-segregation town. The town's commissioner of public safety attacked the young people with fire hoses and police dogs. This brutal suppression of the childrens' protest was caught on television. The sight of it helped drive nationwide opposition to segregation. If not for the great number of children willing to take risks and protest that day, the Civil Rights movement might not have succeeded as much as it did.

Insight

This article illustrates the role young people played at a key moment in the Civil Rights movement. It demonstrates the power of committing to a worthy cause.

SELECTION RESOURCES

- First-Read Guide: Nonfiction
- Close-Read Guide: Nonfiction
- Children of Birmingham: Text Questions
- Audio Summaries
- Selection Audio
- Selection Test

Connection to Essential Question

The Essential Question here is "How can words inspire change?" Raymond Goolsby describes how Martin Luther King, Jr., motivated him and his fellows to pursue the protest. In addition, the impact of these protests on later events cannot be understated.

Connection to Performance-Based Assessment

In addition to the inspiration students took from Dr. King's words, the article describes how they maintained their resolve with freedom songs. These details help us respond to the prompt, "Explain how words have the power to provoke, calm, or inspire."

Text Complexity Rubric: How the Children of Birmingham Changed the Civil-Rights Movement

Quantitative Measures	
Lexile: 1040 **Text Length:** 969 words	
Qualitative Measures	
Knowledge Demands: 3 (scale 1–5)	Content of selection is mostly explained, but it is helpful to have knowledge of the Civil Rights movement, Martin Luther King Jr., segregation, and the idea of civil disobedience.
Structure: 3 (scale 1–5)	Selection follows a journalistic structure. Organization is mostly chronological, but mixes with present-day reflections on past events. Text includes quotes by participants in the Children's Crusade.
Language Conventionality and Clarity: 2 (scale 1–5)	Language is mostly explicit and easy to understand; vocabulary is mostly contemporary and familiar; some sentences have complex grammar constructions.
Levels of Meaning/Purpose: 2 (scale 1–5)	Purpose is explicitly stated, clear, and concrete, but understanding the purpose will sometimes require prior knowledge of unfamiliar events.

SELECTION RESOURCES

- First-Read Guide: Nonfiction
- Close-Read Guide: Nonfiction
- Sheyann Webb: Text Questions
- Audio Summaries
- Selection Audio
- Selection Test

Sheyann Webb *from* Selma, Lord, Selma

Summary

In this narrative nonfiction selection, Frank Sikora interviews Sheyann Webb. She recounts how state troopers attacked a protest she took part in. They rode through the protest on horses, beating anyone they caught. With help from another protestor, Sheyann escaped and made it home. Her father was outraged and wanted revenge for the police's actions, but her mother convinced him to stay. Later that night, others who had been part of the protest began singing freedom songs and marching to the church. The evening's events made Sheyann feel as though they had won that day.

Insight

We so often talk about people who risked their lives for freedom, but rarely see what it's actually like to be afraid for your life. Enduring in the face of brutality and continuing to protest takes immense courage. Maintaining nonviolence in the face of such cruelty was often difficult.

Connection to Essential Question

The Essential Question is "How can words inspire change?" The words exchanged in the panic of the attack did little good. The group's impromptu decision to sing that night brought power back to them, and may have kept the people positive that they could inspire change.

Connection to Performance-Based Assessment

This text shares the fear and later resolve that Sheyann and her family experienced that day. Sheyann's mother successfully calmed her father when he considered resorting to violence. This gives students an angle on the prompt "Explain how words have the power to provoke, calm, or inspire."

Text Complexity Rubric: Sheyann Webb *from* Selma, Lord, Selma

Quantitative Measures	
Lexile: 900 **Text Length:** 1,234 words	
Qualitative Measures	
Knowledge Demands 1 — 2 — **3** — 4 — 5	To understand this book excerpt, students need to have an understanding of the Civil Rights movement and the specific events in Selma, Alabama, in 1965.
Structure 1 — **2** — 3 — 4 — 5	First-hand account by an 11-year-old girl is told chronologically. Events are easy to follow and include a lot of descriptive information.
Language Conventionality and Clarity 1 — **2** — 3 — 4 — 5	Language is familiar, vernacular speech of an 11-year-old telling a first-hand account. Some sentences are lengthy or run-on. Narration switches from past tense to present tense for reporting events in the past.
Levels of Meaning/Purpose 1 — **2** — 3 — 4 — 5	Purpose is straightforward and explicit (describing first-hand experience of events during protest in Selma, Alabama). Many details are included which are concrete and explicit.

DIGITAL PERSPECTIVES

Audio | Video | Document | Annotation Highlights | EL Highlights | Online Assessment

SELECTION RESOURCES

- First-Read Guide: Nonfiction
- Close-Read Guide: Nonfiction
- Hazel Bryan: Text Questions
- Audio Summaries
- Selection Audio
- Selection Test

The Many Lives of Hazel Bryan

Summary

"The Many Lives of Hazel Bryan," a news article by David Margolick, describes the life of Hazel Bryan, a young white woman who was included in a famous 1957 photograph. With others around her, she yelled at Elizabeth Eckford, a young black student entering a white Little Rock, Arkansas, high school for the first time as part of an integration plan. Later in her life, Bryan felt remorse over her actions and the photo. She began to study African-American history and she called Eckford to apologize. The two women became friends and appeared on *The Oprah Winfrey Show.* Despite this reconciliation, there was backlash as people questioned her actions and motives. The friendship became strained. The article shows that this moment has continued to follow her through her life.

Insight

There are two important lessons in this article. The first is that history has few true villains; almost everyone deserves empathy. The second is that the story doesn't end when the media goes away.

Connection to Essential Question

The essential question for this unit is "How can words inspire change?" Hazel Bryan's change came years after a famous photograph was shot. Her remorse and apology led to a change in her actions.

Connection to Performance-Based Assessment

The prompt here is "Explain how words have the power to provoke, calm, or inspire." The photo of Bryan shouting at Eckford is emotionally compelling because of how easy it is to imagine what she is saying, even without hearing the words.

Text Complexity Rubric: The Many Lives of Hazel Bryan

Quantitative Measures	
Lexile: 1220 **Text Length:** 1,724 words	
Qualitative Measures	
Knowledge Demands ① ② **❸** ④ ⑤	Selection is based on content that will be unfamiliar to most readers: Hazel Bryan and Elizabeth Eckford, and racial relations in the 1950s when segregation in schools was outlawed.
Structure ① ② **❸** ④ ⑤	Organization is somewhat sequential, but text is dense, with multiple concepts and pathways. Connection between ideas is not always explicit.
Language Conventionality and Clarity ① ② ③ **❹** ⑤	Complex language with some abstract concepts and rhetorical questions; above-level vocabulary; many complex sentences with multiple clauses.
Levels of Meaning/Purpose ① ② ③ **❹** ⑤	Meaning and purpose are not revealed right away; some concepts are theoretical or abstract; main concepts in each paragraph are not easy to identify.

SELECTION RESOURCES

- First-Review Guide: Media—Video
- Close-Review Guide: Media—Video
- Fannie Lou Hamer: Media Questions
- Audio Summaries
- Selection Video

Fannie Lou Hamer

Summary

This video gives a biography of Fannie Lou Hamer, a 1960s civil rights activist. Hamer was born in the Mississippi Delta. Like most black families in Mississippi, her family worked as sharecroppers. She had to work in the fields from the age of 6. In 1962, at 44 years old, Hamer had an epiphany when a civil rights activist spoke at her church. With a group of volunteers, she went to register to vote and was denied. On the bus ride home, the group was stopped by local police. During this tense road stop, Hamer began to sing, and her voice calmed others. After this she became an activist. During her involvement in the Civil Rights movement, she was imprisoned, beaten, and even shot at, but she didn't give in. Her faith was key to her focus.

Insight

This video shows how a previously politically uninvolved person became an important activist. It also shows the obstacles that the law enforcement of the time posed.

Connection to Essential Question

The Essential Question is "How can words inspire change?" Hearing an activist speak changed Hamer's mind, and directly experiencing political suppression secured her convictions.

Connection to Performance-Based Assessment

The prompt is "Explain how words have the power to provoke, calm, or inspire." Hamer was inspired to protest, and her singing inspired her companions to resist.

Media Complexity Rubric: Fannie Lou Hamer	
Quantitative Measures	
Format and Length: Video, 5 minutes.	
Qualitative Measures	
Knowledge Demands 1 — 2 — **3** — 4 — 5	To fully understand video, it is helpful to have some background information about conditions for African Americans in the South in the early 1900s.
Structure 1 — 2 — **3** — 4 — 5	Multiple images are shown of area (Mississippi Delta, plantations, town and people of Ruleville), but there is low correspondence between images and audio. For example, Fannie Lou, the focus, is not shown until the end, and many significant locations, such as the church and courthouse, are discussed but never shown.
Language Conventionality and Clarity 1 — **2** — 3 — 4 — 5	Narration has clear and concrete descriptions of events and people. Sentences are not complex, though some are lengthy. Pace of narration is slow and diction is clear.
Levels of Meaning/Purpose 1 — 2 — **3** — 4 — 5	Purpose of video is clear and straightforward from audio track. Images support some of the information (town and people of Ruleville, bus driver) but do not add much support to understanding of the story as a whole.

MY NOTES

ADVISING

You may wish to direct students to use the generic **First-Read** and **Close-Read Guides** in the Print Student Edition. Alternatively, you may wish to print copies of the genre-specific **First-Read** and **Close-Read Guides** for students. These are available online in the Interactive Student Edition or Unit Resources.

FIRST READ

Students should perform the steps of the first read independently.

NOTICE: Students should focus on the basic elements of the text to ensure they understand what is happening.

ANNOTATE: Students should mark any passages they wish to revisit during their close read.

CONNECT: Students should increase their understanding by connecting what they've read to other texts or personal experiences.

RESPOND: Students will write a summary to demonstrate their understanding.

Point out to students that while they will always complete the Respond step at the end of the first read, the other steps will probably happen somewhat concurrently. Remind students that they will revisit their first-read annotations during the close read.

After students have completed the First-Read Guide, you may wish to assign the **Text Questions** for the selection that are available in the Digital Teacher's Edition.

Anchor Standards

In the first two sections of the unit, students worked with the whole class and in small groups to gain topical knowledge and greater understanding of the skills required by the anchor standards. In this section, they are asked to work independently, applying what they have learned, and demonstrating increased readiness for college and career.

INDEPENDENT LEARNING

First-Read Guide

Tool Kit
First-Read Guide and Model Annotation

Use this page to record your first-read ideas.

Selection Title: ______________________________

NOTICE

NOTICE new information or ideas you learn about the unit topic as you first read this text.

ANNOTATE

ANNOTATE by marking vocabulary and key passages you want to revisit.

First Read (NOTICE, ANNOTATE, RESPOND, CONNECT)

CONNECT ideas within the selection to other knowledge and the selections you have read.

RESPOND by writing a brief summary of the selection.

CONNECT

RESPOND

STANDARD
Reading Read and comprehend complex literary and informational texts independently and proficiently.

PERSONALIZE FOR LEARNING

Strategic Support

Annotations To help students organize their first-read annotations for a later revisit during the close read, encourage them to annotate words or passages and then apply a code. The codes will differentiate annotations according to their purpose or relationship to the text and/or student. Direct students to the Tool Kit to see a model of the use of the codes.

Annotation Codes

* * Key Idea
* ! I love it!
* ? I have questions
* O Unfamiliar or important word
* ___ Context Clues

Close-Read Guide

Tool Kit
Close-Read Guide and Model Annotation

Use this page to record your close-read ideas.

Selection Title: ______________________________

Close Read the Text

Revisit sections of the text you marked during your first read. Read these sections closely and **annotate** what you notice. Ask yourself **questions** about the text. What can you **conclude?** Write down your ideas.

ANNOTATE · QUESTION · Close Read · CONCLUDE

Analyze the Text

Think about the author's choices of patterns, structure, techniques, and ideas included in the text. Select one, and record your thoughts about what this choice conveys.

QuickWrite

Pick a paragraph from the text that grabbed your interest. Explain the power of this passage.

STANDARD
Reading Read and comprehend complex literary and informational texts independently and proficiently.

DIGITAL PERSPECTIVES

CLOSE READ

Students should begin their close read by revisiting the annotations they made during their first read.

Analyze the Text

Then, students should analyze one of the author's choices regarding the following elements:

- **patterns,** such as repetition or parallelism
- **structure,** such as cause-and-effect or problem-solution
- **techniques,** such as description or dialogue
- **ideas,** such as the author's main idea or claim

Quickwrite

Responses will vary.

MAKE IT INTERACTIVE
Group students according to the selection they have chosen. Then, have students meet to discuss the selection in depth. Their discussions should be guided by their insights and questions.

PERSONALIZE FOR LEARNING

Strategic Support

Analyze the Text Help students complete the Analyze the Text section of the Close-Read Guide. Remind students to study the way that a writer addresses a topic. Suggest that students identify writing-related annotations with these codes:

- **WP:** a writing pattern that is interesting or functional. Remind students to look for word choice, sentence length, or rhythms in the writing.
- **WS:** writing structures that support the genre. For example, students might note the introduction or conclusion, the claims or main ideas, or the key parts of a plot.
- **L:** literary elements or techniques that bring out the art in the writing. Remind students to look for figurative language or other devices that reflect the author's style.
- **I:** Ideas that the author addresses. Ask students to think about the message of the writing.

Once students identify a part of the text, they can then focus on thinking about how that section contributes to the whole.

Share Your Independent Learning

Prepare to Share

Explain to students that sharing what they have learned from their Independent Learning selection provides classmates who read a different selection with an opportunity to consider the text as a source of evidence during the Performance-Based Assessment. As students prepare to share, remind them to highlight how their selection contributed to their knowledge of how words can effect change as well as how the selection connects to the question *How can words inspire change?*

Learn From Your Classmates

As students discuss the Independent Learning selections, direct them to take particular note of how their classmates' chosen selections align with their current position on the Performance-Based Assessment question. Explain how words have the power to provoke, calm, or inspire.

Reflect

Students may want to add their reflection to their Evidence Log, particularly if their insight relates to a specific selection from the unit.

MAKE IT INTERACTIVE

Pair students and have them share their reflections with each other. After each student reads the reflection to his or her partner, encourage them to ask each other the following questions and to have a conversation.

- Do you think your reflection shows you think in a different way about civil rights?
- Let's combine our ideas to show how our selections are different but contribute to the topic of civil rights.

Evidence Log Support students in completing their Evidence Log. This paced activity will help prepare them for the Performance-Based Assessment at the end of the unit.

INDEPENDENT LEARNING

EVIDENCE LOG

Go to your Evidence Log and record what you learned from the text you read.

Share Your Independent Learning

Prepare to Share

How can words inspire change?

Even when you read or learn you learn something independently, you can continue to grow by sharing what you've learned with others. Reflect on the text you explored independently and write notes about its connection to the unit. In your notes, consider why this text belongs in this unit.

Learn From Your Classmates

Discuss It Share your ideas about the text you explored on your own. As you talk with your classmates, jot down ideas that you learn from them.

Reflect

Review your notes and underline the most important insight you gained from these writing and discussion activities. Explain how this idea adds to your understanding of the literature of civil rights.

STANDARDS

Speaking and Listening
Initiate and participate effectively in a range of collaborative discussions with diverse partners on grades 9–10 topics, texts, and issues, building on others' ideas and expressing their own clearly and persuasively.

AUTHOR'S PERSPECTIVE **Ernest Morrell, Ph.D.**

Preparing Students to Be Powerful Speakers Use these suggestions to help students develop the ability to speak confidently in large discussions or presentations:

1. To help students overcome their fear of public speaking, have them visualize success, practice and get feedback on their speech, and exercise briefly before the speech to release stress.
2. Emphasize the importance of speaking loudly and clearly when presenting to the class. The farther away a listener is, the louder a speaker must talk to be heard clearly. Also have students practice speaking with clarity and articulation, paying special attention to not slurring contractions, reversing sounds, omitting letters, and adding letters.
3. As students share in whole groups, remind them to listen carefully and fully before responding, take notes while listening so they can respond on point, and speak with courtesy and respect. They may also wish to draft points for a response quickly before speaking.
4. To field questions, tell students to repeat the question before answering it, as this allows a few seconds to think about a response as well as make sure that everyone hears the question.

PERFORMANCE-BASED ASSESSMENT PREP

Review Evidence for an Informative Essay

At the beginning of the unit, you expressed your ideas in response to the following direction:

Explain how words have the power to provoke, calm, or inspire.

EVIDENCE LOG

Review your Evidence Log and your QuickWrite from the beginning of the unit. Did you learn anything new?

NOTES

Identify at least three pieces of information that interested you about the Civil Rights movement and its literature.

1.

2.

3.

Identify a real-life experience that illustrates one of your revised ideas about literature and the Civil Rights movement:

____

Develop your thoughts into a topic sentence for an informative essay. Complete this sentence starter:
I learned a great deal about the literature of civil rights when

____

Evaluate Your Evidence Consider the information you learned. Did the texts you read expand your knowledge? If not, make a plan.

- ☐ Do more research
- ☐ Talk with my classmates
- ☐ Reread a selection
- ☐ Ask an expert
- ☐ Other: ______________________________

STANDARDS
Writing
Write informative/explanatory texts to examine and convey ideas, concepts, and information clearly and accurately through the effective selection, organization, and analysis of content.

DIGITAL PERSPECTIVES

Review Evidence for an Informative Essay

Evidence Log Students should understand that their ideas could evolve as they learn more about the subject and are exposed to additional points of view. Point out that just because they have formed ideas on the direction *Explain how words have the power to provoke, calm, or inspire* doesn't mean that their ideas can't change after careful consideration of their learning and evidence.

Evaluate the Strength of Your Evidence

Remind students that there are many different types of evidence they can use to support their thesis, including:

- direct quotations from sources
- paraphrases of ideas
- summaries
- anecdotes
- examples

In addition to ensuring they have sufficient evidence to support their thesis, students should evaluate the reliability of their evidence. Discuss the characteristics that make evidence credible:

- reliable sources, including government, educational, and professional organizations
- reputation of the source (i.e., is the person quoted an expert?)
- degree to which experts have reviewed the evidence for accuracy (e.g., some media outlets have rigorous fact-checking)

Writing to Sources: Informative Essay

Students should complete the Performance-Based Assessment independently, with little to no input or feedback during the process. Students should use word processing software to take advantage of editing tools and features.

Prior to beginning the Assessment, ask students to think about ways words have provoked, calmed, or inspired them in their lives.

Review the Elements of an Informational Text

Students can review the work they did earlier in the unit as they complete the Performance-Based Assessment. They may also consult other resources such as:

- the elements of informative text, including a clear thesis statement, facts and evidence from a variety of reliable sources, and a clear introduction, body, and conclusion.
- their Evidence Log
- their Word Network

Although students will use evidence from unit selections for their writing mode, they may need to collect additional evidence, including facts, statistics, anecdotes, quotations from authorities, or examples.

PERFORMANCE-BASED ASSESSMENT

SOURCES

- WHOLE-CLASS SELECTIONS
- SMALL-GROUP SELECTIONS
- INDEPENDENT LEARNING

WORD NETWORK

As you write and revise your informative essay, use your Word Network to help vary your word choices.

STANDARDS

Writing

- Introduce a topic or thesis statement; organize complex ideas, concepts, and information to make important connections and distinctions; include formatting, graphics, and multimedia when useful to aiding comprehension.
- Develop a topic with well-chosen, relevant, and sufficient facts, extended definitions, concrete details, quotations, or other information and examples appropriate to the audience's knowledge of the topic.
- Conduct short as well as more sustained research projects to answer a question (including a self-generated question), or solve a problem; narrow or broaden the inquiry when appropriate; synthesize multiple sources on the subject, demonstrating understanding of the subject under investigation.
- Gather relevant information from multiple authoritative print and digital sources, using advanced searches effectively; assess the usefulness of each source in answering the research question; integrate information into the text selectively to maintain the flow of ideas, avoiding plagiarism and following a standard format for citation including footnotes and endnotes.
- Draw evidence from literary or informational texts to support analysis, reflection, and research.
- Write routinely over extended time frames and shorter time frames for a range of tasks, purposes, and audiences.

PART 1

Writing to Sources: Informative Essay

In this unit, you read about various characters, both real and fictional, who are a part of the struggle for civil rights. Some used words to inspire others and share their own experiences, while others used words as a call to action.

Assignment

Write an **informative essay** on the following:

Explain how words have the power to provoke, calm, or inspire.

Use evidence from at least three of the selections you read and researched in this unit to express and support your thesis. If time permits, do outside research, using credible sources, to support your ideas with examples, facts, and quotations. Ensure that your ideas are fully supported, that you use a formal, objective tone, and that your organization is logical and coherent.

Reread the Assignment Review the assignment to be sure you fully understand it. The task may reference some of the academic words presented at the beginning of the unit. Be sure you understand each of the words given below in order to complete the assignment correctly.

Academic Vocabulary

disrupt	coherent	notation
aggregate	express	

Review the Elements of an Informational Text Before you begin writing, read the Informational Text Rubric. Once you have completed your first draft, check it against the rubric. If one or more of the elements are missing or not as strong as they could be, revise your essay to add or strengthen those components.

AUTHOR'S PERSPECTIVE Kelly Gallagher, M.Ed.

Building a Writing Portfolio With Students Teachers can create a portfolio that enables students to demonstrate the variety of writing they complete over the year. There are three elements of keeping a portfolio—collection of all the writing a student has done, selection of the best pieces, and reflection to evaluate growth.

Teachers can set the criteria using such categories as *Best Argument, Best Narrative Piece, Best Informative Piece, Best On-Demand Writing, Best Poetry, Best Blended Genre, Best Writing from Another Class, Best Model of Revision,* and *Best Single Line You Wrote this Year*. Students should also include a reflective letter at the end of the year. To help them learn to reflect, use questions like this throughout the year.

- Where does your writing still need improvement? How will you improve?
- Reflect on a struggle you faced during this unit. How did you overcome it?
- Discuss a specific writing strategy you used and how it worked for you.
- What strengths have you developed as a writer? Where are those strengths found in this portfolio?

At the end of the year, students can review these pieces to see their growth as writers.

Informative Text Rubric

Score	Focus and Organization	Evidence and Elaboration	Conventions
4	The introduction engages the reader and states a thesis in a compelling way. The informative essay includes a clear introduction, body, and conclusion. The essay uses facts and evidence from a variety of reliable sources. The conclusion summarizes ideas and offers fresh insight into the thesis.	The essay includes specific reasons, details, facts, and quotations from selections and outside resources to support thesis. The tone of the essay is always formal and objective. The language is always precise and appropriate for the audience and purpose.	The essay consistently uses standard English conventions of usage and mechanics.
3	The introduction engages the reader and sets forth the thesis. The essay includes an introduction, body, and conclusion. The essay uses facts and evidence from a variety of sources. The conclusion summarizes ideas.	The essay includes some specific reasons, details, facts, and quotations from selections and outside resources to support the thesis. The tone of the essay is mostly formal and objective. The language is generally precise and appropriate for the audience and purpose.	The essay demonstrates general accuracy in standard English conventions of usage and mechanics.
2	The introduction sets forth the thesis. The essay includes an introduction, body, and conclusion, but one or more parts is weak. The essay uses facts and evidence from a few sources. The conclusion partially summarizes ideas.	The essay includes a few reasons, details, facts, and quotations from selections and outside resources to support the thesis. The tone of the essay is occasionally formal and objective. The language is somewhat precise and appropriate for the audience and purpose.	The essay demonstrates some accuracy in standard English conventions of usage and mechanics.
1	The introduction does not state the thesis clearly. The essay does not include an introduction, body, and conclusion. The essay does not use a variety of facts and evidence. The conclusion does not summarize ideas.	Reliable and relevant evidence is not included. The tone of the essay is not objective or formal. The language used is imprecise and not appropriate for the audience and purpose.	The essay contains mistakes in standard English conventions of usage and mechanics.

DIGITAL PERSPECTIVES

Informative Text Rubric

As you review the Informative Text Rubric with students, remind them that the rubric is a resource that can guide their revisions. Students should pay particular attention to the differences between a conclusion that summarizes ideas (a score of 3) and a conclusion that summarizes ideas and offers fresh insight into the thesis (a score of 4).

Speaking and Listening: Multimedia Presentation

Students should annotate their informative essay in preparation for the multimedia presentation, marking the important elements (a clear thesis statement, cohesive integration, correct grammar and formal style) as well as facts and evidence from a variety of reliable, credited sources.

Remind students that the effectiveness of a multimedia presentation relies on how the speaker establishes credibility with his or her audience. If a speaker comes across as confident and authoritative, it will be easier for the audience to give credence to the speaker's presentation.

Review the Multimedia Presentation Rubric As you review the Multimedia Presentation Rubric with students, remind them that it is a valuable tool that can help them plan their presentation. They should strive to include all of the criteria required to achieve a score of 3. Draw their attention to some of the subtle differences between scores of 2 and 3.

PERFORMANCE-BASED ASSESSMENT

PART 2

Speaking and Listening: Multimedia Presentation

Assignment
After completing the final draft of your informative essay, use it as the foundation for a three-to five-minute **multimedia presentation**.

STANDARDS

Speaking and Listening
- Present information, findings, and supporting evidence clearly, concisely and logically such that listeners can follow the line of reasoning and the organization, development, substance, and style are appropriate to purpose, audience, and task.
- Make strategic use of digital media in presentations to enhance understanding of findings, reasoning, and evidence and to add interest.
- Adapt speech to a variety of contexts and tasks, demonstrating a command of formal English when indicated or appropriate.

Do not simply read your essay aloud. Instead, take the following steps to make your presentation lively and engaging.

- Go back to your essay and annotate the most important ideas and details.
- Choose audio clips and visuals to support your presentation.
- Deliver your presentation with conviction, maintaining eye contact with your audience.

Review the Multimedia Presentation Rubric The criteria by which your multimedia presentation will be evaluated appear in the rubric below. Review these criteria before presenting to ensure that you are prepared.

	Content	Use of Media	Presentation Techniques
3	The introduction engages the audience and establishes the thesis in a compelling way. The presentation provides strong, valid reasons and evidence that support the thesis. The media support the thesis. The conclusion restates thesis and offers fresh insight.	The speaker focuses the right amount of time on each part. The media add interest to the presentation. Media are used evenly throughout the presentation. Listeners can follow presentation.	The speaker maintains eye contact and speaks effectively. Media are audible and visible. The speaker presents with strong conviction and energy.
2	The introduction sets out a thesis. The presentation includes some valid reasons and evidence that support the thesis. The media offer some support for the thesis. The conclusion offers some insight into the thesis.	The speaker focuses the right amount of time on most parts. Media add some interest to the presentation. Media are used in some parts of the presentation but not others. Listeners can mostly follow presentation.	The speaker mostly maintains eye contact and speaks effectively sometimes. Media are mostly audible and visible. The speaker presents with some level of conviction and energy.
1	The introduction does not set out a thesis. The presentation does not include reasons or evidence to support the thesis. The media do not support the thesis. The conclusion does not restate the thesis.	The speaker spends too much time on some parts of the presentation, and too little on others. Media do not add interest to the presentation. Media are used poorly throughout the presentation. Listeners cannot follow presentation.	The speaker does not maintain eye contact or speak effectively. Media are not visible or audible. The speaker presents with little conviction or energy.

DIGITAL PERSPECTIVES

Preparing for Assignment To help students understand what an effective multimedia presentation looks and sounds like, find examples of a Silicon Valley event in which a new product is being unveiled. Note that even though they won't be able to match the high production values of these events, students will still be able to learn something about the characteristics of a strong presentation.

Reflect on the Unit

Now that you've completed the unit, take a few moments to reflect on your learning. Use the questions below to think about where you succeeded, what skills and strategies helped you, and where you can continue to grow in the future.

Reflect on the Unit Goals

Look back at the goals at the beginning of the unit. Use a different colored pen to rate yourself again. Think about readings and activities that contributed the most to the growth of your understanding. Record your thoughts.

Reflect on the Learning Strategies

Discuss It Write a reflection on whether you were able to improve your learning based on your Action Plans. Think about what worked, what didn't, and what you might do to keep working on these strategies. Record your ideas before a class discussion.

Reflect on the Text

Choose a selection that you found challenging and explain what made it difficult.

Explain something that surprised you about a text in the unit.

Which activity taught you the most about the literature of civil rights? What did you learn?

SCAN FOR MULTIMEDIA

Reflect on the Unit

- Have students watch the video on Reflecting on Your Learning.
- A video on this topic is available online in the Professional Development Center.

Reflect on the Unit Goals

Students should re-evaluate how well they met the unit goals now that they have completed the unit. You might ask them to provide a written commentary on the goal they made the most progress with as well as the goal they feel warrants continued focus.

Reflect on the Learning Strategies

Discuss It If you want to make this a digital activity, go online and navigate to the Discussion Board. Alternatively, students can share their learning-strategy reflections in a class discussion.

Reflect on the Text

Consider having students share their text reflections with one another.

MAKE IT INTERACTIVE

Have students prepare one slide using presentation software that summaries their reflection.

Collate student slides into a presentation that can be viewed by the class. Students should be prepared to give a 30-second oral summary for their slide.

Unit Test and Remediation

After students have completed the Performance-Based Assessment, administer the Unit Test. Based on students' performance on the test, assign the resources as indicated on the Interpretation Guide to remediate. Students who take the test online will be automatically assigned remediation, as warranted by test results.

UNIT 4

Star-Crossed Romances

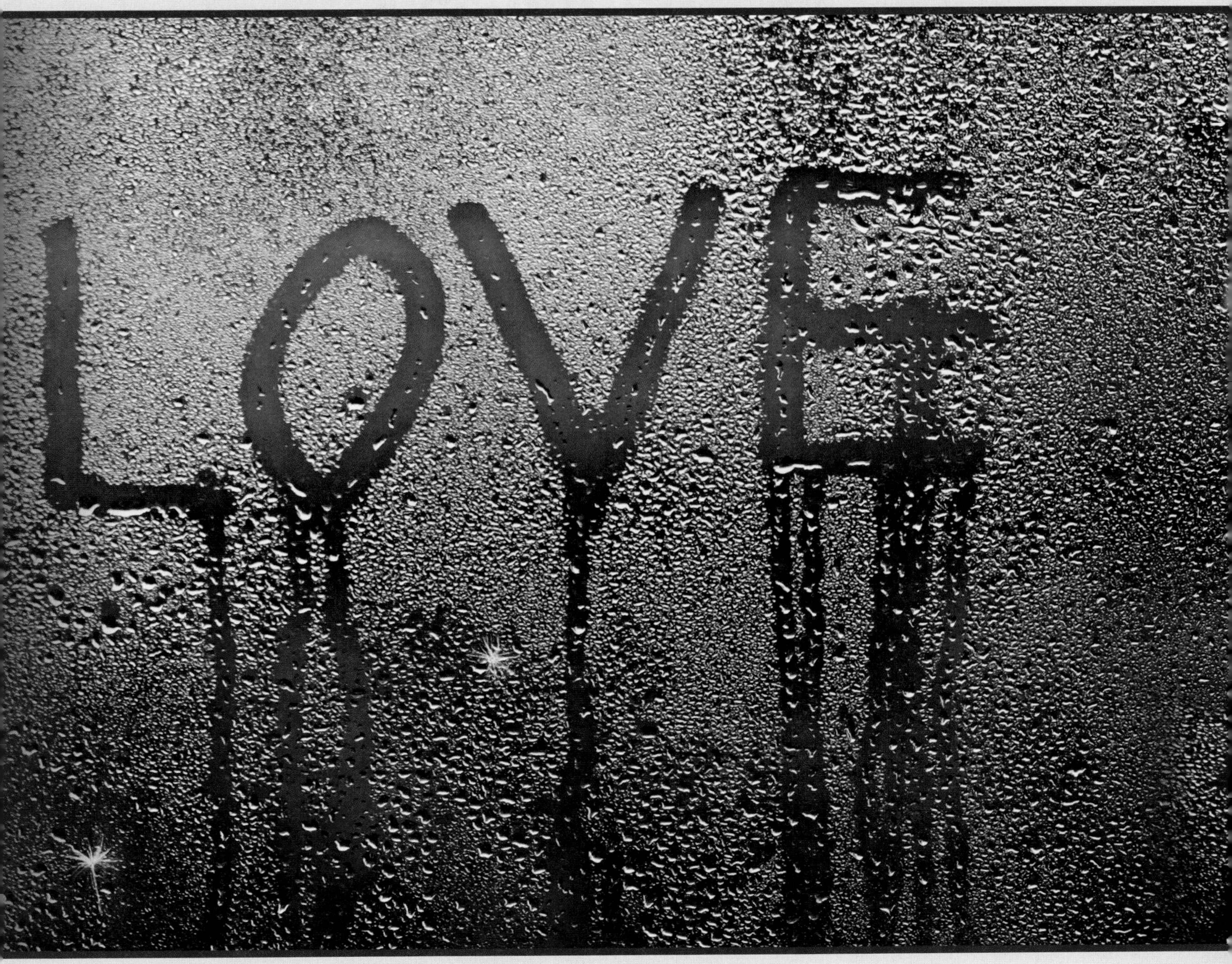

Jump Start

Free will is defined as "the ability to choose how to act; the ability to make choices that are not controlled by fate."

Engage students in a discussion about free will. Ask students, "By exercising free will, can a person change or control his or her fate?" Lead students to compare the meaning and concept of *free will* to the meaning and concept of *fate*.

Star-Crossed Romances

Ask students what the phrase *star-crossed romances* suggests to them. Point out that as they work through this unit, they will read many examples about star-crossed romances.

Video

Project the introduction video in class, ask students to open the video in their interactive textbooks, or have students scan the BouncePage icon with their phones to access the video.

Discuss It If you want to make this a digital activity, go online and navigate to the Discussion Board. Alternatively, students can share their responses in a class discussion.

Block Scheduling

Each day in this pacing calendar represents a 40–50 minute class period. Teachers using block scheduling may combine days to reflect their class schedule. In addition, teachers may revise pacing to differentiate and support core instruction by integrating components and resources as students require.

UNIT 4

Star-Crossed Romances

Do we determine our own direction in life and in love? Or are we simply at the mercy of fate?

A Modern Take on *Romeo and Juliet*

Discuss It How can a centuries-old love story remain relevant for modern audiences?

Write your response before sharing your ideas.

SCAN FOR MULTIMEDIA

356

Pacing Plan

Day	Activity
1	Unit Introduction
2	Introduce Whole-Class Learning
3	Literature and Culture
4–12	*The Tragedy of Romeo and Juliet*, Acts I–V
13	Pyramus and Thisbe
14–15	Performance Task

DIGITAL PERSPECTIVES | Audio | Video | Document | Annotation Highlights | EL Highlights | Online Assessment

UNIT 4

UNIT INTRODUCTION

ESSENTIAL QUESTION: Do we determine our own destinies?

LAUNCH TEXT
ARGUMENT MODEL
Romeo and Juliet: A Tragedy? Or Just a Tragic Misunderstanding?

WHOLE-CLASS LEARNING

LITERATURE AND CULTURE
Historical Context
The Tragedy of Romeo and Juliet

ANCHOR TEXT: DRAMA
The Tragedy of Romeo and Juliet
William Shakespeare
Act I
Act II
Act III
Act IV
Act V
MEDIA CONNECTION: Romeo and Juliet

COMPARE

ANCHOR TEXT: SHORT STORY
Pyramus and Thisbe
Ovid, retold by Edith Hamilton

PERFORMANCE TASK
WRITING FOCUS:
Write an Argument

SMALL-GROUP LEARNING

LITERARY CRITICISM
Romeo and Juliet Is a Terrible Play, and David Leveaux Can't Change That
Alyssa Rosenberg

In Defense of *Romeo and Juliet:* It's Not Childish, It's *About* Childishness
Noah Berlatsky

JOURNALISM
Twenty Years On: The Unfinished Lives of Bosnia's Romeo and Juliet
Gordana Sandić-Hadžihasanović

COMPARE

MEDIA: NEWSCAST
Tragic Romeo and Juliet Offers Bosnia Hope
Nic Robertson

PERFORMANCE TASK
SPEAKING AND LISTENING FOCUS:
Present an Argument

INDEPENDENT LEARNING

MYTH
Popocatepetl and Ixtlaccihuatl
Juliet Piggott Wood

POETRY
Annabel Lee
Edgar Allan Poe

NONFICTION
What's the Rush?: Young Brains Cause Doomed Love
Lexi Tucker

GRAPHIC NOVEL
from William Shakespeare's Romeo & Juliet
artwork by Eli Neugeboren

NEWS ARTICLE
If Romeo and Juliet Had Cell Phones
Misty Harris

PERFORMANCE-BASED ASSESSMENT PREP
Review Evidence for an Argument

PERFORMANCE-BASED ASSESSMENT
Argument: Essay and Multimedia Presentation
PROMPT:
Should the opinions of others affect our own choices or destinies?

357

Do we determine our own destinies?

Introduce the Essential Question and point out that students will respond to related prompts.

- **Whole-Class Learning** *Which has a greater impact on the characters in these texts: destiny or personal choices?*
- **Small-Group Learning** *What is compelling about stories in which people face a tragic destiny?*
- **Performance-Based Assessment** *Should the opinions of others affect our own choices or destinies?*

Using Trade Books

Refer to the Teaching with Trade Books section in this book or online in the Interactive Teacher's Edition for suggestions on how to incorporate the following thematically related novels into this unit.

- *The Fault in Our Stars* by John Green
- *Jane Eyre* by Charlotte Bronte
- *Wuthering Heights* by Emily Bronte

Current Perspectives

To increase student engagement, search online for stories about star-crossed romances, and invite your students to recommend stories they find. Always preview content before sharing it with your class.

- **News Story: "The Most Tragic Love Stories In History,"** by Heather Whipps (LiveScience, February 12, 2009) A look at five historical tragic romances.
- **News Story "A Modern-Day Tale of Romeo and Juliet,"** by Mukul Devichand (BBC News, November 23, 2013) A Yemen couple's love leads to their arrest.

16 — Introduce Small-Group Learning
17, 18, 19 — *Romeo and Juliet* Is a Terrible Play
20, 21, 22 — In Defense of *Romeo and Juliet:* It's Not Childish, It's *About* Childishness
23, 24 — Twenty Years On: The Unfinished Lives of Bosnia's Romeo and Juliet
25 — Media: Tragic Romeo and Juliet Offers Bosnia Hope
26 — Performance Task
27 — Introduce Independent Learning
28 — Independent Learning
29, 30 — Performance-Based Assessment

About the Unit Goals

These unit goals were backward designed from the Performance-Based Assessment at the end of the unit and the Whole-Class and Small-Group Performance Tasks. Students will practice and become proficient in many more standards over the course of this unit.

Unit Goals

Review the goals with students and explain that in this unit, they will improve their skills in reading, writing, research, language, and speaking and listening.

Reading Goals Tell students they will read and evaluate a written argument. They will also read a myth, poetry, and a news article to better understand the ways writers express ideas.

Writing and Research Goals Tell students that they will learn the elements of writing an argument, or taking a position. They will write their own arguments along with organizing and sharing ideas, reflecting on experiences, and gathering evidence. They will conduct research to clarify and explore ideas.

Language Goals Tell students that they will develop a deeper understanding of correctly integrating quotations to convey meaning. They will then practice correctly integrating quotations here in their own writing.

Speaking and Listening Explain to students that they will work together to build ideas, develop consensus, and communicate with one another. They will also learn to incorporate audio, visuals, and text in presentations.

HOME Connection

A Home Connection letter to students' parents or guardians is available in the Interactive Teacher's Edition. The letter explains what students will be learning in this unit and how they will be assessed.

Unit Goals

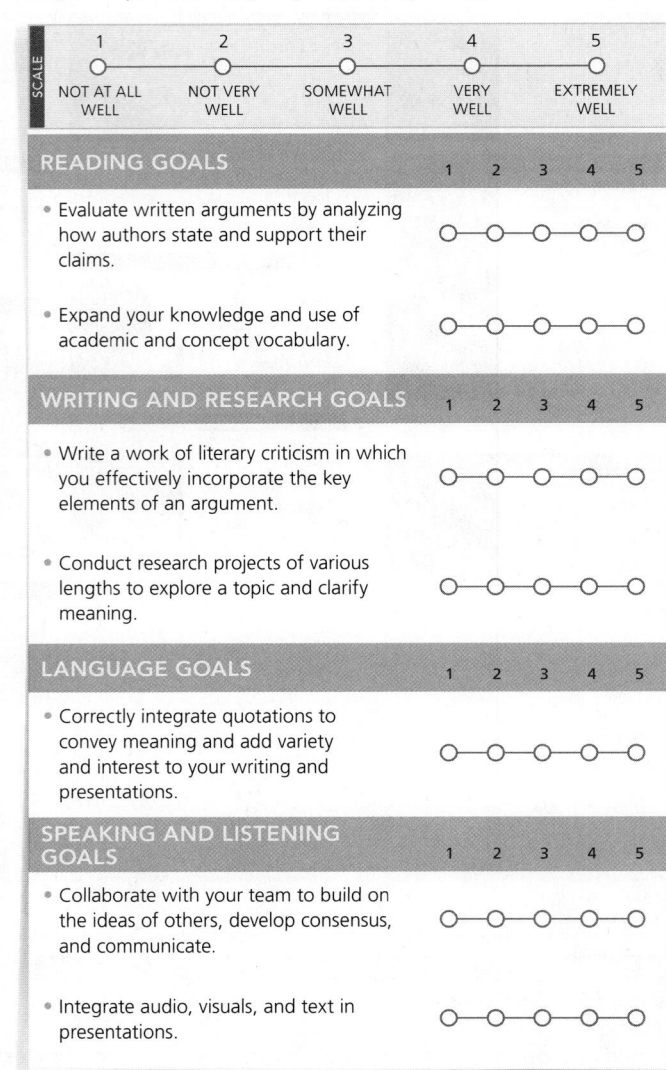

Throughout this unit, you will deepen your understanding of destiny in life and literature by reading, writing, speaking, listening, and presenting. These goals will help you succeed on the Unit Performance-Based Assessment.

Rate how well you meet these goals right now. You will revisit your ratings later when you reflect on your growth during this unit.

SCALE

1	2	3	4	5
NOT AT ALL WELL	NOT VERY WELL	SOMEWHAT WELL	VERY WELL	EXTREMELY WELL

READING GOALS	1	2	3	4	5
• Evaluate written arguments by analyzing how authors state and support their claims.	O	O	O	O	O
• Expand your knowledge and use of academic and concept vocabulary.	O	O	O	O	O

WRITING AND RESEARCH GOALS	1	2	3	4	5
• Write a work of literary criticism in which you effectively incorporate the key elements of an argument.	O	O	O	O	O
• Conduct research projects of various lengths to explore a topic and clarify meaning.	O	O	O	O	O

LANGUAGE GOALS	1	2	3	4	5
• Correctly integrate quotations to convey meaning and add variety and interest to your writing and presentations.	O	O	O	O	O

SPEAKING AND LISTENING GOALS	1	2	3	4	5
• Collaborate with your team to build on the ideas of others, develop consensus, and communicate.	O	O	O	O	O
• Integrate audio, visuals, and text in presentations.	O	O	O	O	O

Language
Acquire and use accurately general academic and domain-specific words and phrases, sufficient for reading, writing, speaking, and listening at the college and career readiness level; demonstrate independence in gathering vocabulary knowledge when considering a word or phrase important to comprehension or expression.

SCAN FOR MULTIMEDIA

AUTHOR'S PERSPECTIVE Ernest Morrell, Ph.D.

Taking Responsibility for Learning Teachers can talk to students about becoming motivated learners. Start by having students reflect on things they are good at outside of class, such as sports, music, and video games. Then have students think about how they take responsibility for their own achievement in these areas, such as having the discipline to practice. Help students further understand the value of becoming independent learners by providing tips on how to do so, such as these:

1. **Be self-motivated and persistent.** Don't be discouraged when faced with minor set-backs.
2. **Develop effective time management skills.** Track assignments and deadlines.
3. **Seek help when necessary.** Don't be afraid to get assistance when you need it.
4. **Set realistic goals.** Then plan ways to achieve your goals.
5. **Believe in yourself.** Visualize success. Recognize that you have the ability to soar.

Encourage students to add to this list to help them focus on strategies for taking ownership of their learning.

Academic Vocabulary: Argument

Academic terms appear in all subjects and can help you read, write, and discuss with more precision. Here are five academic words that will be useful to you in this unit as you analyze and write arguments.

Complete the chart.

1. Review each word, its root, and the mentor sentences.
2. Use the information and your own knowledge to predict the meaning of each word.
3. For each word, list at least two related words.
4. Refer to a dictionary or other resources if needed.

TIP

FOLLOW THROUGH

Study the words in this chart, and highlight them or their forms wherever they appear in the unit.

WORD	MENTOR SENTENCES	PREDICT MEANING	RELATED WORDS
endure ROOT: ***-dur-*** "hard"	1. Just when I thought I couldn't *endure* another minute on the bus, the driver announced that we had arrived. 2. It amazes me that stories from centuries ago continue to *endure*.		endurance; duration
pathos ROOT ***-path-*** "feeling"	1. The novel offers the author's usual blend of humor, drama, and *pathos*. 2. The *pathos* of the drama left audiences in tears.		
compelling ROOT ***-pel-*** "drive"; "push"	1. The jury ruled in favor of the defense because of its *compelling* evidence. 2. When accepting her award, the actress gave a *compelling* speech.		
propose ***-pose-*** "place"	1. At weddings, it is customary for the best man to *propose* a toast to the newly married couple. 2. In his address to Congress, the president will *propose* several new policies and initiatives.		
recurrent ***-curr-*** "run"	1. Hillary has a *recurrent* dream in which she is running and flying at the same time. 2. During the fall, *recurrent* rainstorms led to widespread flooding.		

DIGITAL PERSPECTIVES

Academic Vocabulary: Argument

Introduce the blue academic vocabulary words in the chart on the student page. Point out that the root of each word provides a clue to its meaning. Discuss the mentor sentences to ensure students understand each word's usage. Students should also use the mentor sentences as context to help them predict the meaning of each word. Check that students are able to fill the chart in correctly. Complete pronunciations, parts of speech, and definitions are provided for you. Students are expected only to provide the definition.

Possible responses:

endure *v.* (ehn DUR)
Meaning: to last, to continue; to put up with
Related words: endurance, duration
Additional words related to root *-dur-*: procedure, durable

pathos *n.* (PAY thos)
Meaning: quality that creates a feeling of sadness or pity
Related words: sympathy, sympathetic
Additional words related to root *-path-*: empathy, empathic

compelling *adj.* (kuhm PEHL ihng)
Meaning: interesting and attractive; persuasive
Related words: compelled, compellingly
Additional words related to root *-pel-*: propel, impel

propose *v.* (pruh POHZ)
Meaning: to suggest
Related words: proposition, proposing
Additional words related to root *-pose-*: suppose, impose

recurrent *adj.* (rih KUR uhnt)
Meaning: repeating
Related words: recur, recurrently
Additional words related to root *-curr-*: occurrence, currency

PERSONALIZE FOR LEARNING

English Language Support

Cognates Many of the academic words have Spanish cognates. Use these cognates with students whose home language is Spanish.

recurrent – recurrente   propose – proponer

Not all English learners will recognize and use these cognates automatically. Help students build their cognate awareness by pointing out that these cognates share the same root in both English and Spanish. **ALL LEVELS**

INTRODUCTION

Purpose of the Launch Text

The Launch Text provides students with a common starting point to address the unit topic. After reading the Launch Text, all students will be able to participate in discussions about star-crossed romances.

Lexile: 950 The easier reading level of this selection makes it perfect to assign for homework. Students will need little or no support to understand it.

In addition, "*Romeo and Juliet*: A Tragedy? Or Just a Tragic Misunderstanding?" provides a writing model for the Performance-Based Assessment students complete at the end of the unit.

Launch Text: Argument Model

Illustrate to students the way the author methodically presents the argument throughout the piece, providing a series of examples that build upon the previous points.

Point out that the author quickly, clearly, and concisely presents the argument: "The outcome was not inevitable. Instead, their own bad decisions brought them to that terrible point." From there, the author uses plot details and quotes to make a powerful case. The conclusion then restates the argument.

Encourage students to read this text on their own and annotate unfamiliar words and sections of text they think are particularly important.

AUDIO SUMMARIES

Audio summaries of "*Romeo and Juliet*: A Tragedy? Or Just a Tragic Misunderstanding?" are available in both English and Spanish in the Interactive Teacher's Edition or Unit Resources. Assigning these summaries before students read the Launch Text may help them build additional background knowledge and set a context for their reading.

LAUNCH TEXT | ARGUMENT MODEL

This selection is an example of an **argumentative text,** a type of writing in which an author states and defends a position on a topic. This is the type of writing you will develop in the Performance-Based Assessment at the end of the unit.

As you read, look at the way the writer builds a case. Mark the text to help you answer this question: What is the writer's position, and what evidence supports it?

Romeo and Juliet: A Tragedy? Or Just a Tragic Misunderstanding?

^ Les Ballets de Monte Carlo, Monaco's national ballet company, performs *Romeo and Juliet* at the London Coliseum in 2015.

NOTES

1 The main characters of William Shakespeare's *Romeo and Juliet* have long inspired audiences' pity. For hundreds of years, people have watched as the two characters meet, fall in love, and—both heartbroken—take their last breaths. While the play's ending is tragic, the famous lovers' deaths are the result of their own impulsive decisions. Romeo and Juliet were not destined to die in each other's arms. That outcome was not inevitable. Instead, their own bad decisions brought them to that terrible point.

2 When the play begins, the city of Verona is being battered by a rivalry between two important families: the House of Montague and the House of Capulet. Swordsmen from both families hurl insults at one another and fight in the streets. Romeo, the son of the head of the Montagues, sneaks into the Capulets' party. Here he sees Juliet, daughter of Capulet, and the two fall head-over-heels in love. Even though their families would never accept their union, they are more than willing to throw away everything to be together—having known each other for barely an evening. Indeed, Juliet says as much of their love:

> It is too rash, too unadvised, too sudden;
> Too like the lightning, which doth cease to be
> Ere one can say it lightens. . . .

3 The sheer lack of care with which they pursue their romance is startling. Neither tries to find a way to reconcile their parents to the idea, or even to flee the city. Instead, they hurriedly marry in secret.

4 As the play continues, the drama of poor judgment unfolds. Juliet's cousin Tybalt goads Romeo to fight. Unwilling to fight a relative of

SCAN FOR MULTIMEDIA

AUTHOR'S PERSPECTIVE **Elfrieda Hiebert, Ph.D.**

Rare Words Increasing reading comprehension relies on a connection between fluency and vocabulary. **Rare words** are less frequently used words that represent what might be a common idea. More complex text leads to rarer words to express refined concepts. For example, rather than describing a character as *nervous*, an author might use the word *disconcerted, perturbed,* or *flustered.* Therefore, vocabulary instruction takes different forms across content areas.

Juliet's, Romeo refuses. The situation deteriorates further, eventually leading to Romeo's killing of Tybalt. Throughout these events, Romeo simply reacts in the heat of the moment. He is not guided by principle or clear thinking. The result is that he is forced to leave Verona in exile, a situation that sets up the final deadly outcome.

5 Juliet is shocked when she hears of Romeo's exile. In another example of startling miscalculation, she chooses to fake her own death in order to escape to be with him. She does not even wait to make sure Romeo knows about her plan. At this point, the play proceeds with a cruel irony that ends with Juliet and Romeo taking their own lives.

6 This play features numerous references to the stars, which symbolize destiny or the absence of human choice and control. These references seem to support the idea that Romeo and Juliet never had any influence over the paths their lives would take. They were destined to meet and destined to die. Indeed, the Prologue calls the two leads "star-cross'd lovers," meaning lovers doomed by the stars, or destiny. Romeo suggests as much before he goes to the party where he first meets Juliet:

> I fear, too early; for my mind misgives
> Some consequence yet hanging in the stars

7 When Romeo hears of Juliet's "death," he cries out against fate: "Then, I defy you, stars!" Yet she is not actually dead, nor is the situation controlled by the stars. Romeo does not know this, but the audience does—Juliet's "death" is not a result of destiny but of her own choices. Despite some instances of pure ill fortune, most of the tragic events are the result of Romeo and Juliet's youthful decisions and haste.

8 In short, Romeo and Juliet were not the victims of destiny. Instead, the two stumbled into their own tragedy. Rather than suffering inevitable doom, they made fatal mistakes. The stars may shine above the events of this play, but that is not the true reason for the tragic outcome.

NOTES

WORD NETWORK FOR DESTINY

Vocabulary A Word Network is a collection of words related to a topic. As you read the selections in this unit, identify interesting words related to the idea of destiny and add them to your Word Network. For example, you might begin by adding words from the Launch Text, such as *inevitable, fortune,* and *influence.* Continue to add words as you complete this unit.

Tool Kit
Word Network Model

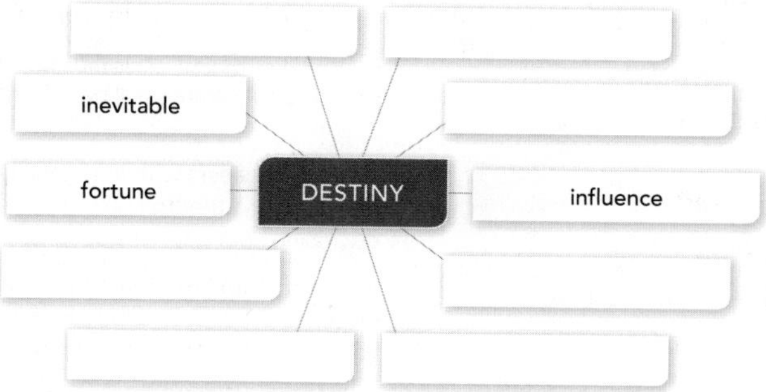

DIGITAL PERSPECTIVES

Word Network for Star-Crossed Romances

Tell students that they can fill in the Word Network as they read texts in the unit, or they can record the words elsewhere and add them later. Point out to students that people may have personal associations with some words. A word that one student thinks is related to star-crossed romances might not be a word another student would pick. However, students should feel free to add any word they personally think is relevant to their Word Network. Each person's Word Network will be unique. If you choose to print the Word Network, distribute it to students at this point so they can use it throughout the rest of the unit.

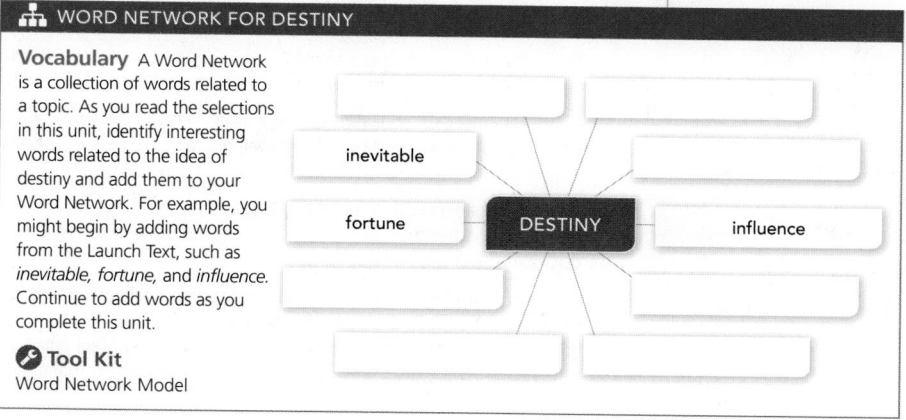

In reading/language arts, for instance, where many rare unknown words pertain to known concepts, teachers should emphasize semantic connections across words. This can be achieved effectively with concept maps or word networks, graphic organizers that help students understand the essential attributes, qualities, or characteristics of a word's meaning. Here's a brief example for the rare word *sluggish:*

heavy	blah	indolent	moony	stiff
inactive	comatose	inert	off	sullen
lethargic	dopey	laid-back	phlegmatic	torpid
listless	languid	pokey	unresponsive	down

Digital tools, including online dictionaries, often have features to help demonstrate the increasing complexity of the spectrum of these words by filtering out levels of complexity.

INTRODUCTION

Summary

Have students read the introductory paragraph. Provide them with tips for writing a summary:

- Write in the present tense.
- Make sure to include the title of the work.
- Be concise: a summary should not be equal in length to the original text.
- If you need to quote the words of the author, use quotation marks.
- Don't put your own opinions, ideas, or interpretations into the summary. The purpose of writing a summary is to accurately represent what the author says, not to provide a critique.

If necessary, students can refer to the Tool Kit for help in understanding the elements of a good summary.

See possible Summary on Student page.

Launch Activity

Explain to students that as they work on this unit they will have many opportunities to discuss the topic of star-crossed romances. Before they begin the launch activity, explain that they are about to conduct an experiment on how people might react when a personal decision is taken out of their hands.

While discussing the decisions they would actually make, you might want to also encourage a discussion about real-life decisions they've made versus ones that were out of their hands.

Summary

Write a summary of "*Romeo and Juliet:* A Tragedy? Or Just a Tragic Misunderstanding?" A **summary** is a concise, complete, and accurate overview of a text. It should not include a statement of your opinion or an analysis.

Possible response: In "Romeo and Juliet: A Tragedy? Or Just a Tragic Misunderstanding?" the author argues that Romeo and Juliet were not destined to die in each other's arms and that their own bad decisions led to their downfall.

The author provides a list of reasons why he believes this to be the case. First, he points out that the characters pursue their romance with an incredible lack of care, marrying in secret instead of attempting to convince their parents it's a good idea. Romeo's poor judgment, including the killing of Tybalt, shows that he can't think clearly. There are other ways in which the two main characters made bad decisions, like when Juliet faked her death.

Put together, the author claims this is evidence of how Romeo and Juliet are responsible for what happened to them.

Launch Activity

Destiny or Choice? Consider these statements. Check the one that most closely aligns to your point of view. Then, explain your reasoning.

☐ The paths we take in life are driven largely by fate.

☐ The paths we take in life are determined mostly by others.

☐ The paths we take in life are primarily the results of our choices.

- Think of a decision you need to make. Perhaps you are deciding whether to take a up a new sport, strike up a new friendship, or study a new subject.
- Choose the decision you want to make. Then, write down your various options on separate small pieces of paper, one piece of paper for each option.
- Trade your papers with a partner. Discuss all of the options. Then, invite your partner to make your decision for you. Reverse the process, discussing your partner's options.
- After you both have shared your options and decisions, shuffle the pieces of paper and randomly choose one. Discuss how you feel when your decision is made by someone else versus how you feel when you let fate decide. Then, discuss which decision you will actually make.

VOCABULARY DEVELOPMENT

Academic Vocabulary Reinforcement Students will benefit from additional examples and practice with the academic vocabulary. Reinforce their comprehension with "show-you-know" sentences. The first part of the sentence uses the vocabulary word in an appropriate context. The second part of the sentence—the "show you know" part—clarifies the first. Model the strategy with this example for *pathos*:

> Following the breakup with Alyssa, the *pathos* that surrounded Mark was unavoidable; the sadness would not lift for quite some time.

Then give students these sentence prompts and coach them in creating the clarification part:

1. He didn't know if he could *endure* another brutal winter; _______.

Possible response: last year's record-breaking snowfall total of nine feet was unbearable.

2. Tyler decided to propose to Nicole; _______.

Possible response: he loved her very much and wanted to spend the rest of his life with her.

QuickWrite

Consider class discussions, presentations, the video, and the Launch Text as you think about the prompt. Record your first thoughts here.

PROMPT: **Should the opinions of others affect our own choices or destinies?**

Possible response: The opinions of other people should affect our choices, but not too much. It's important for a person to take into consideration the thoughts of his family and friends, because they love and care about him. They will often have a thoughtful perspective regarding the decision a person is about to make and the impact it could have on his life.

That said, the decisions a person makes mostly affect just one person, which is why the opinions of others shouldn't have too much of an impact on the choices we make.

EVIDENCE LOG FOR STAR-CROSSED ROMANCES

Review your QuickWrite. Summarize your thoughts in one sentence to record in your Evidence Log. Then, record textual details or evidence from "*Romeo and Juliet:* A Tragedy? Or Just a Tragic Misunderstanding?" that support your initial position.

Prepare for the Performance-Based Assessment at the end of the unit by completing the Evidence Log after each selection.

Tool Kit
Evidence Log Model

Title of Text: ____________________ Date: __________

CONNECTION TO PROMPT	TEXT EVIDENCE/DETAILS	ADDITIONAL NOTES/IDEAS

How does this text change or add to my thinking? Date: __________

SCAN FOR MULTIMEDIA

DIGITAL PERSPECTIVES

QuickWrite

In this QuickWrite, students should present their own response to the prompt based on the material they have read and viewed in the Unit Overview and Introduction. This initial response will help inform their work when they complete the Performance-Based Assessment at the end of the unit. Students should present a clear, strongly stated argument and support it with reasoned evidence. Encourage them to use examples from their own lives.

See possible QuickWrite on Student page.

Evidence Log for Star-Crossed Romances

Students should record their initial position in their Evidence Logs along with evidence from "*Romeo and Juliet*: A Tragedy? Or Just a Tragic Misunderstanding?" that supports this position.

If you choose to print the Evidence Log, distribute it to students at this point so they can use it throughout the rest of the unit.

Performance-Based Assessment: Refining Your Thinking

- Have students watch the video on Refining Your Thinking.
- A video on this topic is available online in the Professional Development Center.

WriteNow Express and Reflect

Write a Play Have students write a short play in which different characters engage in an argument. Suggest that the play take place in a courtroom, since it is a place where different sides present an argument in order to win a legal battle. You might want to cite famous movies that have courtroom scenes, such as *Judgment at Nuremberg, Inherit the Wind, To Kill a Mockingbird,* and *A Few Good Men.*

Explain to students that because the characters will have to take opposing sides, they will need to consider both sides of the argument they are exploring in their play.

WHOLE-CLASS LEARNING

Do we determine our own destinies?

Engage students in discussion about whether they feel we are free to make all decisions and choices in life. How does a person know that he or she is acting with free will and not conforming to what others want? In the case of star-crossed romances, does exercising free will always mean a tragic end? Could it be the reverse, because free will is *not* exercised, there is tragedy?

During Whole-Class Learning, students will read about star-crossed romances, fate, and free will.

Whole-Class Learning Strategies

Review the Learning Strategies with students and explain that as they work through Whole-Class Learning they will develop strategies to work in large-group environments.

- Have students watch the video on Whole-Class Learning Strategies.
- A video on this topic is available online in the Professional Development Center.

Discuss some action items to add to the chart as a class before students complete it on their own. For example, for "Interact and share ideas," solicit the following from students: encourage others to share ideas and possible answers even when they are unsure.

Block Scheduling

Each day in this Pacing Plan represents a 40–50 minute class period. Teachers using block scheduling may combine days to reflect their class schedule. In addition, teachers may revise pacing to differentiate and support core instruction by integrating components and resources as students require.

OVERVIEW: WHOLE-CLASS LEARNING

ESSENTIAL QUESTION:

Do we determine our own destinies?

The idea of destiny was once connected to notions about the stars, which some believed controlled human life. This gave rise to the idea of "star-crossed" lovers—those for whom a sorrowful fate seemed inevitable. While our understanding of the stars has changed, questions about the role destiny plays in our lives remain. You will work with your whole class to explore the idea of destiny. The selections you are going to read present conflicts between destiny and personal choice in two tales of tragic love.

Whole-Class Learning Strategies

Throughout your life, in school, in your community, and in your carer, you will continue to learn and work in large-group environments.

Review these strategies and the actions you can take to practice them as you work with your whole class. Add ideas of your own for each step. Get ready to use these strategies during Whole-Class Learning.

STRATEGY	ACTION PLAN
Listen actively	• Eliminate distractions. For example, put your cell phone away. • Keep your eyes on the speaker. •
Clarify by asking questions	• If you're confused, other people probably are, too. Ask a question to help your whole class. • If you see that you are guessing, ask a question instead. •
Monitor understanding	• Notice what information you already know and be ready to build on it. • Ask for help if you are struggling. •
Interact and share ideas	• Share your ideas and answer questions, even if you are unsure. • Build on the ideas of others by adding details or making a connection. •

SCAN FOR MULTIMEDIA

Pacing Plan

Day	Activity
1	Unit Introduction
2	Introduce Whole-Class Learning
3	Literature and Culture
4–12	*The Tragedy of Romeo and Juliet*, Acts I–V
13	Pyramus and Thisbe
14–15	Performance Task

WHOLE-CLASS LEARNING (Days 2–15)

CONTENTS

LITERATURE AND CULTURE

Historical Context

The Tragedy of Romeo and Juliet

ANCHOR TEXT: DRAMA

The Tragedy of Romeo and Juliet

William Shakespeare

ACT I

Love blossoms despite an old family feud, but can that love last?

ACT II

ACT III

ACT IV

ACT V

▸ MEDIA CONNECTION: Romeo and Juliet

COMPARE

ANCHOR TEXT: SHORT STORY

Pyramus and Thisbe

Ovid,
retold by Edith Hamilton

Deeply in love, a young couple is divided by both real and symbolic walls.

PERFORMANCE TASK

WRITING FOCUS

Write an Argument

The Whole-Class readings are classic tales of true love thwarted by an array of different forces. Both raise questions about individual choice, destiny, and our paths through life. After reading you will write an argument in the form of literary criticism.

Contents

Anchor Texts Preview the anchor texts and media with students to generate interest. Encourage students to discuss other texts they may have read or movies or television shows they may have seen that deal with the issues of star-crossed romances.

You may wish to conduct a poll to determine which selection students think looks more interesting, and discuss the reasons for their preference. Students can return to this poll after they have read the selections to see if their preference changed.

Performance Task

Write an Argument Explain to students that after they have finished reading the selections, they will write an argument, or take a position on individual choice, destiny, and our paths through life. To help them prepare, encourage students to think about the topic as they progress through the selections and as they participate in the Whole-Class Learning experience.

Introduce Small-Group Learning — 16

Romeo and Juliet Is a Terrible Play — 17, 18, 19

In Defense of *Romeo and Juliet*: It's Not Childish, It's *About* Childishness — 20, 21, 22

Twenty Years On: The Unfinished Lives of Bosnia's Romeo and Juliet — 23, 24

Media: Tragic Romeo and Juliet Offers Bosnia Hope — 25

Performance Task — 26

Introduce Independent Learning — 27

Independent Learning — 28

Performance-Based Assessment — 29, 30

The Tragedy of Romeo and Juliet, Act I

AUDIO SUMMARIES
Audio summaries of *The Tragedy of Romeo and Juliet,* Act I are available online in both English and Spanish in the Interactive Teacher's Edition or Unit Resources. Assigning these summaries prior to reading the selection may help students build additional background knowledge and set a context for their first read.

Summary

The Tragedy of Romeo and Juliet, by William Shakespeare, begins with a street fight between the feuding Montague and Capulet families. The prince of the city arrives to break up the fight. He announces that if anyone from these families disturbs the peace again, he will have them put to death. In the next scene, we meet Romeo. He is pining about no longer being loved by a woman named Rosaline. His friend persuades him to go to a party. Juliet goes to the same one. The two meet each other and instantly fall in love but then learn that their families are enemies.

Insight

This classic tragedy examines love and youthful impulsiveness. It is an excellent introduction to Shakespeare.

ESSENTIAL QUESTION:
Do we determine our own destinies?

Connection to Essential Question

The play suggests that Romeo and Juliet were fated to fall in love and die.

WHOLE-CLASS LEARNING PERFORMANCE TASK
Which has a greater impact on the characters in these texts: destiny or personal choices?

UNIT PERFORMANCE-BASED ASSESSMENT
Should the opinions of others affect our own choices or destinies?

Connection to Performance Tasks

Whole-Class Learning Performance Task The text suggests that the protagonists' fates are a matter of destiny. Yet, a reader can easily argue that different choices, or better luck, could have saved them.

Unit Performance-Based Assessment Following their families' advice could have kept Romeo and Juliet alive. But it would not have made them happy.

DIGITAL PERSPECTIVES — Audio | Video | Document | Annotation Highlights | EL Highlights | Online Assessment

LESSON RESOURCES

	Making Meaning	Language Development
Lesson	**First Read** **Close Read** **Analyze the Text** **Analyze Craft and Structure**	**Concept Vocabulary** **Word Study** **Author's Style**
Instructional Standards	**RL.10** By the end of grade 9, read and comprehend literature . . . **RL.3** Analyze how complex characters develop . . . **RL.5** Analyze how an author's choices . . .	**L.4.b** Identify and correctly use patterns of word changes . . . **L.5.a** Interpret figures of speech . . .
STUDENT RESOURCES		
Available online in the Interactive Student Edition or Unit Resources	Selection Audio First-Read Guide: Drama Close-Read Guide: Drama	Evidence Log Word Network
TEACHER RESOURCES		
Selection Resources Available online in the Interactive Teacher's Edition or Unit Resources	Audio Summaries Annotation Highlights EL Highlights English Language Support Lesson: Oxymoron Analyze Craft and Structure: Elements of Drama	Concept Vocabulary and Word Study Author's Style: Figurative Language
Reteach/Practice (RP) Available online in the Interactive Teacher's Edition or Unit Resources	Analyze Craft and Structure: Elements of Drama (RP)	Word Study: Latin Prefix *trans-* (RP) Author's Style: Figurative Language (RP)
Assessment Available online in Assessments	Selection Test	
My Resources	A Unit 4 Answer Key is available online and in the Interactive Teacher's Edition.	

Reading Support

Text Complexity Rubric: *The Tragedy of Romeo and Juliet*, Act I	
Quantitative Measures	
Lexile: NP **Text Length:** 6,105 words	
Qualitative Measures	
Knowledge Demands ① ② ③ ④ **❺**	Students will need information about the historical context. Some of this information is covered in the background information.
Structure ① ② ③ ④ **❺**	The selection is a Shakespearean play written in blank verse. Line breaks will likely be challenging for students.
Language Conventionality and Clarity ① ② ③ ④ **❺**	The selection contains complex sentences, unfamiliar syntax, figurative language, challenging vocabulary, and Elizabethan language.
Levels of Meaning/Purpose ① ② **❸** ④ ⑤	While the classic theme of star-crossed lovers is accessible to students, they may have difficulty identifying that theme as they work to understand the drama's language and structure.

DECIDE AND PLAN

English Language Support

Provide English Learners with support for **Structure and Language** as they read the selection.

Structure Students may have a difficult time keeping track of all the characters. Encourage students to create a chart that sorts Montagues, Capulets, and other characters. Make sure students understand the role of each character before moving on.

Language Students will likely struggle with the Elizabethan language. Make a list of common Elizabethan words: *anon (soon), aye (yes), e'en (even), e'er (ever), hence (away; from here), hither (here), whence (where), wilt (will), withal (in addition), would (wish)*. Help students find sentences with these words and figure out the meaning.

Strategic Support

Provide students with strategic support to ensure that they can successfully read the text.

Knowledge Demands Using the background information, discuss the situation depicted in the story, asking what aspects of it are more likely for people to experience. Discuss that the theme of "star-crossed lovers" is a common one. Discuss other stories with the theme.

Language If students have difficulty with complex sentences, work together to break down sentences into smaller chunks in order to understand their meaning. Ask students to highlight words or phrases that they don't understand. As a group, define some of the terms they find difficult.

Challenge

Provide students who need to be challenged with ideas for how they can go beyond a simple interpretation of the text.

Text Analysis Discuss what it means to use oxymoronic language. Point out that Shakespeare often used oxymorons. For example, Act I, lines 171–175: *Why, then, O brawling love! O loving hate, / O any thing, of nothing first created! / O heavy lightness, serious vanity, / Misshapen chaos of well-seeming forms, / Feather of lead, bright smoke, cold fire, sick health*... Ask students to find other examples of oxymoronic language. Why would an author choose to use this technique? What is the effect?

Written Response Challenge students to write a summary of what they know about Romeo and Juliet at this point. How are their circumstances different? How are they the same? Have students share their ideas in small groups.

TEACH

Read and Respond

Have the class do their first read of the selection. Then have them complete their close read. Finally, work with them on the Making Meaning and Language Development activities.

Standards Support Through Teaching and Learning Cycle

IDENTIFY NEEDS

Analyze results of the Beginning-of-Year Assessment, focusing on the items relating to Unit 4. Also take into consideration student performance to this point and your observations of where particular students struggle.

DECIDE AND PLAN

- If students have performed poorly on items matching these standards, then provide selection scaffolds before assigning them the on-level lesson provided in the Student Edition.
- If students have done well on the Beginning-of-Year Assessment, then challenge them to keep progressing and learning by giving them opportunities to practice the skills in depth.
- Use the Selection Resources listed on the Planning pages for *The Tragedy of Romeo and Juliet*, Act I to help students continually improve their ability to master the standards.

Instructional Standards: *The Tragedy of Romeo and Juliet*, Act I

	Catching Up	This Year	Looking Forward
Reading	You may wish to administer the **Analyze Craft and Structure: Elements of Drama (RP)** worksheet to better familiarize students with dialogue and set directions.	**RL.5** Analyze how an author's choices concerning how to structure a text, order events within it, and manipulate time create such effects as mystery, tension, or surprise.	Challenge students to consider how directors of plays may change stage directions.
Language	You may wish to administer the **Author's Style: Figurative Language (RP)** worksheet to better familiarize students with oxymora. Review the **Word Study: Latin Prefix *trans-* (RP)** worksheet with students to ensure they understand the Latin root word.	**L.5.a** Interpret figures of speech in context and analyze their role in the text. **L.4.b** Identify and correctly use patterns of word changes that indicate different meanings or parts of speech.	Challenge students to think up their own original oxymora. Have students locate other Latin or Greek prefixes they may recognize in the selection.

TEACH

Implement the planned lesson, and gather evidence of student learning.

ANALYZE AND REVISE

- Analyze student work for evidence of student learning.
- Identify whether or not students have met the expectations in the standards.
- Identify implications for future instruction.

LITERATURE AND CULTURE

Historical Context

This section analyzes the key events and characteristics of the time period that led to the Renaissance, including expanding of trade, exploration of new lands, Protestant reformation, and the Civil War. Have students connect these key events and characteristics with the unit topic.

Elizabethan England

Explain that the Renaissance is often called the Elizabethan Age because Queen Elizabeth's rule of England from 1558 to 1603 was so successful. Tell students that "Renaissance" is a French word that means "rebirth." The period is called a rebirth because artists and scholars rejected many of the ideas and philosophies from the Middle Ages. This time after the fall of the Roman Empire was chaotic, and many considered it to be a dark time in human cultural and economic achievement. As part of the rebirth, artists and scholars looked back to the learning and knowledge of ancient Rome and Greece. The Renaissance is often marked as the beginning of the modern age.

The Renaissance in England According to historians, the English Renaissance began about 100 years after the Italian Renaissance began. The English Renaissance and the Italian Renaissance are very similar. The one major difference is that the English Renaissance emphasized music and literature, and the visual arts were not as significant as they were in the Italian Renaissance.

^ Queen Elizabeth ruled from 1558 to 1603, but her reign was so successful that the entire Renaissance in England is often called the Elizabethan Age.

Historical Context

Elizabethan England

The Rebirth of Learning Sometime around the year 1350, at the end of the Middle Ages, Italian city-states, such as Venice and Genoa, began to trade extensively with the East. With trade came more knowledge and growing curiosity about the world. Soon, Italy was leading the way in a flowering of European learning known as the Renaissance (REHN uh sons). Commerce, science, and the arts blossomed as people shifted their focus to the interests and pursuits of human life here on earth. The astronomers Copernicus and Galileo questioned long-held beliefs to prove that the world was round and that it circled the sun, not vice versa. Navigators, including Christopher Columbus and Ferdinand Magellan, braved the seas in tiny boats to explore new lands and seek new trade routes. Religious thinkers, such as Martin Luther and John Calvin, challenged the authority of the Roman Catholic Church and spurred the Protestant Reformation. Artists, including Michelangelo and Leonardo da Vinci, painted and sculpted lifelike human beings. Writers, such as Miguel de Cervantes and William Shakespeare, wrote insightfully about complex human personalities in fiction and drama.

The Renaissance in England The Renaissance was slow to come to England. The delay was caused mainly by civil war between two great families, or houses, claiming the English throne—the House of York and the House of Lancaster. The conflict ended in 1485, when Henry Tudor of the House of Lancaster took the throne as King Henry VII. After a successful rule in which English commerce expanded, he was succeeded by his son Henry VIII, whose reign was filled with turmoil. Henry sought a divorce from the Spanish princess Catherine of Aragon so that he could remarry and possibly have a son. He was convinced that only a male would be strong enough to hold the throne. When the Pope refused to grant the divorce, Henry renounced the Roman Catholic Church and made England a Protestant nation. Ironically, his remarriage, to a woman named Anne Boleyn, produced not a son but a daughter, Elizabeth. Even more ironically, when Elizabeth took the throne, she proved to be one of the strongest monarchs that England has ever known.

QUICK INSIGHT

The symbol of the House of York was a white rose, while the symbol of the House of Lancaster was a red rose. For that reason, the civil wars fought between the two houses were called the Wars of the Roses. Shakespeare wrote several plays about English monarchs involved in these conflicts.

CROSS-CURRICULAR PERSPECTIVES

Science Polish astronomer Nicolaus Copernicus was the first to propose the notion of a heliocentric solar system, one in which Earth and other planets revolve around the sun. Prior to this, it was believed that Earth was the center of the universe. Galileo Galilei used the newly developed telescope to refine Copernicus's theory. Have interested students research the astronomical observations and the conclusions to which his revolutionary evidence led him. Encourage students to develop a monologue in which they play the role of Galileo describing what he saw through his telescope and drawing conclusions about the solar system based on these observations.

The Elizabethan World The reign of Elizabeth I is often seen as a golden age in English history. Treading a moderate and frugal path, Elizabeth brought economic and political stability to the nation, thus allowing commerce and culture to thrive. Advances in mapmaking helped English explorers sail the Old World and claim lands in the New. Practical inventions improved transportation at home. Craft workers created lovely wares for the homes of the wealthy. Musicians composed fine works for the royal court, and literature thrived, peaking with the plays of William Shakespeare.

London became a bustling capital on the busy River Thames (tehmz), where ships from all over the world sailed into port. The city attracted newcomers from the countryside and immigrants from foreign lands. Streets were narrow, dirty, and crowded, but they were also lined with shops where vendors sold merchandise from near and far. English women enjoyed more freedoms than did women elsewhere in Europe, and the class system was more fluid as well. To be sure, those of different ranks led very different lives. Yet even the lowborn were able to attend one of the city's most popular new amusements, the theater.

Elizabeth I and the Spanish Armada

In 1588, King Phillip of Spain sent an armada, or fleet of military ships, to invade England. At the time, Spain was the most powerful nation on earth. Nevertheless, the English soundly defeated the invading forces. The victory cemented Elizabeth's popularity with her people. Prior to the battle, the Queen visited her troops to inspire them to fight. Here is a portion of the speech she delivered:

> . . . And therefore I am come amongst you at this time, not as for my recreation or sport, but being resolved, in the midst and heat of the battle, to live or die amongst you all; to lay down, for my God, and for my kingdom and for my people, my honor and my blood, even the dust. I know I have but the body of a weak and feeble woman; but I have the heart of a king, and of a king of England too . . .

England's defeat of the Spanish Armada was a popular subject in fine art for centuries after the events. This print from 1850 shows one artist's imagining of the scene.

DIGITAL PERSPECTIVES

The Elizabethan World Explain to students that the Elizabethan era, marked by the reign of Elizabeth I (1558–1603), is usually considered the height of the English Renaissance. During this time there was relative peace amongst the religious factions of the nation; the government was effective and organized; the arts flourished; and navigation and exploration of the world began in earnest. During Elizabeth's reign, Sir Francis Drake successfully sailed around the world; Sir Walter Raleigh established the Virginia Colony; and Sir Humphrey Gilbert discovered Newfoundland. Show students a map of the old world. Encourage them to locate the Thames River.

Elizabeth I and the Spanish Armada

Explain to students that Queen Elizabeth I made England's naval strength a high priority during her reign. This era saw many advances in the technology of English shipbuilding. There were many factors that influenced the rising tension between Spain and England. Among them were religion and piracy. Spain was a devoted Catholic nation; England was Protestant. Additionally, English sailors had been encouraged by the English government to plunder Spanish ships. When King Phillip of Spain sent the Spanish fleet to attack and invade England in 1588, the English were heavily outnumbered and outgunned, making their victory even more impressive. Have students analyze Queen Elizabeth's speech to the troops. Ask students to discuss what her speech tells about her character, including her religious beliefs. Discuss how these qualities may have helped England defeat the Spanish.

Theater in Elizabethan England

Explain that during the Middle Ages, acting was not a prestigious occupation. Acting companies had no permanent venue, and actors received little compensation for their performances. During Elizabeth's reign, major acting companies earned permanent homes in the theaters that had been built. However, even these major acting companies were forced to tour whenever the London theaters were shut down because of the Plague.

Explain that a *groundling* is generally a poor spectator who stands in a pit or sits in one of the less expensive seats. In contrast, a noble belongs to a hereditary class with high social or political status. Nobles enjoyed the best seats in the theater.

England's First Theater During Shakespeare's day, acting was still viewed unfavorably by some religious factions. Because of this, theaters had to be built outside the actual city of London, across the River Thames. Women were not permitted to act, and acting companies were all male. Even the roles of women in plays were portrayed by young boys whose voices had not yet begun to change. Encourage students to discuss why officials may have banned plays in London.

Theater in Elizabethan England

Elizabethan audiences included all levels of society, from the "groundlings," who paid a penny entrance fee, to the nobility.

During the Middle Ages, simple religious plays were performed at inns, in castle halls, and on large wagons at pageants. In early Elizabethan times, acting companies still traveled the countryside to perform their plays. However, the best companies acquired noble patrons, or sponsors, who then invited the troupes to perform in their homes. At the same time, Elizabethan dramatists began to use the tragedies and comedies of ancient Greece and Rome as models for their plays. By the end of the sixteenth century, many talented playwrights had emerged, including Christopher Marlowe, Ben Jonson, and of course, William Shakespeare.

England's First Theater England's first successful public theater opened in 1576. Known simply as the Theatre, it was built by an actor named James Burbage. Since officials had banned the performance of plays in London, Burbage built his theater in an area called Shoreditch, just outside the London city walls. Some of Shakespeare's earliest plays were first performed here, including *The Tragedy of Romeo and Juliet,* which probably starred James Burbage's son, Richard, as Romeo.

When the lease on the Theatre expired, Richard Burbage, in charge of the company after his father died, decided to move the company to Southwark (SUHTH uhrk), just across the River Thames from London proper. The Shoreditch landlord had been causing problems, and Southwark was emerging as a popular theater district. Using timbers from the old theater building, Burbage had a newer theater built, bigger and better than the one before. It opened in 1599 and was called the Globe. Under that name it would become the most famous theater in the history of the English stage, for many more of Shakespeare's plays were first performed there.

QUICK INSIGHT

Audience members ate and drank while they watched the plays and apparently made a lot of noise. In 1900, archaeologists found the remains of the foundation of the original Globe Theatre. They also found the discarded shells of the many hazelnuts audiences munched on while watching performances.

QUICK INSIGHT

During Shakespeare's day, acting companies were entirely male. Women did not perform because it was considered improper. The roles of women were usually played by boys of about eleven, or twelve—that is, before their voices changed.

The modern Globe Theatre, rebuilt in the twentieth century a few hundred yards from the original site.

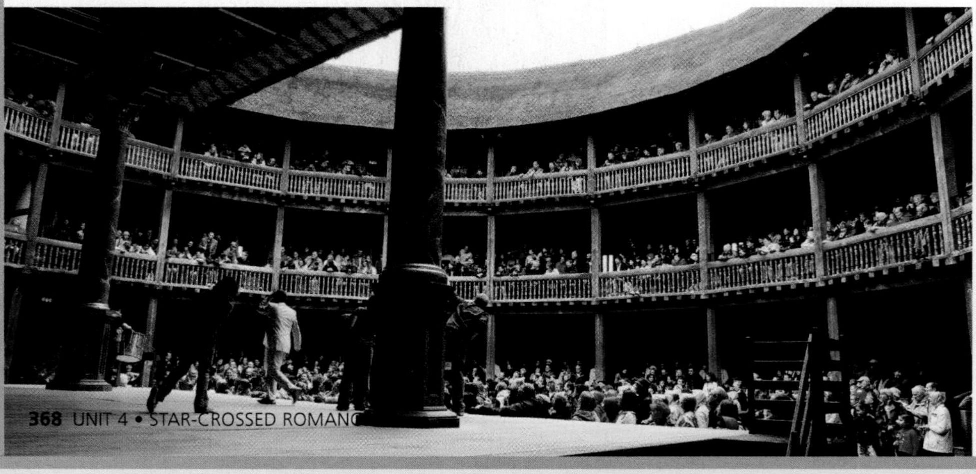

PERSONALIZE FOR LEARNING

English Language Support

False Cognates False cognates, or a pair of words in two different languages that sound similar but have very different meanings, can be confusing to English learners. For example, "city" is a false cognate and could be confusing to Spanish-speaking students because it is similar to the Spanish word "cita," which means an appointment. To help students understand the meaning, explain that "city" means a large town. The Spanish word for "city" is "ciudad." **ALL LEVELS**

Theater Layout No floor plans of the Theatre or the Globe survive, but people's descriptions and sketches of similar buildings suggest what they were like. They were either round or octagonal, with a central stage open to the sky. This stage stretched out into an area called the pit, where theatergoers called groundlings paid just a penny to stand and watch the play. The enclosure surrounding this open area consisted of two or three galleries, or tiers. The galleries accommodated audience members who paid more to watch the play while under shelter from the elements, and with some distance from the groundlings. The galleries probably also included a few elegant box seats, where members of the nobility could both watch the play and be seen by the masses.

Staging the Play The enclosure directly behind the stage was used not for seating but for staging the play. Actors entered and left the stage from doors at stage level. The stage also had a trap door through which mysterious characters, such as ghosts or witches, could disappear suddenly. Some space above the backstage area was used for storage or dressing rooms. The first gallery, however, was visible to the audience and used as a second stage. It would have been on a second stage like this that the famous balcony scene in *The Tragedy of Romeo and Juliet* was performed.

These open-air theaters did not use artificial light. Instead, performances took place in the afternoon, when it was still light outside. There was also no scenery in the theaters of Shakespeare's day. Instead, the setting for each scene was communicated through dialogue. With no need for set changes, scenes could follow one another in rapid succession. Special effects were simple—smoke might billow at the disappearance of a ghost, for example. By contrast, costumes were often elaborate. The result was a fast-paced, colorful production that lasted about two hours.

The Blackfriars In 1609, Shakespeare's acting company began staging plays in the Blackfriars Theatre as well as the Globe. Located in London proper, the Blackfriars was different from the earlier theaters in which Shakespeare's plays were performed. It was an indoor space with no open area for groundlings. Instead, it relied entirely on a wealthier clientele. It was also one of the first English theaters to use artificial lighting, an innovation that allowed for nighttime performances.

The Globe Theatre

The three-story structure, open to the air, could house as many as 3,000 people in the pit and surrounding galleries.

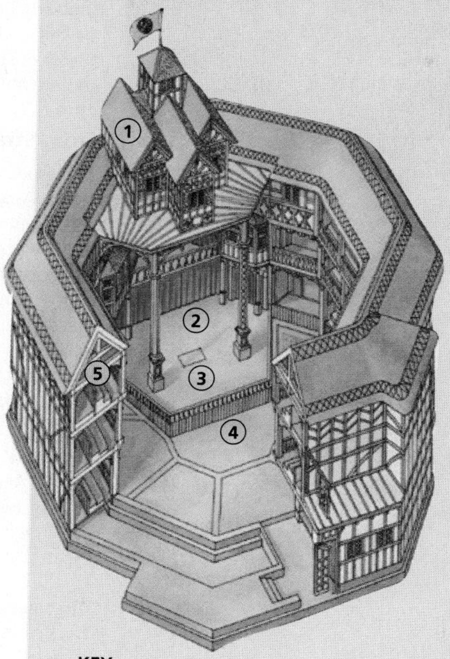

KEY

1. The hut, housing machinery used to lower characters and props to the stage
2. The stage trap, often used for the entrances and exits of special characters, such as ghosts or witches
3. The stage
4. The pit, where groundlings stood to watch the show
5. The galleries

DIGITAL PERSPECTIVES

The Globe Theatre

The original Globe Theatre was built in 1599 and was destroyed by fire in 1613. A second Globe Theatre was constructed on the same site in 1614 and then closed in 1642. In 1990, archaeologists found the remains of the foundation of the original Globe Theatre. They also found discarded shells from the many hazelnuts audience members ate during performances. Reconstruction of a replica Globe Theatre in London was initiated by American actor, director, and producer Sam Wanamaker. It was built approximately 750 feet from the site of the original theater. This modern reconstruction is called Shakespeare's Globe and was officially opened by Queen Elizabeth II in June of 1997. Have students review the illustration and point out where the groundlings and nobles most likely sat in the theater. Then, have students compare and contrast theaters today to those during the Renaissance.

William Shakespeare

Explain to students that very little was written about Shakespeare during his time, leading many to speculate that the glove-maker's son from Stratford was not the actual author of the many plays attributed to him. They argue that other individuals, such as Sir Francis Bacon, English statesman and author; Edward de Vere, 17th Earl of Oxford; Christopher Marlowe, an English playwright and poet; and William Stanley, 6th Earl of Derby, used the pseudonym of William Shakespeare. While historical documents give information about Shakespeare, the debate about who really wrote his plays will likely continue.

William Shakespeare, Playwright and Poet

Shakespeare's plays and poetry are regarded by many as the finest works ever written in English.

William Shakespeare (1564–1616) is widely revered as one of England's greatest writers. Four centuries after his death, his plays are still read and performed every day. Who was this remarkable author of so many masterpieces? In actual fact, we know very little about him.

From Stratford to London

Shakespeare grew up in Stratford-upon-Avon, a busy market town on the Avon River about 75 miles northwest of London. Church and town records indicate that his mother, Mary Arden, was the daughter of a wealthy farmer who owned the land on which Shakespeare's grandfather lived. Shakespeare's father, John, was a prosperous merchant who also served for a time as Stratford's mayor. Shakespeare most likely went to the local grammar school, where he would have studied Latin and Greek as well as English and world history. He would eventually put all those lessons to use in plays about historical figures, such as Julius Caesar and King Henry IV.

In 1582, when he was eighteen, Shakespeare married a woman named Anne Hathaway and had three children with her, including a set of twins. The next decade of his life is a mystery, but by 1592 he had moved to London, where he gravitated to the theater. Starting off an actor, he soon began writing plays as well. By 1594, he had become the principal playwright of the Lord Chamberlain's Men, the Burbages' acting company. Some of the early plays Shakespeare wrote at this time include the romantic comedy *The Taming of the Shrew* and the romantic tragedy *The Tragedy of Romeo and Juliet.*

Shakespeare was not just a performer and a playwright, however; he was also part owner of the theater company. This meant that he earned money in three ways—from fees for his plays, from his acting salary, and from his share of the company's profits. Those profits rose substantially after the Lord Chamberlain's Men moved to the Globe Theatre, where as many as 3,000 people might attend a single performance. It was at the Globe that many of Shakespeare's later masterpieces premiered, probably beginning with *The Tragedy of Julius Caesar* in 1599.

The King's Players In 1603, Queen Elizabeth I died, and her Scottish cousin took the throne as James I. Partial to the theater, James was particularly supportive of the Lord Chamberlain's Men, which had emerged as one of the two best acting companies in the land. Not only did it have a brilliant playwright in William Shakespeare; it also had a fine actor in Richard Burbage, who starred in most of Shakespeare's plays. In 1606, flattered by the

CROSS-CURRICULAR PERSPECTIVES

Social Studies There is no doubt that a man named William Shakespeare was born and died in Stratford-Upon-Avon, married Anne Hathaway, and had three children. These and other facts about his life are well established. Yet a group of literary scholars and amateur detectives are convinced that this William Shakespeare did not write the famous plays with which his name has long been associated. Their evidence differs, but the central question remains the same: How could a middle-class son of a merchant have been the author of such masterpieces? Have students form groups and conduct research on information that supports William Shakespeare as the author and also the possibility that another author was responsible for writing Shakespeare's plays. Invite students to conduct a debate, a mock trial, or a panel discussion to present their evidence.

king's patronage, the company changed its name to the King's Men. It is believed that Shakespeare wrote his great Scottish play, *The Tragedy of Macbeth,* to appeal particularly to James I.

Three years later, the King's Men began performing at the Blackfriars Theatre, using the Globe only in summer months. By using this indoor theater in winter, the King's Men further increased profits. The company did so well that Shakespeare was soon able to retire. In 1610, he moved back to Stratford-upon-Avon, buying one of the finest homes in town. He died of unknown causes in 1616.

Shakespeare Says . . .

Shakespeare's impact on the English language has been enormous. Not only did he coin new words and new meanings for old words, but he also used many expressions that have become part of our everyday speech. Here are a few examples.

EXPRESSION AND SOURCE	MEANING
Eat out of house and home *(Henry VI, Part 2)*	Eat so much that it makes the provider poor
For ever and a day *(The Taming of the Shrew)*	Indefinitely; with no end in sight
Give the devil his due *(Henry IV, Part 1)*	Recognize an opponent's achievement
Greek to me *(Julius Caesar)*	Completely unintelligible to me
Green-eyed monster *(Othello)*	Jealousy
In a pickle *(The Tempest)*	In trouble
In stitches *(Twelfth Night)*	Laughing so hard it hurts
Lay it on with a trowel *(As You Like It)*	Flatter excessively
Makes your hair stand on end *(Hamlet)*	Really frightens you
The milk of human kindness *(Macbeth)*	Compassion
A plague on both your houses *(Romeo and Juliet)*	I'm fed up with both sides (in an argument)
Salad days *(Antony and Cleopatra)*	Green, or naïve, youth
Star-crossed lovers *(Romeo and Juliet)*	Ill-fated lovers
Wear your heart upon your sleeve *(Othello)*	Show your love to all
Won't budge an inch *(The Taming of the Shrew)*	Will not give in; stands firm

DIGITAL PERSPECTIVES

Shakespeare Says . . .

Shakespeare's impact on our language is striking. During his time, the English language was not standardized, and grammar textbooks did not exist yet. This allowed authors and playwrights to have fun with and expand the language. The *Oxford English Dictionary* credits Shakespeare with introducing nearly 3,000 words into the language. He invented many of our words by creating words that had never been heard, combining words that had never been used together before, changing nouns into verbs, and changing verbs into adjectives. Some examples of Shakespeare's "new" words are: *buzzer, elbow, eyeball, label, outbreak, skim milk, unreal,* and *zany*.

How to Read Shakespeare

Shakespeare wrote his plays in Early Modern English, or Elizabethan English, which is linguistically different in grammar and syntax than the contemporary English we use today. It was also different in that many of the words Shakespeare used have either changed in meaning or spelling, or have fallen out of use.

Remind students that even though they might feel at first as though they can't make sense of what they are reading, they can make a guess at meaning if they pay attention to who is speaking, how the characters are behaving, and what is happening in the scene. Students can also refer to notes in the margins for words they don't understand. After they have read through the first act of the play, students will start to notice that some of the same words and phrases are repeated, and the language will become easier to understand.

Shakespeare wrote most of his plays in a meter called iambic pentameter. Simply stated, this is a term for the use of ten-syllable lines that have alternating stressed and unstressed syllables. Shakespeare used pairs of lines that rhymed, which are called couplets, and also unrhymed lines, which is called blank verse. Sometimes, Shakespeare employed prose, or regular spoken language, for depicting lower-class characters.

How to Read Shakespeare

Shakespeare wrote his plays in the language of his time. To the modern ear, however, that language can sound almost foreign. Certain words have changed meaning or fallen out of use. The idioms, slang, and humor of twenty-first-century America are very different from those of Elizabethan England. Even our way of viewing reality has changed. These differences present challenges for modern-day readers of Shakespeare. Here are some strategies for dealing with them.

CHALLENGE: Elizabethan Words

Many words Shakespeare used are now archaic, or outdated. A few types of these words appear here.

TYPE OF WORD	CONTEMPORARY ENGLISH	ELIZABETHAN ENGLISH	EXAMPLE FROM *ROMEO AND JULIET*
pronouns	*you, your, yours*	*thou, thy, thine*	*And if he hear* ***thee, thou*** *wilt anger him. (II.i.22)*
verbs	*come, will, do, has*	*cometh, wilt, doth, hath*	*Verona's summer* ***hath*** *not such a flower. (I.iii.77)*
time words	*morning, evening*	*morrow, even*	*Good* ***morrow****, father. (II.iii.31)*
familiar words used in unfamiliar ways	*if*	*an*	***An*** *I should live a thousand years, / I should never forget it. (I.iii.46–47)*
	fortunate	*happy*	*Oh,* ***happy*** *dagger, / This is thy sheath. (V.iii.182–3)*

STRATEGIES

Familiarize yourself with some of the most common archaic words in Shakespeare.

If a word is completely unfamiliar, look to the marginal notes for a translation. Otherwise, look for clues to the word's meaning in the surrounding text.

CHALLENGE: Elizabethan Syntax

The syntax, or word order, Shakespeare used may also be archaic. In contemporary English, the subject of a sentence usually appears before the verb. Shakespeare often inverts this order, placing the verb before the subject.

Contemporary English Syntax

What do **you** (s) **say** (v)?

Elizabethan English Syntax

What **say** (v) **you** (s)?

STRATEGY

If a sentence uses inverted syntax, identify its subject and verb. Then, rephrase the sentence, placing the subject before the verb.

CHALLENGE: Blank Verse

Shakespeare uses both prose and verse in his plays. The type of verse he wrote is called blank verse. In blank verse, each line has ten syllables, and every unstressed syllable is followed by a stressed one.

If ***ev****er* ***you*** *dis****turb*** *our* ***streets*** *a****gain****,*
Your ***lives*** *shall* ***pay*** *the* ***for****feit* ***of*** *the* ***peace****.* (*Romeo and Juliet*, I.i.87–88)

Often, a single sentence spans more than one line of verse. This is especially true when Shakespeare uses a semicolon to connect two or more clauses.

With love's light wings did I o'erperch these walls;
For stony limits cannot hold love out.... (*Romeo and Juliet*, II.ii.66–67)

STRATEGIES

Look for capital letters and end marks to see where sentences begin and end. Read challenging sentences aloud.

When a sentence is made up of two clauses connected by a semicolon, ask yourself how the ideas in the clauses relate to each other.

PERSONALIZE FOR LEARNING

English Language Support

Unfamiliar Words Non-native speakers may have difficulty understanding some of the vocabulary used in Shakespeare's works. Explain that some words common in English 400 years ago are no longer current or now have different meanings. Prepare students for reading by introducing these words:

against: for; in preparation for; *alack:* alas (an exclamation of sorrow); *e'en*: even; *e'er*: ever; *hence*: away from here; *hie*: hurry; *whence*: where; *wilt*: will; *withal*: in addition; not withstanding

ALL LEVELS

CHALLENGE: Elizabethan Worldview

In Shakespeare's day, society was rigidly organized. The nobility occupied the top rung of the social ladder, and the uneducated peasantry occupied the bottom. It was difficult, if not impossible, to advance from one social class to another.

The ladder of power also existed within families. Children could not determine their own lives or make their own choices; their parents did so for them. Within a marriage, the husband was the master of his wife.

Elizabethan people expected to live shorter, more difficult lives, and they understood the events of a life to be fated. They did not believe they had the power to shape their own destinies as we do today.

STRATEGY

Keep the Elizabethan worldview in mind as you read. If a character's attitude clashes with your own, try to set aside your own ideas and view the situation through the character's eyes. This will help you understand why the character is behaving or speaking in a certain way.

Close Read the Text

Annotating the text as you read can help you tackle the challenges of Shakespearean language. Here are two sample annotations of an excerpt from Act II, Scene ii of *The Tragedy of Romeo and Juliet*—the famous "balcony scene."

Close Read: ANNOTATE · QUESTION · CONCLUDE

ANNOTATE: Two of Romeo's lines end with a dash. Two of Juliet's sentences include a semicolon.

QUESTION: What do these punctuation marks tell me about how the conversation is unfolding?

CONCLUDE: The dashes tell me that Romeo is being interrupted. The first semicolon shows Juliet changing her mind, and the second semicolon shows her expressing her opinion in yet another way. Juliet's interruptions and ramblings make her seem nervous and flirtatious.

Romeo. Lady, by yonder blessèd moon I vow,
That tips with silver all these fruit-tree tops—
Juliet. O, swear not by the moon, th'inconstant moon,
That monthly changes in her circle orb,
Lest that thy love prove likewise variable.
Romeo. What shall I swear by?
Juliet. Do not swear at all;
Or if thou wilt, swear by thy gracious self,
Which is the god of my idolatry,
And I'll believe thee.
Romeo. Heart's dear love—
Juliet. Well, do not swear. Although I joy in thee,
I have no joy of this contract tonight.
It is too rash, too unadvised, too sudden;
Too like the lightning, which doth cease to be
Ere one can say it lightens.

ANNOTATE: This long, complex sentence uses archaic words and syntax.

QUESTION: What is Juliet really saying?

CONCLUDE: If I paraphrase the sentence using modern-day language, it might read like this: *"Don't swear by the inconstant moon, which changes every month in its orbit, in case your love also proves changeable."* Juliet is saying, "The moon comes and goes. I hope you don't!"

Close Read the Text

Review and discuss the sections students have marked. If needed, continue to model close reading by using the Annotation Highlights in the Interactive Teacher's Edition.

Comprehension Check

Ask students to answer these questions independently and to then discuss them in a group.

1. Why is the Renaissance period known as the "birth of learning"?

Possible response: The Renaissance is often referred to as the birth of learning because it was like a rebirth or reawakening after the Middle Ages. Artists and scholars looked back to the learning and knowledge of ancient Rome and Greece to increase their understanding of the world.

2. What was the difference between the English Renaissance and the Italian Renaissance?

Possible response: The English Renaissance began about 100 years after the Italian Renaissance began. Also, the Italian Renaissance emphasized the visual arts more than the English Renaissance did.

3. Why is the reign of Elizabeth I seen as a golden age in English history?

Possible response: The reign of Elizabeth I is seen as a golden age because there was economic and political stability in the nation, and commerce and culture were able to flourish.

4. What are one or two major differences between the Globe Theatre and modern-day theaters?

Possible response: Unlike today's theaters, the Globe Theatre was an open-air theater that did not use artificial lighting. Also, people known as groundlings used to stand in front of the stage at the Globe Theatre, and usually no one stands during modern-day theater performances (unless he or she is at the new Shakespeare's Globe).

5. In what ways has Shakespeare had an impact on culture?

Possible response: William Shakespeare has had a tremendous impact on culture because his plays are still being staged and read 400 years after his death. Also, Shakespeare made major contributions to the English language by introducing new words, creating new meanings for old words, and inventing many expressions we still use.

TEACHING

Jump Start

FIRST READ Many things divide people: genetics, culture, geography, values, and generations. Sometimes the differences between people arise from social interactions. Do our differences define who we are, or are the qualities we have in common more important? Engage students in a discussion about how the differences between people affect relationships to set the context for *The Tragedy of Romeo and Juliet.*

Concept Vocabulary

Support students as they rank their words. Ask if they've ever heard, read, or used them. Reassure them that the definitions for these words are listed in the selection.

FIRST READ

Students should perform the steps of the first read independently.

NOTICE: You may want to encourage students to notice the attitudes of the characters and the results of their interactions.

ANNOTATE: Remind students to mark passages that illuminate the attitudes of the two main characters and the changes they experience as the act progresses.

CONNECT: Encourage students to go beyond the text to make connections with their own experiences. How would they react if they experienced the same events? What would they do differently?

RESPOND: Students will answer questions and write a summary to demonstrate understanding.

Point out to students that while they will always complete the Respond step at the end of the first read, the other steps will probably happen somewhat concurrently. You may wish to print copies of the **First-Read Guide: Fiction** for students to use.

MAKING MEANING

About the Playwright

William Shakespeare (1564–1616) has long been called the greatest writer in the English language. He was born in Stratford-upon-Avon, a town not far from London. In his twenties, he made his name as an actor and a playwright and eventually became a part owner of the Globe theater, where he wrote and produced plays until his late forties. He then retired to the town where he had grown up. For more information, see the Literature and Culture feature.

Tool Kit
First-Read Guide and Model Annotation

STANDARDS
Reading Literature
By the end of grade 9, read and comprehend literature, including stories, dramas, and poems, in the grades 9–10 text complexity band proficiently, with scaffolding as needed at the high end of the range.

The Tragedy of Romeo and Juliet, Act I

Concept Vocabulary

You will encounter the following words as you read Act I of *The Tragedy of Romeo and Juliet.* Before reading, note how familiar you are with each word. Rank the words in order from most familiar (1) to least familiar (3).

WORD	YOUR RANKING
mutiny	
transgression	
heretics	

After completing the first read, come back to the concept vocabulary and review your rankings. Mark changes to your original rankings as needed.

First Read DRAMA

Apply these strategies as you conduct your first read. You will have an opportunity to complete the close-read notes after your first read.

NOTICE *whom* the story is about, *what* happens, *where* and *when* it happens, and *why* those involved react as they do.

ANNOTATE by marking vocabulary and key passages you want to revisit.

CONNECT ideas within the selection to what you already know and what you have already read.

RESPOND by completing the Comprehension Check and by writing a brief summary of the selection.

374 UNIT 4 • STAR-CROSSED ROMANCES

AUTHOR'S PERSPECTIVE **Kelly Gallagher, M.Ed.**

Multi-layered Timeline When students are reading a difficult work for the first time, having them develop a timeline can help them move beyond literal reading into *deep reading,* the process of making inferences. This activity is especially useful for a novel or a play that has an intricate plot or many characters to track. Teachers can start by having students draw a line across two pages in their notebooks.

- First, simply ask students to tell what happens in the story. Closest to the line, have students record the characters and the main events in the plot.
- Next, encourage students to revisit the text by adding layers to the timeline. For example, above the basic characters and plot, encourage students to write questions that arise from their initial reading.
- A third layer might include predictions supported by information from the text.

BACKGROUND FOR THE PLAY

Star-Crossed Lovers

Written in 1594 or 1595, when Shakespeare was still a fairly young man, *The Tragedy of Romeo and Juliet* is a play about young love. The basic plot is simple: Two teenagers from feuding families fall in love and marry against their families' wishes, with tragic results. The story is set in Verona, Italy, and is based on an Italian legend that was fairly well known in England at the time.

Shakespeare's Sources Elizabethan writers deeply respected Italy as the birthplace of the Renaissance and often drew on Italian sources for inspiration. In 1562, an English poet named Arthur Brooke wrote *The Tragicall History of Romeus and Juliet*, a long narrative poem based on the Romeo and Juliet legend. Three years later, a prose version of the legend also appeared in England. Scholars believe, however, that Brooke's poem was Shakespeare's chief source.

That poem contains a great deal of moralizing, stressing the disobedience of the young lovers, along with fate, as the cause of their doom. Shakespeare's portrayal of the young lovers is more sympathetic, but he does stress the strong role that fate plays in their tragedy. In fact, at the very start of the play, the Chorus describes Romeo and Juliet as "star-crossed lovers," indicating that their tragic ending is written in the stars, or fated by forces beyond their control.

The Play Through the Centuries Of all the love stories ever written, *The Tragedy of Romeo and Juliet* may well be the most famous. Acting celebrities down through the centuries have played the leading role—Edwin Booth and Ellen Terry in the nineteenth century, for example, and John Gielgud and Judi Dench in the twentieth. There have been dozens of film versions of the play, numerous works of art depicting its scenes, over twenty operatic versions, a famous ballet version by Tchaikovsky. The play is often adapted to reflect the concerns of different eras: *West Side Story*, for example, adapts the story as a musical set amid the ethnic rivalries of 1950s New York City; *Romanoff and Juliet* is a comedy of the Cold War set during the 1960s. One of the most recent popular adaptations was the 1996 film *Romeo + Juliet* starring Leonardo DiCaprio and Claire Danes, which sets the play in the fictional location of Verona Beach, California.

DIGITAL PERSPECTIVES

The Tragedy of Romeo and Juliet, Act I

Do you believe in love at first sight? Is the approval of one's family in selecting a husband or a wife important? Should love be blind to all differences? Modeling the questions readers might ask as they read *The Tragedy of Romeo and Juliet* for the first time brings the text alive for students and connects it to the Performance Task assignment. Selection audio and print capability for the selection are available in the Interactive Teacher's Edition.

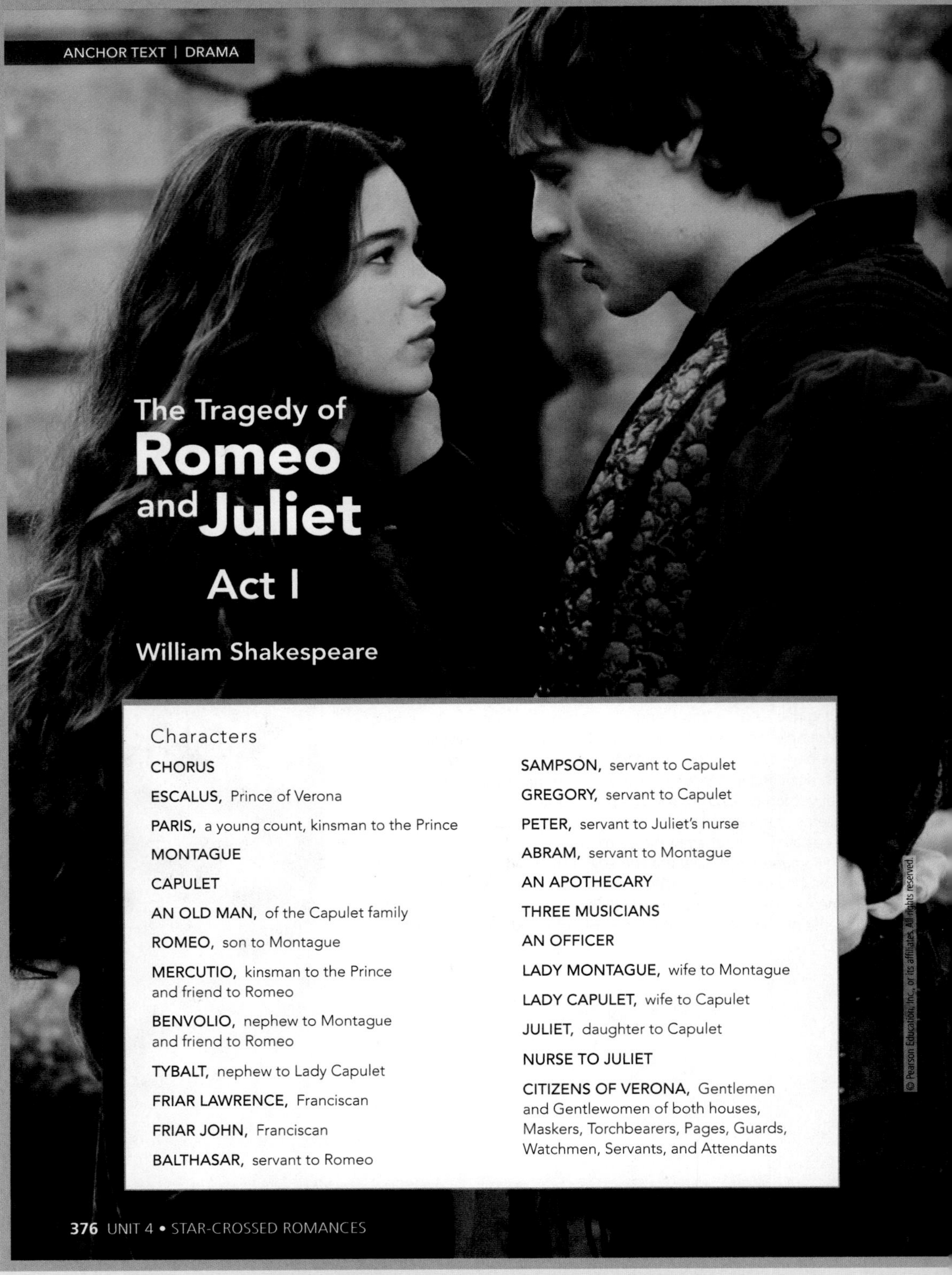

ANCHOR TEXT | DRAMA

The Tragedy of Romeo and Juliet

Act I

William Shakespeare

Characters

CHORUS

ESCALUS, Prince of Verona

PARIS, a young count, kinsman to the Prince

MONTAGUE

CAPULET

AN OLD MAN, of the Capulet family

ROMEO, son to Montague

MERCUTIO, kinsman to the Prince and friend to Romeo

BENVOLIO, nephew to Montague and friend to Romeo

TYBALT, nephew to Lady Capulet

FRIAR LAWRENCE, Franciscan

FRIAR JOHN, Franciscan

BALTHASAR, servant to Romeo

SAMPSON, servant to Capulet

GREGORY, servant to Capulet

PETER, servant to Juliet's nurse

ABRAM, servant to Montague

AN APOTHECARY

THREE MUSICIANS

AN OFFICER

LADY MONTAGUE, wife to Montague

LADY CAPULET, wife to Capulet

JULIET, daughter to Capulet

NURSE TO JULIET

CITIZENS OF VERONA, Gentlemen and Gentlewomen of both houses, Maskers, Torchbearers, Pages, Guards, Watchmen, Servants, and Attendants

PERSONALIZE FOR LEARNING

Background

Students may need help understanding the definitions and roles of some of the characters listed. Explain to them that a *chorus* is a group of twelve or fifteen performers who comment on the action of the play. They are observers who present the *prologue*, which gives background information and describes the conflict, and other hints about what the audience will be watching. A *friar* is a member of a Roman Catholic religious order, such as the Franciscans or the Dominicans. *Apothecary* is a term that was used to describe one who prepared and sold medicines and drugs (like a pharmacist).

SCAN FOR MULTIMEDIA

Prologue

Scene: Verona: Mantua

[*Enter* Chorus.]

Chorus. Two households, both alike in dignity,[1]
In fair Verona, where we lay our scene,
From ancient grudge break to new **mutiny**,
Where civil blood makes civil hands unclean.[2]
From forth the fatal loins of these two foes
A pair of star-crossed[3] lovers take their life;
Whose misadventured piteous overthrows[4]
Doth with their death bury their parents' strife.
The fearful passage of their death-marked love,
And the continuance of their parents' rage,
Which, but[5] their children's end, naught could remove,
Is now the two hours' traffic[6] of our stage;
The which if you with patient ears attend,
What here shall miss, our toil shall strive to mend.[7] [*Exit.*]

NOTES

1. **dignity** *n.* high social rank.

mutiny (MYOO tuh nee) *n.* open rebellion against lawful authority, especially by sailors or soldiers against their officers

2. **Where. . . unclean** in which the blood of citizens stains citizens' hands.
3. **star-crossed** ill-fated by the unfavorable positions of the stars.
4. **Whose . . . overthrows** whose unfortunate, sorrowful destruction.
5. **but** except.
6. **two hours' traffic** two hours' business.
7. **What . . . mend** Whatever is unclear in this prologue we actors shall try to clarify in the course of the play.

⌘ ⌘ ⌘

Act I

Scene i • *Verona. A public place.*

[*Enter* Sampson *and* Gregory, *with swords and bucklers,*[1] *of the house of Capulet.*]

Sampson. Gregory, on my word, we'll not carry coals.[2]

Gregory. No, for then we should be colliers.[3]

Sampson. I mean, an we be in choler, we'll draw.[4]

Gregory. Ay, while you live, draw your neck out of collar.[5]

Sampson. I strike quickly, being moved.

Gregory. But thou art not quickly moved to strike.

Sampson. A dog of the house of Montague moves me.

Gregory. To move is to stir, and to be valiant is to stand. Therefore, if thou art moved, thou run'st away.

Sampson. A dog of that house shall move me to stand. I will take the wall[6] of any man or maid of Montague's.

Gregory. That shows thee a weak slave; for the weakest goes to the wall.

Sampson. 'Tis true; and therefore women, being the weaker

1. **bucklers** *n.* small shields.
2. **carry coals** endure insults.
3. **colliers** *n.* sellers of coal.
4. **an . . . draw** if we are angered, we'll draw our swords.
5. **collar** *n.* hangman's noose.
6. **take the wall** assert superiority by walking nearer the houses and therefore farther from the gutter.

CLOSER LOOK

Analyze Dialogue and Stage Directions

Students may have marked stage directions and dialogue in Scene i, lines 1–11, during their first read. Use these stage directions and dialogue to help students understand how the author reveals information about characters. Encourage them to talk about the annotations that they marked. You may want to model a close read with the class based on the highlights shown in the text.

ANNOTATE: Have students mark details in stage directions and dialogue in lines 1–11 that reveal something about who the characters of Sampson and Gregory are, or have students participate while you highlight them.

QUESTION: Guide students to consider what these details might tell them. Ask what a reader can infer from the details provided in the stage directions and the dialogue, and accept student responses.

Possible response: The details and descriptions imply that Sampson and Gregory are servants of the house of Capulet and that they do not get along with the house of Montague.

CONCLUDE: Help students to formulate conclusions about the importance of these details in the text. Ask students why the author might have included these details.

Possible response: The stage directions and dialogue reveal that Sampson and Gregory are eager to quarrel as they have brought their swords and shields to town and are boasting about fighting. It also indicates that there is some sort of existing hostility or discord between the houses of Montague and Capulet.

Remind students that writers use **dialogue,** or conversation between characters, to reveal character and relationships, to advance the action of the plot, and to develop the conflict. **Stage directions** are notes included in a play to describe how the work is meant to be performed or staged, including where a scene takes place, what it should look and sound like, and how the characters should move and speak. Stage directions don't help only the director, production staff, and actors stage a play. They also help someone reading, rather than watching, a drama visualize everything that's meant to occur on stage.

NOTES

7. **tool** *n.* weapon.

8. **take . . . sides** make sure the law is on our side.

9. **list** please.

10. **bite . . . thumb** make an insulting gesture.

vessels, are ever thrust to the wall. Therefore I will push Montague's men from the wall, and thrust his maids to the wall.

Gregory. The quarrel is between our masters and us their men.

Sampson. 'Tis all one, I will show myself a tyrant. When I have fought with the men, I will be cruel with the maids—I will cut off their heads.

Gregory. The heads of the maids?

Sampson. Ay, the heads of the maids or their maidenheads. Take it in what sense thou wilt.

Gregory. They must take it in sense that feel it.

Sampson. Me they shall feel while I am able to stand: and 'tis known I am a pretty piece of flesh.

Gregory. 'Tis well thou art not fish; if thou hadst, thou hadst been Poor John. Draw thy tool![7] Here comes two of the house of Montagues.

[*Enter two other Servingmen,* Abram *and* Balthasar.]

Sampson. My naked weapon is out. Quarrel! I will back thee.

Gregory. How? Turn thy back and run?

Sampson. Fear me not.

Gregory. No, marry. I fear thee!

Sampson. Let us take the law of our sides;[8] let them begin.

Gregory. I will frown as I pass by, and let them take it as they list.[9]

Sampson. Nay, as they dare. I will bite my thumb[10] at them, which is disgrace to them if they bear it.

Abram. Do you bite your thumb at us, sir?

Sampson. I do bite my thumb, sir.

Abram. Do you bite your thumb at us, sir?

Sampson. [*Aside to* Gregory] Is the law of our side if I say ay?

Gregory. [*Aside to* Sampson] No.

Sampson. No, sir, I do not bite my thumb at you, sir, but I bite my thumb, sir.

Gregory. Do you quarrel, sir?

Abram. Quarrel, sir? No, sir.

Sampson. But if you do, sir, I am for you. I serve as good a man as you.

Abram. No better.

Sampson. Well, sir.

[*Enter* Benvolio.]

PERSONALIZE FOR LEARNING

English Language Support

Complex Syntax Review lines 28–29. Help students analyze the unusual sentence structure of Shakespeare's writing in order to develop a better understanding of conventional English syntax. Point out that because of the constraints of using iambic pentameter, Shakespeare was often forced to reverse words and use a lot of contractions. Additionally, even though Elizabethan English was rapidly changing, Shakespeare still used some archaic pronouns. For example, "thee" and "thou" both mean "you." Explain that in Scene i, lines 28–29, which read *'Tis well thou art not fish; if thou hadst, thou hadst been Poor John* **are basically saying** *It is well you are not fish; if you had, you'd have been Poor John*. Remind students that then as now, poetic writers have more freedom to write outside the conventional rules of English. **ALL LEVELS**

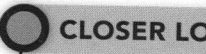

Gregory. [*Aside to* Sampson.] Say "better." Here comes one of my master's kinsmen.

Sampson. Yes, better, sir.

Abram. You lie.

Sampson. Draw, if you be men. Gregory, remember thy swashing[11] blow. [*They fight.*]

Benvolio. Part, fools!
Put up your swords. You know not what you do.
[*Enter* Tybalt.]

Tybalt. What, art thou drawn among these heartless hinds?[12]
Turn thee, Benvolio; look upon thy death.

Benvolio. I do but keep the peace. Put up thy sword,
Or manage it to part these men with me.

Tybalt. What, drawn, and talk of peace! I hate the word
As I hate hell, all Montagues, and thee.
Have at thee, coward! [*They fight.*]

[*Enter an* Officer, *and three or four* Citizens *with clubs or partisans.*[13]]

Officer. Clubs, bills,[14] and partisans! Strike! Beat them down!
Down with the Capulets! Down with the Montagues!

[*Enter old* Capulet *in his gown, and his* Wife.]

Capulet. What noise is this? Give me my long sword, ho!

Lady Capulet. A crutch, a crutch! Why call you for a sword?

Capulet. My sword, I say! Old Montague is come
And flourishes his blade in spite[15] of me.

[*Enter old* Montague *and his* Wife.]

Montague. Thou villain Capulet!—Hold me not; let me go.

Lady Montague. Thou shalt not stir one foot to seek a foe.

[*Enter* Prince Escalus, *with his Train.*[16]]

Prince. Rebellious subjects, enemies to peace,
Profaners[17] of this neighbor-stained steel—
Will they not hear? What, ho! You men, you beasts,
That quench the fire of your pernicious rage
With purple fountains issuing from your veins!
On pain of torture, from those bloody hands
Throw your mistempered[18] weapons to the ground
And hear the sentence of your moved prince.
Three civil brawls, bred of an airy word
By thee, old Capulet, and Montague,
Have thrice disturbed the quiet of our streets
And made Verona's ancient citizens
Cast by their grave beseeming ornaments[19]
To wield old partisans, in hands as old,

NOTES

11. **swashing** *adj.* hard downward swordstroke.

12. **heartless hinds** cowardly servants. *Hind* also means "a female deer."

13. **partisans** *n.* spearlike weapons with broad blades.

14. **bills** *n.* weapons consisting of hook-shaped blades with long handles.

15. **spite** defiance.

16. **Train** *n.* attendants.

17. **Profaners** *n.* those who show disrespect or contempt.

18. **mistempered** *adj.* hardened for a wrong purpose; bad tempered.

19. **Cast . . . ornaments** put aside their dignified and appropriate clothing.

DIGITAL PERSPECTIVES

CLOSER LOOK

Analyze Character

Students may have marked lines 70–75 during their first read. Use these lines to help students understand characterization. Encourage them to talk about the annotations that they marked. You may want to model a close read with the class based on the highlights shown in the text.

ANNOTATE: Have students mark details in lines 70–75 that depict the dialogue of Lord and Lady Capulet and Lord and Lady Montague, or have students participate while you highlight them.

QUESTION: Guide students to consider what these details might tell them. Ask what a reader can infer from the dialogue exchanges between the characters, and accept student responses.

Possible response: The dialogue exchange implies that Lady Capulet thinks Lord Capulet needs a crutch instead of a sword, and Lady Montague wants to restrain her husband.

CONCLUDE: Help students to formulate conclusions about the importance of these details in the text. Ask students why the author might have included these details.

Possible response: The dialogue exchanges reveal that Lord Capulet and Lord Montague are angry men who want to fight even though they are too old. It is also clear that Lady Capulet and Lady Montague do not want their husbands to fight. Perhaps they are tired of the conflict.

Remind students that with **direct characterization,** the author directly states a character's traits. With **indirect characterization,** an author provides clues about a character by describing what a character looks like, does, and says, as well as how other characters react to him or her. It's up to the reader to draw conclusions about the character based on this indirect information.

NOTES

20. **Cank'red hate** rusted from lack of use, to put an end to your malignant feuding.

21. **Who . . . abroach?** Who reopened this old fight?

22. **on . . . part** on one side and the other.

23. **ware** *adj.* aware; wary.

24. **covert** *n.* hidden place.

25. **measuring . . . affections** judging his feelings.

26. **Which . . . found** which wanted to be where there was no one else.

27. **Pursued . . . his** followed my own mind by not following after Romeo.

28. **heavy** *adj.* sad; moody.

Cank'red with peace, to part your cank'red hate.[20]
If ever you disturb our streets again,
Your lives shall pay the forfeit of the peace.
For this time all the rest depart away.
You, Capulet, shall go along with me;
And, Montague, come you this afternoon,
To know our further pleasure in this case,
To old Freetown, our common judgment place.
Once more, on pain of death, all men depart.

[*Exit all but* Montague, *his* Wife, *and* Benvolio.]

Montague. Who set this ancient quarrel new abroach?[21]
Speak, nephew, were you by when it began?

Benvolio. Here were the servants of your adversary
And yours, close fighting ere I did approach.
I drew to part them. In the instant came
The fiery Tybalt, with his sword prepared;
Which, as he breathed defiance to my ears,
He swung about his head and cut the winds,
Who, nothing hurt withal, hissed him in scorn.
While we were interchanging thrusts and blows,
Came more and more, and fought on part and part,[22]
Till the prince came, who parted either part.

Lady Montague. O, where is Romeo? Saw you him today?
Right glad I am he was not at this fray.

Benvolio. Madam, an hour before the worshiped sun
Peered forth the golden window of the East,
A troubled mind drave me to walk abroad:
Where, underneath the grove of sycamore
That westward rooteth from the city side,
So early walking did I see your son.
Towards him I made, but he was ware[23] of me
And stole into the covert[24] of the wood.
I, measuring his affections[25] by my own,
Which then most sought where most might not be found,[26]
Being one too many by my weary self,
Pursued my humor not pursuing his,[27]
And gladly shunned who gladly fled from me.

Montague. Many a morning hath he there been seen,
With tears augmenting the fresh morning's dew,
Adding to clouds more clouds with his deep sighs;
But all so soon as the all-cheering sun
Should in the furthest East begin to draw
The shady curtains from Aurora's bed,
Away from light steals home my heavy[28] son
And private in his chamber pens himself,
Shuts up his windows, locks fair daylight out,

Additional **English Language Support** is available in the Interactive Teacher's Edition.

PERSONALIZE FOR LEARNING

English Language Support

Multiple-Meaning Words Students may struggle with words that have multiple meanings, such as *fiery* (line 104), *blows* (line 108), and *fray* (line 112) in Scene i. To help them understand how the words are used in these lines, explain that in this context, *fiery* is used as an adjective to describe a person having a passionate, quick-tempered nature, *blows* is used as a noun meaning "forcible strokes," and *fray* is used as a noun meaning "a fight or brawl". **ALL LEVELS**

And makes himself an artificial night.
Black and portentous[29] must this humor prove
Unless good counsel may the cause remove.

Benvolio. My noble uncle, do you know the cause?

Montague. I neither know it nor can learn of him.

Benvolio. Have you importuned[30] him by any means?

Montague. Both by myself and many other friends;
But he, his own affections' counselor,
Is to himself—I will not say how true—
But to himself so secret and so close,
So far from sounding[31] and discovery,
As is the bud bit with an envious worm
Ere he can spread his sweet leaves to the air
Or dedicate his beauty to the sun.
Could we but learn from whence his sorrows grow,
We would as willingly give cure as know.

[*Enter* Romeo.]

Benvolio. See, where he comes: so please you, step aside;
I'll know his grievance, or be much denied.

Montague. I would thou wert so happy by thy stay,
To hear true shrift.[32] Come, madam, let's away.

[*Exit* Montague *and* Wife.]

Benvolio. Good-morrow, cousin.

Romeo. Is the day so young?

Benvolio. But new struck nine.

Romeo. Ay me! Sad hours seem long.
Was that my father that went hence so fast?

Benvolio. It was. What sadness lengthens Romeo's hours?

Romeo. Not having that which having makes them short.

Benvolio. In love?

Romeo. Out—

Benvolio. Of love?

Romeo. Out of her favor where I am in love.

Benvolio. Alas, that love, so gentle in his view,[33]
Should be so tyrannous and rough in proof![34]

Romeo. Alas, that love, whose view is muffled still,[35]
Should, without eyes, see pathways to his will!
Where shall we dine? O me! What fray was here?
Yet tell me not, for I have heard it all.
Here's much to do with hate, but more with love.[36]
Why, then, O brawling love! O loving hate,
O any thing, of nothing first created!

NOTES

29. portentous *adj.* promising bad fortune.

30. importuned *v.* questioned deeply.

31. sounding *n.* understanding.

32. I . . . shrift I hope you are lucky enough to hear him confess the truth.

33. view *n.* appearance.

34. in proof when experienced.

35. whose . . . still Cupid is traditionally represented as blindfolded.

36. but . . . love loyalty to family and love of fighting in the following lines, Romeo speaks of love as a series of contradictions—a union of opposites.

DIGITAL PERSPECTIVES

CLOSER LOOK

Analyze Simile

Students may have marked lines 141–150 during their first read. Use these lines to help students understand simile. Encourage them to talk about the annotations that they marked. You may want to model a close read with the class based on the highlights shown in the text.

ANNOTATE: Have students mark details in lines 141–150 in which Lord Montague discusses Romeo and describes his situation and mood, or have students participate while you highlight them.

QUESTION: Guide students to consider what these details might tell them. Ask what a reader can infer from Lord Montague's description of Romeo's situation and mood, and accept student responses.

Possible response: The description indicates that Lord Montague is concerned about his son and feels that he is not living up to his full potential because of some problem that is bothering him.

CONCLUDE: Help students to formulate conclusions about the importance of these details in the text. Ask students why the author might have included this description of Romeo's situation and mood.

Possible response: The author may have included these details as a simile to compare Romeo to a bud that has not been able to grow because it has been bitten by a worm. Romeo's problem has also kept him from living up to his full potential.

Remind students that a **simile** is a figure of speech that compares two apparently unlike things by using *like, as, than,* or *resembles*. Similes reveal the surprising ways in which things that seem dissimilar are often alike.

CLOSE READ

Remind students to focus on how dialogue and word choice reveal character traits, viewpoints, and emotions. You may wish to model the close read using the following think-aloud format. Possible responses to questions on the Student page are included. You may also want to print copies of the **Close-Read Guide: Drama** for students to use.

ANNOTATE: As I read lines 200–211, I notice and highlight the details that relate to war or attacking someone.

QUESTION: I wonder if the author included these details to draw a connection between love and conflict.

CONCLUDE: I can infer from the dialogue exchange that both Romeo and Benvolio view love and women as something to be conquered and won. Romeo describes his courting of a girl with terms that are similar to an attack: *hit, arrow, armed, bow,* and *siege.*

NOTES

O heavy lightness, serious vanity,
Misshapen chaos of well-seeming forms,
Feather of lead, bright smoke, cold fire, sick health,
Still-waking sleep, that is not what it is!
This love feel I, that feel no love in this.
Dost thou not laugh?

Benvolio. No, coz,[37] I rather weep.

Romeo. Good heart, at what?

Benvolio. At thy good heart's oppression.

Romeo. Why, such is love's **transgression**.
Griefs of mine own lie heavy in my breast,
Which thou wilt propagate, to have it prest
With more of thine.[38] This love that thou hast shown
Doth add more grief to too much of mine own.
Love is a smoke raised with the fume of sighs;
Being purged, a fire sparkling in lovers' eyes;
Being vexed, a sea nourished with loving tears.
What is it else? A madness most discreet,[39]
A choking gall,[40] and a preserving sweet.
Farewell, my coz.

Benvolio. Soft![41] I will go along.
And if you leave me so, you do me wrong.

Romeo. Tut! I have lost myself; I am not here;
This is not Romeo, he's some other where.

Benvolio. Tell me in sadness,[42] who is that you love?

Romeo. What, shall I groan and tell thee?

Benvolio. Groan? Why, no;
But sadly tell me who.

Romeo. Bid a sick man in sadness make his will.
Ah, word ill urged to one that is so ill!
In sadness, cousin, I do love a woman.

Benvolio. I aimed so near when I supposed you loved.

Romeo. A right good markman. And she's fair I love.

Benvolio. A right fair mark, fair coz, is soonest hit.

Romeo. Well, in that hit you miss. She'll not be hit
With Cupid's arrow. She hath Dian's wit,[43]
And, in strong proof[44] of chastity well armed,
From Love's weak childish bow she lives uncharmed.
She will not stay[45] the siege of loving terms,
Nor bide th' encounter of assailing eyes,
Nor ope her lap to saint-seducing gold.
O, she is rich in beauty; only poor
That, when she dies, with beauty dies her store.[46]

Benvolio. Then she hath sworn that she will still live chaste?

37. **coz** cousin.

transgression (tranz GREHSH uhn) *n.* the act of breaking a law or command, or committing a sin

38. **Which . . . thine** which griefs you will increase by adding your own sorrow to them.

39. **discreet** *adj.* intelligently sensitive.

40. **gall** *n.* a bitter liquid.

41. **Soft!** Wait!

42. **in sadness** seriously.

43. **Dian's wit** the mind of Diana, goddess of chastity.

44. **proof** *n.* armor.

45. **stay** *v.* endure; put up with.

46. **That . . . store** in that her beauty will die with her if she does not marry and have children.

CLOSE READ

ANNOTATE: In lines 200–211, mark words and phrases that relate to war or attacking someone.

QUESTION: What connection do Benvolio and Romeo seem to be making between love and conflict?

CONCLUDE: What do these references suggest about the ways in which the two characters' view love?

382 UNIT 4 • STAR-CROSSED ROMANCES

Romeo. She hath, and in that sparing make huge waste;
For beauty, starved with her severity,
Cuts beauty off from all posterity.[47]
She is too fair, too wise, wisely too fair
To merit bliss by making me despair.[48]
She hath forsworn[49] to love, and in that vow
Do I live dead that live to tell it now.

Benvolio. Be ruled by me; forget to think of her.

Romeo. O, teach me how I should forget to think!

Benvolio. By giving liberty unto thine eyes.
Examine other beauties.

Romeo. 'Tis the way
To call hers, exquisite, in question more.[50]
These happy masks that kiss fair ladies' brows,
Being black put us in mind they hide the fair.
He that is strucken blind cannot forget
The precious treasure of his eyesight lost.
Show me a mistress that is passing fair:
What doth her beauty serve, but as a note
Where I may read who passed that passing fair?[51]
Farewell. Thou canst not teach me to forget.

Benvolio. I'll pay that doctrine, or else die in debt.[52] [*Exit all.*]

NOTES

47. in . . . posterity By denying herself love and marriage, she wastes her beauty, which will not live on in future generations.

48. She . . . despair She is being too good—she will earn happiness in heaven by dooming me to live without her love.

49. forsworn to sworn not to.

50. 'Tis . . . more That way will only make her beauty more strongly present in my mind.

51. who . . . fair who surpassed in beauty that very beautiful woman.

52. I'll . . . debt I will teach you to forget, or else die trying.

⌘ ⌘ ⌘

Scene ii • *A street.*

[*Enter* Capulet, County Paris, *and the* Clown, *Capulet's servant.*]

Capulet. But Montague is bound as well as I,
In penalty alike; and 'tis not hard, I think,
For men so old as we to keep the peace.

Paris. Of honorable reckoning[1] are you both,
And pity 'tis you lived at odds so long.
But now, my lord, what say you to my suit?

Capulet. But saying o'er what I have said before:
My child is yet a stranger in the world,
She hath not seen the change of fourteen years;
Let two more summers wither in their pride
Ere we may think her ripe to be a bride.

Paris. Younger than she are happy mothers made.

Capulet. And too soon marred are those so early made.
Earth hath swallowed all my hopes[2] but she;
She is the hopeful lady of my earth.[3]

1. reckoning *n.* reputation.

2. hopes *n.* children.

3. She . . . earth My hopes for the future rest in her; she will inherit all that is mine.

CROSS-CURRICULAR PERSPECTIVES

Social Studies In Scene ii, lines 1–37, Paris has come to discuss his proposal of marriage to Juliet with Lord Capulet. Lord Capulet indicates that Juliet is not yet 14 years old and asks Paris to wait another two years. He also says that Juliet is his only surviving child and will inherit all that he owns. Juliet's young age is sometimes a surprise to readers. Have interested students conduct research on the marriage customs and traditions during the Renaissance period and present their findings to the class.

CLOSER LOOK

Analyze Metaphor

Students may have marked lines 24–30 during their first read. Use these lines to help students understand metaphor. Encourage them to talk about the annotations that they marked. You may want to model a close read with the class based on the highlights shown in the text.

ANNOTATE: Have students mark details in lines in which Lord Capulet describes his party and guests to Paris, or have students participate while you highlight them.

QUESTION: Guide students to consider what these details might tell them. Ask what a reader can infer from Lord Capulet's description of the guests who will attend his party, and accept student responses.

Possible response: The details imply that there will be many people present at the party that evening, and that many of them will be beautiful girls.

CONCLUDE: Help students to formulate conclusions about the importance of these details in the text. Ask students why the author might have included Lord Capulet's description of the guests who will attend his party that evening.

Possible response: The author may have included this description as a metaphor to compare all of the young, beautiful girls Paris might encounter at the party to stars from the heavens and fresh fennel buds. Perhaps he makes this comparison and urges Paris to look around at the ladies to make sure that it is really Juliet he wants to marry.

Remind students that a **metaphor** is a figure of speech that compares two apparently unlike things without using the words *like, as, than,* or *resembles*. A metaphor speaks of one thing as if it were the other.

NOTES

4. **An . . . voice** If she agrees, I will consent to and agree with her choice.

5. **Earth-treading stars** young ladies.

6. **Which . . . none** If you look at all the young girls, you may see her as merely one among many, and not worth special admiration.

7. **stay** *v.* await.

8. **shoemaker . . . nets** The servant is confusing workers and their tools. He intends to say that people should stick with what they know.

9. **In good time!** Just in time! The servant has seen Benvolio and Romeo, who can read.

10. **Turn . . . turning** If you are dizzy from turning one way, turn the other way.

11. **plantain leaf** used to stop bleeding.

12. **God-den** good afternoon; good evening.

But woo her, gentle Paris, get her heart;
My will to her consent is but a part.
An she agree, within her scope of choice
Lies my consent and fair according voice.[4]
This night I hold an old accustomed feast,
Whereto I have invited many a guest,
Such as I love; and you among the store,
One more, most welcome, makes my number more.
At my poor house look to behold this night
Earth-treading stars[5] that make dark heaven light.
Such comfort as do lusty young men feel
When well-appareled April on the heel
Of limping Winter treads, even such delight
Among fresh fennel buds shall you this night
Inherit at my house. Hear all, all see,
And like her most whose merit most shall be;
Which, on more view, of many, mine, being one,
May stand in number, though in reck'ning none.[6]
Come, go with me. [*To* Servant, *giving him a paper*]
Go, sirrah, trudge about
Through fair Verona; find those persons out
Whose names are written there, and to them say
My house and welcome on their pleasure stay.[7]

[*Exit with* Paris.]

Servant. Find them out whose names are written here? It is written, that the shoemaker should meddle with his yard and the tailor with his last, the fisher with his pencil and the painter with his nets;[8] but I am sent to find those persons whose names are here writ, and can never find what names the writing person hath here writ. I must to the learned. In good time![9]

[*Enter* Benvolio *and* Romeo.]

Benvolio. Tut, man, one fire burns out another's burning;
One pain is less'ned by another's anguish;
Turn giddy, and be holp by backward turning;[10]
One desperate grief cures with another's languish.
Take thou some new infection to thy eye,
And the rank poison of the old will die.

Romeo. Your plantain leaf[11] is excellent for that.

Benvolio. For what, I pray thee?

Romeo. For your broken shin.

Benvolio. Why, Romeo, art thou mad?

Romeo. Not mad, but bound more than a madman is;
Shut up in prison, kept without my food,
Whipped and tormented and—God-den,[12] good fellow.

VOCABULARY DEVELOPMENT

Concept Vocabulary Reinforcement

To increase familiarity with the concept vocabulary, ask students to use each of the words in a sentence. Reinforce their comprehension with "show-you-know" sentences. The first part of the sentence uses the vocabulary word in an appropriate context. The second part of the sentence—the "show-you-know" part—clarifies the first. Model this example with the word exhausted: I know you must be *exhausted* after your long trip, so I advise you take a nap to regain your energy. Then give students these sentence prompts and coach them to create the clarification parts.

1. Galileo was considered a *heretic* for supporting Copernicus's theory because ________.

Possible response: Galileo was considered a *heretic* for supporting Copernicus's theory because it went against accepted beliefs.

Servant. God gi' go-den. I pray, sir, can you read?

Romeo. Ay, mine own fortune in my misery.

Servant. Perhaps you have learned it without book.
But, I pray, can you read anything you see?

Romeo. Ay, if I know the letters and the language.

Servant. Ye say honestly. Rest you merry.[13]

Romeo. Stay, fellow; I can read. [*He reads the letter.*]
"Signior Martino and his wife and daughters;
County Anselm and his beauteous sisters;
the lady widow of Vitruvio;
Signior Placentio and his lovely nieces;
Mercutio and his brother Valentine;
Mine uncle Capulet, his wife and daughters;
My fair niece Rosaline; Livia;
Signior Valentio and his cousin Tybalt;
Lucio and the lively Helena."
A fair assembly. Whither should they come?

Servant. Up.

Romeo. Whither? To supper?

Servant. To our house.

Romeo. Whose house?

Servant. My master's.

Romeo. Indeed I should have asked you that before.

Servant. Now I'll tell you without asking. My master is the great rich Capulet; and if you be not of the house of Montagues, I pray come and crush a cup of wine. Rest you merry. [*Exit.*]

Benvolio. At this same ancient[14] feast of Capulet's
Sups the fair Rosaline whom thou so loves;
With all the admired beauties of Verona.
Go thither, and with unattainted[15] eye,
Compare her face with some that I shall show,
And I will make thee think thy swan a crow.

Romeo. When the devout religion of mine eye
Maintains such falsehood, then turn tears to fires:
And these, who, often drowned, could never die,
Transparent **heretics**, be burnt for liars![16]
One fairer than my love? The all-seeing sun
Ne'er saw her match since first the world begun.

Benvolio. Tut! You saw her fair, none else being by,
Herself poised with herself in either eye;[17]
But in that crystal scales[18] let there be weighed
Your lady's love against some other maid

NOTES

13. Rest you merry May God keep you happy—a way of saying farewell.

14. ancient *adj.* long-established; traditional.

15. unattainted *adj.* unprejudiced.

heretics (HEHR uh tihks) *n.* people who hold a different belief from the official belief of their church

16. When . . . liars! When I see Rosaline as just a plain-looking girl, may my tears turn to fire and burn my eyes out!

17. Herself . . . eye Rosaline compared with no one else.

18. crystal scales your eyes.

2. He was forgiven for his *transgression* _________.

Possible response: He was forgiven for his *transgression* even though it was a violation of the law.

3. The sailors staged a *mutiny*, and they _________.

Possible response: The sailors staged a *mutiny*, and they refused to obey orders.

That I will show you shining at this feast,
And she shall scant show well that now seems best.

Romeo. I'll go along, no such sight to be shown,
But to rejoice in splendor of mine own.[19] [*Exit all.*]

⌘ ⌘ ⌘

Scene iii • *A room in Capulet's house.*

[*Enter* Capulet's Wife, *and* Nurse.]

Lady Capulet. Nurse, where's my daughter? Call her forth to me.

Nurse. Now, by my maidenhead at twelve year old,
I bade her come. What, lamb! What, ladybird!
God forbid, where's this girl? What, Juliet!

[*Enter* Juliet.]

Juliet. How now? Who calls?

Nurse. Your mother.

Juliet. Madam, I am here.
What is your will?

Lady Capulet. This is the matter—Nurse, give leave[1] awhile;
We must talk in secret. Nurse, come back again.
I have rememb'red me, thou's hear our counsel.[2]
Thou knowest my daughter's of a pretty age.

Nurse. Faith, I can tell her age unto an hour.

Lady Capulet. She's not fourteen.

Nurse. I'll lay fourteen of my teeth—
And yet, to my teen[3] be it spoken, I have but four—
She's not fourteen. How long is it now
To Lammastide?[4]

Lady Capulet. A fortnight and odd days.[5]

Nurse. Even or odd, of all days in the year,
Come Lammas Eve at night shall she be fourteen.
Susan and she (God rest all Christian souls!)
Were of an age.[6] Well, Susan is with God;
She was too good for me. But, as I said,
On Lammas Eve at night shall she be fourteen;
That shall she, marry; I remember it well.
'Tis since the earthquake now eleven years.
And she was weaned (I never shall forget it),
Of all the days of the year, upon that day;
For I had then laid wormwood to my dug,
Sitting in the sun under the dovehouse wall.
My lord and you were then at Mantua.

NOTES

19. **mine own** my own love; Rosaline.

1. **give leave** Leave us alone.

2. **thou's . . . counsel** You shall hear our conference.

3. **teen** *n.* sorrow.

4. **Lammastide** (LAM uhs tyd) August 1, a holiday celebrating the summer harvest.

5. **A fortnight and odd days** two weeks plus a few days.

6. **Susan . . . age** Susan, the Nurse's child, and Juliet were the same age.

DIGITAL PERSPECTIVES

Illuminating the Text To help students comprehend and read Shakespeare's works, which are mostly written in iambic pentameter, it is often helpful to hear the play in spoken form. Find and play audio of scenes from *The Tragedy of Romeo and Juliet.* These are readily available on the Internet. Have students follow along in their texts so they get a better sense of the rhythm and cadence of the language. After students listen to the recording, have them read aloud from parts of the play.

386 UNIT 4 • STAR-CROSSED ROMANCES

Nay, I do bear a brain. But, as I said,
When it did taste the wormwood on the nipple
Of my dug and felt it bitter, pretty fool,
To see it tetchy and fall out with the dug!
Shake, quoth the dovehouse! 'Twas no need, I trow,
To bid me trudge.
And since that time it is eleven years,
For then she could stand high-lone; nay, by th' rood,
She could have run and waddled all about;
For even the day before, she broke her brow;
And then my husband (God be with his soul!
'A was a merry man) took up the child.
"Yea," quoth he, "dost thou fall upon thy face?
Thou wilt fall backward when thou hast more wit;
Wilt thou not, Jule?" and, by my holidam,
The pretty wretch left crying and said "Ay."
To see now how a jest shall come about!
I warrant, and I should live a thousand years,
I never should forget it. "Wilt thou not, Jule?" quoth he,
And, pretty fool, it stinted and said "Ay."

Lady Capulet. Enough of this. I pray thee hold thy peace.

Nurse. Yes, madam. Yet I cannot choose but laugh
To think it should leave crying and say, "Ay."
And yet, I warrant, it had upon it brow
A bump as big as a young cock'rel's stone;
A perilous knock; and it cried bitterly.

NOTES

CLOSE READ

ANNOTATE: In the Nurse's speech starting on line 16, mark contractions, parenthetical statements, and any other deviations from formal speech.

QUESTION: Why does the Nurse's speech have so many asides and digressions?

CONCLUDE: What overall impression of the Nurse does this speech create?

DIGITAL PERSPECTIVES

CLOSE READ

Remind students that authors use dialogue to reveal a lot about a character. You may wish to model the close read using the following think-aloud format. Possible responses to questions on the student page are included.

ANNOTATE: As I read lines 16–48, I notice and highlight the details that are contractions, parenthetical statements, and other deviations from formal speech.

QUESTION: I wonder why the author included so many asides, or digressions, in the Nurse's speech.

CONCLUDE: I think the overall impression this dialogue creates of the Nurse is that she is a little scatter-brained, overly talkative, and, perhaps, less educated than the other characters.

CLOSER LOOK

Analyze Characterization

Students may have marked lines 59–68 during their first read. Use these lines to help students understand characterization. Encourage them to talk about the annotations that they marked. You may want to model a close read with the class based on the highlights shown in the text.

ANNOTATE: Have students mark details in the dialogue from lines 59–68 that indicate something about the nurse's personality and her relationship with Juliet, or have students participate while you highlight them.

QUESTION: Guide students to consider what this dialogue might tell them about the Nurse. Ask what a reader can infer from the dialogue, and accept student responses.

Possible response: The details imply that the Nurse is talkative and is close with Juliet.

CONCLUDE: Help students to formulate conclusions about the importance of these details in the text. Ask students why the author might have included this dialogue.

Possible response: The author may have included this dialogue to reveal the Nurse's character. Through the dialogue exchange, we learn that she is talkative to the point of being annoying, but she genuinely cares about Juliet. We also learn that she has cared for Juliet since Juliet was a baby and is excited that Juliet might get married. Showing this close relationship between the Nurse and Juliet creates a stark contrast with that of Lady Capulet's relationship with her own daughter.

Remind students that with **direct characterization,** the author directly states a character's traits. With **indirect characterization,** an author provides clues about a character by describing what a character looks like, does, and says, as well as how other characters react to him or her. It's up to the reader to draw conclusions about the character based on this indirect information.

NOTES

"Yea," quoth my husband, "fall'st upon thy face?
Thou wilt fall backward when thou comest to age,
Wilt thou not, Jule?" It stinted and said "Ay."

Juliet. And stint thou too. I pray thee, nurse, say I.

Nurse. Peace, I have done. God mark thee to His grace!
Thou wast the prettiest babe that e'er I nursed.
And I might live to see thee married once,
I have my wish.

Lady Capulet. Marry, that "marry" is the very theme
I came to talk of. Tell me, daughter Juliet,
How stands your dispositions to be married?

Juliet. It is an honor that I dream not of.

Nurse. An honor? Were not I thine only nurse,
I would say thou hadst sucked wisdom from thy teat.

Lady Capulet. Well, think of marriage now. Younger than you,
Here in Verona, ladies of esteem,
Are made already mothers. By my count,
I was your mother much upon these years
That you are now a maid.[7] Thus then in brief:
The valiant Paris seeks you for his love.

Nurse. A man, young lady! Lady, such a man
As all the world—Why, he's a man of wax.[8]

Lady Capulet. Verona's summer hath not such a flower.

Nurse. Nay, he's a flower, in faith—a very flower.

Lady Capulet. What say you? Can you love the gentleman?
This night you shall behold him at our feast.
Read o'er the volume of young Paris' face,
And find delight writ there with beauty's pen;
Examine every married lineament,
And see how one another lends content;[9]
And what obscured in this fair volume lies
Find written in the margent[10] of his eyes.
This precious book of love, this unbound lover,
To beautify him only lacks a cover.[11]
The fish lives in the sea, and 'tis much pride
For fair without the fair within to hide.
That book in many's eyes doth share the glory,
That in gold clasps locks in the golden story;
So shall you share all that he doth possess,
By having him making yourself no less.

Nurse. No less? Nay, bigger! Women grow by men.

Lady Capulet. Speak briefly, can you like of Paris' love?

Juliet. I'll look to like, if looking liking move;[12]
But no more deep will I endart mine eye

7. **I . . . maid** I was your mother when I was as old as you are now.

8. **he's . . . wax** He's a model of a man.

9. **Examine . . . content** Examine every harmonious feature of his face, and see how each one enhances every other. Throughout this speech, Lady Capulet compares Paris to a book.

10. **margent** *n.* margin. Paris's eyes are compared to the margin of a book, where whatever is not clear in the text (the rest of his face) can be explained by notes.

11. **cover** metaphor for wife.

12. **I'll . . . move** If looking favorably at someone leads to liking him, I will look at Paris in a way that will lead to liking him.

DIGITAL PERSPECTIVES

Than your consent gives strength to make it fly.[13]
[*Enter* Servingman.]

Servingman. Madam, the guests are come, supper served up, you called, my young lady asked for, the nurse cursed in the pantry, and everything in extremity. I must hence to wait. I beseech you follow straight. [*Exit.*]

Lady Capulet. We follow thee. Juliet, the County stays.[14]

Nurse. Go, girl, seek happy nights to happy days. [*Exit all.*]

⌘ ⌘ ⌘

Scene iv • *A street.*

[*Enter* Romeo, Mercutio, Benvolio, *with five or six other* Maskers; Torchbearers.]

Romeo. What, shall this speech[1] be spoke for our excuse?
Or shall we on without apology?

Benvolio. The date is out of such prolixity.[2]
We'll have no Cupid hoodwinked with a scarf,
Bearing a Tartar's painted bow of lath,
Scaring the ladies like a crowkeeper,
Nor no without-book prologue, faintly spoke
After the prompter, for our entrance;
But, let them measure us by what they will,
We'll measure them a measure and be gone.

Romeo. Give me a torch. I am not for this ambling.
Being but heavy,[3] I will bear the light.

Mercutio. Nay, gentle Romeo, we must have you dance.

Romeo. Not I, believe me. You have dancing shoes
With nimble soles; I have a soul of lead
So stakes me to the ground I cannot move.

Mercutio. You are a lover. Borrow Cupid's wings
And soar with them above a common bound.

Romeo. I am too sore enpiercèd with his shaft
To soar with his light feathers; and so bound
I cannot bound a pitch above dull woe.
Under love's heavy burden do I sink.

Mercutio. And, to sink in it, should you burden love—
Too great oppression for a tender thing.

Romeo. Is love a tender thing? It is too rough,
Too rude, too boist'rous, and it pricks like thorn.

Mercutio. If love be rough with you, be rough with love.
Prick love for pricking, and you beat love down.

NOTES

13. **But . . . fly** But I will not look harder than what you want me to.

14. **the County stays** The Count, Paris, is waiting.

1. **this speech** Romeo asks whether he and his companions, being uninvited guests, should follow custom by announcing their arrival in a speech.

2. **The . . . prolixity** Such wordiness is outdated. In the following lines, Benvolio says, in sum, "Let us forget about announcing our entrance with a show. The other guests can look over as they see fit. We will dance a while, then leave."

3. **heavy** *adj.* weighed down with sadness.

DIGITAL PERSPECTIVES

Illuminating the Text Cupid is referenced twice in this part of the selection, once in line 4 and again in line 17 of Scene iv. For students to understand this part of the selection, they need to know about Cupid and what he represented. Have students conduct online research about Cupid and then discuss their findings. Encourage students to draw conclusions about the repeated references to Cupid and what the author may be trying to show by mentioning him repeatedly.

TEACHING

CLOSE READ

Remind students to focus on the dialogue exchanges between characters. You may wish to model the close read using the following think-aloud format. Possible responses to questions on the student page are included.

ANNOTATE: As I read lines 43–53, I notice and highlight the lines that one character begins but another ends.

QUESTION: I wonder why Shakespeare divides lines between characters. It seems to really break up the text.

CONCLUDE: I think the division of these lines of dialogue shows that Romeo and Mercutio are close friends and enjoy bantering with each other. This writing style emphasizes their relationship.

NOTES

4. **visage** *n.* mask.
5. **A visor . . . visor!** A mask for a mask—which is what my real face is like!
6. **quote deformities** notice my ugly features.
7. **betake . . . legs** start dancing.
8. **Let . . . rushes** Let fun-loving people dance on the floor coverings.
9. **proverbed . . . phrase** directed by an old saying.
10. **The game . . . done** No matter how much enjoyment may be had, I will not have any.
11. **Dun's . . . word!** Lie low like a mouse—that is what a constable waiting to make an arrest might say.
12. **Dun** proverbial name for a horse.
13. **Take . . . wits** Understand my intended meaning. That shows more intelligence than merely following what your senses perceive.

Give me a case to put my visage[4] in.
A visor for a visor![5] What care I
What curious eye doth quote deformities?[6]
Here are the beetle brows shall blush for me.

Benvolio. Come, knock and enter; and no sooner in
But every man betake him to his legs.[7]

Romeo. A torch for me! Let wantons light of heart
Tickle the senseless rushes[8] with their heels;
For I am proverbed with a grandsire phrase,[9]
I'll be a candleholder, and look on;
The game was ne'er so fair, and I am done.[10]

Mercutio. Tut! Dun's the mouse, the constable's own word![11]
If thou art Dun,[12] we'll draw thee from the mire
Of this sir-reverence love, wherein thou stickest
Up to the ears. Come, we burn daylight, ho!

Romeo. Nay, that's not so.

Mercutio. I mean, sir, in delay
We waste our lights in vain, like lights by day.
Take our good meaning, for our judgment sits
Five times in that ere once in our five wits.[13]

Romeo. And we mean well in going to this masque,
But 'tis no wit to go.

Mercutio. Why, may one ask?

Romeo. I dreamt a dream tonight.

Mercutio. And so did I.

Romeo. Well, what was yours?

Mercutio. That dreamers often lie.

Romeo. In bed asleep, while they do dream things true.

Mercutio. O, then, I see Queen Mab[14] hath been with you.
She is the fairies' midwife, and she comes
In shape no bigger than an agate stone
On the forefinger of an alderman,
Drawn with a team of little atomies[15]
Over men's noses as they lie asleep;
Her wagon spokes made of long spinners'[16] legs,
The cover, of the wings of grasshoppers;
Her traces of the smallest spider web;
Her collars, of the moonshine's wat'ry beams;
Her whip, of cricket's bone; the lash, of film;[17]
Her wagoner, a small gray-coated gnat,
Not half so big as a round little worm
Pricked from the lazy finger of a maid;
Her chariot is an empty hazelnut,
Made by the joiner squirrel or old grub,[18]

CLOSE READ

ANNOTATE: In lines 43–53, mark lines that one character begins but another ends.

QUESTION: Why does Shakespeare divide lines between characters?

CONCLUDE: How do these divided lines help to convey the nature of the characters' friendship?

14. **Queen Mab** the queen of fairyland.
15. **atomies** *n.* creatures.
16. **spinners** *n.* spiders.
17. **film** *n.* spider's thread.
18. **old grub** insect that bores holes in nuts.

DIGITAL PERSPECTIVES

Time out o' mind the fairies' coachmakers.
And in this state she gallops night by night
Through lovers' brains, and then they dream of love;
On courtiers' knees, that dream on curtsies straight;
O'er lawyers' fingers, who straight dream on fees;
O'er ladies' lips, who straight on kisses dream,
Which oft the angry Mab with blisters plagues,
Because their breath with sweetmeats[19] tainted are.
Sometimes she gallops o'er a courtier's nose,
And then dreams he of smelling out a suit;[20]
And sometime comes she with a tithe pig's[21] tail
Tickling a parson's nose as 'a lies asleep,
Then he dreams of another benefice.[22]
Sometime she driveth o'er a soldier's neck,
And then dream he of cutting foreign throats,
Of breaches, ambuscadoes,[23] Spanish blades,
Of healths[24] five fathom deep; and then anon
Drums in his ear, at which he starts and wakes,
And being thus frighted, swears a prayer or two
And sleeps again. This is that very Mab
That plats[25] the manes of horses in the night
And bakes the elflocks[26] in foul sluttish hairs,
Which once untangled much misfortune bodes.
This is the hag, when maids lie on their backs,
That presses them and learns them first to bear,
Making them women of good carriage.[27]
This is she—

Romeo. Peace, peace, Mercutio, peace!
Thou talk'st of nothing.

Mercutio. True, I talk of dreams;
Which are the children of an idle brain,
Begot of nothing but vain fantasy;
Which is as thin of substance as the air,
And more inconstant than the wind, who woos
Even now the frozen bosom of the North
And, being angered, puffs away from thence,
Turning his side to the dew-dropping South.

Benvolio. This wind you talk of blows us from ourselves.
Supper is done, and we shall come too late.

Romeo. I fear, too early; for my mind misgives
Some consequence yet hanging in the stars
Shall bitterly begin his fearful date
With this night's revels and expire the term
Of a despisèd life, closed in my breast,
By some vile forfeit of untimely death.[28]
But he that hath the steerage of my course

NOTES

19. **sweetmeats** *n.* candy.

20. **smelling . . . suit** finding someone who has a petition (suit) for the king and who will pay the courtier to gain the king's favor for the petition.

21. **tithe pig** pig donated to a parson.

22. **benefice** *n.* church appointment that included a guaranteed income.

23. **ambuscadoes** *n.* ambushes.

24. **healths** *n.* toasts ("To your health!").

25. **plats** *n.* tangles.

26. **elflocks** *n.* tangled hair.

27. **carriage** *n.* posture.

28. **my mind . . . death** My mind is fearful that some future event, fated by the stars, shall start to run its course tonight and cut my life short.

PERSONALIZE FOR LEARNING

Strategic Support

Imagery Students might struggle to comprehend Mercutio's lengthiest monologue, which is often referred to as the Queen Mab speech. The speech begins on line 53. Explain that Queen Mab was a well-known fairy in Celtic (Irish) folklore who supposedly visited people in their dreams. Mercutio contends that Romeo has been visited by the fairy queen who has made him want something that he is better off not having (Rosaline). Guide students step by step through the vivid images Mercutio provides of Queen Mab. Have them make lists of descriptions that appeal to the sense of sight, sound, and touch. Ask them to consider how the images presented at the start of the monologue differ from those presented toward the end of the monologue and what this may signify in the larger context of the play.

NOTES

1. **trencher** *n.* wooden platter.

2. **marchpane** *n.* marzipan, a confection made of sugar and almonds.

3. **walk a bout** dance a turn.

4. **makes dainty** hesitates; acts shy.

5. **A hall** clear the floor, make room for dancing.

Direct my sail! On, lusty gentlemen!

Benvolio. Strike, drum.

[*They march about the stage, and retire to one side.*]

⌘ ⌘ ⌘

Scene v • *A hall in Capulet's house.*

[Servingmen *come forth with napkins.*]

First Servingman. Where's Potpan, that he helps not to take away? He shift a trencher![1] He scrape a trencher!

Second Servingman. When good manners shall lie all in one or two men's hands, and they unwashed too, 'tis a foul thing.

First Servingman. Away with the joint-stools, remove the court cupboard, look to the plate. Good thou, save me a piece of marchpane,[2] and, as thou loves me, let the porter let in Susan Grindstone and Nell. Anthony and Potpan!

Second Servingman. Ay, boy, ready.

First Servingman. You are looked for and called for, asked for and sought for, in the great chamber.

Third Servingman. We cannot be here and there too. Cheerly, boys! Be brisk awhile, and the longest liver take all.

[*Exit.*]

[*Enter* Capulet, *his* Wife, Juliet, Tybalt, Nurse, *and all the* Guests *and* Gentlewomen *to the* Maskers.]

Capulet. Welcome, gentlemen! Ladies that have their toes
Unplagued with corns will walk a bout[3] with you.
Ah, my mistresses, which of you all
Will now deny to dance? She that makes dainty, [4]
She I'll swear hath corns. Am I come near ye now?
Welcome, gentlemen! I have seen the day
That I have worn a visor and could tell
A whispering tale in a fair lady's ear,
Such as would please. 'Tis gone, 'tis gone, 'tis gone.
You are welcome, gentlemen! Come, musicians, play.

[*Music plays, and they dance.*]

A hall, a hall![5] Give room! And foot it, girls.
More light, you knaves, and turn the tables up,
And quench the fire; the room is grown too hot.
Ah, sirrah, this unlooked-for sport comes well.
Nay, sit; nay, sit, good cousin Capulet;
For you and I are past our dancing days.

PERSONALIZE FOR LEARNING

Strategic Support

Poetic Structures Review Scene v, lines 20 and 21. Explain to students that Shakespeare frequently used enjambment in his plays. Unlike poetry with end-stopped lines, which read almost like sentences, enjambed lines allow for a thought to be stretched from one line to the next. This is called a run-on, or enjambed, line. The term *enjambment* is derived from a French word that means "straddling," and in this case, a single thought may straddle two or more lines. Enjambed lines should be read as one continuous sentence. Instruct students that if they do not encounter a mark of punctuation at the end of a poetic line, such as lines 20 and 21, they should just keep reading, as they would with any sentence, until a mark of punctuation is reached. You might even have students write out a few enjambed lines in sentence format to demonstrate how to read Shakespeare's verse.

How long is't now since last yourself and I
Were in a mask?

Second Capulet. By'r Lady, thirty years.

Capulet. What, man? 'Tis not so much, 'tis not so much;
'Tis since the nuptial of Lucentio,
Come Pentecost as quickly as it will,
Some-five-and-twenty-years, and then we masked.

Second Capulet. 'Tis more, 'tis more. His son is elder, sir;
His son is thirty.

Capulet. Will you tell me that?
His son was but a ward[6] two years ago.

Romeo. [*To a* Servingman] What lady's that which doth enrich the hand
Of yonder knight?

Servingman. I know not, sir.

Romeo. O, she doth teach the torches to burn bright!
It seems she hangs upon the cheek of night
As a rich jewel in an Ethiop's ear—
Beauty too rich for use, for earth too dear!
So shows a snowy dove trooping with crows
As yonder lady o'er her fellows shows.
The measure done, I'll watch her place of stand
And, touching hers, make blessèd my rude hand.
Did my heart love till now? Forswear[7] it, sight!
For I ne'er saw true beauty till this night.

Tybalt. This, by his voice, should be a Montague.
Fetch me my rapier, boy. What! Dares the slave
Come hither, covered with an antic face,[8]
To fleer[9] and scorn at our solemnity?
Now, by the stock and honor of my kin,
To strike him dead I hold it not a sin.

Capulet. Why, how now, kinsman? Wherefore storm you so?

Tybalt. Uncle, this is a Montague, our foe,
A villain, that is hither come in spite
To scorn at our solemnity this night.

Capulet. Young Romeo is it?

Tybalt. 'Tis he, that villain Romeo.

Capulet. Content thee, gentle coz,[10] let him alone.
'A bears him like a portly gentleman,[11]
And, to say truth, Verona brags of him
To be a virtuous and well-governed youth.
I would not for the wealth of all this town
Here in my house do him disparagement.[12]
Therefore be patient; take no note of him.

NOTES

6. **ward** *n.* minor.

7. **Forswear** *v.* deny.

8. **antic face** strange, fantastic mask.

9. **fleer** *v.* mock.

10. **coz** a term of address for a relative.

11. **'A . . . gentleman** He behaves like a dignified gentleman.

12. **disparagement** *n.* insult.

DIGITAL PERSPECTIVES

CLOSER LOOK

Analyze Imagery

Students may have marked lines 44–53 during their first read. Use these lines to help students understand imagery. Encourage them to talk about the annotations that they marked. You may want to model a close read with the class based on the highlights shown in the text.

ANNOTATE: Have students mark details in lines 44–53 that describe light and dark, or have students participate while you highlight them.

QUESTION: Guide students to consider what these details might tell them. Ask what a reader can infer from the descriptions of light and dark, and accept student responses.

Possible response: The details imply that Romeo is struck by Juliet's beauty and describes it by using terms related to light and dark.

CONCLUDE: Help students to formulate conclusions about the importance of these details in the text. Ask students why the author might have included these images of light and dark and what the effect is on the reader.

Possible response: The author may have included these images of light and dark to better describe the huge impact of Juliet's beauty on Romeo the first time he sees her. He repeatedly uses the visual imagery of light in describing her. He says her beauty is brighter than the fire of any torch. He even compares her to a white dove contrasted by the blackness of crows.

Remind students that **images** are words or phrases that appeal to one or more of the senses—sight, hearing, touch, taste, or smell. Writers use images to recreate sensory experiences in words. The term **imagery** is also used to refer to *figurative language* that evokes sensations. Like literal imagery, **figurative imagery** appeals to the senses, but by making imaginative comparisons to things that may not be purely sensory.

CLOSER LOOK

Analyze Poetic Structure

Students may have marked lines 93–106 of Scene v during their first read. Use these lines to help students understand sonnets. Encourage them to talk about the annotations that they marked. You may want to model a close read with the class based on the highlights shown in the text.

ANNOTATE: Have students mark words in lines 93–106 that are end rhymes, or have students participate while you highlight them.

QUESTION: Guide students to consider what these details might tell them. Ask what a reader can infer from the end rhymes, and accept student responses.

Possible response: The end rhymes indicate that there is a distinct pattern being established.

CONCLUDE: Help students to formulate conclusions about the importance of these details in the text. Ask students why the author might have chosen to use these end rhymes.

Possible response: The author may have included these end rhymes to draw attention to these lines of dialogue. The rhymes also create a more poetic structure, similar to a sonnet, with every other line rhyming and the final two lines rhyming with each other.

Remind students that one type of **poetic structure** is a **sonnet**. A sonnet is a fourteen-line lyric poem that is usually written in rhymed iambic pentameter. The English, or Shakespearean, sonnet consists of three *quatrains* (four-line stanzas) and a final *couplet* (two lines), with the rhyme scheme *abab cdcd efef gg*. Each of the three quatrains explores a different aspect of the poem's theme, and then the couplet presents a concluding comment. Shakespeare is acknowledged as the master of the sonnet, and he incorporated many of them into *The Tragedy of Romeo and Juliet.*

NOTES

13. **ill-beseeming semblance** inappropriate appearance.
14. **goodman** term of address for someone below the rank of gentleman.
15. **Go to!** expression of angry impatience.
16. **God . . . soul!** expression of impatience, equivalent to "God save me!"
17. **You will set a cock-a-hoop** You want to swagger like a barnyard rooster.
18. **This . . . you** This trait of yours may turn out to hurt you.
19. **princox** *n.* rude youngster; wise guy.
20. **Patience . . . meeting** enforced self-control mixing with strong anger.
21. **shrine** Juliet's hand
22. **palmers** *n.* pilgrims who at one time carried palm branches from the Holy Land.
23. **move** *v.* initiate involvement in earthly affairs.
24. **O . . . urged!** Romeo is saying, in substance, that he is happy. Juliet calls his kiss a sin, for now he can take it back—by another kiss.

It is my will, the which if thou respect,
Show a fair presence and put off these frowns,
An ill-beseeming semblance[13] for a feast.

Tybalt. It fits, when such a villain is a guest.
I'll not endure him.

Capulet. He shall be endured.
What, goodman[14] boy! I say, he shall. Go to![15]
Am I the master here, or you? Go to!
You'll not endure him, God shall mend my soul![16]
You'll make a mutiny among my guests!
You will set cock-a-hoop.[17] You'll be the man!

Tybalt. Why, uncle, 'tis a shame.

Capulet. Go to, go to!
You are a saucy boy. Is't so, indeed?
This trick may chance to scathe you.[18] I know what.
You must contrary me! Marry, 'tis time—
Well said, my hearts!—You are a princox[19]—go!
Be quiet, or—more light, more light!—For shame!
I'll make you quiet. What!—Cheerly, my hearts!

Tybalt. Patience perforce with willful choler meeting[20]
Makes my flesh tremble in their different greeting.
I will withdraw; but this intrusion shall,
Now seeming sweet, convert to bitt'rest gall. [*Exit.*]

Romeo. If I profane with my unworthiest hand
This holy shrine,[21] the gentle sin is this:
My lips, two blushing pilgrims, ready stand
To smooth that rough touch with a tender kiss.

Juliet. Good pilgrim, you do wrong your hand too much,
Which mannerly devotion shows in this;
For saints have hands that pilgrims' hands do touch
And palm to palm is holy palmers'[22] kiss.

Romeo. Have not saints lips, and holy palmers too?

Juliet. Ay, pilgrim, lips that they must use in prayer.

Romeo. O, then, dear saint, let lips do what hands do!
They pray; grant thou, lest faith turn to despair.

Juliet. Saints do not move,[23] though grant for prayers' sake.

Romeo. Then move not while my prayer's effect I take.
Thus from my lips, by thine my sin is purged.
[*Kisses her.*]

Juliet. Then have my lips the sin that they have took.

Romeo. Sin from my lips? O trespass sweetly urged![24]
Give me my sin again. [*Kisses her.*]

Juliet. You kiss by th' book.[25]

Nurse. Madam, your mother craves a word with you.

Romeo. What is her mother?

Nurse. Marry, bachelor,
Her mother is the lady of the house,
And a good lady, and a wise and virtuous.
I nursed her daughter, that you talked withal.
I tell you, he that can lay hold of her
Shall have the chinks.[26]

Romeo. Is she a Capulet?
O dear account! My life is my foe's debt.[27]

Benvolio. Away, be gone; the sport is at the best.

Romeo. Ay, so I fear; the more is my unrest.

Capulet. Nay, gentlemen, prepare not to be gone;
We have a trifling foolish banquet towards.
Is it e'en so?[28] Why, then, I thank you all.
I thank you, honest gentlemen. Good night.
More torches here! Come on then; let's to bed.
Ah, sirrah, by my fay,[29] it waxes late:
I'll to my rest. [*Exit all but* Juliet *and* Nurse.]

Juliet. Come hither, nurse. What is yond gentleman?

Nurse. The son and heir of old Tiberio.

Juliet. What's he that now is going out of door?

Nurse. Marry, that, I think, be young Petruchio.

Juliet. What's he that follows here, that would not dance?

NOTES

25. by th' book as if you were following a manual of courtly love.

26. chinks *n.* cash.

27. My life . . . debt Since Juliet is a Capulet, Romeo's life is at the mercy of his family.

28. Is . . . so? Is it the case that you really must leave?

29. fay *n.* faith.

PERSONALIZE FOR LEARNING

English Language Support

Syntax Review Scene v, lines 119, through 127. English learners may have difficulty with the syntax of Shakespeare's verse as he often reversed verbs, eliminated verbs, or changed the verb form to fit the iambic pentameter structure. Explain to students that when they encounter lines with odd wording or word orders that seem out of place that they should pause to consider the meanings of each word separately in order to glean meaning. For instance, the line *Away, be gone; the sport is at the best* (line 119) has the verb *be gone* after the adverb *away*. The words *be gone* would normally be stated as the verb *go*. Essentially, this line means *Go away; the sport is at the best.* Similarly, the line *Nay,* 121) also contains reversed words, a skipped verb, and a verb form change. This line means, *No, gentlemen, do not prepare to leave.* Finally, there are examples where verbs were left out. The lines *Come on then; let's to bed* (line 125) and *I'll to my rest* (line 127) mean *Come on then; let's go to bed* and *I'll go to my rest.* **ALL LEVELS**

Comprehension Check

Possible responses:

1. Romeo is troubled and depressed over his unreciprocated love of a girl named Rosaline.
2. Paris is Juliet's potential fiancé. Paris has asked Lord Capulet for her hand in marriage, and Juliet has agreed to meet with Paris at the party.
3. Lord Capulet prevents Tybalt from attacking Romeo at the feast. He tells Tybalt that Romeo is behaving like a gentleman and that he will not allow him to be insulted in his house.
4. Romeo claims that a kiss from Juliet will purge him of his sins because he is comparing Juliet to a saint.
5. Responses will vary, but should include the main events from Act I of the play, including the fight between Montague and Capulet families, followed by the introduction of Romeo, heartsick after being rejected by Rosaline. After Romeo is invited to a party that Rosaline is to attend, he agrees to go and meets Juliet. Romeo and Juliet fall in love instantly, but learn that their families are enemies.

NOTES

Nurse. I know not.

Juliet. Go ask his name—If he is married,
My grave is like to be my wedding bed.

Nurse. His name is Romeo, and a Montague,
The only son of your great enemy.

Juliet. My only love sprung from my only hate!
Too early seen unknown, and known too late!
Prodigious[30] birth of love it is to me
That I must love a loathèd enemy.

Nurse. What's this? What's this?

Juliet. A rhyme I learnt even now.
Of one I danced withal. [*One calls within*, "Juliet."]

Nurse. Anon, anon!
Come, let's away; the strangers all are gone. [*Exit all.*]

30. **Prodigious** *adj.* monstrous; foretelling misfortune.

Comprehension Check

Complete the following items after you finish your first read.

1. What is troubling Romeo at the beginning of the play?
2. What is Paris's relationship to Juliet?
3. What does Lord Capulet stop Tybalt from doing at the feast?
4. What does Romeo say a kiss from Juliet will take from him?
5. **Notebook** Confirm your understanding of the text by writing a summary.

PERSONALIZE FOR LEARNING

Challenge

The Tragedy of Romeo and Juliet has remained popular for 400 years because it addresses some very universal themes, most important, that of teenage love. Just as it was in the late sixteenth century when the play was first staged, there are still pressures today on teenagers with regard to dating. Is there such a thing as love at first sight? Should differences prevent people from dating? Have students write a paragraph or two on how they think the story of Romeo and Juliet connects to the lives of teenagers today.

MAKING MEANING

Close Read the Text

Close Read (Annotate, Question, Conclude)

Reread what the Prince says when he finds the Capulets and Montagues quarreling again (Act I, Scene i, lines 77–89). How does the Prince describe the weapons of the citizens of Verona? What does this show about the feud's effect on the community?

Analyze the Text

CITE TEXTUAL EVIDENCE to support your answers.

Notebook Respond to these questions.

1. (a) What do you know about Romeo's and Juliet's lives at this point in the play? Explain, citing details from the play that support your answer. (b) **Compare and Contrast** How are their circumstances both similar and different? Explain.
2. **Analyze** What threats to Romeo and Juliet's love are evident in Act I? Support your answer with details from the play.
3. (a) What information about the two feuding households is presented in the Prologue? (b) **Connect** How does Juliet's comment in Act I, Scene v, lines 138–141, echo the Prologue? Explain your response.
4. **Essential Question:** ***Do we determine our own destinies?*** What have you learned about destiny by reading Act I of *The Tragedy of Romeo and Juliet*?

LANGUAGE DEVELOPMENT

Concept Vocabulary

mutiny	transgression	heretics

Why These Words? These concept vocabulary words communicate a violation of order or authority. What other words in Act I connect to this concept?

Practice

Notebook Confirm your understanding of these words by using each one in a sentence.

Word Study

Latin Prefix: *trans-* The Latin prefix *trans-* means "across," "beyond," or "through." In the play, Romeo describes his friend's sympathy for him as love's *transgression*. The word suggests that love has crossed a boundary and unfairly involved his friend. Find another word that includes this prefix. Write down the word and its meaning.

THE TRAGEDY OF ROMEO AND JULIET, ACT I

Tool Kit
Close-Read Guide and Model Annotation

WORD NETWORK
Add interesting words related to destiny from the text to your Word Network.

STANDARDS
Language
Identify and correctly use patterns of word changes that indicate different meanings or parts of speech.

DIGITAL PERSPECTIVES

Jump Start

CLOSE READ Have students consider the idea of fate or destiny. Ask them if "star-crossed" love is real and how much control we have over whom we love.

Close Read the Text

Review and discuss the sections students have marked. If needed, continue to model close reading by using the Annotation Highlights in the Interactive Teacher's Edition.

Analyze the Text

1. (a) Romeo's family is feuding with Juliet's. They meet and fall in love. **DOK 1** (b) They know they should be enemies; Romeo has been in love before. **DOK 2**
2. Their love is taboo due to the feud. Tybalt wants to fight Romeo—or any Montague. **DOK 2**
3. (a) The families are feuding over an "ancient grudge." **DOK 2** (b) She says her "only love sprung from my only hate." **DOK 3**
4. Destiny, like their love, is predetermined. **DOK 3**

Concept Vocabulary

Why These Words? Possible responses: *overthrows, rebellious, profaners*

Word Network

Possible words: star-crossed, fatal, misadventured

Practice

Possible responses: The captain worried that his unhappy crew might start a *mutiny*; Society may shun a *heretic* for not conforming to social norms; His latest *transgression* was not taking out the trash.

Word Study

Latin Prefix: *trans-*

If students fail to understand the meaning of the prefix *trans-*, **then** have them search for words that begin with *trans-* and check definitions in a dictionary. For Reteach and Practice, see **Word Study: Latin Prefix *trans-* (RP).**

FORMATIVE ASSESSMENT

Analyze the Text

- **If** students struggle to make the connection between Juliet's dialogue in Act I and the Prologue, **then** have them write her lines in modern English and compare to lines 5–6 in the Prologue.

AUTHOR'S PERSPECTIVE **Elfrieda Hiebert, Ph.D.**

Concept Vocabulary Teachers can help students expand their word networks by using morphemes and cognates.

- **Morphemes** are the smallest grammatical unit of a language that cannot be subdivided into further such elements. Tell students that morphemes can be words or parts of words, such as the words *as, the, write*, or the *–ed* in *stayed*. Many new words are members of morphological families of three to five words. For example, words that come from the Anglo-Saxon layer of English use inflected endings (such as *-s/-es, -ed, -ing*) and *-er* and *-est* for comparisons (such as *big, bigger, biggest*).
- **Cognates** are words that are descended from the same language, such as the English word *family*, the Spanish *familia*, the French *famille*, the Italian *famiglia*, and the German *familie*. Explain to students that knowing cognates can help build language by introducing multiple words and ways to decode unfamiliar words.

Analyze Craft and Structure

Dialogue in drama differs from dialogue in short stories and novels. Drama can be more difficult to read because the natural flow is interrupted with the names of the characters. We see the name of one character followed by what the character says. Then the name of another character appears along with his or her response.

Stage directions are not only important for the reader of drama, but they are also essential for the actors in a drama. They let actors know when to exit the stage, the positions they should take on stage, what actions should be taken with props, what gestures they should make, and even sometimes the emotions they should convey when speaking lines. For more support, see **Analyze Craft and Structure: Elements of Drama.**

Practice

Possible responses:

1. Lines 63–64, when Benovolio says, "I do but keep the peace. Put up thy sword, / Or manage it to part these men with me" and line 103 where he says, "I drew to part them."
2.

CHARACTER	DIALOGUE	WHAT IT REVEALS
Juliet	I'll look to like, if looking liking move; But no more deep will I endart mine eye Than your consent gives strength to make it fly. (lines 97–99)	Juliet is an obedient daughter.
Nurse	Thou wast the prettiest babe that e'er I nursed. And I might live to see thee married once, I have my wish. (lines 60–62)	The Nurse cares very much for Juliet, and they are quite close.
Lady Capulet	This is the matter—Nurse, give leave awhile; We must talk in secret. Nurse, come back again. I have rememb'red me, thou's hear our counsel. Thou knowest my daughter's of a pretty age. (lines 7–10)	The Nurse is closer to Juliet than Lady Capulet is, and Lady Capulet knows this.

3. **(a)** 1. *Enter Sampson and Gregory, with swords and bucklers, of the house of Capulet.* (Act I, scene 1); 2. *They fight.* (Act I, scene 1); 3. *He reads the letter.* (Act I, scene 2). **(b)** 1. This reveals what props the actors are to carry and that they are ready to fight. 2. This reveals that the actors portraying Tybalt and Benvolio are to fight each other and the violent nature of the hostility between the two families. 3. This reveals that the actor portraying Romeo should read the servant's letter and that Romeo is educated.

MAKING MEANING

THE TRAGEDY OF ROMEO AND JULIET, ACT I

STANDARDS

Reading Literature

- Analyze how complex characters develop over the course of a text, interact with other characters, and advance the plot or develop the theme.
- Analyze how an author's choices concerning how to structure a text, order events within it, and manipulate time create such effects as mystery, tension, or surprise

Analyze Craft and Structure

Elements of Drama The two most important elements of drama are **dialogue**, the conversation between the characters, and **stage directions**, the notes that describe how the work should be performed. Each plays an important role in conveying meaning in a drama.

In drama, dialogue generally follows the name of the speaker:

> **Benvolio.** My noble uncle, do you know the cause?
> **Montague.** I neither know it nor can learn of him.

Dialogue reveals characters' personalities and relationships, advances the action, and captures the language of the time and place in which a play is set.

Stage directions describe scenes, lighting, sound, and characters' actions. Stage directions are usually italicized and enclosed in brackets or parentheses.

> *Scene i. Verona. A public place.*
> [*Enter* Sampson *and* Gregory, *with swords and bucklers, of the house of Capulet.*]

As you reread portions of the play, notice how the dialogue and stage directions help you "hear" and "see" the action in your mind.

Practice

CITE TEXTUAL EVIDENCE to support your answers.

Notebook Respond to these questions.

1. Cite two examples of dialogue in Act I, Scene i, that show Benvolio's peace-making personality.
2. Use the chart to analyze what the dialogue among the Nurse, Juliet, and Lady Capulet in Act I, Scene iii, reveals about each character. Record important lines, and determine what those lines reveal about the character speaking them.

CHARACTER	DIALOGUE	WHAT IT REVEALS
Juliet		
Nurse		
Lady Capulet		

3. (a) Identify three examples of stage directions from the text that do more than simply dictate characters' movements on and off stage. (b) Explain what each direction shows about the characters and the action.

FORMATIVE ASSESSMENT

Analyze Craft and Structure

- **If** students are unable to identify dialogue that reveals the characters of Juliet, the Nurse, and Lady Capulet, **then** guide them to examine specific lines and interpret the meanings of those lines.
- **If** students fail to recognize stage directions, **then** have them look for italicized lines in brackets that are not assigned line numbers. For Reteach and Practice, see **Analyze Craft and Structure: Elements of Drama (RP).**

LANGUAGE DEVELOPMENT

Author's Style

Figurative Language An **oxymoron** is a figure of speech that combines contradictory, or opposing, ideas. An oxymoron may help create meaning in a text by communicating a complicated truth, or it can simply display an absurd contradiction for effect. The word *bittersweet* is a perfect example; a bittersweet moment combines feelings of happiness and sadness.

In *The Tragedy of Romeo and Juliet*, Shakespeare uses oxymora (the plural form of *oxymoron*) to help communicate characters' feelings.

OXYMORON	MEANING/EFFECT
Romeo. . . . Why, then, O brawling love! O loving hate, O anything, of nothing first created.	These examples of oxymoron show Romeo's conflicting feelings about love and that love can lead to negative feelings.

Read It

Mark examples of oxymoron in this passage from Act I of *The Tragedy of Romeo and Juliet*. Then, describe what they communicate about love and their effect on the text.

DIALOGUE	MEANING/EFFECT
Romeo. . . . O heavy lightness, serious vanity, Misshapen chaos of well-seeming forms, Feather of lead, bright smoke, cold fire, sick health, Still-waking sleep, that is not what it is!	Romeo thinks love is complex. Some things seem normal that are really chaotic. Romeo thinks love is deceptive. Love is not always what it seems.

Write It

Write a paragraph that includes at least two oxymora you made up on your own.

EVIDENCE LOG

Before moving on to a new selection, go to your Evidence Log and record what you learned from Act I of *The Tragedy of Romeo and Juliet*.

STANDARDS

Language

Interpret figures of speech in context and analyze their role in the text.

DIGITAL PERSPECTIVES

Author's Style

An oxymoron is a figure of speech that juxtaposes ideas that seem contradictory and appear in everyday vocabulary and conversation as well as in purposely crafted literature. A specifically written oxymoron often creates paradoxes, which are statements, ideas, or situations that seem contradictory but on closer inspection turn out to be true. A good example of a paradox is found in Act I, scene v, when Juliet has just discovered Romeo's identity and expresses her distress in the form of a paradox:

My only love, sprung from my only hate!
Too early seen unknown, and known too late!
Prodigious birth of love it is to me
That I must love a loathèd enemy.

While the ideas of oxymoron and paradox seem to be the same thing, they actually are not. An oxymoron is usually just a small phrase consisting of usually just two contradictory words that may express a paradox; whereas, a paradoxical statement is a longer thought that may or may not contain an oxymoron. For more support, see **Author's Style: Figurative Language.**

Read It

See student page for possible responses.

Write It

Possible responses

Answers will vary but students should write two sentences that demonstrate their understanding of an oxymoron.

FORMATIVE ASSESSMENT

Author's Style

- **If** students are unable to identify examples of oxymoron in dialogue, **then** have them search the text for words or ideas that are opposites.
- **If** students are unable to create their own oxymora, **then** have them make lists of opposite nouns and opposite adjectives that they might be able to incorporate into their writing.

For Reteach and Practice, see **Author's Style: Figurative Language (RP).**

PERSONALIZE FOR LEARNING

Strategic Support

Oxymoron If students have difficulty understanding oxymoron and how writers use them to create specific effects, have them each choose a noun such as snow, sun, smile, etc. Then have them list adjectives that could be used to describe the noun they chose, such as cold, bright, or kind. Once they have compiled a list of adjectives, have them consult an online thesaurus to look up antonyms for each of their adjectives.

Finally, have them combine the antonyms with the original nouns to create examples of oxymoron. Have them choose one oxymoron they created and write a sentence that describes what this new oxymoron makes them think of or feel.

Example: *smile* (noun) – *kind* (adjective to describe *smile*) – *cruel* (antonym of *kind*) – *cruel smile* (oxymoron). A *cruel smile* makes me think of a villain.

An expanded **English Language Support Lesson** on Oxymoron is available in the Interactive Teacher's Edition.

The Tragedy of Romeo and Juliet, Act II

AUDIO SUMMARIES
Audio summaries of *The Tragedy of Romeo and Juliet,* Act II are available online in both English and Spanish in the Interactive Teacher's Edition or Unit Resources. Assigning these summaries prior to reading the selection may help students build additional background knowledge and set a context for their first read.

Summary

In Act II of *The Tragedy of Romeo and Juliet,* the young couple pursues their love. After the feast, Romeo sneaks away to look up at the window of Juliet's room. She greets him from the balcony and talks to herself about her love, wishing that he could belong to some other family so that they could be together. He appears and they speak together, playfully teasing each other and then vowing their love. The couple makes preparations to meet up to be married. Friar Lawrence agrees to marry the couple in the hope that the marriage will end the strife between the Capulets and Montagues. At the end of the act, they marry.

Insight

This classic tragedy examines love and youthful impulsiveness. In this scene, two young people marry on the night they meet.

ESSENTIAL QUESTION:
Do we determine our own destinies?

Connection to Essential Question

As students read this play, they will see evidence to argue both sides of the Essential Question, "Do we determine our own destinies?" In this act, the young lovers get married, but the events of the later acts complicate the question. The play suggests that Romeo and Juliet were unavoidably fated to fall in love and die.

WHOLE-CLASS LEARNING PERFORMANCE TASK
Which has a greater impact on the characters in these texts: destiny or personal choices?

UNIT PERFORMANCE-BASED ASSESSMENT
Should the opinions of others affect our own choices or destinies?

Connection to Performance Tasks

Whole-Class Learning Performance Task Ask students to track their ideas about the Performance Task. The full plot line of this play may have them revising their opinions.

Unit Performance-Based Assessment In Act II, the young lovers reject their parents' direction. Students will need to see the events of the story unfold before answering the prompt.

DIGITAL PERSPECTIVES Audio · Video · Document · Annotation Highlights · EL Highlights · Online Assessment

LESSON RESOURCES

	Making Meaning	Language Development	Effective Expression
Lesson	**First Read** **Close Read** **Analyze the Text** **Analyze Craft and Structure**	**Concept Vocabulary** **Word Study**	**Speaking and Listening**
Instructional Standards	**RL.5** Analyze how an author's choices . . . **RL.10** By the end of grade 9, read and comprehend literature . . .	**L.4.b** Identify and correctly use patterns of word changes . . .	**SL.4** Present information, findings, and supporting evidence . . . **SL.6** Adapt speech to a variety of contexts . . .
STUDENT RESOURCES			
Available online in the Interactive Student Edition or Unit Resources	Selection Audio First-Read Guide: Drama Close-Read Guide: Drama	Word Network	Evidence Log
TEACHER RESOURCES			
Selection Resources Available online in the Interactive Teacher's Edition or Unit Resources	Audio Summaries Annotation Highlights EL Highlights English Language Support Lesson: Dramatic Interpretation Analyze Craft and Structure: Poetic Structure	Concept Vocabulary and Word Study	Speaking and Listening: Dramatic Interpretation
Reteach/Practice (RP) Available online in the Interactive Teacher's Edition or Unit Resources	Analyze Craft and Structure: Poetic Structure (RP)	Word Study: Latin Prefix *counter-* (RP)	Speaking and Listening: Dramatic Interpretation (RP)
Assessment Available online in Assessments	Selection Test		
My Resources	A Unit 4 Answer Key is available online and in the Interactive Teacher's Edition.		

Reading Support

Text Complexity Rubric: *The Tragedy of Romeo and Juliet*, Act II	
Quantitative Measures	
Lexile: NP **Text Length:** 5,650 words	
Qualitative Measures	
Knowledge Demands 1—2—3—4—**5**	Students will need information about the historical context of Verona, Italy, during the Renaissance. Some of this information is covered in the background information.
Structure 1—2—3—4—**5**	The selection is a Shakespearean play written primarily in blank verse. Line breaks will likely be challenging for students.
Language Conventionality and Clarity 1—2—3—4—**5**	The selection contains complex sentences, unfamiliar syntax, figurative language, challenging vocabulary, and Elizabethan language.
Levels of Meaning/Purpose 1—2—**3**—4—5	The concept of a classic tale of star-crossed lovers is accessible but will likely be difficult to grasp due to challenging language and structure.

DECIDE AND PLAN

English Language Support

Provide English Learners with support for **Knowledge Demands and Language** as they read the selection.

Knowledge Demands Have students summarize what they know so far. Make sure students understand the main events that have taken place and the primary characters by the end of Act I.

Language Students may struggle with the puns and jokes, particularly in scene iv. Have students listen to an audio version of the scene to try to grasp the spirit of the exchange by listening to the tone and inflection of the speakers. Then discuss the spirit of jokes and puns to help students understand them.

Strategic Support

Provide students with strategic support to ensure that they can successfully read the text.

Knowledge Demands Have students work with a partner to summarize what they know so far. What has happened? Who is involved? Then have students predict what will happen next.

Language If students have difficulty with the challenging vocabulary, ask them to use the glosses that support the archaic language. Ask them to cite clues in the play that may help define the language. Then have them reread and note language that remains unclear. Encourage students to read to get the main idea without struggling to understand every word or phrase.

Challenge

Provide students who need to be challenged with ideas for how they can go beyond a simple interpretation of the text.

Text Analysis Have students note that Shakespeare writes much of the play in blank verse, and often uses rhyming couplets. Have students reread Act II, scene III, in which the Friar speaks in rhymed couplets. Have students discuss why Shakespeare may have chosen to write this scene in rhyme. What is the effect?

Written Response Challenge students to research another work of Shakespeare. Have them compare an aspect of the work to *The Tragedy of Romeo and Juliet*, for example imagery, style of verse, or rhyme scheme. Ask students to share their findings in small groups.

TEACH

Read and Respond

Have students do their first read of the selection. Then have them complete their close read. Finally, work with them on the Making Meaning and Effective Expression activities.

Standards Support Through Teaching and Learning Cycle

IDENTIFY NEEDS

Analyze results of the Beginning-of-Year Assessment, focusing on the items relating to Unit 4. Also take into consideration student performance to this point and your observations of where particular students struggle.

DECIDE AND PLAN

- If students have performed poorly on items matching these standards, then provide selection scaffolds before assigning them the on-level lesson provided in the Student Edition.
- If students have done well on the Beginning-of-Year Assessment, then challenge them to keep progressing and learning by giving them opportunities to practice the skills in depth.
- Use the Selection Resources listed on the Planning pages for *The Tragedy of Romeo and Juliet*, Act II to help students continually improve their ability to master the standards.

Instructional Standards: *The Tragedy of Romeo and Juliet*, Act II

	Catching Up	This Year	Looking Forward
Reading	You may wish to administer the **Analyze Craft and Structure: Poetic Structure (RP)** worksheet to better familiarize students with blank verse.	**RL.5** Analyze how an author's choices concerning how to structure a text, order events within it, and manipulate time create such effects as mystery, tension, or surprise.	Have students discuss whether blank verse makes the play antiquated or timeless.
Speaking and Listening	You may wish to administer the **Speaking and Listening: Dramatic Interpretation (RP)** worksheet to help students prepare for their scenes.	**SL.6** Adapt speech to a variety of contexts and tasks, demonstrating command of formal English when indicated or appropriate.	Challenge students to write and perform an original scene using blank verse.
Language	Review the **Word Study: Latin Prefix *counter-* (RP)** worksheet with students to ensure they understand the Latin prefix.	**L.4.b** Identify and correctly use patterns of word changes that indicate different meanings or parts of speech.	Have students locate other Latin or Greek prefixes they may recognize in the selection.

TEACH

Implement the planned lesson, and gather evidence of student learning.

ANALYZE AND REVISE

- Analyze student work for evidence of student learning.
- Identify whether students have met the expectations in the standards.
- Identify implications for future instruction.

Jump Start

FIRST READ Romeo and Juliet, arguably the world's most famous couple, were only teenagers. Engage the students in a discussion of how seriously they take their relationships. What about their parents and the media—do they feel young love is treated with seriousness or simply as a passing phase?

The Tragedy of Romeo and Juliet, Act II

Who will Romeo and Juliet confide in if they cannot speak of their relationship to their feuding families? Is destiny in some ways toying with them? Modeling the questions readers might ask as they read Act II of *The Tragedy of Romeo and Juliet* brings the text alive for students and connects it to the Whole-Class Performance Task assignment. Selection audio and print capability for the selection are available in the Interactive Teacher's Edition.

Concept Vocabulary

Support students as they rank their words. Ask if they've ever heard, read, or used them. Reassure them that the definitions for these words are listed in the selection.

FIRST READ

Students should perform the steps of the first read independently.

NOTICE: You may want to encourage students to notice how Romeo and Juliet behave and how their relationship develops throughout Act II.

ANNOTATE: Remind students to mark passages that include blank verse and iambic pentameter.

CONNECT: Encourage students to make connections—perhaps they know of other couples who came together in spite of family opposition.

RESPOND: Students will answer questions and write a summary to demonstrate understanding.

Point out to students that while they will always complete the Respond step at the end of the first read, the other steps would probably happen somewhat concurrently. You may wish to print copies of the **First-Read Guide: Fiction** for students to use.

Remind students that during their first read, they should not answer the close-read questions that appear in the selection.

Playwright

William Shakespeare

The Tragedy of Romeo and Juliet, Act II

Concept Vocabulary

You will encounter the following words as you read Act II of *The Tragedy of Romeo and Juliet.* Before reading, note how familiar you are with each word. Then, rank the words in order from most familiar (1) to least familiar (3).

WORD	YOUR RANKING
cunning	
counterfeit	
confidence	

After completing the first read, come back to the concept vocabulary and review your rankings. Mark changes to your original rankings as needed.

Tool Kit
First-Read Guide and Model Annotation

First Read DRAMA

Apply these strategies as you conduct your first read. You will have an opportunity to complete the close-read notes after your first read.

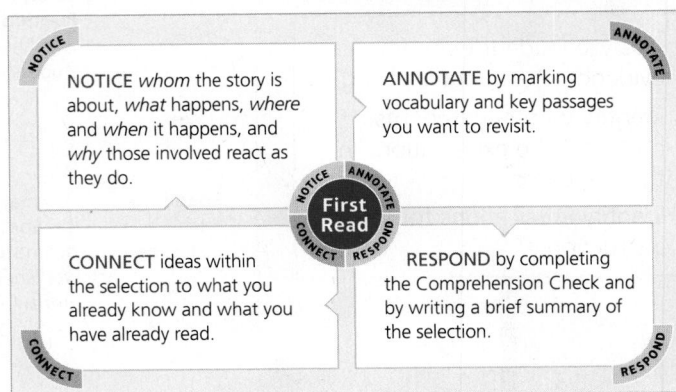

NOTICE *whom* the story is about, *what* happens, *where* and *when* it happens, and *why* those involved react as they do.

ANNOTATE by marking vocabulary and key passages you want to revisit.

CONNECT ideas within the selection to what you already know and what you have already read.

RESPOND by completing the Comprehension Check and by writing a brief summary of the selection.

First Read: NOTICE, ANNOTATE, CONNECT, RESPOND

STANDARDS
Reading Literature
By the end of grade 9, read and comprehend literature, including stories, dramas, and poems, in the grades 9–10 text complexity band proficiently, with scaffolding as needed at the high end of the range.

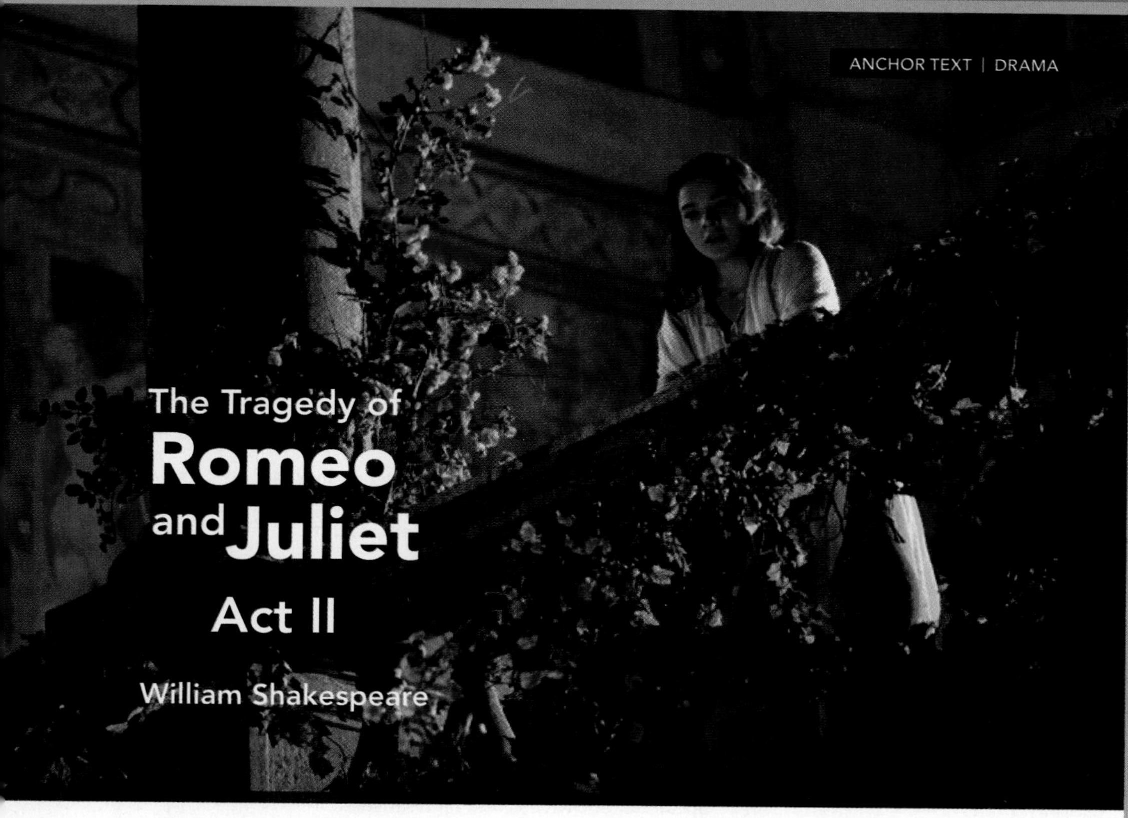

ANCHOR TEXT | DRAMA

The Tragedy of Romeo and Juliet

Act II

William Shakespeare

REVIEW AND ANTICIPATE

Act I reveals a bitter, long-standing feud between the Montagues and the Capulets. It also introduces the play's title characters, who meet at a party and immediately fall in love, only to discover that they come from opposing sides of the feud. As you read Act II, think about the choices Romeo and Juliet make as both their love and the conflicts they face intensify.

SCAN FOR MULTIMEDIA

Prologue

[*Enter* Chorus.]

Chorus. Now old desire[1] doth in his deathbed lie,
And young affection gapes to be his heir.[2]
That fair[3] for which love groaned for and would die,
With tender Juliet matched, is now not fair.
Now Romeo is beloved and loves again,
Alike bewitched[4] by the charm of looks;
But to his foe supposed he must complain,[5]
And she steal love's sweet bait from fearful hooks.
Being held a foe, he may not have access
To breathe such vows as lovers use to swear,

NOTES

1. **old desire** Romeo's love for Rosaline.
2. **young . . . heir** Romeo's new love for Juliet is eager to replace his love for Rosaline.
3. **fair** beautiful woman (Rosaline).
4. **Alike bewitched** Both Romeo and Juliet are enchanted.
5. **complain** *v.* address his words of love.

DIGITAL PERSPECTIVES

CLOSER LOOK

Analyze Chorus

Students may have marked lines 1–5 during their first read of the Prologue. Use this paragraph to help students understand the significance of what the chorus is announcing. Encourage them to talk about the annotations that they marked. You may want to model a close read with the class based on the highlights shown in the text.

ANNOTATE: Have students mark details in the prologue that show the changed state of Romeo's affections from Rosaline to Juliet, or have students participate while you highlight them.

QUESTION: Guide students to consider what these details might tell them. Ask what a reader can infer from these lines about what the chorus is telling us about Romeo, and accept student responses.

Possible response: Romeo has fallen out of love with Rosaline and now both loves and is loved by Juliet.

CONCLUDE: Help students to formulate conclusions about the importance of these details in the text. Ask students why the author might have included these details.

Possible response: Romeo's love for Juliet—someone who is forbidden because of family feuding—sets the stage for this drama. Also, the chorus tells us that Romeo's love for Juliet is returned. This fact changes the destiny of both star-crossed lovers.

Remind students that ancient Greek playwrights developed the Chorus as a crucial part of a drama's structure. The Chorus was a collective of cast members not involved in the plot, who gave the audience background information or inside emotional information about particular characters. They set tone and mood for the audience by giving them necessary information that they wouldn't otherwise have access to.

VOCABULARY DEVELOPMENT

Concept Vocabulary Reinforcement
Students will benefit from practice with Elizabethan vocabulary. Reinforce their comprehension with "show-you-know" sentences. The first part of the sentence uses the vocabulary term in an appropriate context. The second part of the sentence clarifies the vocabulary term. Model the strategy with the vocabulary term *old desire.*

John's *old desire* is parked in the garage as he drives a silver sports car through town; he no longer wants the red pick-up truck he loved as a teenager.

Then give the students these writing prompts and coach them in creating the clarification part:

1. My brother met Sarah at a party and it seems they are *alike bewitched;*

Possible Response: they are enchanted with one another.

2. If you look through this fashion magazine you will only find *fairs*;

Possible Response: every model is a very beautiful woman.

CLOSER LOOK

Identify Iambic Pentameter

Students may have marked Mercutio's lines during their first read of Scene i. Use this paragraph to help students understand iambic pentameter. Encourage them to talk about the annotations that they marked. You may want to model a close read with the class based on the highlights shown in the text.

ANNOTATE: Have students mark lines 19–20, featuring successive rhyming lines in Mercutio's speech, or have students participate while you highlight them.

QUESTION: Guide students to consider what these lines might tell them. Ask what a reader can infer from the meter of Mercutio's speech and accept student responses.

Possible response: The speech is in iambic pentameter, which usually does not rhyme. The sing-song rhyming in these lines suggests that Mercutio might be mocking Romeo's love for Rosaline.

CONCLUDE: Help students to formulate conclusions about the importance of this speech in the text. Ask students why the author might have included Mercutio's thoughts about Rosaline.

Possible response: Mercutio's speech shows what he thinks about Romeo and it also shows what he says when he thinks Romeo is not there.

Remind students that iambic pentameter is five pairs of syllables, with one unstressed syllable followed by a stressed syllable. This meter sounds like natural spoken English, so it often appears in Shakespeare's plays. When the text varies from unrhymed iambic pentameter, the shift in structure signals something important or noteworthy about a character or scene.

NOTES

6. **Temp'ring . . . sweet** easing their difficulties with great delights.

And she as much in love, her means much less
To meet her new belovèd anywhere;
But passion lends them power, time means to meet,
Temp'ring extremities with extreme sweet.[6]
[*Exit.*]

⌘ ⌘ ⌘

Scene i • *Near Capulet's orchard.*

[*Enter* Romeo *alone.*]

Romeo. Can I go forward when my heart is here?
Turn back, dull earth,[1] and find thy center[2] out.
[*Enter* Benvolio *with* Mercutio. Romeo *retires.*]

Benvolio. Romeo! My cousin Romeo! Romeo!

Mercutio. He is wise.
And, on my life, hath stol'n him home to bed.

Benvolio. He ran this way and leapt this orchard wall.
Call, good Mercutio.

Mercutio. Nay, I'll conjure[3] too.
Romeo! Humors! Madman! Passion! Lover!
Appear thou in the likeness of a sigh;
Speak but one rhyme, and I am satisfied!
Cry but "Ay me!" Pronounce but "love" and "dove";
Speak to my gossip[4] Venus one fair word,
One nickname for her purblind son and heir,
Young Abraham Cupid, he that shot so true
When King Cophetua loved the beggar maid!
He heareth not, he stirreth not, he moveth not;
The ape is dead,[5] and I must conjure him.
I conjure thee by Rosaline's bright eyes,
By her high forehead and her scarlet lip,
By her fine foot, straight leg, and quivering thigh,
And the demesnes that there adjacent lie,
That in thy likeness thou appear to us!

Benvolio. And if he hear thee, thou wilt anger him.

Mercutio. This cannot anger him. 'Twould anger him
To raise a spirit in his mistress' circle
Of some strange nature, letting it there stand
Till she had laid it and conjured it down.
That were some spite; my invocation
Is fair and honest; in his mistress' name,
I conjure only but to raise up him.

1. **dull earth** lifeless body.
2. **center** heart, or possibly soul (Juliet).
3. **conjure** *v.* recite a spell to make Romeo appear.
4. **gossip** *n.* good friend
5. **The ape is dead.** Romeo, like a trained monkey, seems to be playing.

PERSONALIZE FOR LEARNING

Strategic Support

Iambic Pentameter If students have difficulty understanding iambic pentameter explain that *iambic pentameter* means there are five pairs of the following pattern: an unstressed syllable followed by a stressed syllable. Use the following example from Christopher Marlowe:

Was this the face that launched a thousand ships?

Have students repeat this line a few times together in their natural speaking rhythm.

Then show them the text with the stressed syllables in bold:

Was ***This*** *the* ***Face*** *that* ***Launched*** *a* ***Thou****sand* ***Ships?***

Have students read it again emphasizing the stressed syllables. Finally have students write this example out and mark it using the iambic symbols (U /). The U stands for Unstressed syllables and the / stands for stressed syllables.

If you have time, ask students to take a line from Mercutio's speech and mark it with the iambic symbols.

DIGITAL PERSPECTIVES

Benvolio. Come, he hath hid himself among these trees
To be consorted[6] with the humorous[7] night.
Blind is his love and best befits the dark.

Mercutio. If love be blind, love cannot hit the mark.
Now will he sit under a medlar[8] tree
And wish his mistress were that kind of fruit
As maids call medlars when they laugh alone.
O, Romeo, that she were, O that she were
And open *et cetera*, thou a pop'rin pear!
Romeo, good night. I'll to my truckle bed;[9]
This field bed is too cold for me to sleep.
Come, shall we go?

Benvolio. Go then, for 'tis in vain
To seek him here that means not to be found.
[*Exit with others.*]

⌘ ⌘ ⌘

Scene ii • *Capulet's orchard.*

Romeo. [*Coming forward*] He jests at scars that never felt a wound.
[*Enter* Juliet *at a window.*]
But soft! What light through yonder window breaks?
It is the East, and Juliet is the sun!
Arise, fair sun, and kill the envious moon,
Who is already sick and pale with grief
That thou her maid art far more fair than she.
Be not her maid, since she is envious.
Her vestal livery[1] is but sick and green,
And none but fools do wear it. Cast it off.
It is my lady! O, it is my love!
O, that she knew she were!
She speaks, yet she says nothing. What of that?
Her eye discourses; I will answer it.
I am too bold; 'tis not to me she speaks.
Two of the fairest stars in all the heaven,
Having some business, do entreat her eyes
To twinkle in their spheres[2] till they return.
What if her eyes were there, they in her head?
The brightness of her cheek would shame those stars
As daylight doth a lamp; her eyes in heaven
Would through the airy region stream so bright
That birds would sing and think it were not night.

NOTES

6. **consorted** *v.* associated.
7. **humorous** *adj.* humid; moody, like a lover.
8. **medlar** *n.* applelike fruit.
9. **truckle bed** trundlebed, placed under a larger bed when not in use.

CLOSE READ

ANNOTATE: In lines 2–22, mark words and phrases that relate to brightness and light.

QUESTION: What connection does this language make between Juliet and the skies?

CONCLUDE: What does this famous speech suggest about Romeo's feelings for Juliet?

1. **livery** *n.* clothing or costume worn by a servant.
2. **spheres** *n.* orbits.

CLOSE READ

Remind students that authors use language to create images and emphasize certain ideas. Point out that students can analyze word choice to help them understand an author's ideas. You may wish to model the close read using the following think-aloud format. Possible responses to questions on the Student page are included.

ANNOTATE: As I read Romeo's lines between 2–22 in Scene ii, I notice and highlight words and phrases that show how Romeo is comparing Juliet to many things light, bright, and celestial.

QUESTION: I can see that this language compares Juliet to the sun, as if her beauty is putting to shame the moon and stars.

CONCLUDE: I can conclude from the images Romeo uses to describe Juliet that he views her beauty and goodness as superior to anyone and anything else. She alone brings joy and light just as the sun brings light to the day.

Additional **English Language Support** is available in the Interactive Teacher's Edition.

PERSONALIZE FOR LEARNING

English Language Support

Extended Metaphor Direct students to Scene ii, line 3, and point out the metaphor *Juliet is the sun*. This metaphor is a comparison between two unlike things, the sun and Juliet, but it does not use "like" or "as." It is an extended metaphor because Romeo continues this comparison throughout multiple lines of verse.
If the figurative language of Romeo's speech is confusing students have them reread Scene ii, lines 2–17, and work in groups to paraphrase each sentence into modern English.

NOTES

See how she leans her cheek upon that hand,
O, that I were a glove upon that hand,
That I might touch that cheek!

Juliet. Ay me!

Romeo. She speaks.
O, speak again, bright angel, for thou art
As glorious to this night, being o'er my head,
As is a winged messenger of heaven
Unto the white-upturned wond'ring eyes
Of mortals that fall back to gaze on him
When he bestrides the lazy puffing clouds
And sails upon the bosom of the air.

Juliet. O Romeo. Romeo! Wherefore art thou Romeo?[3]
Deny thy father and refuse they name;
Or, if thou will not, be but sworn my love,
And I'll no longer be a Capulet.

Romeo. [*Aside*] Shall I hear more, or shall I speak at this?

Juliet. 'Tis but thy name that is my enemy.
Thou art thyself, though not[4] a Montague.
What's Montague? It is nor hand, nor foot,
Nor arm, nor face, nor any other part
Belonging to a man. O, be some other name!
What's in a name? That which we call a rose
By any other name would smell as sweet.
So Romeo would, were he not Romeo called,
Retain that dear perfection which he owes[5]
Without that title. Romeo, doff[6] thy name;
And for thy name, which is no part of thee,
Take all myself.

Romeo. I take thee at thy word.
Call me but love, and I'll be new baptized;
Henceforth I never will be Romeo.

Juliet. What man art thou, thus bescreened in night,
So stumblest on my counsel?[7]

Romeo. By a name
I know not how to tell thee who I am.
My name, dear saint, is hateful to myself
Because it is an enemy to thee.
Had I it written, I would tear the word.

Juliet. My ears have yet not drunk a hundred words
Of thy tongue's uttering, yet I know the sound.
Art thou not Romeo, and a Montague?

Romeo. Neither, fair maid, if either thee dislike.

Juliet. How camest thou hither, tell me, and wherefore?
The orchard walls are high and hard to climb,

3. **Wherefore . . . Romeo?** Why are you Romeo—a Montague?

4. **though not** even if you were not.

5. **owes** *v.* owns; possesses.

6. **doff** *v.* remove.

7. **counsel** *n.* secret thoughts.

WriteNow Express and Reflect

Argument Scene ii, lines 43-44, contain some of Juliet's most famous lines, "What's in a name? That which we call a rose/by any other name would smell as sweet." Juliet feels that only Romeo's last name, Montague, is her enemy. His name ties him to a family, a value system, and old loyalties. Without his last name, Romeo would be someone Juliet could love completely. Have students write a brief argument, taking a position on the claim "A name matters." They should include a counterclaim and evidence, and share their argument.

And the place death, considering who thou art,
If any of my kinsmen find thee here.

Romeo. With love's light wings did I o'erperch[8] these walls;
For stony limits cannot hold love out,
And for what love can do, that dares love attempt.
Therefore thy kinsmen are no stop to me.

Juliet. If they do see thee, they will murder thee.

Romeo. Alack, there lies more peril in thine eye
Than twenty of their swords! Look thou but sweet,
And I am proof[9] against their enmity.

Juliet. I would not for the world they saw thee here.

Romeo. I have night's cloak to hide me from their eyes;
And but[10] thou love me, let them find me here.
My life were better ended by their hate
Than death proroguèd,[11] wanting of thy love.

Juliet. By whose direction found'st thou out this place?

Romeo. By love, that first did prompt me to inquire.
He lent me counsel, and I lent him eyes.
I am no pilot; yet, wert thou as far
As that vast shore washed with the farthest sea,
I should adventure[12] for such merchandise.

Juliet. Thou knowest the mask of night is on my face;
Else would a maiden blush bepaint my cheek
For that which thou hast heard me speak tonight.
Fain would I dwell on form[13]—fain, fain deny
What I have spoke; but farewell compliment![14]
Dost thou love me? I know thou wilt say "Ay";
And I will take thy word. Yet, if thou swear'st,
Thou mayst prove false. At lovers' perjuries,
They say Jove laughs. O gentle Romeo,
If thou dost love, pronounce it faithfully.
Or if thou thinkest I am too quickly won,
I'll frown and be perverse[15] and say thee nay,
So thou wilt woo; but else, not for the world.
In truth, fair Montague, I am too fond,[16]
And therefore thou mayst think my havior light;[17]
But trust me, gentleman, I'll prove more true
Than those that have more **cunning** to be strange.[18]
I should have been more strange, I must confess,
But that thou overheard'st, ere I was ware,
My true-love passion. Therefore pardon me,
And not impute this yielding to light love,
Which the dark night hath so discoverèd.[19]

Romeo. Lady, by yonder blessèd moon I vow,
That tips with silver all these fruit-tree tops—

NOTES

8. **o'erperch** *v.* fly over.

9. **proof** *v.* protected, as by armor.

10. **And but** unless.

11. **proroguèd** (proh ROHG ehd) *v.* postponed.

12. **adventure** *v.* risk a long journey, like a sea adventurer.

13. **Fain . . . form** eagerly would I follow convention (by acting reserved).

14. **compliment** *n.* conventional behavior.

15. **be perverse** act contrary to my true feelings.

16. **fond** *adj.* affectionate.

17. **my havior light** my behavior immodest or unserious.

cunning (KUHN ihng) *n.* skill in deception

18. **strange** *adj.* distant and cold.

19. **discoverèd** *v.* revealed.

DIGITAL PERSPECTIVES

CLOSER LOOK

Identify Theme

Students may have marked Juliet's speech during their first read. Use these lines to help students understand what Juliet is saying and why she feels so bold. Encourage them to talk about the annotations that they marked. You may want to model a close read with the class based on the highlights shown in the text.

ANNOTATE: Have students mark details in Scene ii, lines 83-106, that show how Juliet feels about Romeo, or have students participate while you highlight them.

QUESTION: Guide students to consider what these details might tell them. Ask what a reader can infer from the details of her confession of love, and accept student responses.

Possible response: The cover of night has given Juliet the boldness to speak her true feelings.

CONCLUDE: Help students to formulate conclusions about the importance of these details in the text. Ask students why the author might have included these details.

Possible response: There are consistent mentions in the text of darkness and light. For Juliet, night allows her to speak her mind without showing her blush of embarrassment–darkness and disguise have liberated her. In *The Tragedy of Romeo and Juliet,* light and darkness are important as a theme and a visual motif. Imagine scenes being acted out on the stage under the cover of darkness or in the openness of bright lights.

Remind students a *theme* is the central idea, message, or insight that a literary work reveals. A theme is not the subject of the work, but rather the insight the work reveals about that subject. This central idea can usually be expressed as a generalization about people or life, and it may be directly stated or implied. When the theme is implied, as in most serious literature, the reader has to figure out the work's central idea by analyzing different elements in the text for clues about the writer's meaning. Note that there is usually no single correct statement of a work's theme.

DIGITAL PERSPECTIVES

Enriching the Text This image is from the 2013 film *Romeo and Juliet.* After students have completed their close read, show clips from this film's balcony scene. Have students discuss how watching the scene assists in their understanding of the text. There are many versions of *Romeo and Juliet,* including Franco Zefferelli's film made in 1968 and Baz Luhrmann's production from 1996. You may want to show two film versions of the balcony scene for student comparison. Ask students for any examples of modern romantic movies that have a "balcony" scene of some kind. Point out to students that allusions are frequently made to Shakespeare in both text and film. Preview all videos before showing them in class.

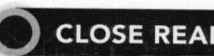

Juliet. O, swear not by the moon, th' inconstant moon,
That monthly changes in her circle orb,
Lest that thy love prove likewise variable.

Romeo. What shall I swear by?

Juliet. Do not swear at all;
Or if thou wilt, swear by thy gracious self,
Which is the god of my idolatry,
And I'll believe thee.

Romeo. If my heart's dear love—

Juliet. Well, do not swear. Although I joy in thee,
I have no joy of this contract[20] tonight.
It is too rash, too unadvised, too sudden;
Too like the lightning, which doth cease to be
Ere one can say it lightens. Sweet, good night!
This bud of love, by summer's ripening breath,
May prove a beauteous flow'r when next we meet.
Good night, good night! As sweet repose and rest
Come to thy heart as that within my breast!

Romeo. O, wilt thou leave me so unsatisfied?

Juliet. What satisfaction canst thou have tonight?

Romeo. Th'exchange of thy love's faithful vow for mine.

Juliet. I gave thee mine before thou didst request it;
And yet I would it were to give again.

Romeo. Wouldst thou withdraw it? For what purpose, love?

Juliet. But to be frank[21] and give it thee again.
And yet I wish but for the thing I have.
My bounty[22] is as boundless as the sea,
My love as deep; the more I give to thee,
The more I have, for both are infinite.

[Nurse *calls within.*]

I hear some noise within. Dear love, adieu!
Anon, good nurse! Sweet Montague, be true.
Stay but a little, I will come again. [*Exit.*]

Romeo. O blessèd, blessèd night! I am afeard,
Being in night, all this is but a dream,
Too flattering-sweet to be substantial.[23]

[*Enter* Juliet *again.*]

Juliet. Three words, dear Romeo, and good night indeed.
If that thy bent[24] of love be honorable,
Thy purpose marriage, send me word tomorrow,
By one that I'll procure to come to thee,
Where and what time thou wilt perform the rite;
And all my fortunes at thy foot I'll lay

NOTES

20. contract *n.* betrothal.

CLOSE READ

ANNOTATE: In lines 116–124, mark repeated words and phrases.

QUESTION: Why do you think Juliet repeats herself so often in this short speech?

CONCLUDE: What is the effect of this repetition?

21. frank *adj.* generous.

22. bounty *n.* what I have to give.

23. substantial *adj.* real.

24. bent *n.* purpose; intention.

DIGITAL PERSPECTIVES

CLOSE READ

Remind students that they are looking for repetition. You may wish to model the close read using the following think-aloud format. Possible responses to questions on the Student page are included.

ANNOTATE: As I read Scene ii, lines 116–124, I notice and highlight the details and phrases that are emphasized by Juliet through repetition.

QUESTION: I can see that Juliet's most often repeated phrase in this short speech is *good night;* she is trying to end her conversation with Romeo. Juliet wants to end their interaction with the tone of love and adoration intact, but she also worries that their love is too "sudden" and might disappear as quickly as the lightning she compares it to.

CONCLUDE: Juliet's repetition of language makes her seem flustered and wavering. As a result of her indecisiveness, Romeo is able to convince her to stay just a few minutes longer and they are able to set their next meeting in motion.

NOTES

25. **By and by** at once.
26. **strife** *n.* efforts.
27. **tassel gentle** male falcon.
28. **Bondage is hoarse** Being bound in by my family restricts my speech.
29. **Echo** In classical mythology, the nymph Echo, unable to win the love of Narcissus, wasted away in a cave until nothing was left of her but her voice.
30. **wanton's** spoiled, playful child's.
31. **gyves** (jyvz) *n.* chains.

And follow thee my lord throughout the world.

Nurse. [*Within*] Madam!

Juliet. I come anon.—But if thou meanest not well,
I do beseech thee—

Nurse. [*Within*] Madam!

Juliet. By and by[25] I come.—
To cease thy strife[26] and leave me to my grief.
Tomorrow I will send.

Romeo. So thrive my soul—

Juliet. A thousand times good night! [*Exit.*]

Romeo. A thousand times the worse, to want thy light!
Love goes toward love as schoolboys from their books;
But love from love, toward school with heavy looks.
[*Enter* Juliet *again.*]

Juliet. Hist! Romeo, hist! O for a falc'ner's voice
To lure this tassel gentle[27] back again!
Bondage is hoarse[28] and may not speak aloud,
Else would I tear the cave where Echo[29] lies
And make her airy tongue more hoarse than mine
With repetition of "My Romeo!"

Romeo. It is my soul that calls upon my name.
How silver-sweet sound lovers' tongues by night,
Like softest music to attending ears!

Juliet. Romeo!

Romeo. My sweet?

Juliet. What o'clock tomorrow
Shall I send to thee?

Romeo. By the hour of nine.

Juliet. I will not fail. 'Tis twenty year till then.
I have forgot why I did call thee back.

Romeo. Let me stand here till thou remember it.

Juliet. I shall forget, to have thee still stand there,
Rememb'ring how I love thy company.

Romeo. And I'll stay, to have thee still forget,
Forgetting any other home but this.

Juliet. 'Tis almost morning. I would have thee gone—
And yet no farther than a wanton's[30] bird,
That lets it hop a little from his hand,
Like a poor prisoner in his twisted gyves,[31]
And with a silken thread plucks it back again,
So loving-jealous of his liberty.

Romeo. I would I were thy bird.

CROSS-CURRICULAR PERSPECTIVES

Social Studies Guide students to Scene ii, line 158, where Juliet mentions *a falc'ner's voice.* She is referring to falconry, or the sport of hunting with falcons. Have students research falcons and draw pictures of this bird of prey. Tell students that falconry was a sport of aristocrats, and a falconer would train the bird to respond to commands, both physical and verbal.

Juliet. Sweet, so would I.
Yet I should kill thee with much cherishing.
Good night, good night! Parting is such sweet sorrow
That I shall say good night till it be morrow. [*Exit.*]

Romeo. Sleep dwell upon thine eyes, peace in thy breast!
Would I were sleep and peace, so sweet to rest!
Hence will I to my ghostly friar's[32] close cell,[33]
His help to crave and my dear hap[34] to tell. [*Exit.*]

NOTES

32. ghostly friar's spiritual father's.

33. close cell small room.

34. dear hap good fortune.

⌘ ⌘ ⌘

Scene iii • *Friar Lawrence's cell.*

[*Enter* Friar Lawrence *alone, with a basket.*]

Friar. The gray-eyed morn smiles on the frowning night,
Check'ring the eastern clouds with streaks of light;
And fleckèd darkness like a drunkard reels
From forth day's path and Titan's burning wheels.
Now, ere the sun advance his burning eye
The day to cheer and night's dank dew to dry,
I must upfill this osier cage of ours
With baleful weeds and precious-juicèd flowers.
The earth that's nature's mother is her tomb.
What is her burying grave, that is her womb;
And from her womb children of divers kind
We sucking on her natural bosom find,
Many for many virtues excellent,
None but for some, and yet all different.
O, mickle[1] is the powerful grace[2] that lies
In plants, herbs, stones, and their true qualities;
For naught so vile that on the earth doth live
But to the earth some special good doth give;
Nor aught so good but, strained[3] from that fair use,
Revolts from true birth,[4] stumbling on abuse.
Virtue itself turns vice, being misapplied,
And vice sometime by action dignified.
[*Enter* Romeo.]

Within the infant rind[5] of this weak flower
Poison hath residence and medicine power;[6]
For this, being smelt, with that part cheers each part;[7]
Being tasted, stays all senses with the heart.[8]
Two such opposèd kings encamp them still[9]
In man as well as herbs—grace and rude will;
And where the worser is predominant,
Full soon the canker[10] death eats up that plant.

CLOSE READ

ANNOTATE: Mark examples of full rhyme at the ends of lines in the Friar's opening speech.

QUESTION: Why does Shakespeare have the Friar speak in rhymed verse?

CONCLUDE: How does the use of rhyme add to the portrayal of the Friar's character?

1. mickle *adj.* great.

2. grace *n.* divine power.

3. strained *v.* turned away.

4. Revolts . . . birth conflicts with its real purpose.

5. infant rind tender skin.

6. and medicine power and medicinal quality has power.

7. with . . . part with that quality—odor—revives each part of the body.

8. stays . . . heart kills (stops the working of the five senses along with the heart).

9. still *adv.* always.

10. canker *n.* destructive caterpillar.

DIGITAL PERSPECTIVES

CLOSE READ

Remind students that character speeches they have read occasionally included rhyming couplets. Have students look for them within Friar Lawrence's lines. You may wish to model the close read using the following think-aloud format. Possible responses to questions on the Student page are included.

ANNOTATE: As I read Scene iii, lines 1–30, I notice and highlight the successive rhyming words.

QUESTION: The style of Friar Lawrence's rhymed verse sets him apart from the other characters. Shakespeare uses blank verse to show the rank of Romeo and Juliet; however, Friar Lawrence is a holy man, and this style gives him distinction.

CONCLUDE: The rhymed lines also serve to show the friar as a character who unifies and brings together. Friar Lawrence is employed by the church, so he is associated with the concepts of spiritual good and evil. He also has knowledge of botany and deals with plants that are both medicinal and poisonous; however, his studies have proven to him that both the "opposed kings" of good and bad have purpose.

NOTES

11. ***Benedicite!*** God bless you!
12. **distemperèd head** troubled mind.
13. **unstuffed** *adj.* not filled with cares.
14. **distemp'rature** illness.
15. **physic** (FIHZ ihk) *n.* medicine.
16. **My . . . foe** my plea also helps my enemy (Juliet, a Capulet).
17. **and . . . drift** and simple in your speech.
18. **Riddling . . . shrift** a confusing confession will get you uncertain forgiveness. The Friar means that unless Romeo speaks clearly, he will not get clear and direct advice.
19. **And . . . save** and we are united in every way, except for (save).
20. **brine** *n.* salt water (tears).

Romeo. Good morrow, father.

Friar. *Benedicite!*[11]
What early tongue so sweet saluteth me?
Young son, it argues a distemperèd head[12]
So soon to bid good morrow to thy bed.
Care keeps his watch in every old man's eye,
And where care lodges, sleep will never lie;
But where unbruisèd youth with unstuffed[13] brain
Doth couch his limbs, there golden sleep doth reign,
Therefore thy earliness doth me assure
Thou art uproused with some distemp'rature;[14]
Or if not so, then here I hit it right—
Our Romeo hath not been in bed tonight.

Romeo. That last is true. The sweeter rest was mine.

Friar. God pardon sin! Wast thou with Rosaline?

Romeo. With Rosaline, my ghostly father? No.
I have forgot that name and that name's woe.

Friar. That's my good son! But where hast thou been then?

Romeo. I'll tell thee ere thou ask it me again.
I have been feasting with mine enemy,
Where on a sudden one hath wounded me
That's by me wounded. Both our remedies
Within thy help and holy physic[15] lies.
I bear no hatred, blessed man, for, lo,
My intercession likewise steads my foe.[16]

Friar. Be plain, good son, and homely in thy drift.[17]
Riddling confession finds but riddling shrift.[18]

Romeo. Then plainly know my heart's dear love is set
On the fair daughter of rich Capulet;
As mine on hers, so hers is set on mine,
And all combined, save[19] what thou must combine
By holy marriage. When and where and how
We met, we wooed, and made exchange of vow,
I'll tell thee as we pass; but this I pray,
That thou consent to marry us today.

Friar. Holy Saint Francis! What a change is here!
Is Rosaline, that thou didst love so dear,
So soon forsaken? Young men's love then lies
Not truly in their hearts, but in their eyes.
Jesu Maria! What a deal of brine[20]
Hath washed thy sallow cheeks for Rosaline!
How much salt water thrown away in waste
To season love, that of it doth not taste!
The sun not yet thy sighs from heaven clears,
Thy old groans ring yet in mine ancient ears.

PERSONALIZE FOR LEARNING

English Language Support

Domain-Specific Vocabulary Call students' attention to Scene iii, line 31. The religious terms and vocabulary that appear in Act II may present a challenge to English learners. Support them in understanding the text by reviewing the following terms:

Friar This comes from the Latin word for brother, and is a term for a member of a Christian religious order. Friars live among the common people of their community and are devoted to preaching, missionary work, and charity.

Benedicite! God bless you!

shrift Confession of sins

Saint Francis A Catholic saint who is generally considered the patron of animals. Also, point out to students that Friar Lawrence refers to Romeo as *son* and Romeo refers to him as *father*. This signifies the relationship they have as spiritual teacher and student.

Have students locate these terms in the text and any others that seem religious in nature. **ALL LEVELS**

Lo, here upon thy cheek the stain doth sit
Of an old tear that is not washed off yet.
If e'er thou wast thyself, and these woes thine,
Thou and these woes were all for Rosaline.
And art thou changed? Pronounce this sentence then:
Women may fall[21] when there's no strength[22] in men.

Romeo. Thou chidst me oft for loving Rosaline.

Friar. For doting,[23] not for loving, pupil mine.

Romeo. And badst[24] me bury love.

Friar. Not in a grave
To lay one in, another out to have.

Romeo. I pray thee chide me not. Her I love now
Doth grace[25] for grace and love for love allow.[26]
The other did not so.

Friar. O, she knew well
Thy love did read by rote, that could not spell.[27]
But come, young waverer, come go with me.
In one respect I'll thy assistant be;
For this alliance may so happy prove
To turn your households' rancor[28] to pure love.

Romeo. O, let us hence! I stand on[29] sudden haste.

Friar. Wisely and slow. They stumble that run fast. [*Exit all.*]

⌘ ⌘ ⌘

Scene iv • *A street.*

[*Enter* Benvolio *and* Mercutio.]

Mercutio. Where the devil should this Romeo be?
Came he not home tonight?

Benvolio. Not to his father's. I spoke with his man.

Mercutio. Why, that same pale hardhearted wench, that Rosaline,
Torments him so that he will sure run mad.

Benvolio. Tybalt, the kinsman to old Capulet,
Hath sent a letter to his father's house.

Mercutio. A challenge, on my life.

Benvolio. Romeo will answer it.

Mercutio. Any man that can write may answer a letter.

Benvolio. Nay, he will answer the letter's master, how he dares, being dared.

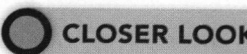

NOTES

21. **fall** *v.* be weak or inconstant.
22. **strength** *n.* constancy; stability.
23. **doting** *v.* being infatuated.
24. **badst** *v.* urged.
25. **grace** *n.* favor.
26. **allow** *v.* give.
27. **Thy . . . spell** your love recited words from memory with no understanding of them.
28. **rancor** *n.* hatred.
29. **stand on** insist on.

DIGITAL PERSPECTIVES

CLOSER LOOK

Analyze Aphorism

Students may have marked some of Friar Lawrence's lines during their first read of Scene iii. Use this to help students understand how the Friar uses aphorisms to advise Romeo. Encourage them to talk about the annotations that they marked. You may want to model a close read with the class based on the highlights shown in the text.

ANNOTATE: Have students mark details in lines 75–94 that show when the Friar is guiding or teaching Romeo with general truths about life, or have students participate while you highlight them.

QUESTION: Guide students to consider what these details might tell them. Ask what a reader can infer from the Friar's message to Romeo, and accept student responses.

Possible response: Details from the text suggest that Romeo and the Friar have a close relationship because Romeo told Friar Lawrence about his love for Rosaline. The Friar is trying to warn Romeo not to be so hasty with his feelings because he is young and very recently had a change of heart.

CONCLUDE: Help students to formulate conclusions about the importance of these details in the text. Ask students why the author might have included these details.

Possible response: As a spiritual mentor and guide, Friar Lawrence uses aphorisms to teach Romeo. This shows the Friar cares for Romeo and is invested in him. Now, the audience must wait to see if Romeo will follow the Friar's advice.

Remind students that an *aphorism* is a brief, memorable saying that expresses a general truth about life. Often both wise and witty, aphorisms appear in many kinds of writing. It is similar to a *proverb*—a traditional wise saying that offers a practical truth about life. As a holy man and adviser of Romeo it makes sense that Friar Lawrence would speak in this way.

NOTES

1. **blind bow-boy's butt-shaft** Cupid's blunt arrow.
2. **Prince of Cats** Tybalt, or a variation of it, is the name of the cat in medieval stories of Reynard the Fox.
3. **captain of compliments** master of formal behavior.
4. **as you sing pricksong** with attention to precision.
5. **rests . . . rests** observes all formalities.
6. **button** *n.* exact spot on the opponent's shirt.
7. **first house** finest school of fencing.
8. **the first and second cause** reasons that would cause a gentleman challenge another to a duel.
9. **passado! . . . punto reverso! . . . hay!** lunge . . . backhanded stroke . . . home thrust.
10. **The pox . . . accent** May the plague strike these absurd characters with their phony manners.
11. **these pardon-me's** these men who are always saying "Pardon me."
12. **Without . . . herring** worn out.
13. **numbers** *n.* verses of love poems.

counterfeit (KOWN tuhr fiht) *n.* something made to deceive

14. **slip** *n.* escape. Slip is also a term for a counterfeit coin.

15. **hams** *n.* hips.

Mercutio. Alas, poor Romeo, he is already dead; stabbed with a white wench's black eye; run through the ear with a love song; the very pin of his heart cleft with the blind bow-boy's butt-shaft;[1] and is he a man to encounter Tybalt?

Benvolio. Why, what is Tybalt?

Mercutio. More than Prince of Cats.[2] O, he's the courageous captain of compliments.[3] He fights as you sing pricksong[4]—keeps time, distance, and proportion; he rests his minim rests,[5] one, two, and the third in your bosom! The very butcher of a silk button,[6] a duelist, a duelist! A gentleman of the very first house,[7] of the first and second cause.[8] Ah, the immortal *passado*! The *punto reverso*! The hay![9]

Benvolio. The what?

Mercutio. The pox of such antic, lisping, affecting fantasticoes—these new tuners of accent![10] "By Jesu, a very good blade! A very tall man! A very good whore!" Why, is not this a lamentable thing, grandsir, that we should be thus afflicted with these strange flies, these fashionmongers, these pardon-me's,[11] who stand so much on the new form that they cannot sit at ease on the old bench? O, their bones, their bones!
[*Enter* Romeo.]

Benvolio. Here comes Romeo! Here comes Romeo!

Mercutio. Without this roe, like a dried herring.[12] O flesh, flesh, how art thou fishified! Now is he for the numbers[13] that Petrarch flowed in. Laura, to his lady, was a kitchen wench (marry, she had a better love to berhyme her), Dido a dowdy, Cleopatra a gypsy, Helen and Hero hildings and harlots, Thisbe a gray eye or so, but not to the purpose. Signior Romeo, *bonjour*! there's a French salutation to your French slop. You gave us the **counterfeit** fairly last night.

Romeo. Good morrow to you both. What counterfeit did I give you?

Mercutio. The slip,[14] sir, the slip. Can you not conceive?

Romeo. Pardon, good Mercutio. My business was great, and in such a case as mine a man may strain courtesy.

Mercutio. That's as much as to say, such a case as yours constrains a man to bow in the hams.[15]

Romeo. Meaning, to curtsy.

Mercutio. Thou hast most kindly hit it.

Romeo. A most courteous exposition.

PERSONALIZE FOR LEARNING

Strategic Support

Language Context If students are struggling with the comprehension of Mercutio's lines, contextualize his words. In Scene iv, lines 19–26, he is insulting his rival Tybalt. This speech is the Elizabethan equivalent of trash talking before a game. Review the insults in the margins with your students and ask them to paraphrase each in modern terms. Remind students to stay appropriate to the classroom setting. Encourage them to get creative with the word choice of this task. Shakespeare is still infamous for witty insults free of the commonly overused curse words of today.

Mercutio. Nay, I am the very pink of courtesy.

Romeo. Pink for flower.

Mercutio. Right.

Romeo. Why, then is my pump[16] well-flowered.

Mercutio. Sure wit, follow me this jest now till thou hast worn out thy pump, that, when the single sole of it is worn, the jest may remain, after the wearing, solely singular.[17]

Romeo. O single-soled jest, solely singular for the singleness![18]

Mercutio. Come between us, good Benvolio! My wits faints.

Romeo. Swits and spurs, swits and spurs; or I'll cry a match.[19]

Mercutio. Nay, if our wits run the wild-goose chase, I am done; for thou hast more of the wild goose in one of thy wits than, I am sure, I have in my whole five. Was I with you there for the goose?

Romeo. Thou wast never with me for anything when thou wast not there for the goose.

Mercutio. I will bite thee by the ear for that jest.

Romeo. Nay, good goose, bite not!

Mercutio. Thy wit is a very bitter sweeting;[20] it is a most sharp sauce.

Romeo. And is it not, then, well served in to a sweet goose?

Mercutio. O, here's a wit of cheveril,[21] that stretches from an inch narrow to an ell broad!

Romeo. I stretch it out for that word "broad," which added to the goose, proves thee far and wide a broad goose.

Mercutio. Why, is not this better now than groaning for love? Now art thou sociable, now art thou Romeo; now art thou what thou art, by art as well as by nature. For this driveling love is like a great natural[22] that runs lolling[23] up and down to hide his bauble[24] in a hole.

Benvolio. Stop there, stop there!

Mercutio. Thou desirest me to stop in my tale against the hair.[25]

Benvolio. Thou wouldst else have made thy tale large.

Mercutio. O, thou art deceived! I would have made it short; for I was come to the whole depth of my tale, and meant indeed to occupy the argument[26] no longer.

Romeo. Here's goodly gear![27]

[*Enter* Nurse *and her Man,* Peter.]

A sail, a sail!

NOTES

16. pump *n.* shoe.

17. when . . . singular the jest will outwear the shoe and will then be all alone.

18. O . . . singleness! O thin joke, unique for only one thing—weakness!

19. Swits . . . match Drive your wit harder to beat me or else I will claim victory in this match of word play.

20. sweeting *n.* kind of apple.

21. cheveril *n.* easily stretched kid leather.

22. natural *n.* idiot.

23. lolling *v.* with tongue hanging out.

24. bauble *n.* toy.

25. the hair natural inclination.

26. occupy the argument talk about the matter.

27. goodly gear good stuff for joking (Romeo sees Nurse approaching).

DIGITAL PERSPECTIVES

CLOSER LOOK

Identify Humor

Students may have marked this page during their first read. Use Scene iv, lines 60-94, to help students understand the humorous and light tone among Romeo, Mercutio, and Benvolio. Encourage them to talk about the annotations that they marked. You may want to model a close read with the class based on the highlights shown in the text.

ANNOTATE: Have students mark details on this page that show the characters joking in the usual manner of teenage boys, or have students participate while you highlight them.

QUESTION: Guide students to consider what these details might tell them. Ask what a reader can infer from the details and accept student responses.

Possible response: Romeo's friends seem to believe he spent the night with Rosaline and are teasing him for disappearing on them.

CONCLUDE: Help students to formulate conclusions about the importance of these details in the text. Ask students why the author might have included these details.

Possible response: Here, amongst his peers, you see a different side of youth and humor in Romeo. The audience also sees his verbal abilities and wit in his battle of words with the clever Mercutio.

Remind students that humor is often used to both entertain and convey a serious theme. Have students consider what Shakespeare might be implying in this scene. Discuss with students how this humorous discussion of love compares to the earnest discussion during the balcony scene.

NOTES

28. **A shirt and a smock** a man and a woman.

29. **fault** *n.* lack.

30. **took** *v.* understood.

confidence (KON fuh duhns) *n.* meeting, especially one held in secret

31. **"Lady . . . lady"** line from an old ballad, "Chaste Susanna."

Mercutio. Two, two! A shirt and a smock.[28]

Nurse. Peter!

Peter. Anon.

Nurse. My fan, Peter.

Mercutio. Good Peter, to hide her face; for her fan's the fairer face.

Nurse. God ye good morrow, gentlemen.

Mercutio. God ye good-den, fair gentlewoman.

Nurse. Is it good-den?

Mercutio. 'Tis no less. I tell ye; for the bawdy hand of the dial is now upon the prick of noon.

Nurse. Out upon you! What a man are you!

Romeo. One, gentlewoman, that God hath made, himself to mar.

Nurse. By my troth, it is well said. "For himself to mar," quoth 'a? Gentlemen, can any of you tell me where I may find the young Romeo?

Romeo. I can tell you; but young Romeo will be older when you have found him than he was when you sought him. I am the youngest of that name, for fault[29] of a worse.

Nurse. You say well.

Mercutio. Yea, is the worst well? Very well took,[30] i' faith! Wisely, wisely.

Nurse. If you be he, sir, I desire some **confidence** with you.

Benvolio. She will endite him to some supper.

Mercutio. A bawd, a bawd, a bawd! So ho!

Romeo. What hast thou found?

Mercutio. No hare, sir; unless a hare, sir, in a lenten pie, that is something stale and hoar ere it be spent.
[*He walks by them and sings.*]
An old hare hoar,
And an old hare hoar,
Is very good meat in Lent;
But a hare that is hoar
Is too much for a score
When it hoars ere it be spent.
Romeo, will you come to your father's? We'll to dinner thither.

Romeo. I will follow you.

Mercutio. Farewell, ancient lady. Farewell, [*singing*] "Lady, lady,[31] lady." [*Exit* Mercutio, Benvolio.]

Nurse. I pray you, sir, what saucy merchant was this that

HOW LANGUAGE WORKS

Blank Verse In all of Shakespeare's plays, including *The Tragedy of Romeo and Juliet,* aristocratic characters speak in blank verse. In contrast, comical or low-ranking characters speak in prose. Prose is writing that is not divided into poetic lines and does not follow a specific meter.

It is important to note that Romeo, Benvolio, and Mercutio are not speaking in blank verse in Scene iv because of all the sexual innuendos they are making in front of Juliet's nurse.

Explain that Shakespeare often uses unrhymed poetry written in a meter called iambic pentameter. A line of iambic pentameter has five stressed syllables, each preceded by an unstressed syllable, as in this example:

But soft! What light through yonder window breaks?

It is the east, and Juliet is the sun!

Have students write down the stressed words or word parts that they hear.

Answer: Soft, light, yon-, win- breaks

Answer: is, east, Jul-, is, sun

was so full of his ropery?[32]

Romeo. A gentleman, nurse, that loves to hear himself talk and will speak more in a minute than he will stand to in a month.

Nurse. And 'a[33] speak anything against me, I'll take him down, and 'a were lustier than he is, and twenty such jacks; and if I cannot, I'll find those that shall. Scurvy knave! I am none of his flirt-gills;[34] I am none of his skainsmates.[35] And thou must stand by too, and suffer every knave to use me at his pleasure!

Peter. I saw no man use you at his pleasure. If I had, my weapon should quickly have been out, I warrant you. I dare draw as soon as another man, if I see occasion in a good quarrel, and the law on my side.

Nurse. Now, afore God, I am so vexed that every part about me quivers. Scurvy knave! Pray you, sir, a word; and, as I told you, my young lady bid me inquire you out. what she bid me say, I will keep to myself; but first let me tell ye, if ye should lead her in a fool's paradise, as they say, it were a very gross kind of behavior, as they say; for the gentlewoman is young; and therefore, if you should deal double with her, truly it were an ill thing to be off'red to any gentlewoman, and very weak[36] dealing.

Romeo. Nurse, commend[37] me to thy lady and mistress. I protest unto thee—

Nurse. Good heart, and i' faith I will tell her as much. Lord, Lord, she will be a joyful woman.

Romeo. What wilt thou tell her, nurse? Thou dost not mark me.

Nurse. I will tell her, sir, that you do protest, which, as I take it, is a gentlemanlike offer.

Romeo. Bid her devise
Some means to come to shrift[38] this afternoon;
And there she shall at Friar Lawrence' cell
Be shrived and married. Here is for thy pains.

Nurse. No, truly, sir; not a penny.

Romeo. Go to! I say you shall.

Nurse. This afternoon, sir? Well, she shall be there.

Romeo. And stay, good nurse, behind the abbey wall.
Within this hour my man shall be with thee
And bring thee cords made like a tackled stair.[39]
Which to the high topgallant[40] of my joy
Must be my convoy[41] in the secret night.

NOTES

32. **ropery** Nurse means "roguery," the talk and conduct of a rascal.

33. **'a** he.

34. **flirt-gills** common girls.

35. **skainsmates** criminals; cutthroats.

36. **weak** *adj.* unmanly.

37. **commend** *v.* convey my respect and best wishes.

38. **shrift** *n.* confession.

39. **tackled stair** rope ladder.

40. **topgallant** *n.* summit.

41. **convoy** *n.* conveyance.

DIGITAL PERSPECTIVES

CLOSER LOOK

Analyze Character

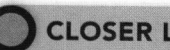

Students may have marked the Nurse's lines during their first read. Use these lines to help students understand how the Nurse and Friar Lawrence differ. Encourage them to talk about the annotations that they marked. You may want to model a close read with the class based on the highlights shown in the text.

ANNOTATE: Have students mark details in Scene iv, lines 150–159, that show the Nurse's character and her relationship with Juliet, or have students participate while you highlight them.

QUESTION: Guide students to consider what these details might tell them. Ask what a reader can infer from the details, and accept student responses.

Possible response: The Nurse is warning Romeo not to hurt Juliet or lead her into "a fool's paradise." She has been Juliet's caretaker and adviser, but she is also willing to help Juliet and Romeo be together.

CONCLUDE: Help students to form conclusions about the importance of these details in the text. Ask students why the author might have included these details.

Possible response: This page reveals much about the Nurse's character, including her unwavering loyalty to Juliet and her nervousness with Romeo. The audience also sees her humanity and flaws because she has yielded to the whims of a teenager and the ideal of love.

Remind students to observe character traits are the qualities, attitudes, and values that a character possesses. A **round character** is complex and multifaceted, showing many different character traits. In contrast, a **flat character** is one-dimensional, exhibiting a single trait. Stories, and particularly novels, usually include both round and flat characters.

NOTES

42. quit *v.* reward; pay you back for.

43. Two . . . away Two can keep a secret if one is ignorant, or out of the way.

44. prating *adj.* babbling.

45. fain . . . aboard eagerly seize Juliet for himself.

46. had as lieve would as willingly.

47. clout *n.* cloth.

48. versal world universe.

49. dog's name *R* sounds like a growl.

50. sententious Nurse means "sentences"—clever, wise sayings.

51. Before, and apace Go ahead of me, and quickly.

Farewell. Be trusty, and I'll quit[42] thy pains.
Farewell. Commend me to thy mistress.

Nurse. Now God in heaven bless thee! Hark you, sir.

Romeo. What say'st thou, my dear nurse?

Nurse. Is your man secret? Did you ne'er hear say,
Two may keep counsel, putting one away?[43]

Romeo. Warrant thee my man's as true as steel.

Nurse. Well, sir, my mistress is the sweetest lady. Lord, Lord! When 'twas a little prating[44] thing—O, there is a nobleman in town, one Paris, that would fain lay knife aboard;[45] but she, good soul, had as lieve[46] see a toad, a very toad, as see him. I anger her sometimes, and tell her that Paris is the properer man; but I'll warrant you, when I say so, she looks as pale as any clout[47] in the versal[48] world. Doth not rosemary and Romeo begin both with a letter?

Romeo. Ay, nurse; what of that? Both with an R.

Nurse. Ah, mocker! That's the dog's name.[49] R is for the—No; I know it begins with some other letter; and she hath the prettiest sententious[50] of it, of you and rosemary, that it would do you good to hear it.

Romeo. Commend me to thy lady.

Nurse. Ay, a thousand times. [*Exit* Romeo.] Peter!

Peter. Anon.

Nurse. Before, and apace.[51] [*Exit, after* Peter.]

⌘ ⌘ ⌘

Scene v • *Capulet's orchard.*

1. low'ring *adj.* darkening.

2. Therefore . . . Love therefore, doves with quick wings pull the chariot of Venus, goddess of love.

[*Enter* Juliet.]

Juliet. The clock struck nine when I did send the nurse;
In half an hour she promised to return.
Perchance she cannot meet him. That's not so.
O, she is lame! Love's heralds should be thoughts,
Which ten times faster glides than the sun's beams
Driving back shadows over low'ring[1] hills.
Therefore do nimble-pinioned doves draw Love.[2]
And therefore hath the wind-swift Cupid wings.
Now is the sun upon the highmost hill
Of this day's journey, and from nine till twelve
Is three long hours; yet she is not come.

PERSONALIZE FOR LEARNING

Strategic Support

Hyperbole is a figure of speech that uses deliberate *overstatement,* or exaggeration—either for comic effect or to express heightened emotion. Engage students in a conversation about when and why they exaggerate in everyday conversation. Have students reread Juliet's lines in Scene v, lines 1–11, and identify her exaggerated statements about love and time.

416 UNIT 4 • STAR-CROSSED ROMANCES

Had she affections and warm youthful blood,
She would be as swift in motion as a ball;
My words would bandy her[3] to my sweet love,
And his to me.
But old folks, many feign[4] as they were dead—
Unwieldy, slow, heavy and pale as lead.
[*Enter* Nurse *and* Peter.]

O God, she comes! O honey nurse, what news?
Hast thou met with him? Send thy man away.

Nurse. Peter, stay at the gate. [*Exit* Peter.]

Juliet. Now, good sweet nurse—O Lord, why lookest thou sad?
Though news be sad, yet tell them merrily;
If good, thou shamest the music of sweet news
By playing it to me with so sour a face.

Nurse. I am aweary, give me leave[5] awhile.
Fie, how my bones ache! What a jaunce[6] have I!

Juliet. I would thou hadst my bones, and I thy news.
Nay, come, I pray thee speak. Good, good nurse, speak.

Nurse. Jesu, what haste? Can you not stay a while?
Do you not see that I am out of breath?

Juliet. How art thou out of breath when thou hast breath
To say to me that thou art out of breath?
The excuse that thou dost make in this delay
Is longer than the tale thou dost excuse.
Is thy news good or bad? Answer to that.
Say either, and I'll stay the circumstance.[7]
Let me be satisfied, is't good or bad?

Nurse. Well, you have made a simple[8] choice; you know not how to choose a man. Romeo? No, not he. Though his face be better than any man's, yet his leg excels all men's; and for a hand and a foot, and a body, though they be not to be talked on, yet they are past compare. He is not the flower of courtesy, but, I'll warrant him, as gentle as a lamb. Go thy ways, wench; serve God. What, have you dined at home?

Juliet. No, no. But all this I did know before.
What says he of our marriage? What of that?

Nurse. Lord, how my head aches! What a head have I!
It beats as it would fall in twenty pieces.
My back a[9] t'other side—ah, my back, my back!
Beshrew[10] your heart for sending me about
To catch my death with jauncing up and down!

Juliet. I' faith, I am sorry that thou art not well.
Sweet, sweet, sweet nurse, tell me, what says my love?

NOTES

3. **bandy her** send her rapidly.

4. **feign** *v.* act.

5. **give me leave** excuse me; give me a moment's rest.

6. **jaunce** *n.* rough trip.

7. **stay the circumstance** wait for the details.

8. **simple** *adj.* foolish; simpleminded.

CLOSE READ

ANNOTATE: In lines 31–65, mark Juliet's questions to the Nurse about Romeo's intentions.

QUESTION: Why does Shakespeare allow the Nurse to take so long to answer Juliet's question?

CONCLUDE: What is the effect of the Nurse's digressions?

9. **a** on.

10. **Beshrew** shame on.

CLOSE READ

Pay attention to the tone of this conversation and what it tells you about the relationship between the Nurse and Juliet. You may wish to model the close read using the following think-aloud format. Possible responses to questions on the Student page are included.

ANNOTATE: As I read Scene v, lines 31–65, I notice and highlight the details that show Juliet's curiosity about Romeo.

QUESTION: I think Shakespeare allows the Nurse to talk so long to draw out Juliet's anticipation and excitement.

CONCLUDE: I think the effect of the Nurse's digression is to allow the audience to get the full of effect of Juliet's feelings. It also allows us to see the familiar and teasing relationship that Juliet and the Nurse have.

NOTES

11. **hot** *adj.* impatient; hot-tempered.
12. **Marry . . . trow** Indeed, cool down, I say.
13. **poultice** *n.* remedy.
14. **coil** *n.* disturbance.
15. **wanton** *adj.* excited.

Nurse. Your love says, like an honest gentleman, and a courteous, and a kind, and a handsome, and, I warrant, a virtuous—Where is your mother?

Juliet. Where is my mother? Why, she is within.
Where would she be? How oddly thou repliest!
"Your love says, like an honest gentleman,
'Where is your mother?'"

Nurse. O God's Lady dear!
Are you so hot?[11] Marry come up, I trow.[12]
Is this the poultice[13] for my aching bones?
Henceforth do your messages yourself.

Juliet. Here's such a coil![14] Come, what says Romeo?

Nurse. Have you got leave to go to shrift today?

Juliet. I have.

Nurse. Then hie you hence to Friar Lawrence' cell;
There stays a husband to make you a wife.
Now comes the wanton[15] blood up in your cheeks:
They'll be in scarlet straight at any news.
Hie you to church: I must another way,
To fetch a ladder, by the which your love
Must climb a bird's nest soon when it is dark.
I am the drudge, and toil in your delight:
But you shall bear the burden soon at night.
Go; I'll to dinner; hie you to the cell.

Juliet. Hie to high fortune! Honest nurse, farewell.

[*Exit all.*]

⌘ ⌘ ⌘

Scene vi • *Friar Lawrence's cell.*

[*Enter* Friar Lawrence *and* Romeo.]

1. **That . . . not!** that the future does not punish us with sorrow.
2. **countervail** *v.* equal.
3. **powder** *n.* gunpowder.

Friar. So smile the heavens upon this holy act
That afterhours with sorrow chide us not![1]

Romeo. Amen, amen! But come what sorrow can,
It cannot countervail[2] the exchange of joy
That one short minute gives me in her sight.
Do thou but close our hands with holy words,
Then love-devouring death do what he dare—
It is enough I may but call her mine.

Friar. These violent delights have violent ends
And in their triumph die, like fire and powder,[3]
Which, as they kiss, consume. The sweetest honey

PERSONALIZE FOR LEARNING

English Language Support

Context Clues The use of the word *Hie* as a verb could confuse English Language Learners. Ask them to underline this word in Scene v, lines 68–77, and use context clues to figure out what this word means.

^ Friar Lawrence weds Romeo and Juliet, while the Nurse looks on.

Is loathsome in his own deliciousness
And in the taste confounds[4] the appetite.
Therefore love moderately; long love doth so;
Too swift arrives as tardy as too slow.
[*Enter* Juliet.]
Here comes the lady. O, so light a foot
Will ne'er wear out the everlasting flint.[5]
A lover may bestride the gossamers[6]
That idles in the wanton summer air,
And yet not fall; so light is vanity.[7]

Juliet. Good even to my ghostly confessor.

Friar. Romeo shall thank thee, daughter, for us both.

Juliet. As much to him,[8] else is his thanks too much.

Romeo. Ah, Juliet, if the measure of thy joy
Be heaped like mine, and that thy skill be more
To blazon it,[9] then sweeten with thy breath
This neighbor air, and let rich music's tongue
Unfold the imagined happiness that both
Receive in either by this dear encounter.

Juliet. Conceit, more rich in matter than in words,
Brags of his substance, not of ornament.[10]

NOTES

4. **confounds** *v.* destroys.

5. **flint** *n.* stone.

6. **gossamers** *n.* spider webs.

7. **vanity** *n.* foolish things that cannot last.

8. **As . . . him** the same greeting to him.

9. **and . . . it** and if you are better to proclaim it.

10. **Conceit . . . ornament** Understanding does not need to be dressed up in words.

DIGITAL PERSPECTIVES

CLOSER LOOK

Analyze Symbolism

Students may have marked Juliet's entrance in lines 16–32 during their first read of Scene vi. Use these lines to help students understand the symbols of Juliet. Encourage them to talk about the annotations that they marked. You may want to model a close read with the class based on the highlights shown in the text.

ANNOTATE: Have students mark details in lines 16–32 that describe Juliet as a bride, or have students participate while you highlight them.

QUESTION: Guide students to consider what these details might tell them. Ask what a reader can infer from what the Friar says about Juliet, and accept student responses.
Possible response: He notices that she is treading lightly like a spider on a web.

CONCLUDE: Help students to formulate conclusions about the importance of these details in the text. Ask students why the author might have included these details.
Possible response: The author's use of symbolism compares Juliet to a spider treading lightly in the summer air. These symbols of nature and season show her youth, purity, and delicacy in her first moments as a bride.

Remind students that a ***symbol*** is anything—an object, person, animal, place, or image—that represents something else. A symbol has its own meaning, but it also stands for something larger than itself, usually an abstract idea.

Comprehension Check

Possible responses:

1. Juliet feels that only Romeo's name is her enemy and if he changes it they will be free to love one another.
2. Friar Lawrence has a basket full of weeds and flowers that had both medicinal and poisonous properties.
3. Friar Lawrence agrees to perform Romeo and Juliet's wedding so that their two feuding households may become unified.
4. Act II, scene iv begins with Mercutio insulting Tybalt – he describes him as a "Prince of Cats," because he is cunning like an animal. He is also a fierce and excellent swordsman who can hit the exact "button" or mark on an opponent.
5. Scene iv takes place in a street.

Research To Clarify If students struggle to come up with research topics suggest a few ideas like falconry, fencing, or Saint Francis.

NOTES

They are but beggars that can count their worth;
But my true love is grown to such excess
I cannot sum up sum of half my wealth.

Friar. Come, come with me, and we will make short work,
For, by your leaves, you shall not stay alone
Till Holy Church incorporate two in one. [*Exit all.*]

Comprehension Check

Complete the following items after you finish your first read.

1. Why does Juliet want Romeo to have a different name?
2. What items does Friar Lawrence carry in his basket when he first appears in the play?
3. What does Friar Lawrence agree to do for Romeo?
4. In Act II, Scene iv, how is Tybalt described?
5. Where does Act II, Scene iv, take place?
6. **Notebook** Confirm your understanding of the text by writing a summary.

RESEARCH

Research to Clarify Choose at least one unfamiliar detail from the text. Briefly research that detail. In what way does the information you learned shed light on an aspect of the drama?

420 UNIT 4 • STAR-CROSSED ROMANCES

PERSONALIZE FOR LEARNING

Challenge

Classroom Debate: Have students make a judgment: Is Juliet committing an act of betrayal by marrying Romeo, or are her actions justified? Once they have chosen a side they must come up with evidence and at least three points in support of their judgment. Act as mediator, calling on students to present a point and others to respond. Allow time for closing remarks and hold an anonymous vote at the end to see if the classroom as a whole believes Juliet to be guilty of betrayal.

MAKING MEANING

Close Read the Text

Close Read (ANNOTATE, QUESTION, CONCLUDE)

Reread what Mercutio says when Benvolio tells him to call for Romeo in Act II, Scene i, lines 7–21. Mark the word that Mercutio uses to "call" for Romeo. How does it help develop the tone in these lines?

THE TRAGEDY OF ROMEO AND JULIET, ACT II

Analyze the Text

CITE TEXTUAL EVIDENCE to support your answers.

Notebook Respond to these questions.

1. (a) When do Romeo and Juliet first mutually declare their love? (b) **Analyze** How does this setting affect what they say to each other?
2. (a) What weakness in Romeo does the Friar point out before agreeing to help? (b) **Compare and Contrast** How do the Friar's motives differ from the couple's motives? Explain your answer based on details from the text.
3. (a) For whom is Juliet waiting in Act II, Scene v? (b) **Analyze** How does she feel as she waits? Use text details to explain your answer.
4. **Essential Question:** ***Do we determine our own destinies?*** What have you learned about destiny by reading Act II of *Romeo and Juliet*?

Tool Kit
Close-Read Guide and Model Annotation

LANGUAGE DEVELOPMENT

Concept Vocabulary

cunning	counterfeit	confidence

Why These Words? These concept vocabulary words relate to secrecy. How does each word contribute to meaning in the text? What other words in the selection connect to this concept?

WORD NETWORK
Add interesting words related to destiny from the text to your Word Network.

Practice

Notebook Confirm your understanding of these words by using each one in a sentence.

Word Study

Notebook **Latin Prefix: *counter-*** The prefix *counter-* comes from the Latin word *contra*, which means "against." In the word *counterfeit*, it is combined with a word part derived from the Latin word *facere*, which means "to make" or "to do." In the word *counterfeit*, *counter-* suggests a substitute, which helps generate its meaning as an "imitation intended to deceive." Using your understanding of the prefix *counter-*, record a definition for each of the following words: *counter*, *counterclaim*, *counterintuitive*.

STANDARDS
Language
Identify and correctly use patterns of word changes that indicate different meanings or parts of speech.

DIGITAL PERSPECTIVES

Jump Start

CLOSE READ Ask students how and why love and secrecy are so entwined. Encourage them to come up with examples of secret love tokens; valentines, messages, locks of hair. Why does secrecy add to love?

Close Read the Text

Mercutio says he will "conjure" Romeo. He is making fun of the spell of love Romeo has fallen under. Review and discuss the sections students have marked. If needed, continue to model close reading by using the Annotation Highlights in the Interactive Teacher's Edition.

Analyze the Text

Possible Responses:

1. (a) Romeo and Juliet first mutually declare their love in Act II, Scene ii, in the balcony scene. **DOK 1** (b) The cover of darkness and the fact that they are not close enough to face each other gives them a freedom and honesty of feeling. **DOK 4**
2. (a) Romeo's weakness is falling in love with Juliet so quickly after Rosaline. **DOK 1** (b) Friar Lawrence agrees to assist Romeo to stop the feud between the families. This is clear in line 92 when he says he wishes to "turn your households' rancor to pure love." **DOK 3**
3. (a) Juliet is waiting for the Nurse. **DOK 1** (b) Her love builds as she waits for she begins to speak of all the ways love's messages could be speedier than "sunbeams" or "shadows." **DOK 4**
4. Student responses will vary. **DOK 3**

Concept Vocabulary

Why These Words? Possible Responses: *Cunning* describes a clever, but sly or sneaky manner; *counterfeit* is something imitation passed off as genuine; saying something in *confidence* is to say it as a secret. Other words: *counsel, messenger, secret, trusty, inquire*.

Practice

1. The *cunning* mouse took cheese from the trap.
2. The *counterfeit* money looked incredibly real.
3. Mom's boss discussed her raise in *confidence*.

For more support, see **Concept Vocabulary and Word Study**

Word Network

Possible words: *bewitched, blessed*

Word Study

counter–against;
counterintuitive–running against what seems obvious

FORMATIVE ASSESSMENT

Concept Vocabulary

If the concept vocabulary is unclear, **then** have students highlight and analyze the lines in the text that contain the words.

Word Study

If students still struggle to grasp the prefix *counter-*, **then** have them seek out further examples of this prefix in the dictionary.

For Reteach and Practice, see **Word Study: Latin Prefix *counter-* (RP).**

Analyze Craft and Structure

Encourage students to be patient in learning iambic pentameter. Recognizing the meter requires careful listening. Have them repeat lines from Shakespeare and to hear where their voice naturally rises and falls with the stressed and unstressed syllables that Shakespeare wrote. For more support, see **Analyze Craft and Structure: Poetic Structure.**

MAKE IT INTERACTIVE

Pair together students for this activity and ask students to try different methods of hearing the syllables; they could clap, tap a pencil, snap, etc. Later ask them what strategy was the most helpful.

Practice

1. Line 1: Stressed syllables fall on I / for- / when / heart / here. The words emphasized are I, forward, when, heart, and here. The emphasis on these words reflects Romeo's feelings of love for Juliet and the conflict with the emotion Romeo feels knowing that Juliet is a Capulet.

   Line 33: Stressed syllables fall on My / love / grown / such / -cess. The words emphasized in this line are my, love, grown, such, excess. The stresses help emphasize what's happening to Juliet and her overwhelming love for Romeo.
2. (a) *Aristocrats:* Chorus, Romeo, Benvolio, Mercutio, Juliet, Friar *Commoners*: Nurse, Peter. (b) Blank version signals seriousness and status. Shifts from verse to prose emphasize mode and tone.

FORMATIVE ASSESSMENT

Analyze Craft and Structure

- **If** students cannot identify key words and meanings, **then** work through this with them showing them key words.

For Reteach and Practice, see **Analyze Craft and Structure: Poetic Structure (RP).**

MAKING MEANING

THE TRAGEDY OF ROMEO AND JULIET, ACT II

STANDARDS

Reading Literature

Analyze how an author's choices concerning how to structure a text, order events within it, and manipulate time create such effects as mystery, tension, or surprise.

Analyze Craft and Structure

Poetic Structure Blank verse is unrhymed poetry written in a meter called **iambic pentameter**. An **iamb** consists of an unstressed syllable followed by a stressed syllable (˘ ´). In **iambic pentameter,** there are five such units, called "feet," in each line. *Romeo and Juliet* is written mainly in blank verse, as shown here:

M̆ethóught Ĭ héard ă vóice crȳ, "Sléep n̆o móre!" (II,ii,34)

In all of Shakespeare's plays, high-ranking, aristocratic characters speak in blank verse. By contrast, comic characters or those of low rank usually speak in prose, which is writing that is not divided into poetic lines and does not follow a specific meter. These two distinct styles clarify characters' social status and contribute to the tone and mood of their interactions.

Practice

CITE TEXTUAL EVIDENCE to support your answers.

1. Use the chart to mark the stressed syllables in each line. (It may help you to read the lines aloud.) For each line, list the words the meter helps to emphasize. Explain how the emphasis created through meter reflects the character's emotions or conflicts.

Line 1 *from Act II, Scene ii*	**Romeo:** Can I go forward when my heart is here? **Emphasized Words:** **How Emphasis Reflects Character's Emotions or Conflicts:**
Line 33 *from Act II, Scene iv*	**Juliet:** But my true love is grown to such excess. **Emphasized Words:** **How Emphasis Reflects Character's Emotions or Conflicts:**

2. (a) Identify the aristocratic and common characters in Act II based on whether they speak in blank verse. (b) Why might Shakespeare have chosen blank verse for the dialogue spoken by aristocrats?

HOW LANGUAGE WORKS

Syllables A syllable is defined as any one of the parts into which a word is naturally divided when it is pronounced. For example, the word *apple* has two syllables; it naturally breaks into two parts when pronounced: *ap-ple*. A quick review of syllabic parts will be very helpful for identifying iambic pentameter.

EFFECTIVE EXPRESSION

Speaking and Listening

Assignment
Work with a partner to choose and analyze a section of dialogue between a commoner and an aristocrat. Present a **dramatic interpretation** of the scene. As you perform the lines, demonstrate the differences between the the commoner's prose speech and the aristocrat's metered speech. After the performance, share your observations about how Shakespeare uses language to suggest character and social status.

1. **Select a Passage** Select an exchange between a commoner and an aristocrat that will work well as a dramatic interpretation. Use the following questions to help you select a passage:
   - What is happening in this passage?
   - How do the characters feel in this passage?
   - How easy or difficult will it be to convey these elements in a dramatic interpretation?
2. **Annotate the Passage** Annotate to better understand what is happening in the passage. Use the following guidelines to help you:
   - Summarize what is happening in the passage.
   - Distinguish between prose and blank verse, and mark the stressed and unstressed syllables in any sections of blank verse.
   - Identify words, phrases, or lines that are funny or convey specific feelings.
3. **Prepare Your Delivery** Practice your performance. Use the following guidelines to plan your delivery:
   - Use emphasis appropriately in both blank verse and prose dialogue.
   - Vary your tone and pace to reflect the characters' emotions or to convey humor.
   - Use facial expressions and gestures to help convey characters' feelings but avoid making them too exaggerated or distracting.
4. **Evaluate Dramatic Interpretations** As your classmates deliver their dramatic interpretations, pay close attention to what they say and do. Use an evaluation guide to analyze their delivery.

PRESENTATION EVALUATION GUIDE

Rate each statement on a scale of 1 (not demonstrated) to 4 (demonstrated).

☐ The speakers conveyed the appropriate actions, if applicable.

☐ The speakers communicated blank verse and prose dialogue appropriately.

☐ The speakers varied their tone and pace appropriately to convey the character's feelings and to convey humor.

☐ The speakers used gestures and other body language effectively to convey the characters' feelings and to convey humor.

EVIDENCE LOG

Before moving on to a new selection, go to your Evidence Log and record what you learned from *The Tragedy of Romeo and Juliet,* Act II.

STANDARDS

Speaking and Listening
- Present information, findings, and supporting evidence clearly, concisely, and logically such that listeners can follow the line of reasoning and the organization, development, substance, and style are appropriate to purpose, audience, and task.
- Adapt speech to a variety of contexts and tasks, demonstrating command of formal English when indicated or appropriate.

DIGITAL PERSPECTIVES

Speaking and Listening

Performance helps improve any experience with Shakespeare's plays. However, not all your students will be as confident with this task. Reassure students that as long as they stick to the guidelines, support their scene partner, and show a real effort to get to know the character that they are representing then their dramatic performance will be satisfactory. Remind students that they may add their own style to this piece as long as the meaning of the scene stays intact. For more support, see **Speaking and Listening: Dramatic Interpretation.**

Evidence Log Support students in completing their Evidence Log. This paced activity will help prepare them for the Performance-Based Assessment at the end of the unit.

FORMATIVE ASSESSMENT

Speaking and Listening

- **If** students struggle to select a passage, **then** ask them for a preferred character and guide them to a selection of interactions between nobles and aristocrats.
- **If** students struggle to annotate a passage, **then** have them summarize the act and briefly review points of blank verse.

For Reteach and Practice, see **Speaking and Listening: Dramatic Interpretation (RP).**

PERSONALIZE FOR LEARNING

English Language Support

Presenting a Dramatic Interpretation Have pairs choose a short excerpt from another Shakespeare play and present a dramatic interpretation to another pair of students. Guide students to ask questions about the emotions Shakespeare is trying to convey in the excerpt. **EMERGING**

Have pairs choose a short excerpt from another Shakespeare play and present a dramatic interpretation to another pair of students. Guide students to ask questions about how Shakespeare uses language to convey emotions and humor where applicable. **EXPANDING**

Have pairs choose a short excerpt from another Shakespeare play and present a dramatic interpretation to another pair of students. Guide students to ask questions about Shakespeare's use of humor, irony, and oxymoron where applicable. **BRIDGING**

An expanded **English Language Support Lesson** on Dramatic Interpretation in Dialogue is available in the Interactive Teacher's Edition.

The Tragedy of Romeo and Juliet, Act III

AUDIO SUMMARIES
Audio summaries of *The Tragedy of Romeo and Juliet,* Act III are available online in both English and Spanish in the Interactive Teacher's Edition or Unit Resources. Assigning these summaries prior to reading the selection may help students build additional background knowledge and set a context for their first read.

Summary

In Act III of *The Tragedy of Romeo and Juliet,* events take a violent turn. Romeo refuses to get into a street fight with Tybalt but when Mercutio is killed, Romeo defends his friend and kills Tybalt. News of the murder spreads quickly, and the Nurse tells Juliet, but there is a miscommunication and Juliet believes Romeo is dead. Once Juliet understands that Romeo is alive but in trouble, the Nurse agrees to get a message to him. Romeo goes to Friar Lawrence where he learns of his punishment. He is banished from Verona and he is devastated. He and the Friar make a plan for Romeo to live in Mantua until news of the marriage can be shared. Meanwhile, Capulet promises Paris that he can marry Juliet on Thursday. Juliet's mother tells her daughter of this news, and Juliet refuses the marriage. Again, the Nurse agrees to take part in another plan.

Insight

This classic tragedy examines love and youthful impulsiveness. This act shows how impulsivity leads to two deaths, and how miscommunication can create havoc.

ESSENTIAL QUESTION:
Do we determine our own destinies?

Connection to Essential Question

Act III provides more to consider as students think about the Essential Question: "Do we determine our own destinies?" In this act, Romeo and Juliet each take actions in which they seem to be taking charge of their futures. The play suggests that Romeo and Juliet were unavoidably fated to fall in love and die.

WHOLE-CLASS LEARNING PERFORMANCE TASK
Which has a greater impact on the characters in these texts: destiny or personal choices?

UNIT PERFORMANCE-BASED ASSESSMENT
Should the opinions of others affect our own choices or destinies?

Connection to Performance Tasks

Whole-Class Learning Performance Task Ask students to track their ideas about the Performance Task. The full plot line of this play may have them revising their opinions.

Unit Performance-Based Assessment In Act III, Juliet explicitly rejects her family's direction and Romeo is devastated by the news of his banishment. Students will need to see the events of the story unfold before addressing the prompt.

DIGITAL PERSPECTIVES — Audio | Video | Document | Annotation Highlights | EL Highlights | Online Assessment

LESSON RESOURCES

	Making Meaning	Language Development	Effective Expression
Lesson	**First Read** **Close Read** **Analyze the Text** **Analyze Craft and Structure**	**Concept Vocabulary** **Word Study**	**Writing to Sources**
Instructional Standards	**RL.10** By the end of grade 9, read and comprehend literature . . . **RL.5** Analyze how an author's choices . . .	**L.4.b** Identify and correctly use patterns of word changes . . .	**W.2** Write informative/explanatory texts . . .
STUDENT RESOURCES			
Available online in the Interactive Student Edition or Unit Resources	Selection Audio First-Read Guide: Drama Close-Read Guide: Drama	Word Network	Evidence Log
TEACHER RESOURCES			
Selection Resources Available online in the Interactive Teacher's Edition or Unit Resources	Audio Summaries Annotation Highlights EL Highlights English Language Support Lesson Analyze Craft and Structure: Dramatic Speeches	Concept Vocabulary and Word Study	Writing: Dual Character Study
Reteach/Practice (RP) Available online in the Interactive Teacher's Edition or Unit Resources	Analyze Craft and Structure: Dramatic Speeches (RP)	Word Study: Latin Prefix *ex-* (RP)	Writing: Dual Character Study (RP)
Assessment Available online in Assessments	Selection Test		
My Resources	A Unit 4 Answer Key is available online and in the Interactive Teacher's Edition.		

Reading Support

Text Complexity Rubric: *The Tragedy of Romeo and Juliet,* Act III	
Quantitative Measures	
Lexile: NP **Text Length:** 6,413 words	
Qualitative Measures	
Knowledge Demands 1—2—3—4—**5**	Students will need information about the historical context of Verona, Italy, during the Renaissance. Some of this information is covered in the background information.
Structure 1—2—3—4—**5**	The selection is a Shakespearean play written primarily in blank verse. Line breaks will likely be challenging for students.
Language Conventionality and Clarity 1—2—3—4—**5**	The selection contains complex sentences, unfamiliar syntax, figurative language, challenging vocabulary, and Elizabethan language.
Levels of Meaning/Purpose 1—2—**3**—4—5	The concept of a classic tale of star-crossed lovers is accessible but will likely be difficult to grasp due to challenging language and structure.

DECIDE AND PLAN

English Language Support

Provide English Learners with support for **Knowledge Demands and Language** as they read the selection.

Knowledge Demands Have students summarize what they know so far. Make sure students understand the main events that have taken place. Ask questions to clarify their understanding, such as *Who is helping to arrange a secret marriage? What did the Friar warn?*

Language If students have difficulty with some of the complex or figurative language, have them break down the sentences into smaller chunks. Then have them highlight any words that cause confusion.

Strategic Support

Provide students with strategic support to ensure that they can successfully read the text.

Knowledge Demands Have students work with a partner to summarize what they know so far. What has happened? Who is involved? Then have students predict what will happen next.

Levels of Meaning/Purpose As students read and listen, ask them to make notes of the main ideas. If students have trouble finding the main ideas, ask them to write questions to direct them to the main ideas.

Challenge

Provide students who need to be challenged with ideas for how they can go beyond a simple interpretation of the text.

Text Analysis Pair students. Have them each take a scene and retell it to their partner, using their own descriptions without reading from the text. Encourage students to include details and descriptive language. They may refer to the text as needed to remember details, but should use their own words.

Written Response Ask students to identify expressions in quotations that are not ones we hear in modern speech. Have them write how we might say the same thing today. Ask partners to read their sentences aloud to compare the different ways they said the same thing.

TEACH

Read and Respond

Have students do their first read of the selection. Then have them complete their close read. Finally, work with them on the Making Meaning and Effective Expression activities.

Standards Support Through Teaching and Learning Cycle

IDENTIFY NEEDS

Analyze results of the Beginning-of-Year Assessment, focusing on the items relating to Unit 4. Also take into consideration student performance to this point and your observations of where particular students struggle.

DECIDE AND PLAN

- If students have performed poorly on items matching these standards, then provide selection scaffolds before assigning them the on-level lesson provided in the Student Edition.
- If students have done well on the Beginning-of-Year Assessment, then challenge them to keep progressing and learning by giving them opportunities to practice the skills in depth.
- Use the Selection Resources listed on the Planning pages for *The Tragedy of Romeo and Juliet,* Act III to help students continually improve their ability to master the standards.

Instructional Standards: *The Tragedy of Romeo and Juliet,* Act III

	Catching Up	This Year	Looking Forward
Reading	You may wish to administer the **Analyze Craft and Structure: Dramatic Speeches (RP)** worksheet to better familiarize students with dramatic speeches.	**RL.5** Analyze how an author's choices concerning how to structure a text, order events within it, and manipulate time create such effects as mystery, tension, or surprise.	Have students identify the three types of dramatic speeches from other works they have read.
Writing	You may wish to administer the **Writing to Sources: Dual Character Study (RP)** worksheet to help students prepare for their explanatory essays.	**W.2** Write informative/explanatory texts to examine and convey complex ideas, concepts, and information clearly and accurately through the effective selection, organization, and analysis of content.	Challenge students to write an optional *triple* character study.
Language	Review the **Word Study: Latin Prefix *ex-* (RP)** worksheet with students to ensure they understand the Latin prefix.	**L.4.b** Identify and correctly use patterns of word changes that indicate different meanings or parts of speech.	Have students locate other Latin or Greek prefixes they may recognize in the selection.

TEACH

Implement the planned lesson, and gather evidence of student learning.

ANALYZE AND REVISE

- Analyze student work for evidence of student learning.
- Identify whether students have met the expectations in the standards.
- Identify implications for future instruction.

Jump Start

FIRST READ Imagine that you have gone on a hike with your brother and your boyfriend, or your sister and girlfriend. All is going well, but near the edge of a cliff the trail gets slippery and they both slide over. As they cling to the side you realize that you are only strong enough to rescue one – whom do you choose?

The Tragedy of Romeo and Juliet, Act III

How powerful are the choices we make? Do our choices allow us full control of our future or is the tricky hand of fate sometimes getting in the way? Modeling the questions a reader might ask as they read *The Tragedy of Romeo and Juliet* for the first time brings the text alive for students and connects it to the Whole-Class Performance Task assignment. Selection audio and print capability for the selection are available in the Interactive Teacher's Edition.

Concept Vocabulary

Support students as they rank their words. Ask if they've ever heard, read, or used them. Reassure them that the definitions for these words are listed in the selection.

FIRST READ

Students should perform the steps of the first read independently.

NOTICE: You may want to encourage students to notice how word choice reveals character.

ANNOTATE: Remind students to mark passages that include figurative language.

CONNECT: Encourage students to go beyond the text to make connections—remind them that they are the same age as Romeo and Juliet and ask if they see themselves in the way either character responds to conflicts with family and friends.

RESPOND: Students will answer questions and write a summary to demonstrate understanding.

Point out to students that while they will always complete the Respond step at the end of the first read, the other steps will probably happen somewhat concurrently. You may wish to print copies of the **First-Read Guide: Fiction** for students to use.

Playwright

William Shakespeare

The Tragedy of Romeo and Juliet, Act III

Concept Vocabulary

You will encounter the following words as you read Act III of *The Tragedy of Romeo and Juliet.* Before reading, note how familiar you are with each word. Then, rank the words in order from most familiar (1) to least familiar (3).

WORD	YOUR RANKING
exile	
banishment	
pardon	

After completing the first read, come back to the concept vocabulary and review your rankings. Mark changes to your original rankings as needed.

First Read DRAMA

Apply these strategies as you conduct your first read. You will have an opportunity to complete the close-read notes after your first read.

NOTICE *whom* the story is about, *what* happens, *where* and *when* it happens, and *why* those involved react as they do.

ANNOTATE by marking vocabulary and key passages you want to revisit.

CONNECT ideas within the selection to what you already know and what you have already read.

RESPOND by completing the Comprehension Check and by writing a brief summary of the selection.

Tool Kit
First-Read Guide and Model Annotation

STANDARDS
Reading Literature
By the end of grade 9, read and comprehend literature, including stories, dramas, and poems, in the grades 9–10 text complexity band proficiently, with scaffolding as needed at the high end of the range.

DIGITAL PERSPECTIVES

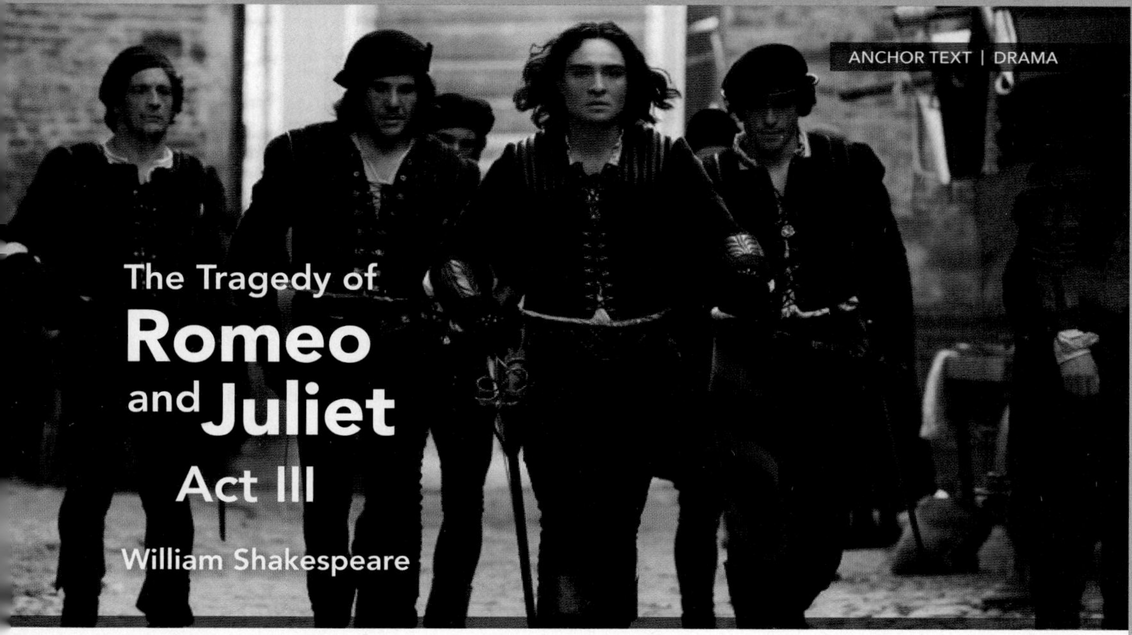

The Tragedy of Romeo and Juliet Act III

William Shakespeare

REVIEW AND ANTICIPATE

In Act II, Romeo and Juliet express their mutual love and enlist the aid of Juliet's nurse and Friar Lawrence to arrange a secret marriage ceremony. As the act closes, the young couple is about to be married. Before performing the ceremony, the Friar warns, "These violent delights have violent ends. . . ." Consider how this statement might hint at events that will occur in Act III or later in the play.

SCAN FOR MULTIMEDIA

Scene i • *A public place.*

[*Enter* Mercutio, Benvolio, *and* Men.]

Benvolio. I pray thee, good Mercutio, let's retire.
The day is hot, the Capulets abroad.
And, if we meet, we shall not 'scape a brawl,
For now, these hot days, is the mad blood stirring.

Mercutio. Thou are like one of these fellows that, when he enters the confines of a tavern, claps me his sword upon the table and says, "God send me no need of thee!" and by the operation of the second cup draws him on the drawer,[1] when Indeed there is no need.

Benvolio. Am I like such a fellow?

Mercutio. Come, come, thou art as hot as a Jack in thy mood as any in Italy; and as soon moved to be moody, and as soon moody to be moved.[2]

Benvolio. And what to?

Mercutio. Nay, and there were two such, we should have none shortly, for one would kill the other. Thou! Why, thou wilt

NOTES

1. **and . . . drawer** and by the effect of the second drink, draws his sword against the waiter.

2. **and . . . moved** and as quickly stirred to anger as you are eager to be so stirred.

CLOSER LOOK

Identify Indirect Characterization

Students may have marked the speeches of Mercutio and Benvolio during their first read. Use lines 1–15 to help students understand how speeches reveal character. Encourage them to talk about the annotations that they marked.

ANNOTATE: Have students mark details in Scene i, lines 1–15, that reveal aspects of each character, or have students participate while you highlight them.

QUESTION: Guide students to consider what these details might tell them. Ask what a reader can infer about Benvolio from Benvolio's own lines and accept student responses.

Possible response: Benvolio tries to avoid conflict, and shows good sense and a cool head as he refuses to be goaded by Mercutio.

CONCLUDE: Help students to formulate conclusions about the importance of these details in the text. Ask students why the author might have included these details.

Possible response: The author included these details to show the contrast between the level-headed Benvolio and the quarrelsome Mercutio.

Remind students that **direct characterization** is what readers are told or given as fact about characters, for example in the prologue. **Indirect Characterization** is what readers learn from the character's appearance and dialogue.

Additional **English Language Support** is available in the Interactive Teacher's Edition.

PERSONALIZE FOR LEARNING

Concept Vocabulary Development

Students will benefit from additional examples and practice with the vocabulary words. Reinforce their comprehension with "show-you-know" sentences. The first part of the sentence uses the vocabulary word in context. The second part of the sentence—the "show-you-know" part—clarifies the first. Model the strategy with this example for *exile* (Scene i, line 185):

The dog was put in *exile* in the garage after eating Mom's shoes; the dog was punished with separation from its family and home. Then give students these sentence prompts and coach them in creating the clarification.

1. Jeremy's *banishment* from the coffee shop will last until he pays for all the broken mugs;

Possible response: He is expelled from the shop until he repays his debt.

2. Please *pardon* the mess in the kitchen we are remodeling;

Possible response: Please forgive and overlook the mess in our kitchen.

CLOSER LOOK

Identify Monologue

Students may have marked Mercutio's lines 15–28 during their first read. Use these lines to help students understand the purpose of the dramatic monologue. Encourage them to talk about the annotations that they marked. You may want to model a close read with the class based on the highlights shown in the text.

ANNOTATE: Explain to students that a monologue is a long speech meant to develop an idea. Have students mark details in Scene i, lines 18–28, that identify them as a monologue and not some other form of dramatic speech, or have students participate while you highlight them.

QUESTION: Guide students to consider what these details might tell them. Ask what a reader can infer from what was marked and accept student responses.

Possible response: Mercutio is deliberately delivering a *speech*—an extensive and highly satirical character study of Benvolio. His intention is to entertain his listeners and to provoke Benvolio. He clearly wants to be heard by Benvolio and anyone else on the street.

CONCLUDE: Help students to formulate conclusions about the importance of these details in the text. Ask students why the author might have included these details.

Possible response: The author includes these details to show that Mercutio is a brilliant verbal performer—he takes the scene over and talks. The only thing he loves more than words is a fight.

Remind students that a **monologue** is a lengthy speech given or *performed* by one character to the other characters onstage.

NOTES

quarrel with a man that hath a hair more or a hair less in his beard than thou hast. Thou wilt quarrel with a man for cracking nuts, having no other reason but because thou hast hazel eyes. What eye but such an eye would spy out such a quarrel? Thy head is as full of quarrels as an egg is full of meat; and yet thy head hath been beaten as addle[3] as an egg for quarreling. Thou hast quarreled with a man for coughing in the street, because he hath wakened thy dog that hath lain asleep in the sun. Didst thou not fall out with a tailor for wearing his new doublet[4] before Easter? With another for tying his new shoes with old riband?[5] And yet thou wilt tutor me from quarreling![6]

Benvolio. And I were so apt to quarrel as thou art, any man should buy the fee simple[7] of my life for an hour and a quarter.[8]

Mercutio. The fee simple? O simple![9]

[*Enter* Tybalt, Petruchio, *and* Others.]

Benvolio. By my head, here comes the Capulets.

Mercutio. By my heel, I care not.

Tybalt. Follow me close, for I will speak to them.
Gentlemen, good-den. A word with one of you.

Mercutio. And but one word with one of us? Couple it with something; make it a word and a blow.

Tybalt. You shall me find me apt enough to that, sir, and you will give me occasion.[10]

Mercutio. Could you not take some occasion without giving?

Tybalt. Mercutio, thou consortest[11] with Romeo.

Mercutio. Consort?[12] What, dost thou make us minstrels? And thou make minstrels of us, look to hear nothing but discords.[13] Here's my fiddlestick; here's that shall make you dance. Zounds,[14] consort!

Benvolio. We talk here in the public haunt of men.
Either withdraw unto some private place,
Or reason coldly of your grievances,
Or else depart. Here all eyes gaze on us.

Mercutio. Men's eyes were made to look, and let them gaze.
I will not budge for no man's pleasure, I.

[*Enter* Romeo.]

Tybalt. Well, peace be with you, sir. Here comes my man.[15]

Mercutio. But I'll be hanged, sir, if he wears your livery.[16]
Marry, go before to field,[17] he'll be your follower!
Your worship in that sense may call him man.

Tybalt. Romeo, the love I bear thee can afford

3. **addle** *adv.* scrambled; crazy.
4. **doublet** *n.* jacket.
5. **riband** *n.* ribbon.
6. **tutor . . . quarreling** instruct me not to quarrel.
7. **fee simple** complete possession.
8. **an hour and a quarter** length of time that a man with Mercutio's fondness for quarreling may be expected to live.
9. **simple!** O stupid!
10. **occasion** *n.* cause; reason.
11. **consortest** *v.* associate with.
12. **Consort** *v.* associate with; *consort* also meant "a group of musicians."
13. **discords** *n.* harsh sounds.
14. **Zounds** exclamation of surprise or anger ("By God's wounds").
15. **man** *n.* man I am looking for; *man* also meant "manservant."
16. **livery** *n.* servant's uniform.
17. **field** *n.* dueling place.

DIGITAL PERSPECTIVES

< Romeo holds Mercutio back from dueling Tybalt.

NOTES

No better term than this: thou art a villain.[18]

Romeo. Tybalt, the reason that I have to love thee
Doth much excuse the appertaining[19] rage
To such a greeting. Villain am I none.
Therefore farewell. I see thou knowest me not.

Tybalt. Boy, this shall not excuse the injuries
That thou hast done me; therefore turn and draw.

Romeo. I do protest I never injured thee,
But love thee better than thou canst devise[20]
Till thou shalt know the reason of my love;
And so, good Capulet, which name I tender[21]
As dearly as my own, be satisfied

Mercutio. O calm, dishonorable, vile submission!
Alla stoccata[22] carries it away. [*Draws.*]
Tybalt, you ratcatcher, will you walk?

Tybalt. What wouldst thou have with me?

Mercutio. Good King of Cats, nothing but one of your nine lives. That I mean to make bold withal,[23] and, as you shall use me here-after, dry-beat[24] the rest of the eight. Will you pluck your sword out of his pilcher[25] by the ears? Make haste, lest mine be about your ears ere it be out.

Tybalt. I am for you. [*Draws.*]

Romeo. Gentle Mercutio, put thy rapier up.

18. **villain** *n.* low, vulgar person.
19. **appertaining** *adj.* appropriate.
20. **devise** *v.* understand; imagine.
21. **tender** *v.* value.
22. ***Alla stoccata*** at the thrust—Italian fencing term that Mercutio uses as a nickname for Tybalt.
23. **make bold withal** make bold with; take.
24. **dry-beat** *v.* thrash.
25. **pilcher** *n.* scabbard.

PERSONALIZE FOR LEARNING

Strategic Support

Cause and Effect Beginning with Act III, scene i, line 1, Shakespeare develops an important conflict. It is important to note what is motivating the actions of each character in this conflict. This conflict is made worse because all three characters are acting on incomplete knowledge and false assumptions. Ask students what has caused Tybalt to seek Romeo out and what the effect was. Allow students to provide responses. Move on to asking students about the cause and effect of Romeo's response towards Tybalt. Then ask them to fill in the boxes for Mercutio on their own.

*You may want to fill in a chart together as a class and leave it posted in the classroom as a living document.

Character	Cause	Effect
Tybalt	**Possible response:** Tybalt thinks Romeo came to mock the Capulet family.	**Possible Response:** He is seeking Romeo out to fight him.
Romeo	**Possible Response:** Romeo went to the party looking for Rosaline. Instead he met and has recently married Juliet.	**Possible Response:** Now that he and Tybalt are cousins he doesn't want to fight him and is trying to prevent their conflict.
Mercutio		

TEACHING

CLOSE READ

Remind students to focus on Mercutio's use of wordplay. You may wish to model the Close Read using the following think-aloud format. Possible responses to questions on the Student page are included.

ANNOTATE: As I read Scene i, lines 90–101, I notice and highlight the details that show Mercutio joking even in the face of his own death.

QUESTION: I believe Shakespeare is being true to Mercutio's character. Mercutio will have only one opportunity to be witty on the subject of his own death, and he seizes it enthusiastically.

CONCLUDE: I think the contrast between Mercutio's wordplay and the plague that he casts on both their houses, humor mixed with bitterness, gives this scene a strong emotional darkness. That feeling takes a strong hold over Romeo right before Tybalt reenters the stage.

NOTES

26. a on.

27. sped *adj.* wounded; done for.

CLOSE READ

ANNOTATE: In lines 90–101, mark examples of Mercutio's wordplay and jokes.

QUESTION: Why does Shakespeare have Mercutio joke around even after he is mortally wounded?

CONCLUDE: What emotional effect does Mercutio's wordplay have in this speech?

28. peppered *adj.* finished off.

29. by . . . arithmetic by formal rules.

30. I have it I have got my deathblow.

31. ally *n.* relative.

32. aspired *v.* climbed to.

33. moe *adj.* more.

34. depend *v.* hang over.

Mercutio. Come, sir, your passado! [*They fight.*]

Romeo. Draw, Benvolio; beat down their weapons.
Gentlemen, for shame! Forbear this outrage!
Tybalt, Mercutio, the Prince expressly hath
Forbid this bandying in Verona streets.
Hold, Tybalt! Good Mercutio!

[Tybalt *under* Romeo's *arm thrusts* Mercutio *in, and flies.*]

Mercutio. I am hurt.
A plague a[26] both your houses! I am sped.[27]
Is he gone and hath nothing?

Benvolio. What, art thou hurt?

Mercutio. Ay, ay, a scratch, a scratch. Marry, 'tis enough.
Where is my page? Go, villain, fetch a surgeon. [*Exit* Page.]

Romeo. Courage, man. The hurt cannot be much.

Mercutio. No, 'tis not so deep as a well, nor so wide as a church door; but 'tis enough, 'twill serve. Ask for me tomorrow, and you shall find me a grave man. I am peppered,[28] I warrant, for this world. A plague a both your houses! Zounds, a dog, a rat, a mouse, a cat, to scratch a man to death! A braggart, a rogue, a villain, that fights by the book of arithmetic![29] Why the devil came you between us? I was hurt under your arm.

Romeo. I thought all for the best.

Mercutio. Help me into some house, Benvolio,
Or I shall faint. A plague a both your houses!
They have made worms' meat of me. I have it,[30]
And soundly too. Your houses!

[*Exit* Mercutio *and* Benvolio]

Romeo. This gentleman, the Prince's near ally,[31]
My very friend, hath got his mortal hurt
In my behalf—my reputation stained
With Tybalt's slander—Tybalt, that an hour
Hath been my cousin. O sweet Juliet,
Thy beauty hath made me effeminate
And in my temper soft'ned valor's steel!

[*Enter* Benvolio.]

Benvolio. O Romeo, Romeo, brave Mercutio is dead!
That gallant spirit hath aspired[32] the clouds,
Which too untimely here did scorn the earth.

Romeo. This day's black fate on moe[33] days doth depend;[34]
This but begins the woe others must end.

[*Enter* Tybalt.]

DIGITAL PERSPECTIVES

Benvolio. Here comes the furious Tybalt back again.

Romeo. Alive in triumph, and Mercutio slain?
Away to heaven respective[35] lenity,
And fire-eyed fury be my conduct[36] now!
Now, Tybalt, take the "villain" back again
That late thou gavest me; for Mercutio's soul
Is but a little way above our heads,
Staying for thine to keep him company.
Either thou or I, or both, must go with him.

Tybalt. Thou, wretched boy, that didst consort him here,
Shalt with him hence.

Romeo. This shall determine that.

[*They fight.* Tybalt *falls.*]

Benvolio. Romeo, away, be gone!
The citizens are up, and Tybalt slain.
Stand not amazed. The Prince will doom thee death
If thou art taken. Hence, be gone, away!

Romeo. O, I am fortune's fool![37]

Benvolio. Why dost thou stay? [*Exit* Romeo.]

[*Enter* Citizens.]

Citizen. Which way ran he that killed Mercutio?
Tybalt, that murderer, which way ran he?

Benvolio. There lies that Tybalt.

Citizen. Up, sir, go with me.
I charge thee in the Prince's name obey.

[*Enter* Prince, Old Montague, Capulet, *their* Wives, *and all.*]

Prince. Where are the vile beginners of this fray?

Benvolio. O noble Prince, I can discover[38] all
The unlucky manage[39] of this fatal brawl.
There lies the man, slain by young Romeo,
That slew thy kinsman, brave Mercutio.

Lady Capulet. Tybalt, my cousin! O my brother's child!
O Prince! O cousin! Husband! O, the blood is spilled
Of my dear kinsman! Prince, as thou art true,
For blood of ours shed blood of Montague.
O cousin, cousin!

Prince. Benvolio, who began this bloody fray?

Benvolio. Tybalt, here slain, whom Romeo's hand did slay,
Romeo, that spoke him fair, bid him bethink
How nice[40] the quarrel was, and urged withal
Your high displeasure. All this—utterèd
With gentle breath, calm look, knees humbly bowed—

NOTES

35. respective lenity thoughtful mercy.

36. conduct *n.* guide.

37. fool *n.* plaything.

38. discover *v.* reveal.

39. manage *n.* course.

40. nice *adj.* trivial.

PERSONALIZE FOR LEARNING

Cross Cultural Connections

Social Studies Act III, scene i, line 82, begins a duel. When Tybalt, Mercutio, and Romeo fence, they fight to kill. Fencing did not become a sport until the late 1700.

The object of fencing is to touch the opponent with a sword and to avoid being touched.

Three different weapons may be used: the *foil*, the *epee*, and the *saber*. These differ in size, weight, and appearance. Now they all include devices to blunt their points for safety, and fencers wear a strong wire-mesh mask and protective clothing to avoid injury.

Have students discuss how dueling scenes would add to a staged play. Have them compare and contrast the dueling scenes in *The Tragedy of Romeo and Juliet* with action scenes in contemporary movies, including car chases, gun scenes, and martial-arts sequences.

NOTES

41. spleen *n.* angry nature.

42. tilts *v.* thrusts.

43. envious *adv.* full of hatred.

44. entertained *v.* considered.

45. His fault . . . Tybalt by killing Tybalt, he did what the law could have done.

exile (EHG zyl) *v.* punish someone by forcing them to leave a place permanently

46. My blood Mercutio was related to the Prince.

47. amerce *v.* punish.

48. attend our will await my decision.

Could not take truce with the unruly spleen[41]
Of Tybalt deaf to peace, but that he tilts[42]
With piercing steel at bold Mercutio's breast;
Who, all as hot, turns deadly point to point,
And, with a martial scorn, with one hand beats
Cold death aside and with the other sends
It back to Tybalt, whose dexterity
Retorts it. Romeo he cries aloud,
"Hold, friends! Friends, part!" and swifter than his tongue,
His agile arm beats down their fatal points,
And 'twixt them rushes; underneath whose arm
An envious[43] thrust from Tybalt hit the life
Of stout Mercutio, and then Tybalt fled;
But by and by comes back to Romeo,
Who had but newly entertained[44] revenge,
And to't they go like lightning; for, ere I
Could draw to part them, was stout Tybalt slain;
And, as he fell, did Romeo turn and fly.
This is the truth, or let Benvolio die.

Lady Capulet. He is a kinsman to the Montague;
Affection makes him false, he speaks not true.
Some twenty of them fought in this black strife,
And all those twenty could but kill one life.
I beg for justice, which thou, Prince, must give.
Romeo slew Tybalt; Romeo must not live.

Prince. Romeo slew him; he slew Mercutio.
Who now the price of his dear blood doth owe?

Montague. Not Romeo, Prince; he was Mercutio's friend;
His fault concludes but what the law should end,
The life of Tybalt.[45]

Prince. And for that offense
Immediately we do **exile** him hence.
I have an interest in your hate's proceeding.
My blood[46] for your rude brawls doth lie a-bleeding;
But I'll amerce[47] you with so strong a fine
That you shall all repent the loss of mine.
I will be deaf to pleading and excuses;
Nor tears nor prayers shall purchase out abuses.
Therefore, use none. Let Romeo hence in haste,
Else, when he is found, that hour is his last.
Bear hence this body and attend our will.[48]
Mercy but murders, pardoning those that kill.

[*Exit with others.*]

WriteNow Express and Reflect

Crime & Punishment In line 184, The Prince presents his punishment. Have students write a one-page essay about whether the Prince's punishment for Romeo was fair. How did his own family play into this decision, and would you recommend a more fair punishment in a society where there are not mandatory trials by jury?

Scene ii • *Capulet's orchard.*

[*Enter* Juliet *alone.*]

Juliet. Gallop apace, you fiery-footed steeds,[1]
Towards Phoebus' lodging![2] Such a wagoner
As Phaëthon[3] would whip you to the west
And bring in cloudy night immediately.
Spread thy close curtain, love-performing night,
That runaways' eyes may wink,[4] and Romeo
Leap to these arms untalked of and unseen.
Lovers can see to do their amorous rites,
And by their own beauties; or, if love be blind,
It best agrees with night. Come, civil night,
Thou sober-suited matron all in black,
And learn me how to lose a winning match,
Played for a pair of stainless maidenhoods.
Hood my unmanned blood, bating in my cheeks,[5]
With thy black mantle till strange[6] love grows bold,
Think true love acted simple modesty,
Come, night; come, Romeo; come, thou day in night;
For thou wilt lie upon the wings of night
Whiter than new snow upon a raven's back.
Come, gentle night; come, loving, black-browed night;
Give me my Romeo; and when I shall die,
Take him and cut him out in little stars,
And he will make the face of heaven so fine
That all the world will be in love with night
And pay no worship to the garish sun.
O, I have bought the mansion of a love,
But not possessed it; and though I am sold,
Not yet enjoyed. So tedious is this day
As is the night before some festival
To some impatient child that hath new robes
And may not wear them. O, here comes my nurse.

[*Enter* Nurse, *with cords.*]

And she brings news; and every tongue that speaks
But Romeo's name speaks heavenly eloquence.
Now, nurse, what news? What hast thou there, the cords
That Romeo bid thee fetch?

Nurse. Ay, ay, the cords.

Juliet. Ay me! What news? Why dost thou wring thy hands?

Nurse. Ah, weraday![7] He's dead, he's dead, he's dead!
We are undone, lady, we are undone!
Alack the day! He's gone, he's killed, he's dead!

NOTES

1. **fiery-footed steeds** horses of the sun god, Phoebus.
2. **Phoebus'** (FEE buhs) **lodging** below the horizon.
3. **Phaëthon** (FAY uh thon) Phoebus' son, who tried to drive his father's horses but was unable to control them.
4. **That runways' eyes may wink** so that the eyes of busybodies may not see.
5. **Hood . . . cheeks** hide the untamed blood that makes me blush.
6. **strange** *adj.* unfamiliar.
7. **Ah, weraday!** alas!

CLOSE READ

ANNOTATE: In lines 1–31 of Scene ii, mark words and phrases that describe the night.

QUESTION: In Juliet's view, what qualities does the night have?

CONCLUDE: How does this language clarify the state of Juliet's emotions?

DIGITAL PERSPECTIVES

CLOSE READ

Remind students to focus on Juliet's wishes. You may wish to model the Close Read using the following think-aloud format. Possible responses to questions on the Student page are included.

ANNOTATE: As I read Scene ii, lines 1–31, I notice and highlight details that describe night.

QUESTION: I see that Juliet refers to the night as "civil" and "sober-suited," "gentle" and "loving." Juliet's descriptions of night reflect both chastity and passion. The night brings her Romeo and so she can see all its positive qualities. Even the *black mantle* of night is allowing her love a cover that allows boldness.

CONCLUDE: I can see that this language shows the state of Juliet's emotions–she is moved with a burning anticipation of love. She believes that "amorous rites" can be observed with "simple modesty." She compares herself to an excited child awaiting a festival. Her excitement and anticipation make all her emotions heightened. To her the night is everything heroic because it brings Romeo and the day is all things dull and tedious.

CLOSER LOOK

Analyze Oxymoron

Students may have marked lines 73–82 during their first read. Use this passage to help students understand Juliet's conflicted emotions about Romeo killing her cousin Tybalt. Encourage them to talk about the annotations that they marked. You may want to model a close read with the class based on the highlights shown in the text.

ANNOTATE: Have students mark details in Scene ii, lines 73–82, that demonstrate the use of adjectives that contradict the nature of the images they describe, or have students participate while you highlight them.

QUESTION: Guide students to consider what these details might tell them. Ask what a reader can infer from these contradictions, and accept student responses.

Possible response: These impossible images give us insight into the conflicting emotions of Juliet.

CONCLUDE: Help students to formulate conclusions about the importance of these details in the text. Ask students why the author might have included these details.

Possible response: Juliet was interrupted from her amorous soliloquy about Romeo to be told that the one she loves so much has killed her cousin. The author uses imagery that expresses and contains contradiction to show that her love is now mixed with anger and each contrasting image shows elements of good and bad. The *damned saint* and *honorable villain* mix up good and evil. This kind of contradiction, expressed in this way, is called an *oxymoron*.

Remind students that an **oxymoron** is a figure of speech in which two opposite ideas are joined to create an effect. It is used primarily to express unresolved conflict.

NOTES

Juliet. Can heaven be so envious?

Nurse. Romeo can,
Though heaven cannot. O Romeo, Romeo!
Who ever would have thought it? Romeo!

Juliet. What devil art thou that dost torment me thus?
This torture should be roared in dismal hell.
Hath Romeo slain himself? Say thou but "Ay,"[8]
And that bare vowel "I" shall poison more
Than the death-darting eye of cockatrice.
I am not I, if there be such an "Ay,"
Or those eyes' shot[9] that makes thee answer "Ay."
If he be slain, say "Ay"; or if not, "No."
Brief sounds determine of my weal or woe.

Nurse. I saw the wound, I saw it with mine eyes,
(God save the mark![10]) here on his manly breast.
A piteous corse,[11] a bloody piteous corse;
Pale, pale as ashes, all bedaubed in blood,
All in gore-blood. I swounded[12] at the sight.

Juliet. O, break, my heart! Poor bankrout,[13] break at once!
To prison, eyes; ne'er look on liberty!
Vile earth, to earth resign;[14] end motion here,
And thou and Romeo press one heavy bier![15]

Nurse. O Tybalt, Tybalt, the best friend I had!
O courteous Tybalt! Honest gentleman!
That ever I should live to see thee dead!

Juliet. What storm is this that blows so contrary?[16]
Is Romeo slaught'red, and is Tybalt dead?
My dearest cousin, and my dearer lord?
Then, dreadful trumpet, sound the general doom![17]
For who is living, if those two are gone?

Nurse. Tybalt is gone, and Romeo banishèd;
Romeo that killed him, he is banishèd.

Juliet. O God! Did Romeo's hand shed Tybalt's blood?

Nurse. It did, it did! Alas the day, it did!

Juliet. O serpent heart, hid with a flow'ring face!
Did ever the dragon keep so fair a cave?
Beautiful tyrant! Fiend angelical!
Dove-feathered raven! Wolvish-ravening lamb!
Despisèd substance of divinest show!
Just opposite to what thou justly seem'st—
A damnèd saint, an honorable villain!
O nature, what hadst thou to do in hell
When thou didst bower the spirit of a fiend
In mortal paradise of such sweet flesh?

8. **"Ay"** yes.

9. **eyes' shot** the Nurse's glance.

10. **God save the mark!** May God save us from evil!

11. **corse** *n.* corpse.

12. **swounded** *v.* swooned; fainted.

13. **bankrout** *n.* bankrupt.

14. **Vile . . . resign** let my body return to the earth.

15. **bier** *n.* platform in which a corpse is displayed before burial.

16. **contrary** *adv.* in opposite directions.

17. **dreadful . . . doom** let the trumpet that announces doomsday be sounded.

Was ever book containing such vile matter
So fairly bound? O, that deceit should dwell
In such a gorgeous palace!

Nurse. There's no trust,
No faith, no honesty in men; all perjured,
All forsworn,[18] all naught, all dissemblers.[19]
Ah, where's my man? Give me some aqua vitae.[20]
These griefs, these woes, these sorrows make me old.
Shame come to Romeo!

Juliet. Blistered by thy tongue
For such a wish! He was not born to shame.
Upon his brow shame is ashamed to sit;
For 'tis a throne where honor may be crowned
Sole monarch of the universal earth.
O, what a beast was I to chide at him!

Nurse. Will you speak well of him that killed your cousin?

Juliet. Shall I speak ill of him that is my husband?
Ah, poor my lord, what tongue shall smooth thy name
When I, thy three-hours wife, have mangled it?
But wherefore, villain, didst thou kill my cousin?
That villain cousin would have killed my husband.
Back, foolish tears, back to your native spring!
Your tributary[21] drops belong to woe,
Which you, mistaking, offer up to joy.
My husband lives, that Tybalt would have slain;
And Tybalt's dead, that would have slain my husband.
All this is comfort; wherefore weep I then?
Some word there was, worser than Tybalt's death,
That murd'red me. I would forget it fain;
But O, it presses to my memory
Like damnèd guilty deeds to sinners' minds!
"Tybalt is dead, and Romeo—banishèd."
That "banishèd," that one word "banishèd,"
Hath slain ten thousand Tybalts. Tybalt's death
Was woe enough, if it had ended there;
Or, if sour woe delights in fellowship
And needly will be ranked with[22] other griefs,
Why followed not, when she said "Tybalt's dead,"
Thy father, or thy mother, nay, or both,
Which modern[23] lamentation might have moved?
But with a rearward[24] following Tybalt's death,
"Romeo is banishèd"—to speak that word
Is father, mother, Tybalt, Romeo, Juliet,
All slain, all dead. "Romeo is banishèd"—
There is no end, no limit, no measure, bound,
In that word's death; no words can that woe sound.

NOTES

18. **forsworn** *v.* are liars.
19. **dissemblers** *n.* hypocrites.
20. **aqua vitae** (AK wuh VY tee) brandy.
21. **tributary** *adj.* contributing; also, honoring.
22. **needly . . . with** must be accompanied by.
23. **modern** *adj.* ordinary.
24. **rearward** *n.* follow up; literally, a rear guard.

PERSONALIZE FOR LEARNING

Strategic Support

Summarize In order for students to understand Juliet's lengthy monologue in Scene ii, lines 97–126, model the process of paraphrasing for students. For example, highlight lines 106–107 "Tybalt's dead that would have slain my husband.... Wherefore weep I then?" for students to paraphrase. Make sure they also restate Scene ii, lines 112–114. What does it mean to Juliet, "that one word 'banishèd,' Hath slain ten thousand Tybalts"? If you have the time call on some students for their responses to this line.

Students should be able to summarize the main ideas; that although the death of her cousin Tybalt is upsetting, Juliet ultimately decides she is more upset that Romeo has been exiled from Verona.

NOTES

banishment (BAN ihsh muhnt) *n.* state of having been banished, or exiled

25. wot *v.* know.

Where is my father and my mother, nurse?

Nurse. Weeping and wailing over Tybalt's corse.
Will you go to them? I will bring you thither.

Juliet. Wash they his wounds with tears? Mine shall be spent,
When theirs are dry, for Romeo's **banishment**.
Take up those cords. Poor ropes, you are beguiled,
Both you and I, for Romeo is exiled.
He made you for a highway to my bed;
But I, a maid, die maiden-widowèd.
Come, cords; come, nurse. I'll to my wedding bed;
And death, not Romeo, take my maidenhead!

Nurse. Hie to your chamber. I'll find Romeo
To comfort you. I wot[25] well where he is.
Hark ye, your Romeo will be here at night.
I'll to him; he is hid at Lawrence' cell.

Juliet. O, find him! Give this ring to my true knight
And bid him come to take his last farewell. [*Exit with* Nurse.]

⌘ ⌘ ⌘

Scene iii • *Friar Lawrence's cell.*

[*Enter* Friar Lawrence.]

Friar. Romeo, come forth; come forth, thou fearful man.
Affliction is enamored of thy parts,[1]
And thou art wedded to calamity.

[*Enter* Romeo.]

Romeo. Father, what news? What is the Prince's doom?
What sorrow craves acquaintance at my hand
That I yet know not?

Friar. Too familiar
Is my dear son with such sour company.
I bring thee tidings of the Prince's doom.[2]

Romeo. What less than doomsday[3] is the Prince's doom?

Friar. A gentler judgment vanished[4] from his lips—
Not body's death, but body's banishment.

Romeo. Ha, banishment? Be merciful, say "death";
For exile hath more terror in his look,
Much more than death. Do not say "banishment."

Friar. Here from Verona art thou banishèd
Be patient, for the world is broad and wide.

1. **Affliction . . . parts** misery is in love with your attractive qualities.
2. **doom** *n.* final decision.
3. **doomsday** *n.* my death.
4. **vanished** *v.* escaped; came forth.

PERSONALIZE FOR LEARNING

English Language Support

Fluency with Reading If students struggle with the pronunciation of words like "banishèd" that appears in line 15, point out the accent mark and read the word aloud. Have students echo you. Clarify that you are emphasizing the accented letter and pronouncing the "ed" as a separate syllable. This is a way in which our pronunciation of English words has changed over time.

Romeo. There is no world without[5] Verona walls,
But purgatory, torture, hell itself.
Hence banishèd is banishèd from the world,
And world's exile is death. Then "banishèd"
Is death mistermed. Calling death "banishèd,"
Thou cut'st my head off with a golden ax
And smilest upon the stroke that murders me.

Friar. O deadly sin! O rude unthankfulness!
Thy fault our law calls death;[6] but the kind Prince,
Taking thy part, hath rushed[7] aside the law,
And turned that black word "death" to "banishment."
This is dear mercy, and thou seest it not.

Romeo. 'Tis torture, and not mercy. Heaven is here,
Where Juliet lives; and every cat and dog
And little mouse, every unworthy thing,
Live here in heaven and may look on her;
But Romeo may not. More validity,[8]
More honorable state, more courtship lives
In carrion flies than Romeo. They may seize
On the white wonder of dear Juliet's hand
And steal immortal blessing from her lips,
Who, even in pure and vestal modesty,
Still blush, as thinking their own kisses sin;
But Romeo may not, he is banishèd.
Flies may do this but I from this must fly;
They are freemen, but I am banishèd.
And sayest thou yet that exile is not death?
Hadst thou no poison mixed, no sharp-ground knife,
No sudden mean[9] of death, though ne'er so mean,[10]
But "banishèd" to kill me—"banishèd"?
O friar, the damnèd use that word in hell;
Howling attends it! How hast thou the heart,
Being a divine, a ghostly confessor,
A sin-absolver, and my friend professed,
To mangle me with that word "banishèd"?

Friar. Thou fond mad man, hear me a little speak.

Romeo. O, thou wilt speak again of banishment.

Friar. I'll give thee armor to keep off that word;
Adversity's sweet milk, philosophy,
To comfort thee, though thou art banishèd.

Romeo. Yet "banishèd"? Hang up philosophy!
Unless philosophy can make a Juliet,
Displant a town, reverse a prince's doom,
It helps not, it prevails not. Talk no more.

Friar. O, then I see that madmen have no ears.

NOTES

5. **without** outside.

6. **Thy fault . . . death** for what you did our law demands the death penalty.

7. **rushed** *v.* pushed.

8. **validity** *v.* value.

9. **mean** *n.* method.

10. **mean** *adj.* humiliating.

DIGITAL PERSPECTIVES

CLOSER LOOK

Analyze Dialogue

Students may have marked lines 17–60 during their first read. Use these lines to help students understand how Romeo is revealing his youthful exuberance and lack of reason in this dialogue with Friar Lawrence. Encourage them to talk about the annotations that they marked. You may want to model a close read with the class based on the highlights shown in the text.

ANNOTATE: Have students mark details in Scene iii, lines 17–60, that show Romeo's youthful fervor regarding his banishment, or have students participate while you highlight them.

QUESTION: Guide students to consider what these details might tell them. Ask what a reader can infer from the details of Romeo's anguish and accept student responses.

Possible response: Romeo is showing his deep desire to be with Juliet but refuses to believe that it could be possible, showing a youthful lack of reason.

CONCLUDE: Help students to formulate conclusions about the importance of these details in the text. Ask students why the author might have included these details.

Possible response: Romeo refuses to see banishment as anything but eternal banishment from Juliet. Friar Lawrence advises him to listen to reason and be hopeful.

Remind students that **dialogue** is a conversation between or among characters. Writers use dialogue to reveal character and relationships, to advance the plot and develop conflict, and to dramatize the interplay of ideas.

NOTES

11. **dispute** *v.* discuss.
12. **estate** *n.* condition; situation.

Romeo. How should they, when that wise men have no eyes?

Friar. Let me dispute[11] with thee of thy estate.[12]

Romeo. Thou canst not speak of that thou dost not feel.
Wert thou as young as I, Juliet thy love,
An hour but married, Tybalt murderèd,
Doting like me, and like me banishèd,
Then mightst thou speak, then mightst thou tear thy hair,
And fall upon the ground, as I do now,
Taking the measure of an unmade grave.

[*Knock.*]

Friar. Arise, one knocks. Good Romeo, hide thyself.

Romeo. Not I; unless the breath of heartsick groans
Mistlike infold me from the search of eyes. [*Knock.*]

Friar. Hark, how they knock! Who's there? Romeo, arise;
Thou wilt be taken.—Stay awhile!—Stand up; [*Knock.*]
Run to my study.—By and by![13]—God's will,
What simpleness[14] is this.—I come, I come! [*Knock.*]
Who knocks so hard? Whence come you? What's your will?

13. **By and by!** In a minute! (said to the person knocking).
14. **simpleness** *n.* silly behavior (Romeo does not move).

[*Enter* Nurse.]

Nurse. Let me come in, and you shall know my errand.
I come from Lady Juliet.

Friar. Welcome then.

Nurse. O holy friar, O, tell me, holy friar,
Where is my lady's lord, where's Romeo?

Friar. There on the ground, with his own tears made drunk.

Nurse. O, he is even in my mistress' case,
Just in her case! O woeful sympathy!
Piteous predicament! Even so lies she,
Blubb'ring and weeping, weeping and blubb'ring.
Stand up, stand up! Stand, and you be a man.
For Juliet's sake, for her sake, rise and stand!
Why should you fall into so deep an O?

Romeo. [*Rises.*] Nurse—

Nurse. Ah sir, ah sir! Death's the end of all.
Romeo. Spakest thou of Juliet? How is it with her?
Doth not she think of me an old murderer,
Now I have stained the childhood of our joy
With blood removed but little from her own?
Where is she? And how doth she? And what says
My concealed lady[15] to our canceled love?

15. **concealed lady** secret bride.

Nurse. O, she says nothing, sir, but weeps and weeps;
And now falls on her bed, and then starts up,
And Tybalt calls; and then on Romeo cries,

PERSONALIZE FOR LEARNING

Strategic Support

Timeline The Nurse visits the Friar in line 79. As the plot continues to get more complex, have students create a basic timeline of all the major events that have occurred in Act III. They will cite all the notable conflicts: the fight, Mercutio's death, Tybalt's death, Romeo's banishment.... Have them leave space so that they may continue to add events to this timeline. Have students illustrate the timeline, giving each event a small symbol, the death of Tybalt may be a skull or a sword. This is a way for students of every reading level to organize the information.

And then down falls again.

Romeo. As if that name,
Shot from the deadly level[16] of a gun,
Did murder her; as that name's cursèd hand
Murdered her kinsman. O, tell me, friar, tell me,
In what vile part of this anatomy
Doth my name lodge? Tell me, that I may sack[17]
The hateful mansion.

[*He offers to stab himself, and* Nurse *snatches the dagger away.*]

Friar. Hold thy desperate hand.
Art thou a man? Thy form cries out thou art;
Thy tears are womanish, thy wild acts denote
The unreasonable fury of a beast.
Unseemly[18] woman in a seeming man!
And ill-beseeming beast in seeming both![19]
Thou hast amazed me. By my holy order,
I thought thy disposition better tempered.
Hast thou slain Tybalt? Wilt thou slay thyself?
And slay thy lady that in thy life lives,
By doing damnèd hate upon thyself?
Why railest thou on thy birth, the heaven, and earth?
Since birth and heaven and earth, all three do meet
In thee at once; which thou at once wouldst lose.
Fie, fie, thou shamest thy shape, thy love, thy wit,[20]
Which, like a usurer,[21] abound'st in all,
And usest none in that true use indeed
Which should bedeck[22] thy shape, thy love, thy wit,
Thy noble shape is but a form of wax,
Digressing from the valor of a man;
Thy dear love sworn but hollow perjury,
Killing that love which thou hast vowed to cherish;
Thy wit, that ornament to shape and love,
Misshapen in the conduct[23] of them both,
Like powder in a skilless soldier's flask,[24]
Is set afire by thine own ignorance,
And thou dismemb'red with thine own defense.[25]
What, rouse thee, man! Thy Juliet is alive,
For whose dear sake thou wast but lately dead.[26]
There art thou happy.[27] Tybalt would kill thee,
But thou slewest Tybalt. There art thou happy.
The law, that threat'ned death, becomes thy friend
And turns it to exile. There art thou happy.
A pack of blessings light upon thy back;
Happiness courts thee in her best array;
But, like a misbehaved and sullen wench,[28]
Thou puts up[29] thy fortune and thy love.

NOTES

16. **level** *n.* aim.

17. **sack** *v.* plunder.

18. **Unseemly** *adj.* inappropriate (because unnatural).

19. **And . . . both!** Romeo has inappropriately lost his human nature because he seems like a man and woman combined.

20. **wit** *n.* mind; intellect.

21. **Which, like a usurer** who, like a rich money-lender.

22. **bedeck** *v.* do honor to.

23. **conduct** *n.* management

24. **flask** *n.* powder flask.

25. **And thou . . . defense** The friar is saying that Romeo's mind, which is now irrational, is destroying rather than aiding him.

26. **but lately dead** only recently declaring yourself dead.

27. **happy** *adj.* fortunate

28. **wench** *n.* low, common girl.

29. **puts up** pouts over.

CLOSER LOOK

Analyze Personification

Students may have marked figurative language in Friar Lawrence's monologue during their first read. Use lines 140–145 to help students understand his use of personification. Encourage them to talk about the annotations that they marked. You may want to model a close read with the class based on the highlights shown in the text.

ANNOTATE: Have students mark details in Scene iii, lines 140–145, that show personification, or have students participate while you highlight them.

QUESTION: Guide students to consider what these details might tell them. Ask what a reader can infer from this use of personification to describe happiness and accept student responses.

Possible response: By personifying happiness as a fine woman who is doing her best to win Romeo over, Friar Lawrence demonstrates the absurdity of his refusal.

CONCLUDE: Help students to formulate conclusions about the importance of these details in the text. Ask students why the author might have included these details.

Possible response: The author is showing that personification can dramatize emotions and give them the power to reason and persuade. Happiness wants Romeo but he rejects her.

Personification is a figure of speech in which a nonhuman subject is given human characteristics ("the wind howled," "the house groaned"). Personification, like other kinds of figurative language, helps readers see the world differently by startling them into fresh perceptions. Effective personification of things or ideas makes them seem vital and alive, as if they were human.

NOTES

30. watch be set watchmen go on duty.

31. blaze *v.* announce publicly.

pardon (PAHR duhn) *n.* forgiveness for a crime

32. apt unto likely to do.

33. chide *v.* rebuke me (for slaying Tybalt).

34. here . . . state this is your situation.

35. Sojourn *v.* remain.

36. signify *v.* let you know.

1. move *v.* discuss your proposal with.

Take heed, take heed, for such die miserable.
Go get thee to thy love, as was decreed,
Ascend her chamber, hence and comfort her.
But look thou stay not till the watch be set,[30]
For then thou canst not pass to Mantua,
Where thou shalt live till we can find a time
To blaze[31] your marriage, reconcile your friends,
Beg **pardon** of the Prince, and call thee back
With twenty hundred thousand times more joy
Than thou went'st forth in lamentation.
Go before, nurse. Commend me to thy lady,
And bid her hasten all the house to bed,
Which heavy sorrow makes them apt[32] unto.
Romeo is coming.

Nurse. O Lord, I could have stayed here all the night
To hear good counsel. O, what learning is!
My lord, I'll tell my lady you will come.

Romeo. Do so, and bid my sweet prepare to chide.[33]

[Nurse *offers to go in and turns again.*]

Nurse. Here, sir, a ring she bid me give you, sir.
Hie you, make haste, for it grows very late. [*Exit.*]

Romeo. How well my comfort is revived by this!

Friar. Go hence; good night; and here stands all your state:[34]
Either be gone before the watch is set,
Or by the break of day disguised from hence.
Sojourn[35] in Mantua. I'll find out your man,
And he shall signify[36] from time to time
Every good hap to you that chances here.
Give me thy hand. 'Tis late. Farewell; good night.

Romeo. But that a joy past joy calls out on me,
It were a grief so brief to part with thee.
Farewell. [*Exit all.*]

⌘ ⌘ ⌘

Scene iv • *A room in Capulet's house.*

[*Enter old* Capulet, *his* Wife, *and* Paris.]

Capulet. Things have fall'n out, sir, so unluckily
That we have had no time to move[1] our daughter.
Look you, she loved her kinsman Tybalt dearly,
And so did I. Well, we were born to die.
'Tis very late; she'll not come down tonight.

PERSONALIZE FOR LEARNING

Strategic Support

For students to understand the action in Act III, scene iii, it is important for them to identify which characters know certain facts and how this could lead to potential conflicts. Review Romeo's comments in line 162. For example, at the same time that Friar Lawrence and the Nurse are planning to announce Romeo and Juliet's marriage and reconcile him to the city, Lord and Lady Capulet are discussing Juliet's engagement to Paris. At the end of scene iv have students fill in the following character chart, paraphrasing information in their own words:

Character	What They Know	What They Don't Know	Potential Conflicts
Friar Lawrence			
The Nurse			
Lord Capulet			
Lady Capulet			
Paris			
Romeo			
Juliet			

I promise you, but for your company,
I would have been abed an hour ago.

Paris. These times of woe afford no times to woo.
Madam, good night. Commend me to your daughter.

Lady Capulet. I will, and know her mind early tomorrow;
Tonight she's mewed up to her heaviness.[2]

Capulet. Sir, Paris, I will make a desperate tender[3]
Of my child's love. I think she will be ruled
In all respects by me; nay more, I doubt it not.
Wife, go you to her ere you go to bed;
Acquaint her here of my son[4] Paris' love
And bid her (mark you me?) on Wednesday next—
But soft! What day is this?

Paris. Monday, my lord.

Capulet. Monday! Ha, ha! Well, Wednesday is too soon.
A[5] Thursday let it be—a Thursday, tell her,
She shall be married to this noble earl.
Will you be ready? Do you like this haste?
We'll keep no great ado[6]—a friend or two;
For hark you, Tybalt being slain so late,
It may be thought we held him carelessly,[7]
Being our kinsman, if we revel much.
Therefore we'll have some half a dozen friends,
And there an end. But what say you to Thursday?

Paris. My lord, I would that Thursday were tomorrow.

Capulet. Well, get you gone. A Thursday be it then.
Go you to Juliet ere you go to bed;
Prepare her, wife, against[8] this wedding day.
Farewell, my lord.—Light to my chamber, ho!
Afore me,[9] it is so very late
That we may call it early by and by.
Good night. [*Exit all.*]

⌘ ⌘ ⌘

Scene v • *Capulet's orchard.*

[*Enter* Romeo *and* Juliet *aloft.*]

Juliet. Wilt thou be gone? It is not yet near day.
It was the nightingale, and not the lark,
That pierced the fearful hollow of thine ear.
Nightly she sings on yond pomegranate tree.
Believe me, love, it was the nightingale.

NOTES

2. **mewed . . . heaviness** locked up with her sorrow.

3. **desperate tender** risky offer.

4. **son** son-in-law.

5. **A** on.

6. **We'll . . . ado** We will not make a great fuss.

7. **held him carelessly** did not respect him enough.

8. **against** for.

9. **Afore me** indeed (a mild oath).

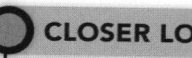

DIGITAL PERSPECTIVES

CLOSER LOOK

Analyze Dramatic Irony

Students may have marked preparations for Juliet's upcoming marriage to Paris during their first read. Use these lines to help students understand dramatic irony. Encourage them to talk about the annotations that they marked. You may want to model a close read with the class based on the highlights shown in the text.

ANNOTATE: Have students mark details in lines 10–35 that show the wedding details, or have students participate while you highlight them.

QUESTION: Guide students to consider what these details might tell them. Ask what a reader can infer from this interaction between the Capulets and Paris, and accept student responses.

Possible response: It seems the Capulets are in a rush to marry off Juliet and turn her mind from the tragic death of their family member Tybalt.

CONCLUDE: Help students to formulate conclusions about the importance of these details in the text. Ask students why the author might have included these details.

Possible response: The Capulets are victims of dramatic irony in not knowing what the audience knows: that Juliet is married to Romeo—Tybalt's killer.

Remind students that dramatic irony refers to a situation where the audience has vital information that one or more characters onstage are lacking (and therefore make mistakes).

NOTES

1. **severing** *adj.* parting.
2. **Night's candles** stars.
3. **exhales** *v.* sends out.
4. **reflex . . . brow** reflection of the moon (Cynthia was a name for the moon goddess.).
5. **sharps** *n.* shrill high notes.
6. **division** *n.* melody.
7. **change eyes** exchange eyes (because the lark has a beautiful body with ugly eyes and the toad has an ugly body with beautiful eyes).
8. **affray** *v.* frighten.
9. **hunt's-up** morning song for hunters.
10. **much in years** much older.

Romeo. It was the lark, the herald of the morn;
No nightingale. Look, love, what envious streaks
Do lace the severing[1] clouds in yonder East.
Night's candles[2] are burnt out, and jocund day
Stands tiptoe on the misty mountaintops.
I must be gone and live, or stay and die.

Juliet. Yond light is not daylight; I know it, I.
It is some meteor that the sun exhales[3]
To be to thee this night a torchbearer
And light thee on thy way to Mantua.
Therefore stay yet; thou need'st not to be gone.

Romeo. Let me be ta'en, let me be put to death.
I am content, so thou wilt have it so.
I'll say yon gray is not the morning's eye,
'Tis but the pale reflex of Cynthia's brow;[4]
Nor that is not the lark whose notes do beat
The vaulty heaven so high above our heads.
I have more care to stay than will to go.
Come, death, and welcome! Juliet wills it so.
How is't, my soul? Let's talk; it is not day.

Juliet. It is, it is! Hie hence, be gone, away!
It is the lark that sings so out of tune,
Straining harsh discords and unpleasing sharps.[5]
Some say the lark makes sweet division;[6]
This doth not so, for she divideth us.
Some say the lark and loathèd toad change eyes;[7]
O, now I would they had changed voices too,
Since arm from arm that voice doth us affray,[8]
Hunting thee hence with hunt's-up[9] to the day.
O, now be gone! More light and light it grows.

Romeo. More light and light—more dark and dark our woes.

[*Enter* Nurse.]

Nurse. Madam!

Juliet. Nurse?

Nurse. Your lady mother is coming to your chamber.
The day is broke; be wary, look about. [*Exit.*]

Juliet. Then, window, let day in, and let life out.

Romeo. Farewell, farewell! One kiss, and I'll descend.

[*He goeth down.*]

Juliet. Art thou gone so, love-lord, ay husband-friend?
I must hear from thee every day in the hour,
For in a minute there are many days.
O, by this count I shall be much in years[10]
Ere I again behold my Romeo!

440 UNIT 4 • STAR-CROSSED ROMANCES

PERSONALIZE FOR LEARNING

Digital Perspectives In Scene v, line 6, Romeo and Juliet have a lovers' quarrel about whether the bird they hear is the lark singing in the morning or a nightingale's song telling them that they may still have the cover of darkness shielding their love from the world for a little while longer. Both birds are used frequently in poetry for their beautiful singing and for their symbolic associations: the nightingale with night and the lark with dawn.

Using your school's media providers of choice, play the calls of the nightingale and the lark for the students. Ask students to compare the two sounds.

Possible Response: Both songs are sweet, just as this is a sweet argument between Romeo and Juliet – both are simply arguing for more time together.

Romeo. Farewell!
I will omit no opportunity
That may convey my greetings, love, to thee.

Juliet. O, think'st thou we shall ever meet again?

Romeo. I doubt it not; and all these woes shall serve
For sweet discourses[11] in our times to come.

Juliet. O God, I have an ill-divining[12] soul!
Methinks I see thee, now thou art so low,
As one dead in the bottom of a tomb.
Either my eyesight fails, or thou lookest pale.

Romeo. And trust me, love, in my eye so do you.
Dry sorrow drinks our blood.[13] Adieu, adieu! [*Exit.*]

Juliet. O Fortune, Fortune! All men call thee fickle.
If thou art fickle, what dost thou[14] with him
That is renowned for faith? Be fickle, Fortune,
For then I hope thou wilt not keep him long
But send him back.

[*Enter* Mother.]

Lady Capulet. Ho, daughter! Are you up?

Juliet. Who is't that calls? It is my lady mother.
Is she not down so late,[15] or up so early?
What unaccustomed cause procures her hither?[16]

Lady Capulet. Why, how now, Juliet?

Juliet. Madam, I am not well.

Lady Capulet. Evermore weeping for your cousin's death?
What, wilt thou wash him from his grave with tears?
An if thou couldst, thou couldst not make him live.
Therefore have done. Some grief shows much of love;
But much of grief shows still some want of wit.

Juliet. Yet let me weep for such a feeling[17] loss.

Lady Capulet. So shall you feel the loss, but not the friend
Which you weep for.

Juliet. Feeling so the loss,
I cannot choose but ever weep the friend.

Lady Capulet. Well, girl, thou weep'st not so much for his death
As that the villain lives which slaughtered him.

Juliet. What villain, madam?

Lady Capulet. That same villain Romeo.

Juliet. [*Aside.*] Villain and he be many miles asunder.[18]—
God pardon him! I do, with all my heart;
And yet no man like he doth grieve my heart.

Lady Capulet. That is because the traitor murderer lives.

NOTES

11. **discourses** *n.* conversations.
12. **ill-divining** *adj.* predicting evil.
13. **Dry sorrow . . . blood** It was once believed that sorrow drained away the blood.
14. **dost thou** do you have to do.
15. **Is she . . . late** Has she stayed up so late?
16. **What . . . hither?** What unusual reason brings her here?
17. **feeling** *adj.* deeply felt.
18. **asunder** *adj.* apart.

DIGITAL PERSPECTIVES

CLOSER LOOK

Analyze Dramatic Speech – The Aside

Students may have marked lines 69–86 during their first read. Use these lines to help students understand the use of the *aside*. Encourage them to talk about the annotations that they marked. You may want to model a close read with the class based on the highlights shown in the text.

ANNOTATE: Have students mark details in lines 69–86 that demonstrate the use of an aside, or have students participate while you highlight them.

QUESTION: Guide students to consider what these details might tell them. Ask what a reader can infer from Juliet's responses to her mother, and accept student responses.

Possible response: Juliet is telling her mother what she wants to hear with vague information that still allows her to be true to her real feelings.

CONCLUDE: Help students to formulate conclusions about the importance of these details in the text. Ask students why the author might have included these details.

Possible response: Juliet uses her aside to share her true emotions of love, forgiveness, and concern for Romeo with the audience.

Remind students that the **aside** is a form of dramatic irony. It expresses a complicity between one character and the audience—they share a secret that nobody else on stage suspects.

CLOSE READ

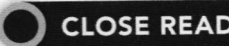

Remind students to focus on Juliet's dialogue. You may wish to model the Close Read using the following think-aloud format. Possible responses to questions on the Student page are included.

ANNOTATE: As I read Scene v, lines 94–125, I notice and highlight details that show Juliet's ironic use of double meaning and puns for the benefit of the audience.

QUESTION: I feel that Juliet believes that lying would dishonor her parents—and the sacred bond between her and Romeo.

CONCLUDE: I believe the wordplay in this scene is similar to Mercutio's in his death scene. Both characters remain true to themselves and defy cruel fortune with a brave and brilliant show of wit.

NOTES

19. runagate *n.* renegade; runaway.

20. unaccustomed dram unexpected dose of poison.

21. dead Juliet is deliberately ambiguous here. Her mother thinks *dead* refers to Romeo. But Juliet is using the word with the following line, in reference to her heart.

22. temper *v.* mix; weaken.

23. wreak (reek) *v.* avenge; express.

24. careful *adj.* considerate

25. sorted out selected.

26. in happy time just in time.

CLOSE READ

ANNOTATE: In lines 94–124, mark Juliet's uses of double meanings and puns.

QUESTION: Why does Shakespeare construct Juliet's lines so that she never directly lies?

CONCLUDE: What purpose does such wordplay, even at critical moments such as this, serve?

27. conduit *n.* water pipe.

Juliet. Ay, madam, from the reach of these my hands,
Would none but I might venge my cousin's death!

Lady Capulet. We will have vengeance for it, fear thou not.
Then weep no more. I'll send to one in Mantua,
Where that same banished runagate[19] doth live,
Shall give him such unaccustomed dram[20]
That he shall soon keep Tybalt company;
And then I hope thou wilt be satisfied.

Juliet. Indeed I never shall be satisfied
With Romeo till I behold him—dead[21]—
Is my poor heart so for a kinsman vexed.
Madam, if you could find out but a man
To bear a poison, I would temper[22] it,
That Romeo should, upon receipt thereof,
Soon sleep in quiet. O, how my heart abhors
To hear him named and cannot come to him,
To wreak[23] the love I bore my cousin
Upon his body that hath slaughtered him!

Lady Capulet. Find thou the means, and I'll find such a man.
But now I'll tell thee joyful tidings, girl.

Juliet. And joy comes well in such a needy time.
What are they, I beseech your ladyship?

Lady Capulet. Well, well, thou hast a careful[24] father, child;
One who, to put thee from thy heaviness,
Hath sorted out[25] a sudden day of joy
That thou expects not nor I looked not for.

Juliet. Madam, in happy time![26] What day is that?

Lady Capulet. Marry, my child, early next Thursday morn
The gallant, young, and noble gentleman,
The County Paris, at Saint Peter's Church,
Shall happily make thee there a joyful bride.

Juliet. Now by Saint Peter's Church, and Peter too,
He shall not make me there a joyful bride!
I wonder at this haste, that I must wed
Ere he that should be husband comes to woo.
I pray you tell my lord and father, madam,
I will not marry yet; and when I do, I swear
It shall be Romeo, whom you know I hate,
Rather than Paris. These are news indeed!

Lady Capulet. Here comes your father. Tell him so yourself,
And see how he will take it at your hands.

[*Enter* Capulet *and* Nurse.]

Capulet. When the sun sets the earth doth drizzle dew,
But for the sunset of my brother's son
It rains downright.
How now? A conduit,[27] girl? What, still in tears?

^ Juliet, the Nurse, and Lady Capulet speak in private.

Evermore show'ring? In one little body
Thou counterfeits a bark,[28] a sea, a wind:
For still thy eyes, which I may call the sea,
Do ebb and flow with tears; the bark thy body is,
Sailing in this salt flood; the winds, thy sighs,
Who, raging with thy tears and they with them,
Without a sudden calm will overset
Thy tempest-tossèd body. How now, wife?
Have you delivered to her our decree?

Lady Capulet. Ay, sir; but she will none, she gives you thanks.[29]
I would the fool were married to her grave!

Capulet. Soft! Take me with you,[30] take me with you, wife.
How? Will she none? Doth she not give us thanks?
Is she not proud?[31] Doth she not count her blest,
Unworthy as she is, that we have wrought[32]
So worthy a gentleman to be her bride?

Juliet. Not proud you have, but thankful that you have.
Proud can I never be of what I hate,
But thankful even for hate that is meant love.

Capulet. How, how, how, how, chopped-logic?[33] What is this?
"Proud"—and "I thank you"—and "I thank you not"—
And yet "not proud"? Mistress minion[34] you,
Thank me no thankings, nor proud me no prouds,
But fettle[35] your fine joints 'gainst Thursday next
To go with Paris to Saint Peter's Church,

NOTES

28. bark *n.* boat.

29. she will none . . . thanks she will have nothing to do with it, thank you.

30. Soft! Take . . . you Wait a minute. Let me understand you.

31. proud *adj.* pleased.

32. wrought *v.* arranged.

33. chopped-logic contradictory, unsound thought and speech.

34. Mistress minion Miss Uppity; overly proud.

35. fettle *v.* prepare.

CLOSER LOOK

Repetition in Dialogue

Students may have marked lines 150–155 during their first read. Use these lines to help students understand the use of repetition in dialogue. Encourage them to talk about the annotations that they marked. You may want to model a close read with the class based on the highlights shown in the text.

ANNOTATE: Have students mark details in lines 150–155 that show repetition, or have students participate while you highlight them.

QUESTION: Guide students to consider what these details might tell them. Ask what a reader can infer from what was marked and accept student responses.

Possible response: Through his repetition of the word *How,* Capulet is showing his impatience and frustration with his daughter's smart and polite evasions.

CONCLUDE: Help students to formulate conclusions about the importance of these details in the text. Ask students why the author might have included these details.

Possible response: This repetition gives dramatic vigor and emphasis to Capulet's frustration and impatience.

Remind students that **repetition** is a manifestly artificial and unnatural use of words for emphasis that is employed to serve an emotional and dramatic truth.

Or I will drag thee on a hurdle[36] thither.
Out, you greensickness carrion![37] Out, you baggage![38]
You tallow-face![39]

Lady Capulet. Fie, fie! What, are you mad?

Juliet. Good father, I beseech you on my knees,
Hear me with patience but to speak a word.

Capulet. Hang thee, young baggage! Disobedient wretch!
I tell thee what—get thee to church a Thursday
Or never after look me in the face.
Speak not, reply not, do not answer me!
My fingers itch. Wife, we scarce thought us blest
That God had lent us but this only child;
But now I see this one is one too much,
And that we have a curse in having her.
Out on her, hilding![40]

Nurse. God in heaven bless her!
You are to blame, my lord, to rate[41] her so.

Capulet. And why, my Lady Wisdom? Hold your tongue,
Good Prudence. Smatter with your gossips, go![42]

Nurse. I speak no treason.

Capulet. O, God-i-god-en!

Nurse. May not one speak?

Capulet. Peace, you mumbling fool!
Utter your gravity[43] o'er a gossip's bowl,
For here we need it not.

Lady Capulet. You are too hot.

Capulet. God's bread![44] It makes me mad.
Day, night; hour, tide, time; work, play;
Alone, in company; still my care hath been
To have her matched; and having now provided
A gentleman of noble parentage,
Of fair demesnes,[45] youthful, and nobly trained,
Stuffed, as they say, with honorable parts,[46]
Proportioned as one's thought would wish a man—
And then to have a wretched puling[47] fool,
A whining mammet,[48] in her fortune's tender,[49]
To answer "I'll not wed, I cannot love;
I am too young, I pray you pardon me"!
But, and you will not wed, I'll pardon you!
Graze where you will, you shall not house with me.
Look to't, think on't; I do not use to jest.
Thursday is near; lay hand on heart, advise:[50]
And you be mine, I'll give you to my friend;
And you be not, hang, beg, starve, die in the streets,
For, by my soul, I'll ne'er acknowledge thee,

NOTES

36. **hurdle** *n.* sled on which prisoners were taken to their execution.
37. **greensickness carrion** anemic lump of flesh.
38. **baggage** *n.* naughty girl.
39. **tallow-face** wax-pale face.
40. **hilding** *n.* worthless person.
41. **rate** *v.* scold; berate.
42. **Smatter . . . go!** Go chatter with the other old women.
43. **gravity** *v.* wisdom.
44. **God's bread!** By the holy Eucharist!
45. **demesnes** (dih MAYNZ) *n.* property.
46. **parts** *n.* qualities.
47. **puling** *adj.* whining.
48. **mammet** *n.* doll.
49. **in . . . tender** when good fortune is offered her.
50. **advise** *v.* consider.

PERSONALIZE FOR LEARNING

English Language Support

Idioms Tell students to be mindful of Capulet's lines because they contain many idioms and sayings. For example, in line 190 of Scene v, Capulet tells Juliet to "Graze where you will, you shall not house with me." Here he is speaking as if she were cattle or a horse grazing grass in the streets of Verona. In reality he is letting her know that if she doesn't marry Paris, she will be seeking her own food and shelter just as one of these animals might.

Challenge English language learners to find other idioms, or sayings not meant literally, on this page and interpret them.

Possible Response: Line 171 – "Hold your tongue," Capulet is telling the Nurse to be quiet, not literally hold her tongue.

Possible Response: Line 183 – "Stuffed, as the say, with honorable parts," Capulet is describing Paris as having many positive and manly qualities. **ALL LEVELS**

Nor what is mine shall never do thee good.
Trust to't. Bethink you. I'll not be forsworn.[51] [*Exit.*]

Juliet. Is there no pity sitting in the clouds
That sees into the bottom of my grief?
O sweet my mother, cast me not away!
Delay this marriage for a month, a week;
Or if you do not, make the bridal bed
In that dim monument where Tybalt lies.

Lady Capulet. Talk not to me, for I'll not speak a word.
Do as thou wilt, for I have done with thee. [*Exit.*]

Juliet. O God!—O nurse, how shall this be prevented?
My husband is on earth, my faith in heaven.[52]
How shall that faith return again to earth
Unless that husband send it me from heaven
By leaving earth?[53] Comfort me, counsel me.
Alack, alack, that heaven should practice stratagems[54]
Upon so soft a subject as myself!
What say'st thou? Hast thou not a word of joy?
Some comfort, nurse.

Nurse. Faith, here it is.
Romeo is banished; and all the world to nothing[55]
That he dares ne'er come back to challenge[56] you;
Or if he do, it needs must be by stealth.
Then, since the case so stands as now it doth,
I think it best you married with the County.
O, he's a lovely gentleman!
Romeo's a dishclout to him.[57] An eagle, madam,
Hath not so green, so quick, so fair an eye
As Paris hath. Beshrew my very heart,
I think you are happy in this second match,
For it excels your first; or if it did not,
Your first is dead—or 'twere as good he were
As living here and you no use of him.

Juliet. Speak'st thou from thy heart?

Nurse. And from my soul too; else beshrew them both.

Juliet. Amen!

Nurse. What?

Juliet. Well, thou hast comforted me marvelous much.
Go in; and tell my lady I am gone,
Having displeased my father, to Lawrence' cell,
To make confession and to be absolved.[58]

Nurse. Marry, I will; and this is wisely done. [*Exit.*]

Juliet. Ancient damnation![59] O most wicked fiend!
Is it more sin to wish me thus forsworn,
Or to dispraise my lord with that same tongue

NOTES

51. forsworn *v.* made to violate my promise.

52. my faith in heaven my marriage vow is recorded in heaven.

53. leaving earth dying.

54. stratagems *n.* tricks; plots.

55. all . . . nothing the odds are overwhelming.

56. challenge *v.* claim.

57. a dishclout to him a dishcloth compared with him.

58. absolved *v.* receive forgiveness for my sins.

59. Ancient damnation! Old devil!

HOW LANGUAGE WORKS

Transitions: On the next page the students will be required to write a summary and complete a challenge. Remind students to be mindful of the use of transitional words and phrases. Suggest students consider the following types of transitions:

Comparison
- in the same way
- similarly

Clarification
- that is to say
- in other words

Cause
- since
- for that reason

Effect
- therefore
- accordingly

Purpose
- in order that
- so that

Comprehension Check

Possible Responses

1. Romeo is already married to Juliet, and Tybalt is her cousin.
2. Romeo is responsible for the death of his friend Mercutio in two ways. He physically prevented him from fighting with Tybalt, which is how Tybalt was able to kill Mercutio through Romeo's arm in such a cowardly manner. He could also have prevented the brawl by letting Mercutio know about his love for Juliet.
3. The prince could have ordered that Romeo be killed as equal payment for Tybalt's life, which is what Lady Capulet wanted. However, he chooses exile for this crime of revenge.
4. Summary: In Act III Romeo and Juliet are married, but nobody else knows about it except Friar Lawrence and the Nurse. Before they can spend their first night together as man and wife, they are both hit with loss. Tybalt, cousin of Juliet, seeks Romeo out to fight for a perceived injustice. When Romeo will not fight Mercutio jumps in and is killed when Romeo tries to break up their fight. In a blind rage Romeo kills Tybalt and is banished from Verona by the Prince. Upon hearing this news Juliet is overcome with emotion—including anger toward Romeo. She quickly decides that their love is more important than her grief for her family. Romeo and she spend their first night together and after he leaves with the lark's first song, Juliet's mother Lady Capulet lets her daughter know she is to be wed to Paris in a few days. As Act III ends, Juliet feels betrayed by her family and the Nurse.

Research to Clarify: If students are struggling coming up with ideas, offer them ideas to assist them in understanding the time period of this play, such as marriage and judicial customs of the Elizabethan period.

NOTES

60. Thou . . . twain You will from now on be separated from my trust

Which she hath praised him with above compare
So many thousand times? Go, counselor!
Thou and my bosom henceforth shall be twain.[60]
I'll to the friar to know his remedy.
If all else fail, myself have power to die. [*Exit.*]

Comprehension Check

Complete the following items after you finish your first read.

1. Why does Romeo refuse to fight with Tybalt?

2. In what two ways is Romeo the cause of Mercutio's death?

3. What punishment could the Prince have ordered for Romeo? What punishment did he order?

4. **Notebook** Confirm your understanding of the text by writing a summary.

RESEARCH

Research to Clarify Choose at least one unfamiliar detail from the text. Briefly research that detail. In what way does the information you learned shed light on an aspect of the play?

PERSONALIZE FOR LEARNING

Challenge

Change the Ending Look at the last line of this act (Scene v, line 244)—where Juliet wants the "power to die," foreshadowing the end of the play. However, in this moment fate has decided nothing. Juliet's actions could change everything. Have students write a summary of their changed ending for Romeo and Juliet from this point on and pair students to collaborate on new endings.

DIGITAL PERSPECTIVES

Close Read the Text

Close Read — ANNOTATE QUESTION CONCLUDE

Reread Benvolio's description of the two fights that lead to Mercutio's and Tybalt's deaths (Act III, Scene i, lines 150–173). Mark words and phrases that describe specific details about the actions of Romeo and Tybalt. Based on these details, what is Benvolio trying to convey in his account to the Prince?

THE TRAGEDY OF ROMEO AND JULIET, ACT III

Analyze the Text

CITE TEXTUAL EVIDENCE to support your answers.

Notebook Respond to these questions.

1. (a) How and why does Romeo kill Tybalt? (b) **Interpret** What does Romeo mean when he says, after killing Tybalt, "I am fortune's fool"?
2. (a) **Analyze** Describe the conflicting emotions Juliet feels when the Nurse reports Tybalt's death and Romeo's punishment. (b) **Compare and Contrast** In what ways are Romeo's and Juliet's reactions to Romeo's banishment similar and different? Explain.
3. (a) **Paraphrase** When you **paraphrase**, you restate a text in your own words. Paraphrase Romeo's thoughts in Act III, Scene iii, lines 29–51. (b) **Criticize** How would you describe Romeo's response in these lines?
4. **Essential Question:** What have you learned about destiny by reading Act III of *The Tragedy of Romeo and Juliet*?

Tool Kit
Close-Read Guide and Model Annotation

LANGUAGE DEVELOPMENT

Concept Vocabulary

exile   banishment   pardon

Why These Words? These concept vocabulary words relate to punishment and forgiveness. How does each word contribute to meaning in the text? What other words in the selection connect to this concept?

Practice

Notebook Confirm your understanding of these words by using each one in a sentence.

Word Study

Notebook Latin Prefix: *ex-* In the word *exile,* the Latin prefix *ex-* means "away" or "out of." In the play, Romeo is exiled, which means he must go away from his home city. Using your understanding of the prefix *ex-*, record a definition for each of the following words: *extract, excavate, export, extension*.

WORD NETWORK
Add interesting words related to destiny from the text to your Word Network.

STANDARDS.
Language
Identify and correctly use patterns of word changes that indicate different meanings or parts of speech.

Jump Start

CLOSE READ Ask students if Romeo and Juliet are to blame for the deaths of Mercutio and Tybalt—and if not, why not?

Close Read the Text

Students may say that Benvolio paints Romeo as a peacemaker and Tybalt as a hothead who provoked him. Then Romeo defends his friend. Review and discuss the sections students have marked. If needed, continue to model close reading by using the Annotation Highlights in the Interactive Teacher's Edition.

Analyze the Text

Possible responses

1. (a) Tybalt struck Mercutio while Romeo was trying to stop the fight. Romeo kills Tybalt to avenge Mercutio's death. **DOK 1** (b) Romeo feels he is a victim of fate. **DOK 2**
2. (a) Juliet is desolated by Tybalt's death, and horrified that Romeo killed him. She is torn between rage and love. **DOK 4** (b) Both Romeo and Juliet react drastically to his banishment. Juliet alludes to suicide and Romeo asserts that separation from Juliet would be worse than death. **DOK 3**
3. (a) Romeo envies the lowest forms of life in Verona—they can see Juliet and he can't. He asks Friar Lawrence to help him die. **DOK 1** (b) I would describe Romeo's response as defeatist, hopeless, and self-pitying. **DOK 3**
4. Responses will vary.

Concept Vocabulary

Why These Words? Possible response: To Romeo, exile means never seeing Juliet again. Banishment means being forbidden to go near her. A pardon from the Prince would allow him to return and live with Juliet. Additional words include *doom, taken, canceled*.

Practice Answers will vary.

Word Study

For more support, see **Concept Vocabulary and Word Study.**

Possible responses

Extract: to draw *out* using force. Excavate: to dig *out*. Export: to send goods or services *away* to another country. Extension: the act of stretching something *out*.

Word Network

Possible words: *fortune, unlucky, doom*

FORMATIVE ASSESSMENT

Concept Vocabulary

If students can't relate the words to the meaning of the text, **then** have them return to the Prince's speech in Scene i and relate them specifically to the content of those lines.

Word Study

If students still don't understand the use of the prefix *ex-*, **then** have them look through the dictionary at other words beginning with *ex-, and* look for *out* and *away* in the definition. For Reteach and Practice, see **Word Study: Latin Prefix *ex-* (RP).**

Analyze Craft and Structure

Engage students in a discussion about the relationship between the characters and the audience. To whom does Juliet address her asides? If the answer is "To us," then who are we? Help students to see the dramatic function of soliloquies.

For more support, see **Analyze Craft and Structure: Dramatic Speeches.**

MAKE IT INTERACTIVE

Before students work on each question individually or in pairs, work with volunteer readers, female and male, on Juliet's soliloquy in Scene ii.

Practice

1. (a) Juliet wants night to come quickly so that she and Romeo can be together. (b) She is appealing to the horses who pull the chariot of the sun god, Phoebus, to run faster—as they once did when Phoebus's son, Phaëton, took over the chariot and lost control of them—so that the day will go more quickly.
2. Friar Lawrence finds Romeo's tears unmanly and his violence bestial (109–115). He reminds him that suicide is a deadly (damnèd) sin and a breach of his vow to cherish his wife (118–129). He fails to see that his life is blessed and full of opportunity: Tybalt would have killed him, exile is better than death, and Juliet is alive (135–144).
3. See possible responses in chart on Student page.

FORMATIVE ASSESSMENT

Analyze Craft and Structure

- **If** students cannot cite textual evidence and identify dramatic speeches, **then** have them reread a dramatic speech and look for clues that show whom the speaker is addressing.
- **If** students cannot complete the chart to analyze Mercutio's speech, **then** have them reread and paraphrase the speech.

For Reteach and Practice, see **Analyze Craft and Structure: Dramatic Speeches (RP).**

THE TRAGEDY OF ROMEO AND JULIET, ACT III

STANDARDS

Reading Literature

Analyze how an author's choices concerning how to structure a text, order events within it, and manipulate time create such effects as mystery, tension, or surprise.

Analyze Craft and Structure

Dramatic Structures In most plays, the dramatic action takes place primarily through **dialogue**—the conversations between characters. Some playwrights use specialized dialogue in the form of these types of **dramatic speeches:**

- **Soliloquy:** a lengthy speech in which a character—usually alone on the stage—expresses his or her true thoughts or feelings.
- **Aside:** a brief remark, often addressed to the audience and unheard by the other characters.
- **Monologue:** a lengthy speech by one character. Unlike a soliloquy or an aside, a monologue is addressed to other characters.

CITE TEXTUAL EVIDENCE to support your answers.

Practice

Notebook Respond to these questions.

1. (a) What thoughts and feelings does Juliet express in the soliloquy that opens Scene ii of Act III? (b) When Juliet makes an allusion to Phoebus and Phaëthon, what is she hoping will happen? Explain.
2. What criticisms of Romeo does the Friar express in his Act III, Scene iii monologue beginning, "Hold thy desperate hand"? Cite details from the monologue in your response.
3. (a) In Act III, Scene v, when her mother refers to Romeo as a villain, Juliet utters the aside, "Villain and he be many miles asunder." What does she mean by this? (b) Why does Juliet speak only to the audience? Explain.
4. Complete the chart to analyze Mercutio's dialogue in Act III, Scene i. (a) In the first row, write the remark regarding the Montagues and the Capulets that Mercutio makes three times as he is dying. (b) In the second row, explain what Mercutio means by this exclamation. (c) In the third row, explain how his remark reinforces ideas set forth in the play's Prologue.

MERCUTIO'S DIALOGUE
"A plague a both your houses!"
MEANING
I curse the Montague family and the Capulet family.
EXPLANATION
As Mercutio is dying, he sees how stupid this feud is, and how wasteful of young life—including his own.

EFFECTIVE EXPRESSION

Writing to Sources

Writings about literature may be called critical writing, literary criticism, or responses to literature. In most literary criticism, you will need to combine explanatory writing with argument. Your aim is to both explain your interpretation of a text and present it in a convincing, persuasive way.

Assignment

Write a **dual character study** in which you show how two characters in the play provide strong contrasts for one another. A character who provides a strong contrast to another character is called a **foil**.

- The foil is usually a secondary character who presents contrasts to a main character.
- The presence of the foil serves to emphasize the main character's distinctive qualities. If a main character is gentle, the foil is aggressive.

In this assignment, consider writing about the following sets of characters:

Romeo and Tybalt / Benvolio and Mercutio

You may also choose another pair of characters that you think work as foils. Regardless of the pair you choose, make sure to describe both characters' qualities and explain how Shakespeare conveys strong contrasts between the two.

Vocabulary Connection In your dual character study, consider including concept vocabulary words.

exile	banishment	pardon

Reflect on Your Writing

After you have written your dual character study, answer these questions.

1. What was the hardest part of creating this dual character study?

2. How might you revise your dual character study to clarify your ideas?

3. **Why These Words?** The words you choose make a difference in your writing. Which words helped you convey contrasts between the two characters in your dual character study?

EVIDENCE LOG

Before moving on to a new selection, go to your Evidence Log and record what you learned from *The Tragedy of Romeo and Juliet*, Act III.

STANDARDS

Writing

Write informative/ explanatory texts to examine and convey complex ideas, concepts, and information clearly and accurately through the effective selection, organization, and analysis of content.

DIGITAL PERSPECTIVES

Writing to Sources

Tell students to begin with the character whose personality most jumps out at them from the text. Then students should identify the character who serves as the first character's opposite and highlight the differences between the two. Shakespeare creates these contrasts in different ways: speech, actions, and descriptions.

Remind students to explore how foils help to mirror flaws and positive character traits.

For more support, see **Writing: Dual Character Study.**

Reflect on Your Writing

1. Student responses will vary. If students struggle with this question ask them which characters seem harder to describe or identify.
2. Student responses will vary. Ask what specifics they need to really improve their analysis of character.

Evidence Log Support students in completing their Evidence Log. This paced activity will help prepare them for the Performance-Based Assessment at the end of the unit.

Why These Words?

Responses will vary, but ask for volunteers who can share words that show real contrasts between their foil characters.

FORMATIVE ASSESSMENT

Writing to Sources

If students struggle to write a dual character study, **then** review the concept of foil characters and have them create lists of character traits to compare. For Reteach and Practice, see **Writing: Dual Character Study (RP).**

PERSONALIZE FOR LEARNING

Support for English Language Learners

Modern Foils In order to complete this writing task, English learners may benefit from more discussion of the term *foil*. Provide modern examples from literature and film. Remind students that foil characters are opposites such as Beauty and The Beast, Lisa and Bart Simpson, or Harry Potter and Draco Malfoy. Encourage students to share their own examples of foils.

The Tragedy of Romeo and Juliet, Act IV

AUDIO SUMMARIES
Audio summaries of *The Tragedy of Romeo and Juliet,* Act IV are available online in both English and Spanish in the Interactive Teacher's Edition or Unit Resources. Assigning these summaries prior to reading the selection may help students build additional background knowledge and set a context for their first read.

Summary

In Act IV of *The Tragedy of Romeo and Juliet,* events continue to move toward a terrible end. Juliet visits Friar Lawrence, the priest who performed the marriage ceremony for her and Romeo, and asks for help. He offers her a potion that will allow her to fake her death. Friar Lawrence tells Juliet that he will send a letter to Romeo so he can play his part in the plan: Juliet will fake her death, the Capulets will place her in the family tomb, and then Romeo will come and free her. Juliet returns home and pretends she plans to marry Paris as her family wishes, convincing them that everything is fine. Then she takes the potion.

Insight

This classic tragedy examines love and youthful impulsiveness. This act shows Juliet is more thoughtful than Romeo. Despite this impulsive act, she works with bravery and planning.

ESSENTIAL QUESTION:
Do we determine our own destinies?

Connection to Essential Question

The play suggests that Romeo and Juliet were unavoidably fated to fall in love and die. The events of Act IV let students see consider the Essential Question from Juliet's point of view. She takes her future into her own hands.

WHOLE-CLASS LEARNING PERFORMANCE TASK
Which has a greater impact on the characters in these texts: destiny or personal choices?

UNIT PERFORMANCE-BASED ASSESSMENT
Should the opinions of others affect our own choices or destinies?

Connection to Performance Tasks

Whole-Class Learning Performance Task Ask students to track their ideas about the Performance Task. The full plot line of this play may have them revising their opinions.

Unit Performance-Based Assessment In Act IV, the young lovers continue to fight the direction of their parents, but they consult other adults. Students may begin to question whether the Friar and the Nurse are truly helping Romeo and Juliet.

DIGITAL PERSPECTIVES: Audio | Video | Document | Annotation Highlights | EL Highlights | Online Assessment

LESSON RESOURCES

	Making Meaning	Language Development	Effective Expression
Lesson	**First Read** **Close Read** **Analyze the Text** **Analyze Craft and Structure**	**Concept Vocabulary** **Word Study**	**Speaking and Listening**
Instructional Standards	**RL.10** By the end of grade 9, read and comprehend literature . . . **RL.5** Analyze how an author's choices . . . **L.5.a** Interpret figures of speech . . .	**L.4.b** Identify and correctly use patterns of word changes . . . **L.5** Demonstrate understanding of figurative language . . .	**W.1** Write arguments . . . **SL.4** Present information, findings, and supporting evidence . . .
STUDENT RESOURCES			
Available online in the Interactive Student Edition or Unit Resources	Selection Audio First-Read Guide: Drama Close-Read Guide: Drama	Word Network	Evidence Log
TEACHER RESOURCES			
Selection Resources Available online in the Interactive Teacher's Edition or Unit Resources	Audio Summaries Annotation Highlights EL Highlights English Language Support Lesson: Classroom Debate Analyze Craft and Structure: Dramatic Elements	Concept Vocabulary and Word Study	Speaking and Listening: Classroom Debate
Reteach/Practice (RP) Available online in the Interactive Teacher's Edition or Unit Resources	Analyze Craft and Structure: Dramatic Elements (RP)	Word Study: Latin Root *-stress-* (RP)	Speaking and Listening: Classroom Debate (RP)
Assessment Available online in Assessments	Selection Test		
My Resources	A Unit 4 Answer Key is available online and in the Interactive Teacher's Edition.		

Reading Support

Text Complexity Rubric: *The Tragedy of Romeo and Juliet*, Act IV	
Quantitative Measures	
Lexile: NP **Text Length:** 3,319 words	
Qualitative Measures	
Knowledge Demands 1—2—3—4—**5**	Students will need information about the historical context of Verona, Italy, during the Renaissance. Some of this information is covered in the background information.
Structure 1—2—3—4—**5**	The selection is a Shakespearean play written primarily in blank verse. Line breaks will likely be challenging for students.
Language Conventionality and Clarity 1—2—3—4—**5**	The selection contains complex sentences, unfamiliar syntax, figurative language, challenging vocabulary, and Elizabethan language.
Levels of Meaning/Purpose 1—2—**3**—4—5	The concept of a classic tale of star-crossed lovers is accessible, but will likely be difficult to grasp due to challenging language and structure.

DECIDE AND PLAN

English Language Support

Provide English Learners with support for Structure and Levels of Meaning/Purpose as they read the selection.

Structure Help students understand the use of soliloquies in the play. Explain that soliloquies are meant to reveal a speaker's thoughts and plans to the audience. Point out Juliet's soliloquy in Act IV, Scene iii. Help students break down the long lines in order to understand them.

Levels of Meaning/Purpose To help students to sort out the events and ideas in the story, suggest that they keep a log of the main events, stating them in their own words. For example, *Friar Lawrence will give Juliet a potion to make her sleep. She will wake when Friar Lawrence brings Romeo to her.*

Strategic Support

Provide students with strategic support to ensure that they can successfully read the text.

Knowledge Demands Have students work with a partner to summarize what they know so far. What has happened? Who is involved? Then have students predict what will happen next.

Language Have students list any Elizabethan language they find difficult. Suggest that the use text aids such as the glossary terms accompanying the text. Review each word to demonstrate correct pronunciation, and clarify meaning if necessary. Have students read the lines with correct pronunciation.

Challenge

Provide students who need to be challenged with ideas for how they can go beyond a simple interpretation of the text.

Text Analysis Ask students to discuss how Juliet's ideas of love differ from her parents' ideas. Have students cite specific text evidence to support their opinions.

Written Response Have students analyze the potential problems with the Friar's plan to save Juliet. Ask students to identify at least three flaws with the plan. Then ask students to write an alternate plan to prevent Juliet's marriage to Paris and to reunite her with Romeo. Have students share their plans in small groups.

TEACH

Read and Respond

Have students do their first read of the selection. Then have them complete their close read. Finally, work with them on the Making Meaning and Effective Expression activities.

Standards Support Through Teaching and Learning Cycle

IDENTIFY NEEDS

Analyze results of the Beginning-of-Year Assessment, focusing on the items relating to Unit 4. Also take into consideration student performance to this point and your observations of where particular students struggle.

DECIDE AND PLAN

- If students have performed poorly on items matching these standards, then provide selection scaffolds before assigning them the on-level lesson provided in the Student Edition.
- If students have done well on the Beginning-of-Year Assessment, then challenge them to keep progressing and learning by giving them opportunities to practice the skills in depth.
- Use the Selection Resources listed on the Planning pages for *The Tragedy of Romeo and Juliet*, Act IV, to help students continually improve their ability to master the standards.

Instructional Standards: *The Tragedy of Romeo and Juliet,* Act IV

	Catching Up	This Year	Looking Forward
Reading	You may wish to administer the **Analyze Craft and Structure: Dramatic Elements (RP)** worksheet to better familiarize students with dramatic irony, comic, relief, and puns.	**RL.5** Analyze how an author's choices concerning how to structure a text, order events within it, and manipulate time create such effects as mystery, tension, or surprise.	Have students identify the three types of dramatic elements from other works they have read.
Speaking and Listening	You may wish to administer the **Speaking and Listening: Classroom Debate (RP)** worksheet to help students prepare for their debate.	**SL.4** Present information, findings, and supporting evidence clearly, concisely, and logically such that listeners can follow the line of reasoning and the organization, development, substance, and style are appropriate to purpose, audience, and task.	Take the debate to the next level by having the whole class debate another class that is also reading *Romeo and Juliet*.
Language	Review the **Word Study: Latin Root *-stress-* (RP)** worksheet with students to ensure they understand the Latin root.	**L.4.b** Identify and correctly use patterns of word changes that indicate different meanings or parts of speech.	Have students locate other Latin or Greek root words they may recognize in the selection.

TEACH

Implement the planned lesson, and gather evidence of student learning.

ANALYZE AND REVISE

- Analyze student work for evidence of student learning.
- Identify whether or not students have met the expectations in the standards.
- Identify implications for future instruction.

TEACHING

Jump Start

FIRST READ Have you ever kept a secret? Engage students in a discussion about the tension of keeping a secret around others who are unaware of the truth, especially when they ask you to do something you know you can't do?

The Tragedy of Romeo and Juliet, Act IV

How will the characters keeping these secrets interact with the other characters who are unaware of the truth? Will their secrets be kept? Will they be found out? What solution could there be to the conundrum faced by Juliet? Modeling questions such as these will help students connect to *The Tragedy of Romeo and Juliet*, Act IV, and to the Performance Task assignment. Selection audio and print capability for the selection are available in the Interactive Teacher's Edition.

Concept Vocabulary

Support students as they rank their words. Ask if they've ever heard, read, or used them. Reassure them that the definitions for these words are listed in the selection.

FIRST READ

Students should perform the steps of the first read independently.

NOTICE: You may want to encourage students to notice the way that characters aware of the secret interact with characters unaware of the secret.

ANNOTATE: Remind students to mark passages that include the characters' efforts at keeping their secret.

CONNECT: Encourage students to think about what they might say and do to safeguard such a secret.

RESPOND: Students will answer questions and write a summary to demonstrate understanding.

Point out to students that while they will always complete the Respond step at the end of the first read, the other steps will probably happen somewhat concurrently. You may wish to print copies of the **First-Read Guide: Fiction** for students to use.

Remind students that during their first read, they should not answer the close-read questions that appear in the selection.

Playwright

William Shakespeare

The Tragedy of Romeo and Juliet, Act IV

Concept Vocabulary

You will encounter the following words as you read Act IV of *The Tragedy of Romeo and Juliet*. Before reading, note how familiar you are with each word. Then, rank the words in order from most familiar (1) to least familiar (3).

WORD	YOUR RANKING
lamentable	
distressed	
melancholy	

After completing your first read, come back to the concept vocabulary and review your rankings. Mark changes to your original rankings as needed.

Tool Kit
First-Read Guide and Model Annotation

First Read DRAMA

Apply these strategies as you conduct your first read. You will have an opportunity to complete the close-read notes after your first read.

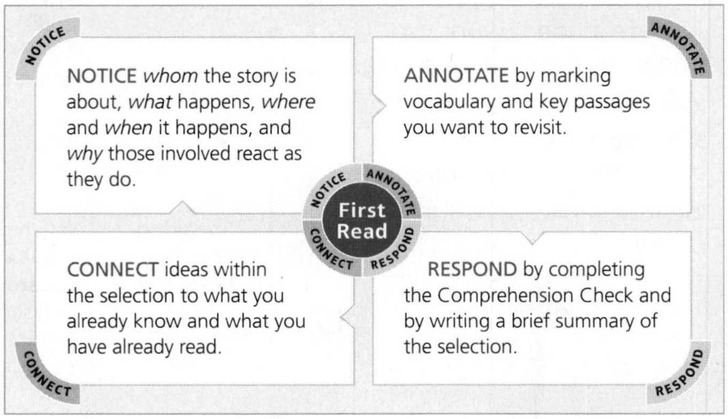
NOTICE
ANNOTATE
NOTICE *whom* the story is about, *what* happens, *where* and *when* it happens, and *why* those involved react as they do.
ANNOTATE by marking vocabulary and key passages you want to revisit.
First Read
CONNECT ideas within the selection to what you already know and what you have already read.
RESPOND by completing the Comprehension Check and by writing a brief summary of the selection.
CONNECT
RESPOND

STANDARDS

Reading Literature
By the end of grade 9, read and comprehend literature, including stories, dramas, and poems, in the grades 9–10 text complexity band proficiently, with scaffolding as needed at the high end of the range.

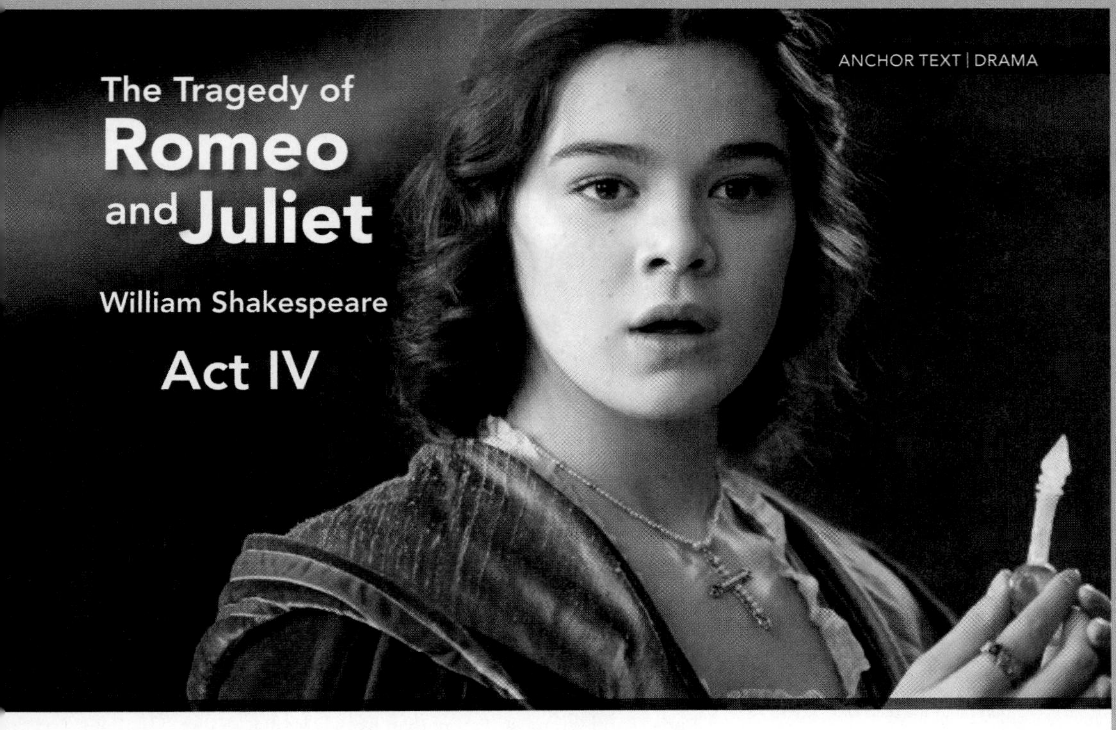

ANCHOR TEXT | DRAMA

The Tragedy of Romeo and Juliet

William Shakespeare

Act IV

DIGITAL PERSPECTIVES

REVIEW AND ANTICIPATE

Romeo and Juliet are married for only a few hours when disaster strikes. In Act III, Juliet's cousin Tybalt kills Mercutio, and then Romeo kills Tybalt. This leads to Romeo's banishment from Verona. To make matters worse, Juliet's parents are determined to marry her to Paris. As you read Act IV, consider the passions and conflicts that motivate Romeo and Juliet as their situation becomes increasingly desperate.

SCAN FOR MULTIMEDIA

Scene i • *Friar Lawrence's cell.*

[*Enter* Friar Lawrence *and* County Paris.]

Friar. On Thursday, sir? The time is very short.

Paris. My father[1] Capulet will have it so,
And I am nothing slow to slack his haste.[2]

Friar. You say you do not know the lady's mind.
Uneven is the course;[3] I like it not.

Paris. Immoderately she weeps for Tybalt's death,
And therefore have I little talked of love;
For Venus smiles not in a house of tears.
Now, sir, her father counts it dangerous
That she do give her sorrow so much sway,
And in his wisdom hastes our marriage
To stop the inundation[4] of her tears,
Which, too much minded[5] by herself alone,
May be put from her by society.
Now do you know the reason of this haste.

NOTES

1. **father** future father-in-law.
2. **I . . . haste** I will not slow him down by being slow myself.
3. **Uneven . . . course** irregular is the plan.
4. **inundation** *n.* flood.
5. **minded** *v.* thought about.

CLOSER LOOK

Analyze Dramatic Irony

Students may have marked lines 1–6 during their first read. Use these lines to help students understand dramatic irony, a form of irony that exists when the reader or audience knows or understands something that a character or speaker does not. Encourage them to talk about the annotations that they marked. You may want to model a close read with the class based on the highlights shown in the text.

ANNOTATE: Have students mark details in lines 1–6 that demonstrate dramatic irony, or have students participate while you highlight them.

QUESTION: Guide students to consider the effect of dramatic irony. Ask students how reading dramatic irony makes them feel, and accept student responses.

Possible response: The reader or audience feels the tension of the characters avoiding the truth.

CONCLUDE: Help students to formulate conclusions about the importance of these details in the text. Ask students why the author might have included these details.

Possible response: Dramatic irony increases the tension in the act.

Remind students that the general term **irony** refers to some type of discrepancy between appearance and reality, expectation and result, or meaning and intention. **Dramatic irony** is one of the three main types of irony, along with **situational irony** and **verbal irony**. Dramatic irony can be a dramatic device in fiction, serving to maintain high tension.

VOCABULARY DEVELOPMENT

Word Forms Expand students' vocabulary by helping them to learn related forms of the concept vocabulary words. Explain to students that each of the vocabulary words also has a word form that fits more than one part of speech. Work with the class to determine the related forms, paying close attention to those forms that fit more than one column. The final chart should look like this:

Noun	Verb	Adjective
lament	lament	lamentable
melancholy	n/a	melancholy
distress	distress/ distressed	distressed

CLOSE READ

Remind students to look at variations in sentence lengths for clues to emotions and moods. You may wish to model the close read using the following think-aloud format. Possible responses to questions on the Student page are included. You may also want to print copies of the **Close-Read Guide: Drama** for students to use.

ANNOTATE: As I read lines 18–38, I notice and highlight the dialogue that is no longer than one sentence.

QUESTION: I notice the quick pace of the dialogue in lines 18–38. Paris is trying to woo her, but Juliet is already married to Romeo, and she does not want to receive his romantic advances or reveal the truth. Her quick responses are an attempt to avoid speaking with him as much as possible.

CONCLUDE: I think that the scene makes the audience feel sorry for Paris because they know what he does not—that Juliet is already married to Romeo and does not want to be his wife.

Additional **English Language Support** is available in the Interactive Teacher's Edition.

NOTES

6. **That's . . . text** That is a certain truth.

CLOSE READ

ANNOTATE: In lines 18–38, mark speeches that are no more than one sentence in length.

QUESTION: Why is Paris and Juliet's conversation composed primarily of short lines?

CONCLUDE: How does this scene make the audience feel about Paris?

7. **price** *n.* value.

8. **before their spite** before the harm that the tears did.

9. **entreat . . . alone** ask to have this time to ourselves.

10. **shield** *v.* forbid.

11. **past . . . wits** beyond the ability of my mind to find a remedy.

12. **prorogue** (proh ROHG) *v.* delay.

13. **presently** *adv.* at once.

Friar. [*Aside*] I would I knew not why it should be slowed.—
Look, sir, here comes the lady towards my cell.
[*Enter* Juliet.]

Paris. Happily met, my lady and my wife!

Juliet. That may be, sir, when I may be a wife.

Paris. That "may be" must be, love, on Thursday next.

Juliet. What must be shall be.

Friar. That's a certain text.[6]

Paris. Come you to make confession to this father?

Juliet. To answer that, I should confess to you.

Paris. Do not deny to him that you love me.

Juliet. I will confess to you that I love him.

Paris. So will ye, I am sure, that you love me.

Juliet. If I do so, it will be of more price,[7]
Being spoke behind your back, than to your face.

Paris. Poor soul, thy face is much abused with tears.

Juliet. The tears have got small victory by that,
For it was bad enough before their spite.[8]

Paris. Thou wrong'st it more than tears with that report.

Juliet. That is no slander, sir, which is a truth;
And what I spake, I spake it to my face.

Paris. Thy face is mine, and thou hast sland'red it.

Juliet. It may be so, for it is not mine own.
Are you at leisure, holy father, now,
Or shall I come to you at evening mass?

Friar. My leisure serves me, pensive daughter, now.
My lord, we must entreat the time alone.[9]

Paris. God shield[10] I should disturb devotion!
Juliet, on Thursday early will I rouse ye.
Till then, adieu, and keep this holy kiss. [*Exit.*]

Juliet. O, shut the door, and when thou hast done so,
Come weep with me—past hope, past cure, past help!

Friar. O Juliet, I already know thy grief;
It strains me past the compass of my wits.[11]
I hear thou must, and nothing may prorogue[12] it,
On Thursday next be married to this County.

Juliet. Tell me not, friar, that thou hearest of this,
Unless thou tell me how I may prevent it.
If in thy wisdom thou canst give no help,
Do thou but call my resolution wise
And with this knife I'll help it presently.[13]
God joined my heart and Romeo's, thou our hands;

And ere this hand, by thee to Romeo's sealed,
Shall be the label to another deed,[14]
Or my true heart with treacherous revolt
Turn to another, this shall slay them both.
Therefore, out of thy long-experienced time,
Give me some present counsel; or, behold,
'Twixt my extremes and me[15] this bloody knife
Shall play the umpire, arbitrating[16] that
Which the commission of thy years and art
Could to no issue of true honor bring.[17]
Be not so long to speak. I long to die
If what thou speak'st speak not of remedy.

Friar. Hold, daughter. I do spy a kind of hope,
Which craves[18] as desperate an execution
As that is desperate which we would prevent.
If, rather than to marry County Paris,
Thou hast the strength of will to slay thyself,
Then is it likely thou wilt undertake
A thing like death to chide away this shame,
That cop'st with death himself to scape from it;[19]
And, if thou darest, I'll give thee remedy.

Juliet. O, bid me leap, rather than marry Paris,
From off the battlements of any tower,
Or walk in thievish ways,[20] or bid me lurk
Where serpents are; chain me with roaring bears,
Or hide me nightly in a charnel house,[21]
O'ercovered quite with dead men's rattling bones,
With reeky[22] shanks and yellow chapless[23] skulls;
Or bid me go into a new-made grave
And hide me with a dead man in his shroud—
Things that, to hear them told, have made me tremble—
And I will do it without fear or doubt,
To live an unstained wife to my sweet love.

Friar. Hold, then. Go home, be merry, give consent
To marry Paris. Wednesday is tomorrow.
Tomorrow night look that thou lie alone;
Let not the nurse lie with thee in thy chamber.
Take thou this vial, being then in bed,
And this distilled liquor drink thou off;
When presently through all thy veins shall run
A cold and drowsy humor,[24] for no pulse
Shall keep his native[25] progress, but surcease;[26]
No warmth, no breath, shall testify thou livest;
The roses in thy lips and cheeks shall fade
To wanny ashes,[27] thy eyes' windows[28] fall
Like death when he shuts up the day of life;
Each part, deprived of supple government,[29]

NOTES

14. **Shall . . . deed** shall give the seal of approval to another marriage contract.

15. **'Twixt . . . me** between my misfortunes and me.

16. **arbitrating** *v.* deciding.

17. **Which . . . bring** which the authority that derives from your age and ability could not solve honorably.

18. **craves** *v.* requires.

19. **That cop'st . . . it** that bargains with death itself to escape from it.

20. **thievish ways** roads where criminals lurk.

21. **charnel house** vault for bones removed from graves to be reused.

22. **reeky** *adj.* foul-smelling.

23. **chapless** *adj.* jawless.

24. **humor** *n.* fluid; liquid.

25. **native** *adj.* natural.

26. **surcease** *v.* stop.

27. **wanny ashes** to the color of pale ashes.

28. **eyes' windows** eyelids.

29. **supple government** ability for maintaining motion.

DIGITAL PERSPECTIVES

Illuminating the Text Have students use the Internet to research the theory of the four humours that was the foundation of medicine during Shakespeare's time. Lead a discussion about the topic. Then, research the etymology of the concept word *melancholy* (Scene v, line 86) that is rooted in this concept. **(Research to Clarify)**

CLOSER LOOK

Identify Suspense

Students may have marked details in lines 103–126 during their first read. Use these lines to help students understand suspense. Encourage them to talk about the annotations that they marked. You may want to model a close read with the class based on the highlights shown in the text.

ANNOTATE: Have students mark details in lines 103–126 that build suspense, or have students participate while you highlight them.

QUESTION: Guide students to consider what these details might tell them. Ask what a reader might feel in response to these lines and accept student responses.

Possible response: Juliet's desperation and Friar Lawrence's plan build suspense. It is a frightening and risky plan; it makes the reader fear for Juliet's safety.

CONCLUDE: Help students to formulate conclusions about the importance of these details in the text. Ask students why the author might have included these details.

Possible response: Shakespeare holds the reader's suspense and continues to build tension. This is the falling action of the plot, but the reader is still held in tight suspense.

Remind students that **suspense** is the growing curiosity, tension, or anxiety the reader feels about the outcome of events in a literary work. Suspense usually builds until the **climax,** the high point of tension in the plot, when the conflict reaches a peak. However, some works employ suspense all the way through to the resolution. The tension of suspense is part of what keeps the reader engaged in a story and anxious to find out what will happen next.

NOTES

Shall, stiff and stark and cold, appear like death;
And in this borrowed likeness of shrunk death
Thou shalt continue two-and-forty hours,
And then awake as from a pleasant sleep.
Now, when the bridegroom in the morning comes
To rouse thee from thy bed, there art thou dead.
Then, as the manner of our country is,
In thy best robes uncovered on the bier[30]
Thou shalt be borne to that same ancient vault
Where all the kindred of the Capulets lie.
In the meantime, against[31] thou shalt awake,
Shall Romeo by my letters know our drift;[32]
And hither shall he come: and he and I
Will watch thy waking, and that very night
Shall Romeo bear thee hence to Mantua.
And this shall free thee from this present shame,
If no inconstant toy[33] nor womanish fear,
Abate thy valor[34] in the acting it.

Juliet. Give me, give me! O, tell not me of fear!

Friar. Hold! Get you gone, be strong and prosperous
In this resolve. I'll send a friar with speed
To Mantua, with my letters to thy lord.

Juliet. Love give me strength! and strength shall help afford.
Farewell, dear father. [*Exit with* Friar.]

30. **uncovered on the bier** (bihr) displayed on the funeral platform.

31. **against** *adv.* before.

32. **drift** *n.* purpose; plan.

33. **inconstant toy** passing whim.

34. **Abate thy valor** Lessen your courage.

⌘ ⌘ ⌘

Scene ii • *Hall in Capulet's house.*

[*Enter* Father Capulet, Mother, Nurse, *and* Servingmen, *two or three.*]

Capulet. So many guests invite as here are writ.
[*Exit a* Servingman.]
Sirrah, go hire me twenty cunning[1] cooks.

Servingman. You shall have none ill, sir; for I'll try[2] if they can lick their fingers.

Capulet. How canst thou try them so?

Servingman. Marry, sir, 'tis an ill cook that cannot lick his own fingers.[3] Therefore he that cannot lick his fingers goes not with me.

Capulet. Go, begone.
[*Exit* Servingman.]
We shall be much unfurnished[4] for this time.
What, is my daughter gone to Friar Laurence?

1. **cunning** *adj.* skillful.

2. **try** *v.* test.

3. **'tis . . . fingers** It is a bad cook who will not taste his own cooking.

4. **unfurnished** *adj.* unprepared.

DIGITAL PERSPECTIVES

Nurse. Ay, forsooth.[5]

Capulet. Well, he may chance to do some good on her.
A peevish self-willed harlotry it is.[6]

[*Enter* Juliet.]

Nurse. See where she comes from shrift with merry look.

Capulet. How now, my headstrong! Where have you been gadding?

Juliet. Where I have learnt me to repent the sin
Of disobedient opposition
To you and your behests,[7] and am enjoined
By holy Lawrence to fall prostrate[8] here
To beg your pardon. Pardon, I beseech you!
Henceforward I am ever ruled by you.

Capulet. Send for the County. Go tell him of this.
I'll have this knot knit up tomorrow morning.

Juliet. I met the youthful lord at Lawrence' cell
And gave him what becomèd[9] love I might,
Not stepping o'er the bounds of modesty.

Capulet. Why, I am glad on't. This is well. Stand up.
This is as't should be. Let me see the County.
Ay, marry, go, I say, and fetch him hither.
Now, afore God, this reverend holy friar,
All our whole city is much bound[10] to him.

Juliet. Nurse, will you go with me into my closet[11]
To help me sort such needful ornaments[12]
As you think fit to furnish me tomorrow?

Lady Capulet. No, not till Thursday. There is time enough.

Capulet. Go, nurse, go with her. We'll to church tomorrow.

[*Exit* Juliet *and* Nurse.]

Lady Capulet. We shall be short in our provision.[13]
'Tis now near night.

Capulet. Tush, I will stir about,
And all things shall be well, I warrant thee, wife.
Go thou to Juliet, help to deck up her.[14]
I'll not to bed tonight; let me alone.
I'll play the housewife for this once. What, ho![15]
They are all forth; well, I will walk myself
To County Paris, to prepare up him
Against tomorrow. My heart is wondrous light,
Since this same wayward girl is so reclaimed.

[*Exit with* Mother.]

⌘ ⌘ ⌘

NOTES

5. **forsooth** *adv.* in truth.
6. **A peevish . . . it is** It is the ill-tempered, selfish behavior of a woman without good breeding.
7. **behests** *v.* requests.
8. **fall prostrate** lie face down in humble submission.
9. **becomèd** *adj.* suitable; proper.
10. **bound** *adj.* indebted.
11. **closet** *n.* private room.
12. **ornaments** *n.* clothes.
13. **short . . . provision** lacking time for preparation.
14. **deck up her** dress her; get her ready.
15. **What, ho!** Capulet is calling one of his servants.

PERSONALIZE FOR LEARNING

Strategic Support

Reading Comprehension Review Juliet's conversation with her father in lines 16–37. Students often find it challenging to comprehend Shakespeare's language. Instruct students to work in pairs to read and summarize one sentence of dialogue at a time, using the notes provided in the section to aid in comprehension. Then, review these summaries as a class to help to clarify meaning.

CLOSE READ

Remind students to mark the questions Juliet asks that include the word *if.* You may wish to model the Close Read using the following think-aloud format. Possible responses to questions on the Student page are included.

ANNOTATE: As I read lines 15–58, I notice and highlight the questions Juliet asks that include the word *if.*

QUESTION: I think that Shakespeare used these lines to help the reader understand the complexity of Juliet's emotions.

CONCLUDE: I think that Juliet is very afraid before she drinks the potion. She is afraid of dying and afraid of being forced to marry Paris if her desperate plan does not work.

NOTES

1. **orisons** (AWR uh zuhnz) *n.* prayers.
2. **state** *n.* condition.
3. **cross** *adj.* selfish; disobedient.
4. **culled** *v.* chosen.
5. **behoveful** *adj.* desirable; appropriate.

CLOSE READ

ANNOTATE: In lines 15–58, mark the questions Juliet asks that include the word *if.*

QUESTION: Why does Shakespeare have Juliet ask this series of questions?

CONCLUDE: What does this series of questions show about Juliet's state of mind as she prepares to drink the potion?

6. **minist'red** *v.* given me.
7. **tried** *v.* proved.
8. **conceit** *n.* idea; thought.

Scene iii • *Juliet's chamber.*

[*Enter* Juliet *and* Nurse.]

Juliet. Ay, those attires are best: but, gentle nurse,
I pray thee, leave me to my self tonight;
For I have need of many orisons[1]
To move the heavens to smile upon my state,[2]
Which, well thou knowest, is cross[3] and full of sin.

[*Enter* Lady Capulet.]

Lady Capulet. What, are you busy, ho? Need you my help?

Juliet. No, madam; we have culled[4] such necessaries
As are behoveful[5] for our state tomorrow.
So please you, let me now be left alone,
And let the nurse this night sit up with you;
For I am sure you have your hands full all
In this so sudden business.

Lady Capulet. Good night.
Get thee to bed, and rest; for thou hast need.

[*Exit* Lady Capulet *and* Nurse.]

Juliet. Farewell! God knows when we shall meet again.
I have a faint cold fear thrills through my veins
That almost freezes up the heat of life.
I'll call them back again to comfort me.
Nurse!—What should she do here?
My dismal scene I needs must act alone.
Come, vial.
What if this mixture do not work at all?
Shall I be married then tomorrow morning?
No, no! This shall forbid it. Lie thou there.

[*Lays down a dagger.*]

What if it be a poison which the friar
Subtly hath minist'red[6] to have me dead,
Lest in this marriage he should be dishonored
Because he married me before to Romeo?
I fear it is; and yet methinks it should not,
For he hath still been tried[7] a holy man.
How if, when I am laid into the tomb,
I wake before the time that Romeo
Come to redeem me? There's a fearful point!
Shall I not then be stifled in the vault,
To whose foul mouth no healthsome air breathes in,
And there die strangled ere my Romeo comes?
Or, if I live, is it not very like
The horrible conceit[8] of death and night,
Together with the terror of the place—
As in a vault, an ancient receptacle

Where for this many hundred years the bones
Of all my buried ancestors are packed;
Where bloody Tybalt, yet but green in earth,[9]
Lies fest'ring in his shroud; where, as they say,
At some hours in the night spirits resort—
Alack, alack, is it not like[10] that I,
So early waking—what with loathsome smells,
And shrieks like mandrakes[11] torn out of the earth,
That living mortals, hearing them, run mad—
O, if I wake, shall I not be distraught,[12]
Environed[13] with all these hideous fears,
And madly play with my forefathers' joints,
And pluck the mangled Tybalt from his shroud,
And, in this rage, with some great kinsman's bone
As with a club dash out my desp'rate brains?
O, look! Methinks I see my cousin's ghost
Seeking out Romeo, that did spit his body
Upon a rapier's point. Stay, Tybalt, stay!
Romeo, Romeo, Romeo, I drink to thee!
[*She falls upon her bed, within the curtains.*]

⌘ ⌘ ⌘

Scene iv • *Hall in Capulet's house.*

[*Enter* Lady of The House *and* Nurse.]

Lady Capulet. Hold, take these keys and fetch more spices, nurse.

Nurse. They call for dates and quinces[1] in the pastry.[2]

[*Enter old* Capulet.]

Capulet. Come, stir, stir, stir! The second cock hath crowed,
The curfew bell hath rung, 'tis three o'clock,

NOTES

9. **green in earth** newly entombed.

10. **like** *adv.* likely.

11. **mandrakes** *n.* plants with forked roots that resemble human legs. The mandrake was believed to shriek when uprooted and cause the hearer to go mad.

12. **distraught** *adj.* insane.

13. **Environed** *v.* surrounded.

1. **quinces** *n.* golden, apple-shaped fruits.

2. **pastry** *n.* baking room.

DIGITAL PERSPECTIVES

CLOSE READ

Remind students to mark details in both spoken lines and stage directions that relate to food, joy, and anticipation. You may wish to model the Close Read using the following think-aloud format. Possible responses to questions on the Student page are included.

ANNOTATE: As I read the lines 5-29, I notice and highlight the dialogue and stage directions that relate to food, joy, and anticipation.

QUESTION: I think Shakespeare includes this happy scene to contrast with Juliet's desperate state and the tragedy of her apparent death.

CONCLUDE: I think that Shakespeare includes this happy scene to give the reader very strong feelings of sympathy for her family. Her family is very excited, expecting that Juliet is on her way to a good life. The audience already knows that is not how the day will end. It helps to keep the tension high.

Look to the baked meats, good Angelica;[3]
Spare not for cost.

Nurse. Go, you cotquean,[4] go,
Get you to bed! Faith, you'll be sick tomorrow
For this night's watching.[5]

Capulet. No, not a whit. What, I have watched ere now
All night for lesser cause, and ne'er been sick.

Lady Capulet. Ay, you have been a mouse hunt[6] in your time;
But I will watch you from such watching now.
[*Exit* Lady *and* Nurse.]

Capulet. A jealous hood, a jealous hood![7]
[*Enter three or four* Fellows *with spits and logs and baskets.*]
Now, fellow,
What is there?

First Fellow. Things for the cook, sir; but I know not what.

Capulet. Make haste, make haste. [*Exit* First Fellow.] Sirrah, fetch drier logs.
Call Peter; he will show thee where they are.

Second Fellow. I have a head, sir, that will find out logs
And never trouble Peter for the matter.

Capulet. Mass,[8] and well said; a merry whoreson, ha!
Thou shalt be loggerhead.[9]
[*Exit* Second Fellow, *with the others.*]
Good faith, 'tis day.
The County will be here with music straight,
For so he said he would. [*Play music.*]
I hear him near.
Nurse! Wife! What, ho! What, nurse, I say!
[*Enter* Nurse.]
Go waken Juliet; go and trim her up.
I'll go and chat with Paris. Hie, make haste,
Make haste! The bridegroom he is come already;
Make haste, I say. [*Exit.*]

⌘ ⌘ ⌘

Scene v • *Juliet's chamber.*

Nurse. Mistress! What, mistress! Juliet! Fast,[1] I warrant her, she.
Why, lamb! Why, lady! Fie, you slugabed![2]
Why, love, I say! Madam; Sweetheart! Why, bride!
What, not a word? You take your pennyworths now;
Sleep for a week; for the next night, I warrant,

NOTES

3. **Angelica** this is probably the Nurse's name.
4. **cotquean** (KOT kween) *n.* man who does housework.
5. **watching** *adj.* staying awake.
6. **mouse hunt** woman chaser.
7. **jealous hood** jealousy.
8. **Mass** by the Mass (an oath).
9. **loggerhead** blockhead.

CLOSE READ

ANNOTATE: Mark details in both spoken lines and stage directions of Scene iv that relate to food, joy, and anticipation.

QUESTION: Why does Shakespeare present such a happy scene?

CONCLUDE: What are the effects of positioning this scene right after Scene iii in which Juliet drinks the potion?

1. **Fast** fast asleep.
2. **slugabed** sleepyhead.

DIGITAL PERSPECTIVES

The County Paris hath set up his rest,
That you shall rest but little. God forgive me!
Marry, and amen. How sound is she asleep!
I must needs wake her. Madam, madam, madam!
Ay, let the County take you in your bed;
He'll fright you up, i' faith. Will it not be?
[*Draws aside the curtains.*]
What, dressed, and in your clothes, and down again?[3]
I must needs wake you. Lady! Lady! Lady!
Alas, alas! Help, help! My lady's dead!
O weraday that ever I was born!
Some aqua vitae, ho! My lord! My lady!
[*Enter* Lady Capulet.]

Lady Capulet. What noise is here?

Nurse. O **lamentable** day!

Lady Capulet. What is the matter?

Nurse. Look, look! O heavy day!

Lady Capulet. O me, O me! My child, my only life!
Revive, look up, or I will die with thee!
Help, help! Call help.

[*Enter* Capulet.]

Capulet. For shame, bring Juliet forth; her lord is come.

Nurse. She's dead, deceased; she's dead, alack the day!

Lady Capulet. Alack the day, she's dead, she's dead, she's dead!

Capulet. Ha! Let me see her. Out alas! She's cold,
Her blood is settled, and her joints are stiff;
Life and these lips have long been separated.
Death lies on her like an untimely frost
Upon the sweetest flower of all the field.

Nurse. O lamentable day!

Lady Capulet. O woeful time!

Capulet. Death, that hath ta'en her hence to make me wail,
Ties up my tongue and will not let me speak.

[*Enter* Friar Laurence *and the* County Paris, *with* Musicians.]

Friar. Come, is the bride ready to go to church?

Capulet. Ready to go, but never to return.
O son, the night before thy wedding day
Hath Death lain with thy wife. There she lies,
Flower as she was, deflowered by him.
Death is my son-in-law, Death is my heir;
My daughter he hath wedded. I will die,

NOTES

3. down again back in bed.

lamentable (luh MEHN tuh buhl) *adj.* grievous; mournful; sorrowful

PERSONALIZE FOR LEARNING

English Language Support

Figurative Language Direct students' attention to Capulet's speech to Paris in Scene v, lines 35–39, *O son, the night before thy wedding day Hath Death lain with thy wife. There she lies, Flower as she was, deflowered by him. Death is my son-in-law, Death is my heir; My daughter he hath wedded.* Explain to students that these lines use **personification**, a type of figurative language in which a nonhuman subject is given human characteristics. In these lines, death is being given human characteristics; the word is even capitalized like a proper noun. Also explain that Juliet was expected to be a virgin until her wedding night and "deflowered" describes the loss of her virginity **through her death**. Discuss the meaning and impact of these lines. Highlight the emotional effect of reminding the audience again of what was intended for Juliet in contrast with how the plot unfolds. **ALL LEVELS**

NOTES

And leave him all. Life, living, all is Death's.

Paris. Have I thought, love, to see this morning's face,
And doth it give me such a sight as this?

Lady Capulet. Accursed, unhappy, wretched, hateful day!
Most miserable hour that e'er time saw
In lasting labor of his pilgrimage!
But one, poor one, one poor and loving child,
But one thing to rejoice and solace[4] in,
And cruel Death hath catched it from my sight.

Nurse. O woe! O woeful, woeful, woeful day!
Most lamentable day, most woeful day,
That ever ever I did yet behold!
O day, O day, O day! O hateful day!
Never was seen so black a day as this.
O woeful day! O woeful day!

Paris. Beguiled,[5] divorcèd, wrongèd, spited, slain!
Most detestable Death, by thee beguiled,
By cruel, cruel thee quite overthrown.
O love! O life!—not life, but love in death!

Capulet. Despised, **distressed**, hated, martyred, killed!
Uncomfortable[6] time, why cam'st thou now
To murder, murder our solemnity?[7]
O child! O child! My soul, and not my child!
Dead art thou—alack, my child is dead,
And with my child my joys are burièd!

Friar. Peace, ho, for shame! Confusion's cure lives not
In these confusions.[8] Heaven and yourself
Had part in this fair maid—now heaven hath all,
And all the better is it for the maid.
Your part in her you could not keep from death,
But heaven keeps his part in eternal life.
The most you sought was her promotion,
For 'twas your heaven she should be advanced;
And weep ye now, seeing she is advanced
Above the clouds, as high as heaven itself?
O, in this love, you love your child so ill
That you run mad, seeing that she is well.[9]
She's not well married that lives married long,
But she's best married that dies married young.
Dry up your tears, and stick your rosemary[10]
On this fair corse, and, as the custom is,
And in her best array bear her to church;
For though fond nature[11] bids us all lament,
Yet nature's tears are reason's merriment.[12]

Capulet. All things that we ordainèd festival[13]
Turn from their office to black funeral—

4. **solace** *v.* find comfort.

5. **Beguiled** *adj.* cheated.

distressed (dihs TREHST) *adj.* full of anxiety and suffering

6. **Uncomfortable** *adj.* painful, upsetting.
7. **solemnity** *n.* solemn rites.
8. **Confusion's . . . confusions** The remedy for this calamity is not to be found in these outcries.
9. **well** *adj.* blessed in heaven.
10. **rosemary** *n.* evergreen herb signifying love and remembrance.
11. **fond nature** mistake-prone human nature.
12. **Yet . . . merriment** While human nature causes us to weep for Juliet, reason should cause us to be happy (since she is in heaven).
13. **ordainèd festival** planned to be part of a celebration.

PERSONALIZE FOR LEARNING

English Language Support

Words with Similar Meanings In lines 43–59, there are adjectives that communicate similar ideas. Ask students to find those words and accept answers. Help students understand how the words are similar and different.

Possible answers: accursed, unhappy, wretched, hateful, and miserable; wronged and spited; detestable and despised; and slain, killed, and martyred. **ALL LEVELS**

Our instruments to **melancholy** bells,
Our wedding cheer to a sad burial feast,
Our solemn hymns to sullen dirges[14] change;
Our bridal flowers serve for a buried corse;
And all things change them to the contrary.

Friar. Sir, go you in; and, madam, go with him;
And go, Sir Paris. Everyone prepare
To follow this fair corse unto her grave.
The heavens do low'r[15] upon you for some ill;
Move them no more by crossing their high will.
[*Exit, casting rosemary on her and shutting the curtains. The* Nurse *and* Musicians *remain.*]

First Musician. Faith, we may put up our pipes and be gone.

Nurse. Honest good fellows, ah, put up, put up!
For well you know this is a pitiful case.[16] [*Exit.*]

First Musician. Ay, by my troth, the case may be amended.
[*Enter* Peter.]

Peter. Musicians, O, musicians, "Heart's ease," "Heart's ease"!
O, and you will have me live, play "Heart's ease."

First Musician. Why "Heart's ease"?

Peter. O, musicians, because my heart itself plays "My heart is full."
O, play me some merry dump[17] to comfort me.

First Musician. Not a dump we! 'Tis no time to play now.

Peter. You will not, then?

First Musician. No.

Peter. I will then give it you soundly.

First Musician. What will you give us?

Peter. No money, on my faith, but the gleek.[18] I will give you[19] the minstrel.[20]

First Musician. Then I will give you the serving-creature.

Peter. Then will I lay the serving-creature's dagger on your pate.
I will carry no crotchets.[21] I'll re you, I'll fa you. Do you note me?

First Musician. And you re us and fa us, you note us.

Second Musician. Pray you put up your dagger, and put out your wit.

Peter. Then have at you with my wit! I will dry-beat you with an iron wit, and put up my iron dagger. Answer me like men.
"When griping grief the heart doth wound,
And doleful dumps the mind oppress,
Then music with her silver sound"—

NOTES

melancholy (MEHL uhn kol ee) *adj.* sad and depressed

14. **dirges** *n.* funeral hymns.

15. **low'r** *v.* frown.

16. **case** *n.* situation; instrument case.

17. **dump** *n.* sad tune.

18. **gleek** *n.* scornful speech.

19. **give you** call you.

20. **minstrel** a contemptuous term (as opposed to "musician").

21. **crochets** *n.* whims; quarter notes.

DIGITAL PERSPECTIVES

CLOSER LOOK

Analyzing Comic Relief

Students may have marked lines 100–121 during their first read. Use these lines to help students understand the technique of comic relief. Explain that comic relief is a humorous scene, speech, or incident that deliberately interrupts a serious literary work. Encourage them to talk about the annotations that they marked. You may want to model a close read with the class based on the highlights shown in the text.

ANNOTATE: Have students mark details in lines 100–121 that demonstrate comic relief, or have students participate while you highlight them.

QUESTION: Guide students to consider what these details might tell them. Ask what a reader can infer about Shakespeare's use of comic relief in this scene.

Possible response: The actions leading up to this point were very emotionally charged, affecting the audience greatly. Including the comic relief at the end of this scene gives the audience a bit of relief, as the name suggests.

CONCLUDE: Help students to formulate conclusions about the importance of these details in the text. Ask students why the author might have included these details.

Possible response: In addition to giving the audience a chance to "catch a breath" emotionally, this comic relief, played out by the servants, demonstrates class difference.

Remind students that **comic relief** is a humorous scene, speech, or incident that deliberately interrupts a serious literary work to lighten the mood and offer the audience some emotional relief. Comic relief is most often found in drama, particularly tragedies.

Comprehension Check

Possible responses:

1. Juliet is prepared to kill herself rather than marry Paris.
2. Juliet tells her father that she is willing to marry Paris so that she will be able to move forward with Friar Lawrence's plan to fake her death and reunite her with Romeo.
3. When Juliet drinks the potion, she falls into a deep sleep that makes her body cold, her joints stiff, and her breath stop. It puts her in a death-like state.
4. Answers will vary. The act begins with Paris making wedding arrangements with Friar Lawrence when Juliet arrives. Paris flirts with Juliet, and she gives him a series of ambiguous answers to avoid the truth. When Paris leaves, Juliet tells Friar Lawrence that she would rather kill herself than marry Paris, so the friar proposes a plan to fake Juliet's death and then sneak her away to be with Romeo. He gives Juliet the potion and then instructs her to pretend that the wedding is still on.

   Back in the Capulet home, Juliet's parents are very happy that she has chosen to marry Paris. Juliet tells the nurse that she prefers to sleep alone so that she may pray. Then she goes to bed to drink the potion.

   The following morning, the house is abuzz with preparation for the wedding when the nurse finds Juliet in her death-like state. The family switches the wedding celebration to preparation for a funeral.

   The act ends with a comic scene in which Peter teases the musicians.

Research to Clarify

If students struggle to come up with a detail to research further, you may want to suggest that they focus on one of the following details: myths about mandrakes or how friars are different from other religious leaders.

NOTES

Why "silver sound"? Why "music with her silver sound?" What say you, Simon Catling?

First Musician. Marry, sir, because silver hath a sweet sound.

Peter. Pretty! What say you, Hugh Rebeck?

Second Musician. I say "silver sound" because musicians sound for silver.

Peter. Pretty too! What say you, James Soundpost?

Third Musician. Faith, I know not what to say.

Peter. O, I cry you mercy,[22] you are the singer. I will say for you. It is "music with her silver sound" because musicians have no gold for sounding.

"Then music with her silver sound
With speedy help doth lend redress." [*Exit.*]

First Musician. What a pestilent knave is this same!

Second Musician. Hang him, Jack! Come, we'll in here, tarry for the mourners, and stay dinner. [*Exit with others.*]

22. **cry you mercy** beg your pardon.

Comprehension Check

Complete the following items after you finish your first read.

1. What is Juliet prepared to do rather than marry Paris?

2. Why does Juliet tell her father she is willing to marry Paris?

3. What happens when Juliet drinks the potion?

4. **Notebook** Confirm your understanding of the text by writing a summary.

RESEARCH

Research to Clarify Choose at least one unfamiliar detail from the text. Briefly research that detail. In what way does the information you learned shed light on an aspect of the play?

PERSONALIZE FOR LEARNING

Challenge

Manipulating Language In Scene i of Act IV, Juliet gives Paris several ambiguous answers in order to keep her secret. She never actually lies, but offers responses that could be interpreted in more than one way. Instruct students to write a brief scene of dialogue in which one character gives ambiguous answers to another character in order to keep a secret.

MAKING MEANING

Close Read the Text

Reread lines 13–20 of Act IV, Scene iii. Mark words and phrases that describe Juliet's thoughts and feelings after the Nurse and Lady Capulet leave. Based on these details, how does Juliet feel about what she is preparing to do?

ANNOTATE QUESTION Close Read CONCLUDE

THE TRAGEDY OF ROMEO AND JULIET, ACT IV

Analyze the Text

CITE TEXTUAL EVIDENCE to support your answers.

Notebook Respond to these questions.

1. (a) What is Friar Lawrence's plan for Juliet? (b) **Analyze** Why do you think Juliet trusts the Friar? Explain your answer using details from the text.
2. (a) What three fears about taking the potion does Juliet reveal in her soliloquy in Act IV, Scene iii? (b) **Interpret** What does the soliloquy reveal about her personality? Explain your response and support it with details from the text.
3. (a) **Summarize** Juliet's words in Act IV, Scene i, lines 50–59. (b) **Interpret** What do Juliet's words indicate about her view of the situation that she finds herself in?
4. **Essential Question:** ***Do we determine our own destinies?*** What have you learned about destiny by reading Act IV of *The Tragedy of Romeo and Juliet?*

Tool Kit
Close-Read Guide and Model Annotation

WORD NETWORK

Add interesting words related to destiny from the text to your Word Network.

LANGUAGE DEVELOPMENT

Concept Vocabulary

lamentable	distressed	melancholy

Why These Words? The concept vocabulary words relate to feelings of sadness. What other words in the selection connect to this concept?

Practice

Notebook Confirm your understanding of these words by using each one in a sentence.

Word Study

Notebook **Latin Root: *-stress-*** The word *distressed* contains the root *-stress-*. This root comes from a Latin word, *stringere*, which means "to draw tight." The roots *-strict-*, in the word *constrict*, and *-strain-* in the word *constrain*, also come from *stringere*. Find several other words that contain *-stress-*, *-strict-*, or *-strain-*. Record the words and their meanings.

STANDARDS.

Language
- Identify and correctly use patterns of word changes that indicate different meanings or parts of speech.
- Demonstrate understanding of figurative language, word relationships, and nuances in word meanings.

DIGITAL PERSPECTIVES

Jump Start

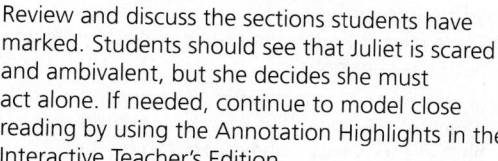

CLOSE READ Ask students to consider Juliet's decision to drink the potion in Act IV, Scene iii. Discuss the two possible outcomes of what Juliet is about to do and what either outcome would mean to her relationship with the important women in her life.

Close Read the Text

Review and discuss the sections students have marked. Students should see that Juliet is scared and ambivalent, but she decides she must act alone. If needed, continue to model close reading by using the Annotation Highlights in the Interactive Teacher's Edition.

Analyze the Text

Possible Responses

1. (a) She will fake her own death and then run away with Romeo. **DOK 1** (b) She puts herself in his hands because he is Romeo's friend and a religious man. **DOK 1**
2. (a) Juliet fears she will have to marry Paris, that the potion will kill her, and that she will be trapped in the tomb. **DOK 2** (b) Juliet is imaginative and brave. **DOK 3**
3. (a) "Tell me there is a way out of this or I will kill myself." (b) Juliet is desperate and determined.
4. Answers will vary.

Concept Vocabulary

Why These Words?

Possible responses

sorrow, weep, woeful, accursed, wretched, miserable

Practice

Answers will vary.

Word Network

Possible words: *accursed, unhappy* ("unlucky"), *faith*

Word Study

For more support, see **Concept Vocabulary and Word Study.**

Possible responses:

restrict, to tighten control or limits; *restrain,* to keep under control; *constrictor,* a snake that tightens its grip on its prey

FORMATIVE ASSESSMENT

Concept Vocabulary

If students fail to see the connection between the concept words, **then** instruct students to use a dictionary to define the words, then compare definitions.

Word Study

If students struggle to find words using the Latin roots given, **then** have them search on the Internet for examples using those roots. For Reteach and Practice, see **Word Study: Latin Root *-stress-* (RP).**

Analyze Craft and Structure

Dramatic Elements To help students understand the effect of comic relief, point out that an audience can get so emotionally drained from dramatic scenes that their emotional response becomes somewhat muted. Comic relief gives the audience a moment to catch a breath, thus preparing people for the full effect of more dramatic action. For more support, see **Analyze Craft and Structure: Dramatic Elements.**

Practice

Possible Responses:

1. The audience knows the truth of Juliet's situation, but Paris does not.
2. (a) See possible responses in chart on student page. (b) It is ironic that Capulet is excited and happy, and we know he is about to be thrown into despair. The audience is in suspense about how and when that will happen.
3. Dramatic irony builds tension as the audience experiences the contrast between the family's joy and the anguish it knows is ahead.
4. (a) Capulet makes jokes and calls the teasing fellows names. (b) The moment lightens the mood, and the actors are probably laughing as Capulet calls the Second Fellow merry.
5. The Nurse makes a pun on the word "case" when the musician says they will put up their pipes (in a case), and she says the case of Juliet is a pitiful one.

FORMATIVE ASSESSMENT

Analyze Craft and Structure

If students struggle to identify examples of comic relief, **then** work as a class to clarify comprehension immediately before, during, and after the examples of comic relief to be sure that they understand the context of these brief breaks in the drama. For Reteach and Practice, see **Analyze Craft and Structure: Dramatic Elements (RP).**

MAKING MEANING

THE TRAGEDY OF ROMEO AND JULIET, ACT IV

STANDARDS

Reading Literature
Analyze how an author's choices concerning how to structure a text, order events within it, and manipulate time create such effects as mystery, tension, or surprise.

Language
Interpret figures of speech in context and analyze their role in the text.

Analyze Craft and Structure

Dramatic Elements The author of a drama may include an element known as dramatic irony. **Dramatic irony** is a contradiction between what a character thinks and what the audience knows to be true. Dramatic irony engages the audience emotionally because it allows tension and suspense to build as the audience waits for the truth to be revealed to the characters. An excellent example of dramatic irony is the scene in which Juliet's family prepares for her wedding celebration while the audience knows that she is lying "dead" in the other room.

In Shakespearean drama, tension and suspense is sometimes broken, at least temporarily, by the use of comic elements such as these:

- **Comic relief** is the introduction of a humorous character or situation into an otherwise tragic sequence of events to lighten the mood and offer the audience some emotional relief.
- A **pun** is a play on words involving either one word that has two different meanings or two words that sound alike but have different meanings. For example, the dying Mercutio makes a pun using the two different meanings of the word *grave*: "Ask for me tomorrow, and you shall find me a grave man."

Practice

CITE TEXTUAL EVIDENCE to support your answers.

Notebook Respond to these questions.

1. Reread Act IV, Scene i, lines 18–43. In what way is Juliet's encounter with Paris in Friar Lawrence's cell an instance of dramatic irony?
2. (a) Based on Capulet's statement in Act IV, Scene iv, line 25, what does the character think? What does the audience know? Record each detail in the chart.

   (b) Use the completed chart to explain why Capulet's statement is an example of dramatic irony. How does this example of dramatic irony build tension and suspense?

WHAT CHARACTER THINKS	WHAT AUDIENCE KNOWS
Capulet thinks the Nurse will get Juliet ready for her wedding.	The audience knows the Nurse will be getting Juliet ready for her funeral.

3. Explain the key role that dramatic irony plays in Act IV, Scene v, lines 1–95.
4. (a) How does Capulet's encounter with the fellows in Act IV, Scene iv, lines 13–21 represent a moment of comic relief? (b) Does this moment effectively lighten the mood? Use text details to support your opinion.
5. Explain the pun in the Nurse's exchange with the First Musician in Act IV, Scene v, lines 97–98. How is the conversation that follows among the musicians and Peter an instance of comic relief? Explain.

Speaking and Listening

Assignment

Hold a **classroom debate** to resolve this question: *Is Juliet's drinking of the potion a brave act or a foolish act?*

- Each debater presents an oral response to the question, stating a claim and supporting it with relevant details from the text.
- A panel of judges or the class as a whole can evaluate the arguments and decide which has the most effective support.

1. **Develop Your Claim and Identify Support** Use the text details you identified to determine how you would respond to the question. Write a clear statement of your claim on a sheet of paper. Then, identify several pieces of supporting evidence from Act IV. Take detailed notes on how each piece of evidence supports your claim.
2. **Develop Your Response** Use your notes to develop your oral response. Decide what points you will make in your response and in what order you will present them.
3. **Prepare Your Delivery** Practice delivering your oral response to the judges. Include the following performance techniques to make your argument convincing:
   - Speak clearly, in an appropriate tone, and at an appropriate volume and rate.
   - Use appropriate facial expressions and gestures to convey your conviction.
   - Maintain regular eye contact with the audience.
4. **Evaluate Responses** Listen carefully as your classmates deliver their responses. Use an evaluation guide like the one shown to evaluate their responses.

EVALUATION GUIDE

Rate each statement on a scale of 1 (not demonstrated) to 4 (demonstrated).

☐ The claim was clearly stated in the response.

☐ The claim was supported with relevant text evidence.

☐ The debater communicated his or her ideas clearly and convincingly.

☐ The debater used appropriate facial expressions, gestures, and eye contact.

EVIDENCE LOG

Before moving on to a new selection, go to your Evidence Log and record what you learned from *The Tragedy of Romeo and Juliet*, Act IV.

STANDARDS

Writing

Write arguments to support claims in an analysis of substantive topics or texts, using valid reasoning and relevant and sufficient evidence.

Speaking and Listening

Present information, findings, and supporting evidence clearly, concisely, and logically such that listeners can follow the line of reasoning and the organization, development, substance, and style are appropriate to purpose, audience, and task.

DIGITAL PERSPECTIVES

Speaking and Listening

Students should annotate Act IV in preparation for their argument, highlighting important details that support their stance on the debate question. Explain that neither answer is the correct answer; either answer could be defended effectively using strongly supported arguments.

Remind students about the definition of parallelism and of how its use helps to strengthen persuasive arguments. Before they begin writing their speeches, and again during the editing stage, encourage students to use parallelism in their debates to clarify their points.

For more support, see **Speaking and Listening: Classroom Debate.**

Evidence Log Support students in completing their Evidence Log. This paced activity will help prepare them for the Performance-Based Assessment at the end of the unit.

FORMATIVE ASSESSMENT

Speaking and Listening

- **If** students fail to support their reasoning, **then** encourage them to use writing maps specifying main idea, supporting details, and examples from the text.
- **If** English Language learners are not yet ready to present an oral debate, **then** pair them with a debating student and encourage them to help to prepare the debating student using the evaluation form.

For Reteach and Practice, see **Speaking and Listening: Classroom Debate (RP).**

Selection Test

Administer the *The Tragedy of Romeo and Juliet*, Act IV Selection Test, which is available, in both print and digital formats online in Assessments.

PERSONALIZE FOR LEARNING

English Language Support

Planning for a Debate Ask small groups of students to choose a topic for a debate and write a list of sample questions that could be asked during the debate. **EMERGING**

Ask small groups of students to choose a topic for a debate, write a list of questions that could be asked, and then hold a mock debate. **EXPANDING**

Have two small groups work together to critique each other's debate. Ask each small group to choose a topic for a debate, write a list of questions that could be asked, and then have a debate while the other group observes. Then the groups trade places and share feedback with each other. **BRIDGING**

An expanded **English Language Support Lesson** on Classroom Debates is available in the Interactive Teacher's Edition.

The Tragedy of Romeo and Juliet, Act V

AUDIO SUMMARIES
Audio summaries of *The Tragedy of Romeo and Juliet,* Act V are available online in both English and Spanish in the Interactive Teacher's Edition or Unit Resources. Assigning these summaries prior to reading the selection may help students build additional background knowledge and set a context for their first read.

Summary

At the beginning of Act V of *The Tragedy of Romeo and Juliet* by William Shakespeare, a messenger tells Romeo that he saw Juliet's body in the Capulet tomb. Romeo leaves to return to Verona and misses Friar Lawrence's letter. Paris is at the tomb, grief-stricken over Juliet's death. When Romeo arrives, Paris blames him. They fight, and Romeo kills Paris. He enters the tomb and, believing that Juliet is dead, poisons himself. Juliet wakes, sees Romeo's body, and stabs herself. The family leaders and the Prince arrive.

Insight

This classic tragedy examines love and youthful impulsiveness. It is an excellent introduction to the writing of Shakespeare.

ESSENTIAL QUESTION:
Do we determine our own destinies?

Connection to Essential Question

Shakespeare's *The Tragedy of Romeo and Juliet* suggests that, rather than determining their own destinies, Romeo and Juliet were fated to fall in love and die.

WHOLE-CLASS LEARNING PERFORMANCE TASK
Which has a greater impact on the characters in these texts: destiny or personal choices?

UNIT PERFORMANCE-BASED ASSESSMENT
Should the opinions of others affect our own choices or destinies?

Connection to Performance Tasks

Whole-Class Learning Performance Task The text suggests that the fates of Romeo and Juliet were due to destiny. Yet, the reader or audience can easily argue that different choices, or different luck, could have saved them.

Unit Performance-Based Assessment Following their families' advice could have kept Romeo and Juliet alive, but it would not have made them happy.

DIGITAL PERSPECTIVES — Audio | Video | Document | Annotation Highlights | EL Highlights | Online Assessment

LESSON RESOURCES

	Making Meaning	Language Development	Effective Expression
Lesson	**First Read** **Close Read** **Analyze the Text** **Analyze Craft and Structure**	**Concept Vocabulary** **Word Study** **Conventions**	**Writing to Sources** **Speaking and Listening**
Instructional Standards	**RL.10** By the end of grade 9, read and comprehend literature . . . **RL.3** Analyze how complex characters develop . . . **RL.5** Analyze how an author's choices . . .	**L.1** Demonstrate command of the conventions . . . **L.1.a** Use parallel structure. **L.5** Demonstrate understanding of figurative language . . .	**W.1** Write arguments . . . **SL.4** Present information, findings, and supporting evidence . . . **RL.7** Analyze the representation of a subject or a key scene . . .
STUDENT RESOURCES			
Available online in the Interactive Student Edition or Unit Resources	Selection Audio First-Read Guide: Drama Close-Read Guide: Drama	Word Network	Evidence Log
TEACHER RESOURCES			
Selection Resources Available online in the Interactive Teacher's Edition or Unit Resources	Audio Summaries Annotation Highlights EL Highlights English Language Support Lesson: Tragic Flaw Analyze Craft and Structure: Tragedy	Concept Vocabulary and Word Study Conventions: Parallelism	Writing to Sources: Persuasive Letter Speaking and Listening: Performance Review
Reteach/Practice (RP) Available online in the Interactive Teacher's Edition or Unit Resources	Analyze Craft and Structure: Tragedy (RP)	Word Study: Word Families (RP) Conventions: Parallelism (RP)	Writing to Sources: Persuasive Letter (RP) Speaking and Listening: Performance Review (RP)
Assessment Available online in Assessments	Selection Test		
My Resources	A Unit 4 Answer Key is available online and in the Interactive Teacher's Edition.		

Reading Support

Text Complexity Rubric: *The Tragedy of Romeo and Juliet*, Act V

Quantitative Measures	
Lexile: NP **Text Length:** 3,474 words	
Qualitative Measures	
Knowledge Demands ①—②—③—④—❺	Students will need information about the historical context of Verona, Italy, and the Renaissance period. Some of this is covered in the background information.
Structure ①—②—③—④—❺	The selection is a Shakespearean play written primarily in blank verse. Line breaks might be challenging for students.
Language Conventionality and Clarity ①—②—③—④—❺	The selection contains complex sentences, unfamiliar syntax, figurative language, challenging vocabulary, and Elizabethan language.
Levels of Meaning/Purpose ①—②—③—❹—⑤	The classic tale of star-crossed lovers is accessible, but the meaning of some passages of dialogue may be difficult to grasp due to challenging language and structure.

DECIDE AND PLAN

English Language Support

Provide English learners with support for Structure and Language as they read the selection.

Structure The final scene is long and complicated, with many characters coming and going and very few stage directions. This may make the action difficult to follow. Have students take notes as they read, noting who is on stage and what events are taking place.

Language Help students reword long and complex sentences. Using the language from the selection, suggest simpler sentences that convey the same meaning. Ask students to read the new sentences and discuss them.

Strategic Support

Provide students with strategic support to ensure that they can successfully read the text.

Knowledge Demands Have students work with a partner to summarize what they know so far. What has happened? Who is involved? Then have students predict what will happen next.

Language If students have difficulty with the dialogue, have them first read to note what goes wrong in this last act and leads to tragedy. Then have students reread and note pieces of dialogue that reveal mistakes being made. Help students work in pairs to clarify their understanding.

Challenge

Provide students who need to be challenged with ideas for how they can go beyond a simple interpretation of the text.

Text Analysis Ask students to reread Act V, Scene i. Point out line 24, when Romeo exclaims, *"Then I defy you, stars!"* What does this line tell you about Romeo? In what way are Romeo's words consistent with what you know about his character?

Written Response Have students select a scene from Act V to perform for their classmates. Tell students to choose either Scene i or Scene iii, then plan and rehearse the scene. Challenge students to use appropriate gestures, body movement, and eye contact to convey the personality of each character.

TEACH

Read and Respond

Have students do their first read of the selection. Then have them complete their close read. Finally, work with them on the Making Meaning, Language Development, and Effective Expression activities.

Standards Support Through Teaching and Learning Cycle

IDENTIFY NEEDS

Analyze results of the Beginning-of-Year Assessment, focusing on the items relating to Unit 4. Also take into consideration student performance to this point and your observations of where particular students struggle.

DECIDE AND PLAN

- If students have performed poorly on items matching these standards, then provide selection scaffolds before assigning them the on-level lesson provided in the Student Edition.
- If students have done well on the Beginning-of-Year Assessment, then challenge them to keep progressing and learning by giving them opportunities to practice the skills in depth.
- Use the Selection Resources listed on the Planning pages for *The Tragedy of Romeo and Juliet*, Act V to help students continually improve their ability to master the standards.

Instructional Standards: ***The Tragedy of Romeo and Juliet*, Act V**

	Catching Up	This Year	Looking Forward
Reading	You may wish to administer the **Analyze Craft and Structure: Tragedy (RP)** worksheet to familiarize students with the elements of tragedy.	**RL.3** Analyze how complex characters develop over the course of a text, interact with other characters, and advance the plot or develop the theme.	Have students identify the elements of tragedy from other works they have read.
Writing	You may wish to administer the **Writing to Sources: Persuasive Letter (RP)** worksheet to prepare them for their letters.	**W.1** Write arguments to support claims in an analysis of substantive topics or texts, using valid reasoning and relevant and sufficient evidence.	Challenge students to write a persuasive letter, using Shakespearean language, urging the Globe Theater to not put on the play for the first time.
Speaking and Listening	You may wish to administer the **Speaking and Listening: Performance Review (RP)** worksheet to help students prepare for their performance review.	**SL.4** Present information, findings, and supporting evidence clearly, concisely, and logically such that listeners can follow the line of reasoning and the organization, development, substance, and style are appropriate to purpose, audience, and task.	Challenge students to write a performance review of a live performance in or near their community.
Language	Review the **Conventions: Parallelism (RP)** worksheet with students to ensure they understand the technique. Review **Word Study: Word Families (RP)** with students to ensure they understand words can share the same root.	**L.1.a** Use parallel structure. **L.5** Demonstrate understanding of figurative language, word relationships, and nuances in word meaning.	Challenge students to list other popular works that use parallelism. Have students identify other common words that share roots.

ANALYZE AND REVISE

- Analyze student work for evidence of student learning.
- Identify whether students have met the expectations in the standards.
- Identify implications for future instruction.

TEACH

Implement the planned lesson, and gather evidence of student learning.

Jump Start

FIRST READ Engage students in a classroom discussion about young people and defiance. What are some possible consequences when young people defy authority figures? Are there instances when it is justified for young people to defy their parents or guardians? This discussion can set the context for reading Act V of *The Tragedy of Romeo and Juliet.*

The Tragedy of Romeo and Juliet, Act V

Will Friar Lawrence's plan work? Will Romeo and Juliet be able to run away together? What will happen to them as the play ends? Modeling questions such as these will help students connect Act V of *The Tragedy of Romeo and Juliet* to the Performance Task assignment. Selection audio and print capability for the selection are available in the Interactive Teacher's Edition.

Concept Vocabulary

Support students as they rank the words. Ask if they've ever heard, read, or used them. Reassure them that the definitions for these words are listed in the selection.

FIRST READ

Students should perform the steps of the first read independently.

NOTICE: Encourage students to notice details that could help them identify the major events that lead to the fate of Romeo and Juliet.

ANNOTATE: Remind students to mark passages that relate to the concept of destiny or fate.

CONNECT: Pose questions to help students go beyond the text and make connections: How would you have counseled Romeo and Juliet if you were Friar Lawrence? How might your choices have affected their final fate?

RESPOND: Students will answer questions and write a summary to demonstrate understanding.

Point out to students that while they will always complete the Respond step at the end of the first read, the other steps will probably happen somewhat concurrently. You may wish to print copies of the **First-Read Guide: Fiction** for students to use.

Remind students that during their first read, they should not answer the close-read questions that appear in the selection.

Playwright

William Shakespeare

The Tragedy of Romeo and Juliet, Act V

Concept Vocabulary

You will encounter the following words as you read Act V of *The Tragedy of Romeo and Juliet.* Before reading, note how familiar you are with each word. Then, rank the words in order from most familiar (1) to least familiar (6).

WORD	YOUR RANKING
desperate	
meager	
misery	
penury	

After completing your first read, come back to the concept vocabulary and review your rankings. Mark changes to your original rankings as needed.

First Read DRAMA

Apply these strategies as you conduct your first read. You will have an opportunity to complete the close-read notes after your first read.

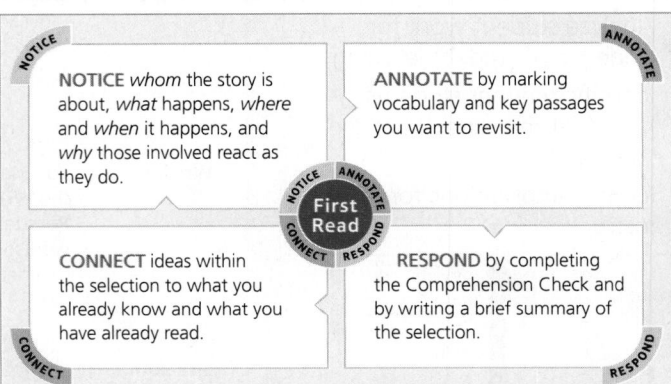

NOTICE *whom* the story is about, *what* happens, *where* and *when* it happens, and *why* those involved react as they do.

ANNOTATE by marking vocabulary and key passages you want to revisit.

CONNECT ideas within the selection to what you already know and what you have already read.

RESPOND by completing the Comprehension Check and by writing a brief summary of the selection.

First Read: NOTICE, ANNOTATE, CONNECT, RESPOND

Tool Kit
First-Read Guide and Model Annotation

STANDARDS
Reading Literature
By the end of grade 9, read and comprehend literature, including stories, dramas, and poems in the grades 9–10 text complexity band proficiently, with scaffolding as needed at the end of the range.

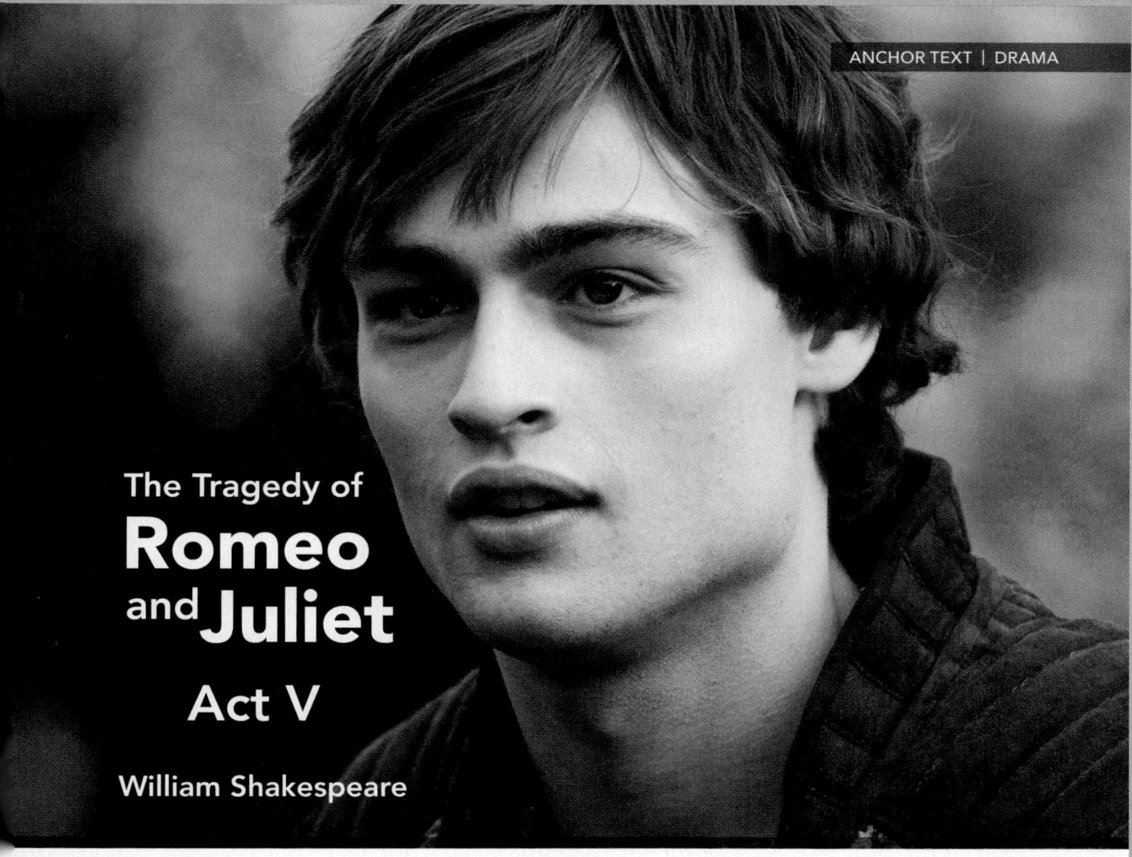

The Tragedy of Romeo and Juliet
Act V
William Shakespeare

DIGITAL PERSPECTIVES

CLOSER LOOK

Analyze Soliloquy

Students may have marked lines 1–8 during their first read. Use this passage to help students understand how the author uses a soliloquy. Encourage them to talk about the annotations that they marked. You may want to model a close read with the class based on the highlights shown in the text.

ANNOTATE: Have students mark details in lines 1–6 that explain Romeo's state of mind, or have students participate while you highlight them.

QUESTION: Guide students to consider what these details might tell them. Ask what a reader can infer from these details,

Possible response: Romeo says that his heart is light. The author conveys Romeo's thoughts and feelings by having him speak to himself as he stands alone on stage.

CONCLUDE: Help students to formulate conclusions about the importance of these details in the text. Ask students why the author might have included these details.

Possible response: Because Romeo is speaking to himself and only himself, we know that what he's saying is true. He feels hopeful that he will soon be with Juliet. Knowing his state of mind is helpful because the audience has information that Romeo does not. They know that Juliet has faked her death. Although there is a plan in motion for Romeo and Juliet to be together, he does not know about it yet, and it could fall apart.

Remind students that a **soliloquy** is a speech in which a character who is alone onstage reveals private thoughts and feelings to the audience.

REVIEW AND ANTICIPATE

To prevent her marriage to Paris, Juliet has taken the Friar's potion, which has placed her in a temporary, deathlike sleep. As Act V begins, her unsuspecting family plans her funeral. Meanwhile, the Friar has sent a messenger to Romeo in Mantua, where he is living in exile. The Friar plans to tell Romeo of the ruse so that he may return and rescue Juliet from the family tomb. As you read Act V, consider how much of the Friar's plan is built on somewhat rickety foundations.

SCAN FOR MULTIMEDIA

Scene i • *Mantua. A Street.*

[*Enter* Romeo.]

Romeo. If I may trust the flattering truth of sleep,[1]
My dreams presage[2] some joyful news at hand.
My bosom's lord[3] sits lightly in his throne,
And all this day an unaccustomed spirit
Lifts me above the ground with cheerful thoughts.
I dreamt my lady came and found me dead
(Strange dream that gives a dead man leave to think!)
And breathed such life with kisses in my lips

NOTES

1. **flattering . . . sleep** pleasing illusions of dreams.
2. **presage** *v.* foretell.
3. **bosom's lord** heart.

VOCABULARY DEVELOPMENT

Concept Vocabulary Reinforcement Students will benefit from additional examples and practice with the concept vocabulary as they encounter the words. Reinforce their comprehension with "show-you-know" sentences. The first part of the sentence uses the vocabulary word in an appropriate context. The second part of the sentence—the show-you-know part—clarifies the first. Model the strategy with this example for *desperate.*

I was *desperate* to catch a cab to the airport because I was losing hope I would make my flight.

Then give students these sentence prompts, and coach them in creating the clarification part.

1. The cat's *meager* appearance ________.
Possible response: was a sign that it had had very little to eat
2. We lived in *misery* ________.
Possible response: after a fire destroyed most of our belongings
3. Two signs of *penury* are ________.
Possible response: homelessness or having very few belongings

NOTES

4. **shadows** *n.* dreams; unreal images.

5. **Capels' monument** the Capulets' burial vault.

6. **presently took post** immediately set out on horseback.

7. **office** *n.* duty.

8. **import / Some misadventure** suggest some misfortune.

desperate (DEHS puhr iht) *adj.* driven to action by a loss of hope

9. **apothecary** (uh POTH uh kehr ee) *n.* one who prepares and sells drugs and medicines.

10. **In tatt'red . . . simples** in torn clothing, with overhanging eyebrows, sorting out herbs.

meager (MEE guhr) *adj.* extremely thin

misery (MIHZ uhr ee) *n.* condition of great wretchedness

11. **beggarly account** small number.

12. **cakes of roses** pressed rose petals (used for perfume).

penury (PEHN yuhr ee) *n.* destitution or poverty

That I revived and was an emperor.
Ah me! How sweet is love itself possessed,
When but love's shadows[4] are so rich in joy!

[*Enter* Romeo's Man, Balthasar, *booted.*]

News from Verona! How now, Balthasar?
Dost thou not bring me letters from the friar?
How doth my lady? Is my father well?
How fares my Juliet? That I ask again,
For nothing can be ill if she be well.

Man. Then she is well, and nothing can be ill.
Her body sleeps in Capels' monument,[5]
And her immortal part with angels lives.
I saw her laid low in her kindred's vault
And presently took post[6] to tell it you.
O, pardon me for bringing these ill news,
Since you did leave it for my office,[7] sir.

Romeo. Is it e'en so? Then I defy you, stars!
Thou knowest my lodging. Get me ink and paper
And hire post horses. I will hence tonight.

Man. I do beseech you, sir, have patience.
Your looks are pale and wild and do import
Some misadventure.[8]

Romeo. Tush, thou art deceived.
Leave me and do the thing I bid thee do.
Hast thou no letters to me from the friar?

Man. No, my good lord.

Romeo. No matter. Get thee gone.
And hire those horses. I'll be with thee straight.

[*Exit* Balthasar.]

Well, Juliet, I will lie with thee tonight.
Let's see for means. O mischief, thou art swift
To enter in the thoughts of **desperate** men!
I do remember an apothecary,[9]
And hereabouts 'a dwells, which late I noted
In tatt'red weeds, with overwhelming brows,
Culling of simples.[10] **Meager** were his looks,
Sharp **misery** had worn him to the bones;
And in his needy shop a tortoise hung,
An alligator stuffed, and other skins
Of ill-shaped fishes; and about his shelves
A beggarly account[11] of empty boxes,
Green earthen pots, bladders, and musty seeds,
Remnants of packthread, and old cakes of roses[12]
Were thinly scattered, to make up a show.
Noting this **penury** to myself I said,

PERSONALIZE FOR LEARNING

Challenge

Apothecary Research For students to understand Scene i of the selection, they will need to know the word *apothecary* in line 37 and what it represents. Have students research the work of apothecaries from history. After they complete their research, lead a class discussion about medical practices long ago. Guide students to compare and contrast the apothecaries of the past to the doctors and pharmacists of today. **(Research to Clarify)**

"And if a man did need a poison now
Whose sale is present death in Mantua,
Here lives a caitiff[13] wretch would sell it him."
O, this same thought did but forerun my need,
And this same needy man must sell it me.
As I remember, this should be the house.
Being holiday, the beggar's shop is shut.
What, ho! Apothecary!

[*Enter* Apothecary.]

Apothecary. Who calls so loud?

Romeo. Come hither, man. I see that thou art poor.
Hold, there is forty ducats.[14] Let me have
A dram of poison, such soon-speeding gear[15]
As will disperse itself through all the veins
That the life-weary taker may fall dead,
And that the trunk[16] may be discharged of breath
As violently as hasty powder fired
Doth hurry from the fatal cannon's womb.

Apothecary. Such mortal drugs I have; but Mantua's law
Is death to any he that utters[17] them.

Romeo. Art thou so bare and full of wretchedness
And fearest to die? Famine is in thy cheeks,
Need and oppression starveth in thy eyes,
Contempt and beggary hangs upon thy back:
The world is not thy friend, nor the world's law;
The world affords no law to make thee rich;
Then be not poor, but break it and take this.

Apothecary. My poverty but not my will consents.

Romeo. I pay thy poverty and not thy will.

Apothecary. Put this in any liquid thing you will
And drink it off, and if you had the strength
Of twenty men, it would dispatch you straight.

Romeo. There is thy gold—worse poison to men's souls,
Doing more murder in this loathsome world,
Than these poor compounds[18] that thou mayst not sell.
I sell thee poison; thou hast sold me none.
Farewell. Buy food and get thyself in flesh.
Come, cordial[19] and not poison, go with me
To Juliet's grave; for there must I use thee. [*Exit all.*]

⌘ ⌘ ⌘

NOTES

13. **caitiff** *adj.* miserable.

14. **ducats** (DUHK uhts) *n.* gold coins.

15. **soon-speeding gear** fast-working stuff.

16. **trunk** *n.* body.

17. **utters** *v.* sells.

CLOSE READ

ANNOTATE: In lines 75–86, mark phrases in which Romeo redefines a word to mean its opposite.

QUESTION: Why does Romeo's dialogue contain so many reversals of meaning?

CONCLUDE: What do these reversals show about Romeo's emotional and mental state?

18. **compounds** *n.* mixtures.

19. **cordial** *n.* health-giving drink.

DIGITAL PERSPECTIVES

CLOSE READ

Remind students to identify a word that Romeo redefines as they read the text. You may wish to model the close read using the following think-aloud format. Possible responses to questions on the Student page are included. You may also want to print copies of the **Close-Read Guide: Drama** for students to use.

ANNOTATE: As I read lines 75–86, I notice that Romeo redefines two words to mean the opposite of their true meaning.

QUESTION: I think Romeo's dialogue includes reversals of meaning to show that his circumstances have drastically changed from one extreme to another.

CONCLUDE: These reversals show that Romeo's emotional state greatly shifted in a very short time. At the beginning of the scene, he was happy and excited to see Juliet again. At the end of the scene, he was determined to poison himself to be with her in death.

CLOSER LOOK

Analyze Plot

Students may have marked lines from Scene ii during their first read. Use this text to help students understand how the plot evolves at this point in the play. Encourage them to talk about the annotations that they marked. You may want to model a close read with the class based on the highlights shown in the text.

ANNOTATE: Have students mark details in Scene ii, lines 14–29, that show how the plot evolves, or have students participate while you highlight them.

QUESTION: Guide students to consider what these details might tell them. Ask what a reader can infer from them about the plot of the play, and accept student responses.

Possible response: At this point in the play, the audience learns why Romeo never received Friar Lawrence's letter. Friar John was mistakenly locked away to prevent an infection from spreading. As a result, he was unable to deliver the letter. Learning this, Friar Lawrence decides to write again to Romeo and hide Juliet until her husband can arrive.

CONCLUDE: Help students to formulate conclusions about the importance of these details in the text. Ask students why the author might have included these details.

Possible response: These details are part of the escalation of the main conflict in the play. Romeo does not receive Friar Lawrence's letter, which means he does not learn about the plan to fake Juliet's death. This event is part of the rising action of the play, as the conflict increases in intensity and nears its tipping point. Romeo and Juliet face an increasing amount of danger, and the audience should sense the plot is close to the climax.

Remind students that **plot** is the sequence of events that makes up a narrative and that usually involves characters in conflict. The sequence of events in a plot is usually divided into five parts: the exposition; the rising action; the climax; the falling action; and the resolution, or denouement.

NOTES

Scene ii • *Friar Lawrence's cell.*

[*Enter* Friar John, calling Friar Lawrence.]

John. Holy Franciscan friar, brother, ho!

[*Enter* Friar Lawrence.]

Lawrence. This same should be the voice of Friar John.
Welcome from Mantua. What says Romeo?
Or, if his mind be writ, give me his letter.

John. Going to find a barefoot brother out,
One of our order, to associate[1] me
Here in this city visiting the sick,
And finding him, the searchers of the town,
Suspecting that we both were in a house
Where the infectious pestilence did reign,
Sealed up the doors, and would not let us forth,
So that my speed to Mantua there was stayed.

Lawrence. Who bare my letter, then, to Romeo?

John. I could not send it—here it is again—
Nor get a messenger to bring it thee,
So fearful were they of infection.

Lawrence. Unhappy fortune! By my brotherhood,
The letter was not nice,[2] but full of charge,
Of dear import;[3] and the neglecting it
May do much danger. Friar John, go hence,
Get me an iron crow and bring it straight
Unto my cell.

John. Brother, I'll go and bring it thee. [*Exit.*]

Lawrence. Now must I to the monument alone.
Within this three hours will fair Juliet wake.
She will beshrew[4] me much that Romeo
Hath had no notice of these accidents;[5]
But I will write again to Mantua,
And keep her at my cell till Romeo come—
Poor living corse, closed in a dead man's tomb! [*Exit.*]

1. **associate** *v.* accompany.
2. **nice** *adj.* trivial.
3. **full of charge, / Of dear import** urgent and important.
4. **beshrew** *v.* blame.
5. **accidents** *n.* happenings.

⌘ ⌘ ⌘

Scene iii • *A churchyard; in it a monument belonging to the Capulets.*

[*Enter* Paris *and his* Page *with flowers and sweet water.*]

Paris. Give me thy torch, boy. Hence, and stand aloof.[1]
Yet put it out, for I would not be seen.

1. **aloof** *adv.* apart.

DIGITAL PERSPECTIVES

Under yond yew trees lay thee all along[2]
Holding thy ear close to the hollow ground.
So shall no foot upon the churchyard tread
(Being loose, unfirm, with digging up of graves)
But thou shalt hear it. Whistle then to me,
As signal that thou hearest something approach.
Give me those flowers. Do as I bid thee, go.

Page. [*Aside*] I am almost afraid to stand alone
Here in the churchyard; yet I will adventure.[3] [*Retires.*]

Paris. Sweet[4] flower, with flowers thy bridal bed I strew
(O woe! thy canopy is dust and stones)
Which with sweet water nightly I will dew;
Or, wanting that, with tears distilled by moans.
The obsequies[5] that I for thee will keep
Nightly shall be to strew thy grave and weep. [Boy *whistles.*]
The boy gives warning something doth approach.
What cursed foot wanders this way tonight
To cross[6] my obsequies and true love's rite?
What, with a torch? Muffle me, night, awhile. [*Retires.*]

[*Enter* Romeo, *and* Balthasar *with a torch, a mattock, and a crow of iron.*]

Romeo. Give me that mattock and the wrenching iron.
Hold, take this letter. Early in the morning
See thou deliver it to my lord and father.
Give me the light. Upon thy life I charge thee,
Whate'er thou hearest or seest, stand all aloof
And do not interrupt me in my course.
Why I descend into this bed of death
Is partly to behold my lady's face,
But chiefly to take thence from her dead finger
A precious ring—a ring that I must use
In dear employment.[7] Therefore hence, be gone.
But if thou, jealous,[8] dost return to pry
In what I farther shall intend to do,
By heaven, I will tear thee joint by joint
And strew this hungry churchyard with thy limbs.
The time and my intents are savage-wild,
More fierce and more inexorable[9] far
Than empty[10] tigers or the roaring sea.

Balthasar. I will be gone, sir, and not trouble ye.

Romeo. So shalt thou show me friendship. Take thou that.
Live, and be prosperous; and farewell, good fellow.

Balthasar. [*Aside*] For all this same, I'll hide me hereabout.
His looks I fear, and his intents I doubt. [*Retires.*]

NOTES

2. **lay . . . along** lie down flat.
3. **adventure** *v.* chance it.
4. **sweet** *adj.* perfumed.
5. **obsequies** (OB suh kweez) *n.* memorial ceremonies.
6. **cross** *v.* interrupt.
7. **dear employment** important business.
8. **jealous** *adj.* curious.
9. **inexorable** *adj.* uncontrollable.
10. **empty** *adj.* hungry.

PERSONALIZE FOR LEARNING

English Language Support

Figurative Language Have students reread lines 37–39 of Scene iii: *The time and my intents are savage-wild, / More fierce and more inexorable far / Than empty tigers or the roaring sea*. Explain to students that these lines use **metaphor**, a type of figurative language in which one thing is compared to another. Romeo compares his intention, or plan, to enter the tomb and join Juliet in death to hungry tigers or the roaring sea. Both hungry tigers and the roaring sea are savage, strong, and unstoppable. By comparing his intention to those two things, Romeo is telling Balthasar he will not be stopped, and anyone who attempts to stop him will be placing himself or herself in danger. **ALL LEVELS**

Romeo. Thou detestable maw,[11] thou womb of death,
Gorged with the dearest morsel of the earth,
Thus I enforce thy rotten jaws to open,
And in despite[12] I'll cram thee with more food.

[Romeo *opens the tomb.*]

Paris. This is that banished haughty Montague
That murd'red my love's cousin—with which grief
It is supposed the fair creature died—
And here is come to do some villainous shame
To the dead bodies. I will apprehend[13] him.
Stop thy unhallowèd toil, vile Montague!
Can vengeance be pursued further than death?
Condemnèd villain, I do apprehend thee.
Obey, and go with me; for thou must die.

Romeo. I must indeed; and therefore came I hither.
Good gentle youth, tempt not a desp'rate man.
Fly hence and leave me. Think upon these gone;
Let them affright thee. I beseech thee, youth,
Put not another sin upon my head
By urging me to fury. O, be gone!
By heaven, I love thee better than myself,
For I come hither armed against myself.
Stay not, be gone. Live, and hereafter say
A madman's mercy bid thee run away.

Paris. I do defy thy conjurations.[14]
And apprehend thee for a felon[15] here.

Romeo. Wilt thou provoke me? Then have at thee, boy!
[*They fight.*]

Page. Lord, they fight! I will go call the watch.

[*Exit.* Paris *falls.*]

Paris. O, I am slain! If thou be merciful,
Open the tomb, lay me with Juliet. [*Dies.*]

Romeo. In faith, I will. Let me peruse[16] this face.
Mercutio's kinsman, noble County Paris!
What said my man when my betossèd[17] soul
Did not attend[18] him as we rode? I think
He told me Paris should have married Juliet.
Said he not so, or did I dream it so?
Or am I mad, hearing him talk of Juliet,
To think it was so? O, give me thy hand,
One writ with me in sour misfortune's book!
I'll bury thee in a triumphant grave.
A grave? O, no, a lanthorn,[19] slaught'red youth,
For here lies Juliet, and her beauty makes
This vault a feasting presence[20] full of light.

NOTES

11. **maw** *n.* stomach.
12. **despite** *n.* scorn.
13. **apprehend** *v.* seize; arrest.
14. **conjurations** *n.* solemn appeals.
15. **felon** *n.* criminal.
16. **peruse** *v.* look over.
17. **betossèd** *adj.* upset.
18. **attend** *v.* give attention to.
19. **lanthorn** (LAN tuhrn) *n.* windowed structure on top of a room to admit light; also, a lantern.
20. **feasting presence** chamber fit for celebration.

PERSONALIZE FOR LEARNING

English Language Support

Syntax Help students analyze the unusual sentence structure of Shakespearean verse in order to develop a better understanding of conventional English syntax. For Scene iii, have students rewrite Paris's speech in lines 49–57 or Romeo's speech in lines 58–67 in prose format, guiding them to remove the line breaks. Ask students to read the rewritten sentences and make observations. Help students understand that the rewritten text contains grammatical errors, such as run-on sentences. Work with them to correct the text to make it acceptable as prose. **ALL LEVELS**

Death, lie thou there, by a dead man interred.

[*Lays him in the tomb.*]

How oft when men are at the point of death
Have they been mercy! Which their keepers[21] call
A lightning before death. O, how may I
Call this a lightning? O my love, my wife!
Death, that hath sucked the honey of thy breath,
Hath had no power yet upon thy beauty.
Thou art not conquered. Beauty's ensign[22] yet
Is crimson in thy lips and in thy cheeks,
And death's pale flag is not advancèd there.
Tybalt, liest thou there in thy bloody sheet?
O, what more favor can I do to thee
Than with that hand that cut thy youth in twain
To sunder[23] his that was thine enemy?
Forgive me, cousin! Ah, dear Juliet,
Why art thou yet so fair? Shall I believe
That unsubstantial Death is amorous,[24]
And that the lean abhorrèd monster keeps
Thee here in dark to be his paramour?
For fear of that I still will stay with thee
And never from this pallet[25] of dim night
Depart again. Here, here will I remain
With worms that are thy chambermaids. O, here
Will I set up my everlasting rest
And shake the yoke of inauspicious[26] stars
From this world-wearied flesh. Eyes, look your last!
Arms, take your last embrace! And, lips, O you
The doors of breath, seal with a righteous kiss
A dateless[27] bargain to engrossing[28] death!
Come, bitter conduct;[29] come, unsavory guide!
Thou desperate pilot,[30] now at once run on
The dashing rocks thy seasick weary bark!
Here's to my love! [*Drinks.*] O true apothecary!
Thy drugs are quick. Thus with a kiss I die. [*Falls.*]

[*Enter* Friar Lawrence, *with lanthorn, crow, and spade.*]

Friar. Saint Francis be my speed![31] How oft tonight
Have my old feet stumbled[32] at graves! Who's there?

Balthasar. Here's one, a friend, and one that knows you well.

Friar. Bliss be upon you! Tell me, good my friend,
What torch is yond that vainly lends his light
To grubs[33] and eyeless skulls? As I discern,
It burneth in the Capels' monument.

Balthasar. It doth so, holy sir; and there's my master,
One that you love.

NOTES

21. keepers *n.* jailers.

CLOSE READ

ANNOTATE: In lines 92–120, mark points at which Romeo speaks of death as having human qualities or speaks to death as though it is a person.

QUESTION: Why does Romeo speak of and to death in this way?

CONCLUDE: What is the effect of Romeo's conversation with death?

22. ensign *n.* banner.

23. sunder *v.* cut off.

24. amorous *adj.* full of love.

25. pallet *n.* bed.

26. inauspicious *adj.* promising misfortune.

27. dateless *adj.* eternal.

28. engrossing *adj.* all-encompassing.

29. conduct *n.* guide (poison).

30. pilot *n.* captain (Romeo himself).

31. speed *n.* help.

32. stumbled *v.* stumbling was thought to be a bad omen.

33. grubs *v.* worms.

DIGITAL PERSPECTIVES

CLOSE READ

Remind students to identify text in lines 92–120 in which Romeo speaks of death as if it were a person. You may wish to model the close read using the following think-aloud format. Possible responses to questions on the Student page are included. You may also want to print copies of the **Close-Read Guide: Drama** for students to use.

ANNOTATE: As I read lines 92–120, I notice that Romeo talks about death as though it were a human. He talks about death taking certain actions that only humans take and speaks with adjectives that could be used to describe people.

QUESTION: I think Romeo speaks of death this way because death has become very real to him. It is as though death were a person he was about to meet.

CONCLUDE: The effect of Romeo's conversation is that death almost feels like another character in the play. By speaking this way, he makes it seem as though death has the ability to affect what happens in the plot just as any other character in the play might.

Additional **English Language Support** is available in the Interactive Teacher's Edition.

CLOSER LOOK

Analyze Dramatic Irony

Students may have marked lines 140–152 during their first read. Use these lines to help students understand dramatic irony, a form of irony that exists when the reader or audience knows or understands something that the characters do not. Encourage them to talk about the annotations that they marked. You may want to model a close read with the class based on the highlights shown in the text.

ANNOTATE: Have students mark details in lines 140–152 that demonstrate dramatic irony, or have students participate while you highlight them.

QUESTION: Guide students to consider the effect of dramatic irony. Ask students how reading dramatic irony makes them feel, and accept student responses.

Possible response: The reader or audience knows the truth and feels the tension of the characters discovering what has taken place.

CONCLUDE: Help students to formulate conclusions about the importance of these details in the text. Ask students why the author might have included these details.

Possible response: Dramatic irony increases the tension in the scene. The audience knows that Juliet will soon discover that Romeo has killed himself and wonders how she will respond. This creates a feeling of concern and suspense.

Remind students that the term **irony** refers to a discrepancy or contradiction between appearance and reality, expectation and result, or meaning and intention. **Dramatic irony** can be used as a device in drama, fiction, or poetry to create suspense or maintain tension.

NOTES

Friar. Who is it?

Balthasar. Romeo.

Friar. How long hath he been there?

Balthasar. Full half an hour.

Friar. Go with me to the vault.

Balthasar. I dare not, sir.
My master knows not but I am gone hence,
And fearfully did menace me with death
If I did stay to look on his intents.

Friar. Stay then; I'll go alone. Fear comes upon me.
O, much I fear some ill unthrifty[34] thing.

Balthasar. As I did sleep under this yew tree here,
I dreamt my master and another fought,
And that my master slew him.

Friar. Romeo!
Alack, alack, what blood is this which stains
The stony entrance of this sepulcher?
What mean these masterless[35] and gory swords
To lie discolored by this place of peace? [*Enters the tomb.*]
Romeo! O, pale! Who else? What, Paris too?
And steeped in blood? Ah, what an unkind[36] hour
Is guilty of this lamentable chance!
The lady stirs. [Juliet *rises.*]

Juliet. O comfortable[37] friar! Where is my lord?
I do remember well where I should be,
And there I am. Where is my Romeo?

Friar. I hear some noise. Lady, come from that nest
Of death, contagion, and unnatural sleep.

34. **unthrifty** *adj.* unlucky.

35. **masterless** *adj.* discarded (without masters).

36. **unkind** *adj.* unnatural.

37. **comfortable** *adj.* comforting.

474 UNIT 4 • STAR-CROSSED ROMANCES

A greater power than we can contradict
Hath thwarted our intents. Come, come away.
Thy husband in thy bosom there lies dead;
And Paris too. Come, I'll dispose of thee
Among a sisterhood of holy nuns.
Stay not to question, for the watch is coming.
Come, go, good Juliet. I dare no longer stay.

Juliet. Go, get thee hence, for I will not away. [*Exit* Friar.]
What's here? A cup, closed in my truelove's hand?
Poison, I see, hath been his timeless[38] end.
O churl![39] Drunk all, and left no friendly drop
To help me after? I will kiss thy lips.
Haply some poison yet doth hang on them
To make me die with a restorative.[40] [*Kisses him.*]
Thy lips are warm!

Chief Watchman. [*Within*] Lead, boy. Which way?

Juliet. Yea, noise? Then I'll be brief. O happy[41] dagger!
[*Snatches* Romeo's *dagger.*]
This is thy sheath; there rust, and let me die.
[*She stabs herself and falls.*]

[*Enter* Paris' Boy *and* Watch.]

Boy. This is the place. There, where the torch doth burn.

Chief Watchman. The ground is bloody. Search about the churchyard.
Go, some of you; whoe'er you find attach.[42]
[*Exit some of the* Watch.]
Pitiful sight! Here lies the County slain;
And Juliet bleeding, warm, and newly dead,
Who here hath lain this two days burièd.
Go, tell the Prince; run to the Capulets;
Raise up the Montagues; some others search.
[*Exit others of the* Watch.]
We see the ground[43] whereon these woes do lie,
But the true ground of all these piteous woes
We cannot without circumstance descry.[44]

[*Enter some of the* Watch, *with* Romeo's Man, Balthasar.]

Second Watchman. Here's Romeo's man. We found him in the churchyard.

Chief Watchman. Hold him in safety till the Prince come hither.

[*Enter* Friar Lawrence *and another* Watchman.]

Third Watchman. Here is a friar that trembles, sighs and weeps.
We took this mattock and this spade from him
As he was coming from this churchyard's side.

Chief Watchman. A great suspicion! Stay the friar too.

NOTES

38. timeless *adj.* untimely; too soon.

39. churl *n.* rude fellow.

40. restorative *n.* medicine.

41. happy *adj.* convenient; opportune.

42. attach *v.* arrest.

43. ground *n.* cause.

44. without circumstance descry see clearly without details.

PERSONALIZE FOR LEARNING

Strategic Support

Theme Review the Chief Watchman's speech, lines 172–181. Students may require support to identify the major themes of the play because a theme is typically implied rather than explicitly stated. Remind students that the theme is not the plot, but rather the "big idea" that the author wants to convey to readers or audience members.

Have students create T-charts. One side should be used to state a theme from *The Tragedy of Romeo and Juliet*. The other side should be used to record details from the text that they used to identify the theme. If students continue to require support, have them identify important details from the play, and ask them to think about how these details relate to one another.

NOTES

[*Enter the* Prince *and* Attendants.]

Prince. What misadventure is so early up,
That calls our person from our morning rest?

[*Enter* Capulet *and his* Wife *with others.*]

Capulet. What should it be, that is so shrieked abroad?

Lady Capulet. O, the people in the street cry "Romeo,"
Some "Juliet," and some "Paris"; and all run
With open outcry toward our monument.

Prince. What fear is this which startles in your ears?

Chief Watchman. Sovereign, here lies the County Paris slain;
And Romeo dead; and Juliet, dead before,
Warm and new killed.

Prince. Search, seek, and know how this foul murder comes.

Chief Watchman. Here is a friar, and slaughtered Romeo's man,
With instruments upon them fit to open
These dead men's tombs.

Capulet. O heavens! O Wife, look how our daughter bleeds!
This dagger hath mista'en, for, lo, his house[45]
Is empty on the back of Montague,
And it missheathèd in my daughter's bosom!

Lady Capulet. O me, this sight of death is as a bell
That warns my old age to a sepulcher.

[*Enter* Montague *and others.*]

Prince. Come, Montague; for thou art early up
To see thy son and heir more early down.

Montague. Alas, my liege,[46] my wife is dead tonight!
Grief of my son's exile hath stopped her breath.
What further woe conspires against mine age?

Prince. Look, and thou shalt see.

Montague. O thou untaught! What manners is in this,
To press before thy father to a grave?

Prince. Seal up the mouth of outrage[47] for a while,
Till we can clear these ambiguities
And know their spring, their head, their true descent;
And then will I be general of your woes[48]
And lead you even to death. Meantime forbear,
And let mischance be slave to patience.[49]
Bring forth the parties of suspicion.

Friar. I am the greatest, able to do least,
Yet most suspected, as the time and place
Doth make against me, of this direful[50] murder;
And here I stand, both to impeach and purge[51]

45. **house** *n.* sheath.

46. **liege** (leej) *n.* lord.

47. **mouth of outrage** violent cries.

48. **general . . . woes** leader in your sorrow.

49. **let . . . patience** be patient in the face of misfortune.

50. **direful** *adj.* terrible.

51. **impeach and purge** accuse and declare blameless.

DIGITAL PERSPECTIVES

Enriching the Text Review the Prince's speech in lines 216–222. Show the class Act V from a filmed version of *The Tragedy of Romeo and Juliet*. After students watch the video, have them compare the video to the written play. How do the filmed scenes add to students' understanding of the play? Were certain elements changed for the film? If so, how did those changes affect the narrative? Be sure to preview any video before showing it to the class.

Myself condemnèd and myself excused.

Prince. Then say at once what thou dost know in this.

Friar. I will be brief, for my short date of breath[52]
Is not so long as is a tedious tale.
Romeo, there dead, was husband to that Juliet;
And she, there dead, that's Romeo's faithful wife.
I married them; and their stol'n marriage day
Was Tybalt's doomsday, whose untimely death
Banished the new-made bridegroom from this city;
For whom, and not for Tybalt, Juliet pined.
You, to remove that siege of grief from her,
Betrothed and would have married her perforce
To County Paris. Then comes she to me
And with wild looks bid me devise some mean
To rid her from this second marriage,
Or in my cell there would she kill herself.
Then gave I her (so tutored by my art)
A sleeping potion; which so took effect
As I intended, for if wrought on her
The form of death. Meantime I writ to Romeo
That he should hither come as[53] this dire night
To help to take her from her borrowed grave,
Being the time the potion's force should cease,
But he which bore my letter, Friar John,
Was stayed by accident, and yesternight
Returned my letter back. Then all alone
At the prefixèd hour of her waking
Came I to take her from her kindred's vault;
Meaning to keep her closely[54] at my cell
Till I conveniently could send to Romeo.
But when I came, some minute ere the time
Of her awakening, here untimely lay
The noble Paris and true Romeo dead.
She wakes; and I entreated her come forth
And bear this work of heaven with patience;
But then a noise did scare me from the tomb,
And she, too desperate, would not go with me.
But, as it seems, did violence on herself.
All this I know, and to the marriage
Her nurse is privy;[55] and if aught in this
Miscarried by my fault, let my old life
Be sacrificed some hour before his time
Unto the rigor[56] of severest law.

Prince. We still have known thee for a holy man.
Where's Romeo's man? What can he say to this?

Balthasar. I brought my master news of Juliet's death;
And then in post he came from Mantua

NOTES

52. date of breath term of life.

53. as on.

54. closely *adv.* hidden; secretly.

55. privy *adj.* secretly informed about.

56. rigor *n.* strictness.

DIGITAL PERSPECTIVES

CLOSER LOOK

Analyze Tragedy

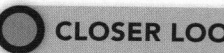

Students may have marked lines 257–264 during their first read. Use this passage to help students understand how the play is an example of a tragedy. Encourage them to talk about the annotations that they marked. You may want to model a close read with the class based on the highlights shown in the text.

ANNOTATE: Have students mark details in the Friar's lines on this page that indicate that the play is an example of a tragedy, or have students participate while you highlight them.

QUESTION: Guide students to consider what these details might tell them. Ask what a reader can infer from the description of the deaths of Romeo and Juliet, and accept student responses.

Possible response: In his speech, Friar Lawrence describes the circumstances that led the two characters to kill themselves. Readers can infer that neither wanted to live without the other.

CONCLUDE: Help students to formulate conclusions about the importance of these details in the text. Ask students why the author might have included these details.

Possible response: As Friar Lawrence explains, Romeo and Juliet died partly as the result of ignorance of crucial information and circumstances beyond their control. This is a common element of tragedies.

Remind students that a **tragedy** is a work of literature, often a play, that shows the downfall or death of the main character. Often, the character's fate is the result of ignorance of some crucial piece of information or even an accident or circumstance beyond his or her control.

NOTES

57. **made your master** was your master doing.

58. **winking at** closing my eyes to.

59. **brace** *n.* pair (Mercutio and Paris).

60. **jointure** *n.* wedding gift; marriage settlement.

61. **rate** *n.* value.

62. **enmity** *n.* hostility.

63. **glooming** *adj.* cloudy; gloomy.

To this same place, to this same monument.
This letter he early bid me give his father,
And threat'ned me with death, going in the vault,
If I departed not and left him there.

Prince. Give me the letter. I will look on it.
Where is the County's page that raised the watch?
Sirrah, what made your master[57] in this place?

Boy. He came with flowers to strew his lady's grave;
And bid me stand aloof, and so I did.
Anon comes one with light to ope the tomb;
And by and by my master drew on him;
And then I ran away to call the watch.

Prince. This letter doth make good the friar's words,
Their course of love, the tidings of her death;
And here he writes that he did buy a poison
Of a poor 'pothecary and therewithal
Came to this vault to die and lie with Juliet.
Where be these enemies? Capulet, Montague,
See what a scourge is laid upon your hate,
That heaven finds means to kill your joys with love.
And I, for winking at[58] your discords too,
Have lost a brace[59] of kinsmen. All are punished.

Capulet. O brother Montague, give me thy hand.
This is my daughter's jointure,[60] for no more
Can I demand.

Montague. But I can give thee more;
For I will raise her statue in pure gold,
That whiles Verona by that name is known,
There shall no figure at such rate[61] be set
As that of true and faithful Juliet.

Capulet. As rich shall Romeo's by his lady's lie—
Poor sacrifices of our enmity![62]

Prince. A glooming[63] peace this morning with it brings.
The sun for sorrow will not show his head.
Go hence, to have more talk of these sad things;
Some shall be pardoned, and some punishèd;
For never was a story of more woe
Than this of Juliet and her Romeo.

⌘ ⌘ ⌘

WriteNow Express and Reflect

Write a Speech Review the Prince's final speech in lines 305–310. At the end of the play, the Prince gives two short speeches about Romeo and Juliet in the form of verse. He recounts the circumstances of their deaths and memorializes them as one might at a funeral. Have students imagine that they are the Prince and ask them to write a short speech to give at a funeral for Romeo or Juliet. They should write about the character's life and death and give a short tribute to honor him or her.

MEDIA CONNECTION

Romeo and Juliet

Discuss It Choose and listen to a scene from Act V of the L.A. Theatre Works production of *The Tragedy of Romeo and Juliet*. As you listen, consider specific ways in which the actors modify their voices and time their deliveries to convey nuances of emotion. Do you find their interpretations of the characters accurate and convincing?

Write your response before sharing your ideas with the class.

SCAN FOR MULTIMEDIA

Comprehension Check

Complete the following items after you finish your first read.

1. How does Romeo get the apothecary to sell him the poison?

2. How was Friar John prevented from delivering Friar Lawrence's letter to Romeo?

3. What is Paris doing at the Capulet vault?

4. **Notebook** Confirm your understanding of the text by writing a summary.

RESEARCH

Research to Clarify Choose at least one unfamiliar detail from the text. Briefly research that detail. In what way does the information you learned shed light on an aspect of the play?

Research to Explore This play may spark your curiosity to read more. Briefly research whether the Montagues and Capulets were real families. You may want to share what you discover with the class.

DIGITAL PERSPECTIVES

Comprehension Check

Possible responses:

1. Romeo gets the apothecary to sell him poison because the man is extremely poor and desperate for money.
2. Friar John was mistakenly locked away to prevent an infection from spreading.
3. Paris comes to the Capulet vault to mourn Juliet's death.
4. Responses will vary, but should include the main events from the fifth act of the play. Romeo hears that Juliet has died, and he decides to kill himself. He buys poison and goes to the tomb where she has been laid. Friar Lawrence learns that Romeo never received his letter. He tries to reach Juliet to save both her and Romeo. At the Capulet vault, Romeo encounters Paris. The two young men fight, and Romeo kills Paris. Romeo takes the poison and dies. Juliet wakes and finds that Romeo is dead. She stabs herself. Their families learn of the deaths, and Friar Lawrence explains the circumstances surrounding their ill-fated love.

Research

Research to Clarify If students struggle to come up with an unfamiliar detail, have them reread the fifth act of the play to notice an idea or concept that might be new to them. Suggest that they find out why the fear of infection was so strong at the time Shakespeare wrote the play.

Research to Explore If students have difficulty researching the Montagues and Capulets, provide a list of key terms to aid their Internet research. Some examples include "famous family feuds," "star-crossed love," and "nobility of Italy."

PERSONALIZE FOR LEARNING

Challenge

Shakespeare's Tragedies Have students research the tragedies of Shakespeare. Ask them to write a brief description of his work. Have them consider the following questions. What were some common themes in his tragic plays? How is *The Tragedy of Romeo and Juliet* similar to other tragedies Shakespeare wrote? How is this play different? How did his tragedies inspire later playwrights? Have students read some of his other works and, if possible, read aloud or play a recording of an excerpt from another Shakespearean tragedy to the class.

Jump Start

CLOSE READ Have students discuss tragic stories. Guide them to consider what makes them interesting to read or watch. Ask students what aspects of *The Tragedy of Romeo and Juliet* are sad or tragic. Talk about how tragic stories affect the reader or audience.

Close Read the Text

Walk students through the annotation model on the Student page. Encourage them to complete items 2 and 3 on their own. Review and discuss the sections students have marked. If needed, continue to model close reading by using the Annotation Highlights in the Interactive Teacher's Edition.

Analyze the Text

Possible responses:

1. (a) Romeo exclaims "Then I defy you, stars" when he hears that Juliet has died. He does not want to accept that she is dead and wants to change the situation. (b) Romeo's words are consistent with his character because he is very brash and has a strong will. **DOK 3**
2. Paris's visit to Juliet's tomb suggests that he genuinely loved her because he appears to be grief-stricken about her death. **DOK 2**
3. Responses will vary, but should relate the concept of destiny to the story of Romeo and Juliet and include details from the text as supporting evidence. **DOK 3**

FORMATIVE ASSESSMENT

Analyze the Text

- **If** students struggle to identify how Romeo's words are consistent with his character, then have students make a list of Romeo's character traits and the reread the quote.

THE TRAGEDY OF ROMEO AND JULIET, ACT V

Close Read the Text

1. This model, from Act V, Scene iii, lines 286–295, shows two sample annotations, along with questions and conclusions. Close read the passage and find another detail to annotate. Then, write a question and your conclusion.

Close Read: ANNOTATE · QUESTION · CONCLUDE

ANNOTATE: The Prince uses this word to describe Romeo's and Juliet's deaths.

QUESTION: Why does the author use this word to describe their deaths?

CONCLUDE: This word helps emphasize that their deaths serve as a punishment for the feud between the Capulets and Montagues.

Prince. This letter doth make good the friar's words, / Their course of love, the tidings of her death; / And here he writes that he did buy a poison / Of a poor 'pothecary and therewithal / Came to this vault to die and lie with Juliet. / Where be these enemies? Capulet, Montague, / See what a scourge is laid upon your hate, / That heaven finds means to kill your joys with love. / And I, for winking at your discords too, / Have lost a brace of kinsmen. All are punished.

ANNOTATE: These two words are opposites.

QUESTION: Why does the author include these words in the Prince's description of Romeo's and Juliet's death?

CONCLUDE: They help create irony. Romeo and Juliet die for their love for each other, not the hatred that has been bred between their families.

2. For more practice, go back into the text, and complete the close-read notes.
3. Revisit a section of the text you found important during your first read. Read this section closely, and **annotate** what you notice. Ask yourself **questions** such as "Why did the author make this choice?" What can you **conclude**?

Tool Kit
Close-Read Guide and Model Annotation

Analyze the Text

CITE TEXTUAL EVIDENCE to support your answers.

Notebook Respond to these questions.

1. (a) **Interpret** In Act V, Scene i, why does Romeo exclaim, "Then I defy you, stars"? (b) **Analyze** In what way are Romeo's words consistent with what you know of his character? Explain.
2. **Analyze** What does Paris's visit to Juliet's tomb suggest about his feelings for her?
3. **Essential Question:** ***Do we determine our own destinies?*** What have you learned about determining one's own destiny by reading Act V of *The Tragedy of Romeo and Juliet*?

STANDARDS

Reading Literature

- Analyze how complex characters develop over the course of a text, interact with other characters, and advance the plot or develop the theme.
- Analyze how an author's choices concerning how to structure a text, order events within it, and manipulate time create such effects as mystery, tension, or surprise.

PERSONALIZE FOR LEARNING

Strategic Support

Central Ideas Have a group of students analyze Scenes i and ii of Act V while a second group analyzes Scene iii. Instruct each group to discuss the main ideas in its scenes. Then agree on one sentence that sums up each scene. When the groups are finished, invite them to share their central ideas. Then ask everyone to work together to create a sentence that sums up the entire fifth act of the play.

Analyze Craft and Structure

Tragedy A **tragedy** is a drama in which the main character, who is of noble stature, meets with great misfortune. Often, the hero's **motives**, or reasons for his or her actions, are good but misguided, and the hero suffers a tragic fate that may seem undeserved. Although tragedies are sad, they also show the nobility of the human spirit.

In Shakespearean tragedies, the hero's doom is the result of fate, a tragic flaw, or a combination of both.

- **Fate** is a destiny over which the hero has little or no control. In some Shakespearean tragedies, errors, the poor judgment of others, or accidents can be interpreted as the workings of fate.
- A **tragic flaw** is a personality defect, such as jealousy, that contributes to the hero's choices and, thus, to his or her tragic downfall.

Practice

CITE TEXTUAL EVIDENCE to support your answers.

Notebook Respond to these questions.

1. (a) What is the Friar's motive for helping Romeo and Juliet? (b) To what extent is he responsible for their tragedy?"
2. (a) Who was responsible for Romeo and Juliet's need for secrecy? (b) To what extent was that a cause of their tragedy?
3. Use the chart below to identify elements that contribute to the play's tragic ending. Consider aspects of Romeo's and Juliet's personalities and elements of fate. Explain which element you think is most responsible for the story's tragic outcome. Support your answer with specific details you gathered.

ROMEO'S AND JULIET'S PERSONALITIES	
ROMEO	JULIET
Romeo has a strong will and loves very deeply. He also is very brash and impulsive. When he impulsively acts to avenge Mercutio's death, it leads to a chain of events that result in his death.	Like Romeo, Juliet loves very deeply. It is this love that causes her to defy her family to be with Romeo. This eventually leads to her downfall.

ELEMENTS OF FATE
Romeo and Juliet have a star-crossed love. Due to the feud between their families, they were never meant to be together. By defying this, they set up a chain of events that led to their deaths.

DIGITAL PERSPECTIVES

Analyze Craft and Structure

Tragedy Discuss with students the different characteristics of tragedies. Explain that although tragedies typically have sad endings, they have other important elements in common. One is the concept of fate, while the other is the hero's tragic flaw. Fate is something the hero cannot escape. Often, a complicated series of events occurs that ensures the main character meets his or her fate. A tragic flaw is often a mistake or bad decision the hero makes that leads to his or her downfall. Sometimes, this mistake results from an accident or a misunderstanding. For more support, see **Analyze Craft and Structure: Tragedy.**

Practice

Possible responses:

1. (a) The Friar helps Romeo and Juliet because he is concerned about them and believes in their love. (b) He is responsible for their tragedy because his plan was too complicated and there were too many opportunities for it to fall apart.
2. (a) The Montagues and the Capulets were responsible for Romeo and Juliet's need for secrecy. Their feud required the couple to keep their love hidden. (b) Having to hide and run away forced Romeo and Juliet to take drastic measures to be together. This was partly the cause of their tragedy.
3. Student responses will vary. See possible responses in chart on Student page.

FORMATIVE ASSESSMENT

Analyze Craft and Structure: Dramatic Elements

If students struggle to identify character traits for Romeo and Juliet, **then** have them talk with a partner to discuss what they liked or did not like about each character. Ask them to consider how their likes and dislikes might relate to the characters' personalities and fate. For Reteach and Practice, see **Analyze Craft and Structure: Tragedy (RP).**

PERSONALIZE FOR LEARNING

English Language Support

Understanding Tragic Flaws Ask pairs of students to reimagine a literary hero, such as Atticus Finch or Huckleberry Finn, as having a tragic flaw. Have students write a few sentences about how the hero's story would change. **EMERGING**

Ask students to reimagine a literary hero, such as Atticus Finch or Huckleberry Finn, as having a tragic flaw. Have students write a paragraph about how the hero's story would change. **EXPANDING**

Ask students to reimagine a literary hero, such as Atticus Finch or Huckleberry Finn, as having a tragic flaw. Have students write a paragraph about how the hero's story would change. Students should include at least three ways that the plot of the story would be different. **BRIDGING**

An expanded **English Language Support Lesson** on Tragic Flaw is available in the Interactive Teacher's Edition.

TEACHING

Concept Vocabulary

Why These Words?

Possible responses:

1. In the last act of the play, Romeo takes actions that are dangerous and foolish and lead to his death. Believing Juliet has died causes him to buy poison illegally to kill himself. This shows that he is *desperate*, or driven to action by a loss of hope.
2. The words *life-weary*, *wretchedness*, and *loathsome* also relate to this concept.

Practice

Possible responses:

1. I was *desperate* to take any job I could find after I was fired. Stranded on an island, he began to take on a *meager* appearance due to the lack of food. This wonderful charity gives aid to homeless people and others in a state of *penury*. Losing a loved one can cause you to feel great sadness and *misery*.
2. **Responses will vary.**

Word Network

Possible words: *misadventure, cursed, inexorable, misfortune, inauspicious*

Word Study

For more support, see **Concept Vocabulary and Word Study.**

Possible words: (1) *despairing, desperateness, desperately;* (2) *miserable, miserably*

FORMATIVE ASSESSMENT

Concept Vocabulary

If students fail to see the connection between the words, **then** have them use each word in a sentence and think about what is similar about the sentences.

Word Study

If students fail to identify a related word, **then** have them work with a partner and a dictionary to find another word in the word family. For Reteach and Practice, see **Word Study: Word Families (RP).**

LANGUAGE DEVELOPMENT

THE TRAGEDY OF ROMEO AND JULIET, ACT V

Concept Vocabulary

desperate	meager	penury	misery

Why These Words? These concept words relate to poverty. Romeo describes the apothecary's apearance as *meager* and says that *misery* has "worn him to the bones." Romeo's observations convince him that the apothecary is poor and will be willing to sell him poison, even though it is illegal.

1. Romeo uses the word *desperate* to describe himself. How does this help the reader understand his actions?

2. What other words in the selection connect to this concept?

Practice

Notebook The concept words appear in Act V of *The Tragedy of Romeo and Juliet*.

1. Use each word in a sentence that demonstrates your understanding of the word's meaning.
2. Work with two classmates, and take turns reading your sentences aloud, leaving out the concept vocabulary words. Have members of your group guess the missing words. Keep taking turns until you each have read all four of your sentences.

WORD NETWORK

Add interesting words related to destiny from the text to your Word Network.

Word Study

Word Families A group of words that share the same root make up a **word family**. The word *desperate*, for example, is part of a word family that includes *despair* and *desperation*. Recognizing that an unfamiliar word may be in the same word family as a familiar word can help you determine its meaning.

1. Identify yet another word that belongs to the same word family as *desperate*, *despair*, and *desperation*.

2. Identify a word that belongs to the same word family as *misery*.

STANDARDS

Language

- Demonstrate command of the conventions of standard English grammar and usage when writing or speaking.
- Use parallel structure.
- Demonstrate understanding of figurative language, word relationships, and nuances in word meanings.

VOCABULARY DEVELOPMENT

Graphic Organizer Help students complete a graphic organizer for the concept vocabulary word *misery.*

Misery	
a state or feeling of great distress or discomfort of mind or body.	Synonyms: *unhappiness, distress, heartache, despair*
The woman was in misery over the death of her husband.	Antonyms: *joyfulness, pleasure, blessing, happiness*

Conventions

Parallelism The use of similar grammatical forms or patterns to express ideas of equal significance is known as **parallelism**. Parallelism creates rhythm and balance in sentences and makes the relationship between ideas in a sentence clear. Shakespeare uses parallelism in Juliet's speech about Romeo's name.

What's Montague? It is nor hand, nor foot
Nor arm, nor face, nor any other part
Belonging to man. O, be some other name!

These lines would be unbalanced and less powerful if they did not include parallel phrases.

Nonparallel: Our work today focused on drafting, reviewing, and to revise a letter.

Parallel: Our work today focused on drafting, reviewing, and revising a letter.

SAMPLE PARALLEL STRUCTURE	
In a Series	The athlete has sharp eyes, strong hands, **and** deft fingers. Sarah walks, bikes, **or** drives to the store on Sundays.
In a Comparison	I like listening to music better **than** watching movies.
With a Coordinating Conjunction	The French **and** the Spanish have rich histories. Laura will pick up her dry cleaning **and** mail a package.
With a Correlative Conjunction	You can **either** walk to the store **or** ride your bike to the store.

Read It

Mark the parallel words or phrases in each sentence.

1. It is easy to see Romeo's romanticism, Mercutio's courage, and Benvolio's loyalty in *The Tragedy of Romeo and Juliet*.
2. Juliet tries to be both a good daughter and a faithful wife.
3. Friar Lawrence advises Romeo and comforts Juliet.

Write It

Notebook Write a paragraph that includes at least three examples of parallelism. In each example, underline the parallel words or phrases.

DIGITAL PERSPECTIVES

Conventions

Parallelism Explain to students that **parallelism** is the repetition of words, phrases, clauses, or sentences that have the same grammatical structure or the same meaning. This device helps to emphasize, link, and balance similar ideas. It also can be used to show the differences between contrasting ideas. Poets writing in verse can use parallelism to create a memorable rhythm. For more support, see **Conventions: Parallelism.**

MAKE IT INTERACTIVE

Have students write a sentence for one of the types of parallel structure (in a series, in a comparison, with a conjunction, with a correlative conjunction). Then have partners swap sentences. Partners should rewrite each other's sentence to make it nonparallel. Then have them discuss the differences and the impact of using parallelism in writing.

Read It

1. It is easy to see Romeo's romanticism, Mercutio's courage, and Benvolio's loyalty in *The Tragedy of Romeo and Juliet.*
2. Juliet tries to be both a good daughter and a faithful wife.
3. Friar Lawrence advises Romeo and comforts Juliet.

Write It

Responses will vary.

FORMATIVE ASSESSMENT

Conventions

If students struggle to complete their paragraphs, **then** have them complete a chart similar to the one on the page that lists one sentence for each type of parallel structure. Students can then use these sentences as a guide or as text to include in their paragraphs. For Reteach and Practice, see **Conventions: Parallelism (RP).**

TEACHING

Writing to Sources

Explain to students that when they write a persuasive text, they must support their argument with strong reasons and evidence. Reasons and evidence should help convince the reader to accept or adopt the writer's argument. As a result, they must be relevant to the topic, clear, and effective.

When drafting a persuasive text, it is also important to include a counterargument, or opposite opinion. The writer should explain why the counterargument is ineffective and should not be supported. This will help to strengthen the writer's own argument and point of view. For more support, see **Writing to Sources: Persuasive Letter.**

Vocabulary and Conventions Connection Have students review the definitions of the concept vocabulary words before they begin writing their persuasive letters. You may wish to have them write one or two examples of sentences with a parallel structure first, then work to incorporate these sentences as they draft their letters.

Reflect on Your Writing

Responses will vary, but students should address the effect of using the concept vocabulary words and parallelism in their writing. Students should also explain how their persuasive letters helped them to better understand the central ideas in *The Tragedy of Romeo and Juliet*.

FORMATIVE ASSESSMENT

Writing to Sources

If students fail to include at least one example of parallelism, **then** have them work with a partner to identify one or two sentences with a nonparallel structure that could be rewritten and revise them together. For Reteach and Practice, see **Writing to Sources: Persuasive Letter (RP).**

EFFECTIVE EXPRESSION

THE TRAGEDY OF ROMEO AND JULIET, ACT V

Writing to Sources

Persuasive writing is a type of argumentation that emphasizes emotions over logic. Indeed, some types of persuasion, such as advertising, include no credible support for a position and rely solely on emotional appeals. That is not the type of persuasion you will write in this activity.

Assignment

Imagine that your school is putting on a play and the students are responsible for deciding which one to perform. Write a **persuasive letter** to your fellow students in which you either encourage them to select *The Tragedy of Romeo and Juliet* or urge them to choose a different play.

- Begin by drafting three to five reasons why you think the student body should or should not choose *The Tragedy of Romeo and Juliet.*
- Provide convincing support for your position. All evidence should be relevant and sufficient to support your claims.
- Recognize that others may feel differently, and explain why your position is preferable.
- Revise to address readers' concerns, create parallelism, and incorporate powerful language.

Vocabulary and Conventions Connection Include several of the concept vocabulary words in your letter. Also, remember to use parallelism in your sentences to provide balance, rhythm, and clarity.

desperate	meager	misery	penury

Reflect on Your Writing

After you have written your persuasive letter, answer these questions.

1. How did writing this letter help you better understand the play's central ideas and themes?

2. What was the most challenging part of writing your letter?

3. **Why These Words?** The words you choose make a difference in your writing. Which words did you choose to add power to your letter?

STANDARDS

Writing
Write arguments to support claims in an analysis of substantive topics or texts, using valid reasoning and relevant and sufficient evidence.

Speaking and Listening
Present information, findings, and supporting evidence clearly, concisely, and logically such that listeners can follow the line of reasoning and the organization, development, substance, and style are appropriate to purpose, audience, and task.

PERSONALIZE FOR LEARNING

Strategic Support

Transitions Some students may have difficulty connecting ideas in their persuasive letters and may require support in using transitions to make an argument. Pair students and have them identify places in each other's letters where a transition word or phrase could be included. Have them work to clarify ideas and improve the flow of the argument. Also have partners consider the specific relationships among ideas. Finally, have students review the suggested transitions and revise their letters as needed.

Speaking and Listening

Assignment

Listen to a scene or act from *The Tragedy of Romeo and Juliet* as presented by L.A. Theatre Works. Then, evaluate the section of the production you heard, and share a **performance review** as a podcast or classroom presentation. Follow these steps to complete the assignment.

1. **Take Notes** As you listen to the performance, take notes about what you hear so that you can cite specific evidence in your review. Use the following questions to guide you as you take notes on the performance:
   - How does the audio performance compare with the text?
   - What do the actors do to bring their characters to life?
   - How does the music contribute to the impact of the performance?
   - What would you have done differently if you were directing an audio version of *The Tragedy of Romeo and Juliet*?
2. **Plan Your Podcast or Presentation** After you listen to the performance, use your notes to draft your review.
   - Write an overall evaluation of the performance, which you will support with your analysis of its key elements.
   - Identify key elements of the performance and offer an analysis of each element.
3. **Record Your Podcast or Deliver Your Presentation** When you have finished writing your review, record your podcast or deliver your presentation.
4. **Evaluate Reviews** As your classmates deliver their reviews, listen attentively. Use the evaluation guide below to analyze their delivery.

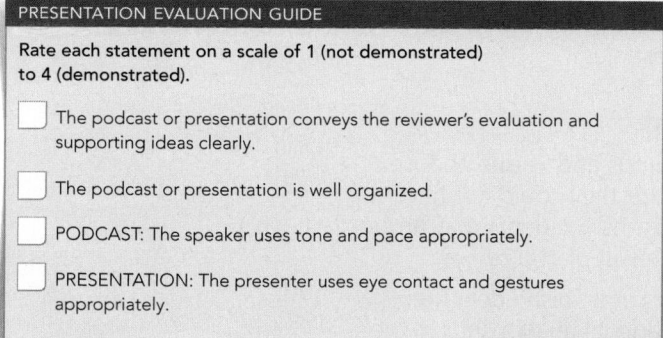

PRESENTATION EVALUATION GUIDE

Rate each statement on a scale of 1 (not demonstrated) to 4 (demonstrated).

- ☐ The podcast or presentation conveys the reviewer's evaluation and supporting ideas clearly.
- ☐ The podcast or presentation is well organized.
- ☐ PODCAST: The speaker uses tone and pace appropriately.
- ☐ PRESENTATION: The presenter uses eye contact and gestures appropriately.

EVIDENCE LOG

Before moving on to a new selection, go to your Evidence Log and record what you learned from Act V of *The Tragedy of Romeo and Juliet.*

STANDARDS

Reading Literature
Analyze the representation of a subject or a key scene in two different artistic mediums, including what is emphasized or absent in each treatment.

SCAN FOR MULTIMEDIA

DIGITAL PERSPECTIVES

Illuminating the Text Have students watch a video or listen to a podcast by a professional critic reviewing a film or theatrical production of *The Tragedy of Romeo and Juliet*. Then hold a class discussion to compare the ideas in the critic's review to students' presentations and podcasts. How did the production seem to compare to the L.A. Theatre Works performance the class watched? How did the students' reviews compare to the professional's review? Preview any videos or podcasts before showing them to the class.

Speaking and Listening

Before students begin, you may wish to provide them with one or two written examples of performance reviews from newspapers or magazines. Discuss the elements that appear in most reviews, including a summary of the plot, an analysis of the performance, and an evaluation of the central ideas. For more support, see **Speaking and Listening: Performance Review.**

1. **Take Notes** Encourage students to listen to the performance at least two times to ensure that they take adequate notes in preparation for their reviews.
2. **Plan Your Podcast or Presentation** Guide students to create an outline based on their notes to help plan their reviews.
3. **Record Your Podcast or Deliver Your Presentation** Remind students to speak clearly, with the appropriate tone and pace. Encourage them to practice before recording their podcasts or delivering their presentations.

Evidence Log Support students in completing their Evidence Log. This paced activity will help prepare them for the Performance-Based Assessment at the end of the unit.

FORMATIVE ASSESSMENT

Speaking and Listening

If students struggle to generate ideas for their performance reviews, **then** have small groups hold discussions about the performance and work together to brainstorm ideas. For Reteach and Practice, see **Speaking and Listening: Performance Review (RP).**

Selection Test

Administer the *The Tragedy of Romeo and Juliet,* Act V Selection Test, which is available in both print and digital formats online in Assessments.

Pyramus and Thisbe

AUDIO SUMMARIES
Audio summaries of "Pyramus and Thisbe" are available online in both English and Spanish in the Interactive Teacher's Edition or Unit Resources. Assigning these summaries prior to reading the selection may help students build additional background knowledge and set a context for their first read.

Summary

Ovid, an ancient Greek poet, wrote "Pyramus and Thisbe" and Edith Hamilton wrote this short story adaptation of the text. Pyramus and Thisbe lived next door to each other and wanted to marry. However, their parents would not allow them. The couple often met at a gap in the wall between their houses to speak to each other. One day, they decided to run away so they could be together. They set a meeting place, but Thisbe got there first and ran into a lion. She escaped the animal, but she lost her cloak while fleeing. Pyramus arrived later, saw Thisbe's torn cloak, and concluded the lion must have killed her. Overwhelmed with grief, he killed himself. Thisbe found him as he died, and killed herself as well.

Insight

This poem prefigures Romeo and Juliet. Its plot is very similar. It introduces students to the influence classical Greek and Roman writers had on later writers, including Shakespeare.

ESSENTIAL QUESTION:
Do we determine our own destinies?

Connection to Essential Question

Pyramus and Thisbe try to meet each other, but circumstances make it impossible for them to reach the happy life they had hoped for. Ultimately, they could not determine their destinies.

WHOLE-CLASS LEARNING PERFORMANCE TASK
Which has a greater impact on the characters in these texts: destiny or personal choices?

UNIT PERFORMANCE-BASED ASSESSMENT
Should the opinions of others affect our own choices or destinies?

Connection to Performance Tasks

Whole-Class Learning Performance Task Pyramus and Thisbe choose to defy their parents' wishes and run away. But they could not have foreseen the coincidences that led to their deaths. Students may argue that the characters' fates are only partly the result of choice.

Unit Performance-Based Assessment Pyramus and Thisbe defy their parents' opinions. As they consider this text and its relationship to the prompt, students may argue whether the characters were right to defy their parents' direction.

DIGITAL PERSPECTIVES: Audio | Video | Document | Annotation Highlights | EL Highlights | Online Assessment

LESSON RESOURCES

	Making Meaning	Language Development	Effective Expression
Lesson	**First Read** **Close Read** **Analyze the Text**	**Concept Vocabulary** **Word Study**	**Writing to Compare**
Instructional Standards	**RL.10** By the end of grade 9, read and comprehend literature . . .	**L.5** Demonstrate understanding of figurative language . . .	**RL.9** Analyze how an author draws on and transforms . . . **W.2** Write informative/explanatory texts . . . **W.9.a** Apply grades 9–10 Reading standards . . .
STUDENT RESOURCES			
Available online in the Interactive Student Edition or Unit Resources	Selection Audio First-Read Guide: Fiction Close-Read Guide: Fiction	Word Network	Evidence Log
TEACHER RESOURCES			
Selection Resources Available online in the Interactive Teacher's Edition or Unit Resources	Audio Summaries Annotation Highlights EL Highlights English Language Support Lesson: Archetypal Plots	Concept Vocabulary and Word Study	Writing to Compare: Analytical Essay
Reteach/Practice (RP) Available online in the Interactive Teacher's Edition or Unit Resources		Word Study: Connotation (RP)	
Assessment Available online in Assessments	Selection Test		
My Resources	A Unit 4 Answer Key is available online and in the Interactive Teacher's Edition.		

Reading Support

Text Complexity Rubric: Pyramus and Thisbe	
Quantitative Measures	
Lexile: 870 **Text Length:** 902 words	
Qualitative Measures	
Knowledge Demands ①—②—❸—④—⑤	The selection may require some historical knowledge of Babylon in ancient times; mythology.
Structure ①—②—❸—④—⑤	The selection is a prose retelling of a poem by Ovid. The story has a straightforward, linear structure.
Language Conventionality and Clarity ①—②—❸—④—⑤	The selection contains mostly short sentences, a few archaic expressions and constructions, and some figurative language.
Levels of Meaning/Purpose ①—❷—③—④—⑤	The meaning is straightforward and easy to grasp. It is a tragic love story.

DECIDE AND PLAN

English Language Support

Provide English Learners with support for Knowledge Demands and Language as they read the selection.

Knowledge Demands If students have difficulty with the setting of the story, have them first read and note events in the story and their causes. Then have them reread and take notes about the setting and how it affects events. Discuss students' notes and provide clarification.

Language Students may get confused reading passages with figurative language, for example *The more that flame is covered up, the hotter it burns.* Ask questions to guide students to understand that this is a figurative rather than literal phrase.

Strategic Support

Provide students with strategic support to ensure that they can successfully read the text.

Knowledge Demands Using the background information discuss the situation depicted in the story, asking what aspects of it sound similar to other stories students have read. Discuss the elements of archetypal stories.

Language Remind students that in the story they are about to read, they will find metaphors and similes. Discuss the difference – similes use the word *like* or *as* to compare, whereas metaphors do not. Give an example from the poem, such as *the deep red berries of the mulberry tree were white as snow,* and ask students to be on the lookout for other such similes or metaphors.

Challenge

Provide students who need to be challenged with ideas for how they can go beyond a simple interpretation of the text.

Text Analysis Ask students to discuss the symbolism of the mulberry tree. Ask them to comment on what the fruit of the mulberry, dyed red by blood, represents. How does this symbol reinforce the story's theme?

Written Response Have students read and report on another story from Ovid's *Metamorphosis*. Ask students to write a comparison and contrast essay that tells how the story is like or unlike Pyramus and Thisbe.

TEACH

Read and Respond

Have students do their first read of the selection. Then have them complete their close read. Finally, work with them on the Making Meaning and Effective Expression activities.

Standards Support Through Teaching and Learning Cycle

IDENTIFY NEEDS

Analyze results of the Beginning-of-Year Assessment, focusing on the items relating to Unit 4. Also take into consideration student performance to this point and your observations of where particular students struggle.

DECIDE AND PLAN

- If students have performed poorly on items matching these standards, then provide selection scaffolds before assigning them the on-level lesson provided in the Student Edition.
- If students have done well on the Beginning-of-Year Assessment, then challenge them to keep progressing and learning by giving them opportunities to practice the skills in depth.
- Use the Selection Resources listed on the Planning pages for "Pyramus and Thisbe" to help students continually improve their ability to master the standards.

Instructional Standards: Pyramus and Thisbe

	Catching Up	This Year	Looking Forward
Language	Review **Word Study: Connotation (RP)** with students to ensure they understand the power of a word's shade of meaning.	**L.5** Demonstrate understanding of figurative language, word relationships, and nuances in word meanings.	Challenge students to write sentences using words with varying connotations. Ask students to discuss the different meanings each sentence conveys.

ANALYZE AND REVISE

- Analyze student work for evidence of student learning.
- Identify whether students have met the expectations in the standards.
- Identify implications for future instruction.

TEACH

Implement the planned lesson, and gather evidence of student learning.

Jump Start

FIRST READ Engage students in a classroom discussion about the idea of secret love. Why might authors want to write about a love that is kept secret or hidden? Why might stories about a secret love interest readers or audiences? What is appealing about this concept? This can set the context for reading "Pyramus and Thisbe."

Pyramus and Thisbe

Who are Pyramus and Thisbe? What is their connection to each other? What is important about them? Modeling the questions readers might ask as they read "Pyramus and Thisbe" for the first time brings the text alive for students and connects it to the Whole-Class Performance Task assignment. Selection audio and print capability for the selection are available in the Interactive Teacher's Edition.

Concept Vocabulary

Support students as they rank their words. Ask if they've ever heard, read, or used them. Reassure them that the definitions for these words are listed in the selection.

FIRST READ

Students should perform the steps of the first read independently.

NOTICE: You may want to encourage students to notice details that could help them identify the theme of the story.

ANNOTATE: Remind students to mark passages that relate to the concept of destiny or fate.

CONNECT: Encourage students to go beyond the text to make connections—how have they responded when they were prevented from doing something that was important to them?

RESPOND: Students will answer questions and write a summary to demonstrate understanding.

Point out to students that while they will always complete the Respond step at the end of the first read, the other steps will probably happen somewhat concurrently. You may wish to print copies of the **First-Read Guide: Fiction** for students to use.

MAKING MEANING

THE TRAGEDY OF ROMEO AND JULIET

Comparing Texts

You will now read the short story "Pyramus and Thisbe." First, complete the first-read and close-read activities. Then, compare the way in which an archetypal, or universal, theme is presented in both the story and Shakespeare's *The Tragedy of Romeo and Juliet.*

PYRAMUS AND THISBE

About the Author

Educated in Rome, **Ovid** (43 B.C.–A.D. 17) began his career writing poems about love and became both popular and successful. For an unknown reason, he fell out of favor with the Emperor Augustus, who banished the poet from Rome. Even though Ovid spent the rest of his life in a remote fishing village, his influence only grew after his death and continues to this day.

Tool Kit
First-Read Guide and Model Annotation

STANDARDS

Reading Literature
By the end of grade 9, read and comprehend literature, including stories, dramas, and poems, in the grades 9–10 text complexity band proficiently, with scaffolding as needed at the end of the range.

Pyramus and Thisbe

Concept Vocabulary

You will encounter the following words as you read "Pyramus and Thisbe." Before reading, note how familiar you are with each word. Then, rank the words in order from most familiar (1) to least familiar (3).

WORD	YOUR RANKING
forbidden	
steal	
tryst	

After completing your first read, come back to the concept vocabulary and review your rankings. Mark changes to your original rankings as needed.

First Read FICTION

Apply these strategies as you conduct your first read. You will have an opportunity to complete the close-read notes after your first read.

NOTICE *whom* the story is about, *what* happens, *where* and *when* it happens, and *why* those involved react the way they do.

ANNOTATE by marking vocabulary and key passages you want to revisit.

CONNECT ideas within the selection to what you already know and what you have already read.

RESPOND by completing the Comprehension Check and by writing a brief summary of the selection.

First Read: NOTICE, ANNOTATE, CONNECT, RESPOND

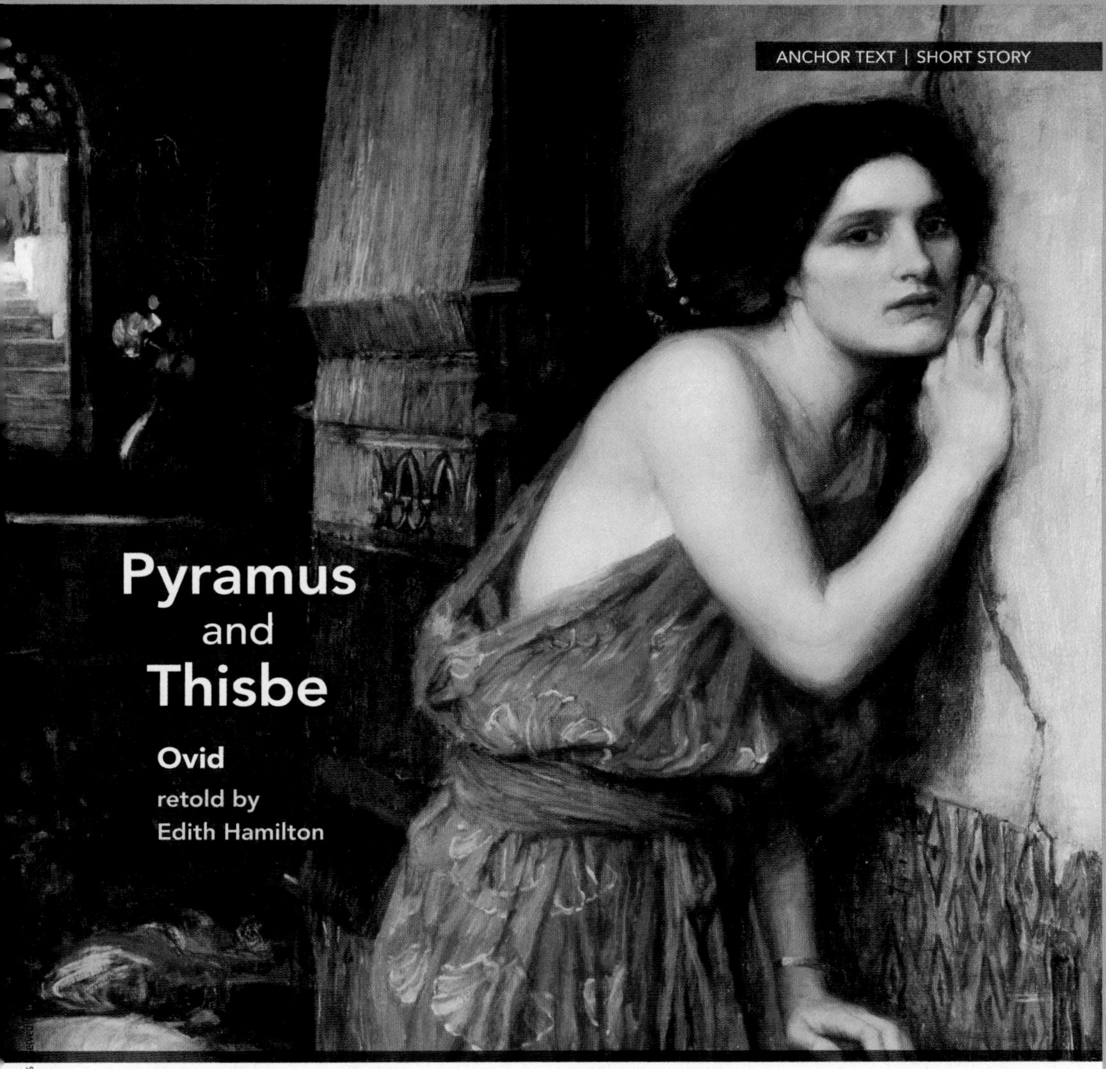

Pyramus and Thisbe

Ovid

retold by Edith Hamilton

BACKGROUND

The tale of Pyramus and Thisbe appears in Book IV of *Metamorphoses,* Ovid's greatest achievement. A poem of nearly 12,000 lines, it tells a series of stories beginning with the creation of the world and ending with the death of Julius Caesar. In each story, someone or something undergoes a transformation. The entire work reads as one long, uninterrupted tale.

SCAN FOR MULTIMEDIA

NOTES

1 Once upon a time the deep red berries of the mulberry tree were white as snow. The change in color came about strangely and sadly. The death of two young lovers was the cause.

2 Pyramus and Thisbe, he the most beautiful youth and she the loveliest maiden of all the East, lived in Babylon, the city of Queen

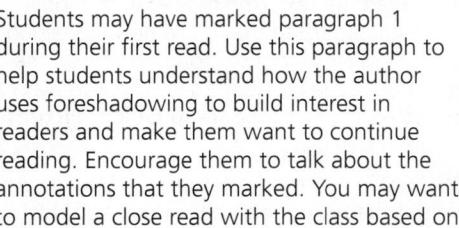

DIGITAL PERSPECTIVES

CLOSER LOOK

Identify Foreshadowing

Students may have marked paragraph 1 during their first read. Use this paragraph to help students understand how the author uses foreshadowing to build interest in readers and make them want to continue reading. Encourage them to talk about the annotations that they marked. You may want to model a close read with the class based on the highlights shown in the text.

ANNOTATE: Have students mark details in paragraph 1 that foreshadow the fate of the main characters and pique readers' interest, or have students participate while you highlight them.

QUESTION: Guide students to consider what these details might tell them. Ask what a reader can infer from the description of the mulberry tree and how it changed, and accept student responses.

Possible response: The author describes a tree with berries that have changed from white to deep red. He states this change was the result of the death of two young lovers. The color deep red could be used to describe blood, suggesting that the characters met a bloody fate.

CONCLUDE: Help students to formulate conclusions about the importance of these details in the text. Ask students why the author might have included these details.

Possible response: The author implies that the young lovers met a tragic fate. He uses this foreshadowing to make readers want to learn how the young lovers died and why the mulberry tree changed.

Remind students that **foreshadowing** is the use of clues to hint at events that will occur later in the plot of a narrative. This technique helps create suspense.

VOCABULARY DEVELOPMENT

Concept Vocabulary Reinforcement To increase familiarity with the concept vocabulary, ask students to use each of the words in a sentence as they encounter them in the text. Encourage students to include context clues in their own sentences to demonstrate their knowledge of the word. If students struggle to create sentences, have them use a thesaurus to identify a synonym that could be used in place of the term. Then using the synonym and the context in the story, have them write a definition for the concept vocabulary word and use it in a sentence.

CLOSE READ

Remind students to focus on spoken dialogue as they read the text. You may wish to model the Close Read using the following think-aloud format. Possible responses to questions on the Student page are included. You may also want to print copies of the **Close-Read Guide: Fiction** for students to use.

ANNOTATE: As I read paragraph 3, I notice and highlight the dialogue that Pyramus and Thisbe speak aloud.

QUESTION: I think the author chooses to let the characters speak for themselves at this point in the story to help readers understand how they talk to each other through the wall.

CONCLUDE: I know that the dialogue helps readers understand that the wall was both an obstacle and a form of communication for Pyramus and Thisbe. Although it kept them apart, it also allowed them to communicate and kept their love alive.

NOTES

forbidden (fuhr BIHD uhn) *adj.* prevented or prohibited

CLOSE READ

ANNOTATE: In paragraph 3, mark the spoken dialogue.

QUESTION: Why does the author choose to let the characters speak for themselves at this point?

CONCLUDE: What is the effect of hearing these lines from Pyramus and Thisbe directly?

steal (steel) *v.* move in a way that is secret or quiet

Semiramis, in houses so close together that one wall was common to both. Growing up thus side by side they learned to love each other. They longed to marry, but their parents forbade. Love, however, cannot be **forbidden**. The more that flame is covered up, the hotter it burns. Also love can always find a way. It was impossible that these two whose hearts were on fire should be kept apart.

3 In the wall both houses shared there was a little chink. No one before had noticed it, but there is nothing a lover does not notice. Our two young people discovered it and through it they were able to whisper sweetly back and forth. Thisbe on one side, Pyramus on the other. The hateful wall that separated them had become their means of reaching each other. "But for you we could touch, kiss," they would say. "But at least you let us speak together. You give a passage for loving words to reach loving ears. We are not ungrateful." So they would talk, and as night came on and they must part, each would press on the wall kisses that could not go through to the lips on the other side.

4 Every morning when the dawn had put out the stars, and the sun's rays had dried the hoarfrost on the grass, they would **steal** to the crack and, standing there, now utter words of burning love and now lament their hard fate, but always in softest whispers. Finally a day came when they could endure no longer. They decided that that very night they would try to slip away and steal out through the city into the open country where at last they could be together in freedom. They agreed to meet at a well-known place, the Tomb of Ninus, under a tree there, a tall mulberry full of snow-white berries, near which a cool spring bubbled up. The plan pleased them and it seemed to them the day would never end.

5 At last the sun sank into the sea and night arose. In the darkness Thisbe crept out and made her way in all secrecy to the tomb. Pyramus had not come; still she waited for him, her love making her bold. But of a sudden she saw by the light of the moon a lioness. The fierce beast had made a kill; her jaws were bloody and she was coming to slake her thirst in the spring. She was still far enough away for Thisbe to escape, but as she fled she dropped her cloak. The lioness came upon it on her way back to her lair and she mouthed it and tore it before disappearing into the woods. That is what Pyramus saw when he appeared a few minutes later. Before him lay the bloodstained shreds of the cloak and clear in the dust were the tracks of the lioness. The conclusion was inevitable. He never doubted that he knew all. Thisbe was dead. He had let his love, a tender maiden,

come alone to a place full of danger, and not been there first to protect her. "It is I who killed you," he said. He lifted up from the trampled dust what was left of the cloak and kissing it again and again carried it to the mulberry tree. "Now," he said, "you shall drink my blood too." He drew his sword and plunged it into his side. The blood spurted up over the berries and dyed them a dark red.

6 Thisbe, although terrified of the lioness, was still more afraid to fail her lover. She ventured to go back to the tree of the **tryst**, the mulberry with the shining white fruit. She could not find it. A tree was there, but not one gleam of white was on the branches. As she stared at it, something moved on the ground beneath. She started back shuddering. But in a moment, peering through the shadows, she saw what was there. It was Pyramus, bathed in blood and dying. She flew to him and threw her arms around him. She kissed his cold lips and begged him to look at her, to speak to her. "It is I, your Thisbe, your dearest," she cried to him. At the sound of her name he opened his heavy eyes for one look. Then death closed them.

7 She saw his sword fallen from his hand and beside it her cloak stained and torn. She understood all. "Your own hand killed you," she said, "and your love for me. I too can be brave. I too can love. Only death would have had the power to separate us. It shall not have that power now." She plunged into her heart the sword that was still wet with his life's blood.

8 The gods were pitiful at the end, and the lovers' parents too. The deep red fruit of the mulberry is the everlasting memorial of these true lovers, and one urn holds the ashes of the two whom not even death could part. ❧

NOTES

tryst (trihst) *n.* secret romantic meeting

Additional **English Language Support** is available in the Interactive Teacher's Edition.

PERSONALIZE FOR LEARNING

Strategic Support

Theme Review paragraph 8 with students. Students may require support to identify the theme of the story because it is implied rather than explicitly stated. Remind students that the theme is not the plot of the story, but rather the "big idea" that the author wants to convey to readers.

Have students create T-charts. One side should be used to state the theme. The other side should be used to record details from the text that they used to identify the theme. If students continue to require support, have them identify important details from the story, and ask them to think about how these details relate to one another.

TEACHING

Comprehension Check

Possible responses:

1. Pyramus's and Thisbe's parents forbid them from seeing one another and getting married.
2. Pyramus and Thisbe are able to communicate through a hole in the wall that separates their two houses. They are the only ones who know about this hole, and as result they are able to talk to each other undiscovered by their parents.
3. Thisbe is at the tomb to meet Pyramus. They had planned to run away together.
4. Responses will vary, but should include the main events from the story's plot. Pyramus and Thisbe are young lovers who have been kept apart by their parents. They communicate in secret through a hole in the wall that separates their houses. They decide to run away together and plan to meet at a tomb. Thisbe arrives first, but runs and hides when she sees a lion approach. The lion rips a cloak that the young woman leaves behind. Pyramus arrives at the tomb and finds the torn cloak and the lion's tracks. Believing Thisbe has been killed, he stabs himself with a sword. Thisbe returns to find her dying lover. She kills herself to be with him in death.

Research

Research to Clarify If students struggle to come up with an unfamiliar detail, suggest that they learn more about Queen Semiramis and the tomb of Ninus. Have them reread the story to notice an idea or concept that might be new to them.

Research to Explore If students have difficulty identifying other stories that have been inspired by "Pyramus and Thisbe," suggest they read one of the following: "The House of the Dead Hand" by Edith Wharton, "Pyramus and Thisbe" from Alexandre Dumas' *The Count of Monte Cristo*, "Thisbe" from *On Famous Women* by Giovanni.

Comprehension Check

Complete the following items after you finish your first read.

1. Who is keeping Pyramus and Thisbe from seeing one another?

2. How are Pyramus and Thisbe able to communicate?

3. Why is Thisbe at the tomb where she meets the lion?

4. **Notebook** Confirm your understanding of the text by writing a summary.

RESEARCH

Research to Clarify Choose at least one unfamiliar detail from the text. Briefly research that detail. In what way does the information you learned shed light on an aspect of the story?

Research to Explore This story may spark your curiosity to read more. Briefly research other stories or plays that may have been inspired by the story of Pyramus and Thisbe. You may want to share what you discover with the class.

PERSONALIZE FOR LEARNING

Challenge

Research Have students research the life of Ovid. Ask them to write a brief biography of the man and a description of his work. Have them consider the following questions. What were some common themes in his poetry? How did his work inspire later authors? Have students read some of his other works and, if possible, read aloud or play a recording of another excerpt from *Metamorphoses* to the class.

Close Read the Text

Close Read — ANNOTATE · QUESTION · CONCLUDE

Reread paragraph 5 of "Pyramus and Thisbe." Mark words and phrases that describe what Pyramus does after finding Thisbe's bloody cloak. How do these details contribute to the mood of the scene?

Analyze the Text

CITE TEXTUAL EVIDENCE to support your answers.

Notebook Respond to these questions.

1. (a) **Interpret** What does "The more that flame is covered up, the hotter it burns" mean? (b) **Analyze** What effect does the author create by comparing love to a fire?
2. (a) Identify at least three events after Thisbe reaches the Ninus' tomb that together cause the tragedy. (b) **Evaluate** Does it make sense for Pyramus to come to the conclusion that Thisbe is dead? Explain.
3. (a) What happens to the mulberries in the tree by the tomb? (b) **Analyze** How does the story explain the color of mulberries today?
4. **Essential Question** *Do we determine our own destinies?* What have you learned about destiny from reading this story?

LANGUAGE DEVELOPMENT

Concept Vocabulary

forbidden	steal	tryst

Why These Words? These concept vocabulary words connote, or are associated with, encounters with risk and secrecy. How does each word contribute to meaning in the text? What other words in the selection connect to this concept?

Practice

Notebook Confirm your understanding of these words by using each one in a sentence.

Word Study

Notebook **Multiple-Meaning Words** Many English words have multiple meanings, or more than one distinct definition. For example, the word *steal* has several different meanings. In paragraph 4 of "Pyramus and Thisbe," it means "to move quietly." However, it can also mean "to take illegally." Find two other multiple-meaning words in the short story. Record the words, and list two definitions for each.

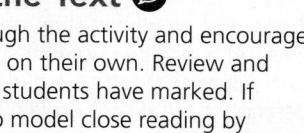

PYRAMUS AND THISBE

Tool Kit
Close-Read Guide and Model Annotation

WORD NETWORK
Add interesting words related to destiny from the text to your Word Network.

STANDARDS
Language
Demonstrate understanding of figurative language, word relationships, and nuances in word meanings.

DIGITAL PERSPECTIVES

Jump Start

CLOSE READ Have students discuss suspenseful stories. Guide them to consider what makes them fun to read or watch. Ask students what aspects of "Pyramus and Thisbe" are suspenseful.

Close Read the Text

Walk students through the activity and encourage them to complete it on their own. Review and discuss the sections students have marked. If needed, continue to model close reading by using the Annotation Highlights in the Interactive Teacher's Edition.

Analyze the Text

Possible Responses:

1. (a) "The more that flame is covered up, the hotter it burns" means that the more Pyramus and Thisbe were forbidden from loving each other, the stronger their feelings became. **DOK 2** (b) Comparing love to a fire suggests that it is a powerful force of nature. **DOK 3**
2. (a) Thisbe sees a lion; she drops her cloak; the lion rips the cloak; Pyramus thinks Thisbe has been killed when he finds the cloak. **DOK 1** (b) Yes, the torn, bloody cloak and the paw prints suggest that an animal has attacked her. **DOK 2**
3. (a) The mulberries in the tree by the tomb turn from snow white to deep red after they become soaked in Pyramus's blood when he stabs himself. **DOK 1** (b) According to the story, the mulberries remain red today to honor the memories of Pyramus and Thisbe. **DOK 2**
4. Responses will vary.

Concept Vocabulary

Why These Words?

Possible Responses:

Forbidden, steal, and *tryst* all suggest that they faced extreme circumstances.

Lament, secrecy, and *inevitable* are words that connect to this concept.

Word Network

Possible words: *impossible, fate, inevitable, everlasting, memorial*

FORMATIVE ASSESSMENT

Concept Vocabulary

If students fail to see the connection between the words, **then** have them use each word in a sentence and identify similarities in the sentences.

Word Study

If students fail to identify more than one meaning of a word, **then** have them consult a dictionary to locate additional definitions.

- If students fail to cite evidence, remind them to support their ideas with specific evidence.

For Reteach and Practice, see **Word Study: Connotation.**

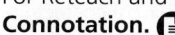

Writing to Compare

Assignment

Explain to students that when they write an analytical essay, they must analyze the major themes of a text. An analysis breaks down the text to explain the big ideas the author presents. It should explain how the author uses the characters, plot, and setting to convey these ideas to readers.

One way a writer can strengthen an analytical essay is to provide quotations from the text. Guide students to include dialogue or descriptions that help explain the theme and the author's intentions. Remind students to use citations to identify the line and page numbers for each quotation. For more support, see **Writing to Compare: Analytical Essay.**

Prewriting

Analyze the Texts

As students analyze the presentation of similar archetypal themes in these two texts, have them think about how each author's background, culture, and purpose for writing are reflected in the theme. Have students review their charts as they prepare to write their analytical essays.

EFFECTIVE EXPRESSION

THE TRAGEDY OF ROMEO AND JULIET

PYRAMUS AND THISBE

STANDARDS

Reading Literature
Analyze how an author draws on and transforms source material in a specific work.

Writing
- Write informative/explanatory texts to examine and convey complex ideas, concepts, and information clearly and accurately through the effective selection, organization, and analysis of content.
- Apply *grades 9–10 Reading standards* to literature.

Writing to Compare

The play and short story you have read in this section center on similar types of characters and plots. In fact, Ovid's story is a foundational source for *The Tragedy of Romeo and Juliet*. Now, deepen your understanding of the texts by comparing and writing about them.

Assignment

An **archetype** is a plot, character, image, symbol, pattern, or setting that appears in literature from all cultures and time periods. The **theme** of a literary work is its central idea, message, or insight about life.

- **Archetypal themes** are ideas about life that are expressed across cultures and time periods. Ill-fated love is one archetypal theme.
- An archetypal theme may also be referred to as a **universal theme**.

Write an **analytical essay** in which you examine the presentation of the archetypal theme of ill-fated love in Shakespeare's *The Tragedy of Romeo and Juliet* and Ovid's "Pyramus and Thisbe." Explain which elements of Ovid's story are used and transformed in Shakespeare's tragic drama.

Prewriting

Analyze the Texts Works of literature can differ for a variety of reasons in their presentations of the same archetypal theme. The values of the work's era, the author's purpose, and the author's culture and language may affect how a writer presents a universal theme. Use the chart to identify similarities and differences between Ovid's "Pyramus and Thisbe" and Shakespeare's *The Tragedy of Romeo and Juliet.*

	SIMILARITIES	DIFFERENCES
Characters		
Settings		
Obstacles Characters Face		
Story Events		

Notebook Respond to these questions.

1. How does the transformation of the mulberry tree at the end of Ovid's tale reflect Roman culture and religion?
2. What kind of memorial, if any, exists for Romeo and Juliet at the end of Shakespeare's play?

PERSONALIZE FOR LEARNING

English Language Support

Using Archetypal Plots Have pairs of students collaborate to choose one of the archetypal plots and write a few sentences describing a character who might be involved in that plot. **EMERGING**

Have students choose one of the archetypal plots and write a paragraph describing a character who might be involved in that plot. **EXPANDING**

Have students choose one of the archetypal plots and write an outline for a story that follows that pattern. Remind students to address main characters, conflict, and resolution in their outline. **BRIDGING**

An expanded **English Language Support Lesson** on Archetypal Plots is available in the Interactive Teacher's Edition.

Drafting

Write a statement of purpose. Determine the specific purpose, or goal, of your essay. Then, write a statement of purpose that you can use in your introduction. Include both the authors' names and titles in your statement. Complete this sentence to get started:

Statement of Purpose: In this essay, I will analyze ________________ and show how ____.

Organize your ideas. In this essay, you need to identify similarities and differences between two works. You also need to consider how Shakespeare drew on elements of Ovid's story to write his play. Decide whether you wish to focus more on the similarities or the differences between the two works. Then, focus your essay by emphasizing the elements you feel matter the most.

Identify passages to use as evidence. Use your Prewriting notes to identify specific passages from the play and the story to use in your essay.

Example Passage: ________________________
Point it will Support:

Example Passage: ________________________
Point it will Support:

Example Passage: ________________________
Point it will Support:

Example Passage: ________________________
Point it will Support:

Provide other supporting details. In addition to example passages, you may include other types of evidence:

- **Summaries,** or brief retellings of the events of a text, can give readers necessary background information. However, make sure not to confuse a summary with deeper analysis and explanation of your ideas.
- **Paraphrases,** or restatements of a text in your own words, can help you clarify someone else's ideas. In this essay, you may want to use paraphrases that interpret Shakespearean language.

Review, Revise and Edit

Once you are done drafting, reread your essay. Make sure your have supported your ideas with clear reasons and evidence. Review each paragraph, marking the main idea. Then, mark sentences that support that idea. If there are sentences that do not support or develop the main idea, consider deleting or rewriting them.

EVIDENCE LOG

Before moving on to a new selection, go to your Evidence Log and record what you have learned from *The Tragedy of Romeo and Juliet* and "Pyramus and Thisbe."

DIGITAL PERSPECTIVES

Drafting

Write a statement of purpose.
Students should think about the goal of their essay before writing a statement of purpose. Remind them that their statement of purpose will be used in the introduction to their essay.

Organize your ideas. Remind students to think about what they want to focus on in their essay and what ideas best support their statement of purpose. They might want to focus on specific similarities or differences between the two texts in order to point out comparisons and contrasts.

Identify passages to use as evidence.
Students will want to note any passages that help illustrate the archetypal theme of ill-fated love. Have them use the notes they took in Prewriting to point out example passages that contain supporting evidence.

Provide other supporting details.
Help students by reminding them to use examples of dialogue, or have them paraphrase the dialogue if it helps with clarifying their ideas. They might also want to include retellings of certain portions of the text.

Review, Revise and Edit

You may want students to work in pairs to review their essays.

Evidence Log Support students in completing their Evidence Logs. This paced activity will help prepare them for the Performance-Based Assessment at the end of the unit.

FORMATIVE ASSESSMENT

Writing to Compare

- **If** students fail to identify an archetypal theme, **then** have them list two or three subjects addressed in the story, such as love or destiny, and name one thing they learned about each from reading "Pyramus and Thisbe."

PERSONALIZE FOR LEARNING

Strategic Support

Finding Evidence If students have difficulty finding evidence from the play and the story to include in their essays, have them work with a partner to discuss the most exciting or interesting moments from each tale. Have them list each of these moments. Then have them write the thesis statement for their essays at the top of the list and place a check mark beside any moments they have noted that help support the thesis.

Jump Start

Have students think about the role that destiny and personal choice plays in their lives. Discuss the decisions they've made, the circumstances into which they were born, and the amount of free will people can have before they go out on their own.

As the discussion progresses, ask them to share specific examples from their lives.

Write an Argument

Have students think about the role of destiny and personal choice in the pieces they read. Students might find that there's a compelling case to be made on both sides of the argument; instruct them to choose the side that resonates more strongly with them.

Students should complete the assignment using word processing software to take advantage of editing tools and features.

Elements of Literary Criticism

Explain to students that literary criticism is a type of argument and that a strong piece of literary criticism incorporates the same elements as a strong argument (e.g., the use of good examples, proper word choice, and appropriate tone).

MAKE IT INTERACTIVE

Project *"Romeo and Juliet:* A Tragedy? Or Just a Tragic Misunderstanding?" and have students identify the elements of literary criticism. To get the discussion started, you might want to point out this example of appropriate tone from paragraph 3: "The sheer lack of care with which they pursue their romance is startling."

Academic Vocabulary

Ask students how the word *compelling* relates to argumentative writing.

WRITING TO SOURCES

- THE TRAGEDY OF ROMEO AND JULIET
- PYRAMUS AND THISBE

Write an Argument

You've read a play and a short story that deal with tragic love. In *The Tragedy of Romeo and Juliet*, two lovers attempt to marry despite a long-standing feud between their families. In "Pyramus and Thisbe," one of the inspirations for *The Tragedy of Romeo and Juliet*, two lovers attempt to cross boundaries in order to be together.

Assignment

Use your knowledge of *The Tragedy of Romeo and Juliet* and "Pyramus and Thisbe" to choose and defend a position on the topic of destiny. Based on those two texts, write an argument in the form of **literary criticism** in response to this question:

> Which has a greater impact on the characters in these texts: destiny or personal choices?

Tool Kit
Student Model of an Argument

ACADEMIC VOCABULARY

As you craft your argument, consider using some of the academic vocabulary you learned in the beginning of this unit.

endure
pathos
compelling
propose
recurrent

Elements of Literary Criticism

One form of argumentative writing is literary criticism.

Literary criticism explores the meaning and techniques of literary works. Like other forms of argument, literary criticism requires the development of a logical line of reasoning and the support of ideas with precise, relevant text evidence.

Effective literary criticism contains these elements:

- an analysis of the work, including its content, organization, and style
- a thesis statement, or precise claim, that expresses your interpretation of the work
- inclusion of a counterclaim, or alternate interpretation, and a discussion of why it is less accurate or less well-supported than your claim(s)
- textual evidence that supports your interpretation
- a logical organization, including a conclusion that follows from and validates your claim
- a formal style and objective tone appropriate for the purpose and audience
- error-free grammar, including standard conventions for the inclusion of quotations

LAUNCH TEXT

Model Literary Criticism For a model of a well-crafted literary criticism, see the Launch Text, *"Romeo and Juliet*: A Tragedy? Or Just a Tragic Misunderstanding?"

Challenge yourself to find all of the elements of an effective literary criticism in the text. You will have an opportunity to review these elements as you prepare to write your own literary criticism.

STANDARDS

Writing

- Write arguments to support claims in an analysis of substantive topics or texts, using valid reasoning and relevant and sufficient evidence.
- Write routinely over extended time frames and shorter time frames for a range of tasks, purposes, and audiences.

AUTHOR'S PERSPECTIVE **Kelly Gallagher, M.Ed.**

Purposeful Editing Many students resist editing because they don't see its value. Explain that **editing**, the process of making things correct, adds power to writing. Teachers can model the process by using the Sentence of the Week (SoW) strategy. Before students enter the classroom each Monday, write three sentences with the same structural, grammatical, or style feature on the board. For example:

1. John, 14, is too young to drive.
2. My girlfriend, who is afraid of snakes, refuses to go to the zoo.
3. The player, exhausted from the long game, collapsed.

Students copy the sentences. Below the sentences, write "What do I notice?" Students might write:

- All the sentences have interruptions.
- All have two commas.
- A comma goes before and after the interruption.
- If you take out the comma, the sentences still make sense.

This activity helps students generate the grammar rules organically and understand the importance of purposeful editing.

Prewriting / Planning

Write a Working Thesis Now that you have read and thought about the selections, write a sentence in which you state your "working" **thesis,** an initial position on the question posed in this assignment. As you continue to write, you may revise your thesis or even change it entirely.

Thesis: ____

____.

Consider Possible Counterclaims Remember that part of your task is to address **counterclaims,** or opposing positions. Complete these sentences to address a counterclaim. Think about reasons and evidence you can use to defend your position.

Another possible interpretation is ______________________________.

However, the majority of the text evidence points to ______________________.

Writing for a Purpose All literary criticism shares similar goals:

- **making connections** within or between works, or between a work of literature and its historical and cultural context
- **making distinctions** or showing differences between elements of a single work or aspects of two or more works
- **achieving insights** that were not apparent from a superficial reading

Gather Evidence These types of evidence you can use in your literary criticism:

- **details from the text:** important ideas from the text that you can describe in your own words
- **quotations from the text:** the exact words of the text, when they are especially relevant or powerful

In the Launch Text, the writer uses both types of evidence as support. For example, the writer uses a quotation from Juliet to demonstrate her awareness of her of own impulsiveness:

> *Even though their families would never accept their union, they are more than willing to throw away everything to be together—having known each other for barely an evening. Indeed, Juliet says as much of their love:*
>
> *It is too rash, too unadvised, too sudden;*
> *Too like the lightning, which doth cease to be*
> *Ere one can say "It lightens."*

Connect Across Texts As you write, use evidence from both texts to develop your claims. Support your ideas with exact quotations from the texts, paraphrases of the texts, or evidence from secondary sources. Consult a style manual to confirm how to incorporate quotations, paraphrases, or outside evidence into your essay correctly.

EVIDENCE LOG

Review your Evidence Log and identify key details you may want to cite in your literary criticism.

STANDARDS

Writing

- Introduce precise claim(s), distinguish the claim(s) from alternate or opposing claims, and create an organization that establishes clear relationships among claim(s), counterclaims, reasons, and evidence.
- Develop claim(s) and counterclaims fairly, supplying evidence for each while pointing out the strengths and limitations of both in a manner that anticipates the audience's knowledge level and concerns.

Language

Write and edit work so that it conforms to the guidelines in a style manual appropriate for the discipline and writing type.

DIGITAL PERSPECTIVES

Prewriting/Planning

Write a Working Thesis Explain to students that the thesis is the building block of a piece of argumentative writing, noting that it's called a "working" thesis because it gives the writer something to work with.

Consider Possible Counterclaims Instruct students to include possible counterclaims in their essay, letting them know that it will strengthen their argument. An astute reader will read with a critical eye, considering counterclaims on their own. Explain that a writer who addresses counterclaims will have more credibility with such a reader.

Writing for a Purpose Encourage students to put a significant amount of thought into their essay, as it will help them gain a greater insight into *The Tragedy of Romeo and Juliet* and "Pyramus and Thisbe." Remind them that writing a well-considered piece of literary criticism will help them to think about the texts in ways they otherwise might not have. Readers of their piece will also gain new insight.

PERSONALIZE FOR LEARNING

Strategic Support

Analyzing Themes Have groups of students analyze the first half of *The Tragedy of Romeo and Juliet,* while other groups analyze the second half. Explain that they're looking for anything that relates to the question of destiny and personal choice and ask groups which plays a greater role in the half they analyzed. Instruct students to agree on one sentence that sums up their analysis. When the groups are finished, invite them to share their analysis.

Drafting

Choose an Effective Organization Point out to students that one reason "*Romeo and Juliet: A Tragedy? Or Just a Tragic Misunderstanding?*" is such an effective piece of literary criticism is because of its clear and compelling organization. Explain how the piece methodically builds toward a crescendo, like a steady drumbeat that gets louder over time. By the end of the text, the author has made an extremely convincing case because the piece expertly organizes the elements of an argument (reasons and evidence, claims, and counterclaims).

Write a First Draft Remind students that their graphic organizer is merely meant to be a guide and that they can deviate from it as they're writing. Students can use the graphic organizer as a tool to support their ideas and to make sure they are including all of the required elements of their argument.

PERFORMANCE TASK: WRITING FOCUS

Drafting

Choose an Effective Organization The organization of an essay is the order in which information is assembled. Organization is especially important in an argumentative essay. A solid organizational structure can help you to unfold a clear analysis and keep your reader on track.

Each section of your literary criticism should connect directly to your main claim and contain sufficient text evidence to support it. Reread the first paragraph of the Launch Text and identify the author's thesis, or claim. Then, read paragraphs 2 and 3. Notice how the writer organizes thoughts and supporting evidence. The writer describes the action of the play, uses, a direct quotation to clarify, and follows the quotation with the the connected argument.

Next, revisit paragraphs 6 and 7 and the different organizational style the author uses. In this section, the author presents an opinion first, followed by quotations to support the argument.

STANDARDS

Reading Literature
Cite strong and thorough textual evidence to support analysis of what the text says explicitly as well as inferences drawn from the text.

Writing
Develop claim(s) and counterclaims fairly, supplying evidence for each while pointing out the strengths and limitations of both in a manner that anticipates the audience's knowledge level and concerns.

Organize Your Argument

Before you draft your essay, use this graphic organizer to identify the points you would like to make, and then find support from the text. Each of your points should be a reason that clearly supports your thesis. Do not include any points that you cannot support with multiple pieces of evidence from each text. Likewise, select evidence from the texts that you can use to address a possible counterclaim in a persuasive way that your audience will understand.

	SUPPORT FROM THE TEXTS
Reason 1	
Counterclaim	
Response to counterclaim	
Reason 2	
Reason 3	

Write a First Draft Use your graphic organizer to write your first draft. Be sure to address the assignment completely by proposing and supporting a clear claim regarding the two texts. Make connections and draw distinctions between the texts. Share the insights you have achieved by reading the texts closely and in relation to each other.

AUTHOR'S PERSPECTIVE **Jim Cummins, Ph.D.**

Transfer of First Language English learners' home languages are valuable cognitive tools that can be tapped to help them improve the quality of their first drafts. Having students write in their home language often produces higher quality writing than when students write only in English because it helps them capture, express, and organize their ideas. Translation software can be useful as a starting point to help students move from their home language draft to an English draft. Obviously, the machine-translated draft will require editing but this can be done collaboratively with help from the teacher and/or the students' classmates. After students have produced their initial drafts in English, teachers can work with them on the revision process, focusing on such key areas as organization, paragraph formation, and coherence. As students revise with teacher input, teachers should encourage them to pay special attention to cognates and genre rules.

LANGUAGE DEVELOPMENT: CONVENTIONS

Supporting Argument: Using Quotations

Text-based analysis and evaluation, such as literary criticism, requires a lot of evidence from sources. **Direct quotations** are passages taken word for word from a work of literature. **Indirect quotations** are paraphrases, or restatements of the ideas in a text. You will use both in your writing.

Setting and Punctuating Direct Quotations All direct quotations in the running text must be enclosed in quotation marks. A comma usually precedes a direct quotation, but sometimes a colon precedes it. Make sure that periods and commas are included inside closing quotation marks. Question marks and exclamation points should be included inside the closing quotation marks only if they are part of the quotation.

Read It

Short Direct Quotations When including a direct quotation that will take up fewer than three lines of your essay, surround it with quotation marks.

When Romeo hears of Juliet's "death," he cries out against fate: "Then, I defy you, stars!"

Block Indentation Use block indentation whenever a direct quotation is four or more lines long, or when you are quoting multiple lines of dialogue from a drama. Introduce such a quotation with a colon, and do not use quotation marks.

Romeo suggests as much before he goes to the party where he first meets Juliet:

I fear, too early: for my mind misgives
Some consequence yet hanging in the stars

Indirect Quotations Use an indirect quotation, or paraphrase, when a restatement of dialogue or events will suffice. Because indirect quotations are paraphrases of the text, you should not put them in quotation marks.

Juliet is shocked when she hears of Romeo's exile.

Write It

Revisit *The Tragedy of Romeo and Juliet* and "Pyramus and Thisbe," and mark passages you would like to include in your essay. Use this chart to record how you will incorporate the evidence into your writing.

SOURCE TEXT TITLE	PARAGRAPH OR LINE NUMBER	TYPE OF QUOTE: RUNNING, BLOCK, OR INDIRECT

STANDARDS

Writing
- Develop claim(s) and counterclaims fairly, supplying evidence for each while pointing out the strengths and limitations of both in a manner that anticipates the audience's knowledge level and concerns.
- Use words, phrases and clauses to link the major sections of the text, create cohesion, and clarify the relationships between claim(s) and reasons, between reasons and evidence, and between claim(s) and counterclaims.

Language
Use a colon to introduce a list or quotation.

DIGITAL PERSPECTIVES

Supporting Argument: Using Quotations

Read It Explain that using quotations is an effective way to illustrate a point. You might want to cite other examples of writing that use quotations, such as journalistic writing, in which an expert will often be quoted. Advise students to avoid using too many direct quotations and to strategically use paraphrasing when direct quotations are too long. Note that using both direct and indirect quotations is another way to add variety to writing.

Write It Instruct students to use a combination of running, block, and indirect quotes as they fill out their charts. Point out that when they begin to write, they might choose to take a different approach, especially if they find that too many direct quotes appear in a row, or if they determine that it would make more sense to paraphrase a quote.

PERSONALIZE FOR LEARNING

English Language Support

Paraphrasing Quotations English learners might require additional support when paraphrasing quotations. Instruct them to write down several lines of dialogue from *The Tragedy of Romeo and Juliet* and then to "translate" it from the Early Modern English it was written in, using this chart as a guide. Then have them summarize their translation. **ALL LEVELS**

Early Modern English	Modern English
Thee, Thou, Thy, and Thine	You, Your
Art	Are
Wherefore	Why
Would	Wish
Aye	Yes

Revising

Evaluating Your Draft

Before students begin revising their writing, they should take some time to review their draft. Remind them that is an opportunity to take a close look at what they've written so that they can determine which areas could be improved. They should make sure that their draft is organized in a logical manner and contains all of the required elements.

Check for Understanding To help students avoid misinterpreting the meaning of the quotations they're using in their essay, you might want to have them first paraphrase the quotations, even if they are planning to use a direct quote. Explain that this will increase the likelihood they fully understand the meaning of the quote.

Revise to Eliminate Unnecessary Information Explain to students that including unnecessary information is a common mistake that even experienced writers make. Let them know that the revision process is an opportunity to tighten an argument, which helps make it stronger.

PERFORMANCE TASK: WRITING FOCUS

Revising

Evaluating Your Draft

Use the checklist to evaluate the effectiveness of your first draft. Then, use your evaluation and the instruction on this page to guide your revision.

FOCUS AND ORGANIZATION	EVIDENCE AND ELABORATION	CONVENTIONS
☐ Introduces a thesis consisting of a claim about the texts.	☐ Develops the thesis fully by analyzing, comparing, contrasting, and offering insights about multiple texts.	☐ Attends to the norms and conventions of the discipline, especially the correct use and punctuation of quotations.
☐ Distinguishes the thesis from opposing claims.	☐ Provides adequate quotations and paraphrases for each major idea.	☐ Establishes and maintains a formal style and an objective tone.
☐ Provides a conclusion that follows from the introduction and argument presented.	☐ Uses vocabulary and word choice that are appropriate for the audience and purpose.	
☐ Establishes a logical organization and situates evidence appropriately to support the thesis and reasons.		
☐ Uses words, phrases, and clauses to clarify the relationships between and among ideas.		

WORD NETWORK

Include interesting words from your Word Network in your literary criticism.

Revising for Focus and Organization

Checking for Understanding Revising is an excellent time to clarify your arguments and support with your audience in mind. If your audience is not knowledgeable about your topic, you may have to revise to define unfamiliar terms for your readers. If your audience is more sophisticated, you can go straight to making sure you carefully outline the strengths and limitation of claims and counterclaims. For example, you might point out where there is not enough evidence to support a specific counterclaim.

Revising for Evidence and Elaboration

Style Literary criticism is written in a formal style even though you are sharing your own original interpretations of the selections. Review your draft. Delete phrases such as "I believe that" and "My interpretation is." Replace them with straightforward claims and explanations, such as "The quote shows . . ."

Revise to Eliminate Unnecessary Information Reread your draft, looking for any words or phrases that are either imprecise or unnecessary. Here are some steps to help you revise ideas and better support your thesis:

- Underline your thesis or claim and the main idea of each paragraph.
- Highlight sentences that do not support your thesis.
- Consider adding or revising details to make a tighter connection to your main idea.
- Eliminate any details that do not clearly contribute to your analysis.

STANDARDS

Writing

- Establish and maintain a formal style and objective tone while attending to the norms and conventions of the discipline in which they are writing.
- Provide a concluding statement or section that follows from and supports the argument presented.

HOW LANGUAGE WORKS

Using Quotations The rules of punctuation for quotations can be difficult to grasp, since the reasoning is often not intuitive. Help students understand when to use a comma or colon to introduce a quote by explaining that a comma is used with singular verbs (e.g., said, questioned, exclaimed); a colon is used before a block quotation and when a statement introduces a quote (e.g, Romeo was happy: "I'll go along, no such sight to be shown, But to rejoice in splendor of mine own."). Instruct students to practice this skill by quoting different parts of *The Tragedy of Romeo and Juliet.*

PEER REVIEW

Exchange papers with a classmate. Use the checklist to evaluate your classmate's literary criticism and provide supportive feedback.

1. Is the thesis clear? Is it obvious what reasons support the thesis?
   ☐ yes ☐ no If no, explain what confused you.
2. Is the thesis supported by evidence from both texts?
   ☐ yes ☐ no If no, point out what needs additional support.
3. Did the literary criticism present the writer's own analysis and insight?
   ☐ yes ☐ no If no, write a brief note explaining what you thought was missing.
4. What is the strongest part of your classmate's paper? Why?

____

____

____

____

Editing and Proofreading

Edit for Conventions Reread your draft for accuracy and consistency. Correct errors in grammar and word usage. When using a direct quotation, make sure that a comma or colon is used to introduce the quotation and that periods and commas are included within the quotation marks.

Proofread for Accuracy Read your draft carefully, looking for errors in spelling and punctuation. Specifically, check the spelling of words in direct quotations. Because *The Tragedy of Romeo and Juliet* and "Pyramus and Thisbe" are older texts, the spelling of the words may be different from the modern spelling. Check the source material for the exact spelling used in the text.

Publishing and Presenting

Create a final version of your essay. Share it with your class so that your classmates can read it and make comments. In turn, review and comment on your classmates' work. Which insights do you find particularly interesting? Which interpretation is the most common? Which is the least common? Consider the ways in which other students' essays are both similar to and different from your own. Always maintain a polite and respectful tone when commenting.

Reflecting

Think about what you learned while writing your literary criticism. What could you do differently the next time you engage in literary criticism to make the writing experience easier and to make your argument stronger?

DIGITAL PERSPECTIVES

Peer Review

Instruct students to read their classmates' essays with a critical eye, encouraging them to consistently ask themselves as they're reading, "Does this make sense? Do I understand what the writer is trying to convey? Am I convinced?" Remind them that the writer will not be well served by a review that is not thorough.

Editing and Proofreading

Acknowledge to students that proofreading can be tedious, but that it is an essential component of the writing process, because mistakes will damage a writer's credibility. Remind students to manually review their work since word processing programs will not always catch every grammar and spelling mistake.

Reflecting

Students should use the reflecting exercise to think about the additional insight into *The Tragedy of Romeo and Juliet* and "Pyramus and Thisbe" they gained from writing their piece of literary criticism.

PERSONALIZE FOR LEARNING

Challenge

Interview Encourage students to shoot a video in which they interview William Shakespeare following the premiere of *The Tragedy of Romeo and Juliet.* In the interview, students should ask whether he thinks his characters were more impacted by destiny or personal choice. Students should ask Shakespeare follow-up questions, like "Why is this theme an important one to you?" and "Which other themes did you cover in the play?"

OVERVIEW

SMALL-GROUP LEARNING

Do we determine our own destinies?

Explain that the concept of free will suggests that a person can make decisions and choices for his or her own life. By making these decisions and choices, is a person then able to determine his or her own destiny? People have differing opinions on this issue. During Small-Group Learning, students will read selections that are concerned with the concepts of free will, fate, and destiny.

Small-Group Learning Strategies

Review the Learning Strategies with students and explain that as they work through Small-Group Learning they will develop strategies to work in small-group environments.

- Have students watch the video on Small-Group Learning Strategies.
- A video on this topic is available online in the Professional Development Center.

You may wish to discuss some action items to add to the chart as a class before students complete it on their own. For example, for "Support others," you might solicit the following actions from students:

- Encourage others in the group and ask them to elaborate on ideas.
- Ask each other questions to show interest and make the discussion more lively.

Block Scheduling

Each day in this Pacing Plan represents a 40–50 minute class period. Teachers using block scheduling may combine days to reflect their class schedule. In addition, teachers may revise pacing to differentiate and support core instruction by integrating components and resources as students require.

OVERVIEW: SMALL-GROUP LEARNING

ESSENTIAL QUESTION:

Do we determine our own destinies?

In both literature and life, questions about who or what is responsible when things go terribly wrong can be painful. You will read selections that examine whether tragic outcomes result from personal decisions or destiny in both fiction and real life. You will work in a group to continue your exploration of the concept of destiny.

Small-Group Learning Strategies

Throughout your life, in school, in your community, and in your career, you will continue to learn and work with others.

Look at these strategies and the actions you can take to practice them as you work in teams. Add ideas of your own for each step. Use these strategies during Small-Group Learning.

STRATEGY	ACTION PLAN
Prepare	• Complete your assignments so that you are prepared for group work. • Organize your thinking so you can contribute to your group's discussions. •
Participate fully	• Make eye contact to signal that you are listening and taking in what is being said. • Use text evidence when making a point. •
Support others	• Build off ideas from others in your group. • Invite others who have not yet spoken to join the discussion. •
Clarify	• Paraphrase the ideas of others to ensure that your understanding is correct. • Ask follow-up questions. •

SCAN FOR MULTIMEDIA

Pacing Plan

Unit Introduction — 1

Introduce Whole-Class Learning — 2

Literature and Culture — 3

The Tragedy of Romeo and Juliet, Act I–V — 4, 5, 6, 7, 8, 9, 10, 11, 12

Pyramus and Thisbe — 13

Performance Task — 14, 15

CONTENTS

LITERARY CRITICISM

Romeo and Juliet Is a Terrible Play, and David Leveaux Can't Change That
Alyssa Rosenberg

In Defense of *Romeo and Juliet:* It's Not Childish, It's *About* Childishness
Noah Berlatsky

Does a classic play stand the test of time?

COMPARE

JOURNALISM

Twenty Years On: The Unfinished Lives of Bosnia's Romeo and Juliet
Gordana Sandić-Hadžihasanović

In a country torn apart by war, love may seem impossible.

MEDIA: NEWSCAST

Tragic Romeo and Juliet Offers Bosnia Hope
Nic Robertson

Can a tragedy bring hope to a country rocked by civil war?

PERFORMANCE TASK

SPEAKING AND LISTENING FOCUS

Present an Argument

The Small-Group readings feature nonfiction writings about tragic love stories, both fictional and real. After reading, your group will plan and deliver a multimedia presentation about the reasons people are drawn to tales of tragic destiny.

DIGITAL PERSPECTIVES

Contents

Selections Circulate among groups as they preview the selections. You might encourage groups to discuss any knowledge they already have about any of the selections or the situations and settings shown in the photographs. Students may wish to take a poll within their group to determine which selections look the most interesting.

Remind students that communicating and collaborating in groups is an important skill that they will use throughout their lives—in school, in their careers, and in their community.

Performance Task

Present an Argument Give groups time to read about and briefly discuss the multimedia presentation they will create after reading. Encourage students to do some preliminary thinking about the types of media they may want to use. This may help focus their subsequent reading and group discussion.

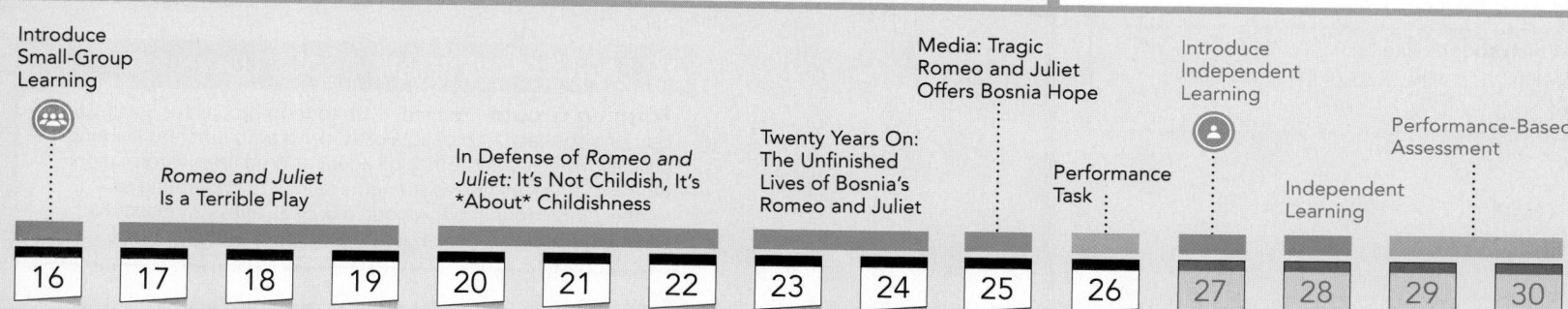

Introduce Small-Group Learning — 16

Romeo and Juliet Is a Terrible Play — 17, 18, 19

In Defense of *Romeo and Juliet:* It's Not Childish, It's *About* Childishness — 20, 21, 22

Twenty Years On: The Unfinished Lives of Bosnia's Romeo and Juliet — 23, 24

Media: Tragic Romeo and Juliet Offers Bosnia Hope — 25

Performance Task — 26

SMALL-GROUP LEARNING

Introduce Independent Learning — 27

Independent Learning — 28

Performance-Based Assessment — 29, 30

OVERVIEW

SMALL-GROUP LEARNING

Working as a Team

1. **Take a Position** Remind groups to let all members share their responses. You may wish to set a time limit for this discussion.
2. **List Your Rules** You may want to have groups share their lists of rules and consolidate them into a master list to be displayed and followed by all groups.
3. **Apply the Rules** As you circulate among the groups, ensure that students are staying on task. Consider a short time limit for this step.
4. **Name Your Group** This task can be creative and fun. If students have trouble coming up with a name, suggest that they think of something related to the unit topic. Encourage groups to share their names with the class.
5. **Create a Communication Plan** Encourage groups to include in their plans agreed-upon times during the day to share ideas. They should also devise a method for recording and saving their communications.

Accountable Talk

Remind students that groups should communicate politely. You can post these Accountable Talk suggestions and encourage students to add their own. Students should:

Remember to . . .
Ask clarifying questions.

Which sounds like . . .
Can you please repeat what you said?
Would you give me an example?
I think you said _____. Did I understand you correctly?

Remember to . . .
Explain your thinking.

Which sounds like . . .
I believe _____ is true because _____.

Remember to . . .
Build on the ideas of others.

Which sounds like . . .
When _____ said _____, it made me think of _____.

OVERVIEW: SMALL-GROUP LEARNING

Working as a Team

1. **Take a Position** In your group, discuss the following question:

   Is luck another way to talk about destiny? Or are luck and destiny totally different concepts?

   As you take turns sharing your positions, be sure to provide reasons for your ideas. After all group members have shared, discuss some of the ways in which characters or people in real life can be lucky or unlucky.

2. **List Your Rules** As a group, decide on the rules that you will follow as you work together. Samples are provided; add two more of your own. You may add or revise rules based on your experience together.
   - Everyone should participate in group discussions.
   - People should not interrupt.
   - ____________________
   - ____________________

3. **Apply the Rules** Practice working as a group. Share what you have learned about destiny. Make sure each person in the group contributes. Take notes and be prepared to share with the class one thing that you heard from another member of your group.

4. **Name Your Group** Choose a name that reflects the unit topic.

   Our group's name: ____________________

5. **Create a Communication Plan** Decide how you want to communicate with one another. For example, you might use online collaboration tools, email, or instant messaging.

   Our group's decision: ____________________

FACILITATING SMALL-GROUP LEARNING

Forming Groups You may wish to form groups for Small-Group Learning so that each consists of students with different learning abilities. Some students may be adept at organizing information whereas others may have strengths related to generating or synthesizing information. A good mix of abilities can make the experience of Small-Group Learning dynamic and productive.

Making a Schedule

First, find out the due dates for the Small-Group activities. Then, preview the texts and activities with your group, and make a schedule for completing the tasks.

SELECTION	ACTIVITIES	DUE DATE
Romeo and Juliet Is a Terrible Play, and David Leveaux Can't Change That In Defense of *Romeo and Juliet:* It's Not Childish, It's *About* Childishness		
Twenty Years On: The Unfinished Lives of Bosnia's Romeo and Juliet		
Tragic Romeo and Juliet Offers Bosnia Hope		

Working on Group Projects

As your group works together, you'll find it more effective if each person has a specific role. Different projects require different roles. Before beginning a project, discuss the necessary roles, and choose one for each group member. Here are some possible roles; add your own ideas.

Project Manager: monitors the schedule and keeps everyone on task

Researcher: organizes research activities

Recorder: takes notes during group meetings

____

____

____

____

____

SCAN FOR MULTIMEDIA

DIGITAL PERSPECTIVES

Making a Schedule

Encourage groups to preview the reading selections and to consider how long it will take them to complete the activities accompanying each selection. Point out that they can adjust the due dates for particular selections as needed as they work on their small-group projects; however, they must complete all assigned tasks before the group Performance Task is due. Encourage groups to review their schedules upon completing the activities for each selection to make sure they are on track to meet the final due date.

Working on Group Projects

Point out to groups that the roles they assign can also be changed later. Students might have to make changes based on who is best at doing what. Try to make sure that there is no favoritism, cliquishness, or stereotyping by gender or other means in the assignment of roles.

Also, you should review the roles each group assigns to its members. Based on your understanding of students' individual strengths, you might find it necessary to suggest some changes.

AUTHOR'S PERSPECTIVE: Ernest Morrell, Ph.D.

Small Group Learning in Higher Education College classrooms are becoming shared discussion spaces, marked by less lecturing and more small groups. That's because college professors increasingly realize that having students work in small groups helps develop higher-level learning and problem-solving skills, increases the success of computer-based instruction, and increases retention rates. As a result, more and more college professors now have small groups lead a portion of class by sharing/presenting what the group has learned. These professors focus on the importance of each group becoming expert at something that they must teach the class. Teachers can point out to students that the project-based small-group learning in colleges is increasingly common in the workplace as well, as collective production is becoming a new norm. Teachers can encourage students to collaborate and develop rubrics to assess how well students are able to work together.

Romeo and Juliet Is a Terrible Play; In Defense of *Romeo and Juliet*

AUDIO SUMMARIES
Audio summaries of "*Romeo and Juliet* Is a Terrible Play" and "In Defense of *Romeo and Juliet*" are available online in both English and Spanish in the Interactive Teacher's Edition or Unit Resources. Assigning these summaries prior to reading the selection may help students build additional background knowledge and set a context for their first read.

Summary

This selection consists of two works of literary criticism.

Alyssa Rosenberg discusses a recent production of *The Tragedy of Romeo and Juliet*, and argues that the text of the play is weak enough that even an interesting staging can't make it much better. The heart of her argument is that *The Tragedy of Romeo and Juliet* is "childish." The characters are immature and reckless in a way that strains plausibility.

Noah Berlatsky argues that the play is not childish, but is *about* childishness. He agrees that the play focuses on themes of young love, and that many characters act unwisely. But he argues that whether the play praises young love is beside the point. Rather, contrasts between youth and age, and the beauty of Shakespeare's language, are the point.

Insight

Students should understand that even a work as canonical as *The Tragedy of Romeo and Juliet* is not beyond critique. Shakespeare's works are open to interpretation and debate.

ESSENTIAL QUESTION:
Do we determine our own destinies?

Connection to Essential Question

According to Rosenberg, the way Romeo and Juliet act is not the way adults act. They could have been more careful, and avoided the misunderstandings that led to their deaths. This suggests that they should have been able to avoid their destinies. Berlatsky argues that many of the characters are similarly reckless, and that people in real life act much the same way.

SMALL-GROUP LEARNING PERFORMANCE TASK
What is compelling about stories in which people face a tragic destiny?

UNIT PERFORMANCE-BASED ASSESSMENT
Should the opinions of others affect our own choices or destinies?

Connection to Performance Tasks

Small-Group Learning Task Berlatsky argues that such stories can be exhilarating. Rosenberg does not find such stories compelling. She is more interested in stories in which people face the consequences of their actions and do the necessary work to get past them.

Unit Performance-Based Assessment Rosenberg questions the characters' judgment not because they ignored their families' opinions, but because they acted incompetently. Berlatsky questions the judgment of their elders as well, suggesting that Juliet shouldn't necessarily have followed the opinions Capulet and the Nurse expressed.

DIGITAL PERSPECTIVES

Audio | Video | Document | Annotation Highlights | EL Highlights | Online Assessment

LESSON RESOURCES

	Making Meaning	Language Development	Effective Expression
Lesson	**First Read** **Close Read** **Analyze the Text** **Analyze Craft and Structure**	**Concept Vocabulary** **Word Study** **Author's Style**	**Writing to Sources**
Instructional Standards	**RL.10** By the end of grade 9, read and comprehend literary nonfiction . . . **RI.8** Delineate and evaluate the argument . . . **L.4.a** Use context as a clue . . .	**L.4.b** Identify and correctly use patterns of word changes . . . **RI.3** Analyze how the author unfolds an analysis . . . **W.2.c** Use appropriate and varied transitions . . .	**RI.8** Delineate and evaluate the argument . . . **W.1.a** Introduce precise claim(s) . . .
STUDENT RESOURCES			
Available online in the Interactive Student Edition or Unit Resources	Selection Audio First-Read Guide: Nonfiction Close-Read Guide: Nonfiction	Word Network	Evidence Log
TEACHER RESOURCES			
Selection Resources Available online in the Interactive Teacher's Edition or Unit Resources	Audio Summaries Annotation Highlights EL Highlights English Language Support Lesson: Criticism *Romeo and Juliet* Is a Terrible Play • In Defense: Text Questions Analyze Craft and Structure: Argumentative Text	Concept Vocabulary and Word Study Author's Style: Organization	Writing to Sources: Criticisms
Reteach/Practice (RP) Available online in the Interactive Teacher's Edition or Unit Resources	Analyze Craft and Structure: Argumentative Text (RP)	Word Study: Latin Root *-cred-* (RP) Author's Style: Organization (RP)	Writing to Sources: Criticisms (RP)
Assessment Available online in Assessments	Selection Test		
My Resources	A Unit 4 Answer Key is available online and in the Interactive Teacher's Edition.		

Reading Support

Text Complexity Rubric: *Romeo and Juliet* Is a Terrible Play • In Defense of *Romeo and Juliet*	
Quantitative Measures	
Lexile: 1310; 1100 **Text Length:** 466 words; 983 words	
Qualitative Measures	
Knowledge Demands ①—②—③—**❹**—⑤	Explores complex analysis of a production of *The Tragedy of Romeo and Juliet* from two different perspectives. Explanation is provided for only some of the complex ideas.
Structure ①—②—**❸**—④—⑤	Organization is evident and sequential, but paragraphs contain information that is not broken up with any headings.
Language Conventionality and Clarity ①—②—③—**❹**—⑤	Selections have complex sentences with embedded clauses, figurative language, and some idiomatic phrases; contains some ironic or sarcastic statements.
Levels of Meaning/Purpose ①—②—③—**❹**—⑤	The main ideas are revealed early, but the concepts may be hard for some to grasp because of sophisticated language and supporting concepts that are complex.

DECIDE AND PLAN

English Language Support

Provide English Learners with support for Language and Levels of Meaning as they read the selection.

Language Help students reword long and complex sentences. Using the language from the selection, suggest simpler sentences that convey the same meaning. For example, for paragraph 2: *Even though I'm happy to see a more diverse cast, the material is horrible*. Ask students to read the new sentences and discuss.

Levels of Meaning/Purpose Help students rephrase main ideas by pulling sentences from the reading or by encouraging them to listen again to key phrases. Write the sentences for reference. For example, *Maybe this works on the page, when we're not forced to watch actors and actresses who are clearly in their 20s and 30s behave like young teenagers.*

Strategic Support

Provide students with strategic support to ensure that they can successfully read the text.

Knowledge Demands After reading the background information, make sure students understand the topic that is the focus of the selection—a new production of *The Tragedy of Romeo and Juliet*. Ask students to discuss some aspects of the play that may be challenging on stage.

Language If students have difficulty with complex sentences, work together to break down sentences into smaller chunks in order to understand their meaning. Ask students to highlight words or phrases that they don't understand. As a group, help to define some of the terms they find difficult.

Challenge

Provide students who need to be challenged with ideas for how they can go beyond a simple interpretation of the text.

Text Analysis Ask students to read aloud paragraph 11 of "In Defense of *Romeo and Juliet*" about youth and age in the play. Ask students to summarize this paragraph in their own words and discuss the author's argument. Do they agree? Disagree?

Written Response Ask students to write a short summary of the main arguments of each writer. Then have them choose which argument they felt was most compelling and explain why it was most convincing.

TEACH

Read and Respond

Have groups read the selection and complete the Making Meaning, Language Development, and Effective Expression activities.

Standards Support Through Teaching and Learning Cycle

IDENTIFY NEEDS

Analyze results of the Beginning-of-Year Assessment, focusing on the items relating to Unit 4. Also take into consideration student performance to this point and your observations of where particular students struggle.

DECIDE AND PLAN

- If students have performed poorly on items matching these standards, then provide selection scaffolds before assigning them the on-level lesson provided in the Student Edition.
- If students have done well on the Beginning-of-Year Assessment, then challenge them to keep progressing and learning by giving them opportunities to practice the skills in depth.
- Use the Selection Resources listed on the Planning pages for "*Romeo and Juliet* Is a Terrible Play" and "In Defense of *Romeo and Juliet*" to help students continually improve their ability to master the standards.

Instructional Standards: "*Romeo and Juliet* Is a Terrible Play" and "In Defense of *Romeo and Juliet*"

	Catching Up	This Year	Looking Forward
Reading	You may wish to administer the **Analyze Craft and Structure: Criticism (RP)** worksheet to help students better understand the craft of criticism.	**RI.8** Delineate and evaluate the argument and specific claims in a text, assessing whether the reasoning is valid and the evidence is relevant and sufficient; identify false statements and fallacious reasoning.	Challenge students to find other criticisms of *The Tragedy of Romeo and Juliet* that either support these critics' claims, or bring new insight.
Writing	You may wish to administer the **Author's Style: Organization (RP)** worksheet to familiarize students with these organizational tools.	**W.2.c** Use appropriate and varied transitions to link the major sections of the text, create and clarify the relationships among the complex ideas and topics.	Challenge students to come up with other ways writers may transition within a text.
Language	Review the **Word Study: Latin Root *-cred-* (RP)** worksheet to familiarize students with the root word.	**L.4.b** Identify and correctly use patterns of word changes that indicate different meanings or parts of speech.	Have students locate other words in the selection that have Latin or Greek root words they may recognize.

TEACH

Implement the planned lesson, and gather evidence of student learning.

ANALYZE AND REVISE

- Analyze student work for evidence of student learning.
- Identify whether students have met the expectations in the standards.
- Identify implications for future instruction.

FACILITATING

Jump Start

FIRST READ Engaging students in a discussion about literary criticisms sets the stage for reading "*Romeo and Juliet* Is a Terrible Play, and David Laveaux Can't Change That" and "In Defense of *Romeo and Juliet*: It's Not Childish, It's *About* Childishness." As students share their thoughts, have them express and defend their own opinions about *The Tragedy of Romeo and Juliet*.

Concept Vocabulary

Ask groups to study the three types of context clues and discuss how they can help clarify meaning. Do they use any of these strategies when they don't know the meaning of a word? Which ones do they find most helpful, and why?

Encourage groups to think of one other type that they might encounter in a text. Possibilities include antonyms, examples, and definitions.

FIRST READ

Students should perform the steps of the first read independently.

NOTICE: You may want to encourage students to notice the differences between the two authors' points of view.

ANNOTATE: Remind students to mark passages that reflect each author's main ideas.

CONNECT: If students cannot make connections to their own lives or other texts, have them consider current news events in the media that might relate.

RESPOND: Students will answer questions and write a summary to demonstrate understanding.

Point out to students that while they will always complete the Respond step at the end of the first read, the other steps will probably happen somewhat concurrently. You may wish to print copies of the **First-Read Guide: Nonfiction** for students to use.

MAKING MEANING

LITERARY CRITICISM

Romeo and Juliet Is a Terrible Play, and David Leveaux Can't Change That

In Defense of *Romeo and Juliet*: It's Not Childish, It's *About* Childishness

Concept Vocabulary

As you perform your first read of these two articles, you will encounter the following words.

intrigued	credulity	indignation

Context Clues If these words are unfamiliar to you, try using **context clues**—other words and phrases that appear in a text—to help you determine their meanings. There are various types of context clues that you may encounter as you read.

Synonyms: This salad is delicious—absolutely **delectable**.

Restatement of Idea: I could give the idea no **credence**. I simply couldn't believe it.

Contrast of Ideas and Topics: Helga is usually responsible, but this time she was completely **unreliable**.

Apply your knowledge of context clues and other vocabulary strategies to determine the meanings of unfamiliar words you encounter during your first read.

First Read NONFICTION

Apply these strategies as you conduct your first read. You will have an opportunity to complete a close read after your first read.

NOTICE the general ideas of each text. *What* is it about? *Who* is involved?

ANNOTATE by marking vocabulary and key passages you want to revisit.

CONNECT ideas within the selection to what you already know and what you have already read.

RESPOND by completing the Comprehension Check and by writing a brief summary of each selection.

First Read: NOTICE, ANNOTATE, CONNECT, RESPOND

STANDARDS

Reading Informational Text
By the end of grade 9, read and comprehend literary nonfiction in the grades 9–10 text complexity band proficiently, with scaffolding as needed at the high end of the range.

Language
Use context as a clue to the meaning of a word or phrase.

AUTHOR'S PERSPECTIVE **Jim Cummins, Ph.D.**

How Language Works Briefly explaining the origins of the English language will help demystify the difference between conversational and academic language. Today's English is a hybrid language, formed from a merger of Anglo-Saxon, spoken in Britain from about 400 to 1000, and French, which derives from Latin and was brought over by the Norman invaders in 1066. Students can see this merger in synonyms of words derived from Anglo-Saxon and Latin/Greek sources: *meet/encounter, ask/inquire, come/arrive*. The Anglo-Saxon words were used by peasants who generally didn't have much education; in contrast, Latin/Greek vocabulary was used by more educated and high-status people and became the language of written text. Today, words with Anglo-Saxon roots are short and commonly used, and words with Latin/Greek roots tend to be low frequency and long. The most common Anglo-Saxon words in English are determiners *(the, a);* prepositions *(of, to, for, etc.);* pronouns *(he, she, I, etc.);* conjunctions *(and, but, etc.);* common verbs, nouns, and adjectives *(think, little, good, etc.)*. Because these words are high frequency and are used daily, they are generally acquired quickly by English learners.

About the Authors

Originally from Massachusetts, **Alyssa Rosenberg** (b. 1984) attended Yale University. She has contributed to many publications, including the *New York Times*, *New York*, the *Daily Beast*, the *New Republic*, and *Salon*. She has been the culture editor at ThinkProgress.com, a columnist at WomenandHollywood.com, and a pop-culture blogger at the *Washington Post*.

Noah Berlatsky (b. 1971) has been working as a freelance writer and editor for more than 20 years. He serves as editor for a comics and culture website. His work has appeared in the *Atlantic*, *Salon*, the *Awl*, *Slate*, and the *Chicago Reader*, as well as other popular blogs and websites. He has also been featured on National Public Radio's news program *All Things Considered*.

Backgrounds

Romeo and Juliet Is a Terrible Play, and David Leveaux Can't Change That

In her critique of David Leveaux's 2013 production of *The Tragedy of Romeo and Juliet,* Alyssa Rosenberg discusses the level of immaturity displayed by the characters in Shakespeare's original play, and how the play holds up when viewed with modern sensibilities.

In Defense of *Romeo and Juliet*: It's Not Childish, It's *About* Childishness

After Alyssa Rosenberg's critique of *The Tragedy of Romeo and Juliet* received a strong reader reaction, Noah Berlatsky responded by describing his experience as an adult rereading the play about young lovers.

DIGITAL PERSPECTIVES

Romeo and Juliet Is a Terrible Play, and David Laveaux Can't Change That

In Defense of *Romeo and Juliet*: It's Not Childish, It's *About* Childishness

Which elements of *The Tragedy of Romeo and Juliet* do you find most interesting, and why? Do you think readers today are able to relate to the characters' story? Is the story believable? Consider modeling the questions a reader might ask as they read "*Romeo and Juliet* Is a Terrible Play, and David Laveaux Can't Change That" and "In Defense of *Romeo and Juliet:* It's Not Childish, It's *About* Childishness." It helps students understand the two authors' perspectives about the play, *The Tragedy of Romeo and Juliet*, and connects it to the Small-Group Performance Task. Selection audio and print capability for the selections are available in the Interactive Teacher's Edition.

FACILITATING SMALL-GROUP CLOSE READING

CLOSE READ: Literary Criticisms Ask students to discuss ways in which the titles of the two literary criticisms suggest what each article is about.

Advise students that as they perform their close read they should look for evidence that might support the titles. Circulate and offer support as needed.

If any group members struggle to identify the kind of supporting evidence that validates each of the author's titles, demonstrate to them that the author uses the title to "hook" the reader, and then uses the body of the article to explain his or her point of view. Throughout the two literary criticisms, supporting evidence appears to help contextualize the authors' opinions.

FACILITATING

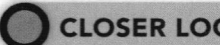

CLOSER LOOK

Infer Tone

Circulate among groups as students conduct their close read. Suggest that groups read paragraph 2. Encourage them to talk about the annotations they mark. If needed, provide the following support.

ANNOTATE: Have students mark details in paragraph 2 that reveal the author's tone, or work with small groups to have students participate as you highlight them together.

QUESTION: Guide students to consider what these details might tell them. Ask what a reader can infer from the author's tone about the original *The Tragedy of Romeo and Juliet*, and accept student responses.

Possible response: The author does not like he original *The Tragedy of Romeo and Juliet* and uses a judgmental tone, calling it childish and depressing.

CONCLUDE: Help students formulate conclusions about the importance of these details in the text. Ask students why the author might have included these details.

Possible response: Even though David Laveaux's adaptation of *The Tragedy of Romeo and Juliet* features a diverse cast, the author's tone reflects that she is disappointed and thinks the original play is terrible; no adaptation could mask the immature ideas about love with which the author struggles.

Remind students that **tone** reveals the author's attitude toward his or her subject and the audience. Tone is established by word choice, or **diction**, and shows the writer's character.

Additional **English Language Support** is available in the Interactive Teacher's Edition.

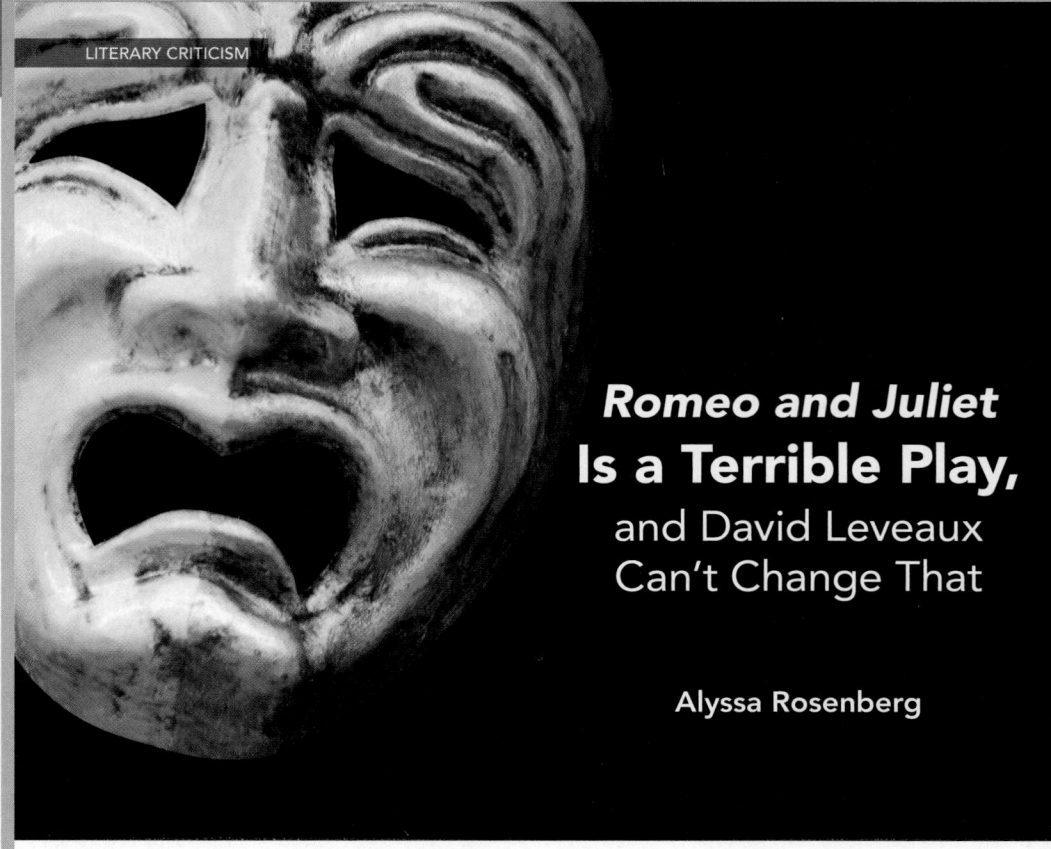

LITERARY CRITICISM

Romeo and Juliet Is a Terrible Play, and David Leveaux Can't Change That

Alyssa Rosenberg

SCAN FOR MULTIMEDIA

NOTES

1 A new, interracial production of *Romeo and Juliet* arrives on Broadway this September, starring Orlando Bloom and Condola Rashad. Director David Leveaux decided to cast the lovers' families in alignment with their races, resulting in a much more diverse production. So why am I not cheering?

2 Because, despite the fact that its latest staging features a 36-year-old actor and a 26-year-old actress, *Romeo and Juliet*—a play about children—is full of terrible, deeply childish ideas about love. And as much as I want to see more interracial couples in pop culture and more diverse casts on stage and screen, I don't want to see them cast in material that is so horribly depressing.

3 *Romeo and Juliet* itself hasn't aged well. The story follows Juliet Capulet, who is 13 when she meets Romeo Montague at a party, falls head over heels in love with him, and marries him within a day of meeting him. Romeo's age isn't specified in the play, but the quickness with which he throws over a former flame for Juliet

doesn't suggest a particularly mature man. Maybe this works on the page, when we're not forced to watch actors and actresses who are clearly in their 20s and 30s behave like early teenagers. But the effect is embarrassing and unsettling for today's theater audiences, perhaps already fretting over suspended adolescence and stunted millennials.

NOTES

4 Update the play to match the aged-up actors in the two main roles, and the plot still doesn't make a lot of sense. Why are the families fighting? What was the inciting incident? The absence of a reason does mean that adaptations can fill in space that Shakespeare left behind, making the warring parties Puerto Rican and Polish-American, for instance, or Israeli and Palestinian. But even then, having the two lovers kill themselves through a series of misunderstandings doesn't translate well in a setting that takes any sort of modern communications for granted. And it's hard to believe the couple, no matter how lovelorn, would lack the patience to wait 24 hours to get hitched—not to mention the savvy to check up on a bad report from Verona.

5 But beyond that, the vision of Romeo and Juliet's deaths uniting their families is an adolescent fantasy of death solving all problems, a "won't they miss me when I'm gone" pout. There's a reason that, in the best modern riff on *Romeo and Juliet*, *West Side Story*, Maria lives after Tony's death to shame the Sharks and the Jets, her survival a seal on the truce between them. Dying is easy. Living to survive the consequences of your actions and to do the actual work of reconciliation is the hard part. An interracial *Romeo and Juliet* is nice, but black actors and actresses deserve richer roles than Romeo and Juliet. ❧

PERSONALIZE FOR LEARNING

English Language Support

Idioms Idioms can be confusing to English Language learners. Explain that the term *hitched* in paragraph 4 is an idiom. To help them understand its usage in the paragraph, ask students to think about the word *hitch*, which has different meanings. The definition that is most relevant here is to fasten, or bring together. Two people cannot literally be fastened together, so this use of the term takes on a more symbolic meaning, which is to join people together through marriage. When two people get hitched, it means they are getting married. **ALL LEVELS**

Concept Vocabulary

INTRIGUED If groups are struggling to define the word *intrigued* in paragraph 2, explain to students that the author restates the idea of being *intrigued* in the sentence. Have students use these context clues to define the word.
Possible response: *Intrigued* must mean "curious."

Concept Vocabulary

CREDULITY If groups are struggling to define the word *credulity* in paragraph 3, explain to students that the author restates the notion of credulity through these ideas. Have students use these context clues to define the word.

Possible response: *Credulity* must mean "gullible, or trusting too easily."

LITERARY CRITICISM

In Defense of *Romeo and Juliet*: It's Not Childish, It's *About* Childishness

Noah Berlatsky

SCAN FOR MULTIMEDIA

NOTES

Mark context clues or indicate another strategy you used that helped you determine meaning.

intrigued (ihn TREEGD) *v.*
MEANING:

credulity (kruh DYOO luh tee) *n.*
MEANING:

1 I haven't read *Romeo and Juliet* since I was in high school 25 years ago. High school is, of course, a time of rampaging hormones and extravagant romantic angst; in theory, the perfect life moment to read *Romeo and Juliet*. In practice . . . eh. I think my favorite character was Mercutio. I thought he was funny.

2 I just reread the play last week, inspired by Alyssa Rosenberg's declaration at *Slate* that "*Romeo and Juliet* is a terrible play." The comments section erupted in howls of outrage . . . but I was **intrigued**. Suddenly, I was curious to find out what I thought of a work I hadn't revisited in more than two decades.

3 Rosenberg argued that "*Romeo and Juliet*—a play about children—is full of terrible, deeply childish ideas about love." Juliet, Rosenberg reminds us, is 13. If you cast someone that age in the role now, the result is queasy. If you cast someone older, you end up with an adult actor behaving like she's a tween. Romeo's age is uncertain, but a lot of what he does is immature, and adolescent as well. The lovers' haste to marry strains **credulity**—it seems (though Rosenberg doesn't quite say this) like a childish fantasy of love at first sight. Similarly, the reconciliation of the lovers' warring families upon their demise reads for Rosenberg as "an adolescent fantasy of death solving all problems."

4 Adolescent or not, though, I sure enjoyed reading it this time through. Romeo and Juliet's first meeting, for example, all by itself validates the romantic comedy genre.

508 UNIT 4 • STAR-CROSSED ROMANCES

Romeo. [*To* Juliet] If I profane with my unworthiest hand
This holy shrine, the gentle fine is this:
My lips, two blushing pilgrims, ready stand
To smooth that rough touch with a tender kiss.

Juliet. Good pilgrim, you do wrong your hand too much,
Which mannerly devotion shows in this;
For saints have hands that pilgrims' hands do touch,
And palm to palm is holy palmers' kiss.

Romeo. Have not saints lips, and holy palmers too?

Juliet. Ay, pilgrim, lips that they must use in prayer.

5 That is some searingly saucy banter, there. "Ay, pilgrim, lips that they must use in prayer" has to be one of the archest lines in all of literature. I'm with Romeo. I'd fall in love with that.

6 In short, now that I'm an adult, I appreciate the young lovers a good bit more than I did when I was their age. This may be counterintuitive . . . but it also seems to be one of the main points of the play itself.

7 A number of Rosenberg's commenters noted that *Romeo and Juliet* is deliberately about young love. This is no doubt true. But the play is also, and insistently, about age. The fact that Juliet is 13, for example, is not just mentioned once. It comes up again and again. Moreover, the first time Juliet appears on stage, her aged comic Nurse launches into a rambling anecdote about when her charge was a toddler, an anecdote that Juliet clearly finds both tedious and embarrassing. Juliet's youth, then, is adamantly established, and also adamantly presented as a source of fascination for the elderly.

8 Old/young remains an obsession throughout the play—but that obsession does not, interestingly, work in any single way. Sometimes, being young means being rash and changeable, as when Romeo switches his hyperbolic affections from Rosalind to Juliet. Sometimes, it means being a hope for the future—as when the Friar marries the couple to try to end the feud between Montagues and Capulets. There are passages where old and young are presented as almost different species, as when Juliet irritably declaims, ". . . old folks, many feign as they were dead; / Unwieldy, slow, heavy and pale as lead."

9 And then there are moments where it seems like old and young don't really act all that differently. Juliet's hasty marriage to Romeo, for example, isn't much more precipitous than Lord Capulet's sudden decision to marry her to Paris. And Romeo's affections aren't any more changeable than those of the Nurse, who, having cheerfully helped Juliet marry Romeo, just as cheerfully advises her to forget that first marriage and turn polyandrist[1] by wedding as her father wishes.

10 Rosenberg might argue that even the adults behave like kids in *Romeo and Juliet* because the play itself is childish. But . . . is Capulet really childish? Is the Nurse? Surely, you don't have to be young

NOTES

1. **polyandrist** (POL ee an drihst) *n.* one who has two or more husbands at the same time.

CLOSER LOOK

Infer Theme

Circulate among groups as students conduct their close read. Suggest that groups close read paragraph 8. Encourage them to talk about the annotations they mark. If needed, provide the following support.

ANNOTATE: Have students mark details in paragraph 8 that reflect the theme of old versus young in *The Tragedy of Romeo and Juliet*, or work with small groups to have students participate as you highlight them together.

QUESTION: Guide students to consider what these details might tell them. Ask what a reader can infer from the theme, and accept student responses.

Possible response: The author appreciates *The Tragedy of Romeo and Juliet* as a play because it addresses how complex the dynamic between the older and younger characters is; all of the characters can learn from each other, no matter their age.

CONCLUDE: Help students to formulate conclusions about why the author might have included these details.

Possible response: The author highlights the distinction between the older and younger characters, in other parts of the story. Sometimes, even the adults act as children.

Remind students that a **theme** is the central idea, message, or an insight that a literary work reveals. This central idea can usually be expressed as a generalization about people or life. The notion of young versus old is a **universal theme** in that it is a message about life that is expressed regularly in many different cultures and time periods.

FACILITATING

Concept Vocabulary

INDIGNATION If groups are struggling to define the word *indignation* in paragraph 11, point out the sentences that have the following phrases: *youth and age seem less like solid, immutable categories than like tropes, they are devices manipulated by Juliet or Romeo to give force*, and *specialness* in paragraph 11. Explain to students that the author offers context clues in these sentences to show the meaning of the word. Have students use these context clues to define the word.

Possible response: *Indignation* must mean "displeasure."

NOTES

Mark context clues or indicate another strategy you used that helped you determine meaning.

indignation (ihn dihg NAY shuhn) *n.*

MEANING:

to be precipitate or fickle. Adults behave like children with some frequency. And . . . vice versa.

11 For *Romeo and Juliet*, in other words, youth and age seem less like solid, immutable categories than like tropes. They're devices manipulated by Juliet or Romeo to give force to their sense of **indignation** or specialness. Or manipulated by the Nurse to give force to her affection and nostalgia. Or manipulated by Shakespeare to sweep (adults?) into a romantic swoon. Or manipulated by Rosenberg, to denigrate[2] that same swooning. From this perspective, the point of the play isn't so much the exhilaration of young love or the dunderheadedness of young love. Rather (as often with Shakespeare) the point is the language itself: the dazzling, disturbing rhetorical force of old/young, corrupt/innocent, experienced/naïve.

12 Rosenberg claims that *Romeo and Juliet* is dated because of the uncomfortable way its childishness, and its child protagonists, sit in our contemporary culture. I'd argue, though, that that uncomfortableness is not a contemporary addition, but is instead one of the things Shakespeare was writing about to begin with. At that first flirtatious meeting, for example, Romeo is masked with friends at a Capulet party. Old Capulet, seeing the maskers, reminisces about when he used to do the same.

Capulet. What, man! 'tis not so much, 'tis not so much:
'Tis since the nuptials of Lucentio,
Come pentecost as quickly as it will,
Some five and twenty years; and then we mask'd.

Second Capulet. 'Tis more, 'tis more, his son is elder, sir;
His son is thirty.

Capulet. Will you tell me that?
His son was but a ward two years ago.

Romeo. [*To a* Servingman] What lady is that, which doth enrich the hand
Of yonder knight?

13 Capulet slips back through time . . . and when he stops slipping, it is Romeo who speaks and goes to woo Juliet. Capulet was Romeo, Romeo is Capulet—and so, by substitution, the lover of the daughter is the father. The mask is a device not so much to enable young love, as to enable the old to imagine young love.

14 In *Romeo and Juliet* play-acting with the categories of adult and child can lead to exhilarating delight, pleasurably moralistic revulsion and, sometimes, to tragedy. If, in our own day, we have pushed the onset of adulthood past the tweens, past the teens, and even to some degree up into the 20s—that makes the play's insights and its sometimes exasperating perversities more relevant, not less. ❧

2. **denigrate** (DEHN uh grayt) *v.* disparage; insult.

DIGITAL PERSPECTIVES

Comprehension Check

Complete the following items after you finish your first read. Review and clarify details with your group.

ROMEO AND JULIET IS A TERRIBLE PLAY

1. What does Rosenberg like about the new production of *The Tragedy of Romeo and Juliet* that she is describing?

2. Why does she object to the ages of the actors?

3. What is Rosenberg's main criticism of the play?

IN DEFENSE OF ROMEO AND JULIET

1. How much time has passed since the author initially read *The Tragedy of Romeo and Juliet?*

2. How does Berlatsky feel about the play now that he is an adult?

3. In Berlatsky's opinion, what makes the play's insights more relevant today?

4. **Notebook** Confirm your understanding by writing a summary of each text.

RESEARCH

Research to Explore Choose something that interested you from one of the texts, and formulate a research question.

PERSONALIZE FOR LEARNING

Challenge

Research Have students research another Shakespeare play, for example, *Hamlet, Othello*, or *Macbeth*, and how the characters in that play deal with love. Ask students to compare and contrast the treatment of love in those plays with that in *The Tragedy of Romeo and Juliet*. How are they similar? How are they different? What messages does Shakespeare convey through each play?

Comprehension Check

Possible responses:

"*Romeo and Juliet* Is a Terrible Play"

1. Rosenberg appreciates the fact that the cast and production is racially diverse.
2. She objects to the ages of the actors because they are adults in their 20s and 30s playing the roles of teenagers.
3. Rosenberg's main criticism is that *The Tragedy of Romeo and Juliet* as a play is not complex or rich enough, and this is exacerbated by the adolescent fantasy that death solves all problems.

"In Defense of *Romeo and Juliet*"

1. 25 years have passed since Berlatsky initially read *The Tragedy of Romeo and Juliet*.
2. Now that he is an adult, Berlatsky appreciates the play even more. He believes that it's more interesting and complex than what he remembers.
3. The play's insights are more relevant today because society has pushed the onset of adulthood past the tweens, teens, and even up into the 20s.
4. **Notebook:** Answers will vary. Possible responses:

"*Romeo and Juliet* Is a Terrible Play"
Rosenberg believes that *The Tragedy of Romeo and Juliet* is a terrible play because not only are the protagonists childish, but also the play itself is about childish things. The author argues that the events in the play are not believable and do not hold up when viewed with modern-day notions of love. She also argues that although David's Leveaux's adaptation of the play is strong because of its racially diverse cast and production team, having actors in their 20s and 30s play teenagers who have "deeply childish ideas about love" is "horribly depressing."

"In Defense of *Romeo and Juliet*"
Berlatsky argues that though it has been 25 years since he read the play initially, he appreciates it more now than he first did because the play is richly complex, and the characters have a sense of humor about them. He argues that though the play is about young love, it is also about age. Throughout the play, Shakespeare obsesses over the notion of old/young and compares and contrasts the behaviors of his youthful and aging characters.

Research to Explore If groups struggle to come up with a research topic, you may want to suggest that they focus on one of the other characters (e.g., Mercutio or the Nurse) and their perception of love, how the adults in the play behave, or how old Romeo was in the original play.

Jump Start

CLOSE READ Ask students to consider the following prompt: Do you agree that *The Tragedy of Romeo and Juliet* is a terrible play, or do you think the play is about childishness? As students discuss the prompt in their groups, have them consider what aspects of the play make it terrible or enjoyable, based on their perspectives.

Close Read the Text

If needed, model close reading by using the Annotation Highlights in the Interactive Teacher's Edition.

Remind students to use Accountable Talk in their discussions and to support one another as they complete the close read.

Analyze the Text

Possible responses:

1. The actors who portray the characters are much older than the characters are in the play, which makes the play unbearable to watch.
2. **Passages will vary by group.** Remind students to explain why they chose the passages they presented to the group members.
3. **Responses will vary by group.**

Concept Vocabulary

Why These Words? Possible response: The words relate to belief or lack of belief; *querulous.*

Practice

- Leah was so *intrigued* by the book that she missed her bus.
- The notion that voters would re-elect the corrupt mayor strains any *credulity*.
- The boy did not hide his *indignation* at what he felt was unfair treatment by his sister.

Word Network

Possible words: *granted, immutable, tragedy*

Word Study

For more support, see **Concept Vocabulary and Word Study.**

1. tendency to believe
2. incredible – not believable; credentials – things showing that someone is to be believed; accredited – certified as trustworthy

MAKING MEANING

SOURCES

- *ROMEO AND JULIET* IS A TERRIBLE PLAY, AND DAVID LEVEAUX CAN'T CHANGE THAT
- IN DEFENSE OF *ROMEO AND JULIET*: IT'S NOT CHILDISH, IT'S *ABOUT* CHILDISHNESS

Close Read the Text

With your group, revisit sections of the texts you marked during your first read. **Annotate** what you notice. What **questions** do you have? What can you **conclude**?

Analyze the Text

CITE TEXTUAL EVIDENCE to support your answers.

Complete the activities.

1. **Review and Clarify** With your group, reread paragraph 3 of "*Romeo and Juliet* is a Terrible Play." Why does the author focus on the ages of the main characters and the actors who portray them?
2. **Present and Discuss** Now, work with your group to share the passages from "*Romeo and Juliet* is a Terrible Play" and "In Defense of *Romeo and Juliet*" that you found especially important. Take turns presenting your passages. Discuss what you notice in the texts, the questions you asked, and the conclusions you reached.
3. **Essential Question** ***Do we determine our own destinies?*** How have these articles contributed to your thinking about destiny? Discuss with your group.

TIP

GROUP DISCUSSION
Start a discussion by expressing your opinion. Then, try to support your opinion with evidence from the article or examples from the play.

LANGUAGE DEVELOPMENT

Concept Vocabulary

intrigued credulity indignation

Why These Words? The three concept vocabulary words are related. With your group, determine what the words have in common. Write your ideas, and add another word that fits the category.

WORD NETWORK

Add interesting words related to destiny from the texts to your Word Network.

Practice

Notebook Confirm your understanding of each vocabulary word by using it in a sentence. Use context clues to help make the meanings clear.

Word Study

Notebook **Latin Root: *-cred-*** The concept vocabulary word *credulity* contains the Latin root *-cred-*, meaning "believe."

1. Write a definition for the word *credulity* that demonstrates how the Latin root *-cred-* contributes to its meaning.
2. Write definitions for these words that also contain the Latin root *-cred-*: *incredible, credentials, accredited*. Consult a dictionary if needed.

STANDARDS

Reading Informational Text
Delineate and evaluate the argument and specific claims in a text, assessing whether the reasoning is valid and the evidence is relevant and sufficient; identify false statements and fallacious reasoning.

Language
Identify and correctly use patterns of word changes that indicate different meanings or parts of speech.

FORMATIVE ASSESSMENT

Analyze the Text

If students struggle to close read the text, **then** provide the ***Romeo and Juliet* Is a Terrible Play • In Defense: Text Questions,** which are available online in the Interactive Teacher's Edition or Unit Resources. Answers and DOK levels are also available.

Concept Vocabulary

If students struggle to identify the concept, **then** have them revisit the context.

Word Study

If students fail to identify other words, **then** have them review the text, or other texts, for the root, *-cred-*.
For Reteach and Practice, see **Word Study: Latin Root *-cred-* (RP).**

Analyze Craft and Structure

Argumentative Text A **criticism** is a type of argumentative writing in which the author expresses an opinion about a created work, such as a book, a film, or a performance. Both "*Romeo and Juliet* Is a Terrible Play" and "In Defense of *Romeo and Juliet*" are examples of criticism.

Effective critical writing includes evidence to support the writer's position and to convince readers that his or her evaluation of the work is valid and correct. Many works of criticism include the following elements:

- background about the work and its significance
- related points about a work's strengths or weaknesses
- relevant and strong examples, quotations, facts, and other evidence presented in a knowledgeable, convincing way
- consideration of opposing points of view or counterclaims; By acknowledging other positions, a writer shows that other claims have been considered, but ultimately his or her argument is the most valid.

TIP

COLLABORATION

It can be helpful to discuss your thoughts with a partner before writing them. Your partner can help by asking you clarifying questions. Together, you can expand the writing.

Practice

CITE TEXTUAL EVIDENCE to support your answers.

Gather information about the arguments that the two articles present by responding to the questions in the chart. Share your responses with the group.

	Romeo and Juliet Is a Terrible Play	In Defense of *Romeo and Juliet*
What is the writer's argument?		
What reasons and evidence does the writer present?		
Is the evidence relevant and sufficient to convince readers? Explain.		
Does the writer effectively acknowledge counterclaims? Explain.		

PERSONALIZE FOR LEARNING

English Language Support

Evaluating an Argument Give students a short argumentative essay to read. Ask them to write down the claim being made, the counterclaim, and one example of relevant evidence. Have them write why it is or isn't convincing. **EMERGING**

An expanded **English Language Support lesson** on Criticism is available in the Interactive Teacher's Edition.

DIGITAL PERSPECTIVES

Analyze Craft and Structure

Argumentative Text

Discuss with students how an author might write a criticism to voice his or her opinion about a text or any other work. Remind students that when writing a criticism, their opinions, or claims, must be backed by substantial evidence. They must also anticipate possible counterarguments, that is, what an opponent might say, and offer evidence that weakens the counterargument.

For more support, see **Analyze Craft and Structure: Argumentative Text.**

Practice

Possible responses:

	Romeo and Juliet Is a Terrible Play…	*In Defense of Romeo and Juliet…*
What is the writer's argument?	Romeo and Juliet is "full of terrible, deeply childish ideas about love." Paragraph 2	The play is not only about love, but also "insistently, about age." Paragraph 7
What reasons and evidence does the writer present?	Romeo falls in love with Juliet at a party and "throws over a former flame." Paragraph 3 Romeo and Juliet can hardly wait 24 hours to get married.	Juliet's age "comes up again and again." Paragraph 7 Juliet's youth is "a source of fascination for the elderly." Paragraph 7
Is the evidence relevant and sufficient to convince readers? Explain.	The evidence is relevant but insufficient because it gives too few examples.	The evidence the writer offers is relevant and sufficient, as it includes quotes, facts, and examples.
Does the writer effectively acknowledge counterclaims?	No, the writer only considers one perspective and doesn't offer opposing views.	Yes, the writer considers multiple perspectives.

FORMATIVE ASSESSMENT

Analyze Craft and Structure

If students struggle with identifying the writers' main ideas and evidence to support their claims, **then** revisit key passages to discuss the ideas presented in each of the literary criticisms, evidence and counterarguments.
For Reteach and Practice, see **Analyze Craft and Structure: Argumentative Text (RP).**

FACILITATING

Author's Style

Organization Discuss with students that transitions facilitate the flow of one's writing. Transitions help the writer make seamless connections between different ideas and help the reader keep track of the various points in the text, which is especially important in argumentative writing.

As you review the examples of transitions with students, consider providing additional examples:

Jack left his wallet at home. *As a result,* he had no money to pay for his coffee.

Alex didn't run for the ice-cream truck; *besides,* he is allergic to dairy.

For more support, see **Author's Style: Organization.**

Read It

Have students write five sentences on a notecard or piece of paper and highlight the transitional word or phrase in each sentence.

See Student page for possible answers.

Write It

Possible responses

Transition words or phrases in the sentences will vary, but make sure that students use them correctly.

- *Likewise*, the reconciliation of the lovers' warring families upon their demise reads for Rosenberg as "an adolescent fantasy of death solving all problems."
- Romeo and Juliet's first meeting, *for instance*, all by itself validates the romantic comedy.
- *All in all*, now that I'm an adult, I appreciate the young lovers a good bit more than I did when I was their age.

FORMATIVE ASSESSMENT

Conventions

If students struggle with using transitions, **then** have them identify sentences that contain transitions throughout the text.
For Reteach and Practice, see **Author's Style: Organization (RP).**

LANGUAGE DEVELOPMENT

SOURCES

- *ROMEO AND JULIET* IS A TERRIBLE PLAY, AND DAVID LEVEAUX CAN'T CHANGE THAT
- IN DEFENSE OF *ROMEO AND JULIET*: IT'S NOT CHILDISH, IT'S *ABOUT* CHILDISHNESS

STANDARDS

Reading Informational Text
Analyze how the author unfolds an analysis or series of ideas or events, including the order in which the points are made, how they are introduced and developed, and the connections that are drawn between them.

Writing
Use appropriate and varied transitions and sentence structures to link the major sections of the text, create cohesion, and clarify the relationships among ideas and concepts.

Author's Style

Organization Writers use **transitions**, or words and phrases that clarify the relationships between ideas, to help organize a text. To create clear paragraphs, transitions can connect ideas and examples or create contrasts within or between sentences. Writers also use transitions to connect paragraphs with related ideas.

For example, in paragraph 2 of "*Romeo and Juliet* is a Terrible Play," Rosenberg uses the transitional word *because* to connect the rhetorical question "So why am I not cheering?" with her answer. With the word *because*, Rosenberg signals a cause-and-effect relationship; the fact that Rosenberg is not cheering about the new casting of *The Tragedy of Romeo and Juliet* is caused by the fact that she believes the play to be "full of terrible, deeply childish ideas about love."

Below are more examples of types of relationships and the transitional words and phrases writers use to establish those relationships.

Comparison: similarly, in comparison, likewise
Contrast: on the other hand, in contrast, however
Cause and Effect: because, inasmuch as, as a result
Addition: also, and, furthermore, in addition
Introducing: for example, for instance, particularly
Summary: in short, to sum up, all in all

Read It

Work individually. Use this chart to identify the transition in each passage from "In Defense of *Romeo and Juliet.*" Explain what relationship the transition shows. When you have finished, discuss with your group.

SELECTION PASSAGE	TRANSITION	TYPE OF RELATIONSHIP
Similarly, the reconciliation of the lovers' warring families upon their demise reads for Rosenberg as "an adolescent fantasy of death solving all problems." (paragraph 3)	Similarly	Comparison
Romeo and Juliet's first meeting, for example, all by itself validates the romantic comedy. (paragraph 4)	for example	Introducing
In short, now that I'm an adult, I appreciate the young lovers a good bit more than I did when I was their age. (paragraph 6)	In short	Summary

Write It

Notebook Rewrite each passage in your notebook. Replace the transition with another one that has the same meaning.

PERSONALIZE FOR LEARNING

Strategic Support

Comparative Research Group members may have difficulty seeing how both sources work together to convey more information about *The Tragedy of Romeo and Juliet.* To help students better understand each writer's argument, have them research other literary criticisms about Shakespeare's famous play and note down key findings. Then, ask students to discuss their research findings in their groups. **(Research to Explore)**

EFFECTIVE EXPRESSION

Writing to Sources

Join the conversation between Rosenberg and Berlatsky by writing responses to these two essays about Shakespeare's play *The Tragedy of Romeo and Juliet*.

Assignment

Remember that **criticism** texts are argumentative texts that express opinions about created works. Write your own criticism using one of the following choices. Your text should include **claims**, or statements that express a position, and evidence that supports these claims. To strengthen your writing, address and refute opposing opinions, called **counterclaims**. Once you have completed the writing, present your work to the class.

- ☐ **Reader Comments** Write comments that could be posted to the blog and website on which these essays appeared. Respond to their ideas and add your own, using textual evidence to support your response.
- ☐ **Speaker Invitation** Write letters to Rosenberg and Berlatsky, inviting them to participate in a school-sponsored Shakespeare festival. State specific reasons you want to include them and support each reason by citing evidence from these essays.
- ☐ **Proposal for Anthology** Write a proposal to create an anthology of critical writings about *The Tragedy of Romeo and Juliet*. Explain whether you wish to include or omit the essays by Rosenberg and Berlatsky.

Analyze Arguments Think carefully about the qualities of each article that worked and did not work as an argument before you write your own criticism. Consult your chart from the Analyze Craft and Structure page to help you analyze the argument in each text. Use the chart below to help you organize your thoughts.

	WHAT WORKED	WHAT DID NOT WORK
Rosenberg		
Berlatzky		

Clarify Ideas and Evidence Use the information you recorded in the chart to determine your claims about each text. Then, identify at least two reasons that support your claim. Finally, identify textual evidence that supports each reason. Discuss your ideas with your group and use their feedback to help you draft your criticism text.

TIP

COLLABORATION

If you are writing a negative comment about someone's writing, be sure to remain polite, especially when you are online. Rude comments reflect badly on the commenter.

EVIDENCE LOG

Before moving on to a new selection, go to your Evidence Log and record what you learned from "*Romeo and Juliet* Is a Terrible Play" and "In Defense of *Romeo and Juliet*."

STANDARDS

Reading Informational Text
Delineate and evaluate the argument and specific claims in a text, assessing whether the reasoning is valid and the evidence is relevant and sufficient; identify false statements and fallacious reasoning.

Writing
Introduce precise claim(s), distinguish the claim(s) from alternate or opposing claims, and create an organization that establishes clear relationships among claim(s), counterclaims, reasons, and evidence.

PERSONALIZE FOR LEARNING

Strategic Support

Understanding Evidence Some groups may require more time to complete the planning process. Be prepared to assist these students in understanding why their evidence represents a claim or counterclaim. Use transitional words and phrases such as *because* and *therefore* as you model for students.

- I think *The Tragedy of Romeo and Juliet* is an interesting play because the characters' behaviors are unpredictable.
- The main characters in *The Tragedy of Romeo and Juliet* both die; therefore, I think the play is terrible.

DIGITAL PERSPECTIVES

Writing to Sources

Explain to students that writing a criticism is like building an argument; they both depend on strong support and aim to sway the reader's point of view. While writing claims may be straightforward for students, constructing a counterclaim may be more of a challenge. Explain that students can address counterclaims in three ways: Present evidence to show that the counterclaim is wrong; to show that the counterclaim is valid, but that their position is as strong; to show that the counterclaim is valid, but that their position is much stronger.

Analyze Arguments Encourage students to include as many kinds of evidence, including facts, examples, and quotes, as possible. Also, have them carefully note their sources, including paragraph numbers from all selections. Remind groups to consult the schedule for Small-Group Activities as they analyze the arguments.

As students write their claims, counterclaims, and supporting evidence for each, they should check to make sure they have quoted all textual citations correctly. Remind students to document any outside sources to avoid plagiarism. For more support, see **Writing to Sources: Criticisms.**

Evidence Log Support students in completing the Evidence Log. This paced activity will help prepare them for the Performance-Based Assessment at the end of the unit.

FORMATIVE ASSESSMENT

Writing to Sources

If students struggle with identifying and writing counterclaims, **then** have them insert the word *not* in the claims to see the other side of the issue. For Reteach and Practice, see **Writing to Sources: Criticisms (RP).**

Selection Test

Administer the "*Romeo and Juliet* Is a Terrible Play, and David Leveaux Can't Change That" and "In Defense of *Romeo and Juliet:* It's Not Childish; It's *About* Childishness" Selection Test, which is available in both print and digital formats online in Assessments.

Twenty Years On: The Unfinished Lives of Bosnia's Romeo and Juliet

AUDIO SUMMARIES
Audio summaries of "Twenty Years On: The Unfinished Lives of Bosnia's Romeo and Juliet" are available online in both English and Spanish in the Interactive Teacher's Edition or Unit Resources. Assigning these summaries prior to reading the selection may help students build additional background knowledge and set a context for their first read.

Summary

"Twenty Years On: The Unfinished Lives of Bosnia's Romeo and Juliet" is a news article by Gordana Sandic-Hadzihasanovic. It begins with the death of a young couple. The couple, a Bosniak and a Serb, were shot by a sniper and died together while trying to leave the city. An eyewitness described the scene; the two of them died embracing each other. No one ever found out who shot them. The story is well-known today, and seen as a parallel that is still relevant to life in the region. Sadly, the city they fell in love in is still very different from the way it once was.

Insight

This selection shows that stories of doomed romance happen in real life. Bosko and Admira had little chance of escaping Sarajevo during the siege. The text also emphasizes that the tragedy of the war is much larger than just one couple. Furthermore, there are more loose ends in reality than in fiction. No one knows who killed them, and the nation has not fully recovered from the war that killed them and so many others.

ESSENTIAL QUESTION:
Do we determine our own destinies?

Connection to Essential Question

Bosko and Admira were unable to escape the war. And yet, the people of the region today may be able to avoid the tensions and violence that led to so much suffering.

SMALL-GROUP LEARNING PERFORMANCE TASK
What is compelling about stories in which people face a tragic destiny?

UNIT PERFORMANCE-BASED ASSESSMENT
Should the opinions of others affect our own choices or destinies?

Connection to Performance Tasks

Small-Group Learning Performance Task Davor Sucic says that the story is compelling because it seems symbolic. It is like a microcosm of the events of the war and has many things in common with life after it, as well.

Unit Performance-Based Assessment Everyone we meet in this selection has a favorable opinion of the couple. And yet, during the war few would have thought so well of them. Widely held opinions change.

DIGITAL PERSPECTIVES Audio | Video | Document | Annotation Highlights | EL Highlights | Online Assessment

LESSON RESOURCES

	Making Meaning	Language Development
Lesson	**First Read** **Close Read** **Analyze the Text** **Analyze Craft and Structure**	**Concept Vocabulary** **Word Study** **Conventions**
Instructional Standards	**RL.10** By the end of grade 9, read and comprehend literary nonfiction . . . **RI.5** Analyze in detail how an author's ideas . . . **L.4.b** Identify and correctly use patterns of word changes . . .	**L.4.b** dentify and correctly use patterns of word changes . . . **L.4.d** Verify the preliminary determination . . . **L.1.b** Use various types of phrases and clauses . . .
STUDENT RESOURCES		
Available online in the Interactive Student Edition or Unit Resources	Selection Audio First-Read Guide: Nonfiction Close-Read Guide: Nonfiction	Word Network
TEACHER RESOURCES		
Selection Resources Available online in the Interactive Teacher's Edition or Unit Resources	Audio Summaries Annotation Highlights EL Highlights English Language Support Lesson: Absolute Phrases The Unfinished Lives of Bosnia's Romeo and Juliet: Text Questions Analyze Craft and Structure: Journalism	Concept Vocabulary and Word Study Conventions: Phrases
Reteach/Practice (RP) Available online in the Interactive Teacher's Edition or Unit Resources	Analyze Craft and Structure: Journalism (RP)	Word Study: Latin Prefix: *inter-* (RP) Conventions: Phrases (RP)
Assessment Available online in Assessments	Selection Test	
My Resources	A Unit 4 Answer Key is available online and in the Interactive Teacher's Edition.	

Reading Support

Text Complexity Rubric: Twenty Years On: The Unfinished Lives of Bosnia's Romeo and Juliet	
Quantitative Measures	
Lexile: 1000 **Text Length:** 671 words	
Qualitative Measures	
Knowledge Demands (1–2–**3**–4–5)	The selection explores a tragic love story from the Bosnian Civil War; explanation is provided for most of the historical references. The references to RFE/RL (Radio Free Europe/Radio Liberty) are not explained.
Structure (1–2–**3**–4–5)	Information in the selection is logically organized, but connections between ideas are not always completely explicit or in a predictable sequence.
Language Conventionality and Clarity (1–2–3–**4**–5)	Some sentences in the explanation are complex, with multiple clauses and difficult vocabulary, but the selection also has many quotations using conversational language.
Levels of Meaning/Purpose (1–2–3–**4**–5)	The concept is accessible (war-time, tragic love story), but will likely be difficult to grasp due to challenging language and structure.

DECIDE AND PLAN

English Language Support

Provide English Learners with support for Knowledge Demands and Language as they read the selection

Knowledge Demands Discuss the meaning and use of the words *cease-fire*, *siege*, and *no-man's land*. Ask students to read sentences in paragraphs 5 and 6 with these words. Help students understand these words and the events that are described.

Language Help students reword long and complex sentences. Using the language from the selection, suggest simpler sentences that convey the same meaning. For example, for paragraph 7: *The deaths of the two lovers made people around the world see the senselessness of the war.* Ask students to read and discuss the new sentences.

Strategic Support

Provide students with strategic support to ensure that they can successfully read the text.

Knowledge Demands Use the background information to discuss the Bosnian Civil War. Determine students' prior knowledge of the war. Provide additional background if needed.

Language If students have difficulty with complex sentences, work together to break down sentences into smaller chunks in order to understand their meaning. Ask students to highlight words or phrases that they don't understand. As a group, help define some of the terms they find difficult.

Challenge

Provide students who need to be challenged with ideas for how they can go beyond a simple interpretation of the text.

Text Analysis Ask students to explain what the selection told them about the ways people cope with the harsh realities of war. How did a rock band respond to the tragedy? How did the young lovers' parents respond?

Written Response Ask students to write a summary of the various ways that the selection describes people reacting to tragedy. Then have them write a fictional but realistic account, putting themselves in that situation and describing how they would respond.

TEACH

Read and Respond

Have students do their first read of the selection. Then have them complete their close read. Finally, work with them on the Making Meaning and Language Development activities.

Standards Support Through Teaching and Learning Cycle

IDENTIFY NEEDS

Analyze results of the Beginning-of-Year Assessment, focusing on the items relating to Unit 4. Also take into consideration student performance to this point and your observations of where particular students struggle.

DECIDE AND PLAN

- If students have performed poorly on items matching these standards, then provide selection scaffolds before assigning them the on-level lesson provided in the Student Edition.
- If students have done well on the Beginning-of-Year Assessment, then challenge them to keep progressing and learning by giving them opportunities to practice the skills in depth.
- Use the Selection Resources listed on the Planning pages for "Twenty Years On: The Unfinished Lives of Bosnia's Romeo and Juliet" to help students continually improve their ability to master the standards.

Instructional Standards: Twenty Years On: The Unfinished Lives of Bosnia's Romeo and Juliet

	Catching Up	This Year	Looking Forward
Reading	You may wish to administer the **Analyze Craft and Structure: Journalism (RP)** worksheet to help students better understand the craft of journalism.	**RI.5** Analyze in detail how an author's ideas or claims are developed and refined by particular sentences, paragraphs, or larger portions of a text.	Challenge students to identify other types of journalism beyond "feature news articles."
Language	Review the **Word Study: Latin Prefix: *inter-* (RP)** worksheet to familiarize students with the root word. Review the **Conventions: Phrases (RP)** worksheet to give students more practice with appositive and absolute phrases.	**L.4.b** Identify and correctly use patterns of word changes that indicate different meanings or parts of speech. **L.1.b** Use various types of phrases and clauses to convey specific meanings and add variety and interest to writing or presentations.	Have students locate other words in the selection that have Latin or Greek prefixes they may recognize. Have students locate appositive and absolute phrases in other works they have read.

ANALYZE AND REVISE

- Analyze student work for evidence of student learning.
- Identify whether students have met the expectations in the standards.
- Identify implications for future instruction.

TEACH

Implement the planned lesson, and gather evidence of student learning.

FACILITATING

Jump Start

FIRST READ "Have you heard any modern-day versions of *The Tragedy of Romeo and Juliet*?" This question provides context for reading "Twenty Years On: The Unfinished Lives of Bosnia's Romeo and Juliet." As students share their ideas, have them explain how the conflicts in those stories are resolved.

Twenty Years On: The Unfinished Lives of Bosnia's Romeo and Juliet

The love story of *The Tragedy of Romeo and Juliet* ends tragically. Why is this story so compelling? Modeling questions readers might ask as they read "Twenty Years On: The Unfinished Lives of Bosnia's Romeo and Juliet" connects the text to the Small-Group Performance Task assignment. Selection audio and print capability for the selection are available in the Interactive Teacher's Edition.

Concept Vocabulary

Ask groups to think of difficult words whose base words have helped them define the words. For example, in the word *entertainment*, the familiar word "inside" the word is *entertain*, which means to provide someone with amusement.

FIRST READ

Students should perform the steps of the first read independently.

NOTICE: You may want to encourage students to notice the key events in the story, from beginning to end.

ANNOTATE: Remind students to mark passages that include vivid details that paint a picture of the events in the story.

CONNECT: If students cannot make connections to their own lives or other texts, have them consider current news events that might relate.

RESPOND: Students will answer questions and write a summary to demonstrate understanding.

Point out to students that while they will always complete the Respond step at the end of the first read, the other steps will probably happen somewhat concurrently. You may wish to print copies of the **First-Read Guide: Nonfiction** for students to use.

MAKING MEANING

TWENTY YEARS ON: THE UNFINISHED LIVES OF BOSNIA'S ROMEO AND JULIET

Comparing Text to Media

In this lesson, you will compare two pieces of journalism—one print and one digital. First, you will complete the first-read and close-read activities for the piece of print journalism. The work you do with your group on this selection will help prepare you for the comparing task.

TRAGIC ROMEO AND JULIET OFFERS BOSNIA HOPE

About the Author

The journalism of **Gordana Sandić-Hadžihasanović** has focused on the plight of refugees. In her program named "I Don't Want Another's, I Want My Own," she interviews approximately 100 refugees about their histories and their attempts to return to their former lives.

Twenty Years On: The Unfinished Lives of Bosnia's Romeo and Juliet

Concept Vocabulary

As you perform your first read of "Twenty Years On: The Unfinished Lives of Bosnia's Romeo and Juliet," you will encounter these words.

besieged surrounding intervened

Base Words If these words are unfamiliar to you, analyze each one to see whether it contains a base word you know. Here is an example of how to apply the strategy.

Unfamiliar Word: *senseless*

Familiar "Inside" Word: *sense*, with meanings including "good reason."

Context: This modern-day "Romeo and Juliet" showed the tragic and **senseless** destruction of the city.

Conclusion: The author thinks that the war did not need to happen. *Senseless* might mean "without a good reason."

Apply your knowledge of base words and other vocabulary strategies to determine the meanings of unfamiliar words you encounter during your first read.

First Read NONFICTION

Apply these strategies as you conduct your first read. You will have an opportunity to complete a close read after your first read.

First Read: NOTICE, ANNOTATE, CONNECT, RESPOND

NOTICE the general ideas of the text. *What* is it about? *Who* is involved?

ANNOTATE by marking vocabulary and key passages you want to revisit.

CONNECT ideas within the selection to what you already know and what you have already read.

RESPOND by completing the Comprehension Check and by writing a brief summary of the selection.

STANDARDS

Reading Informational Text
By the end of grade 9, read and comprehend literary nonfiction in the grades 9–10 text complexity band proficiently, with scaffolding as needed at the high end of the range.

Language
Identify and correctly use patterns of word changes that indicate different meanings or parts of speech.

JOURNALISM

Twenty Years On: The Unfinished Lives of Bosnia's Romeo and Juliet

Gordana Sandić-Hadžihasanović

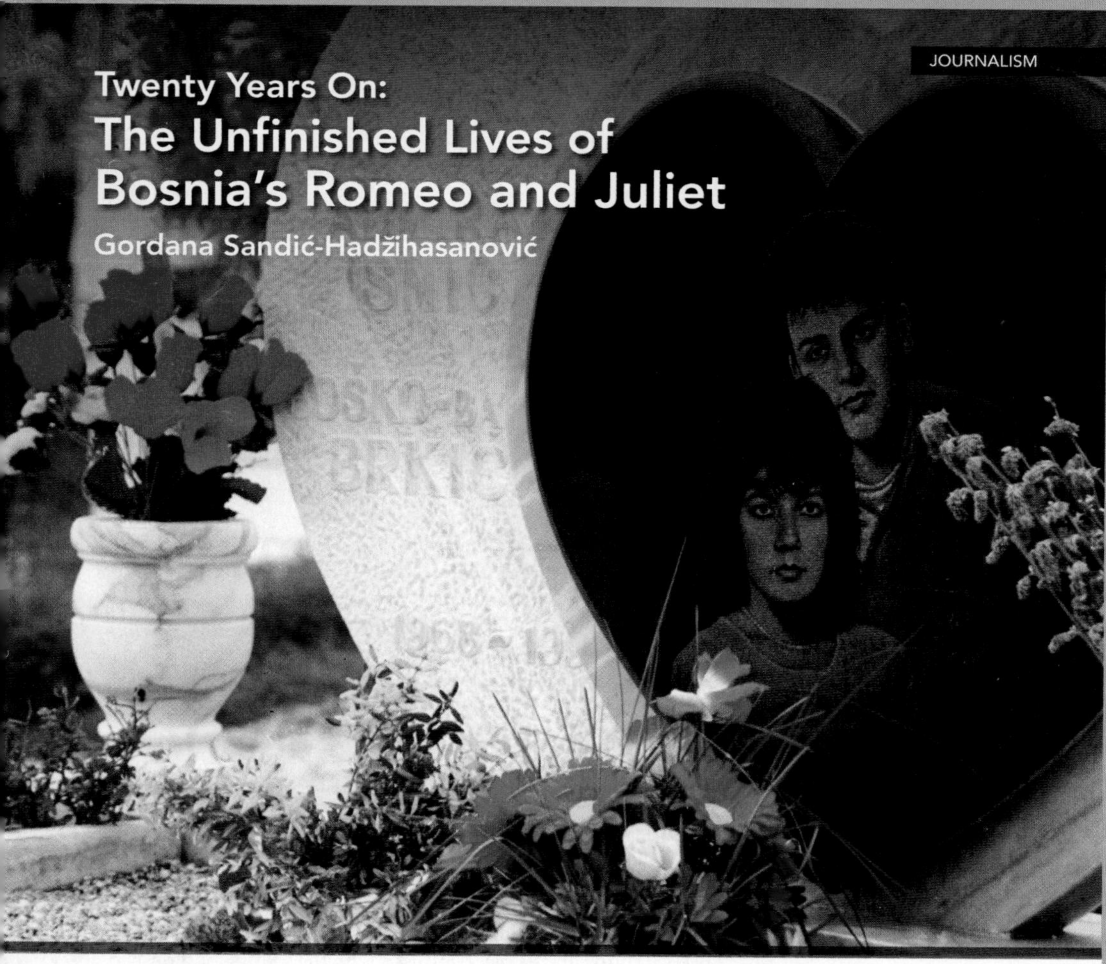

BACKGROUND

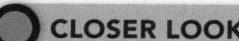

The Bosnian Civil War began in 1992 when Bosnia and Herzegovina, a small country in southeastern Europe, voted for independence from the former Yugoslavia. The primary rival groups included the mostly Christian Serbs and mostly Muslim Bosniaks. The country's capital, Sarajevo, was under siege for nearly four years.

SCAN FOR MULTIMEDIA

SARAJEVO– The story of Bosko Brkic and Admira Ismic ended with two short bursts from a sniper's rifle on a Sarajevo bridge the afternoon of May 19, 1993.

2 Bosko, a 24-year-old ethnic Serb, was killed instantly. Admira, his 25-year-old Bosniak girlfriend, was fatally wounded. She crawled to Bosko and, after about 10 minutes, died with him.

3 One eyewitness described the scene in an interview years later.

4 "The girl was carrying a bag and waving it. They were running and holding hands. It looked like she was dancing," the witness said.

NOTES

DIGITAL PERSPECTIVES

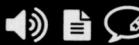

CLOSER LOOK

Infer Flashback

Circulate among groups as students conduct the close read. Suggest that groups read paragraph 4. Encourage them to talk about the annotations they mark. If needed, provide the following support.

ANNOTATE: Have students mark in paragraph 4 a flashback of what happened to Bosko and Admira, or work with small groups to have students participate as you highlight them together.

QUESTION: Guide students to consider what these details might tell them. Ask what a reader can infer from the description of the two lovers based on the eyewitness account, and accept student responses.

Possible response: Based on the eyewitness account, Bosko and Admira are running very quickly and might be trying to flee from something.

CONCLUDE: Help students formulate conclusions about the importance of these details in the text. Ask students why the author might have included these details.

Possible response: The eyewitness reports that Bosko and Admira are running in an attempt to escape the violence and gunshots in their midst. This serves as a flashback to the day of the original event.

Remind students that a **flashback** is a scene within a narrative that interrupts the sequence of events to relate events that occurred in the past. Writers use flashbacks to show what motivates a character or to reveal something about a character's past. In this article, the eyewitness account gives us a glimpse of the day Bosko and Admira are gunned down.

FACILITATING SMALL-GROUP CLOSE READING

Close Read: Nonfiction As groups perform the close read, circulate and offer support as needed.

- Remind groups that when they read a new article or journalistic piece of writing, they should be sure to identify key characters and events.
- If a group is confused about why a particular event is important, remind them to think about the time period and any social, political, or cultural happenings that may have impacted those events.
- Challenge groups to determine the key messages or themes in the article and the specific details that support these messages or themes.

Concept Vocabulary

BESIEGED If groups are struggling to define the word *besieged* in paragraph 5, point out that they can use base words, which are the familiar words that are found "inside" the unfamiliar words. In *besieged*, the familiar word is *siege*. Using the context clues offered in paragraphs 4 and 5: *I heard rifle shots* and *the bodies remained in no-man's land*, you can infer the meaning of siege. It is already known that *be* is a state of something. Therefore, *besieged* must mean the state of being sieged. Have students write their definitions.

Possible response: *Besieged* must mean "under military attack" or "the state of being seized by the military."

SURROUNDING If groups are struggling to define the word *surrounding* in paragraph 5, point out that they can use base words, which are the familiar words that are found "inside" the unfamiliar words. In *surrounding*, the base word is *surround*. Adding an *–ing* to a verb indicates the continuous form of the verb. Based on this, you can infer the meaning of the word *surrounding*.

Possible response: *Surrounding* must mean "encircling" or "gathered around."

NOTES

Mark base words or indicate another strategy you used that helped you determine meaning.

besieged (bih SEEJD) *adj.*

MEANING:

surrounding (suh ROWN dihng) *adj.*

MEANING:

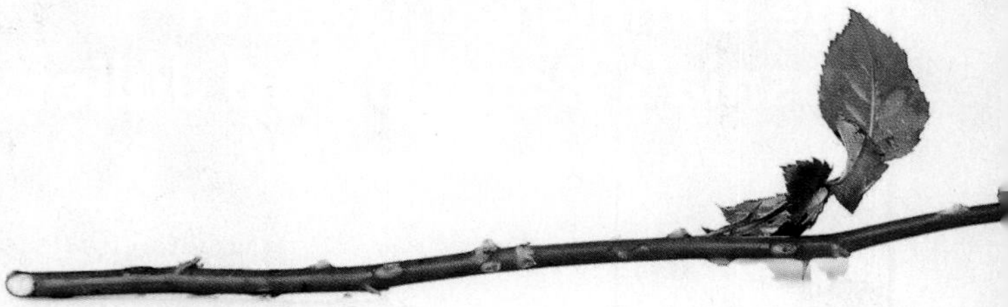

"Suddenly, I heard the rifle shots. They fell to the ground, embracing each other."

5 The bodies remained in the no-man's land of **besieged** Sarajevo for nearly four days before Serbian forces **surrounding** the city sent some Muslim prisoners to gather them.

6 Both sides blamed the other for breaking the shaky cease-fire under which the star-crossed lovers were trying to escape the siege. No definitive conclusions were ever reached.

"Each Other and a Dream"

7 The story flashed around the world in a now-famous dispatch by Reuters correspondent Kurt Schork. For millions around the world, this modern-day "Romeo and Juliet," a love destroyed by the hatred that surrounded it, brought home the tragedy and senselessness of the destruction of Bosnia-Herzegovina's capital.

8 Twenty years later, the classic Yugoslav rock band Zabranjeno Pusenje (No Smoking) has issued a new song and video called starkly "Bosko and Admira," a piece suffused with the sadness and dashed hopes of the original story:

The times get worse around them; they had no chance.
But difficult times always bring great romance.
They weren't from the same tribe, nor did they have the same god.
But they had each other and a dream of escaping out from under it all.

9 "This is [a] well-known Sarajevo story—about Sarajevo's Romeo and Juliet, about Bosko and Admira, young people killed in the war who were trying to find a place for their love and their freedom," Zabranjeno Pusenje front man Davor Sucic tells RFE/RL's Balkan Service. "This is a symbolic story, very relevant, even today. After so many years of peace we are still searching for love and freedom in

this country. In this story, I found a lot of things in common with life today and what is happening to us now."

10 The video was directed by Croatian Zare Batinovic, who tells RFE/RL about the challenges of making the film of a story so intimately tied to a city—the prewar, multiethnic Sarajevo—that essentially no longer exists.

11 "The theme is here. Everyone knows the story," Batinovic says. "So many years have been passed, and it was not easy to evoke the Sarajevo of the 1990s."

Haunting Question

12 If Bosnia's capital little resembles the scarred Sarajevo of 1993, it also remains far from the smiling, confident city that hosted the Winter Olympics in 1984, the year that Bosko and Admira first kissed at a New Year's party at the age of 16.

13 Admira's parents say they plan nothing special to mark the anniversary of their daughter's death beyond visiting the graves and leaving flowers. Her father, Zijo Ismic, still wrestles with the forces that swept over his daughter, his city, his country.

14 "War **intervened** in love—that's the problem," Ismic says. "In such situations, the laws of love do not exist. Only the laws of war."

15 Bosko's mother, Rada Brkic, left Sarajevo during the war and never returned, unable to face the familiar streets and neighborhoods where Bosko and Admira lived and loved.

16 She tells RFE/RL that she tries not to dwell too much on the fact that her son's killers were never identified.

17 "I don't think too much about the person who killed them," she says. "But if I ever saw him, I'd ask: 'Why did you do it?' That's all."

18 Bosko and Admira are buried in Sarajevo's Lion Cemetery along with thousands of other victims of the siege. Schork, who told their story, was killed while on assignment in Sierra Leone in 2000. Half of his ashes were buried next to the grave of Bosko and Admira. ❧

NOTES

Mark base words or indicate another strategy you used that helped you determine meaning.

intervened (ihn tuhr VEEND) *v.*

MEANING:

DIGITAL PERSPECTIVES

Concept Vocabulary

INTERVENED If groups are struggling to define the word *intervened* in paragraph 14, point out that they can use the context clues offered in paragraphs 13 and 14 and infer that war gets in the way of love.

Possible response: *Intervened* must mean "came between" or "got in the way of."

CLOSER LOOK

Infer Historical Context

Circulate among groups as students conduct the close read. Suggest that groups read paragraph 12. Encourage them to talk about the annotations they mark. If needed, provide the following support.

ANNOTATE: Have students mark details in paragraph 12 that compare and contrast the Sarajevo of the 1980s and 1990s, or work with small groups to have students participate as you highlight them together.

QUESTION: Guide students to consider what these details might tell them. Ask what a reader can infer from the description of the two eras in Sarajevo's history, and accept student responses.

Possible response: The Sarajevo of 1984, where people were happy and thriving, was very different from the Sarajevo of the 1990s, right before the civil war began.

CONCLUDE: Help students formulate conclusions about the importance of these details in the text. Ask students why the author might have included these details.

Possible response: When Bosko and Admira fell in love, they lived in a very different world; they could be themselves and love freely. The onset of the civil war in Sarajevo stripped them of this love and freedom, eventually leading to their tragic deaths.

Remind students that the **historical context** of a literary work is the key social, political, or cultural information about the time period in which it is set. When a work is set in the past, knowledge about that historical time period can help the reader better understand the attitudes and actions of its characters. In this case, the article was written twenty years after Bosko and Admira were shot.

Additional **English Language Support** is available in the Interactive Teacher's Edition.

FACILITATING

Comprehension Check

1. Bosko and Admira were trying to escape the siege in Serbia's capital, Sarajevo, when they were shot.
2. During this time period, there was a civil war, which had begun in 1992, between Christian Serbs and Muslim Bosniaks in the city of Sarajevo.
3. Twenty years after the star-crossed lovers were shot, a classic Yugoslav band, Zabranjeno Pusenje (No Smoking), wrote a song and created a video honoring Bosko and Admira.
4. Responses will vary.

   In "Twenty Years On: The Unfinished Lives of Bosnia's Romeo and Juliet," the author details the love of a modern-day Romeo and Juliet, Bosko and Admira, who fall in love when they are 16. Unfortunately, the two come from "different sides of the tracks;" one is a Christian Serb and the other, a Muslim Bosniak. During the Bosnian Civil War in 1992, the two are shot as they try to escape from Sarajevo, the capital. Twenty years later, a classic Yugoslav band writes a song and shoots a video celebrating Bosko and Admira's love, courage, and struggle.

Research

Research to Explore

If groups struggle to come up with a research topic, you may want to suggest that they focus on one of the following topics: Zabranjeno Pusenje, the Civil War in Sarajevo, major differences between the Serbs and Bosniaks, or the former Yugoslavia.

Comprehension Check

Complete the following items after you finish your first read. Review and clarify details with your group.

1. What were Bosko and Admira trying to do when they were shot?

2. What was taking place in the city of Sarajevo during this time period?

3. What happened twenty years later to remind people of Bosko and Admira?

4. **Notebook** Confirm your understanding of the text by writing a summary of the article.

RESEARCH

Research to Explore Choose something that interested you from the text, and formulate a research question.

PERSONALIZE FOR LEARNING

Challenge

Research Have students research modern-day Sarajevo and how it has transformed over the years. Ask students to identify primary sources and eyewitness accounts of events that occurred prewar, during the war, and postwar. How have things changed? How have some things stayed the same? What strategies did people use to help them adapt to their new lives after the war? **(Research to Explore)**

Close Read the Text

With your group, revisit sections of the text you marked during your first read. What do you **notice**? What **questions** do you have? What can you **conclude**?

ANNOTATE QUESTION Close Read CONCLUDE

Analyze the Text

CITE TEXTUAL EVIDENCE to support your answers.

Notebook Complete the activities.

1. **Review and Clarify** With your group, reread paragraphs 1–4 of the text. Discuss with your group the exact events of the afternoon of May 19, 1993. What insight does the eyewitness provide?
2. **Present and Discuss** Now, work with your group to share the passages from the text that you found especially important. Take turns presenting your passages. Discuss what you notice in the text, the questions you asked, and the conclusions you reached.
3. **Essential Question:** ***Do we determine our own destinies?*** What has this text taught you about destiny?

LANGUAGE DEVELOPMENT

Concept Vocabulary

beseiged **surrounding** **intervened**

Why These Words? The three concept vocabulary words are related. With your group, determine what the words have in common. Write your ideas, and add another word that fits the category.

Practice

Notebook Confirm your understanding of the concept vocabulary words from the text by using them in sentences. Share your sentences with members of your group.

Word Study

Notebook **Latin Prefix: *inter-*** The word *intervened* begins with the Latin prefix *inter-*, which means "between" or "among." Complete these activities, and discuss your answers with your group.

1. The Latin root *-ven-* means "to come." Using this fact, write a definition for *intervened* that shows your understanding of the prefix *inter-*.
2. Infer the meaning of *intercultural*, and write a definition. Use a dictionary to verify your answer.

TWENTY YEARS ON: THE UNFINISHED LIVES OF BOSNIA'S ROMEO AND JULIET

TIP

GROUP DISCUSSION

Ask questions to spur discussion. When many members of a group are asking and answering questions, the group is able to come up with more ideas than if only one person is offering ideas.

WORD NETWORK

Add interesting words related to destiny from the text to your Word Network.

STANDARDS

Language
- Identify and correctly use patterns of word changes that indicate different meanings or parts of speech.
- Verify the preliminary determination of the meaning of a word or phrase.

DIGITAL PERSPECTIVES

Jump Start

CLOSE READ Ask students to consider the following prompt: How are Romeo and Juliet similar to Bosko and Admira? How are they different? Which couple's story do you find more interesting or moving, and why?

Close Read the Text

If needed, model close reading by using the Annotation Highlights in the Interactive Teacher's Edition. You may wish to print copies of the **Close Read Guide: Nonfiction** for students to use.

Remind students to use Accountable Talk in their discussions and to support one another as they complete the close read.

Analyze the Text

Possible responses:

1. The eyewitness describes the two "holding hands" and "embracing each other" as they fell to the ground, which conveys how strong their love is. (paragraph 4)
2. Passages will vary by group. Remind students to explain why they chose the passages they presented to the group members.
3. Responses will vary by group.

Concept Vocabulary

Why These Words? Possible response: The words all have to do with attacking or otherwise interfering with something or someone. Another words that fits the category is *accost.*

Practice

Possible responses:

- The Bosnian army *besieged* the city from every corner and took innocent lives.
- The residents in *surrounding* cities were likely too terrified to enter Sarajevo during the war.
- I wonder why other countries did not *intervene* during the war to stop the casualties.

Word Network

Possible words: *star-crossed, chance*

Word Study

For more support, see **Concept Vocabulary and Word Study.**

Possible responses:

1. came between, or inserted oneself into
2. between or among different cultures

FORMATIVE ASSESSMENT

Analyze the Text

If students struggle to close read the text, then provide **The Unfinished Lives of Bosnia's Romeo and Juliet: Text Questions** available online in the Interactive Teacher's Edition or Unit Resources. Answers and DOK levels are also available.

Concept Vocabulary

If students struggle to identify the concept, **then** present them with additional examples of words with recognizable bases.

Word Study

If students fail to use the words in sentences, **then** have them search additional texts for words that have the prefix, *inter-*.

For Reteach and Practice, see **Word Study: Latin Prefix: *inter-* (RP).**

FACILITATING

Analyze Craft and Structure

Journalism Discuss with students how feature news articles are structured to grab the audience's attention. For example, the journalist might use first-hand accounts from eyewitnesses who were present during the event, or include images and details from audio transcripts to ensure that the information presented is as accurate as possible. Also, remind students that the journalist might include specific details about the time and place of the event in order to better contextualize it for the audience. For more support, see **Analyze Craft and Structure: Journalism.**

Practice

See possible responses in Student page.

FORMATIVE ASSESSMENT

Analyze Craft and Structure

If students struggle to determine key details emphasized in the feature news article, **then** revisit key passages to discuss what specific parts of the article are relevant or stand out.

For Reteach and Practice, see **Analyze Craft and Structure: Journalism (RP).**

MAKING MEANING

TWENTY YEARS ON: THE UNFINISHED LIVES OF BOSNIA'S ROMEO AND JULIET

TIP

GROUP DISCUSSION

Sometimes facts that are stated simply can be more powerful and memorable than facts that are stated in a complicated or highly descriptive way.

Analyze Craft and Structure

Journalism News articles and broadcasts make up an important part of journalism, a type of nonfiction writing that focuses on current events and nonfiction subjects of general interest to the public. **Feature articles**, such as "Twenty Years On," are a type of journalism that focuses on a specific event or situation.

Effective journalism grabs readers' attention and emphasizes the most important information in a news story. To do this, the author must first answer the basic questions *who, what, where, when,* and *why* of a story. Authors may answer most of the questions in the first few paragraphs, or lead paragraphs, but they may use the rest of the article to address the *why* questions, since the answer may be more complex. As they answer the *why* questions, authors often include quotations from eyewitnesses or other people related to the story. Authors may also include a paragraph that summarizes the important details and the significance of the event in a "nutshell" paragraph. Finally, authors will conclude with a memorable ending, such as a poignant quotation or a statement that challenges readers to think about what the event may mean for the future. This variety of organizational elements helps journalists convey information logically while also conveying the importance of an event or situation.

Practice

CITE TEXTUAL EVIDENCE to support your answers.

Use the chart to analyze the various elements of a feature article. Then, share your ideas with your group.

FEATURE ARTICLE ELEMENT	DETAILS EMPHASIZED
Headline	Star-Crossed Couple Die Together
Lead Paragraph(s)	Twenty years ago, a modern Romeo and Juliet met their tragic fate on a Sarajevo bridge.
Basic Questions *Who, What, When, Where,* and *Why*	Who: Bosko and Admira What: love, destroyed by war When: May 1993
Quotations	"War intervened in love— that's the problem ... in such situations, the laws of love do not exist."
Nutshell Paragraph	In times of crisis such as war, something as freeing and beautiful as love can be destroyed.
Ending	Bosko and Admira are buried along with thousands of other victims.

STANDARDS

Reading Informational Text

Analyze in detail how an author's ideas or claims are developed and refined by particular sentences, paragraphs, or larger portions of a text.

522 UNIT 4 • STAR-CROSSED ROMANCES

WriteNow Analyze and Interpret

QuickWrite Throughout "Twenty Years On: The Unfinished Lives of Bosnia's Romeo and Juliet," the journalist uses sensory details to create a picture in the reader's mind. Have students write a one-page analysis of these details and how they enhance the story of Bosko and Admira. How does the description of Zabranjeno Pusenje's song about the couple contribute to the overall message?

LANGUAGE DEVELOPMENT

Conventions

Using Phrases to Add Variety Writers may use various types of phrases to clarify the logical relationships among ideas and to add variety to their writing. Two of those types of phrases are appositive phrases and absolute phrases.

An **appositive** is a group of words that identifies, renames, or explains a noun or pronoun. An **appositive phrase** is an appositive along with its own modifiers. An appositive or appositive phrase usually appears directly after the word it is modifying.

An **absolute phrase** features a noun or pronoun and its modifiers. Often, the modifiers include a participle or participial phrase. Rather than modifying an individual word, an absolute phrase modifies an entire clause or sentence.

To strengthen your writing, when two separate sentences are closely related, consider revising to combine them using an appositive phrase or an absolute phrase. This chart shows two examples of this type of revision.

WEAKER WRITING	REVISION USING A PHRASE
Romeo and Juliet is a play by William Shakespeare. It has the archetypal theme of ill-fated love.	Appositive Phrase: *Romeo and Juliet*, **a play by William Shakespeare**, has ill-fated love as a theme.
Bosko and Admira's legend lives long after their death. They are a reminder of senseless loss for the people of Sarajevo.	Absolute Phrase: **Their legend living long after their death**, Bosko and Admira are a reminder of senseless loss for the people of Sarajevo.

Read It

Work individually. Use this chart to identify the appositive phrase or absolute phrase in each sentence.

SENTENCE	APPOSITIVE PHRASE	ABSOLUTE PHRASE
The story of Bosko and Admira takes place in Sarajevo, a town torn by civil war in the early 1990s.	a town that was torn by civil war in the early 1990s	
Their hearts filled with love, Bosko and Admira crossed the bridge between the two halves of the city.		Their hearts filled with love
Zabranjeno Pusenje, a Yugoslav rock band, recently wrote a song about Bosko and Admira.	a Yugoslav rock band	
Many of its buildings rebuilt, the city remains in the shadow of the war.		Many of the buildings rebuilt

Write It

Notebook In your notebook, write one sentence about the article. In your sentence, include either an appositive phrase or an absolute phrase.

EVIDENCE LOG

Before moving on to a new selection, go to your evidence log and record what you've learned from *Twenty Years On: The Unfinished Lives of Bosnia's Romeo and Juliet.*

STANDARDS

Language
Use various types of phrases and clauses to convey specific meanings and add variety and interest to writing or presentations.

DIGITAL PERSPECTIVES

Conventions

Using Phrases to Add Variety Discuss with students that sentences using these types of phrases are common in our everyday speech patterns. Appositive and absolute phrases are often used to add an extra detail, a purpose, or a reason.

As you review the examples of appositive and absolute phrases with students, consider providing additional examples:

appositive phrase:
Bosko and Admira, two young lovers, remind us that there is hope and freedom in love.

absolute phrase:
Having died during a period of unrest, Bosko and Admira are buried with thousands of other victims of the Bosnian Civil War.

For more support, see **Conventions: Phrases (RP).**

Read It

Have students write their own sentences on strips of paper and ask them to add appositive and absolute phrases to different parts of the sentences to determine if their meaning changes.

Write It

Possible responses:
Sentences will vary, but make sure that students include at least one appositive or absolute phrase. Suggest that students use appositive or absolute phrases to elaborate on action, setting, or character details.

Evidence Log Support students in completing the Evidence Log. This paced activity will help prepare them for the Performance-Based Assessment at the end of the unit.

FORMATIVE ASSESSMENT

Conventions

If students are unable to identify appositive or absolute phrases, **then** have them look for nouns or noun phrases that appear right before or follow other nouns directly.

For Reteach and Practice, see **Conventions: Phrases (RP).**

PERSONALIZE FOR LEARNING

English Language Support

Subject-Verb Agreement English learners often struggle with subject-verb agreement when writing. Remind students that the subject and the verb in a sentence need to agree. For example, singular subjects need a singular verb (The sniper shoots.), and plural subjects need a plural verb (The snipers shoot.). Suggest that students review their sentences for subject-verb agreement as part of their editing process. **ALL LEVELS**

Tragic Romeo and Juliet Offers Bosnia Hope

AUDIO SUMMARIES
Audio summaries of "Tragic Romeo and Juliet Offers Bosnia Hope" are available online in both English and Spanish in the Interactive Teacher's Edition or Unit Resources. Assigning these summaries prior to reading the selection may help students build additional background knowledge and set a context for their first read.

Summary

In the video, "Tragic Romeo and Juliet Offers Bosnia Hope," Nic Robertson interviews the parents of Bosko Brkic and Admira Ismic, a young couple who were killed by a sniper's bullets as they were trying to flee Sarajevo during the civil war on May 18, 1993. Admira was Muslim and Bosko was an Eastern Orthodox Serbian. In spite of their love for each other, they were on opposite sides of the ethnic and religious divide that was at the heart of the civil war. The couple's bodies lay for eight days on the bridge where they died until Serbian soldiers buried them. As a Muslim, Admira's mother was not able to cross the front to get to her daughter's burial. The young couple now share a grave in a Sarajevo cemetery. The parents have remained close friends, and they hope that other parents will not have to grieve over the senseless killings of their own children.

Insight

This selection shows that stories of doomed romance do indeed happen in real life. Bosko and Admira had little chance of escaping Sarajevo during the siege. But the two selections also emphasize that the tragedy of the war is much larger than just one couple. Furthermore, there are more loose ends in reality than in fiction. No one knows who killed them, and the nation has not fully recovered from the war that killed them and so many others.

ESSENTIAL QUESTION:
Do we determine our own destinies?

Connection to Essential Question

In their attempt to flee the violence in Sarajevo, Bosko and Admira were trying to determine their own destinies. However, the racial and religious tensions and resulting violence led to a tragic outcome.

SMALL-GROUP LEARNING PERFORMANCE TASK
What is compelling about stories in which people face a tragic destiny?

UNIT PERFORMANCE-BASED ASSESSMENT
Should the opinions of others affect our own choices or destinies?

Connection to Performance Tasks

Small-Group Learning Task The story is compelling because it echoes the way society as a whole tries to bridge its ethnic divides. Also, it is easier to think about the deaths of a couple than the deaths of tens of thousands; tragic stories are a way to get a grip on larger events.

Unit Performance-Based Assessment Everyone we meet in these selections has a favorable opinion of the couple. And yet, during the war few would have thought so well of them. Widely held opinions change.

DIGITAL PERSPECTIVES | Audio | Video | Document | Annotation Highlights | EL Highlights | Online Assessment

Media Complexity Rubric: Tragic Romeo and Juliet Offers Bosnia Hope

Quantitative Measures	
Format and Length: news journal report, 3 minutes and 39 seconds	
Qualitative Measures	
Knowledge Demands ① ② ③ ❹ ⑤	Two young lovers of different religions were killed during the Bosnian civil war of the 1990s. There is little geographical specificity of the "front lines" and the "ethnic divide" that caused the war.
Structure ① ❷ ③ ④ ⑤	Although the killings took place more than twenty years ago, the video is logically organized, though there are jumps between the events of the early 1990s and 2012, when the broadcast originally aired.
Language Conventionality and Clarity ① ② ③ ❹ ⑤	Some terms require a greater knowledge of the history of the war, including "ethnic divide," "front lines," the break up of the "former Yugoslavia." Reference to the "political leaders" is not clarified.
Levels of Meaning/Purpose ① ② ❸ ④ ⑤	The concept of tragic love and the connection between "Bosnia's Romeo and Juliet" and Shakespeare's characters, along with why the couple is a "beacon of hope," may be challenging.

LESSON RESOURCES

	Making Meaning	Language Development	Effective Expression
Lesson	**First Review** **Close Review** **Analyze the Media**	**Media Vocabulary**	**Writing to Compare**
Instructional Standards	**RI.7** Analyze various accounts of a subject . . . **L.6** Acquire and use accurately general academic and domain-specific words and phrases . . .	**L.6** Acquire and use accurately general academic and domain-specific words and phrases . . .	**RI.7** Analyze various accounts of a subject . . . **W.1** Write arguments to support claims . . .
STUDENT RESOURCES			
Available online in the Interactive Student Edition or Unit Resources	Selection Audio First-Review Guide: Media-Video Close-Review Guide: Media-Video	Word Network	Evidence Log
TEACHER RESOURCES			
Selection Resources Available online in the Interactive Teacher's Edition or Unit Resources	Audio Summaries Tragic Romeo and Juliet Offers Bosnia Hope: Media Questions	Media Vocabulary	Writing to Compare: Argument
Assessment Available online in Assessments	Selection Test		
My Resources	A Unit 4 Answer Key is available online and in the Interactive Teacher's Edition.		

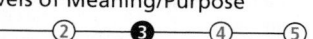

FACILITATING

Jump Start

FIRST REVIEW Engage students in a discussion of the advantages and disadvantages of a variety of formats: print, online print, online news, and television. How might a news story differ depending on whether it is presented as a video or in print?

Tragic Romeo and Juliet Offers Bosnia Hope

What impact can the actions of a few people have on the thoughts, feelings, and/or actions of many? Modeling the questions a reader might ask as they review "Tragic Romeo and Juliet Offers Bosnia Hope" brings the video alive for students and connects it to the Small-Group Performance Task assignment. Selection audio is available in the Interactive Teacher's Edition.

Media Vocabulary

Encourage groups to discuss the media vocabulary. Have they seen the terms in texts before? Do they use any of them in their speech and writing?

Ask groups to consider how the terms relate to each other. Students will notice that three of the terms are video techniques, while the fourth is a type of media that can (but does not always) incorporate the use of those techniques.

FIRST REVIEW

Students should perform the steps of the first review independently.

NOTICE: Remind students to note information provided by the reporter and information provided by other individuals interviewed.

NOTE: Encourage students to note segments of the video that provide information not found in the print story.

CONNECT: Encourage students to make connections beyond the video. If they cannot make connections to their own lives, have them consider other video news stories they have seen.

RESPOND: Students will answer questions and write a summary to demonstrate understanding.

Point out to students that while they will always complete the Respond step at the end of the first read, the other steps will probably happen somewhat concurrently. You may wish to print copies of the **First-Review Guide: Media - Video** for students to use.

MAKING MEANING

Comparing Text to Media

The video "Tragic Romeo and Juliet Offers Bosnia Hope" is from Cable News Network's website. While viewing this selection, you will analyze the differences between how written text and video can tell a story.

About the Narrator

With over twenty years' experience, CNN's Senior International Correspondent **Nic Robertson** (b. 1962) has had a decorated career. He has reported from the war-torn regions of Iraq, Libya, Afghanistan, Yugoslavia, Pakistan, Lebanon, Sudan, and Northern Ireland, among others. His work has won many prestigious awards, including Emmys, Peabodys, and the duPont Award.

STANDARDS

Reading Informational Text
Analyze various accounts of a subject told in different mediums, determining which details are emphasized in each account.

Language
Acquire and use accurately general academic and domain-specific words and phrases, sufficient for reading, writing, speaking and listening at the college and career readiness level; demonstrate independence in gathering vocabulary knowledge when considering a word or phrase important to comprehension or expression.

Tragic Romeo and Juliet Offers Bosnia Hope

Media Vocabulary

These terms will be useful to you as you analyze, discuss, and write about news videos.

Human Interest Story: story that focuses on the personal issues of people	• Human interest stories are often told in a more emotional way than other news stories. • These stories encourage the viewer or listener to identify with the subjects of the stories. • These stories may deal with difficult situations faced by individuals or the achievements of individuals.
Establishing Shot: shot that shows the context of a scene in a film or video	• An establishing shot is often a long shot that shows where a scene takes place.
Reporter Stand-Ups: shot that shows a reporter looking into the camera and delivering information about a story	• Often, reporter stand-ups appear at or near the beginning or the end of a film or video.
Montage: group of images shown quickly, one after another, to create a single impression	• Montages are often used when a director has access to only still images of a person or event. • Montages can be very effective in communicating the personality of a person or the nature of a relationship.

First Review MEDIA: VIDEO

Apply these strategies as you conduct your first review.

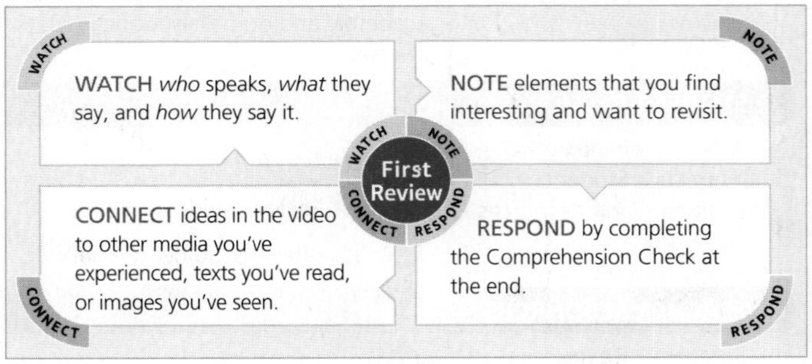

WATCH
WATCH *who* speaks, *what* they say, and *how* they say it.
NOTE
NOTE elements that you find interesting and want to revisit.
First Review
CONNECT
CONNECT ideas in the video to other media you've experienced, texts you've read, or images you've seen.
RESPOND
RESPOND by completing the Comprehension Check at the end.

MEDIA | NEWSCAST

Tragic Romeo and Juliet Offers Bosnia Hope

Nic Robertson

BACKGROUND

During the Bosnian Civil War, the Serbs and the Yugoslav army attacked areas with large Bosniak populations, including the capital city, Sarajevo, in order to control the region. The attack also served as a means of what could be described as "ethnic cleansing." By the end of the war in 1995, about 100,000 people had been killed.

SCAN FOR MULTIMEDIA

NOTES

DIGITAL PERSPECTIVES

CLOSER REVIEW

Analyze Montage

Circulate among groups as students conduct their first reviews. Suggest that groups review the section of video from 00:17 to 00:42. Encourage them to talk about the notes they make. If needed, provide the following support.

NOTE: Have students note the montage in the video that describes the subjects of the video to the viewer, or work with small groups to have students participate while you note them together.

QUESTION: Guide students to consider what these details might tell them. Ask what the photos in the montage have in common, and accept student responses.

Possible response: Most of the photos are of Admira and Bosko together, embracing as a couple.

CONCLUDE: Help students formulate conclusions about the importance of these details in the video. Ask students why the videographer might have included these details.

Possible response: The photos in the montage introduce the viewer to the subjects of the video because they cannot be introduced in person. The videographer uses photos that demonstrate the depth of their relationship because the relationship and its lasting impact is the main focus of the video.

Remind students that a **montage** is often used when live footage is unavailable, such as in cases where a story focuses on a past event or a deceased person.

WriteNow Express and Reflect

Description Throughout the video, references are made to the amount of time that has passed since the deaths of Admira and Bosko. For Admira's parents, the passage of time means that their feelings about and reactions to the event have changed. Have students think of an event from their past that they felt strongly about and write a paragraph describing the feelings they had when it first occurred, as well as their current feelings about the event. Have any of their feelings changed? If so, why do they think those changes occurred? What do they think will happen as even more time passes?

Comprehension Check

Possible responses

1. The filmmakers show Bosko and Admira through the eyes of their parents, who approved of the couple's relationship. This presentation makes the romance even more tragic because unlike Romeo and Juliet, whose families were determined to keep them apart, Bosko and Admira had supportive families and it was society that doomed them.
2. The setting is the bridge where Bosko and Admira were shot nearly 20 years before. The city of Sarajevo is visible in the background.
3. Their bodies were recovered by the Serbian army, which would not allow the Bosnian parents to attend their child's funeral.
4. Summaries will vary; however, students should include elements of the people and events featured and the main ideas expressed in the video broadcast.

Comprehension Check

Complete the following items after you finish your first review. Review and clarify details with your group.

1. Through whose eyes does the newscast show Bosko and Admira?

2. Describe the setting in the reporter stand-up shot near the beginning of the newscast.

3. Why could only one parent attend Bosko and Admira's funeral?

4. **Notebook** Confirm your understanding by writing a summary of the newscast.

PERSONALIZE FOR LEARNING

Challenge

Research Have students research other human interest stories about people who overcame ingrained prejudice in times of conflict. Possible topics for research could include the Holocaust, South African apartheid, ethnic conflict in Rwanda or Palestine, or political conflict in Northern Ireland. Students should provide a brief report on the individuals and situations involved, explaining why they think it was possible to go against the hatred and how that affected the rest of the community.

Close Review

Close Review (REVIEW · QUESTION · CONCLUDE)

With your group, revisit the video and your first-review notes. Record any new observations that seem important. What **questions** do you have? What can you **conclude**?

Analyze the Media

CITE TEXTUAL EVIDENCE to support your answers.

Complete the activities.

1. **Present and Discuss** How does the first shot in the newscast establish a sense of memory and the past? How does this shot convey a sense of loss? Discuss your thoughts with your group.
2. **Review and Synthesize** With your group, review the entire newscast. What does the newscast convey about tragedy, and about hope? Support your ideas with evidence from the media.
3. **Essential Question:** *Do we determine our own destinies?* What has this newscast taught you about destiny? Support your ideas with evidence from the newscast, then discuss them with your group.

LANGUAGE DEVELOPMENT

Media Vocabulary

human interest story	reporter stand-ups
establishing shot	montage

Use the media vocabulary words and phrases in your responses to the questions.

1. How would you describe the opening of the newscast?
2. How would you describe the camera shot that takes place on the bridge?
3. How does the newscast give viewers an idea of what Bosko and Admira were like together?

TRAGIC ROMEO AND JULIET OFFERS BOSNIA HOPE

WORD NETWORK

Add interesting words related to destiny from the video to your Word Network.

STANDARDS

Language

Acquire and use accurately general academic and domain-specific words and phrases, sufficient for reading, writing, speaking, and listening at the college and career readiness level; demonstrate independence in gathering vocabulary knowledge when considering a word or phrase important to comprehension or expression.

DIGITAL PERSPECTIVES

Jump Start

CLOSE REVIEW Ask students to consider the following prompt: *Why is it important for us to revisit past events like the deaths of Bosko and Admira?* As students discuss the prompt, have them consider the following quote: "*Those who cannot remember the past are condemned to repeat it.*" (George Santayana, 1905)

Close Review

If needed, model close reviewing by using the Close Review note for the video. Remind students to clarify anything they did not understand during their first review. You may wish to print the **Close-Review Guide: Media-Video** for students to use.

Remind students to use Accountable Talk in their discussions and to support one another as they complete the close read.

Analyze the Media

Possible Responses

1. The first shot evokes the past by showing Admira's parents looking through a photo album. The sight of parents looking at photographs of the daughter they outlived creates a sense of loss.
2. Answers will vary by group but should include supporting evidence from the video.
3. Answers will vary by group.

Media Vocabulary

For more support, see **Media Vocabulary.**

Possible responses:

1. The opening of the video lets the viewer know that it is a human interest story.
2. The camera shot on the bridge is a reporter stand-up and an establishing shot that shows where the events took place.
3. The video uses a montage of photographs of Bosko and Admira together.

FORMATIVE ASSESSMENT

Analyze the Media

If students struggle to close review the video, **then** provide the **Tragic Romeo and Juliet Offers Bosnia Hope: Media Questions** available online in the Interactive Teacher's Edition or Unit Resources. Answers and DOK levels are also available.

Media Vocabulary

If students struggle to describe the opening of the video, **then** have them review the definition of a *human interest story* and identify elements of the definition as they review the video.

FACILITATING

Writing to Compare

Assignment Explain to students that they will be comparing and contrasting the two works of journalism that they reviewed and read, and that information in each type of journalism is formatted and presented in a different way. Remind students to think about each medium as they make a decision about which writing assignment to choose. Encourage students to make a list of the elements of an effective example of their chosen mode of writing, in addition to the elements of an effective argument. Once students determine the necessary parts for an effective email, opinion article, or blog post, they will be better able to write their argument. For more support, see **Writing to Compare: Argument.**

Analyze the Texts

Have groups analyze both works of journalism and make notes of the facts each report provides. Students should think about how facts are presented and how the mediums differ in terms of the way information is delivered, and whether they think one medium presents facts better than the other.

Possible responses:

1. (a) The article contains the account of the eyewitness. It also mentions the Yugoslav rock band that wrote a song about the couple and includes some of the song's lyrics. (b) In the newscast, we get more quotes from the parents.
2. The author of the article says that Bosko was 24 years old and Admira was 25 years old when they were killed. The newscast says they were both 25 years old when they were killed. The author of the article says that their bodies were left untouched on the bridge "for nearly four days," but the newscast says that it was eight days before the bodies could be reached.
3. The newscast allows viewers to get a visual sense of the bridge where Admira and Bosko were killed and to see the sadness still experienced by their parents.

EFFECTIVE EXPRESSION

TWENTY YEARS ON: THE UNFINISHED LIVES OF BOSNIA'S ROMEO AND JULET

TRAGIC ROMEO AND JULIET OFFERS BOSNIA HOPE

Writing to Compare

You have watched a work of broadcast journalism and read a news article about Bosko and Admira—Sarajevo's "Romeo and Juliet." Now, analyze the texts and consider how the medium, or form, in which the information is delivered affects what you learn and feel about the subject.

Assignment

Write an **argument** in which you compare and contrast the two works of journalism, considering the information each provides and how that information is presented. Explain whether one medium presents more or different facts than the other; delivers information in a more compelling way; or offers richer insights. Choose one of these options.

- ☐ an **email** to a fellow student in which you offer advice about whether to use the article, the video, or both in a presentation
- ☐ an **opinion article** for a website that analyzes the effects of war on individuals
- ☐ a **blog post** that recommends either the article or the video to readers interested in nonfiction about ill-fated love

Analyze the Texts

Notebook Work together to complete the activity and respond to the questions.

Compare Forms of Journalism Gather details from both works of journalism. Identify facts both reports provide. Briefly describe how those facts are presented. Some of the ways in which information can be presented are listed here. Using your observations of the two works, add your own categories to the list.

- reporter relates the information directly
- provides information in an interview
- quotes from another source
- provides information in a camera shot without words
- suggests through descriptive language but does not state directly

1. (a) What information appears in the article but not in the newscast? (b) What information appears in the newscast but not in the article?
2. Which facts or other information appear in both the newscast and the article but are presented differently? Explain.
3. Using your observations, explain the advantages and disadvantages of telling a news story in broadcast form versus print form.

STANDARDS

Reading Informational Text
Analyze various accounts of a subject told in different mediums determining which details are emphasized in each account.

Writing
Write arguments to support claims in an analysis of substantive topics or texts, using valid reasoning and relevant and sufficient evidence.

PERSONALIZE FOR LEARNING

Strategic Support

Self-Analysis Group members may have difficulty analyzing their own experience to determine how each type of media holds their attention. To help them analyze their response to the media, have groups skim their notes from the First Read and First Review. Ask them to consider what they noted as immediately standing out from each piece. Have them think about how and why those elements piqued their interest. Was the style of presentation unique? Was a statement or sentence unexpected?

Planning and Prewriting

Categorize Information and Write a Thesis Work independently to plan and draft your argument. First, review the notes you took as a group. Organize details and observations into logical categories. For example, you might group together one set of details related to facts and another set related to emotional impact. Then, write a working thesis, or claim:

Working Thesis: ______________________________

____

____

Drafting

Provide Varied Details For every claim you make, include evidence to support your ideas.

- **Exact quotations** can illustrate a speaker's attitude.
- **Examples** can help readers visualize a reporter's actions or word choice.
- **Paraphrases,** or restatements in your own words, can help clarify others' ideas.

Establish a Structure Follow this guide to plan the order of your ideas and supporting details.

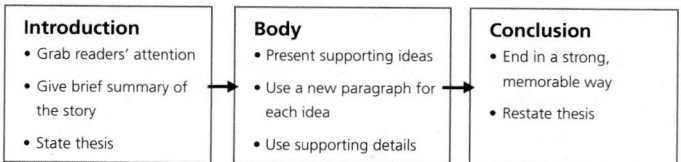

Introduction		Body		Conclusion
• Grab readers' attention • Give brief summary of the story • State thesis	→	• Present supporting ideas • Use a new paragraph for each idea • Use supporting details	→	• End in a strong, memorable way • Restate thesis

Consider Audience Judge your audience's familiarity with the news story and use that judgment to determine how much background information to include.

Review and Revise

Share your writing with your group and review one another's work. Ask for feedback about the clarity of your organization and the strength of your supporting details. Use the feedback to improve any elements that are unclear or ineffective.

EVIDENCE LOG

Before moving on to a new selection, go to your Evidence Log and record what you've learned from "Twenty Years On: The Unfinished Lives of Sarajevo's Romeo and Juliet" and "Tragic Romeo and Juliet Offers Bosnia Hope."

DIGITAL PERSPECTIVES

Planning and Prewriting

Categorize Information and Write a Thesis Students should work independently to plan their argument. Their working thesis should be supported by details and observations they have noted and should clearly state their claim.

Drafting

Provide Varied Details Remind students that they should include a variety of evidence to support claims they make, including quotations, examples from the report, or a restatement of facts or events.

Establish a Structure Encourage students to use the guide on the SE page so that they remember to include a strong introduction, body, and conclusion in their argument. Have them check to make sure they included supporting details for their claims and have organized their ideas in a logical way.

Consider Audience Remind students to think about their audience's level of familiarity with the news story; including some background information at the beginning of their essay could be useful in the setup of their argument.

Review and Revise

Have students share their writing and review another group's essay. Tell students that they can improve their writing by using suggestions and feedback they receive.

Evidence Log Support students in completing the Evidence Log. This paced activity will help prepare them for the Performance-Based Assessment at the end of the unit.

DIGITAL PERSPECTIVES

Illuminating the Standard To help students understand the elements of an effective argument, find two blog posts that make arguments about the same topic, one effective and one ineffective. Review the posts thoroughly beforehand to ensure that all content is appropriate. Show the blog posts to the students, projecting them side by side if possible. Ask students to identify the more effective argument. Then, have them compare and contrast the blog posts, noting the elements of both effective and ineffective arguments.

FORMATIVE ASSESSMENT

Writing to Compare

If groups struggle to provide supporting reasons for their claim, **then** have students review the article, video, and close reads/reviews for ideas.

Present an Argument

Assignment Before groups begin work on their projects, have them clearly differentiate the role each group member will play. Remind groups to consults the schedule for Small-Group Learning to guide their work during the Performance Task.

Students should complete the assignment using presentation software to take advantage of text, graphics, and sound features.

Plan With Your Group

Analyze the Text Remind students that "*Romeo and Juliet* Is a Terrible Play…" and "In Defense of Romeo and Juliet…"discuss the ways in which the characters react to their tragic circumstances and that "Twenty Years On" discusses a real-life tragic romance. Ask students to keep all selections in mind as they develop their multimedia presentation. You might want to guide them with the question "Does the desire to see people overcome overwhelming odds contribute to the compelling nature of a tragedy?"

Remind groups that they might also find evidence to support their argument from other sources. Tell them to provide citations for any source they use, including media.

Gather Evidence and Media Examples Explain that images and other forms of media will help enhance their presentation. Have them brainstorm what types of imagery best illustrates tragedy. You might suggest that they search for images and videos of people looking distraught or upset.

PERFORMANCE TASK: SPEAKING AND LISTENING FOCUS

SOURCES

- *ROMEO AND JULIET* IS A TERRIBLE PLAY, AND DAVID LEVEAUX CAN'T CHANGE THAT
- IN DEFENSE OF *ROMEO AND JULIET*: IT'S NOT CHILDISH, IT'S *ABOUT* CHILDISHNESS
- TWENTY YEARS ON: THE UNFINISHED LIVES OF BOSNIA'S ROMEO AND JULIET
- TRAGIC ROMEO AND JULIET OFFERS BOSNIA HOPE

Present an Argument

Assignment

You have read two works of literary criticism about *The Tragedy of Romeo and Juliet,* and you have also read and viewed accounts of a true-life "Romeo and Juliet." Work with your group to develop and refine a **multimedia presentation** that addresses this question:

What is compelling about stories in which people face a tragic destiny?

Plan With Your Group

Analyze the Text With your group, discuss the various factors that make these kinds of tragic love stories compelling. Why do they hold our attention? What do we learn from them? Use the chart to list your ideas. For each selection, identify examples from the text that help explain each story's significance. Then, come to a consensus about why star-crossed romances have such a profound impact on audiences.

TITLE	WHY IS TRAGIC DESTINY COMPELLING?
Romeo and Juliet Is a Terrible Play, and David Leveaux Can't Change That	
In Defense of *Romeo and Juliet*: It's Not Childish, It's *About* Childishness	
Twenty Years On: The Unfinished Lives of Sarajevo's Romeo and Juliet	
Tragic Romeo and Juliet Offers Bosnia Hope	

Gather Evidence and Media Examples Scan the selections to record specific examples that support your group's claim. Then, brainstorm for types of media you can use to illustrate or elaborate on each example. Consider photographs, illustrations, music, charts, graphs, and video clips that relate to the topic of tragic destiny. For instance, you might use a clip of a tragic scene from a movie or a show that is especially gripping. Allow each group member to make suggestions.

STANDARDS

Speaking and Listening
Present information, findings, and supporting evidence clearly, concisely, and logically such that listeners can follow the line of reasoning and the organization, development, substance, and style are appropriate to purpose, audience, and task.

AUTHOR'S PERSPECTIVE **Ernest Morrell, Ph.D.**

Active Classroom Listening Teachers can help students participate in class more effectively by discussing how to ask critical questions in classroom conversations. Teachers can guide students to determine which questions are most important and will yield good answers by modeling questions that synthesize multiple viewpoints and tap critical thinking skills. Here are some samples to use:

- What are the implications of . . . ?
- What is the difference between . . . and . . . ?
- What is the counterargument for . . . ?
- What are the strengths and weakness of . . . ?
- What is another way to look at . . . ?

Remind students to avoid yes/no questions because they cut off discussion. Teachers can also teach students to use critical listening—weighing what has been said to decide if they agree with it or not. Critical listening can help students identify the salient parts of each question and integrate these parts to formulate an idea or an opinion.

Organize Your Ideas As a group, create a clear statement regarding the appeal of tragic stories. Then, organize your evidence in a logical way, supporting your claim. Choose presentation techniques that will make it clear which point each piece of evidence is related to. Use a storyboard to plan the order of speakers and your use of media.

Rehearse With Your Group

Practice With Your Group As you deliver your portion of the presentation, use this checklist to evaluate the effectiveness of your group's first run-through.

CONTENT	USE OF MEDIA	PRESENTATION TECHNIQUES
☐ The presentation presents a clear claim. ☐ Main ideas are supported with evidence from the texts in Small-Group Learning.	☐ The media support the claim. ☐ Media are used evenly throughout the presentation. ☐ Equipment functions properly.	☐ Media are visible and audible. ☐ Transitions are smooth. ☐ The speaker uses eye contact and speaks clearly.

Fine Tune the Content Review the assignment to make sure that your presentation answers the question completely and with sufficient supporting text evidence.

Improve Your Use of Media Make sure that all included media serve a clear purpose. Vary your use of media as much as possible: alternate video clips with audio, quotations from text, or illustrations. Finally, determine what devices you will need to present your multimedia and check their availability.

Brush Up on Your Presentation Techniques Practice your presentation often so that you are entirely familiar with the material and comfortable responding to questions.

Present and Evaluate

When you present as a group, be sure that each member has taken into account each of the checklist items. As you watch other groups, evaluate how well they meet requirements on the checklist.

STANDARDS

Speaking and Listening
Make strategic use of digital media in presentations to enhance understanding of findings, reasoning, and evidence and to add interest.

DIGITAL PERSPECTIVES

Organize Your Ideas Remind groups that organizing their ideas is an important part of a clear presentation, explaining that the graphic organizer will make this task easier.

Rehearse With Your Group

Practice With Your Group Explain to students that when the different parts of a presentation are put together and rehearsed for the first time, areas for improvement become apparent. They might find, for example, that their pieces of media are all bunched together or that the media aren't visible or audible. Reiterate that even if their rehearsal goes smoothly, there's always room for improvement.

Fine Tune the Content Remind students that sometimes an idea might seem strong when it first comes to mind and is put down on paper, but that upon further review, it might seem less strong. This is an opportunity to refine the presentation and make it better.

Improve Your Use of Media Encourage students to use an appropriate font for the quotes they plan to display, noting that a plain font won't engage the audience as well as an ornate font. Explain that for Shakespearean text, an ornate, old-fashioned font is appropriate for their presentations:

Present and Evaluate

Before beginning the presentations, set the expectations for the audience. You may wish to have students consider these questions as groups present:

- What was the presenting group's claim?
- Which supporting idea was most convincing?
- Was the multimedia used well?
- Do you get the impression the group rehearsed enough?

As students provide feedback to the presenting group, remind them that compliments are just as valuable as constructive criticism.

PERSONALIZE FOR LEARNING

Strategic Support

Transitions Remind students that strong transitions are just as necessary in a presentation as they are in a piece of writing, because in both situations they keep the audience engaged. An audience member might have difficulty following a presentation that lacks strong transitions since disconnected ideas and media segments can cause a person to become confused. Explain that an effective transition carries the viewer from point to point.

INDEPENDENT LEARNING

Do we determine our own destinies?

Encourage students to think carefully about what they have already learned and what more they want to know about the unit topic of star-crossed romances. This is a key first step to previewing and selecting the text they will read in Independent Learning.

Independent Learning Strategies

Review the Learning Strategies with students and explain that as they work through Independent Learning they will develop strategies to work on their own.

- Have students watch the video on Independent Learning Strategies.
- A video on this topic is available online in the Professional Development Center.

Students should include any favorite strategies that they might have devised on their own during Whole-Class and Small-Group Learning. For example, for the strategy "Create a schedule," students might include:

- Keep track of anything you have completed.
- Assess whether you need to adapt your plan to meet all of your goals and deadlines.

Block Scheduling

Each day in this Pacing Plan represents a 40–50 minute class period. Teachers using block scheduling may combine days to reflect their class schedule. In addition, teachers may revise pacing to differentiate and support core instruction by integrating components and resources as students require.

OVERVIEW: INDEPENDENT LEARNING

ESSENTIAL QUESTION:

Do we determine our own destinies?

Throughout history and across all cultures people have had to overcome many struggles to be with their true loves. In this section, you complete your study of star-crossed romances by exploring an additional selection related to the topic. You'll then share what you learn with classmates. To choose a text, follow these steps.

Look Back Think about the selections you have already studied. What more do you want to know about the topic of star-crossed romance?

Look Ahead Preview the texts by reading the descriptions. Which one seems most interesting and appealing to you?

Look Inside Take a few minutes to scan the text you chose. Choose a different one if this text doesn't meet your needs.

Independent-Learning Strategies

Throughout your life, in school, in your community, and in your career, you will need to rely on yourself to learn and work on your own. Review these strategies and the actions you can take to practice them during Independent Learning. Add ideas of your own for each category.

STRATEGY	ACTION PLAN
Create a schedule	• Understand your goals and deadlines. • Make a plan for what to do each day. •
Practice what you've learned	• Use first-read and close-read strategies to deepen your understanding. • After you read, evaluate the usefulness of the evidence to help you understand the topic. • Consider the quality and reliability of the source. •
Take notes	• Record important ideas and information. • Review your notes before preparing to share with a group. •

SCAN FOR MULTIMEDIA

Pacing Plan

Day	Activity
1	Unit Introduction
2	Introduce Whole-Class Learning
3	Literature and Culture
4–12	*The Tragedy of Romeo and Juliet,* Acts I–V
13	Pyramus and Thisbe
14–15	Performance Task

CONTENTS

Choose one selection. Selections are available online only.

MYTH

Popocatepetl and Ixtlaccihuatl

Juliet Piggott Wood

The Mexican myth of a princess and her lover, kept apart from her stubborn father, the emperor.

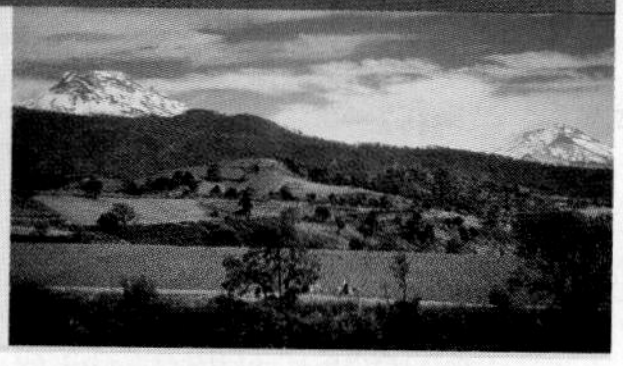

POETRY

Annabel Lee

Edgar Allan Poe

Can death keep lovers apart?

NONFICTION

What's the Rush?: Young Brains Cause Doomed Love

Lexi Tucker

Could brain chemistry be to blame for Romeo and Juliet's demise?

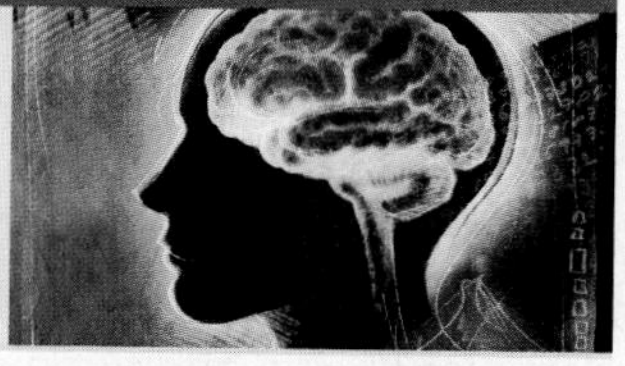

MEDIA: GRAPHIC NOVEL

William Shakespeare's Romeo & Juliet

artwork by Eli Neugeboren

Romeo and Juliet has been adapted for stage and screen countless times, but how would it look as a comic book?

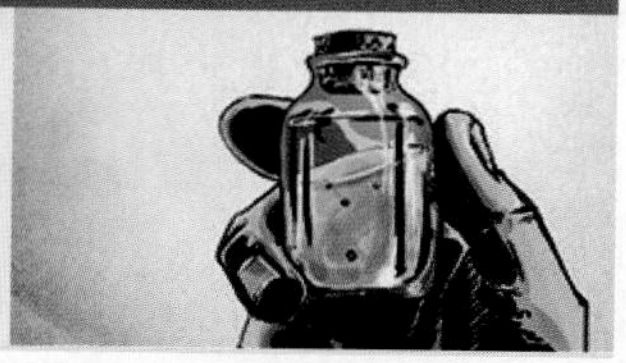

NEWS ARTICLE

If Romeo and Juliet Had Cell Phones

Misty Harris

Could a simple text message have saved the doomed lovers?

PERFORMANCE-BASED ASSESSMENT PREP

Review Evidence for an Argument

Complete your Evidence Log for the unit by evaluating what you've learned and synthesizing the information you have recorded.

SCAN FOR MULTIMEDIA

Contents

Selections Encourage students to scan and preview the selections before choosing the one they would like to read. Suggest that they consider the genre and subject matter of each one before making their decision. You can use the information on the following Planning pages to advise students in making their choice.

Remind students that the selections for Independent Learning are available only in the Interactive Student Edition. Allow students who do not have digital access at home to preview the selections using classroom or computer lab technology. Then have students print the selection they choose or provide a printout for them.

Performance Based-Assessment Prep

Review Evidence for an Argument Point out to students that collecting evidence during Independent Learning is the last step in completing their Evidence Log. After they finish their independent reading, they will synthesize all the evidence they have compiled in the unit.

The evidence students collect will serve as the primary source of information they will use to complete the writing and oral presentation for the Performance-Based Assessment at the end of the unit.

16 Introduce Small-Group Learning

17 18 19 *Romeo and Juliet* Is a Terrible Play

20 21 22 In Defense of *Romeo and Juliet*: It's Not Childish, It's *About* Childishness

23 24 Twenty Years On: The Unfinished Lives of Bosnia's Romeo and Juliet

25 Media: Tragic Romeo and Juliet Offers Bosnia Hope

26 Performance Task

27 Introduce Independent Learning

28 Independent Learning

29 30 Performance-Based Assessment

INDEPENDENT LEARNING

SELECTION RESOURCES

- First-Read Guide: Fiction
- Close-Read Guide: Fiction
- Popocatepetl and Ixtlaccihualtl: Text Questions
- Audio Summaries
- Selection Audio
- Selection Test

Popocatepetl and Ixtlaccihuatl

Summary

"Popocatepetl and Ixtlaccihuatl" is an Aztec myth retold by Juliet Piggot Wood. A powerful emporer ruled the city of Tenochtitlan. The emperor was raising Ixtla, his daughter, to be the next leader. As a result, Ixtla and a great warrior named Popo were in love and they begged for permission to marry. They were always denied. But near the end of his life, the emperor realized his kingdom was in great danger. So that his warriors would fight harder, he said that whoever defeated the kingdom's surrounding enemies could marry Ixtla. Popo succeeded, but a few jealous warriors returned to Tenochtitlan and claimed that Popo was dead. The results were tragic.

Insight

This selection shows that very different cultures often have similar stories. The Aztecs and Elizabethan England were very different. Still, tales of lovers dying after a critical miscommunication cross cultural traditions.

Connection to Essential Question

This myth makes a strong connection to the Essential Question, "Do we determine our own destinies?" Ixtla and Popo strove impressively to be with each other. But powers outside their control — the emperor's stubbornness and the lying warriors — undid all their hard work.

Connection to Performance-Based Assessment

Students will be able to make reference to this myth as they address the prompt, "Should the opinions of others affect our own choices or destinies?" The couple clearly would have been happier if they had been able to marry. Indeed, given Ixtla and Popo's qualifications, the empire probably would have been better off had they taken over late in the emperor's reign.

Text Complexity Rubric: Popocatepetl and Ixtlaccihuatl

Quantitative Measures	
Lexile: 1190 **Text Length:** 2,578 words	
Qualitative Measures	
Knowledge Demands 1 — 2 — **3** — 4 — 5	Unfamiliar and fantastical situation told in an Aztec myth. Though students may not be able to relate it to their own experiences, the situation and the character's feelings are detailed.
Structure 1 — **2** — 3 — 4 — 5	Linear story includes familiar plot elements.
Language Conventionality and Clarity 1 — 2 — **3** — 4 — 5	Selection has lengthy, complex sentences with embedded clauses, and some above-level vocabulary.
Levels of Meaning/Purpose 1 — 2 — **3** — 4 — 5	Multiple levels of meaning; concepts and meanings are mostly explained and easy to grasp. Creation myth explains presence of two volcanoes.

DIGITAL PERSPECTIVES

Audio | Video | Document | Annotation Highlights | EL Highlights | Online Assessment

SELECTION RESOURCES

- First-Read Guide: Poetry
- Close-Read Guide: Poetry
- Annabel Lee: Text Questions
- Audio Summaries
- Selection Audio
- Selection Test

Annabel Lee

Summary

"Annabel Lee" is a poem written by Edgar Allan Poe. The speaker describes a love he shared with a beautiful woman named Annabel Lee. They lived together in a kingdom by the sea. The speaker says that she caught an illness when the angels became jealous of the couple's love and sent a cold wind which made her sick and caused her death. The speaker remains loyal to her, even after her death.

Connection to Essential Question

This poem encourages students to consider the Essential Question, "Do we determine our own destinies?" Outside forces may have slew Annabel Lee. But, the narrator tells us, their love was so strong that even angels and demons could not separate them. Students may also wonder about the speaker's ability to continue his life.

Connection to Performance-Based Assessment

The prompt is "Should the opinions of others affect our own choices or destinies?" The angels' jealousy kills Annabel Lee, but proves unable to sever the love between her and the speaker.

Insight

Like many works of gothic literature, this poem is both beautiful and terrifying. The notion of love beyond death is lovely and sentimental. But it is horrifying when Poe makes it literal, putting the narrator in the tomb with his beloved. The notion of malicious, spiteful angels also seems like an overturning of all that is good.

Students can also benefit from considering an unreliable-narrator interpretation. Is he really linked by love beyond death, or has he gone mad with grief?

Text Complexity Rubric: Annabel Lee	
Quantitative Measures	
Lexile: NP **Text Length:** 41 lines	
Qualitative Measures	
Knowledge Demands 1 — 2 — **3** — 4 — 5	Background information about Edgar Allan Poe will be helpful as this poem contains themes that are similar to his other works; main themes are love and death.
Structure 1 — 2 — **3** — 4 — 5	The selection is a narrative poem that is written in six stanzas with several different poetic techniques including differing rhyme patterns.
Language Conventionality and Clarity 1 — 2 — **3** — 4 — 5	The selection contains imagery, personification, and repetition. Vocabulary is mostly on level.
Levels of Meaning/Purpose 1 — 2 — **3** — 4 — 5	Concepts of love and death are clear, but symbols and imagery may make the meaning difficult to grasp.

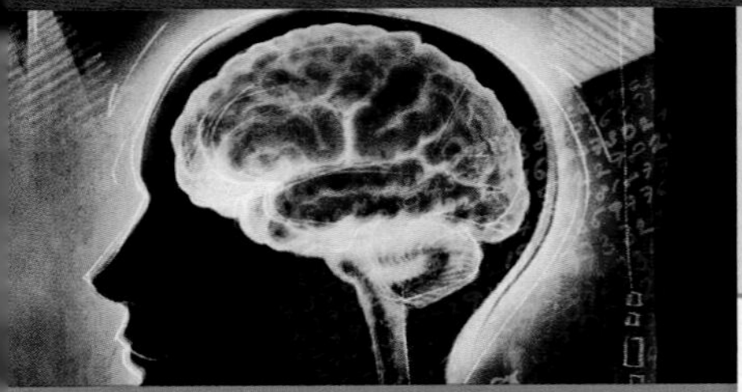

SELECTION RESOURCES

- First-Read Guide: Nonfiction
- Close-Read Guide: Nonfiction
- What's the Rush?: Young Brains Cause Doomed Love: Text Questions
- Audio Summaries
- Selection Audio
- Selection Test

What's the Rush?: Young Brains Cause Doomed Love

Summary

"What's the Rush?: Young Brains Cause Doomed Love" is a nonfiction piece that provides a scientific explanation for Romeo and Juliet's death. The young lovers had poor impulse control, which can be linked to their age. The prefrontal cortex, the part of the brain that helps people plan ahead and anticipate consequences, does not fully develop until age 25. Before then, young people are prone to taking risks that seem unreasonable to older people. The article argues that this isn't all bad; taking some risks lets teenagers learn how to make good choices in serious situations. However, there are some risks that can lead to more serious outcomes.

Insight

This selection may help students understand that they should not always trust their own judgment. Young people tend to make riskier choices than older people. Students may benefit from discussions around what makes something risky and how to determine how big a risk is.

Connection to Essential Question

By offering a scientific approach to the Essential Question "Do we determine our own destinies?" this article discusses how the biology of teenage brain development plays a role in teenage behavior. It suggests that biology, not personality, may prevent teens from making good decisions.

Connection to Performance-Based Assessment

As they prepare to respond to the prompt, "Should the opinions of others affect our own choices or destinies?" students may see that young people are not fully prepared to make life-altering decisions. This article may help them see the importance of parents and other adults in helping them.

Text Complexity Rubric: What's the Rush?: Young Brains Cause Doomed Love

Quantitative Measures	
Lexile: 1100 **Text Length:** 459 words	
Qualitative Measures	
Knowledge Demands 1 — **2** — 3 — 4 — 5	Contains references to neuroscience and the development of the teenaged brain, most of which is explained. Students may need more background about some terms.
Structure 1 — 2 — **3** — 4 — 5	Information in the selection is logically organized, but connections between ideas are not always completely explicit or in a predictable sequence.
Language Conventionality and Clarity 1 — 2 — **3** — 4 — 5	Some informal language is used for figurative power.
Levels of Meaning/Purpose 1 — **2** — 3 — 4 — 5	The main idea is revealed early, and supported with detail. Text may be aimed at a younger audience.

DIGITAL PERSPECTIVES

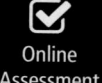

Audio | Video | Document | Annotation Highlights | EL Highlights | Online Assessment

SELECTION RESOURCES

- First-Read Guide: Media Art
- Close-Read Guide: Media Art
- Romeo and Juliet: Media Questions
- Audio Summaries
- Selection Audio
- Selection Test

Romeo and Juliet Graphic Novel

Summary

The graphic novel *Romeo and Juliet* is illustrated by Eli Neugeboren. It tells the story of Romeo and Juliet, with illustrations. The language is taken directly from Shakespeare, and the graphic novel format allows it to tell the story in a way the text alone cannot. This excerpt of the story begins with the prologue, which introduces the conflict between the families. It presents Act I, where Romeo and Juliet are each introduced. They meet at the party, then talk to each other at Juliet's balcony, and then the Friar and the Nurse help them see each other again.

Insight

This selection is useful for seeing how a different format can change the impact of a piece of media. Students should consider the advantages and disadvantages of illustration.

Connection to Essential Question

This retelling of the play should reinforce students' thinking about the tragedy's connection to the Essential Question, "Do we determine our own destinies?" As in the play itself, Romeo and Juliet seem to be swept up by fate.

Connection to Performance-Based Assessment

The Performance-Based Assessment prompt asks students to consider this question, "Should the opinions of others affect our own choices or destinies?" In the play, it is clear that Romeo and Juliet were right to disregard their families' opposition to their love.

Media Complexity Rubric: Romeo and Juliet Graphic Novel	
Quantitative Measures	
Format and Length: graphic novel, 17 pages	
Qualitative Measures	
Knowledge Demands 1 — 2 — **3** — 4 — 5	To fully understand the graphic novel, prior knowledge is needed about the historical setting of Romeo and Juliet, as well as understanding of the original play.
Structure 1 — **2** — 3 — 4 — 5	Each visual contains dialogue from the play making it easy to follow the action.
Language Conventionality and Clarity 1 — 2 — 3 — 4 — **5**	The selection relies on the original text of the play, which contains complex sentences, unfamiliar syntax, challenging vocabulary, and Elizabethan language.
Levels of Meaning/Purpose 1 — 2 — **3** — 4 — 5	The concept is accessible, but may be difficult to grasp due to challenging language. Visuals will help with understanding.

SELECTION RESOURCES

- First-Read Guide: Nonfiction
- Close-Read Guide: Nonfiction
- If Romeo and Juliet Had Cell Phones: Text Questions
- Audio Summaries
- Selection Audio
- Selection Test

If Romeo and Juliet Had Cell Phones

Summary

In the news article "If Romeo and Juliet Had Cell Phones," Misty Harris discusses a sociology research paper by Barry Wellman. The professor says that society has transitioned from tightly knit groups to networks of individuals. The love story of Romeo and Juliet plays out that transition. The couple cross the boundary between their groups to connect as individuals. Wellman also suggests that modern technology could have changed the story. If Romeo and Juliet had been able to communicate remotely, the miscommunications that lead to tragedy would not have happened. In fact, they may not have dated for very long at all.

Insight

This article gives insight into important changes in society. These include greater freedom in relationships across social groups because of the impact of modern communications. The article's conclusion is an interesting twist—Romeo and Juliet would have survived, but probably would have gotten tired of each other.

Connection to Essential Question

Students will consider the Essential Question "Do we determine our own destinies?" This article suggests that modern people have more control over their destinies than people in older eras did.

Connection to Performance-Based Assessment

The Performance-Based Assessment asks students to address this prompt: "Should the opinions of others affect our own choices or destinies?" This article supports the idea that modern society is more individualistic in the past; people are encouraged to make their own choices more often.

Text Complexity Rubric: If Romeo and Juliet Had Cell Phones

Quantitative Measures	
Lexile: 1450 **Text Length:** 499 words	
Qualitative Measures	
Knowledge Demands ① ② ❸ ④ ⑤	The selection is a sociological analysis of the effects of cell phones on society and relationships, specifically the hypothetical idea of Romeo and Juliet having cell phones.
Structure ① ② ❸ ④ ⑤	Information in the selection is logically organized, but connections between ideas are not always completely explicit or in a predictable sequence.
Language Conventionality and Clarity ① ② ③ ❹ ⑤	Many difficult words; many complex sentences; language is used for figurative power without explanation.
Levels of Meaning/Purpose ① ② ❸ ④ ⑤	Meaning is not always explicit; the main idea is clear, but some of the supporting concepts are complicated.

DIGITAL PERSPECTIVES

Audio

Video

Document

Annotation Highlights

EL Highlights

Online Assessment

MY NOTES

ADVISING

You may wish to direct students to use the generic **First-Read** and **Close-Read Guides** in the Print Student Edition. Alternatively, you may wish to print copies of the genre-specific **First-Read** and **Close-Read Guides** for students. Thse are available online in the Interactive Student Edition or Unit Resources.

FIRST READ

Students should perform the steps of the first read independently.

NOTICE: Students should focus on the basic elements of the text to ensure they understand what is happening.

ANNOTATE: Students should mark any passages they wish to revisit during their close read.

CONNECT: Students should increase their understanding by connecting what they've read to other texts or personal experiences.

RESPOND: Students will write a summary to demonstrate their understanding.

Point out to students that while they will always complete the Respond step at the end of the first read, the other steps will probably happen somewhat concurrently. Remind students that they will revisit their first-read annotations during the close read.

After students have completed the First-Read Guide, you may wish to assign the Text Questions for the selection that are available in the Interactive Teacher's Edition.

Anchor Standards

In the first two sections of the unit, students worked with the whole class and in small groups to gain topical knowledge and greater understanding of the skills required by the anchor standards. In this section, they are asked to work independently, applying what they have learned and demonstrating increased readiness for college and career.

INDEPENDENT LEARNING

First-Read Guide

Tool Kit
First-Read Guide and Model Annotation

Use this page to record your first-read ideas.

Selection Title: ______________________________

NOTICE

NOTICE new information or ideas you learn about the unit topic as you first read this text.

ANNOTATE

ANNOTATE by marking vocabulary and key passages you want to revisit.

NOTICE ANNOTATE First Read CONNECT RESPOND

CONNECT ideas within the selection to other knowledge and the selections you have read.

RESPOND by writing a brief summary of the selection.

CONNECT

RESPOND

STANDARD

Reading Read and comprehend complex literary and informational texts independently and proficiently.

PERSONALIZE FOR LEARNING

Strategic Support

Text Connections Help struggling students broaden their awareness of connections to the text. Point out that passages in a text may remind students of memories from their own lives, past reading or media experiences, or general observations they have made about the world. These connections build on what students already know, making a text more accessible to them. As students complete the First-Read Guide, ask them to identify the types of connections they make. Students can indicate these types:

- TS, or "text-to-self," reminds students of a personal memory.
- TTM, or "text-to-text/media," reminds students what they know from earlier reading or media experiences.
- TW, or "text-to-world," represents connections with general ideas they have about people and the world at large.

These codes can help students expand their ability to make connections to texts.

Close-Read Guide

Tool Kit
Close-Read Guide and Model Annotation

Use this page to record your close-read ideas.

Selection Title: ____________________

Close Read the Text

Revisit sections of the text you marked during your first read. Read these sections closely and **annotate** what you notice. Ask yourself **questions** about the text. What can you **conclude**? Write down your ideas.

ANNOTATE · QUESTION · CONCLUDE — Close Read

Analyze the Text

Think about the author's choices of patterns, structure, techniques, and ideas included in the text. Select one and record your thoughts about what this choice conveys.

QuickWrite

Pick a paragraph from the text that grabbed your interest. Explain the power of this passage.

STANDARD
Reading Read and comprehend complex literary and informational texts independently and proficiently.

DIGITAL PERSPECTIVES

CLOSE READ

Students should begin their close read by revisiting the annotations they made during their first read. Then, students should analyze one of the author's choices regarding the following elements:

- **patterns**, such as repetition or parallelism
- **structure**, such as cause-and-effect or problem-solution
- **techniques**, such as description or dialogue
- **ideas**, such as the author's main idea or claim

MAKE IT INTERACTIVE
Group students according to the selection they have chosen. Then, have students meet to discuss the selection in depth. Their discussions should be guided by their insights and questions.

PERSONALIZE FOR LEARNING

Strategic Support
QuickWrite As a prewriting exercise for the QuickWrite, have students work in pairs. Partners should take turns reading aloud the paragraph in the text that will be the focus of their QuickWrite. Encourage students to discuss the paragraph, and address these questions:

- How would you summarize the main idea and supporting details of the paragraph?
- What specific elements interested you? Why?

Part or all of the conversation may facilitate the ideas students will include in their QuickWrite.

ADVISING

Share Your Independent Learning

Prepare to Share

Explain to students that sharing what they learned from their Independent Learning selection provides classmates who read a different selection with an opportunity to consider the text as a source of evidence during the Performance-Based Assessment. As students prepare to share, remind them to highlight how their selection contributed to their knowledge of the concept of survival as well as how the selection connects to the question *Do we determine our own destinies?*

Learn from Your Classmates

As students discuss the Independent Learning selections, direct them to take particular note of how their classmates' chosen selections align with their current position on the Performance-Based Assessment question.

Reflect

Students may want to add their reflection to their Evidence Log, particularly if their insight relates to a specific selection from the unit.

MAKE IT INTERACTIVE

Have students create a four-slide presentation in which they provide reasons why we do determine our own destinies and reasons we don't. The slides should alternate between the pro and con positions. After each student gives the presentation, encourage the class to have a discussion about it. You might want to begin the conversation by asking students which slide they liked the most.

Evidence Log Support students in completing their Evidence Log. This paced activity will help prepare them for the Performance-Based Assessment at the end of the unit.

INDEPENDENT LEARNING

EVIDENCE LOG

Go to your Evidence Log and record what you learned from the text you read.

Share Your Independent Learning

Prepare to Share

Do we determine our own destinies?

Even when you read or learn something independently, you can continue to grow by sharing what you have learned with others. Reflect on the text you explored independently and write notes about its connection to the unit. In your notes, consider why this text belongs in this unit.

Learn from Your Classmates

Discuss It Share your ideas about the text you explored on your own. As you talk with your classmates, jot down ideas that you learn from them.

Reflect

Review your notes, and underline the most important insight you gained from these writing and discussion activities. Explain how this idea adds to your understanding of the topic of star-crossed romances.

AUTHOR'S PERSPECTIVE **Ernest Morrell, Ph.D.**

Self-facing Notes Some students may not believe that they need to take notes because they'll remember what the teacher and their classmates said. However, taking notes can provide more than a memory jog. To reinforce the importance of taking good notes, teachers should remind students that they will need notes to learn effectively from their peers. In addition, self-facing notes may help students in discussion because these notes will help them prepare the key points they want to share. Point out that the Share Your Independent Learning activity will help students in these ways:

- **Provide Feedback:** Making self-facing notes will help students give classmates useful comments about their independent reading, which will result in deeper learning.
- **Share Key Ideas:** Model how to jot down information that is essential to understanding. Focus on identifying the main ideas and critical details. Students can use these notes to help them make valuable discussion contributions.
- **Expand on Other's Ideas:** Explain to students that effective notes help them cut to the heart of the matter and so provide a scaffolding for what others may have noticed in the reading.

PERFORMANCE-BASED ASSESSMENT PREP

Review Evidence for an Argument

At the beginning of this unit, you took a position on the following question:

Should the opinions of others affect our own choices or destinies?

EVIDENCE LOG

Review your Evidence Log and your QuickWrite from the beginning of the unit. Has your position changed?

☐ YES	☐ NO
Identify at least three pieces of evidence that convinced you to change your mind.	Identify at least three pieces of evidence that reinforced your initial position:
1.	**1.**
2.	**2.**
3.	**3.**

State your position now: ____________________

____

____

Identify a possible counterclaim: ____________________

____

____

Evaluate the Strength of Your Evidence Do you have enough evidence to support your claim? Do you have enough evidence to refute a counterargument? If not, make a plan.

☐ Do more research ☐ Talk with my classmates

☐ Reread a selection ☐ Ask an expert

☐ Other: ____________________

STANDARDS

Writing

- Introduce precise claim(s), distinguish the claim(s) from alternate or opposing claims, and create an organization that establishes clear relationships among claim(s), counterclaims, reasons, and evidence.

DIGITAL PERSPECTIVES

Review Evidence for an Argument

Evidence Log Students should understand that their position on an issue could evolve as they learn more about the subject and are exposed to additional points of view. Point out that just because they took an initial position on the question *Do we determine our own destinies?* doesn't mean that their position can't change after careful consideration of their learning and evidence.

Evaluate the Strength of Your Evidence

Remind students that there are many different types of evidence they can use to support their argument, including:

- facts
- statistics
- anecdotes
- quotations from authorities
- examples

Point out that some of these types of evidence work better for certain types of arguments. You might want to explain that for the question in this exercise, using statistics might not be the best approach, since it's difficult to quantify this topic.

Writing to Sources: Argument

Students should complete the Performance-Based Assessment independently, with little to no input or feedback during the process. Students should use word processing software to take advantage of editing tools and features.

Prior to beginning the Assessment, ask students to think about situations in which the opinions of others affected their choices.

Review the Elements of Literary Criticism

Students can review the work they did earlier in the unit as they complete the Performance-Based Assessment. They may also consult other resources such as:

- the elements of literary criticism, including analysis of the work, a thesis statement, and textual evidence that supports the interpretation
- their Evidence Log
- their Word Network

Although students will use evidence from unit selections for their essay, they may need to collect additional evidence, including facts, anecdotes, quotations from authorities, or examples.

SOURCES

- WHOLE-CLASS SELECTIONS
- SMALL-GROUP SELECTIONS
- INDEPENDENT LEARNING

WORD NETWORK

As you write and revise your argumentative essay, use your Word Network to help vary your word choices.

STANDARDS

Writing

- Introduce precise claim(s), distinguish the claim(s) from alternate or opposing claims, and create an organization that establishes clear relationships among claim(s), counterclaims, reasons, and evidence.
- Develop claim(s) and counterclaims fairly, supplying evidence for each while pointing out the strengths and limitations of both in a manner that anticipates the audience's knowledge level and concerns.
- Draw evidence from literary or informational texts to support analysis, reflection, and research.
- Write routinely over extended time frames and shorter time frames for a range of tasks, purposes, and audiences.

PART 1

Writing to Sources: Argument

In this unit, you read about people, both real and fictional, who were kept apart from their lovers because of forces they could not control. Sometimes forbidden love can overcome the obstacles of society, but oftentimes it cannot.

Assignment

Write an argument in the form of a short piece of **literary criticism** that explores how the selections in this unit address the following question:

Should the opinions of others affect our own choices or destinies?

Propose and defend a claim about two or more texts you read in this unit. Acknowledge and address a counterclaim, or possible alternate interpretation of the works. Integrate text evidence from each of the selections you address in your essay and build a compelling argument.

Reread the Assignment Review the assignment to be sure you fully understand it. The task may reference some of the academic words presented at the beginning of the unit. Be sure you understand each of the words given below in order to complete the assignment correctly.

Academic Vocabulary

endure	compelling	recurrent
pathos	propose	

Review the Elements of Literary Criticism Before you begin writing, read the Literary Criticism Rubric. Once you have completed your first draft, check it against the rubric. If one or more of the elements is missing or not as strong as it could be, revise your essay to add or strengthen that component.

Literary Criticism Rubric

	Focus and Organization	Evidence and Elaboration	Conventions
4	The introduction is engaging and establishes the claim in a compelling way. Establishes a clear relationship between the texts and the topic of the assignment. Writer's insights and analysis progress logically, and include a variety of sentence transitions. The conclusion demonstrates deep comprehension and evaluation of the texts.	Sources of evidence are comprehensive and specific and contain relevant information. Textual analysis is supported with appropriate use of direct and indirect quotations. Uses vocabulary strategically and appropriately for the audience and purpose.	The conventions of standard English are used consistently throughout the entire essay. The tone of the essay is formal and objective.
3	The introduction is engaging and establishes the claim. Establishes some relationship between the texts and the topic of the assignment. Writer's insights and analysis progress logically, and include appropriate sentence transitions. The conclusion demonstrates deep comprehension of the texts.	Some direct and indirect quotations are supplied to support textual analysis. Uses vocabulary that is generally appropriate for the audience and purpose.	The conventions of standard English are used throughout most of the essay. The tone of the essay is mostly formal and objective.
2	The introduction establishes the claim. Establishes some similarities or differences between the texts. Writer's insights and analysis progress logically. Transition words and phrases are used. The conclusion demonstrates comprehension of the texts.	Some relevant evidence is used to support textual analysis. Uses vocabulary that is somewhat appropriate for the audience and purpose.	The conventions of standard English are sometimes used in the essay. The tone of the essay is occasionally formal and objective.
1	The claim is not clearly stated. Relationship between the texts, or between the texts and the topic, is not established. Writer's insights and analysis are unclear or hard to follow. Transition words and phrases are not present. The conclusion does not demonstrate comprehension of the texts.	Does not include significant analysis of the texts. Does not include supporting evidence for analysis. The vocabulary is limited or ineffective.	The conventions of standard English are rarely or never used in the essay. The tone of the essay is largely informal.

DIGITAL PERSPECTIVES

Literary Criticism Rubric

As you review the Literary Criticism Rubric with students, remind them that the rubric is a resource that can guide their revisions. Students should pay particular attention to the differences between a conclusion that demonstrates deep comprehension of the texts (a score of 3) and a conclusion that demonstrates deep comprehension and evaluation of the texts (a score of 4).

ASSESSING

Speaking and Listening: Multimedia Presentation

Students should annotate their written literary criticism in preparation for the oral presentation, marking the important elements (a thesis statement, textual evidence, and logical organization) as well as an inclusion of a counterclaim and error-free grammar.

Remind students that the effectiveness of an oral literary criticism relies on how the speaker establishes credibility with his or her audience. If a speaker comes across as confident and authoritative, it will be easier for the audience to give credence to the speaker's presentation.

Review the Multimedia Presentation Rubric As you review the Multimedia Presentation Rubric with students, remind them that it is a valuable tool that can help them plan their presentation. They should strive to include all of the criteria required to achieve a score of 3. Draw their attention to some of the subtle differences between scores of 2 and 3.

PERFORMANCE-BASED ASSESSMENT

SOURCES

- WHOLE-CLASS SELECTIONS
- SMALL-GROUP SELECTIONS
- INDEPENDENT LEARNING SELECTION

PART 2

Speaking and Listening: Multimedia Presentation

Assignment

After completing the final draft of your literary criticism essay, use it as the foundation for a three-to five-minute multimedia presentation.

Your presentation should consist of more than just reading your essay aloud. Take the following steps to make your presentation lively and engaging.

- Go back to your essay and annotate the claim and most important text evidence from your introduction, body paragraphs, and conclusion.
- Choose audio clips and visuals, such as photographs and video, to support your presentation. Mark your text to note audio and visual cues.
- Refer to your annotated text to guide your presentation and keep it focused.
- Deliver your presentation with conviction, speak with adequate volume, and maintain eye contact with your audience.

STANDARDS

Speaking and Listening
- Present information, findings, and supporting evidence clearly, concisely, and logically such that listeners can follow the line of reasoning and the organization, development, substance, and style are appropriate to purpose, audience, and task.
- Make strategic use of digital media in presentations to enhance understanding of findings, reasoning, and evidence and to add interest.
- Adapt speech to a variety of contexts and tasks, demonstrating command of formal English when indicated or appropriate.

Review the Multimedia Presentation Rubric The criteria by which your multimedia presentation will be evaluated appear in the rubric below. Review these criteria before presenting to ensure that you are prepared.

	Content	Use of Media	Presentation Techniques
3	Presentation clearly introduces and supports a claim about the texts and their relationship to the prompt. A counterclaim is acknowledged and refuted. Main claim is well-supported by relevant evidence from multiple sources.	Media has obvious connection to the topic and provides support for the speaker's claim.	Speaker demonstrates understanding of the content and presents it in a way that is easy to understand and engaging. Speaker uses appropriate eye contact, volume, and rate of speech throughout the presentation.
2	Presentation introduces and supports a claim. A counterclaim is mentioned. Main claim is supported by some relevant evidence.	Media is relevant to the claim.	Speaker demonstrates understanding of the content. Speaker uses appropriate eye contact, volume, and rate of speech during some of the presentation.
1	Presentation includes a claim and a counterclaim. Evidence from sources is included.	Media is not present, or is irrelevant.	Speaker does not demonstrate understanding of the content. Speaker does not use appropriate eye contact, volume, or rate of speech.

DIGITAL PERSPECTIVES

Preparing for the Assignment To help students understand how informative text is successfully conveyed in an oral presentation, find examples on the Internet of a compelling news report. You might want to select a radio news story, since that will more closely approximate the presentations students will give, and since they won't have access to the wide variety of imagery that television news stories use. Note how newscasters speak clearly and relatively slowly, to help listeners easily absorb the information that's being fed to them.

Reflect on the Unit

Now that you've completed the unit, take a few moments to reflect on your learning. Use the guidelines below to think about where you succeeded, what skills and strategies helped you, and where you can continue to grow in the future.

Reflect on the Unit Goals

Look back at the goals at the beginning of the unit. Use a different colored pen to rate yourself again. Think about readings and activities that contributed the most to the growth of your understanding. Record your thoughts.

Reflect on the Learning Strategies

Discuss It Write a reflection on whether you were able to improve your learning based on your Action Plans. Think about what worked, what didn't, and what you might do to keep working on these strategies. Record your ideas before a class discussion.

Reflect on the Text

Choose a selection that you found challenging, and explain what made it difficult.

Explain something that surprised you about a text in the unit.

Which activity taught you the most about star-crossed romances? What did you learn?

SCAN FOR MULTIMEDIA

Reflect on the Unit

- Have students watch the video on Reflecting on Your Learning.
- A video on this topic is available online in the Professional Development Center.

Reflect on the Unit Goals

Students should re-evaluate how well they met the unit goals now that they have completed the unit. You might ask them to provide a written commentary on the goal they made the most progress with as well as the goal they feel warrants continued focus.

Reflect on the Learning Strategies

Discuss It If you want to make this a digital activity, go online and navigate to the Discussion Board. Alternatively, students can share their learning strategies reflections in a class discussion.

Reflect on the Text

Consider having students share their text reflections with one another.

MAKE IT INTERACTIVE

After students give their presentation, open the floor to questions. Instruct members of the class to ask the presenters insightful questions about the presentation they saw. You might want to start the questioning by asking presenters why they selected the thesis they did.

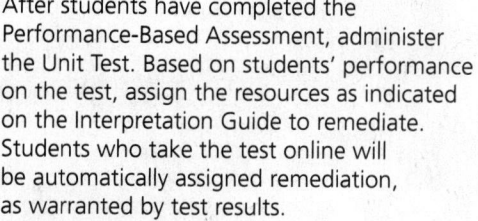

Unit Test and Remediation

After students have completed the Performance-Based Assessment, administer the Unit Test. Based on students' performance on the test, assign the resources as indicated on the Interpretation Guide to remediate. Students who take the test online will be automatically assigned remediation, as warranted by test results.

Journeys of Transformation

UNIT 5

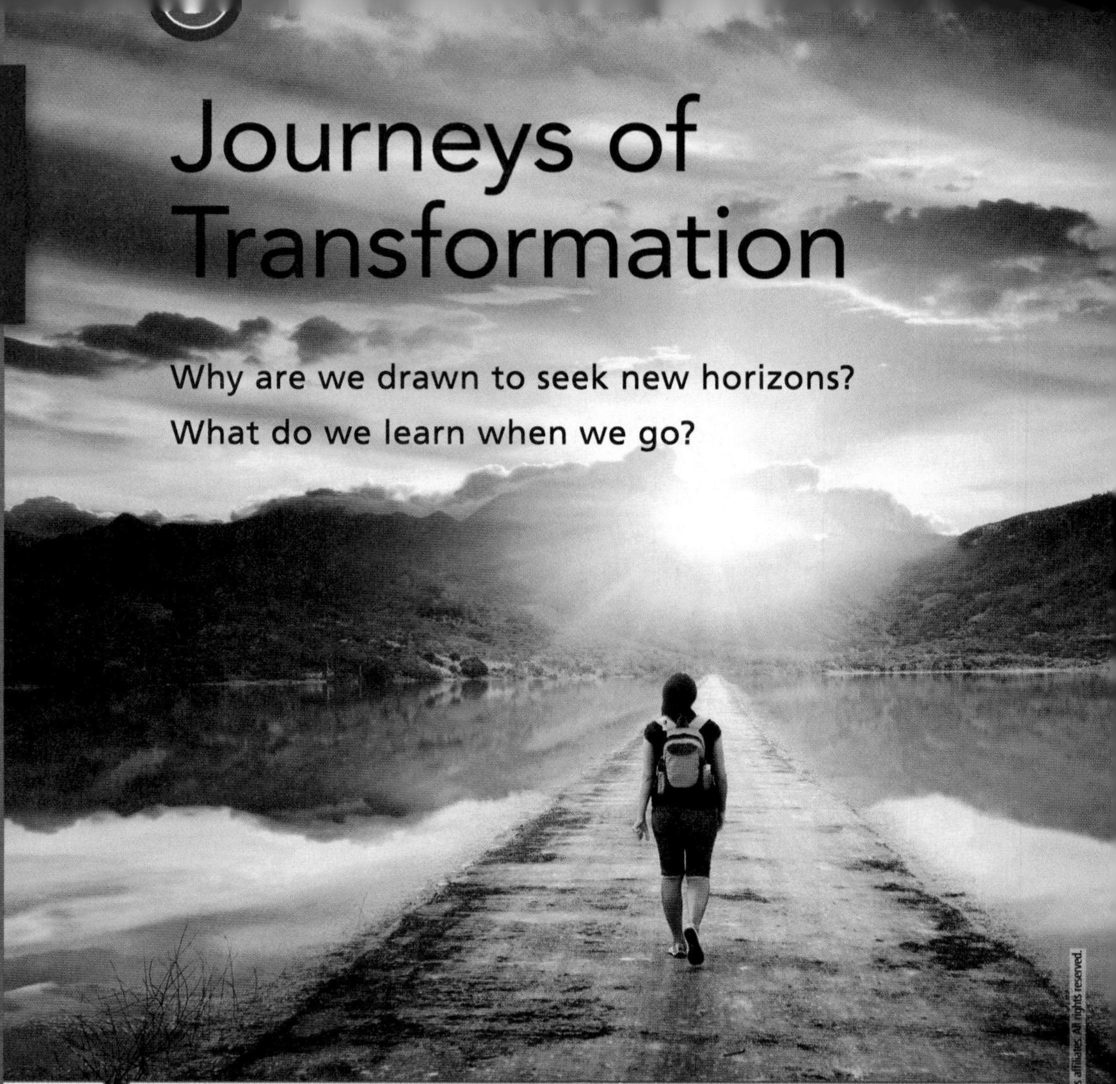

Journeys of Transformation

Why are we drawn to seek new horizons?

What do we learn when we go?

Misty Copeland's Hard-Fought Journey to Ballet Stardom

Discuss It What are the challenges that most people face during their journey to adulthood?

Write your response before sharing your ideas.

542

SCAN FOR MULTIMEDIA

Jump Start

People can travel to a new place across land as well as to new "places" in their minds—or in their understanding of the world. Ask students what might prompt someone to take a "journey of the mind."

Journeys of Transformation

Ask students what the phrase *journeys of transformation* suggests to them. Point out that as they work through this unit, they will read many examples of how people are transformed.

Video

Project the introduction video in class, ask students to open the video in their digital textbooks, or have students scan the Bounce Page icon with their phones to access the video.

Discuss It If you want to make this a digital activity, go online and navigate to the Discussion Board. Alternatively, students can share their responses in a class discussion.

Block Scheduling

Each day in this pacing calendar represents a 40–50 minute class period. Teachers using block scheduling may combine days to reflect their class schedule. In addition, teachers may revise pacing to differentiate and support core instruction by integrating components and resources as students require.

Pacing Plan

Day	Activity
1	Unit Introduction
2	Introduce Whole-Class Learning
3	Literature and Culture
4–6	*from* the Odyssey, Part 1
7–9	*from* the Odyssey, Part 2
10–12	Media: *from* The Odyssey: A Graphic Novel
13	Application for a Mariner's License
14–15	Performance Task

UNIT 5

UNIT INTRODUCTION

ESSENTIAL QUESTION: What can we learn from a journey?

LAUNCH TEXT
EXPLANATORY MODEL
Gone and Back Again: A Traveler's Advice

WHOLE-CLASS LEARNING	SMALL-GROUP LEARNING	INDEPENDENT LEARNING
LITERATURE AND CULTURE Historical Context *The Odyssey*	SHORT STORY The Return *Ngugi wa Thiong'o*	POETRY COLLECTION 2 The Road Not Taken *Robert Frost* Your World *Georgia Douglas Johnson*
ANCHOR TEXT: EPIC POEM *from* the Odyssey, Part 1 *Homer translated by Robert Fitzgerald*	INTERVIEW *from* The Hero's Adventure from The Power of Myth *Joseph Campbell and Bill Moyers*	SHORT STORY The Ugly Duckling *Hans Christian Andersen*
ANCHOR TEXT: EPIC POEM *from* the Odyssey, Part 2 *Homer translated by Robert Fitzgerald*	POETRY COLLECTION 1 Courage *Anne Sexton* Ithaka *C. P. Cavafy translated by Edmund Keeley and Philip Sherrard* *from* The Narrow Road of the Interior *Matsuo Bashō translated by Helen Craig McCullough*	MEDIA: PHOTO ESSAY Thirteen Epic Animal Migrations That Prove Just How Cool Mother Nature Is *Brianna Elliott*
MEDIA: GRAPHIC NOVEL *from* The Odyssey: A Graphic Novel *Gareth Hinds*		MEMOIR *from* Wild *Cheryl Strayed*
FUNCTIONAL WORKPLACE DOCUMENT Application for a Mariner's License *United States Government*		
PERFORMANCE TASK WRITING FOCUS: Write an Explanatory Essay	PERFORMANCE TASK SPEAKING AND LISTENING FOCUS: Deliver a Multimedia Presentation	PERFORMANCE-BASED ASSESSMENT PREP Review Evidence for an Explanatory Essay

COMPARE

PERFORMANCE-BASED ASSESSMENT

Explanatory Text: Essay and Podcast

PROMPT:
When does the journey matter more than the destination?

543

What can we learn from a journey?

Introduce the Essential Question and point out that students will respond to related prompts.

- **Whole-Class Learning** *How do personal strengths and weaknesses shape a journey?*
- **Small-Group Learning** *What different types of journeys are there and how can they transform someone?*
- **Performance-Based Assessment** *When does the journey matter more than the destination?*

Using Trade Books

Refer to the Teaching with Trade Books section in this book or in the Interactive Teacher's Edition for suggestions on how to incorporate the following thematically-related novels into this unit.

- *The Adventures of Huckleberry Finn* by Mark Twain
- *Gulliver's Travels* by Jonathan Swift
- *The Catcher in the Rye* by J. D. Salinger

Current Perspectives

To increase student engagement, search online for stories about journeys of transformation, and invite your students to recommend stories they find. Always preview content before sharing it with your class.

- **News Story: "Can You Still Call Yourself An Adventurer If You Use a GPS Safety Beacon?,"** by Jill Homer (*The Guardian*, August 20, 2015) New GPS technology improves safety for Iditarod teams.
- **Video: "Retracing Shackleton's Epic Journey of Survival,"** by Tim Jarvis (*Vimeo*, 2015) Jarvis recreates Ernest Shackleton's Antarctic voyage in order to raise awareness of climate change.

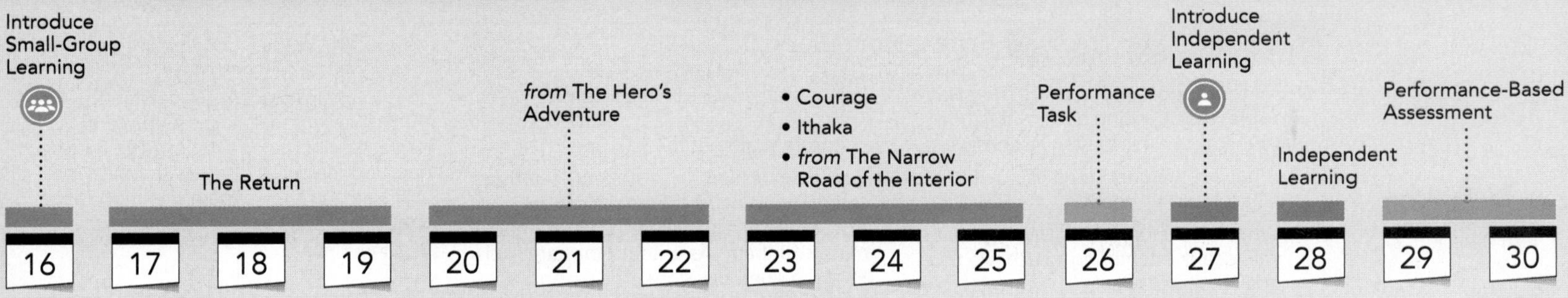

About the Unit Goals

These unit goals were backward designed from the Performance-Based Assessment at the end of the unit and the Whole-Class and Small-Group Performance Tasks. Students will practice and become proficient in many more standards over the course of this unit.

Unit Goals

Review the goals with students and explain that as they read and discuss the selections in this unit, they will improve their skills in reading, writing, research, language, and speaking and listening.

- Have students watch the video on Goal Setting.
- A video on this topic is available online in the Professional Development Center.

Reading Goals Tell students they will read and evaluate an explanatory essay. They will also read fiction, poetry, and an interview to better understand the ways writers express ideas.

Writing and Research Goals Tell students that they will learn elements of explanatory writing. They will also write their own explanatory essay and will write for a number of reasons, including organizing and sharing ideas, reflecting on experiences, and gathering evidence. They will conduct research to clarify and explore ideas.

Language Goal Tell students that they will develop a deeper understanding of using resources to clarify word meanings. They will then practice using resources in their own writing.

Speaking and Listening Goals Explain to students that they will work together to build on one another's ideas, develop consensus, and communicate with one another. They will also learn to incorporate audio, visuals, and text in presentations.

HOME Connection

A Home Connection letter to students' parents or guardians is available in the Interactive Teacher's Edition. The letter explains what students will be learning in this unit and how they will be assessed.

Unit Goals

Throughout the unit you will deepen your perspective of journeys by reading, writing, speaking, listening, and presenting. These goals will help you succeed on the Unit Performance-Based Assessment.

Rate how well you meet these goals right now. You will revisit your ratings later when you reflect on your growth during this unit.

SCALE

1	2	3	4	5
NOT AT ALL WELL	NOT VERY WELL	SOMEWHAT WELL	VERY WELL	EXTREMELY WELL

READING GOALS	1	2	3	4	5
• Evaluate written explanatory texts by analyzing how authors introduce and develop clear central ideas.	○	○	○	○	○
• Expand your knowledge and use of academic and concept vocabulary.	○	○	○	○	○
WRITING AND RESEARCH GOALS	**1**	**2**	**3**	**4**	**5**
• Write an explanatory essay in which you effectively convey complex ideas, concepts, and information.	○	○	○	○	○
• Conduct research projects of various lengths to explore a topic and clarify meaning.	○	○	○	○	○
LANGUAGE GOALS	**1**	**2**	**3**	**4**	**5**
• Use resources, such as a dictionary or thesaurus, to clarify word meanings and improve your writing and presentations.	○	○	○	○	○
SPEAKING AND LISTENING GOALS	**1**	**2**	**3**	**4**	**5**
• Collaborate with your team to build on the ideas of others, develop consensus, and communicate.	○	○	○	○	○
• Integrate audio, visuals, and text in presentations.	○	○	○	○	○

STANDARDS

Language
Acquire and use accurately general academic and domain-specific words and phrases, sufficient for reading, writing, speaking, and listening at the college and career readiness level; demonstrate independence in gathering vocabulary knowledge when considering a word or phrase important to comprehension or expression.

SCAN FOR MULTIMEDIA

AUTHOR'S PERSPECTIVE Ernest Morrell, Ph.D.

How to Support Kids When They Have Trouble When setting goals with students, have them consider these questions:

1. What are the opportunities open to me if I achieve this goal?
2. What are the biggest challenges that I will face in attempting to achieve this goal?
3. What support will I need from others in order to achieve this goal and how will I ensure that I get that support?

The first question helps students see that setting goals helps them take control of their life and focus on the issues that matter to them. As a result, they are likely to make good decisions. The second question helps students understand that achieving goals takes hard work, resilience, and determination. The third question reassures students that help is available and shows them the importance of seeking—and accepting—help when necessary.

Academic Vocabulary: Explanatory Text

Academic terms appear in all subjects and can help you read, write, and discuss with more precision. Here are five academic words that will be useful to you in this unit as you analyze and write explanatory texts.

Complete the chart.

1. Review each word, its root, and the mentor sentences.
2. Use the information and your own knowledge to predict the meaning of each word.
3. For each word, list at least two related words.
4. Refer to a dictionary or other resources if needed.

WORD	MENTOR SENTENCES	PREDICT MEANING	RELATED WORDS
voluntary ROOT: ***-vol-*** "wish"; "will"	1. Cindy made a *voluntary* contribution to the charity because she supported its mission. 2. The teacher told us that the project was *voluntary* and could be done for extra credit.		voluntarily; volunteer
elucidate ROOT: ***-luc-*** "light"	1. Alex was not quite clear about the story's theme, but Aliyah's essay helped to *elucidate* the concept. 2. Current research is helping both to *elucidate* the problems and to find solutions.		
expedite ROOT: ***-ped-*** "foot"	1. In order to make our deadlines, we need to *expedite* matters by splitting up the work. 2. As soon as she was in office, the senator began to *expedite* the projects she had promised her supporters.		
subsequent ROOT: ***-sequ-*** "follow"	1. The baseball team won the first game but lost the *subsequent* game. 2. The editors were able to make corrections in *subsequent* editions of the book.		
procedure ROOT: ***-ced-/ceed-*** "move"; "go"	1. The doctor performed the *procedure* on the patient very carefully. 2. Barry first learned the *procedure* for lining up when he joined our classroom.		

TIP

FOLLOWING THROUGH
Study the words in this chart, and highlight them or their forms wherever they appear in the unit.

Academic Vocabulary: Explanatory Text

Introduce the blue academic vocabulary words in the chart on the student page. Point out that the root of each word provides a clue to its meaning. Discuss the mentor sentences to ensure students understand each word's usage. Students should also use the mentor sentences as context to help them predict the meaning of each word. Check that students are able to fill the chart in correctly. Complete pronunciations, parts of speech, and definitions are provided for you. Students are only expected to provide the definition.

Possible responses:

voluntary *adj.* (VOL uhn tehr ee)
Meaning: something chosen to do freely
Related Words: volunteer, volunteerism
Additional words related to root -*vol*-: volition, volatile, volume

elucidate *v.* (ih LOO suh dayt)
Meaning: to explain, make clear
Related Words: elucidated, elucidates
Additional words related to root -*luc*-: lucid, lucidity

expedite *v.* (EHKS puh dyt)
Meaning: to do more quickly
Related Words: expedient, expediency
Additional words related to root -*ped*-: impediment, pedestrian

subsequent *adj.* (SUHB suh kwuhnt)
Meaning: coming after; following
Related Words: subsequence, subsequently
Additional words related to root -*sequ*-: sequence, sequential

procedure *n.* (pruh SEE juhr)
Meaning: the steps to complete an action
Related Words: process, procedural
related to root –*ced/ceed*-: cede, proceed, recede

PERSONALIZE FOR LEARNING

English Language Support

Cognates Many of the academic words have Spanish cognates. Use these cognates with students whose home language is Spanish.

ALL LEVELS

voluntary - voluntario
elucidate - dilucidar
expedite - acelerar
subsequent - subsecuente
procedure - procedimiento

Purpose of the Launch Text

The Launch Text provides students with a common starting point to address the unit topic. After reading the Launch Text, all students will be able to participate in discussions about journeys of transformation.

Lexile: 830 The easier reading level of this selection makes it perfect to assign for homework. Students will need little or no support to understand it.

Additionally, "Gone and Back Again: A Traveler's Advice" provides a writing model for the Performance-Based Assessment students complete at the end of the unit.

Launch Text: Explanatory Model

Ask students to notice how the author jumps right into the purpose of the piece, which is to explain how to travel and have an enjoyable trip.

Have students pay attention to how the author provides advice on what to do when traveling. They should notice that the author does so in a clear, methodical way to give readers a strong understanding of the keys to a successful trip.

Encourage students to read this text on their own and annotate unfamiliar words and sections of text they think are particularly important.

AUDIO SUMMARIES

Audio summaries of "Gone and Back Again: A Traveler's Advice" are available in both English and Spanish in the Interactive Teacher's Edition or Unit Resources. Assigning these summaries before students read the Launch Text may help them build additional background knowledge and set a context for their reading.

LAUNCH TEXT | EXPLANATORY MODEL

This selection is an example of an **explanatory text**, a type of writing in which the author presents information, discusses ideas, or explains a process. This is the type of writing you will develop in the Performance-Based Assessment at the end of the unit.

As you read, think about how the writer describes the events listed. Mark the text to help you answer this question: How does the order in which the details appear help the reader understand the thesis?

Gone and Back Again: A Traveler's Advice

NOTES

1 Let common sense guide you before you travel and you'll have a better trip. Consider the businesslike details first. Down the road, rich rewards will follow.

2 If you're leaving the country, you'll need backups of all essential documents. Keep both digital and physical copies of your passport, visas, driver's license, birth certificate, health insurance card, serial numbers, and important phone numbers. You may be too young to have some of these items, but if you can read this you're old enough to assist in preparation. Anything can be lost or stolen. Backups might just save you a great deal of international grief.

3 Talk yourself into packing less stuff. The more journeys you take, the sooner you'll discover you don't need as many items as you think. Traveling light makes it easier and faster to get from one place to another, with a more manageable load to lug around. If you really must have a second black sweater, you can probably buy it on the fly.

4 Smart preparations also include shopping wisely from home. There is a wide world of online options for bargain transportation and lodging. Save your money for the experiences you'll be seeking once you get out of your rented bed. Or do a little digging and win major points from your loved ones by helping them save a few bucks.

5 And once you get there, get up early. The light is lovely in the morning. You'll have more tourist attractions to yourself while the layabouts are snoring into their pillows. And you'll run less risk of running into bad experiences: scam artists and other bad actors tend to keep late hours.

SCAN FOR MULTIMEDIA

CROSS-CURRICULAR PERSPECTIVES

Social Studies Have students conduct research about a foreign country that they would like to visit. Ask them to learn about the history of the country and noteworthy places to visit. Have them find out the easiest way to get there.

Then instruct students to create a travel brochure that will entice people to visit the country. Brochures should include a sample itinerary with descriptions of each place listed as well as photos that highlight the country's best features.

6 There is far more practical ground to cover before you take to the skies, the seas, or the road. Do your homework. You'll know you've earned a passing grade when you're having the time of your life.

7 To make the most of your travels, it will also pay to pack a positive attitude. Keep in mind the following suggestions that apply more to what is in your head and heart than your luggage or hip pocket.

8 Keep an open mind. You'll be encountering people whose lifestyles are different from yours. You stop learning when you start judging, and you close yourself off to new experiences. Embrace possibility. Seek opportunity. Ask questions in a spirit of respectful goodwill. There's common ground to be found, no matter where you go.

9 Get lost deliberately. The natives know the cheapest places to eat; the least crowded beaches; the byways and backwaters that are less traveled, that have their own histories and unlikely charms. Hit the pavement on foot. Follow your feet. Stay safe, but seek the unexpected.

10 Slow down occasionally. Take a seat on a park bench or a set of stone steps and watch the local parade go by. The scents and the shades, the tone and feel of a place start to reveal themselves when you put down your guidebook and your smart phone. You never know when you'll be making a memory. Open your senses and let the setting in.

11 And remember to smile, easily and often. In so doing, you will be communicating in the fundamental global language that opens us all up to new people and new experiences. Anna Quindlen said, "The life you have led doesn't need to be the only life you have." Vital moments in that life may be around the next corner. There's no better way to reach out toward those moments than with a hopeful grin.

12 Be prepared. Have fun. The world is ready when you are. Don't forget your toothbrush. ❧

NOTES

WORD NETWORK FOR JOURNEYS OF TRANSFORMATION

Vocabulary A Word Network is a collection of words related to a topic. As you read the selections in this unit, identify interesting words related to the idea of journeys and add them to your Word Network. For example, you might begin by adding words from the Launch Text such as *opportunity*, *transportation*, and *attractions*. Continue to add words as you complete this unit.

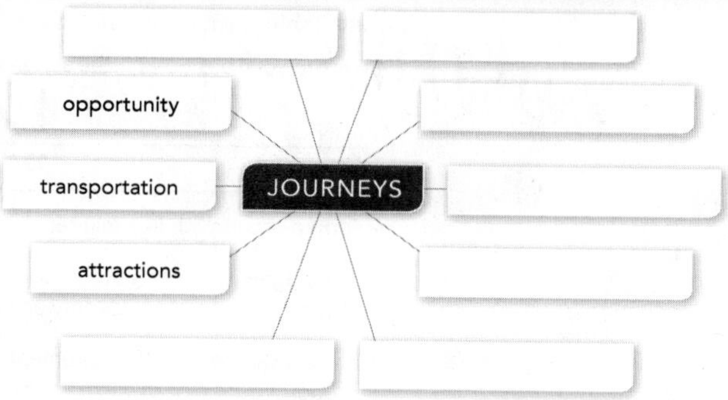

Tool Kit
Word Network Model

Word Network for Journeys of Transformation

Tell students that they can fill in the Word Network as they read texts in the unit, or they can record the words elsewhere and add them later. Point out to students that people may have personal associations with some words. A word that one student thinks is related to journeys of transformation might not be a word another student would pick. However, students should feel free to add any word they personally think is relevant to their Word Network. Each person's Word Network will be unique. If you choose to print the Word Network, distribute it to students at this point so they can use it throughout the rest of the unit.

AUTHOR'S PERSPECTIVE Elfrieda Hiebert, Ph.D.

Rare Words Increasing reading comprehension relies on a connection between fluency and vocabulary. Rare words are less frequently used words that represent what might be a common idea. Instead of calling a character nervous, an author might use disconcerted or flustered. In reading/language arts, where many rare unknown words pertain to known concepts, teachers should emphasize semantic connections across words. This can be achieved effectively with concept maps or word networks that help students understand the essential characteristics of a word's meaning. Here's an example for sluggish:

heavy	blah	indolent	inactive
comatose	inert	off	sullen

Digital tools, including online dictionaries, often have features to help demonstrate the increasing complexity of the spectrum of these words by filtering out levels of complexity.

Gone and Back Again: A Traveler's Advice 547

Summary

Have students read the introductory paragraph. Provide them with tips for writing a summary:

- Write in the present tense.
- Make sure to include the title of the work.
- Be concise: a summary should not be equal in length to the original text.
- If you need to quote the words of the author, use quotation marks.
- Don't put your own opinions, ideas, or interpretations into the summary. The purpose of writing a summary is to accurately represent what the author says, not to provide a critique.

If necessary, students can refer to the Tool Kit for help in understanding the elements of a good summary.

See possible Summary on Student page.

Launch Activity

Explain to students that as they work on this unit, they will have many opportunities to discuss journeys of transformation. Remind them that there is no right or wrong position, but that they should support their position with evidence from their own experiences and prior knowledge.

Encourage students to keep an open mind and really listen to their classmates.

Summary

Write a summary of "Gone and Back Again: A Traveler's Advice." A **summary** is a concise, complete, and accurate overview of a text. It should not include a statement of your opinion or an analysis.

Possible response: In "Gone and Back Again: A Traveler's Advice," the author explains what a traveler should do in order to have a successful trip.

The author includes a lot of advice throughout the essay, explaining what an international traveler should do, how to pack, shopping before the trip, and when to wake up after you've arrived.

The author doesn't just provide advice about what to do. The piece also discusses the proper mindset for travelers, encouraging them to keep an open mind, get lost, and relax occasionally.

Launch Activity

Round Table Consider this statement: **The best way to travel is by train.**

- Record your position on the statement and explain your thinking.
  ☐ Agree ☐ Disagree
  ____
  ____
- Form a group with like-minded students.
- If you agree with the statement, work together to list reasons that support your position. Identify as many reasons as possible.
- If you disagree with the statement, work together to list reasons that support your point of view. For example, you might consider the purpose for a journey, as well as a traveler's age and interests.
- After your discussion, have a representative present a two- to three-minute summary of the group's ideas.

VOCABULARY DEVELOPMENT

Academic Vocabulary Reinforcement Students will benefit from additional examples and practice with academic vocabulary. Reinforce their comprehension with show-you-know sentences. The first part of the sentence uses the vocabulary word in appropriate context. The second part of the sentence—the "show-you-know" part—clarifies the first. Model the strategy with this example for *elucidate*:

Joseph realized he had to *elucidate* his point; his classmates needed a clearer explanation.

Then give the students these sentence prompts and then coach them in creating the clarification part:

1. Going on the trip was not *voluntary*; ______.

Possible response: his parents forced him to go.

2. We need to *expedite* delivery; ______.

Possible response: her birthday is in just a few days.

3. The *procedure* went very well; ______.

Possible response: he shouldn't have any more pain in his abdomen.

QuickWrite

Consider class discussions, presentations, the video, and the Launch Text as you think about the prompt. Record your first thoughts here.

PROMPT: **When does the journey matter more than the destination?**

Possible response: I think that the journey matters more than the destination when there is more satisfaction in the journey itself. For example, people who hike mountains often have to travel many miles to reach the peak. The view at the summit might be beautiful, but the act of getting there is more satisfying.

Even when you are already in a specific place, like a city, the journey through the city can be more satisfying than the destination, like a museum. As the author says in "Gone and Back Again: A Traveler's Advice," "Get lost deliberately" because the byways and backwaters have their own histories and unlikely charms.

EVIDENCE LOG FOR JOURNEYS OF TRANSFORMATION

Review your QuickWrite. Summarize your thoughts in one sentence to record in your Evidence Log. Then, record textual details or evidence from "Gone and Back Again: A Traveler's Advice" that support your thinking.

Prepare for the Performance-Based Assessment at the end of the unit by completing the Evidence Log after each selection.

Tool Kit
Evidence Log Model

Title of Text: ____________ Date: ______

CONNECTION TO PROMPT	TEXT EVIDENCE/DETAILS	ADDITIONAL NOTES/IDEAS

How does this text change or add to my thinking? Date: ______

SCAN FOR MULTIMEDIA

QuickWrite

In this QuickWrite, students should present their own response to the prompt based on the material in the Unit Opener. This initial response will help inform their work when they complete the Performance-Based Assessment at the end of the unit. Students should make sure they state a clear thesis, develop their topic with supporting details, and use transitions to connect ideas.

See possible QuickWrite on Student page.

Evidence Log for Journeys of Transformation

Students should record their initial thinking in their Evidence Logs along with evidence from "Gone and Back Again: A Traveler's Advice" that support this thinking.

If you choose to print the Evidence Log, distribute it to students at this point so they can use it throughout the rest of the unit.

Performance-Based Assessment: Refining Your Thinking

- Have students watch the video on Refining Your Thinking.
- A video on this topic is available online in the Professional Development Center.

OVERVIEW

WHOLE-CLASS LEARNING

What can we learn from a journey?

Have students describe what people might learn from reading about a journey. Tell student that a journey isn't always about moving from one physical place to another. Ask students to suggest other types of journeys. Then ask what they learn from reading about these types of journeys. During Whole-Class Learning, students will read four selections about what certain people learned on their own particular journeys.

Whole-Class Learning Strategies

Explain that as students work through Whole-Class Learning they will develop strategies to work in large-group environments.

- Have students watch the video on Whole-Class Learning Strategies.
- A video on this topic is available online in the Professional Development Center.

You may wish to discuss some action items to add to the chart as a class before students complete it on their own. For example, for "Monitor understanding," you might solicit the following actions from students:

- Make time to research something that is unknown or unclear.
- Review to see if more information would be helpful.

Block Scheduling

Each day in this Pacing Plan represents a 40–50 minute class period. Teachers using block scheduling may combine days to reflect their class schedule. In addition, teachers may revise pacing to differentiate and support core instruction by integrating components and resources as students require.

OVERVIEW: WHOLE-CLASS LEARNING

ESSENTIAL QUESTION:

What can we learn from a journey?

A journey that opens our eyes to something new can take place in an instant or over a lifetime. You will work with your whole class to explore the story of an epic journey and to consider what it says about all journeys. These selections present insights into journeys and their deeper meanings.

Whole-Class Learning Strategies

Throughout your life, in school, in your community, and in your career, you will continue to learn and work in large-group environments.

Review these strategies and the actions you can take to practice them as you work with your whole class. Add ideas of your own for each step. Get ready to use these strategies during Whole-Class Learning.

STRATEGY	ACTION PLAN
Listen actively	• Eliminate distractions. For example, put your cell phone away. • Keep your eyes on the speaker. •
Clarify by asking questions	• If you're confused, other people probably are, too. Ask a question to help your whole class. • If you see that you are guessing, ask a question instead. •
Monitor understanding	• Notice what information you already know and be ready to build on it. • Ask for help if you are struggling. •
Interact and share ideas	• Share your ideas and answer questions, even if you are unsure. • Build on the ideas of others by adding details or making a connection. •

SCAN FOR MULTIMEDIA

Pacing Plan

Day	Activity
1	Unit Introduction
2	Introduce Whole-Class Learning
3	Literature and Culture
4–6	*from* the Odyssey, Part 1
7–9	*from* the Odyssey, Part 2
10–12	Media: *from* The Odyssey: A Graphic Novel
13	Application for a Mariner's License
14–15	Performance Task

WHOLE-CLASS LEARNING (Days 2–15)

CONTENTS

DIGITAL PERSPECTIVES

Contents

Anchor Texts Preview the anchor texts and the graphic novel with students to generate interest. Encourage students to discuss other texts they may have read or movies or television shows they may have seen that deal with journeys of transformation.

You may wish to conduct a poll to determine which selection students think looks most interesting, and discuss the reasons for their preference. Students can return to this poll after they have read the selections to see if their preference changed.

Performance Task

Write an Explanatory Essay Explain to students that after they have finished reading the selections, they will write an explanatory essay about when a journey matters more than a destination. To help them prepare, encourage students to think about the topic as they progress through the selections and as they participate in the Whole-Class Learning experience.

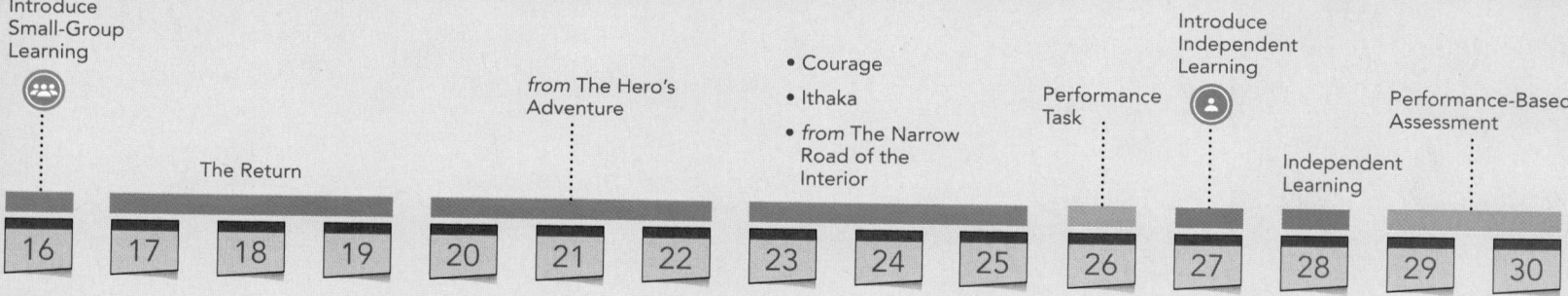

Introduce Small-Group Learning

The Return

from The Hero's Adventure

- Courage
- Ithaka
- *from* The Narrow Road of the Interior

Performance Task

Introduce Independent Learning

Independent Learning

Performance-Based Assessment

16 17 18 19 20 21 22 23 24 25 26 27 28 29 30

from the Odyssey, Part 1

AUDIO SUMMARIES
Audio summaries of this excerpt of the *Odyssey*, Part 1 are available online in both English and Spanish in the Interactive Teacher's Edition or Unit Resources. Assigning these summaries prior to reading the selection may help students build additional background knowledge and set a context for their first read.

Summary

Homer's epic poem the *Odyssey* is a classic adventure story. It combines realistic elements of historical events with wildly imagined scenes of fantastic places and creatures. Odysseus, a leader of courage, daring, and wit, pursues his goal to return home after many years at war. On his journey back home Odysseus encounters many obstacles: the Lotus Eaters, Polyphemus the Cyclops, the deadly Sirens, and the sea monster Scylla. During his journey, he travels to the Land of the Dead to consult the prophet Tiresias about what he needs to do to complete his journey.

Insight

The stories in this excerpt from the *Odyssey*, Part 1, are being retold by Odysseus to Alcinous, ruler of Phaeacia. This selection connects students to one of ancient Greece's most enduring heroes, as well as one of literature's first exciting adventures.

ESSENTIAL QUESTION:
What can we learn from a journey?

Connection to Essential Question

This excerpt, from the *Odyssey,* Part 1, presents a solid connection to the Essential Question, "What can we learn from a journey?" Odysseus encounters a wide array of fascinating characters along the way—some more hospitable than others—as he travels home. The ways in which Odysseus confronts and responds to challenges reveals much about him, including why he refuses to give up.

WHOLE-CLASS LEARNING PERFORMANCE TASK
How are personal strengths and weaknesses magnified during the course of a journey at sea?

UNIT PERFORMANCE-BASED ASSESSMENT
When does the journey matter more than the destination?

Connection to Performance Tasks

Whole-Class Learning Performance Task This selection provides examples of Odysseus' strengths, including his physical prowess and shrewd mind. As easy as it is to root for Odysseus, he is not without weaknesses, such as the indiscretion he shows when taunting the Cyclops after he and his crew escape.

Unit Performance-Based Assessment In this excerpt from the tale of his twenty-year-long adventure home, Odysseus acquires specific and crucial information to navigate adventures along the way. Without the guidance he receives from Circe and later Tiresias, his troubles would have been much worse.

DIGITAL PERSPECTIVES

Audio | Video | Document | Annotation Highlights | EL Highlights | Online Assessment

LESSON RESOURCES

	Making Meaning	Language Development	Effective Expression
Lesson	**First Read** **Close Read** **Analyze the Text** **Analyze Craft and Structure**	**Concept Vocabulary** **Word Study**	**Speaking and Listening**
Instructional Standards	**RL.10** By the end of grade 9, read and comprehend literature . . . **RL.3** Analyze how complex characters develop . . . **RL.5** Analyze how an author's choices . . . **RL.6** Analyze a particular point of view or cultural experience . . .	**L.4.b** Identify and correctly use patterns of word changes . . . **L.5** Demonstrate understanding of figurative language . . .	**SL.1** Initiate and participate effectively in a range of collaborative discussions . . . **SL.1.a** Come to discussions prepared . . . **SL.1.b** Work with peers to set rules . . .
STUDENT RESOURCES			
Available online in the Interactive Student Edition or Unit Resources	Selection Audio First-Read Guide: Poetry Close-Read Guide: Poetry	Word Network	Evidence Log
TEACHER RESOURCES			
Selection Resources Available online in the Interactive Teacher's Edition or Unit Resources	Audio Summaries Annotation Highlights EL Highlights English Language Support Lesson: Discussing Oral Tradition Analyze Craft and Structure: Oral Tradition	Concept Vocabulary and Word Study	Speaking and Listening: Conversation
Reteach/Practice (RP) Available online in the Interactive Teacher's Edition or Unit Resources	Analyze Craft and Structure: Oral Tradition (RP)	Word Study: Word Parts (RP)	Speaking and Listening: Conversation (RP)
Assessment Available online in Assessments	Selection Test		
My Resources	A Unit 5 Answer Key is available online and in the Interactive Teacher's Edition.		

Reading Support

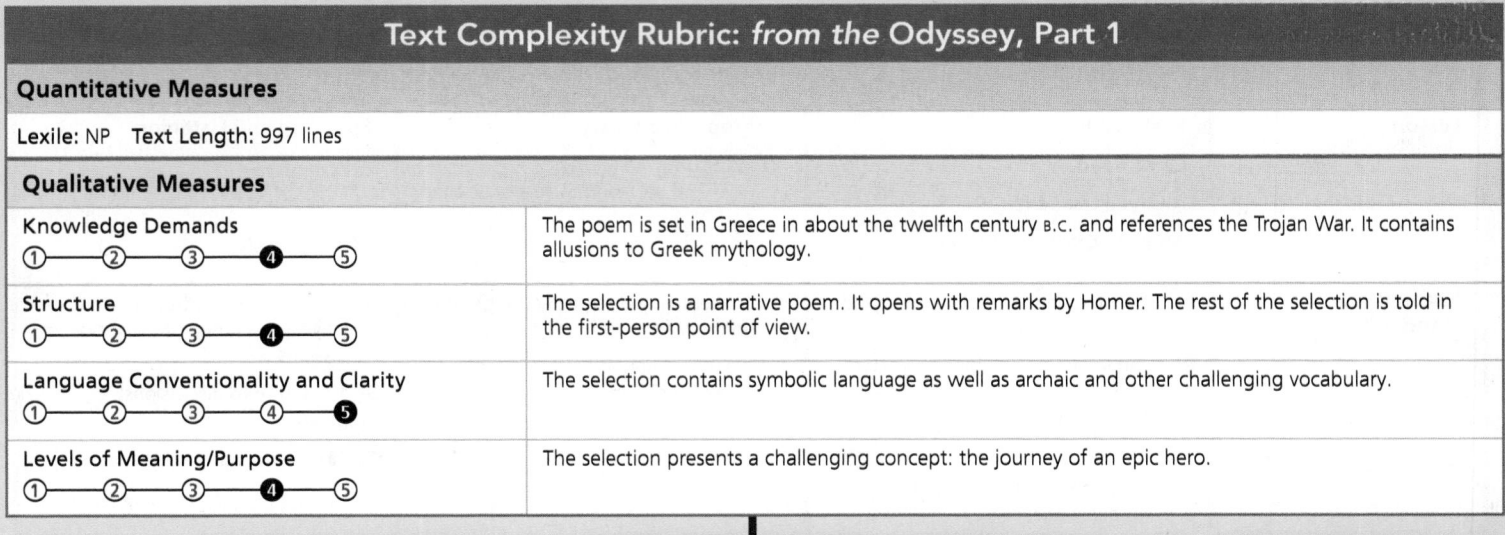

Text Complexity Rubric: *from the* Odyssey, Part 1	
Quantitative Measures	
Lexile: NP **Text Length:** 997 lines	
Qualitative Measures	
Knowledge Demands ①—②—③—❹—⑤	The poem is set in Greece in about the twelfth century B.C. and references the Trojan War. It contains allusions to Greek mythology.
Structure ①—②—③—❹—⑤	The selection is a narrative poem. It opens with remarks by Homer. The rest of the selection is told in the first-person point of view.
Language Conventionality and Clarity ①—②—③—④—❺	The selection contains symbolic language as well as archaic and other challenging vocabulary.
Levels of Meaning/Purpose ①—②—③—❹—⑤	The selection presents a challenging concept: the journey of an epic hero.

DECIDE AND PLAN

English Language Support

Provide English Learners with support for knowledge demands and structure as they read the selection.

Knowledge Demands Review the concept of the oral tradition: before poems were written down they were memorized and recited. Introduce Homer as the supposed author of the *Odyssey* and discuss the "Homeric question": the idea that Homer may have been a group of poets rather than one person. Have students make connections between the mysterious Homer(s) and the modern-day bards: the spoken word and hip-hop artists of today.

Structure Model fluency by reading a section aloud. Remind students that punctuation should guide their reading—not line breaks. Pause after each comma, and markedly after the dashes, colons, and periods. Then have students read aloud.

Strategic Support

Provide students with strategic support to ensure that they can successfully read the text.

Meaning If students have difficulty with meaning and concepts, have them first read the selection and note the main ideas in the plot. Then, have them reread and discuss why Odysseus makes the decisions he does.

Language Help students to understand complex sentences by first breaking them down into parts. Have them summarize each part in their own words. For example, (lines 6 to 9) *He saw the townlands and learned the minds of many distant men, and weathered many bitter nights and days in his deep heart at sea, while he fought only to save his life, to bring his shipmates home.*

Challenge

Provide students who need to be challenged with ideas for how they can go beyond a simple interpretation of the text.

Text Analysis Ask students to read aloud The Siren's Song (lines 719–744). Ask students to explain the purpose of the song.

Written Response Ask students to write a poem based on a heroic cultural icon of their choosing. Have them include details that are central to this person's character and uniqueness. Ask students to read their work to a partner and discuss the poems they wrote.

TEACH

Read and Respond

Have the class do their first read of the selection. Then have them complete their close read. Finally, work with them on the Making Meaning and Effective Expression activities.

Standards Support Through Teaching and Learning Cycle

IDENTIFY NEEDS

Analyze results of the Beginning-of-Year Assessment, focusing on the items relating to Unit 5. Also take into consideration student performance to this point and your observations of where particular students struggle.

DECIDE AND PLAN

- If students have performed poorly on items matching these standards, then provide selection scaffolds before assigning them the on-level lesson provided in the Student Edition.
- If students have done well on the Beginning-of-Year Assessment, then challenge them to keep progressing and learning by giving them opportunities to practice the skills in depth.
- Use the Selection Resources listed on the Planning pages for this excerpt from the *Odyssey*, Part I, to help students continually improve their ability to master the standards.

Instructional Standards: *from* the Odyssey, Part 1

	Catching Up	This Year	Looking Forward
Reading	You may wish to administer the **Analyze Craft and Structure: Oral Tradition (RP)** worksheet to familiarize students with how literature was passed down before books were developed.	**RL.3** Analyze how complex characters develop over the course of a text, interact with other characters, and advance the plot or develop the theme.	Challenge students to consider whether oral tradition still exists today and where it might be found.
Speaking and Listening	You may wish to administer the **Speaking and Listening: Conversation (RP)** worksheet to help students better prepare for their presentations.	**SL.1** Initiate and participate effectively in a range of collaborative discussions with diverse partners on grades 9–10 topics, texts, and issues, building on others' ideas and expressing their own clearly and persuasively.	Allow the students to make Homer one of the characters in the discussion.
Language	Review the **Word Study: Word Parts (RP)** worksheet with students to better familiarize them with word parts.	**L.4.b** Identify and correctly use patterns of word changes that indicate different meanings or parts of speech.	Challenge students to create their own words using the word parts described.

ANALYZE AND REVISE

- Analyze student work for evidence of student learning.
- Identify whether or not students have met the expectations in the standards.
- Identify implications for future instruction.

TEACH

Implement the planned lesson, and gather evidence of student learning.

LITERATURE AND CULTURE

Historical Context

Ancient Greece

This section presents a brief history of ancient Greece, including the fall of the Minoan culture, the rise of the Mycenaean culture, and their conflicts with Troy. Have students discuss why, with today's technology, Linear A has yet to be deciphered. Ask students how they would approach trying to decipher an ancient language.

The Minoans and Mycenaeans Have students analyze why historians think that earthquakes and invasions may have weakened the Minoans. Have them compare what is known about Minoan culture with what is known of the Mycenaeans. Ask students, if they had been Mycenaeans, what aspects of the Minoan culture would have been most useful to adopt? What aspects of the Mycenaean culture might still be useful in our society today?

Legendary Conflicts Remind students that Homer's epic poems, the *Iliad* and the *Odyssey*, use the Trojan War as the reason King Odysseus leaves his homeland of Ithaca. These epic poems were written four hundred years after the actual war. Ask students to discuss why they think Homer used the Trojan War as a basis for his poems. Have students connect movies and books today that use wars that have occurred in the nineteenth and twentieth century as the backdrop of a story.

^ The photograph above shows a reconstruction of one wall of The Palace of Minos at Knossos, Crete.

QUICK INSIGHT

Sir Arthur Evans, the British archaeologist who worked extensively on Crete, named Minoan civilization for King Minos (MY nos), a ruler of Crete in Greek mythology.

Historical Context

Ancient Greece

The world of ancient Greece included the Greek mainland, dipping down from continental Europe, and western Asia Minor, the Asian part of present-day Turkey. It also included hundreds of islands in the Aegean (ee JEE uhn) Sea, the arm of the Mediterranean Sea between mainland Greece and Asia Minor, and in the Ionian (y OH nee uhn) Sea, the arm of the Mediterranean to the west of mainland Greece. Odysseus, the legendary hero of Homer's *Odyssey*, was said to be the ruler of Ithaca, one of the western islands.

The Minoans and Mycenaeans Nearly a thousand years before Odysseus would have lived, Greek civilization rose to greatness on Crete, another island south of the mainland. By about 2000 B.C., a sophisticated society called the Minoan (mih NOH uhn) civilization had developed on Crete. Judging by the archaeological evidence, the Minoans produced elegant stone palaces and fine carvings and metalwork. They also developed a writing system, preserved on a few hundred of the clay tablets on which they wrote. Scholars call that writing system Linear A and have yet to decipher it.

For several centuries, Minoan civilization dominated the Greek world. Then, in about 1450 B.C., it collapsed rather suddenly, perhaps due to earthquakes and invasion. With the weakening of Minoan culture, the Mycenaeans (my suh NEE uhnz) became the dominant force in the Greek world. Originating on mainland Greece, the Mycenaeans had swept south and into Crete. Strongly influenced by Minoan civilization, the Mycenaeans too had a palace culture, an economy based on trade, and a writing system that mostly used clay tablets. Evidence of their writing is found in Knossos and Chania on Crete as well as in Mycenae, Pylos, and Thebes, three of their mainland strongholds. Because the Mycenaeans spoke an archaic, or older, form of Greek, scholars have been able to decipher their writing, known as Linear B. It was used primarily to keep palace records.

Legendary Conflicts The writing and archaeological remains suggest early cities with large central palaces and thick protective walls, each ruled by a *wanax*, or king. Others in society included priests, slaves, workers in trades or crafts, administrative officials, and a warrior class. The Mycenaens wore armor in battle, in which they engaged with apparent frequency. Their warfare with Troy, on the northwest coast of Asia Minor, has become one of the most famous military venues of all time—the Trojan War. If there really was a King Odysseus, he would have been a key player in that conflict.

Scholars date the Trojan War to somewhere around 1200 B.C. Shortly thereafter, Mycenaean civilization collapsed as the Greek world fell into chaos and confusion. For some three hundred years, writing seems to have disappeared in what is often called the Greek Dark Ages. Then, in about 850 B.C., Greece began emerging from this darkness, spurred by flourishing trade throughout the Mediterranean region. Along with the economic boom came a resurgence of the arts and learning that peaked with the epic poems of Homer. These poems—the *Iliad* and the *Odyssey*—chronicle the Trojan War and the subsequent adventures of the hero Odysseus.

The Rise of City-States After Homer's time, Greek civilization grew more organized and sophisticated. Smaller communities organized as city-states—cities that functioned independently, as countries do. Among them were Sparta, known for its military prowess, and Athens, the birthplace of democracy. Through rivalries sometimes led to warfare among city-states, the Greeks still recognized their common heritage as *Hellenes*, as they usually called themselves by that time. They coordinated efforts to defend against their common enemies, such as the Persians. They participated in the Olympic games, which records indicate began in 776 B.C. Together, too, they saw the works of Homer as pillars of their heritage, two great epics that celebrated their common past and its heroes.

QUICK INSIGHT
The Greek word for "city-state" is *polis,* the origin of our words *metropolis* and *politics.*

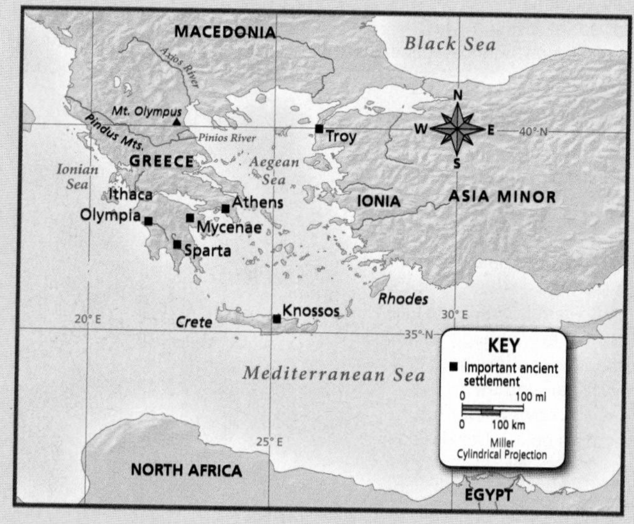

< Ancient Greece included mainland territories and hundreds of islands clustered in the Aegean and Ionian Seas. Odysseus' kingdom of Ithaca is a small island in the Ionian Sea.

DIGITAL PERSPECTIVES

The Rise of the City-States In addition to democracy and the Olympic Games, have students discuss other contributions the culture of the Hellenes contributed to today's world. Do any of these contributions affect or influence their lives directly?

PERSONALIZE FOR LEARNING

Strategic Support

Historic Timelines Open a discussion about historic timelines with a prompt that sparks discussion: *Timelines do much more than show a sequence of events. Can anyone name some of the other things they show?* Accept all reasonable answers that point to the understanding of patterns. Examples should be telling a story (progression of events) or showing how events influence future events (cause and effect).

Greek Mythology and Customs

Explain to students that the gods and goddesses in the religion of the ancient Greeks controlled all aspects of nature, from the sunrise and sunset to hurricanes and earthquakes. Greek mythology was written to explain the gods and goddesses and their powers. Have students choose a natural event in today's world. What myth could they create to explain this phenomenon?

The Titans Are Overthrown Have students discuss why the Greek gods had to "bow to fate" as well. Why do they think the ancient Greeks created stories about such imperfect gods?

Greek Mythology and Customs

All aspects of Greek culture reflected belief in the Olympian gods.

Ancient Greek religion was based on a belief in many gods. Zeus was king of the gods; Hera, his beautiful and powerful wife. Other gods and goddesses were associated with different aspects of nature or human behavior. The most important ones were said to dwell on Mount Olympus, the tallest mountain in Greece, where Zeus sat on a throne of gold.

The Titans Are Overthrown The early poet Hesiod (HEE see uhd) wrote a mythic account of the origin of the gods in *Theogony*, a work the Greeks revered almost as much as Homer's epics. According to that origin myth, first there was Chaos, a dark, empty void. Out of chaos came the Earth, personified as the goddess Gaea. The Earth generated the skies, personified as the god Uranus, who with Gaea produced the giant gods known as Titans. Cronus, the chief Titan, ruled the universe until he was displaced by his three sons, who split the universe among them. Zeus, the most powerful of these sons, became ruler of the heavens. His brother Poseidon became ruler of the seas. The third brother, Hades, became ruler of he underworld, a dark region also called Hades, which was inhabited by the dead.

The Greek gods were powerful, but they were not all-powerful: even Zeus had to bow to fate. The gods displayed many human qualities and were often vengeful and quarrelsome. They were also quick to punish human beings guilty of hubris (HYOO brihs), or excessive pride. To appease the gods, human beings performed sacrifices, which often involved the killing of animals. In the *Odyssey*, Odysseus makes several sacrifices to plead for divine aid on his journey home.

Celebrating the Gods The Greeks worshipped the gods in temples dedicated to many gods or just one. The Parthenon in Athens, for instance, was a temple dedicated to the goddess Athena. The Greeks also celebrated their gods at great festivals such as the Olympic games, which were dedicated to Zeus.

The Greeks believed in prophecy, which they associated with the god Apollo. In the *Odyssey*, Odysseus journeys all the way to the underworld to consult the blind prophet Tiresias (ty REE see uhs), who continues to have the gift of prophecy even though he has died. The Greeks also believed in myths, stories about gods and heroes that they used to explain the world around them. The *Iliad* and the *Odyssey* drew on these myths; however, for future generations of ancient Greeks, Homer's two epics—like Hesiod's *Theogony*—took on the aura of myths themselves.

› a statue of the Greek goddess Athena

DIGITAL PERSPECTIVES

Illuminating the Text Some students may not be familiar with Greek gods and goddesses. To help them visualize these mythological deities, have them view clips from the 2006 documentary *History Channel: Gods and Goddesses*. Remind students that ancient Greeks in general believed that these gods and goddesses existed. Much of their art and culture revolved around their worship of them. After the students have viewed the video, have them discuss how their ability to visualize Greek gods and goddesses has changed. (Research to Explore)

Gods in Greek Mythology

You may be more familiar with the Roman names for the Greek gods. The ancient Romans accepted Greek mythology, but they had their own names for its gods and heroes. For example, they called Odysseus *Ulysses*. For each Greek god listed below, the Roman equivalent is also given.

^ Zeus, or Jupiter

GREEK NAME	DESCRIPTION	ROMAN NAME
Zeus (zoos)	king of the gods and ruler of the heavens	*Jupiter*, sometimes called *Jove*
Hera (HEHR uh)	wife of Zeus and goddess of married women	*Juno*
Poseidon (poh SY duhn)	god of the sea	*Neptune*
Aphrodite (af ruh DY tee)	goddess of love and beauty	*Venus*
Ares (AIR eez)	god of war	*Mars*
Apollo (uh POL oh)	god of prophecy and music; also called Phoebus (FEE buhs)	*Apollo*
Artemis (AHR tuh mihs)	goddess of the hunt and the moon	*Diana*
Athena (uh THEE nuh)	goddess of wisdom, skills, and war	*Minerva*
Hephaestus (hee FEHS tuhs)	god of fire and metalwork	*Vulcan*
Hermes (HUR meez)	god of commerce and cunning; messenger of the gods	*Mercury*
Demeter (dih MEE tuhr)	goddess of the harvest	*Ceres* (SEER eez)
Dionysus (dy uhn Y suhs)	god of wine and revelry, also called Bacchus (BAK uhs)	*Dionysus* or *Bacchus*
Hestia (HEHS tee uh)	goddess of home and hearth	*Vesta*
Helios (HEE lee os)	sun god	*Sol*
Uranus (YOO ruh nuhs)	sky god supplanted by his son Cronus	*Uranus*
Gaea (JEE uh)	earth goddess and mother of the Titans and Cyclopes	*Tellus* or *Terra*
Cronus (KROH nuhs)	Titan who ruled the universe before his son Zeus dethroned him	*Saturn*
Rhea (REE uh)	wife of Cronus and mother of Zeus	*Cybele* (SIHB uh lee)
Cyclops (SY klops)	any one of three Titans who forged thunderbolts for Zeus; plural, Cyclopes (sy KLOH peez)	
The Fates	three goddesses who wove the threads of each person's life; Clotho (KLOH thoh) spun the thread; Lachesis (LAK ih sihs) measured out the amount of thread; Atropos (A truh pohs) snipped the thread	
The Muses (MYOO zihz)	nine goddesses who presided over the arts and sciences, including Calliope (kuh LY uh pee), the Muse of epic poetry	

DIGITAL PERSPECTIVES

Gods in Greek Mythology

Explain to students that the ancient Greeks also worshipped other gods and goddesses besides those listed. Also included in their mythology were demigods, who were half deity and half human.

Discuss with students how ancient Greeks worshipped particular gods and goddesses and built shrines to them. Have students consider the list. Ask them to imagine they are ancient Greeks. Which god or goddess would they associate themselves with and why?

TEACHING

Homer

Ask students to discuss what they have heard about Homer.

Was there really a Homer? Encourage students to discuss the existence of Homer and whether his existence actually matters. If Homer did not write the *Odyssey*, what type of background and knowledge would the author have to possess to have written these epic poems?

Inspiring Poems Have students discuss movies or books that they know are directly or indirectly inspired by the *Odyssey* and the *Iliad*. If they are unfamiliar with both epic poems, have them speculate about what elements the poems must contain to still be read after 3,000 years.

Homer, Epic Poet

The poems attributed to Homer still influence literature and culture today.

Homer is the legendary poet credited with writing the *Iliad* and the *Odyssey*. These epics, known for their sweeping scope, gripping stories, and vivid style, have captured readers' imaginations for almost 3,000 years.

Was there really a Homer? No one can prove his existence with any certainty, for no authentic record of Homer's life exists. Tradition has it that he was born in Ionia in western Asia Minor, perhaps on the island of Chios, and that he was blind. The location is not unreasonable, for Ionia was a center of poetry and learning, where eastern and western cultures met and new intellectual currents were born. Descriptions of Asia Minor in the *Iliad* and the *Odyssey* contain plot elements found in the world's first known epic, *Gilgamesh*, which by Homer's era had traveled from Mesopotamia (present-day Iraq) to become familiar in Asia Minor. For example, the hero *Gilgamesh* visits the underworld, just like the hero of the *Odyssey*; he also has a very good friend who is killed, just like Achilles has in the *Iliad*.

Most efforts to date Homer's life place him somewhere between 850 and 750 B.C. As a Greek oral poet, it is unlikely he lived much later, for by then writing had been reintroduced to Greek culture. The details in Homer's epics make clear that the poems were orally composed and that the *Iliad* was written first—probably some years before the *Odyssey*. The two epics differ in style: the *Iliad* is a single long, highly dramatic narrative, while the *Odyssey* is episodic and reads more like an adventure novel than a drama. For these reasons, some scholars even speculate that the epics were composed by two different poets.

Inspiring Poems Whatever the truth about Homer may be, no one disputes the quality of the two epics with which he is credited. The ancient Greeks revered the *Iliad* and the *Odyssey*. They recited the poems at religious festivals and had children memorize them in school. All the Greek writers and philosophers who came after Homer drew on the two epics. Their influence spread to Rome and beyond, and they became foundational works of western literature. Even in modern times, great works from James Joyce's *Ulysses* to Derek Walcott's *Omeros* have been directly inspired by Homer's verse.

PERSONALIZE FOR LEARNING

English Language Support

Syntax Help students analyze the unusual sentence structure of the *Odyssey* when they first begin reading it. Encourage them to rewrite passages in prose format, removing the line breaks from the epic poem. Ask them to read the rewritten sentences and make observations. Explain that some sentences in the poem may not be grammatically correct, but with poetry the author has more freedom to write outside the conventional rules of English. **ALL LEVELS**

The Epic Form

An **epic** is a long narrative poem that relates important events in the history or folklore of the culture that produced it. Its central character, or epic hero, is a larger-than-life person who embodies traits that the culture values. Typical among those characteristics are physical strength, bravery, high birth, fame, and effective skills as a leader and in a battle.

The *Iliad* and the *Odyssey* influenced virtually all the great western epics that followed them. From the *Aeneid*, the great epic of ancient Rome, to *Beowulf*, the foundational epic of Old English; from *The Divine Comedy*, the masterful epic by the Italian poet Dante, to *Paradise Lost*, the brilliant epic by Britain's John Milton—all had Homer's epics as models. Literary devices in Homer's epics are often imitated in these later works, even though many of the later epics were not orally composed. Influential literary devices found in Homer's epics include the following:

- **Opening invocation to the Muse:** The speaker of the poem asks the Muse for inspiration.
- **Starting the story *in medias res*,** or "in the middle of things": Beginning (after the invocation) with action instead of background information helps capture audience attention.
- **Lofty style:** Elegant language stresses the nobility of the subject.
- **Objective tone:** By keeping an emotional distance, the poet focuses attention on the story.
- **Meter,** or a fixed rhythmic pattern: A strong meter helps the oral poet remember the lines. In the original Greek, the *Odyssey* uses *hexameter*, or six beats to a line, which helps create a fast pace.
- **Epithet,** a characterizing phrase for a person, place, or thing: Recurring epithets are easy to remember and can help fill out the meter. Some examples of Homer's epithets include "rosy-fingered dawn" and "son of Laertes," for Odysseus.
- **Epic simile,** a long comparison over many lines: Such similes were another way to fill out the meter and aid the poet's memory.

^ A view from the ruins of the Temple of Athena in Turkey, on the Acropolis of Assos.

DIGITAL PERSPECTIVES

The Epic Form

Have students discuss why an epic hero of an epic had to come from "high birth." Explain to students that the *Odyssey* in particular was an adventure story that has inspired other adventure stories across the centuries. Encourage students to connect with modern adventure movies and books. Do today's adventure heroes usually come from "high birth"? Do movies or books today usually begin *in medias res,* or do they start from the very beginning of the story? What is an advantage of beginning a story *in medias res*? What is a disadvantage?

Comprehension Check

Ask students to answer these questions independently and then discuss them with the whole class.

1. What happened to the Minoan civilization?

Possible response: The Minoan civilization had been a cultural center, but historians believe that earthquakes and invasions weakened the Minoans, allowing the more militant Mycenaeans to dominate Greek culture.

2. What happened in Greece after the time of Homer?

Possible response: Greek civilization developed into an organization of smaller communities known as city-states. Although these city-states sometimes entered conflicts with one another, the Greeks still recognized their common heritage.

3. What is *hubris*?

Possible response: *Hubris* is excessive pride, a sin punished by the gods.

4. Where did Homer probably come from?

Possible response: Chios, a center of poetry and learning.

5. Where do the great epics usually begin and why?

Possible response: They begin in the middle of things in order to get the audience's attention.

Jump Start

FIRST READ Can you imagine having an adventure that lasted 20 years in which you had to face armies, monsters, and angry gods? What could you learn from this journey?

The *Odyssey*

Which leader would you follow: one who is a master warrior or one who is quick-witted? How long would you feel loyalty to such a leader? Would you be able to serve him or her for 20 years? Modeling the questions readers might ask as they read the *Odyssey* for the first time brings the text alive for students and connects it to the Whole-Class Performance Task assignment. Selection audio and print capability for the selection are available in the Interactive Teacher's Edition.

Concept Vocabulary

Support students as they rank their words. Ask if they've ever heard, read, or used them. Reassure them that the definitions for these words are listed in the selection.

FIRST READ

Have students perform the steps of the first read independently:

NOTICE: Encourage students to notice how the main character uses his imagination when he and his men are at risk.

ANNOTATE: Remind students to mark passages that use vivid detail, figurative language, and suspense to heighten the drama.

CONNECT: Encourage students to go beyond the text to make connections with other stories they know, movies and TV shows they've seen, or with their own personal experiences.

RESPOND: Students will answer questions and write a summary to demonstrate understanding.

Point out to students that while they will always complete the Respond step at the end of the first read, the other steps will probably happen somewhat concurrently. You may wish to print copies of the **First-Read Guide: Fiction** for students to use. Remember that an epic poem has qualities of both poetry and fiction, so the **First-Read Guide: Poetry** may also be beneficial for students.

About the Poet

Homer (approx. 850–750 B.C.) is credited with writing the *Iliad* and the *Odyssey*. For almost 3,000 years, these epic poems have captured readers' imaginations and inspired countless works of art and literature.

from the Odyssey, Part 1

Concept Vocabulary

You will encounter the following words as you read Part I of the *Odyssey*. Before reading, note how familiar you are with each word. Then, rank the words in order from most familiar (1) to least familiar (6).

WORD	YOUR RANKING
plundered	
fugitives	
avenge	
dispatched	
ventured	
tactics	

After completing the first read, come back to the concept vocabulary and review your rankings. Mark changes to your original rankings as needed.

Tool Kit
First-Read Guide and Model Annotation

First Read EPIC POEM

Apply these strategies as you conduct your first read. You will have an opportunity to complete the close-read notes after your first read.

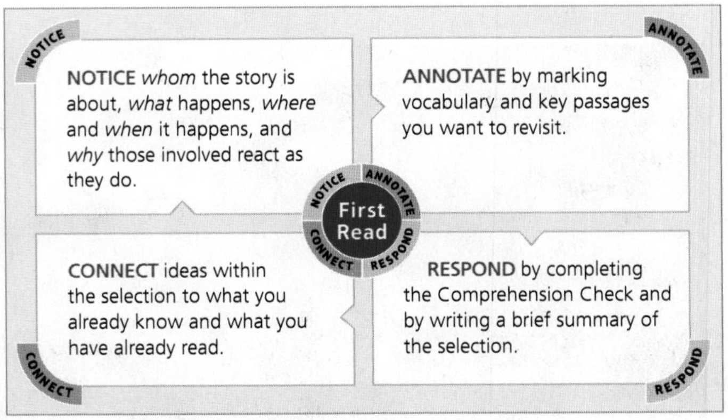
NOTICE
NOTICE *whom* the story is about, *what* happens, *where* and *when* it happens, and *why* those involved react as they do.
ANNOTATE
ANNOTATE by marking vocabulary and key passages you want to revisit.
First Read
CONNECT
CONNECT ideas within the selection to what you already know and what you have already read.
RESPOND
RESPOND by completing the Comprehension Check and by writing a brief summary of the selection.

STANDARDS
Reading Literature
By the end of grade 9, read and comprehend literature, including stories, dramas, and poems, in the grades 9–10 text complexity band proficiently, with scaffolding as needed at the high end of the range.

DIGITAL PERSPECTIVES

BACKGROUND

The Trojan War

In the *Iliad*, Homer focuses on the final year of the Trojan War; in the *Odyssey*, he tells what happened to one of the key warriors afterward.

It Begins With Strife According to legend, the Trojan War began when Eris, goddess of strife, brought among the gods a golden apple inscribed "To the fairest." Hera, Athena, and Aphrodite all wanted that apple. They asked Paris, son of the king of Troy, to decide which of them deserved it. Each tried to bribe him: Hera offered power; Athena, wisdom; and Aphrodite, the world's most beautiful woman. The famous Judgment of Paris was that Aphrodite was the fairest. Soon, on a diplomatic mission to Sparta, Paris met Helen, the world's most beautiful woman and Sparta's queen. With Aphrodite's help, the two fell in love and eloped. When Menelaus (mehn uh LAY uhs), king of Sparta, could not persuade the Trojans to send his wife, Helen, back, he went to his brother Agamemnon, who called on all the Greek rulers to honor a pact and go to Troy to fight to bring Helen home. The Greeks agreed and sailed to Troy. They laid siege to the city but for ten long years could not breach its impregnable walls.

War Crimes and Punishment Agamemnon might have been a more powerful king and Achilles (uh KIHL eez) a superior warrior, but Odysseus, king of Ithaca, was cleverest of them all. He devised a scheme in which the Greeks left a great wooden horse outside the walls of Troy and tricked the Trojans into taking it inside. That night, the Greeks hiding inside the horse—Odysseus among them—slipped out, unlocked the gates of the city, and allowed their fellow warriors to come swarming in to defeat the Trojans and sack the city. The fighting was brutal and destructive. King Priam (PRY uhm), Paris's father, for example, was killed while he was praying. The Greeks' behavior angered many of the gods, who made their voyages home very difficult.

Odysseus was no exception. Following the Greek victory, he set sail for Ithaca but encountered a series of perilous misadventures that made his journey last ten years. It is this difficult, adventure-filled journey that Homer's *Odyssey* recounts.

AUTHOR'S PERSPECTIVE **Kelly Gallagher, M.Ed.**

Reading Reasons Students often ask "Why should I read?" Increasingly, teachers see students who often give up easily when confronted with challenging reading material such as a biology textbook or a state-mandated exam. They are unable, or unwilling, to tackle difficult text. How do teachers turn around this apathy? How do teachers shelter fragile adolescent readers and help them grow into people for whom reading matters? Building reading motivation is complex, as there isn't a single correct motivational tool, but together, many of these techniques send the message that reading is rewarding.

- Give students access to high-interest reading material, which is provided in this program.
- Give students a time and place to read.
- Model the value of reading. Read with students, so they see you enjoying reading. Start a student book club in school.
- Provide structure to the reading program by logging the number of words, pages, and time that students read.

ANCHOR TEXT | EPIC POEM

from the Odyssey

Homer

translated by Robert Fitzgerald

Part I

The Adventures of Odysseus

PERSONALIZE FOR LEARNING

Strategic Support

First-Read Support If students struggle to comprehend the epic poem during the first read, pair them with a partner and have each conduct a think-aloud to explain the thought process as he or she works through the NOTICE, ANNOTATE, CONNECT, and RESPOND steps. For example, the students can isolate the key details and explain what they reveal.

CHARACTERS

Alcinous (al SIHN oh uhs)—king of the Phaeacians, to whom Odysseus tells his story

Odysseus (oh DIHS ee uhs)—king of Ithaca

Calypso (kuh LIHP soh)—sea goddess who loves Odysseus

Circe (SUR see)—enchantress who helps Odysseus

Zeus (zoos)—king of the gods

Apollo (uh POL oh)—god of music, poetry, prophecy, and medicine

Agamemnon (ag uh MEHM non)—king and leader of Greek forces

Poseidon (poh SY duhn)—god of sea, earthquakes, horses, and storms at sea

Athena (uh THEE nuh)—goddess of wisdom, skills, and warfare

Polyphemus (pol ih FEE muhs)—the Cyclops who imprisons Odysseus

Laertes (lay UR teez)—Odysseus' father

Cronus (KROH nuhs)—Titan ruler of the universe; father of Zeus

Perimedes (pehr uh MEE deez)—member of Odysseus' crew

Eurylochus (yoo RIHL uh kuhs)—another member of the crew

Tiresias (ty REE see uhs)—blind prophet who advises Odysseus

Persephone (puhr SEHF uh nee)—wife of Hades

Telemachus (tuh LEHM uh kuhs)—Odysseus and Penelope's son

Sirens (SY ruhnz)—creatures whose songs lure sailors to their deaths

Scylla (SIHL uh)—sea monster of gray rock

Charybdis (kuh RIHB dihs)—enormous and dangerous whirlpool

Lampetia (lahm PEE shuh)—nymph

Hermes (HUR meez)—herald and messenger of the gods

Eumaeus (yoo MEE uhs)—old swineherd and friend of Odysseus

Antinous (ant IHN oh uhs)—leader among the suitors

Eurynome (yoo RIHN uh mee)—housekeeper for Penelope

Penelope (puh NEHL uh pee)—Odysseus' wife

Eurymachus (yoo RIH muh kuhs)—suitor

Amphinomus (am FIHN uh muhs)—suitor

SCAN FOR MULTIMEDIA

In the opening verses, Homer addresses the muse of epic poetry. He asks her help in telling the tale of Odysseus.

Sing in me, Muse,[1] and through me tell the story
of that man skilled in all ways of contending,
the wanderer, harried for years on end,
after he **plundered** the stronghold
on the proud height of Troy.[2]
He saw the townlands
and learned the minds of many distant men,
and weathered many bitter nights and days
in his deep heart at sea, while he fought only
to save his life, to bring his shipmates home.
But not by will nor valor could he save them.
for their own recklessness destroyed them all—

NOTES

1. **Muse** (myooz) any one of the nine goddesses of the arts.

plundered (PLUHN duhrd) *v.* took something by force

2. **Troy** city in northwest Asia Minor; site of the Trojan War.

DIGITAL PERSPECTIVES

CLOSER LOOK

Analyze Blank Verse

Students may have marked lines 1–5 during their first read. Use this paragraph to help students understand the poetic form that the translator uses: a loose form of blank verse. Encourage them to talk about the annotations that they marked. You may want to model a close read with the class based on the highlights shown in the text.

ANNOTATE: Have students mark how many syllables are in each line in lines 1–5 and note whether there are end rhymes or a regular meter, or have students participate while you note these details.

QUESTION: About how long are the lines? Are they rhymed? Is there a regular meter?

Possible response: Most of the lines are 10 or 11 syllables long. There is no end rhyme. Although there are a number of exceptions, the meter is largely iambic. The result is a natural-sounding line, almost like regular speech but more formal than prose or free verse, which has very little structure.

CONCLUDE: Help students to formulate conclusions about the importance of the way the text is written. Ask students why the author might have chosen this form.

Possible response: It's poetry, and it sounds dignified, but it's pretty easy to read and understand.

Remind students that **blank verse** is a form of poetry that combines the dignity and formal quality of poetry with the natural quality of regular speech.

NOTES

3. **Helios** (HEE lee ohs) sun god.

4. **Zeus** (zoos) king of the gods.

5. **Laertes** (LAY ur teez)

6. **guile** (gyl) *n.* craftiness; cunning.

7. **Ithaca** (IHTH uh kuh) island off the west coast of Greece.

8. **Calypso** (kuh LIHP soh) sea goddess who loved Odysseus.

9. **Circe** (SUR see) of Aeaea (EE ee uh)

10. **Ilium** (IHL ee uhm) Troy.

11. **Cicones** (sih KOH neez)

children and fools, they killed and feasted on
the cattle of Lord Helios,[3] the Sun,
and he who moves all day through heaven
took from their eyes the dawn of their return.
Of these adventures, Muse, daughter of Zeus,[4]
tell us in our time, lift the great song again.

Sailing From Troy

Ten years after the Trojan War, Odysseus departs from the goddess Calypso's island. He arrives in Phaeacia, ruled by Alcinous. Alcinous offers a ship to Odysseus and asks him to tell of his adventures.

"I am Laertes'[5] son, Odysseus.
Men hold me
formidable for guile[6] in peace and war:
this fame has gone abroad to the sky's rim.

My home is on the peaked sea-mark of Ithaca[7]
under Mount Neion's wind-blown robe of leaves,
in sight of other islands—Dulichium,
Same, wooded Zacynthus—Ithaca
being most lofty in that coastal sea,
and northwest, while the rest lie east and south.
A rocky isle, but good for a boy's training;
I shall not see on earth a place more dear,
though I have been detained long by Calypso,[8]
loveliest among goddesses, who held me
in her smooth caves to be her heart's delight,
as Circe of Aeaea,[9] the enchantress,
desired me, and detained me in her hall.
But in my heart I never gave consent.
Where shall a man find sweetness to surpass
his own home and his parents? In far lands
he shall not, though he find a house of gold.

What of my sailing, then, from Troy?
What of those years
of rough adventure, weathered under Zeus?
The wind that carried west from Ilium[10]
brought me to Ismarus, on the far shore,
a strongpoint on the coast of Cicones.[11]
I stormed that place and killed the men who fought.
Plunder we took, and we enslaved the women,
to make division, equal shares to all—
but on the spot I told them: 'Back, and quickly!

Additional **English Language Support** is available in the Interactive Teacher's Edition.

PERSONALIZE FOR LEARNING

Strategic Support

Research What books or stories have been influenced by the *Odyssey*? If students are doing their research on the Internet, discuss the importance of search terms. What is the specific information they need to complete the assignment? For example, searching "Odysseus" will result in many interesting links, but will not help them with the specific information needed. Have students try more than one term in their search and evaluate the result. **(Research to Explore)**

Out to sea again!' My men were mutinous,[12]
fools, on stores of wine. Sheep after sheep
they butchered by the surf, and shambling cattle,
feasting,—while **fugitives** went inland, running
to call to arms the main force of Cicones.
This was an army, trained to fight on horseback
or, where the ground required, on foot. They came
with dawn over that terrain like the leaves
and blades of spring. So doom appeared to us,
dark word of Zeus for us, our evil days.
My men stood up and made a fight of it—
backed on the ships, with lances kept in play,
from bright morning through the blaze of noon
holding our beach, although so far outnumbered;
but when the sun passed toward unyoking time,
then the Achaeans,[13] one by one, gave way.
Six benches were left empty in every ship
that evening when we pulled away from death.
And this new grief we bore with us to sea:
our precious lives we had, but not our friends.
No ship made sail next day until some shipmate
had raised a cry, three times, for each poor ghost
unfleshed by the Cicones on that field.

The Lotus-Eaters

Now Zeus the lord of cloud roused in the north
a storm against the ships, and driving veils
of squall moved down like night on land and sea.
The bows went plunging at the gust; sails
cracked and lashed out strips in the big wind.
We saw death in that fury, dropped the yards,
unshipped the oars, and pulled for the nearest lee:[14]
then two long days and nights we lay offshore
worn out and sick at heart, tasting our grief,
until a third Dawn came with ringlets shining.
Then we put up our masts, hauled sail, and rested,
letting the steersmen and the breeze take over.

I might have made it safely home, that time,
but as I came round Malea the current
took me out to sea, and from the north
a fresh gale drove me on, past Cythera.
Nine days I drifted on the teeming sea
before dangerous high winds. Upon the tenth
we came to the coastline of the Lotus-Eaters,
who live upon that flower. We landed there
to take on water. All ships' companies

NOTES

12. mutinous (MYOO tuh nuhs) *adj.* rebellious.

fugitives (FYOO juh tihvz) *n.* group of persons who have run away from danger

CLOSE READ

ANNOTATE: In lines 53–57, mark the words Odysseus uses to describe the enemy army.

QUESTION: What is he expressing about what he and his men felt?

CONCLUDE: How threatening did the enemy appear to Odysseus?

13. Achaeans (uh KEE uhnz) Greeks; here, Odysseus' men.

14. lee *n.* area sheltered from the wind.

DIGITAL PERSPECTIVES

CLOSE READ

Remind students to focus on the words that Odysseus uses to describe the enemy army. You may wish to model the close read using the following think-aloud format. Possible responses to questions on the Student page are included. You may also want to print copies of the **Close-Read Guide: Poetry** for students to use.

ANNOTATE: As I read lines 53–57, I notice and highlight the words that describe the Cicones.

QUESTION: I understand that Odysseus wants to convey the wonder that he and his men felt. It seemed that the enemy army hadn't assembled; it had materialized. Odysseus and his men took it as a sign that they had fallen out of grace with Zeus.

CONCLUDE: I think by using these words, Odysseus shows how threatening the enemy appeared to him and his men and how terrifying the future looked beyond this vast army.

CLOSER LOOK

Examining Alliteration

Students may have marked lines 113–115 during their first read. Use this paragraph to help students understand alliteration. Encourage them to talk about the annotations that they marked. You may want to model a close read with the class based on the highlights shown in the text.

ANNOTATE: Have students mark details in lines 113–115 that show alliteration, or have students participate while you highlight them.

QUESTION: Guide students to consider what these details might tell them. Ask what a reader can infer from the marked words, and accept student responses.

Possible response: There are words that use the same sounds: *gr-* (*ground, grain, grows*); *w-* (*wild, wheat, wine*); and *r-* (*ripen, rains*).

CONCLUDE: Help students to formulate conclusions about the importance of these details in the text. Ask students why the author might have included these details.

Possible response: Words that are connected by the same alliteration are also linked conceptually—"ground," "grain," "grows," and "grapes" are all related to fertility.

Remind students that **alliteration** is the repetition of initial consonant sounds in nearby syllables, particularly stressed syllables (as in "slippery slope" or "weak and weary"). Writers, especially poets, use alliteration to emphasize and link words, to imitate sounds, and to create musical and rhythmic effects.

NOTES

mustered alongside for the mid-day meal.
Then I sent out two picked men and a runner
to learn what race of men that land sustained.
They fell in, soon enough, with Lotus-Eaters,
who showed no will to do us harm, only
offering the sweet Lotus to our friends—
but those who ate this honeyed plant, the Lotus,
never cared to report, nor to return:
they longed to stay forever, browsing on
that native bloom, forgetful of their homeland.
I drove them, all three wailing, to the ships,
tied them down under their rowing benches,
and called the rest: 'All hands aboard;
come, clear the beach and no one taste
the Lotus, or you lose your hope of home.'
Filing in to their places by the rowlocks
my oarsmen dipped their long oars in the surf,
and we moved out again on our sea faring.

The Cyclops

In the next land we found were Cyclopes,[15]
giants, louts, without a law to bless them.
In ignorance leaving the fruitage of the earth in mystery
to the immortal gods, they neither plow
nor sow by hand, nor till the ground, though grain—
wild wheat and barley—grows untended, and
wine-grapes, in clusters, ripen in heaven's rains.
Cyclopes have no muster and no meeting,
no consultation or old tribal ways,
but each one dwells in his own mountain cave
dealing out rough justice to wife and child,
indifferent to what the others do. . . .

As we rowed on, and nearer to the mainland,
at one end of the bay, we saw a cavern
yawning above the water, screened with laurel,
and many rams and goats about the place
inside a sheepfold—made from slabs of stone
earthfast between tall trunks of pine and rugged
towering oak trees.

A prodigious[16] man
slept in this cave alone, and took his flocks
to graze afield—remote from all companions,
knowing none but savage ways, a brute
so huge, he seemed no man at all of those

15. **Cyclopes** (SY kloh peez) *n.* plural form of Cyclops (SY klops), race of giants with one eye in the middle of the forehead.

16. **prodigious** (proh DIHJ uhs) *adj.* enormous.

564 UNIT 5 • JOURNEYS OF TRANSFORMATION

DIGITAL PERSPECTIVES

who eat good wheaten bread; but he seemed rather
a shaggy mountain reared in solitude.
We beached there, and I told the crew
to stand by and keep watch over the ship:
as for myself I took my twelve best fighters
and went ahead. I had a goatskin full
of that sweet liquor that Euanthes' son,
Maron, had given me. He kept Apollo's[17]
holy grove at Ismarus; for kindness
we showed him there, and showed his wife and child,
he gave me seven shining golden talents[18]
perfectly formed, a solid silver winebowl,
and then this liquor—twelve two-handled jars
of brandy, pure and fiery. Not a slave
in Maron's household knew this drink; only
he, his wife, and the storeroom mistress knew;
and they would put one cupful—ruby-colored,
honey-smooth—in twenty more of water,
but still the sweet scent hovered like a fume
over the winebowl. No man turned away
when cups of this came round.

A wineskin full
I brought along, and victuals[19] in a bag,
for in my bones I knew some towering brute
would be upon us soon—all outward power,
a wild man, ignorant of civility.

We climbed, then, briskly to the cave. But Cyclops
had gone afield, to pasture his fat sheep,
so we looked round at everything inside:
a drying rack that sagged with cheeses, pens
crowded with lambs and kids,[20] each in its class:
firstlings apart from middlings, and the 'dewdrops,'
or newborn lambkins, penned apart from both.
And vessels full of whey[21] were brimming there—
bowls of earthenware and pails for milking.
My men came pressing round me, pleading:

'Why not
take these cheeses, get them stowed, come back,
throw open all the pens, and make a run for it?
We'll drive the kids and lambs aboard. We say
put out again on good salt water!'

Ah,
how sound that was! Yet I refused. I wished
to see the cave man, what he had to offer—

NOTES

17. **Apollo** (uh POL oh) god of music, poetry, prophecy, and medicine.

18. **talents** units of money in ancient Greece.

19. **victuals** (viht uhlz) *n.* food or other provisions.

20. **kids** young goats.

21. **whey** (hway) *n.* thin, watery part of milk separated from the thicker curds.

VOCABULARY DEVELOPMENT

Graphic Organizer Have students analyze the word *civility* from line 156, using a four-square diagram. If necessary, guide students as they complete the diagram.

Definition: polite and respectful behavior	**Synonyms:** politeness, courtesy, propriety
Example sentence: My grandmother always treated her houseguests with great civility.	**Other forms using root word:** civil, civic, civilization

CLOSE READ

Remind students to focus on the verb choice in this line. You may wish to model the close read using the following think-aloud format. Possible responses to questions on the Student page are included.

ANNOTATE: As I read lines 178–180, I notice and highlight the verb that Odysseus uses to tell how he and his men moved away from the Cyclops.

QUESTION: I can see that Odysseus uses a verb that evokes an image of panic and disarray—"scattered" suggests insects when they're disturbed.

CONCLUDE: I think by using the verb *scattered*, Odysseus is drawing a strong comparison between the size and power of the Cyclops and the relative insignificance of him and his men.

NOTES

22. boughs (bowz) *n.* tree branches.

CLOSE READ

ANNOTATE: In lines 178–180, mark the verb Odysseus uses to tell how he and his men moved away from Cyclops.

QUESTION: What kind of creature does that verb evoke?

CONCLUDE: What comparison does it suggest between Cyclops and Odysseus and his men?

23. withy (WIHTH ee) *adj.* made from tough, flexible twigs.

24. Agamemnon (ag uh MEHM non) king who led the Greek army during the Trojan War.

avenge (uh VEHNJ) *v.* to get revenge

no pretty sight, it turned out, for my friends.
We lit a fire, burnt an offering,
and took some cheese to eat; then sat in silence
around the embers, waiting. When he came
he had a load of dry boughs[22] on his shoulder
to stoke his fire at suppertime. He dumped it
with a great crash into that hollow cave,
and we all scattered fast to the far wall.
Then over the broad cavern floor he ushered
the ewes he meant to milk. He left his rams
and he-goats in the yard outside, and swung
high overhead a slab of solid rock
to close the cave. Two dozen four-wheeled wagons,
with heaving wagon teams, could not have stirred
the tonnage of that rock from where he wedged it
over the doorsill. Next he took his seat
and milked his bleating ewes. A practiced job
he made of it, giving each ewe her suckling;
thickened his milk, then, into curds and whey,
sieved out the curds to drip in withy[23] baskets,
and poured the whey to stand in bowls
cooling until he drank it for his supper.
When all these chores were done, he poked the fire,
heaping on brushwood. In the glare he saw us.

'Strangers,' he said, 'who are you? And where from?
What brings you here by seaways—a fair traffic?
Or are you wandering rogues, who cast your lives
like dice, and ravage other folk by sea?'

We felt a pressure on our hearts, in dread
of that deep rumble and that mighty man.
But all the same I spoke up in reply:
'We are from Troy, Achaeans, blown off course
by shifting gales on the Great South Sea;
homeward bound, but taking routes and ways
uncommon: so the will of Zeus would have it.
We served under Agamemnon,[24] son of Atreus—
the whole world knows what city
he laid waste, what armies he destroyed.
It was our luck to come here; here we stand,
beholden for your help, or any gifts
you give—as custom is to honor strangers.
We would entreat you, great Sir, have a care
for the gods' courtesy; Zeus will **avenge**
the unoffending guest.'

DIGITAL PERSPECTIVES

NOTES

The Cyclops Polyphemus returns to his cave, where Odysseus and his men are imprisoned.

He answered this
from his brute chest, unmoved:

'You are a ninny,
or else you come from the other end of nowhere,
telling me, mind the gods! We Cyclopes
care not a whistle for your thundering Zeus
or all the gods in bliss; we have more force by far.

I would not let you go for fear of Zeus—
you or your friends—unless I had a whim[25] to.
Tell me, where was it, now, you left your ship—
around the point, or down the shore, I wonder?'

He thought he'd find out, but I saw through this,
And answered with a ready lie:

'My ship?
Poseidon[26] Lord, who sets the earth a-tremble,
broke it up on the rocks at your land's end.
A wind from seaward served him, drove us there.
We are survivors, these good men and I.'

25. whim *n.* sudden thought or wish to do something.

26. Poseidon (poh SY duhn) god of the sea, earthquakes, horses, and storms at sea.

CLOSER LOOK

Identifying Similes

Students may have marked lines 233–238 during their first read. Use this paragraph to demonstrate the use of similes. Encourage them to talk about the annotations that they marked. You may want to model a close read with the class based on the highlights shown in the text.

ANNOTATE: Have students mark details in lines 233–238 that indicate similes, or have students participate while you highlight them.

QUESTION: Guide students to consider what these details might tell them. Ask what a reader can infer from these comparisons, and accept student responses.

Possible response: The men were helpless as puppies, and the Cyclops ate its human prey with the slack-jawed circling motion characteristic of a mountain lion.

CONCLUDE: Help students to formulate conclusions about the importance of these details in the text. Ask students why the author might have included these details.

Possible response: Similes help the reader to visualize the Cyclops's attack on Odysseus's men.

Remind students that a **simile** is a figure of speech that enhances our understanding of something or reveals an unacknowledged truth about it by pointing out its (preferably not obvious) similarity to something else. A simile uses *like, as, than,* or *resembles* to make its point.

NOTES

Neither reply nor pity came from him,
but in one stride he clutched at my companions
and caught two in his hands like squirming puppies
to beat their brain out, spattering the floor.
Then he dismembered them and made his meal,
gaping and crunching like a mountain lion—
everything: innards, flesh, and marrow bones.
We cried aloud, lifting our hands to Zeus,
powerless, looking on at this, appalled;
but Cyclops went on filling up his belly
with manflesh and great gulps of whey,
then lay down like a mast among his sheep.
My heart beat high now at the chance of action,
and drawing the sharp sword from my hip I went
along his flank to stab him where the midriff
holds the liver. I had touched the spot
when sudden fear stayed me: if I killed him
we perished there as well, for we could never
move his ponderous doorway slab aside.
So we were left to groan and wait for morning.

When the young Dawn with fingertips of rose
lit up the world, the Cyclops built a fire
and milked his handsome ewes, all in due order,
putting the sucklings to the mothers. Then,
his chores being all **dispatched**, he caught
another brace[27] of men to make his breakfast,
and whisked away his great door slab
to let his sheep go through—but he, behind,
reset the stone as one would cap a quiver.[28]
There was a din[29] of whistling as the Cyclops
rounded his flock to higher ground, then stillness.
And now I pondered how to hurt him worst,
if but Athena[30] granted what I prayed for.
Here are the means I thought would serve my turn:

a club, or staff, lay there along the fold—
an olive tree, felled green and left to season[31]
for Cyclops' hand. And it was like a mast
a lugger[32] of twenty oars, broad in the beam—
a deep-sea-going craft—might carry:
so long, so big around, it seemed. Now I
chopped out a six foot section of this pole
and set it down before my men, who scraped it;
and when they had it smooth, I hewed again
to make a stake with pointed end. I held this
in the fire's heart and turned it, toughening it,

dispatched (dihs PACHT) *v.* finished something quickly

27. brace *n.* pair.

28. cap a quiver (KWIHV uhr) close a case holding arrows.

29. din *n.* loud, continuous noise; uproar.

30. Athena (uh THEE nuh) goddess of wisdom, skills, and warfare.

31. felled green and left to season chopped down and exposed to the weather to age the wood.

32. lugger *n.* small sailing vessel.

then hid it, well back in the cavern, under
one of the dung piles in profusion there.
Now came the time to toss for it: who **ventured**
along with me? whose hand could bear to thrust
and grind that spike in Cyclops' eye, when mild
sleep had mastered him? As luck would have it,
the men I would have chosen won the toss—
four strong men, and I made five as captain.

At evening came the shepherd with his flock,
his woolly flock. The rams as well, this time,
entered the cave: by some sheepherding whim—
or a god's bidding—none were left outside.
He hefted his great boulder into place
and sat him down to milk the bleating ewes
in proper order, put the lambs to suck,
and swiftly ran through all his evening chores.
Then he caught two more men and feasted on them.
My moment was at hand, and I went forward
holding an ivy bowl of my dark drink,
looking up, saying:

'Cyclops, try some wine.
Here's liquor to wash down your scraps of men.
Taste it, and see the kind of drink we carried
under our planks. I meant it for an offering
if you would help us home. But you are mad,
unbearable, a bloody monster! After this,
will any other traveler come to see you?'

He seized and drained the bowl, and it went down
so fiery and smooth he called for more:

'Give me another, thank you kindly. Tell me,
how are you called? I'll make a gift will please you.
Even Cyclopes know the wine grapes grow
out of grassland and loam in heaven's rain,
but here's a bit of nectar and ambrosia!'[33]

Three bowls I brought him, and he poured them down.
I saw the fuddle and flush come over him,
then I sang out in cordial tones:

'Cyclops,
you ask my honorable name? Remember
the gift you promised me, and I shall tell you.
My name is Nohbdy: mother, father, and friends,
everyone calls me Nohbdy.'

NOTES

ventured (VEHN chuhrd) *v.* tried something dangerous

33. nectar (NEHK tuhr) **and ambrosia** (am BROH zhuh) drink and food of the gods.

WriteNow Inform and Explain

Have students stop reading at the end of line 251. Ask students to imagine they are Odysseus, and then have them write a one-page account of how they would outwit the Cyclops so they could escape with their men. For students who know what happens next in the story, have them write a scheme different from the one Odysseus devises against the Cyclops.

NOTES

And he said:
'Nohbdy's my meat, then, after I eat his friends.
Others come first. There's a noble gift, now.'

Even as he spoke, he reeled and tumbled backward,
his great head lolling to one side; and sleep
took him like any creature. Drunk, hiccuping,
he dribbled streams of liquor and bits of men.

Now, by the gods, I drove my big hand spike
deep in the embers, charring it again,
and cheered my men along with battle talk
to keep their courage up: no quitting now.
The pike of olive, green though it had been,
reddened and glowed as if about to catch.
I drew it from the coals and my four fellows
gave me a hand, lugging it near the Cyclops
as more than natural force nerved them; straight
forward they sprinted, lifted it, and rammed it
deep in his crater eye, and leaned on it
turning it as a shipwright tums a drill
in planking, having men below to swing
the two-handled strap that spins it in the groove.
So with our brand we bored[34] that great eye socket
while blood ran out around the red-hot bar.
Eyelid and lash were seared; the pierced ball
hissed broiling, and the roots popped.

In a smithy
one sees a white-hot axehead or an adze
plunged and wrung in a cold tub, screeching steam—
the way they make soft iron hale and hard—:
just so that eyeball hissed around the spike.
The Cyclops bellowed and the rock roared round him,
and we fell back in fear. Clawing his face
he tugged the bloody spike out of his eye,
threw it away, and his wild hands went groping:
then he set up a howl for Cyclopes
who lived in caves on windy peaks nearby.
Some heard him; and they came by divers[35] ways
to clump around outside and call:

'What ails you,
Polyphemus?[36] Why do you cry so sore
in the starry night? You will not let us sleep.
Sure no man's driving off your flock? No man
has tricked you, ruined you?'

34. bored *v.* made a hole in.

35. divers *adj.* several; various.

36. Polyphemus (pol ih FEE muhs)

DIGITAL PERSPECTIVES

Enriching the Text Have students review the section called "The Cyclops" beginning on line 109. The 1997 Hallmark television miniseries *The Odyssey* contains a scene based on Odysseus's capture by and escape from the Cyclops. After students complete their close read, show the clip from the television miniseries and have students compare it with the written text. How do televised scenes add to students' understanding of the epic poem? Preview all videos before showing them to the class.

Out of the cave
the mammoth Polyphemus roared in answer:

'Nohbdy, Nohbdy's tricked me, Nohbdy's ruined me!'

To this rough shout they made a sage[37] reply:

'Ah well, if nobody has played you foul
there in your lonely bed, we are no use in pain
given by great Zeus. Let it be your father,
Poseidon Lord, to whom you pray.'

So saying
they trailed away. And I was filled with laughter
to see how like a charm the name deceived them.
Now Cyclops, wheezing as the pain came on him,
fumbled to wrench away the great doorstone
and squatted in the breach with arms thrown wide
for any silly beast or man who bolted—
hoping somehow I might be such a fool.
But I kept thinking how to win the game:
death sat there huge; how could we slip away?
I drew on all my wits, and ran through **tactics**,
reasoning as a man will for dear life,
until a trick came—and it pleased me well.
The Cyclops' rams were handsome, fat, with heavy
fleeces, a dark violet.

Three abreast
I tied them silently together, twining
cords of willow from the ogre's bed;
then slung a man under each middle one
to ride there safely, shielded left and right.

So three sheep could convey each man. I took
the woolliest ram, the choicest of the flock,
and hung myself under his kinky belly,
pulled up tight, with fingers twisted deep
in sheepskin ringlets for an iron grip.
So, breathing hard, we waited until morning.

When Dawn spread out her fingertips of rose
the rams began to stir, moving for pasture,
and peals of bleating echoed round the pens
where dams with udders full called for a milking.
Blinded, and sick with pain from his head wound,
the master stroked each ram, then let it pass,
but my men riding on the pectoral[38] fleece
the giant's blind hands blundering never found.

NOTES

37. sage *adj.* wise.

CLOSE READ

ANNOTATE: Mark the verbs Odysseus uses to describe the actions of Cyclops in the sentence beginning on line 366.

QUESTION: What do these verbs suggest about Cyclops' condition?

CONCLUDE: What does this reveal about Cyclops' pain, anger, and remaining strength?

tactics (TAK tihks) *n.* military procedures

38. pectoral (PEHK tuh ruhl) *adj.* located in or on the chest.

DIGITAL PERSPECTIVES

CLOSE READ

Remind students to focus on the verb choices that feature in descriptions of Cyclops's actions. You may wish to model the close read using the following think-aloud format. Possible responses to questions on the Student page are included.

ANNOTATE: As I read lines 366 through 368, I notice and highlight the details that describe Cyclops's movements.

QUESTION: I see that Odysseus uses verbs that suggest Cyclops's clumsy and undignified movements now that he's disabled by blindness and drink.

CONCLUDE: These verbs reveal that Cyclops is in great pain and is angry, but his strength is greatly diminished.

The Cyclops fails to notice the men hidden under the ram.

PERSONALIZE FOR LEARNING

English Language Support

False Cognates False cognates can be confusing to English learners. For example, *blind* on line 436 (*the blind thing*) is a false cognate and could be confusing to Spanish-speaking students. To help them understand the meaning, explain that to be blind means one cannot see, where the Spanish word *blindar* means "to shield oneself." When students read a word that they think might be a cognate, remind them to stop and consider whether or not the word makes sense in context. **ALL LEVELS**

Last of them all my ram, the leader, came,
weighted by wool and me with my meditations.
The Cyclops patted him, and then he said:

'Sweet cousin ram, why lag behind the rest
in the night cave? You never linger so,
but graze before them all, and go afar
to crop sweet grass, and take your stately way
leading along the streams, until at evening
you run to be the first one in the fold.
Why, now, so far behind? Can you be grieving
over your Master's eye? That carrion rogue[39]
and his accurst companions burnt it out
when he had conquered all my wits with wine.
Nohbdy will not get out alive, I swear.
Oh, had you brain and voice to tell
where he may be now, dodging all my fury!
Bashed by this hand and bashed on this rock wall
his brains would strew the floor, and I should have
rest from the outrage Nohbdy worked upon me.'

He sent us into the open, then. Close by,
I dropped and rolled clear of the ram's belly,
going this way and that to untie the men.
With many glances back, we rounded up
his fat, stiff-legged sheep to take aboard,
and drove them down to where the good ship lay.

We saw, as we came near, our fellows' faces
shining; then we saw them turn to grief
tallying those who had not fled from death.
I hushed them, jerking head and eyebrows up,
and in a low voice told them: 'Load this herd:
move fast, and put the ship's head toward the breakers.'
They all pitched in at loading, then embarked
and struck their oars into the sea. Far out,
as far off shore as shouted words would carry,
I sent a few back to the adversary:
'O Cyclops! Would you feast on my companions?
Puny, am I, in a cave man's hands?
How do you like the beating that we gave you,
you damned cannibal? Eater of guests
under your roof! Zeus and the gods have paid you!'

The blind thing in his doubled fury broke
a hilltop in his hands and heaved it after us.
Ahead of our black prow it struck and sank
whelmed in a spuming geyser, a giant wave

NOTES

39. carrion (KAR ee uhn) **rogue** (rohg) repulsive scoundrel.

DIGITAL PERSPECTIVES

CLOSER LOOK

Analyzing Consonance

Students may have marked line 438 during their first read. Use this paragraph to help students understand consonance. Encourage them to talk about the annotations that they marked. You may want to model a close read with the class based on the highlights shown in the text.

ANNOTATE: Have students mark words in line 438 that demonstrate the use of consonance, or have students participate while you highlight them.

QUESTION: Guide students to consider what these details might tell them. Ask what a reader can infer from the use of consonance, and accept student responses.

Possible response: The words that demonstrate the use of consonance are *black*, *struck*, and *sank*. Each word ends with a hard *k* sound.

CONCLUDE: Help students to formulate conclusions about the importance of these details in the text. Ask students why the author might have included these details.

Possible response: The author uses consonance with the repeated sound of a hard *k* to help the reader hear the sound of Cyclops's flying hilltop as it clips the ship's woodwork and crashes into the sea.

Remind students that **consonance** is the repetition of final consonant sounds in stressed syllables that follow different vowel sounds (as in *wind* and *sand, switch* and *clutch, pull* and *fall,* and *like* and *luck*).

CLOSE READ

Remind students to focus on the sense of panic among the crew. You may wish to model the close read using the following think-aloud format. Possible responses to questions on the Student page are included.

ANNOTATE: As I read lines 448–454, I notice and highlight the use of punctuation.

QUESTION: I can see that the translator uses four exclamation points and one question mark in these six lines to indicate to the reader that the crew is extremely alarmed by Odysseus's provocative actions toward Cyclops.

CONCLUDE: The reader has become used to the crew members' being undisciplined and insubordinate in the background. Here they step into the foreground to offer their captain some advice and criticism so urgent that it takes four exclamation marks and a question mark to get it across—and they are of course right. Odysseus is taking crazy risks. The wisest move would be to leave quickly. Odysseus has other plans, however. He is becoming Odysseus the epic hero—and it's not in the nature of epic heroes to always make the wisest move.

NOTES

that washed the ship stern foremost back to shore.
I got the longest boathook out and stood
fending us off, with furious nods to all
to put their backs into a racing stroke—
row, row, or perish. So the long oars bent
kicking the foam sternward, making head
until we drew away, and twice as far.
Now when I cupped my hands I heard the crew
in low voices protesting:

'Godsake, Captain!
Why bait the beast again? Let him alone!'

'That tidal wave he made on the first throw
all but beached us.'

'All but stove us in!'
'Give him our bearing with your trumpeting,
he'll get the range and lob a boulder.'

'Aye
He'll smash our timbers and our heads together!'
I would not heed them in my glorying spirit,
but let my anger flare and yelled:

'Cyclops,
if ever mortal man inquire
how you were put to shame and blinded, tell him
Odysseus, raider of cities, took your eye:
Laertes' son, whose home's on Ithaca!'

At this he gave a mighty sob and rumbled:
'Now comes the weird[40] upon me, spoken of old.
A wizard, grand and wondrous, lived here—Telemus,[41]
a son of Eurymus;[42] great length of days
he had in wizardry among the Cyclopes,
and these things he foretold for time to come:
my great eye lost, and at Odysseus' hands.
Always I had in mind some giant, armed
in giant force, would come against me here.
But this, but you—small, pitiful, and twiggy—
you put me down with wine, you blinded me.
Come back, Odysseus, and I'll treat you well,
praying the god of earthquake[43] to befriend you—
his son I am, for he by his avowal
fathered me, and, if he will, he may
heal me of this black wound—he and no other
of all the happy gods or mortal men.'

CLOSE READ

ANNOTATE: Mark the punctuation in lines 448–454.

QUESTION: What does this punctuation indicate?

CONCLUDE: What does the poet accomplish by letting the reader hear the crew's own voices for the first time?

40. **weird** *n.* fate or destiny.
41. **Telemus** (tehl EH muhs)
42. **Eurymus** (yoo RIHM uhs)
43. **god of earthquake** Poseidon.

574 UNIT 5 • JOURNEYS OF TRANSFORMATION

Few words I shouted in reply to him:

'If I could take your life I would and take
your time away, and hurl you down to hell!
The god of earthquake could not heal you there!'

At this he stretched his hands out in his darkness
toward the sky of stars, and prayed Poseidon:

'O hear me, lord, blue girdler of the islands,
if I am thine indeed, and thou art father:
grant that Odysseus, raider of cities, never
see his home: Laertes' son, I mean,
who kept his hall on Ithaca. Should destiny
intend that he shall see his roof again
among his family in his father land,
far be that day, and dark the years between.

Let him lose all companions, and return
under strange sail to bitter days at home.'
In these words he prayed, and the god heard him.
Now he laid hands upon a bigger stone
and wheeled around, titanic for the cast,
to let it fly in the black-prowed vessel's track.
But it fell short, just aft the steering oar,
and whelming seas rose giant above the stone
to bear us onward toward the island.

There
as we ran in we saw the squadron waiting,
The trim ships drawn up side by side, and all
our troubled friends who waited, looking seaward.
We beached her, grinding keel in the soft sand,
and waded in, ourselves, on the sandy beach.
Then we unloaded all the Cyclops' flock
to make division, share and share alike,
only my fighters voted that my ram,
the prize of all, should go to me. I slew him
by the seaside and burnt his long thighbones
to Zeus beyond the storm cloud, Cronus'[44] son,
who rules the world. But Zeus disdained my offering;
destruction for my ships he had in store
and death for those who sailed them, my companions.
Now all day long until the sun went down
we made our feast on mutton and sweet wine,
till after sunset in the gathering dark
we went to sleep above the wash of ripples.

NOTES

44. Cronus (KROH nuhs) Titan who was ruler of the universe until he was overthrown by his son Zeus.

PERSONALIZE FOR LEARNING

English Language Support

Describing Characters Note the phrase in line 486: *"Odysseus, raider of cities."* Explain to students that this sentence contains an example of a **Homeric epithet**, an adjectival phrase that is routinely used to describe a characteristic quality of that person, thing, or place. Have students do a word search for "Odysseus" in the epic poem to see how often this epithet or one that is similar to it is used to describe Odysseus. Discuss with students that through extensive repetition, Homeric epithets become almost part of the name. Ask students to think of a Homeric epithet to describe themselves, and then have students share their ideas. **ALL LEVELS**

NOTES

45. offing *n.* distant part of the sea visible from the shore.

46. Aeolia (ee OH lee uh) . . . **Aeolus** (EE uh luhs)

47. Laestrygonians (lehs trih GOH nee uhnz)

48. singing nymph . . . hair Circe.

When the young Dawn with fingertips of rose
touched the world, I roused the men, gave orders
to man the ships, cast off the mooring lines;
and filing in to sit beside the rowlocks
oarsmen in line dipped oars in the gray sea.
So we moved out, sad in the vast offing,[45]
having our precious lives, but not our friends.

The Land of the Dead

Odysseus and his men sail to Aeolia, where Aeolus,[46] king of the winds, sends Odysseus on his way with a gift: a sack containing all the winds except the favorable west wind. When they are near home, Odysseus' men open the sack, letting loose a storm that drives them back to Aeolia. Aeolus casts them out, having decided that they are detested by the gods. They sail for seven days and arrive in the land of the Laestrygonians,[47] a race of cannibals. These creatures destroy all of Odysseus' ships except the one he is sailing in.

Odysseus and his reduced crew escape and reach Aeaea, the island ruled by the sorceress-goddess Circe. She transforms half of the men into swine. Protected by a magic herb, Odysseus demands that Circe change his men back into human form. Before Odysseus departs from the island a year later, Circe informs him that in order to reach home he must journey to the land of the dead, Hades, and consult the blind prophet Tiresias.

We bore down on the ship at the sea's edge
and launched her on the salt immortal sea,
stepping our mast and spar in the black ship;
embarked the ram and ewe and went aboard
in tears, with bitter and sore dread upon us.
But now a breeze came up for us astern—
a canvas-bellying landbreeze, hale shipmate
sent by the singing nymph with sunbright hair;[48]
so we made fast the braces, took our thwarts,
and let the wind and steersman work the ship
with full sail spread all day above our coursing,
till the sun dipped, and all the ways grew dark
upon the fathomless unresting sea.
By night
our ship ran onward toward the Ocean's bourne,
the realm and region of the Men of Winter,
hidden in mist and cloud. Never the flaming
eye of Helios lights on those men

PERSONALIZE FOR LEARNING

English Language Support

Domain-Specific Vocabulary The domain-specific vocabulary that appears in the *Odyssey* may present challenges to English learners. Support them in understanding the text by reviewing the following nautical terms from lines 521–523 and 526–537:

cast off unfasten
mooring lines rope used to hold the ship in place (as on a dock)
rowlocks braces that attach the oars to the ship
oars large paddles used to row a ship
oarsmen people who row the oars on a ship
launched to put a boat or ship into water
mast a pole that supports the sails and rigging (the system of masts and lines on ships)
spar wooden pole that supports rigging and sails

ALL LEVELS

at morning, when he climbs the sky of stars,
nor in descending earthward out of heaven;
ruinous night being rove over those wretches.
We made the land, put ram and ewe ashore,
and took our way along the Ocean stream
to find the place foretold for us by Circe.
There Perimedes and Eurylochus[49]
pinioned[50] the sacred beasts. With my drawn blade
I spaded up the votive[51] pit, and poured
libations[52] round it to the unnumbered dead:
sweet milk and honey, then sweet wine, and last
clear water; and I scattered barley down.
Then I addressed the blurred and breathless dead,
vowing to slaughter my best heifer for them
before she calved, at home in Ithaca,
and burn the choice bits on the altar fire;
as for Tiresias,[53] I swore to sacrifice
a black lamb, handsomest of all our flock.
Thus to assuage the nations of the dead
I pledged these rites, then slashed the lamb and ewe,
letting their black blood stream into the wellpit.
Now the souls gathered, stirring out of Erebus,[54]
brides and young men, and men grown old in pain,
and tender girls whose hearts were new to grief;
many were there, too, torn by brazen lanceheads,
battle-slain, bearing still their bloody gear.
From every side they came and sought the pit
with rustling cries; and I grew sick with fear.
But presently I gave command to my officers
to flay those sheep the bronze cut down, and make
burnt offerings of flesh to the gods below—
to sovereign Death, to pale Persephone.[55]
Meanwhile I crouched with my drawn sword to keep
the surging phantoms from the bloody pit
till I should know the presence of Tiresias.

One shade came first—Elpenor, of our company,
who lay unburied still on the wide earth
as we had left him—dead in Circe's hall,
untouched, unmourned, when other cares compelled us.
Now when I saw him there I wept for pity
and called out to him:

'How is this, Elpenor,
how could you journey to the western gloom
swifter afoot than I in the black lugger?'
He sighed, and answered:

NOTES

49. Perimedes (pehr uh MEE deez) **and Eurylochus** (yoo RIHL uh kuhs)

50. pinioned (PIHN yuhnd) *v.* confined or shackled.

51. votive (VOHT ihv) *adj.* done to fulfill a vow or express thanks.

52. libations (ly BAY shuhnz) *n.* wine or other liquids poured upon the ground as a sacrifice or offering.

53. Tiresias (ty REE see uhs)

54. Erebus (EHR uh buhs) dark region under the earth through which the dead pass before entering realm of Hades.

55. Persephone (puhr SEHF uh nee)

CLOSER LOOK

Understanding Mood

Students may have marked lines 551–554 during their first read. Use this paragraph to help students understand the mood, or atmosphere, of the passage. Encourage them to talk about the annotations that they marked. You may want to model a close read with the class based on the highlights shown in the text.

ANNOTATE: Have students mark details in lines 551–554 that describe the preparation of the votive pit and the rituals that take place around it, or have students participate while you highlight them.

QUESTION: Guide students to consider what these details might tell them. Ask what a reader can infer from the details, and accept student responses.

Possible response: The votive pit is dug in order to bury gifts for the dead, and the offerings—milk, honey, wine, clear water, and barley—have ritual value in honoring their service and sacrifice.

CONCLUDE: Help students to formulate conclusions about the importance of these details in the text. Ask students why the author might have included these details.

Possible response: As Odysseus presents offerings to the dead, the author creates a mood of intense solemnity.

Remind students that **mood**, or atmosphere, refers to the emotional setting of an event or a sequence of events in a literary narrative. The author communicates mood to the reader by creating the appropriate emotional resonances with symbolic and figurative language.

NOTES

'Son of great Laertes,
Odysseus, master mariner and soldier,
bad luck shadowed me, and no kindly power;
ignoble death I drank with so much wine.
I slept on Circe's roof, then could not see
the long steep backward ladder, coming down,
and fell that height. My neckbone, buckled under,
snapped, and my spirit found this well of dark.
Now hear the grace I pray for, in the name
of those back in the world, not here—your wife
and father, he who gave you bread in childhood,
and your own child, your only son, Telemachus,[56]
long ago left at home.

When you make sail
and put these lodgings of dim Death behind,
you will moor ship, I know, upon Aeaea Island;
there, O my lord, remember me, I pray,
do not abandon me unwept, unburied,
to tempt the gods' wrath, while you sail for home;
but fire my corpse, and all the gear I had,
and build a cairn[57] for me above the breakers—
an unknown sailor's mark for men to come.
Heap up the mound there, and implant upon it
the oar I pulled in life with my companions.'

He ceased and I replied:

'Unhappy spirit,
I promise you the barrow and the burial.'

So we conversed, and grimly, at a distance,
with my long sword between, guarding the blood,
while the faint image of the lad spoke on.
Now came the soul of Anticlea, dead,
my mother, daughter of Autolycus,[58]
dead now, though living still when I took ship
for holy Troy. Seeing this ghost I grieved,
but held her off, through pang on pang of tears,
till I should know the presence of Tiresias.
Soon from the dark that prince of Thebes[59] came forward
bearing a golden staff; and he addressed me:

'Son of Laertes and the gods of old,
Odysseus, master of landways and seaways,
why leave the blazing sun, O man of woe,
to see the cold dead and the joyless region?
Stand clear, put up your sword;
let me but taste of blood, I shall speak true.'

56. Telemachus (tuh LEHM uh kuhs)

57. cairn (kairn) *n.* conical heap of stones built as a monument.

58. Autolycus (aw TOL ih kuhs)

59. Thebes (theebz)

PERSONALIZE FOR LEARNING

English Language Support

Dependent Clauses Review lines 598–600. Some students may require additional support in distinguishing the difference between dependent and independent clauses. Explain to students that independent clauses consist of a subject and verb or verb phrase that can stand alone and still make grammatical sense. While a dependent clause also has a subject and verb or verb phrase, it begins with a subordinating conjunction.

A dependent clause cannot stand on its own and remain grammatically correct. For example, have students read lines 598–600 as one continuous sentence: *When you make sail and put these lodgings of dim Death behind, you will moor ship, I know, upon Aeaea Island.* Have students determine if the first clause makes sense if the comma after "behind" is changed to a period.

Explain that dependent clauses provide writers a way to connect ideas. Have students practice writing sentences with dependent clauses, using this dependent clause as a start:

While Odysseus tried to get home, ________.

ALL LEVELS

At this I stepped aside, and in the scabbard
let my long sword ring home to the pommel silver,
as he bent down to the somber blood. Then spoke
the prince of those with gift of speech:

'Great captain,
a fair wind and the honey lights of home
are all you seek. But anguish lies ahead;
the god who thunders on the land prepares it,
not to be shaken from your track, implacable,
in rancor for the son whose eye you blinded.
One narrow strait may take you through his blows:
denial of yourself, restraint of shipmates.
When you make landfall on Thrinacia first
and quit the violet sea, dark on the land
you'll find the grazing herds of Helios
by whom all things are seen, all speech is known.
Avoid those kine,[60] hold fast to your intent,
and hard seafaring brings you all to Ithaca.
But if you raid the beeves, I see destruction
for ship and crew. Though you survive alone,
bereft of all companions, lost for years,
under strange sail shall you come home, to find
your own house filled with trouble: insolent men
eating your livestock as they court your lady.
Aye, you shall make those men atone in blood!
But after you have dealt out death—in open
combat or by stealth—to all the suitors,
go overland on foot, and take an oar,
until one day you come where men have lived
with meat unsalted, never known the sea,
nor seen seagoing ships, with crimson bows
and oars that fledge light hulls for dipping flight.
The spot will soon be plain to you, and I
can tell you how: some passerby will say,
"What winnowing fan is that upon your shoulder?"
Halt, and implant your smooth oar in the turf
and make fair sacrifice to Lord Poseidon:
a ram, a bull, a great buck boar; turn back,
and carry out pure hecatombs[61] at home
to all wide heaven's lords, the undying gods,
to each in order. Then a seaborne death
soft as this hand of mist will come upon you
when you are wearied out with rich old age,
your country folk in blessed peace around you.
And all this shall be just as I foretell.'

NOTES

CLOSE READ

ANNOTATE: In lines 632–637, mark the words that describe Odysseus' home and the words that describe what is in his future.

QUESTION: What do these contrasting words express?

CONCLUDE: What can you conclude about Odysseus' goal and what will happen before he reaches it?

60. kine (kyn) *n.* cattle.

61. hecatombs (HEHK uh tohmz) *n.* large-scale sacrifices to the gods in ancient Greece; often, the slaughter of 100 cattle at one time.

DIGITAL PERSPECTIVES

CLOSE READ

Remind students to mark references to Odysseus's home and to his future. You may wish to model the close read using the following think-aloud format. Possible responses to questions on the Student page are included.

ANNOTATE: As I read lines 632–637, I notice and highlight the contrasting words used to describe both Odysseus's home and his future.

QUESTION: I can see that the author creates a contrast between the domestic comforts that he seeks with the intense physical and emotional suffering that awaits him.

CONCLUDE: I think that by using vividly descriptive words, the author wants to contrast the home that Odysseus yearns for with the ordeal he must endure—he must steer a narrow course to survive Poseidon's revenge for killing his son, the Cyclops Polyphemus.

CLOSER LOOK

Analyzing Personification

Students may have marked line 672 during their first read. Use this paragraph to help students understand the use of personification. Encourage them to talk about the annotations that they marked. You may want to model a close read with the class based on the highlights shown in the text.

ANNOTATE: Have students mark details in line 672 that demonstrate the use of personification, or have students participate while you highlight them.

QUESTION: Guide students to consider what these details might tell them. Ask what a reader can infer from these details, and accept student responses.

Possible response: Dawn is imagined as a queen whose "golden throne" is the sun.

CONCLUDE: Help students to formulate conclusions about the importance of these details in the text. Ask students why the author might have included these details.

Possible response: The author included these details of personification to give splendor and majesty to the sunrise.

Remind students that **personification** is a figure of speech in which a nonhuman subject is given human characteristics ("the sea was angry," "the wind was merciless").

NOTES

This nineteenth-century painting by John William Waterhouse shows the Sirens as bird-women, which echoes ancient Greek portrayals of these figures.

The Sirens

Odysseus returns to Circe's island. The goddess reveals his course to him and gives advice on how to avoid the dangers he will face: the Sirens, who lure sailors to their destruction; the Wandering Rocks, sea rocks that destroy even birds in flight: the perils of the sea monster Scylla and, nearby, the whirlpool Charybdis;[62] and the cattle of the sun god, which Tiresias has warned Odysseus not to harm.

62. Charybdis (kuh RIHB dihs)

As Circe spoke, Dawn mounted her golden throne,
and on the first rays Circe left me, taking
her way like a great goddess up the island.
I made straight for the ship, roused up the men
to get aboard and cast off at the stern.
They scrambled to their places by the rowlocks
and all in line dipped oars in the gray sea.
But soon an offshore breeze blew to our liking—
a canvas-bellying breeze, a lusty shipmate
sent by the singing nymph with sunbright hair.
So we made fast the braces, and we rested,
letting the wind and steersman work the ship.
The crew being now silent before me, I
addressed them, sore at heart:

580 UNIT 5 • JOURNEYS OF TRANSFORMATION

NOTES

'Dear friends,
more than one man, or two, should know those things
Circe foresaw for us and shared with me,
so let me tell her forecast: then we die
with our eyes open, if we are going to die,
or know what death we baffle if we can. Sirens
weaving a haunting song over the sea
we are to shun, she said, and their green shore
all sweet with clover; yet she urged that I
alone should listen to their song. Therefore
you are to tie me up, tight as a splint,
erect along the mast, lashed to the mast,
and if I shout and beg to be untied,
take more turns of the rope to muffle me.'

I rather dwelt on this part of the forecast,
while our good ship made time, bound outward down
the wind for the strange island of Sirens.

Then all at once the wind fell, and a calm
came over all the sea, as though some power
lulled the swell.

The crew were on their feet
briskly, to furl the sail, and stow it; then,

CROSS-CURRICULAR PERSPECTIVES

Music Review line 687. Point out that Circe warns Odysseus about the danger of the Sirens' song. Discuss with students what type of music could be so enchanting that listeners would have no control of their actions. Have students write lyrics that they can imagine the Sirens singing as Odysseus's ship sails by them. Remind students that the Sirens' song is described as *haunting* on line 691 and that they should perhaps model their songs after love songs that can also be described as such. When students have finished writing their lyrics, have them share them with the class.

CLOSE READ

Remind students that in this version of the *Odyssey*, Homer's verse is generally, but not always, translated into unrhymed lines that are usually 10 or 11 syllables long. The Sirens' song is one of several exceptions to this general rule. You may wish to model the close read using the following think-aloud format. Possible responses to questions on the Student page are included.

ANNOTATE: As I read the Sirens' song, I notice and highlight the end word of each line.

QUESTION: I see that the translator presents the Sirens' song in the form of four four-line stanzas and two five-line stanzas. The lines are short. The four-line stanzas rhyme ABAB, and the five-line stanzas rhyme ABAAB. Not all the rhymes are exact—the translator often prefers assonance to rhyme.

CONCLUDE: The song is a break from the epic scale of the narrative. Its simplicity is a respite from the intensity and terror of Odysseus's situation. The rhyming creates music and rhythm, and frequent use of assonance creates an effect of seductive vagueness.

NOTES

CLOSE READ

ANNOTATE: In lines 719–744, mark the end words of the lines of several stanzas of the Sirens' song.

QUESTION: What do you notice about these words in relation to each other?

CONCLUDE: How does this contribute to a sense of the Sirens' music?

each in place, they poised the smooth oar blades
and sent the white foam scudding by. I carved
a massive cake of beeswax into bits
and rolled them in my hands until they softened—
no long task, for a burning heat came down
from Helios, lord of high noon. Going forward
I carried wax along the line, and laid it
thick on their ears. They tied me up, then, plumb
amidships, back to the mast, lashed to the mast,
and took themselves again to rowing. Soon,
as we came smartly within hailing distance,
the two Sirens, noting our fast ship
off their point, made ready, and they sang:

This way, oh turn your bows,
Achaea's glory,
As all the world allows—
Moor and be merry.

Sweet coupled airs we sing.
No lonely seafarer
Holds clear of entering
Our green mirror.

Pleased by each purling note
Like honey twining
From her throat and my throat,
Who lies a-pining?

Sea rovers here take joy
Voyaging onward,
As from our song of Troy
Graybeard and rower-boy
Goeth more learnèd.

All feats on that great field
In the long warfare,
Dark days the bright gods willed,
Wounds you bore there,

Argos' old soldiery[63]
On Troy beach teeming,
Charmed out of time we see.
No life on earth can be
Hid from our dreaming.

The lovely voices in ardor appealing over the water
made me crave to listen, and I tried to say
'Untie me!' to the crew, jerking my brows;

63. **Argos' old soldiery** soldiers from Argos, a city in ancient Greece.

but they bent steady to the oars. Then Perimedes
got to his feet, he and Eurylochus,
and passed more line about, to hold me still.
So all rowed on, until the Sirens
dropped under the sea rim, and their singing
dwindled away.

My faithful company
rested on their oars now, peeling off
the wax that I had laid thick on their ears;
then set me free.

Scylla and Charybdis

But scarcely had that island
faded in blue air than I saw smoke
and white water, with sound of waves in tumult—
a sound the men heard, and it terrified them.
Oars flew from their hands; the blades went knocking
wild alongside till the ship lost way,
with no oar blades to drive her through the water.
Well, I walked up and down from bow to stern,
trying to put heart into them, standing over
every oarsman, saying gently,

'Friends,
have we never been in danger before this?
More fearsome, is it now, than when the Cyclops
penned us in his cave? What power he had!
Did I not keep my nerve, and use my wits
to find a way out for us?

Now I say
by hook or crook this peril too shall be
something that we remember.

Heads up, lads!
We must obey the orders as I give them.
Get the oar shafts in your hands, and lay back
hard on your benches; hit these breaking seas.
Zeus help us pull away before we founder.
You at the tiller, listen, and take in
all that I say—the rudders are your duty;
keep her out of the combers and the smoke;[64]
steer for that headland; watch the drift, or we
fetch up in the smother, and you drown us.'

NOTES

64. the combers and the smoke large waves that break on the beach and the ocean spray.

PERSONALIZE FOR LEARNING

Strategic Support

Comparison In lines 766–770, Odysseus tries to calm his men from their fear of Scylla and Charybdis by reminding them how, as their leader, he used his wits to have them escape from the Cyclops. Have students discuss the similarities and the differences between the threat of the Cyclops and that of Scylla and Charybdis. Invite students to place themselves in the position of one of Odysseus's crewmen, and encourage them to share whether or not they are made more confident by Odysseus's speech.

An artist's rendering of the two terrors—Charybdis (the whirlpool) and Scylla (the monster).

NOTES

65. Scylla (SIHL uh)

66. cuirass (kwih RAS) *n.* armor for the upper body.

67. travail (truh VAYL) *n.* very hard work.

68. gorge (gawrj) *n.* throat or gullet.

69. maelstrom (MAYL struhm) *n.* large, violent whirlpool.

That was all, and it brought them round to action.
But as I sent them on toward Scylla,[65] I
told them nothing, as they could do nothing.
They would have dropped their oars again, in panic,
to roll for cover under the decking. Circe's
bidding against arms had slipped my mind,
so I tied on my cuirass[66] and took up
two heavy spears, then made my way along
to the foredeck—thinking to see her first from there,
the monster of the gray rock, harboring
torment for my friends. I strained my eyes
upon the cliffside veiled in cloud, but nowhere
could I catch sight of her.

And all this time,
in travail,[67] sobbing, gaining on the current,
we rowed into the strait—Scylla to port
and on our starboard beam Charybdis, dire
gorge[68] of the salt seatide. By heaven! when she
vomited, all the sea was like a cauldron
seething over intense fire, when the mixture
suddenly heaves and rises.

The shot spume
soared to the landside heights, and fell like rain.
But when she swallowed the sea water down
we saw the funnel of the maelstrom,[69] heard
the rock bellowing all around, and dark

DIGITAL PERSPECTIVES

Enriching the Text Have students review the section titled "Scylla and Charybdis" beginning on line 756. The 1997 Hallmark television miniseries *The Odyssey* contains a scene based on Odysseus's and his crew's encounter with Scylla and Charybdis. After students complete their close read, show the clip from the television miniseries and have students compare it with the written text. How do televised scenes add to students understanding of the epic poem? Preview all videos before showing them to class.

sand raged on the bottom far below.
My men all blanched against the gloom, our eyes
were fixed upon that yawning mouth in fear
of being devoured.

Then Scylla made her strike,
whisking six of my best men from the ship.
I happened to glance aft at ship and oarsmen
and caught sight of their arms and legs, dangling
high overhead. Voices came down to me
in anguish, calling my name for the last time.

A man surfcasting on a point of rock
for bass or mackerel, whipping his long rod
to drop the sinker and the bait far out,
will hook a fish and rip it from the surface
to dangle wriggling through the air:

so these
were borne aloft in spasms toward the cliff.

She ate them as they shrieked there, in her den,
in the dire grapple, reaching still for me—
and deathly pity ran me through
at that sight—far the worst I ever suffered,
questing the passes of the strange sea.

We rowed on.
The Rocks were now behind; Charybdis, too,
and Scylla dropped astern.

The Cattle of the Sun God

In the small hours of the third watch, when stars
that shone out in the first dusk of evening
had gone down to their setting, a giant wind
blew from heaven, and clouds driven by Zeus
shrouded land and sea in a night of storm;
so, just as Dawn with fingertips of rose
touched the windy world, we dragged our ship
to cover in a grotto, a sea cave
where nymphs had chairs of rock and sanded floors.
I mustered all the crew and said:

'Old shipmates,
our stores are in the ship's hold, food and drink;
the cattle here are not for our provision,
or we pay dearly for it.

NOTES

CLOSE READ

ANNOTATE: Mark the words in lines 815–820 that describe a sports activity.

QUESTION: Why does Homer liken this activity to Scylla's actions?

CONCLUDE: What does this comparison suggest about Scylla's power?

DIGITAL PERSPECTIVES

CLOSE READ

Remind students that despite the epic scope of the poem, Homer often makes references to familiar pleasures—particularly to sporting activities. You may wish to model the close read using the following think-aloud format. Possible responses to questions on the Student page are included.

ANNOTATE: As I read lines 815–820, I notice and highlight the details that describe line fishing.

QUESTION: I can see that Odysseus likens Scylla's technique as she catches his men to the long-distance precision of a surfcasting fisherman.

CONCLUDE: I get the impression that Scylla is swift and skilled in her actions, and that she's thoroughly enjoying the sport of killing Odysseus's crew.

NOTES

Fierce the god is
who cherishes these heifers and these sheep:
Helios; and no man avoids his eye.'

To this my fighters nodded. Yes. But now
we had a month of onshore gales, blowing
day in, day out—south winds, or south by east.
As long as bread and good red wine remained
to keep the men up, and appease their craving,
they would not touch the cattle. But in the end,
when all the barley in the ship was gone,
hunger drove them to scour the wild shore
with angling hooks, for fishes and sea fowl,
whatever fell into their hands; and lean days
wore their bellies thin.

The storms continued.
So one day I withdrew to the interior
to pray the gods in solitude, for hope
that one might show me some way of salvation.
Slipping away, I struck across the island
to a sheltered spot, out of the driving gale.
I washed my hands there, and made supplication
to the gods who own Olympus,[70] all the gods—
but they, for answer, only closed my eyes
under slow drops of sleep.
Now on the shore Eurylochus
made his insidious plea:
'Comrades,' he said,
'You've gone through everything; listen to what I say.
All deaths are hateful to us, mortal wretches,
but famine is the most pitiful, the worst
end that a man can come to.

Will you fight it?
Come, we'll cut out the noblest of these cattle
for sacrifice to the gods who own the sky;
and once at home, in the old country of Ithaca,
if ever that day comes—
we'll build a costly temple and adorn it
with every beauty for the Lord of Noon.[71]
But if he flares up over his heifers lost,
wishing our ship destroyed, and if the gods
make cause with him, why, then I say: Better
open your lungs to a big sea once for all
than waste to skin and bones on a lonely island!'

70. Olympus (oh LIHM puhs) Mount Olympus, home of the gods.

71. Lord of Noon Helios.

VOCABULARY DEVELOPMENT

Academic Vocabulary Reinforcement Students will benefit from additional examples and practice with academic vocabulary. Reinforce their comprehension with "show-you-know" sentences. The first part of the sentence uses the vocabulary word in an appropriate context. The second part of the sentence—the "show-you-know" part—clarifies the first. Model the strategy with this example for *appease*.

As long as food was available to *appease* their hunger, Odysseus's crew would not try to kill and eat Helios's cattle.

1. Odysseus made *supplication* to the gods by ________________.

Possible response: praying humbly to them

2. Eurylochus made an *insidious* plea about dying from hunger that was ________________.

Possible response: treacherous in nature

586 UNIT 5 • JOURNEYS OF TRANSFORMATION

Thus Eurylochus; and they murmured 'Aye!'
trooping away at once to round up heifers.
Now, that day tranquil cattle with broad brows
were grazing near, and soon the men drew up
around their chosen beasts in ceremony.
They plucked the leaves that shone on a tall oak—
having no barley meal—to strew the victims,
performed the prayers and ritual, knifed the kine
and flayed each carcass, cutting thighbones free
to wrap in double folds of fat. These offerings,
with strips of meat, were laid upon the fire.
Then, as they had no wine, they made libation
with clear spring water, broiling the entrails first;
and when the bones were burnt and tripes shared,
they spitted the carved meat.
Just then my slumber
left me in a rush, my eyes opened,
and I went down the seaward path. No sooner
had I caught sight of our black hull, than savory
odors of burnt fat eddied around me;
grief took hold of me, and I cried aloud:

'O Father Zeus and gods in bliss forever,
you made me sleep away this day of mischief!
O cruel drowsing, in the evil hour!
Here they sat, and a great work they contrived.'[72]
Lampetia[73] in her long gown meanwhile
had borne swift word to the Overlord of Noon:
'They have killed your kine.'
And the Lord Helios
burst into angry speech amid the immortals:

'O Father Zeus and gods in bliss forever,
punish Odysseus' men! So overweening,
now they have killed my peaceful kine, my joy
at morning when I climbed the sky of stars,
and evening, when I bore westward from heaven.
Restitution or penalty they shall pay—
and pay in full—or I go down forever
to light the dead men in the underworld.'

Then Zeus who drives the stormcloud made reply:
'Peace, Helios: shine on among the gods,
shine over mortals in the fields of grain.
Let me throw down one white-hot bolt, and make
splinters of their ship in the winedark sea.'

NOTES

72. contrived *v.* thought up; devised.

73. Lampetia (lam PEE shuh) a nymph.

DIGITAL PERSPECTIVES

CLOSER LOOK

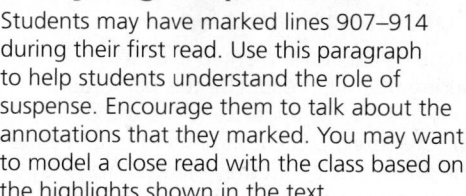

Analyzing Suspense

Students may have marked lines 907–914 during their first read. Use this paragraph to help students understand the role of suspense. Encourage them to talk about the annotations that they marked. You may want to model a close read with the class based on the highlights shown in the text.

ANNOTATE: Have students mark details in lines 907–914 that demonstrate the use of suspense, or have students participate while you highlight them.

QUESTION: Guide students to consider what these details might tell them. Ask what a reader can infer from Helios's speech to the other immortals, and accept student responses.

Possible response: Helios, the sun-god, is seeking the help of Zeus and the other gods in taking revenge against Odysseus's crew for killing his beloved cattle. He addresses Zeus with great respect, but threatens to go down and flood Hades with sunshine if his demand is not granted.

CONCLUDE: Help students to formulate conclusions about the importance of these details in the text. Ask students why the author might have included these details.

Possible response: Homer is raising the stakes to an unforeseen level. Zeus himself is involved in the fate of Odysseus and his crew. The reader is anxious to know Zeus's decision—and Helios's complaint against the crew appears to be well-founded and convincing.

Remind students that **suspense** is the mounting curiosity, tension, or anxiety the reader feels about the outcome of events in a literary work. Suspense builds until the *climax*, the high point of tension in the plot, when the conflict reaches a peak. Suspense is part of what keeps the reader engaged in a story and anxious to find out what will happen next.

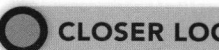

TEACHING

CLOSER LOOK

Understanding Foreshadowing

Students may have marked lines 926–928 during their first read. Use this paragraph to help students understand the use of foreshadowing. Encourage them to talk about the annotations that they marked. You may want to model a close read with the class based on the highlights shown in the text.

ANNOTATE: Have students mark details in lines 926–928 that demonstrate supernatural activity, or have students participate while you highlight them.

QUESTION: Guide students to consider what these details might tell them. Ask what a reader can infer from these details, and accept student responses.

Possible response: A reader can infer that leather that was once the skin of live cattle and meat that was once the muscle and fat of live cattle begin to crawl about and bellow as if they were still living parts of the animals they were torn from.

CONCLUDE: Help students to formulate conclusions about the importance of these details in the text. Ask students why the author might have included these details.

Possible response: Homer is presenting the reader with hideous omens and indications of the horrors in store for Odysseus's crew.

Remind students **foreshadowing** is the use of clues hinting at significant events to come later in a narrative. This technique helps create suspense, the quality in a literary work that keeps the reader anxious to find out what happens next.

NOTES

74. Hermes (HUR meez) *n.* god who serves as herald and messenger of the other gods.

75. beeves (beevz) *n.* alternate plural form of "beef."

76. petrels (PEH truhlz) *n.* small, dark sea birds.

—Calypso later told me of this exchange,
as she declared that Hermes[74] had told her.
Well, when I reached the sea cave and the ship,
I faced each man, and had it out; but where
could any remedy be found? There was none.
The silken beeves[75] of Helios were dead.
The gods, moreover, made queer signs appear:
cowhides began to crawl, and beef, both raw
and roasted, lowed like kine upon the spits.

Now six full days my gallant crew could feast
upon the prime beef they had marked for slaughter
from Helios' herd; and Zeus, the son of Cronus,
added one fine morning.

All the gales
had ceased, blown out, and with an offshore breeze
we launched again, stepping the mast and sail,
to make for the open sea. Astern of us
the island coastline faded, and no land
showed anywhere, but only sea and heaven,
when Zeus Cronion piled a thunderhead
above the ship, while gloom spread on the ocean.
We held our course, but briefly. Then the squall
struck whining from the west, with gale force, breaking
both forestays, and the mast came toppling aft
along the ship's length, so the running rigging
showered into the bilge.

On the afterdeck
the mast had hit the steersman a slant blow
bashing the skull in, knocking him overside,
as the brave soul fled the body, like a diver.
With crack on crack of thunder, Zeus let fly
a bolt against the ship, a direct hit,
so that she bucked, in reeking fumes of sulphur,
and all the men were flung into the sea.
They came up 'round the wreck, bobbing awhile
like petrels[76] on the waves.

No more seafaring
homeward for these, no sweet day of return;
the god had turned his face from them.

I clambered
fore and aft my hulk until a comber
split her, keel from ribs, and the big timber
floated free; the mast, too, broke away.

A backstay floated dangling from it, stout
rawhide rope, and I used this for lashing
mast and keel together. These I straddled,
riding the frightful storm.

Nor had I yet
seen the worst of it: for now the west wind
dropped, and a southeast gale came on—one more
twist of the knife—taking me north again,
straight for Charybdis. All that night I drifted,
and in the sunrise, sure enough, I lay
off Scylla mountain and Charybdis deep.
There, as the whirlpool drank the tide, a billow
tossed me, and I sprang for the great fig tree,
catching on like a bat under a bough.
Nowhere had I to stand, no way of climbing,
The root and bole[77] being far below, and far
above my head the branches and their leaves,
massed, overshadowing Charybdis pool.
But I clung grimly, thinking my mast and keel
would come back to the surface when she spouted.

And ah! how long, with what desire, I waited!
till, at the twilight hour, when one who hears
and judges pleas in the marketplace all day
between contentious men, goes home to supper,
the long poles at last reared from the sea.

Now I let go with hands and feet, plunging
straight into the foam beside the timbers,
pulled astride, and rowed hard with my hands
to pass by Scylla. Never could I have passed her
had not the Father of gods and men,[78] this time,
kept me from her eyes. Once through the strait,
nine days I drifted in the open sea
before I made shore, buoyed up by the gods,
upon Ogygia[79] Isle. The dangerous nymph
Calypso lives and sings there, in her beauty,
and she received me, loved me.

But why tell
the same tale that I told last night in hall
to you and to your lady? Those adventures
made a long evening, and I do not hold
with tiresome repetition of a story."

NOTES

77. **bole** (bohl) *n.* tree trunk.

78. **Father . . . men** Zeus.

79. **Ogygia** (o JIHJ ee uh)

DIGITAL PERSPECTIVES

Enriching the Text To help students understand the concept of the epic hero in literature, ask them to consider the hero of action movies. Show clips of Katniss Everdeen from *The Hunger Games* movies and Frodo from *The Lord of the Rings* movies. Have students note the similarities and differences between Odysseus and these characters. How do modern-day action heroes add to students' understanding of Odysseus as an epic hero? Preview all videos before showing them in class. **(Research to Clarify)**

TEACHING

Comprehension Check

Possible responses:

1. Odysseus leaves his kingdom of Ithaca to honor his pact with other Greek leaders and fight in the Trojan War.
2. Cyclops does not live with other Cyclopes because Cyclopes are not a tribal community and are indifferent to each other's actions as well as to those of the gods.
3. According to Circe, Odysseus has to consult the blind prophet Tiresias in Hades in order to receive advice on how to get home.
4. He speaks to Elpenor, one of his soldiers who died after drinking too much and falling off of a building. He wants to speak to his mother but holds her off until he speaks to Tiresias, who warns Odysseus against letting his men eat Helios' cattle.
5. The *Odyssey* is about a warrior king named Odysseus who, after spending 10 years fighting the Trojan War, embarks on a 10 year journey to return home to his kingdom of Ithaca. Along with his crew and warnings given to him by the enchantress Circe, Odysseus encounters many adversaries and adventures, including rescuing three of his men from the Lotus-Eaters, being trapped by a man-eating Cyclops, traveling to Hades to seek consultation from the prophet Tiresias, tying himself to the mast so he can hear the Sirens' song without wrecking his ship, and navigating past the treacherous monsters Scylla and Charybdis. Odysseus leads his men with wit and cunning, but he is unable to save his crew from Zeus' wrath after they butcher and eat Helios' sacred cattle. Only Odysseus survives the shipwreck caused by Zeus' thunderbolts, and he is left to swim past Scylla and Charybdis again. After nine days on the open sea, he reaches Calypso's island and finds refuge there.

Research to Clarify If students struggle to come up with a research topic, you may choose to suggest that they focus on one of these topics: the importance of following host-guest protocol in ancient Greece; the facts behind the myth of Charybdis; the true history of the Trojan War.

Research to Explore If students struggle to come up with a research topic, you may choose to suggest that they focus on one of these topics: proposed maps of Odysseus' journey; scholarly debate over the location of Ithaca; Sicily, land of the Cyclopes.

Comprehension Check

Complete the following items after you finish your first read.

1. Why does Odysseus leave home?

2. Why does Cyclops live alone in a cave?

3. Why does Odysseus go to Hades, the land of the dead?

4. To whom does Odysseus speak in the land of the dead?

5. **Notebook** Confirm your understanding of the text by writing a summary.

RESEARCH

Research to Clarify Choose at least one unfamiliar detail from the text. Briefly research that detail. In what way does the information you learned shed light on an aspect of the epic?

Research to Explore This epic poem may spark your curiosity to learn more. Briefly research one of the locations mentioned in the poem. You may want to share what you discover with the class.

PERSONALIZE FOR LEARNING

Challenge

Creating an Epic Hero Have students create their own version of an epic hero. First have them present a brief biography of their epic hero in a short essay. Then have students write one adventure in which their epic hero must solve a problem to help other people. Encourage students to have their epic hero use his or her wits to "save the day." Have students share their stories while noting any similar qualities each other's epic heroes may possess.

MAKING MEANING

Close Read the Text

ANNOTATE QUESTION Close Read CONCLUDE

Reread Cyclops' prayer to Poseidon (lines 484–493). Mark his initial request and his alternative request. How do these two requests reflect ancient Greek beliefs about the gods' involvement in the mortal world?

Analyze the Text

CITE TEXTUAL EVIDENCE to support your answers.

Notebook Respond to these questions.

1. (a) What does Odysseus want more than anything else?
   (b) **Analyze** How does this goal give structure to the epic?
2. (a) What two aspects of the life of Cyclopes make Odysseus think that they are uncivilized before he interacts with one?
   (b) **Compare and Contrast** How are the lives of Cyclopes different from the lives of Odysseus and his men?
3. (a) How does Eurylochus convince Odysseus' men to kill Helios' cattle?
   (b) **Analyze** What value do you think Eurylochus is appealing to in his argument?
4. **Essential Question:** *What can we learn from a journey?* What have you learned about the power of journeys by reading Part 1 of the *Odyssey*?

LANGUAGE DEVELOPMENT

Concept Vocabulary

plundered	avenge	ventured
fugitives	dispatched	tactics

Why These Words? These concept vocabulary words relate to actions during war. How does each word contribute to meaning in the text? What other words in the selection connect to this concept?

Practice

Notebook Confirm your understanding of these words from the text by using them in a paragraph. Include context clues that hint at each word's meaning.

Word Study

Notebook **Word Parts** Many English words are formed by adding prefixes, suffixes, or both to existing words. The word *tactic*, for example, is a noun that means "action planned to achieve a certain purpose." Frequently appearing in military contexts, it is often used in the plural. Knowing the meaning of *tactic* can help you figure out that a *tactician* is a person who plans actions to accomplish certain tasks, a valuable person in a war. Divide the following words into their word parts, and use the word parts to write a definition for each word: *marvelous*, *consultation*, *frightful*.

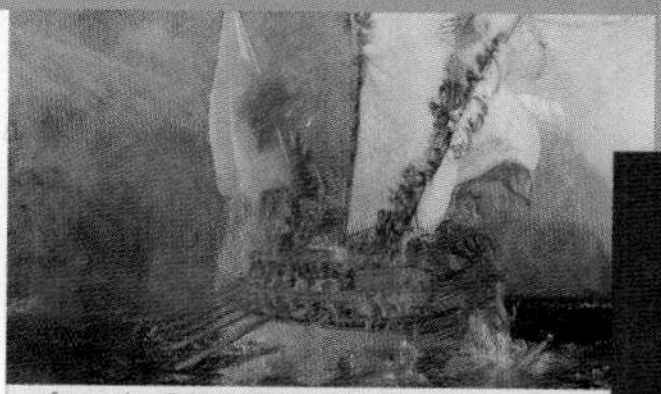
from the ODYSSEY, PART 1

Tool Kit
Close-Read Guide and Model Annotation

WORD NETWORK

Add interesting words related to journeys from the text to your Word Network.

STANDARDS

Language

- Identify and correctly use patterns of word changes that indicate different meanings or parts of speech.
- Demonstrate understanding of figurative language, word relationships, and nuances in word meanings.

DIGITAL PERSPECTIVES

Jump Start

CLOSE READ What drives people to seek revenge? Does revenge resolve a problem or make it worse?

Close Read the Text

Review and discuss the sections students have marked. If needed, continue to model close reading by using the Annotation Highlights in the Interactive Teacher's Edition.

Analyze the Text

Possible responses:

1. (a) To go home. **DOK 1** (b) It creates suspense about if and when he will get home. **DOK 3**
2. (a) They have no laws and beat their families. **DOK 1** (b) Odysseus and his crew work together; the Cyclopes do not support each other. **DOK 2**
3. (a) He says starving slowly would be worse than drowning quickly. **DOK 2** (b) the crew's will to survive **DOK 3**
4. Responses will vary.

Concept Vocabulary

Why These Words? Possible responses: These words provide descriptive details that help the reader visualize the action of the characters. *war, army, lances, squadron*

Practice

Responses will vary but should reflect a connection to the text.

Word Network

Possible words: *odyssey, wanderer, detained*

Word Study

For more support, see **Concept Vocabulary and Word Study.**

Possible responses:
(a) **marvelous**—base word *marvel* (to wonder), suffix *-ous* (full of), meaning "full of wonder" (b) **consultation**—base word *consult* (to ask for advice), suffix *-ation* (act of), meaning "act of asking for advice" (c) **frightful**—base word fright (fear), suffix *-ful* (full of, or causing), meaning "causing fear"

FORMATIVE ASSESSMENT

Concept Vocabulary

If students fail to understand the concept vocabulary, **then** have them look for context clues in the text where these words appear.

Word Study

If students struggle to define the words, **then** have them consider the definition of the base word. For more support, see **Word Study: Word Parts (RP).**

Analyze Craft and Structure

Oral Tradition Explain to students that, when the *Odyssey* was created, the Greeks did not have a written language. Have students think about the advantages and disadvantages of telling stories in the oral tradition. Encourage students to provide examples of times they have heard stories told orally. Have them consider the following prompt: *During what occasions do people usually tell stories?* For more support, see **Analyze Craft and Structure: Oral Tradition.**

Practice

Possible responses:

1. I feel as if he is speaking to me directly. His descriptions of his actions and thoughts make it easier to visualize the story. For example, in lines 809–810, when he says, "Then Scylla made her strike,/whisking six of my best men from the ship," I feel as if I am on the ship and watching Scylla grab men from the crew.
2. Odysseus and crew sail back to Ithaca. Odysseus rescues men from Lotus-Eaters. They are captured by and escape from the Cyclops. The crew releases a gift, all the winds except for the West Wind. Cannibals destroy all but one ship of Odysseus's fleet. Odysseus and crew stay on Circe's island for a year. Circe advises Odysseus how to confront future dangers and to seek counsel with the dead prophet Tiresias. Odysseus consults with Tiresias in Hades. Odysseus listens to Sirens' song while strapped to the mast. Scylla attacks crewmen, and they sail past Charybdis. Crew butchers Helios's cattle, and Helios seeks revenge from Zeus. Zeus sinks the ship and only Odysseus survives. Odysseus is almost killed by Charybdis. He finds safety on Calypso's island.
3. a-b) See possible responses in chart on Student page. c) The ancient Greeks admired people who were intelligent and quick-witted. They also believed in people showing their reverence to the gods and the dead by presenting offerings.

MAKING MEANING

from the ODYSSEY, PART 1

STANDARDS

Reading Literature

- Analyze how complex characters develop over the course of a text, interact with other characters, and advance the plot or develop the theme.
- Analyze how an author's choices concerning how to structure a text, order events within it, and manipulate time create such effects as mystery, tension, or surprise.
- Analyze a particular point of view or cultural experience reflected in a work of literature from outside the United States, drawing on a wide reading of world literature.

Analyze Craft and Structure

Oral Tradition Storytellers and poets of long ago did not write down the tales they told. Instead, they learned the stories and poems of their culture from others and recited them from memory. The term **oral tradition** refers to the literature that was passed down through the ages by word of mouth. Eventually, these spoken stories and poems were retold in writing.

One form of literature that has come from the oral tradition is the **epic**, a long narrative poem that is central to a culture's national identity. The narrative in an epic centers around an **epic hero**, a larger-than-life character who possesses traits that his society values most highly.

Traditional epics like the *Odyssey* use certain plot devices, or structures, that both provide information and allow the story to unfold in an exciting way. Many epics begin ***in medias res***, which means "in the middle of things." Major events occurred before the action of the poem begins, and the audience is thrust into the middle of the story. The hero's adventures are often recounted in a **flashback**, a scene that interrupts a narrative to relate earlier events.

Practice

CITE TEXTUAL EVIDENCE to support your answers.

Notebook Respond to these questions.

1. In this epic, the hero Odysseus recounts his own adventures. In what way does this affect your reaction to the events he describes? Cite an example from the text to support your response.
2. Odysseus recounts most of the action in Part 1 in the form of a flashback. List the events of Part 1 in chronological order, beginning with the end of the Trojan War.
3. (a) Using the chart, identify three actions that Odysseus performs. (b) For each action, identify the character trait that it reveals. (c) Using the results of your analysis, explain which character traits the ancient Greeks admired most.

ACTION	CHARACTER TRAIT
He tells the Cyclops he is named Nohbdy, so when the Cyclops calls for help, the other Cyclopes think nobody has harmed him.	intelligent and quick-witted
He makes offering to the dead in Hades	reverent
He tells his men not to eat Helios' cattle	respectful of host

PERSONALIZE FOR LEARNING

English Language Support

Discussing Oral Tradition Read a Native American folktale to students, or have pairs of students read it together. Ask partners to discuss the folktale.

Ask pairs of students to write a few sentences explaining the lesson that the tale is teaching. **Emerging**

Have each student write a few sentences explaining the lesson that the tale is teaching and citing textual evidence to support their claim. **Expanding**

Have each student write a paragraph explaining the lesson that the tale is teaching. Encourage students to try and think of a modern-day story that has a similar moral to the folktale and mention it in their paragraph. **Bridging**

FORMATIVE ASSESSMENT

Analyze Craft and Structure: Oral Tradition

If students struggle to understand the concept of an epic hero, **then** have them think of action heroes they have read or seen in movies and compare them with Odysseus. For Reteach and Practice, see **Analyze Craft and Structure: Oral Tradition (RP).**

Speaking and Listening

Assignment
With two classmates, write and deliver a **conversation** among ordinary Greeks discussing Odysseus' exploits. Each character's statements should reflect ancient Greek values shown in Part I of the *Odyssey*.

1. **Develop Your Characters** Decide each character's traits and attitude toward Odysseus. For example, one character may admire Odysseus, while another may be critical of his leadership. One may know Odysseus well, while another may have barely heard of him.

Use the chart to make notes about your characters and their attitudes. Each description should include the character's name, age, occupation, and other important information, such as whether he or she knows Odysseus personally.

	FIRST CHARACTER	SECOND CHARACTER	THIRD CHARACTER
Description			
Attitude toward Odysseus			

2. **Plan Your Conversation** As a group, agree on an overall plan for the conversation, but leave room for improvisation.
3. **Prepare Your Delivery** Practice your conversation with your group. Use the following techniques to help communicate ideas clearly and to make your conversation entertaining.
   - As you speak, use verbal techniques—such as varied tone, volume, and pace—to convey different emotions and to make your conversation realistic.
   - In addition, use nonverbal techniques—such as gestures, facial expressions, and eye contact—to help convey your ideas.
4. **Evaluate Conversations** As your classmates deliver their conversations, watch and listen attentively. Use an evaluation guide like the one shown to analyze their delivery.

EVALUATION GUIDE

Rate each statement on a scale of 1 (not demonstrated) to 4 (demonstrated).

☐ The speakers clearly conveyed their characters' traits.

☐ The speakers clearly conveyed their characters' attitudes toward Odysseus.

☐ The speakers used verbal techniques effectively.

☐ The speakers used nonverbal techniques effectively.

TIP

COLLABORATION

One of the rules of improvisation is that you must respond to what your fellow actor says or does, even if it's not what you planned. Remember that as you are presenting your conversation.

EVIDENCE LOG

Before moving on to a new selection, go to your Evidence Log and record what you learned from Part 1 of the *Odyssey*.

STANDARDS

Speaking and Listening
- Initiate and participate effectively in a range of collaborative discussions with diverse partners on *grades 9-10 topics, texts, and issues,* building on others' ideas and expressing their own clearly and persuasively.
- Come to discussions prepared, having read and researched material under study; explicitly draw on that preparation by referring to evidence from texts and other research on the topic or issue to stimulate a thoughtful, well-reasoned exchange of ideas.
- Work with peers to set rules for collegial discussions and decision-making, clear goals and deadlines, and individual roles as needed.

DIGITAL PERSPECTIVES

Speaking and Listening

1. **Develop Your Characters** You may wish to guide students in developing their characters by asking them what character traits and perspectives would make them interesting to others.
2. **Plan Your Conversation** Tell your students that when they conduct their conversation, they should think of how their character would respond and react to the opinions and insights of others.
3. **Prepare Your Delivery** Have trios video-record the conversation. Then have them use the Evaluation Guide to provide feedback to each other prior to presenting to the class.
4. **Evaluate Conversations** Encourage students to make supportive comments about each presentation.

For more support, see **Speaking and Listening: Conversation.**

FORMATIVE ASSESSMENT

Speaking and Listening

If students struggle to understand how to conduct a conversation, **then** have them think of conversations they have had in the past week. For example, have them provide examples of a conversation they had with an adult, a friend, or a fellow student. For Reteach and Practice, see **Speaking and Listening: Conversation (RP)**.

Selection Test

Administer the "*from the* Odyssey, Part 1" Selection Test, which is available in both print and digital formats online in Assessments.

PERSONALIZE FOR LEARNING

Strategic Support

Developing Characters Some students may require additional support in adding variety to their character's conversation. Have each student in the trio provide a brief biography and background of his or her character. Then have all three students in the group consider this information. Have each student suggest the type of phrases and language a person with that age and background would use. Have them discuss the type of experiences the character has had, which would contribute to his or her point of view. Finally, have students review their partners' suggestions as they revise their individual character's profile.

from the Odyssey, Part 2

AUDIO SUMMARIES
Audio summaries of Part 2 of the *Odyssey* are available online in both English and Spanish in the Interactive Teacher's Edition or Unit Resources. Assigning these summaries prior to reading the selection may help students build additional background knowledge and set a context for their first read.

Summary

In Part 2 of the epic poem the *Odyssey*, Odysseus has finally reached his home in Ithaca. After his arrival, Odysseus discovers that his home has been overrun with suitors bidding for Penelope's hand in marriage. Helped by the hidden hand of Athena, Odysseus and Telemachus deliver death to the suitors. Finally, Odysseus must convince his wife that he is indeed her husband, returned to her after twenty years away.

Insight

Reading this excerpt from the *Odyssey* will help students understand the challenges of a journey can include more than just the physical obstacles of travel. For example, Odysseus survives his journey back to Ithaca, but he still must grapple with the consequences of his long absence from home.

ESSENTIAL QUESTION:
What can we learn from a journey?

Connection to Essential Question

In this excerpt from Part 2 of the *Odyssey*, Odysseus discovers that those who were both faithful and loyal to him when he embarked on his journey remain equally devoted twenty years later.

WHOLE-CLASS LEARNING PERFORMANCE TASK
How are personal strengths and weaknesses magnified during the course of a journey at sea?

UNIT PERFORMANCE-BASED ASSESSMENT
When does the journey matter more than the destination?

Connection to Performance Tasks

Whole-Class Learning Performance Task In this Performance Task, students will write an explanatory essay about how personal strengths and weaknesses can shape a journey. In Part 1 of the *Odyssey,* students read several examples of Odysseus's strengths and weakness. In Part 2, however, Homer highlights Odysseus's strengths. Odysseus demonstrates wisdom as he disposes of Penelope's suitors, reclaims his estate, and gains back prominence in Ithaca.

Unit Performance-Based Assessment In this excerpt from the *Odyssey,* the destination of Ithaca matters more than the journey to get there. Odysseus must fight to regain his old life and to protect the people he loves.

DIGITAL PERSPECTIVES — Audio | Video | Document | Annotation Highlights | EL Highlights | Online Assessment

LESSON RESOURCES

	Making Meaning	Language Development	Effective Expression
Lesson	**First Read** **Close Read** **Analyze the Text** **Analyze Craft and Structure**	**Concept Vocabulary** **Word Study** **Author's Style**	**Writing to Sources** **Speaking and Listening**
Instructional Standards	**RL.10** By the end of grade 9, read and comprehend literature . . . **RL.6** Analyze a particular point of view or cultural experience . . .	**L.2** Demonstrate command of the conventions . . . **L.3** Apply knowledge of language . . . **L.4.b** Identify and correctly use patterns of word changes . . .	**W.4** Produce clear and coherent writing . . . **SL.1** Initiate and participate effectively . . . **SL.3** Evaluate a speaker's point of view . . .
STUDENT RESOURCES			
Available online in the Interactive Student Edition or Unit Resources	Selection Audio First-Read Guide: Fiction Close-Read Guide: Fiction	Word Network	Evidence Log
TEACHER RESOURCES			
Selection Resources Available online in the Interactive Teacher's Edition or Unit Resources	Audio Summaries Annotation Highlights EL Highlights English Language Support Lesson: Biography Analyze Craft and Structure: Figurative Language	Concept Vocabulary and Word Study Author's Style: Word Order	Writing to Sources: Biography Speaking and Listening: Debate
Reteach/Practice (RP) Available online in the Interactive Teacher's Edition or Unit Resources	Analyze Craft and Structure: Figurative Language (RP)	Word Study: Latin Root *-sem-* and *-sim-* (RP) Author's Style: Word Order (RP)	Writing to Sources: Biography (RP) Speaking and Listening: Debate (RP)
Assessment Available online in Assessments	Selection Test		
My Resources	A Unit 5 Answer Key is available online and in the Interactive Teacher's Edition.		

Reading Support

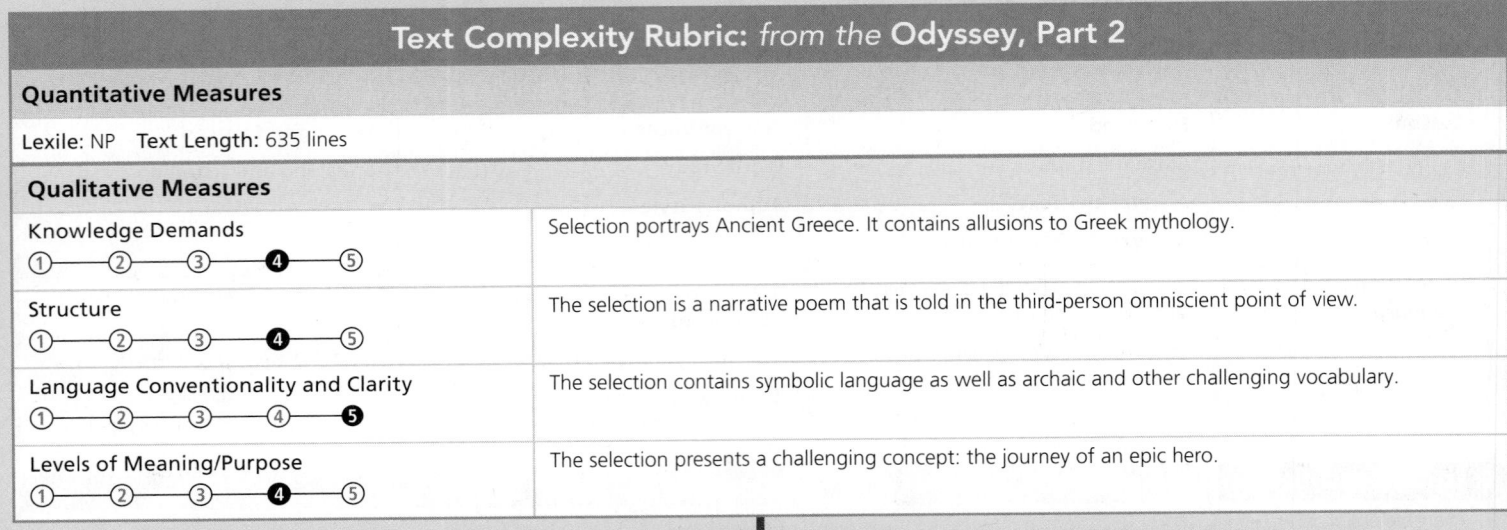

Text Complexity Rubric: *from the* **Odyssey, Part 2**	
Quantitative Measures	
Lexile: NP **Text Length:** 635 lines	
Qualitative Measures	
Knowledge Demands ①—②—③—❹—⑤	Selection portrays Ancient Greece. It contains allusions to Greek mythology.
Structure ①—②—③—❹—⑤	The selection is a narrative poem that is told in the third-person omniscient point of view.
Language Conventionality and Clarity ①—②—③—④—❺	The selection contains symbolic language as well as archaic and other challenging vocabulary.
Levels of Meaning/Purpose ①—②—③—❹—⑤	The selection presents a challenging concept: the journey of an epic hero.

DECIDE AND PLAN

English Language Support

Provide English Learners with support for knowledge demands and language as they read the selection.

Knowledge Demands Before students read this selection, have them review the events of Part 1. Have them recall the major characters and events. Ask them where the first part left off.

Language Students may have difficulty understanding information in the complex sentence and stanza structure. Encourage students to scan for the subject of a stanza. Then ask them to look for verbs that indicate actions. *What is happening to the subject? What is the subject doing?*

Strategic Support

Provide students with strategic support to ensure that they can successfully read the text.

Knowledge Demands Draw on the background information and introduction to discuss what Odysseus will encounter in this next selection. Ask students to predict how Odysseus will react. Make a list of these predictions and review them at the end of the reading.

Structure Discuss how the headings and subheadings aid comprehension of this story. Point out to students that they can reread the selection introduction, headings, and subheadings if they are confused about what is happening. At the end of each section, students may want to summarize it and then compare it to the information in the preceding text features.

Challenge

Provide students who need to be challenged with ideas for how they can go beyond a simple interpretation of the text.

Text Analysis Discuss the use of the third-person omniscient point of view with students. Ask them to consider as they read how this point of view impacts their understanding of Odysseus. Ask students to compare this view with the one they had in the prior section, which used first-person point of view.

Written Response Ask students to speculate on a different future for Odysseus and his family. Have them analyze their individual choices and determine what would have changed if they had chosen differently. Have them rewrite a new ending for the story.

TEACH

Read and Respond

Have the class do their first read of the selection. Then have them complete their close read. Finally, work with them on the Making Meaning, Language Development, and Effective Expression activities.

Standards Support Through Teaching and Learning Cycle

IDENTIFY NEEDS

Analyze results of the Beginning-of-Year Assessment, focusing on the items relating to Unit 5. Also take into consideration student performance to this point and your observations of where particular students struggle.

DECIDE AND PLAN

- If students have performed poorly on items matching these standards, then provide selection scaffolds before assigning them the on-level lesson provided in the Student Edition.
- If students have done well on the Beginning-of-Year Assessment, then challenge them to keep progressing and learning by giving them opportunities to practice the skills in depth.
- Use the Selection Resources listed on the Planning pages for this excerpt from the *Odyssey*, Part 2 to help students continually improve their ability to master the standards.

Instructional Standards: *from* the Odyssey, Part II

	Catching Up	This Year	Looking Forward
Reading	You may wish to administer the **Analyze Craft and Structure: Figurative Language (RP)** worksheet to better familiarize students with Homer's technique.	**RL.6** Analyze a particular point of view or cultural experience reflected in a work of literature from outside the United States, drawing on a wide reading of world literature.	Challenge students to think of other works that contain epic similes or running metaphors.
Writing	You may wish to administer the **Writing to Sources: Biography (RP)** worksheet to help students better prepare for their biographies.	**W.4** Produce clear and coherent writing in which the development, organization, and style are appropriate to task, purpose, and audience.	Challenge students to consider why more than one biography may be written about an historical figure.
Speaking and Listening	You may wish to administer the **Speaking and Listening: Debate (RP)** worksheet to help students better prepare for their debates.	**SL.3** Evaluate a speaker's point of view, reasoning, and use of evidence and rhetoric, identifying any fallacious reasoning or exaggerated or distorted evidence.	Take the debate to the next level by challenging another class in the area who is reading the *Odyssey*.
Language	Review the **Word Study: Latin Root *-sem-* and *-sim-* (RP)** worksheet with students to better familiarize them these Latin roots. Review the **Author's Style: Word Order (RP)** worksheet with students to help them better understand inverted word order.	**L.4.b** Identify and correctly use patterns of word changes that indicate different meanings or parts of speech. **L.3** Apply knowledge of language to understand how language functions in different contexts, to make effective choices for meaning or style, and to comprehend more fully when reading or listening.	Challenge students to think of other Latin roots that are similar but have different meanings. Challenge students to seek out works by contemporary writers that use inverted word order.

TEACH

Implement the planned lesson, and gather evidence of student learning.

ANALYZE AND REVISE

- Analyze student work for evidence of student learning.
- Identify whether or not students have met the expectations in the standards.
- Identify implications for future instruction.

Jump Start

FIRST READ What if you lived in a time period that didn't have convenient communication options such as phones, computers, or postal systems? How would your relationships with family and friends change if you were not able to communicate with them for several years at a time?

The Odyssey

How would you handle coming back from a long journey to find your home full of people you don't know? How would you feel if the people you most loved did not recognize you? How would you convince them of your true identity? Modeling the questions a reader might ask as they read Part 2 of the *Odyssey* for the first time brings the text alive for students and connects it to the Performance Task assignment. Selection audio and print capability for the selection are available in the Interactive Teacher's Edition.

Concept Vocabulary

Support students as they rank their words. Ask if they've ever heard, read, or used them. Reassure them that the definitions for these words are listed in the selection.

FIRST READ

As students read, have them perform the steps of the first read independently:

NOTICE: Encourage students to notice how the main character uses his wit to win back his home.

ANNOTATE: Remind students to mark passages that demonstrate the use of vivid figures of speech.

CONNECT: Encourage students to go beyond the text to make connections with other stories they know, movies and TV shows they've seen, or their own personal experiences.

RESPOND: Students will answer questions and write a summary to demonstrate understanding.

Point out to students that while they will always complete the Respond step at the end of the first read, the other steps will probably happen somewhat concurrently. You may wish to print copies of the **First-Read Guide: Poetry** for students to use. Remember that an epic poem has qualities of both poetry and fiction, so the **First-Read Guide: Fiction** may also be beneficial for students.

About the Poet

Homer (approx. 850–750 B.C.) is credited with writing the *Iliad* and the *Odyssey*. For almost 3,000 years, these epic poems have captured readers' imaginations and inspired countless works of art and literature.

from the Odyssey, Part 2

Concept Vocabulary

You will encounter the following words as you read the *Odyssey*, Part 2. Before reading, note how familiar you are with each word. Then, rank the words in order from most familiar (1) to least familiar (6).

WORD	YOUR RANKING
craft	
dissemble	
incredulity	
bemusing	
guise	
deceived	

After completing the first read, come back to the concept vocabulary and review your rankings. Mark changes to your original rankings as needed.

Tool Kit
First-Read Guide and Model Annotation

First Read EPIC POEM

Apply these strategies as you conduct your first read. You will have an opportunity to complete the close-read notes after your first read.

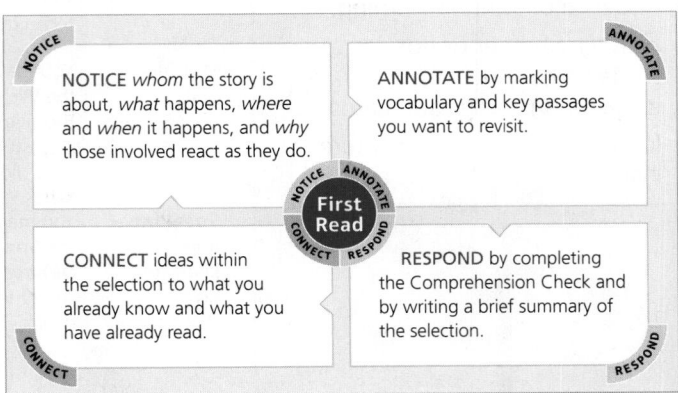

NOTICE *whom* the story is about, *what* happens, *where* and *when* it happens, and *why* those involved react as they do.

ANNOTATE by marking vocabulary and key passages you want to revisit.

First Read

CONNECT ideas within the selection to what you already know and what you have already read.

RESPOND by completing the Comprehension Check and by writing a brief summary of the selection.

STANDARDS

Reading Literature
By the end of grade 9, read and comprehend literature, including stories, dramas, and poems, in the grades 9–10 text complexity band proficiently, with scaffolding as needed at the high end of the range.

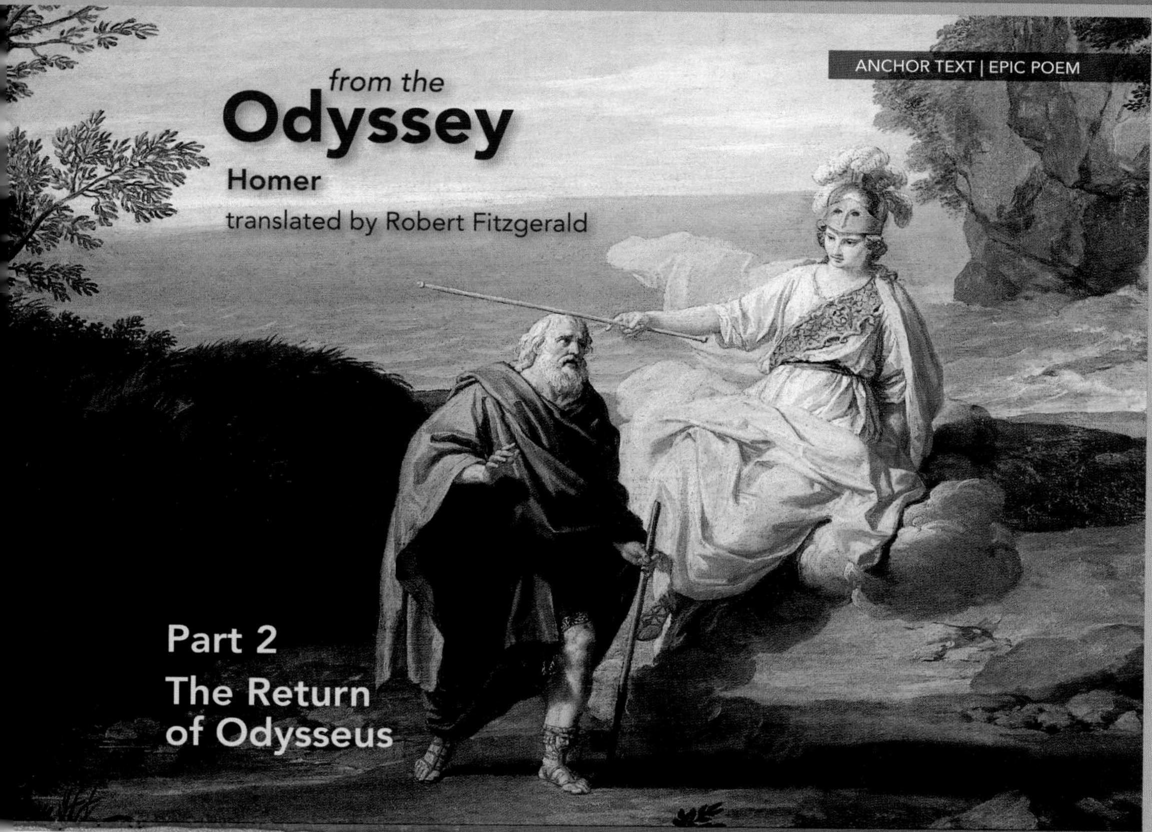

ANCHOR TEXT | EPIC POEM

from the
Odyssey
Homer
translated by Robert Fitzgerald

Part 2
The Return of Odysseus

BACKGROUND
The Greek concept of hospitality, *xenia,* was very important in Greek culture and plays a role in Odysseus' tale. Some scholars believe that this value is based on Greek religious belief. Since the Greek gods could take multiple earthly forms, there was always the possibility that the stranger at the door was a god in disguise. Thus, Greeks opened their homes to strangers. In Part 2, as Odysseus returns home, it is clear that this cultural practice has created some problems.

SCAN FOR MULTIMEDIA

"Twenty years gone, and I am back again . . ."

Odysseus has finished telling his story to the Phaeacians. The next day, young Phaeacian noblemen conduct him home by ship. He arrives in Ithaca after an absence of twenty years. The goddess Athena appears and informs him of the situation at home. Numerous suitors, believing Odysseus to be dead, have been continually seeking the hand of his wife, Penelope, in marriage, while overrunning Odysseus' palace and enjoying themselves at Penelope's expense. Moreover, they are plotting to

NOTES

PERSONALIZE FOR LEARNING

Strategic Support

Research Review the beginning description of Part 2. Have students analyze the presence of Athena and why she is helping Odysseus. Discuss with them the importance of search terms when doing research on the Internet: What specific information do students need to complete the assignment? For example, using only the word *Athena* will result in many interesting links but will not help them find the specific information they need. Have students try more than one term in their search and evaluate the results.

DIGITAL PERSPECTIVES

CLOSER LOOK

Examining Plot

Students may have marked the introductory summary during their first read. Use this paragraph to help students understand Odysseus's position at this point in the poem. Encourage them to talk about the annotations that they marked. You may want to model a close read with the class based on the highlights shown in the text.

ANNOTATE: Have students mark details in introductory summary that explain what has been happening in Ithaca because people thought Odysseus was dead.

QUESTION: Guide students to consider what these details might tell them. Ask what readers can infer from Athena's telling Odysseus what to expect when he returns to his palace, and accept student responses.

Possible response: Penelope has numerous suitors who have inundated Odysseus's palace and are taking advantage of Penelope's hospitality and her status as widow.

CONCLUDE: Help students formulate conclusions about the importance of these details in the text. Ask students why the author might have included these details.

Possible response: The author is setting up a situation where Odysseus must fight to regain control of his palace before he can truly be home again. Athena's warning allows Odysseus to prepare a plan, which is essential to the plot of the poem.

Remind students that the **plot** is the sequence of events that makes up a narrative and usually involves characters in conflict. The sequence of events in a plot is usually divided into five parts: the exposition; the rising action; the climax; the falling action; and the resolution, or denouement.

CLOSE READ

Remind students to focus on Odysseus's encounter with Athena. You may wish to model the close read using the following think-aloud format. Possible responses to questions on the student page are included. You may also want to print copies of the **Close-Read Guide: Poetry** for students to use.

ANNOTATE: As I read lines 1004–1015, I notice and highlight the details that indicate a direct quotation.

QUESTION: I believe Homer wishes to make the goddess's presence and her words more immediate and more dramatic. A direct quotation achieves that effect.

CONCLUDE: The speech suggests that they have a very formal relationship and that the gods have all the authority to direct mortals.

Additional **English Language Support** is available in the Interactive Teacher's Edition.

murder Odysseus' son, Telemachus, before he can inherit his father's lands. Telemachus, who, like Penelope, still hopes for his father's return, has journeyed to Pylos and Sparta to learn what he can about his father's fate. Athena disguises Odysseus as a beggar and directs him to the hut of Eumaeus,[1] his old and faithful swineherd. While Odysseus and Eumaeus are eating breakfast, Telemachus arrives. Athena then appears to Odysseus.

. . . From the air
she walked, taking the form of a tall woman,
handsome and clever at her **craft**, and stood
beyond the gate in plain sight of Odysseus,
unseen, though, by Telemachus, unguessed,
for not to everyone will gods appear.
Odysseus noticed her; so did the dogs,
who cowered whimpering away from her. She only
nodded, signing to him with her brows,
a sign he recognized. Crossing the yard,
he passed out through the gate in the stockade
to face the goddess. There she said to him:
"Son of Laertes and the gods of old,
Odysseus, master of landways and seaways,
dissemble to your son no longer now.
The time has come: tell him how you together
will bring doom on the suitors in the town.
I shall not be far distant then, for I
myself desire battle."

Saying no more,
she tipped her golden wand upon the man,
making his cloak pure white, and the knit tunic
fresh around him. Lithe and young she made him,
ruddy with sun, his jawline clean, the beard
no longer gray upon his chin. And she
withdrew when she had done.

Then Lord Odysseus
reappeared—and his son was thunderstruck.
Fear in his eyes, he looked down and away
As though it were a god, and whispered:

"Stranger,
you are no longer what you were just now!
Your cloak is new; even your skin! You are
one of the gods who rule the sweep of heaven!
Be kind to us, we'll make you fair oblation[2]
and gifts of hammered gold. Have mercy on us!"

NOTES

1. ***Eumaeus*** (yoo MEE uhs)

craft (kraft) *n.* activity that requires skill

dissemble (dih SEHM buhl) *v.* put on an appearance or disguise

CLOSE READ

ANNOTATE: Mark the indications of a direct quotation in lines 1004–1015.

QUESTION: Why does Homer choose to provide Athena's direct words in this passage rather than summarize her speech to Odysseus?

CONCLUDE: What does this speech suggest about the relationship between gods and mortals, especially Odysseus?

2. **oblation** (ob LAY shuhn) *n.* offering to a god.

PERSONALIZE FOR LEARNING

English Language Support

Idioms Idioms can be confusing to English language learners. Point out the idiom *thunderstruck* on line 1022. To help them understand its usage, explain that feeling *thunderstruck* means feeling completely shocked or surprised. Ask students to think of a time they were suddenly surprised by something and what that emotion was like. Since the poet is referring to Telemachus's reaction when he thinks he is witnessing a god revealing himself, explain that the poet is saying that Telemachus was unprepared for such an event. **ALL LEVELS**

The noble and enduring man replied:

"No god. Why take me for a god? No, no.
I am that father whom your boyhood lacked
and suffered pain for lack of. I am he."

Held back too long, the tears ran down his cheeks
as he embraced his son.
Only Telemachus,
uncomprehending, wild
with **incredulity** cried out:
"You cannot
be my father Odysseus! Meddling spirits
conceived this trick to twist the knife in me!
No man of woman born could work these wonders
by his own craft, unless a god came into it
with ease to turn him young or old at will.
I swear you were in rags and old,
and here you stand like one of the immortals!"

Odysseus brought his ranging mind to bear
and said:
"This is not princely, to be swept
away by wonder at your father's presence.
No other Odysseus will ever come,
for he and I are one, the same; his bitter
fortune and his wanderings are mine.
Twenty years gone, and I am back again
on my own island.
As for my change of skin,
that is a charm Athena, Hope of Soldiers,
uses as she will; she has the knack
to make me seem a beggar man sometimes
and sometimes young, with finer clothes about me.
It is no hard things for the gods of heaven
to glorify a man or bring him low."

When he had spoken, down he sat.
Then, throwing
his arms around this marvel of a father
Telemachus began to weep. Salt tears
rose from the wells of longing in both men,
and cries burst from both as keen and fluttering
as those of the great taloned hawk,
whose nestlings farmers take before they fly.
So helplessly they cried, pouring out tears,
and might have gone on weeping so till sundown,
had not Telemachus said:

NOTES

incredulity (ihn kruh DYOO luh tee) *n.* doubt

CLOSE READ

ANNOTATE: In lines 1048–1050, mark words relating to the concept of identity.

QUESTION: Why do you think Homer places such emphasis on the idea of identity?

CONCLUDE: How do these words emphasize Odysseus' message to his son?

DIGITAL PERSPECTIVES

CLOSE READ

Remind students to focus on the reunion between Odysseus and Telemachus. You may wish to model the close read using the following think-aloud format. Possible responses to questions on the student page are included.

ANNOTATE: As I read lines 1048–1050, I notice and highlight the words that indicate identity or identicalness.

QUESTION: Homer places strong emphasis on identity because part of this epic is about what is important to Odysseus.

CONCLUDE: I believe Odysseus is letting his son know that Odysseus's absence from his home and family has been an unhappy one.

NOTES

3. **cutter** *n.* small, swift ship or boat carried aboard a large ship to transport personnel or supplies.

4. **in their prime** in the best or most vigorous stage of their lives.

"Dear father! Tell me
what kind of vessel put you here ashore
on Ithaca? Your sailors, who were they?
I doubt you made it, walking on the sea!"

Then said Odysseus, who had borne the barren sea:

"Only plain truth shall I tell you, child.
Great seafarers, the Phaeacians, gave me passage
as they give other wanderers. By night
over the open ocean, while I slept,
they brought me in their cutter,[3] set me down
on Ithaca, with gifts of bronze and gold
and stores of woven things. By the gods' will
these lie all hidden in a cave. I came
to this wild place, directed by Athena,
so that we might lay plans to kill our enemies.
Count up the suitors for me, let me know
what men at arms are there, how many men.
I must put all my mind to it, to see
if we two by ourselves can take them on
or if we should look round for help."

Telemachus
replied:
"O father, all my life your fame
as a fighting man has echoed in my ears—
your skill with weapons and the tricks of war—
but what you speak of is a staggering thing,
beyond imagining, for me. How can two men
do battle with a houseful in their prime?[4]
For I must tell you this is no affair
of ten or even twice ten men, but scores,
throngs of them. You shall see, here and now.
The number from Dulichium alone
is fifty-two picked men, with armorers,
a half dozen; twenty-four came from Same,
twenty from Zacynthus; our own island
accounts for twelve, high-ranked, and their retainers,
Medon the crier, and the Master Harper,
besides a pair of handymen at feasts.
If we go in against all these
I fear we pay in salt blood for your vengeance.
You must think hard if you would conjure up
the fighting strength to take us through."

Odysseus
who had endured the long war and the sea
answered:

PERSONALIZE FOR LEARNING

Strategic Support

Parenthetical Elements Review line 1088. Remind students that extra detail can be added to a sentence by using a parenthetical element, which is text usually placed within parentheses or between dashes. Explain to students that this information can be deleted from the sentence without affecting the sentence's grammar. Have students read the sentence that begins on line 1088: *O father, all my life your fame / as a fighting man has echoed in my ears— / your skill with weapons and the tricks of war— / but what you speak of is a staggering thing, / beyond imagining, for me.* Have students discuss how the sentence would read differently if the parenthetical element were removed. Then have students write a sentence that uses a parenthetical element set off by dashes and share their work with others in the class.

"I'll tell you now.
Suppose Athena's arm is over us, and Zeus
her father's, must I rack my brains for more?"

Clearheaded Telemachus looked hard and said:

"Those two are great defenders, no one doubts it,
but throned in the serene clouds overhead;
other affairs of men and gods they have
to rule over."

And the hero answered:
"Before long they will stand to right and left of us
in combat, in the shouting, when the test comes—
our nerve against the suitors' in my hall.
Here is your part: at break of day tomorrow
home with you, go mingle with our princes.
The swineherd later on will take me down
the port-side trail—a beggar, by my looks,
hangdog and old. If they make fun of me
in my own courtyard, let your ribs cage up
your springing heart, no matter what I suffer,
no matter if they pull me by the heels
or practice shots at me, to drive me out.
Look on, hold down your anger. You may even
plead with them, by heaven! in gentle terms
to quit their horseplay—not that they will heed you,
rash as they are, facing their day of wrath.
Now fix the next step in your mind.

Athena,
counseling me, will give me word, and I
shall signal to you, nodding: at that point
round up all armor, lances, gear of war
left in our hall, and stow the lot away
back in the vaulted storeroom. When the suitors
miss those arms and question you, be soft
in what you say: answer:

'I thought I'd move them
out of the smoke. They seemed no longer those
bright arms Odysseus left us years ago
when he went off to Troy. Here where the fire's
hot breath came, they had grown black and drear.
One better reason, too, I had from Zeus:
suppose a brawl starts up when you are drunk,

NOTES

CLOSE READ

ANNOTATE: In lines 1120–1132, mark the words Odysseus uses to tell his son what he should do if the suitors abuse Odysseus.

QUESTION: What do these words suggest about Telemachus' emotions?

CONCLUDE: How do these words express Odysseus' sense of his son's love for him?

CLOSE READ

Remind students to focus on the reunion between Odysseus and his son. You may wish to model the close read using the following think-aloud format. Possible responses to questions on the student page are included.

ANNOTATE: As I read lines 1120–1132, I notice and highlight Odysseus's instructions to Telemachus.

QUESTION: I can see these words suggest that Odysseus knows that Telemachus will want to defend his father if the suitors abuse him, but Telemachus must play along with Odysseus's charade for the time being.

CONCLUDE: I believe that by using these words, Odysseus indicates that he is aware that his son loves him and wants to protect him.

NOTES

bemusing (bih MYOOZ ihng) *adj.* confusing; bewildering

5. **shirkers** (SHURK uhrz) *n.* people who get out of doing what needs to be done.

you might be crazed and bloody one another,
and that would stain your feast, your courtship.
Tempered
iron can magnetize a man.'
Say that.
But put aside two broadswords and two spears
for our own use, two oxhide shields nearby
when we go into action. Pallas Athena
and Zeus All-Provident will see you through,
bemusing our young friends.
Now one thing more.
If son of mine you are and blood of mine,
let no one hear Odysseus is about.
Neither Laertes, nor the swineherd here,
nor any slave, nor even Penelope.

But you and I alone must learn how far
the women are corrupted; we should know
how to locate good men among our hands
the loyal and respectful, and the shirkers[5]
who take you lightly, as alone and young."

Argus

Odysseus heads for town with Eumaeus. Outside the palace, Odysseus's old dog, Argus, is lying at rest as his long-absent master approaches.

While he spoke
an old hound, lying near, pricked up his ears
and lifted up his muzzle. This was Argus,
trained as a puppy by Odysseus,
but never taken on a hunt before
his master sailed for Troy. The young men, afterward,
hunted wild goats with him, and hare, and deer,
but he had grown old in his master's absence.
Treated as rubbish now, he lay at last
upon a mass of dung before the gates—
manure of mules and cows, piled there until
fieldhands could spread it on the king's estate.
Abandoned there, and half destroyed with flies,
old Argus lay.
But when he knew he heard
Odysseus's voice nearby, he did his best

DIGITAL PERSPECTIVES

Illuminating the Text To help students analyze the poignancy of Argus being the only one to recognize the disguised Odysseus, have them view video clips from movies such as *Old Yeller* and *Sounder* that express the bond writers have made between a person and a dog. Guide students to evaluate how this bond is portrayed in film. Have them connect these scenes to that of Part II of the *Odyssey*. How do these clips add to the students' understanding of the poem? Preview all videos before showing them in class. **(Research to Explore)**

to wag his tail, nose down, with flattened ears,
having no strength to move nearer his master.
And the man looked away,
wiping a salt tear from his cheek; but he
hid this from Eumaeus. Then he said:

"I marvel that they leave this hound to lie
here on the dung pile;
he would have been a fine dog, from the look of him,
though I can't say as to his power and speed
when he was young. You find the same good build
in house dogs, table dogs landowners keep
all for style."

And you replied, Eumaeus:

"A hunter owned him—but the man is dead
in some far place. If this old hound could show
the form he had when Lord Odysseus left him,
going to Troy, you'd see him swift and strong.
He never shrank from any savage thing
he'd brought to bay in the deep woods; on the scent
no other dog kept up with him. Now misery
has him in leash. His owner died abroad,
and here the women slaves will take no care of him.
You know how servants are: without a master
they have no will to labor, or excel.
For Zeus who views the wide world takes away
half the manhood of a man, that day
he goes into captivity and slavery."

Eumaeus crossed the court and went straight forward
into the megaron[6] among the suitors:
but death and darkness in that instant closed
the eyes of Argus, who had seen his master,
Odysseus, after twenty years.

NOTES

CLOSE READ

ANNOTATE: In lines 1185–1196, mark adjectives and nouns Odysseus and Eumaeus use to describe the dog as he once was.

QUESTION: What do these words have in common?

CONCLUDE: How do they emphasize the sadness of the dog now?

6. **megaron** (MEHG uh ron) *n.* great, central hall of the house, usually containing a center hearth.

DIGITAL PERSPECTIVES

CLOSE READ

Remind students to focus on the questions of identity that run throughout the reunion between Odysseus and Telemachus. You may wish to model the close read using the following think-aloud format. Possible responses to questions on the student page are included.

ANNOTATE: As I read lines 1185–1196, I notice and highlight the adjectives and nouns that describe Argus when he was young.

QUESTION: I see that all the words relating to young Argus are positive and admiring: "a fine dog," "good build," "swift and strong."

CONCLUDE: I think these words emphasize the contrast of how old Argus is "Treated as rubbish now, he lay at last / upon a mass of dung" (lines 1171 and 1172) and not as the "fine dog" (line 1185) he was.

Penelope, Odysseus' wife, in her home overrun with suitors.

WriteNow

Analyze and Interpret Have students write a short analysis of the illustration showing Penelope weaving at her loom. Remind students to include details about her expression, the expression of the other women, and that of the young suitor on the right. Why does the artist depict Penelope standing and not sitting? Have students discuss in their analysis whether they would add or delete elements of the illustration. How would their changes reflect the narrative of the poem?

The Suitors

Still disguised as a beggar, Odysseus enters his home. He is confronted by the haughty[7] suitor Antinous.[8]

But here Antinous broke in, shouting:
"God!
What evil wind blew in this pest?
Get over,
stand in the passage! Nudge my table, will you?
Egyptian whips are sweet
to what you'll come to here, you nosing rat,
making your pitch to everyone!
These men have bread to throw away on you
because it is not theirs. Who cares? Who spares
another's food, when he has more than plenty?"

With guile Odysseus drew away, then said:

"A pity that you have more looks than heart.
You'd grudge a pinch of salt from your own larder
to your own handyman. You sit here, fat
on others' meat, and cannot bring yourself
to rummage out a crust of bread for me!"

Then anger made Antinous' heart beat hard,
and, glowering under his brows, he answered:
"Now!
You think you'll shuffle off and get away
after that impudence?[9] Oh, no you don't!"

The stool he let fly hit the man's right shoulder
on the packed muscle under the shoulder blade—
like solid rock, for all the effect one saw.
Odysseus only shook his head, containing
thoughts of bloody work, as he walked on,
then sat, and dropped his loaded bag again
upon the door sill. Facing the whole crowd
he said, and eyed them all:
"One word only,
my lords, and suitors of the famous queen.
One thing I have to say.
There is no pain, no burden for the heart
when blows come to a man, and he defending
his own cattle—his own cows and lambs.

NOTES

7. **haughty** (HAWT ee) *adj.* arrogant.

8. **Antinous** (an TIHN oh uhs)

9. **impudence** (IHM pyoo duhns) *n.* quality of being shamelessly bold; disrespectfulness

DIGITAL PERSPECTIVES

CLOSER LOOK

Analyze Character

Students may have marked lines 1212 and 1213 during their first read. Use this stanza to help students understand what these words reveal about Antinous's character. Encourage students to talk about the annotations that they marked. You may want to model a close read with the class based on the highlights shown in the text.

ANNOTATE: Have students mark details in lines 1212 and 1213 that may help them to understand the character of Antinous.

QUESTION: Guide students to consider what these details might tell them. Ask what readers can infer about Egyptian whips from this comparison, and accept student responses.

Possible response: Readers can infer that Egyptian whips are notoriously painful.

CONCLUDE: Help students formulate conclusions about the importance of these details in the text. Ask students why the author might have included these details.

Possible response: The poet uses these details to show Antinous as a loud-mouthed bully. The reference to whips rather than weapons indicates his assumption of superiority over Odysseus.

Remind students that **characterization** is how a writer develops and reveals a character's personality and temperament. In **indirect characterization**, the writer can show a character's traits through actions, behavior, dialogue, or thoughts.

CLOSE READ

Remind students to focus on a noun that appears three times and a related verb that appears twice. You may wish to model the close read using the following think-aloud format. Possible responses to questions on the student page are included.

ANNOTATE: As I read lines 1261–1270, I notice and highlight a noun that appears three times and a related verb that appears twice.

QUESTION: I think the reader hears these repetitions as the sound of the single blow travels through the house and is heard separately by both Telemachus and Penelope.

CONCLUDE: I believe the sound of the blow increases Penelope's animosity toward Antinous and her sympathy for the stranger.

NOTES

10. Furies (FYUR eez) *n.* three terrible female spirits who punish the doers of unavenged crimes.

guise (gyz) *n.* outward appearance

CLOSE READ

ANNOTATE: In lines 1261–1270, mark the noun that appears three times. Then, mark its synonym, which appears twice.

QUESTION: What does this repetition emphasize?

CONCLUDE: How does deliberate use of repetition help reveal the feelings of Odysseus' son and wife?

11. Eurynome (yoo RIHN uhm ee)

Here it was otherwise. Antinous
hit me for being driven on by hunger—
how many bitter seas men cross for hunger!
If beggars interest the gods, if there are Furies[10]
pent in the dark to avenge a poor man's wrong, then may
Antinous meet his death before his wedding day!"
Then said Eupeithes's son, Antinous:
"Enough.
Eat and be quiet where you are, or shamble elsewhere,
unless you want these lads to stop your mouth
pulling you by the heels, or hands and feet,
over the whole floor, till your back is peeled!"

But now the rest were mortified, and someone
spoke from the crowd of young bucks to rebuke him:

"A poor show, that—hitting this famished tramp—
bad business, if he happened to be a god.
You know they go in foreign **guise**, the gods do,
looking like strangers, turning up
in towns and settlements to keep an eye
on manners, good or bad."
But at this notion
Antinous only shrugged.
Telemachus,
after the blow his father bore, sat still
without a tear, though his heart felt the blow.
Slowly he shook his head from side to side,
containing murderous thoughts.
Penelope
on the higher level of her room had heard
the blow, and knew who gave it. Now she murmured:

"Would god you could be hit yourself, Antinous—
hit by Apollo's bowshot!"

And Eurynome[11]
her housekeeper, put in:

"He and no other?
If all we pray for came to pass, not one
would live till dawn!"

Her gentle mistress said:

"Oh, Nan, they are a bad lot; they intend
ruin for all of us; but Antinous

604 UNIT 5 • JOURNEYS OF TRANSFORMATION

appears a blacker-hearted hound than any.
Here is a poor man come, a wanderer,
driven by want to beg his bread, and everyone
in hall gave bits, to cram his bag—only
Antinous threw a stool, and banged his shoulder!"

So she described it, sitting in her chamber
among her maids—while her true lord was eating.
Then she called in the forester and said:

"Go to that man on my behalf, Eumaeus,
and send him here, so I can greet and question him.
Abroad in the great world, he may have heard
rumors about Odysseus—may have known him!"

NOTES

Penelope

In the evening, Penelope interrogates the old beggar.

"Friend, let me ask you first of all:
who are you, where do you come from, of what nation
and parents were you born?"
And he replied:
"My lady, never a man in the wide world
should have a fault to find with you. Your name
has gone out under heaven like the sweet
honor of some god-fearing king, who rules
in equity over the strong: his black lands bear
both wheat and barley, fruit trees laden bright,
new lambs at lambing time—and the deep sea
gives great hauls of fish by his good strategy,
so that his folk fare well.

O my dear lady,
this being so, let it suffice to ask me
of other matters—not my blood, my homeland.
Do not enforce me to recall my pain.
My heart is sore; but I must not be found
sitting in tears here, in another's house:
it is not well forever to be grieving.
One of the maids might say—or you might think—
I had got maudlin over cups of wine."

PERSONALIZE FOR LEARNING

English Language Support

Unfamiliar Words Have students read lines 1290–1293: *Your name / has gone out under heaven like the sweet / honor of some god-fearing king, who rules / in equity over the strong.* For students to understand these lines, they will need to know what *equity* means. Have students look up the word in the dictionary and determine which definition applies to the meaning of the word as it is used in the poem. Then have students write a sentence using the word and share their work with others in the class. **ALL LEVELS**

CLOSE READ

Remind students to focus on the reunion of Odysseus and Penelope. You may wish to model the close read using the following think-aloud format. Possible responses to questions on the student page are included.

ANNOTATE: As I read the stanza beginning with line 1335, I notice and highlight the words that have to do with time or duration.

QUESTION: I can see that lines 1135 and 1136 emphasize the amount of time it took for Penelope to complete the shroud. The three short phrases in lines 1338–1140—"me at night," "to finish it," and "at last"— convey the effect of dragging out the time.

CONCLUDE: I believe Penelope confirms her fidelity by telling her husband about her plan to weave and then secretly unweave the shroud for years to keep her suitors away.

And Penelope replied:

"Stranger, my looks,
my face, my carriage,[12] were soon lost or faded
when the Achaeans crossed the sea to Troy,
Odysseus my lord among the rest.
If he returned, if he were here to care for me,
I might be happily renowned!
But grief instead heaven sent me—years of pain.
Sons of the noblest families on the islands,
Dulichium, Same, wooded Zacynthus,[13]
with native Ithacans, are here to court me,
against my wish; and they consume this house.
Can I give proper heed to guest or suppliant
or herald on the realm's affairs?

How could I?
wasted with longing for Odysseus, while here
they press for marriage.

Ruses[14] served my turn
to draw the time out—first a close-grained web
I had the happy thought to set up weaving
on my big loom in hall. I said, that day:
'Young men—my suitors, now my lord is dead,
let me finish my weaving before I marry,
or else my thread will have been spun in vain.
It is a shroud I weave for Lord Laertes
When cold Death comes to lay him on his bier.
The country wives would hold me in dishonor
if he, with all his fortune, lay unshrouded.'
I reached their hearts that way, and they agreed.
So every day I wove on the great loom,
but every night by torchlight I unwove it;
and so for three years I **deceived** the Achaeans.

But when the seasons brought a fourth year on,
as long months waned, and the long days were spent,
through impudent folly in the slinking maids
they caught me—clamored up to me at night;
I had no choice then but to finish it.
And now, as matters stand at last,
I have no strength left to evade a marriage,
cannot find any further way; my parents
urge it upon me, and my son
will not stand by while they eat up his property.
He comprehends it, being a man full-grown,
able to oversee the kind of house
Zeus would endow with honor.

NOTES

12. carriage *n.* posture.

13. Zacynthus (za SIHN thuhs)

14. Ruses (ROOZ ihz) *n.* tricks.

deceived (dih SEEVD) *v.* lied to; tricked

CLOSE READ

ANNOTATE: In the stanza beginning on line 1335, mark the words having to do with time and duration.

QUESTION: What do these words emphasize in Penelope's story?

CONCLUDE: How do they confirm her fidelity to Odysseus?

606 UNIT 5 • JOURNEYS OF TRANSFORMATION

DIGITAL PERSPECTIVES

But you too
confide in me, tell me your ancestry.
You were not born of mythic oak or stone."

Penelope again asks the beggar to tell about himself. He makes up a tale in which Odysseus is mentioned and declares that Penelope's husband will soon be home.

"You see, then, he is alive and well, and headed
homeward now, no more to be abroad
far from his island, his dear wife and son.
Here is my sworn word for it. Witness this,
god of the zenith, noblest of the gods,[15]
and Lord Odysseus's hearthfire, now before me:
I swear these things shall turn out as I say.
Between this present dark and one day's ebb,
after the wane, before the crescent moon,
Odysseus will come."

The Challenge

Pressed by the suitors to choose a husband from among them, Penelope says she will marry the man who can string Odysseus's bow and shoot an arrow through twelve ax handle sockets. The suitors try and fail. Still in disguise, Odysseus asks for a turn and gets it.

And Odysseus took his time,
turning the bow, tapping it, every inch,
for borings that termites might have made
while the master of the weapon was abroad.
The suitors were now watching him, and some
jested among themselves:

"A bow lover!"

"Dealer in old bows!"

"Maybe he has one like it
at home!"

"Or has an itch to make one for himself."

"See how he handles it, the sly old buzzard!"

And one disdainful suitor added this:
"May his fortune grow an inch for every inch he bends it!"

NOTES

15. god of the zenith, noblest of the gods Zeus.

HOW LANGUAGE WORKS

Pronoun-Antecedent Agreement Explain to students that pronouns usually refer to someone or something that was already mentioned in the text. Using pronouns avoids repetition. When a pronoun replaces a noun, the word it refers to is called an antecedent. A pronoun must agree with its antecedent in a number (singular or plural) and gender (male or female).

Note lines 1359–1364: *And Odysseus took his time / turning the bow, tapping it, every inch, / for borings that termites might have made / while the master of the weapon was abroad. / The suitors were now watching him, and some / jested among themselves.* Point out in the last sentence that *him* refers to Odysseus and *themselves* refers to the suitors. Have students write sentences and draw an arrow from each pronoun to its antecedent. Do their pronouns agree with their antecedents?

TEACHING

CLOSE READ

Remind students to focus on Odysseus's reply to Antinous's challenge. You may wish to model the close read using the following think-aloud format. Possible responses to questions on the student page are included.

ANNOTATE: As I read lines 1378–1383, I notice and highlight the words that focus on or indicate sounds.

QUESTION: I think the poet likens the sound of the vibrating bowstring to the high note of a swallow's song to emphasize the string's tautness. A single thunderclap from Zeus indicates something more alarming than an approaching storm.

CONCLUDE: I believe these sounds indicate to Antinous and to everyone else (including readers) that Odysseus is a skilled bowman and may have the gods on his side.

NOTES

CLOSE READ

ANNOTATE: In lines 1378–1383, mark words that indicate or describe sounds.

QUESTION: Why do you think the poet uses these words?

CONCLUDE: How do these words intensify the description of the action?

16. nocked set an arrow into the bowstring.

But the man skilled in all ways of contending,
satisfied by the great bow's look and heft,
like a musician, like a harper, when
with quiet hand upon his instrument
he draws between his thumb and forefinger
a sweet new string upon a peg: so effortlessly
Odysseus in one motion strung the bow.
Then slid his right hand down the cord and plucked it,
so the taut gut vibrating hummed and sang
a swallow's note.
In the hushed hall it smote the suitors
and all their faces changed. Then Zeus thundered
overhead, one loud crack for a sign.
And Odysseus laughed within him that the son
of crooked-minded Cronus had flung that omen down.
He picked one ready arrow from his table
where it lay bare: the rest were waiting still
in the quiver for young men's turn to come.
He nocked[16] it, let it rest across the handgrip,
And drew the string and grooved butt of the arrow,
Aiming from where he sat upon the stool.

Now flashed
arrow from twanging bow clean as a whistle
through every socket ring, and grazed not one,
to thud with heavy brazen head beyond.
Then quietly
Odysseus said:

"Telemachus, the stranger
you welcomed in your hall has not disgraced you.
I did not miss, neither did I take all day
stringing the bow. My hand and eye are sound,
not so contemptible as the young men say.
The hour has come to cook their lordships' mutton—
supper by daylight. Other amusements later,
with song and harping that adorn a feast."

He dropped his eyes and nodded, and the prince
Telemachus, true son of King Odysseus,
belted his sword on, clapped hand to his spear,
and with a clink and glitter of keen bronze
stood by his chair, in the forefront near his father.

DIGITAL PERSPECTIVES

Odysseus begins to take his revenge on Penelope's suitors.

NOTES

Odysseus' Revenge

Now shrugging off his rags the wiliest[17] fighter of the islands
leapt and stood on the broad doorsill, his own bow in his hand.
He poured out at his feet a rain of arrows from the quiver
and spoke to the crowd:

"So much for that. Your clean-cut game is over.
Now watch me hit a target that no man has hit before,
if I can make this shot. Help me, Apollo."

He drew to his fist the cruel head of an arrow for Antinous
just as the young man leaned to lift his beautiful drinking cup,
embossed, two-handled, golden: the cup was in his fingers:
the wine was even at his lips: and did he dream of death?
How could he? In that revelry[18] amid his throng of friends
who would imagine a single foe—though a strong foe indeed—
could dare to bring death's pain on him and darkness on his eyes?
Odysseus's arrow hit him under the chin
and punched up to the feathers through his throat.

17. **wiliest** (WYL ee uhst) *adj.* craftiest; slyest.

CLOSE READ

ANNOTATE: In lines 1412–1414, mark adjectives that describe the drinking cup.

QUESTION: Why do you think the poet describes the cup in such detail and with these words?

CONCLUDE: How does the description heighten the effect of Odysseus' action?

18. **revelry** (REHV uhl ree) *n.* noisy partying.

CLOSE READ

Remind students to focus on the wrongs done to Penelope and Odysseus. You may wish to model the close read using the following think-aloud format. Possible responses to questions on the student page are included.

ANNOTATE: As I read lines 1412–1414, I notice and highlight the words that describe the drinking cup.

QUESTION: The poet describes the beauty of the cup to illustrate the opulence that the suitors were enjoying at Penelope's expense; it also reflects Odysseus's wealth.

CONCLUDE: Its description shows that the suitor is overconfident and not expecting the death that comes with Odysseus's fatal arrow.

NOTES

Backward and down he went, letting the winecup fall
from his shocked hand. Like pipes his nostrils jetted
crimson runnels, a river of mortal red,
and one last kick upset his table
knocking the bread and meat to soak in dusty blood.
Now as they craned to see their champion where he lay
the suitors jostled in uproar down the hall,
everyone on his feet. Wildly they turned and scanned
the walls in the long room for arms; but not a shield,
not a good ashen spear was there for a man to take and
throw.
All they could do was yell in outrage at Odysseus:

"Foul! to shoot at a man! That was your last shot!"
"Your own throat will be slit for this!"
"Our finest lad is down!
You killed the best on Ithaca."
"Buzzards will tear your eyes out!"

For they imagined as they wished—that it was a wild shot,
an unintended killing—fools, not to comprehend
they were already in the grip of death.
But glaring under his brows Odysseus answered:

"You yellow dogs, you thought I'd never make it
home from the land of Troy. You took my house to
plunder . . .
You dared bid for my wife while I was still alive.
Contempt was all you had for the gods who rule wide
heaven,
contempt for what men say of you hereafter.
Your last hour has come. You die in blood."

As they all took this in, sickly green fear
pulled at their entrails, and their eyes flickered
looking for some hatch or hideaway from death.
Eurymachus[19] alone could speak. He said:

"If you are Odysseus of Ithaca come back,
all that you say these men have done is true.
Rash actions, many here, more in the countryside.
But here he lies, the man who cause them all.
Antinous was the ringleader, he whipped us on
to do these things. He cared less for a marriage
than for the power Cronion has denied him
As king of Ithaca. For that
he tried to trap your son and would have killed him.
He is dead now and has his portion. Spare

19. **Eurymachus** (yoo RIH muh kuhs)

VOCABULARY DEVELOPMENT

Graphic Organizer

Have students become more familiar with the word *contempt* in line 1442 by completing a graphic organizer like this one.

Definition in your own words: disrespect for someone or something	Synonyms: disregard disdain scorn
contempt	
Use it in a sentence: He expressed his contempt for peas by scraping them off his dinner plate.	Antonyms: admiration respect regard

610 UNIT 5 • JOURNEYS OF TRANSFORMATION

your own people. As for ourselves, we'll make
restitution of wine and meat consumed,
and add, each one, a tithe of twenty oxen
with gifts of bronze and gold to warm your heart.
Meanwhile we cannot blame you for your anger."

Odysseus glowered under his black brows
and said:
"Not for the whole treasure of your fathers,
all you enjoy, lands, flocks, or any gold
put up by others, would I hold my hand.
There will be killing till the score is paid.
You forced yourselves upon this house. Fight your way out,
or run it, if you think you'll escape death.
I doubt one man of you skins by."

They felt their knees fail, and their hearts—but heard
Eurymachus for the last time rallying them.
"Friends," he said, "the man is implacable.
Now that he's got his hands on bow and quiver
he'll shoot from the big doorstone there
until he kills us to the last man.
Fight, I say,
let's remember the joy of it. Swords out!
Hold up your tables to deflect his arrows.
After me, everyone: rush him where he stands.
If we can budge him from the door, if we can pass
into the town, we'll call out men to chase hm.
This fellow with his bow will shoot no more."

He drew his own sword as he spoke, a broadsword of fine bronze,
honed like a razor on either edge. Then crying hoarse and loud
he hurled himself at Odysseus. But the kingly man let fly
an arrow at that instant, and the quivering feathered butt
sprang to the nipple of his breast as the barb stuck in his liver.
The bright broadsword clanged down. He lurched and fell aside,
pitching across his table. His cup, his bread and meat,
were spilt and scattered far and wide, and his head slammed on the ground.
Revulsion, anguish in his heart, with both feet kicking out,
he downed his chair, while the shrouding wave of mist closed on his eyes.

Amphinomus now came running at Odysseus,
broadsword naked in his hand. He thought to make

NOTES

CLOSE READ

ANNOTATE: Mark the first two sentences of the stanza that begins on line 1484.

QUESTION: How are these lines different from those that go before them?

CONCLUSION: Why do you think the poet made this change when beginning a description of the battle?

DIGITAL PERSPECTIVES

CLOSE READ

Remind students to focus on Eurymachus. You may wish to model the Close Read using the following think-aloud format. Possible responses to questions on the Student page are included.

ANNOTATE: As I read lines 1484–1486, I notice and highlight the first two sentences that begin on line 1484.

QUESTION: I can see that these lines are longer than the lines before them. In fact, these sentences are prose.

CONCLUDE: I believe the poet intends to make the battle scene as fierce and wild as he can, so he abandons the more restrained and rigid poetic line.

NOTES

the great soldier give way at the door.
But with a spear throw from behind Telemachus hit him
between the shoulders, and the lancehead drove
clear through his chest. He left his feet and fell
forward, thudding, forehead against the ground.
Telemachus swerved around him, leaving the long dark spear
planted in Amphinomus. If he paused to yank it out
someone might jump him from behind or cut him down with a sword
at the moment he bent over. So he ran—ran from the tables
to his father's side and halted, panting, saying:

"Father let me bring you a shield and spear,
a pair of spears, a helmet.
I can arm on the run myself: I'll give
outfits to Eumaeus and this cowherd.
Better to have equipment."

Said Odysseus:
"Run then, while I hold them off with arrows
as long as the arrows last. When all are gone
if I'm alone they can dislodge me."
Quick
upon his father's word Telemachus
ran to the room where spears and armor lay.
He caught up four light shields, four pairs of spears,
four helms of war high-plumed with flowing manes,
and ran back, loaded down to his father's side.
He was the first to pull a helmet on
and slide his bare arm in a buckler strap.
The servants armed themselves, and all three took their stand
beside the master of battle.
While he had arrows
he aimed and shot, and every shot brought down
one of his huddling enemies.
But when all barbs had flown from the bowman's fist,
he leaned his bow in the bright entryway
beside the door, and armed: a four-ply shield
hard on his shoulder, and a crested helm,
horsetailed, nodding stormy upon his head,
then took his tough and bronze-shod spears. . . .

Aided by Athena, Odysseus, Telemachus, Eumaeus, and other faithful herdsmen kill all the suitors.

612 UNIT 5 • JOURNEYS OF TRANSFORMATION

DIGITAL PERSPECTIVES

And Odysseus looked around him, narrow-eyed,
for any others who had lain hidden
while death's black fury passed.

In blood and dust
he saw that crowd all fallen, many and many slain.

Think of a catch that fishermen haul in to a half-moon bay
in a fine-meshed net from the whitecaps of the sea:
how all are poured out on the sand, in throes for the salt sea,
twitching their cold lives away in Helios' fiery air:
so lay the suitors heaped on one another.

Penelope's Test

Penelope tests Odysseus to prove he really is her husband.

Greathearted Odysseus, home at last,
was being bathed now by Eurynome
and rubbed with golden oil, and clothed again
in a fresh tunic and a cloak. Athena
lent him beauty, head to foot. She made him
taller, and massive, too, with crisping hair
in curls like petals of wild hyacinth
but all red-golden. Think of gold infused
on silver by a craftsman, whose fine art
Hephaestus[20] taught him, or Athena: one
whose work moves to delight: just so she lavished
beauty over Odysseus' head and shoulders.
He sat then in the same chair by the pillar,
facing his silent wife, and said:

"Strange woman,
the immortals of Olympus made you hard,
harder than any. Who else in the world
would keep aloof as you do from her husband
if he returned to her from years of trouble,
cast on his own land in the twentieth year?

Nurse, make up a bed for me to sleep on.
Her heart is iron in her breast."

Penelope
spoke to Odysseus now. She said:

NOTES

20. **Hephaestus** (hee FEHS tuhs) god of fire and metalworking.

CLOSER LOOK

Analyzing Assonance

Students may have marked lines 1542 and 1543 during their first read. Use these lines to help students understand the use of assonance. Encourage them to talk about the annotations that they marked. You may want to model a close read with the class based on the highlights shown in the text.

ANNOTATE: Have students mark words in lines 1542 and 1543 that have the same vowel sound.

QUESTION: Guide students to consider what these details might tell them. Ask what readers can infer from the words that have the same vowel sound, and accept student responses.

Possible response: The words *golden, clothed,* and *cloak* all have a long *o* sound.

CONCLUDE: Help students formulate conclusions about the importance of these details in the text. Ask students why the author might have included these details.

Possible response: The poet uses words with a long *o* sound to create the soothing effect on Odysseus of the bath, the oils, and the fresh clothes.

Remind students that **assonance** is the repetition of similar vowel sounds in stressed syllables that end with different consonant sounds (as in *blow* and *moan*). Assonance is one device poets use to emphasize meaning, imitate sound, and create musical effects.

NOTES

This illustration shows Odysseus' return to Penelope after an absence of twenty years.

"Strange man,
if man you are . . . This is no pride on my part
nor scorn for you—not even wonder, merely.
I know so well how you—how he—appeared
boarding the ship for Troy. But all the same . . .

Make up his bed for him, Eurycleia.
Place it outside the bedchamber my lord
built with his own hands. Pile the big bed
with fleeces, rugs, and sheets of purest linen."

With this she tried him to the breaking point,
and he turned on her in a flash raging:

"Woman, by heaven you've stung me now!
Who dared to move my bed?
No builder had the skill for that—unless
a god came down to turn the trick. No mortal
in his best days could budge it with a crowbar.
There is our pact and pledge, our secret sign,
built into that bed—my handiwork
and no one else's!

PERSONALIZE FOR LEARNING

English Language Support

Imperative Mood Note lines 1566–1569 in which Penelope gives three commands to her servant: *Make up his bed for him, Eurycleia / Place it outside the bedchamber my lord / built with his own hands. Pile the big bed / with fleeces, rugs, and sheets of purest linen."* Explain to students that these sentences are written in the imperative mood, which is one of three ways a verb can express action or a state of being in a sentence. Point out that imperative sentences express direct requests and commands. The subject for these sentences is always *you.* Even if the word *you* is not included in the sentence, it is still the subject. Explain that an easy check is to place *you* in a sentence and see if it makes sense. (*You make up his bed for him.*) Have students write sentences in the imperative mood and share them with the class. **BRIDGING**

614 UNIT 5 • JOURNEYS OF TRANSFORMATION

An old trunk of olive
grew like a pillar on the building plot,
and I laid out our bedroom round that tree,
lined up the stone walls, built the walls and roof,
gave it a doorway and smooth-fitting doors.
Then I lopped off the silvery leaves and branches,
hewed and shaped that stump from the roots up
into a bedpost, drilled it, let it serve
as model for the rest. I planed them all,
inlaid them all with silver, gold, and ivory,
and stretched a bed between—a pliant web
of oxhide thongs dyed crimson.
There's our sign!
I know no more. Could someone else's hand
have sawn that trunk and dragged the frame away?"

Their secret! as she heard it told, her knees
grew tremulous and weak, her heart failed her.
With eyes brimming tears she ran to him,
throwing her arms around his neck, and kissed him,
murmuring:

NOTES

CLOSER LOOK

Understanding Resolution

Students may have marked lines 1619–1623 during their first read. Use these lines to help students understand the resolution of a plot. Encourage them to talk about the annotations that they marked. You may want to model a close read with the class based on the highlights shown in the text.

ANNOTATE: Have students mark details in lines 1619–1623 that help students understand the resolution of conflict.

QUESTION: Guide students to consider what these details might tell them. Ask what readers can infer from the details that describe the state of Odysseus's and Penelope's lives, and accept student responses.

Possible response: I think these details indicate that Odysseus is once more master of his house and reunited in love with Penelope.

CONCLUDE: Help students formulate conclusions about the importance of these details in the text. Ask students why the author might have included these details.

Possible response: I believe Odysseus's final conflict is resolved.

Remind students that the **resolution** is the part of a plot in which the conflict is resolved. A narrative's **plot,** or sequence of events, is usually divided into five parts: the exposition; the rising action; the climax; the falling action; and the resolution, or denouement. During the **falling action,** the conflict lessens and moves toward the resolution, which affirms a peaceful solution of the conflict.

NOTES

"Do not rage at me, Odysseus!
No one ever matched your caution! Think
what difficulty the gods gave: they denied us
life together in our prime and flowering years,
kept us from crossing into age together.
Forgive me, don't be angry. I could not
welcome you with love on sight! I armed myself
long ago against the frauds of men,
impostors who might come—and all those many
whose underhanded ways bring evil on! . . .
But here and now, what sign could be so clear
as this of our own bed?
No other man has ever laid eyes on it—
only my own slave, Actoris, that my father
sent with me as a gift—she kept our door.
You make my stiff heart know that I am yours."

Now from his breast into his eyes the ache
of longing mounted, and he wept at last,
his dear wife, clear and faithful, in his arms,
longed for as the sunwarmed earth is longed for by a
swimmer
spent in rough water where his ship went down
under Poseidon's blows, gale winds and tons of sea.
Few men can keep alive through a big surf
to crawl, clotted with brine, on kindly beaches
in joy, in joy, knowing the abyss[21] behind:
and so she too rejoiced, her gaze upon her husband,
her white arms round him pressed as though forever.

21. **abyss** (uh BIHS) *n.* ocean depths.

The Ending

Odysseus is reunited with his father. Athena commands that peace prevail between Odysseus and the relatives of the slain suitors. Odysseus has regained his family and his kingdom.

616 UNIT 5 • JOURNEYS OF TRANSFORMATION

Comprehension Check

Complete the following items after you finish your first read.

1. After twenty years, how does Odysseus finally get home?

2. What are Antinous and the others doing in Odysseus' house?

3. What test does Penelope use to choose a husband from among the suitors?

4. Notebook Confirm your understanding of the text by writing a summary.

RESEARCH

Research to Explore This epic poem may spark your curiosity to read more. Briefly research other works by Homer. You may want to share what you discover with the class.

DIGITAL PERSPECTIVES

Comprehension Check

Possible responses:

1. After Odysseus tells his story to the Phaeacians, a Phaeacian nobleman conducts him home by ship.
2. Antinous and the other suitors are seeking Penelope's hand in marriage while they simultaneously overrun Odysseus's palace and enjoy Penelope's food and drink at her expense.
3. Penelope announces that whoever can string Odysseus's bow can marry her. Only the disguised Odysseus is able to accomplish this task.
4. After consulting with Athena, who warns him of the dangers that lie ahead for him, Odysseus returns to Ithaca in disguise as a poor, helpless old man and is recognized only by his faithful dog Argus. After revealing his identity to his son Telemachus, Odysseus shares his plan to fight the suitors who have taken over his home. When the "old man" enters his home, he is abused by the suitors. Penelope tells the "old man" how she has fended off the suitors for two decades, but now must get married to prevent Telemachus from losing his inheritance. Penelope tells the suitors she will marry the man who can string Odysseus's bow. While all the suitors fail at this task, Odysseus is able to string the bow. He pulls off his disguise and begins killing all the suitors with the help of Telemachus and two other servants. Afterward, Penelope, who is not sure if Odysseus is who he says he is, tests him on his knowledge of their marriage bed. Odysseus passes the test and is reunited with his wife.

Research

Research to Explore If students struggle to choose a research topic, you may want to suggest they focus on one of the following topics: Was the *Iliad* really written by Homer? What Homeric influences are included in Virgil's *Aeneid*? Compare monsters in the *Odyssey* and other epic poems, such as *Beowulf*.

PERSONALIZE FOR LEARNING

Challenge

Appearance Appearance plays a key role in Part 2 of the *Odyssey*. Odysseus uses a disguise to gain an advantage over the suitors before his attack. Athena's transformation of him from an older to a more youthful man makes it difficult for Penelope to recognize him, resulting in her testing him with their secret. Have students create images of both appearances of Odysseus, either by hand or on a computer. Encourage them to use authentic details in the clothing. Have them share their images with the class. Invite them to discuss whether someone's appearance should be a judgment of his or her abilities or identity.

Jump Start

CLOSE READ How do you behave when you are a guest in someone's home? How do you expect people to behave when visiting your home? As students discuss the prompt in their groups, remind them that the Greek concept of hospitality was very important in Greek culture. How did this cultural practice influence this part of the *Odyssey*?

Close Read the Text

Walk students through the annotation model on the student page. Encourage them to complete items 2 and 3 on their own. Review and discuss the sections students have marked. If needed, continue to model close reading by using the Annotation Highlights in the Interactive Teacher's Edition.

Analyze the Text

Possible responses:

1. (a) Antinous verbally abuses Odysseus and throws a chair at him, hitting his shoulder. **DOK 1** (b) Odysseus intended on killing the suitors for all their abuses and insults to his home before he even entered the hall. By provoking Antinous, Odysseus is able to validate his killing him without warning. **DOK 3**
2. (a) The suitors plundered his house and pressured Penelope to marry one of them. **DOK 1** (b) Odysseus cares more about his honor being offended than the suitors stealing his food and drink. The suitors offended his honor when they abused their role as guests in his home, squandering his food and pressuring Penelope to marry one of them while Odysseus was still alive. **DOK 2**
3. Responses will vary. **DOK 1**

FORMATIVE ASSESSMENT

Analyze the Text

If students fail to cite evidence, **then** remind them to support their ideas with specific details from the text.

MAKING MEANING

from the *ODYSSEY*, PART 2

Close Read the Text

1. This model, from lines 1116–1132 of the text, shows two sample annotations, along with questions and conclusions. Close read the passage and find another detail to annotate. Then, write a question and your conclusion.

ANNOTATE · QUESTION · Close Read · CONCLUDE

ANNOTATE: Odysseus describes in vivid language what Telemachus should do if the suitors mistreat his father.

QUESTION: What effect does the author's use of vivid language have on the reader?

CONCLUDE: The vivid language helps the reader imagine how Telemachus will feel.

Here is your part: at break of day tomorrow / home with you, go mingle with our princes. / The swineherd later on will take me down / the port-side trail—a beggar, by my looks, / hangdog and old. If they make fun of me / in my own courtyard, let your ribs cage up / your springing heart, no matter what I suffer, / no matter if they pull me by the heels or practice shots at me, to drive me out.

ANNOTATE: This phrase is repeated.

QUESTION: Why does the author repeat the phrase *no matter?*

CONCLUDE: The repetition emphasizes the many types of injustices that Odysseus is likely to face when the suitors mistreat him.

Tool Kit
Close-Read Guide and Model Annotation

2. For more practice, go back into the text and complete the close-read notes.
3. Revisit a section of the text you found important during your first read. Read this section closely, and **annotate** what you notice. Ask yourself **questions** such as "Why did the author make this choice?" What can you **conclude**?

Analyze the Text

CITE TEXTUAL EVIDENCE to support your answers.

Notebook Respond to these questions.

1. (a) Describe Antinous' treatment of Odysseus. (b) **Analyze** Why does Odysseus provoke Antinous to behave badly?
2. (a) What reasons does Odysseus give for taking revenge on the suitors? (b) **Interpret** Did Odysseus care more about what the suitors had stolen from him or about how they offended his honor? Explain.
3. **Essential Question** *What can we learn from a journey?* What have you learned about what a journey can teach people by reading this epic poem?

STANDARDS
Reading Literature
Analyze a particular point of view or cultural experience reflected in a work of literature from outside the United States, drawing on a wide reading of world literature.

PERSONALIZE FOR LEARNING

Strategic Support

Exclamation Points If students are struggling to understand the use of an exclamation point, explain that this punctuation mark is used to express heightened emotion, such as excitement, surprise, and anger. Have students read sentences aloud that use an exclamation point as end punctuation. For example, in lines 1043–1044, Telemachus exclaims, "I swear you were in rags and old, / and here you stand like one of the immortals!" Have students read the sentence with a period as end punctuation and discuss the difference in delivery. Then encourage students to write sentences with and without the exclamation point and compare the differences.

Analyze Craft and Structure

Figurative Language Literature from the oral tradition is full of vivid language that made the works memorable and brought characters, settings, and events alive for listeners. **Figurative language** is language that is used imaginatively rather than literally. There are many types of figurative language, including metaphors, similes, and personification. A special form of simile—the epic simile—is particularly important in Homer's writing.

- A **simile** is a comparison of two fundamentally different things using the words *like* or *as*. For example, you might say that someone's eyes are "as blue as the sky." Similes usually suggest some quality other than the one that is directly stated. In this case, the simile suggests that the eyes are also lovely, like the sky. The same quality of loveliness would not be implied if the eyes were compared to a blue mailbox.
- An **epic simile** is an elaborate simile that may continue for several lines. Unlike a regular simile, which draws a relatively limited comparison and creates a single image, an epic simile might recall an entire place or story. In lines 1061–1065 of Part 2, the poet uses an epic simile to describe the cries of Odysseus and Telemachus when they are reunited.

> Telemachus began to weep. Salt tears
> rose from the wells of longing in both men,
> and cries burst from both as keen and fluttering
> as those of the great taloned hawk,
> whose nestlings farmers take before they fly.

Practice

CITE TEXTUAL EVIDENCE to support your answers.

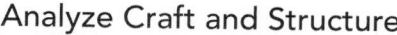

Notebook Respond to these questions.

1. (a) Reread the epic simile in lines 1535–1539. Identify the two things being compared. (b) Explain why this is an effective simile.
2. (a) Use the chart to analyze the epic simile in lines 1613–1623. (b) Explain how Odysseus' feelings are like those of the swimmer.

THINGS BEING COMPARED	DETAILS OF SIMILE	PURPOSE
The safety and warmth of being held in Penelope's arms to the safety and warmth of a beach for a seaman	Odysseus being held in Penelope's arms. Her love is clear and faithful. He is like the swimmer who has finally reached land. The abyss is the sea.	To show how Penelope makes Odysseus feel safe at last from harm.

DIGITAL PERSPECTIVES

Analyze Craft and Structure

Figurative Language In addition to adding depth and power to the narrative, the use of figurative language is common in epic poems that were recited in the oral tradition. Ask students, *How did the epic simile contribute to listeners' understanding of images and actions described in an epic poem?*

Explain to students that an epic simile is also called a Homeric simile. Have students discuss why they think this is so. Encourage students to discuss other poets who use epic similes in their work. For more support, see **Analyze Craft and Structure: Figurative Language**

MAKE IT INTERACTIVE

Have students pick an image they would like to describe in free verse as a class. Have a student write a line on a piece of paper with a simile in it. Then have another student write a second line that continues the simile. Then have a third student continue the simile with a third line, and so on until each student has contributed to the epic simile. Read the poem aloud to the whole class. Encourage students to visualize the image the simile inspires.

Practice

Possible responses:

1. (a) The suitors heaped upon each other are compared to a fisherman's catch spread out on the beach. (b) This is an effective simile because it has an underlying suggestion that both the fish and the suitors are flailing in the throes of death with no ability to change their circumstances.
2. See possible responses in chart on student page.

FORMATIVE ASSESSMENT

Formative Assessment: Analyze Craft and Structure

If students struggle to understand epic simile, **then** have them close read examples from the text. For Reteach and Practice, see **Analyze Craft and Structure: Figurative Language (RP).**

PERSONALIZE FOR LEARNING

English Language Support

Figurative Language Have English learners write an epic simile in free verse. Ask students to explain specific phrases and word choices using figurative language and the different effects these words have on the simile. **EMERGING**

Ask students to explain specific phrases and word choices using figurative language or words with multiple meanings and the different effects these words have on the simile. **EXPANDING**

Ask students to explain different types of phrases and word choices such as hyperbole and the different effects these words have on the simile. **BRIDGING**

To extend the activity, ask students to rewrite their similes for two different audiences—one audience of young children, and another audience of high school students. **ALL LEVELS,**

TEACHING

Concept Vocabulary

Why These Words

Possible responses:

1. All of the concept words mean some form of deceit, whether it be confusing someone (*bemusing*), creating a deceptive plan (*guise*, *craft*), feeling lied to (*deceived*), hiding feelings (*dissemble*); or not being able to believe something (*incredulity*). These words support the plot of deception that Odysseus contrives on his return.
2. honesty: *noble* (line 1030), *true* (line 1280), *honor* (line 1292); dishonesty: *tricks* (line 1090), *corrupted* (line 1160), *secret* (line 1577)

Practice

Possible responses:

1. Responses will vary.
2. Responses will vary.

Word Network

Possible words: *landways, seaways, distant, wanderings, seafarers, passage*

Word Study

For more support, see **Concept Vocabulary and Word Study.**

Possible responses:

1. *Dissemble* means "disguise or conceal."
2. *resemble*: to look like something or someone else; *similar*: nearly the same as something or someone else; *simulation*: something that is made to look or act like something else

---

FORMATIVE ASSESSMENT

Concept Vocabulary

If students struggle to understand the concept vocabulary, **then** have them close read the text where they appear and look for context clues.

Word Study

If students struggle to understand the Latin root *-sem-*, *-sim-*, **then** have them review words in the dictionary with the same Latin root. For Reteach and Practice, see **Word Study: Latin Root *-sem-*, *-sim-* (RP).**

LANGUAGE DEVELOPMENT

from the ODYSSEY, PART 2

Concept Vocabulary

craft	incredulity	guise
dissemble	bemusing	deceived

Why These Words? These concept words relate to ideas about honesty and dishonesty. When Athena tells Odysseus, "*dissemble* to your son no longer," she is telling him to stop pretending that he is a beggar and let his son know the truth. When Homer tells us that Telemachus is "wild with *incredulity*," he is saying that Telemachus cannot believe what Odysseus is telling him.

1. How does the concept vocabulary help readers understand the various layers of pretending and lying in Part 2 of the *Odyssey*?
2. What other words in the selection connect to the concepts of honesty and dishonesty?

Practice

Notebook The concept vocabulary words appear in Part 2 of the *Odyssey*.

1. Use each concept word in a sentence that demonstrates your understanding of the word's meaning.
2. In three of your sentences, challenge yourself to replace the concept word with one or two synonyms. How does the word change affect the meaning of your sentence? For example, which sentence is more descriptive?

WORD NETWORK

Add interesting words related to journeys from the text to your Word Network.

Word Study

Latin Root: *-sem-* *-sim-* The Latin root *-sim-* means "seem" or "like." In a few instances, such as in the word *dissemble*, the root is spelled with an *e* rather than an *i*.

1. Write a definition of *dissemble* based on your understanding of its root and context clues from the text.
2. Define these words that contain the same root: *resemble, similar, simulation*. Use a dictionary to verify your definitions.

STANDARDS

Language

- Demonstrate command of the conventions of standard English grammar and usage when writing or speaking.
- Apply knowledge of language to understand how language functions in different contexts, to make effective choices for meaning or style, and to comprehend more fully when reading or listening.
- Identify and correctly use patterns of word changes that indicate different meanings or parts of speech.

AUTHOR'S PERSPECTIVE Elfrieda Hiebert, Ph.D.

Digital Tools As students develop and expand their word networks, remind them of the digital tools available and of their value. Explain what digital tools offer—pronunciation; audio; word families; definitions; links to synonyms and antonyms; interactive levels of complexity of synonyms and antonyms; words in context sentences. Using digital tools to access word families is especially helpful in a cross-cultural context. A word family for science, for instance, might include the words *botanist, chemist, geneticist, neurologist, nutritionist, physicist, zoologist,* as they all end with the suffix *–ist*. A word family for westward expansion might be organized around the common concept, and so include the words *settler, heritage, mission,* and *manifest destiny.* To conclude, help students understand that digital tools also have drawbacks. For instance, the word family feature doesn't show how the words are related in meaning, only in sound.

Author's Style

Word Order The order of words in a sentence varies from language to language, but it is usually very predictable within a language. In English, the subject of a sentence usually precedes the verb, unless the sentence is a question. Adjectives usually precede the nouns they modify. Adverbs usually follow the verbs they modify.

Most people do not notice word order unless it is changed. Poets often invert words, or reverse their positions, for the sake of meter, rhyme, or emphasis. The reversal of the normal word order in a sentence is known as **inverted word order.**

Both Homer and Robert Fitzgerald, the translator of this version of the epic, sometimes use inverted word order. One of the reasons Fitzgerald's translation of the *Odyssey* is easier to read than other translations is that he does not use inverted word order very often. When he does, he has a purpose. For example, line 1145 states, "One better reason, too, I had from Zeus." In this line, Fitzgerald emphasizes "one better reason" by putting it first.

Read It

Use this chart to identify the word or phrase in each passage from the *Odyssey* that is not in the predictable order.

PASSAGE	WORDS NOT IN PREDICTABLE ORDER
Lithe and young she made him, *ruddy with sun, his jawline clean, the beard* *no longer gray upon his chin.* *(lines 1018–1020)*	Lithe and young she made him
When he had spoken, down he sat. *(line 1059)*	down
They seemed no longer those *bright arms Odysseus left us years ago* *when he went off to Troy.* *(lines 1141–1143)*	seemed no longer
Now flashed *arrow from twanging bow clean as a whistle* *through every socket ring, and grazed not one,* *to thud with heavy brazen head beyond.* *(lines 1389–1392)*	clean as a whistle through every socket ring; with heavy brazen head beyond

Write It

Notebook Rewrite each passage in the chart so that the words are in the usual order. Consider how the rewritten passages are different and whether they have the same power.

DIGITAL PERSPECTIVES

Author's Style

Word Order

Remind students that *syntax* is another term for word order, or the way words are organized. Explain that syntax is especially important to the study of poetry because the poet often experiments with word order to create a particular effect or highlight specific ideas. Tell students that when they first read a poem, they may need to rearrange words to understand what the poet is saying. For more support, see **Author's Style: Word Order.**

MAKE IT INTERACTIVE

Have students write a sentence on index cards, using one card for each word. Then have them move the cards around to invert the order of the words to create a new sentence. Have students share their work with the class.

Read It

See possible responses in chart on student page.

Write It

Possible response:

She made him lithe and young, ruddy with sun, his jawline clean, the beard upon his chin no longer gray. When he had spoken, he sat down. They no longer seemed those bright arms Odysseus left us years ago when he went off to Troy. Now flashed arrow from twanging bow ring clean as a whistle through every socket, and grazed not one, to thud beyond with heavy brazen head. Although the sentences are easier to read, they do not flow as well.

FORMATIVE ASSESSMENT

Author's Style

If students struggle to understand word order, **then** have them locate the subject and the verb to make meaning of the thought. For Reteach and Practice, see **Author's Style: Word Order (RP).**

PERSONALIZE FOR LEARNING

Strategic Support

Compare Explain to students that the *Odyssey* has been translated by many writers. The original Homeric Greek is written in hexameter, or six beats to a line, to create a fast pace. However, Homeric Greek does not translate well into English using that format, so writers have used other forms of poetic verse.

For example, Alexander Pope translated the epic poem in iambic pentameter, or five beats to a line.

Have students do an Internet search on the Project Gutenberg web site for Pope's translation of the *Odyssey*. Then have students compare one stanza by Pope to that of the text they are reading.

Encourage them to discuss which version is easier for them to understand or visualize. Then have students rewrite one stanza from Part 1 or Part 2 of the *Odyssey* in everyday language. Encourage them to use current slang terms. Invite them to share their work with the class.

Writing to Sources

Explain to students that when they write a biography, they should focus on gathering factual information on a person's life. Most biographies are written about famous people—historical and contemporary—but they can also be written about ordinary people.

Remind students that a writer of biographies is called a biographer. One way biographers can strengthen a biography is by including material about their subject's youth, birthplace, and experiences. Discuss with students how examining social and environmental influences on a person helps biographers draw inferences about that person's character and behavior when he or she becomes an adult. Ask students why focusing on key events in a subject's life and examining how that person's response to a crisis might be informative to readers. For more support, see **Writing to Sources: Biography.**

Reflect on Your Writing

Possible responses:

1. **Responses will vary.** If students need support, ask them to consider the insights they gained in understanding Odysseus through his actions and motivations.
2. **Responses will vary.** Be sure that students make connections between the important events in Odysseus's life and the evidence they cite.
3. **Why These Words? Responses will vary.** Have students list specific examples of words they have chosen that add power to their review.

FORMATIVE ASSESSMENT

Writing to Sources

If students struggle to write Odysseus's biography, **then** have them close read the text and make notes of events in Odysseus's life. For Reteach and Practice, see **Writing to Sources: Biography (RP).**

EFFECTIVE EXPRESSION

from the ODYSSEY, PART 2

Writing to Sources

A biography is a type of informative text in which the writer tells the life story of another person. Writers of biographies often include narrative elements such as character development, descriptions of settings, and plot sequences to capture and hold the reader's attention.

Assignment

Write a short **biography** of Odysseus based on details presented in the *Odyssey*. Include the basic facts of the hero's life and adventures, including his important relationships, and hold your reader's attention by describing dramatic situations in detail. Use the following guidelines:

- List events from the *Odyssey* that are suitable for your biography. Focus on events that reveal the character of Odysseus.
- Include quotations from the epic to add detail and depth.
- Share your biography with classmates, and compare the events you each chose to include. In your discussion, consider what makes some events more significant than others.
- Based on your discussion with classmates, consider whether your version of Odysseus' life is complete, accurate, and interesting to readers. Revise your work as needed.

Vocabulary and Conventions Connection Include several of the concept vocabulary words in your biography. Consider using inverted word order at certain points in your biography to call the reader's attention to significant events in Odysseus' life.

craft	incredulity	guise
dissemble	bemusing	deceived

Reflect on Your Writing

After you have written your biography, answer these questions.

1. How do you think writing your biography strengthened your understanding of the epic?
2. What advice would you give to another student writing a biography of a heroic figure?
3. **Why These Words?** The words you choose make a difference in your writing. Which words did you specifically choose to add power to your biography?

STANDARDS

Writing
Produce clear and coherent writing in which the development, organization, and style are appropriate to task, purpose, and audience.

Speaking and Listening
• Initiate and participate effectively in a range of collaborative discussions with diverse partners on *grades 9–10 topics, texts, and issues,* building on others' ideas and expressing their own clearly and persuasively.
• Evaluate a speaker's point of view, reasoning, and use of evidence and rhetoric, identifying any fallacious reasoning or exaggerated or distorted evidence.

PERSONALIZE FOR LEARNING

English Language Support

Planning a Biography Have students write a list of questions that they would ask the subject of a historical biography.

Remind pairs of students about the kinds of information that should be included in a biography. **EMERGING**

Have students write mostly open-ended questions and consider the kinds of contextual information that should be included in a complete biography of the subject. **EXPANDING**

Have pairs of students also create a list of other people they might speak to in order to gather information. Ask partners to then write an outline for the biography. **BRIDGING**

An expanded **English Language Support Lesson** on Biography is available in the Interactive Teacher's Edition.

Speaking and Listening

Assignment

Conduct a **debate** to decide whether Odysseus should be prosecuted for the murders of Penelope's suitors.

- Volunteers should make up opposing teams. One team will argue the affirmative—that Odysseus should be prosecuted—and the other will argue the negative. Each team will present an oral argument, stating its position and supporting it with text evidence.
- A panel of judges or the class as a whole can evaluate the arguments and decide which one has the most effective support.

First, reread the selection. Identify specific text details that relate to the murder of the suitors. Then, follow these steps to complete the assignment.

1. **State and Support the Position** Both affirmative and negative teams should prepare clear position statements and support these statements with strong reasons and relevant evidence from Part 2 of the *Odyssey*.
2. **Refute the Opposing Position** Both teams should also prepare arguments against the opposing team's position, using strong reasons and relevant text evidence to refute the position.
3. **Develop the Argument** Consider how to best organize the information in the argument. Plan to include an introduction to the issue, a body that conveys the main argument, and a conclusion that summarizes the position.
4. **Prepare Your Delivery** Practice delivering the oral argument to the judges. Include the following performance techniques to make the argument convincing:
   - Speak clearly, in an appropriate tone, and at an appropriate volume and rate.
   - Use appropriate facial expressions and gestures to convey your conviction.
5. **Evaluate Responses** Listen carefully as each team delivers its argument. Use an evaluation guide like the one shown to evaluate the argument.

EVALUATION GUIDE

Rate each statement on a scale of 1 (not demonstrated) to 5 (demonstrated).

☐ The position was clearly stated in the oral argument.

☐ The position was supported with relevant text evidence.

☐ The opposing team's position was clearly stated and effectively refuted.

☐ Debaters used appropriate facial expressions, gestures, and eye contact.

EVIDENCE LOG

Before moving on to a new selection, go to your Evidence Log and record what you learned from Part 2 of the *Odyssey*.

PERSONALIZE FOR LEARNING

English Language Support

Have students work in pairs and chose a familiar social or academic topic and research it for a brief oral presentation.

Ask pairs to demonstrate comprehension of oral presentations by each asking and answering questions, with prompting and support. **EMERGING**

Ask pairs to demonstrate comprehension of oral presentations by each answering and asking questions that show thoughtful consideration of ideas and arguments, with minimal prompting and support. **EXPANDING**

Ask pairs to demonstrate comprehension of oral presentations by each answering and asking detailed and complex questions that show thoughtful consideration of ideas and arguments, with light prompting and support. **BRIDGING**

DIGITAL PERSPECTIVES

Speaking and Listening

1. **State and Support the Position** Remind students that when writing their position statements, they should read them aloud to hear if any wording needs to be revised for clarity or meaning.
2. **Refute the Opposing Position** Have students examine every opposing argument before the debate so they will be prepared to refute the opposing position when appropriate. Remind students that debates are designed to be logical in their presentations and arguments. Encourage students to keep composed in their delivery and to avoid emotional pleas or responses.
3. **Develop the Argument** If students struggle to remember their argument, have them take notes on index cards or electronic devices to refer to during the debate.
4. **Prepare Your Delivery** Encourage students to videotape their practice sessions and review them before the debate to see how they can improve their performance.
5. **Evaluate Responses** Encourage students to make at least one supportive comment about each presentation.

For more support, see **Speaking and Listening: Debate.**

Evidence Log Support students in completing their Evidence Log. This paced activity will help prepare them for the Performance-Based Assessment at the end of the unit.

FORMATIVE ASSESSMENT

Speaking and Listening

- **If** students struggle to find supportive evidence for their position, **then** have them close read the text with their position statement in mind.
- **If** students are nervous speaking in front of others, **then** have them practice their debate material in front of friends or family members.

For Reteach and Practice, see **Speaking and Listening: Debate (RP).**

Selection Test

Administer the "*from the* Odyssey, Part 2 (*with an excerpt from* The Odyssey: A Graphic Novel)" Selection Test, which is available in both print and digital formats online in Assessments.

from The Odyssey: A Graphic Novel

AUDIO SUMMARIES
Audio summaries of the excerpt from "The Odyssey: A Graphic Novel" are available online in both English and Spanish in the Interactive Teacher's Edition or Unit Resources. Assigning these summaries prior to reading the selection may help students build additional background knowledge and set a context for their first read.

Summary

In this excerpt from "The Odyssey: A Graphic Novel" by Gareth Hinds, Odysseus has left the company of Circe, a bewitching, powerful immortal who temporarily turned many of Odysseus's men into swine. He and his crew leave for Erebus—or the Land of the Dead—to consult with Tiresias, a long-dead, great seer. Tiresias tells Odysseus that to return to his home in Ithaca, he and his men must not disturb cattle belonging to Helios, the sun god. Tiresias also tells Odysseus what to do once he arrives home. Odysseus must kill the men who have overtaken his home trying to win favor with his wife, Penelope. Then, he must travel inland to a place where men know nothing of ships and the sea and make a sacrifice to Poseidon to make amends for putting out the eye of his son, the Cyclops Polyphemus.

Insight

Reading the excerpt from "The Odyssey: A Graphic Novel" helps students visualize those who reside in the Land of the Dead as well as better understand the struggles and adventures Odysseus encounters as he tries to return home after defeating the Trojans in battle.

ESSENTIAL QUESTION:
What can we learn from a journey?

Connection to Essential Question

This excerpt from "The Odyssey: A Graphic Novel" presents a clear connection to the Essential Question, "What can we learn from a journey?" In this excerpt of the graphic novel, Odysseus literally learns what he must do in order to return home to Ithaca. He also learns steps he must take to live peacefully once he arrives. This information is crucial to Odysseus's return home.

WHOLE-CLASS LEARNING PERFORMANCE TASK
How are personal strengths and weaknesses magnified during the course of a journey at sea?

UNIT PERFORMANCE-BASED ASSESSMENT
When does the journey matter more than the destination?

Connection to Performance Tasks

Whole-Class Learning Performance Task In this Performance Task, students will write an explanatory essay about how personal strengths and weaknesses can shape a journey. This selection shows that Odysseus was capable of following Circe's instructions about how to reach the Land of the Dead and whom to contact—and how—once he arrives. Readers also learn of another one of Odysseus's strengths, his loyalty, as he promises to properly honor his fallen comrade.

Unit Performance-Based Assessment Odysseus's journey and destination are closely linked in this selection, as his years-long journey ultimately involves a series of destinations. This latest destination at the Land of the Dead is where Odysseus learns valuable information for the journey to the final destination on his quest—his home in Ithaca. Odysseus must stop at the Land of the Dead in order to successfully complete the last part of his journey.

DIGITAL PERSPECTIVES | Audio | Video | Document | Annotation Highlights | EL Highlights | Online Assessment

LESSON RESOURCES

	Making Meaning	Language Development	Effective Expression
Lesson	**First Review** **Close Review** **Analyze the Media**	**Media Vocabulary**	**Writing to Compare**
Instructional Standards	**RL.10** By the end of grade 9, read and comprehend literature . . .	**L.6** Acquire and use accurately general academic and domain-specific words and phrases . . .	**RL.7** Analyze the representation of a subject or a key scene . . . **RL.9** Analyze how an author draws on and transforms . . . **W.1.a** Introduce precise claim(s) . . . **W.9.a** Apply grades 9–10 Reading standards . . .
STUDENT RESOURCES			
Available online in the Interactive Student Edition or Unit Resources	Selection Audio First-Review Guide: Media-Art and Photography Close- Review Guide: Media- Art and Photography	Word Network	Evidence Log
TEACHER RESOURCES			
Selection Resources Available online in the Interactive Teacher's Edition or Unit Resources	Audio Summaries	Media Vocabulary	Writing to Compare: Review
Assessment Available online in Assessments	Selection Test		
My Resources	A Unit 5 Answer Key is available online and in the Interactive Teacher's Edition.		

Media Complexity Rubric: *from* The Odyssey: A Graphic Novel

Quantitative Measures	
3-page Graphic Novel	
Qualitative Measures	
Knowledge Demands ① ② ③ **❹** ⑤	To fully understand events shown, students may need additional context about the *Odyssey* and Ancient Greek culture. Selection refers to characters in the epic poem.
Structure ① **❷** ③ ④ ⑤	The selection is an excerpt from a paneled graphic novel. Narrative is presented in a mostly linear fashion with one flashback episode. Details are revealed through dialogue and accompanying illustrations.
Language Conventionality and Clarity ① ② **❸** ④ ⑤	Language is mostly straightforward, literal, and explicit; vocabulary is largely contemporary and familiar, with instances of archaic language and Greek names; multiple sentences have complex constructions.
Levels of Meaning/Purpose ① **❷** ③ ④ ⑤	Purpose is explicit, clear, and concrete; content is narrowly focused on one event.

Jump Start

FIRST REVIEW Ask students to consider the following prompt: How do illustrations affect the way you read a text? Encourage students to think about their personal experiences reading pieces with and without illustrations. Have them discuss whether the presence of illustrations limits the reader's imagination.

from The Odyssey: A Graphic Novel

What is the purpose of adapting a text like the *Odyssey?* How does the adaptation enhance or change your understanding of the text? Modeling the questions readers might ask as they review "The Odyssey: A Graphic Novel" brings the graphic novel alive for students and connects it to the Whole-Class Performance Task assignment. Selection audio is available in the Interactive Teacher's Edition.

Media Vocabulary

Encourage students to discuss the media vocabulary. Have they seen or heard the terms used before? Have they ever used the terms to speak about graphic novels or similar media?

FIRST REVIEW

Have students perform the steps of the first review:

LOOK: Remind students to pay attention to the interaction of text and artwork in panels which contain both.

NOTE: Encourage students to note panels which they find especially visually interesting.

CONNECT: Encourage students to make connections beyond the graphic novel. If they cannot make connections to their own lives, have them consider other graphic novels or comics they may have read.

RESPOND: Students will answer questions and write a summary to demonstrate understanding.

Point out to students that while they will always complete the Respond step at the end of the first read, the other steps will probably happen somewhat concurrently. You may wish to print copies of the **First-Review Guide: Media Art/Photography** for students to use.

MAKING MEANING

from the ODYSSEY

Comparing Texts

The illustrations on the following pages are taken from *The Odyssey: A Graphic Novel*, by Gareth Hinds. While reviewing this selection, you will consider how verbal and visual texts tell a story in different ways.

from THE ODYSSEY: A GRAPHIC NOVEL

About the Author

Gareth Hinds (b. 1971) grew up in Vermont as a self-described "nerdy kid" who drew a lot and was fascinated by mixed martial arts. After graduating from the Parsons School of Design in New York, Hinds began working on video games before turning his attention to writing and illustrating graphic novels, including *Beowulf, King Lear, The Merchant of Venice*, and *Romeo and Juliet*. He is a recipient of the Boston Public Library's "Literary Lights for Children" award.

from The Odyssey: A Graphic Novel

Media Vocabulary

The following words or concepts will be useful to you as you analyze, discuss, and write about graphic novels.

panel: one of the drawings on a page, usually framed by a border	• A single panel usually contains one piece of the action or one bit of information.
splash: large, full-page illustration	• Often, a splash is used to begin a story. • A splash used within a story adds emphasis and visual impact.
tier: row of panels	• A tier can contain several panels or just one.
gutter: space between panels	• A gutter indicates change of place, time, or action.
caption: words in a separate box	• A caption is usually used to contain the words of the narrator, the person who is telling the story.
speech bubble: rounded shape containing a character's words	• The speech bubble usually has a small tail that points to the character that is speaking.

STANDARDS

Reading Literature
By the end of grade 9, read and comprehend literature, including stories, dramas, and poems, in the grades 9–10 text complexity band proficiently, with scaffolding as needed at the high end of the range.

Language
Acquire and use accurately general academic and domain-specific words and phrases, sufficient for reading, writing, speaking, and listening at the college and career readiness level; demonstrate independence in gathering vocabulary knowledge when considering a word or phrase important to comprehension or expression.

First Review MEDIA: GRAPHIC NOVEL

Apply these strategies as you conduct your first review. You will have an opportunity to complete a close review after your first read.

LOOK at each image and determine *whom* or *what* it portrays.

NOTE elements in each panel that you find interesting and want to revisit.

First Review

CONNECT details in the images to other media you've experienced, texts you've read, or images you've seen.

RESPOND by completing the Comprehension Check and by writing a brief summary of the selection.

DIGITAL PERSPECTIVES

CONTENTS

SHORT STORY

The Return

Ngugi wa Thiong'o

After five years as a political prisoner, how will Kamau be welcomed back to his village?

INTERVIEW

from The Hero's Adventure

from The Power of Myth

Joseph Campbell and Bill Moyers

Is the hero's journey one we all experience?

POETRY COLLECTION 1

Courage *Anne Sexton*

Ithaka *C. P. Cavafy, translated by Edmund Keeley and Philip Sherrard*

from The Narrow Road of the Interior

Matsuo Bashō, translated by Helen Craig McCullough

In what ways is life itself a journey into the unknown?

PERFORMANCE TASK

SPEAKING AND LISTENING FOCUS

Deliver a Multimedia Presentation

The Small-Group readings feature journeys that are physical or emotional or both. After reading, your group will plan and deliver a multimedia presentation about journeys that involve no travel.

Contents

Selections Circulate among groups as they preview the selections. You might encourage groups to discuss any knowledge they already have about any of the selections or the situations and settings shown in the photographs. Students may wish to take a poll within their group to determine which selections look the most interesting.

Remind students that communicating and collaborating in groups is an important skill that they will use throughout their lives—in school, in their careers, and in their community.

Performance Task

Deliver a Multimedia Presentation Give groups time to read about and briefly discuss the multimedia presentation they will create after reading. Encourage students to do some preliminary thinking about the types of media they may want to use. This may help focus their subsequent reading and group discussion.

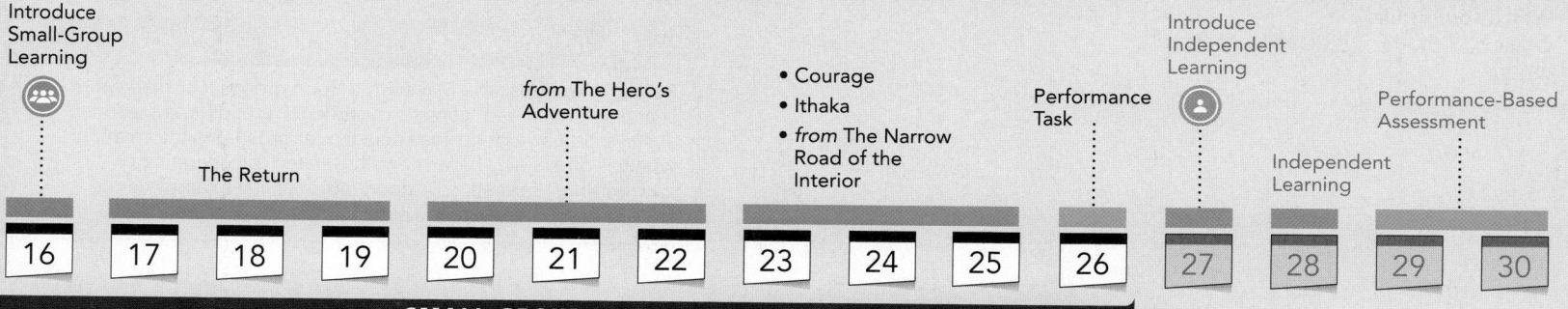

Introduce Small-Group Learning — 16

The Return — 17, 18, 19

from The Hero's Adventure — 20, 21, 22

- Courage
- Ithaka
- *from* The Narrow Road of the Interior

— 23, 24, 25

Performance Task — 26

SMALL-GROUP LEARNING

Introduce Independent Learning — 27

Independent Learning — 28

Performance-Based Assessment — 29, 30

OVERVIEW

SMALL-GROUP LEARNING

Working as a Team

1. **Take a Position** Remind groups to let all members share their responses. You may wish to set a time limit for this discussion.
2. **List Your Rules** You may want to have groups share their lists of rules and consolidate them into a master list to be displayed and followed by all groups.
3. **Apply the Rules** As you circulate among the groups, ensure that students are staying on task. Consider a short time limit for this step.
4. **Name Your Group** This task can be creative and fun. If students have trouble coming up with a name, suggest that they think of something related to the unit topic. Encourage groups to share their names with the class.
5. **Create a Communication Plan** Encourage groups to include in their plans agreed-upon times during the day to share ideas. They should also devise a method for recording and saving their communications.

Accountable Talk

Remind students that groups should communicate politely. You can post these Accountable Talk suggestions and encourage students to add their own. Students should:

Remember to . . .
Ask clarifying questions.

Which sounds like . . .
Can you please repeat what you said?
Would you give me an example?
I think you said _____. Did I understand you correctly?

Remember to . . .
Explain your thinking.

Which sounds like . . .
I believe _____ is true because _____.

Remember to . . .
Build on the ideas of others.

Which sounds like . . .
When _____ said _____, it made me think of _____.

OVERVIEW: SMALL-GROUP LEARNING

Working as a Team

1. **Take a Position** In your group, discuss the following question:

   Why are some people reluctant to make a journey?

   As you take turns sharing your positions, be sure to provide reasons that support your ideas. After all group members have shared, discuss some of the reasons people have for their choices to start—or to avoid—a travel adventure.

2. **List Your Rules** As a group, decide on the rules that you will follow as you work together. Samples are provided; add two more of your own. You may add or revise rules based on your experience together.
   - Everyone should participate in group discussions.
   - People should not interrupt.
   - ______________________________
   - ______________________________

3. **Apply the Rules** Practice working as a group. Share what you have learned about journeys. Make sure each person in the group contributes. Take notes, and be prepared to share with the class one thing that you heard from another member of your group.

4. **Name Your Group** Choose a name that reflects the unit topic.

   Our group's name: ______________________________

5. **Create a Communication Plan** Decide how you want to communicate with one another. For example, you might use online collaboration tools, email, or instant messaging.

   Our group's decision: ______________________________

FACILITATING SMALL-GROUP LEARNING

Forming Groups You may wish to form groups for Small-Group Learning so that each consists of students with different learning abilities. Some students may be adept at organizing information whereas others may have strengths related to generating or synthesizing information. A good mix of abilities can make the experience of Small-Group Learning dynamic and productive.

Making a Schedule

First, find out the due dates for the small-group activities. Then, preview the texts and activities with your group, and make a schedule for completing the tasks.

SELECTION	ACTIVITIES	DUE DATE
The Return		
from The Hero's Adventure		
Courage Ithaka *from* The Narrow Road of the Interior		

Working on Group Projects

As your group works together, you'll find it more effective if each person has a specific role. Different projects require different roles. Before beginning a project, discuss the necessary roles, and choose one for each group member. Here are some possible roles; add your own ideas.

Project Manager: monitors the schedule and keeps everyone on task
Researcher: organizes research activities
Recorder: takes notes during group meetings

____

____

____

____

____

SCAN FOR MULTIMEDIA

DIGITAL PERSPECTIVES

Making a Schedule

Encourage groups to preview the reading selections and to consider how long it will take them to complete the activities accompanying each selection. Point out that they can adjust the due dates for particular selections as needed as they work on their small-group projects. However, they must complete all assigned tasks before the group Performance Task is due. Encourage groups to review their schedules upon the completion of the activities for each selection to make sure they are on track to meet the final due date.

Working on Group Projects

Point out to groups that different projects have different requirements. They should discuss roles assigned on previous projects and evaluate their usefulness. Groups should consider deleting one role or assigning at least one new role for this project. Review the importance of avoiding stereotyping and favoritism, then have students finalize the assigned roles within each group. Remind groups that they can re-evaluate and re-assign as they move toward completion of the project.

AUTHOR'S PERSPECTIVE **Kelly Gallagher, M.Ed.**

Accountability in Group Work The teacher's role during group work is to serve as the facilitator rather than as the leader. This means that the teacher should support the thinking and discussion, but not provide the answers or content direction. Problems can arise if a group is unfocused, if the task is not meaningful, or if there is no accountability. To help groups work together well, achieve their goals, and ensure accountability, teachers can follow these three steps:

1. First, define and clarify the task. Explain why it is valuable, and make sure students know what they are expected to do.
2. Provide strategies for accountability. Make sure that students clearly understand how they will be held responsible.
3. Pull the whole class back together to share back information and to check learning.

If groups struggle, teachers can prod them with questions that support how they will get to the answer. For example, if they are unable to find the main point of the essay, ask them: "*Where* might you find the main idea?"

The Return

AUDIO SUMMARIES
Audio summaries of "The Return" are available online in both English and Spanish and can be assigned to students in the Interactive Teacher's Edition or Unit Resources. Assigning these summaries prior to reading the selection may help students build additional background knowledge and set a context for their first read.

Summary

In this short story by Ngugi wa Thiong'o, Kamau returns home upon his release from a government prison camp. He walks wearily down roads that lead to his house outside of Nairobi, waiting for a familiar sign, finding none. Women who recognize him behave in a way that shows there is something he doesn't know. He hurries home, eager to see his wife, whom he had been married to for only a short while before his arrest, but he does not receive the reception he expects.

Insight

Kamau learns an important lesson about how upsetting change can be at first. He expects his life to be just as he left it, but he has to realize how his actions have affected others and brought about change he wasn't expecting.

ESSENTIAL QUESTION:
What can we learn from a journey?

Connection to Essential Question

"The Return" provides an interesting perspective on the Essential Question. Through his journey back to his hometown, Kamau has to reconcile his expectations with the reality of life in the village he has been absent from for years. This teaches him to accept change.

SMALL-GROUP LEARNING PERFORMANCE TASK
What different types of journeys are there and how can they transform someone?

UNIT PERFORMANCE-BASED ASSESSMENT
When does the journey matter more than the destination?

Connection to Performance Tasks

Small-Group Learning Task In this Performance Task, students will consider different types of journeys and how they can be transformative. Kamau's journey is really about learning to accept change, not learning from the physical journey itself.

Unit Performance-Based Assessment This selection will contribute to students' understanding of when a journey matters more than the destination. As he makes his way to his family, Kamau has to realize just how much his village has changed. When he finds his family, he receives very disappointing news. Dealing with his disappointment and accepting change becomes more important for Kamau than simply returning home.

DIGITAL PERSPECTIVES

Audio | Video | Document | Annotation Highlights | EL Highlights | Online Assessment

LESSON RESOURCES

	Making Meaning	Language Development	Effective Expression
Lesson	**First Read** **Close Read** **Analyze the Text** **Analyze Craft and Structure**	**Concept Vocabulary** **Word Study** **Conventions**	**Writing to Sources**
Instructional Standards	**RL.10** By the end of grade 9, read and comprehend literature . . . **RL.5** Analyze how an author's choices . . . **RL.6** Analyze a particular point of view or cultural experience . . .	**L.4** Determine or clarify the meaning of unknown and multiple-meaning words and phrases . . . **L.4.b** Identify and correctly use patterns of word changes . . . **L.5** Demonstrate understanding of figurative language . . . **L.1** Demonstrate command of the conventions . . .	**W.2** Write informative/ explanatory texts . . .
STUDENT RESOURCES			
Available online in the Interactive Student Edition or Unit Resources	Selection Audio First-Read Guide: Fiction	Word Network	Evidence Log
TEACHER RESOURCES			
Selection Resources Available online in the Interactive Teacher's Edition or Unit Resources	Audio Summaries Annotation Highlights EL Highlights English Language Support Lesson: Using Active and Passive Voice The Return: Text Question Analyze Craft and Structure: Plot Devices	Conventions: Active and Passive Voice Concept Vocabulary and Word Study	Writing to Sources
Reteach/Practice (RP) Available online in the Interactive Teacher's Edition or Unit Resources	Analyze Craft and Structure: Plot Devices (RP)	Conventions: Active and Passive Voice (RP) Word Study: Etymology: Suffix *-ine* (RP)	Writing to Sources (RP)
Assessment Available online in Assessments	Selection Test		
My Resources	A Unit 5 Answer Key is available online and in the Interactive Teacher's Edition.		

Reading Support

Text Complexity Rubric: The Return	
Quantitative Measures	
Lexile: 670 **Text Length:** 2,116 words	
Qualitative Measures	
Knowledge Demands ① ② ❸ ④ ⑤	A political conflict in rural Africa is at the center of the selection. Students may need additional context about African geography and history; however, characters reveal some information through dialogue and background information.
Structure ① ❷ ③ ④ ⑤	Story is told in a linear third-person narrative. The plot is simple; however, it refers to some past events.
Language Conventionality and Clarity ① ② ❸ ④ ⑤	Selection contains mostly literal and familiar language, with some figurative language. Complex sentence structures appear throughout the selection.
Levels of Meaning/Purpose ① ② ❸ ④ ⑤	The main idea of the selection is relatively easy to grasp. However, students must interpret a symbolic event.

DECIDE AND PLAN

English Language Support

Provide English Learners with support for structure and language as they read the selection.

Structure Complex sentences run throughout the text. If students have difficulty understanding complex sentences, reinforce the concept that combining clauses connects ideas in the text. This would be a good opportunity to review the conjunction *and*.

Language Work with students to help them understand how adjectives are included in noun phrases. These phrases, such as "monotonous murmurs," "homeward journey," and "serpentine movement," help create detailed sentences. Have students explain how the adjectives in these examples change how they understand the nouns in the text.

Strategic Support

Provide students with strategic support to ensure that they can successfully read the text.

Language Help students unpack lengthy sentences by asking them to summarize each part. For example, in paragraph 2, the narrator states, "He made quick, springing steps, his left hand dangling freely by the side of his once white coat, now torn and worn out." This sentence could be summarized using the following sentences: He is walking quickly and casually. He is wearing an old coat.

Meaning Discuss how setting creates meaning within a story. Work with students to identify descriptions of the setting and then link them to the main character's feelings and actions.

Challenge

Provide students who need to be challenged with ideas for how they can go beyond a simple interpretation of the text.

Text Analysis Have students identify words in the text that are related to political conflict, such as *detainee* and *detention*. Ask them how these words relate to the main character's experiences.

Written Response Ask students to create a different ending for the story based on the idea that the main character's wife stayed home. How would his feelings have changed? What might he do at the end of the story instead?

TEACH

Read and Respond

Have the groups read the selection and complete the Making Meaning, Language Development, and Effective Expression activities.

Standards Support Through Teaching and Learning Cycle

IDENTIFY NEEDS

Analyze results of the Beginning-of-Year Assessment, focusing on the items relating to Unit 5. Also take into consideration student performance to this point and your observations of where particular students struggle.

DECIDE AND PLAN

- If students have performed poorly on items matching these standards, then provide selection scaffolds before assigning them the on-level lesson provided in the Student Edition.
- If students have done well on the Beginning-of-Year Assessment, then challenge them to keep progressing and learning by giving them opportunities to practice the skills in depth.
- Use the Selection Resources listed on the Planning pages for "The Return" to help students continually improve their ability to master the standards.

Instructional Standards: The Return

	Catching Up	This Year	Looking Forward
Reading	You may wish to administer the **Analyze Craft and Structure: Plot Devices (RP)** worksheet to better familiarize students with the literary technique of plot devices.	**RL.5** Analyze how an author's choices concerning how to structure a text, order events within it, and manipulate time create such effects as mystery, tension, or surprise.	Have students identify other works they are familiar with that use plot devices. Then, have them compare the aesthetic impacts of those to this text.
Writing	You may wish to administer the **Writing to Sources (RP)** worksheet to help students better prepare for their assignment.	**W.2** Write informative/explanatory texts to examine and convey complex ideas, concepts, and information clearly and accurately through the effective selection, organization, and analysis of content.	Challenge students to write using mostly sensory details and see the effect it has on their writing.
Language	You may wish to administer the **Word Study: Etymology: Suffix *-ine* (RP)** worksheet to better familiarize students with the root word. You may wish to administer the **Conventions: Active and Passive Voice (RP)** worksheet to help students better understand the difference between active and passive voice.	**L.4.b** Identify and correctly use patterns of word changes that indicate different meanings or parts of speech. **L.1** Demonstrate command of the conventions of standard English grammar and usage when writing or speaking.	Have students locate other words in the text that have Latin or Greek roots they recognize. Challenge students to write a short story and then go back and edit the story to eliminate passive voice.

TEACH

Implement the planned lesson, and gather evidence of student learning.

ANALYZE AND REVISE

- Analyze student work for evidence of student learning.
- Identify whether or not students have met the expectations in the standards.
- Identify implications for future instruction.

FACILITATING

Jump Start

FIRST READ Is it easier to leave loved ones behind or to stay home while a loved one is away? Have students discuss a time when they went away for a while or a time when a loved one went away for a while.

The Return

What kind of reception do you think Kamau expects his village to give him? What does he hope for? What did he learn in the end? Modeling the questions readers might ask as they read "The Return" for the first time brings the text alive for students and connects it to the Small-Group Performance Task assignment. Selection audio and print capability for the selection are available in the Interactive Teacher's Edition.

Concept Vocabulary

Encourage groups to discuss the vocabulary words and their base words. Challenge them to work with their groups to come up with other words that use the same base word and discuss how the words are related.

FIRST READ

Have students perform the steps of the first read independently:

NOTICE: Encourage students to notice Kamau's outlook on life and what has happened to him to make him feel this way.

ANNOTATE: Remind students to mark passages that contain flashbacks and descriptive language.

CONNECT: Encourage students to connect the text to events in their own lives. Challenge them to think of a time when they were disappointed by something or someone. What were their expectations, and why did they hold them?

RESPOND: Students will answer questions and write a summary to demonstrate understanding.

Point out to students that while they will always complete the Respond step at the end of the first read, the other steps will probably happen somewhat concurrently. You may wish to print copies of the **First-Read Guide: Fiction** for students to use.

MAKING MEANING

About the Author

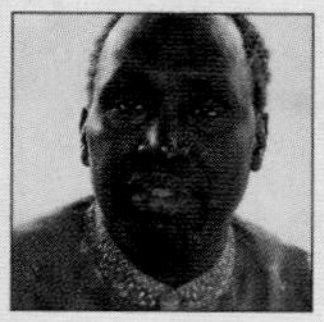

Ngugi wa Thiong'o (b. 1938) was born in Kenya and as a young boy lived through the Mau Mau Rebellion. His first play, *The Black Hermit*, was a major success. His unsparing but accurate account of life in the dictatorship of postcolonial Kenya, *Petals of Blood*, landed him in prison in 1977. After his release, the government reissued a warrant for his arrest. Ngugi chose exile instead, and fled to the United States. Ngugi has received numerous honors and taught at a number of major universities.

The Return

Concept Vocabulary

As you perform your first read of "The Return," you will encounter the following words.

sprawling serpentine compact

Base Words If these words are unfamiliar to you, analyze each one to see whether it contains a base word you know. Then, use your knowledge of the "inside" word and any prefix or suffix, along with context, to determine a meaning for the concept word. Here is an example of how to apply the strategy.

Unfamiliar Word: *detainee*

Familiar "Inside" Word: *detain*, which means "keep" or "confine."

Context: One day he was working next to another **detainee** from Muranga.

Conclusion: *Detainee* is referring to a person in this sentence. It might mean "one who has been detained, or confined."

Apply your knowledge of base words and other vocabulary strategies to determine the meanings of unfamiliar words you encounter during your first read.

First Read FICTION

Apply these strategies as you conduct your first read. You will have an opportunity to complete a close read after your first read.

NOTICE *whom* the story is about, *what* happens, *where* and *when* it happens, and *why* those involved react as they do.

ANNOTATE by marking vocabulary and key passages you want to revisit.

First Read

CONNECT ideas within the selection to what you already know and what you have already read.

RESPOND by completing the Comprehension Check and by writing a brief summary of the selection.

STANDARDS

Reading Literature
By the end of grade 9, read and comprehend literature, including stories, dramas, and poems, in the grades 9–10 text complexity band proficiently, with scaffolding as needed at the high end of the range.

Language
• Determine or clarify the meaning of unknown and multiple-meaning words and phrases based on *grades 9–10 reading and content*, choosing flexibly from a range of strategies.
• Identify and correctly use patterns of word changes that indicate different meanings or parts of speech.

AUTHOR'S PERSPECTIVE **Jim Cummins, Ph.D.**

Language Awareness Vocabulary knowledge is an extremely robust predictor of students' reading comprehension. The Frayer model is an effective tool for enabling students to extend their vocabulary knowledge in a systematic way. The tool aims to deepen students' knowledge of words and concepts by focusing their attention not only on simple definitions but also on characteristics of the concept and examples and non-examples of it.

SHORT STORY

The Return

Ngugi wa Thiong'o

BACKGROUND

The British colonial government controlled Kenya, the setting of this story, from the late nineteenth century until 1963. In 1952, this government declared a state of emergency in order to violently suppress the Mau Mau Rebellion, an anti-British uprising by the Gikuyu ethnic group. Over 20,000 Gikuyu were imprisoned by the government, and over 10,000 people lost their lives during the fighting.

SCAN FOR MULTIMEDIA

1 The road was long. Whenever he took a step forward, little clouds of dust rose, whirled angrily behind him, and then slowly settled again. But a thin train of dust was left in the air, moving like smoke. He walked on, however, unmindful of the dust and ground under his feet. Yet with every step he seemed more and more conscious of the hardness and apparent animosity of the road. Not that he looked down; on the contrary, he looked straight ahead as if he would, any time now, see a familiar object that would hail him as a friend and tell him that he was near home. But the road stretched on.

2 He made quick, springing steps, his left hand dangling freely by the side of his once white coat, now torn and worn out. His right hand, bent at the elbow, held onto a string tied to a small bundle on his slightly drooping back. The bundle, well wrapped with a cotton cloth that had once been printed with red flowers now faded out, swung from side to side in harmony with the rhythm of his steps. The bundle held the bitterness and hardships of the years spent in detention camps. Now and then he looked at the sun on its homeward journey. Sometimes he darted quick side-glances at the small hedged strips of land which, with their sickly-looking crops, maize, beans, and peas, appeared much as everything else did—unfriendly. The whole country was dull and seemed weary. To Kamau, this was nothing new. He remembered that, even before the Mau Mau emergency, the overtilled Gikuyu holdings wore haggard looks in contrast to the **sprawling** green fields in the settled area.

3 A path branched to the left. He hesitated for a moment and then made up his mind. For the first time, his eyes brightened a little as he went along the path that would take him down the valley and then

NOTES

Mark base words or indicate another strategy you used that helped you determine meaning.

sprawling (SPRAWL ihng) *adj.*

MEANING:

DIGITAL PERSPECTIVES

Concept Vocabulary

SPRAWLING If groups are struggling to define *sprawling* in paragraph 2, point out that *sprawl* means "to spread out." Students can use this definition to conclude that "sprawling green fields" are wide, open areas of green grass.

Possible response: *Sprawling* must mean "spread out."

Possible response: The descriptive language helps to establish the setting and creates a sense of unease for the reader.

Remind students that descriptive language uses images that appeal to the senses: sight, hearing, taste, smell, and touch.

CLOSER LOOK

Analyzing Descriptive Language

Circulate among groups as students conduct their close read. Suggest that groups close read paragraph 2. Encourage them to talk about the annotations that they mark. If needed, provide the following support.

ANNOTATE: Have students mark details in paragraph 2 that show descriptive language, or work with small groups to have students participate while you highlight them together.

QUESTION: Guide students to consider what these details might tell them. Ask what a reader can infer from these sensory details, and accept student responses.

Possible response: The sensory details help communicate how much time has passed and how much has changed during that time.

CONCLUDE: Help students to formulate conclusions about the importance of these details in the text. Ask students why the author might have included these details.

Additional **English Language Support** is available in the Interactive Teacher's Edition.

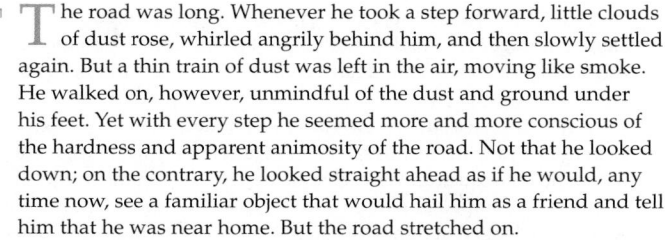

Definition	Image
Target Word:	
Synonym and/or antonym	Sentence

Create an electronic template and have students work in groups of "language detectives" to enter new and interesting words onto the group's template. If time allows, encourage students to compile two to five words each day. Where multiple home languages are represented in a group, students could take turns entering the L1 word in their home language, and all members of the group could learn that word. At the end of each week, the teacher could compile the words into a class quiz.

FACILITATING

Concept Vocabulary

SERPENTINE If groups are struggling to define the word *serpentine* in paragraph 3, point out that the root word is *serpent*, which means "snake." The suffix *-ine* generally means "like." If something is *serpentine*, that means that it is "like a snake." In this case, Kamau is referring to the river, so we can conclude that the river is curving around and moving through the land in a winding pattern, which resembles the movement of a snake.

Possible response: *Serpentine* means "moving like a snake."

NOTES

Mark base words or indicate another strategy you used that helped you determine meaning.

serpentine (SUR puhn teen) *adj.*

MEANING:

to the village. At last home was near and, with that realization, the faraway look of a weary traveler seemed to desert him for a while. The valley and the vegetation along it were in deep contrast to the surrounding country. For here green bush and trees thrived. This could only mean one thing: Honia River still flowed. He quickened his steps as if he could scarcely believe this to be true till he had actually set his eyes on the river. It was there; it still flowed. Honia, where so often he had taken a bath, plunging stark naked into its cool living water, warmed his heart as he watched its **serpentine** movement around the rocks and heard its slight murmurs. A painful exhilaration passed all over him and for a moment he longed for those days. He sighed. Perhaps the river would not recognize in his hardened features that same boy to whom the riverside world had meant everything. Yet as he approached Honia, he felt more akin to it than he had felt to anything else since his release.

4 A group of women were drawing water. He was excited, for he could recognize one or two from his ridge. There was the middle-aged Wanjiku, whose deaf son had been killed by the Security Forces just before he himself was arrested. She had always been a darling of the village, having a smile for everyone and food for all. Would they receive him? Would they give him a "hero's welcome"? He thought so. Had he not always been a favorite all along the ridge? And had he not fought for the land? He wanted to run and shout: "Here I am. I have come back to you." But he desisted. He was a man.

5 "Is it well with you?" A few voices responded. The other women, with tired and worn features, looked at him mutely as if his greeting was of no consequence. Why! Had he been so long in the camp? His spirits were damped as he feebly asked: "Do you not remember me?" Again they looked at him. They stared at him with cold, hard looks; like everything else, they seemed to be deliberately refusing to know or own him. It was Wanjiku who at last recognized him. But there was neither warmth nor enthusiasm in her voice as she said, "Oh, is it you, Kamau? We thought you—" She did not continue. Only now he noticed something else—surprise? fear? He could not tell. He saw their quick glances dart at him and he knew for certain that a secret from which he was excluded bound them together.

6 "Perhaps I am no longer one of them!" he bitterly reflected. But they told him of the new village. The old village of scattered huts spread thinly over the ridge was no more.

7 He left them, feeling embittered and cheated. The old village had not even waited for him. And suddenly he felt a strong nostalgia for his old home, friends and surroundings. He thought of his father, mother and—and—he dared not think about her. But for all that, Muthoni, just as she had been in the old days, came back to his mind. His heart beat faster. He felt desire and a warmth thrilled through him. He quickened his step. He forgot the village women as he remembered his wife. He had stayed with her for a mere two weeks;

PERSONALIZE FOR LEARNING

Strategic Support

Personification Students may not notice the personification in paragraph 3. Point out that *personification* means "to give human qualities to an inanimate object." Sometimes authors do this to give special meaning to an object or to give it agency in the story. Discuss with the class why the author chose to include the following sentence: "Perhaps the river would not recognize in his hardened features that same boy to whom the riverside world had meant everything." Why does the river's opinion matter so much to Kamau?

then he had been swept away by the colonial forces. Like many others, he had been hurriedly screened and then taken to detention without trial. And all that time he had thought of nothing but the village and his beautiful woman.

8 The others had been like him. They had talked of nothing but their homes. One day he was working next to another detainee from Muranga.[1] Suddenly the detainee, Njoroge, stopped breaking stones. He sighed heavily. His worn-out eyes had a faraway look.

9 "What's wrong, man? What's the matter with you?" Kamau asked.

10 "It is my wife. I left her expecting a baby. I have no idea what has happened to her."

11 Another detainee put in: "For me, I left my woman with a baby. She had just been delivered. We were all happy. But on the same day, I was arrested . . ."

12 And so they went on. All of them longed for one day—the day of their return home. Then life would begin anew.

13 Kamau himself had left his wife without a child. He had not even finished paying the bride price. But now he would go, seek work in Nairobi, and pay off the remainder to Muthoni's parents. Life would indeed begin anew. They would have a son and bring him up in their own home. With these prospects before his eyes, he quickened his steps. He wanted to run—no, fly to hasten his return. He was now nearing the top of the hill. He wished he could suddenly meet his brothers and sisters. Would they ask him questions? He would, at any rate, not tell them all: the beating, the screening, and the work on roads and in quarries with an askari[2] always nearby ready to kick him if he relaxed. Yes. He had suffered many humiliations, and he had not resisted. Was there any need? But his soul and all the vigor of his manhood had rebelled and bled with rage and bitterness.

14 One day these wazungu[3] would go!

15 One day his people would be free! Then, then—he did not know what he would do. However, he bitterly assured himself no one would ever flout his manhood again.

16 He mounted the hill and then stopped. The whole plain lay below. The new village was before him—rows and rows of **compact** mud huts, crouching on the plain under the fast-vanishing sun. Dark blue smoke curled upward from various huts, to form a dark mist that hovered over the village. Beyond, the deep, blood-red sinking sun sent out fingerlike streaks of light that thinned outward and mingled with the gray mist shrouding the distant hills.

17 In the village, he moved from street to street, meeting new faces. He inquired. He found his home. He stopped at the entrance to the yard and breathed hard and full. This was the moment of his return home. His father sat huddled up on a three-legged stool. He was now very aged and Kamau pitied the old man. But he had been spared—yes, spared to see his son's return—

1. **Muranga** (moo RAHN gah) town in Kenya.
2. **askari** (ahs KAH ree) *n.* local soldier employed by the British Empire in colonial Africa.
3. **wazungu** (wah ZOON goo) *n.* people of European descent.

NOTES

Mark base words or indicate another strategy you used that helped you determine meaning.

compact (kuhm PAKT) *adj.*

MEANING:

DIGITAL PERSPECTIVES

CLOSER LOOK

Understanding Flashbacks

Circulate among groups as students conduct their close read. Suggest that groups close read paragraphs 8–12. Encourage them to talk about the annotations they mark. If needed, provide the following support.

ANNOTATE: Have students mark details in these paragraphs that demonstrate the use of flashback, or work with small groups to have students participate while you highlight them together.

QUESTION: Guide students to consider what these details might tell them. Ask what a reader can infer from these flashbacks and accept student responses.

Possible response: The author wants the reader to understand what motivates Kamau's desire to return home.

CONCLUDE: Help students to formulate conclusions about the importance of these details in the text. Ask students why the author might have included these details.

Possible response: The detainees are reminiscing about their homes and families, which instills a sense of hope in Kamau. He dreams of seeing his wife again and continuing his life with her.

A **flashback** is a scene within a narrative that interrupts the sequence of events to relate events that occurred in the past. Writers use flashbacks to show what motivates a character or to reveal something about a character's past. A writer may present a flashback as a character's memory, as part of an account or story told by a character, as a dream or a daydream, or as a dramatic transition by the narrator.

Concept Vocabulary

COMPACT If groups are struggling to define *compact* in paragraph 15, point out that the root word is *com*, which means "together." Using context clues from the text, such as "rows and rows," we can infer that the word *compact* means "tightly grouped together."

CLOSER LOOK

Evaluating Cultural Context

Circulate among groups as students conduct their close read. Suggest that groups close read paragraph 28. Encourage them to talk about the annotations they mark. If needed, provide the following support.

ANNOTATE: Have students mark details in this paragraph that show cultural context, or work with small groups to have students participate while you highlight them together.

QUESTION: Guide students to consider what these details might tell them. Ask what a reader can infer from these details, and accept student responses.

Possible response: Kamau expected Muthoni to wait for him because she was married to him, and his family ended up letting her leave with Karanja because he grew up with Kamau.

CONCLUDE: Help students to formulate conclusions about the importance of these details in the text. Ask students why the author might have included these details.

Possible response: We can conclude that wives were expected to stay committed to their husbands, even in their husbands' absence. Muthoni stayed with Kamau's family for as long as she believed that he was alive, but once they heard of his death, his family let her leave with Karanja because they couldn't afford to keep her. They trusted him because he grew up in the same group of children as their son.

Remind students that the **cultural context** of a literary work refers to the economic, social, and historical environment that its characters inhabit, including the attitudes and customs of that culture and historical period. The term cultural context also encompasses the cultural attitudes and ideologies of the period in which the writer lived (which may be different from the period in which the literary work is set) because those beliefs may also be reflected in the work, either consciously or unconsciously.

NOTES

18 "Father!"

19 The old man did not answer. He just looked at Kamau with strange vacant eyes. Kamau was impatient. He felt annoyed and irritated. Did he not see him? Would he behave like the women Kamau had met by the river?

20 In the street, naked and half-naked children were playing, throwing dust at one another. The sun had already set and it looked as if there would be moonlight.

21 "Father, don't you remember me?" Hope was sinking in him. He felt tired. Then he saw his father suddenly start and tremble like a leaf. He saw him stare with unbelieving eyes. Fear was discernible in those eyes. His mother came, and his brothers too. They crowded around him. His aged mother clung to him and sobbed hard.

22 "I knew my son would come. I knew he was not dead."

23 "Why, who told you I was dead?"

24 "That Karanja, son of Njogu."

25 And then Kamau understood. He understood his trembling father. He understood the women at the river. But one thing puzzled him: he had never been in the same detention camp with Karanja. Anyway he had come back. He wanted now to see Muthoni. Why had she not come out? He wanted to shout, "I have come, Muthoni; I am here." He looked around. His mother understood him. She quickly darted a glance at her man and then simply said:

26 "Muthoni went away."

27 Kamau felt something cold settle in his stomach. He looked at the village huts and the dullness of the land. He wanted to ask many questions but he dared not. He could not yet believe that Muthoni had gone. But he knew by the look of the women at the river, by the look of his parents, that she was gone.

28 "She was a good daughter to us," his mother was explaining. "She waited for you and patiently bore all the ills of the land. Then Karanja came and said that you were dead. Your father believed him. She believed him too and keened[4] for a month. Karanja constantly paid us visits. He was of your Rika,[5] you know. Then she got a child. We could have kept her. But where is the land? Where is the food? Ever since land consolidation,[6] our last security was taken away. We let Karanja go with her. Other women have done worse—gone to town. Only the infirm and the old have been left here."

29 He was not listening; the coldness in his stomach slowly changed to bitterness. He felt bitter against all, all the people including his father and mother. They had betrayed him. They had leagued against him, and Karanja had always been his rival. Five years was admittedly not a short time. But why did she go? Why did they allow her to go? He wanted to speak. Yes, speak and denounce

4. **keened** *v.* wailed in mourning.
5. **Rika** (REE kah) *n.* group of Gikuyu children that are the same age.
6. **land consolidation** British policy of seizing Gikuyu land to make large farms for cash crops.

654 UNIT 5 • JOURNEYS OF TRANSFORMATION

everything—the women by the river, the village, and the people who dwelled there. But he could not. This bitter thing was choking him.

30 "You—you gave my own away?" he whispered.

31 "Listen, child, child . . ."

32 The big yellow moon dominated the horizon. He hurried away bitter and blind, and only stopped when he came to the Honia River.

33 And standing at the bank, he saw not the river, but his hopes dashed on the ground instead. The river moved swiftly, making ceaseless monotonous murmurs. In the forest the crickets and other insects kept up an incessant buzz. And above, the moon shone bright. He tried to remove his coat, and the small bundle he had held onto so firmly fell. It rolled down the bank and before Kamau knew what was happening, it was floating swiftly down the river. For a time he was shocked and wanted to retrieve it. What would he show his—Oh, had he forgotten so soon? His wife had gone. And the little things that had so strangely reminded him of her and that he had guarded all those years, had gone! He did not know why, but somehow he felt relieved. Thoughts of drowning himself dispersed. He began to put on his coat, murmuring to himself, "Why should she have waited for me? Why should all the changes have waited for my return?" ❧

NOTES

Comprehension Check

Complete the following items after you finish your first read. Review and clarify details with your group.

1. Where has Kamau been for the five years preceding the events in the story?

2. Where is Kamau going as the story begins?

3. How does Kamau's mother feel about Kamau's wife, Muthoni?

4. **Notebook** To confirm your understanding, write a summary of the story.

RESEARCH

Research to Clarify Choose an unfamiliar detail from the text. Briefly research that detail. How has the information you learned shed light on an aspect of the story?

DIGITAL PERSPECTIVES

Comprehension Check

Possible responses:

1. Kamau has been imprisoned by the government for the past five years.
2. When the story begins, Kamau is going back home to see his family in Honia, the village by the river where he grew up.
3. Kamau's mother accepts Muthoni's decision to leave, stating, "She was a good daughter to us." Muthoni left with Karanja because Kamau's family didn't have enough money and food to keep her, and they trusted Karanja because he was Kamau's childhood friend.
4. A man named Kamau was released from imprisonment and journeys home to receive an unpleasant reception. His family believed he was dead and let his wife leave with his childhood friend because they couldn't afford to keep her. Kamau is very upset, but in the end, he realizes that things change whether you are around to see them or not.

Research to Clarify If groups struggle to find a topic to research, suggest one of the following topics: the British colonization of Kenya, the Kenyan African Union (KAU), or the Mau Mau Rebellion.

PERSONALIZE FOR LEARNING

Challenge

Research To help students understand the cultural context and meaning of this story, have them research the Gikuyu people, particularly in the 1888–1963 time frame. They should find that the area was involved in several conflicts during that time period. When Kamau is released from imprisonment, he symbolizes the path towards peace. When we know about the hostile context of the setting, we learn that the story can represent the sacrifices that are sometimes made in order to bring about change.

Jump Start

CLOSE READ Why does Kamau believe he will get a grand welcome when he gets home? Do you think he should have this expectation? Discuss with the class why Kamau believes everything will be the same when he returns and how his opinion changes in the end.

Close Read the Text

If needed, model close reading by using the Annotation Highlights in the Interactive Teacher's Edition. Remind students to use Accountable Talk in their discussions and to support one another as they complete the close read.

Analyze the Text

1. **Possible response:** The women at the river do not greet Kamau warmly. They instead look at him coldly and hesitantly. The "secret" that they are hiding is that his wife is gone and everyone thinks he is dead.
2. **Passages will vary by group.** Remind students to explain why they chose the passage they presented to group members.
3. **Responses will vary by group.**

Concept Vocabulary

Why These Words? Possible response: The words all describe the terrain of the land Kamau is from. The word choice helps paint a visual picture of the setting for the reader.

Practice

Possible responses: The **sprawling** mansion had six bedrooms, a theater, a gym, and a swimming pool. **Serpentine** roads twisted around the mountains on the way up. All of the pieces were **compact,** so they fit neatly in the little box.

Word Network

Possible words: *homeward, traveler, nostalgia*

Word Study

For more support, see **Concept Vocabulary and Word Study.**

Possible responses:

1. Serpentine means "snakelike." Some rivers are windy, like the shape of a snake in motion.
2. bovine – cow; leonine – lion; porcine – pig

MAKING MEANING

THE RETURN

Close Read the Text

With your group, revisit sections of the text you marked during your first read. **Annotate** details that you notice. What **questions** do you have? What can you **conclude**?

Close Read

TIP

GROUP DISCUSSION
As your group discusses the story, try to build upon each other's ideas so that you can deepen your understanding of the text.

Analyze the Text

CITE TEXTUAL EVIDENCE to support your answers.

Complete the activities.

1. **Review and Clarify** With your group, reread paragraphs 4–6. Discuss the reaction to Kamau that the three women at the river have. What is the "secret" that he feels is binding them together?
2. **Present and Discuss** Work with your group to share other key passages from the selection. What passage did you focus on? What made you choose this particular passage? Take turns presenting your choices.
3. **Essential Question:** ***What can we learn from a journey?*** What has this selection taught you about journeys? Discuss with your group.

LANGUAGE DEVELOPMENT

Concept Vocabulary

sprawling serpentine compact

Why These Words? The three concept vocabulary words are related. With your group, determine what the words have in common. How do these word choices enhance the impact of the text?

WORD NETWORK
Add interesting words related to journeys from the text to your Word Network.

Practice

Notebook Confirm your understanding of these words from the text by using them in sentences. Provide context clues to each word's meaning.

STANDARDS
Reading Literature
- Analyze how an author's choices concerning how to structure a text, order events within it, and manipulate time create such effects as mystery, tension, or surprise.
- Analyze a particular point of view or cultural experience reflected in a work of literature from outside the United States, drawing on a wide reading of world literature.

Language
- Identify and correctly use patterns of word changes that indicate different meanings or parts of speech.
- Demonstrate understanding of figurative language, word relationships, and nuances in word meanings.

Word Study

Latin Suffix: *-ine* In "The Return," the author describes the Honia River's movement as *serpentine.* The word *serpentine* ends with the Latin suffix *-ine,* which means "of," "like," or "related to." The suffix appears in many adjectives that describe animals or animal-like qualities. For instance, you may be familiar with *canine,* meaning "related to dogs."

1. Explain why the word *serpentine* may be a fitting word to describe a river.
2. Use a college-level dictionary to look up these words that end with the suffix *-ine: bovine, leonine, porcine.* Write the animal to which each word refers.

FORMATIVE ASSESSMENT

Analyze the Text

If students struggle to close read the text, **then** provide the **The Return: Text Questions** available online in the Interactive Teacher's Edition or Unit Resources. Answers and DOK levels are also available.

Word Study

If students struggle to determine the meaning of words ending in *-ine,* **then** help them look up the word and analyze its parts.
For Reteach and Practice, see **Word Study: Etymology: Suffix *-ine* (RP).**

Concept Vocabulary

If students struggle to identify the concept, **then** suggest they reread the sentences.

Analyze Craft and Structure

Author's Choices: Plot Devices Short story authors draw on various literary devices to build suspense and add meaning to their narratives. Two essential devices in "The Return" are *foreshadowing* and *situational irony.*

Foreshadowing is the use of clues carefully placed throughout a story that hint at later events. For example, in "The Return," the strange behavior of the women at the river raises questions in readers' minds about how Kamau will be received at home. These clues help to pull readers through the story, and make the sequence of events feel logical and unified.

Situational irony also plays with readers' expectations. **Situational irony** occurs when events in a story directly challenge readers' or characters' expectations. Authors use situational irony to interest and surprise readers and to emphasize and deepen meaning.

Practice

CITE TEXTUAL EVIDENCE to support your answers.

With your group, review "The Return" to identify elements of foreshadowing and situational irony in the story. Then, individually, complete the charts to understand how foreshadowing sets up expectations that affect situational irony. Finally, gauge the impact of situational irony on what the story says about homecomings.

FORESHADOWING IN "THE RETURN"

STORY CLUES	QUESTIONS RAISED	WHAT THE CLUES SUGGEST
The women at the river exchange knowing glances when they realize who Kamau is.	What do the women know about Kamau that he does not know?	Kamau will have a surprise in store after he returns to his village.
Kamau remembers a conversation with detainees about going back home and seeing families	What will Kamau find when he returns home?	What Kamau expects, and what he actually finds when he returns may not be the same thing.

SITUATIONAL IRONY IN "THE RETURN"

EXPECTATIONS	WHAT ACTUALLY HAPPENS	CONNECTION TO THE STORY'S MEANING
Kamau expects a reunion with his wife.	His wife believed he had died, and eventually left with another man.	Kamau has to learn to accept his new situation.

DIGITAL PERSPECTIVES

Analyze Craft and Structure

Foreshadowing Discuss with students ways in which foreshadowing might help an author better tell his or her story. Explain that foreshadowing can also build suspense and can make a story more compelling and intriguing.

Situational Irony Explain to students that irony is a sharp difference or contradiction between expectation and outcome, appearance or reality, or meaning and intention. Situational irony helps keep readers' attention and often surprises them at the last moment.

Prompt students to discuss the connections between foreshadowing and situational irony. For more support, see **Analyze Craft and Structure: Plot Devices.**

See possible responses in chart on Student page.

FORMATIVE ASSESSMENT

Analyze Craft and Structure

If students have trouble identifying examples of foreshadowing, **then** have them re-read the text with the knowledge of the full outcome and look for clues to the ending.

For Reteach and Practice, see **Analyze Craft and Structure: Plot Devices (RP).**

PERSONALIZE FOR LEARNING

English Language Support

Sentence Starters Provide sentence starters to help students organize their ideas before completing the chart. Suggest they format their answers in a way that addresses the expectations and the outcome of the situations, such as, "The expectation is that _____, but ____ happens instead." Have students work together to complete their answers. **ALL LEVELS**

Conventions

Active and Passive Voice Discuss with the class why writing in active voice tends to create a more engaging experience for a reader. Is it more fun to read about someone doing something or having something done to them? Why would this matter? For more support, see **Conventions: Active and Passive Voice.**

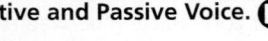

MAKE IT INTERACTIVE

Have students create a list of sentences using the passive voice and challenge their classmates to rewrite the sentences using active voice.

Read It

Possible responses:

1. was left; passive
2. held; active
3. felt; active
4. was taken (away); passive
5. dominated; active

Write It

Possible responses:

"Only the infirm and the old have been left here." *They have only left the infirm and old here.* "Karanja constantly paid us visits." *We were constantly visited by Karanja.* The active voice creates a tone of interest, while the passive voice creates a complacent tone.

FORMATIVE ASSESSMENT

Conventions

If students have trouble identifying active voice and passive voice, **then** show them examples of both types of sentences and challenge them to identify the difference between the verbs.

For Reteach and Practice, see **Conventions: Active and Passive Voice (RP).**

THE RETURN

Conventions

Active and Passive Voice The **voice** of a verb indicates whether the subject is performing the action or is being acted upon. A verb is in the **active voice** if its subject performs the action. A verb is in the **passive voice** if its action is performed upon the subject. A passive verb is always a verb phrase made from a form of *to be* plus the past participle of a verb—for instance, *is eaten, has been deceived,* or *will be sung.*

Passive Voice: The mouse was trapped by the cat.

Active Voice: The cat trapped the mouse.

The active voice tends to be more direct and economical. However, the passive voice does have two important uses. Writers use the passive voice to emphasize the receiver of an action rather than the performer. They also use the passive voice to point out the receiver of an action when the performer is not important or not easily identified.

Read It

Work individually. Read each of these passages from "The Return." Mark each verb or verb phrase. Then, write whether the passage is in the active voice or the passive voice. When you are done, discuss your answers with your group. Resolve any differences in your answers.

1. But a thin train of dust was left in the air. . . .
2. The bundle held the bitterness and hardships of the years. . . .
3. And suddenly he felt a strong nostalgia for his old home, friends and surroundings.
4. Ever since land consolidation, our last security was taken away.
5. The big yellow moon dominated the horizon.

Write It

Notebook Work individually. Write two sentences about "The Return" in the passive voice. Then, revise those sentences so that they are in the active voice. When you are done, share your sentences with your group. Discuss the effect your revisions had on the impact of your sentences.

STANDARDS

Writing
Write informative/explanatory texts to examine and convey complex ideas, concepts, and information clearly and accurately through the effective selection, organization, and analysis of content.

Language
Demonstrate command of the conventions of standard English grammar and usage when writing or speaking.

PERSONALIZE FOR LEARNING

English Language Support

Using Active and Passive Voice Have pairs of students work together to write two sentences that describe the selection. One sentence should use the active voice and one should use the passive voice. **EMERGING**

Have students write a few sentences that address irony in the selection. One sentence should use the active voice and one should use the passive voice. **EXPANDING**

Have students write a brief paragraph that addresses the kind of irony used in the selection. Remind them to use sentences that feature both active and passive forms of their verbs. **BRIDGING**

An expanded **English Language Support Lesson** on Active and Passive Voice is available in the Digital Teacher's Edition.

EFFECTIVE EXPRESSION

Writing to Sources

Assignment

Writing can help you understand and explain your response to a story. Choose from the following projects.

- ☐ Write a **chat board post** in which you explain your response to the story. Identify the moment or moments that had the greatest impact on you, and explain the reasons they were effective. You may assume that your readers have read the story.
- ☐ "The Return" presents many details specific to the Kenyan cultural experience. Do these details make the story more or less universal? Support your answer by writing a **short essay** explaining the effect of specific details on the reader.
- ☐ Imagine that you are a film director. Draft an **adaptation proposal** for the story to create a short film. Describe the devices you will use to reflect specific effects achieved by the author.

Project Plan Before you begin, make a list of the tasks you will need to accomplish in order to complete your chosen assignment. Develop your central idea and write it so that it will guide the rest of your work. Review the selection or conduct research as needed to complete the tasks you have listed. Then, assign individual group members to each task. Finally, determine how you will make decisions about choices of images, text, and the overall design of your project.

Sensory Details Words and phrases that appeal to the senses have a strong impact on readers. Similarly, film writers choose images and sounds for the impact they will have on the audience. Use the chart below to record some sensory details you want to be sure to use in your writing.

SENSORY DETAIL	EFFECT ON READER/AUDIENCE

EVIDENCE LOG

Before moving on to a new selection, go to your Evidence Log and record what you learned from "The Return."

DIGITAL PERSPECTIVES

Writing to Sources

Lead a discussion with the class about the moments in the story that most impacted them. Which scenes were the most surprising or meaningful? Perhaps they connected with Kamau's disappointment in his family and neighbors, the irony of his experience, or the nostalgic feeling of wanting to go home. Prompt students to think about Kamau's journey and write about what they think they were meant to take away from the piece.

Project Plan Suggest that students collaborate on their central idea and split up the tasks of their project evenly. Guide them through brainstorming their ideas and narrowing them down before assigning tasks.

Sensory Details Guide students in thinking about which sensory details were most important to them as readers and the effect those details had on the story's impact. For more support, see **Writing to Sources.**

Evidence Log Support students in completing their Evidence Log. This paced activity will help prepare them for the Performance-Based Assessment at the end of the unit.

FORMATIVE ASSESSMENT

Writing to Sources

If students struggle to come up with a topic for their assignment, **then** help them brainstorm which parts of the text most appealed to them and their own experiences. For Reteach and Practice, see **Writing to Sources (RP).**

Selection Test

Administer the "The Return" Selection Test, which is available in both print and digital formats online in Assessments.

DIGITAL PERSPECTIVES

Illuminating the Standard To help students understand the best way of narrowing down their ideas, show them some examples of brainstorming charts online, such as bubble maps or idea trees. Guide them in filling out their own brainstorming charts and selecting their best ideas. (Research to Clarify)

from The Hero's Adventure

AUDIO SUMMARIES
Audio summaries of the excerpt from *The Hero's Adventure* are available online in both English and Spanish in the Interactive Teacher's Edition or Unit Resources. Assigning these summaries prior to reading the selection may help students build additional background knowledge and set a context for their first read.

Summary

In this interview, journalist Bill Moyers speaks with author Joseph Campbell about different types of heroes. As Campbell explains to Moyers, different societies have different heroes. Campbell says that a hero is someone who has given his or her life over to something that is greater than himself or herself. There are heroes who perform courageous acts, such as saving a life, and there are heroes who experience a supernormal range of spiritual life and return with a message. The men also discuss how a journey helps transform a person into a hero.

Insight

Reading the excerpt from the "The Hero's Adventure" will help students understand that being a hero or heroine might be less extraordinary than it seems. By focusing on the importance of a transformation, Campbell makes a hero's transformation more relatable.

ESSENTIAL QUESTION:
What can we learn from a journey?

Connection to Essential Question

"The Hero's Adventure" provides a different perspective on the Essential Question. Campbell argues that by undergoing a journey of some sort, a person proves that he or she has the courage, knowledge, and capacity to be a hero.

SMALL-GROUP LEARNING PERFORMANCE TASK
What different types of journeys are there and how can they transform someone?

UNIT PERFORMANCE-BASED ASSESSMENT
When does the journey matter more than the destination?

Connection to Performance Tasks

Small-Group Learning Task In this Performance Task, students will create a multimedia presentation that addresses how a journey can be transformative. In "The Hero's Adventure," Joseph Campbell mentions journeys of transformation, such as the psychological transformation from dependency on others to the mature self and the journey from maiden to mother.

Unit Performance-Based Assessment In this selection, Joseph Campbell suggests that the journey to becoming a hero matters much more than being declared one. Campbell would argue that without the journey, there can be no hero.

DIGITAL PERSPECTIVES — Audio | Video | Document | Annotation Highlights | EL Highlights | Online Assessment

LESSON RESOURCES

	Making Meaning	Language Development	Effective Expression
Lesson	**First Read** **Close Read** **Analyze the Text** **Analyze Craft and Structure**	**Concept Vocabulary** **Word Study** **Conventions**	**Research**
Instructional Standards	**RL.10** By the end of grade 9, read and comprehend literary nonfiction . . . **RI.3** Analyze how the author unfolds an analysis . . .	**L.4.a** Use context as a clue . . . **L.4.c** Consult general and specialized reference materials . . . **L.5** Demonstrate understanding of figurative language . . . **L.1** Demonstrate command of the conventions . . . **L.1.b** Use various types of phrases and clauses . . .	**W.7** Conduct short as well as more sustained research projects . . . **W.9** Draw evidence from literary or informational texts . . .
STUDENT RESOURCES			
Available online in the Interactive Student Edition or Unit Resources	Selection Audio First-Read Guide: Nonfiction	Word Network	Evidence Log
TEACHER RESOURCES			
Selection Resources Available online in the Interactive Teacher's Edition or Unit Resources	Audio Summaries Annotation Highlights EL Highlights English Language Support Lesson: Writing Interview Questions The Hero's Adventure: Text Questions Analyze Craft and Structure: Development of Ideas	Conventions: Gerunds Concept Vocabulary and Word Study	Research: Multimedia Presentation
Reteach/Practice (RP) Available online in the Interactive Teacher's Edition or Unit Resources	Analyze Craft and Structure: Development of Ideas (RP)	Conventions: Gerunds (RP) Word Study: Etymology: Greek Names (RP)	Research: Multimedia Presentation (RP)
Assessment Available online in Assessments	Selection Test		
My Resources	A Unit 5 Answer Key is available online and in the Interactive Teacher's Edition.		

Reading Support

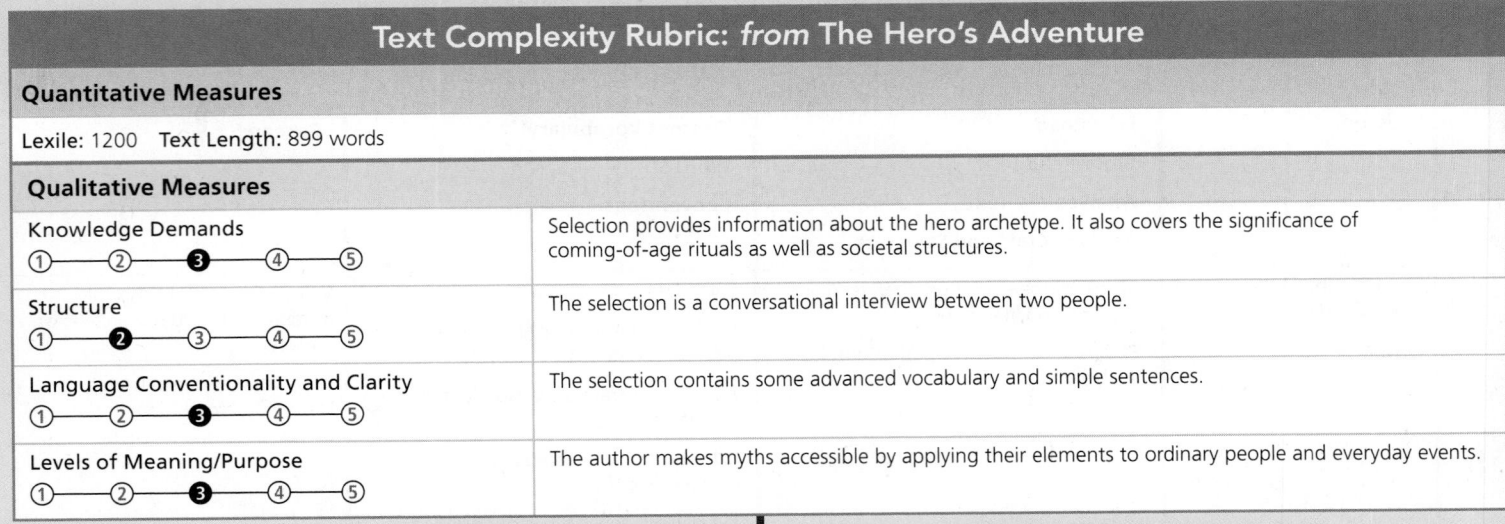

Text Complexity Rubric: *from* The Hero's Adventure	
Quantitative Measures	
Lexile: 1200 **Text Length:** 899 words	
Qualitative Measures	
Knowledge Demands ① ② ❸ ④ ⑤	Selection provides information about the hero archetype. It also covers the significance of coming-of-age rituals as well as societal structures.
Structure ① ❷ ③ ④ ⑤	The selection is a conversational interview between two people.
Language Conventionality and Clarity ① ② ❸ ④ ⑤	The selection contains some advanced vocabulary and simple sentences.
Levels of Meaning/Purpose ① ② ❸ ④ ⑤	The author makes myths accessible by applying their elements to ordinary people and everyday events.

DECIDE AND PLAN

English Language Support

Provide English Learners with support for structure and meaning as they read the selection.

Structure Help students understand that colons are commonly used in written question-and-answer interviews instead of quotation marks. Point out how colons set off Bill Moyers' questions and Joseph Campbell's answers.

Meaning Work with students to help them understand why heroes and heroines are central to mythology. Engage students in a discussion about popular myths, identifying the heroic characters and describing how each one has "given his or her life to something bigger than oneself."

Strategic Support

Provide students with strategic support to ensure that they can successfully read the text.

Knowledge Demands Make a list of challenging words that students will encounter in the selection, such as *initiation, deemed, undertaken, transformation, self-responsibility,* and *intentions*. Ask students to fill in what they know about these words or take educated guesses about their meanings. Review the correct definitions and have students refer to this list as they read.

Meaning If students have difficulty with levels of meaning, have them first read to identify examples of everyday heroes. Then, have them reread while taking notes on their heroic qualities or deeds.

Challenge

Provide students who need to be challenged with ideas for how they can go beyond a simple interpretation of the text.

Text Analysis Have students evaluate Campbell's ideas about heroes and their adventures. As a class, discuss why students think Campbell's reasoning is or is not sound.

Written Response Ask students to draft a character sketch for a heroic character. Have them detail the character's physical and personality traits. Ask students to compare and contrast their characters to those in mythology.

TEACH

Read and Respond

Have groups read the selection and complete the Making Meaning, Language Development, and Effective Expression activities.

Standards Support Through Teaching and Learning Cycle

IDENTIFY NEEDS

Analyze results of the Beginning-of-Year Assessment, focusing on the items relating to Unit 5. Also take into consideration student performance to this point and your observations of where particular students struggle.

DECIDE AND PLAN

- If students have performed poorly on items matching these standards, then provide selection scaffolds before assigning them the on-level lesson provided in the Student Edition.
- If students have done well on the Beginning-of-Year Assessment, then challenge them to keep progressing and learning by giving them opportunities to practice the skills in depth.
- Use the Selection Resources listed on the Planning pages for "The Hero's Adventure" to help students continually improve their ability to master the standards.

Instructional Standards: *from* The Hero's Adventure

	Catching Up	This Year	Looking Forward
Reading	You may wish to administer the **Analyze Craft and Structure: Development of Ideas (RP)** worksheet to better familiarize students with the Q&A format.	**RI.3** Analyze how the author unfolds an analysis or series of ideas or events, including the order in which the points are made, how they are introduced and developed, and the connections that are drawn between them.	Have students analyze the development of ideas in an interview of their choosing.
Writing	You may wish to administer the **Research: Multimedia Presentation (RP)** worksheet to help students better prepare for their presentations.	**W.7** Conduct short as well as more sustained research projects to answer a question (including a self-generated question) or solve a problem; narrow or broaden the inquiry when appropriate; synthesize multiple sources on the subject, demonstrating understanding of the subject under investigation.	Challenge students to compare and contrast this interview with another work that addresses some of the same topics.
Language	You may wish to administer the **Word Study: Etymology Greek Names (RP)** worksheet to help students understand words that were derived from Greek names. You may wish to administer the **Conventions: Gerunds (RP)** worksheet to help students understand gerunds.	**L.5** Demonstrate understanding of figurative language, word relationships, and nuances in word meaning. **L.1** Demonstrate command of the conventions of standard English grammar and usage when writing or speaking.	Have students locate other words in the text that have Greek roots they recognize. Challenge students to rewrite sentences from the selection using gerunds.

TEACH

Implement the planned lesson, and gather evidence of student learning.

ANALYZE AND REVISE

- Analyze student work for evidence of student learning.
- Identify whether or not students have met the expectations in the standards.
- Identify implications for future instruction.

FACILITATING

Jump Start

FIRST READ What kinds of myths have you heard about? Do you believe in myths? What is your definition of a hero? Can heroes only exist in myths, or can they exist in real life? Who are some real-life heroes?

from The Hero's Adventure

Why does Joseph Campbell write about heroes? Does he believe that all heroes are alike, or that some are different? Modeling the questions readers might ask as they read *The Hero's Adventure* for the first time brings the text alive for students and connects it to the Small-Group Performance Task assignment. Selection audio and print capability for the selection are available in the Interactive Teacher's Edition.

Concept Vocabulary

Ask groups to study context clues by looking at sentences and words that surround unfamiliar words or phrases. Encourage groups to think of other types of vocabulary strategies that can be used to infer meanings of unfamiliar words.

FIRST READ

Have students perform the steps of the first read independently:

NOTICE: Encourage students to take notice of the vocabulary the author uses when he describes heroes.

ANNOTATE: Remind students to mark passages that are strong examples of the author's use of diction when describing heroes in mythological stories.

CONNECT: Encourage students to explore the ways in which heroic values are different from their own.

RESPOND: Students will answer questions and write a summary to demonstrate understanding.

Point out to students that while they will always complete the Respond step at the end of the first read, the other steps will probably happen somewhat concurrently. You may wish to print copies of the **First-Read Guide: Nonfiction** for students to use.

MAKING MEANING

About the Authors

Joseph Campbell (1904–1987) At the age of seven, Joseph Campbell attended Buffalo Bill's Wild West show and became enamored with all things Native American. His curiosity led him to an interest in anthropology and English literature. Through those disciplines, Campbell developed new insights into heroes and myths, which he shared in his acclaimed book *The Hero With a Thousand Faces*.

Bill Moyers (b. 1934) A publisher, writer, press secretary, presidential assistant, deputy director of the Peace Corps, and broadcast journalist, Bill Moyers has expanded the tradition of television journalism to include not only political discussion but also conversations with some of the world's leading thinkers. Moyers worked for both CBS and PBS starting in the 1970s, and he continues to work for PBS.

from The Hero's Adventure

Concept Vocabulary

As you perform your first read of the excerpt from "The Hero's Adventure," you will encounter these words.

infantile	psyche	dependency

Context Clues To infer the meaning of an unfamiliar word, look to its context—the words and sentences that surround it.

Example: Sammy complained that he was experiencing **vertigo** and could not seem to get his balance.

Explanation: The underlined context clues provide hints that *vertigo* means "state of being dizzy or off balance."

Example: The senator told his **constituents,** "If you vote for me in the next election, I will make our state great again!"

Explanation: The underlined context clues help you to infer that *constituents* refers to the people who are able to vote for the senator and determine his reelection. *Constituents* must mean "people represented by a public official."

Apply your knowledge of context clues and other vocabulary strategies to determine the meanings of unfamiliar words you encounter during your first read.

First Read NONFICTION

Apply these strategies as you conduct your first read. You will have an opportunity to complete a close read after your first read.

NOTICE the general ideas of the text. *What* is it about? *Who* is involved?

ANNOTATE by marking vocabulary and key passages you want to revisit.

CONNECT ideas within the selection to what you have already read.

RESPOND by completing the Comprehension Check and by writing a brief summary of the selection.

STANDARDS

Reading Informational Text
By the end of grade 9, read and comprehend literary nonfiction in the grades 9–10 text complexity band proficiently, with scaffolding as needed at the high end of the range.

Language
Use context as a clue to the meaning of a word or phrase.

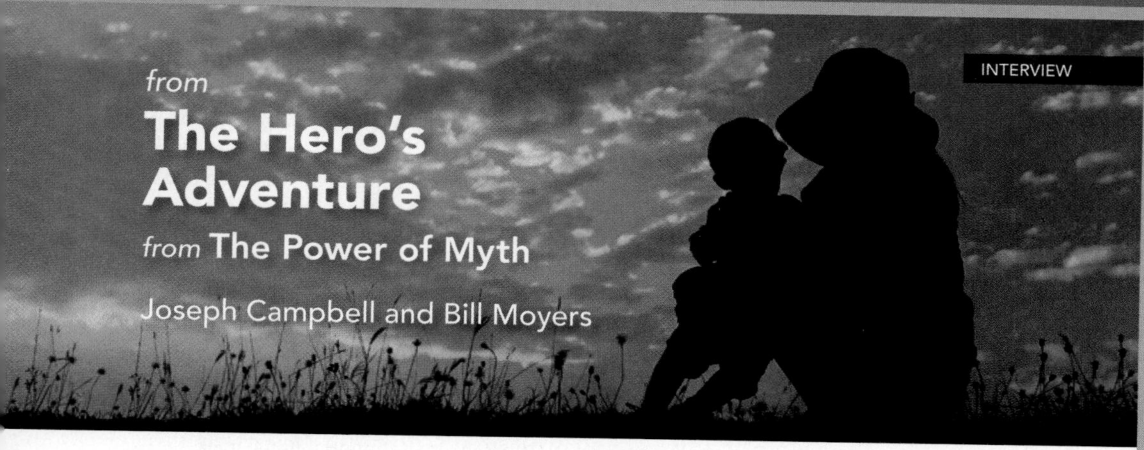

INTERVIEW

from

The Hero's Adventure

from The Power of Myth

Joseph Campbell and Bill Moyers

DIGITAL PERSPECTIVES

Concept Vocabulary

INFANTILE If groups are struggling to define *infantile* in paragraph 6, point out the words and phrases used before and after it in the text. The author includes *child* and *childish*. In addition, part of the word *infantile* is *infant*, which also suggests its meaning.
Possible response: *Infantile* must mean "childish."

PSYCHE If groups are struggling to define *psyche* in paragraph 6, point out the surrounding words in the text, such as *personality* and *psychological*. By understanding what these words mean, you can determine the meaning of *psyche*.
Possible response: *Psyche* must mean "a person's mind or soul."

DEPENDENCY If groups are struggling to define *dependency* in paragraph 6, point out that the sentence provides an explanation of the word by discussing how children need protection and supervision.
Possible response: *Dependency* must mean "needing someone or something."

BACKGROUND

Joseph Campbell first published his theories about the structure of myth in his 1949 book *The Hero With A Thousand Faces*. In it, he describes the monomyth, a single central myth that he believes is present in all human societies. This interview is a brief excerpt of a famous series of conversations between Campbell and Bill Moyers.

SCAN FOR MULTIMEDIA

1 **Moyers:** Why are there so many stories of the hero in mythology?

2 **Campbell:** Because that's what's worth writing about. Even in popular novels, the main character is a hero or heroine who has found or done something beyond the normal range of achievement and experience. A hero is someone who has given his or her life to something bigger than oneself.

3 **Moyers:** So in all of these cultures, whatever the local costume the hero might be wearing, what is the deed?

4 **Campbell:** Well, there are two types of deed. One is the physical deed, in which the hero performs a courageous act in battle or saves a life. The other kind is the spiritual deed, in which the hero learns to experience the supernormal range of human spiritual life and then comes back with a message.

5 The usual hero adventure begins with someone from whom something has been taken, or who feels there's something lacking in the normal experiences available or permitted to the members of his society. This person then takes off on a series of adventures beyond the ordinary, either to recover what has been lost or to discover some life-giving elixir. It's usually a cycle, a going and a returning.

6 But the structure and something of the spiritual sense of this adventure can be seen already anticipated in the puberty or initiation rituals of early tribal societies, through which a child is compelled to give up its childhood and become an adult—to die, you might say, to its **infantile** personality and **psyche** and come back as a responsible adult. This is a fundamental psychological transformation that everyone has to undergo. We are in childhood in a condition of **dependency** under someone's protection and supervision for some

NOTES

Mark context clues or indicate another strategy you used that helped you determine meaning.

infantile (IHN fuhn tyl) *adj.*
MEANING:

psyche (SY kee) *n.*
MEANING:

dependency (dih PEHN duhn see) *n.*
MEANING:

FACILITATING SMALL-GROUP CLOSE LEARNING

CLOSE READ: Interviews As groups perform the close review, circulate among them and offer support as needed. Emphasize that this is an unusual piece because it is an interview in which the author discusses his rationale for writing about heroes. What is an advantage of reading an interview with the author? How does this help you interpret the text? Remind students to think about what authors want their readers to know about their work and what they want readers to interpret for themselves. Are there any drawbacks to hearing what the author has to say about his or her work?

CLOSER LOOK

Analyze Comparisons

Circulate among groups as students conduct their close read. Suggest that groups close read paragraph 10. Encourage them to talk about the annotations they mark. If needed, provide the following support.

ANNOTATE: Have students mark details in this paragraph that are used to make stark comparisons between two different kinds of events, or work with small groups to have students participate while you highlight them together.

QUESTION: Guide students to consider what these details might tell them. Ask what a reader can infer from the author's comparison, and accept student responses.
Possible response: The author equates dying in childbirth with dying in battle, defining them both as heroic acts worthy of the ultimate reward of admittance to heaven. He also notes the mother's part in the heroic act of birth.

CONCLUDE: Help students to formulate conclusions about the importance of these details in the text. Ask students why the author might have included these details.
Possible response: The author indicates that men and women are capable of performing different but equally heroic acts.

Remind students that by comparing and contrasting, an author helps the reader better understand each of the ideas, events, or objects he or she is comparing and their relationship.

Additional **English Language Support** is available in the Interactive Teacher's Edition.

NOTES

fourteen to twenty-one years—and if you're going on for your Ph.D., this may continue to perhaps thirty-five. You are in no way a self-responsible, free agent, but an obedient dependent, expecting and receiving punishments and rewards. To evolve out of this position of psychological immaturity to the courage of self-responsibility and assurance requires a death and a resurrection. That's the basic motif of the universal hero's journey—leaving one condition and finding the source of life to bring you forth into a richer or mature condition.

7 **Moyers:** So even if we happen not to be heroes in the grand sense of redeeming society, we still have to take that journey inside ourselves, spiritually and psychologically.

8 **Campbell:** That's right. Otto Rank in his important little book *The Myth of the Birth of the Hero* declares that everyone is a hero in birth, where he undergoes a tremendous psychological as well as physical transformation, from the condition of a little water creature living in a realm of amniotic fluid into an air-breathing mammal which ultimately will be standing. That's an enormous transformation, and had it been consciously undertaken, it would have been, indeed, a heroic act. And there was a heroic act on the mother's part, as well, who had brought this all about.

9 **Moyers:** Then heroes are not all men?

10 **Campbell:** Oh, no. The male usually has the more conspicuous role, just because of the conditions of life. He is out there in the world, and the woman is in the home. But among the Aztecs, for example, who had a number of heavens to which people's souls would be assigned according to the conditions of their death, the heaven for warriors killed in battle was the same for mothers who died in childbirth. Giving birth is definitely a heroic deed, in that it is the giving over of oneself to the life of another.

11 **Moyers:** Don't you think we've lost that truth in this society of ours, where it's deemed more heroic to go out into the world and make a lot of money than it is to raise children?

12 **Campbell:** Making money gets more advertisement. You know the old saying: if a dog bites a man, that's not a story, but if a man bites a dog, you've got a story there. So the thing that happens and happens and happens, no matter how heroic it may be, is not news. Motherhood has lost its novelty, you might say.

13 **Moyers:** That's a wonderful image, though—the mother as hero.

14 **Campbell:** It has always seemed so to me. That's something I learned from reading these myths.

15 **Moyers:** It's a journey—you have to move out of the known, conventional safety of your life to undertake this.

16 **Campbell:** You have to be transformed from a maiden to a mother. That's a big change, involving many dangers.

17 **Moyers:** And when you come back from your journey, with the child, you've brought something for the world.

18 **Campbell:** Not only that, you've got a life job ahead of you. Otto Rank makes the point that there is a world of people who think that their heroic act in being born qualifies them for the respect and support of their whole community.

19 **Moyers:** But there's still a journey to be taken after that.

20 **Campbell:** There's a large journey to be taken, of many trials.

21 **Moyers:** What's the significance of the trials, and tests, and ordeals of the hero?

22 **Campbell:** If you want to put it in terms of intentions, the trials are designed to see to it that the intending hero should be really a hero. Is he really a match for this task? Can he overcome the dangers? Does he have the courage, the knowledge, the capacity, to enable him to serve? ❧

NOTES

Comprehension Check

Complete the following items after you finish your first read. Review and clarify details with your group.

1. How does Campbell define a hero?

2. What are the two types of deeds that make up the hero's journey?

3. Describe the main stages in a typical hero's adventure.

4. **Notebook** Write a five-sentence summary of "The Hero's Adventure."

RESEARCH

Research to Clarify Choose at least one unfamiliar detail from the text. Briefly research that detail. In what way does the information you learned shed light on an aspect of the interview?

DIGITAL PERSPECTIVES

Comprehension Check

Possible responses:

1. Campbell defines a hero as someone who has given his or her life to something bigger than himself or herself.
2. The two types of deeds that make up a hero's journey are physical and spiritual deeds.
3. A hero's adventure usually begins with someone from whom something has been taken or someone who feels he or she has been wronged in some way. The person goes through a transformation and evolves psychologically and physically. This adventure unfolds beyond the ordinary as the person seeks to recover what was lost or gain some sort of balance.
4. "The Hero's Adventure" is about the qualities that make a hero. A hero is someone who does something extraordinary. Joseph Campbell describes to Bill Moyers the elements of a hero and explains why both men and women are heroes. He also emphasizes the importance of taking a journey. The journey tests a person's true ability to be a hero.

Research

Research to Clarify If groups struggle to identify a detail to research, you may want to suggest one of the following topics: Aztec heavens or Otto Rank's *The Myth of the Birth of the Hero*.

PERSONALIZE FOR LEARNING

Challenge

Relating to Personal Experiences Ask students to think about real-life heroes they may have met personally or have heard about through family, friends, or the media. What made that individual a hero? What heroic act did he or she partake in? Discuss how the heroes influenced or inspired the students. What did they learn from these heroic acts? What does this say about the definition and role of a hero?

Jump Start

CLOSE READ Have students close read the excerpt from *The Hero's Adventure*. Ask them to consider what kinds of stories contain heroes. Then have groups talk about where they may see heroes in everyday life.

Close Read the Text

If needed, model close reading by using the Annotation Highlights in the Interactive Teacher's Edition. Remind students to use Accountable Talk in their discussions and to support one another as they complete the close read.

Analyze the Text

1. **Possible response:** Each person is capable of acting in a heroic way. Behaving in a heroic way might not make everyone a hero. Therefore, this statement might water down the idea of heroism.
2. **Passages will vary by group.** Remind students to explain why they chose the passage they presented to group members.
3. **Responses will vary by group.**

Concept Vocabulary

Why These Words? Possible response: These words all have to do with people's minds and behaviors.

Practice

Possible responses:

- Bullying had a negative effect on Ana's *psyche.*
- She was getting tired of his *infantile* behavior.
- Sarah could see that her best friend showed a lot of *dependency* on her parents.

Word Network

Possible words: *discover, undertake, adventures*

Word Study

For more support, see **Concept Vocabulary and Word Study.**

Possible responses:

- *Draconian* comes from Draco, the first legislator of Athens known for his harsh rule of law.
- *Herculean* comes from Hercules, a Greek mythological hero with enormous strength.
- *Iridescent* comes from Iris, a goddess in Greek mythology who was seen as a rainbow.
- *Lethargic* comes from the Greek mythological river Lethe, also known as the river of forgetfulness.

MAKING MEANING

from THE HERO'S ADVENTURE

Close Read the Text

Close Read (ANNOTATE · QUESTION · CONCLUDE)

With your group, revisit sections of the text you marked during your First Read. **Annotate** details that you notice. What **questions** do you have? What can you **conclude**?

Analyze the Text

CITE TEXTUAL EVIDENCE to support your answers.

Complete the activities.

1. **Review and Clarify** With your group, reread paragraphs 4–8 of the interview. Discuss the idea that "everyone is a hero." Does this concept grant dignity to every individual, or does it weaken the idea of heroism?
2. **Present and Discuss** Now, work with your group to share the passages from the selection that you found especially important. Discuss what you notice in the selection, what questions you asked, and what conclusions you reached.
3. **Essential Question:** *What can we learn from a journey?* What has this text taught you about journeys? Discuss with your group.

TIP

GROUP DISCUSSION
Consider "trying on" opinions that are different from your own by expressing and defending opposite viewpoints as clearly and strongly as possible. This technique can help you understand other points of view and may lead you to modify or expand your own response.

LANGUAGE DEVELOPMENT

Concept Vocabulary

infantile   psyche   dependency

Why These Words? The three concept vocabulary words are related. With your group, determine what the words have in common. Write your ideas, and add another word that fits the category.

Practice

Notebook Confirm your understanding of these words by writing sentences as a team. One group member begins with a single word. Take turns adding one word at a time until you have a complete sentence that uses one concept vocabulary word. Evaluate the sentence as a group to make sure the word is used correctly. Repeat for the other two concept vocabulary words.

WORD NETWORK

Add interesting words related to journeys from the text to your Word Network.

Word Study

Notebook **Etymology: Greek Names** A word's origins are called its **etymology**. The word *psyche* comes from a name from Greek mythology. Psyche was a young woman who fell in love with the god Eros. As a result of their relationship, she became closely identified with the soul—a connection still reflected in the meaning of the English word *psyche.*

1. Research the etymology of each of these other words that come from Greek mythology: *draconian, herculean, iridescent, lethargic.*
2. Share with your group information about the original Greek names, and discuss how the words' origins are reflected in their English meanings.

STANDARDS

Reading Informational Text
Analyze how the author unfolds an analysis or series of ideas or events, including the order in which the points are made, how they are introduced and developed, and the connections that are drawn between them.

Language
- Consult general and specialized reference materials, both print and digital, to find the pronunciation of a word or determine or clarify its precise meaning, its part of speech, or its etymology.
- Demonstrate understanding of figurative language, word relationships, and nuances in word meanings.

664 UNIT 5 • JOURNEYS OF TRANSFORMATION

FORMATIVE ASSESSMENT

Analyze the Text

If students struggle to close read the text, **then** provide the **The Hero's Adventure: Text Questions** available online in the Interactive Teacher's Edition or Unit Resources. Answers and DOK levels are also available.

Concept Vocabulary

If students struggle to identify the concept, **then** have students reread the words in context and think again about how they are related.

Word Study

If students fail to identify a word's etymology, **then** help them research the word's origins. For Reteach and Practice, see **Word Study: Greek Names (RP).**

Analyze Craft and Structure

Development of Ideas An **interview** is an exchange of ideas between an interviewer and an expert or someone who has had a unique experience. The basic structure of an interview is the **Q&A** (question-and-answer) **format**. A good interviewer does not simply follow a script of prepared questions, wait for an answer, and proceed to the next question. Instead, interviewers use different types of questions and statements to create a fluid exchange of ideas. The interviewer builds on and clarifies the interviewee's ideas during the conversation, resulting in a smooth progression of anecdotes and ideas that informs and engages the audience. In most cases, interviews are edited for organization and consistency before publication.

Interviews may include these techniques to develop and communicate ideas:

- **Follow-up questions** build on the interview subject's response, clarifying and deepening answers.
- **Restatements,** or paraphrases, help an interviewer make sure the audience understands the main point the interviewee is communicating.
- **Clarifications** focus on a specific part of a response, sometimes simplifying the original idea and other times providing more detail.

TIP

COLLABORATION

When analyzing the structure of a text as a group, have each group member scan the text for one technique or strategy. Then, share your analyses to draw conclusions about which strategies are used most frequently and most effectively.

Practice

CITE TEXTUAL EVIDENCE to support your answers.

Working as a group, use the chart to analyze how ideas are introduced and developed in "The Hero's Adventure." Cite an example of each technique listed. Then, explain how the technique is used to introduce, build on, or clarify an idea.

TECHNIQUE	EXAMPLES	EXPLANATION
Initial Question	"Why are there so many stories of the hero in mythology?" from paragraph 1	This initiates a conversation about where the concept of a "hero" originated and what it means to be a hero.
Follow-Up Question	"Then heroes are not all men?" from paragraph 9	The interviewer is following up on Campbell's previous statement.
Restatement	"So even if we happen not to be heroes in the grand sense of redeeming society, we still have to take that journey inside ourselves, spiritually and psychologically." from paragraph 7	The interviewer restates Campbell's philosophy about heroes and their physical and spiritual journeys.
Clarification	"It's a journey—you have to move out of the known, conventional safety of your life to undertake this." from paragraph 15	The interviewer uses clarification to simplify the concept of a hero's journey

DIGITAL PERSPECTIVES

Analyze Craft and Structure

Development of Ideas Discuss with students that authors often develop their ideas in an interview using a question and answer format. Whether or not ideas are developed properly depends on the skill set of the interviewer. A poor interviewer might not draw out the interviewee's ideas. A good, skilled interviewer will know what questions to ask to extract the most engaging information from the interviewee. Additional ways to develop ideas through interviews include asking follow-up questions, making restatements (or paraphrases), and clarifying information that the interviewee provides. For more support, see **Analyze Craft and Structure: Development of Ideas.**

See possible responses in chart on Student page.

FORMATIVE ASSESSMENT

Analyze Craft and Structure

If students fail to understand the development of ideas, **then** have them reread the interview and indicate the techniques the interviewer uses.

For Reteach and Practice, see **Analyze Craft and Structure: Development of Ideas (RP).**

PERSONALIZE FOR LEARNING

English Language Support

Writing Interview Questions Have students write additional questions that they would like to ask Joseph Campbell, the man who is interviewed in the selection.

Have pairs of students write two additional open-ended questions. **EMERGING**

Have students write two open-ended questions and one closed question and explain why they want to ask them. **EXPANDING**

Have students write two closed questions and three open-ended questions. Have students explain the kinds of information they would want to gather from their questions. **BRIDGING**

An expanded **English Language Support Lesson** on Interviews is available in the Digital Teacher's Edition.

FACILITATING

Conventions

Remind students of the definition of gerund, and give them examples. As you review the interview with students, identify gerunds in the text. Encourage students to think about the difference between nouns and verbs as you discuss which words in the the text are gerunds.

MAKE IT INTERACTIVE

Have students write the example sentences on sentence strips and instruct them to underline the gerund. Then, have them identify how the gerund is used in the sentence.

Read It

See possible responses in chart on Student page.

Write It

Possible response:

In the interview, Campbell and Moyers discuss the meaning of a hero and the elements found in heroic stories. Campbell discusses his strategy for structuring a heroic adventure, while Moyers drives the conversation with questions and clarifying statements that help the audience follow along. Several examples of heroes are given, including comparisons between male and female heroes and their heroic acts. Campbell also discusses the importance of going on a journey. Then they discuss the significance of the hero's journey.

FORMATIVE ASSESSMENT

Conventions

If students are unable to differentiate between verbs and gerunds, **then** have them look through the transcript of the interview to identify verbs that end in *-ing* and then discuss what role each word serves in the sentence. For Reteach and Practice, see **Conventions: Gerunds (RP).**

LANGUAGE DEVELOPMENT

from THE HERO'S ADVENTURE

Conventions

Gerunds and Gerund Phrases A **gerund** is a form of a verb that ends in *-ing* and acts as a noun. A **gerund phrase** is a gerund and its modifiers, objects, or complements, all acting together as a noun.

This box shows examples of the ways a gerund or gerund phrase can function in a sentence. The gerunds are italicized, and the gerund phrases are underlined.

Subject: *Surfing* is Heather's hobby.

Direct Object: Yan enjoys *floating* slowly down the river.

Predicate Noun: Ahmed's greatest talent is *playing* the piano.

Object of a Preposition: Wei never gets tired of *playing* boardgames.

Appositive Phrase: I am putting off the worst chore, *cleaning* the kitchen.

Read It

Work individually. Read these sentences from "The Hero's Adventure." In the chart, identify each gerund phrase and its function in the sentence. Discuss your answers with your group.

SENTENCE	GERUND PHRASE	FUNCTION
So even if we happen not to be heroes in the grand sense of redeeming society . . . (paragraph 7)	redeeming society	object of a preposition
Making money gets more advertisement. (paragraph 7)	making money	subject
. . . it is the giving over of oneself to the life of another. (paragraph 10)	giving over of oneself to the life of another	predicate noun
That's the basic motif of the universal hero's journey—leaving one condition. . . . (paragraph 6)	leaving one condition	appositive phrase

Write It

Notebook Write a paragraph summarizing what Campbell and Moyers talked about in the interview. In your paragraph, use at least two gerund phrases.

STANDARDS

Writing

- Conduct short as well as more sustained research projects to answer a question or solve a problem; narrow or broaden the inquiry when appropriate; synthesize multiple sources on the subject, demonstrating understanding of the subject under investigation.
- Draw evidence from literary or informational texts to support analysis, reflection, and research.

Language

- Demonstrate command of the conventions of standard English grammar and usage when writing or speaking.
- Use various types of phrases and clauses to convey specific meanings and add variety and interest to writing or presentations.

EFFECTIVE EXPRESSION

Research

Assignment

With your group, create a **multimedia presentation** in which you incorporate charts, images, video, music, or any other media that help convey your ideas effectively to explain a subject. Choose from the following options:

- ☐ Research and present the "origin story" of a hero from literature, film, television, or another narrative choice. Incorporate Campbell's theories about what heroism is.
- ☐ Joseph Campbell's philosophy is often summarized in his quote "Follow your bliss." Research what Campbell means by this quotation and consider whether or not this belief is consistent with the ideas he expresses in the interview.
- ☐ Moyers and Campbell discuss one way that women can be heroes. Research three different cultural perspectives on female heroes and relate them to the concept of the hero's journey.

Project Plan Make a list of tasks that your group will need to carry out. Assign individual group members to carry out each task. Determine how you will obtain or create multimedia items for your presentation, which may include text, charts, images, video, music, and other media. Use this chart to organize your plans.

Working Title: ______________________________

TASK	WHO	QUESTIONS TO ASK

Practice Practice your presentation before you present it to your class. Include the following performance techniques to help you achieve the desired effect.

- Speak clearly and comfortably without rushing.
- Vary the tone and pitch of your voice in order to convey meaning and add interest. Avoid speaking in a flat, monotone style.
- Use appropriate and effective body language. Maintain eye contact to keep your audience's attention.
- Ensure that you can present your media smoothly, without technical problems.

EVIDENCE LOG

Before moving on to a new selection, go to your Evidence Log and record what you learned from "The Hero's Adventure."

DIGITAL PERSPECTIVES

Research

Project Plan Remind students to consult the project plan chart to ensure that each person in the group fulfills his or her assigned role.

Practice Assign time limits to student presentations and encourage students to time their presentations as they practice to ensure that they will be able to deliver their entire presentation and maintain a consistent pace. For more support, see **Research: Multimedia Presentation.**

Evidence Log Support students in completing their Evidence Log. This paced activity will help prepare them for the Performance-Based Assessment at the end of the unit.

FORMATIVE ASSESSMENT

Research

If students are unable to select an assignment, have them select the topic they thought was least developed in the interview.

For Reteach and Practice, see **Research: Multimedia Presentation (RP).**

Selection Test

Administer *The Hero's Adventure* Selection Test, which is available in both print and digital formats online in Assessments.

DIGITAL PERSPECTIVES

Enriching the Text Show students clips of movies or real-life interviews that depict heroes. Be sure to preview the clips in advance to make sure the content is appropriate for your class.

After students have viewed the clips, have them discuss how they relate to the author's description and definition of heroes. After showing the clips, have students discuss whether they agree or disagree with the author's definition of a hero and why. (Research to Explore)

Courage • Ithaka • *from* The Narrow Road of the Interior

AUDIO SUMMARIES
Audio summaries of "Courage,' "Ithaka," and the excerpt from "The Narrow Road of the Interior" are available online in both English and Spanish in the Interactive Teacher's Edition or Unit Resources. Assigning these summaries prior to reading the selection may help students build additional background knowledge and set a context for their first read.

Summary

These three texts contrast the grand and mundane in travel.

Anne Sexton's poem "Courage" looks at life as a series of journeys, through childhood and onward. It emphasizes the connection between bravery and love.

C.P. Cavafy's poem "Ithaka" plays on the myth of the hero Odysseus, and emphasizes that what one gains on the journey may be much greater than what one finds at the destination.

The excerpt from Matsuo Bashō's "The Narrow Road of the Interior," a travelogue with embedded poetry, compares the sun, the moon, and the years gone by as travelers. The author finds a desire to be as rootless as these entities. He lives for a while near a riverside, until spring arrives, and he gives away his home, realizing it is time to move on once again.

Insight

These texts show the significance even a seemingly small journey can have. "Courage" focuses on the heroism of going through life. "Ithaka" puts particular emphasis on what one can gain along the way. The excerpt from "The Narrow Road of the Interior" looks at travel as a means of healing so that one may settle down in peace again.

ESSENTIAL QUESTION:
What can we learn from a journey?

Connection to Essential Question

These three selections provide differing perspectives on the Essential Question. "Courage" discusses how life teaches us to be brave. "Ithaka" concludes with how experience can change our perception of value—Ithaka is poorer than other places Odysseus went, but as his hometown it has a deeper value. The excerpt from "The Narrow Road of the Interior" shows how a voyage can teach you to live with yourself.

SMALL-GROUP LEARNING PERFORMANCE TASK
What different types of journeys are there and how can they transform someone?

UNIT PERFORMANCE-BASED ASSESSMENT
When does the journey matter more than the destination?

Connection to Performance Tasks

Small-Group Learning Task In this Performance Task students will consider how a journey can be transformative. "Courage" and "The Narrow Road of the Interior" focus on the transformation we go though as we journey across life and time. "Ithaka" speaks to the transformation that occurs when taking a journey over a period of time. In "Courage" and the excerpt from "The Narrow Road of the Interior" the passage of time is itself a journey, even if one does not leave home.

Unit Performance-Based Assessment These selections all speak to the idea that the journey is as important if not more important than the destination. "Ithaka" is an interesting case, in that the journey teaches the true significance of the destination even as it makes the destination seem small and poor.

LESSON RESOURCES

	Making Meaning	Language Development	Effective Expression
Lesson	**First Read** **Close Read** **Analyze the Text** **Analyze Craft and Structure**	**Concept Vocabulary** **Word Study** **Author's Style**	**Speaking and Listening**
Instructional Standards	**RL.10** By the end of grade 9, read and comprehend literature . . . **L.5** Demonstrate understanding of figurative language . . .	**L.4.a** Use context as a clue . . . **L.4.d** Verify the preliminary determination . . . **L.4.b** Identify and correctly use patterns of word changes . . . **RL.4** Determine the meaning of words and phrases . . . **L.1** Demonstrate command of the conventions . . .	**SL.1** Initiate and participate effectively in a range of collaborative discussions . . .
STUDENT RESOURCES			
Available online in the Interactive Student Edition or Unit Resources	Selection Audio First-Read Guide: Poetry Close-Read Guide: Poetry	Word Network	Evidence Log
TEACHER RESOURCES			
Selection Resources Available online in the Interactive Teacher's Edition or Unit Resources	Audio Summaries Annotation Highlights EL Highlights English Language Support Lesson: Point of View Poetry Collection: Text Questions Analyze Craft and Structure: Figurative Language	Concept Vocabulary and Word Study Author's Style: Point of View	Speaking and Listening: Group Discussion
Reteach/Practice (RP) Available online in the Interactive Teacher's Edition or Unit Resources	Analyze Craft and Structure: Figurative Language (RP)	Word Study: Old English Suffix *-some* (RP) Author's Style: Point of View (RP)	Speaking and Listening: Group Discussion (RP)
Assessment Available online in Assessments	Selection Test		
My Resources	A Unit 5 Answer Key is available online and in the Interactive Teacher's Edition.		

Reading Support

Text Complexity Rubric: Poetry	
Quantitative Measures	
Lexile: NP; NP; 1210 **Text Length:** 47 lines; 37 lines; 216 words	
Qualitative Measures	
Knowledge Demands ①—②—❸—④—⑤	"Courage" contains the familiar themes of childhood along with references to war and old age. For "Ithaka" and the excerpt from "The Narrow Road of the Interior," students may need additional context about Ancient Greece and Japanese culture.
Structure ①—❷—③—④—⑤	"Courage" and "Ithaka" use conventional forms of free-verse poetry. The excerpt from "The Narrow Road of the Interior" contains prose and haiku.
Language Conventionality and Clarity ①—②—③—❹—⑤	Selections contain above-level words and figurative language. "Ithaka" contains Greek words and the excerpt from "The Narrow Road of the Interior" contains Japanese words.
Levels of Meaning/Purpose ①—②—❸—④—⑤	"Courage" and "Ithaka" contain ideas that are developed through the use of symbolism. Students will encounter real and metaphorical journeys within the selections.

DECIDE AND PLAN

English Language Support

Provide English Learners with support for language and meaning as they read the selection.

Language Students may need help with figurative language. Review metaphors and similes such as *your courage was a small coal* and *love as simple as shaving soap*. Discuss that similes use *like* or *as* to compare while metaphors do not. Ask students to develop a metaphor or simile that expresses love.

Meaning Discuss literal and figurative meanings. For example, *picking the scabs off your heart; what joy, you come into harbors seen for the first time;* and *had I swept away the old cobwebs from my dilapidated riverside hermitage*. Ask students to infer the meanings of these lines. What is real? What is imagined? What might be both?

Strategic Support

Provide students with strategic support to ensure that they can successfully read the text.

Knowledge Demands Have students research the history of how haiku emerged from the poetic form of renga. Ask students to explore how renga and haiku arose from collaborative environments. Have students connect this background information to what they read in the excerpt from "The Narrow Road of the Interior."

Structure Discuss the differences between the free-verse structure of the first two selections in comparison to the meter contained within the haiku. Have students consider: *Are formal structures more limiting? Do the words used in free-verse poetry have as much importance as the ones in haiku?*

Challenge

Provide students who need to be challenged with ideas for how they can go beyond a simple interpretation of the text.

Text Analysis Have students identify words in the text that are related to real and metaphorical journeys. Ask students to analyze lines such as: *hope the journey is a long one* and *but do not hurry the journey at all*.

Written Response Ask students to review the excerpt from "The Narrow Road of the Interior." Discuss how it is filled with imagery about Bashō's experiences. Have students use their knowledge of the haiku form to write haiku based on Bashō's journey.

TEACH

Read and Respond

Have the class do their first read of the selection. Then have them complete their close read. Finally, work with them on the Making Meaning and Effective Expression activities.

Standards Support Through Teaching and Learning Cycle

IDENTIFY NEEDS

Analyze results of the Beginning-of-Year Assessment, focusing on the items relating to Unit 5. Also take into consideration student performance to this point and your observations of where particular students struggle.

DECIDE AND PLAN

- If students have performed poorly on items matching these standards, then provide selection scaffolds before assigning them the on-level lesson provided in the Student Edition.
- If students have done well on the Beginning-of-Year Assessment, then challenge them to keep progressing and learning by giving them opportunities to practice the skills in depth.
- Use the Selection Resources listed on the Planning pages for "Courage," "Ithaka," and the excerpt from "The Narrow Road of the Interior" to help students continually improve their ability to master the standards.

Instructional Standards: Courage • Ithaka • *from* The Narrow Road of the Interior

	Catching Up	This Year	Looking Forward
Reading	You may wish to administer the **Author's Style: Point of View (RP)** worksheet to better familiarize students with point of view.	**RL.4** Determine the meaning of words and phrases as they are used in the text, including figurative and connotative meanings; analyze the cumulative impact of specific word choices on meaning and tone.	Challenge students to rewrite a selection using a different point of view. Then have them analyze the author's choice.
Speaking and Listening	You may wish to administer the **Speaking and Listening: Group Discussion (RP)** worksheet to better prepare students for their presentations.	**SL.1** Initiate and participate effectively in a range of collaborative discussions with diverse partners on grades 9-10 topics, texts, and issues, building on others' ideas and expressing their own clearly and persuasively.	Challenge students to refer back to other texts from this unit in their presentations.
Language	Review the **Word Study: Old English Suffix *-some* (RP)** worksheet with students to better familiarize them with the suffix. You may wish to administer the **Analyze Craft and Structure: Figurative Language (RP)** worksheet to better familiarize students with similes, metaphors and extended metaphors.	**L.4.b** Identify and correctly use patterns of word changes that indicate different meanings or parts of speech. **L.5** Demonstrate understanding of figurative language, word relationships, and nuances in word meaning.	Have students locate other words in the text that came from Old English. Challenge students to identify whether the poets' uses of figurative language are universal; in other words, are they archetypes?

TEACH

Implement the planned lesson, and gather evidence of student learning.

ANALYZE AND REVISE

- Analyze student work for evidence of student learning.
- Identify whether or not students have met the expectations in the standards.
- Identify implications for future instruction.

Jump Start

FIRST READ Ask students to consider the following prompt: *What makes a journey an adventure?* Engage students in a discussion about what can be learned along a journey in order to set the context for reading "Poetry Collection 1." As students share their thoughts, have them explain the reasons for their opinion.

Concept Vocabulary

Ask groups to study the three types of context clues and discuss how they can help clarify meaning. Encourage groups to think of one other type that they might encounter in a text. Possibilities include antonyms, examples, and definitions.

FIRST READ

Have students perform the steps of the first read independently:

NOTICE: Encourage students to notice the differences and similarities in each author's approach to journeys and voyages.

ANNOTATE: Tell students to mark lines that interest them for any reason and that they wish to examine in greater depth.

CONNECT: Encourage students to make connections to their own experiences or to texts they have read, as well as to accounts they have heard from others.

RESPOND: Students will answer questions to demonstrate understanding.

Point out to students that while they will always complete the Respond step at the end of the first read, the other steps will probably happen somewhat concurrently. You may wish to print copies of the **First-Read Guide: Poetry** for students to use.

POETRY COLLECTION 1

Courage
Ithaka
from The Narrow Road of the Interior

Concept Vocabulary

As you perform your first read of these three poems, you will encounter the following words.

awesome	destined	eternal

Context Clues If these words are unfamiliar to you, try using context clues to help you determine their meanings. There are various types of context clues that you may encounter as you read.

Synonyms: The house was terribly shabby, really **dilapidated**.

Restatement of Ideas: The **convoluted** explanation confused the children, who were not accustomed to someone speaking in a rambling, disconnected way.

Contrast of Ideas: I really like to stay home, but she gets **wanderlust** every time she sees a train.

Apply your knowledge of context clues and other vocabulary strategies to determine the meanings of unfamiliar words you encounter during your first read. If necessary, verify the meaning you infer using a dictionary.

First Read POETRY

Apply these strategies as you conduct your first read. You will have an opportunity to complete a close read after your first read.

NOTICE who or what is "speaking" the poem and whether the poem tells a story or describes a single moment.

ANNOTATE by marking vocabulary and key passages you want to revisit.

CONNECT ideas within the selection to what you already know and what you have already read.

RESPOND by completing the Comprehension Check.

First Read

STANDARDS

Reading Literature
By the end of grade 9, read and comprehend literature, including stories, dramas, and poems, in the grades 9–10 text complexity band proficiently, with scaffolding as needed at the high end of the range.

Language
- Use context as a clue to the meaning of a word or phrase.
- Verify the preliminary determination of the meaning of a word or phrase.

About the Poets

Anne Sexton (1928–1974) had a difficult childhood growing up in Massachusetts. She attended boarding school, married at nineteen to a soldier serving in the Korean War, and later found work as a model. Sexton's work is considered to be part of the "confessional" movement in American poetry. Emerging in the 1950s and including poets such as Sylvia Plath and John Berryman, confessional poetry emphasized intensely personal experiences in a way not previously seen in American literature.

Of Greek descent, **C. P. Cavafy** (1863–1933) was born in Egypt to parents who worked in the import-export business. After the death of his father, Cavafy's family relocated to Liverpool, England, where Cavafy spent most of his teenage years. An obscure poet during his lifetime, Cavafy is now regarded as one of Greece's greatest writers.

Widely regarded as the seventeenth-century master of haiku, **Matsuo Bashō** (1644–1694) became interested in literature as a child and soon began writing poems in collaboration with others. After losing his home to a fire, Basho walked over 1,200 miles for more than five months and described his travels in some of his best-known poems, including "Travelogue of Weather-Beaten Bones."

Backgrounds

Courage

Anne Sexton's life and work were intimately tied together. She struggled with mental illness but found in poetry a way to confront and release her fears. Perhaps it was her daily struggle with fear that inspired this poem about courage.

Ithaka

Ithaka (or Ithaca), a part of Greece, is a real island in the Ionian sea. It is also the fabled island home to which Odysseus, the epic hero of the *Odyssey*, struggles to return. It is this second meaning that drives the symbolism of this poem.

from The Narrow Road of the Interior

This is an excerpt from Bashō's famous *haibun*, a classical Japanese form of literature that combines elements of prose with *haiku*. Haiku are unrhymed verses arranged into three lines of five, seven, and five syllables. The haiku poet often uses a striking image from nature to convey a strong emotion.

DIGITAL PERSPECTIVES

Courage • Ithaka • *from* The Narrow Road of the Interior

What are some reasons people choose to travel? How does one prepare to take a long journey to a new place? What may be gained from such a trip? Modeling the questions readers might ask as they read the poetry collection for the first time brings the text alive for students and connects it to the Small-Group Performance Task assignment. Selection audio and print capability for the selection are available in the Interactive Teacher's Edition.

FACILITATING SMALL-GROUP CLOSE LEARNING

CLOSE READ: Poetry As groups perform the close read, circulate and offer support as needed.

- Remind groups that when they read poetry, they should pay particular attention to the figurative language.
- If a group is confused about the poem's meaning, suggest that they consider each word the poet uses and think about every possible meaning the word may have.
- Challenge group members to debate the poems' meanings to develop a deeper understanding about the message in each poem. Encourage student to compare the poems.

POETRY

Courage

Anne Sexton

PERSONALIZE FOR LEARNING

Strategic Support

Theme As students work to read "Courage," they may require support to identify the theme because it is implied rather than explicitly stated. Have students review line 1 and the way the rest of the lines support it. Remind students that a text's theme is not the topic of the text, but rather the "big idea" about life that the author trying to convey.

Have students create T-charts with one side for identifying the theme, and the other for recording details that prove the theme. If students continue to need support, have them identify important details from the poem and ask them to think about how those details relate to one another.

SCAN FOR MULTIMEDIA

It is in the small things we see it.
The child's first step,
as **awesome** as an earthquake.
The first time you rode a bike,
wallowing up the sidewalk.
The first spanking when your heart
went on a journey all alone.
When they called you crybaby
or poor or fatty or crazy
and made you into an alien,
you drank their acid
and concealed it.
Later,
if you faced the death of bombs and bullets
you did not do it with a banner,
you did it with only a hat to
cover your heart.
You did not fondle the weakness inside you
though it was there.
Your courage was a small coal
that you kept swallowing.
If your buddy saved you
and died himself in so doing,
then his courage was not courage,
it was love; love as simple as shaving soap.
Later,
if you have endured a great despair,
then you did it alone,
getting a transfusion from the fire,
picking the scabs off your heart,
then wringing it out like a sock.
Next, my kinsman, you powdered your sorrow,
you gave it a back rub
and then you covered it with a blanket
and after it had slept a while
it woke to the wings of the roses
and was transformed.
Later,
when you face old age and its natural conclusion
your courage will still be shown in the little ways,
each spring will be a sword you'll sharpen,
those you love will live in a fever of love,
and you'll bargain with the calendar
and at the last moment
when death opens the back door
you'll put on your carpet slippers
and stride out.

NOTES

Mark context clues or indicate another strategy you used that helped you determine meaning.

awesome (AW suhm) *adj.*

MEANING:

DIGITAL PERSPECTIVES

Concept Vocabulary

AWESOME If groups struggle to define the word *awesome* in line 3, point out the phrases "first step" and "first time" in lines 2 and 4. These are important events, and the earthquake metaphor shows that the effect is enormous. Have students use these context clues to define the word.

Possible response: *Awesome* means "amazing."

CLOSER LOOK

Infer Personification

Circulate among groups as students conduct their close read. Suggest that groups close read lines 32–37 of "Courage." Encourage them to talk about the annotations they mark. If needed, provide the following support.

ANNOTATE: Have students mark details in lines 32–37 that attribute human qualities to the concept of "sorrow," or work with small groups to have students participate as you highlight them together.

QUESTION: Guide students to consider what these details might tell them. Ask what a reader can infer from the author's word choice, and accept student responses.

Possible response: The author likens sorrow to a medicine that can heal.

CONCLUDE: Help students draw conclusions about the importance of these details in the text. Ask students why the author might have included these details.

Possible response: The speaker personifies despair by speaking about it as if it were a baby. This use of personification shows that the speaker is sensitive to his or her own despair and has learned to use it as a source of power over all human suffering.

Remind students that **personification** is a figure of speech in which a nonhuman subject is given human characteristics to make the nonhuman elements more familiar.

Additional **English Language Support** is available in the Interactive Teacher's Edition.

FACILITATING

CLOSER LOOK

Analyze Parallelism

Circulate among groups as students conduct their close read. Suggest that groups close read lines 1–14 of "Ithaka." Encourage them to talk about the annotations they mark. If needed, provide the following support.

ANNOTATE: Have students mark details in lines 1–14 that show repeated words or phrases, or work with small groups to have students participate as you highlight them together.

QUESTION: Guide students to consider what these details might tell them. Ask what a reader can infer from the author's use of repetitious language and structures, and accept student responses.

Possible response: The author repeats phrases in a parallel structure to explain and emphasize what the reader requires to transform the voyage into an adventure.

CONCLUDE: Help students to formulate conclusions about the importance of these details in the text. Ask students why the author might have included these details.

Possible response: These details are expressed by the author using a parallel structure to emphasize their importance. For example, the repeated language structures emphasize the need for "hope" and the fact that the voyage will be "long."

Remind students that **parallelism** is the repetition of words, phrases, clauses, or sentences that have the same grammatical structure or the same meaning. This device, also known as parallel structure, is used to emphasize, link, and balance related ideas—or to juxtapose contrasting ones. Poets often use parallelism to create a rhythm in which words and meanings may be emphasized.

POETRY

Ithaka

C. P. Cavafy

translated by Edmund Keeley and Philip Sherrard

SCAN FOR MULTIMEDIA

NOTES

As you set out for Ithaka
hope the voyage is a long one,
full of adventure, full of discovery.
Laistrygonians[1] and Cyclops,
angry Poseidon—don't be afraid of them:
you'll never find things like that on your way
as long as you keep your thoughts raised high,
as long as a rare excitement
stirs your spirit and your body.
Laistrygonians and Cyclops,
wild Poseidon—you won't encounter them
unless you bring them along inside your soul,
unless your soul sets them up in front of you.

1. **Laistrygonians** (lehs trih GOH nee uhnz) cannibals who destroy all of Odysseus' ships except his own and kill the crews.

Hope the voyage is a long one.
May there be many a summer morning when,
with what pleasure, what joy,
you come into harbors seen for the first time;
may you stop at Phoenician trading stations
to buy fine things,
mother of pearl and coral, amber and ebony,
sensual perfume of every kind—
as many sensual perfumes as you can;
and may you visit many Egyptian cities
to gather stores of knowledge from their scholars.

Keep Ithaka always in your mind.
Arriving there is what you are **destined** for.
But do not hurry the journey at all.
Better if it lasts for years,
so you are old by the time you reach the island,
wealthy with all you have gained on the way,
not expecting Ithaka to make you rich.

Ithaka gave you the marvelous journey.
Without her you would not have set out.
She has nothing left to give you now.

And if you find her poor, Ithaka won't have fooled you.
Wise as you will have become, so full of experience,
you will have understood by then what these Ithakas mean.

NOTES

Mark context clues or indicate another strategy you used that helped you determine meaning.

destined (DEHS tihnd) *adj.*

MEANING:

DIGITAL PERSPECTIVES

Concept Vocabulary

DESTINED If groups are struggling to define the word *destined* in line 26, point out the lines with the phrases *always in your mind, do not hurry the journey,* and *all you have gained on the way.* Have students use these context clues to define the word.

Possible response: *Destined* must mean "predetermined, or meant to be."

VOCABULARY DEVELOPMENT

Concept Vocabulary Reinforcement To increase familiarity with the concept vocabulary, ask students to use each of the words in a sentence. Encourage students to include context clues in their own sentences to demonstrate their knowledge of the word. If students are still struggling with the word, encourage them to identify the base word in each term, look up the base word in the dictionary, and then use the definition to come up with the meaning of the concept vocabulary word.

FACILITATING

The Narrow Road of the Interior

This text, "The Narrow Road of the Interior," is a travelogue with embedded poetry. Point out that in this text, the author is telling the story of his travels and includes a haiku related to his experience. Use this question to spark discussion: *Why does poetry fit well in a travelogue format?*

Possible response: Travelogues, journals, and diaries are personal writing. When traveling, people see new things, taste new foods, and meet new people. Writers may feel inspired to experiment with different habits, and poetry might express an emotion more effectively than prose.

POETRY

from

The Narrow Road of the Interior

Matsuo Bashō
translated by Helen Craig McCullough

PERSONALIZE FOR LEARNING

English Language Support

Figurative Language Note this sentence in paragraph 2 of "The Narrow Road of the Interior": *I myself fell prey to wanderlust some years ago, desiring nothing better than to be a vagrant cloud scudding before the wind.* Explain to students that this sentence contains an example of **metaphor**, a type of **figurative language** that compares one thing to another, often using colorful terms. The author compares himself traveling around to a lonesome cloud moving or bouncing about ahead of the wind. Make sure students understand the meaning of *wanderlust* as a longing to travel, and the idiom "to fall prey to" as a giving in to something. Ask students why they think the author chose to describe his wish to travel using a variety of types of figurative language and imagery. (Possible response: The author's use of metaphor and other figurative language creates an image of traveling as carefree and desirable.) **ALL LEVELS**

SCAN FOR MULTIMEDIA

1 The sun and the moon are **eternal** voyagers; the years that come and go are travelers too. For those whose lives float away on boats, for those who greet old age with hands clasping the lead ropes of horses, travel is life, travel is home. And many are the men of old who have perished as they journeyed.

2 I myself fell prey to wanderlust some years ago, desiring nothing better than to be a vagrant cloud scudding before the wind. Only last autumn, after having drifted along the seashore for a time, had I swept away the old cobwebs from my dilapidated riverside hermitage. But the year ended before I knew it, and I found myself looking at hazy spring skies and thinking of crossing Shirakawa Barrier.[1] Bewitched by the god of restlessness, I lost my peace of mind; summoned by the spirits of the road, I felt unable to settle down to anything. By the time I had mended my torn trousers, put a new cord on my hat, and cauterized my legs with moxa,[2] I was thinking only of the moon at Matsushima.[3] I turned over my dwelling to others, moved to a house belonging to Sanpū,[4] and affixed the initial page of a linked-verse sequence to one of the pillars at my cottage.

kusa no to mo sumikawaru yo zo hana no ie	Even my grass-thatched hut will have new occupants now: a display of dolls.

1. **Shirakawa** (shee rah kah wah) **Barrier** ancient gate between the northern and southern regions of Honshu, the largest island of Japan.
2. **moxa** *n.* traditional medicine treatment similar to acupuncture, using burning herbs.
3. **Matsushima** (mah tsoo shee mah) group of Japanese islands known for their scenic views.
4. **Sanpū** (sahn poo) Sanpū Sugiyama, patron of Matsuo Bashō.

NOTES

Mark context clues or indicate another strategy you used that helped you determine meaning.

eternal (ih TUR nuhl) *adj.*

MEANING:

DIGITAL PERSPECTIVES

Concept Vocabulary

ETERNAL If groups are struggling to define the word *eternal* in line 1, point out the contrast of terms in the first paragraph, "the sun and the moon" and "the years that come and go." Have students use this context clue to define the word.

Possible response: *Eternal* means "without a beginning or end."

CLOSER LOOK

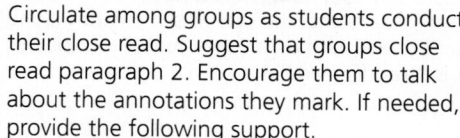

Infer Antithesis

Circulate among groups as students conduct their close read. Suggest that groups close read paragraph 2. Encourage them to talk about the annotations they mark. If needed, provide the following support.

ANNOTATE: Have students mark details in paragraph 2 that show contrasting images or ideas in the travelogue, or work with small groups to highlight them together.

QUESTION: Guide students to consider what these details indicate. Ask what a reader can infer from the description of settling down and then wanting to travel again, and accept student responses.

Possible response: The author appears restless and unable to stay in one place for very long. The cobwebs and dilapidation imply that he spends more time traveling than at his riverside hermitage.

CONCLUDE: Help students draw conclusions about the importance of these details in the text. Ask students why the author might have included these details.

Possible response: The author uses **antithesis** to emphasize the contrast between his brief stay at home and his desire to travel again, using strong language such as "bewitched by the god" and "summoned by the spirits" to stress the power of this urge.

FACILITATING

Comprehension Check

Courage

Possible responses:

1. The speaker of the poem uses the word *you* to refer both to the reader and to her own experiences because they are described so vividly that only someone who has been through the emotions herself could describe them in such detail.
2. The speaker says name calling causes someone to hide his or her true feelings and hurt.
3. The speaker tells how sorrow from a great loss causes someone to feel great pain, with "scabs" on the heart, until the person can comfort it and put it to bed with a "blanket" until it dissipates, or is "transformed."

Ithaka

Possible responses:

1. The speaker thinks when encountering Cyclops and Poseidon, a traveler should not feel afraid and in fact, should not expect to encounter them at all if the traveler remains in good spirits along the journey.
2. The speaker hopes the traveler has a long journey, full of discovery and new places and experiences.
3. The speaker tells the traveler he will be wealthy from all he has "gained on the way" in the richness of experience and beauty.

Comprehension Check

Complete the following items after you finish your first read. Review and clarify details with your group.

COURAGE

1. When the speaker of the poem says "you," is it meant to refer to only the readers' experiences—or the speaker's experiences as well? How do you know?

2. What effect does name calling have on its targets, according to the speaker?

3. According to the speaker, how does sorrow affect those who suffer a great loss?

ITHAKA

1. How does the speaker believe the traveler should react when encountering Cyclops and Poseidon?

2. What type of journey does the speaker hope the traveler has?

3. What does the speaker say will make the traveler wealthy?

from THE NARROW ROAD OF THE INTERIOR

1. In what way are the sun, the moon, and time similar to the speaker?

2. What does restlessness prevent the speaker from doing?

3. What becomes of the first page of verse the speaker writes after moving to a new home?

RESEARCH

Research to Explore The Cavafy and Bashō pieces may spark your curiosity to learn more. Briefly research a location mentioned in one of the poems. How does your newfound knowledge add to your appreciation of the text?

DIGITAL PERSPECTIVES

Comprehension Check

from The Narrow Road of the Interior

Possible responses:

1. The author connects the sun, the moon, and the passing of time by saying they are all eternal.
2. The author's restlessness prevents him from staying in any one place for very long.
3. The author posts the verse he writes to the pillar of the home he left behind.

Research

Research to Explore If groups struggle to come up with a research topic, you may want to suggest that they focus on one of the following locations: the Greek island of Ithaka (Ithaca), the Shirakawa Barrier, or the Matsushima Islands off the coast of Japan.

PERSONALIZE FOR LEARNING

Challenge

Conclusions Ask students to reflect on the impact of the three texts. Point out that often the end of a poem will include a conclusion or "take-away," although sometimes this will be derived from the entire poem. Reread the ending lines of the first two poems and the haiku included in the travelogue, and ask students to discuss how the ending lines relate to each text's meaning as a whole. Then have students write a short essay to compare and contrast the conclusions of the three texts. What do the texts have in common? How are they different?

Jump Start

CLOSE READ Ask students to consider the following prompt: *What type of journey would you most like to take?* As students discuss the prompt with their groups, have them consider the benefits they could receive from a life-changing traveling experience.

Close Read the Text

If needed, model close reading by using the Annotation Highlights in the Interactive Teacher's Edition. Remind students to use Accountable Talk in their discussions and to support one another as they complete the close read.

Analyze the Text

Possible responses:

1. The speaker in "Courage" mentions a child's first step, first time riding a bike, first spanking and name calling as specific events on the journey of life. The speaker in "Ithaka" mentions a long voyage of adventure and discovery in which one should not feel afraid of Laistrygonians, Cyclops and Poseidon, which can be euphemisms for life's challenges and emotions. **DOK 1**
2. **Passages will vary by group.** Remind students to explain why they chose the passages they presented to the group members. **DOK 2**
3. Responses will vary by group. **DOK 3**

Concept Vocabulary

Why These Words?

Possible response:

The words all describe something larger than life. Another possible word is *marvelous*.

Practice

Possible response:

If you reach the top of the cliff, you are *destined* to have an *awesome* view of the ocean's *eternal* beauty.

Word Network

Possible words: *transformed, encounter, vagrant.*

Word Study

For more support, see **Concept Vocabulary and Word Study.**

Possible responses:

1. We were astounded by the awesome size of the whale.
2. *troublesome* – causing trouble; *quarrelsome* – causing an argument; *fearsome* – causing fear; *adventuresome* – bringing on adventure.

MAKING MEANING

POETRY COLLECTION 1

Close Read the Text

Close Read — ANNOTATE · QUESTION · CONCLUDE

With your group, revisit sections of the text you marked during your first read. **Annotate** details that you notice. What **questions** do you have? What can you **conclude**?

Analyze the Text

CITE TEXTUAL EVIDENCE to support your answers.

Complete the activities.

1. **Review and Clarify** With your group, reread the first stanzas of "Courage" and "Ithaka." Discuss the way the two speakers talk about the journey of life. What specific events does each speaker mention?
2. **Present and Discuss** Now, work with your group to share the passages from the text that you found especially important. Take turns presenting your passages. Discuss what you notice in the text, what questions you asked, and what conclusions you reached.
3. **Essential Question:** *What can we learn from a journey?* What have these texts taught you about journeys? Discuss with your group.

TIP

GROUP DISCUSSION

Some group members may have good contributions to make to the discussion but find it difficult to speak up. To make sure that you hear all the best ideas, reach out to quieter group members by asking them questions.

LANGUAGE DEVELOPMENT

Concept Vocabulary

awesome · destined · eternal

Why These Words? The three concept vocabulary words are related. With your group, determine what the words have in common. Write your ideas, and add another word that fits the category.

Practice

Notebook Confirm your understanding of these words from the text by using all three of them in a single sentence. Try several variations. Use context clues to help you make the meanings clear.

WORD NETWORK

Add interesting words related to journeys from the text to your Word Network.

Word Study

Anglo-Saxon Suffix: *-some* In "Courage," the speaker describes a child's first step as "awesome as an earthquake." The word *awesome* ends with the Anglo-Saxon suffix *-some*, which means "causing," "tending to," or "to a considerable degree" and is used to form adjectives from nouns, verbs, and other adjectives.

1. Write a definition for the word *awesome* that demonstrates your understanding of the suffix *-some*.
2. Write definitions for these words ending with the suffix *-some: troublesome, fearsome, quarrelsome*. Consult a dictionary if necessary.

STANDARDS

Language

- Identify and correctly use patterns of word changes that indicate different meanings or parts of speech.
- Demonstrate understanding of figurative language, word relationships, and nuances in word meaning.

FORMATIVE ASSESSMENT

Analyze the Text

If students struggle to close read the text, **then** provide the **Poetry Collection: Text Questions** available online in the Interactive Teacher's Edition or Unit Resources. Answers and DOK levels are also available.

Concept Vocabulary

If students struggle to identify the concept, **then** have them revisit the context in which the words were used in the text.

Word Study

If students fail to identify the meanings of the words, **then** have them look in a dictionary for the meanings of other words with the suffix *-some*. For Reteach and Practice, see **Word Study: The Old English Suffix *-some* (RP).**

Analyze Craft and Structure

Figurative Language Language used imaginatively rather than literally is referred to as **figurative language**. Its meaning is not what it appears to be. To say that a person's smile is "as warm as the sun," is not to say that a thermometer put next to his or her face would register thousands of degrees. This phrase means that the person's smile makes you feel good, the way a nice, warm, sunny day does. Figurative language often compares two things—like the sun and the smile—that are essentially different. Simile and metaphor are two examples of this.

- A **simile** is a comparison that uses a connecting word, either *like* or *as*. The example given above of the sun and the smile is a simile.
- A **metaphor** is a comparison that does not use a connecting word. Instead, the comparison is either implied or directly stated: "All the world's a stage."
- An **extended metaphor** is also called a **sustained metaphor**. It involves a metaphorical comparison that is developed through multiple references and layers of meaning.

Figurative language is especially useful for poets because it allows them to express complex emotions and ideas in vivid, powerful ways.

Practice

CITE TEXTUAL EVIDENCE to support your answers.

Working individually, use this chart to record and analyze three metaphors or similes from the poems. Compare and discuss your responses with your group

METAPHOR OR SIMILE	THINGS COMPARED	EFFECT ON THE READER
"when your heart went on a journey all alone"	your heart / traveler	The author uses this metaphor to show the lonely feeling a child may experience during a first spanking.
"And if you find her poor, Ithaka won't have fooled you."	Ithaka / a person	The author expresses adulation for Ithaka throughout the poem, so here in the end, Ithaka is personified.
"travel is life, travel is home"	travel / life and home	Travel takes on two different comparisons both to life and to home, which implies the author's passion for travel.

DIGITAL PERSPECTIVES

Analyze Craft and Structure

Figurative Language Poets use language to create images in the mind of the reader. This language takes many forms that make it different from everyday speech and add to the expressiveness of a poem.

For more support, see **Analyze Craft and Structure: Figurative Language.**

See possible responses in chart on Student page.

FORMATIVE ASSESSMENT

Analyze Craft and Structure

If students fail to see the significance of the metaphor or simile, **then** have them review the figurative language in context and ask how it contributes to the meaning of the text. For Reteach and Practice, see **Analyze Craft and Structure: Figurative Language (RP).**

PERSONALIZE FOR LEARNING

English Language Support

Figurative Language Review the definitions of the figurative language devices referenced in this lesson (simile, metaphor, extended metaphor). Have students identify an example of each, and use their examples in sentences. Allow students to share their examples for additional support in learning the terms. **ALL LEVELS**

FACILITATING

Author's Style

Point of View Discuss with students that **point of view** refers to the vantage point from which a story or poem is told. There are generally three types of points of view used to narrate a story:

- **First-person:** The narrator or speaker uses the pronoun "I" when speaking, and the reader learns only what this narrator or speaker reveals through his or her point of view.
- **Third-person:** The narrator or speaker is not a character in the story or poem and makes use of **third-person pronouns**, such as *he*, *she*, or *they*. The narrator or speaker can have a limited point of view through the eyes of a single character or can be omniscient, an all-knowing observer who can describe the thoughts and feelings of all the characters.
- **Second-person:** This narration is less common and uses **direct address**, referring to the reader as "you."

For more support, see **Author's Style: Point of View.**

Read It

See possible responses in chart on Student page.

Write It

Responses will vary, but should include an original paragraph which appropriately utilizes either the first-person or the second-person point of view.

FORMATIVE ASSESSMENT

Author's Style

If students struggle to identify the point of view, **then** have them review each text and identify the pronouns used within the text. For Reteach and Practice, see **Author's Style: Point of View (RP).**

LANGUAGE DEVELOPMENT

POETRY COLLECTION 1

Author's Style

Point of View The **point of view** of a piece of literature is the perspective from which a story or poem is narrated, spoken, or told. The point of view affects every aspect of a story or poem. The two most familiar and commonly used points of view are **first person** and **third person**. In first-person point of view, the narrator or speaker is a character in the story or poem who uses pronouns such as *I*, *me*, *we*, and *us* and **reflexive pronouns** such as *myself*. In third-person point of view, the narrator or speaker is a voice outside the work who uses third-person pronouns such as *he*, *she*, *they*, *them*, *him*, and *her*. A first-person narrator/speaker may refer to other characters using third-person pronouns, but a third-person narrator/speaker will never use a first-person pronoun.

The more unusual **second-person** narrator/speaker uses **direct address**, speaking directly to the reader and using second-person pronouns such as *you* and *your*. This point of view is rarely used in fiction, but it is often used in advertisements, handbooks, and song lyrics. It is frequently used in poetry. It focuses attention not on the person writing or speaking, and not on a character in a story, but on the person being spoken to.

First-person point of view: "I stepped around the corner and saw my destiny."

Second-person point of view: "You need to hold your hand very steady."

Third-person point of view: "He watched the sun fade from the sky."

Read It

Work individually. Use this chart to identify the point of view used in each of the poems. Quote evidence from the poems to support your choice.

SELECTION	POINT OF VIEW	EVIDENCE
Courage	second-person	• When they called you crybaby..." • "when death opens the back door you'll put on your carpet slippers..."
Ithaka	second-person	• "As you set out for Ithaka..." • "Arriving there is what you are destined for."
The Narrow Road of the Interior	first-person	• "I myself fell prey to wanderlust some years ago, ..." • "I turned over my dwelling to others, ..."

Write It

Notebook Write a paragraph using either the first-person or the second-person point of view.

STANDARDS

Reading Literature
Determine the meaning of words and phrases as they are used in the text, including figurative and connotative meanings; analyze the cumulative impact of specific word choices on meaning and tone.

Language
Demonstrate command of the conventions of standard English grammar and usage when writing or speaking.

PERSONALIZE FOR LEARNING

English Language Support

Considering Different Points of View Have students make a list of ways that differing points of view affect "Ithaka" and "The Narrow Road of the Interior."

Have pairs of students focus on how the points of view affect the tone and mood of each selection. **EMERGING**

Have students focus on how the points of view affect the tone, mood, and information that the reader can gather from the texts. **EXPANDING**

Have students focus on how the points of view affect the information that the reader can gather from the texts. Ask students to also include which point of view they prefer and why. **BRIDGING**

An expanded **English Language Support Lesson** on Point of View is available in the Interactive Teacher's Edition.

Speaking and Listening

Assignment

With your group, explore the ideas expressed in "Courage," "Ithaka," and "The Narrow Road of the Interior." Choose from the following options.

- ☐ **Nomination** Imagine that you are on a committee that will present student achievers with an engraved plaque featuring a poem. Discuss which of these poems you would recommend and why. You might also consider whether to include the entire poem or only a section.
- ☐ **Debate** Are some ideas better expressed through poetry than through prose? Choose your position, and defend it with examples from the poems.
- ☐ **Radio Broadcast** Present a radio show in which a caller asks for advice on a specific life issue. Respond with advice supported by a key theme or message of one of the poems. Quote relevant lines, and give examples.

Project Plan After you have selected an option, work with your group to determine what additional preparation is necessary. Review your group's rules for discussion: What methods do you have in place for taking and holding the floor? How do you ensure that diverse perspectives are represented in discussion? Decide how you will assign discussion roles to group members, and use this chart to record the responsibilities of each.

DISCUSSION ROLE	TASKS	GROUP MEMBER

EVIDENCE LOG

Before moving on to a new selection, go to your Evidence Log and record what you learned from "Courage," "Ithaka," and "The Narrow Road of the Interior."

STANDARDS

Speaking and Listening
Initiate and participate effectively in a range of collaborative discussions with diverse partners on grades 9–10 topics, texts, and issues, building on others' ideas and expressing their own clearly and persuasively.

DIGITAL PERSPECTIVES

Speaking and Listening

Remind students to focus on the central ideas presented in each of the texts as they choose a task to complete with their group. Have the students review the three options and then discuss with their group whether to choose a nomination, a debate, or a radio broadcast to develop.

Project Plan Explain to students that when discussing the task with their group, they should assume a role in the discussion and follow the group rules. For more support, see **Speaking and Listening: Group Discussion.**

Evidence Log Support students in completing their Evidence Log. This paced activity will help prepare them for the Performance-Based Assessment at the end of the unit.

FORMATIVE ASSESSMENT

Speaking and Listening

If students struggle to understand the ideas in the three texts and apply them to one of the options to discuss, **then** have them reread the texts and apply a text to each option before selecting. For Reteach and Practice, see **Speaking and Listening: Group Discussion (RP).**

Selection Test

Administer the "Poetry Collection 1" Selection Test, which is available in both print and digital formats online in Assessments.

DIGITAL PERSPECTIVES

Illuminating the Text Have students find photos and videos on the Internet of travelogues about places they might like to visit. Encourage students to take notes on the appealing features of a few locations, paying particular attention to sensory details. Ask students to write a short poem about an imaginary journey to one of the places they researched. Students should use a single point of view to narrate their poem and include figurative language to emphasize key ideas. Have students present their poems to fellow group members. (Research to Explore)

FACILITATING

Deliver a Multimedia Presentation

Assignment Before groups begin work on their projects, have them clearly differentiate the role each group member will play. Remind groups to consult the schedule for Small-Group Learning to guide their work during the Performance Task.

Students should complete the assignment using presentation software to take advantage of text, graphics, and sound features.

Plan With Your Group

Analyze the Text Have groups think about the different types of journeys discussed in the reading selections. Instruct them to consider them all as they think about the answer to the question: "What different types of journeys are there and how can they transform someone?"

Remind groups that they can incorporate ideas from other sources, including their own experiences. Have them think about the journeys that characters from their favorite movies or books have taken. You might want to mention that personal growth is often considered a journey.

Gather Evidence and Media Examples Suggest that groups include both literal and nonliteral representations of journeys. As groups create their research plans, they should discuss or write down whether each piece of media assigned is meant to illustrate or symbolize an aspect of a journey, a theme developed in the texts, or a specific example from one of the texts.

Assist students in identifying and acquiring the devices or equipment their multimedia presentations will require.

PERFORMANCE TASK: SPEAKING AND LISTENING FOCUS

SOURCES

- THE RETURN
- *from* THE HERO'S ADVENTURE
- COURAGE
- ITHAKA
- *from* THE NARROW ROAD OF THE INTERIOR

Deliver a Multimedia Presentation

Assignment

You have read a short story, an interview, and three poems that deal with different perspectives of journeys. Work with your group to develop, refine, and present a **multimedia presentation** in which you explain your answer to this question:

What different types of journeys are there, and how can they transform someone?

Plan with Your Group

Analyze the Text With your group, analyze the question, and decide how you will define the key terms *journeys* and *transform*. This will help you create a precise thesis on the topic of personal transformation and develop your ideas with evidence from the selections.

Next, discuss key information and themes at work in the selections you have read. Think about how each writer presents the idea of a journey. Make sure that your group expands its thinking beyond just physical journeys. Identify specific examples from the selections to support your group's ideas. Use a graphic organizer to list your ideas and textual evidence.

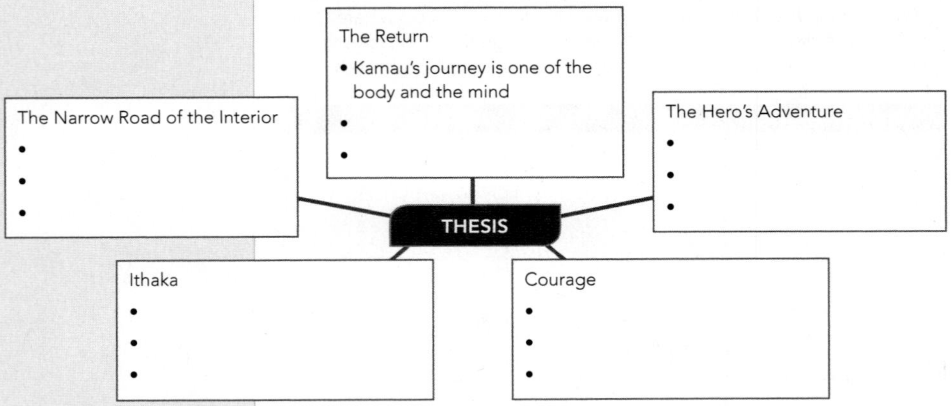

STANDARDS

Speaking and Listening
Present information, findings, and supporting evidence clearly, concisely and logically such that listeners can follow the line of reasoning and the organization, development, substance, and style are appropriate to purpose, audience, and task

Gather Evidence and Media Examples As a group, brainstorm for types of media you can use to illustrate each example. Consider photographs, paintings or drawings, music, charts, graphs, and video. Next, make a research plan. Each group member should be assigned pieces of media to acquire. If possible, use your local library or media center. After you have gathered your text evidence and media, determine what equipment your presentation will require.

AUTHOR'S PERSPECTIVE **Ernest Morrell, Ph.D.**

Digital Speech Since "a picture is worth a thousand words," help students find and use effective images for oral presentations. Remind students to give full credit to visual sources, as they would for print ones. Teachers can guide students to create rhetorically powerful digital presentations such as slideshows, blogs, and online forums using these suggestions:

- *Keep it simple.* Choose one striking image rather than several smaller ones. Position the visual carefully, allowing "white space" to make the image stand out.
- *Go for quality.* Choose clear, high-quality images or take high-resolution photos.
- *Limit bullet points and text.* The most effective slideshows have limited text. Suggest that slides should have no more than six words across and six lines down of text.
- *Choose color and font carefully.* Cool colors (blues, greens) work best for backgrounds; warm colors (orange, red) work best for objects in the foreground. Use a simple, standard font such as Arial or Helvetica.

Last, teachers can help students create a rubric to assess presentations.

Organize Your Ideas As a group, organize the script for your presentation. You may use the Multimedia Presentation Script shown here. Decide who will do what job in each part of the presentation. Also note when multimedia will be used.

MULTIMEDIA PRESENTATION SCRIPT		
	Media Cues	Script
Presenter 1		
Presenter 2		
Presenter 3		

Rehearse with Your Group

Practice with Your Group Use this checklist to evaluate the effectiveness of your group's first run-through. Then, use your evaluation and the instructions here to guide your revision.

CONTENT	USE OF MEDIA	PRESENTATION TECHNIQUES
☐ The presentation presents a clear thesis. ☐ Main ideas are supported with evidence from the texts in Small-Group Learning.	☐ The media support the thesis. ☐ The media communicate key ideas. ☐ Media are used evenly throughout the presentation. ☐ Equipment functions properly.	☐ Media are visible and audible. ☐ Transitions between media segments are smooth. ☐ The speaker uses eye contact and speaks clearly.

Fine-Tune the Content To make your explanation of the topic clearer or more thorough, you may need to go back into the texts to find more support for your main ideas. Alternately, you may need to add or replace some of your multimedia content. Check with your group to identify key details that are not clear to listeners. Find new or additional examples, definitions, or quotations to include.

Improve Your Use of Media Double-check that everything is in working order and make a back-up plan in case your equipment fails. If the media are not well distributed through the presentation, work to change the pacing.

Make sure you consider your audience and their interest level with your use of media. For instance, media can often add drama or visual interest to a wordy description.

Present and Evaluate

When you present as a group, be sure that each member has taken into account each of the checklist items. As you watch other groups, evaluate how well they meet the requirements on the checklist.

STANDARDS
Speaking and Listening
• Make strategic use of digital media in presentations to enhance understanding of findings, reasoning, and evidence and to add interest.
• Adapt speech to a variety of contexts and tasks, demonstrating a command of formal English when indicated or appropriate.

DIGITAL PERSPECTIVES

Rehearse With Your Group

Practice With Your Group Remind students that practicing their parts ahead of time will reduce the likelihood that they'll make a mistake when they give the presentation.

Fine-Tune the Content Encourage groups to avoid falling into the trap of being overly content with the "first draft" of their presentation. To avoid doing more work, they might make only minor revisions, but tell them that the first take is never the best take. Remind them to remain actively engaged with their content; they are bound to come up with new, better ideas. Tell groups they should practice their presentations. Have students give each other constructive feedback and encouragement.

Improve Your Use of Media Have students double check that any equipment they plan to use is in working order and that they understand how to operate it.

Present and Evaluate

Before beginning the presentations, set the expectations for the audience. You may wish to have students consider these questions as groups present.

- What was the presenting group's thesis?
- Which examples from the selections or from their personal lives best supported the thesis?
- Which multimedia best illustrated their key ideas? Why?
- What did you enjoy most about the presentation?

As students provide feedback to the presenting group, remind them that evaluation does not refer only to finding flaws. Letting a group know what they have done well will help them to repeat their successes, and provide a positive model for other groups.

DIGITAL PERSPECTIVES

Explanatory Presentations Consider finding examples of explanatory videos on the Internet to give students some ideas for their presentations. You could show them a travelogue about a foreign country in which the host discusses things to prepare for and places to see, or a documentary about a historic event. Point out that in these examples, the presenters are clearly explaining a topic or an idea, an approach that groups should take when creating their presentations. Always preview videos before sharing with the class.

OVERVIEW

INDEPENDENT LEARNING

What can we learn from a journey?

Encourage students to think carefully about what they have already learned and what more they want to know about the unit topic of Journeys of Transformation. This is a key first step to previewing and selecting the text or media they will read or review in Independent Learning.

Independent Learning Strategies

Review the Learning Strategies with students and explain that as they work through Independent Learning they will develop strategies to work on their own.

- Have students watch the video on Independent Learning Strategies.
- A video on this topic is available online in the Professional Development Center.

Students should include any favorite strategies that they might have devised on their own during Whole-Class and Small-Group Learning. For example, for the strategy "Practice what you have learned," students might include:

- For practice, apply some of the strategies you have learned for reviewing evidence to another topic.
- Pair up with a group member and review all of your strategies and evidence together.

Block Scheduling

Each day in this Pacing Plan represents a 40–50 minute class period. Teachers using block scheduling may combine days to reflect their class schedule. In addition, teachers may revise pacing to differentiate and support core instruction by integrating components and resources as students require.

OVERVIEW: INDEPENDENT LEARNING

ESSENTIAL QUESTION:

What can we learn from a journey?

Reading about others' journeys can help us reflect on our own. In this section, you will complete your study of journeys of transformation by exploring an additional selection related to the topic. You'll then share what you learn with classmates. To choose a text, follow these steps.

Look Back Think about the selections you have already studied. What more do you want to know about the topic of journeys of transformation?

Look Ahead Preview the texts by reading the descriptions. Which one seems most interesting and appealing to you?

Look Inside Take a few minutes to scan the text you chose. Choose a different one if this text doesn't meet your needs.

Independent Learning Strategies

Throughout your life, in school, in your community, and in your career, you will need to rely on yourself to learn and work on your own. Review these strategies and the actions you can take to practice them during Independent Learning. Add ideas of your own to each category.

STRATEGY	ACTION PLAN
Create a schedule	• Understand your goals and deadlines. • Make a plan for what to do each day. •
Practice what you have learned	• Use first-read and close-read strategies to deepen your understanding. • After you read, evaluate the usefulness of the evidence to help you understand the topic. • Consider the quality and reliability of the source. •
Take notes	• Record important ideas and information • Review your notes before preparing to share with a group. •

SCAN FOR MULTIMEDIA

Pacing Plan

Introduce Whole-Class Learning (2)

Application for a Mariner's License (13)

Unit Introduction	Literature and Culture	*from* the Odyssey, Part 1	*from* the Odyssey, Part 2	Media: *from* The Odyssey: A Graphic Novel	Application for a Mariner's License	Performance Task
1, 2	3	4, 5, 6	7, 8, 9	10, 11, 12	13	14, 15

CONTENTS

Choose one selection. Selections are available online only.

SCAN FOR MULTIMEDIA

Contents

Selections Encourage students to scan and preview the selections before choosing the one they would like to read or review. Suggest that they consider the genre and subject matter of each one before making their decision. You can use the information on the following Planning pages to advise students in making their choice.

Remind students that the selections for Independent Learning are only available in the Interactive Student Edition. Allow students who do not have digital access at home to preview the selections or review the media selection using classroom or computer lab technology. Then either have students print the selection they choose or provide a printout for them.

Performance Based-Assessment Prep

Review Evidence for an Explanatory Text Point out to students that collecting evidence during Independent Learning is the last step in completing their Evidence Log. After they finish their independent reading, they will synthesize all the evidence they have compiled in the unit.

The evidence students collect will serve as the primary source of information they will use to complete the writing and oral presentation for the Performance-Based Assessment at the end of the unit.

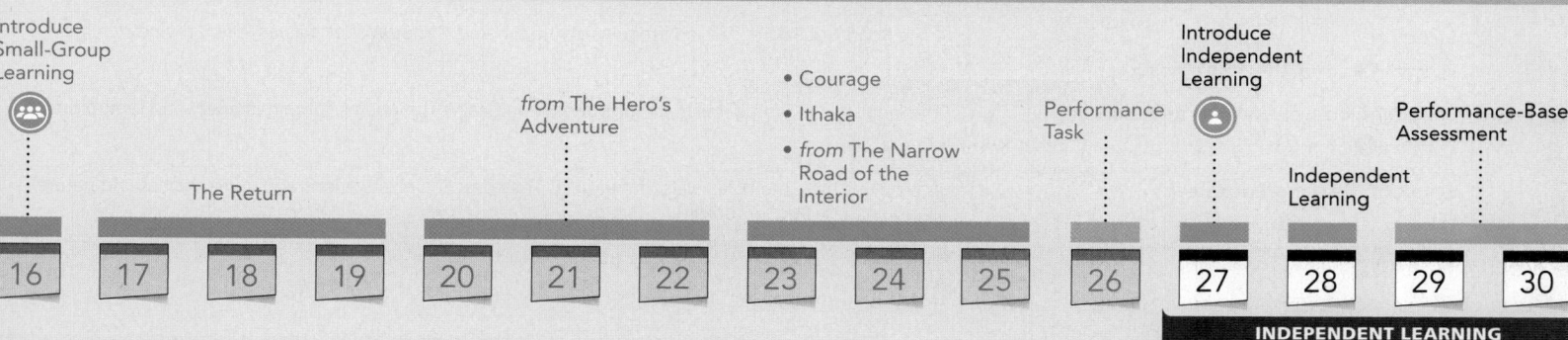

Introduce Small-Group Learning (16)

The Return (17–19)

from The Hero's Adventure (20–22)

- Courage
- Ithaka
- *from* The Narrow Road of the Interior

(23–25)

Performance Task (26)

Introduce Independent Learning (27)

Independent Learning (28)

Performance-Based Assessment (29–30)

16 17 18 19 20 21 22 23 24 25 26 27 28 29 30

INDEPENDENT LEARNING

The Road Not Taken • Your World

Summary

Robert Frost's poem "The Road Not Taken" describes a traveler's choice. The speaker is standing at a fork in the road, comparing the two paths he might choose. One path has had more use, but neither has been walked on that day. After considering each, the speaker makes his choice.

Georgia Douglas Johnson's poem "Your World" encourages exploration. The speaker says that she used to stay in a very small, confined space. But then she saw the distant horizon and wanted to travel across this big space. She knocked down the barriers around her and flew to the farthest points.

Insight

These poems are both about the value of travel. Frost talks about making choices about which path to take, while Johnson talks about going to many places that you can see from afar.

SELECTION RESOURCES

- First-Read Guide: Poetry
- Close-Read Guide: Poetry
- Poetry Collection 2: Text Questions
- Audio Summaries
- Selection Audio
- Selection Test

Connection to Essential Question

The Essential Question is "What can we learn from a journey?" The speakers of both poems tell us that their own decisions about their journeys have made a great difference. Frost is more enigmatic about what changed. Johnson is clear about how she transformed from sheltered and confined to soaring.

Connection to Performance-Based Assessment

These poems help students consider the prompt, "When does the journey matter more than the destination?" Here, the journeys matter because of the ways in which they changed the person who went on them. Exactly where they went is irrelevant, the journey itself is what matters.

Text Complexity Rubric: The Road Not Taken • Your World

Quantitative Measures	
Lexile: NP; NP **Text Length:** 20 lines; 12 lines	
Qualitative Measures	
Knowledge Demands 1 — **2** — 3 — 4 — 5	These poems require minor knowledge of a forest setting and the idea of travel.
Structure 1 — **2** — 3 — 4 — 5	"The Road Not Taken" has an irregular rhyme scheme. "Your World" has an ABCB rhyme scheme.
Language Conventionality and Clarity 1 — **2** — 3 — 4 — 5	The language in the poems is straightforward and easy. The poems contain imagery and symbolism.
Levels of Meaning/Purpose 1 — 2 — **3** — 4 — 5	The poems have multiple levels of meaning. They describe observations about life choices and nature using imagery and symbolism.

DIGITAL PERSPECTIVES

Audio | Video | Document | Annotation Highlights | EL Highlights | Online Assessment

SELECTION RESOURCES

- First-Read Guide: Fiction
- Close-Read Guide: Fiction
- The Ugly Duckling: Text Questions
- Audio Summary
- Selection Audio
- Selection Test

The Ugly Duckling

Summary

"The Ugly Duckling" is a well-known children's story by Hans Christian Andersen about a family of ducks. One day, a group of ducklings hatched from eggs, except for one that didn't hatch until later. When it did, the bird that hatched from it was uglier than the rest. Though his mother accepted him, the other ducks he lived with did not. Treated badly, the bird decided to leave and go to a different pond. He was cast out everywhere he went. But after many misadventures, he came to find where he belonged, and what he really was.

Insight

This story shows how people can find their place in the world. Its lasting message is that troubles tend to be temporary. Someone may feel like an ugly duckling now, but in enough time or in a different place that person will be a beautiful swan.

Connection to Essential Question

The Essential Question is "What can we learn from a journey?" At its lowest point, the bird realizes it is no longer ugly. Its view of itself completely changes.

Connection to Performance-Based Assessment

The prompt is "When does the journey matter more than the destination?" The duckling had to take an inner journey in order to find a new perspective. So the "destination" of acceptance was not possible without the trials of the journey.

Text Complexity Rubric: The Ugly Duckling	
Quantitative Measures	
Lexile: 1020 **Text Length:** 3,772 words	
Qualitative Measures	
Knowledge Demands ① ❷ ③ ④ ⑤	The selection is a familiar, classic fairy tale about identity and fitting in.
Structure ① ❷ ③ ④ ⑤	The story is linear and contains some long paragraphs and dialogue.
Language Conventionality and Clarity ① ❷ ③ ④ ⑤	The selection has some long, complex sentences, on-level vocabulary, and simple language.
Levels of Meaning/Purpose ① ② ❸ ④ ⑤	The importance of personal transformation is clear and accessible.

Thirteen Epic Animal Migrations That Prove Just How Cool Mother Nature Is

SELECTION RESOURCES

- First-Read Guide: Media Art/Photography
- Close-Read Guide: Media Art/Photography
- Thirteen Epic Animal Migrations: Media Questions
- Audio Summary
- Selection Audio
- Selection Test

Summary

This photo essay by Brianna Elliot is about the journeys of animals. Animals migrate for a number of reasons, including avoiding dangerous weather, going to where food is more plentiful, and giving birth. Some living things take advantage of the way the world around them moves: they let waves or wind carry them to their destination. Migratory animals tend to move in enormous groups. The distances they move vary wildly, from across a single island to across continents.

Insight

This photo essay helps illustrate why it is important to conserve large areas: many animals need large areas to survive and thrive. What happens in one place can have a significant effect on migratory animals that normally live in another place. Wind and waves can carry animals—and pollution—far and wide.

Connection to Essential Question

The Essential Question is "What can we learn from a journey?" Here, students can learn about the journeys animals seem hardwired to make.

Connection to Performance-Based Assessment

The prompt is "When does the journey matter more than the destination?" To the animals, the goals they seek are more important. To people, much of the beauty is in the way the animals make their journey.

Media Complexity Rubric: Thirteen Animal Migrations That Prove Just How Cool Mother Nature Is	
Quantitative Measures	
Format and Length Photo Essay including 13 photos	
Qualitative Measures	
Knowledge Demands ① ❷ ③ ④ ⑤	The selection details migratory habits of several different animal species. Captions clearly explain the photos.
Structure ① ❷ ③ ④ ⑤	The selection is a photo essay that includes 13 photos with captions to describe them. Each caption includes the same type of information.
Language Conventionality and Clarity ① ❷ ③ ④ ⑤	The language is accessible and clear with conventional syntax.
Levels of Meaning/Purpose ① ❷ ③ ④ ⑤	Meaning and concepts are straightforward and easy to understand.

DIGITAL PERSPECTIVES — Audio | Video | Document | Annotation Highlights | EL Highlights | Online Assessment

SELECTION RESOURCES

- First-Read Guide: Nonfiction
- Close-Read Guide: Nonfiction
- from Wild: Text Questions
- Audio Summary
- Selection Audio
- Selection Test

from Wild

Summary

This selection is from *Wild*, a memoir by Cheryl Strayed. She tells a story about hiking in the mountains, nearby but separate from her companion Greg. The trail is hidden beneath the snow, and she becomes lost. Eventually she finds herself back on the trail and sees some skiers in the distance. She yells to them, but the communication is challenging. With the path so unclear, she must rely on the descriptions in her guidebook. She is often uncertain whether she is on the path or not, finding it and then losing it again. But despite her uncertainty, the effort of moving forward feels right.

Insight

This selection shows how a journey can help someone heal and become stronger, learning through difficulty to cope with problems. The end of this selection involves an encounter with a fox, an encounter that exemplifies Strayed's awe of nature.

Connection to Essential Question

The Essential Question is "What can we learn from a journey?" Strayed feels great uncertainty, but it is clear to her that she belongs on the journey she is taking.

Connection to Performance-Based Assessment

The prompt is "When does the journey matter more than the destination?" Strayed considers going back to Sierra City and catching a ride farther north instead of hiking. But she does not want to get there the easy way. She wants to make the journey on her own, even if it is difficult.

Text Complexity Rubric: *from* Wild

Quantitative Measures	
Lexile: 1110 **Text Length:** 3,591 words	
Qualitative Measures	
Knowledge Demands ①—②—❸—④—⑤	Students will not be familiar with the situation, but emotions and events are clearly explained. Background information about Cheryl Strayed's memoir *Wild* will be helpful.
Structure ①—②—❸—④—⑤	The selection is an excerpt from a memoir. The first-person narration is clear and easy to follow.
Language Conventionality and Clarity ①—②—❸—④—⑤	The selection contains some long, descriptive sentences. Language is used for figurative power.
Levels of Meaning/Purpose ①—②—❸—④—⑤	Concepts and meanings are mostly explained and easy to grasp. The main purpose of the selection is to convey a transformative journey in the wilderness.

MY NOTES

DIGITAL PERSPECTIVES

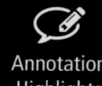

Audio Video Document Annotation Highlights EL Highlights Online Assessment

MY NOTES

ADVISING

You may wish to direct students to use the generic **First-Read** and **Close-Read Guides** in the Print Student Edition. Alternatively, you may wish to print copies of the genre-specific **First-Read** and **Close-Read Guides** for students. These are available online in the Interactive Student Edition or Unit Resources.

FIRST READ

Students should perform the steps of the first read independently:

NOTICE: Students should focus on the basic elements of the text to ensure they understand what is happening.

ANNOTATE: Students should mark any passages they wish to revisit during their close read.

CONNECT: Students should increase their understanding by connecting what they've read to other texts or personal experiences.

RESPOND: Students will write a summary to demonstrate their understanding.

Point out to students that while they will always complete the Respond step at the end of the first read, the other steps will probably happen somewhat concurrently. Remind students that they will revisit their first-read annotations during the close read. You may wish to print copies of the First-Read Guide for students to use.

After students have completed the First-Read Guide, you may wish to assign the **Text Questions** for the selection that are available in the Interactive Teacher's Edition.

Anchor Standards

In the first two sections of the unit, students worked with the whole class and in small groups to gain topical knowledge and greater understanding of the skills required by the anchor standards. In this section, they are asked to work independently, applying what they have learned and demonstrating increased readiness for college and career.

INDEPENDENT LEARNING

First-Read Guide

Tool Kit
First-Read Guide and Model Annotation

Use this page to record your first-read ideas.

Selection Title: ________________________________

NOTICE new information or ideas you learn about the unit topic as you first read this text.

ANNOTATE by marking vocabulary and key passages you want to revisit.

First Read: NOTICE, ANNOTATE, CONNECT, RESPOND

CONNECT ideas within the selection to other knowledge and the selections you have read.

RESPOND by writing a brief summary of the selection.

STANDARD
Reading Read and comprehend complex literary and informational texts independently and proficiently.

PERSONALIZE FOR LEARNING

Strategic Support

Writing a Summary Support students who struggle to write a summary. Have them use their first-read coded annotations for key ideas ("*") to help them write a text summary. Remind students of these guidelines for writing summaries:

- Along with the text title and author, students should briefly restate the author's ideas in their own words.
- Summaries should present the main ideas for nonfiction texts and descriptions of important elements for literary texts (i.e., main characters, plot, point of view, tone, author's style, literary techniques).
- Students should use transitional words and phrases to signal the relationships among ideas. For instance, summaries often include words or phrases that signal the order of events or order of importance.

Have students work with partners to review their summaries for the main ideas and important details, as well as to make suggestions for the use of transitions.

Close-Read Guide

Tool Kit
Close-Read Guide and Model Annotation

Use this page to record your close-read ideas.

Selection Title: ______________________________

Close Read the Text

Revisit sections of the text you marked during your first read. Read these sections closely and **annotate** what you notice. Ask yourself **questions** about the text. What can you **conclude**? Write down your ideas.

ANNOTATE · QUESTION · Close Read · CONCLUDE

Analyze the Text

Think about the author's choices of patterns, structure, techniques, and ideas included in the text. Select one and record your thoughts about what this choice conveys.

QuickWrite

Pick a paragraph from the text that grabbed your interest. Explain the power of this passage.

STANDARD
Reading Read and comprehend complex literary and informational texts independently and proficiently.

DIGITAL PERSPECTIVES

CLOSE READ

Students should begin their close read by revisiting the annotations they made during their first read. Then, students should analyze one of the author's choices regarding the following elements:

- **patterns,** such as repetition or parallelism
- **structure,** such as cause-and-effect or problem-solution
- **techniques,** such as description or dialogue
- **ideas,** such as the author's main idea or theme

MAKE IT INTERACTIVE
Group students according to the selection they have chosen. Then, have students meet to discuss the selection in depth. Their discussions should be guided by their insights and questions.

PERSONALIZE FOR LEARNING

Challenge

Sharing in Pairs Extend the independent reading experience for students who are ready. Have students work with partners who have selected a different independent reading text. Student pairs can take turns talking about the texts they read. Encourage students to reference their First-Read Guide summaries and their Close-Read Guide entries as they share their ideas. Ask students to discuss the annotations that helped them unlock text meaning. Once students have introduced each text, ask partners to compare and contrast their texts in terms of the topic or genre, main ideas and details, text structure, or author's craft. You may wish to have student pairs report their text comparisons to the rest of the class, inviting participation and additional ideas from other students.

ADVISING

Share Your Independent Learning

Prepare to Share

Explain to students that sharing what they learned from their Independent Learning selection provides classmates who read a different selection with an opportunity to consider the text as a source of evidence during the Performance-Based Assessment. As students prepare to share, remind them to highlight how their selection contributed to their knowledge of the concept of transformative journeys as well as how the selection connects to the question *What can we learn from a journey?*

Learn From Your Classmates

As students discuss the Independent Learning selections, direct them to take particular note of how their classmates' chosen selections align with their current position on the Performance-Based Assessment question.

MAKE IT INTERACTIVE

Have students create a short comic book about a person who is taking a journey. Each page of the comic book should include a thought bubble in which the character thinks about what he has learned thus far on his journey. Arrange the comic books around the room and have students circulate. When they're finished looking at all the comic books in the room, have them write a short essay about the fresh insights they gained.

Reflect

Have students create presentation slides illustrating their most important insights about the relationship between journeys and personal change. Project the slides for the class and guide students to give 30-second oral summaries then participate in a brief question and answer session.

Evidence Log Support students in completing their Evidence Log. This paced activity will help prepare them for the Performance-Based Assessment at the end of the unit.

INDEPENDENT LEARNING

EVIDENCE LOG

Go to your Evidence Log and record what you learned from the text you read.

Share Your Independent Learning

Prepare to Share

What can we learn from a journey?

Even when you read or learn something independently, you can continue to grow by sharing what you have learned with others. Reflect on the text you explored independently, and write notes about its connection to the unit. In your notes, consider why this text belongs in this unit.

Learn From Your Classmates

Discuss It Share your ideas about the text you explored on your own. As you talk with your classmates, jot down ideas that you learn from them.

Reflect

Review your notes, and underline the most important insight you gained from these writing and discussion activities. Explain how this idea adds to your understanding of the topic of journeys of transformation.

STANDARDS

Speaking and Listening
Initiate and participate effectively in a range of collaborative discussions with diverse partners on grades 9-10 *topics, texts, and issues*, building on others' ideas and expressing their own clearly and persuasively.

AUTHOR'S PERSPECTIVE Ernest Morrell, Ph.D.

Powerful Speaking in Small Groups Explain to students that learning how to speak with confidence, without overcompensating, will help them make and/or defend an argument and point of view in a small group. Point out that their goal is to be convincing, but not argumentative. To help build this skill, provide students with the following guidelines:

1. **Earn credibility.** Speakers who are prepared with evidence tailored to their audience's needs will sway their audience with the power of their proof. As a result, these speakers will have no need to try to harass or intimidate their listeners.
2. **Choose words carefully.** Effective speakers use the exact words they need, words that convey their precise meaning. Further, effective speakers avoid "loaded words" that attempt to sway an audience by appealing to stereotypes.
3. **Be audible, not loud.** Speakers who avoid shouting convey their point with greater confidence than those who do raise their voices.

PERFORMANCE-BASED ASSESSMENT PREP

Review Evidence for an Explanatory Essay

At the beginning of the unit, you wrote a response to the following question:

When does the journey matter more than the destination?

EVIDENCE LOG

Review your Evidence Log and your QuickWrite from the beginning of the unit. Did you learn anything new?

☐ YES	☐ NO
Identify at least three ideas, definitions, or examples that stood out to you related to the topic of journeys of transformation.	Identify at least three ideas, definitions, or examples that reinforced your original ideas related to journeys of transformation.
1.	1.
2.	2.
3.	3.

Identify a fact or detail that relates to one of your revised ideas about journeys of transformation: ______________________________

____

Develop your thoughts into a topic sentence for an explanatory essay. Complete this sentence starter:

The journey matters more than the destination when

____

Evaluate Your Evidence Consider what information you learned. Did the texts you read expand your knowledge? If not, make a plan.

☐ Do more research ☐ Talk with my classmates

☐ Reread a selection ☐ Ask an expert

☐ Other: ______________________________

STANDARDS

Writing

Write informative/ explanatory texts to examine and convey ideas, concepts, and information clearly and accurately through the effective selection, organization, and analysis of content.

DIGITAL PERSPECTIVES

Review Evidence for an Explanatory Essay

Evidence Log Students should understand that their thinking on an issue could evolve as they learn more about the subject and are exposed to additional points of view. Point out that just because they took an initial position on the question *When does the journey matter more than the destination?* doesn't mean that their thinking can't change after careful consideration of evidence.

Evaluate Your Evidence Remind students that there are many different types of evidence they can use to support their thesis, including:

- concrete details
- facts or definitions
- physical descriptions
- actions
- quotations

In addition to ensuring they have sufficient evidence to support their thesis, students should evaluate the reliability of their evidence. Discuss the characteristics that make evidence credible:

- reliable sources, including government, educational, and professional organizations
- reputation of the source (i.e., is the person quoted an expert?)
- degree to which experts have reviewed the evidence for accuracy (e.g., some media outlets have rigorous fact-checking)

Writing to Sources: Explanatory Essay

Students should complete the Performance-Based Assessment independently, with little to no input or feedback during the process. Students should use word processing software to take advantage of editing tools and features.

Prior to beginning the Assessment, ask students to think about journeys they've taken (literal or metaphorical) that have provided more fulfillment than reaching the destination.

Review the Elements of Effective Explanatory Essays Students can review the work they did earlier in the unit as they complete the Performance-Based Assessment. They may also consult other resources such as:

- the elements of explanatory text, including a clear thesis statement, details to support the thesis, and correct spelling and grammar.
- their Evidence Log
- their Word Network

Although students will use evidence from unit selections for their explanatory text, they may need to collect additional evidence, including facts, statistics, anecdotes, quotations from authorities, and examples.

SOURCES

- WHOLE-CLASS SELECTIONS
- SMALL-GROUP SELECTIONS
- INDEPENDENT LEARNING

PART 1

Writing to Sources: Explanatory Essay

In this unit, you read about the journeys of various people and characters. When they reached their destination, these characters learned something new about themselves and the world.

Assignment

Write an **explanatory essay** in which you examine a topic and convey ideas, concepts, procedures, and information related to the following question:

When does the journey matter more than the destination?

Use relevant evidence from at least three of the selections you read and researched in this unit to elucidate your ideas. Ensure that you introduce your topic, develop the topic with sufficient facts, details, and quotes, and use appropriate and varied transitions.

Reread the Assignment Review the assignment to be sure you fully understand it. The task may reference some of the academic words presented at the beginning of the unit. Be sure you understand each of the words here in order to complete the assignment correctly.

Academic Vocabulary

voluntary	expedite	procedure
elucidate	subsequent	

Review the Elements of Effective Explanatory Essays
Before you begin writing, review the Explanatory Rubric. Once you have completed your first draft, check it against the rubric. If one or more of the elements is missing or not as strong as it could be, revise your essay to add or strengthen that component.

WORD NETWORK

As you write and revise your explanatory text, use your Word Network to help vary your word choices.

STANDARDS

Writing

- Write informative/explanatory texts to examine and convey complex ideas, concepts, and information clearly and accurately through the effective selection, organization, and analysis of content.
- Write routinely over extended time frames and shorter time frames for a range of tasks, purposes, and audiences.

Explanatory Rubric

	Focus and Organization	Evidence and Elaboration	Conventions
4	The introduction engages the reader and states a thesis in a very effective way. The essay's organization is clear and well-suited to its topic. The conclusion summarizes ideas and offers fresh insight into the thesis.	The tone of the essay is always formal and objective. The topic is developed with well-chosen, relevant, and sufficient facts, extended definitions, concrete details, quotations, or other information appropriate to the audience's knowledge of the topic. The language is always precise and appropriate for the audience and purpose.	The essay consistently uses standard English conventions of usage and mechanics. Transitions are appropriately varied to link major sections of the text, create cohesion, and clarify the relationships among complex ideas and concepts.
3	The introduction engages the reader and sets forth the thesis. The essay's organization is mostly clear and suited to its topic. The conclusion offers some insight into the claim and summarizes ideas.	The tone of the essay is mostly formal and objective. The topic is mostly developed with well-chosen, relevant, and sufficient facts, extended definitions, concrete details, quotations, or other information appropriate to the audience's knowledge of the topic. The language is mostly precise and appropriate for the audience and purpose.	The essay demonstrates general accuracy in standard English conventions of usage and mechanics. Transitions are mostly varied to link major sections of the text, create cohesion, and clarify the relationships among complex ideas and concepts.
2	The introduction states a thesis, but does not engage the reader. The essay's organization is sometimes unclear and does not fully support its topic. The conclusion restates information.	The tone of the essay switches from formal to informal at times. The topic is developed with adequate relevant facts, definitions, details, quotations, or other information appropriate to the audience's knowledge of the topic. The language is rarely precise and appropriate for the audience and purpose.	The essay contains some mistakes in standard English conventions of usage and mechanics. Transitions are sometimes used to link major sections of the text, create cohesion, and clarify the relationships among complex ideas and concepts, but are sometimes used incorrectly.
1	The introduction does not state a thesis. The essay does not have a logical organization. The conclusion does not summarize ideas, or is missing completely.	The tone of the essay is informal and expresses personal opinions. The topic is developed primarily with opinions; contains no well-chosen, relevant, and sufficient facts, definitions, details, quotations, or other information appropriate to the audience's knowledge of the topic. The language is imprecise and confusing to the audience.	The essay contains many mistakes in standard English conventions of usage and mechanics. The essay lacks appropriate transitions.

DIGITAL PERSPECTIVES

Explanatory Rubric

As you review the Explanatory Rubric with students, remind them that the rubric is a resource that can guide their revisions. Students should pay particular attention to the differences between an essay with a tone that is mostly formal and objective (a score of 3) and an essay with a tone that is always formal and objective (a score of 4).

PERSONALIZE FOR LEARNING

Challenge

Journeys Ask students to review the unit contents and determine which selections, if any, were about destinations rather than journeys. Challenge them to speculate about why the unit includes the works that it does. Have them consider that rationale as they prepare to complete this assignment.

Speaking and Listening: Podcast

Students should annotate their written explanatory essay in preparation for creating their podcast, marking the important elements (a clear thesis, a clear introduction, and strong details) as well as proper grammar, a formal style, and an objective tone.

Remind students that the effectiveness of a podcast relies on how well it holds a listener's attention. Encourage them to imagine what would interest them most if they were listening to their explanatory text, and to develop or emphasize that aspect in their podcast.

Review the Podcast Rubric As you review the Podcast Rubric with students, remind them that it is a valuable tool that can help them plan their presentation. They should strive to include all of the criteria required to achieve a score of 3. Draw their attention to some of the subtle differences between scores of 2 and 3.

PART 2

Speaking and Listening: Podcast

Assignment

After completing the final draft of your explanatory essay, use it as the foundation for a three- to five-minute **podcast**.

Take the following steps to make your podcast lively and engaging. If possible, record your podcast and distribute it within your school.

- Podcasts come in many different forms. Choose the type that you find interesting. Some examples include: interviews, individual or multiple people telling a story, or a performance of a dramatic scene.
- Choose one of the supporting details from your explanatory essay, and expand upon it with greater description of the characters, events, and settings. Consider using sound effects or other media to enhance your podcast.

STANDARDS

Speaking and Listening

Present information, findings, and supporting evidence clearly, concisely, and logically such that listeners can follow the line of reasoning and the organization, development, substance, and style are appropriate to purpose, audience, and task.

Review the Rubric The criteria by which your oral podcast will be evaluated appear in this rubric. Review these criteria before presenting to ensure that you are prepared.

	Content	Use of Media	Presentation Technique
3	The podcast has a clear focus that is well developed with details. The language is always precise and appropriate for the audience and purpose. The podcast has a clear, logical organization that suits its overall purpose.	The speaker uses time very effectively by spending the right amount of time on each part. Sound effects, recorded audio, and other media effectively develop and clarify the topic and ideas.	The speaker(s) engages the listener with dialogue relevant to the thesis. The speaker(s) speaks clearly and at an appropriate pace. The speaker(s) presents with strong conviction and energy.
2	The podcast has a clear focus that is supported with some details. The language is sometimes precise and appropriate for the audience and purpose. The podcast has a somewhat effective organizational structure.	The speaker uses time effectively by spending the right amount of time on most parts. Sound effects, recorded audio, and other media mostly develop and clarify the topic and ideas.	The speaker(s) provides some support of the thesis, but is occasionally off-topic. The speaker(s) mostly speaks clearly and at an appropriate pace. The speaker(s) presents with some conviction and energy.
1	The podcast lacks a clear focus. The language is not precise or appropriate for the audience and purpose. The podcast has no organizational structure.	The speaker does not allot time effectively. Sound effects, recorded audio, and other media fail to develop and clarify the topic and ideas.	The speaker(s) does not support the thesis. The speaker(s) does not speak clearly or at an appropriate pace. The speaker(s) lack energy.

DIGITAL PERSPECTIVES

Preparing for the Assignment Encourage students to listen to a podcast about a topic of interest to them (e.g., sports, pop culture, humor, music, news), taking notes about engaging aspects of the presentation. Have them use their notes to guide them as they produce their own podcasts.

Reflect on the Unit

Now that you've completed the unit, take a few moments to reflect on your learning. Use the questions below to think about where you succeeded, what skills and strategies helped you, and where you can continue to grow in the future.

Reflect on the Unit Goals

Look back at the goals at the beginning of the unit. Use a different colored pen to rate yourself again. Think about readings and activities that contributed the most to the growth of your understanding. Record your thoughts.

Reflect on the Learning Strategies

Discuss It Write a reflection on whether you were able to improve your learning based on your Action Plans. Think about what worked, what didn't, and what you might do to keep working on these strategies. Record your ideas before a class discussion.

Reflect on the Text

Choose a selection that you found challenging, and explain what made it difficult.

Explain something that surprised you about a text in the unit.

Which activity taught you the most about journeys of transformation? What did you learn?

STANDARDS

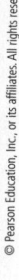

Speaking and Listening

Present information, findings, and supporting evidence clearly, concisely, and logically such that listeners can follow the line of reasoning and the organization, development, substance, and style are appropriate to purpose, audience, and task.

SCAN FOR MULTIMEDIA

DIGITAL PERSPECTIVES

Reflect on the Unit

- Have students watch the video on Reflecting on Your Learning.
- A video on this topic is available online in the Professional Development Center

Reflect on the Unit Goals

Students should re-evaluate how well they met the unit goals now that they have completed the unit. You might ask them to provide a written commentary on the goal they made the most progress with as well as the goal they feel warrants continued focus.

Reflect on the Learning Strategies

Discuss It If you want to make this a digital activity, go online and navigate to the Discussion Board. Alternatively, students can share their learning strategies reflections in a class discussion.

Reflect on the Text

Consider having students share their text reflections with one another.

MAKE IT INTERACTIVE

Have students create a logo and a short description for their podcast, explaining that every podcast available for download on a smartphone is accompanied by a logo and a description.

You might want to share some logos and descriptions of popular podcasts to give them ideas.

Unit Test and Remediation

After students have completed the Performance-Based Assessment, administer the Unit Test. Based on students' performance on the test, assign the resources as indicated on the Interpretation Guide to remediate. Students who take the test online will be automatically assigned remediation, as warranted by test results.

DANGER

UNIT 6

World's End

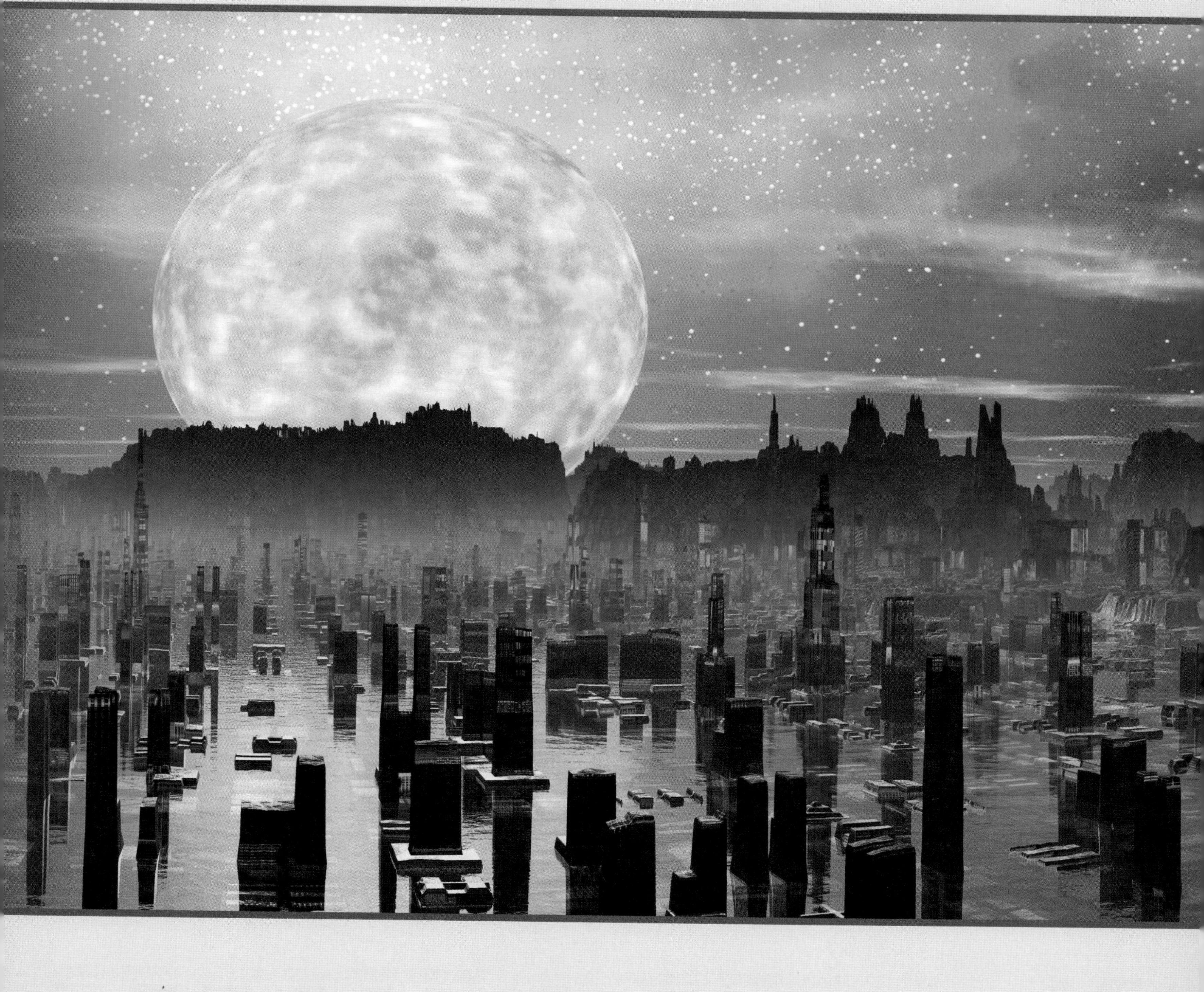

INTRODUCTION

Jump Start

Many people wonder what the end of the world might be like. The writers of science fiction, with their imaginations set on "future," provide us with some fascinating possibilities.

World's End

Ask students what the phrase *world's end* suggests to them. Point out that as they work through this unit, they will read many examples about people imagining how the world might end.

Video

Project the introduction video in class, ask students to open the video in their digital textbooks, or have students scan the Bounce Page icon with their phones to access the video.

Discuss It If you want to make this a digital activity, go online and navigate to the Discussion Board. Alternatively, students can share their responses in a class discussion.

Block Scheduling

Each day in this pacing calendar represents a 40–50 minute class period. Teachers using block scheduling may combine days to reflect their class schedule. In addition, teachers may revise pacing to differentiate and support core instruction by integrating components and resources as students require.

UNIT 6

World's End

What draws us to imagine doomsday scenarios? And why are they so entertaining?

"Doomsday" Plane Ready for Nuclear Attack

Discuss It Should the government keep a "Doomsday" plane or similar resource in continuous operation?

SCAN FOR MULTIMEDIA

694

Pacing Plan

Day	Activity
1	Unit Introduction
2	Introduce Whole-Class Learning
3–8	By the Waters of Babylon
9–13	There Will Come Soft Rains
14–15	Performance Task

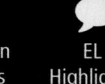

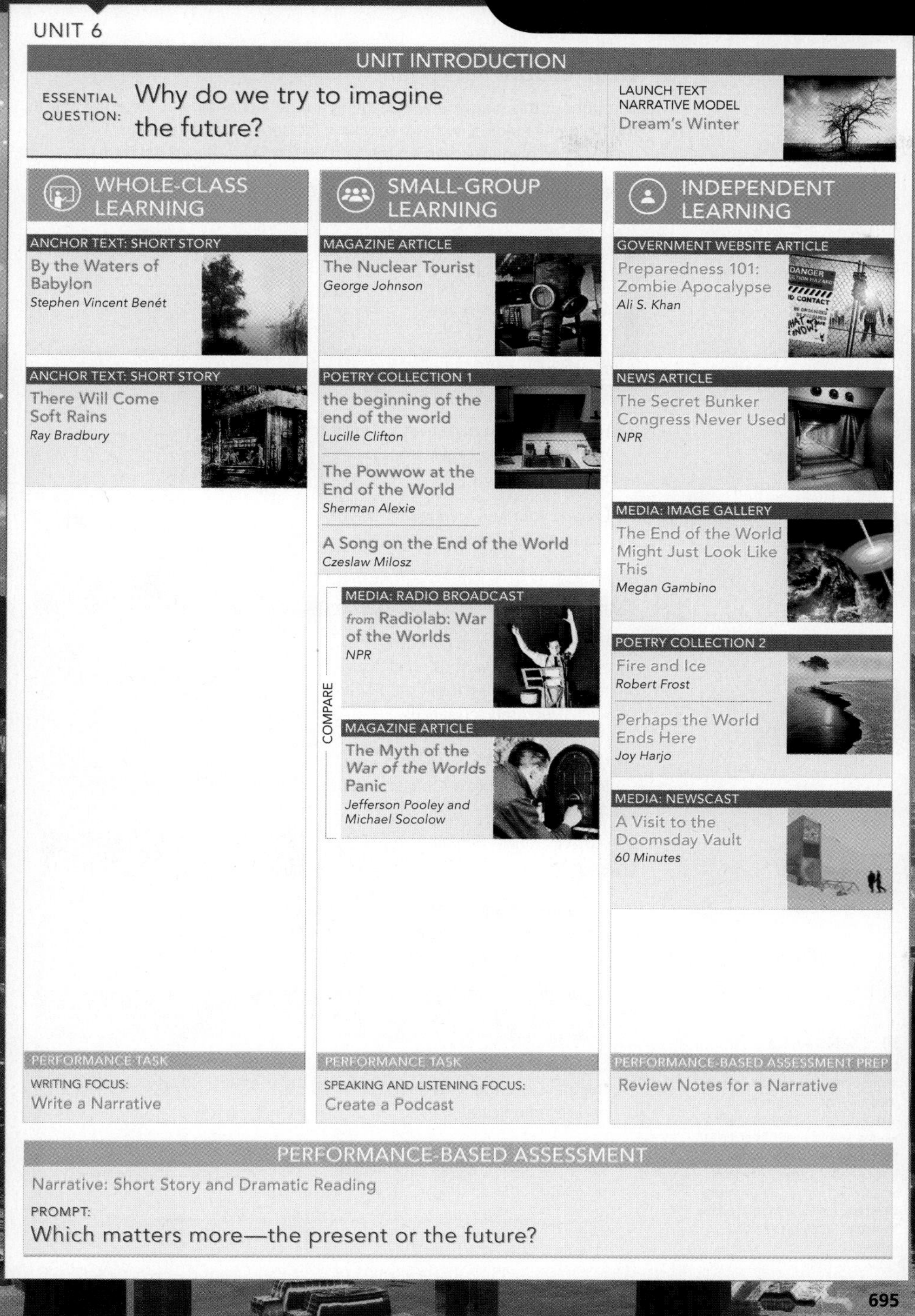
UNIT 6

UNIT INTRODUCTION

ESSENTIAL QUESTION: Why do we try to imagine the future?

LAUNCH TEXT
NARRATIVE MODEL
Dream's Winter

WHOLE-CLASS LEARNING	SMALL-GROUP LEARNING	INDEPENDENT LEARNING
ANCHOR TEXT: SHORT STORY By the Waters of Babylon *Stephen Vincent Benét*	MAGAZINE ARTICLE The Nuclear Tourist *George Johnson*	GOVERNMENT WEBSITE ARTICLE Preparedness 101: Zombie Apocalypse *Ali S. Khan*
ANCHOR TEXT: SHORT STORY There Will Come Soft Rains *Ray Bradbury*	POETRY COLLECTION 1 the beginning of the end of the world *Lucille Clifton* The Powwow at the End of the World *Sherman Alexie* A Song on the End of the World *Czeslaw Milosz*	NEWS ARTICLE The Secret Bunker Congress Never Used *NPR*
	COMPARE: MEDIA: RADIO BROADCAST *from* Radiolab: War of the Worlds *NPR*	MEDIA: IMAGE GALLERY The End of the World Might Just Look Like This *Megan Gambino*
	COMPARE: MAGAZINE ARTICLE The Myth of the *War of the Worlds* Panic *Jefferson Pooley and Michael Socolow*	POETRY COLLECTION 2 Fire and Ice *Robert Frost* Perhaps the World Ends Here *Joy Harjo*
		MEDIA: NEWSCAST A Visit to the Doomsday Vault *60 Minutes*
PERFORMANCE TASK WRITING FOCUS: Write a Narrative	PERFORMANCE TASK SPEAKING AND LISTENING FOCUS: Create a Podcast	PERFORMANCE-BASED ASSESSMENT PREP Review Notes for a Narrative

PERFORMANCE-BASED ASSESSMENT

Narrative: Short Story and Dramatic Reading

PROMPT:
Which matters more—the present or the future?

695

Why do we try to imagine the future?

Introduce the Essential Question and point out that students will respond to related prompts.

- **Whole-Class Learning** *At the end of the world, how do we begin anew?*
- **Small-Group Learning** *What do stories about the future say about the present?*
- **Performance-Based Assessment** *Which matters more—the present or the future?*

Using Trade Books

Refer to the Teaching with Trade Books section in this book or online in myPerspectives+ for suggestions on how to incorporate the following thematically-related novels into this unit.

- *The Road* by Cormac McCarthy
- *Fahrenheit 451* by Ray Bradbury
- *Paradise Lost & Paradise Regained* by John Milton

Current Perspectives

To increase student engagement, search online for stories about what people have considered the end of the world might be like, and invite your students to recommend stories they find. Always preview content before sharing it with your class.

- **News Story: "10 Science Fiction Novels That Correctly Predicted The Future,"** (Business Insider) Ten science-fiction novels offer compelling and accurate predictions of the future.
- **Video: "Asimov's Predictions From the 60s Are Spot On,"** (DNews 2014) A discussion of one of the leading sci-fi writer's legacy.

Day	Activity
16	Introduce Small-Group Learning
17–19	The Nuclear Tourist
20–21	• the beginning of the end of the world • The Powwow at the End of the World • A Song on the End of the World
22–23	Media: *from* Radiolab: War of the Worlds
24–25	The Myth of the War of the Worlds Panic
26	Performance Task
27	Introduce Independent Learning
28	Independent Learning
29–30	Performance-Based Assessment

About the Unit Goals

These unit goals were backward designed from the Performance-Based Assessment at the end of the unit and the Whole-Class and Small-Group Performance Tasks. Students will practice and become proficient in many more standards over the course of this unit.

Unit Goals

Review the goals with students and explain that as they read and discuss the selections, they will improve their skills in reading, writing, research, language, and speaking and listening.

- Have students watch the video on Goal Setting.
- A video on this topic is available online in the Professional Development Center.

Reading Goals Tell students they will read and evaluate written narratives and poetry.

Writing and Research Goals Tell students that they will learn the elements of writing a narrative. Students will write to reflect on experiences. They will gather evidence and conduct research.

Language Goals Tell students that they will develop a deeper understanding of using adverbials and other types of clauses to convey precise meaning. They will then practice using adverbials and other types of clauses in their writing.

Speaking and Listening Explain to students that they will work together to build on one another's ideas and communicate with one another. They will also learn to incorporate audio, visuals, and text in presentations.

HOME Connection

A Home Connection letter to students' parents or guardians is available in myPerspectives+. The letter explains what students will be learning in this unit and how they will be assessed.

Unit Goals

Throughout this unit, you will deepen your understanding of literature about the future by reading, writing, speaking, presenting, and listening. These goals will help you succeed on the Unit Performance-Based Assessment.

Rate how well you meet these goals right now. You will revisit your ratings later when you reflect on your growth during this unit.

SCALE	1	2	3	4	5
	NOT AT ALL WELL	NOT VERY WELL	SOMEWHAT WELL	VERY WELL	EXTREMELY WELL

READING GOALS	1	2	3	4	5
• Evaluate written narratives by analyzing how authors craft their stories.	○	○	○	○	○
• Expand your knowledge and use of academic and concept vocabulary.	○	○	○	○	○

WRITING AND RESEARCH GOALS	1	2	3	4	5
• Write a narrative to convey an experience or event using effective techniques, well-chosen details, and well-structured sequences.	○	○	○	○	○
• Conduct research projects of various lengths to explore a topic and clarify meaning.	○	○	○	○	○

LANGUAGE GOALS	1	2	3	4	5
• Use adverbial and other types of clauses to convey precise meaning and add sentence variety to your writing and presentations.	○	○	○	○	○

SPEAKING AND LISTENING GOALS	1	2	3	4	5
• Collaborate with your team to build on the ideas of others, develop consensus, and communicate.	○	○	○	○	○
• Integrate audio, visuals, and text in presentations.	○	○	○	○	○

STANDARDS

Language
Acquire and use accurately general academic and domain-specific words and phrases, sufficient for reading, writing, speaking, and listening at the college and career readiness level; demonstrate independence in gathering vocabulary knowledge when considering a word or phrase important to comprehension or expression.

AUTHOR'S PERSPECTIVE Ernest Morrell, Ph.D.

When Students Feel They Can't Reach Their Goals People often get discouraged when they can't reach their goals, and this feeling can be especially difficult for students. Teachers can help students overcome their pessimism about setting and meeting goals with these strategies:

- **Offer occasions for students to revisit and revise their goals.** Explain that this step in the process is common and important. Remind students that sometimes the goals we set are unrealistic and they will need to be revised.
- **Help break down the goals into smaller steps.** Building intermediate steps into goals may make them more manageable. For example, when students are setting long-term goals, have them identify a first step. Ask them what they can do immediately, over the next few days. Help students identify the steps they'll need to take to achieve a goal and encourage them to take them one at a time.

Academic Vocabulary: Narrative

Academic terms appear in all subjects and can help you read, write, and discuss with more precision. Here are five academic words that will be useful to you in this unit as you analyze and write narratives.

Complete the chart.

1. Review each word, its root, and the mentor sentences.
2. Use the information and your own knowledge to predict the meaning of each word.
3. For each word, list at least two related words.
4. Refer to a dictionary or other resources if needed.

TIP

FOLLOW THROUGH

Study the words in this chart, and highlight them or their forms wherever they appear in the unit.

WORD	MENTOR SENTENCES	PREDICT MEANING	RELATED WORDS
innovate ROOT: ***-nov-*** "new"	1. American musicians have shown that they can *innovate* and create new musical forms. 2. When you work on a project, *innovate* and avoid repeating the same old ideas.		innovation; innovative; innovatively
technique ROOT: ***-tech-*** "skill"; "craft"	1. The statue demonstrates the artist's impressive *technique* and skill in working with marble. 2. A singer's emotional power can be more important than vocal *technique*.		
depiction ROOT: ***-pict-*** "paint"	1. The new president's vision for America is a *depiction* of peace, equality, and prosperity. 2. Your proposal for the new playground should include some sort of *depiction*, such as a drawing or map.		
introspective ROOT: ***-spec-*** "see"	1. Amanda likes action stories more than *introspective* dramas. 2. Michaela's father worries that she is too *introspective* and thinks too much.		
conjecture ROOT: ***-jec-*** "throw"	1. Any notion of what might happen in the future is just *conjecture*. 2. I can only *conjecture* that Willis will do well because he studied so hard.		

DIGITAL PERSPECTIVES

Academic Vocabulary: Narrative

Introduce the blue academic vocabulary words in the chart on the student page. Point out that the root of each word provides a clue to its meaning. Discuss the mentor sentences to ensure students understand each word's usage. Students should also use the mentor sentences as context to help them predict the meaning of each word. Check that students are able to fill the chart in correctly. Complete pronunciations, parts of speech, and definitions are provided for you. Students are only expected to provide the definition.

Possible responses:

innovate *v.* (IHN uh vayt)
Meaning: to make changes; to introduce something new
Related words: innovation; innovative, innovatively
Additional words related to root *-nov-*: novel, novice, novelty, renovation

technique *n.* (tehk NEEK)
Meaning: special method or skill
Related words: techniques
Additional words related to root *-techni-*: technical, technically, technology, biotech

depiction *n.* (dih PIHK shuhn)
Meaning: a picture, description, or explanation of something
Related words: depicted, depict
Additional words related to root *-pict-*: picture, pictograph

introspective *adj.* (ihn truh SPEHK tihv)
Meaning: having the habit of examining of one's own thoughts and feelings
Related word: introspection
Additional words related to root *-spec-*: spectacle, respect, retrospective, inspection

conjecture *n., v.* (kuhn JEHK chuhr)
Meaning: *n.* guess; v. to guess
Related words: conjecturer, misconjecture
Additional words related to root *-jec-*: interjection, objective, reject, inject

PERSONALIZE FOR LEARNING

English Language Support

Cognates Many of the academic words have Spanish cognates. Use these cognates with students whose home language is Spanish.
ALL LEVELS

innovate – innovar
technique – técnica
depiction – representación
introspective – introspectivo
conjecture – conjetura

Purpose of the Launch Text

The Launch Text provides students with a common starting point to address the unit topic. After reading the Launch Text, all students will be able to participate in discussions about literature and ideas that imagine the world's end.

Lexile: 520 The easier reading level of this selection makes it perfect to assign for homework. Students will need little or no support to understand it.

Additionally, "Dream's Winter" provides a writing model for the Performance-Based Assessment students complete at the end of the unit

Launch Text: Narrative Model

Ask students to think about the story the author is telling and how details are used to weave a vivid and meaningful narrative.

Have students pay attention to the way the author uses the opening sentence of "Dream's Winter" to set the scene, establishing that the setting is dreary and perhaps even apocalyptic. They should notice that the third paragraph indicates that football no longer exists, suggesting that the story takes place in the future.

Encourage students to read this text on their own and annotate unfamiliar words and sections of text they think are particularly important.

AUDIO SUMMARIES

Audio summaries of "Dream's Winter" are available in both English and Spanish in the Interactive Teacher's Edition or Unit Resources. Assigning these summaries before students read the Launch Text may help them build additional background knowledge and set a context for their reading.

LAUNCH TEXT | NARRATIVE MODEL

This selection is an example of a **narrative text,** a type of writing in which the author tells a story. This is the type of writing you will develop in the Performance-Based Assessment at the end of the unit.

As you read, think about how the writer uses the elements of character, time, and setting. Mark the text to help you answer the question: How do specific details add to the portrayal of characters and events?

Dream's Winter

NOTES

1 Chase sat with his back to the old dead tree, scratching at a patch of hard, blackened earth with his compass.

2 "So what do you dream of, kid?"

3 The Tribe on the Hill operates the way a football team did, back when there was such a thing. They're an elite unit, comprised of specialists. It wasn't long ago they took me in. They were impressed with my skills as a sneak: I got through two and a half layers of security before they nabbed me, nine paces from the Shed.

4 They accepted me because I'm a good shot—with a rock, a makeshift spear, or a rifle. But they're not about to trust me with the latter. I wouldn't expect them to.

5 Chase is a scrounge. He has status here. I don't. One wrong word, one errant move, and they could throw me back down the hill, to waste away from starvation and thirst.

6 So I stared at a pill bug on its back, little gray legs flailing, trying to right itself. I'm not touching this one, or that one either.

7 Chase has a face that seems hacked out of flint, like an actor whose name I can't remember. He's old enough to be my father, I guess. That kind of thing doesn't matter like it used to.

8 "I dream of snow," he said, staring at me. Looking past me. I stretched my legs. The pill bug stopped scrabbling.

9 "Kids playing in snow," he said. "Rosy cheeks. Little smiles. Like the kids on the old soup cans."

10 The bug turned itself over. It started to run, then got near my left foot and stopped.

SCAN FOR MULTIMEDIA

CROSS-CURRICULAR PERSPECTIVES

Science Provide students with a list of the following insects and ask them to conduct research to determine which orders they belong to: cockroaches, beetles, butterflies, grasshoppers, dragonflies, and pill bugs. Once they've finished this part of the assignment, have them select one of the insects from the list and write a short report about it. Instruct students to include information about where the insects are commonly found, their morphology and physiology, and their senses.

11 "I'm watching them through a tall, narrow window," he said. Out of the corner of my eye, I saw him bend his head. I think he wanted me to look up. His eyes were so dark they seemed to be all pupils. They're too bright for my liking, but not harsh.

12 "My dining room used to have windows like that. Do you remember dining rooms, kid?"

13 I lifted my heel so it was poised above the bug. Roly-polies, they also call them. It curled into a ball, its shell a series of overlapping blackish-brown wedges.

14 "Then there's the flash," Chase said. "Boom!" Something shook in the pit of my gut, from down beneath uneasiness and hunger.

15 "Then it goes black," he said. "I stare out the window. I can still hear the kids. I can't see them. They're saying something. Whispering and laughing. For the life of me, I can't make it out."

16 He stood up. I flicked the bug away. Pill bugs have blue blood. I remember reading that a few years ago in a book I pulled out of a ditch, but I didn't need to see this proved.

17 Chase tried driving his stick into the crusty earth, as if he were planting a flag. It snapped at a weak spot. He studied the broken end protruding from his fist as if it were trying to tell him something.

18 "I used to wake up in a sweat every time I heard the bang," he said. "Now I don't. Now I stay in the dream, straining… straining in sleep, to hear what those kids out there are saying."

19 I looked up at him. His mouth had gone small, pulled to one side. He chewed at his inner lip. His eyes were wet. He tried to make them steely.

20 "The water bottles come out in a while," he said. "Be ready. No one's going to call you."

21 My foot had missed the bug. It took off, following Chase, as if it heard and understood about the water.

22 John Carradine. That's the actor's name. I think I might have read that somewhere too. ❧

NOTES

WORD NETWORK FOR WORLD'S END

Vocabulary A Word Network is a collection of words related to a topic. As you read the selections in this unit, identify interesting words related to the end of the world, and add them to your Word Network. For example, you might begin by adding words from the Launch Text, such as *compass, makeshift,* and *scrounge*. Continue to add words as you complete this unit.

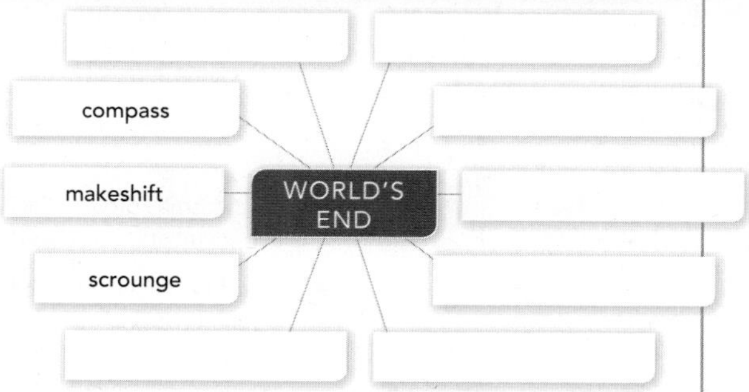

Tool Kit
Word Network Model

DIGITAL PERSPECTIVES

Word Network for World's End

Tell students that they can fill in the Word Network as they read texts in the unit, or they can record the words elsewhere and add them later. Point out to students that people may have personal associations with some words. A word that one student thinks is related to the world's end might not be a word another student would pick. However, students should feel free to add any word they personally think is relevant to their Word Network. Each person's Word Network will be unique. If you choose to print the Word Network, distribute it to students at this point so they can use it throughout the rest of the unit.

AUTHOR'S PERSPECTIVE **Elfrieda Hiebert, Ph.D.**

Multiple Meaning Words A word can have different meanings across content groups. Therefore, the same word will appear in different content maps. It may appear in more than one concept group: some words with multiple meanings even appear in many concept groups.

For example, when the word *channel* is used as a noun in geology, it refers to the bed of a river or other waterway; a navigable route between two bodies of a wide strait; or the deeper part of a waterway. When used as a noun in the field of communication, it refers to the specific, official course or means of discourse. Further, when *channel* is used as a verb in biology ("channel your energy,") economics ("channel money into the program,") or geology ("channel water in the fields"), its meaning changes yet again. As a result, the word *channel* has a place in a variety of concept maps.

Work with students to increase their awareness of multiple meaning words. Seeing words in their various contexts used across subject areas can help build their vocabulary knowledge.

Dream's Winter 699

Summary

Have students read the introductory paragraph. Provide them with tips for writing a summary:

- Write in the present tense.
- Make sure to include the title of the work.
- Be concise: a summary should not be equal in length to the original text.
- If you need to quote the words of the author, use quotation marks.
- Don't put your own opinions, ideas, or interpretations into the summary. The purpose of writing a summary is to accurately represent what the author says, not to provide a critique. If necessary, students can refer to the Tool Kit for help in understanding the elements of a good summary.

See possible summary on student page.

Launch Activity

Explain to students that as they work on this unit, they will have many opportunities to discuss the world's end. Remind them that the end of the world could take many forms and that it doesn't have to match the depictions they've seen at the movies or on TV or that they've read about. Reiterate that imaginations are flexible and that thoughts or ideas don't need to match preconceived notions.

Summary

Write a summary of "Dream's Winter." A **summary** is a concise, complete, and accurate overview of a text. It should not include a statement of your opinion or an analysis.

Possible response: In the narrative "Dream's Winter," the author tells an apocalyptic tale set in the future about a world that's experiencing a nuclear winter.

Throughout the story, the narrator is having a conversation with a character named Chase, someone who has earned high status amongst a group of bandits called The Tribe on the Hill because of his ability to work in a futuristic, dead landscape. Chase talks about his dreams about life in the past, when kids played outside in the snow, before the flash and boom of the nuclear blast. At the end, Chase mentions that the water is about to arrive, indicating that it's a scarce resource.

Launch Activity

Conduct a Small-Group Discussion Consider this question: **Is it possible to imagine the end of the world?**

- Record your thoughts on the question in relation to the Launch Text, books you have read, and movies or programs you have watched. Explain your thinking.

  ____

  ____

- Gather in small groups. Each group should discuss the question, and group members should explain their thoughts and reasoning.
- Bring all the small groups together, and have a representative from each describe the group's responses.
- Discuss as a class the different responses. Is it possible to imagine the end of the world? Why or why not?

VOCABULARY DEVELOPMENT

Academic Vocabulary Reinforcement Have students analyze the word *technique* using a three-column chart. If necessary, guide students as they complete the chart. After they're finished, ask them to share their sample sentences with the class.

Definition: the way in which an expert in a profession or artistic field employs the skills needed to perform in that endeavor.

Synonyms: approach, method

Example sentence: His guitar-playing technique was masterful.

QuickWrite

Consider class discussions, presentations, the video, and the Launch Text as you think about the prompt. Record your first thoughts here.

PROMPT: **Which matters more—the present or the future?**

Possible response: I think the present matters more than the future because the present affects both people who live on the planet now and people who will live on it in the future. By thinking about the present, we can make sure that the future is as great as it can be.

The future represents potential and possibility, but we first must get there. When the nuclear blast discussed in "Dream's Winter" happened, it took place during the present and had a lasting effect on the future.

EVIDENCE LOG FOR WORLD'S END

Review your QuickWrite. Summarize your thoughts in one sentence to record in your Evidence Log. Then, record textual details or evidence from "Dream's Winter" that support your thinking.

Prepare for the Performance-Based Assessment at the end of the unit by completing the Evidence Log after each selection.

Tool Kit
Evidence Log Model

Title of Text: ________ Date: ________

CONNECTION TO PROMPT	TEXT EVIDENCE/DETAILS	ADDITIONAL NOTES/IDEAS

How does this text change or add to my thinking? Date: ________

DIGITAL PERSPECTIVES

QuickWrite

In this QuickWrite, students should present their own response to the prompt based on the material they have read and viewed in the Unit Overview and Introduction. This initial response will help inform their work when they complete the Performance-Based Assessment at the end of the unit. Students should present their thinking and support it with clear, well-reasoned ideas and strong evidence.

See possible QuickWrite on student page.

Evidence Log for World's End

Students should record their initial thinking in their Evidence Logs along with evidence from "Dream's Winter" that supports this thinking.

If you choose to print the Evidence Log, distribute it to students at this point so they can use it throughout the rest of the unit.

Performance-Based Assessment: Refining Your Thinking

- Have students watch the video on Refining Your Thinking.
- A video on this topic is available online in the Professional Development Center.

WriteNow Express and Reflect

Short Story In "Dream's Winter," the narrator and Chase are talking about life in the past. Have students write a short story about a character who is imagining the future, reminding them to include details about what life is like that illustrate how the world has changed. Instruct students to include strong, interesting people in the story, telling them that compelling characters help readers connect to a narrative and that boring characters could cause them to lose interest.

OVERVIEW

WHOLE-CLASS LEARNING

Why do we try to imagine the future?

The science-fiction genre offers a wealth of fictional possibilities. It can be very rewarding and enlightening to read these stories and imagine a future world. During Whole-Class Learning, students will read selections about what the future might be like.

Whole-Class Learning Strategies

Review the Learning Strategies with students and explain that as they work through Whole-Class Learning they will develop strategies to work in large-group environments.

- Have students watch the video on Whole-Class Learning Strategies.
- A video on this topic is available online in the Professional Development Center.

You may wish to discuss some action items to add to the chart as a class before students complete it on their own. For example, for "Monitor understanding," you might suggest these strategies:

- As a group, students can take the time to research something that is unknown or unclear.
- Students might check with others to be sure everyone is following along.

Block Scheduling

Each day in this Pacing Plan represents a 40–50 minute class period. Teachers using block scheduling may combine days to reflect their class schedule. In addition, teachers may revise pacing to differentiate and support core instruction by integrating components and resources as students require.

OVERVIEW: WHOLE-CLASS LEARNING

ESSENTIAL QUESTION:

Why do we try to imagine the future?

Human beings are curious. We are explorers, unwilling to step back and let questions remain unanswered. Yet, there are limits to what we can know. For example, we cannot visit the future, no matter how hard we try. Instead, in literature, in movies, and in science, we work to imagine it. The stories that we tell as a result are sometimes reassuring and sometimes frightening. As you read, you will work with your whole class to explore literary visions of the world's end. The selections you are going to read present two writers' conceptions of a troubled future.

Whole-Class Learning Strategies

Throughout your life, in school, in your community, and in your career, you will continue to learn and work in large-group environments.

Review these strategies and the actions you can take to practice them as you work with your whole class. Add ideas of your own for each category.

STRATEGY	ACTION PLAN
Listen actively	• Eliminate distractions. For example, put your cellphone away. • Keep your eyes on the speaker. •
Clarify by asking questions	• If you're confused, other people probably are, too. Ask a question to help your whole class. • If you see that you are guessing, ask a question instead. •
Monitor understanding	• Notice what information you already know and be ready to build on it. • Ask for help if you are struggling. •
Interact and share ideas	• Share your ideas and answer questions, even if you are unsure. • Build on the ideas of others by adding details or making a connection. •

SCAN FOR MULTIMEDIA

Pacing Plan

Unit Introduction: 1
Introduce Whole-Class Learning: 2
By the Waters of Babylon: 3, 4, 5, 6, 7, 8
There Will Come Soft Rains: 9, 10, 11, 12, 13
Performance Task: 14, 15

WHOLE-CLASS LEARNING

CONTENTS

ANCHOR TEXT: SHORT STORY

By the Waters of Babylon

Stephen Vincent Benét

What will John find when he travels to the Dead Places?

ANCHOR TEXT: SHORT STORY

There Will Come Soft Rains

Ray Bradbury

In the aftermath of destruction, what do we leave behind?

PERFORMANCE TASK

WRITING FOCUS

Write a Narrative

The Whole-Class readings illustrate the world after catastrophe has struck. After reading, you will write your own narrative about the world that remains in the wake of a similar catastrophe.

Contents

Anchor Texts Preview the anchor texts and media with students to generate interest. Encourage students to discuss other texts they may have read or movies or television shows they may have seen that deal with the issues of people's ideas about what the end of the world might be like.

You may wish to conduct a poll to determine which selection students think looks more interesting, and discuss the reasons for their preference. Students can return to this poll after they have read the selections to see if their preference changed.

Performance Task

Write a Narrative Explain to students that after they have finished reading the selections, they will write a narrative about what the world might be like after catastrophe has struck. To help them prepare, encourage students to think about the topic as they progress through the selections and as they participate in the Whole-Class Learning experience.

Introduce Small-Group Learning — 16

The Nuclear Tourist — 17, 18, 19

- the beginning of the end of the world
- The Powwow at the End of the World
- A Song on the End of the World

— 20, 21

Media: *from* Radiolab: War of the Worlds — 22, 23

The Myth of the War of the Worlds Panic — 24, 25

Performance Task — 26

Introduce Independent Learning — 27

Independent Learning — 28

Performance-Based Assessment — 29, 30

By the Waters of Babylon

AUDIO SUMMARIES
Audio summaries of "By the Waters of Babylon" are available online in both English and Spanish in the Interactive Teacher's Edition or Unit Resources. Assigning these summaries prior to reading the selection may help students build additional background knowledge and set a context for their first read.

Summary

In this science-fiction short story, written by Stephen Vincent Benét, the narrator is a member of a tribe living in the hills. The unnamed narrator is the son of a priest, and has learned to read and write the "language of the gods," as well as how to hunt, how to survive in the wilderness, and how to scavenge metal tools from dead places. The gods built these, but are long dead. The narrator grows to adulthood in his tribe, and decides that he must travel on a long journey east to the forbidden Place of the Gods. Though threatened by predators such as wild dogs, he travels to the Place of the Gods, an immense city of empty buildings, broken by the war that killed the gods. There, he has a vision of the gods.

Insight

The story ultimately reveals that the "Place of the Gods" is New York City, destroyed in an apocalyptic war that reduced civilization to hunter-gatherer tribes. This reveal is a classic twist in science fiction, and various details throughout the story hint at it before it is explicitly stated.

ESSENTIAL QUESTION:
Why do we try to imagine the future?

Connection to Essential Question

The future imagined in this selection warns that humanity may well have the tools to destroy civilization, and that we may do so. However, it offers hope that the human spirit will survive, and that people will rebuild civilization, even if such a disaster occurs.

WHOLE-CLASS LEARNING PERFORMANCE TASK
At the end of the world, how do we begin anew?

UNIT PERFORMANCE-BASED ASSESSMENT
Which matters more—the present or the future?

Connection to Performance Tasks

Whole-Class Learning Performance Task The story may give students several ideas to consider as they prepare to address the prompt. The story is set long after the end of the world, depicting the first stage of rebuilding civilization. Further, the story is about learning the truth about the end of the world and promising the eventual recovery of humanity.

Unit Performance-Based Assessment The story clearly considers the future—and the reconstruction of society—to be more important than the present concerns of humanity. However, it also places the blame for the end of civilization on the present. As such, in this story, the present is important as the root of the future.

DIGITAL PERSPECTIVES — Audio | Video | Document | Annotation Highlights | EL Highlights | Online Assessment

LESSON RESOURCES

	Making Meaning	Language Development	Effective Expression
Lesson	**First Read** **Close Read** **Analyze the Text** **Analyze Craft and Structure**	**Concept Vocabulary** **Word Study** **Author's Style**	**Writing to Sources** **Speaking and Listening**
Instructional Standards	**RL.10** By the end of grade 9, read and comprehend literature . . . **RL.5** Analyze how an author's choices concerning how to structure a text . . .	**RL.3** Analyze how complex characters develop . . . **L.2** Demonstrate command of the conventions of standard English . . . **L.4.b** Identify and correctly use patterns of word changes . . . **L.5** Demonstrate understanding of figurative language . . .	**W.3** Write narratives to develop real or imagined experiences . . . **W.3.b** Use narrative techniques . . . **SL.2** Integrate multiple sources of information . . . **SL.4** Present information, findings . . . **SL.5** Make strategic use of digital media . . .
STUDENT RESOURCES			
Available online in the Interactive Student Edition or Unit Resources	Selection Audio First-Read Guide: Fiction Close-Read Guide: Fiction	Word Network	Evidence Log
TEACHER RESOURCES			
Selection Resources Available online in the Interactive Teacher's Edition or Unit Resources	Audio Summaries Annotation Highlights EL Highlights English Language Support Lesson: Multimedia Timeline Analyze Craft and Structure: Narrative Elements	Concept Vocabulary and Word Study Author's Style: Character Development	Writing to Sources: Sequel Speaking and Listening: Multimedia Timeline
Reteach/Practice (RP) Available online in the Interactive Teacher's Edition or Unit Resources	Analyze Craft and Structure: Narrative Elements (RP)	Word Study: Word Families (RP) Author's Style: Character Development (RP)	Writing to Sources: Sequel (RP) Speaking and Listening: Multimedia Timeline (RP)
Assessment Available online in Assessments	Selection Test		
My Resources	A Unit 6 Answer Key is available online and in the Interactive Teacher's Edition.		

Reading Support

Text Complexity Rubric: By the Waters of Babylon	
Quantitative Measures	
Lexile: 810 **Text Length:** 5,662 words	
Qualitative Measures	
Knowledge Demands ① ② **❸** ④ ⑤	The selection is a post-apocalyptic short story. Context information and some knowledge of New York will be helpful.
Structure ① **❷** ③ ④ ⑤	The selection is a first-person short story with linear organization.
Language Conventionality and Clarity ① **❷** ③ ④ ⑤	The selection is mostly simple sentences with formal language and on-level vocabulary. Language is sometimes used for figurative power.
Levels of Meaning/Purpose ① **❷** ③ ④ ⑤	The meaning is mostly straightforward. Themes include coming-of-age and the detriment of war. Superstitious elements may be confusing.

DECIDE AND PLAN

English Language Support

Provide English Learners with support for **Knowledge Demands and Language** as they read the selection.

Knowledge Demands Invite students to listen actively as you share information about the text. Tell students that this short story is set in a post-apocalyptic world and the people are very superstitious. They should expect to see language that describes rituals and beliefs, including references to purification and spirits.

Language Students may find the unconventional capitalization of certain words confusing. Explain that the author often capitalizes words that have significant meaning to the people in the story, including Great Burning and Dead Places.

Strategic Support

Provide students with strategic support to ensure that they can successfully read the text.

Knowledge Demands Use the background information to discuss the context of the story. Determine students' prior knowledge and experience with post-apocalyptic stories. Provide additional background information as needed.

Levels of Meaning/Purpose If students have difficulty with the superstitious elements of the story, have them first summarize the events that are taking place. Then have them reread each sentence to try to determine the significance.

Challenge

Provide students who need to be challenged with ideas for how they can go beyond a simple interpretation of the text.

Text Analysis Have students discuss the simple sentence structure the author uses. What effect does this structure have on the tone of the story? What impression do students have of the narrator, John?

Written Response Challenge students to write a short story about their own version of a post-apocalyptic world. Encourage them to include detailed descriptions of the setting, characters, and events.

TEACH

Read and Respond

Have the class do their first read of the selection. Then have them complete their close read. Finally, work with them on the Making Meaning, Language Development, and Effective Expression activities.

Standards Support Through Teaching and Learning Cycle

IDENTIFY NEEDS

Analyze results of the Beginning-of-Year Assessment, focusing on the items relating to Unit 6. Also take into consideration student performance to this point and your observations of where particular students struggle.

DECIDE AND PLAN

- If students have performed poorly on items matching these standards, then provide selection scaffolds before assigning them the on-level lesson provided in the Student Edition.
- If students have done well on the Beginning-of-Year Assessment, then challenge them to keep progressing and learning by giving them opportunities to practice the skills in depth.
- Use the Selection Resources listed on the Planning pages for "By the Waters of Babylon" to help students continually improve their ability to master the standards.

Instructional Standards: By the Waters of Babylon

	Catching Up	This Year	Looking Forward
Reading	You may wish to administer the **Analyze Craft and Structure: Narrative Elements (RP)** worksheet to help students better understand how writers use these elements.	**RL.5** Analyze how an author's choices concerning how to structure a text, order events within it, and manipulate time create such effects as mystery, tension, or surprise.	Challenge students to compare use of dramatic irony in this text to other examples they have read.
Writing	You may wish to administer the **Writing to Sources: Sequel (RP)** worksheet to better prepare students for their writing.	**W.3.b** Use narrative techniques, such as dialogue, pacing, description, reflection, and multiple plot lines, to develop experiences, events, and/or characters.	Challenge students to adapt their original sequels into short plays or film scripts.
Speaking and Listening	You may wish to administer the **Speaking and Listening: Multimedia Timeline (RP)** worksheet to help students better prepare for their presentations.	**SL.2** Integrate multiple sources of information presented in diverse media or formats evaluating the credibility and accuracy of each source.	Challenge students to create their own media for the presentation instead of repurposing media found from other sources.
Language	Review the **Word Study: Word Families (RP)** worksheet to better familiarize students with word families. You may wish to administer the **Author's Style: Character Development (RP)** worksheet to help students better understand how these conventions inform character.	**L.4.b** Identify and correctly use patterns of word changes that indicate different meanings or parts of speech **RL.3** Analyze how complex characters develop over the course of a text, interact with other characters, and advance the plot or develop the theme.	Have students locate words in the text that are also part of word families. Challenge students to apply the Author's Style character development chart to another text they have read.

TEACH

Implement the planned lesson, and gather evidence of student learning.

ANALYZE AND REVISE

- Analyze student work for evidence of student learning.
- Identify whether or not students have met the expectations in the standards.
- Identify implications for future instruction.

Jump Start

FIRST READ According to the website *Livescience*, in the last 100 years, humans have gotten taller, fatter, and older than at any time in history. Ask students to think about how humanity will change (physically, morally, intellectually) in the next 100 years. Engaging students in a discussion about changes the future will bring can set the context for reading "By the Waters of Babylon."

By the Waters of Babylon

What would you risk to "boldly go where no man has gone before"? Who gets to decide whether you can take that risk? Modeling the questions readers might ask as they read "By the Waters of Babylon" for the first time brings the text alive for students and connects it to the Whole-Class Performance Task assignment. Selection audio and print capability for the selection are available in the Interactive Teacher's Edition.

Concept Vocabulary

Support students as they rank their words. Ask if they've ever heard, read, or used them. Reassure them that the definitions for these words are listed in the selection.

FIRST READ

Have students perform the steps of the first read independently:

NOTICE: You may want to encourage students to notice the time period in which the story takes place and the year that the story was written.

ANNOTATE: Remind students to mark passages that they want to revisit and passages that can be interpreted in more than one way.

CONNECT: Ask students to list other stories or movies they know that present post–apocalyptic worlds.

RESPOND: Students will answer questions and write a summary to demonstrate understanding.

Point out to students that while they will always complete the Respond step at the end of the first read, the other steps will probably happen somewhat concurrently. You may wish to print copies of the **First-Read Guide: Fiction** for students to use.

About the Author

Stephen Vincent Benét (1898–1943) and his two siblings were clearly influenced by their father's love of literature, as they all grew up to be writers. Much of Benét's work centers on American history and folklore, including his most famous story, "The Devil and Daniel Webster," and his epic poem about the Civil War, *John Brown's Body*. The latter work won the Pulitzer Prize in 1929. At the time of his death, Benét was at work on a second epic poem, *Western Star,* which he planned to write as a narrative that would span five books. He finished only the first volume, which posthumously won him a second Pulitzer Prize when it was published in 1944.

Tool Kit
First-Read Guide and Model Annotation

STANDARDS
Reading Literature
By the end of grade 9, read and comprehend literature, including stories, dramas, and poems, in the grades 9–10 text complexity band proficiently, with scaffolding as needed at the high end of the range.

By the Waters of Babylon

Concept Vocabulary

You will encounter the following words as you read "By the Waters of Babylon." Before reading, note how familiar you are with each word. Then, rank the words in order from most familiar (1) to least familiar (6).

WORD	YOUR RANKING
purified	
bade	
stern	
fasting	
customs	
summoned	

After completing the first read, come back to the concept vocabulary and review your rankings. Mark changes to your original rankings as needed.

First Read FICTION

Apply these strategies as you conduct your first read. You will have an opportunity to complete the close-read notes after your first read.

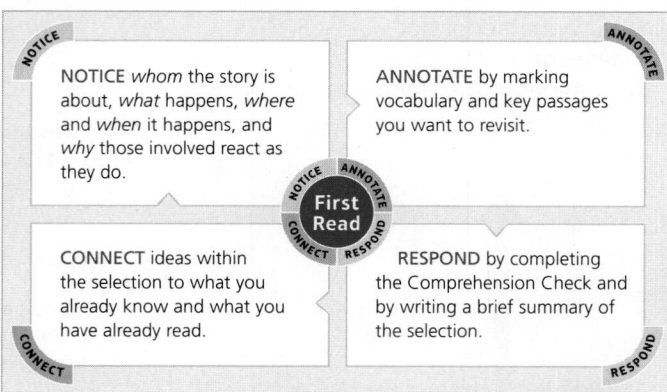

NOTICE *whom* the story is about, *what* happens, *where* and *when* it happens, and *why* those involved react as they do.

ANNOTATE by marking vocabulary and key passages you want to revisit.

CONNECT ideas within the selection to what you already know and what you have already read.

RESPOND by completing the Comprehension Check and by writing a brief summary of the selection.

ANCHOR TEXT | SHORT STORY

By the Waters of Babylon

Stephen Vincent Benét

BACKGROUND

Stephen Vincent Benét published this story in 1937, just after the devastating bombing of Guernica in Spain, in which hundreds of defenseless civilians were killed. During this time, people were afraid of the increasingly destructive power of modern weaponry. A few short years after this story was published, World War II would erupt, and the nuclear bomb would be invented. The title of the story is an allusion, or reference, to a line from Psalm 137, which describes the yearning of the Jews for their homeland after they were exiled by the Babylonians.

SCAN FOR MULTIMEDIA

1 The north and the west and the south are good hunting ground, but it is forbidden to go east. It is forbidden to go to any of the Dead Places except to search for metal, and then he who touches the metal must be a priest or the son of a priest. Afterwards, both the man and the metal must be **purified**! These are the rules and the laws: they are well made. It is forbidden to cross the great river and look upon the place that was the Place of the Gods—this is most strictly forbidden. We do not even say its name though we know its name. It is there that spirits live, and demons—it is there that there are the ashes of the Great Burning. These things are forbidden—they have been forbidden since the beginning of time.

2 My father is a priest; I am the son of a priest. I have been in the Dead Places near us, with my father—at first, I was afraid. When my father went into the house to search for the metal, I stood by the door and my heart felt small and weak. It was a dead man's house, a spirit house. It did not have the smell of man, though there were old bones in a corner. But it is not fitting that a priest's son should show fear. I looked at the bones in the shadow and kept my voice still.

NOTES

purified (PYUR uh fyd)
v. cleaned by removing harmful or unwanted materials or qualities

CLOSE READ

ANNOTATE: In paragraph 1, mark a key word that the narrator repeats.

QUESTION: What emotional quality or **tone** does this repetition create?

CONCLUDE: What does this repeated word suggest about the narrator and his society?

DIGITAL PERSPECTIVES

CLOSE READ

Remind students to focus on the narrator's use of repetition. You may wish to model the Close Read using the following think-aloud format. Possible responses to questions on the Student page are included. You may also want to print copies of the **Close-Read Guide: Fiction** for students to use.

ANNOTATE: As I read paragraph 1, I notice and highlight the word "forbidden," which is repeated six times.

QUESTION: The use of this word suggests religion or ritual, and it creates a formal tone.

CONCLUDE: The repeated word shows that there are many rules and expectations that govern life. It also shows that the narrator follows these rules.

AUTHOR'S PERSPECTIVE Kelly Gallagher, M.Ed.

Ten Reasons to Read Students often question why they should read; after all, so much information is now available in audio and video. Students are also likely to say that reading is dull and difficult, especially regarding canonical and traditional texts. Teachers can counter these claims by providing students with these ten reasons to read. Revisit these reasons throughout the year, asking students to discuss and to write about them.

1. Reading is rewarding.
2. Reading builds a mature vocabulary, which fights "word poverty."
3. Reading makes you a better writer.
4. Reading is "hard," and "hard" is necessary.
5. Reading makes you smarter.
6. Reading prepares you for the world of work.
7. Reading is financially rewarding.
8. Reading opens the door to college and beyond.
9. Reading arms you against oppression.
10. Reading leads you to a deeper understanding of the world.

NOTES

3 Then my father came out with the metal—a good, strong piece. He looked at me with both eyes but I had not run away. He gave me the metal to hold—I took it and did not die. So he knew that I was truly his son and would be a priest in my time. That was when I was very young—nevertheless, my brothers would not have done it, though they are good hunters. After that, they gave me the good piece of meat and the warm corner by the fire. My father watched over me—he was glad that I should be a priest. But when I boasted or wept without a reason, he punished me more strictly than my brothers. That was right.

4 After a time, I myself was allowed to go into the dead houses and search for metal. So I learned the ways of those houses—and if I saw bones, I was no longer afraid. The bones are light and old—sometimes they will fall into dust if you touch them. But that is a great sin.

5 I was taught the chants and the spells—I was taught how to stop the running of blood from a wound and many secrets. A priest must know many secrets—that was what my father said. If the hunters think we do all things by chants and spells, they may believe so—it does not hurt them. I was taught how to read in the old books and how to make the old writings—that was hard and took a long time. My knowledge made me happy—it was like a fire in my heart. Most of all, I liked to hear of the Old Days and the stories of the gods. I asked myself many questions that I could not answer, but it was good to ask them. At night, I would lie awake and listen to the wind—it seemed to me that it was the voice of the gods as they flew through the air.

6 We are not ignorant like the Forest People—our women spin wool on the wheel, our priests wear a white robe. We do not eat grubs from the tree, we have not forgotten the old writings, although they are hard to understand. Nevertheless, my knowledge and my lack of knowledge burned in me—I wished to know more. When I was a man at last, I came to my father and said, "It is time for me to go on my journey. Give me your leave."

7 He looked at me for a long time, stroking his beard, then he said at last, "Yes. It is time." That night, in the house of the priesthood, I asked for and received purification. My body hurt but my spirit was a cool stone. It was my father himself who questioned me about my dreams.

8 He **bade** me look into the smoke of the fire and see—I saw and told what I saw. It was what I have always seen—a river, and, beyond it, a great Dead Place and in it the gods walking. I have always thought about that. His eyes were **stern** when I told him—he was no longer my father but a priest. He said, "This is a strong dream."

9 "It is mine," I said, while the smoke waved and my head felt light. They were singing the Star song in the outer chamber and it was like the buzzing of bees in my head.

10 He asked me how the gods were dressed and I told him how they were dressed. We know how they were dressed from the book, but

bade (bayd) *v.* past tense of *bid;* requested

stern (sturn) *adj.* strict; severe

CROSS-CURRICULAR PERSPECTIVES

Science In paragraph 5, John says that he was taught how to stop the running of blood from a wound—the Forest People thought it was accomplished by chants and spells. Have students do research on ways to stop bleeding from a wound. Address the following questions:

What purpose is served by bleeding?

What condition results when the bleeding is under the skin?

What can happen when you bleed excessively?

When should you seek medical care for a cut or wound?

Have volunteers share their research with the class.

I saw them as if they were before me. When I had finished, he threw the sticks three times and studied them as they fell.

11 "This is a very strong dream," he said. "It may eat you up."

12 "I am not afraid," I said and looked at him with both eyes. My voice sounded thin in my ears but that was because of the smoke.

13 He touched me on the breast and the forehead. He gave me the bow and the three arrows.

14 "Take them," he said. "It is forbidden to travel east. It is forbidden to cross the river. It is forbidden to go to the Place of the Gods. All these things are forbidden."

15 "All these things are forbidden," I said, but it was my voice that spoke and not my spirit. He looked at me again.

16 "My son," he said. "Once I had young dreams. If your dreams do not eat you up, you may be a great priest. If they eat you, you are still my son. Now go on your journey."

17 I went **fasting**, as is the law. My body hurt, but not my heart. When the dawn came, I was out of sight of the village. I prayed and purified myself, waiting for a sign. That sign was an eagle. It flew east.

18 Sometimes signs are sent by bad spirits. I waited again on the flat rock, fasting, taking no food. I was very still—I could feel the sky above me and the earth beneath. I waited till the sun was beginning to sink. Then three deer passed in the valley, going east—they did not mind me or see me. There was a white fawn with them—a very great sign.

19 I followed them, at a distance, waiting for what would happen. My heart was troubled about going east, yet I knew that I must go. My head hummed with my fasting—I did not even see the panther spring upon the white fawn. But, before I knew it, the bow was in my hand. I shouted and the panther lifted his head from the fawn. It is not easy to kill a panther with one arrow but the arrow went through his eye and into his brain. He died as he tried to spring—he rolled over, tearing at the ground. Then I knew I was meant to go east—I knew that was my journey. When the night came, I made my fire and roasted meat.

20 It is eight suns' journey to the east and a man passes by many Dead Places. The Forest People are afraid of them but I am not. Once I made my fire on the edge of a Dead Place at night and, next morning, in the dead house, I found a good knife, little rusted. That was small to what came afterward, but it made my heart feel big. Always when I looked for game, it was in front of my arrow, and twice I passed hunting parties of the Forest People without their knowing. So I knew my magic was strong and my journey clean, in spite of the law.

21 Toward the setting of the eighth sun, I came to the banks of the great river. It was half-a-day's journey after I had left the god-road—we do not use the god-roads now for they are falling apart into great blocks of stone, and the forest is safer going. A long way off, I had seen the water through trees but the trees were thick. At last, I came out upon an open place at the top of a cliff. There was the

NOTES

CLOSE READ

ANNOTATE: In paragraphs 13–16, mark examples of repetition.

QUESTION: Why has the author chosen to repeat words and word patterns?

CONCLUDE: What overall effect does the use of repetition create?

fasting (FAS tihng) *v.* intentionally not eating, often for religious or spiritual reasons

DIGITAL PERSPECTIVES

CLOSE READ

Remind students to focus on the writer's tone or attitude. You may wish to model the Close Read using the following think-aloud format. Possible responses to questions on the Student page are included.

ANNOTATE: As I read paragraphs 13–16, I notice and highlight words that are repeated.

QUESTION: I think the repetition of words and word patterns emphasizes that there are many things that John's society does not allow him to do.

CONCLUDE: The repetition creates a somber effect. It may also create a feeling of fear or worry in the reader.

PERSONALIZE FOR LEARNING

Strategic Support

Rites of Passage Explain that many stories include rites of passage, or events that mark the transition between one phase of life and another. In this section of the story beginning with paragraph 11, John journeys to learn more about his society and himself. If he is successful, he will become a priest, which will allow him to take his place in the society. Have students look for examples in the text that show that this journey is significant as a rite of passage. **Possible responses:** He fasts, he prays, he undergoes purification rituals, and he travels by himself. The trip is more than 8 days long.

CLOSE READ

Have students focus on contrasting details that represent conflict in this passage. You may wish to model the Close Read using the following think-aloud format. Possible responses to questions on the Student page are included.

ANNOTATE: As I read John's song in paragraph 25, I notice and highlight the details that present contrasting ideas.

QUESTION: The author is emphasizing the contrast between what John was forbidden to do and what he has done.

CONCLUDE: The song reveals a lot about John. I think John could not be at peace with himself if he did not continue his journey, and he could not have learned his strengths if he had stayed within the confines of his home and culture. This contrast results in both external and internal conflict. I notice, however, that in both instances John says what he has done, not what he intends to do. This gives his disobedience a sense of the inevitable.

NOTES

great river below, like a giant in the sun. It is very long, very wide. It could eat all the streams we know and still be thirsty. Its name is Ou-dis-sun, the Sacred, the Long. No man of my tribe had seen it, not even my father, the priest. It was magic and I prayed.

22 Then I raised my eyes and looked south. It was there, the Place of the Gods.

23 How can I tell you what it was like—you do not know. It was there, in the red light, and they were too big to be houses. It was there with the red light upon it, mighty and ruined. I knew that in another moment the gods would see me. I covered my eyes with my hands and crept back into the forest.

24 Surely, that was enough to do, and live. Surely it was enough to spend the night upon the cliff. The Forest People themselves do not come near. Yet, all through the night, I knew that I should have to cross the river and walk in the places of the gods, although the gods ate me up. My magic did not help me at all and yet there was a fire in my bowels, a fire in my mind. When the sun rose I thought, "My journey has been clean. Now I will go home from my journey." But, even as I thought so, I knew I could not. If I went to the place of the gods, I would surely die, but, if I did not go, I could never be at peace with my spirit again. It is better to lose one's life than one's spirit, if one is a priest and the son of a priest.

If I went to the place of the gods, I would surely die, . . .

25 Nevertheless, as I made the raft, the tears ran out of my eyes. The Forest People could have killed me without a fight, if they had come upon me then, but they did not come. When the raft was made, I said the sayings for the dead and painted myself for death. My heart was cold as a frog and my knees like water, but the burning in my mind would not let me have peace. As I pushed the raft from the shore, I began my death song—I had the right. It was a fine song.

"I am John, son of John," I sang. "My people are the Hill People. They are the men.
I go into the Dead Places but I am not slain.
I take the metal from the Dead Places but I am not blasted.
I travel upon the god-roads and am not afraid. E-yah! I have killed the panther. I have killed the fawn!
E-yah! I have come to the great river. No man has come there before.
It is forbidden to go east, but I have gone, forbidden to go on the great river, but I am there.
Open your hearts, you spirits, and hear my song.
Now I go to the Place of the Gods. I shall not return.
My body is painted for death and my limbs weak, but my heart is big as I go to the Place of the Gods!"

26 All the same, when I came to the Place of the Gods. I was afraid, afraid. The current of the great river is very strong—it gripped my

CLOSE READ

ANNOTATE: In paragraph 25, mark contrasting details in John's song.

QUESTION: Why has the author chosen to emphasize contrasting ideas?

CONCLUDE: What can you conclude about John from his song?

DIGITAL PERSPECTIVES

raft with its hands. That was magic, for the river itself is wide and calm. I could feel evil spirits about me, in the bright morning: I could feel their breath on my neck as I was swept down the stream. Never have I been so much alone—I tried to think of my knowledge, but it was a squirrel's heap of winter nuts. There was no strength in my knowledge any more, and I felt small and naked as a new-hatched bird—alone upon the great river, the servant of the gods.

27 Yet, after a while, my eyes were opened and I saw both banks of the river—I saw that once there had been god-roads across it, though now they were broken and fallen like broken vines. Very great they were, and wonderful and broken—broken in the time of the Great Burning when the fire fell out of the sky. And always the current took me nearer to the Place of the Gods, and the huge ruins rose before my eyes.

28 I do not know the **customs** of rivers—we are the People of the Hills. I tried to guide my raft with the pole but it spun around, I thought the river meant to take me past the Place of the Gods and out into the Bitter Water of the legends. I grew angry then—my heart felt strong. I said aloud, "I am a priest and the son of a priest!" The gods heard me—they showed me how to paddle with the pole on one side of the raft. The current changed itself—I drew near to the Place of the Gods.

29 When I was very near, my raft struck and turned over. I can swim in our lakes—I swam to the shore. There was a great spike or rusted metal sticking out into the river—I hauled myself up upon it and sat there, panting. I had saved my bow and two arrows and the knife I found in the Dead Place but that was all. My raft went whirling downstream toward the Bitter Water. I looked after it, and thought if it had trod me under, at least I would be safely dead. Nevertheless, when I had dried my bow-string and restrung it, I walked forward to the Place of the Gods.

30 It felt like ground underfoot; it did not burn me. It is not true what some of the tales say, that the ground there burns forever, for I have been there. Here and there were the marks and stains of the Great Burning, on the ruins, that is true. But they were old marks and old stains. It is not true either, what some of our priests say, that it is an island covered with fogs and enchantments. It is not. It is a great Dead Place—greater than any Dead Place we know. Everywhere in it there are god-roads, though most are cracked and broken. Everywhere there are the ruins of the high towers of the gods.

31 How shall I tell what I saw? I went carefully, my strung bow in my hand, my skin ready for danger. There should have been the wailings of spirits and the shrieks of demons, but there were not. It was very silent and sunny where I had landed—the wind and the rain and the birds that drop seeds had done their work—the grass grew in the cracks of the broken stone. It is a fair island—no wonder the gods built there. If I had come there, a god, I also would have built.

NOTES

customs (KUHS tuhmz) *n.* traditions; actions that are commonly done by a group of people

CLOSE READ

ANNOTATE: Mark the first sentence in paragraphs 31, 32, and 33.

QUESTION: Why does the narrator start each paragraph with the same question?

CONCLUDE: What is the narrator trying to communicate about his experience by asking these questions?

CLOSE READ

Remind students to note the writer's use of rhetorical questions. You may wish to model the Close Read using the following think-aloud format. Possible responses to questions on the Student page are included.

ANNOTATE: As I read paragraphs 31–33, I notice and highlight the first sentence in each.

QUESTION: I think the question is repeated because the narrator is still contemplating the question in his own mind.

CONCLUDE: I think that John is communicating that the things he has experienced are almost too much for him to believe; he is incredulous. He has discovered that many things he has been taught all his life are not true. These rhetorical questions, understandably, reflect how emotional he is over his experience.

Explain that **rhetorical questions** are just one rhetorical device commonly used by writers to add style and energy to narratives. Other devices that utilize special word patterns or idea patterns are *parallelism, restatement, repetition, and antithesis*. Rhetorical questions can make the audience feel personally and emotionally involved.

Additional **English Language Support** is available in the Interactive Teacher's Edition.

NOTES

32 How shall I tell what I saw? The towers are not all broken—here and there one still stands, like a great tree in a forest, and the birds nest high. But the towers themselves look blind, for the gods are gone. I saw a fish-hawk, catching fish in the river. I saw a little dance of white butterflies over a great heap of broken stones and columns. I went there and looked about me—there was a carved stone with cut-letters, broken in half. I can read letters but I could not understand these. They said UBTREAS. There was also the shattered image of a man or a god. It had been made of white stone and he wore his hair tied back like a woman's. His name was ASHING, as I read on the cracked half of a stone. I thought it wise to pray to ASHING, though I do not know that god.

33 How shall I tell what I saw? There was no smell of man left, on stone or metal. Nor were there many trees in that wilderness of stone. There are many pigeons, nesting and dropping in the towers—the gods must have loved them, or, perhaps, they used them for sacrifices. There are wild cats that roam the god-roads, green-eyed, unafraid of man. At night they wail like demons, but they are not demons. The wild dogs are more dangerous, for they hunt in a pack, but them I did not meet till later. Everywhere there are the carved stones carved with magical numbers or words.

34 I went North—I did not try to hide myself. When a god or a demon saw me, then I would die, but meanwhile I was no longer afraid. My hunger for knowledge burned in me—there was so much that I could not understand. After a while, I knew that my belly was hungry. I could have hunted for my meat, but I did not hunt. It is known that the gods did not hunt as we do—they got their food from enchanted boxes and jars. Sometimes these are still found in the Dead Places—once, when I was a child and foolish, I opened such a jar and tasted it and found the food sweet. But my father found out and punished me for it strictly, for, often, that food is death. Now, though, I had long gone past what was forbidden, and I entered the likeliest towers, looking for the food of the gods.

35 I found it at last in the ruins of a great temple in the mid-city. A mighty temple it must have been, for the roof was painted like the sky at night with its stars—that much I could see, though the colors were faint and dim. It went down into great caves and tunnels— perhaps they kept their slaves there. But when I started to climb down, I heard the squeaking of rats, so I did not go—rats are unclean, and there must have been many tribes of them, from the squeaking. But near there, I found food, in the heart of a ruin, behind a door that still opened. I ate only the fruits from the jar—they had a very sweet taste. There was drink, too, in bottles of glass— the drink of the gods was strong and made my head swim. After I had eaten and drunk, I slept on the top of a stone, my bow at my side.

36 When I woke, the sun was low. Looking down from where I lay, I saw a dog sitting on his haunches. His tongue was hanging out of his mouth; he looked as if he were laughing. He was a big dog,

PERSONALIZE FOR LEARNING

English Language Support

Idioms Idioms can be confusing to English Language learners, as in paragraph 35 when John says, "My hunger for knowledge burned in me…" Explain to students that John felt like he needed mental and intellectual stimulation just like he needed physical food. He compared a lack of knowledge to a hunger. Ask students to discuss how this idiom helps them to understand the strength of his desire to learn. **ALL LEVELS**

DIGITAL PERSPECTIVES

NOTES

with a gray-brown coat, as big as a wolf. I sprang up and shouted at him but he did not move—he just sat there as if he were laughing. I did not like that. When I reached for a stone to throw, he moved swiftly out of the way of the stone. He was not afraid of me; he looked at me as if I were meat. No doubt I could have killed him with an arrow, but I did not know if there were others. Moreover, night was falling.

37 I looked about me—not far away there was a great broken god-road, leading North. The towers were high enough, but not so high, and while many of the dead-houses were wrecked, there were some that stood. I went toward this god-road, keeping to the heights of the ruins, while the dog followed. When I had reached the god-road. I saw that there were others behind him. If I had slept later, they would have come upon me asleep and torn out my throat. As it was, they were sure enough of me; they did not hurry. When I went into the dead-house, they kept watch at the entrance—doubtless they thought they would have a fine hunt. But a dog cannot open a door and I knew from the books, that the gods did not like to live on the ground but on high.

38 I had just found a door I could open when the dogs decided to rush. Ha! They were surprised when I shut the door in their faces—it was a good door, of strong metal. I could hear their foolish baying beyond it, but I did not stop to answer them. I was in darkness—I found stairs and climbed. There were many stairs, turning around till my head was dizzy. At the top was another door—I found the knob and opened it. I was in a long small chamber—on one side of it was a bronze door that could not be opened, for it had no handle. Perhaps there was a magic word to open it, but l did not have the word. I turned to the door in the opposite side of the wall. The lock of it was broken and I opened it and went in.

CLOSE READ

ANNOTATE: In paragraphs 36–38, mark details that characterize or describe the dogs.

QUESTION: Why does the author provide so much detail about John's encounter with the dogs?

CONCLUDE: What can you conclude about the ways in which John's world differs from that of the reader?

CLOSE READ

Remind students to focus on the structure of the sentences in this passage. You may wish to model the Close Read using the following think-aloud format. Possible responses to questions on the Student page are included.

ANNOTATE: As I read paragraphs 36, 37, and 38, I notice and highlight the details that describe the dogs.

QUESTION: I think the author spends time developing the encounter with the dogs to create suspense and to show the potential danger that John is in.

CONCLUDE: This description shows that John's world is overrun by wild animals. He is exploring a place where there seem to be no people and the animals are the only life. This is in stark contrast to the world of the reader.

CLOSER LOOK

Analyze Rhythm

Students may have marked paragraph 40 during their first read. Use this paragraph to help students understand parallelism as a rhetorical device. Encourage them to discuss the annotations that they marked. You may want to model a close read with the class based on the highlights shown in the text.

ANNOTATE: Have students mark details in paragraph 40 that are examples of rhythm, or have students participate while you highlight them.

QUESTION: Guide students to consider what these details might tell them. Ask what a reader can infer from the things that John describes, and accept student responses.

Possible response: John expresses his puzzlement as a series of contradictions. In every instance the structure is the same. Each expresses a contradiction which confuses John.

CONCLUDE: Help students to formulate conclusions about the importance of these details in the text. Ask students why the author might have included these details.

Possible response: The objects John sees represent tools that support basic human life—cooking, washing, and lighting dark places. John may not have been familiar with the details of this time and place, but he could recognize the common thread. The contradictions between these objects and John's expectations are expressed in sentences that take the form of parallel structures: *There was this but not that*. The rhythm created by parallel sentences emphasizes the pattern. John sees an object he recognizes, but there is a central difference which prevents him from understanding it.

Remind students that **rhythm** is the pattern of weak and strong beats in spoken or written language. Though often associated with poetry, prose can also have rhythm, usually in a much looser and irregular pattern. The rhythm of a passage can make it memorable.

NOTES

39 Within, there was a place of great riches. The god who lived there must have been a powerful god. The first room was a small anteroom—I waited there for some time, telling the spirits of the place that I came in peace and not as a robber. When it seemed to me that they had had time to hear me, I went on. Ah, what riches! Few, even, of the windows had been broken—it was all as it had been. The great windows that looked over the city had not been broken at all though they were dusty and streaked with many years. There were coverings on the floors, the colors not greatly faded, and the chairs were soft, and deep. There were pictures upon the walls, very strange, very wonderful—I remember one of a bunch of flowers in a jar—if you came close to it, you could see nothing but bits of color, but if you stood away from it, the flowers might have been picked yesterday. It made my heart feel strange to look at this picture—and to look at the figure of a bird, in some hard clay, on a table and see it so like our birds. Everywhere there were books and writings, many in tongues that I could not read. The god who lived there must have been a wise god and full of knowledge. I felt I had right there, as I sought knowledge also.

Everywhere there were books and writings, many in tongues that I could not read.

40 Nevertheless, it was strange. There was a washing-place but no water—perhaps the gods washed in air. There was a cooking-place but no wood, and though there was a machine to cook food, there was no place to put fire in it. Nor were there candles or lamps—there were things that looked like lamps but they had neither oil nor wick. All these things were magic, but I touched them and lived—the magic had gone out of them. Let me tell one thing to show. In the washing-place, a thing said "Hot" but it was not hot to the touch—another thing said "Cold" but it was not cold. This must have been a strong magic but the magic was gone. I do not understand—they had ways—I wish that I knew.

41 It was close and dry and dusty in their house of the gods. I have said the magic was gone but that is not true—it had gone from the magic things but it had not gone from the place. I felt the spirits about me, weighing upon me. Nor had I ever slept in a Dead Place before—and yet, tonight, I must sleep there. When I thought of it, my tongue felt dry in my throat, in spite of my wish for knowledge. Almost I would have gone down again and faced the dogs, but I did not.

42 I had not gone through all the rooms when the darkness fell. When it fell, I went back to the big room looking over the city and made fire. There was a place to make fire and a box with wood in it, though I do not think they cooked there. I wrapped myself in a floorcovering and slept in front of the fire—I was very tired.

43 Now I tell what is very strong magic. I woke in the midst of the night. When I woke, the fire had gone out and I was cold. It seemed to me that all around me there were whisperings and voices. I closed my eyes to shut them out. Some will say that I slept again, but I do not think that I slept. I could feel the spirits drawing my spirit out of my body as a fish is drawn on a line.

DIGITAL PERSPECTIVES

44 Why should I lie about it? I am a priest and the son of a priest. If there are spirits, as they say, in the small Dead Places near us, what spirits must there not be in that great Place of the Gods? And would not they wish to speak? After such long years? I know that I felt myself drawn as a fish is drawn on a line. I had stepped out of my body—I could see my body asleep in front of the cold fire, but it was not I. I was drawn to look out upon the city of the gods.

45 It should have been dark, for it was night, but it was not dark. Everywhere there were lights—lines of lights—-circles and blurs of light—ten thousand torches would not have been the same. The sky itself was alight—you could barely see the stars for the glow in the sky. I thought to myself "This is strong magic" and trembled. There was a roaring in my ears like the rushing of rivers. Then my eyes grew used to the light and my ears to the sound. I knew that I was seeing the city as it had been when the gods were alive.

46 That was a sight indeed—yes, that was a sight: I could not have seen it in the body—my body would have died. Everywhere went the gods, on foot and in chariots—there were gods beyond number and counting, and their chariots blocked the streets. They had turned night to day for their pleasure—they did not sleep with the sun. The noise of their coming and going was the noise of many waters. It was magic what they could do—it was magic what they did.

47 I looked out of another window—the great vines of their bridges were mended and the god-roads went East and West. Restless, restless, were the gods and always in motion! They burrowed tunnels under rivers—they flew in the air. With unbelievable tools they did giant works—no part of the earth was safe from them, for, if they wished for a thing, they **summoned** it from the other side of the world. And always, as they labored and rested, as they feasted and made love, there was a drum in their ears—the pulse of the giant city, beating and beating like a man's heart.

48 Were they happy? What is happiness to the gods? They were great, they were mighty, they were wonderful and terrible. As I looked upon them and their magic, I felt like a child—but a little more, it seemed to me, and they would pull down the moon from the sky. I saw them with wisdom beyond wisdom and knowledge beyond knowledge. And yet not all they did was well done—even I could see that—and yet their wisdom could not but grow until all was peace.

49 Then I saw their fate come upon them and that was terrible past speech. It came upon them as they walked the streets of their city. I have been in the fights with the Forest People—I have seen men die. But this was not like that. When gods war with gods, they use weapons we do not know. It was fire falling out of the sky and a mist that poisoned. It was the time of the Great Burning and the Destruction. They ran about like ants in the streets of their city—poor gods, poor gods! Then the towers began to fall. A few escaped—yes, a few. The legends tell it. But, even after the city had become a Dead Place, for

NOTES

summoned (SUHM uhnd) *v.* ordered someone or something to come to a place

PERSONALIZE FOR LEARNING

English Language Support

Simile A simile is figurative language that compares two apparently unlike things using connecting words such as *like, as, than,* or *resembles*. Help students analyze the simile in paragraph 48 when John says, "As I looked upon them and their magic, I felt *like a child*..." Explain to students that, even though John was not a child, when he had his vision of what happened to the Place of the Gods, he felt small and helpless as a child might. Ask students to consider what other child-like qualities John might be feeling. **Possible response:** awe and confusion at the power of adults. **ALL LEVELS**

CLOSE READ

Remind students to focus on ideas that may be repeated in the story. You may wish to model the Close Read using the following think-aloud format. Possible responses to questions on the Student page are included.

ANNOTATE: As I read paragraph 51, I notice a very frequent use of dashes.

QUESTION: The pattern seems to suggest that the narrator is trying to describe a scene that he may have found overwhelming. It looks like the second part of each sentence reflects a second thought built off the first one.

CONCLUDE: This choice shows that the narrator is thoughtful and trying to make sense of a scene that he did expect to see.

NOTES

many years the poison was still in the ground. I saw it happen, I saw the last of them die. It was darkness over the broken city, and I wept.

50 All this, I saw. I saw it as I have told it, though not in the body. When I woke in the morning. I was hungry, but I did not think first of my hunger, for my heart was perplexed and confused. I know the reason for the Dead Places but I did not see why it had happened. It seemed to me it should not have happened, with all the magic they had. I went through the house looking for an answer. There was so much in the house I could not understand—and yet I am a priest and the son of a priest. It was like being on one side of the great river, at night, with no light to show the way.

51 Then I saw the dead god. He was sitting in his chair, by the window, in a room I had not entered before and, for the first moment, I thought that he was alive. Then I saw the skin on the back of his hand—it was like dry leather. The room was shut, hot and dry—no doubt that had kept him as he was. At first I was afraid to approach him—then the fear left me. He was sitting looking out over the city—he was dressed in the clothes of the gods. His age was neither young nor old—I could not tell his age. But there was wisdom in his face and great sadness. You could see that he would have not run away. He had sat at his window, watching his city die—then he himself had died. But it is better to lose one's life than one's spirit— and you could see from the face that his spirit had not been lost. I knew that if I touched him, he would fall into dust—and yet, there was something unconquered in the face.

52 That is all of my story, for then I knew he was a man—I knew then that they had been men, neither gods nor demons. It is a great knowledge, hard to tell and believe. They were men—they went a dark road, but they were men. I had no fear after that—I had no fear going home, though twice I fought off the dogs and once I was hunted for two days by the Forest People. When I saw my father again, I prayed and was purified. He touched my lips and my breast, he said, "You went a boy. You come back a man and a priest." I said, "Father, they were men! I have been to the Place of the Gods and seen it! Now slay me, if it is the law—but still I know they were men."

53 He looked at me out of both eyes. He said, "The law is not always the same shape—you have done what you have done. I could not have done it in my time but you come after me. Tell!"

54 I told and he listened. After that, I wished to tell all the people but he showed me otherwise. He said, "Truth is a hard deer to hunt. If you eat too much truth at once, you may die of the truth. It was not idly that our fathers forbade the Dead Places." He was right—it is better the truth should come little by little. I have learned that, being a priest. Perhaps, in the old days, they ate knowledge too fast.

55 Nevertheless, we make a beginning. It is not for the metal alone we go to the Dead Places now—there are the books and the writings. They are hard to learn. And the magic tools are broken—but we can look at them and wonder. At least, we make a beginning. And, when

CLOSE READ

ANNOTATE: Mark the uses of dashes and commas in paragraph 51, and take note of the groupings of words contained within dashes.

QUESTION: Why do you think the author has chosen to create sentences that sometimes break off into new thoughts that are separated by dashes?

CONCLUDE: What effect does the author's choice create? In what way does this choice help you better understand the narrator?

714 UNIT 6 • WORLD'S END

I am chief priest we shall go beyond the great river. We shall go to the Place of the Gods—the place newyork—not one man but a company. We shall look for the images of the gods and find the god ASHING and the others—the gods Lincoln and Biltmore[1] and Moses.[2] But they were men who built the city, not gods or demons. They were men. I remember the dead man's face. They were men who were here before us. We must build again. ❧

NOTES

1. **Biltmore** hotel in New York City.
2. **Moses** Robert Moses (1888–1981), former New York City municipal official who oversaw many large construction projects.

Comprehension Check

Complete the following items after you finish your first read.

1. After what type of event is this story set?

2. What sets the narrator and his father apart from the people surrounding them?

3. How does the narrator arrive at his insight about who the gods of the Dead Places were?

4. What advice about sharing knowledge does John's father give him at the end of the story?

5. **Notebook** To confirm your understanding, write a summary of the story.

RESEARCH

Research to Clarify Choose at least one unfamiliar detail from the text. Briefly research that detail. In what way does the information you learned shed light on an aspect of the story?

Research to Explore Benét wrote this story in response to the bombing of the Basque town of Guernica on April 25, 1937, during the Spanish Civil War. Conduct research to find out more about this event and consider how it influenced Benét's story. Share your findings and conclusions with the class.

DIGITAL PERSPECTIVES

Comprehension Check

Possible responses

1. The story takes place after destructive, apocalyptic-type events on the Earth.
2. The narrator's father is a priest; the narrator is son of the priest—a priest in training. They are People of the Hills surrounded by Forest People.
3. John discovers the clothed body of a dead man sitting in his apartment. He looks at his skin and into his face and realizes that he is a human, not a god.
4. John's father tells him that truth should be taught a little at a time.
5. A young man sets out to explore the world around him, and finds that many of his long-held beliefs are based on ignorance of the facts. Generations of his people have lived in isolation because of war and the destruction of civilization. With his newly acquired knowledge, he vows to spearhead the rebuilding of civilization and help his community avoid the devastating mistakes of generations past.

Research

Research to Clarify If students struggle to choose an unfamiliar detail from the text to research, you may want to suggest one of the following: ancient Babylon as a world power; process of purifying metal.

Research to Explore Students may discover that Guernica was attacked by bombers on a market day, when it was most heavily populated and more people were likely to be killed. The methodical, relentless bombardment lasted for more than three hours. Fires burned for days; a third of the civilian population was killed; 70% of the city was destroyed. Guernica, the cultural center of the region, was reduced to rubble and ashes, which the writer may have correlated to the Place of the Gods, now home to the "dead places." The bombing of the city inspired a mural that is one of Pablo Picasso's better known works.

PERSONALIZE FOR LEARNING

Challenge

Title Research Encourage interested students to learn more about the allusion in the title of the story. Students may study Psalm 137 and then draw a connection between the two texts. Ask students to share their findings with the class.

TEACHING

Jump Start

CLOSE READ Have students close read the title "By the Waters of Babylon." Explain that while the ancient city was considered one of the earliest cradles of civilization and the birthplace of writing and literature, the modern city is essentially in ruins near Baghdad in the country of Iraq. Ask students to make a comparison between Babylon and the Place of the Gods.

Close Read the Text

Walk students through the annotation model on the student page. Encourage them to complete items 2 and 3 on their own. Review and discuss the sections students have marked. If needed, continue to model close reading by using the Annotation Highlights in the Interactive Teacher's Edition.

Analyze the Text

Possible responses

1. (a) John describes the Forest People as ignorant. **DOK 1** (b) The Hill People view the Forest People as inferior. **DOK 2**
2. (a) John compares his knowledge to a squirrel's heap of winter nuts. **DOK 1** (b) John felt that his knowledge was useless in the place he was. He could not rely on his experiences. **DOK 2**
3. (a) John observes his clothing, his skin, and the look on his face. **DOK 2** (b) John is no longer afraid because he realizes that this is a dead man, not a god; he was a man like John is a man. **DOK 3**
4. (a) John repeats the phrase, "They were men." **DOK 1** (b) This repetition suggests an epiphany, a sudden flash of insight on his part. **DOK 2**
5. Students may conclude that some world's end literature includes apocalyptic visions as this story presents. **DOK 3**

FORMATIVE ASSESSMENT

Analyze the Text

If students fail to cite evidence, **then** remind them to support their ideas with specific information.

If students struggle to interpret the metaphor in paragraph 26, **then** discuss the term *metaphor* and give examples.

MAKING MEANING

BY THE WATERS OF BABYLON

Close Read the Text

1. This model, from paragraph 1 of the text, shows two sample annotations, along with questions and conclusions. Close read the passage, and find another detail to annotate. Then, write a question and your conclusion.

ANNOTATE: These words are repeated.

QUESTION: What effect does the repetition create?

CONCLUDE: The repetition gives the text a formal, solemn, and religious tone.

It is there that spirits live, and demons—it is there that there are the ashes of the Great Burning. These things are forbidden—they have been forbidden since the beginning of time.

ANNOTATE: These words are capitalized.

QUESTION: What does the capitalization tell a reader?

CONCLUDE: The capitalization shows that this event has become one of historical significance for the narrator's people.

2. For more practice, go back into the text, and complete the close-read notes.
3. Revisit a section of the text you found important during your first read. Read this section closely, and **annotate** what you notice. Ask yourself **questions** such as "Why did the author make this choice?" What can you **conclude**?

Tool Kit
Close-Read Guide and Model Annotation

Analyze the Text

CITE TEXTUAL EVIDENCE to support your answers.

Notebook **Respond to these questions.**

1. (a) In paragraph 6, what word does John, one of the Hill People, use to describe the Forest People? (b) **Make Inferences** What does this suggest about how the Hill People view the Forest People?
2. (a) What does John compare his knowledge to in paragraph 26? (b) **Interpret** How does this metaphor help you understand how John feels at this point in the story?
3. (a) **Summarize** In paragraph 51, what does John observe about the "dead god"? (b) **Analyze** Why do these observations free John from fear?
4. (a) What phrase does John repeat in the beginning of paragraph 52? (b) **Interpret** What does this repetition suggest about his realizations in that particular moment? Explain.
5. **Essential Question:** *Why do we try to imagine the future?* What have you learned about world's end literature from reading this story?

STANDARDS

Reading Literature

- Analyze how an author's choices concerning how to structure a text, order events within it, and manipulate time create such effects as mystery, tension, or surprise.
- Cite strong and thorough textual evidence to support analysis of what the text says explicitly as well as inferences drawn from the text.

Analyze Craft and Structure

Author's Choices: Narrative Elements Fiction writers choose a specific **narrative point of view**, or vantage point, from which to tell a story. In "By the Waters of Babylon," Stephen Vincent Benét uses a first-person narrator, John, who is a character in the story and speaks in the first person, using the pronoun *I*.

Benét's use of the first-person point of view in this story contributes to the development of **dramatic irony**, a device that involves a contrast between what a character thinks to be true and what the reader knows to be true. In this story, readers can see the meaning in certain details, such as the name of the river John crosses, but John himself cannot. The first-person point of view allows the reader to connect textual clues to build an understanding of events that John only realizes later.

Practice

CITE TEXTUAL EVIDENCE to support your answers.

Notebook Respond to these questions.

1. (a) Reread paragraphs 1 and 2. How does the author introduce the narrative point of view? (b) How might the narrative be different if told by a third-person narrator who is not a character in the story?
2. Record in the chart examples of dramatic irony by comparing John's beliefs with the reader's understanding.

WHAT JOHN BELIEVES	WHAT THE READER KNOWS
John believes that holding a piece of metal will kill him if he is not a priest or the son of a priest.	The reader understands that there is no inherent magic in a piece of metal.
John believes the ruined structures that spanned bodies of water were god-roads.	The reader understands that these were bridges built and used by people.
John believes the "gods" who lived in the city loved pigeons or used them for sacrifices.	The reader understands that pigeons (and their droppings) in New York are a nuisance.

3. At what point in the story does John's understanding catch up to the reader's? Explain.
4. (a) How does the use of dramatic irony in this story suggest the loss of knowledge that may occur when a civilization fails? (b) What does this irony suggest about our own understanding of past civilizations?

DIGITAL PERSPECTIVES

Analyze Craft and Structure

Explain to students that the first-person narrative tells a personal experience of the narrator. Discuss other pronouns that are used in a first-person narrative, including those used when recounting a shared personal experience, such as *me, mine, myself, we, us, ours, ourselves*. For more support, see **Analyze Craft and Structure: Narrative Elements.**

MAKE IT INTERACTIVE

By story's end, John is determined to return to the Place of the Gods to find the god *ASHING*. Have students use clues in the story to help discover the true identity of *ASHING*. Have students draw something that they know about ASHING which contrasts with what John thinks to be true. Students should label their drawings with a description that includes ASHING's full name. (For example, a drawing of a group of soldiers in a small boat on a river would be labeled "George Washington crossing the Delaware"; a drawing of a boy with a hatchet and a tree would be labeled "George Washington chops down a cherry tree.")

Practice

Possible responses:

1. (a) The author introduces the first-person point of view by using first person pronouns: *we* (plural first person) in paragraph 1, then *I* in paragraph 2. (b) In paragraph 2, a third-person narrator would have to describe how *he*—John—felt (small, weak, afraid).
2. See answers in chart on student page.
3. John's understanding does not catch up to the reader's until he realizes that the dead body in the apartment is a man and not a god. Then he says, "I knew then that they had been men, neither gods nor demons" in paragraph 52.
4. (a) The story is futuristic, and readers might expect the civilization would be advanced. However, characters lack much of the knowledge held by prior generations. (b) Past civilizations may have been more advanced than we have perceived them to be.

PERSONALIZE FOR LEARNING

English Language Support

Subject-Verb Agreement Use the literature to support students' mastery of subject-verb agreement. English learners may struggle to understand subject-verb agreement since an *-s* is added to singular verbs, not plural verbs. An example of plural subject-verb agreement is in paragraph 6, "our *women spin* wool on the wheel, our *priests wear* a white robe." If these were singular subjects and singular verbs, this sentence would read "our *woman spins* wool on the wheel, our *priest wears* a white robe." Invite students to work with partners to find and confirm subject-verb agreement in the selection. Monitor student discussion for support. **ALL LEVELS**

FORMATIVE ASSESSMENT

Analyze Craft and Structure

- **If** students struggle to chart examples of dramatic irony, **then** model an example for the class.
- **If** students cannot identify the point at which John's understanding converges with the reader's, **then** have them reread paragraph 52.

For Reteach and Practice, see **Analyze Craft and Structure: Narrative Elements (RP).**

TEACHING

Concept Vocabulary

Why These Words

Possible responses:

1. The words help emphasize that John's culture is centered around spirituality and religious rites.
2. *spirits, demons, gods, priest, forbidden, chants.*

Practice

Possible responses:

1. I would know a material has been purified if it is clean. If I *bade* someone to take a specific action, I would give him an order. A *stern* teacher might be quite unfriendly with her students. I would feel hungry after *fasting* for 24 hours. Observing Mardi Gras and having a jazz funeral are two *customs* practiced in my culture. If I *summoned* my dog, I would expect him to come to me.
2. Responses will vary.

Word Network

Possible words: *heap, dead, shattered, terrible.*

Word Study

For more support, see **Concept Vocabulary and Word Study**

Possible responses:

1. purify, purity, purely
2. custom, customer, accustomed

FORMATIVE ASSESSMENT

Concept Vocabulary

If students fail to see the connection between the words, **then** have them review the definition of each word and think about what is similar about them.

Word Study

If students need additional help identifying word families, **then** explain that *bade* is part of a word family with *bid* and *bidding.* For Reteach and Practice, see **Word Study: Word Families (RP).**

LANGUAGE DEVELOPMENT

BY THE WATERS OF BABYLON

Concept Vocabulary

purified	stern	customs
bade	fasting	summoned

Why These Words? These concept words all help to describe the elaborate ceremonies and rituals that John's people have created. For example, in the opening paragraph, the narrator explains that metal gathered from the Dead Places must be *purified*, or cleansed. Later, John mentions that he "asked for and received purification" before his solo journey. The idea of purification has religious connotations, emphasizing the removal of unclean or impure thoughts, as well as physical poisons.

1. How does the concept vocabulary help readers understand John's culture?
2. What other words in the selection connect to this concept?

WORD NETWORK

Add interesting words related to the world's end from the text to your Word Network.

Practice

Notebook The concept words appear in "By the Waters of Babylon."

1. Demonstrate your understanding of the concept words' meanings by using each word in a sentence to answer these questions.
   - How might you tell whether or not a material has been *purified*?
   - If you *bade* another person to take action to resolve a problem, what is it that you did?
   - How might a *stern* teacher act toward students?
   - How might you feel after *fasting* for 24 hours?
   - What are two *customs* that reflect your cultural heritage?
   - If you *summoned* your dog, what would you expect the animal to do?
2. Create fill-in-the-blank puzzles for others to solve. First, write a sentence that demonstrates the meaning of each concept word. Then, rewrite each sentence, but replace the concept word with a blank. Challenge your classmates to fill in the missing words.

STANDARDS

Reading Literature

Analyze how complex characters develop over the course of a text, interact with other characters, and advance the plot or develop the theme.

Language

- Demonstrate command of the conventions of standard English capitalization, punctuation, and spelling when writing.
- Identify and correctly use patterns of word changes that indicate different meanings or parts of speech.
- Demonstrate understanding of figurative language, word relationships, and nuances in word meanings.

Word Study

Word Families A **word family** is a group of words that share the same origin or that were all formed from a common base word. For instance, the words *purified* and *purification,* which appear in "By the Waters of Babylon," are part of the same word family as the word *pure.*

1. Identify two other words that belong to the same word family as *purified, purification,* and *pure.*
2. Identify two words that belong to the same word family as *customs.*

AUTHOR'S PERSPECTIVE Elfrieda Hiebert, Ph.D.

Collocation Teachers can explain to students that many words often occur together, a process called *collocation*. Point out examples: the words "stormy" and "weather" go together, as do "adverse weather conditions"—"adverse" is not used to describe other nouns such as "assignments." Other examples of weather collocation include "a change in the weather" and "to weather the storm." Teachers can have students share and discuss the following examples. Focus on the fact that although the underlined words are synonyms, they are not interchangeable:

<u>warm</u> greeting	but not	a <u>hot</u> greeting
<u>tall</u> people	but not	<u>high</u> people

Author's Style

Character Development Benét uses a variety of elements to develop the character of John, the narrator of "By the Waters of Babylon." The author's choices help readers understand both John's personality and the culture that helped form it.

ELEMENT	EXAMPLE	ANALYSIS
Punctuation: marks (other than letters) that are used to organize writing and make its meaning clear	*These things are forbidden—they have been forbidden since the beginning of time.* (paragraph 1)	The use of a dash (—) emphasizes the connection between ideas and creates the feeling that John is truly speaking the story.
Diction: a writer's or speaker's word choice—the type of vocabulary, the vividness of the language, and the appropriateness of the words	*It did not have the smell of man, though there were old bones in a corner. But it is not fitting that a priest's son should show fear.* (paragraph 2)	John's vocabulary is relatively limited. He uses formal diction characterized by an absence of contractions, which suggests that John is unfamiliar with colloquial language. It might also suggest that he is concerned with presenting himself correctly and does not use language carelessly.
Syntax: the way that words are organized, such as their order in a sentence or phrase	*He gave me the metal to hold—I took it and did not die.* (paragraph 3)	John speaks in simple sentences that reflect his formality and might suggest a lack of familiarity or comfort with informal language.

Read It

1. Mark the punctuation in this excerpt from paragraph 5 of "By the Waters of Babylon." How does the author use this punctuation to develop John's character?

   I was taught the chants and the spells—I was taught how to stop the running of blood from a wound and many secrets. A priest must know many secrets—that was what my father said. If the hunters think we do all things by chants and spells, they may believe so—it does not hurt them.

2. Read John's "death song" in paragraph 26 aloud. Listen carefully to John's diction and syntax. Explain how the diction and syntax in his "fine song" help you understand and appreciate both John's character and his culture.

Write It

Notebook Revise the punctuation, diction, and syntax in this paragraph to make it sound more like John's narration in "By the Waters of Babylon."

Everyone's always telling me I need to follow the rules, but I know better. I'm sure that I was totally right to travel east, even though everybody says you shouldn't go there. It was definitely worth it even though I can't share what I learned now that I'm back home. The others can't handle the truth right now, but maybe someday they'll be ready.

DIGITAL PERSPECTIVES

Author's Style

Character Development Explain that writers often provide indirect clues and rely on the reader to make inferences and draw conclusions about a character. If a writer provides enough information to help us understand a character's motivation, readers may feel that the character is believable. For more support, see **Author's Style: Character Development.**

Read It

Possible Responses:

1. See responses in paragraph on student page. This punctuation makes John sound rigid and formal.
2. John's vivid language shows he is proud of his bravery and has shown himself unafraid of man and beast; these characteristics are prized by his culture. John's sentence structure shows him to be part of a simplistic culture.

Write It

Possible Response: The rules and the laws must be followed—but my spirit will not let me. It is forbidden to travel east—but I traveled east and I did not die. My journey has been a fine one, but I must keep hold on my truth. I have made a beginning. The people will also eat knowledge, but slowly—in time.

FORMATIVE ASSESSMENT

Author's Style

If students cannot explain the importance of diction and syntax, **then** provide examples of text with different styles and discuss the power of diction and syntax to set tone.

If students cannot rewrite the sample paragraph to sound more like the selection, **then** have them make note of those punctuation marks that are used extensively in the text. For Reteach and Practice, see **Author's Style: Character Development (RP).**

Guiding students to collect words that collocate can support them in becoming flexible in the use of language. Further, learning collocation provides a store of ready-made expressions, helping students express language concisely. Help students learn more about collocation by using the Academic Collocation List developed by Pearson, posted at http://pearsonpte.com/research/academic-collocation-list/.

PERSONALIZE FOR LEARNING

English Language Support

Sentence Starters Provide sentence starters to help students learn the principles of effective punctuation, syntax, and diction. Remind students that the author's style choice informs the reader about who the character is. For example, *When the character uses speech that is stiff and formal, it may indicate that he is* ____________________.

ALL LEVELS

TEACHING

Writing to Sources

Explain that a sequel is a unique kind of story that may have a built-in audience. Writing a sequel may sound risky, but remind students that their audience has already invested in the original story and characters to the extent that they want to read more. Encourage students to keep some constancy between the character in the original and the character in a sequel, but ask them to depict the characters in ways that show they have grown and changed. For more support, see **Writing to Sources: Sequel.**

Reflect on Your Writing

Responses for all will vary:

1. If students need support, have them think about what things they did not understand when they initially read the original story.
2. Have students think about primary details that drive their sequel and secondary details that play a supportive role.
3. Students should provide examples of words that they used for a specific effect.

FORMATIVE ASSESSMENT

Writing to Sources

If students struggle to write their sequel, **then** have them think about those things in the original story that they think need further explanation or exploration. For Reteach and Practice, see **Writing to Sources: Sequel (RP).**

EFFECTIVE EXPRESSION

BY THE WATERS OF BABYLON

Writing to Sources

A great story ends with a satisfying conclusion that resolves the main conflicts. However, some narratives leave questions open for readers to interpret. Writing a sequel can help readers imagine the events that take place after a story is over.

Assignment

Write a **sequel** that begins after the last sentence of "By the Waters of Babylon." Consider these questions as you plan your writing:

- What happens when John rejoins his people?
- What truths does he begin to share with them, and how does he do so?
- What does John's community do with this new knowledge? How do they change their culture and start to rebuild?
- How might John's people avoid repeating the errors of the past?

Your sequel should include:

- A clear narrative with a beginning, a middle, and an end
- Realistic dialogue that reflects characters' personalities
- Detailed descriptions of characters, settings, and events
- Pacing that speeds up or slows down the action

Vocabulary and Style Connection Include several of the concept vocabulary words in your sequel to show how rituals changed for John's people after the end of the story. Develop characters through careful choices in diction, syntax, and punctuation.

purified	stern	customs
bade	fasting	summoned

Reflect on Your Writing

After you have written your sequel, answer these questions.

1. How did writing a sequel help you understand and appreciate the events of the original story?
2. What details from the original story helped you create an effective sequel?
3. **Why These Words?** The words you choose make a difference in your writing. Which words did you use to achieve a specific effect in your sequel?

STANDARDS

Writing

- Write narratives to develop real or imagined experiences or events using effective technique, well-chosen details, and well-structured event sequences.
- Use narrative techniques, such as dialogue, pacing, description, reflection, and multiple plot lines, to develop experiences, events, and/or characters.

Speaking and Listening

- Integrate multiple sources of information presented in diverse media or formats evaluating the credibility and accuracy of each source.
- Present information, findings, and supporting evidence clearly, concisely and logically such that listeners can follow the line of reasoning and the organization, development, substance, and style are appropriate to purpose, audience, and task.
- Make strategic use of digital media in presentations to enhance understanding of findings, reasoning, and evidence and to add interest.

720 UNIT 6 • WORLD'S END

DIGITAL PERSPECTIVES

Illuminating the Text Find and show video clips about the bombing of Guernica as well as modern-day Guernica. This will help students understand the chilling effect that the Spanish Civil War had on citizens of the world, including Spanish artist Pablo Picasso and American author Stephen Benét. Have students relate the conclusion of "By the Waters of Babylon" with what is seen in Guernica today. (*Rick Steves' Europe,* (PBS), has a clip featuring modern-day Guernica, which has gloriously risen from the ashes, much like John's vision for his people's future.)

Speaking and Listening

Assignment

Create and present a **multimedia timeline** of the story that includes information about events that took place before the beginning of John's narration. Include images, videos, audio, or other media elements in your timeline to enhance your audience's understanding of the events. First, reread the selection. Then, follow these steps to complete the assignment.

1. **Identify and Order Events** First, list the key story events. Then, look for clues in the story that tell what happened in the past and how those events affected the society in which John lives during the time of the story. List these "prequel" events. Finally, order the events chronologically.
2. **Write Timeline Labels** After you identify and order events, write concise timeline labels to describe them. Most events should be described in one sentence. Consider how to shorten long labels without losing crucial details.
3. **Select Appropriate Media** Review each timeline event, and consider which type of media element would best support it. Remember, you will be presenting your entire timeline, so make sure that individual media elements are relatively short.
4. **Prepare Your Delivery** Practice presenting your completed timeline. Consider how to pace your presentation. Develop a planning script that shows how much time you will spend discussing each event. Remember to include the time needed to screen videos or play audio recordings.
5. **Evaluate Timelines** As your classmates share their timelines, listen attentively. Use the evaluation guide to analyze their timelines.

EVALUATION GUIDE

Rate each statement on a scale of 1 (not demonstrated) to 4 (demonstrated).

☐ The timeline includes, in chronological order, key events from before and during the action of the story.

☐ Events are described briefly and clearly.

☐ Media elements effectively support the timeline.

☐ The presenter used time wisely and fully explained each event.

EVIDENCE LOG

Before moving on to a new selection, go to your Evidence Log and record what you learned from "By the Waters of Babylon."

DIGITAL PERSPECTIVES

Speaking and Listening

1. Remind students that ordering story events chronologically means to put them in order according to how they happened.
2. Tell students they can shorten their timeline descriptions by eliminating unnecessary adverbs, adjectives, and gerunds.
3. Encourage students to have at hand a list of all the media available to them. This will help when they make assignments.
4. Students should keep the time limit in mind. As they practice, they might use the stopwatch feature on a smartphone.
5. Encourage students to listen with the goal of making a supportive comment about each presentation.

For more support, see **Speaking and Listening: Multimedia Timeline.**

Evidence Log Support students in completing their Evidence Log. This paced activity will help prepare them for the Performance-Based Assessment at the end of the unit.

FORMATIVE ASSESSMENT

Speaking and Listening

- **If** students struggle to shorten their timelines, **then** remind them that it may help to eliminate *–ing* from the verbs used.
- **If** students struggle with shyness about making a presentation, **then** remind them that a smartphone can usually be used to record their practice sessions so they can hear what they sound like to others.

For Reteach and Practice, see **Speaking and Listening: Multimedia Timeline (RP).**

Selection Test

Administer the "By the Waters of Babylon" Selection Test, which is available in both print and digital formats online in Assessments.

PERSONALIZE FOR LEARNING

English Language Support

Creating a Timeline Have students create a simple timeline.

Tell students to create a timeline of their lives as students. Have them think of the most important milestones, and ask them to include them in their timelines. **EMERGING**

Have students think of a story (a book or a movie) that has a chronological plot. Then ask them to create a timeline of the events in the story. **EXPANDING**

Tell students to create a timeline showing the history of their families before and after they came to the United States. Ask them to include the most important moments of their family history. **BRIDGING**

An expanded **English Language Support Lesson** on Multimedia Timelines is available in the Interactive Teacher's Edition.

There Will Come Soft Rains

AUDIO SUMMARIES
Audio summaries of "There Will Come Soft Rains" are available online in both English and Spanish in the Interactive Teacher's Edition or Unit Resources. Assigning these summaries prior to reading the selection may help students build additional background knowledge and set a context for their first read.

Summary

In "There Will Come Soft Rains," a classic science-fiction short story, Ray Bradbury describes the automated functions of a house coming on in the morning. First, the alarm-clock rings, the kitchen automatically prepares breakfast, and the house calendar reads out the schedule for the day. However, the house is empty. The breakfast goes uneaten and is discarded by the house, which is kept clean by tiny machines. The house keeps up with its daily routines, despite the fact that the city has been destroyed. The day continues, with the automated systems responding to various problems and enacting various daily rituals, despite the death of everyone who once lived there.

Insight

This story is considered a classic of post-apocalyptic science fiction, both for its eerie, lyrical quality and for the pessimistic tone it takes. The house collapses in fire at the end, and the animals seen in the story are endangered, raising questions about how technology might outlive the people who create it.

ESSENTIAL QUESTION:
Why do we try to imagine the future?

Connection to Essential Question

This story presents a bleak answer to the Essential Question. In this case, the motivation for imagining such a future is presumably anti-war. The nuclear apocalypse imagined in the story has not spared humans, and nothing else survives.

WHOLE-CLASS LEARNING PERFORMANCE TASK
At the end of the world, how do we begin anew?

UNIT PERFORMANCE-BASED ASSESSMENT
Which matters more—the present or the future?

Connection to Performance Tasks

Whole-Class Learning Performance Task The story begins with the nuclear apocalypse that eliminated the family, and continues some time after, as a coda or epilogue to the larger story of the end of the world. The story is in some sense the final stage of the end of the world, as the last house burns down. There is no suggestion of hope for rebirth.

Unit Performance-Based Assessment In this story, the present matters more than the future. While the death of the house is tragic, without its inhabitants, it was already a pointless and doomed building. This story presents no future.

DIGITAL PERSPECTIVES — Audio | Video | Document | Annotation Highlights | EL Highlights | Online Assessment

LESSON RESOURCES

	Making Meaning	Language Development	Effective Expression
Lesson	**First Read** **Close Read** **Analyze the Text** **Analyze Craft and Structure**	**Concept Vocabulary** **Word Study** **Conventions**	**Writing to Sources** **Speaking and Listening**
Instructional Standards	**RL.10** By the end of grade 9, read and comprehend literature... **RL.4** Determine the meaning of words and phrases... **RL.5** Analyze how an author's choices... **L.5** Demonstrate understanding of figurative language...	**L.1** Demonstrate command of the conventions of standard English grammar and usage . . . **L.1.a** Use parallel structure. **L.4.b** Identify and correctly use patterns of word changes . . . **L.4.d** Verify the preliminary determination . . .	**W.3** Write narratives to develop real or imagined experiences . . . **W.3.d** Use precise words and phrases . . . **SL.4** Present information, findings, and supporting evidence . . .
STUDENT RESOURCES			
Available online in the Interactive Student Edition or Unit Resources	Selection Audio First-Read Guide: Fiction Close-Read Guide: Fiction	Word Network	Evidence Log
TEACHER RESOURCES			
Selection Resources Available online in the Interactive Teacher's Edition or Unit Resources	Audio Summaries Annotation Highlights EL Highlights English Language Support Lesson: Setting and Personification Analyze Craft and Structure: Setting	Concept Vocabulary and Word Study Author's Style: Parallelism	Writing to Sources: Short Story Speaking and Listening: Oral Recitation
Reteach/Practice (RP) Available online in the Interactive Teacher's Edition or Unit Resources	Analyze Craft and Structure: Setting (RP)	Word Study: Latin Root *-man-* (RP) Author's Style: Parallelism (RP)	Writing to Sources: Short Story (RP) Speaking and Listening: Oral Recitation (RP)
Assessment Available online in Assessments	Selection Test		
My Resources	A Unit 6 Answer Key is available online and in the Interactive Teacher's Edition.		

Reading Support

Text Complexity Rubric: There Will Come Soft Rains	
Quantitative Measures	
Lexile: 920 **Text Length:** 2,102 words	
Qualitative Measures	
Knowledge Demands ① ❷ ③ ④ ⑤	The selection is a post-apocalyptic story written during the Cold War period. Historical context will be helpful, but students should be able to follow the story's events.
Structure ① ❷ ③ ④ ⑤	The selection is a short story with a linear structure.
Language Conventionality and Clarity ① ❷ ③ ④ ⑤	The selection contains figurative language and personification. The vocabulary is mostly on-level, and sentence structure is mostly conventional.
Levels of Meaning/Purpose ① ② ❸ ④ ⑤	The selection contains a lot of symbolism, but references to man's destruction after nuclear war are fairly easy to grasp.

DECIDE AND PLAN

English Language Support

Provide English Learners with support for Knowledge Demands and Language as they read the selection.

Knowledge Demands Invite students to listen actively as you share background information about the text. Tell students that this selection is a short story that was written during the Cold War period. Help students to understand the context of the story. You may also want to discuss the idea of automation at the heart of this story.

Language Students may find the use of sensory language difficult to grasp. Explain that the author often uses words in a figurative way to create feelings or sensations. Figurative language is language that is used imaginatively rather than literally. Such expressions can be difficult for second-language learners.

Strategic Support

Provide students with strategic support to ensure that they can successfully read the text.

Knowledge Demands Using the background information for the selection, discuss what the Cold War was. Ask students to share their prior knowledge about the Cold War. Provide additional background if needed.

Language Help students to understand the author's use of personification in the story. Guide students to see that the author uses this technique to make the house the main character in the story.

Challenge

Provide students who need to be challenged with ideas for how they can go beyond a simple interpretation of the text.

Text Analysis Have students analyze the text in paragraphs 34–36 describing the nursery. Ask students what the description says about the human connection to nature in this world.

Written Response Challenge students to write an essay that addresses the idea of technology as religion. Point out paragraph 16: *The house was an altar with ten thousand attendants, big, small, servicing, attending, in choirs. But the gods had gone away, and the ritual of the religion continued senselessly, uselessly.* How can technology be like a religion? Has our relationship to technology changed since this was written? For better or for worse?

TEACH

Read and Respond

Have the class do their first read of the selection. Then have them complete their close read. Finally, work with them on the Making Meaning, Language Development, and Effective Expression activities.

Standards Support Through Teaching and Learning Cycle

IDENTIFY NEEDS

Analyze results of the Beginning-of-Year Assessment, focusing on the items relating to Unit 6. Also take into consideration student performance to this point and your observations of where particular students struggle.

DECIDE AND PLAN

- If students have performed poorly on items matching these standards, then provide selection scaffolds before assigning them the on-level lesson provided in the Student Edition.
- If students have done well on the Beginning-of-Year Assessment, then challenge them to keep progressing and learning by giving them opportunities to practice the skills in depth.
- Use the Selection Resources listed on the Planning pages for "There Will Come Soft Rains" to help students continually improve their ability to master the standards.

Instructional Standards: There Will Come Soft Rains

	Catching Up	This Year	Looking Forward
Reading	You may wish to administer the **Analyze Craft and Structure: Setting (RP)** worksheet to better familiarize students with setting and personification.	**RL.5** Analyze how an author's choices concerning how to structure a text, order events within it and manipulate time create such effects as mystery, tension, or surprise.	Have students compare the personification to examples of this technique in other works they are familiar with.
Writing	You may wish to administer the **Writing to Sources: Short Story (RP)** worksheet to better prepare students for their writing.	**W.3** Write narratives to develop real or imagined experiences or events using effective technique, well-chosen details, and well-structured event sequences.	Challenge students to write a short story that includes one or more of the characters from "By the Waters of Babylon."
Speaking and Listening	You may wish to administer the **Speaking and Listening: Oral Recitation (RP)** worksheet to help students better prepare for their performances.	**SL.4** Present information, findings, and supporting evidence clearly, concisely, and logically such that listeners can follow the line of reasoning and the organization, development, substance, and style are appropriate to purpose, audience, and task.	Challenge students to integrate media, music, lighting, and any other kind of theatrics to punch up their performances.
Language	Review **Word Study: Latin Root *-man-* (RP)** worksheet to better familiarize students with the root word. You may wish to administer the **Author's Style: Parallelism (RP)** worksheet to help students better understand how the technique of parallelism works.	**L.4.b** Identify and correctly use patterns of word changes that indicate different meanings or parts of speech. **L.1.a** Use parallel structure.	Have students locate words in the text that have roots they recognize. Have students discuss why parallelism is an effective and popular technique.

TEACH

Implement the planned lesson, and gather evidence of student learning.

ANALYZE AND REVISE

- Analyze student work for evidence of student learning.
- Identify whether or not students have met the expectations in the standards.
- Identify implications for future instruction.

Jump Start

FIRST READ Engage students in a discussion about how much we rely on our electronic devices. This can set the context for reading "There Will Come Soft Rains."

There Will Come Soft Rains

Do we pay more attention to advancing technology than developing human relationships? Are we relying on technology to secure mankind's future? Modeling the questions readers might ask as they read "There Will Come Soft Rains" for the first time brings the text alive for students and connects it to the Whole-Class Performance Task assignment. Selection audio and print capability for the selection are available in the Interactive Teacher's Edition.

Concept Vocabulary

Support students as they rank their words. Ask if they've ever heard, read, or used them. Reassure them that the definitions for these words are listed in the selection.

FIRST READ

As they read, students should perform the steps of the first read:

NOTICE: You may want to encourage students to notice hints that may indicate what has happened to the human inhabitants of the house.

ANNOTATE: Remind students to mark passages that include sensory language.

CONNECT: Encourage students to think about elements of the story that were "futuristic" at the time of writing, and are still futuristic today. Ask students to consider other futuristic stories or movies they know.

RESPOND: Students will answer questions and write a summary to demonstrate understanding.

Point out to students that while they will always complete the Respond step at the end of the first read, the other steps will probably happen somewhat concurrently. You may wish to print copies of the **First-Read Guide: Fiction** for students to use.

Remind students that during their first read, they should not answer the close-read questions that appear in the selection.

About the Author

Ray Bradbury (1920–2012) developed a fascination with horror movies and futuristic fantasies. As a teenager, he decided to become a writer and to use fiction to "live forever." He published his first novel, *The Martian Chronicles*, in 1950, and his novel *Fahrenheit 451* became an instant bestseller when it was published in 1953. In 2007, Bradbury won a special Pulitzer Prize for his "distinguished, prolific, and deeply influential career as an unmatched author of science fiction and fantasy."

Tool Kit
First-Read Guide and Model Annotation

STANDARDS
Reading Literature
By the end of grade 9, read and comprehend literature, including stories, dramas, and poems, in the grades 9–10 text complexity band proficiently, with scaffolding as needed at the high end of the range.

There Will Come Soft Rains

Concept Vocabulary

You will encounter the following words as you read "There Will Come Soft Rains." Before reading, note how familiar you are with each word. Then, rank the words in order from most familiar (1) to least familiar (6).

WORD	YOUR RANKING
chimed	
attending	
delicately	
fluttered	
manipulated	
tremulous	

After completing the first read, come back to the concept vocabulary and review your rankings. Mark changes to your original rankings as needed.

First Read FICTION

Apply these strategies as you conduct your first read. You will have an opportunity to complete the close-read notes after your first read.

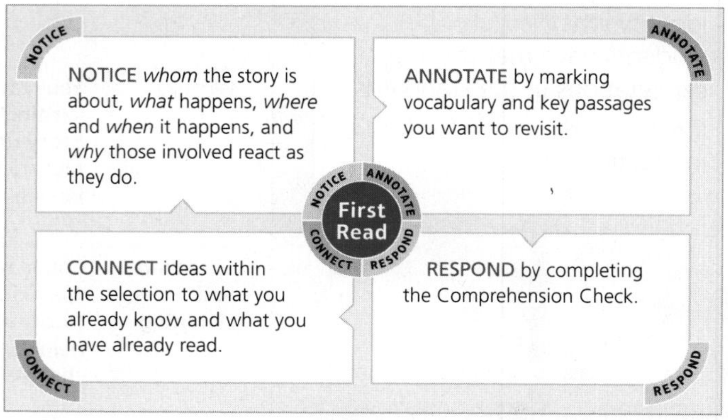

NOTICE
NOTICE *whom* the story is about, *what* happens, *where* and *when* it happens, and *why* those involved react as they do.
ANNOTATE
ANNOTATE by marking vocabulary and key passages you want to revisit.
First Read
CONNECT ideas within the selection to what you already know and what you have already read.
RESPOND by completing the Comprehension Check.
CONNECT
RESPOND

ANCHOR TEXT | SHORT STORY

There Will Come Soft Rains

Ray Bradbury

DIGITAL PERSPECTIVES

CLOSE READ

Remind students to focus on sound devices that the writer uses. You may wish to model the Close Read using the following think-aloud format. Possible responses to questions on the Student page are included. You may also want to print copies of the **Close-Read Guide: Fiction** for students to use.

ANNOTATE: As I read paragraph 1, I notice some language that sounds like a nursery rhyme.

QUESTION: The use of this kind of language may seem inviting. The author sets up the voice-clock as a character from the start.

CONCLUDE: The sing-song language sets a friendly tone for the story.

Additional **English Language Support** is available in the Interactive Teacher's Edition.

BACKGROUND

This story was written in 1950 during a period known as the Cold War, a mostly non-military conflict that occurred between the United States and the Soviet Union. Each side became increasingly focused on developing more nuclear weapons to discourage the other side from using its own bombs. This, coupled with the fact that the United States had dropped two atomic bombs on Japan during World War II, created a widespread fear of nuclear war.

SCAN FOR MULTIMEDIA

1 In the living room the voice-clock sang, *Tick-tock, seven o'clock, time to get up, time to get up, seven o'clock!* as if it were afraid nobody would. The morning house lay empty. The clock ticked on, repeating and repeating its sounds into the emptiness. *Seven-nine, breakfast time, seven-nine!*

2 In the kitchen the breakfast stove gave a hissing sigh and ejected from its warm interior eight pieces of perfectly browned toast, eight eggs sunnyside up, sixteen slices of bacon, two coffees, and two cool glasses of milk.

3 "Today is August 4, 2026," said a second voice from the kitchen ceiling, "in the city of Allendale, California." It repeated the date three times for memory's sake. "Today is Mr. Featherstone's birthday.

NOTES

CLOSE READ

ANNOTATE: In paragraph 1, mark examples of sing-song language.

QUESTION: Why does the author include this language in the opening scene?

CONCLUDE: What mood, or emotional quality, does the sing-song language create?

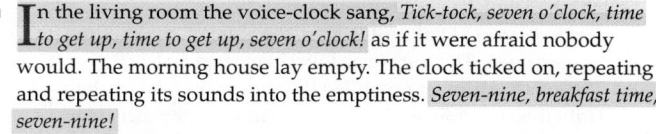

PERSONALIZE FOR LEARNING

Strategic Support

Zoom In To help students who are visually impaired, project onto a screen the illustration that opens the story so that the image is enlarged. Lead a discussion about those elements that contrast sharply with the happy-sounding description of the activity inside the house beginning in paragraph 1. For example, the image includes the shells of destroyed buildings, the outlines of charred trees, the stark looking exterior of the house, the sickly-looking morning sky punctuated with dark, and ominous clouds.

CLOSE READ

Remind students to focus on how sensory language makes use of imagery. You may wish to model the Close Read using the following think-aloud format. Possible responses to questions on the Student page are included.

ANNOTATE: As I read paragraphs 11 and 12, I notice and highlight the words that describe the shapes formed by the five spots of paint.

QUESTION: I see that the house was earlier described as being busily and continually cleaned inside. Now I see the outside of the house charred and burned evenly, free of white paint except for these five places. Paragraph 11 shows the family alive and active. I also notice that paragraph 12 includes very stark language. Finally, these two paragraphs are quite different from the busy excitement of the earlier parts of the story.

CONCLUDE: I believe the author describes the shapes to tell the reader who the house's inhabitants were. The fact that all of these shapes describe humans caught in mid-movement as they work and play emphasizes that the obliteration of this family was unexpected and sudden. The author's use of plain, blunt language to describe the death of the family may slow readers down to imagine it.

NOTES

Today is the anniversary of Tilita's marriage. Insurance is payable, as are the water, gas, and light bills."

4 Somewhere in the walls, relays clicked, memory tapes glided under electric eyes.

5 *Eight-one, tick-tock, eight-one o'clock, off to school, off to work, run, run, eight-one!* But no doors slammed, no carpets took the soft tread of rubber heels. It was raining outside. The weather box on the front door sang quietly: "Rain, rain, go away; rubbers, raincoats for today . . ." And the rain tapped on the empty house, echoing.

6 Outside, the garage **chimed** and lifted its door to reveal the waiting car. After a long wait the door swung down again.

chimed (chymd) *v.* rang; made the sound of a bell

7 At eight-thirty the eggs were shriveled and the toast was like stone. An aluminum wedge scraped them into the sink, where hot water whiled them down a metal throat which digested and flushed them away to the distant sea. The dirty dishes were dropped into a hot washer and emerged twinkling dry.

8 *Nine-fifteen*, sang the clock, *time to clean.*

9 Out of warrens in the wall, tiny robot mice darted. The rooms were acrawl with the small cleaning animals, all rubber and metal. They thudded against chairs, whirling their mustached runners, kneading the rug nap, sucking gently at hidden dust. Then, like mysterious invaders, they popped into their burrows. Their pink electric eye faded. The house was clean.

10 *Ten o'clock.* The sun came out from behind the rain. The house stood alone in a city of rubble and ashes. This was the one house left standing. At night the ruined city gave off a radioactive glow which could be seen for miles.

11 *Ten-fifteen.* The garden sprinklers whirled up in golden founts, filling the soft morning air with scatterings of brightness. The water pelted windowpanes, running down the charred west side where the house had been burned evenly free of its white paint. The entire west face of the house was black, save for five places. Here the silhouette[1] in paint of a man mowing a lawn. Here, as in a photograph, a woman bent to pick flowers. Still farther over, their images burned on wood in one titanic instant, a small boy, hands flung into the air; higher up, the image of a thrown ball, and opposite him a girl, hand raised to catch a ball which never came down.

12 The five spots of paint—the man, the woman, the children, the ball—remained. The rest was a thin charcoaled layer.

13 The gentle sprinkler rain filled the garden with falling light.

14 Until this day, how well the house had kept its peace. How carefully it had inquired, "Who goes there? What's the password?" and, getting no answer from the lonely foxes and whining cats, it had shut up its windows and drawn shades in an old-maidenly preoccupation with self-protection which bordered on a mechanical paranoia.

CLOSE READ

ANNOTATE: Mark the words in paragraphs 11 and 12 that describe the "five spots of paint."

QUESTION: How do these descriptions differ from the earlier descriptions of the house?

CONCLUDE: What idea does the author emphasize by carefully selecting sensory language?

1. **silhouette** (sihl uh WEHT) *n.* outline of a figure, filled in with a solid color.

DIGITAL PERSPECTIVES

15 It quivered at each sound, the house did. If a sparrow brushed a window, the shade snapped up. The bird, startled, flew off! No, not even a bird must touch the house!

16 The house was an altar with ten thousand attendants, big, small, servicing, **attending**, in choirs. But the gods had gone away, and the ritual of the religion continued senselessly, uselessly.

17 *Twelve noon.*

18 A dog whined, shivering, on the front porch.

19 The front door recognized the dog voice and opened. The dog, once huge and fleshy, but now gone to bone and covered with sores, moved in and through the house, tracking mud. Behind it whirred angry mice, angry at having to pick up mud, angry at inconvenience.

20 For not a leaf fragment blew under the door but what the wall panels flipped open and the copper scrap rats flashed swiftly out. The offending dust, hair, or paper, seized in miniature steel jaws, was raced back to the burrows. There, down tubes which fed into the cellar, it was dropped into the sighing vent of an incinerator which sat like evil Baal[2] in a dark corner.

21 The dog ran upstairs, hysterically yelping to each door, at last realizing, as the house realized, that only silence was here.

22 It sniffed the air and scratched the kitchen door. Behind the door, the stove was making pancakes which filled the house with a rich baked odor and the scent of maple syrup.

23 The dog frothed at the mouth, lying at the door, sniffing, its eyes turned to fire. It ran wildly in circles, biting at its tail, spun in a frenzy, and died. It lay in the parlor for an hour.

24 *Two o'clock*, sang a voice.

25 **Delicately** sensing decay at last, the regiments of mice hummed out as softly as blown gray leaves in an electrical wind.

26 *Two-fifteen.*

27 The dog was gone.

28 In the cellar, the incinerator glowed suddenly and a whirl of sparks leaped up the chimney.

29 *Two thirty-five.*

30 Bridge tables sprouted from patio walls. Playing cards **fluttered** onto pads in a shower of pips. Glasses manifested on an oaken bench with egg salad sandwiches. Music played.

31 But the tables were silent and the cards untouched.

32 At four o'clock the tables folded like great butterflies back through the paneled walls.

33 *Four-thirty.*

34 The nursery walls glowed.

35 Animals took shape: yellow giraffes, blue lions, pink antelopes, lilac panthers cavorting in crystal substance. The walls were glass. They looked out upon color and fantasy. Hidden films clocked though the well-oiled sprockets, and the walls lived. The nursery

2. **Baal** (BAY uhl) ancient Near Eastern deity, later associated with evil.

NOTES

attending (uh TEHND ihng) *adj.* being present; taking care of things

delicately (DEHL uh kiht lee) *adv.* carefully; with grace and gentleness

fluttered (FLUH tuhrd) *v.* waved gently

PERSONALIZE FOR LEARNING

English Language Support

Figurative Language Note this sentence in paragraph 16: "The house was an altar with ten thousand attendants, big, small, servicing, attending, in choirs." Explain to students that this sentence contains an example of a *metaphor*, which compares two apparently unlike things by speaking of one thing as if it were the other. Spanish speakers will know that the word *altar* has a religious connotation (the same is true in English), which is carried throughout the rest of the paragraph. The writer is comparing the house to an altar, a place where sacrifices are made. Ask students to think about the kinds of things the author thinks have been sacrificed by those who lived in this house and the other houses that have been destroyed. Ask students to evaluate this use of figurative language. **ALL LEVELS**

CLOSER LOOK

Infer Author's Purpose

Students may have marked paragraph 44 during their first read. Use this paragraph to help students understand the author's purpose in writing this story. Encourage them to talk about the annotations that they marked. You may want to model a close read with the class based on the highlights shown in the text.

ANNOTATE: Have students mark details in paragraph 44 that show the triumph of nature over technology, or have students participate while you highlight them.

QUESTION: Guide students to consider what these details might tell them. Ask what a reader can infer from the author's inclusion of this poem, and accept student responses.

Possible response: Readers can infer that this poem, which gives the story its name, had a significant presence in the author's mind when he wrote the story. Since it is quoted in full, readers can also infer that the author wishes the poem to have a significant presence in their minds, too, as they go on with the story.

CONCLUDE: Help students to formulate conclusions about the importance of these details in the text. Ask students why the author might have included these details.

Possible response: The author quotes Sara Teasdale's poem (written during World War I) as a warning that humans are in danger of annihilating themselves—and that if they do, the earth will not miss them. It expresses the author's purpose in writing this story about nuclear annihilation.

Remind students that an **author's purpose** is his or her reasons for writing. Some texts are written to entertain, educate, inform, or warn, and other texts are written to meet a combination of these purposes. The details a writer uses, as well as the tone and diction of a piece, will help a writer achieve a specific purpose.

NOTES

floor was woven to resemble a crisp cereal meadow. Over this ran aluminum roaches and iron crickets, and in the hot still air butterflies of delicate red tissue wavered among the sharp aroma of animal spoors![3] There was the sound like a great matted yellow hive of bees within a dark bellows, the lazy bumble of a purring lion. And there was the patter of okapi[4] feet and the murmur of a fresh jungle rain, like other hoofs falling upon the summer-starched grass. Now the walls dissolved into distances of parched weed, mile on mile, and warm endless sky. The animals drew away into thorn brakes and water holes.

36 It was the children's hour.

37 *Five o'clock.* The bath filled with clear hot water.

manipulated (muh NIHP yuh layt ihd) *v.* managed or controlled through clever moves

38 *Six, seven, eight o'clock.* The dinner dishes **manipulated** like magic tricks, and in the study a click. In the metal stand opposite the hearth a fire now blazed up warmly.

39 *Nine o'clock.* The beds warmed their hidden circuits, for nights were cool here.

40 *Nine-five.* A voice spoke from the study ceiling:

41 "Mrs. McClellan, which poem would you like this evening?"

42 The house was silent.

43 The voice said at last, "Since you express no preference, I shall select a poem at random." Quiet music rose to back the voice. "Sara Teasdale. As I recall, your favorite . . .

tremulous (TREHM yuh luhs) *adj.* trembling; quivering; timid; fearful

44
There will come soft rains and the smell of the ground,
And swallows circling with their shimmering sound;

And frogs in the pools singing at night,
And wild plum trees in **tremulous** *white;*

Robins will wear their feathery fire,
Whistling their whims on a low fence-wire;

And not one will know of the war, not one
Will care at last when it is done.

Not one would mind, neither bird nor tree,
If mankind perished utterly;

And Spring herself, when she woke at dawn
Would scarcely know that we were gone."

45 The fire burned on the stone hearth. The empty chairs faced each other between the silent walls, and the music played.

46 At ten o'clock the house began to die.

47 The wind blew. A falling tree bough crashed through the kitchen window. Cleaning solvent, bottled, shattered over the stove. The room was ablaze in an instant!

48 "Fire!" screamed a voice. The house lights flashed, water pumps shot water from the ceilings. But the solvent spread on the linoleum,

3. **spoors** (spurz) *n.* droppings of wild animals.
4. **okapi** (oh KAH pee) *n.* African animal related to the giraffe but with a much shorter neck.

licking, eating, under the kitchen door, while the voices took it up in chorus: "Fire, fire, fire!"

49 The house tried to save itself. Doors sprang tightly shut, but the windows were broken by the heat and the wind blew and sucked upon the fire.

50 The house gave ground as the fire in ten billion angry sparks moved with flaming ease from room to room and then up the stairs. While scurrying water rats squeaked from the walls, pistoled their water, and ran for more. And the wall sprays let down showers of mechanical rain.

51 But too late. Somewhere, sighing, a pump shrugged to a stop. The quenching rain ceased. The reserve water supply which filled the baths and washed the dishes for many quiet days was gone.

52 The fire crackled up the stairs. It fed upon Picassos and Matisses[5] in the upper halls, like delicacies, baking off the oily flesh, tenderly crisping the canvases into black shavings.

53 Now the fire lay in beds, stood in windows, changed the colors of drapes!

54 And then, reinforcements.

55 From attic trapdoors, blind robot faces peered down with faucet mouths gushing green chemical.

NOTES

5. **Picassos** (pih KAH sohz) **and Matisses** (mah TEES ihz) paintings by the celebrated modern painters Pablo Picasso (1881–1973) and Henri Matisse (1869–1954).

HOW LANGUAGE WORKS

Parallelism Review paragraph 51 with students. Remind students that parallel structure is the repetition of patterns of words in a sentence. Parallel structure creates balanced sentences, giving two or more ideas equal importance. Therefore, verb tenses must match and place each idea in the same chronological time period. In paragraph 51, the parallel structure is demonstrated with the use of verb phrases in the past tense: *The reserve water supply which **filled the baths** and **washed the dishes** for many quiet days was gone.*

This example balances two verb phrases. Each is written in the past tense and includes an object. Ask students to suggest two more phrases that would fit the parallel pattern. **Possible response:** *flooded the floor, burned the countertops.*

CLOSE READ

Remind students to look for adjective and adverb descriptors. You may wish to model the Close Read using the following think-aloud format. Possible responses to questions on the Student page are included.

ANNOTATE: As I read paragraphs 61 and 63, I notice and highlight the details that express extreme mental states.

QUESTION: I think these words emphasize the nonsensical, mindless, and urgent state that the house seems to be in.

CONCLUDE: This choice of descriptive language raises the tempo of the writing, conveying the panic of the situation to the reader.

NOTES

CLOSE READ

ANNOTATE: In paragraphs 61 and 63, mark words and phrases that relate to extreme mental states.

QUESTION: What do these words show about the process the house is undergoing?

CONCLUDE: What is the effect of the author's choice to portray the house in this way?

56 The fire backed off, as even an elephant must at the sight of a dead snake. Now there were twenty snakes whipping over the floor, killing the fire with a clear cold venom of green froth.

57 But the fire was clever. It had sent flames outside the house, up through the attic to the pumps there. An explosion! The attic brain which directed the pumps was shattered into bronze shrapnel on the beams.

58 The fire rushed back into every closet and felt of the clothes that hung there.

59 The house shuddered, oak bone on bone, its bared skeleton cringing from the heat, its wire, its nerves revealed as if a surgeon had torn the skin off to let the red veins and capillaries quiver in the scalded air. Help, help! Fire! Run, run! Heat snapped mirrors like the first brittle winter ice. And the voices wailed Fire, fire, run, run, like a tragic nursery rhyme, a dozen voices, high, low, like children dying in a forest, alone, alone. And the voices fading as the wires popped their sheathings like hot chestnuts. One, two, three, four, five voices died.

60 In the nursery the jungle burned. Blue lions roared, purple giraffes bounded off. The panthers ran in circles, changing color, and ten million animals, running before the fire, vanished off toward a distant steaming river . . .

61 Ten more voices died. In the last instant under the fire avalanche, other choruses, oblivious, could be heard announcing the time, playing music, cutting the lawn by remote-control mower, or setting an umbrella frantically out and in the slamming and opening front door, a thousand things happening, like a clock shop when each clock strikes the hour insanely before or after the other, a scene of maniac confusion, yet unity; singing, screaming, a few last cleaning mice darting bravely out to carry the horrid ashes away! And one voice, with sublime disregard for the situation, read poetry aloud all in the fiery study, until all the film spools burned, until all the wires withered and the circuits cracked.

62 The fire burst the house and let it slam flat down, puffing out skirts of spark and smoke.

63 In the kitchen, an instant before the rain of fire and timber, the stove could be seen making breakfasts at a psychopathic rate, ten dozen eggs, six loaves of toast, twenty dozen bacon strips, which, eaten by fire, started the stove working again, hysterically hissing!

64 The crash. The attic smashing into the kitchen and parlor. The parlor into cellar, cellar into subcellar. Deep freeze, armchair, film tapes, circuits, beds, and all like skeletons thrown in a cluttered mound deep under.

65 Smoke and silence. A great quantity of smoke.

66 Dawn showed faintly in the east. Among the ruins, one wall stood alone. Within the wall, a last voice said, over and over again and again, even as the sun rose to shine upon the heaped rubble and steam:

67 "Today is August 5, 2026, today is August 5, 2026, today is . . ." ❧

Comprehension Check

Complete the following items after you finish your first read.

1. What is the daily routine of the automated house?

2. What has happened to the rest of the houses in the neighborhood?

3. What are the five spots of paint on the exterior of the house?

4. By the end of the story, what happens to the house?

5. **Notebook** Create a storyboard that summarizes the sequence of events in "There Will Come Soft Rains."

RESEARCH

Research to Clarify Choose at least one unfamiliar detail from the text. Briefly research that detail. In what way does the information you learned shed light on an aspect of the story?

Research to Explore Bradbury published this story in 1950. Conduct research about modern "smart houses" to find out which of the technologies he described exist today. Share your findings with the class.

DIGITAL PERSPECTIVES

Comprehension Check

Possible responses:

1. The house wakes the family up, tells events on the family calendar as well as the weather, prepares meals and snacks and puts them on the table, cleans the house, turns on the sprinkler system, runs baths and warms the beds, turns on the fireplace, plays music, and reads to the family.
2. The other houses in the city have been destroyed by a bomb.
3. The five spots of paint are the images of the mother, father, son, daughter, and ball that have been left on the side of the house after the nuclear explosion.
4. The house catches fire and is destroyed, but, at the end of the story, one wall is still standing.
5. Responses will vary.

Research

Research to Clarify If students struggle to choose an unfamiliar detail, you may want to suggest the following: the poetry of Sara Teasdale; nuclear bombs.

Research to Explore Students should discover that smart houses today can be voice controlled and programmed to assess systems and turn them on and off at a specified time. The systems communicate with each other via computer and cameras. Current technology includes robot vacuums and electrically controlled garage doors.

PERSONALIZE FOR LEARNING

Challenge

Text-to-World Connection "There Will Come Soft Rains" is a work of fiction, but author Ray Bradbury was inspired by the historical occurrences in Hiroshima and Nagasaki, Japan during World War II. Have students research radioactivity to learn more about the effects of atomic bombs. Students may research these questions: What are some modern applications of technology that expose people to radioactivity? What are the benefits and dangers? Ask students to share their findings with the class.

Jump Start

CLOSE READ Have students close read the title, "There Will Come Soft Rains." Ask students to discuss whether the title prepared them for the tone and mood of the story.

Close Read the Text

Walk students through the annotation model on the student page. Encourage them to complete items 2 and 3 on their own. Review and discuss the sections students have marked. If needed, continue to model close reading by using the Annotation Highlights in the Interactive Teacher's Edition.

Analyze the Text

Possible responses:

1. (a) The automated voice sounds afraid that no one will answer; Paragraph 1. **DOK 1** (b) This tone suggests that technology has humanlike feelings. **DOK 3**
2. (a) The gods are the people who lived in the house. **DOK 2** (b) The house was operating as if all was normal, but the reality was that the "gods" had gone away, and the rituals were useless. **DOK 2**
3. (a) The lady of the house is named Mrs. McClellan; she likes to hear poems read by the voice. **DOK 2** (b) The author may be trying to emphasize the automation of the daily routine. The late introduction of a person suggests she is not that important. **DOK 2**
4. The story is somewhat a retelling of the poem in that, after the nuclear devastation, radiation will dissipate with time and the land will again support life. Once man is gone, he won't be missed and nature can be at peace. **DOK 2**
5. Responses will vary.

FORMATIVE ASSESSMENT

Analyze the Text

- **If** students fail to cite evidence, **then** remind them to support their ideas with specific information.
- **If** students struggle to formulate a hypothesis for question 3, **then** remind them that there is not necessarily a right or wrong answer.

THERE WILL COME SOFT RAINS

Close Read the Text

1. This model, from paragraph 5 of the text, shows two sample annotations, along with questions and conclusions. Close read the passage, and find another detail to annotate. Then, write a question and your conclusion.

ANNOTATE: This unusually exact time is repeated in rapid succession.

QUESTION: What effect does the rapid repetition of *"eight-one"* create?

CONCLUDE: It suggests a relentless technology that may be unnecessarily precise and does not allow for flexibility.

Eight-one, tick-tock, eight-one o'clock, off to school, off to work, run, run, eight-one! But no doors slammed, no carpets took the soft tread of rubber heels. It was raining outside. The weather box on the front door sang quietly: "Rain, rain, go away; rubbers, raincoats for today . . ."

ANNOTATE: These sing-song rhymes are childish.

QUESTION: Why does the author include these lines?

CONCLUDE: The house's technology treated all inhabitants, including the adults, like children.

Tool Kit
Close-Read Guide and Model Annotation

2. For more practice, go back into the text, and complete the close-read notes.
3. Revisit a section of the text you found important during your first read. Read this section closely, and **annotate** what you notice. Ask yourself **questions** such as "Why did the author make this choice?" What can you **conclude**?

Analyze the Text

CITE TEXTUAL EVIDENCE to support your answers.

Notebook Respond to these questions.

1. (a) **Analyze** What tone, or attitude, does the automated voice use to address the missing inhabitants? (b) **Draw Conclusions** What idea about technology does this tone suggest?
2. Reread paragraph 16. (a) **Interpret** Who are the "gods" that have gone away? (b) **Contrast** What contrast does this passage set up between the house's behavior and the new reality?
3. (a) **Summarize** In paragraphs 40–42, what personal information is given about one of the house's former inhabitants? (b) **Hypothesize** Why does the author wait until this point in the story to provide specific information about one of the people who lived in the house?
4. **Evaluate** Reread the poem in paragraph 44. Is the story a "retelling" of the poem? Explain.
5. **Essential Question:** *Why do we try to imagine the future?* What have you learned about people's attempts to imagine the future from reading this story?

STANDARDS

Reading Literature
- Determine the meaning of words and phrases as they are used in the text, including figurative and connotative meanings; analyze the cumulative impact of specific word choices on meaning and tone.
- Analyze how an author's choices concerning how to structure a text, order events within it, and manipulate time create such effects as mystery, tension, or surprise.

Language
Demonstrate understanding of figurative language, word relationships, and nuances in word meanings.

Analyze Craft and Structure

Author's Choices: Setting In many stories, the **setting**, or time and place of the action, merely provides a backdrop for the action. However, in stories such as "There Will Come Soft Rains," the setting serves a much more central function. Since there are no living characters in this story, the setting of the automated house also functions as a character through an extended form of **personification**, a figure of speech in which a nonhuman subject is given human characteristics.

Bradbury introduces this device in the opening sentence:

> In the living room the voice-clock sang, *Tick-tock, seven o'clock, time to get up, time to get up, seven o'clock!* as if it were afraid nobody would.

The verb *sang* is usually reserved for humans, not machines. Also, the idea that the house itself has emotions such as fear launches the personification that will be extended and deepened throughout the story.

Practice

CITE TEXTUAL EVIDENCE to support your answers.

Notebook Respond to these questions.

1. (a) Record in the chart specific examples of personification from the story.
(b) Review each example and write a brief analysis of how it gives a particular human characteristic to the automated house.

EXAMPLE OF PERSONIFICATION	ANALYSIS OF EXAMPLE
voice from the kitchen ceiling (paragraph 3)	makes the house seem like it could speak
the weather box sang (paragraph 5)	makes the house seem like it could sing
metal throat digested the breakfast (paragraph 7)	makes the house seem like it could eat
the house had carefully inquired (paragraph 14)	makes the house seem like it could think
the house quivered at each sound (paragraph 3)	makes the house seem like it could feel emotion

2. Review the details in your completed chart. How does the use of personification add to the emotional quality of the story?
3. In what ways is the house personified as a dynamic character—that is, a character who develops during the course of the story?

DIGITAL PERSPECTIVES

Analyze Craft and Structure

The time established by the setting can go beyond a general past, present, or future. It can be a specific year, season, or time of day. The place may not only involve the country, state, or town but also the social or cultural environment. We see all of these elements in "There Will Come Soft Rains." For more support, see **Analyze Craft and Structure: Setting.**

Practice

Possible responses:

1. See possible responses in chart on student page.
2. Personification makes us sympathetic to the plight of the house.
3. The house develops when it tries to save itself from the fire, then compensates for the empty water reserves, and finally has no choice but to succumb to the fire.

FORMATIVE ASSESSMENT

Analyze Craft and Structure

- **If** students fail to analyze examples of personification, **then** work through one or two examples with the class.
- **If** students struggle to see how the house is a dynamic character, **then** remind them that a dynamic character is different at the end of the story from what it is at the beginning. For Reteach and Practice, see **Analyze Craft and Structure: Setting (RP).**

PERSONALIZE FOR LEARNING

English Language Support

Identifying Setting and Personification Have students write a sentence describing the setting of "There Will Come Soft Rains." **EMERGING**

Have students describe the setting and locate and explain an example of personification in "There Will Come Soft Rains." **EXPANDING**

Ask students to write a short paragraph explaining how Bradbury uses personification of the automated house to tell the story of what happened after an atomic bomb. **BRIDGING**

An expanded **English Language Support Lesson** on Setting and Personification is available in the Interactive Teacher's Edition.

Concept Vocabulary

Why These Words

Possible responses:

1. The concept vocabulary connotes grace and gentility. The house has been created to make life easier and more pleasant for the people who live there. Society at that time is looking for someone or something else to handle the messy and mundane things of life.
2. twinkling; quivered; softly; quietly; cavorting; sublime; crystal

Practice

Possible responses:

1. The clock *chimed* at the top of every hour. She opened her mouth so that the snow fell *delicately* on her tongue. The baker *manipulated* the dough into a plait. She was busy *attending* to the refreshments. Her eyelashes *fluttered* flirtatiously. Praying not to spill it, he passed the wine with *tremulous* hands.
2. The clock *rang* at the top of every hour. She opened her mouth so that the snow fell *gently* on her tongue. The baker *formed* the dough into a plait. She was busy *caring* for the refreshments. Her eyelashes *flickered* flirtatiously. Praying not to spill it, he passed the wine with *trembling* hands.

   Student discussions will vary, but should note that each word carries a different shade of meaning.

Word Network

Possible words: slammed, titanic, burned, radioactive, paranoia, incinerator, crisping, rubble

Word Study

For more support, see **Concept Vocabulary and Word Study**

Possible responses:

1. *manual:* completed by hand
   manuscript: a document written by hand
   manifest: obvious, easily understood
2. *manicure:* caring for the hands and nails
   manufacture: to make by hand or machine

FORMATIVE ASSESSMENT

Concept Vocabulary

If students struggle to find synonyms for the concept vocabulary words, **then** encourage them to use a thesaurus.

Word Study

If students cannot relate the definition of a word to its root, **then** explore the word origins.
For Reteach and Practice, see **Word Study: Latin Root –*man*– (RP).**

LANGUAGE DEVELOPMENT

THERE WILL COME SOFT RAINS

Concept Vocabulary

chimed	delicately	manipulated
attending	fluttered	tremulous

Why These Words? These concept words relate to delicacy and carefulness. For example, consider the description "the garage chimed and lifted its door." The verb *chimed* has connotations of softness and grace, suggesting a sound that is more delicate than the loud clang of a bell or an alarm. Later, the house is described as *attending* to chores, suggesting that it is a loyal servant to its inhabitants.

1. How does the concept vocabulary help readers understand both the automated house and the society that created it?
2. What other words in the selection connect to this concept?

Practice

Notebook The concept words appear in "There Will Come Soft Rains."

1. Use each concept word in a sentence that demonstrates your understanding of the word's meaning.
2. Rewrite the sentences, replacing each concept word with a synonym. Exchange sentences with a partner. Identify the synonym in each of your partner's sentences, as well as the concept word that the synonym replaced. Discuss with your partner how each synonym differs slightly in meaning from the concept word that it replaced.

WORD NETWORK

Add interesting words related to the world's end from the text to your Word Network.

Word Study

Latin Root: *-man-* Many English words contain the root *-man-*, which is derived from the Latin word *manus*, meaning "hand." In "There Will Come Soft Rains," the verb *manipulated* means "managed or controlled through clever moves"—as though being moved by skillful hands.

1. Using your knowledge of the root *-man-,* record definitions of the words *manual*, *manuscript*, and *manifest*. Use a college-level dictionary to verify your answers.
2. Use reliable print or online reference materials to find two more words that contain the root *-man-*. Briefly define each one in your own words.

STANDARDS

Language

- Demonstrate command of the conventions of standard English grammar and usage when writing or speaking.
- Use parallel structure.
- Identify and correctly use patterns of word changes that indicate different meanings or parts of speech.
- Verify the preliminary determination of the meaning of a word or phrase.

Author's Style

Parallelism Ray Bradbury uses the literary device of parallelism to describe many events in "There Will Come Soft Rains." **Parallelism** is the use of similar grammatical forms or patterns to express similar ideas. Effective use of parallelism adds rhythm and balance to writing and strengthens connections among ideas.

The chart shows types of parallel elements, along with examples from "There Will Come Soft Rains."

TYPE OF PARALLEL ELEMENT	EXAMPLE
adjectives—words that describe nouns or pronouns	*Animals took shape: yellow giraffes, blue lions, pink antelopes, lilac panthers cavorting in crystal substance.* (paragraph 35)
adverbs—words that modify verbs, adjectives, or other adverbs	*But the gods had gone away, and the ritual of the religion continued senselessly, uselessly.* (paragraph 16)
adjective phrases—groups of words that function as adjectives	*They thudded against chairs, whirling their mustached runners, kneading the rug nap, sucking gently at hidden dust.* (paragraph 9)
adverb phrases—groups of words that function as adverbs	*Until this day, how well the house had kept its peace. How carefully it had inquired, "Who goes there? What's the password?"* (paragraph 14)
verb phrases—main and helping verbs that describe actions	*The offending dust, hair, or paper, seized in miniature steel jaws, was raced back to the burrows. There, down tubes which fed into the cellar, it was dropped into the sighing vent of an incinerator which sat like evil Baal in a dark corner.* (paragraph 20)

Read It

Read this paragraph about "There Will Come Soft Rains." Mark and classify the parallel elements in each sentence.

> The small whirring robots cleaned under rugs, inside drawers, on top of counters, and over doorways. They took care of thinly layered dust, entirely uneaten meals, and almost-imaginary dirt. As they worked, they whistled contentedly, purposefully. When they were done, the house was spotless, gleaming, and empty.

Write It

Notebook Add details to this paragraph, using parallel structures. Include one set of parallel adjectives or adjective phrases and one set of parallel adverbs or verb phrases.

> As night began to fall, the house prepared for dinner. Mechanical arms set the table while kitchen appliances cooked a three-course meal. The dining-room chairs stood empty while each dish was conveyed to the table. Finally, the meal was removed and thrown away.

PERSONALIZE FOR LEARNING

English Language Support

Parts of Speech Students may need support with grammatical terms before addressing parallel structure in this activity. First, work with students to help them notice the parallel patterns. Then, as students can recognize the balanced language, introduce definitions to support the activity. Review the definitions of the parts of speech referenced in this lesson (verb phrase, adjective, adjective phrase, adverb, adverb phrase). This will provide additional assistance to those students who may have difficulty classifying the parallel structures in the selected passage and providing parallel structure details in their own writing. **ALL LEVELS**

DIGITAL PERSPECTIVES

Author's Style

Parallelism Discuss the definition of parallelism with students. Explain that parallelism can involve degrees of variation. Sometimes, for emphasis, a writer will restate an idea in subsequent lines using slightly different wording. Review the examples of parallelism and define the following terms as needed:

emphasize – to stress or clearly define

juxtapose – to place close together, usually side-by-side, for comparison or contrast

For more support, see **Author's Style: Parallelism.**

MAKE IT INTERACTIVE

Have students rewrite the sample sentences using a different colored marker for each type of phrase or part of speech: adjective, adjective phrase, adverb, adverb phrase, and verb phrase.

Read It

Possible responses:

- under rugs, inside drawers, on top of counters, over doorways (adverb phrases)
- thinly layered dust, entirely uneaten meals, almost-imaginary dirt (adjective phrases and nouns)
- contentedly, purposefully (adverbs)
- spotless, gleaming, empty (adjectives)

Write It

Possible responses:

As night began to fall, the conscientious house prepared for a sumptuous dinner. Mechanical arms set the table while kitchen appliances cooked a three-course meal; how precise this was. The dining-room chairs stood empty while each dish was conveyed to the table; how puzzling this was. Finally, the meal was removed and thrown away; how sad this was. (adjectives/adverb phrases)

FORMATIVE ASSESSMENT

Author's Style

- **If** students can't classify the parallel structures, **then** remind them that adjectives describe a noun or pronoun, while adverbs answer *where, when, how,* or *to what extent.*
- **If** students struggle to add details using parallel structure, **then** encourage them to think of information that would make the passage more descriptive or colorful. Then, they can revise for parallel structure.

For Reteach and Practice, see **Author's Style: Parallelism (RP).**

TEACHING

Writing to Sources

Explain to students that *narration* is writing that tells a story. The narrative is usually told in chronological order—the order in which the events occurred in time. Encourage students to create a quick timeline to help them identify the events of their story. In addition, suggest that students review the story to find details they can include in their narrative. For more support, see **Writing to Sources: Short Story.**

Reflect on Your Writing.

Responses will vary.

1. If students need support, ask them to consider if there are things they understand now about the original story that they did not understand initially.
2. If students need support, have them think about those elements that were most important to them when they created the voice of the house.
3. Have students list specific examples of words they chose that define the house's character.

FORMATIVE ASSESSMENT

Writing to Sources

If students struggle to use the vocabulary words in their story, **then** have them review the definitions of the words to make sure they know the meanings. For Reteach and Practice, see **Writing to Sources: Short Story (RP).**

EFFECTIVE EXPRESSION

THERE WILL COME SOFT RAINS

Writing to Sources

Like longer works of fiction, short stories include the narrative elements of character, setting, and plot. However, short stories usually have fewer characters than longer fictional works do, as well as simpler plots, and often just one setting. Short stories also tend to reveal character at a crucial moment rather than developing it over time and through many incidents.

Assignment

Imagine that the house in this story can speak. Write a **short story** in which the house describes a day in the life of its family before the bombs fell. Incorporate details from "There Will Come Soft Rains" that suggest what the house does for its living inhabitants and how it feels while performing these tasks.

Your story should include:

- a clear first-person narrative with a beginning, middle, and end
- precise words and phrases that capture how the house speaks
- relevant descriptive details to explain events
- sensory language that develops the character of the house

Vocabulary and Style Connection Include several of the concept vocabulary words in your story. Also, use parallelism to create detailed descriptions of the routines that the house carries out on the day in which your story takes place.

chimed	delicately	manipulated
attending	fluttered	tremulous

Reflect on Your Writing

After you have written your story, answer these questions.

1. How did writing a story from the house's point of view deepen your understanding of the original story?
2. What details from the story helped you effectively create the voice of the house?
3. **Why These Words?** The words you choose make a difference in your writing. Which words did you use to give the house a specific quality or characteristic?

STANDARDS

Writing
- Write narratives to develop real or imagined experiences or events using effective technique, well-chosen details, and well-structured event sequences.
- Use precise words and phrases, telling details, and sensory language to convey a vivid picture of the experiences, events, setting, and/or characters.

Speaking and Listening
Present information, findings, and supporting evidence clearly, concisely, and logically such that listeners can follow the line of reasoning and the organization, development, substance, and style are appropriate to purpose, audience, and task.

Speaking and Listening

Assignment

Work with a partner to prepare and deliver an **oral recitation and interpretation** of the Sara Teasdale poem included in "There Will Come Soft Rains." Structure your presentation to include:

- an oral recitation of the poem
- an explanation of whether or not the world that Teasdale's poem predicts actually emerges in the story.

First, reread the selection. Then, follow these steps to complete the assignment.

1. **Memorize the Poem** Use the following ideas to help you memorize the poem.
   - Copy the poem, and read it aloud numerous times, varying your tone of voice, the your reading pace, and your speaking volume. Make notes on the poem to mark your most effective choices. For example, you might add double slashes (//) to indicate places where you will pause and underline words you will emphasize.
   - Use the poem's rhythms and rhymes to help you remember the words.
   - Have your partner follow along with your marked-up copy of the poem as you read it aloud so that he or she can tell you if you have dropped, changed, or added any words. Make corrections as needed.
2. **Plan Your Interpretation** Discuss with your partner the interpretation of the poem that you would like to share with the class. Use this question to focus your thinking: Does the poem accurately predict what happens in the story? State your position in writing, and gather supporting evidence from both the poem and the story.
3. **Prepare Your Delivery** Practice reciting the poem from memory and delivering your interpretation of the poem. Include the following performance techniques to make the oral recitation and interpretation compelling.
   - Speak clearly, in an appropriate tone, and at an appropriate volume and rate.
   - Use appropriate facial expressions and gestures to convey the poem's power and your interpretation of the work.
   - Maintain regular eye contact with the audience.
4. **Evaluate Oral Recitations and Interpretations** As your classmates deliver their recitations and interpretations, listen attentively, and take notes. Afterward, write a brief analysis of each classmate's delivery. List specific examples of what each speaker did well and suggestions for how the recitation could be improved.

EVIDENCE LOG

Before moving on to a new selection, go to your Evidence Log and record what you learned from "There Will Come Soft Rains."

DIGITAL PERSPECTIVES

Speaking and Listening

1. **Memorize the Poem** Tell students that listening to a looped recording of the poem, along with reading it aloud, may help them to memorize it.
2. **Plan Your Interpretation** To support students as they interpret the poem, you may want to suggest that they conduct research to find a variety of interpretations. Then, encourage students to consider what they have read in order to arrive at their own ideas.
3. **Prepare Your Delivery** Remind students to practice until they are comfortable. Some students may need more support in presenting before a large group.
4. **Evaluate Oral Recitations and Interpretations** Encourage students to make one supportive comment about each presentation.

For more support, see **Speaking and Listening: Oral Recitation.**

Evidence Log Support students in completing their Evidence Log. This paced activity will help prepare them for the Performance-Based Assessment at the end of the unit.

FORMATIVE ASSESSMENT

Speaking and Listening

- **If** students struggle to memorize the poem, **then** remind them to work closely with and rely on their partner to help them.
- **If** students struggle with preparing their delivery, **then** have them use the performance techniques provided.

For Reteach and Practice, see **Speaking and Listening: Oral Recitation (RP).**

Selection Test

Administer the "There Will Come Soft Rains" Selection Test, which is available in both print and digital formats online in Assessments.

PERSONALIZE FOR LEARNING

Strategic Support

Irony Explain to students that Sara Teasdale's "There Will Come Soft Rains" is filled with verbal irony. The writer makes scathing judgments and observations about the fate of mankind, but does so in a calm, detached, and genteel way. The reader is presented with a pleasant, idyllic scene where humanity does not trespass because it has obliterated itself by warfare. And Mother Nature is just fine with that. Have students consider why this method of presentation is so effective.

DIGITAL PERSPECTIVES

Illuminating the Standard To prepare students for their poetry recitation, play video clips of poetry being recited. Watching others recite stirring poems can show the subtle ways that speakers vary the tone and style of their presentations to match their message.

Jump Start

What does an apocalyptic future look like?

After students have read "By the Waters of Babylon" and "There Will Come Soft Rains," ask them to write three descriptions of a civilization that has been destroyed by extremely powerful weaponry. You might want to encourage them to write a list of words that come to mind.

Then, ask students to share their descriptions in a class discussion before they begin to write their own end-of-world narratives.

Write a Narrative

Make sure students understand they are being asked to imagine a world that has not literally ceased to exist, but whose population has either been wiped from the planet or has been mostly killed off. This assignment asks students to write about what happens next.

Students should complete the assignment using word processing software to take advantage of editing tools and features.

Elements of a Narrative

Remind students that an effective narrative such as "Dream's Winter" includes all the required elements, flows well, establishes a connection with the audience by having strong characters, and uses word choice and tone to create a mood.

MAKE IT INTERACTIVE

Project "Dream's Winter" from the Interactive Teacher's Edition and have students identify the elements of a narrative. To get the discussion started, you might want to point out how the author sets the tone of the story in the opening paragraph.

Academic Vocabulary

Ask students to explain why a person might become *introspective* after surviving a nuclear war.

WRITING TO SOURCES

- BY THE WATERS OF BABYLON
- THERE WILL COME SOFT RAINS

Write a Narrative

You have read two short stories that address the topic of the end of the world. "By the Waters of Babylon" presents the journey of a young narrator who belongs to a tribe that remains after a catastrophic event has befallen humankind. "There Will Come Soft Rains" describes an ordinary household in the aftermath of an apocalyptic event. Each story deals with the concept of the world's end in its own way. Now you will use what you have learned to write your own narrative about the end of the world.

Assignment

Use your knowledge of "By the Waters of Babylon" and "There Will Come Soft Rains" as inspiration to write a **narrative** that answers this question:

After the end of the world, how do we begin again?

Elements of a Narrative

A **narrative** is any type of writing that tells a story, whether it is fiction, nonfiction, poetry, or drama.

An effective narrative connects specific incidents with larger themes and includes these elements:

- an introduction to the characters and the situation they face
- a specific perspective or point of view from which the story is told
- events and characters developed though narrative techniques such as dialogue, pacing, and description
- a smooth and logical sequence of events
- precise words and phrases, descriptive details, and sensory language
- an ending that conveys the significance of story events

Model Narrative For a model of a well-crafted narrative, see the Launch Text, "Dream's Winter."

Challenge yourself to find all of the elements of an effective narrative in the text. You will have an opportunity to review these elements as you prepare to write your own narrative.

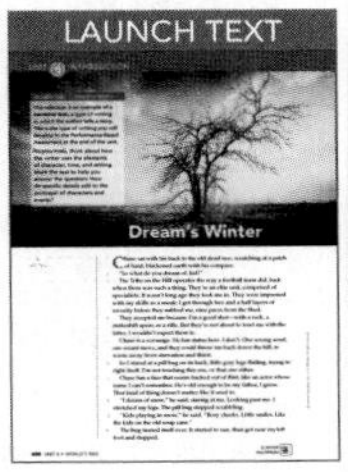

Tool Kit
Student Model of a Narrative

ACADEMIC VOCABULARY

As you craft your narrative, consider using some of the academic vocabulary you learned in the beginning of the unit.

innovate
technique
depiction
introspective
conjecture

STANDARDS

Writing

- Write narratives to develop real or imagined experiences or events using effective technique, well-chosen details, and well-structured event sequences.
- Write routinely over extended time frames and shorter time frames for a range of tasks, purposes, and audiences.

AUTHOR'S PERSPECTIVE **Kelly Gallagher, M.Ed.**

Drafting Like reading, writing is not a "one and done" activity. Teachers can use a surfing metaphor to reinforce the importance of drafting, of evaluating ideas to find the best ones. Explain that ideas come in sets of waves. Remind students that a surfer can sit in the water for ten minutes or longer, waiting for a new set of waves to come in. When a wave finally comes in, an inexperienced surfer might catch it immediately, but a more experienced surfer recognizes that waves come in sets. The second wave in the set is usually larger than the first one, the third wave may be even larger, and so on. Likewise, often the student's best idea is not the first one that comes to mind.

As tempting as that first wave may be, the experienced surfer looks for the best wave in the set, just as a skilled writer sifts ideas and evaluates drafts, looking for the best ones. Encourage students to draft, and then consider additional ideas that can improve their writing.

Prewriting / Planning

Establish a Situation You need to establish a situation at the outset of your narrative to engage and orient the reader. First, review "By the Waters of Babylon" and "There Will Come Soft Rains" to determine how the authors establish the situations in their stories. Then, answer these questions to establish an engaging situation for your own narrative.

- Who are the characters?
- Where and when do the events take place?
- What are the characters trying to achieve?
- What obstacle(s) will they have to overcome to achieve their goal(s)?
- What happens in the end?

Write a sentence describing the situation: ______________________________

____

Establish Point of View A story's **point of view** is the perspective from which it is told. Point of view is determined by what type of **narrator**, or voice, is telling the story. Will your story be told from the point of view of a character that speaks in the first person, or a narrator who is not a story character? Will your story have multiple points of view? Complete this sentence to establish the point of view in your story.

My story will be told from the point of view of ______________________________

Gather Details There are different narrative techniques you can use to develop experiences, events, and characters in your story:

- **dialogue:** conversation between or among characters
- **pacing:** speed at which a narrative unfolds
- **description:** portrait in words of a person, place, or thing

Using a variety of narrative techniques can help you craft a compelling narrative. Brainstorm to generate details to use in dialogue and description. For example, in the Launch Text, the writer uses vivid description to help the reader visualize a character.

> *Chase has a face that seems hacked out of flint, like an actor whose name I can't remember.*
>
> –"Dream's Winter"

EVIDENCE LOG

Review your Evidence Log and identify key details you may want to cite in your narrative.

STANDARDS

Writing

Engage and orient the reader by setting out a problem, situation, or observation, establishing one or multiple point(s) of view, and introducing a narrator and/or characters; create a smooth progression of experiences or events.

DIGITAL PERSPECTIVES

Prewriting/Planning

Establish a Situation Ask students to think about the way one of their favorite movies begins. Note that the screenwriter chose to open the film in this way not only because it got the plot moving, but also because it set the tone of the movie. Explain that this exposition sets up the way a story feels. It helps the viewer anticipate the kind of story about to unfold. The same idea applies to a written narrative like a short story.

Establish Point of View Review the strengths and weaknesses of a first-person narrator as compared to a third-person narrator who stands outside the action. Help students decide which point of view will be best for their purposes.

Gather Details Encourage students to try to give characters different voices in their dialogue, acknowledging that making each character sound distinct is a difficult challenge for writers.

PERSONALIZE FOR LEARNING

Strategic Support

Pacing Some students might not understand the concept of pacing. Pacing is the speed of the narrative, and it is based on amount of description, dialogue, new events, and even sentence length. Explain that writers can employ a variety of techniques to establish strong pacing. For example, short sentences and snappy dialogue create a feeling of intensity and speed, whereas longer sentences and extended conversations create a leisurely feeling. Encourage students to vary their pacing so that the reader doesn't get bored. Have a class discussion about the various pacing techniques that have been used in popular movies. As the discussion progresses, introduce the idea that the same techniques apply to written story-tellling.

TEACHING

Organize Your Narrative

Explain to students that the best stories strike a strong balance between plot and character development. Point out that readers will be more interested in plot developments if they care about the characters. At the same time, readers will be more likely to care about the characters if the plot is compelling.

Drafting

Write a First Draft Remind students that the main goal of the first draft is to get their ideas on paper, incorporating all the elements of narrative fiction. Instruct them to include details that will compel readers to want to keep reading. Encourage students to grab the reader's attention by beginning the narrative with an especially interesting detail.

PERFORMANCE TASK: WRITING FOCUS

Organize Your Narrative

The sequence of related events in a narrative is known as **plot**. There are five elements of plot:

- the **exposition** introduces the setting, the characters, and the basic situation
- the **rising action** introduces and develops the central conflict, or problem
- the **climax**, or turning point, is the highest point of the action and tension
- the **falling action** shows how the conflict lessens in intensity
- the **resolution** shows how the conflict is resolved, ties up loose ends, and often conveys an insight or change by the main character

Use the graphic organizer to take notes on how you will include the plot elements in your own narrative.

EXPOSITION
↓
RISING ACTION
↓
CLIMAX
↓
FALLING ACTION
↓
RESOLUTION

STANDARDS

Writing

- Use narrative techniques, such as dialogue, pacing, description, reflection, and multiple plot lines, to develop experiences, events, and/or characters.
- Use a variety of techniques to sequence events so that they build on one another to create a coherent whole.

Drafting

Write a First Draft Use your completed graphic organizer to write your first draft. Begin by introducing your narrator and other characters, the situation they face, and the setting. Develop the characters, setting, and plot though narrative techniques such as dialogue, pacing, and description. Aim to present a smooth and logical sequence of events. Use precise words and phrases, descriptive details, and sensory language to make your narrative engaging. End with a resolution that conveys the significance of story events.

AUTHOR'S PERSPECTIVE **Jim Cummins, Ph.D.**

Writing Vibrant Sentences Having students focus on writing more expressive sentences encourages them to pay attention to how ideas are conveyed in the texts they read. Students will develop an enhanced awareness of how to control rich descriptive language when teachers draw their attention to vivid descriptions in the texts they are reading. Teachers can point to "strong sentences" in these passages in order to sensitize students to ways in which meanings can be expressed powerfully and imaginatively.

Step 1: Select an expressive sentence from the text to use as a model.

Step 2: Draw students' attention to the range of adjectives, adverbs, nouns, and verbs in the sentence that enabled the author to create lively images of what is being described.

Step 3: Show students how to expand simple nouns into noun phrases that provide additional information about what is being described.

LANGUAGE DEVELOPMENT: CONVENTIONS

Add Variety: Use Adverbial Clauses to Combine Sentences

Adverbial Clauses A **clause** is a group of words that contains a subject and a verb. An **adverbial clause** is a type of clause that begins with a subordinating conjunction and functions as an adverb in a sentence. It tells *where, when, in what way, to what extent, how much, under what condition,* or *why.* Adverbial clauses can be used to combine sentences, clarifying the relationships between ideas and adding variety to writing.

Some Common Subordinating Conjunctions

after	as though	since	when
although	because	so that	whenever
as	before	than	where
as if	even though	unless	wherever
as long as	if	until	while

Read It

These sentences from the Launch Text use adverbial clauses to link related ideas and show the relationship between them.

- *I got through two and a half layers of security* ***before*** *they nabbed me. . . .* **(tells *when*)**
- *They accepted me* ***because*** *I'm a good shot. . . .* **(tells *why*)**
- *Chase tried driving his stick into the crusty earth,* ***as if*** *he were planting a flag.* **(tells *in what way*)**

Write It

As you draft your narrative, think about how you can use adverbial clauses to combine sentences that contain related ideas. First, identify the relationship between the ideas in the sentences. Then, select a subordinating conjunction that clarifies that relationship, and use it to turn information in one sentence into an adverbial clause. Put the adverbial clause at the beginning or end of the combined sentence.

If you want to...	consider using one of these conjunctions.
tell where	*where, wherever*
tell when	*after, before, until, when, whenever, while*
tell in what way	*as, as if, as though*
tell under what condition	*if, unless*
tell why	*because, since, so that*

TIP

PUNCTUATION

Make sure to punctuate sentences that contain adverbial clauses correctly. When an adverbial clause begins a sentence, put a comma after the clause.

STANDARDS

Writing
Use precise words, and phrases, telling details, and sensory language to convey a vivid picture of the experiences, events, setting, and/or characters.

Language
Use various types of phrases and clauses to convey specific meanings and add variety and interest to writing or presentations.

DIGITAL PERSPECTIVES

Add Variety: Use Adverbial Clauses to Combine Sentences

Adverbial Clauses Encourage students to use adverbial clauses to add an element of sophistication to their narratives. Adverbial clauses allow students to vary sentence length and style. Use this as an example: "Hannah enjoyed her summer, even though she went through a difficult breakup with her boyfriend."

Read It

Emphasize that without adverbial clauses, writing would often feel choppy. Have a few students remove the adverbial phrases from the examples and ask them to read them aloud, asking them to evalaute what is left. Students may say that shorter sentences establish a regular pattern that might become dull.

Write It

Remind students to think carefully before deciding which subordinating conjunctions to use. Explain that if they misuse them, readers will probably be confused, since they expect certain subordinating conjunctions to suggest a specific idea or tone.

Review this example from the launch text: *It took off, following Chase,* ***as if*** *it heard and understood about the water.*

Next, replace "as if" with "unless:" *It took off, following Chase,* ***unless*** *it heard and understood about the water.*

Discuss with students the effect of this change.

PERSONALIZE FOR LEARNING

English Language Support

Understanding Meaning Some English learners might have difficulty understanding the subtle differences in meaning among different subordinating conjunctions. Review the conjunctions by presenting sample sentences that use each correctly. Ask pairs of students to practice writing sentences that use the conjunctions.

Help students to see that use of these conjunctions is one way to condense ideas. Students may also compound verbs:
She saw and accepted the challenge.
An additional way to condense ideas is to create more precise and detailed sentences:
She accepted the interviewer's challenge and explained her success in finance.
ALL LEVELS

Revising

Evaluating Your Draft Before students begin revising their writing, they should first evaluate their draft to determine it contains all the required elements, is organized well, and adheres to the norms and conventions of narrative fiction.

Logical Organization Explain to students that writers can take more liberties with organization in narrative fiction than they can with forms of nonfiction writing, such as expository and informational writing. However, remind students that the structure must be clear to readers.

Use Narrative Techniques Have students review the passages where they introduced dialogue. Students may ask themselves questions such as these: *Does it contribute to the plot or character development? Does it sound realistic?* Students may use their answers to these questions to guide the revision.

PERFORMANCE TASK: WRITING FOCUS

Revising

Evaluating Your Draft

Use the following checklist to evaluate the effectiveness of your draft. Then, use your evaluation and the instruction on this page to guide your revision.

FOCUS AND ORGANIZATION	DEVELOPMENT OF IDEAS/ELABORATION	CONVENTIONS
☐ Begins with an introduction that clearly establishes the situation and point of view.	☐ Develops events and characters through narrative techniques such as dialogue, pacing, and description.	☐ Spells all words correctly, using a print or online dictionary as needed.
☐ Organizes the sequence of events smoothly and logically through the use of the five stages of plot.	☐ Includes precise words and phrases, descriptive details, and sensory language to engage the reader.	☐ Attends to the norms and conventions of the discipline, especially the correct use of adverbial clauses in sentences.
☐ Ends with a conclusion that shows the resolution of the conflict and conveys the significance of story events.		

Revising for Focus and Organization

Logical Organization Reread your narrative. Are the events organized smoothly and logically into a coherent whole through the use of the five stages of plot? If not, review the five elements, and determine which ones are missing or could be strengthened in your draft. Revise parts of your narrative as needed.

Revising for Ideas and Elaboration

Use Narrative Techniques Remember that narrative techniques such as dialogue, pacing, and description can help to develop the events and characters in a story. Review your draft and ask yourself these questions:

- Are there sections where adding a conversation between or among characters could convey ideas more clearly? If so, how?
- Are there sections where the speed of the story seems to be too fast or too slow? If so, how can the pacing be improved?
- Are there sections where a person, place, or thing could be described in more detail? What specific details could be included in the description?

Mark these sections in your draft, and revise them as needed.

Use Vivid Details Reread your draft, and mark your use of descriptive details. Ask yourself these questions:

- Have I relied too much on adjectives? If so, would nouns that are more specific work better?
- Have I repeated too many verbs? If so, would varying my choice of verbs or adding adverbs provide more interest and color to my story?

Continue to review your word choices, and revise as needed.

WORD NETWORK

Include interesting words from your Word Network in your narrative.

STANDARDS

Writing
Use a variety of techniques to sequence events so that they build on one another to create a coherent whole.

Language
- Demonstrate command of the conventions of standard English grammar and usage when writing or speaking.
- Spell correctly.

HOW LANGUAGE WORKS

Subordinating Conjunctions As students revise their narratives, remind them to use subordinating conjunctions to show the relationship between ideas and to add variety to their writing. Have them look at the list in the Language Development lesson. They may also consider using the additional adverbial clauses in this chart.

Tell when	as soon as, since
Tell in what way	even if, even though, whether
Tell under what condition	although, whereas
Tell why	now that, so

PEER REVIEW

Exchange papers with a classmate. Use the checklist to evaluate your classmate's narrative and provide supportive feedback.

1. Are the situation and point of view clearly established?
☐ yes ☐ no If no, suggest how the writer might clarify them.

2. Is there a clear sequence of events that unfolds smoothly and logically?
☐ yes ☐ no If no, explain what confused you.

3. Does the narrative end with a conclusion that conveys the significance of story events?
☐ yes ☐ no If no, tell what you think might be missing.

4. What is the strongest part of your classmate's paper? Why?

____

____

Editing and Proofreading

Edit for Conventions Reread your draft for accuracy and consistency. Correct errors in grammar and word usage. Be sure you have included a variety of sentence structures that add variety and interest to your narrative and reflect your unique voice.

Proofread for Accuracy Read your draft carefully, correcting errors in spelling and punctuation. As you proofread, make sure that any dialogue is enclosed in quotation marks. Review your draft closely for instances of split dialogue—that is, dialogue in which a quotation is split up by additional information, such as the identification of the speaker. Make sure these instances of split dialogue are punctuated correctly with quotation marks.

Publishing and Presenting

Create a final version of your narrative. Share it with a small group so that your classmates can read it and make comments. In turn, review and comment on your classmates' work. As a group, discuss what your narratives have in common and the ways in which they are different. Always maintain a polite and respectful tone when commenting.

Reflecting

Reflect on what you learned as you wrote your narrative. In what ways did writing about imagined experiences and events relating to the end of the world enhance your understanding of the topic? What was the most challenging aspect of composing your narrative? Did you learn something from reviewing the work of others and discussing your narrative with your classmates that might inform your narrative writing process in the future?

DIGITAL PERSPECTIVES

Peer Review

Before they begin their peer review, set guidelines for review for students. Remind them to review the story in front of them. They should provide feedback on how well the story is told, not suggest a level of change that would require a complete rewrite. The peer review checklist provided will help keep students focused.

Editing and Proofreading

As students proofread, they should check for grammar, spelling, and punctuation errors. Remind them that they should not rely on word processing programs to find all mistakes, as programs may fail to recognize that the wrong form of a homonym was used, for example. Students should also be aware that it's easy to misspell names of people and places.

Reflecting

Explain that by reflecting on their narrative and the comments from their peers, students can gain a new appreciation for the significance of the story they told. Tell them that by hearing the perspectives of others, they may think of something that had never occurred to them. It is also helpful for students to review which strategies helped them so that they may use them again.

PERSONALIZE FOR LEARNING

Challenge

Write a Screenplay Invite students to adapt their narratives into screenplays. Explain that books are often adapted into movies. Students will be familiar with series like *The Hunger Games* and *Harry Potter*, which were translated from print for the screen. Note that since a screenplay doesn't usually have a narrator, the story must be told solely through dialogue, acting, setting, and camera work. Encourage students to describe the setting of various scenes and to include stage direction that guides actors in delivering lines with the proper emotion.

OVERVIEW

SMALL-GROUP LEARNING

Why do we try to imagine the future?

Scientists seek to explain a likely future for Earth and its inhabitants. In a few billion years, our sun will run out of hydrogen to burn. Will that mean the end of the world? What else might happen in that time? During Small-Group Learning, students will read selections that pose ideas for what might happen to our world.

Small-Group Learning Strategies

Review the Learning Strategies with students and explain that they will develop strategies to work in small-group environments.

- Have students watch the video on Small-Group Learning Strategies.
- A video on this topic is available online in the Professional Development Center.

Discuss some action items to add to the chart before students complete it on their own. For example, for "Clarify," you might suggest:

- Use resources to confirm vocabulary or background information.
- As a group, review meeting notes to make sure everyone is in agreement about next steps.

Block Scheduling

Each day in this Pacing Plan represents a 40–50 minute class period. Teachers using block scheduling may combine days to reflect their class schedule. In addition, teachers may revise pacing to differentiate and support core instruction by integrating components and resources as students require.

OVERVIEW: SMALL-GROUP LEARNING

ESSENTIAL QUESTION:

Why do we try to imagine the future?

Some stories about a doomed future capture people's anxieties about the world right now. You will read selections featuring situations that seem futuristic but affect people in the present. You will work in a group to continue your exploration of literature about the world's end.

Small-Group Learning Strategies

Throughout your life, in school, in your community, and in your career, you will continue to learn and work with others.

Review these strategies and the actions you can take to practice them as you work in teams. Add ideas of your own for each step. Use these strategies during Small-Group Learning.

STRATEGY	ACTION PLAN
Prepare	• Complete your assignments so that you are prepared for group work. • Organize your thinking so you can contribute to your group's discussions. •
Participate fully	• Make eye contact to signal that you are listening and taking in what is being said. • Use text evidence when making a point. •
Support others	• Build off ideas from others in your group. • Invite others who have not yet spoken to join the discussion. •
Clarify	• Paraphrase the ideas of others to ensure that your understanding is correct. • Ask follow-up questions. •

SCAN FOR MULTIMEDIA

Pacing Plan

Unit Introduction: 1
Introduce Whole-Class Learning: 2
By the Waters of Babylon: 3, 4, 5, 6, 7, 8
There Will Come Soft Rains: 9, 10, 11, 12, 13
Performance Task: 14, 15

CONTENTS

MAGAZINE ARTICLE

The Nuclear Tourist

George Johnson

The worst nuclear power plant disaster in history took place in Chernobyl in 1986. What does Chernobyl look like today?

POETRY COLLECTION 1

the beginning of the end of the world

Lucille Clifton

The Powwow at the End of the World

Sherman Alexie

A Song on the End of the World

Czeslaw Milosz

What can poetry teach us about the end of the world?

COMPARE

MEDIA: RADIO BROADCAST

from Radiolab: War of the Worlds

NPR

What effect did a radio drama about a Martian invasion have when it was presented as breaking news?

MAGAZINE ARTICLE

The Myth of the *War of the Worlds* Panic

Jefferson Pooley and Michael Socolow

Did people in 1938 really believe that killer Martians had invaded Earth?

PERFORMANCE TASK

SPEAKING AND LISTENING FOCUS

Create a Podcast

The Small-Group readings present scenes, both real and imagined, of doomsday events. After reading, your group will plan and deliver a narrative that suggests what our visions of the future tell us about our concerns in the present.

DIGITAL PERSPECTIVES

Contents

Selections Circulate among groups as they preview the selections. You might encourage groups to discuss any knowledge they already have about any of the selections or the situations and settings shown in the photographs. Students may wish to take a poll within their group to determine which selections look the most interesting.

Remind students that communicating and collaborating in groups is an important skill that they will use throughout their lives—in school, in their careers, and in their community.

Performance Task

Create a Podcast Give groups time to read about and briefly discuss the podcast they will need to develop. They should consider what their narrative might cover and how they will create their podcast after reading. Encourage students to do some preliminary thinking about the types of media they may want to use. This may help focus their subsequent reading and group discussion.

SMALL-GROUP LEARNING

- 16: Introduce Small-Group Learning
- 17, 18, 19: The Nuclear Tourist
- 20, 21:
  - the beginning of the end of the world
  - The Powwow at the End of the World
  - A Song on the End of the World
- 22, 23: Media: *from* Radiolab: War of the Worlds
- 24, 25: The Myth of the War of the Worlds Panic
- 26: Performance Task
- 27: Introduce Independent Learning
- 28: Independent Learning
- 29, 30: Performance-Based Assessment

SMALL-GROUP LEARNING

Working as a Team

1. **Take a Position** Remind groups to let all members share their responses. You may wish to set a time limit for this discussion.
2. **List Your Rules** You may want to have groups share their lists of rules and consolidate them into a master list to be displayed and followed by all groups.
3. **Apply the Rules** As you circulate among the groups, ensure that students are staying on task. Consider a short time limit for this step.
4. **Name Your Group** This task can be creative and fun. If students have trouble coming up with a name, suggest that they think of something related to the unit topic. Encourage groups to share their names with the class.
5. **Create a Communication Plan** Encourage groups to include in their plans times during the day to share ideas. They should also devise a method for recording and saving their communications.

Accountable Talk

Remind students that groups should communicate politely. You can post these Accountable Talk suggestions and encourage students to add their own. Students should:

Remember to . . .
Ask clarifying questions.

Which sounds like . . .
Can you please repeat what you said?
Would you give me an example?
I think you said _____. Did I understand you correctly?

Remember to . . .
Explain your thinking.

Which sounds like . . .
I believe _____ is true because _____.

Remember to . . .
Build on the ideas of others.

Which sounds like . . .
When _____ said _____, it made me think of _____.

OVERVIEW: SMALL-GROUP LEARNING

Working as a Team

1. **Take a Position** In your group, discuss the following question:

   What is one thing people can do today to make the world a better place tomorrow?

   As you take turns sharing your ideas, provide reasons that support them. After all group members have shared, discuss similarities and differences among the various suggestions.

2. **List Your Rules** As a group, decide on the rules that you will follow as you work together. Samples are provided; add two more of your own. You may add or revise rules based on your experience together.
   - Everyone should participate in group discussions.
   - People should not interrupt.
   - ______________________________
   - ______________________________

3. **Apply the Rules** Practice working as a group. Share what you have learned about world's end stories. Make sure each person in the group contributes. Take notes and be prepared to share with the class one thing that you heard from another member of your group.

4. **Name Your Group** Choose a name that reflects the unit topic.

   Our group's name: ______________________________

5. **Create a Communication Plan** Decide how you want to communicate with one another. For example, you might use online collaboration tools, email, or instant messaging.

   Our group's decision: ______________________________

FACILITATING SMALL-GROUP LEARNING

Forming Groups You may wish to form groups for Small-Group Learning so that each consists of students with different learning abilities. Some students may be adept at organizing information, whereas others may have strengths related to generating or synthesizing information. A good mix of abilities can make the experience of Small-Group Learning dynamic and productive.

Making a Schedule

First, find out the due dates for the small-group activities. Then, preview the texts and activities with your group, and make a schedule for completing the tasks.

SELECTION	ACTIVITIES	DUE DATE
The Nuclear Tourist		
the beginning of the end of the world The Powwow at the End of the World A Song on the End of the World		
from Radiolab: War of the Worlds The Myth of the *War of the Worlds* Panic		

Working on Group Projects

As your group works together, you'll find it more effective if each person has a specific role. Different projects require different roles. Before beginning a project, discuss the necessary roles, and choose one for each group member. Here are some possible roles; add your own ideas.

Project Manager: monitors the schedule and keeps everyone on task

Researcher: organizes research activities

Recorder: takes notes during group meetings

____

____

____

____

____

SCAN FOR MULTIMEDIA

DIGITAL PERSPECTIVES

Making a Schedule

Encourage groups to preview the reading selections and to consider how long it will take them to complete the activities accompanying each selection. Point out that they can adjust the due dates for particular selections as needed as they work on their small-group projects; however, they must complete all assigned tasks before the group Performance Task is due. Encourage groups to review their schedules upon completing the activities for each selection to make sure they are on track to meet the final due date.

Working on Group Projects

Point out to groups that the roles they assign can also be changed later. Students might have to make changes based on who is best at doing what. Try to make sure that there is no favoritism, cliquishness, or stereotyping by gender or other means in the assignment of roles.

Also, you should review the roles each group assigns to its members. Based on your understanding of students' individual strengths, you might find it necessary to suggest some changes.

AUTHOR'S PERSPECTIVE Ernest Morrell, Ph.D.

Supporting Groups As students work in groups, they may need some help to resolve issues and move ahead. Teachers can use these suggestions:

- If groups get stuck on a trivial point or a bone of contention, encourage members to move on so that they will get their work done. Intense discussions are fine, but they shouldn't be a substitute for getting work done.
- If the group has not realized that the issue has more than one side and that all sides deserve consideration, teachers might step in and play devil's advocate by arguing an unpopular position so that students can take it into consideration.
- If the group has reached too easy a consensus and not thoughtfully weighed all aspects of the issue, teachers can push groups who need a challenge.

As a facilitators in the room, teachers can encourage students to move beyond their comfort zone and go the extra mile to exceed expectations and do their best work.

The Nuclear Tourist

AUDIO SUMMARIES
Audio summaries of "The Nuclear Tourist" are available online in both English and Spanish in the Interactive Teacher's Edition or Unit Resources. Assigning these summaries prior to reading the selection may help students build additional background knowledge and set a context for their first read.

Summary

"The Nuclear Tourist" is a magazine article by George Johnson, who traveled to Chernobyl twenty-eight years after the nuclear power plant disaster there. The writer describes a trip into the radioactive region, a place which has been abandoned since the 1986 accident. Johnson travels into the zone with guides who explain how to minimize risk. On the way into the zone, they encounter a resident—someone who refused to evacuate the zone and has lived there for years. Continuing into the zone, the team approaches the deserted city of Pripyat, where empty schools and apartment buildings have decayed, and the area has become overrun with wildlife. The author recounts the events of the Chernobyl disaster and the sight-seeing trip through Pripyat. He is amazed by the adventure seekers who come to places like Chernobyl where radiation danger was once very high.

Insight

The irony of this article, juxtaposing the amount of radiation in the Chernobyl exclusion zone with the normal amount encountered in life, characterizes its tone of melancholy, rather than fear. This image of apocalyptic collapse is far more sedate than worrying.

ESSENTIAL QUESTION:
Why do we try to imagine the future?

Connection to Essential Question

This article offers valuable information about a real-life answer to the essential question—one that does not require imagination. The future envisioned by the first responders to the disaster at Chernobyl was not the quiet wilderness of modern Pripyat; however, we can use the exclusion zone's example to imagine a future without humanity.

SMALL-GROUP LEARNING PERFORMANCE TASK
What do stories about the future say about the present?

UNIT PERFORMANCE-BASED ASSESSMENT
Which matters more—the present or the future?

Connection to Performance Tasks

Small-Group Learning Task The article offers a certain consolation that disasters which endanger humanity are not necessarily capable of destroying nature itself.

Unit Performance-Based Assessment While there are currently people living in the radioactive zone, the question raised by the article is what will happen to the region over time. Students may consider this article as they prepare for the Performance-Based Assessment. They may wonder if the region will someday be more habitable or whether it will simply remain a wilderness forever.

DIGITAL PERSPECTIVES — Audio | Video | Document | Annotation Highlights | EL Highlights | Online Assessment

LESSON RESOURCES

	Making Meaning	Language Development	Effective Expression
Lesson	**First Read** **Close Read** **Analyze the Text** **Analyze Craft and Structure**	**Concept Vocabulary** **Word Study** **Author's Style**	**Research**
Instructional Standards	**RI.10** By the end of grade 9, read and comprehend literary nonfiction . . . **RI.1** Cite strong and thorough textual evidence . . .	**L.4.a** Use context as a clue . . . **L.4.b** Identify and correctly use patterns . . . **L.4.c** Consult general and specialized reference materials . . . **L.3** Apply knowledge of language . . . **L.6** Acquire and use accurately general academic and domain-specific words and phrases . . .	**W.7** Conduct short as well as more sustained research projects . . . **W.8** Gather relevant information from multiple authoritative print and digital sources . . . **W.9** Draw evidence from literary or informational texts . . .
STUDENT RESOURCES			
Available online in the Interactive Student Edition or Unit Resources	Selection Audio First-Read Guide: Nonficition Close-Read Guide: Nonfiction	Word Network	Evidence Log
TEACHER RESOURCES			
Selection Resources Available online in the Interactive Teacher's Edition or Unit Resources	Audio Summaries Annotation Highlights EL Highlights The Nuclear Tourist: Text Questions English Language Support Lesson: Travel Journalism Analyze Craft and Structure: Literary Nonfiction	Concept Vocabulary and Word Study Author's Style: Diction	Research: Present Findings
Reteach/Practice (RP) Available online in the Interactive Teacher's Edition or Unit Resources	Analyze Craft and Structure: Literary Nonfiction (RP)	Word Study: Latin Root *-spec-* (RP) Author's Style: Diction (RP)	Research: Present Findings (RP)
Assessment Available online in Assessments	Selection Test		
My Resources	A Unit 6 Answer Key is available online and in the Interactive Teacher's Edition.		

Reading Support

Text Complexity Rubric: The Nuclear Tourist	
Quantitative Measures	
Lexile 1130 **Text Length** 2,248 words	
Qualitative Measures	
Knowledge Demands ① ② ❸ ④ ⑤	The selection tells about the new industry of nuclear tourism; explanation is provided for most of the complex ideas. Students may need support in understanding the effects of the Chernobyl disaster.
Structure ① ② ❸ ④ ⑤	Information in the selection is logically organized, but connections between ideas are not always, completely explicit or in a predictable sequence.
Language Conventionality and Clarity ① ② ❸ ④ ⑤	The selection contains many long, descriptive sentences and scientific language. Language is used for figurative power.
Levels of Meaning/Purpose ① ② ❸ ④ ⑤	The purpose of the article is at least two-fold. First, the writer describes the after-effects of the accident at Chernobyl, providing history and context. Second, the article describes the newly-popular interest in visiting areas of disaster.

DECIDE AND PLAN

English Language Support

Provide English Learners with support for Knowledge Demands and Language as they read the selection.

Knowledge Demands Invite students to listen actively as you share this background information. Tell students that this selection is about a nuclear accident site. Introduce subject-specific vocabulary including *sieverts, radiation,* and *reactor*.

Language Prepare students for the mix of personal narrative and scientific detail in the article. Ask students to describe various field trips or tours of historic places they have taken. As they read, ask students to take note of details in the text which reflect science and history and which details describe the writer's personal experiences.

Strategic Support

Provide students with strategic support to ensure that they can successfully read the text.

Knowledge Demands Use the background information to discuss the Chernobyl disaster. Determine students' prior knowledge of nuclear disasters. Provide additional background if needed.

Language If students have difficulty with complex sentences, work together to break down sentences into smaller chunks in order to understand their meaning. Ask students to highlight words or phrases that they don't understand. As a group, help to define some of the terms they find difficult.

Challenge

Provide students who need to be challenged with ideas for how they can go beyond a simple interpretation of the text.

Text Analysis Ask students to reread paragraphs 5 and 12 about some of the people the author speaks with on his trip. Use these questions to prompt discussion: *Why does the author include these meetings in his story? What impact does it have on the reader?*

Written Response Challenge students to research one of the other nuclear tourist sites the author mentions. Have students write an essay about the site and share their findings in small groups.

TEACH

Read and Respond

Have groups read the selection and complete the Making Meaning, Language Development, and Effective Expression activities.

Standards Support Through Teaching and Learning Cycle

IDENTIFY NEEDS

Analyze results of the Beginning-of-Year Assessment, focusing on the items relating to Unit 6. Also take into consideration student performance to this point and your observations of where particular students struggle.

DECIDE AND PLAN

- If students have performed poorly on items matching these standards, then provide selection scaffolds before assigning them the on-level lesson provided in the Student Edition.
- If students have done well on the Beginning-of-Year Assessment, then challenge them to keep progressing and learning by giving them opportunities to practice the skills in depth.
- Use the Selection Resources listed on the Planning pages for "The Nuclear Tourist" to help students continually improve their ability to master the standards.

Instructional Standards: The Nuclear Tourist

	Catching Up	This Year	Looking Forward
Reading	You may wish to administer the **Analyze Craft and Structure: Literary Nonfiction (RP)** worksheet to better familiarize students with literary nonfiction and travel writing.	**RI.1** Cite strong and thorough textual evidence to support analysis of what the text says explicitly as well as inferences drawn from the text.	Challenge students to make a chart of the different subgenres of literary nonfiction.
Writing	You may wish to administer the **Research: Present Findings (RP)** worksheet to better prepare students for their research.	**W.7** Conduct short as well as more sustained research projects to answer a question (including a self-generated question) or solve a problem; narrow or broaden the inquiry when appropriate; synthesize multiple sources on the subject, demonstrating understanding of the subject under investigation.	Challenge students to come up with a fourth, equally thought-provoking prompt for their research presentations.
Language	Review the **Word Study: The Latin Root *-spec-* (RP)** worksheet to better familiarize students with the root word. You may wish to administer the **Author's Style: Diction (RP)** worksheet to help students better understand how writers use diction.	**L.4.b** Identify and correctly use patterns of word changes that indicate different meanings or parts of speech. **L.3** Apply knowledge of language to understand how language functions in different contexts, to make effective choices for meaning or style, and to comprehend more fully when reading or listening.	Have students locate words in the text that have roots they recognize. Have students discuss informative texts they have read which did not use diction effectively.

ANALYZE AND REVISE

- Analyze student work for evidence of student learning.
- Identify whether or not students have met the expectations in the standards.
- Identify implications for future instruction.

TEACH

Implement the planned lesson, and gather evidence of student learning.

Jump Start

FIRST READ Engage students in a discussion of their knowledge of nuclear reactor meltdowns. Ask students to share what they know about the short-term and long-term effects of an accident such as the one that occurred at Chernobyl in order to set the context for reading "The Nuclear Tourist."

The Nuclear Tourist

What lessons can be learned from disasters at nuclear plants? How can safety measures be made foolproof to avoid another terrible accident? Modeling the questions readers might ask as they read "The Nuclear Tourist" brings the text alive for students and connects it to the Small-Group Performance Task assignment. Selection audio and print capability for the selection are available in the Interactive Teacher's Edition.

Concept Vocabulary

Ask groups to study the three types of context clues and discuss how they can help clarify meaning. Encourage groups to think of one other type that they might encounter in a text. Possibilities include restatement, antonyms, and definitions.

FIRST READ

Have students perform the steps of the first read independently:

NOTICE: Encourage students to notice the author's attitude as he narrates the experience of his journey.

ANNOTATE: Have students mark places where the language evokes a response in them.

CONNECT: Encourage students to make connections to their own experiences or to texts they have read, as well as to accounts of nuclear accidents they have seen or heard in the news.

RESPOND: Students will answer questions and write a summary to demonstrate understanding.

Point out to students that while they will always complete the Respond step at the end of the first read, the other steps will probably happen somewhat concurrently. You may wish to print copies of the **First-Read Guide: Nonfiction** for students to use.

About the Author

George Johnson (b. 1952) is a science writer who writes for the *New York Times, Slate, National Geographic*, and several other publications. Johnson is the author of nine books, three of which were finalists for the Royal Society Winton Prize for Science Books. In 2014, he won the AAAS Kavli Science Journalism Award for three of his articles.

The Nuclear Tourist

Concept Vocabulary

As you perform your first read of "The Nuclear Tourist," you will encounter these words.

macabre　eerily　specter

Context Clues If these words are unfamiliar to you, try using **context clues**—other words and phrases that appear in a text—to help you determine their meanings. There are various types of context clues that you may encounter as you read.

Synonyms: Extreme **valor** in the face of danger earned the firefighters commendations for bravery.

Elaborating Details: Her parents were **ecstatic** about her grades, heaping praise on her for her excellent work.

Contrast of Ideas: The **immaculate** silverware stood out against the filthy tablecloth and uncleaned plates.

Apply your knowledge of context clues and other vocabulary strategies to determine the meanings of unfamiliar words you encounter during your first read.

First Read NONFICTION

Apply these strategies as you conduct your first read. You will have an opportunity to complete a close read after your first read.

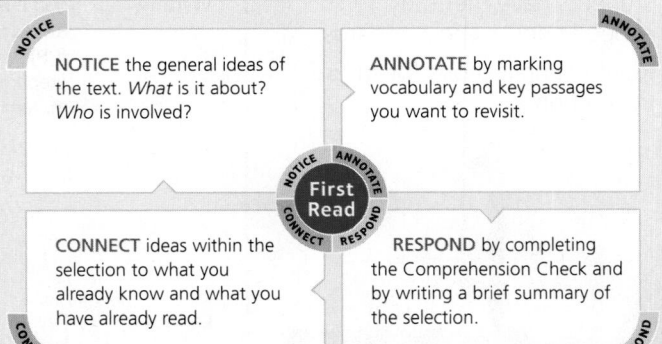

NOTICE the general ideas of the text. *What* is it about? *Who* is involved?

ANNOTATE by marking vocabulary and key passages you want to revisit.

CONNECT ideas within the selection to what you already know and what you have already read.

RESPOND by completing the Comprehension Check and by writing a brief summary of the selection.

STANDARDS

Reading Informational Text
By the end of grade 9, read and comprehend literary nonfiction in the grades 9–10 text complexity band proficiently, with scaffolding as needed at the high end of the range.

Language
Use context as a clue to the meaning of a word or phrase.

AUTHOR'S PERSPECTIVE **Jim Cummins, Ph.D.**

Language Tasks Teachers can reinforce students' grasp of how academic language works by explicitly identifying the functions that language serves in different kinds of texts. Possibilities include *describing, comparing, contrasting, sequencing, choosing, classifying*, and *evaluating*. Teachers can scaffold students' understanding of these language functions by using graphic organizers. Note these examples:

DIGITAL PERSPECTIVES

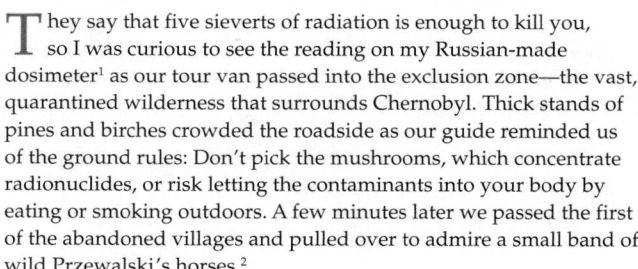

MAGAZINE ARTICLE

The Nuclear Tourist

George Johnson

BACKGROUND

On April 26, 1986, during a routine test, a power surge caused an explosion in one of the reactors at the Chernobyl Nuclear Power Plant in Pripyat, Ukraine. To date, the Chernobyl incident is the worst nuclear power plant disaster in history, exceeding other incidents such as the 1979 Three Mile Island disaster in Pennsylvania. The Chernobyl explosion is one of only two incidents that have been classified as Level 7 events on the International Nuclear Event Scale, the highest possible rating in terms of destruction.

SCAN FOR MULTIMEDIA

NOTES

1 They say that five sieverts of radiation is enough to kill you, so I was curious to see the reading on my Russian-made dosimeter[1] as our tour van passed into the exclusion zone—the vast, quarantined wilderness that surrounds Chernobyl. Thick stands of pines and birches crowded the roadside as our guide reminded us of the ground rules: Don't pick the mushrooms, which concentrate radionuclides, or risk letting the contaminants into your body by eating or smoking outdoors. A few minutes later we passed the first of the abandoned villages and pulled over to admire a small band of wild Przewalski's horses.[2]

1. **dosimeter** (doh SIHM uh tuhr) *n.* device used to measure the total absorbed dose from radiation exposure.
2. **Przewalski's** (shuh VOL skeez) **horses** endangered wild horses native to central Asia.

Language Tasks	Related Key Visuals/ Graphic Organizers
Identifying	Tables
Describing	Diagrams
Comparing	T-charts
Contrasting	Pictures, plans, drawings

These language demands can be applied across the curriculum. Teachers might provide an example for biology ("Compare the structure and function of plant and animal cells") and one for social studies ("Analyze similarities and differences in social values and aspects of life between present-day city-dwellers and those who lived in cities between 1900–1950"). Following this process helps students see what steps they need to take and helps them achieve greater reading success.

Concept Vocabulary

MACABRE If groups are struggling to define the word *macabre*, point out the descriptive phrases in paragraph 4 that surround the word: "suspended by the neck as if with an executioner's noose" and "gas masks hanging from trees." Students should be able to infer from the descriptions of these upsetting images that things are not pleasant or ordinary in the village. The abandoned and unkempt dolls and toys give the reader a feeling of loss and sadness, particularly because these images refer to children who once played there. Students can use their understanding of restatement to recognize that the phrase a "lost, quiet horror" can signify the meaning of *macabre*.

Possible response: *Macabre* must mean "frightening and horrible in an unnatural way."

Additional **English Language Support** is available in the Interactive Teacher's Edition.

NOTES

Mark context clues or indicate another strategy you used that helped you determine meaning.

macabre (muh KAH bruh) *adj.*

MEANING:

2 Twenty-eight years after the explosion of a nuclear reactor at Chernobyl, the zone, all but devoid of people, has been seized and occupied by wildlife. There are bison, boars, moose, wolves, beavers, falcons. In the ghost city of Pripyat, eagles roost atop deserted Soviet-era apartment blocks. The horses—a rare, endangered breed—were let loose here a decade after the accident, when the radiation was considered tolerable, giving them more than a thousand square miles to roam.

3 I glanced at my meter: 0.19 microsieverts per hour—a fraction of a millionth of a single sievert, a measure of radiation exposure. Nothing to worry about yet. The highest levels I had seen so far on my trip to Ukraine were on the transatlantic flight from Chicago—spikes of 3.5 microsieverts per hour as we flew 40,000 feet over Greenland, cosmic rays penetrating the plane and passengers. Scientists studying Chernobyl remain divided over the long-term effects of the radiation on the flora and fauna. So far they have been surprisingly subtle. More threatening to the animals are the poachers, who sneak into the zone with guns.

4 A few minutes later we reached Zalesye, an old farming village, and wandered among empty houses. Broken windows, peeling paint, crumbling plaster. On the floor of one home a discarded picture of Lenin[3]—pointy beard, jutting chin—stared sternly at nothing, and hanging by a cord on a bedroom wall was a child's doll. It had been suspended by the neck as if with an executioner's noose. Outside, another doll sat next to the remains of a broken stroller. These were the first of the **macabre** tributes we saw during our two days in the zone. Dolls sprawling half dressed in cribs, gas masks hanging from trees—tableaux placed by visitors, here legally or otherwise, signifying a lost, quiet horror.

5 Farther down the road we were surprised by an inhabitant. Dressed in a scarf, a red sweater, and a winter vest, Rosalia is one of what officials call the "returnees"—stubborn old people, women mostly, who insist on living out their lives in the place they call home. She seemed happy for the company. Prompted by our guide, she told us of worse hardships. The lands around Chernobyl (or Chornobyl, as it is known in Ukraine) are part of the Pripyat Marshes on the eastern front, where the bloodiest battles of World War II were fought. She remembers the German soldiers and the hardships under Stalin.[4]

6 "You can't see radiation," she said in Ukrainian. Anyway, she added, she is not planning to have children. She lives with five cats. Before we departed, she showed us her vegetable garden and said her biggest problem now is Colorado potato bugs.

3. **Lenin** (LEHN ihn) Vladimir Lenin (1870–1924), leader of the Russian Communist revolution of 1917 and first premier of the Soviet Union.
4. **Stalin** (STAH lihn) Joseph Stalin (1879–1953), leader of the Soviet Union from 1922 to 1953. Under Stalin's rule, the Soviet Union became a world power, but millions of people were imprisoned in labor camps, died from famine, or were executed.

7 There is something deeply rooted in the human soul that draws us to sites of unimaginable disaster. Pompeii, Antietam, Auschwitz, and Treblinka—all **eerily** quiet now. But in the 21st century we hold a special awe for the aftermath of nuclear destruction. The splitting of the atom almost a hundred years ago promised to be the most important human advance since the discovery of fire. Unleashing the forces bound inside atomic nuclei would bring the world nearly limitless energy. Inevitably it was first used in warfare, but after Hiroshima and Nagasaki[5] a grand effort began to provide electricity "too cheap to meter," freeing the world from its dependence on fossil fuels.

8 More than half a century later the swirling symbol of the atom, once the emblem of progress and the triumph of technology, has become a bewitching death's-head, associated in people's minds with destruction and Cold War fear. Every spring visitors head for Stallion Gate in southern New Mexico for an open house at Trinity Site, where the first atomic bomb was detonated—a preview of what was to come when the bombers reached Japan. Monthly tours to the Nevada Test Site in the Mojave Desert, where more than a thousand nuclear weapons were exploded during the Cold War, are booked solid through 2014.

9 Then there is the **specter** of nuclear meltdown. In 2011, Chernobyl, site of the world's worst catastrophe at a nuclear power plant, was officially declared a tourist attraction.

10 Nuclear tourism. Coming around the time of the Fukushima disaster,[6] the idea seems absurd. And that is what drew me, along with the wonder of seeing towns and a whole city—almost 50,000 people lived in Pripyat—that had been abandoned in a rush, left to the devices of nature.

11 Sixty miles away in Kiev, Ukraine's capital city, weeks of bloody demonstrations had led in February to the expulsion of the president and the installation of a new government. In response to the upheaval Russia had occupied Crimea, the peninsula that juts from southern Ukraine into the Black Sea. Russian troops were massing on Ukraine's eastern border. In a crazy way, Chernobyl felt like the safest place to be.

12 The other diehards in the van had come for their own reasons. John, a young man from London, was into "extreme tourism." For his next adventure he had booked a tour of North Korea and was looking into options for bungee jumping from a helicopter. Gavin from Australia and Georg from Vienna were working together on a performance piece about the phenomenon of quarantine. We are used to thinking of sick people quarantined from the general population. Here it was the land itself that was contagious.

13 Of all my fellow travelers, the most striking was Anna, a quiet young woman from Moscow. She was dressed all in black with

5. **Hiroshima** (hee roh shee mah) **and Nagasaki** (nah gah sah kee) Japanese cities upon which the United States dropped nuclear bombs during World War II.

6. **Fukushima** (foo koo shee mah) **disaster** In 2011, a nuclear power plant in Fukushima, Japan, overheated and leaked radiation after a powerful earthquake and tsunami struck the area.

NOTES

Mark context clues or indicate another strategy you used that helped you determine meaning.

eerily (EER uh lee) *adv.*

MEANING:

Mark context clues or indicate another strategy you used that helped you determine meaning.

specter (SPEHK tuhr) *n.*

MEANING:

DIGITAL PERSPECTIVES

Concept Vocabulary

EERILY If groups are struggling to define the word *eerily*, point out the surrounding words in paragraph 7, "quiet" and "unimaginable." Students should be able to infer that the events seem strange. Students can use their knowledge of base words to find the meaning of "eerie" and apply the meaning of the suffix *-ly*.

Possible response: *Eerily* must mean "mysteriously."

SPECTER If groups are struggling to define the word *specter*, point out the contrary ideas in paragraph 9, "world's worst catastrophe" and "a tourist attraction." Students can use their knowledge of the Chernobyl "nuclear meltdown" over twenty-eight years ago to infer the meaning of *specter*.

Possible response: *Specter* must mean "ghost" or "spirit."

PERSONALIZE FOR LEARNING

English Language Support

Idioms Idioms can be confusing to English Language Learners. "The Nuclear Tourist" is full of idiomatic language. Help students understand usage of some of the words and phrases in paragraphs 8–12.

- Explain that the symbol of the atom is described as a "bewitching death's-head" because of its association with the deadly atomic bomb.
- The term "nuclear tourism" is an odd juxtaposition signaling an attraction for visitors that is not the usual happy venue.
- Explain that the "diehards" on the tour are devoted tourists who want to see unusual sites and those who participate in "extreme tourism" are most adventurous. Have students think of more examples of activities that might be described in this manner.

ALL LEVELS

CLOSER LOOK

Analyze Diction

Circulate among groups as students conduct their close read. Suggest that groups close read paragraphs 17–18 of "The Nuclear Tourist." Encourage them to talk about the annotations they mark. If needed, provide the following support.

ANNOTATE: Have students mark details in paragraphs 17–18 that show the author's purposeful use of word choice, or work with small groups to have students participate as you highlight them together.

QUESTION: Guide students to consider what these details might tell them. Ask what a reader can infer from the author's use of specific vocabulary and sentence structure, and accept student responses.

Possible response: The author's journal combines accuracy of description with use of the correct technical terms.

CONCLUDE: Help students to formulate conclusions about the importance of these details in the text. Ask students why the author might have included these details.

Possible response: The author does not "dramatize" events. Instead, it is because of the precision of his journal record that the reader is able to sense the drama, urgency, and terror of the unfolding disaster.

Remind students that **diction** is a writer's or speaker's word choice. When analyzing diction, students should note the type of vocabulary, the vividness of the language, and the appropriateness of the words. Diction is part of a writer's style and may be described in such categories as formal or informal, plain or ornate, abstract or concrete, and ordinary or technical.

NOTES

fur-lined boots, her long dark hair streaked with a flash of magenta. It reminded me of radioactivity. This was her third time at Chernobyl, and she had just signed up for another five-day tour later in the year.

14 "I'm drawn to abandoned places that have fallen apart and decayed," she said. Mostly she loved the silence and the wildlife—this accidental wilderness. On her T-shirt was a picture of a wolf.

15 "'Radioactive Wolves'?" I asked. It was the name of a documentary I'd seen on PBS's *Nature* about Chernobyl. "It's my favorite film," she said.

16 In the early hours of April 26, 1986, during a scheduled shutdown for routine maintenance, the night shift at Chernobyl's reactor number four was left to carry out an important test of the safety systems—one delayed from the day before, when a full, more experienced staff had been on hand.

17 Within 40 seconds a power surge severely overheated the reactor, rupturing some of the fuel assemblies and quickly setting off two explosions. The asphalt roof of the plant began burning, and, much more threatening, so did the graphite blocks that made up the reactor's core. A plume of smoke and radioactive debris rose high into the atmosphere and began bearing north toward Belarus and Scandinavia. Within days the fallout had spread across most of Europe.

18 Throughout the night firefighters and rescue crews confronted the immediate dangers—flames, smoke, burning chunks of graphite. What they couldn't see or feel—until hours or days later when the sickness set in—were the invisible poisons. Isotopes of cesium, iodine, strontium, plutonium.[7] The exposures they received totaled as much as 16 sieverts—not micro or milli but whole sieverts, vastly more radiation than a body can bear. From the high-rises of Pripyat, less than two miles away, Chernobyl workers and their families stood on balconies and watched the glow.

19 In the morning—it was the weekend before May Day[8]—they went about their routines of shopping, Saturday morning classes, picnics in the park. It was not until 36 hours after the accident that the evacuation began. The residents were told to bring enough supplies for three to five days and to leave their pets behind. The implication was that after a quick cleanup they would return home. That didn't happen. Crews of liquidators quickly moved in and began bulldozing buildings and burying topsoil. Packs of dogs were shot on sight. Nearly 200 villages were evacuated.

20 The immediate death toll was surprisingly small. Three workers died during the explosion, and 28 within a year from radiation poisoning. But most of the effects were slow in unfolding. So far, some 6,000 people who were exposed as children to irradiated

7. **Isotopes of cesium, iodine, strontium, plutonium** versions of these elements that are radioactive.
8. **May Day** holiday for laborers and the working class celebrated in the Soviet Union and other countries.

DIGITAL PERSPECTIVES

An abandoned school in the small city of Pripyat. Evacuated on April 27, 1986, the city remains largely untouched to this day.

milk and other food have had thyroid cancer. Based on data from Hiroshima and Nagasaki, the overall mortality rate from cancer may rise by a few percent among the 600,000 workers and residents who received the highest doses, possibly resulting in thousands of premature deaths.

21 After the accident a concrete and steel structure—the sarcophagus—was hastily erected to contain the damaged reactor. As the sarcophagus crumbled and leaked, work began on what has been optimistically named the New Safe Confinement, a 32,000-ton arch, built on tracks so it can be slid into place when fully assembled. Latest estimate: 2017. Meanwhile the cleanup continues. According to plans by the Ukrainian government, the reactors will be dismantled and the site cleared by 2065. Everything about this place seems like science fiction. Will there even be a Ukraine?

22 What I remember most about the hours we spent in Pripyat is the sound and feel of walking on broken glass. Through the dilapidated hospital wards with the empty beds and cribs and the junk-strewn operating rooms. Through the school hallways, treading across mounds of broken-back books. Mounted over the door of an old science class was an educational poster illustrating the spectrum of electromagnetic radiation. Heat to visible light to x-rays and gamma rays—the kind that break molecular bonds and mutate DNA. How abstract that must have seemed to the schoolkids before the evacuation began.

23 In another room gas masks hung from the ceiling and were piled in heaps on the floor. They were probably left there, our guides told us, by "stalkers"—surreptitious visitors who sneak into the zone. At

NOTES

PERSONALIZE FOR LEARNING

Strategic Support

Description Students may require support to make the connection between the dramatic explosion of 1986 and the remains that the writer describes in paragraphs 21–22. Ask students to explore the connotation of the words used to describe the physical remains of the location near the reactor, including "sarcophagus," "science fiction," "dilapidated," "junk-strewn," and "broken-back." If students continue to need support, have them identify surrounding context clues for each of the words, and ask them to think about how those details support the meaning of the word.

CLOSER LOOK

Infer Author's Attitude

Circulate among groups as students conduct their close read. Suggest that groups close read paragraphs 27–28 of "The Nuclear Tourist." Encourage them to talk about the annotations they mark. If needed, provide the following support.

ANNOTATE: Have students mark details in paragraphs 27–28 that show words or phrases that appear to violate common sense and invite danger, or work with small groups to have students participate as you highlight them together.

QUESTION: Guide students to consider what these details might tell them. Ask what a reader can infer from the author's descriptions of events that seem to contradict the serious tone of the text, and accept student responses.

Possible response: The author explains how proximity to the disaster site over time encourages a relaxed and even playful attitude to the deadly danger. The guide and the visitors play a Chernobyl version of dares. The author records but doesn't comment on this surprising behavior—except to make a factual comparison between the levels of radiation that they recorded and the much higher levels that the emergency services faced at the time of the accident.

CONCLUDE: Help students to formulate conclusions about the importance of these details in the text. Ask students why the author might have included these details.

Possible response: These details are a matter of recorded fact in the author's journal. His attitude is neutral—he expresses neither shame nor pride in joining in such behavior. The author records how the guide and visitors exhibited characteristically human attitudes as they joke and play games, faced with real tragedy and the presence of a deadly threat.

Remind students that the **author's attitude** is the bias and opinions that the writer brings to a text. George Johnson's narrative seems to reflect a true journalistic concern for recording his experiences, but he conveys a level of surprise about the group's attitude toward the danger.

NOTES

first they came to scavenge, later for the thrill. They drink from the Pripyat River and swim in Pripyat bay, daring the radiation and the guards to get them. A stalker I met later in Kiev said he'd been to Chernobyl a hundred times. "I imagined the zone to be a vast, burnt-out place—empty, horrible," he told me. Instead he found forests and rivers, all this contaminated beauty.

24 Our tour group walked along the edge of a bone-dry public swimming pool, its high dive and racing clock still intact, and across the rotting floor of a gymnasium. Building after building, all decomposing. We visited the ruins of the Palace of Culture, imagining it alive with music and laughter, and the small amusement park with its big yellow Ferris wheel. Walking up 16 flights of steps—more glass crunching underfoot—we reached the top of one of the highest apartment buildings. The metal handrails had been stripped away for salvage. Jimmied doors opened onto gaping elevator shafts. I kept thinking how unlikely a tour like this would be in the United States. It was refreshing really. We were not even wearing hard hats.

25 From the rooftop we looked out at what had once been grand, landscaped avenues and parks—all overgrown now. Pripyat, once hailed as a model Soviet city, a worker's paradise, is slowly being reabsorbed by the earth.

26 We spent the night in the town of Chernobyl. Eight centuries older than Pripyat, it now has the look of a Cold War military base, the center for the endless containment operation. My hotel room with its stark accommodations was like a set piece in a museum of life in Soviet times. One of the guides later told me that the vintage furnishings were salvaged from Pripyat. I wasn't able to confirm that officially. The radiation levels in my room were no greater than what I've measured back home.

27 By the next morning we were becoming almost cavalier about the exposure risk. Standing beneath the remains of a cooling tower, our guide, hurrying us along, exclaimed, "Oh, over here is a high-radiation spot! Let's go see!" as casually as if she were pointing us toward a new exhibit in a wax museum. She pulled up a board covering the hot spot, and we stooped down holding our meters—they were frantically beeping—in a friendly competition to see who could detect the highest amount. My device read 112 microsieverts per hour—30 times as high as I had measured on the flight. We stayed for only a minute.

28 The hottest spot we measured that day was on the blade of a rusting earthmover that had been used to plow under the radioactive topsoil: 186 microsieverts per hour—too high to linger but nothing compared with what those poor firemen and liquidators got.

29 On the drive back to Kiev our guide tallied up our accumulated count—ten microsieverts during the entire weekend visit.

30 I'd probably receive more than that on the flight back home. ❧

Comprehension Check

Complete the following items after you finish your first read. Review and clarify details with your group.

1. What is the exclusion zone?

2. What are some characteristics that draw tourists to areas like Chernobyl?

3. What elements caused the explosion at Chernobyl in 1986?

4. What is the current condition of the towns of Pripyat and Chernobyl?

5. **Notebook** Confirm your understanding of the text by writing a summary.

RESEARCH

Research to Clarify Choose at least one unfamiliar detail from the text. Briefly research that detail. In what way does the information you learned shed light on an aspect of the article?

Research to Explore This essay may spark your curiosity to learn more. Briefly research a topic that interests you. You may want to share what you discover with your group.

DIGITAL PERSPECTIVES

Comprehension Check

Possible responses:

1. The exclusion zone is a quarantined area around Chernobyl that contains protected plants and wildlife.
2. Tourists are drawn to Chernobyl to experience the chilling results of a nuclear accident and a small slice of what the atomic bomb produced in Hiroshima and Nagasaki.
3. The explosion was caused when a scheduled safety test experienced a power surge and overheated the reactor.
4. At the time the article was written, Pripyat is full of broken glass on the ground, abandoned buildings, and materials from the reactor explosion, while Chernobyl houses simple buildings where the tourists and others can stay.
5. Answers will vary.

Research

Research to Clarify If groups struggle to come up with an unfamiliar detail in the article, you may want to suggest that they focus on one of the following topics: the Ukraine, the effect of radiation on plants and wildlife, Hiroshima, and Nagasaki.

Research to Explore If groups struggle to come up with a research topic, you may want to suggest that they focus on one of the following topics: history of nuclear power accidents, the discovery of nuclear energy, or unusual travel destinations.

PERSONALIZE FOR LEARNING

Challenge

Research Have students research some of the personal stories of survivors of the Chernobyl accident. Students can find information on the Internet about power plant workers who survived the explosion, as well as nearby citizens who witnessed the aftermath. Ask students to identify the emotions of the people both during the time of the accident and as they recall the events many years later. After reading several survivor stories, have students express their opinions on the safety and value of maintaining nuclear power plants around the world.

FACILITATING

Jump Start

CLOSE READ Ask students to consider the following prompt: *What would it be like to visit an abandoned site that was destroyed by a disaster?* As students discuss the prompt in their groups, have them consider whether they would want to visit such a place and, if so, what things they might look for on such a visit.

Close Read the Text

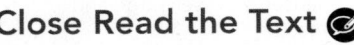

If needed, model close reading by using the Annotation Highlights in the Interactive Teacher's Edition. Remind students to use Accountable Talk in their discussions and to support one another as they complete the close read.

Analyze the Text

Possible responses:

1. **Possible response:** Students may agree that people may be compelled to visit a place like Chernobyl based on a deep-rooted feeling of sorrow, guilt, or regret over the tragedy.
2. **Passages will vary by group.** Remind students to explain why they chose the passages they presented to the group members.
3. **Responses will vary by group.**

Concept Vocabulary

Why These Words? Possible response: The words describe something sinister, deadly, or surreal. Another word is *morbid*.

Practice

Possible responses:

- There was definitely something *macabre* about meeting at the cemetery in the dark.
- The wolf's eyes glowed *eerily* in the darkness.
- The *specter* of suspension kept him from participating in the Senior Prank.

Word Network

Possible words: *contaminants, abandoned*

Word Study

For more support, see **Concept Vocabulary and Word Study.**

Possible responses:

1. *spectrum:* an array organized from greatest to least
2. *inspection:* the act of looking at something carefully; *spectacles:* glasses to help improve sight; *aspect:* appearance to the eye

MAKING MEANING

THE NUCLEAR TOURIST

Close Read the Text

With your group, revisit sections of the text you marked during your first read. **Annotate** details that you notice. What **questions** do you have? What can you **conclude**?

ANNOTATE · QUESTION · Close Read · CONCLUDE

Analyze the Text

CITE TEXTUAL EVIDENCE to support your answers.

Complete the activities.

1. **Review and Clarify** With your group, reread paragraphs 7–10 of the selection. Do you agree or disagree with the author that "There is something deeply rooted in the human soul" that compels people to visit places like Chernobyl? Explain.
2. **Present and Discuss** Now, work with your group to share the passages from the selection that you found especially important. Discuss what you noticed in the selection, the questions you asked, and the conclusions you reached.
3. **Essential Question:** ***Why do we try to imagine the future?*** What has this article taught you about world's end literature? Discuss with your group.

LANGUAGE DEVELOPMENT

Concept Vocabulary

macabre	eerily	specter

Why These Words? The three concept vocabulary words are related. With your group, determine what the words have in common. Write your ideas, and add another word that fits the category.

Practice

Notebook Write a sentence using each of the concept vocabulary words. How did the words make your sentences more vivid? Discuss.

Word Study

Notebook **Latin Root: *-spec-*** In "The Nuclear Tourist," Johnson explains "the specter of nuclear meltdown." The word *specter* contains the Latin root *-spec-*, meaning "to see" or "to look." Work individually to complete the following activities. Then, discuss your responses with your group.

1. Reread paragraph 22 of "The Nuclear Tourist." Identify a word that contains the root *-spec-*. Look the word up in an online dictionary, and write its definition.
2. Find and write definitions for these words that contain the root *-spec-*: *inspection, spectacles, aspect.*

WORD NETWORK

Add interesting words related to the world's end from the text to your Word Network.

STANDARDS

Reading Informational Text
Cite strong and thorough textual evidence to support analysis of what the text says explicitly as well as inferences drawn from the text.

Language
- Identify and correctly use patterns of word changes that indicate different meanings or parts of speech.
- Consult general and specialized reference materials, both print and digital, to find the pronunciation of a word or determine or clarify its precise meaning, its part of speech, or its etymology.

FORMATIVE ASSESSMENT

Analyze the Text

- **If** students struggle to close read the text, **then** provide the worksheet **The Nuclear Tourist: Text Questions,** available online in the Interactive Teacher's Edition or Unit Resources. Answers and DOK levels are also available.

Concept Vocabulary

If students struggle to identify the concept, **then** have them revisit the context in which the words were used in the passage.

Word Study

If students fail to identify the meanings of the words, **then** have them look in a dictionary for the meaning of the root *-spec-*. For Reteach and Practice, see **Word Study: Latin Root *-spec-* (RP).**

Analyze Craft and Structure

Literary Nonfiction In literary nonfiction, authors use traditional fiction-writing techniques to bring true stories and real locations to life for readers. **Travel journalism** is a type of literary nonfiction in which the writer describes what it is like to visit a particular place.

Effective travel journalism captures the reader's interest and gives the reader a vivid impression of a specific location or journey. To accomplish this goal, the writer does the following:

- includes fact-based information about the place. This information can include the place's location, how to get there, and key historical events that happened there.
- adds personal observations about the place, such as what the writer saw, heard, felt, tasted, and smelled. These observations are *subjective*, or based on personal opinion, but they also offer an impression of the place beyond what readers may get from straightforward facts.
- employs literary techniques, such as a story-like sequence of events, figurative language, and dialogue. With these literary techniques, writers set the scene for readers, allowing them to imagine what they might see, hear, or experience as if they had traveled with the writer.

Practice

Work independently to analyze elements of travel journalism in "The Nuclear Tourist." Then, discuss your findings with your group.

FEATURE	EXAMPLES FROM THE ARTICLE	HOW THEY HELP READERS IMAGINE CHERNOBYL
fact-based information	• power surge overheats the reactor • fallout spreads within days	provides details about how the accident occurred
personal observations	• author describes woman who lives in the area • description of operating rooms and abandoned classrooms	provides details about the emotions associated with visiting the site years after the accident
literary techniques	• description of the sound and feel of broken glass • dialogue	evokes emotion and response of reader

TIP

GROUP DISCUSSION
There is no wrong way to think about a particular place, but travel journalism has to be based on real experiences that happened in that location. Members of your group might have different ideas about similar places. Talk out differing opinions, and learn more about why group members feel a certain way about an area.

DIGITAL PERSPECTIVES

Analyze Craft and Structure

Travel Journalism Explain to students that travel journalism is just one form of literary nonfiction. The genre of literary nonficton was pioneered by Truman Capote in 1966 with *In Cold Blood,* the story of four senseless murders in Kansas. Today, literary nonfiction is used in true crime, history, and many other types of books. While individual authors' styles vary widely, the term *literary nonfiction* is generally applied to any work in which the content is factual but the format is more like that of a novel, with quoted dialogue, scenic descriptions, and careful attention to quality writing. For more support, see **Analyze Craft and Structure: Literary Nonfiction.**

Practice

See possible responses in chart on student page.

FORMATIVE ASSESSMENT

Analyze Craft and Structure

If students struggle to determine the characteristics of literary nonfiction, **then** revisit key passages to discuss specific details and personal observations the author includes. For Reteach and Practice, see **Analyze Craft and Structure: Literary Nonfiction (RP)**

PERSONALIZE FOR LEARNING

English Language Support

Distinguishing Fact from Subjective Observation Help students analyze text to differentiate between fact-based writing and personal observation. Display the following sentences.

There is a store that sells local products. It's a charming store with a wide variety of interesting trinkets.

Ask students to identify which of the sentences is based on fact and which one is a subjective observation. Have them justify their answers. **EMERGING**

Have students write two more sentences that could be part of a travel article describing a place they have visited. At least one sentence should be fact-based and one sentence should present a subjective observation. **EXPANDING**

Ask students to write a short paragraph for a travel article describing a place they have visited. The paragraph should include both fact-based information and subjective information. **BRIDGING**

An expanded **English Language Support Lesson** on Travel Journalism is available in the Digital Teacher's Edition.

Author's Style

Help students get a feel for differences in diction. Using the passages on the student page as models, have students write their own examples. Ask students to select a sentence from the text that contains scientific or technical terms and rewrite it without those terms.

Use the questions to guide discussion:

- Are the revised passages more interesting?
- Can they convey the same information?
- Which sentences do they prefer?

For more support, see **Author's Style: Diction.**

Read It

See possible responses in chart on student page.

Write It

Possible response:

1. My meter told me that I had been exposed to 2 microsieverts per hour.
2. Our guide told us that we could be harmed just from picking the mushrooms called the Death Cap, which concentrate amatoxins.

FORMATIVE ASSESSMENT

Author's Style

If students struggle to identify technical vocabulary, **then** show them a video of a weather forecast and point out the specialized language meteorologists use. For Reteach and Practice, see **Author's Style: Diction (RP).**

LANGUAGE DEVELOPMENT

THE NUCLEAR TOURIST

Author's Style

Diction Word choice, or **diction,** is a key element of a writer's style, helping to express his or her voice and purpose. A writer's diction also reflects the topic. For example, articles about history will include diction particular to that study. Likewise, writings about science or technology will include **scientific and technical terms,** or words and phrases with precise scientific or technical meanings. Consider passages A and B, both of which are based on paragraph 3 of the article.

Passage A: *I glanced at my device: The dial had moved past zero—this indicated that I was being exposed to some measure of danger. Nothing to worry about yet.*

Passage B: *I glanced at my meter: 0.19 microsieverts per hour—a fraction of a millionth of a single sievert, a measure of radiation exposure. Nothing to worry about yet.*

Passage A provides information, but it is not specific. The reader does not learn what type of danger the author is in nor how he is measuring it. In contrast, Passage B uses scientific and technical terms, such as *radiation exposure* and *sieverts*, that have precise meanings. These terms communicate specific information in an efficient way.

The use of scientific and technical terms allows writers to quantify critical information and make it exact. However, these terms can be challenging for general readers.

STANDARDS

Language

- Apply knowledge of language to understand how language functions in different contexts, to make effective choices for meaning or style, and to comprehend more fully when reading or listening.
- Acquire and use accurately general academic and domain-specific words and phrases, sufficient for reading, writing, speaking, and listening at the college and career readiness level; demonstrate independence in gathering vocabulary knowledge when considering a word or phrase important to comprehension or expression.

Read It

Work individually. Use this chart to record examples of scientific and technical terms from the selection. Define each term by using context clues and verifying definitions in a dictionary. Then, discuss with your group how each term helps the author communicate precise information in an efficient way.

SCIENTIFIC/TECHNICAL TERM	DEFINITION	HOW IT IMPROVES UNDERSTANDING
sievert	unit for measuring dosage of radiation	helps reader understand author's concern and constant monitoring of radioactivity near the site of the accident
nuclear reactor	a device that generates power through nuclear fission	explains the types of plants that are used as an energy source with a potential for danger
sarcophagus	generally, a stone coffin	descriptive language that creates an image; shows how the reactor was protected

Write It

Notebook Rewrite the sentences so that each includes a scientific or technical term.

1. My device told me that I had been exposed to some radiation.
2. Our guide told us that we could be harmed just from picking mushrooms, which concentrate poisons.

PERSONALIZE FOR LEARNING

English Language Support

Technical Terms and Parts of Speech This magazine article includes technical vocabulary that English Learners may find difficult. Explain to students that knowing the part of speech and how each word functions in a sentence can help them interpret text with unfamiliar vocabulary. Review the definitions of the various parts of speech (noun, verb, adjective), and have students identify which part of speech is represented by the following scientific terms in the text: *nuclear, explosion, quarantine, radiation*. Have students reread to use context clues to help understand the meaning of the terms. Then, ask students to work in pairs to write sentences using these words correctly. **ALL LEVELS**

EFFECTIVE EXPRESSION

Research

"The Nuclear Tourist" touches on the effects of Chernobyl and looks at what it was like to visit the area decades after the disaster. Learn more about Chernobyl by completing the following research assignment.

Assignment

With your group, research the Chernobyl disaster. Focus on finding out about what happened before, during, and after the accident.

Once your research is complete, present your findings in one of the following formats. Remember that scientific and technical terms help clarify important concepts, so consider using those terms to support ideas in your writing.

- ☐ Assume the identity of a journalist stationed in the Soviet Union in 1986. Write a series of three **newspaper reports** that correspond to before, during, and after the accident.
- ☐ Assume the identity of a citizen who lives in Chernobyl in 1986. Write three **journal entries** that describe what life was like before, during, and after the accident.
- ☐ Assume the identity of a local government official who lives in Chernobyl in 1986. Write three **reports** that might have been issued by the government before, during, and after the accident.

Project Plan Before you begin, make a list of the tasks you will need to accomplish to complete your research. Then, assign individual group members to each task. Finally, determine how you will make decisions about what sources you will use, what information and details to include, and how you will present your information.

Finding Sources When researching, consult a variety of reliable and trustworthy sources such as newspapers, peer-reviewed magazine and journal articles, encyclopedias, and books written about the subject. When searching on the Internet, look for articles and studies that list their own sources. Then, verify the credibility of those sources. Use the checklist to determine the quality and usefulness of the sources you find. You should be able to check the "Yes" boxes for all sources you choose to use.

Source Checklist

☐ Yes	☐ No	Does the source have a good reputation?
☐ Yes	☐ No	Does the source avoid bias or a political agenda?
☐ Yes	☐ No	Is the content well-written and clearly designed?
☐ Yes	☐ No	Does the source accurately cite information from other sources?
☐ Yes	☐ No	Does the source address questions you have about the subject, either directly or through textual details?

EVIDENCE LOG

Before moving on to a new selection, go to your Evidence Log and record what you learned from "The Nuclear Tourist."

STANDARDS

Writing

- Conduct short as well as more sustained research projects to answer a question or solve a problem; narrow or broaden the inquiry when appropriate; synthesize multiple sources on the subject, demonstrating understanding of the subject under investigation.
- Gather relevant information from multiple authoritative print and digital sources, using advanced searches effectively; assess the usefulness of each source in answering the research question; integrate information into the text selectively to maintain the flow of ideas, avoiding plagiarism and following a standard format for citation.
- Draw evidence from literary or informational texts to support analysis, reflection, and research.

DIGITAL PERSPECTIVES

Research

Guide students through the steps of researching the topic for the assignment. Remind students to focus on the events that happened before, during, and after the accident at Chernobyl. Encourage students to discuss the three formats for presenting their information. Have students consider the group contributions depending on whether they select **newspaper reports, journal entries,** or the series of government **reports.**

Project Plan Explain to students that when discussing the task with their group, they should each assume a role in the discussion and follow the group rules. Have students assign tasks to individual members based on interest and skills.

Finding Sources Help students find appropriate sources for their research on the Internet or in magazines or books. Have students take notes and write up their research in preparation for presenting their findings in their chosen format. For more support, see **Research: Present Findings.**

Evidence Log Support students in completing their Evidence Log. This paced activity will help prepare them for the Performance-Based Assessment at the end of the unit.

DIGITAL PERSPECTIVES

Illuminating the Text To help students understand the process of using nuclear fission to produce energy, have them search the Internet for science videos on atomic energy. Explain to students how the initial discovery of nuclear energy was directed toward explosives, while using it as a cleaner energy source than fossil fuels was a later idea. Ask students to search for video footage on nuclear power plant operations to understand the safety procedures in place to prevent another accident like the one that happened at Chernobyl.

FORMATIVE ASSESSMENT

Research

If students struggle to find sources for their research, **then** have them conduct an Internet search for "Chernobyl nuclear accident" to find links. For Reteach and Practice, see **Research: Present Findings (RP).**

Selection Test

Administer the "The Nuclear Tourist" Selection Test, which is available in both print and digital formats online in Assessments.

the beginning of the end of the world • The Powwow at the End of the World • A Song on the End of the World

AUDIO SUMMARIES
Audio summaries of these poems are available online in both English and Spanish in the Interactive Teacher's Edition or Unit Resources. Assigning these summaries prior to reading the selections may help students build additional background knowledge and set a context for their first read.

Summary

Lucille Clifton's "the beginning of the end of the world" describes cockroaches coming up kitchen drains before solemnly leaving to parts unknown. The speaker wonders if they are a symptom of the end of the world.

"The Powwow at the End of the World," by Sherman Alexie, presents the argument of a Native American speaker who identifies several events that would have to happen for him to forgive others for their responsibility for damaging the environment. His list includes a gathering of other Native Americans as they celebrate a reunion at the end of the world.

The third poem, "A Song on the End of the World," by Czeslaw Milosz, describes a perfectly normal day as the end of the world. The speaker says that those who expected lightning and thunder would be disappointed by the average events of the last day.

Insight

Clifton and Alexie's poems each present a specific cultural and personal context as it relates to the end of the world. Alexie expresses a desire for a certain apocalypse as a moral event. Milosz' end of the world, meanwhile, is a moment in time like any other, emphasizing that the world's end may be subtle and unexpected.

ESSENTIAL QUESTION:
Why do we try to imagine the future?

Connection to Essential Question

These poems present different perspectives on the Essential Question. Clifton's imagined future suggests that cockroaches, the insects that are expected to live through all kinds of disasters, will hold the warning to humans about the end of the world. Alexie, meanwhile, describes a future of political or national victory and revenge. Milosz imagines the future as a continuation of the present, suggesting the future will not be so different from today.

SMALL-GROUP LEARNING PERFORMANCE TASK
What do stories about the future say about the present?

UNIT PERFORMANCE-BASED ASSESSMENT
Which matters more – the present or the future?

Connection to Performance Tasks

Small-Group Learning Task Clifton's poem suggests that humans may not be paying enough attention and might miss signs of the end of the world. Alexie's poem clearly expresses his resentments about the present, stating that he will only forgive when the end of the world sweeps away the current order. Milosz's poem describes the present and the future together, as something sedate and alive and impossible to imagine ending.

Unit Performance-Based Assessment All three poems rely on the state of the present to make their imagined end-of-world depictions comprehensible or meaningful.

DIGITAL PERSPECTIVES — Audio · Video · Document · Annotation Highlights · EL Highlights · Online Assessment

LESSON RESOURCES

	Making Meaning	Language Development	Effective Expression
Lesson	**First Read** **Close Read** **Analyze the Text** **Analyze Craft and Structure**	**Concept Vocabulary** **Word Study** **Author's Style**	**Speaking and Listening**
Instructional Standards	**RL.10** By the end of grade 9, read and comprehend literature . . . **RL.2** Determine a t heme or central idea of a text . . .	**L.4.b** Identify and correctly use patterns . . . **L.4.c** Consult general and specialized reference materials . . . **RL.5** Analyze how an author's choices . . .	**W.3** Write narratives . . . **SL.2** Integrate multiple sources of information . . . **SL.4** Present information, findings, and supporting evidence . . .
STUDENT RESOURCES			
Available online in the Interactive Student Edition or Unit Resources	Selection Audio First-Read Guide: Poetry Close-Read Guide: Poetry	Word Network	Evidence Log
TEACHER RESOURCES			
Selection Resources Available online in the Interactive Teacher's Edition or Unit Resources	Audio Summaries Annotation Highlights Poetry Collection 1: Text Questions EL Highlights English Language Support Lesson: Suffixes *-ful* and *-less* Analyze Craft and Structure: Theme and Poetic Structure	Concept Vocabulary and Word Study Author's Style: Use of Language	Speaking and Listening: Oral Presentation
Reteach/Practice (RP) Available online in the Interactive Teacher's Edition or Unit Resources	Analyze Craft and Structure: Theme and Poetic Structure (RP)	Word Study: Anglo Saxon Suffixes *-ful* and *-less* (RP) Author's Style: Use of Language (RP)	Speaking and Listening: Oral Presentation (RP)
Assessment Available online in Assessments	Selection Test		
My Resources	A Unit 6 Answer Key is available online and in the Interactive Teacher's Edition.		

Reading Support

Text Complexity Rubric: the beginning of the end of the world • The Powwow at the End of the World • A Song on the End of the World

Quantitative Measures

Lexile: NP **Text Length:** 21 lines; 27 lines; 27 lines; 54 words; 356 words; 195 words

Qualitative Measures	
Knowledge Demands ① ② **❸** ④ ⑤	The poems explore end-of-world themes. While students may not be familiar with the specifics in each poem, the ideas are mostly accessible. Alexie's poem may require some knowledge of Native American themes.
Structure ① **❷** ③ ④ ⑤	The selections are free verse poems.
Language Conventionality and Clarity ① ② **❸** ④ ⑤	The selections contain figurative language and mostly on-level vocabulary. "the beginning of the end of the world" contains unconventional syntax and regional language.
Levels of Meaning/Purpose ① ② **❸** ④ ⑤	The main ideas are mostly accessible, though may be challenging for some due to figurative language. Each poem includes literal and deeper levels of meaning.

DECIDE AND PLAN

English Language Support

Provide English Learners with support for Language and Meaning as they read the selection.

Language Students may struggle to read passages with figurative language. Ask questions to guide students to understand that some of the text in the poems present figurative rather than literal phrases. Students may find it easier to approach Alexie's poem by rewriting the poem with the multiple lines of repetition.

Knowledge Demands Invite students to listen actively as you share background information about the struggle between native people and industrialists who take steps to invade nature.

Strategic Support

Provide students with strategic support to ensure that they can successfully read the text.

Language Remind students that in these poems, they will find metaphors and similes. Discuss the difference — similes use the word *like* or *as* to compare, whereas metaphors do not. Give an example from the poems and ask students to be on the lookout for other such similes or metaphors.

Levels of Meaning / Purpose If students have difficulty understanding the multiple levels of meaning, focus on individual lines. Ask students to first state what they understand. Then ask them to reread the stanza to determine what feelings or ideas are conveyed by the words.

Challenge

Provide students who need to be challenged with ideas for how they can go beyond a simple interpretation of the text.

Text Analysis Ask students to make a list of all the metaphors and similes they find in the poems. Pair students, and have them analyze the figurative language and how it contributes to the overall meaning of each poem.

Written Response Using the similes and metaphors in the poems, ask students to write their own. For example, ask them what other images they could use to convey the end of the world.

TEACH

Read and Respond

Have groups read the selection and complete the Making Meaning, Language Development, and Effective Expression activities.

Standards Support Through Teaching and Learning Cycle

IDENTIFY NEEDS

Analyze results of the Beginning-of-Year Assessment, focusing on the items relating to Unit 6. Also take into consideration student performance to this point and your observations of where particular students struggle.

DECIDE AND PLAN

- If students have performed poorly on items matching these standards, then provide selection scaffolds before assigning them the on-level lesson provided in the Student Edition.
- If students have done well on the Beginning-of-Year Assessment, then challenge them to keep progressing and learning by giving them opportunities to practice the skills in depth.
- Use the Selection Resources listed on the Planning pages for "the beginning of the end of the world," "The Powwow at the End of the World," and "A Song on the End of the World" to help students continually improve their ability to master the standards.

Instructional Standards: the beginning of the end of the world • The Powwow at the End of the World •A Song on the End of the World

	Catching Up	This Year	Looking Forward
Reading	You may wish to administer the **Analyze Craft and Structure: Theme and Poetic Structure (RP)** worksheet to have a clearer understanding of the organization of poetry.	**RL.2** Determine a theme or central idea of a text and analyze in detail its development over the course of the text, including how it emerges and is shaped and refined by specific details; provide an objective summary of the text.	Have students seek out other poems that deal with the same themes, but with different structures than the selections.
Speaking and Listening	You may wish to administer the **Speaking and Listening: Oral Presentation (RP)** worksheet to practice speaking to a group.	**SL.4** Present information, findings, and supporting evidence clearly, concisely, and logically such that listeners can follow the line of reasoning and the organization, development, substance, and style are appropriate to purpose, audience, and task.	Have students create a skit about the world ending.
Language	You may wish to administer the **Author's Style: Use of Language (RP)** worksheet to better familiarize students with the language an author uses.	**RL.5** Analyze how an author's choices concerning how to structure a text, order events within it, and manipulate time create such effects as mystery, tension, or surprise.	Have students search out another poem and identify the author's use of language.

TEACH

Implement the planned lesson, and gather evidence of student learning.

ANALYZE AND REVISE

- Analyze student work for evidence of student learning.
- Identify whether or not students have met the expectations in the standards.
- Identify implications for future instruction.

FACILITATING

Jump Start

FIRST READ Writers, philosophers, and artists have long contemplated the end of the world. Ask students to consider what the last day on earth might be like. Do they think it will happen many years in the future?

Engage students in a discussion about the end of the world to help set the context for reading "the beginning of the end of the world," "The Powwow at the End of the World," and "A Song on the End of the World."

Concept Vocabulary

Encourage groups to discuss the three concept vocabulary words. Have they seen the words in texts before? Do they use any of the words in their speech and writing? Do they recognize any word parts, such as a root word, a prefix, or a suffix?

Ask students to look closely at word parts, the roots and suffixes, and discuss how these types of clues can help clarify meaning. Encourage groups to think of one other type of word part that they might encounter in a word (prefixes).

FIRST READ

As they read, students should perform the steps of the first read:

NOTICE: Encourage students to notice the main ideas expressed in each poem.

ANNOTATE: Remind students to mark words, phrases, lines, or stanzas they would like to revisit in order to enhance comprehension or to increase their aesthetic appreciation.

CONNECT: Encourage students to make connections between the poems and to compare the ways they relate to the idea of "the end of the world."

RESPOND: Students will answer questions to demonstrate understanding.

Point out to students that while they will always complete the Respond step at the end of the first read, the other steps will probably happen somewhat concurrently. You may wish to print copies of the **First-Read Guide: Poetry** for students to use.

MAKING MEANING

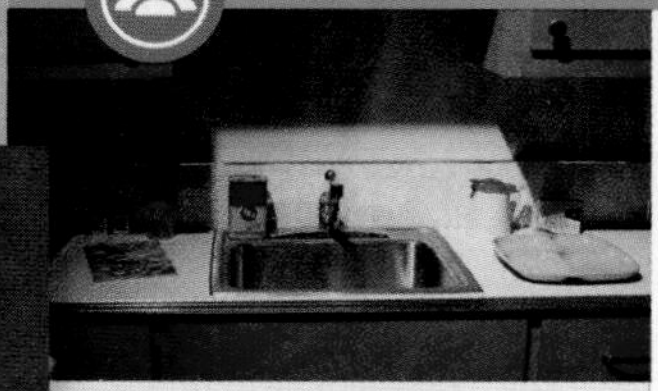

POETRY COLLECTION 1

the beginning of the end of the world
The Powwow at the End of the World
A Song on the End of the World

Concept Vocabulary

As you perform your first read, you will encounter these words.

prayerful **faithless** **prophet**

Base Words If these words are unfamiliar to you, analyze each one to see whether it contains a base word you know. Then, use your knowledge of the "inside" word, along with context, to determine the meaning of the concept word. Here is an example of how to apply the strategy.

Unfamiliar Word in Context: . . . until [the salmon] arrives in the shallows of a secret bay on the **reservation** where I wait alone.

Familiar "Inside" Word: *reserve*, with meanings including "to save for future use."

Conclusion: The speaker is waiting in a secret area, so *reservation* may refer to land that has been set aside for a specific purpose.

Apply your knowledge of base words and other vocabulary strategies to help you determine the meanings of unfamiliar words you encounter during your first read.

First Read POETRY

Apply these strategies as you conduct your first read. You will have an opportunity to complete a close read after your first read.

NOTICE *who* or *what* is "speaking" the poem and whether the poem tells a story or describes a single moment.

ANNOTATE by marking vocabulary and key passages you want to revisit.

CONNECT ideas within the selection to what you already know and what you have already read.

RESPOND by completing the Comprehension Check.

First Read: NOTICE, ANNOTATE, CONNECT, RESPOND

STANDARDS

Reading Literature
By the end of grade 9, read and comprehend literature, including stories, dramas, and poems, in the grades 9–10 text complexity band proficiently, with scaffolding as needed at the high end of the range.

Language
Identify and correctly use patterns of word changes that indicate different meanings or parts of speech.

DIGITAL PERSPECTIVES

About the Poets

Lucille Clifton (1936–2010) grew up in New York State and worked in government agencies until shortly after her first book was published. From there, Clifton authored many critically acclaimed collections of poetry. Her many honors include an Emmy Award, the National Book Award, the Coretta Scott King Award, and the Ruth Lilly Prize for Poetry.

Sherman Alexie (b. 1966) grew up on the Spokane Indian Reservation in Washington State. As a child, Alexie suffered from seizures and spent much of his time in bed reading. After he finished college, his career as a writer took off. Since then, Alexie has won numerous awards for his novels, stories, screenplays, and poems.

Czeslaw Milosz (1911–2004) was born in Lithuania before the revolution brought the Soviets to power in 1918. Milosz spent the World War II years working for underground presses, then came to the United States as an embassy official for the communist Polish government. In 1951, Milosz defected to the United States and began writing books, ultimately receiving the Nobel Prize in 1980.

Backgrounds

the beginning of the end of the world

Cockroaches have been around for 300 million years. They easily outlived the dinosaurs, and time will tell if they will outlast people as well. It is often said that only cockroaches could survive a nuclear war. That may be an exaggeration, but they are resilient creatures—a cockroach can withstand ten times as much radiation as a person can.

The Powwow at the End of the World

The Grand Coulee Dam spans the Columbia River and stands 550 feet tall and over 5,000 feet long. Completed in 1942, the dam was built to provide jobs and generate massive amounts of electricity for the region. However, the dam has been controversial—its creation flooded Native American communities and forced thousands to relocate. Furthermore, the dam has blocked salmon migration and was used to supply energy for the production of the first atomic bombs.

A Song on the End of the World

Warsaw, Poland, was one of many cities devastated by the Nazi regime during World War II. For most of the war, the Nazis occupied the city. Polish Jews were rounded up in ghettos, sent to concentration camps, and executed. In 1944, the Polish Home Army staged an uprising against the Nazis. Civilian casualties were in the hundreds of thousands. The Nazis eventually overcame the uprising and went on to destroy much of the city.

FACILITATING SMALL-GROUP CLOSE READING

CLOSE READ: Poetry As groups perform their close read, circulate and offer support as needed.

- Remind groups that when they read poetry, they should identify the speaker and pay attention to the figurative language.
- If a group is confused about a poem's meaning, suggest that they examine each stanza and discuss what is taking place or being described in each one.
- Challenge group members to discuss the poem's overall meaning to develop an understanding of the theme or message.

POETRY

the beginning of the end of the world

Lucille Clifton

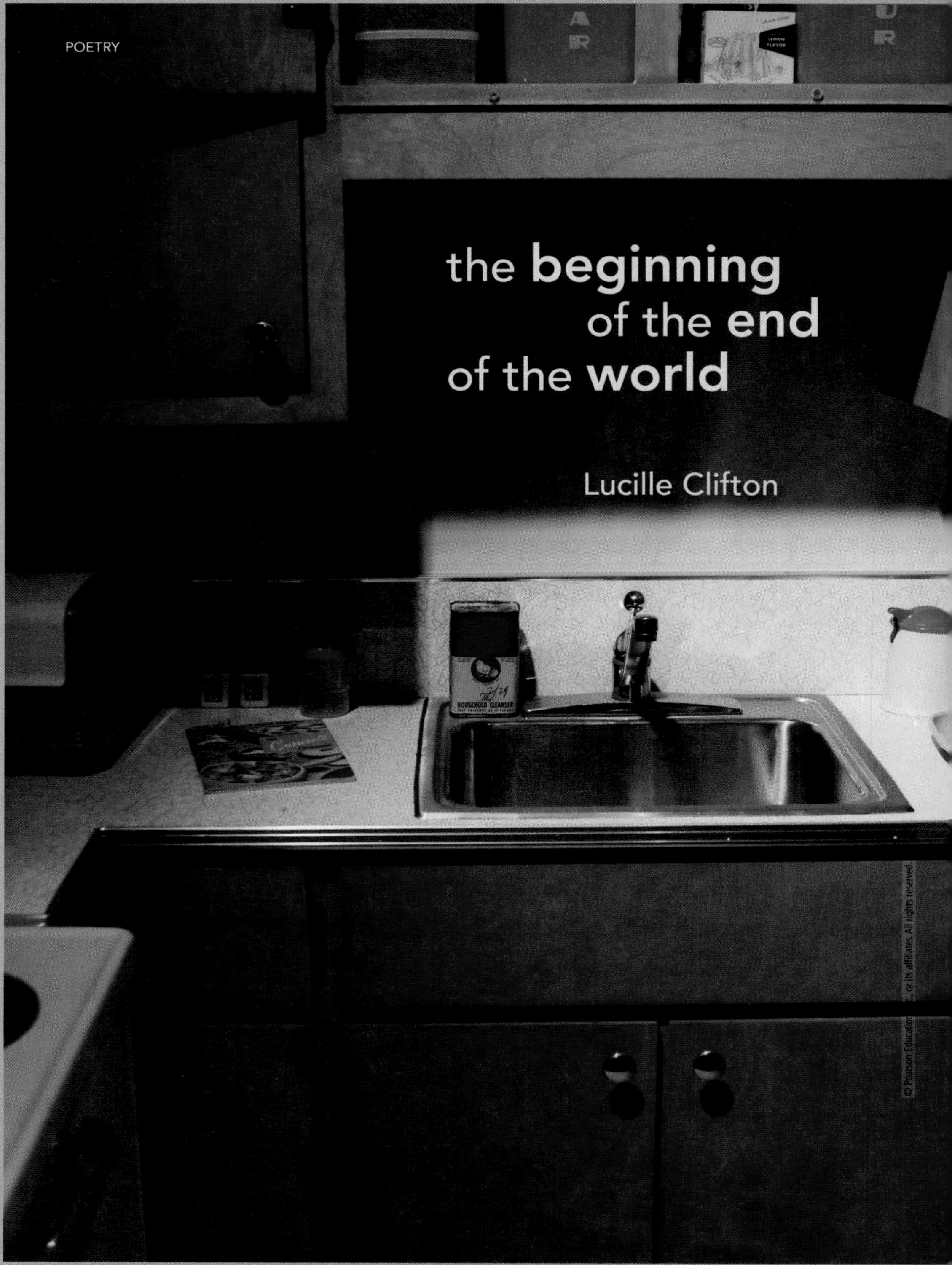

PERSONALIZE FOR LEARNING

Strategic Support

Enjambment Students may require support to read and comprehend the unusual sentence structure of poetry that employs enjambment, or run-on lines. Students will encounter their first example of enjambment in line 1 of Clifton's poem. Remind students that a *run-on line* is one in which the grammatical structure and sense continue past the end of the line. A run-on line ends in the middle of a statement, and readers should go on to the next line without pausing to complete the meaning. The poet's choice to use end-stopped or run-on lines—or a combination of both—affects the poem's rhythm and tone. To assist students in comprehending run-on lines, ask them to rewrite a few of the poem's lines in prose format, removing the line breaks from within the poetry. Have them read the rewritten lines aloud.

SCAN FOR MULTIMEDIA

cockroach population possibly declining
—news report

maybe the morning the roaches
walked into the kitchen
bold with they bad selves
marching up out of the drains
not like soldiers   like priests
grim and patient in the sink
and when we ran the water
trying to drown them as if they were
soldiers   they seemed to bow their
sad heads   for us not at us
and march single file away

maybe then   the morning we rose
from our beds as always
listening for the bang of the end
of the world   maybe then
when we heard only the tiny tapping
and saw them dark and **prayerful**
in the kitchen   maybe then
when we watched them turn from us
faithless at last
and walk in a long line away

NOTES

Mark base words or indicate another strategy you used that helped you determine meaning.

prayerful (PRAIR fuhl) *adj.*

MEANING:

faithless (FAYTH lihs) *adj.*

MEANING:

DIGITAL PERSPECTIVES

Concept Vocabulary

PRAYERFUL If groups are struggling to define the word *prayerful* in line 17, point out that it contains the base word *prayer*, with meanings including "a solemn request for help or expression of thanks addressed to God or an object of worship." Combined with the meaning of the base word, they can use the suffix *–ful*, which means full of or characterized by, to determine the meaning of the word.

Possible response: In this context, *prayerful* is an adjective meaning "full of prayer."

FAITHLESS If groups are struggling to define the word *faithless* in line 20, point out that it contains the base word *faith*, with meanings including "complete trust or confidence in someone or something." Combined with the meaning of the base word, they can use the suffix *–less*, which means "without," to determine the meaning of the word.

Possible response: In this context, *faithless* is an adjective meaning "without faith, or non-believing."

Additional **English Language Support** is available in the Interactive Teacher's Edition.

PERSONALIZE FOR LEARNING

English Language Support

Syntax Lines written in dialect can be confusing to English learners. For example, line 3 of the poem, which states "bold with they bad selves," is written in dialect. To help students understand dialect, explain that it is the form of a language spoken by people in a particular region or group, and that dialects differ from one another in grammar, syntax, vocabulary, and pronunciation.

Tell students that dialect is not the kind of English they are expected to use in formal writing, but that writers often use it to make characters sound more realistic and to create local color in a literary work. In this instance, "bold with they bad selves" is dialect that simply means the roaches were bold and self-confident.

ALL LEVELS

POETRY

The Powwow at the End of the World

Sherman Alexie

SCAN FOR MULTIMEDIA

NOTES

I am told by many of you that I must forgive and so I shall
after an Indian woman puts her shoulder to the Grand Coulee Dam
and topples it. I am told by many of you that I must forgive
and so I shall after the floodwaters burst each successive dam
downriver from the Grand Coulee. I am told by many of you
that I must forgive and so I shall after the floodwaters find
their way to the mouth of the Columbia River as it enters the Pacific
and causes all of it to rise. I am told by many of you that I must forgive
and so I shall after the first drop of floodwater is swallowed by that salmon
waiting in the Pacific. I am told by many of you that I must forgive and so I shall
after that salmon swims upstream, through the mouth of the Columbia
and then past the flooded cities, broken dams and abandoned reactors
of Hanford.* I am told by many of you that I must forgive and so I shall

* **Hanford** nuclear production site in southeastern Washington State where the plutonium for the atomic bomb that ended World War II was made.

DIGITAL PERSPECTIVES

Illuminating the Text Beginning in line 2, the poem includes references to structures students may not know. They may not be familiar with the Grand Coulee Dam on the Columbia River, the Hanford project, or the various Native American reservations in the states of Washington and Oregon which were directly affected by both of these man-made structures. To help them visualize these references in the poem, find and project maps and images of these items. Additionally, have students go online to find information on how both The Grand Coulee Dam and the nuclear activities at the Hanford Site negatively affected Native Americans. Have the students consider how viewing these images and learning this information helps them understand the sentiments expressed in the poem.

after that salmon swims through the mouth of the Spokane River
as it meets the Columbia, then upstream, until it arrives
in the shallows of a secret bay on the reservation where I wait alone.
I am told by many of you that I must forgive and so I shall after
that salmon leaps into the night air above the water, throws
a lightning bolt at the brush near my feet, and starts the fire
which will lead all of the lost Indians home. I am told
by many of you that I must forgive and so I shall
after we Indians have gathered around the fire with that salmon
who has three stories it must tell before sunrise: one story will teach us
how to pray; another story will make us laugh for hours;
the third story will give us reason to dance. I am told by many
of you that I must forgive and so I shall when I am dancing
with my tribe during the powwow at the end of the world.

NOTES

DIGITAL PERSPECTIVES

CLOSER LOOK

Analyze Parallel Structure

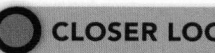

Circulate among groups as students conduct their close read. Suggest that groups close read lines 17 to 27 of *The Powwow at the End of the World.* Encourage them to talk about the annotations they mark. If needed, provide the following support.

ANNOTATE: Have students mark details in the poem where the words repeat, or work with small groups to have students participate as you highlight them together.

QUESTION: Guide students to consider what these details might tell them. Ask what a reader can infer from the way every sentence is introduced with the same sixteen words, and accept student responses.

Possible response: At the start of each sentence the author asserts that he is ready to forgive the building of the Grand Coulee as long as a certain condition is met.

CONCLUDE: Help students to formulate conclusions about the importance of these details in the text. Ask students why the author might have included these details.

Possible response: The author uses parallel structure to emphasize his willingness to forgive. He states it nine times, and the repetition of those words is the structuring principle of the poem. Each time, the words are used to introduce a condition that must be met before forgiveness is possible. Each condition demands in different ways the reinstatement of something that was lost or destroyed. Parallel statement reinforces the impossibility of his demands ever being met—and, in turn, his inability to forgive.

Remind students that **parallel structure** can involve the repeated use of phrases, clauses, or other grammatical elements, or of a particular form of words in a series of sentences. It can be used to emphasize meaning or belief, and as a structuring principle in speeches, poems, or other texts. It can create music and introduce recurring patterns of rhythm, both of which can add to a text's impact.

CLOSER LOOK

Analyze Alliteration

Circulate among groups as students conduct their close read. Suggest that groups close read stanza 2 (lines 7-13) of *A Song on the End of the World.* Encourage them to talk about the annotations they mark. If needed, provide the following support.

ANNOTATE: Have students mark details in stanza 2 that demonstrate deliberate use of language for sound purposes, or work with small groups to have students participate as you highlight them together.

QUESTION: Guide students to consider what these details might tell them. Ask what a reader can infer from the noticeable pattern in some of the words, and accept student responses.

Possible response: The speaker uses alliteration as he describes what's happening around him on the day the world ends. "Women" and "walk" both begin with "w"; "voice" and "violin" both begin with "v"; "lead" and "last" both begin with "l."

CONCLUDE: Help students to formulate conclusions about the importance of these details in the text. Ask students why the author might have included these details.

Possible response: The author included these elements of alliteration to emphasize ordinary words that describe ordinary activities. The language adds musicality to the description of an average day, which may lull the reader into a sense of security despite the poem's topic.

Remind students that **alliteration** is the repetition of initial consonant sounds in nearby syllables, as in "slippery slope" or "weak and weary." Writers, especially poets, use alliteration to emphasize and link words, reinforce meaning, imitate sounds, and create music and rhythm.

Concept Vocabulary

PROPHET If groups are struggling to define the word *prophet* in line 22, point out that it contains the Greek root word *phet*, which means "speak." They can use the prefix *pro-,* which means "advancing or projecting forward," in combination with the root word to determine the meaning of the word.

Possible response: *Prophet* is a noun that means "one who foretells future events."

POETRY

A Song on the End of the World

Czeslaw Milosz

SCAN FOR MULTIMEDIA

NOTES

Mark base words or indicate another strategy you used that helped you determine meaning.

prophet (PROF iht) *n.*

MEANING:

On the day the world ends
A bee circles a clover,
A fisherman mends a glimmering net.
Happy porpoises jump in the sea,
By the rainspout young sparrows are playing
And the snake is gold-skinned as it should always be.

On the day the world ends
Women walk through the fields under their umbrellas,
A drunkard grows sleepy at the edge of a lawn,
Vegetable peddlers shout in the street
And a yellow-sailed boat comes nearer the island,
The voice of a violin lasts in the air
And leads into a starry night.

And those who expected lightning and thunder
Are disappointed.
And those who expected signs and archangels' trumps*
Do not believe it is happening now.
As long as the sun and the moon are above,
As long as the bumblebee visits a rose,
As long as rosy infants are born
No one believes it is happening now.

Only a white-haired old man, who would be a **prophet**
Yet is not a prophet, for he's much too busy,
Repeats while he binds his tomatoes:
There will be no other end of the world,
There will be no other end of the world.

Warsaw, 1944

* **trumps** trumpets.

Comprehension Check

Complete the following items after you finish your first read. Review and clarify details with your group.

1. How does the speaker try to get rid of the roaches in "the beginning of the end of the world"?

2. What causes the Pacific Ocean to rise in "The Powwow at the End of the World"?

3. In "The Powwow at the End of the World," how will each of the three stories the salmon tells affect listeners?

4. In "A Song on the End of the World," why are some people disappointed?

5. **Notebook** Confirm your understanding by writing a brief description of each poem.

RESEARCH

Research to Clarify Choose at least one unfamiliar detail from one of the poems. Briefly research that detail. In what way does the information you learned shed light on an aspect of the poem?

DIGITAL PERSPECTIVES

Comprehension Check

Possible responses:

1. The speaker tries to drown the roaches by running water on them in the sink.
2. Floodwaters from the Columbia River enter the Pacific and cause it to rise.
3. The salmon will tell a story to teach people how to pray, a story to make people laugh, and a story that will give people reason to dance.
4. Some people are disappointed because they expected lightning and thunder at the end of the world.
5. In "the beginning of the end of the world," the unusual behavior of cockroaches might be an important sign to humans. In "The Powwow at the End of the World," the speaker identifies a list of actions that would have to take place for him to be able to forgive. All these actions involve a chain of events which follow the tumbling down of the Grand Coulee Dam, and end with the reunion of Native Americans who celebrate before the end of the world. "A Song on the End of the World" describes an ordinary day as the last day, disappointing those who may have expected lightning and thunder.

Research

Research to Clarify If students have trouble coming up with a detail to research, suggest these options: cockroaches, the Grand Coulee Dam, or Warsaw in 1944. Each of these details play an important part in the poems.

PERSONALIZE FOR LEARNING

Challenge

Poem Invite students to write their own imitative poem about the end of the world modeled on one of the three poems they read. They might choose to focus on a mundane object in life that they encounter every day, such as the roaches in "the beginning of the end of the world." They may choose to focus on a specific idea, such as the concept of holding a grudge and only forgiving someone at the end of days, as in "The Powwow at the End of the World." Finally, they could choose to focus on admiring nature and every day activities, as in "A Song on the End of the World." Encourage students to use figures of speech, such as repetition, simile, alliteration, or dialect, as the poets do. As students share their poems, guide listeners to identify the focus of the poems and the literary devices used by their fellow student writers.

FACILITATING

Jump Start

CLOSE READ *What would you do if it were your last day on Earth?* As groups discuss the prompt, remind them that people have predicted the end of the world for centuries.

Close Read the Text

If needed, model close reading by using the Annotation Highlights in the Interactive Teacher's Edition.

Analyze the Text

1. The speaker must forgive people who have wronged Native Americans; the conditions make forgiveness impossible.
2. Responses will vary by group.
3. Responses will vary by group.

Concept Vocabulary

Why These Words? Possible response: The words can all be used to describe religion.

Practice

1. Responses will vary.
2. Responses will vary.
3. Responses will vary.

Word Network

Possible words: *topples, declining, flooded*

Word Study

For more support, see **Concept Vocabulary and Word Study.**

Possible responses:

1. having faith or belief
2. proud

FORMATIVE ASSESSMENT

Analyze the Text

If students struggle to close read the text, **then** provide the **Poetry Collection 1: Text Questions** available online in the Interactive Teacher's Edition or Unit Resources. Answers and DOK levels are also available.

Concept Vocabulary

If students struggle to identify the concept, **then** have them revisit the context in which the words were used in the poems.

Word Study

If students fail to define the words, **then** provide more practice with these suffixes. For Reteach and Practice, see **Word Study: Anglo-Saxon Suffixes -*ful* and -*less* (RP).**

MAKING MEANING

POETRY COLLECTION 1

Close Read the Text

With your group, revisit sections of the poems you marked during your first read. **Annotate** details that you notice. What **questions** do you have? What can you **conclude**?

Close Read — ANNOTATE · QUESTION · CONCLUDE

TIP

GROUP DISCUSSION
Keep in mind that the members of your group have had diverse experiences. Listen to each other's experiences with an open mind. Use empathy so that you can learn from and relate to one another.

Analyze the Text

CITE TEXTUAL EVIDENCE to support your answers.

Complete the activities.

1. **Review and Clarify** With your group, reread "The Powwow at the End of the World." Who or what must the speaker forgive? Under what conditions will the speaker completely forgive? Explain.
2. **Present and Discuss** Now, work with your group to share the passages from the poems that you found especially important. Discuss what you noticed in the poems, the questions you asked, and the conclusions you reached.
3. **Essential Question:** ***Why do we try to imagine the future?*** What have these poems taught you about world's end literature? Discuss.

LANGUAGE DEVELOPMENT

Concept Vocabulary

prayerful faithless prophet

Why These Words? The three concept vocabulary words are related. With your group, determine what the words have in common. Write your ideas, and add another word that fits the category.

WORD NETWORK
Add interesting words related to the world's end from the texts to your Word Network.

Practice

Notebook Use a dictionary to confirm the definitions of these words. Write a sentence using each word. How did these words improve the clarity and meaning of the sentences you wrote? Discuss with your group.

STANDARDS

Reading Literature
Determine a theme or central idea of a text and analyze in detail its development over the course of the text, including how it emerges and is shaped and refined by specific details; provide an objective summary of the text.

Language
- Identify and correctly use patterns of word changes that indicate different meanings or parts of speech.
- Consult general and specialized reference materials, both print and digital, to find the pronunciation of a word or determine or clarify its precise meaning, its part of speech, or its etymology.

Word Study

Notebook **Anglo-Saxon Suffixes: -*ful* and -*less*** In "the beginning of the end of the world," Clifton uses the words *prayerful* and *faithless*. These two words end in Anglo-Saxon suffixes that have opposite meanings. The suffix -*ful* means "full of" or "having," whereas the suffix -*less* means "without" or "lacking." Many base words can take either suffix, forming a pair of antonyms. Work individually to complete these activities.

1. Using your understanding of these two suffixes, write a definition for the word *faithful*, an antonym of *faithless*.
2. Write a synonym for the word *prideful*. Consult a thesaurus if needed.

PERSONALIZE FOR LEARNING

English Language Support

Using Anglo-Saxon Suffixes –*ful*, –*less* Display the following words: *use, pain, fear, care, joy.* Have students use the suffixes –*ful* and –*less* to convert these nouns into adjectives.

Tell students to pick one adjective with each suffix and write their definition. Ask them to use a dictionary if they need help. **EMERGING**

Have students pick two adjectives with each suffix and use each in a sentence. **EXPANDING**

Have students come up with three more nouns that could be converted to adjectives using the suffixes –*ful*, and –*less*. **BRIDGING**

An expanded **English Language Support Lesson** on the Saxon suffixes –*ful* and –*less* is available in the Interactive Teacher's Edition.

Analyze Craft and Structure

Theme and Poetic Structure A **theme** is a central idea or message about life revealed through a literary work. Sometimes, poets state themes directly. More often, however, messages are implied. When themes are implied, readers make connections among the events, details, and images in order to figure out the poem's larger message.

One literary element that can reinforce a poem's theme is **poetic structure,** the way in which lines and stanzas of the poem are organized. A **stanza** is a group of lines in a poem that is separated from other stanzas by space. Like a paragraph in prose, a stanza often expresses a single main idea. Poems vary widely in structure. They may have short lines, long lines, short stanzas, long stanzas, and so on. These choices support the flow of the poet's ideas and are clues to the theme.

TIP

GROUP DISCUSSION
Discuss each group member's interpretations of the poems. Through this discussion, determine possible themes for each poem. Remember to be respectful of other students' interpretations during discussion.

Practice

CITE TEXTUAL EVIDENCE to support your answers.

Notebook Work with your group to answer the questions.

1. What is the end of the world like in each poem? For example, is it terrible, peaceful, or uneventful? Explain.
2. (a) What message are the cockroaches trying to communicate in Clifton's poem? (b) Do the people understand that message? Explain.
3. Why might Alexie have chosen to use one continuous stanza? What effect does that choice have?
4. Work together to identify elements of each poem that suggest its theme. Capture your notes in the chart. Then, for each poem, propose and discuss possible themes.

	EVENTS	DETAILS/IMAGES	POSSIBLE THEMES
the beginning of the end of the world	Roaches rise from drains	Soldiers, tiny tapping like prayerful priests	The insects know the universe; we should pay attention.
The Powwow at the End of the World	Woman breaks dam, causes flood; salmon saves Native Americans	Floods, abandoned cities, fire, nature, dancing, laughter	Native Americans can regain their power.
A Song on the End of the World	An average day	People doing everyday tasks, flowers, birth; sun, moon	The end will be very average.

DIGITAL PERSPECTIVES

Analyze Craft and Structure

Theme Explain the difference between **theme** and main idea. The main idea is what a story or poem is actually about. The theme, however, is the underlying message the author wants to convey.

Poetic Structure Remind students that authors group related thoughts. In this way, the **stanza** in poetry is similar to the paragraph in prose. The word *stanza* is an Italian word meaning "room." Each room in a house is used for a different purpose, and it is the same with stanzas in poetry. For more support, see **Analyze Craft and Structure: Theme and Poetic Structure.**

Possible responses:

1. "the beginning of the end of the world": unexpected; quiet. "The Powwow at the End of the World": celebratory. "A Song on the End of the World": ordinary; uneventful.
2. (a) The cockroaches try to warn that something has changed. (b) The people do not understand; they did not notice this small change.
3. He might have written in a single stanza to convey all the things that have to happen for him to be able to forgive.
4. See responses in chart on student page.

FORMATIVE ASSESSMENT

Analyze Craft and Structure

If students struggle to identify theme, **then** revisit key passages to discuss the messages they convey. For Reteach and Practice, see **Analyze Craft and Structure: Theme and Poetic Structure (RP).**

PERSONALIZE FOR LEARNING

Strategic Support

Theme Guide students through the literal meaning of each stanza. After this review of each poem in full, ask students to think about what the author might have wanted readers to take away from the poem. Students may need to study some of each author's specific choices.

- What is the importance of the cockroaches, and why do they "bow their sad heads / not for us but at us?"
- Who has told the speaker he must forgive? Will he be able to?
- What is the importance of the reference to Warsaw, 1944, at the end of the last poem?

FACILITATING

Author's Style

Use of Language Explain to students that poets use a limited number of words to convey meaning to readers. As such, each of their stylistic choices is extremely important. These choices have a huge impact on the way in which readers make meaning from the poem. For example, lack of punctuation may signal that the poem is meant to be read as one full thought. Repetition can be used to create a soothing, rhythmic sound or a discordant one. Remind students that each of these choices is purposeful. For more support, see **Author's Style: Use of Language.**

Read It

1. See answers in chart on student page.
2. Responses will vary.

Write It

Possible responses:

Paragraphs will vary, but make sure that students include discussion of rhythmic devices, line breaks, punctuation, and images. As you evaluate student writing, look for attention to details.

LANGUAGE DEVELOPMENT

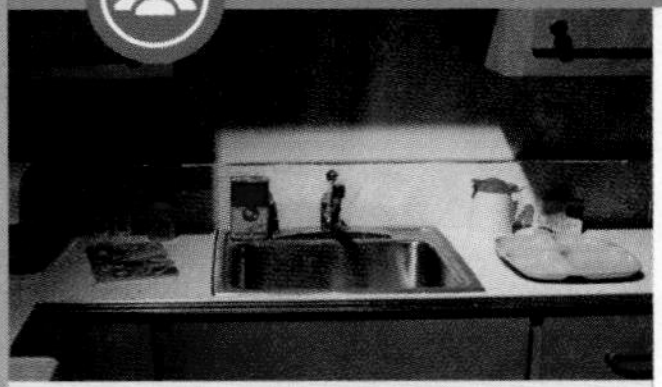

POETRY COLLECTION 1

Author's Style

Use of Language Some poems are organized in set patterns, a quality that is often evident from the way they look. Poetry that follows a defined structure is called formal verse. **Free verse** poems, like those in this collection, are poems that do not follow specific set patterns. While free verse poems may have a looser appearance, they, too, use formal elements, such as sound devices, to build meaning.

Sound devices are uses of language that emphasize the sound relationships among words. Rhyme is one type of sound device, but there are others:

- **Alliteration:** repetition of initial consonant sounds in nearby syllables, particularly stressed syllables (as in ***n**early **n**apping*)
- **Consonance:** repetition of final consonant sounds in stressed syllables that follow different vowel sounds (as in *si**t*** and *ca**t***)
- **Assonance:** repetition of similar vowel sounds in stressed syllables that end with different consonant sounds (as in ***s**ea**l*** and *m**ee**t*)

All sound devices create musical and emotional effects, heighten the sense of unity in a poem, and emphasize meaning.

Read It

1. Work together to identify examples of alliteration, consonance, and assonance in each of the three poems. Use the chart to gather your observations.

POEM	ALLITERATION	CONSONANCE	ASSONANCE
the beginning of the end of the world	maybe /morning bold / bad tiny tapping	Bold /bad Sad heads	grim/sink
The Powwow at the End of the World	floodwaters find salmon swims where I wait lead lost	causes/ rise swims upstream arrives/shallows	**drop/floodwaters** **swallowed/salmon**
A Song on the End of the World	world/women walk voice/violin will/world	world ends sun/moon expected/disappointed	those/long who would

2. Choose one example from each poem, and explain how it emphasizes meaning, creates a sense of unity, or adds a musical effect.

Write It

Notebook Working independently, write three phrases or poetic lines. Use alliteration in one, consonance in the second, and assonance in the third.

STANDARDS

Reading Literature

Analyze how an author's choices concerning how to structure a text, order events within it, and manipulate time create such effects as mystery, tension, or surprise.

FORMATIVE ASSESSMENT

Author's Style

If students are unable to identify rhythmic devices, **then** have them search the text for repeated initial consonants, words, or phrases. For Reteach and Practice, see **Author's Style: Use of Language (RP).**

PERSONALIZE FOR LEARNING

English Language Support

Domain-Specific Vocabulary Support students understanding of literary terms that describe poetry. Review the terms *free verse*, *stanza*, *line break*, and *rhythmic device.* In small groups, encourage students to apply these terms to the poems in this grouping. Encourage them to use any new vocabulary they discovered while reading the poems. **ALL LEVELS**

EFFECTIVE EXPRESSION

Speaking and Listening

The poems in this collection all relate to the idea of the world's end. Explore this idea further by writing and presenting an original literary work.

Assignment

With your group, choose one of the following prompts. Discuss the poem related to your prompt, and refer to your notes about the author's style and the poem's themes. As a group, use your discussion to craft an original literary piece, which you will deliver in an **oral presentation** to the class.

- ☐ In "the beginning of the end of the world," the cockroaches are sad for and eventually become disappointed in the speaker. Write a **poem** from the cockroaches' point of view in which they are able to say in words what they cannot communicate in the poem.
- ☐ In "The Powwow at the End of the World," the speaker says that he or she will forgive when the speaker and all the lost Indians sit around a fire and listen to a salmon tell three stories. Use information from the poem to write and tell the **three stories** that the salmon relates.
- ☐ In "A Song on the End of the World," what might the disappointed people in the third stanza wish to tell the white-haired prophet? Write a **dialogue** between the two parties that addresses the poem's ideas about the expectations and realities of the end of the world.

Project Plan Before you begin, make a list of the tasks you will need to accomplish in order to complete the assignment. Then, assign individual group members to each task. Finally, determine how you will make decisions about what themes you want to convey, what images and word choice to use, and how you will use literary structure to present your ideas.

Revise Before you present, read your writing aloud as a group. Consider your stylistic choices, and make changes as needed in order to emphasize the words, images, and lines that are the most important to convey the meaning of your work. Make sure all group members have a role to play in the presentation.

Present Once your group is satisfied with your work, practice your presentation, and provide constructive feedback. Strive to make the presentation seamless and smooth.

EVIDENCE LOG

Before moving on to a new selection, go to your Evidence Log and record what you learned from "the beginning of the end of the world," "The Powwow at the End of the World," and "A Song on the End of the World."

STANDARDS

Writing

Write narratives to develop real or imagined experiences or events using effective techniques, well-chosen details, and well-structured event sequences.

Speaking and Listening

- Integrate multiple sources of information presented in diverse media or formats evaluating the credibility and accuracy of each source.
- Present information, findings, and supporting evidence clearly, concisely, and logically such that listeners can follow the line of reasoning and the organization, development, substance, and style are appropriate to purpose, audience, and task.

DIGITAL PERSPECTIVES

Speaking and Listening

You may wish to explain to students that understanding point of view is essential for approaching the oral presentation assignment.

- The poems "the beginning of the end of the world" and The "Powwow at the End of the World" are both told from the first-person point of view and use pronouns such as *I* and *we*.
- The poem "A Song on the End of the World" is told from the third-person point of view. Some first-person texts include more intimate information as the speaker may be more directly involved in the action. For this assignment, students will be retelling the poem from the vantage point of another character, but they must also decide on which point of view they plan on using in their own poems.

Project Plan Remind groups to consult the schedule for Small-Group Activities as they create their Project Plan. Check to make sure each group has made assignments and that the work is divided evenly among group members.

Present Remind students that each group member must have a role in the presentation. Group members should practice their parts ahead of time to ensure that each student is intimately familiar with the material. For more support, see **Speaking and Listening: Oral Presentation.**

Evidence Log Support students in completing their Evidence Log. This paced activity will help prepare them for the Performance-Based Assessment at the end of the unit.

FORMATIVE ASSESSMENT

Speaking and Listening

If students are unable to choose the poem upon which to base their presentations, **then** have them consider which poem evoked more feelings or images for them upon the first read. For Reteach and Practice, see **Speaking and Listening: Oral Presentation (RP).**

Selection Test

Administer the "the beginning of the end of the world; The Powwow at the End of the World; A Song on the End of the World" Selection Test, which is available in both print and digital formats online in Assessments.

from Radiolab: War of the Worlds

AUDIO SUMMARIES
Audio summaries of "Radiolab: War of the Worlds." are available online in both English and Spanish in the Interactive Teacher's Edition or Unit Resources. Assigning these summaries prior to listening to the selection may help students build additional background knowledge and set a context for their first review.

Summary

This radio broadcast "Radiolab: War of the Worlds," discusses the famous 1938 broadcast of "War of the Worlds." The hosts explain that there was a panic that followed the broadcast. The radioplay was based on a older story that most people knew, but the producers added some new elements to update it for a 1938 audience. For example, they began with a musical program and interrupted the music to bring the news of an invasion from Mars. 1938 radio audiences were familiar with these types of interruptions because of the approaching war in Europe. These news bulletins made the production sound less like a play. In addition, the production included multiple interruptions, sounds of chaos, interviews with experts live on the scene, and problems with field transmissions. All these details led some people to worry that the Martian attack was real. In their panic, they called the police or ran into the streets. The Radiolab hosts describe later studies of the panic— people reported seeing smoke and Martians. Some thought the country was being invaded by Germany. Later, Orson Welles, the producer, was surprised that the broadcast had caused trouble. He explained that they had meant to provide a holiday offering in the spirit of Halloween.

Insight

This selection includes discussion of the effect of "War of the Worlds" on the public and the context the broadcast occurred in; the broadcast itself mimics a style of news broadcast that is no longer current.

ESSENTIAL QUESTION:
Why do we try to imagine the future?

Connection to Essential Question

This analysis of the famous 1938 broadcast may help students address the Essential Question. By reviewing the impact of a classic science-fiction radio play, the hosts of Radiolab help show the a level of fear in imagining the unknown. Even in 1938, Americans struggled to understand whether there was life beyond our planet.

SMALL-GROUP LEARNING PERFORMANCE TASK
What do stories about the future say about the present?

UNIT PERFORMANCE-BASED ASSESSMENT
Which matters more—the present or the future?

Connection to Performance Tasks

Small-Group Learning Task The War of the World broadcast is an imagined event that, while originally set in 1898 by H.G. Wells, was updated and transformed to fit the style of 1938 when it aired. The Radiolab hosts suggest the the 1938 audiences were more primed for fear because of the events of their world, including news bulletins that began to interrupt programming, and the reality of living with gas masks and potential attacks.

Unit Performance-Based Assessment The question of the future of humanity is a major preoccupation of the War of the Worlds story. The concern it raises is human extinction at the hands of the Martians. Still, the broadcast created anxiety, and listeners seemed to have been more concerned about the immediate present's survivability.

DIGITAL PERSPECTIVES — Audio | Video | Document | Annotation Highlights | EL Highlights | Online Assessment

Media Complexity Rubric: *from* Radiolab: War of the Worlds	
Quantitative Measures	
Format and Length	Radio Broadcast excerpt; approximately 22 minutes
Qualitative Measures	
Knowledge Demands ① ② ③ **4** ⑤	To fully understand the radio broadcast, prior knowledge is needed about the 1930's radio play, "War of the Worlds," as well as historical background information. The excerpt provides this context.
Structure ① ② ③ **4** ⑤	The radio broadcast often includes clips from other interviews and historical bulletins. The broadcast hosts introduce and explain these clips.
Language Conventionality and Clarity ① ② **3** ④ ⑤	The language in the broadcast is conversational, but some of the historical clips may be difficult to understand.
Levels of Meaning/Purpose ① ② **3** ④ ⑤	The tone of the Radiolab is often lighthearted and humorous, but the content is serious. Listeners should evaluate the message of the broadcast to understand its purpose.

LESSON RESOURCES

	Making Meaning	Language Development	Effective Expression
Lesson	**First Review** **Close Review** **Analyze the Media**	**Media Vocabulary**	**Writing to Sources**
Instructional Standards	**L.6** Acquire and use accurately general academic and domain-specific words and phrases . . .	**L.6** Acquire and use accurately general academic and domain-specific words and phrases . . .	**RI.1** Cite strong and thorough textual evidence . . . **RI.2** Determine a central idea of a text . . . **RI.3** Analyze how the author unfolds an analysis . . .
STUDENT RESOURCES			
Available online in the Interactive Student Edition or Unit Resources	Selection Audio First-Review Guide: Audio Close- Review Guide: Audio	Word Network	Evidence Log
TEACHER RESOURCES			
Selection Resources Available online in the Interactive Teacher's Edition or Unit Resources	Audio Summaries Radiolab: War of the Worlds: Media Questions	Media Vocabulary	Writing to Sources: Broadcast Outline
Assessment Available online in Assessments	Selection Test		
My Resources	A Unit 6 Answer Key is available online and in the Interactive Teacher's Edition.		

Jump Start

FIRST REVIEW Ask students to discuss this prompt: *Why do stories and hoaxes spread virally online, no matter how outlandish or untrue they might be?*

from Radiolab: War of the Worlds

Have you ever believed a story only to find out later that it definitely was not true? Modeling the questions readers might ask as they review "Radiolab: War of the Worlds" brings the broadcast alive for students and connects it to the Small-Group Performance Task assignment. Selection audio is available in the Interactive Teacher's Edition.

Media Vocabulary

Encourage groups to discuss the media vocabulary. Have they seen the terms in texts before? Do they use any of them in their speech and writing?

Ask groups to look closely at the four terms to see what they have in common. Students will notice that some of the terms are applicable not only to media, such as radio broadcasts and podcasts, but also to other speaking events.

FIRST REVIEW

Have students perform the steps of the first review independently:

LISTEN: Ask students to track the events the hosts describe to get the main idea of the broadcast.

NOTE: Encourage students to take note of specific segments of the broadcast they wish to revisit during their close review.

CONNECT: Encourage students to make connections between the subject of this broadcast and other similar media stories that have gone "viral" and had a significant cultural impact.

RESPOND: Students will answer questions to demonstrate understanding.

Point out to students that while they will always complete the Respond step at the end of the first read, the other steps will probably happen somewhat concurrently. You may wish to print copies of the **First-Review Guide: Media: Audio** for students to use.

MAKING MEANING

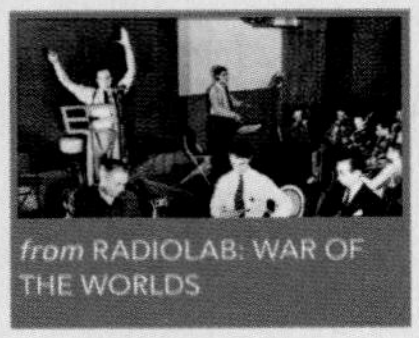

from RADIOLAB: WAR OF THE WORLDS

Comparing Media to Text

In this lesson, you will compare two different takes on the famous "War of the Worlds" radio broadcast of 1938. First, you will complete the first-review and close-review activities for a clip from an episode of the NPR show *Radiolab*.

THE MYTH OF THE *WAR OF THE WORLDS* PANIC

About the Narrators

Jad Abumrad (b. 1973) came up with the idea for *Radiolab* while working for the radio station WNYC. He now cohosts the Peabody Award–winning radio program with **Robert Krulwich**, a television and radio journalist with more than 20 years of experience. Each month, more than four million people tune in to listen to the show, which focuses on the intersections of science, philosophy, and human experience.

from Radiolab: War of the Worlds

Media Vocabulary

The following words or concepts will be useful to you as you analyze, discuss, and write about radio broadcasts.

archival audio: sound recorded from radio broadcasts, television shows, or films of past decades	• For historical documentation, archival audio is considered to be a primary source. • Archival audio is converted to and preserved in digital format.
tone: attitude a speaker takes toward a subject	• Tone can vary from friendly, breezy, gentle, or playful to serious, intense, solemn, or even aggressive.
understatement: downplaying a topic to make it seem less important	• Radio show hosts often use understatement to establish a humorous or ironic tone.
banter: friendly exchange between speakers	• Banter often includes wordplay, jokes, and other witty remarks.

First Review MEDIA: AUDIO

Apply these strategies as you conduct your first review. You will have the opportunity to complete a close review after your first review.

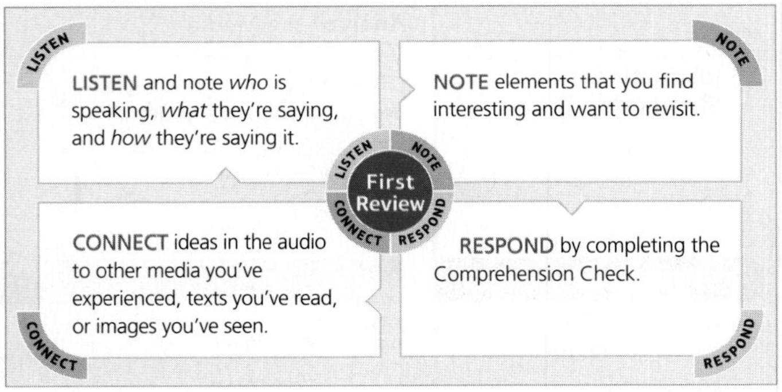

LISTEN
NOTE
CONNECT
RESPOND
LISTEN and note *who* is speaking, *what* they're saying, and *how* they're saying it.
NOTE elements that you find interesting and want to revisit.
First Review
CONNECT ideas in the audio to other media you've experienced, texts you've read, or images you've seen.
RESPOND by completing the Comprehension Check.

STANDARDS

Language

Acquire and use accurately general academic and domain-specific words and phrases, sufficient for reading, writing, speaking, and listening at the college and career readiness level; demonstrate independence in gathering vocabulary knowledge when considering a word or phrase important to comprehension or expression.

FACILITATING SMALL-GROUP CLOSE REVIEWING

CLOSE REVIEW: Radio Broadcast As groups perform the close review, circulate and offer support as needed.

- Remind groups that when they listen to audio, they should actively listen to be sure to identify the subject and main points being discussed.
- If a group is confused about the importance of the topic being discussed in this broadcast, remind them to consider the cultural impact the multiple broadcasts of "War of the Worlds" have had.
- Remind students that broadcasts may often include several different voices. Encourage them to track the various speakers and what perspective they each bring to the work.

from Radiolab: War of the Worlds

NPR

BACKGROUND

In the photo, director Orson Welles is seen rehearsing his broadcast of a radio play based on H. G. Wells's classic novel *The War of the Worlds*. The broadcast aired the night before Halloween in 1938, causing a controversy that remains to this day. Starting in the early 1920s, radio was a major source of news and entertainment for many Americans. Radio offered a full array of programs, including music and variety shows, news and journalism, and plays in every genre. The rise in popularity of television during the 1950s pushed radio to the sidelines, but it remains an important media source today.

SCAN FOR MULTIMEDIA

NOTES

DIGITAL PERSPECTIVES

CLOSER REVIEW

Analyze Cultural Context

Circulate among groups as students conduct their first review. Suggest that groups close review the parts of the broadcast that deal with the original 1938 broadcast. Encourage them to talk about the notes they make. If needed, provide the following support.

NOTE: Have students note the details that provide information on world events at the time of the 1938 broadcast, or work with small groups to have students participate while you note them together.

Possible response: In 1938, CBS journalists used special bulletins to cover Hitler's actions.

QUESTION: Guide students to consider what these details might tell them. Ask students what impact these 1938 current events might have had on the populace and accept student responses.

Possible response: Events in Europe revealed Hitler's plans of conquest. This worried Americans and created a fearful sense of approaching danger.

CONCLUDE: Help students to formulate conclusions about the importance of these details in the broadcast. Ask students why the commentators might have included these details.

Possible response: These details might have been included to provide cultural context for the original radio broadcast so that modern audiences have a better understanding of why radio audiences of 1938 would have been so easily persuaded that the events being described in the original radio broadcast were real.

Remind students that **cultural context** can be relevant to literary works as well as to media events. The cultural context is the economic, social, and historical environment in which a story or media event takes place. It can also apply to the cultural attitudes and ideologies of the period in which the writer lived or in which a literary work or piece of media is presented.

PERSONALIZE FOR LEARNING

English Language Support

Domain-Specific Vocabulary The domain-specific vocabulary associated with "Radiolab: War of the Worlds" may present challenges to English learners. Support them in understanding the text and broadcast by reviewing the following radio terms.

broadcast: the presentation of a radio or television show. *We watched a broadcast of the awards show.* (Note that broadcast can also be a verb synonymous with *aired*.)

aired: released a program or have made it available to the public at a specific time. *This story aired on Tuesday night.*

mass media: methods of distributing information widely to reach millions of people. *Television, radio, and national magazines are examples of mass media.*

Have students locate these terms in the text or make note of them in the audio selection. Then have them use these words as they discuss the selection.

ALL LEVELS

FACILITATING

Jump Start

CLOSE REVIEW Ask students to discuss this prompt in groups: *What would you do if you heard on the radio or TV that Martians had landed on Earth? Would you believe it, or would you wait to see how others reacted?* As student discuss these questions in their groups, have them consider why people in the first part of the twentieth century may have reacted differently.

Comprehension Check

1. The first indication in the 1938 broadcast that something unusual was taking place was the frequent special bulletin interruptions.
2. In the 1938 broadcast, the Martians landed in Grover's Mill, New Jersey, and many listeners panicked.
3. Newspapers of the time reported that the public's response to the 1938 broadcast was that of panic. Some thought the Germans were attacking, and some thought they were going to perish.

Close Review

Remind students to use Accountable Talk in their discussions and to support one another as they complete the close read.

Analyze the Media

Possible responses:

1. Responses will vary by group.
2. Responses will vary by group, but be sure that students discuss the topic of special bulletins.
3. Responses will vary by group.

Media Vocabulary

Possible responses:

1. They use archival audio.
2. They use tone of voice, banter, and questions.

For more support, see **Media Vocabulary**

Word Network

Possible words: *hysteria, crisis, panic, destroy, meteorite, terrifying*

MAKING MEANING

Comprehension Check

Complete the following items after you finish your first listen. Review and clarify details with your group.

1. What is the first indication in the 1938 broadcast that something unusual is taking place?
2. In the 1938 broadcast, where do the Martians land, and what response do Americans have to their landing?
3. **Notebook** According to the *Radiolab* episode, what did newspapers of the time report about the public's response to the 1938 broadcast?

WORD NETWORK

Add interesting words related to the world's end from the broadcast to your Word Network.

Close Review

Listen to the radio broadcast again. What **questions** do you have? What can you **conclude**?

Close Review — REVIEW · QUESTION · CONCLUDE

Analyze the Media

Complete the activities.

1. **Present and Discuss** Now, work with your group to share the segments of the broadcast you found especially important. Discuss the questions you asked and the conclusions you reached.
2. **Review and Synthesize** With your group, listen to the segment that describes the innovation that Edward R. Murrow introduced. How do the audio clips help you understand listeners' responses to the broadcast?
3. **Notebook** **Essential Question:** *Why do we try to imagine the future?* What has this broadcast taught you about world's end literature?

STANDARDS

Language

Acquire and use accurately general academic and domain-specific words and phrases, sufficient for reading, writing, speaking, and listening at the college and career readiness level; demonstrate independence in gathering vocabulary knowledge when considering a word or phrase important to comprehension or expression.

LANGUAGE DEVELOPMENT

Media Vocabulary

understatement | banter | archival audio | tone

Notebook Use these vocabulary words in your responses.

1. What techniques do the hosts use to recreate a listener's experience of Welles's adaptation of H. G. Wells's *The War of the Worlds*?
2. How do the hosts convey their feelings about the broadcast?

FORMATIVE ASSESSMENT

Analyze the Media

If students struggle to close review the broadcast, **then** provide the **Radiolab: War of the Worlds: Media Questions** available online in the Interactive Teacher's Edition or Unit Resources. Answers and DOK levels are also available.

Media Vocabulary

If students fail to identify the effect of tone in a radio broadcast, **then** have them review the definition of tone and revisit excerpts of the broadcast containing archival audio from the original 1938 broadcast to listen to the different tones the announcers, reporters, and experts use.

EFFECTIVE EXPRESSION

Writing to Sources

Assignment

With your group, discuss the central ideas of the clip from the *Radiolab* "War of the Worlds" broadcast, and consider how the hosts convey them to listeners. Then, create a **broadcast outline** in which you trace how the hosts introduce, develop, and support ideas in this section of the show.

Discuss the Broadcast Listen to the entire excerpt again before you hold your discussion. As you discuss the broadcast, keep in mind that it might not follow a linear structure. The hosts might not state central ideas directly, and you may have to infer them from the hosts' conversation and their use of evidence.

Create an Outline After you have discussed the broadcast with your group, use the chart to create an outline of the key ideas, the ways in which the hosts introduce and develop those ideas, and the evidence they use to support them.

RADIOLAB: WAR OF THE WORLDS	
INTRODUCTION:	
KEY IDEA:	The use of news bulletins in the presentation of "War of the Worlds" made the radio play seem realistic.
Introduction	
Development	
Evidence	
KEY IDEA:	
Introduction	
Development	
Evidence	

from RADIOLAB: WAR OF THE WORLDS

EVIDENCE LOG

Before moving on to a new selection, go to your Evidence Log and record what you learned from the *Radiolab* "War of the Worlds" broadcast.

STANDARDS

Reading Informational Text

- Cite strong and thorough textual evidence to support analysis of what the text says explicitly as well as inferences drawn from the text.
- Determine a central idea of a text and analyze its development over the course of the text, including how it emerges and is shaped and refined by specific details; provide an objective summary of the text.
- Analyze how the author unfolds an analysis or series of ideas or events, including the order in which the points are made, how they are introduced and developed, and the connections that are drawn between them.

DIGITAL PERSPECTIVES

Writing to Sources

Discuss the Broadcast Remind students that as with themes in literature, central ideas in audio presentations are not always stated directly. Remind students that the central idea is not the topic of the broadcast; rather, it is the overall message or insight about life that the broadcast conveys.

Create an Outline For more support, see **Writing to Sources: Broadcast Outline.**

Possible responses:

Student responses will vary but should include the idea that the broadcast led to an unusual reaction among the public and the media. Responses should include specific evidence from the broadcast.

Evidence Log Support students in completing their Evidence Log. This paced activity will help prepare them for the Performance-Based Assessment at the end of the unit.

FORMATIVE ASSESSMENT

Writing to Sources

If students are unable to provide specific key ideas and evidence, **then** direct them to consider what elements of the initial broadcast stood out to them.

PERSONALIZE FOR LEARNING

Strategic Support

Using Transcripts and Supporting the Hearing Impaired To help students who are hearing impaired, provide transcripts of the broadcast so that they can follow along with the class. In small group settings, use circular seating arrangements so that the hearing-impaired student can easily see all participants. Finally, encourage group members to take turns speaking, and offer strategies to encourage full participation from all group members.

The Myth of the *War of the Worlds* Panic

AUDIO SUMMARIES
Audio summaries of "The Myth of the *War of the Worlds* Panic" are available online in both English and Spanish in the Interactive Teacher's Edition or Unit Resources. Assigning these summaries prior to reading the selection may help students build additional background knowledge and set a context for their first read.

Summary

In "The Myth of the *War of the Worlds* Panic," Jefferson Pooley and Michael J. Socolow argue that the "War of the Worlds" broadcast caused almost no panic at all. The writers claim that newspapers exaggerated the panic so they could damage the growing popularity of radio news. At the time, newspapers were worried about losing readers to radio. The article includes information about a small number of people listening to the broadcast. The writers discuss a RadioLab broadcast and another current review of the "War of the Worlds" broadcast, arguing that these documentaries miss some important facts, including that the 1938 broadcast was not even aired in certain cities.

Insight

This article explicitly challenges the previous selection, depicting it as biased. This comparison requires the reader to weigh the selections against each other to determine what is most likely to be true.

ESSENTIAL QUESTION:
Why do we try to imagine the future?

Connection to Essential Question

This article presents a different angle on the Essential Question, suggesting the answer might be economic. The writers argue that the *War of the Worlds* broadcast panic was a result of print journalists' fear of radio's dominance in the future.

SMALL-GROUP LEARNING PERFORMANCE TASK
What do stories about the future say about the present?

UNIT PERFORMANCE-BASED ASSESSMENT
Which matters more – the present or the future?

Connection to Performance Tasks

Small-Group Learning Task This article provides interesting background on the performance task prompt. Students may be surprised to hear that a story they might have been familiar with may not be exactly what they thought. They may decide that the message of the panic was mis-reported, and that critical thinking is important in helping analyze what is known about the past, present, and future.

Unit Performance-Based Assessment The article clearly suggests that the decisions of one time period can create inaccurate understandings in a future time period.

DIGITAL PERSPECTIVES — Audio | Video | Document | Annotation Highlights | EL Highlights | Online Assessment

LESSON RESOURCES

	Making Meaning	Language Development	Effective Expression
Lesson	**First Read** **Close Read** **Analyze the Text**	**Concept Vocabulary** **Word Study**	**Writing to Compare**
Instructional Standards	**RI.10** By the end of grade 9, read and comprehend literary nonfiction... **L.4.a** Use context as a clue . . .	**L.4.a** Use context as a clue...	**RI.7** Analyze various accounts of a subject... **W.9.b** Apply grades 9–10 Reading standards... **SL.5** Make strategic use of digital media... **W.1** Write arguments to support claims . . . **W.9** Draw evidence from literary or informational texts . . . **SL.4** Present information, findings, and supporting evidence . . .
STUDENT RESOURCES			
Available online in the Interactive Student Edition or Unit Resources	Selection Audio First-Read Guide: Nonfiction Close-Read Guide: Nonfiction	Word Network	Evidence Log
TEACHER RESOURCES			
Selection Resources Available online in the Interactive Teacher's Edition or Unit Resources	Audio Summaries Annotation Highlights EL Highlights The Myth of *The War of the Worlds* Panic: Text Questions	Concept Vocabulary and Word Study	Writing to Compare: Script
Reteach/Practice (RP) Available online in the Interactive Teacher's Edition or Unit Resources		Word Study: Word Families (RP)	
Assessment Available online in Assessments	Selection Test		
My Resources	A Unit 6 Answer Key is available online and in the Interactive Teacher's Edition.		

Reading Support

Text Complexity Rubric: The Myth of the *War of the Worlds* Panic	
Quantitative Measures	
Lexile: 1280 **Text Length:** 699 words	
Qualitative Measures	
Knowledge Demands ① — ② — ❸ — ④ — ⑤	The selection is a counter-argument to the uproar over the 1930's radio play, the *War of the Worlds* media hoax. Reading this after the RadioLab broadcast will be helpful.
Structure ① — ② — ❸ — ④ — ⑤	Information in the selection is logically organized, but connections between ideas are not always completely explicit or in a predictable sequence.
Language Conventionality and Clarity ① — ② — ❸ — ④ — ⑤	Some sentences in the explanation are complex, with multiple clauses and difficult vocabulary, but the selection also has conversational language.
Levels of Meaning/Purpose ① — ② — ❸ — ④ — ⑤	Selection has only one level of meaning. The main concept and supporting ideas are clearly stated when reading or listening.

DECIDE AND PLAN

English Language Support

Provide English Learners with support for Knowledge Demands and Meaning as they read the selection.

Knowledge Demands Invite students to listen actively while you share background information. Tell students that this selection is a counter-argument about the panic that set in after the broadcast of *The War of the Worlds*. Review the RadioLab broadcast to help set the context.

Levels of Meaning/Purpose Help students to rephrase main ideas by pulling sentences from the reading or by encouraging them to listen again to key phrases. Write the sentences for reference.

Strategic Support

Provide students with strategic support to ensure that they can successfully read the text.

Knowledge Demands Use the background information and the RadioLab broadcast to discuss the original legend of the media hoax. Determine students' prior knowledge and experience with the radio broadcast. Provide additional background as needed.

Levels of Meaning/Purpose As students read, ask them to make notes of the main ideas. If students have trouble finding the main ideas, ask them to find the text that they find challenging and to read those sections carefully, paraphrasing the text.

Challenge

Provide students who need to be challenged with ideas for how they can go beyond a simple interpretation of the text.

Text Analysis Ask students to explain what the selection told them about media reliability. Ask students to use text evidence to support their ideas.

Written Response Challenge students to research another urban legend, for example the Roswell UFO incident. Have students write an essay that presents the arguments regarding the incident. Then ask students to share their essays with the class.

TEACH

Read and Respond

Have groups read the selection and complete the Making Meaning, Language Development, and Effective Expression activities.

Standards Support Through Teaching and Learning Cycle

IDENTIFY NEEDS

Analyze results of the Beginning-of-Year Assessment, focusing on the items relating to Unit 6. Also take into consideration student performance to this point and your observations of where particular students struggle.

DECIDE AND PLAN

- If students have performed poorly on items matching these standards, then provide selection scaffolds before assigning them the on-level lesson provided in the Student Edition.
- If students have done well on the Beginning-of-Year Assessment, then challenge them to keep progressing and learning by giving them opportunities to practice the skills in depth.
- Use the Selection Resources listed on the Planning pages for "The Myth of the *War of the Worlds* Panic" to help students continually improve their ability to master the standards.

Instructional Standards: The Myth of the *War of the Worlds* Panic

	Catching Up	This Year	Looking Forward
Language	You may wish to administer the **Word Study: Word Families (RP)** worksheet to help students understand that many English words are part of a word family derived from a single root word.	**L.4.a** Use context as a clue to the meaning of a word or phrase.	Have students find another base word, and ask them to identify the words that belong to each base's word family.

ANALYZE AND REVISE

- Analyze student work for evidence of student learning.
- Identify whether or not students have met the expectations in the standards.
- Identify implications for future instruction.

TEACH

Implement the planned lesson, and gather evidence of student learning.

FACILITATING

Jump Start

FIRST READ Use this prompt to start discussion in groups: *Have you ever heard a news report that created some form of hysteria?* Invite students to share their stories regarding personal experiences with news reports. Engaging students in a discussion about mass panic and the media sets the context for reading "The Myth of the *War of the Worlds* Panic."

The Myth of the *War of the Worlds* Panic

What happens when the masses panic as a result of news in the media? What kind of impact does this have on society? Modeling the questions readers might ask as they read "The Myth of the *War of the Worlds* Panic" for the first time brings the text alive for students and connects it to the Small-Group Performance Task assignment. Selection audio and print capability for the selection are available in the Interactive Teacher's Edition.

Concept Vocabulary

Ask groups to study the instruction on context clues and discuss how it helps them clarify meaning. Encourage groups to think of other types of context clues they might encounter in a text, such as definitions and connotations.

FIRST READ

Have students perform the steps of the first read independently:

NOTICE: Encourage students to notice significant details that help them understand the subject of the piece.

ANNOTATE: Remind students to mark key passages that support the main idea of the text.

CONNECT: If students cannot make connections to their own lives or other texts, have them consider current or recent news events that might relate to concepts of widespread panic.

RESPOND: Students will answer questions and write a summary to demonstrate understanding.

Point out to students that while they will always complete the Respond step at the end of the first read, the other steps will probably happen somewhat concurrently. You may wish to print copies of the **First-Read Guide: Nonfiction** for students to use.

MAKING MEANING

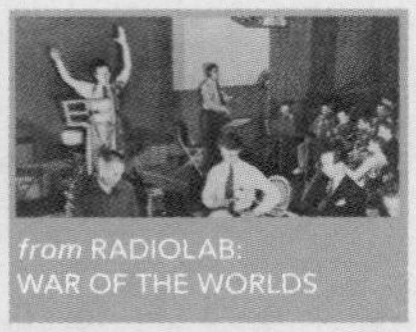
from RADIOLAB: WAR OF THE WORLDS

Comparing Media to Text

So far, you have been presented with one view of the 1938 "War of the Worlds" broadcast. As you read this next selection, you will consider whether there was more to the "War of the Worlds" broadcast than people have been led to believe.

THE MYTH OF THE *WAR OF THE WORLDS* PANIC

About the Authors

Jefferson Pooley (b. 1976) is the chairman of the Media and Communications department at Muhlenberg College in Allentown, Pennsylvania. He has written widely on consumer culture, as well as on the impact of social media on culture.

Michael J. Socolow (b. 1969) is a media historian who specializes in the analysis of the first radio networks that arose in America during the 1920s and 1930s. Socolow is especially interested in how the early radio networks gained control of popular media and what they did with their control once they obtained it.

The Myth of the *War of the Worlds* Panic

Concept Vocabulary

As you perform your first read of the article, you will encounter these words.

sensationalized **apocryphal** **salient**

Context Clues To infer the meaning of unfamiliar words, analyze how they are used within their context. Consider this line from the selection.

So the papers seized the opportunity presented by Welles' program to ***discredit*** *radio as a source of news.*

- The word *discredit* is used as a verb and consists of the prefix *dis-*, meaning "not," plus the root word *credit*, meaning "to acknowledge or praise."
- Since the newspapers were upset that radio had siphoned off ad revenues, it makes sense that *discredit* means "to insult or dishonor."

First Read NONFICTION

Apply these strategies as you conduct your first read. You will have an opportunity to complete a close read after your first read.

NOTICE the general ideas of the text. *What* is it about? *Who* is involved?

ANNOTATE by marking vocabulary and key passages you want to revisit.

CONNECT ideas within the selection to what you already know and what you have already read.

RESPOND by completing the Comprehension Check.

First Read

STANDARDS

Reading Informational Text
By the end of grade 9, read and comprehend literary nonfiction in the grades 9–10 text complexity band proficiently, with scaffolding as needed at the high end of the range.

Language
Use context as a clue to the meaning of a word or phrase.

MAGAZINE ARTICLE

The Myth of the *War of the Worlds* Panic

Jefferson Pooley and Michael J. Socolow

BACKGROUND

H. G. Wells's sensational 1898 novel *The War of the Worlds* was one of the first to depict a Martian invasion of Earth. In 1938, director and actor Orson Welles adapted the novel into a radio play, which was produced to sound like an actual news broadcast instead of a work of fiction. The popular legend is that when the program first aired, many listeners believed a real alien invasion was happening, causing mass panic.

SCAN FOR MULTIMEDIA

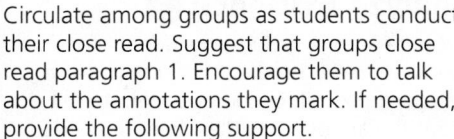

1 How did the story of panicked listeners begin? Blame America's newspapers. Radio had siphoned off advertising revenue from print during the Depression,[1] badly damaging the newspaper industry. So the papers seized the opportunity presented by Welles' program to discredit radio as a source of news. The newspaper industry **sensationalized** the panic to prove to advertisers, and regulators, that radio management was irresponsible and not to be trusted. In an editorial titled "Terror by Radio," the *New York Times*

1. **the Depression** period of economic downturn in the United States that lasted from 1929 through the 1930s.

NOTES

Mark context clues or indicate another strategy you used that helped you determine meaning.

sensationalized (sehn SAY shuh nuh lyzd) *v.*

MEANING:

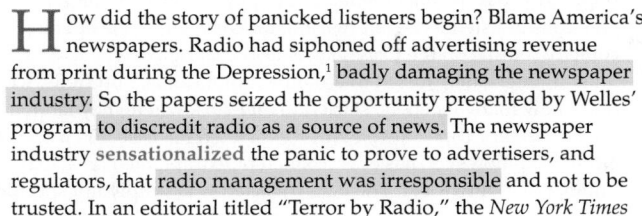

FACILITATING SMALL-GROUP LEARNING

CLOSE READ: Argument As groups perform the close read, circulate and offer support as needed.

- Remind groups that when they read an argument, they should identify the claim and how the claim is supported.
- If a group is confused about the author's claim, point out that the claim is not always in the first paragraph of a text.
- Challenge groups to find all the types of evidence the author uses (facts, statistics, anecdotes, quotations from authorities, or examples).

DIGITAL PERSPECTIVES

Concept Vocabulary

SENSATIONALIZED If groups are struggling to define the word *sensationalized* in paragraph 1, point out that many of the surrounding words and phrases provide context to help show the use of the word. For instance, the sentence tells readers that the newspaper industry was trying to prove that radio management was irresponsible.

Possible response: *Sensationalized* means "presented information in a way that creates excitement."

CLOSER LOOK

Infer Author's Purpose

Circulate among groups as students conduct their close read. Suggest that groups close read paragraph 1. Encourage them to talk about the annotations they mark. If needed, provide the following support.

ANNOTATE: Have students mark details in paragraph 1 that include negative language, or work with small groups to have students participate as you highlight them together.

QUESTION: Guide students to consider what these details might tell them. Ask what a reader can infer from the language the author uses, and accept student responses.

Possible response: The authors use language that shows they think newspapers distorted news about the *War of the Worlds* panic.

CONCLUDE: Help students to formulate conclusions about the importance of these details in the text. Ask students why the author might have included these details.

Possible response: The authors show their purpose by using words and phrases that are powerfully negative to try to persuade readers that the newspaper industry was attacking radio.

Remind students that the language an author uses can help reveal an **author's purpose,** his or her main reason for writing. An author may want to entertain, inform, or persuade the reader. Sometimes an author is trying to teach a moral lesson or reflect on an experience.

FACILITATING

Concept Vocabulary

APOCRYPHAL If groups are struggling to define the word *apocryphal* in paragraph 3, point out that many of the surrounding words and phrases provide context to help students understand the use of the word. For instance, the words "curious" and "phenomenon" can help students understand the meaning of *apocryphal*.

Possible response: *Apocryphal* means "of doubtful authenticity or reality."

CLOSER LOOK

Analyze Evidence

Circulate among groups as students conduct their close read. Suggest that groups close read paragraph 4. Encourage them to talk about the annotations they mark. If needed, provide the following support.

ANNOTATE: Have students mark details in paragraph 4 that provide evidence to support the claim that few people were watching, or work with small groups to have students participate as you highlight them together.

QUESTION: Guide students to consider what these details might tell them. Ask what a reader can infer from the author's language, and accept student responses.

Possible response: The author provides precise statistical support for his assertion that very few people actually listened to the radio broadcast.

CONCLUDE: Help students to formulate conclusions about the importance of these details in the text. Ask students why the author might have included these details.

Possible response: The author included these details to persuade the reader that only a tiny number of people actually heard the broadcast—fewer by far than claims after the event would suggest.

Remind students that **evidence** is an important element of argumentative writing. Authors must provide reasons, facts, and details to support their ideas. This paragraph includes statistics to help support the writer's claim that the panic did not actually happen.

NOTES

reproached "radio officials" for approving the interweaving of "blood-curdling fiction" with news flashes "offered in exactly the manner that real news would have been given." Warned *Editor and Publisher*, the newspaper industry's trade journal, "The nation as a whole continues to face the danger of incomplete, misunderstood news over a medium which has yet to prove . . . that it is competent to perform the news job."

2 The contrast between how newspaper journalists experienced the supposed panic, and what they reported, could be stark. In 1954, Ben Gross, the *New York Daily News'* radio editor, published a memoir in which he recalled the streets of Manhattan being deserted as his taxi sped to CBS headquarters just as *War of the Worlds* was ending. Yet that observation failed to stop the *Daily News* from splashing the panic story across the cover a few hours later.

Mark context clues or indicate another strategy you used that helped you determine meaning.

apocryphal
(uh POK ruh fuhl) *adj.*
MEANING:

3 From these initial newspaper items on Oct. 31, 1938, the **apocryphal** apocalypse only grew in the retelling. A curious (but predictable) phenomenon occurred: As the show receded in time and became more infamous, more and more people claimed to have heard it. As weeks, months, and years passed, the audience's size swelled to such an extent that you might actually believe most of America was tuned to CBS that night. But that was hardly the case.

4 Far fewer people heard the broadcast—and fewer still panicked—than most people believe today. How do we know? The night the program aired, the C. E. Hooper ratings service telephoned 5,000 households for its national ratings survey. "To what program are you listening?" the service asked respondents. Only 2 percent answered a radio "play" or "the Orson Welles program," or something similar indicating CBS. None said a "news broadcast," according to a summary published in *Broadcasting*. In other words, 98 percent of those surveyed were listening to something else, or nothing at all, on Oct. 30, 1938. This miniscule rating is not surprising. Welles' program was scheduled against one of the most popular national programs at the time—ventriloquist Edgar Bergen's *Chase and Sanborn Hour*, a comedy-variety show.

5 The new PBS documentary allows that, "of the tens of millions of Americans listening to their radios that Sunday evening, few were tuned to the *War of the Worlds*" when it began, due to Bergen's popularity. But the documentary's script goes on to claim that "millions of listeners began twirling the dial" when the opening comedy routine on the *Chase and Sanborn Hour* gave way to a musical interlude. "Just at that moment thousands, hundreds, we don't how many listeners, started to dial-surf, where they landed on the *Mercury Theatre on the Air*,"[2] explained *Radiolab* this weekend. No scholar, however, has ever isolated or extrapolated an actual number of dial twirlers. The data collected was simply not specific

2. ***Mercury Theatre on the Air*** weekly radio show created by Orson Welles that broadcast the "War of the Worlds" radio play.

PERSONALIZE FOR LEARNING

English Language Support

Abbreviations Abbreviations can be confusing to English language learners. For example, in the article, the author uses CBS in paragraphs 2 and 3. He references PBS in paragraph 5. Explain to students that when they encounter abbreviations that they do not recognize, they can use context clues to help determine their meaning.

Guide students through a questioning strategy to understand that the abbreviations represent news stations. For example, PBS presented a documentary, whereas CBS was covering footage. **ALL LEVELS**

enough for us to know how many listeners might have switched over to Welles—just as we can't estimate how many people turned their radios off, or switched from *Mercury Theatre on the Air* over to NBC's *Chase and Sanborn Hour* either. (*Radiolab* played the *Chase and Sanborn Hour's* musical interlude for its audience, as if the song itself constituted evidence that people of course switched to Welles' broadcast.)

6 Both *American Experience* and *Radiolab* also omit the **salient** fact that several important CBS affiliates (including Boston's WEEI) pre-empted Welles' broadcast in favor of local commercial programming, further shrinking its audience. CBS commissioned a nationwide survey the day after the broadcast, and network executives were relieved to discover just how few people actually tuned in. "In the first place, most people didn't hear it," CBS's Frank Stanton recalled later. "But those who did hear it, looked at it as a prank and accepted it that way." ❧

NOTES

Mark context clues or indicate another strategy you used that helped you determine meaning.

salient (SAY lee uhnt) *adj.*

MEANING:

DIGITAL PERSPECTIVES

Concept Vocabulary

SALIENT If groups are struggling to define the word *salient* in paragraph 6, point out that many of the surrounding words and phrases provide context to help understand the use of the word. For instance, the phrase "several important CBS affiliates" can help students come to the meaning of the word.

Possible response: *Salient* means "critical," or "very important."

PERSONALIZE FOR LEARNING

Strategic Support

Unfamiliar Words For students to understand the point the writer makes in paragraph 6, they will need to know the word *pre-empted.* Have students find the word in a dictionary, and then discuss their own experiences with programs being pre-empted. Ask students what other things, besides a broadcast, can be "pre-empted."

FACILITATING

Comprehension Check

Possible responses:

1. Of 5000 homes surveyed, only 2% reported listening to the program.
2. The authors say the newspaper industry was to blame for sensationalizing the panic.
3. There is no specific data ever collected to account for how many dial-turners there were.
4. Some affiliates pre-empted the program in favor of local commercial programming.

Research

Research to Clarify If groups struggle to come up with an unfamiliar detail, you may suggest they research ratings services, *Mercury Theatre on the Air,* or the *Chase and Sanborn Radio Hour.*

Research to Explore If groups struggle to formulate an effective research question, you may want to suggest that they focus on one of the following topics: mass media, widespread panic stories, or Orson Welles.

Comprehension Check

Complete the following items after you finish your first read. Review and clarify details with your group.

1. According to the authors, what was the size of the audience that listened to the "War of the Worlds" broadcast?

2. According to these authors, the "panic" that took place on the night of the broadcast was greatly exaggerated. Whom do the authors blame for this exaggeration?

3. According to the authors, why is it inaccurate to assume there were a large number of "dial-turners" the night of the incident?

4. What action by some CBS affiliates further reduced the size of Welles's audience that night?

RESEARCH

Research to Clarify Choose at least one unfamiliar detail from the text. Briefly research that detail. In what way does the information you learned shed light on an aspect of the article?

Research to Explore Choose something from the text that interests you, and formulate a research question.

PERSONALIZE FOR LEARNING

Challenge

Relating to Personal Experience Ask students to think about how people respond to widespread panic caused by mass media. Have them identify examples of recent news stories that caused some kind of panic. Discuss how these events were handled by the media, how they impacted audiences, and how people responded to them. Invite students to discuss what role social media plays in the spread of information and panic.

MAKING MEANING

Close Read the Text

With your group, revisit sections of the text you marked during your first read. **Annotate** details that you notice. What **questions** do you have? What can you **conclude**?

Close Read (ANNOTATE, QUESTION, CONCLUDE)

Analyze the Text

CITE TEXTUAL EVIDENCE to support your answers.

Complete the activities.

1. **Review and Clarify** With your group, reread paragraphs 4 and 6 of the selection. What important pieces of evidence do the authors include to support their claim that the audience for Welles's radio play was much smaller than people believe?
2. **Present and Discuss** Now, work with your group to share the passages from the text that you found especially important. Take turns presenting your passages. Discuss what you noticed in the text, the questions you asked, and the conclusions you reached.
3. **Essential Question:** *Why do we try to imagine the future?* What has this article taught you about world's end literature? Discuss with your group.

LANGUAGE DEVELOPMENT

Concept Vocabulary

sensationalized   salient   apocryphal

Why These Words? The three concept vocabulary words are related. With your group, determine what the words have in common. Write your ideas, and add another word that fits the category.

Practice

Notebook Confirm your understanding of these words by using each one in a sentence. Be sure to include context clues that hint at each word's meaning.

Word Study

Notebook **Word Families** Many English words are part of a word family, or a group of words derived from a single base word. The word *sensationalized*, for example, belongs to the family of words derived from *sense*. The word *sense* usually refers to sight, hearing, smell, taste, or touch, but it can also suggest "good judgment" or "meaning that is conveyed." Use your understanding of the word *sense* to determine a definition for the following words: *sensation, sensationally, nonsense*. Then, use a dictionary to check your definitions.

THE MYTH OF THE *WAR OF THE WORLDS* PANIC

TIP

GROUP DISCUSSION
Keep in mind that finding the truth in a controversy such as this one can be challenging. Be sure to consider the significance of the data and the historical context the authors offer as you discuss the article.

WORD NETWORK
Add interesting words related to the world's end from the text to your Word Network.

DIGITAL PERSPECTIVES

Jump Start

CLOSE READ Ask students to consider the following prompt: *How would you respond to a news report or broadcast that pledged the end of the world was looming?* As students discuss the prompt in their groups, have them consider what character traits people would need, depending on their response to the news.

Close Read the Text

If needed, model close reading by using the Annotation Highlights in the Interactive Teacher's Edition.

Remind students to use Accountable Talk in their discussions and to support one another as they complete the close read.

Analyze the Text

Possible responses

1. The authors present statistics to show data as to how many people were tuned into the program that night. This data serves as important evidence.
2. Passages will vary by group.
3. Responses will vary by group.

Concept Vocabulary

Why These Words? Possible response: The words can all be used to describe the credibility of the events in the text.

Practice

Possible responses

- The movie *sensationalized* the breakup of the rock star's marriage.
- The report *skewed* the data so that it was closer to the results that the science team hoped to find.
- The story about the woman's dog saving a fully grown bear was *apocryphal*.

Word Network

Possible words: *panicked, blood-curdling, apocalypse*

Word Study

For more support, see **Concept Vocabulary and Word Study**

Possible responses
sensation – a feeling
sensationally – extremely exciting or arousing
nonsense – having no meaning; ridiculous

FORMATIVE ASSESSMENT

Analyze the Text

If students struggle to close read the text, then provide the **The Myth of The *War of the Worlds* Panic: Text Questions** available online in the Interactive Teacher's Edition or Unit Resources. Answers and DOK levels are also available.

Concept Vocabulary

If students struggle to identify the concept, **then** have them revisit the context in which the words were used in the article.

Word Study

If students fail to properly define the words, **then** have them identify more word families.

For Reteach and Practice, see **Word Study: Word Families (RP).**

FACILITATING

Writing to Compare

As students prepare to compare two accounts of *The War of the Worlds,* they will consider the two different ways that the reporters explain what happened when the radio broadcast was first presented. Groups will study the prompt and then develop an audio production to evaluate the accounts.

Analyze the Texts

See responses on chart on student page.

1. (a) The radio show includes actual broadcasts to show what the public was hearing at the same time that this broadcast was aired. It included quotations from people who panicked. (b) The article includes information about the experience of newspaper journalists.
2. The broadcast can present sound bites; the article cannot.
3. Responses will vary.

EFFECTIVE EXPRESSION

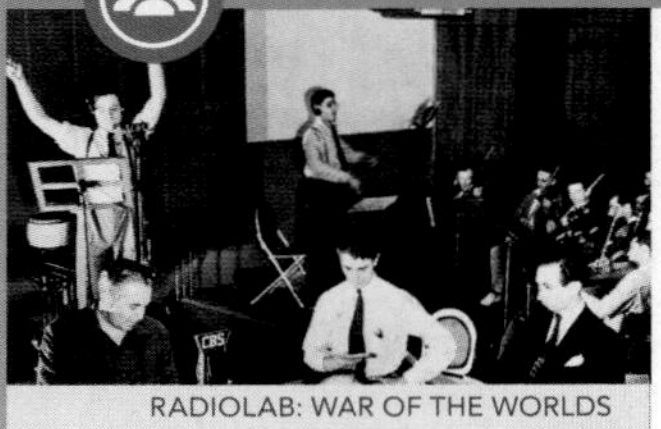

RADIOLAB: WAR OF THE WORLDS

THE MYTH OF THE *WAR OF THE WORLDS* PANIC

Writing to Compare

You have studied two accounts of Orson Welles's radio play based on H. G. Wells's *The War of the Worlds*. Now, analyze the selections, and consider how the medium of each one shapes its message.

Assignment

Both accounts of the 1938 radio broadcast offer a **claim**, or main idea, supported by **evidence**, or supporting details. Compare and contrast the claims and evidence in each. Then, create a **script** for an audio production that answers the following question: Did the 1938 radio broadcast cause mass hysteria? Choose from the following options:

- ☐ a radio essay
- ☐ a radio play
- ☐ a podcast

Include details from both the *Radiolab* episode and the magazine article in your production. You may deliver your production live or, if possible, record and post it for your class.

Analyze the Texts

Compare the Broadcast and Article With your group, consider how the *Radiolab* episode and the magazine article convey information. Use the chart to identify a claim each selection makes. Then, analyze the types of evidence used to support the claim.

ACCOUNT	CLAIM	TYPES OF EVIDENCE / HOW THEY SUPPORT CLAIM
Radiolab: War of the Worlds	The time period was ripe for fear.	News interruptions had just begun; people adjusting to this. (Facts) People in England had been hearing about gas masks. (Example)
The Myth of the *War of the Worlds* Panic	Newspaper created story of panic.	Actually few listeners. (Statistics) Story gained momentum over time. (Facts)

STANDARDS

Reading Informational Text
Analyze various accounts of a subject told in different mediums, determining which details are emphasized in each account.

Writing
Apply *grades 9–10 Reading standards* to literary nonfiction.

Speaking and Listening
Make strategic use of digital media in presentations to enhance understanding of findings, reasoning, and evidence and to add interest.

Notebook Respond to these questions.

1. **(a)** What types of evidence does the radio broadcast include that the magazine article does not? **(b)** What types of evidence does the magazine article include that the radio broadcast does not?
2. In what ways does the medium of each selection affect the types of evidence it uses?
3. Does one account do a better job than the other of supporting its claim? Explain.

PERSONALIZE FOR LEARNING

Strategic Support

Comparison Group members may have difficulty seeing how the sources work together to convey more information about the events of the Martian's invasion. To help them learn more about how the sources work together, have students stop to discuss the claims and evidence presented in each source, one at a time. Make sure students take notes. Then, they will be able to compare their notes to complete their comparison of the texts.

Planning and Prewriting

Organize Tasks Make a list of tasks you will have to accomplish as you prepare for the production and then record it or present it live. Assign the tasks to individual group members. You may add to or modify this list as needed.

TASK LIST

Conduct Research: Decide whether you need more information about the 1938 "War of the Worlds" broadcast. If you do, research that content.

Assigned To: ______________________

Locate Audio Files: Consider whether you need audio files. For example, you may want to use archival recordings from 1930s radio, sound effects, or period music.

Assigned To: ______________________

Cast the Production: Assign the roles each group member will take on during the recording or live presentation. Consider the following jobs:

Recording Engineer
Assigned To: ______________________

Narrator / Actors / Hosts
Assigned To: ______________________

Sound–Effects Person
Assigned To: ______________________

Write a Working Outline: Prepare a sequence for your content. You may always change it later.

Assigned To: ______________________

Drafting

Include Cues Write your script in play form, clearly indicating speaking parts, as well as cues to play music or add sound effects.

Answer the Question Your production should be both entertaining and informative. Answer the question posed in the assignment, and draw evidence from both the radio broadcast and the magazine article.

Reviewing and Revising

Make sure your script is clearly organized so that information flows logically and no one is confused about what he or she is saying or doing. If necessary, simplify your use of audio or sound effects to make your presentation more manageable.

EVIDENCE LOG

Before moving on to a new selection, go to your Evidence Log and record what you learned from the *Radiolab* "War of the Worlds" episode and "The Myth of the *War of the Worlds* Panic."

STANDARDS

Writing
- Write arguments to support claims in an analysis of substantive topics or texts, using valid reasoning and relevant and sufficient evidence.
- Draw evidence from literary or informational texts to support analysis, reflection, and research.

Speaking and Listening
- Present information, findings, and supporting evidence clearly, concisely and logically such that listeners can follow the line of reasoning and the organization, development, substance, and style are appropriate to purpose, audience, and task.
- Make strategic use of digital media in presentations to enhance understanding of findings, reasoning, and evidence and to add interest.

DIGITAL PERSPECTIVES

Planning and Prewriting

Organize Tasks Support students as they select appropriate tasks, and encourage students to look for ways to build in accountability. Remind students to refer to the work they did in the Small Group Overview to help them ensure that everyone is participating fully.

Drafting

Include Cues You may suggest that students use different colors to differentiate the part of the script to be read aloud from any sound effects or sound clips they plan to use. Multiple colors will help students include transitional language to introduce sound, where necessary.

Answer the Question Remind the groups to assign one student to track the group's ability to address the prompt. That student may evaluate whether their work includes a balanced number of references to each account.

Reviewing and Revising

As students review their audio productions, ask them to decide if the hand-offs to various speakers go smoothly, if the flow of the narrative makes sense, and if the sound quality is clear. Have groups share their work with classmates.

FORMATIVE ASSESSMENT

Writing to Compare

If students are unable to form claims, **then** have students think about opinions that they have regarding the events of the *War of the Worlds* broadcast, which they can use as a foundation for building claims. For Reteach and Practice, **Writing to Compare: Script.**

PERSONALIZE FOR LEARNING

Strategic Support

Finding Evidence If students have difficulty finding persuasive outside sources concerning the events of the *War of the Worlds* broadcast, suggest they refine their search terms to open up more possible resources and statistics.

FACILITATING

Create a Podcast

Assignment Before groups begin work on their projects, have them clearly differentiate the role each group member will play. Remind groups to consult the schedule for Small-Group Learning to guide their work during the Performance Task.

Students should complete the assignment using presentation software to take advantage of text, graphics, and sound features.

Plan With Your Group

Analyze the Text Instruct students to thoroughly think about the different points of view that are presented in reading selections regarding catastrophic events, and the way they reflect the fear people feel about the end of the world. Each author has a unique perspective, and the readings present a variety of perspectives on the end times.

Remind students that they can include stories about the future or catastrophic events from other sources. If they have read books or short stories about a dystopian future, they might want to include quotations or ideas from them.

Gather Evidence and Media Examples Explain that images and other forms of media will help students enhance their presentation. Have them brainstorm what types of imagery best illustrate the present and future. You might suggest that they search for images and videos of a classically designed building and one that looks futuristic.

PERFORMANCE TASK: SPEAKING AND LISTENING FOCUS

SOURCES

- THE NUCLEAR TOURIST
- THE BEGINNING OF THE END OF THE WORLD
- THE POWWOW AT THE END OF THE WORLD
- A SONG ON THE END OF THE WORLD
- *from* RADIOLAB: WAR OF THE WORLDS
- THE MYTH OF THE *WAR OF THE WORLDS* PANIC

Create a Podcast

Assignment

You have read or listened to two magazine articles, three poems, and a radio broadcast that explore how people respond, or might respond, to catastrophic events. Work with your group to develop a podcast that addresses this question:

What do stories about the future say about the present?

Plan With Your Group

Analyze the Text With your group, discuss key ideas and themes from each text. Use the chart to list your ideas. As a group, discuss your notes about the selections. Use these notes to begin your discussion on how stories about the future reflect the present. Then, come to a consensus about which ideas about the present reflected in stories about the future are most significant. You will discuss these ideas in your podcast.

TITLE	KEY IDEAS/THEMES
The Nuclear Tourist	
the beginning of the end of the world	
The Powwow at the End of the World	
A Song on the End of the World	
from Radiolab: War of the Worlds	
The Myth of the *War of the Worlds* Panic	

STANDARDS

Speaking and Listening
Present information, findings, and supporting evidence clearly, concisely and logically such that listeners can follow the line of reasoning and the organization, development, substance, and style are appropriate to purpose, audience, and task.

Gather Evidence and Media Examples Identify specific examples from the selections to support your group's ideas. Then, brainstorm ideas for types of audio you can use to help convey your ideas. Consider using audio clips of actors or authors reading the selections. You may also include your own readings of passages, music, and other sound effects. Allow each group member to make suggestions.

AUTHOR'S PERSPECTIVE **Ernest Morrell, Ph.D.**

Fielding Questions When students give presentations that have question and answer portions, they should be prepared to field questions confidently and to defend their positions without being defensive. Teachers can share the following techniques with students for answering difficult questions.

- Speakers should show that they understand the questioner's point of view by restating the question before offering an answer.
- Speakers should not make up answers. If they don't know the answer, they should say so and say, "Let me get back to you." Teachers should emphasize that it is critical that speakers do indeed return with an answer, as this establishes trust and credibility.
- Presenters should keep answers simple without adding too much technical language. If the question might take the speaker away from the central topic, the speaker can provide a brief answer and offer to talk to the questioner after the presentation.
- If the question is difficult and if the speaker feels it is intended to attack, the speaker should answer calmly and move on to the next question as quickly as possible.

Organize Your Ideas Organize the script for your podcast. Assign roles for each part of the podcast, including the introduction and the conclusion. Allow each member of the team the opportunity to perform. Note when each segment will begin, and record what each speaker will say. Plan where you will place audio clips.

PODCAST SCRIPT		
	Audio	Script
Speaker: 1	1	1
Speaker: 2	2	2
Speaker: 3	3	3

Rehearse With Your Group

Practice with Your Group As you work through the script for your podcast, use this checklist to evaluate the effectiveness of your group's first run-through. Then, use your evaluation and the instruction here to guide your revision.

CONTENT	USE OF AUDIO	PRESENTATION TECHNIQUES
☐ The podcast has a clear introduction, explaining the topic. ☐ The podcast presents clear ideas about the topic. ☐ Ideas are supported with evidence from the texts.	☐ The audio helps communicate key ideas. ☐ Media clips are used appropriately and effectively.	☐ Podcast is audible. ☐ Transitions between speakers' segments and other audio clips are smooth. ☐ Each speaker speaks clearly.

Fine-Tune the Content To make your podcast stronger, you may need to review each speaker's segment to make sure it relates to the prompt. Check with your group to identify key ideas that are not clear to listeners. Find another way to word these ideas.

Improve Your Use of Audio Review all audio clips and sound effects to make sure they communicate key ideas and help create cohesion. Ensure that the equipment is working properly to record and play your podcast.

Brush Up on Your Presentation Techniques Practice reading your script before recording anything. Review your recorded podcast so that you can rerecord anything that is not audible.

Present and Evaluate

Before you play your podcast for the class, be sure that each member has taken into account each of the checklist items. As you listen to other groups' podcasts, evaluate how well they meet requirements on the checklist.

STANDARDS

Speaking and Listening

- Make strategic use of digital media in presentations to enhance understanding of findings, reasoning, and evidence and to add interest.
- Adapt speech to a variety of contexts and tasks, demonstrating command of formal English when indicated or appropriate.

DIGITAL PERSPECTIVES

Organize Your Ideas Let students know that a strong podcast uses a conversational tone that helps the listener connect to the podcast hosts.

Rehearse With Your Group

Practice With Your Group Remind students that practicing their parts ahead of time will reduce the likelihood that they'll make a mistake when they "record" their podcast. Rehearsal will also allow them to detect areas where the script copy is awkward and doesn't flow.

Improve Your Use of Audio Groups might find that the media they've chosen does little to enhance the presentation. Remind them that this is an opportunity to explore other options.

Brush Up on Your Presentation Techniques Encourage students to practice the pacing of their podcast. They should avoid speaking too quickly. One technique to improve presentation speaking is to mark words students want to stress. They can then practice reading those words with more emphasis.

Present and Evaluate

Before beginning the presentations, set the expectations for the audience. You may wish to have students consider these questions as groups present.

- What are the groups saying about the present?
- What are the groups saying about the future?
- Is the multimedia enhancing the presentations?
- What areas of the presentation are strong? Which might need more practice?

Remind students that positive feedback is as valuable as constructive criticism.

PERSONALIZE FOR LEARNING

Strategic Support

Analyze Podcasts Explain to students that this is considered to be the golden age of podcasting. Have them search for a podcast about a topic that's of interest to them (e.g., sports, culture, music, science, news) and listen to an episode. Ask students to analyze the episode as they're listening, taking notes about the characteristics that make it interesting. Ask students to listen to the way the host talks, the background music that might be used, the ease with which the information is presented, and the way the podcast is structured.

OVERVIEW

INDEPENDENT LEARNING

Why do we try to imagine the future?

Encourage students to think about what they have learned and what they want to know about why people imagine the end of the world. This is a key step to previewing the selection they will read or review in Independent Learning.

Independent Learning Strategies

Review the Learning Strategies with students and explain that they will develop strategies to work on their own.

- Have students watch the video on Independent Learning Strategies.
- A video on this topic is available online in the Professional Development Center.

Students should include any favorite strategies that they might have devised on their own during Whole-Class and Small-Group Learning. For example, for the strategy "Create a schedule," students might include:

- Plan a periodic review of their project status and adapt their schedule accordingly.
- Schedule their time in small increments. Each segment can have a different focus.

Block Scheduling

Each day in this Pacing Plan represents a 40–50 minute class period. Teachers using block scheduling may combine days to reflect their class schedule. In addition, teachers may revise pacing to differentiate and support core instruction by integrating components and resources as students require.

OVERVIEW: INDEPENDENT LEARNING

ESSENTIAL QUESTION:

Why do we try to imagine the future?

Our fears and hopes lead us to prepare for whatever the future may bring. In this section, you will complete your study of world's end literature by exploring an additional selection related to the topic. You'll then share what you learn with classmates. To choose a text, follow these steps.

Look Back Think about the selections you have already studied. What more do you want to know about world's end literature?

Look Ahead Preview the texts by reading the descriptions. Which one seems more interesting and appealing to you?

Look Inside Take a few minutes to scan the text you chose. Choose a different one if this text doesn't meet your needs.

Independent Learning Strategies

Throughout your life, in school, in your community, and in your career, you will need to rely on yourself to learn and work on your own. Review these strategies and the actions you can take to practice them during Independent Learning. Add ideas of your own to each category.

STRATEGY	ACTION PLAN
Create a schedule	• Understand your goals and deadlines. • Make a plan for what to do each day. •
Practice what you have learned	• Use first-read and close-read strategies to deepen your understanding. • After you read, evaluate the usefulness of the evidence to help you understand the topic. • Consider the quality and reliability of the source. •
Take notes	• Record important ideas and information. • Review your notes before preparing to share with a group. •

SCAN FOR MULTIMEDIA

Pacing Plan

Introduce Whole-Class Learning

Unit Introduction

By the Waters of Babylon

There Will Come Soft Rains

Performance Task

1 2 3 4 5 6 7 8 9 10 11 12 13 14 15

DIGITAL PERSPECTIVES

CONTENTS

Choose one selection. Selections are available online only.

SCAN FOR MULTIMEDIA

Contents

Selections Encourage students to scan and preview the selections before choosing the one they would like to read or review. Suggest that they consider the genre and subject matter of each one before making their decision. You can use the information on the following Planning pages to advise students in making their choice.

Remind students that the selections for Independent Learning are only available in the Interactive Student Edition. Allow students who do not have digital access at home to preview the selections or review the media selections using classroom or computer lab technology. Then either have students print the selection they choose, or provide a printout for them.

Performance Based-Assessment Prep

Review Evidence for a Narrative Point out to students that collecting evidence during Independent Learning is the last step in completing their Evidence Log. After they finish their independent reading, they will synthesize all the evidence they have compiled in the unit.

The evidence students collect will serve as the primary source of information they will use to complete the writing and oral presentation for the Performance-Based Assessment at the end of the unit.

- 16: Introduce Small-Group Learning
- 17–19: The Nuclear Tourist
- 20–21: • the beginning of the end of the world • The Powwow at the End of the World • A Song on the End of the World
- 22–23: Media: *from* Radiolab: War of the Worlds
- 24–25: The Myth of the War of the Worlds Panic
- 26: Performance Task
- 27: Introduce Independent Learning
- 28: Independent Learning
- 29–30: Performance-Based Assessment

INDEPENDENT LEARNING

SELECTION RESOURCES

- First-Read Guide: Nonfiction
- Close-Read Guide: Nonfiction
- Preparedness 101: Zombie Apocalypse: Text Questions
- Audio Summaries
- Selection Audio
- Selection Test

Preparedness 101: Zombie Apocalypse

Summary

This public document, "Preparedness 101: Zombie Apocalypse" was written by Ali S. Khan and published by the U.S. government. It begins by describing the rising popularity of zombies in popular movies and television shows and then defines zombies. Next, it outlines advice about surviving a zombie apocalypse. Most of the document educates people on how to prepare for a real emergency. There is a list of supplies people should keep on hand in case of hurricane, pandemic, or tornado. This list includes water, food, medications, tools, important documents, and a first-aid kit. The writer provides information for developing an emergency plan based on the type of emergency. Plans should include a meeting place for each family, a list of emergency contacts, and a planned evacuation route. The document also assures readers that the CDC is available to study disease outbreaks related to zombies or other true-life emergencies.

Insight

Despite the goofy and nonsensical name of the document, the true goal of the Centers for Disease Control and Prevention is to get families prepared for a natural disaster in their area.

Connection to Essential Question

This selection connects to the Essential Question, "Why do we try to imagine the future?," by teaching students about emergency preparedness. In case of an emergency or natural disaster, the CDC instructs people to gather supplies and develop a plan.

Connection to Performance-Based Assessment

The selection connects to the prompt, "Which matters more—the present or the future?," by instructing people to use the present to prepare for the future. In the case of a natural disaster, the link between past, present, and future is critical.

Text Complexity Rubric: Preparedness 101: Zombie Apocalypse

Quantitative Measures	
Lexile: 1310 **Text Length:** 839 words	
Qualitative Measures	
Knowledge Demands ① ❷ ③ ④ ⑤	The main premise of emergency preparedness may not be familiar to all students, but the concepts are clearly explained. Many references to zombie pop culture.
Structure ① ❷ ③ ④ ⑤	The selection is told in a straightforward, entertaining way; conversational language and headings break up the text.
Language Conventionality and Clarity ① ❷ ③ ④ ⑤	The selection contains sentence structure and vocabulary that are on-level.
Levels of Meaning/Purpose ① ❷ ③ ④ ⑤	Selection has only one level of meaning. The main concept and supporting ideas are clearly stated when reading or listening. Students may need to understand the use of humor to state an important message.

The Secret Bunker Congress Never Used

Summary

"The Secret Bunker Congress Never Used" is a news article broadcast by National Public Radio. The writer sheds light on a secret bunker Congress built for itself inside the Greenbrier, a luxury hotel four hours north of Washington, D.C. The underground shelter was conceived and built in the 1950s, when talk of atomic warfare was common. At the time, many people were building private bomb shelters for their families. Though never used, the structure was carefully maintained for more than thirty years. Inside were rows of hundreds of metal bunk beds as well as a six-month supply of food and water. Through the years, locals may have suspected something, but no rumors were ever confirmed. Once the Washington Post exposed its location, it was confirmed that the bunker would never be used.

Insight

How does one go about building a "secret" bomb shelter that can sleep 1,100 people without even the resort's official historian noticing? The Greenbrier's bunker was added as part of an expansion that included a conference hall. Through the years, all of the bunker's beds were assigned to someone, though it's possible not even members of Congress knew there was a bed reserved for them.

SELECTION RESOURCES

- First-Read Guide: Nonfiction
- Close-Read Guide: Nonfiction
- The Secret Bunker Congress Never Used: Text Questions
- Audio Summaries
- Selection Audio
- Selection Test

Connection to Essential Question

This selection connects to the Essential Question, "Why do we try to imagine the future?," by helping students understand the planning that takes place to prepare for dire situations. Not only was the bunker equipped with beds and many men's restrooms, but for thirty years the food and water supply were continuously restocked for freshness.

Connection to Performance-Based Assessment

The selection connects to the prompt, "Which matters more—the present or the future?," by describing the work that went in to planning for a future nuclear attack. This kind of planning links the past, present, and future to protect a nation's survival.

Text Complexity Rubric: The Secret Bunker Congress Never Used

Quantitative Measures	
Lexile: 1110 **Text Length:** 990 words	
Qualitative Measures	
Knowledge Demands 1 — **2** — 3 — 4 — 5	The selection tells about a secret government bunker that was created during the Cold War period. Historical context will be needed.
Structure 1 — **2** — 3 — 4 — 5	Information in the selection is logically organized and connections between ideas are clear.
Language Conventionality and Clarity 1 — 2 — **3** — 4 — 5	Some sentences in the explanation are complex, with multiple clauses and difficult vocabulary, but the selection also has many quotations using conversational language.
Levels of Meaning/Purpose 1 — **2** — 3 — 4 — 5	Selection has only one level of meaning. The main concept and supporting ideas are clearly stated.

SELECTION RESOURCES

- First-Review Guide: Media - Art
- Close-Review Guide: Media - Art
- The End of the World Might Just Look Like This: Media Questions
- Audio Summaries
- Selection Audio
- Selection Test

The End of the World Might Just Look Like This

Summary

In "The End of the World Might Just Look Like This," writer Megan Gambino uses an image gallery by digital artist Ron Miller to explain what the end of the world might look like. The article includes seven different scenes. In one, a blackhole swallows a fiery planet. In the next, hundreds of feet of ash rise to the chins of the four presidents carved into Mount Rushmore. One picture shows the flooding of London. Another shows a meteor hitting New York City. Another piece of Miller's work shows the Statue of Liberty being tossed in a tsunami. In the last two images, the sun turns into a red giant and a gamma ray causes high-energy particles to raise the temperatures on the planet. Each image includes Miller's commentary, explaining that so little is known about what might happen.

Insight

The collection of this artist's work may help students to imagine various scenarios in a way the texts have not.

Connection to Essential Question

This selection connects to the Essential Question, "Why do we try to imagine the future?," by helping students visualize what familiar places would look like should natural disasters that occurred thousands of years ago happen again today. Ron Miller's artwork is beautiful but eerie, and his commentary suggests the difficulty of making any accurate predictions.

Connection to Performance-Based Assessment

The selection connects to the prompt, "Which matters more—the present or the future?," by showing what well-known locations might look like in disastrous situations. Students may say that, given the chance of these kinds of endings, the present is more important. Others may say that humans have the power to change behaviors that might cause the destruction seen in the images.

Text Complexity Rubric: The End of the World Might Just Look Like This

Quantitative Measures

Lexile: 1020 **Text Length:** 1,142 words

Qualitative Measures	
Knowledge Demands ①—②—❸—④—⑤	The selection is about an illustrator who creates end-of-the-world art. Some scientific terms and scenarios may need to be explained.
Structure ①—❷—③—④—⑤	The selection is organized by the artist's work, with explanations and quotes from the artist.
Language Conventionality and Clarity ①—②—❸—④—⑤	The selection is written in conversational style and contains some subject-specific vocabulary.
Levels of Meaning/Purpose ①—❷—③—④—⑤	The main idea of the selection is straightforward. Some of the scientific concepts may be challenging.

SELECTION RESOURCES

- First-Read Guide: Poetry
- Close-Read Guide: Poetry
- Poetry Collection: Fire and Ice • Perhaps the World Ends Here: Text Questions
- Audio Summaries
- Selection Audio
- Selection Test

Fire and Ice • Perhaps the World Ends Here

Summary

In Robert Frost's poem "Fire and Ice," the speaker wonders how the world will end. He says some say it will end in fire and others say in ice. He says that fire is like desire which would be a powerful end. Then he considers that hate is like ice, and equally destructive. In the end, he says that both options would be enough to end the world.

Joy Harjo's poem, "Perhaps the World Ends Here," describes the importance of the kitchen table in daily life. The speaker provides a list of all the actions that happen at this table, from eating, to raising families, to making friends and sharing fears. The speaker suggests that the world might end at the kitchen table while people are getting the last bits of life together.

Insight

The Frost poem is considered a classic, and despite its short length and bare style, it makes strong claims about the nature of emotions. Similarly, the kitchen table metaphor in Harjo's poem is understated, but seeks to describe human emotion in general.

Connection to Essential Question

Both of these selections imagine the end of the world, and more generally the future, in terms of human emotions and human experience. These futures are not worldly and grand, but personal.

Connection to Performance-Based Assessment

These selections do not particularly address the present as opposed to the future; however, they do consider life in a timeless, abstract sense. In that sense, they imply the importance of the future, as the result of timeless truths, as much or more than the present.

Text Complexity Rubric: Fire and Ice • Perhaps the World Ends Here

Quantitative Measures	
Lexile: NP **Text Length:** 9 lines; 11 lines	
Qualitative Measures	
Knowledge Demands ① ❷ ③ ④ ⑤	The selections are poems about the end of the world.
Structure ① ❷ ③ ④ ⑤	"Fire and Ice" has an irregular rhyme scheme, and "Perhaps the World Ends Here" is written in free verse.
Language Conventionality and Clarity ① ❷ ③ ④ ⑤	The selections contain simple language and syntax.
Levels of Meaning/Purpose ① ❷ ③ ④ ⑤	The meaning of the poems is straightforward and easy to grasp.

SELECTION RESOURCES

- First-Review Guide: Media - Video
- Close-Review Guide: Media - Video
- A Visit to the Doomsday Vault: Media Questions
- Audio Summaries
- Selection Audio
- Selection Test

A Visit to the Doomsday Vault

Summary

In this newcast, "A Visit to the Doomsday Vault," journalist Scott Pelley reports on a building intended to survive for ten thousand years. It is on an icy island in the north of Norway, a place with more polar bears than people. The purpose of the vault is to serve as a seed bank for as many species of plants that scientists can gather. The bank is meant to protect against crop extinction, growing world population, and global warming. Many food crops are at risk of going extinct. The vault preserves seeds of those crops in case we need them in the future. Many plants have unique genetic characteristics that may be helpful in the future, such as resisting particular crop diseases. Some countries have their own seed banks, which are at risk of damage from the effects of war or weather. This vault built in the polar region may be safer because it is far away from most risk.

Insight

This selection may reveal a plan for a problem that most people have never considered. Countries have worked together to prepare for potential disaster.

Connection to Essential Question

The Essential Question is "Why do we try to imagine the future?" Here, actions taken by scientists around the world anticipate possible future catastrophe.

Connection to Performance-Based Assessment

The prompt is "Which matters more – the present or the future?" Students will see that the present and the future are linked. Preparations taken now may allow humanity to overcome an agricultural disaster in the future.

Media Complexity Rubric: A Visit to the Doomsday Vault	
Quantitative Measures	
Format: Video **Length:** 12:41	
Qualitative Measures	
Knowledge Demands (rated 3 of 5)	Requires knowledge of the idea of complete crop failure or of the idea of seed banks. Clear explanations are made of most of the elements in the selection.
Structure (rated 2 of 5)	The presentation has a conversational structure with questions, answers, and commentary. There are many quotations.
Language Conventionality and Clarity (rated 2 of 5)	The video contains conventional syntax and on-level vocabulary supported by images.
Levels of Meaning/Purpose (rated 2 of 5)	The meaning and concepts are straightforward.

DIGITAL PERSPECTIVES

Audio | Video | Document | Annotation Highlights | EL Highlights | Online Assessment

MY NOTES

ADVISING

You may wish to direct students to use the generic **First-Read** and **Close-Read Guides** in the Print Student Edition. Alternatively, you may wish to print copies of the genre-specific **First-Read** and **Close-Read Guides** for students. These are available online in the Interactive Student Edition or Unit Resources.

FIRST READ

Students should perform the steps of the first read independently.

NOTICE: Students should focus on the basic elements of the text to ensure they understand what is happening.

ANNOTATE: Students should mark any passages they wish to revisit during their close read.

CONNECT: Students should increase their understanding by connecting what they've read to other texts or personal experiences.

RESPOND: Students will write a summary to demonstrate their understanding.

Point out to students that while they will always complete the Respond step at the end of the first read, the other steps will probably happen somewhat concurrently. Remind students that they will revisit their first-read annotations during the close read. You may wish to print copies of the First-Read Guide for students to use.

After students have completed the First-Read Guide, you may wish to assign the the Text Questions for the selection that are available in the Interactive Teacher's Edition.

Anchor Standards

In the first two sections of the unit, students worked with the whole class and in small groups to gain topical knowledge and greater understanding of the skills required by the anchor standards. In this section, they are asked to work independently, applying what they have learned and demonstrating increased readiness for college and career.

INDEPENDENT LEARNING

First-Read Guide

Tool Kit
First-Read Guide
and Model Annotation

Use this page to record your first-read ideas.

Selection Title: ______________________________

NOTICE

NOTICE new information or ideas you learn about the unit topic as you first read this text.

ANNOTATE

ANNOTATE by marking vocabulary and key passages you want to revisit.

CONNECT

CONNECT ideas within the selection to other knowledge and the selections you have read.

RESPOND

RESPOND by writing a brief summary of the selection.

STANDARD
Reading Read and comprehend complex literary and informational texts independently and proficiently.

PERSONALIZE FOR LEARNING

Challenge

Additional Questions To help students reflect on their first read and prepare for the close read, encourage them to think about what more they would like to know about a text. Ask students to write two to three questions they have about the text. Then, students can meet in small groups with others who have read the same text. Each group can share First-Read Guides and their additional questions before proceeding to the close read.

Close-Read Guide

Use this page to record your close-read ideas.

Tool Kit
Close-Read Guide and Model Annotation

Selection Title: ______________________________

Close Read the Text

Revisit sections of the text you marked during your first read. Read these sections closely and **annotate** what you notice. Ask yourself **questions** about the text. What can you **conclude**? Write down your ideas.

Close Read: ANNOTATE · QUESTION · CONCLUDE

Analyze the Text

Think about the author's choices of patterns, structure, techniques, and ideas included in the text. Select one and record your thoughts about what this choice conveys.

QuickWrite

Pick a paragraph from the text that grabbed your interest. Explain the power of this passage.

STANDARD
Reading Read and comprehend complex literary and informational texts independently and proficiently.

DIGITAL PERSPECTIVES

CLOSE READ

Students should begin their close read by revisiting the annotations they made during their first read. Then, students should analyze one of the author's choices regarding the following elements:

- **patterns,** such as repetition or parallelism
- **structure,** such as cause-and-effect or problem-solution
- **techniques,** such as description or dialogue
- **ideas,** such as the author's main idea or claim

MAKE IT INTERACTIVE
Group students according to the selection they have chosen. Then, have students meet to discuss the selection in depth. Their discussions should be guided by their insights and questions.

PERSONALIZE FOR LEARNING

Challenge

Research Those students who seek a challenge may want to develop a question about the text or the author that they can answer by conducting brief research. Allow time for students to conduct research in print and/or on the Internet. Students should take notes on their findings, list the sources they used, and cite the sources when paraphrasing or quoting directly. Provide some class time for students to present their findings in informal oral reports. In a follow-up class discussion, ask presenters how further research related to the texts or authors helped them better understand the texts or appreciate writing choices the authors made.

ADVISING

Share Your Independent Learning

Prepare to Share

Explain to students that sharing what they learned from their Independent Learning selection provides classmates who read a different selection with an opportunity to consider the text as a source of evidence during the Performance-Based Assessment. As students prepare to share, remind them to highlight how their selection contributed to their knowledge of the concept of survival as well as how the selection connects to the question *Why do we try to imagine the future?*

Learn From Your Classmates

As students discuss the Independent Learning selections, direct them to take particular note of how their classmates' chosen selections align with their current position on the Performance-Based Assessment question.

Reflect

Students may want to add their reflection to their Evidence Log, particularly if their insight relates to a specific selection from the unit.

MAKE IT INTERACTIVE

After students independently answer the question, ask them to form pairs of two people. Then have students discuss the question with their partner and share their ideas and/or contrasting opinions. After the pairs are finished discussing the question, ask some of them to talk about what they learned from their discussion.

Evidence Log Support students in completing their Evidence Log. This paced activity will help prepare them for the Performance-Based Assessment at the end of the unit.

INDEPENDENT LEARNING

EVIDENCE LOG

Go to your Evidence Log and record what you learned from the text you read.

Share Your Independent Learning

Prepare to Share

Why do we try to imagine the future?

Even when you read or learn something independently, you can continue to grow by sharing what you have learned. Reflect on the text you explored independently, and write notes about its connection to the unit. In your notes, consider why this text belongs in this unit.

Learn From Your Classmates

Discuss It Share your ideas about the text you explored on your own. As you talk with your classmates, jot down ideas that you learn from them.

Reflect

Review your notes, and underline the most important insight you gained from these writing and discussion activities. Explain how this idea adds to your understanding of the topic of the world's end.

STANDARDS

Speaking and Listening
Initiate and participate effectively in a range of collaborative discussions with diverse partners on *grades 9–10 topics, texts, and issues*, building on others' ideas and expressing their own clearly and persuasively.

AUTHOR'S PERSPECTIVE **Ernest Morrell, Ph.D.**

Asking Good Questions Students may not know how to ask effective questions, a critical component in learning from others. To teach this skill, teachers can explain that effective questioners always show respect, clarify the goals of the discussion, and solicit everyone's ideas. In addition, effective questions are open-ended rather than yes/no requests, so they allow group members to express more extensive and complex responses and solicit follow-up responses. Teachers can use these models of effective questions to model the skill:

- **Ask to clarify:** Sample questions include: "Can you give an example?"; "Where in the text do you see that?"; and "How did you reach this conclusion?"
- **Ask to start a discussion:** Sample techniques include taking the opposite opinion and setting up a "What If?" situation.
- **Push for the larger idea:** Sample questions include: "Is it always this way?"; "Why do we believe this?"; and "How has this changed our thinking?"

Review Notes for a Narrative

At the beginning of this unit, you took a position on the following question:

Which matters more—the present or the future?

EVIDENCE LOG

Review your Evidence Log and your QuickWrite from the beginning of the unit. Has your position changed?

☐ YES	☐ NO
Identify at least three pieces of evidence that convinced you to change your mind.	Identify at least three pieces of evidence that reinforced your initial position.
1.	**1.**
2.	**2.**
3.	**3.**

State your position now: ____________________

Use that position to write a theme for your narrative: ____________________

Use the evidence in your chart to develop important details about the setting, plot, or characters in a narrative that develops this theme: ____________________

Evaluate Your Ideas Do you have enough ideas to write a narrative that develops your theme? If not, make a plan.

- ☐ Do more research
- ☐ Reread a selection
- ☐ Talk with my classmates
- ☐ Ask an expert
- ☐ Other: ____________________

DIGITAL PERSPECTIVES

Review Notes for a Narrative

Evidence Log Students should understand that their thinking on an issue could evolve as they learn more about the subject and are exposed to additional points of view. Point out that just because they took an initial position on the question *What matters more—the present, or the future?* doesn't mean that their thinking can't change after careful consideration of their learning and evidence.

Evaluate Your Ideas

Remind students that there are many different ways to write a narrative that develops their theme:

- strong dialogue
- good pacing
- vivid descriptions
- interesting situation

In addition to ensuring their narrative develops their theme sufficiently and compellingly, students should evaluate the strength of their characters. Discuss the narrative elements that are necessary for writing strong characters:

- realistic dialogue
- well-chosen details about their personality
- showing, not telling

Writing to Sources: Narrative

Students should complete the Performance-Based Assessment independently, with little to no input or feedback during the process. Students should use word processing software to take advantage of editing tools and features.

Prior to beginning the Assessment, ask students to think about whether they put more thought into the present or the future.

Review the Elements of Effective Narrative Students can review the work they did earlier in the unit as they complete the Performance-Based Assessment. They may also consult other resources such as:

- the elements of narrative fiction, including an introduction with a situation, character development, and narrative techniques such as dialogue, pacing, and description.
- their Evidence Log
- their Word Network

Although students will use evidence from unit selections for their writing mode, they may need to collect additional evidence, including facts, statistics, anecdotes, quotations from authorities, or examples.

SOURCES

- WHOLE-CLASS SELECTIONS
- SMALL-GROUP SELECTIONS
- INDEPENDENT LEARNING

PART 1

Writing to Sources: Narrative

In this unit, you read fictional accounts of the world's demise. You also read about responses to catastrophic disasters—real and fictional. Each story teaches us something new about the world and about ourselves.

Assignment

Write a **short story** in which you develop a theme related to the following question:

Which matters more—the present or the future?

First, introduce a main character and a situation or problem, and establish the narrator's point of view. Then, create a sequence of events in which you show how the characters address the situation or problem in an innovative way. Be sure that your conclusion provides a logical and meaningful resolution to the conflict. As you write your narrative, use a variety of techniques and descriptive language to depict the setting, events, and characters. Incorporate ideas from the texts in this unit to help develop details in your story.

Reread the Assignment Review the assignment to be sure you fully understand it. The task may reference some of the academic words presented at the beginning of the unit. Be sure you understand each of the words here in order to complete the assignment correctly.

Academic Vocabulary

innovate	depiction	conjecture
technique	introspective	

Review the Elements of Effective Narrative Before you begin writing, read the Narrative Rubric. Once you have completed your first draft, check it against the rubric. If one or more of the elements is missing or not as strong as it could be, revise your narrative to add or strengthen that component.

WORD NETWORK

As your write and revise your narrative, use your Word Network to help vary your word choices.

STANDARDS

Writing

- Write narratives to develop real or imagined experiences or events using effective technique, well-chosen details, and well-structured event sequences.
- Write routinely over extended time frames and shorter time frames for a range of tasks, purposes, and audiences.

Narrative Rubric

	Focus and Organization	Development of Ideas/Elaboration	Conventions
4	The introduction establishes a clear situation and establishes the narrator's point of view. Events are presented in a logical sequence, and the progression from one event to another is smooth. The conclusion resolves the situation or problem and clearly conveys the significance of the events in the story.	Narrative techniques such as dialogue, pacing, and description are used effectively to develop characters and events. Descriptive details, sensory language, and precise words and phrases are used effectively to engage the reader.	The narrative intentionally uses standard English conventions of usage and mechanics, except where language is manipulated for effect.
3	The introduction establishes the situation and point of view but leaves some details unclear. Events are presented logically, but the progression from one event to another is sometimes unclear. The conclusion resolves the situation or problem but does not clearly convey the significance of the events in the story.	Narrative techniques such as dialogue, pacing, and description are used occasionally. Descriptive details, sensory language, and precise words and phrases are used occasionally.	The narrative consistently uses standard English conventions of usage and mechanics.
2	The introduction provides little description of the situation or the point of view. The event sequence is evident, but the progression from one event to another is unclear. The conclusion comes abruptly and provides little or no reflection on the experiences related in the narrative.	Narrative techniques such as dialogue, pacing, and description are used sparingly, or the narrative relies too heavily on one technique. The story contains few examples of descriptive details, precise words and phrases, and sensory language.	The narrative contains some errors in standard English conventions of usage and mechanics.
1	The introduction does not introduce the situation and does not establish the narrator's point of view. The sequence of events is unclear and hard to follow. The narrative does not have a conclusion.	The narrative is not developed with dialogue, pacing, and description. The narrative lacks descriptive details and sensory language.	The narrative contains many errors in standard English conventions of usage and mechanics.

DIGITAL PERSPECTIVES

Narrative Rubric

As you review the Narrative Rubric with students, remind them that the rubric is a resource that can guide their revisions. Students should pay particular attention to the differences between a story that uses descriptive details, sensory language, and precise words and phrases occasionally (a score of 3) and a story that uses descriptive details, sensory language, and precise words and phrases effectively to engage the reader (a score of 4).

ASSESSING

Speaking and Listening: Dramatic Reading

Students should annotate their written writing mode in preparation for the oral presentation, marking the important elements (an introduction to the narrator, a situation, and a conclusion) as well as dialogue, pacing, and description.

Remind students that the effectiveness of an oral writing mode relies on how the speaker establishes credibility with his or her audience. If a speaker comes across as confident and authoritative, it will be easier for the audience to give credence to the speaker's presentation.

Review the Dramatic Reading Rubric As you review the Dramatic Reading Rubric with students, remind them that it is a valuable tool that can help them plan their presentation. They should strive to include all of the criteria required to achieve a score of 3. Draw their attention to some of the subtle differences between scores of 2 and 3.

PERFORMANCE-BASED ASSESSMENT

PART 2

Speaking and Listening: Dramatic Reading

Assignment

After completing the final draft of your narrative, record a **dramatic reading** of your narrative to present to the class.

Instead of simply reading your narrative, take the following steps to make your dramatic reading engaging:

- Use music and sound effects to enhance the narrative.
- Use effective pacing as you build your story to the climax. Vary your speed and tone to build suspense and drama.

STANDARDS

Speaking and Listening

Make strategic use of digital media in presentations to enhance understanding of findings, reasoning, and evidence and to add interest.

Review the Rubric The criteria by which your dramatic reading will be evaluated appear in the rubric below. Review these criteria before presenting or recording your narrative to ensure that you are prepared.

	Content	Organization	Presentation Technique
3	The introduction establishes a clear situation and establishes the narrator's point of view. Events are presented in an understandable sequence, and the progression from one event to another is smooth. The conclusion conveys the significance of the events in the story.	Audio is very effective in communicating ideas from the narrative. The use of audio is consistent.	The speaker uses tone and pace effectively. The narration and dialogue are clear throughout the entire presentation or recording.
2	The introduction establishes some setting. Point of view is established, though not detailed. The event sequence is logical, but the progression from one event to another may be unclear. The conclusion is logical, but does not conveys the significance of the events in the story clearly.	Audio is somewhat effective in communicating ideas from the narrative. The use of audio is somewhat consistent.	The speaker uses tone and pace somewhat effectively. The narration and dialogue are clear throughout most of the presentation or recording.
1	The introduction does not establish the situation, and the narrator's point of view is unclear. The sequence of events is hard to follow. The conclusion is abrupt and does not convey the significance of the events in the story.	Audio is ineffective in communicating ideas from the narrative. The use of audio is inconsistent.	The speaker does not use tone and pace effectively. The narration and dialogue are unclear in the presentation or recording.

DIGITAL PERSPECTIVES

Preparing for the Assignment To help students understand how music can be used to make a reading sound more dramatic, find examples on the Internet of beat poets from the 1950s reading over a jazz soundtrack. You can also play them a clip from a podcast, many of which use music for dramatic effect. After sharing these examples, have a class discussion in which you talk about why the music adds drama.

Reflect on the Unit

Now that you've completed the unit, take a few moments to reflect on your learning. Use the questions below to think about where you succeeded, what skills and strategies helped you, and where you can continue to grow in the future.

Reflect on the Unit Goals

Look back at the goals at the beginning of the unit. Use a different colored pen to rate yourself again. Think about readings and activities that contributed the most to the growth of your understanding. Record your thoughts.

Reflect on the Learning Strategies

Discuss It Write a reflection on whether you were able to improve your learning based on your Action Plans. Think about what worked, what didn't, and what you might do to keep working on these strategies. Record your ideas before a class discussion.

Reflect on the Text

Choose a selection that you found challenging, and explain what made it difficult.

Explain something that surprised you about a text in the unit.

Which activity taught you the most about visions of the world's end? What did you learn?

SCAN FOR MULTIMEDIA

DIGITAL PERSPECTIVES

Reflect on the Unit

- Have students watch the video on Reflecting on Your Learning
- A video on this topic is available online in the Professional Development Center

Reflect on the Unit Goals

Students should re-evaluate how well they met the unit goals now that they have completed the unit. You might ask them to provide a written commentary on the goal they made the most progress with, as well as the goal they feel warrants continued focus.

Reflect on the Learning Strategies

Discuss It If you want to make this a digital activity, go online and navigate to the Discussion Board. Alternatively, students can share their learning strategies reflections in a class discussion.

Reflect on the Text

Consider having students share their text reflections with one another.

Unit Test and Remediation
After students have completed the Performance-Based Assessment, administer the Unit Test. Based on students' performance on the test, assign the resources as indicated on the Interpretation Guide to remediate. Students who take the test online will be automatically assigned remediation, as warranted by test results.

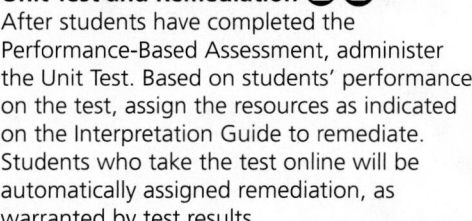

RESOURCES

CONTENTS

Marking the Text: Strategies and Tips for Annotation

When you close read a text, you read for comprehension and then reread to unlock layers of meaning and to analyze a writer's style and techniques. Marking a text as you read it enables you to participate more fully in the close-reading process.

Following are some strategies for text mark-ups, along with samples of how the strategies can be applied. These mark-ups are suggestions; you and your teacher may want to use other mark-up strategies.

- * Key Idea
- ! I love it!
- ? I have questions
- ◯ Unfamiliar or important word
- ---- Context Clues

Suggested Mark-Up Notations

WHAT I NOTICE	HOW TO MARK UP	QUESTIONS TO ASK
Key Ideas and Details	• Highlight key ideas or claims. • Underline supporting details or evidence.	• What does the text say? What does it leave unsaid? • What inferences do you need to make? • What details lead you to make your inferences?
Word Choice	• Circle unfamiliar words. • Put a dotted line under context clues, if any exist. • Put an exclamation point beside especially rich or poetic passages.	• What inferences about word meaning can you make? • What tone and mood are created by word choice? • What alternate word choices might the author have made?
Text Structure	• Highlight passages that show key details supporting the main idea. • Use arrows to indicate how sentences and paragraphs work together to build ideas. • Use a right-facing arrow to indicate foreshadowing. • Use a left-facing arrow to indicate flashback.	• Is the text logically structured? • What emotional impact do the structural choices create?
Author's Craft	• Circle or highlight instances of repetition, either of words, phrases, consonants, or vowel sounds. • Mark rhythmic beats in poetry using checkmarks and slashes. • Underline instances of symbolism or figurative language.	• Does the author's style enrich or detract from the reading experience? • What levels of meaning are created by the author's techniques?

CLOSE READING

First Read: Notice, Annotate, Connect, Respond

- * Key Idea
- ! I love it!
- ? I have questions
- ◯ Unfamiliar or important word
- ---- Context Clues

NOTES

In a first read, work to get a sense of the main idea of a text. Look for key details and ideas that help you understand what the author conveys to you. Mark passages that prompt a strong response from you.

Here is how one reader marked up this text.

MODEL

INFORMATIONAL TEXT

from Classifying the Stars

Cecilia H. Payne

1 Sunlight and starlight are composed of waves of various lengths, which the eye, even aided by a telescope, is unable to separate. We must use more than a telescope. In order to sort out the component colors, the light must be dispersed by a prism, or split up by some other means. For instance, sunbeams passing through rain drops, are transformed into the myriad-tinted rainbow. The familiar rainbow spanning the sky is Nature's most glorious demonstration that light is composed of many colors.

2 The very beginning of our knowledge of the nature of a star dates back to 1672, when Isaac Newton gave to the world the results of his experiments on passing sunlight through a prism. To describe the beautiful band of rainbow tints, produced when sunlight was dispersed by his three-cornered piece of glass, he took from the Latin the word *spectrum*, meaning an appearance. The rainbow is the spectrum of the Sun. . . .

3 In 1814, more than a century after Newton, the spectrum of the Sun was obtained in such purity that an amazing detail was seen and studied by the German optician, Fraunhofer. He saw that the multiple spectral tints, ranging from delicate violet to deep red, were crossed by hundreds of fine dark lines. In other words, there were narrow gaps in the spectrum where certain shades were wholly blotted out. We must remember that the word spectrum is applied not only to sunlight, but also to the light of any glowing substance when its rays are sorted out by a prism or a grating.

MODEL

First-Read Guide

You may want to use a guide like this to organize your thoughts after you read. Here is how a reader completed a First-Read Guide.

Use this page to record your first-read ideas.

Selection Title: Classifying the Stars

NOTICE

NOTICE new information or ideas you learned about the unit topic as you first read this text.

Light = different waves of colors. (Spectrum)

Newton - the first person to observe these waves using a prism.

Faunhofer saw gaps in the spectrum.

ANNOTATE

ANNOTATE by marking vocabulary and key passages you want to revisit.

Vocabulary

- myriad
- grating
- component colors

Different light types = different lengths

Isaac Newton also worked theories of gravity.

Multiple spectral tints? "colors of various appearance"

Key Passage:
Paragraph 3 shows that Fraunhofer discovered more about the nature of light spectrums: he saw the spaces in between the tints.

NOTICE ANNOTATE First Read CONNECT RESPOND

CONNECT ideas within the selection to other knowledge and the selections you have read.

I remember learning about prisms in science class.

Double rainbows! My favorite. How are they made?

CONNECT

RESPOND by writing a brief summary of the selection.

Science allows us to see things not visible to the naked eye. What we see as sunlight is really a spectrum of colors. By using tools, such as prisms, we can see the components of sunlight and other light. They appear as single colors or as multiple colors separated by gaps of no color. White light contains a rainbow of colors.

RESPOND

CLOSE READING

ANNOTATE · QUESTION · Close Read · CONCLUDE

In a close read, go back into the text to study it in greater detail. Take the time to analyze not only the author's ideas but the way that those ideas are conveyed. Consider the genre of the text, the author's word choice, the writer's unique style, and the message of the text.

Here is how one reader close read this text.

- ✱ Key Idea
- ! I love it!
- ? I have questions
- ◯ Unfamiliar or important word
- ---- Context Clues

MODEL

INFORMATIONAL TEXT

from Classifying the Stars

Cecilia H. Payne

NOTES

- explanation of sunlight and starlight
- What is light and where do the colors come from?
- This paragraph is about Newton and the prism.
- What discoveries helped us understand light?
- Fraunhofer and gaps in spectrum

1 Sunlight and starlight are composed of waves of various lengths, which the eye, even aided by a telescope, is unable to separate. We must use more than a telescope. In order to sort out the component colors, the light must be dispersed by a prism, or split up by some other means. For instance, sunbeams passing through rain drops, are transformed into the myriad-tinted rainbow. The familiar rainbow spanning the sky is Nature's most glorious demonstration that light is composed of many colors.

2 The very beginning of our knowledge of the nature of a star dates back to 1672, when Isaac Newton gave to the world the results of his experiments on passing sunlight through a prism. To describe the beautiful band of rainbow tints, produced when sunlight was dispersed by his three-cornered piece of glass, he took from the Latin the word *spectrum*, meaning an appearance. The rainbow is the spectrum of the Sun. . . .

3 In 1814, more than a century after Newton, the spectrum of the Sun was obtained in such purity that an amazing detail was seen and studied by the German optician, Fraunhofer. He saw that the multiple spectral tints, ranging from delicate violet to deep red, were crossed by hundreds of fine dark lines. In other words, there were narrow gaps in the spectrum where certain shades were wholly blotted out. We must remember that the word spectrum is applied not only to sunlight, but also to the light of any glowing substance when its rays are sorted out by a prism or a grating.

MODEL

Close-Read Guide

You can use the Close-Read Guide to help you dig deeper into the text. Here is how a reader completed a Close-Read Guide.

Use this page to record your close-read ideas.

Selection Title: Classifying the Stars

Close Read the Text

Revisit sections of the text you marked during your first read. Read these sections closely and **annotate** what you notice. Ask yourself **questions** about the text. What can you **conclude?** Write down your ideas.

Paragraph 3: Light is composed of waves of various lengths. Prisms let us see different colors in light. This is called the spectrum. Fraunhofer proved that there are gaps in the spectrum, where certain shades are blotted out.

More than one researcher studied this and each built off the ideas that were already discovered.

Analyze the Text

Think about the author's choices of patterns, structure, techniques, and ideas included in the text. Select one, and record your thoughts about what this choice conveys.

The author showed the development of human knowledge of the spectrum chronologically. Helped me see how ideas were built upon earlier understandings. Used dates and "more than a century after Newton" to show time.

QuickWrite

Pick a paragraph from the text that grabbed your interest. Explain the power of this passage.

The first paragraph grabbed my attention, specifically the sentence "The familiar rainbow spanning the sky is Nature's most glorious demonstration that light is composed of many colors." The paragraph began as a straightforward scientific explanation. When I read the word "glorious," I had to stop and deeply consider what was being said. It is a word loaded with personal feelings. With that one word, the author let the reader know what was important to her.

WRITING

Argument

When you think of the word *argument*, you might think of a disagreement between two people, but an argument is more than that. An argument is a logical way of presenting a belief, conclusion, or stance. A good argument is supported with reasoning and evidence.

Argument writing can be used for many purposes, such as to change a reader's point of view or opinion or to bring about an action or a response from a reader.

Elements of an Argumentative Text

An **argument** is a logical way of presenting a viewpoint, belief, or stand on an issue. A well-written argument may convince the reader, change the reader's mind, or motivate the reader to take a certain action.

An effective argument contains these elements:

- a precise claim
- consideration of counterclaims, or opposing positions, and a discussion of their strengths and weaknesses
- logical organization that makes clear connections among claim, counterclaim, reasons, and evidence
- valid reasoning and evidence
- a concluding statement or section that logically completes the argument
- formal and objective language and tone
- error-free grammar, including accurate use of transitions

MODEL

ARGUMENT: SCORE 1

Selfies, Photoshop, and You: Superficial Image Culture is Hurtful for Teens

Selfies are kind of cool, also kind of annoying, and some say they might be bad for you if you take too many. Selfies of celebrities and ordinary people are everywhere. People always try to smile and look good, and they take a lot of selfies when they are somewhere special, like at the zoo or at a fair. Some people spend so much time taking selfies they forget to just go ahead and have fun.

> The writer does not clearly state the claim in the introduction.

TV and other media are full of beautiful people. Looking at all those model's and celebrities can make kids feel bad about their one bodies, even when they are actually totally normal and fine and beautiful they way they are. Kids start to think they should look like the folks on TV which is mostly impossible. It's also a cheat because lots of the photos we see of celebrities and model's have been edited so they look even better.

> The argument contains mistakes in standard English conventions of usage and mechanics.

Selfies make people feel even worse about the way they look. They're always comparing themselves and feeling that maybe they aren't as good as they should be. Selfies can make teens feel bad about their faces and bodies, and the stuff they are doing every day.

Regular people edit and change things before they post their pictures. That means, the pictures are kind of fake and it's impossible to compete with something that is fake. It's sad to think that teens can start to hate themselves and feel depressed just because they don't and can't look like a faked photo of a movie star.

> The tone of the argument is informal, and the vocabulary is limited or ineffective.

Kids and teens post selfies to hear what others think about them, to show off, and to see how they compare with others. It can be kind of full of pressure always having to look great and smile. Even if you get positive comments about a selfie that you post, and everyone says you look beautiful, that feeling only lasts for a few minutes. After all, what you look like is just something on the outside. What's more important is what you are on the inside and what you do.

It's great for those few minutes, but then what? If you keep posting, people will not want to keep writing nice comments. Kids and teens should take a break from posting selfies all the time. It's better to go out and have fun rather than always keeping on posting selfies.

> The writer does not address counterclaims.

> The conclusion does not restate any information that is important.

TOOL KIT: WRITING

TOOL KIT: WRITING

MODEL

ARGUMENT: SCORE 2

Selfies and You: Superficial Image Culture is Hurtful for Teens

Selfies are bad for teens and everyone else. Selfies of celebrities and ordinary people are everywhere. It seems like taking and posting selfies is not such a big deal and not harmful, but that's not really true. Actually, taking too many selfies can be really bad.

> The introduction establishes the writer's claim.

TV and other media are full of beautiful people. Looking at all those models and celebrities can make kids feel bad about their own bodies. Kids start to think they should look like the folks on TV which is mostly impossible. It's also a cheat because lots of the photos we see of celebrities and model's have been edited so they look even better.

> The tone of the argument is occasionally formal and objective.

Regular people use image editing software as well. They edit and change things before they post their pictures. That means, the pictures are kind of fake and it's impossible to compete with something that is fake.

Selfies make people feel even worse about the way they look. They're always comparing themselves and feeling that maybe they aren't as good as they should be. Selfies can make teens feel bad about their faces and bodies.

But maybe selfies are just a fun way to stay in touch, but that's not really how people use selfies, I don't think. Kids and teens post selfies show off. It can be full of pressure always having to look great and smile.

> The writer briefly acknowledges one counterclaim.

Sometimes posting a selfie can make you feel good if it gets lots of 'likes' and positive comments. But you can never tell. Someone also might say something mean. Also, even if you get positive comments and everyone says you look beautiful, that feeling only lasts for a few minutes. It's great for those few minutes, but then what? If you keep posting and posting, people will not want to keep writing nice comments.

The selfie culture today is just too much. Kids and teens can't be happy when they are always comparing themselves and worrying about what they look like. It's better to go out and have fun rather than always keeping on posting selfies.

> The conclusion offers some insight into the claim and restates information.

MODEL

ARGUMENT: SCORE 3

Selfies and You: Superficial Image Culture is Hurtful for Teens

Selfies are everywhere. Check out any social media site and you'll see an endless parade of perfect smiles on both celebrities and ordinary people. It may seem as if this flood of seflies is harmless, but sadly that is not true. Selfies promote a superficial image culture that is harmful and dangerous for teens.

The problem starts with the unrealistic: idealized images teens are exposed to in the media. Most models and celebrities are impossibly beautiful and thin. Even young children can feel that there is something wrong with they way they look. According to one research group, more than half of girls and one third of boys ages 6-8 feel their ideal body is thinner than their current body weight. Negative body image can result in serious physical and mental health problems.

When teens look at selfies they automatically make comparisons with the idealized images they have in their minds. This can make them feel inadequate and sad about themselves, their bodies, and their lives. And with social media sites accessible 24/7, it's difficult to get a break from the constant comparisons, competition, and judgment.

Image editing software plays a role too. A recent study carried out by the Renfrew Center Foundation said that about 50% of people edit pictures of themselves before posting. They take away blemishes, change skin tone, maybe even make themselves look thinner. And why not? Even the photos of models and celebrities are heavily edited. Teens can start to hate themselves and feel depressed just because they don't and can't look like a faked photo of a movie star.

Some say that posting a selfie is like sending a postcard to your friends and family, but that's not how selfies are used: teens post selfies to get feedback, to compare themselves with others, and to present a false image to the world. There is a lot of pressure to look great and appear happy.

It's true that sometimes a selfie posted on social media gets 'likes' and positive comments that can make a person feel pretty. However, the boost you get from feeling pretty for five minutes doesn't last.

A million selfies are posted every day—and that's way too many. Selfies promote a superficial image culture that is harmful to teens. In the end, the selfie life is not a healthy way to have fun. Let's hope the fad will fade.

The argument's claim is clearly stated.

The tone of the argument is mostly formal and objective.

The writer includes reasons and evidence that address and support claims.

The ideas progress logically, and the writer includes sentence transitions that connect the reader to the argument.

The conclusion restates important information.

WRITING

MODEL

ARGUMENT: SCORE 4

Selfies and You: Superficial Image Culture Is Hurtful for Teens

Smile, Snap, Edit, Post—Repeat! That's the selfie life, and it's everywhere. A million selfies are posted every day. But this **tsunami** of self-portraits is not as harmless as it appears. Selfies promote a superficial image culture that is hurtful and dangerous for teens.

It all starts with the unrealistic: When teens look at selfies they automatically make comparisons with the idealized images they have in their minds. This can cause them to feel inadequate and sad about themselves, their bodies, and their lives. According to Common Sense Media, more than half of girls and one third of boys ages 6-8 feel their ideal body is thinner than their current body weight. Negative body image can result in serious physical and mental health problems such as anorexia and other eating disorders.

To make matter worse, many or even most selfies have been edited. A recent study carried out by the Renfrew Center Foundation concluded that about 50% of people edit their own images before posting. They use image-editing software to take away blemishes, change skin tone, maybe even make themselves look thinner. And why not? Even the photos of models and celebrities are heavily edited.

Some say that selfies are a harmless and enjoyable way to communicate: posting a selfie is like sending a postcard to your friends and family, inviting them to share in your fun. But that is not how selfies are used: teens post selfies to get feedback, to compare themselves with others, and to present an (often false) image to the world.

It's true that posting a selfie on social media can generate 'likes' and positive comments that can make a person feel good.

However, the boost one gets from feeling pretty for five minutes is like junk food: it tastes good but it is not nourishing.

The selfie culture that is the norm today is out of control. The superficial image culture promoted by selfies is probably behind the recent 20 percent increase in plastic surgery—something with its own dangers and drawbacks. Let's hope the fad will fade, and look forward to a future where people are too busy enjoying life to spend so much time taking, editing, and posting pictures of themselves.

The introduction is engaging, and the writer's claim is clearly stated at the end of the paragraph.

The writer has included a variety of sentence transitions such as "To make matters worse…" "Some say…" "Another claim…" "It is true that…"

The sources of evidence are specific and contain relevant information.

The writer clearly acknowledges counterclaims.

The conclusion offers fresh insights into the claim.

Argument Rubric

	Focus and Organization	Evidence and Elaboration	Conventions
4	The introduction engages the reader and establishes a claim in a compelling way. The argument includes valid reasons and evidence that address and support the claim while clearly acknowledging counterclaims. The ideas progress logically, and transitions make connections among ideas clear. The conclusion offers fresh insight into the claim.	The sources of evidence are comprehensive and specific and contain relevant information. The tone of the argument is always formal and objective. The vocabulary is always appropriate for the audience and purpose.	The argument intentionally uses standard English conventions of usage and mechanics.
3	The introduction engages the reader and establishes the claim. The argument includes reasons and evidence that address and support my claim while acknowledging counterclaims. The ideas progress logically, and some transitions are used to help make connections among ideas clear. The conclusion restates the claim and important information.	The sources of evidence contain relevant information. The tone of the argument is mostly formal and objective. The vocabulary is generally appropriate for the audience and purpose.	The argument demonstrates general accuracy in standard English conventions of usage and mechanics.
2	The introduction establishes a claim. The argument includes some reasons and evidence that address and support the claim while briefly acknowledging counterclaims. The ideas progress somewhat logically. A few sentence transitions are used that connect readers to the argument. The conclusion offers some insight into the claim and restates information.	The sources of evidence contain some relevant information. The tone of the argument is occasionally formal and objective. The vocabulary is somewhat appropriate for the audience and purpose.	The argument demonstrates some accuracy in standard English conventions of usage and mechanics.
1	The introduction does not clearly state the claim. The argument does not include reasons or evidence for the claim. No counterclaims are acknowledged. The ideas do not progress logically. Transitions are not included to connect ideas. The conclusion does not restate any information that is important.	Reliable and relevant evidence is not included. The vocabulary used is limited or ineffective. The tone of the argument is not objective or formal.	The argument contains mistakes in standard English conventions of usage and mechanics.

R11

WRITING

Informative/Explanatory Texts

Informative and explanatory writing should rely on facts to inform or explain. Informative writing can serve several purposes: to increase readers' knowledge of a subject, to help readers better understand a procedure or process, or to provide readers with an enhanced comprehension of a concept. It should also feature a clear introduction, body, and conclusion.

Elements of Informative/Explanatory Texts

Informative/explanatory texts present facts, details, data, and other kinds of evidence to give information about a topic. Readers turn to informational and explanatory texts when they wish to learn about a specific idea, concept, or subject area, or if they want to learn how to do something.

An effective informative/explanatory text contains these elements:

- a topic sentence or thesis statement that introduces the concept or subject
- relevant facts, examples, and details that expand upon a topic
- definitions, quotations, and/or graphics that support the information given
- headings (if desired) to separate sections of the essay
- a structure that presents information in a direct, clear manner
- clear transitions that link sections of the essay
- precise words and technical vocabulary where appropriate
- formal and object language and tone
- a conclusion that supports the information given and provides fresh insights

MODEL

INFORMATIVE/EXPLANATORY: SCORE 1

Moai: The Giant Statues of Easter Island

Easter Island is a tiny Island. It's far out in the middle of the pacific ocean, 2200 miles off the coast. The closest country is Chile, in south america. The nearest island where people live is called Pitcairn, and that's about 1,300 miles away, and only about 60 people live so their most of the time. Easter island is much bigger than Pitcairn, and lots more people live there now—about 5,000-6,000. Although in the past there were times when only about 111 people lived there.

Even if you don't really know what it is, you've probably seen pictures of the easter island Statues. You'd recognize one if you saw it, with big heads and no smiles. Their lots of them on the island. Almost 900 of them. But some were never finished They're called *moai.* They are all different sizes. All the sizes together average out to about 13 feet tall and 14 tons of heavy.

Scientists know that Polynesians settled Easter Island (it's also called Rapa Nui, and the people are called the Rapanui people). Polynesians were very good at boats. And they went big distances across the Pacific. When these Polynesians arrived was probably 300, but it was probably 900 or 1200.

The island was covered with forests. They can tell by looking at pollin in lakes. The Rapanui people cut trees, to build houses. They didn't know that they wood run out of wood). They also carved *moai.*

The *moai* were made for important chiefs. They were made with only stone tools. They have large heads and narrow bodies. No 2 are the same. Although they look the same as far as their faces are concerned. They are very big and impressive and special.

Over the years, many of the statues were tipped over and broken. But some years ago scientists began to fix some of them and stand them up again. They look more better like that. The ones that have been fixed up are probably the ones you remember seeing in photographs.

The essay does not include a thesis statement.

The writer includes many details that are not relevant to the topic of the essay.

The essay has many errors in grammar, spelling, capitalization, punctuation. The errors detract from the fluency and effectiveness of the essay.

The sentences are often not purposeful, varied, or well controlled.

The essay ends abruptly and lacks a conclusion.

TOOL KIT: WRITING

MODEL

INFORMATIVE/EXPLANATORY: SCORE 2

Moai: The Giant Statues of Easter Island

Easter Island is a tiny Island. It's far out in the middle of the pacific ocean, 2200 miles off the coast. The closest South American country is Chile. The nearest island where people live is called Pitcairn, and that's almost 1,300 miles away. Even if don't know much about it, you've probably seen pictures of the Easter Island statues. You'd recognize one if you saw it. They're almost 900 of them. They're called *moai*. The average one is about 13 feet high (that's tall) and weighs a lot—almost 14 tons.

Scientists know that Polynesians settled Easter Island (it's also called Rapa Nui, and the people are called the Rapanui). Polynesians were very good sailers. And they traveled big distances across the Pacific. Even so, nobody really can say exactly *when* these Polynesians arrived and settled on the Island. Some say 300 A.D., while others say maybe as late as 900 or even 1200 A.D.

Scientists can tell that when the settlers first arrived, the island was covered with forests of palm and hardwood. They can tell by looking at pollin deposits in lakes on the island. The Rapanui people cut trees, built houses, planted crops, and a thriving culture. They didn't know that cutting so many trees would cause problems later on (like running out of wood). They also began to carve *moai*.

The *moai* were built to honor important Rapanui ancestors or chiefs. The statutes all have large heads and narrow bodies, but no too are exactly the same. There faces are all similar. Some have places where eyes could be inserted.

Why did the Rapanui stopped making *moai*? Part of it might have been because there were no more trees and no more of the wood needed to transport them. Part of it was maybe because the people were busy fighting each other because food and other necessary things were running out. In any case, they stopped making moai and started tipping over and breaking the ones that were there already. Later on, archeologists began to try to restore some of the statues and set them up again. But even now that some have been set up again, we still don't know a lot about them. I guess some things just have to remain a mystery!

> The writer does not include a thesis statement.

> Some of the ideas are reasonably well developed.

> The essay has many errors in grammar, spelling, capitalization, punctuation. The errors decrease the effectiveness of the essay.

> The writer's word choice shows that he is not fully aware of the essay's purpose and tone.

> The writer does not include a clear conclusion.

TOOL KIT: WRITING

MODEL

INFORMATIVE/EXPLANATORY: SCORE 3

Moai: The Giant Statues of Easter Island

Easter Island is a tiny place, far out in the middle of the Pacific Ocean, 2200 miles off the coast of South America. Another name for the island is Rapa Nui. Even if you don't know much about it, you would probably recognize the colossal head-and-torso carvings known as *moai*. Even after years of research by scientists, many questions about these extraordinary statues remain unanswered.

The thesis statement is clearly stated.

Scientists now agree that it was Polynesians who settled Easter Island. Earlier some argued South American voyagers were the first. But the Polynesians were expert sailors and navigators known to have traveled huge distances across the Pacific Ocean. However, scientists do not agree about *when* the settlers arrived. Some say A.D. 300, while others suggest as late as between A.D. 900 and 1200.

Scientists say that when the settlers first arrived on Rapa Nui, the island was covered with forests of palm and hardwood. They can tell by looking at the layers of pollen deposited over the years in the lakes on the island. The Rapa Nui began to carve *moai*. They developed a unique artistic and architectural tradition all of their own.

The essay has many interesting details, but some do not relate directly to the topic.

Archeologists agree that the *moai* were created to honor ancestor's or chief's. Most *moai* are made from a soft rock called *tuff* that's formed from hardened volcanic ash. The statues all have large heads on top of narrow bodies, but no two are exactly the same. Some have indented eye sockets where eyes could be inserted.

There are very few errors in grammar, usage, and punctuation. These errors do not interrupt the fluency and effectiveness of the essay.

At some point, the Rapanui stopped making *moai*. Why? Was it because there were no more trees and no longer enough wood needed to transport them? Was it because the people were too busy fighting each other over resources which had begun to run out? No one can say for sure. Rival groups began toppling their enemys' *moai* and breaking them. By the 19th century, most of the statues were tipped over, and many were destroyed. It wasn't until many years later that archeologists began to restore some of the statues.

The *moai* of Easter Island are one of the most awe-inspiring human achievements ever. Thanks to scientific studies, we know much more about the *moai, ahu,* and Rapanui people than we ever did in the past. But some questions remain unanswered. At least for now, the *moai* are keeping their mouths shut, doing a good job of guarding their secrets.

The writer's conclusion sums up the main points of the essay and supports the thesis statement.

MODEL

INFORMATIVE/EXPLANATORY: SCORE 4

Moai: The Giant Statues of Easter Island

Easter Island, 2200 miles off the coast of South America, is "the most remote inhabited island on the planet." Few have visited this speck in the middle of the vast Pacific Ocean, but we all recognize the colossal statues that bring this tiny island its fame: the head-and-torso carvings known as *moai*. Yet even after years of research by scientists, many questions about the *moai* remain unanswered.

The thesis statement of is clearly stated in an engaging manner.

Scientists now agree that it was Polynesians, not South Americans, who settled Easter Island (also known as Rapa Nui). Polynesians were expert sailors and navigators known to have traveled huge distances across the Pacific Ocean. Even so, there is little agreement about *when* the settlers arrived. Some say A.D. 300, while others suggest as late as between A.D. 900 and 1200.

The ideas in the essay relate to the thesis statement and focus on the topic.

Most archeologists agree that the *moai* were created to honor ancestors, chiefs, or other important people. Most *moai* are made from a soft rock called *tuff* that's formed from hardened volcanic ash. The statues have large heads atop narrow torsos, with eyes wide open and lips tightly closed. While the moai share these basic characteristics, no two are exactly the same: while all are huge, some are bigger than others. Some are decorated with carvings. Some have indented eye sockets where white coral eyes could be inserted. It's possible that the eyes were only put in for special occasions.

The writer includes many specific and well-chosen details that add substance to the essay.

In the late 1600s, the Rapanui stopped carving *moai*. Was it because the forests had been depleted and there was no longer enough wood needed to transport them? Was it because they were too busy fighting each other over dwindling resources? No one can say for sure. What is known is that rival groups began toppling their enemies' *moai* and breaking them. By the 19th century, most of the statues were tipped over, and many were destroyed. It wasn't until many years later that archeologists began restoration efforts.

The *moai* of Easter Island are one of humanity's most awe-inspiring cultural and artistic achievements. Part of Rapa Nui was designated as a World Heritage Site in 1995 to recognize and protect these extraordinary creations. Thanks to scientific studies, we know much more about the *moai* than we ever did in the past. But some questions remain unanswered, some mysteries unsolved. Don't bother asking the *moai*: their lips are sealed.

The fluency of the writing and effectiveness of the essay are unaffected by errors.

The conclusion relates to the thesis statement and is creative and memorable.

TOOL KIT: WRITING

Informative/Explanatory Rubric

	Focus and Organization	Evidence and Elaboration	Conventions
4	The introduction engages the reader and states a thesis in a compelling way. The informative essay includes a clear introduction, body, and conclusion. The conclusion summarizes ideas and offers fresh insight into the thesis.	The essay includes specific reasons, details, facts, and quotations from selections and outside resources to support thesis. The tone of the essay is always formal and objective. The language is always precise and appropriate for the audience and purpose.	The essay uses standard English conventions of usage and mechanics. The essay contains no spelling errors.
3	The introduction engages the reader and sets forth the thesis. The essay includes an introduction, body, and conclusion. The conclusion summarizes ideas and supports the thesis.	The research includes some specific reasons, details, facts, and quotations from selections and outside resources to support the thesis. The tone of the research is mostly formal and objective. The language is generally precise and appropriate for the audience and purpose.	The essay demonstrates general accuracy in standard English conventions of usage and mechanics. The essay contains few spelling errors.
2	The introduction sets forth the thesis. The essay includes an introduction, body, and conclusion, but one or more parts is weak. The conclusion partially summarizes ideas but may not provide strong support of the thesis.	The research includes a few reasons, details, facts, and quotations from selections and outside resources to support the thesis. The tone of the research is occasionally formal and objective. The language is somewhat precise and appropriate for the audience and purpose.	The presentations demonstrates some accuracy in standard English conventions of usage and mechanics. The essay contains some spelling errors.
1	The introduction does not state the thesis clearly. The essay does not include an introduction, body, and conclusion. The conclusion does not summarize ideas and may not relate to the thesis.	Reliable and relevant evidence is not included. The tone of the essay is not objective or formal. The language used is imprecise and not appropriate for the audience and purpose.	The essay contains mistakes in standard English conventions of usage and mechanics. The essay contains many spelling errors.

WRITING

Narration

Narrative writing conveys experience, either real or imaginary, and uses time to provide structure. It can be used to inform, instruct, persuade, or entertain. Whenever writers tell a story, they are using narrative writing. Most types of narrative writing share certain elements, such as characters, setting, a sequence of events, and, often, a theme.

Elements of a Narrative Text

A **narrative** is any type of writing that tells a story, whether it is fiction, nonfiction, poetry, or drama.

An effective nonfiction narrative usually contains these elements:

- an engaging beginning in which characters and setting are established
- characters who participate in the story events
- a well-structured, logical sequence of events
- details that show time and place
- effective story elements such as dialogue, description, and reflection
- the narrator's thoughts, feelings, or views about the significance of events
- use of language that brings the characters and setting to life

An effective fictional narrative usually contains these elements:

- an engaging beginning in which characters, setting, or a main conflict is introduced
- a main character and supporting characters who participate in the story events
- a narrator who relates the events of the plot from a particular point of view
- details that show time and place
- conflict that is resolved in the course of the narrative
- narrative techniques such as dialogue, description, and suspense
- use of language that vividly brings to life characters and events

MODEL

NARRATIVE: SCORE 1

The Remark-a-Ball

Eddie decided to invent a Remark-a-Ball. Eddie thought Barnaby should be able to speak to him.

That's when he invited the Remark-a-Ball.

Barnaby had a rubber ball. It could make a bunchs of sounds that made Barnaby bark. It had always seemed that Barnaby was using his squeaky toy to talk, almost.

This was before Barnaby got hit by a car and died. This was a big deal. He took his chemistry set and worked real hard to created a thing that would make the toy ball talk for Barnaby, his dog.

Eddie made a Remark-a-Ball that worked a little too well, tho. Barnaby could say anything he wanted too. And now he said complaints—his bed didn't feel good, he wanted to be walks, he wanted to eat food.

Barnaby became bossy to Eddy to take him on walks or wake up. It was like he became his boss. Like my dad's boss. Eddy didn't like having a mean boss for a dog.

Eddy wished he hadn't invented the Remark-a-Ball.

The story's beginning is choppy and vague.

The sequence of events is unclear and hard to follow.

The narrative lacks descriptive details and sensory language.

The narrative contains many errors in standard English conventions of usage and mechanics.

The conclusion is abrupt and unsatisfying.

WRITING

MODEL

NARRATIVE: SCORE 2

The Remark-a-Ball

Eddie couldn't understand what his dog was barking about, so he decided to invent a Remark-a-Ball. Eddie thought Barnaby should be able to speak to him.

That's when he invented the Remark-a-Ball.

Barnaby had a rubber ball the size of an orange. It could make a bunch of sounds that made Barnaby bark. It had always seemed to Eddie that Barnaby was almost talking with his squeaky toy.

This was a big deal. Eddy would be the first human ever to talk to a dog, which was a big deal! He took his chemistry set and worked real hard to created a thing that would make the toy ball talk for Barnaby, his dog.

Eddie made a Remark-a-Ball that worked a little too well, tho. Barnaby could say anything he wanted now. And now he mostly said complaints—his bed didn't feel good, he wanted to be walked all the time, he wanted to eat people food.

Barnaby became bossy to Eddy to take him on walks or wake him up. It was like he became his boss. His really mean boss, like my dad's boss. Eddy didn't like having a mean boss for a dog.

Eddy started to ignore his best friend, which used to be his dog named Barnaby. He started tot think maybe dogs shouldn't be able to talk.

Things were much better when Barnaby went back to barking

The story's beginning provides few details to establish the situation.

Narrative techniques such as dialogue, pacing, and description are used sparingly.

The narrative contains some errors in standard English conventions of usage and mechanics.

The conclusion comes abruptly and provides little insight about the story's meaning.

TOOL KIT: WRITING

MODEL

NARRATIVE: SCORE 3

The Remark-a-Ball

Any bark could mean anything: *I'm hungry, Take me outside,* or *There's that dog again*. Eddie thought Barnaby should be able to speak to him.

And that's how the Remark-a-Ball was born.

Barnaby had a rubber ball the size of an orange. It could make a wide range of sounds that made Barnaby howl. It had always seemed to Eddie that Barnaby was almost communicating with his squeaky toy.

This was big. This was epic. He would be the first human ever to bridge the communication gap between species! He dusted off his old chemistry set and, through trial and error, created a liquid bath that would greatly increase the toy's flexibility, resilience, and mouth-feel.

Eddie had a prototype that worked—perhaps too well. Barnaby was ready to speak his mind. This unleashed a torrent of complaints—his bed was lumpy, he couldn't *possibly* exist on just three walks a day, he wanted table food like the poodle next door.

Barnaby made increasingly specific demands to Eddie to take him on walks or wake him up. This kind of conversation did not bring them closer, as Eddie had thought, but instead it drove them apart.

Eddie started to avoid his former best friend, and he came to the realization that there is a good reason different species don't have a common language.

So Eddie quit letting Barnaby use the toy.

"Hey, Barn, want to go outside?" Eddie would say, and the dog, as if a switch was turned on, would shake, wag, pant, run in circles, and bark—just like he used to.

The story's beginning establishes the situation and the narrator's point of view but leaves some details unclear.

The narrative consistently uses standard English conventions of usage and mechanics.

Narrative techniques such as dialogue and description are used occasionally.

The conclusion resolves the situation or problem, but does not clearly convey the significance of the events in the story.

WRITING

MODEL

NARRATIVE: SCORE 4

The Remark-a-Ball

Barnaby, for no apparent reason, leapt up and began to bark like a maniac. "Why are you barking?" asked Eddie, holding the leash tight. But Barnaby, being a dog, couldn't say. It could have been anything—a dead bird, a half-eaten sandwich, the Taj Mahal.

The story's beginning is engaging, sets up a point of view, and establishes characters and tone.

This was one of those times Eddie wished that Barnaby could talk. Any bark could mean anything: *I'm hungry, Take me outside,* or *There's that dog again*. Eddie thought, as buddies, they should be able to understand each other.

And that's how the Remark-a-Ball was born.

The narrative uses standard English conventions of usage and mechanics, except where language is manipulated for effect.

Barnaby had a squeaky toy—a rubber ball the size of an orange. It could emit a wide range of sounds. It made Barnaby howl even as he was squeaking it. And it had always seemed to Eddie that through this process Barnaby was almost communicating.

This was big. This was epic. He, Edward C. Reyes III, would be the first human ever to bridge the communication gap between species! He dusted off his old chemistry set and, through trial and error, created a liquid bath that would greatly increase the toy's flexibility, resilience, and mouth-feel.

By the end of the week Eddie had a prototype that worked—perhaps too well. Barnaby was ready to speak his mind. This unleashed a torrent of complaints—his bed was lumpy, he couldn't *possibly* exist on just three walks a day, he wanted table food like the poodle next door.

Events are presented in a logical sequence, and the progression from one even to another is smooth.

Barnaby made increasingly specific demands, such as "Wake me in ten minutes," and "I want filtered water." This kind of conversation did not bring them closer, as Eddie had thought, but instead it drove them apart.

Narrative techniques are used effectively to develop characters and events.

Eddie started to avoid his former best friend, and he came to the realization that there is a good reason different species don't have a common language. It didn't take long for the invention to be relegated to the very bottom of Barnaby's toy chest, too far down for him to get.

There followed a period of transition, after which Eddie and Barnaby returned to their former mode of communication, which worked out just fine.

"Hey, Barn, want to go outside?" Eddie would say, and the dog, as if a switch was turned on, would shake, wag, pant, run in circles, and bark—just like he used to.

The conclusion resolves the situation or problem and clearly conveys the significance of the events in the story.

"You're a good boy, Barnaby," Eddie would say, scratching him behind the ears.

TOOL KIT: WRITING

Narrative Rubric

	Focus and Organization	Development of Ideas/ Elaboration	Conventions
4	The introduction establishes a clear context and point of view. Events are presented in a clear sequence, building to a climax, then moving towards the conclusion. The conclusion follows from and reflects on the events and experiences in the narrative.	Narrative techniques such as dialogue, pacing, and description are used effectively to develop characters, events, and strengths. Descriptive details, sensory language, and precise words and phrases are used to convey the experiences in the narrative and to help the reader imagine the characters and setting. Voice is established through word choice, sentence structure, and tone.	The narrative uses standard English conventions of usage and mechanics; deviations from standard English are intentional and serve the purpose of the narrative. Rules of spelling and punctuation are followed.
3	The introduction gives the reader some context and sets the point of view. Events are presented logically, though there are some jumps in time. The conclusion logically ends the story, but provides only some reflection on the experiences related in the story.	Narrative techniques such as dialogue, pacing, and description are used occasionally. Description details, sensory language, and precise words and phrases are used occasionally. Voice is established through word choice, sentence structure, and tone occasionally, though not evenly.	The narrative mostly uses standard English conventions of usage and mechanics, though there are some errors. There are few errors in spelling and punctuation.
2	The introduction provides some description of a place. The point of view can be unclear at times. Transitions between events are occasionally unclear. The conclusion comes abruptly and provides only a small amount of reflection on the experiences related in the narrative.	Narrative techniques such as dialogue, pacing, and description are used sparingly. The story contains few examples of descriptive details and sensory language. Voice is not established for characters, so that it becomes difficult to determine who is speaking.	The narrative contains some errors in standard English conventions of usage and mechanics. There are many errors in spelling and punctuation.
1	The introduction fails to set a scene or is omitted altogether. The point of view is not always clear. The events are not in a clear sequence, and events that would clarify the narrative may not appear. The conclusion does not follow from the narrative or is omitted altogether.	Appropriate narrative techniques such as dialogue, pacing, or reflection, are not used. Details are vague or missing. No sensory language is included. Voice has not been developed.	The text contains mistakes in standard English conventions of usage and mechanics. Rules of spelling and punctuation have not been followed.

Conducting Research

We are lucky to live in an age when information is accessible and plentiful. However, not all information is equally useful, or even accurate. Strong research skills will help you locate and evaluate information.

Narrowing or Broadening a Topic

The first step of any research project is determining your topic. Consider the scope of your project and choose a topic that is narrow enough to address completely and effectively. If you can name your topic in just one or two words, it is probably too broad. Topics such as Shakespeare, jazz, or science fiction are too broad to cover in a single report. Narrow a broad topic into smaller subcategories.

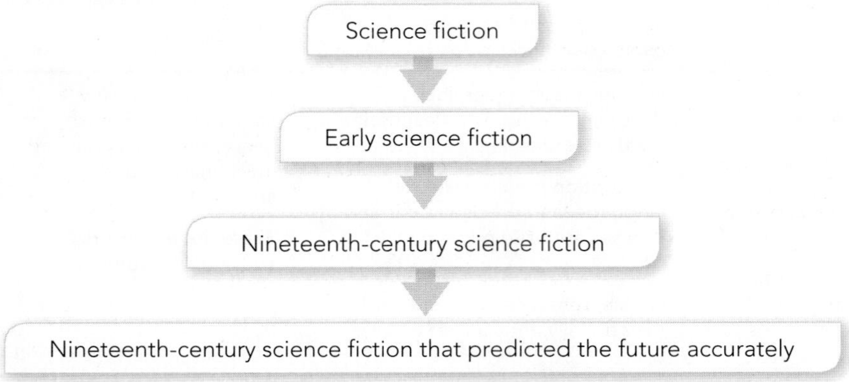

When you begin to research a topic, pay attention to the amount of information available. If you feel overwhelmed by the number of relevant sources, you may need to narrow your topic further.

If there isn't enough information available as your research, you might need to broaden your topic. A topic is too narrow when it can be thoroughly presented in less space than the required size of your assignment. It might also be too narrow if you can find little or no information in library and media sources, so consider broadening your topic to include other related ideas.

Generating Research Questions

Use research questions to focus your research. Specific questions can help you avoid time-wasting digressions. For example, instead of simply hunting for information about Mark Twain, you might ask, "What jobs did Mark Twain have, other than being a writer?" or "Which of Twain's books was most popular during his lifetime?"

In a research report, your research question often becomes your thesis statement, or may lead up to it. The question will also help you focus your research into a comprehensive but flexible search plan, as well as prevent you from gathering unnecessary details. As your research teaches you more about your topic, you may find it necessary to refocus your original question.

Consulting Print and Digital Sources

Effective research combines information from several sources, and does not rely too heavily on a single source. The creativity and originality of your research depends on how you combine ideas from multiple sources. Plan to consult a variety of resources, such as the following:

- **Primary and Secondary Sources:** To get a thorough view of your topic, use primary sources (firsthand or original accounts, such as interview transcripts, eyewitness reports, and newspaper articles) and secondary sources (accounts, created after an event occurred, such as encyclopedia entries).
- **Print and Digital Resources:** The Internet allows fast access to data, but print resources are often edited more carefully. Use both print and digital resources in order to guarantee the accuracy of your findings.
- **Media Resources:** You can find valuable information in media resources such as documentaries, television programs, podcasts, and museum exhibitions. Consider attending public lectures given by experts to gain an even more in-depth view of your topic.
- **Original Research:** Depending on your topic, you may wish to conduct original research to include among your sources. For example, you might interview experts or eyewitnesses, or conduct a survey of people in your community.

Using Online Encyclopedias

Online encyclopedias are often written by anonymous contributors who are not required to fact-check information. These sites can be very useful as a launching point for research, but should not be considered accurate. Look for footnotes, endnotes, or hyperlinks that support facts with reliable sources that have been carefully checked by editors.

Evaluating Sources It is important to evaluate the credibility, validity, and accuracy of any information you find, as well as its appropriateness for your purpose and audience. You may find the information you need to answer your research question in specialized and authoritative sources, such as almanacs (for social, cultural, and natural statistics), government publications (for law, government programs, and subjects such as agriculture), and information services. Also, consider consumer, workplace, and public documents.

Ask yourself questions such as these to evaluate these additional sources:

- **Authority:** Is the author well known? What are the author's credentials? Does the source include references to other reliable sources? Does the author's tone win your confidence? Why or why not?
- **Bias:** Does the author have any obvious biases? What is the author's purpose for writing? Who is the target audience?
- **Currency:** When was the work created? Has it been revised? Is there more current information available?

RESEARCH

Using Search Terms

Finding information on the Internet can be both easy and challenging. Type a word or phrase into a general search engine and you will probably get hundreds—or thousands—of results. However, those results are not guaranteed to be relevant or accurate.

These strategies can help you find information from the Internet:

- Create a list of keywords that apply to your topic before you begin using a search engine. Consult a thesaurus to expand your list.
- Enter six to eight keywords.
- Choose precise nouns. Most search engines ignore articles and prepositions. Verbs may be used in multiple contexts, leading to sources that are not relevant. Use modifiers, such as adjectives, when necessary to specify a category.
- Use quotation marks to focus a search. Place a phrase in quotation marks to find pages that include exactly that phrase. Add several phrases in quotation marks to narrow your results.
- Spell carefully. Many search engines autocorrect spelling, but they cannot produce accurate results for all spelling errors.
- Scan search results before you click them. The first result isn't always the most relevant. Read the text and consider the domain before make a choice.
- Utilize more than one search engine.

Evaluating Internet Domains

Not everything you read on the Internet is true, so you have to evaluate sources carefully. The last three letters of an Internet URL identify the Website's domain, which can help you evaluate the information of the site.

- **.gov**—Government sites are sponsored by a branch of the United States federal government, such as the Census Bureau, Supreme Court, or Congress. These sites are considered reliable.
- **.edu**—Education domains include schools from kindergartens to universities. Information from an educational research center or department is likely to be carefully checked. However, education domains can also include student pages that are not edited or monitored.
- **.org**—Organizations are nonprofit groups and usually maintain a high level of credibility. Keep in mind that some organizations may express strong biases.
- **.com** and **.net**—Commercial sites exist to make a profit. Information may be biased to show a product or service in a good light. The company may be providing information to encourage sales or promote a positive image.

Taking Notes

Take notes as you locate and connect useful information from multiple sources, and keep a reference list of every source you use. This will help you make distinctions between the relative value and significance of specific data, facts, and ideas.

For long-term research projects, create source cards and notecards to keep track of information gathered from multiple resources.

Source Cards
Create a card that identifies each source.

- For print materials, list the author, title, publisher, date of publication, and relevant page numbers.
- For Internet sources, record the name and Web address of the site, and the date you accessed the information.
- For media sources, list the title, person, or group credited with creating the media, and the year of production.

Source Card [A]

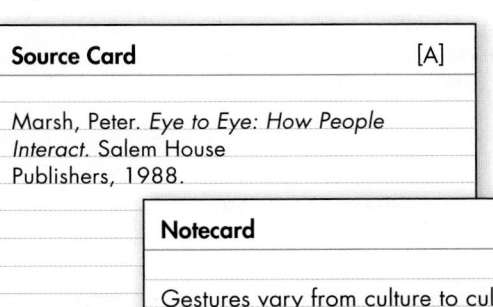

Marsh, Peter. *Eye to Eye: How People Interact.* Salem House Publishers, 1988.

Notecards
Create a separate notecard for each item of information.

- Include the fact or idea, the letter of the related source card, and the specific page(s) on which the fact or idea appears.
- Use quotation marks around words and phrases taken directly from print or media resources.
- Mark particularly useful or relevant details using your own annotation method, such as stars, underlining, or colored highlighting.

Notecard

Gestures vary from culture to culture. The American "OK" symbol (thumb and forefinger) is considered insulting in Greece and Turkey.

Source Card: A, p. 54.

Quote Accurately Responsible research begins with the first note you take. Be sure to quote and paraphrase your sources accurately so you can identify these sources later. In your notes, circle all quotations and paraphrases to distinguish them from your own comments. When photocopying from a source, include the copyright information. When printing out information from an online source, include the Web address.

Reviewing Research Findings

While conducting research, you will need to review your findings, checking that you have collected enough accurate and appropriate information.

Considering Audience and Purpose

Always keep your audience in mind as you gather information, since different audiences may have very different needs. For example, if you are writing an in-depth analysis of a text that your entire class has read together and you are writing for your audience, you will not need to gather background information that has been thoroughly discussed in class. However, if you are writing the same analysis for a national student magazine, you cannot assume that all of your readers have the same background information. You will need to provide facts from reliable sources to help orient these readers to your subject. When considering whether or not your research will satisfy your audience, ask yourself:

- Who are my readers? For whom am I writing?
- Have I collected enough information to explain my topic to this audience?
- Are there details in my research that I can omit because they are already familiar to my audience?

Your purpose for writing will also influence your review of research. If you are researching a question to satisfy your own curiosity, you can stop researching when you feel you understand the answer completely. If you are writing a research report that will be graded, you need to consider the criteria of the assignment. When considering whether or not you have enough information, ask yourself:

- What is my purpose for writing?
- Will the information I have gathered be enough to achieve my purpose?
- If I need more information, where might I find it?

Synthesizing Sources

Effective research writing does not merely present facts and details; it synthesizes—gathers, orders, and interprets—them. These strategies will help you synthesize information effectively:

- Review your notes and look for connections and patterns among the details you have collected.
- Arrange notes or notecards in different ways to help you decide how to best combine related details and present them in a logical way.
- Pay close attention to details that support one other, emphasizing the same main idea.
- Also look for details that challenge each other, highlighting ideas about which there is no single, or consensus, opinion. You might decide to conduct additional research to help you decide which side of the issue has more support.

Types of Evidence

When reviewing your research, also consider the kinds of evidence you have collected. The strongest writing contains a variety of evidence effectively. This chart describes three of the most common types of evidence: statistical, testimonial, and anecdotal.

TYPE OF EVIDENCE	DESCRIPTION	EXAMPLE
Statistical evidence includes facts and other numerical data used to support a claim or explain a topic.	Examples of statistical evidence include historical dates and information, quantitative analyses, poll results, and quantitative descriptions.	"Although it went on to become a hugely popular novel, the first edition of William Goldman's book sold fewer than 3,000 copies."
Testimonial evidence includes any ideas or opinions presented by others, especially experts in a field.	Firsthand testimonies present ideas from eyewitnesses to events or subjects being discussed.	"The ground rose and fell like an ocean at ebb tide." —Fred J. Hewitt, eyewitness to the 1906 San Francisco earthquake
	Secondary testimonies include commentaries on events by people who were not involved. You might quote a well-known literary critic when discussing a writer's most famous novel, or a prominent historian when discussing the effects of an important event	Gladys Hansen insists that "there was plenty of water in hydrants throughout [San Francisco] . . . The problem was this fire got away."
Anecdotal evidence presents one person's view of the world, often by describing specific events or incidents.	Compelling research should not rely solely on this form of evidence, but it can be very useful for adding personal insights and refuting inaccurate generalizations. An individual's experience can be used with other forms of evidence to present complete and persuasive support.	Although many critics claim the novel is universally beloved, at least one reader "threw the book against a wall because it made me so angry."

RESEARCH

Incorporating Research Into Writing

Avoiding Plagiarism

Plagiarism is the unethical presentation of someone else's ideas as your own. You must cite sources for direct quotations, paraphrased information, or facts that are specific to a single source. When you are drafting and revising, circle any words or ideas that are not your own. Follow the instructions on pages R32 and R33 to correctly cite those passages.

Review for Plagiarism Always take time to review your writing for unintentional plagiarism. Read what you have written and take note of any phrases or sentences that do not have your personal writing voice. Compare those passages with your resource materials. You might have copied them without remembering the exact source. Add a correct citation to give credit to the original author. If you cannot find the questionable phrase in your notes, revise it to ensure that your final report reflects your own thinking and not someone else's work.

Quoting and Paraphrasing

When including ideas from research into your writing, you will decide to quote directly or paraphrase.

Direct Quotation Use the author's exact words when they are interesting or persuasive. You might decide to include direct quotations for these reasons:

- to share an especially clear and relevant statement
- to reference a historically significant passage
- to show that an expert agrees with your position
- to present an argument that you will counter in your writing.

Include complete quotations, without deleting or changing words. If you need to omit words for space or clarity, use ellipsis points to indicate the omission. Enclose direct quotations in quotation marks and indicate the author's name.

Paraphrase A paraphrase restates an author's ideas in your own words. Be careful to paraphrase accurately. Beware of making sweeping generalizations in a paraphrase that were not made by the original author. You may use some words from the original source, but a legitimate paraphrase does more than simply rearrange an author's phrases, or replace a few words with synonyms.

Original Text	"*The Tempest* was written as a farewell to art and the artist's life, just before the completion of his forty-ninth year, and everything in the play bespeaks the touch of autumn." Brandes, Georg. "Analogies Between *The Tempest* and *A Midsummer Night's Dream*." *The Tempest*, by William Shakespeare, William Heinemann, 1904, p. 668.
Patchwork Plagiarism phrases from the original are rearranged, but too closely follows the original text.	A farewell to art, Shakespeare's play, *The Tempest*, was finished just before the completion of his forty-ninth year. The artist's life was to end within three years. The touch of autumn is apparent in nearly everything in the play.
Good Paraphrase	Images of autumn occur throughout *The Tempest*, which Shakespeare wrote as a way of saying goodbye to both his craft and his own life.

Maintaining the Flow of Ideas

Effective research writing is much more that just a list of facts. Be sure to maintain the flow of ideas by connecting research information to your own ideas. Instead of simply stating a piece of evidence, use transition words and phrases to explain the connection between information you found from outside resources and your own ideas and purpose for writing. The following transitions can be used to introduce, compare, contrast, and clarify.

Useful Transitions

When providing examples:

for example   for instance   to illustrate   in [name of resource], [author]

When comparing and contrasting ideas or information:

in the same way   similarly   however   on the other hand

When clarifying ideas or opinions:

in other words   that is   to explain   to put it another way

Choosing an effective organizational structure for your writing will help you create a logical flow of ideas. Once you have established a clear organizational structure, insert facts and details from your research in appropriate places to provide evidence and support for your writing.

ORGANIZATIONAL STRUCTURE	USES
Chronological order presents information in the sequence in which it happens.	historical topics; science experiments; analysis of narratives
Part-to-whole order examines how several categories affect a larger subject.	analysis of social issues; historical topics
Order of importance presents information in order of increasing or decreasing importance.	persuasive arguments; supporting a bold or challenging thesis
Comparison-and-contrast organization outlines the similarities and differences of a given topic.	addressing two or more subjects

RESEARCH

Formats for Citing Sources

In research writing, cite your sources. In the body of your paper, provide a footnote, an endnote, or a parenthetical citation, identifying the sources of facts, opinions, or quotations. At the end of your paper, provide a bibliography or a Works Cited list, a list of all the sources referred to in your research. Follow an established format, such as Modern Language Association (MLA) style.

Parenthetical Citations (MLA Style) A parenthetical citation briefly identifies the source from which you have taken a specific quotation, factual claim, or opinion. It refers readers to one of the entries on your Works Cited list. A parenthetical citation has the following features:

- It appears in parentheses.
- It identifies the source by the last name of the author, editor, or translator, or by the title (for a lengthy title, list the first word only).
- It provides a page reference, the page(s) of the source on which the information cited can be found.

A parenthetical citation generally falls outside a closing quotation mark but within the final punctuation of a clause or sentence. For a long quotation set off from the rest of your text, place the citation at the end of the excerpt without any punctuation following.

Sample Parenthetical Citations

It makes sense that baleen whales such as the blue whale, the bowhead whale, the humpback whale, and the sei whale (to name just a few) grow to immense sizes (Carwardine et al. 19–21). The blue whale has grooves running from under its chin to partway along the length of its underbelly. As in some other whales, these grooves expand and allow even more food and water to be taken in (Ellis 18–21).

Authors' last names

Page numbers where information can be found

Works Cited List (MLA Style) A Works Cited list must contain accurate information to enable a reader to locate each source you cite. The basic components of an entry are as follows:

- name of the author, editor, translator, and/or group responsible for the work
- title of the work
- publisher
- date of publication

For print materials, the information for a citation generally appears on the copyright and title pages. For the format of a Works Cited list, consult the examples on this page and in the MLA Style for Listing Sources chart.

Sample Works Cited List (MLA 8th Edition)

Carwardine, Mark, et al. *The Nature Company Guides: Whales, Dolphins, and Porpoises.* Time-Life, 1998.

"Discovering Whales." *Whales on the Net.* Whales in Danger, 1998, www.whales.org.au/discover/index.html. Accessed 11 Apr. 2017.

Neruda, Pablo. "Ode to Spring." *Odes to Opposites*, translated by Ken Krabbenhoft, edited and illustrated by Ferris Cook, Little, 1995, p. 16.

The Saga of the Volsungs. Translated by Jesse L. Byock, Penguin, 1990.

List an anonymous work by title.

List both the title of the work and the collection in which it is found.

Works Cited List or Bibliography?

A Works Cited list includes only those sources you paraphrased or quoted directly in your research paper. By contrast, a bibliography lists all the sources you consulted during research—even those you did not cite.

MLA (8th Edition) Style for Listing Sources

Book with one author	Pyles, Thomas. *The Origins and Development of the English Language.* 2nd ed., Harcourt Brace Jovanovich, 1971. [Indicate the edition or version number when relevant.]
Book with two authors	Pyles, Thomas, and John Algeo. *The Origins and Development of the English Language.* 5th ed., Cengage Learning, 2004.
Book with three or more authors	Donald, Robert B., et al. *Writing Clear Essays.* Prentice Hall, 1983.
Book with an editor	Truth, Sojourner. *Narrative of Sojourner Truth.* Edited by Margaret Washington, Vintage Books, 1993.
Introduction to a work in a published edition	Washington, Margaret. Introduction. *Narrative of Sojourner Truth,* by Sojourner Truth, edited by Washington, Vintage Books, 1993, pp. v–xi.
Single work in an anthology	Hawthorne, Nathaniel. "Young Goodman Brown." *Literature: An Introduction to Reading and Writing,* edited by Edgar V. Roberts and Henry E. Jacobs, 5th ed., Prentice Hall, 1998, pp. 376–385. [Indicate pages for the entire selection.]
Signed article from an encyclopedia	Askeland, Donald R. "Welding." *World Book Encyclopedia,* vol. 21, World Book, 1991, p. 58.
Signed article in a weekly magazine	Wallace, Charles. "A Vodacious Deal." *Time,* 14 Feb. 2000, p. 63.
Signed article in a monthly magazine	Gustaitis, Joseph. "The Sticky History of Chewing Gum." *American History,* Oct. 1998, pp. 30–38.
Newspaper article	Thurow, Roger. "South Africans Who Fought for Sanctions Now Scrap for Investors." *Wall Street Journal,* 11 Feb. 2000, pp. A1+. [For a multipage article that does not appear on consecutive pages, write only the first page number on which it appears, followed by the plus sign.]
Unsigned editorial or story	"Selective Silence." Editorial. *Wall Street Journal,* 11 Feb. 2000, p. A14. [If the editorial or story is signed, begin with the author's name.]
Signed pamphlet or brochure	[Treat the pamphlet as though it were a book.]
Work from a library subscription service	Ertman, Earl L. "Nefertiti's Eyes." *Archaeology,* Mar.–Apr. 2008, pp. 28–32. *Kids Search,* EBSCO, New York Public Library. Accessed 7 Jan. 2017. [Indicating the date you accessed the information is optional but recommended.]
Filmstrips, slide programs, videocassettes, DVDs, and other audiovisual media	*The Diary of Anne Frank.* 1959. Directed by George Stevens, performances by Millie Perkins, Shelley Winters, Joseph Schildkraut, Lou Jacobi, and Richard Beymer, Twentieth Century Fox, 2004. [Indicating the original release date after the title is optional but recommended.]
CD-ROM (with multiple publishers)	Simms, James, editor. *Romeo and Juliet.* By William Shakespeare, Attica Cybernetics / BBC Education / Harper, 1995.
Radio or television program transcript	"Washington's Crossing of the Delaware." *Weekend Edition Sunday,* National Public Radio, 23 Dec. 2013. Transcript.
Web page	"Fun Facts About Gum." ICGA, 2005–2017, www.gumassociation.org/index.cfm/facts-figures/fun-facts-about-gum. Accessed 19 Feb. 2017. [Indicating the date you accessed the information is optional but recommended.]
Personal interview	Smith, Jane. Personal interview, 10 Feb. 2017.

All examples follow the style given in the MLA Handbook, 8th edition, published in 2016.

MODEL

Evidence Log

Unit Title: Discovery

Perfomance-Based Assessment Prompt:
Do all discoveries benefit humanity?

My initial thoughts:
Yes - all knowledge moves us forward.

As you read multiple texts about a topic, your thinking may change. Use an Evidence Log like this one to record your thoughts, to track details you might use in later writing or discussion, and to make further connections.

Here is a sample to show how one reader's ideas deepened as she read two texts.

Title of Text: Classifying the Stars — Date: Sept. 17

CONNECTION TO THE PROMPT	TEXT EVIDENCE/DETAILS	ADDITIONAL NOTES/IDEAS
Newton shared his discoveries and then other scientists built on his discoveries.	Paragraph 2: "Isaac Newton gave to the world the results of his experiments on passing sunlight through a prism." Paragraph 3: "In 1814 . . . the German optician, Fraunhofer . . . saw that the multiple spectral tints . . . were crossed by hundreds of fine dark lines."	It's not always clear how a discovery might benefit humanity in the future.

How does this text change or add to my thinking? This confirms what I think. — Date: Sept. 20

Title of Text: Cell Phone Mania — Date: Sept. 21

CONNECTION TO THE PROMPT	TEXT EVIDENCE/DETAILS	ADDITIONAL NOTES/IDEAS
Cell phones have made some forms of communication easier, but people don't talk to each other as much as they did in the past.	Paragraph 7: "Over 80% of young adults state that texting is their primary method of communicating with friends. This contrasts with older adults who state that they prefer a phone call."	Is it good that we don't talk to each other as much? Look for article about social media to learn more about this question.

How does this text change or add to my thinking? — Date: Sept. 25
Maybe there are some downsides to discoveries. I still think that knowledge moves us forward, but there are sometimes unintended negative effects.

MODEL

Word Network

A word network is a collection of words related to a topic. As you read the selections in a unit, identify interesting theme-related words and build your vocabulary by adding them to your Word Network.

Use your Word Network as a resource for your discussions and writings. Here is an example:

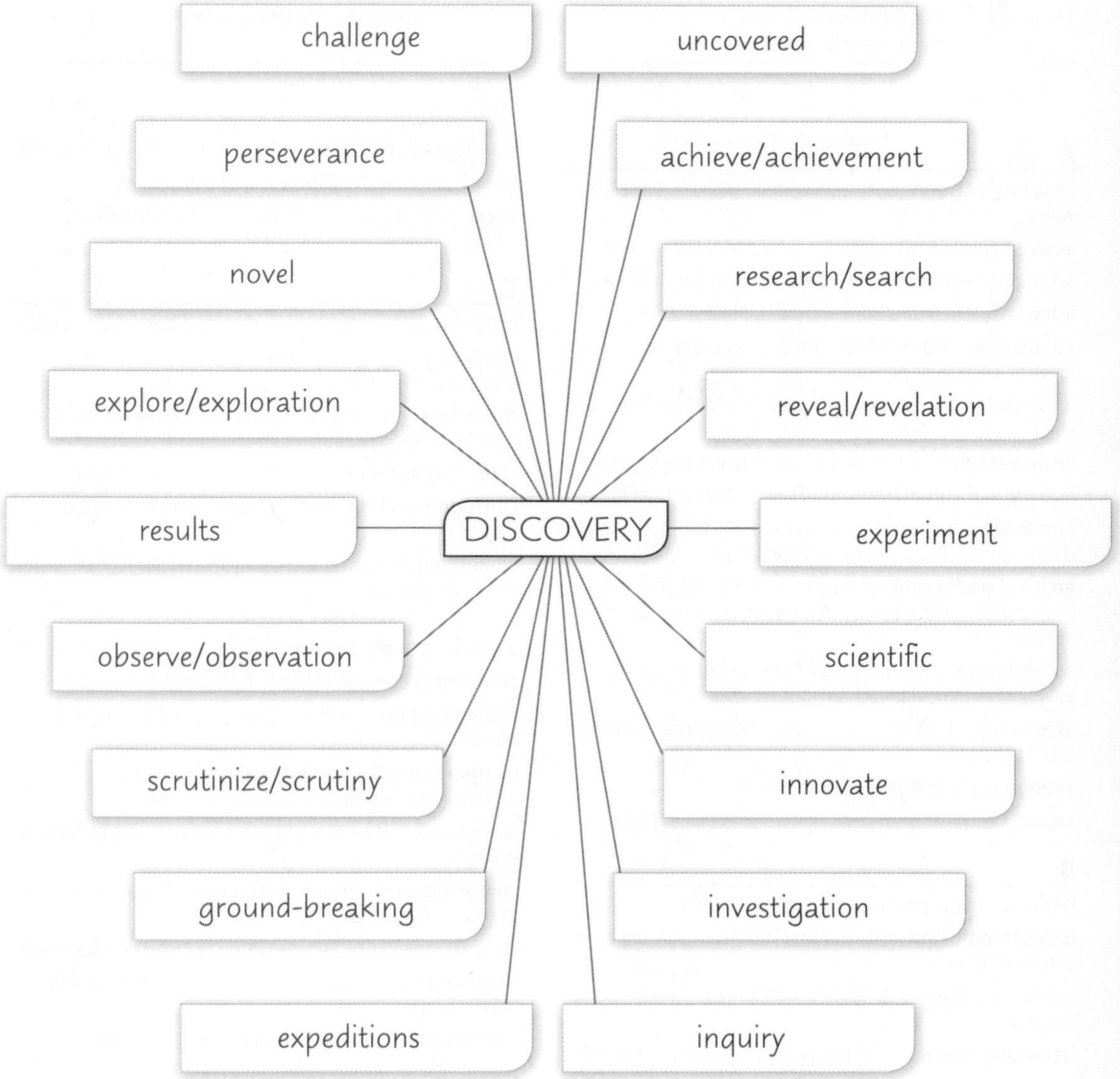

TOOL KIT: PROGRAM RESOURCES

ACADEMIC / CONCEPT VOCABULARY

Academic vocabulary appears in **blue type**.

Pronunciation Key

Symbol	Sample Words	Symbol	Sample Words
a	***at, catapult, Alabama***	oo	***boot, soup, crucial***
ah	***father, charms, argue***	ow	***now, stout, flounder***
ai	***care, various, hair***	oy	***boy, toil, oyster***
aw	***law, maraud, caution***	s	***say, nice, press***
awr	***pour, organism, forewarn***	sh	***she, abolition, motion***
ay	***ape, sails, implication***	u	***full, put, book***
ee	***even, teeth, really***	uh	***ago, focus, contemplation***
eh	***ten, repel, elephant***	ur	***bird, urgent. perforation***
ehr	***merry, verify, terribly***	y	***by, delight, identify***
ih	***it, pin, hymn***	yoo	***music, confuse, few***
o	***shot, hopscotch, condo***	zh	***pleasure, treasure, vision***
oh	***own, parole, rowboat***		

A

absolute (AB suh loot) *adj.* certain; positive; perfectly whole

activist (AK tuh vihst) *n.* active supporter of a cause

adamant (AD uh muhnt) *adj.* not giving in; stubborn

adversary (AD vuhr sehr ee) *n.* opponent; enemy

advocating (AD vuh kayt ihng) *v.* speaking or writing in favor of a cause or person

aggregate (AG ruh giht) *n.* collection; sum of many parts

anticipated (an TIHS uh payt ihd) *v.* eagerly expected

apocryphal (uh POK ruh fuhl) *adj.* fake; not genuine

applicant information (AP luh kuhnt) (ihn fuhr MAY shuhn) *n.* data about a person applying for a job

archival audio (ahr KY vuhl) (AW dee oh) *n.* sound recorded from radio broadcasts, television shows, or films of past decades

assimilation (uh sihm uh LAY shuhn) *n.* process of adapting to the culture of an adopted country

attending (uh TEHND ihng) *adj.* being present; taking care of things

avenge (uh VEHNJ) *v.* get revenge for

awesome (AW suhm) *adj.* impressive; causing awe

B

bade (bayd) *v.* past tense of *bid;* requested

banishment (BAN ihsh muhnt) *n.* state of having been banished, or exiled

banter (BAN tuhr) *n.* friendly exchange between speakers

bemusing (bih MYOOZ ihng) *adj.* confusing; bewildering

besieged (bih SEEJD) *adj.* under military attack

bewildered (bih WIHL duhrd) *adj.* confused completely

blundering (BLUHN duhr ihng) *adj.* clumsy

burden (BUR duhn) *n.* something that is carried with difficulty or obligation

C

cadence (KAY duhns) *n.* rhythm and flow of language

caption (KAP shuhn) *n.* words in a separate box in a graphic novel or comic strip

check box (chehk) (boks) *n.* place on a form to indicate "yes," signifying that a certain statement is true

chimed (chymd) *v.* rang; made the sound of a bell

chirruped (CHIHR uhpt) *v.* made bird-like chirping sounds

coalescing (koh uh LEHS ihng) *n.* coming together in one body or place

coherent (koh HIHR ihnt) *adj.* sticking together; holding together; logically consistent

compact (kuhm PAKT) *adj.* firmly packed

compelling (kuhm PEHL ihng) *adj.* interesting and attractive; persuasive

complacency (kuhm PLAY suhn see) *n.* state of unthinking or satisfied acceptance

composed (kuhm POHZD) *n.* created music or literary work

composition (kom puh ZIHSH uhn) *n.* arrangement of the parts of a picture

concessions (kuhn SEHSH uhnz) *n.* special allowances

confidence (KON fuh duhns) *n.* meeting, especially one held in secret

conflict (KON flihkt) *n.* struggle; problem; fight

conjecture (kuhn JEHK chuhr) *n.* guess; *v.* guess

conscience (KON shuhns) *n.* inner sense of what is morally right or wrong in one's actions

correspondents (kawr uh SPON duhnts) *n.* reporters who send news from far away or on a special subject

counterfeit (KOWN tuhr fiht) *n.* something made to deceive

craft (kraft) *n.* activity that requires skill

credible (KREHD uh buhl) *adj.* believable; convincing

credulity (kruh DYOO luh tee) *n.* readiness to believe

culpability (kuhl puh BIHL uh tee) *n.* guilt or blame that is deserved; blameworthiness

cunning (KUHN ihng) *n.* skill in deception

customs (KUHS tuhmz) *n.* traditions; actions that are commonly done by a group of people

D

deceived (dih SEEVD) *v.* lied to; tricked

deftly (DEHFT lee) *adv.* in a way that is skillfull and quick

delicately (DEHL uh kiht lee) *adv.* carefully; with grace and gentleness

delivery (dih LIHV uhr ee) *n.* manner in which a speaker gives a speech

dependency (dih PEHN duhn see) *n.* act of leaning on another for support or help

depiction (dih PIHK shuhn) *n.* picture, description, or explanation

descendants (dih SEHN duhnts) *n.* people who are the offspring of an ancestor

description (dih SKRIHP shuhn) *n.* writing or speech that tells about something

desperate (DEHS puhr iht) *adj.* involving extreme danger or disaster; driven to action by a loss of hope

destined (DEHS tihnd) *adj.* caused by fate; meant to do; meant for

devoted (dih VOHT ihd) *adj.* loving, loyal, and concerned with another's well-being

dialogue (DY uh log) *n.* conversation between characters in writing, film, or drama

discordant (dihs KAWR duhnt) *adj.* unrelated; out of place

disparate (DIHS puhr iht) *adj.* essentially different in kind

dispatched (dihs PACHT) *v.* finished something quickly

disrupt (dihs RUHPT) *v.* break up; upset; interrupt

dissemble (dih SEHM buhl) *v.* put on an appearance or disguise

distressed (dihs TREHST) *adj.* full of anxiety and suffering

diversity (duh VUR suh tee) *n.* variety of different ethnic or cultural groups

E

eerily (EER uh lee) *adv.* strangely; weirdly

elation (ih LAY shuhn) *n.* great happiness and excitement

elucidate (ih LOO suh dayt) *v.* explain; make clear

empathic (ehm PATH ihk) *adj.* characterized by empathy, the ability to identify with the feelings or thoughts of others

endure (ehn DUR) *v.* last; continue; put up with

enthralled (ehn THRAWLD) *v.* captivated

entranced (ehn TRANST) *adj.* in a state of wonder or amazement

entrusted (ehn TRUHST ihd) *v.* given the responsibility of doing something or caring for someone or something

establishing shot (ehs TAB lihsh ihng) (shot) *n.* shot that shows the context of a scene in a film or video

eternal (ih TUR nuhl) *adj.* timeless; everlasting

evidence (EHV uh duhns) *n.* facts or details that support a position or claim

exalted (ehg ZAWL tihd) *adj.* elevated

exile (EHG zyl) *v.* punish someone by forcing that person to leave a place permanently

expedite (EHKS puh dyt) *v.* make easy and quick; do quickly

expert commentary (EHKS purht) (KOM ehn tair ee) *n.* information delivered by a person who has special knowledge of the subject

exposition (ehks spuh ZIH shuhn) *n.* writing or speech that explains or shows

express (ehks PREHS) *v.* say; convey; reveal

eyewitness (Y wiht nihs) *n.* someone who has firsthand experience of an event

F

factions (FAK shuhnz) *n.* groups of people inside a political party, club, government, etc., working against another group

faithless (FAYTH lihs) *adj.* without faith; unbelieving

fasting (FAS tihng) *v.* intentionally not eating, often for religious or spiritual reasons

fluttered (FLUH tuhrd) *v.* waved gently

forbidden (fuhr BIHD uhn) *adj.* prevented or prohibited

formulate (FAWR myuh layt) *v.* build; state definitely; develop

fugitives (FYOO juh tihvz) *n.* group of persons who have run away from danger

G

gesture (JEHS chuhr) *n.* movement of the hands or body that conveys meaning

guise (gyz) *n.* outward appearance

gutter (GUHT uhr) *n.* space between panels in a graphic novel

GLOSSARY: ACADEMIC / CONCEPT VOCABULARY

H

hallowed (HAL ohd) *adj.* holy; sacred

hallucination (huh loo suh NAY shuhn) *n.* something perceived that has no reality

heretics (HEHR uh tihks) *n.* people who hold a different belief from the official belief of their church

human interest story (HYOO muhn) (IHN trihst) (STAWR ee) *n.* story that focuses on the personal issues of people

I

idly (YD lee) *adv.* lazily; without taking action

impulse (IHM puhls) *n.* sudden urge to act or do something

incredulity (ihn kruh DYOO luh tee) *n.* doubt

indignation (ihn dihg NAY shuhn) *n.* righteous anger; hostility

inevitable (ihn EHV uh tuh buhl) *adj.* certain to occur; unavoidable

infantile (IHN fuhn tyl) *adj.* babyish; childish

infatuated (ihn FACH oo ayt ihd) *adj.* briefly but intensely in love

innovate (IHN uh vayt) *v.* make changes; introduce something new

inscribed (ihn SKRYBD) *adj.* written or engraved upon

interpreter (ihn TUR pruh tuhr) *n.* person who changes the words of one language into another for the benefit of listeners

intervened (ihn tuhr VEEND) *v.* came between groups

interwoven (ihn tuhr WOH vuhn) *adj.* intermingled; combined

intrigued (ihn TREEGD) *v.* interested and curious

introduction (ihn truh DUHK shuhn) *n.* context and background information about the topic of a radio broadcast, provided at its beginning

introspective (ihn truh SPEHK tihv) *adj.* having the habit of examining one's own thoughts and feelings

iridescent (ihr uh DEHS uhnt) *adj.* changing in color when seen from different angles

irresolvable (ihr ih ZOL vuh buhl) *adj.* impossible to resolve or settle

L

lamentable (luh MEHN tuh buhl) *adj.* grievous; mournful; sorrowful

languished (LANG gwihsht) *v.* grown weak; lived under distressing conditions

lighting and color (LY tihng) (KUHL uhr) *n.* use of light, shadow, and color in a picture

logical (LOJ uh kuhl) *adj.* based on reason or sound judgment

luminous (LOO muh nuhs) *adj.* shining; radiating light

M

macabre (muh KAH bruh) *adj.* grim and horrible

manipulated (muh NIHP yuh layt ihd) *v.* managed or controlled through clever moves

meager (MEE guhr) *adj.* extremely thin

meditative (MEHD uh tay tihv) *adj.* given to extended thought

melancholy (MEHL uhn kol ee) *adj.* sad and depressed

memento (muh MEHN toh) *n.* souvenir; keepsake

minority (muh NAWR uh tee) *n.* group of people that differs in some way from the larger population

misery (MIHZ uhr ee) *n.* condition of great wretchedness

montage (mon TOZH) *n.* group of images shown quickly, one after another, to create a single impression

mortality (mawr TAL uh tee) *n.* condition of being sure to die sometime

mutiny (MYOO tuh nee) *n.* open rebellion against lawful authority, especially by sailors or soldiers against their officers

N

naturalization (nach uhr uh luh ZAY shuhn) *n.* process of becoming a citizen

notation (noh TAY shuhn) *n.* brief note added to a text to explain, elaborate, remind, etc.

O

oppression (uh PREHSH uhn) *n.* cruel or unjust treatment

oratory (AWR uh tawr ee) *n.* formal public speaking

P

panel (PAN uhl) *n.* one of the drawings on a page, usually framed by a border

pardon (PAHR duhn) *n.* forgiveness for a crime

pathos (PAY thos) *n.* quality that creates a feeling of sadness or pity

penury (PEHN yuhr ee) *n.* destitution or poverty

perspective or angle (puhr SPEHK tihv) (ANG guhl) *n.* vantage point from which a photo is taken

physiology (fihz ee OL uh jee) *n.* all functions and activites of living things and their parts

pipes (pyps) *v.* says in a loud, clear, or shrill voice

pitched (pihcht) *v.* moved up and down

plotted (PLOT ihd) *v.* planned a strategy or activity

plundered (PLUHN duhrd) *v.* took something by force

pluralistic (pluhr uh LIHS tihk) *adj.* having multiple parts or aspects

point of view (poynt) (uhv) (vyoo) *n.* perspective from which the creators of a media piece approach a topic

postpone (pohst POHN) *v.* delay

prayerful (PRAIR fuhl) *adj.* appearing as if praying

predatory (PREHD uh tawr ee) *adj.* living by capturing and feeding on other animals

premonition (prehm uh NIHSH uhn) *n.* feeling that something bad will happen

primary source (PRY mehr ee) (sawrs) *n.* document, recording, image, or other source that was created at the same time as the events it describes or shows

privacy statement (PRY vuh see) (STAYT muhnt) *n.* statement from an institution that guarantees personal information will not be given out

procedure (pruh SEE juhr) *n.* steps to complete an action

profound (pruh FOWND) *adj.* intense; deep

prophet (PROF iht) *n.* person who predicts the future

propose (pruh POHZ) *v.* suggest

prosperity (pros PEHR uh tee) *n.* good fortune; success

proximity (prok SIHM uh tee) *n.* quality of being near or close to

psyche (SY kee) *n.* human mind or spirit

purified (PYUR uh fyd) *v.* cleaned by removing harmful or unwanted materials or qualities

R

radical (RAD uh kuhl) *adj.* extreme; fundamental

recurrent (rih KUR uhnt) *adj.* repeating

redemptive (rih DEHMP tihv) *adj.* serving to deliver from sorrow, make amends, or pay back

reeling (REE lihng) *adj.* going around and around in a whirling motion

reincarnation (ree ihn kahr NAY shuhn) *n.* belief that the soul reappears after death in another bodily form

relented (rih LEHNT ihd) *v.* agreed to do something after resisting it before

remorse (rih MAWRS) *n.* deep sense of regret for having done wrong

reporter stand-ups (rih POHR tuhr) (STAND uhps) *n.* shots that show a reporter looking into the camera and delivering information about a story

retaliating (rih TAL ee ayt ihng) *v.* paying back for injury; returning evil for evil

S

salient (SAY lee uhnt) *adj.* noticeable; prominent

secondary source (SEHK uhn dehr ee) (sawrs) *n.* document, recording, image, or other source that is written or created after an event by someone who did not witness it firsthand

sensationalized (sehn SAY shuh nuh lyzd) *v.* exaggerated for effect

sequence (SEE kwuhns) *n.* order, as a linear order of steps or events

serpentine (SUR puhn teen) *adj.* twisting; winding; like a serpent

sheer (sheer) *adj.* absolute; complete; utter

specter (SPEHK tuhr) *n.* ghost

speech bubble (speech) (BUHB uhl) *n.* rounded shape containing a character's words

splash (splash) *n.* large, full-page illustration

sprawling (SPRAWL ihng) *adj.* spread out

stagnation (stag NAY shuhn) *n.* state of being inactive and not moving or changing

steal (steel) *v.* move in a way that is secret or quiet

stern (sturn) *adj.* strict; severe

stock (stok) *n.* descendants of a particular individual or ethnic group; family or lineage

subsequent (SUHB suh kwuhnt) *adj.* coming after; following

summoned (SUHM uhnd) *v.* ordered someone or something to come to a place

surrounding (suh ROWN dihng) *adj.* enclosing on all sides

T

tactics (TAK tihks) *n.* military procedures

teased (teezd) *v.* made an affectionate, good-humored personal joke

technique (tehk NEEK) *n.* special method or skill

tier (tihr) *n.* row of panels in a graphic novel

tone (tohn) *n.* attitude a speaker takes toward a subject

transgression (tranz GREHSH uhn) *n.* act of breaking a law or command, or of committing a sin

treasure (TREHZH uhr) *v.* value greatly; cherish

trembling (TREHM blihng) *v.* shaking because of fear, excitement, or weakness, etc.

tremulous (TREHM yuh luhs) *adj.* trembling; quivering; timid; fearful

tribulations (trihb yuh LAY shuhnz) *n.* great trouble or misery

tryst (trihst) *n.* secret romantic meeting

U

understatement (UHN duhr stayt muhnt) *n.* downplaying a topic to make it seem less important

upheaval (uhp HEE vuhl) *n.* a lifting up

V

valid (VAL ihd) *adj.* well-founded; sound; effective

ventured (VEHN chuhrd) *v.* tried something dangerous

voluntary (VOL uhn tehr ee) *adj.* done freely

Y

yearning (YUR nihng) *n.* strong desire; longing

VOCABULARIO ACADÉMICO/ VOCABULARIO DE CONCEPTOS

A

absolute / absoluto *adj.* innegable; definitivo; completo

activist / activista *s.* partidario o defensor activo de una causa

adamant / inflexible *adj.* firme; terco

adversary / adversario *s.* oponente; enemigo

advocating / abogar *v.* hablar o escribir en favor de una causa o persona

aggregate / total *s.* conjunto; suma de varias partes

anticipated / esperado *adj.* deseado con ansias

apocryphal / apócrifo *adj.* falso; no legítimo

applicant information / información sobre el solicitante *s.* datos de una persona que está solicitando un trabajo

archival audio / grabación de archivo *s.* sonido grabado de programas de radio, televisión o películas de décadas pasadas

assimilation / asimilación *s.* proceso de adaptación a la cultura del país de adopción

attending / asistir *v.* estar presente; ocuparse de atender a alguien o algo

avenge / vengar *v.* tomar revancha; vengarse

awesome / impresionante *adj.* imponente; que causa asombro

B

bade / demandó *v.* pasado de *demandar*; pidió; requirió

banishment / destierro *s.* el estado de encontrarse desterrado o exiliado

banter / cotorreo *s.* intercambio amistoso entre dos interlocutores

bemusing / desconcertante *adj.* que confunde mucho; que deja perplejo

besieged / sitiado *adj.* bajo ataque militar

bewildered / perplejo *adj.* profundamente confundido

blundering / torpe *adj.* desmañado, inhábil

burden / carga *s.* algo que se hace o se lleva con dificultad o por obligación

C

cadence / cadencia *s.* el ritmo y la fluidez del lenguaje

caption / cartela *s.* texto que está en un recuadro aparte en las novelas gráficas o en los cómics

check box / casillero de verificación *s.* espacio en un formulario para indicar "sí", y que señala que un enunciado es verdadero

chimed / repicó *v.* sonó del modo en que suena una campana

chirruped / gorjeó *v.* hizo un sonido similar al gorjeo de un pájaro

coalescing / fusión *s.* acto de fundirse o juntarse en un solo cuerpo o lugar

coherent / cohesivo *adj.* que produce adherencia; que junta o pega

compact / compacto *adj.* denso, abarrotado

compelling / cautivador *adj.* interesante y atractivo; convincente

complacency / complacencia *s.* estado de aceptación despreocupada o irreflexiva

composed / compuesta *adj* escrita, creada, especialmente cuando se refiere a una obra musical o literaria

composition/ composición *s.* distribución o arreglo de las partes de un cuadro

concessions / concesiones *s.* permisos o prestaciones especiales

confidence / confianza *s.* reunión, especialmente la que se lleva a cabo en secreto

conflict / conflicto *s.* lucha; problema; pelea

conjecture / conjetura *s.* suposición; *v.* adivinar

conscience / conciencia *s.* sentido interior de lo que es moralmente correcto o incorrecto en nuestras acciones

correspondents / corresponsales *s.* reporteros que envían noticias sobre un determinado tema desde lugares lejanos

counterfeit / falsificación *s.* algo hecho para engañar

craft / oficio *s.* actividad que requiere ciertas destrezas

credible / creíble *adj.* verosímil; convincente

credulity / credulidad *s.* diposición a creer

culpability / culpabilidad *s.* culpa o responsabilidad en algún hecho censurable; reprobabilidad

cunning / astucia *s.* habilidad para mentir o engañar

customs / costumbres *s.* tradiciones; las acciones que por lo general realizan un grupo de personas

D

deceived / engañar *v.* mentir; burlarse de

deftly / hábilmente *adv.* de manera diestra y rápida

delicately / delicadamente *adv.* cuidadosamente; con gracia y suavidad

delivery / presentación oral *s.* la manera en que un orador pronuncia su discurso

dependency / dependencia *s.* condición de necesitar el apoyo o ayuda de otra persona

depiction / representación *s.* retrato, descripción o explicación de algo

descendants / descendientes *s.* las personas que son sucesoras de un ancentro

description / descripción *s.* texto o discurso que informa acerca de algo

desperate / desesperado *adj.* que implica algún desastre o peligro extremo ; que toma acción al perder la esperanza

destined / destinado *adj.* causado por el destino; llamado a hacer; nacido para realizar algo

devoted / dedicado *adj.* cariñoso, leal y preocupado por el bienestar de otra persona

dialogue / diálogo *s.* conversación entre los personajes de un texto, película u obra de teatro

discordant / discordante *adj.* no relacionado; fuera de lugar

disparate / dispar *adj.* de un tipo esencialmente distinto

dispatched / despachar *v.* terminar algo rápidamente

disrupt / irrumpir *v.* interrumpir; perturbar

dissemble / disimular *v.* simular, pretender

distressed / angustiado *adj.* lleno de ansiedad y preocupación

diversity / diversidad *s.* una variedad de distintos grupos étnicos o culturales

E

eerily / misteriosamente *adv.* extrañamente; inquietantemente o siniestramente

elation / euforia *s.* gran felicidad y entusiasmo

elucidate / elucidar *v.* explicar, aclarar

empathic / empático *adj.* que se caracteriza por la empatía, es decir, por la habilidad de identificarse con los sentimientos o pensamientos de otras personas

endure / perdurar *v.* durar, continuar; aguantar o tolerar algo

enthralled / embelesado *adj.* cautivado o fascinado

entranced / extasiado *adj.* maravillado o asombrado

entrusted / encargado *adj.* que se le ha asignado la responsabilidad de hacer algo o de cuidar de alguien o de algo

establishing shot / plano de situación *s.* plano que muestra el contexto de una escena en una película o video

eternal / eterno *adj.* sin final; perpetuo

evidence / evidencia *s.* datos o detalles que respaldan una posición o reclamo

exalted / exaltado *adj.* elevado

exile / exiliar *v.* castigar a una persona forzándola a abandonar un lugar de manera permanente

expedite / acelerar *v.* facilitar algo; hacer algo rápidamente

expert commentary / comentario experto *s.* información ofrecida por una persona con conocimiento especial sobre un tema

exposition / presentación *s.* texto o discurso que explica o muestra algo

express / expresar *v.* decir; transmitir; revelar

eyewitness / testigo presencial *s.* persona que ha presenciado un evento directamenete

F

factions / facciones *s.* grupos de personas que pertenecen a un partido político, club, gobierno, etc. y que se oponen a las posturas de otros grupos

faithless / ateo *adj.* que no profesa una fe religiosa; no creyente

fasting / ayunar *v.* privarse voluntariamente de la comida, generalmente por razones religiosas o espirituales

fluttered / aleteó *v.* ondeó suavemente

forbidden / prohibido *adj.* que se impide o se veta

formulate / formular *v.* construir; enunciar de forma precisa; desarrollar

framework script / borrador de guión *s.* se usa para bosquejar escenas de una película o video

fugitives / fugitivos *s.* personas que escaparon de un peligro

G

gesture / gesto *s.* movimiento de las manos o de otras partes del cuerpo que comunica algo

guise / aspecto *s.* apariencia exterior

gutter / canaleta *s.* en una novela gráfica, el espacio entre dos viñetas

H

hallowed / santificado *adj.* sagrado

hallucination / alucinación *s.* algo que se percibe pero que no tiene una existencia real

heretics / herejes *s.* personas que tienen creencias distintas de las aceptadas por su religión

human interest story / relato de interés humano *s.* una historia que se centra en los problemas personales de la gente

I

idly / descuidadamente *adv.* perezosamente; sin tomar acción

impulse / impulso *s.* súbita urgencia de actuar o de hacer algo

incredulity / incredulidad *s.* duda

indignation / indignación *s.* ira justificada; hostilidad

inevitable / inevitable *adj.* que ocurrirá; que no puede evitarse

infantile / infantil *adj.* ingenuo; propio de un niño pequeño

infatuated / prendado *adj.* estar breve pero intensamente enamorado

innovate / innovar *v.* hacer cambios; introducir algo nuevo

inscribed / inscripto *adj.* escrito o grabado

interpreter / intérprete *s.* persona que traduce de una lengua a otra de forma oral

intervened / intervino *v.* que terció entre dos grupos para ayudar a resolver diferencias

interwoven / entretejido *adj.* entrelazado; combinado

intrigued / intrigado *adj.* interesado, curioso

introduction / presentación *s.* contexto e información sobre el tema al inicio de un programa de radio

introspective / introspectivo *adj.* que tiene por costumbre analizar sus propios pensamientos y sentimientos

iridescent / iridiscente *adj.* que cambia de color cuando se lo mira desde distintos ángulos

irresolvable / irresoluble *adj.* que no se puede resolver o solucionar

L

lamentable / lamentable *adj.* penoso; doloroso; lastimoso

languished / languideció *v.* se debilitó poco a poco bajo condiciones angustiosas

lighting and color / luz y color *s.* uso de la luz, la sombra y el color en un cuadro

logical / lógico *adj.* que se basa en la razón o en un juicio sensato

luminous / luminoso *adj.* brillante, que irradia luz

M

macabre / macabro *adj.* lúgubre y horroroso

manipulated / manipulado *adj.* manejado o controlado por medio de movimientos atinados

meager / raquítico *adj.* sumamente delgado

meditative / meditativo *adj.* que tiende a pensar prolongadamente

melancholy / melancólico *adj.* triste y deprimido

memento / recuerdo *s.* souvenir; objeto que se da como recuerdo

minority / minoría *s.* grupo de personas que se distingue de alguna manera de la mayor parte de la población

misery / miseria *s.* estado de gran infortunio o desgracia

montage / montaje *s.* grupo de imágenes que se muestran rápidamente, una tras otra, para dar la impresión de que es una sola imagen

mortality / mortalidad *s.* seguridad de que en algún momento se va a morir

mutiny / motín *s.* rebelión o revuelta contra la autoridad legítima, especialmente la llevada a cabo por los marineros o los soldados contra los oficiales

N

naturalization / naturalización *s.* proceso de hacerse ciudadano de un país que no es el de su nacimiento

notation / anotación *s.* apunte; información que se pone por escrito

O

oppression / opresión *s.* tratamiento cruel o injusto

oratory / oratoria *s.* arte formal de hablar en público

P

panel / viñeta *s.* cada dibujo de una página, por lo general enmarcado por un borde

pardon / perdón *s.* indulto de un delito

pathos / patetismo *s.* cualidad que produce un sentimiento de tristeza o de compasión

penury / penuria *s.* indigencia o pobreza

perspective or angle / ángulo o perspectiva *s.* punto desde el cual se toma una foto

physiology / fisiología *s.* conjunto de funciones y actividades de los seres vivos y sus partes

pipes / chillar *v.* hablar en voz alta, clara o muy aguda

pitched / cabeceó *v.* se movió hacia arriba y hacia abajo

plotted / tramó *v.* planificó una estrategia o actividad

plundered / saqueó *v.* tomó algo por la fuerza

pluralistic / pluralista *adj.* que tiene múltiples partes o aspectos

point of view / punto de vista *s.* perspectiva desde la cual se observa lo que se narra

postpone / posponer *v.* retrasar

prayerful / piadoso *adj.* que parece que estuviera rezando

predatory / predatorio *adj.* que se alimenta de los animales que captura

premonition / premonición *s.* sensación de que algo malo va a pasar

primary source / fuente primaria *s.* documento, grabación, imagen u otra fuente original creada al mismo tiempo que los eventos que describe o muestra

privacy statement / aviso de privacidad *s.* garantía de una institución de que no se compartirá información personal

procedure / procedimiento *s.* conjunto de pasos para realizar una acción

profound / profundo *adj.* intenso; hondo

prophet / profeta *s.* persona que predice el futuro

propose / proponer *v.* sugerir

prosperity / prosperidad *s.* buena suerte; éxito

proximity / proximidad *s.* cualidad de estar cerca o próximo a algo

psyche / psiquis *s.* espíritu o mente humana

purified / purificado *adj.* limpio de todo atributo o materia dañina o no deseada

R

radical / radical *adj.* muy cambiado

recurrent / recurrente *adj.* que se repite

redemptive / redentor *adj.* que sirve para librar del dolor, para reparar o compensar

reeling / girar *v.* dar vueltas y más vueltas en un movimiento circular

reincarnation / reencarnación *s.* creencia de que, después de la muerte, el alma reaparece en otro cuerpo o forma material

relented / cedió *v.* accedió a hacer algo a lo que se había negado en el pasado

remorse / remordimiento *s.* un profundo sentido de arrepentimiento por haber hecho algo malo

reporter stand-ups / reportero *in situ* *s.* toma que muestra al reportero mirando a la cámara e informando sobre el evento que está cubriendo

retaliating / tomar represalias *v.* vengarse por un daño recibido; devolver un perjuicio con otro

S

salient / sobresaliente *adj.* notable, prominente

secondary source / fuente secundaria *s.* documento, grabación, imagen u otra fuente escrita o creada después de un evento por alguien que no lo presenció

sensationalized / hacer sensacionalismo *v.* exagerar una situación para provocar un efecto sensacionalista o tremendista

sequence / secuencia *s.* serie u orden lineal de pasos o sucesos

serpentine / serpentino *adj.* sinuoso; serpenteante, como el movimiento de una serpiente

sheer / transparente *adj.* muy fino; cuerpo a través del cual se puede ver

specter / espectro *s.* fantasma

speech bubble / globo (historieta) *s.* forma circular que contiene las palabras de los personajes

splash / *splash page* *s.* en una novela gráfica o cómic un dibujo de toda una página

sprawling / expandido *adj.* extendido

stagnation / estancamiento *s.* estado de inactividad, de no moverse ni cambiar

steal / escabullirse *v.* moverse en secreto o silenciosamente

stern / estricto *adj.* rígido; severo

stock / linaje *s.* línea de descendencia de un determinado individuo o grupo étnico; familia o antepasados

subsequent / subsecuente *adj.* que viene después; siguiente

summoned / convocó *v.* le ordenó a alguien o algo que fuera a un lugar determinado

surrounding / rodear *adj.* encerrando por todos lados

T

tactics / tácticas *s.* métodos militares

teased / bromeó *v.* hizo un chiste afectuoso, con buen humor

technique / técnica *s.* destreza o método especial

tier / hilera *s.* cada fila de viñetas de una novela gráfica

tone / tono *s.* la actitud que toma el hablante hacia su tema

transgression / transgresión *s.* la acción de violar una ley o un mandato, o de cometer un pecado

treasure / atesorar *v.* valorar enormemente; estimar mucho

trembling / tembloroso *adj.* que se agita o tirita por temor, entusiasmo, debilidad, etc.

tremulous / trémulo *adj.* tembloroso; estremecido; tímido; temeroso

tribulations / tribulaciones *s.* conjunto de adversidades o penurias

tryst / cita *s.* encuentro amoroso secreto

U

understatement / subestimación *s.* la acción de minimizar un tema para que parezca menos importante

upheaval / revuelta *s.* levantamiento

valid / válido *adj.* bien fundamentado; sensato; efectivo

ventured / arriesgó *v.* intentó algo peligroso

voluntary / voluntario *adj.* hecho libremente

Y

yearning / anhelo *s.* deseo profundo; añoranza

LITERARY TERMS HANDBOOK

ADAPTATION An ***adaptation*** is a work of art that uses the characters and tells the story originally presented in another work of art. Often, the adaptation is in a different form. A novel or play becomes a film, for example, or a poem becomes a story.

ALLITERATION ***Alliteration*** is the repetition of initial consonant sounds. Writers use alliteration to give emphasis to words, to imitate sounds, and to create musical effects.

ALLUSION An ***allusion*** is a reference to a well-known person, place, event, literary work, or work of art.

ANALOGY An ***analogy*** makes a comparison between two or more things that are similar in some ways but otherwise unalike.

ANECDOTE An ***anecdote*** is a brief story about an interesting, amusing, or strange event told to entertain or to make a point.

ANTAGONIST An ***antagonist*** is a character or force in conflict with a main character, or protagonist.

ANTITHESIS ***Antithesis*** is a form of parallelism that emphasizes strong contrasts.

ARCHETYPE An ***archetype*** is is a type of character, detail, image, or situation that appears in literature throughout history. Some critics believe that archetypes reveal deep truths about human experience.

ARGUMENT An ***argument*** is writing or speech that attempts to convince the reader to adopt a particular opinion or course of action. An argument is a logical way of presenting a belief, conclusion, or stance. A good argument is supported with reasoning and evidence.

ASIDE An ***aside*** is a short speech delivered by a character in a play in order to express his or her true thoughts and feelings. Traditionally, the aside is directed to the audience and is presumed to be inaudible to the other actors.

ASSONANCE ***Assonance*** is the repetition of vowel sounds followed by different consonants in two or more stressed syllables.

AUTHOR'S PURPOSE An ***author's purpose*** is his or her reason for writing. The four general purposes for writing are to inform, to persuade, to entertain, and to reflect.

AUTOBIOGRAPHICAL WRITING ***Autobiographical writing*** is any type of nonfiction in which an author tells his or her own story.

AUTOBIOGRAPHY An ***autobiography*** is a form of nonfiction in which a writer tells his or her own life story. An autobiography may tell about the person's whole life or only a part of it.

BIBLIOGRAPHY A ***bibliography*** or "works cited" lists all research sources used for an informative essay in an approved style.

BIOGRAPHY A ***biography*** is a form of nonfiction in which a writer tells the life story of another person. Biographies have been written about many famous people, historical and contemporary, but they can also be written about "ordinary" people.

BLANK VERSE ***Blank verse*** is poetry written in unrhymed iambic pentameter lines. This verse form was widely used by William Shakespeare.

CAUSE-AND-EFFECT CHAIN A single cause, which results in an effect, which leads to a second effect, which causes a third effect, and so on, is a ***cause-and-effect chain.***

CAUSE-AND-EFFECT RELATIONSHIP A cause-and-effect relationship shows how one event or situation leads to another.

CENTRAL IDEA The ***central idea*** is the main idea the author wants the audience to understand and remember

CHARACTER A ***character*** is a person or an animal that takes part in the action of a literary work. The main character, or protagonist, is the most important character in a story. This character often changes in some important way as a result of the story's events.

Characters are sometimes classified as round or flat, dynamic or static. A complex, or *round character*, shows many different traits—faults as well as virtues. A *flat character* shows only one trait. A *dynamic character* develops and grows during the course of the story; a *static character* does not change.

CHARACTERIZATION ***Characterization*** is the act of creating and developing a character. In ***direct characterization,*** the author directly states a character's traits.

In ***indirect characterization,*** an author provides clues about a character by describing what a character looks like, does, and says, as well as how other characters react to him or her. It is up to the reader to draw conclusions about the character based on this indirect information.

The most effective indirect characterizations usually result from showing characters acting or speaking.

CHARGED LANGUAGE Words or phrases that evoke strong positive or negative reactions are referred to as ***charged language.***

CLAIM The ***claim*** of a text is the key message that the writer wants to communicate about a topic.

CLARIFICATION A ***clarification*** focuses on a specific part of a response, sometimes simplifying the original idea and other times providing more detail.

COMIC RELIEF ***Comic relief*** is a technique that is used to interrupt a serious part of a literary work by introducing a humorous character or situation.

CONFLICT A ***conflict*** is a struggle between opposing forces. Characters in conflict form the basis of stories, novels, and plays.

There are two kinds of conflict: external and internal. In an ***external conflict,*** the main character struggles against an outside force.

An ***internal conflict*** involves a character in conflict with himself or herself.

CONNOTATION The ***connotation*** of a word is the set of ideas associated with it in addition to its explicit meaning.

CONSONANCE ***Consonance*** is the repetition of final consonant sounds in stressed syllables with different vowel sounds, as in *hat* and *sit*.

COUPLET A ***couplet*** is a pair of rhyming lines, usually of the same length and meter. Couplets are often found in poems and in plays written in verse.

CRITICISM ***Criticism*** is a form of argumentative writing in which an author expresses an opinion about a created work, such as a book, a film, or a performance.

DENOTATION The ***denotation*** of a word is its dictionary meaning, independent of other associations that the word may have.

DESCRIPTION A ***description*** is a portrait in words of a person, a place, or an object. Descriptive writing uses sensory details, those that appeal to the senses: sight, hearing, taste, smell, and touch. Description can be found in all types of writing. Rudolfo Anaya's essay "A Celebration of Grandfathers" contains descriptive passages.

DIALOGUE A ***dialogue*** is a conversation between characters that may reveal their traits and advance the action of a narrative. In fiction or nonfiction, quotation marks indicate a speaker's exact words, and a new paragraph usually indicates a change of speaker.

DICTION ***Diction*** refers to an author's choice of words, especially with regard to range of vocabulary, use of slang and colloquial language, and level of formality.

DRAMA A ***drama*** is a story written to be performed by actors. The script of a drama is made up of ***dialogue***—the words the actors say—and ***stage directions,*** which are comments on how and where action happens.

The drama's ***setting*** is the time and place in which the action occurs. It is indicated by one or more sets, including furniture and backdrops, that suggest interior or exterior scenes. *Props* are objects, such as a sword or a cup of tea, that are used onstage.

At the beginning of most plays, a brief ***exposition*** gives the audience some background information about the characters and the situation. Just as in a story or novel, the plot of a drama is built around characters in conflict.

Dramas are divided into large units called ***acts,*** which are divided into smaller units called ***scenes***. A long play may include many sets that change with the scenes, or it may indicate a change of scene with lighting.

DRAMATIC IRONY ***Dramatic irony*** is a contradiction between what a character thinks and what the audience knows to be true. For example: If a character tries desperately to crack a safe when the audience already knows the safe is empty, dramatic irony is created, causing humor or tension.

ELLIPSES ***Ellipses*** are used to show omitted words or sentences in quoted texts.

END-STOPPED LINE An ***end-stopped line*** is one in which both the grammatical structure and sense are complete at the end of the line.

EPIC An ***epic*** is a long narrative poem about the deeds of gods or heroes.

An epic is elevated in style and usually follows certain patterns. The poet begins by announcing the subject and asking a Muse—one of the nine goddesses of the arts, literature, and sciences—to help. An *epic hero* is the larger-than-life central character in an epic. Through behavior and deeds, the epic hero displays qualities that are valued by the society in which the epic originated.

See also ***Epic Simile*** and ***Narrative Poem.***

EPIC SIMILE An ***epic simile,*** also called ***Homeric simile,*** is an elaborate comparison of unlike subjects.

ESSAY An ***essay*** is a short nonfiction work about a particular subject. While classification is difficult, four types of essays are sometimes identified.

A *descriptive essay* seeks to convey an impression about a person, place, or object.

A *narrative essay* tells a true story.

An *expository essay* gives information, discusses ideas, or explains a process.

An *explanatory* essay describes and summarizes information gathered from a number of sources on a concept.

A *persuasive essay* tries to convince readers to do something or to accept the writer's point of view.

EXPOSITION ***Exposition*** is writing or speech that explains a process or presents information. In the plot of a story or drama, the exposition is the part of the work that introduces the characters, the setting, and the basic situation.

EXTENDED METAPHOR In an ***extended metaphor,*** as in regular metaphor, a writer speaks or writes of a subject as though it were something else. An extended metaphor sustains the comparison for several lines or for an entire poem.

FATE ***Fate*** is a destiny over which a hero has little or no control.

FEATURE ARTICLES ***Feature articles*** are a type of journalism that focuses on a specific event or situation.

FICTION ***Fiction*** is prose writing that tells about imaginary characters and events. The term is usually used for novels and short stories, but it also applies to dramas and narrative poetry. Some writers rely on their imaginations alone to create their works of fiction. Others base their fiction on actual events and people, to which they add invented characters, dialogue, and plot situations.

FIGURATIVE LANGUAGE ***Figurative language*** is writing or speech not meant to be interpreted literally. It is often used to create vivid impressions by setting up comparisons between dissimilar things.

Some frequently used figures of speech are ***metaphors, similes,*** and ***personifications.***

FLASHBACK A ***flashback*** is a means by which authors present material that occurred earlier than the present tense of the narrative. Authors may include this material in a character's memories, dreams, or accounts of past events.

FOIL A ***foil*** is a character who provides a contrast to another character. In *Romeo and Juliet*, the fiery temper of Tybalt serves as a foil to the good nature of Benvolio.

FOLLOW-UP QUESTION A ***follow-up question*** builds on the interview subject's response, clarifying and deepening answers.

FORESHADOWING ***Foreshadowing*** is the use in a literary work of clues that suggest events that have yet to occur. This technique helps create suspense, keeping readers wondering about what will happen next.

FRAME STORY A ***frame story*** is a story that brackets—or frames—another story or group of stories. This device creates a story-within-a-story narrative structure.

FREE VERSE ***Free verse*** is poetry not written in a regular pattern of meter or rhyme.

GENRE A ***genre*** is a category or type of literature. Literature is commonly divided into three major genres: poetry, prose, and drama. Each major genre is in turn divided into smaller genres, as follows:

1. **Poetry:** Lyric Poetry, Concrete Poetry, Dramatic Poetry, Narrative Poetry, and Epic Poetry
2. **Prose:** Fiction (Novels and Short Stories) and Nonfiction (Biography, Autobiography, Letters, Essays, and Reports)
3. **Drama:** Serious Drama and Tragedy, Comic Drama, Melodrama, and Farce

HYPERBOLE A ***hyperbole*** is a deliberate exaggeration or overstatement.

IAMB An ***iamb*** is an unstressed syllable followed by a stressed syllable.

IAMBIC PENTAMETER Blank verse written in ***iambic pentameter*** has five iambs, called "feet," in each line.

IN MEDIA RES In media res means "in the middle of things."

IDIOM An ***idiom*** is an expression that is characteristic of a language, region, community, or class of people. *Idiomatic expressions* often arise from figures of speech and therefore cannot be understood literally.

INTERVIEW An ***interview*** is an exchange of ideas between an interviewer and an expert or someone who has had a unique experience. The basic structure of an interview is the Q&A (question and answer) format.

IMAGE An ***image*** is a word or phrase that appeals to one or more of the five senses—sight, hearing, touch, taste, or smell. Writers use images to re-create sensory experiences in words.

IMAGERY ***Imagery*** is the descriptive or figurative language used in literature to create word pictures for the reader. These pictures, or images, are created by details of sight, sound, taste, touch, smell, or movement.

INTERNAL MONOLOGUE To show a character's thoughts with more dimension, an author uses ***internal monologue,*** a kind of "conversation" a character has with himself or herself.

INTERVIEW An ***interview*** is an exchange of ideas between an interviewer and an expert or someone who has had a unique experience.

IRONY ***Irony*** is the general term for literary techniques that portray differences between appearance and reality, or expectation and result. In ***verbal irony,*** words are used to suggest the opposite of what is meant. In ***dramatic irony,*** there is a contradiction between what a character thinks and what the reader or audience knows to be true. In ***situational irony,*** an event occurs that directly contradicts the expectations of the characters, the reader, or the audience.

JOURNALISM ***Journalism*** is a type of nonfiction writing that focuses on current events and nonfiction subjects of general interest to the public.

LYRIC POEM A ***lyric poem*** is a highly musical verse that expresses the thoughts, observations, and feelings of a single speaker.

MEMOIR A ***memoir*** is a limited kind of autobiographical writing that focuses on one period or aspect of the writer's life.

METAPHOR A ***metaphor*** is a figure of speech in which one thing is spoken of as though it were something else. Unlike a simile, which compares two things using *like* or *as,* a metaphor implies a comparison between them.

MONOLOGUE A ***monologue*** in a play is a speech by one character that, unlike a ***soliloquy,*** is addressed to another character or characters.

MOOD ***Mood,*** or ***atmosphere,*** is the feeling created in the reader by a literary work or passage. The mood is often suggested by descriptive details. Often the mood can be described in a single word, such as lighthearted, frightening, or despairing.

MOTIVE A ***motive*** is a reason for an action.

NARRATION ***Narration*** is writing that tells a story. The act of telling a story in speech is also called narration. Novels and short stories are fictional narratives. Nonfiction works—such as news stories, biographies, and autobiographies—are also narratives. A narrative poem tells a story in verse.

NARRATIVE A ***narrative*** is a story told in fiction, nonfiction, poetry, or drama.

NARRATIVE NONFICTION Writing that tells a real-life story is called ***narrative nonfiction.***

NARRATIVE POINT OF VIEW A ***narrative point of view*** is the vantage point from which a fiction writer chooses to tell a story.

NARRATOR A ***narrator*** is a speaker or character who tells a story. The writer's choice of narrator determines the story's ***point of view***, which directs the type and amount of information the writer reveals.

When a character in the story tells the story, that character is a *first-person narrator*. This narrator may be a major character, a minor character, or just a witness. Readers see only what this character sees, hear only what he or she hears, and so on. The first-person narrator may or may not be reliable.

When a voice outside the story narrates, the story has a third-person narrator. An omniscient, or all-knowing, third-person narrator can tell readers what any character thinks and feels. A limited third-person narrator sees the world through one character's eyes and reveals only that character's thoughts.

NONFICTION ***Nonfiction*** is prose writing that presents and explains ideas or that tells about real people, places, ideas, or events. To be classified as nonfiction, a work must be true. "Single Room, Earth View" is a nonfictional account of the view of Earth from space.

NOVEL A ***novel*** is a long work of fiction. It has a plot that explores characters in conflict. A novel may also have one or more subplots, or minor stories, and several themes.

ONOMATOPOEIA ***Onomatopoeia*** is the use of words that imitate sounds. *Whirr, thud,* and *hiss* are examples.

ORAL TRADITION The ***oral tradition*** is the passing of songs, stories, and poems from generation to generation by word of mouth. Many folk songs, ballads, fairy tales, legends, and myths originated in the oral tradition.

See also *Myth.*

OXYMORON An ***oxymoron*** is a combination of words, or parts of words, that contradict each other. Examples are "deafening silence," "honest thief," "wise fool," and "bittersweet."

PANTOUM A ***pantoum*** is an old, formal poetic structure consisting of a series of quatrains, or four-line stanzas.

PARADOX A ***paradox*** is a statement that seems contradictory but may actually be true. Because a paradox is surprising, it catches the reader's attention.

PARALLELISM ***Parallelism*** is the repetition of a grammatical structure in order to create a rhythm and make words more memorable.

PARAPHRASE A ***paraphrase*** is a restatement of a passage from an original text

PERSONIFICATION ***Personification*** is a type of figurative language in which a nonhuman subject is given human characteristics.

PERSUASION ***Persuasion*** is writing or speech that attempts to convince the reader to adopt a particular opinion or course of action. An ***argument*** is a logical way of presenting a belief, conclusion, or stance. A good argument is supported with reasoning and evidence.

PERSUASIVE APPEALS ***Persuasive appeals*** are methods of informing or convincing readers to see something in a new way.

PERSUASIVE ESSAY A ***persuasive essay*** is a short nonfiction work in which a writer seeks to convince the reader to think or act in a certain way.

PERSUASIVE SPEECH In a ***persuasive speech,*** the speaker uses rhetoric, logic, and oral-presentation techniques to convince listeners to think or act in a certain way.

PLOT ***Plot*** is the sequence of events in a literary work. In most novels, dramas, short stories, and narrative poems, the plot involves both characters and a central conflict. The plot usually begins with an ***exposition*** that introduces the setting, the characters, and the basic situation. This is followed by the ***inciting incident***, which introduces the central conflict. The conflict then increases during the ***development*** until it reaches a high point of interest or suspense, the ***climax***. All the events leading up to the climax make up the ***rising action***. The climax is followed by the ***falling action***, which leads to the ***denouement***, or ***resolution***, in which a general insight or change is conveyed.

POETIC STRUCTURE The basic structures of poetry are lines and stanzas. A ***line*** is a group of words arranged in a row. A line of poetry may break, or end, in different ways. An ***end-stopped line*** is one in which both the grammatical structure and sense are complete at the end of the line. A ***run-on,*** or ***enjambed, line*** is one in which both the grammatical structure and sense continue past the end of the line.

POETRY ***Poetry*** is one of the three major types of literature, the others being prose and drama. Most poems make use of highly concise, musical, and emotionally charged language. Many also make use of imagery, figurative language, and special devices of sound such as rhyme. Poems are often divided into lines and stanzas and often employ regular rhythmical patterns, or meters. However, some poems are written out just like prose, while others are written in free verse.

POINT OF VIEW An author's ***point of view*** is the perspective from which events are told or described.

PRIMARY SOURCE A ***primary source*** is raw material or first-hand information about what is being studied.

PROSE ***Prose*** is the ordinary form of written language. Most writing that is not poetry, drama, or song is considered prose. Prose is one of the major genres of literature and occurs in two forms: fiction and nonfiction.

PUN A ***pun*** is a play on words involving a word with two or more different meanings or two words that sound alike but have different meanings. In *Romeo and Juliet*, the dying Mercutio makes a pun involving two meanings of the word *grave*, "serious" and "burial site": "Ask for me tomorrow, and you shall find me a grave man" (Act III, Scene i, lines 92–93).

QUATRAIN A ***quatrain*** is a stanza or poem made up of four lines, usually with a definite rhythm and rhyme scheme.

QUOTATION A speaker's exact words are a ***direct quotation*** and are shown using quotation marks.

REPETITION ***Repetition*** is the use of any element of language—a sound, a word, a phrase, a clause, or a sentence—more than once.

Poets use many kinds of repetition. Alliteration, assonance, rhyme, and rhythm are repetitions of certain sounds and sound patterns. A refrain is a repeated line or group of lines. In both prose and poetry, repetition is used for musical effects and for emphasis.

RESTATEMENT ***Restatements,*** or paraphrases, help an interviewer make sure the audience understands the main point the interviewee is communicating.

RHETORIC ***Rhetoric*** refers to language devices, especially the art of speaking or writing effectively.

RHETORICAL DEVICES ***Rhetorical devices*** are special patterns of words and ideas that create emphasis and stir emotion, especially in speeches or other oral presentations. ***Parallelism,*** for example, is the repetition of a grammatical structure in order to create a rhythm and make words more memorable.

Other common rhetorical devices include: ***analogy***, drawing comparisions between two unlike things; ***charged language***, words that appeal to the emotions; ***restatement***, expressing the same idea in different words; and ***rhetorical questions***, questions with obvious answers.

RUN-ON, OR ENJAMBED, LINE A ***run-on, or enjambed, line*** is one in which both the grammatical structure and sense continue past the end of the line.

See also ***Meter***.

SCIENCE FICTION ***Science fiction*** is writing that tells about imaginary events involving science or technology. Many science-fiction stories are set in the future.

SENSORY LANGUAGE ***Sensory language*** is writing or speech that uses details to appeal to one or more of the senses.

SETTING The ***setting*** of a literary work is the time and lace of the action. Time can include not only the historical period—past, present, or future—but also a specific year, season, or time of day. Place may involve not only the geographical place—a region, country, state, or town—but also the social, economic, or cultural environment.

In some stories, setting serves merely as a backdrop for action, a context in which the characters move and speak. In others, however, setting is a crucial element.

SHORT STORY A ***short story*** is a brief work of fiction. In most short stories, one main character faces a conflict that is resolved in the plot of the story. Great craftsmanship must go into the writing of a good story, for it has to accomplish its purpose in relatively few words.

SIMILE A ***simile*** is a figure of speech in which the words *like* or *as* are used to compare two apparently dissimilar items. The comparison, however, surprises the reader into a fresh perception by finding an unexpected likeness.

SITUATIONAL IRONY ***Situational irony*** occurs when events in a story go directly against the expectations of the main characters or the readers.

SOCIAL AND HISTORICAL CONTEXT The circumstances of the time and place in which a story occurs are referred to as ***social and historical context.***

SOLILOQUY A ***soliloquy*** is a long speech expressing the thoughts of a character alone on stage.

SOUND DEVICES A ***sound device*** is a technique used by a poets and writers to emphasize the sound relationships among words in order to create musical and emotional effects and emphasize a poem's meaning. These devices include ***alliteration, consonance, assonance, onomatopoeia,*** and ***rhyme.***

SPEAKER The ***speaker*** is the imaginary voice assumed by the writer of a poem. In many poems, the speaker is not identified by name, and may be may be a person, an animal, a thing, or an abstraction.

SPECIFIC DETAILS ***Specific details*** are used by both fiction and nonfiction writers to support and develop a central idea or theme.

STAGE DIRECTIONS ***Stage directions*** are notes included in a drama to describe how the work is to be performed or staged. These instructions are printed in italics and are not spoken aloud. They are used to describe sets, lighting, sound effects, and the appearance, personalities, and movements of characters.

STANZA A ***stanza*** is a repeated grouping of two or more lines in a poem that often share a pattern of rhythm and rhyme. Stanzas are sometimes named according to the number of lines they have—for example, a ***couplet,*** two lines; a ***quatrain,*** four lines; a ***sestet,*** six lines; and an ***octave***, eight lines.

STYLE ***Style*** refers to an author's unique way of writing. Elements determining style include diction; tone; characteristic use of figurative language, dialect, or rhythmic devices; and syntax.

SUMMARY A ***summary*** is a concise, complete, and accurate overview of a text.

SUPPORTING DETAILS Pieces of information that illustrate, expand on, or prove an author's ideas are called ***supporting details.*** Supporting details can validate an argument, provide information, or add interest.

SYMBOL A ***symbol*** is anything that stands for something else. In addition to having its own meaning and reality, a symbol also represents abstract ideas. For example, a flag is a piece of cloth, but it also represents the idea of a country.

THEME A ***theme*** is a central message or insight into life revealed through a literary work. The theme of a literary work may be stated directly or implied. When the theme of a work is implied, readers think about what the work suggests about people or life.

Archetypal themes are those that occur in folklore and literature across the world and throughout history.

TONE The ***tone*** of a literary work is the writer's attitude toward his or her audience and subject.

TRAGEDY A ***tragedy*** is a work of literature, especially a play, that results in a catastrophe or great misfortune for the main character, or *tragic hero*. In ancient Greek drama, the main character was always a significant person—a king or a hero—and the cause of the tragedy was a *tragic flaw,* or weakness, in his or her character. In modern drama, the main character can be an ordinary person, and the cause of the tragedy can be some evil in society itself.

TRAGIC FLAW A ***tragic flaw*** is a personality defect that contributes to a hero's choice, and thus, to his or her tragic downfall.

TRAVEL JOURNALISM ***Travel journalism*** is a type of literary nonfiction in which a writer describes the experience of visiting a particular place.

VISUAL ESSAY A ***visual essay*** is an exploration of a topic that conveys its ideas through visual elements as well as language. Like a standard essay, a visual essay presents an author's views of a single topic. Unlike other essays, however, much of the meaning in a visual essay is conveyed through illustrations or photographs.

VIVID LANGUAGE ***Vivid language*** is strong, precise words that bring ideas to life.

VOICE ***Voice*** is a writer's distinctive "sound" or way of "speaking" on the page. It is related to such elements as word choice, sentence structure, and tone. It is similar to an individual's speech style and can be described in the same way—fast, slow, blunt, meandering, breathless, and so on.

Voice resembles ***style,*** an author's typical way of writing, but style usually refers to a quality that can be found throughout an author's body of work, while an author's voice may sometimes vary from work to work.

MANUAL DE TÉRMINOS LITERARIOS

ADAPTACIÓN Una ***adaptación*** es una obra de arte que incluye los personajes y cuenta la misma historia que se presentó originalmente en otra obra de arte. A menudo, la adaptación adopta una forma diferente. Una novela u obra de teatro puede transformarse en una película, por ejemplo, o un poema puede transformarse en un cuento.

ALITERACIÓN La ***aliteración*** es la repetición de los sonidos consonantes iniciales. Los escritores usan la aliteración para dar énfasis a las palabras, para imitar sonidos y para crear efectos de musicalida.

ALUSIÓN Una ***alusión*** es una referencia a una persona, lugar, hecho, obra literaria u obra de arte muy conocida.

ANALOGÍA Una ***analogía*** establece una comparación entre dos o más cosas que son parecidas en algunos aspectos pero se diferencian en otros.

ANÉCDOTA Una ***anécdota*** es un relato breve sobre un hecho interesante, divertido o extraño, que se narra con el fin de entretener o decir algo importante.

ANTAGONISTA Un ***antagonista*** es un personaje o fuerza en conflicto con el personaje principal o protagonista.

ANTÍTESIS Una ***antítesis*** es una forma de paralelismo que enfatiza los contrastes más importantes.

ARQUETIPO Un ***arquetipo*** es un tipo de personaje, detalle, imagen o situación que reaparece en la literatura a través de la historia. Algunos críticos piensan que los arquetipos revelan verdades profundas sobre la experiencia humana.

ARGUMENTO Un ***argumento*** es un escrito o discurso que trata de convencer al lector para que siga una acción o adopte una opinión en particular. Un argumento es una manera lógica de presentar una creencia, una conclusión o una postura. Un buen argumento se respalda con razonamientos y pruebas.

APARTE Un ***aparte*** es un parlamento breve en boca de un personaje en una obra de teatro, en el que expresa sus verdaderos pensamientos y sentimientos. Tradicionalmente, los apartes se dirigen a la audiencia y se suponen inaudibles a los otros personajes.

ASONANCIA La ***asonancia*** es la repetición de los sonidos vocálicos seguidos de distintas consonantes en dos o más sílabas acentuadas.

PROPÓSITO DEL AUTOR El ***propósito del autor*** es su razón para escribir. Los cuatro propósitos generales del autor son: informar, persuadir, entretener y reflexionar.

ESCRITURA AUTOBIOGRÁFICA La ***escritura autobiográfica*** es cualquier forma de no-ficción en la que el autor narra la historia de su vida

AUTOBIOGRAFÍA Una ***autobiografía*** es una forma de no-ficción en la que el escritor cuenta su propia vida. Una autobiografía puede contar toda la vida de una persona o solo una parte de ella.

BIBLIOGRAFÍA Una ***bibliografía*** o lista de "obras citadas" enumera todas las fuentes de investigación usadas para escribir un ensayo informativo en un estilo aprobado.

BIOGRAFÍA Una ***biografía*** es una forma de no-ficción en la que un escritor cuenta la vida de otra persona. Se han escrito biografías de muchas personas famosas de la historia o del mundo contemporáneo, pero también pueden escribirse biografías de personas comunes.

VERSO BLANCO El ***verso blanco*** es poesía escrita en líneas de pentámetros yámbicos sin rima. Esta forma de verso fue muy utilizada por William Shakespeare.

CADENA DE CAUSA Y CONSECUENCIA Una causa única, que tiene como resultado una consecuencia, la cual lleva a una segunda consecuencia, que a su vez causa una tercera consecuencia, etcétera, constituye una ***cadena de causa y consecuencia.***

RELACIÓN DE CAUSA Y CONSECUENCIA Una ***relación de causa y consecuencia*** muestra como un suceso o situación lleva a otro.

IDEA CENTRAL La ***idea central*** es la idea principal que el autor quiere que la audiencia comprenda y recuerde.

PERSONAJE Un ***personaje*** es una persona o animal que participa de la acción en una obra literaria. El personaje principal, o protagonista, es el personaje más importante del relato. Este personaje a menudo cambia de una manera importante como resultado de los eventos que se suceden en el cuento.

Los personajes a veces son clasificados como complejos o chatos, dinámicos o estáticos. Un *personaje complejo* muestra muchos rasgos diferentes—tanto faltas como virtudes. Un *personaje chato* muestra solo un rasgo. Un *personaje dinámico* se desarrolla y crece en el curso del relato; mientras que un *personaje estático* no cambia.

CARACTERIZACIÓN La ***caracterización*** es el acto de crear y desarrollar un personaje. En una ***caracterización directa,*** el autor expresa explícitamente los rasgos de un personaje. En una ***caracterización indirecta,*** el autor proporciona claves sobre el personaje, describiendo el aspecto del personaje, qué hace, qué dice, así como la manera en que otros personajes lo ven y reaccionan a él. Al lector le corresponde sacar conclusiones sobre los personajes basándose en información indirecta.

La caracterización indirecta más efectiva resulta por lo general de mostrar cómo hablan y actúan los personajes.

LENGUAJE EMOCIONALMENTE CARGADO Se conoce como ***lenguaje emocionalmente cargado*** a las palabras o frases que evocan reacciones intensas, ya sean positivas o negativas.

AFIRMACIÓN La ***afirmación*** de un texto es el mensaje clave que el escritor quiere comunicar acerca de un tema.

ACLARACIÓN La ***aclaración*** se centra en una parte determinada de la respuesta, simplificando la idea original o aportando más detalles.

ALIVIO CÓMICO El ***alivio cómico*** es una técnica que se usa para interrumpir una parte seria de una obra literaria introduciendo personajes o situaciones jocosas.

CONFLICTO Un ***conflicto*** es una lucha entre fuerzas opuestas. Los personajes en conflicto forman la base de cuentos, novelas y obras de teatro.

Hay dos tipos de conflicto: externos e internos. En un ***conflicto externo***, el personaje principal lucha contra una fuerza externa.

Un ***conflicto interno*** atañe a un personaje que entra en conflicto consigo mismo.

CONNOTACIÓN La ***connotación*** de una palabra es el conjunto de ideas que se asocian a ella, además de su significado explícito.

CONSONANCIA La ***consonancia*** es la repetición de los sonidos consonantes finales de sílabas acentuadas con distintos sonidos vocálicos, como en *hat* and *sit*.

PAREADO Un ***dístico*** o ***pareado*** es un par de versos rimados, por lo general de la misma extensión y metro. Por lo general, los pareados se usan en poemas y en obras de teatro escritas en verso.

CRÍTICA La ***crítica*** es un texto argumentativo en el que un autor expresa su opinión acerca de una obra como, por ejemplo, un libro, una película o una actuación.

DENOTACIÓN La ***denotación*** de una palabra es su significado en un diccionario, independientemente de otras asociaciones que la palabra suscita.

DESCRIPCIÓN Una ***descripción*** es un retrato en palabras de una persona, un lugar o un objeto. La escritura descriptiva utiliza detalles sensoriales, es decir, aquellos que apelan a los sentidos: la vista, el oído, el gusto, el olfato y el tacto. La descripción puede encontrarse en todo tipo de escritores. El ensayo de Rudolfo Anaya, "Una celebración de los abuelos" incluye pasajes descriptivos.

DIÁLOGO Un ***diálogo*** es una conversación entre personajes que puede revelar sus rasgos y hacer progresar la acción de un relato. Ya sea en un género de ficción o de no ficción —en inglés— las comillas reproducen las palabras exactas de un personaje, y un nuevo párrafo indica un cambio de personaje.

DICCIÓN La ***dicción*** comprende la elección de palabras que hace el autor, especialmente en relación a un abanico de posibilidades, al uso de un lenguaje coloquial o jerga, y al nivel de formalidad que utilizan tanto el narrador como los personajes.

DRAMA Un ***drama*** es una historia escrita para ser representada por actores. El guión de un drama está constituido por ***diálogo*** —las palabras que dicen los actores— y por ***direcciones escénicas***, que son los comentarios acerca de cómo y dónde se sitúa la acción.

La ***ambientación*** es la época y el lugar donde sucedes la acción. Se indica a través de una o varias escenografías, que incluyen el mobiliario y el fondo, o telón de fondo, que sugieren si las escenas son interiores o exteriores. La *tramoya o utilería* son los objetos, tales como una espada o una taza de té, que se usan en escena.

Al principio de la mayoría de los dramas, una breve ***exposición*** le da a la audiencia cierta información de contexto sobre los personajes y la situación. Al igual que en un cuento o una novela, el argumento o trama de una obra dramática se construye a partir de personajes en conflicto.

Los dramas se dividen a grandes unidades llamadas ***actos***, que a su vez se dividen en unidades más breves llamadas ***escenas***. Un drama de cierta extensión puede incluir muchas escenografías que cambian con las escenas, o pueden indicar un cambio de escena por medio de la iluminación.

IRONÍA DRAMÁTICA La ***ironía dramática*** es una contradicción entre lo que el personaje cree y lo que la audiencia sabe. Por ejemplo: se produce ironía dramática que provoca humor o tensión si el personaje intenta desesperadamente forzar una caja fuerte cuando la audiencia ya sabe que la caja está vacía.

PUNTOS SUSPENSIVOS Los ***puntos suspensivos*** se usan para indicar que se han omitido palabras u oraciones de un texto que se cita.

VERSO NO ENCABALGADO Un ***verso no encabalgado*** es aquel en el que tanto la estructura gramatical como el sentido se completan al final del renglón.

ÉPICA Un ***poema épico*** es un poema narrativo extenso sobre las hazañas de dioses o héroes.

Los poemas épicos son de estilo elevado y por lo general siguen ciertos patrones. El poeta comienza por anunciar el tema y le pide ayuda a la Musa—una de las nueve diosas de las artes, la literatura y las ciencias. Un *héroe épico* es el personaje principal de un poema épico y suele tener características sobrehumanas. A través de su conducta y sus hazañas, el héroe épico demuestra tener cualidades muy valoradas por la sociedad en la que se originó el poema.

Ver también ***Comparativo épico*** **y** ***Poema narrativo***

GLOSARIO: MANUAL DE TÉRMINOS LITERARIOS

COMPARATIVO ÉPICO El ***comparativo épico***, también llamado ***comparativo homérico***, es una comparación muy elaborada de dos objetos disímiles.

ENSAYO Un ***ensayo*** es una obra breve de no-ficción sobre un tema en particular. Si bien es difícil llegar a una clasificación, suelen diferenciarse cinco tipos de ensayos.

El *ensayo descriptivo* se propone transmitir una impresión acerca de una persona, un lugar o un objeto.

El *ensayo narrativo* narra una historia real.

El *ensayo expositivo* proporciona información, discute ideas o explica un proceso.

El *ensayo explicativo* describe y resume información sobre un determinado concepto recogida de cierto número de fuentes.

El *ensayo persuasivo* intenta convencer a los lectores de que hagan algo o que acepten el punto de vista del escritor.

EXPOSICIÓN Una ***exposición*** es un escrito o un discurso que explica un proceso o presenta información. En un cuento o un drama, la exposición es la parte donde se presenta a los personajes, la ambientación y la situación básica.

METÁFORA EXTENDIDA En una ***metáfora extendida***, al igual que en una metáfora habitual, el escritor escribe o habla de algo como si fuera otra cosa. Una metáfora extendida prolonga la comparación a lo largo de varios versos o de un poema entero.

DESTINO El ***destino*** es la suerte del héroe, algo sobre lo que no tiene control.

ARTÍCULOS DESTACADOS Los ***artículos destacados*** son una forma de periodismo que se centra en una situación o suceso específico.

FICCIÓN Una obra de ***ficción*** es un escrito en prosa que cuenta algo sobre personajes y hechos imaginarios. El término se usa por lo general para referirse a novelas y cuentos, pero también se aplica a dramas y poemas narrativos. Algunos escritores se basan solamente en su imaginación para crear sus obras de ficción. Otros basan su ficción en hechos y personas reales, a las que agregan personajes, diálogos y situationes de su propia invención.

LENGUAJE FIGURADO El ***lenguaje figurado*** es un escrito o discurso que no se debe interpretar literalmente. A menudo se usa para crear impresiones vívidas, estableciendo comparaciones entre cosas disímiles.

Algunas de las formas más usadas del lenguaje figurado son las ***metáforas***, los ***símiles*** y las ***personificaciones***.

FLASHBACK Un ***flashback*** o ***escena retrospectiva*** es una de las maneras a través de las que los autores presentan materiales de algo que ocurrió antes del tiempo presente del relato. Los autores pueden incluir estos materiales en los recuerdos o sueños de un personaje, o como relatos de hechos pasados

PERSONAJE COMPLEMENTARIO Un ***personaje complementario*** es un personaje que se presenta como la contraposición de otro. En *Romeo y Julieta*, el mal carácter de Teobaldo sirve de complementario a la buena disposición de Benvolio.

PREGUNTA COMPLEMENTARIA En las entrevistas, una ***pregunta complementaria*** clarifica y profundiza en las respuestas del entrevistado.

PREFIGURACIÓN La ***prefiguración*** es el uso, en una obra literaria, de claves que sugieren hechos que van a suceder. Esta técnica ayuda a crear suspenso, manteniendo a los lectores interesados preguntándose qué sucederá.

CUENTO DE ENMARQUE Un ***cuento de enmarque*** es un relato dentro del cual se incluyen otros relatos. Este recurso permite crear una estructura narrativa del tipo "cuento dentro del cuento".

VERSO LIBRE El ***verso libre*** es una forma poética en la que no se sigue un patrón regular de metro ni de rima.

GÉNERO Un ***género*** es una categoría o tipo de literatura. La literatura se divide por lo general en tres géneros principales: poesía, prosa y drama. Cada uno de estos géneros principales se dividen a su vez en géneros más pequeños. Por ejemplo:

1. **Poesía:** Poesía lírica, Poesía concreta, Poesía dramática, Poesía narrativa y Poesía épica.
2. **Prosa:** Ficción (Novelas y Cuentos) y No-ficción (Biografía, Autobiografía, Cartas, Ensayos, Artículos).
3. **Drama:** Drama serio y Tragedia, Comedia dramática, Melodrama y Farsa.

HIPÉRBOLE Una ***hipérbole*** es una exageración o magnificación deliberada.

YAMBO Una sílaba átona seguida por una tónica constituyen un ***yambo.***

PENTÁMETRO YÁMBICO El verso libre escrito en ***pentámetro yámbico*** tiene cinco yambos, llamados "pies", en cada verso.

EXPRESIÓN IDIOMÁTICA Una ***expresión idiomática*** es una expresión propia de una lengua, región, comunidad, o clase de personas. Las *expresiones idiomáticas* surgen a menudo a partir de expresiones del lenguaje figurado y por lo tanto no pueden entenderse literalmente.

IN MEDIA RES La frase ***in media res*** significa "en el medio de las cosas".

ENTREVISTA Una ***entrevista*** es un intercambio de ideas entre un entrevistador y un experto o alguien que ha tenido una experiencia inusual. La estructura básica de una entrevista es una sucesión de preguntas y respuestas.

IMAGEN Una ***imagen*** es una palabra o frase que apela a uno o más de los cinco sentidos: la vista, el oído, el tacto, el gusto y el olfato. Los escritores usan imágenes para recrear en palabras las experiencias sensoriales.

IMÁGENES Las ***imágenes*** son el lenguaje figurado o descriptivo que se usa en la literatura para crear una descripción verbal para los lectores. Estas descripciones verbales, o imágenes, se crean incluyendo detalles visuales, auditivos, gustativos, táctiles, olfativos o de movimiento.

MONÓLOGO INTERIOR Para mostrar los pensamientos de un personaje con mayor profundidad, los autores usan ***monólogo interior,*** una especie de "conversación" que el personaje tiene consigo mismo.

ENTREVISTA Una ***entrevista*** es un intercambio de ideas entre el entrevistador y un experto o alguien que haya tenido una experiencia singular.

IRONÍA ***Ironía*** es un término general para distintas técnicas literarias que subrayan las diferencias entre apariencia y realidad, o entre expectativas y resultado. En una ***ironía verbal***, las palabras se usan para sugerir lo opuesto a los que se dice. En la ***ironía dramática*** hay una contradicción entre los que el personaje piensa y lo que el lector o la audiencia sabe que es verdad. En una ***ironía situacional,*** ocurre un suceso que contradice directamente las expectativas de los personajes, y del lector o la audiencia.

PERIODISMO El ***periodismo*** es un fipo de escritura de no-ficción que se centra en hechos presentes y en temas de no-ficción de interés general.

POEMA LÍRICO Un ***poema lírico*** es una sucesión de versos de mucha musicalidad que expresan los pensamientos, observaciones y sentimientos de un único hablante.

MEMORIAS Un libro de ***memorias*** es un tipo limitado de escrito autobiográfico que se centra en un período o aspecto de la vida del autor.

METÁFORA Una ***metáfora*** es una figura retórica en la que el escritor se refiere a algo como si fuera otra cosa. Al contrario del símil, que compara dos cosas con las palabras *como* o *tal como*, la metáfora insinúa la comparación.

MONÓLOGO Un ***monólogo*** en una obra de teatro es un parlamento por parte de un personaje que, a diferencia del ***soliloquio***, se dirige a otro u otros personajes.

TONO El ***tono*** o la ***atmósfera*** es la sensación que un pasaje u obra literaria crea en el lector. Por lo general, el tono se crea a partir de detalles descriptivos. A menudo puede ser descrito con una sola palabra, tal como desenfadado, aterrador o desesperante.

MOTIVO El ***motivo*** es la razón de una acción.

NARRACIÓN Una ***narración*** es un escrito que cuenta una historia. El acto de contar una historia de forma oral también se llama narración. Las novelas y los cuentos son obras narrativas de ficción. Las obras de no-ficción, como las noticias, las biografías y las autobiografías, también son narraciones. Un poema narrativo cuenta una historia en verso.

RELATO Se llama ***relato*** a la historia que se narra, en una obra de ficción, de no-ficción, en un poema o en un drama.

RELATO DE NO-FICCIÓN Se le llama ***relato de no-ficción*** al escrito que cuenta una historia de la vida real.

PUNTO DE VISTA NARRATIVO El ***punto de vista narrativo*** es la perspectiva desde la que el escritor de ficción cuenta la historia.

NARRADOR Un ***narrador*** es el hablante o el personaje que cuenta una historia. La elección del narrador por parte del autor determina el ***punto de vista*** desde el que se va a narrar la historia, lo que determina el tipo y la cantidad de información que se revelará.

Cuando el que cuenta la historia es uno de los personajes, a ese personaje se lo llama *narrador en primera persona*. Este narrador puede ser uno de los personajes principales, un personaje menor, o solo un testigo. Los lectores ven solo lo que este personaje ve, oyen solo lo que este personaje oye, etc. El narrador en primera persona puede ser confiable o no.

Cuando la que cuenta la historia es una voz exterior a la historia, hablamos de un *narrador en tercera persona*. Un narrador en tercera persona, omnisciente —es decir, que todo lo sabe— puede decirles a los lectores lo que cualquier personaje piensa o siente. Un narrador en tercera persona limitado ve el mundo a través de los ojos de un solo personaje y revela solo los pensamientos de ese personaje.

NO-FICCIÓN La ***no-ficción*** es un escrito en prosa que presenta y explica ideas o cuenta algo acerca de personas, lugares, ideas o hechos reales. Para ser clasificado como no-ficción un escrito debe ser verdadero. "Single Room, Earth View" es un relato no ficcional acerca de cómo se ve la Tierra desde el espacio.

NOVELA Una ***novela*** es una obra extensa de ficción. Tiene una trama que explora los personajes en conflicto. Una novela también puede tener una o más tramas secundarias —es decir, historias de menor importancia—, así como tocar varios temas.

ONOMATOPEYA La ***onomatopeya*** es el uso de palabras que imitan sonidos, tales como *pío-pío, tic-tac* o susurro.

TRADICIÓN ORAL La ***tradición oral*** es la transmisión de canciones, cuentos y poemas de una generación a otra, de boca a boca. Muchas canciones folklóricas, baladas, cuentos de hadas, leyendas y mitos se originaron en la tradición oral.

OXÍMORON Un ***oxímoron*** es una combinación de palabras, o partes de palabras, que se contradicen mutuamente. Por ejemplo, "un silencio ensordecedor", "un ladrón honesto", "la música callada".

CUARTETAS ENCADENADAS Las ***cuartetas encadenadas*** son una antigua estructura poética que consiste en un serie de cuartetas, o estrofas de cuatro versos.

PARADOJA Una ***paradoja*** es un enunciado que parece contradictorio, pero que sin embargo puede ser verdadero. Por ser siempre sorpresiva, la paradoja suele captar la atención de los lectores.

PARALELISMO El ***paralelismo*** es la repetición de una estructura gramatical con el fin de crear un ritmo y que las palabras resulten más memorables.

PARÁFRASIS La ***paráfrasis*** es reescribir o volver a contar una historia con nuestras propias palabras.

PERSONIFICACIÓN La ***personificación*** es un tipo de figura retórica en la que se dota a una instancia no humana de rasgos y actitudes humanas.

PERSUASIÓN La ***persuasión*** es un recurso escrito u oral por el que se intenta convencer al lector de que adopte una opinión o actúe de determinada manera. Un ***argumento*** es una manera lógica de presentar una creencia, una conclusión o una postura. Un buen argumento se respalda con razones y evidencias.

APELACIONES PERSUASIVAS Las ***apelaciones persuasivas*** son métodos que se utilizan para informar o convencer a los lectores de que vean algo desde una nueva perspectiva.

ENSAYO PERSUASIVO Un ***ensayo persuasivo*** es una obra corta de no-ficción en la que el escritor tiene como objetivo convencer al lector para que piense o actúe de una manera determinada.

DISCURSO PERSUASIVO En un ***discurso persuasivo*** el hablante utiliza técnicas de la retórica, la lógica y las presentaciones orales para convencer a los oyentes de que piensen o actúen de una manera determinada.

TRAMA o ARGUMENTO La ***trama*** o ***argumento*** es la secuencia de los eventos que suceden en una obra literaria. En la mayoría de las novelas, dramas, cuentos y poemas narrativos, la trama implica tanto a los personajes como al conflicto central. La trama por lo general empieza con una ***exposición*** que introduce la ambientación, los personajes y la situación básica. A ello le sigue el ***suceso desencadenante***, que introduce el conflicto central. Este conflicto aumenta durante el ***desarrollo*** hasta que alcanza el punto más alto de interés o suspenso, llamado ***clímax***. Todos los sucesos que conducen al clímax contribuyen a la ***acción dramática creciente***. Al clímax le sigue la ***acción dramática decreciente*** que conduce al ***desenlace***, o ***resolución***, en el que se produce un cambio significativo.

ESTRUCTURA POÉTICA Las ***estructuras poéticas*** básicas son los versos y las estrofas. Un verso es un grupo de palabras ordenadas en una misma hilera. Un verso puede terminar, o cortarse, de distintas maneras. En un ***verso no encabalgado*** la estructura gramatical y el sentido se completan al final de esa línea. En un verso encabalgado tanto la estructura gramatical como el sentido de una línea continúa en el verso que sigue.

POESÍA La ***poesía*** es uno de los tres géneros literarios más importantes. Los otros dos son la prosa y el drama. La mayoría de los poemas están escritos en un lenguaje altamente conciso, musical y emocionalmente rico. Muchos también hacen uso de imágenes, de figuras retóricas y de recursos especiales de sonido, tales como la rima. Los poemas a menudo se dividen en versos y estrofas y emplean patrones rítmicos regulares, llamados metros. Sin embargo, algunos poemas están escritos en un lenguaje similar al de la prosa, mientras que otros están escritos en verso libre.

PUNTO DE VISTA El ***punto de vista*** es la perspectiva desde la cual se narran o describen los hechos.

FUENTE PRIMARIA Una ***fuente primaria*** es el material o la información de primera mano acerca de lo que se estudia.

PROSA La ***prosa*** es la forma común del lenguaje escrito. La mayoría de los escritos que no son poesía, ni drama, ni canciones, se consideran prosa. La prosa es uno de los géneros literarios más importantes y puede ser de dos formas: de ficción y de no-ficción.

JUEGO DE PALABRAS Un ***juego de palabras*** es una frase que comprende una palabra con dos o más significados distintos, o dos palabras que suenan igual pero tienen distinto significado. En *Romeo y Julieta*, Mercurio, moribundo, hace un juego de palabras a partir de los dos sentidos que tiene en inglés la palabra "grave" (serio y tumba): "Pregunta por mí mañana, y me encontrarás serio/ enterrado". (Acto 3, Escena i, versos 92–93).

CUARTETA Una ***cuarteta*** es una estrofa o poema de cuatro versos, por lo general con un esquema de ritmo y rima determinados.

CITA Las palabras exactas que pronuncia un hablante constituyen una ***cita directa*** y se indican encerrándolas entre comillas.

REPETICIÓN La ***repetición*** es el uso de cualquier elemento del lenguaje —un sonido, una palabra, una frase, una cláusula o una oración— más de una vez.

Los poetas usan muchos tipos de repeticiones. La aliteración, la asonancia, la rima y el ritmo son repeticiones de ciertos sonidos o patrones sonoros. Un estribillo es un verso o grupo de versos que se repiten. Tanto en prosa como en poesía, la repetición se usa tanto para lograr efectos de musicalidad como para dar énfasis.

REAFIRMACIÓN Las ***reafirmaciones*** o paráfrasis le ayudan al entrevistador a asegurarse de que la audiencia entienda el mensaje del entrevistado.

RETÓRICA La ***retórica*** se refiere a recursos lingüísticos, en especial el arte de hablar o escribir eficazmente.

FIGURAS RETÓRICAS Las ***figuras retóricas*** son patrones especiales de palabras e ideas que dan énfasis y producen emoción, especialmente en discursos y otras presentaciones orales. El ***paralelismo***, por ejemplo, es la repetición de una estructura gramatical con el propósito de crear un ritmo y hacer que las palabras resulten más memorables.

Otras figuras retóricas muy frecuentes son: la ***analogía***, que establece una comparación entre dos cosas diferentes; el ***lenguaje emocionalmente cargado***, en el que las palabras apelan a las emociones; la ***reafirmación***, en la que se expresa la misma idea con distintas palabras y las ***preguntas retóricas***, que son preguntas cuyas respuestas son obvias.

VERSO ENCABALGADO Un ***verso encabalgado*** es aquel en el que tanto la estructura gramatical como el sentido no se completan al final del verso, sino que continúan en el verso siguiente.

CIENCIA FICCIÓN La ***ciencia ficción*** es un escrito que narra hechos imaginarios relacionados con la ciencia o la tecnología. Muchos relatos de ciencia ficción están ambientados en el futuro.

LENGUAJE SENSORIAL El ***lenguaje sensorial*** es un escrito o discurso que incluye detalles que apelan a uno o más de los sentidos.

AMBIENTACIÓN La ***ambientación*** de una obra literaria es la época y el lugar en el que se desarrolla la acción. La época incluye no solo el período histórico —pasado, presente o futuro—, sino también el año específico, la estación, la hora del día. El lugar puede incluir no solo el espacio geográfico —una región, un país, un estado, un pueblo— sino también el entorno social, económico o cultural.

En algunos cuentos, la ambientación sirve solo como un telón de fondo para la acción, un contexto en el que los personajes se mueven y hablan. En otros casos, en cambio, la ambientación es un elemento crucial.

CUENTO Un ***cuento*** es una obra breve de ficción. En la mayoría de los cuentos, un personaje principal se enfrenta a un conflicto que se resuelve a lo largo de la trama. Para escribir un buen cuento se necesita mucho dominio técnico, porque el cuento debe cumplir su cometido en relativamente pocas palabras.

SÍMIL Un ***símil*** es una figura retórica en la que se usa la palabra *como* para establecer una comparación entre dos cosas aparentemente disímiles. La comparación sorprende al lector permitiéndole una nueva percepción que se deriva de descubrir una semejanza inesperada.

IRONÍA SITUACIONAL La ***ironía situacional*** tiene lugar cuando los eventos de una historia suceden de manera opuesta a lo esperado por los personajes principales o los lectores.

CONTEXTO SOCIAL E HISTÓRICO Se conoce como ***contexto social e histórico*** a las circunstancias de tiempo y lugar en las que se desarrolla la historia.

SOLILOQUIO Un ***soliloquio*** es un largo parlamento en el que un personaje, solo en escena, expresa sus sentimientos.

RECURSOS SONOROS Un ***recurso sonoro*** es una técnica usada por poetas y prosistas para enfatizar la relación sonora entre las palabras con el fin de crear efectos musicales y emotivos, y de subrayar el significado del texto. Estos recursos incluyen la ***aliteración***, la ***consonancia***, la ***asonancia***, la ***onomatopeya*** y la ***rima***.

HABLANTE El ***hablante*** es la voz imaginaria que asume el escritor en un poema. En muchos poemas, el hablante no se identifica con un nombre. Al leer un poema, recuerda que el hablante que habla en el poema puede ser una persona, un animal, un objeto, o una abstracción.

DETALLES ESPECÍFICOS Tanto los escritores de ficción como los de no-ficción utilizan ***detalles específicos*** para respaldar una idea central o un tema.

DIRECCIONES ESCÉNICAS Las ***direcciones escénicas*** son notas que se incluyen en una obra de teatro para describir cómo debe ser actuada o puesta en escena. Estas instrucciones aparecen en itálicas y no se pronuncian durante la representación. Se usan para describir decorados, la iluminación, los efectos sonoros y el aspecto, la personalidad y los movimientos de los personajes.

ESTROFA Una ***estrofa*** es un grupo de dos o más versos cuya estructura se repite. Las distintas estrofas de un poema suelen seguir un mismo patrón de ritmo y de rima. Las estrofas a menudo reciben su nombre del número de versos que las componen. Por ejemplo, un ***dístico*** o ***pareado*** (dos versos), una ***cuarteta*** (cuatro versos), una ***sextina*** (seis versos), una ***octava real*** (ocho versos endecasílabos).

ESTILO El ***estilo*** es la manera particular en que escribe un autor. Los elementos que determinan el estilo son: la dicción, el tono; el uso característico de ciertas figuras retóricas, del dialecto, o de los recursos rítmicos; y la sintaxis, es decir, los patrones y estructuras gramaticales que usa con más fecuencia.

RESUMEN Un ***resumen*** es una síntesis concisa, completa y precisa de un texto.

DETALLES DE APOYO Se conoce como ***detalles de apoyo*** a la información que explica, amplía o demuestra las ideas del autor. Los detalles de apoyo validan un argumento, informan o añaden interés al texto.

SÍMBOLO Un ***símbolo*** es algo que representa otra cosa. Además de tener su propio significado y realidad, un símbolo también representa ideas abstractas. Por ejemplo, una bandera es un trozo de tela, pero también representa la idea de un país. Los escritores a veces usan símbolos convencionales como las banderas. Con frecuencia, sin embargo, crean sus propios símbolos, a veces a través del énfasis o la repetición.

TEMA Un ***tema*** es el mensaje central o la concepción de la vida que revela una obra literaria.

El tema de una obra literaria puede estar implícito o bien puede expresarse directamente. Cuando el tema de una obra está implícito, los lectores piensan qué sugiere la obra acerca de la vida o la gente.

Los ***temas arquetípicos*** son aquellos temas que aparecen en el folklore y en la literatura de todo el mundo, y a lo largo de toda la historia.

TONO El ***tono*** de una obra literaria es la actitud del escritor hacia su tema y su audiencia.

TRAGEDIA Una ***tragedia*** es una obra literaria, por lo general una obra de teatro, que termina en una catástrofe, un desastre o un gran infortunio para el personaje principal, también llamado *héroe trágico*. En el drama de la antigua Grecia, el personaje principal siempre era una persona importante —un rey o un héroe— y la causa de la tragedia era un *error trágico,* una debilidad de su carácter. En el drama moderno, el personaje principal puede ser una persona común, y la causa de la tragedia puede ser algún problema o falla de la sociedad misma. La tragedia no solo despierta miedo y piedad en la audiencia, sino también, en algunos casos, transmite un sentido de la majestuosidad y la nobleza del espíritu humano.

ERROR TRÁGICO Un ***error trágico*** es un defecto de la personalidad que contribuye a las decisiones del héroe y, por lo tanto, a su ruina.

PERIODISMO DE VIAJES El ***periodismo de viajes*** es un tipo de literatura de no-ficción en la que el escritor describe la experiencia de visitar un lugar determinado.

ENSAYO VISUAL Un ***ensayo visual*** es una exploración de un tema que transmite sus ideas tanto con el lenguaje como con los elementos visuales. Al igual que un ensayo estándar, un ensayo visual presenta las opiniones del autor acerca de un tema en particular. A diferencia de otros tipos de ensayos, sin embargo, gran parte del sentido del ensayo visual se expresa en las ilustraciones o fotografías.

LENGUAJE VÍVIDO Las palabras convincentes y precisas que dan vida a las ideas y las comunican de manera contundente constituyen ***lenguaje vívido.***

VOZ La ***voz*** es el "sonido" distintivo de un escritor, o la manera en que "habla" en la página. Se relaciona a elementos tales como la elección del vocabulario, la estructura de las oraciones y el tono. Es similar al estilo en que habla un individuo y puede describirse de la misma manera: rápida, lenta, directa, dispersa, entrecortadamente, etc.

La voz se parece al ***estilo***, es decir, a la manera típica en que escribe un autor, pero el estilo por lo general se refiere a una cualidad que puede encontrarse a lo largo de toda la obra de un autor, mientras que la voz de un autor puede variar de una obra a otra.

PARTS OF SPEECH

Every English word, depending on its meaning and its use in a sentence, can be identified as one of the eight parts of speech. These are nouns, pronouns, verbs, adjectives, adverbs, prepositions, conjunctions, and interjections. Understanding the parts of speech will help you learn the rules of English grammar and usage.

Nouns A **noun** names a person, place, or thing. A **common noun** names any one of a class of persons, places, or things. A **proper noun** names a specific person, place, or thing.

Common Noun	Proper Noun
writer, country, novel	Charles Dickens, Great Britain, *Hard Times*

Pronouns A **pronoun** is a word that stands for one or more nouns. The word to which a pronoun refers (whose place it takes) is the **antecedent** of the pronoun.

A **personal pronoun** refers to the person speaking (first person); the person spoken to (second person); or the person, place, or thing spoken about (third person).

	Singular	Plural
First Person	I, me, my, mine	we, us, our, ours
Second Person	you, your, yours	you, your, yours
Third Person	he, him, his, she, her, hers, it, its	they, them, their, theirs

A **reflexive pronoun** reflects the action of a verb back on its subject. It indicates that the person or thing performing the action also is receiving the action.

I keep *myself* fit by taking a walk every day.

An **intensive pronoun** adds emphasis to a noun or pronoun.

It took the work of the president *himself* to pass the law.

A **demonstrative** pronoun points out a specific person(s), place(s), or thing(s).

this, that, these, those

A **relative pronoun** begins a subordinate clause and connects it to another idea in the sentence.

that, which, who, whom, whose

An **interrogative pronoun** begins a question.

what, which, who, whom, whose

An **indefinite pronoun** refers to a person, place, or thing that may or may not be specifically named.

all, another, any, both, each, everyone, few, most, none, no one, somebody

Verbs A **verb** expresses action or the existence of a state or condition.

An **action verb** tells what action someone or something is performing.

gather, read, work, jump, imagine, analyze, conclude

A **linking verb** connects the subject with another word that identifies or describes the subject. The most common linking verb is *be*.

appear, be, become, feel, look, remain, seem, smell, sound, stay, taste

A **helping verb,** or **auxiliary verb,** is added to a main verb to make a verb phrase.

be, do, have, should, can, could, may, might, must, will, would

Adjectives An **adjective** modifies a noun or pronoun by describing it or giving it a more specific meaning. An adjective answers the questions:

What kind?	*purple* hat, *happy* face, *loud* sound
Which one?	*this* bowl
How many?	*three* cars
How much?	*enough* food

The articles *the, a,* and *an* are adjectives.

A **proper adjective** is an adjective derived from a proper noun.

French, Shakespearean

Adverbs An **adverb** modifies a verb, an adjective, or another adverb by telling *where, when, how,* or *to what extent.*

will answer *soon, extremely* sad, calls *more* often

Prepositions A **preposition** relates a noun or pronoun that appears with it to another word in the sentence.

Dad made a meal *for* us. We talked *till* dusk. Bo missed school *because of* his illness.

Conjunctions A **conjunction** connects words or groups of words. A **coordinating conjunction** joins words or groups of words of equal rank.

bread *and* cheese, brief *but* powerful

Correlative conjunctions are used in pairs to connect words or groups of words of equal importance.

both Luis *and* Rosa, *neither* you *nor* I

Subordinating conjunctions indicate the connection between two ideas by placing one below the other in rank or importance. A subordinating conjunction introduces a subordinate, or dependent, clause.

We will miss her *if* she leaves. Hank shrieked *when* he slipped on the ice.

Interjections An **interjection** expresses feeling or emotion. It is not related to other words in the sentence.

ah, hey, ouch, well, yippee

PHRASES AND CLAUSES

Phrases A **phrase** is a group of words that does not have both a subject and a verb and that functions as one part of speech. A phrase expresses an idea but cannot stand alone.

Prepositional Phrases A **prepositional phrase** is a group of words that begins with a preposition and ends with a noun or pronoun that is the **object of the preposition.**

before dawn   as a result of the rain

An **adjective phrase** is a prepositional phrase that modifies a noun or pronoun.

Eliza appreciates the beauty **of a well-crafted poem.**

An **adverb phrase** is a prepositional phrase that modifies a verb, an adjective, or an adverb.

She reads Spenser's sonnets **with great pleasure.**

Appositive Phrases An **appositive** is a noun or pronoun placed next to another noun or pronoun to add information about it. An **appositive phrase** consists of an appositive and its modifiers.

Mr. Roth, **my music teacher**, is sick.

Verbal Phrases A **verbal** is a verb form that functions as a different part of speech (not as a verb) in a sentence. **Participles, gerunds,** and **infinitives** are verbals.

A **verbal phrase** includes a verbal and any modifiers or complements it may have. Verbal phrases may function as nouns, as adjectives, or as adverbs.

A **participle** is a verb form that can act as an adjective. Present participles end in *-ing;* past participles of regular verbs end in *-ed*.

A **participial phrase** consists of a participle and its modifiers or complements. The entire phrase acts as an adjective.

Jenna's backpack, **loaded with equipment,** was heavy.

Barking incessantly, the dogs chased the squirrels out of sight.

A **gerund** is a verb form that ends in *-ing* and is used as a noun.

A **gerund phrase** consists of a gerund with any modifiers or complements, all acting together as a noun.

Taking photographs of wildlife is her main hobby. [acts as subject]

We always enjoy **listening to live music.** [acts as object]

An **infinitive** is a verb form, usually preceded by *to,* that can act as a noun, an adjective, or an adverb.

An **infinitive phrase** consists of an infinitive and its modifiers or complements, and sometimes its subject, all acting together as a single part of speech.

She tries **to get out into the wilderness often.** [acts as a noun; direct object of *tries*]

The Tigers are the team **to beat.** [acts as an adjective; describes *team*]

I drove twenty miles **to witness the event.** [acts as an adverb; tells why I drove]

Clauses A **clause** is a group of words with its own subject and verb.

Independent Clauses An independent clause can stand by itself as a complete sentence.

George Orwell wrote with extraordinary insight.

Subordinate Clauses A subordinate clause, also called a dependent clause, cannot stand by itself as a complete sentence. Subordinate clauses always appear connected in some way with one or more independent clauses.

George Orwell, **who wrote with extraordinary insight,** produced many politically relevant works.

An **adjective clause** is a subordinate clause that acts as an adjective. It modifies a noun or a pronoun by telling *what kind* or *which one.* Also called relative clauses, adjective clauses usually begin with a **relative pronoun:** *who, which, that, whom, or whose.*

"The Lamb" is the poem **that I memorized for class.**

An **adverb clause** is a subordinate clause that, like an adverb, modifies a verb, an adjective, or an adverb. An adverb clause tells *where, when, in what way, to what extent, under what condition,* or *why.*

PHRASES AND CLAUSES continued

The students will read another poetry collection **if their schedule allows.**

When I recited the poem, Mr. Lopez was impressed.

A **noun clause** is a subordinate clause that acts as a noun.

William Blake survived on **whatever he made as an engraver.**

SENTENCE STRUCTURE

Subject and Predicate A **sentence** is a group of words that expresses a complete thought. A sentence has two main parts: a *subject* and a *predicate*.

A **fragment** is a group of words that does not express a complete thought. It lacks an independent clause.

The **subject** tells *whom* or *what* the sentence is about. The **predicate** tells what the subject of the sentence does or is.

A subject or a predicate can consist of a single word or of many words. All the words in the subject make up the **complete subject.** All the words in the predicate make up the **complete predicate.**

Complete Subject **Complete Predicate**
Both of those girls | have already read *Macbeth*.

The **simple subject** is the essential noun, pronoun, or group of words acting as a noun that cannot be left out of the complete subject. The **simple predicate** is the essential verb or verb phrase that cannot be left out of the complete predicate.

Both of those girls | **have** already **read** *Macbeth*.
[Simple subject: *Both;* simple predicate: *have read*]

A **compound subject** is two or more subjects that have the same verb and are joined by a conjunction.

Neither the horse nor the driver looked tired.

A **compound predicate** is two or more verbs that have the same subject and are joined by a conjunction.

She **sneezed and coughed** throughout the trip.

Complements A **complement** is a word or word group that completes the meaning of the subject or verb in a sentence. There are four kinds of complements: *direct objects, indirect objects, objective complements,* and *subject complements.*

A **direct object** is a noun, a pronoun, or a group of words acting as a noun that receives the action of a transitive verb.

We watched the **liftoff**.
She drove **Zach** to the launch site.

An **indirect object** is a noun or pronoun that appears with a direct object and names the person or thing to which or for which something is done.

He sold the **family** a mirror. [The direct object is *mirror.*]

An **objective complement** is an adjective or noun that appears with a direct object and describes or renames it.

The decision made her **unhappy**.
[The direct object is *her.*]
Many consider Shakespeare the greatest **playwright.** [The direct object is *Shakespeare.*]

A **subject complement** follows a linking verb and tells something about the subject. There are two kinds: *predicate nominatives* and *predicate adjectives.*

A **predicate nominative** is a noun or pronoun that follows a linking verb and identifies or renames the subject.

"A Modest Proposal" is a **pamphlet.**

A **predicate adjective** is an adjective that follows a linking verb and describes the subject of the sentence.

"A Modest Proposal" is **satirical.**

Classifying Sentences by Structure

Sentences can be classified according to the kind and number of clauses they contain. The four basic sentence structures are *simple, compound, complex,* and *compound-complex.*

A **simple sentence** consists of one independent clause.

Terrence enjoys modern British literature.

A **compound sentence** consists of two or more independent clauses. The clauses are joined by a conjunction or a semicolon.

Terrence enjoys modern British literature, but his brother prefers the classics.

A **complex sentence** consists of one independent clause and one or more subordinate clauses.

Terrence, who reads voraciously, enjoys modern British literature.

A **compound-complex sentence** consists of two or more independent clauses and one or more subordinate clauses.

Terrence, who reads voraciously, enjoys modern British literature, but his brother prefers the classics.

Classifying Sentences by Function

Sentences can be classified according to their function or purpose. The four types are *declarative, interrogative, imperative,* and *exclamatory.*

SENTENCE STRUCTURE continued

A **declarative sentence** states an idea and ends with a period.

An **interrogative sentence** asks a question and ends with a question mark.

An **imperative sentence** gives an order or a direction and ends with either a period or an exclamation mark.

An **exclamatory sentence** conveys a strong emotion and ends with an exclamation mark.

PARAGRAPH STRUCTURE

An effective paragraph is organized around one **main idea,** which is often stated in a **topic sentence.** The other sentences support the main idea. To give the paragraph **unity,** make sure the connection between each sentence and the main idea is clear.

Unnecessary Shift in Person

Do not change needlessly from one grammatical person to another. Keep the person consistent in your sentences.

Max went to the bakery, but **you** can't buy mints there. [shift from third person to second person]

Max went to the bakery, but **he** can't buy mints there. [consistent]

Unnecessary Shift in Voice

Do not change needlessly from active voice to passive voice in your use of verbs.

Elena and I **searched** the trail for evidence, but no clues **were found.** [shift from active voice to passive voice]

Elena and I **searched** the trail for evidence, but we **found** no clues. [consistent]

AGREEMENT

Subject and Verb Agreement

A singular subject must have a singular verb. A plural subject must have a plural verb.

Dr. Boone uses a telescope to view the night sky.

The **students use** a telescope to view the night sky.

A verb always agrees with its subject, not its object.

Incorrect: The best part of the show were the jugglers.

Correct: The best part of the show was the jugglers.

A phrase or clause that comes between a subject and verb does not affect subject-verb agreement.

His **theory**, as well as his claims, **lacks** support.

Two subjects joined by *and* usually take a plural verb.

The **dog** and the **cat are** healthy.

Two singular subjects joined by *or* or *nor* take a singular verb.

The **dog** or the **cat is** hiding.

Two plural subjects joined by *or* or *nor* take a plural verb.

The **dogs** or the **cats are** coming home with us.

When a singular and a plural subject are joined by *or* or *nor,* the verb agrees with the closer subject.

Either the **dogs** or the **cat is** behind the door.

Either the **cat** or the **dogs are** behind the door.

Pronoun and Antecedent Agreement

Pronouns must agree with their antecedents in number and gender. Use singular pronouns with singular antecedents and plural pronouns with plural antecedents.

Doris Lessing uses **her** writing to challenge ideas about women's roles.

Writers often use **their** skills to promote social change.

Use a singular pronoun when the antecedent is a singular indefinite pronoun such as *anybody, each, either, everybody, neither, no one, one, or someone.*

Judge **each** of the articles on **its** merits.

Use a plural pronoun when the antecedent is a plural indefinite pronoun such as *both, few, many,* or *several.*

Both of the articles have **their** flaws.

The indefinite pronouns *all, any, more, most, none,* and *some* can be singular or plural depending on the number of the word to which they refer.

Most of the *books* are in **their** proper places.

Most of the *book* has been torn from **its** binding.

USING VERBS

Principal Parts of Regular and Irregular Verbs

A verb has four principal parts:

Present	Present Participle	Past	Past Participle
learn	learning	learned	learned
discuss	discussing	discussed	discussed
stand	standing	stood	stood
begin	beginning	began	begun

Regular verbs such as *learn* and *discuss* form the past and past participle by adding *-ed* to the present form. **Irregular verbs** such as *stand* and *begin* form the past and past participle in other ways. If you are in doubt about the principal parts of an irregular verb, check a dictionary.

The Tenses of Verbs

The different tenses of verbs indicate the time an action or condition occurs.

The **present tense** expresses an action that happens regularly or states a current condition or general truth.

Tourists **flock** to the site yearly.

Daily exercise **is** good for your heallth.

The **past tense** expresses a completed action or a condition that is no longer true.

The squirrel **dropped** the nut and **ran** up the tree.

I **was** very tired last night by 9:00.

The **future tense** indicates an action that will happen in the future or a condition that will be true.

The Glazers **will visit** us tomorrow.

They **will be** glad to arrive from their long journey.

The **present perfect tense** expresses an action that happened at an indefinite time in the past or an action that began in the past and continues into the present.

Someone **has cleaned** the trash from the park.

The puppy **has been** under the bed all day.

The **past perfect tense** shows an action that was completed before another action in the past.

Gerard **had revised** his essay before he turned it in.

The **future perfect tense** indicates an action that will have been completed before another action takes place.

Mimi **will have painted** the kitchen by the time we finish the shutters.

USING MODIFIERS

Degrees of Comparison

Adjectives and adverbs take different forms to show the three degrees of comparison: the *positive*, the *comparative*, and the *superlative*.

Positive	Comparative	Superlative
fast	faster	fastest
crafty	craftier	craftiest
abruptly	more abruptly	most abruptly
badly	worse	worst

Using Comparative and Superlative Adjectives and Adverbs

Use comparative adjectives and adverbs to compare two things. Use superlative adjectives and adverbs to compare three or more things.

This season's weather was **drier** than last year's.

This season has been one of the **driest** on record.

Jake practices **more often** than Jamal.

Of everyone in the band, Jake practices **most often.**

USING PRONOUNS

Pronoun Case

The **case** of a pronoun is the form it takes to show its function in a sentence. There are three pronoun cases: *nominative*, *objective*, and *possessive*.

Nominative	Objective	Possessive
I, you, he, she, it, we, you, they	me, you, him, her, it, us, you, them	my, your, yours, his, her, hers, its, our, ours, their, theirs

Use the **nominative case** when a pronoun functions as a *subject* or as a *predicate nominative.*

They are going to the movies. [subject]

The biggest movie fan is **she.** [predicate nominative]

Use the **objective case** for a pronoun acting as a *direct object*, an *indirect object*, or the *object of a preposition.*

The ending of the play surprised **me**. [direct object]

Mary gave **us** two tickets to the play. [indirect object]

The audience cheered for **him.** [object of preposition]

Use the **possessive case** to show ownership.

The red suitcase is **hers.**

GLOSSARY: GRAMMAR HANDBOOK

COMMONLY CONFUSED WORDS

Diction The words you choose contribute to the overall effectiveness of your writing. **Diction** refers to word choice and to the clearness and correctness of those words. You can improve one aspect of your diction by choosing carefully between commonly confused words, such as the pairs listed below.

accept, except

Accept is a verb that means "to receive" or "to agree to." *Except* is a preposition that means "other than" or "leaving out."

Please **accept** my offer to buy you lunch this weekend.

He is busy every day **except** the weekends.

affect, effect

Affect is normally a verb meaning "to influence" or "to bring about a change in." *Effect* is usually a noun meaning "result."

The distractions outside **affect** Steven's ability to concentrate.

The teacher's remedies had a positive **effect** on Steven's ability to concentrate.

among, between

Among is usually used with three or more items, and it emphasizes collective relationships or indicates distribution. *Between* is generally used with only two items, but it can be used with more than two if the emphasis is on individual (one-to-one) relationships within the group.

I had to choose a snack **among** the various vegetables.

He handed out the booklets **among** the conference participants.

Our school is **between** a park and an old barn.

The tournament included matches **between** France, Spain, Mexico, and the United States.

amount, number

Amount refers to overall quantity and is mainly used with mass nouns (those that can't be counted). *Number* refers to individual items that can be counted.

The **amount** of attention that great writers have paid to Shakespeare is remarkable.

A **number** of important English writers have been fascinated by the legend of King Arthur.

assure, ensure, insure

Assure means "to convince [someone of something]; to guarantee." *Ensure* means "to make certain [that something happens]." *Insure* means "to arrange for payment in case of loss."

The attorney **assured** us we'd win the case.

The rules **ensure** that no one gets treated unfairly.

Many professional musicians **insure** their valuable instruments.

bad, badly

Use the adjective *bad* before a noun or after linking verbs such as *feel, look,* and *seem*. Use *badly* whenever an adverb is required.

The situation may seem **bad**, but it will improve over time.

Though our team played **badly** today, we will focus on practicing for the next match.

beside, besides

Beside means "at the side of" or "close to." *Besides* means "in addition to."

The stapler sits **beside** the pencil sharpener in our classroom.

Besides being very clean, the classroom is also very organized.

can, may

The helping verb *can* generally refers to the ability to do something. The helping verb *may* generally refers to permission to do something.

I **can** run one mile in six minutes.

May we have a race during recess?

complement, compliment

The verb *complement* means "to enhance"; the verb *compliment* means "to praise."

Online exercises **complement** the textbook lessons.

Ms. Lewis **complimented** our team on our excellent debate.

compose, comprise

Compose means "to make up; constitute." *Comprise* means "to include or contain." Remember that the whole comprises its parts or is composed of its parts, and the parts compose the whole.

The assignment **comprises** three different tasks.

The assignment is **composed** of three different tasks.

Three different tasks **compose** the assignment.

different from, different than

Different from is generally preferred over *different than,* but *different than* can be used before a clause. Always use *different from* before a noun or pronoun.

Your point of view is so **different from** mine.

His idea was so **different from** [or **different than**] what we had expected.

farther, further

Use *farther* to refer to distance. Use *further* to mean "to a greater degree or extent" or "additional."

Chiang has traveled **farther** than anybody else in the class.

If I want **further** details about his travels, I can read his blog.

fewer, less

Use *fewer* for things that can be counted. Use *less* for amounts or quantities that cannot be counted. *Fewer* must be followed by a plural noun.

Fewer students drive to school since the weather improved.

There is **less** noise outside in the mornings.

good, well

Use the adjective *good* before a noun or after a linking verb. Use *well* whenever an adverb is required, such as when modifying a verb.

I feel **good** after sleeping for eight hours.

I did **well** on my test, and my soccer team played **well** in that afternoon's game. It was a **good** day!

its, it's

The word *its* with no apostrophe is a possessive pronoun. The word *it's* is a contraction of "it is."

Angelica will try to fix the computer and **its** keyboard.

It's a difficult job, but she can do it.

lay, lie

Lay is a transitive verb meaning "to set or put something down." Its principal parts are *lay, laying, laid, laid. Lie* is an intransitive verb meaning "to recline" or "to exist in a certain place." Its principal parts are *lie, lying, lay, lain.*

Please **lay** that box down and help me with the sofa.

When we are done moving, I am going to **lie** down.

My hometown **lies** sixty miles north of here.

like, as

Like is a preposition that usually means "similar to" and precedes a noun or pronoun. The conjunction *as* means "in the way that" and usually precedes a clause.

Like the other students, I was prepared for a quiz.

As I said yesterday, we expect to finish before noon.

Use **such as,** not **like,** before a series of examples.

Foods **such as** apples, nuts, and pretzels make good snacks.

of, have

Do not use *of* in place of *have* after auxiliary verbs such as *would, could, should, may, might,* or *must.* The contraction of *have* is formed by adding *-ve* after these verbs.

I **would have** stayed after school today, but I had to help cook at home.

Mom **must've** called while I was still in the gym.

principal, principle

Principal can be an adjective meaning "main; most important." It can also be a noun meaning "chief officer of a school." *Principle* is a noun meaning "moral rule" or "fundamental truth."

His strange behavior was the **principal** reason for our concern.

Democratic **principles** form the basis of our country's laws.

raise, rise

Raise is a transitive verb that usually takes a direct object. *Rise* is intransitive and never takes a direct object.

Iliana and Josef **raise** the flag every morning.

They **rise** from their seats and volunteer immediately whenever help is needed.

than, then

The conjunction *than* is used to connect the two parts of a comparison. The adverb *then* usually refers to time.

My backpack is heavier **than** hers.

I will finish my homework and **then** meet my friends at the park.

that, which, who

Use the relative pronoun *that* to refer to things or people. Use *which* only for things and *who* only for people.

That introduces a restrictive phrase or clause, that is, one that is essential to the meaning of the sentence. *Which* introduces a nonrestrictive phrase or clause—one that adds information but could be deleted from the sentence—and is preceded by a comma.

Ben ran to the park **that** just reopened.

The park, **which** just reopened, has many attractions.

The man **who** built the park loves to see people smiling.

when, where, why

Do not use *when, where,* or *why* directly after a linking verb, such as *is*. Reword the sentence.

Incorrect: The morning is when he left for the beach.

Correct: He left for the beach in the morning.

who, whom

In formal writing, use *who* only as a subject in clauses and sentences. Use *whom* only as the object of a verb or of a preposition.

Who paid for the tickets?

Whom should I pay for the tickets?

I can't recall to **whom** I gave the money for the tickets.

your, you're

Your is a possessive pronoun expressing ownership. *You're* is the contraction of "you are."

Have you finished writing **your** informative essay?

You're supposed to turn it in tomorrow. If **you're** late, **your** grade will be affected.

Capitalization

First Words

Capitalize the first word of a sentence.

Stories about knights and their deeds interest me.

Capitalize the first word of direct speech.

Sharon asked, "**D**o you like stories about knights?"

Capitalize the first word of a quotation that is a complete sentence.

Einstein said, "**A**nyone who has never made a mistake has never tried anything new."

Proper Nouns and Proper Adjectives

Capitalize all proper nouns, including geographical names, historical events and periods, and names of organizations.

Thames **R**iver **J**ohn **K**eats the **R**enaissance
United **N**ations **W**orld **W**ar II **S**ierra **N**evada

Capitalize all proper adjectives.

Shakespearean play **B**ritish invaision
American citizen **L**atin **A**merican literature

Academic Course Names

Capitalize course names only if they are language courses, are followed by a number, or are preceded by a proper noun or adjective.

Spanish **H**onors **C**hemistry **H**istory 101
geology **a**lgebra **s**ocial **s**tudies

Titles

Capitalize personal titles when followed by the person's name.

Ms. Hughes **D**r. Perez **K**ing George

Capitalize titles showing family relationships when they are followed by a specific person's name, unless they are preceded by a possessive noun or pronoun.

Uncle Oscar Mangan's **s**ister his **a**unt Tessa

Capitalize the first word and all other key words in the titles of books, stories, songs, and other works of art.

Frankenstein "**S**hooting an **E**lephant"

Punctuation

End Marks

Use a **period** to end a declarative sentence or an imperative sentence.

We are studying the structure of sonnets.
Read the biography of Mary Shelley.

Use periods with initials and abbreviations.

D. H. Lawrence Mrs. Browning
Mt. Everest Maple St.

Use a **question mark** to end an interrogative sentence.

What is Macbeth's fatal flaw?

Use an **exclamation mark** after an exclamatory sentence or a forceful imperative sentence.

That's a beautiful painting! Let me go now!

Commas

Use a **comma** before a coordinating conjunction to separate two independent clauses in a compound sentence.

The game was very close, but we were victorious.

Use commas to separate three or more words, phrases, or clauses in a series.

William Blake was a writer, artist, and printer.

Use commas to separate coordinate adjectives.

It was a witty, amusing novel.

Use a comma after an introductory word, phrase, or clause.

When the novelist finished his book, he celebrated with his family.

Use commas to set off nonessential expressions.

Old English, of course, requires translation.

Use commas with places and dates.

Coventry, England September 1, 1939

Semicolons

Use a **semicolon** to join closely related independent clauses that are not already joined by a conjunction.

Tanya likes to write poetry; Heather prefers prose.

Use semicolons to avoid confusion when items in a series contain commas.

They traveled to London, England; Madrid, Spain; and Rome, Italy.

Colons

Use a **colon** before a list of items following an independent clause.

Notable Victorian poets include the following: Tennyson, Arnold, Housman, and Hopkins.

Use a colon to introduce information that summarizes or explains the independent clause before it.

She just wanted to do one thing: rest.
Malcolm loves volunteering: He reads to sick children every Saturday afternoon.

Quotation Marks

Use **quotation marks** to enclose a direct quotation.

"Short stories," Ms. Hildebrand said, "should have rich, well-developed characters."

An **indirect quotation** does not require quotation marks.

Ms. Hildebrand said that short stories should have well-developed characters.

Use quotation marks around the titles of short written works, episodes in a series, songs, and works mentioned as parts of collections.

"The Lagoon" "Boswell Meets Johnson"

Italics

Italicize the titles of long written works, movies, television and radio shows, lengthy works of music, paintings, and sculptures.

Howards End *60 Minutes* *Guernica*

For handwritten material, you can use underlining instead of italics.

The Princess Bride Mona Lisa

Dashes

Use **dashes** to indicate an abrupt change of thought, a dramatic interrupting idea, or a summary statement.

I read the entire first act of *Macbeth*—you won't believe what happens next.
The director—what's her name again?—attended the movie premiere.

Hyphens

Use a **hyphen** with certain numbers, after certain prefixes, with two or more words used as one word, and with a compound modifier that comes before a noun.

seventy-two
self-esteem
president-elect
five-year contract

Parentheses

Use **parentheses** to set off asides and explanations when the material is not essential or when it consists of one or more sentences. When the sentence in parentheses interrupts the larger sentence, it does not have a capital letter or a period.

He listened intently (it was too dark to see who was speaking) to try to identify the voices.

When a sentence in parentheses falls between two other complete sentences, it should start with a capital letter and end with a period.

The quarterback threw three touchdown passes. (We knew he could do it.) Our team won the game by two points.

Apostrophes

Add an **apostrophe** and an *s* to show the possessive case of most singular nouns and of plural nouns that do not end in *-s* or *-es*.

Blake's poems the mice's whiskers

Names ending in *s* form their possessives in the same way, except for classical and biblical names, which add only an apostrophe to form the possessive.

Dickens's Hercules'

Add an apostrophe to show the possessive case of plural nouns ending in *-s* and *-es*.

the girls' songs the Ortizes' car

Use an apostrophe in a contraction to indicate the position of the missing letter or letters.

She's never read a Coleridge poem she didn't like.

Brackets

Use **brackets** to enclose clarifying information inserted within a quotation.

Columbus's journal entry from October 21, 1492, begins as follows: "At 10 o'clock, we arrived at a cape of the island [San Salvador], and anchored, the other vessels in company."

Ellipses

Use three ellipsis points, also known as an **ellipsis,** to indicate where you have omitted words from quoted material.

Wollestonecraft wrote, "The education of women has of late been more attended to than formerly; yet they are still . . . ridiculed or pitied. . . ."

In the example above, the four dots at the end of the sentence are the three ellipsis points plus the period from the original sentence.

Use an ellipsis to indicate a pause or interruption in speech.

"When he told me the news," said the coach,
"I was . . . I was shocked . . . completely shocked."

Spelling

Spelling Rules

Learning the rules of English spelling will help you make **generalizations** about how to spell words.

Word Parts

The three word parts that can combine to form a word are roots, prefixes, and suffixes. Many of these word parts come from the Greek, Latin, and Anglo-Saxon languages.

The **root word** carries a word's basic meaning.

Root and Origin	Meaning	Examples
-leg- (-log-) [Gr.]	to say, speak	*legal, logic*
-pon- (-pos-) [L.]	to put, place	*postpone, deposit*

A **prefix** is one or more syllables added to the beginning of a word that alter the meaning of the root.

Prefix and Origin	Meaning	Example
anti- [Gr.]	against	*antipathy*
inter- [L.]	between	*international*
mis- [A.S.]	wrong	*misplace*

A **suffix** is a letter or group of letters added to the end of a root word that changes the word's meaning or part of speech.

Suffix and Origin	Meaning and Example	Part of Speech
-ful [A.S.]	full of: *scornful*	adjective
-ity [L.]	state of being: *adversity*	noun
-ize (-ise) [Gr.]	to make: *idolize*	verb
-ly [A.S.]	in a manner: *calmly*	adverb

Rules for Adding Suffixes to Root Words

When adding a suffix to a root word ending in *y* preceded by a consonant, change *y* to *i* unless the suffix begins with *i*.

ply + -able = pliable   happy + -ness = happiness
defy + -ing = defying   cry + -ing = crying

For a root word ending in *e*, drop the *e* when adding a suffix beginning with a vowel.

drive + -ing = driving   move + -able = movable
SOME EXCEPTIONS: traceable, seeing, dyeing

For root words ending with a consonant + vowel + consonant in a stressed syllable, double the final consonant when adding a suffix that begins with a vowel.

mud + -y = muddy   submit + -ed = submitted
SOME EXCEPTIONS: mixing, fixed

Rules for Adding Prefixes to Root Words

When a prefix is added to a root word, the spelling of the root remains the same.

un- + certain = uncertain   mis- + spell = misspell

With some prefixes, the spelling of the prefix changes when joined to the root to make the pronunciation easier.

in- + mortal = immortal   ad- + vert = avert

Orthographic Patterns

Certain letter combinations in English make certain sounds. For instance, *ph* sounds like *f*, *eigh* usually makes a long *a* sound, and the *k* before an *n* is often silent.

pharmacy   n**eigh**bor   **k**nowledge

Understanding **orthographic patterns** such as these can help you improve your spelling.

Forming Plurals

The plural form of most nouns is formed by adding *-s* to the singular.

computers   gadgets   Washingtons

For words ending in *s, ss, x, z, sh,* or *ch,* add *-es*.

circus**es**   tax**es**   wish**es**   bench**es**

For words ending in *y* or *o* preceded by a vowel, add *-s*.

key**s**   patio**s**

For words ending in *y* preceded by a consonant, change the *y* to an *i* and add *-es*.

cit**ies**   enem**ies**   troph**ies**

For most words ending in *o* preceded by a consonant, add *-es*.

echo**es**   tomato**es**

Some words form the plural in irregular ways.

women   oxen   children   teeth   deer

Foreign Words Used in English

Some words used in English are actually foreign words that have been adopted. Learning to spell these words requires memorization. When in doubt, check a dictionary.

sushi   enchilada   au pair   fiancé
laissez faire   croissant

INDEX OF SKILLS

Boldface numbers indicate pages where terms are defined.

Analyzing Text

R68

Assessment

Language Conventions

Research

Speaking and Listening

R69

Vocabulary

INDEX OF SKILLS

INDEX OF SKILLS

Writing

INDEX OF SKILLS

R72

INDEX OF AUTHORS AND TITLES

The following authors and titles appear in the print and online versions of *my*Perspectives.

R74

R75

ADDITIONAL SELECTIONS: AUTHOR AND TITLE INDEX

The following authors and titles appear in the Online Literature Library.

ACKNOWLEDGMENTS AND CREDITS

Acknowledgments

The following selections appear in this grade level (Grade 9) of *my*Perspectives. Some selections appear online only.

ABC News - Permissions Dept. "Amazing Stories of Rescues and Survival in Nepal" ©ABC News; "Misty Copeland's Hard-Fought Journey to Ballet Stardom" ©ABC News; "Doomsday Plane Ready for Nuclear Attack" ©ABC News.

Abner Stein. "Rules of the Game" by Amy Tan, from *The Joy Luck Club.* Used with permission of Abner Stein.

Alfred A. Knopf. "The Seventh Man" by Haruki Murakami, translated by Jay Rubin; from *Blind Willow Sleeping Woman* by Haruki Murakami and translated by Philip Gabriel and Jay Rubin, copyright © 2006 by Haruki Murakami. Used by permission of Alfred A. Knopf, an imprint of the Knopf Doubleday Publishing Group, a division of Penguin Random House LLC. All rights reserved. Any third party use of this material, outside of this publication, is prohibited. Interested parties must apply directly to Penguin Random House LLC for permission; "The Voyage of the James Caird" from *The Endurance: Shackleton's Legendary Antarctic Expedition* by Caroline Alexander, copyright © 1998 by Caroline Alexander. Used by permission of Alfred A. Knopf, an imprint of the Knopf Doubleday Publishing Group, a division of Penguin Random House LLC. All rights reserved. Any third party use of this material, outside of this publication, is prohibited. Interested parties must apply directly to Penguin Random House LLC for permission.

Apostrophe S Productions, Inc. "The Hero's Adventure" from *The Power of Myth* by Joseph Campbell. Used with permission of Apostrophe S Productions.

Arte Publico Press. "Legal Alien" is reprinted with permission from the publisher of *Chants* by Pat Mora ©1994 Arte Publico Press - University of Houston).

BBC Worldwide Americas, Inc. "Grace Abbott and the Fight for Immigrant Rights in America" ©BBC Worldwide Learning; "Civil Rights Movement and the MLK Assassination" ©BBC Worldwide Learning; "Fannie Lou Hamer" ©BBC Worldwide Learning; "A Modern Take on Romeo and Juliet" ©BBC Worldwide Learning.

BOA Editions, Ltd. Lucille Clifton, excerpt from "mulberry fields" from *The Collected Poems of LucilleClifton*. Copyright © 2004 by Lucille Clifton. Reprinted with the permission of The Permissions Company, Inc. on behalf of BOA Editions Ltd.; Lucille Clifton, "the beginning of the end of the world" from *The Collected Poems of Lucille Clifton*. Copyright ©1991 by Lucille Clifton. Reprinted with the permission of The Permissions Company, Inc. on behalf of BOA Editions Ltd.

Brandt & Hochman Literary Agents Inc. "The Most Dangerous Game" by Richard Connell. Copyright ©1924 by Richard Connell. Copyright renewed © 1952 by Louise Fox Connell. Used by permission of Brandt & Hochman Literary Agents, Inc. Any copying or distribution of this text is expressly forbidden. All rights reserved.; "By the Waters of Babylon" by Stephen Vincent Benet. Copyright ©1937 by Stephen Vincent Benet Copyright renewed ©1965 by Thomas C. Benet, Stephanie Mahin and Rachel B. Lewis. Used by permission of Brandt & Hochman Literary Agents, Inc. Any copying or distribution of this text is expressly forbidden. All rights reserved.

Candlewick Press. *The Odyssey.* Copyright © 2010 by Gareth Hinds. Reproduced by permission of the publisher, Candlewick Press, Somerville, MA.

Canongate Books Limited. *From The Life of Pi.* Used with permission of Canongate Books Ltd.; Used with permission of Canongate Books Ltd.

Carnegie Mellon University Press. Gregory Djanikian, "Immigrant Picnic" from *So I Will Till the Ground.* Originally published in Poetry (July 1999). Copyright ©1999, 2007 by Gregory Djanikian. Reprinted with the permission of The Permissions Company, Inc., on behalf of Carnegie Mellon University Press.

CBS News. "A Visit to the Doomsday Vault," CBS, 60 Minutes. Used with permission of CBS News.

CBS Rights & Permissions. "A Visit to the Doomsday Vault," CBS, 60 Minutes, Copyright ©2008.

Center for Disease Control. "Preparedness 101: Zombie Apocalypse" by Ali S. Khan (CDC, 2011).

Cesar Chavez Foundation. "Lessons of Dr. Martin Luther King, Jr." TM/©2015 The Cesar Chavez Foundation.

CNN ImageSource. CNN newscast of "Tragic Romeo and Juliet Offers Bosnia Hope" ©CNN.

Copyright Clearance Center. "Ithaka" republished with permission of Princeton University Press, from *Collected Poems* by C.P. Cavafy, translated by Keeyley & Sherrard, 1992; permission conveyed through Copyright Clearance Center, Inc.

Define American. "Define American." Hiep Le, Culver City, CA ©Define American.

Don Congdon Associates. "There Will Come Soft Rains." Reprinted by permission of Don Congdon Associates, Inc. Copyright ©1950 by the Crowell Collier Publishing Company, renewed 1977 by Ray Bradbury.

Dunbar, Paul Laurence. "We Wear the Mask" by Paul Laurence Dunbar.

Dungy, Camille. "The Writing on the Wall." First published on Harriet, the blog for the Poetry Foundation. Reprinted with permission of the author.

Farrar, Straus and Giroux. "Traveling" from *Just as I Thought* by Grace Paley. Copyright ©1998 by Grace Paley. Reprinted by permission Farrar, Straus and Giroux, LLC. CAUTION: Users are warned that this work is protected under copyright laws and downloading is strictly prohibited. The right to reproduce or transfer the work via any medium must be secured with Farrar, Straus and Giroux, LLC.; Excerpts from *The Odyssey* by Homer, translated by Robert Fitzgerald. Copyright ©1961, 1963 by Robert Fitzgerald. Copyright renewed 1989 by Benedict R.C. Fitzgerald, on behalf of the Fitzgerald children. Reprinted by permission of Farrar, Straus and Giroux, LLC. CAUTION: Users are warned that this work is protected under copyright laws and downloading is strictly prohibited. The right to reproduce or transfer the work via any medium must be secured with Farrar, Straus and Giroux, LLC.

Farrell, Joanna. "Popocatepetl and Ixtlaccihuatl" by permission of Mrs. J.S.E. Farrell.

Fitzgerald, Benedict. From *The Odyssey* translated by Robert Fitzgerald. Reprinted with permission of Benedict R.C. Fitzgerald.

Frost, Robert. "Fire and Ice" by Robert Frost (1920).

Hanging Loose Press. "The Powwow at the End of the World." Reprinted from *The Summer of Black Widows* ©1996 by Sherman Alexie, by permission of Hanging Loose Press.

HarperCollins Publishers. Chapter 5: "The Immigrant Contribution" [pp. 32–5: 1500 words] from *A Nation of Immigrants* by John F. Kennedy. Copyright ©1964, 2008 by Anti-Defamation League of B'nai B'rith. Reprinted by permission of HarperCollins Publishers; "A Song on the End of the World" from *New and Collected Poems: 1931–2001* by Czeslaw Milosz. Copyright ©1988, 1991, 1995, 2001 by Czeslaw Milosz Royalties, Inc. Reprinted by permission of HarperCollins Publishers.

HarperCollins Publishers Ltd. From *Unbroken.* Reprinted by permission of HarperCollins Publishers Ltd. ©Laura Hillenbrand.

Hill Nadell Literary Agency. "With a Little Help From My Friends." Copyright ©2003 Firouzeh Dumas. Used by permission of the author.

Hinds, Gareth. *The Odyssey.* Copyright ©2010 by Gareth Hinds. Reproduced by permission of the publisher, Candlewick Press, Somerville, MA.

Holy Cow! Press. Roberta Hill Whiteman "Morning Talk" from *Philadelphia Flowers.* Copyright ©1996 by Roberta Hill Whiteman. Reprinted with the permission of The Permissions Company, Inc., on behalf of Holy Cow! Press, www.holycowpress.org.

Houghton Mifflin Harcourt Publishing Co. Excerpts from *Life of Pi:* A Novel by Yann Martel. Copyright ©2001 by Yann Martel. Reprinted by permission of Houghton Mifflin Publishing Company. All rights reserved; "The Writer" from *The Mind-Reader* by Richard WIlbur. Copyright ©1971, and renewed 1999 by Richard Wilbur. Reprinted by permission of Houghton Mifflin Harcourt Publishing Company. All rights reserved; "Incident" from *Native Guard: Poems* by Natasha Trethewey. Copyright ©2006 by Natasha Trethewey. Reprinted by permission of Houghton Mifflin Company. All rights reserved; "Courage" from *The Awful Rowing Toward God* by Anne Sexton. Copyright ©1975 by Loring Conant, Jr., Executor of the Estate of Anne Sexton. Reprinted by permission of Houghton Mifflin Harcourt Publishing Company. All rights reserved.

ICM. "A Quilt of a Country" ©[2001] by Anna Quindlen. Used by Permission. All rights reserved; "The Seventh Man" ©2006 by Haruki Murakami. Used by Permission. All rights reserved.

Knopf Doubleday Publishing Group (Alfred A. Knopf). "The Hero's Adventure." Excerpt(s) from *The Power of Myth* by Joseph Campbell, copyright ©1988 by Apostrophe S Productions, Inc., and Bill Moyers and Alfred Van der Marck Editions, Inc., for itself and the estate of Joseph Campbell. Used by permission of Doubleday, an imprint of the Knopf Doubleday Publishing Group, a division of Penguin Random House LLC. All rights reserved. Any third party use of this material, outside of this publication, is prohibited. Interested parties must apply directly to Penguin Random House LLC for permission.

LA Theatre Works. LA Theatre Works' *Romeo and Juliet* by William Shakespeare ©LA Theatre Works.

Little, Brown and Co. (New York). "Pyramus and Thisbe" from *Mythology* by Edith Hamilton. Copyright 1940, 1942 by Edith Hamilton, renewed ©1969 by Doris Fielding Reid, Executrix of the will of Edith Hamilton. Reprinted with the permission of Little, Brown and Company. All rights reserved.

London, Jack. London, Jack. "To Build a Fire."

MacNeil/Lehrer Productions. "Remembering Civil Rights History: When Words Meant Everything" ©2014 NewsHour Productions LLC.

Mekko Productions. "Perhaps the World Ends Here," from *The Woman Who Fell From the Sky* by Joy Harjo. Copyright ©1994 by Joe Harjo. Used by permission of W.W. Norton & Company, Inc. and by the author.

Moorland-Spingarn Research Centers. "Your World" by Georgia Douglas Johnson. Used with permission of Moorland-Spingam Research Center, Howard University.

National Archives. Robert F. Kennedy's remarks on the assassination of Martin Luther ©National Archives.

National Geographic Society. "The Nuclear Tourist," *National Geographic,* October 2014. ©Johnson, George L./National Geographic Creative.

National Park Service. "Survival Is Your Own Responsibility: Thoughts from a Retired Mountaineering Ranger" by Daryl R. Miller.

New Directions Publishing Corp. "I Am Offering This Poem" by Jimmy Santiago Baca, from *Immigrants in Our Own Land,* Copyright ©1979 by Jimmy Santiago Baca. Reprinted by permission of New Directions Publishing Corp.

New York Public Radio. Podcast of "War of the Worlds" from Radiolab ©New York Public Radio.

New York Times. "The Moral Logic of Survival Guilt" from *The New York Times,* July 16, 2008 ©2008 The New York Times. All rights reserved. Used by permission and protected by the Copyright Laws of the United States. The printing, copying, redistribution, or retransmission of this Content without express written permission is prohibited.

NPR. "The Secret Bunker Congress Never Used" ©2011 National Public Radio, Inc. News report titled "The Secret Bunker Congress Never Used" by NPR Staff was originally published on NPR.org on March 26, 2011, and is used with the permission of NPR. Any unauthorized duplication is strictly prohibited.

NPR (National Public Radio). "The Key To Disaster Survival? Friends And Neighbors" ©2011 National Public Radio, Inc. News report titled "The Key To Disaster Survival? Friends And Neighbors" was originally broadcast on NPR's All Things Considered on July 4, 2011, and is used with the permission of NPR. Any unauthorized duplication is strictly prohibited.

Outside Magazine. "The Value of a Sherpa Life" by Grayson Schaffer, from *Outside,* April 18, 2014. Used with permission of Outside Magazine.

PARS International Corporation. "In New York with Six Weeks to Adapt to America" from *New York Times,* August 26, 2012 ©2012 The New York Times. All rights reserved. Used by permission and protected by the Copyright Laws of the United States. The printing, copying, redistribution, or retransmission of this Content without express written permission is prohibited."; "How the Children of Birmingham Changed the Civil-Rights Movement" from *The Daily Beast,* May 2, 2013 ©2013 The Daily Beast Company LLC. All rights reserved. Used by permission and protected by the Copyright Laws of the United States. The printing, copying, redistribution, or retransmission of this Content without express written permission is prohibited; "The Myth of the *War of the Worlds* Panic" from *Slate,* October 28, 2013 ©2013 The Slate Group. All rights reserved. Used by permission and protected by the Copyright Laws of the United States. The printing, copying, redistribution, or retransmission of this Content without express written permission is prohibited; "Romeo and Juliet is a Terrible Play, and David Leveaux Can't Change That" from *Slate*, April 2, 2013 ©2013 The Slate Group. All rights reserved.

Used by permission and protected by the Copyright Laws of the United States. The printing, copying, redistribution, or retransmission of this Content without express written permission is prohibited; "13 Epic Animal Migrations That Prove Just How Cool Mother Nature Is" from *The Huffington Post*, April 2, 2014 ©2014 AOL Inc. All rights reserved. Used by permission and protected by the Copyright Laws of the United States. The printing, copying, redistribution, or retransmission of this Content without express written permission is prohibited.

Penguin Books, Ltd. (UK). "A Song on the End of the World" taken from *New and Collected Poems: 1931–2001* by Czeslaw Milosz (Penguin Classics 2005) Copyright ©Czeslaw Milosz Royalties Inc., 1988, 1991, 1995, 2001. Reproduced by permission of Penguin Books Ltd.

Penguin Publishing Group. "Rules of the Game," from *The Joy Luck Club* by Amy Tan, copyright ©1989 by Amy Tan. Used by permission of G. P. Putnam's Sons, an imprint of Penguin Publishing Group, a division of Penguin Random House LLC.

Penguin Random House Canada Limited (McClelland & Stewart). From *Life of Pi* excerpted from *Life of Pi: A Novel* by Yann Martel. Copyright (C)2001 by Yann Martel. Reprinted by permission of Alfred A. Knopf Canada, a division of Penguin Random House Canada Limited.

Perseus Books Group (direct). From *When I Was Puerto Rican* by Esmeralda Santiago, copyright ©1993. Reprinted by permission of Da Capo Press, a member of The Perseus Books Group.

Postmedia Network, Inc. "If Romeo and Juliet Had Cell Phones" by Misty Harris, from Canada.com, January 30, 2013. Material reprinted with the express permission of: Postmedia News, a division of Postmedia Network Inc.

Random House Group Ltd., Permissions Department. "Ithaka" from *Collected Poems* by C. P. Cavafy (translated by Edmund Keeley and Philip Sherrard). Published by The Hogarth Press. Reprinted by permission of The Random House Group Limited.

Random House, Inc. "With a Little Help from My Friends" from *Funny in Farsi: A Memoir of Growing Up Iranian in America* by Firoozeh Dumas, copyright ©2003 by Firoozeh Dumas. Used by permission of Villard Books, an imprint of Random House, a division of Penguin Random House LLC. All rights reserved. Any third party use of this material, outside of this publication, is prohibited. Interested parties must apply directly to Penguin Random House LLC for permission; "Chapter Fifteen: Sharks and Bullets," and "Chapter Sixteen: Singing in the Clouds" from *Unbroken: A World War II Story of Survival, Resilience, and Redemption* by Laura Hillenbrand, copyright ©2010 by Laura Hillenbrand. Used by permission of Random House, an imprint and division of Penguin Random House LLC. All rights reserved. Any third party use of this material, outside of this publication, is prohibited. Interested parties must apply directly to Penguin Random House LLC for permission; Excerpt(s) from *Wild: From Lost to Found on the Pacific Crest Trail* by Cheryl Strayed, copyright ©2012 by Cheryl Strayed. Used by permission of Alfred A. Knopf, an imprint of the Knopf Doubleday Publishing Group, a division of Penguin Random House LLC. All rights reserved. Any third party use of this material, outside of this publication, is prohibited. Interested parties must apply directly to Penguin Random House LLC for permission.

RFE/RL. "Twenty Years On—The Unfinished Lives of Bosnia's Romeo and Juliet" Copyright ©2015. RFE/RL, Inc. Reprinted with the permission of Radio Free Europe/Radio Liberty, 1201 Connecticut Ave NW, Ste 400, Washington DC 20036.

Rogers, Coleridge and White Ltd. "Ithaka" from *Collected Poems* by C. P. Cavafy. Published by Princeton University Press, 1990. Copyright ©C. P. Cavafy. Reproduced by permission of the Estate of C. P. Cavafy c/o Rogers, Coleridge & White., 20 Powis Mews, London W11 1JN.

Sheil Land Associates Ltd. "The Voyage of the James Caird." Extract from *Endurance* by F. A. Worsley. ©The Estate of F. A. Worsle, 1931. Reproduced by permission of Sheil Land Associates Ltd.

Shihab Nye, Naomi. "Hugging the Jukebox" by permission of the author, Naomi Shihab Nye, 2015.

Smithsonian Enterprises. "The End of the World May Look Like This" by Megan Gambino, from *Smithsonian*, July 18, 2013. Copyright 2013 Smithsonian Institution. Reprinted with permission from Smithsonian Enterprises. All rights reserved. Reproduction in any medium is strictly prohibited without permission from Smithsonian Institution.

Stanford University Press. "Narrow Road of the Interior" by Matsuo Basho. From *Classical Japanese Prose: An Anthology*, compiled and edited by Helen Craig McCullough. Copyright ©1990 by the Board of Trustees of the Leland Stanford Jr., University. All rights reserved. With the permission of Stanford University Press.

Sterling Lord Literistic, Inc. "Courage" from *The Awful Rowing Toward God* by Anne Sexton. Copyright ©1975 by Loring Conant, Jr., Executor of the Estate of Anne Sexton. Reprinted by permission of SLL/Sterling Lord Literistic, Inc.

Time Magazine. "Titanic vs. Lusitania: How People Behave in a Disaster" ©2010 Time Inc. All rights reserved. Reprinted/Translated from TIME and published with permission of Time Inc. Reproduction in any manner in any language in whole or in part without written permission is prohibited. TIME and the TIME logo are registered trademarks of Time Inc. used under license.

Tribune Content Agency, LLC. "In Defense of Romeo and Juliet" ©2013 The Atlantic Media Co., as first published in *The Atlantic Magazine*. All rights reserved. Distributed by Tribune Content Agency, LLC.

Tsai, Diane. "Finding a Voice: A Taiwanese Family Adapts to America" from Immigrant Connect. Used with permission of Diane Tsai.

Union Literary. "Traveling" from *Just As I Thought* by Grace Paley. Used with permission of Union Literary.

United States Department of Homeland Security. Application for a Mariner's License (U.S. Department of Homeland Security).

University of Alabama Press. Excerpt, pp 95–106, from *Selma, Lord, Selma: Girlhood Memories of the Civil-Rights Days* by Sheyann Webb and Rachel West Nelson, as told to Frank Sikora. ©1980, The University of Alabama Press. Reprinted with permission.

University of Georgia Press. "American History" from *The Latin Deli* by Judith Ortiz Cofer. Copyright ©1992 by Judith Ortiz Cofer. Reprinted by permission of University of Georgia Press; "For My People" by Margaret Walker from *This is My Century: New and Collected Poems.* Copyright ©1989. Used with permission of University of Georgia Press.

University of Washington Press. "The Writing on the Wall." Lai, Him Mark, Genny Lim, and Judy Yung, eds. *Island: Poetry and History of Chinese Immigrants on Angel Island, 1910–1940* ©1991. Reprinted with permission of the University of Washington Press.

W. W. Norton & Co. "The Voyage of the James Caird" from *Endurance: An Epic of Polar Adventure* by F. A. Worsley. Copyright ©1931 by the Estate of F. A. Worsley. Used by permission of W.W. Norton & Company, Inc.; "Perhaps the World Ends Here," from *The Woman Who Fell From the Sky* by Joy Harjo. Copyright ©1994 by Joe Harjo. Used by permission of W.W. Norton & Company, Inc.

Watkins/Loomis Agency. "The Return" from *Secret Lives* by Ngugi wa Thiong'o. Reprinted by Permission of Ngugi wa' Thiong'o and the Watkins Loomis Agency.

Westwood Creative Artists. From *Life of Pi* by Yann Martel (Harcourt, 2001). Copyright ©2001 Yann Martel. With permission of the author.

Writers House LLC. "I Have a Dream" / "Letter From a Birmingham City Jail"—Reprinted by arrangement with The Heirs to the Estate of Martin Luther King Jr., c/o Writers House as agent for the proprietor New York, NY; Reprinted by arrangement with the Heirs to the Estate of Martin Luther King Jr., c/o Writers House as agent for the proprietor New York, NY. Copyright ©1963 Dr. Martin Luther King, Jr. Copyright renewed 1991 Coretta Scott King; Reprinted by arrangement with The Heirs to the Estate of Martin Luther King Jr., c/o Writers House as agent for the proprietor New York, NY. Copyright ©1963 Dr. Martin Luther King, Jr. Copyright renewed 1991 Coretta Scott King.

WUNC. "Franklin McCain Dies—Helped Start Sit-In Movement At Greensboro Lunch Counter" ©National Public Radio, Inc.

Wylie Agency. "A Song on the End of the World" by Czeslaw Milosz, collected in *New and Collected Poems: 1931–2001*. Copyright ©1988, 1991, 1995, 2001 by Czeslaw Milosz Royalties, Inc., used by permission of The Wylie Agency LLC.

Yale University Press. "The Many Lives of Hazel Bryan" from *Elizabeth & Hazel: Two Women of Little Rock* by David Margolick. Copyright ©2011. Used with permission of the publisher, Yale University Press.

YGS Group. "Seven Steps to Surviving a Disaster" used with permission of Bloomberg L.P. Copyright ©2015. All rights reserved.

Zachary Shuster Harmsworth Literary Agency. From *Wild* by Cheryl Strayed; copyright ©2012 by Cheryl Strayed. Used by permission of Zachary Shuster Harmsworth Literary Agency.

Credits

Photo locators denoted as follows: Top (T), Center (C), Bottom (B), Left (L), Right (R), Background (Bkgd)

vi P_Wei/Getty Images; **viii** All Canada Photos/Alamy: **x** William James Warren/Getty Images; **xii** Archivart/Alamy; **xiv** Soft_light/Shutterstock; **2** P_Wei/Getty Images; **3** (BC) Gary Carter/Corbis, (BL) Roni Ben Ishay/ Shutterstock, (B) Don Mason/Blend Images/Corbis, (CL) Everett Historical/ Shutterstock, (CT) Brant Ward/San Francisco Chronicle/Corbis, (T) Juanmonino/Getty Images, (C) Zerophoto/Fotolia, (TL) Blvdone/ Shutterstock; 6 Juanmonino/Getty Images; **11**(B) Roni Ben Ishay/ Shutterstock, (C) Everett Historical/Shutterstock, (T) Blvdone/ Shutterstock; **12** (CL) Dpa picture alliance/Alamy, (TL) Blvdone/ Shutterstock, (TR) Everett Historical/Shutterstock; **13, 18, 20** Blvdone/ Shutterstock; **22** (CL) National Archives/Handout/Hulton Archive/Getty Images, (TL) Blvdone/Shutterstock, (TR) Everett Historical/Shutterstock; **23** Everett Historical/Shutterstock; **25** Everett Historical/Shutterstock; **30, 32, 34** Everett Historical/Shutterstock; **36** Photo by Tanya Cofer; 37 Roni Ben Ishay/Shutterstock; **41** Peopleimages/Getty Images; **46, 48, 50** Roni Ben Ishay/Shutterstock; **59** (B) Gary Carter/Corbis, (CB) Don Mason/ Blend Images/Corbis, (CT) Brant Ward/San Francisco Chronicle/Corbis, (T) Zerophoto/Fotolia; **62** J.J. GUILLEN/EPA/Newscom; **63** Zerophoto/Fotolia; **69** Peter Dazeley/Getty Images; **74** Zerophoto/Fotolia; **76** Zerophoto/ Fotolia; **78** Frazer Harrison/Getty Images; **79** Brant Ward/San Francisco Chronicle/Corbis; **81** Camille Dungy; **82** Kurt Rogers/San Francisco Chronicle/Corbis; **84, 86** Brant Ward/San Francisco Chronicle/Corbis; **88** Lynn Goldsmith/Corbis; **89, 96** Don Mason/Blend Images/Corbis; **98** Gary Carter/Corbis; **99** (C) Alysa Bennett, (T) Chris Felver/Getty Images; **100** Gary Carter/Corbis; **102** Lauri Patterson/Getty Images;**122** All Canada Photos/Alamy, (BCL) Wonderlust/Photonica/Getty Images, (C) AF archive/ Alamy, (L) Guylain Doyle/AGE fotostock; (BL) FUKUSHIMA MINPO/AFP/ Getty Images, (T) Scazza/Fotolia, (TC) Dmytro Pylypenko/Shutterstock, (TCL) Deposit Photos/Glow Images, (TL) Water Rights/SuperStock; **131** (B) FUKUSHIMA MINPO/AFP/Getty Images, **131** (C) Deposit Photos/Glow Images, (T) Water Rights/SuperStock; **132** Jeremy sutton hibbert/Alamy; **133** Water Rights/SuperStock; **137** Olga Ptashko/Shutterstock; **142** Vetryanaya/o/Shutterstock; **146, 148, 150** Water Rights/SuperStock; **152** Patrick McMullan Co/McMullan/Sipa USA/Newscom; **153, 158, 160, 162** Deposit Photos/Glow Images; **165** FUKUSHIMA MINPO/AFP/Getty Images; **168** Scazza/Fotolia; **175** (B) Wonderlust/Photonica/Getty Images, (BC) Guylain Doyle/AGE footstock, (C) AF archive/Alamy; (T) Dmytro Pylypenko/Shutterstock; **178** (CL) Janette Beckman/Getty Images, (TL) Dmytro Pylypenko/Shutterstock, (TR) Library of Congress Prints and Photographs Division [LC 3a11347u]; **183** Nejron/123RF; **187** Maksimilian/Shutterstock; **191, 194** Dmytro Pylypenko/Shutterstock; **194** (CL) Hulton Deutsch Collection/Corbis, (TR) Library of Congress Prints and Photographs Division [LC 3a11347u]; **195** Library of Congress Prints and Photographs Division [LC 3a11347u]; **196** (B) Library of Congress Prints and Photographs Division [LC 3a12748u], (T) Library of Congress Prints and Photographs Division [LC 3a19377u]; **197** (B) Library of Congress Prints and Photographs Division [LC 3a11986u], (T) Hulton Archive/Getty Images; **198** Library of Congress Prints and Photographs Division [LC 3a12746u]; **199** Library of Congress Prints and Photographs Division [LC 3a11347u]; **200** (B) Library of Congress Prints and Photographs Division [LC 3a11347u], (TL) Dmytro Pylypenko/ Shutterstock; **202** Rachel Torres/Alamy; **207** Alistair Hobbs/Shutterstock; **210** Danté Fenolio/Science Source; **212, 214** AF archive/Alamy; **217** Guylain Doyle/AGE fotostock; **220** Guylain Doyle/AGE fotostock; **222** Guylain Doyle/AGE fotostock; **224** Wonderlust/Photonica/Getty Images; **225** (BL) Handout/KRT/Newscom, (CL) Oscar White/Corbis, (TL) Christopher Felver/Corbis; **226** Wonderlust/Photonica/Getty Images; **228** Yulkapopkova/Vetta/Getty Images; **230** Icetray/123RF; **251**(BC) Jack Delano/PhotoQuest/Getty Images, (B) Bettmann/Corbis; (CL) Everett Collection Inc/Alamy, (CT) Everett Collection Historical/Alamy, (T) Charles Moore/Black Star/Alamy, (TL) Photoshot; **254** Charles Moore/Black Star/ Alamy; **259** (B) National Archives, (C) Everett Collection Inc/Alamy, (T) Photoshot; **260** Stephen F. Somerstein/Getty Images; **260** (TL) Photoshot; **266** Photoshot; **268** Photoshot; **270** Stephen F. Somerstein/Getty Image; **275** Bettmann/Corbis; **280** Bob Adelman/Corbis; **288** Everett Collection Inc/Alamy; **290** Everett Collection Inc/Alamy; **292** Everett Collection Inc/ Alamy; **294** PhotoQuest/Getty Images; **295** National Archives; **297** National Archives; **305** (B) Jack Delano/PhotoQuest/Getty Images, (BC) Bettmann/Corbis, (CT) Everett Collection Historical/Alamy; **308** Andrea Jacobson, The Observatory. MacNeil/Lehrer Productions; **312** Everett Collection Historical/Alamy; **313** (B) Everett Collection Historical/Alamy, (T) Bill O'Leary/The Washington Post/Getty Images; **314** Everett Collection Historical/Alamy; **316** Thall/iStock/Getty Images; **318** Everett Collection Historical/Alamy; **320** Everett Collection Historical/Alamy; **322** ZUMA Press, Inc./Alamy; **323** Bettmann/Corbis; **327** Viramontes, Xavier (1947) ©Copyright Smithsonian American Art Museum, Washington, DC/Art Resource, NY; **327** Xavier Viramontes; **330** Bettmann/Corbis; **332** Bettmann/Corbis; **334** Chris Felver/Getty Images; **335** Jack Delano/ PhotoQuest/Getty Images; **337** AP Images; **340** Jack Delano/PhotoQuest/ Getty Images; **342** Jack Delano/PhotoQuest/Getty Images; **365** Sotheby's/ akg images/Newscom; **374** GL Archive/Alamy; **356** Kichigin/Shutterstock; **357** (BL) Sotheby's/akg images/Newscom, (C) Reuters, (CL) Relativity Media/courtesy Everett Collection, (T) Leo Mason/Leo Mason/Corbis, (TC) Ben Welsh/age fotostock/Alamy, (TL) GL Archive/Alamy; **360** Leo Mason/ Leo Mason/Corbis; **365** (BL) Relativity Media/courtesy Everett Collection, **365** (CBL) Relativity Media/courtesy Everett Collection; **365** (CL) Relativity Media/courtesy Everett Collection, (TR) Georgios Kollidas/Shutterstock, (R) GL Archive/Alamy; **367** The Print Collector/Corbis; **368** Peter Phipp/ Britain On View/Getty Images; **369** Hugo Philpott/Epa/Newscom; **370** GL Archive/Alamy; **375** Sergii Figurnyi/Fotolia; **376** Relativity Media/courtesy Everett Collection; **400** GL Archive/Alamy; **401** Relativity Media/courtesy Everett Collection; **450** GL Archive/Alamy; **457** BHE FILMS/DINO DE LAURENTIIS CINEMATOGRAFICA/VERONA PROD/Ronald Grant Archive/ Mary Evans; **466** GL Archive/Alamy; **479** Cantonatty/Shutterstock; **480** Relativity Media/courtesy Everett Collection; **486** (B) ZU_09/Getty Images, (L) Relativity Media/courtesy Everett Collection, (R) Sotheby''s/ akg images/Newscom; **501**(B) Courtesy CNN, (C) Reuters, (T) Ben Welsh/ age fotostock/Alamy; **504** Ben Welsh/age fotostock/Alamy; **505** Frederick M. Brown/Getty Images; **506** Ben Welsh/age fotostock/Alamy; **508** Ben Welsh/age fotostock/Alamy; **516**(L) Reuters,(R) Courtesy CNN; **517** Reuters; **518** Snvv/Shutterstock; **521** Reuters; **522** Reuters; **524**(B) Nicolas Khayat/KRT/Newscom, (L) Reuters, (R) Courtesy CNN; **528** Courtesy CNN; **529**(B) Courtesy CNN, (T) Reuters; Dinka Jurkovic, Radio Free Europe/Radio Liberty; **542** Soft_light/Shutterstock; **543**(BL) Oleksandr Kalinichenko/Shutterstock, (C) FWStudio/Shutterstock, (BC) A.G.A/Shutterstock, (CL) De Agostini Picture Lib./A. Dagli Orti/akg images, (CTL) Archivart/Alamy, (T)cunaplus/Shutterstock, (TC) Galyna Andrushko/Shutterstock, (TL) Beerkoff/Fotolia; **546** cunaplus/ Shutterstock; **551**(B) Oleksandr Kalinichenko/Shutterstock, (CT) De Agostini Picture Lib./A. Dagli Orti/akg images, (T) Beerkoff/Fotolia Kichigin/Shutterstock; **552** Beerkoff/Fotolia; **554** Roman replica of the Athena Farnese (marble), Phidias (c.500 c.432 BC) Museo Archeologico Nazionale, Naples, Italy/Bridgeman Images; **555** Statue of Zeus at Oympia, English School, (20th century)/Private Collection / © Look and Learn/Bridgeman Images; **556** GeoM/Fotolia; **558** Hulton Archive/ Handout/Getty Images; **559** The Siege of Troy (oil on canvas), French School, (17th century)/Musee des Beaux Arts, Blois, France/Bridgeman Art Images; **559** The Siege of Troy (oil on canvas), French School, (17th century)/Musee des Beaux Arts, Blois, France/Bridgeman Images; **567** Ivy Close Images/Alamy; **560** Archivart/Alamy; **572** Mary Evans Picture Library/Alamy; **580 581** JOHN WILLIAM/akg images; **584** Scylla attacking Olysseus's ship, Payne, Roger (b.1934)/Private Collection/Look and Learn/ Bridgeman Art Images; **584** Scylla attacking Olysseus's ship, Payne, Roger (b.1934)/Private Collection/Look and Learn/Bridgeman Images; **591** Archivart/Alamy; **592** Archivart/Alamy; **594** Hulton Archive/Handout/ Getty Images; **595** De Agostini Picture Lib./A. Dagli Orti/akg images; **602** Penelope and the Suitors, 1900 (oil on canvas), Robertson, Victor John (fl.1892 1903)/Private Collection/Photo © Peter Nahum at The Leicester Galleries, London/Bridgeman Art Images; **609** Odysseus punishes the suitors (colour litho), Robinson, Thomas Heath (1869 1954)/Private Collection/The Stapleton Collection/Bridgeman Art Images; **614** North Wind Picture Archives/Alamy; **618** De Agostini Picture Lib./ A. Dagli Orti/akg images; **620** De Agostini Picture Lib./A. Dagli Orti/akg images; **622** De Agostini Picture Lib./A. Dagli Orti/akg images;

624 (B) Photo by Scott LaPierre, (T) Archivart/Alamy; **632** Archivart/Alamy; **635** Oleksandr Kalinichenko/Shutterstock; **636** USCG; **639** Oleksandr Kalinichenko/Shutterstock; **647** Galyna Andrushko/Shutterstock; **650** Colin McPherson/Corbis; **651** Galyna Andrushko/Shutterstock; **656** Galyna Andrushko/Shutterstock; **658** Galyna Andrushko/Shutterstock; **660**(R) Marc Bryan Brown/WireImage/Getty Images, (TL) Matthew Naythons/The LIFE Images Collection/Getty images; **666** FWStudio/Shutterstock; **668** A.G.A/Shutterstock; **661** FWStudio/Shutterstock; **669**(B) Tony Mcnicol/Alamy, (C) P Anastasselis/REX/Newscom; (T) Everett Collection Historical/Alamy; **670** A.G.A/Shutterstock; **672** Kovalenko Inna/Fotolia; **674** Shukaylova Zinaida/Shutterstock; **694** Angela Harburn/fotolia; **695** (BC) Everett Collection/Shutterstock, (C) World History Archive/Alamy,(TC) B Christopher/Alamy, (T)djgis/Shutterstock, (TCL) Liukov/Shutterstock, (TL) Falcon Eyes/Shutterstock; **703** Falcon Eyes/Shutterstock; **704** Pirie MacDonald/Corbis; Eyes/Shutterstock; **711** Dezi/Shutterstock; **722** Everett Collection Inc/Alamy; **743**(B) Everett Collection/Shutterstock, (BC)World History Archive/Alamy, (T) Liukov/Shutterstock, (TR) B Christopher/Alamy; **746** Photo by Kerry Sherck; **747** Liukov/Shutterstock; **751** Iryna Rasko/Shutterstock; **754** Liukov/Shutterstock; **759**(B) Louis Monier/Gamma Rapho/Getty Images, (T) Mark Lennihan/AP Images; **760** (B) Christopher/Alamy; **762** Cultura RM/Art Wolfe Stock/Cultura/Getty Images; **764** Inkwelldodo/Fotolia; **770**(B) Sam Simmonds/Polaris/Newscom; (TL) World History Archive/Alamy, (TR) Everett Collection/Shutterstock; **771** World History Archive/Alamy; **773** World History Archive/Alamy; **774**(B) Michael Tran/Contributor/FilmMagic/Getty Images, (TL) World History Archive/Alamy, (TR) Everett Collection/Shutterstock; **784** World History Archive/Alamy; Courtesy of University of Maine.

Credits for Images in Interactive Student Edition Only

Unit 1

BBC Worldwide Americas, Inc.; BBC Worldwide Learning; Bettmann/Corbis; Charles Eshelman/Getty Images; lithian/Shutterstock; Pat Mora

Unit 2

Amos Chapple/Lonely Planet Images/Getty Images; Antonio Busiello/Moment Open/Getty Images; B.Stefanov/Fotolia; Daryl Miller; Dean Lambert/Alamy; Fotosearch/Getty Images; James A. Parcell/The Washington Post/Getty Images; Oriontrail/iStockphoto/Getty Images; Richard A McMillin/Shutterstock; Saez Pascal/SIPA/Newscom; Saul Loeb/AFP/Getty Images; Serezniy/123RF; Stephen Frink/Corbis; Ullstein bild/Getty Images; AS400 DB/Corbis

Unit 3

John G. Moebes/Corbis; Bettmann/Corbis; David Margolick; Hulton Archive/Getty Images; Mark Bennington; Sheyann Webb Christburg; WUNC

Unit 4

DeAgostini/Getty Images; Elizabeth I, Armada Portrait, c.1588 (oil on panel), Gower, George (1540 96) (attr. to)/Woburn Abbey, Bedfordshire, UK/Bridgeman Art Library; Elizabeth I, Armada Portrait, c.1588 (oil on panel), Gower, George (1540 96) (attr. to)/Woburn Abbey, Bedfordshire, UK/Bridgeman Images; Misty Harris;

Unit 5

Courtesy National Park Service; David Nunuk/All Canada Photos/Getty Images; Doug Allan/Oxford Scientific/Getty Images; Epa european pressphoto agency b.v./Alamy; Frans Lanting/Mint Images/Getty Images; James R.D. Scott/Moment/Getty Images; Owen Newman/Oxford Scientific/Getty Images; Paul Popper/Popperfoto/Getty Images; Perrine Doug/Perspectives/Getty Images; readyimage/Shutterstock; Richard Ellis/Getty Images; Rodney Ungwiluk, Jr./Getty Images; Schomburg Center, NYPL/Art Resource, NY; Sue Flood/Photodisc/Getty Images; Wayne Lynch/All Canada Photos/Getty Images

Unit 6

Solarseven/Shutterstock; Chris Felver/Archive Photos/Getty Images; Dennis Van Tine/ABACAUSA.COM/Newscom; Eric Francis/Getty Images; Eric Schaal/The LIFE Picture Collection/Getty Images; Ron Miller; S_Photo/Shutterstock; Smithsonian Magazine